THE OXFORD COMPANION TO
AMERICAN MILITARY HISTORY

THE OXFORD COMPANION TO
AMERICAN MILITARY HISTORY

EDITOR IN CHIEF

John Whiteclay Chambers II

EDITORS

Fred Anderson

Lynn Eden

Joseph T. Glatthaar

Ronald H. Spector

CONSULTING EDITOR

G. Kurt Piehler

OXFORD
UNIVERSITY PRESS

1999

OXFORD

UNIVERSITY PRESS

Oxford   New York

Athens   Auckland   Bangkok   Bogotá   Buenos Aires   Calcutta
Cape Town   Chennai   Dar es Salaam   Delhi   Florence   Hong Kong
Istanbul   Karachi   Kuala Lumpur   Madrid   Melbourne   Mexico City   Mumbai
Nairobi   Paris   São Paulo   Singapore   Taipei   Tokyo   Toronto   Warsaw

and associated companies in
Berlin   Ibadan

Copyright © 1999 by Oxford University Press, Inc.

Published by Oxford University Press, Inc.,
198 Madison Avenue, New York, New York 10016–4314

Library of Congress Cataloging-in-Publication Data

The Oxford companion to American military history /
editor in chief, John Whiteclay Chambers II.
p.   cm.
Includes bibliographical references and index.
ISBN 0-19-507198-0 (alk. paper)
1. United States—History, Military Dictionaries.
I. Chambers, John Whiteclay.
II. Title: American military history.
E181.094   1999
355'.00973—dc21   99-21181

1 3 5 7 9 8 6 4 2

Printed in the United States of America
on acid-free paper

CONTENTS

INTRODUCTION

"It is well that war is so terrible, or we would grow too fond of it." As Gen. Robert E. Lee observed at Fredericksburg in 1862, battle can produce spectacular pageantry, bravery, and exhilaration, but it also yields mangled bodies and bloated corpses. That is war's eternal paradox. In it, brutality, cynicism, tragedy, and absurdity are accompanied by courage, comradeship, self-sacrifice, and noble purpose. The continuing popularity of books and films from *All Quiet on the Western Front* (1930) to *Saving Private Ryan* (1998) demonstrates that, for all its contradictions, war has its fascinations.

War is central to the way the United States has developed as a nation and a society. The use of military force attended the conquest of the Indians, the expulsion of French and then British power, the birth of the republic, western expansion, the preservation of the Union, the creation of an island empire, and the triumph of the United States in two world wars. The use and the threat of using military force accompanied the emergence of the United States as a global superpower.

Warlike images form part of the national memory: the Minutemen with farmers' muskets and tricornered hats standing up to the king's red-coated soldiers at Lexington and Concord, Andrew Jackson and his buck-skinned frontiersmen blasting the British regulars at New Orleans, the masses of blue- and gray-clad citizen-soldiers firing volley after volley at each other in the Civil War, Theodore Roosevelt and his Rough Riders charging up San Juan Hill (and the oft-forgotten black regulars alongside them), khaki-clad doughboys slashing through the Argonne Forest in World War I.

Who can forget the iconography of World War II, from the burning ships in Pearl Harbor to the Japanese surrender on the deck of the USS *Missouri* in Tokyo Bay? Photographers immortalized Douglas MacArthur wading ashore returning to the Philippines, the Marines raising the flag on Iwo Jima, the B-17s dropping sticks of bombs over Germany, and the deadly mushroom cloud spiraling above Hiroshima. The American memory of that war also contains pictures of Gen. George Patton and his ivory-handled pistols, Dwight D. Eisenhower meeting paratroopers bound for Normandy, Robert Capa's blurred photos of G.I.s struggling ashore at Omaha Beach, and the haunting images of skeletal survivors as the Allies liberated German death camps.

War certainly has its dark side—one emphasized since World War II. The cold, bone-weary faces of American G.I.s haunt David Duncan's photos of the Korean War. Following them are the fiery images of burning villages and screaming civilians in the Vietnam War, and the emotive pictures of American body bags and amputees coming home from Southeast Asia, Eddie Adams's picture of a summary execution in the streets of Saigon in 1968. Some twenty years later, fear of massive American casualties accompanied the deployment of U.S. troops in the Persian Gulf War—a fear only alleviated by the success of America's high-technology weaponry and combat-ready forces, which destroyed many of Saddam Hussein's military units and installations in Iraq and occupied Kuwait.

With the end of the Cold War, international conflict and the military are once again in transition. Gone are the minuscule standing forces in peacetime and the old mass armies of wartime draftees and volunteers. Replacing them are highly mobile, professional, all-volunteer forces now increasingly combining active duty and reserve troops. War too has changed. The world wars and threat of global conflict that characterized much of the twentieth century seem to be a thing of the past. The Persian Gulf War of 1991 showed that intensive regional wars may certainly continue. Retaining the ability to project massive power overseas, American armed forces at the beginning of the twenty-first century have been assigned new missions, such as acting against regional threats involving the use of weapons of mass destruction. But the U.S. military has also returned to an old mission involving constabulary duties. Now, however, these include border security, counter-terrorism, and, in a world increasingly torn by internal and sectarian strife, peacekeeping.

As U.S. experiences in Somalia and Bosnia show, the multinational use of outside armed forces in dangerous areas to separate previously warring groups and encourage the development of sta-ble peaceful conditions is a complex and difficult mission. Yet this role is rooted in historic Amer-ican relationships among war, peace, and the military. For Americans often seek to use the mili-tary for idealistic purposes—from "the war to end all wars" in 1917–18 to the rescue mission of the Berlin Airlift in 1948–49—and in recent years, the United States has been a major supporter of the idea of collective security and peacekeeping through the United Nations and NATO.

Of course, peace and peace movements are also important in U.S. history. Traditionally, Ameri-cans see themselves as a peace-loving people and war as an aberration. As a people, they are com-mitted not to Old World conquest or balance-of-power politics, but to the expansion of their po-litical and economic ideals expressed in terms of life, liberty, justice, and democracy. Only a few Americans have been absolute pacifists, like the Quakers, but many have led in struggles for non-violence and social justice, among them, William Lloyd Garrison, Jane Addams, and Martin Luther King, Jr. They also believed in an internationalism without violence. Other internationalists cham-pioned collective security for a world of peace and justice, such as Presidents Woodrow Wilson and Franklin Roosevelt. Both kinds of internationalists reacted against traditional American isolation-ism; indeed, isolationists usually opposed the deployment or use of U.S. troops overseas.

Increased popular interest in the role of war, peace, and the military in U.S. history is evident in films, books, commemorations, reenactments, and other aspects of popular culture. This coin-cides with a transformation in scholarship in the field. In the last two generations, a variety of new scholarly approaches has augmented the old "drum and trumpet" school of refighting bat-tles. The new military history first shifted attention to the evolution of military institutions, en-gaging not simply historians but sociologists, economists, anthropologists, and political scien-tists. Some scholars then began to explore the wider relationship between war, the military, and society. Others probe the nexus with science and technology. Scholars in cultural history as well as in psychology, literary criticism, film studies, and gender studies explore cultural dimensions of war, peace, and the military. The comparatively new field of peace history is producing works on peace and antiwar movements and their relationship to politics and culture. Building on a broad conception of national defense, some historians, political scientists, sociologists, and econ-omists examine relationships among the military, the economy, and governmental policy either in the short run or in long-term interpretations of the rise and decline of particular nations. In a different direction, but equally as influential, is a renewed attention on battle. This new combat history, however, shifts the focus away from the perspective of top commanders to the battle ex-periences of the common soldiers, airmen, sailors, or Marines.

Drawing on the most current scholarship in the field and in a number of cases advancing that scholarship, *The Oxford Companion to American Military History* provides a comprehensive, one-volume guide to the study of war, peace, and the military throughout American history. Through more than 1,000 alphabetically arranged entries, each written and signed by a specialist in the field, this work examines America's military past from the colonial era to the present. It focuses not only on wars, battles, and military institutions but also on their relationship to the social, eco-nomic, political, and cultural milieu. In recognition of this broader understanding of military history and the history of war and peace in America, the volume also examines peace and antiwar movements, efforts at arms reduction, and limitations on the size and use of the armed forces.

In entries ranging from brief essays to extensive analyses, the *Companion* covers the various armed conflicts, institutions, policies, weapons, organizations, individuals, and issues that have together made up the American experience with war, peace, and the military. Although its primary focus is historical—particularly military history, war and society studies, peace history, and the history of international relations—the work uses an interdisciplinary approach. It includes concepts and research from such other fields as art history, cultural anthropology, economics, film studies, gender studies, literary criticism, minority studies, political science, and sociology.

Like the shadows on a parade field, the military reflects the larger society that creates it. The primary goal of this reference work is to explore the *changing* nature of war and the military and, in the process, to explain how and why the United States developed its military institutions, weapons, and national security policies. It seeks to understand the impact of war on American society and the state, and the influence of American politics, culture, and society on the nature of war and military organization. Taken as a whole, the *Companion* seeks to answer several key thematic questions: How has the military evolved in American history? How has it prepared for and carried out its missions? What have been the role and impact of war and the military? What has been the relationship of war, weaponry, and the military to U.S. foreign policy and to American society, including various social and economic groups, the political system, and the national culture and pluralistic subcultures? How have these groups, institutions, policies, and values helped to shape one another? What has caused and characterized the evolution of movements for arms limitation, peace, and reduction of the armed forces?

Included in the *Companion* are broad, interpretive entries designed to further several goals. One aim is to provide historical insight into particular wars and military organizations. "Composite" pieces composed of integrated essays separate these large topics into manageable areas. For example, articles on each major war are divided into essays that deal with the war's causes, military and diplomatic events, domestic course, postwar impact, and changing interpretations. Other composite articles break into chronological periods the history of each major service— U.S. Army, Navy, Air Force, and Marine Corps. Another aim is to provide theoretical as well as historical understanding of the military's structure and missions, and of the social, political, economic, technological, cultural, and strategic context in which these have evolved.

Within the space available, this book provides a comprehensive guide to the history and current circumstances of the U.S. armed services, as well as American ideas about war, peace, and national security. It does so through an alphabetical organization that comprises several broad categories of entries. These categories were designed to reveal the connections and relationships among the topics under consideration. In planning articles, the criteria for inclusion always began with the question: What is the overall significance of this subject within the context of war, peace, and the military in American history?

Conceptual categories include:

Historical Actions and Events. More than 300 articles examine historical actions and events. Varying in length from a few hundred to several thousand words, these entries deal with wars (from King Philip's War of 1675–1677 to the Persian Gulf War of 1991), battles and sieges (such as Bunker Hill, Gettysburg, Normandy, Inchon, and the Tet Offensive), overviews of air and naval operations in specific wars or campaigns (such as U.S. Naval Operations in the Pacific in World War II and U.S. Air Operations in the Korean War), armed insurrections (like the Whiskey Rebellion of 1794 or the New York City Antidraft Riots of 1863), and international incidents and crises (from the Samoan Crisis of 1888–89 to the Kosovo Crisis of 1999). They include acts of Congress (like the G.I. Bill and the War Powers Resolution) and executive orders, court cases and decisions, international conferences and agreements, and overviews of U.S. military involvement in other countries or regions (from Canada to the United Kingdom, the Caribbean to the Middle East).

Concepts. War, peace, and the military cannot be adequately understood without the concepts that underlie them. Thus, the *Companion* provides extensive articles on such major relevant concepts as Foreign Policy, War, Peace, National Security, Military Doctrine, and the State. More than two dozen middle-length entries on related concepts, among them Collective Security, Command and Control, Deterrence, Operational Art, the Order of Battle, Principles of War, the Rules of Engagement, Victory, and Defeat, as well as Pacifism, Peacekeeping, Nonviolence, Just War Theory, and the Laws of War. There are also composite articles, combining a cluster of connected entries. The composite entry on Strategy, for example, is divided among articles on the Fundamentals of Strategy and Historical Development, and then three separate articles on the application of Strategy to Land, Sea, and Air warfare. Due to the differences they entail, there are also entries on nearly two dozen different kinds of warfare (such as Airborne Warfare, Amphibious Warfare, Napoleonic Warfare, Privateering, and Trench Warfare).

The Armed Services. A special emphasis of the work is on explaining the nature and historical evolution of the armed services as institutions and their relationship to American society, polity, culture, and international relations. Each has, of course, influenced the other. Institutional entries provide historical perspective on such topics as the individual U.S. armed services, plus each of their combat branches. A composite entry on the U.S. Army, for example, contains an overview article, accompanied by five chronological articles covering the Colonial and Revolutionary Eras, and the periods 1783–1865, 1866–1899, 1900–1941, and since 1941. Another composite article explores the Army Combat Branches, with entries on Infantry, Artillery, Cavalry, Armor, and Aviation. For more information about the weapons of these branches, the reader can consult generic articles on, for example, Artillery, Machine Guns, Standard Infantry Side Arms, Tanks. There are similar composite chronological and combat branch articles on the navy, air force, and Marine Corps, as well as a general article on the Coast Guard. Other entries explain the development of the militia and the National Guard and of the other reserves. The myriad aspects of military life in war and peace are explored in scores of different articles: these include overviews of the nature of Gender and Identity in the Military, Mobilization, Rank and Hierarchy in the Military, Recruitment, and Training and Indoctrination, as well as Concepts of Military Leadership. There are also articles on Careers in the Military, Casualties, the Changing Experience of Combat, Combat Effectiveness, Combat Support, Prisoners of War, and Troop Morale.

Weaponry and Material. Weapons systems, and instruments of detection, observation, communication, and supply essential components of the armed forces. The *Companion* encompasses a wide variety of articles here, ranging from specific weapons and other instruments to generic categories. The aim is not simply to describe and explain their function but to give their historical military significance and, when pertinent, to situate them within a larger political and economic context. Interpretive overview articles place developments in multidimensional perspective (there are long entries, for example, on the Evolution of Weapons, on Nuclear Weapons, and on the Arms Race, as well as separate overviews on the Weaponry of the U.S. Air Force, the army, the navy, the U.S. Air Force, and the Marine Corps). Other articles of varying length explain the evolving forms and usage of such support functions as Intelligence (with separate articles on the roles of MAGIC and ULTRA in World War II), Coding and Decoding, Covert Operations, Engineering, Logistics, Maintenance, and Transportation, as well as such detection systems as Radar, Sonar, AWACS aircraft, AEGIS ships, U-2 Spy Planes, Reconnaissance Satellites, and Heat-Seeking Technology.

State and Society. The armed forces are, of course, instruments of the state, but they—and war itself—reflect and affect the larger society. Responding to new scholarship on war and society, as well as producing new scholarship itself, the *Companion* includes substantial articles on social perspectives, economic perspectives (from the economy and war to procurement in various defense industries), and political perspectives (Congress, War, and the Military; the News Media,

War, and the Military; the President as Commander in Chief; Public Opinion, War, and the Military; and the Supreme Court, War, and the Military). There are also articles about rebellions against state power: an extensive one on Colonial Rebellions and Armed Civil Unrest (1607–1775), and specific articles on Bacon's Rebellion (1676), Shays's Rebellion (1786–87), and the Whiskey Rebellion (1794), as well as the internal strife known as Bleeding Kansas (1854–58).

Law and Ethics. Because of the purpose of the armed forces and the nature of war, the military's system of law and its professional ethics have often differed from those of the larger civilian society. Particularly in twentieth-century America, however, with the increased sense of individual rights, egalitarianism, and civil liberty, more confluence has evolved between military and civilian systems of law and ethics. In this work, the nature and evolution of military law, which has focused more on maintaining discipline than achieving justice, and of military ethics, increasingly delineated, are treated in a number of entries. Among these is a large composite article on Military Justice, plus shorter articles on the Right to Bear Arms, Civil Liberties and War, and the Constitutional and Political Basis of War and the Military. There are also individual articles on such topics as Atrocities, Ethical Issues Involving Nuclear Weapons, Genocide, the U.S. War Effort and the Holocaust, and War Crimes.

Dissent. War and the military have sometimes provoked vigorous dissent in American history. Responding to broadening scholarship on peace, arms reduction movements, and alternative views of national security, the *Companion* includes articles on such groups and movements. Sizable interpretive entries examine Conscientious Objection, Draft Resistance and Evasion, Nuclear Protest Movements, Peace and Antiwar Movements, and the Vietnam Antiwar Movement. Individual groups, ranging from Quakers to the War Resisters League, merit smaller entries.

Popular Culture and the Military. Cultural perspectives are important in understanding the relationship of war and the military to society. Consequently, a number of pioneering articles explore various interrelationships between war and the military and American culture, including historically oriented entries dealing with such diverse topics as Commemoration and Public Ritual, Military Reenactments, and Paramilitary Groups. Separate articles appear on War and the Military in Film; Illustration, and Photography; Literature; Music; Sermons and Orations; and Textbooks. There is even an article on Military Influences on Fashion.

Biographies. Some 300 biographical entries explore the lives of individuals of particular importance to war, peace, and the military in American history. These include 25 U.S. presidents and many other civilian public officials, more than 100 generals and admirals (from Nathanael Greene to Colin Powell), plus other military figures (from Molly Pitcher to Sergeant Alvin York). You will find biographies of military theorists, inventors, scientists (such as Carl von Clausewitz, Alfred T. Mahan, Giulio Douhet, Robert Fulton, Samuel Colt, John Dahlgren, John Holland, Orville and Wilbur Wright, John von Neumann); pacifists and social activists (William Penn, Henry David Thoreau, and Emily Greene Balch); and other nonmilitary public figures (among them Clara Barton, Frederick Douglass, W. E. B. Du Bois, Charles Lindbergh, Bill Mauldin, Ernie Pyle, and Norman Thomas). There are Native American warrior chiefs, and several foreign leaders, friend or foe (from George III to Saddam Hussein).

Combining clear, lively prose with the latest scholarship, *The Oxford Companion to American Military History* is a reference source that students, teachers, journalists, military history buffs, and general readers will find indispensable.

HOW TO USE THIS *COMPANION*

As you begin the intellectual adventure of exploring and using this work, you will rapidly discover that it is designed for both specific reference and sustained browsing. Wide exploration of related topics is encouraged by several features:

• *Alphabetical arrangement* of entries provides the quickest way to locate a significant person or topic. You can plunge right into the book by selecting something that interests you and go from there. Perhaps it is an individual—King Philip (Metacomet), Molly Pitcher (Mary Hays Ludwig), George Washington, Tecumseh, Winfield Scott, Robert E. Lee, Ulysses S. Grant, Abraham Lincoln, or maybe George Custer, Emory Upton, George Patton, Hyman Rickover, Robert McNamara, or Bill Clinton. It could be an adversary: Charles Cornwallis, Antonio Lopez de Santa Anna, Isoroku Yamamoto, Erwin Rommel, Adolf Hitler, or Vo Nguyen Giap. Maybe it is a specific battle or war or a particular type of weapon (Sailing Warships, Battleships, Stealth Aircraft, or Rifled Musket, Gatling Gun, the M-16 Rifle). It might be a particular branch of the service such as Special Operations Forces: U.S. Navy SEALS, or historical organizations like the Continental Army and Navy, the Union Army and Navy, the U.S. Colored Troops, or the Confederate Army and Navy. It could be the Militia and National Guard. There are midlength historical articles on various aspects of military life, from Uniforms, Insignia, Interservice Rivalry to Medical Practice, Military Families, and Sexual Harassment. Longer thematic essays probe such topics as Native Americans in the Military; War: Nature of War; Nuclear Weapons and War, Popular Images of; Pacifism; and Terrorism and Counterterrorism. There are historical overviews of U.S. Military Involvement in the Caribbean and Latin America as well as the Middle East—or any one of nearly two dozen other regions or specific countries.

• The *index* is a good place to start a more systematic search, for it offers the most effective way to discover a wide variety of persons, events, organizations, institutions, doctrines, and weapons, whether they have their own entries or are embedded in a larger article. For example, the index references to Gen. Billy Mitchell will not only guide the reader to his alphabetically listed biographical entry; they will also indicate references to this controversial advocate of airpower in articles on the predecessors of the U.S. Air Force, 1907–46; on Strategy: Air Warfare Strategy; and, because of his court-martial, to the entry on Civil-Military Relations. Or, since there is no alphabetical entry for the Pequot War (1636–37), a description of this conflict can be found via the index in the article on Native American Wars: Wars Between Native Americans and Europeans.

• *Blind entries* appear within the alphabetical range of headwords. For synonyms, related subjects, and inverted terms, they refer the reader to the entry under which the topic is discussed. For example, the blind entry on "Manassas, Battles of" refers the reader to entries listed as "Bull Run, First Battle of (1861)" and "Bull Run, Second Battle of (1862)." In some cases, the blind entry will refer to another entry that discusses the topic as part of a broader category. The blind entry "Atomic Bomb," for example, directs the reader to "Atomic Scientists," "Hiroshima and Nagasaki, Bombings of (1945)," "Manhattan Project," and "Nuclear Weapons."

• *Asterisks* in the body of an article denote cross-references. Topics marked can be found elsewhere in the volume as separate entries. Asterisks can direct the reader to more detailed treatments of specific battles, weapons, commanders, laws, or court cases. For example, the article on "Civil-Military Relations: Civilian Control of the Military" is cross-referenced to more than half a dozen acts or events, from the "Newburgh 'Conspiracy' (1783)" to the "Goldwater-Nichols Act (1986)." Or, the cross-references can place a more limited topic within a larger context. For example, the entries on the "D-Day Landing (1944)" and "St. Lô, Breakout at (1944)," both refer the reader to the larger campaign of which they were a part: the article on "Normandy, Invasion of (1944)."

• *Cross-references* also appear in the section entitled "See also" that follows many entries. For example, in the article on "Bacon's Rebellion (1676)," there are such cross-references to larger entries on "Colonial Rebellions and Armed Civil Unrest," as well as "Native American Wars: Wars Between Native Americans and Europeans." In the entry on "Benedict Arnold," the reader is also directed to such larger topics as the "Revolutionary War: Military and Diplomatic Course" and

"Treason." From the "War of 1812," cross-references lead to conceptual entries on "Neutrality" and on "Trade, Foreign," which were major causes of the war. Similarly, the entry on the "Emancipation Proclamation" also directs the reader to related broader topics such as "African Americans in the Military" and "Civil War: Domestic Course."

Suggestions for further reading at the end of most articles are useful to learn more about the topic. The length of these reading lists varies, with the longest included with the most comprehensive essays. While every effort has been made to include the most recent, nontechnical, and widely available books, inevitably some topics require more specialized reading, and their bibliographies reflect this fact. Finally, the name of the contributor of the entry appears either at the end of the text or after the bibliography. A section in the front of the book lists individual contributors and their institutional affiliations.

The history of America's wars and the military can be made more understandable by graphics. Consequently, the *Companion* includes tables on wartime mobilization and casualties, charts indicating the ranks and accompanying insignia in the armed forces, and maps of the Revolutionary War, Civil War, World War II, and the Vietnam War. These are located in an appendix at the end of the book for the reader's reference.

ACKNOWLEDGMENTS

Initially conceived in conjunction with Linda J. Halvorson of Oxford University Press in 1990, this *Companion* has been an extensive project. Nearly a decade in the making, it involved the work of hundreds of scholars and other professionals, whose efforts I greatly appreciate. First, for their invaluable assistance, I want to thank my fellow section editors—Fred Anderson, Lynn Eden, Joseph T. Glatthaar, and Ronald H. Spector. In addition, members of the Advisory Board offered extraordinarily helpful advice as we sought to bring to a broad audience the latest scholarship from a wide range of fields.

Planning and implementing such an undertaking benefited not simply from the knowledge of those on the *Companion*'s Editorial and Advisory Boards and from Oxford University Press, but also from numerous other scholars. We often drew upon those in the Army's Center of Military History, the Inter-University Seminar on the Armed Forces and Society, the Marine Corps Historical Center, the Navy Historical Center, the Office of Air Force History, the Organization of American Historians, the Peace History Society, the Society for Historians of American Foreign Relations, and the Society for Military History. We called upon independent scholars, members of the armed forces, and faculty at college and universities around the world. A number of individuals interrupted their own work to provide invaluable advice on the project whenever needed. Among these stalwarts were Dean C. Allard, Harriet Hyman Alonso, Stephen E. Ambrose, Edward M. Coffman, Graham A. Cosmas, Richard H. Kohn, Allan R. Millett, Charles C. Moskos, Carol M. Petillo, Alex Roland, and Edwin Howard Simmons. At a crucial period, G. Kurt Piehler helped out by serving as consulting editor.

Hundreds of authors contributed the over 1,000 articles in this volume. A separate list of contributors provides the names and institutional affiliations of these authors, whose scholarship, learning, and erudition made this volume possible. This book is a tribute to the strong support that colleagues in many different branches, fields, and disciplines gave to the project.

Coordinating such an enterprise and shepherding it through to production required a sustained effort by the Trade Reference Department of Oxford University Press (USA). After the initial exploration of the concept and systematic entry development with Linda Halvorson, then executive editor, and Marion Osmun, the first development editor assigned to the project, progress over the next nine years was guided sequentially by developmental editors Mark Cummings, John Drexel, and Liz Sonneborn, and then by a series of project editors: Anita Vanca, Hannah Borgeson, and, in 1998–99, Catherine E. Carter, who completed the monumental task of bringing the manuscript into production. Anne Adelman did the copyediting; Suzanne Gilad and Maine Proofreading Services read the proofs; Mary Neal Meador designed and typeset the interior of the book; Sonny Mui designed the cover; Gary S. Tong created the maps; Adam B. Bohannon, Elizabeth Szaluta, and Kelly Trezza guided it through the final stages of production. I would also like to thank Marjorie Mueller, Director of Subsidiary Rights at Oxford. In 1998, Nancy Toff succeeded Linda Halvorson as head of Oxford's Trade Reference Department and provided overall supervision for the final publication of the book in November 1999. Sincerest thanks to all who worked on making this volume an important contribution to the understanding of war, peace, and the military in American history.

John Whiteclay Chambers II
Editor in Chief
May 1999

ABOUT THE EDITORS

EDITOR IN CHIEF

John Whiteclay Chambers II is Professor of History and former Chair of the History Department at Rutgers University, New Brunswick, New Jersey. He received his Ph.D. in History from Columbia University (1973), where he then taught for ten years. He has written *To Raise an Army: The Draft Comes to Modern America* (1987), which won the Distinguished Book Award from the Society for Military History, and *The Tyranny of Change: America in the Progressive Era, 1890–1920* (1992); he is completing a book titled *All Quiet on the Western Front: The 1930 Motion Picture and the Image of World War I* (forthcoming, 2000). He is the editor or co-editor of *Three Generals on War* (1973); *Draftees or Volunteers* (1975); *American History* (1983); *The Eagle and the Dove* (1991); *The New Conscientious Objection* (1993); *World War II, Film, and History* (1996); and *Major Problems in American Military History* (1998).

EDITORS

Fred Anderson is Associate Professor of History at the University of Colorado, Boulder. He served in the U.S. Army from 1973 to 1975 and in 1981 received his Ph.D. from Harvard University. He is the author of several scholarly articles and two books—*A People's Army: Massachusetts Soldiers and Society in the Seven Years' War* (1984) and *The Crucible of War: The Seven Years' War and the Fate of Empire in British North America, 1754–1766* (forthcoming, 2000).

Lynn Eden is Senior Research Scholar at the Center for International Security and Cooperation, Stanford University. She received her Ph.D. in Sociology from the University of Michigan (1985), was a Social Science Research Council–MacArthur Foundation Fellow in International Peace and Security (1986–87), and taught in the Department of History at Carnegie Mellon University. Eden has written *Crisis in Watertown: The Polarizaion of an American Community* (1972; nominated for the 1973 National Book Award); co-authored *Witness in Philadelphia* (1977; Book-of-the-Month-Club alternate selection); and co-edited *Nuclear Arguments: Understanding the Strategic Nuclear Arms and Arms Controls Debates* (1989). She is completing a book entitled *Constructing Deconstruction: Organizations, Knowledge, and the Effects of Nuclear Weapons* (forthcoming).

Joseph T. Glatthaar is Professor of History at the University of Houston. He received his Ph.D. in History from the University of Wisconsin-Madison and is the author of numerous articles and three books—*Forged in Battle* (1991), *Partners in Command* (1993), and *The March to the Sea and Beyond* (1995). He has also taught at the U.S. Army Command and General Staff College and the U.S. Army War College.

Ronald H. Spector is Professor of History and International Relations at George Washington University. He has been a senior Fulbright Lecturer in India and Israel. During 1995–96 he was Distinguished Visiting Professor of Strategy at the National War College. He is the author of five books, the most recent of which are *Eagle Against the Sun: The American War With Japan* (1985) and *After Tet: The Bloodiest Year in Vietnam* (1994). Professor Spector is a retired Lieutenant Colonel in the U.S. Marine Corps Reserve.

CONSULTING EDITOR

G. Kurt Piehler is Assistant Professor of History and Director of the Center for the study of War and Society at the University of Tennessee, Knoxville. He is author of *Remembering War the American Way* (1995) and co-editor of *Major Problems in American Military History* (1999). His articles have appeared in *History of Education Quarterly, Journal of the Rutgers University Libraries,* and the anthology *Commemorations: The Politics of National Identity* (1994). As director (1994–98) of the Rutgers Oral History Archives of World War II, he conducted over 200 interviews with veterans of this conflict. His televised lecture "The War That Transformed a Generation," which drew on the Oral History Archives, appeared on the History Channel in 1997. A Phi Beta Kappa graduate of Drew University (1982), he received his Ph.D. from Rutgers in 1990.

DIRECTORY OF CONTRIBUTORS

James L. Abrahamson, *Colonel, U.S. Army (Ret); Professor of History, American Military University, Manassas Park, Virginia*
ARMY, U.S.: 1900–1941; ECONOMY AND WAR; STRATEGY: FUNDAMENTALS; STRATEGY: LAND WARFARE STRATEGY

Matthew Abramovitz, *Department of History, Cornell University, Ithaca, New York*
PANAMA, U.S. MILITARY INVOLVEMENT IN

Larry H. Addington, *Professor of History Emeritus, The Citadel, Charleston, South Carolina*
ARMY REORGANIZATION ACT (1950)

Brian Adkins, *Ph.D. candidate, American History, Rutgers University, New Brunswick, New Jersey*
DREW, CHARLES; MCNAMARA, ROBERT S. (co-author)

Regina T. Akers, *Archivist, Specialist in the History of Minorities in the Military, Operational Archives, Naval Historical Center, Washington, D.C.*
WAVES

Stephen J. Allie, *Director, Frontier Army Museum, Fort Leavenworth, Kansas*
SPRINGFIELD MODEL 1903

Robert J. Allison, *Assistant Professor of History, Suffolk University, Boston, Massachusetts*
ALIEN AND SEDITION ACTS (1798); FRANCE, UNDECLARED NAVAL WAR WITH (1798–1800); JEFFERSON, THOMAS; TRIPOLITAN WAR (1801–1805)

Harriet Hyman Alonso, *Professor of History and Associate Dean and Director of the Center for Worker Education, City College of New York*
GARRISON, WILLIAM LLOYD; VILLARD, OSWALD AND FANNY GARRISON

Stephen E. Ambrose, *Boyd Professor of History Emeritus, University of New Orleans; Founder of the National D-Day Museum; Director Emeritus of the Eisenhower Center, New Orleans, Louisiana*
D-DAY LANDING (1944)

Lloyd E. Ambrosius, *Professor of History, University of Nebraska, Lincoln*
COLLECTIVE SECURITY; WORLD WAR I (1914–1918): POSTWAR IMPACT

David L. Anderson, *Professor of History, University of Indianapolis, Indianapolis, Indiana*
BATAAN AND CORREGIDOR, BATTLES OF (1942); LODGE, HENRY CABOT; MAYAGUEZ INCIDENT (1975); SEATO (EST. 1954); VIETNAM WAR (1960–1975): MILITARY AND DIPLOMATIC COURSE

Fred Anderson, *Associate Professor of History, University of Colorado at Boulder*
REVOLUTIONARY WAR (1775–1783): CAUSES; REVOLUTIONARY WAR (1775–1783): MILITARY AND DIPLOMATIC COURSE

Richard Anderson, *Associate Professor of History, Bloomsburg University, Bloomsburg, Pennsylvania*
GERMANY, BATTLE FOR (1945)

William L. Anderson, *Professor of History and Director of Cherokee Studies, Western Carolina University, Cullowhee, North Carolina*
TRAIL OF TEARS (1838–1839)

David A. Armstrong, *Director for Joint History, Joint History Office, Office of the Chairman, Joint Chiefs of Staff, Pentagon, Washington, D.C.*
MACHINE GUNS

Ben Arnold, *Associate Professor and Chair of Music, Emory University, Atlanta, Georgia*
MUSIC, WAR AND THE MILITARY IN

James R. Arnold, *Writer, Burro Station, Lexington, Virginia*
BUSH, GEORGE

Cynthia J. Arnson, *Assistant Director, Latin American Program, Woodrow Wilson Center, Washington, D.C.*
HELSINKI WATCH (1978); IRAN-CONTRA AFFAIR (1986)

William F. Atwater, *Director, U.S. Army Ordnance Museum, Aberdeen Proving Ground, Maryland*
GRENADES AND GRENADE LAUNCHERS; MINES, LAND; MORTARS

John D. Auger, *Colonel, U.S. Army (Ret), Carlisle, Pennsylvania*
WAR: LEVELS OF WAR

Andrew J. Bacevich, *Professor of International Relations, Boston University, Boston, Massachusetts*
WOOD, LEONARD

Arthur D. Baker III, *Editor, Combat Fleets of the World, U.S. Naval Institute, Annapolis, Maryland*
NAVY COMBAT BRANCHES: SUBMARINE FORCES

William C. Baldwin, *Historian, Office of History, Headquarters, U.S. Army Corps of Engineers, Alexandria, Virginia*
ENGINEERING, MILITARY

Jeffrey G. Barlow, *Historian, Contemporary History Branch, U.S. Naval Historical Center, Washington, D.C.*
RADFORD, ARTHUR

William L. Barney, *Professor of History, University of North Carolina at Chapel Hill*
CIVIL WAR (1861–1865): CAUSES

Michael Barnhart, *Professor of History, State University of New York at Stonybrook*
JAPAN, PEACE TREATY WITH (1952)

Merrill L. Bartlett, *Author; Historian, Vashon Island, Washington*
MARINE CORPS COMBAT BRANCHES: GROUND FORCES

Omer Bartov, *Professor of History, Rutgers University, New Brunswick, New Jersey*
HITLER, ADOLF; ROMMEL, ERWIN

Alan Harris Bath, *Captain, U.S. Navy (Ret); Independent Scholar, Houston, Texas*
SUPPORT SHIPS

Donald R. Baucom, *Historian, Department of Defense, Ballistic Missile Defense Organization, Pentagon, Washington, D.C.*
AWARDS, DECORATIONS, AND HONORS; STRATEGIC DEFENSE INITIATIVE

Colin F. Baxter, *Professor of History, East Tennessee State University, Johnson City*
MONTGOMERY, BERNARD LAW

Daniel R. Beaver, *Professor of History, University of Cincinnati, Cincinnati, Ohio*
BAKER, NEWTON D.; PROCUREMENT: MILITARY VEHICLES AND DURABLE GOODS INDUSTRY

Robert L. Beisner, *Professor of History Emeritus, American University, Washington, D.C.*
ACHESON, DEAN

Aaron Belkin, *Assistant Professor of Political Science; Director, Center for the Study of Sexual Minorities in the Military, University of California, Santa Barbara*
GAY MEN AND LESBIANS IN THE MILITARY

Frederic A. Bergerson, *Professor of Political Science, Whittier College, Whittier, California*
HELICOPTERS (co-author)

Eric Bergerud, *Professor of History, Lincoln University, San Francisco, California*
EASTER OFFENSIVE (1972); LOW-INTENSITY CONFLICT

Volker R. Berghahn, *Seth Low Professor of History, Columbia University, New York, New York*
WORLD WAR I (1914–1918): CAUSES

Jonathan M. Berkey, *Ph.D. Candidate, American History, Penn State University, University Park, Pennsylvania*
BULL RUN, FIRST BATTLE OF (1861); BULL RUN, SECOND BATTLE OF (1862)

Alison R. Bernstein, *Vice President, Education, Media, Arts & Culture Program, The Ford Foundation, New York, New York*
NATIVE AMERICANS IN THE MILITARY

Irving Bernstein, *Writer; Professor Emeritus of Political Science, University of California at Los Angeles*
JOHNSON, LYNDON B.

Gary Dean Best, *Professor of History, University of Hawaii, Hilo*
HOOVER, HERBERT C.

Geoffrey Best, *Senior Associate Member, St. Antony's College, Oxford University, Oxford, England*
GENEVA CONVENTIONS (1864); LAWS OF WAR

Tami Davis Biddle, *Assistant Professor of History, Duke University, Durham, North Carolina*
AIR FORCE, U.S.: PREDECESSORS OF, 1907–1946

Donald F. Bittner, *Professor of Military History, Marine Corps Command and Staff College, Quantico, Virginia*
HISTORY, MILITARY USE OF

Allida Black, *Department of History, The George Washington University, Washington, D.C.*
ROOSEVELT, ELEANOR

Jennifer Blanck, *Director of Communications, Center for Security Strategies and Operations, TECHMATICS, Arlington, Virginia*
USO

Daniel K. Blewett, *Government Documents Librarian and Bibliographer for History and Political Science, The Elizabeth M. Cudahy Memorial Library, Loyola University, Chicago, Illinois*
REFERENCE BOOKS ON WAR, PEACE, AND THE MILITARY

Martin Blumenson, *Professorial Lecturer in International Affairs (Ret), The George Washington University, Washington, D.C.*
ANZIO, BATTLE OF (1944); PATTON, GEORGE S.

James D. Blundell, *Colonel, U.S. Army (Ret); Director of Programs, Institute of Land Warfare, Association of the U.S. Army, Arlington, Virginia*
LAND WARFARE; RANK AND HIERARCHY: ARMY

Brian Bond, *Professor of Military History, Department of War Studies, King's College, London, England*
LIDDELL HART, BASIL H.

Suzanne Borghei
ELLIS, "PETE" EARL HANCOCK (co-author)

Stephen Bowman, *Colonel, U.S. Army (Ret); Associate Professor of History, American Military University, Manassas Park, Virginia*
TACTICS: FUNDAMENTALS

Paul S. Boyer, *Merle Curti Professor of History; Director, Institute for Research in the Humanities, University of Wisconsin, Madison*
BRYAN, WILLIAM JENNINGS; NUCLEAR WEAPONS AND WAR, POPULAR IMAGES OF

Walter J. Boyne, *Colonel, U.S. Air Force (Ret); Chairman, "Wingspan" the Air and Space Channel, Ashburn, Virginia*
MISSILES

Paul Bracken, *Professor of Political Science, Yale University, New Haven, Connecticut*
SOCIETY, MILITARY ORGANIZATION AND

James C. Bradford, *Associate Professor of History, Texas A & M University, College Station*
PERRY, MATTHEW

Walter H. Bradford, *Museum Curator and Chief Planner, Army Museum, U.S. Army Center of Military History, Washington, D.C.*
UNIFORMS

Paul F. Braim, *Professor of History, Embry Riddle University, Daytona Beach, Florida*
BELLEAU WOOD, BATTLE OF (1918); MARNE, SECOND BATTLE OF THE (1918); MEUSE-ARGONNE OFFENSIVE (1918); ST. MIHIEL, BATTLE OF (1918)

H. W. Brands, *Professor of History, Texas A & M University, College Station*
DISCIPLINARY VIEWS OF WAR: DIPLOMATIC HISTORY

T. R. Brereton, *Assistant Professor of History, University of Louisville, Louisville, Kentucky*
GATLING GUN; GOETHALS, GEORGE W.; LEADERSHIP, CONCEPTS OF MILITARY; MEIGS, MONTGOMERY; MUSKET, RIFLED; SEVEN DAYS' BATTLE (1862)

John W. Brinsfield, *Chaplain, U.S. Army War College, Carlisle, Pennsylvania*
RELIGION IN THE MILITARY

Charles E. Brodine, Jr., *Historian, Early History Branch, Naval Historical Center, Washington Navy Yard Washington, D.C.*
BANCROFT, GEORGE

Edwin B. Bronner, *Professor of History Emeritus, Librarian and Curator of the Quaker Collection (Ret), Haverford, Pennsylvania*
QUAKERS

Robert S. Browning III, *Chief, Office of History, 37th Training Wing, Lackland Air Force Base, San Antonio, Texas*
FORTIFICATIONS

W. Elliot Brownlee, *Professor of History, University of California at Santa Barbara*
PUBLIC FINANCING AND BUDGETING FOR WAR

Rock Brynner, *Novelist and Historian, Pawling, New York*
SHAYS'S REBELLION (1786–1787)

Arden Bucholz, *Professor of History, State University of New York at Brockport*
WILHELM II

George E. Buker, *Professor Emeritus of History, Jacksonville University, Jacksonville, Florida*
ERICSSON, JOHN; HAMPTON ROADS, BATTLE OF (1862); WELLES, GIDEON

George Bunn, *Consulting Professor, Center for International Security and Cooperation, Stanford University Institute for International Studies, Stanford, California*
ARMS CONTROL AND DISARMAMENT: NUCLEAR; LIMITED TEST BAN TREATY (1963); NON-PROLIFERATION OF NUCLEAR WEAPONS, TREATY ON THE (1968)

Donald S. Burke, *Professor, Department of International Health, Johns Hopkins University, Baltimore, Maryland*
AIDS

Stewart Burns, *Independent Historian and Director, Center for Social Healing, Mendocino, California*
ELLSBERG, DANIEL

William Burr, *Senior Analyst, The National Security Archive, Washington, D.C.*
BERLIN CRISES (1958, 1962); BROWN, HAROLD; CLIFFORD, CLARK; NATIONAL SECURITY COUNCIL; NATIONAL SECURITY COUNCIL MEMORANDA

John Sibley Butler, *The Dallas TACA Centennial Professor of Liberal Arts. The Arthur James Douglass Centennial Professor of Small Business and Entrepreneurship, University of Texas at Austin*
AFRICAN AMERICANS IN THE MILITARY

Bruce J. Calder, *Associate Professor of History, University of Illinois at Chicago*
DOMINICAN REPUBLIC, U.S. MILITARY INVOLVEMENT IN THE

Mary P. Callahan, *Assistant Professor, Jackson School of International Studies, University of Washington, Seattle*
CITIZEN-SOLDIER; WOMEN IN THE MILITARY

Colin G. Calloway, *Professor of History and Native American Studies and John Sloan Dickey Third Century Professor in the Social Sciences, Dartmouth College, Hanover, New Hampshire*
TECUMSEH

Craig M. Cameron, *Associate Professor of History, Old Dominion University, Norfolk, Virginia*
GENDER: MALE IDENTITY AND THE MILITARY

Susan Canedy, *Historian and Special Assistant to the Commanding General, HQ U.S. Army Training and Doctrine Command, Fort Monroe, Virginia*
DEMOBILIZATION; MOBILIZATION; RECRUITMENT

Mark Cannon, *Lieutenant Colonel, U.S. Army (Ret), Melbourne, Florida*
VERTICAL TAKEOFF AND LANDING AIRCRAFT

Clayborne Carson, *Professor of History, Stanford University, Stanford, California*
KING, MARTIN LUTHER, JR.

Andrew R. L. Cayton, *Professor of History, Miami University, Oxford, Ohio*
NORTHWEST TERRITORY, MILITARY ACTIONS IN THE OLD (1783–1794); WHISKEY REBELLION (1794)

William H. Chafe, *Dean of the Faculty of Arts and Sciences and Alice Mary Baldwin Professor of History, Duke University, Durham, North Carolina*
COLD WAR (1945–1991): DOMESTIC COURSE

John Whiteclay Chambers II, *Professor of History, Rutgers University, New Brunswick, New Jersey*
ACADEMIES, SERVICE: OVERVIEW; ARMY CORPS OF ENGINEERS, U.S.; ASPIN, LES, JR.; BARUCH, BERNARD M.; BASES, MILITARY: DEVELOPMENT OF; BODY ARMOR; BOSNIAN CRISIS (1990s); CARIBBEAN AND LATIN AMERICA, U.S. MILITARY INVOLVEMENT IN; CARTER, JIMMY; CARTER DOCTRINE (1980); CHENEY, RICHARD; CIVIL-MILITARY RELATIONS: MILITARY GOVERNMENT AND OCCUPATION; CLARK, MARK; CLAY, LUCIUS; CLINTON, BILL; CONSCIENTIOUS OBJECTION; CONSCRIPTION; COUNTERINSURGENCY; DEFENSE REORGANIZATION ACTS (1950, 1953, 1958); DESERTION; FORD, HENRY; GENEVA PROTOCOL ON CHEMICAL WARFARE (1925); HAIG, ALEXANDER MEIGS; JACKSON, "SCOOP" [HENRY]; JUSTICE, MILITARY: MILITARY POLICE; JUSTICE, MILITARY: MILITARY PRISONS; KING, ERNEST J.; KOREA, U.S. MILITARY INVOLVEMENT IN; KOREAN WAR, U.S. NAVAL OPERATIONS IN; KOSOVO CRISIS (1999); MARINE CORPS, U.S.: 1775–1865; MARSHALL, S. L. A.; MCNAMARA, ROBERT S. (co-author); MINES, NAVAL; MUSTE, ABRAHAM J.; NATIONAL DEFENSE ACTS (1916, 1920); NUNN, SAM; PANAY INCIDENT (1937); PENNYPACKER, GALUSHA; PENTAGON, THE; PORTER, DAVID DIXON; ROTC; SAMOAN INCIDENT (1888–89); SCHWARZKOPF, H. NORMAN; SELECTIVE DRAFT CASES (1918); SHOUP, DAVID; SURVEILLANCE, DOMESTIC; TAFT, ROBERT; VINSON, CARL; VINSON-TRAMMEL ACT (1934); VOLUNTEERS, U.S.; WAR: AMERICAN WAY OF WAR; WARSAW PACT (EST. 1955); WEAPONRY, EVOLUTION OF; WORLD WAR I (1914–1918): CAUSES OF U.S. ENTRY; YORK, ALVIN

Gordon H. Chang, *Associate Professor of History, Stanford University, Stanford, California*
TAIWAN STRAITS CRISES (1955; 1958)

Charles Chatfield, *H. Orth Hirt Professor of History, Emeritus, Wittenberg University, Springfield, Ohio*
AMERICAN PEACE SOCIETY;PEACE AND ANTIWAR MOVEMENTS;THOMAS, NORMAN

Frederick J. Chiaventone, *Colonel, U.S. Army (Ret); Professor of International Security Affairs, Office of Strategic Studies, Department of Joint and Combined Operations, U.S. Army Command and General Staff College, Fort Leavenworth, Kansas*
ARCTIC WARFARE; DESERT WARFARE; GUERRILLA WARFARE; JUNGLE WARFARE

Donald D. Chipman, *Professor of Military Studies, United States Air Force, Air University, Montgomery, Alabama*
HALSEY, WILLIAM F.; PRINCIPLES OF WAR; WORLD WAR II, U.S. NAVAL OPERATIONS IN: THE NORTH ATLANTIC

Thomas Christianson, *Lieutenant Colonel, U.S. Army, University of Wisconsin, Madison*
M-1 RIFLE; M-16 RIFLE

Christopher G. Clark, *Major, U.S. Army (Ret), Peachtree City, Georgia*
ARMORED VEHICLES

James L. Clayton, *Professor of History, University of Utah, Salt Lake City*
INDUSTRY AND WAR; WAR: EFFECTS OF WAR ON THE ECONOMY

Kendrick A. Clements, *Professor of History, University of South Carolina, Columbia*
WILSON, WOODROW

J. Garry Clifford, *Professor of Political Science, University of Connecticut at Storrs*
DESTROYERS-FOR-BASES AGREEMENT (1940); HOPKINS, HARRY; LEND-LEASE ACT AND AGREEMENTS (1941); ROOSEVELT, FRANKLIN D.

Edward M. Coffman, *Professor of History Emeritus, University of Wisconsin, Madison*
MARCH, PEYTON C.

Jon T. Coleman, *PhD. candidate, American History, Yale University, New Haven, Connecticut*
AMHERST, JEFFREY; ARNOLD, BENEDICT; BACON'S REBELLION (1676); CLINTON, SIR HENRY; GAGE, THOMAS; GEORGE III;HOWE, SIR WILLIAM;JONES, JOHN PAUL

James L. Collins, Jr., *Brigadier General, U.S. Army (Ret), U.S. Commission on Military History, Washington, D.C.*
NORMANDY, INVASION OF (1944); ST. LÔ, BREAKOUT AT (1944)

Mary Ellen Condon-Rall, *Historian, Histories Branch, U.S. Army Center of Military History, Washington, D.C.*
DISEASE, TROPICAL

Owen Connelly, *McKissick Dial Professor of History, University of South Carolina, Columbia*
RANGERS, U.S. ARMY

John W. Coogan, *Associate Professor of History, Michigan State University, East Lansing*
NEUTRALITY; NEUTRALITY ACTS (1930s)

Blanche Wiesen Cook, *Distinguished Professor, Department of History, John Jay College of Criminal Justice, City University of New York*
EASTMAN, CRYSTAL

B. Franklin Cooling, *Professor of History, Industrial College of the Armed Forces; Research Director, U.S. Department of Energy, Washington, D.C.*
TRACY, BENJAMIN F.

Carolyn C. Cooper, *Research Affiliate in History of Technology, Economics Department, Yale University, New Haven, Connecticut*
WHITNEY, ELI

Jerry Cooper, *Professor of History, University of Missouri—St. Louis*
ARMY RESERVES AND NATIONAL GUARD; LOGAN, JOHN; MILITIA ACTS; MILITIA AND NATIONAL GUARD; POSSE COMITATUS ACT (1878)

William J. Cooper, *Boyd Professor of History, Louisiana State University, Baton Rouge*
DAVIS, JEFFERSON

Anthony H. Cordesman, *Senior Fellow for Strategic Assessment, Center for Strategic and International Studies; Professor of National Security Studies, Georgetown University, Washington, D.C.*
PERSIAN GULF WAR (1991)

David Cortright, *President, Fourth Freedom Forum, Goshen, Indiana; Research Fellow, Joan B. Kroc Institute for International Peace Studies, University of Notre Dame, Notre Dame, Indiana*
LA ROQUE, GENE

Graham A. Cosmas, *Chief, Histories Branch, U.S. Army Center of Military History, Washington, D.C.*
ARMY, U.S.: OVERVIEW; ARMY, U.S.: SINCE 1941; SANTIAGO, BATTLE OF (1898)

Edward Countryman, *Professor of History, Southern Methodist University, Dallas, Texas*
COLONIAL REBELLIONS AND ARMED CIVIL UNREST (1607–1775)

David L. Cowen, *Professor Emeritus of History, Rutgers University, New Brunswick, New Jersey*
DIX, DOROTHEA

Conrad C. Crane, *Professor of History, U.S. Military Academy, West Point, New York*
AIR FORCE, U.S.: SINCE 1947; WORLD WAR II, U.S. AIR OPERATIONS IN: THE AIR WAR AGAINST JAPAN

James Grant Crawford, *Instructor, Department of History, University of North Carolina at Chapel Hill*
AGUINALDO, EMILIO; ATROCITIES

Robin J. Crews, *Visiting Associate Professor of Peace Studies, Haverford College, Haverford, Pennsylvania*
PEACE

James E. Crisp, *Associate Professor of History, North Carolina State University, Raleigh*
GUADALUPE-HIDALGO, TREATY OF (1848)

Victor J. Croizat, *Colonel, U.S. Marine Corps (Ret), Santa Monica, California*
ELLIS, "PETE" EARL HANCOCK (co-author)

Tom D. Crouch, *Senior Curator, Aeronautics Department, National Air and Space Museum, Smithsonian Institution, Washington, D.C.*
WRIGHT, ORVILLE AND WILBUR

David Culbert, *Professor of History, Louisiana State University, Baton Rouge*
FILM, WAR AND THE MILITARY IN: NEWSFILMS AND DOCUMENTARIES; PROPAGANDA AND PUBLIC RELATIONS, GOVERNMENT; PSYCHOLOGICAL WARFARE

Thomas W. Cutrer, *Professor of American Studies, Arizona State University West, Phoenix*
CONFEDERATE ARMY

Boyd L. Dastrup, *Command Historian, U.S. Army Field Artillery Center and Fort Sill, Fort Sill, Oklahoma*
ARMY COMBAT BRANCHES: ARTILLERY; ARTILLERY

Cori Dauber, *Associate Professor of Communication Studies, University of North Carolina, Chapel Hill*
LANGUAGE, MILITARY: OFFICIAL TERMINOLOGY; LANGUAGE, MILITARY: INFORMAL SPEECH

Leo J. Daugherty III, *Undergraduate Chair of Military History, American Military University, Manassas Park, Virginia*
RANK AND HIERARCHY: MARINE CORPS

Calvin D. Davis, *Professor Emeritus of History, Duke University, Durham, North Carolina*
HAGUE PEACE CONFERENCES (1899, 1907)

Richard G. Davis, *Senior Historian, U.S. Air Force History Support Office, Washington, D.C.*
ARNOLD, "HAP" [H. H.]; DOOLITTLE, JAMES; LEMAY, CURTIS E.; SPAATZ, CARL A.; TWINING, NATHAN; VANDENBERG, HOYT; WORLD WAR II, U.S. AIR OPERATIONS IN: EUROPE

Joseph G. Dawson III, *Associate Professor of History and Director of the Military Studies Institute, Texas A & M University, College Station*
ARMY, U.S.: 1866–1899; MEXICAN WAR (1846–1848); SHERIDAN, PHILIP H.

Eric T. Dean, Jr., *Independent Scholar, New Haven, Connecticut*
MCCLELLAN, GEORGE B.

John Morgan Dederer, *Adjunct Professor, Housatonic Community Technical College, Bridgeport, Connecticut*
GREENE, NATHANAEL; GUILFORD COURTHOUSE, BATTLE OF (1781); SIDE ARMS, STANDARD INFANTRY

Carlo D'Este, *Lieutenant Colonel, U.S. Army (Ret), Mashpee, Massachusetts*
ITALY, INVASION AND CONQUEST OF (1943–45)

Ron Dick, *CB, FRAeS, RAF (Ret); Writer and Lecturer in Aviation and Military History, Woodbridge, Virginia*
BOMBER AIRCRAFT; BOMBS; WEAPONRY, AIR FORCE

Steve E. Dietrich, *Lieutenant Colonel, U.S. Army (Ret); Alumnus, U.S. Army Center of Military History, Washington, D.C.*
ARMY COMBAT BRANCHES: ARMOR

John M. Dobson, *Professor of History and Dean, Oklahoma State University, Stillwater*
MCKINLEY, WILLIAM

Saki Dockrill, *Senior Lecturer in History and War Studies, Department of War Studies, King's College, London, England*
TOJO, HIDEKI

Justus D. Doenecke, *Professor of American History, New College of the University of South Florida, Sarasota*
ISOLATIONISM; NYE, GERALD P.; WORLD WAR II (1939–1945): CHANGING INTERPRETATIONS

Michael D. Doubler, *Lieutenant Colonel, U.S. Army National Guard, Arlington, Virginia*
AIRBORNE WARFARE; FRANCE, LIBERATION OF (1944–45)

Robert A. Doughty, *Professor and Head, Department of History, U.S. Military Academy, West Point, New York*
TACTICS: LAND WARFARE TACTICS

Gregory Evans Dowd, *Associate Professor of History, University of Notre Dame, Notre Dame, Indiana*
PONTIAC; PONTIAC'S REBELLION (1763–1766)

George W. Downs, *Professor of Politics, New York University, New York*
ARMS RACE: OVERVIEW

Robert C. Doyle, *Historical Consultant, Joint SERE Agency (Ft. Belvoir, Virginia), Steubenville, Ohio*
PRISONERS OF WAR: U.S. SOLDIERS AS POWS; PRISONERS OF WAR: ENEMY POWS; PRISONERS OF WAR: THE POW EXPERIENCE

James D. Drake, *Assistant Professor of History, Metropolitan State College of Denver, Denver, Colorado*
BRANT, JOSEPH; LEWIS AND CLARK EXPEDITION (1804–1806); NATIVE AMERICAN WARS: WARFARE IN NATIVE AMERICAN SOCIETIES; NATIVE AMERICAN WARS: WARS AMONG NATIVE AMERICANS; NATIVE AMERICAN WARS: WARS BETWEEN NATIVE AMERICANS AND EUROPEANS AND EURO-AMERICANS

Edward J. Drea, *Historian, Fairfax, Virginia*
ULTRA

Sidney Drell, *Professor Emeritus of the Stanford Linear Accelerator Center; Hoover Fellow, Stanford University, Stanford, California*
NUCLEAR WEAPONS

John S. Duffield, *Assistant Professor of Political Science, University of Georgia, Athens*
LISBON AGREEMENT ON NATO FORCE LEVELS (1952)

Simon Duke, *Associate Professor, European Institute of Public Administration, Maastricht, Netherlands*
UNITED KINGDOM, U.S. MILITARY INVOLVEMENT IN THE

Russell Duncan, *Associate Professor of History, University of Copenhagen, Denmark*
FORT PILLOW, BATTLE OF (1864); FORT WAGNER, SIEGE OF (1863)

Charles J. Dunlap, Jr., *Colonel, U.S. Air Force; Staff Judge Advocate, U.S. Central Command Air Forces, Shaw Air Force Base, South Carolina*
ARMS, RIGHT TO BEAR

Paul M. Edwards, *Professor, Park College, Independence, Missouri*
RIDGWAY, MATTHEW B.

Keith E. Eiler, *Research Fellow, Hoover Institution on War, Revolution and Peace, Stanford University, Stanford, California*
WEDEMEYER, ALBERT C.

Arthur A. Ekirch, Jr., *Professor of History Emeritus, State University of New York, Albany*
MILITARISM AND ANTIMILITARISM

Trudie Eklund, *Military Historian (Ret), Dover, Delaware*
NATO

Jean Bethke Elshtain, *The Laura Spelman Rockefeller Professor of Social and Political Ethics, The Divinity School, University of Chicago, Chicago, Illinois*
ADDAMS, JANE

Cynthia Enloe, *Professor of Government, Clark University, Worcester, Massachusetts*
SCHROEDER, PATRICIA

Andrew P.N. Erdmann, *Department of History, Harvard University, Cambridge, Massachusetts*
VICTORY

*Jeffrey L. Ethell
INSIGNIA

Keith Eubank, *Professor of History Emeritus, Queens College, The City University of New York, Flushing*
YALTA CONFERENCE (1945)

David C. Evans, *Professor of History and Associate Dean, School of Arts and Sciences, University of Richmond, Richmond, Virginia*
YAMAMOTO, ISOROKU

Dana Eyre, *Assistant Professor, Department of National Security Affairs, Naval Postgraduate School, Monterey, California*
LOBBIES, MILITARY; PEACEKEEPING

Luther Faggart, *Ph.D. candidate, Department of History, University of South Carolina, Columbia*
RIVERS, L. MENDEL

Richard Falkenrath, *Assistant Professor of Public Policy, John F. Kennedy School of Government, Harvard University, Cambridge, Massachusetts*
CFE TREATY (1990)

Mary J. Farmer, *Instructor and Ph.D. candidate in History, Bowling Green State University, Bowling Green, Ohio*
HABEAS CORPUS ACT (1863); MERRYMAN, EX PARTE (1861); MILLIGAN, EX PARTE (1866)

*Byron Farwell, *Author, Fellow of the Royal Society of Literature, Hillsboro, Virginia*
JACKSON, "STONEWALL" [THOMAS]

Elizabeth Faue, *Associate Professor of History, Wayne State University, Detroit, Michigan*
LABOR AND WAR; VETERANS OF FOREIGN WARS

Michael Fellman, *Professor of History, Simon Fraser University, Vancouver, British Columbia, Canada*
SHERMAN'S MARCH TO THE SEA (1864–1865)

John Ferling, *Professor of History, State University of West Georgia, Carrollton*
ADAMS, JOHN; CHURCH, BENJAMIN

Robert H. Ferrell, *Professor of History Emeritus, Indiana University, Bloomington*
WORLD WAR I (1914–1918): CHANGING INTERPRETATIONS

Ernest F. Fisher, *Colonel, U.S. Army (Ret), Arlington, Virginia*
BULGE, BATTLE OF THE (1944–45)

Louis Fisher, *Senior Specialist in Separation of Powers, Congressional Research Service, Library of Congress, Washington, D.C.*
CONSTITUTIONAL AND POLITICAL BASIS OF WAR AND THE MILITARY

Michael S. Fitzgerald, *Associate Professor of History, Pikeville College, Pikeville, Kentucky*
ADAMS-ONÍS TREATY (1819)

Roy K. Flint, *Brigadier General, U.S. Army (Ret), Valle Crucis, North Carolina*
KOREAN WAR (1950–1953)

David S. Foglesong, *Associate Professor of History, Rutgers University, New Brunswick, New Jersey*
RUSSIA, U.S. MILITARY INTERVENTION IN, 1917–20

Carrie Foster, *Associate Professor of History, Miami University, Hamilton, Ohio*
WOMEN'S INTERNATIONAL LEAGUE FOR PEACE AND FREEDOM

Gaines M. Foster, *Associate Professor of History, Louisiana State University, Baton Rouge*
DEFEAT

William Fowler, Jr., *Director, Massachusetts Historical Society, Boston*
CONTINENTAL NAVY

Andrew K. Frank, *Assistant Professor of History, California State University, Los Angeles*
REGIONALISM AND THE MILITARY

Benis M. Frank, *Retired Chief Historian of the Marine Corps, Marine Corps Historical Center, Washington, D.C.*
IWO JIMA, BATTLE OF (1945); SPECIAL OPERATIONS FORCES: MARINE SPECIAL UNITS; TARAWA, BATTLE OF (1943)

Richard B. Frank, *Independent Historian, Washington, D.C.*
GUADALCANAL, BATTLE OF (1942–1943)

Louis D. F. Frasché, *Colonel, U.S. Army (Ret), Leavenworth, Kansas*
MARION, FRANCIS

Raymond H. Fredette, *Lieutenant Colonel, U.S. Air Force (Ret), Alexandria, Virginia*
LINDBERGH, CHARLES

Lawrence Freedman, *Professor of War Studies, King's College, University of London, London, England*
ARMS RACE: NUCLEAR ARMS RACE; UNITED KINGDOM

Christopher R. Gabel, *Historian, Combat Studies Institute, U.S. Army Command and General Staff College, Fort Leavenworth, Kansas*
TANK DESTROYERS

Marc Gallicchio, *Associate Professor of History, Villanova University, Villanova, Pennsylvania*
CHINA, U.S. MILITARY INVOLVEMENT IN

J. Matthew Gallman, *Henry R. Luce Professor of the Civil War Era, Departments of History and Interdepartmental Studies, Gettysburg College, Gettysburg, Pennsylvania*
CIVIL WAR (1861–1865): DOMESTIC COURSE; SANITARY COMMISSION, U.S. (1861–65)

Larry Gara, *Professor of History Emeritus, Wilmington College, Wilmington, Ohio*
WAR RESISTERS LEAGUE

Albert N. Garland, *Lieutenant Colonel Infantry, U.S. Army (Ret), Columbus, Georgia*
ARMY COMBAT BRANCHES: INFANTRY

Dee Garrison, *Professor of History, Rutgers University, New Brunswick, New Jersey*
CIVIL DEFENSE

Raymond L. Garthoff, *Senior Fellow, Retired, The Brookings Institution; Ambassador of the United States (Ret), Washington, D.C.*
RUSSIA, U.S. MILITARY INVOLVEMENT IN, 1921–95; SALT TREATIES (1972; 1979); STALIN, JOSEF; START

Norman Gelb
NORTH AFRICA CAMPAIGN (1942–1943); SICILY, INVASION OF (1943)

Louis S. Gerteis, *Professor of History, University of Missouri, St. Louis*
EMANCIPATION PROCLAMATION (1863)

Jeffrey G. Giauque, *Visiting Assistant Professor of 20th Century European History and International Studies, Miami University, Oxford, Ohio*
FRANCO-AMERICAN ALLIANCE (1778–1800)

Patrick F. Gilbo, *Chief Historian, American Red Cross, Washington, D.C.*
RED CROSS, AMERICAN

Mary C. Gillett, *Historian (Ret), U.S. Army Center of Military History, Washington, D.C.*
REED, WALTER

Robert L. Goldich, *Specialist in National Defense, Congressional Research Service, Library of Congress, Washington, D.C.*
GOLDWATER-NICHOLS ACT (1986); NAVAL RESERVE

Emily O. Goldman, *Associate Professor of Political Science and Director of International Relations, University of California at Davis*
ARMS CONTROL AND DISARMAMENT: NONNUCLEAR

Donald M. Goldstein, *Professor of Public and International Affairs, Graduate School of Public and International Affairs, University of Pittsburgh, Pittsburgh, Pennsylvania*
PEARL HARBOR, ATTACK ON (1941)

RitaVictoria Gomez, *Assistant Professor, Anne Arundel Community College, Arnold, Maryland*
HOBBY, OVETA CULP

Allan E. Goodman, *President and CEO, Institute of International Education, New York, New York*
GENEVA AGREEMENT ON INDOCHINA (1954); PARIS PEACE AGREEMENT (1973)

James Gormly, *Professor of History, Washington and Jefferson College, Washington, Pennsylvania*
POTSDAM CONFERENCE (1945)

Van Gosse, *Co-Chair, Radical History Review, Alexandria,Virginia*
EL SALVADOR, U.S. MILITARY INVOLVEMENT IN

Lewis L. Gould, *Eugene C. Barker Centennial Professor Emeritus, University of Texas, Austin*
PARIS, TREATY OF (1783); PARIS, TREATY OF (1898)

Norman A. Graebner, *Randolph P. Compton Professor of History and Public Affairs, Emeritus, University of Virginia at Charlottesville*
EXPANSIONISM; INTERNATIONALISM

J. L. Granatstein, *Director and CEO, Canadian War Museum, Ottawa, Ontario, Canada*
CANADA, U.S. MILITARY INVOLVEMENT IN

Mark R. Grandstaff, *Associate Professor of History, Brigham Young University, Provo, Utah*
CAREERS IN THE MILITARY; RANK AND HIERARCHY: AIR FORCE

Steven C. Gravlin, *Lieutenant Colonel, U.S. Army; Formerly Assistant Professor of History, United States Military Academy, West Point, New York*
ACADEMIES, SERVICE: U.S. MILITARY ACADEMY; LUCE, STEPHEN B.; MAINE, SINKING OF THE USS (1898)

John Robert Greene, *Distinguished Professor of History and Communication, Cazenovia College, Cazenovia, New York*
FORD, GERALD

Mark Grimsley, *Associate Professor of History, Ohio State University, Columbus*
ENEMY, VIEWS OF THE; PETERSBURG, SIEGE OF (1864); UNION ARMY

Alan L. Gropman, *Chair, Department of Grand Strategy and Mobilization, Industrial College of the Armed Forces, National Defense University, Fort McNair, Washington, D.C.*
AIR FORCE, U.S.: OVERVIEW

Charles J. Gross, *Chief, Air National Guard History, Historical Services Division, National Guard Bureau, Washington, D.C.*
AIR NATIONAL GUARD; ARMED FORCES RESERVE ACT (1952); RESERVE FORCES ACT (1955)

Dave Grossman, *Lieutenant Colonel, U.S. Army (Ret); Author, Jonesboro, Arkansas*
AGGRESSION AND VIOLENCE

Michael L. Grumelli, *Professor of War Theory and Military History, Air Command and Staff College, Montgomery, Alabama*
DOUHET, GIULIO; MITCHELL, BILLY [WILLIAM]

Allen C. Guelzo, *Dean, The Templeton Honors College, Eastern College, St. Davids, Pennsylvania*
CIVIL WAR (1861–1865): CHANGING INTERPRETATIONS

John F. Guilmartin, Jr., *Associate Professor of History, Ohio State University, Columbus*
AIR WARFARE; STRATEGY: AIR WARFARE STRATEGY

Kurt Henry Hackemer, *Assistant Professor of History, University of South Dakota, Vermillion, South Dakota*
RODMAN, THOMAS JACKSON

Barton C. Hacker, *Curator, Armed Forces History, Smithsonian Institution, Washington, D.C.*
LASERS; NATIONAL LABORATORIES; TOXIC AGENTS: ATOMIC RADIATION EXPOSURE

R. Cargill Hall, *Chief Historian, National Reconnaissance Office, Chantilly, Virginia*
SATELLITES, RECONNAISSANCE; SPACE PROGRAM, MILITARY INVOLVEMENT IN THE

Richard P. Hallion, *Air Force Historian, Bolling Air Force Base, Washington, D.C.*
AWACS AND E-3s; FIGHTER AIRCRAFT; STEALTH AIRCRAFT

Kenneth E. Hamburger, *Colonel, U.S. Army (Ret), Bellvale, New York*
KOREAN WAR, U.S. AIR OPERATIONS IN THE; OPERATIONAL ART

Paul Y. Hammond, *Distinguished Service Professor of Public and International Affairs, University of Pittsburgh, Pittsburgh, Pennsylvania*
STATE, THE

William M. Hammond, *Historian, Histories Division, U.S. Army Center of Military History, Washington, D.C.*
PENTAGON PAPERS (1971)

Joseph P. Harahan, *Public Historian, U.S. Department of Defense, Washington, D.C.*
ON-SITE INSPECTION AGENCY

Herbert M. Hart, *Colonel, U.S. Marine Corps (Ret); Executive Director, Council on America's Military Past, Fort Myer, Virginia*
BATTLEFIELDS, ENCAMPMENTS, AND FORTS AS PUBLIC SITES

John M. Hart, *Professor of History, University of Houston, Houston, Texas*
DONIPHAN, ALEXANDER; KEARNY, STEPHEN WATTS; MEXICAN REVOLUTION, U.S. MILITARY INVOLVEMENT IN THE; SCOTT, WINFIELD; TAYLOR, ZACHARY

Tom Hatley, *Director, Southern Appalachian Forest Coalition, Asheville, North Carolina*
CHEROKEE WAR (1759–1761)

Herman Hattaway, *Professor of History, University of Missouri at Kansas City, Kansas City, Missouri*
CIVIL WAR (1861–1865): MILITARY AND DIPLOMATIC COURSE (co-author)

Richard F. Haynes, *Professor of American History and Department Head, Department of History and Government, Monroe, Louisiana*
TRUMAN, HARRY S.

William Head, *Chief, Office of History, Warner Robins Air Logistics Center, U.S. Air Force, Robins Air Force Base, Georgia*
HIROSHIMA AND NAGASAKI, BOMBINGS OF (1945)

William Darryl Henderson, *Owner, Henco LLC; Colonel, U.S. Army (Ret), Saratoga, California*
FRAGGING

James A. Henretta, *Priscilla Alden Burke Professor of History, University of Maryland, College Park*
REVOLUTIONARY WAR (1775–1783): DOMESTIC COURSE

Jan Herman, *Historian, Navy Medical Department, Navy Bureau of Medicine and Surgery, Washington, D.C.*
NURSE CORPS, ARMY AND NAVY (co-author)

Earl J. Hess, *Associate Professor of History, Lincoln Memorial University, Cumberland Gap, Tennessee*
PEA RIDGE, BATTLE OF (1862); STONES RIVER, BATTLE OF (1862–1863)

Lawrence Lee Hewitt, *Professor of History, Southeastern Louisiana University (Ret), Chicago, Illinois*
NEW ORLEANS, SIEGE OF (1862); VICKSBURG, SIEGE OF (1862–1863)

Donald R. Hickey, *Professor of History, Wayne State College, Wayne, Nebraska*
DECATUR, STEPHEN; JACKSON, ANDREW; PERRY, OLIVER HAZARD

Don Higginbotham, *Dowd Professor of History, University of North Carolina, Chapel Hill*
ARMY, U.S.: COLONIAL AND REVOLUTIONARY ERAS; MORGAN, DANIEL; WASHINGTON, GEORGE

Robin Higham, *Professor of Military History Emeritus, Kansas State University, Manhattan*
BERLIN AIRLIFT (1948–1949)

Margaret Higonnet, *Professor of English and Comparative Literature, University of Connecticut at Storrs*
DISCIPLINARY VIEWS OF WAR: FEMINIST AND GENDER STUDIES

Trenton E. Hizer, *Local Archivist, Library of Virginia, Richmond*
CALHOUN, JOHN C.

Godfrey Hodgson, *Director, Reuter Foundation Programme, University of Oxford, Oxford, England*
STIMSON, HENRY L.

Jon T. Hoffman, *Lieutenant Colonel, U.S. Marine Corps Reserve, Durham, North Carolina*
MARINE CORPS, U.S.: 1914–1945

David W. Hogan, Jr., *Historian, Histories Division, U.S. Army Center of Military History, Washington, D.C.*
CHINA-BURMA-INDIA THEATER (1941–45)

I. B. Holley, Jr., *Major General, U.S. Air Force (Ret); Professor of History Emeritus, Duke University, Durham, North Carolina*
PALMER, JOHN MCAULEY

Tom Holm, *Professor of American Indian Studies, University of Arizona, Tucson*
INDIAN TREATIES AND CONGRESSES; NATIVE AMERICANS, U.S. MILITARY RELATIONS WITH

Kevin C. Holzimmer, *Temple University, Philadelphia, Pennsylvania, Ph.D. in American History, 1999*
NEW GUINEA CAMPAIGN (1942–44)

Gregory Hooks, *Associate Professor of Sociology, Washington State University, Pullman*
AGRICULTURE AND WAR

Townsend Hoopes, *Distinguished International Executive School of Public Affairs, University of Maryland, College Park*
FORRESTAL, JAMES V.

Sir Michael Howard, *Robert A. Lovett Professor Emeritus of Military and Naval History, Yale University, New Haven, Connecticut*
DISCIPLINARY VIEWS OF WAR: MILITARY HISTORY

Charles F. Howlett, *Social Studies Department, Amityville Memorial High School, Amityville, New York*
DISCIPLINARY VIEWS OF WAR: PEACE HISTORY; FELLOWSHIP OF RECONCILIATION

John T. Hubbell, *Director, The Kent State University Press, Kent, Ohio*
LINCOLN, ABRAHAM

Wayne P. Hughes, Jr., *Captain, U.S. Navy (Ret); Professor of Operations Research, Naval Postgraduate School, Monterey, California*
TACTICS: NAVAL WARFARE TACTICS

Richard A. Hunt, *Senior Historian, United States Army Center of Military History, Washington, D.C.*
BUNKER, ELLSWORTH

Wallace S. Hutcheon, Jr., *Commander, U.S.N.R. (Ret); Professor of History, Northern Virginia Community College, Annandale*
FULTON, ROBERT

Joseph E. Illick, *Professor of History, San Francisco State University, San Francisco, California*
PENN, WILLIAM

Richard H. Immerman, *Professor of History, Temple University, Philadelphia, Pennsylvania*
DULLES, ALLEN WELSH; DULLES, JOHN FOSTER

Lorna S. Jaffe, *Historian, Joint History Office, Office of the Chairman of the Joint Chiefs of Staff, Washington, D.C.*
POWELL, COLIN

Perry D. Jamieson, *Historian, Analysis Team, Air Force History Support Office, Bolling Air Force Base, Washington, D.C.*
FORT SUMTER, CAPTURE OF (1861)

Reese V. Jenkins, *Professor of History, Rutgers University, New Brunswick, New Jersey*
EDISON, THOMAS ALVA

James Turner Johnson, *Professor of Religion, Rutgers University, New Brunswick, New Jersey*
BOMBING, ETHICS OF; JUST WAR THEORY

Manfred Jonas, *John Bigelow Professor of History Emeritus, Union College, Schenectady, New York*
CONANT, JAMES B.; GERMANY, U.S. MILITARY INVOLVEMENT IN; SEWARD, WILLIAM H.

Archer Jones, *Professor Emeritus of History, North Dakota State University, Fargo*
JOMINI, ANTOINE-HENRI

Howard Jones, *Chairman and University Research Professor, Department of History, University of Alabama, Tuscaloosa*
TRUMAN DOCTRINE (1947)

Ervin L. Jordan, Jr., *Associate Professor and Curator of Technical Services, Civil War Historian, Special Collections Department, University of Virginia Library, Charlottesville*
EWELL, RICHARD STODDERT; GORGAS, WILLIAM C.; HILL, A. P.

James C. Juhnke, *Professor of History, Bethany College, North Newton, Kansas*
PACIFISM

Kenneth C. Kan, *Historian, Headquarters Air Force Reserve Command, Robins Air Force Base, Georgia*
AIR FORCE RESERVE

Zachary Karabell, *Research Associate, Miller Center, University of Virginia, Charlottesville*
COLD WAR (1945–1991): EXTERNAL COURSE

Efraim Karsh, *Professor of Mediterranean Studies and Head, Mediterranean Studies Programme, King's College, London, England*
HUSSEIN, SADDAM

Peter Karsten, *Professor of History, University of Pittsburgh, Pittsburgh, Pennsylvania*
CULTURE, WAR, AND THE MILITARY

Milton S. Katz, *Professor of Humanities, Chair of the Liberal Arts Department, Kansas City Art Institute, Kansas City, Missouri*
NATIONAL COMMITTEE FOR A SANE NUCLEAR POLICY

Robert Gordon Kaufman, *Associate Professor of Political Science, University of Vermont, Burlington*
WASHINGTON NAVAL ARMS LIMITATION TREATY (1922)

John Keegan, *Author, Historian; Defense Editor of the London Daily Telegraph; Formerly Senior Lecturer at the Royal Military Academy at Sandhurst, England*
COMBAT, CHANGING EXPERIENCE OF

Jennifer D. Keene, *Assistant Professor of History, University of Redlands, Redlands, California*
ARMED SERVICES LOBBYING ASSOCIATIONS; LEAVES AND FURLOUGHS; NAVAL MILITIA

Charles W. Kegley, Jr., *Pearce Professor of International Relations, University of South Carolina, Columbia*
FOREIGN POLICY

Kathleen F. Kellner, *Assistant Professor of History, Kent State University, Kent, Ohio*
LEMNITZER, LYMAN

Edward Keynes, *Professor of Political Science, Pennsylvania State University, University Park*
CURTISS-WRIGHT, UNITED STATES V. (1936); SUPREME COURT, WAR, AND THE MILITARY

Irving H. King, *Professor of History, U.S. Coast Guard Academy, New London, Connecticut*
ACADEMIES, SERVICE: U.S. COAST GUARD ACADEMY

Cole C. Kingseed, *Professor of History, U.S. Military Academy, West Point, New York*
EISENHOWER DOCTRINE (1957)

Douglas Kinnard, *Emeritus Professor of Political Science, University of Vermont; Brigadier General, U.S. Army (Ret), Alexandria, Virginia*
TAYLOR, MAXWELL

Faris R. Kirkland, *Historian, Bryn Mawr, Pennsylvania*
PSYCHIATRY, MILITARY; SUBSTANCE ABUSE; VETERANS: VIETNAM WAR

Michael T. Klare, *Professor, Five College Program in Peace and World Security Studies, Hampshire College, Amherst, Massachusetts*
ARMS TRANSFERS

George Knapp, *Major, U.S. Army (Ret), Leavenworth, Kansas*
FLAMETHROWERS

Thomas J. Knock, *Associate Professor of History, Southern Methodist University, Dallas, Texas*
FOURTEEN POINTS (1918); LEAGUE OF NATIONS (1919–46); VERSAILLES, TREATY OF (1919)

Abigail A. Kohn, *Ph.D. candidate, Medical Anthropology Program, University of California, San Francisco*
PARAMILITARY GROUPS

Richard H. Kohn, *Chair, Curriculum in Peace, War and Defense, and Professor of History, University of North Carolina, Chapel Hill*
CIVIL-MILITARY RELATIONS: CIVILIAN CONTROL OF THE MILITARY

Paul A. C. Koistinen, *Professor of History, California State University, Northridge*
WILSON, CHARLES E.

Lawrence Korb, *Director of Studies, Council on Foreign Relations, New York, New York*
BROWN, GEORGE; LIMITED WAR, JOINT CHIEFS OF STAFF AND

Daniel T. Kuehl, *Lieutenant Colonel, U.S. Air Force (Ret);*
Professor of Military History and Strategy, National Defense
University, Fort McNair, Washington, D.C.
RADAR

James Kurth, *Claude C. Smith Professor of Political Science,*
Swarthmore College, Swarthmore, Pennsylvania
MILITARY-INDUSTRIAL COMPLEX; RIVALRY,
INTERSERVICE

Paul D. Lack, *Vice President for Academic Affairs, McMurry*
University, Abilene, Texas
SAN JACINTO, BATTLE OF (1836); SANTA ANNA,
ANTONIO LOPEZ DE; TEXAS WAR OF INDEPENDENCE
(1836)

William Lanouette, *Writer, Public Policy Analyst, Washington,*
D.C.
SZILARD, LEO

Stephen S. Large, *Reader in Modern Japanese History, University*
of Cambridge, Cambridge, England
HIROHITO

Roger D. Launius, *Chief Historian, National Aeronautics and*
Space Administration (NASA), Washington, D.C.
AIR AND SPACE DEFENSE

William M. Leary, *E. Merton Coulter Professor of History,*
University of Georgia, Athens
COVERT OPERATIONS

Richard Ned Lebow, *Director, Mershon Center; Professor of*
Political Science, History, and Psychology, The Ohio State
University, Columbus
NATIONAL SECURITY IN THE NUCLEAR AGE

Russell E. Lee, *Curator, Aeronautics, National Air and Space*
Museum, Washington, D.C.
SEVERSKY, ALEXANDER DE

John Lehman, *Former Secretary of the Navy, New York,*
New York
NAVY, U.S.: SINCE 1946; SEA WARFARE

Stuart Leibiger, *Assistant Professor of History, La Salle University,*
Philadelphia, Pennsylvania
HAMILTON, ALEXANDER; LEE, CHARLES; LEE, HENRY;
MADISON, JAMES

David Levering Lewis, *Martin Luther King, Jr., University*
Professor in the Department of History, Rutgers University, New
Brunswick, New Jersey
DU BOIS, W. E. B.

Guenter Lewy
MY LAI MASSACRE (1968)

Lawrence W. Lichty, *Professor, Department of Radio/Television/*
Film, Northwestern University, Evanston, Illinois
WESTMORELAND V. CBS (1985)

Roy Licklider, *Professor of Political Science, Rutgers University,*
New Brunswick, New Jersey
SOMALIA, U.S. MILITARY INVOLVEMENT IN

James M. Lindsay, *Professor of Political Science, University of*
Iowa, Iowa City
CONGRESS, WAR, AND THE MILITARY

Edward T. Linenthal, *Professor of Religion and American*
Culture, University of Wisconsin, Oshkosh
REENACTMENTS, MILITARY

Brian M. Linn, *Professor of History, Texas A & M University,*
College Station
PHILIPPINE WAR (1899–1902)

Douglas Little, *Professor of History, Clark University, Worcester,*
Massachusetts
CAMP DAVID ACCORDS (1978); MIDDLE EAST, U.S.
MILITARY INVOLVEMENT IN THE

Greg Lockhart, *Writer and Historian, Sydney, Australia*
GIAP, VO NGUYEN; HO CHI MINH

James W. Loewen, *Sociologist; Author, Lies My Teacher Told*
Me: Everything Your American History Textbook Got Wrong,
Washington, D.C.
TEXTBOOKS, WAR AND THE MILITARY IN

Timothy J. Lomperis, *Professor and Chair, Department of*
Political Science, St. Louis University, St. Louis, Missouri
ABRAMS, CREIGHTON

F. M. Lorenz, *Colonel, U.S. Marines; Professor of Political Science,*
Industrial College of the Armed Forces, Washington, D.C.
RULES OF ENGAGEMENT

Christopher Losson, *Adjunct Professor of History, Missouri*
Western State College, St. Joseph
PERRYVILLE, BATTLE OF (1862); SHILOH, BATTLE OF
(1862)

Pedro Loureiro, *Curator, Pacific Basin Institute, Pomona College,*
Claremont, California
MAGIC

Mark M. Lowenthal, *President, Open Source Solutions, U.S.A.,*
Arlington, Virginia
DEFENSE INTELLIGENCE AGENCY; INTELLIGENCE,
MILITARY AND POLITICAL; NATIONAL SECURITY ACT
(1947); NATIONAL SECURITY AGENCY

Philip Karl Lundeberg, *Curator Emeritus, Armed Forces History*
Collections, National Museum of American History, Smithsonian
Institution, Washington, D.C.
HOLLAND, JOHN; MUSEUMS, MILITARY HISTORY;
TORPEDO BOATS

John B. Lundstrom, *Curator of American and Military History,*
Milwaukee Public Museum, Milwaukee, Wisconsin
CORAL SEA, BATTLE OF THE (1942)

Jonathan Lurie, *Professor of History, Rutgers University, Newark,*
New Jersey; Historian, United States Court of Appeals for the
Armed Forces, Washington, D.C.
INTERNMENT OF ENEMY ALIENS; JUSTICE, MILITARY:
UNIFORM CODE OF MILITARY JUSTICE

Edward N. Luttwak, *Senior Fellow, Former Holder of Arleigh*
Burke Chair in Strategy, Center for Strategic and International
Studies, Washington, D.C.
STRATEGY: HISTORICAL DEVELOPMENT

Michael A. Lutzker, *Associate Professor of History, New York*
University, New York
CARNEGIE ENDOWMENT FOR INTERNATIONAL PEACE

Mark H. Lytle, *Professor of History, Bard College, Annandale,*
New York
IRAN, U.S. MILITARY INVOLVEMENT IN

David MacIsaac, *Lieutenant Colonel, U.S. Air Force (Ret.),*
Montgomery, Alabama; member History Department, U.S. Air
Force Academy, 1964–78
STRATEGY: NUCLEAR WARFARE STRATEGY AND WAR
PLANS

John K. Mahon, *Professor of History, Emeritus, University of Florida, Gainesville*
SEMINOLE WARS (1818; 1835–1842; 1855–1858)

Patrick M. Malone, *Associate Professor of American Civilization and Urban Studies, Brown University, Providence, Rhode Island*
KING PHILIP'S WAR (1675–1677); PHILIP

Robert Mann, *Baton Rouge, Louisiana*
RUSSELL, RICHARD

Norman Markowitz, *Associate Professor of History, Rutgers University, New Brunswick, New Jersey*
DEBS, EUGENE V.

Frederick W. Marks III, *Essayist and Historian, Forest Hills, New York*
ROOSEVELT COROLLARY TO THE MONROE DOCTRINE (1928)

Ann Markusen, *Director, Project on Regional and Industrial Economics, and Professor, Rutgers, University, New Brunswick, New Jersey*
PROCUREMENT: AEROSPACE;
INDUSTRYPROCUREMENT: INFLUENCE ON INDUSTRY

Edward J. Marolda, *Senior Historian, Naval Historical Center, Washington, D.C.*
PUEBLO INCIDENT (1968); VIETNAM WAR, U.S. NAVAL OPERATIONS IN THE

John F. Marszalek, *William L. Giles Distinguished Professor of History, Mississippi State University, Mississippi State*
HOOKER, JOSEPH; SHERMAN, WILLIAM TECUMSEH

Jerome V. Martin, *Lieutenant Colonel, U.S.Air Force (Ret); Vice President for Academic Affairs, Peru State College, Peru, Nebraska*
AIR FORCE COMBAT ORGANIZATIONS: TACTICAL AIR FORCES

Richard Martin, *Curator, Costume Institute, The Metropolitan Museum of Art, New York, New York*
FASHION, MILITARY INFLUENCES ON

Lloyd J. Matthews, *Colonel, U.S. Army (Ret) and Editor (Ret), Parameters: Journal of U.S. Army War College, Carlisle, Pennsylvania*
IDEALS, MILITARY

Holly A. Mayer, *Associate Professor of History, Duquesne University, Pittsburgh, Pennsylvania*
"CAMP FOLLOWERS"; PITCHER, MOLLY

William M. McBride, *Associate Professor of History, United States Naval Academy, Annapolis, Maryland*
DESTROYERS AND DESTROYER ESCORTS

James M. McCaffrey, *Associate Professor of History, University of Houston—Downtown, Houston, Texas*
ALAMO, BATTLE OF THE (1836); BROWNING AUTOMATIC RIFLE; BUENA VISTA, BATTLE OF (1847); CHAPULTEPEC, BATTLE OF, AND CAPTURE OF MEXICO CITY (1847)

Stuart McConnell, *Professor of History, Pitzer College, Claremont, California*
GRAND ARMY OF THE REPUBLIC; VETERANS: OVERVIEW; VETERANS: CIVIL WAR

Stephen McFarland, *Professor of History and Associate Dean of the Graduate School, Auburn University, Auburn, Alabama*
AIR FORCE COMBAT ORGANIZATIONS: STRATEGIC AIR FORCES

Robert J. McMahon, *Professor of History, University of Florida, Gainesville*
VIETNAM WAR (1960–1975): CHANGING INTERPRETATIONS

Thomas L. McNaugher, *Deputy Director, RAND Arroyo Center, Washington, D.C.*
PROCUREMENT: OVERVIEW

James C. McNaughton, *Command Historian, Defense Language Institute Foreign Language Center, Presidio of Monterey, California*
SPECIAL OPERATIONS FORCES: AIR FORCE SPECIAL FORCES

Patricia McNeal, *Associate Professor, Director of Women's Studies, Indiana University South Bend, Indiana*
BERRIGAN, DANIEL AND PHILIP; PAX CHRISTI USA

William H. McNeill, *Professor of History, Emeritus, University of Chicago, Chicago, Illinois*
DEMOGRAPHY AND WAR

Peter J. McNelis, *Organizational and Program Development Consultant; Colonel, U.S. Army (Ret); Director/Professor, Military Family Institute, Boothbay Harbor, Maine*
BASES, MILITARY: LIFE ON; BOHR, NIELS; FERMI, ENRICO; OPPENHEIMER, J. ROBERT

James M. McPherson, *George Henry Davis '86 Professor of American History, Princeton University, Princeton New Jersey*
ANTIETAM, BATTLE OF (1862)

Alexander Medlicott, Jr., *Retired Professor of English; Institute for Lifelong Education at Dartmouth College, Hanover, New Hampshire*
LITERATURE, WAR AND THE MILITARY IN

Stanley Meisler, *Writer, Bethesda, Maryland*
UNITED NATIONS (EST. 1945)

Richard B. Meixsel, *Assistant Professor of History, James Madison University, Harrisonburg, Virginia*
PHILIPPINES, LIBERATION OF THE (1944–45); PHILIPPINE SCOUTS AND CONSTABULARY

David Mendeloff, *Department of Political Science, Massachusetts Institute of Technology, Cambridge*
WAR: CAUSES OF WAR (co-author)

Leisa D. Meyer, *Associate Professor of History, Director of Women's Studies, The College of William and Mary, Williamsburg, Virginia*
GENDER AND WAR

David E. Michlovitz, *U.S. Media/Public Relations Manager, Jane's Information Group, Alexandria, Virginia*
PRECISION-GUIDED MUNITIONS; SONAR

Laura L. Miller, *Assistant Professor of Sociology, University of California, Los Angeles*
SEXUAL HARASSMENT

Stuart Creighton Miller, *Professor of Social Science and History Emeritus, San Francisco State University, Mill Valley, California*
PHILIPPINES, U.S. MILITARY INVOLVEMENT IN THE

Allan R. Millett, *General Raymond E. Mason, Jr. Professor of Military History, The Ohio State University, Columbus, Ohio*
COMBAT EFFECTIVENESS; CUBA, U.S. MILITARY INVOLVEMENT IN; LEJEUNE, JOHN A.; MARINE CORPS, U.S.: OVERVIEW; MARINE CORPS RESERVE

David A. Mindell, *Frances and David Dibner Assistant Professor of the History of Engineering and Manufacturing Program in Science, Technology, and Society, Massachusetts Institute of Technology, Cambridge*
DETECTION, OBSERVATION, AND FIRE CONTROL SYSTEMS; PROCUREMENT: GOVERNMENT ARSENALS

Max M. Mintz, *Professor of History, Southern Connecticut State University, New Haven*
BURGOYNE, JOHN; GATES, HORATIO; SARATOGA, BATTLES OF (1777)

Thomas J. Misa, *Associate Professor of History, Illinois Institute of Technology, Chicago*
PROCUREMENT: STEEL AND ARMOR PLATE INDUSTRY (1865–1918)

Wilson D. Miscamble, *Associate Professor of History, University of Notre Dame, Notre Dame, Indiana*
KENNAN, GEORGE F.

Vance O. Mitchell, *Senior Historian, East Inc., Chantilly, Virginia*
U-2 INCIDENT (1960); U-2 SPY PLANES

Gregory L. Mixon, *Assistant Professor of History, University of North Carolina, Charlotte*
YOUNG, CHARLES

Edwin E. Moise, *Professor of History, Clemson University, Clemson, South Carolina*
GULF OF TONKIN INCIDENTS (1964)

John Ellis van Courtland Moon, *Professor Emeritus of History, Fitchburg State College, Fitchburg, Massachusetts*
CHEMICAL AND BIOLOGICAL WEAPONS AND WARFARE

Constance J. Moore, *ANC Historian, U.S. Army Center of Military History, Washington, D.C.*
NURSE CORPS, ARMY AND NAVY (co-author)

Daniel Moran, *Professor, National Security Affairs, Naval Postgraduate School, Monterey, California*
ARMS RACE: NAVAL ARMS RACE; CLAUSEWITZ, CARL VON; GUERRE DE COURSE; NAVAL GUNS; THEORISTS OF WAR

Bettie J. Morden , *Colonel, U.S. Army (Ret), Arlington, Virginia*
WAC

George J. Mordica II, *Major, U.S. Army (Ret); Combat Operations Analyst, Center for Army Lessons Learned, Fort Leavenworth, Kansas*
TANKS

Madeline H. Morris, *Professor of Law, Duke University School of Law, Durham, North Carolina*
RAPE BY MILITARY PERSONNEL

James L. Morrison Jr., *Professor of History Emeritus, York College of Pennsylvania; Colonel, U.S. Army (Ret), Luray, Virginia*
THAYER, SYLVANUS

John Morrow, *Franklin Professor of History, University of Georgia, Athens*
WORLD WAR I, U.S. AIR OPERATIONS IN

Paul J. Morton, *Associate Professor of History, Covenant College, Lookout Mountain, Georgia*
BLEEDING KANSAS (1854–1858)

Charles Moskos, *Professor of Sociology, Northwestern University, Evanston, Illinois*
NATIONAL SERVICE

John Mueller, *Professor of Political Science, University of Rochester, Rochester, New York*
PUBLIC OPINION, WAR, AND THE MILITARY

Elizabeth Muenger
ACADEMIES, SERVICE: U.S. AIR FORCE ACADEMY

Malcolm Muir, Jr., *Chair, Department of History and Philosophy, and Professor of History, Austin Peay State University, Clarksville, Tennessee*
BATTLESHIPS; CRUISERS; LEYTE GULF, BATTLE OF (1944); NAVY, U.S.: 1866–1898; NAVY, U.S.: 1899–1945; NAVY COMBAT BRANCHES: SURFACE FORCES; TORPEDOES

Justin D. Murphy, *Director, Douglas MacArthur Academy of Freedom Honors Program, Howard Payne University, Brownwood, Texas*
RANKIN, JEANETTE

*Paul L. Murphy, *Former Regents' Professor of American History, University of Minnesota, Minneapolis*
CIVIL LIBERTIES AND WAR; ESPIONAGE AND SEDITION ACTS OF WORLD WAR I (1917, 1918); MARTIAL LAW; SCHENCK AND ABRAMS CASES (1919)

John M. Murrin, *Professor of History, Princeton University, Princeton, New Jersey*
NATIONALISM; PATRIOTISM

Timothy J. Naftali, *International Security Studies, Yale University, New Haven, Connecticut*
COUNTERINTELLIGENCE

Bernard C. Nalty, *Historian, Retired from the Office of Air Force History, Washington, D.C.*
BLIMPS AND DIRIGIBLES; CHENNAULT, CLAIRE; MARINE CORPS COMBAT BRANCHES: AVIATION FORCES

Jonathan Nashel, *Assistant Professor of History, Indiana University, South Bend*
COLD WAR (1945–1991): CHANGING INTERPRETATIONS; LANSDALE, EDWARD G.

Michelle L. Nelson, *Research Analyst, SAIC, McLean, Virginia*
HEAT-SEEKING TECHNOLOGY

Paul David Nelson
CORNWALLIS, CHARLES; WAYNE, ANTHONY

Ralph Nichols, *Professor of Military Science, University of Central Arkansas, Conway*
HOUSING, MILITARY

Roger L. Nichols, *Professor of History, University of Arizona, Tucson*
BLACK HAWK; BLACK HAWK WAR (1832)

Brooke Nihart, *Colonel, U.S. Marine Corps (Ret); former head, Marine Corps Museums; Founder and Director, Marine Corps Historical Foundation, McLean, Virginia*
WEAPONRY, MARINE CORPS

Alan T. Nolan, *Chair, Board of Trustees, Indiana Historical Society, Indianapolis*
LEE, ROBERT E.

Mark A. Noll, *McManis Professor of Christian Thought, Wheaton College, Wheaton, Illinois*
RELIGION AND WAR

Michael Noone, *Professor of Law, The Columbus School of Law, The Catholic University of America, Washington, D.C.*
JUSTICE, MILITARY: ARTICLES OF WAR; JUSTICE, MILITARY: MILITARY CRIMES; JUSTICE, MILITARY: MILITARY COURTS; JUSTICE, MILITARY: MILITARY PUNISHMENT; RIGHTS IN THE MILITARY, CITIZENS'

Elizabeth Nuxoll, *Project Director and Co-Editor, The Papers of Robert Morris, Queens College of The City University of New York, Flushing*
MORRIS, ROBERT

John Kennedy Ohl, *Professor of History, Mesa Community College, Mesa, Arizona*
PROCUREMENT: ORDNANCE AND ARMS INDUSTRY

Gary Y. Okihiro, *Professor of International and Public Affairs, Columbia University, New York, New York*
JAPANESE-AMERICAN INTERNMENT CASES (1942)

Sterling P. Olmsted, *Provost Emeritus and Professor of English, Wilmington College, Wilmington, Ohio*
WOOLMAN, JOHN

Barry O'Neill, *Visiting Professor, Center for Rationality, Hebrew University of Jerusalem, Israel*
GAME THEORY; NEUMANN, JOHN VON; OPERATIONS RESEARCH

William L. O'Neill, *Professor of History, Rutgers University, New Brunswick, New Jersey*
WORLD WAR II (1939–1945): DOMESTIC COURSE

David Osher, *Senior Research Fellow, American Institutes for Research, Washington, D.C.*
RACE RELATIONS AND WAR

Matthew Oyos, *Assistant Professor of History, Radford University, Radford, Virginia*
GENERAL STAFF ACT (1903); ROOSEVELT, THEODORE; ROOT, ELIHU

Chester J. Pach Jr., *Associate Professor of History, Ohio University, Athens*
MUTUAL DEFENSE ASSISTANCE ACT (1949); MUTUAL SECURITY ACT (1951)

Michael A. Palmer, *Associate Professor of History, East Carolina Unversity, Greenville, North Carolina*
NAVY, U.S.: 1783–1865

Sarandis Papadopoulos, *Department of History, The George Washington University, Washington, D.C.*
SUBMARINES; SUBMARINE WARFARE

Herbert S. Parmet, *Distinguished Professor of History Emeritus, City University of New York*
NIXON DOCTRINE (1969)

Rod Paschall, *Colonel, U.S. Army (Ret); Editor, MHQ: The Quarterly Journal of Military History, Carlisle, Pennsylvania*
CODING AND DECODING; LEBANON, U.S. MILITARY INVOLVEMENT IN; MEDICAL PRACTICE IN THE MILITARY; SPECIAL OPERATIONS FORCES: OVERVIEW; SPECIAL OPERATIONS FORCES: ARMY SPECIAL FORCES; SPECIAL OPERATIONS FORCES: NAVY SEALS; SPRUANCE, RAYMOND A.; WAR CRIMES; WESTMORELAND, WILLIAM C.

Thomas G. Paterson, *Professor of History Emeritus, University of Connecticut at Storrs*
KENNEDY, JOHN F.

John J. Patrick, *Senior Analyst, Center for Security Strategies and Operations, Techmatics Division, Anteon Corporation, Arlington, Virginia*
WEAPONRY, NAVAL

Stephen E. Patterson, *Professor of History, University of New Brunswick, Fredericton, New Brunswick, Canada*
REVOLUTIONARY WAR (1775–1783): POSTWAR IMPACT

William Pencak, *Professor of History, Pennsylvania State University, University Park*
AMERICAN LEGION; VETERANS: WORLD WAR I

Carol Morris Petillo, *Associate Professor of History, Boston College, Chestnut Hill, Massachusetts*
FAMILIES, MILITARY

William B. Pickett, *Professor of History, Rose-Hulman Institute of Technology, Terre Haute, Indiana*
EISENHOWER, DWIGHT D.

G. Kurt Piehler, *Assistant Professor of History and Director of the Center for the Study of War and Society, University of Tennessee, Knoxville*
CEMETERIES, MILITARY; CINCINNATI, SOCIETY OF THE; COMMEMORATION AND PUBLIC RITUAL; GETTYSBURG NATIONAL MILITARY PARK; G.I. BILL (1944); MAULDIN, BILL [WILLIAM]; MAXIM, HIRAM; MORGENTHAU, HENRY, JR.; PEARL HARBOR NATIONAL MONUMENT; PYLE, ERNIE; STILWELL, JOSEPH; VETERANS: REVOLUTIONARY WAR; VETERANS: WORLD WAR II; VETERANS: KOREAN WAR; VETERANS ADMINISTRATION; WAINWRIGHT, JONATHAN

Richard M. Pious, *Adolph and Effie Ochs Professor of American Studies, Barnard College, Columbia University, New York, New York*
COMMANDER IN CHIEF, PRESIDENT AS; WAR POWERS RESOLUTION (1973)

William Garrett Piston, *Professor of History, Southwest Missouri State University, Springfield*
LONGSTREET, JAMES

Anne Marie Pois, *Instructor of History and Women's Studies, History Department and Women's Studies Program, University of Colorado at Boulder*
BALCH, EMILY GREENE

Mark R. Polelle
LAIRD, MELVIN R.; TELLER, EDWARD

Norman Polmar
RICKOVER, HYMAN G.

Walter S. Poole, *Chief, Joint Staff History Branch, Joint History Office, Department of Defense, Washington, D.C.*
BRADLEY, OMAR N.

Jerrold M. Post, *Professor of Psychiatry, Political Psychology, and International Affairs; Director of the Political Psychology Program, The George Washington University, Washington, D.C.*
TERRORISM AND COUNTERTERRORISM (co-author)

*E. B. Potter, *Professor of History, Emeritus, U.S. Naval Academy, Annapolis, Maryland*
NIMITZ, CHESTER

John Prados, *Author, Washington, D.C.*
KHE SANH, SIEGE OF (1968)

Clement Alexander Price, *Professor of History, Chair of the Department of Afro-American Studies, and Director of the Institute on Ethnicity, Culture, and the Modern Experience, Rutgers University, Newark, New Jersey*
DAVIS, BENJAMIN O., JR.; DAVIS, BENJAMIN O., SR.; RANDOLPH, A. PHILIP

Stephen G. Rabe, *Professor of History, University of Texas— Dallas, Richardson*
INTER-AMERICAN TREATY OF RECIPROCAL ASSISTANCE (1947); OAS (EST. 1948)

George C. Rable, *Charles Summersell Professor of History, University of Alabama, Tuscaloosa*
BURNSIDE, AMBROSE; FREDERICKSBURG, BATTLE OF (1862)

Ethan S. Rafuse, *Ph.D. candidate in History and Political Science, University of Missouri at Kansas City*
CIVIL WAR (1861–1865): MILITARY AND DIPLOMATIC COURSE

Edward D. Ragan, *Department of History, Syracuse University, Syracuse, New York*
SERMONS AND ORATIONS, WAR AND THE MILITARY IN

Edgar F. Raines, Jr., *Historian, Histories Branch, U.S. Army Center of Military History, Washington, D.C.*
ARMY COMBAT BRANCHES: AVIATION

Harry Howe Ransom, *Professor of Political Science Emeritus, Vanderbilt University, Nashville, Tennessee*
CENTRAL INTELLIGENCE AGENCY

Eugene L. Rasor, *Professor of History Emeritus, Emory and Henry College, Emory, Virginia*
STEAMSHIPS

George W. Rathjens, *Professor Emeritus of Political Science, Center for International Studies, Massachusetts Institute of Technology; Secretary General, Pugwash Conferences on Science and World Affairs, American Academy of Arts and Sciences, Cambridge*
NUCLEAR WINTER

Richard S. Rauschkolb
CROWE, WILLIAM

Walton H. Rawls, *Author and Editor, Atlanta, Georgia*
ILLUSTRATION, WAR AND THE MILITARY IN

Steven L. Rearden, *Defense Consultant and Historian, Washington, D.C.*
BUNDY, MCGEORGE; CONSULTANTS; DEFENSE, DEPARTMENT OF; JOHNSON, LOUIS; KEY WEST AGREEMENT (1948); NITZE, PAUL H.

Carol Reardon, *Associate Professor of History, Pennsylvania State University, University Park*
SCHOOLS, PRIVATE MILITARY; UPTON, EMORY

Joseph P. Reidy, *Professor of History, Howard University, Washington, D.C.*
CIVIL WAR (1861–1865): POSTWAR IMPACT

Dan Reiter, *Assistant Professor of Political Science, Emory University, Atlanta, Georgia*
NUCLEAR WAR, PREVENTION OF ACCIDENTAL

Clark G. Reynolds, *Professor of History, University of Charleston, Charleston, South Carolina*
AIRCRAFT CARRIERS; CARRIER WARFARE; MOFFETT, WILLIAM A.; NAVY COMBAT BRANCHES: NAVAL AIR FORCES; SHERMAN, FORREST

Gordon C. Rhea, *Independent Historian, Mount Pleasant, South Carolina*
WILDERNESS, BATTLE OF THE (1864); WILDERNESS TO PETERSBURG CAMPAIGN (1864)

Edward Rhodes, *Associate Professor of Political Science and Director, Center for Global Security and Democracy, Rutgers University, New Brunswick, New Jersey*
DETERRENCE

Rob S. Rice, *Professor, The American Military University, Manassas Park, Virginia*
SAILING WARSHIPS

James I. Robertson, Jr., *Alumni Distinguished Professor in History, Virginia Polytechnic Institute and State University, Blacksburg, Virginia*
PRISONER-OF-WAR CAMPS, CIVIL WAR

William Glenn Robertson, *Professor of History and Deputy Director, Combat Studies Institute, U.S. Army Command and General Staff College, Fort Leavenworth, Kansas*
CHICKAMAUGA, BATTLE OF (1863); HOWARD, O. O.; ROSECRANS, WILLIAM S.; THOMAS, GEORGE H.

Hugh Rockoff, *Professor of Economics, Rutgers University, New Brunswick, New Jersey*
DISCIPLINARY VIEWS OF WAR: ECONOMICS

Jorge Rodríguez Beruff, *Professor of Politics, General Studies Faculty, University of Puerto Rico, Rio Piedras*
PUERTO RICAN UNITS; TELLER AMENDMENT (1898)

Alex Roland, *Chair and Professor of History, Duke University, Durham, North Carolina*
DISCIPLINARY VIEWS OF WAR: CAUSES-OF-WAR STUDIES; DISCIPLINARY VIEWS OF WAR: HISTORY OF SCIENCE AND TECHNOLOGY; SCIENCE, TECHNOLOGY, WAR, AND THE MILITARY

Andrew Rolle, *Research Scholar, Huntington Library, San Marino, California*
FRÉMONT, JOHN C.

Elihu Rose, *Adjunct Associate Professor of History, New York University, New York*
MUTINY

David Alan Rosenberg, *Admiral Harry W. Hill Professor of Maritime Strategy, The National War College, Washington, D.C. Senior Strategic Researcher, Naval War College, Newport, Rhode Island; Associate Professor of History, Temple University, Philadelphia, Pennsylvania*
BURKE, ARLEIGH

Steven T. Ross, *Professor, Strategy and Policy Department, Naval War College, Newport, Rhode Island*
WAR PLANS

Gunther E. Rothenberg, *Professor, Military History, Department of History, Purdue University, West Lafayette, Indiana; Research Associate, Monash University, Clayton, Victoria, Australia*
NAPOLEONIC WARFARE

Andrew J. Rotter, *Chairman, Department of History, Colgate University, Hamilton, New York*
VIETNAM WAR (1960–1975): CAUSES

Keven G. Ruby
TERRORISM AND COUNTERTERRORISM (co-author)

George L. Rueckert
INF TREATY (1987)

Paul J. Sanborn, *Associate Professor of Intelligence, American Military University, Manassas Park, Virginia*
REVOLUTIONARY WAR (1775–1783): CHANGING INTERPRETATIONS

Nicholas Evan Sarantakes, *Assistant Professor, Department of History, Texas A & M University, Commerce*
ARMY COMBAT BRANCHES: CAVALRY

Ronald Schaffer, *Professor of History Emeritus, California State University, Northridge*
WORLD WAR I (1914–1918): DOMESTIC COURSE

Michael Schaller, *Professor of History, University of Arizona, Tucson*
JAPAN, U.S. MILITARY INVOLVEMENT IN; MACARTHUR, DOUGLAS; REAGAN, RONALD

Herbert Y. Schandler, *Colonel, U.S. Army (Ret); Professor of History, Industrial College of the Armed Force, Fort McNair, Washington, D.C.*
BALL, GEORGE; ROSTOW, WALT W.; WHEELER, EARLE G.

Georg Schild, *Lecturer, Department of Political Science, University of Bonn, Bonn, Germany*
WORLD BANK (EST. 1944)

Hans R. Schmidt, *Independent Scholar, Ormond Beach, Florida*
BUTLER, SMEDLEY

David F. Schmitz, *Professor of History, Whitman College. Walla Walla, Washington*
CASE-CHURCH AMENDMENT (1973); COLD WAR (1945–1991): CAUSES; COOPER-CHURCH AMENDMENT (1970); NICARAGUA, U.S. MILITARY INVOLVEMENT IN

Robert J. Schneller, Jr., *Historian, Contemporary History Branch, Naval Historical Center, Washington, D.C.*
DAHLGREN, JOHN

R. L. Schreadley, *Commander, U.S. Navy (Ret), Charleston, South Carolina*
RIVER CRAFT; SWIFT BOATS; ZUMWALT, ELMO

John H. Schroeder, *Professor of History, University of Wisconsin—Milwaukee*
POLK, JAMES K.; THOREAU, HENRY DAVID

Frank N. Schubert, *Chief, Joint Operational History, Office of the Chairman, Joint Chiefs of Staff, Washington, D.C.*
"BUFFALO" SOLDIERS

Robert D. Schulzinger, *Professor of History, University of Colorado at Boulder*
KISSINGER, HENRY

Barry Schwartz, *Professor of Sociology, University of Georgia, Athens*
MEMORIALS, WAR

Thomas A. Schwartz, *Associate Professor of History, Vanderbilt University, Nashville, Tennessee*
MARSHALL PLAN (1948–52); MCCLOY, JOHN J.

Eileen Scully, *Assistant Professor of History, Princeton University, Princeton, New Jersey*
CHINA RELIEF EXPEDITION (1900)

Larry Seaquist, *Captain, U.S. Navy (Ret); Chairman, The Strategy Group, Washington, D.C.*
STRATEGY: NAVAL WARFARE STRATEGY

James E. Sefton, *Professor of History, California State University at Northridge*
JOHNSON, ANDREW; PHOTOGRAPHY, WAR AND THE MILITARY IN; RECONSTRUCTION; TENURE OF OFFICE ACT (1867); WORLD WAR II, U.S. NAVAL OPERATIONS IN: THE PACIFIC

David R. Segal, *Director, Center for Research on Military Organization, and Professor of Sociology and of Government and Politics, University of Maryland, College Park*
ALL-VOLUNTEER FORCE; STRATIFICATION AND LABOR MARKET DYNAMICS IN THE MILITARY

Harold E. Selesky, *Associate Professor and Director of the Maxwell Program in Military History, University of Alabama, Tuscaloosa*
BUNKER HILL, BATTLE OF (1775); CHARLESTON, SIEGE OF (1780); CONTINENTAL ARMY; COWPENS, BATTLE OF (1781); KINGS MOUNTAIN, BATTLE OF (1780); LEXINGTON AND CONCORD, BATTLES OF (1775); MONMOUTH, BATTLE OF (1778); NEWBURGH "CONSPIRACY" (1783); NEW YORK, BATTLE OF (1776); TRENTON AND PRINCETON, BATTLES OF (1776–1777); YORKTOWN, BATTLE OF (1781)

Martin Shaw, *Professor of International Relations and Politics, University of Sussex, Brighton, England*
DISCIPLINARY VIEWS OF WAR: SOCIETY STUDIES

Michael S. Sherry, *Professor of History, Northwestern University, Evanston, Illinois*
BOMBING OF CIVILIANS; WORLD WAR II (1939–1945): POSTWAR IMPACT

John Darrell Sherwood, *Historian, Naval Historical Center, Washington, D.C.*
VIETNAM WAR, U.S. AIR OPERATIONS IN THE

Dennis E. Showalter, *Professor of History, Colorado College, Colorado Springs*
HINDENBURG, PAUL VON; LUDENDORFF, ERICH

Charles R. Shrader, *Independent Scholar, Carlisle, Pennsylvania*
CASUALTIES; COMBAT SUPPORT; EDUCATION, MILITARY; FRIENDLY FIRE; LOGISTICS; MAINTENANCE; SCHOOLS, POSTGRADUATE SERVICE; TRANSPORTATION

Jack Shulimson, *Head, Histories Section, Marine Corps Historical Center, Washington, D.C.*
MARINE CORPS, U.S.: 1865–1914

Mark R. Shulman, *Military Historian and Author, New York, New York*
CHILEAN CRISIS (1891); MAHAN, ALFRED T.; NAVY, U.S.: OVERVIEW

Nina Silber, *Associate Professor of History, Boston University, Boston, Massachusetts*
BARTON, CLARA

Joel H. Silbey, *President White Professor of History, Cornell University, Ithaca, New York*
VALLANDIGHAM, CLEMENT L.

Edwin Howard Simmons, *Brigadier General, U.S. Marine Corps (Ret); Director Emeritus, Marine Corps History, Alexandria, Virginia*
AMPHIBIOUS WARFARE; CHOSIN RESERVOIR, BATTLE OF THE (1950); INCHON LANDING (1950); MARINE CORPS, U.S.: SINCE 1945; OKINAWA, BATTLE OF (1945)

John Y. Simon, *Professor of History, Southern Illinois University at Carbondale; Executive Director and Managing Editor, Ulysses S. Grant Association*
GRANT, ULYSSES S.

Harvard Sitkoff, *Professor of History, University of New Hampshire, Durham*
VIETNAM WAR (1960–1975): POSTWAR IMPACT

William B. Skelton, *Professor of History, University of Wisconsin at Stevens Point*
ARMY, U.S.: 1783–1865

Jane Slaughter, *Associate Professor of History, University of New Mexico, Albuquerque*
SEX AND THE MILITARY

Melvin Small, *Professor of History, Wayne State University, Detroit, Michigan*
NEWS MEDIA, WAR, AND THE MILITARY; STUDENTS FOR A DEMOCRATIC SOCIETY; VIETNAM WAR (1960–1975): DOMESTIC COURSE

John Kenly Smith, *Associate Professor of History, Lehigh University, Bethlehem, Pennsylvania*
PROCUREMENT: MUNITIONS AND CHEMICAL INDUSTRY

Merritt Roe Smith, *Cutten Professor of The History of Technology, Massachusetts Institute of Technology, Cambridge*
COLT, SAMUEL

Richard K. Smith
TRANSPORT AND SUPPLY AIRCRAFT

William D. Smith, *Admiral, U.S. Navy (Ret); Senior Fellow, Center for Naval Analyses, Alexandria, Virginia*
ANTISUBMARINE WARFARE SYSTEMS; INCIDENTS-AT-SEA TREATY, U.S.-SOVIET (1972); PROCUREMENT: SHIPBUILDING INDUSTRY

Lewis Sorley, *Military Historian, Potomac, Maryland*
SCHLESINGER, JAMES R.

Ronald H. Spector, *Chairman and Professor of History, The George Washington University, Washington, D.C.*
DEWEY, GEORGE; MANILA BAY, BATTLE OF (1898)

Roger Spiller, *George C. Marshall Professor of Military History, U.S. Army Command and General Staff College, Fort Leavenworth, Kansas*
DOCTRINE, MILITARY; MURPHY, AUDIE

J. C. A. Stagg, *Professor of History and Editor in Chief of The Papers of James Madison, University of Virginia, Charlottesville*
MONROE, JAMES; MONROE DOCTRINE (1823); NEW ORLEANS, BATTLE OF (1815); WAR OF 1812 (1812–1815)

Donn A. Starry, *General, U.S. Army (Ret); Senior Fellow, Armed Forces Staff College, Norfolk, Virginia*
ANTITANK WEAPONS; HAMBURGER HILL, BATTLE OF (1969)

Ervin Staub, *Professor of Psychology, University of Massachusetts, Amherst*
GENOCIDE

Ian K. Steele, *Professor of History, University of Western Ontario, London, Ontario, Canada*
BRADDOCK, EDWARD; BRADDOCK'S DEFEAT (1755); FRENCH AND INDIAN WAR (1754–1763); IMPERIAL WARS; LOUISBOURG SIEGE (1745); PRISONERS AND CAPTIVES OF WAR, COLONIAL; QUEBEC, BATTLE OF (1759)

Keir B. Sterling, *Command Historian, U.S. Army Combined Arms Support Command, Fort Lee, Virginia*
ANTIPERSONNEL WEAPONS

Judith Hicks Stiehm, *Professor of Political Science, Florida International University, Miami*
GENDER: FEMALE IDENTITY AND THE MILITARY

Carol E. Stokes, *Command Historian, U.S. Army Signal Corps (Ret), Fort Gordon, Georgia*
COMMUNICATIONS

Mark A. Stoler, *Professor of History, University of Vermont, Burlington*
JOINT CHIEFS OF STAFF; MARSHALL, GEORGE C.; WORLD WAR II (1939–1945): MILITARY AND DIPLOMATIC COURSE

Clifford L. Stott, *Independent Scholar and Author; Fellow, American Society of Genealogists, Orem, Utah*
MORMON "WAR" (1857–1858)

Mary V. Stremlow, *Colonel, U.S. Marine Corps Reserve (Ret), Lakeview, New York*
MARINE CORPS WOMEN'S RESERVE, U.S.

Lawrence Suid, *Military Historian and Author, Greenbelt, Maryland*
FILM, WAR AND THE MILITARY IN: FEATURE FILMS; RADIO AND TELEVISION SERVICE, ARMED FORCES

Harry G. Summers Jr., *Distinguished Fellow, U.S. Army War College; Colonel, U.S. Army (Ret); and Editor, Vietnam Magazine, Leesburg, Virginia*
IA DRANG VALLEY, BATTLE OF THE (1965)

Martin Summers, *Assistant Professor of History, New Jersey Institute of Technology, Newark*
COLORED TROOPS, U.S.; DOUGLASS, FREDERICK; RUSTIN, BAYARD

Daniel E. Sutherland, *Professor of History, University of Arkansas, Fayetteville*
BRANDY STATION, BATTLE OF (1864)

Carl E. Swanson, *Associate Professor of History, East Carolina University, Greenville, North Carolina*
PRIVATEERING

Craig Swanson, *Major, United States Marine Corps Reserve; Historian, Field Operations Branch, History and Museums Division, U.S. Marine Corps University, Bowie, Maryland*
GRENADA, U.S. INTERVENTION IN (1983)

Peter M. Swartz, *Captain, U.S. Navy (Ret); Center for Naval Analyses, Alexandria, Virginia*
MOORER, THOMAS

John Talbott, *Professor of History, University of California, Santa Barbara*
COMBAT TRAUMA

William R. Tanner, *Professor of History Emeritus, Humboldt State University, Arcata, California*
MCCARRAN INTERNAL SECURITY ACT (1950)

Terry Terriff, *Senior Lecturer in International Security, University of Birmingham, Birmingham, England*
NIXON, RICHARD M.

Daniel C. Thomas, *Assistant Professor of Political Science, University of Illinois at Chicago; Jean Monnet Fellow, European University Institute, Florence, Italy*
CONFERENCE ON SECURITY AND COOPERATION IN EUROPE

Gerald C. Thomas, Jr., *Colonel, U.S. Marine Corps (Ret); Former Research Assistant, Marine Corps Research Center, The Plains, Virginia*
AMPHIBIOUS SHIPS AND LANDING CRAFT; LEBANON CRISIS (1958); PULLER, "CHESTY" [LEWIS B.]

Thomas A. Thomas
VALLEY FORGE NATIONAL PARK

J. Mark Thompson
BOSTON MASSACRE (1770); KALB, JOHANN [BARON DE]; KNOX, HENRY; KOSCIUSZKO, THADDEUS; LAFAYETTE, MARQUIS DE; STEUBEN, FRIEDRICH WILHELM VON [BARON]

John A. Tilley, *Associate Professor of History, East Carolina University, Greenville, North Carolina*
COAST GUARD, U.S.; COAST GUARD RESERVE; SPARS

James W. Tollefson, *Professor of English, University of Washington, Seattle*
DRAFT RESISTANCE AND EVASION

Barbara Brooks Tomblin, *Lecturer, Rutgers University, New Brunswick, New Jersey*
ACADEMIES, SERVICE: U.S. NAVAL ACADEMY; AEGIS; RANK AND HIERARCHY: NAVY

John Lawrence Tone, *Associate Professor of History, School of History, Technology and Society, Georgia Institute of Technology, Atlanta*
PLATT AMENDMENT (1901)

Edmund C. Tramont, *Colonel (Ret) MC USA; Professor and Associate Director, Institute of Human Virology, University of Maryland at Baltimore*
DISEASES, SEXUALLY TRANSMITTED

David F. Trask, *Chief of Military History, retired, U.S. Army Center of Military History, Washington, D.C.*
LUSITANIA, SINKING OF THE (1915); SAMPSON, WILLIAM; SAN JUAN HILL, BATTLE OF (1898); SIMS, WILLIAM S.; SPANISH-AMERICAN WAR (1898); WORLD WAR I, U.S. NAVAL OPERATIONS IN

Roger R. Trask, *Former Deputy Historian, Office of the Secretary of Defense, Chief Historian, U.S. General Accounting Office (Ret), Locust Grove, Virginia*
WEINBERGER, CASPAR

Tim Travers, *Professor of History, University of Calgary, Calgary, Alberta, Canada*
TRENCH WARFARE

Hans L. Trefousse, *Distinguished Professor of History, Brooklyn College and Graduate Center, City University, Brooklyn, New York*
BUTLER, BENJAMIN F.;NEW YORK CITY ANTI-DRAFT RIOTS (1863);STEVENS, THADDEUS;WADE, BENJAMIN FRANKLIN

Jason E. Trumpler, *Austin, Texas*
HELICOPTERS (co-author)

William S. Turley, *Professor of Political Science, Southern Illinois University, Carbondale*
TET OFFENSIVE (1968)

Maxine T. Turner, *Independent Scholar; Professor Emerita of Literature and Communication, Georgia Institute of Technology, Atlanta*
CONFEDERATE NAVY; FARRAGUT, DAVID; MOBILE BAY, BATTLE OF (1864); UNION NAVY

Frank Uhlig, Jr., *Editor Emeritus, Naval War College Review, U.S. Naval War College, Newport, Rhode Island*
BLOCKADES; MIDWAY, BATTLE OF (1942)

Michael E. Unsworth, *Bibliographer, Library, and Assistant Director of Canadian Studies, Canadian Studies Centre, Michigan State University, East Lansing*
PERIODICAL PUBLICATIONS ON WAR AND THE MILITARY; SERVICE ASSOCIATIONS

Robert M. Utley, *Historian, Georgetown, Texas*
CRAZY HORSE; CUSTER, GEORGE ARMSTRONG; GERONIMO; JOSEPH, CHIEF; LITTLE BIGHORN, BATTLE OF THE (1876); PLAINS INDIAN WARS (1854–1890); SAND CREEK MASSACRE (1864); SITTING BULL; WOUNDED KNEE, BATTLE OF (1890)

Martin van Creveld, *Professor of History, Hebrew University, Jerusalem, Israel*
WAR: NATURE OF WAR

Stephen Van Evera, *Associate Professor of Political Science and Member, Security Studies Program, Massachusetts Institute of Technology, Cambridge*
WAR: CAUSES OF WAR (co-author)

Jacob Vander Meulen, *Assistant Professor of History, Dalhousie University, Halifax, Nova Scotia, Canada*
AIRCRAFT INDUSTRIALISTS

Frank E. Vandiver, *Distinguished University Professor and Sara and John Lindsey Chair in Humanities, Texas A & M University, College Station*
BEAUREGARD, P. G. T.; BRAGG, BRAXTON; CHANCELLORSVILLE, BATTLE OF (1863); GETTYSBURG, BATTLE OF (1863); JOHNSTON, JOSEPH E.; MEADE, GEORGE GORDON; PERSHING, JOHN J.; RICKENBACKER, EDDIE; STANTON, EDWIN M.

John A. Vasquez, *Professor of Political Science, Vanderbilt University, Nashville, Tennessee*
DISCIPLINARY VIEWS OF WAR: POLITICAL SCIENCE AND INTERNATIONAL RELATIONS

Milan Vego, *Professor of Operations, U.S. Naval War College, Newport, Rhode Island*
COMMAND AND CONTROL

Anne Cipriano Venzon, *Historian, Publisher, Bethesda, Maryland*
HAITI, U.S. MILITARY INVOLVEMENT IN

Dennis D. Wainstock
Associate Professor of History, Salem-Teikyo University, Salem, West Virginia
MANHATTAN PROJECT

Arthur Waldron, *Lauder Professor of International Relations, University of Pennsylvania, Philadelphia; Director of Asian Studies, American Enterprise Institute, Washington, D.C.*
CHINESE CIVIL WAR, U.S. INVOLVEMENT IN THE (1945–1949)

Samuel Walker, *Professor of Criminal Justice, University of Nebraska at Omaha*
AMERICAN CIVIL LIBERTIES UNION

William O. Walker III, *Professor of History and International Relations, Florida International University, Miami*
NORIEGA, MANUEL

*Joseph F. Wall, *Professor of History, Grinnell College*
CARNEGIE, ANDREW

Robert J. Watson, *Former Chief, Historical Division, Joint Chiefs of Staff and Former Historian, Office of the Secretary of Defense, Arlington, Virginia*
GATES, THOMAS, MCELROY, NEIL

Donald Cameron Watt, *Emeritus Professor of International History, Department of International History, London School of Economics and Political Science, London, England*
WORLD WAR II (1939–1945): CAUSES

Willard J. Webb, *Former Chief, Historical Office, Joint Chiefs of Staff, Arlington, Virginia*
JONES, DAVID, VESSEY, JOHN

William Earl Weeks, *Lecturer in History, San Diego State University, San Diego, California*
TREASON

Paul Wehr, *Associate Professor of Sociology, University of Colorado, Boulder*
NONVIOLENCE

William J. Weida, *Professor of Economics and Business, Colorado College, Colorado Springs*
PROCUREMENT: NUCLEAR WEAPONS INDUSTRY

David A. Welch, *Associate Professor of Political Science, University of Toronto, Toronto, Ontario, Canada*
CUBAN MISSILE CRISIS (1962–1963)

Mark K. Wells, *Colonel, United States Air Force; Senior Military Professor and Acting Head, Department of History, United States Air Force Academy, Colorado Springs, Colorado*
MORALE, TROOP, TACTICS: AIR WARFARE TACTICS

Tom Wells, *Author; Visiting Scholar, University of California at Berkeley*
VIETNAM ANTIWAR MOVEMENT

Michael Wessells, *Professor of Psychology, Randolph-Macon College, Ashland, Virginia*
DISCIPLINARY VIEWS OF WAR: PSYCHOLOGY

Gerald E. Wheeler, *Professor of History Emeritus, San Jose State University, San Jose, California*
KINKAID, THOMAS C.

Bruce White, *Associate Professor of American History, Erindale College, University of Toronto, Mississauga, Ontario, Canada*
ETHNICITY AND RACE IN THE MILITARY, ETHNICITY AND WAR

Neil L. Whitehead, *Associate Professor of Anthropology, University of Wisconsin, Madison*
DISCIPLINARY VIEWS OF WAR: ANTHROPOLOGY

Patricia R. Wickman, *Director, Department of Anthropology and Genealogy, Seminole Tribe of Florida, Hollywood, Florida*
OSCEOLA

Fred A. Wilcox, *Associate Professor of Writing, Ithaca College, Ithaca, New York*
TOXIC AGENTS: AGENT ORANGE EXPOSURE

Brian S. Wills, *Chairman and Associate Professor of History, Clinch Valley College of the University of Virginia, Wise*
CONFEDERACY, THE MILITARY IN THE, STUART, J. E. B.

Theodore Wilson, *Professor of History, University of Kansas, Lawrence*
TRAINING AND INDOCTRINATION

Jay M. Winter, *Reader in Modern History and Fellow of Pembroke College, Cambridge University, Cambridge, England*
DISCIPLINARY VIEWS OF WAR: CULTURAL HISTORY, SOCIETY AND WAR

Harold R. Winton, *Professor of Military History and Theory, School of Advanced Airpower Studies, Air University, Montgomery, Alabama*
WEAPONRY, ARMY

James J. Wirtz, *Associate Professor of National Security Affairs, Naval Postgraduate School, Monterey, California*
GENEVA AGREEMENT ON LAOS (1962), ORDER OF BATTLE, PACIFICATION, SAIGON, BATTLE FOR (1968)

Lawrence S. Wittner, *Professor of History, State University of New York, Albany*
NUCLEAR PROTEST MOVEMENTS

David R. Woodward, *Professor of History, Marshall University, Huntington, West Virginia*
WORLD WAR I (1914–1918): MILITARY AND DIPLOMATIC COURSE

Steven E. Woodworth, *Assistant Professor of History, Texas Christian University, Fort Worth*
ATLANTA, BATTLE OF (1864), FORREST, NATHAN BEDFORD, FRANKLIN, BATTLE OF (1864), HOOD, JOHN BELL; MISSIONARY RIDGE, BATTLE OF (1863); NASHVILLE, BATTLE OF (1864)

Robert Wooster, *Professor of History and Chair, Department of Humanities, Texas A & M University at Corpus Christi*
RED CLOUD

David S. Wyman, *Josiah DuBois Professor of History Emeritus, University of Massachusetts, Amherst*
HOLOCAUST, U.S. WAR EFFORT AND THE

William T. Y'Blood, *Historian, Air Force History Support Office, Bolling Air Force Base, Washington, D.C.*
PHILIPPINE SEA, BATTLE OF THE (1944)

Adam Yarmolinsky, *Regents Professor of Public Policy, University of Maryland, Baltimore*
ATOMIC SCIENTISTS; FLEXIBLE RESPONSE

John W. Young, *Chair of Politics, University of Leicester, Leicester, England*
CHURCHILL, WINSTON S.

G. Pascal Zachary, *Independent Scholar and Author, Berkeley, California*
BUSH, VANNEVAR

Thomas W. Zeiler, *Associate Professor of History, University of Colorado at Boulder*
RUSH-BAGOT AGREEMENT (1817), TRADE, FOREIGN: WARTIME, TRADE, FOREIGN: TRADE RESTRICTIONS, TRADE, FOREIGN: NEUTRAL TRADE

Caroline F. Ziemke, *Research Staff Member, Institute for Defense Analyses, Alexandria, Virginia*
GROUND ATTACK AIRCRAFT

*deceased

THE OXFORD COMPANION TO

AMERICAN MILITARY HISTORY

A

ABM TREATY (1972). *See* Salt Treaties (1972; 1979).

ABRAMS, CREIGHTON W. (1914–1974), one of the leading American generals of the twentieth century.

From a humble background, in Springfield, Massachusetts, he earned an appointment to West Point in 1932 and graduated in the famous class in 1936 that produced 60 wartime generals. "Abe" Abrams commanded an armored battalion in World War II, and, astride his tank "Thunderbolt," led the column that relieved American forces in Bastogne during the Battle of the *Bulge.

Considered the best tactical leader in the army, he was placed in charge of armored forces in Germany during the Berlin Crisis of 1961. He also earned the respect of President John F. *Kennedy for his sensitive handling of federal troops in racial disturbances in Alabama. Sent to Vietnam as deputy to General William C. *Westmoreland, he succeeded Westmoreland in 1968. Under President Richard M. *Nixon's strategy of "Vietnamization," Abrams sought to train and equip South Vietnamese troops to fight on their own.

In the last two years of his life, as Army Chief of Staff (1972–74), he was determined to rebuild the army in a way that would ensure its decisive use in future engagements. His vision is widely credited with creating the foundation for the 1991 Desert Storm victory over Iraq during the *Persian Gulf War. His insistence on joining superbly trained soldiers to multiple and synergistically devastating equipment led to the development of the Air Land Battle, the strategy that produced the most lopsided military victory in history in 1991.

• Lewis Sorley, *Thunderbolt: General Creighton Abrams and the Army of His Times,* 1992. Robert H. Scales, ed., *Certain Victory: The U.S. Army in the Gulf War,* 1993.
——Timothy J. Lomperis

ACADEMIES, SERVICE
Overview
U.S. Military Academy
U.S. Naval Academy
U.S. Air Force Academy
U.S. Coast Guard Academy

ACADEMIES, SERVICE: OVERVIEW

The primary function of the military service academies is to educate and train professional officers for the nation's standing armed forces.

With the development of modern standing armies and more complex military technology, the modern military academy originated in Western Europe in the eighteenth century, established by royal governments to train younger sons of the nobility or veterans as line officers. Other academies trained middle-class officers for the technical services: *artillery, military *engineering, and *logistics. In the nineteenth century, preparation of naval officers shifted to shore-based naval academies, and in the twentieth century, air force academies were established.

Unlike those in some other nations, U.S. service academies are not narrowly vocational, but offer a broad education in the liberal arts and sciences, as well as engineering, management, and the military sciences, while emphasizing, of course, leadership, duty, responsibility, and loyalty. The requirements for admission are similar to those of other undergraduate schools, although the academies stress physical ability, character, and leadership potential.

Appointments to the service academies (except for the Coast Guard Academy) are made by members of Congress, a requirement designed to ensure a representative geographical distribution of the officer corps. In return for the government-provided college education, the newly commissioned graduates are required to serve five years of active duty.

From the early republic, some Americans partly viewed national military academies and the regular officer corps as potential aristocratic threats to democracy. Consequently, Congress has periodically adopted measures to ensure the representativeness of the academies and the officer corps. For example, blacks were admitted to West Point beginning in the 1870s (although only in token numbers at first); women were admitted to all the service academies beginning in the 1970s.

The officer corps in the United States is prepared at public and private military academies (the latter including such state-supported institutions as Virginia Military Institute and The Citadel in South Carolina) as well as at Officer Candidate School and in the campus-based Reserve Officer Training Corps (*ROTC). However, although only a minority of U.S. military officers graduate from service academies, their connections, training in military technology, and leadership qualities have promoted their careers, including selection for positions of high command.

[*See also* Education, Military; Leadership, Concepts of Military.]
——John Whiteclay Chambers II

ACADEMIES, SERVICE: U.S. MILITARY ACADEMY

The U.S. Military Academy (USMA) at West Point, New York, located fifty miles north of New York City on the west bank of the Hudson River, originated as a *Revolutionary War fortress. After the war it became a military stores depot. George *Washington, however, advocated a military academy to train professional officers, and

Thomas *Jefferson saw an academy as a way to create a "republican" officer corps. On 16 March 1802, Jefferson signed the act establishing a military academy at West Point, the first American school of engineering.

West Point's existence remained tenuous until Sylvanus *Thayer arrived as superintendent in 1817. Thayer studied European military academies after the *War of 1812 and modeled USMA on the French Ecole Polytechnique. Under Thayer, the "Father of the Military Academy," West Point became the nation's premier school for civil engineering. Thayer established a four-year curriculum and annual examinations. The books he secured in Europe became America's first technical library. His insistence upon strict discipline, integrity, small classes, and daily recitations placed the burden for learning upon cadets. Thayer's "system," copied throughout the United States, survives at West Point today.

West Point was criticized by many during its early years as being wasteful and aristocratic. Alden Partridge, an 1807 graduate and later superintendent, became an unrelenting critic of both USMA and Thayer, who had replaced him. Instead, Partridge advocated regional military schools like Norwich, which he founded after leaving the army. Other critics included Congressman Davy Crockett of Tennessee, who claimed that West Point taught undemocratic values and was too expensive. Fortunately, West Point enjoyed support from other influential Americans, including President Andrew *Jackson, who declared it to be "the best school in the world."

The critics were mostly silenced by the performance of the academy's graduates. When American expansion demanded engineers for internal improvements, West Point provided them. Most railroad lines built before the *Civil War involved academy graduates. Others mapped new territory, and supervised roadbuilding, canal construction, and harbor improvements. However, West Pointers mainly achieved fame in battle, beginning with the *Mexican War, where junior officers like Robert E. *Lee, Ulysses S. *Grant, and Thomas "Stonewall" *Jackson practiced what they had studied under Professor Dennis Hart Mahan, a disciple of the Swiss war philosopher, Antoine Henri *Jomini.

Despite its superintendents' efforts, including those of Lee, the growing rift between North and South disrupted West Point life. When the Civil War began, most Southern cadets resigned and most Southern alumni sided with their native region. West Point graduates dominated in the Civil War, commanding both sides in fifty-five of the sixty major battles and one side or the other in the other five. West Pointer Jefferson *Davis served as president of the Confederacy; the contesting armies were commanded by the likes of Lee, "Stonewall" Jackson, Joseph E. *Johnston, Grant, William Tecumseh *Sherman, Philip H. *Sheridan, George B. *McClellan, and George Gordon *Meade.

West Point stagnated after the Civil War, as the army was reduced to frontier constabulary duties. But America's colonial expansion after the *Spanish-American War and entry in World War I returned USMA graduates to prominence. Col. George W. *Goethals supervised the building of the Panama Canal. John J. *Pershing led the American Expeditionary Force in France and Chief of Staff Peyton C. *March mobilized and trained the army. March also revitalized the academy by appointing Douglas *MacArthur superintendent in 1919. MacArthur introduced curricular and other reforms, liberalizing USMA's course of study for the first time in a century and insisting upon every cadet being an athlete.

The Reserve Officer Training Corps and Officer Candidate Schools bolstered the army's officer corps in World War II, but West Point continued to furnish many of the highest ranking officers for the army and air force. Four of the five men promoted to five-star General of the Army rank—MacArthur, Dwight D. *Eisenhower, "Hap" *Arnold, and Omar *Bradley—were West Pointers. Over 85 percent of living West Point graduates served in the armed forces during World War II, 10 percent as general officers, including George S. *Patton, Joseph *Stilwell, and Mark *Clark.

The advent of *nuclear weapons and the *Cold War limited warfare in scope and resources. Difficult conflicts tested West Pointers MacArthur, Matthew B. *Ridgway, and Maxwell *Taylor in Korea, and William C. *Westmoreland and Creighton *Abrams in Vietnam. These experiences also changed the academy's curriculum, broadening cadets' education in humanities. Reform superintendents, like Taylor and Garrison Davidson, pointed to military governors such as Lucius *Clay in Germany and Douglas MacArthur in Japan to justify requiring more history, languages, economics, political science, and international relations. A 1960s building program supported doubling the Corps of Cadets, to over 4,000.

Although Henry O. Flipper, the first black graduate of West Point, graduated in 1877, black cadets were not treated well generally and only three African Americans graduated from West Point before 1941. These attitudes began to change following the integration of the armed forces after World War II, and minority recruitment increased significantly in the 1960s. After much controversy, USMA also admitted its first women cadets in 1976. Since the end of the Cold War, graduates have participated in expeditionary warfare, as in the *Persian Gulf War, where Gen. H. Norman *Schwarzkopf commanded Coalition Forces against Iraq.

The U.S. Military Academy's mission remains essentially as in 1802: to provide leaders of character, imbued with the academy's motto, "Duty, Honor, Country," to serve the common defense. In 1994, the academy produced its 50,000th graduate.

[See also African Americans in the Military; Education, Military; Leadership, Concepts of Military; Women in the Military.]

• Stephen E. Ambrose, Duty, Honor, Country: A History of West Point, 1966. Dave Richard Palmer, The River and the Rock, 1969. John P. Lovell, Neither Athens Nor Sparta? The American Service Academies in Transition, 1979. James L. Morrison, Jr., "The Best School in the World," 1986. Theodore J. Crackel, The Illustrated History of West Point, 1991. George S. Pappas, To The Point: The United States Military Academy, 1802–1902, 1993.

—Steven C. Gravlin

ACADEMIES, SERVICE: U.S. NAVAL ACADEMY

The U.S. Naval Academy is a four-year undergraduate institution whose mission is to educate and train officers for the U.S. *Navy and U.S. *Marine Corps. The academy was founded in 1845 by Secretary of the Navy George *Bancroft. He overcame years of congressional opposition to a naval school by transferring Fort Severn, an old army post on the banks of the Severn River in Annapolis, Maryland, to the navy for a naval school. Earlier, American naval officers were trained on shipboard by schoolmasters or chaplains, but the inefficiency of this system led to appeals for a naval school ashore. The Naval School opened 10 October 1845 with fifty-six midshipmen and seven faculty members under the direction of the first superintendent, Franklin Buchanan. Five years later, with a new four-year curriculum, summer cruises, and major improvements to the physical plant, the school became known as the U.S. Naval Academy.

Over its 152-year history, the U.S. Naval Academy has expanded from the original 10 acres and antiquated buildings of Fort Severn to a modern, 338-acre campus designed by Ernest Flagg in 1894. His French Renaissance buildings, including Bancroft Hall and the Naval Academy Chapel, were completed early in the century, but complemented in the 1960s by the addition of three classroom buildings, the Nimitz Library, Halsey Auditorium, and recently a Brigade Activity Center.

The Naval Academy program is supervised by a board of visitors and administered by an academic board composed of the superintendent, commandant, academic dean, and division directors. Once called "naval cadets," since 1902 students have been referred to as "midshipmen," a name originating in the days of sail. A need for more junior officers just prior to World War I prompted expansion of the student body to a regiment of 1,240 men. Today, the Brigade of Midshipmen numbers about 4,600, including women, who were first admitted in 1976 and now comprise about 10 percent of each class. Three African Americans entered the academy in the 1870s, but the first to graduate was Wesley A. Brown, Class of 1949. The number of minorities was increased from 9 midshipmen in 1965 to 178 by 1974; today, minority midshipmen compose about a fifth of each entering class.

Applicants to the academy must qualify scholastically, physically, and medically, and obtain an executive nomination. Once admitted, midshipmen are educated at government expense in a four-year program taught by a civilian-military faculty. In the 1960s, Superintendents Charles C. Kirkpatrick and James F. Calvert expanded the core curriculum with the Trident Scholar independent study program, elective majors, and more professional courses. Midshipmen are under military discipline and are bound by the honor concept, which states: "A Midshipman may not lie, cheat, or steal."

Athletics, first encouraged as intramurals by Adm. David Dixon *Porter, superintendent after the *Civil War, remain important to the academy program, and all midshipmen are required to participate in year-round sports. A navy football team was organized in 1882 and played the first Army-Navy football game at West Point on 29 November 1890. Blue and gold colors were chosen in 1893 and a navy team mascot, Bill the Goat, was first adopted by Commandant of Cadets Cmdr. Colby M. Chester (Class of 1864) in 1890.

U.S. Naval Academy graduates are awarded a bachelor of science degree, first given in 1933, and commissioned as ensigns in the U.S. Navy or as second lieutenants in the U.S. Marine Corps. Because their education is paid for by the government, they are required to serve five years on active duty following graduation. Although the academy provides only a fraction of the navy's officers, many senior naval officers have been or are Annapolis graduates. Distinguished graduates include Admirals George *Dewey and William *Sampson; Fleet Admirals Ernest J. *King, Chester *Nimitz, and William F. *Halsey; Nobel Prize winner Albert Michelson; historian Alfred T. *Mahan; inventor Bradley Fiske; Adm. Arleigh *Burke; and President Jimmy *Carter.

[See also Education, Military; Leadership, Concepts of Military.]

• Jack Sweetman, The U.S. Naval Academy: An Illustrated History, 1979. United States Naval Academy Catalogue, 1988–89.
—Barbara Brooks Tomblin

ACADEMIES, SERVICE: U.S. AIR FORCE ACADEMY

In 1947, when the *Air Force was established as a separate service, the question of how to educate potential career Air Force officers was one which followed immediately. It seemed to Air Force leaders that since there was a clear distinction between the challenges of an Army career and an Air Force career, it was also important to create a distinct education process for an Air Force officer. In 1948 the Stearns-Eisenhower Board, studying military education, recommended the creation of a separate Air Force Academy, but not until the *Korean War was over was legislation for an Academy presented in Congress. On April 1, 1954, President Dwight D. *Eisenhower, who had been an early supporter of the idea, signed the bill that created the academy.

Colorado Springs, Colorado, was chosen as the academy's home. Availability of land and water, a supportive community, an aesthetic environment, weather, flying conditions and real estate value were important factors considered. While the new institution was being constructed, the Class of 1959 began their Academy education at Lowry Air Force Base in Denver, moving to the permanent site for their final year.

Much planning went into the curriculum of the institution, and many of the principles behind a West Point education were adapted at the Air Force Academy. A military faculty was deemed important, as well as a core curriculum providing a strong concentration in the sciences. An introduction to flying was considered crucial. Development of character, intellectual and physical development, and professional military development form the basis of an Air Force Academy education; the second lieutenant graduated by the Academy is expected to meet demanding standards in each of these areas.

In 1965 Congressional action increased the size of the cadet wing to 4400, almost doubling it. In 1976 the first women entered the cadet wing; their numbers have steadily increased in the succeeding decades.

[See also Academies, Service: Overview; Air Force, U.S.: Overview.]

• John P. Lovell, Neither Athens Nor Sparta? The American Service Academies in Transition, 1979. George V. Fagan, The Air Force Academy: An Illustrated History, 1988.   —Elizabeth A. Muenger

ACADEMIES, SERVICE: U.S. COAST GUARD ACADEMY

The U.S. Coast Guard Academy located in New London, Connecticut, was founded in 1876. It educates young men and women for a career as Coast Guard officers. Admission is based upon academic competition without congressional appointment. In the 1995–96 school year 862 cadets were enrolled. The student body included 24 percent women, 21 percent minorities.

The curriculum is designed to meet the needs of the service. In addition to teaching professional skills, providing practical seagoing experience, and ensuring that cadets learn integrity, maritime law, and the importance of public service, the curriculum provides humanistic, scientific, and technical knowledge. An emphasis on interactive learning assures that tomorrow's graduates will have the analytical skills needed to cope with a changing international maritime world.

The faculty consists of a mix of permanently assigned commissioned officers, rotating officers, and civilians. They provide a stable base of academic excellence and continuous interaction with the operational Coast Guard.

Cadets concentrate in one of eight majors (civil, electrical, mechanical, or marine engineering; government; management; operations research; or marine science) and graduate with a bachelor of science degree and a commission as an ensign in the U.S. Coast Guard.

[See also Coast Guard, U.S.; Coast Guard Reserve.]

• Paul Johnson and Bill Earle, "U.S. Coast Guard Academy," *The Bulletin*, Centennial Issue (1976). Irving H. King, *The Coast Guard Expands, 1865–1915*, 1996.   —Irving H. King

ACHESON, DEAN (1893–1971), lawyer, statesman, secretary of state. After holding lower State Department posts from 1941 to 1947, Acheson became secretary of state under President Harry S. *Truman in January 1949, serving until January 1953. As a diplomatic official, Acheson held strong views about how, when, and why to use armed force in international affairs.

Acheson was a hawkish interventionist before U.S. entry into World War II. After the war, in 1945–46, he advocated an agreement with the USSR on control of nuclear arms (embodied in the Acheson-Lilienthal Plan). In 1949, when the Soviets first exploded an atomic bomb, Acheson feared it would neutralize the West's nuclear weapons. In response, he consistently advocated building strong conventional U.S. and NATO military forces. Acheson thought an East-West war unlikely, but should it occur, he wanted a military that could stop aggression before the Soviets could conquer Western Europe. With some ambivalence, he always favored keeping a powerful American nuclear arsenal, and in 1950 as an adviser he recommended to President Truman that the United States build the hydrogen bomb. He worked to keep the *Korean War from becoming a general war, but used the sense of resulting urgency to push for greater *NATO forces, including the rearmament of West Germany.

Advising Presidents Kennedy, Johnson, and Nixon after 1953, he consistently took hard-line defense positions, especially in the Berlin Crisis of 1961, the *Cuban Missile Crisis of 1962, and the early stages of the *Vietnam War. However, by 1968 he became an influential advocate of ending the war in Vietnam.

Acheson's key strategic concepts focused on the efficacy of various forms of power, the importance of "strategic reach" to project the first line of U.S. defense far from American shores, and developing "positions of strength" before engaging in negotiations with potential adversaries.

[See also Berlin Crisis.]

• Dean Acheson, *Present at the Creation: My Years in the State Department*, 1969. Gaddis Smith, *Dean Acheson*, 1972. Douglas Brinkley, *Dean Acheson: The Cold War Years, 1953–71*, 1992. Melvyn P. Leffler, *A Preponderance of Power: National Security, the Truman Administration, and the Cold War*, 1992.   —Robert L. Beisher

ACLU. See American Civil Liberties Union.

ADAMS, JOHN (1735–1826), member of the Continental Congress, diplomat, vice president, and second president of the United States. John Adams never soldiered, but throughout his public life he repeatedly faced issues of war and peace.

In June 1775, at the beginning of the *Revolutionary War, Adams nominated George *Washington to command the Continental army, and in October and November 1775, as a member of the Continental Congress's Naval Committee, he was instrumental in creating the U.S. Navy and Marines. From June 1776 until November 1777, Adams chaired the Board of War and Ordnance, Congress's committee to oversee the Continental army and the conduct of the war. As a U.S. diplomat in Europe after 1778, Adams repeatedly implored France to make a greater military commitment. He emphasized the need for concerted action by Washington's army and the French Navy, a formula that eventually led to victory at the Battle of *Yorktown.

Later, faced by the Undeclared Naval War with *France (1798–1800) during his presidency, Adams sought to avoid hostilities, fearful that the fragile new nation might not endure another war. He took steps to strengthen the Union's defenses, but also dispatched to Paris the envoys who ultimately negotiated the accord that prevented war. His action split the Federalist Party and contributed to his defeat in the 1800 election. Reflecting on his public career in 1815, Adams said that his greatest achievement had been the preservation of peace during his presidency.

• Page Smith, *John Adams*, 1962. John Ferling, *John Adams: A Life*, 1988.   —John Ferling

ADAMS-ONÍS TREATY (1819) This agreement, also called the Transcontinental Treaty, was made during the administration of President James *Monroe and settled long-standing disputes between the United States and Spain. Madrid ceded East Florida to the Americans, while Washington surrendered its claims to Texas and agreed to assume payment of American financial claims against the Spanish up to $5 million. The treaty established definitive western boundaries for the Louisiana Purchase, following the Sabine, Red, and Arkansas Rivers to the 42nd parallel, and running along that line to the Pacific. The United States also secured Spanish claims to Oregon.

Historians have variously interpreted the treaty's significance. Samuel F. Bemis stressed the establishment of the first American claims to territory bordering the Pacific. More recently, William E. Weeks emphasized that the treaty consummated the first phase of the United States's aggressive, nineteenth-century territorial expansion. Strategically speaking, the Florida cession closed a vulnerable point in American coastal defenses. European powers welcomed the treaty because it ended the possibility of war between the United States and Spain. Some westerners protested the loss of Texas, but otherwise, there was little domestic opposition. The agreement was named for its principal negotiators—Secretary of State John Quincy Adams and Spain's minister to the United States, Don Luis de Onís.

[*See also* Expansionism.]

• Charles C. Griffin, *The United States and the Disruption of the Spanish Empire, 1810–1822*, 1937. Philip C. Brooks, *Diplomacy and the Borderlands: The Adams-Onís Treaty of 1819*, 1939. Samuel Flagg Bemis, *John Quincy Adams and the Foundations of American Foreign Policy*, 1949. William E. Weeks, *John Quincy Adams and American Global Empire*, 1992.   —Michael S. Fitzgerald

ADDAMS, JANE (1860–1935), American social reformer, settlement house founder, pacifist, and writer. Addams was born 6 September 1860 in Cedarville, Illinois. Heir to her father's political sensibilities, Jane Addams's early heroes were Abraham *Lincoln and Giuseppe Mazzini. A member of the first generation of college women, she found a way to put her social gospel and piety directly to work with the founding (with Ellen Gates Starr) of Hull House, a settlement house in Chicago's immigrant ghetto. In 1889, Addams claimed that democratic political governance was, in fact, a form of civic housekeeping: she became a leading social reformer of the era and a founder of modern social work.

Jane Addams's world was turned upside down with the outbreak of World War I. Her defense of radicals and anarchists, her brave and often lonely devotion to *pacifism and opposition to "the idea of war" as well as its terrible reality, placed her outside the American mainstream and brought down derision and abuse. In 1915, Addams, Emily Greene *Balch, and others helped to create the Woman's Peace Party, which called for "continuous mediation." This was the forerunner to the *Women's International League for Peace and Freedom, founded in 1919, of which Jane Addams was a founding mother and president from its inception in 1915 to her death. An advocate of women's suffrage, Addams in her articles, speeches, and books traced the powerful role women must play in promoting peace as an imperative to preserve human life. Her understanding of feminism set it in "unalterable" opposition to militarism.

Unfairly and inaccurately called a traitor and a Bolshevik, Addams never reneged on her commitments to civil liberties or to pacifism. Her joint recognition (with Nicholas Murray Butler) for the Nobel Peace Prize in 1931 and her embodiment of the notion of service helped restore her stature as one of America's foremost humanitarians.

• Christopher Lasch, ed., *The Social Thought of Jane Addams*, 1965. Daniel Levine, *Jane Addams and the Liberal Tradition*, 1980.
           —Jean Bethke Elshtain

AEGIS. The AEGIS Combat System is a sophisticated shipborne target detection and tracking system developed by the U.S. *Navy and currently installed in twenty-eight *Ticonderoga*-class guided missile cruisers and eighteen *Arleigh *Burke–class fleet escorts.

The U.S. Navy developed AEGIS in the 1970s in response to the Soviet threat of saturation missile attacks against American carrier forces. Conventional rotating radars cannot rapidly track and process multiple targets, but AEGIS planar arrays are able to track an unlimited number of targets and relay the data instantaneously to a main computer in the ship's combat information center. The system then rapidly prioritizes the target data received from its SPY-1 phased array radars and assigns targets to the ship's weapons systems. Superior to more conventional radar systems and highly resistant to electronic counter-

measures, AEGIS has also enhanced the target collection and processing capability of *Ticonderoga*-class cruisers serving as flagships for battle groups.

Budget limitations prompted the navy, which originally intended AEGIS for nuclear-powered escorts, to substitute the less expensive, but proven, oil-fired *Spruance*-class design for its new guided missile cruisers In 1988, the first of an AEGIS-equipped class of fleet escorts, USS *Arleigh Burke* (DDG 51), was launched, and to date twenty-eight have been completed.

To support joint and coalition operations against adversaries in littoral areas, the U.S. Navy has offered the AEGIS system to allied navies. Japan already has a significant AEGIS capability and Spain plans to install the lighter, more compact SPY-1F arrays in its new F-100 class frigates.

[*See also* Radar.]

• David Miller and Chris Miller, *Modern Naval Combat*, 1986. Dennis M. Bailey, *Aegis Guided Missile Cruiser*, 1991. Robert Gardner, ed., *Conway's All the World's Fighting Ships 1947–1995*, 1995. John Jordan, *An Illustrated Guide to the Modern U.S. Navy*, 1992. Dr. Robin Laird, "The Challenges of Internationalization," *Seapower* (September 1997).   —Barbara Brooks Tomblin

AFRICAN AMERICANS IN THE MILITARY. Americans of African descent have participated in all the wars of the United States, serving their country and themselves, for military service has offered African Americans a means of economic, social, and political as well as military advancement. Black participation thus must be understood in the context of the importance of racial issues that developed as early as the colonial era, issues that have shaped the unique expansion of African Americans in the American military.

During the colonial period, the largest numbers of free blacks were in the northern colonies. These colonies were much more willing to include Americans of African descent in their militia than were the southern colonies, which held the majority of slaves, although some colonies used blacks in labor units for militia expeditions. But in cases of dire need, even colonies like South Carolina, where slaves greatly outnumbered whites, would arm slaves to fight in exchange for their freedom, as in the victorious campaign against the Yamasee Indians in 1715.

Following the 1739 slave revolt in Stono, South Carolina, however, most of the colonies excluded all blacks from military service. Laws for black exclusion were repealed in the North for freed blacks and often overlooked in the South, where despite the official policy of exclusion, free Americans of African descent were still armed during conflicts with the Indians and the French, and even slaves served as scouts, wagoners, laborers, and servants.

In the American Revolution, African Americans served with the New England "Minute Men" at Lexington and Concord and helped fire the "shot heard 'round the world." Although blacks had served in the colonial wars before the revolution and still served in northern militias, when the *Revolutionary War began in 1775, they were not at first welcomed into the *Continental army because of the influence of the slave states in the new national government. It was not until after November 1775, when the British started to recruit blacks into their forces, that African Americans were officially allowed to join the Continental army. By 1776, faced with increasing shortages of volunteers, Gen.

George *Washington disagreed with the Continental Congress and declared that he could depart from the resolution that barred participation by blacks. Because Congress did not challenge Washington's action, more than 5,000 Americans of African descent served in integrated units in the Continental forces. Most of the southern states officially refused to use blacks in the military except as laborers, but in practice, some Southern black slaves were sent as substitutes. African Americans participated in many battles, including those of Bunker Hill, New York, Trenton and Princeton, Savannah, Monmouth, and Yorktown.

Following the Revolutionary War, the new United States virtually eliminated its army and navy. The U.S. Army was soon established and accepted blacks; the U.S. Navy was created in 1798, accepting black sailors as it had during the revolution and continuing to do so throughout the nineteenth century. The smaller U.S. Marine Corps excluded blacks from its inception in 1798 until 1942. Black soldiers served in the War of 1812, but in 1820, Secretary of War John C. *Calhoun of South Carolina, responding to Southern slaveowners, banned any further enlistment by African Americans. As black veterans left, the U.S. Army became exclusively white until the *Civil War.

The Civil War, a conflict over slavery as well as the nature of the Union, also raised the issue of black military service. The Confederacy, which used the black slaves as the basic agricultural labor force and which feared slave rebellion, refused to recruit blacks until 1865, when it was too late. In the North, the U.S. War Department in 1861 continued its policy of rejecting black enlistment, but in 1862 as slaves flocked to the Northern armies invading the South, some abolitionist Union generals began training them to fight. Official policy did not change until after the *Emancipation Proclamation took effect, 1 January 1863; then, when volunteering had slackened in the North and it had become a war to free the slaves, the Northern states and the federal government began recruiting the eager freedmen into black regiments with black noncommissioned officers (NCOs) and mostly white commissioned officers.

Eventually, 186,000 Americans of African descent fought for their freedom in the *Union army (and another 30,000 in the *Union navy), winning fourteen Congressional Medals of Honor in the process. Units of the U.S. *Colored Troops fought in a number of major battles, including the 54th Massachusetts Regiment's assault during the siege of *Fort Wagner at Charleston and the attack of the black Fourth Division of the Ninth Corps at the Battle of the Crater in the siege of Petersburg, Virginia. Confederates often refused to take black prisoners, and they killed a number of them at the *Fort Pillow massacre in Tennessee. Although the black soldiers were paid less than the whites, their wartime service and heroism were cited as one reason for giving black men the vote in *Reconstruction.

After the Civil War, there were black militia units in the southern states until the end of Reconstruction, and in some northern cities well into the twentieth century. Congress added four black regiments to the regular army (the 9th and 10th Cavalry and the 24th and 25th Infantry). These *"Buffalo" Soldiers, as they were called by the Indians, served mainly in the West, but they also saw combat in the *Spanish-American War and Philippine insurrection, as well as in the Mexican Punitive Expedition of 1916. Most of their officers were white, like John J. *Pershing.

Only three African Americans graduated from West Point, 1865–98; one of them, Charles *Young (Class of 1884), remained the army's sole black officer until he was joined by Benjamin O. *Davis, Sr.

With the increased segregation, disfranchisement, and lynching of black Americans at the turn of the century, race became an issue in the U.S. *mobilization for World War I. NAACP leader W. E. B. *Du Bois urged black men to join the military in order to regain the rights of citizenship and he obtained commissions for a few black junior officers (Col. Charles Young was forced into retirement). The southern-dominated Wilson administration supported the army's insistence on continuation of racially segregated units, and, after a race riot in Houston in August 1917, limited these to eight black combat regiments. *Conscription and voluntarism brought 380,000 Americans of African descent into the wartime army, but 89 percent were assigned to labor units and only 11 percent to the two combat divisions. Although the 93rd Division, which included the black National Guard units like the 369th New York (the "Harlem Hell Fighters"), distinguished itself fighting alongside French troops, after the armistice, the War Department concluded that in future wars, black soldiers should mainly serve as laborers. It cut back the one black regular regiment (the 25th Infantry) and excluded blacks from new specialties like aviation. By 1940, there were only 5,000 black soldiers (2 percent of the force) and five black officers in the army. The navy had been accepting fewer blacks since its changeover from sail to steampower in the later nineteenth century (there were only 441 black sailors in 1934); the Marines continued their all-white policy.

At the outbreak of World War II, America reverted to its practice of turning to African Americans when it needed more troops. In 1940, President Franklin D. *Roosevelt appointed Col. Benjamin O. Davis, Sr., to be the army's first black brigadier general, and opened the Army Air Corps to black pilots. These "Black Eagles," including Davis's son, Benjamin O. *Davis, Jr., who trained at Tuskegee, Alabama, served in all-black units. In 1941, black labor leader A. Philip *Randolph threatened a protest march on Washington for equal opportunity in the defense workforce and the military. Civil rights activist Bayard *Rustin and Black Muslim leader Elijah Muhammad dramatized such concerns by going to prison.

Most of the 900,000 blacks who served in the armed forces in World War II were in segregated units, chiefly in the army (and including black women, who served in segregated units of the *WACs and the Army and Navy *Nurse Corps). However, wartime demands for increased numbers of service people as well as the ideology of a war against Nazi racism contributed to some integration. The Coast Guard began racial integration on shipboard, and the navy followed on some fleet auxiliary ships. Army units were segregated for most of the war, but beginning with the Battle of the *Bulge, when the army suffered shortages of white infantrymen, some 4,500 men from black service units volunteered and formed black platoons in formerly all-white combat companies. Although the Marine Corps accepted a few black recruits, it largely maintained its racial segregation. Black service people, like other veterans, benefited after the war from the *G.I. Bill.

In the postwar era, the armed forces initially sought to avoid integration, delaying even in the face of President Harry S. *Truman's 1948 election-year order (Executive

Order 9981) for an end to segregation in the military—the armed forces were directed to provide equal treatment and opportunity regardless of race. The U.S. Air Force, however, had moved toward integration in 1949 after achieving independent status in 1947. Beginning in 1951, the reverses of the *Korean War led to the end of all-black units in the army and Marines, and moved all the services toward racial integration in the enlisted ranks for greater efficiency. Black and white service people now fought side by side, dined in the same mess hall, and slept in the same barracks. Nevertheless, the officer corps remained white, with black officers representing only 3 percent of the army's officers and 1 percent of the air force, navy, and Marine officer corps.

The *Vietnam War saw the highest proportion of blacks ever to serve in an American war. During the height of the U.S. involvement, 1965–69, blacks, who formed 11 percent of the American population, made up 12.6 percent of the soldiers in Vietnam. The majority of these were in the infantry, and although authorities differ on the figures, the percentage of black combat fatalities in that period was a staggering 14.9 percent, a proportion that subsequently declined. Volunteers and draftees included many frustrated blacks whose impatience with the war and the delays in racial progress in America led to race riots on a number of ships and military bases, beginning in 1968, and the services' response in creating interracial councils and racial sensitivity training.

The Nixon administration ended the Vietnam War and the draft in 1973, and the *All-Volunteer Force (AVF) soon included a disproportionate number of African Americans. By 1983, blacks represented 33 percent of the army, 22 percent of the Marine Corps, 14 percent of the air force, and 12 percent of the navy. Black senior NCOs in the army increased from 14 percent in 1970 to 26 percent in 1980, and 31 percent in 1990. Blacks also increased in the officer corps; by 1983, the army had almost 10 percent, the air force 5 percent, the Marine Corps 4 percent, and the navy 3 percent. Black women were an important component of the influx of women into the AVF, beginning in the 1970s; by 1983, they comprised 17 percent of the army's officers and 20 percent of its enlisted women. For the air force, the figures were 11 and 20; the Marine Corps, 5 and 23; and the navy, 5 and 18 percent.

In 1977, Clifford Alexander was appointed the first black secretary of the army, and in 1989, Army Gen. Colin *Powell was appointed the first black chairman of the *Joint Chiefs of Staff, the head of the uniformed services. Powell oversaw the *Persian Gulf War of 1991, in which 24 percent of the 500,000 U.S. service people deployed to the Middle East (30 percent of the soldiers) were Americans of African descent. Significant percentages of African American troops also participated in peacekeeping operations in Somalia, Haiti, and Bosnia and Kosovo in the 1990s.

The participation of Americans of African descent in the U.S. military has a long and distinguished history. But although African Americans have participated in all American wars, they have sometimes faced almost as bitter a hostility from their fellow Americans as from the enemy. Nevertheless, particularly since the 1970s, the U.S. military has made a serious effort at racial integration, and while much remains to be done, the military has achieved a degree of success in this area that surpasses most civilian institutions.

[See also Ethnicity and Race in the Military.]

• Dudley Taylor Cornish, *The Sable Arm: Negro Troops in the Union Army, 1861–1865*, 1956. Ulysses Lee, *The United States Army in World War II; Special Studies: The Employment of Negro Troops*, 1966. William H. Leckie, *The Buffalo Soldiers: A Narrative of the Negro Cavalry in the West*, 1967. Richard M. Dalfiume, *Desegregation of the U.S. Armed Forces: Fighting on Two Fronts, 1939–1953*, 1969. Otis A. Singletary, *The Negro Militia and Reconstruction*, 1971. Arthur E. Barbeau, and Florette Henri, *The Unknown Soldiers: Black American Troops in World War I*, 1974. Marvin E. Fletcher, *The Black Soldier and Officer in the United States Army, 1891–1917*, 1974. Henry I. Shaw, Jr., and Ralph N. Donnelly, *Blacks in the Marine Corps*, 1975. Robert V. Hayes, *A Night of Violence: The Houston Riot of 1917*, 1976. Alan L. Gropman, *The Air Force Integrates, 1945–1964*, 1977. Morris J. MacGregor, and Bernard C. Nalty, eds., *Blacks in the United States Armed Forces: Basic Documents*, 13 vols., 1977. Alan M. Osur, *Blacks in the Army Air Forces during World War II*, 1977. Morris J. MacGregor, *Defense Studies: Integration of the Armed Forces, 1940–1965*, 1981. Martin Binkin, and Mark J. Eitelberg, *Blacks and the Military*, 1982. Bernard C. Nalty, *Strength for the Fight: A History of Black Americans in the Military*, 1986. Charles C. Moskos, and John Sibley Butler, *All That We Can Be: Black Leadership and Racial Integration the Army Way*, 1996.

—John Sibley Butler

AGGRESSION AND VIOLENCE. To understand the nature of aggression and violence on the battlefield, it must first be recognized that most participants in close combat are literally "frightened out of their wits." Once the bullets start flying, most combatants stop thinking with the forebrain (that portion of the brain that makes us human) and start thinking with the midbrain (the primitive portion of our brain, which is indistinguishable from that of an animal).

In conflict situations, this primitive, midbrain processing can be observed in the existence of a powerful resistance to killing one's own kind. Animals with antlers and horns slam together in a relatively harmless head-to-head fashion, and piranha fish fight their own kind with flicks of the tail, but against any other species these creatures unleash their horns and teeth without restraint. This is an essential survival mechanism that prevents a species from destroying itself during territorial and mating rituals.

One major modern revelation in the field of military psychology is the observation that such resistance to killing one's own species is also a key factor in human combat. Brig. Gen. S. L. A. *Marshall first observed this during his work as an official U.S. Army historian in the Pacific and European theaters of operations in World War II. Based on his postcombat interviews, Marshall concluded in his book *Men Against Fire* (1946, 1978) that only 15 to 20 percent of the individual riflemen in World War II fired their own weapons at an exposed enemy soldier. Key weapons, such as *flamethrowers, were usually fired. Crew-served weapons, such as *machine guns, almost always were fired. And action would increase greatly if a nearby leader demanded that the soldier fire. But when left on their own, the great majority of individual combatants appear to have been unable or unwilling to kill.

Marshall's findings were and have remained controversial. Faced with scholarly concern about a researcher's methodology and conclusions, the scientific method involves replicating the research. In Marshall's case, every available parallel, scholarly study validates his basic findings. Ardant du Picq's surveys of French officers in the

1860s and his observations about ancient battles (*Battle Studies,* 1946), John Keegan and Richard Holmes's numerous accounts of ineffectual firing throughout history (*Soldiers,* 1985), Holmes's assessment of Argentine firing rates in the Falklands War (*Acts of War,* 1985), Paddy Griffith's data on the extraordinarily low firing rate among Napoleonic and American *Civil War regiments (*Battle Tactics of the American Civil War,* 1989), the British army's laser reenactments of historical battles, the FBI's studies of nonfiring rates among law enforcement officers in the 1950s and 1960s, and countless other individual and anecdotal observations, all confirm Marshall's fundamental conclusion that human beings are not, by nature, killers. Indeed, from a psychological perspective, the history of warfare can be viewed as a series of successively more effective tactical and mechanical mechanisms to enable or force combatants to overcome their resistance to killing other human beings, even when defined as the enemy.

By 1946, the U.S. Army had accepted Marshall's conclusions, and the Human Resources Research Office of the U.S. Army subsequently pioneered a revolution in combat training, which eventually replaced firing at targets with deeply ingrained "conditioning," using realistic, man-shaped pop-up targets that fall when hit. Psychologists assert that this kind of powerful "operant conditioning" is the only technique that will reliably influence the primitive, midbrain processing of a frightened human being. Fire drills condition schoolchildren to respond properly even when terrified during a fire. Conditioning in flight simulators enables pilots to respond reflexively to emergency situations even when frightened. And similar application and perfection of basic conditioning techniques increased the rate of fire to approximately 55 percent in Korea and around 95 percent in Vietnam.

Equally high rates of fire resulting from modern conditioning techniques can be seen in Holmes's observation of British firing rates in the Falklands, and FBI data on law enforcement firing rates since the nationwide introduction of modern conditioning techniques in the late 1960s.

The extraordinarily high firing rate resulting from these processes was a key factor in the American ability to claim that the United States never lost a major engagement in Vietnam. But conditioning that overrides such a powerful, innate resistance has enormous potential for psychological backlash. Every warrior society has a "purification ritual" to help the returning warrior deal with his "blood guilt" and to reassure him that what he did in combat was "good." In primitive tribes, this generally involves ritual bathing, ritual separation (which serves as a cooling-off and "group therapy" session), and a ceremony embracing the veteran back into the tribe. Modern Western rituals traditionally involve long separation while marching or sailing home, parades, monuments, and the unconditional acceptance of society and family.

In the *Vietnam War, this purification ritual was turned on its head. The returning American veteran was attacked and condemned in an unprecedented manner. The traditional horrors of combat were magnified by modern conditioning techniques, and this combined with societal condemnation to create a circumstance that resulted in .5 to 1.5 million cases of Post-Traumatic Stress Disorder (PTSD) in Vietnam veterans. The mass incidence of psychiatric disorders among Vietnam veterans resulted in the "discov-

ery" of PTSD, a condition that we now know traditionally occurred as a result of warfare, but never in such quantity.

PTSD seldom results in violent criminal acts, and upon returning to society, the recipient of modern military conditioning is statistically no more likely to engage in violent crime than a nonveteran of the same age. The key safeguard in this process appears to be the deeply ingrained discipline that the combat soldier internalizes with his military training. However, with the advent of interactive "point-and-shoot" arcade and video games, there is significant concern that society is aping military conditioning, but without the vital safeguard of discipline. There is strong evidence to indicate that the indiscriminate civilian application of combat conditioning techniques as entertainment may be a factor in worldwide, skyrocketing violent crime rates, including a sevenfold increase in per capita aggravated assaults in America since 1956. Thus, the latest chapter in American military history may be occurring in the city streets.

[*See also* Combat, Changing Experience of; Combat Trauma; Disciplinary Views of War: Psychology; Psychiatry, Military; Training and Indoctrination.]

• Konrad Lorenz, *On Aggression,* 1963. John Keegan, *The Face of Battle,* 1976. Jim Goodwin, *Post-Traumatic Stress Disorders: A Handbook for Clinicians,* 1988. Dave Grossman, *On Killing: The Psychological Cost of Learning to Kill in War and Society,* 1995. Dave Grossman, *On Killing: The Psychological Cost of Learning to Kill in War and Society,* 8th ed., 1996. Dave Grossman and Gloria DeGaetano, *Teaching Our Kids to Kill: A Call to Action Against TV, Movie, and Video Game Violence,* 1999.   —Dave Grossman

AGRICULTURE AND WAR. War and agriculture have often been intertwined during the nation's history. Although this usually involved arable land and farm production, there were times when agricultural trade was at issue.

The American Revolution, for example, stemmed in part from British mercantilist regulations, including the requirements that the colonies ship certain commodities, such as tobacco, only to England, and that the English have a monopoly of the American market on certain foodstuffs such as tea. During the *Revolutionary War, agriculture helped to feed the American forces, and in the Continental Congress it saw U.S. commodity exports as a major lever in building alliances with other nations, creating the model Commercial Treaty of 1777 (Jefferson later sought to use the curtailment of American agriculture exports, the embargo, to force Britain and France to change their maritime policies toward the United States). Land was the major resource of the new government, which often offered it as enlistment bounty to soldiers during the revolution. The peace treaty of 1783 provided the new United States with land as far west as the Mississippi River.

Westward expansion of agriculture intensified the pressures on American Indian nations and fueled intermittent wars with them. The westward expansion of American agriculture was founded on military conquest and the displacement of Native Americans. The *Mexican War of 1846–48 also involved westward expansion, this time at the expense of Mexicans as well as Indians.

The *Civil War was partly caused by the expansion into those new lands and the debate over whether the agricultural workforce there would be slave or free. Secessionists dedicated to slavery believed that demand for southern cotton would force Great Britain and other countries to support the Confederacy. Southern agriculture continued during much of the war, maintained by slave labor; the main change was diversification from large cotton crops to corn and other foodstuffs as the South was cut off from Northern wheat supplies. In the North, many rural young men went into the *Union army, creating a great shortage on the farms when foodstuffs were bringing high prices because of inflation and increased demands at home and abroad. Immigration and use of farm machines was expanded—to horse-powered cultivators, mowers, and reapers—to resolve the dilemma.

In 1862, the Republican Congress enacted a number of the party's programs for agriculture. Among these were the Homestead Act, promoting western agricultural expansion by granting family-sized farms free to settlers; the Morrill Act, offering states public lands to sell for endowing land-grant agricultural colleges; and the establishment of the U.S. Department of Agriculture (USDA). Congress also adopted high protective tariffs for industry, which meant rural consumers would pay higher prices for manufactured goods.

American agriculture boomed in World War I when the United States in essence fed the Allied nations as well as its own wartime armed forces. In 1914–18, American wheat production rose to an average of about 870 million bushels and cotton exports also increased, although corn production remained relatively stable. Farmers and much farm labor received draft deferments; encouraged by soaring commodity prices, they increased their production through purchase of gasoline-powered machinery and the cultivation of additional land. In 1918, grain production reached into the most arid section of the Great Plains. The wholesale price index of farm products more than doubled, from 100 to 208 between 1914 and 1918. When the wartime foreign and military demands declined after the war, export markets collapsed, and American agriculture, already heavily in debt from the wartime expansion, plunged into a severe economic depression in 1921, which lasted for more than a decade.

During the 1930s, the Roosevelt administration responded to the depression in agriculture with commodity support programs that provided benefits to the more affluent commercial farmers, especially midwestern corn growers and southern cotton producers. At the same time, the New Deal in agriculture included a land-use planning effort in which USDA officials worked with less affluent farmers at the local level in pursuit of a reformist program. New Deal reform initiatives for agriculture, as in many other areas, were overwhelmed by the World War II economic mobilization. President Franklin D. *Roosevelt's wartime administration relied on the commodity support programs—not the land-use planning infrastructure—to guide wartime production. By guaranteeing high prices, the wartime program generated high output of crops that were not needed, overproduction of important crops, and a sharp rise in food prices. In pushing land-use planning to the margins of the mobilization, these wartime decisions determined the outlines of the agricultural policies that would dominate the postwar period. The postwar U.S. Department of Agriculture distributed commodity support payments according to the total output and landholdings of farmers; marginal producers received less and were

thereby encouraged (in many cases forced) to leave farming. Whereas the mobilization for the Civil War gave birth to the Department of Agriculture, the mobilization for World War II ensured the demise of reformist planning efforts that had characterized the Department of Agriculture during the New Deal of the 1930s.

During the war, farmers received draft deferments as well as loans for increasing production through mechanization, land acquisition, and increased use of fertilizers. The index of gross farm production (with 1939 at 100) rose from 108 in 1940 to 126 in 1946. Cash receipts from farm products doubled, from $9 billion in 1940 to $22 billion in 1945.

The federal government sought to limit domestic civilian demand by rationing certain products, including sugar, coffee, meat, fats and cooking oils, butter, cheese, and processed foods. Wheat and cotton both tripled in price; wheat from 90 cents a bushel in 1940 to $2.88 in 1948; cotton from 9 cents per pound in 1940 to 32 cents in 1947. Beef cattle prices also increased dramatically. During World War II, the American Farm Bureau Federation, created in 1920 among affluent, commercial farmers, worked actively to protect those farmers' interests under price controls and in directing programs necessary in the war effort.

In the post–World War II period, the changing technologies and logistics of war sharply reduced the strategic importance of agriculture. During the 1940s and 1950s, the national security doctrine asserted the need for the United States to maintain a preponderance of power—power that was not based solely upon strategic *nuclear weapons. National security required the United States to maintain a lead in industrial production and access to raw materials. Even with this expansive definition of national security, agricultural goods were at the margins of U.S. military planning.

Yet while diminishing in its direct relevance to the military, agriculture played an important role in the *Cold War. The damage to European agriculture in World War II and extensive aid given through the *Marshall Plan to deter the expansion of communism led Washington to fund the marketing of American agricultural surpluses in Europe in the late 1940s and early 1950s. With American agriculture continuing to produce more than was consumed by the domestic market, the Agricultural Trade Development Act of 1954 authorized the secretary of agriculture to accept up to $700 million in foreign currency as repayment for commodities shipped overseas to nations deemed friendly to the United States.

In the 1960s, the Food for Peace program administered by George McGovern was one of the Kennedy administration's efforts to counter communism in Third World countries while assisting American farmers in finding foreign markets. The 1960s and 1970s saw a shift away from price supports and instead an expanded role for American farmers and agribusiness in producing foodstuffs under government subsidies for export to Third World nations.

In the hegemonic role the United States played during the Cold War, a major strategy was to liberalize world trade in manufactured goods, especially through the General Agreement on Tariffs and Trade (GATT) system. But under pressure from the farm interests, Washington in the 1950s obtained an exclusion of agricultural products from GATT, allowing the U.S. government to use import quotas to protect commercial farmers. Not until the late 1980s, when the more heavily subsidized farmers of Japan and the European Community would bear more of the cost of trade liberalization, did Washington include agriculture within the GATT.

Agricultural goods were necessary to sustain the mass industrial armies of the twentieth century, but these supplies represented a shrinking portion of all munitions. In the Franco-Prussian War of 1870, for example, foodstuffs constituted the largest portion of military supplies (for soldiers and for horses), while ammunition constituted only 1 percent of the total. During World War II, food and clothing comprised approximately 10 percent of military supplies, while petroleum and ammunition constituted the largest share of military supplies.

Even during the Korean and Vietnam Wars, procuring agricultural goods to feed and clothe the armed forces did not require specialized agencies and governmental controls. In the 1990s, as the nation entered the post–Cold War era, the separation of the military and agriculture seemed likely to widen further. Military planners project a significantly smaller force structure and procuring the necessary agricultural goods is increasingly taken for granted. If this projected diminution of agriculture's strategic importance does occur, it should not obscure the intimate ties between the U.S. military and agriculture in the foundation and early development of the nation.

[See also, Economy and War; Expansionism; War: Effects of War on the Economy.]

• Murray R. Benedict, *Farm Policies of the United States 1790–1950: A Study of Their Origins and Development,* 1953. Richard Kirkendall, *Social Scientists and Farm Politics in the Age of Roosevelt,* 1966. Martin van Creveld, *Supplying War: Logistics from Wallenstein to Patton,* 1977. Gregory Hooks, "From an Autonomous to a Captured State Agency: The Decline of the New Deal in Agriculture," *American Sociological Review,* vol. 55, no. 1 (1990), pp. 29–43. Gregory Hooks, *Forging the Military-Industrial Complex: World War II's Battle of the Potomac,* 1991. Renee Marlin-Bennett, *Food Fights: International Regimens and the Politics of Agricultural Trade Disputes,* 1993.   —Gregory Hooks

AGUINALDO, EMILIO (1869–1964), revolutionary and statesman of the Philippines. During the *Spanish-American War, Emilio Aguinaldo y Famy consolidated a strong nationalist movement against Spain only to face a stronger opponent of Filipino independence, the U.S. government. Though initially aided by U.S. Navy and consular agents, Aguinaldo's provisional government became the primary obstacle to the annexation policy of President William *McKinley after Spain capitulated in August 1898. Six months later, U.S. troops drove Filipino militias from Manila and pursued them into the countryside. With his political council divided between accommodationists and die-hard nationalists, and his regiments poorly trained and ill-equipped, Aguinaldo's was perhaps a doomed effort. Nevertheless, he used guerrilla tactics and clandestine political organization to resist, retreating from redoubt to redoubt until his capture by Brig. Gen. Frederick Funston on 31 March, 1901. Accepting defeat, he swore allegiance to the United States and retired to his plantation. In 1935, he lost a bid for the presidency of the Philippine Commonwealth. After supporting Japanese occupation during World War II, Aguinaldo was imprisoned in 1945, but re-

ceived amnesty. He died in 1964, a tragic but beloved Philippine national hero.

[*See also* Philippine War (1899–1902).]

• Stuart C. Miller, *Benevolent Assimilation,* 1986. Glenn A. May, *Battle for Batangas,* 1992.   —James Grant Crawford

AIDS. Shortly after the first cases of acquired immunodeficiency syndrome (AIDS) were recognized among civilians in 1981, early forms of the disease (AIDS-related complex and lymphadenopathy syndrome) were detected among active duty personnel. The causative virus (now called the human immunodeficiency virus, HIV) was first isolated from ill soldiers and their asymptomatic but nonetheless infected wives in 1984. These military studies provided the first proof that HIV could be transmitted through heterosexual intercourse. Nationwide blood bank testing for HIV began in June 1985. Shortly thereafter, in October 1985, the Department of *Defense (DoD) began screening all civilian applicants for military service; those who tested positive for the virus were medically disqualified from service. Overall, 1 in 650 applicants was found to be infected, but prevalence rates in various geographic and demographic subpopulations varied from as low as 1 in 20,000 in the upper Midwest to 1 in 50 in northeastern urban centers. The HIV screening program was the first population-based screening program in the United States, and provided the first hard data that the epidemic had already spread silently throughout the country by the mid-1980s.

HIV screening of active duty military personnel began in 1986. Based largely on the recommendations of the Armed Forces Epidemiological Board, policies for HIV infection were established to be comparable to those for any other chronic medical condition. Infected military personnel were to remain on active duty, to lodge in military quarters, and to continue work in their duty assignment. Implemented at a time when fear of HIV contagion was widespread in the United States, these policies were far-sighted and courageous. All DoD HIV-positive personnel were to be medically evaluated periodically, and those with advanced disease were honorably discharged with medical disability and benefits. HIV-infected personnel were restricted from overseas deployment, from health care jobs where potentially risky procedures were performed, and from sensitive Personal Reliability Program (e.g., nuclear missile) positions. In an effort to decrease HIV transmission, HIV-infected active duty personnel were counseled by their commanders that if they knowingly put others at risk of infection through sexual intercourse, they could be prosecuted through the military justice system. Overall, DoD policies were designed to reflect fair and rational public health principles.

Screening was originally undertaken annually for all active duty personnel, but this interval has gradually lengthened with a number of new service-specific regulations. For example, testing takes place every five years for all air force personnel, or for the following clinically indicated reasons: during pregnancy; on entry into a drug/alcohol rehabilitation program; on presenting at a STD (sexually-transmitted disease) clinic; on deployment overseas; on PCS (Permanent Change of Station) overseas. However, all personnel must be proven negative within six months of any overseas deployment.

The U.S. military HIV research program began in 1986, when Congress provided $40 million for this purpose. The U.S. Army Medical Research and Development Command, as the lead agency for infectious disease research, managed the tri-service program. Major accomplishments include the following firsts: definition of antibody test criteria for a diagnosis of HIV (criteria used worldwide today); evidence that HIV was becoming a serious problem among minorities; detection of transmission of drug-resistant HIV strains; tracking the global spread of genetic variants; vaccine therapy trials; and international preventive vaccine trials.

At the heart of the controversy over HIV/AIDS research is the question of its relevance to the military. HIV/AIDS has little or no direct impact on readiness or combat operations for U.S. forces. However, recent studies have shown very high HIV prevalences among some African (one in four) and Asian (one in ten) military populations. From a broader national security point of view, the global pandemic is a threat requiring maximal efforts by all capable U.S. agencies.

Rates for new infections have decreased; in 1995, the DoD's total of infections among active duty personnel was approximately 300. In 1996, an amendment to the department's authorization bill ruled that all HIV-infected personnel on active duty must be involuntarily separated, regardless of their fitness for duty or years of service; however, as of 1999, the policy was not to separate HIV-infected personnel who were physically fit. The impact of this legislation on the effectiveness of public health control of HIV within the military remains to be determined.

[See also Diseases, Sexually Transmitted; Medical Practice in the Military.]   —Donald S. Burke

AIR AND SPACE DEFENSE. Recognizing that the two great oceans that had protected the United States from invasion for more than a century could now, at least in theory, be overcome through aerial assault, the administration of President Franklin D. *Roosevelt after the outbreak of World War II in September 1939 began to rearm the nation. A sizable investment in this effort went to the Army Air Corps, which was woefully inadequate to meet the needs of national defense. In April 1939, when Congress passed the National Defense Act of 1940, it authorized the Army Air Corps to develop and procure 6,000 new airplanes, to increase personnel to 3,203 officers and 45,000 enlisted, and to spend $300 million, much of it directly earmarked for defense of U.S. territory. As a result, the aviation forces received $70.6 million, 15.7 percent of the army's direct appropriations. This number and the percentage continued to climb during the early 1940s.

After the attack on *Pearl Harbor of 7 December 1941, the ability of the Japanese Navy to strike American forces on the West Coast could not be dismissed. On 9 December, Gen. "Hap" *Arnold, commanding the U.S. Army Air Corps, directed that all aircraft on the West Coast be dispersed so that a single attack could not destroy significant military capability. He also placed air squadrons along the borders on alert, relocated most support infrastructure to the interior, and set into motion the modern approach to defense of the nation's perimeter.

During World War II, coastal aerial attacks on the United States were limited to a few Japanese balloons carrying bombs over the West Coast in 1944 and 1945. However, the effect of World War II on thinking about U.S. national defense proved crucial. Two major technological developments rendered the nation particularly vulnerable to outside attack: the long-range strategic bomber (especially if carrying atomic bombs), and the ballistic missile, which had enormous potential for intercontinental attack (also with atomic warheads). During World War II, the strategic bombing campaigns in Europe and Asia represented for many the "creation of Armageddon"; estimates well in excess of 100,000 deaths took place in the two atomic bombings of *Hiroshima and Nagasaki, Japan. Likewise, the German V-2 rocket demonstrated the potential of missiles for long-range attack. As the first true ballistic missile, the V-2 flew at speeds of over 3,500 miles per hour and delivered a 2,200-pound warhead 500 miles away. First flown in October 1942, it was employed against targets in Britain beginning in September 1944. By the end of the war, 1,155 had been fired against England and another 1,675 had been launched against Antwerp and other Continental targets. The guidance system for these missiles was imperfect and many did not reach their targets, but they struck without warning and there was no defense against them. As a result, the V-2 had a terror factor far beyond its capabilities.

Following World War II, despite postwar *demobilization, the *Cold War precipitated a continuation of the expansion of military aerospace activities and fostered the search for a truly effective air and space defense for the United States. In the process, the air arm became an independent service, the U.S. *Air Force, in 1947. The military air and space component during the Cold War involved a broad range of activities: training, equipping, and employment of aerospace power extended from aircraft to missiles to satellites to other systems, both passive and active. Much of this, such as satellite reconnaissance, was carried out in a highly classified environment, with neither details nor records of government available for ready inspection. All has been justified as a means of maintaining integrity against an aggressive threat from Russia and other global rivals.

In this context, U.S. air and space defense strategy developed in two distinct ways. First was the development of offensive strategic nuclear forces capable of deterring any attack on the United States—either by striking an enemy before it had a chance to inflict significant damage, or by being able to retaliate massively in response to a strike.

To execute this deterrent mission, the *Department of Defense (DoD) created such organizations as the Strategic Air Command (SAC) in the late 1940s, and placed in command Gen. Curtis E. *LeMay, as rough and irascible an officer as the air force had, but he got results. LeMay fully understood that the nation's first line of defense—indeed, in many respects its only line of defense—was the nuclear deterrent that SAC was charged with maintaining. The command, he knew, had to be prepared to carry out its nuclear mission at any time for the deterrent to have viability. He therefore refined the procedures for strategic bombardment, both with intercontinental ballistic missiles (ICBMs) and strategic bombers, and he made them increasingly more effective. The preparedness of SAC to execute its mission became legendary and set standards of excellence still sought after within the air force, as SAC maintained a state of extreme readiness from the late 1940s through the early 1980s.

More broadly, this strategy ensured the development of what was know as the *nuclear triad:* U.S. continental-based, long-range strategic bombers; U.S. continental-based intercontinental ballistic missiles (ICBMs); and sea-launched intercontinental ballistic missiles (SLBMs) carried on *submarines and therefore mobile. All of these could strike the Soviet Union—or anywhere else on the globe—with *nuclear weapons and therefore ensure an enemy's destruction despite a United States in ruins. Sometimes referred to as mutual assured destruction, this doctrine was known by the most appropriate acronym ever coined by the military: MAD.

Second, perhaps more critical to air and space defense, was the development of early warning and interception systems by the United States. The first successful one was the DEW (distant early warning) Line, approved by President Harry S. *Truman in 1952, across Alaska, Canada, and Greenland. Its purpose was to provide *radar and other electronic surveillance of the Soviet Union to monitor technological progress and, more important, any possible hostile actions against the United States and its allies. The capability of this string of listening posts across the arctic was to be 100 percent detection for all weapons up to 100,000 feet in altitude, which would therefore handle ballistic missiles and bombers. A joint project, the United States provided the funding and supervision of the construction. The Canadians, with a similar system already in place in certain parts of their nation, would link with the DEW Line for an unbroken surveillance sequence in the arctic. This system was constructed quickly in the next two years, coming on line in 1957, and served its purpose throughout the Cold War. It was still operational, although its capabilities had been upgraded, at the close of the century.

To manage the DEW Line, and to respond to any threat detected, the United States and Canada created the North American Air Defense Command (NORAD) in 1957 ("Aerospace" was substituted for "Air" in the title in 1981). Based at Cheyenne Mountain a few miles outside Colorado Springs, for more than three decades NORAD provided integrated command of air and space defense forces of the two nations. It directed dedicated interceptors, other fighters, surface-to-air missiles, air and space detection and control centers, and other facilities to defend the continent against attack.

A U.S. service-backed antiballistic missile (ABM) program was accelerated in 1967. But by the early 1970s, Russian work on an ABM system of ultra-high-speed missiles and phased array radars threatened to destabilize deterrence. In 1972, one of President Richard M. *Nixon's arms control agreements was an ABM treaty limiting deployment to two ABM sites.

Another major component in the U.S. air and space defense system was the strategic reconnaissance efforts of space satellites. Under development in the late 1950s, Project CORONA was the first successful reconnaissance satellite program. Essentially, the objective was to obtain high-quality satellite photographs of the Soviet Union and thereby ensure that the United States would never suffer another Pearl Harbor–like surprise attack. As part of this effort, the first satellite, launched 18 August 1960, reached orbit and then correctly returned its reentry vehicle containing photographs of the Soviet ICBM base at Plesetsk

and the bomber base at Mys Schmidta. The satellite was plucked from the Pacific Ocean by U.S. Navy frogmen. After this flight, CORONA became an operational mission and functioned through 1973, when it was succeeded by later generation reconnaissance satellite projects.

But strategic deterrence, satellite reconnaissance, and NORAD's warning and response capability were insufficient to guarantee safety against a determined enemy, and this prompted national security officials to seek an ultimate shield. The result was the *Strategic Defense Initiative (SDI), unveiled by President Ronald *Reagan in March 1983. An expansive, technologically complex, and exceptionally expensive research and development (R&D) program, SDI's aim was to create an array of space-based technologies that could track and destroy incoming missiles. The project immediately became controversial because of its technical complexity, its high price tag, and because it would upset the strategic nuclear balance of power between the United States and the USSR that had succeeded in avoiding superpower war. With the collapse of the Soviet Union in 1989 and the end of the Cold War, SDI declined in importance and survived only as a modest R&D effort within the DoD in the mid-1990s.

Indeed, with the end of the Cold War in the early 1990s, the U.S. air and space defense system underwent substantial changes. NORAD continues to exist, but as a component of U.S. Space Command and its mandate has been narrowed since there is no major strategic threat. Some of its response component has been transferred from the active military force to the Air National Guard. Some nuclear forces of the DoD have been taken off alert, some nuclear weapons destroyed, and SAC inactivated, and targeting of Russia has been deemphasized. The DoD component managing SDI has been reduced in size and funding and renamed the Ballistic Missile Defense Organization. Finally, public conceptions of air and space defense, such as civil defense in its various capacities, have been minimized.

[*See also* Arms Control and Disarmament; Canada, U.S. Military Involvement in; Deterrence; Missiles; Satellites, Reconnaissance.]

• Benson D. Adams, *Ballistic Missile Defense,* 1971. *Astronautics and Aeronautics: A Chronology of Science, Technology, and Events* (covers 1915–85), 24 vols., 1962–90. Ernest J. Yanarella, *The Missile Defense Controversy: Strategy, Technology, and Politics, 1955–1972,* 1977. Paul B. Stares, *The Militarization of Space: U.S. Policy, 1945–1984,* 1985. William E. Burrows, *Deep Black: Space Espionage and National Security,* 1987. Robert F. Futrell, *Ideas, Concepts, Doctrine: A History of Basic Thinking in the United States Air Force,* 2 vols., 1987; Michael S. Sherry, *The Rise of American Air Power: The Creation of Armageddon,* 1987. Matthew Evangelista, *Innovation and the Arms Race: How the United States and the Soviet Union Develop New Military Technologies,* 1988. H. Bruce Franklin, *Star Wars: The Superweapon and the American Imagination,* 1988. Sanford A. Lakoff and Herbert A. York, *A Shield in Space? Technology, Policy, and the Strategic Defense Initiative,* 1989. Jeffrey Richelson, *U.S. Military Uses of Space, 1945–1991,* microfiche documents, 1991. Donald R. Baucom, *The Origins of SDI, 1944–1983,* 1992. Kevin C. Ruffner, ed., *Corona: America's First Satellite Program,* 1995.

—Roger D. Launius

AIRBORNE WARFARE. The first concept for the use of American airborne troops occurred during World War I in 1918, when Gen. Billy *Mitchell proposed a mass drop of paratroopers against German trenches on the western front. The following year, Gen. John J. *Pershing endorsed Mitchell's plan, but the armistice of November 1918 made the airborne assault unnecessary. *Isolationism and small budgets between the world wars prevented the development of an airborne force, but the U.S. *Army kept a close eye on developments in the Soviet Union and Germany where paratrooper and glider units participated in large training exercises. The dramatic, successful assault in May 1940 on Fort Eben Emael in Belgium by German parachute and glider troops, followed by a successful German mass airborne assault against Crete in 1941, convinced military planners that America needed an airborne capability for the coming war.

On 16 August 1940, a test platoon of U.S. paratroopers made their first jump at Fort Benning, Georgia, and by April 1942, four months after U.S. entry into World War II, a parachute school was in full operation. In August 1942, the army formed its first two airborne divisions, the 82nd and the 101st. Their mission was vertical envelopment: to land behind enemy lines in order to disrupt command, control, and communications and to impede the enemy's ability to fight. From the beginning, U.S. paratroopers exhibited characteristics that remain central to the airborne fighting spirit. All were volunteers, physically and mentally tough, filled with esprit de corps, and capable of acting alone in a crisis.

The U.S. Army formed six airborne divisions of parachute and glider regiments during World War II, and the most famous exploits of these elite units under commanders such as Maxwell D. *Taylor, James M. Gavin, and Matthew B. *Ridgway occurred in Europe. The first combat action took place in November 1942, during the *North Africa campaign, followed by a larger airborne assault during the invasion of *Sicily in July 1943. Early airborne operations had significant problems; but in September 1943, paratroopers proved their worth when the 82nd Airborne made an emergency jump into the beachhead at Salerno, Italy, and helped prevent a potential Allied debacle. The 82nd and 101st Airborne Divisions were among the best in the war and fought valiantly in June 1944 as the airborne vanguard of the *D-Day landing. Despite some units being dropped in the wrong place, they captured key bridges and road junctures and impeded the German Army's ability to react to the amphibious assault. In August, a provisional division of airborne and glider troops supported Operation Dragoon, the invasion of southern France. The 82nd and 101st Airborne jumped again that September and fought at Eindhoven and Nijmegen in Holland as part of Field Marshal Bernard Law *Montgomery's abortive British Operation Market-Garden to seize the Arnhem Bridge on the Rhine. During the Battle of the *Bulge, the 82nd Airborne helped to defend the northern shoulder of the German salient near St. Vith. Meanwhile, the 101st rushed to Bastogne by truck and fought a dogged defense of the village, denying the Germans control of an important road junction even while surrounded. In March 1945, the 17th Airborne Division participated in Operation Varsity, the airborne assault supporting the British crossing of the Rhine River in northern Germany. The 11th Airborne Division fought in several campaigns in the Pacific and distinguished itself in 1945 during the liberation of the *Philippines.

The *Cold War saw a dramatic transformation in airborne forces. Significant reductions in airborne units occurred after World War II. During the *Korean War, the 187th Airborne Regimental Combat Team made two jumps in an effort to cut off retreating North Korean forces at Sukchon in October 1950 and at Musan-ni in March 1951. The Korean War saw a greater use of *helicopters, and in 1952 the army formed its first helicopter battalions for vertical envelopment and soon eliminated all glider units.

The unconventional nature of the *Vietnam War precluded normal airborne operations and led to air-mobile warfare in which helicopters transported soldiers to the battlefield. The army's first air-mobile division, the 1st Cavalry Division, deployed to Vietnam in August 1965 and fought the war's initial, major air-mobile Battle of the *Ia Drang Valley in November 1965. Later, the 101st Airborne Division converted from parachutes to helicopters, and air-mobile "search and destroy" missions came to dominate U.S. operations. The 173rd Airborne Brigade conducted the only major parachute drop of the Vietnam War near Tay Ninh City in February 1967.

In the post–Vietnam War era, airborne and air-mobile forces remain vital to the U.S. military. The 82nd Airborne and the 101st Airborne (Air Assault) Divisions deployed to Saudi Arabia in 1990 and saw action during the *Persian Gulf War. In 1994, the 82nd Airborne was en route from North Carolina to a parachute drop to help overthrow the military junta in Haiti, but was recalled in the air due to successful political negotiations. Today, the 82nd Airborne and the 101st Airborne (Air Assault) Divisions retain their elite status, maintain a high level of readiness, and possess the strategic mobility to respond rapidly to crises across the globe.

[See also Army Combat Branches: Aviation.]

• S.L.A. Marshall, Night Drop, 1962. John R. Galvin, Air Assault, 1969. James M. Gavin, On to Berlin, 1978. Gerard M. Devlin, Paratrooper!, 1979. Clay Blair, Ridgway's Paratroopers, 1985. William B. Breuer, Geronimo!, 1989.   —Michael D. Doubler

AIRBORNE WARNING AND CONTROL SYSTEMS. See AWACS and E-3s.

AIRCRAFT. See AWACS and E-3S; Bombers; Blimps and Dirigibles; Ground Attack Planes; Helicopters; Stealth Aircraft; Transport Planes; U-2 Spy Planes; Vertical Take-off and Landing Aircraft.

AIRCRAFT CARRIERS. Invented by the British during World War I, the aircraft carrier was adopted by the United States and Japan as an experimental weapon to augment the battle line. In contrast to the Japanese, whose fleet and carriers were designed for defensive operations in the western Pacific, the U.S. Navy planned for an offensive, transpacific war all the way to Japan and created the long-legged "fast" (33-knot) carrier to operate over those great distances. The navy first converted a collier (coaling ship) into the 11,050-ton carrier Langley (CV-1 "V" being the symbol for heavier-than-air craft), commissioned in 1922. Then it converted two battle-cruiser hulls, as allowed by the *Washington Naval Arms Limitation Treaty, into 36,000-ton fast carriers of the Lexington class. While the 542-foot Langley experimented with fighter and scout planes in fleet maneuvers during the 1920s, the navy developed *dive-bombers and *torpedo planes for the new 888-

foot-long carriers. As soon as the *Lexington* and the *Saratoga* joined the fleet, Adm. Joseph Mason Reeves placed squadrons of all four plane types aboard them, a total of eighty planes per carrier. With the *Saratoga,* he launched a successful surprise mock attack on the Panama Canal during Fleet Problem IX in 1929. This demonstration of offensive carrier air power established the foundation of U.S. carrier aviation for the rest of the century.

During the war games of the 1930s, similar aggressive attacks struck the Hawaiian Islands, including Pearl Harbor; West Coast seaports; and defending fleets and land-based air forces. Traditional battleship admirals often minimized these achievements and argued for using the carriers with the battle line, but this only inhibited their mobility and made them vulnerable to air, ship, and submarine attacks. The *Lexington*-class carriers mounted a defensive battery of eight 8-inch and twelve 5-inch guns. In fact, their own fighter planes and escorting gunships provided the surest defense. So newer carriers, built from the keel up as carriers, mounted only eight 5-inch guns. Flight decks were made of wood so that *bombs would not explode until they struck the hangar deck, enabling planes to keep operating during battle.

The stunning Japanese attack on *Pearl Harbor by planes from six Japanese carriers on 7 December 1941 proved decisively the offensive power of fast carriers. It was, however, uncharacteristic of Japanese warships to operate so far from home waters. Adm. Ernest J. *King, commander in chief of the U.S. Fleet, therefore instituted wide-ranging offensive hit-and-run raids with the six available carriers to keep the Japanese off balance. Their most aggressive leader was Adm. William F. *Halsey, who even launched James *Doolittle's army bombers from the *Hornet* to strike Tokyo in April 1942. U.S. carriers won naval victories at the Battle of the *Coral Sea in May, the Battle of *Midway in June, and the battles around *Guadalcanal between August and November, sinking several Japanese carriers—four at Midway alone. But one by one all U.S. carriers were sunk except for the *Saratoga* and the *Enterprise,* and even these two were heavily damaged. The reasons included imperfect tactics and damage control, inferior aircraft, inadequate numbers of fighter planes, ships, and antiaircraft guns, and insufficient reconnaissance.

These lessons were applied to the construction of two dozen new fast carriers of the *Essex* class, which entered the fleet in 1943. At 27,100 tons, the 872-foot *Essexes* each embarked an air group of three squadrons: thirty-six fighters, the superior F6F Hellcat; thirty-six dive-bombers, first the SBD Dauntless and later the SB2C Helldiver; and eighteen torpedo bombers, the TBF/TBM Avenger. All three types performed scouting functions too, but the greatest innovation for detecting enemy planes was the installation of shipboard search *radar, enabling fighter director officers to coordinate their fighters out to 100 miles from the carrier. In addition, antiaircraft defenses included twelve 5-inch/.38-caliber guns and numerous 40mm and 20mm batteries on each carrier. Nine 11,000-ton light carriers (CVL) of the 31-knot Independence class, converted from cruiser hulls between 1941 and 1943, added additional offensive punch; each operated twenty-four fighters and nine torpedo bombers. Circular screens of new escorting fast *battleships, *cruisers, and *destroyers, all bristling with antiaircraft guns, surrounded the carriers in each tactical formation.

Organized in the Fast Carrier Task Force of some fifteen carriers and 1,000 planes, these carriers provided the overwhelming firepower that spearheaded the Central Pacific offensive of 1943–45. Their optimum effectiveness occurred under the sagacious leadership of Adm. Marc A. Mitscher as the fast carriers overcame virtually all enemy opposition. The only major changes were the introduction of four-plane night fighter teams aboard each *Essex,* three carriers equipped primarily for night operations, and an increase of fighters, including the F4U Corsair, over bombing planes to counter the kamikazes, Japanese suicide planes. Only one of the new fast carriers was sunk, the light carrier *Princeton,* off Leyte.

In the Atlantic, to defeat Germany's U-boats, the navy depended on small, slow 18-knot escort carriers (CVE), eighty-four of which were commissioned. There were four major classes of CVEs, some converted from oilers but most mass-produced; they varied in size between 7,800 and 11,400 tons, and each carried a composite air group of nine fighters and twelve torpedo bombers. Operating primarily as an independent hunter-killer group, each escort carrier worked in concert with its five destroyers and destroyer escorts to track down and sink most of the U-boats destroyed between 1943 and 1945. Many of them also operated in the Pacific, where fighters outnumbered torpedo bombers in providing close air support during amphibious assaults. Light construction made the escort carriers especially vulnerable, and several were sunk by bombs, gunfire, submarine torpedoes, or kamikazes.

Three large (CVB) 45,000-ton, *Midway*-class carriers, commissioned after the war ended, featured armored flight decks in order to nullify bomb hits. Each had a 986-foot flight deck and a 137-plane air group of fighters and dive-bombers. The future of the carrier and its vulnerability to nuclear weapons became a cause of bitter controversy in the late 1940s, a controversy complicated by interservice *rivalry. The navy depended upon the older *Essexes* in the Korean War (1950–53). Their air groups were comprised of F4U fighter bombers, F9F jet fighters, and piston-engine AD (later A-1) Skyraider attack planes. Atomic bombs were first deployed aboard carriers in the early 1950s.

The *Korean War and the menace of the Soviet Union served to stimulate new carrier construction. During the 1950s and 1960s eight attack carriers (CVA, later CV again) belonging to the *Forrestal* and *Kitty Hawk/America* classes were built. Each displaced 56,000 to 61,000 tons and had 1,046-foot flight decks to accommodate new and heavier planes. Air groups (later air wings) were comprised of up to 100 fighters and attack planes, mostly jets. The major fighters were F-8 Crusaders and F-4 Phantoms IIs, the bombers A-1s, A-3 Skywarriors, A-4 Skyhawks, A-6 Intruders, and A-7 Corsair IIs. Cruising endurance was greatly increased with the commissioning in 1961 of the first nuclear-powered carrier (CVN), the 75,700-ton *Enterprise,* which did not require refueling at sea. To deal with the large Soviet submarine force, thirteen *Essexes* were redesignated as antisubmarine carriers (CVS) between 1954 and 1973; these operated S-2 Tracker pison-engine search planes and H-34 Seabat and H-3 Sea King antisub *helicopters. All of these carrier types and planes supported ground operations during the *Vietnam War (1965–73). In addition, three converted Essexes acted as amphibious-assault helicopter personnel carriers (LPH) during the 1960s, until superseded by the *Iwo Jima* (LPH) and *Tarawa*

(LPA) classes (landing platform, helicopter or assault) built specifically for that purpose.

During the 1970s, doctrinal confusion and criticism over retention of the large and seemingly vulnerable attack carriers continued. They were retained because of repeated crises in the Middle East and the growing Soviet surface fleet, which though basically defensive, included a few carriers. Eight 81,600-ton nuclear-powered carriers of the Nimitz class with 1,089-foot flight decks were added between the late 1960s and late 1990s to begin replacing older oil-fueled ships. Each was accompanied by a protective screen of missile-bearing escort ships and formed a carrier battle group. They provided the core of the offensive power projection that effectively deterred the Soviet Navy. F-14 Tomcat fighters and F/A-18 Hornet fighter attack planes joined the carriers during the 1970s and 1980s, respectively, along with S-3 Viking antisub jet search planes to augment E-2 long-range early warning radar carrier aircraft.

Throughout the *Cold War, attack carrier strength remained fairly constant between twelve and fifteen, but even the collapse of the Soviet Union in 1989–90 did not diminish the need for carriers to help deter and quell global tensions. Thus, six carriers participated during 1990–91 in the *Persian Gulf War. The continuing requirement for such large numbers of these extremely versatile carriers has been governed by the fact that, generally, for every carrier operating on station, one is home-ported undergoing refit and overhaul, and another is in transit to or from the operating area. In this way, the United States has maintained the long-legged global reach of its naval power.

[See also Fighter Aircraft; Navy Combat Branches: Surface Forces; Navy Combat Branches: Naval Air Forces.]

• Stefan Terzibaschitsch, Aircraft Carriers of the U.S. Navy, 1980. Norman Friedman, Carrier Air Power, 1981. Stefan Terzibaschitsch, Escort Carriers and Aviation Support Ships of the U.S. Navy, 1980. Norman Friedman, U.S. Aircraft Carriers: An Illustrated Design History, 1983. Clark G. Reynolds, The Fighting Lady: The New Yorktown in the Pacific War, 1986. George C. Wilson, Supercarrier, 1986. Edward P. Stafford, The Big E, 1988 repr. Clark G. Reynolds, "The U.S. Fleet-in-Being Strategy of 1942," The Journal of Military History, Vol. 58 (1994), pp. 103–118. Theodore Taylor, The Magnificent Mitscher, 1991 repr.   —Clark G. Reynolds

AIRCRAFT INDUSTRIALISTS. Among the ever-widening links between military and social institutions, few have been as extensive or dynamic as the relationship between the U.S. military and the aircraft industry. From the industry's origins before World War I through the early *Cold War period, this relationship, though heavily mediated by Congress, was made up of army and navy officers and individual aircraft industrialists who for the most part owned and operated independent firms. These firms performed research and development for new military aircraft and also manufactured them. During the interwar years, suggestions that the aircraft industry be nationalized were occasionally heard but never really challenged the consensus that the industry ought to remain in private hands and that the military ought to relate to aircraft firms on contractual business terms kept as distant and impartial as possible.

From the first flight at Kitty Hawk in 1903 through World War I, the aircraft industry was dominated by two firms named after this technology's pioneers, the brothers Orville and Wilbur *Wright and Glenn Curtiss. When the U.S. Army, U.S. Navy, and Congress pushed for large-scale airpower during World War I, other firms entered the industry to try to meet the enormous demand. Most notable were two automobile companies, Fisher Body and Willys-Overland. The Ford Motor Company also engaged briefly in large-scale production of the Liberty aircraft engine. But despite the expenditure of hundreds of millions of taxpayer dollars, wartime military aircraft production proved a fiasco, mainly because of the misguided effort to mass-produce air frames according to the automobile industry's assembly-line manufacturing methods. Nevertheless, many blamed an "Aircraft Trust," supposedly composed of corrupt corporate executives and military contracting officers who profited enormously but failed to produce aircraft. The U.S. Congress imposed a punishing postwar business environment for military aircraft that meant unprofitability for the industry. Worried about possible collusion, Congress also blocked efforts to streamline the industry's dealings with the military.

Throughout the interwar years, military aircraft design and manufacture remained highly competitive, despite severely limited military spending. Congress maintained easy access for new entries through price-competitive contract laws, which military officers were obliged to follow. Low start-up and capital costs also eased entry for the many aircraft entrepreneurs who wanted to be part of the exciting new technology despite business risks. The energies of this group of competitive entrepreneurs/industrialists, many of whom were independently wealthy and willing to absorb steady losses, were key to the industry's viability until mass demand developed during World War II. They maintained an airpower supply base that was inferior to, but at least comparable with, those of the world's leading military powers.

In this period, tiny new companies emerged to give the aircraft/aerospace industry many of its familiar names. Glenn Martin, William Boeing, Donald Douglas, Chance Vought, Charles Lawrence, and Clyde Cessna found plenty of room to compete with the two larger firms under the Wright and Curtiss names. Three other lesser-known but significant figures also entered the industry during the early 1920s. In 1923, Reuben Fleet established Consolidated Aircraft in Buffalo, New York, and moved it to San Diego in 1935, where it eventually became an important part of General Dynamics. In 1926, Frederick Rentschler reorganized Pratt & Whitney into a major supplier of aircraft engines. The most prominent aircraft industrialist during the 1920s was Clement Keys, a Wall Street financier deeply committed to aeronautics. He bought Curtiss Aeroplane in 1920 and arranged the Curtiss-Wright merger in 1928, which combined aircraft and engine production and became a critical airpower supplier during World War II.

Aviation companies became a focus for much of the investment frenzy of the 1927–29 stock market boom. Some aircraft firms merged, but new, independent ones also appeared. All found access to new investment capital that helped sustain a competitive industry during the early depression years. Most notable among the new entries were Leroy Grumman, John Northrop, Igor Sikorsky, Sherman Fairchild, Lawrence Bell, and Alexander de *Seversky. Seversky's firm was reorganized as Republic Aircraft in 1938. North American Aviation, controlled by General Motors, was incorporated in Baltimore and moved to Los Angeles in 1935 under the guidance of James Kindleberger. The Loughead brothers established a company, but changed its name to Lockheed because it was so often mispronounced. In 1931, two entrepreneurs from Boston, Robert and Courtland Gross, bought Lockheed and made it an important innovator in Los Angeles. During the 1930s, Howard Hughes also began competing from Los Angeles. In 1939, James McDonnell established a company in St. Louis.

In the 1930s and even during World War II, the industry remained fragmented, highly competitive, and geographically dispersed. Companies pursued resolutely independent business and technological strategies. Most snubbed he industry's trade association in Washington, D.C., unwilling to suspend their separate interests for a common industry front that might alter the debilitating contracting rules they all faced in their dealings with army and navy officers. In 1940, Congress authorized cost-plus contracts and advance payments. But even after these reforms and the massive new demand for warplanes, the industrialists remained highly independent and wary of one another and the government. Some giant aircraft corporate combines expanded or emerged during the war, such as Curtiss-Wright and Consolidated-Vultee (Convair), and automobile companies—General Motors, Ford, and Chrysler—entered the industry on a large scale. But aircraft manufacture still did not become heavily concentrated.

The industry's relations with the military also remained erratic, ad hoc, and unpredictable. The early aircraft industry scarcely resembled a common perception of military industries as appendages of a "warfare state" or a state-centered *military-industrial complex. The government had no overall plan or coordinated approach for mobilizing the aircraft industry or demobilizing it in 1945. It relied on the independent strengths and abilities of the manufacturers. The military's involvement with firms rarely went beyond issuing aircraft specifications and contracts, providing financing, and selecting sites for new factories. Industrialists continued to give only nominal support to their trade association. They plotted individual competitive strategies for the postwar military and civilian market. Relations between firms and the air force and navy became more integrated only when the industry's viability seemed threatened by balance sheet crises during the late 1940s and the *Korean War. Rapid technological development meant far greater complexity in aircraft design and production and also seemed to mandate more stable, predictable, and longer-term relations.

[See also Air Force, U.S.: Overview; Procurement: Aerospace Industry.]

• I.B. Holley, Jr., Buying Aircraft: Materiel Procurement for the Army Air Forces, 1962. John B. Rae, Climb to Greatness: The American Aircraft Industry, 1920–1960, 1968. Roger E. Bilstein, The American Aerospace Industry: From Workshop to Global Enterprise, 1996. Jacob Vander Meulen, The Politics of Aircraft: Building an American Military Industry, 1991.
—Jacob Vander Meulen

AIR FORCE, U.S.

Overview
Predecessors of, 1907–46
Since 1947

AIR FORCE, U.S.: OVERVIEW

The U.S. Air Force, the world's most powerful air arm, was not always the most potent. The force dates its beginnings from 1907 as an organization of three men and no operational aircraft within the U.S. Army. During and immediately after World War I, the Army Air Service remained much smaller and less capable than European air forces. However, as the Army Air Forces, it grew during World War II to become the mightiest air force in the world, with 2.4 million uniformed people in 1944 and nearly 100,000 operational aircraft. In 1947, as the U.S. Air Force (USAF), it finally became an independent service, reaching its maximum size in 1955 during the *Cold War era (960,000 people). By 1998 it had "downsized" to 381,100 active duty, uniformed personnel (plus 184,000 in the *Air Force Reserve and *Air National Guard). But today's force, with its 580 intercontinental ballistic missiles, 4,700 aircraft (another 1,900 in the Air Force Reserve and Air National Guard), and numerous space-based reconnaissance *satellites, has much greater range, capability, mobility, and flexibility than the numerically larger Army Air Force of World War II.

The USAF provides its aircrews with more flying hours and more realistic training than any other comparable force in the world, and its equipment is unmatched technologically. Those that can compete with USAF crews in skill are all regional: Israel, the United Kingdom, Germany, France, and Australia retain motivated, capable air forces, but all are range-limited and considerably smaller. Although some air forces approach the size of the USAF in aircraft numbers (e.g., China's), all of them are range-restricted and most of their aircraft are obsolete. The Soviet Union came closest to possessing a large, global air force, but since 1991 Russia's airpower has greatly deteriorated.

The American air forces have been reorganized several times. From 1907 to 1947, the force was part of the U.S. Army. Within the army, it became sequentially the Aeronautical Division of the U.S. Signal Corps (1907–14), the Aviation Section of the Signal Corps (1914–18), the Army Air Service (1918–26), the Army Air Corps (1926–41), and the Army Air Forces (1941–47). Since 1947, the force has been on a par with the army and navy.

Through 1918, its primary mission was reconnaissance, although some air supremacy fighting and ground attack did occur during World War I. It was not until 1923 that army doctrine officially recognized combat strike uses for airplanes. During the 1920s and 1930s, the Army Air Corps developed the strategic bombing doctrine in which "air power" was envisaged as being decisive in war: an enemy's vital targets would be bombed, and the war could end before ground or naval forces became engaged.

The idea of strategic bombing dominated air force thinking and force structure through World War II and for twenty-five years thereafter. In the 1930s, the Army Air Corps developed robust four-engine bombers, but poor *fighter-aircraft, because fighters were seen as unnecessary for escorting the defensively armed and armored bombers that it was believed "would always get through." It was thought a war would end before fighters became necessary to support ground forces. The Army Air Forces (together with Britain's Bomber Command) blasted German cities into rubble using mainly B-24 and B-17 heavy *bomber aircraft, but the war in Europe ended only when Allied armies occupied Germany's territory. The Army Air Forces achieved more decisive results in the Pacific, but only after the army, navy, and *Marine Corps captured enough territory to bring very long range B-29 bombers within range of Japan. Massive bombardment in 1945, culminating in the atomic bombings of *Hiroshima and Nagasaki, was probably the most important factor causing Japan to surrender without an invasion.

Convinced that aerial bombardment had won both the European and the Pacific Wars, air force leaders developed a huge strategic bombing force during the 1950s that would deter the Soviet Union, or defeat it should war occur. While the USAF developed superior interceptor aircraft, it discounted the value of tactical aircraft for supporting ground forces. The *Korean War did not dramatically alter this situation, nor did the growing power of the Soviet ground forces in the 1950s. Today's air force, however, is more flexibly equipped.

Its current mission is to control air and space in order to provide freedom of action for air, sea, and ground forces to secure national security objectives. And the USAF is more capable of performing multiple missions than in the past. One can track the change in doctrinal emphases from the *Vietnam War, when the emphasis on strategic bombing gave way to increased emphasis on tactical operations. Since 1982, six consecutive air force chiefs of staff have been fighter pilots, none of whom had any flying time as strategic bomber crew members. In 1992, with the collapse of the Soviet Union, the Strategic Air Command (SAC), the command most identified with strategic bombing, was disestablished. SAC's nuclear strategic missions were placed in a new joint (multiservice) command, the Strategic Command. (SAC's conventional missions went to other organizations.)

Today's balanced air force is divided into eight major commands, thirty-eight field operating agencies, and three direct reporting units. The eight major commands contain almost 94 percent of the uniformed personnel. Air Combat Command is the largest, with 28 percent of the people. It has fighters (F-15s, F-16s, F-117s, A-10s, etc.) and bombers (B-52s, B-1s, B-2s). Two other commands also possess fighters. U.S. Air Forces in Europe and Pacific Air Forces (combined, 16% of the air force) would both be supplemented by Air Combat Command aircraft if needed. The Air Education and Training Command, about 17 percent of personnel, is equipped with training aircraft (T-37s and T-38s, etc.), and is responsible for training and most professional education. The Air Mobility Command (about 15%) has aerial refueling tankers (KC-135s and KC-10s) and transports (C-130s, C-141s, C-5s, and C-17s). The Space Command (6%) maintains the strategic missile forces during peacetime and the space-based satellites. The Special Operations Command (2%) is equipped with *helicopters, some specially equipped C-130s, and gunships. The Materiel Command (10%) equips the force through research, development, and acquisition of systems, and sustains it through maintenance and supply.

The thirty-eight field operating agencies, such as the Air Weather Service, contain 5 percent of personnel. Finally, the three direct reporting units (e.g., Air Force Academy) contain about 1 percent of personnel.

The USAF today is engaged in missions around the world, demonstrating daily its global power and reach.

[See also Academies, Service: U.S. Air Force Academy; Air and Space Defense; Air Force Combat Organizations; Special Operations Forces: Air Force Special Forces; Strategy: Air Warfare Strategy; Tactics: Air Warfare Tactics.]

• Wesley Frank Craven and James Lea Cate, editors, *The Army Air Forces in World War II*, 7 vol., 1948–1958. Irving B. Holley, Jr., *Ideas and Weapons: Exploitation of the Aerial Weapons by the United States during World War I; A Study in the Relationship of Technological Advance, Military Doctrine, and the Development of Weapons*, 1971. Robert F. Futrell, *Ideas, Concepts, Doctrine: A History of Basic Thinking in the United States Air Force 1907–1964*, 1974. United States Air Force, *The United States Air Force in Southeast Asia*, 5 vol., 1981–1983. Robert F. Futrell, *The United States Air Force in Korea 1950–1953*, 1983. Thomas A. Keaney and Eliot A. Cohen, *Gulf War Air Power Survey Summary Report*, 1993.   —Alan Gropman

AIR FORCE, U.S.: PREDECESSORS OF, 1907–46

On 1 August 1907, the U.S. Army's chief signal officer established an Aeronautical Division within the Signal Corps. Two years later the Signal Corps accepted an airplane from the Wright brothers, and by 1911 Lt. Thomas DeWitt Milling had begun early experimentation with an aircraft bombsight. Despite these developments, army attitudes to aircraft remained conservative: the role of aircraft, like that of dirigibles, would be to assist in observation and reconnaissance. Most army officers remained unmoved by the extensive body of predictive literature—of which H. G. Wells's novel, *The War in the Air* (1908), was only one example—which assumed that aircraft would be the most important tools in the wars of the future.

Between Orville and Wilbur *Wright's triumph in 1903 and the beginning of World War I, the Europeans generally outpaced the Americans in aviation. The U.S. Army failed to use aircraft successfully in its 1916 attempt to punish Mexican outlaw Pancho Villa, exposing the inadequate nature of its aerial program. Nonetheless, upon entry into World War I in 1917, the Americans quickly developed plans to produce a major air force. But such plans turned out to be overambitious since they implicitly assumed that essential technological and bureaucratic structures might be put into place almost overnight. Ultimately the Americans were able to supply trainer airplanes, aircraft engines, and pilots—but they had to rely heavily on the Europeans for material and expertise.

The most important World War I air action for the Americans took place in September 1918, when Gen. Billy *Mitchell, of the Air Service of the American Expeditionary Force, commanded American, British, and French squadrons in support of the U.S. First Army at St. Mihiel. This action brought the Americans important experience in the realm of tactical—or battlefield—aviation, but they did not have an opportunity to develop similar experience in what was then called "strategical" (later strategic) bombing, which focused on the use of long-range bombers to fly over the heads of an opposing army and directly undermine the enemy's capacity and will to fight.

Nonetheless, the Americans were able to observe European efforts and even developed a plan for the future use of long-range bombers—though it leaned heavily on the work of a leading British planner, Lord Tiverton. Indeed, the Americans were interested enough to undertake their own postwar survey of long-range bomb damage in Europe. Heeding the arguments of the British Air Staff, the Americans concluded that the most effective planning would be achieved by making a careful study of the enemy's war economy, identifying those industries most vital to its continued functioning, and aiming to destroy them.

Without direct experience of aviation other than for purposes of reconnaissance and battlefield support, American airmen were not in a strong position to push for postwar independence from the army. The determined aerial stunts of General Mitchell raised the public profile of aviation, but his insistent demand for service independence angered army leadership and brought his career to a premature end. In the 1920s, when military budgets were tight and the nation's foreign policy was isolationist, American airmen were compelled to keep their more futuristic ideas to themselves. Despite a number of interwar congressional bills proposing a separate service, the airmen remained part of the army. Gradual change commenced in 1926, when new legislation transformed the Air Service into the slightly more autonomous Air Corps. In the early 1930s, the Air Corps Tactical School (ACTS) gained a new home at Maxwell Air Force Base, Alabama. The 1931 MacArthur-Pratt agreement divided land-based and naval aviation between the army and the navy, and gave the former an officially sanctioned use for long-range bombers: defenders of the American coastline. Increasingly, instructors at ACTS defied army ideological constraints by developing a set of ideas about the independent use of long-range bombers against an enemy's industrial economy; these ideas ultimately would serve as the foundation of American bombing strategy in World War II.

Viewing advanced industrial societies as complex and interdependent entities subject to economic disruption, American air planners sought out those "bottleneck" targets that might be central to an enemy's functioning in wartime. They posited that if these could be attacked with swiftness and precision, then the enemy might be defeated. This theory was bolstered by the development of new technologies that seemed to make the plan feasible, specifically the B-17 long-range bomber and the Norden bombsight. Both the B-17 and the Norden bombsight (a product of the navy's in-house designer, Carl Norden) were originally designed to help the United States defend itself from hostile threats at sea. Being able to hit a hostile target at sea naturally put a premium on accuracy, and this in turn reinforced American confidence in the notion of what would come to be referred to, optimistically, as "precision bombing."

As the threat of war loomed increasingly large in the summer of 1941, President Franklin D. *Roosevelt decided to invest heavily in the newly renamed U.S. Army Air Forces (USAAF). His decision, not unlike the decision undertaken on America's entry into World War I, probably rested on the appeal of a high-technology mode of war fighting, which seemed to promise reduced *casualties and quicker results. In August 1941, a handful of American air planners (former instructors at ACTS) devised a plan for massed bombers to fly in daylight against critical targets in the German war economy. Like their British Allies, the Americans generally had come to believe that the bomber "would always get through." They assumed that the speed and multiple guns of the B-17 "Flying Fortress" would enable them to fly in self-defending groups—without long-range fighters to fly alongside as protective escorts.

As in World War I, gearing up for total warfare proved to be more complicated and time-consuming than anticipated. It took most of 1942 for the Americans to train the pilots, and to build the planes and infrastructure for a large-scale bombing offensive. In the meantime, the efforts of Britain's Bomber Command had increased steadily in scale and destructiveness. The British had discovered that strategic bombing was a difficult and complicated enterprise. The unexpected effectiveness of German defense forced them to fly under cover of night, and the difficulty of finding targets led them to concentrate on those places they could find reliably: cities. Fearful that the Americans would experience the same problems, Prime Minister Winston *Churchill urged his ally to join the night bombing offensive. Stubbornly clinging to their theory of air warfare, the Americans resisted.

American faith in the self-defending bomber was badly shaken in the summer and fall of 1943. In two separate raids against ball bearings factories deep in German territory at Schweinfurt, the Americans suffered huge losses. The USAAF was now forced to make changes, too. Still wedded to the idea of daylight "precision" bombing, the Americans sought to solve their problem by bringing large numbers of escort aircraft into the European theater. Equipped with jettisonable fuel tanks for range, these could fly over enemy territory with the bombers, and engage German defensive aircraft head-on. American bombers drew German fighters into the air, and through the winter and spring of 1944 the two air forces fought ferocious battles of attrition. In the end, the Americans were able badly to erode Luftwaffe strength—a result that greatly facilitated the Anglo-American *D-Day landing at Normandy in June, and exposed German factories and cities to the full weight of Allied bombardment.

By the autumn of 1944 and continuing into 1945, Bomber Command and the USAAF were in a position to pummel targets in Germany with near impunity. In heavy strikes against railway lines and synthetic oil plants, the Allied air forces sought to halt the German war effort by crippling its ability to move men and supplies, and by eliminating its fuel supply. Convinced that the Germans would capitulate in the face of vast destruction, Bomber Command chief Sir Arthur Harris chose to continue attacks on cities as well. But if Harris and the Americans differed over priorities, the line between British "area bombing" and American "precision bombing" was not always so clean as the Americans claimed. On those frequent occasions when they were forced to bomb through cloud (rather than visually), the Americans achieved accuracy rates not much different from—indeed, sometimes rather worse than—the British. And in the Pacific theater, the Americans ultimately adopted bombing tactics which had much in common with Bomber Command's incendiary raids on German cities.

In the Far East, the Americans initially tried to use the same "precision" tactics they had employed in Europe. But heavy, incessant cloud cover prevailed over Japan, and the strong winds of the Pacific jet stream bedeviled formation flying. By the winter of 1944–45, the American bomber fleet (equipped with powerful B-29 bombers) had little to show for its efforts. Abandoning their preferred tactics, the Americans—now under the field command of Gen. Curtis E. *LeMay—began to fly low-level, nighttime incendiary attacks against Japanese cities. Some sixty-six Japanese cities were firebombed in the months prior to the atomic bombings of *Hiroshima and Nagasaki. In concert with the navy's blockade of Japan and mining of its harbors, the objective of the devastating air campaign was to weaken the enemy army and the entire nation prior to invasion, and, if possible, bring about Japanese capitulation. Because of the often indiscriminate nature of strategic bombing during World War II, the Anglo-American air campaigns have been the subject of emotional postwar debate.

Members of the USAAF believed that their performance in World War II put them in a strong position to argue for independence from the army. In addition, their new role as the first service able to deliver atomic bombs moved them to a position of central importance in the postwar American defense establishment. The precise nature and organization of that establishment, however, remained to be determined. Its initial form was hammered out in lengthy and often acrimonious debates—held from from 1945 to 1947—in which the navy fought hard to resist a centralized defense department, and to maintain authority over aircraft with sea-related missions. American airmen finally achieved their long-standing goal of autonomy when the *National Security Act of July 1947 gave the newly named United States Air Force co-equal status with the army and the navy within the broader framework of a national military establishment headed by a civilian secretary. The act was a problematical compromise, though, and had to be amended in 1949. The amendments strengthened the power of the secretary of defense over the services, but did not end the debates, which continue to this day, over roles and missions, and how the services should divide up control over the aircraft they need for their individual tasks.

[See also Department of Defense; Strategy: Air Warfare Strategy; Tactics: Air Warfare Tactics.]

• Thomas Greer, *The Development of Air Doctrine in the Army Air Arm, 1917–1941*, 1955. Alfred Goldberg, *A History of the United States Air Force, 1907–1957*, 1957. Eugene Emme, *The Impact of Air Power*, 1959. Robert Frank Futrell, *Ideas, Concepts, Doctrine: A History of Basic Thinking in the United States Air Force, 1907–1964*, 1971. Robin Higham, *Air Power: A Concise History*, 1972. Michael Sherry, *The Rise of American Air Power*, 1987. Richard G. Davis, *Carl A. Spaatz and the Air War in Europe*, 1993. John Gooch, ed., *Air Power: Theory and Practice*, 1995.   —Tami Davis Biddle

AIR FORCE, U.S.: SINCE 1947

The United States Air Force (USAF) was formally established by the *National Security Act of July 1947. The creators of the USAF envisioned a service capable of winning wars independently by destroying the enemy's warmaking capability. This has remained the primary focus of the air force, whether through the use of *nuclear weapons or precision conventional strikes. The air force has been characterized as well by a concentration on the development and employment of new technology to a higher degree than any of the other services.

As early as 1942, leaders of the predecessor organization, the Army Air Forces (AAF), realized that World War II gave them the opportunity to justify their status as a co-equal service with the army and navy. Commanding Gen. "Hap" *Arnold nevertheless restrained his more outspoken subordinates. He intended to earn postwar independence in recognition of a decisive AAF contribution to victory, as well as through the support he garnered from a close relationship with Army Chief of Staff Gen. George C. *Marshall. Arnold demanded maximum efforts from his commanders, and secured ample publicity for those operations. The AAF received increasing autonomy as the war went on, and Arnold's campaign was finally rewarded

with army support for air force independence after the war. The harmony between the two services was also strengthened by the fact that Arnold's successor in 1946, Gen. Carl A. *Spaatz, had been the principal air commander in Europe for the new army chief of staff, Gen. Dwight D. *Eisenhower.

Arnold put his stamp on the air force in a number of specific ways. He emphasized the decisive nature of air warfare and the importance of anticipating and exploiting new technology. Spaatz followed by reorganizing the postwar AAF into three major functionally defined combat commands based in the United States—Strategic Air Command (SAC), Tactical Air Command (TAC), and Air Defense Command (ADC)—in addition to separate commands for training and support. Overseas theaters had their own air commands as well. This structure worked well enough to be retained by the new USAF when, after a two-year battle with the navy, which retained naval aviation, it finally achieved independence.

Interservice *rivalry continued, however, as postwar military forces and defense budgets were reduced. The *Key West Agreement—a gentleman's agreement between the services on roles and missions—of 1948 gave the air force sole responsibility for strategic airpower, but that consensus soon dissolved in budget squabbles. Cutbacks of a strategic "supercarrier" and in naval aviation brought on the "Revolt of the Admirals" in 1949. The navy particularly questioned USAF capability to perform its strategic mission with the massive B-36 bomber. The navy also argued that atomic attacks on cities were immoral, a claim it conveniently forgot when it established its own potent nuclear forces later.

In the meantime, the development of the air force's combat commands was hampered by budget constraints and personality conflicts. Defense cuts reduced the organization from a planned seventy air groups to only forty-eight by 1950, and eventually Secretary of the Air Force Stuart Symington resigned in protest. The AAF had had more than 2.5 million personnel on V-J Day, but by May 1947, its strength was down to 303,600 military and 110,000 civilians. Emphasis on strategic airpower ensured SAC would get support, but it initially languished under Gen. George Kenney, whose leadership style caused low morale and training readiness at SAC. Not until Chief of Staff Gen. Hoyt *Vandenberg relieved Kenney and replaced him with Curtis E. *LeMay in 1948 did SAC begin to evolve into an elite force.

LeMay's dynamic leadership and personality would keep the USAF primarily focused on its strategic mission for the next two decades. TAC was temporarily absorbed into Continental Air Command in 1949, but was reactivated in 1950 and began to expand its responsibilities to include delivering tactical *nuclear weapons. ADC was always a low priority, and though it had established the distant early warning (DEW) Line by 1955, it was slow to get adequate aircraft or personnel. By the time its fighters, *missiles, and *radar were integrated into an effective homeland defense system, the threat of the Soviets' manned bomber had declined, and it was eventually deactivated in 1980.

Vandenberg's skillful lobbying and the exigencies of the *Korean War helped sustain the USAF through the early 1950s. The depleted service was initially forced to rely on many World War II aircraft. By the end of the war, however, most bombing missions were being conducted by jet fighter-bombers. The most glamorous and challenging roles were filled by the F-86 interceptor pilots battling MiG-15s for air superiority, and Sabre jet aces soon became America's—and the air force's—idols. Each service drew very different aerial lessons from its experience. The navy emphasized the failure of interdiction and problems with *command and control of joint air operations. The army was dissatisfied with the amount and conduct of close air support. In contrast, the air force trumpeted that airpower had ultimately been successful, claiming its "air pressure" campaign had finally forced the enemy to sign the armistice.

In the decade after the Korean conflict, the emphasis of the air force in the *Coldwar remained on deterring and winning a general war against the Soviet Union. SAC's aging B-29s had been driven out of the daylight skies over North Korea in October 1951, but by the mid-1950s its B-47 medium and B-52 heavy *bomber aircraft were the most advanced jet planes of their type in the world. The 1952 budget authorized ninety-five air force wings, a full third of them to SAC, which was the centerpiece of President Eisenhower's "New Look." By 1960, it had over 2,000 bombers. Service strength had peaked at 960,000 in 1955, but it was still over 800,000 five years later. Air force interests were also furthered by the selection of Gen. Nathan *Twining as first USAF chairman of the *Joint Chiefs of Staff (JCS) in 1957.

As the new decade opened, another technology was becoming the cornerstone of America's deterrent—missiles. Under the capable leadership of Gen. Bernard Schriever, the USAF Ballistic Missile Division guided the service and the missile industry through the completion of four separate launch systems in 1955–62: Atlas, Thor, Titan, and Minuteman. The first SAC missile wing was activated on 1 January 1958; within five years, 13 Atlas squadrons with 127 missiles had been deployed. Along with the new technology came a new way of thinking about general war. Most of the analysis of American nuclear strategy during the 1950s was being conducted by the RAND Corporation, a civilian "think tank" created by the air force after World War II that was independent in title but contracted to do service research. USAF has always led the way in the use of civilian experts and systems analysis to evaluate its technology and operations.

LeMay became USAF chief of staff in 1961, ensuring the predominance of strategic bomber proponents over more tactically focused "fighter jockeys" (a schism that affects most air services, with air transporters the lowest-ranking members of the flying caste) until the beginnings of the *Vietnam War. As a result, in the 1960s USAF found itself again with the wrong aircraft and tactics to meet the needs of a limited war. In Vietnam as in Korea, it chafed under political constraints, had problems with joint air control, and failed in its interdiction campaign. However, the late success of Operation Linebacker II enabled air force leaders to claim they had again brought an enemy to the peace table, and to use it to justify their performance as an example of what could have been accomplished if airpower had been applied with less restraint.

Despite such confident rhetoric, the air force did much to reform itself after Vietnam as it entered the trying decade of the 1970s. SAC's influence declined, and the ser-

vice focused more on its other missions. USAF strength hovered around 800,000 throughout the 1960s, but by 1975 it had declined by 200,000, and it was down to close to 550,000 by 1980. USAF provided two chairmen of the JCS during that time: Gen. George Brown, who as USAF chief of staff had changed regulations so others besides pilots could hold important commands; and Gen. David *Jones, later instrumental in creating the *Goldwater-Nichols Act. The service also began to consider the use of space, eventually creating its own Space Command in 1983, and providing the impetus for the unified U.S. Space Command established by the Department of *Defense, despite navy objections, in 1984. Though it was a difficult period for military budgets and programs, air force leaders proved very farsighted in developing technologies. They fielded the capable F-15 Eagle and supplemented it with the lighter and cheaper F-16; developed a specialized close air support aircraft in the A-10 as well as a new strategic missile, the Peacekeeper; and laid the foundations for Tomahawk cruise missiles, new strategic bombers like the B-1, and *stealth aircraft like the F-117. The appearance of the C-5A Galaxy significantly expanded national airlift capabilities.

Structural reforms also would have important future implications. Innovative training programs such as Red Flag honed the skills of active duty combat flyers, while the USAF response to Secretary of Defense James Schlesinger's call for a "Total Force" in 1973 considerably increased the readiness of the *Air National Guard and *Air Force Reserve. The air force has remained the most successful of all the services in keeping reserve elements prepared and integrating them into active plans and operations.

A new set of thinkers typified by Col. John Warden began to consider the proper application of this new force and technology, including *precision-guided munitions first used in Vietnam. The "smart" bombs employed against the Iraqis in the *Persian Gulf War of 1991 demonstrated a combination of accuracy and penetrating power unique in the history of warfare. The service also coordinated more closely with the army in developing doctrinal concepts of "Air-Land Battle." Though the USAF was down to 530,000 personnel as the Cold War came to an end, the defense buildup under President Ronald *Reagan had created the best trained and most technologically advanced air service in the world.

All the aforementioned factors came to bear in the impressive USAF performance in the Persian Gulf War. Aerial operations also demonstrated great improvement in the command and control of joint airpower, though the navy and Marines continued to resist the complete integration of their assets under a joint forces air component commander. Again air force leaders claimed the decisive role in winning the war. Service historians even claimed that airpower could now seize and hold ground without ground support. Media images were misleading, however, and the Gulf War Air Power Survey commissioned by USAF to verify its claims revealed numerous flaws in the conduct and results of the air campaign.

Disputes about the decisiveness of airpower swirled throughout the budget battles of the early 1990s, as Chief of Staff Gen. Merrill McPeak oversaw a reduction and reorganization of his service. By late 1997, active duty strength was down to around 370,000, supplemented by more than 155,000 civilians. SAC and TAC were disbanded, as their nuclear forces came under the new unified Strategic Command, while a new USAF Air Combat Command absorbed everything else. As air force leaders fought to get more B-2 stealth strategic bombers and the new F-22 to replace the F-15 and F-16, strategic airlift assets of the Air Mobility Command received increased funding in recognition of the increased need for Continental United States (CONUS) deployments as overseas bases closed. Plans to replace the A-10 with multirole F-16s made economic sense to the air force, but awoke old fears in the army that close air support was being relegated to a low priority. As USAF tried to exploit a perceived revolution in military affairs with continued emphasis on precision and the exploitation of new information technologies, it also had to come to grips with reduced budgets and a lack of appreciation for the strategic airpower that had been its raison d'être. The future holds much promise and many challenges for the premier air force in the world.

[See also Air and Space Defense; Air Force: Combat Organizations; Strategy: Air Warfare Strategy; Strategy: Nuclear Warfare Strategy.]

• Fred Kaplan, The Wizards of Armageddon, 1983. Herman S. Wolk, Planning and Organizing the Postwar Air Force, 1943–1947, 1984. John L. Frisbee, ed., Makers of the United States Air Force, 1989. Robert Frank Futrell, Ideas, Concepts, Doctrine, 2 vols., 1989. Allan R. Millett and Peter Maslowski, For the Common Defense: A Military History of the United States of America, 1984; rev. and exp. ed. 1994. Walton S. Moody, Building a Strategic Air Force, 1996. Walter J. Boyne, Beyond the Wild Blue: A History of the United States Air Force, 1947–1997, 1997.   —Conrad C. Crane

AIR FORCE COMBAT ORGANIZATIONS: TACTICAL AIR FORCES.

Tactical air forces are air combat forces that are organized to conduct operations within a theater of war in support of military campaign and possibly national objectives. The traditional view of these forces is that they provide offensive and defensive support to ground and naval surface forces. However, after its creation in 1947, the United States *Air Force (USAF) increasingly viewed tactical air power as a potentially decisive factor in modern warfare that should be organized and used as an independent combat force whenever possible. The differing views on the proper roles of air power have often generated significant debates between the USAF (and its predecessors) and the other three armed services. The other services—*army, *navy, and *Marines—tend to view air power as a subordinate and supporting capability.

The modern USAF tactical air force structure has been built upon the framework of the early military aviation units and the experiences of air power in combat. The earliest basic U.S. aviation tactical unit was an aerosquadron, later called a squadron. As its role evolved, squadrons were characterized by a specific combat function and were normally equipped with a single type of aircraft. Squadrons were often subdivided into "flights." Squadrons remain the basic operational unit in the modern USAF. In the early years of U.S. military aviation, when used in combat, squadrons were assigned directly to ground units. This situation reflected the view of aviation units as primarily support for surface units, a role that was also illustrated by aviation's overall subordination as the Aeronautical Division or Aviation section within the Signal Corps until 1918.

The experience of *World War I led to the formation of a somewhat more independent organization, the Division

of Military Aeronautics of the U.S. Army, in 1918. The First World War experience also defined the basic roles of tactical air power: reconnaissance and observation, air superiority (control of the air—the most critical function of air power—through offensive and defensive action, normally by pursuit or fighter aircraft), attack (support for friendly surface forces either through close air support or interdiction), and bombardment (deep attacks on enemy surface forces and support capabilities). Air forces also showed promise for other missions, including emergency logistic support and tactical movement of ground forces. Many air leaders extrapolated from the experience and envisioned even greater roles for air power in future conflict. As a minimum, these leaders, like Gen. Billy *Mitchell, envisioned air power as a key to breaking away from the bloody trench warfare of the past war, and many believed that air power could change the very nature of future wars.

The debates on the role of air power that emerged during and after World War I have continued into the post–Cold War period. The more revolutionary perspective of air power potential has focused on the concept of strategic bombardment, meaning direct attacks on the enemy's homeland and his ability, as well as willingness, to support continued combat operations. Although strategic bombardment became the focal point of the effort to define the role of air power in modern warfare, many air leaders believed that the capabilities of air power must be used in a decisive manner in tactical operations as well. Air power advocates believed that air power, tactical as well as strategic, must be organized centrally under the control of airmen who understood the inherent abilities of air power as well as its limitations. This centralized control would allow air forces commanders to exploit the inherent offensive capability and flexibility of air power, to focus on air assets on potentially decisive targets, and to respond rapidly to changing combat conditions.

During the inter-war period, Army leaders maintained overall control of aviation forces, although the push for greater independence by air leaders led to the creation of the Army Air Service in 1920 and the Army Air Corps in 1926. Even more importantly, in 1935, the Army created General Headquarters (GHQ) Air Force to control all combat forces in the continental United States. In 1941, the Army created the Army Air Forces in recognition of the increasingly important role of the aviation branch. Along with the evolution of the higher command and control organizations, the operational forces also evolved. Squadrons remained the key tactical units, and were normally organized into groups, which in turn were organized into wings. A group normally included several squadrons and also controlled the support functions needed to operate an air base and sustain the operational forces stationed at the base.

During *World War II, wings contained several groups and were organized into numbered air forces (e.g. Eighth Air Force, Ninth Air Force, or Fifth Air Force). As needed, intermediate organizations, including divisions and commands, were formed under the air forces to meet theater or campaign requirements. The most important of these for theater operations was the tactical air command or TAC (e.g. IX TAC or XIX TAC), which was specifically formed to provide offensive and defensive support for surface forces. Air Force leaders believed that the experiences in Europe and the Southwest Pacific validated the value of tactical air power as a coequal combat power with the surface forces. Army commanders generally concurred that air power had been a critical factor, but they viewed aviation as a supporting, indeed subordinate, capability, not a coequal force.

The creation of an independent USAF in 1947 and the associated changes in the national defense structure incorporated an increased emphasis on independent air power. The flight, squadron, and wing structure of the tactical forces remained the foundation of the combat capabilities. (Following the creation of the USAF, the wing replaced the group as the standard base-level unit controlling all the base activities, including the combat squadron.) Until the collapse of the Soviet Union, the strategic mission tended to dominate the image and the force structure of the USAF. But, centrally controlled tactical forces also provided important combat capabilities to the U.S. military. Due in part to the competition imposed by limited budgets, the other services aggressively criticized the USAF for both its emphasis on strategic operations and for its emphasis on centralized control in theater operation and for independent operations.

The USAF theater capabilities were organized to support the unified commanders within the U.S. national command and control structure. Each regional commander had a USAF component command—organizationally equal to the surface components—that was also a major command for the USAF. For example, in Europe, the air forces were commanded by the U.S. Air Forces in Europe (USAFE) and in the Pacific by first the Far East Air Forces (FEAF) and then Pacific Air Forces (PACAF). In the continental United States, the tactical forces were controlled by the Tactical Air Command (TAC) for most of the post–World War II period—replaced by the Air Combat Command (ACC) in the post–Cold War era. TAC trained forces, developed doctrine, and provided combat forces to overseas commanders. Within the major commands, the key subordinate organizations were number air forces, with air divisions providing another management level above the wings.

As the unified command structure matured and concepts of joint operations evolved, the theater command and control system developed to include a joint forces air component commander (JFACC), who controlled all air assets from all services involved in theater operations. The JFACC position represents the maturation of the concept of centralized control of theater air power. In the perspective of the USAF, the JFACC concept and the modern role of theater air power was validated in Operation Desert Storm against Iraq, in which air assets were used in a combination of strategic and tactical operations to independently create the conditions of victory. The interpretation of this experience varies: the other U.S. military services continue to argue that air power still primarily supports surface operations, while the USAF continues to claim that air power is indeed decisive in modern warfare, including theater or tactical operations, and must not be tied too tightly to surface force concepts.

[See also Air Force Combat Organizations: Strategic Air Forces; Air Force, U.S.: Overview; Air Force, U.S.: The Predecessors of, 1907 to 1946; Air Force, U.S.: Since 1947; Army Combat Branches: Aviation, Persian Gulf War, 1991.]

• William W. Momyer, Air Power in Three Wars, 1978. Maurer Maurer. Aviation in the U.S. Army, 1919–1939, 1987. John A. Warden, Jr., The Air Campaign: Planning for Combat, 1988. Richard P. Hallion, Strike from the Sky: The History of Battlefield Attack, 1919—1945, 1989. James A. Winnefield and Dana J. Johnson, Joint Air Operations: Pursuit of Unity in Command and Control, 1942–1991, 1993. Steven J. McNamara, Air Power's Gordian Knot: Centralized Versus Organic Control, 1994.
                                                      —Jerome V. Martin

AIR FORCE COMBAT ORGANIZATIONS: STRATEGIC AIR FORCES. First introduced as auxiliaries in support of ground and naval forces, aircraft offered a potential technological solution to the problems of warfare in the industrial age. Aerial forces could fly over defending armies and navies, which were tactical targets, and directly attack the strategic sources of an enemy's warmaking capability—factories, *communications, *transportation, workers, and urban concentrations—without the need for bloody ground campaigns. A product of the airmen's special perspective from on high and the American love of technology, this strategic view of air war received its first expression in the United States from pioneer aviator Lt. Benjamin Foulois's proposal in 1907 that military aviation focus on targets behind enemy armies. In 1917, airpower prophet Lt. Col. Billy *Mitchell sought to divide American air units on the western front into tactical and strategic air forces, the former to support ground forces, the latter to attack "enemy material of all kinds behind the lines." Inadequate resources and the opposition of his staff encouraged Gen. John J. *Pershing, commanding the American Expeditionary Force (AEF) in France, to reject both Mitchell's proposal and a detailed plan to bomb "commercial centers and the lines of communications" by Mitchell's technical chief, Maj. Edgar Gorrell. Other nations engaged in strategic bombing in World War I, but the U.S. Army Air Service, America's wartime air force, remained a tactical force in support of army ground operations under the AEF.

In the interwar period, the Air Service and its successor, the Air Corps, struggled to win an independent role for army aviation by emphasizing strategic operations behind the army's battle lines. Opposed by the army and navy, General Mitchell, General Foulois, and World War II air commander "Hap" *Arnold nevertheless worked out the tactics, training, and technology of strategic bombing. Officers at the Air Corps Tactical School developed a strategic bombing doctrine based on high-altitude, daylight, precision attacks on an enemy's industrial infrastructure or "fabric," in contrast to European plans to employ airpower in support of armies or to attack cities. The appearance of the B-17 "Flying Fortress" bomber and the Norden bombsight, coupled with Adolf *Hitler's successful use of bombers to intimidate foes in the 1930s, convinced President Franklin D. *Roosevelt and army chief George C. *Marshall to support a strategic bombing campaign against Axis enemies in World War II.

For the war the Army Air Forces established America's first strategic bombing organizations, The Eighth and Fifteenth Air Forces against Germany and the Twentieth Air Force against Japan, to bomb primarily oil and transportation links, but also aircraft production, ball bearings, and other industries. Thirty-one months of strategic operations against Germany saw most bombs aimed at industry, while ten months against Japan brought mostly area attacks against urban concentrations. Though assigned the role of bombing the sources of enemy power under the unified command of airmen, American air forces in Europe remained subordinate to ground commanders in pursuit of war objectives. Only against Japan did the Twentieth Air Force carry out an independent strategic air campaign.

During the *Cold War, the threat of strategic attack using *nuclear weapons dominated air force war planning. The Strategic Air Command (SAC), established on 21 March 1946, had the mission of conducting "long-range offensive operations in any part of the world," but its primary responsibility was to maintain a credible threat of assured destruction—any nation attacking the United States or its Western European allies would suffer an overwhelming counterattack. Based initially on manned bombers (the B-29 and B-36 to start, though primarily the B-52 from 1955 into the 1990s) and later intercontinental ballistic missiles (starting with the Atlas in 1958, followed by the Titan, Minuteman, and Peacekeeper) carrying thermonuclear hydrogen bombs and warheads, SAC war plans evolved from area attacks on Soviet urban industrial concentrations in the late 1940s to attacks on specific governmental, industrial, and military targets in the decades following.

Under the leadership of the hard-driving Gen. Curtis E. *LeMay from 1948 to 1957, SAC became an elite force that consumed a major portion of America's defense budget. LeMay and SAC's dominating influence also caused America's defense planning to focus on nuclear war preparations to the detriment of preparations for limited conventional war. Involvement in Korea and Vietnam propelled an unprepared USAF into strategic bombing operations using nonnuclear weapons. Targets remained consistent with 1930s doctrine—industrial infrastructure. In both wars, however, the vital industrial centers supporting enemy war efforts were in the Soviet Union and China, put beyond the range of strategic bombers by political considerations. The dearth of industrial targets in North Korea and North Vietnam, and the presence of strong defenses against air attack, created the ironic situation of strategic bombers attacking tactical targets in safer areas while more maneuverable tactical fighter-bombers went after the few strategic targets available.

In the *Persian Gulf War of 1991, tactical fighters such as the F-117 stealth aircraft replaced large strategic bombers such as the B-52 in carrying out a strategic bombing campaign against Iraq because of the need for greater accuracy and the dangers posed by Iraqi antiaircraft defenses. A new bombing doctrine, building on the experience in the *Vietnam War, moved beyond the industrial focus of earlier strategies to envision Iraq's warmaking capability as a synergy between leadership, communication, industrial production, transportation, and military forces, merging tactical and strategic air warfare into a unified air campaign. Five weeks of intensive bombing aimed at Iraq's military, industrial, and governmental complex paved the way for a successful four-day ground offensive.

Doctrinal and technological developments so blurred the boundary between tactical and strategic bombing in the 1980s and 1990s that the USAF redefined the former as joint operations involving conventional weapons and the latter as independent operations involving nuclear weapons. Reflecting this change, the United States integrated its strategic nuclear forces, including land- and sea-based ballistic missiles and manned bombers, under the U.S. Strategic Command on 1 June 1992, simultaneously

disbanding SAC. At the same time, air force conventional bombing forces, including traditionally defined tactical and nonnuclear strategic bombers, reorganized as Air Combat Command.

[*See also* Strategy: Air Warfare Strategy.]

• Lee Kennett, *A History of Strategic Bombing*, 1982. Michael S. Sherry, *The Rise of American Air Power: The Creation of Armageddon*, 1987. Jacob Neufeld, *The Development of Ballistic Missiles in the United States Air Force, 1945–1960*, 1990. Norman Polmar and Timothy M. Laur, eds., *Strategic Air Command: People, Aircraft, and Missiles*, 1990. Earl H. Tilford, Jr., *Crosswinds: The Air Force's Setup in Vietnam*, 1993. Stephen L. McFarland, *America's Pursuit of Precision Bombing, 1910–1945*, 1995.   —Stephen L. McFarland

AIR FORCE RESERVE. The U.S. Air Force Reserve was established on 14 April 1948. This and the activation of the Continental Air Command on 1 December 1948 to oversee the reserve unit program represented the air force's desire to achieve greater coherence in its federal reserve component program, which in various guises dated back to 1916.

Air Force Reservists first participated in combat in the *Korean War. All 25 flying wings of the reserve, a total of 30,000 personnel, were mobilized, plus nearly 119,000 individual reservists. The Air Force Reserve emerged from its wartime service with significant program problems, and the air force spent the remainder of the 1950s rebuilding it. Key milestones included the establishment of the Air Reserve Personnel Center and the implementation of an Air Reserve Technician program, which established a full-time cadre of civil servants who were also military personnel in Air Force Reserve units.

During the 1960s, the Air Force Reserve demonstrated its operational readiness and underwent further organizational changes. Reservists participated in numerous *Cold War events, including the 1961–62 Berlin Crisis and the Korea and Vietnam mobilizations of 1968–69. The Department of *Defense sought to merge reserve and National Guard components, but this was halted by Congress in the Reserve Forces Bill of Rights and Vitalization Act of 1967. The act also established the Office of Air Force Reserve as part of the Air Staff. On 1 August 1968, Headquarters Air Force Reserve replaced the Continental Air Command, and assumed responsibility for Air Force Reserve unit program.

By the 1970s, air force officials increasingly called upon the reserve to support a variety of national security objectives. With the establishment of the Total Force policy in 1973, reservist and *Air National Guard personnel were trained to active duty operational readiness standards. More than 23,500 Air Force Reservists took part in the 1991 *Persian Gulf War. Other post-Cold war operations included participating in United Nations and *NATO-sponsored relief and peacekeeping missions in Africa and the Balkans.

• Gerald T. Cantwell, *The Air Force Reserve: From Flying Club to Total Force*, 1996.   —Kenneth C. Kan

AIR NATIONAL GUARD. The Air National Guard (ANG) was established as a separate reserve component of the U.S. *Air Force (USAF) by the *National Security Act of 1947. The Guard's involvement in aviation began before World War I, when a few states established small but poorly funded flying programs. In 1915, the first viable National Guard aviation unit—the First Aero Company of New York—was organized, and a year later it was mobilized during the border crisis with Mexico. All-Guard aviation units were disbanded by the War Department in 1917. Instead, Guardsmen played important leadership and combat aviation roles as individual volunteers in the U.S. Army Air Service.

After World War I, despite War Department opposition, Guard aviation was placed on a permanent footing. The army organized twenty-nine Guard observation squadrons during the interwar period. Those units, with 4,800 experienced personnel, were mobilized in 1940–41. Although many remained intact, they lost the majority of their personnel to other units of the Army Air Forces (AAF) during World War II, when Guard aviators served in every operational theater.

A reluctant AAF was compelled by political pressure from National Guard interests to develop a dual-component postwar reserve system consisting of the ANG, a force with federal and state roles, and the Air Force Reserve (AFRES), an organization with a strictly federal role. At first, the ANG was little more than a poorly trained and equipped flying club.

The *Korean War (1950–53) proved a turning point for the ANG. Some 45,000 Air Guard personnel, 80 percent of the force, were called into federal service, but they were unprepared for combat. Eventually, ANG units and individual Guardsmen contributed substantially in the air war in Korea and the USAF's global buildup. *Mobilization problems and political controversy forced the USAF to revamp its reserve programs. In 1951, the USAF included the ANG in its war plans. Two years later, ANG units began augmenting the nation's air defense runway alert forces. That program integrated training and operational support of the USAF by the ANG on a daily basis. The innovation served as a precursor for the Total Force policy implemented in 1973 by the Department of *Defense.

ANG units gradually improved their readiness after the *Korean War and were integrated into a widening circle of planning activities, exercises, and operational missions. The ANG became a mixed force of fighters, airlifters, tankers, and support units.

Mobilization performance continued to improve in the Berlin crisis (1961) and the USS Pueblo and *Tet Offensive crises (1968). From 1967 to 1977, ANG volunteers operated a tanker task force in Europe on a continuous basis, foreshadowing the extensive use of reserve forces abroad in a nonmobilized status. During the 1970s, significant numbers of women and minorities began to enter the ANG, and with the draft's end in 1973, it became an *All-Volunteer Force. The ANG evolved into a well-equipped force capable of rapid global deployment. During the Persian Gulf crisis (1990–91), over 12,000 Air Guard members performed ably. Since then, the ANG has assumed a growing share of the USAF's missions.

[*See also* Militia and National Guard.]

• Charles J. Gross, *The Air National Guard and the Persian Gulf Crisis: From Shield to Storm*, 1995. Charles J. Gross, *Militiaman, Volunteer, and Professional; The Air National Guard and the American Military Tradition*, 1996.   —Charles J. Gross

AIR WARFARE. Despite having given birth to the airplane in 1903, the United States was slow to explore the military applications of aviation and had effectively no air arm when war broke out in August 1914. By contrast, Germany, France, and Britain went to war with remarkably efficient aviation establishments, and even Austria-Hungary and Russia possessed useful air arms. Limited by feeble engines and drag-producing, externally braced structures, few aircraft in 1914 could carry more than a pilot and an observer. Nevertheless, they played a pivotal role in key early battles, notably the Marne, where British Royal Flying Corps reconnaissance reports were instrumental in turning the Germans back from Paris.

The value of visual reconnaissance was evident from the outset, but when the war deadlocked in the trenches, new missions emerged as designers and manufacturers struggled to improve aircraft performance. By 1916, aerial photography was a crucial element of intelligence: photo mapping provided the detailed charts needed for operational planning; and spotting and adjustment of artillery fire by radio-equipped aircraft was essential to the massive barrages that dominated the land war on the western front.

The advantages of denying the air to an enemy were obvious, but the first effective means of doing so appeared only in April 1915, when French pilot Roland Garros fielded a device that enabled a machine gun mounted on the engine cowling to fire through the propeller arc, turning his aircraft into a flying gun, a *fighter aircraft. After a brief string of aerial victories, Garros was forced down and captured along with his aircraft. Concerned at Garros's success, the German High Command asked Dutch designer Anthony Fokker to copy his device. Instead, Fokker designed his own mechanical synchronization gear (Garros's device was unreliable, relying on steel deflector plates on the blades), which Fokker fitted to his single-place E-III monoplane. Fokker's *Eindekkers* soon reached the front, launching a "Fokker scourge" that lasted until the following spring when superior French Nieuport and British De Havilland fighters appeared. The Germans responded with Albatros scouts, initiating the struggle for air superiority that was central to both world wars.

By the time America entered the war in April 1917, aviation was crucial to victory, particularly on the western front where the opposing industrial powers squared off. The German High Command implicitly recognized this by allocating high-performance aero engines top production priority in their *Amerika Program,* designed to produce victory before America's industrial might could be brought to bear. In the event, British and French aircraft production far surpassed Germany's producing air superiority over the trenches and guiding the devastating artillery barrages that broke the German Army. Despite enormous productive capacity, America's intervention in the air war was disappointing. Aside from a handful of Curtiss "Big America" flying boats, America produced no one battleworthy aircraft. The vaunted Liberty engine was produced in impressive numbers, but had mediocre performance and arrived too late. The air component of the American Expeditionary Forces fought well, but mostly in cast-off French aircraft.

America's most impressive achievement was in training large numbers of aviators and mechanics, but they too arrived late. Most American pilots who saw combat were French-trained. An important consequence of the U.S. commitment to the air war was the release on the postwar economy of huge numbers of surplus Liberty engines and Curtiss JN-2 "Jenny" trainers. The results were mixed: on the one hand, the availability of cheap engines and aircraft exposed large numbers of Americans to aviation, notably in the form of touring "flying circuses"; on the other, cheap surplus materiel rendered the civil aviation industry temporarily moribund and stifled technical innovation.

America's huge expanse and thin rail net intervened, creating a larger civil aviation market than the rest of the world combined. The competitive nature of that market led to steady advances in aircraft design, and by the mid-1930s the best U.S. civil transports could outperform first-line European bombers and fighters in speed, range, and—most important—useful load as a function of empty weight. This was particularly impressive since, in contrast to Europe and Japan, military aviation subsidies in the United States had all but ceased with the Great Depression.

During the interwar years aerial bombardment was used widely in colonial wars, with the Spanish in Morocco and the Italians in Libya and Ethiopia dropping poison gas on a large scale. U.S. Navy and Marine Corps experiments in the 1920s led to the development of one type of *bomber aircraft, the dive-bomber. These and specialized torpedo bombers comprised the attack complement of *aircraft carriers commissioned by the British, American, and Japanese navies. The 1936–39 Spanish Civil War served as a testing ground for aerial combat, with Nazi Germany and Fascist Italy pitted against Soviet Russia. The Luftwaffe perfected its ground support doctrine and revolutionized air-to-air tactics with voice radio-equipped fighters. At the beginning of the conflict, German Ju-52 transports ferried Spanish regular troops from Morocco to secure Andalusia for the Nationalist rebels in the first decisive use of *transport and supply aircraft.

By the late 1930s, few doubted that war was imminent and that airpower would play a major role in its outcome. In 1938, some 80 percent of all aircraft in the world were American civil craft, reflecting the robustness of an industrial and social base that would produce prodigious quantities of aircraft and, of at least equal importance, an inexhaustible flood of pilots, aircrew, and mechanics. But that robustness represented only potential, for the United States possessed only one world-quality warplane, the Boeing B-17 bomber, and that only in prototype. At the time of the Japanese attack on *Pearl Harbor, America's only battleworthy fighter in service was the Navy F4F Wildcat: not until 1943 did U.S. fighters routinely take the measure of their Axis opponents. In contrast, Britain, Germany, and Japan all entered the war with world-class fighters, and if prewar Axis bombers lacked the payload-to-weight ratios of their American equivalents, they had been battle-tested in China and Spain.

Only three air forces entered World War II with coherent strategic doctrines: the Luftwaffe with an embryonic theory of strategic bombardment; the Royal Air Force with an air defense doctrine based on radar-directed intercepts; and the United States Army Air Forces (USAAF) with a well-articulated theory of strategic daylight precision bombardment. The Luftwaffe, Japanese Navy Air Force (JNAF), and the U.S. Navy's air arm were well trained and equipped to support surface operations; the Royal Navy's Fleet Air Arm was superbly trained, but had mediocre aircraft. Of the rest, the French Armée de l' Air had high standards of training and some good aircraft, but was shackled to obsolete tactical support doctrine and caught in the middle of a major reequipment program when Germany invaded in May 1940; the Soviet Union's Red Air Force was enormous, but had obsolescent aircraft, mediocre training, and, in the wake of Josef *Stalin's purges, a shortage of competent leaders; the Italian Regia Aeronautica was well trained, but with obsolescent equipment and an inadequate industrial base; the Japanese Army Air Force (JAAF) was well trained, but possessed indifferent equipment.

The strategic initiative, sound tactical doctrine, and battleworthy materiel carried the day for Germany and Japan in the initial clashes of the air war, punctuated only by British victory in the Battle of Britain. The Luftwaffe virtually obliterated the Red Air Force at the start of Operation Barbarossa, and Japanese carrier aviation went from victory to victory during the first six months of the Pacific War. The tide turned in the summer of 1942, when U.S. carrier aviation blunted the JNAF's cutting edge at the Battle of *Midway just as the British, with copious American aid, were wresting superiority from the Luftwaffe in the Mediterranean. By the eve of the *D-Day landing, heavy losses at Stalingrad, in North Africa, at Kursk, and in Italy had forced the Luftwaffe to concede air superiority everywhere save over Germany, where the hammer blows of RAF Lancaster and Halifax bombers by night and USAAF B-17s and B-24s by day forced a maximum defensive effort. The cost in aircraft (which could be replaced) and skilled aircrew (who could not) broke the back of the Luftwaffe. Meanwhile, the JNAF had been destroyed in the Solomons, and the JAAF ruined in the New Guinea. The critical losses were in trained aircrew. Japanese aircraft production increased dramatically and showed remarkable resilience under heavy bombing, but U.S. air superiority was never seriously threatened thereafter, the shock of kamikaze attacks on warships notwithstanding. There is not doubt that airpower was crucial to the defeat of the Axis, but just how and why was—and is—a matter of debate.

Strategic bombing advocates, notably the leaders of the USAAF and its successor, the U.S. Air Force, argued that Germany and Japan were defeated by strategic bombing, or, in the case of Germany, could have been with different targeting priorities. Detractors argued that Nazi Germany fell only to ground invasion, and pointed to the effects of naval blockade on Japan, a resource-poor island nation, attributing Japanese surrender to shock at the awesome power of the atomic bomb rather than to the economic effects of bombing. Focus on this argument, which formed the backdrop to public debate over America's *Cold War military priorities, has obscured awareness of other elements of airpower, notably transport and antisubmarine aviation, both of which were pivotal in World War II; and flight training, which was arguably decisive.

The reality of nuclear *deterrence made World War II the last war in which industrialized nations actually tried to destroy one another from the air, and the few massive air campaigns since have been mounted against nonnuclear states by a superpower, a superpower-led coalition, or a superpower client. The classic early examples are Korea and Vietnam, in which U.S. *bombs were pitted against enemy troops and lines of communication. The Soviet Union did commit first-line equipment and personnel to combat against American air forces—MiG-15 jet fighters in Korea, and SA-2 surface-to-air missiles plus MiG-17, MiG-19, and MiG-21 fighters in Vietnam—but did so discreetly to avoid overt confrontation. The provision of British and American shoulder-launched, heat-seeking antiaircraft *missiles to the mujahiddin in opposition to the Soviet invasion of Afghanistan is a parallel example. Israel's air campaigns against its enemies fall into the same category, particularly the 1973 Yom Kippur War, in which U.S.-provided Israeli aircraft were pitted against Soviet-designed SA-6 surface-to-air missiles and SPU 23-4 mobile gun systems which amounted to a technical and tactical extension of the air war over North Vietnam. The most recent example is the coalition air campaign in the 1991 *Persian Gulf War.

The operational and tactical parameters of air warfare have changed enormously since 1945 as a result of jet propulsion; *helicopters; guided air-to-air, surface-to-air, and air-to-surface *missiles; *precision-guided munitions; and, from the 1970s, infrared technology, micro-miniaturized, transistor-based, flight control, guidance, and navigation systems; and, finally, *stealth aircraft. Indeed, the differences between the attritional air campaigns of World War II, Korea, and Vietnam, and that of the 1991 Gulf War, in which all the elements of change enumerated above came into play for the first time, are so stark that some have argued that the latter represents a revolution in military affairs.

Be that as it may, elements of continuity stemming from the robustness of America's aviation industry are arguably of equal importance. The engineering skill, productive capacity, and the underlying market forces that swamped Axis airpower in World War II are still very much in evidence. To make the point by example, the Boeing B-52, arguably the most successful bomber ever built, entered service in 1955, played a major role in the Cold War and Vietnam War, and is slated to remain in service into the 2040s. Its immediate predecessor was the Boeing B-47, a bomber of radical design powered by six jet engines suspended on pylons beneath its thin, swept wings. The B-47 inspired not only the B-52s, but the Boeing 707, the first truly successful jet airliner and ancestor of the Boeing airliners that dominate world air traffic today. Many of the high-capacity civilian air transports called to duty in the 1991 Gulf War as part of the U.S. Civil Reserve Air Fleet were Boeing 747 jumbo jets, descendants of the B-17 of World War II.

[See also Aircraft Industrialists; Air Force, U.S.: Overview; Procurement: Aerospace Industry; Strategy: Air Warfare Strategy; Tactics: Air Warfare Tactics.]

—John F. Guilmartin, Jr.

ALAMO, BATTLE OF THE

ALAMO, BATTLE OF THE (1836). In fall 1835, a political revolution broke out among the North American settlers in Mexican Texas. After the colonists ousted the Mexican garrison from San Antonio in December, the Mexican president, Gen. Antonio López de *Santa Anna, led an army northward to avenge the loss. Texan commander Sam Houston recognized that San Antonio had no strategic value and ordered Texans there to evacuate to the east.

Approximately 150 men decided to stay and fortify the abandoned mission known as the Alamo. By 24 February 1836, Mexican troops initiated a siege. Texas Col. William Barrett Travis sent out messages pleading for reinforcements, but only thirty-two men responded.

On 6 March, Santa Anna launched an overwhelming assault with about 1,800 troops. The defenders fought desperately, killing or wounding some 600 Mexicans, but by sunup, the approximately 180 defenders, including Travis and David Crockett, were dead.

Word quickly reached the American settlements of Texas, and the slogan "Remember the Alamo!" helped mo-

tivate the remainder of the Texas army. On 21 April Sam Houston led his men to victory over Santa Anna at the Battle of *San Jacinto—thus guaranteeing Texas independence.

[See also Texas War of Independence.]

• Walter Lord, *A Time to Stand*, 1961. Jeff Long, *Duel of Eagles: The Mexican and U.S. Fight for the Alamo*, 1990.

—James M. McCaffrey

ALCOHOLISM. *See* Substance Abuse.

ALIEN AND SEDITION ACTS (1798). In 1798, the Federalist Congress passed four laws to check a perceived French threat during the Undeclared Naval War with *France. The Naturalization Act (18 June) extended required residence from five to fourteen years before an alien could become a citizen. The Alien Friends Act (25 June) allowed the president to deport any alien deemed dangerous to "peace and safety" and the Alien Enemies Act (July 6) allowed the deportation of any alien from a country at war with the United States. The Sedition Act (14 July) rendered it a crime to make statements intended to defame or bring the president, Congress, or government into contempt or disrepute. Those convicted could be fined up to $2,000 and jailed for two years. The Naturalization and Enemies Acts were permanent; the Alien Friends Act would expire in 1800, and the Sedition Act in 1801. Not vigorously enforced, the Alien Acts convinced many aliens to leave the United States.

Ultimately twenty-one people were indicted for sedition, and eleven were convicted, receiving sentences of up to eighteen months and fines of $1,000 or more. Influential Republican editors and leaders were the main targets, but any criticism was a federal crime. The Federalists argued that by allowing truth as a defense, the Sedition Act advanced civil liberties. Federal judges at sedition cases, however, interpreted the law so as to guarantee convictions: the accused must prove the truth of their opinions.

In November 1798, Vice President Thomas *Jefferson and former congressman James *Madison secretly drafted resolutions adopted by the Kentucky and Virginia legislatures challenging the Alien and Sedition Acts. These resolutions argued that the states had not delegated power to punish libel to the federal government, and that free government rested on the people's free opinions. As president (1801), Jefferson pardoned all convicted under the Sedition Act and helped pay their fines.

[See also Adams, John; Civil Liberties and War.]

• James Morton Smith, *Freedom's Fetters: The Alien and Sedition Laws and American Civil Liberties*, 1956. —Robert J. Allison

ALL-VOLUNTEER FORCE. In 1973, Defense Secretary Melvin *Laird announced the formation of the All-Volunteer Force (AVF) and the end of the conscription that had been the major basis of America's *Cold War army. Although volunteerism had been America's peacetime military tradition prior to 1940, the AVF represented the nation's first attempt to maintain a standing force on a completely voluntary basis.

The blueprint for the AVF was prepared by President Richard M. *Nixon's Commission on an All-Volunteer Armed Force, appointed in 1969. Driven by political pressure to end the draft and an ideological commitment to free market forces, the commission headed by Thomas *Gates had concluded that a volunteer force, supported by the potential to reintroduce the draft, was preferable to a mixed force of conscripts and volunteers, and that, based on labor market dynamics, it was economically feasible to raise a volunteer army. The Gates Commission also believed that the end of conscription would have no major effect on racial or gender composition of the service.

In 1973, the American economy was troubled, youth unemployment was high, entry-level military pay was comparable to civilian pay, and the All-Volunteer Force initially appeared to be a success. There were major increases in the representation of African Americans and women. A standby structure for conscription was retained, but the military became more dependent on the reserve components as its primary base for *mobilization. These too experienced major increases in women and minority personnel.

During the late 1970s, funding for recruiting was cut, and the purchasing power of the average enlisted person declined. In 1976, the *G. I. Bill ended; simultaneously, a new selection and classification test, which had been miscalibrated, was introduced. Recruit quality declined, and in 1979, the army fell 17,000 soldiers short of its recruiting goal: the worst recruiting year in postwar history. During this period, the force was decried as a "hollow army."

A recovery in the early 1980s was driven by pay increases and new educational incentives for enlistment. In 1983, on the tenth anniversary of the All-Volunteer Force, Defense Secretary Caspar *Weinberger announced that on the basis of this success, the Department of *Defense would no longer use the title "All-Volunteer Armed Forces," but merely "Armed Forces." In the subsequent decade, the recruiting environment remained relatively poor, and recruit quality was at best stable, in an increasingly smaller force.

The army in 1973 had about 800,000 soldiers; in 1990 it still had 732,000. After the end of the Cold War, President Bill *Clinton proposed to bring the army down to 491,000 soldiers by 1999. The total AVF dropped from 2 million in 1975 to 1.5 million in 1996. The smaller volunteer force has been involved in an expanded number of operations in recent years, including the use of 30,000 troops in the 1989 invasion of Panama to seize Manuel *Noriega and some 650,000 American personnel (active and reserve) in the *Persian Gulf War in 1990–91.

[See also Conscription.]

• Jerald G. Bachman, John D. Blair, and David R. Segal, The All-Volunteer Force, 1977. John B. Keeley, ed., The All-Volunteer Force and American Society, 1978. William Bowman, Roger Little, and G. Thomas Sicilia, eds., The All-Volunteer Force After a Decade, 1986.
—David R. Segal

AMERICAN CIVIL LIBERTIES UNION. The American Civil Liberties Union (ACLU), founded in 1920, is a nonprofit organization devoted to the defense of individual rights under the U.S. Constitution. The ACLU was an outgrowth of the National Civil Liberties Bureau, founded (1917) to provide assistance to conscientious objectors (COs) and to defend the free speech rights of critics of U.S. involvement in World War I. Roger Baldwin, founder and executive director of the ACLU from 1920 to 1950, was a pacifist as well as a civil libertarian, as were many other early ACLU leaders. Defending the right of individuals to criticize the government, even during wartime, became the cornerstone of the ACLU's approach to civil liberties.

In the 1920s and 1930s, the organization opposed compulsory military training in public schools and colleges. During World War II, the ACLU helped establish the National Committee on Conscientious Objectors to provide assistance to COs. It also provided legal assistance in Supreme Court cases challenging the president's order directing the military to relocate and intern Japanese Americans on the West Coast.

During the *Vietnam War, the ACLU assisted COs and defended the free speech rights of opponents of the war. In 1970, it declared the U.S. military involvement unconstitutional on the grounds that Congress had not officially declared war. The ACLU and its New York State affiliate provided legal counsel in several cases challenging the legality of the war. The organization strongly supported the 1973 *War Powers Resolution, which sought to limit the presidential power to send U.S. military forces into combat without congressional approval.

[See also Conscientious Objection.]

• Leon Friedman and Burt Neuborne, Unquestioning Obedience to the President, 1972. Samuel Walker, In Defense of American Liberties: A History of the ACLU, 1990.   —Samuel Walker

AMERICAN LEGION. The American Legion was founded in 1919 by World War I veterans seeking to preserve comradeship fostered in service, to obtain medical care and compensation for the disabled, and to combat postwar radicalism during the Red Scare. It immediately became the largest veterans' organization in U.S. history: membership varied between 600,000 and 1.1 million from 1919 to 1941, and has remained over 2.5 million since 1945. Unlike the *Veterans of Foreign Wars, the Legion admits all veterans of periods of conflict, regardless of whether they served in a theater of combat. More than 10,000 local posts elect delegates to state and national conventions. The Legion lobbied to create the precursor of the *Veterans Administration in 1921 to pay adjusted compensation of the veteran "bonus" ahead of schedule in 1936, and later to provide a *G.I. Bill of benefits for World War II veterans.

Domestically, the Legion has been a major force for national defense and against radicalism. A number of posts resorted to vigilante tactics during the Red Scare of 1919 and against industrial unionization in the 1930s. The Legion is known for community service and disaster relief, Legion baseball, and for an interest in patriotic school curricula. Although politically conservative, the organization has always supported representative democracy, welcoming a diverse ethnic and religious membership and embracing no economic programs besides veterans benefits. Its aging members disagreed initially with many of the younger veterans of the *Vietnam War.

[See also Veterans: Vietnam War; Veterans: World War I; Veterans: World War II.]

• William Pencak, For God and Country: The American Legion, 1919–1941, 1989. Thomas A. Rumer, The American Legion, 1991.
—William Pencak

AMERICAN PEACE SOCIETY. The American Peace Society (APS) was formed in 1828 out of the Massachusetts Peace Society (1815) and other local and state groups. Its principal organizers, William Ladd (1778–1841) and George Beckwith (1800–1870), recruited members, edited its journal—*The Advocate of Peace*—and publicized Ladd's idea of a league of nations with an international court of arbitration. The society embraced peace advocates of every persuasion, although in the 1840s it found the attraction of absolute *pacifism very strong. It opposed the *Mexican War of 1846–48, but endorsed the *Civil War.

In the last quarter of the century, the APS returned to an international campaign for arbitration treaties. A coalition with other peace societies was shattered by World War I (which the society endorsed), and by the postwar debate over the *League of Nations (which the society rejected insofar as it was designed to enforce peace).

The APS never resumed a vigorous advocacy role. In 1932 its journal, now factually oriented, was renamed *World Affairs*. After a flurry of activity during the 1940s on behalf of a *United Nations, the society limited its activity to publication.

[*See also* Peace; Peace and Antiwar Movements.]

• Edson L. Whitney, *The American Peace Society: A Centennial History*, 1928. Merle E. Curti, *The American Peace Crusade: 1815–1860*, 1929.   —E. Charles Chatfield

AMERICAN REVOLUTION. *See* Revolutionary War.

AMERICAN WAY OF WAR. *See* War: American Way of War.

AMHERST, JEFFREY (1717–1797), British general and governor-general, British North America. Born in Kent, England, Amherst used his family's political connections to secure a commission in the British army in 1731. Rising in rank by strategic aide-de-camp appointments, he served as Gen. John Ligonier's aide and later joined the earl of Cumberland's staff. In 1758, William Pitt, acting on Ligonier's advice, promoted Amherst to major-general and sent him to America to take command of 14,000 men during the siege of Louisbourg, on Cape Breton Island. This victory seemingly shifted the momentum of the French and Indian War, and convinced Pitt to make Amherst commander in chief in North America. Amherst captured Ticonderoga and Crown Point in 1759, and accepted the surrender of New France at Montréal in 1760.

Appointed Governor-general of British North America in 1761, Amherst inherited a tense relationship with the Indians of the Ohio Region, then aggravated matters by cutting off diplomatic gifts to the western tribes, forbidding alcohol sales, and altering the terms of trade. The western Indians rebelled in 1763, and Amherst was recalled to Britain. Within a few years, however, he regained his stature, eventually becoming a field marshal and commander in chief of the British army.

[*See also* French and Indian War.]

• John C. Long, *Lord Jeffrey Amherst*, 1933.

—Jon T. Coleman

AMPHIBIOUS SHIPS AND LANDING CRAFT. Amphibious operations—large-scale attacks of hostile shores by combined naval and land forces—were a special feature of World War II. The need for special craft to support amphibious assault had been clearly foreseen and U.S. Fleet maneuvers of the 1920s and 1930s tested designs for boats to carry artillery, tanks, and assault troops. In the thirties two commercial designs emerged: the "Eureka," designed

by Andrew C. Higgins for work in the Louisiana swamps; and the "Alligator," Donald Roebling's track-laying rescue vehicle for the Florida Everglades. These became the workhorses of the U.S. forces—the Landing Craft Vehicle Personnel and Landing Craft Mechanized (LCVP, LCM) from the Higgins boat and the Landing Vehicle Tracked (LVT, in later development redesignated Assault Amphibian Vehicle, AAV) from the Alligator. The LCVP had a capacity of 36 troops or 8,100 pounds of cargo; the LCM carried 30 tons; and the LVT 24 troops.

The design for larger landing ships was spurred by the need to transport and land large mechanized forces in the European theater. Two general types derived from British designs (1940–41) were conceived: the Landing Ship Tank (LST), which beached, opened its bow doors, and let down a ramp to rapidly offload tanks and other vehicles; and the Dock Landing Ship (LSD), a combination troop transport and floating dry dock capable of transporting the largest landing craft in its well deck and launching them by opening a stern gate.

Other British designs adopted for American use were the Landing Craft Tank (LCT; in later development Landing Craft Utility, LCU) and the Landing Craft Infantry (LCI). The LCT was equipped with a bow ramp and the largest model carried up to three 50-ton tanks; the largest LCI carried 200 troops, who debarked on deployable gangways. The most important U.S. Army development was the DUKW, a 6×6 cargo truck surrounded by a boat-shaped flotation hull; it was propelled in water by a stern propeller and on land by its truck wheels.

U.S. wartime developments included attack transports (APA), attack cargo ships (AKA), and amphibious command ships (AGC), all more suitable for operating in forward battle areas than prewar troop transports; the APA and AKA were capable of carrying large numbers of deck-loaded landing craft. Many other modifications to ships and craft throughout the war added a variety of guns, armor, communications, and other special capabilities. In all, some fourteen types of personnel landing craft, twenty-one types of vehicle and tank landing craft, twenty types of landing ships, and three types of amphibian vehicles were in use by the Allies by the end of the war.

After World War II, amphibious forces were retained, and, with embarked Marine combat units, soon became a standard feature of the forward-deployed naval forces of the *Cold War. The most notable use of amphibious forces was the dramatic landing at *Inchon, which reversed the course of the *Korean War. Other operations were *Lebanon in 1958, the *Dominican Republic in 1965, and the initial combat troop deployments to Vietnam. Throughout that war, special landing forces were employed in the I Corps area and numerous landing craft were adapted for riverine warfare in IV Corps. Early in the war, a new class of dock transport (LPD) was developed to add a small helicopter flight deck and hangar, allowing it to carry up to six medium helicopters. Ultimately, fifteen of this class were built.

The most important postwar development in amphibious ships was the creation of three new classes of assault ships: the seven-ship, 18,000-ton *Iwo Jima* class (LPH) in 1961; the five-ship, 39,300-ton *Tarawa* class (LHA) in 1976; and—the world's largest amphibious ships—the five-ship, 40,500-ton *Wasp* class (LHD) in 1989. All are fully capable aircraft carriers, with hangar decks and elevators able to operate twenty medium helicopters in the *Iwo Jima* and *Tarawa* classes and thirty in the *Wasp* class. The latter two classes have well decks to accommodate the navy's new air cushion landing craft (LCAC). Rapid surface assault to complement helicopter assault is now a reality with the 40-knot, 60-ton payload LCAC.

The U.S. Navy plans a total of ninety-one LCACs. Four of the *Tarawa-* and all of the *Wasp*-class ships can accommodate up to eight Harrier jet attack aircraft, as well as helicopters, adding a new dimension. These amphibious assault ships with their embarked Marines have proved important in every large operation of the 1990s and their role into the next century seems assured.

[*See also* Amphibious Warfare.]

• James C. Fahey, *The Ships and Aircraft of the U.S. Fleet*, 6th ed., 1950. Kenneth J. Clifford, *Progress and Purpose: A Developmental History of the United States Marine Corps*, 1973. Kenneth J. Clifford, *Amphibious Warfare Development in Britain and America 1920–1940*, 1983. Samuel E. Morison and John S. Rowe, *The Ships and Aircraft of the U.S. Fleet*, 10th ed., 1975. Norman Polmar, *Ships and Aircraft of the U.S. Fleet*, 16th ed., 1996.

—Gerald C. Thomas, Jr.

AMPHIBIOUS WARFARE is the projection, transition, or movement of military force from sea against a hostile shore. As a form of warfare, it is as old as seaworthy ships.

Britain's grasp of amphibious warfare was one of the secrets of its empire-building. The American colonies had ample exposure to its uses prior to the Revolution. Not surprisingly, the Continental Congress foresaw amphibious as well as shipboard uses for Marines and authorized the raising of two Marine battalions on 10 November 1775 for a never-executed operation against Nova Scotia. The British, however, repeatedly moved amphibiously against the Americans, but the one large-scale operation attempted by the Americans against Fort George at Penobscot, Maine, in July 1779, was a failure, chiefly because of squabbling between the naval and land force commanders. More successful were amphibious raids conducted by the *Continental navy against the British in the Caribbean and even against the British home isles.

The British gave the Americans further lessons in amphibious warfare in the *War of 1812 with their harrying of the Atlantic Coast, which included the burning of Washington and the failed attack against Baltimore. The war would see, however, the humiliating defeat of Britain's largest amphibious expedition of the war. Sir Edward Pakenham executed a technically superb landing and approach to New Orleans in December 1814, but in a final, overconfident attack against Andrew *Jackson in January 1815, he met his own death and disastrous defeat.

In the *Mexican War (1846–48), the United States made singularly enlightened use of amphibious warfare. Not only were there a series of highly successful amphibious raids and lodgments against the California and Gulf coasts of Mexico, but the conclusive operation of the war hinged on the landing of Winfield *Scott's army at Vera Cruz in March 1847.

Most of the amphibious lessons learned in the Mexican War were forgotten by the time of the *Civil War, less than a generation later. Landing operations, often ineptly conducted, against Confederate forts and positions on the Atlantic and Gulf coasts were an inevitable extension of the Union blockade. As the war went on, successful Union

lodgments increased. The final large amphibious operation was the assault against Fort Fisher, which guarded the river approaches to Wilmington, North Carolina, the Confederacy's last remaining major port. The first assault, made in December 1864, failed. The second assault, in January 1865, after Grant's personal intervention in matters of command, was an overwhelming success.

During the remainder of the nineteenth century, the United States, increasingly involved in foreign affairs, found its navy making dozens of landings, amphibious operations in very rudimentary form, to "protect American lives and property" around the globe.

The *Spanish-American War (1898), because of the insular nature of Spain's colonial possessions in the Caribbean and the Far East, was largely naval and amphibious in nature.

Thereafter, the United States increasingly involved itself in interventions, in such places as China, Cuba, Haiti, Nicaragua, and Santo Domingo, of much longer duration than the transitory landings of the previous century. The experience of the Spanish-American War and the increasing professionalization of their officer corps caused the U.S. Navy and Marine Corps to give at least some attention to the development of the doctrine, tactics, and techniques needed for modern amphibious warfare. These largely experimental studies had an almost comic opera testing in the April 1914 landing at Vera Cruz.

In World War I with secure bases available in France, there was no requirement for amphibious operations to introduce the American Expeditionary Forces to the European battlefields. The sole great amphibious operation of that war, the Franco-British landing at Gallipoli in 1915, had ended in disaster for the invaders.

The experience of the first two decades of the twentieth century seemed to leave the U.S. Marine Corps with two destinies: to provide colonial infantry for the garrisoning of such places as Haiti and Santo Domingo, and to provide cloned augmentation of the U.S. Army in larger wars. Some Marine officers, most notably Lt. Col. Earl H. "Pete" *Ellis, and some fewer Navy officers studied War Plan Orange, the long-lived plan for the eventuality of a war with Japan, coupled with a study of the British failure at Gallipoli, and saw a need for specialized amphibious ships and troops and a doctrine to manage their use.

In 1934, a *Tentative Manual for Landing Operations* was published by the Marine Corps Schools at Quantico, Virginia. In the few years that remained before the entry of the United States into World War II, this tentative manual, tested in fleet exercises, was refined into a doctrine accepted by the U.S. Navy, the U.S. Army, and perforce all the Allies. The amphibious ships and landing craft needed to make the doctrine work also evolved, and were built in huge quantities.

The reentry of the Allies into Europe was predicated on a series of amphibious invasions, first of North Africa, then of Italy, and then of Normandy and the South of France. In the Pacific, with its vast watery spaces and limited land areas, amphibious operations were more often seizures rather than invasions. The abrupt end to the war precluded the planned amphibious invasion of the Japanese home islands.

The *Korean War saw not only the amphibious triumph of *Inchon Landing (September 1950) but also the very successful amphibious withdrawal of the X Corps from Hungnam (December 1950).

In the *Vietnam War, there were no great amphibious assaults of defended beaches. The possibility of a great turning movement in the manner of Inchon, perhaps at Vinh, North Vietnam, was much discussed but never ventured. Amphibious techniques were used to land American ground forces in South Vietnam as a substitute for adequate port facilities, and there were many minor landings that attempted to catch the elusive Viet Cong along the coast.

The next large use of amphibious techniques was in the *Persian Gulf War during the buildup of American and Coalition forces in Operation Desert Shield (1990). When Desert Shield became Desert Storm and the allies went on the offensive to recapture Kuwait, U.S. Navy and Marine forces afloat in the Persian Gulf, although unused, posed a palpable threat to Iraq's seaward flank.

[See also Amphibious Ships and Landing Craft; Lejeune, John A.; Marine Corps, U.S.]

• Alfred Vagts, Landing Operations, 1946. Jeter A. Isley and Philip A. Crowl, The U.S. Marines and Amphibious War, 1951. Alan Moorehead, Gallipoli, 1956. Merrill R. Bartlett, ed., Assault from the Sea, 1983. Kenneth J. Clifford, Amphibious Warfare Development in Britain and America from 1920–1940, 1983. Edwin Howard Simmons, The United States Marines: A History, 3rd ed., 1998.

—Edwin Howard Simmons

ANTIETAM, BATTLE OF (1862). The appointment of Gen. Robert E. *Lee as commander of the Army of Northern Virginia on 1 June 1862 helped reverse the momentum of the Civil War. Union armies and naval forces had won impressive victories along the South Atlantic and Gulf coasts and the river systems of Tennessee, Mississippi, Louisiana, and Arkansas, overrunning some 50,000 square miles of the Confederacy. In Virginia, Maj. Gen. George B. *McClellan's large and well-equipped Army of the Potomac had advanced westward up the Virginia Peninsula to within six miles of Richmond. The Confederate States of America seemed doomed. But during Lee's first three months in command, he launched a series of counteroffensives. In the Seven Days' battles and the battles of Cedar Mountain and Second Manassas, Southern victories shifted the war in Virginia from the gates of Richmond to the environs of Washington. Hoping to strike a knockout blow that would force the Lincoln administration to sue for peace, Lee decided to invade Maryland.

Great possibilities rode with the Army of Northern Virginia as it began crossing the Potomac River northwest of Washington on 4 September 1862. The most powerful nations in the world, Britain and France, were considering diplomatic recognition of the Confederacy; one more military victory would win that crucial goal. A large faction in the Northern Democratic Party wanted peace negotiations; another Union defeat might enable them to capture the House of Representatives in the fall. President Abraham *Lincoln had decided in July to issue a proclamation to free the slaves in Confederate states and was awaiting a Union military victory to announce it.

After the defeat at Second Manassas (Bull Run), Lincoln had merged the Union Army of Virginia into the Army of the Potomac and given McClellan command, ordering him to "destroy the rebel army." Cautious as always, McClellan probed northward along the Potomac. On 13 Sep-

tember at Frederick, Maryland, he had extraordinary luck: two Union soldiers found a copy of Lee's invasion orders wrapped around some cigars lost by a Confederate staff officer. Lee had divided his army into five parts, sending three under "Stonewall" *Jackson to capture the Union garrison at Harpers Ferry, which lay athwart Lee's line of communications with the Shenandoah Valley. If he moved quickly, McClellan could destroy the separated units piecemeal. He did not move quickly. Union attacks did overrun Confederate defenders in the South Mountain gaps west of Frederick on 14 September, but failed to save the 12,000 Union troops at Harpers Ferry, which surrendered to Jackson on 15 September. McClellan's tardiness enabled Lee to reunite most of his army along high ground east of the village of Sharpsburg—his left flank on the Potomac and his right on Antietam Creek. Although he outnumbered Lee by about 80,000 troops to 45,000, McClellan assumed that the enemy outnumbered him.

After deliberate preparations that gave Lee time to unite his army, McClellan attacked at dawn on 17 September. His plan called for a one-two punch against the Confederate left and right, followed by reserves to exploit whatever breakthrough might occur. The Union attacks were uncoordinated, enabling Lee to shift troops from quiet sectors to threatened points. During the early morning hours, assaults by six Union divisions on Jackson's corps were contained in vicious fighting in locales that became forever famous: the Cornfield, the West Woods, and the Dunkard Church. Meanwhile, the commander on the Union left flank, Maj. Gen. Ambrose *Burnside, tried to force his troops across a bridge over the Antietam instead of fording that shallow stream. In the center at midday, two Union divisions broke through Confederate defenses along a sunken farm road known ever after as Bloody Lane, but McClellan failed to exploit this success because he feared Lee's nonexistent reserves. Burnside finally punched across the Antietam in early afternoon and advanced toward Sharpsburg, threatening Lee's rear and his retreat route across the Potomac. But at about 4:00 P.M. Maj. Gen. A. P. *Hill's Confederate division arrived after a forced march from Harpers Ferry and hit Burnside's flank, halting the Union advance.

The sun set on the deadliest single day in the Civil War—indeed, in all of American history. Some 6,000 men lay dead or dying, and another 16,000 were wounded. The fighting was not renewed next day, and that night Lee retreated to Virginia. McClellan failed to follow up, but nevertheless claimed a victory. Britain and France did not recognize the Confederacy. Republicans retained control of the House in November. And five days after the battle, Lincoln issued his preliminary *Emancipation Proclamation.

[See also Civil War: Military and Diplomatic Course.]

• James V. Murfin, The Gleam of Bayonets: The Battle of Antietam and the Maryland Campaign of 1862, 1965. Stephen W. Sears, Landscape Turned Red: The Battle of Antietam, 1983. Gary W. Gallagher, ed., Antietam: Essays on the 1862 Maryland Campaign, 1989.

—James M. McPherson

ANTIMILITARISM. See Militarism and Antimilitarism.

ANTIPERSONNEL WEAPONS have been defined as being "designed to destroy or obstruct personnel." The first antipersonnel (AP) mine device activated by human foot pressure, a *fladdermine*, was described by a German author in 1726. During the American *Civil War, Gabriel Rains (1803–1881) devised step mines activated by foot pressure and small AP devices set off when attractive items laid on the ground activated a cord attached to the buried mine. Despite outraged objections from critics in both the North and South, work on AP devices continued during that war. In World War I, the *tretmine,* or step-on mine, containing shrapnel, was used mainly in *trench warfare. Most early twentieth-century AP mines were intended to dissuade enemy personnel from disabling heavier antitank mines.

All modern mines have fuses, detonators, booster and principal charges, and a case; but they come in a variety of types. *Bounding fragmentation mines,* such as the German S-Mine (1935), sprang up to 2 yards above the ground before they exploded, effectively spewing metal to a radius of some 150 feet, though injuries were possible up to several thousand feet. The M-2 was the first U.S. mine of this type (1942). The M-3 *fixed,* or *nondirectional fragmentation mine* (1943) was an early example of a weapon that effectively spewed metal fragments to a distance of 30 feet, though some shards might travel for several hundred more. The Claymore mine, developed by the American Norman A. MacLeod in the early 1950s, was a *directional fragmentation mine,* utilizing several pounds of explosive to disseminate hundreds of irregularly shaped steel cubes. Lighter types were utilized by infantrymen in the *Vietnam War.

Blast mines achieve results through their bursting effect. Some of these are very lightweight, can be fabricated in the field, and have increasingly been made of plastic, glass, wood, and other nonmetallic substances, with nonmetallic fuses, rendering them virtually impossible to detect. The *wide area antipersonnel mine* (WAAPM) was a flanged metal sphere with tripwires spread by springs. Scatterable blast-kill, tripwire-activated mines, dispensed from magazines or drums on truck trailers, have seen much use since the 1970s. By 1996, there were some 2500 different types of AP mine and fuse combinations worldwide.

Detection of mines by hand or by hand-held detectors is still the most effective method, but it is labor-intensive. Vehicular clearing methods have entailed the use of flails, plows, and lightweight rollers. Breaching of minefields can also be done by electronic means, or by the use of explosives. By the late 1980s, more than 90 percent of casualties due to AP mines worldwide were civilians. And by 1995, approximately 110 million AP mines had been deployed around the world. In 1992, the U.S. Congress enacted a moratorium on the sale of AP mines, and the *United Nations and other nations have since done the same. In 1997, the United States refused to sign a multinational treaty banning the use of antipersonnel land mines because the U.S. Army uses such devices to protect American troops on the Korean peninsula.

[*See also* Mines, Land.]

• The Arms Project of Human Rights and Physicians for Human Rights, *Landmines: A Deadly Legacy,* 1993. Eric Prokosch, *The Technology of Killing,* 1995.
—Keir B. Sterling

ANTISUBMARINE WARFARE SYSTEMS are designed to defeat the warmaking use of enemy submarines. This is done through the destruction of submarine bases or construction facilities, and most commonly by seeking out and destroying hostile submarines themselves.

There are two operational approaches to antisubmarine warfare. The most direct is to detect, classify, locate, track, and attack hostile submarines. The more indirect is to deny hostile submarines access to their targets.

Actual antisubmarine warfare occurred mainly during the two world wars, although planning and practice operations have been a major part of U.S. naval operations in the *Cold War. Antisubmarine warfare in World War I was conducted particularly by the British and American navies against German U-boats. The British use of barriers of mines in the English Channel in 1917–18 was relatively ineffective in destroying German submarines, but it apparently forced them to take the more distant North Sea route to the Atlantic. Nor did the Royal Navy's shelling of U-boat bases on the Belgian coast do much damage. Much more effective was the combination in 1917–18 of the replacement of individual merchant ship sailings with the protected convoy system, plus the use of aerial and surface surveillance and then the destruction of submarines by British and American destroyers, frigates, and small subchasers dropping depth charges. The majority of the 159 German U-boats destroyed in enemy action were sunk by surface ships. By the summer of 1917, the British and Americans had greatly limited the effectiveness of the German submarine campaign.

During World War II, British and American efforts against German submarines were more sophisticated and much more extensive. Allied bombers raided U-boat bases, particularly on the French and Norwegian coasts, but failed to penetrate the concrete-roofed submarine shelters. However, after extensive German operations in the Atlantic in 1940–42, the Allies became increasingly effective in locating and destroying German submarines in the Atlantic, largely curtailing the U-boat menace by the end of the war. In part this was due to the protected convoy system, but in large part it resulted from the Allied decryption of the German submarine fleet's cipher (through *ULTRA) and the interception and location of U-boat radio traffic through high-frequency direction-finding equipment. Particularly effective was the Allied campaign to locate and destroy the "Milk Cows"—fuel replenishment submarines for the German underwater "wolf packs." The development of *radar and improvement of *sonar detection also aided the blimps and airplanes, frigates, and destroyers as they sought out enemy submarines and attacked them with depth charges. More than half of the 728 German U-boats destroyed in action were sunk by aircraft. In the Pacific, the U.S. *Navy sank 124 Japanese submarines (most of them by surface ships), while ineffective Japanese action resulted in the sinking of only 44 U.S. submarines. The Japanese proved unable to prevent American undersea vessels from imposing against Japan the most effective submarine blockade in history.

During the Cold War, the increased stealth provided by the development of nuclear-powered and quiet-running submarines posed major challenges. This became even more important when submarine-launched ballistic *missiles made the undersea boats a major factor in nuclear warfare. The U.S. Navy and other *NATO forces prepared major plans and weapons systems to detect and destroy Soviet submarines. Systems were stationed at particular strategic positions to track or deter Soviet submarines, for example, outside their bases or in the entrance to the North Atlantic between Iceland and Greenland.

Modern antisubmarine warfare is conducted by three major naval platforms: hunter-killer submarines; surface ships such as frigates and destroyers; and maritime patrol aircraft. Hunter-killer submarines use hull-mounted sonar as well as towed arrays to detect enemy submarines (by permitting listening at some distance from the noise of the ship itself); their principal weapons to destroy other submarines are heavy-homing *torpedoes. Modern frigates also have hull-mounted sonar and passive towed arrays, as well as depth charges to destroy submarines. However, the frigates also employ *helicopters, which can use dipping sonar and dropped sonobuoys (radio-equipped buoys) for detection, and which can attack the submarines with light-weight honing torpedoes. Aircraft use sonobuoys and magnetic anomaly detectors for locating submarines and lightweight torpedoes for destroying them. Against submarine, as well as aircraft or missile, attack, modern U.S. naval carrier task forces rely particularly on protection in depth, with an outer ring of detection and destruction systems provided on, above, and under the sea.

[*See also* Submarines; Submarine Warfare.]

• R. M. Grant, *U-boats Destroyed: The Effect of Anti-Submarine Warfare, 1914–1918,* 1964. J. R. Hill, *Anti-Submarine Warfare,* 1984. D. Daniel, *Anti-Submarine Warfare and Superpower Stability,* 1986. W. J. R. Gardner, *Anti-Submarine Warfare,* 1996. *Jane's Underwater Warfare Systems, 1995–1996,* 1996.   —William D. Smith

ANTITANK WEAPONS. Tanks first appeared in battle in *World War I. Their bolted armor plate protected crews, weapons, power train, on-board ammunition, and fuel against machine gun and artillery fire. Firepower was provided by artillery cannon and *machine guns. Full tracked, tractor-like chassis provided mobility to both weapons and armor, but mobility was considerably inhibited by trenches, shell craters, and Western Front mud. No antitank weapons specifically designed for that purpose were employed against 1917–18 tanks.

By *World War II, antitank weapons included rounds from high velocity cannon, shaped charge warheads on shoulder fired rockets, and antitank mines. Cannon, on towed mounts, tanks, or motorized gun carriages, were adaptations of artillery or air defense weapons. Cannon sought to defeat armor using explosive (blast energy), high velocity (kinetic energy), or shaped charge (chemical energy) warheads. Kinetic energy from high velocity rounds is a function of half the projectile mass multiplied by the square of projectile velocity. Shaped charge cannon warheads, similar to those of portable shoulder fired antitank rockets, are designed to defeat armor with a high velocity jet of extremely small particles formed from detonation of a cone-shaped explosive charge. Since penetration by shaped charge is a function of the diameter of the explosive cone, larger diameter charges promise greater penetration than smaller diameter warheads, where size and weight are limited by cannon caliber or the need for man-portability. Finally, antitank mines are designed to immobilize tanks, principally by damaging track and suspension gear. Armor had been improved to counter new antitank weapons. Welded seams replaced riveted joints, cast or rolled homogenous armor replaced boiler plate; all served to limit antitank lethality to ranges of about 1100 meters.

By the 1991 *Persian Gulf War, large diameter long range antitank guided *missiles, with acronyms like SAGGER, TOW, HOT, MILAN, and HELLFIRE, guided by wire, radio, or laser, fired from vehicles or aircraft, with effective hit-kill ranges of four kilometers or more, had been fielded. Shaped charge antitank mines, and small, self-forging penetrator warheads were employed for attack of less well protected areas, e.g. belly, sides, and tops of armored vehicles. Tank cannon rounds featured more powerful kinetic energy penetrators which, for the first time, were competitive with shaped charge warheads. Together with vastly improved fire control, day and night, these weapons more than quadrupled World War II lethal tank gun engagement ranges. To counter more lethal antiarmor weapons, armored vehicles featured armor with tougher penetration resistant materials, including ceramics and depleted uranium, and more effective, less penetrable, geometries, all logical extensions of the never-ending armor/antiarmor competition.

• Robert M. Citino, *Armored Forces: History and Sourcebook,* 1994.
                                                        —Donn A. Starry

ANTIWAR MOVEMENTS. *See* Peace and Antiwar Movements, Vietnam Antiwar Movement.

ANZIO, BATTLE OF (1944). In the skillfully defended terrain of southern Italy, the Allies in November 1943 during World War II were advancing so slowly that they decided to go around the German defenses by sea, hoping to speed progress to Rome. In December, they canceled the planned amphibious venture because Anzio was too far ahead of the front to guarantee swift overland linkup with an isolated, vulnerable beachhead. Also, they doubted whether the ships remaining in the Mediterranean after a sizable number was transferred to England for Operation Overlord, the cross-Channel attack, could sustain the attack.

Prime Minister Winston *Churchill, who favored the Italian campaign over Overlord, received permission from President Franklin D. *Roosevelt to hold the ships scheduled to depart and in January 1944, reinstated the enterprise. By now, instead of depositing 14,000 men just ahead of the front, 110,000 were to land deep in hostile territory.

The different outlooks of Gen. Sir Harold Alexander, the British Army Group commander, and Lieut. Gen. Mark *Clark, the Fifth U.S. Army commander, confused expectations. As other units of the Fifth Army tried vainly to cross the Rapido River and penetrate the Gustav Line in order to start the cross-country movement to Anzio, troops of Maj. Gen. John Lucas's U.S. Corps achieved surprise at Anzio and waded ashore on 22 January 1944.

Should Lucas have driven inland 20 miles to the Alban Hills, the last natural barrier on the southern approaches to Rome and tried to enter the undefended capital, as Alexander desired? Or should he, as he would choose to do, have built up port and depot facilities to secure supplies coming by sea from Naples, as Clark wished? The questions inspire controversy today.

German troops rushed from northern Italy, the Balkans, southern France, and Germany contained the beachhead, then attacked to eliminate it. From the Alban heights, they had excellent observation of the Anzio plain, and their artillery and aircraft pounded Allied positions and the ships offshore. In fierce and close range fighting, the Germans pushed back the VI Corps almost to the water's edge. Reinforcements from the main front enabled the Allies to hang on.

Four months later, Alexander brought most of the

British Eighth Army across the Apennines to bolster Clark's forces, then launched a massive offensive on 11 May. These units made contact on 25 May with the VI Corps, now commanded by Maj. Gen. Lucian Truscott, Jr. As the two fronts joined, the Germans gave way, and the Allies entered Rome on 4 June, two days before the Overlord D-Day.

Allied *casualties in the Anzio beachhead numbered around 25,000; losses in the forces advancing to join the beachhead totaled an additional 25,000.

[See also Italy, Invasion and Conquest of.]

• Wynford Vaughan-Thomas, Anzio, 1961. Martin Blumenson, Anzio: The Gamble That Failed, 1963.   —Martin Blumenson

ARCTIC WARFARE. Characterized by subzero temperatures, rapidly shifting weather fronts, and vast expanses of tundra or icefields, the arctic is an especially hostile environment in which to conduct combat operations. The severity of conditions dictates that military operations differ markedly from those in more temperate regions. Virtually all operations are performed by highly trained, specially equipped light infantry units, skilled in the use of skis, snowshoes, *ahkios* (sledges, either man- or dog-drawn), and, more recently, snowmobiles and tracked personnel carriers.

Prior to 1941, the U.S. military had little experience of arctic warfare. However, in World War II, the military established outposts in Newfoundland, Danish Greenland, and Iceland, from which aircraft were transported to Europe and from which air and sea patrols provided escort, weather intelligence, and early warning for convoys bound for Britain and the Soviet ports of Archangel and Murmansk. In the Pacific theater, some 58,000 troops were stationed in Alaska and islands of the Aleutian chain located along the shortest route from the United States to Japan in terms of defense, and to Vladivostock in terms of Lend-Lease shipping headed to the USSR.

In June 1942, a Japanese invasion force under Adm. Kakuji Kakuta launched air raids on the U.S. base at Dutch Harbor on Unalaska Island, and captured the islands of Attu and Kiska. Not until May 1943 did a joint U.S. task force under Adm. Thomas C. *Kincaid and Maj. Gen. Eugene Landrum recapture the island of Attu after almost a month of heavy fighting. Of 2,300 Japanese defenders, only 29 survived; many took their own lives. U.S. losses totaled 549 killed and 1,148 wounded in action. The Japanese garrison on Kiska evacuated without a fight.

During the *Cold War, the United States saw the arctic regions as a first line of defense against aerial attack from the Soviet Union across the pole, and undertook the construction (1950s) of remote *radar detection sites close to the Arctic Circle. The DEW Line, a chain of fifty-seven radar sites stretching from Iceland to Alaska, was designed to provide distant early warning (DEW) of manned bomber or intercontinental ballistic missile (ICBM) attacks. The DEW Line (1957) supplemented the Mid-Canada or McGill Line (1955) of microwave detection sites and the Pine Tree Line (1954) of thirty-four radar stations that straddled the U.S.-Canada border. These defenses were supplemented (1958–60) by ballistic missile early warning (BMEW) sites at Thule, Greenland, and Clear, Alaska. The Strategic Air Command also established forward-placed bomber and interceptor bases in Thule and in Elmendorf, Alaska.

The U.S. Army in the 1980s and 1990s maintained arctic training facilities at Alaskan Forts Wainwright and Richardson and reactivated the 10th Mountain Division—specially trained in winter warfare techniques—at Fort Drum, New York.

[See also Canada, U.S. Military Involvement in; Lend-Lease Act and Agreements.]

• John Toland, But Not in Shame, 1961. U.S. Army Field Manual 37–71, Northern Operations, 1971. Kenneth Schaffel, The Emerging Shield: The Air Force and the Evolution of Continental Air Defense 1945–1960, 1991.
          —Frederick J. Chiaventone

ARMED FORCES RESERVE ACT (1952). The Armed Forces Reserve Act of 1952 was a response to the severe weaknesses in the U.S. reserve forces and inequities for veterans revealed by the partial *mobilization during the *Korean War. Pressured by reserve and veterans' organizations, Congress sought to improve reserve organization and most immediately to restrict the vulnerability of Korean War veterans to future service. The act established three categories of reserve forces—ready, standby, and retired—subject to different liabilities for mobilization. The most important of those categories, the ready reserve, was authorized a strength of 1.5 million personnel, including the entire National Guard. The ready reserve could be mobilized in a national emergency declared by the president. The act allowed individual reservists and Guardsmen to volunteer for active duty. That enabled the armed forces to use them in routine peacetime operations and contingencies without incurring the political and diplomatic risks associated with mobilizations. The act strengthened the influence of reserve and Guard officers in the military planning process.

• Eileen Galloway, "History of U.S. Military Policy on Reserve Forces, 1775–1957," 1957. Charles J. Gross, Prelude to the Total Force: The Air National Guard, 1943–1969, 1985.
          —Charles J. Gross

ARMED SERVICES LOBBYING ASSOCIATIONS. Voluntary organizations designed to support a specific branch of the American military have always existed in the United States. In the nineteenth century, many groups organized along specialist lines to publish professional journals and bring together active duty and retired military personnel. Real influence on military policy did not come until the twentieth century, when lobbying associations were formed for each armed service. These modern associations defined their primary purpose as lobbying Congress, explaining defense issues to the public, and working in close alliance with the branch of the armed services they represent. Such private, dues-collecting organizations often brought intraservice rivalries into the political arena. By the 1960s, they were considered part of the *military-industrial complex, allowing defense industry advertising to subsidize their publications. Though their opponents tended to exaggerate their power to influence policy, reserve organizations served as critical links between the service branches, the public, and Congress during times of open debate over military policy.

The nation's oldest military lobbying association is the National Guard Association (NGA). Maj. Gen. Dabney H. Maury, a former Confederate officer, organized the NGA in 1878 after the militiamen of the West Virginia National Guard refused to fire on strikers in the Great Railroad

Strike of 1877. The NGA, an organization of National Guard officers, had two early goals: better training and funding for internal policing duties and recognition of the National Guard as the country's main ready reserve for national defense. At first the boost in funding came primarily from state governments, though the federal government gave the Guard substantial grants-in-aid by loaning materiel for training camps. Federal funding increased when Congress recognized the Guard as the first line military reserve in the Dick Act of 1903 and other *Militia Acts, and in the *National Defense Acts of 1916 and 1920. The NGA lobbied successfully throughout the twentieth century to preserve this reserve status, though the cost has been increased supervision and control by branches of the federal armed forces.

The Navy League organized in 1902 when similar professional groups designed to unite civilians and others interested in naval issues appeared throughout Europe. Never numbering more than 19,000 in its first 50 years, the Navy League had many prominent businessmen and industrialists as members. The League pressed continuously for larger naval appropriations and often provided sympathetic members of Congress with critical statistics when naval legislation was pending. The U.S. *Navy depended heavily on the Navy League to defend its policies. During the isolationist 1920s and 1930s, the League recorded its greatest success by keeping interest in a naval shipbuilding program alive. In the *Cold War, the Navy League promoted the navy's concerns about the policy of massive retaliation and its competition for appropriations with the army and air force.

The Air Force Association (AFA) was founded in 1946 by Gen. "Hap" *Arnold to provide the Army Air Force with an effective lobbying group. The new organization drew on well-known war heroes, such as Gen. James *Doolittle and Hollywood actor James Stewart, to bring attention to the importance of airpower issues. The AFA enjoyed an immediate victory when the independent U.S. Air Force separated from the army in 1947. Two years later, the AFA successfully opposed the navy during the "Revolt of the Admirals" against the cancellation of their supercarrier in favor of the B-36 bomber. More recently, AFA opposition to a controversial 1995 Smithsonian exhibit on the atomic bombings of *Hiroshima and Nagasaki initiated a highly publicized debate. This led to a complete reorganization of the exhibit, which the AFA and its supporters in Congress charged was too sympathetic to Japanese victims of the atomic bomb blast and failed to present the full horror of Japanese *aggression and violence in Asia. Membership in the AFA has ranged from a low of 40,000 in the mid-1950s to a high of 230,000 in the late 1980s.

The Association of the U.S. Army (AUSA) was founded in 1950 when two of the army's older organizations, the Infantry and Field Artillery Associations, merged. Senior army leaders feared that branch parochialism was undermining funding for an adequate land force, and wanted an organization that would help the army speak with one voice to Congress. AUSA absorbed the Antiaircraft Association in 1955. The 100,000-member association drew retired army generals to its board, and until 1956, AUSA leadership consisted of uniformed soldiers. The difficulty confronting active duty personnel in openly debating army policy with Congress caused the AUSA to restrict key lobbying and policy positions to nonactive duty members.

Like the AFA and Navy League, the AUSA publishes a professional magazine to evaluate contemporary doctrinal and funding issues, organizes local chapters, holds annual conventions, and provides experts to testify at congressional hearings.

[See also Lobbies, Military; Militia and National Guard; Service Associations.]

· Morris Janowitz, *The Professional Soldier: A Social and Political Portrait,* 1960. Armin Rappaport, *The Navy League of the United States,* 1962. Jim Dan Hill, *The Minute Man in Peace and War: A History of the National Guard,* 1964. "Fifty Years of AFA," *Air Force,* 79 (February 1996), pp. 35–45. Association of the U.S. Army, *AUSA Background Brief,* 76 (September 1997).   —Jennifer D. Keene

ARMORED VEHICLES. The evolution of armored vehicles, cars, and personnel carriers has paralleled the development of the tank. In World War I, to overcome the stalemate of the western front, and break through the mud, barbed wire, and *machine guns, the British and French developed a fully tracked, armored, heavily armed vehicle—the tank—in 1916. This was followed closely by the armored car and other hybrid car/track combinations. Though the tank might provide shock value, it lacked the speed and mobility for reconnaissance and patrol; other armored vehicles would take over these traditional roles of cavalry. Lightly armored cars equipped with machine guns were used successfully by the British in Mesopotamia.

Between the wars, the U.S. Army began to develop armored vehicles. Brig. Gen. Adna Chaffee in particular saw armored cars as part of a greater effort to mechanize cavalry functions. Some results of this experimentation were the M8 Scout Car and the M3 Armored Half-Track that the U.S. Army would use in World War II in cavalry, tank, infantry, and artillery units. The M8 (wt: 7,485 kg [16,500 lbs]; spd: 90 kmh [55 mph]; arm: 37mm gun/2x mgs, 7.62 and 12.7 mm), manufactured by Ford, was a wheeled, lightly armored reconnaissance vehicle that was one of the first effective replacements of light horse cavalry. It was adopted in 1943. The M3 Armored Half-Track (wt: 8,872 kg [19,558 lbs]; spd: 70 kmh [45 mph]; arm: 2x mgs, 12.7 and 7.62mm), manufactured by Autocom, Diamond T, International Harvester, and White, was a revolutionary vehicle in that it represented an early armored personnel carrier for U.S. infantry. An all-purpose weapons carrier, the M3 would carry a variety of weapons and was adopted by the U.S. Army in 1940. Mechanically as well, the M3 was novel in that it had wheels mounted in front used to guide the vehicle while rear-mounted tracks provided propulsion.

Since the end of World War II the U.S. military has been at the forefront in armored vehicle development, which centers on two areas: cavalry and infantry. These vehicles are lighter than tanks, speedy, lightly armed and armored, and less expensive to purchase and maintain. Two vehicles in particular have been revolutionary in their impact on armored warfare in the late twentieth century. The M113 Armored Personnel Carrier and the M2/3 Cavalry/Infantry Fighting Vehicle (Bradley). The M113, currently manufactured by United Defense, was a product of the 1950s, one of the first successful fully armored infantry vehicles; over 74,000 were produced worldwide. The Bradley M2/3 (wt: 29,940 kg [65,868 lbs]; spd: 61 kmh [38 mph]; arm: 25mm gun, 7.62mm mg, tube-launched, optically-tracked, wire-guided weapon system), manufactured by FMC Corporation, holds nine infantry or five cavalrymen and was adopted by the U.S. Army in 1981, replacing the M113 series. Despite early fears of compatibility and problems with transmissions and weight, the Bradley proved its worth in the *Persian Gulf War.

[*See also* Tank Destroyers; Tanks.]

• A. J. Barker, *The Bastard War, The Mesopotamian Campaign of 1914–1915*, 1967. Christopher Foss, ed., *Jane's Armour and Artillery, 1994*, 1994.   —Christopher G. Clark

ARMS, RIGHT TO BEAR. The Second Amendment's brief but tangled declaration that "[a] well regulated Militia, being necessary to the security of a free State, the right of the people to keep and bear Arms, shall not be infringed" remains among the Constitution's most controversial provisions.

The modern debate centers on whether the amendment safeguards individual rights or whether it merely preserves a state's right to maintain militia forces (the "collectivist theory"). English antecedents not only allowed the possession of arms by the male citizenry, but also frequently compelled it, and many American colonies followed suit.

The amendment itself, however, arose out of Antifederalists' fears about the oppressive potential of a central government protected by a standing army. Cognizant that standing armies often aided European tyrants, and recalling the repression British regulars enforced prior to the revolution, the framers were leery of professional militaries. They were also concerned about the enormous expense of sustaining a full-time force.

Nevertheless, influential leaders like George *Washington insisted that some professional forces were required. The compromise reflected in the Constitution provides for both a full-time national military and part-time state-based militias. The Second Amendment, the Supreme Court said in *U.S.* v. *Miller* (1939), was intended to "assure the continuation and render possible the effectiveness" of these militia, which were meant to counterbalance the dangers of a standing army, as well as to provide a cost-effective supplement to the nation's defense.

According to the Supreme Court in *Miller*, the amendment extends only to "ordinary" militia arms. The Militia Act of 1792, for example, required the maintenance of little more than a musket and bayonet, small arms that the ordinary male citizen would have at home in the 1780s and could physically "bear."

Eighteenth-century warfare was organized around the massed effect of such relatively simple personal weapons. Over the next two centuries, however, the nature of warfare shifted and the strategic value of small arms declined. Today, civilians equipped with small arms hardly counterbalance the heavy weaponry of military professionals.

Twentieth-century American laws limiting the right to bear arms are largely a response to the rise in firearm-related crime and are usually upheld by the courts. Many follow the collectivist theory and hold that the amendment only shields state-organized militias. Others, like the *Miller* decision, find that an individual's possession of a particular weapon is unrelated to a militia's "preservation or efficiency" and can therefore be controlled. Following the Supreme Court in *Presser* v. *Illinois* (1886), most courts sanction state firearms restrictions by declaring that the amendment bars only federal interference.

Despite these rulings, polls show that an overwhelming number of Americans believe the U.S. Constitution guarantees them the right to own a gun. Indeed, 80 million Americans own firearms, primarily for sporting or safety purposes. The absence of any recent Supreme Court cases addressing the Second Amendment, as well as new arguments in the 1990s that a right to bear arms might exist in the penumbra of the Ninth or Tenth Amendments, seems to assure that the nature and scope of the right to bear arms will remain contentious in the United States.

[*See also* Citizen-Soldier; Militia and National Guard; Supreme Court, War, and the Military.]

• Ellen Alderman and Caroline Kennedy, *In Our Defense: The Bill of Rights in Action*, 1991. "Second Amendment Symposium Issue," *Tennessee Law Review*, 62 (Spring 1995).

—Charles J. Dunlap, Jr.

ARMS CONTROL AND DISARMAMENT: NONNUCLEAR. "Arms control," or "arms limitation," generally refers to efforts to refigure arsenals or to limit their growth. "Disarmament" refers to more ambitious efforts to reduce or eliminate certain weapons. Historically, disarmament efforts came first. The *Rush-Bagot Agreement of 1817 between Great Britain and the United States disarmed the Great Lakes and gradually made the U.S.-Canadian boundary the longest undefended border in the world.

The idea of negotiating disarmament among sovereign nations in peacetime is relatively recent. In 1899 and 1907, Czar Nicholas II of Russia instigated The *Hague Peace Conference with the declared aim of ensuring universal peace and reducing excessive armaments. The Czar's motives were not entirely altruistic. He hoped to freeze the military modernization efforts of the Austro-Hungarian and German empires and cause them to spend on industry and commerce, not armaments. The Conferences outlawed the use of dumdum bullets and asphyxiating gases; regulated the use of underwater mines; improved arbitration procedures; and codified certain laws of war. However, the disarmament goals were unfulfilled because of fears of eroding national sovereignty and suspicions that others would gain strategic advantage.

Following *World War I, assertive, widely supported *peace and antiwar movements emerged, dedicated to promoting general disarmament among the major powers. The public drew the lesson from the prewar Anglo-German naval race that arms races led to war. Disarmament would eliminate the means to wage war and also restrain weapons manufacturers, at the time called "merchants of death," who were thought to profit from and to stimulate war. In the United States, an unprecedented movement to disarm emerged. The idea that maintaining peace required arms reductions was enshrined in President Woodrow *Wilson's famous *Fourteen Points (1918).

The *Treaty of Versailles, negotiated after the war, imposed on Germany the most complete and rigorous disarmament in modern history. It severely restricted Germany's army and navy, forbade aircraft and *submarines, and drastically curtailed the manufacture, import, and storage of arms. However, general disarmament did not occur.

The first extended effort to limit arms in the history of the United States were the treaties negotiated to end the naval competition among the United States, Great Britain, and Japan in Washington in 1922 (the *Washington Naval Arms Limitation Treaty), and the London Conferences of

1930 and 1936. In 1921–1922, invoking the analogy of the Anglo-German pre–World War I naval race, Republican Senator William Borah generated passionate public support for naval limitation to halt a competition in building among the three great naval powers. Borah argued that the arms race was the basic cause of World War I and of war in general. Borah's views echoed popular conceptions. They also meshed with demands for economy and sound fiscal policy. Businessmen welcomed arms limitations to reduce spending and lower taxes. Isolationists were attracted to the prospect of arms reduction without alliance or the *League of Nations. There was even some support with the U.S. naval establishment that helped to mute the impact of naval opposition. Naval limitation fit well with America's desire for peace and a strong economy, and with its isolationist sentiments. Over the course of fifteen years, the leading naval powers limited their navies, established spheres of influence in the Pacific, and pledged to uphold the territorial and administrative integrity of China, the naval treaties initially diffused tensions but cooperation began to collapse by the late 1920s under the pressures of worldwide depression, the Nationalist unification of China, and German rearmament.

Further the 1932 Geneva World Disarmament Conference fell victim to European politics. France would not disarm for fear of losing military superiority over Germany. After France conceded to arms equality with Germany, Adolf *Hitler became Chancellor of Germany, scuttling any hopes for disarmament.

Given the failure of disarmament efforts in the 1920s, 1930s, and after *World War II, the idea of disarmament fell from favor. In the late 1950s and 1960s, "new thinking" on arms control emerged, chiefly in the United States, partly in response to early failures at disarmament within the United Nations framework. "Arms control" diverged from traditional disarmament doctrine in its emphasis on managing the U.S.-Soviet rivalry and fostering strategic stability between superpowers with growing arsenals. The goals were to reduce the probability of war, reduce the destructiveness of war should it occur, and to save money. Arms control might or might not reduce levels of armaments. Arms control also came to encompass measures to verify compliance, to build confidence among states through measures that increase transparency over military exercises, deployments, budgets, and doctrine, and to reduce the risk of accidental war.

Post–World War II conventional arms control was overshadowed by its nuclear counterpart, emerging on the east-west agenda only in 1973 with the Mutual Balanced Force Reduction (MBFR) talks. In 1966, U.S. Senator Mike Mansfield called for unilateral reduction in U.S. forces stationed in Europe and this catalyzed both U.S. and Soviet leaders. The *Nixon administration feared the impact on western defense and *NATO's viability; Soviet leaders feared that large-scale reduction in U.S. forces would lead to an increase in German forces. MBFR, however, was largely a stalemated process, foundering as past conventional arms control efforts had on the difficulty of defining parity given asymmetries in geography, force structure, and doctrine, and of constructing a verification regime, particularly for manpower. The Soviet Union opposed Western calls for asymmetric troop reductions to compensate for geographic proximity. Not surprisingly, more progress was made in promoting "soft" arms control, or

confidence and security building measures, under the Conference for Security and Cooperation in Europe (CSCE) process launched in 1975.

The Conventional Forces in Europe (CFE) negotiations produced more rapid progress. Begun in 1989, one month after the MBFR talks ended, CFE successfully concluded with the signing of *CFE Treaty in Paris in 1990. The treaty is the first significant conventional arms control agreement to cover most of Europe from the Atlantic to the Urals. CFE benefited from the MBFR experience, but success stemmed largely from Soviet desires to address their dire economic situation and to close a perceived technological gap with the West. The treaty was modified after the break-up of the Soviet Union with the Oslo Document, and follow-up negotiations concluded with the CFE-1A Agreement of 1992. Despite its successes, CFE still confronts several thorny issues, particularly turmoil along Russia's borders, which have raised Russian concerns about flank limitations. CFE will also have to adapt to newly emerging European security issues including NATO enlargement, Russian and Turkish policy in the North Caucasus, Russia's future relations with former states of the Soviet Union, Russia's developing relationship with the West, and Russia's domestic political problems.

[See also Arms Control and Disarmament: Nuclear; Arms Race: Overview; Arms Race: Naval Arms Race; Cold War: External Course; World War I: Postwar Impact.]

—Emily O. Goldman

ARMS CONTROL AND DISARMAMENT: NUCLEAR.

During the Cold War, at the same time that the United States and the Soviet Union were engaged in a massive *nuclear weapons arms race, the two countries negotiated to limit that race. In the beginning, there was hope that these negotiations would, first, reduce the destructiveness of any war between the two; second, reduce their defense budgets; and, third, reduce the risks of war between them. Until the Cold War ended, however, only the last of these purposes was clearly served: The negotiations did help to manage the rivalry between the Soviet Union and the United States, to slow the global spread of nuclear weapons to other countries, to produce Soviet-American cooperation in fields other than arms control, and, eventually, to achieve detente and an end to the Cold War.

After the failure of the Baruch Plan in the Truman administration, serious negotiations began during the administrations of President Dwight D. *Eisenhower and Premier Nikita Khrushchev in 1958. Except for a brief period at the beginning, little progress was made until after the *Cuban Missile Crisis of October 1962. Then, having come close to an exchange of nuclear-tipped missiles, Khrushchev and President John F. *Kennedy made a determined search for ways to reduce the future risk of nuclear war. Because they had experienced dangerous delays in exchanging messages relating to the crisis, their first agreement was to install a "hot line" between Moscow and Washington for crisis communications.

Their next was to limit nuclear testing. Testing was essential for designing new weapons and had come to symbolize the nuclear arms race. Moreover, if no new countries learned how to make nuclear weapons because of a ban on testing, the chances of such weapons ever being used by others would clearly be decreased.

Gaining Soviet agreement to "on-site" inspection to

make sure a test ban was observed was a problem from the beginning. Because inspections were unnecessary to verify a ban on tests above ground, American negotiators proposed a ban on all tests *except* those underground. The Soviets at first rejected this as an inadequate alternative to a "comprehensive" ban on all testing. After Kennedy wrote to Khrushchev, appealed to the Soviets publicly in his famous American University speech of June 1963, and sent a personal representative to Moscow for negotiations, Khrushchev relented and agreed to ban all but underground tests. In 1996, long after the end of the Cold War, a comprehensive ban on all tests with provisions for inspections to assure compliance was finally agreed.

Efforts to find common ground continued under President Lyndon B. *Johnson (1963–69) and Premier A. N. Kosygin, despite their assistance to opposing sides in the *Vietnam War. Their common interest in preventing the spread of nuclear weapons to additional countries again produced agreement, this time in the Treaty on the *Nonproliferation of Nuclear Weapons of 1968. Made permanent in 1995, the treaty now has as many members as the UN Charter. In it, nonnuclear countries promise not to acquire nuclear weapons and the five avowed nuclear powers—Britain, China, France, Russia, and the United States—promise not to transfer them.

Then came efforts to slow the U.S.-Soviet nuclear arms race by freezing the levels of intercontinental ballistic missiles and by prohibiting defenses against such missiles. Each side had sufficient weapons with which to retaliate against a first strike by the other and to cause "unacceptable damage" in retaliation. As a result, each was restrained from striking first by the risk of mutual suicide. However, if an effective defense against missiles could be built, the side having such a system (called an anti-ballistic missile system) could strike first without fear of a devastating missile retaliation by the other. Thus, both sides would race to build a missile defense and, if both did, neither would be better off.

Agreements to prevent this were negotiated during the Nixon administration (1969–74). In his inaugural address, President Richard M. *Nixon announced an "era of negotiations." He and his national security adviser Henry *Kissinger came to see Strategic Arms Limitation Talks (SALT) as a major element in a broad strategy of detente to reduce the risk of nuclear war, curb military budgets, and gain Soviet help in resolving disputes in regions of conflict such as Vietnam and the Middle East. The Soviets were not as cooperative on all these subjects as Nixon and Kissinger hoped, but they also wanted to reduce the risk of nuclear war. Negotiations produced improved relations between the two countries and a period of detente resulted. The biggest arms control achievements were the Anti-Ballistic Missile Treaty of 1972, permitting only limited missile defenses on each side, and a five-year SALT I interim agreement freezing the number of missiles and aircraft on each side capable of delivering nuclear weapons to the other.

Detente continued under President Ford but came to an end under President Jimmy *Carter (1977–81). Carter had the opportunity to turn a Ford-Brezhnev agreement "in principle" into a SALT II treaty with more effective limits on warheads than SALT I. However, he wanted much more. He combined idealism about deep nuclear reductions with righteousness about Soviet failure to respect human rights and inexperience in both foreign affairs and Washington politics. He tried for too much and botched the job—managing to alienate both the Soviet leaders and conservatives in the U.S. Senate whose support he needed to gain approval for the SALT II Treaty he negotiated. While the treaty was pending in the Senate, the Soviets invaded Afghanistan. Senate approval became not just doubtful but impossible.

President Ronald *Reagan (1981–89) pursued a major defense buildup rather than arms control. He called the Soviet Union an "evil empire" and proposed a "Star Wars" high-tech antiballistic defense known formally as the *Strategic Defense Initiative (SDI). His administration argued that the Anti-Ballistic Missile Treaty of 1972 did not apply because the technology of Star Wars was far different from that of 1972. Although, like Carter, Reagan was inexperienced in both foreign affairs and Washington's ways, unlike Carter, he opposed arms control negotiations with the Soviets. And he was very successful in gaining approval from Congress for a major anti-Soviet defense buildup.

Reagan was finally persuaded to begin arms control negotiations over Soviet missiles aimed at Europe rather than the United States, negotiations that had been promised to *NATO allies by Carter. Soviet leaders had deployed new accurate, intermediate-range missiles aimed at Europe without serious consideration of the possible European reaction, and were then outraged when their deployment produced a NATO consensus favoring U.S. deployment of new, accurate, intermediate-range missiles in Europe aimed at the Soviet Union.

By the end of 1985, Reagan was persuaded that a new Soviet leader, Mikhail Gorbachev, was a man Americans could do business with on arms control. This came about as the result of Gorbachev's "new thinking," plus the effective work of Reagan's secretary of state, George Shultz, and personal communications and meetings between Gorbachev and Reagan. Part of Gorbachev's new thinking was to understand that Soviet deployment of new missiles aimed at Europe was a great mistake because it reduced Soviet security by producing new, accurate American missiles that reduced the warning time to ten minutes for Soviet leaders to implement a retaliatory strike and get to bomb shelters.

The first Gorbachev-Reagan summit produced a joint communiqué agreeing that nuclear war could not be won and must never be fought. Eventually, the two sides agreed to eliminate all missiles with "intermediate" ranges (i.e., from 300 to 3,300 miles). The Intermediate Nuclear Forces Treaty of 1987 became the first true nuclear arms reduction treaty between the two countries. It cemented a new era of U.S.-Soviet friendship. Detente returned and cooperation in other fields was renewed.

Negotiations to reduce long-range (strategic) nuclear aircraft and missiles also started up again. These came to be known as *START, the Strategic Arms Reduction Talks. Again, Gorbachev was responsible for concessions that made agreement possible. But the treaty was not completed until after the fall of the Berlin Wall in 1989, an event that came to symbolize the end of the Cold War.

The START Treaty of 1991 was the first to reduce long-range nuclear aircraft and missiles. It was signed shortly before the attempted August 1991 coup by Soviet conservatives against Gorbachev. Seeing a much weakened central Soviet government and aware that Soviet nuclear weapons were dispersed in parts of the Soviet Union that might seek independence, President George *Bush (1989–93) acted quickly to deal with short-range American and Soviet nuclear weapons, more widely dispersed around the world than the long-range weapons that had been the subject of the SALT and START agreements. Bush announced a global American withdrawal of nuclear weapons for artillery, and for ground-launched and ship-launched missiles wherever deployed in the world. He called upon Gorbachev to reciprocate.

Gorbachev matched Bush and went beyond him. For example, the short-range nuclear shells, bombs, and warheads withdrawn to Russia would total about 12,000 as compared with the Americans' 4,000. As a result, all short-range nuclear weapons were moved out of the territories of Soviet republics that later declared independence.

By 1996, however, legislators hostile to nuclear arms control treaties were in control of both the U.S. Senate and the Russian Duma, approval by both of which was necessary for treaties to become fully effective. By early 1999, the Duma had not approved START II, signed six years earlier by Bush and President Boris Yeltsin. And President Bill *Clinton had been unable to persuade the Senate to approve the Comprehensive Test Ban, negotiated during his administration and signed by him in 1996. This treaty, sought by Presidents Eisenhower, Kennedy, John, and Carter, as well as Clinton, would ban all future nuclear weapons tests.

Though slow-moving before the end of the Cold War, arms control negotiations clearly helped reduce the risk of nuclear conflict and bring an end to the Cold War. What their future will be in the post-Cold War world only time will tell.

[See also Arms Race; Baruch, Bernard; Cold War: External Course; SALT Treaties.]

• Henry Kissinger, White House Years, 1979. Strobe Talbott, Endgame: The Inside Story of SALT II, 1979. Gerard Smith, Double Talk: The Story of SALT I, 1980. Raymond Garthoff, Detente and Confrontation: American-Soviet Relations from Nixon to Reagan, 1985. Glenn T. Seaborg with Benjamin S. Loeb, Stemming the Tide: Arms Control in the Johnson Years, 1987. Lynn Eden and Steven E. Miller, eds., Nuclear Arguments: Understanding the Strategic Nuclear Arms and Arms Control Debates, 1989. George Bunn, Arms Control by Committee: Managing Negotiations with the Russians, 1992. James A. Baker, The Politics of Diplomacy: Revolution, War and Peace, 1989–1992, 1995. Anatoly Dobrynin, In Confidence: Moscow's Ambassador to America's Six Cold War Presidents, 1995. Institute for Defense and Disarmament Studies, The Arms Control Reporter: A Chronicle of Treaties, Negotiations, Proposals, Weapons and Policy, 1999. —George Bunn

ARMS LIMITATION AND MANAGEMENT. See Arms Race: Nuclear Arms Race.

ARMS RACE

Overview
Naval Arms Race
Nuclear Arms Race

ARMS RACE: OVERVIEW

The term *arms race* has been used since the 1850s to describe periodic competitions between states to shift (or preserve) the balance of power between them by modernizing their weaponry and increasing the magnitude of various arms stocks. However, it was not until the end of World War I that arms races were viewed as a special pathology of interstate behavior that required explanation. At a loss to account for a war whose duration and horror seemed inexplicable by the logics of political or strategic calculation, both politicians and the public seized upon the idea that arms competitions could assume a deterministic dynamic that made war inevitable. It followed that the best way for states to ensure that conflicts of this sort would not occur in the future was to regulate the building of armaments or, as it is known today, to practice arms control. President Woodrow *Wilson fought to include a commitment to arms control in the *League of Nations Covenant, and his sentiments received widespread bipartisan support. Even Senator William Borah, an ardent opponent of the League, argued that the postwar naval competition between the United States, Great Britain, and Japan had already begun to take on the characteristics of the prewar Anglo-German naval race. If not contained, it would lead to a cycle of threats and counterthreats that would eventually spiral upward into war, as fear and mutual hostility increased in proportion to the size of each side's arsenal.

The situation in which a state's attempt to achieve greater security by expanding its arsenals can, at the same time, decrease the security of its rival is known as the "security dilemma." The increasingly uncontrollable and volatile process of arms growth that can ensue as each state reacts to its rival's arms increases with increased suspiciousness about the rival's motives and an even greater increase of its own is termed the *spiral model*.

In 1960, Lewis Fry Richardson gave formal expression to this blind action-reaction vision of an arms race in a mathematical model that remains influential today. His model postulates that the rate of each side's arms increases is a simple function of its rival's increase in the previous period. Depending on the magnitude of each side's response, arms production either manages to achieve a stable rate of growth or accelerates until it can no longer be sustained, at which time war ensues. In keeping with the absence of foresight that animates the security dilemma, Richardson's model is basically deterministic: states react to each other as automatons.

In the 1970s and 1980s, theorists attempted to formulate a richer, psychological account of the spiral model's dynamics. They argued that the real key to the perverse cycle of action and reaction lay in the operation of suboptimal decision-making biases and heuristics that are fundamental to human cognition. These cognitive limitations lead state leaders (1) to underestimate systematically the extent to which their rival's arms increases are driven by defensive concerns and internal, "pork barrel" politics and to assume that they are motivated exclusively by aggressive aspirations; and (2) to assume that the rival will appreciate the fact that it was forced to increase its military capacity as a defensive necessity. This leads to a psychologically driven propensity to interpret the rival's behavior as indicating growing hostility without showing any corresponding sensitivity to the implications of one's own actions. As a result, both sides' incentive to engage in preemptive or preventative war increases.

In the last twenty years, the emphasis of researchers has shifted from psychological biases to strategic calculation as the principal inspiration for arms races. Investigators looking at the nineteenth-century naval competitions between the British and the French; the naval competition between the United States, the Japanese, and to a lesser extent the British after World War I; and even the pre–World War I Anglo-German naval race—archetype of the spiral model—found each to be a calculated competition between a militarily weaker challenger state trying to increase its relative power and another militarily stronger state committed to defending the status quo. This rationalistic view of the arms race is partly corroborated by the fact that the state leaders involved often speak in terms of maintaining the balance of power and publicly commit themselves to not pursuing an open-ended building program. For example, in the U.S.-Japanese naval race of 1916–22, President Wilson emphasized that the U.S. building program would be discontinued as soon as an arms limitation agreement was achieved.

*Game theory, with its emphasis on rational expectations and complicated reciprocal effects, is a logical extension of the strategic calculation school, and its stylized models now underlie most theoretical work on arms races. Game theorists play down the role of psychological variables and argue that arms races are most frequently driven by a confluence of three factors: (1) the anarchic nature of the state system; (2) the presence of resources that permit both states to respond to the competitive incentives that it creates; and (3) uncertainty about the resources and motives of the rival state. Arms spirals tend to be seen as the product of severe (but rational) uncertainty regarding the ambitions and actions of the rival state.

Interestingly, given their close relationship with the "dismal science" of economics, game theorists tend to be more optimistic than their counterparts in the psychological or Richardsonian schools. Their most commonly used model, the repeated "Prisoners' Dilemma," suggests that states in protracted arms races, such as that between the United States and the Soviet Union, will eventually learn about the attributes and motivations of their rival and devise strategies that take advantage of the cooperative benefits offered by arms control. Game theorists even offer strategies by which a state can induce its opponent to slow or terminate an arms race. For example, they recommend demonstrating a resolve to build an amount of arms that effectively cancels out any advantage the opponent would gain, but no more. Unfortunately, there is little evidence to believe that every arms race is driven by the logic of the repeated Prisoners' Dilemma. History suggests that different historical arms races are driven by "games," or patterns of incentives, and not every type responds to a single strategy.

[See also Arms Control and Disarmament; Strategy: Fundamentals; Disciplinary Views of War: Causes-of-War Studies.]

• Charles E. Osgood, An Alternative to War or Surrender, 1962. Lewis F. Richardson, Arms and Insecurity, 1962. Robert Jervis, Perception and Misperception in International Politics, 1976. Walter Isard, Arms Races, Arms Control, and Conflict Analysis, 1988. George W. Downs and David M. Rocke, Arms Races, Arms Control, and Tacit Bargaining, 1990. Colin S. Gray, Weapons Don't Make War, 1993.
—George W. Downs

ARMS RACE: NAVAL ARMS RACE

Defined as intensive peacetime competition in the design and production of warships, naval arms races aimed at altering the balance of naval power between or among the states involved. All such arms races attempt to exploit changing economic and technological conditions to gain military advantage. In the nineteenth and early twentieth centuries, most have sought to undermine the maritime supremacy of Great Britain until the Soviet naval challenge to the U.S. Navy in the 1960s and 1970s.

The ascendancy of the Royal Navy in the early nineteenth century rested upon geographical, social, and economic factors that no adversary could match by programmatic effort: an insular position astride the waters linking Northern Europe to the world's oceans; a population inured to seafaring and shipbuilding, and thus a reliable source of naval manpower (the demands of military seamanship being, in this era, little different from those of maritime commerce); and a system of state finance tailored to ensure that the proceeds of Britain's commercial economy would be available to support the king's ships. The agrarian economies of the European Continent, and the mature technologies of naval warfare in the age of sail, offered scant leverage against such advantages.

In a tactical environment so stable that a well-maintained warship had a useful fighting life of half a century, the idea of a naval arms race could have no meaning. Even if a rival could contrive to outspend Britain on naval armaments for a period of years—a virtual impossibility for any state in need of a large army—the results would mean little when measured against the totality of such long-accumulated assets. The Industrial Revolution made naval arms races possible, in the first instance, by radically depreciating those assets. It destabilized a tactical consensus two centuries in the making, and raised the prospect that warships could be rendered obsolete by improvements in ship design or weapons technology. It also narrowed the gap in economic performance that separated Britain from its rivals, and increased the incentives for all advanced countries to maintain strong navies, by heightening the importance of trade and empire as elements of national success.

Observers first applied the metaphor of a "race" to naval arms production in the early 1890s. The principal contestants were thought to be Great Britain and its main rivals in the pursuit of empire, France and Russia—though many other nations, including the United States, embarked on naval building programs during this period. Most did so less from a desire to outbuild prospective rivals than because admiralties everywhere were finally achieving clarity about the optimal characteristics of modern warships. By the middle of the 1880s, thirty years of chaotic technological advance had transformed the battle fleets of the major maritime states into menageries of incongruent types, operating under a doctrine that envisioned fleet action as an impossible combination of disciplined gun duel and ramming mêlée. Uncertainty about virtually every aspect of naval armament and ship design was compounded by sharply rising costs. Construction of larger ships had fallen off everywhere, and disproportionately so in Great Britain, whose frustrations reached a climax in 1886 when the Admiralty suspended orders for new capital ships until their vulnerability to *torpedoes could be resolved.

The naval building programs of the 1890s marked an intensification of long-standing rivalries, driven by rising self-confidence that in turn rested upon a convergence of technical and doctrinal solutions to a number of long-standing problems of gun design, ships armor, fleet tactics, and particularly to producing modern *battleships. If the results were interpreted, a little too simply, as a "race" among a few prime contestants, it was at least partly owing to the existence of a simple means of keeping score. Britain's Naval Defense Bill, put forward in 1889 in the wake of a study about the requirements for war with France, formally embraced the customary principle that Britain would maintain a navy "at least equal to the strength of any two other countries." "Strength," however, was now no longer a matter of informed professional judgment. It was to be measured directly, by counting the number of capital ships "of the newest type and most approved design"—a striking innovation reflecting the new sense of clarity that had descended upon naval affairs. The bill accordingly called for ten such battleships to be built over the next five years, along with forty-two *cruisers and eighteen torpedo gunboats, at a cost that doubled the annual rate of expenditure during the previous decade.

The Naval Defense Bill was intended to discourage Britain's rivals from embarking on building programs of their own. It failed. France announced new construction of similar scale and proportions in 1891 (its first major program since 1872). Russia, having laid down five new battleships between 1886 and 1889 (the first since the 1860s), added two more after 1890.

Britain included an eleventh battleship in its naval estimates for 1891–92, and two more in 1893–94—additions that still left the Royal Navy two ships short of its "two-power standard." The gap was finally closed in 1894–95 with the inauguration of a second five-year plan, calling for 7 new battleships (raised to 12 in 1895–96), 20 cruisers, and over 100 smaller craft. Thereafter, the British lead in capital ships was beyond the combined reach of France and Russia—though both continued to expand their navies for another ten years, until the ententes of 1904 and 1907 brought an end to the colonial rivalries that had given the contest its purpose.

The United States was at first less a participant in the race than an interested observer. It laid down three first-class battleships (its first) in 1890, though Congress insisted that the range of the ships be limited, so that no taint of imperialism attached to them. War with Spain in 1898 seemed to confirm the importance of a modern fleet, however, and thereafter naval building increased steadily, thanks in part to the strong support of President Theodore *Roosevelt. U.S. naval expenditures, which amounted to 7 percent of total federal spending in 1890, consumed 21 percent in 1905. By the eve of World War I, the U.S. fleet was third in the world.

It had been intended that it be second, behind only Great Britain. In the meantime, however, a new and unexpected rival had emerged in the form of the German High Seas Fleet. In contrast to the multilateral building programs of the early 1890s, which in retrospect resemble less a race than a festival of competitive modernization, the German effort was conceived from the start as a kind of marathon, whose distant finish line was defined by a bold and quixotic strategic calculus. To deter Britain from involving itself in a European war, contemporary theories of naval combat held that Germany would need a fleet of capital ships two-thirds as large—the smallest force deemed capable of winning a defensive fleet action. Beginning in 1898, Germany set out, on the basis of no experience whatsoever as a maritime power, to build such a fleet. Its naval leadership planned to lay down three ships per year for twenty years, with a program of regular replacements thereafter. By 1918, Germany would dispose in perpetuity of a fleet of sixty modern battleships. To keep up, Britain would need to build ninety of its own, a burden that was judged impossible to bear, once the commitments required to sustain the empire were added to it. Other states reacted as well: one of the justifications for the expanded U.S. building program during these years was the need to deter German designs on South America.

The soundness of Germany's approach depended entirely on whether its calculations were correct, and whether they would remain correct for the two decades required to win the race. In the event, neither the economics nor the technology of naval armaments proved sufficiently constant. The building programs of the early 1890s had been helped by cost-cutting improvements in key shipbuilding components, above all, armor plate. By 1900, however, the cost of capital ship construction was again rising sharply, as naval guns, and the hulls and mountings needed to carry them, grew bigger and heavier. The price of a first-class battleship increased by about 20 percent between 1900 and 1905, an especially unwelcome development for Germany because, despite its inherent economic strength, its system of state finance remained hostage to social groups averse to the kinds of taxation needed to weather such increases.

These problems were made markedly worse by the launching, in 1906, of the HMS *Dreadnought*, a super battleship of radically new (and even more expensive) design that rendered all existing battleships obsolete. Compelled, in essence, to start over, and confronted by costs far higher than had originally been foreseen, there was little hope that the 2:3 force ratio required by German strategy could be achieved. In 1909, a German government went down to defeat in the Reichstag because it could not pass the tax reforms necessary to finance the construction of three Dreadnoughts per year. A few months earlier, Britain had declared its intention to build eight (a compromise, as Winston *Churchill remarked, between the Conservative demand for six and the Liberal demand for four). Although the race as such did not end, its outcome was increasingly foreseeable. When war came in 1914, Britain had twenty Dreadnoughts, Germany thirteen.

Particularly under President Theodore *Roosevelt, the United States joined the naval arms race. U.S. naval expenditures rose from 7 percent of total federal spending in 1890 to 21 percent in 1905. Focusing on battleships, the battle line of the U.S. Fleet had grown to thirty six ships by 1913 and ranked only behind both Britain and Germany in size.

The Great War brought an end to naval arms races. Navies have continued, in myriad ways, to try to outdo each other, but their efforts have never replicated the kind of tit-for-tat pattern that prevailed for a quarter century before 1914. A new naval race might easily have broken out in East Asia in the 1920s, involving Britain, the United States, and Japan, but all three nations quickly concluded that the costs would far outweigh gains that recent history suggested would be illusive at best. The result was the *Washington Naval Arms Limitation Treaty of 1922, the first successful arms control agreement. More recently, naval arms buildups, like that embarked upon by the Soviet navy in the 1960s and 1970s in challenge to American naval supremacy, have been viewed not as independent phenomena, but as elements of broader military competition—a pattern that is likely to continue as the capabilities of land, sea, and air forces grow increasingly interdependent.

[See also Arms Control and Disarmament: Nonnuclear; Navy, U.S.: 1899–1945; Procurement: Shipbuilding Industry.]

• Paul M. Kennedy, The Rise and Fall of British Naval Mastery, 1976. Andrew Lambert, Battleships in Transition, 1984. Christopher Hall, Britain, America, and Arms Control, 1921–37, 1987. Richard W. Fieldhouse, Superpowers at Sea, 1989. Jon Tetsuro Sumida, In Defence of Naval Supremacy, 1989. B.J.C. McKercher, ed., Arms Limitation and Disarmament, 1992. C.I. Hamilton, The Anglo-French Naval Rivalry, 1840–1870, 1993. Volker Berghahn, Germany and the Approach of War in 1914, 1993. George W. Baer, One Hundred Years of Sea Power, 1994.
                                                —Daniel Moran

ARMS RACE: NUCLEAR ARMS RACE

The United States, with Britain, developed atomic weapons during World War II and used them as a means to force Japan's early surrender. The first (and so far last) use of these weapons in hostilities came in August 1945 with the atomic bombings of *Hiroshima and Nagasaki. By then the seeds of the *Cold War were being sown as the two superpowers argued about the political reconstruction of postwar Europe. If the United States hoped that the Soviet Union would be sufficiently impressed by the destructive potential of a single bomb to become more conciliatory in its foreign policy, it was soon disappointed. Josef *Stalin recognized that troops on the ground would determine the distribution of political influence in Europe and Asia, and he acted accordingly. By the time of Hiroshima he was already well informed about the American nuclear program, from sympathizers working within it, and he pushed forward with a Soviet program.

Suspicions between the two superpowers were too great for significant cooperation to prevent a nuclear arms race. They defeated an American scheme to place nuclear energy under international control (known as the "Baruch Plan"), presented to the *United Nations in 1946. As the Cold War intensified, the manufacture of American atomic bombs increased. In August 1949, far earlier than expected, the Soviet Union tested its first atomic device. From then on the United States could not escape the sensation of being in some sort of race, and this sensation influenced all decisions. The course of the nuclear age was no longer simply a matter of Western decision.

The first effect of the new situation was the decision to move from atomic weapons, based on nuclear fission, to hydrogen weapons, based on fusion. There were no obvious limits to the destructive capacity of thermonuclear weapons. Fearful of an inexorable march toward weapons and strategies of mass destruction, many of the most influential *atomic scientists opposed their development. President Harry S. *Truman overruled them, for now he could not be sure that Stalin would match any American restraint. In the event the first successful Soviet test of an H-bomb came not long after the first American test.

This did not mean that the Truman administration was convinced that nuclear weapons could play a domineering role in national strategy. Though the United States was on the verge of virtual mass production of nuclear weapons, when the *Korean War started in June 1950, stocks were still small and were not used in this conflict. The Truman administration saw nuclear superiority as a diminishing asset, for the Soviet Union would inevitably catch up. For this reason, with the new North Atlantic Treaty Organization (*NATO), it set in motion a program of conventional rearmament.

This proved to be too expensive to implement completely. In January 1954, Secretary of State John Foster *Dulles announced what became known as the doctrine of massive retaliation. Dulles did not believe it was either feasible or desirable to develop local forces to counter Communist aggression at any of the many points where it might occur. He therefore argued the need to "depend primarily upon a great capacity to retaliate, instantly, by means and at places of our own choosing," implying nuclear attacks against Soviet cities.

The basic idea was to counter perceived Soviet advantages in conventional forces with American nuclear superiority, at least so long as it lasted. A couple of years later, Americans had good reason to believe that the period of their superiority was drawing abruptly to a close. Until now the United States had deployed its nuclear weapons on its powerful bomber force, to the point where the commitment of the USAF to the manned bomber had held back the development of long-range missiles. The Soviet Union had adopted a different approach, putting few resources into bombers and concentrating instead on missiles. In June 1957, it tested the first intercontinental ballistic missile (ICBM), but its program gained American attention with the world's first artificial earth satellite, Sputnik 1, launched in October 1957. This punctured American self-confidence in its technological advantages. For a while there was panic (from which President Dwight D. *Eisenhower remained commendably immune) as alarms were raised about an impending "missile gap." Now the Americans no longer had the luxury of wondering how to exploit their superiority, but the worry of what the Russians might do with theirs. In the event, and despite some embarrassing failures in tests, the American missile program surged ahead of the Russian (which was based on cumbersome designs) so that by the start of the Kennedy administration in 1961, the "gap" was in the other direction, with U.S. superiority.

John F. *Kennedy, and his energetic secretary of defense, Robert S. *McNamara, wished to back away from the doctrine of massive retaliation. They were reinforced in this view by their experience of the two most dangerous crises in the nuclear age. For some time the Soviet Union had been putting pressure on the West to abandon the outpost of West Berlin, situated in the East German heartland and a constant source of aggravation, as it was used as an escape route by disaffected East Germans. Kennedy resisted this pressure. In August 1961, a wall was constructed, dividing Berlin. While causing outrage in the West, it also eased the immediate crisis caused by the flow of refugees. The next year the discovery of Soviet missiles in Cuba led Kennedy to risk war by demanding their removal. After a tense week, the Russians backed down. Both sides were now deeply aware of the dangers of nuclear confrontation.

However, it was not so easy to reduce NATO's dependence on nuclear deterrence. As part of the earlier attempt to match *Warsaw Pact conventional strength, West Germany had been allowed to rearm. Germany had no intention of joining NATO in order to provide a battleground, so it required that its territory be defended at the East German border. If this could not be achieved through a conventional defense, then the task would fall to nuclear deterrence. The prospect now loomed of Armageddon being triggered by any Warsaw Pact incursion from East to West Germany. American strategy was torn between an unaffordable conventional defense and an incredible nuclear deterrent.

Eventually a compromise was reached in the form of NATO's doctrine of *flexible response. The basic idea was that the alliance should not move immediately to nuclear use but would do so if Soviet aggression could not be stopped by conventional military or political means. Before large-scale nuclear exchanges would be tried, it was envisaged that "tactical" nuclear weapons would be employed first.

Small nuclear weapons for battlefield use had been introduced during the 1950s and integrated with NATO's general purpose forces. At the time they represented an area of Western superiority, while the Soviet Union caught up with strategic weapons. It was hoped that concentrated enemy invasion forces would provide lucrative targets, but it soon became apparent that the same weapons could also help a Communist offense blast a way through NATO defenses. Nor would they be used "as if" they were merely hyperefficient conventional firepower. Exercises in the mid-1950s indicated that use on a substantial scale by NATO alone would cause enormous *casualties among the population supposedly being defended. Later efforts by weapons' designers to reduce the collateral damage with more "tailored" munitions did not get round this problem. The main consequence would be as likely to start the processes of nuclear escalation a little earlier rather than restrict them to a limited level.

Winning a nuclear war would require disarming the enemy in a surprise, preemptive attack, destroying as much as possible of his means of retaliation on the ground, and intercepting any bombers or missiles that escaped before they reached their targets. The ability to execute such an attack was described as a *first-strike* capability; the capacity to absorb such an attack and then retaliate, a *second-strike capability*. A first strike would be the most demanding task ever to face a military planner. A first strike would fail if critical targets were not located or were not attacked effectively or if enemy missiles were launched on warning of an impending attack. Defenses might be able to cope with a limited second strike, but they would soon be overwhelmed by anything substantial. At all stages the devastating power of individual nuclear weapons left little room for a margin of error.

The development of the first submarine-launched ballistic missiles (SLBMs) in the late 1950s in the American Polaris program effectively defeated the first-strike concept. Submarines remained difficult to spot, track, and destroy. Even with advances in *antisubmarine warfare systems, the increased range of the missiles meant that *submarines could choose their patrol areas to maximize the problems faced by any attacker. By the end of the 1960s, the invention of multiple independently targeted reentry vehicles (MIRVs), a technique by which a large number of warheads could be put on top of a single missile, multiplied the problems that would be faced by ballistic-missile defenses.

The fear that the other side might obtain a first-strike capability, as much as a push for a national capability, began to drive the arms race. Instead of a competition to accumulate raw destructive power, national capability was now seen to be largely technological in nature, and geared to gaining a decisive strategic advantage. Not only did this lead to constant and expensive innovation in weapons design and force structures; with both sides trying to anticipate each other's next moves, this could lead to them both fearing an imminent surprise attack in a crisis. As it became evident that neither side could achieve a first-strike capability, it became possible to think in terms of a stable nuclear balance. McNamara described the essential objective for U.S. strategic forces to be an *assured destruction capability*, which would leave no doubt that the result of a nuclear war would be the elimination of the enemy as a twentieth-century society. This set limits on the force levels required and the type of forces required. To achieve stability, both sides would need to follow the same approach, creating a condition of *mutual assured destruction*—which inevitably became known as MAD.

The situation was recognized through the strategic arms limitation talks, which began between the Soviet Union and the United States in November 1969 and produced agreements in May 1972. The Strategic Arms Limitation Treaty (SALT) of 1972 froze the number of missiles at current levels—at the time some 1,700 for the United States, but some 2,300 for the Soviet Union, which had been engaged in a major buildup in ICBMs since the mid-1960s and was beginning to overtake the United States in SLBMs. While these raw numbers did not recognize American technological advantages (and did not include the U.S. bomber fleet), they created a damaging impression that the process favored Moscow. This dogged efforts to conclude a second SALT agreement, and even when one was agreed in 1979, it was never ratified by the U.S. Senate because of a revival in Cold War tensions (and in particular the Soviet invasion of Afghanistan). President Ronald *Reagan was more ambitious, renaming the negotiations the Strategic Arms Reduction Talks (*START). They did not produce the dramatic cuts he sought until the Cold War was over.

In 1972, President Richard M. Nixon and Leonid Brezhnev had also signed the Antiballistic Missile (ABM) Treaty, which imposed strict limits on the number of defensive systems either side could deploy (no more than 100 launchers). In 1983, President Reagan appeared prepared to challenge the logic of this treaty when he launched his *Strategic Defense Initiative (SDI), to provide a shield against a nuclear attack. The technological problem he posed was not solved. As important was the president's view of SDI as an alternative to dependence on nuclear deterrence. Would it not be better, he asked, to "protect than to avenge." Unfortunately, SDI could also appear as an attempt to develop a first-strike capability and so a likely result was just another round in the arms race.

SDI was another symptom of a growing unease with the condition of mutual assured destruction. For the same reason, there was also an exploration of the possibilities of partial first strikes. One proposal was to aim for the enemy's political and military *command and control centers in so-called *decapitation* attacks, in the hope that leaderless forces would not launch their weapons. Assuming that such an attack could be executed, there would be risks of leaving the other side leaderless. With whom would it then be possible to negotiate an end to the war?

Another idea was to attack only land-based missiles in a *counterforce* attack, in the hope that it would remove the most formidable part of the enemy arsenal with minimal civilian damage. However, such attacks would still cause massive civilian damage and so stimulate a ferocious retaliation. Furthermore, technological developments were improving bombers, cruise missiles, and SLBMs, so that even if ICBMs were lost, powerful and versatile forces would remain. Cruise missiles were pilotless aircraft, the descendants of the German V-1, suddenly rendered more potent by developments in engine design, miniaturization, and precision guidance.

The currency given to ideas such as these during the 1970s and 1980s in the United States reflected a fear that the Soviet Union had never accepted MAD and was seeking a real nuclear superiority. This was a particular problem given that it was the West that was most dependent upon a credible nuclear strategy, as a means of countering the perceived strength of the Soviet conventional forces facing NATO. Certainly Soviet thinking appeared to be based on the possibility of using the conventional phase of a war in Europe in order to prepare the basis (for example, by destroying NATO nuclear assets) for a decisive nuclear strike. The risk to the Soviet homeland (but not that of other members of the Warsaw Pact) would be limited by seeking an implicit deal by which the territories of both superpowers could be established as sanctuaries. If it looked as if the United States was preparing to strike at the Soviet Union, then Soviet doctrine would argue for a preemptive attack in order to limit the damage.

Soviet ideas for a "winnable" nuclear war were no more practicable than American, but they nonetheless prompted a Western response. The *countervailing* strategy was designed to deny the Soviet Union confidence that at any point in the ladder of escalation from crisis to all-out nuclear war, it could expect to so dominate the fighting that it would force NATO to surrender. In line with this, intermediate-range nuclear forces, including cruise missiles, were introduced into Europe. These stimulated powerful protest movements in Western Europe before their deployment began in 1983. However, not long after this, reformer Mikhail Gorbachev achieved dominance. Alarmed by the expense of the arms race, and anxious to improve relations with the West, Gorbachev in 1987 signed the INF (Intermediate-range Nuclear Forces) Treaty with President Reagan, which eliminated this whole category of missiles, including Soviet SS-20 missiles.

Two years later, in 1989, the Cold War was effectively over. By this time, both sides had over 10,000 strategic nuclear warheads. The political conditions were now propitious for more radical arms control. Moreover, with Russia now vulnerable to economic and political chaos, there was an incentive to decommission as many nuclear warheads as possible lest they become prone to accident or unauthorized use. By 1993, the START process was pointing to ceilings of 3,000 to 3,500 for each side. In 1997, further reductions of 1,000 were agreed. But by this time, the collapse in Russia's conventional strength meant that its parliament was reluctant to ratify such large cuts, and its military doctrine was moving to greater reliance upon nuclear threats.

The United States had become the most substantial conventional military power and had no need to resort to nuclear threats. For the same reason, potential enemies saw weapons of mass destruction as one of their few means of neutralizing this power. The United States was still unable to escape from the practice of deterrence.

[See also Cold War: External Course; Cuban Missile Crisis; Deterrence; Nuclear Weapons; SALT Treaties.]

• Thomas Schelling, Arms and Influence, 1966. Alain C. Enthoven and Wayne K. Smith, How Much Is Enough? Shaping the Defense Program 1961–1969, 1971. John Newhouse, Cold Dawn: The Story of SALT, 1973. Patrick Morgan, Deterrence: A Conceptual Analysis, 1977. Fred Kaplan, The Wizards of Armageddon, 1983. David Rosenberg, "The Origins of Overkill: Nuclear Weapons and American Strategy, 1945–1960," International Security 7:4, Spring 1983. Strobe Talbott, Deadly Gambits, 1984. Gregg Herken, Counsels of War, 1985. Philip Bobbitt, Lawrence Freedman, and Greg Treverton, U.S. Nuclear Strategy: A Reader, 1989. Lawrence Freedman, Evolution of Nuclear Strategy, 1989. Ivo Daalder, The Nature and Practice of Flexible Response: NATO Strategy and Theater Nuclear Forces Since 1967, 1991. Michael J. Mazarr, "Virtual Nuclear Arsenals," Survival, Autumn 1995. Scott Sagan and Kenneth Waltz, The Spread of Nuclear Weapons: A Debate, 1995.

—Lawrence Freedman

ARMS TRANSFERS. Arms transfers—both imports and exports—have played a major role in American military history and defense policy since the founding of the nation. Initially lacking the capacity to produce all but the simplest of weapons, the American colonies and later the infant republic relied on imported European arms for their basic military needs. Guns supplied by France in 1778–83 helped to secure the American victory during the *Revolutionary War, and despite the subsequent development of indigenous arms industries, European arms continued to find service with American forces (including both sides during the *Civil War) until well into the nineteenth century. By 1900, however, the United States had become a major producer of all types of munitions, and, since then, it has been more a supplier to international arms markets than a recipient—a fact that has provoked periodic debate over the value, significance, and morality of arms transfers.

The debate over arms sales began in earnest during the interwar period following World War I. Prior to 1914, the United States exported relatively small quantities of munitions, and the private firms that dominated this traffic were subjected to few restraints by the government. In 1915, however, the United States began to produce vast quantities of weapons for foreign consumption—by one estimate, U.S. military exports rose from $40 million in 1914 to $1.3 billion in 1916 and $2.3 billion in the succeeding nineteen months. At first, this remarkable effort was lauded as a significant contribution to the Allied war campaign; but later, as the immense scale of the carnage in Europe became known, many people concluded that the arms makers' desire for profit was itself a cause of conflict.

As the guns were stilled in Europe, world leaders set out to create a new international order based on consensus and negotiation—a task that was assumed to require curbs on the global arms traffic. Although the United States did not join the *League of Nations, fearing that membership would result in periodic entanglement in overseas conflicts, it did participate in a League-sponsored Disarmament Conference (1932–37) aimed at reducing global arms production. At the same time, antiwar organizations like the *Women's International League for Peace and Freedom campaigned for a public investigation into the munitions trade. Critical books and articles—most notably The Merchants of Death (1934), by Helmuth Engelbrecht and Frank Hanighen—further aroused public opinion. Finally, in 1934, Congress established a Munitions Investigating Committee under the leadership of Senator Gerald *Nye of North Dakota to consider charges that American and European arms producers had conspired to instigate World War I in order to stimulate the demand for weapons.

The Nye Committee, as it was called, revealed that U.S. arms manufacturers often spread tales of imminent hostilities in order to play one buyer off against another; it failed, however, to demonstrate that they had conspired to ignite World War I or force the United States into the war. Although the investigation did not result in any legal action against American arms merchants, it did contribute to the mood of isolationism then sweeping the country, and helped ensure passage of the *Neutrality Act of 1935 (which compelled the president to impose an arms embargo on nations at war).

Although widely popular, the Neutrality Act and other expressions of isolationism appeared increasingly constrictive to President Franklin D. *Roosevelt as the Nazis in Germany began their quest for world domination. Roosevelt argued against repeal of the arms embargo in early 1939, but reversed his stance in September, when Germany invaded Poland. Two months later, when Congress repealed the embargo, Roosevelt authorized a series of "cash and carry" sales of U.S. arms to the European democracies. In 1940, he proposed a more ambitious program of arms transfers, under which the U.S. government would lend, lease, or donate military equipment to the nations fighting Adolf *Hitler. Our goal, he told the nation on 29 December 1940, is to make America "the great arsenal of democracy."

Ultimately, it was the commitment of American soldiers, rather than of American weapons, that was to turn the tide of war in Europe and the Pacific. But U.S. arms transfers under the Lend-Lease program (1941–45) enabled America's Allies—including the Soviet Union—to hold out for two years of unrelenting combat while American troops were trained for combat. All told, some $50 billion worth of U.S. military equipment was furnished through this program, representing a vital contribution to the Allied victory.

The Cold War and Beyond. World War II was not followed, as World War I had been, by a wave of popular revulsion against American makers. Instead, U.S. military industries were viewed as a major source of America's overall strength. Thus, when U.S. allies in Europe began to feel threatened by growing Soviet aggressiveness, most members of Congress were prepared to support a new round of arms transfers along the lines of the Lend-Lease program. After the famous "*Truman Doctrine" speech of March 1947 by President Harry S. *Truman on the need to resist Soviet *expansionism, Congress voted $400 million in emergency military aid to Greece and Turkey. This outlay was soon followed by similar grants to other likely targets of Communist action, producing a stream of conventional military equipment to overseas friends and allies that was to continue undiminished for forty years. (Except for some technical assistance to Britain and France, the United States has not exported nuclear weapons or technology to any foreign country.)

In the first few decades of the *Cold War, U.S. arms aid was largely furnished to the *NATO countries in Europe and to key allies in Asia and the western Pacific (notably Australia, Japan, New Zealand, South Korea, and National-

ist China). Between 1950 and 1967, the United States supplied friendly countries with $33.4 billion in arms and services under the Military Assistance Program (MAP), and another $3.3 billion worth of surplus weaponry. The U.S. government also sold these countries $11.3 billion worth of military equipment through its Foreign Military Sales (FMS) program—but the emphasis, in those early years of the Cold War, was on direct military assistance, not on sales.

Although the basic premise of American arms programs—to bolster the defenses of U.S. allies facing a military threat from the Soviet bloc—did not change over the years, many aspects of these programs were significantly altered. Whereas initially the bulk of U.S. weaponry was funneled to the industrialized powers of Europe and the Pacific, by the 1960s an increasing portion of it was being supplied to Middle Eastern and Third World countries. The primary impetus for this shift was the apparent Soviet success in using arms transfers to establish military links with Egypt (beginning in 1954), Syria (in 1955), Iraq (in 1958), and other developing countries. In order to combat the growing Soviet presence in the Middle East and Asia, Washington began supplying vast quantities of arms and ammunition to its own friends and allies in these areas—thereby stimulating fresh Soviet arms transfers to its allies, and so on, in what was to become an ongoing pattern of U.S.-Soviet competition.

At first, most of the U.S. and Soviet arms aid went to the Middle East. In the early 1960s, however, Washington began to focus considerable attention on Southeast Asia, where Communist insurgents had grown increasingly strong. As part of its effort to combat these guerrillas (and their supporters in North Vietnam), the United States provided $18 billion worth of arms and military equipment in 1965–75 to the governments of Cambodia, Laos, South Vietnam, and Thailand. Substantial aid was also provided to South Korea and the Philippines in return for their agreement to supply troops for the U.S.-led counterguerrilla campaign in South Vietnam.

Although Washington was prepared to provide arms at no cost to its allies in Southeast Asia, it was not prepared to do so in other areas where key allies were capable of paying for their military imports. In order to stimulate overseas purchases of U.S. munitions—thereby diminishing America's balance-of-payments deficit and recouping some of its investment in weapons research—the Nixon administration barred grant aid to the industrialized countries and aggressively marketed U.S. arms through the FMS program. This new emphasis on military sales was first directed toward the states of Western Europe (which had by then recovered from the destruction of World War II) and later extended to the wealthier nations of Asia and the Middle East.

The continuing U.S. quest for allies and the growing emphasis on military sales soon led to a particular focus on Iran, then ruled by Shah Mohammed Reza Pahlavi. Eager to enhance his nation's regional power position while maintaining close relations with Washington, Shah Pahlavi ordered $20 billion worth of U.S. arms between 1970 and 1978—at that time a record for military purchases by a developing nation. Iranian arms purchases were so massive that many in Congress became troubled by the scale of the U.S. sales program and its potential for abuse. Indeed, a 1976 report by the Senate Foreign Relations Committee concluded that U.S. arms sales to Iran were "out of control." This report, and others like it, led Congress—for the first time since the 1930s—to impose significant restrictions on U.S. arms exports (under the Arms Export Control Act of 1976).

The more restrictive approach favored by many in Congress was then adopted by President Jimmy *Carter when he assumed office in 1977. Arguing that the uncontrolled spread of conventional weaponry "threatens stability in every region of the world," Carter announced a policy of "arms restraint" on 19 May 1977. During the next three years, he imposed a "ceiling" on the dollar value of U.S. arms exports to non-NATO countries. But growing tensions with Moscow (prompted, in particular, by the Soviets' 1979 invasion of Afghanistan), coupled with the growing U.S. military commitment to Israel and Egypt, led Carter to abandon the ceiling in 1980.

Ronald *Reagan, who became president in 1981, repudiated what remained of Carter's arms restraint policy and authorized stepped-up military aid to threatened allies abroad. "This Administration believes that arms transfers, judiciously applied, can complement and supplement our own defense efforts," Undersecretary of State James Buckley explained in May 1981. In addition to aiding established U.S. allies through normal military channels, the Reagan administration (or elements thereof) also conducted clandestine arms transfers to Iran (then supposedly subject to an American embargo for its role in the Iran-Iraq War of 1980–88) and to anti-Communist insurgents in Nicaragua (after 1984 barred by Congress from receiving U.S. aid)—an endeavor that, when exposed in 1986, resulted in the scandal known as the "*Iran-Contra Affair."

Throughout this period, U.S. arms exports were largely governed by Cold War priorities and a desire to reap the economic benefits of military sales. Between 1981 and 1990, the United States sold $110.3 billion worth of arms to foreign buyers—far more than in the previous thirty years combined. But, once again, international events were to call these policies into question. When Iraq invaded Kuwait in August 1990, employing a massive array of imported weapons, many policymakers concluded that it was necessary to impose multilateral controls on the arms trade. With the support of President George *Bush, representatives of the five permanent members of the UN Security Council (the "P-5" powers) met in various locales in 1991–92 to develop mutual restraints on conventional arms exports.

Although initially supportive of the P-5 talks, President Bush drove them into limbo in September 1992 by announcing the sale of 150 F-16 *fighter aircraft to Taiwan—a move that prompted China to withdraw from the negotiations, which have not reconvened since. Bush then announced a number of other major transactions, raising U.S. arms exports to record levels. In approving these sales, Bush asserted that military exports were as important to the American economy as they were to American national security—an argument that had never been made so explicit before.

As a candidate for president, Bill *Clinton had voiced concern over the growth in American arms exports. Once in office, however, he embraced the more pragmatic stance initiated by his predecessor, arguing that arms sales were vital to U.S. economic health. On 17 February 1995, he announced a "Conventional Arms Transfer Policy" that specifically identified economic concerns as a factor in arms export decision making. This announcement was followed by a series of major military sales to long-standing U.S. clients, including Egypt, Israel, Saudi Arabia, Turkey, and the United Arab Emirates.

Although, in the mid-1990s, American policymakers generally favored a relaxed policy on arms transfers, the historic U.S. concern over the moral aspects of such exports had not disappeared altogether. Many peace and religious organizations continued to argue that arms sales undermined American values and interests by enhancing the repressive capabilities of authoritarian governments, by fueling local arms races, and by encouraging states to seek military rather than negotiated solutions to their disputes with others. These concerns surfaced in a number of legislative proposals introduced by sympathetic members of Congress, and in occasional newspaper editorials. Whether they will have any impact on future policy remains to be seen, but such efforts are likely to continue as a significant feature of the national debate over foreign policy.

[See also Arms Control and Disarmament; Lend-Lease Act and Agreements; Neutrality Acts; Weaponry, Air Force; Weaponry, Army; Weaponry, Naval.]

• George Thayer, The War Business, 1969. Robert E. Harkavy, The Arms Trade and International Systems, 1975. Andrew J. Pierre, The Global Politics of Arms Sales, 1982. Paul Y. Hammond, David J. Louscher, et al., The Reluctant Supplier: U.S. Decisionmaking for Arms Sales, 1983. Michael T. Klare, American Arms Supermarket, 1984. Keith Krause, Arms and the State: Patterns of Military Production and Trade, 1992. Edward J. Laurance, The International Arms Trade, 1992. William D. Hartung, And Weapons for All, 1994.
—Michael T. Klare

ARMY, U.S. This entry consists of six articles that provide an overview and trace the basic history of the U.S. Army. The individual essays are:

Army, U.S.: Overview
Army, U.S.: Colonial and Revolutionary Eras
Army, U.S.: 1783–1865
Army, U.S.: 1866–99
Army, U.S.: 1900–41
Army, U.S.: Since 1941

The overview outlines the basic characteristics of the U.S. Army. Subsequent articles describe the development of the army—its organization, personnel, equipment, doctrines, and actions—in five chronological periods. Extensive cross-references within and appended to these articles lead to more detailed information.

ARMY, U.S.: OVERVIEW

The principal land force of the United States, the U.S. Army traces its origins to the *Continental army of the *Revolutionary War. That army, a "national" force raised by the Continental Congress, had the mission of engaging British and Hessian regulars in essentially European-style combat, and was composed, insofar as its leaders could manage it, of long-serving volunteers. In these characteristics—an orientation toward conventional combat and a long-serving enlisted force—the Continental army set the pattern for its successor under the U.S. Constitution. The Army of the Constitution—the true United States Army—came into existence during the 1790s, amid bitter political warfare between Federalists and Democratic-Republicans primarily to meet the needs of frontier policing and defense. From that time, the existence of the U.S. Army has been continuous, although its strength has fluctuated widely.

From the Revolution, the American army included two components: the federally controlled professional "Continental" or "regular" army and the state militias of part-time citizen-soldiers. Most debates over American military policy centered on the relationship between these components and what role each should play in peace and war. States' rights and populist parties and movements tended to favor the militia; conservative, nationalistic elements supported the regulars. Complicating the issue was the fact that the militia of the eighteenth and nineteenth centuries was not a true army reserve. During wartime, its units turned out only for short-term local defense while furnishing men to temporary forces of U.S. *Volunteers, which campaigned alongside the regulars and in fact constituted the majority of the wartime army in the nineteenth century. During the last decades of the century, the volunteer state militia, the National Guard, began campaigning for the status of a genuine national reserve force, a status regulars were reluctant to concede as long as the Guard remained essentially under state control.

Beginning with the Dick Act of 1903 and especially the *National Defense Acts of 1916 and 1920, this issue was resolved through gradual federalization of the National Guard and other reserve components, culminating in today's "Total Army" concept. To some extent during the *Civil War, and more thoroughly during the two world wars and most of the *Cold War, the United States resorted to *conscription to fill all components of the army. In peacetime, however, volunteer military service has been the norm—a pattern reestablished with the end of the Cold War draft and the creation of the *All-Volunteer Force in the aftermath of the *Vietnam War.

Throughout its history, command of the army has been based on the principle of civilian control. During the nineteenth century, the president exercised his constitutional power as commander in chief through a civilian secretary of war who headed a War Department composed of a number of staff bureaus. The army lacked an effective uniformed head until 1903, when Secretary of War Elihu *Root persuaded Congress to create a chief of staff subordinate to the secretary of war but with authority over the staff bureaus as well as the line. Root also established a General Staff to provide the army with central planning and operational direction.

This system, although significantly revised and expanded during two world wars, persisted until the *National Security Act of 1947. Under that act and subsequent amendments, the War Department lost cabinet status to the new Department of *Defense and became the Department of the Army, with the mission of providing forces to multiservice joint commanders reporting to the *Joint Chiefs of Staff, of which the army chief of staff now was a member. As the army became increasingly enmeshed in a joint defense system, its internal administrative structure also changed, with the old bureaus disappearing into broader functional commands.

Throughout its history, the army has displayed doctrinal and tactical eclecticism and a command of *logistics. Strategically, it has tried to adapt effectively to the demands of both limited and total war; indeed, American officers understood the close relationship between policy and military strategy long before they began reading Carl von *Clausewitz in translation in the mid-twentieth century. In tactics and technology, the army until after World War II took its cues from Europe but adapted what it learned to the unique requirements of American campaigning. It kept abreast of and sought with varying success to assimilate the changing technologies of warfare, from the repeating rifle to *tanks, airplanes, and *missiles. Since World War II, the U.S. Army has led rather than followed in the evolution of military art and science, as attested by its success in complex combined arms warfare in the *Persian Gulf War of 1991. Faced from its earliest years with the need to support troops across the vast, economically undeveloped distances of North America, the army emphasized logistics and achieved a unique capacity for force projection. That capacity enabled it to discharge truly global missions during two world wars, the Cold War, and beyond.

The U.S. Army prides itself on being a "jack of all trades" among military services, able to do everything from waging continentwide warfare to feeding and housing disaster victims. In fact, it has done all those things and more besides. During most of its history, the peacetime standing army functioned primarily as a constabulary. It policed the frontier, maintained law and order, enforced *Reconstruction, governed overseas colonies, and responded to natural disasters. Its officers often were in the forefront of civilian as well as military scientific developments, for example, in engineering, medicine, and surgery. Yet its officer corps always kept sufficiently current in the art of *war to be able to raise citizen armies and lead them to victory in the nation's nineteenth- and twentieth-century conflicts. During the Cold War, the army received complex global missions, including forward defense and *deterrence in Europe and Asia, the waging of major local wars in Korea and Vietnam, and the provision of military advice and support to allies on every continent.

The end of the Cold War brought declining forces and budgets but no reduction in the variety of missions. The U.S. Army today continues to try to balance preparation for war fighting against the demands of international *peacekeeping and humanitarian intervention.

[See also Army Reserves and National Guard; Citizen-Soldier; Civil-Military Relations: Civilian Control of the Military; Land Warfare; Militia and National Guard; Weaponry, Army.]

• Russell F. Weigley, Towards an American Army: Military Thought from Washington to Marshall, 1962. Richard H. Kohn, Eagle and Sword: The Federalists and the Creation of the Military Establishment in America, 1975. Russell F. Weigley, History of the United States Army, enl. ed., 1984. Edward M. Coffman, The Old Army: A Portrait of the American Army in Peacetime, 1784–1898, 1986. Kenneth J. Hagan and William R. Roberts, eds., Against All Enemies: Interpretations of American Military History from Colonial Times to the Present, 1986. Robert E. Scales, Jr., et al., Certain Victory: The United States Army in the Gulf War, 1993.   —Graham A. Cosmas

ARMY, U.S.: COLONIAL AND REVOLUTIONARY ERAS

In military terms, England's colonies moved slowly but steadily from amateurism to a kind of military semiprofessionalism in the century before the American Revolution. The militia, though often effective for social control and police functions, proved inadequate for participating in the eighteenth-century imperial wars, since they were poorly trained, sometimes even lacking firearms, and were restricted by law to brief duty within their own colonies. The term *semiprofessional,* as used here, means forces that constituted a hybrid between the militia and a standing army. They comprised men who enlisted for a year or more in return for a bounty, served if necessary outside their own provinces, and faced stricter military law than that applied to the militia. They performed under officers who might aspire to military expertise, having read European treatises on training and tactics and having sought to learn firsthand from observing British officers in the field. Such provincial units, including Col. George *Washington's Virginia Regiment in the 1750s, were called upon to join intercolonial expeditions, possibly assigned to cooperate with British armies against French and Spanish citadels in the New World.

In some respects, the *Continental army during the *Revolutionary War at first appeared to resemble an extension of semiprofessional colonial forces. Except for several former British regular officers, most of its general officers had held provincial commissions in the final imperial conflict. In military justice, its Articles of War were less harsh than those of the British army. Its soldiers were enlisted for a year or less. But in 1776, the evolution of an American professional army continued, a process that saw it increasingly look like European military establishments of the day. These changes included longer enlistments, stricter martial law, more uniform tactical arrangements, and employment of Prussian and French military procedures and personnel. Friedrich Wilhelm von *Steuben, as inspector general, and Louis Duportail, head of the U.S. *Army Corps of Engineers, played critical roles in these developments.

Certainly, one reason that Washington and his abler subordinates learned quickly and had less to comprehend than would be true of commanders in a later age was that the nature of warfare scarcely changed in the mid-eighteenth century. Armies continued to move from column to line, employing linear formations in open battle, and engaging in siege operations when moving against fortresses and cities. (In a sense the War of Independence began with the siege of Boston and ended with the siege of Yorktown; and the most one-sided American defeat resulted from the successful British siege of *Charleston.) Moreover, British commanders who opposed American generals had been relatively junior officers themselves in the Seven Years' War (the *French and Indian War) and had seen hardly any active duty between the wars.

Nor did the Revolutionary War produce any new seminal military literature on either side. Officers still lacked a body of strategic doctrine to analyze a problem in systematic fashion. We find no parallel to what transpired in Prussia in the concluding stages of the Napoleonic era, where the War Academy stimulated the first modern analytical studies of conflict, highlighted by Carl von *Clausewitz's *On War.*

American army administration hardly anticipated future trends. The command system illustrates this point. Washington, as commander in chief, acted as the principal conduit of information between the army and its superiors in the Continental Congress. Always deferential to Congress and committed to civil control, the Virginian nonetheless remained candid with the lawmakers, even to voicing his disagreements with them. Since Washington

could hardly direct all theaters of operations, Congress created various regional departments as needed: New England, the northern, the middle, the southern, and the western. Congressional experiments with administrative oversight proved less than successful. The Board of War, in fact, received attacks from some in the army and in Congress for allegedly being hostile to Washington and wishing to replace him with Gen. Horatio *Gates, the victor at Saratoga in an overexaggerated episode known as the Conway Cabal.

Finally, in 1781, Congress created a war department, first headed by Gen. Benjamin Lincoln; but its powers were weak. Even so, it evolved into a substantial post late in the Confederation years. The second person to serve as war secretary, Gen. Henry *Knox, continued in that office under the new constitutional government in 1789.

If the army over eight and a half years—the longest American conflict before the *Vietnam War—displayed staying power, it scarcely hid its resentments toward Congress and American society, believing its sacrifices unappreciated. Lagging enlistments and *desertion led authorities to accept British prisoners, white servants, and African Americans in the service. Restlessness in the ranks grew worse because of inadequate provisions, clothing, and pay. Several regiments mutinied during the last years of the war. American leaders voiced more serious concern over the officers' discontent about Congress's failure to provide back pay and to make firm assurances of postwar pensions or lump-sum mustering-out bonuses. The senior officers remained loyal to the Revolution—with the notable exception of Benedict *Arnold—and this fact, along with Washington's shrewd response to the most vocal dissidents, explains the failure of the still somewhat mysterious *Newburgh "Conspiracy" in early 1783; but the rumblings and threats, mostly among field-grade officers, evaporated when Congress promised to move quickly on the officers' concerns.

With the end of the war in late 1783, the army disbanded peacefully. The principle of civil control of the military remained intact. That, unlike the results of so many revolutions, emerged as a great legacy of the American Revolution. And Washington, in this respect, proved a successful model for future American military officers.

[*See also* Citizen-Soldier; Civil-Military Relations: Civilian Control of the Military; Militia and National Guard; Weaponry, Army.]

• Charles Royster, *A Revolutionary People at War: The Continental Army and American Character, 1775–1783,* 1979. James Kirby Martin and Mark Edward Lender, *A Respectable Army: The Military Origins of the Republic, 1763–1789,* 1982. Robert K. Wright, Jr., *The Continental Army,* 1983. E. Wayne Carp, *To Starve the Army at Pleasure: Continental Army Administration and American Political Culture, 1775–1783,* 1984. Ronald Hoffman and Peter J. Albert, eds., *Arms and Independence: The Military Character of the American Revolution,* 1984. Don Higginbotham, *George Washington and the American Military Tradition,* 1985.   —Don Higginbotham

ARMY, U.S.: 1783–1865

The U.S. Army as a permanent institution began on 3 June 1784, when the Confederation Congress approved a resolution to establish a regiment of 700 officers and men. Intended as a force to assert federal authority in the Ohio River Valley, the regiment deployed at a string of posts along the Ohio where it functioned as a frontier constabulary during the last years of the Articles of Confederation era.

Congress adopted this tiny force after the reorganization of the government under the Constitution in 1789. Responding to the outbreak of Indian war in the Old Northwest—and especially to St. Clair's defeat in 1791, the worst setback at Indian hands in the army's history—the government expanded the military establishment to over 5,000 in 1792. Organized as the "American Legion" and commanded by Maj. Gen. Anthony *Wayne, the army defeated the northwestern tribes at Fallen Timbers in 1794. During the same year, in response to European threats, the government launched a program of seacoast *fortifications and added a corps of artillerists and engineers to build and man them.

The army became the center of intense partisan controversy with the rise of political parties and conflicting ideologies. Federalists sought to maintain a relatively large regular force, while Democratic-Republicans opposed a sizable standing army that might require high taxes and threaten liberty. The result was a period of extreme instability in the army's size and structure. In 1796, the government reduced the army to 3,359. Two years later, however, the Undeclared Naval War with *France led the Federalist Congress to expand the authorized level to over 14,000. Alexander *Hamilton, appointed as inspector general and de facto commander of the army in 1798–99, strove to transform this force into a permanent, European-style standing army, capable of checking domestic opposition. This political role aroused intense suspicion, and in 1800, following the diplomatic settlement with France, Congress reduced the army to 4,436. After Thomas *Jefferson and the Republicans won the election of 1800, they fixed the peace establishment at two regiments of infantry, one of artillery, and a tiny U.S. *Army Corps of Engineers—a total official strength of 3,287. In 1802, they also established the U.S. Military Academy at West Point, New York, primarily to train future officers in military engineering.

Throughout Jefferson's administration, the War Department and the small regular army performed a variety of constabulary tasks: administering the Louisiana Purchase; regulating Indian-white relations; conducting diplomatic relations in the Spanish borderlands; and policing the Embargo Act against Great Britain and Napoleonic France. Meanwhile, deteriorating relations with Britain and France caused the Republicans to reassess their traditional antimilitarism, and in 1808, Congress authorized an increase to 9,921 officers and men. The onset of the *War of 1812 continued the buildup, as the inadequacy of the militia for offensive operations left President James *Madison little alternative but to expand the regular forces. The army's official authorized size reached 62,674 in 1814, although actual troop strength fell well short of this level.

The War of 1812 marked a major transition in the army's history. Until then, its dominant characteristics had been fluctuating size and organization, a high rate of turnover in the officer corps, and the absence of a clear sense of mission—conditions reflected in the poor military performance of the early war years. By 1814, however, the army's performance was improving, largely because of the rise of young, combat-proven commanders to high and middle rank, exemplified by Jacob Jennings Brown, Winfield *Scott, and Alexander Macomb.

Although Congress cut the army to 12,383 in 1815,

many veterans remained in service, and they came to share a conviction that the army's chief mission should be preparation for a future war with a major European power. With the support of the Madison and Monroe administrations, they rationalized military management through permanent general staff bureaus, adopted uniform tactical manuals and regulations, launched a new and more systematic program of coastal fortification, and, under the direction of Capt. Sylvanus *Thayer, revitalized the U.S. Military Academy. When Congress reduced the army to 6,126 in 1821, it tacitly followed a plan proposed by Secretary of War John C. *Calhoun that called for a cadre organization: the retention of a high ratio of officers to enlisted men as a way to preserve military expertise and provide a framework for a rapid and efficient expansion in case of war (Skelton, 1992).

The reduction of 1821 was the last major cutback and reorganization of the army's basic establishment in the nineteenth century. It left a force of eleven line regiments under a major general with the title of commanding general of the army (a position held by Winfield Scott from 1841 to 1861), supported by a group of general staff bureaus—quartermaster, engineers, subsistence, ordnance, medical, and pay—reporting directly to the secretary of war. During the decades that followed, the army was usually dispersed at small garrisons along the frontiers and the Atlantic seaboard, where it continued to perform its customary constabulary duties. In particular, regulars enforced the Indian trade and intercourse laws and served as the government's principal instrument for conducting Indian removal. The latter duty produced one of the army's most most tragic assignments—the removal of the Cherokee Indians in the so-called *Trail of Tears (1838–39)—and the army's most frustrating experience of the antebellum era—the long guerrilla conflict in Florida of the *Seminole Wars (1818, 1835–42, 1855–58).

The demands of national *expansionism brought occasional increases in army strength, including the reintroduction of mounted regiments in 1833 and 1836, the first since the War of 1812. With the outbreak of the *Mexican War in 1846, the army's basic establishment swelled to 17,812, achieved mainly by filling the understrength units with recruits; Congress supplemented this force with 10 temporary regular regiments and over 70,000 citizen-soldiers raised as U.S. *Volunteers. Although the postwar *demobilization left the army at 10,317, the occupation of the newly acquired western territories soon renewed the buildup. The government added 4 permanent regiments in 1855, bringing the total to 19; on the eve of the *Civil War, the regular army's actual strength stood at 16,367 officers and men.

Within the army, the most notable development of the antebellum period was the professionalization of the officer corps. Beginning in 1821, West Point graduates received the vast majority of officers' commissions, and the stabilization of military organization encouraged growing numbers of regulars to make the service a long-term career. Despite the pressures of constabulary duty, many regulars took a serious interest in such professional topics as *tactics, *weaponry, fortification, and military *education, and the era brought a steady infusion of European military thought into the army. Officers developed a service ethic— a collective image of the army as a politically neutral instrument of the government, performing sometimes unpleasant but essential tasks for the public welfare. In the Mexican War, the reformed army—officered largely by West Pointers and armed with elite batteries of light artillery—passed its first major combat test, validating the cadre concept and formal military education.

A yawning social chasm separated the officer corps from the enlisted ranks of the antebellum army. The great majority of enlisted men were urban laborers and journeyman artisans who enlisted for economic reasons. Although some *African Americans in the military served in regular units in the later stages of the War of 1812, most were discharged in the postwar *demobilization, and blacks were officially barred by a War Department order of 1820. On the other hand, white immigrants (mainly Irish and Germans) composed a sizable segment of the enlisted regulars throughout the period, and they reached two-thirds of the total with the great wave of immigration in the late 1840s and 1850s. Because of low troop *morale and harsh living conditions at frontier posts, *desertion and other disciplinary problems were common, and the officers countered with a severe and often arbitrary regime of physical punishment. Such treatment merely aggravated the problem of discipline and the result was chronic tension along the officer-enlisted boundary.

The Civil War confronted the army with a crisis of loyalty, and about one-quarter of the officer corps left to support the Confederacy. U.S. president Abraham *Lincoln drew mainly on state organized and federally funded ad hoc units of U.S. volunteers to raise the vast wartime army, which reached approximately 1 million in 1865. However, Congress expanded the regular establishment to 30 regiments in 1861 and increased the enlisted strength of all units, bringing the official level to 39,278. The War Department kept these units relatively intact, resisting pressures to scatter experienced personnel through the volunteer forces. Nevertheless, hundreds of active duty and former officers did obtain volunteer commissions, and regulars dominated the high command levels of the Union forces. The traditions, procedures, and identities of the antebellum army pervaded the war effort and shaped in numerous ways the conduct of the struggle: *strategy, tactics, *logistics, administration, and civil-military relations.

[See also, Academies, Service: U.S. Military Academy; Army Combat Branches; Ethnicity and Race in the Military; Northwest Territory, Military Actions in the Old.]

• Russell F. Weigley, History of the United States Army, 1967. Francis Paul Prucha, The Sword of the Republic: The United States Army on the Frontier, 1783–1846, 1969. Richard H. Kohn, Eagle and Sword: The Beginnings of the Military Establishment in America, 1783–1802, 1975. Edward M. Coffman, The Old Army: A Portrait of the American Army in Peacetime, 1784–1898, 1986. William B. Skelton, An American Profession of Arms: The Army Officer Corps, 1784–1861, 1992.   —William B. Skelton

ARMY, U.S.: 1866–99

In the post–Civil War era, the 1-million-man *Union army was reduced by 1871 to a U.S. Army of 29,000, remaining around that level until the *Spanish-American War in 1898, when the wartime force grew to nearly 200,000 regulars and *U.S. Volunteers. It fell to about 80,000 by the end of 1899. From 1866 to 1898, the small regular army fulfilled its traditional primary task as a constabulary force on the Indian frontier, but it also took on new duties of military occupation during *Reconstruction and of suppressing labor strife in industrial areas.

No other agency had the personnel to carry out federal Reconstruction policies in the South. In addition to *peacekeeping there, the army performed such civil functions as opening schools, operating railroads, rebuilding bridges, supervising banks, and holding courts of law. When President Andrew *Johnson and the Republican majority in Congress disagreed, Congress in 1867 passed Military Reconstruction Acts over Johnson's vetoes. The acts divided the former Confederate states into five military districts, each governed by a major general, and initiated the process for new state constitutions that declared slavery illegal, disavowed secession, and enfranchised African American men. The process was completed between 1868 and 1870. Thereafter, Southern Republican governors called on the army as a posse comitatus to protect freed blacks and others loyal to the Union, by guarding polling places and controlling paramilitary organizations like the Ku Klux Klan. Thus, the U.S. Army was involved in postwar politics in the South until the end of Reconstruction in 1877.

During Reconstruction, Congress for the first time authorized permanent units of black soldiers (albeit with white officers) for the army. In 1866, six such regiments were recruited, later reduced to four. Separate black regiments continued to exist until the *Korean War in the 1950s. In the 1870s, black soldiers patrolled the frontier and participated in campaigns against the Indians, who called them *"Buffalo" Soldiers. Some Indian scouts were employed. The majority of enlisted ranks were white soldiers, many of them recent immigrants.

The Indian-fighting army of the *Plains Indians Wars later became legendary in fiction and film, but its service was controversial. The federal government ordered the army to restrain or fight Indian tribes in order to open the West. Desire for the Indians' lands meant that conflict was inevitable. Gen. William Tecumseh Sherman and Gen. Philip H. *Sheridan supervised campaigns that inflicted defeats on the Indians. Indian noncombatants were killed in some campaigns. The Indians won a few battles, most notably the Battle of the *Little Bighorn (1876), but were never victorious in a campaign. The tribes were forced to sign treaties restricting them to reservations.

Historians debate whether the army was isolated from society in the Gilded Age. Senior officers hobnobbed in the East with political and economic leaders, while the majority of enlisted men and line officers served at isolated frontier posts. Several times between 1877 and 1899, the government sent army units to quell labor strikes in northern cities, along railroad routes, and in western mining camps. By 1890, several of the army's posts were located near large cities. The debate over the army's alleged "isolation" begs the questions of when, where, and which portions of the army may have been isolated from society.

In part reacting to European developments after the Franco-Prussian War of 1870–71, army officers sought modernization and reforms. In 1881, General Sherman established the Command and General Staff School at Leavenworth, Kansas. Sherman's protégé, Col. Emory *Upton, studied armies in other nations. Upton's classic, Military Policy of the United States, unfinished when he committed suicide in 1881, was not published until 1904. Upton's criticism of the traditional civilian control of the military and of the *citizen-soldier, and his desire for pre-trained, European-style reserves, meant that he gained little influence outside the regular army.

The Ordnance Department, showing its inherent conservatism, was reluctant to acquire repeating rifles, like the lever action Winchester, that would rapidly consume ammunition. Ordnance adopted the breech-loading *Springfield Model 1873 rifle to replace the Union army's muzzleloader, but both were single-shot weapons using black powder. Not until 1892 did Ordnance adopt a smokeless powder rifle, the bolt action Krag-Jorgensen, based on a Danish design; but it was still less effective than European clip-fed rifles. In 1898, due to shortages of ammunition and cleaning kits, Krags were not issued to the U.S. Volunteers at the beginning of the *Spanish-American War; consequently, most of them carried the obsolete Model 1873 into battle.

The army was not well prepared when Congress declared war against Spain, and the lawmakers bypassed the regulars plans by authorizing massive numbers of U.S. Volunteers. Pushed to act by President William *McKinley, the War Department cobbled together expeditions to the Spanish colonies of Cuba, Puerto Rico, and the Philippine Islands. Combining aggressiveness and luck, the Americans (regulars supplemented with U.S. Volunteers) won campaigns against larger if demoralized Spanish garrisons in all of the contested colonies. The Treaty of *Paris (1898) ending the war awarded the United States possession of Puerto Rico, Guam, the Philippines, and temporary control of Cuba. The army administered military governments in Cuba and the Philippines and continued to fight in the *Philippine War (1899–1902) against Filipino insurgents who sought independence. Responsibilities for garrisoning a new island empire, acting as the constabulary on a new overseas frontier, would occupy an expanded U.S. Army in the early twentieth century, even as the army sought to modernize and prepare for wars against other expanding world powers.

[See also African Americans in the Military; Army Combat Branches; Ethnicity and Race in the Military; Side Arms, Standard Infantry; Weaponry, Army.]

• Stephen E. Ambrose, Upton and the Army, 1964. William H. Leckie, The Buffalo Soldiers: A Narrative of the Negro Cavalry in the West, 1967. James E. Sefton, The United States Army and Reconstruction, 1865–1877, 1967. Robert M. Utley, Frontier Regulars: The United States Army and the Indian, 1866–1890, 1973. Jerry M. Cooper, The Army and Civil Disorder, 1980. David F. Trask, The War with Spain in 1898, 1981. Joseph G. Dawson III, Army Generals and Reconstruction: Louisiana, 1862–1877, 1982. Paul A. Hutton, Phil Sheridan and His Army, 1985. Edward M. Coffman, The Old Army, 1986.
—Joseph G. Dawson III

ARMY, U.S.: 1900–41

During the transitional period prior to 1920, the army abandoned its traditional constabulary duties on the Indian frontier to pursue preparation for modern warfare—adapting its organization, training, and doctrine for projection of American power abroad, fighting one world war, and preparing for another.

In the new century's first years, progressive officers convinced Secretary of War Elihu *Root that the nation must create a "war army" prepared for conflict with other great powers. The resulting Root reforms included an army war college; a strengthened system of officer education; a four-

fold increase in regular forces; improvement of the National Guard; and the *General Staff Act (1903).

Although the last seemed to clarify the relation of the commanding general (the line or field forces) and the bureau chiefs (the administrative and technical staffs) to one another and to the secretary of war, traditional line-staff rivalries persisted in new form as bureau chiefs battled the chief of the General Staff for the right, in the name of the war secretary, to control the army.

Other events during Root's secretaryship—the *Philippine War, U.S. military involvement in the *Caribbean and Latin America, and the China Relief Expedition—continued the army's constabulary role, if in new locations, as its units overseas reflected the Progressive Era's spirit by keeping order, sponsoring local government, conquering yellow fever, and building roads, sewers, schools, and water systems.

Fear of an expanding Germany and Japan, however, aided advocates of a "war army," and during the secretaryships of Root and Henry L. *Stimson, the army resumed annual maneuvers. Congress appropriated modest sums for modern rifles (the *Springfield Model 1903), *artillery, and field telephones, and for experimentation with aircraft, motor transport, and *machine guns. At the urging of Chief of Staff Leonard *Wood, Stimson established the nation's first peacetime divisions: self-contained and self-supporting fighting units of approximately 10,000 men.

The Preparedness movement—prompted by the outbreak of World War I—contributed to further land force modernization, which included attempts to resolve the long-standing debate over how to raise trained manpower sufficient to match the armies of Europe. The resulting National Defense Act of 1916 sought gradually to expand both regular forces and the National Guard, strengthen the latter, and lay the foundations of *ROTC (Reserve Officer Training Corps).

The army nevertheless remained unprepared for World War I, and when Gen. John J. *Pershing sailed for France in June 1917 at the head of the *American Expeditionary Force, he took with him trained personnel sorely needed to manage an 18-month expansion of the army from just over 100,000 regulars to a wartime force of almost 4 million men, more than two-thirds of whom were draftees.

The strains of economic *mobilization finally prompted Secretary Newton D. *Baker to appoint a vigorous new chief of staff—Gen. Peyton C. *March—and use the powers granted by the Overman Act of 1918 to strengthen the General Staff, reorganize the supply bureaus under Gen. George W. *Goethals, and cooperate with the War Industries Board. Even so, soldiers of the world's leading industrial power went into battle using many French or British weapons.

The postwar National Defense Act of 1920 returned to a peacetime, volunteer army, enlarged the General Staff, and confirmed the authority of its chief. As chief of staff after 1921, Pershing created the structure—personnel, intelligence, training/operations, supply, and war plans divisions—that the General Staff would carry into World War II. The army also studied the Great War's economic demands and produced a series of industrial mobilization plans in the 1930s that improved upon the work of the prewar Council of National Defense.

In 1920, Congress rejected General March's proposal of

a half-million-man expandable regular force backed by reservists given three months of compulsory military training. Instead, Congress authorized a ready-to-fight regular
army roughly half that size and a program of voluntary
training for an expanded National Guard and organized
reserve.

By 1922, a budget-conscious Congress reduced the regulars to 150,000. The National Guard and enlisted Reserve
Corps remained far below authorized strengths. Mistakenly keeping the 1920 act's sprawling organizational structure intact, and abetted by a Congress unwilling to fund
new weapons, the army maintained a poorly armed skeletal force incapable of rapid deployment, and, by the mid-
1930s, lacked a single combat-ready division.

Unwisely assigning its *tanks to the infantry rather than
the cavalry, the interwar army was hampered by more
than a lack of funds from creating a modern armored
force. Although the Army Air Corps received funding
for new aircraft, doctrinal battles highlighted by the court-
martial of Gen. Billy *Mitchell emphasized strategic
*bomber aircraft, and left it without planes, doctrine, or
procedures for tactical close air support of ground
troops or even adequate fighters to escort the strategic
bombers.

In the interwar years, the army turned to extensive planning and officer education to keep alive skills needed for future warfare. This included joint planning by army and
navy officers for war with potential enemies. In addition,
at the Infantry School (1927–32), Col. George C. *Marshall
emphasized education as he revolutionized infantry tactics and troop-leading procedures. Two hundred of the
school's faculty and graduates would become general officers in World War II. Branch schools, the General Service
School (Leavenworth), The Army War College, even army
posts became scenes of intense activity led by spelling of
such dedicated officers as Fox Conner, George S. *Patton,
and Dwight D. *Eisenhower. Nevertheless, the army did not
hold its first genuine corps-sized maneuver until April
1940.

Beginning in 1935, Congress gradually increased the
army's size and soon authorized an ammunition reserve
and "educational" contracts—small orders for new
weapons to encourage industry to obtain machine tools
and develop techniques for a rapid, emergency increase in
arms production. Even with the outbreak of war in Europe
in September 1939, however, President Franklin D. *Roosevelt refused to implement army plans for industrial *mobilization. The German defeat of France in June 1940 led
to further expansion of the regular forces, federalization of
the National Guard, a reserve call-up, and the nation's first
peacetime *conscription, with the aim of creating, by mid-
1941, a better-armed field force of 1.5 million organized
into thirty-four semimotorized triangular divisions and
thirty-five air groups.

Military planning made a further shift by 1941 when
adoption of a "Germany First" strategy, Anglo-American
coordination, the American occupation of Greenland and
Iceland, and the navy's escorting of convoys as a result of
the *Lend-Lease Act and Agreements (1941) to Britain.
These brought the United States to a de facto if still limited
military involvement in the European War—a limitation
abandoned following Japan's attack on *Pearl Harbor in
1941 and Hitler's subsequent declaration of war upon the
United States.

[See also Army Combat Branches; Militia Acts; Militia
and National Guard; National Defense Acts; Weaponry,
Army.]

• Forrest C. Pogue, George C. Marshall: Education of a General,
1880–1939, 1963. Edward M. Coffman, The Hilt of the Sword: The
Career of Peyton C. March, 1966. Russell F. Weigley, History of the
United States Army, 1967. Allan R. Millett, The General: Robert L.
Bullard and Officership in the United States Army, 1881–1925, 1975.
James L. Abrahamson, America Arms for a New Century: The Mak-
ing of a Great Military Power, 1981. John W. Chambers, To Raise an
Army: The Draft Comes to Modern America, 1987. David F. Trask,
The AEF and Coalition Warmaking, 1917–1918, 1993. Carlo D'Este,
Patton: A Genius for War, 1995.   —James L. Abrahamson

ARMY, U.S.: SINCE 1941

During World War II, the U.S. Army developed into a powerful and flexible war machine. Numbering over 8 million
officers and men, its ranks filled by a comprehensive draft,
the army fielded ninety-eight combat divisions, as well as a
large tactical and strategic air force and the service troops
needed to sustain worldwide deployments. The most
highly mechanized of World War II ground forces, the
army fought effectively in a wide variety of environments.
It also mastered joint operations, culminating in the *D-
Day landing in the invasion of *Normandy. Backed by
American industry, the army established a global logistical
system that sustained forces over vast distances with a lav-
ishness unprecedented in history. The U.S. Army accomplished its basic mission: the total defeat of Nazi Germany
and Imperial Japan.

After V-J Day, 2 September 1945, the World War II
army quickly melted away. By mid-1950, army strength
totaled about 590,000 in 10 understrength divisions.
However, the beginning of the *Cold War with the
Soviet Union, the U.S. commitment to the North Atlantic
Treaty Organization (*NATO), and the outbreak of open
hostilities in Korea soon brought renewed expansion
sustained by *Conscription and draft-induced volunteers. The Cold War army fluctuated in strength from 1.5
million at the height of the *Korean War, to 873,000 under
the President Dwight D. *Eisenhower "New Look," to
just over 1 million under President John F. *Kennedy's
*Flexible Response. After the 1950s, it was no longer a
racially segregated force, but integrated *African Americans in the military.

Until the *Vietnam War, the largest concentrations of
army troops were in three areas: Europe, where they
formed a major component of NATO's ground forces; Korea, where they guarded against renewed North Korean attack; and the United States, where a pool of divisions was
available to reinforce the overseas theaters or respond to
new contingencies. Under the National Defense Acts of
1947, 1949, and 1958, the Department of the Army—now
part of the Department of *Defense and no longer with
cabinet status—organized, trained, and supplied these
forces for regional joint commands but no longer itself directed combat operations. The army's chief of staff served
as a member of the *Joint Chiefs of Staff, along with the
heads of the navy and Marine Corps and of the air force,
which had been separated from the army in 1947. The
army command and staff meanwhile underwent repeated
reorganizations, all tending to eliminate the old War
Department bureaus in favor of broad functional commands such as the Strike Command, Continental Army

Command, Air Defense Command, and Material Command, all created in 1963.

In the so-called joint arena, where the services competed for funding, roles, and missions, the army had mixed fortunes. Under Eisenhower's post-Korea "New Look," which emphasized nuclear *deterrence, the air force and the navy received budgetary priority. The army seemed in danger of being relegated to serving as a nuclear trip-wire in Europe and dealing with minor "brushfire" conflicts elsewhere. Under President Kennedy, who sought other than nuclear means of preventing Communist inroads, the army moved back to center stage as the principal agency for conventional defense in Europe and for *counterinsurgency against Communist revolutionary warfare in the Third World.

These fluctuations of emphasis notwithstanding, the basic tasks of the Cold War army remained throughout forward defense and deterrence in Europe and Korea; conduct of short-of-war interventions, as in the *Lebanon Crisis (1958) and the Dominican Republic (1965); and the provision of arms, training, and assistance to America's allies around the world. Additionally, during the domestic racial and social upheavals of the late fifties and the sixties, the army repeatedly was called on to help control civil disturbances at home.

Weaponry and tactical organization were in a state of transition in the 1950s and early 1960s. Under the "New Look," the army developed a family of tactical *nuclear weapons and competed with the air force in the emerging field of ballistic missile research and development. It reorganized its divisions on the "Pentomic" pattern of five battle groups, supposedly able to operate effectively on a nuclear battlefield. More productively in the long run, the army experimented with *helicopters as a means of both troop transport and fire support. Under Flexible Response, the army modernized its material for nonnuclear warfare. It acquired new models of *tanks and *armored vehicles, adopted new standard infantry *sidearms, and brought air mobile tactics to full development. The service restructured its divisions on the ROAD (Reorganization Objective Army Division) pattern of three task-organized brigades, a formation adaptable to both nuclear and nonnuclear operations. To assist American allies in counterinsurgency, the army organized its green beret–wearing *Special Operations Forces.

When Presidents Kennedy and Lyndon B. *Johnson committed the army to the Vietnam War, the service was at a peak in training, administrative efficiency, *troop morale, and popular acceptance. The long, inconclusive Vietnam conflict ended this state of affairs and brought the army to the edge of disintegration. Not all was failure. Most of the army's draftee and volunteer soldiers fought bravely; the ROAD division performed well; and the helicopter and air mobility revolutionized the conduct of ground operations. Yet *victory proved elusive. The army had to fight a major war without the *Army Reserves and National Guard, under budgets inadequate both to sustain the conflict and maintain its worldwide commitments.

As the war absorbed men and materiel, army forces in Europe and the United States became hollow shells, lacking *combat effectiveness. The quality of leadership and discipline deteriorated; racial violence, drug abuse, assaults on officers and NCOs, and general defiance of authority proliferated in Vietnam and worldwide. Scandals, such as the *My Lai Massacre (1968) and its cover-up within the chain of command, tarnished the army's public image and undermined its self-esteem. The war alienated the army from much of the American public. Responding to antiwar, antimilitary sentiment, President Richard M. *Nixon ended the draft, leaving the army with a whole new set of manpower procurement problems.

During the two decades after the end of the Vietnam War, a dedicated cadre of leaders pulled the army back together. Accepting the challenge of creating an *All-Volunteer Force with a strength fixed at about 780,000, they overcame the service's race, drug, and discipline problems, and adopted programs to bring well-educated young people into the ranks. In the process, they integrated women into the service until they could be found in all but the highest general officer ranks and in every specialty except direct ground combat. Helped by the generous defense budgets of President Ronald *Reagan's administration, army leaders made up for lost time in securing new weapons and equipment in the 1980s. They radically revamped army training and tactics in the light of the lessons of the 1973 Arab-Israeli War, evolving the concept of a highly mechanized, fast-moving "AirLand Battle." Their objective was to create an army ready to fight and win the first battle against Soviet forces superior in numbers and very nearly equal in technology. The rebuilt army successfully met the test of combat during the U.S. intervention in *Grenada (1983) and in Panama. During the *Persian Gulf War (1991), it outmaneuvered and outfought what had been thought to be a formidable Iraqi opponent.

Yet victory over Iraq was followed by new challenges. With the end of the Soviet Union and the Cold War, America's army had to cope with declining budgets and the painful necessity of reducing a force of professionals who had expected to make the service a career. Lacking a dominant threat on which to center their plans and programs, army leaders contemplated a range of new missions and contingencies. Throughout, they expressed their determination to maintain a high level of readiness and retain their technological advantage over any likely enemy.

[See also African Americans in the Military; Army Combat Branches; Strategy: Land Warfare Strategy; Tactics: Land Warfare Tactics; Vietnam Antiwar Movement; Weaponry, Army; Women in the Military; World War II: Military and Diplomatic Course.]

• William L. Hauser, America's Army in Crisis, 1973. Paul H. Herbert, Deciding What Has to Be Done: General William E. DePuy and the 1976 Edition of FM 100-5 Operations, 1984. John L. Romjue, From Active Defense to Airland Battle: The Development of Army Doctrine 1973–1982, 1984. Russell F. Weigley, History of the United States Army, enl. ed., 1984. Ronald H. Spector, "The Vietnam War and the Army's Self-Image," in John Schlight, ed., Second Indochina War Symposium: Papers and Commentary, 1986. Geoffrey Perret, There's a War to Be Won: The United States Army in World War II, 1991. Robert E. Scales, Jr., et al., Certain Victory: The United States Army in the Gulf War, 1993.   —Graham A. Cosmas

ARMY AIR CORPS, U.S. See Air Force, U.S.: Predecessors of, 1907–1946.

ARMY COMBAT BRANCHES: INFANTRY. The infantry is the oldest and most important of the U.S. Army's combat arms. Its insignia consists of crossed muskets, Model

1795; its motto is "Follow Me." Its primary mission is to close with and destroy or capture the enemy.

The infantry does not fight alone. It often fights with, sometimes supports, but more frequently is supported by the army's other arms and services, and by the air force, the navy, and the Marine Corps.

Although the infantryman can arrive on a battlefield in a variety of ways, he is always a ground combat soldier, who fights on foot with the weapons and ammunition he can carry. He can fight from *armored vehicles when the situation demands. His basic weapon is the rifle and bayonet, although he has used *grenades and *grenade launchers, *machine guns, *mortars, *flamethrowers, and some hand-held *antitank weapons to bolster his combat effectiveness.

On 14 June 1775, the Second Continental Congress authorized the raising of ten companies of riflemen to be part of George *Washington's new *Continental Army besieging Boston at the outset of the *Revolutionary War. There, these companies were grouped into regiments, an organization that for the next 181 years remained the infantry's primary tactical and administrative unit.

Over time, the regimental structure underwent several changes. Until the *Spanish-American War, infantry regiments consisted of ten companies grouped under one headquarters. In 1898, each regiment was given two battalions, each battalion consisting of four companies. The battalion then became the primary tactical organization while the regiment retained administrative and tactical oversight functions.

When the United States entered World War I in 1917, the number of battalions in each regiment was increased to three, each battalion still containing four companies. This remained the standard regimental structure until 1956, when the entire regimental structure was done away with, to be replaced by the Pentomic battle group—a unit smaller than a regiment but larger than a battalion. The army's leaders had become convinced that a different type of unit was needed to meet the demands posed by growing *nuclear weapons and chemical warfare threats.

The Pentomic structure lasted only a few years; in 1961, a new organizational concept was introduced: Reorganization Objective Army Division (ROAD). ROAD eliminated the infantry battle group and brought back the battalion, but not the regiment, as the infantry's primary tactical and administrative organization, a position it still holds. Despite the U.S. Army's attempts to perpetuate regimental traditions, honors, and lineages through the Combat Arms Regimental System (CARS), the infantry community has never fully recovered from the loss of the regiment, the traditional key unit in the British army and many other forces.

Various types of infantry units have been developed over the years to permit the American infantry better to accomplish its mission in various parts of the world and on differing types of terrain, among these specialized forms of infantry are the following: light, airborne, air assault, mechanized, and ranger. In the process, the infantry has become the most mobile and flexible of the army's combat arms.

Despite furnishing the bulk of the United States's men and suffering by far the greatest number of battle *casualties, infantry service, at least until World War II, was never considered choice military duty. U.S. Military Academy graduates, for example, invariably chose the U.S. *Army Corps of Engineers, the cavalry, or the artillery before the infantry. Even today, service with line infantry units is not considered choice duty. Service with airborne or ranger infantry units, though, is deemed necessary for infantry officers who hope to reach flag rank.

As a result of this attitude, after years of struggle, the infantry was finally given its own home base and training school at Fort Benning, Georgia, in 1918. Until then, infantry officers and noncommissioned officers were given special training, if at all, at other service schools or on the fields of battle.

Many outstanding U.S. military leaders and warriors have come from the infantry's ranks, Robert Rogers, George Washington, Joshua Chamberlain, Nelson Miles, Alvin *York, Audie *Murphy, George C. *Marshall, and Dwight D. *Eisenhower among them.

Despite the technological advances that have marked the army's progress in recent years, the role of the infantryman on the future battlefield will not change but will remain as important to future success as it has been in the past.

[See also Army, U.S.; Land Warfare: Side Arms, Standard Infantry; Tactics.]

• John K. Mahon and Romana Danysh, *Army Lineage Series, Infantry, Part I: Regular Army*, 1972. The Department of the Army Manual, December 1980, Section V, pp. 6–19. Gregory J. W. Urwin, *The United States Infantry: An Illustrated History, 1775–1918*, 1988.

—Albert N. Garland

ARMY COMBAT BRANCHES: ARTILLERY. Beginning in colonial times, American *artillery has served as coast artillery to defend the coasts, siege artillery to bombard *fortifications, garrison artillery to defend land fortifications, and field artillery to support infantry and cavalry. Although artillery made an early appearance with the initial English settlement in Jamestown in 1607, it played a minor role in military operations during colonial times.

The *Revolutionary War of 1775–83, however, encouraged the Americans to broaden the employment of their artillery. During that war, they used light, mobile cannons as field artillery and heavier pieces as siege, garrison, or coast artillery. Early in 1776, American siege and field artillery bombarded the British in Boston and caused them to sail for Halifax, Nova Scotia, in defeat. Two years later, in June 1778, Americans massed field artillery fire to help defeat the British at the Battle of *Monmouth, New Jersey. In October 1781, American and French field and siege artillery destroyed British defenses in the Battle of *Yorktown, Virginia, and induced the British to surrender. Henry *Knox, who commanded the *Continental army's artillery during most of the war, later became secretary of war.

By the mid-nineteenth century, the Americans had bronze field artillery and cast-iron siege, garrison, and coast artillery, as well as *mortars and rockets. During the *Mexican War of 1846–48, U.S. artillery, much more modern than that of the Mexicans, played a critical role in many battles. At Palo Alto in May 1846 and the Battle of *Buena Vista in February 1847, U.S. Army gun crews boldly pushed field guns within range (300–400 yards) of numerically superior Mexican forces and raked them with devastating antipersonnel canister fire. In 1848, U.S. siege batteries, composed of howitzers, guns, and *mortars, proved essential in the Battle of *Chapultepec and the capture of Mexico City.

The introduction of the rifled *musket in the 1850s

with ranges greater than canister altered the role of field artillery. Field artillerymen learned early in the *Civil War that they could no longer safely push their field guns within canister range of the enemy. To protect themselves and their guns, they had to site them out of range of small-arms fire. Although during the Civil War this transformed field artillery's role from an offensive to a largely defensive one, massed fire from Union field and siege artillery at Malvern Hill in 1862 demonstrated the lethality of rifled and smoothbore field and siege artillery on the defensive, while siege and field artillery contributed to a Union victory in the siege of *Vicksburg (1862–63).

Recoil systems, breech-loading systems, cartridge ammunition, and high explosives dramatically enhanced the lethality of artillery during the latter decades of the nineteenth century. Recoil systems and cartridge ammunition increased rates of fire of breech-loading weapons over that of muzzleloaders, while high explosives produced ranges greater than black powder artillery did. The Americans armed their coastal fortifications in the United States, Cuba, Panama, and the Philippine Islands with rifled coast artillery for harbor defense, while the field artillery introduced its first rapid-fire field gun during the first decade of the twentieth century.

World War I provided an opportunity for the Americans to employ their new rifled artillery in battle. Requiring more firepower to destroy sophisticated German fortifications along the western front, the Americans also mounted coast artillery guns on railcars. During the Battle of *St. Mihiel and the *Meuse-Argonne offensive in 1918, American gun crews employed field, siege, and coast artillery to destroy complex German defenses and contributed to Allied victories.

Seeking to avoid a repetition of *trench warfare, Americans improved the mobility of their artillery during the two decades following World War I. By the 1940s, they had adopted towed and self-propelled field artillery, antiaircraft artillery, and towed and self-propelled antitank artillery. Because of the requirement for tremendous amounts of firepower during World War II, Americans often employed antiaircraft artillery, antitank artillery, and coastal artillery in a field artillery role. At the siege of Metz in 1944, during the liberation of *France, for example, heavy coast artillery pieces and field guns shelled the fortresses there. Later, in the *Korean War, vintage artillery from World War II saw action supporting infantry and armor.

After World War II, the Americans made significant changes in their artillery. Because aerial *bombs and high-velocity naval guns could easily destroy concrete coastal fortifications, the coast artillery was abolished as a branch of artillery; it consolidated its antiaircraft mission with the field artillery in 1950. During the 1950s, in their drive for more firepower, Americans adopted cannon, rocket, and guided missile artillery that carried nuclear and conventional warheads to complement their conventional artillery for possible battle in Europe in the *Cold War.

However, the new artillery with conventional munitions saw its first combat in Southeast Asia in the early 1960s. During the *Vietnam War, American field artillery, sited in fire bases, provided effective close support to the infantry, while air defense artillery, composed of guns and surface-to-air missiles, played a minor role because the enemy lacked aircraft to attack American forces.

In the 1970s and 1980s, Americans introduced new artillery systems. Field artillery and air defense artillery fire adopted computers to calculate fire direction and precision-guided munitions. The first opportunity to employ the new technology came during the *Persian Gulf War of 1991. In that war, precision-guided munitions from American field artillery destroyed Iraqi bunkers and command and control centers, while the Patriot air defense missiles downed many Iraqi Scud missiles launched against Israeli and Saudi-Arabian targets.

[See also Army, U.S.; Weaponry, Army.]

• Albert Manucy, Artillery Through the Ages: A Short Illustrated History of Cannon, Emphasizing Types Used in America, 1949. Fairfax Downey, Sound of the Guns: The Story of the American Artillery, 1955. Harold L. Peterson, Round Shot and Rammers, 1969. Ian Hogg, Artillery 2000, 1990. Boyd L. Dastrup, King of Battle: A Branch History of the U.S. Army's Field Artillery, 1992.

—Boyd L. Dastrup

ARMY COMBAT BRANCHES: CAVALRY. Starting with the colonial militias, the cavalry has always had an elite status in the American military. Despite its prestige, however, this branch has played a secondary role to the artillery and infantry in combat operations. Traditionally, there were several utilizations of the mounted warrior in combat. Heavy cavalry could charge enemy positions in force or pursue retreating units, using pistols, swords, lance, and the intimidating power of massed horses to overwhelm soldiers on foot. Light cavalry units were used for picket duty, reconnaissance, and raiding.

Cavalry units were elite organizations in colonial times, partly because of the financial costs involved in acquiring, feeding, and housing the horses, but also because of traditional images of aristocratic daring. George *Washington has been criticized for making little effort to employ cavalry during the *Revolutionary War, even though the terrain of most battle sites was appropriate for its use. Washington's indifference stemmed largely from his early military experience as an officer in the *French and Indian War, when he commanded units in wooded, hilly terrain, where the cavalry had limited utility. During the Revolution, in the southern colonies (outside Washington's area), American partisans used the horse as mounted infantry. These so-called dragoons would ride into combat, and then dismount and fight on foot.

Building on this heritage, the U.S. Army later utilized horse soldiers in combat as dragoons during the period of the early republic. Between 1802 and 1808, however, the army briefly did away with horse units altogether. This represented partly a Jeffersonian reaction against the social and economic elite status of the cavalry, but to a larger extent it was a cost-cutting measure that eliminated an element of the military that then had little utility. The main mission of the U.S. Army during this period was Indian fighting. The heavily wooded terrain of the western frontier was not appropriate for cavalry units. Nevertheless, the army published Col. Pierce Darrow's Cavalry Tactics in 1822, the first official tactical manual for the cavalry. Cavalry was little used in the *Mexican War.

During the *Civil War, both the *Union army and the *Confederate army used cavalry, mainly in reconnaissance and raiding roles. Technological innovations limited the utility of heavy cavalry. The rifled *musket allowed infantrymen to direct accurate fire at large targets long before the cavalry closed in, preventing the shock and force of massed cavalry. The light firepower of cavalry units, armed with carbines and pistols, also made it difficult for a mounted force to hold positions against infantry attack or counterattack. Commanders on each side, however, like J. E. B. *Stuart and George Armstrong *Custer, made a name for themselves leading or directing units performing the functions of light cavalry.

The *Plains Indians Wars were unique. Cavalry was of fundamental military importance in these conflicts. Once they moved to the plains, the Indians adopted the horse, which had been brought to the Americas by Europeans, and made it central to their culture. These nomadic peoples used the horse to travel across the plains in search of the American bison, which provided the material underpinning of their societies. The warriors of the plains fought primarily on horseback, performing functions similar to light cavalry. The U.S. Army used a similar force organized into cavalry regiments to fight the Plains Indians, and conducted many of the campaigns in the winter months when the lack of foliage available for grazing would weaken Indian ponies. Although the cavalry played a key military role in these conflicts, the force of demographics and the destruction of the "buffalo" herds played a larger role in the ultimate conquest of the Indians.

Toward the end of the nineteenth century, technological innovations again made the future of cavalry questionable. *Machine guns allowed infantry soldiers to direct heavy fire at an opponent, making direct cavalry charges futile. Indeed, no U.S. units fought as cavalry in Europe during World War I. Instead, *tanks and *armored vehicles, which were developed during the war, assumed the ability to perform many of the cavalry functions. Armored units could act with the speed and shock of cavalry, and the staying power of infantry. Armored vehicles could perform wide ranging reconnaissance.

During the interwar period, the chiefs of the cavalry branch of the U.S. Army fought innovation, seeing the advocates of the tank as individuals who sought mainly to destroy the cavalry. The National Defense Act of 1920 created the position of branch chief, and made the officer serving in that position responsible for tactical doctrine for each combat branch. This authority allowed the proponents of the horse cavalry to reject the new weapon, the tank. By the late 1930s, some cavalrymen, such as George S. *Patton, supported armored warfare. In 1940, the success of German Panzer units in France, and the inadequacy of horse units against armor units, overcame even the most dedicated cavalryman's resistance. During World War II, the First Cavalry Division (1st Cav), still technically a mounted force in matters of structure, was the only cavalry unit to see combat in the war but fought as an armored unit without its horses. The horse cavalry and the cavalry branch were formally abolished with the reorganization following the *National Security Act of 1947, although the First Cavalry Division, first with armor and then air mobile via *helicopters, retained the insignia and designation.

[See also Army, U.S.: 1866–99; National Defense Acts.]

• Russell F. Weigley, History of the United States Army, 1967. Lucian K. Truscott, Jr., The Twilight of the U.S. Cavalry: Life in the Old Army, 1917–1942, 1989.   —Nicholas Evan Sarantakes

ARMY COMBAT BRANCHES: ARMOR. The motto of the U.S. Army's armor branch is "The Combat Arm of Decision." Equipped with *tanks and supported by infantry,

*artillery, *helicopters, and air forces, armor units close with and destroy enemy forces using maneuver, protected firepower, and shock.

Though armor only became a separate branch with the U.S. *Army Reorganization Act of 1950, American armor saw combat during World War I. Inspired by British and French tanks, Gen. John J. *Pershing in 1916 approved plans for an overseas U.S. Army Tank Corps. On 10 November 1917, Capt. George S. *Patton, Jr., became the first soldier assigned to the new Tank Corps, which would be headed by Col. Samuel D. Rockenbach. During the war, 1,235 officers and 18,977 enlisted men served in the Tank Corps, two-thirds of their overseas forces. While Patton organized the light tank school and its two battalions in France, the 301st Heavy Tank Battalion trained at a British tank school.

Equipped with 144 French-supplied Renault tanks, Patton's was the first U.S. tank unit into battle on 12 September 1918 in the Battle of *St. Mihiel. The U.S. heavy tank brigade first fought on 29 September, using forty-seven British-supplied Mark V tanks. American-made tanks, modified from French and British designs, did not reach Europe during the war.

After World War I, U.S. tank forces all but vanished in the midst of strong and widespread antimilitary sentiments. The National Defense Act of 1920 disbanded the Tank Corps and transferred responsibility for tanks to the chief of infantry who broke the corps into separate tank companies, assigning one per infantry division. During the 1920s, while far-sighted American officers like Patton, Dwight D. *Eisenhower, Daniel Van Voorhis, Robert W. Grow, Bradford G. Chenoweth, and Adna R. Chaffee followed the armor doctrine evolving in Europe through Britain's Basil H. *Liddell Hart and J. F. C. Fuller, France's Charles de Gaulle, and Germany's Heinz Guderian, the U.S. War Department viewed tanks simply as support for advancing infantrymen.

In 1931, after becoming chief of staff, Gen. Douglas *MacArthur directed each branch of the army to pursue mechanization on its own. The cavalry took over the mechanized force, then at Fort Eustis, Virginia, moved it to Fort Knox, Kentucky, and formed it into the Seventh Cavalry Brigade (Mechanized). It developed annually about two experimental "Combat Cars"—a euphemism for cavalry's light and medium tanks, since the law allowed only the infantry branch to have tanks. These experiments included the high-speed vehicle developed by J. Walter Christie, which America abandoned but the Soviet Union adopted as the concept behind its highly successful main battle tank of World War II, the T-34. The U.S. cavalry's M1 and M2 Combat Cars became the basis for the Light Tank M3, the Stuart, which was designed in the spring of 1940 and saw U.S. and British service in World War II. The infantry formed a provisional tank brigade at Fort Benning, Georgia, and carried out its own limited experiments.

On 15 July 1940, in reaction to the stunning German armored successes in Poland and France and its own experiments with armor units, the U.S. War Department created the Armored Force under Chaffee, earning him the title, "Father of the American Armored Force." The Fort Knox and Fort Benning brigades formed the nuclei for two new armored divisions assigned to an armored corps. From this small beginning, the Armored Force grew during World

War II to sixteen armored divisions, which fought in Europe (armor played only a minor role in the Pacific theater). Five armored regiments and 119 tank battalions saw combat. Starting in 1940 with under 1,000 obsolete World War I–era tanks and only 28 new ones, the United States produced nearly 90,000 tanks by 1945. Cavalry units also used tanks. By mid-1942, the Armored Force had nearly 150,000 men.

The workhorse of U.S. armor units in World War II was the M4 Sherman tank and its numerous variants. This medium tank was relatively fast and agile, combining armored protection, speed, and firepower. It was outmatched, however, by Germany's heavy Panther and Tiger tanks. In February 1945, the United States fielded in Europe the first 20 of 200 T26E3 Pershing heavy tanks, which were nearly a match for the Tiger. The Pershing also saw action on Okinawa in the Pacific.

Additionally, World War II units of thin-skinned, self-propelled, fully tracked *tank destroyers—created to defeat enemy tanks—peaked in early 1943 at 106 battalions with about 100,000 men. Battlefield experience showed that tanks were superior to the vulnerable tank destroyers, and the U.S. Army abandoned tank destroyers shortly after the war.

Using doctrine that emphasized their mobility, protected firepower, and shock effect, tank units sliced through weak points, dashed around enemy flanks to strike deep into the enemy rear, or sped to plug gaps and blunt attacks. Armor employed in mass proved an effective way to exploit success. The dash of Patton's Third Army across the countryside in the liberation of *France in 1944 exemplified these tactics, with the Fourth Armored Division's encirclement of German forces at the city of Nancy in Lorraine, a classic example.

In the *Army Reorganization Act (1950), Congress designated armor a new branch. The cavalry was merged into it, and Congress directed that the new branch be considered "a continuation of the cavalry." The new armor branch assumed responsibility for traditional cavalry missions—reconnaissance, scouting, security, covering force operations, and pursuit, in addition to new missions of penetration, counterarmor, and infantry support.

After World War II the active army divisions were cut from ninety-two to ten, the sixteen armored divisions down to one. With the outbreak of the *Korean War in June 1950, there were no U.S. tanks in the Far East that could match the enemy's Soviet-made T34s. The first U.S. tanks into Korea were light, thin-skinned M24 Chaffees. In early August, the United States sent to Korea three hastily cobbled together tank battalions with a hodgepodge of about 200 M4A3E8 Shermans, M26 Pershings, and untested M46 Patton heavy tanks.

By January 1951, there were over 600 American tanks in Korea. At the 1953 armistice, there were also a few new seventy-five M47 Pattons and T41E (experimental) Walker Bulldog tanks. This mishmash of obsolescent and untested experimental tanks seriously degraded the effectiveness of American armor in the war.

Armor units also fought in the *Vietnam War, though they did not play a major role. The main battle tank used in Vietnam was the M48A3 Patton; nearly two were sent there. More important was the lightly armored M551 Sheridan Armored Reconnaissance Airborne Assault Vehicle, which weighed only 16.5 tons and was amphibious and air-droppable. It fired a guided antitank missile in addition to conventional tank rounds and a special antipersonnel round containing thousands of tiny dartlike flechettes. The Sheridan arrived in Vietnam in 1969; by late 1970, over 200 were issued to almost every ground cavalry unit there. Armor in Vietnam was primarily employed piecemeal and used mainly to clear roads, protect logistical areas, and as reaction forces.

In Europe during the *Cold War, both sides expended considerable resources on armored formations. The United States increased its *NATO divisions to sixteen (four armored, six mechanized, and six infantry) with three armored cavalry regiments. The 1967 and 1973 Arab-Israeli wars, where armor played a key role, showed the need for new American equipment, doctrine, and more realistic armor training. The result was the M1 Abrams tank, fielded in 1980, the squad-carrying Bradley infantry and cavalry fighting vehicle, and other modern battlefield systems key to the execution of the new "AirLand Battle" doctrine. The new doctrine, designed to defeat a *Warsaw Pact attack into Central Europe, deemphasized defensive operations and stressed offensive reaction and the combined effects of rapid maneuver, surprise, firepower, and airpower to bypass enemy strengths and to strike deep into the enemy's rear.

During the *Persian Gulf War in 1991, the U.S. Army deployed 3 armored divisions and 2 mechanized infantry divisions equipped with nearly 2,000 Abrams tanks and another 1,600 Bradley infantry and cavalry fighting vehicles. The Soviet-modeled Iraqi Army proved no match for these formations.

By the 1990s, however, the U.S. Army had downsized to ten divisions and two armored cavalry regiments. Among the ten were two armored and four mechanized divisions which contained the remaining twenty-nine armor battalions. In the twenty-first century, the armored forces faced an uncertain future, and their usefulness in *peacekeeping operations, such as Somalia and the *Bosnian Crisis, remained an open question.

[See also Army, U.S.; National Defense Acts (1916, 1920); Tactics: Land Warfare Tactics; Weaponry, Army.]

• Timothy K. Nenninger, "The World War I Experience," Armor, vol. 78, no. 1 (January–February 1969), pp. 46–51, and "The Tank Corps Reorganized," Armor, Vol. 78, no. 2 (March–April 1969), pp. 34–38. Mary Lee Stubbs and Stanley Russell Connor, Armor-Cavalry: Part I: Regular Army and Army Reserve, 1969. Charles M. Bailey, Faint Praise: American Tanks and Tank Destroyers During World War II, 1983. Dale E. Wilson, Treat 'Em Rough!: The Birth of American Armor, 1917–20, 1989. Robert M. Citano, Armored Forces: History and Sourcebook, 1994.
—Steve E. Dietrich

ARMY COMBAT BRANCHES: AVIATION. The army aviation combat branch consists of those aircraft so essential to the day-to-day operations of ground forces that they are placed under the command and control of a ground commander. In the United States, modern army aviation dates from the efforts of the field artillery to obtain adequate aerial observation just before *World War II. The War Department approved the air-observation-post program on June 6, 1942. Each firing battalion of field artillery received an artillery air section of two light planes, usually L-4s, flown and maintained by field artillerymen. Eventually, air sections of varying strength joined all field artillery staff echelons from division to theater level. The Department of

Air Training at the Field Artillery School, Fort Sill, Oklahoma, provided advanced training for field artillery pilots and aviation mechanics. Air observation posts, as the Army designated the aircraft, were most important in providing observed fire for field artillery and transportation for commanders and staff officers in the battle zone.

The success of the program led the War Department to expand it to the other ground combat branches in July 1945. Renamed Army Ground Forces light aviation, it received legislative sanction in the *National Security Act of 1947, which also created an independent Air Force. In 1949 the Department of the Army renamed the program Army aviation. Not until 1983 did the specialty become a separate branch of the Army.

During the late 1940s, the Army obtained limited numbers of helicopters as well as a slightly larger fixed-wing aircraft. The Army used *helicopters during the *Korean War to perform front-line evacuation of wounded soldiers. A controversy with the *Air Force over the procurement of cargo helicopters, however, delayed until December 1952 the deployment of the first of two transportation helicopter companies that eventually saw service in Korea. During this period, the Army expanded its aviation training base. In January 1953 the Department of Air Training became the Army Aviation School. It moved to Fort Rucker, Alabama, in 1954. In the aftermath of the war, the Army experimented with armed helicopters. The development of turbine-powered helicopters made possible the creation of an airmobile division, recommended by the Howze Board in 1962.

After testing the concept, the Army deployed the 1st Cavalry Division (Airmobile) to Vietnam during the summer of 1965. Helicopters gave the U.S. Army great tactical flexibility, but were not sufficient in themselves to win the war. Army pilots refined techniques of aeromedical evacuation and developed new skills in all-weather and night flying. The armed helicopter proved itself as a close fire-support weapon and in the waning stages of the *Vietnam War demonstrated an ability to kill *tanks when outfitted with anti-armor rockets.

This development and the invention of techniques that allowed helicopters to survive in areas with significant anti-aircraft defenses were among the factors that led the Army to adopt its Air-Land battle doctrine. Helicopters played a significant role in post-Vietnam operations in *Grenada, *Panama, and *Somalia.

[See also Airborne Warfare; Transport and Supply Aircraft.]

• Christopher C. S. Cheng, Air Mobility: The Development of a Doctrine, 1994. Edgar F. Raines, Jr., "Maytag Messerschmidts" and "Biscuit Bombers": The Origins of Modern Army Aviation During World War II, forthcoming.   —Edgar F. Raines, Jr.

ARMY CORPS OF ENGINEERS, U.S. With the tasks of facilitating military movement by the construction of roads, bridges, and bases, and of protecting troops or territory through fortification, military engineering has been part of warfare since ancient times. The U.S. Army Corps of Engineers has supervised most of the construction for the U.S. Army and, after 1947, for the U.S. Air Force (the navy has its own construction agencies). It has also had important, if sometimes controversial, civil works responsibilities.

The U.S. Army Corps of Engineers originated on 16 June 1775, when Gen. George *Washington appointed Col. Richard Gridley as the first chief engineer of the *Continental army. Later, Gridley was succeeded by several French officers, most notably Gen. Louis du Portail (American spelling Duportail) in 1777. A Corps of Engineers was established by Congress as a component of the Continental army in 1779.

The engineers' fortifications played an important role in many *Revolutionary War battles, such as the Battle of *Bunker Hill and the Battles of *Saratoga, and the engineers' siegecraft, including sapper and mining operations, contributed to the victory at the Battle of *Yorktown. Like most of the Continental army, they were mustered out after the war. A combined Corps of Artillerists and Engineers was created in 1794, but it was short-lived.

In 1802, recognizing the need for a national engineering capability, civil as well as military, Congress, supported by President Thomas *Jefferson, established the U.S. Military Academy at West Point, New York. For more than a quarter century, West Point remained the only engineering school in the country. Congress also established the U.S. Army Corps of Engineers, which dates its continuous origin from 1802, and stationed the Corps at West Point. Until 1866, the academy superintendent was a military engineer.

The nation repeatedly called upon the Army Engineers to perform civil works as well as military engineering projects. During the nineteenth century, the Corps supervised construction of extensive coastal fortifications and built lighthouses, piers, and jetties, as well as mapping navigation channels. After the Supreme Court's Gibbons v. Ogden decision that federal authority over interstate commerce included river navigation, the General Survey Act of 1824 led to the Corps of Engineers' assignment to survey routes for roads and canals. Another act the same year authorized the Corps to dredge and make other navigation improvements on the nation's waterways. This was the origin of the Corps' responsibilities in river and harbor improvements, and it eventually led to the Corps' reorganization into a series of local district and regional division offices, all under the Office of the Chief of Engineers. A Corps of Topographical Engineers, a separate unit in 1838–63, helped explore, survey, and map many regions of the West.

During the *Mexican War and *Civil War, in addition to supplying many important commanders such as Robert E. *Lee, George *McClellan, and George Gordon *Meade, the Corps of Engineers played important roles in mapping, road and bridge construction, *fortifications, and siegecraft. The 2,170-foot pontoon bridge built across the James River in June 1864 was the longest floating bridge erected before World War II.

Army Engineers continued the construction and modernization of coastal fortifications in the second half of the nineteenth century on the Pacific Coast and on the overseas territories acquired in the *Spanish-American War. They also continued river and harbor improvements. One of the Army engineers, George W. *Goethals, supervised the construction of the Panama Canal. In World War I, the Quartermaster Corps constructed training cantonments in the United States while the Corps of Engineers built bridges, roads, railroads, and buildings for the American Expeditionary Forces in France.

In the 1930s disastrous floods led Congress, through a series of measures culminating in the Flood Control Act of 1936, to declare flood control a function of the federal government and to authorize the Corps of Engineers to build levees, dams, and reservoirs to supervise such projects on the Mississippi, Missouri, and other rivers. The Flood Control Act of 1944, authorized the Corps to construct multipurpose dams that provided flood control, irrigation, navigation, water supply, hydroelectric power, and recreational areas.

During World War II, the Corps of Engineers was given responsibility for all U.S. Army and Army Air Forces construction, as the Quartermaster Corps concentrated on its other responsibilities. In the United States and around the world, army engineers built airfields, roads, bridges, ports, petroleum pipelines, military camps and cantonments, warehouses, hospitals, and dozens of other facilities, including the *Pentagon, the world's largest office building, completed in 1942. Among the most acclaimed of the combat engineers' achievements were the Alcan Highway to Alaska, the Ledo and Burma Roads through the mountains and jungles of Asia, and the clearing of mines and underwater obstacles from the beaches before the invasion of *Normandy. The Manhattan District of the Corps of Engineers supervised the *Manhattan Project, the construction of the atomic bomb.

During the *Cold War, the Corps of Engineers engaged in a major construction program as part of the military buildup of the early 1950s, erecting U.S. Army and U.S. Air Force bases in the United States and throughout the world, from the deserts of North Africa to the permafrost of the arctic. To protect the United States, the Corps erected extensive *radar early warning systems across northern Canada, and NIKE and other antiaircraft missile sites in the United States. In the missile age, the Corps constructed ICBM silos, ballistic missile early warning systems (BMEWs), and part of the NASA facilities at Cape Kennedy.

During the *Korean War, combat engineers destroyed bridges over the Naktong River and built fortifications that helped stop the North Korean assault at the Pusan perimeter. In the *Vietnam War, army engineers built military bases and roads in Southeast Asia. To cut through the jungle in support of U.S. "search and destroy" missions, the engineers also introduced the Rome plow, a military tractor equipped with a protective cab and a special tree-cutting blade.

The Corps of Engineers engaged in varied civil works, including construction of *Veterans Administration hospitals, post offices, and bulk mail facilities. The Corps' dam construction and other flood control work came under attack, particularly in the 1960s and 1980s, when critics accused it of being overly responsive to "pork barrel" projects of the Congress. Paradoxically, when the federal government responded to the environmental movement in the 1970s, the executive branch turned first for protection of the nation's wetlands and waterways from pollution to the Corps of Engineers, whose regulatory authority under the 1899 Rivers and Harbors Act was expanded under the Federal Water Pollution Control Act Amendments of 1972.

The change in public attitudes of the 1980s, however, led to the Water Resources Act of 1986, which signified a major change in water resources planning. The new direction was toward shifting responsibility away from the federal government, which indicated a diminished civil works role for the Corps of Engineers. But the military role of the Corps continued, as seen in its construction of army and air force facilities in the buildup of the 1980s, the Corps'

roles in Operations Desert Shield and Desert Storm in the *Persian Gulf War in 1990–91, and its erection of military facilities for *peacekeeping operations in Somalia, Haiti, and Bosnia and Kosovo throughout the 1990s.

[See also Academies, Service: U.S. Military Academy; Bases, Military: Development of; Engineering, Military.]

• Forest G. R. Hill, Rails and Waterways: The Army Engineers and Early Transportation, 1957. Blanche D. Coll, et al., The Corps of Engineers: Troops and Equipment, in Office of the Chief of Military History, U.S. Army in World War II: The Technical Services, 1958. William H. Goetzmann, Army Exploration in the American West, 1803–1863, 1959. Karl C. Dod, The Corps of Engineers: The War Against Japan, in Office of the Chief of Military History, U.S. Army in World War II: The Technical Services, 1966. Lenore Fine and Jesse Remington, The Corps of Engineers: Constructions in the United States in Office of the Chief of Military History, U.S. Army in World War II, 1972. Vincent C. Jones, Manhattan: The Army and the Atomic Bomb, 1985. Martin Reuss and Charles Hendricks, U.S. Army Corps of Engineers: A Brief History, 1997.

—John Whiteclay Chambers II

ARMY REORGANIZATION ACT (1950). In part, the 1950 Reorganization Act was intended to regularize the new relationship provided by the National Security Act of 1947, which created an Office of the Secretary of Defense, at cabinet level, and the World War II creation of the *Joint Chiefs of Staff. The act also abolished the old statutory limits on the size of the Army General Staff, providing an undersecretary of the army and four assistant secretaries (reduced to three after 1958). Infantry, Artillery, and Armor were recognized as the component arms of the army, while the Coast Artillery, already largely defunct, was formally abolished, and the Air Defense Artillery (technically a sub-branch of the Coast Artillery) was merged with the Field Artillery in a single artillery arm. The act recognized fourteen technical services, and, as a quasi-arm, Army Aviation was authorized fixed-wing and rotary-wing aircraft for support and medical purposes.

[See also Army, U.S.: Since 1941.]

• Russell F. Weigley, History of the United States Army, 1967; enlarged ed., 1984. Larry H. Addington, "The U.S. Coast Artillery and the Problem of Artillery Organization, 1907–1954," Military Affairs: The Journal of Military History, vol. 30, no. 1 (February 1976).

—Larry H. Addington

ARMY RESERVES AND NATIONAL GUARD. The Army Reserve originated in the *National Defense Act of 1916, which established the Officers' Reserve Corps (ORC), the Reserve Officer Training Corps (*ROTC), and an Enlisted Reserve Corps (ERC). This reserve represented a federal force long sought by the army. A 1920 congressional amendment incorporated the ORC and ERC in the Organized Reserves. Finally, the *Armed Forces Reserve Act of 1952 renamed the organization the Army Reserve.

When the nation entered World War I, only 8,000 ORC officers were ready to serve; another 80,000 men earned reserve commissions during the war. From 1916 through 1941, officers dominated the reserve, with only 3,233 ERC men in a total strength of 120,000. World War I veterans, joined by ROTC graduates and civilian appointees, manned the ORC during the 1920s and 1930s. Lack of funding hampered the force, for without money or men it could not maintain units. ORC members received no drill pay and few had the opportunity to take active duty training. Reserve officers contributed significantly to the World War II effort by providing thousands of company and battalion officers to army and National Guard divisions.

From its creation in 1916 to the late 1940s, the ORC functioned as a rarely trained inactive force. Given the lack of funding, only the understrength and poorly equipped National Guard functioned as an active reserve. World War II produced an Officers' Reserve Corps of 200,000. It also created a pool of nearly 3 million enlisted men with a nominal reserve obligation. While 50 percent of demobilized officers took ORC commissions, few enlisted men signed up. The postwar years posed many problems for the armed forces. Foreign policy led to a permanent American presence overseas and probable military intervention, but defense spending forced sharp cuts in the regular forces and left little money for the reserves.

Under these conditions, the U.S. Army struggled to devise a viable reserve policy. It had a reserve force of its own, nearly 600,000 in 1949, but no policy to use it. The reserve muddle posed serious problems with the 1950 intervention in Korea. Army plans, such as they were, assumed total mobilization for a mass war. Korea was a limited war requiring only a partial reserve call-up. The army was reluctant to mobilize the National Guard. It decided instead to activate individual reservists to reinforce understrength regular units. The *mobilization fell heavily on World War II veterans, which generated much hard feeling, and led to the Armed Forces Reserve Act of 1952. Just over 241,000 reservists were called, whereas 138,000 Guardsmen, also largely veterans, served.

The army continued its quest for a viable reserve policy through the 1950s. Defense policy now provided increased spending, larger active forces, and selective service. The draft took in thousands of men annually for two years of active duty, followed by a reserve obligation. However, the army could not devise ways to compel these men to join a reserve unit. It failed to commit funds to maintain drill pay units to take them anyway. In 1956, for example, the Army Reserve manned its authorized units at a 32 percent level.

The reserve muddle persisted because army leaders realized belatedly that under the nuclear umbrella, planning for mass war and total mobilization seemed increasingly unlikely. By the end of President Dwight D. *Eisenhower's second term, the Department of *Defense began to consider reducing both the Army Reserve and the Army National Guard. Secretary of Defense Robert *McNamara continued the reassessment into the 1960s. He sought to create a genuine ready reserve by manning Guard and reserve units at near full strength while equipping and training them properly.

McNamara erred badly with his proposal to merge the Army Reserve into the National Guard. He encountered a potent lobby in the Reserve Officers Association and reserve units with strong local ties similar to those of the established National Guard. However, McNamara succeeded in reducing Guard and reserve strengths and units even while improving readiness. The 1960s reserve reorganizations may be seen as the time when the Army Reserve came of age. McNamara's reforms gave the reserve a mobilization function: to provide combat and service support. The emphasis on readiness and full manning also heightened reserve unit identity and ensured its permanent status. The Army Reserve still provided individual ready reservists

but its units would no longer be stripped of fillers for the active army.

The *Vietnam War delayed implementation of the new policy. It also distorted Army Reserve and National Guard development by flooding both with recruits eager to avoid the draft and possible duty in Vietnam. President Lyndon B. *Johnson, despite the advice of the *Joint Chiefs of Staff, refused to mobilize reserve components. Johnson relented with a limited call-up in 1968. Forty-two Army Reserve units answered the call (nearly 8,000 men), 32 of which went to Vietnam. Nearly all the units were detachments or companies providing support services.

The 1960s reserve reforms went into effect after the Vietnam War. Defense Department leaders adopted a Total Force policy that included reserve and National units. The policy eased the impact of defense cuts and ensured use of reserve components in future wars. Larger reserves fielding combat support and service support units allowed the active army to maintain more combat units. The army structured the National Guard to provide most of the combat reserve (71% of its force) and gave the bulk of service units to the Army Reserve (81% of its composition). With the end of the draft the reserve witnessed a dramatic drop in strength—from 1,294,256 men in the ready reserve in 1972 to a low of 338,847 in 1979.

Aggressive recruiting and attractive benefits brought recovery in less than a decade. In 1988, the Army Reserve boasted 600,000 ready reservists and 286,000 individual ready reservists, a dramatic rebound from the 1979 nadir. Total Force policy was designed so that the nation could not fight a war without a reserve mobilization. The *Persian Gulf War put the policy to the test. By all accounts Army Reserve support units performed their duties well in 1990–91, deploying 39,000 men and women to the gulf, 6,000 more than the National Guard. Despite the limited nature of the Gulf War and the limited call-up, this war stands as the highlight in Army Reserve history. Reservists went to war in identifiable units, received media attention, and came home to a heroes' welcome.

[See also Militia Acts; Militia and National Guard.]

• Russell F. Weigley, *Towards an American Army: Military Thought from Washington to Marshall*, 1962. William F. Levantrosser, *Congress and the Citizen Soldier: Legislative Policy-Making for the Federal Armed Forces Reserve*, 1967. Richard B. Crossland and James T. Currie, *Twice the Citizen: A History of the Army Reserve, 1908–1983*, 1984. David R. Segal, *Recruiting for Uncle Sam: Citizenship and Military Manpower*, 1984. Eliot A. Cohen, *Citizens and Soldiers: The Dilemma of Military Service*, 1985. Bennie J. Wilson III, ed., *The Guard and Reserve in the Total Force: The First Decade, 1973–1983*, 1985. Martin Binkin and William W. Kaufman, *U.S. Army Guard and Reserve: Rhetoric, Realities, Risks*, 1989. Martin Binkin, *Who Will Fight the Next War? The Changing Face of the American Military*, 1993.

—Jerry Cooper

ARNOLD, BENEDICT (1741–1801), *Continental army general and traitor. In 1755, at sixteen, Arnold fled his dysfunctional family in Norwich, Connecticut, and joined the provincial army of New York. Arnold soon tired of military life and deserted, as he did after a second enlistment in 1760, anticipating a lifelong pattern of abandoning military allegiances that failed to produce wealth, status, or fame.

A prominent merchant in New Haven, Arnold in April 1775 led his militia company to Massachusetts. In May,

Massachusetts authorities commissioned him a colonel, and he helped lead the expedition that captured Fort Ticonderoga. In September, he led an army through Maine toward Quebec. The conquest of Canada failed, but Arnold's wilderness march and his later defense of Lake Champlain secured his reputation as a dashing, talented leader. After being wounded at the Battle of *Saratoga (1777), Arnold commanded the Philadelphia garrison in 1778. Rampant corruption in Arnold's command led to his court-martial in 1779, and a reprimand from Washington. Furious, and desperate for money to support a lavish lifestyle, Arnold plotted to betray West Point to the British for £20,000. The plot was uncovered in 1780. Arnold fled to the British, who commissioned him a brigadier general and gave him command of a corps of deserters, the American Legion, which he led on raids in Virginia and Connecticut (1780–81). His name remains a symbol of treason in U.S. national history.

[See also Revolutionary War: Military and Diplomatic Course; Treason.]

• James Thomas Flexner, The Traitor and the Spy, 1953; 2d ed., 1975. Clare Brandt, The Man in the Mirror: A Life of Benedict Arnold, 1994. James Kirby Martin, Benedict Arnold, Revolutionary Hero: An American Warrior Reconsidered, 1997.

—Jon T. Coleman

ARNOLD, "HAP" [HENRY HARLEY] (1886–1950), aviator and World War II general. A 1907 graduate of the U.S. Military Academy, Arnold joined the Aviation Section in 1911, receiving his flight training from Orville and Wilbur *Wright. As an aviation pioneer, he set altitude records and won the initial Mackay Trophy in 1912. During *World War I, he served in Washington as the head of flight training. The haphazard aviation programs of the war gave him useful insight into future efforts. After the war, he continued to advance the cause of military aviation. He testified for Col. Billy *Mitchell and violated regulations in soliciting reservists for support of legislation. This action exiled him to Fort Riley, Kansas, in 1926. He persevered, however, rising to the rank of brigadier general in 1935. Arnold developed and exploited relationships with aviation entrepreneurs, scientists at the California Institute of Technology, Hollywood celebrities, and senior Army officers, and frequently served as the logistics and organization officer in air maneuvers.

In 1938, Arnold became Chief of the Air Corps. Simultaneously, President Franklin D. *Roosevelt inaugurated U.S. rearmament, with emphasis on aircraft. In the next seven years, Arnold oversaw the creation of the world's most powerful air force—243 combat groups, 2.5 million men, and 63,000 aircraft at its height—which was his most significant contribution to the Allied victory in *World War II. Although slowed by two heart attacks, he attended most of the meetings of the Combined Chiefs of Staff and *Joint Chiefs of Staff, where he championed the interests of the U.S. Army Air Forces and demonstrated that air power required representation at the highest levels. He deferred the fight for an independent air arm until after the war, but his loyal wartime support of both Army Chief of Staff Gen. George C. *Marshall and European Theater Commander Gen. Dwight D. *Eisenhower helped to ensure postwar army support for independence. In December 1944, he achieved five-star rank and, with the creation of the U.S. *Air Force in 1947, became the only General of the Air Force.

• Arnold H. H., Global Mission, 1949.

—Richard G. Davis

ARTICLES OF WAR. See Justice, Military: Articles of War.

ARTILLERY. Artillery has played a critical role in providing close support to the infantry, bombarding *fortifications, defending coasts, and, in the twentieth century, attacking tanks and aircraft. Beginning with the initial settlements, English colonists in North America, like Europeans, employed smoothbore, muzzle-loading, black powder, cast-bronze cannons and howitzers. Cannons, also called guns by the nineteenth century, had powerful, flat trajectories to batter down fortification walls or to shatter troop formations, while howitzers had curved trajectories for lobbing projectiles over fortification walls or into troop formations. Colonial artillery fired several types of projectiles, among them: solid shot, an exploding shell that was detonated by a fuse; canister, which was a can filled with musket balls; and grapeshot, a cluster of iron balls grouped around a wooden spindle and covered by a heavy cloth netting.

English colonists gave their artillery colorful names, such as falcon, saker, demiculverin, and culverin, to name a few. A falcon shot a 2- to 3-pound projectile; a culverin fired a 15- to 22-pound projectile. During the seventeenth century, however, Europeans and Americans started designating their artillery by the size of the projectile that they threw. For example, a cannon that shot a 4-pound projectile was known as a 4-pounder. Besides classifying their howitzers by the size of the projectile that it shot, Europeans and Americans also labeled them by the size of the bore, such as a 5.5-inch howitzer.

Meanwhile, most European armies began to classify their artillery as field, siege, garrison, and coast artillery. Light pieces, usually 3- to 12-pounders, served as field artillery to support the infantry and cavalry, while heavier and less maneuverable pieces were employed as siege, garrison, and coast artillery where mobility was not critical.

Unlike the Europeans, colonists had little use for arranging their artillery functionally by size. First, the rugged North American terrain limited artillery to siege operations along coasts or to the defense of a fortification because even the lightest pieces were too heavy to drag across the roadless terrain. Second, Native American warfare was too mobile for artillery of any size.

Although the colonists did not employ artillery extensively or standardize it, they had a diverse assortment composed primarily of French and British pieces. At the outbreak of the *Revolutionary War in 1775, the colonists had thirteen different calibers of artillery, ranging from 3- to 24-pounder cannons and 5.5- to 8-inch howitzers. Cut off from their sources of artillery at the beginning of the war, the Americans started casting their own iron and bronze artillery in foundries in Philadelphia by 1775. Under the guidance of Henry *Knox, who commanded the Continental army's artillery throughout most of the Revolution, they developed a system of field, garrison, siege, and coast artillery of 3- to 32-pounders. Colonial field artillery could hit targets at between 500 and 1,000 yards, while garrison, siege, and coast artillery had ranges of 2,000–3,000 yards.

After the Revolution, the Americans retained their categories of artillery. For coast artillery, which also doubled as siege artillery and garrison artillery, the Americans used 18-, 24-, and 32-pounder cannons. Bronze and cast-iron field artillery armed frontier forts but seldom saw action during the *Native American wars. Later, in the 1840s, the

Americans adopted rockets with explosive and incendiary warheads for use against personnel and fortifications at ranges of around 3,000 yards. Although rockets provided greater firepower than cannon artillery, developments with more accurate rifled artillery in the 1840s and 1850s caused rocket artillery to fall out of favor.

American smoothbore bronze artillery experienced its apogee in the middle of the nineteenth century. Designed by Maj. Alfred Mordecai of the army during the 1840s, the field artillery system had 6- and 12-pounder guns to support the infantry and cavalry, and 12-, 24-, and 32-pounder howitzers to bombard temporary field and permanent fortifications. For coastal defense, the army employed Columbiad cannons of 10 to 15 inches designed by Col. George Bomford.

Improved metallurgy and advancements in machining permitted significant breakthroughs with rifled muzzle-loading and breech-loading artillery. In the 1840s, the Italian Army produced the first workable rifled fieldpiece. Ranges of rifled artillery were twice that of smoothbore artillery—sometimes up to 4,000 yards.

Although rifled artillery promised to make smoothbore artillery obsolete, Union and Confederate armies during the *Civil War of 1861–65 did not abandon their muzzle-loading smoothbores for rifled breechloaders or muzzle-loaders. Prominent siege pieces included 10-, 20-, 30-, 60-, 100-, 200-, and 300-pounder rifled artillery produced by Robert P. Parrott of the United States. Other important siege and coast artillery pieces were smoothbores developed by Capt. Thomas J. *Rodman of the army. Some of the most popular rifled fieldpieces were the muzzle-loading, wrought-iron M1861 3-inch rifle and muzzle-loading 3- to 10-inch rifled guns. The latter, again manufactured by Robert P. Parrott, were of cast iron, with a wrought-iron hoop around the breech to prevent the weapon from bursting upon being fired. Like their smoothbore counterparts, rifled artillery fired solid shot, exploding shell, canister, and occasionally grapeshot, and used black powder as a propelling and bursting charge. However, smoothbore fieldpieces, especially the M1857 12-pounder Napoleon, remained the favorite because direct fire (also called line-of-sight fire direction) and the difficult terrain of Civil War battlefields prevented gun crews from engaging targets beyond human eyesight of about one mile and forced them to fire at targets at relatively short ranges.

A surplus of Civil War artillery and engagement in wars with Native Americans stalled new ordnance developments between 1865 and 1900. Early in the 1900s, Americans adopted breech-loading, rifled steel field artillery with recoil systems that allowed the gun tube to recoil on the carriage and return into battery without moving the carriage. At the same time the Americans started using high-explosive powder as a propelling and a bursting charge for steel shell and shrapnel, a projectile that was filled with iron balls. These high-explosive powders increased ranges and diminished the amount of smoke produced when the cannon was fired; the M1903 3-inch field gun, for example, had a range of almost 7,000 yards. For coastal defense, Americans introduced steel, rifled artillery mounted on disappearing carriages. Upon being fired, the gun moved back for some distance before swinging down behind the parapet to permit the gun crew to load the weapon out of sight of enemy guns.

Coupled with these advancements, Americans adopted indirect fire for their field artillery early in the twentieth century. This arching fire permitted concealing the field gun behind cover to protect it from counterbattery fire and small-arms fire, and engaging targets beyond human eyesight. By World War I, all combatants were using indirect fire, locating their guns several miles behind the infantry line; they acquired targets by using forward observers, who relayed target information back to the batteries by telegraphy, telephone, and even human runners.

Even though the Americans went into World War I with distinct classifications of field, siege, and coast artillery, the war obscured the differences. Requiring heavy guns to batter down elaborate German earthworks and concrete fortifications along the western front, the U.S. Army frequently employed heavy coast and siege artillery pieces; some were mounted on railroad tracks in a field artillery role to help 75mm guns, 105mm howitzers, 155mm guns and howitzers, and 240mm, 8-inch and 9.2-inch howitzers shatter enemy positions. The army also introduced antiaircraft artillery, assigning it to the Coast Artillery branch.

During World War II, multiple rocket launchers mounted on trucks were used to lay down heavy concentrations of fire rapidly. The army even employed a recoilless rifle designed to fire the same size of projectile as light fieldpieces to engage tanks, enemy bunkers, and lightly armored vehicles. Ninety mm antiaircraft guns and shells with proximity fuses were employed to shoot down aircraft detected by *radar or the human eye. The main U.S. artillery pieces in World War II were the 105mm howitzer, with a range of 12,500 yards; the 155mm howitzer, with a range of 16,350 yards; and the 155mm gun, with a range of 25,500 yards. All were later utilized in the *Korean War.

The advent of nuclear cannon artillery, rockets, and guided missiles during the 1950s and 1960s transformed the field artillery. First fired in May 1953 at Frenchman's Flat, Nevada, the 280mm cannon, known as "Atomic Annie," shot a 200-pound nuclear projectile up to 20 miles. Later, the army also developed nuclear warheads for 8-inch and 155mm artillery pieces. In the 1950s, it introduced the "Honest John," a first-generation free flight rocket with a range of about 24 miles, to carry either a conventional or a nuclear warhead; and the medium-range Redstone, Corporal, and Sergeant guided missiles, with nuclear and conventional warheads and ranges between 75 and 200 miles.

Aircraft and high-velocity naval guns made concrete coastal fortifications vulnerable and obsolete; the Coast Artillery branch was abolished in 1950, and succeeded in 1968 by the Air Defense artillery. Antiaircraft missile artillery included large, immobile surface-to-air missiles such as the radar-guided Nike Ajax with a range of 100 miles; they defended American cities. The Nike Hawk, with a range of 25 miles, was a mobile antiaircraft missile. The Redeye, with a range of 3,300 yards, was a lightweight, man-portable antiaircraft missile.

Also beginning in the 1960s, the U.S. Army introduced new field artillery for the tactical nuclear battlefield to replace World War II pieces. These new weapons included the M102 105mm howitzer, with a range of 16,500 yards; the M109 155mm self-propelled artillery with a range of 19,700 yards; and the M110 8-inch artillery, with a range of 18,400 yards. Although intended for the European battlefield, these field guns saw service in Vietnam.

From the mid-1970s onward, high technology improved U.S. artillery. Field and air defense artillery employed computers for fire direction and adopted *precision-guided munitions (PGMs). The highly sophisticated

Patriot air defense missile with a range of 65 miles replaced the Nike Hercules and Nike Hawk missiles, while the Redeye was replaced by the shoulder-fired Stinger, with a range of 3 miles homed in on heat emitted from the aircraft target. The army fielded the nuclear Pershing II missile with a range of 1,000 miles in Europe in the mid-1980s and the Multiple-Launch Rocket System with a range of 15 miles in the field artillery and simultaneously improved the M109 self-propelled 155mm howitzer. Both the howitzer and the rocket system were employed by some *NATO armies in the 1970s and 1980s.

In the 1990s, the U.S. Army started laying the foundations to introduce leap-ahead artillery technology. It would include digital command, control, and communication systems; fire-and-forget munitions; and new propellants to give unprecedented ranges.

Although artillery technology had changed greatly since the colonial era, the basic role of artillery on the battlefield remained constant. Field artillery still provided close support of infantry and now armor (replacing cavalry). Coastal artillery had become obsolete due to high-velocity naval ordnance and especially aircraft and missiles. Yet air defense artillery had emerged to take on a defensive mission against the new skyborne weapons.

[See also Army Combat Branches: Artillery; Nuclear Weapons; Weaponry, Army.]

• Albert Manucy, Artillery Through the Ages: A Short Illustrated History of Cannon, Emphasizing Types Used in America, 1949. Fairfax Downey, Sound of the Guns: The Story of American Artillery, 1956. Kenneth P. Werrell, Archie, Flak, AAA, and Sam, 1988. Boyd L. Dastrup, King of Battle: A Branch History of the U.S. Army's Field Artillery, 1992. Bruce I. Gudmundson, On Artillery, 1993. Boyd L. Dastrup, Modernizing the King of Battle: 1973–1991, 1994.
—Boyd L. Dastrup

ASPIN, LES, JR. (1938–1995), member of Congress, secretary of defense. Aspin was a loyalist critic of the U.S. defense establishment. Born in Milwaukee, the son of a British immigrant, he earned degrees at Yale, Oxford, and MIT. In 1966–68, he worked as a policy analyst for Secretary of Defense Robert *McNamara. Aspin became convinced that the *Pentagon was making many mistakes in Vietnam and in Washington.

Returning to Wisconsin, he taught briefly at Marquette University, then won election to the House of Representatives as a liberal, anti–*Vietnam War Democrat. Serving in the House from 1971 to 1993, Aspin found and publicized evidence of waste, mismanagement, and fraud, exposing evidence of Pentagon cost overruns, corruption, and abuse of privileges. In 1975, he helped overthrow autocratic F. Edward Hébert as head of the House Armed Forces Committee.

Unlike most liberal, antiwar Democrats, however, Aspin was committed to strengthening the military, not diminishing it. As he became more conservative, he broke with many liberals and supported a 5 percent annual growth in military spending, as well as draft registration, and the MX missile. In 1985, Aspin became chair of the Armed Forces Committee, continuing his drive to streamline defense spending and curtail procurement abuses while encouraging modernization. He was a key supporter of President George *Bush's decision to fight Iraq in 1991.

Appointed President Clinton's first secretary of defense in 1993, Aspin was forced out after a controversial year involving Somalia, gays in the military, and a "bottom up" review of U.S. defense strategy and structure. He died two years later of a stroke.

[See also Defense, Department of.]
—John Whiteclay Chambers II

ASTRONAUTS. See Space Program, Military Involvement in the.

ATLANTA, BATTLE OF (1864). Throughout May, June, and early July 1864, the *Union army of Maj. Gen. William Tecumseh *Sherman advanced through northern Georgia toward Atlanta while the Confederate army of Gen. Joseph E. *Johnston, to the increasing alarm of the Richmond authorities, retreated in front of it. Finally, on 17 July, President Jefferson *Davis acted, replacing Johnston with the aggressive Gen. John Bell *Hood.

By this time the *Confederate army was backed into the very outskirts of Atlanta, and Hood had no choice but to fight or abandon the city. On 20 July, he attacked Federal troops under Maj. Gen. George H. *Thomas near Peachtree Creek (the Battle of Peachtree Creek). Hood's plan went awry and the result was a bloody repulse.

Two days later, Hood struck again, in what is called the Battle of Atlanta. His target this time was a Federal force under Maj. Gen. James B. McPherson. Hood's plan was a good one, a flanking maneuver of his own, and this time it was tolerably well executed. Lt. Gen. William J. Hardee led his Confederate force on a long, tiring night march to gain the Federal rear. While he attacked from that direction, Confederates under Maj. Gen. Benjamin F. Cheatham were to attack the Union front. Hood, who was hampered by a crippled arm and a missing leg, was not personally present on the battlefield, and afterward he complained that Hardee had not positioned his troops as directed. Hardee, who resented being passed over in favor of Hood, was sometimes uncooperative. Still, Confederates struck hard at McPherson's Federals in a fierce day-long battle. The result went against the Southerners. Two Union divisions of Maj. Gen. Grenville Dodge's corps had, the night before, taken up a position that allowed them to blunt Hardee's attack. That, along with exceptionally hard fighting on the part of McPherson's men, produced Hood's defeat, but not before McPherson himself had been killed and John A. Logan had taken his place. On the Confederate side, Maj. Gen. William H. T. Walker was killed. Just over 30,000 Federals were engaged against nearly 40,000 Confederates. Federal *casualties were 3,722; Confederate losses are harder to pinpoint, but the best estimate is 7,000.

Six days later, Sherman tried yet another turning maneuver, and Hood responded again, attacking the Federals at the Battle of Ezra Church and again suffering a bloody repulse. After that, operations settled down to a quasi-siege of Atlanta. Hood's three sorties had cost him heavily in casualties and failed to gain battlefield success. Nevertheless, they had prevented Sherman from taking the city that month and forced the Union commander to show more caution in his future operations. Though Atlanta fell to Sherman on 2 September 1864, it is likely that Hood's installation as commander had delayed that event six weeks beyond the time it would have happened had Johnston remained in command.

[See also Civil War: Military and Diplomatic Course.]

• Richard M. McMurry, *John Bell Hood and the War for Southern Independence,* 1982. Albert Castel, *Decision in the West: The Atlanta Campaign of 1864,* 1992.
                                                    —Steven E. Woodworth

ATOMIC BOMB. *See* Nuclear Weapons; Hiroshima and Nagasaki, Bombings of (1945); Atomic Scientists; Manhattan Project.

ATOMIC SCIENTISTS. From the moment when Albert Einstein in 1940 suggested to President Franklin D. *Roosevelt, that a new and decisive military weapon, the atom bomb, might be developed from the phenomenon of the nuclear chain reaction, atomic scientists assumed a critical role in the development of weaponry that would change the nature of modern warfare. Important scientists involved at this early stage included the physicists Niels *Bohr and Leo *Szilard, and some of them opposed the use of *nuclear weapons against Japan in 1945. The scientific knowledge and skills required to create such weapons— first the atom bomb and then the hydrogen bomb—separated this small group of scientists from their fellows, initially because of the extraordinary security requirements of the *Manhattan Project, the program to design and build the first atomic bomb. Later, the weight of responsibility for creating a device that could for the first time destroy civilization led them to become involved in the most fundamental issues of international policy.

In 1953, J. Robert *Oppenheimer, the scientific leader of the Manhattan Project, had his security clearances revoked by President Dwight D. *Eisenhower, ostensibly because of admitted violations of security procedures; however, it was generally believed that the action was taken because of Oppenheimer's opposition to the development of the even more destructive hydrogen bomb, which was vigorously pressed by the chairman of the Atomic Energy Commission, Adm. Lewis Strauss. During the security proceeding before the commission, Oppenheimer's colleague and close associate, the physicist Edward *Teller, testified against him. As a result, Teller himself was ostracized by a large part of the atomic science community, symbolizing a fundamental division of opinion on nuclear weapons policy.

Other scientists prominent in the development of the atomic bomb included the physicists Hans Bethe and Enrico *Fermi, the chemist George Kistiakowsky, and the mathematician John von *Neumann, whose invention of the high-speed computer was critical in the development process.

As the nuclear policy concerns of government policymakers have moved from building a nuclear arsenal to assuring that many atomic weapons could survive an attack and then retaliate (a "secure second strike capability"), to negotiating international agreements to reduce the likelihood of a nuclear exchange and control the spread of nuclear weapons, and now to the eventual abolition of nuclear weapons, atomic scientists have been involved at every stage. They served as technical experts but also as proponents of policy options. The creation of the office of science adviser to the president, and of the president's Science Advisory Committee, provided significant input on nuclear policy, particularly during the incumbency as science advisers of George Kistiakowsky under President Eisenhower, and Jerome Wiesner under President John F. *Kennedy.

The atomic science community has tended to support more severe constraints on the use of nuclear weapons, somewhat in contrast to the attitudes of political scientists, who seem more willing, in Herman Kahn's phrase, to think about the unthinkable. Even before the end of the Cold War, and in the face of rigorous security arrangements, atomic scientists in the West were able to develop working relationships with Soviet colleagues concerned about avoiding nuclear holocaust. On the other hand, the scientists on the staff of the nuclear weapons laboratories have persisted, perhaps understandably, in arguing and lobbying for continued testing of nuclear weapons, even in the face of international agreement on the Comprehensive Test Ban Treaty.

With the parallel development of fissionable materials as a potential source of energy for peacetime use, atomic scientists have also been involved in discussions on how to minimize the production of weapons-grade materials, as byproducts of nuclear reactors, and how to deal with the problem of nuclear waste.

The creation of the first atom bomb called for the highest levels of scientific creativity; but it is generally acknowledged that today, many well-named scientists would be able to fabricate at least a crude nuclear device. The focus of concern within the atomic science community has therefore shifted to more sophisticated technical problems of delivery, reliability, and control, with a consequent splintering of scientific expertise. The dynamic that continues to exert most force on the community is the awareness of the destructive power that their science has unleashed.

[*See also* Bush, Vannevar; Cold War: Domestic Course.]

• Charles P. Curtis, *The Oppenheimer Case,* 1955. Gene M. Lyons and Louis Morton, *Schools for Strategy,* 1965. George Kistiakowsky, *A Scientist in the White House,* 1976. Gregg Herken, *The Winning Weapon,* 1980. Fred Kaplan, *The Wizards of Armageddon,* 1983.
                                                    —Adam Yarmolinsky

ATROCITIES are acts of wartime violence whose cruelty or brutality exceeds martial necessity. Such acts include looting, torture, rape, and massacre—the killing of captive troops or civilians. The contentious issue of atrocity has arisen in all American wars, typically as a rallying cry against enemies, but also when American troops have committed unmerciful acts.

Beginning with the 1637 Pequot War, conflicts with eastern Native Americans were bloody. Punishing the Pequots for the death of an English trader, Massachusetts militia attacked men, women, and children at the stockaded Mystic village, setting it ablaze and shooting escapees. Celebrating their rivals' destruction, the victors set an enduring pattern in Indian-white relations. Anglo-Americans decried Mohawk, Miami, Seminole, or Creek attacks on their settlements or troops as massacres, but praised no less brutal strikes against Indian villages as just.

Distrust of English rule grew after the *Boston Massacre, in which royal soldiers fatally shot five members of a protest mob in 1770. During the *Revolutionary War, when bayonet-wielding British troops ambushed and routed sleeping colonial militia at Paoli in 1777, some Americans retaliated by denying quarter to their foe at Germantown. Frontier fighting between patriots and loyalists, especially in the South, was particularly ruthless.

Mid-nineteenth-century wars saw efforts to curb atrocity. But in 1836, Mexican troops killed all 187 defenders in the Battle of the *Alamo and executed 330 prisoners at Goliad. Thus, when vengeful Texans under Sam Houston overran the Mexicans at the Battle of *San Jacinto, they shot, clubbed, and stabbed to death enemy soldiers (some wounded) begging for mercy. During the 1846 U.S. invasion of Mexico, newspapers reported pillage, rape, and murder of civilians by Gen. Zachary *Taylor's soldiers. Consequently, Gen. Winfield *Scott set a code of conduct enforceable by military courts.

In the *Civil War, the federal government issued General Order 100 to limit battlefield excesses. The first man executed under it was Confederate Henry C. Wirz, commandant of the most infamous of Civil War *prisoner-of-war camps—Andersonville. Public outrage over the deaths of thousands of Union soldiers by starvation, exposure, and disease overrode evidence that Wirz did everything in his power to improve conditions. In another controversial case, a Confederate brigade under Nathan Bedford *Forrest overwhelmed a Union garrison in the Battle of *Fort Pillow, Tennessee, in 1864, slaying 60 percent of the defenders. Sparing one-half of the white Federals but killing over four-fifths of the black soldiers, Forrest's men seemingly committed a calculated racist massacre. Congressional hearings yielded contradictory testimony, but prompted no trials.

Late nineteenth-century authorities contended that laws governing combat between "civilized" powers did not apply to irregular warfare and "uncivilized" foes. The Colorado volunteer militia's 1864 *Sand Creek Massacre of 105 Cheyenne women and children inspired Indian depredations against settlers and the dismemberment of 81 U.S. soldiers in the 1866 Fetterman Massacre. In Gen. George Armstrong *Custer's 1868 Washita raid, only 13 of 103 Cheyenne killed were warriors. Thwarting a U.S. raid at the Battle of the *Little Bighorn in 1876, Sioux and Cheyenne braves took no prisoners, killing Custer and 265 of his men. At the Battle of *Wounded Knee, 1890, the Seventh Cavalry ended the cycle of retribution by slaughtering 200 Sioux refugees.

During the 1899–1902 *Philippine War, some American commanders allegedly condoned atrocities, including denying quarter, indiscriminate burnings, and torture of prisoners and civilians. Reacting to the 1901 Balangiga massacre, in which Filipino guerrillas hacked to death thirty-nine U.S. soldiers, Gen. Jacob Smith told officers to make the island of Samar a "howling wilderness" and kill any males over the age of ten. Though not implemented as policy, his directive exonerated one subordinate who illegally executed civilians.

Reaction to atrocity contributed to U.S. involvement in both world wars and in *war crimes tribunals. In 1915, Americans shuddered at reports of Germany's ruthless Belgian occupation (made even more lurid by British reportage) and Berlin's use of *submarines—most notably the sinking of the *Lusitania, a British passenger liner, in which 1,200 passengers (128 of them Americans) died. The 1937 "Rape of Nanjing" (260,000 Chinese civilians and POWs were killed and as many as 30,000 women sexually assaulted) helped fix the Japanese government in the American mind as a rogue regime. The attack on *Pearl Harbor and the April 1942 Bataan Death March, in which 15,000 American and Filipino prisoners died from abuse and starvation in the Philippines, seemed to confirm the perception of Japanese barbarity. Even more horrific was the genocidal policy of Nazi Germany, whose systematic liquidation of millions of civilians, including two-thirds of

European Jews, shocked global opinion into united action. After 1945, international courts convicted and executed many Axis officials for war crimes against humanity.

In the *Vietnam War, U.S. officials emphasized the Communist insurgents' campaigns of kidnapping and assassination, but downplayed atrocities of their Saigon allies. U.S. Army suppression of reports of American participation in the *My Lai Massacre inflamed national anger at the 1968 slaughter of 200 unarmed villagers, damaging public confidence in the war effort. A 1971 court-martial condemned Lt. William L. Calley to life in prison for the crime, a sentence later commuted.

Charges of atrocity justified U.S. military involvement in *Somalia, Bosnia, and Kosovo, as well as the *Persian Gulf War. Reported abuse of civilians during Iraq's 1990 occupation of Kuwait galvanized an international coalition to reverse the invasion and attempt to supervise the elimination of Saddam *Hussein's offensive arsenals. Seeking to end the deplorable famine and factional violence in Somalia, U.S. troops safeguarded relief efforts in 1992–93, but could not stop the vicious fighting. Outrages in the *Bosnian Crisis ("ethnic cleansing" and the use of *land mines, *artillery, and snipers against civilians) eventually led to 20,000 U.S. troops joining *NATO forces to police that area of the former Yugoslavia. The same occurred in the *Kosovo Crisis (1999).

[See also Geneva Conventions; Genocide; Holocaust, U.S. War Effort and the; Native American Wars: Wars Between Native Americans and Europeans and Euro-Americans.]

• Leon Friedman, The Law and War: A Documentary History, 2 vols., 1972. Richard R. Lael, The Yamashita Precedent: War Crimes and Command Responsibility, 1982.

—James Grant Crawford

AVF. See All-Volunteer Force.

AWACS AND E-3S. The AWACS—for Airborne Warning and Control System—is a specialized military aircraft intended for long-range air surveillance and control. Development of the AWACS—more specifically known as the Boeing E-3 Sentry—began in 1961, as the latest in a long line of previous *radar-equipped early warning aircraft. But unlike these earlier aircraft, intended primarily to operate over the ocean, the E-3 was to operate over land and in much more integrated fashion with supporting *fighter aircraft. These two requirements demanded refinements in radar development and *communications far beyond what had been expected of earlier airborne warning aircraft.

Airborne warning aircraft were first developed as a response to the threat of Japan's kamikaze attackers in the later Pacific War. The U.S. Navy acquired a small number of Boeing B-17 Flying Fortresses, removed the bomb bay from the aircraft, and replaced it with a belly-mounted radar, designating the new airplane the PB-1. It foreshadowed a number of subsequent aircraft, both large and small, for the early warning and air control role. One notable example was the air force Lockheed C-121 Warning Star aircraft, which helped direct air operations over North Vietnam and, in particular, warn American strike aircraft of the presence, location, and strength of opposing North Vietnamese MiG fighters.

Development of the AWACS took over a decade. Boeing flew the first AWACS testbed in 1972, based on a modified jet transport. At the same time, Westinghouse won a competition to produce the critical airborne radar that would perch above the transport, giving it a vaguely "flying saucer" shape. The first production E-3 entered service with the U.S. Air Force in 1977. Subsequently, advanced models of the aircraft have been sold to the air force, as well as to *NATO, Great Britain, France, and Saudi Arabia.

Key to the AWACS, in addition to its radar, is its comprehensive electronic equipment, including the Have Quick secure voice communications system, the Joint Tactical Information Display System (JTIDS), the Mark XV Identification Friend or Foe (IFF) radar, and the Navstar Global Position System space-based location system. Over twenty crewmen operate the AWACS systems in flight, and it is data-linked to other aircraft and to ground stations.

The value of AWACS was clearly demonstrated during the *Persian Gulf War (1991). In that conflict, AWACS aircraft operated by the U.S. Air Force and the Royal Saudi Air Force managed and controlled over 3,000 coalition aircraft sorties per day. They detected Iraqi threats, and helped pair targets with strike aircraft. They "deconflicted" the air war, preventing so-called "blue-on-blue" attacks. Further, their comprehensive control capabilities enabled the coalition to conduct the war without a single aircraft lost due to a midair collision.

[*See also* Intelligence, Military and Political.]

• Benson, Lawrence R. "Sentries Over Europe: First Decade of the E-3 Airborne Warning and Control System in NATO Europe." HQ USAF Europe, Office of History, February 10, 1983. Breslin, Vincent C. "Development of the Airborne Warning and Control System and the E-3A Brassboard, 1961–1972." Hanscom AFB, MA: AFSC ESD History Office, June 1983. In AF Historical Research Agency Archives, Maxwell AFB, Ala, as Call No. K243.016. Sun, Jack K. "AWACS Radar Program: "The Eyes of the Eagle." Westinghouse Corporation, June 1, 1985. Tessmer, Arnold Lee. "The Politics of Compromise: A Study of NATO AWACS." Washington: NDU Research Directorate, March 19, 1982. Document 1272A, Archive No. 0171A. Williams, George K. "AWACS and JSTARS," in Jacob Neufeld, and George M. Watson, Jr., eds., *Technology and the Air Force: A Retrospective Assessment,* Washington, DC: AF History and Museums Program, 1997. ——Richard P. Hallion

AWARDS, DECORATIONS, AND HONORS. One of the oldest traditions in the profession of arms is the recognition of heroic feats of arms against an armed enemy. The ancient Greeks awarded crowns, the Romans torques and decorative discs. This ancient tradition is carried on in the U.S. awards and decorations system, which includes six medals that recognize heroism on the field of battle. To these are added two other types of awards, one recognizing meritorious service that is a response to the importance of administrative and logistical efficiency in modern warfare; the other recognizing participation in campaigns and completion of overseas tours.

The American system of decorations began in 1782, when George *Washington established the Badge of Military Merit to recognize "instances of unusual gallantry" as well as "extraordinary fidelity" and "essential service." The actual decoration was a heart-shaped piece of purple cloth that was sewn to the recipient's uniform coat. Largely forgotten after the *Revolutionary War, this decoration was revived by the War Department as the Purple Heart in 1932, the 200th anniversary of Washington's Birthday. In its new form, this decoration recognizes military personnel

wounded or killed in combat and does not in itself constitute an award for heroic action.

America's highest award for gallantry, the Medal of Honor (often mistakenly called the Congressional Medal of Honor), was established during the *Civil War. Originally, it was used to recognize both gallantry in combat and meritorious performance, but by the end of the nineteenth century the standard for awarding this medal had become "conspicuous gallantry and intrepidity at the risk of life above and beyond the call of duty."

During World War I, two more decorations for heroism were added. The Distinguished Service Cross (Army), the Navy Cross, and the Air Force Cross (added in 1960) all recognize bravery that falls short of that required for the Medal of Honor. The second medal, the Silver Star, is awarded by all service for gallantry that is less noteworthy than that required for a service cross.

Finally, there are three other decorations that recognize varying degrees of gallantry in combat: the Distinguished Flying Cross (authorized by Congress in 1926); the Bronze Star (authorized by executive order in 1944); and the Air Medal (established by executive order in 1942). All three of these medals may also be used to recognize outstanding service or special achievements that do not necessarily entail bravery in the face of an armed enemy. When the Bronze Star is awarded for heroic action, it is worn with a small bronze "V" device that stands for valor. Without the V, the Bronze Star recognizes meritorious service in support of combat operations. Multiple awards of all decorations are indicated through a system of small metallic oak clusters and stars that are affixed to medals.

In addition to medals recognizing heroism in combat, each service has a decoration for heroism and risk of life outside of combat: the Soldier's Medal, the Navy and Marine Corps Medal, and the Airman's Medal.

Modern combat units became increasingly dependent upon support forces, whose personnel came to outnumber those in combat commands by nearly ten to one. Moreover, throughout the *Cold War, crews manning strategic weapons systems endured long hours on alert or patrol with virtually no opportunity to perform a heroic feat of arms. The need to recognize the contributions of personnel serving in noncombat roles gave rise to a second set of military decorations.

The highest-ranking award in this second set is the Defense Distinguished Service Medal, bestowed by the secretary of defense. Just below this decoration are the Army Distinguished Service Medal (DSM) and the Navy DSM, established by Congress in 1918 and 1919, respectively; an air force version was added in 1960. These medals call for "specially meritorious service to the Government in a duty of great responsibility." Rounding out this set of awards are several other Department of *Defense decorations and military service medals that recognize lower levels of achievement and meritorious service. Finally, the Air Force Combat Readiness Medal was established to recognize the sacrifice of service members who spent much, if not all, of their professional careers in roles related to deterring nuclear war.

The expansion of U.S. overseas service requirements was accompanied by a steady rise in the number of decorations recognizing such factors as participation in a campaign and completion of an overseas deployment, even in peacetime. This began in 1898, when the Dewey Medal was authorized for those who participated in the Battle of *Manila Bay. Another form of participatory award is the unit citation, which recognizes those who serve in a unit that accomplished its mission in a superior manner. An example of this type of award is the Presidential Unit Citation.

Medals are usually worn only on ceremonial occasions. For routine, daily wear, each medal comes with a small oblong swatch that matches the pattern of the suspension ribbon.

Napoleon's comment to the effect that soldiers will risk their lives for a little piece of colored ribbon indicates the extreme importance the military attaches to its decorations for combat heroism. However, the criteria for awarding medals are highly subjective. Controversies relating to U.S. military decorations can be traced back as far as the *Civil War, when the Medal of Honor was awarded under questionable circumstances on several occasions. During World War II, the number of decorations awarded raised serious questions about the significance of medals. In the course of this war, the army (which still included the Army Air Forces, AAF) gave out a total of 1,800,739 medals. Of these, 1,314,000, or 73 percent, went to personnel of the AAF although they accounted for only 28 percent of the total personnel strength of the army. Similar problems have occurred right down to the *Persian Gulf War of 1991.

As the ratio of support forces to combat forces increased dramatically in the twentieth century, new awards to recognize and motivate support personnel proliferated, skewing the awards and decorations system toward meritorious service and mere participation in military activities. By the mid-1990s, the situation had reached the point where medals recognizing heroic combat service were often lost among the multiple rows of ribbons worn by virtually every career member of the armed services, the vast majority of whom had never been subjected to enemy fire. The U.S. awards and decorations system had yielded much of its traditional function of recognizing those who demonstrated extraordinary courage in combat.

[*See also* Commemoration and Public Ritual; Ideals, Military; Insignia; Uniforms.]

• Robert E. Wyllie, *Orders, Decorations and Insignia, Military and Civil,* 1921. Robert Werlich, *Orders and Decorations of All Nations: Ancient and Modern; Civilian and Military,* 1964. Evans E. Kerrigan, *American War Medals and Decorations,* 1990.

—Donald Baucom

B

BACON'S REBELLION (1676). Nathaniel Bacon arrived in Virginia in 1674 with money for land and impeccable connections to the colony's elite. Two years later he died of swamp fever, the leader of a rebel army made up of former indentured servants. Bacon's transformation from gentleman planter to rebel ringleader united two potent animosities in colonial Virginia: the colonists' hatred of Indians and small freeholders' hatred of land-monopolizing gentry.

Smallholders on Virginia's frontier had long-running disputes with the Susquehannocks north of the James River and with the colony's elite. The sources of the freemen's anger converged in 1676 when Governor William Berkeley, fearing the outbreak of Indian war, discountenanced Bacon's plans to lead a frontier army against the Indians and refused him a commission. Bacon planned to exterminate the Indians in the colony, and attack those beyond its border; Berkeley reasonably insisted on distinguishing between friendly and hostile Indians. In June, Bacon and five hundred men traveled to Jamestown to confront Berkeley. The governor eventually granted the commission and authorized Bacon to raise an army; Berkeley then fled Jamestown and sent to England for troops.

While Bacon's followers sought out Indians to enslave or massacre, Berkeley and Bacon waged a recruiting war, vying for the loyalty of servants and small landowners. In October, Bacon died and his rebellion fizzled. British troops arriving in 1677 confronted a puny rebel force: eighty slaves and twenty servants.

A class brawl within an Indian conflict, Bacon's Rebellion revealed the mixed motivations and tangled outcomes of warfare in colonial America. The revolt changed little within the colony; gentlemen continued to monopolize the best land, the highest offices, and the most slaves. The Indians suffered the most. Those within the colony lost population and land; the Susquehannocks to the north were decimated by Iroquois warriors, who seized the opportunity to attack. By the 1680s, the Susquehannocks existed only as Iroquois dependents, and the Iroquois were free to sell their lands to colonial planters.

[*See also* Colonial Rebellions and Armed Civil Unrest; Native American Wars: Wars Between Native Americans and Europeans and Euro-Americans.]

• Wilcomb E. Washburn, *The Governor and the Rebel*, 1957. Edmund S. Morgan, *American Slavery, American Freedom*, 1975.
　　　　　　　　　　　　　　　　　　—Jon T. Coleman

BAKER, NEWTON D. (1871–1937), urban reformer, secretary of war. The career of Newton D. Baker, Woodrow *Wilson's second secretary of war (1916–21), was paradoxical. A compassionate man, he balanced concern for justice with commitment to order. A man of peace, he became an accomplished warmaker. A social reformer, he did little to combat wartime racial and political prejudice in the army. An antimilitarist, he supported national *conscription. A man with no experience in foreign affairs, he supervised the movement of the *American Expeditionary Forces (AEF) to France and protected their independence against the French and British who attempted to amalgamate them with their own armies. The rather unimposing, bespectacled, owlish-looking cabinet officer thus gave President Wilson a strong hand at the peace table and achieved recognition as a successful secretary of war.

A lawyer and reform Democratic mayor of Cleveland, Baker had a reputation as a pacifist as well as an efficient administrator when Wilson appointed him to succeed Lindley Garrison in March 1916 on the eve of the U.S. Punitive Expedition into Mexico. Unlike Garrison, who had been won over by the generals and the Republican-based Preparedness movement, Baker always remained loyal to Wilson. In the War Department he was a conciliator and kept congenial connections between his office, the General Staff, and the army's bureau chiefs as long as possible. Even during the war production and transportation crisis in the winter of 1917–18 he refused to act hastily; it was April 1918 before authority was adequately concentrated in the General Staff and the War Industries Board. Baker also refused to resolve command issues between the War Department and the AEF. In the struggle between Gen. John J. *Pershing and Chief of Staff Peyton C. *March for the control of military policy, Baker did not decide in March's favor until the war was nearly over. The secretary believed that most problems were resolved if left alone. After the war, he remained an outspoken Wilsonian internationalist and was a candidate for the Democratic presidential nomination in 1924.

[*See also* World War I: Domestic Course.]

• Frederick Palmer, *Newton D. Baker: America at War*, 2 vols., 1933. Daniel R. Beaver, *Newton D. Baker and the American War Effort 1917–1918*, 1966.
　　　　　　　　　　　　　　　　　—Daniel R. Beaver

BALCH, EMILY GREENE (1867–1961), pacifist, feminist, and Nobel Peace Prize winner. Born in Massachusetts, educated at Bryn Mawr College, Balch became an economics professor at Wellesley College until 1919, when she was fired for her antiwar activities during World War I. She was one of the founders and leaders of the Woman's Peace Party (1915–19) and the *Women's International League for Peace and Freedom (WILPF), founded in Zurich in 1919. She served as WILPF's international secretary from 1919 to 1922 and in a number of other leadership positions until her retirement in 1950. Her belief in transnational ideals, *nonviolence, and justice, as well as her commitment to women's equality and freedom, shaped her approach to peace activism. A "practical" pacifist and feminist, Balch held that, as responsible citizens, women must work to end war by promoting just and nonviolent alternatives such as disarmament and peaceful international processes for conflict resolution and for meeting human needs. Believing most strongly that cooperative international endeavors offered the first steps toward peace, Balch proposed plans for mediation of the conflicts in Manchuria and Spain during the 1930s. She was one of two recipients of the Nobel Peace Prize in 1946.

[See also Addams, Jane; Pacifism.]

• Mercedes M. Randall, Improper Bostonian: Emily Greene Balch, 1964. Mercedes M. Randall, ed., Beyond Nationalism: The Social Thought of Emily Greene Balch, 1972. Anne Marie Pois, "Foreshadowing: Jane Addams, Emily Greene Balch, and the Ecofeminism/Pacifist Feminism of the 1980s," Peace & Change: A Journal of Peace Research, Vol. 20, No. 4 (October 1995): 439–465.

—Anne Marie Pois

BALL, GEORGE (1909–1994), undersecretary of state. As undersecretary of state (1961–66) under Presidents Kennedy and Johnson, George W. Ball achieved his greatest prominence as the highest-ranking U.S. official to oppose, consistently but unsuccessfully, the decisions to increase the American military role during the *Vietnam War.

President Kennedy appointed him assistant secretary of state for economic affairs in 1961. After the Bay of Pigs disaster, Ball was promoted to undersecretary of state. He took issue with the Taylor-Rostow mission in 1961, which advocated the introduction of U.S. combat troops into Vietnam. Ball saw the United States becoming involved in a revolutionary war with little hope of eventual success; he argued that U.S. military resources were better deployed in Europe.

Ball's opposition to American involvement in the war continued throughout the Johnson administration, but this opposition proved futile, and he left the administration in 1966 to return to his law practice. He remained personally and publicly loyal to the president, and his determined opposition to American involvement in the war became widely known only after the publication of the *Pentagon Papers in 1971. He later served as U.S. delegate to the *United Nations and as an adviser on Iran to President Jimmy *Carter.

• Lyndon B. Johnson, The Vantage Point: Perspectives of the Presidency, 1963–1969, 1971. George W. Ball, The Past Has Another Pattern: Memoirs, 1982.

—Herbert Y. Schandler

BANCROFT, GEORGE (1800–1891), historian, secretary of the navy, diplomat. Appointed James K. Polk's first secretary of the U.S. *Navy in March 1845, Bancroft initiated a number of important reforms of the naval service during his seventeen months in office. The most important of these was the establishment of a permanent naval academy for the education and training of young officers. In a feat of administrative legerdemain, Bancroft found funds, teachers, and a site for a school without resort to Congress. It opened 10 October 1845 with lawmakers agreeing to fund the new academy the following year. Bancroft took other steps to rehabilitate an officer corps grown moribund in

the decades following the *War of 1812. He argued for promotions based on merit rather than seniority; he sought legislation for removing old and unfit officers from the ranks; and he ordered candidates for certain officers' grades to demonstrate their fitness for appointment by passing examinations. Though not all of Bancroft's attempts at reform met with success, his efforts laid the foundation for a better-trained, more professional officer corps. Bancroft also provided vigorous and able direction of the navy's initial efforts during the *Mexican War. On his orders, navy squadrons blockaded Mexico, occupied several Pacific Coast towns, and provided valuable assistance to American land forces. In September 1846, Bancroft left the secretaryship to become minister to Great Britain.

[See also Academies, Service: U.S. Naval Academy.]

• Mark Anthony de Wolf Howe, Life and Letters of George Bancroft, 2 vols., 1908. Lilian Handlin, George Bancroft: The Intellectual as Democrat, 1984.

—Charles E. Brodine, Jr.

BARTON, CLARA (1821–1912), *Civil War nurse, relief worker, and founder of the American *Red Cross. Raised in a quiet New England family, Clara Barton taught, founded a public school in New Jersey, and in 1854 became a copyist in the U.S. Patent Office. In 1861, the Civil War catapulted her to national prominence. During the first two years, Barton functioned as a one-woman relief agency. Relying on the assistance of a few sympathetic politicians and friends, and shunning official channels of the U.S. *Sanitary Commission and Dorothea *Dix's nursing corps, Barton brought supplies and relief to thousands of suffering Union soldiers on fields in the Eastern theater. Her timely arrivals from *Fredericksburg to *Antietam earned her the nickname "Angel of the Battlefield." In June 1864, she agreed to serve as head nurse in the Army of the James.

As the Civil War, especially early on, afforded few official roles for women, Barton could carve out an independent niche and use her status to bypass the formidable military bureaucracy. Throughout, she sought to bring humanity and personal dignity to the war; to counteract the brutal and dehumanizing affects of modern, large-scale carnage. Although her relief activities abated somewhat later in the war, she began in February 1865 the herculean effort of identifying missing men. Much of her attention focused on the unknown dead of Andersonville Prison, securing the identification of nearly 11,000 in that infamous pen.

When the Civil War ended, Barton continued her mission of humanizing the horrors of military suffering. She worked tirelessly for U.S. ratification of the *Geneva Conventions of 1864 (conferring neutrality on wounded and hospital personnel in war), and in 1881, organized the American Association of the Red Cross. In 1898, she personally led Red Cross relief efforts in Cuba during the *Spanish-American War.

• Rev. William E. Barton, Life of Clara Barton, 2 vols., 1922. Stephen Oates, A Woman of Valor: Clara Barton and the Civil War, 1994.

—Nina Silber

BARUCH, BERNARD M. (1870–1965), financier and political adviser. In matters of war and national security, Baruch was a major administrator during World War I, an important influence on Democratic congressional leaders from 1918 to 1948, and an intermittent consultant to

Democratic presidents. Son of a German Jewish immigrant and his southern wife, Baruch was born in Camden, South Carolina, but moved with his family to New York City, where he graduated from City College in 1889. Successful on Wall Street, he was a millionaire by the age of thirty.

Baruch became a friend of Woodrow *Wilson and many Democrats in Congress. In World War I, Wilson appointed Baruch to several *mobilization posts, most importantly (1918) chair of the War Industries Board (WIB), then designated the major civilian agency for industrial mobilization. Not the "czar" described in the press, Baruch worked largely by persuasion rather than coercion. Furthermore, there were other agencies, and the military retained independent contracting authority. Nevertheless, at the WIB and on the President's War Council, Baruch was at the center of the government's mobilization. The WIB's success established Baruch's reputation as an industrial statesman. Wilson took him as an economic adviser to the Paris peace talks.

In the interwar years, Baruch—who believed in business-government cooperation—encouraged industrial-military planning through the new Army Industrial College and through the War Department's Industrial Mobilization Plan of 1930 and its subsequent revisions.

During World War II, Baruch urged a new WIB, but President Roosevelt, concerned with his own prerogatives, ignored this advice. Denied administrative power, Baruch still maintained political influence, primarily through his influence in Congress and friendships with the heads of mobilization agencies.

In 1946, President Truman asked Baruch to formulate a postwar international policy for atomic energy. The Baruch Plan proposed guarding America's atomic secrets and its production of atomic bombs until an international agency, over which the USSR would not have a veto, established full control of manufacturing plants anywhere in the world. The Soviet Union rejected it. During the *Korean War, Baruch, fearful of inflation, tried unsuccessfully to get the Truman administration to impose price and wage controls. By then, however, Baruch had lost his great influence.

[See also Industry and War.]

• Bernard M. Baruch, *Baruch: My Own Story,* 1957. Bernard M. Baruch, *Baruch: The Public Years,* 1960. Jordan A. Schwarz, *The Speculator: Bernard M. Baruch in Washington, 1917–1965,* 1981.
—John Whiteclay Chambers II

BASES, MILITARY: DEVELOPMENT OF. Providing a secure site from which to operate, military bases can be temporary wartime installations or long-term facilities. Strategic planning drives their necessity, but other considerations often determine their location, particularly in peacetime.

With the creation of a permanent U.S. *Army after the *Revolutionary War, the primary bases for the standing army and its supplies were established at West Point, New York, and at Fort Pitt (later Fort Fayette), at what is now Pittsburgh, Pennsylvania, an indication of the regular army's missions of coastal and frontier defense. Bases served as military headquarters, barracks, training fields, and storage depots. Later bases would be created in a number of the seacoast *fortifications such as Fort Jay (1794)

on Governors Island in New York Harbor and Fortress Monroe (1823) at Point Comfort on Hampton Roads, Virginia, where the Coastal Artillery School was situated.

U.S. expansion in the first half of the nineteenth century saw the establishment of a string of army outposts across the country, including Jefferson Barracks, St. Louis, Missouri (1826), where the Infantry School was established, Fort Leavenworth, Kansas (1827), which later became the site for both the military prison and the Command and General Staff College; and Carlisle Barracks, in Carlisle, Pennsylvania (1842), site of the Army War College in the twentieth century.

When the U.S. *Navy was established in 1794, permanent navy yards were soon created in Boston, Brooklyn, Philadelphia, Washington, and Norfolk, for the construction, repair, and berthing of ships and their preparation for sea duty. Mindful of the political and economic benefits of these bases, Congress made sure that the navy yards were dispersed among New England, the Mid-Atlantic, and the South.

When not serving afloat, members of the U.S. *Marine Corps, created in 1798, guarded navy yards, drilled, and maintained discipline. In 1800, the Marine Corps commandant was relocated from Philadelphia to Washington, D.C. Consequently, Marine barracks were established there and at the other navy yards.

Acquisition of Florida, Texas, Oregon, and the Mexican territories led to the construction of new army posts, naval bases, and Marine barracks on the Gulf and West Coasts. Among these new bases were navy yards created at Pensacola, Florida, in 1825, and Mare Island, San Francisco Bay, in 1853 (the Marine barracks founded on Mare Island in 1862 is the oldest permanent Marine Corps installation on the West Coast).

In the *Plains Indians Wars, infantry and mounted troops were quartered in wooden and adobe forts dotting the West and Southwest. Among the most famous were Fort Bliss, Texas (established 1849); Fort Bridger, Wyoming (1857); Fort Riley, Kansas (1852); Fort Laramie, Wyoming (1849); Fort Sam Houston, Texas (1876); and Fort Sill, Oklahoma (1869). Long after the Indians had been conquered, however, the economic benefit to rural congressional districts of scores of small posts prevented the army from abandoning them until just before World War I.

America's outward thrust and acquisition of an island empire after the *Spanish-American War led to the establishment of the first permanent U.S. military bases overseas. Congress was reluctant to spend outside its constituencies, and the army and navy often disagreed over the best location (for example, in the Philippines), so the major expansion of naval bases took place within the continental United States. Nevertheless, naval installations were created in Cuba, Guam, the Philippines, Hawaii (Pearl Harbor, Oahu, was designated the navy's major forward base in the Pacific in 1911), and, after 1914, in the U.S. Panama Canal Zone. By 1916, the navy had ten major continental bases (with particularly significant facilities at Newport, Rhode Island, and Norfolk, Virginia), including two new navy yards, created largely through congressional influence, at Charleston, South Carolina, and Bremerton, Washington. After 1920, the main part of the fleet was moved from the Atlantic to the Pacific; consequently, the navy bases at San Diego, Los Angeles, and Pearl Harbor grew in importance.

World War I and the creation of massive wartime armies led to the proliferation of military training camps. Although the majority of Americans lived in the North of the country, climate and congressional influence meant that a majority of training cantonments were erected in the South. Among the most important training facilities of 1917–18 were Fort Benning, Georgia (1918), which later became the nation's largest infantry training center and home of the army's Infantry School; Fort Bragg, North Carolina (1918), later the army's main airborne training center and site of the Special Warfare School; Fort Dix, New Jersey (1917), later, in World War II, to become the largest army training center in the United States; Fort George G. Meade, Maryland (1917); and Fort Knox, Kentucky (1917), which later also served as the U.S. gold depository. The Marines established a basic training camp at Parris Island, South Carolina (1917), and an officers' training camp at Quantico, Virginia (1917).

Many of these bases remained in operation or were reactivated and modernized in World War II, but new training centers were also created for that. Among the new facilities, the largest were the army's Fort Leonard Wood, Missouri (1940), and Fort Hood, Texas (1942); and the Marines' training center at Camp Lejeune, North Carolina (1942), subsequently the largest Marine base in the eastern United States.

The Army Air Service had established Langley Field, Virginia, in 1916; today, as headquarters of the Air Combat Command, it remains the oldest continuously active air force base in the United States. Other early air bases (initially called fields) for the Army Air Corps, 1926–41, included Wright-Patterson Field, Ohio (1917); Bolling Field, Washington, D.C. (1918); and Maxwell Field, Alabama (1918). Maxwell housed the Air Corps Tactical School, a major flight training center in World War II and the Air University after the war. In the 1930s, Wheeler and Hickam Fields, Hawaii, and Clark Field, in the Philippines, were created.

The Army Air Forces, 1941–47, established a number of air bases in the United States, including Andrews Army Air Base, Maryland (1942); Dover Army Air Base, Delaware (1941); and Muroc Army Base, California (1942), a combat training and experimental test site renamed Edwards Air Force Base in 1949.

It was only during World War II and the *Cold War that the United States established a network of long-term overseas bases in foreign countries. Since sovereignty resided with the host nation, major diplomatic negotiations were required for U.S. forces to be stationed there permanently or on long-term leases. Negotiations also involved issues of military necessity and use, economic compensation, legal jurisdiction, and even social fraternization. One of the first of these was the *Destroyers-for-Bases Agreement (1940), which provided for ninety-nine-year leases for U.S. naval and air bases in Newfoundland, Bermuda, and five British islands in the Caribbean.

During the war, the United States obtained other basing rights in Iceland, the Azores, Brazil, Morocco, and Great Britain. These bases supported the antisubmarine war, the ferrying of aircraft and other supplies to Britain and the Soviet Union, and ultimately the Allied invasions of North Africa, Italy, and France. In the Pacific, after the loss of Guam and the Philippines, the U.S. military established advanced bases in Australia and New Zealand for the war against Japan. The Army Air Forces created major bomber bases in Britain, North Africa, and Italy, as well as in China and in Pacific islands like Tinian. The logistics of training and supplying an army of more than 11 million were enormous and involved scores of bases throughout the world.

*Cold War containment of communism and global defense of U.S. interests during the *Korean War and the *Vietnam War led to a proliferation of major American bases overseas in the 1950s and 1960s. With its air-atomic offensive capability, the U.S. Air Force's Strategic Air Command (SAC), headquartered at Offutt Air Force Base, Nebraska (1948), was America's principal instrument of *deterrence and potential offensive operations against the Soviet Union. As part of the containment of the Soviet Union, Congress authorized an extensive system of overseas bases after the outbreak of the Korean War in 1950. SAC increased the deployment of its bombers from nineteen to thirty bases in the United States and from one to eleven bases overseas, including forward bases in England, Morocco, Spain, Libya, Greenland, Korea, and the Philippines. But when the Soviets developed *missiles in the late 1950s, and domestic dissent arose in many of the host countries, the overseas SAC bases became increasingly vulnerable both militarily and politically. Consequently, the SAC strike force was withdrawn, primarily to air bases and intercontinental ballistic missile bases in the western hemisphere.

The North Atlantic Treaty Organization (*NATO) had been expanded in 1951 to include rearmament and ground defense of West Germany; as a result, the United States stationed army divisions at bases in Heidelberg, Würzburg, and Bad Kreuznach, and aircraft at air bases at Ramstein and Rhein-Main Air Force Base near Frankfurt. The U.S. Navy's Sixth Fleet operated in the Mediterranean from a forward Italian base at Gaeta, north of Naples. In the Pacific, the navy took over the old Imperial Japanese naval yard at Yokosuka on Tokyo Bay as the forward base for the Seventh Fleet. The Third Fleet remained based at San Diego and the Second Fleet at Norfolk. The army and air force also retained major facilities in South Korea and in Japan, and particularly on the southernmost Japanese island of Okinawa, as well as Hickam Air Force Base and Schofield Barracks on Hawaii. The Marine Expeditionary Forces were based at Camps Lejeune, North Carolina; Pendleton, California; and Butler, Okinawa.

During the Vietnam War, Okinawa, Guam, and Subic Bay on Luzon in the Philippines became major advanced bases for supplying the U.S. military effort. In 1965, the United States established one of the largest military facilities in South Vietnam at Cam Ranh Bay.

As major U.S. military concerns shifted to the unstable, oil-rich Persian Gulf, an advanced U.S. naval base was established at Diego Garcia, a British atoll in the Indian Ocean. This was augmented by a new system of prepositioned, commercially leased supply ships loaded with heavy equipment and supplies, stationed in various regions. In the *Persian Gulf War of 1991, unlike the previous overseas buildups, adequate port and air facilities for the allied Coalition forces already existed.

At the end of the Cold War, downsizing of the armed forces was accompanied by major closing of bases and installations. Domestically, this politically difficult task was accomplished through a bipartisan commission, headed by former member of Congress James Courter. Its recommendations were presented to Congress on an all-or-nothing basis. Overseas, often under local pressure to withdraw or renegotiate existing treaties, the United States closed some of its oldest and largest bases, including, in the Philippines, Clark Air Force Base in 1991 after it was extensively damaged by a volcanic eruption, and Subic Bay Naval Base in 1992.

In the late 1990s, the United States came under increasing pressure to withdraw from Okinawa, which had succeeded the Philippines as the largest U.S. military base in the western Pacific. At the end of the twentieth century, it remained an open question how much further the U.S. overseas and domestic base system would be reduced.

[*See also* Bases, Military: Life on; Canada, U.S. Military Involvement in; Germany, U.S. Military Involvement in; Japan, U.S. Military Involvement in; Korea, U.S. Military Involvement in; Philippines, U.S. Military Involvement in; United Kingdom, U.S. Military Involvement in.]

• Francis Paul Prucha, *A Guide to the Military Posts of the United States, 1789–1895,* 1964. Robert W. Frazer, *Forts of the West,* 1965. Paolo E. Coletta, ed., *United States Navy and Marine Corps Bases,* 2 vols., 1985. Edward M. Coffman, *The Old Army,* 1986. Simon Duke, *U.S. Defence Bases in the United Kingdom,* 1987. William E. Berry, Jr., *U.S. Bases in the Philippines: The Evolution of the Special Relationship,* 1989. Simon Duke, *United States Military Forces and Installations in Europe,* 1989. James R. Blaker, *United States Overseas Basing: An Anatomy of the Dilemma,* 1990. "Guide to Major Air Force Installations Worldwide," *Air Force* (May 1990), pp. 122–33. Charles D. Bright, ed., *Historical Dictionary of the U.S. Air Force,* 1992.　　　　　　　　　　　　　—John Whiteclay Chambers II

BASES, MILITARY: LIFE ON. At 0600 hours (6:00 A.M.) on most U.S. military bases around the world, people are stirred from sleep by the muffled, deep-throated boom of a cannon and a rousing wake-up Reveille. Although most residents have been on duty during the night, the majority are now beginning their day. Junior enlisted personnel and their noncommissioned officers soon head for some form of physical exercise, to be followed by showers, breakfast, and a day filled with varied training experiences.

Enter that base through one of its several, often guarded, gates and you enter a world very different from civilian life and community. Certainly, it has changed over the years, but it still represents one of the earliest and most comprehensive examples of planned communities in the United States. Just as in Reston, Virginia, or Columbia, Maryland, on a military base you can work, play, shop, give birth, and bank in the place where you live. But there are many significant differences. The military base is, in a sense, a "company town" where the employer is at once landlord, sheriff, fire department, and grocer.

The residents, clustered by rank (and indirectly by income), are all part of an institution whose mission, as statutorily defined, is to maintain the common defense and, if necessary, to wage war successfully. All of the operations and activities of the base are intended to support that mission and to increase the service members' identification with, and loyalty to, the units that comprise it. A wide and responsive array of family support services—including medical care, reasonable housing, highly competitive grocery stores (commissaries), clubs, and recreational activities—is designed to meet the needs of family members and to assure the soldier, sailor, Marine, or airman that

their spouses and children will be looked after if they have to deploy to some trouble spot in the world.

If you live on a base for even a few short weeks, you will notice that you and your neighbors in general differ in some surprising ways from civilian counterparts outside the gates. You are younger (98% under forty years of age), healthier, and better educated (99.7% have at least a high school degree and approximately 70% some college education), and you are in a relatively stable marriage (over 62% are married; 78% for the first time, 15% for the second time, 3% three or more times). Furthermore, you can expect that the incidence rates of local crime will be less and that you can still count on your neighbor to get involved should your home or family be threatened by an intruder.

If you happen to be a member of a minority racial or ethnic group on that military installation, you are not alone. Although the majority are white (69.5%), black, Hispanic, and Asian/Pacific Island members of the armed forces are often disproportionately represented compared to their numbers in the civilian population (black members comprise 27% of the army population). The racial and ethnic demographics of the military reflect the attraction it has for citizens seeking equal opportunity to advance. Although much remains to be done for race relations, life within the military neighborhood or barracks is characterized by a respect based upon performance, and by the fact that the military has had years of experience at the leading edge of integration in the United States.

Women comprise only 20 percent of the active duty force, yet their numbers, seniority, and the variety of roles they may play in the force structure have increased dramatically over the past decade. Today, women are excluded only from the most direct combat-related roles, and even there, the decision is often justified on strength considerations rather than gender or social/sexual stereotypes.

At the workplace itself, there are also a number of differences. On duty clothing considerations are circumscribed; there are prescribed *uniforms for the work to be done. Once at work, an eight-hour day is the norm, but personnel will be expected to remain on the job, with no overtime pay, for as long as it takes to complete the task assigned. A military career is still considered by many to be a vocation (versus an occupation); it calls upon its members willingly to do the extraordinary in the service of their country. In return, the tangible and intangible rewards are many, including regular recognition ceremonies and a sense of ritual; an opportunity to advance based upon performance; a family-oriented social and health care safety net; and retirement after twenty (or fewer) years of service.

At the end of the duty day, around 1700 hours (5:00 P.M.), all of the civilian workforce, and perhaps 50 percent of the uniformed personnel, head to their off-base homes; the remainder walk or ride to their quarters somewhere on the installation. Everyone, however, will stop when the cannon again roars and a bugle is heard sounding the first notes of Retreat. If you are in a car, you dismount and face the flag. If you are in uniform, you stand at attention and salute. The world comes to a stop for a few moments as the flag is lowered, folded, and put away for another day, as it has always been in the military.

In the evening, if time permits, you and your family might enjoy an on-base Little League game, a bowling tournament, a shopping expedition, or even a movie at the base theater. At the theater, you will not be surprised when the strains of the national anthem are heard prior to the performance and everyone rises respectfully.

Although certainly reflecting the civilian society that surrounds it, life on a military base has a character and pulse of its own . . . and Reveille is just a few hours away.

[See also African Americans in the Military; Careers in the Military; Class and the Military; Families, Military; Housing, Military; Women in the Military.]

• Ward S. Just, Military Men, 1970. Charles C. Moskos and Frank R. Wood, eds., The Military: More Than Just a Job?, 1988. Mary Edwards Wertsch, Military Brats, 1991. Office of the Assistant Secretary of Defense, Family Status and Initial Term of Service (December 1993). 1992 Department of Defense Surveys of Officers and Enlisted Personnel and their Spouses, 1994. Navy Personnel Research and Development Center, Quality of Life in the Navy, Findings from 1990 to 1992: The Navy-wide Personnel Survey (October 1994). Peter Grier, "The Quality of Military Life," Air Force (December 1995), pp. 30–35.   —Peter J. McNelis

BATAAN AND CORREGIDOR, BATTLES OF (1942). From December 1941 to May 1942, after the entry of the United States into World War II, U.S. and Philippine forces fought desperate and ultimately doomed battles to resist the Japanese invasion of the main island of Luzon. Implementing one of the U.S. *war plans—War Plan Orange— Gen. Douglas *MacArthur, commander of all U.S. and Philippine forces, chose to make the stand against the invaders on the Bataan Peninsula and on the island fortress of Corregidor in Manila Bay. Well before the Japanese Fourteenth Army under Lt. Gen. Homma Masaharu made its main landing on 22 December at Lingayen Gulf, north of Bataan, MacArthur had suffered two major setbacks. On 8 December, Japanese air raids had destroyed over half of the U.S. B-17 bombers and P-40 fighters on the ground at Clark Field on Luzon. The subject of much subsequent controversy (MacArthur had not thought Japanese planes had such range), this disaster gave Japan local air superiority. Second, MacArthur initially dispersed his forces and supplies to try to repulse the Japanese on the beaches, but when he eventually reverted to the original plan to pull back to defend Bataan, tons of valuable materiel were abandoned.

Dangerously short of food, medicine, and ammunition, the U.S. forces still put up a furious defense of the peninsula. "The Battling Bastards of Bataan" and the defenders of "the Rock"—Corregidor—provided a tremendous morale boost after U.S. losses suffered in the attack on *Pearl Harbor, Guam, and Wake Island. Heeding direct orders from President Franklin D. *Roosevelt, MacArthur and his family escaped from Corregidor by PT boat on 11 March 1942, and upon arrival in Australia, MacArthur made his famous "I shall return" promise. By 9 April, the Japanese controlled Bataan and besieged Corregidor. On 6 May 1942, Lt. Gen. Jonathan *Wainwright, commanding an ill and starving garrison, surrendered. In the infamous Bataan Death March that followed, more than 600 American and 5,000 to 10,000 Filipino and many Australian and British prisoners of war died from disease, malnourishment, and abuse as they were taken to Japanese prisoner-of-war camps. As with Pearl Harbor, this atrocity became a powerful motivational symbol for Americans in the war against the Japanese empire.

[See also Prisoners of War: U.S. Soldiers as POWs; World War II, U.S. Naval Operations in: The Pacific.]

• D. Clayton James, The Years of MacArthur. Vol. 2, 1941–1945, 1975. Ronald H. Spector, Eagle Against the Sun: The American War with Japan, 1985.   —David L. Anderson

BATTLEFIELDS, ENCAMPMENTS, AND FORTS AS PUBLIC SITES. Usually in the forefront of expansion are the sites of military posts and encampments that protected advancing explorers or soldiers. At or near many posts are the locations of battles that took place. In general, such places are called forts, used interchangeably with other terms, such as camp, post, garrison, cantonment, barracks, presidio, and the like. Many have been preserved for the public as symbols of American history.

Europeans usually built defensive stockades immediately upon arrival in the New World in order to protect their foothold on the shore. The earliest of these is probably Fort San Marcos and San Felipe II at the settlement of Santa Elena, established in 1566 at what is now the Marine Corps Base at Parris Island, South Carolina. James Fort, established by the settlers of Jamestown, Virginia, in 1607 was the first permanent English settlement in the New World.

The establishment of forts marked the movement westward from the eastern seaboard. The exceptions are those in the Far West, such as the Spanish presidios, and Fort Ross, north of San Francisco, the Russian trade and colonization attempt south from Alaska.

In the East, rough stockades were built to protect settlements or such strategic locations as roads or river crossings. The *French and Indian War (1754–63) resulted in a line of forts in western Pennsylvania, northern Ohio, and Indiana. The *Revolutionary War brought about the construction of numerous forts throughout the eastern United States from earthworks or stockades at many towns to major construction protecting the harbors.

Fort Stanwix in the center of Rome, New York, is a full-scale replica constructed by the National Park Service in 1977 to recognize this stockaded structure that played a role in the French and Indian War and the American Revolution.

There are a number of other preserved examples of eighteenth-century *fortifications in the East, some of them military, others nonmilitary. One of the latter is Fort Western (1754–69) at Augusta, Maine, built as part of the defenses of the Kennebec River during the French and Indian War.

Further south near Orlando, Florida, is the replica of Fort Christmas, representative of the many forts built during the *Seminole Wars. The original post was established on Christmas Day, 1835, and abandoned in 1845. More than 135 years later, the Orange County Parks Department undertook its reconstruction. Another reproduction from the eighteenth century is Fort St. Jean Baptiste (1737), a palisaded square fort near Natchitoches, Louisiana. It was garrisoned by French troops, although in Spanish territory until the Louisiana Purchase. The U.S. *Army abandoned its use in 1819, but it has risen again in a ten-building reconstruction near Northwestern State University that opened in 1982 as part of Louisiana's tricentennial.

A most unusual reconstruction is that of Fort de Chartres (1753–56), four miles from the Mississippi River town of Prairie du Rocher, Illinois. The four-acre fort had stone walls 18 feet high and more than 2 feet thick. In 1765 it became the seat of British rule in the Illinois country until it was leveled in 1772. Fort de Chartres became a state park in 1915, and most of the buildings were reconstructed on the original stone foundations.

A strategic location of French and British authority was the point between Lakes Michigan and Huron at the Straits of Mackinac, separating Upper and Lower Michigan. In 1712, Fort Michilimackinac—a palisade of pointed logs and blockhouses surrounding log buildings—was built by the French on the southern side of the straits as a fortified trading post. The British took over in 1761, but two years later the fort was attacked by Indians and most of the thirty-five-man garrison massacred. The British reoccupied the ruined fort in 1764; it remained the only British-occupied post on the Great Lakes above Detroit until near the end of the American Revolution. In 1780, the garrison moved to Mackinac Island. Here Fort Mackinac was built on the high bluff with stone ramparts and three blockhouses that remain today in a state park. At the Michilimackinac site, the trading post stockade was restored in 1959 with a full-scale replica that has 20-foot-high log walls surrounding barracks, officers' quarters, storehouse, French church, British trader cabins, and blockhouses.

Also in the Northwest is privately constructed and maintained Fort St. Charles, one of the most isolated posts in the country. Set in the political incongruity of the Northwest Angle—a tiny Minnesota peninsula on Lake of the Woods that is separated by a strip of Canadian territory—the stockade was a trading post erected in 1732 by the French explorer Pierre LaVerendrye. Twenty miles away, in 1736, Indians massacred and beheaded a twenty-one-man party led by LaVerendrye's son; parts of their mutilated bodies were buried at the fort. Abandoned in 1763, the fort was soon forgotten. But in 1951–68 it was reconstructed by the Knights of Columbus. The double-deep log palisade, with its two blockhouses, chapel, and outlined buildings, can be visited by boat from resorts in the Northwest Angle on Lake Superior.

The Great Lakes were strategically important in eighteenth-century relationships first between the French and British, then the Americans, and forts were built at important points along the shores, usually in direct opposition to each other. Thus Fort Malden at Amhertsburg, Canada, faces Fort Wayne at Detroit; and Fort George, on the Niagara River and Lake Ontario, faces Fort Niagara on the opposite shore of the river.

By the mid-1790s, the federal government realized that the war in Europe might pose a threat to the United States and a plan was approved to fortify twenty ports along the Atlantic seaboard from Portland, Maine, to Savannah, Georgia. The construction that took place under this so-called First System of Fortification (1794–1804) consisted primarily of sodded earthworks over which a dozen or so guns could fire.

The appropriations for the First System totaled $172,000 initially in 1794, with an additional $250,000 in 1798. Increased funding made improvements possible, and masonry was introduced at some, including still-existent Fort McHenry at Baltimore and Fort Mifflin across the Delaware River from Philadelphia.

The Second System of Fortification was precipitated by growing antagonism with England, which exposed the disrepair of the early construction. In 1807, Congress began a five-year program funded by more than $3 million in appropriations. This Second System included some open earthen batteries, but more were of partial or full masonry construction. A design that characterized the forts of this era was the circular or elliptical masonry bastion: Fort Norfolk in Norfolk, Virginia, is one of the few remaining examples. The use of multitiered masonry casemates as part of the construction permitted the firing of heavy sea-coast guns from within the forts instead of from on top of the walls. Castle Williams on Governors Island is a prime example, with four levels in a circular design mounting 102 guns.

The Third System, begun in 1817, could be accomplished systematically. Looking for a "permanent" defense of the country, a board of officers planned and supervised all aspects of a long-term program—a board that continued in existence under various names until World War II.

In 1821, the board recommended that fifty defensive works be constructed, but termed only eighteen of the first class as urgently necessary. By 1850, the plan had been expanded to recommend about 200 coastal works. In actuality, the effort concentrated on upgrading the protection of the principal harbors in the East, with Florida and the Gulf Coast the main locations for new forts of the Third System. Although most of these forts were constructed simply of brick- or stone-backed earthen uncovered parapets, some were elaborate structures. Examples still standing today include Sumter, South Carolina; Monroe, Virginia; Adams, Rhode Island; Morgan, Alabama; Pulaski, Georgia; Jackson, Louisiana; Jefferson at the tip of the Florida Keys; and Fort Point in San Francisco Bay. Most of these are now preserved and interpreted as part of the National Park Service or that of their parent states. One, Fort Monroe, is still an active army post.

Protection of the coasts of the country looked toward an enemy coming from Europe. To protect the movement of explorers, missionaries, and settlers westward, the army established forts at key locations and along trails and waterways through the frontier. Sometimes these were log cabins, surrounded by upright log stockades—the traditional design accepted by romanticists and the entertainment industry; more often they were just collections of structures built of locally available materials without stockaded walls.

Several of the early frontier forts were actually trading posts but now are preserved as replicas constructed and maintained by the National Park Service. Fort Union, North Dakota, and Bent's Fort, Colorado, both built by the National Park Service, are good examples.

South of Bismarck, North Dakota, is the site of Fort Abraham Lincoln (1872–91), the fort from which Lt. Col. George Armstrong *Custer led his Seventh Cavalry to the fatal Battle of the *Little Bighorn in 1876. Reconstruction of the buildings of the fort began in 1989 in a project that was supported from the proceeds of legalized gambling in North Dakota.

Fort Sisseton (1864–89) near Lake City, South Dakota, is one of the best preserved forts, with original buildings because of its past as a hunting club and the work of the Civilian Conservation Corps in the 1930s. It is now a state park. Fort Hartsuff (1874–81) near Ord, Nebraska, was privately owned after the army left until the state accepted it as a park.

There is no real estimate of the number of forts and camps established in the United States. That might also be said of battlefields. The *French and Indian War, the

*Revolutionary War, *War of 1812, *Mexican War, *Civil War, various Indian wars, and the Mexican border incidents of 1916 left battle sites throughout the country. World War II had a few battlesites in the United States, Pearl Harbor being the most famous.

Hundreds of battlefields are preserved as federal, state, or local historic parks around the country. They range from many Revolutionary War sites in the Northeast and South, such as those of the battles of *Bunker Hill, Massachusetts; *Monmouth, New Jersey; and the Brandywine (and encampment commemorated now at Valley Forge National Park) in Pennsylvania; to those in the Southwest in the *Texas War of Independence (the Battle of the *Alamo), and Far West in the *Plains Indian Wars (such as the Battle of the *Little Bighorn). The most visited battlefields are clearly those of the Civil War, particularly the National Battlefields and Military Parks maintained by the U.S. Park Service, especially those at Gettysburg, Pennsylvania; and in Virginia at Manassas, Chancellorsville, Spotsylvania, Fredericksburg, and Petersburg. Efforts are being made to expand additional sites and protect them from encroaching development.

The Civil War had demonstrated the inadequacy of the old coastal forts. In 1886, an army-navy study recommended vast increases in defensive works and firepower. It called for fortifications to be built at twenty-six coastal localities and three on the Great Lakes, for a total of 1,300 guns and mortars of heavy caliber; in fact, only about half ultimately were installed. These new forts were made of reinforced concrete buried in the ground so as to minimize their silhouette and blend with the landscape. Their main vulnerability was that they were open from the rear and, more so, from above. With the advent of the airplane, the army realized that the traditional coastal defense fortification had become obsolete.

Many of these structures still stand on the seacoasts of the East, the West, and the Gulf of Mexico—some because they were historic; more because of the difficulty of destroying the tons of reinforced concrete that withstand even advanced technology.

There are forts and battlefield sites in every state of the Union. Many are preserved and open to the public; many more are just sites, some marked, most forgotten. The National Park Service has 365 sites in its system, of which several hundred could be considered military in nature, either because of a fort or a battlefield, or sometimes both.

[See also Bases, Military: Development of; Cemeteries, Military; Gettysburg National Military Park; Pearl Harbor National Monument.]

• Herbert M. Hart, Historic Western Military Posts (1963–1967), 4 vols. Francis Paul Prucha, A Guide to the Military Posts of the United States, 1780–1895, 1964. Herbert M. Hart, Tour Guide to Old Western Forts: The Posts and Camps of the Army, Navy and Marines on the Western Frontier, 1804–1916, 1980. Craig L. Symonds, A Battlefield Atlas of the American Revolution, 1986. Robert B. Roberts, Encyclopedia of Historic Forts: The Military, Pioneer, and Trading Posts of the United States, 1988. Joseph E. Stevens, America's National Battlefield Parks, 1990. Alice Cromie, A Tour Guide to the Civil War, 4th ed., 1992. A. Wilson Greene and Gary W. Gallagher, National Geographic Guide to the Civil War National Battlefield Parks, 1992. Frank E. Vandiver, Civil War Battlefields and Landmarks: A Guide to National Park Sites, 1996.
—Herbert M. Hart

BATTLESHIPS. Descended from the wooden ship of the line in the age of sailing warships, the steel battleship in the U.S. *Navy was usually distinguished from its foreign counterparts in the nineteenth and twentieth centuries by its heavy gun armament, sturdy protection, and relatively slow speed. Although initially ordered by Congress for coastal defense in the 1890s, battleships soon took on the mission of control of the seas, which they held until eclipsed by *aircraft carriers during World War II. Denounced for decades as obsolete, the battleship ultimately survived in the navy until 1995 by adapting to other roles.

U.S. battleships fell into three distinct subtypes: the twenty-seven mixed-battery ships (typically with four 12-inch and eight 8-inch guns, 18 knots speed), constructed between 1888 and 1908; the twenty-two all-big-gun "dreadnoughts" (with armaments from eight 12-inch to eight 16-inch guns, 18 to 21 knots) completed between 1910 and 1923; and the ten fast *battleships (nine 16-inch guns, 27 to 33 knots) built in 1937 to 1944. In addition to these vessels, Congress authorized seven dreadnoughts in 1916 and seven fast battleships in 1940, none of which was finished.

Technically, American battleship designers pioneered the "all-or-nothing" scheme for armor protection with the Nevada class of 1912. Light armor plating, which would serve only to detonate armor-piercing shells, was deleted, and the weight saved used for thicker protection of vital areas. Later, the ten fast battleships were in advance of their foreign contemporaries in mounting dual-purpose secondary batteries effective against both antisurface and antiaircraft targets.

Operationally, the early mixed-battery ships saw little combat as a type. Aside from the Maine, which exploded (probably accidentally) in February 1898, only five had been completed in time for the *Spanish-American War. Although not seriously tested, their performance at Santiago was judged impressive enough to justify an accelerated program of battleship construction. Sixteen of these warships flexed America's muscles during the cruise of the Great White Fleet (1907–09), but returned home already outmoded by the revolution in battleship design wrought by HMS Dreadnought. Dispensing with all medium-caliber guns in favor of ten 12-inch rifles, the Dreadnought gained weight of fire and long-range accuracy through simplified fire control. During World War I, the obsolete vessels of the Great White Fleet were relegated to training and convoy duty. By 1923, all had been retired from active duty.

The "dreadnoughts" of the World War I era played a much more active role in the nation's defense. Eight served in British waters during 1918; fifteen were on hand in 1941. Except for the Arizona and the Oklahoma, both sunk in the attack on *Pearl Harbor, all were modernized, and some were virtually reconstructed with the most modern antiaircraft armament, *radar, and fire control equipment. Six of these veteran warships won at Surigao Strait during the Battle of *Leyte Gulf on 25 October 1944, the last action between big-gun warships; but their most significant contribution was artillery support for amphibious assaults from Attu and Tarawa to Normandy and Okinawa. So impressive were the dreadnoughts in this role that five were maintained in the U.S. Navy's reserve fleet through the 1950s.

As for the ten fast battleships completed during World War II, only two engaged their opposite numbers when, at the Battle of *Guadalcanal on the night of 14–15 November 1942, Washington and South Dakota inflicted mortal damage on the Imperial Japanese Navy's *Kirishima*, helping prevent the Japanese from landing substantial reinforcements on the island. But the fast battleships proved themselves useful in many other roles: as logistics support ships for smaller combatants, as flagships, as antiaircraft escorts for aircraft carriers, and especially as shore bombardment vessels. Indeed, the last four ships of the *Iowa* class would see action in five separate conflicts over a half century—an unprecedented record. Well-protected, maneuverable, carrying up to 150 antiaircraft guns, and the fastest battleships ever with their speed of 33 knots, the *Iowas* were the finest big-gun ships built by any navy.

Despite these merits, the battleship as a type had obviously yielded pride of place by the end of World War II to the carriers as the "backbone of the fleet." In the subsequent great *demobilization, only the *Missouri* remained on active duty by 1949. The *Korean War brought back the other three *Iowa*-class ships for shore bombardment duties during which they fired many more rounds than in World War II. Their effective performance in this role kept them in the reserve fleet after their decommissioning later in the decade when all their earlier cousins had become museum ships or scrap.

With the *Vietnam War, the *New Jersey,* after an "austere" modernization, made one combat tour in 1968. Much praised by soldiers ashore for the effectiveness of her gunfire, the *New Jersey* nonetheless returned to mothballs in 1969 with the diminution of the American role in the war.

Narrowly escaping the cutter's torch during the 1970s, the four *Iowas* then became a controversial element in the Reagan administration's buildup of the navy. Recommissioned with upgraded electronics and long-range cruise *missiles, the battleships served as the centerpieces of surface warfare action groups. The debate over their reactivation flared with questions about the accuracy of the *New Jersey*'s gunnery during the Lebanon crisis of 1983–84 and the reasons for the *Iowa*'s lethal turret explosion in 1989.

Battleship proponents found vindication with the performance of the *Missouri* and *Wisconsin,* which fired both missiles and big guns to much effect during the *Persian Gulf War in 1991. Unfortunately, the large size of their crews told against them during the downsizing of the military; all four were once again in mothballs by 1992 and were ordered stricken from the navy's lists in January 1995.

Thus, the U.S. Navy had carried battleships on its rosters for little more than a century. For most of that time, they drew opposition, especially from airpower advocates, for their size and expense. During their first fifty years, they probably did take up too much of the navy's attention and resources at the expense of smaller vessels (such as carriers, cruisers, and *destroyers) and other missions (such as antisubmarine warfare). But wartime experience proved them tough ships–only three of the fifty-nine (*Maine, Oklahoma,* and *Arizona*) were permanently sunk. As ship killers, the battleships saw little action; yet they ultimately justified their existence in important subsidiary missions, the most significant being gunfire support for troops ashore.

[*See also* Mahan, Alfred T.; Navy Combat Branches.]

• John C. Reilly, Jr. and Robert L. Scheina, *American Battleships 1886–1923,* 1980. Norman Friedman, *U.S. Battleships,* 1985. Paul Stillwell, *Battleship New Jersey,* 1986. Malcolm Muir, Jr., *The Iowa Class Battleships,* 1987. Jonathan G. Utley, *An American Battleship at Peace and War: The USS Tennessee,* 1991. William H. Garzke, Jr. and Robert O. Dulin, Jr., *Battleships: United States Battleships, 1935–1992,* 2nd ed., 1994.   —Malcolm Muir, Jr.

BEAVER WARS. *See* Native American Wars: Warfare in Native-American Societies; Native American Wars: Wars among Native Americans.

BELLEAU WOOD, BATTLE OF (1918). Belleau Wood was a significant U.S. action of World War I, attack by a Marine brigade of the U.S. Second Division in woods west of Château Thierry, France. Having participated in stopping the German offensive on the Marne River, the Marines were eager to attack. The brigade was tasked to clear the woods and retake the nearby town of Boursches. Beginning on 6 June and attacking in linear formations, with poor artillery fire support coordination, the Marines immediately began taking heavy *casualties; they then shifted to short rushes by small groups, engaging in hand-to-hand fighting in a maze of woods, and heavy undergrowth. Several German counterattacks were beaten off, and the Marines advanced into raking machine-gun fire and well-adjusted artillery. "Come on, you sonsabitches, do you want to live forever?" shouted Sgt. Dan Daly, leading his Marines into the woods—and into U.S. *Marine Corps history. The Americans finally cleared the woods on 26 June, as much by courage and determination as by fighting skill. It was a bloody fight, the bloodiest in Marine Corps history to that date. The Marines suffered 5,200 casualties, more than half their strength. But they gained the respect of the Allies and the Germans.

[*See also* Marne, Second Battle of the; World War I: Military and Diplomatic Course.]

• Robert B. Asprey, *At Belleau Wood,* 1965. John Toland, *No Man's Land,* 1980.   —Paul F. Braim

BEAUREGARD, P. G. T. (1818–1893), known as the "Great Creole," became the Confederacy's first field commander. A Louisianian, he graduated second of forty-five in the U.S. Military Academy Class of 1838. An engineer, Beauregard was brevetted for gallantry in the *Mexican War, and in January 1861 became superintendent of the U.S. Military Academy. Relieved because of Southern sympathies, he accepted a commission as brigadier general in the Confederacy's Provisional army on 1 March 1861.

Beauregard commanded rebel forces at Fort Sumter and at First Manassas. Promoted to full general, he assumed command of the Southern army after Gen. Albert Sidney Johnston's death during the Battle of *Shiloh, and had to retreat. He defended Charleston brilliantly from late 1862 to 1864. In May 1864, he defeated Union Gen. Benjamin F. *Butler in front of Petersburg, then became commander of the Division of the West and fought under Gen. Joseph E. *Johnston at war's end.

After the war, Beauregard became a railroad company president and recouped his fortunes as manager of the Louisiana lottery and head of New Orleans's public works. He wrote frequently about the war and ghost-wrote a biography of himself.

Disliked by President Jefferson *Davis, Beauregard's talents were wasted and he ranks as a "first-rate second rater"—but his reputation is rising.

[*See also* Bull Run, First Battle of; Civil War: Military and Diplomatic Course; Fort Sumter, Capture of.]

• Alfred Roman, *The Military Operations of General Beauregard*, 2 vols., 1884. T. Harry Williams, *P. G. T. Beauregard*, 1954. Frank E. Vandiver, *Blood Brothers: A Short History of the Civil War*, 1992.
—Frank E. Vandiver

BERLIN AIRLIFT (1948–49). The Soviet blockade of Berlin was triggered by Allied currency reforms opposed by Josef *Stalin as a step toward unification and reindustrialization of the American, British, and French occupation zones of Germany. The blockade started on 22 June 1948, when the Soviets shut off ground access from the west to the occupation zones in Berlin. It triggered a vast airlift to supply the estimated 4,500 tons needed daily to maintain the West Berlin industry and population of 2 million.

An ad hoc effort by the USAF, using C-47 transport planes, and aided by the RAF, developed into an armada of service and civilian planes, two-thirds U.S. and one-third British. The backbone of the movement became four-engined American C-54s, and British Yorks and Hermes manned by World War II–qualified aircrews. U.S. operations began under Curtis E. *LeMay, USAF Europe commander, but he was succeeded by Maj. Gen. William N. Tunner, who had commanded the American airlift over "the Hump" between India and China in World War II. To keep the planes and supplies moving, loading was cut to 1 hour 25 minutes, while unloading in Berlin took a mere 49 minutes. Soviet fighters harassed the cargo planes, but did not shoot. Most hazardous was the weather; this was overcome by ground-controlled approaches handled by *radar operators who reduced landing gaps to three minutes rain or shine, and by the use of Rebecca/Eureka homing radar, as well as new Calvert sodium approach lights. With a roundtrip distance of 274–565 miles, depending upon the base and corridor used, planes did not have to refuel in Berlin.

By September 1948, the American effort was handled by 319 C-54 Skymasters—225 in service and the rest undergoing maintenance or repair. The British No. 46 Group operated a more mixed force, including Sunderland flying boats, from eight airfields and one water base. The Americans operated out of Frankfurt and Wiesbaden; both Gatow and Tempelhof in Berlin, as well as bases in the west, had to be rapidly expanded. By 12 May 1949, when the Soviets lifted the blockade, 1,783,000 tons had been flown with a loss of thirty-one U.S. lives in twelve fatal accidents. Flights totaling 250,000 continued on into October to build up stocks for the coming winter.

The Berlin Airlift proved the West would maintain its position in Berlin even at the risk of war. The airlift was a public relations victory for the peaceful use of airpower, heightening the reputation of the U.S. Military Airlift Command and of Generals LeMay and Tunner.

[*See also* Berlin Crises; Cold War: External Course; Germany, U.S. Military Involvement in.]

• Charles D. Bright, *Historical Dictionary of the U.S. Air Force*, 1992.
—Robin Higham

BERLIN CRISES (1958, 1962). The Berlin Crises involved mounting tension between the Soviet Union and the Western Allies over West Berlin. Since the 1948–49 blockade, West Berlin had become a symbol of U.S. guarantees for Western European security and a platform for Western intelligence operations. In November 1958, Soviet premier Nikita S. Khrushchev launched a campaign to terminate the Allied presence in West Berlin and to prompt the West to recognize the German Democratic Republic (GDR). He hoped to reduce the GDR's isolated diplomatic position; some analysts argue that Moscow also feared U.S. plans for nuclear sharing with West Germany.

Without Western concessions, Moscow declared it would turn over its responsibilities in East Berlin to the GDR and allow East German officials to regulate civilian and Allied military traffic between West Berlin and West Germany. Khrushchev did not want to risk nuclear war; Presidents Eisenhower (1959) and Kennedy (1961–62) were willing to negotiate, but neither would grant the concessions he sought.

In the event of a military confrontation, Eisenhower and the Allies authorized U.S. Commander-in-Chief Europe (CINCEUR) Gen. Lauris Norstad to create a secret planning group—code-named "Live Oak"—to develop contingency plans. Yet Eisenhower ruled out a conventional U.S.-Soviet war over in Germany; he considered U.S. capabilities for massive nuclear strikes as sufficient both for deterring a serious crisis and for war-fighting. When the Kennedy administration came to power, however, its emphasis on nonnuclear and limited nuclear options prompted Pentagon and Live Oak planners to develop plans for conventional warfare in Central Europe. In addition, the Live Oak group was attached to *NATO, with West German membership.

The Berlin crisis became most intense after the Kennedy–Khrushchev summit at Vienna in June 1961. Khrushchev set a six-month deadline for a settlement. Kennedy authorized a U.S.-NATO conventional buildup, heightened nuclear alert, and accelerated contingency planning. To staunch a tremendous outflow of East German refugees, Khrushchev in mid-August supported GDR leader Walter Ulbricht's efforts to close the East-West Berlin sector borders, first with barbed wire, then with a concrete wall. The Western Allies condemned this new border closing.

The only military confrontation of the second Berlin crisis, the "Checkpoint Charlie" incident, occurred in late October 1961 when tank deployments on both sides of the Wall followed U.S. challenges of GDR restrictions on official travel to East Berlin. However, both sides carefully regulated this brief confrontation. Meanwhile, pressured by Britain and neutral powers, Kennedy had initiated diplomatic contacts in late September and Khrushchev withdrew his deadline. Negotiations stalemated during 1962 and U.S. officials worried about major Soviet moves, but a crisis occurred over Cuba, not Berlin. The shock of the missile crisis, however, may have lowered tensions over Berlin; also easing the situation, some scholars argue, was Bonn's signature on the *Limited Test Ban Treaty (1963), which reduced Moscow's concerns about a nuclear Germany. Nevertheless, divided Berlin remained a Cold War flash point and the Live Oak group remained in existence in the event that an access crisis occurred. Live Oak disbanded, however, in 1990, when Germany reunified and Berlin's occupation ended.

[*See also* Berlin Airlift; Cold War: External Course; Germany, U.S. Military Involvement in.]

• Jack Schick, *The Berlin Crisis, 1958–1962*, 1971. Marc Trachtenberg, *A Constructed Peace: The Making of the European Settlement, 1945–1963*, 1999. U.S. Department of State, *Foreign Relations of the United States, 1958–1960*, ed. David Baehler and Charles S.

Sampson, 1993. U.S. Department of State, *Foreign Relations of the United States, 1961–1963*, Vols. 14 and 15, ed. Charles S. Sampson, 1994. Anatoly Dobrynin, *In Confidence: Moscow's Ambassador to America's Six Cold War Presidents*, 1995. William Burr, "Avoiding the Slippery Slope: Eisenhower and the Berlin Crisis, November 1958–January 1959," *Diplomatic History* 18 (Spring 1994): 177–206.

—William Burr

BERRIGAN, DANIEL (1921) AND PHILIP (1923). The Berrigan brothers—Daniel, a Jesuit priest, and Philip, of the Josephite order—led the antiwar and antidraft movements during the *Vietnam War. Philip served in the U.S. Army in World War II, becoming a priest in 1955. Daniel, the intellectual and theologian, ordained in 1952, complements his brother's activism, acquired in assignments to black parishes in New Orleans and Baltimore.

In May 1968, the two brothers, along with seven other Catholic protesters, burned the records of the Catonsville, Maryland, draft board with homemade napalm. Their arrest, trial, and sentence to 3 years in prison propelled the Berrigans to national prominence. They helped found the Catholic resistance movement: estimates for draft board raids range from 53 to 250. Having lost their appeals, Philip reported to jail, in April 1970, but Daniel became a fugitive. Captured by FBI agents in August, he joined his brother in Danbury Prison. In January 1971, the Nixon administration indicted the Berrigans and others for conspiracy, including bizarre charges of planning to kidnap Henry *Kissinger and blow up heating tunnels in federal buildings in Washington, D.C. After sixty hours of deliberation, the jury could not reach a verdict, forcing the judge to declare a mistrial.

After Vietnam, the brothers continued the Catholic resistance with a new focus on nuclear disarmament. In September 1980, they led a group into a GE plant in King of Prussia, Pennsylvania, that damaged the nose cones for Mark 12A nuclear warheads and poured blood on company records. They were sentenced to 3 to 10 years, but their appeal stretched across the 1980s; eventually the case was brought before a lenient judge who sentenced them to twenty-three months' probation.

The Berrigan brothers' radical antiwar activism reflected increased alienation from government and American society.

[*See also* Peace and Antiwar Movements.]

• Francine du Plessix Gray, *Divine Disobedience: Profiles in Catholic Radicalism*, 1970. Patricia McNeal, *Harder Than War: Catholic Peacemaking in Twentieth-century America*, 1992.

—Patricia McNeal

BIOLOGICAL WEAPONS AND WARFARE. *See* Chemical and Biological Weapons and Warfare.

BLACK HAWK (1767?–1838), Illinois Sauk Indian warrior and leader. Born at the village of Saukenuk in west-central Illinois, Black Hawk as a young man acquired a reputation for bravery, good leadership, and cultural conservatism. Although never a village chief, he was a respected leader.

During the *War of 1812, he led many Sauks to join the British. In 1813 they fought at the Battle of Frenchtown and in the sieges of Fort Meigs and Fort Stephenson. In Black Hawk's absence young Keokuk became the recognized war chief of their village, leading to long-term competition and bitterness between the two men. The warriors

returned to Illinois (1814), where they defeated U.S. forces near Rock Island twice.

After the war, the Sauks tried to resume their peacetime activities, but increasing confrontations with the pioneers occurred. By 1830, Black Hawk had become a leader for those Sauks determined to occupy their traditional Illinois lands, while Keokuk accepted the need to migrate west. Dissident Sauks, Mesquakies, and Kickapoos coalesced in early 1832 into the British Band, who considered Black Hawk an elder statesman. He encouraged them to return to Illinois, which precipitated the Black Hawk War. For his role in those events, authorities imprisoned him. He returned to Iowa in 1833 and died there in 1838.

Black Hawk's life spanned an era of transition from relative freedom for midwestern tribes to their total subjugation by the federal government. Sauk actions illustrated the limited choices Indians had in the early nineteenth century, and demonstrated how the inflexible demands Americans made of their tribal neighbors brought disaster.

[*See also* Black Hawk War.]

• Donald Jackson, ed., *Black Hawk: An Autobiography*, 1955. Roger L. Nichols, *Black Hawk and the Warrior's Path*, 1992.

—Roger L. Nichols

BLACK HAWK WAR (1832). This conflict was the last armed resistance in the Midwest to cause federal removal of the eastern Indians beyond the Mississippi River. It resulted from a disputed 1804 treaty signed by a few Sauks unauthorized to take such action. Though the tribe disavowed the treaty, federal officials acted upon it, opening lands in Illinois for settlement.

The conflict began in April 1832, encouraged by *Black Hauk, a Sauk leader, when nearly 2,000 Sauks and Mesquakies crossed the Mississippi River, moving into Illinois. That brought about the mobilization of the state militia and the movement of the U.S. Sixth Infantry, commanded by Col. Henry Atkinson, from Jefferson Barracks, Missouri, north into Illinois. There the troops pursued the migrating Indians up the Rock River Valley. On 14 May 1832, militiamen under Col. Isaiah Stillman attacked Indians trying to parley, triggering the actual combat. For much of the summer the troops hunted for the fleeing Indians as they moved north into Wisconsin and west toward the Mississippi. On 2 August, Atkinson's force overtook their exhausted quarry at the mouth of the Bad Axe River, killing or capturing most of the Indians.

Fighting that summer consisted of frequent small-scale raids by groups of warriors and pursuit by the militiamen. The campaign demonstrated the need for mounted troops in similar campaigns, and led to the establishment of the dragoons a few years later. The war persuaded other tribes that they must move west or face destruction.

[*See also* Native American Wars: Wars Between Native Americans and Europeans and Euro-Americans.]

• Roger L. Nichols, *General Henry Atkinson: A Western Military Career*, 1965. Roger L. Nichols, *Black Hawk and the Warrior's Path*, 1992.

—Roger L. Nichols

BLEEDING KANSAS (1854–58) refers to the violent civil disturbances in Kansas over the question of whether the territory would be slave or free. Slavery was prohibited in land north of 36°, 30′ under the Missouri Compromise. But in 1854, Democratic Senator Stephen Douglas of

Illinois put forward legislation to organize the Kansas-Nebraska Territory. To gain support from southern senators, the bill repealed the Missouri Compromise and called for popular sovereignty to determine the question of slavery. After a bitter struggle, the act passed in 1854, prompting many northern Democrats to defect to the newly formed Republican Party, which opposed the extension of slavery.

The Kansas-Nebraska Act injected the debate over slavery into western settlement. Emigrants quickly moved into Kansas—some primarily motivated to make the territory free, others to make it a slave state. By the end of 1855, there were two rival governments in Kansas. A pro-slavery territorial legislature recognized by President Franklin Pierce's administration was fraudulently elected through the votes of border "ruffians" from Missouri. Free Soil settlers rejected this government, wrote a free state constitution, and established a rival government in Topeka.

The calm in Kansas was shattered in May 1856 by two events that began a small civil war. On 21 May, the Free Soil town of Lawrence was sacked by an armed pro-slavery force. A few days later, the abolitionist John Brown and six followers executed five men along the Pottawatomie Creek in retaliation. May through October witnessed numerous skirmishes between armed bands of pro-slavery and Free Soil men. The U.S. Army had two garrisons in Kansas, the First Cavalry Regiment at Fort Leavenworth and the Second Dragoons and sixth Infantry at Fort Riley.

The territorial governor tried to stem the violence and maintain peace by policing Kansas with federal troops. He had small detachments sent to assist civil officers and to disperse any unauthorized armed force. The worst of the violence ended in October 1856 as neither Free Soil nor pro-slavery forces wanted to clash with the federal army. By early November, most federal troops had returned to Forts Leavenworth and Riley.

The governor's action to station federal troops across Kansas during the 1857 October elections for territory offices was the last extensive use of the army during the period of civil strife. Most of Kansas was at peace by the end of 1857, except for an area in the extreme southeast on the Missouri border. Between 1857 and 1861, small detachments of federal troops periodically went into this area for *pacification purposes. One soldier was killed in action during the domestic disorder, which claimed about 200 civilian lives.

The civil conflict in Kansas was a product of the political fight over slavery. Federal troops were not used to decide a political question, but they were used by successive territorial governors to pacify the territory so that the political question of slavery in Kansas could finally be decided by peaceful, legal, and political means.

[See also Civil War: Causes.]

• Allan Nevins, Ordeal of the Nation, Vol. 2: A House Dividing, 1852–1857, 1947. Allan Nevins, The Emergence of Lincoln, Vol. 1: Douglas, Buchanan, and Party Chaos, 1857–1859, 1950. Robert W. Coakley, The Role of Federal Military Forces in Domestic Disorders, 1789–1878, 1988. James M. McPherson, Battle Cry of Freedom, 1988.
                                                                    —Paul J. Morton

BLIMPS AND DIRIGIBLES differ in their size and construction. The blimp consists of a gas-filled inflatable bag, pressurized to retain its aerodynamic shape, and attached to a rigid keel that supports a crew compartment and en-

gines. The dirigible, roughly three times larger but otherwise similar in appearance, has vanished from the skies. It had a rigid aluminum frame that embraced several gas cells, maintained the ship's shape, and anchored the control cabin and engine pods, suspended outside a fabric-covered hull.

In 1908, the U.S. Army purchased its first steerable, gasoline-powered airship; with a heavy keel attached to the cigar-shaped gas bag, it foreshadowed the blimp. The program lapsed in 1912, and during World War I the service employed only tethered observation balloons. The postwar army's Italian-built blimp Roma, inflated with inflammable hydrogen, exploded in 1922. The use of helium, a noninflammable lifting gas, prevented further explosions, but the army gradually lost interest in lighter-than-air craft, except for tethered observation or barrage balloons, and in 1938 handed over its last blimps to the navy.

The U.S. Navy acquired its first blimps in 1917 and used them for coastal patrol during World War I. Navy interest soon shifted to the dirigible, a craft that seemed ideal for over-ocean reconnaissance because its lifting gas enhanced aerodynamic efficiency: it could cruise up to 6,000 miles before refueling. Some dirigibles were over 750 feet long and could launch and recover small scouting airplanes, further extending their range.

The navy's dirigible program, encouraged by Rear Adm. William A. *Moffett, began with a disaster. The first craft—modeled on a German design, built in Britain, and filled with hydrogen—exploded in 1921 while being test-flown by an Anglo-American crew. Misfortune plagued the navy's program. Shenandoah (1923–25) broke up in a thunderstorm, as did Akron (1931–33). Macon (1933–35) crashed because of structural failure. In effect, the destruction of Macon in 1935 signaled the end of the dirigible program. The navy's General Board rejected a five-year procurement plan (1937–41) that would have replaced both Akron and Macon and built a new metal-clad airship.

Navy blimps, some of them 253 feet in length, escorted coastal convoys during World War II, operating over the Pacific, the Gulf of Mexico, the Caribbean, the Atlantic, and the Mediterranean. The airships used *radar to locate surfaced *submarines and magnetic detectors to spot submerged U-boats; their number peaked in March 1944 at 119. The blimp continued maritime reconnaissance after the war, and in 1956 radar-equipped versions began guarding against possible aerial attack. Plans called for one early warning squadron on the Atlantic Coast and another on the Pacific, but only the unit based at Lakehurst, New Jersey, was actually commissioned. In October 1961, all blimp operations, including air defense missions, came to an end, though experimental flights continued until 31 August 1962. Proposals to revive the airship as a tool of war have surfaced since 1962, but none has evoked more than passing interest.

• Douglas H. Robinson and Charles L. Keller, "Up Ship": A History of the U.S. Navy's Rigid Airships, 1919–1935, 1982. William F. Althoff, Sky Ships: A History of Airships in the United States Navy, 1990.
                                                                    —Bernard C. Nalty

BLOCKADES. A blockade in its most common form—the naval blockade—is intended to prevent the passage of ships in and out of an enemy's harbors. It can be defensive, focusing on the enemy's warships; offensive, focusing on his commercial and military supply ships; or it can be both. A blockade can restrain just traffic flying the enemy's flag, or it can halt neutral shipping as well. It can halt the passage of only specified items, or it can halt all. It can last for only a few weeks, or for years. The idea of blockade is the antithesis of the idea of freedom of the seas.

By the time of the *French and Indian War (1754–63), the blockade had become one of Britain's major instruments of war. But when the American *Revolutionary War began (1775), the Royal Navy was too weak to blockade distant colonial ports. The entry of France and Spain into the war worsened the British position. In 1781, a brief blockade of Chesapeake Bay by a French fleet played an important role in bringing about the surrender of a British army at the Battle of *Yorktown, and as a result, the end of the war.

After an arduous campaign in the southern states, Gen. Charles *Cornwallis moved his army to Yorktown, Virginia, on the Chesapeake, where the British fleet could resupply and reinforce it easily or, if necessary, evacuate it entirely. As the colonial and French armies under George *Washington and count de Rochambeau marched south from New York and Newport to strengthen the small force besieging Cornwallis, ships bearing the French artillery and supplies sailed in convoy from Newport toward the same destination. The British fleet under Adm. Thomas Graves departed New York in order to intercept the French ships as they approached the Chesapeake. The French ships Graves found, however, were those of Adm. count de Grasse's fighting fleet recently arrived from the Caribbean. They had Cornwallis under blockade. In a long but not very bloody fight, de Grasse repulsed Graves and sent him back to New York. The convoy from Newport arrived safely, the allied armies besieged Cornwallis closely, and de Grasse forestalled any British attempt to rescue the trapped army. His situation hopeless, Cornwallis surrendered. The war petered out, and the colonies gained their collective independence. By itself de Grasse's blockade would not have led to that result, but in combination with the effective work of the allied armies, it served perfectly.

The next American experience with blockade, during the *War of 1812, was grim. By this time the British Fleet had long regained its strength and more, and it had had nearly twenty years of experience in blockading enemy ports in the wars of the French Revolution and Napoleon. Most of the famous American frigate victories in this war took place in the early months, before the British could deploy forces sufficient to lock the ships of the small U.S. Navy into whatever port they happened to be. As the blockade grew tighter and extended further, American foreign trade dried up. So did American domestic trade, most of which went by water. Farmers could not sell their crops; merchants lost their businesses, employees their jobs. Moreover, without tariffs on imports, the government had little money. In addition, the U.S. invasion of Canada had failed; British warships sailed the Chesapeake; and British troops had burned Washington. Despite American successes on Lakes Erie and Champlain, and spectacular raids by American privateers upon British shipping, the American people were ready for peace. So were the British, who had been at war almost without a break since 1793. In December 1814, the opponents signed a treaty of peace.

Soon after the outbreak of the *Civil War, President Abraham *Lincoln, knowing that the Southern states man-ufactured little, ordered the U.S. Navy to blockade the Southern ports so as to prevent them from importing arms and other goods from Europe. This the navy attempted, first by using armed commercial steamers and then by adding new ships built for the task. The blockaders drove sailing ships, mostly neutral, out of the trade with the South. But those ships were replaced by swift steamers, again mostly neutral, which sailed from Bermuda and the Bahamas mainly toward Charleston, South Carolina, and Wilmington, North Carolina. By war's end in 1865, the blockaders had driven ashore, sunk, or captured three-quarters of the 300 blockade-running steamers. But the latter kept the Southern armies supplied with arms until early in 1865, when Northern forces took Charleston from inland and seized the sea approaches to Wilmington. That spring, Gen. Robert E. *Lee surrendered, but not for lack of arms. It is easy to quantify the effort expended on the blockade, but difficult to judge its contribution to the North's eventual success.

Early in the twentieth century, developments in naval *mines, torpedo craft, and coast artillery made it plain to the Royal Navy that close blockade was no longer possible. Hence, when World War I broke out in 1914, the Grand Fleet took station at Scapa Flow, north of Scotland, whence, in conjunction with forces in the Channel, it kept the German High Seas Fleet locked uselessly in the North Sea. Protected by the Grand Fleet, old warships and armed merchant cruisers as well as minefields effectively carried out a commercial blockade against both belligerent and neutral merchant ships trying to enter not only Germany's ports but also those of its neighbors.

The Germans responded with a counterblockade against shipping attempting entry into or exit from Allied ports, especially those of Britain. Their instrument was the submarine, a small warship that could sail surprising distances, could hide under the water when attacking or in danger, and that carried the most deadly of naval weapons: *torpedoes and mines. By the spring of 1917, when—partly as a result of the brutality of the submarine campaign—the United States joined in the war against Germany, that campaign was driving Britain, the last strong combatant among the Allies, to defeat. The Allied decision to convoy merchant ships rather than to let them continue sailing singly, combined with the arrival of enough U.S. destroyers to make convoy possible, defeated the *submarines. The sailing of 2 million American troops to France made possible by this success gave the Allies the edge in strength to halt and then reverse the German offensives in 1918, and that in turn led directly to the end of the war.

The Allies were more vulnerable to blockade than the Germans, but although the submarines were beaten, the Allied blockaders kept their stranglehold on Germany's economy months after the war had ended.

By its nature the submarine, unable to rescue its victims, brought a new savagery to a hitherto not very bloody form of war. Aircraft, soon to join in the war at sea, suffered from the same shortcoming and the savagery worsened.

So far as blockade and counterblockade went, World War II in the Atlantic and Mediterranean followed the pattern of the preceding war. The chief difference was that both sides were better prepared than before to resist the other's blockade. In the Mediterranean and the narrow seas of Europe, aircraft took a leading part in the conduct of blockade. In the Pacific War, the Japanese made no particular effort either to attack enemy shipping or to protect their own. In contrast, the Americans, led by their submarines, destroyed Japanese shipping. This meant that the empire's troops often perished when being moved to where they were needed. For lack of fuel, Japan's pilots could not be trained adequately, and toward the end, its fighting ships could not sail. The blockade was the primary contributor to the defeat of Japan.

In more recent conflicts, blockades have again played significant roles. But in the long struggle against North Vietnam (1965–73), because of an implied (or inferred) threat of Soviet retaliation, the United States imposed no blockade on North Vietnam during the first seven years U.S. combat forces were engaged in that war. As a result, three-quarters of the arms, ammunition, and fuel that the North used in the *Vietnam War entered by sea in ships from the Soviet Union. Finally, in 1972, the United States mined the approaches to North Vietnam's harbors, and the traffic stopped. This, combined with hard fighting on the ground and in the air that used up the North's arms stocks, particularly its surface-to-air *missiles, led to a peace agreement between that country and the United States that permitted the withdrawal of U.S. forces. These events illustrate both the value of blockade under the conditions of that war and the ease by which an interested and more clever government was able to forestall for years the imposition of a blockade on the Soviet Union's client state.

In itself, blockade is not often likely to achieve much. Used wisely and unremittingly against a foe dependent on sea traffic, however, and in tandem with vigorous action elsewhere, it can be a highly effective instrument of war.

[See also Submarine Warfare.]

• Sir Julian S. Corbett, Some Principles of Maritime Strategy, 1911; repr. 1972. S. W. Roskill, White Ensign: The British Navy at War, 1939–1945, 1960. G. J. Marcus, The Age of Nelson: The Royal Navy, 1793–1815, 1971. Clay Blair, Silent Victory: The U.S. Submarine War Against Japan, 1976. Paul M. Kennedy, The Rise and Fall of British Naval Mastery, 1976. Stephen R. Wise, Lifeline of the Confederacy: Blockade Running During the Civil War, 1988. John B. Hattendorf, ed., Mahan on Naval Strategy: Selections from the Writings of Rear Admiral Alfred Thayer Mahan, 1991. Frank Uhlig, Jr., How Navies Fight: The U.S. Navy and Its Allies, 1993. Paul G. Halpern, A Naval History of World War I, 1994.   —Frank Uhlig, Jr.

BODY ARMOR. Protective covering and other equipment designed to guard individuals in combat dates back to early warfare. Rocks, clubs, and arrows were deflected by hand-held shields, later augmented by helmets and coverings for the chest, arms, and legs. Protective coverings were made of leather, wood, shells, or basketwork, later replaced by bronze, iron, and steel. The mounted knights of medieval Europe were clad in chain mail, armor plate, and helmets; their horses, too, were partially encased.

Some soldiers in the early North American colonies wore metal helmets and breastplates, but these proved cumbersome in the woodlands and were soon abandoned. Gunpowder cannon and small arms, and the increasing mobility of warfare, diminished the importance of personal armor, which finally disappeared by the end of the seventeenth century.

Steel helmets reappeared in the twentieth century largely to protect against shrapnel and fragments from artillery shells. In World War I, the Americans adopted the shallow British "tin hat," but the U.S. Army developed its own deeper helmet for World War II. A new configuration, including more neck protection, was adopted in the 1980s.

The French and Germans experimented with metal cuirasses for machine gunners in World War I; the Americans did not adopt chest armor until World War II, when some bomber crews were provided with "flak jackets."

Beginning in the *Vietnam War, American combat infantrymen wore protective vests made of new composite materials, such as kevlar, covered by fabric. The vests, which provided relative flexibility and low heat retention, were designed to protect against blast fragments and antipersonnel, small-arms "ball" ammunition. Crews of ground vehicles, *helicopters, and other aircraft today wear heavier vests made of metal (often titanium), or ceramic tiles contained in the pockets; these prove bulkier but more efficient against small-caliber armor-piercing ammunition.   —John Whiteclay Chambers II

BOHR, NIELS (1885–1962), along with Einstein, one of the two most influential physicists of the twentieth century. Bohr was born in Copenhagen, Denmark to affluent, well-educated parents (his father was a professor of philosophy at the University of Copenhagen). Bohr became a professor at the University of Copenhagen in 1916 and in 1920 established the Institute for Theoretical Physics there, which quickly became a world-recognized think tank frequented by the best scientific minds of the time. From this institute a new comprehension of the physical world emerged, which would have a profound impact on the remainder of the century and beyond: the observed and the observer were seen to interact; nature was both wave and particle; and philosophy and physics shared subject matter as issues of causality and interdeterminism were raised when Bohr and others deepened their understanding of nuclear fission.

In 1939, Bohr fled Denmark, accepting an invitation from the United States to participate in the *Manhattan Project in Los Alamos, New Mexico. There he was instrumental in the development of the atomic bomb but ambivalent about its use as a weapon of mass destruction. Bohr spent the remainder of his life called for international control of *nuclear weapons and the peaceful use of atomic energy.

[See also Arms Control and Disarmament: Nuclear; Atomic Scientists.]

• Ruth Moore, Niels Bohr: The Man, His Science, and the World He Changed, 1966. Abraham Pais, Niels Bohr's Times: In Physics, Philosophy, and Polity, 1991.   —Peter J. McNelis

BOMBER AIRCRAFT. The generic term bomber can be applied to any aircraft that has as its primary role the delivery of *bombs against an enemy target. As military aircraft have evolved, attempts have been made periodically to classify bombers more precisely by adding a variety of adjectives like "night," "day," "light," "medium," "heavy," "dive," "tactical," "strategic," "conventional," or "nuclear." Time and circumstance have often proved such categories temporary or artificial, and the lines of distinction have become blurred, with "night" bombers being used in daylight, or "strategic" bombers attacking "tactical" targets. With the technological advances of the late twentieth century, it has become possible to make aircraft that are capable of performing well in several different combat roles and the need for specialized *bomber aircraft has diminished. Even so, there are still aircraft in which the delivery of bombs or air-to-ground *missiles is clearly the primary role.

The U.S. Army Air Service had no combat aircraft when the United States declared war on Germany in April 1917, nor was it possible for the fragmented American aircraft industry to provide any. Arrangements were made for the Air Service to acquire British, French, and Italian aircraft, and for American industry to build selected European types. The principal bombers chosen were the French Breguet-14, the Italian Caproni CA-33, and the British Airco DH-4 and Handley Page 0/100. Plans were made to have the British and Italian aircraft built in the United States, but only the DH-4 went into quantity production before the end of the war.

American airmen gained most of their bombardment experience in World War I in Brequet-14s and DH-4s. These single-engined, two-seat biplanes were of limited range and carrying capacity, but they were used to some effect against battlefield targets, and close behind the front lines, against supply centers and troop concentrations. Most of the operations were carried out in daylight, sometimes at low level, and both enemy *fighter aircraft and ground fire caused high losses. A few Americans also experienced "strategic" bombing with the Italians, flying Capronis against targets deep inside Austrian territory. Given the primitive navigation and bombing equipment, and the fact that they were bombing from 12,000 feet or higher, in open cockpits without oxygen, it is hardly surprising that the crews had difficulty in finding, never mind hitting, their targets.

In 1917, Brig. Gen. Billy *Mitchell, who rose to command the combat aircraft of the American Expeditionary Force, met and was strongly influenced by Britain's Maj. Gen. Hugh Trenchard, one of the foremost prophets of strategic airpower. Trenchard's views on the use of large numbers of heavy bombers against targets deep inside enemy territory had a marked effect on Mitchell.

The United States began its pursuit of a strategic capability in 1917 by asking the Martin Company to develop a heavy bomber. The best of the Martin series was the MB-2, but with a top speed of only 100 mph and a range of not much more than 500 miles, it was a long way from meeting Mitchell's expectations. However, it did serve as the instrument for his dramatic airpower demonstration in 1921, during his tenure as Assistant Chief of the Air Service. Undeterred by scathing criticism, particularly from the U.S. Navy, Mitchell's MB-2s conducted several bombing trials against warships, concluding with the spectacular destruction of two *battleships, the old German *Ostfriesland* and the obsolete USS *Alabama*.

Another disappointment for Mitchell was the Barling Bomber, a massive American triplane that flew in 1923 and managed to lift over 6,000 pounds of bombs; but with such a load its top speed was just 95 mph, its range only 170 miles, and it proved incapable of climbing over the Appalachians. Technology had not caught up with ideas and the intended "superbomber" was scrapped.

The first significant steps on the road to a U.S. strategic air force were taken with the appearance of Boeing's YB-9, a single-engine, all-metal monoplane, in 1931. Within a year, the YB-9 was overshadowed by the Martin B-10, a twin-engine, all-metal monoplane with retractable under-carriage, with the added features of internal bomb stowage, enclosed crew positions, wing flaps, wheel brakes, and variable pitch propellers. With a top speed of over 200 mph, the B-10 could outstrip most fighters of the day, it could reach 25,000 feet, and its range with 1,000 pounds of bombs was 700 miles. It was "one of the most significant advances in the history of military aircraft." Encouraged by its experience with the B-10, the Army Air Corps pursued its ideal of a truly strategic bomber. In 1934, Boeing was awarded a contract for a "superbomber" with a 5,000-mile range, a top speed of at least 200 mph, and a payload of 2,000 pounds. Produced as the XB-15, engines of sufficient power were not available for the monster bomber and the project was canceled. But information was gathered about the structural and aerodynamic problems of very large aircraft, all of which would prove valuable some years later.

Boeing also bid for a second contract, intended to provide for the aerial defense of the United States against enemy fleets. This aircraft, the Boeing Model 299, became the B-17 "Flying Fortress," the most celebrated bomber ever flown by U.S. air forces. Developed and used operationally as a strategic bomber, especially in the World War II air assault on Germany, it became the embodiment of the beliefs Billy Mitchell had promoted so fiercely until his death in 1936. In its early days, the B-17 was said to be able to fly fast and high enough to outrun most enemy fighters, and to be so heavily armed that it could defend itself even if intercepted, but these assumptions were rapidly proven false in the heat of combat. Out of over 12,000 B-17s of all models built, nearly 5,000 were lost in combat, and almost 4,000 more in accidents.

In Europe, its principal theater of operation, the B-17 was used by the U.S. 8th Air Force together with the Consolidated B-24 "Liberator" for day bombing, while RAF bombers undertook the night operations of a "round-the-clock" combined bomber offensive. Although flown in large formations to increase the firepower brought to bear on attacking fighters, the U.S. bombers suffered intolerable losses until the arrival of long-range escort fighters like the P-51D "Mustang." The B-17s and B-24s bombed in formation from above 20,000 feet, releasing together when the lead aircraft's bombs dropped. This precision bombing method was intended to ensure great accuracy and target saturation. (As opposed to the night area bombing of the RAF, in which specific aiming points were chosen for the bomber crews, but it was accepted that the targets were whole German cities.) Unfortunately, combat and the European weather combined to degrade results and some commanders later described their operations rather ruefully as "area bombing of precision targets." By the end of World War II, the combined bomber offensive had effectively destroyed most German industrial cities, with particularly catastrophic effects in Hamburg and Dresden.

At the tactical level, in operations aimed at influencing the surface campaign directly, twin-engine bombers like the North American B-25 "Mitchell," Martin B-26 "Marauder," Douglas A-20 "Havoc" and A-26 "Invader" were used at medium and low level during World War II against specific targets such as rail junctions, bridges, supply depots, and troops concentrations. A-20s and B-25s also operated to particular effect against Japanese shipping during the Pacific War, notably during the destruction of a Japanese invasion fleet in the Battle of the Bismarck Sea. By contrast, in April 1942, B-25s were used in a unique operation that had a strategic purpose. Lt. Col. James (Jimmy) *Doolittle's B-25 squadron was launched from the deck of the aircraft carrier *Hornet* to strike a symbolic blow against Tokyo.

The technique of dive-bombing, intended for use against targets where great accuracy was essential, was promoted in the 1920s by the U.S. *Navy and *Marine Corps, and brought to fruition in combat by the German Luftwaffe in the 1930s. The Junkers 87-B Stuka was a vital part of the German *Blitzkrieg* that led to the fall of France in 1940. The devastating effects of determined dive-bombing were most graphically demonstrated by the U.S. Navy's Douglas SBD-1 "Dauntless" dive-bombers at the Battle of *Midway in 1942, when they sank four Japanese *aircraft carriers to shift the balance of power in the Pacific permanently in favor of the United States.

In 1944, Boeing's B-29 "Superfortress" flew its first combat operations. Its internal bombload was 20,000 pounds, over three times that of the B-17, and its combat range of 3,000 miles plus more than doubled that of its predecessor. Equipped with a pressurized cabin, a B-29 crew could operate in comfort up to 30,000 feet. In the closing months of the war, B-29s were used in massive raids on Japan, dropping enormous quantities of incendiaries to burn Japanese cities. The most destructive raid of World War II took place on the night of 9 March 1945, when more than 300 B-29s bombed and burned Tokyo. An estimated 84,000 people died and more than 1 million were made homeless. The firebombing of Japan continued until August, when two single B-29s, named *Enola Gay* and *Bockscar,* ended World War II with the atomic bombings of *Hiroshima and Nagasaki, respectively. The postwar period then saw the development of the policy of *deterrence, in which the threatened use of *nuclear weapons was intended to deter war, and the start of the unending public debate on the morality of using strategic airpower, either conventional or nuclear, to attack enemy populations.

After World War II, the jet engine revolutionized bomber aircraft. In the late 1940s, the USAF's first truly intercontinental bomber, the massive Boeing B-36, improved performance by the addition of four jets to its six piston engines. The first U.S. bombers to usher in the pure jet age, however, were the North American B-45 and the Boeing B-47 in 1947. The B-45 was built before swept-wing theory was understood and was quickly overshadowed by the B-47, which introduced thin, swept-back wings, six axial-flow jet engines mounted in pods, and "bicycle" main landing gear. In 1952, Boeing added the eight-jet B-52 "Stratofortress," a huge bomber that has remained an impressive instrument of war since its introduction. Originally conceived for the delivery of free fall nuclear bombs, the B-52 was for many years the backbone of the twenty-four-hour-a-day alert flown by the USAF's Strategic Air Command (SAC). Progressive modifications have added the capability to carry cruise missiles and conventional high-explosive bombs in various combinations. The B-52's 5,000-mile combat radius can be extended as required by air-to-air refueling, and it has the capacity to lift a total weapon load of over 60,000 pounds, as much as the maximum weight of a loaded B-17 in World War II. During both the *Vietnam War and the *Persian Gulf War, the B-52's internal stowage of eighty-four 500-pound bombs made it a formidable offensive weapon.

In the late 1950s, the USAF acquired a supersonic strategic bomber in the Convair B-58, a delta-winged aircraft that could exceed Mach 2. Its impressive performance allowed it to set numerous international records, but its high cost of operations led to withdrawal in 1970.

Designated as fighters (F), many of the smaller USAF jets were fitted with bomb-carrying pylons under the wings and the association of aircraft types with specific roles became less certain. These multirole aircraft included the North American F-100 and the McDonnell-Douglas F-4 Phantom. The Republic F-105 and the General Dynamics F-111 were both conceived for low- and medium-altitude penetration of defenses, and were designed with internal weapons bays. All four types saw action in Vietnam with a variety of conventional ordnance, and all were capable of nuclear weapon delivery. The F-111 also later carried out a successful strike against Libya. In the 1970s, the USAF began taking delivery of the McDonnell-Douglas F-15 and the General Dynamics F-16. Both aircraft are capable of multirole operations and demonstrated the effectiveness of the new generation of "smart" weapons (guided bombs, stand-off missiles, etc.) in the Gulf War.

Naval aircraft have followed a similar path in their development since World War II. The Douglas A-3D "Skywarrior" and the North American A-5 "Vigilante" were both designed as carrier-borne strategic bombers, and the Douglas A-4, Grumman A-6, Vought A-7, and McDonnell-Douglas F-18 are all tactical aircraft with multirole capabilities. The McDonnell Douglas/British Aeropsace AV-8B Harrier is a more specialized close support attack aircraft, uniquely capable of vertical takeoff and landing, which is flown by the U.S. Marine Corps and can be used to deliver a variety of bombs and missiles.

In the mid-1980s, the USAF received the first of its Rockwell International B-1Bs, a supersonic strategic aircraft with both conventional and nuclear capability in bombs and cruise missiles. Sophisticated electronics provide the defensive systems and the B-1B can achieve near sonic speeds at low level. Even further advances have been made with the introduction of "stealth" technology, which reduces both the *radar and infrared signatures of an aircraft dramatically. The Lockheed F-117A demonstrated the effectiveness of its stealth design when it penetrated Iraqi airspace at will during the Gulf War, destroying critical *command and control facilities with "smart" bombs. One F-117A frequently accomplished what would have required several hundred B-17s in World War II.

The next page of the "stealth" story was turned with the first flight of the Northrop B-2 in 1989. The aircraft is a "flying wing" with no vertical surfaces, masked engine intakes and exhausts, and internal weapons stowage for nuclear weapons or up to eighty 500-pound bombs. In a world dominated by multirole aircraft, the USAF's futuristic B-2 is the closest approach to the classic "bomber" as Billy Mitchell would have understood the term—an aircraft of intercontinental range, which can leap over armies and navies, penetrate the defenses of an enemy nation, and strike devastating blows from the air.

[*See also* Airborne Warfare; Bombing, Ethics of; Bombing of Civilians; Korean War: U.S. Air Operations in the; Strategy: Air Warfare Strategy; Vietnam War: U.S. Air Operations in the; World War I: Air Operations in; World War II, U.S. Air Operations in.]

• Edward Jablonski, *Air War*, 1979. Enzo Angelucci, *The Rand McNally Encyclopedia of Military Aircraft*, 1983. Bill Gunston, *American Warplanes*, 1986. David Wragg, *The Offensive Weapon*, 1986. Robin Cross, *The Bombers*, 1987. Michael S. Sherry, *The Rise of American Air Power*, 1987. Richard Hallion, *Strike from the Sky*, 1989. Ron Dick, *American Eagles: a History of the United States Air Force*, 1997. Daniel March & Chris Bishop, eds., *The Aerospace Encyclopedia of Air Warfare*, 1997.   —Ron Dick

BOMBING, ETHICS OF. Debate over the ethics of bombing focuses largely on strategic bombing: attacks carried out by strikes into the enemy nation for such purposes as impeding production, disrupting *transportation and *communications, and lowering civilian support for the war effort. Strategic bombing is morally problematic because by its nature it involves harm (intentional or not) to nonmilitary targets, while tactical bombing aims only at military targets. As originally conceived by Giulio *Douhet and Billy *Mitchell in the 1920s, strategic bombing was intended to target population centers so as to disrupt the social fabric of the enemy nation and thereby destroy its ability to wage war effectively. Less extreme advocates of airpower, beginning in the 1930s, argued for a conception of strategic bombing by which the actual targets were defined as military bases and means of production, transport, and communication in direct support of military activity, though these might be located in or near population centers.

In terms of ethical analysis, while tactical bombing engages only the ethical principle of proportionality (no destruction beyond that necessary for the tactical purpose), strategic bombing engages both proportion and the principle of discrimination or noncombatant immunity. Two historical contexts have largely focused the ethical debate: the experience of strategic bombing of cities in Britain, Germany, and Japan during World War II, and the development of strategic nuclear targeting in the period 1945–89. Three distinct kinds of ethical argument against such bombing have been advanced.

First is an argument framed in terms of the obligation to protect noncombatants—understood as persons not engaged in the fighting or in providing functional support of the military effort—from direct, intentional harm by acts of war. This is the classic argument from *Just War theory, applied long before the age of aerial warfare to earlier forms of attack directed against noncombatant or mixed combatant-noncombatant targets, such as the artillery bombardment of enemy cities during sieges. The influential early modern theorist Francisco de Vitoria reasoned that this argument accepted bombardment of a fortified city as a sometimes necessary part of just warfare, but insisted that only the fortifications and the combatant forces in such a city can rightly be targeted. Collateral harm to noncombatants is justified only if it is an indirect and unintentional effect of such legitimate acts of war (the "rule of double effect"). The total damage caused must, moreover, not be disproportionate to the justifiable ends achieved. In the seventeenth and eighteenth centuries, such writers as John Locke and Emmerich de Vattel extended the traditional idea of noncombatant immunity to prohibit acts of war aimed at civilian property and values of common benefit to humanity.

The codification of positive international law on war,

beginning in the late nineteenth century, incorporated this established ethical understanding of noncombatant immunity. The 1907 *Hague Convention IV on land warfare explicitly prohibited attacks or bombardment against undefended "towns, villages, dwellings, or buildings," and required that "all necessary steps must be taken to spare" various specific kinds of noncombatant property. Similar provisions were laid out in Convention IX on naval bombardment. The 1923 Hague Rules of Aerial Warfare extended these restrictions to aerial bombardment, adding an explicit prohibition of such bombardment "for the purpose of terrorizing the civilian population, of destroying or damaging private property not of military character, or of injuring non-combatants." These provisions remain the letter of positive international law on war, though their application has been the subject of both legal and ethical dispute.

Curiously, in the context of World War II, arguments for the need to avoid harm to noncombatants in strategic bombing appear more in debates within military circles than in ethical discussion. A prominent and influential exception was an article (1944) by Fr. John C. Ford, S.J., applying this form of moral reasoning to "obliteration bombing." Ford's position was essentially that of Vitoria, updated to address strategic air bombardment. In recent ethical debate, such influential thinkers as Paul Ramsey and Michael Walzer have forcefully stated the argument against strategic targeting of noncombatants, with Ramsey—drawing on Ford but giving a new basis to his argument—reasoning from the duty of nonmaleficence, as defined by the Christian ideal of love, and Walzer focusing on the inherent right of noncombatants not to be harmed directly and intentionally by acts of war. Both accept the moral "rule of double effect" that allows genuinely unintended, indirect harm to noncombatants from an otherwise justified act of war, subject to a judgement as to its proportionality. There is some question as to whether bombardment by *nuclear weapons can ever meet these tests. For example, the American Catholic bishops in their 1983 pastoral letter explicitly rejected the use of nuclear weapons as inherently causing indiscriminate and disproportionate collateral destruction even when targeted directly at military targets within populated areas. Various authors in recent moral debate have applied similar reasoning to condemn retroactively incendiary and atomic bombing in World War II.

The second line of argument over the ethics of bombing is posed in terms of a proportional calculus of the goods achieved versus those lost and the evils done versus those averted. In contrast to the first line, which depends on an ethical distinction between combatants and noncombatants, this second argument generally assumes that in modern warfare every member of a belligerent society is in some sense complicit and thus may be targeted by acts of war. With the combatant-noncombatant distinction sharply diminished, or denied altogether, whether and how far to target civilians depends on the relative utility of doing so in prosecuting the war. In practice, this argument typically has reduced the ethical calculus to a counting of the actual or potential lives lost and casualties inflicted by strategic bombing versus the cost in lives and casualties of other military means without such bombing. Such an argument, reflecting Douhet and Mitchell, was widely used in the British and American debate over the strategic bombing of Germany and Japan in World War II (including the use of atomic bombs against Japan, where the decision was explicitly to choose targets of a mixed civilian-military nature), and it carried over into early debates about American strategic nuclear targeting. Generally, the moral force of this argument lies in the claim that strategic bombing shortens the conflict and therefore saves lives. Thus President Truman justified the atomic bombing of *Hiroshima and Nagasaki by its inducing Japan to end the war, reasoning echoed by such recent authors as Paul Fussell and given wide popular voice in the debate over the *Enola Gay* exhibit at the Smithsonian Institution. In the context of strategic nuclear targeting, deterrence theorists extended this reasoning into the concept that the threat of such bombing by nuclear weapons can prevent the beginning of war.

The third type of argument has been named "supreme emergency" by Walzer. It holds in principle to the morality of the combatant-noncombatant distinction and other forms of restraint in war, but maintains that a particular threat may be so grave that if the enemy won, these and all other forms of moral order upheld by the vanquished society would be lost. Under such extreme circumstances, it is seen as justifiable to use means that temporarily violate the accepted ethical restraints in order to protect and preserve them for the future. Walzer identifies this as the argument used in justifying the indiscriminate bombing of German cities by British Bomber Command in World War II. However, overtones of similar reasoning can be found in debates over the ethics of nuclear targeting, for example, in early postwar arguments justifying atomic counter-city strikes to punish the "crime" of aggression, and later arguments over nuclear strategy that took as their premise the moral superiority of the United States over the Soviet Union.

In World War II and during much of the *Cold War, the technology of aerial bombardment did not allow for close operational discrimination between combatant and noncombatant targets. In this context, the moral argument based on the combatant-noncombatant distinction was dismissed by advocates of the second line of argument as an unattainable ideal and thus irrelevant to the actual conduct of war, leaving only moral reasoning based in proportionality. At the same time, so-called modern war pacifists attacked the first line of argument from another direction, criticizing the rule of double effect as leading in practice to removing the protection of noncombatants living or working close to military targets. For these, too, the critical moral test of targeting doctrine was proportionality.

In contrast to these positions, both international law and contemporary American military doctrine explicitly hold to the combatant-noncombatant distinction that is central to the first form of ethical reasoning about strategic bombing. The present context, however, has changed significantly as targeting and delivery technology for "smart" bombs and both cruise and ballistic *missiles have greatly improved in accuracy, allowing targeting decisions that can realistically discriminate between combatants and noncombatants even when the two are in close proximity. Though on the face of the matter this means that ethical argument depending on a combatant-noncombatant distinction can no longer be criticized as setting an impossibly high ethical standard for warfare, it is also true that such increased accuracy allows for less destructive war-

heads, so that the ethical criterion of proportionality is also more likely to be satisfied when such weapons are employed for strategic bombardment.

In the final analysis, the three ethical arguments defined above are not divided by what is operationally possible in any given context, but by sharply differing normative concepts of what matters in the conduct of war. A conception of war in which discrimination between combatants and noncombatants is a binding moral obligation differs fundamentally from one in which all the citizens of the enemy nation may equally be targeted, subject only to concerns of proportionality, and both differ from a conception in which "supreme emergency" may justify temporary suspension of all moral rules for fighting. Thus, ethical debate over strategic bombing may be expected to continue so long as these differing conceptions of war persist.

[*See also* Bombing of Civilians; Bombs; Strategy: Air Warfare Strategy; Vietnam War, U.S. Air Operations in the; World War II, U.S. Air Operations in.]

• Edward Meade Earle, ed., *Makers of Modern Strategy*, 1943; repr. 1971. Paul Ramsey, *War and the Christian Conscience*, 1961. James Turner Johnson, *Ideology, Reason, and the Limitation of War*, 1975. Michael Walzer, *Just and Unjust Wars*, 1977. William V. O'Brien, *The Conduct of Just and Limited War*, 1981. National Conference of Catholic Bishops, *The Challenge of Peace*, 1983. James Turner Johnson, *Can Modern War Be Just?*, 1984.

—James Turner Johnson

BOMBING OF CIVILIANS. The practice of attacking civilians is as old as warfare itself. Shelling cities by naval or land artillery, for example, long has been commonplace; it continued in the modern-day sieges of Leningrad and Berlin during World War II and of Sarajevo in the 1990s. Aerial bombardment of civilians—widely predicted even before it began, eagerly by pundits who saw it as a way to avert protracted wars—extended that practice. In the 1930s, Fascists in Spain, Italians in Ethiopia, and Japanese in China offered notable examples, ones condemned by American leaders. Imperial powers also bombed civilians in efforts to curb challenges to their rule. In World War I and at the start of World War II, Germany and Great Britain were primarily responsible for initiating deliberate bombing of cities. As embodied in agreements like the *Hague Conventions of 1899 and 1907, legal prohibitions of such practices were clear but unenforceable. The constraints instead were political (fear of condemnation), strategic (fear of retaliation), or operational (lack of resources or bases).

Although a latecomer to the practice, the United States had the history, resources, and attitudes to employ it with unmatched vigor. In operations against Indians, fellow Americans in the *Civil War, and Filipino insurgents, earlier American forces often attacked noncombatants. Before and during World War II, the Army Air Corps's doctrine of precision bombing, and widespread media celebration of it, disguised the nation's ability and willingness to bomb enemy civilians, a practice that President Franklin D. *Roosevelt supported vigorously, if mostly in private. Though hardly peculiar to Americans, notions of total war obliterated distinctions between enemy soldiers and noncombatants. With bombers like the B-17 and the B-29, the United States was technologically supreme in bombing cities and invulnerable to retaliation in kind. Most Americans understood Axis atrocities to provide moral sanction for such actions, which presumably would punish the enemy, forestall his further misdeeds, or hasten war's end. Racial fury against the Japanese further loosened restraints on American forces in the Pacific. Bad weather and technological limitations undercut efforts to strike more limited targets. Some army and navy leaders criticized the bombing that ensued but lacked the power or keen desire to stop it. With notable exceptions, Air Corps leaders, eager for the air force to win the war, worried only when bombing civilians threatened their public image.

As a result, American bombing of civilians escalated during World War II, although British forces attacked cities more zealously in Europe, largely unleashing the famous firestorms at Hamburg (1943) and Dresden (1945). The American contribution came in destroying some sixty Japanese cities, first by incendiary raids and then by two atomic attacks. Over 80,000 Japanese—most civilians—died in one great fire raid on Tokyo in March 1945, with similar death tolls in the August atomic attacks. To the end, official policy maintained the fiction that American forces sought only industrial and military targets: firebombing simply continued the "basic policy of . . . pin-point bombing," the Air Corps insisted; "the first atomic bomb was dropped on Hiroshima, a military base," claimed President Harry S. *Truman's public statement, as if no city were there at all. The majority of Americans accepted the bombing of civilians as an act of justifiable revenge or regrettable necessity, and bombing Japan's cities did hasten its surrender, though by how much historians disagree.

After World War II, U.S. ability to bomb civilians swelled, but the practice of doing so diminished. *Nuclear weapons supremely suited that purpose, as American war plans made clear, but in part because Soviet forces presumably could reply in kind, deterring rather than waging nuclear war dominated American doctrine. In the Korean War, American forces again firebombed enemy cities, but in Vietnam, America's bombs struck civilians of its ally, South Vietnam, more often than North Vietnamese. Congress's decision in 1973 to bar further bombing of Cambodia was a reminder that in the United States, the primary legal restraint on attacking civilians was Congress's power of the purse (the House considered but set aside an article of impeachment against President Richard Nixon for his secret bombing of Cambodia). Technological improvements in the design and delivery of aerial ordinance also diminished attacks on civilians, though less so than American leaders often claimed. Above all, such attacks diminished because no new world war—with all the ferocity, unlimited stakes, and sense of necessity such a war entails—erupted. Perhaps one reason it did not was the chilling record of bombing civilians in earlier wars.

[See also Bombing, Ethics of; Bombs; Hiroshima and Nagasaki, Bombings of; Korean War, U.S. Air Operations in the; Vietnam War, Air Operations in the; World War II, U.S. Air Operations in.]

• Lee Kennett, A History of Strategic Bombing, 1982. Ronald Schaffer, Wings of Judgment: American Bombing in World War II, 1985. Michael S. Sherry, The Rise of American Air Power: The Creation of Armageddon, 1987. Robert Jay Lifton and Greg Mitchell, Hiroshima in America: Fifty Years of Denial, 1995. Stephen L. McFarland, America's Pursuit of Precision Bombing, 1910–1945, 1995.
—Michael S. Sherry

BOMBS. In aerial warfare, the term *bomb* is applied to a wide range of containers filled with explosive, incendiary, or fissile material, or with chemical/biological agents, and designed for use as air-delivered offensive weapons. Fusing and detonating devices are included, and external fins are usually fitted for directional stability. In the late twentieth century, particular attention has been given to the aerodynamics of bombs, and to devising methods of delivering them accurately.

When World War I began in 1914, little thought had been given by the military of Britain, France, or the United States to an air offensive. Most airplane bombs weighed about 20 pounds and were hand-held. German airships, however, were equipped with racks that carried bombs of 110 pounds, and both Russia and Italy had built large aircraft capable of carrying total loads of over 1,000 pounds of bombs. From 1915 on, the first strategic bombing offensive was conducted by Germany against Britain, using airships and later large aircraft carrying bombs of up to 2,200 pounds. The material damage suffered was random and relatively slight, but the morale of the civil population was badly affected. As a result, assumptions were made about the drastic effects of strategic bombing on civilian morale, which proved unjustified in World War II.

At the tactical level, both on the battlefield and immediately behind it, aircraft carrying bombs typically of 112 or 230 pounds were, by 1918, providing effective support to the Allied armies. The U.S. Air Service became heavily involved in the air offensive after 1917, but lacked American equipment and had to rely upon aircraft and weapons of British or French design.

Between the wars, minimal defense budgets precluded significant weapons development, but the impetus of World War II produced remarkable advances. By 1945, the U.S. services were using bombs ranging from 100 to 4,000 pounds. (An experimental bomb weighing 42,000 pounds existed.) Also in the inventory were fragmentation, incendiary, and chemical bombs, some equipped with retarding parachutes for low-level delivery. Armor-piercing bombs were available, particularly for use against warships, and work had been done on fuel/air explosive weapons, which produced catastrophic blast effects by scattering and then detonating large clouds of combustible material. Dramatic demonstrations of the destructive capacity of conventional bombs were given by the Allied air forces in such cities as Hamburg (45,000 dead, 40,000 wounded), Dresden (approximately 60,000 dead), and Tokyo (over 80,000 dead), where firestorms were started by the combined effects of high explosive and incendiaries, killing people by the tens of thousands and effectively destroying the area bombed. Contrary to the interwar predictions, such destruction did not, by itself, bring about the collapse of the attacked state.

High degrees of accuracy were seldom achieved, despite the use of advanced bombsights, *radar, and radio bombing aids, and a host of target-marking techniques. Even the U.S. Army Air Force, which was committed to a policy of "precision" bombing, needed to drop very large numbers of bombs to ensure the destruction of a target. This was not true of bombs delivered at low level from a dive. The destruction of the Japanese carrier force at the Battle of *Midway, for example, was accomplished by a relatively small number of bombs dropped by U.S. Navy dive-bombers.

In August 1945, World War II was brought to an end when USAAF B-29 bombers dropped two atomic bombs on Japan. The first ("Little Boy," Uranium 235) fell on Hiroshima, and the second ("Fat Man," Plutonium 239) on Nagasaki. Each target city was destroyed by a release of nuclear energy that was the equivalent of 20 kilotons of TNT. With this vast increase in the destructive capacity of single bombs, strategic bombing finally reached a point that matched the dire predictions of the interwar strategists. Subsequently, new theories of *deterrence evolved to take account of the awesome power of nuclear weapons and to portray war at the highest level as an unacceptable risk for any nation.

Since World War II, high-yield nuclear bombs have diminished in size while rising in destructive capacity into the multimegaton range, and smaller yield "tactical" nuclear weapons have been introduced. The range of conventional bombs now includes containers filled with napalm (petroleum jelly) and others carrying numerous small bomblets that can be used against vehicles and personnel, or to deny an area like an airfield to enemy use. Technological advances, including *lasers, television, and radar guidance, allow guided—or "smart"—bombs to be delivered at a distance from the target and with great accuracy, hugely magnifying the effectiveness of conventional bombs. During the *Persian Gulf War between the United Nations' forces and Iraq in 1991, the U.S. forces and their allies used guided bombs to great effect in crippling Iraqi command and control systems, one bomb often achieving the same damage as hundreds would have done in World War II.

[See also Air Force Combat Organizations: Strategic Air Forces; Air Force Combat Organizations: Tactical Air Forces; Bomber Aircraft; Bombing of Civilians; Hiroshima and Nagasaki, Bombings of; Korean War, U.S. Operations in the; Kosovo Crisis (1999); Nuclear Weapons; Persian Gulf War; Strategy: Air Warfare Strategy; Vietnam War, U.S. Air Operations in the; World War II, U.S. Air Operations in.]

• D. Lennox, ed., Jane's Air-Launched Weapons, annual. John W. R. Taylor, A History of Aerial Warfare, 1974. Edward Jablonski, Air War, 1979. Bill Gunston, The Illustrated Encyclopedia of Aircraft Armament, 1988. Martin Middlebrook, The Bomber Command War Diaries, 1990. Ron Dick, American Eagles, 1997.

—Ron Dick

BOSNIAN CRISIS (1990s). As the *Cold War ended, the disintegration of the former Yugoslavia, contributing to bloody civil war in Bosnia (1991–95), ultimately led to a *NATO-led peacekeeping mission that constituted the largest military operation in Europe since World War II.

Created from several Balkan states in 1918, Serbian-dominated Yugoslavia began to unravel after the death of Communist leader Tito (Josip Broz) in 1980. In June 1991, the Yugoslav republics of Slovenia and Croatia declared their independence, which was quickly recognized in an extraordinary unilateral move by the newly unified Germany, an old ally. Germany pressured the European Union, including Britain and France, old allies of Serbia, to recognize the breakaway republics.

On 15 October 1991, the parliament of the Yugoslav republic of Bosnia-Herzegovina adopted a declaration of sovereignty, and a majority of the voters opted for independence in a referendum held on 29 February 1992. The Bosnian population was approximately 44 percent Muslim, 31 percent Serb, 17 percent Croat, 8 percent other; and in general, the Muslims and Croats supported secession (although many Croats favored joining Croatia), while Bosnian Serbs objected.

The Bosnian Serbs began to carve out enclaves for themselves, and with the help of the largely Serbian Yugoslav army, the Bosnian Serbs, led by Radovan Karadzíc and Gen. Ratko Mladic, took the offensive, laying siege to a number of cities, most prominently the Bosnian capital of Sarajevo. Their shelling and sniping resulted in many civilian deaths. By the end of August 1992, the ethnic Serbs had extended their control from 60 to approximately 70 percent of Bosnia. Reports of massacres, mass rapes, and "ethnic cleansing" (the expulsion of Muslims and other non-Serbs from areas under Bosnian Serb control) led to public demands for Western intervention. In 1991, the *United Nations Security Council imposed an arms embargo on all the republics; and in 1992, it ordered economic sanctions against Yugoslavia, holding the Belgrade government of President Slobodan Milosevic responsible for actions of the Bosnian Serbs.

Fueled by media coverage, public pressure mounted in the West, but the major European governments were reluctant to act. President Bill *Clinton's administration condemned Belgrade and the Bosnian Serbs as the aggressors and supported an arms embargo but declined to commit U.S. forces. The military feared a Vietnam-like quagmire in the mountains of Bosnia, and much of the public and Congress believed that the Europeans should resolve the matter.

But the only effective multinational military force in Europe was NATO, and any NATO action required U.S. leadership. That began haltingly with NATO's agreement in July 1992 to monitor a UN arms embargo to stop Belgrade from supplying the Bosnian Serbs. Britain, France, and several other countries sent some soldiers as UN monitors. In March 1994, the Bosnian Muslims and Croats linked their territories into a single federation, and an international peace plan proposed dividing control of Bosnia in half between the federation and the Bosnian Serbs. But it was rejected by the Bosnian Serbs, and the fighting continued.

A Bosnian Serb offensive in 1995—especially the capture of the alleged "safe havens" of Sebrenica and Zepa—together with more reports of large-scale atrocities, led the Clinton administration to commit NATO airpower against the Bosnian Serbs. A rebuilt Croatian army, joined by Bosnian Muslim forces armed by Iran and other Muslim nations, launched major ground attacks and successfully pushed back the Bosnian Serbs. In combination with a NATO air campaign, this gain changed the balance of power and forced the Bosnian Serbs to reduce their territorial ambitions.

The Clinton administration now took the lead, obtaining a cease-fire on 5 October 1995, and a month later bringing the three Balkan presidents—Alija Izetbegovic of Bosnia-Herzegovina, Slobodan Milosevic of Serbia, and Franjo Tudjman of Croatia—to Wright-Patterson Air Force Base in Dayton, Ohio, for peace talks. Three weeks of negotiations resulted in the three presidents initialing the Dayton peace agreements on 21 November. This was followed by a lifting of the UN economic sanctions against Yugoslavia. Signed in Paris on 14 December 1995, the peace treaty ended the four-year civil war. It also sought to establish a Bosnian republic of two "entities" divided 49 percent for the Bosnian Serbs and 51 percent for the Muslim-Croat federation. The 42 months of warfare had left 250,000 people dead and driven more than 1 million from their homes.

A 60,000-strong international Implementation Force (I-For), under command of NATO, would replace the UN monitoring force to provide for implementation of the agreement. The largest contingents included the United States with 20,000 troops, Britain with 13,000, and France with 8,000; but more than two dozen countries sent soldiers, including Russia with 2,000 troops. Congress gave basic approval on 13 December 1995, and the United States ended its arms embargo and began to upgrade the Bosnian Army. The U.S. occupation sector was in eastern Bosnia, around Tuzla. The soldiers deployed in late December and early January 1996, and quickly established a 2.5-mile-wide buffer zone between the opposing forces. The American soldiers lived in newly constructed army camps, staffed checkpoints, and went out on heavily protected patrols.

The U.S.-instituted Dayton Accords envisioned a sovereign, multi-ethnic Bosnian republic composed of Croats, Muslims, and Serbs. Thus the peacekeeping force's mission was not simply to prevent the resumption of the civil war, which it did, but also to protect the return of refugees and the conduct of free local elections as important steps in rebuilding the new republic. This was a lofty goal, which the peacekeeping force was unable to achieve because of feuding among Bosnian Serbs, Muslims, and Croats. The Western governments and the international stabilization force were reluctant to act as local police or to try to arrest persons for *war crimes. Indeed, the West was divided, as Britain and France differed with the United States by offering greater support for Serbia as a continuing power in the region and allowing partitioning of Bosnia into Serb, Croat, and Muslim sectors.

Under the Dayton agreements, the NATO-led implementation force was to be in Bosnia for one year. But in December 1996, this deadline was extended, although I-For was succeeded by a "follow-on" force (the International Stabilization Force) and reduced to 30,000. The United States still had 6,000 troops in Bosnia in 1999. It remained far from certain whether the internally secure, multiethnic Bosnian republic envisioned by the United States in the Dayton agreements would be sustained or whether the country would fragment along hostile ethnic lines, leading to a partitioning of Bosnia into Muslim, Serb, and Croat sectors. In 1998–99, when the Yugoslavian government's increased control of Kosovo province was challenged by ethnic Albanian rebels and bloody fighting resulted, NATO agreed to send a peacekeeping contingent of nearly 30,000 troops, to which President Clinton contributed 4,000 U.S. peacekeepers, if the warring Serbs and ethnic Albanians could not reach a peace agreement.

[See also Kosovo Crisis (1999); Peacekeeping.]

• Rebecca West, Black Lamb and Grey Falcon: A Journey Through Yugoslavia, 1941; repr. 1968. Misha Glenny, The Fall of Yugoslavia: The Third Balkan War, 1992. Edgar O'Ballance, Civil War in Bosnia, 1992–94, 1995. David Rieff, Slaughterhouse: Bosnia and the Failure of the West, 1995. Laura Silber and Allan Little, eds., The Death of Yugoslavia, 1995. Susan L. Woodward, Balkan Tragedy: Chaos and Dissolution After the Cold War, 1995.

—John Whiteclay Chambers II

BOSTON MASSACRE (1770). The Boston Massacre, a pivotal event of the Revolutionary era, emerged from Britain's attempts to assert greater control over its North American colonies after the *French and Indian War. When customs officials complained about abusive Bostonians, the British government assigned four regiments to garrison the town.

The troops' arrival in October 1768 heightened political conflict and exacerbated local economic pressures, as off-duty soldiers competed for jobs on the docks; but the situation eventually stabilized sufficiently that two regiments could be withdrawn. Soldiers and civilians maintained a strained but generally peaceful relationship until 5 March 1770, when nervous redcoats fired into a crowd taunting them and throwing iceballs at them. Five townspeople died, instantly becoming martyrs to British "tyranny." Even though Gen. Thomas *Gage removed the troops from Boston and a local jury acquitted all but two redcoats involved, the consequences were significant.

The so-called massacre embarrassed the British ministry and fed anti-British sentiment in the American colonies. It also, more than any other event, galvanized a growing anti–standing army sentiment among Americans.

[See also Adams, John; Civil-Military Relations: Civilian Control of the Military; Revolutionary War: Causes.]

• John Shy, Toward Lexington: The Role of the British Army in the Coming of the American Revolution, 1965. Hiller Zober, The Boston Massacre, 1970.

—J. Mark Thompson

BOXER REBELLION. See China Relief Expedition (1900).

BRADDOCK, EDWARD (1695–1755). British Maj. Gen. Edward Braddock had served in Flanders and commanded at Gibraltar, but had no battle command experience when sent with two understrength regiments to repel French "encroachments" in North America. From his arrival in Hampton Roads, Virginia, on 20 February 1755, this gruff but humane disciplinarian led the colonial governors in organizing an unexpectedly ambitious campaign involving four independent expeditions against Fort Beauséjour, Fort St. Frédéric, Fort Niagara, and Fort Duquesne.

Braddock personally, and efficiently, commanded the expedition to Fort Duquesne in western Pennsylvania in the face of major transport shortages, minimal Indian support, and mountainous terrain that hindered movement of his heavy artillery. His army advanced 150 miles from Alexandria to Little Meadows; then Braddock led a force of 1,450 that reached the Monongahela River on 8 July. The next day, this column was surprised, completely disorganized, and defeated by a force of 783 French, Canadians, and Indians. Severely wounded after having several horses killed under him, Braddock died four days later. Although not personally culpable for the defeat, he came to bear the opprobrium that accompanied this disaster.

[See also Braddock's Defeat; French and Indian War.]

• Lee McCardell, Ill-Starred General, 1958.

—Ian K. Steele

BRADDOCK'S DEFEAT (1755). At the outset of the *French and Indian War, a 1,450-man advance column of Gen. Edward *Braddock's army of British and American soldiers had, by July 1755, marched for three weeks without incident, to within seven miles of Fort Duquesne. The advance party, apparently lulled into overlooking routine precautions, failed to detect an approaching force of 783 French, Canadians, and Indians.

The equally surprised French *troupes de la marine* blocked the twelve-foot-wide forest roadway with effective musketry. Braddock's column did not receive—or did not hear—the order to halt, and infantry, artillery, and baggage train telescoped into each other in confusion. Indians and Canadians immediately used Indian tactics of "moving fire" along both flanks of the disrupted column. The British lost 977 wounded and killed, while their opponents sustained only 39 casualties.

The British sought revenge, committing unprecedented funds and regulars to the war. Indian victors, gathering rich booty, encouraged dozens of tribes to assist in the successful French campaigns of 1756 and 1757. Braddock's defeat also provoked Indian raids that disrupted the Pennsylvania and Virginia frontiers. In American mythology, "Braddock's Defeat" became a convenient synonym for the superiority of frontiersmen over European regulars.

• Paul E. Kopperman, *Braddock at the Monongahela*, 1977.

—Ian K. Steele

BRADLEY, OMAR N. (1893–1981), World War II commander and first chairman of the *Joint Chiefs of Staff (JCS). Born in Clark, Missouri, and graduating from West Point, Bradley served in World War I, then spent most of the interwar years as student or instructor. In 1942, he trained the 28th and 82nd Divisions and took combat command in spring 1943 of II Corps in the *North Africa campaign and the subsequent invasion of *Sicily. Bradley led the First Army in the invasion of *Normandy and on 1 August 1944 took charge of 12th Army Group, which by V-E Day included four U.S. armies with forty-three divisions. Gen. Dwight D. *Eisenhower rated Bradley as a battle-line commander without peer, but controversies continue about his approval of close-in carpet bombing to facilitate the breakout at *St. Lô in Normandy; his failure to close the Falaise-Argentan gap; his advocacy of a broad-front approach to the battle for *Germany; his failure to foresee the Germans' surprise counteroffensive in the Battle of the *Bulge; as well as his tense relations with the British field marshal, Bernard Law *Montgomery.

Bradley served as head of the *Veterans Administration (1945–47), then became army chief of staff in February 1948, and served as first permanent chairman of the JCS (1949–53). He was made four-star General of the Army in September 1950. As JCS chairman, Bradley supported President Harry S. *Truman's rejection of the navy's supercarrier in 1949 and helped oversee the *Cold War defense buildup after 1950. In the *Korean War, Bradley recommended sending troops to oppose North Korea's invasion in 1950, favored confining hostilities after the Chinese intervention in November, and supported Truman's decision to relieve Gen. Douglas *MacArthur in 1951. Speaking for the JCS that year, he testified that the Soviet Union posed the main threat and that conflict with China—which MacArthur seemed willing to widen—would be "the wrong war, at the wrong place, at the wrong time, and with the wrong enemy." Bradley retired in 1953; he died in 1981.

[*See also* World War II: Military and Diplomatic Course.]

—Walter S. Poole

BRAGG, BRAXTON (1817–1876), Confederate general. Bragg was born in North Carolina and graduated from West Point in 1837. He fought in the *Seminole Wars and the *Mexican War and was a Louisiana sugar planter from 1856 until 1861. Appointed a Confederate brigadier during the Civil War by his friend Jefferson *Davis in March 1861, Bragg trained volunteers at Pensacola and became a major general in September. Sent to aid A. S. Johnston's army in February 1862, Bragg fought well at the Battle of *Shiloh.

A full general commanding the western department in April 1862, Bragg invaded Kentucky but gained little. He fought the indecisive Battle of *Perryville, 8 October 1862, then retreated to Tennessee. On 31 December, he fought Gen. W. S. *Rosecrans at Murfreesboro, with initial success. Persistent Union resistance drained Bragg's confidence, and on 2 January 1863 he retreated to Tullahoma. Rosecrans flanked him from Chattanooga on 9 September 1863.

Doubting subordinates foiled Bragg's plans to attack below Chattanooga, but on 19 and 20 September—reinforced by Gen. James *Longstreet's corps from the Army of Northern Virginia—he attacked successfully at the Battle of *Chickamauga and besieged the beaten Federals in Chattanooga.

Bragg quarreled with his subordinates while Gen. Ulysses S. *Grant replaced Rosecrans. Grant routed Bragg's Army of the Tennessee from *Missionary Ridge on 23–25 November.

Davis accepted Bragg's resignation, but in February 1864 called him to Richmond as military adviser—a job he performed well because of administrative skills. Bragg, though, used malign influence to get Joseph E. *Johnston removed from command of the army at Atlanta—with dire results.

In October 1864, Bragg's command indecision lost the Confederacy's last blockade-running port, Wilmington, North Carolina. He served under Joseph Johnston at the end of the war, was captured on 9 May 1865, paroled, and died in Galveston, Texas.

Probably the most controversial Confederate general, his abilities thwarted by a thorny personality and odd moments of dereliction, Bragg did much to defeat his cause.

[*See also* Civil War: Military and Diplomatic Course.]

• Grady McWhiney, *Braxton Bragg and Confederate Defeat*, Vol. 1, 1969; repr. 1991. Steven E. Woodworth, *Jefferson Davis and His Generals: The Failure of Confederate Command in the West*, 1990. Judith Lee Hallock, *Braxton Bragg and Confederate Defeat*, Vol. 2, 1991.

—Frank E. Vandiver

BRANDY STATION, BATTLE OF (1863). This battle, fought just south of the Rappahannock River in Culpeper County, Virginia, stands as the largest clash of cavalry in North America. While not strategically important, the battle had long-range consequences for cavalry operations during the second half of the Civil War.

Robert E. *Lee intended to launch his Gettysburg campaign from Culpeper County on the morning of 9 June 1863. Gen. James E. B. *Stuart, commanding five cavalry brigades and five artillery batteries (9,700 men), had orders to screen the infantry's line of march northward from Union forces under Gen. Joseph *Hooker. Stuart had encamped his men on a north-south line ten miles long and midway between Lee's infantry at Culpeper Courthouse and the Rappahannock River. The approximate center of his line was Brandy Station, on the Orange & Alexandria Railroad.

Gen. Alfred Pleasonton, cavalry chief of the Army of the

Potomac, moved first. Benefiting from reforms enacted the previous February by Hooker, Federal cavalry was beginning to take a more aggressive role in the war. Pleasonton on this day had orders to cross the Rappahannock with three cavalry divisions, two infantry brigades, and six artillery batteries, and destroy whatever Confederate forces he found in Culpeper. Unfortunately, Pleasonton did not know the precise location or size of those forces, which he erroneously assumed would be encamped around Culpeper Courthouse, eleven miles west of the river.

Following instructions from Hooker, Pleasonton divided his force on 9 June. The right wing (5,418 men) under Gen. John Buford crossed the river at Beverly's Ford around 5:00 A.M. The left wing (5,563 men) under Gen. David M. Gregg crossed at Kelly's Ford, six miles below Beverly's Ford, an hour later. The two wings were to rendezvous at Brandy Station and move west toward the courthouse. Buford was surprised to encounter rebel resistance near the river, but he advanced swiftly toward the brigade camp of Gen. William E. "Grumble" Jones, near St. James's Church and two miles north of Brandy Station. Jones established a strong defensive line, composed largely of artillery and dismounted cavalry, that repulsed repeated assaults by Buford. The line was soon reinforced and extended in the shape of a crescent by the arrival of Gen. Wade Hampton's brigade on Jones's right flank and Gen. W. H. F. "Rooney" Lee's brigade on his left, along the base of Yew Ridge.

By that time, however, around 11:00 A.M., the Federal left wing was approaching Stuart's rear. Gregg's command, consisting primarily of his own cavalry division and a cavalry division under Col. Alfred N. A. Duffie, had overwhelmed pickets at Kelly's Ford. Gregg's division circumvented Gen. Beverly Robertson's brigade and was poised to seize Fleetwood Hill, just north of Brandy and the site of Stuart's headquarters, before Stuart appreciated the danger. In this second and most famous phase of the battle, thousands of mounted cavalry launched charge after countercharge seeking to control the heights of Fleetwood. At the same time, a third phase of the fight unfolded near Stevensburg, four miles south of Brandy, where Duffie, who had been dispatched toward Culpeper Courthouse, battled two Confederate regiments. Duffie, with nearly 2,000 horsemen, outnumbered his opponents four to one, but his overly cautious nature prohibited him from breaking through to join Buford and Gregg.

By 4:00 P.M., Pleasonton, who had accompanied Buford's wing, had ordered his command to recross the Rappahannock. Federal retreat was accelerated by a final Confederate attack. As troops were withdrawn from the fighting around St. James's to engage on Fleetwood, Buford had slowly pushed back Rooney Lee. Now the brigades of Rooney Lee and Fitzhugh Lee rallied to slam into the Union right flank as Pleasonton's entire line faded back toward the river.

Stuart would never admit to being taken by surprise at Brandy Station, and he could, in fact, claim a tactical victory. He had held his ground, and Confederate casualties amounted to only 485, compared to Federal losses of 866. The heaviest fighting and the lion's share of the casualties came around St. James's. But Federal cavalrymen believed they had earned a stalemate deep in rebel territory. This sense of accomplishment, combined with the new Federal strategy that gave them a larger combat role, enhanced their confidence and morale. Stuart, say some authorities,

stung by public criticism of his performance at Brandy Station, tried to atone with an ill-conceived raid during the Gettysburg campaign, a raid that left Robert E. Lee blind during the early, critical stages of that campaign and battle.

[See also Civil War: Military and Diplomatic Course; Gettysburg, Battle of.]

• Stephen Z. Starr, The Union Cavalry in the Civil War, 3 vols., 1979–85. Emory M. Thomas, Bold Dragoon: The Life of J. E. B. Stuart, 1986. Clark B. Hall, "The Battle of Brandy Station," Civil War Times Illustrated, 19 (June 1990), pp. 32–42, 45. Clark B. Hall, "'Long and Desperate Encounter': Buford at Brandy Station," Civil War, 8 (July–August 1990), pp. 12–17, 66–67. Gary W. Gallagher, "Brandy Station: The Civil War's Bloodiest Arena of Mounted Combat," Blue & Gray Magazine, 8 (October 1990), pp. 8–22, 44–53. Daniel E. Sutherland, Seasons of War: The Ordeal of a Confederate Community, 1995.   —Daniel E. Sutherland

BRANT, JOSEPH (1742–1807), British army officer and Mohawk leader. Brant was the son of a Mohawk chief and a woman of mixed English and Indian descent. After his father's death, Brant lived with his sister's husband, William Johnson, superintendent of Indian affairs north of the Ohio River from 1755 to 1774. This experience, combined with attendance at a Christian school in Connecticut, prepared him for work as a bicultural mediator between the English and Iroquois in the years leading up to the American Revolution.

When the *Revolutionary War broke out, Brant traveled to England, and was commissioned captain, and expressed his allegiance to the British crown. He returned to the Hudson River Valley and rallied the Iroquois to the loyalist cause, leading highly effective expeditions against Americans living in the region. These brought harsh retaliation from American forces under Gen. John Sullivan in 1779. Brant continued to resist even after British troops ceased hostilities. The English rewarded him and a number of Mohawks for their services with a tract of land in Ontario, where Brant eventually died. Brant's leadership and skills as a mediator enabled him and his followers to carve out a degree of autonomy while facing Anglo-American expansionist pressures.

• Barbara Graymont, The Iroquois in the American Revolution, 1972. Isabel Thompson Kelsay, Joseph Brant, 1743–1807: Man of Two Worlds, 1984.   —James D. Drake

BREED'S HILL, BATTLE OF. See Bunker Hill, Battle of (1776).

BROWN, GEORGE (1918–1978), chairman of the *Joint Chiefs of Staff, 1974–78. George Brown served on the Joint Chiefs of Staff (JCS) for five years: one year as air force chief of staff (1973–74), and four years as chairman. Although General Brown fought in three wars and served with distinction in high-level positions in the *Pentagon, he is best known for a series of myopic and offensive public remarks made during his tenure as chairman. Brown complained about Israel's undue influence on Congress, and ascribed that influence to the "fact" that the Jewish people in the United States control the banks and newspapers. He also said that the American commitment to Israel was a burden on the United States, and vigorously defended the right of the government to spy on American citizens in order to protect national security. Normally, such statements by a high government official would have resulted in dismissal by the president.

Brown was not relieved by either President Ford or Carter simply because he was too valuable as chairman of the JCS. Brown's value came from three sources. First, he was a superb military strategist with great expertise on the complex issues involved in the *Strategic Arms Limitation Talks (SALT) with the Soviet Union. Second, Brown held a balanced analytical view of the military situation between the United States and the USSR. Unlike some of his contemporaries, he was inclined neither to overstate the Soviet military threat nor to understate America's military capabilities. Third, Brown was held in high regard by his military colleagues for his honesty and expertise. He was also highly regarded for helping the U.S. military adjust to the post-Vietnam draw down.

• Lawrence Korb, *The Joint Chiefs of Staff: The First Twenty-Five Years.* 1976. Lawrence Korb, *The Fall and Rise of the Pentagon,* 1979.
—Lawrence Korb

BROWN, HAROLD (1927–), nuclear physicist and weapons designer; secretary of the air force and secretary of defense; defense consultant. The first scientist to become secretary of defense, Harold Brown's career epitomizes the linkages between scientific, educational, and military institutions that developed during the *Cold War. A high school graduate at age fifteen, Brown received his Ph.D. in physics from Columbia University in 1949, at twenty-one. After working at the Lawrence Radiation Laboratory at the University of California, Berkeley, in 1952 Brown joined the newly created Lawrence Livermore Laboratory, where he worked on controlled fusion and nuclear explosives. Before becoming laboratory director (1960), he had played a leading role in the design of the Polaris missile warhead and taken part in discussions on Project Plowshare (peaceful uses of *nuclear weapons). Brown joined the Kennedy administration in May 1961 as director of the Division of Research and Engineering (DDR&E) within the Department of *Defense. As DDR&E, he scrutinized service proposals for new weapons systems, rejecting some, such as the Skybolt missile and the B-70 bomber, while backing others, such as highly accurate multiple independently targetable reentry vehicles (MIRVs) and the TFX fighter-bomber.

From 1965 to 1968, Brown was secretary of the air Force. Initially a supporter of the *Vietnam War, he was an architect of the bombing program, but became a supporter of deescalation. Appointed president of California Institute of Technology (1969), Brown served the Nixon administration as a member of the SALT I delegation. When Jimmy *Carter was elected president in 1976, he appointed Brown secretary of defense. A strong secretary, who was committed to sustaining a strategic nuclear edge over the Soviet Union, Brown left his stamp upon the administration's defense programs, including the MX missile, SALT II, and nuclear strategy (Presidential Directive 59). Brown also presided over defense budget increases, especially after the invasion of Afghanistan (1979), although his rationale—a purportedly increased rate of Soviet military investment—remains contested. To bolster containment of the Soviet Union, Brown promoted military and intelligence cooperation with China, an initiative that he cemented with a major trip to Beijing (1980). During the 1980s, Brown became an investment banker but also held posts at Johns Hopkins University and the Center for International Strategic Studies.

[*See also* SALT Treaties.]

• *Current Biography,* 1961, pp. 76–78. *Current Biography,* 1977, pp. 86–89. Bernard Weinraub, "The Browning of the Pentagon," *New York Times:* 29 January 1977. Raymond Garthoff, *Detente and Confrontation: U.S.-Soviet Relations from Nixon to Reagan,* 1994. Olav Njølstad, *Peacekeeper and Troublemaker: The Containment Policy of Jimmy Carter,* 1995.
—William Burr

BROWNING AUTOMATIC RIFLE. Responding to the need to counter massed German *machine guns in World War I, renowned American arms inventor John M. Browning developed his Browning Automatic Rifle (BAR) in 1918. This was a 16-pound, gas-operated weapon that fired .30-caliber bullets from a twenty-round detachable box magazine. The BAR had a selector switch that allowed the user to fire individual shots or in a fully automatic mode that would empty the magazine in about two seconds. The muzzle tended to rise during automatic fire, making it difficult to stay on target. Sustained automatic fire also tended to overheat the barrel.

Various firms produced some 85,000 BARs during World War I. By World War II, modifications had increased its weight to almost 20 pounds, but it remained in use as the principal squad automatic weapon of the U.S. Army during World War II and Korea. Some indigenous forces on both sides during the *Vietnam War also used these weapons.

• Joseph E. Smith and W. H. B. Smith, *Small Arms of the World,* 9th rev. ed., 1969. Ian V. Hogg and John Weeks, *Military Small Arms of the 20th Century,* 4th rev. ed., 1981.
—James M. McCaffrey

BRYAN, WILLIAM JENNINGS (1860–1925), politician and secretary of state. Reared in Illinois, Bryan attended Illinois College and Chicago's Union College of Law. In 1887 he moved to Nebraska, entering Democratic politics as a champion of agrarian reform. Elected to Congress in 1890, defeated in a Senate bid four years later, he won the Democratic presidential nomination in 1896 but lost to Republican William *McKinley. He ran again in 1900 and 1908—both times unsuccessfully.

Having supported Woodrow *Wilson in 1912, Bryan became his secretary of state. A pacifist and anti-imperialist with no diplomatic experience, Bryan negotiated conciliation treaties with some thirty nations providing for the submission of disputes to investigative commissions.

The outbreak of war in 1914 tested Bryan's *pacifism. Embracing Wilson's call for U.S. *neutrality, he opposed loans to the Allies and travel on belligerent ships by U.S. citizens; he also called on U.S. vessels to observe Germany's U-boat blockade of Great Britain. President Wilson, by contrast, saw the German blockade as a violation of neutral rights.

In May 1915, a German U-boat sank the British liner *Lusitania* (heavily loaded with munitions), killing 1,198 people, including 128 Americans. Wilson repeatedly demanded that Germany pay reparations, disavow U-boat warfare, and accept his interpretation of neutral rights. Bryan resigned, believing Wilson was treating the German and British maritime *blockades unequally; he also deplored the president's preempting of his role. He was succeeded by the colorless Robert Lansing, who proved highly favorable to the Allies.

Out of office, Bryan opposed the militaristic "Preparedness" campaign but endorsed Wilson in 1916. Personally opposed to U.S. entry into the war in 1917, he refused to speak out.

As a diplomat, Bryan shared Wilson's moralistic approach to world affairs, but the two men's basic principles differed: Bryan valued peace above all; Wilson insisted that Germany accept his view of neutral rights. Bryan's resignation reflected the conflict of wills that often ensues when a president seeks to conduct his own foreign policy—a conflict that has more than once upset the course of U.S. diplomacy.

[See also Lusitania, Sinking of the; World War I: Causes.]

• Merle Curti, Bryan and World Peace, 1931; repr. 1969. Paolo E. Coletta, Bryan: A Political Biography, 1971. Kendrick A. Clements, William Jennings Bryan: Missionary Isolationist, 1982.

—Paul S. Boyer

BUDGETING FOR WAR. See Public Financing and Budgeting for War.

BUENA VISTA, BATTLE OF (1847). Maj. Gen. Zachary *Taylor's small army had been victorious in all three of its *Mexican War battles by the end of 1846. After the Battle of Monterrey in September, many of his troops were assigned to Maj. Gen. Winfield *Scott for a proposed attack on the Mexican coastal town of Veracruz.

Antonio López de *Santa Anna commanded Mexican forces, and he knew from captured dispatches that Scott had siphoned off Taylor's best troops. In late January 1847, therefore, he led 21,000 troops northward to attack Taylor's weakened force of about 5,000. The U.S. forces positioned themselves near the Hacienda San Juan de la Buena Vista, where the road passed between mountains.

The Mexican Army, reduced to about 15,000 men by death, disease, and desertion, reached the U.S. position on 22 February. After Taylor refused Santa Anna's invitation to surrender, the Mexicans attacked. The fighting was brisk but inconclusive. It ended at sunset.

Santa Anna reopened the battle the next morning. Mexican cavalry rode around the U.S. position and toward its supply base at the hacienda. Col. Jefferson *Davis formed his Mississippi volunteers and an Indiana regiment into a large V. When the Mexican horsemen rode into the mouth of this V, they were shot to pieces. Meanwhile, superbly handled U.S. artillery held off Mexican infantry advancing straight up the valley.

Nightfall again ended the fighting, but this time Santa Anna used the darkness to mask his retreat. He had lost over 3,500 men in the two-day fight. U.S. *casualties were also heavy; over 600 had fallen.

The Battle of Buena Vista was the last major battle of the war in northern Mexico. Within two weeks, General Scott landed at Veracruz, and Santa Anna hastened southward to try to protect his nation's capital city from this new threat. Had the Mexicans won at Buena Vista, Scott's attack probably would have been postponed or even canceled.

• K. Jack Bauer, The Mexican War, 1846–1848, 1974. John S. D. Eisenhower, So Far From God: The U.S. War with Mexico 1846–1848, 1989.

—James M. McCaffrey

"BUFFALO" SOLDIERS. In the post–*Civil War regular army, Congress set aside six regiments for black enlisted men in the reorganization act of 28 July 1866. These were the 9th and 10th Cavalry and the 38th, 39th, 40th, and 41st Infantry Regiments. The act marked the first inclusion of black units in the regular army. It was seen as recognition of the contribution black units of the *Union army had made in the *Civil War. In the spring of 1869, the 38th and 41st were merged into the 24th Infantry Regiment; the 39th and 40th became the 25th. Commissioned officers of the black units were white (the only exceptions before 1901 were Henry Flipper, Charles *Young, and John Alexander).

Until the 1890s, the black regiments served almost entirely at remote western frontier posts. Comprised initially of mostly illiterate former slaves, they overcame their shortcomings and the army's initial tendency to supply them with cast-off equipment. They also faced considerable racial hostility and occasional violence from white civilians throughout their frontier service.

All saw action against hostile Indians. Sergeant Emanuel Stance of the Ninth Cavalry was the first of eighteen black soldiers to receive the Medal of Honor during the Indian Wars between 1870 and 1890. Both cavalry regiments played prominent roles in the brutal Apache wars of 1877–81; they suffered more *casualties than all the other frontier campaigns. They also fought in Cuba, in the *Philippine War (1899–1902), and in Mexican border skirmishes (1915–16).

The sobriquet "Buffalo" Soldiers was applied first to the 10th Regiment around 1870. The term apparently originated with the Cheyenne Indians, who may have seen a similarity between the curly hair and the dark skin of the soldiers and the buffalo. Soon the Ninth's troopers also became known as buffalo soldiers, and ultimately the infantrymen too came to be considered buffalo soldiers. Many writers contend that the name reflected the Indians' respect for the soldiers, but Native American commentators disagree.

[See also African Americans in the Military; Army, U.S.: 1866–99; Plains Indians Wars.]

• William H. Leckie, The Buffalo Soldiers: A Narrative of the Negro Cavalry in the West, 1967. Arlen L. Fowler, The Black Infantry in the West 1869–1891, 1971. Frank N. Schubert, On the Trail of the Buffalo Soldier: Biographies of African Americans in the U.S. Army, 1866–1917, 1995.

—Frank N. Schubert

BULGE, BATTLE OF THE (1944–45). Also known as the Ardennes Campaign of World War II, this was Adolf *Hitler's last counteroffensive in the West, an attempt to break the Allied lines at the Ardennes Forest, drive a wedge between the American and British armies, capture the Belgian port of Antwerp, disrupt logistics, trap Allied forces, and perhaps achieve a negotiated peace in the West.

Spearheading the thrust were two German Panzer (armored) armies—the Sixth SS Panzer Army and Fifth Panzer Army—plus the Seventh Army composed primarily of volksgrenadier replacement units, plus paratroopers who were to be dropped ahead to capture bridges and block reinforcements. The total German strike force included 38 divisions with perhaps 250,000 troops, supported by nearly 1,000 aircraft.

Surprise was crucial to Hitler's plan, so the Germans used deceptive techniques; even Field Marshal Gerd von Rundstedt, the German theater commander, was initially misled about the concentration of troops, which he and the Allies (listening through *ULTRA since the Germans used landlines rather than radio transmissions within Germany) thought were for defensive purposes to block the next Allied offensive north and south of the Ardennes. Tactically, the Germans also imposed strict radio silence. They were aided by the inclement winter weather, which prevented aerial reconnaissance.

The Germans achieved complete surprise when they launched the massive offensive on 16 December 1944. Facing them were some 83,000 American troops in five divisions from Gen. Courtney H. Hodges's First U.S. Army, largely new or recuperating divisions, since Hodges's main force was north near Aachen preparing to attack the Roer Dams. In fog and then snow, the Germans tanks and infantry, most of them armed with automatic weapons, pushed forward, their artillery severing communication lines. A handful of English-speaking German soldiers in American uniforms and vehicles sowed confusion and apprehension.

The Germans achieved breakthroughs in half a dozen places, and for two weeks, it appeared that they might reach at least the Meuse River (a penetration of more than seventy miles). Although the Americans continued to hold the shoulders of the growing salient (the "bulge"), the 58th Panzer Corps and the 47th Corps poured through the gap created by the collapse of the U.S. 28th and the newly arrived and untested 106th Infantry Divisions.

At his headquarters in Paris, Supreme Allied Commander Gen. Dwight D. *Eisenhower conferred with Gen. Omar N. *Bradley, head of the 12th Army Group. Bradley believed it a spoiling attack, but Eisenhower sensed its scope. Yet Eisenhower's broad-front strategy denied him the reserves to meet such an attack. Thus on 19 December, he ordered General Hodges on the north and Gen. George S. *Patton on the south of the salient to pivot the First and Third U.S. Armies and redirect their offensives to cut off the German salient at its base. He also ordered the 82nd and 101st U.S. Airborne Division sent in by truck, and all available U.S. reserves in Europe to be put into action. This meant that black platoons went into combat at the company level with white units, fighting their mutual enemy.

The vital road center of Bastogne was soon surrounded by the advancing Germans. But calling themselves the "Battered Bastards of Bastogne," the 101st U.S. Airborne Division refused to surrender—Brig. Gen. Anthony C. McAuliffe's answer to a German delegation was "Nuts"—and held down five German divisions. The 82nd Airborne Division also thwarted the Germans at Houffalize, and Americans put up major resistance at St. Vith. Many were angered by true reports that the SS had executed captured G.I.s at Malmédy.

On 24 December, the German Panzers reached their limit, blocked three miles from the Meuse by Gen. James "Lightning" Collins's 2nd Armored Division. The previous day, clearing skies enabled 2,000 Allied planes to begin attacking enemy columns and supply lines. The Luftwaffe counterattacked, destroying more than 150 Allied planes, but lost 300 themselves and never recovered. U.S. and British airplanes shattered the German offensive, which was already running short of fuel and ammunition.

The Army Air Force also began on 23 December to resupply the besieged American paratroopers. The first reinforcements reached Bastogne the day after Christmas.

With the German offensive blunted, the U.S. First and Third Armies began their pincer movements on 3 January 1944, but deep snow prevented their closing on Houffalize until 16 January. By then many of the Germans had escaped.

Although the German counteroffensive had been defeated, it was a costly victory. Allied *casualties totaled 77,000 men, which included 8,000 killed in action, 48,000 wounded in action, and 21,000 as prisoners of war or missing in action. Exact figures for German casualties are impossible to determine, but estimates suggest that the Germans lost over 200,000 men, including 110,000 as prisoners of war. In addition, they lost 1,400 tanks and 600 other vehicles.

Hitler's decision for the massive counteroffensive, rather than the traditional delaying actions and defense, also cost the Germans their last reserves in veteran troops, *tanks, and mechanized artillery and vehicles. Despite some desperate moments, the "Battle of the Bulge" ultimately proved to be the beginning of the invasion of the Third Reich from the West.

[See also France, Liberation of; World War II: Military and Diplomatic Course.]

• Robert E. Merriam, Dark December, 1947. Leonard Rapport and Arthur Northwood, Jr., Rendezvous with Destiny. A History of the 101st Airborne Division, 1948. John Toland, Battle: The Story of the Bulge, 1959. Hugh M. Cole, The Ardennes: Battle of the Bulge, 1965. John S. D. Eisenhower, The Bitter Woods, 1969. Charles B. MacDonald, The Last Offensive, 1973. Russell F. Weigley, Eisenhower's Lieutenants: The Campaigns of France and Germany, 1944–45, 1981. Charles B. MacDonald, A Time for Trumpets. The Untold Story of the Battle of the Bulge, 1985.
—Ernest F. Fisher

BULL RUN, FIRST BATTLE OF (1861). The first major land battle of the Civil War occurred at Bull Run Creek (near the town of Manassas, Virginia) Virginia, on 21 July 1861. Brig. Gen. P. G. T. *Beauregard, the hero of Fort Sumter, commanded the *Confederate army. His force of 20,000 protected a rail link that led to Brig. Gen. Joseph E. *Johnston's army in the lower Shenandoah Valley. Johnston's 12,000 men faced a Federal force of 18,000 commanded by the aged Robert Patterson, a veteran of the *War of 1812.

Beauregard deployed his force along a stream called Bull Run; it was crossable only at a number of fords and one stone bridge. Henry Hill commanded the bridge and the fords around it, thus forming the key to the Confederate position. Believing the Federals would attack his right, Beauregard posted most of his force there. Meanwhile, on 18 July, Johnston was ordered to join Beauregard at Manassas; for the first time in the history of warfare, the Confederates used railroads operationally, over the next two days sending Johnston's men sixty miles from the Shenandoah Valley to reach Beauregard's army.

Under intense public pressure to capture Richmond, Union Brig. Gen. Irvin McDowell planned to move from Centreville with 30,000 men to turn the Confederate left flank, isolating Beauregard from Johnston and making his strong defensive line along Bull Run untenable.

On the morning of 21 July, the Federals attacked the stone bridge. Confederate Capt. Nathan G. "Shanks" Evans perceived that the Federal attack in his front was merely a feint; in the first battlefield use of the wigwag telegraph system, Capt. E. P. Alexander signaled to Evans that his left flank was turned. With his left threatened, Beauregard rushed his forces toward Henry Hill to support Evans.

That afternoon, the Federals launched several piecemeal assaults against Henry House Hill. At one intense moment of fighting Brig. Gen. Barnard E. Bee rallied his Alabamians by declaring, "There is Jackson standing like a stone wall." His comment gave Brig. Gen. "Stonewall" *Jackson his immortal nickname. The attacks on Henry House Hill continued for about two hours, with neither side gaining a decisive advantage.

At around 4:00 P.M., fresh troops from Beauregard's army under Col. Jubal A. Early and Brig. Gen. E. Kirby Smith arrived on the field and began to roll up the Federal right. The Union units withdrew, and some panic ensued—it was impossible to rally the army, which began a retreat all the way back to Washington, D.C. Similar confusion reigned on the Confederate side, allowing the Federals to escape unmolested.

The losses in the largest battle yet fought in North America were considered heavy, though by the following year they would be eclipsed frequently: the Confederates suffered 1,982 *casualties, while the Union suffered 2,896. In the humiliation of defeat Northerners realized that blind enthusiasm was not enough to win the war; many felt a renewed sense of purpose in the Union's war effort. The victory reinforced Southern views of their martial superiority.

[See also Civil War: Military and Diplomatic Course.]

• Russell H. Beattie, Jr., Road to Manassas, 1961. William C. Davis, Battle at Bull Run, 1977.   —Jonathan M. Berkey

BULL RUN, SECOND BATTLE OF (1862). On 26 June 1862, Civil War Union Maj. Gen. John Pope assumed command of the Army of Virginia, a collection of three formerly independent armies that had recently suffered humiliating defeats at the hands of Maj. Gen. "Stonewall" *Jackson in the Shenandoah Valley. Pope brashly assured his troops that they would no longer be concerned with lines of retreat. He planned to attack Richmond from the north after receiving reinforcements from the Army of the Potomac, which was still on the Virginia Peninsula following an unsuccessful campaign.

The Federal plan put Confederate Gen. Robert E. *Lee in a tough position. If the Federal armies united, he would be outnumbered two to one. With this in mind, he devised one of the most daring campaigns of the war: Leaving a small force to defend Richmond, Lee moved the rest of his army to join Jackson, who had clashed with an isolated Union corps at Cedar Mountain on 9 August. Lee hoped to destroy Pope's army before it could be reinforced.

Once in front of Pope, Lee divided his army. While Maj. Gen. James *Longstreet faced Pope across the Rappahannock River, 24,000 men under Jackson would march around Pope's right and cut the Federal supply line along the Orange & Alexandria Railroad. Once Jackson accomplished his objective, Longstreet would march to join him. In two days, Jackson marched fifty miles and captured several hundred Federals and massive amounts of supplies at Manassas Junction. As Pope ordered his 66,000 men back and forth to find the Confederates, Jackson moved north of the old Bull Run battlefield and hid his men in an abandoned railroad cut.

On 28 August, Jackson revealed his position by fighting a Federal division to a stalemate at Groveton. The Federals converged on Jackson, determined to destroy his force. The next day, Jackson held his ground with great difficulty against several uncoordinated Federal attacks.

Unbeknownst to Pope, Longstreet had established contact with Jackson on the afternoon of 29 August. The next day Maj. Gen. Fitz John Porter launched an unsuccessful attack that featured part of the Confederate line tossing rocks at the Federals after running out of ammunition. At 4:00 P.M., Longstreet began a massive attack on the lightly defended Federal left flank. His successful assault assured Confederate victory; a Federal attack at Chantilly on 1 September ended Jackson's attempt to cut off the Union retreat, but also resulted in the death of Maj. Gen. Philip Kearney.

The Second Bull Run campaign marked the emergence of Lee as an army commander. He inflicted 14,500 *casualties on the Federals while suffering about 9,500 of his own. Although the campaign demonstrated Lee's operational brilliance, it did not reflect well on his Union counterpart. Often indecisive, Pope could not envision the campaign from his opponent's perspective. He blamed his failure on Porter, who was court-martialed for disobeying orders. His cashiering inaugurated a battle of ink—before 1890, probably no battle, including Gettysburg, would receive more attention.

[See also Bull Run, First Battle of; Civil War: Military and Diplomatic Course.]

• Otto Eisenschmil, The Celebrated Case of Fitz John Porter, 1950. John J. Hennessy, Return to Bull Run, 1993.

—Jonathan M. Berkey

BUNDY, McGEORGE (1919–1996), historian, educator, U.S. government official. Though associated with academic affairs and philanthropic enterprises for most of his career, McGeorge Bundy is best remembered for his years (1961–66) as special assistant for national security affairs to Presidents John F. *Kennedy and Lyndon B. *Johnson. During that time Bundy participated in many crucial foreign policy episodes, and effectively transformed the role of national security assistant from that of a behind-the-scenes coordinator, as it had developed in the 1950s, into a policy adviser operating on a par with cabinet officials.

Born into Boston Brahmin society, Bundy was educated at Groton School, Yale College, and Harvard University. Deemed unfit for military service because of nearsightedness, he memorized the eye chart in order to join the army as a private and rose to become a captain by the end of World War II. In 1949 he joined the Harvard government department, teaching a popular world affairs course, and in 1953, at age thirty-four, he became dean of Harvard's Faculty of Arts and Sciences. He was a foreign policy consultant to Kennedy's 1960 presidential campaign, and afterwards accepted Kennedy's invitation to come to Washington to reorganize and oversee the *National Security Council (NSC).

At Kennedy's request, Bundy adopted a broad view of his responsibilities at the NSC, and came to enjoy a close working relationship with the president and other senior officials. As a result, Bundy was at the center of practically all major foreign policy deliberations, including Kennedy's decision to launch the ill-fated Bay of Pigs invasion of Cuba, the Berlin Wall episode, the *Cuban Missile Crisis, and the escalation of U.S. involvement in Southeast Asia.

As the United States became involved in *Vietnam War, Bundy emerged as a leading advocate of "sustained reprisals" against North Vietnam. When in January 1965 it appeared that the South Vietnamese were nearing collapse, he joined with Secretary of Defense Robert S. *McNamara in urging President Johnson to step up the use of U.S. military power and to expand the air war against the North. Many historians have since come to see this as a major turning point, setting the stage for the large-scale U.S. intervention later that year. Much criticized for his role in Vietnam policy, Bundy left government in 1966 to become president of the Ford Foundation. In later years, Bundy devoted himself to research and writing on the threat of nuclear war and ways of curbing it.

• David Halberstam, *The Best and the Brightest*, 1969. McGeorge Bundy, *Danger and Survival: Choices About the Bomb in the First Fifty Years*, 1988. Kai Bird, *The Color of Truth: McGeorge and William Bundy, Brothers in Arms*, 1998.

—Steven L. Rearden

BUNKER, ELLSWORTH (1894–1984), U.S. diplomat and businessman. Born into a well-to-do family, Ellsworth Bunker looked after his family's sugar interests after graduating from Yale University in 1916, and served as director (1927–66) and chairman of the board (1948–51) of the National Sugar Refining Company. Throughout his long, productive life, Bunker balanced accomplishments in business with a distinguished record of public service.

He made his mark on American history in two key assignments. As American representative to the Organization of American States, Bunker was instrumental in resolving the 1965 Dominican Republic crisis. He persuaded two political rivals, Juan Bosch and Joaquin Balaquer, to agree to compete in open democratic elections, which averted the threat of rule by a military junta or a Communist regime. As ambassador to South Vietnam from 1967 to 1973, Bunker gave stronger direction to the nonmilitary side of the *Vietnam War and worked to integrate American civil and military programs there. He helped arrange a compromise between South Vietnamese political rivals Nguyen Van Thieu and Nguyen Cao Ky. Bunker also played a key role in helping mobilize South Vietnam's post–*Tet Offensive recovery effort of 1968. Before leaving Saigon, he presided over the U.S. mission during the *Paris peace agreements, the withdrawal of American military forces from Vietnam, and North Vietnam's 1972 Easter invasion against South Vietnam.

• Bruce Palmer, *Intervention in the Caribbean: The Dominican crisis of 1965*, 1989. Richard A. Hunt, *Pacification: The American Struggle for Vietnam's Hearts and Minds*, 1995.   —Richard A. Hunt

BUNKER HILL, BATTLE OF (1775). Two months after the *Revolutionary War began, on the night of 16–17 June 1775, about 1,200 Massachusetts soldiers set out to fortify Bunker Hill on the Charlestown peninsula, across the Charles River from Boston; by fortifying a position overlooking Boston, they intended to force the British to evacuate the town. In the dark, they mistakenly erected a redoubt on Breed's Hill, closer to Boston than planned. Later in the day, about 2,000 men from New Hampshire and Connecticut reinforced them. Shocked by this display of audacity, Maj. Gen. Thomas *Gage, the British commander in Boston, sent Maj. Gen. Sir William *Howe with 1,500 men (later reinforced to 2,500) to oust the Rebels. Howe planned to feign an attack on the redoubt while sending a strong force around its northeast flank on the low land along the Mystic River.

Howe underestimated the military capacity of his opponent. Thanks to the leadership of *French and Indian War veterans, the Americans blunted his plan. John Stark and his New Hampshire men destroyed the outflanking force

on the Mystic River beach, forcing Howe to convert the feint in front of the redoubt into a full attack. Three times he led his troops up the slope, and twice from behind their earthwork William Prescott's soldiers forced the British to retreat. With the Americans running out of ammunition, the third British attack overran the redoubt and forced the Rebels off the peninsula.

Victory cost the British over 1000 *casualties, 40 percent, a loss, Gage wrote, "greater than we can bear." The New Englanders suffered over 400 casualties, heaviest among the defenders of the redoubt. Their skill and tenacity reassured colonists everywhere that the Revolution would not be strangled in its cradle.

• Allen French, *The First Year of the American Revolution*, 1934. Thomas J. Fleming, *Now We Are Enemies*, 1960. Richard M. Ketchum, *The Battle for Bunker Hill*, 1962.

—Harold E. Selesky

BURGOYNE, JOHN (1723–1792), British Revolutionary War general. Burgoyne was rumored to be the natural son of Lord Bingley. His Seven Years' War exploits in France and Portugal (and his marriage to the Earl of Derby's daughter) propelled him to major general by 1772. Assigned to help Gen. Thomas *Gage put down the New England rebellion in 1775, he directed artillery fire from Boston at the Battle of *Bunker Hill; he then intrigued against Gage and politicked for command of an army to invade from Canada, isolating New England from the Middle Colonies.

In spring 1777, Burgoyne took command of an expeditionary force of about 8,000, planning to meet a force that was to march north from New York City at Albany. He captured Fort Ticonderoga, but failed to seize supplies at Bennington and lost contact with his Canadian base of supply when he crossed the Hudson (13 September) dismantling the bridge of boats behind him. Burgoyne marched on, hoping to join the forces of Maj. Gen. Sir Henry *Clinton. Instead, he confronted Horatio *Gates's army at the two Battles of *Saratoga, and surrendered on 17 October 1777. Burgoyne was allowed to return to England, where he resumed his seat in Parliament and blamed Secretary of State for the colonies Lord George Germain for his defeat. A commander of unusual humanity, Burgoyne pioneered the employment of light cavalry; as a strategist, he (like many British officers) unwisely underrated American determination.

[*See also* Revolutionary War: Military and Diplomatic Course.]

• Gerald Howson, *Burgoyne of Saratoga*, 1979. Richard J. Hargrove, Jr., *General John Burgoyne*, 1983.   —Max M. Mintz

BURKE, ARLEIGH (1901–1996), legendary World War II destroyer skipper and Cold War naval strategist.

Born on a farm near Boulder, Colorado, Arleigh Burke never completed high school but won appointment to the U.S. Naval Academy. Graduating 7 June 1923, he married Roberta "Bobbie" Gorsuch the same day. After five years in battleship *Arizona*, Burke chose an ordnance specialty. He earned a master's degree in chemical engineering from the University of Michigan in 1931. A skilled pre–World War II and wartime commander and tactical innovator, Burke received national attention and the nickname "31 Knot Burke" in November 1943 when his Destroyer Squadron

23 decisively defeated a Japanese force in the Battle of Cape St. George in the Solomon Islands. Burke subsequently served as Vice Adm. Marc A. Mitscher's chief of staff in Fast Carrier Task Force 58/38 during the Marianas, Philippines, Iwo Jima, and Okinawa operations.

After the war, Burke prepared the navy's first postwar long-range plan, helped coordinate the service's testimony before Congress during the 1949 "Admirals' Revolt" hearings on defense unification and strategy, and served on the first *United Nations Truce Negotiation Team during the *Korean War. Eisenhower appointed Rear Admiral Burke in 1955 over ninety-two more senior admirals to become chief of naval operations (CNO). He served an unprecedented three terms through August 1961.

As CNO, Burke fought against increased unification and restriction of command authority in the armed forces, and for maintenance of a balanced, flexible fleet capable of responding quickly and effectively to crises and limited wars. He also accelerated the development of innovative weapons systems, championing development of the Polaris submarine-based ballistic missile, deployed in 1960, as a national nuclear deterrent system. Burke overruled advisers concerned about Polaris's cost and feasibility because he believed that a small, relatively invulnerable force of missile *submarines could deter war and ensure a controlled response to Soviet attack. Burke linked the navy's strategy of "finite deterrence, controlled retaliation" to the need to prepare for limited as well as general war. He led one of the few serious challenges to massive retaliation and nuclear buildup during the first decades of the Cold War.

[See also Cold War.]

• David Alan Rosenberg, "Arleigh Albert Burke," in *The Chiefs of Naval Operations,* ed. Robert William Love, Jr., 1980. David Alan Rosenberg, "Admiral Arleigh A. Burke," in *Men-of-War, Great Naval Leaders of World War II,* ed. Stephen Howarth, 1993.

—David Alan Rosenberg

BURNSIDE, AMBROSE (1824–1881), Civil War general. Burnside graduated from West Point in 1847 and served as an artillery officer in the *Mexican War. He resigned in 1853 to manufacture the breech-loading rifle he had invented. After this venture failed, George B. *McClellan hired him to work for the Illinois Central Railroad.

At the beginning of the *Civil War, Burnside organized the First Rhode Island Infantry Regiment. Quickly promoted to brigadier general, he led the Federal campaign against Roanoke Island (February 1862) and became a major general. Joining the Army of the Potomac in July, Burnside fought at the Battle of *Antietam, where his slow crossing of Antietam Creek has caused historical controversy. After McClellan's removal that November, Burnside reluctantly assumed command of the Army of the Potomac. The unsuccessful Fredericksburg campaign gave Burnside the reputation of a man unsuited to command an army. His move to Fredericksburg had merit, but a bureaucratic snarl over pontoon bridges, uncooperative subordinates, and his own fuzzy battle orders contributed to a stunning defeat. He was relieved from command after the unsuccessful "Mud March" up the Rappahannock River. He later successfully defended Knoxville, Tennessee, against a Confederate attack. Returning east, Burnside commanded the Ninth Corps in the Overland Company. His role in the Battle of the Crater near Petersburg provoked more controversy. Resigning near the end of the war, Burnside remained active in business and Rhode Island politics.

• William Marvel, *Burnside,* 1991. Gary W. Gallagher, ed., *Decision on the Rappahannock: Causes and Consequences of the Fredericksburg Campaign,* 1995. —George C. Rable

BUSH, GEORGE (1924–), forty-first president of the United States. Born into a wealthy, privileged family, Bush accepted his father's belief that such people have an obligation to give something back to society. On his eighteenth birthday in June 1942, he enlisted in the U.S. Navy, becoming its youngest pilot. During wartime service in the Pacific, he flew fifty-eight combat missions.

Elected as a Texas Republican congressman in 1966, he supported the *Vietnam War. Thereafter, he served as ambassador to the United Nations (1971–73), director of the *Central Intelligence Agency (1976–77), and vice president under Ronald *Reagan (1981–89). He won the presidency in 1988. Ill at ease in the contentious environment of domestic politics, Bush relished foreign policy. In response to the harassment of American military personnel, he committed U.S. forces to the 20 December 1989 invasion of Panama. The four-day campaign ended successfully with the capture of the Panamanian dictator Gen. Manuel *Noriega. Following communism's collapse in Russia, Bush and Soviet leader Mikhail Gorbachev signed a historic accord in November 1990 that marked the end of the Cold War. Bush claimed that the treaty signaled "the new world order."

That order received a profound challenge when Iraq invaded Kuwait on 2 August 1990. After declaring that the invasion "shall not stand," Bush skillfully cobbled together an international coalition to resist Iraq. He proved less interested and able to explain to the American public why war was necessary. After an economic embargo failed, Bush launched Operation Desert Storm on 17 January 1991. Ten days later, with Iraqi forces in full rout, he suspended hostilities. Pleased, he claimed the quick victory had "licked the Vietnam syndrome." The national perception that the war had been halted too soon contributed to Bush's electoral defeat in 1992. As war leader, he developed strategy and then left its implementation in military hands. He failed clearly to articulate the objective, namely, what constituted "victory" against Iraq.

[See also Cold War: Changing Interpretations; Persian Gulf War.]

• Roger Hilsman, *George Bush vs. Saddam Hussein,* 1992. Rick Atkinson, *Crusade: The Untold Story of the Persian Gulf War,* 1993. —James R. Arnold

BUSH, VANNEVAR (1890–1974), engineer, developer of military technology, and defense analyst. Bush graduated from Tufts University in 1913 and later taught electrical engineering at the Massachusetts Institute of Technology. While still at MIT, he cofounded a successful radio tube company: Raytheon. Over the next decade, Bush designed a series of mechanical calculators, termed *differential analyzers,* that were initially useful for simulating the operations of electric power grids, but by the mid-thirties became widely seen as the world's most powerful computers. He was named president (1939) of the Carnegie Institution.

In June 1940, Bush persuaded President Franklin D. *Roosevelt to name him chief of a new federal agency charged with coordinating civilian research on military problems. As chief of the National Defense Research Council (and later its parent agency, the Organization for Scientific Research and Development), Bush oversaw the creation of hundreds of military technologies, most notably *radar and the proximity fuse. He neutralized skeptics within the Army and Navy Departments by relying on his direct line to Roosevelt. And he relied on experts to set technical priorities.

Bush at first thought atomic weapons might not play a part in World War II. But he changed his mind in the fall of 1941 and set in motion creation of the *Manhattan Project, choosing the army to direct the crash program because he mistrusted the navy for disparaging him and other scientists. Among the first in government to foresee the darker implications of atomic weapons, Bush warned Secretary of War Henry L. *Stimson in September 1944 of the possibility of "a secret arms race" that might result in the United States losing its "temporary advantage" in atomic weapons. Such race might be avoided, he suggested, "by complete international scientific and technical interchange on this subject." Yet in summer 1945, Bush recommended that atomic bombs be dropped on Japan.

From 1945 through 1948, Bush sought to create a civilian-dominated directorate within the U.S. military establishment that would rationalize research, setting priorities for the individual branches and limiting duplication. The services, by then intent on building their own research organizations, resisted centralized planning, but Bush succeeded in creating a Research and Development Board (RDB) within the Pentagon whose chairman (initially Bush) reported directly to the secretary of defense. The RDB laid a foundation for later, more effective coordination of military research.

[See also Atomic Scientists; Conant, James; Science, Technology, War, and the Military.]

• G. Paschal Zachary, Endless Frontier: Vannevar Bush, Engineer of the American Century, 1997.　　　　　—G. Paschal Zachary

BUTLER, BENJAMIN F. (1818–1893), *Civil War general and politician. A prominent Democratic lawyer in Lowell, Massachusetts, militia Brigadier General Butler was given command of the state's troops in 1861 in order to rally Democrats to the Union cause. After relieving Washington by way of Annapolis, he secured Baltimore, was promoted to major general in command at Fortress Monroe, and won popularity by declaring fugitive slaves used by the enemy against the United States contraband of war. He lost the Battle of Big Bethel, only to recoup his fortunes by participating in the navy's seizure of Fort Hatteras.

In April 1862, Butler accompanied Flag Officer David *Farragut in the seizure of New Orleans, a city where he proved his agility as an administrator. Although he maintained order and prevented an outbreak of yellow fever, Southerners called him "Beast" because he hanged a Confederate who had torn down the American flag and issued General Order No. 28 threatening to treat females who insulted his soldiers as "women of the town plying their avocation." Rumors of corruption and controversies with foreign consuls caused him to be recalled in December. In 1863, he was given command of the Department of Virginia and North Carolina, which he exercised in his usual controversial manner.

In 1864, leading the Army of the James against Richmond from the coast, Butler found himself "bottled up" at Bermuda Hundred and suffered a defeat at Drury's Bluff. After failing to take Fort Fisher (Wilmington, North Carolina) in December, he was finally recalled.

After the war, Butler proved an arch-radical congressman during *Reconstruction and a firm supporter of President Ulysses S. *Grant. He was a sharp critic of West Point. Elected Democratic governor of Massachusetts in 1882, he ran as an unsuccessful third-party candidate for the presidency in 1884. His military career furnishes a good example of the strengths and weaknesses of political generals, while his championship of black troops deserves to be remembered.

• Hans L. Trefousse, Ben Butler: The South Called Him Beast, 1957. Richard S. West, Jr., Lincoln's Scapegoat General: A Life of Benjamin F. Butler 1818–1893, 1965.　　　　　—Hans L. Trefousse

BUTLER, SMEDLEY (1881–1940), Marine officer, antiwar crusader. Born into an old Pennsylvania Quaker family, Butler nevertheless joined the Marines as a lieutenant when the *Spanish-American War broke out in 1898. The campaigned in expeditions and military occupations from 1898 onward, spanning the transition from colonial punitive warfare to mediatory peacekeeping: Cuba, the Philippines (1899, 1905–07), China (1900), Honduras (1903), Panama (1903, 1909–14), Nicaragua (1910–12), Mexico (1914), Haiti (1915–18), France (1917–18), and finally China again as commander of the Marine peacekeeping force (1927–29). Winner of two Congressional Medals of Honor, "Old Gimlet-Eye," as he was called, promoted a warrior-style Marine Corps mystique of physical stridency and anti-intellectual egalitarianism, contrary to contemporary trends toward elitist, bookish professionalism.

Drawing upon his experience organizing colonial constabularies, Butler attempted to militarize Philadelphia's police force as its director (1924–25) during the Prohibition era, and became a leading proponent of national paramilitary police reform in the late twenties and early thirties. After premature retirement from the Marines as a major general in 1931, he renounced war and imperialism, becoming the most prominent leader of the formidable veterans' antiwar movement during the isolationist era of the mid- and late 1930s.

[See also Marine Corps, U.S.: 1865–1914 and 1914–45.]

• Smedley D. Butler, War Is a Racket, 1935. Hans Schmidt, Maverick Marine: General Smedley D. Butler and the Contradictions of American Military History, 1987.　　　　　—Hans R. Schmidt

C

CALHOUN, JOHN C. (1782–1850), congressman, secretary of war, vice president, senator, and secretary of state. When James Monroe appointed Congressman John C. Calhoun secretary of war in 1817, the South Carolinian discovered a department mired in financial irresponsibility and managerial incompetence. Calhoun eliminated economic waste, initiated a series of coastal defenses, tightened the army command structure, and improved the curriculum at West Point. He continued the standing policy of negotiating treaties for Indian land and Indian removal, and sent out expeditions to explore the country's vast western expanse. Calhoun, however, struggled to get along with his generals, especially the headstrong Andrew *Jackson.

Government retrenchment due to the Panic of 1819 sidetracked many of his initiatives, eliminating his improved transportation system. In 1820 to avoid the disastrous impact of a huge cut in the army, Calhoun proposed his ingenious Expandable Army Plan. The reduction would come among privates; officer and noncommissioned officer strength would remain. In crisis, the army could expand by recruiting privates to serve under experienced leadership. A penurious Congress rejected the scheme. The South Carolinian was, however, able to implement another of his plans, the prohibition of the recruitment of blacks into the U.S. Army, an order that remained in effect from 1820 until the *Civil War.

When Calhoun left office in 1825, he had accomplished much less than he had desired. However, he had restored some fiscal responsibility and some order to a department found in chaos. Though better known for his later political career, Calhoun was an influential secretary of war.

[See also African Americans in the Military; Army, U.S.: 1783–1865.]

• Charles M. Wiltse, *John C. Calhoun*, 3 vols. 1944–51. Irving H. Bartlett, *John C. Calhoun, A Biography*, 1993.

—Trenton E. Hizer

CAMP DAVID ACCORDS (1978). The Camp David Accords, which outlined a framework for a comprehensive Middle East peace, were initialed on 17 September 1978 by U.S. president Jimmy *Carter, Israeli prime minister Menachem Begin, and Egyptian president Anwar Sadat following a two-week conference at Camp David, the presidential retreat in Maryland's Catoctin Mountains. The Camp David process began in November 1977, when Sadat made an unprecedented visit to Israel, where he told Israeli leaders that Egypt was willing to make a lasting peace if they were willing to withdraw from Arab territory occupied during the 1967 and 1973 wars. Despite encouragement from Washington, the Israeli-Egyptian negotiations stalled during the spring of 1978, prompting Carter to invite Sadat and Begin to Camp David in September.

Adopting a low-key approach, Carter was able to make surprising progress on the bilateral Israeli-Egyptian front. The Israelis indicated that, in return for a formal peace treaty with Egypt, they would pull their troops out of the Sinai Desert and would also dismantle the handful of Jewish settlements recently established in the troubled isthmus. The major sticking point was the fate of the Israeli-occupied West Bank, an oblong bulge of Jordanian territory that 800,000 Palestinians called home. Fearing that he would be branded a traitor who had sold out the Arab cause if he agreed to a bilateral Egyptian-Israeli peace treaty without resolving the Palestinian dilemma, Sadat insisted that Begin agree to autonomy for the West Bank Arabs. Unwilling to abandon territory that had been part of ancient Israel and that was now also home to several thousand Jewish settlers, Begin adamantly refused to accept the principle of Palestinian self-determination on the West Bank. With the two sides deadlocked and the Camp David conference on the verge of collapse, Carter brokered an eleventh-hour compromise by arranging two parallel but separate agreements, one on the Sinai and the other on the West Bank. Sadat pledged to recognize Israel and to sign a formal peace treaty with Begin in return for an Israeli promise to withdraw from the Sinai. Begin agreed temporarily to suspend Israeli settlements on the West Bank and promised to negotiate "new arrangements" with "representatives of the Palestinian people."

Implementing the Camp David Accords, however, proved more difficult than Carter and his advisers had imagined. To be sure, the lure of a multi-billion-dollar U.S. aid package and the promise that several hundred American troops would monitor the Sinai frontier helped persuade Sadat and Begin to sign a peace treaty in Washington on 26 March 1979, and within three years all Israeli troops and settlers had departed from Egyptian soil. But the West Bank negotiations were stillborn, largely because the Palestinian clauses in the Camp David agreements were subject to radically different interpretations by the Israelis, the Arabs, and the Americans. During the next decade, Begin and his successor, Yitzhak Shamir, expanded the number of Israeli settlements on the West Bank dramatically; the Palestinians responded by launching an uprising—the *Intifada*—in late 1987, and the peace process stalemated, resuming in earnest only after Yitzhak Rabin was elected prime minister in 1992. The Oslo peace accords hammered out between 1993 to 1995, whereby the Israelis agreed ultimately to grant self-government to the Palestinians on the West Bank, had their roots in the Camp David Accords of 1978.

[*See also* Middle East, U.S. Involvement in the.]

• Jimmy Carter, *Keeping Faith: Memoirs of a President*, 1982. Steven Spiegel, *The Other Arab-Israeli Conflict: Making America's Middle East Policy from Truman to Reagan*, 1985. William Quandt, *Camp David: Peacemaking and Politics*, 1986.   —Douglas Little

"CAMP FOLLOWERS." Although this expression has been corrupted into a synonym for prostitutes who follow army camps, it historically referred to all civilians, male and female, associated with the military. Followers accompanied military units to pursue profit, find employment, or remain with loved ones. American military forces have always had such followers; their number, kind, activities, and administration, however, have changed over time.

Camp followers helped the *Continental army during the *Revolutionary War. Sutlers—those merchants authorized to peddle provisions in camp—sold such merchandise as soap, thread, and liquor. They served both morale and supply functions. Family followers also affected a soldier's welfare and his will to fight. Finally, an assortment of civilians served the army in key staff and logistics positions, releasing soldiers and officers for combat.

Followers continued to be important to the maintenance and morale of military forces in the nineteenth and twentieth centuries. Authorized merchants suttled goods at posts established across the continent; in the twentieth century, suttling became big business in the form of base exchanges. Spouses and children endured hardships to maintain their families, and in so doing provided a civilian—some might say civilized—context to military life.

Civilian employees also continued their labors in the military. During the *Civil War, they clerked, drove teams, nursed, spied, and operated telegraphs; since then the services have experimented with the civilian-military mix in attempts to find the most efficient, cost-effective formula.

As camp followers could hinder as well as help the military, they had to be controlled. Although not subject to military law, these civilians did have to conform to regulations and were liable for punishment—generally revocation of privileges or banishment—if they did not. The legal basis for such control was established via a clause in the first American Articles of War and maintained in subsequent revisions, including, in a modified form, the Uniform Code of Military Justice that replaced the articles in 1950.

[*See also* Bases, Military: Life On; Families, Military; Justice, Military; Logistics; Women in the Military.]

• Edward M. Coffman, *The Old Army: A Portrait of the American Army in Peacetime, 1784–1898*, 1986. Betty Sowers Alt and Bonnie Domrose Stone, *Campfollowing: A History of the Military Wife*, 1991.   —Holly A. Mayer

CANADA, U.S. MILITARY INVOLVEMENT IN. "The undefended border" is the cliché that still governs Canada–United States military relations. Most clichés are true, but for most of North American history not this one. Before American independence, the French and their native allies in Québec warred against New York and New England from the early seventeenth century to the fall of New France in 1760 in the *French and Indian War. Congress's project for 1775, during the *Revolutionary War, was an attack on Canada and, though Montreal fell, the venture failed. Again in the *War of 1812, American forces attacked Canada, the fighting especially fierce along the Niagara frontier. The resulting stalemate meant Canadian survival. The *Rush-Bagot Agreement of 1817 put limits on the number of naval vessels Britain and the United States could station on the Great Lakes and Lake Champlain, but land fortifications proceeded apace. Then, after the 1837–38 Canadian rebellions against British authoritarianism, there were supportive "Patriot" incursions from the United States, but these were no more successful than U.S. calls for "54 40 or Fight" in the Oregon Territory border dispute or the 1860s Fenian raids that sped Canadian Confederation. During the *Civil War, some 40,000 Canadians served in Union blue, while U.S. draft evaders hid in Canada.

After Canadian Confederation in 1867, the frequently aggressive-sounding United States continued to be perceived as a military threat to the new dominion. Repeated war scares in the 1870s and 1890s produced bursts of Canadian martial enthusiasm, but economic and social intercourse made such talk increasingly unreal.

The two countries cooperated militarily in 1917–18. Each provided pilot training to the other's nationals; the U.S. Navy lent materiel for the Canadian antisubmarine war; and military-industrial cooperation flourished. President Roosevelt was close to Prime Minister Mackenzie King, and in 1940 they created the Permanent Joint Board on Defense. Agreements to maximize war production followed; there were joint operations in the Aleutians, and U.S. troops built and manned air and other installations in northern Canada. After 1945, these were purchased by sovereignty-conscious Ottawa.

During the Cold War, the new Soviet threat forced continued cooperation. U.S. bases in Newfoundland, acquired in 1941, remained a sore point, and joint northern *radar lines were contentious projects, especially when the Dew Line (distant early warning) bases forbade entry to members of the Canadian Parliament. Nonetheless, air defenses were combined in the NORAD (North American Air Defense) Agreement (1957–58). The Conservative government of Prime Minister John Diefenbaker undertook to acquire nuclear weapons for its NORAD and *NATO forces, but it delayed and was toppled in Parliament in 1963. Some charged that the administration of President John F. *Kennedy had connived at its downfall; certainly, the successor Canadian government under Prime Minister Lester B. Pearson accepted the weapons. Ottawa was less accommodating during the *Vietnam War, when Canada provided haven to perhaps 100,000 American deserters or draft evaders and Prime Minister Pearson was occasionally critical of U.S. policy. Nonetheless, military cooperation between the two nations remained close in North America, Europe, and the Middle East. Canadian forces relied on U.S. equipment, they trained with American forces, and Canada's *United Nations peacekeeping frequently served U.S. interests, as in Haiti in the 1990s. Not without domestic opposition, Canada permitted cruise missile testing over its territory, and it participated in the U.S.-led coalition in the *Persian Gulf War. The myth of the undefended border had been replaced by close defense cooperation.

[*See also* Arctic Warfare; Cold War; Destroyers-for-Bases Agreement.]

• J. L. Granatstein and Norman Hillmer, *For Better or for Worse: Canada and the United States to the 1990s*, 1991. Desmond Morton, *A Military History of Canada: From Champlain to the Gulf War*, 1992.   —J. L. Granatstein

CAREERS IN THE MILITARY. Since the early 1780s, careers in the American military have been varied and demanding. Over the last 200 years, the requirements of the military to be variously a constabulary, combatant, occupational force, diplomatic corps, and deterrent have ensured that both the officer and the enlisted person master several skills to carry out their different missions. Particularly in the twentieth century, the rate of technological change has frequently resulted in highly specialized training early in a military person's career and more generalist education later.

During the nineteenth century, army, navy, and Marine officers entered a career either through a direct commission or from one of the service *academies (West Point or Annapolis). At the service academy, cadets were taught the rudiments of mathematics, history, and engineering, and were thoroughly immersed in military culture. Following this experience, officers were often delayed from entering active duty until older officers retired, resigned, or were cashiered. Once on active duty, junior officers were sent for further training to a regiment (the army) or to a ship (the navy or Marines). Because of a stiflingly slow promotion rate, these apprenticeships could last well over a decade. None of the military jobs was particularly challenging once mastered. Thus, it was not unusual for men to become thoroughly proficient as an infantry, cavalry, or deck officer in a short time and then languish in some isolated frontier post or ship of the line. One bright spot was that an officer could take extended leave of absence to visit family, pursue advanced civilian education, or even talk personally to the secretary of war or navy about future assignments. Ultimately, however, an officer's career was one of classical and technical education, followed by apprenticeship or a frontier, seagoing, or staff assignment, while waiting for senior officers to retire in order to be promoted.

By 1885, a series of educational reforms added additional requirements during an officer's career. The creation of branch schools for the infantry and artillery, along with the formation of professional lyceums at army posts and the establishment of a Naval War College, set a precedent for advanced professional education. Citing technological advances in weapon systems, the professional militaries of European powers, and a growing desire on behalf of many Americans to establish the United States as a world power, many officers argued that they were members of a modern profession whose responsibility it was to protect the country's interests. It followed that if the military was a profession that called for an inordinate amount of expertise in warmaking, then it was incumbent upon the military officer to study war throughout his or her life. By the turn of the century, the expectation that officers required professional education throughout their careers shaped what a military career would mean in the modern world. After World War II, all branches of service had established professional schools to teach leadership, military strategy and tactics, and personnel management.

The increasing pace of technological advancement continued to shape military careers in the late nineteenth and twentieth centuries. The emergence of steam-driven, steel-plated warships created the need for specialized engineering officers in the navy. The early twentieth-century army developed motorized transportation and developed new weapons such as *tanks and aircraft. These innovations created new career paths for officers. The airplane would

eventually form the basis of a completely new military service (the air force), while advances in landing craft provided a new amphibious mission for the Marines.

By the 1950s, an officer who planned to serve a twenty-to thirty-year career initially received a service college education or a Reserve Officer Training Corps (*ROTC) commission through a civilian university. After commissioning, he or she attended a military specialty school to receive training for a combat, combat support, engineering, aviation, or surface warfare career. Thereafter, the young lieutenant or ensign was sent to a regiment or sea assignment to gain practical and leadership experience. At the fourth to sixth year in service, the newly promoted captain might be selected to attend an advanced course at the Amphibious Warfare School at Quantico, Virginia, or a more generalized professional military course such as the air force's Squadron Officer School at Montgomery, Alabama. Such training prepared officers for further specialization or tours as instructors or staff officers at higher echelons. After a series of operational and staff assignments, officers distanced themselves from technical specialties as they moved toward positions of command. This movement toward becoming a "generalist" meant additional school assignments at postgraduate service *schools and war colleges, as well as broadening assignments overseas or to joint commands and schools within the United States. Thus, military education throughout periods of an officer's career, combined with the need for technical specialization, formalized the career path for the rest of this century.

Evolving since 1861, officer non-disability retirement legislation for all services was combined for the first time in the Officer Personnel Act of 1947. This act specified the length of an officers's career (between twenty and thirty years based on time-in-service and time-in-grade requirements) as well as when the individual must leave the service due to inadequate performance. Officers serving for twenty years or more would receive a minimum of 50 percent and a maximum of 75 percent (thirty years' service) of their base pay for life upon retirement.

Military careers for enlisted personnel are a product of the mid-twentieth century. In earlier times, the enlisted person's life was a physically arduous, dirty, and thankless job. People who were willing to put up with the hardships of military life were accepted for duty; there was little training and few opportunities for improvement below decks or at isolated forts. For much of the nineteenth and early twentieth century, the enlisted men of the regular forces had a significant number of illiterates, alcoholics, and foreign-born immigrants in their ranks. Duties during peacetime were routine and required little talent. The classic portrait of an enlisted person during this time was that of an outcast who needed to be kept on the margins of society. Many refused to remain in the service for more than a few years, others were promoted to noncommissioned officer (NCO) ranks and served as specialist-craftsmen in a variety of jobs from saddler to sailmaker to boatswain's mate. Without such skills, some stayed in the ranks as "career" privates.

The rapid pace of technological innovation during the twentieth century caused significant changes in all this. By the end of World War I, the military identified many enlisted personnel as occupational specialists who operated or repaired the newer weapons systems—airplanes, tanks, *submarines—or the new *communications devices. By the end of World War II, the need for technicians and maintenance personnel exceeded the need for enlisted combatants. In 1942, there were only two army enlisted specializations in the *radar and fire control field; by 1958, there were twenty-seven, plus seventy-two specializations in guided *missiles and nine in atomic weapons.

The need to separate traditional military specialties from technicians began before World War I and would climax in the 1950s. Even as early as 1918, the army established specialist grades to separate technicians from NCO grades and combat career fields. However, during World War II, the army integrated technical specialists into the NCO grades. After the war, the army again separated the technical specialists from the NCO grades and combat specialties. The more technically oriented navy and air force did not distinguish between technical specialist and traditional military specialties. An enlisted person was expected to be a specialist and a noncommissioned officer. Eventually, all the services opted to pattern an enlisted career much like that for officers: enlisted personnel obtained specialty training, became proficient in it, were promoted on the basis of technical skill and military bearing, and gradually moved toward supervisory positions during the course of a career.

Congress passed enlisted retirement legislation for the first time in 1885. The act authorized voluntary retirement at thirty years and a retirement pay of 75 percent of the active duty pay. By 1948, all the military branches adopted the twenty year voluntary retirement as legislated in the Army and Air Force Vitalization and Retirement Equalization Act (1948). Like their officer counterparts, enlisted personnel could now retire at twenty years with 50 percent active duty pay for life to reach a maximum of 75 percent for thirty years' service. Changes in the percentage of retirement pay an officer or enlisted person receives has undergone several revisions since its establishment and is a continual source of congressional scrutiny.

In the early 1950s, the services established separate professional military education schools for NCOs. These schools offered subjects formerly reserved for officers such as leadership, world affairs, and management. Like commissioned officers, NCOs were now expected to attend professional schools throughout their careers. Promotions eventually became dependent on the amount of technical training and professional education an enlisted person received and demonstrated.

Fortunately, a career in the military can mean a variety of work experiences and responsible positions. Upon retirement after twenty or thirty years, some find that their training proves useful and rewarding in civilian life; others, especially those in combat roles, may find it difficult to move to a second career. Typically, officers have skills that translate into the realms of consulting, business, engineering, and politics. Enlisted personnel often pursue a college degree, teach in public or vocational schools, work in skilled trades, or manage small businesses. Officer and enlisted personnel who do not remain on active duty for a full career may choose to go into a civilian occupation and remain in the reserves. Given America's dependence on a well-trained reserve for wartime augmentation of the regular force, reservists can continue in a part-time military career that closely resembles their active duty counterpart. Retirement from the reserves is similar to active duty— twenty to thirty years' service. Unlike the active duty re-

tiree, who will receive remuneration for the rest of his or her life from the date of retirement, the reservist will not receive such compensation until at least age sixty-two.

• Morris Janowitz, *The Professional Soldier, A Social and Political Portrait*, 1960. Peter Karsten, *The Naval Aristocracy: The Golden Age of Annapolis and the Emergence of Modern American Navalism*, 1972. Frederick S. Harrod, *Manning the New Navy: The Development of a Modern Naval Enlisted Force, 1899–1940*, 1978. Edward M. Coffman, *The Old Army: A Portrait of the American Army in Peacetime, 1784–1898*, 1986. Christopher McKee, *A Gentlemanly and Honorable Profession: The Creation of the U.S. Naval Officer Corps, 1794–1815*, 1991. William B. Skelton, *An American Profession of Arms: The Army Officer Corps, 1784–1815*, 1992. Jack Shulimson, *The Marine Corps' Search for a Mission, 1880–1898*, 1993. Ernest F. Fisher, *Guardians of the Republic: A History of the Noncommissioned Officer Corps of the U.S. Army*, 1994. Mark R. Grandstaff, *Foundation of the Force: Air Force Enlisted Personnel Policy, 1907–1956*, 1996. Vance O. Mitchell, *Air Force Officers: Personnel Policy Development, 1944–1974*, 1996.

—Mark R. Grandstaff

CARIBBEAN AND LATIN AMERICA, U.S. MILITARY INVOLVEMENT IN THE. Since the enunciation of the *Monroe Doctrine (1823), U.S. policy towards the countries to the south has reflected the tensions between a self-interested appraisal of North American economic and military interests and an idealistic declaration of commitment to democracy. As the Monroe Doctrine indicates, the United States has viewed the New World as superior to the Old World, and the United States itself as the leader and protector of the Western Hemisphere. Yet the ideas of a common moral, political, and economic superiority in the New World and U.S. responsibility for the region have often produced impatience with the pace and direction of development in the Caribbean and Latin America. When impatience led to U.S. military intervention, the use of force was sometimes aimed at advancing the economic interests or national security of the United States and sometimes directed at keeping European influence out of the region.

As part of its *expansionism, the United States government caused the *Mexican War (1846–1848) and annexed the northern third of Mexico. In the middle of the nineteenth century, adventurers or "filibusters" like William Walker led privately armed groups into Nicaragua and other Central American and Caribbean countries with the hope of luring the United States government into annexing them. They were blocked, however, by local resistance as well as northern opposition to the expansion of the slave South before the Civil War.

For most of the nineteenth century, the United States viewed the newly independent Latin American countries as struggling underdeveloped nations. Projecting their own biases, North Americans believed that this economic underdevelopment was a result of what they considered to be racial inferiority, enervating tropical climate, and a restrictive Spanish cultural heritage in Latin America.

Although there were a few incidents that might have served as pretexts for war, such as the *Chilean Crisis (1891) and the Venezuelan Crisis (1895), it was not until 1898 that the United States joined the European race for formal colonies. As a result of the *Spanish-American-Cuban War (1898) and the *Philippine War (1899–1902), the United States conquered and annexed the former

Spanish colonies of Puerto Rico, Guam, and the Philippines. It also made Cuba a protectorate, administering it directly through U.S. military governors from 1898 to 1902.

It was not primarily through formal colonies, however, but through economic, cultural, and strategic influence backed up when deemed necessary by military force that the United States exercised its hegemony in the region. President Theodore *Roosevelt encouraged and protected the Panamanian revolt against Colombia with a U.S. warship. With the construction of the Panama Canal (1904–14), the Caribbean and Central America came to be seen as vital to U.S. national security. The U.S. Army directly governed the U.S. Canal Zone. The goal of U.S. hegemony had been announced in the *Roosevelt Corollary to the Monroe Doctrine (1904), authorizing U.S. intervention ostensibly to prevent European intervention. The Panama Canal and Roosevelt's doctrine provided the reason and the rationale for the United States's "protectorate policy" toward the region. On nearly twenty occasions in the first three decades of the twentieth century, U.S. presidents sent troops into Caribbean and Central American countries, most often the Dominican Republic, Haiti, Nicaragua, and Mexico. Historians differ over whether the primary motive of Roosevelt, William Howard Taft, and Woodrow *Wilson was to make the area safe for U.S. business, preclude European competition and intervention, or to maintain stability to protect U.S. strategic interests.

In the first half of the twentieth century, North Americans came to believe that economic underdevelopment in Latin America was less a result of indigenous factors than exploitative control of agriculture, mining, and transportation by European nations. This attitude and World War I helped North Americans replace Europeans as the major investors in the region. After the war, as the United States reduced its military role overseas, the Marines were withdrawn from the Caribbean basin, but they often left behind a U.S.-trained national guard to help maintain order and governments favorable to the United States. In his Good Neighbor policy, announced in 1933, President Franklin D. *Roosevelt formally ended the "protectorate policy" and accepted the principle of nonintervention. His emphasis on mutual respect built on reciprocal trade agreements helped to build a healthy new relationship that produced hemispheric solidarity against Germany and Japan in World War II.

The United States leadership continued after World War II through new organizations. These included global institutions such as the General Agreement on Tariffs and Trade (GATT), the International Monetary Fund (IMF) and the World Bank, and the *United Nations. They also included strictly regional bodies and agreements, most importantly the *Organization of American States (OAS) and the mutual defense agreement, the *Inter-American Treaty of Reciprocal Assistance (1947), which, like the 1949 North Atlantic Treaty (NATO), declared an attack against one to be an attack against all.

During the *Cold War, from 1947 until the collapse of the Soviet Union in 1991, U.S. national security policy toward Latin America was directed against the spread of communism. At the Caracas meeting in 1954, a majority of the OAS foreign ministers supported a U.S. resolution declaring communism incompatible with the inter-American system. President Dwight D. *Eisenhower

authorized a covert action program run by the *Central Intelligence Agency, which later that year overthrew the leftist, Guatemalan democratic regime of President Jacobo Arbenz, whose land reform had threatened the United Fruit Company and who was believed to be closely associated with communists. With the support of Eisenhower and his successor, President John F. *Kennedy, the CIA developed a plan to overthrow Fidel Castro, who had led a successful takeover in Cuba in 1959 and had then launched a sweeping socialist revolution under his own rule with increasingly close ties with the Soviet Union. The CIA-sponsored invasion by Cuban exiles at the Bay of Pigs in 1961 proved a disastrous failure.

As a result of the Soviet-Cuban threat of expanding communism in the Western Hemisphere, the United States developed major economic and security measures. The Alliance for Progress was designed to promote economic development and democracy (the "modernization" theory that undergirded it was, however, criticized by many Latin Americans as controlled "dependency"). Although it stimulated some economic development, it did not promote either democracy or social reform. The United States also engaged in increased anti-communist military activities.

In the *Cuban Missile Crisis (1962–63), triggered by the Soviet introduction of nuclear weapons to the island, Kennedy imposed a successful naval *blockade of Cuba, and the missiles were withdrawn in exchange for a U.S. pledge not to invade. Although ending the blockade, the United States continued to use some covert means but primarily economic embargos to undermine Castro, who, nevertheless, continued to rule one of the few remaining communist nations at the end of the century.

During the Cold War, fear of communism had led to considerable U.S. military involvement in the region. In part this involved the training of Latin American military officers in counterinsurgency techniques at schools on U.S. Army installations in the Panama Canal Zone and in the United States. Sometimes it involved direct use of U.S. forces, as in 1966, when President Lyndon B. *Johnson sent troops into the Dominican Republic, fearing, inaccurately most scholars agree, that instability there might lead to a communist takeover. Sometimes it was CIA activity rather than direct U.S. military involvement, as in 1973, when President Richard M. *Nixon authorized covert operations to help topple the Marxist president of Chile, Salvador Allende Gossens, who was overthrown by Gen. Augusto Pinochet in a bloody coup. Emphasizing human rights, President Jimmy *Carter reduced aid to authoritarian governments such as those in Argentina, Brazil, and Chile and refused to use military force to defend the Somoza regime in Nicaragua against leftist rebels. Following Panamanian riots, Carter also negotiated the treaties (1978) transferring control of the U.S.-built and -defended canal to Panama in 2000.

In 1979–80, leftist revolutions in Nicaragua, Grenada, and El Salvador raised the possibility of expanded communist influence and led to increased U.S. military involvement. President Ronald *Reagan built up the U.S. armed forces and often threatened force, but although he provided Army advisers and military and economic assistance to hard-line, anti-communists in Nicaragua and El Salvador, he sent troops into battle in the region only once, in the liberation of the island of Grenada in 1983 following a left-wing coup there.

The end of the Cold War enabled President George *Bush to depoliticize the North American perceptions of threats to U.S. security in Nicaragua and El Salvador and to join with other nations in negotiating peace and free elections there. He and his successor President Bill *Clinton reduced Latin American debt and encouraged trade liberalization through the creation of a North American Free Trade Agreement (1993) among the United States, Canada, and Mexico. However, direct U.S. military force was used by Bush in 1989 to capture Panamanian strongman General Manuel *Noriega, who was connected with Colombian drug traffickers. In 1994, Clinton dispatched U.S. troops to overthrow the military junta which had overthrown the president of Haiti, but a last-minute settlement led U.S. forces to arrive as transition peacekeepers rather than an invading force.

At the end of the twentieth century, although the U.S. provided aid against leftist guerrillas in Colombia, the main involvement of the U.S. military in Caribbean and Latin American countries focused on a relatively new role for the armed forces: trying to prevent the flow of illegal drugs into the United States. This mission was performed directly through the protection of U.S. borders and approaching air corridors and indirectly through the provision of U.S. equipment and military advisers to countries believed to be sources or transit routes for illegal drugs bound for the United States..

[See also Cuba: U.S. Military Involvement in; Cuban Missile Crisis (1962–1963); El Salvador, U.S. Military Involvement in; Grenada, U.S. Military Involvement in; Haiti, U.S. Military Involvement in; Iran-Contra Affair (1986); Mexican Revolution, U.S. Military Involvement in the; Nicaragua, U.S. Military Involvement in; Panama, U.S. Military Involvement in.]

• J. Child, Unequal Balance: The Inter-American Military System, 1938–1978, 1980; Cole Blasier, The Hovering Giant: U.S. Responses to Revolutionary Change in Latin America, 1910–1985, 1985; David Healy, Drive to Hegemony: The United States in the Caribbean, 1898–1917, 1988; Robert A. Pastor, Whirlpool: U.S. Foreign Policy Toward Latin America and the Caribbean, 1992; Walter LaFeber, Inevitable Revolutions, 2nd ed., 1993; John A. Britton, Revolution and Ideology: Images of the Mexican Revolution in the United States, 1995; and James William Park, Latin American Underdevelopment: A History of Perspectives in the United States, 1870–1965, 1995.

—John Whiteclay Chambers II

CARNEGIE, ANDREW (1835–1919), steel magnate, philanthropist, and pacifist. Born in Dunfermline, Scotland, Carnegie was indoctrinated in the democratic, pacifistic tenets of his father, a Chartist radical. The Carnegies emigrated to Pittsburgh in 1848, where the boy became a telegrapher for Thomas Scott of the Pennsylvania Railroad. He accompanied Scott to Washington at the outbreak of the *Civil War to supervise the extension of telegraph lines to the Union forces. In 1865, Carnegie left the Pennsylvania Railroad to enter a variety of business activities before devoting his full attention to the manufacture of steel. By the 1880s, he was America's king of steel.

Although opposed to militarism, Carnegie justified his providing armor plate for the naval expansion program of the 1890s as defensive, not offensive, in purpose. He supported the *Spanish-American War for Cuban independence, but became a leader in opposing the acquisition of the Philippines, even offering to pay Spain a higher sum than that proposed by the United States in order to give the islands their independence.

Carnegie sold his steel empire in 1901 for $400 million. He funded a variety of philanthropic enterprises, but after 1904 largely concentrated upon securing world peace through the establishment of foundations to promote this goal: the Carnegie Hero Fund; the *Carnegie Endowment for International Peace; and the Church Peace Union. He also funded the building of three "Temples of Peace": the International Court of Justice at the Hague; the Pan American Union Building in Washington, D.C.; and the Central American Court of Justice in Costa Rica. In the naive belief that peace could be purchased, he authorized the trustees of his foundations to eradicate other social ills after world peace had been secured. Not even World War I could crush his hopes. Carnegie died believing that Woodrow *Wilson's *League of Nations and his money would soon render war as morally unacceptable as cannibalism.

[See also Peace and Antiwar Movements.]

• Simon Goodenough, The Greatest Good Fortune: Andrew Carnegie's Gift for Today, 1985. Joseph Frazier Wall, Andrew Carnegie, 2nd ed. 1989.   —Joseph F. Wall

CARNEGIE ENDOWMENT FOR INTERNATIONAL PEACE. In 1910, retired steelmaker and philanthropist Andrew *Carnegie, a longtime supporter of peace societies, established the Carnegie Endowment for International Peace with a donation of $10 million, making it the wealthiest organization in the resurgent American peace movement of the early twentieth century. Like other peace advocates, Carnegie wanted America to be a world leader in promoting international arbitration to settle disputes among nations.

Carnegie's most influential advisers, elder statesman Elihu *Root, and the president of Columbia University, Nicholas Murray Butler, chose as trustees leading businessmen, influential members of Congress, and notable educators, bypassing longtime, more outspoken peace advocates. The politically conservative Endowment leaders, Root and Butler, thus created an organization for "scientific research" rather than active advocacy of peace. In World War I, the endowment curtailed its activities instead of advocating U.S. mediation or nonintervention.

The endowment's accomplishments in the areas of research and publication during the interwar period were impressive. Its projects included a monumental study, Economic and Social History of the World War (more than 100 volumes); many other studies of economics and international law; financing of overseas exchange visits by educators and journalists; creation of "International Mind" alcoves in libraries; and the endowing of university chairs in International Relations. The endowment published the scholarly journal International Conciliation until 1972, when the organization became associated with Foreign Policy magazine. After World War II, the endowment gave support and encouragement to the work of the *United Nations.

The endowment's trustees were always careful to avoid controversy. At its founding, many in the peace movement hoped Carnegie's gift would establish a powerful advocacy organization; instead, it became an early prototype of the policy research institute.

[See also Peace; Peace and Antiwar Movements.]

• Carnegie Endowment for International Peace, *Yearbooks* (1910–). Michael A. Lutzker, "The Formation of the Carnegie Endowment for International Peace: A Study of the Establishment-Centered Peace Movement, 1910–1914," in *Building the Organizational Society*, ed. Jerry Israel, 1972.   —Michael A. Lutzker

CARRIER WARFARE. The U.S. Navy has dominated aircraft carrier warfare since the 1920s. Conceived to provide scouting "eyes" for the fleet, the carrier evolved an attack capability that rivaled that of the *battleships during the interwar period. Offensive tactics were developed during annual "fleet problems" by innovative admirals, notably Joseph Mason Reeves, and a small cadre of younger naval aviators led by John H. Towers. In World War II, the carrier became the major arbiter of American seapower, a role more or less perpetuated during and after the *Cold War.

U.S. carrier forces have engaged in five principal roles and missions of varying priority according to operational objectives: (1) *fleet support,* using scouting planes for reconnaissance and fighter planes as defensive interceptors; (2) *destruction of the enemy fleet,* especially opposing carriers, with attack planes (bombers); (3) *protection of merchant shipping* as defensive convoy escorts or offensively in hunter-killer groups, against *submarines; (4) *destruction of enemy merchant shipping* at sea or at anchor; and (5) *projecting aerial firepower inland.* The function of the latter objective has been twofold: *supporting amphibious assaults* with close air support of infantry over the beach, protective fighter cover against enemy planes, and interdiction of enemy transportation systems (bridges, roads, rail lines) in order to isolate the beachhead; and *striking strategic targets*—airfields, army installations, port facilities, and industrial plants.

The sine qua non of carrier warfare is fleet support. The symbiotic interrelationship between carriers and gun ships exists in their mutual defense against enemy air, submarine, and surface ship attacks. The carriers provide combat air patrol fighters and antisubmarine and antiship patrol searches; the escorting gun ships (*destroyers, *cruisers, battleships) supply antiair, antisub, and antiship guns and missiles.

Tactically, the vulnerability of World War II carrier forces exposed to air attack caused them to disperse in order to split enemy attacks—during 1942–43 against Japan in the Pacific when U.S. carrier strength was weak, and again during the Cold War due to the threat of nuclear attack by Soviet submarines. Nevertheless, several carriers were temporarily concentrated during the 1942 naval battles at the Coral Sea, Midway, and around Guadalcanal. In overwhelming strength, carriers were concentrated permanently for the Central Pacific War campaign of 1943–45 and in the limited wars thereafter.

At the Battle of *Midway, three U.S. carriers, superbly coordinated by Adm. Raymond A. *Spruance, sank all four Japanese carriers to the loss of one American "flattop." Otherwise, carrier strength on both sides was whittled down while supporting amphibious and island struggles in the Coral Sea–Guadalcanal region. When a powerful Fast Carrier Attack Force was created late in 1943 for the offensive, it was organized into three or four task groups, each made up of three or four carriers plus escorting gun ships in a circular screen. The carriers' simultaneous but conflicting missions of supporting amphibious forces and seeking out the Japanese fleet led to confusion and missed opportunities during invasions of the Gilbert Islands, the Marians, and Leyte. Nevertheless, under the brilliant tactical command of Adm. Marc A. Mitscher, the fast carriers neutralized Japan's air and naval bases at Rabaul and Truk, annihilated its carrier planes in the Battle of the *Philippine Sea, and sank its last operational carriers at the Battle of *Leyte Gulf.

In all subsequent amphibious campaigns—Luzon, Iwo Jima, Okinawa—the carriers battled land-based Japanese kamikazes, striking their airfields and other strategic targets. Most close air support in the Pacific, and North Africa and the Mediterranean as well, was provided by the small, slower escort carriers.

U.S. carriers helped defeat Germany's U-boats in the Battle of the Atlantic by utilizing antisubmarine hunter-killer groups, each an independent force of one escort carrier and a screen of destroyers. Similarly, from the mid-1950s to the mid-1970s, specially designated antisubmarine carriers patrolled against Soviet submarines until this mission was reassigned to the attack carriers. During the limited wars and crises of Korea, Vietnam, and the Middle East, American carriers operated virtually free from enemy interference. Carriers also played a Cold War deterrent role by carrying *nuclear weapons. The emergence of a large Soviet surface fleet and carriers by the 1970s led to a revived doctrine for fighting naval battles, including the projected use of carriers against the Russian fleet in the North Atlantic according to the unofficial "Maritime Strategy" of the 1980s. But the Soviet collapse nullified it.

The major controversies over carrier warfare have been caused by opponents within the U.S. Navy, the U.S. Air Force, and Congress claiming the carrier to be vulnerable to air and submarine attacks and thus a waste of defense expenditures. These arguments have yet to be proven.

[See also Aircraft Carriers; Naval Combat Branches: Naval Air Forces.]

• Samuel Eliot Morison, *History of U.S. Naval Operations in World War II: The Atlantic Battle Won,* Vol. 10, 1956. Richard P. Hallion, *The Naval Air War in Korea,* 1986. John B. Nichols and Barrett Tillman, *On Yankee Station: The Naval Air War Over Vietnam,* 1987. Clark G. Reynolds, *Admiral John H. Towers: The Struggle for Naval Air Supremacy,* 1991. Clark G. Reynolds, *The Fast Carriers: The Forging of an Air Navy,* 1968, repr. 1992. E. T. Woodridge, ed., *Carrier Warfare in the Pacific: An Oral History Collection,* 1993.
                     —Clark G. Reynolds

CARTER, JIMMY (1924–), naval officer, farm business operator, governor, president of the United States. Born in Plains, Georgia, Carter graduated from the U.S. Naval Academy in 1946 and became a nuclear submarine officer. After his father's death (1953), he returned to manage the family's farming enterprises. Active in the local Baptist church and state politics, Carter was a state senator (1963–67) and governor of Georgia (1971–75). In 1974, he narrowly defeated President Gerald *Ford.

As president, Carter characterized himself as nonideological, a social liberal and fiscal conservative. He had a strong sense of morality and equity. A rational and diligent manager, Carter proved a technician rather than a logrolling politician or a highly inspiring leader. He experienced only a mixed success in foreign and defense matters, a result of circumstances and of Carter himself.

Diplomatically, the Carter administration negotiated and secured a divided Senate's ratification of the Panama

Canal treaties, completed normalization of relations with the People's Republic of China, and spectacularly achieved a peace treaty, the *Camp David Accords (1978), between Israel and Egypt.

Carter was also confronted with major challenges over which he had little control, although he was criticized for lurching between weak and hard-line policies. Soviet intervention in Cuba and the Horn of Africa and Russian military occupation of Afghanistan led the administration to support a military buildup. Carter ended his opposition to increases in the military budget, approved construction of the MX missile, abandoned his SALT II Treaty, canceled U.S. participation in the Summer Olympics in Moscow, and resumed compulsory draft registration. In the "*Carter Doctrine," he pledged protection of the oil-rich Persian Gulf region and established a rapid deployment force to enforce it.

Seizure of U.S. Embassy hostages in November 1979 by successful Iranian revolutionaries led Carter to impose diplomatic and economic sanctions against Iran. In April 1980, an ill-fated military rescue attempt was aborted at the "Desert One" site south of Tehran after three of the eight helicopters malfunctioned. Another helicopter and a C-130 transport plane collided in the nighttime lift-off. Government released the hostages in January 1981 when Ronald *Reagan became president.

Out of office, Carter pursued his own agenda, involving human rights, social welfare, and international mediation. He played particularly important, if often controversial, roles in easing later conflicts with Nicaragua, North Korea, and Haiti.

[See also Conscription; Iran, U.S. Military Involvement in; Panama, U.S. Military Involvement in; SALT Treaties.]

• Burton I. Kaufman, The Presidency of James Earl Carter, Jr., 1993. Gary M. Fink and Hush Davis Graham, eds., The Carter Presidency, 1998.   —John Whiteclay Chambers II

CARTER DOCTRINE (1980). Announced by President Jimmy *Carter on 24 January 1980, the "Carter Doctrine" extended U.S. containment policy to the Persian Gulf region. Under pressure from containment advocates, Carter concluded that the 1979 Soviet invasion of Afghanistan might be the first step in a threat to the Persian Gulf oil resources. Furthermore, with the overthrow of the shah of Iran (and seizure of American hostages) by militant Islamic revolutionaries earlier in 1979, the United States had lost its primary military ally in the gulf.

To ensure protection of Middle East oil, Carter declared that the United States would consider any attempt by an outside force (the Soviet Union) to gain control of the gulf region an assault on U.S. vital interests that would be repelled by military force if necessary. Consequently, Carter expanded military aid to Saudi Arabia, Egypt, Israel, and Pakistan, and went beyond surrogate forces to create a U.S. Rapid Deployment Joint Task Force (RDF).

From its new headquarters, the RDF could call upon 200,000 troops from all services to meet emergencies in the gulf. It also acquired air and naval basing rights at Diego Garcia, a British atoll in the Indian Ocean, for positioning more than a dozen preloaded merchant ships to support any initial deployment. Additional basing rights were sought in several East African countries. Many of these were later used in the *Persian Gulf War of 1991.

[See also Middle East, U.S. Military Involvement in the.]

• Gaddis Smith, Morality, Reason, and Power: American Diplomacy in the Carter Years, 1986. Burton I. Kaufman, The Presidency of James Earl Carter, Jr., 1993.   —John Whiteclay Chambers II

CASE-CHURCH AMENDMENT (1973). The signing of the *Paris Peace Agreement in January 1973 brought a final withdrawal of American military forces from Vietnam following the *Vietnam War. Many believed, however, that the peace agreement only marked a temporary respite in the fighting. The question was what would the administration of President Richard M. *Nixon do once the inevitable renewal of hostilities between the North and South Vietnamese forces began? In order to prevent a reintroduction of United States forces into the conflict, Senators Clifford Case (R-NJ) and Frank Church (D-ID) introduced on 26 January 1973 a bill that barred any future use of American forces in Vietnam, Laos, and Cambodia without the authorization of the Congress. The inclusion of Cambodia was crucial because the Paris agreement did not cover the continued fighting there, and American air power continued to be employed in bombing the Khmer Rouge.

The Senate passed the amendment for the first time on 14 June. While awaiting action in the House of Representatives, Nixon vetoed separate legislation that would have ended the bombing in Cambodia. Finally, a modified Case-Church amendment was passed by the Senate on 29 June by a 63–26 vote. It allowed the bombing in Cambodia to continue until 15 August. After that date, all use of the American military was prohibited in Southeast Asia unless the president secured Congressional approval in advance. The proponents of the ban did not know that Nixon had, in fact, secretly promised South Vietnam's president Nguyen Van Thieu that the United States would resume bombing in North and South Vietnam if he determined it necessary to enforce the peace settlement. The Case-Church amendment, therefore, marked the final end to direct American military involvement in Southeast Asia.

• LeRoy Ashby and Rod Gramer, Fighting the Odds: The Life of Senator Frank Church, 1994.   —David F. Schmitz

CASUALTIES. Casualties—soldiers killed or rendered unable to fight by enemy weapons, disease, or accident—reduce combat strength and sap the morale of those personnel who remain fit for service. The outcomes of battles, campaigns, and even wars have often been determined by the casualties suffered by one side or the other.

Casualties may be classified as either battle or nonbattle. Battle casualties include personnel killed in action, wounded in action, captured, or missing in action; nonbattle casualties include those killed or disabled by disease or accident, as well as those incapacitated by psychiatric illnesses (known variously as shell shock, battle fatigue, or Post-Traumatic Stress Disorder) induced by the stresses of military service.

Since 1775, weapons have become more lethal, and with increased lethality has come an increase in both the number of casualties and the severity of wounds. Before 1850, about half of all battle casualties were caused by artillery. The introduction of the conoidal bullet in the mid-nineteenth century greatly increased the range, accuracy, and striking power of small-arms fire, and in the *Civil

War rifle fire accounted for most battle casualties. By World War I, better recoil mechanisms (which improved the rapidity and accuracy of fire), the introduction of indirect firing techniques, and advances in high explosives and shell design made artillery once again the most destructive force on the battlefield. More recently, landmines and aerial attack (bombardment, strafing, and napalm) have produced significant casualties. The huge number of weapons systems on the modern battlefield and their more rapid rate of fire has also increased casualties, and chemical, nuclear, and biological weapons pose even greater threats to survival.

Prevailing tactical doctrines and practices significantly influence the proportion of soldiers who become casualties. Until the end of the nineteenth century, the dominant tactical methods involved close-packed linear formations and frontal assaults, both of which exposed attackers to the full effect of defenders' weapons. Since World War I, the wider dispersion of forces on the battlefield and the increased use of cover and concealment have reduced exposure to enemy fire. On the other hand, modern battles involve continuous combat over extended periods, and thus the number of casualties, particularly those due to fatigue and combat stress, has tended to increase.

The assurance of rapid evacuation and effective treatment of the wounded is a major factor in maintaining military morale and the willingness to endure combat. The speed at which the wounded soldier reaches medical treatment is the key element in his chances of surviving his wounds and avoiding permanent disability. Few soldiers who suffer severe wounds will survive unless they receive adequate medical care within six hours.

The principles of military medical evacuation employed by most modern armies were devised by U.S. Army Maj. Jonathan Letterman during the Civil War. Letterman reorganized the existing system of field hospitals, established an ambulance corps, and laid down the principle that rear echelons should be responsible for sending forward the men and transport to evacuate casualties to medical facilities well behind the battle line. Letterman's system reduced both the confusion attendant to the handling of battle casualties and the time required to get the wounded to definitive medical care.

Refinement of Letterman's system and more rapid means of transport further reduced the time required for evacuation in World Wars I and II, but the helicopter dramatically transformed battlefield evacuation. A few primitive helicopters were used in World War II for evacuating sick and wounded soldiers from remote locations. Such use was expanded during the *Korean War, and in Vietnam the medical evacuation helicopter all but replaced ground evacuation. The result was a significant reduction in the time required to get a battle casualty to life-saving treatment. In Vietnam, for example, the average time required for the evacuation of a casualty by helicopter was only 35 minutes. Consequently, the number of wounded soldiers who died was substantially reduced and the chances of avoiding permanent disability or disfigurement improved considerably.

Major improvements in battlefield evacuation since 1860 have been accompanied by equally striking advances in diagnostic techniques, surgery, drugs, and preventive medicine. Before the Civil War, some advances were made in surgical techniques, the use of anesthetics (chloroform),

and camp sanitation. However, the half century between the Civil War and World War I saw astounding progress in medical science. Louis Pasteur's germ theory, Jacob Lister's concept of antisepsis, and Wilhelm Roentgen's X-ray process enabled major steps forward. Surgical techniques improved greatly, and the use of more effective anesthetics became general, as did more potent painkillers such as morphine. Inoculation against infectious diseases, particularly those (typhoid, for example) that severely threatened massed military forces operating under poor sanitary conditions, also became routine.

American military physicians made major contributions to the advance of medical science in the late nineteenth and early twentieth century. Antiseptic surgery was practiced in U.S. Army hospitals as early as 1883, well before Lister's theories were generally accepted. George Miller Sternberg, army surgeon general in 1893–1902, was a recognized pioneer in the field of bacteriology and promoted the work of other military physicians who sought the causes of communicable diseases such as cholera, typhoid, and typhus. Under Sternberg's patronage, Maj. Walter *Reed identified the mosquito as the vector for yellow fever, and the subsequent efforts of Col. William C. *Gorgas to control malaria and yellow fever made possible the construction of the Panama Canal and the reduction of those diseases worldwide.

The frightful casualties resulting from more destructive weapons in World War I spurred the development of improved surgical techniques and better management of infection. Further advances significantly reduced mortality in World War II and set the pace for even greater progress in medical science after 1945. Effective new drugs, such as sulfa and penicillin, were introduced; X-ray techniques and equipment were improved; and the use of blood plasma to prevent shock and replace blood volume saved thousands of lives, military and civilian. The global deployment of American forces also prompted research into the causes, prevention, and treatment of a variety of diseases until then little known or understood. Malaria and other endemic diseases were eradicated in certain areas as part of the American military public health efforts.

Medical science has continued to advance since 1945, and the resources now available to the military physician far surpass anything available in World War II. The surgical laser, greatly improved diagnostic technology, and modern antibiotics make diagnosis and treatment more efficient and effective. Recent advances in bioelectronic and biomechanical devices have also substantially improved the chances of restoring to wounded soldiers the nearly full use of damaged limbs and organs.

The rate of death from wounds has fallen significantly in the last 150 years. In the *Mexican War (1846–48), 14.9 percent of all battle casualties died from their wounds. The rate fell slightly—to 14.1 percent—in the Civil War, and then declined sharply to only 6.7 percent in the *Spanish-American War. Mortality rose to 8.1 percent in World War I (exclusive of gas casualties), due to the greater destructiveness of modern weapons, but subsequently fell even more sharply. The rate of deaths from wounds after reaching medical treatment was 4.5 percent in World War II and 2.4 percent in Korea. In the *Vietnam War, 97.5 percent of the wounded survived, and 80 percent of those later returned to duty.

Until well into the twentieth century, disease, rather

than the effects of enemy weapons, was the single most important producer of casualties. In the *Revolutionary War, 90 out of every 100 deaths were due to disease. As late as 1865, more soldiers died from disease, shock, or secondary infection of wounds than died from the direct effects of weapons. Even in Vietnam, 75 percent of all hospital admissions were for the treatment of disease rather than wounds. However, the effect of progress in preventive medicine and the treatment of disease on the survival rates of sick and wounded soldiers was profound. In the Mexican War, the rate of death from disease was 103.9 per 1,000 men. The rate fell to 71.4 per 1,000 in the Civil War and then to 34.0 per 1,000 in the Spanish-American War. In World War I, the rate was only 16.5 per 1,000, and in World War II it fell to just 0.6 per 1,000.

Although the weapons of war continue to grow more destructive, improved tactical doctrine, more efficient evacuation, and advances in medical technology and techniques promise continued reduction in the number of casualties and continued increase in the rate of survival for the sick and wounded. Today, military personnel are healthier and less likely to die from their wounds or from disease than ever before.

[See also Combat Trauma; Medical Practice and the Military.]

• Albert G. Love, Eugene L. Hamilton, and Ida Levin Hellman, *Tabulating Equipment and Army Medical Statistics*, 1958. Rose C. Engleman, ed., *A Decade of Progress: The United States Army Medical Department, 1959–1969*, 1971. Mary C. Gillett, *The Army Medical Department, 1775–1818*, 1981. Albert E. Cowdrey, *The Medic's War*, 1987. Trevor N. Dupuy, "Attrition: Personnel Casualties," in Trevor N. Dupuy, et al., *International Military and Defense Encyclopedia*, Vol. 1, 1993. N. T. P. Murphy, "Casualties: Evacuation and Treatment," in Trevor N. Dupuy, et al., *International Military and Defense Encyclopedia*, Vol. 2, 1993. U.S. Department of Defense, "Service and Casualties in Major Wars and Conflicts (as of Sept. 30, 1993)," *Defense 94—Almanac*, Issue 5 (September–October 1994).
—Charles R. Shrader

CAVALRY. *See* Army Combat Branches: Cavalry.

CEMETERIES, MILITARY. Few provisions were made prior to the *Civil War for the maintenance of permanent cemeteries for Americans who died in military service. After battle, the dead were buried in hastily dug graves on the site or at nearby civilian cemeteries. In peacetime, commanders at many forts and outposts, such as Fort Leavenworth, Kansas, in the 1840s, established burial grounds for soldiers who died. In the aftermath of the *Mexican War, the United States established a cemetery in Mexico City for U.S. soldiers killed during the capture of that city.

During the Civil War, the U.S. government established a permanent national cemetery system in 1862 for uniformed personnel. Most of these army-maintained cemeteries were located near a military hospital or major battlefield, although the battle dead were still frequently buried in scores of smaller, scattered plots, and the dead of losing sides were often interred in mass graves. After 1865, the Quartermaster Corps removed the bodies of Union soldiers from many of these smaller burial sites and placed them in large, more centralized cemeteries with standard markers for officers and enlisted men. It was at the dedication of the national military cemetery at Gettysburg (later *Gettysburg National Military Park), only weeks

after the battle, that President Abraham *Lincoln gave his famous Gettysburg Address defining the nature of American democracy.

In the aftermath of the Civil War, the national military cemetery system for the Union dead served as an important site of both individual and collective mourning, especially on Memorial Day—a national day of mourning for the Union dead designated by the *Grand Army of the Republic in 1868 and by Congress in 1887. In these national military cemeteries, state governments, veterans' groups, and other organizations erected memorials commemorating particular units, states, or other entities. By the late nineteenth century, Civil War cemeteries at Antietam, Gettysburg, and Shiloh served as the nucleus of a system of national military parks. In 1872, Congress extended the right of burial in national military cemeteries to all Union *veterans of the Civil War. To foster sectional reconciliation, the federal government in 1912 allowed burial rights to Confederate veterans in Arlington National Cemetery (originally established in 1864).

There still remained, however, strong local and regional patterns of mourning that militated against having all the war dead buried in national cemeteries. Families retained the right to reclaim bodies. The bodies of service members who had died in most subsequent foreign wars were returned by the federal government to the United States. During the *Spanish-American War and the *Philippine War, the army created the Quartermaster Burial Corps to disinter those who died overseas and to return their bodies to the United States.

In contrast, World War I brought significant support among internationalists to create permanent U.S. military cemeteries overseas to symbolize the American commitment to Europe. This proposal aroused considerable opposition from families who wanted the fallen buried in home-town cemeteries and from isolationists who feared that the European cemeteries would commit America to defend those countries in the future. In response to such disagreements, Congress and the War Department affirmed the right of each family to decide where a soldier would be buried. In 1923, Congress created the American Battle Monuments Commission to build and maintain permanent cemeteries abroad to cover U.S. participation in World War I. After World War II, this authority would be extended to cemeteries in battle grounds in Europe, North Africa, and Asia.

No overseas cemeteries were established for either the *Korean War or the *Vietnam War. Initially, Americans killed in the Korean War were buried in overseas cemeteries in Korea, but even before the war ended, Washington decided to bring all the bodies back to the United States. This practice differed from that of almost all other major nations, such as Great Britain, which buried soldiers on or near the battlefield. During the Vietnam War, the bodies of the American dead were flown immediately to the United States for burial in either national or private cemeteries.

In the twentieth century, Veterans' groups like the *American Legion were active in ensuring that veterans and their spouses were accorded the option of burial in the national military cemeteries, especially Arlington National Cemetery. Since many of the cemeteries were established near the sites of Civil War battlefields or hospitals, they were widely dispersed. With some success—often over the opposition of funeral directors, private cemetery managers, and the national government—veterans' organizations pressured Congress to create smaller military cemeteries nearer to major population centers. The army finally agreed. Only a limited number of new cemeteries were added in the immediate post–World War II period, generally after sufficient pressure was placed on Congress by veterans' groups and local leadership. In 1962, during John F. *Kennedy's administration, the army officially abandoned any plans for a new system of military cemeteries for 16 million veterans and their eligible dependents.

The army had held full control over the national cemeteries until 1933, when eleven Civil War battlefields near national military parks were transferred to the control of the National Park Service. Veterans' groups opposed to the policy of nonexpansion lobbied Congress to transfer jurisdiction of the national cemetery system away from the army and place it with the more sympathetic *Veterans Administration (VA). In 1973, the VA gained control of most national cemeteries—except for Arlington.

National cemeteries have served as important sites for *commemoration and public ritual, especially during Memorial and Veterans Days. American presidents have visited overseas national cemeteries to underscore U.S. commitments abroad. In the twentieth century, Arlington National Cemetery evolved into a powerful site of national collective memory with the creation of the Tomb of the Unknowns, the Memorial Amphitheater, and the burial of a number of prominent civilian leaders, most notably John F. and Robert Kennedy.

[See also Battlefields, Encampments, and Forts as Public Sites; Memorials, War.]

• James M. Mayo, War Memorials As Political Landscape, 1988. David Charles Sloane, The Last Great Necessity: Cemeteries in American History, 1991. Dean W. Holt, American National Cemeteries, 1992. Garry Wills, Lincoln at Gettysburg, 1992. G. Kurt Piehler, Remembering War the American Way, 1995.   —G. Kurt Piehler

The **CENTRAL INTELLIGENCE AGENCY,** (CIA) was created by Congress in the *National Security Act of 1947, recognizing strategic intelligence as a first line of defense and a crucial instrument in warfare. The attack on *Pearl Harbor in 1941 had demonstrated the need to gather and coordinate intelligence information. Significantly, the CIA was created the year President Harry S. *Truman announced the containment doctrine at the beginning of the *Cold War.

Truman abolished the wartime Office of Strategic Services (OSS) in 1945, transferring some of its intelligence-gathering functions to the State Department and the army and some to a new Central Intelligence Group, created in January 1946. The CIA was established by Congress, not the president, and as an independent agency; the director (DCI) would report directly to the president. It operated under the *National Security Council (NSC), a newly established presidential advisory board, and had legal access to the intelligence information of all other civilian and military agencies.

Concerns about an all-powerful secret police spying on Americans led Congress to prohibit the CIA from "police, subpoena, law enforcement powers or internal-security" functions. Domestic counterintelligence was to remain the preserve of the FBI.

The CIA's leaders, many of them former OSS officers, quickly became involved in bureaucratic struggles over jurisdiction and resources with nearly a dozen other military and civilian agencies, and the State Department required that the CIA's overseas personnel come under the jurisdiction of the U.S. ambassador in that country. The first DCI, Rear Adm. Roscoe H. Hillenkoetter (1947–50), lacked influence. Under his successors, Army Gen. Walter Bedell Smith (1950–53) and Allen Welsh *Dulles (1953–61), the CIA became a powerful agency. Yet it never achieved anywhere near total control over U.S. intelligence policy because too many other departments retained their own sources of intelligence, especially those under the secretary of defense.

The 1947 National Security Act authorized the CIA to collect, correlate, and evaluate intelligence relating to national security, and to disseminate that information to appropriate agencies within the government. It was also authorized to perform "other functions and duties related to intelligence affecting the national security." Although the agency's charter did not mention "espionage," "counterespionage," or "covert action," the broad language became the source for later expansion of the CIA's activities.

Within a year, the agency—often called "the company" by its personnel—had expanded its roles under NSC directives to include covert activities. These included secret *psychological warfare as well as undercover political, economic, and paramilitary operations overseas. Originally, most of these anti-Communist operations were in Europe, designed to be secret and planned and executed in such a way that the U.S. government could "plausibly disclaim any responsibility for them."

In large part because of such clandestine operations Congress amended the statute (1949) to permit the CIA to receive funds secretly under budget cover of other federal agencies. Under the so-called black budget, the director was given extraordinary authority to spend money and to impose absolute secrecy for sources and methods. The justification was to prevent foreign governments from learning the scope of the CIA's activities, but this secrecy also protected the CIA from domestic budgetary and accounting agencies.

The *Korean War, and the massive national security buildup that accompanied it, led to a huge expansion of the CIA. The U.S. intelligence community's failure to anticipate the North Korean invasion of South Korea, like the Pearl Harbor attack, demonstrated the failure of intelligence gathering and coordination of information. The CIA was finally given access to military signals intelligence, and Truman replaced Hillenkoetter with Smith (1953), who had been Eisenhower's chief of staff during World War II. With increased funding and mandate, Smith largely created the CIA in its modern form. By 1953, the agency had more than 10,000 employees, including nearly 3,000 in the Office of Policy Coordination (which ran the covert operations), and more than 3,000 additional personnel serving overseas. Headquarters were moved to Langley, Virginia, in 1963.

Allen Dulles, former OSS officer, deputy director, and brother of Secretary of State John Foster *Dulles, was the first civilian to head the CIA; under his leadership, the agency reached a peak strength of 18,000. The CIA created and ran Radio Liberty and Radio Free Europe as propaganda services beamed at Eastern Europe and the USSR.

NSC directives in the 1950s expanded the agency's

*covert operations, which came to overshadow information-gathering functions. While covert actions by definition remained secret and presidents were given plausible deniability, secrecy was undermined in major cases when its coups achieved success, for example, Iran (1953) and Guatemala (1954). Most of the public controversy about the CIA involved covert foreign interventions where policy as well as secrecy failed, especially the Bay of Pigs invasion (1961). Although photo reconnaissance increased dramatically in the 1950s with the high-flying U-2 "spy" planes, the agency and the Eisenhower administration were publicly embarrassed when a plane was shot down over the USSR in May 1960 and the pilot captured. The public came to know of many intelligence failures, too, most dramatically the failure to predict the onset of the Korean War.

Dulles was replaced by John A. McCone (1961–65), a former chair of the Atomic Energy Commission, who shifted emphasis from covert operations to intelligence gathering and analysis. Through human intelligence gathering (HUMINT) by a Soviet military officer, Col. Oleg Penkovsky, and photoimage intelligence (IMINT) U-2 flights over Cuba, the CIA learned in 1962 about Soviet missile technology and the deployment of nuclear-tipped, medium-range *missiles in Cuba. The agency continued its covert operations, for example in a successful coup in Guyana in the early 1960s.

The CIA was hard hit during the *Vietnam War. Pessimistic about conventional forces winning a guerrilla war, its own covert and counterintelligence operations in Southeast Asia became increasingly controversial. President Lyndon B. *Johnson appointed Vice Adm. William F. Raborn, Jr. (ret.) as DCI, but he was soon replaced by Richard M. Helms (1966–73), the first career intelligence officer to head the agency. Neither Johnson nor President Richard M. *Nixon paid much attention to intelligence reports that contradicted their views, and Nixon and his NSC adviser, Henry *Kissinger, tended to fashion their own intelligence estimates.

In the 1970s, in the wake of Watergate and Vietnam, the media and Congress launched major investigations into illegal or inappropriate activities by the CIA. These revealed that under orders from the Johnson and Nixon administrations, the CIA had violated its charter through surveillance (Operation Chaos) of domestic opponents of the Vietnam War, and that some U.S. intelligence officials had been involved in programs since the early 1960s to assassinate Communist leaders, most prominently Fidel Castro and the Congo's Patrice Lumumba.

Such revelations, especially by the investigating committee headed by Senator Frank Church, contributed to calls for abolition of the agency. Instead, the investigation precipitated reforms begun under DCIs James R. Schlesinger, William E. Colby, and George *Bush. Assassination plots in peacetime were prohibited by executive order (1975) by President Gerald *Ford, who also created an Intelligence Oversight Board and reinvigorated the President's Foreign Intelligence Advisory Board. In 1976–77, Congress created permanent intelligence committees in both houses to oversee all aspect of intelligence. President Jimmy *Carter appointed Adm. Stanfield Turner, an active duty naval officer, as DCI (1977–81); under Turner, the agency shrank by more than one-third of its peak size.

With the U.S. defense buildup that began in 1980, and

especially under President Ronald *Reagan and his first director, William J. Casey (1981–87)—a former OSS station chief, successful lawyer, and Reagan's 1980 campaign manager—the CIA was "unleashed," its budget increased and clandestine operations reemphasized, especially in Afghanistan, Angola, and Nicaragua. The Intelligence Reform Act (1980) freed the CIA from earlier restraints: although presidential approval of covert operations was required, in "extraordinary circumstances" congressional oversight committees might be notified only later. New photo and satellite imagery and signals/communications intelligence (SIGINT) increased U.S. information on Soviet military capability. But tensions over covert operations grew between the Republican president and the Democratic Congress, culminating in the *Iran-Contra Affair (1986), which revealed that the CIA had violated congressional restraints. Following Casey's death, FBI director William H. Webster became DCI (1987–91). The Intelligence Authorization Acts (1991, 1992) tightened legislative oversight and required prior notice for all covert actions.

With the dissolution of the Soviet Union, which the agency had failed to predict, fundamental questions were raised about the future of the CIA, widely perceived as a Cold War institution. The agency's reputation was further hurt when CIA officer Aldrich H. Ames was exposed (1994) as a "mole" who had sold secrets to the Soviets for nearly a decade, causing the deaths of a dozen foreign agents. In 1997 a former CIA station chief, Harold Nicholson, was convicted of spying for Russia.

Robert Gates, R. James Woolsey, Jr., John M. Deutch, and George J. Tenet sought to find new roles for the CIA, especially technological surveillance for economic and ecological as well as security purposes, and monitoring drug traffic and terrorist threats. At century's end the future of the CIA remained uncertain.

[See also Intelligence, Military and Political; Pentagon, The.]

• U.S. Senate, 94th Congress, Select Committee (Church Committee) to Study Government Operations with Respect to Intelligence Activities, *Hearings and Reports*, 1975–76. Anne Karalekas, *History of the Central Intelligence Agency*, 1977. Harry Rositzke, *The CIA's Secret Operations: Espionage, Counterespionage, and Cover Action*, 1977. Robert M. Gates, *From the Shadows: The Ultimate Insider's Story of Five Presidents and How They Won the Cold War*, 1996. Loch K. Johnson, *Secret Agencies: U.S. Intelligence in a Hostile World*, 1996. Commission on the Roles and Capabilities of the U.S. Intelligence Community, *Report*, "Preparing for the 21st Century: An Appraisal of the U.S. Intelligence Community," 1996.

—Harry Howe Ransom

CFE TREATY. The Treaty on Conventional Armed Forces in Europe (CFE) was signed in Paris on 19 November 1990 by the heads of state of the then-members of *NATO and the Warsaw Treaty Organization (WTO, or *Warsaw Pact). The treaty's system of equal and verified quantitative ceilings on conventional weaponry (main battle *tanks, *artillery, *armored vehicles, strike aircraft, and attack *helicopters) was designed to impose a stable military balance on the *Cold War's two opposing alliances. In practice, however, the most pronounced effect of the CFE Treaty was to mandate steep reductions in the overall size and forward deployment of the Soviet armed forces; NATO forces were little affected. Such an outcome would have been inconceivable if the Cold War were not already well near its close by the time the CFE Treaty was ready for signature.

The origins of the treaty lie in a perception that was widely shared by the strategists of the NATO Alliance after the 1960s, when the alliance adopted a strategy of *Flexible Response: the Warsaw Pact's gross preponderance of conventional military equipment in Central Europe meant that NATO would quickly be forced to resort to tactical *nuclear weapons to halt a conventional offensive by the Warsaw Pact. Though possibly exaggerated, the belief that NATO's conventional inferiority to the Warsaw Pact had lowered the nuclear threshold in Europe gave rise to great interest in conventional arms control, especially in NATO's front-line states, such as Germany. The first practical manifestation of this interest was the Mutual and Balanced Force Reduction (MBFR) talks, which ground on inconclusively between 1973 and 1987. By the time the Intermediate Nuclear Forces (*INF) Treaty was signed in December 1987, righting the conventional balance in Europe had become one of the alliance's highest strategic priorities.

The CFE Treaty was made possible principally by the foreign policy reforms of Soviet president Mikhail Gorbachev, whose willingness to overrule the Soviet General Staff in the course of the negotiations attested to his determination to end the costly military standoff in Central Europe as quickly as possible.

The mandate talks, which began in Vienna on 17 February 1987, concluded on 14 January 1989, five weeks after Gorbachev had announced sweeping unilateral reductions in Soviet forces before the *United Nations General Assembly. The negotiations themselves, beginning 9 March 1989, coincided with the fall of the Communist regimes in Eastern Europe (mid-1988 through December 1989), the fall of the Berlin Wall (9 November 1989), full German unification (3 October 1990), the effective collapse of the Warsaw Pact as a military alliance, and Moscow's decision to withdraw all Soviet forces from Eastern Europe. Thus, the CFE Treaty codified a new political-military reality in Europe that probably would have emerged in any case, albeit without solemn treaty-based undertakings.

The treaty entered into force on 9 November 1992, after a difficult ratification process that was complicated by the collapse of the Soviet Union in December 1991. Eight of the former Soviet republics acceded to the treaty as the Soviet Union's successor states. When the treaty's numerical ceilings became binding on 19 November 1995, most of the thirty states-parties were in compliance with its provisions. However, the Russian Federation, while in overall compliance with the treaty's ceilings, was in violation of the regional ceiling on the "flank zone," an area that encompassed the Caucasus. This issue was resolved at the May 1996 CFE Treaty Review Conference, at which the parties to the treaty agreed to remove four Russian military districts (Pskov, Volgograd, Rostov, and Astrakhan) from the flank zone, thereby allowing Russia to meet the zone's original numerical ceilings on tanks, armored combat vehicles, and artillery pieces. According to this agreement, which entered into force in May 1997, Russia had until May 1999 to comply with the numerical limits on the reduced flank zone.

At the Lisbon summit of the Organization for Security and Cooperation in Europe in December 1996, the parties to the CFE Treaty agreed to begin a new round of negotiations aimed to "adapt" the CFE Treaty to new geopolitical realities of post–Cold War Europe. These negotiations were motivated in large part by NATO enlargement and sought to eliminate the treaty's bloc-to-bloc character. CFE adaptation talks began in Vienna in January 1997 and were expected to run at least until 1999.

[See also Arms Control and Disarmament: Nonnuclear; Berlin Crises.]

• Jane M. O. Sharp, "Conventional Arms Control in Europe," in SIPRI Yearbook 1991: World Armaments and Disarmament, 1991. Richard A. Falkenrath, Shaping Europe's Military Order: The Origins and Consequences of the CFE Treaty, Center for Science and International Affairs. Studies in International Security No. 6, 1995.

—Richard Falkenrath

CHANCELLORSVILLE, BATTLE OF (1863). After the *Civil War Battle of *Fredericksburg, President Abraham *Lincoln gave Gen. Joseph *Hooker command of the Army of the Potomac. Hooker planned an aggressive spring campaign to turn the left flank of Gen. Robert E. *Lee's Army of Northern Virginia. On 29 April 1863, Hooker left Gen. John Sedgwick with 40,000 men to hold Lee at Fredericksburg and took 90,000 across the Rappahannock River into the densely wooded Virginia Wilderness.

With only 60,000 men, Lee left Gen. Jubal Early at Fredericksburg with 10,000, and sent Gen. "Stonewall" *Jackson's Corps to meet Hooker. When Union and Confederate troops clashed in the woods, Hooker faltered, ordered a halt, and later confessed that "for once I lost confidence in Hooker."

While Hooker pondered at Chancellorsville, Jackson, at 8:00 A.M. on 1 May, attacked Federals in the Wilderness; noting weak resistance, he concluded Hooker would retreat. Lee disagreed, and wanted to hit the Yankees tangled in the woodland. Frontal attacks were unfeasible. If Hooker's right flank could be turned, Lee would divide his force yet again and attack the enemy front and rear. Scouts sought a screened flanking route.

Rumors of Rebels on the right bothered the Federals throughout that day. Hooker convinced himself that the rumored Rebels proved Lee was retreating. Gen. Oliver O. *Howard's XI Corps held Hooker's right and its own flank was unprotected. Many warnings of a flanking attack were ignored at Hooker's headquarters—Lee was retreating.

Early on 2 May, a usable road was reported and Lee agreed to let Jackson take 28,000 men on a flank march, leaving 14,000 to pin Hooker down. About 8:00 A.M., Jackson started a fifteen-mile trek. His columns crossed part of Hooker's front, were once attacked, but by late afternoon were deployed athwart the Old Turnpike that ran into Chancellorsville behind the Union lines. At 5:15 P.M. Jackson's men attacked, overwhelmed hapless XI Corps outposts, and began "rolling up" Hooker's front. Hooker, occupied by Lee's heavy skirmishing during the afternoon, desperately tried to regroup.

Nightfall and confusion stalled the Confederates and Jackson rode ahead of his lines to find the enemy. Locating the fiercely entrenching Federals, Jackson and aides turned back and, mistaken for Union cavalry, were fired on by a North Carolina regiment. Jackson, mortally wounded, fell from his horse and was carried from the field. Gen. J. E. B. *Stuart took command, and hoped to join Lee in a crushing attack on 3 May.

On the 3rd, Sedgwick drove Early from Fredericksburg and tried to reach Chancellorsville. Judging Hooker inert,

Lee took 25,000 men to join Early and perhaps capture Sedgwick's corps. Sedgwick barely escaped back across the Rappahannock on 4 May.

With 17,000 *casualties, Hooker still outnumbered Lee by two to one; but, psychologically beaten, he retreated across the Rappahannock on 5 May. Lincoln anguished: "My God.... What will the country say?"

Chancellorsville was Lee's greatest and costliest triumph. Thirteen thousand Confederates fell, and on 10 May 1863, Stonewall Jackson died.

• John Bigelow, *The Campaign of Chancellorsville*, 1910. Stephen W. Sears, *Chancellorsville*, 1998. Carl Smith (Adam Hook, illus.), *Chancellorsville 1863: Jackson's Lightning Strike*, 1998.

—Frank E. Vandiver

CHAPULTEPEC, BATTLE OF, AND CAPTURE OF MEX-ICO CITY (1847). By 12 September 1847, the *Mexican War was almost over; the Americans had been victorious in every major engagement, New Mexico had surrendered, U.S. forces had subdued Upper California, and Maj. Gen. Winfield *Scott and 7,000 U.S. troops were camped outside Mexico City.

The Mexican capital was built in an ancient lakebed and could only be approached on raised causeways that passed through sizable gateways into the walled city. Just southwest of the city, on a 200-foot-high hill, the castle of Chapultepec commanded key causeways and was the site of a military college. Scott decided to storm Chapultepec first. On 12 September, in order to keep Mexican commander Gen. Antonio López de *Santa Anna and his 15,000 troops unsure of his ultimate plans, Scott ordered part of his force to demonstrate south and southeast of the capital while his artillery began to hammer at Chapultepec. U.S. infantry attacked, scaling the rocky summit with ladders and pickaxes early the next morning. Within two hours, Scott's troops had overrun the castle. Among the 1,000 defenders were 100 boy cadets who died defending their college and Mexican honor. "Los Niños" became Mexican national heroes.

From Chapultepec, some of the victorious U.S. soldiers swarmed onto the causeway leading to the gates at the southwest corner of Mexico City, and others attacked the gateway near the northwest corner. The soldiers and a battalion of U.S. Marines broke through the walls. Mexican resistance was fierce. When nightfall stopped the fighting for the day, U.S. troops were inside the Mexico City, but only barely. Luckily, Mexican authorities decided not to contest further the U.S. attempt to capture the city, and Santa Anna withdrew his army during the night. The next day, General Scott triumphantly entered the city. U.S. troops suffered over 860 *casualties; Mexican losses are estimated to have been at least twice that many.

The capture of Mexico City did not immediately end the war. Santa Anna led his army eastward and helped lay siege to the U.S. garrison at Puebla, but within a month U.S. reinforcements had lifted the siege and the fighting was over.

• K. Jack Bauer, *The Mexican War, 1846–1848*, 1974. John S. D. Eisenhower, *So Far From God: The U.S. War with Mexico 1846–1848*, 1989. —James M. McCaffrey

CHARLESTON, SIEGE OF (1780). In June 1776, early in the *Revolutionary War, a British expedition under Sir Henry *Clinton failed to seize Charleston, South Carolina's

principal port and the largest city in the South. Less than four years later, Clinton returned with overwhelming force and a plan to make the South the centerpiece of British strategy to subdue the colonies. France's recognition of American independence and its declaration of war on Britain in May 1778 altered the character of the war, turning a colonial revolt into a worldwide war. Britain, seeking to maximize results on its now over-stretched resources, intended to use the army to eliminate rebel activity and reestablish royal authority, then turn control over to the loyalists and move on to repeat the process against rebels further north.

This southern strategy began well. Leaving 10,000 men to defend New York, Clinton sailed south with about 8,700 men. Despite damage caused by a storm en route, he landed 6,000 men thirty miles south of Charleston on 12 February 1780. The remaining troops rejoined him in late March, and another 2,500 men arrived from New York in late April. Benjamin Lincoln initially defended Charleston with 1,600 South Carolina and Virginia Continentals and 2,000 militia; 1,500 North Carolina and Virginia Continentals soon reinforced them. Conserving his army, Clinton moved methodically to lay siege, giving Lincoln time to withdraw; political considerations, however, dictated that Lincoln defend the city. The British began investing Charleston on 1 April, and cut off the last escape route on 14 April. With no hope of timely relief and local civilian leaders clamoring to save their city from further damage, Lincoln surrendered on 12 May. It was the largest disaster suffered by any American army during the war.

Clinton followed up his success by defeating the remaining American forces at the battles of the Waxhaws and Camden, ending organized military resistance in South Carolina. Politically, he was less successful. The loyalists, restored to power by a British army they hoped would never leave, refused to treat defeated rebels leniently in return for a renewal of their allegiance. Loyalist abuses rekindled the civil war that nullified Britain's southern strategy and dissipated the fruits of Clinton's greatest victory.

• Piers Mackesy, *The War for America*, 1964. William B. Willcox, *Portrait of a General: Sir Henry Clinton in the War of Independence*, 1964. David Mattern, *Benjamin Lincoln*, 1995.

—Harold E. Selesky

CHATEAU THIERRY, BATTLE OF (1918). *See* Marne, Second Battle of the (1918).

CHEMICAL AND BIOLOGICAL WEAPONS AND WAR-FARE. *Chemical warfare* is the military use of lethal, harassing, or incapacitating chemicals specifically designed to harm or to kill; *biological warfare* is the use of disease-causing bacteria, viruses, rickettsia, or fungi; *toxin warfare* is the use of poisonous chemical substances naturally produced by living organisms, such as the highly lethal cobra toxin. These agents can be used to target humans, animals, and plants. The use of all such weapons has been condemned in customary and international law. Although allegations are numerous, confirmed or extensive use has been limited to a few conflicts in the twentieth century: notably World War I (1914–18), the Ethiopian-Italian War (1935–36), and the Iran-Iraq War (1980–88).

In World War I, lethal chemical warfare began on 22 April 1915 with the German release of chlorine gas at

Ypres on the Flanders front. By the time U.S. troops entered combat, its technology was fully developed. New agents, notably phosgene (an asphyxiating agent) and mustard (a blister agent called a *vesicant*), had been developed and used. Cylinders, projectors, and shells were the means of delivery. Gas masks protected soldiers against asphyxiating agents, but no adequate protection had yet been found against mustard gas, which attacked the skin.

After the war, widespread revulsion against gas, combined with the fear that in future conflicts it would be used against civilian populations, led to attempts to ban it. Notable success came with the *Geneva Protocol on chemical and bacteriological (1925), which prohibited the use in war of "asphyxiating, poisonous or other gases and of bacteriological methods of warfare." Most major powers hedged their accession, reserving the right of retaliation, thereby rendering the Geneva Protocol a "no first use" treaty. In the United States, the ratification debate dramatized the division between proponents and opponents of chemical warfare. The proponents, led by Gen. Amos Fries, chief of the Chemical Warfare Service, argued that gas was a relatively humane weapon and that ratification of the Geneva Protocol would seriously affect national security. Their opponents argued that gas was an indiscriminate, immoral, and inhumane weapon. The national security argument prevailed in the Senate. The United States did not ratify the protocol until 1975.

During the opening phases of World War II, it was widely expected that chemical weapons would be used. The use of mustard gas by the Italian Air Force against Ethiopian soldiers and civilians was regarded as an anticipatory prelude to massive aerial gas attacks against Western cities. However, except for Japanese operations against the Chinese, gas was not used in combat during World War II. Most of the belligerents were initially unprepared to use it and reluctant to expose their civilian populations to a gas attack from the air. Strategic restraint dictated tactical restraint. President Franklin D. *Roosevelt, who had an abhorrence for gas warfare, committed the United States to a policy of retaliation, throwing a deterrent shield around his more vulnerable allies. During the war, although it undertook a biological warfare program, the United States did not mass-produce lethal antipersonnel agents.

The wisdom of Allied restraint was confirmed by the discovery in Germany (1945) of stocks of nerve gases (tabun, sarin, and soman), which kill by attacking the nervous system. These agents, far more lethal than any in the Allies' arsenal, went undetected by Allied intelligence during the course of the war. Chemical weapons now could be considered "weapons of mass destruction," especially if the new agents were wedded to *missiles. Moreover, the potential development of an operational capability for biological weapons posed an even greater threat to the security of the United States.

American policy in the postwar period was characterized by cyclical shifts determined largely by the political rhythms of the *Cold War. In periods of confrontation, intensified by mutual suspicion, emphasis fell upon chemical and biological warfare preparedness. In periods of detente, emphasis fell upon the furthering of security through arms control and disarmament. These two trends, however, were not mutually exclusive. From 1946 to the early 1950s, when the policy of retaliation only was being reexamined by government committees, American preparedness efforts lagged. In 1956, the *National Security Council reversed its policy: in the future, the decision on chemical and biological weapons would be based on "military effectiveness." During the Kennedy and Johnson administrations, funding increased significantly, reaching its maximum in fiscal year 1965: the nerve agents sarin and VX; mustard gas; irritant, incapacitating, and defoliant agents all were stockpiled, and approximately thirteen biological and toxin agents (including anthrax and botulin) were produced. The United States developed a multitude of delivery systems, ranging from multiple rocket launchers to missiles.

U.S. use of defoliants and riot control agents during the *Vietnam War led to condemnation by the international community and by scientists who saw the use of these "nonlethal" agents as a contravention of the Geneva Protocol, posing a danger of escalation to the use of lethal agents. This political backlash, along with expert consensus that biological weapons capability was militarily unreliable and not essential to national security, led President Richard M. *Nixon in 1969 to renounce that option and to order the destruction of the American stockpile. In 1970, he also ordered the destruction of toxin stocks. This unilateral renunciation of biological and toxin warfare by the United States spurred the completion of the 1972 Convention on the Prohibition of the Development, Production and Stockpiling of Bacteriological (Biological) and Toxin Weapons (BTWC), which entered into force in 1975.

The period of detente that characterized the Nixon and Carter administrations was ended by the Soviet invasion of Afghanistan (1979). Subsequently, the United States charged that the Soviet Union operated a biological weapons facility at Sverdlovsk in violation of the BTWC, and that Communist forces were waging chemical and biological warfare in Kampuchea, Laos, and Afghanistan: the so-called Yellow Rain allegations, which centered on the aerial dispersion of tricothecenes—fungal toxin agents. These allegations were hotly debated. Matthew Meselson and other leading scientists argued convincingly that the government had mistaken bee feces for toxin agents. However, alarmed by the possibility that the Soviet Union was contemplating the development of new biological agents through genetic engineering, and convinced that the Soviets enjoyed overwhelming superiority in chemical weapons, the administration secured additional funding for defensive research, which rose steeply in the 1980s, peaking in fiscal year 1985, and won congressional approval in 1985 for a new binary chemical weapons production program. (Binary munitions, which are far safer to store than unitary munitions, combine two chemicals that mix upon firing.)

The second Reagan administration and the Bush administration saw a return toward disarmament. The thaw in Soviet-American relations, concern on both sides regarding the dangers of proliferation, accentuated by the use of chemical weapons in the Iran-Iraq War, led to bilateral agreements between the United States and the USSR on the mutual reduction of chemical weapons stockpiles. Multinational negotiations in the Conference on Disarmament led to the conclusion in 1992 of the Chemical Weapons Convention, which, unlike the Biological and Toxin Convention, contained strict provisions for verification and challenge inspections. The convention entered into force in 1997; it has been ratified by the United States and Russia.

Across these favorable developments in arms control and disarmament falls the shadow of the *Persian Gulf War (1991). The war was preceded by fears, fueled by the precedent of the Iran-Iraq War, that the Iraqis would use chemical agents against Coalition forces. Those fears were not realized. The stern American warnings to the regime about the consequences of such use, the folly of using these weapons against nuclear-armed powers, and the blitzkrieg conduct of the coalition land operations militated against their use. The defeat of Iraq by Coalition forces, led by the United States, and the subsequent investigation of Iraq's facilities and capabilities by the UN Special Commission, revealed the extensive nature of Iraq's biological and chemical weapons programs, highlighting the continuing dangers of proliferation.

Despite the elimination of Iraq's weapons of mass destruction and the completion of the Chemical Weapons Convention, major problems remain in implementing any regime banning chemical and biological warfare: intelligence and verification, proliferation, terrorism, destruction, *deterrence, and enforcement. If the Chemical Weapons Convention is successfully implemented, intelligence problems will be eased; however, the Biological and Toxin Convention, despite recent efforts to strengthen it, is still based on trust, and the task of verifying compliance, given the number of laboratories throughout the world, remains formidable. The list of potential proliferators in the Third World stands at approximately fifteen. The use of sarin in the Tokyo subway by the Aum Shinrikyo terrorists (1995) highlighted the vulnerability of modern societies to state-sponsored or cult terrorism. The destruction of chemical agents is proving difficult, especially in Russia, because of its cost and environmental concerns. A new Chemical Weapons Convention, prohibiting the production, storage, and use of poison gas, and providing for monitoring of the civilian chemical industry with systematic and surprise inspections was signed by President George *Bush in January 1993 after ten years of negotiations. Pressed by President Bill *Clinton and Senate Majority Leader Trent Lott (R.-Miss.), the U.S. Senate overrode concerns from the chemical industry and conservatives worried about North Korea, Iran, Iraq, and Syria, and ratified the treaty 74–26 on 24 April 1997. With seventy-five nations approving the treaty it went into effect on 29 April 1997. By adhering to the Chemical Weapons Convention, the parties to the treaty are renouncing retaliation in kind. Deterrence therefore will depend upon the threat to punish violators by other means—nuclear or conventional. Relying on the former will threaten the developing structure of nuclear arms control. Finally, no treaty is stronger than the willingness of its adherents to enforce it.

[See also Arms Control and Disarmament; Nonproliferation of Nuclear Weapons, Treaty on the; Terrorism and Counterterrorism; Toxic Agents: Chemical Weapons Exposure; Toxic Agents: Agent Orange Exposure.]

• Frederic J. Brown, Chemical Warfare: A Study in Restraints, 1968. Stockholm International Peace Research Institute, The Problem of Chemical and Biological Warfare: A Study of the Historical, Technical, Military, Legal and Political Aspects of CBW, and Possible Disarmament Measures, 6 vols., 1971–75. Matthew Meselson and Julian Perry Robinson, "Chemical Warfare and Chemical Disarmament," Scientific American, vol. 242, no. 4 (April 1980), pp. 38–47. Erhard Geissler, ed., Biological and Toxin Weapons Today, 1986. Ludwig F. Haber, The Poisonous Cloud: Chemical Warfare in the First World War, 1986. Susan Wright, ed., Preventing a Biological Arms Race, 1990. Gordon M. Burck and Charles C. Floweree, International Handbook on Chemical Weapons Proliferation, 1991. Edward M. Spiers, Chemical and Biological Weapons: A Study of Proliferation, 1994. Richard M. Price, The Chemical Weapons Taboo, 1997.
—John Ellis van Courtland Moon

CHENEY, RICHARD (1941–), member of Congress, secretary of defense. Born in Lincoln, Nebraska, the son of a federal soil conservation agent, Cheney grew up in Casper, Wyoming, and attended Yale and the Universities of Wyoming and Wisconsin. Appointed a congressional fellow in 1968, he served as assistant to Donald Rumsfeld in various positions in the Nixon and Ford administrations. In 1975–77, Cheney was President Gerald *Ford's chief of staff. Then, in 1979–89, Cheney served in the House of Representatives as a staunch but pragmatic conservative Republican from Wyoming. As minority whip, he actively supported President Ronald *Reagan's defense buildup and aid to the Nicaraguan Contras.

President George *Bush appointed Cheney secretary of defense after the Senate rejected John Tower. Cheney had no military service, having obtained deferments during the *Vietnam War, but as defense secretary (1989–93), despite his skepticism about reformist Soviet leader Mikhail Gorbachev, Cheney followed Bush's instructions to downsize the U.S. military. A Washington insider, he challenged the *Pentagon's lobbying, reformed procurement, and curtailed a number of weapons programs. But the new chairman of the *Joint Chiefs of Staff, Gen. Colin *Powell, on his own authority devised the plan for the post–Cold War U.S. military.

Although General Powell kept tightly in his own hands operational planning and control of the U.S. military response to the Iraqi invasion of Kuwait in August 1990, Cheney helped persuade the Saudi government to accept U.S. military forces and to join the Allied Coalition that achieved successful liberation of Kuwait from control of Saddam *Hussein.

[See also Arms Control and Disarmament; Defense, Department of; Persian Gulf War.]

• Richard B. and Lynne A. Cheney, Kings of the Hill, 1983. Michael R. Gordon, and Bernard F. Trainor, The General's War, 1995.
—John Whiteclay Chambers II

CHENNAULT, CLAIRE (1893–1958), aviator. Chennault grew up in Louisiana, joined the army in April 1917, earned a reserve commission, and completed pilot training in 1919. After a taste of civilian life, he obtained a regular commission in 1920. Until his retirement as a captain in 1937 because of physical disability, he specialized in tactical pursuit aviation at a time when the army air arm emphasized strategic bombardment instead.

Chennault became aviation adviser to the Chinese government in 1937, and in 1941 organized the American Volunteer Group, the "Flying Tigers," to fight for China against the Japanese invaders. After the Japanese attack on *Pearl Harbor, Chennault rejoined the U.S. Army Air Forces, became a major general in February 1943, and took command of the new Fourteenth Air Force in China. Communicating with President Franklin D. *Roosevelt, he undercut his superior, Lieut. Gen. Joseph W. *Stilwell, with whom he disagreed about strategy and the apportionment of scarce supplies. An inspirational leader as well as a difficult subordinate, Chennault won aerial victories but could not achieve his ambition of defeating the Japanese in China exclusively through airpower.

Having retired again in 1945, he helped launch Civil Air Transport, China's national airline. The airline moved to Taiwan when the Communists conquered the mainland, and by the time of Chennault's death had undertaken numerous missions for the *Central Intelligence Agency.

[See also China, U.S. Military Involvement in.]

• Claire L. Chennault, *Way of a Fighter*, ed. Robert W. Hotz, 1949. Martha Byrd, *Chennault: Giving Wings to the Tiger*, 1987. Daniel Ford, *Flying Tigers: Claire Chennault and the American Volunteer Group*, 1991.   —Bernard C. Nalty

CHEROKEE WAR (1759–61). The Cherokee War consisted of three campaigns from South Carolina against the Cherokees Indian nations. Colonial ambitions, backcountry misunderstandings that caused killings on both sides, and the undertow of *French and Indian War hostilities to the north, all tangled, leading South Carolina to act against its neighbor and trading partner in the southern Appalachian Mountains. The first campaign saw colonial regiments march resistantly under an arrogant royal governor, only to be turned back by an outbreak of smallpox. The second and third, in 1760 and 1761, saw British regulars lead resentful militiamen. The Cherokees successfully rebuffed attack in 1760; this was followed by an equivocal concession in 1761. Meanwhile, the Cherokees fought sporadic engagements against other native peoples on their western and northern mountain flanks. The campaigns left deep scars and provoked anxieties with the young generation of both colonists and Cherokees alike.

The Cherokee War, on the colonial side, was a revolt against the idea of the Cherokees as the "key" to westward expansion, and a response to Carolinians' own weak place within the empire. For the Cherokees, the scorched-earth campaigns and disease besieged their economy, destabilized conventional intertribal politics, and split their towns. The "Indian War" of 1775, led by South Carolina, ended over a decade of trouble between the Cherokee War and the *Revolutionary War. The Cherokee War and its decade marked the removal of the Cherokees from the pivot of regional geopolitics, and the beginning of a revolutionary era of change for both peoples.

• Tom Hatley, *The Dividing Paths: Cherokees and South Carolinians Through the Era of Revolution*, 1993.   —Tom Hatley

CHICKAMAUGA, BATTLE OF (1863). After maneuvering Confederate Gen. Braxton *Bragg's Army of Tennessee from its namesake state in midsummer 1863, U.S. Gen. William S. *Rosecrans and the Army of the Cumberland paused only briefly before resuming their drive upon Chattanooga, Tennessee. In late August, Rosecrans feinted upstream while crossing the Tennessee River unopposed in four places below Chattanooga; subsequently he began an advance south and east of the city to threaten Bragg's line of communication to Atlanta. In response, Bragg on 8 September evacuated Chattanooga and concentrated his army, now reinforced by James *Longstreet's corps from the Army of Northern Virginia, around LaFayette, Georgia. Supremely overconfident, Rosecrans imprudently ordered a general pursuit by his widely separated forces. Only after

the XIV Corps barely escaped a trap in McLemore's Cove on 11 September did Rosecrans order a consolidation of his army near Chattanooga.

For the next week, Rosecrans scrambled to gather his command while Bragg struggled to defeat the Federals in detail. Late on 18 September, when the two armies stumbled together by accident along Chickamauga Creek, Rosecrans had almost completed his concentration. In heavy but confused fighting the following day, neither side gained any significant advantage. A coordinated Confederate attack on 20 September made little progress until an exhausted Rosecrans mistakenly ordered a Federal division out of line, permitting a massive Confederate column to rush through the gap. In the resulting debacle, Rosecrans and one-third of his army fled ignominiously. However, Gen. George H. *Thomas rallied the remaining Federals around Snodgrass Hill. After nightfall, Thomas withdrew safely without Confederate pursuit. In this, the largest *Civil War battle in the western theater, the opposing forces were nearly equal: approximately 62,000 Federals to 65,000 Confederates. Over 16,000 Federals and 18,000 Confederates became *casualties. Although a major Confederate success, Chickamauga was a barren victory because the Union Army of the Cumberland was neither destroyed nor forced to relinquish Chattanooga.

• Peter Cozzens, *This Terrible Sound: The Battle of Chickamauga*, 1992. William Glenn Robertson, *The Battle of Chickamauga*, 1995.

—William Glenn Robertson

CHILEAN CRISIS (1891). The Chilean Crisis (or *Baltimore* Affair) was one in a string of late nineteenth-century naval crises. Despite U.S. efforts to support the old regime, a Chilean revolution succeeded in the summer of 1891. U.S. antipathy to the new regime notwithstanding, the new, light (protected) cruiser USS *Baltimore* remained in the Chilean port of Valparaiso, near Santiago. On 16 October, Cdr. Winfield S. Schley permitted some of his crew long-overdue leave, and several became involved in a saloon brawl. An ensuing riot left two U.S. sailors dead and seventeen injured.

The Navy Department ordered the *Baltimore* replaced by the *Yorktown* under Robley D. "Fighting Bob" Evans, who waited impatiently for negotiations on restitution— or war. Secretary of State James Blaine and Timothy Egan, U.S. minister in Santiago, evinced little interest in peaceful reconciliation. President Benjamin Harrison increased pressure on the Chilean government, issuing a virtual ultimatum on 25 January 1892.

Some North Americans were concerned, noting that the Chilean Navy was technically larger than that of the United States and might threaten West Coast cities. Nonetheless, the Chilean government quickly offered a complete apology and $75,000 in restitution. At the last minute, war had been averted.

Other naval crises continued apace: Honolulu in 1893, Guiana in 1895, and Havana in 1898. After a decade of naval buildup, the United States was quickly and frequently involved in the type of disputes other great powers knew well. North Americans soon forgot an event that Chileans would long remember.

• Joyce Goldberg, *The Baltimore Affair*, 1986. Mark R. Shulman, *Navalism and the Emergence of American Sea Power*, 1995.

—Mark R. Shulman

CHINA, U.S. MILITARY INVOLVEMENT IN. The United States maintained a military presence in China or its territorial waters from 1835, when it established the East Indies Squadron, through the 1950s, when it actively supported the defense of the Republic of China on Taiwan against an attack from the Communist-led People's Republic of China (PRC).

From the 1830s to 1911, American forces came into contact with a declining empire, dispatching Marines ashore to protect American missionaries and businesspeople, establishing in 1891 the Yangtze River patrol, and during the Boxer Uprising in 1900 contributing three regiments to a multinational force to relieve foreign legations in Peking (now Beijing). When in 1911 a revolution overthrew the Manchus and ended imperial rule in China, the United States between 1911 and 1914 used two infantry regiments and units of Marines to defend U.S. treaty rights and protect American lives and property.

Following World War I, the U.S. Asiatic Squadron was upgraded to a fleet, and the army increased its interest in China. American forces faced a grave challenge in 1927 when the Nationalists (Kuomintang), led by Chiang Kai-shek, marched north from Canton to unify the country. Fearing antiforeign attacks, the United States eventually put 5,000 American soldiers and Marines in China. The Japanese Army seized Manchuria in 1931 and invaded China south of the Great Wall in 1937. As conditions in China worsened, the U.S. Army's 15th Infantry Regiment, in China since 1912, left Tientsin in 1938. After the *Panay incident, American gunboats ceased patrolling the Yangtze River in late 1940. The 4th Marines, which had become a symbol of the American commitment to the "open door" in China since 1927, left Shanghai in November 1941.

During World War II, U.S. Army officers like Gen. Joseph *Stilwell pushed their Chinese allies to build and use the army to repulse the Japanese. Stilwell's first priority was the opening of the Burma Supply Road into China. U.S. Gen. Claire *Chennault, commander of the Fourteenth Air Force, touted airpower as the key to victory in China. Chiang preferred Chennault's strategy for political reasons. As Stilwell predicted, the Japanese responded to Chennault's attacks by overrunning the poorly defended airfields. Stilwell was mistaken, however, in believing that the Pacific War would be won in China. By 1944, American advances in the Pacific made China a strategic backwater. Gen. Albert C. *Wedemeyer replaced Stilwell later the same year.

In September 1945, after Japan's surrender, approximately 46,000 Marines occupied Tientsin and Tsingtao in northern China to repatriate Japanese troops and civilians and to prevent the Chinese Communists from seizing North China until Kuomintang troops could arrive from the southwest, transported by American planes and ships. Following *V-J Day, the U.S. Army and Navy created the Military Advisory Group in China to continue the modernization of Nationalist forces. To avert full-scale civil war between Nationalists and Communists, President Truman dispatched retired Gen. George C. *Marshall, who negotiated an uneasy truce.

In early 1947, the truce broke down. Chiang believed that American support would be unstinting. The Communists, led by Mao Zedong, distrusted the Americans. As the Communists overwhelmed Kuomintang forces, the Truman administration concluded that the Nationalists were beyond help. Most of the Marines left China in 1948, and Chiang, defeated, fled to Taiwan in 1949.

The third phase of American involvement began with the outbreak of the *Korean War in June 1950 and lasted until the early 1970s. After the North Korean invasion of the South, President Truman ordered the Seventh Fleet to "neutralize" the Taiwan Strait to prevent the capture by the Communists of Chiang's Republic of China (ROC) on Taiwan. In December 1950, after U.S.-led UN forces drove the North Koreans back to the Chinese border, Chinese Communist "volunteers" intervened, driving back American troops and freezing Sino-American relations in a state of implacable hostility for nearly two decades. Subsequently, the United States resumed its advisory mission on Taiwan. In 1954, in the midst of the first offshore islands crisis, the two governments concluded a mutual defense treaty. In 1958, during the second attempt by the PRC to seize the Nationalist-held islands of Quemoy and Matsu, the Seventh Fleet alerted 140 ships for possible action in the strait. But Nationalist pilots, flying F-86 Saber jets armed with modern sidewinder *missiles, eliminated any possibility of a Communist attack.

During the 1960s, the looming presence of the PRC, which exploded its first nuclear device in 1964, led the U.S. government to restrict its operations in the *Vietnam War. The process of detente, begun in 1972 by President Nixon, was completed with U.S. recognition of the PRC in 1979. During the 1980s, the United States sold the PRC military equipment to help modernize its forces. The Chinese also began building a "blue-water" navy, augmented after 1991 by purchases from the former Soviet Union. The Soviet Union's collapse, growing trade friction with China, and Beijing's ambitious military program reawakened U.S. fears of PRC dominance in Asia.

In 1995, renewed U.S. arms sales to the ROC and political developments on Taiwan led the PRC to hold threatening military exercises in the Taiwan Strait. Although the U.S. defense commitment to Taiwan had ended in 1979, Washington placed the Seventh Fleet on alert for possible action in the strait. By early 1996, tensions had decreased. But the nettlesome Taiwan problem and the PRC's expanding military power raised troubling questions.

[See also China-Burma-India Theater; China Relief Expedition; Chinese Civil War, U.S. Involvement in the.]

• Charles Romanus and Riley Sunderland, *Time Runs Out in CBI,* 1959. Joe C. Dixon, ed., *The American Military and the Far East: Proceedings of the Ninth Military History Symposium,* 1980. Marc Gallicchio, *The Cold War Begins in Asia: American East Asian Policy and the Fall of the Japanese Empire,* 1988. Warren I. Cohen, *America's Response to China: A History of Sino-American Relations,* 1990. Dennis L. Noble, *Eagle and Dragon: The U.S. Military in China, 1901–1937,* 1991. Rosemary Foot, *U.S. Relations with China Since 1949,* 1995.

—Marc Gallicchio

CHINA-BURMA-INDIA THEATER (1941–45). The China-Burma-India (CBI) theater has been dubbed "the forgotten theater" of World War II. Once the United States entered the war, American strategy called for building up China as a source of manpower, as a base for bombers and the eventual invasion of Japan, and as a pro-American regional power in the postwar era.

After Japanese occupation of Burma and the April 1942 closure of the Burma Road, China's last overland link with its allies, two years passed before the Allies could make a major effort to reopen the route. Vast distances, rugged terrain, few roads, heavy rainfall, and diseases made Burma a horrendous place for a campaign. Given the "Germany First" strategy, the CBI theater lay far down the Allies' list of priorities. Although the British wanted to recover Burma and their other Far Eastern colonies, they shared little of the American sense of urgency for aiding China. The Nationalist leader Chiang Kai-shek, anxious to conserve his forces for the postwar showdown with Mao Zedong's Chinese Communists, was wary of major commitments. Consequently, the Americans built up their logistical structure and examined alternative strategies. From airbases near Dinjan in Assam Province (northeastern Indian), C-46 and C-47 transport planes flew supplies 500 miles through the Himalayas over "the Hump" to Kunming, China. In December 1942, the U.S. Army Corps of Engineers took over construction of a road from Ledo to join the Burma Road. Searching for alternatives, Roosevelt and Chiang were drawn to Maj. Gen. Claire *Chennault's extravagant promise that with 150 planes and priority on "Hump" tonnage, he could defeat Japan. The Allies also tied intelligence gathering to Kachin guerrillas rescuing downed Allied fliers by Detachment 101 of the U.S. Office of Strategic Services (OSS) and deep raids by British Brig. Orde C. Wingate's "Chindits."

At the Cairo Conference in November and December 1943, Allied leaders could not agree on a major 1944 offensive into Burma by Adm. Lord Louis Mountbatten's new Southeast Asia Command, but Lt. Gen. Joseph *Stilwell had his own ideas. The able but acerbic Stilwell was American theater commander, Mountbatten's deputy, Chiang's chief of staff, and commander of the Chinese Army in India. Determined to proceed with his three U.S.-trained Chinese divisions and "Merrill's Marauders"—3,000 air-supplied, American light infantrymen originally assigned to Wingate—Stilwell sent the Marauders on deep flanking marches into the rear of the Japanese 18th Division while the Chinese attacked in front. By mid-April 1944, Stilwell's forces had advanced to sixty-five miles from Myitkyina, a key transportation center and air base in North Burma. To the south, a drive by three Japanese divisions into Assam threatened Stilwell's communications; but in June, Lt. Gen. William J. Slim's British Fourteenth Army badly defeated the Japanese at Imphal. Meanwhile, the Marauders seized the airfield at Myitkyina in a surprise attack on 17 May. Worn down by *casualties and disease, they and the Chinese could not take the city, which held out until 3 August. In October, the Allies resumed their offensive. The Fourteenth Army advanced to the Chindwin River, and the Chinese and Mars Task Force, including the revived Marauders, pushed on Bhamo and Lashio. On 20 January 1945, patrols of the 38th Chinese Division from India linked up with Chinese troops from Yunnan on the Burma Road, and on 29 January the first convoy from Ledo passed the linkup en route to Kunming.

By then, the war had passed by CBI. Since the Cairo Conference, Roosevelt and his advisers had become increasingly disillusioned with Chiang and his inability or unwillingness to drive back the Japanese. American strategy became oriented toward the Pacific, limiting CBI's role largely to diverting Japanese divisions. In June 1944, the Twentieth U.S. Air Force had launched B-29 raids from Chengtu, China, against Japan, but after ten months of disappointing results and logistical problems, the B-29s were shifted to the Mariana Islands in the Pacific. Chennault's strategy also proved a disappointment, as the Japanese Army, fulfilling Stilwell's predictions, seized the Fourteenth Air Force's bases once its operations began to affect them. Stilwell could take little satisfaction, for on 18 October 1944, Roosevelt, bowing to increased pressure from Chiang, relieved him. CBI split into an India-Burma theater with about 184,000 U.S. forces under Lt. Gen. Daniel I. Sultan and a China theater with about 28,000 Americans under Gen. Albert C. *Wedemeyer, who prepared ambitious plans for a rejuvenated Chinese Army to drive to the China coast by 1946. To coordinate a Chinese offensive against the Japanese, an OSS delegation, the "Dixie Mission," even visited Mao in Yenan Province, Northwest China, but U.S. Ambassador Patrick Hurley, fearing the impact on Communist-Nationalist negotiations, vetoed cooperation with the Communist forces. Wedemeyer's offensive in July 1945 came too late to affect the war's outcome.

CBI produced some of the most impressive feats of engineering and logistics in American military history. Yet, despite the best efforts of numerous Americans, it contributed little to Japan's defeat, except perhaps to keep China in the war and thereby tie up sizable Japanese forces on the Asian mainland.

[See also China, U.S. Military Involvement in; Chinese Civil War, U.S. Military Involvement in the, World War II, U.S. Air Operations in: The Air War Against Japan.]

• Charles F. Romanus and Riley Sunderland, *Stilwell's Mission to China,* 1953. Charles F. Romanus and Riley Sunderland, *Stilwell's Command Problems,* 1956. Charlton Ogburn, Jr., *The Marauders,* 1959. Charles F. Romanus and Riley Sunderland, *Time Runs Out in CBI,* 1959. Barbara W. Tuchman, *Stilwell and the American Experience in China, 1911–1945,* 1970. Warren I. Cohen, *America's Response to China: An Interpretive History of Sino-American Relations,* 1971.
—David W. Hogan, Jr.

CHINA RELIEF EXPEDITION (1900). In summer 1900, a multinational expeditionary force including U.S. troops under overall British command arrived in northern China to suppress the Nationalist, antiforeign Boxer Rebellion and break the siege of the foreign Legation Quarter, Peking (now Beijing).

In May 1900, responding to escalating violence, 450 foreign troops—including about 115 Americans—reinforced the legations in Peking. As the Ch'ing government of the Manchu dynasty moved to support the Boxers and the legations came under siege, a relief force of 2,080 troops under British Vice Adm. Edward Seymour (including a small force of American sailors and Marines) set out from Tientsin on the coast. However, it was held at bay. A larger relief force of troops from Britain, France, Germany, Japan, Russia, and America was then organized under British Gen. Alfred Gaselee. On 16 June, the United States diverted substantial forces from the Philippines to participate in this effort, including the 9th and 14th Infantry Regiments, 1st Marines, and an army artillery unit. The Sixth Cavalry Regiment came directly from America. U.S. forces, eventually numbering about 2,500 out of 18,000, were commanded by Maj. Gen. Adna Chaffee. On 3 July, Secretary of State John Hay reiterated the U.S. "open door" policy of preserving China's territorial entity.

The Battle of Peking, 14–16 August 1900—in which "Reilly's Battalion" gave covering fire to British troops advancing on the Legation Quarter—broke the 55-day siege of the legations. The defeat of the Boxers led to the signing of the Boxer Protocols in September 1901, providing a $332 million indemnity. Most of the U.S. share was remitted to educate Chinese students in the United States.

[See also China, U.S. Military Involvement in.]

• Aaron S. Daggett, *America in the China Relief Expedition*, 1903. Reginald Hargreaves, "Comrades in Arms," *Marine Corps Gazette*, vol. 48, no. 10 (1964), pp. 50–55. Michael H. Hunt, "The Forgotten Occupation: Peking, 1900–1901," *Pacific Historical Review*, vol. 48, no. 4 (1979), pp. 501–29.   —Eileen Scully

CHINESE CIVIL WAR, U.S. INVOLVEMENT IN THE

(1945–49). Beginning with the ambiguous *Yalta Conference (1945), the United States and the Soviet Union failed to agree on the future political shape of Asia or to control their Asian allies and clients (as they did in postwar Europe). Manchuria, which Yalta had effectively awarded to the USSR, played the pebble that starts an avalanche.

After the Japanese surrender, the U.S. transport moved Chinese government armies from the southwest to key cities such as Peking, Tientsin, and Shanghai, and 50,000 U.S. troops landed in China proper. The Soviets who arrived in Manchuria in August 1945 excluded Nationalist forces and helped bring Chinese Communist main forces there from Northwest China.

Fearing deep involvement in China, the United States attempted to deal with this and other issues primarily by negotiations between Nationalists and Communists, sponsored first by Ambassador Patrick Hurley (1945) and then by Gen. George C. *Marshall (1945–47). Unrealistic to begin with, this approach was further undermined by a clear American tilt toward the Nationalists, made worse by the abandonment of the direct U.S. contact with the Communists that had been provided, for example, by the military "Dixie Mission" of 1944.

The Chinese Communists' concentration on civil administration rather than military preparation in Manchuria suggests that they expected an East European–style outcome: a stable partition and the establishment of a "Red China" in Manchuria under Soviet tutelage. Their calculations were upset by Soviet withdrawal and by the unexpected initiation, in early 1946, of a massive Nationalist offensive that saw American-equipped elite Nationalist divisions quickly throw the Communists into full retreat. The Communists in Manchuria were saved when Marshall evidently pressured Chinese Nationalist leader Chiang Kai-shek to stop the offensive, in June 1946, just short of Harbin.

Thereafter the tide of war shifted toward the Communists, and American public opinion became increasingly concerned. In October 1947, an Army Advisory Group was formed to counsel Chiang and $27.7 million in aid was supplied. The Nationalists requested far more and eventually another $400 million was paid, but only in 1948, long after the Truman administration had lost faith in Chiang's Nationalist government. In 1949, after Truman won reelection, he refused further aid and ordered the U.S. ambassador not to follow the retreating Nationalists to Taiwan but rather to remain in Nanking to establish contact with the Communists.

[See also China-Burma-India Theater; China, U.S. Military Involvement in.]

• Edward L. Dreyer, *China at War: 1901–1949*, 1995.
                      —Arthur Waldron

CHOSIN RESERVOIR, BATTLE OF THE (1950). After

the liberation of Seoul in September 1950, Gen. Douglas *MacArthur opened an offensive aimed at ending the *Korean War. The independent U.S. X Corps, separated from the Eighth Army by a mountain range, was stretched out on Korea's east coast. At the midway point, the First Marine Division was echeloned from Hungnam to the northwest along a mountain road to the Chosin Reservoir, an important hydroelectric plant.

On 24 November, MacArthur began an "end-the-war" attack to the Yalu. Days later, a massive Chinese counteroffensive erupted. The First Marine Division, its 5th and 7th Regiments now at Yudam-ni north of the reservoir, was ordered to shift its attack to the west to shore up the collapsed right flank of the Eighth Army. Overwhelming Chinese forces quickly brought the Marine advance to a halt. Temperatures had dropped to -25° Fahrenheit.

The 1st Marines, the division's third infantry regiment, held positions in battalion strength at Hagaru-ri, Koto-ri, and Chinhung-ni along the only road leading south from Yudam-ni. Maj. Gen. Oliver P. Smith, the division commander, pulled the 5th and 7th Marines back to Hagaru-ri. The breakout from there began on 6 December. Immeasurably helped by close air support and aerial resupply, the division reached Hungnam six days later. Of the some 15,000 Marines engaged, 4,400 were battle *casualties. Almost all the Marines suffered some degree of frostbite. The Chinese had lost perhaps 25,000 dead and did not oppose the evacuation of Hungnam by X Corps, which was accomplished by Christmas.

• Lynn Montross and Nicholas A. Canzona, *The Chosin Reservoir Campaign*, 1957. Roy E. Appleman, *Escaping the Trap*, 1990.
                      —Edwin Howard Simmons

CHURCH, BENJAMIN (1639–1718), colonial soldier. A

farmer in Plymouth-Colony, Benjamin Church soldiered in three wars. The son of a veteran of the Pequot War, he served as a provincial captain during *King Philip's War. In December 1675, Church was a member of a New England army which struck a fortified Narragansett settlement in the Great Swamp in Rhode Island. The surprise attack succeeded, killing more than 600 Indians and destroying the village. Church was wounded in the engagement. The following summer, he led a force into the Mount Hope swamp in Rhode Island, where the Wampanoag chieftain, Metacom, dwelled. The raid caught Metacom by surprise, and he was killed in the brief battle. Church emerged as a New England hero for having destroyed the settlers' adversary. He additionally achieved a reputation as a skilled Indian fighter, a soldier who learned from the tactics of his foe and who refused to be bound by European-style warfare. In King William's War in the 1690s, Church led expeditions against the Abenaki in Maine and the French in Acadia. In 1704, during Queen Anne's War, he commanded a Massachusetts invasion of Acadia, which failed in absence of naval assistance.

[See also Philip.]

• Thomas Church, *Entertaining Passages Relating to King Philip's War*, 1716. H. M. Dexter, ed., *The History of the Eastern Expeditions of 1689, 1692, 1696, and 1704*, 1867.   —John Ferling

CHURCHILL, WINSTON S. (1874–1965), British soldier,

politician, and prime minister. Son of an English statesman, Lord Randolph Churchill, and an American, Jennie

Jerome, Winston Churchill served as a cavalry officer and worked as a war correspondent before entering Parliament. A conservative, he joined the cabinet in 1908, and, at the start of World War I as first lord of the Admiralty, was in charge of the Royal Navy, with general oversight of the policy of searching neutral, including American, ships. Blamed for the ill-fated Gallipoli expedition, he left government to serve on the western front. In 1919, back as minister of war, he was an advocate of military intervention in the Russian civil war. Falling out with his party leaders, Churchill spent most of the 1930s as a backbench member of Parliament, but he made his name once more as an opponent of appeasement of Nazi Germany, and again took charge of the navy in 1939. With his great experience of war and government, he was a natural choice as war leader in May 1940.

As prime minister, Churchill's rousing oratory and determination embodied Britain's will to win, but he could also be impatient and arrogant, overworking himself and others. He believed it vital to work closely with the United States, to forge a personal link to President Franklin D. *Roosevelt, and to create a long-term "special relationship" between the two countries. Taking an active part in military planning with U.S. and British commanders, he especially advocated a "Mediterranean Strategy," designed to attack Germany through what he called the "soft underbelly" of Europe while preserving British Imperial interests. Defeated by the Labour Party in the July 1945 election, and replaced at the *Potsdam Conference by Clement Attlee, Churchill nonetheless urged resistance to Soviet communism with the 1946 "Iron Curtain" speech at Fulton, Missouri. As prime minister once more in 1951–55, he visited America three times and took a great interest in nuclear developments, reaching an agreement in January 1952 on the use of British air bases by American nuclear bombers. His aim was always to maintain Britain as a great power.

[See also D-Day Landing, World War II: Military and Diplomatic Course.]

• Martin Gilbert, *Churchill: A Life,* 1991. Norman Rose, *Churchill: An Unruly Life,* 1994. Warren Kimball, *Roosevelt, Churchill, and the Second World War,* 1997.
—John W. Young

CIA. *See* Central Intelligence Agency.

SOCIETY OF THE CINCINNATI. In 1783, at the end of the *Revolutionary War and before the *Continental army disbanded, Gen. Henry *Knox and other officers founded the Society of the Cincinnati at Newburgh, New York, to continue the ties of comradeship among the officer corps in peacetime and to press their pension claims before the national government. Named after Cincinnatus, venerated statesmen in the ancient Roman Republic, the society excluded enlisted men, and membership could be passed to the eldest male descendant. In the 1780s, Thomas *Jefferson and other civilian leaders feared that the nationalistic fraternal organization represented an attempt to establish an aristocratic order posing a potential threat to republican values.

With chapters in all thirteen states, the Cincinnati was one of the young republic's earliest national institutions. Most state chapters met annually on the Fourth of July, holding banquets for members and sponsoring public orations. After the death of the Revolutionary generation by the 1830s, many state chapters lapsed into inactivity. The Centennial of 1876 and renewed public interest in the Revolution led to the revival of several dormant state chapters in the East and the founding of new chapters in the West. The society continued to restrict membership to the eldest male descendants of Continental army officers, contributing to the founding of the Sons of the American Revolution in 1877 by the descendants of enlisted personnel and the *Daughters of the American Revolution in 1890 by female descendants of those who served in the War for Independence.

[See also Veterans: Revolutionary War.]

• Minor Myers, Jr., *Liberty Without Anarchy: A History of the Society of the Cincinnati,* 1983.
—G. Kurt Piehler

CITIZEN-SOLDIER. The concept of the "citizen-soldier" is based on the notion that citizens have the obligation to arm themselves to defend their communities or nations from foreign invaders and from domestic tyrants. Usually associated with republicanism, it is best understood in opposition to other forms of military organization, particularly the practices of hiring mercenaries or establishing professional standing armies of the state. In the latter two cases, soldiers and officers are isolated from society and can represent a praetorian challenge to legitimate rule. By contrast, the citizen-soldiers embody the will of the people directly because they are the people. They have a stake in preserving liberties and rights in a society, hence supplying a check on tyranny and corruption of governments.

In American history, the concept gained widespread popularity in the decade before the *Revolutionary War and became associated with colonial militia. Philosophically grounded in more than a century of Whig antimilitarism brought over from England, calls for citizen-soldiering spread throughout the colonies, especially after the *Boston Massacre in 1770 (in which regular soldiers in the British army killed five civilians in the streets). Pamphleteers whipped up American hatred of the British "standing army," which became a catch phrase associated with all colonial grievances. The Declaration of Independence repeatedly charged King George II with abusing his power through the use of his standing army of non-citizen-soldiers: "He has kept among us ... standing armies"; "He has affected to render the military independent of and superior to the civil power...."

In the early years after independence, the concepts of the citizen-soldier and the standing army also became identified with the larger struggle for political power between the states and the central government. Federalist politicians, many of whom had fought in the *Continental army in the Revolutionary War and had firsthand experience with the indiscipline and inefficiency of militia soldiers, pressed for the establishment of a strong, standing army under the direct command of the central government. However, Anti-Federalists claimed that such an army could be used by a national government to oppress the citizenry and argued for the continued maintenance of state-raised and state-commanded militias of citizen-soldiers; their concern was that in a nation as large as the United States, the central government could become dislocated from its citizens and enforce its authority only by use of its army. A compromise emerged in which the Constitution allows Congress "to raise and support armies" as necessary, but the Second Amendment also allows states to maintain militias.

Throughout history, the problem of the "citizen-soldier" has been that it represented an ideal abstraction rather than an operationally efficient strategy in anything but the most local kinds of community defense. In the United States, the concept evolved through the militia and the U.S. *Volunteers, and lives on in the form of the National Guard.

[See also Arms, Right to Bear; Army Reserves and National Guard; Civil-Military Relations.]

• Richard H. Kohn, *Eagle and Sword*, 1975. Allan R. Millett, *The American Political System and Civilian Control of the Military*, 1979. Eliot A. Cohen, *Citizens and Soldiers: The Dilemmas of Military Service*, 1990.   —Mary P. Callahan

CIVIL DEFENSE. Even after the advent of *nuclear weapons, the civil defense program did not begin in earnest in the United States until 1951, reaching an initial peak of federal interest in the early 1960s, and a second peak in the early 1980s. In both periods, a nuclear civil defense program, whenever it moved beyond mere rhetoric to be seriously supported by high federal officials, immediately elicited general hostility, set the scientific and political elite to arguing in public, and energized peace groups into successful action to discredit the program and return it to its usual marginal status in American life.

President Truman resisted significant funding for civil defense, preferring to save money for weapons, but the beginning of the *Korean War and the Soviet Union's development of an atomic bomb led to the creation of the Federal Civil Defense Administration (FCDA) in 1951. Congress continually cut FCDA funding requests by at least half. The agency concentrated on producing propaganda, which it termed "educational material." A flood of booklets, films, television shows, and media stories sought to convince the American public they could survive a nuclear attack with minor preparations. Meanwhile, many public schools initiated atomic air-raid drills, teaching children to "Duck and Cover!" in case of nuclear war.

In the Eisenhower era, a series of nuclear bomb tests, in both the Pacific and the American West, dramatized the danger of blast and radioactive fallout. The creation of the H-bomb convinced many Americans that civil defense was useless. The FCDA shifted from a shelter program to a policy of evacuation of the cities, which was met with public ridicule. From 1955 to 1962, national air-raid drills called "Operation Alert" were held each year in dozens of major cities. These drills set off major protests nationwide, especially in New York City, where between 1955 and 1961 thousands of people participated in well-organized civil disobedience efforts to discredit civil defense as a solution to the threat of nuclear annihilation. Several large cities refused to participate in Operation Alert drills, and millions of citizens simply ignored them. In 1958, President Eisenhower, who fully understood the horrific effect of nuclear exchange, ignored a call for a hugely expensive civil defense program issued by his FCDA director and supported by Cold War conservatives. He cut civil defense funds and shut down the FCDA. Despite lack of government financial support, a brief shelter craze occurred in the late fifties and early sixties, largely stimulated by the press and construction firms.

Presidential support for civil defense peaked in the Kennedy administration. Partly because of Kennedy's desire for a "macho" stand, but mostly because of his rivalry with Nelson Rockefeller—a strong supporter of civil defense and Kennedy's expected rival in the election of 1964—Kennedy transferred responsibility for civil defense to the *Pentagon and called for an expanded shelter program. Congress appropriated the largest amount ever, $208 million in 1961, for marking and stocking existing shelter spaces such as basements and subways. Unnerved by the dissent and public excitement, Kennedy downplayed civil defense in 1962, especially after Governor Rockefeller's civil defense program was defeated in New York State. The growing peace movement argued effectively that civil defense offered no protection against nuclear *missiles and fueled the *arms race and the threat of nuclear war. Critics of civil defense also noted the chief function of civil defense propaganda—to legitimate both deterrence policy and the hugely expensive underground shelters reserved for the political, military, and economic elite.

After the *Limited Test Ban Treaty of 1963, civil defense all but disappeared, not to be resurrected until 1979 when President Carter, apparently motivated by a false report that the USSR was building a large civil defense program, combined all civil defense actions, including protection against natural disasters, into a new organization called the Federal Emergency Management Agency (FEMA). In the 1980s, during the Reagan years, high federal officials again called for a large civil defense program that would sponsor a mass evacuation of people into rural areas if war seemed imminent. As in the early 1960s, the plan quickly faded in the wake of massive public resistance.

[See also Nuclear Strategy; Peace and Antiwar Movements; Propaganda and Public Relations, Government.]

• Robert Scheer, *With Enough Shovels: Reagan, Bush and Nuclear War*, 1982. Thomas J. Kerr, *Civil Defense in the U.S.: Bandaid for a Holocaust?*, 1983. Paul Boyer, *By the Bomb's Early Light: American Thought and Culture at the Dawn of the Atomic Age*, 1985. Elaine May, *Homeward Bound: American Families in the Cold War Era*, 1986. Allan M. Winkler, *Life Under a Cloud: American Anxiety About the Atom*, 1993. Dee Garrison, "'Our Skirts Gave Them Courage': The Civil Defense Protest Movement in New York City, 1955–1961," in Joanne Meyerowitz, ed., *Not June Cleaver: Women and Gender in Postwar America, 1945–1960*, 1994. Guy Oakes, *The Imaginary War: Civil Defense and American Cold War Culture*, 1994.   —Dee Garrison

CIVIL LIBERTIES AND WAR. From the outset of the new American government under the Articles of Confederation, the need for striking a delicate balance between authority and liberty was essential. Fear of powerful central control was stated clearly regarding the English king in the U.S. Declaration of Independence. It remained an ongoing concern under the Constitution. Indeed, a Bill of Rights limiting the new central government was adopted, which from its First Amendment assumed that the main enemy of liberty was Congress, which was admonished to "make no law abridging freedom of speech and of the press." Further, the amendment went on to protect freedom of assembly and the right to petition, along with its initial statement of religious freedom.

The very nature of republican government, James *Madison stated in 1792, required that "the censorial power be in the people over the government, and not in the government over the people." Actual war intensified the issue, and the early Federalists felt its dangers required national security legislation. Hence the *Alien and Sedition Acts, which sought to sharply curtail freedom of speech and press as long as the Undeclared Naval War with *France of 1798–1800 was underway. With all three branches of the national government controlled by the Federalists, the libertarian Jeffersonians found their voices silenced, as most Anti-Federalist editors were jailed. This produced negative backlash and Jefferson's election to the presidency in 1800. It also resulted in a movement headed by political writers to define more precisely the permissible limits of free speech and press. The *War of 1812 with England, highly unpopular in Federalist New England, not only elicited bitter criticism of Republican president James Madison but produced discussions by some Federalists at the Hartford Convention regarding secession. Madison prosecuted none, but deplored many.

The *Mexican War of the 1840s carried with it so many subtle moral and political issues that formal legalistic civil liberties issues took a backseat. Congressmen, including Abraham *Lincoln, worried aloud how slavery could be further curtailed so as not to destroy the union. Henry David *Thoreau denounced the war and refused to pay taxes to support it, but also called for civil disobedience and noncompliance with wartime actions that might result in obtaining more slave territory. Gen. Winfield *Scott appeased some critics by seeking to protect Mexican property rights by setting up military commissions that would develop a form of due process of law for citizens subjected to unruly behavior by occupying U.S. soldiers. Even though this did not restrain the U.S. Army, it brought a new technique of controlling the more extreme abuses of the military in its dealing with civilian populations.

The *Civil War saw important crises in civil liberties developed ultimately out of the White House as President Abraham *Lincoln claimed a body of Presidential War Powers which had the force of law and which frequently sublimated civil liberties to national security. This sprang from presidential initiative, but was then followed by congressional approval or acquiescence. Lincoln consolidated state militias into one force, summoned volunteers for active service, increased the size of the army and navy without legislative authority, paid money from the Treasury without an appropriation, and closed the Post Office to "treasonable correspondence."

In addition, Lincoln and his generals in the field were not reluctant to use censorship to protect wartime secrecy considered necessary to assure victory. Translated informally, this led to various orders for control of the press and curtailment of disloyal utterances. The army was to control reporters and take action against incorrect reports and inadvertent leaking of strategic and military secrets. Feeling that more control was needed, an effort was made to exclude from the mails printed material that was calculated to interfere with the war policy. Dissenters were threatened with arrest and trial before a court-martial.

Congress's *conscription legislation (1863, 1864) penalized those who counseled resistance to the draft. This followed its 1862 Treason Act, which was never held to cover the expression of disloyal sentiments. But through the temporary wartime suspension of the writ of habeas corpus, the government found ways of striking at those who might interfere with the president's duty to ensure that the

laws were faithfully executed. These actions, plus the use of martial law against critical civilians, constituted a kind of prior restraint and drew strong negative public reaction.

It was not until the war was over that the Supreme Court ruled on such restrictions of constitutional liberties. In an 1866 case, Ex Parte *Milligan, the Court struck hard at the suspension of the writ of habeas corpus and further proclaimed that martial law could not be justified by a threatened invasion.

Lincoln's pattern was repeated in World War I, when President Woodrow Wilson initially closed German wireless stations and later created a host of administrative boards and agencies to monitor war criticism. Yet the Civil War experience had not provided the federal government with the kind of legal weapons, such as statutory instruments of suppression, that it needed to control public discourse on a massive scale in wartime. With the formal declaration of war in April 1917, Congress passed an Espionage Act, and a Trading with the Enemies Act, which created a Censorship Board to coordinate and make recommendations about censorship. It condoned censorship of mail or any other kind of communication with foreign countries and gave the Postmaster General almost absolute censorship power over the American foreign-language press. Included also was a Sedition Act, 1918, which sought to repress anarchists, socialists, pacifists, agrarian radicals, and especially the Non-Partisan League, which had taken over North Dakota at the time. The Alien Act of 1918 empowered the government to deport "any alien who, at the time of entering the United States was found to have been a member of an anarchist organization."

Other forms of war restriction raised civil liberties concerns. The Selective Service Act (1917) elicited legal challenge. In the 1918 *Selective Draft Cases, a unanimous Supreme Court found the constitutional authority to impose compulsory military service in Congress's power to declare war and to "raise and support armies."

Critics complained that much of this legislation was a threat to freedom. But except for conscription, the Supreme Court did not pass judgment on the constitutionality of any of it pending the end of the war itself. In the 1919 *Schenck and Abrams cases, wartime prosecutions were upheld, much to the distress of a number of loyal Americans who feared this was laying the basis for a surveillance state. From these decisions arose the "clear and present danger" test, and also the *American Civil Liberties Union in 1920, to preserve the Bill of Rights.

But there were those who found the strong new federal government a blessing in disguise. Private power groups, which had greatly distrusted burgeoning regulatory authority in the economic field, now seemed pleased to accept such federal authority when applied to stifling the ideas and expression of their critics. In fact, they were delighted to have the national government play this role since federal authorities could rationalize such actions as essential to victory in a war to preserve international liberal capitalism without incurring the criticism and stigma that private groups would have elicited had they attempted to crush their enemies in such a fashion.

This new role of the state, however, produced strong negative reactions. It seemed to be progressivism gone wrong. Its critics rejected the war emergency rationalization as a dubious justification for such a radical departure in governmental policy. Critics particularly questioned the grounds for giving new federal agencies—from the Committee on Public Information and the Federal Bureau of Investigation to the newly swollen Justice and Post Office Departments—discretionary power to limit Americans' use of their individual freedom. Further, they deplored the absence of legal remedies for innocent citizens whose rights were violated by the excessive zeal of agents of these organizations.

Civil liberties in World War II took a different form. President Franklin D. *Roosevelt had been in the Wilson government, and vowed that should war come, his administration would not repeat the repression of the World War I years. But Roosevelt was also aware that domestic groups and individuals had ties with Germany and the Axis powers, and in the late 1930s he alerted the FBI to begin domestic surveillance in the name of national security and the avoidance of sabotage. Meanwhile, conservatives in Congress set up the Dies Committee to investigate the loyalty of the Roosevelt administration. The result was that the World War I Espionage Act was reenacted, and Congress also passed the Smith Alien Registration Act (1940), instructing the government to search out and expose disloyal Americans, and to begin the practice of denaturalizing citizens who expressed sympathy with Nazi Germany. Attorney General Francis Biddle disagreed with both policies and took cases to the Supreme Court (*Hartzel* v. *U.S.,* 1944; *Baumgartner* v. *U.S.,* 1944) sharply curtailing both measures. The previous year, 1943, had seen the Court reverse a 1940 ruling by granting First Amendment protection to Jehovah's Witness children freeing them from compulsory flag salute policies on the ground that the state laws violated the free exercise of religion clause. The wartime period also saw a rare use of the treason clause (*Haupt* v. *U.S.,* 1947), with the government facilitating several treason prosecutions of U.S. nationals for allegedly assisting the Germans and the Japanese during the war.

The most flagrant wartime violation of civil liberties in American history involved the Japanese Americans living on the West Coast, the majority of whom—70,000 of 112,000—were American citizens. Rounded up by the military after Pearl Harbor, they were first subjected to a curfew, then banned from coastal areas, and subsequently shipped to inland detention camps, known as relocation centers. In the process they were punished without indictment or trial, and since this action was called for by the military in the name of national security, the Supreme Court in the *Japanese American Internment Cases hesitated to interfere. In the *Hirabayshi* case (1943), the Court ruled the curfew constitutional on the excuse that it was wartime. A year later, the Court did uphold the right of loyal Americans to leave the camps through a writ of habeas corpus. It was never willing to examine the constitutionality of the relocation program itself, thereby leaving future wartime restraint unresolved.

The war in Korea was technically not a war, but a *United Nations "police action" without a formal declaration. Coming during the McCarthy era, when the Truman administration was being criticized for being "soft on communism," little was done to curtail negative expression for fear of right-wing backlash. However, in the *Dennis* case (1951), the Supreme Court sustained the Smith Act, jailing and silencing leaders of the American Communist Party with an extremely narrow interpretation of the clear and present danger test.

The *Vietnam War was a sharp contrast. Again, there was no formal war declaration. But a half million American troops eventually fought with meager success and mounting domestic protest, particularly from student organizations such as the *Students for a Democratic Society, and angered civil rights leaders, questioning national priorities. Some criminal prosecutions and conspiracy trials were launched against war resisters, but with limited success. The Supreme Court was reluctant to curtail such expression. It expanded the right of *conscientious objection. It struck down the Nixon administration's attempt to halt the publication of the *Pentagon Papers (*New York Times* v. *U.S.,* 1971) a critical study of the origins and early history of the Vietnam conflict. Significantly, it was in this period that the Court finally clarified the true permissible limits of freedom of expression. In the landmark case of *Brandenburg* v. *Ohio* (1969), a unanimous Court held that the government in order to limit free expression was required to prove that its danger was real and immediate, not imaginary. Even threatening speech was now guaranteed, said the Court, unless the state could prove that the advocacy was directed to inciting or producing imminent lawless action and was likely to incite or produce such action.

Some Americans blamed the defeat in Vietnam on the war critics, who critics said should have been silenced, or at the least denied access to certain information. This questionable view was embraced by the military and applied during the Reagan and Bush administrations, especially regarding paramilitary operations in Central America and the Caribbean, and particularly during the *Persian Gulf War of 1991. Tight control was placed on "strategic" information, and also on reporters attempting to cover the hostilities. Information was to come only through military briefings. Later information, available following investigations of the health of military personnel and civilians, raised questions about such limited briefings and denial of access to contemporary data that the public had a right to know.

[*See also* Conscientious Objection; Draft Resistance and Evasion; Espionage and Sedition Acts of World War I; Habeas Corpus Act; Martial Law; Surveillance, Domestic; Treason; Vietnam Antiwar Movement.]

• Paul L. Murphy, *The Constitution in Crisis Times, 1918–1969,* 1972. Paul L. Murphy, *World War I and the Origins of Civil Liberties in the United States,* 1979. Leonard W. Levy, *Emergency of a Free Press,* 1985. Harry Kalven, Jr., *A Worthy Tradition: Freedom of Speech in America,* 1988. James G. Randall, *Constitutional Problems Under Lincoln,* 1997. David M. Rabban, *Free Speech in Its Forgotten Years,* 1998.   —Paul L. Murphy

CIVIL-MILITARY RELATIONS: CIVILIAN CONTROL OF THE MILITARY. By the time that the United States became an independent nation, civilian control of the military was already firmly established as an axiom of government. On the basis of history and political theory, Americans considered standing armies to be instruments of despotism as well as defense. With their weapons and discipline, soldiers possessed the means to overthrow a government and destroy liberty. In the state constitutions written after independence, in the Articles of Confederation, and in the Constitution of 1787, the generation that founded the United States explicitly subordinated military forces to elected officials so that all the great decisions relating to *war and *peace, to raising and organizing armies and navies, to governing them internally, and to their use and support, rested in the hands of the representatives of the people, or those appointed by them to administer military affairs.

The system adopted at the end of the eighteenth century derived from English practice and American colonial experience. At the time of settlement in the early 1600s, military forces belonged to the crown. During and after the English Civil War of the 1640s, when Parliament sought control of the armed forces, executed the king who resisted this claim, and was then replaced by a military dictatorship under Oliver Cromwell, civilian control broke down. The Stuart monarchs who were restored to the throne after 1660 reasserted military command, but seemed to threaten arbitrary rule by using the new standing army as their instrument. In the constitutional settlement of the Glorious Revolution of 1688–89, Parliament took control of military finance and discipline in what proved to be a watershed for English liberty. Henceforth, civilian control rested on dividing authority over the military between Crown and Commons so that neither could rule by force: Parliament would approve the existence of a military establishment through its power of the purse (appropriating money annually) and by passage of a mutiny act to govern the internal order of the forces. The monarchy retained command, deployed the regiments and ships, and raised and administered them in peace and in war.

In the century before independence, the colonies experienced a similar struggle between legislative and executive. Legislatures created militias or authorized the raising of *volunteers or conscripts, voting the funds and setting the conditions of service by law, while command and administration rested with the governors. Gradually, using mostly the power of appropriation, the assemblies increased their influence when governors, desperate for forces for defense against European and Native American foes, compromised their authority in return for money, supplies, and permission to raise men. The governors, many of whom were military officers, wielded great influence, but fear of military rule was muted because local defense depended on militia or citizen volunteers—the adult white male population, officered by members of the local elite who rarely had reason to attempt to overturn the established order. During the struggles with France beginning in 1689, however, conflict with the British army, friction with the population, and the regulars' disdain for provincial forces all reinforced colonial antipathy to royal forces. By the time of the Revolution, the standing army had become a symbol of repressive authority and arbitrary rule. The *Boston Massacre in 1770, when redcoats fired into a threatening mob, killing five civilians, and the imposition of military government in Massachusetts under the Coercive Acts in 1774, engraved a century's concern with controlling military force into the American political tradition, confirming the belief that the safest way to defend a free people was to rely on citizen-soldiers.

During the *Revolutionary War, military and civilian leaders took care to ensure civilian control of the forces raised. As commander of the *Continental army, George *Washington conspicuously deferred to Congress's authority. Throughout the war, he treated state and local officials with respect, working to minimize conflict. Even during the most desperate periods, there was no serious consideration of suspending civilian rule. And at the end, in spite of intense bitterness over the prospect of *demobilization without back pay or promised pensions, the officers at the main cantonment near Newburgh, New York, rejected a call to revolt or resign en masse in the so-called *Newburgh "Conspiracy." Washington's intervention in the crisis, the refusal of the officers to defy civilian authority, and Washington's solemn return of his commission to Congress a few months later, began a national tradition of loyalty and subordination that has characterized American military forces ever since.

The Constitution of 1787, following English and American custom, provided for civilian control by distributing authority over the military to the three branches of government and to the states, so that none could use force to seize power. Congress could "raise and support Armies," "provide and maintain a Navy," and specify their organization and governance, but appropriations for the army were limited to two years, forcing every new Congress to consent to land forces. As commander in chief, the president would command and deploy the nation's armed forces and conduct war once Congress declared it, but Congress must approve all the president's nominations of officers and even, if desired, their assignments to duty. While Congress could "provide for organizing, arming, and disciplining the Militia," the states appointed officers and retained authority over the forces unless called into federal service. Because the military operated under law, and the national government acted directly on the citizenry rather than on the states as under the Articles of Confederation, the judiciary could hold members of the military personally accountable. Finally, supposing that an armed citizenry provided the ultimate safeguard against an army overthrowing republicanism, the Second Amendment guaranteed "the right . . . to keep and bear Arms," preventing the government from destroying the militia by disarming the population.

For the next century and a half under this constitutional arrangement, the nation's military forces remained subordinate to civilian authority in spite of frequent tension and occasional conflict. Geographic separation from Europe and disentanglement from great power rivalry allowed the United States to keep its regular military forces very small, and devoted largely to exploration, patrolling against Indians and pirates, and other constabulary activities. Defense rested upon mobilizing the population behind a shield of coast artillery and naval forces, with the regulars providing training, leadership, and weapons for the citizen forces raised. Congress exercised its powers under the Constitution in laws specifying the size, shape, organization, character, funding, and function of the armed forces (including in part the state militias), periodically expanding and contracting the forces, authorizing new installations and weapons, investigating problems, and generally dictating the broader policies and procedures under which the military operated. On a day-to-day basis, civilian control became an administrative matter, carried out by the secretaries of war and of the navy, who directed the armed services with the help (and sometimes over the resistance) of senior military officers commanding forces or managing bureaus in the two cabinet departments.

Most important, civilian control functioned successfully because it was assumed by the public and internalized within the armed forces. Belief in the rule of law, combined with reverence for the Constitution as the legitimate foundation of civic society, meant that any open disobedience would fail and invoke punishment—or plunge the country into crisis. As part of their professionalization during the first half of the nineteenth century, the officer corps of the navy and army began to disassociate themselves from partisan politics, viewing the armed services as the neutral instruments of the state and themselves as soldiers or sailors loyal to the government regardless of which party held sway. During the political upheavals of *Reconstruction and the labor disorders of the last quarter of the nineteenth century, when the army ruled the South and was dragged into riot duty and law enforcement, Congress (with officers' blessing) in the *Posse Comitatus Act (1878) prohibited the use of the regular army to execute the laws or to act under the command of local or federal officials other than the military chain of command as specified in the Constitution or law. The willing subordination of a nonpartisan military establishment has assured civilian supremacy down to the present day.

Yet beneath a seemingly placid surface, the peacetime relationship between the military and civilian leadership was filled with discord and struggles for influence that sometimes flared into open conflict. After the *War of 1812, strong secretaries of war and of the navy had to establish the supremacy of their offices in confrontations with uniformed leaders. Top army generals fought with cabinet secretaries and with Congress over issues as personal as rank and as significant as their own authority, or the organization and funding of their armed service. Occasionally, the senior general and secretary were not even on speaking terms. Agitation by naval officers in the 1880s, by reform-minded army officers in the 1890s, and by army airpower advocates in the 1920s and 1930s were catalysts in the modernization of both services, but at the same time provoked schisms inside the officer corps and in Congress and the executive branch. In the case of Billy *Mitchell, the controversy led to a spectacular trial for insubordination.

Between the *Civil War and World War II, officers grew gradually more estranged from American society, which they viewed as undisciplined, unprincipled, and preoccupied with commercialism. In peacetime, the armed forces suffered lean budgets, pork barrel expenditures, skeletal forces, deteriorating equipment, and low combat readiness. But at the same time the increasing participation of the United States in world politics, and the growing complexity of warmaking, particularly logistics and operations, gave professional officers greater influence in military affairs. And the maturation of the armed services into cohesive institutions, configured on the basis of doctrines of war fighting and attuned to their own organizational needs, gave their advice—now institutionalized in staffs and agencies in Washington—more authority.

War tended to mute the friction, but it never disappeared. After a weak beginning in the War of 1812, the dominance of the president in wartime was established by Presidents James K. *Polk and Abraham *Lincoln: managing *mobilization, overseeing *strategy, negotiating with allies and enemies, and even on occasion ordering operations. Except for a brief effort to oversee the conduct of the *Civil War, Congress deferred to presidents, supporting requests for larger forces, new weapons, increased appropriations, and expanded executive authority. Disagreement between military and civilian leaders, largely over strategy,

generally remained out of public view. Except for rare instances, such as the struggle between Lincoln and Gen. George B. *McClellan over taking the offensive during the Civil War, military commanders acceded to presidential wishes even when opposed to a particular policy or course of action. Presidents understood how quickly wartime heroes could become presidential aspirants (as numerous generals from Andrew *Jackson through Dwight D. *Eisenhower have done) and how difficult they could be to manage, which contributed to the tension. Polk, Lincoln, William *McKinley, and Woodrow *Wilson kept a tight rein over the direction of their conflicts, Wilson personally making overall policy while leaving the details of implementation, tactics, and fighting to the military.

The mobilization for World War II that began in 1940 spread the influence of the military more deeply into the fabric of American society than ever before. When the government, applying its World War I experience and plans readied during the interwar years, took control of society by drafting men into the armed forces, converting production to munitions, controlling raw materials and wages and prices, and harnessing virtually all activity to achieving *victory over the Axis, the military became powerful arbiters in American life. Franklin D. *Roosevelt never ceded any authority; he directed the war effort in broad outline and sometimes in small detail. But the needs of the military forces and the judgments of the uniformed leadership framed many choices, and extended deeply into foreign policy and economic life. In ways both obvious and subtle, the power and prestige of the professional military reached a zenith in the American experience.

The creation of a permanent military establishment in the 1950s to contain the Soviet Union and deter nuclear war overloaded the traditional procedures by which civilian control functioned. The military institutions were simply too large, their activities too diverse, and their influence too pervasive for effective oversight by the legislative and bureaucratic procedures historically used by civilians on Capitol Hill and in the executive branch. Vicious struggles broke out between the armed services over roles, missions, strategy, and budgets, which the civilians, struggling to balance military needs with finite financial resources and lacking any consensus about how to meet the threat, could not contain, even under the new, more unified organizational structure of the Department of *Defense (DoD). The need to control atomic weapons and to harmonize military operations with broad national objectives, particularly to keep limited wars from escalating into a general conflagration, drove civilians to invade what had become the customary prerogatives of military commanders in the field. In 1951, in the most public civil-military confrontation in American history, President Harry S. *Truman relieved Douglas *MacArthur, one of the century's most celebrated commanders, for openly opposing the administration's effort to keep the war in Korea limited to the peninsula and to conventional weapons. By 1961, the century's only professional soldier-president, Dwight D. Eisenhower, had become so concerned about restraining defense spending and conflicts with (and between) the armed services that he left office warning about a "*military-industrial complex" whose "influence, whether sought or unsought," had the "potential for the disastrous rise of misplaced power."

The Kennedy and Johnson administrations reasserted

civilian control by installing new bureaucratic procedures in the *Pentagon to unite strategy and policy with force structure and budgets, and by imposing special instructions or operational restrictions on commanders, notably during the *Cuban Missile Crisis and the fighting in Southeast Asia. But over the next three decades—partly in reaction to the disaster in Vietnam, partly in response to Secretary of Defense Robert S. *McNamara's peremptory rule, and partly because the Republicans, dominating the presidency, became such vocal champions of national defense—influence over military affairs began gradually to shift back toward the uniformed leadership. Congress, controlled for most of the period by the Democrats, added staff and began to exert more power through appropriations and directives in legislation. But the *Goldwater-Nichols Act (1986), a defense reorganization law, gave the chairman of the *Joint Chiefs of Staff (JCS) and senior commanders in the field more weight inside the DoD. Successful interventions abroad, especially the *Persian Gulf War, restored the military's prestige. And a new generation of officers—more determined to resist policies that would damage military effectiveness or involve U.S. forces in quagmires abroad, less sensitive to the historical restraints involved in subordination to civilian authority, and more adept at political maneuvering inside the bureaucracy and on Capitol Hill—gained greater success in promulgating their views in policy and decision making, even after the end of the *Cold War. During the 1990s, after losing a public battle with the military and Congress over permitting homosexuals to serve openly in the armed forces, President Bill *Clinton's administration relinquished much of its power over the military establishment in the areas of budget, organization, and strategy. Only in foreign interventions did the president assert his authority, and then within limits negotiated with a military leadership wary of deploying American forces abroad.

Thus, at the close of the century, civilian control remained the same sometimes smooth, sometimes awkward, but always situational process it had been throughout American history: shaped by the issues and personalities of the moment; characterized by consultation but also negotiation, tension, and conflict; and measured by the relative influence of the professional military and civilian authorities in policy and decision making. Congress and the president continued to pass the laws and decide upon war and peace, and the military to operate under law and civilian authority. At the same time, military and civilian leaders struggled in uneasy partnership to reconcile frequently diverging perspectives in pursuit of the common defense, in an increasingly uncertain world.

[See also Conscription; Gay Men and Lesbians in the Military; Militia Acts; Militia and National Guard; Commander in Chief, President as.]

• Louis Smith, American Democracy and Military Power: A Study of Civil Control of the Military Power in the United States, 1951. Arthur A. Ekirch, Jr., The Civilian and the Military, 1956. Samuel P. Huntington, The Soldier and the State: The Theory and Politics of Civil-Military Relations, 1957. Morris Janowitz, The Professional Soldier: A Social and Political Portrait, 1960. Ernest R. May, ed., The Ultimate Decision: The President as Commander in Chief, 1960. Richard K. Betts, Soldiers, Statesmen, and Cold War Crises, 1977. Allan R. Millett, The American Political System and Civilian Control of the Military: A Historical Perspective [Mershon Center Position Papers in the Policy Sciences, 4], 1979. Richard H. Kohn, ed., The United States Military Under the Constitution of the United States, 1789–1989, 1991. Russell F. Weigley, "The American Military and the Principle of Civilian Control from McClellan to Powell," Journal of Military History, vol. 57, no. 5 (October 1993), pp. 27–59. Richard H. Kohn, "Out of Control: The Crisis in Civil-Military Relations," The National Interest, 35 (Spring 1994), pp. 3–17.

—Richard H. Kohn

CIVIL-MILITARY RELATIONS: MILITARY GOVERNMENT AND OCCUPATION.

Americans have traditionally been suspicious of military governance, a distrust that stems from their belief in individual liberty, representative government, and civilian control of the military. That view was reinforced during the *Revolutionary War when the British army occupied and established military rule in a number of American cities. As the new republic expanded westward, the U.S. government's policy was to put new territory under civilian administration as rapidly as possible. Nevertheless, the U.S. military has often acted as an occupying and governing force.

As the U.S. Army marched through Mexico during the *Mexican War (1846–48), Gen. Winfield *Scott, faced with the need to deal with Mexican civilians, issued General Order No. 20 on 19 February 1847, providing a code of conduct that emphasized respect for the rights and property of innocent civilians. In his sensible and humanitarian guidelines, Scott ordered U.S. military governors to rule through local officials where possible.

During the *Civil War, as it occupied increasing areas of the Confederacy, the *Union army had to control a hostile civilian population, protect freed slaves and friendly Unionists, and ensure essential services. The broad aim of military government was to restore the Union by suppressing the secession and establishing loyal state governments. To guide the army, the War Department issued General Order No. 100, 23 April 1863, later published as an army manual, Instructions for the Government of Armies of the United States in the Field, the first formal attempt by a national government to codify the "*laws of war."

The Union army became the major instrument of the U.S. government in the occupied South during the war and through most of *Reconstruction. In 1867, the Republican Congress divided the conquered South into five military districts. Each state had to guarantee suffrage to adult black males and ratify the Fourteenth Amendment before military rule was ended in 1870.

Following the *Spanish-American War, the far-flung empire obtained by the United States was initially governed by the military occupation forces. The army governed Cuba, 1898–1903 (again in 1906–09); Puerto Rico, 1898–1900; and the Philippine Islands, 1899–1901. The U.S. Navy governed Guam, 1899–1950; and American Samoa, 1899–1951. In the Caribbean, naval and Marine forces governed—sometimes directly, sometimes through local leaders—in Haiti, 1915–34; the Dominican Republic, 1916–24; Honduras, 1924–25; and Nicaragua, 1909–10, 1912–25, and 1926–33. The army's governance of the Panama Canal Zone began in 1903 and was scheduled to end in 2000.

World War I led to the first U.S. military occupation in Europe: after the armistice in 1918, the U.S. Army was assigned an Allied occupation sector in the Rhineland. Despite French pleas to remain, the U.S. force was rapidly reduced and its role ended in 1923.

America's world role during and after World War II was accompanied by unprecedented responsibilities in military occupation and governance. Before U.S. entry into the war, the army prepared two field manuals on the subject: *The Rules of Land Warfare* (1939) and *Military Government* (1940). Because of the initial wartime experience, another manual, *Army-Navy Manual of Military Government and Civil Affairs* (1943), emphasized assisting military operations rather than winning over the population. U.S. policy, however, continued to insist on "just and reasonable" treatment of civilians and prompt rehabilitation of the civilian economy.

In Europe, Gen. Dwight D. *Eisenhower allowed considerable independence to his field commanders over occupation and governance policies. In Italy, the policy favored rapid reconstruction of local and regional governments and the civil service, drawing upon all except original and clearly committed Fascists. In Germany and Austria, the U.S. Army played a role in aiding millions of refugees, in arranging for reparations, in conducting a denazification program, and in prosecuting *war crimes.

Because of the *Cold War, U.S. military government continued in Europe long after the German surrender in May 1945. Although the Allied military occupation of Italy ended in 1947 with the signing of a peace treaty there, Germany remained divided into separate military occupation zones. The U.S. Zone was in the south, plus part of jointly occupied Berlin; in 1945–49, it was governed by Gen. Lucius *Clay. With the containment policy beginning in 1947, the United States and Britain merged their two zones, first economically, and then, along with the French, entirely in order to create the Federal Republic of Germany in 1949. (In East Germany, West Berlin remained an Allied occupation zone.) However, U.S. occupation and governance, under High Commissioner John J. McCloy, did not end until the Federal Republic rearmed and joined *NATO in 1955; the occupation of Austria ended the same year.

In contrast to General Eisenhower's decentralized occupation policy, Gen. Douglas *MacArthur established highly centralized control of occupied Japan in 1945. The United States was also the sole occupying force in Micronesia (the Carolines, Marianas, and Marshalls), Okinawa, and Iwo Jima.

Supported by President Harry S. *Truman, MacArthur planned to "reform" Japan and replace its militaristic roots with centrist Western liberalism. MacArthur's military government expanded civil rights, broadened the franchise, officially emancipated women, established new political parties and labor unions, created land reform, and began antitrust proceedings against giant Japanese conglomerates. Furthermore, an International Military Tribunal tried Japanese war criminals. After the Communists gained power in China in 1949, however, the emphasis shifted to building up Japan as a bastion against communism. A formal peace treaty in 1951 ended U.S. military occupation and governance, although not American military bases.

U.S. military government in Korea south of the 38th parallel (1945–46) was followed by a staunch anti-Communist civilian government headed by Syngman Rhee. The United States had removed most of its forces by the time of the North Korean invasion in 1950.

The active global role pursued by the United States after World War II led to a number of military interventions, some followed by occupation and governance, and some-times serious attempts at remolding local government or creating entirely new political institutions. Such attempts in South Vietnam ultimately failed with the North's victory. However, the U.S. military was successful in its intervention and occupations in Grenada (1983) and Panama (1989–90).

Although the United States did not set up a military government during the *Persian Gulf War of 1991, the army did mount its largest military–civil affairs operation since World War II in Kuwait, seeking to restore the shattered country.

Results were mixed in other missions involving U.S. occupation and direct or assisted military governance. As part of a *United Nations force in Somalia (1992–93), the U.S. military expanded areas of humanitarian relief and order; but the overall effort to end the civil war was a failure.

Much more effective, at least initially, was the U.S. military involvement in *Haiti, beginning in 1994. After the resignation of the military junta, Haiti's elected president, Jean-Bertrand Aristide, was reinstalled and order restored.

In the *Bosnian Crisis, a U.S. force joined a *peacekeeping occupation in Bosnia in December 1995, and in early 1999, President Bill *Clinton prepared to send another to the Yugoslavian province of Kosovo. It was not clear to what extent the American military would also engage in forms of governance and state building in that region of the former Yugoslavia.

Over the past century, American military occupation, reflecting military and foreign policy goals, has emphasized restrained use of force, and the reliance instead upon local elites, using political, economic, and cultural means to shift occupied populations toward U.S. policies. From the Civil War to the Cold War and beyond, occupation and governance have thus reflected dominant American attitudes and values as well as civil and military policy.

[*See also* Caribbean and Latin America, U.S. Military Involvement in the; Germany, U.S. Military Involvement in; Grenada, U.S. Intervention in; Japan, U.S. Military Involvement in; Kosovo Crisis (1999); Panama, U.S. Military Involvement in; Philippines, U.S. Military Involvement in the; Somalia, U.S. Military Involvement in.]

• E. Grant Meade, *American Military Government in Korea,* 1951. James E. Sefton, *The U.S. Army and Reconstruction,* 1967. John Morgan Gates, *Schoolbooks and Krags: The United States Army in the Philippines, 1898–1902,* 1973. Keith L. Nelson, *Victors Divided: America and the Allies in Germany, 1918–1923,* 1975. Robert Wolfe, ed., *Americans as Proconsuls: U.S. Military Government in Germany and Japan, 1944–1952,* 1984. Michael Schaller, *The American Occupation of Japan: The Origins of the Cold War in Asia,* 1985. Thomas A. Schwartz, *America's Germany: John J. McCloy and the Federal Republic of Germany,* 1991. John T. Fishel, "Taking Responsibility for Our Actions? Establishing Order and Stability in Panama," *Military Review,* 71 (April 1992), pp. 66–78.

—John Whiteclay Chambers II

CIVIL WAR (1861–65)

Causes
Military and Diplomatic Course
Domestic Course
Postwar Impact
Changing Interpretations

CIVIL WAR (1861–65): CAUSES

The election of the Republican Abraham *Lincoln to the presidency in November 1860 triggered a chain of events that within six months shattered the Union and culminated in the outbreak of the Civil War. The coming to power of a Republican and Northern administration committed to prohibiting the expansion of slavery struck at the vital interests of the slave South; it was the signal eagerly awaited by the proponents of Southern independence to launch a secession movement. Tensions over slavery and the struggles to perpetuate or end the institution that dated back to the incomplete American Revolution of 1776 had now become so polarized along sectional lines that the North and South lacked common ground on which to compromise the issue.

The Roots of Sectional Conflict. The democratic revolution in which the United States gained its independence from Britain rested on a profound paradox. The Revolution produced both the world's leading model of political democracy and one of its greatest slaveholding powers. Freedom for whites coexisted uneasily with bondage for African Americans, some 20 percent of the population. The federal Union crafted at the Constitutional Convention in 1787 also embodied this contradiction when the U.S. Constitution recognized the right of a state to regulate slavery within its jurisdiction. Indeed, without this express acknowledgment of their sovereign power over slavery, the slave states would never have joined the proposed Union. Thus, white liberty and black slavery were constitutionally joined in the very creation of the federal Union.

Within a generation of the Revolution, all the states north of Maryland embarked on programs of gradual emancipation. By the early nineteenth century, slavery was almost exclusively a sectional institution confined to the South, home to over 90 percent of American blacks. At the same time as the North was moving away from slavery, the invention of the cotton gin and rising demand in English textile factories for raw cotton were stimulating the westward expansion of slavery throughout the southeastern United States.

As social and economic patterns of development diverged sharply along sectional lines, the South's national share of political power began to slip. From a rough balance of power with the North in 1790, the South held only 42 percent of the votes in the House of Representatives by 1820. Worried over their growing minority status, and enraged over the attempt of the North to force emancipation upon Missouri when it applied for admission as a slave state in 1819, white southerners for the first time threatened secession during the debates that resulted in the Missouri Compromise of 1820. The heart of the compromise was the drawing of a line through the Louisiana Purchase territory that prohibited slavery north of the latitude 36°30′ and allowed it to the south.

In addition to proclaiming their right to an equal share of the expanding West, southern proponents of slavery protested protective tariffs that they insisted sacrificed the agricultural export economy of the South on behalf of northern manufacturers. This issue precipitated the sectional crisis of 1832–33 in which South Carolina planters, led by John C. *Calhoun, held that a state could constitutionally nullify federal legislation that it determined violated its interests.

President Andrew *Jackson forced the Nullifiers to back down, but of greater concern in the 1830s to southerners anxious over the future of slavery was the sudden emergence of an abolitionist movement in the North. Inspired by northern evangelical Protestantism and a belief in the right of African Americans to freedom and self-betterment, the abolitionists denounced slavery as the nation's greatest moral abomination and urged all Americans to begin immediately the work of emancipation. Skillful at spreading their message, the abolitionists launched a major propaganda campaign in the mid-1830s and deluged Congress with antislavery petitions.

The agitation of the slavery issue by the abolitionists predisposed many northerners to see in the admission of the slave republic of Texas in 1845 and the outbreak of the *Mexican War in 1846 the fearful designs of a conspiracy of slaveholders—the "slave power"—to expand slavery throughout new regions in the West and thereby deprive northern farmers and workers of the opportunity to settle the West for their social and economic advancement. When northern congressmen rallied behind the Wilmot Proviso in 1846 in an effort to bar slavery from any territories gained in the Mexican War, southerners formed their own sectional bloc and forced the ultimate defeat of the proviso. The divisive issue of the expansion of slavery had moved to center stage in American politics and would continue to dominate it through the 1850s.

Rising Sectional Tensions in the 1850s. Whether measured by rates of industrialization, urbanization, and immigration, or the cultural willingness to embrace reforms such as public education aimed at promoting social improvement, the free and slave states were set apart far more significantly by the mid-nineteenth century than at the birth of the Union. The North was growing and evolving at a more rapid pace than the predominantly agrarian South. Most ominously for slaveholders, a northern majority was forming that viewed slavery as a moral wrong that should be set on the road to extinction. Northerners also now saw slavery as a barbaric relic from the past, a barrier to secular and Christian progress that contradicted the ideals of the Declaration of Independence and degraded the free labor aspirations of northern society.

Since slavery within the states was protected by the Constitution, antislavery sentiment focused on keeping it out of the territories. Southerners, arguing that the territories were the common property of all the states, insisted on what they deemed their constitutional right to carry slaves into the territories. Furthermore, slaves and land were the major sources of wealth in the South, particularly with the cotton boom. The result was a decade of sectional strife.

A complex constitutional agreement, the congressional Compromise of 1850, permitted California to enter the Union as a free state. The remaining land won in the Mexican War was divided into the territories of Utah and New Mexico with no conditions placed on the status of slavery. In 1854, the Kansas-Nebraska Act reopened the entire controversy. In order to gain essential southern support for his bill organizing the remaining Louisiana Purchase territory north of 36°30′, Democratic senator Stephen A. Douglas of Illinois had to revoke the Missouri Compromise restriction on slavery. Northerners reacted by charging that the Slave Power was moving to monopolize the territories for slavery at the expense of free labor.

The Whig Party split and collapsed in the storm of northern protest over the Kansas-Nebraska Act, and a sectionalized Republican Party quickly formed around the core principle of blocking the expansion of slavery. The major Protestant denominations had already split into sectional wings over the slavery issue, and only the Democratic Party now remained as an important national institution that represented northern and southern interests. Democratic unity, however, shattered during the administration of James Buchanan (1857–61). The ruling of the Supreme Court in the *Dred Scott* decision of 1857 that Congress had no constitutional authority to prohibit slavery in the territory further polarized sectional attitudes, and northern Democrats led by Douglas lost the trust of the southern wing of the party when they joined Republicans in blocking the admission of Kansas as a slave state.

The decade came to a close with abolitionist John Brown's raid against the federal arsenal at Harpers Ferry, Virginia, in October 1859. Brown's unsuccessful attempt to incite a slave rebellion sent paroxysms of fear and anger through the South and touched off rumors of conspiracies and slave uprisings. Brown was hanged, and although the Republicans denounced him as a wild-eyed fanatic, many white southerners were convinced that the Republican Party was dominated by abolitionists and plotting with them to unleash a bloodbath in the slave states.

Lincoln's Election and the Secession Crisis. Vowing to use federal power both to keep slavery in check and to promote the free labor economy of the North through protective tariffs, subsidies for railroads, and free homesteads in the West, the Republicans ran Abraham Lincoln of Illinois for the presidency in 1860. His victory over three rivals—Stephen Douglas for the Northern Democrats, John C. Breckinridge for the Southern Democrats, and John Bell, the candidate of former Whigs in the Upper South—was achieved with no basis of support in the South. Rather than accept Republican rule, Southern radicals immediately provoked a crisis by organizing a campaign for secession.

Pushing the constitutional doctrine of states' rights to its logical extreme, the secessionists held that individual states retained ultimate sovereignty within the Union and could peacefully leave the Union the same way they had entered it through special state conventions. Rejecting any plan of prior cooperation among the slave states, they pursued a strategy of separate state action, accurately predicting that the momentum of secession would force wavering states to join those that had already gone out.

South Carolina took the lead on 20 December 1860, and within six weeks seven states from the Lower South left the Union. Delegates from these states set up the provisional government of the Confederate States of America at Montgomery, Alabama, in February 1861. This original Confederacy represented those states with the heaviest concentration of slaves and the highest percentage of white families owning slaves. Planters were in the forefront of secession. What opposition they encountered from the majority of nonslaveholding farmers took the form of cooperationism, the argument that secession should be delayed until a united bloc of Southern states agreed to go out together. The cooperationists polled about 40 percent of the vote in the secession elections, but in the end they followed the leadership of the secessionist planters.

Fort Sumter and the Outbreak of War. Northerners rejected the doctrine of secession. Believing that the Union was sovereign and perpetual, they viewed secession as illegal, indeed, revolutionary. They equated secession with anarchy and feared that it would lead quickly to a fragmentation of the United States and an end to America's mission of serving as a beacon of free government to the rest of the world. Still, no consensus existed on using coercion to force the seceded states back into the Union. In particular, Democrats were against coercion and favored negotiations to heal the sectional rift, even with the continuation of slavery. At the same time, the Unionists in the Upper South who had turned back secession in their slave states had hedged their Unionism by proclaiming that they would resist any Republican use of military force against a seceded state.

When inaugurated on 4 March 1861, Lincoln thus faced a dilemma. If he took no action against the Confederacy, he risked demoralizing his party and subjecting his administration to the same derision that had pilloried the outgoing Buchanan Democrats for standing by while the secessionists broke up the Union. On the other hand, any forceful step against the seceded states threatened to divide the North and drive the Upper South into the Confederacy.

Realizing that he could not afford to be locked into an endless policy of drift and delay, Lincoln decided to take a stand for the Union over Fort Sumter in Charleston Harbor, the most visible installation in the Confederacy that was still under federal control. Aware that the garrison at Fort Sumter would be forced to surrender for lack of supplies sometime in early April, he ordered a relief expedition to the fort on 6 April. He stressed that the fort would be supplied "with provisions only; and that, if such attempt be not resisted, no effort to throw in men, arms, or ammunition, will be made, without further notice, or in case of an attack upon the Fort."

Lincoln in effect placed the decision for war in the hands of Confederate authorities. The government of Confederate president Jefferson *Davis accepted that burden as the price it had to pay to establish the Confederacy as a sovereign power. On 9 April, Davis ordered Gen. P. G. T. *Beauregard to demand the immediate surrender of Fort Sumter. Fearful of Union duplicity and anxious to avoid any possibility of having to fight two Union forces at the same time, Davis wanted Sumter in Confederate hands before the relief expedition arrived.

In the predawn hours of 12 April 1861, Confederate batteries opened fire on Fort Sumter. The capture of *Fort Sumter occurred on April 13 and Maj. Robert Anderson surrendered the fort on 14 April. The next day, Lincoln issued a call for 75,000 state militia to put down what he defined as an insurrection. Virginia, Arkansas, Tennessee, and North Carolina scornfully rejected Lincoln's call for troops and joined the Confederacy in the next five weeks. Still, Lincoln now had a Northern majority behind the goal of preserving the Union with force. The Confederacy was cast as the aggressor that had fired the first shot of the Civil War, and the Northern crusade to save the Union persisted through four agonizing years of war.

[*See also* War: Causes of War.]

• Roy F. Nichols, *The Disruption of American Democracy*, 1948. Kenneth M. Stampp, *And War Came*, 1950. Eric Foner, *Free Soil, Free Labor, Free Men*, 1970. William L. Barney, *The Road to Secession*, 1972. Michael F. Holt, *The Political Crisis of the 1850s*, 1973. David M. Potter, *The Impending Crisis, 1848–1861*, 1976. J. Mills Thornton III, *Politics and Power in a Slave Society*, 1978. Daniel W. Crofts, *Reluctant Confederates*, 1989. Bruce Levine, *Half Slave and Half Free*, 1992.

—William L. Barney

CIVIL WAR (1861–65):
MILITARY AND DIPLOMATIC COURSE

The war between the North and South that followed Abraham *Lincoln's election to the presidency in 1860 claimed over 600,000 American lives and seriously threatened the balance of power in the Western Hemisphere. When Lincoln called for 75,000 troops to suppress the southern rebellion after the fall of *Fort Sumter in April 1861, the federal government possessed overwhelming superiority in manpower and the material resources needed to conduct war in an industrial age. The Confederacy had a number of factors in its favor, however. To win, the North had to conquer vast territories and break the will of the Southern people. Furthermore, the railroads that made it possible to supply the large military forces it would take to occupy and conquer the South restricted the strategic flexibility of Union commanders. Finally, Southern armies enjoyed the advantage of operating in sympathetic and supportive territory.

The South also benefitted, although not to a crucial extent, from a generally superior level of military leadership. The traditional notion that a Southern dominance prevailed at West Point and the antebellum army has an element of truth to it, but should not be exaggerated. On the whole, Northern students tended to perform better at the technically oriented Military Academy. Consequently, after graduation they were assigned to the more prestigious artillery and engineering units, rather than the cavalry and infantry branches. There lesser-performing Southern graduates tended to dominate, and the Civil War would be an infantryman's war.

The status of the West Point–trained military officer would be a source of friction for both sides throughout the war. The Union and the Confederacy benefitted immeasurably from the professional knowledge and expertise of the West Pointers. Yet neither society completely appreciated nor understood the specialized skills and standards the professionals deemed essential for conducting a modern war. In the North, suspicion of professional officers was further inflamed by the number of Southern officers who joined the *Confederate army; in the South, by the clear preference President Jefferson *Davis accorded West Pointers. For their part, professional officers often let their contempt for politics and civilians manifest itself in a haughty cliquishness and were at times unduly harsh in their efforts to impose military discipline.

Even the professionals were inadequately prepared for the revolution in warfare brought about by innovations in military technology. They did not appreciate how the dramatic enhancement of firepower provided by the widespread use of rifled *muskets gave an overwhelming advantage to forces operating on the tactical defensive and rendered traditional assault tactics obsolete. And although West Pointers recognized the importance of field fortifications, none really anticipated the extent to which Civil War armies would employ them.

Both sides also encountered significant strategic problems. In the western theater (primarily the area between the Mississippi River and the Appalachian Mountains), three major rivers, the Cumberland, Tennessee, and Mississippi, provided Northern armies with excellent invasion routes. However, they would be vulnerable to raids and turning movements any time they operated away from river supply lines. In the east, Union and Confederate armies, for the most part, focused on the direct overland route between the two capitals, Washington and Richmond, through Fredericksburg Virginia. Yet both sides were capable of conducting strategic turning movements. The North, with its overwhelming naval superiority, could operate from the lower Chesapeake Bay along the rivers

that reached into the Virginia heartland, which it did with some success in 1862 and 1864. The Shenandoah Valley could be used for the same purpose by the Confederate armies, and was in 1862, 1863, and 1864.

Although the war was ultimately decided on the battlefield, the diplomatic contest was no less important. By 1860 a state of detente prevailed between the United States and the European powers. The most important of these, Great Britain and France, valued the United States as a check against the ambitions of other European powers in the Western Hemisphere. Both countries also had strong ties of economic interdependence with North and South. Not only did both Britain and France need southern cotton to feed their textile industries, they also had heavy investments in northern land, railroads, and public securities.

Southerners nonetheless went to war confident of success in the diplomatic arena. The European powers, they surmised, would find it difficult to resist the opportunity presented by the rebellion to diminish U.S. power in the hemisphere. To assuage European fears of an overweening Confederacy, southern diplomats and statesmen continually emphasized their limited war aims, and portrayed themselves as a people merely seeking freedom from Yankee tyranny. British freetraders were also expected to resent protectionist trade policies a Republican administration was certain to implement.

However, the Confederate cause overseas was compromised during the early months of the war, when the European powers were establishing their initial policies, by overconfidence in their ability to achieve military success and a lack of a seasoned diplomatic corps. The South also underestimated Europe's determination to avoid involvement. Although sympathetic to the Southern struggle for self-determination, and confident that the Union cause would ultimately fail, Europe was unwilling to recognize the Confederacy without some demonstration of its viability as a nation. Yet if the South could meet this test, why, European statesmen could fairly ask, antagonize the North by getting involved if the Confederacy was going to win anyway?

The North had the advantage of merely advocating preservation of the status quo, which the European powers, especially Great Britain, had a powerful interest in maintaining. If sufficiently aroused, British statesmen feared the North might attempt to seize Canada. There was also the danger that diminution of American power might promote instability in the Americas, and compel a diversion of energy, resources, and attention away from affairs on the European Continent. Finally, British statesmen had to take into account the fact that their constituents were highly dubious of foreign adventures in the wake of the Crimean War.

This did not mean the North would have an easy time diplomatically. The British prime minister, Lord Viscount Palmerston, held a deep antipathy toward republican government in general, and Americans in particular. Furthermore, Palmerston viewed the war as a pointless one. Secession was in his mind an irrevocable fait accompli, and he doubted the Lincoln administration had either the means or the will necessary to restore the Union. To Palmerston, the question was not whether the South would win her independence, but whether the North would give up the fight before too much death and destruction had occurred. Britain's role, as he saw it, was to keep a pointless war from threatening the peace and stability upon which British imperial interests depended.

Responsibility for the North's diplomatic efforts rested with Secretary of State William H. *Seward, a crafty and pragmatic politician who recognized the value of bluster in diplomacy. His sincere advocacy of a war against European intrusions in the Caribbean during the Fort Sumter crisis to revitalize southern Unionism shocked the diplomatic corps in Washington. Although Lincoln rejected the idea of a foreign war, Seward's actions during this critical period successfully fostered an image of American bellicosity that reinforced British and French caution in their dealings with the South.

The Union also benefitted immensely from the skill of the American Minister in Great Britain, Charles Francis Adams. His handling of affairs played a major role in settling a number of crises that threatened the Union war effort. The issue of slavery helped the North. Although European statesmen consistently approached the "American question" from a purely pragmatic standpoint, they and their constituents were unenthusiastic about supporting a nation founded in part to protect the institution of slavery.

In April 1861, however, Lincoln committed a grave blunder by declaring a *blockade, which, according to international law, implied the existence of a conflict between two independent states. Britain responded with a proclamation of neutrality—in effect implying belligerent status on the Confederacy. Seward responded with a harsh warning that further steps in favor of the South would lead to a serious breach in U.S.–British relations. In London, Adams toned down Seward's message without losing its essence, and obtained assurances from Palmerston that he had no present intention of recognizing the Confederacy. Although both the proclamations of neutrality and the blockade would remain sources of friction, the North, by fixing the British and French into noninterventionist positions at the outset, had won a major diplomatic victory.

When Lincoln issued his call for volunteers after Fort Sumter, he made it clear that the North was fighting solely for the Union. No effort would be made to molest Southern civilians, their property or institutions, nor would any attempt be made to abolish slavery where it then existed. The president adopted this position for two reasons. First, he realized he needed a broad coalition of support in the North for the war. Adopting radical war aims might alienate more conservative elements of public opinion, particularly in those slave states that remained loyal. Lincoln also believed that the vast majority of Southerners were lukewarm about independence and had been forced to accept secession by irresponsible political leaders. To declare war on Southern institutions would, Lincoln and most northerners feared in 1861, unite the white South behind secession.

The task of developing a military strategy to achieve these political goals feel upon Gen. Winfield *Scott, commander of all the Union armies. Scott put forth a two-part plan, dubbed the "Anaconda" by the press, after the strangling snake, that represented both his and Lincoln's desire for an easy reconciliation between the sections. First, the Union navy would establish a complete blockade of the Southern states. Second, a combined army-navy force of 80,000 men would capture the Mississippi Valley. Cut off from the outside world, Scott believed economic pressure would lead Southerners to reassert their natural loyalty to the Union with a minimum of bloodshed. Lincoln, however, felt Scott's plan would take too much time to implement and perhaps years to produce desirable results. Despite vigorous protests from many of his professional military advisers, Lincoln ordered an advance on the Confederate position near Manassas Junction, Virginia.

On 26 July 1861, the South won a close, but decisive, victory at the First Battle of *Bull Run (Manassas). A chastened Lincoln called Gen. George B. *McClellan to Washington and appointed him commander of Union forces around the capital. McClellan's magnetic personality, success building the Army of the Potomac, and record of military victories in western Virginia impressed the president. On 1 November 1861, McClellan replaced Scott as general-in-chief of the *Union army.

Rejecting the idea that large-scale fighting could be avoided, McClellan advocated taking the time to assemble, organize, and train an overwhelming military force to render Southern resistance futile. At the same time, he championed a lenient policy toward the South and slavery to make returning to the Union as attractive as possible. McClellan's operational strategy called for the main land offensive to be made in Virginia against Richmond, the Southern capital and industrial center. Supporting operations would be undertaken into East Tennessee to liberate the loyal population there and break the railroad that connected the eastern Confederacy with the west, and along the Mississippi River. Finally, McClellan wanted the navy to establish enclaves along the Southern coastline to support the blockade and pin down Confederate troops that might otherwise be sent to resist Union operations in Virginia.

In November 1861, however, only McClellan's Army was anywhere near ready to commence operations. To give Gen. Henry W. Halleck in Missouri and Gen. Don Carlos Buell in Kentucky time to organize their forces, McClellan decided to postpone offensive operations until the spring of 1862. By the time spring came, however, dissatisfaction with military delay had dramatically eroded McClellan's personal prestige with the Northern public and his relations with the President.

Among the sources of discontent with military inactivity in the winter of 1861–62 was a crisis in U.S.–British relations. In November 1861, a British mail steamer, the *Trent*, was stopped by a Union warship that took into custody two Confederate emissaries, James Mason and John Slidell. The Palmerston government was enraged, and quickly made it clear that if the Lincoln administration did not apologize and release Mason and Slidell, there would be serious consequences. To bolster the threat, the British began active military preparations in Canada. After several tense weeks the Lincoln administration backed down and surrendered the two emissaries in late December.

Responsibility for the formation of Southern military strategy fell upon President Davis, a West Pointer, Mexican War hero, and former secretary of war. On the surface, the Confederacy's strategic problem appeared much simpler: Southerners merely had to offer sufficient resistance to convince the North it could not be conquered. However, geography and political factors imposed serious limitations on strategic planning. The location of the Confederacy's small industrial base and vital agricultural areas in the upper South ruled out the adoption of a Fabian strategy. Such a strategy would also have placed the institution of slavery at risk, as the sight of Union armies marching through the South would have undermined the moral authority of the master class and served as a haven for runaway slaves. Perhaps even more important than these material considerations in shaping Southern strategy was a too widely espoused belief that as a point of honor the Confederacy should defend every inch of its soil.

Also widely espoused was a belief that Europe's voracious appetite for cotton would compel intervention. Although not officially sanctioned by the Confederate government, Southerners imposed an effective embargo on cotton exports to increase demand for the crop overseas. "King Cotton diplomacy" proved a disastrous failure, however. Bumper crops in 1857–60 had left British mills with more than enough cotton to process for an already satiated market. By the time the lack of cotton might have seriously affected the British economy, alternative sources in Egypt and India had been developed, and they more than made up the difference. Furthermore, poor harvests during the first two years of the war increased European demand for Northern food crops, making King Corn as important to European statesmen as King Cotton.

In January 1862, Confederate forces west of the Mississippi, under the command of Gen. Albert S. Johnston, held a badly overextended line that stretched from Columbus, Kentucky, on the Mississippi River to Mill Springs in eastern Kentucky. At the center of the line stood Fort Henry on the Tennessee River and Fort Donelson on the Cumberland. In February, both fell to a joint army-navy force commanded by Gen. Ulysses S. *Grant. This opened the Confederate heartland to invasion. With his flanks exposed by the penetration of his center, Johnston abandoned Kentucky and most of Tennessee. The industrial center of Nashville fell, and Union forces moved quickly up the Tennessee and Cumberland Rivers.

Political pressure and a belief that the burden of simultaneously serving as field commander and general in chief was too much led Lincoln to remove McClellan from the latter post in March 1862. Lincoln named no replacement, and instead intended to perform the functions of general in chief himself. He did, however, combine the western departments and appoint Henry Halleck as their overall commander. Upon assuming this position, Halleck decided to concentrate his forces for an operation against the strategic rail point at Corinth, Mississippi. Before Halleck could complete his concentration, Johnston, on 6 April 1862, attacked unprepared Union forces under Grant near Shiloh Church by the Tennessee River. Grant's army managed to hold on despite extremely heavy losses, and, reinforced by forces under Buell, launched a successful counterattack the next day. The Confederates retreated to Corinth, having lost the Battle of *Shiloh; Johnston, who had been mortally wounded; and their bid to reverse Southern fortunes in western Tennessee.

In March, McClellan launched a combined navy-army campaign from the lower Chesapeake Bay. After a month-long siege before Yorktown, McClellan commenced a steady advance toward Richmond in the Peninsular Campaign. By early June, the Army of the Potomac was within ten miles of the Confederate capital, and the end of the rebellion appeared at hand.

But then two men emerged who would transform the war in Virginia, Gen. Robert E. *Lee and his lieutenant, "Stonewall" *Jackson. They recognized that if the Confederacy remained wholly on the defensive and continued to concede the strategic initiative, it would inevitably be crushed by superior numbers. To prevent this, they decided to seize the initiative by assuming the strategic and tactical offensive while attempting to defend the South.

It has been argued that Lee's aggressive strategy led him into tactical blunders and high casualties that bled the Confederacy white. Clearly, in retrospect, the ultimate objective of an offensive strategy, the destruction of the opposing army in battle, was a practical impossibility given the size and firepower of Civil War armies. Yet Lee recognized that if the South could only frustrate Northern military operations until the 1864 elections, the Northern public might replace the Lincoln administration with one more amenable to Southern independence. In May and June 1862, Jackson, with Lee's active support and encouragement, conducted a brilliant campaign in the Shenandoah Valley that induced the Lincoln administration to hold back reinforcements from McClellan's army. Lee then called Jackson's force to Richmond, and took the offensive. In the *Seven Days' Battle of 25 June–1 July 1862, McClellan responded to Lee's and Jackson's attack by conducting a successful fighting retreat to a new position on the James River.

The setback on the Peninsula and the tremendous casualties suffered by McClellan and by Grant at Shiloh had a profound effect on Northern opinion. Until the Seven Days' Battle, Lincoln had resisted calls for a more radical approach out of fear that it would stimulate Southern resistance. In July 1862, however, Lincoln saw little evidence that the conservative policy was convincing many southerners to lay down their arms. Lincoln also perceived a hardening of Northern public opinion, and began moving toward a more radical position on the war. In July, he read to his cabinet a draft of a proclamation emancipating the slaves in the Confederacy, but was persuaded to await a military victory before issuing it.

To achieve that victory, Lincoln organized a new army in Virginia and placed it under the command of John Pope, who issued a series of orders promulgating a tougher policy toward Southern property and civilians. Next, Lincoln restored the position of general in chief and appointed Halleck to the post. Finally, Lincoln then, through Halleck, ordered McClellan's army back to Washington to unite with Pope's forces. But Pope proved no match for Lee. In a brilliant campaign, Lee forced Pope back to the old battlefield of Bull Run before all of McClellan's army could join him, and, on 29–30 August 1862, won a crushing victory at the Second Battle of *Bull Run.

Lee then decided to cross the Potomac River into Maryland. Lee did this hoping to feed his army in Maryland rather than Virginia, recruit Marylanders into his army, and win a decisive victory on Union soil that would bring the North to the peace table. Lincoln reluctantly restored McClellan to command. The speed with which McClellan got his army reorganized and on the march surprised Lee, who had divided his army, and allowed the Federal commander to seize the strategic initiative. Compelled to abandon his plan of pushing into Pennsylvania, Lee reconcentrated his army near Sharpsburg, Maryland. There, on 17 September 1862, the two armies fought the battle of *Antietam, the bloodiest single day of combat in American military history. Although McClellan and his subordinates mismanaged the battle and failed fully to commit their superior forces, Lee was forced to return to Virginia.

While Lee was in Maryland, Confederates under Gen. Braxton *Bragg were on the offensive in the West. After the capture of Corinth, a force under Buell was pushed east toward Chattanooga and East Tennessee. To counter this, Bragg decided to seize the strategic initiative by invading Kentucky. The invasion began well, but a drought that had plagued Buell's advance on Chattanooga also took a severe toll on Bragg's army and slowed its advance, giving Buell time to return to Kentucky. The two armies met in the Battle of *Perryville, Kentucky, on 8 October 1862. Neither side gained a decisive victory, but Bragg, with his supply line overextended, was compelled to retreat to Tennessee.

Confederate victories in the summer of 1862 reinforced the Palmerston government's conviction that the Union could not be restored. Furthermore, suffering among British textile workers was increasing as the lack of cotton started to pinch. Consequently, after Second Bull Run, Palmerston began to seriously ponder an effort to bring the North and South to the negotiating table. It was hoped that an offer of mediation that did not explicitly recognize Confederate independence, would be amenable to the North now that the impossibility of the task of conquering the South had been proven. To facilitate the process of bringing the combatants to the table, the British sought partners in the venture abroad. France, although facing a crisis in Italy, had long been sympathetic to the Southern cause. But Russia, a staunch supporter of the north, was much cooler to the proposal for mediation.

On 22 September 1862, Lincoln finally issued his Preliminary *Emancipation Proclamation expecting that it, in combination with the victory at Antietam, would demonstrate both the Union's ability to achieve success on the battlefield and, by making the war one between slavery and freedom, destroy British interest in intervention. He was wrong on both counts, at least in the short term. The stalemated condition of the war after Antietam seemed only to demonstrate that even if the North could win battles, it could never do so in so overwhelming a fashion as to conquer the South, and that some form of outside intervention was necessary to stop the war. More importantly, the Palmerston government feared the Emancipation Proclamation would incite slave insurrections in the South and make restoration of a stable political, social, and economic environment in North America impossible. Consequently, Palmerston allowed members of his government to seriously discuss an armistice plan put forward by France.

Republican defeats in the 1862 congressional elections, however, were not significant enough to suggest the North's commitment to military victory had eroded to the point where an offer of mediation would be accepted. If Britain was to bring the North to the negotiating table, clearly there would have to be some coercion involved. At this point Secretary for War George Lewis brought a memorandum before the cabinet. Lewis shared Palmerston's view that the Union could not be restored by force of arms, and that the purpose of the Emancipation Proclamation was to foment servile insurrection in the South. Yet in his memorandum, Lewis concluded that the South had yet to earn recognition. More importantly, Lewis gave a pessimistic assessment of Britain's ability to compel the North to accept an armistice or develop a workable solution that both sides would accept. Lewis's arguments carried the day. The British pulled back, and the crisis ended.

After Antietam and Perryville the Union high command attempted to impose an element of coordination among its main armies. In December, major operations were undertaken by Union armies at *Fredericksburg in Virginia, Chickasaw Bayou in Mississippi, and Murfreesboro in Tennessee. Neither side achieved a decisive success, however, and as 1862 ended, the war settled into a stalemate.

The armies went into winter quarters and the Union high command adjusted its overall strategy. In Halleck, Lincoln had a man who would carry out his wishes without the acrimony and conflict that had characterized his relationship with McClellan. Halleck helped shape Lincoln's strategic thought and translated the president's wishes into military strategy. Both agreed that in making the Confederate capital the main target of strategic planning, McClellan had given insufficient priority to the security of Washington. They decided the Army of the Potomac would operate along the overland route with its focus more on defending Washington and neutralizing Lee's army than capturing Richmond. As long as it did not uncover Washington, the Army of the Potomac was to keep Lee's army busy to prevent it from detaching forces to reinforce Confederate armies in the west, and, if possible, catch Lee in a tactical or strategical mistake. Although willing to accept the prospect of stalemate in Virginia, Lincoln understood that Lee's aggressive generalship had offered an opportunity in Maryland to achieve a decisive *victory. Such an opportunity might come again.

With the shift to a defensive strategy in the east and the change in Northern war aims, operations in the west took on greater importance and received greater priority. Halleck and Lincoln recognized that the adoption of emancipation as a war aim raised the stakes for the Confederacy, and dramatically reduced the chances for a quick end to the war. Despite its political, psychological, and material importance to the Confederacy, simply capturing Richmond would not end the rebellion. The entire South would have to be conquered. Halleck and Lincoln gambled that the Union armies could either win the war by 1864, or at least gain enough victories in the west to sustain popular support for the Lincoln administration and ensure its reelection that year.

By 1863, the Union had established control of the entire Mississippi Valley except for a stretch between Vicksburg, Mississippi, and Port Hudson, Louisiana. A Union army-navy expedition in 1862 had reached Vicksburg, but had been unable to take the town. In the summer of 1863, Grant, in a brilliant campaign, captured that fortified city commanding the Mississippi. Marching overland on the Louisiana side, and crossing the Mississippi below town, Grant moved quickly inland, drove off a force sent to assist the army defending Vicksburg, then turned back toward the town. After victories at Champion's Hill on 16 May and the Big Black River on 17 May, Grant drove the Confederate army back into the defenses of Vicksburg. On 4 July 1863, after a month-long siege, Vicksburg surrendered, followed by Port Hudson less than a week later; thus allowing the Mississippi, in Lincoln's words, to flow "unvexed to the sea." The Confederacy was divided in two.

After the Union defeat at the Battle of Fredericksburg, Lincoln appointed Gen. Joseph *Hooker commander of the Army of the Potomac. Hooker did a magnificent job reinvigorating the army, but in the field he proved no match for Lee and Jackson. In his tactical masterpiece, although outnumbered two-to-one, Lee won a brilliant victory at the *Chancellorsville, Virginia in May 1863. The victory came at a tremendous cost, however. Jackson died after being accidentally shot by his own men.

Lee then embarked on another invasion of the North, this time into Pennsylvania. Lincoln recognized that Lee's action provided a second opportunity to catch the rebel army far from its base and administer the crippling blow McClellan had failed to deliver at Antietam. Having lost faith in Hooker, Lincoln replaced him with Gen. George Gordon *Meade on 30 June 1863. Two days later the armies came into contact near Gettysburg, Pennsylvania. For three days—1–3 July 1863—Lee attacked the Union army in quest of decisive victory. Meade held his ground and the rebel army was compelled to return to Virginia. It had suffered such severe losses at the Battle of *Gettysburg that it would never be the same again. The war in the east returned to a state of stalemate, with the two armies engaging in a war of maneuver that produced no major results.

Gettysburg and Vicksburg greatly diminished Southern prospects overseas. Beginning in 1863, the North's campaign to prevent intervention also benefitted from Great Britain and France's preoccupation with events in Europe, including the Polish insurrection of 1863 and the controversy over Schleswig-Holstein in 1864. Yet in violation of the *Monroe Doctrine, the French government of Napoleon III, in 1863, took advantage of the U.S. Civil War to install a puppet regime in Mexico under Emperor Ferdinand Maximilian. Confederate agents offered to recognize the new Mexican government in exchange for French recognition of Southern independence. Napoleon, however, remained unwilling to do this without Britain.

The French enterprise in Mexico did not go unnoticed by the Lincoln administration. After the capture of Vicksburg and Port Hudson, Nathaniel Banks was directed to conduct operations in the Trans-Mississippi West, in part to capture cotton in that region, but also to show the flag. Although a campaign along the Red River in Louisiana failed, Banks was able to occupy Brownsville, Texas. After Lee's surrender at Appomattox in April 1865, the federal government sent 50,000 soldiers to the Mexican border. But by then Napoleon had already begun scaling back his enterprise. In 1867, the French misadventure collapsed, and Maximilian was executed by the Mexicans.

The most serious controversy on the diplomatic front during the last two years of the war was prompted by the efforts of Confederate Secretary of the Navy Stephen Mallory to obtain ironclad ships in Europe to break the Union blockade. The British government facilitated this enterprise by applying a narrow interpretation of a law that prohibited the construction and arming of warships in British territory. The Southern agent, James D. Bulloch, exploited this loophole by arranging for ships to be built unarmed in Britain, whence they would be sent to the Bahamas to complete construction. In 1862, Bulloch was able to acquire the steam and sail *cruisers Florida and Alabama; both would enjoy productive careers as commerce raiders.

Bulloch then contracted with the Laird firm in Britain for two new vessels with rams to break the blockade. As they neared completion in the summer of 1863, Union minister Adams issued a series of hotly worded protests to the British Foreign Office warning of the consequences of allowing the ships to be released. Palmerston resented the tone of Adams's protests, but, with the Polish insurrection threatening the peace of Europe, could not afford a conflict

with the United States. In September, his government ordered the detention of the ships.

In addition to its diplomatic triumphs, the Union achieved a second major military objective in 1863, the occupation of East Tennessee. That summer Union Gen. William S. Rosecrans conducted a brilliant campaign of maneuver and seized East Tennessee without a fight. After pausing briefly at Chattanooga, Rosecrans pushed on into Georgia. In September Bragg brought the Confederate retreat to a halt, and, his force augmented by reinforcements from Virginia, prepared a counterstroke to crush one of Rosecrans's three widely separated wings. Rosecrans awakened to the danger in the nick of time and quickly reconcentrated his army near Chickamauga Creek. However, a blunder by one of Rosencrans's subordinates allowed the Confederate army to win a smashing victory on 20 September 1863. Instead of following up his victory at the Battle of *Chickamauga with a vigorous attack, Bragg decided to lay siege to the Union army in Chattanooga. Washington reacted to the crisis by placing Grant in command of all Union forces west of the Appalachian Mountains, and sent him two corps from the Army of the Potomac. After reestablishing a secure line of supplies, Grant smashed the Confederate line at Lookout Mountain and *Missionary Ridge near Chattanooga on 24–25 November 1863.

In early 1864, Grant was called to Washington and promoted to general-in-chief. Grant appointed Gen. William Tecumseh *Sherman to replace him as overall commander in the western theater, and assigned him the task of bringing Bragg's army, now under the command of Gen. Joseph E. *Johnston, to battle by campaigning against Atlanta. Grant would accompany Meade's army as it campaigned against Lee. Supporting movements would be made in the Shenandoah Valley and along the James River. To prevent the Confederacy, as it had at Chickamauga, from exploiting its interior lines, the Union armies would all begin their campaigns at the same time.

On 4 May 1864, the Army of the Potomac began its sixth campaign against Richmond. Over the next few weeks the Virginia theater endured the bloodiest month of the war, as the two armies fought the Battle of the *Wilderness and the battles at *Spotsylvania, the North Anna River, and *Cold Harbor. Grant continually maneuvered in an effort to force Lee out of his entrenchments. Lee successfully countered all of Grant's moves, leading the Union commander to adopt a strategy of attrition. Willing to accept tremendous casualties, Grant, by pinning Lee in his entrenchments, made it impossible for the rebel commander to attempt another of the brilliant counteroffensives that had disrupted earlier Union campaigns.

After a futile attempt to break Lee's lines at Cold Harbor, Grant crossed the James River in June 1864, bypassing Richmond in hopes of seizing Petersburg and the railroads supplying Lee's army. When commanders on the scene failed vigorously to attack the lightly guarded town, Lee was able to bring his army down to defend Petersburg. The armies then settled into the Siege of *Petersburg, a campaign of siegecraft that presaged the trench warfare of World War I. Throughout the fall and winter of 1864–65, Grant continually extended his left flank to the west, one by one seizing the railroads leading into Petersburg and inexorably forcing Lee to stretch his lines ever more thin.

Meanwhile, after a several-weeks campaign of maneuver, Sherman's army reached the outskirts of Atlanta in

July 1864. However, he had not "bagged" Johnston's army, nor did the town's capitulation appear in any way certain. Northern morale plummeted as Grant and Sherman's grand offensive, which had began with such promise, bogged down in frustrating and bloody stalemate before Petersburg and Atlanta.

But Confederate leaders were not encouraged by the situation. Uncomfortable with the idea of allowing Grant and Sherman to maintain their grip on Petersburg and Atlanta, they decided to take the offensive. Realizing Grant's army was too strong for them to attack directly, Confederate leaders sent a force under Gen. Jubal Early on a raid in the Shenandoah Valley. In the west, the cautious and defensive-minded Johnston was replaced on President Davis's orders by Gen. John Bell *Hood, an aggressive young corps commander. Early reached the outskirts of Washington, but, after Grant sent back a full army corps to defend the capital, Early was forced to return to the valley. The Union forces around the capital and in the valley were then organized into a single force under the command of Gen. Philip H. *Sheridan. Sheridan then pursued Early into the Shenandoah Valley, winning battles at Winchester, Fisher's Hill, and Cedar Creek in September and October 1864. Sheridan then undertook a campaign to destroy the valley, burning crops and any other resources that could be of use to the Confederate war effort.

In Georgia, Hood launched a series of costly and unsuccessful attacks on the Union army during the last week of July 1864. Afterwards, the Confederate army retreated to the defenses of Atlanta, but was forced to abandon the town in September 1864. The fall of Atlanta, combined with Sheridan's victories in the Shenandoah Valley, and a victory by naval forces under David *Farragut at *Mobile Bay in August, reinvigorated Northern morale and set the stage for Lincoln's reelection that November.

Sherman then obtained Grant's approval for a type of operation the two had been experimenting with for some time—large-scale raids using army-size forces. Recognizing that Southern civilians and their resources were as important as Southern armies in sustaining the rebellion, Sherman made them the objective of his campaign. The famous (or infamous, depending on one's viewpoint) *Sherman's March to the Sea cut a sixty-mile wide trail of destruction through Georgia. Not only was severe damage inflicted on Southern resources, but the fact that the North could morally and materially undertake such an operation had a severe impact on Confederate morale.

After reaching the coast at Savannah, Georgia, in December 1864, Sherman turned northward to join Grant for the final battle of the war. That same month, a desperate attempt by Hood to invade Tennessee ended with the destruction of his army at the Battles of *Franklin and *Nashville. Johnston was restored to command to resist Sherman's movement through the Carolinas, but lacked the resources or manpower to be effective. Before Sherman could reach Virginia, Grant captured the last Confederate supply line at the Battle of Five Forks on 1 April 1865. Lee evacuated Richmond and Petersburg and made a bold attempt to link up with Johnston. Grant cut off Lee's retreat near a small crossroads town called Appomattox, Virginia. There Lee surrendered on 9 April. A few days later, Johnston surrendered to Sherman at Raleigh, North Carolina. With the surrender of the two major field armies resistance throughout the South ended despite the pleas of President Davis. The war was over, and with the sectional conflict finally settled, the United States was free to complete the task of conquering the continent and move toward realizing its destiny as one of the great nations of the world.

[See also Army Combat Branches; Army, U.S.: 1783–1865; Commander in Chief, President as; Confederacy, the Military in the; Marine Corps, U.S.: 1775–1865; Navy, U.S.: 1783–1865.]

• David P. Crook, The North, the South, and the Powers 1861–1865, 1974. Grady McWhiney and Perry D. Jamieson, Attack and Die: Civil War Military Tactics and the Southern Heritage, 1982. Herman Hattaway and Archer Jones, How the North Won: A Military History of the Civil War, 1983. Edward Hagerman, The American Civil War and the Origins of Modern Warfare: Ideas, Organization, and Field Command, 1988. Richard M. McMurray, Two Great Rebel Armies: An Essay in Confederate Military History, 1989. Steven E. Woodworth, Jefferson Davis and His Generals: The Failure of Confederate Command in the West, 1990. Howard E. Jones, Union in Peril: The Crisi over British Intervention in the Civil War,1992. Mark Grimsley, The Hard Hand of War: Union Military Policy Toward Southern Civilians, 1861–1865, 1995. Robert May, ed., The Union, the Confederacy, and the Atlantic Rim, 1995. Herman Hattaway, Shades of Blue and Gray: An Introductory Military History of the Civil War, 1997. Charles Hubbard, The Burden of Confederate Diplomacy, 1997. Joseph L. Harsh, Confederate Tide Rising: Robert E. Lee and the Making of Confederate Strategy, 1861–1862, 1998. Steven E. Woodworth, ed., Civil War Generals in Defeat, 1999.

—Herman Hattaway and Ethan Rafuse

CIVIL WAR (1861–65): DOMESTIC COURSE

In the days following the capture of *Fort Sumter, few Americans anticipated a lengthy conflict. President Abraham *Lincoln responded to the crisis by calling for 75,000 90-day volunteers, reflecting his confidence that the war would not last the summer. But, of course, such optimism proved ill-founded. By any measure, the next four years would be the bloodiest in American history. How did the men and women on the home front respond to the war's enormous challenges?

In some fundamental ways, the North and the South faced very similar situations in April 1861. The outbreak of open hostilities, after months of uncertainty and division, prompted most citizens above and below the border states to "rally 'round" their flag. Town dignitaries delivered bellicose speeches with puffed chests; editorials urged readers to new patriotic heights; bands blared. Military recruiters had no trouble obtaining volunteers in such an atmosphere; those who persisted in dissent generally maintained a judicious silence.

The Union and the Confederacy also faced comparable obstacles. Neither side was remotely prepared to fight a major war. The federal army only numbered about 16,000 men. The Confederacy had to start with nothing, although it did have the advantage of a more military-oriented population, including compulsory military service and a disproportionate share of the nation's *Mexican War veterans. And despite all the excitement, mid-nineteenth-century Americans had little familiarity with—and less enthusiasm for—the sort of activist central government a long war might require. These similarities notwithstanding, both sides went to war with dissimilar material and human resources. Moreover, the Confederate government was constructed in a society committed to states' rights and lacking a functioning two-party system. Such differences helped mold distinctive patterns of wartime *mobilization, and as the war dragged on, they created quite different home front experiences.

Manpower. At the outset, mobilization in both North and South took on an almost carnival air. The young men rushed to volunteer for hastily organized companies, anxious to get in on the glory while there was still time. Before long, both sides discovered that they could no longer rely on such unfettered passion, and thus they turned—in stages—to various strategies initially to coax young men into *uniform in the *Union army or the *Confederate army. The North enjoyed a huge numerical advantage. The free Union states had a total population of 19 million; the slaves states that stayed with the Union—Delaware, Kentucky, Maryland, and Missouri—added another 3.2 million, although that number included many Southern sympathizers. The eleven Confederate states totaled just over 9 million people. These numbers understate the Union's numerical superiority by including the Confederacy's 3.5 million black slaves, who were central to the Southern economy and war effort but not deemed fit for military service. Furthermore, roughly 800,000 foreign immigrants arrived in the North during the war.

Both central governments initially relied on the states and localities to orchestrate recruiting. When Abraham Lincoln and Jefferson *Davis called for volunteers, each state received a quota to fill. By the time the three-month recruits were returning home in late summer 1861, the North had issued calls for three-year volunteers that yielded more than 700,000 men. The infant Confederacy had already requested 100,000 men before the capture of *Fort Sumter in April and added another 400,000 the following month.

With winter approaching and the most willing recruits already in uniform, the Confederate Congress offered bounties and furloughs to convince volunteers to reenlist. In April 1862, the Confederacy passed the first national draft legislation, making white men between ages eighteen and thirty-five eligible for *conscription. The North was not too far behind. In June 1862, Lincoln called for 300,000 more three-year volunteers. When the citizenry responded slowly, Congress passed the Militia Act giving state governors the power to draft men. That August, the Union implemented this new legislation by requisitioning 300,000 nine-month militiamen, with the provision that states failing to meet their quota would be subject to a draft. In March 1863, the North replaced the controversial state militia drafts with federal conscription measures that were more on a par with the Confederacy's system.

The initial conscription legislation in both the Union and the Confederacy provided military-aged men with ample opportunities for avoiding service. In addition to excluding men with certain disabilities, the Confederate legislation exempted a long list of professions, ranging from political and judicial officers to teachers and clergymen to workers in war-related occupations. A later act exempted one white man from every plantation with twenty or more slaves. Each of these provisions could be defended in the name of military necessity or domestic stability, but together they triggered angry complaints of class legislation from nonslave owning Southern whites. The North's federal draft act had no occupational exemptions, but it did exclude men with numerous medical ailments or certain family obligations, as well as unnatural-ized aliens. Most controversial were the provisions enabling wealthier conscripts simply to buy their way out of service. Following long-standing European tradition, both sides allowed draftees to send substitutes in their place, the North permitting conscripts to pay a commutation fee of $300 (an amount equal to a worker's annual wages) rather than serving.

As the war dragged on, the Confederacy was forced to widen its conscription net. The list of exemptions gradually shrank; the Southern Congress repealed the substitute clause and made all those who had furnished substitutes eligible for the draft; and the age parameters expanded to include white males between seventeen and fifty. The more populous North tinkered with its rules but made fewer substantial revisions other than restricting the controversial commutation clause to members of certain religious groups. (As many had feared, this resulted in a steady increase in the market price for substitutes.)

Despite the superficially similar rules, conscription played different roles in the two nations. Only about eight percent of Union soldiers were conscripts or substitutes. The four federal drafts were really designed to encourage enthusiastic local recruiting rather than to put conscripts into uniform. The Union army's provost marshal general announced draft days long in advance, giving communities every opportunity to fill their quotas and avoid a draft. Cities and towns responded by raising large bounty funds—which supplemented existing federal and state bounties—to encourage enlistment. The poorer South soon exhausted funds available for enlistment bounties, limiting the effectiveness of pre-draft recruiting. Roughly one in five Confederate soldiers was either a draftee or a substitute.

In 1863, the North tapped a further manpower advantage when it decided to accept *African Americans in the military. Blacks had served in both the *Revolutionary War and the *War of 1812, but black enlistment was prohibited in 1820. Many Northern blacks offered their services to the Union, but for long months racist assumptions about the ability of African American troops and political qualms about the costs of arming black volunteers conspired to keep black men out of uniform (although thousands did serve in the navy). The 1862 Militia Act allowed Lincoln to accept black volunteers, but it was not until after the 1 January 1863 *Emancipation Proclamation that the North aggressively recruited black volunteers. By the end of the Civil War, 179,000 African American men had served in 166 black regiments of the U.S. *Colored Troops. The North commissioned few black officers and persisted in giving black regiments inferior wages, equipment, and assignments. In the war's waning months the Confederate Congress voted to accept black soldiers, but this legislation was passed too late to be tested in practice.

By the end of the war, roughly half of the North's military-aged white men had served in uniform, as compared with nearly four-fifths of Southern white males of military age. Some critics at the time and some later historians charged that the war became "A Rich Man's War But a Poor Man's Fight," yet comparisons of the occupational distribution of sampled soldiers with data from the 1860 census indicate that both armies were surprisingly representative of the white male populations. The Northern army was also not, as sometimes suggested, dominated by foreign mercenaries; immigrants were actually underrepresented in the Union ranks.

Economic Mobilization and Its Effects. The North enjoyed enormous economic advantages over its weaker adversary. In 1860, roughly 90 percent of the nation's manufacturing output was from the Northern states. The Union's economic superiority was particularly pronounced in key war-related sectors, such as textiles, boots and shoes, iron, and firearms. Moreover, the North had a near monopoly in railroads and shipping. The agrarian South was even behind its Northern neighbor in some critical foodstuffs. In 1860, Northern agriculture was producing half the nation's corn and four-fifths of its wheat.

With a few key exceptions, the Union was able to outfit its armies through private contracting rather than establishing federally owned factories. Unlike modern conflicts, this war did not call for the vast production of uniquely military goods. Most of the items needed to feed, outfit, and arm a soldier could be provided by existing farms and factories; a few government arsenals produced the rest. Lacking an established industrial base, the Confederacy found itself in far more challenging circumstances.

Here was one of the war's many ironies. Whereas the Union could rely on private enterprise, the states' rights–oriented Confederacy was forced to build nationally owned factories, subsidize private enterprises, regulate prices, and impress goods and services (including slave labor) to meet the war's economic needs. With the passage of time, the South's economic deficiencies became more glaring. The Union blockade limited Confederate access to foreign ports, and the North's military successes destabilized portions of the Southern economy. Above all, Southerners learned to reuse materials where they could and to manage with less wherever possible.

The Northern war effort cost an estimated $2.3 billion; the smaller Confederacy spent roughly $1 billion. As he developed strategies to fund the war, U.S. Secretary of the Treasury Salmon P. Chase had a host of advantages over his Confederate counterpart, Christopher G. Memminger. In many senses, the fiscal history of the war runs parallel to the mobilization of the armies, with both sides employing similar strategies tailored in distinctive ways to meet their individual needs. The wealthier North funded most of its costs through the sale of interest-bearing bonds. These bonds, sold largely under the enthusiastic direction of Philadelphia banker Jay Cooke, enabled the Union, effectively, to "borrow" roughly two-thirds of its military expenses from its own citizens or from foreign investors. The North covered an additional 20 percent of its expenses through a assortment of import duties and taxes, including a modest federal income tax. It paid for the war's remaining costs by issuing "greenbacks," printed notes not backed by specie or any precious metal.

This new currency, which was authorized by the Legal Tender Act of 1862, proved crucial to the smooth functioning of the wartime economy while passing on part of the war's costs to consumers in the form of relatively high inflation. The South, with less disposable wealth and a poorly developed financial structure, could fund only about 40 percent of its costs through taxation and the sale of bonds. Instead, the Confederacy had to rely on massive issues of paper money, triggering a disastrously high inflation.

The war's economic strains fell unevenly on different groups across the home front. The booming Northern economy assured low unemployment, but soon wage earners chafed at the burden of rising prices. The more skilled urban artisans managed to organize and negotiate comfortable raises; the less skilled, including scores of women who worked for unscrupulous military subcontractors, for example, in the manufacture of *uniforms, suffered through declining real wages. Federal forces only intervened in a handful of labor conflicts, and then only under the guise of claimed military necessity. Heavy wartime demands for food, poor European harvests, and disproportionately high enlistment rates among agricultural workers combined to produce a variety of results: unusually high profits for farm owners; increased wages for the agricultural workers who remained at home; and unprecedented investment in agricultural machinery. Women and men on the Confederate home front felt the war's economic pains even more acutely. By mid-1863, the combination of high prices and food shortages had driven many Southerners into open dissent. In April, an angry mob composed largely of women destroyed much of Richmond's shopping district after their appeals for relief from inflated food prices had gone unanswered.

Richmond's "bread riots" underscored the war's effect on women and children on the home front. In the prosperous North, some benevolent institutions reported proportionally greater demands from women, perhaps reflecting the combined weight of more economic opportunities for male workers and soldiers and the loss of family income when men fell on the battlefield. Cities and towns across the North collected special funds for the "families of volunteers," providing much needed relief while adding further incentives to reluctant enlistees. Southern women bore the brunt of the Confederacy's economic ills without much opportunity for relief. When private charities ran dry, Southerners turned to unprecedented public welfare measures, at the local, state, and national levels. But inflation, inefficiency, and overwhelming numbers conspired to limit the effectiveness of these initiatives.

For some women, the Civil War's economic challenges brought new opportunities. Although the Union's military demands did not produce an army of nineteenth-century factory women, the war did accelerate the movement of Northern women into positions as clerks, teachers, and nurses. In both the North and the South, white women took on expanded agricultural roles when white men left for the front. This was particularly true in the Confederacy, where women often acted independently of any male influence. Wartime necessity also forced Southern women into new positions, but they continued to run up against cultural barriers. The North, for instance, proved more receptive to the use of female nurses.

For Southern blacks, there was no such ambiguity. Long before the war ended, hundreds of thousands of slaves had won their freedom. The story of wartime emancipation reflects the complexity of national, local, and individual forces. As official Northern policy slowly inched its way toward Lincoln's Emancipation Proclamation, which took effect 1 January 1863, individual slaves responded to their own circumstances, pursuing freedom when absent masters or approaching Union troops provided the best opportunities. Many of these freed slaves remained in the South, finding refuge behind Union lines, while others fled to the North. The process of piecemeal emancipation left much of the Southern agricultural economy in disarray while laying the groundwork for various wartime experiments with the ramifications of free labor.

Politics and Dissent. Four years of war produced serious strains on domestic politics in both the Union and the Confederacy. In most fundamental ways the Confederate leaders modeled their new constitution and government after the nation that they had abandoned. After all, the seceding states had insisted that they were the true heirs to the founders of the republic. Beneath the structural similarities, however, lay important political differences. Whereas Lincoln entered a political arena with a strong two-party system, Davis presided over a nation that would be torn by factionalism but without any party mechanisms to register (and control) dissent. Moreover, many of the Confederacy's leaders had worked during the antebellum decades as political dissenters, resisting perceived challenges to states' rights.

From his first days in office, Lincoln had to navigate between the radical Republicans in his own party, such as Thaddeus *Stevens, and an increasingly vocal array of dissenting Peace Democrats. The relative unanimity that followed the outbreak of hostilities quickly dissolved as Northerners debated a series of controversial war measures including the *Habeas Corpus Act, conscription, greenbacks, and, above all, emancipation. Even Unionist War Democrats in Washington and across the North criticized policies that they claimed enacted an unconstitutional Republican agenda.

The administration countered with aggressive measures to silence the most dangerous dissent, the Peace Democrats. Soon after the capture of *Fort Sumter, Lincoln ordered the suspension of the writ of habeas corpus in the border states. This set in motion a critical series of events in Maryland: military authorities threw several prominent local figures, including wealthy secessionist John Merryman, in jail; in *Ex Parte *Merryman* (1861), U.S. Supreme Court Chief Justice Roger Taney of Maryland responded by ordering Merryman's release; and Lincoln refused to yield, leaving it to history to judge his actions. The following year, with the state militia drafts underway, federal officials arrested several hundred vocal draft resisters and five dissenting newspaper editors while suspending publication of several opposition newspapers. By 1863, the Northern "Copperheads"—the antiwar wing of the Democratic Party—had won important strongholds across the Midwest and in some areas of the East. In May, Maj. Gen. Ambrose *Burnside ordered the arrest of dissenting Ohio congressman Clement L. *Vallandigham, triggering another round of angry outbursts.

As the election of 1864 approached, Lincoln had every reason to fear that he would lose to the Democratic challenger, Maj. Gen. George B. *McClellan. McClellan, long a thorn in the president's side, had repeatedly criticized emancipation, the loss of civil liberties, and Lincoln's overall handling of the war. When the votes were counted, Lincoln had managed to garner 55 percent, aided by Gen. William Tecumseh *Sherman's recent successes in the South and the overwhelming support of absentee ballots from the Union Army.

Historians have often compared Lincoln with Jefferson Davis, generally finding the Confederate president lacking. The South's material disadvantages forced Davis into a series of measures that dramatically expanded the central government while placing him in the center of controversy.

This process of central government growth, which Emory Thomas (1979) has termed a "political revolution," included the continent's first draft legislation, impressment of goods and labor, the suspension of civil liberties, and a wide range of ventures into economic control. Davis faced heated opposition from strong-minded state governors as well as attacks from much closer to home, often led by his vice president, the surly Georgian Alexander Stephens. Davis, like Lincoln, used his authority to declare martial law in sensitive areas, but civil liberties for whites may have in fact fared better in the Confederacy (for instance, freedom of the press survived unscathed in the South).

Much of the most rigorous wartime dissent was voiced beyond the boundaries of normal political discourse. Northerners fretted over secret societies, such as the notorious Knights of the Golden Circle, which reputedly conspired against the Union. Portions of the nonslave hill country and mountain region in the South remained bastions of pro-Union sympathy throughout the conflict. The North's worst internal violence followed tension-filled conscription days, but often reflected broader tensions. In July 1863, disgruntled conscripts attacked a draft office, triggering four days of *New York City antidraft riots, which led to much carnage. Many of the rioters were Irish immigrants who took out their hostilities on African Americans.

In addition to periodic food riots, portions of the Confederacy experienced violence at the hands of roving companies of guerrillas. Some of these groups had at least passing connections to formal military bodies, but others were little more than desperate bands of hungry deserters. Even where the South did not divide into open warfare, declining *troop morale eventually took a tremendous toll, inciting soldiers to flee the army and accelerating the demise of the Confederacy.

Supporting the War Effort. For most people on the home front, the "citizens' war" provided a wealth of opportunities to assist the war effort. In the North, women and men labored in a wide variety of voluntary societies designed to fill the gaps in the official governmental machinery. Local women's groups sewed clothing, rolled bandages, visited hospitals, fed traveling soldiers, and provided refuge for escaped slaves. Fund-raising concerts and fairs, modeled on antebellum practices, enabled the volunteers to mail packages off to distant soldiers. Two national bodies—the U.S. *Sanitary Commission and the U.S. Christian Commission—emerged to organize and direct some of these benevolent efforts. Confederate women threw themselves into war work with equal vigor. White women of all classes gathered at sewing circles to produce all manner of goods for the men in gray. As the Confederacy faced financial ruin, Southern women demonstrated their *patriotism by staging fund-raisers or sacrificing heirlooms. Even in its heyday, Southern voluntarism did not spawn bodies comparable to the North's national commissions, and long before the war had ended the South had exhausted whatever funds the volunteers could raise.

Civil War voluntarism raises important questions of gender for historians. Women in both the North and South earned widespread notice and praise for their "noble" wartime sacrifices. Sacrifice for larger benevolent causes was nothing new for American women, but the scale of wartime activities and the paucity of civilian men (at least white men in the South) enabled some women to go beyond established practices. Southern historians—weighing the economic, political, and voluntaristic experiences of Confederate women—remain divided over how much, and for how long, the war opened the door to changing gender roles.

A few Northern women such as Clara *Barton rose to positions of national prominence, but the Sanitary Commission and the Christian Commission remained largely under male direction. Nevertheless, women in some communities (Chicago, for instance) took on unfamiliar authority, and the organizational skills and theories that scores of volunteers developed at the grassroots level proved crucial in molding the postwar activities of a key cohort of female activists. Overall, the conflict helped expand the range of experiences for many women while probably doing little to alter commonly held assumptions about *gender and war.

In addition to providing material and emotional assistance to the soldiers, home front volunteers sought to affect public opinion and otherwise contribute to wartime discourse. Most of the organized Civil War "propaganda" emerged from a handful of Northern publication societies. The first few years of the war saw the occasional printing of partisan pamphlets by interested individuals, a practice that had a long American tradition. In 1863, the Democrats raised the stakes with the establishment of the Society for the Diffusion of Useful Political Knowledge. Soon Philadelphia's Union League had countered with its own Board of Publications while the equally partisan Loyal Publication Society began operations in New York City. These, and a few other smaller bodies, flooded the North with millions of copies of several hundred political publications, many of which aimed to sway the electorate in 1864. Some authors wrote extremely sophisticated pamphlets, examining esoteric constitutional issues; others aimed their rhetoric at a broader, less educated, audience. Taken together, these Northern pamphlets provided members of the Union League and their antagonists with a crucial vehicle for reaching a broad audience outside formal party politics. So did patriotic songs such as "Dixie" and "Battle Hymn of the Republic."

Conclusions. The Civil War home front offers a host of perspectives. The military historian can find seeds of success and failure in the goings-on behind the lines. For instance, although the South was outmanned and outgunned, a strong case can be made that the Confederacy's fall owed much to the loss of civilian morale. Scholars of race, gender, and class have mined the war years for evidence of both changing relationships and stubborn continuities. Emancipation forever reshaped American race relations, but racial inequalities persisted in both the North and South. Although wartime women earned approval for their highly public patriotic efforts, suffragists had to wait three more generations for the vote. Economic historians have dismissed the notion that the war launched a "takeoff" into postwar industrial growth, while stressing the importance of emancipation in reducing Southern agriculture.

The political and institutional history of the home front is full of interesting ironies. Focusing on the North, it is tempting to tell a tale of Lincoln and the Republican Party using the pressures of war to promote sweeping national reform. After all, the legislative litany includes taxation, greenbacks, banking reform, conscription, and emancipation. But if we widen our lens to include the Confederacy—the bastion of militant individualism and states' rights—we find far more evidence of an expanded national state, including more aggressive conscription and a much greater federal role in economic affairs. In truth, both regions remained devoted to tradition and localism throughout the war. Jefferson Davis and the Confederacy went further than the Union in using the machinery of a central government to support the war effort, but only because conditions required it.

[*See also* Agriculture and War; Civil Liberties and War; Congress, War, and the Military; Economy and War; Industry and War; Labor and War; Race Relations and War; Society and War.]

• Emory Thomas, *The Confederate Nation: 1861–1865*, 1979. Phillip Shaw Paludan, *"A People's Contest": The Union and the Civil War, 1861–1865*, 1988. George C. Rable, *Civil Wars: Women and the Crisis of Southern Nationalism*, 1989. Roger Ransom, *Conflict and Compromise: The Political Economy of Slavery, Emancipation and the American Civil War*, 1989. Richard F. Bensel, *Yankee Leviathan: The Origins of Central State Authority in America, 1859–1877*, 1990. Maris A. Vinovskis, ed., *Toward a Social History of the American Civil War: Exploratory Essays*, 1990. James W. Geary, *We Need Men: The Union Draft in the Civil War*, 1991. Mark E. Neely, *The Fate of Liberty: Abraham Lincoln and Civil Liberties*, 1991. Catherine Clinton and Nina Silber, eds., *Divided Houses: Gender and the Civil War*, 1992. James M. McPherson, *Ordeal By Fire: The Civil War and Reconstruction*, 1982; 2nd ed. 1992. J. Matthew Gallman, *The North Fights the Civil War: The Home Front*, 1994. Drew Faust, *Mothers of Invention*, 1996.
                                                    —J. Matthew Gallman

CIVIL WAR (1861–65): POSTWAR IMPACT

By their very nature, civil wars leave open wounds and unsettled scores behind. Despite the recently rejuvenated notion that the Civil War of 1861–65 created modern America, the legacy is far more ambiguous and complex. The war stifled the Confederacy's bid for national independence and destroyed the institution of slavery upon which it rested. The ensuing peace—specifically, the Radical *Reconstruction crafted by the Republican Party—reunited the nation economically and politically, yet did so on terms that not just the defeated Confederates came to resent. Small wonder that each generation has assessed the war through the prism of its own central political concerns.

The veterans from both sides were the first and probably the most partisan revisionists. On some points they found near unanimity: Northern *veterans believed they had saved the Union and given a new birth to freedom; Confederate veterans believed they had fought nobly for independence and might well have prevailed had their resources not given out. But both argued endlessly over the specifics.

The legions of popular and academic authors who have studied the war have discerned no clearer pattern of grand truths from the clutter of documented facts. Moreover, today, thousands of ordinary citizens not only retrace the soldiers' steps literally across preserved battlefields but claim expertise about the war as they do for no other event in U.S. history. Partly because of and partly in spite of such interest, attempting to understand the long-term impact of the Civil War has produced as much conflict as consensus.

From a strictly military standpoint, the war appears to many historians as the first modern war. A technological explosion around midcentury accounted for such innovations as rifled small arms and ordnance, armor-plated steam vessels, and primitive *machine guns and *submarines. Corresponding changes in *transportation and *communications helped make the Civil War more like World War I than *Napoleonic warfare. Yet old-fashioned tactics retained grisly currency, and both armies depended upon animal power—mules for supply and horses for tactical mobility—to the very end. Clearly, this was a transitional time wherein elements of the old and the new were mixed.

In its unprecedented requirements for men and goods, the Civil War called forth novel administrative skills and structures. The Confederate central government took a commanding role in these affairs, largely due to the comparatively underdeveloped industrial and transportation infrastructure in the plantation states before the war. Although the U.S. government in Washington increased dramatically in size, and expenditures during Abraham *Lincoln's presidency surpassed those of all his predecessors combined, Northern officials relied upon conventional market mechanisms and the lure of profits rather than coercion to meet their need for supplies. Whereas early in the war, bureaucrats with extensive administrative experience—such as Edwin M. *Stanton, whom Lincoln appointed secretary of war—were in short supply, the crucible of war quickly changed that.

From the standpoint of manpower, both sides departed sharply from precedent in resorting to *conscription to replenish their ranks. Precisely because conscription was so European a practice, Americans had abhorred it from the time of the *Revolutionary War. Citizens of the Confederate states, who adopted the draft a year before their Yankee counterparts did, also suffered levies upon food, wagons, work animals, and other militarily useful supplies. Although Northerners escaped such material tolls and their demoralizing consequences, they found much to criticize in the draft of men. The *New York City anti-draft riots of July 1863 epitomized the opposition. Even apart from the disturbances that it produced, the Union's draft worked poorly. As a result, the military-run, undemocratic conscription served largely as a negative example for the future.

The North's other major overture toward filling the ranks, the recruitment of *African Americans in the military, left a much more significant legacy. This policy reflected the North's commitment to destroying slavery, as best expressed in the *Emancipation Proclamation of 1 January 1863. Besides its grant of freedom to slaves in the Confederate states, the proclamation also provided for the wholesale incorporation of black men into the *Union army.

Like most other innovations of the Civil War years, the legacy of this *mobilization was mixed. On the negative side of the ledger, African American soldiers endured separate and unequal treatment to the end. When the demographics of *demobilization dictated that they would play a major role in occupying the defeated South, Washington forestalled that opportunity by assigning black regulars to positions along the Atlantic coast and the border with Mexico, far removed from possible contact with former slaves. And for their part, black sailors soon found themselves again subjected to the prewar quota system (5% of total enlistments) and consigned systematically to the ratings of cook and steward.

On the positive side of the ledger, African Americans won a permanent—though neither undisputed nor uncheckered—place in the armed forces of the reunited nation. The all-black 24th and 25th Infantry and 9th and 10th Cavalry Regiments (the fabled "*Buffalo" Soldiers) created a legacy of loyalty and sacrifice that persisted well into the twentieth century. Even more important, the service of nearly 200,000 black soldiers and sailors—the overwhelming majority of whom were former slaves—established a claim for citizenship rights that the nation attempted to satisfy in the Thirteenth, Fourteenth, and Fifteenth Amendments to the U.S. Constitution. Participation by former slaves in the political life of the ex-Confederate states followed. Affiliation with the Republican Party, the party of Lincoln, persisted among black voters until the 1930s. Union army veterans played an important part in this allegiance.

The war conferred a similarly mixed legacy upon the officer corps of the army and the navy. Although most volunteer officers returned to civilian life after the war, men who opted for continued service encountered considerable frustration. Reduced from their inflated if temporary (brevet) rank to the more prosaic regular rank in the shrunken regular army, officers faced an abundance of boredom and danger but little glory on the western frontier. Naval officers likewise languished in the smaller postwar navy, often spending years at the same grade with little hope of promotion in a fleet a mere shadow of its wartime counterpart. In part because of their isolation from civilian life, officers in both branches cultivated a strong sense of professionalism. Postwar military school systems helped the officer corps regain the collective confidence it had enjoyed at the end of the Civil War.

Scholars have assessed the impact of the war on the national government variously over the years. Early studies stressed the transformation of the prewar state of limited constitutional authority into a powerful centralized government, which the metamorphosis of "the United States" from a plural to a singular construction neatly captures. During the past generation, social scientists from various disciplines have examined the Civil War from the standpoint of state formation. Often they employ a comparative method that likens the process of national consolidation in the United States with that in late nineteenth-century Germany, Italy, Japan, and Brazil. Whereas some scholars take the approach that centralized bureaucratic states are the functional byproducts of industrial society, most insist that historically specific considerations determine the evolution of the state in relation to society. From the latter perspective, the Civil War presents a treasure trove of insights.

With nearly monopolistic control over the wartime government in Washington, the Republican Party enacted pivotal measures regarding homesteads, banking and the currency, education, railroads, and the freed slaves. But even in such circumstances, policymakers found it easier to prosecute military victory than to secure the peace. Amid increasingly rancorous debate, congressional Republicans seized the Reconstruction process from President Andrew *Johnson, guaranteed the freedom and citizenship of the former slaves, and imposed temporary military rule on the South. Obstinate opposition from white southerners coupled with growing disenchantment among white northerners soon fragmented the Republican coalition. Party moderates backed away from guaranteeing citizenship rights, from supporting the elected Republican governments in the former Confederate states, and from radically transforming the southern economy. Content in the knowledge that the South (like the West) was subject to the economic dominion of the Northeast, Washington acquiesced in southern "home rule." Former Confederate soldiers led the way in forcibly removing freedmen from public life.

If students of the late nineteenth-century South tend to view the consequences of the war as devastating to the regional economy, students of the national economy show far less unanimity over the effects of the Civil War. Some seventy years ago, historians Charles R. and Mary A. Beard (1927) declared that the war constituted "The Second American Revolution," which removed southern agrarians from national power and thereby made possible the industrial transformation of the nation after 1865. Historians who have examined this thesis using assorted interpretive frameworks and techniques have reached no firm consensus. Whereas some would confirm the Beards' assertion that the war ushered in the industrial transformation, others perceive it as a retardant force. Given the accelerating pace of industrialization before the war, the critics argue, the war in fact slowed development, largely due to the diversion of human and material resources. Yet statistics of economic performance do not tell the whole tale.

The true measure of the war's economic impact lies in its consolidation of federal dominion over the North American landmass the United States had accumulated during the first half of the nineteenth century. Just as reconstructing the South was key to this objective—even if remaking the southern economy along demonstrably northern lines was of secondary importance—controlling the Indians of the Great Plains figured prominently in the larger scheme. Although the wartime and postwar conflicts between Anglo-Americans and Native Americans grew out of grievances present in such encounters from the seventeenth century onward, there were many new factors in the equation.

Aside from the growing desire of white homesteaders and prospectors for access to Indian lands, railroad interests laden with federal land grants increased the demand. Missionaries and officials of the Bureau of Indian Affairs made strong overtures on behalf of "civilizing the savages," all of which strengthened the federal commitment to confining each tribe to a specific reservation (and by 1887 produced the Dawes Severalty Act and the fixation with individual land allotments). Civil War politics further complicated the mix, the most famous instances being the "disloyalty" of the Five Civilized Tribes in the Indian Territory and the violent rebellions undertaken by the Sioux on the northern plains and the Comanches in the southwest desert. When in the late 1860s, Gen. William Tecumseh *Sherman and Gen. Philip H. *Sheridan set out to subdue the Indians' resistance to federal authority, they took full advantage of the new weaponry and means of transportation that the Civil War had proven. Their use of the new tactics of unconditional surrender—winter campaigns, making war on women and children, and destroying villages and crops in the *Plains Indians Wars forced the Native Americans to succumb.

In sum, the Civil War has left a mixed, even contentious, legacy in the different sections of the nation and among the different sectors of the population. Moreover, as each generation born since the war has found—alternately to its delight and its dismay—that legacy is not fixed and immutable. Instead, it is subject to reinterpretation. Perhaps the recurrent controversy that surrounds the public display of the Confederate battle flag best illustrates a key interpretive insight: though struggles over the legacy of the war may degenerate into mere skirmishes or escalate into full-scale wars, their guns, unlike those of 1861–65, will never fall completely silent.

[*See also* Economy and War; Industry and War; Society and War; State, The.]

• Charles A. and Mary R. Beard, *The Rise of American Civilization,* 2 vols., 1927. Jay Luvaas, *The Military Legacy of the Civil War,* 1959. Emory M. Thomas, *The Confederacy as a Revolutionary Experience,* 1971. Robert M. Utley, *Frontier Regulars: The United States Army and the Indian, 1866–1890,* 1973. Ira Berlin, Joseph P. Reidy, and Leslie S. Rowland, eds., *The Black Military Experience,* 1982. Edward Hagerman, *The American Civil War and the Origins of Modern Warfare,* 1988. Philip Shaw Paludan, *"A People's Contest": The Union and Civil War, 1861–1865,* 1988. Richard Franklin Bensel, *Yankee Leviathan: The Origins of Central State Authority in America, 1859–1877,* 1990. Theda Skocpol, *Protecting Soldiers and Mothers: The Political Origins of Social Policy in the United States,* 1992.
—Joseph P. Reidy

CIVIL WAR (1861–65): CHANGING INTERPRETATIONS

The Civil War had not even ended before it was being interpreted, although in many cases, the earliest interpretations of the war sprang directly out of the justifications Northerners and Southerners had offered for beginning and sustaining it. Resentful Southerners like Edward Pollard in *The Lost Cause* (1867) announced that the South had waged the war in defense of a genteel, noncompetitive agrarian society, and only the brute force of Northern numbers and weapons had defeated it. Confederate leaders like Jefferson *Davis and Alexander H. Stephens defined the "Lost Cause" as a political one, in which the Confederacy stood for a strict reading of the federal Constitution and resistance to the centralization of power in the national government. The place of slavery in these Southern interpretations was reduced to a pretext Northerners had seized upon for provoking the war.

By contrast, Northerners in the first two decades after the war interpreted it primarily as a moral crusade against slavery. Isaac N. Arnold in his *History of Abraham Lincoln and the Overthrow of Slavery* (1866), John W. Draper in his *History of the American Civil War* (1868–70), and former Senator Henry Wilson in his *History of the Rise and Fall of the Slave Power* (1872–77) all insisted that the war had been caused by the wicked ambitions of a "slave power" conspiracy to subvert American republican virtue.

By the end of the century, as Americans were faced with the problems of industrialization, immigration, and labor unrest, it became easier to downplay the divisiveness of the war and recast it as the painful but necessary forge in which a single, unshakable American national identity was created. Academic historians, from James Ford Rhodes—*History of the United States from the Compromise of 1850* (1893–1919) to Arthur C. Cole—*The Irrepressible Conflict, 1850–1865* (1934), urged that slavery be seen as an institutional problem which the war removed in the interest of achieving national unification, rather than as the basis for a conspiratorial "slave power." However, professional historians who were shaped by the economic Progressive tradition and the horrors of World War I took this as evidence that the moral rhetoric of the war, whether for abolitionism or the "Lost Cause," had been hollow from the start. In Avery Craven's *The Repressible Conflict, 1830–1861* (1939) and James G. Randall's multivolume history of the Lincoln administration and his long-lived textbook, *The Civil War and Reconstruction* (1937), the war became a needless conflict, triggered by a generation of blundering politicians, since slavery would have eventually proven economically unprofitable, they argued. Or worse than that, Charles and Mary Beard, in *The Rise of American Civilization* (1927), declared that the real agenda of the war had been the dominance of the national economy by Northern industry and finance. Southern historians like Charles Ramsdell and Frank L. Owsley, who were inspired by the unrepentant anticapitalism of the Southern agrarian movement of the 1930s, converted the Beards's thesis into an unintended echo of the "Lost Cause" myth, in which the South appeared as a helpless victim of Northern cultural and economic aggression.

The economic emphasis of the Progressive historians was itself challenged by the moral commitments of World War II. The defeat of totalitarian ideologies abroad, and later the power of the civil rights movement to shake the conscience of the nation, once again made it possible to see the Civil War as a moral moment. Kenneth Stampp's *And the War Came: The North and the Secession Crisis, 1860–1861* (1950) defiantly insisted that the moral argument over slavery was, after all, the vital element in the making of the war. Allan Nevius, over the course of his multivolume *Ordeal of the Union* (1947–50) and *The War for the Union* (1959–60), also gradually moved slavery back to the center of the war's meaning. James M. McPherson's two single-volume histories, *Ordeal by Fire: The Civil War and Reconstruction* (1982) and *Battle Cry of Freedom: The Civil War Era* (1988), similarly shifted from treating the war as a Beardian conflict between a "modernizing" North and an underdeveloped South to describing it as the solution to the ideological contradiction of slavery in a liberal republic.

The tremendous upsurge in Civil War literature which began shortly before the centennial of the war in 1961, and which was renewed in the late 1970s and 1980s, encouraged the exploration of a number of new interpretations of specific aspects of the war. Grady McWhiney and Perry D. Jamieson resurrected the older arguments about the South's cultural uniqueness and applied them controversially to Southern military tactics, arguing that the South's "Celtic" culture explained the Confederacy's propensity for costly head-on offensives. By contrast, political and intellectual historians argued that the Confederacy had not been unique enough: David Donald, Drew Faust, Paul Escott, Emory Thomas, and the authors of *Why the South Lost the Civil War* (Richard Beringer, Herman Hattaway, Archer Jones, and William N. Still) inverted the old nationalist argument and claimed that the Confederacy was as much an example as the North of an experiment in nation-building. George Rable, in *The Confederate Republic: A Revolution Against Politics* (1994), argued that the Confederacy actually saw its political experiment in the war as a struggle to resist ideological uniqueness and reassert the pristine virtues of eighteenth-century republicanism.

The question of the Civil War's significance in military terms has taken on particularly new force in recent studies. The impact of British military social historians like John Keegan in the 1970s set off calls for the application of a "face of battle" interpretation to Civil War combat studies, and helped produce innovative studies of Civil War soldier behavior from Reid Mitchell and Gerald Linderman. Much more subject to debate were challenges to two cherished notions about the overall strategic significance of the war. One of these, beginning with David Donald and T. Harry Williams, claimed that Civil War field strategy had been dominated by the ideological lessons of Antoine Henri *Jomini and Dennis Hart Mahan, both of which fostered a passion for Napoleonic-style headlong offensive that had been rendered out-of-date by the rifled *musket. Both Williams and Donald believed that a handful of federal generals, headed by Ulysses S. *Grant, learned to ignore Jomini and Mahan, and to master the new lessons of industrial technology and *communications sufficiently to lead the North to victory.

A second and related interpretation of Civil War strategy located the center of the Civil War's "modernity" in its development into a "total" war. From T. Harry Williams in *Lincoln and His Generals* (1952) up through McPherson's *Battle Cry of Freedom* and Philip S. Paludan's *"A People's Contest": The Union and the Civil War* (1988), the Civil War was repeatedly portrayed as the first example of warfare consciously directed at civilian as well as military targets.

Both of these views, however, came under strenuous criticism during the late 1980s: Edward Hagerman's *The American Civil War and the Origins of Modern Warfare* (1988) and the authors of the massive 1983 study *How the North Won: A Military History of the Civil War* (Herman Hattaway and Archer Jones) downplayed the extent of Jomini's influence on Civil War strategy. Paddy Griffith, a British military historian, argued that technology, whether in the form of the rifled *musket or the railroads, could have made little difference on the small-scale battlefields of North America, where, he said, the decisive factor was the sheer amateurism of Union and Confederate officers and volunteers. Above all, Mark Neely sharply criticized the notion that the Civil War had involved "total" warfare by questioning whether the Civil War had ever involved in any significant way the targeted destruction of enemy civilian lives and property or the curtailment of domestic civilian civil rights by the military.

One last major debate has concerned the quality and substance of Civil War military leadership. Robert E. *Lee and Grant had been held up in many popular histories as antitheses in Civil War leadership, with Lee cast in Douglas S. Freeman's four-volume *R. E. Lee* (1934–35) as a defensive patrician who carefully hoarded the Confederacy's limited human resources, and Grant portrayed in biographies like William S. McFeely's *Grant: A Biography* (1981) as an unimaginative "butcher," willing to achieve victory by using the North's numerical superiority to grind down the Confederate armies through attrition. Lee's image, however, began to crumble in 1977 with Thomas Connelly's *The Marble Man: Robert E. Lee and His Image in American Society*, which portrayed Lee as a fatalist always willing to yield to aggressive and costly impulses for the offensive. Grant, by comparison, was defended by biographers as diverse as Bruce Catton and Brooks Simpson as a swift-moving strategic thinker, whose triumph over Lee in

1865 was a demonstration of superior management and operational skill.

Similarly, comparative evaluations of Presidents Jefferson Davis and Abraham *Lincoln as commanders in chief have usually favored Lincoln as the better overall strategist, with David Potter and T. Harry Williams holding up Lincoln as a model of strategic wisdom and even the head of the first "modern" staff system. But throughout the 1980s, Jefferson Davis's star rose considerably, with Ludwell Johnson, Hattaway and Jones, and Steven E. Woodworth all underscoring that Davis was an intelligent risk taker who ably managed and cooperated with his generals.

The controlling factor in these interpretations, apart from the debates over the merits of certain commanders or the details of specific battles, has been the place and understanding accorded slavery. The weight given to the motives of leaders, the role of economic conflict, and even the significance of civilian and troop morale, have all in the end contained judgments about the role of slavery. In the interpretation of a war so charged with political meaning, and which so clearly involved political direction-giving, this not likely to change.

[See also Commander in Chief, President as; Disciplinary Views of War: Military History.]

• Thomas J. Pressly, Americans Interpret Their Civil War, 1954. David Donald, ed., Why The North Won the Civil War, 1960. Marvin R. Cain, "A 'Face of Battle' Needed: An Assessment of Motives and Men in Civil War Historiography," Civil War History, 28 (March 1982), pp. 5–27. Joseph T. Glatthaar, "The 'New' Civil War History: An Overview," Pennsylvania Magazine of History and Biography, 115 (July 1991), pp. 339–69. Gabor Boritt, Why the Confederacy Lost, 1992. Gabor Boritt, ed., Lincoln the War President: The Gettysburg Lectures, 1992. Gary W. Gallagher, The Confederate War, 1997. Allen C. Guelzo, The Crisis of the American Republic: A History of the Civil War and Reconstruction, 1994.
—Allen C. Guelzo

CLARK, MARK (1896–1984), general, and one of five top U.S. Army commanders in World War II. A third-generation soldier, Clark was born in Madison Barracks, New York, the son of an army colonel. Graduating from West Point in 1917, Clark became an infantry captain and was wounded in France. During the interwar period he served at various military posts, and graduated from the Command and General Staff School and the Army War College.

In World War II, General Clark played a major role in preparing the invasion of North Africa, including leading a successful secret mission by submarine to gain the cooperation of Vichy French officials. Such collaboration drew criticism, but it was defended as military expediency, and resistance to the invasion in November 1942 proved minimal.

Clark then trained and led the U.S. Fifth Army in the invasion and conquest of *Italy in 1943–45. The Allied campaign up the mountainous Italian Peninsula was arduous, and its tactics drew some serious criticism. As U.S. commander and, after December 1944, Allied commander in Italy, Clark bore much of the controversy, including that over the Battle of *Anzio, the bombing of the abbey on Monte Cassino, and the bloody defeat of the 36th (Texas) Division, which lost 2,100 men in 24 hours attempting to cross the Rapido River.

In June 1944, Clark led his forces into Rome. Some postwar critics, including Dan Kurzman in The Race for Rome (1975), argued that Clark's desire to be the first to seize an Axis capital took precedence over the more important objective of cutting off and entrapping retreating German forces. The Germans built a new line that held until April 1945.

After the war, Clark as a four-star general, commanded U.S. occupation forces in Austria (1945–47). During the *Korean War, he succeeded Matthew B. *Ridgway in April 1952 in command of *United Nations forces. In July 1953, he signed the armistice and initiated the difficult prisoner exchange.

Retiring from the army, Clark served as president of The Citadel Military College of South Carolina (1953–65). Thereafter, he championed continued *Conscription and expanded U.S. military effort during the *Vietnam War.

Mark Clark's military career was frequently embroiled in dispute, in part due to his readiness to take controversial positions in difficult circumstances. Additionally, although an individual of undeniable courage and commitment, Clark lacked the personal aura of the other top U.S. Army commanders of World War II.

• Mark W. Clark, Calculated Risk, 1950. Mark W. Clark, From the Danube to the Yalu, 1954. Martin Blumenson, Mark Clark, 1984.
—John Whiteclay Chambers II

CLAUSEWITZ, CARL VON (1780–1831), Prussian general and theorist of war. Clausewitz's On War (1832) is the most important general study of war. Incomplete and in need of revision at the time of Clausewitz's death, its sometimes disconnected arguments are typically remembered as relatively simple propositions, which do not always reflect the complexity of the reasoning that produced them. Among these are: that war is not an autonomous phenomenon, but a political instrument; that the violence of war knows no theoretical limit, and is prone to escalate; that war's theoretically boundless violence is tempered in practice by the political goals of the belligerents, and by the "friction" to which military operations are subject; that armed forces possess "centers of gravity," whose successful attack promises the most decisive military results; that all attacks lose impetus as they proceed; and that the defensive is the stronger form of war. These and similar insights, although by no means universally accepted, are well established as foundational elements of serious strategic theory in the United States and throughout the world.

Clausewitz's work first attracted widespread attention among English-speaking readers in the aftermath of Germany's victory over France in 1871, a success that Prussia's chief of staff, Helmuth von Moltke, attributed in part to the influence of Clausewitz's ideas. The first English translation of On War appeared two years later, and thereafter Clausewitz acquired a growing reputation among military professionals as a proponent of operations that were swift, violent, offensive, and decisive in character to overcome the strength of defense conducted with modern weapons—an interpretation that owed more to the perceived requirements of industrialized warfare than to a close reading of his work. After 1914, Clausewitz's writings were studied for clues to German military conduct, and increasingly misread as harbingers of Prussian militarism. By the outbreak of World War II, it was not unusual for American authors to find significant links between Clausewitz and Hitler.

This baleful trend was checked primarily by the work of German expatriates like Herbert Rosinski and Hans Rothfels, who presented Clausewitz's ideas with greater comprehensiveness, and greater attention to their original context, than most of their Anglo-American counterparts had done. Of special significance was Rothfels's contribution to the first edition of *Makers of Modern Strategy* (1943), which demonstrated the analytic power of Clausewitz's identification of war as a political instrument, and also the fundamental significance of what Clausewitz called the "dual nature" of war, by which he had sought to reconcile the historical preponderance of limited war with the theoretically unlimited violence of war as such. Rothfels also portrayed Clausewitz himself as a figure of great intellectual integrity, striving for a disinterested and universally valid understanding of war.

Rothfels's essay set a new intellectual standard and a new direction for Clausewitz scholarship in English, which reached a culminating point in 1976 with the simultaneous appearance of Peter Paret's magisterial *Clausewitz and the State*, and a new translation of *On War* by Paret and Michael Howard. Clausewitz's insistence on war's political nature acquired special resonance in the nuclear era, when the means of organized violence so often threatened to dwarf the aims of policy; while his emphasis on the preeminence of limited war throughout history spoke directly to those who had endured the frustrations of Korea and Vietnam. At the end of the twentieth century, Clausewitz's ideas permeated the professional education and outlook of American military officers. When Michael Howard, writing in the wake of the *Persian Gulf War (1991), nominated Clausewitz (in the *New York Times*) as "Man of the Year," the proposal was rightly seen less as a jest than as tacit acknowledgment that, 160 years after his death, Clausewitz's influence and reputation had never been greater.

[*See also* War: Nature of War.]

• Raymond Aron, *Clausewitz: Philosopher of War,* 1976; English ed. 1983. Peter Paret and Daniel Moran, eds. and trans., *Carl von Clausewitz: Historical and Political Writings,* 1992.

—Daniel Moran

CLAY, LUCIUS (1897–1978), army general and diplomat. Born in Marietta, Georgia, Clay graduated from West Point in 1918 as a military engineer. His career departed from the routine with assignments to the International Naval Conference in Brussels in 1934 and to the staff of Gen. Douglas *MacArthur in the Philippines in 1937.

During World War II, Clay became deputy director of the Office of War Mobilization and Reconversion (1944). In 1945, he served briefly as deputy to Gen. Dwight *Eisenhower, and then as deputy military governor of the U.S. zone in Germany. From 1947 to 1949 he served as commander of U.S. forces in Europe, and as U.S. military governor in Germany. Clay won acclaim for his direction of operations including the *Berlin Airlift in the American response to the Soviets' blockade of the western access routes to Berlin in 1948–49. His determination and his blunt criticism of the Soviets made him a symbol of the U.S. support for West Berlin. He retired from the army as a full general in May 1949, and served as chairman of the board of Continental Can Company from 1950 to 1962.

At the time of the Berlin Wall crisis of 1961, President John F. *Kennedy recalled Clay to active duty to symbolize

U.S. commitment to the city. Clay served from September 1961 to May 1962 as Kennedy's personal representative in Berlin, with the rank of ambassador. The crisis reached a flashpoint in October 1961, when, with Kennedy's permission to take a strong stance, Clay ordered ten M-48 tanks to the entrypoint of the wall, "Checkpoint Charlie," where they were met with a similar Soviet armored force. Kennedy made a secret appeal to Soviet premier Nikita Khrushchev to defuse the crisis, and both sides withdrew their *tanks after the show of force.

[*See also* Berlin Crises; Germany, U.S. Military Involvement in.]

• Lucius D. Clay, *Decision in Germany,* 1950. Lucius D. Clay, *The Papers of General Lucius D. Clay: Germany 1945–1949,* 2 vols., ed. Jean Edward Smith, 1974. John H. Backer, *Winds of History: The German Years of Lucius DuBignon Clay,* 1983.

—John Whiteclay Chambers II

CLIFFORD, CLARK (1906–1998), longtime presidential adviser and secretary of defense. In his role as adviser to many Democratic presidents, the Washington lawyer Clark Clifford was extraordinarily influential at decisive moments of the *Cold War. As special White House counsel during President Harry S. *Truman's first term, the Missourian worked with George Elsey in 1946 on a key top-secret report to Truman, assessing U.S. Soviet relations. Explaining Soviet policy as a quest for domination, Clifford and Elsey recommended expanded military programs and foreign aid efforts to support potential allies overseas. Clifford also helped draft the *National Security Act of 1947 that created the Department of *Defense and the *National Security Council. Early in 1948, he played a key role in the debate over Palestine by supporting partition and U.S. recognition of the state of Israel.

Resuming private law practice in 1949, Clifford developed an important corporate clientele that made him one of the wealthiest and most influential attorneys in Washington for decades, through the 1980s. Moreover, he developed close personal, advisory, and legal relationships with leading Democratic politicians, including John F. *Kennedy. During the Kennedy-Johnson administrations, he served as a member, and then chairman, of the President's Foreign Intelligence Advisory Board (PFIAB), where he strongly supported efforts to modernize intelligence collection capabilities by adopting the latest electronic and satellite technologies.

As an informal adviser to President Lyndon B. *Johnson, Clifford was highly critical of escalating the Vietnam War, which he believed could not be won. Johnson initially rejected his recommendations for a negotiated settlement, but Clifford kept his access to the White House by publicly supporting the war. When Robert S. *McNamara left his position as secretary of defense, Johnson appointed Clifford his successor on 18 January 1968; his official tenure lasted from March 1968 to January 1969.

As Clifford began his work at the *Pentagon, the Vietnamese Communists launched the *Tet Offensive, a development that confirmed Clifford's growing pessimism about the war. Worried that the "bottomless pit" of war could wreck America's social fabric, he began strongly to advocate disengagement. By the end of 1968, he had helped convince the president to stop the bombing of North Vietnam, begin negotiations with the Viet Cong, and support a greater South Vietnamese role in the fighting—a move that presaged Richard M. *Nixon's later "Vietnamization" policy.

Clifford also played a central role in another Johnson initiative renewed by the Nixon administration: an attempt to begin strategic arms limitation negotiations with Moscow, which foundered when the Soviets invaded Czechoslovakia in August 1968. However, Clifford contributed to escalation of the *arms race by approving air force programs to test multiple independently targetable reentry vehicle (MIRVs), also in August 1968. Returning to private law practice after he left the Pentagon in January 1969, Clifford remained a Washington influential, although financial scandal tarnished his reputation at the end of his life.

[See also Vietnam War: Domestic Course; Vietnam War: Changing Interpretations.]

• Clark M. Clifford, Counsel to the President: A Memoir, 1991.

—William Burr

CLINTON, BILL (1946–), forty-second president of the United States. William Jefferson (Bill) Clinton was born in Hope, Arkansas, graduated from Georgetown University in 1968, went to Oxford University as a Rhodes Scholar (1968–70), and then Yale Law School. With the exception of 1981–83, he served as Democratic governor of Arkansas from 1979 until 1993 when he became president, defeating the Republican incumbent George *Bush and a third-party candidate, Ross Perot.

From the beginning, President Clinton had a rocky relationship with the military. During the campaign, it was alleged that as a college student he had dodged the draft and publicly protested the *Vietnam War. As president, his first policy action was to pledge to end the ban on *gay men and lesbians in the military. The attempt to allow homosexuals to serve openly in the armed forces faced vigorous opposition in the *Pentagon and the Congress. Clinton ultimately accepted a compromise dubbed the "don't ask, don't tell" policy.

Clinton's first secretary of defense, former representative Les *Aspin, Jr., initiated a "bottom-up" review of the post–*Cold War military. His successor, William Perry, further reduced the armed forces by closing bases, capping expenditures, and emphasizing reservists. Active duty personnel declined in Clinton's first term from 1.7 million to under 1.5 million. William Cohen became secretary of defense after Clinton's reelection in 1996. The former Republican senator from Maine sought to maintain a 1.4 million active duty force while boosting weapons spending by 50 percent and simultaneously keeping the defense budget at about $255 billion. Skeptics predicted more troop and procurement cuts instead.

In his foreign policy, Clinton often combined brinkmanship with indecision over the use of military force. He escalated the use of force in Somalia, then withdrew in 1994 after the killing of U.S. Army *Rangers. Later that year, however, his brinkmanship with North Korea contributed to Pyongyang's agreement to dismantle the reactors that could make *nuclear weapons. His vacillating policy on the military junta in Haiti ultimately led in September 1994 to the dispatch of an airborne invasion force, recalled only at the last minute when a negotiating team, led by former President Jimmy *Carter, convinced the junta to step down. A combined *United Nations/U.S. oc-

cupation force landed peacefully and ensured the return of Haiti's democratically elected president. In the *Bosnian Crisis, Clinton avoided ground intervention until the peace accord of 1995, then included 20,000 Americans in the UN peacekeeping force, which was still in Bosnia four years later.

After a terrorist bombing of U.S. embassies in Nairobi and Khartoum, he ordered sea-launched missile attacks on a plant in the Sudan and a terrorist camp in Afghanistan in August 1998. Faced with Saddam *Hussein's blocking of UN weapons inspectors and challenging of U.S. air surveillance, Clinton ordered sporadic American air attacks against Iraqi military targets beginning in December 1998. Domestically, in January 1999, Clinton was acquitted in a Senate trial on House impeachment charges involving a sex scandal. In March 1999, he brought the Czech Republic, Hungary, and Poland into *NATO. In the Balkans, Clinton announced on 23 March 1999, a decision to use force to halt Serbian aggression against ethnic Albanians in the *Kosovo Crisis; the next day, NATO began air strikes against the Serbs. The war lasted 78 days.

[See also Commander in Chief, President as; Haiti, U.S. Military Intervention in; Middle East, U.S. Military Intervention in; Somalia, U.S. Military Intervention in.]

• David Maraniss, First in His Class: A Biography of Bill Clinton, 1995. Colin Campbell and Bert A. Rockman, eds., The Clinton Presidency: First Appraisals, 1995. Stanley Allen Renshon, High Hopes: The Clinton Presidency and the Politics of Ambition, 1996. Thomas H. Henrikson, Clinton's Foreign Policy in Somalia, Bosnia, Haiti, and North Korea, 1996.   —John Whiteclay Chambers II

CLINTON, SIR HENRY (1730–1795), British general. Sir Henry Clinton succeeded Sir William *Howe as commander in chief of British forces in the American colonies in 1778. Clinton inherited an army demoralized by Burgoyne's defeat at the Battles of *Saratoga and a war radically altered by France's 1778 alliance with the Americans. An aggressive and annoying junior officer, Clinton had continually bombarded Howe with ambitious plans to crush the *Continental army. As commander in chief, however, Clinton acquired Howe's caution. He fought the Continental army only once in 1778, at the Battle of *Monmouth. In 1779, his army saw only limited action that included taking two minor American forts. The next year, Clinton captured Charleston. This brilliant victory, however, could not overcome his reputation for caution. London named a more aggressive general, Lord Charles *Cornwallis, his second in command in 1779; now Clinton was ordered back to New York and Cornwallis took over in the South. Powerless to intervene in Cornwallis's campaigns, Clinton nevertheless became the scapegoat for Cornwallis's devastating defeat at the Battle of *Yorktown in 1781. Replaced by Gen. Guy Carleton in 1782, the embittered Clinton returned to England. He devoted the rest of his life to defending his tattered reputation.

[See also Revolutionary War: Military and Diplomatic Course.]

• William B. Willcox, Portrait of a General: Sir Henry Clinton in the War of Independence, 1964. George A. Billias, George Washington's Opponents, 1969.   —Jon T. Coleman

COAST GUARD, U.S. The Coast Guard has existed in various forms since 1790, although its name dates from 1915.

On 4 August 1790, President George *Washington signed an act of Congress "to regulate the collection of the duties imposed by law on the tonnage of ships or vessels, and on goods, wares, and merchandise, imported into the United States." Ten boats, "for securing the collection of the revenue," were to be built, and forty officers and men would be hired to operate them. In 1799, during the Undeclared Naval War with *France, Congress authorized the president to place the Revenue-Cutter Service (or "Revenue Marine," as it was often called in its early days) under the U.S. Navy in time of war or other national emergency.

In that capacity revenue cutters gained their first combat experience. In 1799 and 1800, they captured fifteen French vessels. During the *War of 1812, the Revenue Marine took several British prizes, though four of its vessels surrendered to British warships. Revenue cutters searched the Caribbean for pirates and slavers throughout the early nineteenth century, and patrolled the coast of Florida during the Seminole War of 1836—the only "Indian War" in which naval forces took part.

In 1843, the Treasury Department set up a Revenue Marine Bureau, headed by Capt. Alexander Fraser. He initiated a series of administrative reforms that made the service function on a military basis. In the *Mexican War of 1846–48 the Revenue Marine participated in the blockade of Mexico.

The Coast Guard cutter *Harriet Lane* took part in the first Union victories of the *Civil War: the operations against Forts Clark and Hatteras. The service assisted the *Union navy with the blockade of the Southern ports and the protection of northern shipping.

In 1876, Congress authorized the establishment of the Revenue-Cutter Service School of Instruction on board a training ship. (The school would move in 1918 to New London, Connecticut, becoming the nucleus of the U.S. Coast Guard Academy.)

In 1880, the service inaugurated the Bering Sea Patrol. The Coast Guard cutter *Bear* became a familiar sight in Alaskan waters, rescuing icebound whalers, providing medical services for the Eskimos, and enforcing the international seal protection treaty. Several scientists made oceanographic expeditions to the arctic in revenue cutters.

Thirteen revenue cutters served with the Union navy during the *Spanish-American War. The *McCulloch* participated in the Battle of *Manila Bay, and the *Hudson* towed a disabled navy torpedo boat out from under enemy fire in the Battle of Cardenas Bay.

In 1914, two years after the *Titanic* sank after hitting an iceberg, a Convention for the Safety of Life at Sea held in London established the International Ice Patrol, to be carried out by revenue cutters with financial support from the other signing countries.

The following year, President Woodrow *Wilson signed a law amalgamating the Revenue Cutter Service and the coastline Life-Saving Service, a civilian agency of the Treasury Department. The new service was headed by Commandant Ellsworth Price Bertholf. The government accepted his suggestion that "'Coast Guard' is the logical name for the old Revenue Cutter Service as well as the new combination." It was to "constitute a part of the military forces of the United States ... under the Treasury Department in time of peace and [to] operate as a part of the Navy, subject to the orders of the Secretary of the Navy, in time of war or when the President shall so direct."

During World War I, the Coast Guard was responsible for policing the massive shipping traffic that passed through American seaports. Several cutters served as convoy escorts. One, the *Tampa,* was sunk by a German submarine; two others were destroyed in collisions.

In 1924, Congress appropriated funds for the first Coast Guard aviation stations at Cape May, New Jersey, and Gloucester, Massachusetts. The airplane proved useful for search and rescue operations. Coast Guard cutters and aircraft formed the federal government's front-line defense during the Prohibition era against liquor smugglers.

In 1939, the Coast Guard expanded again when it absorbed the U.S. Lighthouse Service. On 1 November 1941, with U.S. entry into World War II imminent, President Roosevelt transferred the Coast Guard to the Navy Department.

World War II presented the Coast Guard with the most rigorous set of challenges it had faced yet. Wartime recruiting swelled the service's ranks to 171,000—including 12,000 members of the Women's Reserve (*SPARS). More than 51,000 volunteers enrolled in the Coast Guard Reserve. The Beach Patrol waged a tedious war against German espionage and sabateurs, and the Port Security program absorbed 20 percent of the service's personnel.

Coast Guard cutters and patrol boats traded their peacetime white paint for wartime camouflage; armed with depth charges, sonar gear, and substantial optimism, they were renamed convoy escorts and submarine chasers. The Coast Guard manned 351 navy vessels, ranging from troop transports to landing craft, and 288 vessels of the Army Transportation Corps. Primarily as landing craft operators, Coast Guardsmen took part in most of the amphibious campaigns in the Pacific, the Mediterranean and in the *D-Day landing. During the invasion of *Normandy, 60 Coast Guard patrol boats pulled some 150 survivors from the English Channel.

One of the Coast Guard's most vexing, if least publicized, wartime assignments was to patrol the waters around Greenland. Lt. Cdr. Edward H. "Iceberg" Smith took command of the Greenland Patrol, a handful of cutters, tugs, and smaller vessels. The *Northland* made the first American naval capture of the war by seizing a radio-equipped German trawler in September 1941.

Several converted merchant ships in Coast Guard service added significant footnotes to naval history. The *Cobb* was the site in June 1944 of the first landing of a helicopter on board a ship, and the *Sea Cloud,* a yacht converted to a weather ship, became in 1943 the first racially integrated vessel in U.S. naval service.

On 1 March 1942, the Bureau of Marine Inspection and Navigation was transferred from the Department of Commerce to the Coast Guard. That arrangement completed the administrative structure of the Coast Guard as it exists today.

During World War II, twenty-eight Coast Guard and Coast Guard–manned vessels were sunk. The service's wartime deaths totaled 1,030, including 572 killed in action. Coast Guard cutters and Coast Guard–manned naval vessels sank eleven enemy *submarines; a twelfth was sunk by a Coast Guard aircraft. Coast Guardsmen rescued more than 4,000 survivors from sinking of sunken vessels.

In 1945, the Coast Guard resumed its peacetime law enforcement and search and rescue functions. In 1948, Congress gave the service responsibility for operating the chain of LORAN (LOng-RAnge-Navigation) electronic aids to navigation. High-endurance cutters cruised the Ocean Stations—designated spots in the Atlantic and Pacific from which they radioed weather reports, collected scientific data, and assisted foundering ships and aircraft.

During the Red Scare of the 1950s, the Treasury Department ordered the Coast Guard to withhold licenses from merchant sailors suspected of subversive activity. Several labor unions filed protests against the Coast Guard in federal courts and before the United Nations.

Fidel Castro's takeover of Cuba confronted the Coast Guard with a major refugee problem, an exasperating one that was to continue for decades. In each Caribbean crisis, Coast Guard cutters have had the duty of intercepting refugees, and in accordance with the current edicts of the State Department, either escorting them to the United States or turning them away.

Coast Guard icebreakers have cruised to both poles, and break paths for shipping in the Great Lakes and other inland bodies of water each winter. In 1957, the cutters *Storis, Bramble,* and *Spar* forced their way from Bellot Strait on the west coast of Canada to Baffin Bay on the east coast, demonstrating the feasibility of a mercantile route north of North America.

In 1965 during the *Vietnam War, seventeen Coast Guard patrol craft helped inaugurate Operation Market Time, the navy's ongoing effort to sever the supply lines from North Vietnam to Viet Cong guerrillas in the South. More than 50 Coast Guard vessels and 8,000 Coast Guardsmen took part in the "brown-water" war in Vietnam destroying nearly 2,000 vessels at a cost in American casualties of 7 deaths and 53 wounded.

On 1 April 1967, the Coast Guard was transferred from the Department of the Treasury to the newly created Department of Transportation.

In 1996, women comprised about 7 percent of the Coast Guard's 37,000 active duty personnel. New London was the first service academy to accept female applicants, and in 1988, Lt. (J. G.) Beverly Kelly became the first woman to command a U.S. naval vessel, the patrol boat *Cape Newagen.*

The Coast Guard has seven peacetime missions: the enforcement of recreational boating safety regulations; search and rescue operations; the maintenance of aids to navigation; the enforcement of Merchant Marine safety regulations; environmental protection; the enforcement of fisheries, customs, and immigration laws; and port safety.

The commandant of the Coast Guard presides over the Eastern and Western Coast Guard Areas, which are subdivided into ten Coast Guard districts. The service is supported by a Coast Guard Reserve and the Coast Guard Auxiliary, which conducts recreational boat inspections, teaches boating courses, and assists in search and rescue missions.

The service's motto is *Semper paratus*—"Always ready."

[*See also* Coast Guard Reserve; Seminole Wars.]

• Stephen H. Evans, *The United States Coast Guard, 1790–1915: A Definitive History,* 1949. Malcolm F. Willoughby, *The U.S. Coast Guard in World War II,* 1957. Irving H. King, *George Washington's Coast Guard: Origins of the U.S. Revenue Cutter Service, 1789–1801,* 1978. Robert L. Scheina, *U.S. Coast Guard Cutters and Craft of World War II,* 1982. Robert E. Johnson, *Guardians of the Sea: History of the United States Coast Guard, 1915 to the Present,* 1987. Irving H. King, *The Coast Guard Under Sail: The United States Revenue Cutter Service, 1789–1865,* 1989. Arthur Pearcy, *A History of U.S. Coast Guard Aviation,* 1989. Robert L. Scheina, *U.S. Coast Guard Cutters and Craft, 1946–1990,* 1990. Donald L. Canney, *U.S. Coast Guard and Revenue Cutters, 1790–1935,* 1995.

—John A. Tilley

COAST GUARD RESERVE. The Coast Guard Reserve Act of 1939 was a response to the booming hobby of pleasure boating. The law created an organization of civilian boat owners who volunteered to assist the U.S. *Coast Guard in such activities as patrolling regattas and promoting marine safety.

On 19 February 1941, Congress passed a law restructuring the Coast Guard Reserve. The existing civilian organization was renamed the Coast Guard Auxiliary. A new Coast Guard Reserve would function as a source of military manpower, like the reserves of the other armed services.

Coast Guard reservists were divided into two categories. "Regular Reservists" were paid for their services and could be assigned to any duty. A "Temporary Reservist," or "Coast Guard TR," was an unpaid volunteer who served part time in some designated geographic area.

During World War II, the Coast Guard itself suspended regular enlistments; virtually all of the approximately 115,000 people who joined the service during the war served as reservists. That figure includes 51,000 temporary reservists and 12,000 members of the Women's Reserve, called *SPARS.

The Coast Guard Reserve and the Coast Guard Auxiliary became permanent institutions after the war. In 1994, the reserve had a strength of about 12,000 and auxiliary membership stood at about 34,000.

[*See also* Air Force Reserve; Navy Combat Branches.]

• Malcolm F. Willoughby, *The U.S. Coast Guard in World War II,* 1957. Robert E. Johnson, *Guardians of the Sea: History of the United States Coast Guard, 1915 to the Present,* 1987.

—John A. Tilley

CODING AND DECODING. *Cryptography,* the art of creating or deciphering secret writing, is an ancient military process with a rich history in the American military experience. U.S. coding and decoding expertise trailed that of European nations, particularly Britain, until World War II, but America became the premier cryptographic power during the Cold War and has maintained a lead in this field ever since. While military cryptography has been a powerful tool for uniformed leaders in obtaining information about an enemy's capabilities, limitations, and intentions, it is just as important to the commander in masking his own powers, vulnerabilities, and plans. In the rare case, such as the naval Battle of *Midway in 1942, American deciphering abilities have proven decisive. Cryptography normally supplies only partial solutions for military intelligence and counterintelligence problems. Coding and decoding is and has always been a "cat and mouse" game, the coder occasionally gaining a temporary advantage on those who intercept and decode, only to experience the shock of a role reversal at other times.

From the outset of U.S. military operations, cryptography was practiced, but the security of American codes and the ability to read an enemy's secret writing lagged behind the U.S. *Army and U.S. *Navy's mentors, the British. Codes and ciphers were personally used in the *Revolutionary War by both Gen. George Washington and the Continental Congress's Secret Committee. However,

British agents were quite successful in penetrating Washington's headquarters as well as gaining knowledge of Benjamin Franklin's diplomatic operations in Paris. American cryptographic skills made little difference in the outcome of the Revolutionary War.

During the nineteenth century, American military cryptography suffered from the same ills that plagued U.S. military and political *intelligence in general. There would be a flurry of coding and decoding activity in time of war, but with the coming of peace, cryptographic knowledge and skills would atrophy and have to be relearned again at the next outbreak of hostilities. The entire U.S. intelligence capability in this era can best be described as primitive. Those Americans who engaged in the craft were invariably amateurs.

This cycle was broken during the twentieth century through the efforts of Herbert O. Yardley, a State Department code clerk who demonstrated a capability to break foreign ciphers before World War I. During that war, Yardley was used as an instructor and organizer for U.S. military cryptography. Afterward, he resumed his State Department work in the 1920s, and much to the advantage of U.S. negotiators, broke the Japanese diplomatic code during the Washington Conference that led to the *Washington Naval Arms Limitation Treaty of 1922. When the State Department discontinued this work, Yardley retired and wrote *The American Black Chamber* (1931), exposing his feats and causing foreign nations to manufacture ciphers that were far more difficult to decode.

The next master American codebreaker was the War Department's William F. Friedman, who managed to create a machine that could decipher much of the Japanese Foreign Office's "Purple" Code in 1940. Army and navy intelligence officers coordinated the placement of radio intercept stations, exchanged information, and produced signals intelligence known as *MAGIC even before the Japanese attack on *Pearl Harbor in December 1941. However, the Japanese main naval code was not broken until early 1942. During World War II, the army and navy became adept at both signals intelligence and the ability to create codes that were nearly impossible for the Axis powers to decipher. But American intercept and deciphering capabilities were no panacea; for example, in late 1944 there was a rapid decline in the quality of U.S. Army intelligence as American forces approached the German border. Telephonic *communications of the German Army had been monitored and reported to the Allies by the French Resistance. Learning or suspecting this, Germans defending France were forced to use their radios more often than they would have liked and these coded radio messages were intercepted (as they had been since 1940) by the British and decided through the process called *ULTRA. But as the German forces withdrew into Germany in late 1944, they traded radio communications for the comparatively secure German telephone system, and other land lines. The concentration of troops that led to the rapid and initially successful German thrust into Belgium in December 1944 in the Battle of the *Bulge was not detected by a U.S. intelligence system that had grown too reliant on communications intelligence.

Following World War II, the Department of *Defense (DoD) combined army and navy cryptography and in 1952 designated the resulting organization the *National Security Agency (NSA). Headed by a military officer and making its headquarters in Fort Meade, Maryland, NSA kept a low profile during the Cold War. By the 1990s, it had created over 2,000 air, land, sea, and space-based intercept sites. During this period, it gained the largest budget and the most personnel of any element of the U.S. intelligence community, including the *Central Intelligence Agency. Much of the reason for this size and expense stems from the fact that NSA's work is not only dependent on the latest technology, it is also labor-intensive. Cryptanalysis, particularly work in breaking some of America's adversaries' high-level codes, requires large numbers of people who must endlessly toil to decipher critical foreign communications for the use of U.S. decision makers. The same applies to the creation of secure communications for the U.S. government. Secure communications also demands manpower and equipment. And NSA's work is not limited to creating or deciphering "secure" communications between people. As the missile age developed from the 1950s on, telemetry between instruments, guidance systems, and detection systems was increasingly deciphered or encoded.

Since most industrialized nations have created sophisticated codes for use in their most sensitive communications, NSA cannot quickly decipher an opponent's high-level messages. Lower-level codes, those associated with typical military units, are somewhat easier to break; but here some of the best information may be which units are communicating with a particular headquarters. This "traffic analysis," the art of associating one organization with another in time and space, is a specialty of military intelligence analysts and has contributed to several American military successes, particularly before and during the *Persian Gulf War, 1990–91. But as U.S. cryptographic achievements have become known, opponents have avoided radio communications, relying on face-to-face meetings or the simple use of messengers. Electronic intercept is only one of several components the American military intelligence community uses to provide their commanders with the best information about an adversary.

[*See also* Cold War: External Course; Cold War: Domestic Course.]

• Herbert O. Yardley, *The American Black Chamber,* 1931. Fletcher Pratt, *Secret and Urgent: The Story of Codes and Ciphers,* 1939. David Kahn, *The Codebreakers: The Story of Secret Writing,* 1967. Ronald W. Clark, *The Man Who Broke Purple: The Life of Colonel William F. Friedman,* 1977. U.S. Army Security Agency, *The History of Codes and Ciphers in the United States Prior to World War I,* 1978. U.S. Army Security Agency, *The History of Codes and Ciphers in the United States During World War I,* 1979. James Bamford, *The Puzzle Palace: A Report on NSA, America's Most Secret Agency,* 1982. Thomas Parrish, *The American Codebreakers: The U.S. Role in UL-TRA,* 1986.
—Rod Paschall

COLD HARBOR, BATTLE OF. See Wilderness to Petersburg Campaign (1864).

COLD WAR (1945–91)

Causes
External Course
Domestic Course
Changing Interpretations

COLD WAR (1945–91): CAUSES

The Grand Alliance of the United States, Great Britain, and the Soviet Union was the indirect creation of Adolf *Hitler. Only such a challenge as Nazi Germany could bring together the world's leading capitalist democracy, the world's greatest colonial empire, and the world's major Communist state. Relations between the Anglo-Americans and the Russians, moreover, had been marked by ideological clash and distrust since the Bolshevik Revolution. The Western powers had intervened in the Russian civil war against the Bolsheviks, and the United States had refused to recognize the Soviet Union from 1917 to 1933. Prewar diplomacy, particularly Western appeasement of Hitler and rejection of collective security with the Soviet Union, followed by the Nazi-Soviet Pact in August 1939, led each side to be wary of the other's intentions and motives.

During World War II, President Franklin D. *Roosevelt set forth two parallel strategies for postwar peace. The first was the continuation of the Grand Alliance. Best symbolized by the *United Nations, this path sought continued cooperation with the Soviet Union, great power control over different spheres of influence, and incorporation of socialist economies into a world trade system. The other strategy was based on American power, the "open door," policy, and unilateral planning. It was best represented by the development of the atomic bomb, which Roosevelt refused to share with the Russians. Though Roosevelt wished for continued cooperation with the Soviets, he was also willing to hedge his bets and keep his options open. Underlying both approaches was Roosevelt's tactic of delaying the major decisions on boundaries, governments, occupation policies, and reparations and reconstruction aid until the end of the war, when American power would be at its height. With his characteristic optimism, Roosevelt believed that time would allow the conflicts in these approaches to be worked out.

The *Yalta Conference in February 1945 appeared to expose the problems and contradictions of Roosevelt's two-track approach. The Allies clashed over the composition of Poland's government, and could not reach firm agreements on the crucial questions of the occupation of Germany and postwar reparations and loans. Roosevelt, believing any truly representative government in Warsaw would be anti-Soviet, accepted a vague compromise that allowed the Soviet-imposed government to maintain control without technically violating the agreement. Four zones of occupation were established for Germany, and $10 billion was adopted as a working figure for German reparations to the Soviet Union, with the details to be settled later. Still, Roosevelt saw the common desire to prevent a resurgence of German power, along with Soviet needs for postwar reconstruction, to be firm roads to continued cooperation among the Big Three (the United States, the United Kingdom, and the USSR). He believed that concessions to Soviet security concerns in Eastern Europe were necessary in the short run until the West could demonstrate its good faith through American economic aid and guarantees against German remilitarization. Once Soviet dictator Josef *Stalin was persuaded that the West did not intend to allow Germany again to threaten Europe's peace, and that it would assist the Soviet Union in its recovery, Moscow would no longer need to dominate its neighbors. The Soviet Union would find its security protected within the collective arrangements of the United Nations Security Council.

Roosevelt's hopes of resolving the contradictions of his policy died with him on 12 April 1945. The new president, Harry S. *Truman, was by all accounts unaware of

Roosevelt's plans, generally uninformed about foreign policy and military matters, and therefore initially reliant upon a set of advisers that included Ambassador to the Soviet Union Averell Harriman, Secretary of War Henry L. *Stimson, and Truman's choice for secretary of state, James Brynes. This group tended to take a harder line toward the Soviet Union than had Roosevelt. Truman believed in cooperation, but he thought it should be on American terms. He stated that he did not expect to get his way every time, but he did believe "we should be able to get eighty-five percent." In his first meeting with the Soviet foreign minister, V. M. Molotov, in late April 1945, Truman used blunt language in accusing the Soviets of failing to carry out their promise of establishing a democratic government in Poland. In July, when Truman learned of the successful testing of the atomic bomb, he wrote privately that he now had an "ace in the hole," which he could use to end the war in the Pacific and in negotiations with the Soviets. The unilateral approach was winning out over cooperation and negotiation.

The bombings of *Hiroshima and Nagasaki did indeed add to Soviet distrust of the United States, but Soviet leaders in the Kremlin continued in 1945 to seek cooperation with the West. The reasons for this were compelling. The devastation of the Soviet Union by the Germans was unprecedented. Over 20 million Soviet citizens died during the war, and over 1,700 cities, 70,000 villages, and 31,000 factories were destroyed. To ensure more secure borders, rebuild, and prevent a future resurgence of German strength seemed to demand continued good relations with the United States. Only Washington could ensure Soviet security through its occupation policies and provide funds for reconstruction. Cooperation, for Stalin, was a means to ensure the Soviet sphere of influence, control Germany, and secure vital economic aid.

Yet, from Washington's perspective Soviet actions in Eastern Europe more and more came to be seen not as necessary steps for security but as aggressive actions that threatened American plans for postwar peace and prosperity. From the outset of World War II, officials in the Roosevelt administration were determined that the United States would seize its "second chance" (the first chance had been lost after World War I) to shape the postwar world in such a way as to promote American interests and peace. It was an article of faith for advocates of American *internationalism that the United States had an obligation to accept responsibility for postwar leadership and to see to it that the world adopted American ideas of self-determination, free trade, arms limitations, and collective security. These were not only good for the United States but beneficial to all nations. With *isolationism discredited, the objective was to maintain the principles of the Grand Alliance as set out in the Atlantic Charter. The United States had fought the war in part to protect self-determination and open trade.

It was therefore necessary to combat spheres of influence and closed trading systems. No one nation or group of powers could be allowed to establish a competing system to the one the U.S. government envisioned for the world. Truman and his advisers believed that political and economic freedoms were interrelated and necessary for American prosperity and international *peace. Any restrictions of trade or exclusive economic spheres would lead to a repetition of the 1930s. As Truman declared in 1947, "peace, freedom, and world trade" were inseparable; "the grave lessons of the past have proved it." Limiting a Soviet sphere of influence was perceived as necessary to postwar peace. This understanding led to great fears among American officials that if they did not respond to Soviet actions, the United States would find itself once again in a world of trade blocs and international competition. To compel the Soviets to accept American interpretations of agreements, the Truman administration denounced Soviet behavior in Poland, Romania, and elsewhere, threatened action over Soviet involvement in Iran, and held up economic assistance until the Soviets demonstrated their willingness to cooperate on American terms. Truman, believing he had either the power to force Soviet compliance or the ability to achieve American goals without the Kremlin's cooperation, was convinced by the end of 1945 that it was time to "stop babying the Soviets." "Unless Russia is faced with an iron fist and strong language," he said, "another war is in the making."

The arrival of George F. *Kennan's Long Telegram from Moscow in February 1946 served to provide coherence to the developing hard line against the Soviets. Kennan argued that the Soviet Union was motivated by a combination of traditional Russian desires to expand and by Marxist ideology that taught there could be no cooperation with capitalist states. There was therefore no room for compromise and negotiation. The Soviets would take advantage of all sincere efforts at peace and only honor agreements when it was expedient to their goals. He portrayed Stalin as acting on a coherent design, rather than as a man responding to events in the interests of his nation. The obvious conclusion for Kennan—and the one drawn by the Truman administration—was that the Soviets had no legitimate grievances. There was thus no need to try to understand and meet Soviet concerns. Rather, a policy of opposition and the containment of Soviet power was necessary.

A few weeks later in Fulton, Missouri, former British prime minister Winston S. *Churchill delivered his "Iron Curtain" speech sounding the call for an Anglo-American alliance against the Soviets, whom he said had established a dictatorial regime behind an "iron curtain" from "Stettin in the Baltic to Trieste in the Adriatic." Problems seemed to be multiplying around the world, and from the White House it appeared that more often than not the source of the difficulties was the Soviet Union. In Asia, revolutionary nationalist movements, often headed by Communists, were fighting against the restoration of Europe's colonial empires, while civil war between the Nationalists and Communists resumed in China. In Europe, economic recovery was slow, food and other essential goods short, and Communist parties, particularly in France and Italy, were gaining ground. Truman's advisers warned him that time was running short. The Soviet strategy, they argued, was to weaken the position of the United States in Europe and Asia to create confusion and collapse. The threat was not necessarily a military one, but a political and economic challenge.

Other apparent challenges appeared in Turkey and Iran. In 1946, the Soviets pushed for access to the strategic Dardanelles Straits while simultaneously delaying the removal of troops from Iran's northern provinces.

The event that spurred Truman to action was the British government's announcement in February 1947 that it was pulling out of Greece. It could no longer afford to finance the Greek royalist forces in their civil war against a Communist-led rebellion. Rather than viewing the war as a civil conflict revolving around Greek issues, American policymakers incorrectly interpreted it as a Soviet effort. Secretary of State Dean *Acheson told congressional leaders that the "Soviet Union was playing one of the greatest gambles in history at minimal cost" in an effort to expand into the Middle East, Asia, and Africa. The United States alone could stop this. In March 1947, the president announced the *Truman Doctrine. It "must be the policy of the United States," Truman declared, "to support free peoples who are resisting attempted subjugation by armed minorities or outside pressures." This was followed in June by the *Marshall Plan (1948–52), a pledge of economic assistance to Europe to stimulate recovery and trade.

By 1947, U.S. policy was predicated on the containment of the Soviet Union. In its efforts to establish a postwar order based upon American institutions and ideals, the Truman administration came to see the Soviet Union as a threat to U.S. interests. In the late 1940s, containment and anticommunism were globalized to include Asia, Africa, and Latin America. Competing security and economic demand in Europe shattered the Grand Alliance and brought about the Cold War.

[See also Russia, U.S. Military Involvement in, 1917–20; Russia, U.S. Military Involvement in, 1921–95.]

• John Lewis Gaddis, *The United States and the Origins of the Cold War, 1941–1947,* 1972. Daniel Yergin, *Shattered Peace: The Origins of the Cold War and the National Security State,* 1977. Thomas Paterson, *On Every Front: The Making of the Cold War,* 1979. Fraser Harbutt, *The Iron Curtain: Churchill, American and the Origins of the Cold War,* 1986. Michael Hogan, *The Marshall Plan,* 1987. Melvyn Leffler, *A Preponderance of Power: National Security, the Truman Administration, and the Cold War,* 1992. Lloyd Gardner, *Spheres of Influence,* 1993. Carolyn Eisenberg, *Drawing the Line: The American Decision to Divide Germany, 1944–49,* 1996.
—David F. Schmitz

COLD WAR (1945–91): EXTERNAL COURSE

The most famous image to emerge from the *Yalta Conference in 1945 is a picture of Winston S. *Churchill, Franklin D. *Roosevelt, and Josef *Stalin seated outdoors, wearing their overcoats, Churchill with his trademark cigar and Stalin with his marshal's cap. The three look pleased, almost jovial. The war in Europe had turned decisively against Nazi Germany and the Allied leaders knew that victory was near.

When the Allied leaders next met, in July 1945, Roosevelt had died, replaced by his vice president, Harry S. *Truman. A man of scant foreign policy experience, Truman arrived at the *Potsdam Conference, near Berlin, with the knowledge that an atomic bomb had been successfully detonated in New Mexico. He was hopeful about a future U.S.-Soviet detente, but the relationship was marked by suspicion and distrust on both sides. At some point before 1947, it deteriorated to the point where the two superpowers became locked in a global struggle that stopped short of direct armed conflict.

The Role of Nuclear Weapons. By 1949, both countries possessed *nuclear weapons. There has been much debate over the exact role of these weapons in the Cold War. Many historians argue that the only reason the Cold War never became "hot" was that the fear of nuclear annihilation effectively deterred each side from directly attacking the other. Others disagree, pointing to the fact that the Cold War had already reached a fever pitch before the Soviets had nuclear weapons, and that until the widespread development of hydrogen bombs in the 1950s, atomic weapons were only slightly more deadly than the most concentrated conventional attacks.

Without question, nuclear weapons were an integral aspect of the Cold War, and it is impossible to understand the history of the conflict without an appreciation for how large the threat of these weapons loomed, not just over Washington and Moscow but throughout the world. The rapid growth of nuclear arsenals altered the nature of international relations and made both nuclear superpowers far more wary of military confrontation with one another than they might otherwise have been.

After the *Cuban Missile Crisis in October 1962, both sides made strenuous efforts to establish a modus vivendi. A period of detente continued until 1979, when the Soviet invasion of Afghanistan contributed to renewed American military spending and to the election of President Ronald *Reagan, who pursued what is sometimes known as the "second Cold War." This lasted from 1979 to 1986, when Reagan and the reform-minded Soviet premier, Mikhail Gorbachev, came to an agreement in Iceland. The final years, between 1986 and 1991, saw the rapid dissolution of the Soviet Union. Its collapse in December 1991 marked the end of a Cold War that had all but sputtered out in the previous five years.

Phase One: 1945–46. After Potsdam, the United States and the Soviet Union approached each other warily. Throughout the fall of 1945, the two countries shifted attention from the European and Asian wars that had consumed them for the past five years. As they did so, they found that their visions for a post–Cold War world differed, most noticeably in Poland and occupied Germany. The United States envisioned a world dominated by democracy and free market economics, while the USSR saw that vision as a thinly veiled strategy to dominate the Soviet Union. By the end of 1946, the level of antagonism between the two nations had risen precipitously. Each viewed the other as the primary foreign policy threat, and both governments mobilized resources and planned strategy with one goal in mind: maximizing their own influence and minimizing that of the other.

Phase Two: 1947–62. The second phase was the most intensive of the Cold War, and the most dangerous. During this period, the United States and the Soviet Union constructed formidable nuclear arsenals and enormous conventional forces, and at several points the two countries nearly came to blows.

In 1947, the U.S. government reorganized. The *National Security Act created a unified Department of *Defense, a *Central Intelligence Agency (CIA), and a *National Security Council. These would be the primary bureaucracies for American policy in the Cold War. Responding to a Communist insurgency in Greece and to Stalin's pressure on Turkey to allow Soviet military access to the straits connecting the Black Sea to the Mediterranean, Truman requested Congress to authorize a $400 million aid program. In order to mobilize isolationists in the Republican Congress, the Democratic president heightened the rhetorical stakes, painting the Cold War as a contest between "free institutions and representative

government" and those who were forcibly ruled by "the will of the minority." The struggle between the two sides in the Cold War was more than military, strategic, or economic; it was also profoundly ideological, with each side presenting the other as the embodiment of evil.

The *Truman Doctrine was followed by an announcement of European aid by Secretary of State George C. *Marshall, in June 1947. The twin policies of the Truman Doctrine and the *Marshall Plan led to billions in economic and military aid to Western Europe and the eastern Mediterranean. With American assistance, the Greek military defeated the insurgents, and the Christian Democrats in Italy defeated the powerful Communist-Socialist alliance in the elections of 1948.

At the same time, tension over Germany grew. Unable to agree on a partition of Germany, both Soviet and U.S. troops remained in Berlin, and in an attempt to force the Americans out, the Soviets blockaded Berlin in the summer of 1948. Rather than backing down, the United States orchestrated the *Berlin airlift of supplies to Berlin, which lasted nearly a year until Stalin realized that his blockade had failed in its aims.

The year 1949 saw three developments that deepened the conflict. In April, a Western military alliance, the North Atlantic Treaty Organization (*NATO), was created, and it bound the United States to the defense of Western Europe. In September, the Soviet Union successfully tested a nuclear weapon; and in October, the Communist forces of Mao Zedong defeated the last remnant of the Nationalist Army and took power in China. In response to these events, the National Security Council in Washington drew up a plan in early 1950 known as NSC 68, which called for a massive buildup of American conventional and nuclear forces and an aggressive military response to Communist *expansionism throughout the world.

When war erupted between North and South Korea in June 1950, Truman and his advisers barely hesitated before acting on NSC 68 and sending U.S. troops to bolster South Korea. By late fall, more than 1 million Chinese troops crossed the Yalu River in North Korea and entered the *Korean War against American, South Korean, and other *United Nations troops. The war turned into a stalemate that lasted until an armistice in 1953 that returned Korea essentially to its pre-1950 dividing line.

The inauguration of Dwight D. *Eisenhower as president in January 1953 and the death of Josef Stalin that March shifted the dynamic of the Cold War somewhat. Eisenhower and his secretary of state, John Foster *Dulles, initiated the "New Look" strategy, which called for a greater reliance on nuclear weapons to deter China and the Soviet Union. Dulles enunciated a doctrine of massive retaliation that called for a severe American response to any Soviet *aggression and violence, and the "New Look" also drew the United States more closely into Third World politics. The Soviets, now led by Nikita Khrushchev, moved away from the depredations of Stalinism, but in foreign policy they remained dedicated to global competition with the United States.

The Cold War in Europe settled into an uneasy armed truce, with NATO troops stationed in West Germany and *Warsaw Pact and Soviet forces stationed throughout Eastern Europe. In 1956, the Soviets invaded Hungary rather than allow the Hungarians to move out of the Soviet orbit.

Berlin remained divided and contested, and in 1961, the East Germans erected a wall to prevent their citizens from fleeing to West Berlin.

The other arena for the Cold War during the 1950s was the Third World, where nationalist movements in countries such as Guatemala, Iran, and the Philippines were often allied with or led by Communist groups. The United States and the Soviet Union began to compete by proxy in the Third World, and the U.S. government utilized the CIA as well as various forms of *covert operations in order to remove certain Third World governments and support others. Third World countries reacted by rejecting the impetus to choose sides in the Cold War. At Bandung, Indonesia, in 1955, dozens of Third World governments gathered and resolved on staying out of the Cold War. This resolve culminated with the creation of the Non-Aligned movement in 1961.

During the 1950s, the Soviets and the Americans created a new generation of nuclear weapons—hydrogen *bombs—which magnified exponentially the potential damage of nuclear war. In the late 1950s, the Soviets launched the first of the reconnaissance *satellites, Sputnik, while the United States developed *U-2 spy planes. Both innovations soon led to aerial reconnaissance, allowing Cold War adversaries to gain a clearer picture of the military strength of the other.

But in 1960, U.S. reconnaissance did not prevent the CIA and the American military from overestimating the strength of the Soviet military. During the presidential election of 1960, John F. *Kennedy criticized the Eisenhower administration for allowing an alleged "missile gap" to develop with the Soviet Union, even though in reality the United States was ahead of the Soviets in *missiles, in particular, intercontinental missile development. On his inauguration as president, Kennedy promised that the United States would not fall behind the Soviet Union in military strength.

Kennedy and Khrushchev held a summit in Vienna in June 1961, but it did not go well. Kennedy felt bullied, and Khrushchev felt that Kennedy was a weak man surrounded by hawkish advisers. At the same time, Khrushchev knew that the only missile gap was on the Soviet side, and he intended to redress that imbalance. In the summer of 1962, Khrushchev decided to station nuclear missiles in Cuba, where the anti-American Fidel Castro had recently come to power and thwarted a CIA-sponsored invasion by Cuban exiles. An American U-2 overflight of Cuba detected these missiles, and that discovery set off what has since become known as the *Cuban Missile Crisis.

For thirteen days in October 1962, Kennedy and Khrushchev played a deadly game of "chicken," each threatening to escalate the crisis to the brink of nuclear war. After a tense standoff, Khrushchev decided to withdraw the weapons from Cuba in return for a pledge from Kennedy that the United States would not invade the island. Though the crisis was a victory for Kennedy, it signaled to both the United States and the Soviet Union that the cost of direct confrontation in an era of nuclear weapons was greater than any potential gain. In 1963, the two countries agreed on a *Limited Test Ban Treaty, which marked the first step toward normalization of relations.

Phase Three: 1963–79. After 1963, the United States and the Soviet Union entered the period that came to be known as *detente*. Ideological passions gradually dissipated in favor of a more pragmatic approach to international politics. The United States turned its attention to the *Vietnam War, and until 1973, it remained mired there. The civil war in Vietnam was part of the Cold War insofar as it was the logical outgrowth of American policies of containment and rollback, but with its military attention locked on Vietnam and beset by severe domestic unrest, the administration of Lyndon B. *Johnson focused less on Moscow. President Richard M. *Nixon, while disengaging from Vietnam, worked assiduously to establish a diplomatic rapport with the Soviets, aided in that task by his chief foreign policy official, Henry *Kissinger.

The Soviets until the very end of this period focused on their bitter rivalry with Mao's China; after Khrushchev's ouster in 1964, the Soviet leadership turned inward to attend to the many domestic problems that plagued the Soviet Union. Soviet rulers such as Alexei Kosygin and Leonid Brezhnev warily embraced the notion of detente, although like the Americans they continued to expend considerable energies trying to win various Third World states to their side.

The year 1972 was the apogee of detente. Nixon and Kissinger orchestrated a stunning and secretive rapprochement with Communist China. For their part, the Chinese had sought improved relations with the Americans in order to gain advantage over the Soviets. In February, Nixon traveled to the Forbidden City in Beijing and met with Mao and Chou En-Lai. Then, in June, Nixon and Kissinger met with Brezhnev and Soviet military officials in Moscow. The result was the first of the *SALT Treaties (an acronym for Strategic Arms Limitation Talks), which pledged the United States and the USSR to limit the deployment of antiballistic missiles and set restrictions on offensive nuclear missiles as well. SALT I was followed in 1974 by SALT II, which went even further in specifying numbers of warheads each side could possess.

President Jimmy *Carter came into office in 1977 with SALT II unratified, and he announced that his administration would make human rights a central concern. Carter had great success brokering a Middle East peace agreement between Israel and Egypt, the *Camp David Accords (1979). However, though relations with the Soviets and the Chinese were civil, the spirit of detente began to dissipate. In December 1979, Brezhnev ordered Soviet troops to invade Afghanistan to support a tottering pro-Moscow regime. The U.S. Embassy in Teheran, Iran, had been seized a month earlier by Islamic militant students allied with the Ayatollah Khomeini, and the American hostages were held until the day Ronald Reagan was inaugurated in January 1980. The dual effects of the Iranian hostage crisis and the Soviet invasion of Afghanistan led to a significant increase in U.S. military spending in Carter's last year, to the election of Reagan, and to the end of detente.

Phase Four: 1980–86. Reagan arrived in office determined to restore American pride and power. He and his advisers believed that both the realpolitik of Kissinger and the weakness of Carter had sacrificed America's ideological and strategic advantage in the Cold War. Calling the Soviet Union an "evil empire," Reagan embarked on a huge military buildup that ranged from new aircraft carrier groups to research for a space missile defense system known as the *Strategic Defense Initiative (or "Star Wars"). The most visible manifestation of Reagan's renewed Cold War fervor was the support given to the Contra rebels in Nicaragua, who were fighting a guerrilla war against the Communist Sandinista government.

The Soviets attempted to match Reagan's military spending. But the war in Afghanistan deteriorated, and Moscow discovered that the ailing industry and economy of the Soviet Union simply could not keep pace with the Americans. In 1985, a young, dynamic Mikhail Gorbachev became premier, and he instituted a series of domestic reforms known as *glasnost* (openness) and *perestroika* (restructuring the economy).

At first, the Reagan administration saw these initiatives as a ruse. They were not. Meeting with Gorbachev in Reykjavik, Iceland, in October 1986, Reagan made what was for him a leap of faith, agreeing to both the *INF Treaty (Intermediate Nuclear Forces) and the *START Treaty (Strategic Arms Reduction, the stepchild of SALT II). At Reykjavik, the Cold War began to thaw.

Phase Five: 1987–91. Few could have predicted how quickly the ice would melt. Although *glasnost* was designed to save and strengthen the Soviet Union, it helped cause the Soviet system to collapse. The economy was in shambles, and the pressures of war in Afghanistan and deep structural reform were simply more than the system could bear. In 1989, taking their cue from Moscow, people throughout the Eastern bloc demanded change. In Poland, Hungary, East Germany, and Czechoslovakia, Communist regimes fell and were replaced by interim governments dedicated to democracy and the free market. At the same time, in the Soviet Union itself, the Baltic states declared their independence, and Gorbachev significantly refused to authorize the use of the military to force either Eastern European or the Baltics back into the Soviet fold.

The end came in 1991. In August, Gorbachev survived a coup attempt by hard-liners opposed to any further reforms, but he survived largely because the newly elected Russian president, Boris Yeltsin, rallied army units and crowds to oppose the coup in Moscow. Gorbachev returned, but only for a brief time, before the Ukraine, Belarus, and the Russian Federation declared their independence. In December 1991, Gorbachev resigned as president of the defunct Soviet Union.

Assessment. The end of the Cold War came as a surprise to Moscow, Washington, and to the world. Almost no one had thought that the conflict would end so suddenly with one side collapsing internally. Both the Americans and the Western Europeans were unprepared for the rapid demise of Soviet military and economic power, and in the years after 1991, the major players in the Cold War tried to find a new strategic template that would organize their foreign policy. With the possible exception of China, that template proved elusive in the 1990s.

Like the Westphalian system in 1648 after the Thirty Year's War, and that of the Congress of Vienna in 1815 after the Napoleonic Wars, the Cold War was as much an international system following a major war as it was a struggle between two nuclear superpowers. It was a system that dominated all aspects of world politics between 1945 and 1991, and one that both exacerbated conflict in the Third World and prevented armed nuclear confrontation between the United States and the Soviet Union.

[*See also* Arms Control and Disarmament; China, U.S. Military Involvement in; Deterrence; Iran, U.S. Military Involvement in; Nicaragua, U.S. Military Involvement in; Russia, U.S. Military Involvement in, 1921–95.]

• Walter Lafeber, *America, Russia, and the Cold War,* first publ. 1972; 7th ed. 1993. John Lewis Gaddis, *Strategies of Containment: A Critical Appraisal of Postwar American National Security Policy,* 1982. McGeorge Bundy, *Danger and Survival: Choices About the Bomb in the First Fifty Years,* 1988. Gabriel Kolko, *Confronting the Third World: United States Foreign Policy, 1945–1990,* 1988. Walter Laqueur, *Europe in Our Time: A History, 1945–1992,* 1992. Martin Walker, *The Cold War: A History,* 1993. Vladislav Zubok and Constantine Pleshakov, *Inside the Kremlim's Cold War: From Stalin to Khrushchev,* 1996. Aleksandr Fursenko and Timothy Naftali, *"One Hell of a Gamble": Khrushchev, Castro and Kennedy, 1958–1964,* 1997.
—Zachary Karabell

COLD WAR (1945–91): DOMESTIC COURSE

It was no accident that nine days after Harry S. *Truman asked Congress to enact a massive aid program to fight communism in Turkey and Greece—the *Truman Doctrine—he issued Executive Order 9835 creating the Federal Employee Loyalty Program with a mandate to purge America's own government of any hint of political deviance. With these two actions in March 1947, the president put into place the twin pillars of foreign and domestic policy that would determine the structure of American political discourse for the ensuing four decades. Just as Truman made it virtually impossible for any American political leader to question fighting the "Red menace" wherever it threatened—this, after all, was a battle between freedom and slavery, atheistic communism and God-fearing democracy—he also made deeply suspect any American politician who appeared overcritical of the nation's social and economic fabric, or who advocated reforms, such as national health insurance, that could be characterized as "socialistic." No one, on either the foreign policy or the domestic front, could afford to be accused of being "soft on communism." It was the ultimate political anathema, hence the boundary line of permissible political debate.

The implications of this new hegemony of anticommunism became crystal clear during 1947 and 1948, well before the vaunted rise of "McCarthyism" in the early 1950s. The chilling effect on cultural freedom became manifest when in 1947 the House Committee on Un-American Activities (known popularly by the acronym HUAC) sought to blacklist any actors, playwrights, or producers who refused to "name names" and list Communists or "fellow travelers" they might have met in the course of their work or political activities. The HUAC's technique was insidious. Under the guise of inquiring about a Hollywood personality's own beliefs, the committee insisted that its witnesses list all other people who might have attended a meeting of a "subversive" group in the 1930s or 1940s. The only recourse for someone who wished to avoid betraying friends who could or could not have entertained a sympathy for socialism was to "take the Fifth" Amendment and refuse to answer—at which point, of course, "taking the Fifth" became synonymous with being a traitor, hence someone who could not be employed lest the contagion of disloyalty spread.

The exact same process occurred in electoral politics during the 1948 presidential election when President Truman denounced Henry Wallace—his main opponent on the left, and the former vice president—for his "Communist" sympathies. Wallace had urged a softer stance toward

Russia and a bolder commitment to social welfare measures at home. It did not take other politicians long to learn from that exchange the degree to which one could be excluded from the political dialogue simply by being accused of sympathy toward communism. When Senator Joseph McCarthy turned that mode of debate into a political art form in the 1950s with his insistence that the State Department (and other agencies) was infested with Communists, he was simply carrying to its extreme a pattern already imbedded in the political process.

One major result of the politics of anticommunism, therefore, was to shrink the political spectrum in the United States. In Britain, France, Germany, Italy, and Scandinavia, there were political parties on the left that advocated social democratic policies such as universal health insurance, generous maternity leaves, and high unemployment benefits. Yet precisely because these political groups identified themselves with some socialist ideas, they had no counterparts in America, where expressing even toleration for such ideas was *verboten*. American politics thus became a dialogue between the Center and the Right, rather than the Left and the Right. Everything began with the premise of anticommunism and a faith in the virtues of capitalism as an engine of positive change. Incremental reforms in the status quo could be considered—for example, a hike in the minimum wage or in Social Security benefits—but anything more radical never made it to the negotiating table.

This shrunken political spectrum limited substantially the tactics and mobilization strategies of civil rights and labor groups. FBI agents questioned African Americans who boldly criticized the U.S. government, and interrogated whites who fraternized with such radicals. In the thirties and early forties, an alliance had begun to develop between civil rights groups and more "progressive" or radical unions such as the electrical and auto workers. Now, civil rights groups retreated to a more legalistic strategy of challenging segregation in the courts and seeking incremental reforms through modest congressional legislation—at least until the 1960s. Labor, in turn, moved away from pushing for a model of shared management/labor control toward "business unionism," in which unions traded a share in decision making for higher wages and benefits. At the same time, organized labor purged its ranks of any Communist or Left-leaning leadership in 1948 and 1949. Much of labor's success in organizing industrial unions—autos, rubber, the electrical industry—came from the energies of left-of-center activists. Now, these voices were stilled.

A similar insistence on conformity affected American family life and sexual norms during the postwar era. World War II had generated significant social changes. Millions of women, most of them married, had entered the labor force and found they enjoyed their work outside the home. Now, with the return of peace, government and civic leaders, magazine publishers and advertisers joined in a crusade to urge women back to a life of "normality" as housewives and mothers. The three- and four-child suburban family became a new standard of "success" for women, with a life of segregated sexual spheres a domestic version, in the historian Elaine Tyler May's words, of the "containment" policy practiced by America toward world communism. Traditional roles for women became America's answer to the free love, antifamily, collectivist social policies of the Soviet Union. Not surprisingly, Vice President Richard M. *Nixon

used such traditional roles as his trump card in the famous "kitchen debate" he held with Nikita Khrushchev in 1958 to celebrate America's superiority in competition with the Soviet Union.

Similarly, gay and lesbian Americans experienced a substantial increase of official and unofficial pressure to conform to heterosexual norms. During the war, increased travel, military experience, and access to more anonymous environments had made it possible for some homosexuals openly to express their sexual preference. The politics of anticommunism, on the other hand, now placed a premium on conformity to traditional masculine and feminine roles. Denunciations of "pinko queers" went hand-in-hand with efforts to purge the federal bureaucracy of anyone suspected of deviance, whether political or personal. Any affirmation of civil liberties or civil rights had to take place within a framework of pledging loyalty to all the ingredients of 100 percent Americanism, including total support of heterosexuality.

In the context of this narrowed political and cultural spectrum, an enormous amount of ferment continued to develop. The musical rebellion of rock 'n' roll and rhythm and blues signaled a growing restlessness among the young; so too did the plays of Tennessee Williams, the poetry of Allen Ginsberg, the novels of Jack Kerouac, and the rising religious commitment of young people who felt called to something more than another tract house in a suburban community. But ironically, it was still the Cold War—and the fear of losing it—that prompted the most obvious social changes of the 1950s. The Interstate Highway system emerged primarily as a means of facilitating *mobilization and response to a military threat; the National Defense Education Act, with its cutting-edge role in providing government support for scholars in graduate school, responded to the terror Americans experienced after the Russians were the first to conquer space with Sputnik; and the civil rights gains of the *Brown* v. *Board of Education* decision, and the Civil Rights Acts of 1957 and 1960 were at least in part a response to America's embarrassment in the face of Russia's Cold War propaganda accusing the United States of being hypocritical in its defense of freedom.

Yet, appropriately, it was the civil rights movement that provided the wedge for finally undermining the dominance of Cold War cultural politics. Based on the simple and patriotic claim to equal treatment for blacks and whites under the law, the civil rights movement insisted on dramatic change. Armed with the powerful religious appeal of the Judeo-Christian tradition, Martin Luther *King, Jr., and his colleagues mobilized millions to criticize the status quo. The ethical call to join in the quest for a better America galvanized all the other groups in America seeking a way of expressing their frustration with the doctrines of conformity and false pride in the status quo—women, Chicanos, gays, students, Vietnam antiwar activists. It may have been only a small segment of each group of critics who seized public attention; but the attention they secured focused the entire nation on a different perspective toward the values, behaviors, and political norms that had reigned unchallenged for the preceding two decades.

The Cold War remained central to American society and politics all the way through the 1980s. Arguably, it remains central today, even though the actual conflict has ended. But after the successful challenge of the civil rights movement in the early and mid-1960s, the ubiquitous hold of Cold War culture and politics was broken, providing at least the opportunity for a different kind of individual and group expression of dissent.

[See also Culture, War, and the Military; Civil-Military Relations: Civilian Control of the Military; McCarran Internal Security Act (1950); Military-Industrial Complex; Nuclear Protest Movements; Nuclear Weapons, Popular Images of; Propaganda and Public Relations, Government; Society and War; Surveillance, Domestic.]

• David M. Oshinsky, A Conspiracy So Immense: The World of Joe McCarthy, 1983; Elaine Tyler May, Homeward Bound: American Families in the Cold War, 1988; Richard M. Fried, Nightmare in Red: The McCarthy Era in Perspective, 1990; Thomas Byrne Edsall and Mary D. Edsall, Chain Reaction: The Impact of Race, Rights, and Taxes on American Politics, 1991; Kevin P. Phillips, Boiling Point: Republicans, Democrats, and the Decline of Middle-Class Prosperity, 1993; Charles M. Payne, I've Got the Light of Freedom: The Organizing Tradition and the Mississippi Freedom Struggle, 1995; David Halberstam, The Children, 1998; Robert Dallek, Flawed Giant: Lyndon Johnson and His Times, 1961–1973, 1998; and William H. Chafe, Unfinished Journey: America since 1945, 4th ed., 1999.

—William H. Chafe

COLD WAR (1945–91): CHANGING INTERPRETATIONS

The Cold War generated two often indistinct battles: the first being the actual struggle between the West and Communism; the second being the continuing battles among historians, political scientists, and journalists—not to mention laymen—as to the origins and nature of, as well as the blame for, the Cold War. At the core of debates has been the contention that one side, either the Soviet Union or the United States (depending on one's interpretation), was primarily responsible for beginning the Cold War and the havoc it wreaked. The debates first focused on the origins of the Cold War, but the stakes were soon raised. Scholars would also blame the responsible party for the *arms race and the proliferation of *nuclear weapons, as well as apportioning an overriding share of the blame for a series of local wars around the world.

Since scholars immediately after World War II did not have access to top-secret documents from American and Soviet policymakers, almost all Western writers took as their cue Winston S. *Churchill's famous declaration in 1946 that the Soviet Union had dropped an "iron curtain" over Eastern Europe, and that the West needed to do everything in its power to prevent further loss of liberty. To almost all American commentators at the time—with the noticeable exception of the journalist Walter Lippmann—the United States had no choice but to challenge this new enemy; after fighting the Nazis, the United States then had to take on the Soviet Union, now compared to the Nazis by the common use of the terms Red fascism and increasingly totalitarianism.

Scholars who argued from this perspective came to be known as the "orthodox" (or "traditional") school and generally viewed U.S. actions as being virtuous and sincere. George F. *Kennan, in his Long Telegram to the State Department and later writing as "Mr. X" in his article "The Sources of Soviet Conduct" in Foreign Affairs (July 1947), remains the classic formulator of this argument. He noted that Soviet actions were inexorably expansionist, antidemocratic, and posed a very real threat to the United States

and its allies. The United States therefore needed to adopt a policy of "containment" toward the Soviet Union. Kennan expanded upon this argument in his American Diplomacy (1951). To Kennan and other traditionalists, the United States was facing a new type of enemy and had to adapt accordingly. Hans Morgenthau, Jr., continued this form of interpretation in his classic In Defense of the National Interest: A Critical Examination of American Foreign Policy (1951). Herbert Feis's Roosevelt-Churchill-Stalin (1957) remains the best summary of this position, with its unapologetic championing of the West and its hysterical condemnation of Soviet premier Josef *Stalin.

Arthur Schlesinger, Jr., is another renowned historian who worked within this framework. His influential essay "The Origins of the Cold War" (Foreign Affairs, October 1967) built on Kennan's and Morganthau's apportioning of blame, and further, argued that the Cold War emanated not only from Soviet imperialism but from Stalin's paranoid psychological profile. To Schlesinger, Stalin's adherence to Communist doctrine and his alleged mental illness combined to make the Soviet state both imperialistic and unstable. Unlike other members of this school of thought, Schlesinger acknowledged that the United States had global economic interests and was not always sensitive to the needs of peoples in the Third World. Yet he was at pains to note that the United States had almost single-handedly ensured economic and political freedoms throughout the postwar world. In sum, the orthodox perspective viewed the United States as innocent of any political nefariousness and simply acting at the invitation of beleaguered nations. An updated version of this interpretation is Geir Lundestad's "Moralism, Presentism, Exceptionalism, Provincialism, and Other Extravagances in American Writings on the Early Cold War Years" in Diplomatic History (Fall 1989).

The orthodox interpretation remained the dominant mode of historical thought until the 1960s—and it continues in various forms to this day. Beginning in 1959, though, an alternative approach appeared when William Appleman Williams published The Tragedy of American Diplomacy. This work challenged a number of long-held assumptions made by the orthodox interpretation and American Cold War policies in general. Williams's work became an instant classic (or a notorious act of disloyalty, depending upon one's politics). Williams argued here and later in revised editions of the book that Americans had been far from innocent actors upon the world stage and in fact had always been an empire-building people, even as they fiercely denied it. So incendiary was this charge that Williams was accused of disloyalty and even treasonous behavior by those who saw U.S. actions in the Cold War as just. However, Williams's work deeply influenced others, and within ten years' time it generated an entire school of historical thought known as revisionism—one that sought to reexamine all aspects of American foreign relations, but was especially concerned with defining the nature of the Cold War.

One of the intriguing qualities of Williams's work was his use of lengthy quotes from American policymakers to support his interpretation. To Williams, these statements were the documented proof that these people were far more honest when they spoke among themselves about an "American Empire" than in the explanations of policy to the public. Leaders like Franklin D. *Roosevelt and Harry

S. *Truman and their advisers were therefore seen as far-sighted and lacking any naïveté in considering American foreign policy objectives. According to Williams and many of his followers, these policymakers shared an overriding desire to maintain capitalism at home; in order to ensure this goal, they advocated the "open door" policy abroad, which would therefore increase access to foreign markets for American business and agriculture. This in turn would create a healthy economic climate at home and the propagation of American power abroad.

Williams's overall argument gained currency throughout the 1960s as a new group of historians sought to explain the roots of American foreign policy, especially as it related to the origins of American involvement in the *Vietnam War. Though a school of thought invariably contains differences between individual scholars, one of the most intriguing claims of the revisionist school is that the classic definition is mistaken in claiming that the Cold War began after World War II. Historians in such works as N. Gordon Levin's *Woodrow Wilson and World Politics: America's Response to War and Revolution* (1968), Walter LaFeber's *America, Russia, and the Cold War* (1972), and David Foglesong's *America's Secret War Against Bolshevism: U.S. Intervention in the Russian Civil War, 1917–1920* (1995), point to the century-old conflicts between the two powers, and especially to the conflict after the Bolshevik triumph in the 1917 Russian Revolution. It was the domestic policy of the United States—visceral anticommunism dating from the early twentieth century—that helped shape American Cold War policy as much as any foreign event.

Other revisionists have pointed out provocative Soviet actions such as installing puppet regimes in Eastern Europe. Yet Gar Alperovitz in his influential *Atomic Diplomacy: Hiroshima and Potsdam* (1965) places much of the blame on the Cold War on President Truman's calculated use of the atomic bomb. Alperovitz's updated version, *The Decision to Use the Atomic Bomb and the Architecture of an American Myth* (1995) extends his argument, while Michael Hogan's edited collection, *Hiroshima in History and Memory* (1996), finds problems with his analysis. According to Alperovitz, the bomb was unnecessary in defeating Japan, and was intended instead as a provocative signal to the Soviets that the United States would use such a weapon to fashion a postwar world accessible to American interests. A more moderate revisionist view of this position was put forth by Lloyd Gardner. His *Architects of Illusion* (1970) offered a slight modification of Williams's and Alperovitz's insistent critique of U.S. foreign policy, but still found America's overarching belief in economic expansion the key to understanding America's hostile view of the Soviet Union. An even harsher indictment of U.S. foreign policy appealed in Joyce and Gabriel Kolko's *The Limits of Power: The World and U.S. Foreign Policy, 1945–1954* (1972), in which the United States's Cold War policy was seen as both reflexively anti-Communist and counterrevolutionary. Any form of challenge to the American form of politics or economics was controlled by either covert or military means.

Not surprisingly, each new historical interpretation of the Cold War begat another—one that built on the earlier findings even as it contradicted them. For an early but still cogent breakdown of these historical camps, see Warren Kimball, "The Cold War Warmed Over," *American Historical Review* (October 1974). An example of this process at work is John Lewis Gaddis's *The United States and the Origins of the Cold War, 1941–1947* (1972). It was immediately hailed as ushering in a new interpretative approach, *postrevisionism*, which claimed to synthesize a variety of interpretations. Gaddis's work did not simply blame the Americans or the Soviets for their postwar actions; it also mentioned the economic motives of the West in regard to Eastern Europe. But the tenor of Gaddis's argument was clear: the Soviets were definitively more responsible for the origins of the Cold War, through their aggressive and anti-democratic policies in Eastern Europe. Interestingly, Gaddis's position seems to have become more antagonistic over time; his essay, "The Tragedy of Cold War History" (in *Diplomatic History* [Winter 1993]), is a not too subtle attack on Williams and the revisionist school in general for refusing wholly to indict Soviet policy. Gaddis's "post-revisionist synthesis" remains highly contentious, as indicated by the caustic critique of it in Bruce Cumings's "Revising Postrevisionism," *Diplomatic History* (Fall 1993).

The battles over the origins of the Cold War continue; but they are not as fierce, given the dissolution of the Soviet Union in 1991. Selective releases from Soviet archives have, however, continued to fuel debates. Many of these documents have been translated and can be found in the volumes of the *Cold War International History Project*. For a survey of differing interpretations, see Melvin Leffler and David Painter's edited collection, *Origins of the Cold War: An International History* (1994). Further, Melvin Leffler's *A Preponderance of Power: National Security, the Truman Administration and the Cold War* (1992) is an important work, for it built on Gaddis's ideas but changed the focus of the debate from issues of imperialism and morality to a more searching critique of U.S. notions of national security. Howard Jones and Randall Woods believe that some kind of national security synthesis is now possible, given the United States's ability to fuse the insights of both the orthodox and revisionist interpretations. However, other historians such as Emily Rosenberg, Anders Stephanson, and Barton Bernstein continue to disagree. For an exchange on these views, see "Origins of the Cold War in Europe and the Near East," and the successive commentaries in *Diplomatic History* (Spring 1993). Finally, Michael Hogan's edited collection, *The End of the Cold War: Its Meaning and Implications* (1996), summarizes a variety of viewpoints now that the Cold War is history.

—Jonathan Nashel

COLLECTIVE SECURITY. The term collective security was coined in the 1930s, but the concept that each nation's security depended upon that of all other nations, that peace was universal and indivisible, was not new. Earlier advocates, especially President Woodrow *Wilson, had affirmed this concept during World War I. The victorious Allies had institutionalized it in the postwar *League of Nations. Despite the Senate's rejection of the League, and the League's failures to stop aggression during the 1930s, Wilson's legacy—his vision of a "new world order"—continued to shape U.S. foreign policy throughout the twentieth century. As one of the world's great powers, the United States by midcentury abandoned its earlier policy of neutrality in favor of collective security.

Wilsonian collective security presupposed U.S. hegemony. Drafting the Covenant for the postwar League at the Paris Peace Conference of 1919, Wilson ensured that it would conform to his vision of world order. He viewed the League as the worldwide extension of the *Monroe Doctrine. He expected the United States to control the League so that it would extend U.S. influence abroad without jeopardizing U.S. independence. A veto over potentially unacceptable decisions by the League Council would guarantee that its actions would coincide with U.S. preferences.

Rejecting Wilson's globalism, Republican senators doubted that the United States could control the League. Led by Henry Cabot Lodge, they feared that the League would endanger U.S. independence and entangle the United States indiscriminately in foreign wars. They did not want Wilson or any president to use the League to involve the United States in foreign wars without congressional approval. Although most had supported war against Germany in 1917, these senators repudiated the Wilsonian vision of collective security.

After World War I, Republican presidents largely shunned the League in Geneva, Switzerland. The closest they came to global collective security was the Kellogg-Briand Pact of 1928 and the Hoover-Stimson Doctrine of 1932. President Calvin Coolidge approved the multilateral treaty that Secretary of State Frank Kellogg had negotiated with French foreign minister Aristide Briand to renounce war except for self-defense. The Kellogg-Briand Pact did not, however, prevent Japanese aggression against China in Manchuria in 1931. In response, Secretary of State Henry Stimson announced his and President Herbert Hoover's doctrine of nonrecognition. The United States rejected forceful changes in the territorial and political independence of nations, but it also eschewed both unilateral and collective action to enforce the avowed right of national self-determination.

During World War II, President Franklin D. *Roosevelt revived the Wilsonian idea of collective security. In the 1930s, the United States had attempted neutrality while Fascist Italy, Nazi Germany, and Imperial Japan committed aggression against their neighbors in Europe, Africa, and Asia. After the 1938 Munich Agreement failed to preserve peace, Roosevelt and other U.S. policymakers concluded that the nation could not protect its security alone. In 1939–41, the United States formed an alliance with the United Kingdom and the Soviet Union, and also China. This alliance served as FDR's model for a postwar *United Nations to replace the discredited League. Like Wilson earlier, he expected the victorious powers—the world's policemen—to dominate world affairs. Five nations, eventually including France, would each have the right to veto the UN Security Council's decisions.

The United Nations failed to fulfill its Wilsonian promise. FDR's secretaries of state, first Cordell Hull at Dumbarton Oaks in 1944 and then Edward Stettinius at Yalta in 1945, helped to draft the new UN Charter. Their efforts culminated in 1945 at the San Francisco Conference, where President Harry S. *Truman, after FDR's death, reaffirmed Wilson's legacy. However, this revived concept of global collective security, involving cooperation among the great powers, soon succumbed to the *Cold War. The Soviet Union and the United States divided the world into competing spheres of influence, creating a new balance of power rather than universal collective security.

Only once during the Cold War did the United Nations provide collective security as FDR and Truman had hoped. In 1950, after North Korea attacked South Korea, the United Nations responded with collective defense against aggression. Because the Soviets were temporarily absent, the United States obtained the Security Council's approval for the use of military force to defend South Korea from aggression. From the *Korean War to the end of the Cold War, the United Nations served as an international forum for U.S.-Soviet rivalry rather than as an organization for collective security. U.S. presidents, frustrated by their lack of control over the United Nations, routinely criticized it for failing to fulfill its original intent.

As an alternative throughout the Cold War, the United States pursued regional collective security, which the UN Charter permitted. Under the 1947 *Inter-American Treaty of Reciprocal Assistance, the United States committed itself to defend Latin American nations. The 1949 North Atlantic Treaty ended American isolationism by involving the United States in a long-term military alliance with western European states (*NATO). Other mutual security treaties extended the U.S. network of alliances to the Pacific and Asia, including Australia and New Zealand in 1951 (ANZUS), Southeast Asia in 1954 (*SEATO), and bilateral treaties with the Philippines, Japan, Taiwan, and Korea. Claiming authorization under these mutual security treaties, the United States intervened in various countries to sustain allies and prevent Communist victory, most notably in Vietnam from the 1950s to 1975. This unilateral form of regional collective security epitomized U.S. involvement in the Cold War.

The end of the Cold War opened another opportunity for the United States to use the United Nations for collective security. After Iraq's invasion of Kuwait in 1990, President George *Bush organized a broad coalition, including the Soviet Union, to stop this aggression and restore Kuwait's sovereignty. For the first time since the Korean War, now that the United States was the world's only superpower, it could provide leadership in the United Nations to use military force in the Persian Gulf. During the *Persian Gulf War of 1991, Bush proclaimed a "new world order" of global collective security. Thus the Wilsonian legacy still influenced U.S. foreign policy in the post-Cold War world.

President Bill *Clinton extended collective security into the Balkans, involving both the United Nations and NATO in conflicts arising from the breakup of Yugoslavia, the *Bosnian Crisis. In 1995, the United States and its NATO allies retaliated with air attacks against Serbia to enforce UN resolutions calling for the end of Serb aggression and ethnic cleansing in Bosnia-Herzegovina. NATO intervention enabled the United States and its UN partners to negotiate the 1995 Dayton Peace Accords, which established an international peacekeeping regime in Bosnia-Herzegovina and ended most fighting in the region. Three years later, after Serbia resorted to ethnic cleansing of Albanians in its province of Kosovo, the United States and its NATO allies threatened military reprisal against Serbia to force it to comply with UN demands. This collective action curtailed Serbia's attacks and facilitated the negotiation of the 1998 Kosovo Accords, which required Serbia to remove some armed forces and accept international supervision in Kosovo, even within its own province. This was enforced in the *Kosovo Crisis (1999). Thus the United States, along with its partners in the United Nations and NATO, continued to pursue collective security in the post-Cold War world.

[See also Peacekeeping.]

• Roland N. Stromberg, *Collective Security and American Foreign Policy: From the League of Nations to NATO*, 1963. Lloyd E. Ambrosius, *Woodrow Wilson and the American Diplomatic Tradition: The Treaty Fight in Perspective*, 1987. Lawrence S. Kaplan, *NATO and the United States: The Enduring Alliance*, 1988. Robert C. Hilderbrand, *Dumbarton Oaks: The Origins of the United Nations and the Search for Postwar Security*, 1990. Robert W. Tucker and David C. Hendrickson, *The Imperial Temptation: The New World Order and America's Purpose*, 1992. Thomas G. Weiss, David P. Forsythe, and Roger A. Coate, *The United Nations and Changing World Politics*, 1994. Townsend Hoopes and Douglas Brinkley, *FDR and the Creation of the UN*, 1997.
—Lloyd E. Ambrosius

COLONIAL REBELLIONS AND ARMED CIVIL UNREST (1607–1775).

Rebellions and armed unrest did not so much punctuate as define the history of colonial British America. All three of colonial society's constituent groups—Native Americans, Africans, and Europeans—took part. The Stono Rebellion by South Carolina slaves in 1739 and the New York City slave conspiracies in 1712 and 1741 were important points in setting the terms of black-white relations. "Frontier" warfare was not so much a matter of continuous Indian dispossession as a means by which Indians and whites dealt with one another within a social order they shared.

Unrest stemmed in part, then, from the unprecedented encounter of three groups, each ignorant of the others, that created "early American" society. In part, too, it arose from the character of colonial social organization. "Mobs, a sort of them at least, are constitutional," commented Thomas Hutchinson in 1768, three years after he had seen his own house thoroughly sacked by his fellow Bostonians. But he knew that a volunteer fire company, a militia unit, or a posse was just a "mob" drawn into ranks and given official standing.

In this sense white Americans and Europeans shared a great deal. For both, popular uprisings could be a means of negotiation across class and community lines, within a framework that recognized "liberties" but made no pretense of equality. Such was the "Knowles Riot" in Boston in 1747, named for the British naval officer who ordered the impressment of Bostonians despite local procedures and customs. For merchant sailors and fishermen, resisting the press meant protecting their own lives. For community leaders, it meant protecting the town, because during a press neither merchant nor fishing vessels would sail. Similarly, a community might respond to food shortage by forcing merchants to release reserves of grain at "just" prices, or prevent pestilence by keeping smallpox victims away. Such uprisings rested on three assumptions. First, local customs bound rulers and ruled, rich and poor alike. Second, both official actions and uprisings offered means by which "society" rightly controlled its members. Third, the subject could usually be negotiated. A press gang might withdraw, releasing its victims. The price of salt, bread, or grain could be adjusted.

This dimension of colonial-era uprisings fit perfectly with the *ancien régime* in Europe. One historian has described the same thing in England as "the moral economy of the crowd"; another has written about "the reasons of misrule" and "the rites of violence" in early modern France. Marie Antoinette's suggestion that Parisians protesting the absence of bread might "eat cake" showed her profound ignorance of what obligations a time of shortage imposed upon her class. Thomas Hutchinson knew better.

Rural upheaval was another matter. Among the major events were mid-eighteenth-century land rioting in New Jersey and New York, the Green Mountain Boys' insurrection that led to the creation of Vermont, and separate 1760s "Regulator" movements in the two Carolinas.

Uncertainty about the basic conditions of rural life, especially landholding, underpinned all of these episodes. Who would hold and develop the land could not be compromised among whites, any more than between whites and Indians. Colonial-era land distribution was extremely haphazard. A grantee could "locate" land almost at choice, with virtually none of the regularity that the national-era grid system was intended to provide. The ultimate example was how Kentucky became "shingled" four times over with conflicting claims.

Individual claims had their counterpart in ill-drawn provincial boundaries. A map of 1774 shows Massachusetts towns extending into New York and New York manors reaching into New England. Charter grants overlapped, as Connecticut's claim to the Wyoming Valley of Pennsylvania and the claim of both New Hampshire and New York to the Green Mountains showed. In such circumstances would-be owners clashed repeatedly over possession, typically creating extended movements rather than short-lived risings.

Of the movements, only the Green Mountain Boys achieved all they wanted. They originated among Yankee settlers who had New Hampshire titles to lands between the Upper Connecticut River and Lake Champlain and who proposed to organize the region in New England style. New York also claimed the territory, perhaps with the better title, and imposed its own system of counties and of large estates where "amiable and innocent tenants" would toil. The New England migrants created a countergovernment and found the chance in 1777 to claim statehood.

Others traveled the same path, but not so far. Hudson Valley land rioters denied the validity of the region's great manorial land grants, broke jails open, and flourished rhetoric about mobs overcoming kings. In 1766, they staged a great rising between New York City and Albany. New Jersey rioters who claimed land under Indian titles established their own courts and "a gaol [jail] back in the woods." Authorities responded as strongly as they could, with laws that condemned known rioters, like Vermont's Ethan Allen, to death by name. New York officials sent British troops against the Hudson Valley rioters in 1766.

The southern situation offers a variation on this theme. North Carolina's huge land grants were the subject of contention. But the problem both there and in South Carolina was as much poor government as poorly defined land claims. The immediate subject that sparked the North Carolina Regulation was Tryon's Palace—an elaborate mansion constructed at public expense for the royal governor. Like northern land riots, this turned into a dispute about public power, as perhaps 8,000 Piedmont farmers resisted the taxes and closed courts to prevent collection. The authorities responded with strong force, crushing the armed rebels in 1771 at the Battle of the Alamance. The South Carolina Regulators did not come to blows with government. Aspiring farmers who wanted to develop a stable slave society, they claimed that colonial authorities did nothing to protect them against mixed-race bandits, and set up their own institutions to remedy the problem. Those bandits themselves present a case of a colonial rising that still awaits its historian.

[See also Bacon's Rebellion.]

• Peter Wood, Black Majority: Negroes in South Carolina from 1670 Through the Stone Rebellion, 1974. William Pencak and John Lax, "The Knowles Riot and the Crisis of the 1740s in Massachusetts," Perspectives in American History, 10 (1976), pp. 163–214. Dirk Hoerder, Crowd Action in Revolutionary Massachusetts, 1977. Edward Countryman, A People in Revolution: The American Revolution and Political Society in New York, 1760–1790, 1981. A. Roger Ekirch, "Poor Carolina": Politics and Society in Colonial North Carolina, 1729–1776, 1981. Thomas L. Purvis, "Origins and Patterns of Agrarian Unrest in New Jersey, 1735–1754," William and Mary Quarterly, 39 (1982), pp. 600–27. Rachel Klein, Unification of a Slave State: The Rise of a Planter Class in the South Carolina Backcountry, 1760–1808, 1990. Michael Bellesiles, Revolutionary Outlaws: Ethan Allen and the Struggle for Independence on the Early American Frontier, 1993.   —Edward Countryman

COLORED TROOPS, U.S. From the beginning of the *Civil War, concern over the use of black soldiers pervaded Union military policy. In order to avoid alienating slaveholding states that had not seceded, the federal government did not sanction the black volunteer regiments that were organized in South Carolina, Kansas, and Louisiana during the early years of the war. By 1863, the federal government needed manpower and passed a national *conscription act, subsequently authorizing the recruitment of black soldiers, particularly in the South. In May 1863, the War Department established the Bureau of Colored Troops to oversee the organization of black regiments. These regiments formed the United States Colored Troops (USCT).

By the end of the war, the USCT consisted of over 140 regiments (infantry, cavalry, heavy and light artillery) with troop strength numbering almost 180,000 enlisted men and 7,000 officers. The bulk of the enlisted soldiers were Southern free blacks and freedmen, although the North provided some 30,000 men. Nearly all of the USCT's commissioned officer corps was white; only 100 or so blacks ever received commissions. Literate black soldiers became noncommissioned officers, largely to serve as intermediaries between white officers and their mostly illiterate troops. Training, esprit de corps, and presence on the battlefield varied among regiments, often influenced by the preconceptions of a particular unit's officers. Saddled with racial stereotypes of blacks as incapable of self-discipline and possessing the character of children, many officers tailored their training methods to fit these prejudices. USCT regiments received a simpler training manual from the War Department, along with substandard weapons and equipment, and until March 1865, lower wages than white soldiers. Many regimental commanders, however, circumvented this unequal treatment and potentially low morale by training their troops under standard military protocol. The racial predispositions of military policies were also counterbalanced by the enthusiasm of black soldiers. The opportunity to strike a blow against slavery and racism, along with expected recognition of their citizenship, drove most USCT recruits to master the art of soldiering.

Initially, USCT regiments were mustered into service as labor and support units. The War Department and a substantial amount of the Northern public did not think that black troops could withstand the rigors of combat. Once they fought, black regiments dispelled that notion. In the spring and summer of 1863, USCT units engaged in three major battles. The 1st and 3rd Louisiana Guards participated in an assault on the Confederate stronghold of Port Hudson on the Mississippi River in May. Although they did not break through the Confederate defenses and lost almost 20 percent of their men, the regiments proved their mettle on the battlefield. Black troops, facing a Confederate force nearly twice as large, held their position at Milliken's Bend, Louisiana, in June, despite horrendous *casualties. In July, men of the 54th Massachusetts Infantry, under the command of Col. Robert Gould Shaw, proved their courage in the siege of *Fort Wagner, South Carolina, although they lost over 40 percent of their regiment, including Shaw. Overall, USCT troops fought in more than 400 battles, including 39 major engagements. Other significant fighting took place at the Battle of *Fort Pillow, Tennessee, in April 1864; the Battle of Chaffin's Farm, Virginia, in September 1864, where fourteen blacks received Congressional Medals of Honor; the Battle of *Nashville in December 1864, where the Confederacy's Tennessee campaign was halted; and the Battle of Fort Blakely, Alabama, in April 1865, one of the last major battles of the war. By war's end, USCT fatalities totaled almost 38,000. Most regiments were disbanded after the war, but six all-black regiments (four infantry and two cavalry) were organized as regular army units. Eventually, two infantry regiments were decommissioned and the resulting four (the 24th and 25th Infantry and the 9th and 10th Cavalry) were stationed west of the Mississippi, where they participated in the Indian wars and the federal suppression of strikes.

Whether the Union would have won the war without the aid of the black troops was heatedly debated by Northerners and Southerners alike. The consensus among historians is that the USCT played an integral role in the Union's victory. More important, the USCT started a precedent in the American military's use of black soldiers, characterized by a reluctance to employ them, unequal treatment, and a grudging acknowledgment of their indispensable service. As blacks displayed their loyalty to the U.S. government and performed the highest duty of citizenship, limited gains in civil rights among the entire black community usually followed military crises.

[See also African Americans in the Military.]

• Dudley Taylor Cornish, The Sable Arm: Black Troops in the Union Army, 1861–1865, 1956; repr. 1987. James M. McPherson, The Negro's Civil War, 1965; repr. 1991. Jack D. Foner, Blacks and the Military in American History, 1974. Mary Frances Berry, Military Necessity and Civil Rights Policy: Black Citizenship and the Constitution, 1861–1868, 1977. Joseph T. Glatthaar, Forged in Battle: The Civil War Alliance of Black Soldiers and White Officers, 1990.

                    —Martin Summers

COLT, SAMUEL (1814–1862), inventor and manufacturer. The flamboyant Samuel Colt was best known for his patented revolving pistols, called *six-shooters*. After an abortive attempt to manufacture an early version of his pistol, Colt turned to other pursuits—including the development of a submarine battery and a submarine telegraph—before going back to manufacture an improved version of his pistol at the outbreak of the *Mexican War (1846–48). Provided with U.S. Army contracts, as well as an expanding market for his product in Europe and the

COMBAT, CHANGING EXPERIENCE OF 159

American West, Colt's business thrived to such an extent that in 1854–55 he constructed a large state-of-the-art armory at Hartford, Connecticut. Equipped with the latest tools and machinery, "Coltsville" became a showplace of American industry and the training ground of numerous inventor-entrepreneurs. During the *Civil War, the Colt armory approached mass-production levels, producing over 400,000 pistols and 85,000 rifles, second only in quantity to the output of the U.S. government–owned Springfield Armory.

By the 1870s, Colt firearms (including the *Gatling gun) could be found in virtually every part of the world. Moreover, former Colt workers proved instrumental in transferring the machine-based technology initially developed in the small-arms industry to technically related industries making such consumer durables as sewing machines, typewriters, business machines, bicycles, and, eventually, motorcycles and automobiles. Though many gifted individuals contributed to what, by the 1850s, became known as the "American system of manufactures," Samuel Colt was the system's most vocal spokesman. Few other manufacturers achieved greater prominence or exerted greater influence on the developing American economy during the age of the first Industrial Revolution (c. 1815–76).

• William B. Edwards, *The Story of Colt's Revolver*, 1953. R. L. Wilson, *Colt, An American Legend*, 1985. William Hosley, *Colt: The Making of an American Legend*, 1996.   —Merritt Roe Smith

COMBAT, CHANGING EXPERIENCE OF. The English settlers of North America twice made principled attempts to detach themselves from the world of war altogether. Many of the Puritans who arrived in the early seventeenth century hoped to lead a peaceful life in the New World. The founding fathers of the eighteenth-century republic, George *Washington foremost among them, wanted to create a society in which war as Europe knew it would have no place. Indeed, the United States tried at the outset to dispense with an army as an instrument of government, even though it was through a successful war that its independence from European rule had been won.

Both efforts to create an America liberated from the imperatives of combat failed. The Puritans, who had first sought peace with the Native Americans, quickly fell into conflict with them. The young United States found it could not govern its territory without an instrument of force. Two military institutions were the outcome of these disappointments. The first was the militia of the original colonies. The second, which had its origins in the colonies' militias, was the U.S. *Army.

Americans, when called upon to perform military duty, proved adept at its discharge. The early colonists created an effective military frontier against the Indians, and despite some setbacks, successfully protected their settlements against raiding. Their successors in the later seventeenth and eighteenth centuries contributed importantly to the defense of the colonies against French power in North America. Using techniques learned from the Indians in forest fighting, they played a major part in King William's War, King George's War, and the *French and Indian War, the conflicts in which the British eventually triumphed over the French in the New World.

The colonial militias were transplants from England, modeled on the home defense forces successively raised

and reformed under the Tudors, the Stuarts, and the Hanoverians. They were not a regular force and the crown raised none in the colonies for their defense. The Royal Americans, formed during the French and Indian War, was a unit of the British army (it survives today as part of the Royal Greenjackets, having in the interim been known as the 60th Regiment and the King's Royal Rifle Corps), while Roger's Rangers, a truly local formation, was an irregular body, albeit the precursor of the U.S. Army *Rangers. Both the Royal Americans and the Rangers, nevertheless, were a valuable leaven in the crown's forces during the French-Indian War, bringing to its conduct a skill in "Indian" or "American" warfare the redcoats shipped across the Atlantic did not possess. The redcoats further benefited from the local knowledge and expertise of militia officers, George Washington prominent among them, in forest and backcountry operations.

"Indian" or "American" warfare was a bloody business, if only because the Europeans who fought it—French and British alike—did so hand-in-glove with their Indian allies. Its central techniques were those of the raid and the ambush, in which there were no formal tactics and little quarter was given. "American" tactics subsequently made their way back into European warfare, through the raising by both the British and French of irregular units modeled on those that had proved so successful in the American forests.

"American" warfare also contributed greatly to the eventual victory of the colonists over the crown in the *Revolutionary War. At the outset, the colonial militias, which provided the Revolution with its first military force, attempted to overcome the redcoats on their own terms, fighting in fixed lines on open battlefields. They were not up to the task and were beaten at the Battle of *Bunker Hill and the Battle of *New York. When Washington, appointed commander of the *Continental army, withdrew his force to more distant regions in New Jersey and Pennsylvania, his army achieved greater success by appearing when not expected on small battlefields, such as Trenton and Princeton, close to its sanctuaries, and often in bad weather. Nevertheless, Washington was eventually reduced to withdrawing his army into a secure sanctuary near the frontier in the hope of waiting out a better turn of events.

The better turn came when the British despaired of bringing Washington's army to battle on conventional terms and transferred their main force into the southern colonies, where they expected wider loyalist support. In that roadless, heavily forested, and sometimes swampy terrain, it was their enemies who in practice achieved superiority, by reverting to a form of American warfare. Their guerrilla tactics overcame the superior force the British deployed, obliging the redcoats to abandon their southern strongholds and retreat northward to the shores of Chesapeake Bay in the hope finding support from the British Fleet. They did not, and at the battle of *Yorktown they lost a final conventional battle in defense of formal *fortifications.

Having won a war of independence in part by unconventional tactics, which they had also exported to the Old World, the Americans found themselves in their own civil war obliged to relearn contemporary tactics from Europe. This was largely because the conditions that had made so-called "American" warfare so effective against *George III's army no longer prevailed in most of the theater of operations between 1861 and 1865. The forest east of the

Appalachians had largely gone, to be replaced by pasture and plowland, and had been severely reduced between the mountains and the Mississippi. In open country, both North and South had to fight European-style, in closed formations, supported by *artillery.

This not to say that there was not something distinctively American about the way the *Civil War was fought. Indeed, there was, and its Americanness would eventually be transmitted to Europe, though with little acknowledgment by European armies of who had pioneered the new developments. The most important innovation was the dismissal of cavalry from the line of battle. North and South learned early on that horsed formations could not charge ranks of infantry armed with the new rifled *musket, and they relegated cavalry to scouting and raiding roles. They also learned the importance of massing artillery forward in direct support of the infantry. They further learned the importance of leadership by example by senior officers—a practice that produced the exceptionally high level of *casualties suffered by generals on both sides. Finally, they demonstrated that infantry, if strongly motivated and well led, could carry positions or sustain attack even at the cost of unprecedently high casualties inflicted by long-range, accurate rifle fire. The Americans were the first soldiers to undergo the experience of the attrition battle and to overcome the ordeal.

Because the armies of the Civil War were largely amateur, their achievements were not noted in Europe, or, if noted, were dismissed as irrelevant to the demands of warfare between professional forces. This lack of appreciation of the significance of Civil War combat obliged the European armies, during World War I, to relearn its lessons at terrible cost. In that war, the American Expeditionary Force, when it began to deploy in strength on French battlefields, also suffered grievously. By attacking in Civil War style, however, it achieved a moral superiority over the German Army, dispirited by four years of attrition, that contributed greatly to the Allied victory.

World War II compelled the U.S. Army once again to adapt its tactics to a new form of combat, as it had had to do in 1861. Mechanized warfare in Europe, *amphibious warfare in the Pacific required novel responses, all the more difficult to make because of the parsimony with which the armed forces had been funded in the interwar years. The earliest success was achieved in amphibious operations, thanks chiefly to the prescience of the leadership of the U.S. Marine Corps, which during the 1920s had worked out the fundamental principles of cross-beach attack and designed the essential equipment, in particular, the first practicable landing craft, the Higgins boat. The principles and the equipment were to underlie Allied success in the amphibious operations of the Mediterranean, European, and Pacific campaigns. Without the Marine Corps experiments the *D-Day landing would not have worked.

American forces lagged behind those of Europe, particularly the German, in mechanized operations and in the ancillary field of airborne operations. They proved, thankfully, quick learners. After an uncertain start in the *North African campaign, the American expeditionary armies developed in the invasion and conquest of *Italy a formidable expertise in airborne and conventional ground operations. But their greatest success came in Northwest Europe, the theater in which they first deployed a large mass of armor. Profiting in part from a stalemate in the invasion

of *Normandy that drew German armor into a battle of attrition with the British and Canadian forces, the Americans were able eventually to achieve an enormous superiority in numbers of *tanks over the Germans at their section of the bridgehead, and to stage a breakout at *St. Lô into open country that culminated first in the encirclement of the enemy and then in a headlong advance to the frontiers of Germany.

By the time of the coming of *victory in May 1945, the American soldier had unarguably established his distinctive combat style. Flexible and adaptive, particularly to varied conditions of combat, it was characterized above all by a ruthlessly decision-oriented ethos and, as long as victory promised, a hardheaded disregard for casualties. Americans fought to win—and to win as quickly as possible—even at heavy cost to their own side.

Little in U.S. military history since the victory of 1945 vitiates that judgment of American military style. The *Korean War continued the tradition. Even at the gloomiest periods of the *Vietnam War, many front-line units continued to soldier with courage and dedication, however ill-supported by domestic opinion. In the *Persian Gulf War of 1991, American combat expertise was seen at its best. The outcome established the American armed forces as without peer in the contemporary world, and that reputation is likely to be preserved for the foreseeable future.

[See also Militia and National Guard; Native American Wars; World War II: Military and Diplomatic Course.]
—John Keegan

COMBAT EFFECTIVENESS. The mystery of why men fight has always tantalized students of warfare. Explanations usually reflect cultural and military-institutional prejudices. Men have fought—and died—against all instincts for survival because of many factors: tribal loyalties, charismatic leaders, ethnic and cultural characteristics, strict military discipline, demanding training, superior physical condition, hatred and revenge, advanced weapons, love of God or gods, belief in an afterlife that favors slain warriors, fate, sexual and biological imperatives, loot, and national *patriotism. Not until the nineteenth century did military commanders and planners begin to study the phenomenon, assisted in the last 100 years by social scientists and psychologists. Despite a brief confidence that unit cohesion and peer pressure determined combat performance, the question of combat motivation remains elusive, subject to the interaction of many characteristics of military units and the conditions of particular types of warfare.

Combat effectiveness should be seen, first, as only a part of a general framework of military effectiveness. National defense politics produces the resources for the armed forces: leadership, manpower (and now womanpower) in quality and quantity, advanced weapons, logistical support, public support, a sense of legitimacy and purpose, and a promise of rewards and compensation for the service member and his or her immediate family, especially as dependent survivors of dead or permanently incapacitated veterans. Political effectiveness is not within the province of the armed forces—except in a military dictatorship—but it certainly can be affected by how well or poorly resources are transformed into capable military forces by the nation's military leadership. Linked to political effectiveness is strategic effectiveness, or the general framework for the employment of military forces in the pursuit of war aims or the deterrence of war. Sound strategy always considers the relationship of means to ends, and the issues of appropriateness and proportionality, when examining the use of real or threatened violence as a political instrument. The history of warfare is strewn with examples in which flawed strategy doomed combat-effective forces to eventual defeat, the most recent being the experience of Germany and Japan in World War II.

Combat effectiveness is a combination of operational and tactical effectiveness, which is the performance of military units in direct contact with the enemy. Questions of operational effectiveness usually focus on the integration of forces of different combat specializations (land, air, sea) and nationality (allies); logistical sustainability for a campaign extended in time and/or distance; provisions for effective higher command in both the personal and the technical sense; the identification of fundamental enemy weaknesses; and the maximum combination of overwhelming firepower and surprising maneuver. Tactical effectiveness concentrates on the actual performance of combatant forces (infantry, armor, artillery, warships, combat aviation units) in engagements with the enemy. Operational and tactical effectiveness have an organic relationship; neither in isolation is likely to bring battlefield victory. For example, a sound operational concept like the attack by U.S. Navy *submarines on Japanese commerce (1942–1945) can be ruined (it wasn't) by poor submarine employment, faulty *torpedoes, and timorous officers and crews—all tactical considerations.

The American experience in identifying fundamental truths about combat effectiveness and transforming theory into training practice has undergone substantial change since the creation of the U.S. armed forces. It has also varied by service, since the army and Marine Corps have always worried about the special trials of ground combat, while the air force (and its predecessors) and the navy have argued that their combat functions have unique characteristics that differentiate them from ground combat units. Until the twentieth century, the normative questions about combat effectiveness concentrated on training, discipline, and mental conditioning. For wartime ground forces, the issue became avoiding the fatal combination of untrained volunteer officers with untrained militia and volunteers. Lack of peacetime military training for citizens meant that few emergency units could fight Indian warriors, European troops (i.e., the British), or even each other (the Civil War) with any prospect of success with acceptable casualties. In fact, the *citizen-soldier showed that he could fight well—if properly led and deployed in the tactical defense. Citizen-officers, on the other hand, showed little understanding of the demands of command until they had been awakened by losing a battle or two. In the early twentieth century, the problem of officership in wartime armies was addressed by providing peacetime training for prospective officers in special summer camps and at land-grant universities, and after 1916 in the Reserve Officers' Training Corps (*ROTC).

The U.S. Navy viewed its combat efficiency problems differently since its peacetime maritime constabulary missions provided it with at least a cadre of trained mariners around which to build wartime naval forces. As long as the United States had a large merchant marine—a condition that lasted into the second half of the nineteenth century—the navy could draw merchant seamen and officers into uniform for wartime service in adequate numbers and skills. The *Union navy of the Civil War represented the high point of this policy. Merchant seamen might need additional training in gunnery, but they already knew discipline and seamanship from their civilian occupations. Only when the navy had to depend upon landsmen for recruits did it worry about recruit and advanced training; most officers came from the Naval Academy and needed little more than practical experience to function well. For the navy, the major challenge became training all its personnel in the technological advances that eliminated sails and muzzle-loaded broadside guns late in the nineteenth century. New demands came from steam engines, fire direction systems, advanced turret ordnance, torpedoes, and (eventually) radar-defined and then electronic naval combat effectiveness; the introduction of aircraft and submarines only accelerated the concern for technical competence as the foundation of combat performance.

The entry of aircraft as weapons over land and sea created another approach to combat effectiveness that combined technical training with elite personnel selection—a common approach in the armies and navies of all the belligerents in World War I, and continued by separate or integrated air forces thereafter. The U.S. Army Air Service determined that the requirements of technical training, hurried under wartime conditions, meant that it had to recruit young men of bold temperament, exceptional physical skill and conditioning, and the highest intellectual acuity, with an emphasis on academic performance in formal schooling. This argument that air combat demanded the best human potential was extended to all other aircrews and even to ground service personnel. Pilots, who would almost always be officers, were promised extra pay, symbols of skill (winged insignia) and daring, freedom from ordinary military discipline, exceptional living conditions, special medical attention, and organizational preference in matters of command and training. The public fascination with aviation, as well as potential employment in the civilian aviation industry, simply reinforced the cult of the pilot. The only real modification of his ethos has been the realization that flying skill does not perish with youth and that successful combat pilots are experienced in terms of hours flown, not chronological age or prime physical condition. The spiraling demands of aviation technology and the increase of multiperson aircrews—even for superior fighters like the F-4 and F-14—also reinforced the experience of World War II (high-quality recruits still needed much flying to be combat effective). The cost of such flight training remains a concern, but the U.S. Air Force has substituted virtual reality simulator training with some success.

In the classic tradition, observers of human performance in combat from Ardant du Picq to S. L. A. *Marshall have stressed the importance of group cohesion and collective values, but the issue is complicated and in a sense exaggerated in American experience by other factors. First, a ship's crew may or may not be happy, but its fate is certainly collective: stricken warships almost always produce superhuman, selfless behavior on the part of some crewmen. The issue there, however, is not killing the enemy but saving comrades. In combat, shipboard organization stresses teamwork and a social context of cooperation and trust, based on repetitive training. The U.S. Navy has used demanding psychological testing in selecting submariners since World War II, but the screening process emphasizes adjustment to claustrophobic living rather than combat performance. Physical ability is less important than steadiness under stress and keen technical skills, a condition that also applies to aircrew service. The navy and the air force also understand the effects of fatigue, poor health, sustained tension, mental exhaustion, and eating habits on effectiveness, and expend special effort to address these problems, which make them the envy of ground forces.

Since the nineteenth century, American ground forces had plenty of group cohesion—they fought or ran in groups—and the army did not worry about the problem until World War I, when *conscription produced combat units that lacked such with civilian bonds as ethnic homogeneity, community identification, religious preference, common occupation, and self-selected leadership. In the *Civil War, volunteer infantry regiments like the 69th New York, the 1st Minnesota, the 15th New Jersey, the 20th Maine, the 4th Alabama, the 26th North Carolina, and the 27th Virginia needed no social scientist to tell them about the importance of group cohesion in combat. The introduction of conscription and the use of individual replacements by the army in every war since 1917 produced serious concern that the army would have to create group cohesiveness where none existed. The Marine Corps, never homogeneous, used one approach: complete institutional socialization from boot camp to battlefield. Smaller in number (the Marine Corps has never been larger than one-fifth the size of the army), Marines found their inspiration in limited occupational specialization ("every Marine is a rifleman") and dedication to the Corps, not some part of it. This organizational loyalty centers on the commitment to combat. The army, on the other hand, found that it had a special problem in keeping infantry units effective in wartime (America's enemies have consistently rated U.S. Army artillery and aviation as more fearsome than its foot soldiers). The issue emerged in the late stages of World War I when the divisions of the *American Expeditionary Forces endured a lack of trained replacements, of effective junior leaders, of healthy troops untouched by bad weather and the flu epidemic, and of superior firepower. That experience reshaped army definitions of combat effectiveness in World War II and thereafter.

The ground forces in World War II showed weakness in almost every aspect of combat effectiveness, especially in infantry units from divisions to squads. Arguing that they required high-quality personnel, the army air forces and navy took more than their fair share of the ablest men; the army ground forces made the wound self-inflicted when they placed similar talent into support units in excessive numbers. Combat divisions received personnel on the basis of physical condition, not maturity and intelligence, and casualties quickly thinned the ranks of junior leaders. Elite units (airborne divisions, ranger battalions) enjoyed substantial training periods, as well as quality personnel; but the average infantry and armor division had little relief from combat, especially in the European theater. Divisions that entered combat in 1942 stayed in action until the end of the war; divisions committed in June 1944 never really had an opportunity thereafter to rest and retrain.

The army's own decision to cap the wartime ground forces at eighty-nine divisions had much to do with the difficulty of maintaining combat effectiveness. This condition could not be remedied, even with the infusion of quality

(but untrained) troops from service units late in 1944. Ground combat analysts also reported that excessive fatigue caused by overloading, poor weapons training, and a lack of good junior officers and NCOs reduced combat effectiveness. The relative aggressiveness and skill of German infantry suggested a new stress upon the factor of peer pressure, based on studies by sociologists Edward Shils and Morris Janowitz as well as the work on American soldiers by a team of psychologists organized by Samuel Stouffer and the observations of former journalist S. L. A. Marshall, the latter a persuasive, self-promoting reserve officer who wrote convincingly if controversially of his after-action interviews with infantry units. The research on the Wehrmacht did indeed show that German personnel assignment and training produced good infantrymen and cohesive units, but Shils and Janowitz underestimated the influence of Nazi ideology and the German Army's practice of field executions for desertion or non-performance. Marshall stressed weapons employment and argued, without real statistical evidence, that the great majority of American soldiers did not shoot their rifles in combat—a conclusion partially supported by other analysis but also hotly contested. Marshall did identify real problems like overloading and fatigue, and he saw that the Germans stressed the use of crew-served machine guns and mortars, which demanded teamwork and produced large enemy casualties.

The postwar army sought ways to improve the performance of its ground forces—especially infantry—through a variety of reforms and succeeded within tactical definitions under its control. One policy (adopted by all the services) was to rotate personnel on and off active operations. Aviation units had begun this practice in World War II for sound operational reasons. Ships also required periodic relief from operations for service and repair, and their crews benefitted.

The idea that large numbers of ground troops, especially enlisted men, would rotate out of combat, and even leave the service before a war ended, emerged during the *Korean War (1950–51). In retrospect, combat effectiveness had little to do with the rotation policy. Equity in exposure to death and domestic politics had a great deal to do with the policy of limited liability, which was subsequently extended to the *Vietnam War. Only about one-third of the mobilized armed forces actually reached the Korean War theater; the rest remained in training in the United States or deployed to Europe. Individual reservists, especially World War II veterans, went off to fight, while National Guard and reserve units (with some exceptions) only served elsewhere. Sociologists like Janowitz and Charles Moskos reinforced the views of senior army officers that rotation weakened group cohesion and performance, but the policy was an effect, not a cause, of fighting an undeclared war with limited public support for limited goals and a negotiated (not imposed) armistice. Casualties reduce group cohesion, not rotation. The practice of conserving infantrymen by calling for deluges of artillery fire and close air support paradoxically produced excessive American casualties from so-called *friendly fire. Such a reliance also allowed many infantry units to avoid serious training and combat experience. One useful change by the army was the wider use of crew-served weapons and the internal reorganization of squads into fire teams.

Problems that went unsolved in Korea returned in the Vietnam conflict, but as long as soldiers saw some prospect of victory, they fought well. The conduct of American soldiers and Marines well into 1969 showed superior training and commitment, even in a dubious cause. Limiting Vietnam tours of duty to twelve months gave some prospect of relief, though not much for infantrymen. It was hard for "grunts" to survive a year in the "bush" under the pressures of combat and disease. The most invidious policy was rotating officers out of infantry companies after six months when grunts had no such option. Committed warriors often actually extended their combat tours, but did so most often if they belonged to elite special forces or reconnaissance units, the ground equivalent of aviation fighter squadrons. Personnel policies that reduced group cohesion may have been counterproductive. The root cause, however, of undiscipline, malingering, drug use, and soldier crime against each other and civilians was the lack of belief in the war's value, and the widespread demoralization and even incompetence in the officer corps. Just how to deal with this potential problem remains unresolved, since post-1975 operations in Grenada, Panama, and Kuwait did not last long enough or produce enough casualties to test group cohesion under sustained combat. Instead, the prevailing view is that sophisticated technology, massive firepower, low casualties, and unambiguous causes now characterize the American Way of *War. Whether this combination constitutes combat effectiveness in every instance remains to be seen.

[*See also* Combat, Changing Experience of; Combat Support; Morale, Troop; Training and Indoctrination.]

• Allan R. Millett and Williamson Murray, *Military Effectiveness*, 3 vols., 1988. Allan R. Millett and Peter Maslowski, *For the Common Defense: The Military History of the United States of America*, 1984; rev. ed., 1994.
—Allan R. Millett

COMBAT ETHICS. *See* Just War Theory.

COMBAT SUPPORT. Land warfare is the mission of the U.S. Army, and army forces are divided into three categories according to their function on the battlefield: *combat, combat support,* and *combat service support. Combat* forces engage in direct confrontation with enemy forces to kill or capture them, to break their will to continue the fight, and to seize and hold terrain or to deny it to the enemy. *Combat support* forces provide direct support of the forces on the battlefield by providing intelligence, communications, engineering, and chemical warfare services of immediate impact on the course of the battle. *Combat service support* forces provide administrative and technical (logistical) services to ensure that the combat and combat support forces are adequately manned, armed, fed, fueled, maintained, and moved as required. This division of forces into three functional groups applies specifically to the army, but navy, Marine Corps, and air force units and personnel fall into the same general categories.

With the exception of general officers, every officer, soldier, and unit of the army is assigned to one of the army's twenty-five basic and special branches. The basic branches are: Armor, Artillery, Air Defense Artillery, Aviation, Infantry, Military Intelligence, and Special Forces; the Corps of Engineers; and the Adjutant General's, Chemical, Finance, Military Police, Ordnance, Quartermaster, Signal, and Transportation Corps. The special branches include the Chaplain's and Judge Advocate General's Corps and the six branches of the Army Medical Service (the Medical,

Dental, Veterinary, Army Nurse, Army Medical Service, and Medical Specialist Corps). The Adjutant General's, Chaplain's, Finance, Judge Advocate General's, and Military Police Corps are considered administrative services. Technical services include the Corps of Engineers, Army Medical Service, and the Chemical, Ordnance, Quartermaster, Signal, and Transportation Corps. One additional special branch, Civil Affairs, is found only in the reserve components. The General Staff Corps and the Inspector General's Corps are not in fact separate branches at all, even though they have distinctive insignia. Rather, officers and enlisted personnel are detailed to the General Staff Corps or Inspector General's Corps for limited periods and then return to their basic branch.

The basic and special branches of the army are aligned with the three functional categories. The combat arms (branches) are Infantry, Armor, Artillery, Air Defense Artillery, Aviation, and Special Forces. The combat support branches include the Corps of Engineers, the Military Intelligence Corps, the Chemical Corps, and the Signal Corps. The U.S. *Army Corps of Engineers is considered both a combat arm and a combat support branch in that engineers perform direct combat missions as well as support functions. In many respects, the Signal Corps and the Chemical Corps also perform both functions. Finally, the combat service support branches include the Adjutant General's Corps, the Chaplain's Corps, the Finance Corps, the Judge Advocate General's Corps, the Military Police Corps, the Ordnance Corps, the Quartermaster Corps, the Transportation Corps, and the six branches of the Army Medical Service.

The Combat Service Support Mission. According to the official armed forces definition, combat service support covers "the essential logistic functions, activities, and tasks necessary to sustain all elements of operating forces in an area of operations. At the tactical level of war, it includes but is not limited to that support rendered by service troops in ensuring the operational and tactical aspects of supply, maintenance, transportation, health services, and other services required by aviation and ground combat troops to permit those units to accomplish their missions in combat." Thus, combat service support incorporates those functions necessary to man, arm, feed, fuel, maintain, and move the fighting forces and their equipment in the field. Its forces provide immediate support as organic elements of the forward combat units (battalions, brigades, divisions, and corps), as well as administrative and technical services in rear areas and at the highest national level. Members of the combat service support branches, like their comrades in the other branches, prepare plans, estimates, and orders; participate in the development of doctrine and materiel; and conduct training in their respective specialties.

The combat service support forces form the "tail" in the often-cited "tooth-to-tail" ratio. In fact, the analogy is a poor one. A somewhat better characterization of a field army as a living organism would be to consider the staff the brain; the combat arms, the arms and legs; the combat support branches, the eyes, ears, and nervous system; and the combat service support forces as the heart and circulatory system, which provide nourishment to the other elements.

Although the bulk of combat service support is provided out of direct contact with the enemy, these troops on the modern battlefield often become engaged in direct combat with the enemy. Soldiers receive basic combat training, and with the exception of army medical personnel and chaplains, are armed. No small percentage of the Medals of Honor and other decorations awarded for gallantry on the battlefield have been given to combat service support soldiers.

Evolution of Combat Service Support Forces. The process by which our armed forces create combat service support forces reacts to the same stimuli that influence the structuring of the combat forces themselves (namely, changing organization, doctrine, and technology). The process is especially sensitive to new developments in technology and to the ever-increasing scope and scale of modern war. Over the past two centuries, the evolution of the army's support structure has followed general trends in warfare. Four main factors have emerged: increasing complexity and scale; increasing specialization; an increasing proportion of manpower required for combat service support functions; and an increasing proportion of civilians.

Combat service support forces have been an integral and important part of the army since its creation in 1775. As the size and technological sophistication of the forces have grown, so too have the size and technological sophistication of the combat service support elements of the army. Most of the present-day support branches were established in 1818 in the aftermath of the *War of 1812, and evolved alongside the combat arms and combat support branches through the *Mexican War, the *Civil War, the *Spanish-American War, and the two world wars. Until 1912, the army had a separate Commissary of Subsistence Department, which handled the procurement and distribution of rations. However, in 1912 the Subsistence Department was merged with the Quartermaster Department. In 1950, the secretary of the army received authority to determine the number and strength of the various combat arms and services. The Infantry was retained as the premier combat arm; Armor replaced Cavalry; the Field Artillery, Coast Artillery, and Antiaircraft Artillery were consolidated in one artillery branch; the Transportation Corps and Military Police Corps were made permanent; and the six medical branches were consolidated in the Army Medical Service. A Military Intelligence branch was created in 1962, and in 1971 the Artillery was redivided into separate Artillery and Air Defense Artillery branches. The Women's Army Corps (*WAC), made a permanent part of the army establishment by the Women's Armed Services Integration Act of 12 June 1948, was discontinued in October 1978, and all women in the army were assigned to one of the twenty-five basic or special branches. The Army Air Corps, which had become the independent U.S. Air Force in 1947, was revived in 1983 as the Aviation branch. The Special Forces branch was created in 1987 by the transfer of officers and soldiers from several other basic and special branches.

Since the end of the *Vietnam War, two important developments in the organization and employment of combat service support forces have taken place. First, the proportion of female soldiers assigned to service support units of all types has increased dramatically. Second, in the Total Force concept since the 1980s, most of the army's combat service support force structure has been taken out of the active (regular) army and assigned to the reserve components. Thus, in the *Persian Gulf War (1991), over 70 percent of the army's combat service support forces deployed to the region came from the Army Reserve and National Guard.

Traditionally, the combat service support forces have occupied a status seen as somewhat inferior to those of the other two categories. Even today, many army leaders give lip service to the importance of combat service support on the modern battlefield but still fail correctly to assess its contribution to the overall equation of victory. In modern warfare such a faulty appreciation can no longer be sustained in view of the ample evidence of the importance of administrative and logistical matters.

[*See also* Army Combat Branches; Communications; Engineering, Military; Intelligence, Military and Political; Logistics; Maintenance; Transportation.]

• Headquarters, Department of the Army, *The Department of the Army*, 1977. Robert H. Scales, Jr., *Certain Victory: The U.S. Army in the Gulf War*, 1994. Charles R. Shrader, ed., *Reference Guide to United States Military History*, Vol. 5: *1945 to the Present*, 1994. United States, Office of the Joint Chiefs of Staff, *Joint Pub 1–02: Department of Defense Dictionary of Military and Associated Terms*, 1994.
—Charles R. Shrader

COMBAT TRAUMA. That war can wound minds as well as bodies was not recognized for many years. Military physicians often diagnosed combat trauma as malingering; high-ranking officers regarded it as a threat to discipline and combat effectiveness. Some of the soldiers executed as cowards during the *Civil War probably suffered from combat trauma. Not until the 1980s did the U.S. government unequivocally recognize psychic injury as a legitimate service-related disability.

Symptoms of combat trauma have almost always been similar to those of a heart attack: involuntary trembling, exaggerated startle response (usually with respect to noises), outbursts of uncontrollable anger, nightmares, flashbacks, emotional numbing, restlessness, depression, and alcoholism. Combat trauma might persist for days or months; it can also haunt a lifetime.

Chronologically, such labels as "soldier's heart," "shell shock," "battle fatigue," "Post-Traumatic Stress Disorder" hint at the different medical and cultural assumptions of the times in which they were devised. The mid-nineteenth-century conviction that mental disease had an organic origin gave way to the notion that wounds to the mind have psychological causes. Recently, the pendulum has swung in the direction of biopsychological explanations for mental disorder.

Civil War surgeons were almost wholly preoccupied with amputating arms and legs, a form of higher butchery that left little time and no patience for the treatment of combat trauma—had its existence been recognized. Countless Union veterans bore psychic injuries of greater or lesser severity long into the peace—among them the jurist Oliver Wendell Holmes, Jr., and the writer Ambrose Bierce—but neither government nor society recognized this in any direct way. And in all likelihood, many ex-soldiers themselves probably did not understand the cause of their troubles.

In the early months of World War I, combat trauma took British medical officers by surprise. At first ascribed to the concussive effect of exploding artillery rounds on the brain, "shell shock" was soon seen as an emotional response to the overwhelming and sustained life-threatening character of modern warfare. Some medical officers prescribed "disciplinary therapy"—electric shock treatments—betraying their conviction that combat trauma was a form of malingering; others resorted to psychotherapy, the still-novel "talking cure."

Fully a year before the entry of the United States into the war in April 1917, the Rockefeller Foundation sponsored an inquiry by the psychiatrist Thomas Salmon into the Allies' methods of dealing with shell shock. By the time elements of the American Expeditionary Forces began landing in France, Salmon had established a psychiatric field hospital. The Americans emulated the French, treating psychiatric casualties at aid stations near the front rather than waiting, as the British did, until they had reached the rear. A medical officer's military duties tended to override his obligations to his patients. Treatment aimed at returning psychically wounded men to the front. As Sigmund Freud noted: "The physicians had to play a role somewhat like that of a machine gun behind the front line, that of driving back those who fled."

The leading postwar veterans group, the *American Legion, called for welcoming shell-shocked veterans back into society and lobbied successfully to see them compensated, at least in part, for a war-related disability. Within the armed forces, combat trauma was largely disregarded because medical and military authorities had come to believe that psychological testing provided an effective preventive measure against it. The prevailing degeneration theory held that mental disorders were inheritable; they were discernible at an early age. Men likely to break down in combat could be weeded out before they ever put on a uniform.

In World War II, the American armed forces swelled to enormous size; psychological testing itself was put to the test, and its premises with respect to combat trauma were found to be false. Military psychiatrists were soon convinced that *any* infantryman exposed to prolonged fighting would eventually break down. "There is no such thing as 'getting used to combat,'" an official study found. If the incidence of combat trauma was likely to be highest among foot soldiers, it was by no means unknown to sailors and airmen. The crews of ships targeted by kamikazes during the Okinawa campaign (April–June 1945) sustained numerous psychiatric casualties; Joseph Heller's absurdist war novel *Catch-22* (1961) rests on the premise about what it took, in terms of a diagnosis for combat trauma, to be relieved of flying bombing raids over enemy territory.

If all wars are fearful, each is fearful in different ways. In World War I, for instance, the prevalence of shell shock was ascribed to the lethality of the western front. In the *Vietnam War, however, the risk of getting killed was lower than it had been in 1917–18, but the incidence of combat trauma was higher. In Vietnam, perhaps the elusiveness of the enemy and the absence of a front inspired fears similar to those that the low odds on surviving had inspired in *trench warfare. Yet in provoking combat trauma, all modern wars display common elements. The terror peculiar to undergoing sustained artillery fire, for instance, unites combat soldiers in the field at Fredericksburg in 1862 with their counterparts in the trenches of 1917, on Okinawa in 1945, and in the rice paddies of Vietnam in 1968.

Post-Traumatic Stress Disorder (PTSD) was a postVietnam creation. The outcome of the successful lobbying of Congress and the *Veterans Administration by veterans' interest groups, PTSD also expressed the shifting balance of influence within the psychiatric profession: away from psychodynamic psychotherapy toward biopsychiatric, pharmacological approaches to the treatment of mental illness. So far, however, the great increase in the explanatory power of biomedical stories about combat trauma has not been accompanied by a commensurate increase in the efficacy of therapies directed against it. By altering minds, the horrific experiences of combat have reshaped lives—drastically shortening some, blighting the promise of others, ruining still others. Psychiatric casualties are implicated in what the medical anthropologist Arthur Kleinman calls "social suffering," a web in which the woes of one person engender woes for many.

[*See also* Aggression and Violence; Casualties; Combat, Changing Experiences of; Combat Effectiveness; Morale; Troop; Psychiatry, Military.]

• Abram Kardiner, *The Traumatic Neuroses of War,* 1940. Paul Fussell, *Wartime: Understanding and Behavior in the Second World War,* 1989. Jonathan Shay, *Achilles in Vietnam,* 1994. David Grossman, *On Killing: The Psychological Cost of Learning to Kill in War and Society,* 1995. Allan Young, *The Harmony of Illusions: Inventing Post-Traumatic Stress Disorder,* 1995. Samuel Hynes, *The Soldiers' Tale: Bearing Witness to Modern War,* 1997. Eric T. Dean, Jr., *Shook Over Hell: Post-Traumatic Stress, Vietnam, and the Civil War,* 1997.

—John Talbott

COMMAND AND CONTROL. In the military, the term *command and control (C2)* means a process (not the systems, as often thought) that commanders, including command organizations, use to plan, direct, coordinate, and control their own and friendly forces and assets to ensure mission accomplishment. Command and control of U.S. armed forces today is the result of a long historical evolution. From 1775 to 1947, there was no common superior to the War and Navy Departments and their respective military services, except for the president of the United States, who was commander in chief of the army and navy under the Constitution. Only in 1947 were all the military departments and services unified in principle.

The rudiments of U.S. national military command and control emerged in 1775, when the American colonists challenged the government in London and ultimately obtained independence from the mother country. Initially, the American colonists were loosely organized and lacked a recognized military commander. The Second Continental Congress convened in Philadelphia and on 15 June 1775 named Gen. George *Washington commander in chief "of all the continental forces raised, or to be raised, for the defense of American liberty."

After 1776, the Continental Congress acted as the principal coordinator of the war effort of the American colonies. It organized an army and navy and appointed commanders of these forces. However, there was no clear direction as to whether Congress or the commander in chief was to devise strategy. Unwilling to put a single person in charge of the war effort, Congress appointed a committee, the Board of War and Ordnance, in June 1776. But the board did not work satisfactorily, and Congress kept close watch on the military and its commanders. The war proved the need for strong, central direction and the subordination of state to national interests.

The new Constitution of 1789 created a separate executive branch, but declaring war, raising armies, and providing for a navy was assigned exclusively to Congress. In March 1789, Washington became the first president under this Constitution, and as such he was also designated commander in chief of the army and navy. The Department of War was established on 7 August 1789; the secretary of war headed the War Department and was a deputy to the president in military matters. The Navy Department was not created until 30 April 1798.

In the *War of 1812, the lack of a senior line officer in the chain of command to act as adviser to the secretary of war and the president proved a serious deficiency. Command and control of the U.S. Army and Navy remained essentially unchanged between 1821 and the beginning of the *Civil War in 1861. The president was commander in chief of the army and navy, while his two civilian deputies ran the War Department and the Navy Department. In command of army troops after 1821 was the senior army officer, the commanding general or general in chief. However, his duties were left undefined. There was no corresponding position for the navy.

In the aftermath of the Civil War, the Commanding general of the army was made responsible for the efficiency, discipline, and conduct of the troops, while the secretary of war was responsible for the administrative and technical services. The latter also controlled budget, and all the army bureau chiefs reported to him. The secretary of war was a civilian, often with very little military experience, and he depended for guidance on bureau chiefs. Hence, Gen. Ulysses S. *Grant proposed in 1866 to place the Adjutant General under the control of the commanding general of the army, who was to be responsible directly to the president through the secretary of the army in all army matters. No action was taken until 1869, when General Grant became the president and issued an order putting his proposal into effect.

The *Spanish-American War exemplified all the worst features of the archaic U.S. system of military command and control. The lack of military planning and very poor coordination between the services led to general confusion and inefficiency. Nonetheless, the war was successful, due to the initiative, courage, and endurance of the American soldier and his immediate superiors.

The underlying cause of friction and confusion in the War Department was between the commanding general of the army and the bureau chiefs. The new secretary of war, Elihu *Root, proposed to abolish the position of commanding general, and the new position of chief of staff of the army was created. That officer was to be in charge of all army forces and the staff departments, and directly responsible to the secretary of war. The chief of staff would act as adviser and executive agent of the president through the secretary of war. Congress adopted Root's proposal in February 1903. Another significant change proposed by Root and approved by Congress was the creation of a General Staff Corps (patterned after the Prussian system but greatly reduced) of forty-four officers to prepare plans for the national defense and for the mobilization of the military forces.

The disruptive experiences of attempted navy-army cooperation during the Spanish-American War led to an attempt in 1903 to improve matters by institutionalizing coordination between the two services through a Joint Army and Navy Board, consisting of four army and four Navy officers. However, the Joint Board did not have a group of officers to do the planning. Its work was suspended by President Woodrow *Wilson in 1914, and it did not play any role during World War I.

National command and control underwent some changes in the 1920s. The National Defense Act of June 1920 remained the principal piece of legislation pertaining to the U.S. Army until 1950. The Joint Board was reestablished in 1919 and its membership increased to six. In contrast to its predecessor, the newly reestablished board acted continuously. It was also provided for the first time with a subordinate staff group: the Joint Planning Committee.

In 1922, the Joint Committee on the Reorganization of Government Departments proposed that the army and navy be unified into a Department of *Defense under a single cabinet secretary, who would be assisted by undersecretaries for the army, the navy, and for national resources. Nothing came of these efforts because the two military departments opposed unification. A further attempt by Congress at unification failed in April 1932.

In 1939, President Franklin D. *Roosevelt placed the Joint Board, the Joint Economy Board, the Aeronautical Board, and the Army-Navy Munitions Board under his own direction as commander in chief. The Joint Board of the Army and Navy was never organized as a body to provide strategic direction; its meetings were held only once a month, while its Joint Planning Committee met twice a month. A more serious problem was that any decision of the Joint Board required the approval of the secretaries of war and the navy before it could be effected. By May 1941, the Joint Board established a Joint Strategical Committee as a part of the existing planning committee. Its major responsibility was to draft joint war plans. In July, the Joint Board began to meet weekly.

The Joint Board evolved into the *Joint Chiefs of Staff (JCS) as a result of a visit by British prime minister Winston S. *Churchill and his military advisers who came to Washington in late December 1941 to confer with President Roosevelt about collaboration in the war against the Axis powers. By early 1942, a decision was made that the Combined Chiefs of Staffs (CCS)—a collective term for the U.S. and the British chiefs of staff—were to provide strategic direction for all operations under Anglo-American responsibility. The first formal meeting of the CCS took place on 23 January 1942.

The chiefs of staff of the various U.S. armed services held their first meeting on 9 February 1942. Afterward, the chiefs of staffs constituted themselves with tacit approval of the president as Joint Chiefs of Staff. The Joint Board for all practical purposes ceased to operate. Initially, the JCS served as the U.S. representative of the CCS and as the coordinating agency for the war efforts of the army and navy, directly responsible to the president. The JCS was also in the direct chain of command of each U.S. theater commander. No legislative or executive action was taken to formalize the JCS until the *National Security Act (NSA) of 1947 was adopted. This proved to be an advantage, because it allowed a great deal of flexibility and innovation in the work. The act created the National Military Establishment (NME) and the civilian secretary. It unified all the services and created co-equal cabinet-level secretaries for the new Departments of the Army, Navy, and Air Force. The roles and missions of the military services were specified in an executive order (Congress did not do the same until 1958). The NSA also legalized both the JCS and its Joint Staff. For the first time it defined the term *combatant command*. The "unified" combatant command was defined as a command composed of forces from more than a single military department and with one broad, continuing mission.

The act became effective when Secretary of Defense James V. *Forrestal took the oath of office on 18 December 1948. The act also established the *National Security Council (NSC) as the principal forum to consider national security issues that require presidential decision. NSA was subsequently supplemented or amended by several other pieces of legislation and executive agreement. The *Key West Agreement of 1948 clarified the residual roles left to the military departments. It also allowed members of the JCS to serve as executive agents for unified commands—a responsibility that enabled them to originate a direct communication with the combatant command. (This authority was canceled by a 1953 amendment to NSA.)

The NSA was amended in 1949 and the name of the NME changed to Department of *Defense (DoD). The secretary of defense's position was strengthened by his appointment as the head of an executive department. The authority of military department heads was reduced, and they assumed budgeting responsibilities. In 1953, the president and secretary of defense agreed to designate military departments to function as "executive agents" for the unified commands. Also, the chairman of the JCS was not to exercise any command over theater forces. The Reorganization Act of 1958 further clarified the direction, authority, and control of the secretary of defense; moreover, the act clarified the operational chain of command by stipulating that it ran from the president and the secretary of defense to the combatant forces, thereby removing military departments from the operational chain of command and redefining their support and administrative responsibilities.

The most important piece of legislation on national defense since 1947 was the *Goldwater-Nichols Act of 1986. It was specifically aimed to enhance cohesion between the services, clarify the chain of command, and further strengthen civilian control over the U.S. military. It also strengthened the position and authority of the CJCS. The chairman became principal military adviser to the president, secretary of defense, and NSC. However, in presenting his advice, the CJCS was required to present the range of advice and opinions he had received, along with any individual comments of the other JCS members.

The 1986 act also created a new position, vice chairman of the JCS, and two new directors of the Joint Staff. The size of the Joint Staff was expanded but limited to 1,627 personnel. The vice chairman is the second-ranking member of the armed forces and replaces the CJCS in his absence. The National Defense Authorization Act (1993) vested the vice chairman as a full voting member of the JCS.

In legal terms, the National Command Authorities (NCA)—that is, the president and the secretary of defense or their duly deputized alternates or successors—retain ultimate authority and responsibility for U.S. national security. The DoD Reorganization Act (1986) reiterated that the chain of command runs from the president to the secretary, and from the latter to the combatant commanders. A provision permits the president to authorize communications through the CJCS. Presidential directive 5100.1 of 25 September 1987 placed the CJCS in the communications chain of command. Communications between the National Command Authorities and the combatant command pass through the CJCS. Directly subordinate to the NCA in the operational chain of command are five geographical combatant commands (Atlantic, Central, European, Pacific, and Southern) and three functional combatant commands (Strategic, Space, and Transportation).

U.S. national military command control today is much more effective than it was only a decade ago. Civilian control of the military is preserved and strengthened. The operational chain of command is simple and clear. And the geographic combatant commanders possess the necessary resources and authority to accomplish their assigned missions.

[*See also* Civil-Military Relations: Civilian Control of the Military; Commander in Chief, President as.]

• Louis Smith, *American Democracy and Military Power: A Study of Civil Control of the Military Power in the United States*, 1951. Maurice Matloff, ed., *American Military History*, 1956. Harry T. Williams, *Americans at War: The Development of the American Military System*, 1956. Samuel P. Huntington, *The Soldier and the State: The Theory and the Politics of Civil Military Relations*, 1957. Demetrios Caraley, *The Politics of Military Unification. A Study of Conflict and the Policy Process*, 1966. Edward Kolodziej, *The Uncommon Defense and Congress 1945–1963*, 1966. C. W. Borkland, *The Department of Defense*, 1968. Russell F. Weigley, *The American Way of War. A History of United States Military Policy and Strategy*, 1973. Mark D. Mandeles, Thomas C. Hone, and Sanford S. Terry, *Managing "Command and Control" in the Persian Gulf War*, 1996.

—Milan Vego

COMMANDER IN CHIEF, PRESIDENT AS. The Constitution (Article II, section 2) specifies that "The President shall be Commander in Chief of the Army and Navy of the United States, and of the Militia of the several states, when called into the actual Service of the United States." This language provides the president with constitutional powers over the armed forces, powers shared with Congress; but the constitutional framework leaves several unsettling questions unanswered. May the president use force if he believed an attack were imminent; use force without a declaration of war; defend American lives and property abroad; execute treaty obligations involving the armed forces; or engage in "coercive diplomacy" to get leaders of other nations to accede to his wishes?

The president's most important duty as commander in chief is to defend the United States, its territories and possessions and its armed forces, from attack. Domestically, this may mean using or threatening to use force to make sure that laws are faithfully executed, as George *Washington did when he rode out at the head of a column of troops to put down the Whiskey Rebellion, as Andrew *Jackson did in 1832 when he threatened to use force against South Carolina if it did not permit collection of the tariff, and as Abraham *Lincoln did to end the secession of Southern states. Presidents may also use the armed forces to maintain "the peace of the United States," as several presidents in the late nineteenth and early twentieth centuries did in enforcing district court injunctions against striking miners and railway workers.

Presidents are not expected to march at the heads of their armed forces. Some, such as Franklin D. *Roosevelt, Lyndon B. *Johnson, and George *Bush, maintained close control over military operations, not only reviewing strategy but controlling the details of specific missions. They communicated directly with key theater commanders. Others, such as Woodrow *Wilson and Harry S. Truman, set overall parameters, but tended to rely more on going through channels and trusting the judgment of their top commanders. As Lincoln discovered during the *Civil War, the most important war power the president possesses is the power to hire and fire those commanders.

The most controversial constitutional issue involves presidential warmaking without a declaration from Congress, when presidents depend solely on their constitutional prerogative as commander in chief. Outside the United States, presidents have used the armed forces without congressional declarations of war in more than 230 instances, relying on that constitutional prerogative. Fewer than half of these instances involved prior legislative authorization. Almost all use of force by presidents in the nineteenth century without a declaration of war involved minor incidents—mostly against pirates and bandits. Uses of force in hostilities without congressional sanction in the twentieth century, however, have involved much wider operations against organized governments. With large numbers of American soldiers killed or wounded in pursuit of foreign policy goals, such actions raised serious questions of constitutionality.

Uses of force based on the commander in chief's power include gaining additional territory for the United States, such as Florida (actions of James *Monroe and John Quincy Adams), the American Southwest (during the *Mexican War), and Hawaii. Presidents may order actions against politically unorganized pirates and bandits, drug smugglers, and terrorists that may involve limited incursion into another state or its airspace or territorial waters. Presidents may order the evacuation of U.S. citizens and interventions to protect American lives and property during disorders in foreign nations. In some situations, the United States may be involved unilaterally or multilaterally in efforts to restore law and order in other nations. During the last half of the nineteenth century, the U.S. Army fought frontier wars against Indian tribes. In the early twentieth century, presidents ordered U.S. forces to intervene in Caribbean nations to administer their assets on behalf of their creditors; these included Haiti, *Nicaragua, the Dominican Republic, and Cuba. Presidents have used force to topple regimes unfriendly to the United States, such as the Dominican Republic (1965), Grenada (1982), Panama (1989), and Haiti (1994).

Presidents have enforced *blockades and quarantines, for example, the quarantine of Cuba during the *Cuban Missile Crisis (1962–63); the blockade of Iraq in 1990 to attempt to pressure that nation to withdraw from Kuwait; the subsequent blockade designed to ensure acquiescence in *United Nations resolutions; and the blockade of Haiti in 1993 in an effort to force a change in government. Since the early 1950s, presidents have had the capacity to launch preemptive or retaliatory nuclear strikes in the event of all-out nuclear war, or to order a nuclear "first use" against an enemy in the process of defeating U.S. conventional forces. The exigencies of the use of nuclear weapons make it highly unlikely that Congress could be part of such a decision. More recently, presidents have used U.S. forces for United Nations' or other multilateral *peacekeeping, humanitarian, or monitoring operations, such as the protection of foreign aid workers in Somalia in 1992–93, the re-

lief of famine in Rwanda in 1994, and the *NATO peacekeeping mission in Bosnia beginning in 1995.

The most controversial use of presidential power has involved deployment of U.S. forces in major hostilities without a declaration of war. Three major instances come to mind: North Korea (1950–53), North Vietnam (1964–73), and Iraq (1991). In the Korean and Iraq hostilities, Presidents Truman and Bush cited UN authorization. However, Truman used force prior to obtaining UN authorization, and neither president followed the procedures set down by Congress in the UN Participation Act (1945), which required congressional approval for commitments of force in UN operations. In the *Vietnam War, President Johnson claimed he was executing provisions of *SEATO, yet the relevant provisions required consultation with other signatory nations and did not specify the use of military force to deal with a civil war between two "military regroupment zones" (i.e., North and South Vietnam). In all three cases, presidents acted according to their prerogative power, and in Korea and Vietnam, no hostilities were authorized by Congress (though the Gulf of Tonkin Resolution did authorize Johnson to use necessary measures to protect U.S. forces). Indeed, the *War Powers Resolution of 1973 sought to impose Congressional approval for committing U.S. troops to combat. In 1991, Bush lobbied Congress for authorization to use force to implement UN resolutions; but in his signing statement once a resolution had been passed, the president refused to concede that he had needed such authorization, claiming instead that he had "constitutional authority to use the Armed Forces to defend vital U.S. interests." Congress passed a second resolution reiterating its understanding that the president had been required to obtain prior authorization from Congress before using force against Iraq, leaving the two institutions at loggerheads about the authority of the president to engage in military actions to implement UN resolutions.

Use of the armed forces exposes the incumbent to significant political risk. Presidents Truman and Johnson became so unpopular because of mounting casualties during the Korean and Vietnam Wars, both decided not to run for second elected terms. Studies have shown that there is a direct correlation between increased *casualties in congressional districts and a drop in approval for the war—and for the commander in chief who authorized it. To minimize this political risk, presidents in the post–Vietnam era have authorized operations that involve overwhelming force against weak opponents—the operations in Grenada, Panama, and Haiti—and have tightly controlled the media so that reportage emphasizes military successes rather than any operational failures. Such quick operations have been highly successful politically, resulting in a "rally 'round the flag" effect and an upward surge in popularity for the commander in chief. Presidents have also been reluctant to remain involved in operations with significant American casualties. President Reagan withdrew American forces from Lebanon after 240 Marines were killed in a bombing of the American barracks; President Clinton withdrew forces from Somalia after eighteen army Rangers were killed in military operations.

With the end of the *Cold War, the commander in chief's power focuses on the use of armed forces for humanitarian, policing, and peacekeeping operations. Does the president have the power to assign U.S. forces to foreign command? Can Congress prohibit or regulate such assignments? Republicans in their 1994 "Contract with America" proposed a National Security Restoration Act to prohibit such assignments, in a replay of the partisan controversy over a Democratic president's power to do so during the Korean War (when U.S. troops were nominally under UN command). Although such a prohibition did not pass, the constitutional questions involving presidential use of force remain open in the post–Cold War era.

[See also Civil-Military Relations: Civilian Control of the Military; Congress, War, and the Military; Constitutional and Political Basis of War and the Military; National Defense Acts; Peacekeeping.]

• Clinton Rossiter and Richard Longaker, The Supreme Court and the Commander in Chief, 1976. Richard Pious, The American Presidency, 1979. Francis Wormuth and Arthur Firmage, To Chain the Dog of War, 1986; 2nd ed. 1989. Joseph Dawson, ed., Commanders in Chief, 1993. Gary M. Stern and Morton H. Halperin, eds., The U.S. Constitution and the Power to Go to War, 1993. Louis Fisher, The Presidential War Powers, 1995.   —Richard M. Pious

COMMEMORATION AND PUBLIC RITUAL. The memory of past wars has played a central role in creating and defining American national identity. After the signing of the Declaration of Independence in 1776, Independence Day became the new republic's preeminent national holiday, even before the United States won the armed struggle against Great Britain. Neither the Continental Congress nor succeeding federal Congresses ever mandated rituals for the day, but certain patterns emerged culturally that lasted into the twentieth century. In many communities, Fourth of July observances centered on public orations, readings of the Declaration of Independence, religious services, parades, public dinners, and fireworks. Local governments often sponsored Independence Day ceremonies, but this was by no means universal.

The Fourth of July has often been contested as dominant and dissenting groups have created rituals to bolster their ideologies and social positions. During the 1790s, for example, Federalists and Jeffersonian Republicans held separate, competing celebrations. Whereas Federalists went so far as to drop the reading of the Declaration of Independence in order to diminish Thomas *Jefferson's crucial role, Republicans made the reading of this text a central part of their ceremonies.

During the nineteenth century, especially in larger urban centers, the Independence Day parade developed into a broad-based celebration that included virtually every major group in the locality. Strong traditions of popular participation still fostered dissenting groups' tendencies to use Fourth of July ceremonies to advance their aims. Ethnic, religious, labor, and other groups commonly sponsored their own observances. Susan B. Anthony, Frederick Douglass, Charles Sumner, and other speakers used Independence Day orations to protest injustices; such speeches were frequently published, thus reaching substantial regional and national audiences.

The militia also played an important ritualistic role in the commemoration of the Revolution, especially on Independence Day. Militia units, particularly elite volunteer regiments, used the occasion to march in parades and display their military prowess and social standing. In the 1820s and 1830s, volunteer militia staged some of the first reenactments of Revolutionary battles.

To honor and later memorialize George *Washington and successive generations of war leaders, Americans created a range of holidays, many of them transitory. As early as the 1780s, Americans commemorated the birth of Washington. During his presidency, Federalists lit bonfires and held balls in his honor, carrying over earlier British practices of honoring the birthday of the sovereign. Jeffersonian Republicans disapproved; only after the demise of the Federalist Party in the 1820s did Washington's Birthday observances lose their partisanship and evolve into the permanent holiday that eventually gained federal recognition. Later in the nineteenth century, Andrew *Jackson, Abraham *Lincoln, Jefferson *Davis, Robert E. *Lee, and George *Dewey all had their birthdays or other days associated with them commemorated. Jackson Day, celebrating his victory at the Battle of *New Orleans on 8 January 1815, was always a partisan affair. Lee's and Davis's birthdays remained southern holidays, while Lincoln's birthday too had regional overtones; most southern states never made it an official holiday.

The passing of the Revolutionary generation in the 1820s and 1830s gave impetus to the creation of new forms of commemoration. By the antebellum period, monuments—controversial in the 1790s because of their association with monarchical Europe—became widely accepted. Usually funded by private organizations, the inauguration and completion of such monuments could be marked by lavish celebrations. In 1824, the Marquis de Lafayette laid the cornerstone of many Revolutionary memorials, including the Bunker Hill Obelisk.

The *Civil War led to a democratization and an emphasis on rituals that remembered the sacrifice of average *citizen-soldiers. In both North and South during the late 1860s, cemeteries became the focal point of a new holiday—Memorial Day, often known as Decoration Day. This holiday, which developed concurrently in both regions, centered on decorating the graves of the war dead with flowers and holding religious services, parades, and other ceremonies. Veterans' organizations, especially the *Grand Army of the Republic, played a crucial role in organizing and promoting these observances.

Reconciliation, but also continued sectional bitterness, emerged as competing themes in the rituals commemorating the Civil War. Memorial Day orators often stressed the need to honor the fallen from both sides and early accounts of the holiday emphasized decorating the graves of soldiers, regardless of the army in which they fought. Nonetheless, in the North, the Memorial Day observance took place on 30 May whereas most Southerners (except for African Americans) commemorated Confederate Memorial Day on varying dates in the spring. Ladies' Memorial Associations and later the Daughters of the Confederacy played a crucial role in organizing Confederate holiday activities.

Most Civil War *veterans never joined any veterans' organization, but a significant number became members of either the Grand Army of the Republic or the United Confederate Veterans, the two dominant societies to emerge after the war. Encampments on old battlefields or in or near major cities remained a central activity for these organizations. "Blue-Gray" reunions, joint gatherings of participants from opposing armies, began as early as the 1870s, but took place with greater frequency during the Gilded Age and Progressive Era. Participants in the Battle of *Gettysburg gathered under federal sponsorship on its fiftieth and seventy-fifth anniversaries. Both Woodrow *Wilson (1913) and Franklin D. *Roosevelt (1938) addressed these reunions, stressing national unity and sectional reconciliation.

In the late nineteenth century, federal and state governments joined private organizations in sustained, if uncoordinated, efforts to preserve battlefields, homes, and other sites associated with past American wars. Under pressure from veterans' organizations, the federal government began acquiring Civil War battlefields. During the twentieth century, while continuing to purchase Civil War sites, congress added locations associated with the *Revolutionary War, The *War of 1812, and Indian wars to a growing list of national military parks. These sites had already been important places for memorial services, reunions, and tourism, and the National Park Service, from the 1930s onward, promoted their use for a range of ceremonies, including battlefield reenactments.

After *World War I, members of both major political parties sought to diminish ethnic, racial, class, and gender divisions by instituting national rituals of remembrance. In response to a conflict marked by antiwar resistance and an ambiguous peace, these commemorative activities were intended to reassure Americans that the United States's participation in the war had been necessary. As in the post–Civil War era, the war dead remained a central symbol. The federal government maintained cemeteries and monuments in Europe, but also responded to pressures from families and localist groups by allowing next-of-kin to decide whether the fallen should be repatriated or remain in these newly created overseas burial grounds.

To represent the sacrifice of the average soldier, Congress followed British and other European precedents in authorizing the burial of an Unknown Soldier in a place of honor in Arlington National Cemetery. The remains of unknown soldiers from *World War II, the *Korean War, and the *Vietnam War have since been interred there. The Tomb of the Unknown Solider, visited by presidents and other high officials to lay wreaths and to participate in ceremonies at the Arlington National Amphitheater, has become an important site of commemorative ritual.

In the 1920s, Armistice Day emerged as holiday to mark the anniversary of the end of World War I, and an occasion to honor not only the fallen but all of the veterans who had served. The *American Legion promoted community observances, including parades, orations, and memorial services; many citizens joined veterans in observing two minutes of silence on the eleventh of hour of the eleventh day of the eleventh month to mark the exact time the war ended and to mourn its dead. In 1938, the American Legion convinced Congress to make Armistice Day an official federal holiday.

Despite its epic nature, World War II led to few significant changes in the American pattern of remembrance. Only Arkansas and Rhode Island made V-J Day—the anniversary of the end of the conflict—into a holiday. Renamed Veterans' Day, Armistice Day evolved in the 1940s and 1950s into a holiday that honored veterans of all wars.

The post–World War II era witnessed a decline in public rituals centered on remembrance of the past. The concurrent growth of suburbia, the mass media (especially television), and a consumer culture all diminished attendance at public commemorative events. In 1968, Congress recog-

nized the fact that holidays had become days of leisure and consumption by decreeing that the official celebrations of civic holidays, except for Independence Day and Thanksgiving, would take place on the Monday nearest their customary dates. In the 1970s, veterans' groups successfully lobbied Congress and state legislatures to return the commemoration of Veterans' Day to 11 November.

Meanwhile, the federal government under took a more active role in planning and organizing commemorative rituals. Created in 1957, the Civil War Centennial Commission sponsored national commemorations and encouraged states and local communities to organize their own observances. Controversy embroiled this commission, especially over its policy of segregation in the South and the widespread use of battlefield reenactments to mark major events of the war. Critics assailed the commission, as well as a number of state and local organizations, for commercializing centennial activities. Even under nationally organized commissions, however, localist traditions still predominated: the American Revolution Bicentennial Commission, for instance, maintained that its central role was to encourage state and local community observances.

In the late 1970s and 1980s, Americans memorialized the Vietnam War in monuments that rejected classicism and embraced modernism, as well as a more pluralistic depiction of American society. Critics, especially on the right, often derided these memorials as "anti-monuments." Maya Lin's highly influential design—two stark black granite walls inscribed with the names of all those killed in Vietnam—for the national Vietnam Veterans' Memorial on the Mall in Washington, D.C., aroused considerable opposition. Critics forced the addition in 1984 of a more traditional statue and a flagpole. Even after its dedication in 1982, controversy still dogged the Vietnam Memorial over its failure to recognize the contribution of women. Responding to appeals from women veterans, Congress mandated in 1989 that a statue honoring their service be added to the memorial. Despite such criticism, the Vietnam Memorial emerged in the 1980s as one of most visited sites in the nation's capital. The scores of poems, letters, and artifacts left each day by visitors testify to the monument's power to evoke collective and personal grief.

As America entered the closing decade of the twentieth century, a renewed interest in both rituals and monuments emerged. In the late 1980s, a number of communities staged long-delayed welcome home parades for Vietnam veterans. After the Persian Gulf War in 1991, several major cities held victory parades to honor both the combatants of this conflict and those who served in Vietnam. Responding to the success of the Vietnam Memorial, the American Battle Monuments Commission received congressional authorization for a national Korean War Veterans' Memorial in 1995, also in the Mall in Washington. A monument commemorating World War II is proposed for completion by the close of the twentieth century.

[See also Battlefields, Encampments, and Forts as Public Sites; Cemeteries, Military; Culture, War, and the Military; Patriotism.]

• Wallace Evan Davies, *Patriotism on Parade: The Story of Veterans' and Hereditary Organizations, 1783–1900*, 1955. Jan C. Scruggs and Joel L. Swerdlow, *To Heal a Nation: The Vietnam Veterans Memorial*, 1985. Susan G. Davis, *Parades and Power: Street Theatre in Nineteenth-Century Philadelphia*, 1986. Gaines M. Foster, *Ghosts of the Confederacy: Defeat, the Lost Cause, and the Emergence of the New*

South, 1865–1913, 1987. Edward Tabor Linenthal, *Sacred Ground: Americans and Their Battlefields,* 1991. John Bodnar, *Remaking America: Public Memory, Commemoration, and Patriotism in the Twentieth Century,* 1992. Garry Wills, *Lincoln at Gettysburg,* 1992. Jim Cullen, *The Civil War in Popular Culture: A Reusable Past,* 1995. G. Kurt Piehler, *Remembering War the American Way,* 1995.
—G. Kurt Piehler

COMMUNICATIONS. From the *Revolutionary War to the present, the American military has used communications in order to command and control its forces and other assets, but the technology has changed dramatically. Methods employed during the nation's war for independence (messengers, signal lights, and voice commands) differed little from those used by ancient armies.

During the *Civil War, visual signaling remained the primary communications method. The utility of the electric telegraph (invented 1837) had been amply demonstrated by European armies since the 1850s; but Albert J. Myer gave it little attention when designing the nation's first military communications organization, the U.S. Army Signal Corps. Established by an act of Congress on 21 June 1860, the Signal Corps employed Myer's "wigwag" system. Using an adaptation of the Bain telegraph code, movements of flags (and at night, torches) transmitted tactical communications within visual range. Although army signalers operated "telegraph trains" (communications wagons with telegraphs and field wire), fixed wire communications were beyond Myer's purview. With regular trips to the War Department, President Lincoln read the latest telegraphic reports on the progress of the war. The conduit for that information, more than likely, was the rival U.S. Military Telegraph, a contract firm that used commercial lines and civilian employees to meet the administrative and strategic needs of the army.

After the war, the Signal Corps assumed responsibility for the electric telegraph and used it to create a national weather service as well as a military communications network. Although visual signaling—wigwag, sun-powered heliograph, and observation balloons—remained important to the U.S. military, the *Spanish-American War found commercial and military telegraph enjoying extensive use. Commanders in widely dispersed theaters of war—Cuba, Puerto Rico, and the Philippines—made use of both military and commercial telegraph. Telegraph and ocean cable connected the front lines of Cuba with defense planners in Washington. Wire communications facilities across the Philippine Islands linked the archipelago by submarine cable. At the same time, Adolphus W. Greely (chief signal officer 1887–1906) adapted and equipped the army with emerging late nineteenth-century technology, such as the telephone (invented 1876) to command and control its forces. Its use was demonstrated by the telephone system in Cuba that enabled Gen. William Shafter's Fifth Army to communicate within yards of the front line, as well as with the admiral of the U.S. Fleet.

While providing a communications network and trying to quell the *Philippine War (1899–1902), the Signal Corps simultaneously supported the army on another frontier. Signal Corps celebrities such as then Lt. Billy *Mitchell helped to construct the Washington-Alaska Military Cable and Telegraph System (WAMCATS). The network, which connected the region's isolated military posts, helped the army coordinate its peacekeeping efforts in the

territory during the Alaska gold rush. Renamed the Alaska Communication System in 1936, it remained under military control for over sixty years. Radio replaced Alaska's telegraph system in 1928, owing much to the efforts of George Owen Squier (chief signal officer 1917–24), who tested Marconi's invention, the wireless (1895), for military use.

The U.S. Army and the U.S. Navy both employed the wireless. In 1904, a radio station in the Boston Navy Yard transmitted the first official Naval Observatory time. Although experimentation continued and the navy employed wireless to transmit time and weather reports, the navy's admirals had little faith in its tactical uses.

The Army Signal Corps introduced the first portable wireless sets into the field in 1906, and began experimenting with radio telephony (voice radio) the following year. In 1914, it tested a radio set mounted in an automobile. Parallel efforts by the navy during this period included in-house experimentation and support of the commercial development of radio. Regarded as a novelty, however, radio remained largely unused. Army land forces in *World War I relied on the telephone, telegraph, and even homing pigeons for communications in the era of trench warfare.

Supporting the American Expeditionary Forces, the army was also responsible for combat photography and aviation. Nevertheless, the Signal Corps' grandest achievement was the establishment of a massive wire communications system that ran from the seacoast to the American battle zone in France. The system consisted of literally thousands of miles of administrative and combat lines: 134 permanent telegraph offices and 273 telephone exchanges, facilitated by 200 bilingual American telephone operators. Multiplex printing telegraph equipment linked Tours, Chaumont, Paris, and London.

The army's communications arm also oversaw the adaptation of the airplane to military use. With its genesis in Civil War and Spanish-American War observation balloons, the Signal Corps purchased a Wright brothers' flying machine in 1908. James Allen (chief signal officer 1906–13) and his immediate successors perceived the airplane as an observation platform and vehicle for courier service. When aviation's role as a fighting and bombing force expanded during World War I, the army created the Army Air Service (1918), separating aviation from the Signal Corps.

Experimentation before and during World War I contributed to the Signal Corps' development of radio for military purposes. Stepping stones included the achievements of Signal Corps captain (later major) Edwin H. Armstrong. Armstrong invented a major component of amplitude modulated (AM) radio—the superhetrodyne circuit—during World War I. His next invention, frequency modulated (FM) radio, came during the interwar years. Chief Signal Officer Squier facilitated the standardization and mass production of vacuum tubes. He established the first Signal Corps Laboratory at Camp Alfred Vail, New Jersey. Introduction of the SCR-68, an airborne radio telephone, and its companion ground set, the SCR-67, were significant steps in the development of radio communications.

During the interwar years, developments in both wire and radio technology set the stage for communications support for *World War II. Naval research included experimentation with the radio compass, airborne radio, and radio remote control. The teletype, remarkable for its accuracy, speed, and simplicity of operation, came into the arsenal in the 1930s. The battery-powered field telephone was developed as the Germans improved both the switchboard and communications cable. The War Department Radio Net (established 1922) became the genesis for an elaborate command and control communications system that enveloped both army forces and navy ships during World War II. About the same time, the International Radio Convention (1927) adopted the navy's plan for worldwide frequency allocation.

A 25-pound army walkie-talkie, developed in 1934, made its debut in the army maneuvers of 1939. A truck-mounted long-range radio, with a 100-mile voice range and several times greater range for Morse Code, was introduced in the 1940 Louisiana maneuvers. Captain Armstrong helped Col. Roger Colton develop his invention into the army's first FM pushbutton, crystal-controlled, tactical radio in the Signal Corps Laboratory at Fort Monmouth, New Jersey. Although the army's armor and artillery branches communicated via FM radio (proven feasible by 1936), the infantry (as well as the navy) failed to integrate the new technology until after World War II.

Numerous countries claimed ownership of *radar, developed during the 1930s. Its significance in World War II communications cannot be overstated. By 1943, the Germans were effectively using radar as an early warning and weapons-directional device. In the United States, navy research and development paralleled that of the Army Signal Corps. Prewar, the navy installed it on ships (1940), while the army used it as a short-range radio locator for directing searchlights. A new, long-range aircraft detector radar, on Oahu, Hawaii, issued a warning (unfortunately ignored) when Japanese aircraft approached the island on 7 December 1941. By early 1942, the Signal Corps SCR-517 microwave radar was used in aircraft to search for ships in the Atlantic. In 1944, a microwave SCR-584 helped aim U.S. weapons in combat at Anzio, Italy. By the end of the war, such communications advances as the bi-service advancement of radar, navy perfection of sonar, army development of FM radio, and overall miniaturization of electronic components laid the groundwork for the electronics and space ages to follow.

The Signal Corps used a modified SCR-271 long-range radar set (1946) to bounce radar signals off the Moon to test the properties of radio communications in space. Postwar navy technological achievements included over-horizon VHF radio communications, the use of radar waves to reflect signals off the Moon (1951), and Moon relayed messages between Honolulu, Hawaii, and Washington (1956). Both services contributed to the development of artificial space satellites and communications. By the 1960s, rockets of the U.S. Air Force were sending manned and unmanned vehicles into space.

Improved radar supported land and air forces and naval batteries in the conduct of the *Korean War. The Signal Corps played a major supporting role in that conflict. Although doctrine dictated wire as the primary means of communication, the exigencies of Korea—distance, terrain, primitive roads—led to a dependence on very high frequency (VHF) radio. VHF, effective far beyond its 25-mile range, carried teletype as well as voice traffic. It proved adaptable to the frequent infantry moves characteristic of the fighting in the first two years of the conflict. But line-of-sight properties restricted its usage; VHF station components, weighing hundreds of pounds, often required transportation to—and operation and maintenance from—high, remote communication sites. In spite of the difficulties, army communicators proclaimed VHF the backbone of communications during the Korean War.

Between Korea and Vietnam, military efforts again focused on the peaceful uses of communications. The army, in 1958, used its technology to explore outer space. The Signal Corps' Space Sentry bounced signals from the Moon, developing the ability to ensure the close tracking of satellites. The same year, Vanguard II's infrared scanning devices mapped the cloud cover over the Earth.

Technological advances in communications during the *Vietnam War were the end product of twenty years of research and experimentation by the army, navy, and air force. Miniaturized electronic components increased the payloads of U.S. communications satellites propelled into space by air force boosters. One notable benefit was initiation of the first operational satellite communications system in history when the Army Satellite Communications Command established two clear channels from Tan Son Nhut, South Vietnam, to Hawaii (1964).

Radio transmission had improved as well. Line-of-sight wave transmission was surpassed by tropospheric scatter or troposcatter propagation radio with a maximum 400-mile range. The new technology enabled radio waves to travel long distances by using special antennas to bounce them off clouds of ionized particles in the higher ionosphere before they returned to Earth hundreds of miles away.

Military communications support in Southeast Asia proved that advanced electronics could master the geography. Although Vietnam's Integrated Wideband Communications System (established and funded by the air force and operated jointly with the army) never fulfilled the promise of a regional civil-military network, it demonstrated the need and effectiveness of a high-capacity area telecommunications system in an undeveloped region. More important, the wideband system reflected a permanent move to an area-oriented communications doctrine. Improved technology was directly responsible for the shift in focus.

As a joint-services endeavor, Vietnam communications included numerous examples of inter-service cooperation. For example, army field commanders enjoyed rapid aircraft response because of connectivity with air force support centers. Joint army-navy mobile riverine forces, using command and communications boats, had well established internal as well as external communications with the South Vietnamese army. A continuing problem in Vietnam, security was addressed first by the navy's "Talk Quick" system which preceded the army's automatic secure voice system (1967).

Major communications systems in Vietnam included the 1st Signal Brigade's Southeast Asia Defense Communications System and the Southeast Asia Automatic Telephone Service (1968). The latter comprised 9 switches connected to 54 automatic army, navy, and air force dial exchanges. Overall, communications support for the Vietnam war could be characterized as the beginning of an ongoing trend toward the use of commercial-type facilities for both strategic and tactical communications. While mobile multichannel radios, switchboards, and teletype centers linked headquarters throughout the chain of command, strategic and administrative networks comprised a variety of commercial sets.

Changes in military strategy and tactics such as the

long-range and heavy logistical requirements of modern weapons, and reliance on coordinated air-ground operations, both prevalent in Vietnam, dictated more flexible and extensive communications support than that offered by traditional chains of command. Technical advances in communications made it possible—indeed, imperative—to create interconnecting area networks. The merger of tactical and strategic communications became official in 1966 with the formation of the 1st Signal Brigade. As part of the Strategic Communications Command, area networks linked fighters with intelligence, personnel, and logistical centers in the United States. At the same time, combat commanders kept organic tactical communications to respond to military requirements.

Higher-echelon advances did little to change Vietnam's combat communications from those of previous conflicts. Field telephones connected by single-strand wire linked artillery battery, guns, fire direction centers, and commanders. Infantry platoon command posts used small field switchboards and wire lines to connect squads, sentries, and listening posts. The 173rd Airborne Brigade, in 1965, deemed the PRC-25 (transistorized FM voice radio) its greatest communications device. Hand-held, vehicle-, and aircraft-mounted PRC-25s were the primary means of combat communication for army units from squads through division level.

The Vietnam conflict demonstrated the interdependence of the army, navy, and air forces in the conduct of mid-twentieth-century warfare. The secretary of defense acknowledged this fact in such cooperative efforts as the Joint Tactical Satellite Research and Development Program (1965). At the same time, the communications arms of the various military branches continued to invest in their own unique information systems.

Post-Vietnam technology further changed the face of military communications. The 1970s development of the semiconductor dramatically decreased size and power requirements of communications systems. The microprocessor revolution, in turn, led to the development of modules rather than discrete systems. Miniaturization, greater standardization, and modules all made commercial equipment cheaper, more adaptable, mobile, and secure.

The U.S. military's post–*Cold War operations revealed major weaknesses in the Department of *Defense's (DoD) efforts to weld its various communications assets into a cohesive whole. Communicators in Operation Urgent Fury (Grenada, 1983) encountered major obstacles in the coordination and provision of support for the Joint Task Force. Both the DoD and Congress took positive steps to strengthen cooperation among the various service components—DoD through the establishment of the Joint Tactical Command Control and Communications Agency (1984) and Congress with the *Goldwater-Nichols Act (1986). The positive results of these and other actions became clear in Operation Just Cause (Panama, 1989–90).

Operation Desert Storm (1990–91), a major joint operation directed by the U.S. Central Command, provided a true test of service cooperation. The *Persian Gulf War demonstrated that military communications had expanded and transformed into information technology. In the few years between Panama and the gulf, joint training had become the rule.

As information systems achieved equal footing with military hardware in the conduct of the Gulf War, all of the services incorporated numerous commercially produced systems. The Army Signal Corps' network, connected with those of the other services and Allied Coalition forces, spanned the geographic area with commercially developed cellular telephone and a single-channel ground and airborne radio system.

Operation Desert Storm left little doubt that late twentieth-century military communications embraced all aspects of information management. Using multimedia sources, communicators need to get the right information to the right people almost instantaneously. At the end of the twentieth century, information activities in war have equaled and in some cases supplanted industrial activities.

Military communication—or more accurately, information management—presents a seamless network on the late twentieth-century battlefield. As a result of technological advancements, the centerpiece of the battlefield is no longer simply the weapons platforms but also an information grid into which weapons are plugged.

Information technology will continue to transform military communications. Because the value of information increases exponentially through dissemination, its potential is virtually limitless.

[See also Combat Support; Command and Control; Satellites, Reconnaissance.]

• U.S. Naval Communications Chronological History, 1961. Carroll V. Glines, Jr. Compact History of the United States Air Force, 1973. Paul J. Scheips, Military Signal Communications, 2 vols., 1980. John D. Bergen, A Test For Technology, 1986. John G. Westover, Combat Support in Korea, 1987. Kathy R. Coker and Carol E. Stokes, A Concise History of the U.S. Army Signal Corps, 1995. Rebecca Robbins Raines, Getting the Message Through, 1996.

—Carol E. Stokes

COMPREHENSIVE TEST BAN TREATY. See Limited Test Ban Treaty.

CONANT, JAMES B. (1893–1978), scientist, educator, and diplomat who played a key role in the development of the atomic bomb. Conant received his Ph.D. in chemistry at Harvard in 1916. During *World War I, he joined the Chemical Warfare Service, where he directed the Organic Research Unit in the production of mustard gas. He subsequently taught at Harvard, became chair of the chemistry department, and in 1933, the university's president. In the depth of the depression, his dealings with conservative and radical groups on campus led him to take positions in national politics. He generally opposed New Deal programs, but also the isolationist views that dominated in his own Republican Party.

When *World War II broke out, Conant advocated aid to the democracies and worked through the National Defense Research Committee to enlist U.S. scientists in war preparations. Later, with the Office of Scientific Research and Development, he played a key role in coordinating atomic research with Great Britain and setting up the *Manhattan Project. His June 1945 suggestion to drop the newly completed atomic bomb on a Japanese war plant and its populated environs in order to shorten the war was taken up by President Harry S. *Truman, who targeted Hiroshima, a sizable city, an army headquarters, a rail center, and a major producer of material. From 1946 to 1962, Conant served as adviser to the Atomic Energy Commission.

The outbreak of the *Korean War in 1950 convinced

him of the magnitude of the Soviet threat, and he soon headed the Committee on the Present Danger, which urged the United States to station up to 1 million troops in Europe under *NATO command. An appreciative President Dwight D. *Eisenhower named Conant U.S. high commissioner for occupied western Germany in 1953, and, after the occupation ended in 1955, first U.S. ambassador to the Federal Republic of Germany. During his four years in Bonn, Conant aided in the transformation of Germany into a democratic state and a dependable military ally against communism.

After his return to the United States, Conant devoted his reforming energies primarily to the field of education, heading a Carnegie Foundation study of American secondary schools (1957–62) and publishing a number of important works on education.

[See also Atomic Scientists; Bush, Vannevar; Hiroshima and Nagasaki, Bombings of; Science, Technology, War, and the Military.]

• James B. Conant, My Several Lives: Memoirs of a Social Inventor, 1970. James Hershberg, James B. Conant: Harvard to Hiroshima and the Making of the Nuclear Age, 1993.   —Manfred Jonas

CONFEDERACY, THE MILITARY IN THE. From the moment the representatives of the seceded Southern states met in Montgomery, Alabama, on 4 February 1861, they sought to defend the South. As a former military officer and secretary of war, the provisional president, Jefferson *Davis, seemed to possess impeccable credentials for that task.

The Confederate War Department had the specific responsibility of assembling an army using state militia units and volunteers. The governors of the states would then transfer those units to Confederate service, and thus create a national army. Hastily organized units soon bombarded the War Department for requisitions and instructions; with limited resources, the government could not provide the necessary arms and accoutrements for its troops. Even so, by April 1861, the Confederate states could boast some 70,000 men in the field.

After the Confederate capture of *Fort Sumter on 12 April 1861, U.S. president Abraham *Lincoln issued a call for 75,000 volunteers to suppress the rebellion. Davis countered with a call for 100,000 men.

But if the Confederates had established the basis for a military, significant problems remained. That military had to be supported and maintained adequately. It had to be deployed properly and employed effectively. All of this demanded a coherent war *strategy.

The closest the Confederate hierarchy came to such a plan was an implicit belief in the defensive nature of their war. Rather than subjugate the North, the Confederacy relied on the fact that it could win simply by continuing to exist and that its people would be waging war in defense of their homes. Even so, the South could not afford to conduct a completely passive defense, thereby exposing its citizens to the ravages of war.

Instead, Davis planned to implement an "offensive-defensive" strategy. This overall defensive scheme would allow the Confederate forces to exploit their interior lines of communication and supply and concentrate Southern forces against invading Union columns. The South could shift troops to repel a threat at a time and place of its own choosing.

Unfortunately, Davis faced political demands that greatly hampered his plan. In addition to his personal difficulties with some generals, the Confederacy's creation of a rigid departmental command structure militated against this strategy. Thus, Davis and the War Department confronted localized pressures from governors, such as Joseph E. Brown of Georgia and Zebulon Vance of North Carolina, and from various generals more concerned with protecting their own interests than with cooperating with others.

Despite the South's defensive strategy, Confederate armies did mount several major offensive operations into Union territory, including the Maryland campaign of Gen. Robert E. *Lee in 1862, the Kentucky campaign of Gen. Braxton *Bragg, also in 1862, and Lee's invasion of Pennsylvania in 1863. All of them failed, depleting the South's offensive power.

Manpower shortages in particular prevented the Confederacy from engaging in further grand offensives. Such concerns had led to the implementation of *conscription, or the draft, in April 1862. Initially designed to include able-bodied men between the ages of eighteen and thirty-five, conscription was expanded to men between seventeen and fifty, and exemptions were sharply reduced. Finally, in 1865, the Confederate government authorized the arming of slaves, but the war ended with the program only in its initial phases.

The Confederate government ultimately attempted to establish a unified command structure under General Lee. Unfortunately, by then—February 1865—the Confederacy was in its death throes. Lee's army and the rest of the main Confederate field armies would surrender in a matter of months.

Debates continue to rage over the relative importance of the eastern and western theaters of operations and the Civil War's role as a "total" or "modern" war.

[See also Civil War: Military and Diplomatic Course; Civil War: Changing Interpretations.]   —Brian S. Wills

CONFEDERATE ARMY. On 19 February 1861, President Jefferson *Davis appointed Leroy P. Walker of Alabama secretary of war of the newly formed Confederate States of America—the first of the five men to serve in that troubled office—and on 6 March, the Confederate Congress authorized an army of 100,000 volunteers to serve for twelve months. In May 1861, following the outbreak of war, Congress authorized the further enlistment of as many as 400,000 volunteers for three-year terms.

The white male population of the eleven Confederate states, aged fifteen to thirty-nine, was approximately 1 million. The best estimates of total Confederate enlistments range from 850,000 to 900,000. Less than 2,000 men served in the regular army; nearly all were in the Provisional army, a force intended to be disbanded at the end of the war.

At the outset, the South had more volunteers than it could arm and equip, forcing the army to turn away some 200,000 volunteers that it would soon sorely miss. In June 1863, the army peaked at almost 475,000 men; it declined steadily thereafter. By comparison, some 2.3 million men served in the Union army, with more than 1 million in uniform in 1865. As martial enthusiasm waned in late 1861, the Confederate government was forced to resort to conscription for the first national draft in American history. On 16 April 1862, the Confederate Congress enacted the

First Conscription Act, which declared all able-bodied, unmarried white men between the ages of eighteen and thirty-five liable for the draft. One-year volunteers already in the army were enjoined to serve for two additional years but were allowed to return home on a sixty-day furlough and to elect new field- and company-grade officers. The Second Conscription Act of September 1862 and the Third Conscription Act, adopted seventeen months later, extended the ages of liability from seventeen to fifty, although exemptions greatly weakened the draft law. The stigma of conscription induced potential draftees to volunteer before they were called, so that only 82,000 were actually conscripted.

In the spring of 1861, seceding states consolidated their militia companies into regiments, mustered them into Confederate service, and sent them where the need seemed greatest, without reference to higher organization. Soon, however, President Davis began to pattern the Confederate States Army after the armed forces of the old Union during the *Mexican War. A full-strength regiment consisted of 10 companies of 100 men each, although many regiments began with far fewer than 1,000 men and their numbers dwindled throughout the war due to *casualties, disease, and desertions. Each regiment, upon muster into Confederate service, received a numerical designation in chronological order of organization, such as the 3rd Louisiana Volunteer Infantry or the Eighth Texas Cavalry. From three to five regiments, ideally from the same state, formed a brigade. The brigade's commander, a brigadier general, was appointed by the president, subject to Senate confirmation, from the unit's home state. Three brigades, in turn, combined to form a division commanded by a major general; and two or more divisions, commanded by a lieutenant general, would become an army corps. Ideally, two or more corps constituted an army.

Confederate territory was organized into military departments, usually named for the state or states in which it operated. A general officer commanded each department, with responsibility for all military administration, resources, and operations within it. By this definition, the Confederacy fielded at least forty "armies," yet most departmental forces were such in name only.

Although the states recruited and organized regiments for the army, the Confederate government was responsible for their rations, uniforms, training, arms, equipment, and pay—at the rate of $11 per month for privates. The South's underdeveloped industrial and transportation systems were, however, never able to overcome the army's logistical and supply problems. Quartermaster General Abraham Myers struggled to provide the necessary material to wage a modern war, and Commissary General Lucius B. Northrop proved grossly incompetent at supplying rations. Josiah Gorgas, chief of the Bureau of Ordnance, was the one high-ranking Confederate supply officer who excelled in his job, improvising the manufacture of gunpowder, cannons, and rifles in sufficient numbers and quality.

The South selected cadet gray as its official uniform color—in tribute to "the long gray line" at West Point—but the War Department could not begin to supply so many shell jackets and trousers. Consequently, Rebel armies, from beginning to end, were clad in everything from state militia uniforms to "butternut"-dyed homespun to captured Union apparel. Before the Confederacy could provide Southern soldiers with modern rifles, many volunteers relied on sporting rifles, shotguns, revolvers, and even Bowie knives brought from home. Moreover, Confederate soldiers provided their own horses, which contributed materially to the decline in the superiority of Rebel cavalry and the further disadvantage of Rebel artillery after 1862.

Volunteers were mustered in so-called camps of instruction, but their training was minimal, consisting mainly of the manual of arms and basic squad, company, and regimental drill. Regiments sometimes went into combat within three weeks of their organization, aggravating the chaos of the typical Civil War battlefield and the consequent appalling casualty figures. By 1862 or 1863, those who survived had become veteran soldiers, with fighting skills as formidable as any army on record. Confederate troops, however, from first to last were notorious for their resistance to formal discipline.

Southerners viewed the soldier's profession as an especially honored one, and a disproportionate number of Southern-born officers held high rank in the U.S. Army in 1860. Three hundred and thirteen officers—nearly one-third of the West Point–trained officers on active duty at the outbreak of war—resigned to join the Confederacy, contributing crucial leadership to the Southern armies.

This infusion, however vital, did not begin to fill the need for officers. As American volunteers had always done, Confederate troops elected their own company-grade officers, while governors generally appointed regimental officers. This practice often undermined discipline and morale, replacing efficient officers with those who promised to enforce a less rigorous military regimen. On the other hand, soldiers were generally a canny lot and chose intelligently. Since units were recruited from communities, the men had often known candidates all of their lives and judged their potential as leaders shrewdly. Too, the men usually selected officers with some military training or experience, either from a military academy—notably Virginia Military Institute in Lexington and The Citadel in Charleston—or in the war with Mexico, or at least in an antebellum militia company. To weed out the incompetents, in October 1862 the War Department established examining boards for officers.

Jefferson Davis, a graduate of the U.S. Military Academy, favored West Point–educated professionals for high command, leading to bitter complaints of a "West Point clique" monopolizing promotions. Occasionally, a general appointed from civilian life, such as Richard Taylor and Nathan Bedford *Forrest, rose to high rank and performed admirably. To a remarkable degree, untrained officers at company or field grade overcame their deficiencies by studying *Hardee's Tactics* and by setting an example in camp and field. Leading from the front, the Confederate officer corps absorbed appalling casualties—15 percent higher than those suffered by their enlisted men—and generals enjoyed a 50 percent greater chance of dying in battle than those they led.

Confederate *casualties, sustained during four years of heavy fighting, were enormous. Within a year of its organization, a typical regiment was reduced to half or less of its original number by sickness, battle casualties, and desertions, and by 1865 many regiments mustered fewer than two hundred men. More than 250,000 Confederate solders died of wounds or disease; 200,000 or more men were wounded in the course of the war. At least 100,000 Southern soldiers deserted during the course of the war, most in

1865. At the end of the war, 359,000 names appeared on Confederate muster rolls, but only 160,000 were on active duty, and of those, only 126,000 were present for duty.

Despite poor to nonexistent pay, uniforms, food, training, and equipment; the bane of amateur officers; and horrific casualties, the Rebel soldier maintained a remarkably high level of morale—at least until the closing months of the war, when Union invasion and the destruction of civilian property sapped the fighting spirit of the army and desertion increased.

Moreover, the Confederate army performed remarkably well in the field, especially in the eastern theater, where the Army of Northern Virginia under Gen. Robert E. *Lee won a string of stunning victories. The Army of Tennessee, assigned the task of defense of the Confederate heartland, was less fortunate. Plagued by poor leadership, accorded only cursory attention from Richmond, and expected to hold a vast area, it was doomed to four years of frustration. It nevertheless maintained a high level of morale and remained a potent fighting force until squandered by John Bell *Hood at Atlanta, Franklin, and Nashville. In the trans-Mississippi region—the darkest corner of the Confederacy—makeshift Rebel armies often overcame even greater neglect, especially during the 1864 Red River campaign that saved Texas and Northwest Louisiana from Union occupation.

[See also Civil War: Military and Diplomatic Course; Civil War: Domestic Course; Confederate Navy; Conscription; Union Army.]

• Douglas S. Freeman, Lee's Lieutenants: A Study in Command, 3 vols., 1942–44. Thomas L. Connelly, Army of the Heartland: The Army of Tennessee, 1861–1862, 1967. Thomas L. Connelly, Autumn of Glory: The Army of Tennessee, 1862–1865, 1971. Robert L. Kerby, Kirby Smith's Confederacy: The Trans-Mississippi South, 1863–1865, 1972. James M. McPherson, Battle Cry of Freedom: The Civil War Era, 1988. Richard M. McMurry, Two Great Rebel Armies, 1989.

—Thomas W. Cutrer

CONFEDERATE NAVY. Confederate navy secretary Stephen R. Mallory of Florida, who had chaired the U.S. Senate Naval Affairs Committee, assessed his navy's ten ships and fifteen guns in 1861: "The Union have a navy; we have a navy to construct." That construction would take place in a region where strategic resources were largely untapped, and agriculture dominated an undiversified economy. Foreign carriers shipped Southern raw materials in exchange for manufactured goods—and Southerners foresaw no interruption of that commerce. Those assumptions held for about two months between the inauguration of the Confederate states in February 1861 and Lincoln's declaration of the Union *blockade after the capture of *Fort Sumter in April.

The Confederacy needed merchant ships and transports along with warships to defend its harbors and rivers. It also needed ships capable of breaking the blockade. And as a daring strategy, the Confederacy commissioned raiders to disrupt and destroy Union merchant shipping, hoping this would draw Union naval strength away from the Confederate coast.

The Confederacy's major asset for meeting those needs for a navy resided in some 300 officers who had left the Union to join the Confederacy. Although some were aged admirals, others were brilliant officers whose careers had been mired in an antiquated seniority system. Matthew

Fontaine Maury, already an internationally respected naval scientist, had chafed against the bureaucracy; he would pioneer the use of *torpedoes, or mines. John Mercer Brooke was to design a naval cannon, the Brooke rifle, which was superior to the Union standard designed by his commander, John *Dahlgren. Another "scientific sailor" who was to command the Virginia in the first battle of ironclads was Catesby ap R. Jones. These and dozens of other officers added to their experience a wealth of innovative spirit.

To build a serviceable merchant and transport fleet, the Confederacy purchased and, in some cases, commandeered ships in Southern ports. By the fall of 1861, the Navy Department let numerous contracts to private builders to construct small wooden gunboats. In keeping with the need to develop industry, the navy also considered these wartime contracts an investment in postwar industries.

In actual practice, the gunboat policy was plagued by inexperience at every level. It was said that ships were built along any stretch of river with banks level enough to work on. There was slave labor available, but shipwrights, machinists, sailmakers, and all the skilled trades required in shipbuilding were in critically short supply. An increasingly effective Union blockade reduced the availability of ships' machinery and even such items as nails and spikes. Only a fraction of ships laid down were ever fully operational.

The blockade prodded the Confederate navy to devise new means of overcoming the Union's overwhelming advantage. Blockade runners, which could retract a funnel and change profile or burn nearly smokeless coal, were sleek and fast, more like seagoing yachts than transports of guns, ammunition, and medicines.

Seeking to overcome numbers with technology, the Confederates constructed an ironclad on the burned hulk of the Merrimack and rechristened it Virginia. The battle with Monitor in March 1862 changed the course of naval history. During the war, the Confederacy completed twenty-two ironclads; as with the wooden gunboat projects, however, steam engines were makeshift affairs. There were insufficient supplies of iron for armor, and designs at one site or another were so individually eccentric that mass production was impossible.

One pervasive power of the ironclads was their psychological effect upon Union blockading crews: "ram fever" caused endless anxiety, and even a floating log could send all hands scrambling to battle stations. The semisubmerged torpedo boat, or "David," also had a powerful effect upon Union blockaders. This small craft was designed to steer in under the guns of a man-of-war and detonate a torpedo against the hull below the waterline. Mines, too, were a hazard when deployed in rivers and harbors, and more effective against Union ships than any other weapon.

Confederate innovative technology culminated in the submarine Hunley, first employed at Mobile and then at Charleston. Called a "Peripetetic coffin" because of the crews killed in its operations, Hunley was lost in a mission against the U.S.S. Housatonic, but became the first submarine to sink a ship in battle.

Operating in a rather loosely structured administration that cast about in search of some means to overcome the Union advantage, Confederate naval forces went further in devising strategies. On the Mississippi, cotton was used as armor on the river defense fleet. Raiders in small boats would launch surprise attacks against Union blockaders; capturing the Union Underwriter was one success. A scheme elaborately planned but unsuccessful was a large-scale covert operation in Canada. The plan was to disrupt rail shipments along the Great Lakes, capture vessels and disrupt shipping on the lakes, and rescue Confederate prisoners in Ohio.

The Confederate navy was spectacularly successful with its commerce raiders, which harassed and destroyed Union ships in global warfare. *Alabama* was built in England, secretly commissioned in the South Atlantic, and set free under the command of Raphael Semmes to detain and destroy Union merchantmen in the Atlantic, around Africa into the Indian Ocean, and as far east as Singapore. Before being sunk by the Union *Kearsarge* in a famous battle off Cherbourg in the English Channel, *Alabama* took sixty-five ships.

Sumter, *Tallahassee*, and *Florida* had briefer careers. The more famous *Shenandoah* wreaked havoc in the Pacific where American whalers harvested critical supplies of oil. Considered pirates by the Union, these ships captured the world's imagination, and the willingness of neutral ports to welcome the ships and lionize their crews resulted in U.S. claims against England in the 1870s.

Deficiencies in industrial strength, scarcities in raw materials and skilled labor, and the overwhelming numbers of Union vessels express in naval terms the same disadvantages that helped to defeat Confederate armies. In ships, they were outnumbered more than three to one; in enlisted ranks, more than ten to one; yet the Confederate navy employed technologies that, in time, became essential to naval warfare.

[*See also* Confederate Army, Union Army; Union Navy.]

• J. Thomas Scharf, *History of the Confederate States Navy*, 1887. Joseph T. Durkin, *Stephen R. Mallory, Confederate Navy Chief*, 1954. Milton F. Perry, *Infernal Machines, the Story of Confederate Submarine and Mine Warfare*, 1965. William N. Still, Jr., *Iron Afloat, the Story of the Confederate Armorclads*, 1971. Tom H. Wells, *The Confederate Navy, a Study in Organization*, 1971. Stephen R. Wise, *Lifeline of the Confederacy*, 1988. John M. Taylor, *Confederate Raider, Raphael Semmes of the Alabama*, 1994. Raimondo Luraghi, *A History of the Confederate Navy*, 1996.   —Maxine T. Turner

The **CONFERENCE ON SECURITY AND COOPERATION IN EUROPE** (CSCE) involved thirty-three European states plus the United States and Canada in a series of negotiations bridging the East-West divide through the 1970s and 1980s. Washington linked initial U.S. participation to settlement of the status of Berlin and Soviet agreement to parallel talks on conventional force reductions (the MBFR). The CSCE Final Act, signed in Helsinki on 1 August 1975, codified the diplomatic "rules of the road" for the remainder of the *Cold War, including the inviolability of frontiers, nonintervention, and respect for human rights.

Publication of the Final Act catalyzed an upsurge of activity for human rights and in opposition to totalitarianism across the Soviet Union and Eastern Europe in the mid-late 1970s. CSCE review meetings in Belgrade (1977–78), Madrid (1980–83), and Vienna (1986–89) focused on implementation and extension of the Final Act, especially in the areas of human rights and military confidence-building measures. By 1989, the political principles established by the Final Act were widely credited with contributing to the collapse of Communist rule in Eastern Europe.

After the *Cold War, the CSCE established a permanent Secretariat in Prague, a Conflict Prevention Center in Vienna, an Office for Democratic Institutions and Human Rights in Warsaw, and an Office on National Minorities in the Hague. With the breakup of the Soviet Union, Czechoslovakia, and Yugoslavia, and the accession of Albania, membership in the CSCE increased from thirty-five to fifty-three states. In 1994, it was renamed the Organization for Security and Cooperation in Europe (OSCE). Since then, the OSCE has supervised democratic elections, promoted respect for human rights in new laws and constitutions, and negotiated and monitored cease-fires throughout Eastern Europe and the former Soviet Union.

[*See also* Helsinki Watch.]

• John J. Maresca, *To Helsinki: The Conference on Security and Cooperation in Europe, 1972–1975*, 1987. Daniel C. Thomas, *The Power of International Norms: Human Rights, the Helsinki Accords and the Demise of Communism*, forthcoming 2000.
—Daniel C. Thomas

CONGRESS, WAR, AND THE MILITARY. Article I, section 8, of the U.S. Constitution states that Congress has the power to "provide for the common Defence," "To declare War," "To raise and support Armies," and "To provide and maintain a Navy." In theory, these enumerated grants of power give Congress extensive (but not unlimited) power over the preparation and use of U.S. military forces. In practice, Congress has found its ability to control the military, and especially its ability to dictate when and where military force will be used, challenged by the executive branch.

Declaration of War. Congress's role in decisions to go to war has changed dramatically since the early days of the republic. Traditionally, congressional authorization was seen as necessary for any offensive use of military force, but following World War II presidents began to claim that their role as commander in chief gave them independent authority to order U.S. troops into combat. In 1973, Congress tried to reclaim its war powers by passing the War Powers Resolution, but the question of when (or even if) congressional authorization is needed to use force remains a continuing controversy.

The delegates to the constitutional convention clearly intended to lodge the war power with Congress rather than the president. They explicitly rejected a proposal to give the president the power to declare war, and while they designated the president as commander in chief, they saw the position simply as an office and not as an independent source of warmaking authority. The delegates expected that it would be the exclusive province of Congress to decide whether to move the nation from a state of peace to a state of war. Presidents were empowered to send U.S. troops into combat without congressional authorization only to repel sudden attacks on the United States.

The founders' views on the war power largely guided political practice over the next one 150 years. Congress passed formal declarations of war four times: the *War of 1812 (1812); the *Spanish-American War (1898); *World War I (1917); and *World War II (1941). In the case of the *Mexican War (1846–1848), Congress did not formally declare war but rather passed a resolution recognizing that a state of war existed. (The *Civil War was undeclared because a declaration of war would have recognized the legitimacy of the Confederate government.) On other occasions, Congress authorized, or refused to authorize, the president to use force in situations short of full-scale war. Moreover, in the 150 years before World War II, presidents repeatedly acknowledged the need for Congress to authorize offensive military actions.

Of course, the original intent of the founders was not always followed in practice. The U.S. military on occasion—the exact number is a matter of some dispute—used force without congressional sanction. Yet most of these incidents involved relatively inconsequential attacks on nonstate actors such as brigands and pirates, and they frequently occurred without the benefit of either congressional or presidential authorization. When presidents did violate congressional prerogatives, they typically drew sharp criticism. In 1848, the House of Representatives censured President James K. *Polk for "unnecessarily and unconstitutionally" provoking war with Mexico.

The willingness of presidents to order the use of force against sovereign states on their own authority grew after World War II. When North Korea invaded South Korea in June 1950, President Harry S. *Truman decided against asking Congress to declare war because he thought his critics might filibuster the resolution and thereby dilute its symbolic effect. Over the next four decades, presidents used Truman's precedent to argue that the commander-in-chief clause empowers them to send U.S. troops into combat without congressional authorization. In August 1964, Congress passed with only two dissenting votes the Tonkin Gulf Resolution, which approved President Lyndon B. *Johnson's decision to use force to prevent further Communist aggression in South Vietnam. Although legal scholars differ over whether the resolution constituted an adequate legal basis for American military involvement in the *Vietnam War, Johnson and Richard M. *Nixon both argued that they had full authority to prosecute the war without congressional authorization. Congress repealed the resolution in January 1971, but American involvement in Vietnam continued.

The experience in Vietnam soured many in Congress on the wisdom of giving presidents wide berth to send U.S. troops into combat. In 1973 Congress passed, over President Nixon's veto, the *War Powers Resolution. The resolution stipulates (among other things) that the president can send troops into situations of imminent or actual hostilities for no more than sixty days (ninety days in some circumstances) unless Congress authorizes the deployment.

During its first two decades in operation, the War Powers Resolution failed to check the president's use of force. Every president but Jimmy *Carter and Bill *Clinton denied its constitutionality, and successive administrations exploited ambiguities in the law to prevent the sixty-day clock from starting. President Ronald *Reagan did sign a 1983 bill that gave him authority to keep U.S. troops in Lebanon for eighteen months, but in doing so he repeated the claim that the War Powers Resolution is unconstitutional. (No court has ruled on the constitutionality issue.) The resolution did not figure in the invasions of Grenada in 1983 and Panama in 1989, the intervention in Haiti in 1994, or the peacekeeping missions in Somalia in 1992 or Bosnia in 1995.

In the case of the *Persian Gulf War of 1991, President George *Bush refused to invoke the War Powers Resolution, and he argued that he did not need congressional authorization to order U.S. troops to liberate Kuwait. Public opinion, however, eventually forced Bush to seek the approval of Congress. The authorizing resolution, which did not mention the War Powers Resolution, passed in the Senate with five votes to spare.

The circumstances in which presidents can initiate the use of military force without congressional authorization remain an open constitutional question. The federal courts have generally declined to hear lawsuits challenging the president's right to use military force, either on the grounds that such suits raise political and not legal questions or that it is up to Congress and not the courts to preserve congressional prerogatives. The net effect of the courts' reluctance to settle the issue has been to diminish the war powers of Congress and to enhance those of the president.

Conduct and Termination of War. Congress has no direct constitutional authority over the conduct of war. The founders expected that once the United States was at war, the command and direction of the military would fall to the president, pursuant to his role as commander in chief. Indeed, to make clear that the president and not Congress would direct military operations, the delegates to the Constitutional Convention voted to substitute the phrase "to declare War" for the phrase "to make War" in the initial draft of the Constitution.

The Constitution fails to say which branch of government has the power to make peace, and there is no evidence that the delegates to the convention discussed the matter. As a matter of custom, presidents are not required to gain congressional approval for a peace settlement. President Nixon, for example, handled U.S. withdrawal from the *Vietnam War through an executive agreement that was not submitted to Congress. In theory, Congress can use its appropriations power to terminate American participation in a war, though no such cases exist. Any formal peace treaty is not binding, of course, until the Senate gives its "advice and consent" by a two-thirds majority.

Deployment of Troops. The executive power and commander-in-chief clauses of the Constitution give the president broad authority to deploy troops overseas where combat is not anticipated. Congress itself recognized this authority when it passed the War Powers Resolution. Unlike the case of imminent or actual hostilities, the resolution places no time limits on presidential decisions to send U.S. troops overseas during peacetime, even if those troops are equipped for combat. Thus, President Clinton did not need congressional authorization for his decision in 1995 to send U.S. troops to Bosnia as peacekeepers. The one undecided constitutional question is whether Congress can, through its appropriations power, bar the president from deploying troops to a specific country or theater of operations. The federal courts have never decided the issue, and legal scholars are divided on the matter.

Military Alliances. U.S. participation in formal military alliances is handled through treaties, which under the U.S. Constitution must be approved by two-thirds of the Senate. Despite frequent claims that U.S. alliance commitments render Congress's war power obsolete, no alliance in which the United States is involved requires the automatic commitment of troops once war begins. Instead, most treaties of alliance follow the precedent set by the North Atlantic Treaty of 1949, which states that the signatories will take the actions they deem necessary under the treaty "in accordance with their respective constitutional processes." On occasion, and especially in the 1950s and 1960s, presidents have used executive agreements to commit the United States to defend other countries against aggression. Such agreements are not submitted for congressional approval, and in most cases the commitment was initially kept secret. These commitments are of dubious constitutional validity.

Appropriations Power. Article 1, section 9, of the U.S. Constitution stipulates that "No Money shall be drawn from the Treasury, but in Consequence of Appropriations made by Law." This appropriations power, in conjunction with the more specific constitutional charges to "raise and support Armies" and "provide and maintain a Navy," gives Congress tremendous say over the budgets, structures, and duties of the armed forces. The Constitution forbids Congress from making defense appropriations more than two years in advance, and by custom appropriations laws are passed annually. In addition to using the appropriations power to determine how much the armed services may spend, Congress can use the appropriations power to bar the armed services from undertaking specified programs or operations. The Supreme Court has never struck down any use of the appropriations power as an unconstitutional infringement on executive authority, which is why it stands as Congress's foremost instrument for shaping military policy.

The funding of defense programs follows a twin-track process on Capitol Hill. First, defense programs must be authorized, a process spearheaded in the Senate by the Armed Services Committee and in the House by the National Security Committee. Second, the funds for defense programs must be appropriated, a process spearheaded in each house by the Appropriations Committee. In theory, the authorizers focus on policy issues and the appropriators on budgetary issues, but in practice the line between the two is heavily blurred. The authorization requirement is rooted in congressional rules rather than the Constitution, and thus Congress may, if it so chooses, dispense with the requirement that defense programs be authorized before any money for them is appropriated.

The tremendous size of the U.S. military establishment means that as a practical matter Congress writes its defense authorization and appropriations bills in close consultation with the executive branch. By both tradition and law, the executive branch has some flexibility to reprogram the monies appropriated by Congress across defense accounts, as well as to spend funds to meet unanticipated military contingencies. At times, presidents have used their reprogramming authority and contingency funds to frustrate congressional efforts to dictate military policy.

Oversight. Oversight of the U.S. military is a long-standing congressional power that dates back to the House of Representatives' inquiry into Gen. Arthur St. Clair's disastrous defeat at the hands of the Wabash Indians in 1791. Most oversight activities are conducted by standing committees such as the Senate Armed Services Committee and the House National Security Committee. Special congressional panels, such as one convened to investigate the *Iran-Contra Affair, may also be convened to hold hearings on matters of special interest.

The Constitution gives Congress wide powers over the American military. In many respects, though, Congress finds its ability to exercise these powers frustrated by what Alexander Hamilton in *Federalist* No. 70 called the president's inherent advantages of "decision, activity, secrecy,

and dispatch." The ability of Congress to override these inherent advantages depends ultimately on the wisdom and the political popularity of what the president seeks to accomplish.

[*See also* Commander in Chief, President As; Constitutional and Political Basis of War and the Military; Supreme Court, War, and the Military.]

• A. D. Sofaer, *War, Foreign Affairs, and Constitutional Power: The Origins,* 1976. F. D. Wormuth and E. B. Firmage, *To Chain the Dog of War: The War Power of Congress in History and Law,* 1986; 2nd ed., 1989. M. J. Glennon, *Constitutional Diplomacy,* 1990. W. C. Banks and P. Raven-Hansen, *National Security Law and the Power of the Purse,* 1994. J. M. Lindsay, *Congress and the Politics of U.S. Foreign Policy,* 1994. L. Fisher, *Presidential War,* 1995.

—James M. Lindsay

CONSCIENTIOUS OBJECTION. Whenever government in America has employed compulsory military training or service, it has been confronted by those who, on principle, refuse to bear arms. The early colonists included many members of pacifist Protestant sects—*Quakers, Mennonites, Brethren—who believed the Bible and the teachings of Jesus of Nazareth prohibited them from participating in war or engaging in any violence against other human beings. Colonial officials fined them for refusing to serve in the militia, but since they were economically productive and otherwise law-abiding, most colonial governments eventually exempted them from personally bearing arms.

In the *Revolutionary War some objectors were forced into militia service, but several states recognized religious conscientious objection as a right and excused objectors if they paid a special tax. In 1790, James *Madison sought to include protection for religious objectors in the Bill of Rights, a measure that passed the House, but failed in the Senate.

Both the North and South dealt with religious objectors in the *Civil War. Some suffered severely, but ultimately both sides recognized their sincerity and stubbornness. Drafted members of the historic peace sects were allowed to purchase an exemption or hire a substitute. When some refused, the Lincoln administration gave them the option of aiding in the care of wounded soldiers or former slaves.

In World War I, the Selective Draft Act of 1917 recognized only members of the historical peace churches as "conscientious objectors" (COs), but required them to serve in the military in non-arms-bearing roles. Some 64,700 men, most of them not members of the pacifist sects, claimed CO status on religious or political grounds. Local draft boards classified 57,000 as COs, and 20,900 COs were inducted into the army. In the training camps, 80 percent abandoned their objections. Some 4,000 remained COs; ultimately most were furloughed into agricultural work, and 1,300 others served in the medical corps. But 450 "absolutists," who refused to cooperate in any way, were court-martialed and sent to military prisons.

The harsh and fumbling experience with COs during World War I contributed to a more liberal policy in World War II. The Selective Service Act of 1940 provided CO status for all religious objectors. It also allowed them to choose non-arms-bearing military service or alternative civilian service. In 1940–45, 50,000 draftees were classified as COs, most serving in the military, primarily the medical corps. Some 12,000 chose civilian alternative service, working without pay on soil erosion control, reforestation, and agricultural experimentation in one of seventy Civilian Public Service (CPS) camps operated for the Selective Service System by the historic peace churches. Another 2,000 COs worked in mental hospitals and 500 volunteered as subjects for medical experiments on disease. Some 5,000 absolutists refused to cooperate and went to federal prison—a majority of them Jehovah's Witnesses, but also some pacifist social activists such as A. J. *Muste, Bayard *Rustin, and David Dellinger.

The 1948 draft law in effect reiterated the 1940 CO provisions throughout the *Cold War; but with no CPS camps, most of the 35,000 COs performing alternative service between 1951 and 1965 worked in local hospitals or mental institutions. During the *Korean War, the percentage of inductees exempted as COs grew to nearly 1.5 percent, compared with 0.15 percent in each world war.

In the *Vietnam War, the traditionally small group of religious objectors was succeeded by massive numbers of secular and religious young men applying for CO status or simply refusing to cooperate in the draft. The new COs tended to come from better-educated and higher socioeconomic groups. They received support from mainline religions—Protestant, Jewish, and Catholic—plus antiwar and antidraft groups. Established antidraft organizations included the War Resisters League (founded 1919); the National Interreligious Service Board for Conscientious Objectors (1940); and the Central Committee for Conscientious Objectors (1948). Numbers of African Americans applied as COs, most prominently Muhammad Ali, a Black Muslim and heavyweight boxing champion, who was sent to prison when he refused military service after his CO claim was rejected.

The Supreme Court, in the *Seeger* (1965) and *Welsh* (1970) decisions, expanded the criteria for CO status from religious to secular moral or ethical beliefs. More than 170,000 registrants were classified as COs between 1965 and 1970. CO exemptions granted to registrants as compared to actual inductions soared from 8 percent of inductions in 1967 to 43 percent in 1971, to three times that ratio in 1972, when more people were being exempted as COs than were being drafted into the army. Additionally, between 1965 and 1973, approximately 17,500 members of the armed forces applied for noncombatant status or discharge as COs.

Compulsory draft registration was reactivated in 1980. When 500,000 failed to register between 1982 and 1984, the Reagan administration prosecuted a few of those who publicly proclaimed their refusal to register. The Justice Department soon abandoned such an approach. Instead, Congress, adopting an amendment by Representative Gerald Solomon (Rep.-N.Y.) penalized nonregistrants by denying them student financial assistance from federal funds.

Within the armed services, even without conscription, conscientious objection became a public issue again during the preparation for the *Persian Gulf War, when between 1,500 and 2,000 persons in reserve and regular military units applied for discharge as COs. The army eventually reassigned or released these soldiers, but the Marine Corps court-martialed and imprisoned nearly fifty Marine COs.

In the 1990s, the right of conscientious objection in many other Western nations was being expanded to include recognition of secular and religious COs in and out of uniform and in some countries, selective objection. Derived from the Vietnam War and new directions in Western political and ethical thought, this trend demonstrated that the tension between concepts of freedom of conscience and the *citizen-soldier continued to redefine conscientious objection in America.

[*See also* Conscription; Draft Resistance and Evasion; Pacifism; Peace and Antiwar Movements; Selective Draft Cases.]

• Edward Needles Wright, *Conscientious Objectors in the Civil War*, 1931. Mulford Q. Sibley and Philip E. Jacob, *Conscription of Conscience: The American State and the Conscientious Objector, 1940–1947*, 1952. Lillian Schlissel, *Conscience in America: A Documentary History of Conscientious Objection in America, 1757–1967*, 1968. Michael F. Noone, Jr., ed., *Selective Conscientious Objection: Accommodating Conscience and Security*, 1989. Cynthia Eller, *Conscientious Objectors and the Second World War*, 1991. Charles C. Moskos and John Whiteclay Chambers II, eds., *The New Conscientious Objection: From Sacred to Secular Resistance*, 1993. James W. Tollefson, *The Strength Not to Fight: An Oral History of Conscientious Objectors of the Vietnam War*, 1993. Heather T. Frazer and John O'Sullivan, *"We Have Just Begun to Fight": An Oral History of Conscientious Objectors in Civilian Public Service During World War II*, 1996. Rachel Goossen, *Women Against the Good War: Conscientious Objection and Gender on the American Home Front, 1941–1947*, 1997.   —John Whiteclay Chambers II

CONSCRIPTION. Compulsory military service has played a periodic and often controversial role in raising America's wartime forces. It has only rarely been used in peacetime in America.

English colonists revitalized the county militia system of compulsory, short-term training and service for local defense. However, in the eighteenth century for longer-term forces most colonies turned to ad hoc units composed primarily of volunteers with occasional draftees and legally hired substitutes.

During the *Revolutionary War, state governments assumed the colonies' authority to raise their short-term militias through drafts if necessary. They sometimes extended this to state units in the *Continental Army, but they denied Gen. George *Washington's request that the central government be empowered to conscript. As the initial volunteering slackened, states boosted enlistment bounties and held occasional drafts, producing more hired substitutes than actual draftees.

The Constitution neither mentioned nor prohibited national conscription, simply providing Congress with the power "to raise and support armies." Most of the framers apparently believed that the United States, like England, would enlist rather than conscript its soldiers, paying for them through federal taxes.

For much of the nineteenth century, the United States relied upon a small, all-volunteer regular army, augmented in wartime by the militia (renamed the National Guard) and by large numbers of temporary, locally organized, federally funded units—the U.S. *Volunteers. During the *War of 1812, however, the Madison administration tried unsuccessfully to adopt a national draft (which Daniel Webster, a New England Federalist, denounced as "Napoleonic despotism").

National conscription came to America in the *Civil War. With fewer people, the South adopted conscription in 1862, eventually applying it to white males seventeen to fifty years of age. Conscription raised 21 percent of the 1 million Confederate soldiers. But because it violated individual liberty and states' rights and included unpopular class-based occupational exemptions, such as for overseers on large plantations, it eroded some popular support for the Confederacy.

The North adopted the draft in 1863, making it applicable to males twenty to forty-five. Avoiding unpopular occupational exemptions, Congress permitted draftees to hire a substitute or pay a commutation fee of $300, then comparable to a worker's annual wages. Peace Democrats denounced it as a "rich man's war but a poor man's fight," and thousands evaded or resisted when military provost marshals began conscripting. Bloody draft riots erupted New York and other cities.

Four federal drafts produced only 46,000 conscripts and 118,000 substitutes (2 and 6%, respectively, of the 2.1 million Union troops). Most soldiers were U.S. Volunteers. However, the draft was credited, along with $600 million in enlistment bounties, with prodding volunteers, encouraging reenlistments, and demonstrating political will.

Not until *World War I did the United States rely primarily upon conscription. A civilian-led "Preparedness" movement helped persuade many Americans that national compulsion was more equitable and efficient than local voluntarism for an industrial society to raise a mass army. President Woodrow *Wilson overcame considerable opposition—particularly from agrarian isolationists and ethnic and ideological opponents of U.S. involvement—to obtain a temporary wartime, national, selective draft.

The Selective Service Act of 1917 prohibited enlistment bounties and hiring substitutes but authorized deferments on the grounds of dependency or essential work in industry or agriculture. The draft was implemented by a Selective Service System composed of a national headquarters commanded by Gen. Enoch Crowder and some 4,000 local draft boards staffed by civilian volunteers. The boards decided, within overall national guidelines, on the induction or deferment of particular individuals.

In 1917–18, Selective Service registered and classified 23.9 million men, eighteen to forty-five, and drafted 2.8 million of them. In all, 72 percent of the 3.5 million-man wartime army were draftees. Despite the initial divisions over the war, there were no draft riots. Authorities arrested those who counseled draft resistance, including the anarchist Emma Goldman and Socialist Party leader Eugene V. *Debs. Except for a few rural incidents, opposition took the form of draft evasion or registration as conscientious objectors (COs). Apparently between 2 and 3 million men never registered, and 338,000 (12% of those drafted) failed to report when called or deserted after arrival at training camp. In addition, 64,700 registrants sought CO status. The U.S. Supreme Court upheld the draft law in 1918.

In *World War II, following the German defeat of France, Congress in 1940 adopted the nation's first prewar conscription act, the result of a campaign headed by old "Preparedness" leaders. The draft system was set to operate through 1945, but because of intense opposition from isolationists, Congress obligated the 1940 draftees to serve only one year, for training purposes. A year later, the lawmakers voted (203–202 in the House) to retain the 600,000 draftees. After Pearl Harbor, the Congress extended the draft to men aged eighteen to thirty-eight (and briefly to forty-five), and prolonged military duty for the duration.

Headed by Gen. Lewis Hershey, Selective Service drafted a total of 10.1 million men in World War II, the majority for the army. Nearly 6 million other men and women joined voluntarily, primarily in the Army Air Corps, the navy, and the Marines. Deferments were limited primarily to war industries, hardship cases, and agriculture.

Still there was dissent, reflected in the 72,000 registrants who applied for CO status and in antidraft incidents in Chicago and other cities. The latter included protests by African Americans against discrimination and segregation in the armed forces. In addition, the Justice Department investigated 373,000 cases of draft evasion; 16,000 evaders were convicted.

After the war, until Congress let the induction authority expire in 1947, conscription was extended to help maintain the much-reduced military. Escalation of *Cold War tensions led Congress to adopt a new draft law in 1948. It required twenty-one months of military training and service by individuals selected by their local draft boards. The Cold War military was composed of volunteers, draftees, and draft-induced volunteers.

During the *Korean War, 1.5 million men, eighteen to twenty-five, were drafted; another 1.3 million volunteered, primarily for the navy and air force. Discontent led to an increase in the number of COs, and there were 80,000 reported cases of draft evasion.

Cold War conscription became a casualty of the *Vietnam War. The draft enabled President Lyndon B. *Johnson to build up U.S. forces in Vietnam between 1964 and 1968 from 23,000 military advisers to 543,000 troops. In 1964–66, annual draft calls soared from 100,000 to 400,000.

Although draftees were a small minority (16%) in the U.S. armed forces, they comprised the bulk of infantry riflemen in Vietnam (88% in 1969). They accounted for more than half the army's battle deaths. Because of student and other deferments, the draft and the casualties fell disproportionately upon working-class youths, black and white.

Dissent increased, along with soaring draft calls and casualty rates. Supported by an antiwar coalition of students, pacifists, and clergy, and many liberal and radical groups, draft evasion and resistance increased dramatically. There were antidraft demonstrations, draft card burnings, sit-ins at induction centers, break-ins and destruction of records at a dozen local draft boards.

In 1965–75, confronted with well over 100,000 instances of draft evasion or resistance, the federal government indicted 22,500 persons. Some 8,800 were convicted and 4,000 imprisoned. As the Supreme Court expanded the criteria for conscientious objection, CO exemptions rose to more than 170,000 between 1965 and 1970.

An estimated 571,000 young men illegally evaded the draft. Of these, 360,000 were never caught, and another 198,000 had their cases dismissed, but some 9,000 were convicted and 4,000 sent to prison. Between 30,000 and 50,000 others fled into exile, mainly to Canada, Britain, and Sweden.

Congress came under pressure to reform or eliminate the draft. With conservative support, however, General Hershey, Selective Service director since 1941, blocked any significant changes, including recommendations for national uniformity by a 1967 presidential commission headed by former Assistant Attorney General Burke Marshall.

Having criticized the draft in his 1968 campaign, President Richard M. *Nixon removed Hershey, ended new occupational and dependency deferments, and initiated an annual draft lottery in 1969 among eighteen-year-olds (to reduce prolonged uncertainty). He also appointed a commission, headed by former Secretary of Defense Thomas *Gates, which in 1970 recommended an *All-Volunteer Force (AVF), with a standby draft for emergency use.

President Nixon reduced draft calls while gradually withdrawing troops from Vietnam. However, his dispatch of American units into Cambodia in 1970 triggered massive new public protests. Only reluctantly did Congress in 1971 extend the draft for two more years. The lawmakers also eliminated student deferments, deemed a class-based privilege, and voted a major pay increase ($2.4 million) for the lower ranks of the military to achieve an AVF by mid-1973. During the 1972 election campaign, Nixon cut draft calls to 50,000 and stopped requiring draftees to go to Vietnam. On 27 January 1973, the day a cease-fire was announced, the administration stopped drafting, six months before induction authority expired on 1 July 1973.

Even without induction, Selective Service maintained compulsory draft registration until 1975, when President Ford suspended the process. President Jimmy *Carter resumed it in 1980 in response to the Soviet invasion of Afghanistan. With local draft boards dismantled, Selective Service headquarters directed the program. In response to a suit that women, as equal citizens, should also have to register, the Supreme Court upheld the constitutionality of male-only draft registration. In 1980–84, half a million young men did not register, and under President Ronald *Reagan the Justice Department prosecuted a few of those who publicly refused to register.

In the post-Vietnam era, the military relied entirely on volunteers. However, in the 1990 buildup for the *Persian Gulf War, Selective Service headquarters prepared contingency plans to call up 100,000 men in 30 days if reactivation of the draft was required to obtain replacements if there were massive American casualties. In November 1990, Secretary of Defense Richard *Cheney issued orders preventing any military personnel from leaving even if their enlistment contracts had expired, in effect, making the AVF temporarily less voluntary. The quick victory against Iraq in 1991 did not produce massive American casualties; the draft was not reactivated; and after the war, military personnel were allowed to leave the service.

By 1991, with the collapse of the Soviet Union and the end of the Cold War, debate resumed over whether to maintain even a semblance of Selective Service. The House of Representatives voted in 1993 to eliminate Selective Service headquarters and end compulsory draft registration, but the Defense Department successfully argued the need to retain Selective Service and draft registration, and the measure to end them died in the Senate. Appropriations were reduced in the 1990s and evaders were not prosecuted.

[See also Conscientious Objection; Draft Resistance and Evasion; New York City Draft Riots; Peace and Antiwar Movements; Selective Draft Cases; Volunteers, U.S.]

• Albert B. Moore, Conscription and Conflict in the Confederacy, 1924. Eugene C. Murdock, Patriotism Limited, 1862–1865: The Civil War Draft and the Bounty System, 1967. Eugene C. Murdock, One Million Men: The Civil War Draft in the North, 1971. John Whiteclay Chambers II, ed., Draftees or Volunteers: A Documentary History of the Debate Over Military Conscription in the United States, 1787–1973, 1975. Lawrence M. Baskir and William A. Strauss, Chance and Circumstance: The Draft, the War and the Vietnam Generation, 1978. John O'Sullivan, From Voluntarism to Conscription: Congress and Selective Service, 1940–1945, 1982. Eliot A. Cohen, Citizens and Soldiers: The Dilemmas of Military Service, 1985. George Q. Flynn, Mr. Selective Service: Lewis B. Hershey, 1985. John Garry Clifford and Samuel R. Spencer, Jr., The First Peacetime Draft, 1986. John Whiteclay Chambers II, To Raise an Army: The Draft Comes to Modern America, 1987. James W. Geary, We Need Men: The Union Draft in the Civil War, 1991. George Q. Flynn, America and the Draft, 1940–1973, 1993.

—John Whiteclay Chambers II

CONSTITUTIONAL AND POLITICAL BASIS OF WAR AND THE MILITARY. When the framers met in Philadelphia to draft the U.S. Constitution, they were aware that existing models of government placed the war power squarely in the hands of the king. John Locke, William Blackstone, and other writers on government regarded the power to go to war as a monarchical prerogative. But when America declared its independence from England, all executive powers were placed in the Continental Congress. The first national constitution, the Articles of Confederation, also concentrated all powers of government in a legislative branch.

By the time the Constitution was completed in Philadelphia, many of the executive prerogatives envisioned by Locke and Blackstone had been vested in Congress, such as the power to declare war, to raise and regulate fleets and armies, and the power over foreign commerce. Unlike Blackstone's model, the president had no power to issue letters of marque and reprisal (authorizing private citizens to undertake military actions). That power was reserved to Congress. Other powers, including treaties and the power to appoint ambassadors, were shared with the Senate.

The reason for breaking decisively with Locke and Blackstone is clearly explained in the debates at Philadelphia, the ratification debates in the states, and The Federalist Papers written by Alexander *Hamilton, John Jay, and James *Madison. James Wilson told his colleagues in Philadelphia that it was incorrect to consider "the Prerogatives of the British Monarch as a proper guide in defining the Executive powers. Some of these prerogatives were of a Legislative nature. Among others that of war & peace &c." In Federalist No. 69, Hamilton pointed out that the British king "is the sole possessor of the power of making treaties," whereas the U.S. Constitution shared that power with the Senate. The power of the king, he said, "extends to the declaring of war and to the raising and regulating of fleets and armies," powers now entrusted to Congress. Madison later remarked: "The constitution supposes, what the History of all Govts demonstrates, that the Ex[ecutive] is the branch of power most interested in war, & most prone to it. It has accordingly with studied care, vested the question of war in the Legisl[ative]."

The framers empowered the president to be commander in chief, but that title relates to responsibilities authorized by Congress. The language in the Constitution reads: "The President shall be Commander in Chief of the Army and Navy of the United States, and of the Militia of the several States, when called into the actual Service of the United States." Congress, not the president, does the calling. Article 1 gives to Congress the power to provide "for calling forth the Militia to execute the Laws of the Union, suppress Insurrections and repel invasions."

The debates at the Philadelphia convention include a revealing discussion of Congress's power to declare war. The early draft empowered Congress to "make war." Charles Pinckney, who expected Congress to meet only once a year, objected that legislative proceedings "were too slow" for the safety of the country in an emergency. Madison and Elbridge Gerry recommended that "declare" be substituted for "make," leaving to the president "the power to repel sudden attacks." Their motion carried.

The president's authority was carefully constrained. The power to repel sudden attacks represented an emergency measure that allowed the president, when Congress was not in session, to take actions necessary to repel sudden attacks either against the mainland of the United States or against American troops abroad. It did not authorize the president to take the country into full-scale war or mount an offensive attack against another nation.

Remarks on the Madison-Gerry amendment clarify the framers' intent. In support of the amendment, Roger Sherman said that the president should be able "to repel and not to commence war." George Mason spoke "ag[ain]st giving the power of the war to the Executive, because not [safely] to be trusted with it.... He was for clogging rather than facilitating war." At the Pennsylvania ratification convention, James Wilson expressed the prevailing sentiment that the system of checks and balances "will not hurry us into war; it is calculated to guard against it. It will not be in the power of a single man, or a single body of men, to involve us in such distress; for the important power of declaring war is vested in the legislature at large."

Madison insisted that the power of commander in chief be kept separate from the power to take the nation to war: "Those who are to *conduct a war* cannot in the nature of things, be proper or safe judges, whether *a war ought* to be *commenced, continued,* or *concluded.* They are barred from the latter functions by a great principle in free government, analogous to that which separates the sword from the purse, or the power of executing from the power of enacting laws."

Early Precedents. Presidential use of force during the first few decades conformed closely to the expectations of the framers that the decision to take the country to war was lodged solely in Congress. Whether involving military actions against Indian tribes, the *Whiskey Rebellion, or the Undeclared Naval War with *France from 1798 to 1800, presidential actions were based on authority granted by statute. Two decisions by the Supreme Court in 1800 (*Bas* v. *Tingy*) and 1801 (*Talbot* v. *Seeman*) recognized that Congress could authorize hostilities either by a formal declaration of war or by a statute that authorized an undeclared war. In the second case, Chief Justice John Marshall wrote for the Court: "The whole powers of war being, by the constitution of the United States, vested in congress, the acts of that body can alone be resorted to as our guides in this inquiry." The Barbary Wars during the administrations of Thomas *Jefferson and James Madison were repeatedly authorized by Congress. The *War of 1812 against England was declared by Congress.

The power of the president as commander in chief is at its low point when there is no standing army and Congress must act to raise troops. But when a standing army exists, ready to move at the president's command, the balance of power can shift decisively. The capacity of the president to put the nation at war is illustrated by the actions of President James K. *Polk in 1846, when he ordered Gen. Zachary *Taylor to occupy disputed territory on the Texas-Mexico border. The order provoked a clash between American and Mexican soldiers, prompting Polk to tell Congress a few weeks later that "war exists." After a few days of debate, Congress declared war against Mexico, recognizing that "a state of war exists." In 1848 the House of Representatives censured Polk's actions as a war "unnecessarily and unconstitutionally begun by the President of the United States."

One of the members of the House who voted for this censure was Abraham *Lincoln, who some years later would exercise military force during the *Civil War without first obtaining authority from Congress. In April 1861, with Congress in recess, he issued proclamations calling forth the state militia, suspending the writ of habeas corpus, and placing a blockade on the rebellious states. However, Lincoln never claimed that he had full authority to act as he did. He conceded to Congress that he had probably overstepped the constitutional boundaries established for the president and thus needed congressional sanction. Legislators debated this issue at length, eventually passing legislation "approving, legalizing, and making valid all the acts, proclamations, and orders of the President, etc., as if they had been issued and done under the previous express authority and direction of the Congress of the United States." Presidents have used force unilaterally a number of times, but the actions were relatively small in scope and duration.

Aside from Polk's initiatives in Mexico and Lincoln's emergency actions during the Civil War, the power of war remained in the hands of Congress during the nineteenth century, and the first half of the twentieth. The *Spanish-American War of 1898, *World War I, and *World War II were all formally declared by Congress.

The UN Charter and Korea. In June 1950, President Harry S. *Truman ordered U.S. troops to Korea without first requesting congressional authority. For legal footing he cited resolutions passed by the United Nations Security Council, but the history of the UN Charter and its implementing legislation demonstrates that UN machinery is not a legal substitute for congressional action. If it were, the president and the Senate, through treaty action, could strip from the House of Representatives its constitutional role in deciding questions of war.

In adopting the Charter, all parties in the executive and legislative branches understood that the decision to use military force through the United Nations required prior approval from both Houses of Congress. In response to any threat to the peace, breach of the peace, or act of aggression, the Security Council may decide under Article 41 of the Charter to recommend "measures not involving the use of armed force." If those measures prove inadequate, Article 43 provides that all members of the United Nations shall undertake to make available to the Security Council, "on its call and in accordance with a special agreement or agreements," armed forces and other assistance. These agreements spell out the numbers and types of forces, their degree of readiness and general location, and the nature of the facilities and assistance to be provided. Article 43 further states that the special agreements shall be ratified by each nation "in accordance with their respective constitutional processes."

The meaning of constitutional processes within the U.S. system was defined by Congress when it passed the UN Participation Act of 1945. The statute clearly provides that special agreements "shall be subject to the approval of the Congress by appropriate Act or joint resolution." The legislative history of the Participation Act underscores the need to protect congressional interests by obtaining legislative approval in advance.

Notwithstanding the UN Charter and the Participation Act, President Truman acted militarily in Korea without ever coming to Congress for approval. He circumvented Congress by never entering into special agreements with the Security Council. The very procedural safeguard carefully enacted into law to protect the constitutional prerogatives of Congress thus amounted to nothing. No special agreement has ever been entered into under the UN Charter, although there have been many UN military actions.

From the War Powers Resolution to Bosnia. In an effort to restore its powers over war and peace, Congress enacted the *War Powers Resolution of 1973. The purpose was to provide for the "collective judgment" of both Congress and the president before U.S. troops are sent into combat. Because of ambiguities in the statute and Congress's failure to protect its institutional interests, presidents from Gerald *Ford to Bill *Clinton have taken a range of military actions with little involvement by Congress.

Military actions in the years immediately after the War Powers Resolution were modest, ranging from President Ford's evacuation of Americans and foreign nationals in Southeast Asia to efforts by President Jimmy *Carter to rescue American hostages in Iran. Congressional efforts to restrict the Reagan administration's assistance to the Contras in Nicaragua caused a major clash between executive and legislative branches, beginning in 1982. Although the administration testified repeatedly that it was complying with these statutory directives, executive branch officials actively solicited funds from private parties and from foreign governments to assist the Contras. When these activities surfaced in November 1986, as the *Iran-Contra Affair, Congress passed several statutes to tighten controls over covert operations.

Another confrontation occurred in 1990 when President Bush claimed that he could take offensive action against Iraq, after its invasion of Kuwait, without authorization from Congress. The Bush administration regarded a UN Security Council resolution of 29 November 1990 as sufficient legal basis. On 8 January 1991, President Bush decided to ask Congress to pass legislation supporting his policy in the Persian Gulf. A day later, however, when reporters asked him whether he needed a resolution from Congress, he replied: "I don't think I need it.... I feel that I have the authority to fully implement the United Nations resolution." A potential constitutional crisis was averted when Congress debated, and passed, legislation authorizing the military action against Iraq.

President Clinton repeatedly insisted that he could use military force against other nations without seeking authority from Congress. While threatening to invade Haiti in 1994, he encouraged the UN Security Council to adopt a resolution "inviting" all states, particularly those in the region of Haiti, to use "all necessary means" to remove the military leadership in that island. By a vote of 100 to zero, the Senate passed a "sense of the Senate" amendment stating that the Security Council resolution "does not constitute authorization for the deployment of United States Armed Forces in Haiti under the Constitution of the United States or pursuant to the War Powers Resolution."

A few weeks later, Clinton "welcomed" the support of Congress for an invasion of Haiti, adding: "Like my predecessors of both parties, I have not agreed that I was constitutionally mandated to get it." In a televised address in September, he told the American public that he was prepared to use military force to invade Haiti, referring to the Security Council resolution as authority, and stating his willingness to lead a multilateral force "to carry out the will of the United Nations." Several votes by the House and the Senate to deny funds for the contemplated military action failed. An invasion became unnecessary when former president Jimmy Carter negotiated an agreement in which the military leaders agreed to step down to permit the return of ousted President Jean-Bertrand Aristide. Both Houses of Congress resolved that "the President should have sought and welcomed Congressional approval before deploying United States Forces to Haiti."

President Clinton also used air strikes against the Bosnian Serbs and sent 20,000 ground troops to Bosnia-Herzegovina without obtaining authority from Congress. In 1993, he acted in concert with the United Nations and *NATO to authorize humanitarian airdrops of food, helped to enforce the no-fly zone (a ban on unauthorized flights) over Bosnia-Herzegovina, and supported an arms embargo on that region. The next year, while contemplating air strikes in Bosnia, he looked not to Congress for authority but solely to the Security Council and to NATO. In response to a reporter's question whether he had decided to use air strikes to retaliate against shellings in Sarajevo, Clinton referred to UN and NATO authority. At no time did he acknowledge a need to obtain congressional authorization.

In late February 1994, U.S. jets shot down four Serbian bombers over Bosnia. The United Nation and NATO, not Congress, became the authorizing bodies. Other air strikes occurred throughout 1994 and 1995. At the end of August 1995, after NATO aircraft had carried out the war's biggest air raid, Clinton announced that the bombing attacks "were authorized by the United Nations." In proposing the introduction of U.S. ground troops into Bosnia, he welcomed the "support" of Congress without conceding that he needed its authority. Congress passed several nonbinding resolutions to withhold funds for ground troops to Bosnia unless the president first obtained legislative approval, but never employed binding statutory language. In the end, President Clinton dispatched the troops to Bosnia.

Presidential war power has expanded dramatically since 1950 because of a combination of factors: presidents pressing their powers to the limit and the passivity and acquiescence of Congress. The courts have tended to remain above the fray when members of Congress have objected that presidents have violated the War Powers Resolution or the Constitution. Federal judges have regularly told legislators that if they want to check the president, they must exercise the considerable powers within their arsenal. They should not expect courts to do Congress's job for it. That message is well stated and soundly based, but legislators have consistently failed to protect their institutional prerogatives.

Members of Congress continue to use the power of the purse to direct the president in foreign affairs and war, but increasingly seem to lack the institutional self-confidence to function as a coequal branch. In 1973, Congress succeeded in invoking its power of the purse to end the *Vietnam War, but only after escalating financial costs and military casualties tore the country apart. At various points legislators could have used the purse to constrain or terminate the war, but generally allowed the president to define the scope of hostilities. Only sustained public opinion forced Congress to vote for a cutoff in funds. Efforts to use the power of the purse to prevent military operations in Haiti and Bosnia came to naught.

Arguments about presidential war power that would have been astonishing fifty years ago are now routinely accepted as plausible, credible, and well within the bounds of reason. The political and constitutional costs are heavy. Instead of the two branches working in concert to create a program that has broad public support and understanding, presidents unilaterally offer various forms of economic and military assistance to other countries, consigning legislators to the backseat. In this era of executive hegemony it may take a major crisis to restore respect for the constitutional allocation of war-making authority, and the principle of checks and balances.

[See also Civil-Military Relations; Commander in Chief, President as; Congress, War, and the Military; Supreme Court, War, and the Military.]

• Thomas M. Franck, ed., The Tethered Presidency: Congressional Restraints on Executive Power, 1981. Francis D. Wormuth and Edwin B. Firmage, To Chain the Dog of War: The War Powers of Congress in History and Law, 1989. Michael J. Glennon, Constitutional Diplomacy, 1990. Harold Hongju Koh, The National Security Constitution: Sharing Power After the Iran-Contra Affair, 1990. Louis Henkin, ed., Foreign Affairs and the Constitution, 1990. Theodore Draper, A Very Thin Line: The Iran-Contra Affairs, 1991. John Hart Ely, War and Responsibility, 1993. William C. Banks and Peter Raven-Hansen, National Security Law and the Power of the Purse, 1994. Gary M. Stern and Morton H. Halperin, eds., The U.S. Constitution and the Power to Go to War, 1994. Louis Fisher, Presidential War Power, 1995. David Gray Adler and Larry N. George, eds., The Constitution and the Conduct of American Foreign Policy, 1996.
—Louis Fisher

CONSULTANTS. An important but often controversial part of the post–World War II defense establishment was the contracting-consulting industry, which grew apace amid deteriorating relations with the Soviet Union and rising levels of *Cold War military spending. Traditionally, contracting denoted mainly construction and procurement functions, while consulting involved the occasional services of individuals (usually skilled professionals) outside the military. However, from 1945 on, as national security came to rest on expensive high-tech weaponry, the military's need for outside expert advice and technical evaluation services increased dramatically. Demand was heaviest in the areas of science and technology, though cost-effectiveness, logistical, and operations analyses figured prominently as well.

During the 1950s, as the military competition between East and West intensified, the use of consultants hired by the Department of *Defense (DoD) on a contractual basis became increasingly institutionalized through the establishment of nonprofit "think tanks," later known as federally funded research and development centers (FFRDC). These organizations owed their principal source of funding to annual contract subsidies from the DoD. Most engaged in research and development of one sort or another; rarely did they actually produce a manufactured item. FFRDCs had two distinct advantages: they bypassed low government pay scales in the hiring of expert technical and scientific personnel; and they provided relatively easy and direct access to the industrial, academic, and scientific communities which had the knowledge and expertise the military services needed. Two early examples of such collaboration were the development in *World War II of the proximity fuse, a joint endeavor of the navy and the Applied Physics Laboratory of the Johns Hopkins University; and the systematic application of operations research to air warfare through Project RAND, started in 1945 by Douglas Aircraft and reconstituted as a nonprofit corporation funded by the air force in 1948.

The next decade witnessed a veritable explosion in the number of FFRDCs, reaching a total of thirty-nine by the early 1960s. Among the larger and more prominent were the Institute for Defense Analyses (IDA), founded in 1956, to help support the Weapons Systems Evaluation Group under the *Joint Chiefs of Staff; Analytic Services (ANSER), created in 1958, to provide specialized operations analysis for the air force; MITRE (1958), another air force–sponsored technical organization, which grew out of the Lincoln Laboratory of the Massachusetts Institute of Technology; Aerospace Corporation (1960), which initially specialized in ballistic missile systems; Research Analysis Corporation (RAC), the 1961 successor to the Operations Research Office (ORO), which had performed technical evaluations for the army since 1948 under contract with Johns Hopkins; and the Center for Naval Analyses (CNA), established in 1962 to consolidate scattered navy-sponsored technical research activities.

Accompanying the growth in FFRDCs was an increase in the number of for-profit contracting and consulting firms in the private sector. The greatest opportunities generally awaited contractors involved in hardware development and production, but a growing number of profit companies also emerged in direct competition with the FFRDCs. Many of these new companies moved into the burgeoning field of "systems analysis" that Secretary of Defense Robert S. *McNamara introduced in the 1960s in an effort to streamline and improve Pentagon planning and fiscal management through the application of computerized models.

Criticism by Congress and public interest groups that the Defense Department was becoming overly dependent on outside consultants and contractors led to periodic investigations and calls for reform. Initially targeted were the FFRDCs, whose activities their rivals in the private sector often strenuously lobbied to have curbed. At one point Congress imposed a funding ceiling on FFRDCs, until DoD agreed in 1972 to exercise closer controls and to shed all but ten FFRDCs from the military budget. In 1976, a task force of the Defense Science Board concluded that consulting arrangements with profit and nonprofit companies alike were an essential part of the Defense Department's operations. However, a year later, amid continuing controversy, President Jimmy *Carter ordered a governmentwide crackdown on what he termed "the excessively large volume of consulting and expert services."

Over the years Congress frequently debated legislation to curtail the use of consultants and contractors and the jobs they could perform. Congress tried to halt one alleged abuse—the so-called "revolving door"—when in 1985 it barred presidential appointees for two years from taking related jobs in the private sector. But as a rule efforts to legislate reform produced few dramatic changes in the system, due largely to the difficulty of finding workable definitions for terms like *consulting* and *consulting services.* Though it was clear that the number of consultants and contractors had increased enormously since World War II, no one was ever able to say with certainty how many there were, who they were, or how much DoD was spending on their services. According to a General Accounting Office audit in 1988, the Department of Defense devoted anywhere between $2.8 and $15.9 billion for consulting services in fiscal year 1987, excluding individual consultants earning under $25,000 per year.

Despite criticism, consultants and contractors performed functions that the military departments found difficult and expensive to do on their own. One appealing feature of "contracting out" was that it was less costly and more efficient in certain cases—small jobs especially—than doing the work in house; and in 1994, responding to recommendations from a task force headed by Vice President Albert Gore, Jr., Congress enacted legislation relaxing the rules and paperwork so that DoD and other government agencies could make freer use of contractors.

[*See also* National Laboratories; Science, Technology, War, and the Military.]

• H. L. Nieburg, *In the Name of Science,* 1966. Daniel Guttman and Barry Willner, *The Shadow Government,* 1976. James A. Smith, *The Idea Brokers: Think Tanks and the Rise of the New Policy Elite,* 1991. David M. Ricci, *The Transformation of American Politics: The New Washington and the Rise of Think Tanks,* 1993.

—Steven L. Rearden

CONTAINMENT. *See* Truman Doctrine.

CONTINENTAL ARMY. Americans used various forms of military organization in the Revolutionary War, the most prominent of which was the set of traditional forms and innovative solutions called the "Continental army." The name meant more as the military expression of a collective political resistance than as a description of the variety of forces fighting in scattered theaters.

In simplest terms, the Continental army was the military force that delegates to the Continental Congress agreed to support financially by requisitions on the states. Each state raised a segment of the army, called its "Continental Line" because the troops were to be trained to fight according to European linear tactics. States reinforced, reorganized, and re-created their lines many times in response to the enormous demand for armed forces during the war; they retained the responsibility for raising, clothing, feeding, and paying their own troops. Congress annually assigned each state a quota of men, leaving each legislature to decide how to fill it. Without effective central management, levels of recruitment and support varied widely. No state raised all the Continentals that Congress thought were required.

At the start of the conflict, Americans raised the same kinds of units they had previously used to fight French, Spanish, and Indian enemies. These units were separate from the militia, which remained responsible for home defense, local political control, and funneling manpower into active service units. The first "Continental" army was born on 15 June 1775, when Congress adopted the thirty-six regiments the four New England governments had created in late April to maintain the siege of Boston after the militia, which had besieged the town after Lexington and Concord, went home. These regiments (plus one from Pennsylvania) so closely resembled their *French and Indian War predecessors that the first campaign of the new conflict was, in terms of the composition of American forces, the last colonial war.

New England soldiers were volunteers who expected to be paid wages comparable to what they would receive in civilian employments, and expected to serve for only a single campaign. (Virginia in late 1775 raised troops for three years as had been its practice during the French and Indian War.) Most soldiers expected to go home in November or early December, and viewed their enlistment as a contract, the terms of which they expected their governments strictly to observe. Recruits enlisted to serve under men they knew, and disciplinary problems arose whenever the men in a unit lost confidence in an officer; discipline was based more on collective agreement among the soldiers than on anything imposed from above. Legislatures selected officers who could persuade their neighbors to enlist incorporated combat veterans of the French and Indian War in the mix of officers. By force of character and example, these men created an army out of an armed mob, and were the principal reason why New England soldiers performed so well at Bunker Hill on 17 June, two weeks before their "Continental" commander arrived from Philadelphia.

The most important military decision Congress made was to appoint George *Washington as commander in chief. Regiments from every state except South Carolina and Georgia served at one time or another under Washington's command, and although many units served in other theaters, the name "Continental" army is most closely associated with the force Washington superintended from early July 1775 through late fall 1783. Washington, a veteran of French and Indian War service, insisted that officers act as gentlemen, soldiers obey those whom Congress had set over them, and the army be subordinate to civil authority. He wanted a force modeled after the British army, and capable of defeating the British with linear tactics. He disliked the militia: incapable of remaining in service long enough to be trained in linear tactics, profligate of arms and accoutrements, and unsuited to fulfilling his aspirations to military respectability (sniping at the enemy from behind stone walls was no way to earn a place among the civilized nations of Europe), militiamen remained throughout the war the bane of Washington's existence.

Washington begged Congress to enlist men for more than one year at a time. A minimum of three years of service, he argued, was required to build a proficient army. Congress, more attuned to the ideological problems that standing armies posed, and the practical difficulty of inducing their constituents to serve over the winter, never gave Washington all he wanted. In 1776, it opted again for annual enlistments, although it did expand the term of service from 1 January through 31 December and emphasized the army's "Continental" pretensions by numbering New England regiments sequentially. In late 1776, Congress authorized the states to raise eighty-eight regiments "for three years or the war," from 1 January 1777; thereafter, these were the officially preferred terms of enlistment. Massachusetts and Virginia were assigned the most regiments, eighteen apiece, Delaware only one.

Some states raised more Continentals than did others. Massachusetts, with roughly the same total white population as Pennsylvania and Virginia (about 310,000 in 1775), raised perhaps 34,000 men—over twice as many as its two peers in population. Connecticut, with roughly 195,000 white people in 1775, raised more proportionally, and ranked second with about 16,000 Continentals. Virginia probably raised less than 15,000 and North Carolina fewer than 6,000. Of course, states raised men differently—southern states relied more on militiamen than did their northern counterparts—but as these figures indicate, New Englanders and Pennsylvanians predominated in the main army.

As the war dragged on, it became more difficult to find soldiers. States increased bounties, shortened terms, and reluctantly forced men to serve. But conscription was such a distasteful and dangerous exercise of state power that legislatures would use it only in extreme circumstances. More frequently, legislatures tried to reinforce the army with men drawn by incentive or compulsion from the militia for only a few months of summer service. The army's composition thus reflected a bewildering variety of enlistment terms. After 1779, for example, a Connecticut company might have eight or ten privates serving for three years or the war, and twice or three times that number enlisted only for the summer. Washington's complaints to Congress have obscured his genius in building an effective army out of the limited service most Americans were willing to undertake.

Because Congress reckoned military service by individual enlistments—one man serving one time for terms that ranged from one day in the militia to "during the war" in the Continentals—it is impossible to know precisely how many men served in the Continental army. Multiple and consecutive enlistments were commonplace; men crossed from Continental to militia units and back again; record-keeping left much to be desired during intense campaigning; many muster rolls were lost around New York in 1776, Canada in 1775–76, and in the South in 1780–81. Francis Heitman, an early twentieth-century authority, estimated that 250,000 individuals performed military service supporting American independence during the war, or about one in four white men (African American men also served in significant numbers in New England units, especially regiments from Rhode Island). Perhaps as many as 120,000 men served in some part of the Continental army. The largest number of Continentals in Washington's army at one time was probably 32,000 men in November 1778; of these, only 21,500 men were fit for duty. The core of the army—men who repeatedly reenlisted and officers who served for several consecutive years—probably numbered less than 15,000 men. Washington's Continentals always had to be reinforced by summertime recruits or militiamen before they could take the field.

A Continental soldier's service record could be extremely complex. In Massachusetts, for instance, a minuteman might enlist for the rest of 1775 in what became the Continental army, reenlist in 1776, again in 1777 for three years, again in 1780 for a year, and again in 1781 for the war. Or, tired of continuous Continental service, another 1775 veteran might serve in the militia in 1776 and 1777, and, because he knew his experience was a valuable commodity, enlist in the Continental army for nine months in 1778, nine months in 1779, and six months in 1780, each time collecting the bounty money offered by a government increasingly desperate to fill its quota. A third veteran of 1775 might eschew Continental service altogether and serve in the militia sent to Rhode Island or the Northern army, lending his experience to units that might otherwise appear to have little military value. Similar patterns elsewhere, many even more complex in southern states, illustrate the amalgam of tradition and innovation that was the Continental army.

Who served? Because enthusiasm was highest in 1775, the earlier units offered a better social, economic, and ethnic cross section of society than later units. American society was never perfectly reflected in its army: the colonies had traditionally left the fighting to men willing to accept money to serve, whether voluntarily or under threat of compulsion. As in late colonial armies, some soldiers came from economically disadvantaged groups (including free blacks and Indians), and enlisted because the army offered the best prospects of survival. But the Continental army was not drawn from the dregs of society; nor was it intended to be. Many young men viewed military service, and especially enlistment bounties, as a means to accumulate money. When inflation eroded the value of currency, towns used creative methods to recruit, among others, young men just entering the manpower pool. In Massachusetts in early 1781, for instance, an eighteen-year-old who agreed to serve for three years in the Continental army received an enlistment bounty of a few dollars in specie and several hundred dollars in paper money, plus six three-year-old cattle to be delivered when he completed his service. The town thus paid him with cattle not yet born, which he might not live to collect!

The quest for economic advancement does not imply lack of patriotism; if the discontinuous character of Continental army service was a nightmare for recruiting officers and Washington, it allowed soldiers the flexibility to combine self-interest with commitment to the cause. Moreover, many men enlisted and reenlisted in the Continental army for reasons that had less to do with economic or ideological motives than with adventure, camaraderie, and the opportunity for more responsibilities than they might exercise as a civilian—all the factors that have motivated soldiers at other times and in other wars.

Despite its continual turnover in personnel, the Continental army became an effective fighting force. It became a sophisticated, mobile human community, with a population that during the summer campaigning season in most years was exceeded only by Philadelphia, New York, and Boston. The army absorbed tremendous amounts of money and resources to feed, cloth, equip, house, train, transport, and pay its members, and to build and maintain its own infrastructure, including services like baking bread, butchering cattle, constructing shelter, and repairing clothing. Later in the war, especially in 1778–81, a corps of light infantry, formed each year from the best soldiers from each regiment, furnished much of its fighting power. Under Anthony *Wayne, light infantrymen captured Stony Point with great élan in 1779; at Yorktown in 1781, ten companies under Alexander *Hamilton demonstrated that the American army could field forces equal to the best of Europe. American soldiers did not always look the part. In the South, especially in 1780–81, Continental soldiers counted themselves lucky to have even threadbare uniforms. But their clean muskets, neat cartridge boxes, and quick response to battlefield commands showed them to be the equal of their opponent. Out of sometimes unpromising elements, Americans had crafted a unique military force, one that in the end performed the tasks demanded of it.

[See also Army, U.S.: Colonial and Revolutionary Eras; Conscription; Continental Navy; Revolutionary War: Military and Diplomatic Course.]

• Charles Royster, *A Revolutionary People at War: The Continental Army and the American Character,* 1979. Robert K. Wright, Jr., *The Continental Army,* 1983.   —Harold E. Selesky

CONTINENTAL NAVY. The first vessel to sail under authority of the Continental Congress was the schooner *Hannah.* Shortly after taking command of the *Continental army at Cambridge, George *Washington realized the usefulness of interdicting British supply vessels entering Boston as a means of tormenting the enemy and supplying his own troops. *Hannah* went to sea on 5 September 1775.

Hannah's success encouraged the Congress to take further action. At the urging of Rhode Island and other colonies, Congress on 13 October 1775 authorized the fitting out of a "swift vessel to carry ten carriage guns" and formed a committee to oversee this task, as well as to find additional vessels and bring in an estimate of the expense. This legislation marked the official launching of the Continental navy.

As often happened with the Continental Congress, ambition exceeded resources. Spurred by dreams of naval glory and an exaggerated opinion of American capabilities, Congress eventually authorized the construction of twenty frigates (thirteen in December 1775), three ships of the line, and at least two smaller vessels. Some of these vessels were never built and many never got to sea. Almost all of those that did set sail were captured or destroyed by the British.

Nevertheless, the Continental navy made important contributions to American victory. Continental vessels harassed British trade, carried American diplomats to foreign posts, and forced the Royal Navy to stretch its resources further than they would otherwise have been required to do.

Among the earliest accomplishments of the Continental navy was Commodore Esek Hopkins's capture of the Bahamas Islands. Sailing from Philadelphia in mid-February 1776, Hopkins's squadron captured Nassau, remaining only long enough to load cannon from the fort before returning to Connecticut. En route Hopkins's squadron encountered the British frigate *Glasgow,* which managed to inflict considerable damage on its pursuers and then escape. This unhappy engagement cast a pall over what had until that moment been an important accomplishment. Hopkins came under heavy criticism and Congress later dismissed him from the service.

Among the chief achievements of the Continental navy was to bring the war to Europe. Both Capt. Lambert Wickes and Gustavus Conyngham sailed in British home waters, capturing several enemy vessels and generally embarrassing the Royal Navy. The most famous Continental captain to sail these waters, however, was John Paul *Jones.

Having sailed the Continental sloop of war *Ranger* to France, Jones lobbied the French for the loan of a large warship. Thanks to help from Benjamin Franklin, the French provided him with an old East Indiaman, *Duc de Duras,* which he renamed *Bon Homme Richard* in honor of his friend Franklin. Jones took his ship, sailed around the British Isles, and on 23 September 1779, in a bravely fought battle, defeated the British frigate HMS *Serapis* off Flamborough Head. It was the most celebrated American naval victory of the Revolution.

While Jones, Conyngham, and other captains brought fame to the American navy, in home waters the story was less encouraging. A few weeks before Flamborough Head, a combined expedition of Continental navy and state naval vessels, with reinforcements of privateers, suffered a disastrous defeat at Penobscot Bay on the Maine coast. Sent to dislodge the British from that area, the expedition was surprised by the Royal Navy and completely destroyed. Less than a year later at Charleston, South Carolina, the Continental navy lost four additional vessels when that city fell to the enemy.

When Gen. Charles *Cornwallis surrendered in mid-October 1781 at the Battle of *Yorktown, the Continental navy had been reduced to two frigates, *Alliance* and *Deane.* In November 1782, after innumerable delays, the Continental navy launched its first and only ship of the line, *America,* at Portsmouth, New Hampshire. Eager to economize, Congress quickly presented her to the French to replace a ship of the line that had run aground in Boston.

By early in 1783, only *Deane* and *Alliance* remained in service; at the end of the year *Alliance* was the sole American warship left. She remained in commission but inactive until 1785, when she too was sold out of the service.

The federal Constitution of 1787 stipulated (Art. I, sec. 8) that Congress might "provide and maintain a Navy," and made the president its commander in chief (Art. II, sec. 2). It was not until 1794, however, that the new government authorized a navy; and not until 1797 were the first ships launched. Several captains from the Revolution, including John Barry and Silas Talbot, received commissions in the new navy.

In addition to the vessels that sailed under the authority of the Continental Congress all of the states also authorized public warships. Most of these vessels remained close to their own states and were used primarily to defend local commerce. Far more numerous than public warships were privateers. Commissioned by either the Continental Congress or the state governments, several hundred of these vessels sailed during the Revolution. Although they captured hundreds of enemy merchant vessels they did not have a dramatic effect on the war. As the Royal Navy dispatched more warships to American waters many privateers were either trapped in port or captured at sea.

Although not a direct part of the naval effort American sailors did make a contribution to Washington's army. During the escape from Manhattan sailors from Marblehead, Massachusetts manned the small boats that evacuated American troops. They were also important later in that same year when Washington depended upon them to help his army cross the Delaware River.

[See also Commander in Chief, President as; Revolutionary War.]

• Gardner W. Allen, *A Naval History of the American Revolution,* 2 vols., 1913. William James Morgan, ed., *Naval Documents of the*

American Revolution, 9 vols., 1964. William M. Fowler, Jr., *Rebels Under Sail*, 1976.

—William Fowler, Jr.

CONVENTIONAL ARMED FORCES IN EUROPE, TREATY OF (1990). *See* CFE Treaty.

COOPER-CHURCH AMENDMENT (1970). During the *Vietnam War, President Richard M. *Nixon on 30 April 1970 ordered American and South Vietnamese troops to invade Cambodia in order to attack North Vietnamese and National Liberation Front sanctuaries. Nixon defended his action as necessary to carry out his Vietnamization program. In protest, Senators John Sherman Cooper (R-Ky.) and Frank Church (D-Idaho) introduced a bipartisan amendment to the Foreign Military Sales Act to prohibit the use of American forces in Cambodia after 30 June 1970.

By 1970, the nation was deeply divided concerning the wisdom of the war in Southeast Asia. Senate opposition had been building since 1965, but most members of Congress still yielded to the president. The invasion of Cambodia proved to be the pivotal point for change. In addition to the time limit for withdrawal of U.S. forces from Cambodia, the Cooper-Church Amendment barred the reintroduction of forces into that nation without express congressional approval. The Nixon administration strove to limit the impact of the proposal, chiefly through a series of modifications sponsored by Robert Dole (R-Kans.) and Robert Byrd (D-W. Va.) that would have allowed broad presidential discretion over the deployment of military forces. However, on 30 June the Senate adopted the original amendment in a historic vote of 58 to 37. Under heavy pressure from the White House to weaken the amendment, the House of Representatives did approve a weakened measure in December. The passage of the Cooper-Church Amendment was a milestone in congressional-presidential relations, the first time that the Congress had restricted the deployment of U.S. troops during a war. After 1970, congressional debate was now not on whether to withdraw troops from the Vietnam War, but when.

• LeRoy Ashby and Rod Gramer, *Fighting the Odds: The Life of Senator Frank Church*, 1994. Randall Bennett Woods, *Fulbright*, 1995.

—David F. Schmitz

CORAL SEA, BATTLE OF THE (1942). The first confrontation during *World War II between American and Japanese aircraft carriers occurred on 7–8 May 1942 in the Southwest Pacific. Imperial Japanese naval forces under Vice Adm. Shigeyoshi Inoue, Fourth Fleet commander, sought to capture Port Moresby in southeastern New Guinea and Tulagi in the Solomon Islands in order to threaten Australia to the south across the Coral Sea. The fleet carriers *Shokaku* and *Zuikaku* under Vice Adm. Takeo Takagi and the light carrier *Shoho* with 140 planes covered the invasion forces.

Warned in April by naval code breaking of *ULTRA intelligence, Adm. Chester W. *Nimitz, Commander of the U.S. Pacific Fleet, hurriedly deployed Rear Adm. Frank Jack Fletcher's Task Force 17 with the carriers *Lexington* and *Yorktown* (a total of 138 planes) to the Coral Sea. In support were Australian and American naval and air forces from Gen. Douglas *MacArthur's Southwest Pacific Area.

Tulagi fell on 3 May. The Port Moresby landing was scheduled for 10 May. However, Fletcher attacked the invasion force on 7 May and sank *Shoho*. That morning Takagi failed to find the American carriers, but sank the fleet oiler *Neosho* and destroyer *Sims*. On 8 May in the main carrier duel, Fletcher lost *Lexington* and 66 planes and suffered damage to *Yorktown*, in return for damaging *Shokaku*. Although Fletcher withdrew, Inoue canceled the Port Moresby invasion due to high Japanese carrier plane losses (73 aircraft). *Shokaku* and *Zuikaku* missed the Battle of *Midway in June, but *Yorktown* contributed decisively to the victory.

The Battle of the Coral Sea was the first naval battle in which opposing forces fought solely with carrier aircraft. Although it achieved a tactical *victory, Japan also suffered its first strategic defeat of the Pacific War.

[*See also* World War II, U.S. Air Operations in; World War II, U.S. Naval Operations in.]

• Samuel E. Morison, *History of United States Naval Operations in World War II, Vol. IV: Coral Sea, Midway, and Submarine Actions May 1942–August 1942*, 1950. John B. Lundstrom, *The First South Pacific Campaign*, 1976. John B. Lundstrom, *The First Team: Pacific Naval Air Combat from Pearl Harbor to Midway*, 1984; 2nd ed., 1990.

—John B. Lundstrom

CORNWALLIS, CHARLES (1738–1805), British soldier. Favored with distinguished ancestry and a good education, Cornwallis rose rapidly in the British army. By age twenty-nine, he was colonel of the 33rd Regiment, having performed with *éclat* in Europe during the Seven Years' War. In the *Revolutionary War, with Henry *Clinton at Charleston in June 1776, he joined Sir William *Howe in New York for the Battle of Long Island, 7 August, and a series of campaigns in New Jersey in the winter of 1776–77. In 1777, he campaigned in Pennsylvania, and performed well at Monmouth, 28 June 1778. He served under Clinton at the capture of Charleston on 12 May 1780. Although he and Clinton despised each other, Clinton nonetheless placed him in command in the South before returning to New York. Routing Horatio *Gates at Camden on 16 August 1780, Cornwallis pursued Nathanael *Greene into North Carolina the following year, winning, but failing to destroy Greene's army. Ordered by Clinton to Virginia, and then entrapped at the battle of *Yorktown because of his own lackluster performance, he surrendered on 19 October 1781. Back in England, Cornwallis blamed Clinton for the disaster. Later, he redeemed his reputation by serving with distinction in India.

• William B. Wilcox, *Portrait of a General: Sir Henry Clinton in the War of Independence*, 1964. Franklin and Mary Wickwire, *Cornwallis: The American Adventure*, 1970.

—Paul David Nelson

COUNTERINSURGENCY. *Counterinsurgency* was the name given in the 1960s to a U.S. political-military doctrine designed to defeat Communist-influenced insurgencies, what Soviet premier Nikita Khrushchev called "wars of national liberation" in the process of decolonization. The word *counterinsurgency* was used instead of *counterrevolution* since *revolution* had a more favorable, even heroic connotation to Americans.

Actually, insurgency and counterinsurgency are as old as empires and rebellions, as familiar as the Romans' harsh repression of uprisings within their empire. The Spanish insurgency against Napoleon's conquest gave birth to the term *guerrilla warfare*. In the nineteenth century European empires fought what they called "small wars" against indigenous forces and frequently employed "antiguerrilla" and "antirevolutionary" warfare techniques. These were primarily attempts to keep armed insurgents from obtaining support from civilians in villages, often by isolating the villagers, and then tracking down and destroying the insurgents.

Separation of villagers and the use of brutal interrogation methods characterized many of the efforts to suppress armed rebellions. In Cuba in the late nineteenth century, the Spanish used a *reconcentrado* policy of herding rural dwellers into makeshift camps to prevent support for the Cuban rebels; the result, as almost always in makeshift arrangements, was widespread disease and death. The British used active antiguerrilla methods in the Boer War (1899–1902), including the establishment of internment camps in which thousands of Afrikaner men, women, and children died. In the *Philippine War, the U.S. Army, in response to guerrilla warfare by Filipino nationalists, isolated villages and sought to obtain information about rebel locations through various means, including the "water cure" (forcibly swelling suspects with water until they yielded information). Totalitarian governments in World War II used widespread executions and mass terror as part of their suppression of insurgent resistance movements.

In the post–World War II era, as colonial empires faced independence movements and insurgencies around the world, Britain, France, and Belgium in particular used counterrevolutionary warfare against Communist or simply nationalist insurgents. Britain isolated villages and set up internment camps successfully in Malaya in the 1950s. The American helped the Filipino government defeat the Communist-led Hukbalahap (Huk) rebellion in central Luzon in 1954. In Indochina, France fought a losing battle against multiparty independence forces led by the Communist *Ho Chi Minh; subsequently the French lost to insurgent urban guerrillas in Algeria.

American "counterinsurgency doctrine" was developed in the 1960s in an effort to counter guerrilla movements seen by the government as antithetical to U.S. interests. Although it originated as a response to Khrushchev's call for Communist-led wars of national liberation in the decolonizing Third World, it could be used against insurgency by any political group. In practice, however, it was employed mainly against Communist and left to left-center insurgencies.

American counterinsurgency doctrine sought to defeat the insurgents through both military and psychological means. Recognizing that such uprisings were based in part on the discontent of poor rural and urban Third World peoples with unresponsive political and economic institutions, American planners thought the discontent could be contained through "nation-building" or "modernization" programs, while military efforts sought out and eliminated insurgent units and leadership.

The U.S. Army established a Psychological Warfare Center at Fort Bragg, North Carolina, in 1952 to study psychological and unconventional warfare, and a Special Forces Group was created there that same year as the operational force. In 1961, President John F. *Kennedy, emphasizing the need to counter Communist guerrillas, particularly in Southeast Asia, ordered the buildup of Special Forces (and authorized their distinctive headgear, a green beret) and the development of counterinsurgency doctrine and training in special warfare.

U.S. doctrine included emphasis on isolating the insurgents from the population and resources, and the use of patrols and other means to maintain pressure on insurgent groups. The Special Forces underwent vigorous military training, including ranger and airborne training, guerrilla operations, intelligence gathering, demolition, communications, and hand-to-hand combat. But engagement with the civilian population was also emphasized, and therefore included training in indigenous languages, preventive medicine, and village sanitation.

Counterinsurgency was employed with U.S. assistance during the 1960s and 1970s in a number of Latin American countries—Bolivia, Columbia, Guatemala, Peru, and Venezuela—as well as in the 1980s in Guatemala and El Salvador.

The primary U.S. counterinsurgency effort, however, was in the *Vietnam War during the 1960s and early 1970s. The Special Forces grew to about 12,000 soldiers during that period, although they declined to about 4,000 by 1985. In Vietnam, both civilian and military U.S. agencies were involved in counterinsurgency, which was emphasized by the CIA and the Marine Corps (the latter through its Combined Action Program) and initially by the U.S. Army. But under Gen. William C. *Westmoreland, the army subsequently focused on a conventional strategy of searching for and then destroying enemy units with massive firepower. The counterinsurgency effort in Vietnam sought to isolate the villagers from the Communist Viet Cong through the "strategic hamlet" program, and to link the South Vietnamese government with positive programs involving medical care, local political and land reform, and agricultural development. Eventually these nation-building efforts were coordinated through the Office of Civil Operations and Rural Development Support (CORDS) under the supervision of the U.S. Military Assistance Command Vietnam (MACV). But these had inadequate support, and genuine rural politicization and land redistribution were opposed by both the Saigon government and the South Vietnamese Army. Partly in response to Communist terrorism in 1967, CORDS created Operation Phoenix, in which joint "provincial reconnaissance units" used ambushes and raids to kill, capture, or co-opt persons believed to be members of Communist cadres. In the end, the U.S. counterinsurgency and *pacification programs in Vietnam failed in their major aims of undermining the Communists' political-military organization and strengthening the link between the rural population and the government of South Vietnam.

During the 1980s, when Soviet client states in Angola, Mozambique, and Ethiopia faced ethnic uprisings, their Communist Soviet Cuban military protectors proved no better at counterinsurgency than had the French or the Americans in Vietnam. Nor were the Communist Vietnamese successful in suppressing Cambodian resistance after their invasion of Cambodia in 1978. The Russians also failed in their attempt to conquer Afghan guerrillas in the 1970s or Chechin insurgents in the 1990s.

The importance of U.S. counterinsurgency doctrine should not be overemphasized in terms of the *Cold War. Conceptually, there was little new in the idea, other than the emphasis on political reform and nation-building. It failed in Vietnam, its greatest test. And successes in Bolivia, Colombia, Guatemala, and Peru stemmed less from the success of the American doctrine than from the weakness of communism in those countries.

[See also Central Intelligence Agency; Guerrilla Warfare; Covert Operations; Low–Intensity Warfare; Psychological Warfare; Rangers, U.S. Army; Special Operations Forces.]

• Douglas Blaufarb, The Counterinsurgency Era: U.S. Doctrine and Performance, 1950 to the Present, 1977; Lawrence M. Greenberg, The Hukbalahap Insurgency: A Case Study of a Successful Anti–Insurgency Operation in the Philippines, 1946–1955, 1986; John Prados, Presidents' Secret Wars: CIA and Pentagon Covert Operations Since World War II, 1986; Aaron Bank, From OSS to Green Berets, 1986; Sam Sarkesian, The New Battlefield: The United States and Unconventional Conflicts, 1986; Michael Lee Lannaing, Inside the LRRP: Rangers in Vietnam, 1988; Brian M. Linn, The U.S. Army and Counterinsurgency in the Philippine War, 1899–1902, 1989; Bob Newman, Guerrillas in the Mist: A Battlefield Guide to Clandestine Warfare, 1997.   —John Whiteclay Chambers II

COUNTERINTELLIGENCE. Throughout U.S. military history, the term counterintelligence has referred to both an activity and a type of secret information. As the former, counterintelligence is designed to neutralize information gathering by foreign powers. In its guise as a kind of intelligence, counterintelligence consists of data on the personalities and modus operandi of other espionage services and systems. There is an important distinction between security and counterintelligence. Security involves monitoring and closing channels by which state secrets might reach unauthorized individuals or groups; whereas counterintelligence implies the use of such channels to identify, mislead, and frustrate foreign intelligence services seeking to gather those secrets. Counterespionage, the study and combatting of foreign spies, is a subset of counterintelligence.

Counterintelligence was not unknown to the founding fathers. The case of Benedict *Arnold, for example, helped to shape republican ideas about loyalty and treason. Yet the Secret Service was the only counterintelligence institution to emerge from U.S. military experiences from the *Revolutionary War through the *Civil War. Allan Pinkerton, the chief of the Secret Service, served as President Abraham *Lincoln's security officer before joining the staff of Gen. George B. *McClellan. Following the war, Congress provided a legal foundation for Pinkerton's Secret Service. But loath to retain a presidential or even a military police force, Congress placed the Secret Service in the treasury department and restricted its operations to security against counterfeiting. Only in 1908 would the Secret Service again assume responsibility for protecting the president.

For most of the nineteenth century, the *army and *navy shared the view held by Congress that counterintelligence was a form of detective work which was incompatible with the American military tradition. So deeply held was this belief that the military reforms of the 1880s that created the first peacetime military intelligence bureaus— the Office of Naval Intelligence (ONI) and the Military Intelligence Division (MID)—did not produce any counterintelligence units within the services. Even with the host of new threats that accompanied the rise of the United States as a world power at the end of the nineteenth century, the army and the navy preferred to contract out counterintelligence work instead of risking institutional contamination.

During the *Spanish-American War and the 1907 war scare with Japan, the services engaged Secret Service officers to investigate possible foreign espionage activity. The sole exception was the counterespionage mission undertaken by the U.S. army as part of its pacification of the *Philippines.

The traditional obstacles to counterintelligence eroded in *World War I. Suspicious explosions like Black Tom at munitions facilities and the advent of energetic advocates of counterespionage were the cause. For the first time, the U.S. army and the navy created separate "negative" bureaus for counterintelligence and a Counterintelligence Police (CIP) was recruited to protect Gen. John Pershing's American Expeditionary Force. Interest in institutionalizing counterintelligence work emerged throughout the federal government. The Justice Department set up a General Intelligence Division (GID) under an ambitious young lawyer, J. Edgar Hoover, to investigate radicalism and subversion in the U.S., and Woodrow Wilson asked the State Department to coordinate these new federal counterespionage programs.

Although World War I had institutionalized counterespionage in the military, no federal agency, civilian or military, considered foreign spying enough of a threat to warrant having a peacetime counterespionage service. Following the excesses of the Red Scare of 1919, the Justice Department closed its GID. Meanwhile the Office of Naval Intelligence (ONI) and the Military Intelligence Division (MID) were reduced in size, and the Counterintelligence Police (CIP) nearly disappeared entirely. Consequently when the U.S. government confronted the problem of German spying in the late 1930s, none of the established members of the national security state had a counterespionage program.

Counterintelligence was the first field of secret activity addressed by the Roosevelt administration when it took stock of an increasingly hostile world in 1938. Consistent with his general philosophy of leadership, President Franklin D. *Roosevelt chose to divide responsibility for counterintelligence between the FBI, which coordinated it at home and throughout most of the Western hemisphere, and the army and navy. The army received exclusive responsibility for counterintelligence on army bases, the Panama Canal Zone, and the Philippines. Aside from fleet security, the navy received the nod for Hawaii and Guam. Otherwise the services had an overlapping interest in all of the Eastern hemisphere. The entry of the Office of Strategic Services (OSS) into the U.S. intelligence system in 1942 did nothing to improve coordination among the existing services. Ultimately creating its own counterintelligence service in 1943, the OSS went into competition with the army's Counterintelligence Corps and the Office of Naval Intelligence.

The debate following *World War II involved not whether there should be counterespionage in peacetime but who should control it and what its targets should be. In 1947 the National Security Council subordinated all U.S. foreign intelligence and counterintelligence to the newly created Director of Central Intelligence, whose responsibilities included running the *Central Intelligence Agency and directing Washington's nascent intelligence community. National Security Council Intelligence Directive-5, which established DCI leadership in foreign clandestine activities, removed the responsibility for counterintelligence in the Western hemisphere from the FBI and limited the military to conducting counterintelligence only as required to protect military installations and operations.

The new position of DCI threatened what the military considered to be its traditional prerogatives in wartime. With the intensification of the Cold War following the successful detonation of the Soviet Union's first nuclear device in 1949, the *Joint Chiefs of Staff sought to establish the principle that all foreign clandestine activity, including counterintelligence, would be transferred to its authority in wartime. In 1951, at the height of the *Korean War, the Joint Chiefs made their most serious effort to revise NSCID-5 to permit them to supervise U.S. clandestine activities as they had OSS operations between 1942 and 1945. The DCI, Gen. Walter Bedell Smith, successfully turned away these efforts.

As the *Cold War continued, the military services grew increasingly reluctant to accept a secondary position in overseas counterintelligence. Secretary of Defense Robert S. *McNamara's 1961 initiative to reform military intelligence coincided with another attempt by the services to weaken the CIA's authority in counterintelligence. The U.S. military recommended the formation of a security subcommittee of the United States Intelligence Board, the executive oversight organization for intelligence, in the hope of acquiring more of a voice in setting counterintelligence policy.

The military had more than institutional interests at heart. The CIA's counterintelligence efforts in its first decade had not been well regarded. The CIA's earliest operations in Eastern Europe were riddled with penetrations, and its tiny counterintelligence force had few successful exploitations of double agents to its credit. Even the agency's counterespionage experts considered their specialty but the stepchild of the organization. Notwithstanding this less-than-brilliant reputation in counterintelligence, the CIA was able to fend off military challenges to its supervisory control.

As president, Richard M. *Nixon responded to the weaknesses in U.S. counterintelligence with the so-called Huston plan, which envisioned White House coordination of these activities. Nixon believed that a more efficient federal program would produce evidence of Soviet assistance to the *peace and antiwar movements. The military counterintelligence units had maintained domestic operations on and off since World War I. In the 1960s, domestic counterintelligence operations by the U.S. army grew and coordination with other services became a problem. Opposition from J. Edgar Hoover at the FBI, however, thwarted the Nixon reforms and responsibility for counterespionage remained divided. The spate of spy cases in the 1980s, culminating in the "Year of the Spy" of 1985, brought the creation of a counterintelligence subcommittee in the *National Security Council.

[See also Intelligence, Military and Political; National Security Act (1947).]

• Jeffrey M. Dorwart, The Office of Naval Intelligence: The Birth of America's First Intelligence Agency, 1965–1918, 1979. Thomas F. Troy, Donovan and the CIA: A History of the Establishment of the Central Intelligence Agency, 1981. Robert J. Lamphere, with Tom Shachtman, The FBI-KGB War: A Special Agent's Story, 1986. Roy Talbert, Jr., Negative Intelligence: The Army and the American Left, 1917–1941, 1991.
—Timothy J. Naftali

COVERT OPERATIONS. In June 1948, National Security Council Directive 10/2 defined covert operations as actions conducted by the United States against foreign states "which are so planned and executed that any U.S. Government responsibility for them is not evident to unauthorized persons and that if uncovered the U.S. Government can plausibly disclaim any responsibility for them." It then authorized the *Central Intelligence Agency (CIA) to undertake such clandestine activities, including "propaganda, economic warfare; preventive direct action, including sabotage, anti-sabotage, demolition and evacuation measures; subversion against hostile states, including assistance to underground resistance movements, guerrillas and refugee liberations groups, and support of indigenous anti-communist elements in threatened countries of the free world."

Long before the CIA became involved in covert operations, however, the United States had used similar clandestine methods to achieve national objectives. President George *Washington, for example, who had a keen appreciation for the role of intelligence in both war and peace, persuaded Congress in July 1790 to establish the Contingent Fund of Foreign Intercourse. Known as the Secret Service fund, this money was spent by Washington (without a requirement for detailed accounting) in a covert operation to ransom Americans held hostage by the Barbary states.

During the nineteenth century, American presidents authorized covert operations on an infrequent, ad hoc basis. Although the United States remained isolated for the most part from international power politics, various administrations found cause to initiate covert operations in Canada, Cuba, Hawaii, and Central America. For the most part, the State Department maintained control over these clandestine activities. At no time did the government consider establishing a professional foreign intelligence service.

The increasing involvement of the United States in world affairs during the twentieth century led inexorably to the creation of a permanent intelligence service with the capability to undertake covert operations. Presidents Woodrow *Wilson and Franklin D. *Roosevelt both became deeply immersed in clandestine intelligence activities while fighting global wars. Indeed, the most immediate precedent for the CIA's covert operations can be found in World War II's Office of Strategic Services (OSS), an organization that combined intelligence gathering with paramilitary covert action. The OSS provided assistance to resistance and guerrilla groups from France to Burma. Although "plausible deniability" was not required for these wartime activities, the methods and techniques—and many of the personnel—that were used by Gen. William Donovan's clandestine fighters were passed on to the CIA.

After World War II, policymakers in Washington recognized the need for an option beyond diplomacy but short of war as they grew apprehensive about the emergence of an aggressive Soviet Union that seemed to threaten American interests around the world. The *National Security Act (1947), which created the CIA, gave the new organization not only the mission to collect and evaluate intelligence but also a vaguely worded duty "to perform such other functions and duties related to intelligence affecting the national security as the National Security Council may from time to time direct." At the end of 1947, the *National Security Council (NSC) first defined these "other functions and duties" when it made the CIA responsible for covert psychological operations. Directive 10/2 went much further, creating the Office of Special Projects (later, Office of Policy Coordination), headed by Frank Wisner to conduct a wide variety of covert operations.

The first clandestine project undertaken by the CIA was an attempt through psychological warfare and political covert action to influence the elections of 1948 in Western Europe. Paramilitary covert operations began with the *Korean War. By 1952, the budget of the Office of Policy Coordination had grown from $4.7 million (1949) to $82 million. At the same time, personnel assigned to this covert action agency increased from 302 to 2,812 (plus 3,142 overseas contract personnel).

The presidency of Dwight D. *Eisenhower (1953–61) marked the "golden age" of covert operations. More than any other chief executive in the postwar era, Eisenhower made covert action a major part of his foreign policy. The CIA, led by Allen Welsh *Dulles, undertook a variety of clandestine activities at presidential direction, including the successful overthrow of unfriendly governments in Iran and Guatemala, and a failed attempt to topple the government of Indonesia. During the Eisenhower-Dulles era, clandestine collection and covert action accounted for 54 percent of the CIA's total annual budget.

Although the disastrous attempt to invade Cuba at the Bay of Pigs in 1961 painfully revealed the limits of the CIA's capability for cover paramilitary action and led to the dismissal of Dulles, presidents during the 1960s continued to utilize covert operations with undiminished enthusiasm, most notably in the Caribbean, Africa, and Southeast Asia. The CIA was especially active in Laos, where between 1961 and 1973 it directed local troops against major Communist forces in the largest covert paramilitary operation in the agency's history. As a result of these activities, the budget of the clandestine service remained at over 50 percent of the CIA's total budget in the sixties.

By this time, the original concept of "plausible deniability" had been broadened to include the presidency. Assassination plots against such foreign leaders as Cuba's Fidel Castro and the Congo's Patrice Lumumba by the Eisenhower and Kennedy administrations, for example, were structured in such a way that the president could deny responsibility for the activities.

Covert operations declined precipitously during the 1970s as a series of congressional investigations, especially the 1975–76 inquiry Senate's Select Committee on Intelligence (or Church Committee), led to greater skepticism about, and oversight of, intelligence activities. By 1977, the proportion of the CIA's budget allocated to covert action fell to less than 5 percent of the total budget, the lowest figure since 1948.

Congress, which had played little role in what was considered a prerogative of the executive branch, began to exercise tighter control of CIA clandestine activities with the Hughes-Ryan Act (1974). This amendment to the Foreign Assistance Act prohibited the CIA from spending money for operations in foreign countries (other than for the collection of intelligence) "unless and until the President finds that each such operation is important to the national security of the United States and reports, in a timely fashion, a description and scope of each operation to the appropriate committees of Congress." The Intelligence Oversight Act (1980) further expanded the role of Congress in monitoring covert operations. Indeed, by the 1980s, congressional committees not only exercised oversight over intelligence operations but also became part of the decision-making process for covert action.

President Reagan and his CIA director, William Casey, placed renewed emphasis on covert operations as an instrument of national policy, especially in Nicaragua and Afghanistan. Their efforts, including the use of the staff of the NSC to conduct covert action, led to the Iran-Contra investigation, and increased congressional watchfulness over the executive branch's use of clandestine action. By the 1990s, covert operations, which could be conducted only under carefully controlled and fully reviewed conditions, had declined to a low ebb.

[See also Caribbean and Latin America, U.S. Military Involvement in the; Central Intelligence Agency; Counterinsurgency; Intelligence, Military and Political; Iran, U.S. Military Involvement in; Iran-Contra Affair.]

• Rhodri Jeffreys-Jones, American Espionage: From Secret Service to CIA, 1977. William M. Leary, ed., The Central Intelligence Agency: History and Documents, 1984. John Prados, Presidents' Secret Wars: CIA and Pentagon Covert Operations Since World War II, 1986. Loch K. Johnson, America's Secret Power: The CIA in a Democratic Society, 1989. Christopher Andrews, For the President's Eyes Only: Secret Intelligence and the American Presidency from Washington to Bush, 1995.
—William M. Leary

COWPENS, BATTLE OF (1781). Daniel *Morgan and his 1,100-man American army defeated Banastre Tarleton and 1,100 British and loyalist troops at the Cowpens in northwestern South Carolina on 17 January 1781 in the tactical masterpiece of the *Revolutionary War—a classic demonstration of a commander's ability to exploit the resources at hand. The Battle of *King's Mountain on 7 October 1780 demonstrated that British and loyalist forces in the backcountry could be overwhelmed by temporary concentrations of Rebel militia. But the aggressive Tarleton had little interest in caution; when he crossed the trail of the last regular American force in the South, he worried only that it might escape, and pressed forward without knowing his enemy's number or location. On the morning of 17 January, he fell headlong into Daniel Morgan's trap.

Morgan had picked unpromising ground, a rolling tree-dotted meadow used to winter cattle, which seemed to give Tarleton's cavalry the opportunity to outflank his force; the Broad River, five miles to the north, would impede any American withdrawal. But Morgan had planned to take advantage both of the impetuosity of Tarleton and the variable abilities of his own soldiers. Positioning his relatively untrained militia in the first two of three lines, he ordered them to shoot at British officers three times before withdrawing to the rear. This ensured that by the time the British reached his third line, made up of Maryland, Virginia, and Delaware Continentals, the enemy would be disorganized and leaderless. Lastly, behind a small ridge to his rear, Morgan stationed 100 horsemen under William Washington.

As Tarleton attacked, everything seemed to unfold as he expected. But when his troops encountered the third line, Washington's horsemen plowed into their right while the re-formed militia struck their left. Tarleton's force disintegrated in the midst of a double envelopment; Tarleton fled to avoid capture. Together, King's Mountain and Cowpens stripped the British army in the South of its most mobile troops, and thus severely diminished its ability to defeat the Americans.

• Robert D. Bass, *The Green Dragoon: The Lives of Banastre Tarleton and Mary Robinson,* 1957. Don Higginbotham, *Daniel Morgan: Revolutionary Rifleman,* 1961. Lawrence E. Babits, *A Devil of a Whipping: The Battle of Cowpens,* 1998.

—Harold E. Selesky

CRAZY HORSE (1840?–1877), war leader of the Oglala Lakota Sioux. Crazy Horse achieved renown in intertribal warfare on the northern Great Plains and in conflict with the U.S. Army. Introverted, mystical, and eccentric in dress and deportment, he excelled at hit-and-run tactics. Between 1866 and 1876, he gained distinction in combat with U.S. soldiers. On 21 December 1866, he led the decoy party that enticed Capt. William J. Fetterman and eighty soldiers to their destruction near Fort Phil Kearny, Wyoming. He also participated in the Wagon Box Fight nearby on 2 August 1867. His greatest fame, however, arose from his role in the Battle of the *Little Bighorn, 25 June 1876, when he and other warriors wiped out an entire unit of Lt. Col. George Armstrong *Custer's 7th Cavalry Regiment. The Indian victory prompted decisive military reaction, and on 6 May 1877, Crazy Horse surrendered at Camp Robinson, Nebraska. On 7 September, resisting confinement in the post guardhouse, he received a fatal wound from a soldier's bayonet. His people buried him at an unknown spot on the plains. He is remembered as the greatest of all Sioux war leaders.

• Mari Sandoz, *Crazy Horse, Strange Man of the Oglalas,* 1942.

—Robert M. Utley

CROWE, WILLIAM (1925–), career naval officer and eleventh chairman of the Joint Chiefs of Staff. Crowe is a Naval Academy graduate (1947), a Stanford M.A. (1956), and a Princeton Ph.D. (1965). He pursued an unusual naval career path by combining political-military assignments with command. Crowe rose through the ranks to become Commander in Chief of Pacific Command (1983). He became the first chairman to serve under the *Goldwater-Nichols Act (1986), which made the chairman the nation's principal military adviser and mandated increased cooperation among the armed services. Crowe's career spanned major events of the *Cold War, and as chairman his principal contribution was to aid in decreasing American-Soviet rivalry at the end of the Cold War.

Following the Intermediate Nuclear Forces Treaty (1987), he developed on his own initiative military-to-military agreements and exchanges with his Soviet counterpart. In the Middle East, Crowe oversaw America's military responses to the hijacking of the cruise liner *Achille Lauro* by Palestinian terrorists (1985), hostilities with Libya (1986), the reflagging and escorting of Kuwaiti tankers in the Persian Gulf (1987), and the shootdown of an Iranian civilian airliner by the USS *Vincennes* (1988). After retirement, Crowe encouraged a cautious approach in dealing with Iraq's invasion of Kuwait (1990) and endorsed Bill *Clinton for president (1992). He was named ambassador to the United Kingdom in 1994 and retired from that position in 1997.

• William J. Crowe, Jr., with David Chanoff, *The Line of Fire: From Washington to the Gulf, the Politics and Battles of the New Military,* 1993.

—Richard S. Rauschkolb

CRUISERS. Successor to the sailing frigate, the cruiser inherited the earlier ship's missions: scouting and screening for the battle fleet, commerce raiding, or protecting trade. U.S. cruisers often provided flagship facilities for officers commanding destroyer flotillas or even entire fleets. In peacetime, cruisers frequently maintained a naval presence in troubled areas. To operate alone, cruisers carried substantial armament, were protected by armor of medium thickness, and possessed high speed, great range, and good seakeeping qualities. Thus, U.S. cruisers were sizable ships (from 3,000 to 35,000 tons), with crews of 300 to 1,700 men.

Because the traditional American strategy had been one of commerce raiding, when the United States began rebuilding its navy in the early 1880s, the first warships ordered were the steel cruisers *Atlanta, Boston,* and *Chicago,* beginning the tradition of naming them after cities. Over the next decade, the navy settled on a sustained program of cruiser construction, adding fifteen ships.

The successes of American cruisers (most famously George *Dewey's flagship *Olympia*) in the *Spanish-American War brought additional orders, culminating in ten very large cruisers (14,500 tons each). As the navy reoriented its strategy increasingly to the battleship during Theodore *Roosevelt's presidency, however, cruiser construction fell into abeyance.

World War I demonstrated anew the merits of the type, and in 1916, Congress authorized ten fast scout cruisers of the *Omaha* class, plus six huge battle cruisers of 35,000 tons armed with ten 14-inch guns. After U.S. entry into the war, cruisers performed important services by patrolling and escorting convoys (the *San Diego* was lost to a mine off Fire Island).

After the war, the U.S. *Navy confronted a reorientation to the Pacific and the limitations imposed by the *Washington Naval Arms Limitation Treaty, which limited cruiser size and armament. The six battle cruisers were scrapped on the ways or their hulls converted to aircraft carriers; the new scout cruisers were too short-legged (short-ranged) for Pacific work.

During the interwar years, the navy built long-range cruisers armed with nine or ten 8-inch guns, designated "heavy cruisers" for their gun caliber under the treaty provisions. Eighteen were commissioned prior to Pearl Harbor; they were reinforced by nine new "light cruisers" of the *Brooklyn* class, armed with fifteen 6-inch pieces. As aircraft increased in capability, the navy began construction of four ships designed for antiaircraft defense: the *Atlanta* class (of 6,718 tons), armed with a dual-purpose battery of sixteen 5-inch guns.

When *World War II broke out in Europe, Congress funded the most ambitious cruiser-building program in history. Authorized by 1943 were seven additional *Atlantas.* Two new designs were ordered in quantity: the Baltimore-class heavy cruisers (14,472 tons, nine 8-inch guns) of which fourteen entered service, and the Cleveland-class light cruisers (11,744 tons, twelve 6-inch guns) of which twenty-seven were built, making them the largest class of cruisers ever. The navy also ordered six ships classified as "large cruisers"—the *Alaska* class, of 29,779 tons and nine 12-inch guns. Intended as "cruiser killers," only the first two ships were completed.

Cruisers proved valuable in a number of wartime missions: antiaircraft escort, shore bombardment, and especially night surface action against enemy vessels. Off Guadalcanal, American cruisers fought numerous engagements and even mortally damaged the Japanese battleship *Hiei*. During the war, the navy lost ten cruisers: two (*Juneau* and *Indianapolis*) to submarine torpedoes, one to air attack, and seven (*Houston, Astoria, Quincy, Vincennes, Atlanta, Northampton*, and *Helena*) to surface ship gunfire and torpedoes. Other cruisers (e.g., *Minneapolis, Salt Lake City, San Francisco*, and *Savannah*) proved their ruggedness by surviving damage from almost every type of weapon, including a German glide bomb. *Indianapolis* served as Fifth Fleet flagship for Vice Admiral Raymond A. *Spruance in 1943. On several occasions in peacetime, that ship carried President Franklin D. *Roosevelt.

To compensate for losses, the navy ordered slightly modified versions of the *Cleveland* and *Baltimore* types, although only two of the *Fargo* class and three of *Oregon City* class were finished postwar. More advanced cruisers were also begun: the *Worcester* class (two finished), with a 6-inch antiaircraft battery, and the *Des Moines*-class heavy cruisers (three commissioned) with rapid-firing 8-inch guns.

In the changed defense environment of the atomic age, the navy put most of its cruisers into mothballs, keeping only a few operational for flag duty or amphibious support. To counter aerial threat to the carriers, the navy began conversion during the 1950s of nine of the extant light and heavy cruisers to carry the new Talos or Terrier missile systems.

Two unique cruisers were also completed in this period. The *Northampton*, begun as a heavy cruiser, was converted into a command ship to provide accommodations and communications for the president and other *national* leaders in the event of nuclear war. Then, in 1961, the navy commissioned the futuristic *Long Beach*, armed only with guided missiles and propelled by nuclear power.

The *Vietnam War once again proved the usefulness of cruisers, for both shore bombardment and antiaircraft duties. In 1968, *Long Beach* was the first vessel in history to destroy an enemy aircraft with guided missiles. Nonetheless, nuclear warships were extremely expensive, and construction of more advanced ships, called "strike cruisers," was halted, mid-1970s, for budgetary reasons.

The dividing line between cruisers and lesser vessels now had so blurred that the navy reclassified as "cruisers" (1975) twenty-six larger surface warships earlier categorized as guided missile frigates or destroyers. Similarly, the twenty-seven ships of the new *Ticonderoga* class, ordered originally as guided missile destroyers, were labeled "cruisers" in 1980 to reflect their costs and capabilities. The breakdown in identity was further reflected in the naming of cruisers for states, battles, or individuals. The navy has contended that the old distinctions between cruisers and lesser ships are today irrelevant, given enhanced capabilities and similarities of mission between the types.

[*See also* Battleships.]

• Naval Historical Center, *Dictionary of American Naval Fighting Ships*, 8 vols., 1959–91. Samuel E. Morison, *The Two Ocean War*, 1963. Norman Friedman, *U.S. Cruisers*, 1984. Stefan Terzibaschitsch, *Cruisers of the U.S. Navy, 1922–1962*, 1984. M. J. Whitley, *Cruisers of World War Two*, 1996.
—Malcolm Muir, Jr.

CUBA, U.S. MILITARY INVOLVEMENT IN. "So far from God, so close to the United States," one Cuban historian despaired. Proximity alone, however, did not determine the varied nature of U.S. military deployments to Cuba,

and the Cubans themselves bear part of the responsibility for *yanqui* military appearance. Fighting the Spaniards or themselves, they often asked for U.S. troops, then complained when they arrived.

Reflecting upon their defeat in the Ten Year War (1868–78), the Cuban political elite swore that the next rebellion against Spain would draw the United States into the war. Their failure to incite American military intervention had doomed their struggle for independence. Through media manipulation and careful political cultivation, Cuban rebels created popular support in the United States when they again "took to the field" in 1895. In the presidential campaign of 1896, all three major parties (Republican, Democratic, and Populist) called for Cuban independence, by force of arms if necessary. Stung by Spanish intransigence, atrocities, and the sinking of the USS *Maine* by an unexplained explosion in Havana Harbor, the Congress pressured President McKinley to lead the nation into the *Spanish–American War in April 1898. The goal was to free Cuba from Spain.

Rejecting one scheme to invest Havana, the U.S. Army and U.S. Navy agreed to blockade Cuba to turn back reinforcements, defeat any Spanish naval forces in the Caribbean, and join the Cuban rebel army in eastern Cuba and defeat the Spanish garrisons in detail. Two American expeditionary forces went to Oriente Province. A Marine battalion of 650 seized a fleet operating base at Guantanamo Bay. The army's Fifth Corps then landed to the west at Daiquiri and, 17,000 strong in regulars of the U.S. Army and wartime volunteers, marched toward Santiago to besiege the city and capture the Spanish naval squadron in refuge there. The advance guard fought Spanish outposts at Las Guasimas, and the whole force made a spirited if awkward twin assault on the Spanish fortifications at Kettle and San Juan Hills and El Caney. Despite 1,400 casualties, the Americans in the Battle of *Santiago forced the Spanish to surrender on 17 July, two weeks after an American squadron destroyed the Spanish squadron in its desperate flight. A general capitulation and peace negotiations soon followed.

Although the United States rejected annexation and agreed to limit its own economic penetration, it occupied Cuba until May 1902, and the ultimate agreement to withdraw contained a provision (the *Platt Amendment) that the United States reserved the right of future intervention in order to preserve republican government in Cuba and prevent European interference. Cuba also agreed to continue the social, economic, and educational reforms begun by the American military.

To keep internal peace, the United States formed the *Guardia Rural* (a national police), but no army. The first Cuban president, Tomás Estrada Palma, tried to rig his own reelection in 1906, and his opponents started a mild guerrilla war. President Theodore *Roosevelt refused to send troops to reinforce the ineffective Cuban constabulary, but agreed to assume temporary control of the government until a second election produced a new government. An expeditionary force of 5,000 soldiers and 1,000 Marines occupied Cuba without incident, remaining until 1909.

The Second Intervention of 1906–09, however, produced enough frustration for the United States that subsequent administrations chose to back the incumbent Cuban regime rather than adjudicate revolts. U.S. troops generally replaced Cubans around economic targets, not just to protect foreign property but to prevent the rebels from using destruction to spark wider war and deeper intervention. A Marine brigade of 800 helped the Cuban Army suppress electoral revolts in 1912 and 1917. Marine detachments aboard navy warships provided small landing parties for short-term security duties. In most instances, the rebels avoided Marine outposts while the Marine companies did not seek out the enemy. The last security force departed in 1922.

The next threatened use of U.S. military occupation in 1933–34 had a major influence on Cuban politics, for President Franklin D. *Roosevelt wanted the oppressive regime of Gerardo Machado overthrown (which happened) and a legitimate, moderate, democratic regime to replace him (which it did not). Dismayed by the radical reformism of President Ramón Grau San Martín, the State Department negotiated an end to the Platt Amendment and signaled its willingness to accept a substitute regime. The result was a wave of military coups that produced a military-dominated authoritarian government headed by a former sergeant, Fulgencio Batista. Fearing Axis and Communist influence in the Caribbean and Mexico, the United States did not challenge either Batista's indirect rule (1934–59) or actual term as president (1940–44), nor his coup of 1952.

The Communist-led revolution of 1957–59 made Cuba a serious political and strategic problem for the United States for the first time in history. Alarmed by a U.S.-sponsored invasion by 1,300 Cuban exiles on 17–19 April 1961, President Fidel Castro turned to the Soviet Union for massive military assistance. Even though he overwhelmed Brigade 2506 at the Bahia de los Cochinos (Bay of Pigs) with 20,000 militiamen in one day's battle, Castro saw the continuing danger of invasion and insurrection. He allowed the Russians to use Cuba as a naval base, intelligence platform, and nuclear missile base. Castro welcomed a Russian Army combined arms task force of 40,000 to Cuba in 1962. Acutely aware that a navy-Marine task force had been minutes away from supporting the Cuban exile brigade, Castro even allowed the Russians to build launch sites for eighty-some offensive nuclear missiles, surrounded by antiaircraft missiles. In the *Cuban Missile Crisis of October 1962, President John F. *Kennedy and Soviet Premier Nikita Khrushchev both retreated, but not before the Navy blockaded the island and 400,000 American servicemen deployed for an invasion of Cuba. This expeditionary force would have faced a Cuban army of over 100,000 and the 40,000 Russians armed with tactical nuclear weapons.

Since 1962, the United States has not put significant military pressure on Cuba, even after the collapse of Russian support after 1989; but it deployed special operations forces and paramilitary covert action teams to counter Cuban revolutionary campaigns in Angola, Haiti, Bolivia, Nicaragua, and El Salvador. Paramilitary Cuban exile groups still conduct occasional raids and sabotage against the island itself. No Cuba-watcher would predict that U.S. military intervention has become only a historical phenomenon.

[*See also* Caribbean and Latin America, U.S. Military Involvement in the.]

• Lester Langley, *The Cuban Policy of the United States*, 1968. Hugh Thomas, *Cuba: The Pursuit of Freedom*, 1971. Louis A. Pérez, Jr., *Army Politics in Cuba, 1898–1958*, 1976. Lester Langley, *The Banana Wars: An Inner History of American Empire, 1900–1934*, 1983.

Allan R. Millett and Peter Maslowski, *For the Common Defense: A Military History of the United States of America*, rev. ed. 1994.

—Allan R. Millett

CUBAN MISSILE CRISIS (1962–63). On 15 October, 1962, U.S. intelligence discovered Soviet strategic nuclear missile bases under construction in Cuba, leading to the most dramatic and dangerous crisis of the nuclear age. After a week of secret deliberation with a group of advisers (the Executive Committee of the *National Security Council, or ExComm), President John F. *Kennedy demanded that the missiles be withdrawn and imposed a naval "quarantine" on shipments of "offensive" weapons to Cuba. Kennedy ordered a massive redeployment of U.S. forces to the Caribbean and placed the Strategic Air Command (SAC) on heightened alert.

Soviet premier Nikita Khrushchev was furious at what he considered Kennedy's flagrant interference in Soviet-Cuban affairs and his violation of freedom of navigation. But by the time the quarantine took effect on the morning of 24 October—after a unanimous endorsement by the Organization of American States—Khrushchev ordered Soviet ships not to challenge the blockade. For several days a settlement proved elusive and pressure built for more decisive action.

Neither Kennedy nor Khrushchev wanted to risk nuclear war over the issue, and both became increasingly concerned that an accident or inadvertent military action might trigger escalation. An apparent break in the tension came on 26 October, when, in a rambling, emotional letter, Khrushchev offered to withdraw the missiles in return for a U.S. pledge not to invade Cuba. But in a second, tougher letter received the following morning, Khrushchev demanded that Kennedy withdraw analogous Jupiter missiles from Turkey (deployed under the aegis of *NATO). Most of Kennedy's advisers argued strongly against this, on the ground that it would be interpreted by the Soviets as evidence of American weakness, and by NATO as betrayal of an ally. Kennedy decided to ignore Khrushchev's latest demand and accept his earlier offer.

As the ExComm deliberated on 27 October, word reached the White House that an American U-2 reconnaissance plane had been shot down over Cuba, and that another had inadvertently strayed over Siberian air space, narrowly avoiding a similar fate. Kennedy resolved to bring the crisis to an end. Ignoring the ExComm's advice, he secretly agreed that the United States would withdraw its missiles from Turkey "within a few months" as a private quid pro quo to a UN-verified withdrawal of Soviet missiles from Cuba. Kennedy would also pledge publicly not to invade Cuba. Khrushchev accepted, and on 28 October the acute phase of the crisis came to an end.

Castro, feeling betrayed by his Soviet patron, refused to allow *United Nations inspectors on Cuban soil to verify the withdrawal. But satisfied by aerial photography that the Soviets had withdrawn the weapons the United States considered offensive, Kennedy issued a proclamation terminating the quarantine on 21 November.

The causes of the crisis have long been debated. Khrushchev conceived the deployment in the late spring of 1962, after a hasty and uncritical decision-making process involving only a small group of advisers. His goals appear to have been to deter a feared American invasion of Cuba; to redress the United States's massive superiority in strategic *nuclear weapons, publicly revealed by the United States in October 1961, exploding the myth of a "missile gap" favoring the Soviet Union; and less importantly, to reciprocate the Jupiter deployment in Turkey.

The crisis provides textbook illustrations of important misperceptions and miscalculations. The U.S. government had calculated that the Soviet Union would not deploy nuclear weapons to Cuba because such a move would be inconsistent with past Soviet behavior, and because it seemed obvious that it would trigger a major confrontation. The Kennedy administration also failed to appreciate the extent to which the public demolition of the missile gap myth heightened the Soviets' sense of vulnerability; the strength of Soviet and Cuban fears of a U.S. invasion of Cuba (heightened by the abortive Bay of Pigs invasion of the previous year); and the strength and sincerity of the Soviet view that if the United States had the right to deploy missiles in Turkey, the Soviet Union had the right to deploy missiles in Cuba. Consequently, Kennedy failed to deter the move in a timely fashion, issuing stern warnings against it only in September 1962, when the secret deployment was well underway.

Similarly, Khrushchev grossly overestimated the willingness of Kennedy and the American people to tolerate a major disruption in the hemispheric status quo; underestimated the likelihood that American intelligence would discover the missiles prematurely; and failed to appreciate that the secrecy and deception surrounding the deployment would inflame American passions. Consequently, Khrushchev underestimated the risks of the deployment.

Although scholars differ in their assessment, some consider the Cuban Missile Crisis a classic case of prudent crisis management. Kennedy and Khrushchev prevented the conflict from escalating while they sought and found a mutually satisfactory solution. They did so by avoiding irreversible steps, curtailing unwarranted bluster, and avoiding backing each other into a corner. Other scholars have criticized the handling of the crisis as being too timid or too reckless. Kennedy's critics on the right lament his unwillingness to seize the opportunity to destroy Castro; his critics on the other side of the spectrum condemn his willingness to risk nuclear war merely to delay the inevitable—the vulnerability of the American homeland to Soviet nuclear weapons. Hard-liners in the Soviet military severely criticized Khrushchev for yielding to U.S. pressure. New information on intelligence failures, *command and control breakdowns, and near accidents suggest that both leaders' fears of uncertainty, misperception, misjudgment, accident, and unauthorized military action provided a critical degree of caution and circumspection that prevented the crisis from escalating even further.

Paradoxically, the Cuban Missile Crisis led to an immediate improvement in U.S.-Soviet relations. A series of agreements intended to restrain the *arms race and improve crisis stability followed, most notably the Hot-Line Agreement and *Limited Test Ban Treaty of 1963. Over the following decades, the superpowers crafted a modus vivendi designed to prevent a similar occurrence whereby the Soviet Union refrained from deploying military equipment with offensive capabilities to Cuba, and the United States acquiesced in a Communist-controlled Cuba with close ties to the USSR.

[See also Arms Control and Disarmament; Cold War: External Course; Cold War: Changing Interpretations; U-2 Spy Planes.]

• Raymond L. Garthoff, *Reflections on the Cuban Missile Crisis*, 1987; rev. ed. 1989. James G. Blight, Bruce J. Allyn, and David A. Welch, *Cuba on the Brink: Castro, the Missile Crisis, and the Soviet Collapse*, 1993. James G. Blight, and David A. Welch, "Risking 'The Destruction of Nations': Lessons of the Cuban Missile Crisis for New and Aspiring Nuclear States," *Security Studies*, 4 (Summer 1994), pp. 811–50. Anatoli I. Gribkov, and William Y. Smith, *Operation Anadyr: U.S. and Soviet Generals Recount the Cuban Missile Crisis*, 1994. Richard Ned Lebow and Janice Gross Stein, *We All Lost the Cold War*, 1994. Ernest R. May and Philip D. Zelikow, *Inside the White House during the Cuban Missile Crisis*, 1997. James G. Blight and David A. Welch, eds., *Intelligence and the Cuban Missile Crisis*, 1998.
—David A. Welch

CULTURE, WAR, AND THE MILITARY. Critiquing Clausewitz's aphorism that war is the continuation of politics by other means, John Keegan argues to the contrary in *A History of Warfare* (1993) that "war embraces much more than politics . . . it is always an expression of culture, often a determinant of cultural forms, in some societies the culture itself." This applies to the American experience no less than it does to Keegan's examples in the Cossack steppes or the Himalayan foothills.

Exactly how has American culture shaped and defined American military institutions and the ways that Americans have waged war? Was there significant "feedback"— moments when the nature of those institutions or that warfare affected or altered the culture in significant ways? Defining the "culture" of a place as vast and differentiated as the United States at any period, let alone for over three centuries, is a daunting task; but some generalizations are clearly more warranted than others.

By the mid-nineteenth century, both Americans themselves and a number of insightful European visitors appeared to agree that American culture could be described by the use of such terms as *individualism, egalitarianism*, *"get-aheadism*," a respect for "rights" and "liberties," a diverse *religiosity*, much *local boosterism*, and a tendency to join private associations of one sort or another. With the exception of the last two, these characteristics were not consistent with military service. Hence it is not surprising that President Andrew *Jackson's secretary of war, John Eaton, complained in his annual report for 1830 of his department's inability to recruit even the modest number of soldiers the Congress had authorized. "A country possessing 12 millions of people ought surely to be able at all times" to find and enlist 6,000 acceptable recruits "obtained upon principles of fair contract," he wrote. "If this can not be effected then will it be better to rely on some other mode of defense, rather than resort to the expedient of obtaining a discontented and besotted soldiery."

Secretary Eaton did not have compulsory military service in mind. American culture has been averse to the drafting of young men (let alone young women) for most of our past. "Draughts stretch the strings of government too violently to be adopted," Edmund Randolph told his colleagues at the Constitutional Convention in Philadelphia, May 1787, a view echoed by Horace Greeley, editor of the *New York Tribune*, in 1863 when he wrote to War Secretary Edwin Stanton: "Drafting is an anomaly in a free State; it oppresses the masses." Like imprisonment for debt, it had no place in "our system of political economy." A limited draft was imposed by Congress in that year, to be sure, but it was designed to force individuals and communities to protect themselves against compulsory service with self-insurance schemes to purchase substitutes or pay commutation fees, like those that had come into being in the British Isles in 1757 and the 1790s when draft laws were passed by Parliament.

Opposition to the draft was pronounced in areas where "the party of personal liberty" (the Democratic Party) was strong. "If citizens do not choose to preserve the government, what right has the government to compel them to do so against their will?" asked D. A. Mahony, an Indiana Democrat and journalist. In Pennsylvania, the three Democrats who constituted the majority of the Supreme Court of that state simply declared the federal draft law unconstitutional, though after the by-election in November 1863, one Democratic member was replaced by a Republican, and the new Republican majority reconsidered the case and declared the act to be within constitutional bounds.

John Chambers's *To Raise an Army: The Draft Comes to Modern America* (1987) provides an account of the draft and resistance of Americans to drafts throughout the years before 1917 and the difficulties that advocates of Selective Service faced in 1917, 1940, and in the *Vietnam War. By 1973, this relatively brief venture in compulsion had ended.

Secretary Eaton's problem was somewhat different: He was not in charge of a draft; he was simply in charge of a *regular* army, and that was bad enough. American culture in the nineteenth and most of the twentieth centuries celebrated wartime volunteers, not regulars. Most self-respecting young men would not stoop to the low pay, regimented life, isolation, and boredom of the regulars unless they found themselves in the direst of straits. Moreover, the regulars were the "standing army" that the majority culture had feared and reviled since at least the mid-eighteenth century—a force that flourished at society's expense in a land where yeomen, tradesmen, and artisan volunteers were expected to defend their own freedoms with their own lives and honor.

But to say that compulsory service was anathema and that the regular army was not a popular occupational choice or a revered institution for much of our history is not to say that American culture rejected military service. There has always been a small pacifist subculture in America, and many other, nonpacifist youth have been indifferent to the call of fife and drum. But a substantial fraction of young American men have responded to the allure of what the editor of *Youth's Companion* called "the war-spirit." A. A. Livermore referred in 1850 to "the wooden sword, and the tin drum of boyhood," to "the training and the annual muster" of the militia and the volunteer companies, to "the red uniform and the white plume, and the prancing steed," to "the ballads of Robin Hood, and the stories of Napoleon, and the 'Tales of the Crusaders,'" to "the example of the father and the consent of the mother," to "the blood of youth, and the pride of manhood, and stories of revolutionary sires," the "love of excitement" and "the bubble of glory." "By one and all," he wrote, "the heart of the community is educated for war, from the cradle to the coffin."

What made these youth inaccessible to Secretary Eaton or many other secretaries of war was that they preferred to do their soldiering in local, volunteer companies. Whether we look to the "covenanted" militia units of seventeenth-century New England, the volunteers of the *French and Indian War or the War, for Independence, the antebellum drill companies in both North and South, the volunteers of the *Civil War and *Spanish-American War, or the National Guard and reserve units that dotted the twentieth-century urban and suburban landscape, the process was essentially the same: Surprisingly large percentages of young men have been prepared to don uniforms and shoulder arms, often for little or no pay, under commanders and in settings of their choosing throughout the course of American history. Before the advent of public high schools and colleges, before football cheers and fraternities, there were volunteer military companies with fancy drill teams and cadence chants that served a similar social purpose for those in their late teens and early twenties, as Marcus Cunliffe's *Soldiers and Civilians* (1969) has shown.

When units like these joined the colors upon the outbreak of war, their contractarian and egalitarian nature puzzled and annoyed many regular army officers, whether the town militias during *King Philip's War in 1675–76, the volunteer companies of the *French and Indian War and War for Independence, or the volunteer units from midwestern towns during the *Spanish-American War. The story of the captain of one such group during the American Revolution who appeared before a quartermaster seeking pay and provisions may be apocryphal, but it rings true: "How many men do you command?" the quartermaster asked. "I command no one," the captain replied. "I am commanded by eighty."

When the regular army secured its own local volunteers (the Army Reserves) in the twentieth century and gained greater supervisory and regulatory control from the Congress over the nonregular local volunteers (the National Guard units), sparks sometimes flew. Later, in 1961, Secretary of Defense Robert S. *McNamara mobilized some 148,000 reservists during a Cold War crisis concerning Berlin. After several weeks of garrison service, many of these reservists became restless, organized mass rallies calling for their own demobilization, and generally behaved in ways the regulars regarded as mutinous. Reservists had formed important parts of American mobilizations for the *Korean War in 1950, but after these incidents in 1961, there would be fewer reservists in the next major mobilization, for Vietnam.

The modern, regular-led military responded relatively effectively to several mandates designed to address problems of racism, sexism, and drug use imported by recruits, draftees, and officers alike. The racial integration of the services beginning in the early 1950s successfully confounded critics of that measure who incorrectly predicted that white soldiers would never accept black soldiers as equals; later, in the 1960s, the McNamara Pentagon effectively saw to the integration of housing in southern communities where military bases were located as the price of obtaining military customers for rental units and realty. Simultaneously, the services, responding to changes taking place in the greater business culture, shifted their leadership style from coercion to "persuasion"—a process that accelerated after the Selective Service System was made moribund in 1973 and the *All-Volunteer Force became the order of the day. It was one thing to require young men to shave their heads and "do as I say" in the days of the draft; it was quite another to expect that of badly needed electronics technicians in an all-volunteer army, navy, or air force.

In *The American Way of War* (1973), Russell Weigley argues that since the Civil War, American strategic planners have consistently promoted an "*American way of war,'" one that relied on firepower and massive use of force. This emphasis on the "annihilation" of enemy strength is to be distinguished from the hit-and-run "attrition" strategy practiced by American forces during the American Revolution, when the nation's new leaders lacked the financial and bureaucratic resources to fight in any other fashion, and when its military leaders were comfortable with a Cincinnatus-like "maneuver" strategy. The leaders who rose to the fore while America industrialized in the nineteenth and twentieth centuries were committed to the use of men and machines in massive direct attack to achieve "victory," and they grew increasingly impatient with wars of maneuver and negotiation designed to achieve acceptable political outcomes short of the complete destruction of the enemy's will. The strategic bombing raids during World War II on cities in Germany and Japan produced what W. Darrell Gertch calls a "mutation in American values" as attacks upon population centers became less and less remarkable.

But no sooner had the day of "total" war arrived than it began to lose its appeal for American policymakers. Once intercontinental bombers became operational in the late 1940s, to be followed in short order by intercontinental ballistic missiles, and once the Soviet Union acquired nuclear weapons and the capacity to deliver them on American targets, a century and a half of "free security" (provided by the combined British and American fleets and some 3,000 miles of Atlantic Ocean) came to an end, and America entered a forty-year era of Cold War apprehension. Some would insist on the "rollback" of Soviet power in proper "annihilation" fashion; others on its "containment" in more limited fashion.

Thus when Gen. Douglas *MacArthur was dismissed in 1951 by President Harry S. *Truman, and MacArthur's strategy of "no substitute for victory" gave way to the "attrition" and limited warfare policies of his successor, Gen. Matthew B. *Ridgway, it took some time for Congress and the general public to accept the verdict. The problem would resurface in Vietnam, the *Persian Gulf War, and the humanitarian and peacekeeping missions in Somalia and Bosnia. Has the greater American culture adopted itself to the new peace-keeping strategy as thoroughly as the leadership of the U.S. military has?

In the centuries before the advent of "total" war, it was possible for those who served as well as those who remained on what came to be known as "the home front" to find uplifting social and moral lessons in tales from the battlefield of self-sacrifice and valor. The dying were sometimes reported to have composed themselves in dignity, drawing their hands across their chests; official reports of action were expected to note at least one example of selfless or courageous behavior. Those too old to serve celebrated these feats and victories in poems (such as Herman Melville's "On the Photograph of a Corps Commander," 1866) paintings and prints (such as those produced by Currier & Ives during the Civil War), and sculpture (still found today in squares or beside courthouses throughout

the land). During the Civil War, as George Fredrickson tells us in *The Inner Civil War* (1965), a number of New England Brahmins who had been of a Trancendentalist persuasion abandoned that antistatist perspective for the more nationalist patriotism of the Union League clubs once the war began. War and culture were interrelated and sometimes war helped to shape culture.

As the battlefields grew larger and the battles longer in duration and more lethal, in the 1860s, 1918, the 1940s, and thereafter, those Americans who faced death found the experience more daunting than their predecessors, and discovered that their perception of combat as a "testing of mettle," a rite of passage to full manhood, was hard to maintain, given the impersonal, random nature of the carnage they witnessed all about them. In *Embattled Courage: The Experience of Combat in the American Civil War* (1987), Gerald Linderman had described this loss of innocence, as have Stanley Cooperman in *World War I and the American Novel* (1967), Paul Fussell in *Wartime: Understanding and Behavior in the Second World War* (1989), and Lloyd Lewis in *The Tainted War: Culture and Identity in Vietnam War Narratives* (1985). Men who entered Vietnam, for example, often did so with a Hollywood-induced notion of what the war was about, how American forces would fare, and what they could accomplish (what Lewis, quoting veterans, calls a "John Wayne Wet Dream Syndrome"). But they soon acquired what many observers were to style "the thousand yard stare"—a symptom of combat stress that army psychiatrists encountered in each of the wars Americans engaged in throughout the twentieth century. And many of these young men would later experience Post-Traumatic Stress Disorder.

The horror of war and incompetent leadership would be the theme of many novels produced by veterans of World Wars I and II and Vietnam. The cynicism and anger bubbling up in John Dos Passos's *Three Soldiers* (1919), e. e. cummings's *The Enormous Room* (1922), Thomas Boyd's *Through the Wheat* (1923), William Faulkner's *Soldier's Pay* (1926), Ernest Hemingway's *A Farewell to Arms* (1929), Humphrey Cobb's *Paths of Glory* (1935), Dalton Trumbo's *Johnny Got His Gun* (1939), Norman Mailer's *The Naked and the Dead* (1948), James Jones's *From Here to Eternity* (1951), Joseph Heller's *Catch-22* (1962), Tim O'Brien's *Going After Cacciato* (1975), and James Webb's *Fields of Fire* (1978) stand in stark contrast to the more "heroic" war novels written by older nonveterans like Arthur Train (*Earthquake*, 1918), Edith Wharton (*The Marne*, 1918), and Willa Cather (*One of Ours*, 1922). Early Hollywood filmmakers and song writers like George M. Cohan or Irving Berlin celebrated American military efforts and the men who "won't come back till it's over over there." They now shared the stage with trench-bred tunes like "Home, Boys, Home," "I Don't Want to Join the Army," antiwar numbers like Country Joe & the Fish's "Fixin' to Die Rag," and films like Michael Cimino's *The Deer Hunter* (1978), Francis Coppola's *Apocalypse Now* (1979), and Oliver Stone's *Platoon* (1986). This new, more critical perspective on warfare and the American military did not sweep the field or emerge as the dominant paradigm, as it did in some European countries; there was still a place in the hearts and minds of many Americans, for example, for John Wayne's role *The Green Berets* and Barry Sadler's song "The Ballad of the Green Berets" as the Vietnam War ground to its bitter end. But the cultural terrain was now a contested one, just as the concept of what constituted "the American way of war" had become contested.

In this new cultural battlefield, a further skirmish was underway by the 1950s: a skirmish over the new masterpieces of the "annihilation" strategy, nuclear weapons. These quickly acquired their champion on the Hollywood scene in Jimmy Stewart's portrayal of an SAC pilot in *Strategic Air Command.* The alternative view was limned by Peter Sellers's three characters in Stanley Kubrick's *Dr. Strangelove,* and the contest was joined—a contest fortunately confined to celluloid.

[*See also* Clausewitz, Carl von; Cold War: Changing Interpretations; Conscription; Disciplinary Views of War: Causes-of-War Studies; Pacifism; War: American Way of War.]

• S. Kaplan, "Rank and Status Among Massachusetts Continental Line Officers," *American Historical Review,* LVI (1950–51), pp. 318–26. Edmund Wilson, *Patriotic Gore: Studies in the Literature of the American Civil War,* 1962. Marcus Cunliffe, *Soldiers and Civilians: The Martial Spirit in America, 1775–1865,* 1968. W. D. Gertch, "The Strategic Air Offensive and the Mutation of American Values, 1937–1945," *Rocky Mountain Social Science Journal,* XI (1974), pp. 37–50. Gerald Linderman, *The Mirror of War: American Society and the Spanish-American War,* 1974. Robert Gross, *The Minutemen and Their* World, 1976. Peter Karsten, "Consent and the American Soldier: Theory versus Reality," *Parameters: Journal of the U.S. Army War College,* XII (1982), pp. 42–49. Peter Karsten, ed., *The Military in America from Colonial Times to the Present,* 1986. Michael Sherry, *The Rise of American Air Power: The Creation of Armageddon,* 1987.
—Peter Karsten

CURTISS-WRIGHT v. *UNITED STATES* (1936). Using authority granted by a congressional joint resolution in May 1934, President Roosevelt embargoed all U.S. arms shipments to Paraguay and Bolivia in an effort to end their military conflict. In January 1935, the Justice Department indicted the Curtiss-Wright Corporation for selling machine guns in violation of the embargo. The company countered that the resolution was an unconstitutional delegation of power giving the executive uncontrolled discretion to make policy.

In 1936, the Supreme Court upheld the resolution and the president's action. Justice George Sutherland's opinion held that in foreign affairs, unlike domestic affairs, Congress had authority to delegate broad power to the executive. Moreover, Sutherland claimed, the president exercised inherent, extraconstitutional powers derived from international law and practice—to promote national interest and survival. This sweeping assertion of presidential supremacy in international affairs came, paradoxically, at a time when the Court sought to limit executive power in the domestic arena. Sutherland's opinion is often cited to support the president's authority, as commander in chief,

to commit U.S. armed forces to combat without Congressional authorization. However, in Reid v. Covert (1956), Justice Hugo Black's majority opinion suggested that all power, domestic and foreign, must flow from the Constitution. Black's opinion vitiated the argument for inherent executive authority in foreign affairs.

[*See also* Commander in Chief, President as; Supreme Court, War, and the Military.]

• Clinton Rossiter, *The Supreme Court and the Commander in Chief,* 1951. Edward Keynes, *Undeclared War: Twilight Zone of Constitutional Power,* repr. 1991.
—Edward Keynes

CUSTER, GEORGE ARMSTRONG (1839–1876), U.S. military leader in the Civil War and Indian wars. An 1861 West Point graduate, Custer rose to fame and high rank during the Civil War as a flamboyant and successful cavalry chief. He ended the war a major general at the age of twenty-five. In the postwar regular army he was a lieutenant colonel in command of the 7th Cavalry. His introduction to the Plains Indians Wars came in Kansas in 1867. The campaign ended in failure and court-martial on charges of misconduct. Sentenced to a year's suspension, Custer was recalled in the fall of 1868 by Maj. Gen. Philip H. *Sheridan to lead his regiment in a winter campaign against the southern Plains tribes. At the Battle of the Washita, 27 November 1868, Custer surprised and destroyed Black Kettle's Cheyenne village and laid the groundwork for his reputation as an Indian fighter.

Assigned to Fort Abraham Lincoln in Dakota Territory, Custer led the 7th in the Yellowstone Expedition of 1873, protecting surveyors of the Northern Pacific Railroad; he fought two actions with Sitting Bull's Sioux. In 1874, Custer's Black Hills Expedition discovered gold. The rush to the hills, part of the Great Sioux Reservation, inflamed the Sioux and led to the Sioux War of 1876. The 7th Cavalry formed part of Brig. Gen. Alfred H. Terry's column, one of three converging on the Indians. On 25 June, Custer attacked a large camp of Sioux and Cheyennes at the Battle of the *Little Bighorn. He and the five companies under his immediate command, about 225 men, were wiped out. The other seven companies, under Maj. Marcus A. Reno, held out on a hilltop four miles away until relieved two days later. Custer's actions at the Little Bighorn were and remain bitterly controversial, but he and his "last stand" gained lasting renown.

[*See also* Crazy Horse; Sitting Bull.]

• Robert M. Utley, *Cavalier in Buckskin: George Armstrong Custer and the Western Military Frontier,* 1988. Paul Andrew Hutton, ed., *The Custer Reader,* 1992.
—Robert M. Utley

CUSTER'S LAST STAND. *See* Little Bighorn, Battle of the (1876).

D

DAHLGREN, JOHN (1809–1870), naval ordnance innovator and commander of the South Atlantic Blockading Squadron during the Civil War. Dahlgren joined the navy in 1826. Service on the U.S. Coast Survey (1834–37) distinguished his early career. In 1847, Lieutenant Dahlgren was assigned to ordnance duty at the Washington Navy Yard. Over the next fifteen years, he invented and developed bronze boat guns, heavy smoothbore shell guns, and rifled ordnance. He also created the first sustained weapons R&D program and organization in U.S. naval history. For these achievements, Dahlgren became known as the "father of American naval ordnance." His heavy smoothbores, characterized by their unusual bottle shape, derived from scientific research in ballistics and metallurgy, manufactured and tested under the most comprehensive program of quality control in the navy to that time, and were the navy's standard shipboard armament during the *Civil War. Promoted to commander in 1855, captain in 1862, and rear admiral in 1863, he became commandant of the Washington Navy Yard in 1861 and chief of the Bureau of Ordnance in 1862. With help from his friend President Abraham *Lincoln, Dahlgren took command of the South Atlantic Blockading Squadron in July 1863, and for the next two years led naval forces besieging Charleston, in the Union navy's most frustrating campaign. After the war, he commanded the South Pacific Squadron, then returned to the command of the Bureau of Ordnance and the Washington Navy Yard.

[*See also* Civil War: Military and Diplomatic Course; Navy, U.S.: 1783–1865; Rodman, Thomas; Union Navy.]

• Madeleine Vinton Dahlgren, *Memoir of John A. Dahlgren, Rear-Admiral United States Navy*, 1882. Robert J. Schneller, Jr., *A Quest for Glory: A Biography of Rear Admiral John A. Dahlgren*, 1996.
—Robert J. Schneller, Jr.

DAVIS, BENJAMIN O., JR. (1912–), first black lieutenant general. Born in Washington, D.C., the son of a black army officer, Benjamin O. *Davis, Sr., young Benjamin Davis attended school in Tuskegee, Alabama, and Cleveland, Ohio, and the University of Chicago, before entering the all-white U.S. Military Academy at West Point, where the last African American had graduated in the 1880s. Davis graduated in 1936 (35th in a class of 276). His request for assignment to the Army Air Corps was refused because there were no black aviation units; instead, he was assigned to an all-black infantry regiment and then to Tuskegee Institute as an instructor. In 1941, the War Department finally allowed blacks into the Air Corps, although in segregated units. Davis established a flight program at Tuskegee, and as a lieutenant colonel took command of the 99th Pursuit Squadron (the "Black Eagles"), the first black air unit.

In 1943, during World War II, he led the unit to North Africa. Subsequently, he commanded the 332nd Fighter Group, a larger all-black flying unit, and as a colonel, flew sixty combat missions in the Italian theater. In 1948, following President Harry S. *Truman's desegregation order, Davis designed the implementation program for the U.S. *Air Force. In 1954, he was promoted to brigadier general, in 1959 to major general, and in 1965, he became America's first black lieutenant general, serving with the air force in Germany and the Philippines during the *Vietnam War before his retirement in 1970. Afterward, he served in the early 1970s in the U.S. Department of Transportation on issues involving air hijacking and aviation safety.

[*See also* African Americans in the Military.]

• Bernard C. Nalty, *Strength for the Fight: A History of Black Americans in the Military*, 1986. Benjamin O. Davis, Jr., *American: An Autobiography*, 1991.
—Clement Alexander Price

DAVIS, BENJAMIN O., SR. (1880–1970), first black general. Born the son of a U.S. government worker in Washington, D.C., Davis attended Howard University, then in the *Spanish-American War helped recruit a company for the 8th U.S. Volunteer Infantry as a lieutenant. In 1899, after *demobilization, he enlisted as a private in one of the army's traditional black cavalry units. Two years later, he passed a competitive examination and was commissioned a lieutenant in a black regiment. For the next three decades, Davis served in a number of positions—most of them designed to keep him from commanding white officers or white troops in the segregated army. These assignments included military attaché to Liberia, military science instructor at Wilberforce University and at Tuskegee Institute, and instructor with the Ohio and New York National Guard.

In 1930, Davis became the first black colonel. One week before the 1940 presidential election, President Franklin D. *Roosevelt appointed Davis a brigadier general, the army's first black general. In World War II, Davis headed a special section of the Inspector General's Department dealing with racial issues involving U.S. troops. During the Battle of the *Bulge in December 1944, he convinced Gen. Dwight D. *Eisenhower to accept the integration of black platoons into white units, a temporary breakthrough in the army's traditional segregation by regiment.

Davis retired in 1948 after fifty years of service. His son, Benjamin O. *Davis, Jr., became America's first black lieutenant general. In 1998, the 85-year-old retired general was awarded a fourth star by President Bill *Clinton.

[*See also* African Americans in the Military.]

• Bernard C. Nalty, *Strength for the Fight: A History of Black Americans in the Military*, 1986. Marvin E. Fletcher, *America's First Black General: Benjamin O. Davis, Sr., 1880–1970*, 1989.

—Clement Alexander Price

DAVIS, JEFFERSON (1808–1889), soldier, senator, U.S. secretary of war, and the only president of the Confederate States of America. Jefferson Davis was born in Kentucky on 3 June 1808, and the family moved to Mississippi when he was an infant. In 1828, he graduated from West Point with a modest record and an infantry commission. He served in a variety of posts in Missouri, Oklahoma, and the Old Northwest, resigning in 1835 as a first lieutenant of dragoons.

Receiving a Mississippi cotton plantation from an older brother, Davis married the daughter of Gen. Zachary *Taylor, but she died three months later. In 1845, he married Varina Howell and began a political career with election to the House of Representatives.

During the *Mexican War, Davis commanded a Mississippi regiment with distinction at the Battle of Monterrey (1846) and the Battle of *Buena Vista (1847), where he was wounded. Returning a hero, he was appointed U.S. senator in 1847, resigning to run unsuccessfully for governor in 1851. Under fellow Democrat Franklin Pierce, he served effectively as secretary of war, 1853–57, adopting improved rifled muskets; increasing pay; and obtaining four new regiments from Congress, which doubled the size of the regular army to protect western expansion.

A staunch states' rights Democrat as well as the owner of many slaves, Davis justified black slavery and championed Southern economic and territorial expansion to counter growing Northern influence. Returning to the Senate in 1857, Davis became a leader of the Southern bloc as well as head of the Military Affairs Committee. In the crisis following Lincoln's election, Davis was not a secession leader, but he resigned the Senate when Mississippi seceded in January 1861, and was immediately given command of his state's militia as a major general.

Chosen as president by the Confederate provisional government established at Montgomery, Alabama, Davis was inaugurated in February 1861. Subsequently, he was elected to a six-year term as president of the Confederate States of America and inaugurated at Richmond, Virginia, in February 1862.

As president of the Confederacy and commander in chief of its armed forces, Davis led the South's military effort in the *Civil War and also tried to deal with wartime economic and political matters. Despite his dedication to the task, Davis did not prove as politically able or publicly inspiring a war leader as U.S. President Abraham *Lincoln. Both presidents realized increased centralization was necessary for the war effort, but the South was much more resistant to such reduction of states' rights. As the war dragged on with diminishing hope and increasing deprivation, domestic political opposition mounted against Davis, who seemed politically and temperamentally hard put to deal with the rising dissent in the Confederate Congress and the Southern statehouses.

As a commander in chief who was also a West Pointer, war hero, and former secretary of war, Davis had considerable confidence in his own military judgment. He was closely involved with the army, particularly its organization and strategy, and became engaged in arguments with many of his generals. In his assignments, Davis made some

excellent choices, such as Robert E. *Lee, and some poor ones, such as Braxton *Bragg. For a long time, Davis failed to have a general in chief at Richmond to administer the army, and the burdens of personally performing that task contributed to his debilitation.

Strategically, Davis believed that the Southern forces must protect all of the Confederacy, east and west, and preserve territory rather than overthrow enemy armies. He sought to divide the South's outnumbered military resources to block logical avenues of approach, and to concentrate two or more large commands—particularly via railroads—to confront any major Union advance. It was a strategy that was ultimately overwhelmed by simultaneous advances from numerous numerically superior Union armies. Despite the claims of his contemporary critics, most experts consider Davis to have been a sound strategist and a competent commander in chief under extremely adverse circumstances.

With the Confederacy collapsing, Generals Lee and Joseph E. *Johnston surrendered their armies in April 1865 against the wishes of Davis, who wanted to continue the war. Fleeing south, the Confederate president was captured at Irwinville, Georgia, in May, and imprisoned in Fortress Monroe on charges of treason. He was released on bail in May 1867 after his physical and emotional health had deteriorated. Davis refused to take the oath of allegiance, and in 1881 published a history of the Confederacy. He died in 1889.

[*See also* Civil War, Military and Diplomatic Course; Confederacy, the Military in the; Confederate Army.]

• Lynda L. Crist, et al., eds., *The Papers of Jefferson Davis*, 9 vols., 1971– . Clement Eaton, *Jefferson Davis*, 1977. Paul D. Escott, *After Secession: Jefferson Davis and the Failure of Confederate Nationalism*, 1978. William C. Davis, *Jefferson Davis: The Man and His Hour*, 1991.

—William J. Cooper

D-DAY LANDING (1944). Operation Overlord was the greatest amphibious attack in history. Nearly 175,000 American, Canadian, and British troops landed in Normandy on D-Day, 6 June 1944, supported by 6,000 aircraft and 6,000 naval vessels ranging in size from battleships to 32-foot landing craft. The object of the attack was to win a beachhead in France in order to open a second front against Hitler's armies and to use the beachhead as a springboard for the liberation of France and Belgium, and the eventual conquest of Nazi Germany.

Planning began in earnest early in 1943. The critical need for the Allies was to gain surprise, because they would be taking the offensive with nine divisions, none armored, against an enemy with fifty-five divisions in France, nine of them armored. Gen. Gerd von Rundstedt, commanding the German forces in the west, and Gen. Erwin *Rommel, commanding the forces in France, assumed that the Allies would have to gain a major port in the initial assault, so they strengthened the "Atlantic Wall" around the French ports, especially Calais, which was on the direct line London-Dover-Calais-Belgium-Cologne-Berlin. The Allied supreme commander, Gen. Dwight D. *Eisenhower, achieved surprise by attacking straight south rather than east, and by going ashore in Normandy, where there were no significant ports. An elaborate and highly successful deception plan (Operation Fortitude) kept the German attention centered on Calais.

D-Day was set for 5 June, but a storm that day precluded amphibious operations. At the height of the storm, at 0430 on 5 June, Eisenhower's weather expert predicted that it would soon ease off and that conditions would be acceptable. Eisenhower decided to go for it.

The attack consisted of division-strength assaults on five beaches, two British (code-named "Gold" and "Sword"), two American ("Omaha" and "Utah"), one Canadian ("Juno"), preceded by a night assault of three airborne divisions to protect the flanks (one British on the left and two American on the right).

The night operation on 5/6 June caused great confusion among both attackers and defenders. The American paratroopers were scattered over the countryside and very few managed to hook up with their units before daylight. But the Germans were confused by reports of paratroopers and gliders landing here, there, everywhere. Meanwhile, small groups of airborne troops destroyed bridges and gun emplacements, and captured crossroads and routes inland from Utah Beach.

At dawn, before the 0630 first-wave attack, there was a tremendous air and sea bombardment, which was highly effective at all the beaches except Omaha, where most of the shells and bombs landed far inland. At Omaha, the first wave was decimated, the follow-up waves badly pounded. Those troops still alive huddled against the seawall, pinned down by fierce German fire. They had expected support from amphibious tanks (Shermans supported by rubber skirts and equipped with a propeller), but at Omaha the tanks were launched too far out in too-rough seas and thirty-two of thirty-four sank. At midmorning, Gen. Omar *Bradley, commanding the U.S. First Army, contemplated withdrawing from the beach. But thanks to heroic action by individual soldiers, who led the way up the bluff, the crisis was overcome.

By nightfall, the Allies were ashore on a beachhead that stretched fifty-five miles. The cost was some 4,900 casualties, half of them at Omaha. German losses were not calculated, but they must have been considerably higher. Hitler's Atlantic Wall, built at enormous expense, had not held up the Allied landings for even one day.

[See also France, Liberation of; Normandy, Invasion of.]

• Dwight D. Eisenhower, *Crusade in Europe*, 1948. Forrest Pogue, *The Supreme Command*, 1954. S. L. A. Marshall, *Night Drop: The American Airborne Invasion of Normandy*, 1962. S. E. Ambrose, *D-Day: The Climactic Battle of World War II*, 1994. Ronald J. Drez, ed., *Voices of D-Day*, 1994.   —Stephen E. Ambrose

DEBS, EUGENE V. (1855–1926), Socialist, presidential candidate, war opponent. Born of French immigrant parents in Terre Haute, Indiana, Debs became active in the labor movement in the 1870s and created the American Railway Union (ARU), an industrial union, in 1893. Following the federal government's smashing of the ARU-led Pullman Strike (1894), Debs slowly became convinced that corporate or monopoly capitalism could not be reformed, gravitated toward the socialist movement, and became its best-known leader and five-time presidential candidate of the Socialist Party of America.

In 1917, Debs led the socialist opposition to U.S. entry into *World War I, which he condemned as an imperialist war fought for the interests of the trusts. Arrested for an antiwar, antidraft speech at Canton, Ohio, on 15 June 1918, Debs began serving a ten-year sentence at the Atlanta Federal Penitentiary in April 1919. Still in prison, he re-

ceived nearly 1 million votes as the Socialist Party's presidential candidate in 1920, and was pardoned by President Harding on Christmas Day, 1921. He remained a committed socialist.

Debs's attitude toward war was best expressed in this widely quoted statement: "I am not a capitalist soldier; I am a proletarian revolutionist. I am opposed to every war but one; I am for that war with heart and soul, and that is the world-wide war of the social revolution."

[*See also* Peace and Antiwar Movements.]

• Ray Ginger, *The Bending Cross: A Biography of Eugene Victor Debs*, 1949. Nick Salvatore, *Eugene V. Debs: Citizen and Socialist*, 1982.
          —Norman Markowitz

DECATUR, STEPHEN (1779–1820), U.S. naval officer. Raised in a seafaring and naval family, Stephen Decatur served as midshipman and acting lieutenant during the Undeclared Naval War with *France (1798–1800) and as a first lieutenant and captain during the Tripolitan War (1801–05). In 1804, he commanded the party that burned the USS *Philadelphia*, which had fallen into enemy hands; then he led attacks on several Tripolitan vessels. Decatur's exploits, which entailed fierce hand-to-hand combat, won him great acclaim. After the Tripolitan War, he helped enforce the embargo. During the *War of 1812 he took part in two notable engagements: the celebrated victory of USS *United States* over HMS *Macedonian* in 1812, and the 1815 surrender of USS *President* to a British squadron. He commanded the flagship *Guerrière* in the Algerine War (1815), capturing or destroying several enemy vessels before extracting treaties from Algiers, Tripoli, and Tunis. Upon returning to the United States, he served on the Board of Navy Commissioners.

Decatur had served on the court-martial of James Barron after the *Chesapeake* affair of 1807, and enmity between the two led to a duel in 1820 in which Decatur was killed. A symbol of the reckless bravery and bold nationalism of the young Republic, Decatur was particularly remembered for his toast: "Our country! In her intercourse with foreign nations may she always be in the right; but our country, right or wrong!"

• Alexander S. Mackenzie, *Life of Stephen Decatur, A Commodore in the Navy of the United States*, 1846. Gardner W. Allen, *Our Navy and the Barbary Corsairs*, 1905. Lewis, Charles L., *Romantic Decatur*, 1937; rpt. 1971.   —Donald R. Hickey

DECODING. See Coding and Decoding.

DECORATIONS, MILITARY. *See* Awards, Decorations, and Honors.

DEFEAT. Until the 1970s, Americans did not think much about defeat. U.S. military leaders usually defined war aims in terms of total victory, and the civilian culture they defended assumed that God guided the nation's fate and ensured its success. With a profound innocence, Americans denied those defeats that did occur and assumed their invincibility.

This sense of innocence and invincibility had deep roots in American history. During the *Revolutionary War, the American revolutionaries met with defeat and in many ways failed to live up to their own ideals. Led by the *Continental army, Americans still won their independence. Once they did, they gave little credit to the army or to

French aid, rarely dwelt on their defeats, but instead portrayed their victory as testimony to their own and the nation's virtue. The *War of 1812 offered a greater challenge to Americans' mythmaking powers. The military met frequent defeat in battle and the outcome of the war could at best be labeled a draw. Nevertheless, Americans came to remember this war too as a victory.

In the century and a half that followed, the United States sometimes endured defeat on the battlefield, but won its wars. In the Mexican, Civil, Indian, and Spanish-American Wars, the United States achieved the near-total victories its strategists sought. This persistent success deepened Americans' faith in their innocence, invincibility, and special favor in God's sight. After World War I, some Americans, disillusioned by the peace as well as by the war, questioned whether U.S. intervention had been wise; but World War II, with its total, if hard-earned, victory over foes Americans found evil, reaffirmed their conviction of invincibility and virtue. In the two decades that followed, the United States's sense of its power and rectitude never seemed surer.

Writing in the midst of this collective sense of American innocence, the historian C. Vann Woodward challenged it by pointing to the history of the American South. Unlike other Americans, Woodward argued, white Southerners had experienced military defeat. The loss of the *Civil War, along with poverty, guilt, and other frustrations, could have created a unique southern identity, one that would have offered an important corrective to the sense of innocence and invincibility that dominated American culture as a whole. Many southern intellectuals embraced Woodward's view and maintained that southern culture had been chastened, yet ennobled, by defeat. Other historians questioned such assumptions. They found that white Southerners interpreted the loss of the war as a sign of God's favor, blamed defeat on factors outside of their control, and celebrated the heroism, nobility, and fighting ability of Confederates. Defeat did not force them to reexamine old myths and assumptions; rather, like other Americans, Southerners celebrated a glorious, military achievement. And in the *Spanish-American War, they demonstrated their continued faith in American invincibility and inevitable victory. They did as well, as Woodward himself noted, in their involvement in and support for the Vietnam War.

American defeat in Vietnam, though, forced Americans, North and South, to confront their assumptions of invincibility. A few Americans, including some political leaders, at times claimed that the United States had never really been defeated on the field of battle. But this time the mythmaking seemed to fail; most Americans accepted the reality of what they saw as America's first defeat in war. Others, especially those in the military, searched for the cause of this defeat. Some blamed it on antiwar protesters or the press; others questioned American strategy or pointed to mistakes made by the military. Almost all agreed that the absence of a national consensus in favor of the war and the policy of phased escalation contributed to America's failure.

The latter lesson of defeat, the importance of delivering massive amounts of force at the beginning of the war, clearly shaped military strategy in the United States's next "major" military confrontation, the *Persian Gulf War. The military employed overwhelming airpower and as many soldiers as had served in Vietnam at its height to win the war in days. In the wake of the victory, some talked of having buried the ghosts of Vietnam, by which they apparently meant not just America's post-Vietnam hesitancy to use military force abroad but also doubts about American innocence and invincibility as well. Whether the Gulf War has revived those myths remains to be seen, as does just how profoundly defeat in Vietnam has affected American attitudes toward war and its sense of providential blessing.

[See also War: American Way of War; Vietnam War: Changing Interpretations; Victory.]

• C. Vann Woodward, The Burden of Southern History, 1960; 3rd rev. ed. 1993. Russell F. Weigley, The American Way of War: A History of United States Military Strategy and Policy, 1973. Charles Royster, A Revolutionary People at War: The Continental Army and American Character, 1775–1783, 1979. Gaines M. Foster, Ghosts of the Confederacy: Defeat, the Lost Cause, and the Emergence of the New South, 1865–1913, 1987. Gaines M. Foster, "Coming to Terms with Defeat: Post-Vietnam America and the Post–Civil War South," Virginia Quarterly Review, 66 (Winter 1990), pp. 17–35.

—Gaines M. Foster

DEFENSE, DEPARTMENT OF. Created in 1949, the Department of Defense was an outgrowth of the *National Security Act of 1947, which had "unified" the armed services. The debate in Congress leading up to the 1947 legislation had its origins in the experiences of World War II, which, despite the overall success, had revealed numerous problems in command and control and the allocation of resources. Aiming to avoid similar situations in the future, President Harry S. *Truman recommended a War Department plan calling for a highly centralized and closely unified structure, including a separate air force, under a single secretary of defense. The navy worried that such a setup would threaten the future of naval aviation and the independence of the Marine Corps, and urged that instead of unification, attention be given to improving high-level policy coordination, with Britain's Committee of Imperial Defence serving as the model.

The resulting compromise, enshrined in the National Security Act of 1947, borrowed from both sides. Congress wanted the savings promised by unification, but it was afraid that an overly centralized system would produce a "Prussian-style general staff," reducing congressional and civilian control over the military. In enacting legislation, it leaned more toward the navy concept, with emphasis on a loosely unified defense establishment, a secretary of defense with limited authority, and new coordinating machinery, including a *National Security Council to advise the president on policy questions, a *Central Intelligence Agency for the coordination of intelligence gathering and analysis, and a National Security Resources Board to plan the management of resources.

The unique feature of the act was its handling of service unification. In the preamble to the law, Congress stated that its purpose was to unify the services but "not to merge them." Its vehicle was a hybrid organization it called the National Military Establishment (NME). Although the secretary of defense was designated the NME's senior presiding official, he exercised only "general direction, authority, and control" over the military services, which retained the status of "individual executive departments," but without cabinet status. The Navy Department remained the same, while the War Department became the Department of the Army. To placate airpower advocates, the act established a new Department of the Air Force, organized from what had been the Army Air Forces. As part of the NME, the act gave statutory standing to the *Joint Chiefs of Staff (JCS), which had operated without a formal charter since their creation in 1942; and it established a Munitions Board for interservice coordination of logistical planning, a Research and Development Board to do the same in the areas of science and technology, and a senior-level War Council (renamed the Armed Forces Policy Council in 1949) to help coordinate overall NME policy.

Early Development. The first secretary of defense, James *Forrestal (1947–49), took office on 17 September 1947. For staff support he had but three special assistants whose statutory authority was unclear. As secretary of the navy during the unification debate, Forrestal had been a reluctant convert to service unification and had assured Congress that there would be no need for a large bureaucracy in the Office of the Secretary of Defense (OSD). Once installed in his new job, he adopted a go-slow approach—"evolution, not revolution"—toward integrating service activities, but did not receive what he considered sufficient support or cooperation from within the *Pentagon. An added handicap was President Truman's practice of setting rigid budget ceilings, an untoward consequence of which was to encourage interservice competition and feuding over the allocation of funds. At critical conferences in 1948—Key West in March and Newport in August— Forrestal tried to convince the services, especially the navy and the air force, to set aside their differences and work together. But he found it impossible to overcome their resistance with reason and persuasion.

Forrestal eventually concluded that the secretary's powers and staff support needed legislative strengthening. His successor, Louis *Johnson (1949–50), believed he already had the power and authority he needed, but acquired even more when in August 1949 Congress amended the National Security Act. The 1949 amendments converted the NME into a full-scale executive department, the Department of Defense (DoD), and designated the secretary of defense as "the principal assistant to the President in all matters relating to the Department of Defense." The services were downgraded to the status of "military departments," but with the proviso that they remain "separately administered," and the qualification of "general" to describe the secretary's powers and authority was dropped. The secretary also acquired a deputy (previously an undersecretary deriving from special legislation enacted in April 1949) and the special assistants became assistant secretaries of defense, one of whom was designated comptroller, while a nonvoting chairman was added to the Joint Chiefs. The secretary of defense thus emerged as a true executive, not the *primus inter pares* (first among equals) he had been under the original law. With unencumbered powers and a strengthened staff, he became the focal point of an increasingly centralized administrative system.

From this point on, challenges to the secretary's authority became rarer, but did not cease immediately. The most serious assault occurred in the summer and autumn of 1949 during the "Revolt of the Admirals," in which senior navy officers, reeling from Johnson's economy measures and imposition of authority, openly attacked the wisdom and impact of service unification and the growing reliance in U.S. defense policy on air-atomic power as the country's first line of defense. But following the across-the-board military buildup precipitated by the outbreak of the *Korean War in June 1950, the stresses and strains on interservice relations eased as money for defense became more plentiful.

The 1953 and 1958 Reorganizations. The Korean War revealed that true unification still had far to go. As defense spending surged, jumping from approximately $14 billion in fiscal year (FY) 1950 to $49 billion in FY 1953, it put growing pressure on the secretary to effect sound departmental policies. A common complaint in Congress was that the services continued to mismanage and squander resources while unnecessarily duplicating functions. In November 1952, the outgoing secretary of defense, Robert A. Lovett (1951–53), sent President Truman a detailed letter pointing out flaws in the existing setup. Lovett thought the secretary should have more explicit authority over the services; a military staff of his own to augment the Joint Chiefs; and greater flexibility to deal with the problems of supply and logistics.

Lovett was only one of many who felt that defense organization could be improved, and with the change of administrations in January 1953, reforms came quickly. As a first step, President Dwight D. *Eisenhower named a committee headed by Nelson A. Rockefeller to review DoD's organizational needs. Eisenhower had long favored a more closely unified defense establishment, and it was with this goal in mind that the Rockefeller Committee framed its findings. Guided by the committee's report, Lovett's letter, and his own instincts, Eisenhower issued an executive order, Reorganization Plan No. 6, to provide a "quick fix" that avoided the need for legislation. Implemented in April 1953, the reorganization eliminated the Munitions Board and the Research and Development Board, transferring their functions to the secretary of defense. It also created six additional assistant secretaries of defense and a general counsel, and empowered the chairman of the Joint Chiefs to manage the Joint Staff (the JCS bureaucracy). Eisenhower had wanted to go further, especially in strengthening the powers of the JCS chairman, but his soundings among members of Congress convinced him that the time was not yet ripe.

In 1958, after the Soviet success in launching the first space satellite, Sputnik, and amid chronic interservice bickering and competition over the U.S. guided missile program, Eisenhower sent Congress additional proposals for defense reform, which this time would require legislative authority. Arguing that "separate ground, sea, and air warfare is gone forever," Eisenhower asked for further changes that he hoped would dampen interservice rivalry, blend their efforts more efficiently and effectively, and streamline command and control mechanisms to meet the new demands of the atomic era. Criticism of the proposed changes came mostly from the navy, fearing more loss of autonomy, and from its supporters in Congress, led by Representative Carl *Vinson, chairman of the House Armed Services Committee. But the predominant sentiment among legislators favored the more centralized and unified defense establishment the president wanted.

The Defense Reorganization Act of 1958 amended the 1947 law by taking the unification process about as far as it could go without abandoning the concept of individual military services. The main changes were a significant clarification of the secretary's authority, including the power to transfer, reassign, abolish, and consolidate service functions; the addition of a new senior official, the director of defense research and engineering (DDR&E), to oversee research and development matters; a new chain of command, running from the president through the secretary of defense to the unified field commanders, thus bypassing the service secretaries; and increased authority for the chairman of the Joint Chiefs, who could now participate as an equal in their deliberations. Instead of being separately administered as in the past, the military departments were to be "separately organized"—a gesture toward preserving service autonomy but a distinct departure from the days when the departments had functioned as sovereign entities. Though the 1949 amendments had already largely settled the matter of the secretary's authority, the 1958 reorganization removed any lingering doubt and made it possible to consolidate and centralize activities with an unimpeded mandate.

McNamara's Impact. The first secretary of defense to make full use of the increased powers bestowed by the 1958 reorganization was Robert S. *McNamara (1961–68). A former president of the Ford Motor Company, McNamara entered office with a formidable background in business techniques that emphasized statistical analysis and close program management. His advent would, as it turned out, usher in some of the most far-reaching changes the DoD had yet experienced, earning him both high praise and summary condemnation. His initial task was to fulfill President Kennedy's campaign promise of overcoming purported inadequacies in the country's defenses—weakened conventional forces owing to an overreliance on nuclear weapons in the 1950s, and a dangerous "missile gap" in which preliminary evidence suggested that the Soviet Union was outproducing the United States in intercontinental ballistic missiles (ICBMs). Further intelligence confirmed that missile gap worries were unfounded, but as a precaution against expected Soviet increases, McNamara set in motion a strategic buildup, which by the end of his tenure encompassed a triad of strategic forces consisting of 1,054 ICBM launchers, a fluctuating number of long-range bombers, and 41 fleet ballistic missile submarines—the basic structure of the strategic deterrent until the 1980s.

Though Kennedy usually gave McNamara a free hand running the department, it was with the understanding that improved efficiency and toughened cost controls would offset much of the increase in expenditures for new missiles and other weapons systems. Defense spending at the outset of the 1960s consumed nearly 10 percent of the gross national product, and it was not Kennedy's intention that it should get any larger. Accordingly, McNamara introduced a variety of reforms, including mission-oriented budgeting with five-year expenditure projections, the use of "systems analysis" techniques that relied on computer-driven models to evaluate the cost-effectiveness of weapons, and a highly publicized cost reduction program. In addition, he expanded the practice, begun in the 1950s, of consolidating key functions by creating new DoD-wide agencies for supply, intelligence, and contract auditing. Not all of McNamara's unification measures turned out as he planned, however. A case in point was his abortive effort to cut aircraft procurement costs by developing a single fighter-bomber, the TFX (F-111), for both the air force and the navy. But compared with previous secretaries of defense, he achieved an unprecedented degree of centralized civilian control.

Under McNamara, Defense also acquired a more prominent role in foreign affairs through its "little State Department," the Office of International Security Affairs (ISA), headed in the 1960s by a succession of able assistant secretaries, including Paul H. *Nitze, John McNaughton, and Paul Warnke. During a decade dominated by volatile national security issues—the Berlin Wall Crisis, the *Cuban Missile Crisis, the Dominican Republic, nuclear strategy, arms control, and Vietnam—McNamara and ISA were a conspicuous and influential part of the response. One of McNamara's most impressive accomplishments in foreign affairs was to convince *NATO to reduce its reliance on nuclear weapons and to develop a more balanced defense posture known as "flexible response." But his successes with NATO contrasted sharply with the debacle in Southeast Asia. Secretaries of defense had customarily stayed out of the operational side of military affairs, leaving them to the professionals, but McNamara inserted himself directly into many of the details of running the *Vietnam War. Initially a strong proponent of American involvement in Vietnam, he gradually came to have doubts and left office counseling stepped-up efforts at negotiations and disengagement.

Post-McNamara Changes. After McNamara came a reaction to centralized authority. Most of the managerial and budgeting techniques he had pioneered more or less survived, but his use of civilians in roles traditionally reserved for military professionals had aroused too much resentment among the services and too much skepticism in Congress for his successors to do likewise. Heeding the critics, President Nixon appointed a Blue Ribbon Defense Panel to review the department's procedures. The panel's report of July 1970 condemned the McNamara style of highly centralized decision making as "inherently inadequate to manage the spectrum of activities required of the Department of Defense," and urged that the military departments be restored to greater authority and responsibility. Few formal changes actually resulted, but in deference to the services' sensitivities, Secretary of Defense Melvin *Laird (1969–73) took steps to reinvolve the military in key decisions, notably budget planning, and to reduce the high profile that ISA and systems analysis experts had enjoyed in McNamara's time.

Meanwhile, the unpopularity of the Vietnam War had seriously eroded the military's prestige and credibility, and as the war wound down, cutbacks in military spending followed, leaving what some considered a "hollow" and demoralized force more in need of unified direction than at any time since the late 1940s. At Laird's suggestion, Congress in 1972 authorized a second deputy secretary of defense, though the post remained vacant until 1975. The role of the deputy had traditionally been that of the secretary's "alter ego" (Forrestal's concept), and having two in that job proved awkward and redundant. In 1977, in an effort to streamline functions, Congress abolished the second deputy slot and created two new under secretaries with broad responsibilities—one for policy, to supervise such tasks as strategic planning, military assistance, and international security affairs; and a second for research and engineering. President Carter wanted to go further and initiated a major defense organization study, completed in 1980, which recommended strengthening the role of the Joint Chiefs and upgrading the management responsibilities of the service secretaries. But after Carter lost the 1980 election, the study was largely forgotten.

The Goldwater-Nichols Reforms of 1986. By the mid-1980s, organizational reform of the Defense Department was again a topic of intense discussion, with the initiative this time coming from Congress rather than the executive. President Ronald *Reagan was determined to reverse what he considered a decade of neglect of the armed forces, but the sustained buildup he launched in 1981 also gave rise to congressional criticism of waste, abuse, and cost overruns. Endeavoring to ease congressional anxieties, the administration in 1982 reluctantly accepted legislation creating an inspector general for the Defense Department. Reagan and Secretary of Defense Caspar *Weinberger (1981–87) opposed more extensive organizational change and tried to dissuade Congress from acting precipitously by forming an advisory commission on defense management headed by David Packard, a former deputy secretary of defense. One of the commission's main findings was that procurement procedures needed a drastic overhaul, starting with appointment of a high-level procurement "czar." Congress needed little nudging, and in the summer of 1986 it created the post of under secretary for acquisition, later giving it the same pay grade as the deputy secretary and potentially sweeping authority over nearly all facets of the procurement process.

More extensive reforms followed with the passage of the Defense Reorganization Act of 1986, a bipartisan measure spearheaded by Senator Barry Goldwater and Representative William Nichols. The goal of the *Goldwater-Nichols Act was to revitalize the Organization of the Joint Chiefs of Staff, whose stature and effectiveness had diminished steadily over the past several decades. In an attempt to reverse this trend, the law gave the JCS chairman added advisory powers and administrative authority over the Joint Staff; established a vice chairman to help oversee JCS business; and assigned more responsibility to the combatant (i.e., unified) commands. The idea was to encourage more "jointness" among the services, not just in Washington but in the field and at the various service schools, and in so doing, presumably, to improve planning and combat readiness. Although the performance of U.S. forces in the *Persian Gulf War (1991) seemed to bear out the soundness of the new emphasis on joint doctrine, subsequent misadventures in Somalia and command and control problems in the Middle East suggested a need for further refinements.

For the Department of Defense, the major challenge by the 1990s was to readjust to an international environment in which the dangers of Soviet military power no longer overshadowed all other security problems. The ending of the Cold War and the collapse of the Soviet Union in 1991 brought respite from the continuous tensions of the previous four decades, but also increased pressure from Congress and the public to curb military spending. This meant thinking differently about defense needs, and, as a congressional commission on military roles and missions pointed out in May 1995, more sharing of service responsibilities. In these circumstances, the demands on the secretary of defense to provide unified strategic and programmatic guidance were, if anything, apt to increase. Centralization of authority around the secretary of defense, though often unpopular with the services, had grown to be a practical necessity.

[*See also* Cold War; Defense Reorganization Acts; Rivalry, Interservice; World War II: Postwar Impact.]

• Steven L. Rearden, *History of the Office of the Secretary of Defense: The Formative Years, 1947–1950,* 1984. Robert J. Art, Vincent Davis, and Samuel P. Huntington, eds., *Reorganizing America's Defense,* 1985. Doris M. Condit, *History of the Office of the Secretary of Defense: The Test of War, 1950–1953,* 1988. James A. Blackwell, Jr., and Barry M. Blechman, eds., *Making Defense Reform Work,* 1990. Roger Trask and Alfred Goldberg, *The Department of Defense, 1947–1997,* 1997. Robert J. Watson, *History of the Office of the Secretary of Defense: Into the Missile Age, 1956–1961,* 1997.
—Steven L. Rearden

DEFENSE INTELLIGENCE AGENCY. Creation of a unified Department of *Defense (DoD) in 1947–49 was not accompanied by the unification of defense intelligence activities. Each of the military services maintained its own intelligence organization; indeed, maintaining these distinct capabilities had been a major demand of the military during deliberations over the creation of the CIA. But there were also a number of intelligence requirements that were either interservice or departmentwide. Thus, additional intelligence organizations designed existed to meet these broader needs.

In 1961, Secretary of Defense Robert S. *McNamara decided to rationalize much of the DoD's structure, and to improve resource management for broader defense intelligence efforts. The result was the Defense Intelligence Agency (DIA). Each service continued to argue, however, that it had unique intelligence needs that could not be met by a "joint" agency, and so the separate service units survived as well.

DIA is headed by a three-star military officer, a position filled by rotation among the services. DIA has been through several major reorganizations in the past few years, although its major functions remain the same: the collection and analysis of intelligence specifically related to military requirements. Collection is carried out overtly by defense attachés and covertly by the relatively new Defense HUMINT (Human Intelligence) Service (DHS). The functions of attachés remain known to host governments; DHS collectors operate under cover. DIA produces independent analyses and contributes to communitywide intelligence estimates. It is one of three "all-source" intelligence analysis centers (along with CIA and the State Department's Bureau of Intelligence and Research).

The DIA has sometimes found itself torn between its military customers (the *Joint Chiefs of Staff and their organization) and civilian customers in the DoD. The Joint Chiefs may seek analysis to support specific or preferred positions; the civilians may prove skeptical of military-produced analysis, which often tends toward more pessimistic assumptions about conflict and combat.

Competition with the military service intelligence units is less of a problem. But DIA has been among the intelligence agencies most severely hit by the end of the *Cold War, which led to a 25 percent reduction in its personnel.

[*See also* Central Intelligence Agency; Intelligence, Military and Political.]

• Mark M. Lowenthal, *U.S. Intelligence: Evolution and Anatomy,* 1984; 2nd ed. 1992. Patrick Mescall, "The Birth of the Defense Intelligence Agency," in Rhodri Jeffrey-Jones and Andrew Lownie, eds., *North American Spies: New Revisionist Essays,* 1991.
—Mark M. Lowenthal

DEFENSE REORGANIZATION ACTS (1950, 1953, 1958). Following quasi-unification of the armed forces in the Department of *Defense, created by the *National Security Act of 1947, Congress passed the Army Reorganization Act of 1950 to achieve simplicity and flexibility in the army's statutory organization. The law revised provisions, some of which dated back to the *War of 1812, and confirmed many of the changes made by executive action during World War II. It made the secretary of the army, now aided by an expanded staff, directly responsible for conducting all the affairs of the army. Congress abandoned appropriating funds directly to each technical service, and instead authorized the secretary of the army to make the allocations and to determine the number and relative strengths of the arms and services. In 1950, those included three combat arms: Infantry, Armor, and Artillery (including the old Field Artillery, Coast Defense, and Air Defense), and fourteen services, from the Chemical Corps to the Women's Army Corps.

Following the coordinating and centralizing efforts in the National Security Act of 1947, and its 1949 amendments, Congress, on the recommendations of the Rockefeller Committee and President Eisenhower, adopted the Defense Reorganization Acts in 1953 and 1958 designed to reduce service obstacles to coordinated defense planning and management. These acts strengthened the Office of the Secretary of Defense (OSD) by more than tripling its size and by giving it additional authority; they also somewhat enhanced the Office of the Chairman of the *Joint Chiefs of Staff (JCS). However, Congress continued to allow individual service chiefs to take their opinions directly to Capitol Hill.

The 1953 and 1958 reforms did not prevent open disagreement among the services nor the JCS from making split recommendations. Nor did they curtail budget requests or weapons procurement. They did, however, provide some additional centralized direction.

Individual secretaries of defense, chairmen of the JCS, and service chiefs continued to struggle over interservice *rivalry and coordination within this framework up to and even after the *Goldwater-Nichols Defense Reorganization Act of 1986, the most thorough revision of statutes governing DoD organization since the National Security Act of 1947.   —John Whiteclay Chambers II

DEMOBILIZATION is the release or "draw down" of wartime military forces as the nation resumes peacetime status following a war or major buildup. It is, then, the opposing process of *mobilization,* which is the assembling and organizing of troops, materiel, and equipment for active military service in time of war or other national emergency. The extent of the process of demobilization depends upon the mobilization that preceded it. Factors include the size, duration, and location of conflict, as well as the level of technology and state of the industrial base and degree of public support. These factors, in turn, determine the number of men mobilized, the duration of service, the distance they move, and the equipment they use. Demobilization is as tumultuous and as fraught with change as mobilization, for after mobilization, and after the conflict, while there can be a normalizing, there cannot be a return to normality. Over the course of American history, demobilization has been a largely haphazard and rela-

tively unplanned process, reflecting a nation whose emphasis has been on peacetime pursuits while maintaining a small standing army.

For the United States, the history of demobilization begins, in modern terms, with the *Civil War. Previous conflicts had involved forces small enough to make demobilization relatively invisible. Over the course of the *Revolutionary War, for example, demobilization was a continual, and relatively informal, process. The Continental Congress had limited authority over the troops; soldiers were allowed to return home at the end of their enlistment, desertions were frequent, and men were often unceremoniously sent home after a campaign. With the cessation of hostilities, the Continental army was virtually disbanded. Men wandered home without medical examinations, outprocessing, written discharges, or pay.

The reasons for this are apparent after 200 years. The United States barely existed; the Continental Congress had little power; the army, composed of Continental troops and militia, was small and considered temporary; no bureaucracy existed to process or track either mobilization or demobilization. Significantly, there was strong distrust of standing armies during times of peace. That distrust was not only for the armed force itself, but the government that would control it. A standing force, it was felt, would contribute to a more centralized and more powerful government than many thought wise.

The *War of 1812 and even the *Mexican War changed this situation and sentiment very little. As during the Revolutionary War, men were continually inducted into service even as large numbers who had served out their enlistments were discharged. Terms of enlistment were short, from one to twenty months, and the total number of troops at any given time was relatively small for both conflicts. The Mexican War witnessed a movement to permanent enlistments, a precedent that would not be adopted again until the *Spanish-American War. At the end of each war, the army returned to a peacetime basis by disbanding all excess regiments and consolidating remaining ones with regiments in the active force. Demobilization could remain unorganized and informal because the forces were not large.

The Civil War changed the policy of demobilization, just as it changed warfare, public understanding of war, and almost everything else. True to tradition, prior to the end of the Civil War, little thought was given to how the war would end, much less to the processes of disbandment. As before, troops were continuously discharged after completing their terms of enlistment. With Lee's surrender in 1865, and a general public feeling that demobilization should be immediate, the Union faced the task of outprocessing over 1 million Federal troops. Demobilization directives were hastily drawn up and issued in May 1865.

The Union plan called for the movement of large units to rendezvous areas within the former Confederacy and the border states. This served both to facilitate the demobilization process and to position Union forces for reconstruction duties. Troops were marched to the rendezvous areas where they camped while muster rolls and payrolls were prepared. Units were mustered out of federal service and men were sent to their home state to be individually mustered out. Mustering out took time, and boredom and homesickness caused a mass of desertions. Payment for service was not uniform from state to state.

Meanwhile, Lee's Confederate army stacked its weapons, signed a pledge not to take up arms against the government, and marched home without pay. As word spread, many troops simply left without signing anything. Demilitarization of the South proceeded slowly and unevenly.

Because of the large numbers of troops who were recruited, fought, and were subsequently mustered out, America took some lessons on demobilization and applied them. The Spanish-American War was a foreign war, which set it apart from the country's preceding experience; as in previous conflicts, the armed forces consisted of regulars and volunteers. No volunteer units were mustered out of the service during the conduct of operations. At war's end, most nonregular units were returned to their home state and demobilized. The federal government required that soldiers be transported to their respective state camps. There they were furloughed while their records were prepared. They returned for separation and pay. The exception was those units that were held over for occupation duty in the Philippines.

With the turn of the century, defense organization and legislation changed the face of the military establishment. The new Army General Staff lent the services a guiding structure; the Militia Act (1903) set the National Guard's relationship to the federal government. This represented a serious attempt to professionalize the military establishment. Each was intended to contribute to the ability of the services—and hence the nation—to mobilize for war and demobilize afterward.

The army that fought World War I was composed of regulars, National Guardsmen, and individual volunteers. Volunteer units were no longer called; most of the ranks were filled through conscription, which was passed in the summer of 1917. During this war, all troops under enlistment served for the duration of the conflict. Unfortunately, despite the existence of the General Staff, the end of the Great War found the United States as unprepared to demobilize as it had been to wage war. When Congress declared war in April 1917, the armed forces numbered almost 300,000. Nineteen months later, over 2 million men were serving in France, yet planning for demobilization began only a month before hostilities ceased. The army, relying on the draft, had greater problems with demobilization than the navy or Marines, of which most were volunteers.

The traditional unit demobilization began with the war's conclusion. Some units were still required to man the ports of debarkation, demobilization centers, supply depots, hospitals, and various garrisons. Due to strong public outcry, however, the War Department accelerated demobilization by discharging individuals, generally before deactivating their units. The discharge was carried out at demobilization centers throughout the country, where physical exams were conducted, financial claims made, and administrative details gathered. The centers were primarily designed to accommodate troops returning from overseas. Soldiers were discharged at camps closest to their homes; physical needs were attended to; coal miners, railroad employees, and railway mail clerks were discharged immediately. Units were demobilized according to plan, with replacement battalions first and combat divisions following. Because of the number of men under arms, the demobilization process affected society in general: communities with war industries experienced an immediate labor surplus when those industries closed down, and the large numbers of returning soldiers added to the unemployment problem.

In World War II, formal planning for demobilization began two years before the end of the war with Germany. For the first time in American history, demobilization was done primarily by individual rather than by unit. Demobilization by unit had previously been the standard for the army, and had worked well with small forces, for it allowed units to retain their integrity and combat effectiveness. The individual method, however, allowed for faster mustering out with acknowledgment paid to individual service—both of which were popular in American society. A service score plan was devised whereby individual soldiers were assigned points as credit for length of service, time spent overseas, time spent in combat, number of wounds sustained, and number of children at home. America began partial demobilization of its ground and air forces in May 1945 with over 8 million men under arms. The navy began demobilization on V-J Day with a strength of approximately 4 million. Demobilization took from 1945 to 1947, and was characterized by upheaval, waste, and confusion. By June 1947, the total strength of the army was just over 900,000.

This immense demobilization affected all phases of American life. The army, after having been perhaps the most powerful military machine in Western history, dwindled to a state of near impotence, impairing national security and limiting the flexibility of foreign policy. Demobilization also adversely affected supply, maintenance, and storage of munitions; experts in those fields were normally in rear areas during fighting and among the first to leave the service. The army thus was left with not only an absence of manpower to tackle the job of organizing and mastering demobilization and reorganization but also a low level of expertise in many significant fields. Waste was incredibly high; thousands of items of equipment worth millions of dollars were left to rust in place. The mass exodus of men from units overseas caused a complete turnover in leadership. In some cases, whole units disappeared, to be replaced by untrained and untried fillers. Throughout the process, congressional criticism was intense, made particularly acute by upcoming congressional elections in which candidates demanded swift, if not immediate, dismantling of the military.

With the war's end, debate again resurfaced over the issue of universal military training. Late in 1945, President Harry S. *Truman asked Congress for legislation requiring male citizens to undergo a year of military training. Proponents believed this would permit a quick expansion of the force when mobilization was necessary. Although this idea became the subject of extensive debate, American citizenry did not accept it, and reinforcement of the regular forces would continue to depend on the reserve forces. Interestingly, the draft, enacted in 1940, was maintained, although not without debate of its own, until 1973.

From the end of World War II until 1989, America was preoccupied by the *Cold War, as a result of which it maintained a relatively large standing army for the first time in its history. Conscription was enforced until 1973 to ensure that strength was held at that high level. The draft ended in 1973; since then, all services have been filled by enlistments alone. Over the Cold War period, no large conflict erupted between the superpowers. The United States did participate in limited hostilities, however, including the *Korean

War and the *Vietnam War. Both of these required the armed forces to be built up to fight on foreign soil; neither, however, resulted in mass mobilization or demobilization. During the Vietnam conflict, the United States returned to the earlier policy of "rolling" demobilization—recruits served in Vietnam for thirteen months (including one month of R&R) rather than for the duration, America's earlier pattern of demobilization.

[See also Militia and National Guard; Mobilization; Recruitment.]

• William A. Ganoe, *History of the United States Army,* 1936. Oliver L. Spaulding, *The United States Army in War and Peace,* 1937. Kent R. Greenfield, *The Organization of Ground Combat Troops,* 1947. John C. Sparrow, *History of Personnel Demobilization in the United States Army,* 1951. Russell F. Weigley, *History of the United States Army,* 1967.
—Susan Canedy

DEMOGRAPHY AND WAR. Rapidly growing populations are often aggressive. They both enjoy and suffer from an abundance of young men seeking new places for themselves in the world because a plurality of sons cannot all inherit a father's property without suffering an unacceptable decline of living standards. As long as the majority of Americans lived on farms and had lots of children, this circumstance fueled rapid frontier expansion at the expense of Indian peoples. Easy victories in sporadic warfare were essential to the expansion of American settlement, beginning in the 1630s and lasting until 1890, when the final armed clash between the U.S. Army and an Indian people took place at the Battle of *Wounded Knee, South Dakota (1895). American military successes in turn reflected an abundance of armed men—militiamen in colonial times supplemented after independence by professional soldiers—who were willing and ready to invade Indian territory and seize new lands from the occupants.

Nonetheless, the demographic disasters that crippled the Indian population of North America were not primarily due to warfare. Indian communities were disrupted instead by repeated exposures to lethal diseases imported from the Old World, to which they initially had no inherited resistance. The result was a vicious circle: epidemic disease deaths weakened, when they did not paralyze, armed resistance; and sporadic defeats in war deprived survivors of any chance of recovery.

The upshot was a drastic repeopling of the broad swathe of the North American continent that frontier expansion brought within the boundaries of the United States. Starting from two tiny shoreline footholds in 1607 and 1620, English colonists quickly achieved rapid rates of population growth that carried the frontier across the Appalachians in the late eighteenth century, and across the Rockies some sixty years later. Africans, who crossed the ocean as slaves, and immigrants from Europe, who came initially as indentured servants, added additional strands to the repeopling of the country.

Throughout the colonial period, local militias conducted sporadic local offensives against Indians with only occasional regard for British imperial policy. But when imperial wars broke out in the Americas, colonial militiamen played a significant support role, and on several occasions (1710, capture of Port Royal; 1745, capture of Louisburg) carried through successful offensive operations. French and Spanish colonists in America were too few to support their home governments with comparably numerous or well-organized military units. This was a factor—though scarcely the primary factor—in British successes in the decisive *French and Indian War of 1754–63 that added Canada and Florida to Great Britain's American empire.

But, almost at once, their remarkable demographic expansion allowed the colonists to leave their European rivals behind and (with help from France) to break their political bond with Great Britain in the *Revolutionary War. Former imperial restraints on frontier expansion and military aggression against the Indians were removed after the United States became sovereign. As a result, rapid population growth together with improvements in transport raised the westward movement to flood proportions during the first half of the nineteenth century. Local militiamen continued to play the principal role in Indian fighting and frontier expansion until the *Mexican War (1846–48), when regulars of the U.S. Army fought their way to Mexico City and compelled the Mexicans to cede California and the rest of their northern territories to the victors.

The *Civil War was by far the most costly conflict ever fought by Americans. The North enjoyed a definite demographic advantage from the start, with a total population of about 21 million opposing about 9 million Southerners, of whom 3.5 million were black slaves. More than 1.5 million soldiers served in the Union army, and suffered an official total of 359,528 deaths from lethal infections and battlefield casualties. The Confederates enrolled some 800,000 soldiers, and suffered about 258,000 deaths, so that the combined loss of life from the war exceeded 600,000. Such a trauma slowed but did not stop population growth for the nation as a whole, but aftereffects kept the South depressed and backward for the following two generations. The North suffered proportionately less, and an increasing flow of European immigrants more than made up for wartime losses.

A fundamental change in American demography and warfare set in between 1870 and 1890 when land suitable for pioneer cultivation disappeared after the frontier of settlement encountered the dry landscapes of the high plains. As a result, by about 1890, when the U.S. Census report announced that the open frontier had disappeared, the demographic regime that had sustained white territorial expansion at Indian expense for the preceding 270 years broke down. Instead of seeking new land to cultivate, surplus children from rural families headed into town, where industrial manufacturing and service jobs presented them with a radically different style of life—whether they arrived from American farms or from European villages across the ocean. Consequently, in 1920 the U.S. Census recorded an urban majority for the first time, and in ensuing decades the American countryside emptied out so that fewer than 5 percent of the population are today employed as farmers.

Wars fought by the United States since 1898 both reflected and affected these demographic and social changes. Superficially, the *Spanish-American War (1898) looked like the translation of old-fashioned frontier war to Cuban soil; but the aggressive dynamic of American rural society was already slackening. As a result, after the familiar sort of easy victory, the United States refrained from annexing Cuba, and despite an uneasy conscience, settled for annexing Puerto Rico and the Philippines. Overseas islands, already occupied by farming populations, were not available for frontier settlement in the old way, and the drive for territorial expansion was therefore far weaker than before.

World Wars I and II were far more serious engagements, and provoked more thorough mobilization of the entire nation than had been possible during the Civil War, when a majority of the population had to remain working in the fields in traditional ways to assure sufficient food. About 4 million men were recruited undrafted into the army during *World War I and a total of 1.2 million crossed the ocean to France. But these figures were dwarfed during *World War II, when about 15 million men and women served in many different theaters of war and remained in uniform for a longer time than had been necessary in 1917–18. Yet military deaths in both wars totaled less than 410,000, almost a third fewer than in the Civil War—a tribute, more than anything else, to advances in military medicine that had taken place since 1890.

Wartime experience for so many millions in 1917–19 and again in 1941–45 had dramatic demographic impacts. Postwar baby booms were in both cases succeeded by an accelerated decline in birth rates, so that by 1990, births in the United States was just about at the replacement level—2.1 children per woman of childbearing age. Total population continued to grow rapidly, thanks to the relaxation of legal barriers to immigration after World War II; but without the inflow of newcomers, the population of the United States would no longer replace itself.

Many factors contributed to this radical departure from the earlier pattern of American demographic expansion—urbanization chief among them. But informal exposure to a long-standing professional military tradition of sexual habits designed to prevent unwanted births, supplemented by official medical efforts at inhibiting the spread of venereal disease, affected the behavior of millions of conscripted soldiers. This wartime experience surely (but secretly) carried over into civilian life, altering sexual habits and expectations much more rapidly than could otherwise have occurred. Birth rates plummeted to less than half of what they had been in the colonial era.

A second aspect of wartime mobilization, 1917–19 and 1941–45, confirmed and extended this basic demographic shift. Wartime labor shortages allowed and invited millions of women to start working outside the home; and not all of them resumed a merely domestic style of life when peace returned. By the 1960s, earning their own money by working for wages became a badge of women's liberation, and the costs of childbearing and infant nurture became correspondingly harder to bear. This kept birth rates low, opening the United States to newcomers from crowded rural communities in Latin America and elsewhere.

The repeopling of America, begun so radically in 1607, thus assumed a new guise in the 1960s. Except for an influx of Vietnamese refugees after the U.S. forces left the Vietnam war in 1973, warfare has had little significance, at least so far, for this second chapter in the exceptional demographic instability that distinguished the British North American colonies and the United States of America throughout their history.

[See also Casualties; Mobilization; Society and War.]

• Richard E. Easterlin, "Population Change and Farm Settlement in the Northern United States," *Journal of Economic History*, 36 (1976), pp. 45–75. Rudy Ray Seward, *The American Family: A Demographic History*, 1978. Lawrence Delbert Cress, *Citizens in Arms: The Army and Militia in American Society to the War of 1812*, 1982. John E. Ferling, *A Wilderness of Misery: War and Warriors in Early America*, 1980. Robert M. Utley, *The Indian Frontier of the American West, 1846–1890*, 1982. William H. Chafe, *The Paradox of Change: American Women in the Twentieth Century*, 1991.

—William H. McNeill

DESEGREGATION, RACIAL, IN THE MILITARY. See African Americans in the Military.

DESERTION. Under American military law, *desertion* is the act of leaving one's service or duty without the intention of returning or being absent without authorization for more than a month.

In peacetime, desertion has been a continuing phenomenon in American military history, at least through the early twentieth century, although its extent has varied widely depending upon the circumstances facing the service people. Unlike European nations, the U.S. government had little control over its citizens, and deserters could escape relatively easily, particularly into the rural and frontier regions of the country. Low pay and poor conditions have contributed significantly to peacetime desertions.

The armed forces require enlisted men and women to serve tours of duty of specific duration. Unlike commissioned officers, enlisted personnel are not legally permitted to resign unilaterally. Thus, desertion constitutes an enlisted person's repudiation of his or her legal obligation.

A correlation has existed in peacetime between desertion rates and the business cycle. When the country experienced economic depression and high unemployment, fewer people abandoned the service. Yet in an expanding economy, with workers in demand and wage scales increasing, many more service men and women have forsaken the high job security but lesser monetary rewards of the military.

The highest peacetime desertion rates in American history were reached during periods of economic growth in the 1820s, early 1850s, early 1870s, the 1880s, early 1900s, and the 1920s, when the annual flow of deserters averaged between 7 and 15 percent of the U.S. Army. A peak of 32.6 percent was recorded in 1871, when 8,800 of the 27,010 enlisted men deserted in protest against a pay cut. (By contrast, the desertion rate in the British army was only about 2 percent.) Lured by higher civilian wages and prodded by miserable living conditions—low pay, poor food, inadequate amenities, and boredom—on many frontier western outposts, a total of 88,475 soldiers (one-third of the men recruited by the army) deserted between 1867 and 1891.

The peacetime navy had its own desertion problems. In the nineteenth century, many of the enlisted men had grim personal backgrounds or criminal records or were foreigners with little loyalty to the United States. A rigid class system and iron discipline contributed to high rates of alcoholism and desertion. In 1880, there were 1,000 desertions from an enlisted force of 8,500 seamen.

During wartime, desertion rates in all the military services have varied widely but have generally been lower than in peacetime—perhaps reflecting the increased numbers of service people, national spirit, and more severe penalties prescribed for combat desertion. The end of hostilities, however, generally was accompanied by a dramatic flight from the military. After almost every war, the desertion rate doubled temporarily as many regular enlisted personnel joined other Americans in returning to peace-time pursuits. The variation in wartime desertion rates seems to result from differences in public sentiment and prospects for military success. Although many factors are involved, generally the more swift and victorious the campaign and the more popular the conflict, the lower the desertion rate. Defeat and disagreement or disillusionment about a war have been accompanied by a higher incidence of desertion.

In the *Revolutionary War, desertion depleted both the state militias and the Continental army after such reverses as the British seizures of New York City and Philadelphia; at spring planting or fall harvesting times, when farmer-soldiers returned to their fields; and as veterans deserted in order to reenlist, seeking the increased bounties of cash or land that the states offered new enlistees. Widespread desertion, even in the midst of battle, plagued the military during the setbacks of the *War of 1812. In the *Mexican War, 6,825 men, or nearly 7 percent of the army, deserted; and one unit of the Mexican Army, the San Patricio Artillery Battalion, was composed of American deserters.

The *Civil War produced the highest American wartime desertion rates because of its bloody battles, new enlistment bounties, and the relative ease with which deserters could escape capture, particularly in the mountain regions. The Union armies recorded 278,644 cases of desertion, representing 11 percent of the troops. As the Confederate military situation deteriorated, desertion reached epidemic proportions. The Appalachian Mountains, Florida swamps, and Texas chaparral became the domain of armed bands of Southern deserters. In the final year of the war, whole companies and regiments, sometimes with most of their officers, left together to return to their homes. In all, Confederate deserters numbered 104,428, or 10 percent of the South's armies.

The brief and successful *Spanish-American War resulted in 5,285 desertions, or less than 2 percent of the armed forces in 1898. However, the rate climbed to 4 percent during the long and arduous *Philippine War between 1900 and 1902. In World War I, because *conscription regulations classified any draftee failing to report for induction at the prescribed time as a deserter, the records of 1917–18 showed 363,022 deserters, who would have been more appropriately designated draft evaders. Traditionally defined deserters amounted to 21,282, or less than 1 percent of the army in World War I.

In World War II, desertion rates reached 6.3 percent of the armed forces in 1944, and during the American reverses at the Battle of the *Bulge, the army executed one American soldier, Private Ernie Slovik, for desertion in the face of the enemy as an example to other troops. Desertion rates dropped to 4.5 percent in 1945. During the *Korean War, the use of short-term service and the rotation system helped keep desertion rates down to 1.4 percent of the armed forces in fiscal year (FY) 1951 and to 2.2 percent or 31,041 in FY 1953.

The divisive *Vietnam War generated the highest percentage of wartime desertion since the Civil War. From 13,177 cases—or 1.6 percent of the armed forces—in FY 1965, the annual desertion statistics mounted to 2.9 percent in FY 1968, 4.2 percent in FY 1969, 5.2 percent in FY 1970, and 7.4 percent (79,027 incidents of desertion) in FY 1971. Like the draft resisters from this same war, many deserters sought sanctuary in Canada, Mexico, or Sweden. In 1974, the Defense Department reported that between 1 July 1966 and 31 December 1973, there had been 503,926 incidents of desertion in all services during the Vietnam War.

The end of the draft and the Vietnam War, together with the enhancement of pay and living conditions in the *All-Volunteer Force, dramatically reduced desertions, although there was somewhat of another upsurge during the *Persian Gulf War (1991).

[See also Military Justice; Morale, Troop.]

• Ella Lonn, Desertion During the Civil War, 1928, 1966; William B. Huie, The Execution of Private Slovik, 1954, 1991; Russell F. Weigley, History of the United States Army, 1967; Jack D. Foner, The United States Soldier between the Two Wars: Army Life and Reforms, 1865–1898, 1968; Thomas L. Hayes, American Deserters in Sweden, 1971; Robert L. Alotta, Stop the Evil: A Civil War History of Desertion and Murder, 1978; Edward M. Coffman, The Old Army: A Portrait of the American Army in Peacetime, 1784–1898, 1986.

—John Whiteclay Chambers II

DESERT SHIELD. See Persian Gulf War (1991).

DESERT STORM. See Persian Gulf War (1991).

DESERT WARFARE. The nature of deserts—arid, barren regions lacking sources of fresh water—makes combat operations there particularly demanding on troops and equipment. Additionally, deserts frequently lack readily identifiable landmarks, making map reading and navigation very difficult. Though visibility tends to be excellent at extreme ranges, cover and concealment are minimal. Thus, modern desert warfare tends to mean armored and mechanized warfare.

For many years U.S. doctrine failed to address desert warfare. During World War II, U.S. forces suffered heavy losses in the opening phase of the *North Africa Campaign (1942–43) at the hands of German and Italian troops at Sidi-bou-Zid and the Kasserine Pass in Tunisia. Stung by these defeats, American forces learned quickly and fared somewhat better later.

After the war, American military doctrine focused on the defense of Europe, and desert warfare was again ignored—until the Arab-Israeli War of 1973. Stunned by Israel's initially heavy losses to wire-guided *antitank weapons, and impressed by the Israelis' rapid recovery and counterattack, the U.S. military began to reevaluate its approach to armored warfare in the desert. A national training center was established in the Mojave Desert at Fort Irwin, California (1981)—the army's premier combat training center. All combat units were required to rotate through a warfare training cycle at Fort Irwin in the 1980s and 1990s, which pitted them against an opposing force (OPFOR) that until the 1990s employed *Warsaw Pact–style equipment and tactics.

The U.S. guiding principles in conducting desert operations may be summarized as find, fix (immobilize), and destroy the enemy at extreme long range. Typically, satellite imagery is used to gather intelligence on enemy force dispositions. Long-range air strikes are then launched to destroy these forces—as well as their communications infrastructure—to disrupt the enemy's system of command and control and deny him the ability to maneuver. Ground maneuver units of heavy armor and mechanized infantry punch through or bypass enemy positions, using sophisticated fire control systems to destroy enemy assets at extremely long ranges (up to two and one-half miles in direct fire mode). This method was essentially employed successfully by the U.S. and Coalition forces during Operation Desert Storm in February 1991. Field Manual 90-3, *Desert Operations* (1993), incorporated the "lessons learned" during the *Persian Gulf War (1991).

[*See also* Middle East, U.S. Military Involvement in the.]

• U.S. Field Manual 90-3/FMFM 7-27, *Desert Operations,* 1993. Gen. Robert H. Scales, *Certain Victory: The U.S. Army in the Gulf War,* 1994. Richard M. Swain, *Lucky War: Third Army in Desert Storm,* 1995.
—Frederick J. Chiaventone

DESTROYERS-FOR-BASES AGREEMENT (1940). On 3 September 1940, after intricate negotiations, President Franklin D. *Roosevelt announced that he was transferring fifty destroyers of World War I vintage to England—already at war with Germany—in exchange for ninety-nine-year leases to seven British air and naval bases in the western hemisphere (Newfoundland, Bermuda, several Caribbean islands, and British Guiana). Prime Minister Winston S. *Churchill had first asked for the warships to replenish British losses in the Norwegian campaign. Despite his promise that spring to support England with "the material resources of this nation," Roosevelt waited as Britain continued the war against Nazi Germany after France's surrender. Private groups like the Committee to Defend America by Aiding the Allies worked to arouse public opinion in support of Britain, while FDR sought assurances that Churchill would never surrender the Royal Navy, even if Hitler occupied the British Isles.

Not until intelligence in August 1940 during the air Battle of Britain indicated that Britain had better than a fifty-fifty chance of defeating a German invasion did Roosevelt finally act. By obtaining valuable bases in exchange, he persuaded a reluctant chief of naval operations, Adm. Harold R. Stark, to certify, as required by law, that the destroyers were no longer essential to national defense. The President bypassed Congress by concluding the arrangement through an executive agreement, an action challenged by isolationists but justified legally by Attorney General Robert Jackson. Because most of the old vessels needed extensive repairs and refitting, the actual military value of the Destroyers-for-Bases-Agreement proved less important than the diplomatic implications. What Roosevelt called the most important "reinforcement of our defense ... since the Louisiana Purchase," Churchill considered "a decidedly unneutral act" that inaugurated the Anglo-American alliance of World War II.

[*See also* Lend-Lease Act and Agreements; World War II, U.S. Naval Operations in: The North Atlantic.]

• David Reynolds, *The Creation of the Anglo-American Alliance, 1937–1941,* 1981. Robert Shogan, *Hard Bargain,* 1995.
—J. Garry Clifford

DESTROYERS AND DESTROYER ESCORTS. The modern destroyer (DD) is a general purpose warship capable of surface, subsurface, and antiair warfare. Destroyers evolved from ships designed to destroy torpedo boats that threatened battleships at the end of the nineteenth century. Much like the horizontal expansion of fortifications around castles to protect them from cannons, torpedo boat destroyers formed a defensive ring around capital ships and engaged torpedo boats beyond torpedo range. By the turn of the century, destroyers mounted torpedoes and replaced the torpedo boat.

The introduction of the submarine during World War I resulted in the need for destroyers to escort convoys and hunt *submarines. A destroyer shortage led to a conflict over U.S. shipbuilding resources. Adm. William S. *Sims, commander of U.S. naval forces in Europe, disagreed with the chief of naval operations (CNO), Adm. William S. Benson, over the continued allocation of shipbuilding resources to capital ships. These battleships would provide the United States with naval superiority over Britain—considered by Benson to be a postwar rival. The anglophilic Sims successfully argued that the first priority was victory in the Atlantic, and resources were shifted to construct destroyers and other antisubmarine ships.

After the war, the battleship remained the standard of naval power. Since no modern battleship had been sunk by a submarine, submarines were largely discounted. The destroyer returned to its prewar mission of torpedo attack and defense. When President Franklin D. *Roosevelt restarted warship construction under the National Industrial Recovery Act (1933), Adm. William V. Pratt, the CNO, identified destroyers as the first construction priority since those built during World War I were approaching obsolescence and construction of capital ships was prohibited by the *Washington Naval Arms Limitation (1922) and the London Naval Treaty (1930). The U.S. Navy commissioned 114 interwar destroyers in three major classes prior to the attack on *Pearl Harbor in December 1941; another 67 of these 1930s designs were completed during the first two years of the war.

In fall 1939, the navy began design work on "Destroyer 1941"—the 175-ship *Fletcher* class that would bear the brunt of World War II destroyer action. The *Fletchers* were large ships, designed as torpedo attack vessels, with a secondary mission of antisubmarine defense of the battle fleet. Many senior officers were concerned over the increasing size of such destroyers, but increased capability required larger ships. In addition to their torpedoes, *Fletchers* were equipped with dual-purpose (antiair and antisurface) 5-inch guns, as well as 40mm and 20mm antiaircraft guns to enhance their survival in a war in which the airplane was demonstrating its ascendancy.

Referred to as "tin cans" due to an absence of armor, destroyers relied on their high speed (up to 40 knots) for survival. But speed had failed to protect British battle cruisers at the 1916 Battle of Jutland, and unarmored destroyers proved equally vulnerable to gunfire, *torpedoes, bombs, and kamikaze attacks during World War II. Seventy-one U.S. destroyers were sunk. By 1944, the *Fletchers* were joined by larger *Gearing/Summer*–class ships with even more emphasis on air defense.

In the post-1945 U.S. Navy, the destroyer continued to protect the capital ship—now the aircraft carrier—which came with more emphasis on antiair warfare and secondary emphasis on antisubmarine warfare. The development of surface-to-air *missiles and sensors drove up the size of postwar destroyer designs. The *Forrest Sherman*–class destroyers (1953) displaced almost 5,000 tons, approximately a fivefold increase over the mass-produced destroyers of World War I. The *Charles F. Adams* class of guided missile destroyers (1958) were nearly as large.

Adm. Hyman *Rickover pushed for a nuclear-propelled

navy, which led to the construction of nuclear-powered destroyers (DLGNs) and cruisers to escort the new nuclear-powered aircraft carriers. Adm. Elmo *Zumwalt, CNO in 1970–74, viewed the increasing complexity, size, and cost of U.S. destroyers (now approaching the size of World War II cruisers) with alarm. Zumwalt advocated a "high-low" mix of ships but ran afoul of Rickover's political clout. Zumwalt was able to shepherd the "low-end" FFG-7 class of guided missile frigates (ships smaller than destroyers and designed for convoy escort) into production. But "purebred" destroyers continued to increase in size and cost. The *Spruance* class (1975) weighed in at 7,800 tons, and its hull design was large enough to be used for the CG-47 class of Aegis air defense cruisers.

The navy's most recent destroyers, the *Arleigh Burke* (DDG-51) class (1991), are large, capable ships, and like the *Fletchers* that Adm. Arleigh *Burke commanded during World War II, are designed for three-dimensional warfare, using sophisticated sensors and weapons, including cruise missiles, to strike targets above, on, and under the sea.

[*See also* Aircraft Carriers; Battleships; Cruisers; Torpedo Boats; World War I: Naval Operations in: World War II: Naval Operations in.]

• Theodore Roscoe, *United States Destroyer Operations in World War II*, 1953. Norman Friedman, *The U.S. Destroyer: An Illustrated Design History*, 1982. William M. McBride, *Good Night Officially: The Pacific War Letters of a Destroyer Sailor*, 1994. Don Sheppard, *Bluewater Sailor: The Memoir of a Destroyer Officer*, 1996.

—William M. McBride

DETECTION, OBSERVATION, AND FIRE CONTROL SYSTEMS. Hitting a distant moving target requires observing its range and bearing, estimating its speed and direction, extrapolating into the future to compute the lead, and then calculating ballistics (that is, how to set a gun with the proper angle and elevation to hit a target at a particular range and bearing). Before the twentieth century, gunners performed these tasks manually or aided by small instruments, observing with optical telescopes and rangefinders, looking up ballistics in firing tables, and setting guns by hand. Beginning around World War I, however, these operations became progressively automated and combined into specialized fire control systems. The apparatus integrated target detection and tracking, ballistics calculation, and gun command into a connected set of machines. For much of the twentieth century, fire control ranked among the most secret and delicate technologies in the American arsenal.

Automated fire control began in the navy with the adoption of "director firing," which controlled all guns on a ship from a centralized location. Before World War I, Arthur Hungerford Pollen designed an early automated plotting system for British ships. In America, the Sperry Gyroscope Company connected instruments that collected observed data about a target into a central plotting room. An automatic plotter drew the paths of both the firing ship and the target ship on paper, from which a gunnery officer could read the range and bearing for the guns to fire. He then electrically transmitted these data to gunners in the turrets. In 1915, Sperry's chief designer, Hannibal Ford, left to start the Ford Instrument Company and introduced the Ford Rangekeeper, which both incorporated British technology and added new mechanisms of Ford design. The Rangekeeper, a mechanical analog computer, estimated the

course and speed of a target ship based on repeated observations of range and bearing, continually updating the estimate in accord with new observations. The U.S. Navy enthusiastically adopted the Ford Rangekeeper, at first for *battleships and then for *destroyers and *cruisers. Before World War II, the secret and novel military-industrial alliance of the Bureau of Ordnance and the Ford Instrument Company, the Arma Engineering Company, and General Electric built nearly all fire control systems for the navy. Ford Rangekeepers, in numerous updates and modifications, directed guns on American warships into the 1990s. Arma also designed the famous Torpedo Data Computer (TDC) for *submarines and surface ships. Sperry and another spinoff, Carl Norden Inc., began building bombsights, a technology similar to Rangekeepers that played a critical role in World War II.

Naval fire control systems achieved a certain technical maturity between the world wars, but the critical problem in fire control shifted from hitting surface targets to a new challenge: aircraft. This problem, including all the difficulty of surface fire but at higher speed and in three dimensions, pushed fire control technology to its limits. Both the army and the navy developed antiaircraft directors, which tracked airplanes (at first with telescopes and then with radar), calculated the "lead," and directed guns to proper aiming positions. During World War II, lightweight, low-cost "lead computing sights," mounted directly on manually controlled guns, approximated the solution for close-in attacks. An extensive research program under the National Defense Research Committee extended the scope and sophistication of fire control technology, covering theory, electronics, bombsights, fuses, radar, fire control for aerial guns, and automation. This led not only to new fire control technologies but also to fundamental advances in computers, including work by Norbert Wiener (founder of cybernetics), Claude Shannon (founder of information theory), and George Stibitz (builder of the first digital computers). Automated, radar-directed fire control systems achieved critical successes during the war, especially against the German V-1 "buzz bombs" in Britain, and against Japanese air attacks in the western Pacific. Still, researchers never adequately solved the general problem of hitting rapidly maneuvering targets with ballistic shells (although the current Phalanx system does so at short ranges). Engineers, then, moved the control system into the projectile itself so it could continue to observe the target and control the shell during flight. The proximity fuse, developed during World War II for antiaircraft munitions, accomplished this control in a single dimension, detecting a target with a miniature radio transmitter and detonating the shell at the optimum time. Extending control to further dimensions and adding rocket motors for propulsion produced guided missiles.

Today, numerous military systems, including tanks, aircraft, and submarines, have their own specialized fire control systems. Guided missiles rely on fire control to find, track, and select targets. Large, computerized command and control systems, such as Sage and BMEWs for air defense, and NTDS and *Aegis for naval warfare, also inherited the legacy of fire control and made significant contributions to computer science. The problem of directing fire against rapidly moving targets still drives military technology, even in public perception. The *Stark* and *Vincennes* incidents in the Persian Gulf in the 1980s, the questionable performance of the Patriot missile system in the *Persian Gulf War (1991), and the continuing controversy over ballistic missile defenses such as the *Strategic Defense Initiative all illustrate that fire control remains a critical and difficult component of American technological warfare.

[*See also* Consultants; Heat-Seeking Technology; Lasers; Missiles; Radar; Sonar.]

• United States Navy, *Administrative History of the U.S. Navy in World War II*, Vol. 79: *Fire Control*, 1946. Buford Rowland and William B. Boyd, *U.S. Navy Bureau of Ordnance in World War II*, 1953. Norman Friedman, *U.S. Naval Weapons: Every Gun, Missile, Mine and Torpedo Used by the U.S. Navy from 1883 to the Present Day*, 1983. John Tetsuro Sumida, *In Defense of Naval Supremacy: Finance, Technology, and British Naval Policy 1889–1914*, 1989. Donald MacKenzie, *Inventing Accuracy: A Historical Sociology of Nuclear Missile Guidance*, 1990. Stephen L. McFarland, *America's Pursuit of Precision Bombing 1910–1914*, 1995.   —David A. Mindell

DETERRENCE is an exercise in coercion: it involves the use of threats and/or promises to dissuade an adversary from undertaking some action it might otherwise have taken. In political science terms, one entity, A, is said to have deterred another entity, B, if B, influenced by A's explicit or implicit threats or promises, chooses to refrain from certain activities. From A's perspective, deterrence represents an effort to achieve A's goal of preserving some aspect of the status quo by obtaining B's compliance, rather than by physically preventing an alteration in that status quo. From B's perspective, deterrence represents A's deliberate manipulation of B's calculation of costs and benefits to make acceptance of the status quo more attractive than challenging it.

For deterrence to operate, two conditions must exist. First, A must possess an effective coercive strategy—some combination of negative and positive sanctions large enough to shift B's evaluation of the desirability of a particular action. Negative sanctions for noncompliance may be of three sorts: denial of benefits; retaliation; or punishment. Second, A must be able credibly to commit itself to carrying out its effective coercive strategy. Because imposing negative or positive sanctions is unlikely to be cost-free for A, A's capacity credibly to commit itself may be problematic. Credible commitment to threats and promises can be established in three ways: by taking steps, *ex ante*, to ensure that the costs of failing to carry out threats and promises exceed the costs of carrying them out; by arranging for the threats and promises to be carried out automatically (as in "Dr. Strangelove's" fictional doomsday machine); or by ensuring, *ex ante*, that decisions to execute sanctions will be made irrationally, without due attention to costs and benefits.

Though both are exercises in coercion, deterrence differs from *compellence* in what A demands of B. In deterrence, A seeks to convince B not to undertake particular actions. In compellence, A seeks to force B to undertake particular actions. The distinction is between coercion aimed at preserving the status quo and coercion aimed at changing it. Deterrence is likely to be easier to accomplish than compellence because deterrence does not involve a deadline for action and is less likely to involve a visible and humiliating act of compliance, and because, whereas deterrence simply maintains the status quo, in compellence it is unclear where A's demands will end once B begins to make concessions.

Deterrence and compellence both involve coercive uses of power by A to achieve its goals indirectly, by obtaining B's compliance. They differ from direct uses of power aimed at achieving A's desired outcome regardless of B's behavior. This difference yields the distinction between deterrence and *defense*. Deterrence aims to reduce or eliminate B's interest in undertaking certain actions, and its success rests on A's capacity credibly to commit itself to harm B. Defense aims to reduce or eliminate B's capacity to hurt A or A's interests: its success rests on A's capacity to disarm, defeat, or protect against B. A's ability to limit or eliminate B's physical capacity to impose pain on A is irrelevant to deterrence, but is the essential element of defense. Measures aimed at defense may be *preemptive* (that is, may involve destroying or neutralizing B's capabilities before B has an opportunity to use them); *active* (defeating, repulsing, or blunting B's actions); or *passive* (protecting items of value against the consequences of B's successful actions).

The distinction between deterrence and defense is evident in alternative *Cold War strategies developed for dealing with the possibility of a Soviet nuclear attack. The Assured Destruction and Mutual Assured Destruction (MAD) doctrines enunciated by Secretary of Defense Robert S. *McNamara, and the various strategies of controlled nuclear retaliation developed after the early 1960s, reflect the logic of deterrence: they acknowledged the vulnerability of American society to a Soviet attack, but aimed to protect the territory of the United States by credibly committing it to exact appropriate retribution. By contrast, *active* defenses like the proposed Sentinel thin area defense antiballistic missile (ABM) program of the late 1960s, or broad missile defenses like those envisioned in President Ronald *Reagan's 1984 *Strategic Defense Initiative (SDI), reflect the idea of defending against, rather than deterring, an attack.

Though deterrence has always coexisted with defense as an element in American military policy, the development by the end of World War II of effective long-range airpower, missile technology, and atomic weapons simultaneously rendered defense more difficult and increased national capacity to threaten an adversary with massive suffering. Insightful observers like Bernard Brodie noted almost immediately the basic implications of these technological developments for American security policy. The Eisenhower administration's explicit incorporation of nuclear deterrence—"massive retaliation"—into U.S. defense planning in 1954 as part of its "New Look" in national security policy sharply accelerated the development of deterrence theory, principally by civilian analysts and scholars.

The early theorizing of the immediate postwar period was supplemented in the late 1950s and early 1960s by careful analyses by Brodie, Herman Kahn, William Kaufman, Klaus Knorr, Thomas Schelling, Glenn Snyder, and Albert Wohlstetter, among others, who explored the problems of achieving credible commitment, assuring "second-strike" capability, enhancing stability in situations of mutual vulnerability, using threats of limited and controlled retaliation to make nuclear deterrence credible even while American cities remained hostage, and employing arms control to enhance crisis management and arms race stability. This theorizing provided the blueprint for American nuclear strategy and arms control policy from the mid-1960s until the administration of Ronald *Reagan. With SDI and particularly with the end of the

Cold War, the focus of U.S. nuclear policy shifted increasingly from the problem of deterrence to the problems of defense against limited nuclear attacks, as well as nuclear proliferation.

[See also Arms Control and Disarmament; Game Theory; Missiles; Nuclear Weapons; Nuclear War, Prevention of Accidental; Strategy: Fundamentals; Strategy: Nuclear Warfare Strategy.]

• Bernard Brodie, *Strategy in the Missile Age,* 1959. Thomas C. Schelling, *Arms and Influence,* 1966. Glenn H. Snyder, *Deterrence and Defense,* 1961. Alexander L. George and Richard Smoke, *Deterrence in American Foreign Policy,* 1974. Robert Jervis, *The Illogic of American Nuclear Strategy,* 1984. Edward Rhodes, *Power and MADness: The Logic of Nuclear Coercion,* 1989. Ted Hopf, *Peripheral Visions: Deterrence Theory and American Foreign Policy in the Third World, 1965–1990,* 1994.   —Edward Rhodes

DEWEY, GEORGE (1837–1917), American admiral and popular naval hero. Dewey was born in Montpelier, Vermont, in 1837 and graduated from the U.S. Naval Academy in 1858. He served with distinction at the battles of New Orleans and Port Hudson during the *Civil War and ended the war as a lieutenant commander. He served in varying peacetime assignments, including command of the sloops *Pensacola* and *Narragansett.* Dewey spent the 1890s in Washington as chief of the Bureau of Equipment, president of the Lighthouse Board, and president of the Board of Inspection and Survey. In 1897, with the support of his Vermont senator, Redfield Procter, and Assistant Secretary of the Navy Theodore *Roosevelt, Dewey was appointed to command the Asiatic Squadron, based in the Far East.

Dewey's squadron was at Hong Kong when the *Spanish-American War began in April 1898. The U.S. Navy had long-standing plans to attack the Philippines in the event of war with Spain, and on 1 May 1895, Dewey led his squadron boldly into Manila Bay, disregarding reports of sea *mines at its narrow entrance. In a few hours Dewey had destroyed the antiquated Spanish squadron in the Philippines and blockaded Manila. News of the dramatic victory in the Battle of *Manila Bay, achieved without the loss of a single American life, made Dewey a popular hero and set in motion a chain of events leading to the U.S. annexation of the Philippines.

Following his return to the United States, Dewey, now promoted to the rank of admiral of the navy, flirted briefly with a run for the presidency, then settled down to preside over the General Board, the navy's first military planning organization. Under Dewey's stewardship, the board prepared plans for possible war with Germany and Japan and dealt with such questions as the location of naval bases in the Pacific, ship characteristics, and Navy Department organization. He died in January 1917 having served as a trusted naval adviser to three presidents.

[See also: Navy, U.S.: 1866–98; Philippines, U.S. Military Involvement in the.]   —Ronald H. Spector

DIEN BIEN PHU, SIEGE OF (1954). See Vietnam War (1960–1975).

DIRIGIBLES. See Blimps and Dirigibles.

DISARMAMENT. See Arms Control and Disarmament.

DISCIPLINARY VIEWS OF WAR

Anthropology
Cultural History
Causes-of-War Studies
Diplomatic History
Economics
Feminist and Gender Studies
History of Science and Technology
Military History
Peace History
Political Science and International Relations
Psychology
Society Studies

DISCIPLINARY VIEWS OF WAR: ANTHROPOLOGY

Anthropology seeks the type of comparative explanations that are lacking in histories of specific wars or in the synchronic analyses of social and political science. Because of anthropology's access to the archeological and ethnographic data, it is well placed to analyze not only the causes of specific wars but also the origins of warfare itself.

The definitions of warfare anthropology uses to achieve this special focus are a source of continuing debate; in part because of these problems in defining *war, some anthropologists turn to the study of *peace, seeing war only as socially dysfunctional. However, most definitions of war draw attention to its collective and socially sanctioned nature, allowing its distinction from the great variety of human behaviors that demonstrate *aggression and violence.

How, and with what causal significance, individual motivations, biological predispositions, and sociocultural purposes are manifest in warfare is therefore the substance of anthropological debate. In addition, anthropology's perspective allows special investigation of the persistence, positive consequences, and sociocultural variation in the practice of war. Traditionally, anthropology concentrated on the first two issues, and a number of derived causal models dominated the literature.

Biological models stressed the links between human and other primate violence, as well as the putative links between success in war and success in reproduction. The inference was that violent conflict was a critical factor in shaping human evolution and that this *natural* selection produced a *cultural* predilection for "war" (Napoleon Chagnon, in Haas, 1990). More recently, biological anthropology is beginning to decouple small-scale human warfare from simplistic evolutionary models (Knauft, 1991), but the problem remains that even if genetic selection were occurring in war, this still wouldn't explain why or how a change from war to peace occurs.

Ecological models suggested that war has a positive feedback for smaller-scale societies by playing a hidden role in mediating relationships with the environment. Warfare was ethnographically noted to maintain space between settlements and so prevent resource degradation, or to provide a means to ensure the fluidity of settlement patterns critical to the practice of low-intensity agriculture or nomadic pastoralism.

Social-structural models developed the idea that certain types of social organization (or the lack thereof) impelled people to war. The antagonistic constitution of clan and lineage groupings, or the lack of any overarching authority in nonstate societies, were observed to create perennial tensions that might erupt into war.

However, the shortcomings of such models become very apparent when trying to explain the particular motivations and meanings that warriors give to their acts. The reductive nature of these models thus made many aspects of warfare—especially such phenomena as torture, cannibalism, or head-hunting—even more obscure, something to be assigned to the "primitive savagery" of tribal societies. Yet, cultural values clearly affect the pragmatics of war. Hermeneutic approaches have revealed the symbolic and ritual influences that modulate modes and intensities of armed conflict. Case studies show the importance of ritual performance in forms of reciprocal warring, as well as illuminating the links between symbolic schema and the practices of cannibalism and trophy taking.

This kind of approach leads to wider debate on "cultures of resistance," where the study of violent conflict in tribal societies is integrated with the study of terrorism, state repression, or *guerrilla warfare. It is important to note that such approaches suggest that external linkages often underlie internal cultural patterns of conflict and violence; this is particularly evident during the regional intrusion of colonial powers or the local collapse of state authority.

Such recognition represents the starting point for the other main strand of current anthropological theory, which stresses diachronic processes. Like the hermeneutic approaches, historical anthropology suggests that there is no one cause for war, and that the specific circumstance of conflict must condition our explanations. Commitment to historical explanation means that questions are also asked about the origins of observed levels of conflict, and about the factors underlying their persistence. Previously, anthropology generally accepted the premise that tribal war was a given, part of what must be a long-standing pattern of behavior. Recent work reacts against this presumption and through the concept of the "tribal zone" brings together a nuanced analysis of the hermeneutic approach with a historical appreciation of how external relations are critical in patterning a given war complex.

A tribal zone is defined as a spatial and conceptual arena affected by the proximity of state systems, but not under direct state control. European global colonialism is an obvious context in which this has occurred, but the implosion of a nation-state is also an important context.

The consequence of being located within a tribal zone is rapid sociocultural transformation, occurring through the linked processes of militarization and tribalization. Militarization refers to the growth in armed collective violence, whose purpose, conduct, and technology rapidly adapts to the threat of state expansion or collapse. This often leads to the emergence of ethnic soldiering, whereby collective identities become indissolubly linked to military capabilities—either as specialists in state armies, or as guerrillas in opposition to them. Tribalization is the social corollary of this process, through which collective sentiments are transformed into overt political principles, as seen in the emergence of authoritarian or charismatic leaders during times of war. There is also an increasing rigidity in sociocultural boundaries and a burgeoning economic dependency on an intrusive state system or transnational institutions.

The main implications of these recent theoretical innovations for the future anthropological study of war are,

first, that the militarizing effects of state expansion or collapse typically precede ethnographic or journalistic accounts of local warfare, and so cannot be taken as direct evidence of other people's predilection for war. Second, that state systems tend to intensify existing local levels of conflict and rarely suppress them, except through an even deadlier application of force. Third, that tribe/state interactions, not just existing indigenous cultural patterns, produce observed levels of warfare. In turn, local warfare may be transformed through these external links into new forms of violence emerging as banditry, terrorism, or guerrilla conflict. Ethnic sentiment is not the direct cause of war but can itself be a consequence of those extraneous factors that structure many "tribal" conflicts, or those wherein nation-states confront ethnic minorities.

[See also: Agriculture and War; Ethnicity and War; Society and War; Terrorism and Counterterrorism.]

• R. Rosaldo, Ilongot Headhunting, 1883–1974, 1980. Raymond C. Kelly, The Nuer Conquest. The Structure and Development of an Expansionist System, 1985. J. Haas, The Anthropology of War, 1990. B. Knauft, "Violence and Sociality in Human Evolution," Current Anthropology, 32 (1991), pp. 391–428. R. B. Ferguson and N. L. Whitehead, War in the Tribal Zone. Expanding States and Indigenous Warfare, 1992. E. Viveiros de Castro, From the Enemy's Point of View, 1992.
—Neil L. Whitehead

DISCIPLINARY VIEWS OF WAR: CULTURAL HISTORY

The study of the cultural history of war is the analysis of the ways groups and individuals ascribe meaning to military conflict: in anticipation, during such conflict, or in its aftermath.

Research has concentrated on four specific areas. The first focuses on the role in military history of popular culture, understood as the codes, gestures, and forms of voluntary associations and collectives, elaborated not through the *state but in civil society and through the marketplace. These associations engage in leisure activities at home while war goes on elsewhere. Through such activities they expresses commonly held notions about the rights and wrongs of military conflict, the nature of military service, and views of the *enemy. In every war, entrepreneurs sell items or services that derive from these forms of expression. Profit and *patriotism frequently go hand in hand. Here the emphasis is on the evolution of propaganda, not necessarily manipulated from above, but consonant with prewar cultural forms and modes of expression, like music hall, organized sports, or the cinema. The destination is a deeper understanding of what may be termed wartime culture, or the negotiation of consent through entertainment or other cultural activities.

Examples of this kind of research include the analysis of the intersection of the history of motion pictures with the two world wars. Newsreels are usually manipulated forms of disseminated information. Cultural historians recognize this area, but turn more frequently to the commercial film industry and its indirect messages, which by that very fact makes them subtler and more powerful carriers of ideas about war than officially produced films or newsreels.

The second area of research concerns the impact of war on cultural forms. Here the emphasis is on writers, artists, and other workers in the field of cultural reproduction. Many are deeply affected by their own military service, and spend years elaborating the echoes and nightmares that inhabit their imagination. Others turn to political activism and use their art to convey messages about war to the yet unknowing world.

Edmund Wilson's study of American writing after the *Civil War, *Patriotic Gore,* is a case in point. Here the echoes of the *Civil War were heard in areas of American cultural life not usually associated with the conflict. Oliver Wendell Holmes's "cosmic skepticism" is one kind of cultural outcome of war with consequences far beyond the field of military affairs.

The third area well developed in this field is the analysis of the *indirect effects* of war on other cultural forms, such as notions of gender, insanity, or race. Here the focus is less on war and its representations than on the way war highlights or deflects notions of difference between classes, races, ethnic groups, or men and women.

Much attention has been focused on the "overfeminization" of women in wartime, their relegation to a maternal role less threatening to patriarchy than their continued participation after the war in industrial employment. Notions of racial injustice have also been explored in the aftermath of maltreatment of African Americans or other racial and ethnic groups while in uniform, or simply as suspect groups in wartime. The mass incarceration of Japanese Americans during World War II is a subject that highlights the effect of war on preexisting racial and ethnic prejudices.

The history of Post Traumatic Stress Disorder (PTSD), in existence long before it was recognized as a medical syndrome in 1980, is a subject that has drawn many scholars in the field of cultural studies and medical history. It throws considerable light on the way we understand mental illness and on the evolution of its treatment.

The fourth area of research is the study of *sites associated with war.* The Tomb of the Unknown Soldier in Arlington National Cemetery and Maya Lin's Vietnam Veterans' Memorial are just two such sites; thousands exist in towns and parks surrounding battlefields. The iconography, preparation, and reception of these sites are central parts of American cultural history.

[*See also:* Film, War and the Military in; Gender and War; Memorials, War; Propaganda and Public Relations, Government.]

• Edmund Wilson, *Patriot Gore: Studies in the Literature of the American Civil War,* 1962. Paul Fussell, *The Great War and Modern Memory,* 1977. Paul Fussell, *Wartime: Understanding and Behavior in the Second World,* 1990. Maya Lin, et al., *Grounds for Remembering,* 1995. Samuel Hynes, *The Soldier's Tale. Bearing Witness to Modern War,* 1997.
　　　　　　　　　　　　　　　　　　　　　—Jay Winter

DISCIPLINARY VIEWS OF WAR: CAUSES-OF-WAR STUDIES

The causes of war have puzzled Western thinkers since Thucydides attributed the Peloponnesian War to fear of the growing power of Athens. Machiavelli thought that war was the natural order of things and fighting the first business of the prince. Immanuel Kant noted that states with republican regimes were more peaceful than other states, an insight that anticipated a flurry of scholarship at the end of the *Cold War.

The systematic study of the causes of war, however, emerged only in the twentieth century. The greatest achievement in the field was stimulated by World War I. Following that unexpectedly costly and protracted war,

scholars sought its causes in biology, psychiatry, politics, statistics, anthropology, history, and other disciplines. A group of scholars at the University of Chicago sought to synthesize these disciplinary analyses. Working from 1926 to 1942, they produced the monumental *A Study of War* under the authorship of political scientist Quincy Wright.

Wright developed a four-tier model of the causes and nature of war. Animal warfare, he believed, was driven by biological instincts. Primitive war was driven by the nature of society. What he called civilized war, that is, war among states after the appearance of civilizations, was driven by the nature of the international system. And modern war, war after 1500, was driven by technology. The primary drive in each era, he believed, dominated the shaping of war but did not entirely eliminate the drives still extant from previous eras.

Historians and political scientists have taken the lead since Wright in exploring the causes of war. Kenneth Waltz influenced many successors with *Man, the State, and War* (1954), a three-tier model similar to Wright's but without animal warfare. Subsequent literature in the field may be divided among those that look for the causes of war in individual behavior or decision making, the political imperatives of individual states, or the anarchy of the international system. As yet, no general theory has captured a consensus. Historians such as Michael Howard—*The Causes of War* (1983)—and John Stoessinger—*Why Nations Go to War* (1974)—have attempted to generalize from specific cases without reducing their conclusions to theory. Neither political science nor historical discipline has succeeded in integrating theories and explanations of nuclear war with those of conventional war.

Scholars in other disciplines have also continued to study the causes of war. Anthropologists, sociologists, biologists, psychologists, and economists have all advanced theories. Whole new disciplines, such as conflict resolution and peace studies, have grown up around the topic. One tendency within this scholarship has been to define war more broadly than heretofore and to seek to understand the nature of all large-scale, organized intergroup violence. Yet little interdisciplinary work has followed in the tradition of Quincy Wright. With the end of the Cold War, two scholarly communities, one at Rutgers University and another at Duke University and the University of North Carolina at Chapel Hill, have turned their attention to interdisciplinary study of this topic.

[*See also* Clausewitz, Carl von; Disciplinary Views of War: Political Science and International Relations; Peace and Antiwar Movements; War.]
　　　　　　　　　　　　　　　　　　　　　—Alex Roland

DISCIPLINARY VIEWS OF WAR: DIPLOMATIC HISTORY

In a simpler time, diplomatic historians wrote about what diplomats did. And in that simpler time, *war was war, *peace was peace, and the twain met only when countries exchanged declarations of belligerence or negotiated armistices and surrenders. Consequently, although the diplomatic historians had much to relate regarding how wars began and how they ended, they had little to offer about war per se. They covered events up to the moment the antagonists broke diplomatic relations, and resumed the story when the belligerents began suing for peace. Alliance diplomacy, in those cases when the United States had allies, gave them partial employment for the duration.

But just as the diplomats left the fighting itself to the generals, so the diplomatic historians left war to the military historians. For every chapter the diplomatic historians devoted to American participation in World War I, they wrote a dozen on the period of American *neutrality or on Wilsonian peacemaking. The road to Pearl Harbor quickly grew crowded with diplomatic historians explaining how the United States got itself to 7 December 1941; the same generation of diplomatic historians found far less to say about the global conflict that followed.

But the traditional treatment broke down under the unusual circumstances of the *Cold War. The superpower struggle belied the conventional dichotomy between war and peace; Americans now found themselves in a chronic condition that was neither one nor quite the other. Moreover, the principal U.S. armed conflicts of the Cold War—in Korea and Vietnam—were undeclared, partially proxy contests, and never provoked the United States and the Soviet Union to break diplomatic relations. (Relation breaking—the traditional precursor to belligerence—had been another reason the diplomats left war to the generals: wars put them out of business.) But the diplomats found themselves busier than ever during the Korean and Vietnam Wars, struggling to keep those limited conflicts limited. Diplomatic historians, who habitually shadowed diplomats at a distance of five to thirty years, found themselves necessarily drawn into this no-man's-land.

In addition, even as the context of diplomacy was changing during the Cold War, so was the context of diplomatic history. Starting in the 1960s, the American historical profession experienced a revolt against elitism. The study of governing groups and ruling classes gave way to investigations into the lives of common people. Women and racial and ethnic minorities were judged more interesting than white males. Political history was supplanted by social and cultural history. On nearly all points, traditional diplomatic history came under attack: its subjects were overwhelmingly white and male; they operated, even if they didn't always originate, as an exclusive elite; and their actions were frequently quite removed from the concerns of ordinary folks.

It was a toss-up whether the assault from within the academy or the changing reality of the Cold War was the more responsible, but between the two influences the diplomatic historians altered their approach to war. It certainly was not coincidental that the alteration accelerated with the souring of the American intervention in Vietnam—the single event of the Cold War that went farthest toward discrediting diplomatic elites and rebutting received notions regarding the nature of war. Quite obviously, the diplomats had got things horribly wrong. The diplomatic historians, in order to understand the error and prevent its repetition, needed to lift themselves to a higher plane of understanding. The diplomats had misconceived the social and cultural roots of Vietnamese resistance; the diplomatic historians must make such social and cultural roots central elements of a new, more inclusive, and presumably more enlightening diplomatic history.

The earliest reexamination involved the origins of the Cold War. Historians being the reflexive regressionists they are, this in turn provoked a fresh look at previous wars. Radical revisionists like Gabriel Kolko saw the Cold War as the inevitable outgrowth of decisions made during World War II; John Lewis Gaddis and other moderate "postrevisionists" interpreted the outgrowth as not exactly inevitable but still strongly influenced by developments of the war years. Atomic revisionist Gar Alperowitz was even more explicit in describing the last shots of World War II as the first shots of the Cold War. Others among the new generation of diplomatic historians (now often restyled "historians of American foreign relations," a label designed to encompass unofficial relations as well as the official ones dear to the diplomats) applied the revisionist analysis to World War I. N. Gordon Levin, Jr., found the battle between the belligerents in the Great War to be less instructive than the jockeying for position between Woodrow *Wilson and Lenin; Lloyd C. Gardner perceived the war as part of a larger American drive for ideological hegemony.

The first wave of revisionists typically stayed within the bounds of traditional diplomatic history, if not within the traditional lines of war and peace; gradually, however, the culturally inclined exponents of the "new diplomatic history" gained a voice. Foremost among these was Akira Iriye, who interpreted the Pacific War less as a clash of American and Japanese arms than as a long-building collision between American and Japanese cultures. Iriye was comparatively highbrow, as the culturalists went, concentrating on the more literate representatives of the Pacific Rim cultures. John W. Dower took a lower road, -examining popular wartime stereotypes in all their scurrilousness. An entire school of interpretation adopted the same tack for the *Vietnam War: the failure of American culture, it was discovered, predestined the United States to defeat in Indochina.

The cultural-egalitarian approach didn't convince all diplomatic historians, many of whom pointed out that whether one liked it or not, elites wielded power, especially over foreign policy. Yet, unwilling, in an age of academic multiculturalism, to be seen as apologists for tradition, some diplomatic historians adopted what amounted to an elitist alternative to multiculturalism, namely, multiarchivalism. These researchers deliberately decentered the debate and deprivileged the United States, traveling to foreign archives and taking pains to write from the perspective of foreign governments. Pains were indeed often required, since few foreign governments granted anything like the access to internal records that Washington did (although the end of the Cold War resulted in opened archives in certain formerly Communist countries). That most international conflict of the Cold War—the *Korean War—was a natural candidate for the internationalist approach. Strikingly, the insights the internationalists provided forced only modest revisions of traditional views on the subject.

[See also Cold War: Changing Interpretations; Vietnam War: Changing Interpretations.]

• Herbert Feis, The Road to Pearl Harbor, 1950. Gar Alperowitz, Atomic Diplomacy, 1965. Gabriel Kolko, The Politics of War, 1968. N. Gordon Levin, Jr., Woodrow Wilson and World Politics, 1968. John Lewis Gaddis, The United States and the Origins of the Cold War, 1972. Lloyd C. Gardner, Safe for Democracy, 1984. Loren Baritz, Backfire: A History of How American Culture Led Us into Vietnam and Made Us Fight the Way We Did, 1985. John W. Dower, War Without Mercy, 1986. Akira Iriye, The Origins of the Second World War in Asia and the Pacific, 1987. H. W. Brands, The Devil We Knew: Americans and the Cold War, 1993. William Stueck, The Korean War: An International History, 1995.   —H. W. Brands

DISCIPLINARY VIEWS OF WAR: ECONOMICS

Wars are often assumed to be special cases in which the normal principles of economics do not apply. In fact, however, economics has much to say about wars, and much to learn from them.

Consider first the financing of wars. There are numerous ways of raising the necessary resources. The government can, for example, simply commandeer resources from its own citizens or from its enemies. *Conscription has been the most important example of commandeering in the United States. But in terms of financial resources, three have been predominant: borrowing, taxing, and printing money.

But which source, or combination of sources, of finance is best? In his *Wealth of Nations* (1776), Adam Smith argued that when a war is financed by debt, there is only a small increase in taxes: the increase needed to meet the interest on the debt. The smallness of the increase, Smith argued, conceals the cost of the war and weakens opposition to it. Raising taxes high enough to pay expenses as they are incurred ("pay-as-you go") would mean that wars were accompanied by sharp increases in taxes, and that "Wars would be in general more speedily concluded and less wantonly undertaken."

For almost two centuries this was the orthodox view. It was challenged in the 1940s and 1950s by Keynesian economists, but the major challenge is more recent. A number of economists, including Robert Lucas and Marvin Goodfriend, have argued that high wartime taxes distort the allocation of resources. Governments, according to these economists, should smooth tax rates over time by issuing debt during a war and gradually retiring afterwards. Economics has come full circle: the policy that Smith rejected is the new orthodoxy.

What about simply printing money? There has been no reversal on this question: economists, with few exceptions, have rejected it. First, printing money produces painful, and undesirable redistributions of wealth—the classic problem of widows and orphans living on fixed incomes. Second, inflation produces attempts to economize on use of cash that reduce efficiency. In the extreme case, barter replaces the use of money. But printing money has its advantages. First, printing money, unlike taxing, does not require an administrative bureaucracy. This explains why printing money was the primary source of finance in the Revolutionary War and for the South in the *Civil War. Second, the government may be able to blame "shortages" or "war profiteers" for the inflation, thus concealing the costs of war. Finally, the distortions produced by a moderate inflation may be similar to those produced by various taxes. For these reasons, printing money has been used to finance part of all wars in the United States.

Economists have also been concerned with how labor is procured for the armed forces. Smith, and the economists who followed him, argued that the state should rely on a paid professional army because normally it could defeat even a much larger part-time militia, another example of the increased efficiency produced by the specialization of labor.

Modern economists have continued to prefer paid professional forces. During the Vietnam era, economists such as Milton Friedman and Walter Oi took an active role in the debate over the draft. One of their points was that the budgetary savings from conscription are illusory. What the taxpayer saves—the difference between what a conscript would have to be paid to induce him or her to serve voluntarily and the pay the conscript actually receives—does not go unpaid; it is paid by the conscript. Hiring military personnel, moreover, reduces the output loss in the civilian sector because the most highly paid, and therefore most productive, workers remain in the private sector. Thus, the draft illustrates the conflict between efficiency and equity. Efficiency calls for paid professionals, but the result may be a "rich man's war and a poor man's fight." In the Revolutionary War and the Civil War, draftees were allowed to hire substitutes. This reduced the output loss in the civilian economy, but produced bitter resentment. In the twentieth century, the United States chose conscription combined with exemptions designed, in part, to minimize damage to the civilian sector.

During nineteenth-century wars, the United States generally left the allocation of resources within the private sector to the market. In World Wars I and II and the *Korean War, however, the government tried to control the private sector with price controls, rationing, and bureaucratic controls over investment. Partly, these policies reflected the loss of confidence in the market. Some economists argued that wars were a special case in which benefits of planning outweighed the costs. During a war, for example, one of the strengths of a market economy, its ability to generate information about the tastes and preferences of the public, is of great importance. Whether in fact the array of controls imposed during these wars improved the equity or efficiency of the economy is a matter of debate.

Economists have also contributed by measuring the long-term costs and benefits of *war. The main point is to look beyond government budgets to the losses in physical and human capital. In the North during the Civil War, and in the two world wars, the United States suffered little direct damage to its physical capital. In World War II, moreover, it is not even clear that the capital stock was less at the end of the war than it would have been if peace had continued, because the war restored full employment and the government invested directly in new plant and equipment that was useful in peacetime. Losses in human capital have been even harder to assess. One complicating factor is that the United States has been able to make good much of its wartime losses of human capital by altering its immigration policies.

In addition, economists have attended to the institutional legacy of wars. At one time it was believed that the Civil War created an array of institutional changes (freedom for the slaves, transcontinental railroads, a national banking system, and so on) that produced rapid industrialization after the war. That thesis, however, has been challenged and the case remains open. Similarly, it has been argued that World War II left the United States in a unique position in the world economy, which created the basis for rapid expansion until the 1970s. This case also remains open.

These examples may be sufficient to illustrate the value of economics in the study of war, and the challenges that still await economists and economic historians.

[*See also* Economics and War; Public Financing and Budgeting for War.]

• John Kenneth Galbraith, *A Theory of Price Control*, 1952. Stanley E. Engerman, "The Economic Impact of the Civil War," in Stanley

E. Engerman and Robert W. Fogel, eds., *The Reinterpretation of American Economic History*, 1971. Alan S. Millward, *War, Economy and Society, 1939–45*, 1979. Hugh Rockoff, *Drastic Measures: A History of Wage and Price Controls in the United States*, 1984. Harold G. Vatter, *The U.S. Economy in World War II*, 1985. Robert Higgs, *Crisis and Leviathan: Critical Issues in the Emergence of the Mixed Economy*, 1986. Roger L. Ransom, *Conflict and Compromise: The Political Economy of Slavery, Emancipation, and the American Civil War*, 1989. Geofrey Mills and Hugh Rockoff, eds., *The Sinews of War: Essays on the Economic History of World War II*, 1993.

—Hugh Rockoff

DISCIPLINARY VIEWS OF WAR: FEMINIST AND GENDER STUDIES

Feminist questions about *war and *peace challenge a number of basic definitions, identifications, and exclusions. These challenges are both theoretical and archival; they have changed the way that we understand men's as well as women's experiences.

The traditional doctrine of "separate spheres" for men and women assumed that war was men's business, peace that of women; men were "just warriors," while women were "beautiful souls" (see Jean Bethke Elshtain). As Harriet Hyman Alonso has shown, some women pacifists have embraced the view that the experience or concept of maternity inclines them to pacifism. Combat belonged to the public arena, and was opposed to the private hearth for which war was allegedly waged. In an extension of this paradigm that has sometimes fostered misogyny, men were understood to be at the battle front, while women remained safe at the home front.

These assumptions have all been challenged by feminist studies such as Cynthia Enloe's *Does Khaki Become You? The Militarization of Women's Lives* (1983), the double issue on women's peace studies of *Women's Studies Quarterly* (1995), and "Twentieth-Century Women in Wartime," a special issue of the *International History Review* (1997).

One of the factors enabling a reassessment of the relationship between war and the construction of gender has been the shift by historians from a study of events to the study of social structures, the economy, and mentalities. Feminist historians have as a rule rejected the understanding of war as a set of material or political facts. Critical to their analysis has been the distinction between *military combat*, which in most Western cultures has been an exclusively or predominantly male activity, and the larger phenomenon of *war*, which involves political structures, economic organization, and social hierarchies, and thus affects noncombatants as well as combatants, women as well as men.

Conventional views hold that the knowledge of combat divides male soldiers from women and other civilians. The line is drawn not only in fiction by men, but in that by women, from Edith Wharton's *A Son at the Front* (1923) to Bobbie Ann Mason's *In Country* (1985). This view, however, does not allow for the nature of modern warfare, with blanket bombing, group massacres, and increasingly remote technology that blurs the line between men pushing buttons and women assembling electronic weaponry.

Historians now argue that women's wartime experiences carry them across most of these theoretical lines. Undercutting the distinction between battle front and home front, scholars like Enloe have shown that women of different kinds have always been at "the front," as sutlers selling provisions, "*Camp followers," nurses, wives, or as victims of theft and violence by occupying forces, and sometimes as fighters themselves. In the study of women in the military, interest has revived in controversial women who cross-dressed in order to fight, reaching back to such figures as Deborah Sampson, who fought during the *Revolutionary War; Loreta Janeta Velasquez, whose *The Woman in Battle* (1876) recalled her service as a lieutenant in the *Confederate army; and Emma Edmonds, whose autobiography, *Nurse and Spy in the Union Army* (1865), supported her subsequent campaign for a pension. Women, in short, have not been exclusively passive, pacific, or victimized. The line between battle and home front is also complicated by the *mobilization of noncombatants for military purposes (e.g., in munitions, *communications, and auxiliary services).

A further fundamental challenge comes from feminist work on the coexistence of military structures with peacetime politics. The sharp distinction between war and peace has been eroded. So has that between a formally constituted military force and the network of informal, linked institutions such as prostitution or industrial suppliers. This erosion has necessarily revised the temporal definition of war experience. The aim of war to inflict pain (see Elaine Scarry), forces the examination of the long-term consequences of wartime violence both for those firing guns under fire and for their victims. Once we recognize pain as a goal of warfare, we can better understand the impact of war on women. The memorializing of war in museums tends to fetishize weaponry, but work on the trauma of Holocaust survivors and of Vietnam *veterans (including nurses as well as soldiers) brings us closer to the ramifications of war.

By distinguishing between the social reality and the symbolic construction of gender roles, some scholars have explored how significant social and economic shifts in women's assigned roles during wartime could fail to endure in the postwar period (see Higonnet, et al.). Women have drawn on traditional images of their role as moral (endorsing abolitionism, pacifism, or maternalism) in order to justify wartime entry into the public sphere. World War II images of Rosie the Riveter anchor the heterosexual order while permitting women to enter a male world, according to Maureen Honey and others. The feminist interest in the representation of masculinity and femininity has also fostered fresh work on the wartime gendering of the enemy (as effeminate), of politicians (as impotent), and of women (as unsexed), by feminist scholars such as Susan Jeffords. This turn to questions of language has been accompanied by a renewed study of the eroticization of aggression and violence.

Revisionist historians argue that the variety of women's wartime experiences behind the lines depends on their class, ethnicity, geographic location, or political alignment. The *Civil War contributions of Northern and Southern women, for example, are now distinguished by such scholars as Elizabeth D. Leonard, in *Yankee Women* (1994), Catherine Clinton, in *Tara Revisited: Women, War and the Plantation Legend* (1995), and Drew Gilpin Faust, in *Mothers of Invention: Women of the Slaveholding South in the American Civil War* (1996).

In order to explore this variety, feminist historians have also turned to new kinds of resources—not only memoirs or letters but oral history interviews, as in Sherna Gluck's

Rosie the Riveter Revisited (1987). While earlier histories focused on elites, this new work extends the reach of history to women of the working classes, including women of different ethnicities, whose lack of literacy, leisure, and a forum prevented them from recording their experiences. These new methodologies aim to revise former exclusions and broaden our understanding of the scope of war.

[*See also:* Gender; Gender and War; Pacifism; Women in the Military.]

• Maureen Honey, *Creating Rosie the Riveter,* 1984. Elaine Scarry, *The Body in Pain,* 1985. Jean Bethke Elshtain, *Women and War,* 1987. Margaret R. Higonet, et al., eds., *Behind the Lines: Gender and the Two World Wars,* 1987. Susan Jeffords, *The Remasculinizing of America,* 1989. Harriet Hyman Alonso, *Peace as a Woman's Issue: A History of the U.S. Movement for World Peace and Women's Rights,* 1993.
　　　　　　　　　　　　　　　　　　　—Margaret Higonnet

DISCIPLINARY VIEWS OF WAR:
HISTORY OF SCIENCE AND TECHNOLOGY

The history of science had its roots in intellectual history; it studied the ideas of great men. George Sarton launched the field on its modern, independent trajectory with the creation of the journal *Isis* in 1912 and the History of Science Society in 1924. The history of technology had its roots both in the history of science and in economic history. Its autonomy as a field began with the founding of the Society for the History of Technology (SHOT) and the journal *Technology and Culture* in 1958.

Until World War II, historians of science paid little attention to *war and the military, in spite of the fact that both loomed large in the lives and work of scientists as disparate and renowned as Archimedes, Galileo, and Lavoisier. The few exceptions, such as Robert Merton's classic *Science, Technology and Society in Seventeenth-Century England* (1938), prove the rule; Merton, in fact, was a sociologist. In contrast, historians of technology appreciated the importance of military topics before the creation of SHOT. For example, the standard multivolume reference works all have extensive coverage of military topics: Charles J. Singer, et al., *A History of Technology,* 8 vols. (1954–84); Maurice Daumas, ed., *Historie général des techniques,* English trans. by Eileen B. Hennessy, 3 vols. (1970); and Melvin Kranzberg and Carroll Pursell, eds., *Technology in Western Civilization,* 2 vols. (1967). The last work actually was sponsored by the Department of *Defense.

Lewis Mumford's *Technics and Civilization* (1932) established a benchmark among pre–World War II studies. In this synthetic, richly interpretive overview of Western experience, Mumford identified four loci of what he saw as the deterioration of civilization from its natural, organic state to a perverse, mechanistic, artificial corruption that had set in during the modern era. These loci were the soldier, the miner, the cleric, and the accountant. The solder was responsible, in Mumford's view, for the regimentation of life and work and the subordination of the individual to the group.

In 1932, Mumford had hoped that the twentieth century, a period he called the *neotechnic era,* would witness a return to natural, organic values. Instead, civilization continued to disappoint him, prompting his two-volume study, *The Myth of the Machine* (1967–70). In the second volume, *The Pentagon of Power,* Mumford portrayed the *military-industrial complex as the sad culmination of the mechanistic, authoritarian tendencies he had first identified in *Technics and Civilization.* The greening of civilization had failed to materialize.

Other works appearing in Mumford's prime were less judgmental. For example, Carlo Cipolla, an economic historian, argued in *Guns, Sails, and Empire* (1965) that the West had established hegemony over the world's littoral in the early modern period by exploiting the superior military technology of the heavy cannon and the side-gunned sailing ship. Lynn White, Jr., argued in *Medieval Technology and Social Change* (1962) that the introduction of the stirrup in eighth-century Europe empowered the mounted warrior and thus catalyzed the feudal system. Both books have been interpreted as indulging in technological determinism. This claim places them in the same category as Jacques Ellul's *The Technological Society* (1964), an alarmist tract lamenting the loss of human agency in the face of increasingly autonomous technological imperatives.

Against this interpretation has emerged a school of thought generally described as *social constructivist.* Adherents of this school, whose roots are in European sociology, argue that all technologies are socially constructed, that is, they take their form and their role in society from human decisions. An excellent example of this kind of analysis is Donald MacKenzie's *Inventing Accuracy: An Historical Sociology of Nuclear Missiles and Guidance* (1990). That the debate between these two schools remains unsettled is manifest in Merritt Roe Smith and Leo Marx, eds., *Does Technology Determine History? The Dilemma of Technological Determinism* (1994).

Many important works have escaped this controversy. For example, Merritt Roe Smith's *Harpers Ferry Armory and the New Technology: The Challenge of Change* (1977) explored the revolution in small arms manufacture that lay behind the so-called American System. In the process he called into question America's purported love affair with technology.

A related issue, military conservatism, received its most influential treatment in Elting Morison's *Men, Machines, and Modern Times* (1966), especially in his seminal essay "Gunfire at Sea." Morison eschewed the temptation to stereotype the military, arguing instead that "military organizations are really societies, more rigidly structured, more highly integrated, than most communities, but still societies." Their response to technological change, he believed, differed in degree but not in kind from that of other societies. Military officers in general and naval officers in particular had good reasons to cherish proven technologies and to resist innovation; after all, they risked their lives and the lives of their subordinates on that technology. Arms and equipment that had been proven in battle were bound to appear more secure and trustworthy than new technology yet to win its spurs. Morison went so far as to argue in another article that we would do well to recognize "the destructive energy in machinery." His examination of the navy's skepticism about the revolutionary warship *Wampanoag* after the *Civil War presents naval conservatism in a new light, almost as an early aversion to the dangers of autonomous technology.

The great irony about traditional military conservatism toward technological change is that it reversed itself completely after World War II. This was the first war in which the weapons deployed at the end were significantly different from those with which it was launched; the most familiar examples are jet aircraft, ballistic *missiles, proximity fuses, and, of course, the atomic bomb. These developments convinced the services that the desideratum of modern war was shifting from industrial production to technological development. The next war would be won in the research laboratory fully as much as the factory. Thus began the hothouse environment of military research and development that produced a new *arms race, military-industrial complexes in the United States and abroad, and the expansion of military interest and funds into new realms, such as computers, *communications, space flight, microelectronics, astrophysics, and a host of other fields.

Many scholars writing in this environment found their views and conclusions shaped by the *Cold War and the military-industrial complex. Perhaps the most influential was William H. McNeill, whose The Pursuit of Power: Technology, Armed Force, and Society Since A.D. 1000 (1982) explored the relationship between technology and war through the second millennium. McNeill believed that free enterprise had driven the explosion of military technology in the late Middle Ages and early modern periods, only to be replaced by command economies in the twentieth century. Under state direction, these economies drove the nuclear arms race, which threatened human survival. Implicit in McNeill's work was a belief that historians should understand, expose, and perhaps deflect a military-technical trajectory that seemed headed to Armageddon.

The topic has attracted historians of science as well. Following the lead of scientists themselves, historians of science turned increasingly after World War II to military topics in general, and the moral and political implications of *nuclear weapons in particular. The ethical concerns about developing weapons that some scientists have had throughout history were magnified in the twentieth century as scientific knowledge and expertise were bent on producing weapons of mass destruction—gas in World War I and most especially the atomic bomb in World War II.

Between 1950 and 1990, a significant body of scholarship explored the military-industrial complex, the making of science policy, the ethical position of the scientist, and the militarization of universities and other centers of scientific and technical research. Paul Forman provided a benchmark in this scholarship with his seminal study, "Behind Quantum Electronics: National Security as Basis for Physical Research in the United States, 1940–1960," Historical Studies in the Physical and Biological Sciences, 18 (1987). Others have expressed many of the same concerns. Michael Sherry's The Rise of American Airpower (1987) finds "technological fanaticism" in the infatuation with strategic bombing that gripped American air force officers after 1930. In Forces of Production (1984), David Noble demonstrates the ways in which military imperatives shaped the development of numerically controlled machine tools in the United States. Stuart W. Leslie saw a perverse military influence on two of America's leading research universities in The Cold War and American Science: The Military-Industrial Complex at MIT and Stanford (1993). The end of the Cold War seems to have shrunken this branch of scholarship, but it is unlikely to entirely disappear.

Meanwhile, the best scholarship in the history of science and technology combines solid grounding in the technical material with rich contextualization. For example, Hugh G. J. Aitken's Taylorism at Watertown Arsenal: Scientific Management in Action (1960) explores the military roots of American technological and industrial practice. Daniel Kevles's The Physicists (1964) reveals the ways in which physics and war shaped each other in the United States. Richard Rhodes examines the Making of the Atomic Bomb (1986) with unprecedented insight and precision, virtues also present in his sequel, Dark Sun: The Making of the Hydrogen Bomb (1995). As the Cold War recedes into history, it may be expected that historians of science and technology will be less influenced by the passions of that conflict and even more inclined to see war and the military as important contextual issues.

[See also: Society and War.]   —Alex Roland

DISCIPLINARY VIEWS OF WAR: MILITARY HISTORY

Certainly in Western Society, given the frequency of warfare, it could be said with only slight exaggeration that before the eighteenth century little history of any kind was written that was not "military" history, and in antiquity virtually none. Homer might claim to be the first military historian, and Thucydides is still often considered the greatest, while the Anabasis of Xenophon continued to be read until the eighteenth century, not only for the heroic story it had to tell of the Greco-Persian conflict, but also for its shrewd advice about the conduct of war. The work of the Romans Polybius, Livy, and of course Julius Caesar also survived the so-called Dark Ages to be revived in the Renaissance for their didactic value, as were the more analytic works of Aelian and Vegetius. Medieval military studies were of less value to the practical soldier. They had consisted, on the one hand, of heroic epics such as the Song of Roland, and the anecdotes of the Crusades put together under the title Gesta Dei per Francos, or, a little later, the chronicles of Holinshed and Froissart (to name only the best known); or, on the other, of handbooks of chivalric practice that bore little relation to the grim reality of medieval warfare. It is not surprising that serious students of *war in the sixteenth century turned back to antiquity for guidance, as did Niccolò Machiavelli with his Discourses on Livy, and the Netherlander Justus Lipsius, whose studies of Polybius laid the foundation for the military reforms introduced into Europe by the house of Orange-Nassau that were to transform the conduct of war until the age of Napoleon.

The military historiography of Europe in the sixteenth and early seventeenth centuries was as diffuse and episodic as the nature of warfare itself. It was not until the middle years of the seventeenth century that the simplification of the chaotic Thirty Years' War into a century-long contest between the power of France and the Habsburg Empire made it possible to write histories that were more than chronicles of episodic sieges or, very infrequently, of battles. The works of that epoch that have worn best are the memoirs of the remarkably literate and civilized aristocrats who conducted the wars. In 1660, the vicomte de Turenne published his Memoirs, and the vicomte de Puységur his historically based Instructions Militaires. In 1680, Count Montecuccoli produced his own account of the campaigns he had conducted against the Turks. In these works, historical narrative combined with strategic and tactical analysis to lay the foundation for military history as it was to be understood for the next 200 years.

By the eighteenth century, historians were beginning to study contemporary campaigns as they had previously studied those of classical antiquity, as a guide to military action in the future. The foundation by all major European powers of military colleges for the training of officers created a steady demand for their works. Frederick the Great produced dry but useful accounts of his own campaigns, but the first serious analytic study is usually considered to be that of Henry Humphrey Lloyd on the Seven Years' War, *A History of the Late Wars in Germany,* which was published in 1766 and was translated into German with an extended commentary by G. F. von Tempelhoff in 1783. But this was overtaken in the 1790s by the years of almost continuous warfare unleashed on Europe by the French Revolution and then the Napoleonic era, which was to be accompanied by a deluge of military history that even now shows little sign of diminishing.

To single out any single work on the Napoleonic wars would be invidious, although for English-speaking readers William Napier's *History of the War in the Peninsula* (1828–40) will always enjoy pride of place for its spectacular narratives. The most influential near-contemporary study embracing the whole period, however, was certainly that of Antoine Henri *Jomini, whose *Traité des grandes opérations militaires,* initiated in 1804 and constantly revised until 1851, not only covered the Revolutionary and Napoleonic wars in their entirety but collated them with the campaigns of Frederick the Great in a single synoptic overview of "modern war" that was to be immensely influential throughout the nineteenth century. The historical studies of his contemporary and rival Carl von *Clausewitz, mainly published after that writer's death in 1832 and written primarily as preparatory studies for his subsequent masterpiece On War, made less impact, even within his native Prussia, until his disciple Gen. Helmuth von Moltke made them compulsory reading for the Prussian General Staff beginning in the 1870s.

With von Moltke (1800–1891), the writing of military history underwent a transformation, which was itself part of the general historiographical revolution initiated in Prussia in the nineteenth century by Leopold von Ranke and his followers. The task of the military historian, in the eyes of von Moltke, was to be of service to the military profession, and that historian's primary duty was to discover exactly what had happened in war; a task, in major warfare, of almost impossible complexity. In Moltke's view, all attempts to glorify armies and their commanders, to recreate the horror and splendor of battle, even to draw broad didactic conclusions, had to be subordinated to the precise, scientific description and analysis of events; a task best carried out, not by individuals—certainly not civilian individuals—but by professional research teams under the auspices of the General Staff. The first such study was that which Moltke commissioned, and very largely wrote himself, on the Franco-Austrian War of 1859, which was followed by immensely detailed works on the Austro-Prussian War of 1866 and the Franco-Prussian War of 1870. Thereafter, the War-Historical Section of the German General Staff earned its keep by detailed archival studies of Prussia's earlier wars, until the turn of the century brought it new wars to study, particularly the Anglo-Boer War of 1899–1901 and the Russo-Japanese War of 1904–05.

In this as in all other military matters, Germany set the standards for other military powers. European armies established Historical Sections in their General Staffs to study their own and others' campaigns on a documentary basis, producing works as massive as they are now unreadable. Those of the French are an exception: their studies of military developments in the eighteenth century were models of analysis and readability, and some of their writers, notably Jean Colin, emerged as major military historians in their own right. Colin's *Les transformations de la guerre* (1912) remains one of the best surveys of the development of warfare from antiquity to the twentieth century yet written.

By the beginning of the twentieth century a huge gap had thus opened up in Continental Europe between the narrowly specialized military histories written by military professionals and those addressed to wider audiences by civilian writers, who were often not professional historians at all. It was a highly professional historian who first attempted to reverse the trend, the German Hans Delbrück; who criticized the specialized approach of his military colleagues; and who in 1900 published the first volume of his *Geschichte der Kriegskunst im Rahmen der politische Geschichte (History of the Art of War in the Framework of Military History).* He aroused the wrath both of his academic colleagues and of the German High Command, who were united in the belief that civilians had no business to be meddling in military matters. But his work reintroduced military history into the mainstream of general historiography. Although it would take the best part of half a century for this fully to take effect.

In Britain and the United States, military history never became quite so narrowly specialized as in Continental Europe, for the obvious reason that in those countries the military, let alone its General Staff, commanded far less influence. In Britain it is true that a Historical Section was established at the beginning of the twentieth century under the Committee for Imperial Defence. It published exhaustive studies of the South African and the Russo-Japanese Wars, and did the same with a multivolume history of World War I. Of the latter, the monographs by F. Aspinall Oglander on the Gallipoli and by Cyril Falls on the Salonika Campaigns have some value, but the sheer weight of material overwhelmed the authors of the volumes on the western front, which are now of value only for the source material they provide. In the United States, the War Department first dealt with the history of the *Civil War in a multivolume work, *The War of the Rebellion ... The Official Records of the Union and Confederate Armies* (1880–1901), an invaluable documentary collection that the editors wisely did not attempt to turn into a history, official or otherwise.

Ample material about U.S. military historiography will be found elsewhere in this volume. Here it must suffice to say that, even more than in Britain, military history was regarded as too serious a matter to be left to the military, and even when the U.S. armed forces initiated their massive multivolume surveys of World War II, they employed civilian historians to edit and write them. In both countries the best military history was often written by men of letters who were neither military men nor necessarily academic. For Britain one need only cite Thomas Babington Lord Macaulay's *History of England* (1858–62), with its account of King William's Wars, continued by his great-nephew George Macaulay Trevelyan in *England Under Queen Anne* (1930–34), and the still definitive study of *Marlborough,*

His Life and Times by Winston S. *Churchill (1933–34). In the same genre one can cite the works of Francis Parkman on *France and England in North America* (1865–92). The more general work of George Bancroft and Benjamin Lossing also comes into this category. Academic historians who specialized in the history of war, as did Sir Charles Oman at Oxford with his pioneer studies of war in the Middle Ages and the sixteenth century, were rare, and in universities the study of military history remained marginal.

The most prolific military historians in the early part of the twentieth century, especially in Britain, thus tended to be serving or retired military men; and three of these, Col. G. F. R. Henderson, Col. J. F. C. Fuller, and Capt. B. H. Liddell Hart, were responsible for influential historical studies of the American Civil War. Teaching at the British Staff College at the turn of the century, Henderson focused on the Civil War as the best model for the British military to follow in their future campaigns, and in 1903 published a detailed two-volume study of the campaigns of "Stonewall" *Jackson to show how small forces skillfully led could defeat larger ones. In 1929, Fuller, as part of a project for devising a new theory of war for the industrial age, published a work on *The Generalship of Ulysses S. *Grant;* and the same year Liddell Hart, in vindication of his own theory of "The Indirect Approach," produced a study of William Tecumseh *Sherman. Both these writers, however, were too concerned with promoting their own new approaches to military *strategy to write entirely dispassionate appraisals.

After World War II such detailed and didactic analyzes fell out of favor. The scope of that war was too vast to be covered by detailed campaign histories; and although these appeared in plenty from both official and unofficial authors, the planners of both the American and the British official histories arranged to cover political, economic, and social aspects of the war as well. The official German history, *Das Deutsche Reich und der Zweiten Weltkrieg,* which began to appear in 1979 and is also written by civilian historians, is even more eclectic in its approach. These cooperative projects not only broadened the scope of military history; they introduced the subject to many young professional historians who were later to make it their life study.

It was now that Delbrück was to come into his own. *Military history* became almost too narrow a term to embrace the expanded studies of war that were written by professional historians after World War II. Seminal was Karl Ritter's four-volume study of the German military before and during World War I, *Staatskunst und Kriegshandwerk* (1954–68), which followed Delbrück in placing the history of the German army in its political and social context. Also influential was a new translation of Clausewitz's *On War* (published by Princeton in 1976), which revived interest not only in Clausewitz's definition of war as a political act, but in his reminder that the conduct of war varies, chameleonlike, with differences in national and regional culture. In Britain and the United States, military historians cooperated with their colleagues in the political and social sciences in joint projects of war studies, strategic studies, war and society studies, and even peace studies. In the disturbed international environment of the *Cold War, some of those attracted the support of the armed forces and of private foundations.

Past eras were reexamined to discover, not so much how wars were fought as why they were fought in the way that they were, and how warfare influenced and was influenced by the structure and ideology of the societies that fought them. The work of Geoffrey Parker on Europe in the early seventeenth century, of André Corvisier on France in the *ancien régime,* of Peter Paret on Prussia in the Revolutionary and Napoleonic era, are only a few examples of what was becoming known in the United States as "the New Military History." The old military history, however, did not fall out of favor, as much of the huge quantity of studies published about the Civil War during and after the centenary of that conflict bears ample witness. Meanwhile, British military historians continue to rake over the embers of the campaigns of World War II in search of relics of their nation's era as a great military power. Recently, however, military historians of various nationalities have been devoting increasing attention to the complex and tragic campaigns of World War I, while writers of American military history have also reexamined the Korean and Vietnam Wars.

Military history, in fact, for long an area neglected by professional historians, has now become a nucleus whose splitting and expansion is causing an explosion, the creative potential of which is still far from being exhausted.

[*See also:* Napoleonic Warfare; War: Nature of War.]

—Michael Howard

DISCIPLINARY VIEWS OF WAR: PEACE HISTORY

Only recently have some historians begun to integrate peace research into scholarship as a legitimate alternative perspective on the past. Previously, to the extent that pacifists, peace advocates, and peace movements were even included in historical monographs and textbooks, they were usually treated negatively—denounced as misguided idealism or even traitorous.

Since the 1960s, however, the number of peace history scholars has grown significantly. The field itself—defined as the historical study of nonviolent efforts for peace and social justice—has become widely recognized, accepted as a subfield of the discipline of history, and as part of a larger multidisciplinary approach known as Peace Studies.

In 1995, the primary professional association, the Peace History Society (PHS; formerly the Conference on Peace Research in History) had nearly 300 members, mainly in the United States and Canada. Founded in 1964 after the *Cuban Missile Crisis, the organization grew during the *Vietnam War, and again during the international tensions of the late 1970s and early 1980s. An affiliate of the American Historical Association, recognized as a significant nongovernmental organization by the *United Nations, the Peace History Society sponsors sessions at the annual conferences of leading historical associations. It also publishes a newsletter and a quarterly journal, *Peace & Change: A Journal of Peace Research.*

Peace historians generally see themselves as engaged scholars, involved in the study of *peace and *war, and in efforts to eliminate or at least restrict armaments, *conscription, nuclear proliferation, colonialism, racism, sexism, and war. As a social reform movement, the work of peace historians presents alternatives to the policies they oppose.

Peace history can be classified into three categories. First, *conflict management,* which involves achieving peace through negotiation, mediation, arbitration, international law, and *arms control and disarmament. Second, *social* *reform*, which involves changing political and economic structures and traditional ways of thinking. Third, a *world order transformation*, which incorporates world federation, better economic and environmental relationships, and a common feeling of security.

The discipline's basic focus has been historical analysis of *peace and antiwar movements and individuals, international relations, and the causes of war and peace. Two pioneering works in the field were Merle Curti, *Peace or War: The American Struggle, 1636–1936* (1936), and Arthur A. Ekirch, Jr., *The Civilian and the Military: A History of the American Antimilitarist Tradition* (1956).

In the 1960s, a new generation of peace historians, seeking to understand and legitimate past movements for peace and social justice, produced monographs about peace movements and biographies of pacifists and other social activists. Among the pathbreaking works were the 328-volume reprint series, *The Garland Library of War and Peace* (1973–75), edited by Charles Chatfield, Blanche Wiesen Cook, and Sandi Cooper; Peter Brock's study of religious sectarian views, *Pacifism in the United States: From the Colonial Era to the First World War* (1968); Sondra R. Herman's study of peace advocates, *Eleven Against War* (1969); Charles Chatfield, *For Peace and Justice: Pacifism in America, 1914–1941* (1971); Lawrence S. Wittner, *Rebels Against War: The American Peace Movement, 1933–1983* (1969, 2nd ed. 1984); and the PHS-sponsored reference work, *Biographical Dictionary of Peace Leaders* (1985), edited by Harold Josephson.

Numerous monographs surveyed the secular and religious peace movements in the United States in the decades between the 1880s and the 1960s. One of the most prolific authors was Charles DeBenedetti. Before his early death, DeBenedetti edited a work about *Peace Heroes in Twentieth-Century America* (1986); wrote a synthesis and textbook, *The Peace Reform in American History* (1980); and started a study of the *Vietnam antiwar movement, *An American Ordeal* (1990), (completed by Charles Chatfield). A memorial conference to DeBenedetti resulted in Melvin Small and William D. Hoover, eds., *Give Peace a Chance: Exploring the Vietnam Antiwar Movement* (1992).

New subspecialties have appeared in the 1990s, including studies of women and peace, such as Harriet Hyman Alonso, *Peace as a Women's Issue* (1993); and studies of *conscientious objection, such as Charles C. Moskos and John Whiteclay Chambers II, *The New Conscientious Objection* (1993).

The new frontiers in the field today also include transnational studies such as Lawrence S. Wittner's trilogy, *The Struggle Against the Bomb: A History of the World Nuclear Disarmament Movement Through 1953*, 3 vols. (1993–); the relationship between political culture and peace movements, as in Charles Chatfield and Peter van den Dungen, eds., *Peace Movements and Political Cultures* (1988); and the linking of peace movements with social movement theory, as in Charles Chatfield with Robert Kleidman, *American Peace Movement* (1992).

A recent debate, initiated in the January 1995 issue of *Peace & Change*, involves the degree of influence peace history has had on foreign policy or attitudes toward international relations, and whether peace history should seek greater acceptance and influence within mainstream American history or emphasize a separate, activist ethos.

[*See also*: Pacifism.]

• Blanche Wiesen Cook, ed., *Bibliography on Peace Research in History*, 1969. John Whiteclay Chambers II, ed., *The Eagle and the Dove: The American Peace Movement and United States Foreign Policy, 1900–1922*, 1976; 2nd ed. 1991. Berenice Carroll, Jane E. Mohraz, and Clinton Fink, eds, *Peace and War: Guide to Bibliographies*, 1982. Merle Curti, "Reflections on the Genesis and Growth of Peace History," *Peace & Change* (Spring 1985). Charles F. Howlett, *The American Peace Movement: History and Historiography*, 1985. Charles F. Howlett, *The American Peace Movement: References and Resources*, 1991. Charles Chatfield, ed., "Peacemaking in American History," *OAH Magazine of History* (Spring 1994). Frances Early, *A World Without War: How U.S. Feminists and Pacifists Resisted World War I*, 1997.
—Charles F. Howlett

DISCIPLINARY VIEWS OF WAR: POLITICAL SCIENCE AND INTERNATIONAL RELATIONS

The study of *war in the West goes back to the time of Thucydides, who averred that the cause of the Peloponnesian War was "the growth of Athenian power and the fear this caused in Sparta." The founding of the modern discipline of international relations, however, did not occur until the end of World War I with the endowment of the world's first chair in International Politics at Aberystwyth, Wales. This institutionalization of the field was a result of Wilsonian thinking prevalent at the end of the war that through the use of reason and the spread of education the causes of war could be discovered and eliminated. The rise of Nazi Germany and militaristic Japan led to the collapse of the *League of Nations and the emergence of a "realist" school, which criticized the "idealists" for failing to understand and use power. The credit for shifting the field of international relations from idealist advocacy to realist analysis is usually given to Hans J. Morgenthau's *Politics Among Nations* (1948).

Explanations that emphasize the shifts in power and the struggle for power are the hallmark of the realist school of international relations, which claims Thucydides, Machiavelli, Hobbes, and Carl Von *Clausewitz as its forebears. Realists tend to see war as endemic and a natural occurrence with shifts in power often associated with the onset of war. In the contemporary period, Hans J. Morgenthau, Kenneth N. Waltz, and Robert Gilpin represent the most important thinkers of this school, but none of them has a precise explanation of war. Waltz sees the anarchic nature of the international system (the absence of some form of world governing structure) as a "permissive" cause of war, that is, there is nothing in the system to prevent states from resorting to war any time they choose. But what brings about war in any given instance is not specified. Gilpin comes closest to stipulating the conditions that lead to war by maintaining that the largest wars come about when a rising ascendent *state challenges the dominant hegemony of the system. However, he sees this as only a necessary condition of war, which means that the sufficient conditions are unspecified. Likewise, his explanation leaves unexplained the vast number of interstate wars that do not involve the two strongest states in the system.

Realist work often tends to support its explanations with argumentation and historical analysis. In the late 1950s and early 1960s, the behavioral movement in political science criticized this approach because it tended to "ransack history" by looking for cases that would support its explanations while ignoring evidence that contradicted them. These "behavioralists" wanted to apply the scientific method to the search for the causes of war. They were inspired by the early work of Lewis F. Richardson, who pioneered the use of mathematical models and statistical data analysis to study war and by Quincy Wright, who employed a broad interdisciplinary approach in his seminal study on the causes of war. J. David Singer founded the Correlates of War project and, building on the efforts of Richardson and Wright, began collecting data on war, capability, and alliances in the hopes that empirical research would be able to delineate patterns as a step toward constructing scientific explanations. A number of other researchers developed and tested scientific explanations of war focusing on capability. These included Organski and Kugler's *power transition,* Modelski and Thompson's *long cycle,* Charles Doran's *power cycle,* and Bueno de Mesquita's *expected utility models* (see Midlarsky, 2000).

Empirical research has produced a number of findings that have not been supportive of simple realist explanations, particularly the notion that a balance of power is associated with peace, or that a disruption of it is associated with war. Singer, Bremer, and Stuckey (in Singer, 1979) find that parity (relative balance) in the international system is associated with a *low magnitude* of war in the nineteenth century, but with a *high magnitude* of war in the twentieth century. Neither parity nor a preponderance of power in the system is associated with the complete absence of war. A follow-up study by Bueno de Mesquita (1981) found no relationship between capability distribution and periods of war or peace in either century. The evidence overall implies that while capability distributions may in certain contexts be associated with wars of high or low magnitude, no particular type of capability distribution is associated with *peace. One of the reasons for this, as Bueno de Mesquita points out, is that a balance of power usually implies a fifty-fifty chance of winning a war, and thus will only inhibit risk-averse leaders. Later work by Bueno de Mesquita and Lalman demonstrates the importance of supplementing power calculations with an analysis of domestic political factors in order to explain the decision to go to war.

Realists often assert that alliance making, because it is usually a result of attempts to balance power, can be a force for peace. The research of Jack Levy (1981) raises questions about this claim since he finds that from 1495 to 1975, with the exception of the nineteenth century, most great power alliances (56 percent to 100 percent) have been followed by war within five years. An even more pernicious effect of alliances uncovered by researchers focusing on the post-1815 period is that once war breaks out, alliances can act as a contagion mechanism to expand war.

Among the major states, war does not usually break out with the first crisis. Leng (1983) and Brecher and Wilkenfeld (1997) show that as states go from one crisis to the next, the probability of war goes way up. To date, empirical research has found that the crises that escalate tend to have the following characteristics: they are triggered by physical threats to vital issues; they are one in a series of repeated confrontations, with realpolitik tactics becoming more coercive; a hostile interaction spiral emerges; and there is an ongoing *arms race.

Of these findings, the most controversial is that linking arms races and crisis escalation, first enunciated by Michael Wallace. Paul Diehl (1983) has questioned the validity and reliability of Wallace's (1982) arms race index and was unable to replicate it. Nevertheless, Diehl's own research shows a relationship between escalation to war and some sort of measure of military buildup and defense burden. Subsequent research by Susan Semple (1997), using Diehl's index shows that, except for where nuclear weapons are present, most disputes occurring in the presence of an ongoing mutual military build up will result in war within five years. She, as with others, also finds that it is extremely rare for disputes in the absence of a military buildup escalate to war.

The findings on alliances, crises, and military buildups have led Vasquez (1993) to argue that power politics itself constitutes a series of steps to war, each of which when taken increases the probability of war between equal states. This suggests that in order to bring about a peaceful system, states must transcend the power politics game and develop ways of making authoritative decisions in the absence of government on some basis other than coercive diplomacy. Research that tries to identify the characteristics of peaceful systems has shown that such systems exhibit efforts to develop a set of "rules of the game" among major states, and embody an acceptance of the *pacta sunt servanda* (agreements must be kept) norm in international law. This suggests, contrary to realism, that the world is not always in a constant war of all against all.

Other research shows that war may be confined to states that have a certain kind of relationship or contend over certain types of issues. Research by Russett (1993) and by Ray (1995) has shown that democracies rarely fight each other. This is thought to be a result of domestic constraints placed on democratic governments by their publics and/or that democratic states develop norms in dealing with each other that promote the resolution of conflict without resorting to armed force. This set of findings supports the idea of a liberal peace promulgated by Kant and recently articulated by Michael Doyle.

Such findings raise the possibility that there might be other zones of peace. Most interstate wars are fought between neighbors; in fact, the only wars not fought between neighbors are those involving major states. For some, this finding suggests that states fight primarily over territorial issues (see Hensel, 1996) and that the probability of war is highest when territorial disputes between equals are handled in a power politics fashion. Vasquez predicts that once neighbors settle their border claims, the probability of their fighting will go way down even if other contentious issues arise.

Research on the termination and impact of war has produced clearer findings than those on the causes of war. States with more revenue have won almost 80 percent of their wars, and states that have suffered a lower percentage of battle deaths in proportion to their population have won about 75 percent of their wars. Being both wealthier and having lost a lower percent of population increases the probability of *victory to 84 percent. Typically, major states defeated in world wars recover, in terms of economic power, in about fifteen to twenty years. World wars are frequently associated with shifts in global leadership, with third parties sometimes benefiting the most. Domestically, world wars tend to increase the power and size of the state, giving it a permanent increase in its tax revenue and expanding its expenditures (Rasler and Thompson, 1989).

[*See also* Disciplinary Views of War: Causes-of-War Studies.]

• Quincy Wright, *A Study of War*, 1942. Lewis F. Richardson, *Statistics of Deadly Quarrels*, 1960. David Singer, ed., *The Correlates of War*, Vols. 1 and 2, 1979, 1980. Bruce Bueno de Mesquita, "Risk, Power Distributions, and the Likelihood of War," *International Studies Quarterly*, 25 (December 1981), pp. 541–68. Jack S. Levy, "Alliance Formation and War Behavior," *Journal of Conflict Resolution*, 25 (December 1981), pp. 581–613. Michael D. Wallace, "Armaments and Escalation: Two Competing Hypotheses," *International Studies Quarterly*, 26 (March 1982), pp. 37–56. Paul F. Diehl, "Armaments and Escalation: A Closer Look," *Journal of Peace Research*, vol. 20, no. 3 (1983), pp. 205–12. Russell J. Leng, "When Will They Ever Learn?" *Journal of Conflict Resolution*, 27 (September 1983), pp. 379–419. Michael Doyle, "Liberalism and World Politics," *American Political Science Review*, 80 (December 1986), pp. 1151–69. Karen Rasler and William R. Thompson, *War and State Making*, 1989. Bruce Bueno de Mesquita and David Lalman, *War and Reason*, 1992. Bruce Russett, *Grasping the Democratic Peace*, 1993. John A. Vasquez, *The War Puzzle*, 1993. James Lee Ray, *Democracy and International Conflict*, 1995. Paul F. Hensel, "Charting a Course to Conflict: Territorial Issues and Interstate Conflict, 1816–1992," *Conflict Management and Peace Science*, 15 (Spring 1996), pp. 43–73. Michael Brecher and Jonathan Wilkenfeld, *A Study of Crisis*, 1997. Susan G. Semple, "Arms Races and Dispute Escalation: Resolving the Debate," *Journal of Peace Research*, 34 (February 1997), pp. 7–22. Manus Midlarsky, ed., *Handbook of War Studies*, 2nd ed., 2000.   —John A. Vasquez

DISCIPLINARY VIEWS OF WAR: PSYCHOLOGY

Psychology in the United States became a recognized discipline mainly through work during World War I with the War Department, which needed psychological tests to identify trainable recruits. Work to support American military efforts continued in subsequent decades, particularly during World War II, on such issues as personnel selection, combat training, psychological warfare, and therapy for war-affected soldiers. After 1945, researchers increasingly analyzed the psychological origins of *war. Psychological study of war has expanded recently in part because of the brutality and pervasiveness of ethnopolitical wars, which have powerful emotional dimensions.

Such studies of the origins of war and paths toward *peace employ diverse methodologies. Although much research has focused on individual leaders and their decisions, questions have been raised about the accuracy of psychohistorical studies; the limits of retrospective case studies, interview methods, and content analyses of archival documents; the difficulties of extrapolating from laboratory studies and computer simulations to the real world; and the problems of separating individual actors from the multifaceted, institutional context in which they function. To move beyond individual analyses, psychologists have adopted more appropriate strategies of conducting actual field experiments and case studies of groups, or of measuring attitudes and group behavior in situations of armed conflict. Political psychologists have emphasized the need to embed psychological analysis in a multidisciplinary matrix.

Reflecting the "nature-nurture" controversy that has pervaded psychology, research has examined whether human aggression and war are biologically determined or rooted in learning and political socialization. Studies suggest a universal tendency to separate the in group from the out group and to favor the former while derogating the latter. Some individual *aggression and violence stems from genetic factors, although these interact extensively with ex-

periential factors throughout life. Yet little evidence supports the universality of war, as nearly 20 percent of preindustrial societies neither fight wars nor engage in preparations for war.

Controversy exists over the extent to which destructive conflict arises through competition over scarce resources. Henri Tajfel established that destructive conflict also stems from social categorizations that order one's social world and define one's identity and place in society. Social identity theory posits that people strive for a positive identity and compare their in group with relevant out groups, creating status competition that animates conflict. The quest for positive social identity helps to fuel *nationalism. These theories may be integrated into a more comprehensive framework, since groups compete both for positive identity and status and for scarce resources. Groups often compete for legitimacy, too, and violence may result when a group's identity needs go unmet. Morton Deutsch has integrated cognitive and social competition processes by establishing that conflicting groups often create a malignant social process characterized by excessive competition, cognitive rigidity, misjudgments and unwitting commitments, self-fulfilling prophecies, and vicious, escalating spirals.

Socially constructed memories and perceptions also contribute to inter-group tensions and war. Vamik Volkan noted that unjustly treated groups often enshrine their victimization in chosen traumas that are passed down through generations and that invite future conflict.

Misperceptions contribute to tensions and war. Although real divergences of interest and enmities fuel wars and arms races, biased perceptions often lead to exaggerated fear, hostility, and enmity. In *Fearful Warriors*, Ralph K. White established that strong fears on both sides during the *Cold War created images that portrayed the other as thoroughly diabolical, aggressive, and untrustworthy. Enemy images encouraged the attribution of hostile motives for diverse behaviors, blocked empathy, dehumanized the other, enabled blaming and human rights abrogations, and provided a tool for politicians to stir public fears and rally support for sustained, high levels of military spending. This suggests that it is psychologically advantageous to have enemies, leading people to create enemies even where none exist in reality. When fear and dehumanization are particularly strong, groups may exclude their adversaries from the moral universe, thereby removing restraints that ordinarily limit atrocities. Still, some have criticized White for emphasizing perceptions over hard realities in a Hobbesian environment and for privileging fear over power as the dominant motive behind war.

Diverse processes can skew a leader's decision making particularly under conditions of high stress and uncertainty. Flawed decisions often reflect cognitive limitations, which lead people to use mental heuristics or shortcuts. For example, in the *availability* strategy, one judges a current situation by comparing it with a well-established, readily available pattern in memory. Thus, leaders concerned over the appeasement of Adolf *Hitler at the Munich Conference and his escalating demands might interpret present crises in terms of that pattern, even if the new case does not actually apply. Because of memory limitations, human beings often function as "cognitive misers," who oversimplify and draw lessons from history on a highly selective basis.

Robert Jervis, Richard Ned Lebow, and Janice Gross

Stein have criticized nuclear *deterrence policies by showing that leaders frequently make biased estimates of their adversary's strength, intent, and willingness to fight. However, Philip Tetlock noted that debates about nuclear deterrence are highly speculative since they typically rely on counterfactual arguments such as "What would have happened if event X had or had not occurred?" Much debate continues about whether psychological research is policy-relevant and when it is legitimate for scientists to advocate particular policies.

The interplay of cognitive and small group processes was emphasized by Irving Janis, who showed how U.S. leaders sometimes succumbed to making flawed decisions (e.g., the Bay of Pigs invasion) due to groupthink—a group process in which there is an illusion of invulnerability, unquestioned belief in the group's morality, censorship of dissent, and premature quest for consensus, among other factors. Although Janis underestimated subtle political influences on decision makers' judgments, he identified significant, preventable sources of bad decisions.

Recently, significant growth has occurred in the nascent field of peace psychology, which seeks to prevent destructive conflict at all levels. Scholar-practitioners such as Herbert Kelman have pioneered the use of problem-solving workshops to advance the nonviolent resolution of the Israeli-Palestinian conflict. Recognizing that victims often become perpetrators of violence, some psychologists have developed interventions for healing psychological wounds of war and for promoting collective forgiveness and reconciliation. Interested readers should consult *Peace and Conflict: Journal of Peace Psychology*.

[*See also:* Enemy, Views of the; Psychological Warfare.]

• Henri Tajfel and John Turner, "An Integrative Theory of Intergroup Conflict," in W.G. Austin and S. Worchel, eds., *The Social Psychology of Intergroup Relations*, 1979. Irving Janis, *Victims of Groupthink*, 1982. Morton Deutsch, "Preventing World War III: A Psychological Perspective," *Political Psychology*, 3 (1983), pp. 3–31. Ralph K. White, *Fearful Warriors*, 1984. Robert Jervis, Richard Ned Lebow, and Janice Gross Stein, *Psychology and Deterrence*, 1985. Ralph K. White, ed., *Psychology and the Prevention of Nuclear War*, 1986. Steven Kull, *Minds at War: Nuclear Reality and the Inner Conflicts of Defense Policymakers*, 1988. Philip E. Tetlock, Charles B. McGuire, and Gregory Mitchell, "Psychological Perspectives on Nuclear Deterrence," *Annual Review of Psychology*, 1991. Herbert H. Blumberg and Christopher C. French, *Peace Abstracts of the Psychological and Behavioral Literature 1967–1990*, 1992. Herbert H. Kelman, "The Interactive Problem-Solving Approach," in Chester A. Crocker, Fen Osler Hampson, and Pamela Aall, eds., *Managing Global Chaos*, 1996, pp. 501–20. Vamik Volkan, *Bloodlines*, 1997.

—Michael Wessells

DISCIPLINARY VIEWS OF WAR: SOCIETY STUDIES

Although *war is one of the most important human social activities, the study of war in its social context has remained marginal to both sociology and war studies. Sociology has tended to treat war as an abnormal intrusion into the regularities of social life, rather than a major social institution in its own right. War studies have tended to focus on political, military-strategic, and technological aspects more than on the social or cultural aspects of war.

War and society represents an interdisciplinary area with diverse inputs, and the body of theory is diffuse in origin. Classic strategic thought contains important sociological insights, notably in Carl von *Clausewitz's presentation of war as a type of social action with a distinct logic centering on the mobilization of aggression and violence. He saw war as a unique means of pursuing political goals, but also as analogous to commerce—war is produced in the social organization of men and weapons, which have to be tested in battle rather as the value of commodities has to be realized in the marketplace.

Few social theorists have followed Clausewitz in addressing the character of war as a social activity. Rare exceptions include the Marxian approach of Mary Kaldor, in her study of the oversophistication of Western military technology, *The Baroque Arsenal* (1982), and Martin Shaw's *Dialectics of War* (1988). More orthodox Marxists have tended to reduce war to its political and economic context—looking for social causes—rather than understanding the peculiarities of the kind of social action that war involves. Major sociological theorists of the late twentieth century, such as Theda Skocpol, *States and Revolutions* (1979), Anthony Giddens, *The Nation-State and Violence* (1985), and Michael Mann, *The Sources of Social Power* (1986 and 1993), have also followed this trend by addressing the role of war in the development of states, rather than the nature of armed violence.

More empirically, the field of military sociology has examined military organizations as social institutions. Originating in sociological and psychological studies during World War II, this field burgeoned from the 1960s as Western militaries began the transition from mass armies to an *All-Volunteer force, with such seminal works as Morris Janowitz's *The Professional Soldier* (1961) and Jacques van Doorn's *The Soldier and Social Change* (1975). Military sociology is institutionalized in an international network, the Inter-University Seminar on Armed Forces and Society, which promotes institutionally focused comparative research. It deals less with issues of the wider influence of military values in society, explored for example, in Shaw's *Post-Military Society* (1991).

The majority of war and society studies are historical in character. A few major synthetic social histories, such as William H. MacNeill's *The Pursuit of Power* (1982), have demonstrated the relationships between military organization and weaponry and social, economic, and political change over the modern period as a whole. Some military historians, such as Michael Howard, have written about war in a way that emphasizes its social contexts. Rarely, sociologists have also applied their theoretical insights to past conflicts, as in Tony Ashworth's *Trench Warfare 1914–18: The Live-and-Let-Live System* (1982).

Most historical work is by social historians specializing in a particular period, and concerned with the social effects rather than the causes of war. The largest number of works concerns the two world wars, especially World War II. A central concern is the role of war in causing or accelerating socioeconomic transformations. In a series of works including *War and Social Change* (1974), Arthur Marwick has made a wide-ranging and influential exploration of these relationships. More specialist authors have addressed particular issues such as propaganda, media and culture, and the changes in the status of women and ethnic minorities through participation in war. Feminist historians have particularly contested the assertion of a positive relationship between war and social change, in respect of gender roles.

This assertion is, in any case, a culturally specific

notion, strongly linked to experiences of war in societies like America and Britain that were victorious and uninvaded in both global conflicts. Other experiences of world war—notably in Continental Europe and East and Southeast Asia—were manifestly more disastrous for social groups and entire national societies. The links between total war and *genocide, not only in the politically calculated mass murders of the Nazis and others but also in the technological mass killings of strategic and atomic bombing, bring into question many of the assumptions in studies based on Anglo-American experiences.

A similar problem is manifest in the general absence of studies of post-1945 conflicts. Because these wars have occurred mainly in the so-called Third World and outside advanced Western countries, less academic attention has been devoted to relationships between war and social change here. During the *Cold War period, distant conflicts were mainly of interest for their strategic relevance to the central world division.

Since 1989, it has become evident that wars, in the former Yugoslavia and Soviet Union as well as in Africa, concern complex ethnic, religious, and other social divisions as well as the rivalries of political and military elites. The relationship between war and genocide has once more come to the fore. The role of mass media—not only as propaganda machines in combatant states, but as sources of critical information propelling Western states and the *United Nations into action—has been the subject of numerous studies. This reflects the central fact that for Western societies, wars are no longer arenas of mass *mobilization and direct participation, but mediated experiences.

With the end of the Cold War, therefore, military studies and international relations have partially shifted their focus from strategic and weapons-related issues to the broader social and political context of armed conflict. In this sense, a broadly sociological approach has become more widely influential. The more disciplinary based sociological or sociohistorical study of war, however, remains concentrated on past conflicts and has yet to show much of its relevance to contemporary wars.

[See also: Bombing of Civilians; Gender; Gender and War; Propaganda and Public Relations, Government; Society and War.]
—Martin Shaw

DISEASE, TROPICAL. Tropical disease has plagued American forces from the colonial period to modern times. Malaria, dysentery, dengue, and yellow fever (all endemic to the United States), as well as schistosomiasis, yaws, leishmaniasis, filariasis, and scrub typhus (all from other areas), have decimated garrisons and overwhelmed combat troops. To conquer or contain tropical disease, the U.S. military, sometimes cooperating with civilian scientists, developed preventive techniques, therapies, and cures. Collaborative research controlled and even vanquished most tropical diseases except for malaria, whose parasite became immune to traditional antimalarials, and whose prevention and cure remain elusive.

The military historically follows standard civilian practice regarding contagion, diagnosis, and treatment. Before the *Civil War, physicians did not suspect mosquitoes as transmitters, blamed fever on the climate or air, and often could not distinguish one fever from another, treating them with emetics, chinchona bark, bleeding, mercury,

wine, aromatics, snakeroot, or arsenic compounds. During the *Mexican War, physicians at the Veracruz hospital treated yellow fever with quinine sulfate, first extracted from chinchona bark in 1820, to reduce the fever; mustard plasters and baths to help the circulation; and mercurials to evacuate the bowels. About 28 percent of victims died in the spring and summer of 1847. More prevalent was diarrhea or dysentery, which accounted for one-third of all hospital admissions. Quinine proved highly beneficial in treating malaria. During the Civil War, the *Union army had plenty of quinine, but the disease scourged the *Confederate army, which occupied infested areas and had limited supplies. Better sanitation in the post–Civil War period helped curtail communicable disease among troops.

The *Spanish-American War (1898) forced the U.S. Army to lead a fight against tropical disease. American forces could not garrison the islands they had won without controlling yellow fever, typhoid, malaria, and dengue. The work of Maj. William C. *Gorgas of the Medical Corps in Havana (1899) and (as colonel) in Panama (1904–06) in preventive medicine halted epidemics of typhoid, dysentery, and yellow fever, and made possible construction of the Panama Canal. Maj. Walter *Reed and the Army Medical Board in the autumn and winter of 1900–1901 proved scientifically that the mosquito served as intermediate host for the yellow fever parasite. Reed was indebted to Dr. Carlos Finlay of Cuba, Sir Patrick Manson of Britain, and Maj. Ronald Ross of the British army, each of whom had helped prove that the mosquito was the carrier of disease. Their research pioneered the science of tropical medicine. During the early twentieth century, army medical research boards, such as the Philippine Tropical Disease Board, conducted investigations and began control measures that drastically reduced disease around U.S. bases at home and overseas.

By World War II, the development of vaccines, due largely to support from the Rockefeller Foundation, had eliminated yellow fever and typhus. Improvement of field sanitation controlled the dysenteries. Wartime research under the aegis of the National Research Council improved chemotherapy for the prevention and treatment of malaria and secured development of a powerful insecticide: DDT. Those advances, plus the work of army and navy malaria control units, and the enforcement of malaria discipline by personnel (taking atabrine tablets and wearing protective clothing) reduced incidence to historic lows. In the Southwest Pacific, monthly rates fell from 251 per 1,000 in December 1943 to 62 per 1,000 in November 1944: malaria no longer impeded campaigns.

During the *Vietnam War, however, despite research to find better antimalarial drugs or a vaccine, chloroquine-resistent falciparum malaria from Southeast Asia threatened the U.S. armed forces. Drug-resistant malaria continues to be the most important military medical problem of the tropics.

[See also Caribbean and Latin America, U.S. Military Involvement in the; Casualties.]

• E. C. Andrus et al., eds., *Advances in Military Medicine Made by American Investigators Working Under the Sponsorsphip of the Committee on Medical Research*, 1948. John Z. Bowers and Elizabeth F. Purcell, eds., *Advances in American Medicine: Essays at the Bicentennial*, vols. 1, and 2, 1976. François Delaporte, *The History of Yellow Fever. An Essay on the Birth of Tropical Medicine*, 1991. Mary Ellen

Condon-Rall and Albert E. Cowdrey, *The Medical Department: Medical Service in the War Against Japan,* 1998.
—Mary Ellen Condon-Rall

DISEASES, SEXUALLY TRANSMITTED. Venereal diseases, or as the military currently defines them, sexually transmitted diseases (STDs), occur most often in sexually active people less than twenty-four years of age. Because military forces historically have consisted of mostly young people, predominantly young men, often sexually active, the incidence of STD in military personnel has always been two to three times that of a similar matched group of civilians. This rate can rise five to eight times higher during wartime.

Some form of STDs seems to have plagued military forces from earliest recorded history. Herodotus in the fifth century B.C.E. wrote that Scythian soldiers who pillaged the Celestial Temple of Venus were infected with a "female disease" that afflicted all of their descendants. The first recorded cases of syphilis appeared in Europe in 1493 supposedly among Spanish sailors returning from the New World. Spanish and French armies soon spread what was called the "Neapolitan disease" or the "French pox" throughout Europe.

Historically, two methods have been advocated for controlling rates of STDs in the U.S. military: punishment of soldiers and support for regulation of civilian conveyors of the disease through regular examination and treatment of prostitutes. Traditionally when rates became high, particularly in wartime, regulation was enforced; when rates returned to baseline levels, the military either ignored the problem or relied upon punitive action. Such shifts in policy occurred during the *Civil War, the *Spanish-American War, and World War I. The primary reason was that the methods of treatment, which consisted chiefly of local applications of antiseptics (containing arsenic, mercury, and bismuth), were only marginally effective. In addition, infected soldiers often did not develop a persistent and immediately debilitating illness, although they often became asymptomatic and infectious carriers. During World War I, the military public health authorities sought to eliminate prostitution in the areas around U.S. military and naval bases.

During World War II, the public health authorities encouraged publicity about venereal disease, breaking a long taboo on public discussion. The advent of antibiotics, especially penicillin, had a dramatic impact on STDs, primarily gonorrhea and syphilis. Another effective preventive measure was the use of condoms, which were distributed to all members of the armed forces.

STDs reemerged as a major problem in the military in the 1960s and 1970s as a result of several new developments. In the wider society, the "sexual revolution" in attitudes and behavior meant that sexual encounters were more readily accepted as a social norm. There was also indiscriminate use of antibiotics, thus reducing their effectiveness. And in 1976, new resistant strains of gonorrhea emerged first in the Far East, then in the United States which within a decade rendered many antibiotic treatments useless. Further, new sexually-transmitted viral agents emerged: herpes; venereal warts (Papilloma virus); hepatitis B; and the deadly *AIDS virus, HIV.

STDs have always been a problem for the military. Attempts to control them by changing behavior have had a significant, if temporary, impact. But recent resistant microorganisms and new STDs threaten to bring back the high prevalence rate that existed before antibiotics.

[*See also* Casualties; Demography and War.]

• U.S. Army, Medical Department, *Preventive Medicine in World War II,* Vol. V: *Communicable Diseases,* ed. John B. Coates, Ebbe C. Haff, and Phebe M. Hoff, 1960. Stanhope Bayne-Jones, *The Evolution of Preventive Medicine in the United States Army, 1606–1939,* 1968. Edmund C. Tramont, "AIDS and Its Impact on Medical Readiness," *Military Review,* 6 (1990), pp. 48–58.
—Edmund C. Tramont

DIX, DOROTHEA (1802–1887), humanitarian, Union Superintendent of Women Nurses in the *Civil War. Born in Hampden, Maine, Dix spent her life as a social activist, dedicated to improving the care and treatment of the insane. Beginning in 1841, she spearheaded the movement to establish asylums—as a social responsibility and financed by public funds—to replace the jails and almshouses in which the mentally impaired were confined. She was responsible, through her remarkable ability to influence people and legislatures, for the founding or enlarging of more than thirty mental hospitals in the United States and abroad.

With the outbreak of the Civil War she offered her services, gratis, to the secretary of war in April 1861. She was given the responsibility "to select and assign women nurses to general and permanent military hospitals." Two months later, she was named Superintendent of Women Nurses.

Dix rented a house in Washington at her own expense, advertised nationally for volunteers, and weeded out those she thought physically or morally unsuitable. She accepted only nurses over thirty years of age and refused to allow Roman Catholic nuns or other religious orders to serve. Independent, autocratic, eccentric, working outside of established lines of authority and assuming powers beyond her responsibility, she antagonized the medical establishment. Military doctors, supported by the U.S. Sanitary Commission, resented her domineering intrusions. Although her authority was reaffirmed by Surgeon General William A. Hammond in July 1862, in October of that year Secretary of War Edwin M. *Stanton issued an order that gave the appointment, assignment, and control of nurses to hospital surgeons and medical directors. Dix was left without authority. She continued to work in the hospitals in the Washington area, however, and did not relinquish her title as superintendent until September 1866.

Dix returned to her interest in the insane. In 1881, ill, she accepted an apartment offered to her at the New Jersey State Hospital in Trenton, where she lived until her death.

[*See also* Sanitary Commission, U.S.]

• Francis Tiffany, *Life of Dorothea Lynde Dix,* 1890. David Gollaher, *Voice for the Mad: The Life of Dorothea Dix,* 1995.
—David L. Cowen

DOCTRINE, MILITARY. In any modern army's hierarchy of professional concerns, military doctrine is ranked near the top. Theoretically, a nation's grand strategy sets the terms of reference for its military strategy, which in turn dictates the character of its military doctrines. As a practical matter, however, doctrine behaves much like any other complex of ideas and is governed by the same considerations as those that influence evolving schools of thought. Framed in this way by its historical and strategic context, military doctrine aims at prescribing the manner in which an armed force will fight.

Fighting doctrines always have been expressions of their time and place, much as any other artifact of military history. Any armed force operates in accordance with a conception of war that evolves as a consequence of its history, the state of military knowledge available to it, the technology at hand, the objectives to which the force expects to be committed, and, not least, the caliber of those who must attempt to give it life on the battlefield. Although modern soldiers expect their doctrines to be explicit, professionally authoritative, and officially sanctioned, for the greater part of American military history the doctrines under which soldiers fought were rarely so all-encompassing, prescriptive, or explicit as they are today. These earlier doctrines are best regarded as loose collections of military folkways. The history of U.S. military doctrine describes a rough evolution from these folkways toward its contemporary forms.

The military doctrines that were brought to America during the colonial period reflected the orthodox European military interests of the day: limited dynastic wars emphasizing sieges and battles between drilled formations of soldiers armed with pike and musket. Important early colonists—John Smith, Roger Williams, John Underhill, and Lion Gardiner among them—had learned their military skills on the Continent.

Implicit in their military orthodoxy was the assumption that one's enemies were mostly like oneself. Colonial warfare against Native Americans permitted no such assumption, however. American Indians possessed their own military habits, most of which were at great variance from those of their European enemies. Native doctrines reflected their tribal origins, in which individual rather than collective purpose governed action. Most often, natives fought for the achievement or preservation of honor or self-esteem within the tribe, and not the kind of state policy war so familiar to the Europeans. Native American warfare favored fighting to satisfy individual aims: skirmish, raid, and ambush; single rather than the collective, orchestrated combat his enemies attempted. And although both sides did militarily acculturate themselves, the Europeans were loathe to forsake their Continental military heritage. The colonial experience thus induced a certain schizophrenia, where a tension persisted between the new world of warfare and the traditions of European orthodoxy.

George *Washington and Nathanael *Greene embodied this tension during the *Revolutionary War. It was Washington's ambition to transform the tiny American Army into one that could stand against British regulars in the stylized tactical fashions of the day. Greene was happier with practicality: he would fight in the orthodox mode when the occasion suited, but he was not so enamored of the European style as his general in chief. Greene developed a form of guerrilla warfare in the south. Washington pined for the climactic, war-winning battle.

The Americans' quest for military respectability led to the appearance of military doctrine in a form that modern soldiers would recognize. In 1778–79, Friedrich Wilhelm von *Steuben, Washington's Inspector General, wrote his *Regulations for the Order and Discipline of the Troops of the United States,* a drill manual that would ever after be known simply as "The Blue Book." Von Steuben based his drills on those he had learned in the Prussian Army, but he tried to tailor them to the particular needs and character of the American soldier. The practical results never quite produced the army Washington wanted, but "The Blue Book" represented the European military ideal for a generation, until in 1812 it was finally superseded by a French manual of arms.

The advent of French military texts in America coincided roughly with the Napoleonic Wars, when the few professional military officers in America began seriously to study the arts of war. The French style became the fashion and remained so for the next several decades. After the *War of 1812, Gen. Winfield *Scott published the first edition of his *Tactics,* generously indebted to French tactical manuals, which held sway until the eve of the Civil War. *Tactics* hardly acknowledged the realities of war in America, nor did the other tactical manuals produced in the United States during the antebellum years. The dichotomy between European orthodoxy and American necessity achieved its fullest expression when in 1836 Scott himself attempted to employ Napoleonic tactics during the First Seminole War—with predictably dismal results.

American doctrinal thought exhibited a certain retrograde character during the years before the *Civil War. Very like their European colleagues, American officers looked nostalgically over their shoulders at Napoleon even as the conduct of battle was changing before their eyes. Technological progress improved the speed, range, and deadliness of small-arms and artillery fire. However, American military writers—Henry Halleck and Dennis Hart Mahan among them—took little notice of these advances. When William J. Hardee's *Rifle and Light Infantry Tactics* finally replaced Scott's *Tactics* in the 1850s, troops were to be arranged in the same close orders as before: Hardee's remedy for the new, deadlier battlefield was to move the troops faster, and his *Tactics* was the definitive Civil War text for citizen officers on both sides.

American soldiers of both armies entered the Civil War thus ready to fight a version of war more than half a century old. A few officers applied themselves to rectifying the disjuncture between doctrine and reality, among them Emory *Upton. A reactionary military aesthete, Upton understood the essential tactical problem of his day: how to advance across the fire-beaten zone to close with the enemy. Upton understood that formations must disperse themselves more widely if they were to survive the assault. But dispersing or "opening" formations meant surrendering one's tactical control. Close formations cost casualties; open formations threatened purposeless action. In either case, tactical failure awaited.

Upton was the first to offer solutions. Two years after Appomattox, an army board approved his *Tactics,* the most notable feature of which was his "system of fours," combat groupings of eight or twelve soldiers—forerunner of the modern infantry squad. Upton's "fours" forced combat direction toward the lower ranks.

For the rest of the nineteenth century and well into the next, professional soldiers argued over the proper balance of firepower, mobility, and shock. Where one stood on this question fixed one's views on a host of subordinate issues: whether the offense or the defense was superior in modern war; the benefits of individual marksmanship versus those of massed volley fire; whether formations should be dense and "robust," or whether they should be "fragile," articulated organizations susceptible to precise tactical control. Such concerns were by no means confined to Americans alone. In all of the advanced industrial nations, soldiers worried over the new shapes of battle.

Some would grumble at the pedantry of these debates, but this intellectual foment also gave rise to schools of higher military education and an institutional home for doctrinal studies. At Fort Leavenworth in the School of Application for Cavalry and Infantry, doctrine boards produced field manuals that culminated in 1891 with the publication of *Infantry Drill Regulations*, as well as manuals for artillery and cavalry. These boards set a new course for field manuals, which previously had aimed only to prepare troops to fight; the new manuals also addressed how to fight. Too, earlier manuals had been known by the names of their authors. The new manuals were regarded as the product of the corporate mind of the army, officially approved and sanctioned, a point driven home in the 1905 edition of *Field Service Regulations* that first carried the imprimature of the army's newly formed General Staff.

Meanwhile, nearly three centuries of frontier soldiering had produced its own unique school of practices, few of which were reduced to formal knowledge. Horseborne warfare and western geography lent a different character to frontier conflicts after the Civil War, but the clash of military cultures was every bit as dangerous as when Europeans and Native Americans had first met in combat. Although much professional energy was devoted to codifying orthodox military knowledge, frontier doctrines remained mostly implicit, the kind of knowledge communicated informally in garrison and in the saddle, over campfire and on the trail. A collection of beliefs and prejudices, tricks of the trade, fieldcraft, and frontier field doctrine was wholly vocational and often quite ephemeral. There was precious little theory in it.

For all that, it would have been a rare soldier (or sailor) before World War I who could have provided a definition of doctrine or its functions. In truth, the nature of military doctrine was being transformed in those years. Only a few perceived that armies might create doctrine as an expression of their operational philosophy. Navy commander Dudley Knox, and Army captain John McAuley *Palmer were exceptions who did grasp the larger potential of doctrine. As early as 1914, Knox wrote that the "object of military doctrine is to furnish a basis for prompt and harmonious conduct by the subordinate commanders of a large military force, in accordance with the intentions of the commander-in-chief." Palmer, a pivotal figure in the army, saw how modern warfare demanded a doctrine that transcended training routines. Knox and Palmer agreed that doctrine ought to provide a common basis of understanding and communication for professional soldiers. Palmer especially thought that one dividend of regularly returning General Staff officers to line units was to "spread a common doctrine as to the purposes and ends of training, the means to be employed, and the results to be attained."

Despite such high-minded sentiments, Americans soldiers wrote practical, vocational manuals during World War I. Driven by the necessities of industrialized warfare, twentieth-century armies were forced to learn new technical tasks. The grafting of millions of civilians upon the old professional army demanded instructional literature free of the empty formalism all too typical of earlier field manuals. The means by which technical military knowledge was rendered into doctrine was already in place, however, dominated by the various branches and their schools, as well as the staff and war colleges and the General Staff itself. The progressive doctrine that Knox and Palmer had envisioned was out of the question. By war's end, doctrine had been thoroughly domesticated: its role was not so much the advancement of military thought and practice as the ratification of orthodoxy.

Thus, military knowledge after World War I advanced without the assistance of doctrine. In only one particular could doctrine be said to have lent itself to innovation. The 1921 edition of *War Department Regulations No. 10-5* contained a list of nine "principles of war." For nearly a generation, Western military thinkers had been calling for a "scientific" approach to the study and practice of war. This, they believed, would lead them to battle's universal characteristics, said to have been embodied in the "principles" of war. The British military historian J. F. C. Fuller had noted them as early as 1914 and after the war had codified eight such principles. Fuller and others held that these were immutable, and that although their actions had always guided the conduct of war, only now had military knowledge advanced sufficiently to recognize and appreciate their existence.

However compelling the scientific analogy, the principles of war kept changing, both in number and content, from edition to edition of American field manuals. This approach to understanding war, while no doubt appalling to philosophers, was highly attractive and deeply satisfying to soldiers. And although the precise meaning of each "principle" was subject to an infinity of interpretations, their most appealing feature was that one could possess in shorthand the military wisdom of the ages.

After World War I, doctrine was of marginal importance to military innovation, becoming instead the creature of anonymous official boards and committees, far from "the best available thought that can be defended by reason"—as one official definition had it. Whether addressing subjects grand or mundane, doctrine was aimed at providing not the best available thought, but the most acceptable thought. By the time a solution to any important question of theory or practice was committed to doctrine—and there were many between the world wars—it bore the army's stamp of official approval. Military intellectuals might have disapproved of chaining doctrine to orthodoxy, but doctrine had become the means by which the army established and enforced military standards. "Doing it by the book" became a figure of speech, and "the book," the field manual was always available if imagination failed, specifying in detail the minimum acceptable standard.

Thus one may read official army doctrines after World War II as a text from which the intellectual state of the army may be deduced. The advent of nuclear weapons quite naturally posed the most extreme challenge to concepts of land warfare and the doctrines that might implement them. But the army failed to offer a credible vision of how it might conduct itself in a nuclear battlefield. The army's chief of staff in the late 1950s, Maxwell *Taylor, was forced to "conjure up" a specious concept whose name was more important than its substance: his "Pentomic" army was merely a reorganization scheme with a Madison Avenue adjective attached. Within five years, even the army was unable to sustain the fiction that Pentomia had doctrinal credibility.

The Pentomic reorganization might have been the low point in the postwar history of doctrine but for the war in Vietnam, where the U.S. Army clung to the orthodoxies of conventional warfare. The army was reluctant to contend with the doctrinal problems of guerrilla war: that belonged to the class of unorthodox conflict for which it had never felt much affinity. As early as 1962, President Kennedy had directed the army to pay more attention to these forms of conflict. But during the first few years of the Southeast Asian conflict, the military leaders still focused upon the defense of Europe. When the army did finally commit its orthodox forces to Vietnam, it turned a war it did not approve of into one that it did. The agency of this transformation was the heliborne "air cavalry" division, whose innovative design and striking mobility were offset by the stolid manner in which it was employed, applying conventional tactics more quickly. The unreality of this doctrine in the final years of the war contributed importantly to one of the darkest and most frustrating periods in the history of the U.S. Army.

In the aftermath of the *Vietnam War, strategic retrenchment narrowed the scope of American interests once again toward European defense. Against this backdrop, the Arab-Israeli War (1973) offered a glimpse of what might be expected in modern, orthodox warfare: combined arms conflict, characterized by armored speed, high lethality, and precisely guided munitions. That war also seemed to show how far out of date the U.S. Army had become during its years in Vietnam. A group of American generals led by William E. DePuy began a decade-long campaign to modernize the army and, not incidentally, erase the legacy of the lost war in Southeast Asia. DePuy believed military doctrine might be one important means of rejuvenating an army that, everyone agreed, was an institutional wreck.

This high-ranking interest in doctrine in the 1970s and 1980s heralded a new conception of its nature and functions. DePuy and his colleagues harnessed doctrine to several purposes. Doctrine would be made to serve its traditional role of describing how an army fights. But doctrine would also establish the army's public and operational raison d'etre. Like Dudley Knox and John McAuley Palmer, nearly a century earlier, DePuy thought that doctrine could be progressive, that it could promote the army's modernization, both materially and intellectually. DePuy and his colleagues took a direct, sometimes peremptory, hand in doctrinal reforms from the beginning, and often wrote it themselves. They called their new doctrine "the Active Defense." Doctrine had become generals' business.

It had also become everyone else's business—including civilian scholars and military writers. Because the army had elevated the Active Defense to such a prominent role in its modernization campaign, it achieved an unprecedented degree of public exposure in the late 1970s. The flowering of doctrinal debate did not sit well with DePuy and his colleagues, but the new doctrine, which was widely criticized as unimaginative, and as a defensive prescription for disaster, did galvanize public attention.

Doctrine was no longer of negligible importance in the professional lives of American soldiers. Perhaps inevitably, reaction set in. More than any other American soldier since Upton, DePuy's name was associated with military

doctrine; evidence suggests that part of the reaction against it was reaction to DePuy himself. When DePuy retired in 1978, the critics hoped his doctrine would be overturned. DePuy's successors nevertheless did manage to exercise control over the next doctrinal evolution, which was to be named "AirLand battle."

That new doctrine was published in FM 100-5 to generally favorable reviews in service and defense journals in 1982. The AirLand battle was imagined as a sophisticated, highly orchestrated application of all the army's combat power in conjunction with that of the air force in order to build a chain of successful engagements all pointed toward one operational objective. As a doctrine, AirLand battle was more sophisticated, certainly more attuned to the sort of enemy the U.S. Army might have to face in the years ahead, and it was not so exclusively fixed upon European defense. Ideally, it was hoped, many of its precepts could be utilized anywhere the army might fight. Intellectually, the new doctrine was the product of a cadre of young military intellectuals that had collected at the staff college during the late 1970s. And while the highest-ranking officers of the army acted as the doctrine's patrons, the new field manual was regarded as much less the result of one man's passion.

AirLand battle doctrine has not been substantially revised since 1982. The success of American arms in the *Persian Gulf War, many have argued, can be directly traced to the doctrinal "renaissance" of the 1970s. Modern American soldiers do have a certain appreciation for a fighting doctrine that enjoys credibility and authority; but none would go so far as to argue that doctrine alone can win a war, any more than doctrine alone could lose one.

[See also Clausewitz, Carl von; Deterrence; Education, Military; Strategy; Tactics; Theorists of War.]

• Russell F. Weigley, History of the United States Army, 1967, rev. ed. 1984. Russell F. Weigley, The American Way of War: A History of United States Military Policy, 1973. John I. Alger, the Quest for Victory: The History of the Principles of War, 1982. Brian Holden Reid, J. F. C. Fuller, Military Thinker, 1987. Paul Herbert, Deciding What Has to Be Done: General William E. DePuy and the 1976 Edition of FM 100-5, Operations, 1988. William B. Skelton, An American Profession of Arms: The Army Officer Corps, 1784–1861, 1992. Robert H. Scales, Jr., et al., Certain Victory: The U.S. Army in the Gulf War, 1993. Perry D. Jamieson, Crossing the Deadly Ground: United States Army Tactics, 1865–1899, 1994. Virgil Ney, The Evolution of the United States Army Field Manual, Valley Forge to Vietnam, 1996.
—Roger Spiller

DOMINICAN REPUBLIC, U.S. MILITARY INVOLVEMENT IN THE.

The Dominican Republic, a colony of Spain until the early nineteenth century, shares the Caribbean island of Hispaniola with the republic of Haiti, with which it has had a long rivalry. The two principal U.S. military incursions into the Dominican Republic were the occupation of 1916–24 and the invasion of 1965. The first was integral to the increasing U.S. involvement in the Caribbean, resulting from economic expansion and strategic concerns. The Dominican Republic figured centrally in this process, with its near annexation by the United States in 1871, the announcement of the *Roosevelt Corollary to the Monroe Doctrine (1904) as a foil to the European influence in Dominican affairs and the gradual imposition of U.S. control over the republic's internal political and economic affairs. U.S. corporations had taken over much of the republic's large sugar industry and increasingly dominated its trade. When U.S. efforts at direct control over Dominican internal affairs were thwarted, Washington responded with military threats and actual intervention. Brief armed incursions occurred in 1904, 1905, 1912, and 1914, under Presidents Theodore *Roosevelt, William Howard Taft, and Woodrow *Wilson.

The occupation of 1916–24, initiated by Wilson and his secretary of the navy, Josephus Daniels, was inspired both by previous policy and by growing U.S. fears of Germany's influence in the Caribbean. A military government headed by U.S. Navy and Marine officers, backed by several thousand Marines, displaced the constitutional Dominican government in 1916. Although there was limited resistance initially, opposition became important later in two distinct forms. The first involved a political struggle waged by nationalist elements of the elite and middle class. The second was a five-year guerilla war (1917–22) fought by peasants in the country's eastern region. The event bought the first use of U.S. military aircraft in a guerrilla conflict. Both types of resistance, plus the general unpopularity of U.S. interventionist policy in Latin America and elsewhere, helped cause Washington to negotiate a withdrawal in 1924.

The U.S. occupation government, pursuing goals of stability and development, had implemented various reforms. The principal efforts involved education, public health, public works, and improvement of the weak and highly politicized military. Though serious problems affected all these endeavors, the two most successful were the creation of a modern road network and of a more effective but still politicized military. Both of these accomplishments became crucial to the creation of a dictatorship in 1930, by Gen. Rafael Trujillo, who had risen to power in the mid–1920s within the U.S.-created Dominican military, the National Guard.

There were differences within the U.S. government over Trujillo. Some members of the Congress and elements of the Marine Corps were enthusiastic supporters, with several ex–Marine officers actually holding influential positions in his government. However, the State Department frequently opposed Trujillo, at least until the 1950s when his unconditional support for U.S. positions during the *Cold War led Washington to ignore the abuses and megalomania characteristic of his regime. About 1960, following the Cuban revolution, the inauguration of President John F. *Kennedy, and the formation of internal Dominican forces of resistance, the U.S.–Trujillo relationship shifted. In 1961, Trujillo was assassinated by Dominicans aided by the *Central Intelligence Agency.

In April 1965, a rebellion meant to restore the short-lived (1963) constitutional government of President Juan Bosch was suppressed by the intervention of nearly 23,000 U.S. Marine and Army troops. President Lyndon B. *Johnson's decision to intervene, like Wilson's in 1916, had strategic and economic roots, with the difference that the anti–Communist fears of U.S. national security policymakers led Johnson to exaggerate the possibility of the Dominican Republic becoming a "second Cuba." The intervention was unilateral, although Washington soon pressured the Organization of American States to create an Inter-American Defense Force, to which six Latin American countries contributed token forces.

The U.S. role in the events of 1965 remains disputed. The State Department claimed to act as a neutral broker by separating the warring factions and arranging for elections; yet most scholars conclude that U.S. actions distinctly favored more conservative elements. Their triumph in the 1966 elections, followed by the withdrawal of foreign troops, led to stable but repressive civilian rule. A U.S. Military Advisory and Assistance Group (MAAG) has maintained close ties with the Dominican military since the early 1960s. This relationship has proved important in recent decades as Washington has used its influence to pressure the Dominican military, and its civilian allies, to accept a policy of stability, gradual democratization, and strengthened ties to the U.S. economy.

[See also: Cuba, U.S. Military Involvement in; Haiti, U.S. Military Involvement in.]

• Abraham F. Lowenthal, The Dominican Intervention, 1972. Piero Gleijeses, The Dominican Crisis: the 1965 Constitutionalist Revolt and American Intervention, 1978. Bruce J. Calder, The Impact of Intervention: The Dominican Republic During the U.S. Occupation of 1916–1924, 1984. Eric Paul Roorda, The Dictator Next Door: The Good Neighbor Policy and the Trujillo Regime in the Dominican Republic, 1930–1945, 1998.   —Bruce J. Calder

DONIPHAN, ALEXANDER (1808–1887), lawyer, soldier, and statesman. Born in Kentucky, Doniphan became a prominent attorney there and after 1833 in Missouri. At the beginning of the Mexican-American War, he organized the 1st Regiment of Missouri Volunteers and was elected its colonel.

During a campaign that began in late October 1846 at Santa Fe, New Mexico, and would end at Saltillo, Coahuila, in late April 1847, Colonel Doniphan led an American force that seized control of the capital of the Mexican state of Chihuahua. He also marched into Navajo Territory and obtained a treaty recognizing the U.S. government.

Doniphan then led his troops back to the Rio Grande, on to Socorro and toward El Paso. On Christmas Day, his troops, numbering 856, fought a Mexican force at Tamascalitos outside El Paso del Norte, killing 43 and wounding 150 Mexican soldiers. His force suffered only seven wounded. On 27 December they occupied the city.

On 8 February 1847, Doniphan marched south toward Chihuahua City. On 28 February, he routed the Mexican army in the Battle of Rio de Sacramento and occupied the state capital the next day. The Mexicans suffered 300 killed. After occupying the capital for nearly two months, Doniphan and his men departed for Saltillo on 28 April. They then returned to New Orleans by ship via Brazos Santiago. In one year, Doniphan and his men had covered 3,600 miles by land and 2,000 by water—one of the most successful military marches in U.S. history.

[See also: Kearny, Stephen Watts; Mexican-American War.]

• Jacob S. Robinson, A Journal of the Sante Fe Expedition Under Colonel Doniphan, 1932. K. Jack Bauer, The Mexican War, 1974.
                                                        —John M. Hart

DOOLITTLE, JAMES (1896–1993), Army Air Force Officer. Doolittle, a man of brilliant scientific ability, received one of the first U.S. doctorates in aeronautical engineering from MIT in 1925. He also possessed immense physical and moral courage. After joining the air service in 1917, he transferred to the reserves in 1930. He pioneered instrument flying and won several airplane races. In the 1930s, as a manager in Shell Petroleum, "Jimmy" Doolittle pushed the development of high-octane aviation fuels, which permitted the creation of the advanced piston engines powering World War II U.S. combat aircraft. He continued to fly as a test and racing pilot, establishing flight time and speed records. After returning him to active duty in 1940, the Army Air Forces in January 1942 selected him to lead the first bombing mission against Japan. The "Doolittle Raid" on Tokyo by B-25 bombers launched from U.S. *aircraft carriers earned him a jump in rank to brig. general and a Medal of Honor. It helped convince the Japanese to launch their disastrous Midway.

In November 1942, Doolittle led the U.S. Twelfth Air Force into North Africa, and in November 1943 he headed the Fifteenth Air Force in Italy. In January 1944, he took command of the Eighth Air Force in Britain, which he controlled until V-E Day. His promotion of aggressive fighter escort tactics gained the Americans air superiority over Germany. After the war, he served on numerous government commissions.

• Lowell Thomas and Edward Jablonski, *Doolittle: A Biography,* 1976. James H. Doolittle, with Carroll V. Glines, *I Could Never Be So Lucky Again: An Autobiography by General James H. "Jimmy" Doolittle,* 1991. —Richard G. Davis

DOUGLASS, FREDERICK (1818–1895), abolitionist, journalist, and orator. Born in bondage on the eastern shore of Maryland, Douglass worked for several different slaveholders in both eastern Maryland and Baltimore between 1818 and 1838. During his youth, Douglass became proficiently literate by reading the Bible and classic orations and listening to the sermons of antislavery black preachers and *Quakers. These experiences later contributed to his unyielding abolitionism and fierce egalitarianism. In 1838, while a ship caulker's apprentice, Douglass acquired free seaman papers and escaped to New York City. He then moved to Massachusetts and became involved in antislavery activism, under the tutelage of William Lloyd *Garrison. Eventually rejecting the apolitical nature of Garrisonian abolitionism, Douglass moved to Rochester, New York, and founded his own abolition journal, *The North Star.* Between 1847 and 1863, he edited that journal and subsequently the *Douglass Monthly.*

A tireless abolitionist, Douglass campaigned for the Liberty, Free Soil, and Republican parties in the 1840s and 1850s, although he opposed a nonextension, gradualist approach to slavery. His activist approach to abolition contributed to his hawkish position once the slaveholding states seceded in 1860 and 1861. Douglass stressed the importance of black loyalty during the *Civil War and actively recruited Northern blacks—including his two sons, who volunteered for the 54th Massachusetts Infantry—for the Union effort. His egalitarianism, however, led to his criticism of the discriminatory pay and promotion practices of the Federal army. Nevertheless, Douglass's investment in assimilation through self-help and racial uplift undergirded his conviction that the rights of citizenship would accompany black military participation—a rationale that, according to one of his intellectual biographers, anticipated W. E. B. *Du Bois's "Close Ranks" argument concerning World War I and the "Double Victory" campaign of the black press during World War II.

[*See also* Colored Troops, U.S.]

• David W. Blight, *Frederick Douglass' Civil War,* 1989. William S. McFeely, *Frederick Douglass,* 1991. —Martin Summers

DOUHET, GIULIO (1869–1930), Italian general and early air power theorist. Giulio Douhet is remembered best for propounding a doctrine of offensive strategic air attack as a preferable, even more humane, form of warfare than the massive battles of attrition that marked World War I. His bold ideas about *air warfare injected a tremendous energy into the usual strategic discussions of nations able to produce, or procure, such advanced technology. Although it would be incorrect to say that this approach to armed conflict originated with Douhet, his ability to integrate a rapidly expanding body of concepts about aerial warfare provided airpower advocates with a cogent theoretical foundation upon which to build.

Like American airpower adherent Billy *Mitchell (1879–1936), Douhet began his army career at an early age and during a period of national transition. In addition, both men were moved by their advocacy of aviation to dissent vigorously, at times even recklessly, from military orthodoxy. This course eventually led to court-martial, suspension from active duty, and in Douhet's case imprisonment for one year. Unlike Mitchell, however, World War I resurrected Douhet's career. In 1918, he was made chief of the Italian Army's Central Aeronautical Board, a post he held until retiring from service as a general in 1921. Also in 1921, his seminal work on aerial warfare, *The Command of the Air,* was published. In 1922, the Fascist leader Benito Mussolini appointed him head of Italy's aviation program.

Douhet's central argument that future conflicts would be decided by the nation most able to destroy an opponent's means and will to resist through airpower still engenders much debate. Moreover, the ongoing struggle to validate or refute the concepts set forth in *The Command of the Air* suggests a transcendent quality unmatched by other air war theorists. For airmen, in particular, his views gave rise to a tenacious search for the enemy's "vital center"—the perfect target set.

• Giulio Douhet, *The Command of the Air,* 1942; rept. 1938. —Michael L. Grumelli

DRAFT. *See* Conscription.

DRAFT RESISTANCE AND EVASION. Draft resistance in American history has taken many forms, including deliberate lawbreaking for the sake of conscience (*civil disobedience*); direct action to disrupt the draft; noncooperation; and individual efforts to avoid military service (*draft evasion*).

Draft resisters in America have emerged from several distinct traditions. These have included *Quakers, and other religious pacifists, who have been active since the colonial period; abolitionists, who opposed slavery from 1815 until the *Civil War; the social progressive movements from 1880 until World War II; the trade union movement from the turn of the century until the 1950s; and the civil rights and *peace and antiwar movements after World War II.

The Colonial Period and the American Revolution. In the colonial period and the early days of the republic, middle- and upper-class unwillingness to serve in the military was widespread. Despite George *Washington's frequent complaints about his inability to raise an adequate army, the early Congresses refused to institute a national draft. At the state level, state militias were staffed largely by volunteers, but during specific emergencies such as the Indian wars and the *Revolutionary War, coercive methods were also used. However, men who could afford it could pay fees or hire substitutes to fight in their place.

It was in response to local and state militias that the first draft resisters appeared. The earliest resisters were primarily from religious groups, including the Quakers, who arrived in the 1650s; the Mennonites, including the Amish and Hutterites (1683); and the Brethren (1719). These early religious pacifists refused to fight in the *Native American Wars. Widely considered to be heretics, they suffered many forms of punishment, including fines, whippings, and occasionally executions. Gradually, however, their consistent commitment to nonviolence won grudging acknowledgment from colonial legislatures, which increasingly permitted them exemption from service in militias—Massachusetts in 1661, Rhode Island in 1673, and Pennsylvania in 1757. Such exemptions began the tradition that continued until the 1960s of providing legal exemptions for religious groups while denying them to secular objectors.

The Abolitionist Movement and the Civil War. Opposition to war and a compulsory draft remained widespread in the early days of America, exemplified in the Madison administration's unsuccessful attempt at a national draft for the *War of 1812. From 1812 to 1860, abolitionist organizations such as the American Anti-Slavery Society (1833) and the New England Non-Resistance Society (1838), as well as pacifist organizations such as the Massachusetts Peace Society (1812) and the American Peace Society (1828), included many individuals who opposed war and conscription. During this period, all states and territories required men who wanted to avoid military service in the militias to pay fees or to hire substitutes.

An important influence on draft resistance was Henry Thoreau's article on "Civil Disobedience" (1849). Written during the *Mexican War, the essay was a classic analysis of the individual's duty to refuse to cooperate with immoral government policies.

The Civil War brought the first national draft, with both the North and the South passing *conscription laws. A popular means of avoiding military service was physical disability: of almost 777,000 names drawn in four Northern drafts in 1863 and 1864, 159,400 men gained physical exemptions. Draftees could also hire a substitute or pay a commutation fee ($500 in the South, $300 in the North). In the North, 86,700 men paid the fee, while 73,600 provided substitutes. But the most common form of evasion was failing to report. More than 161,000 of the 777,000 draftees simply did not show up for service.

The system of fees and exemptions meant that most soldiers were recent immigrants and the poor. Such a system met violent resistance, most significantly in the 1863 antidraft riots, the worst rioting in the nation's history, in which armed resistance to the draft and to government authority erupted in New York City, Boston, Albany, and elsewhere from the East Coast to the Midwest. Hundreds were killed, including thirty-eight federal draft officials. In the *New York City antidraft riots, poor and working-class immigrants overwhelmed the police for four days, finally re-treating only when six regiments of troops brought from the Battle of *Gettysburg arrived to restore order.

An additional form of evasion was flight to Canada. Although the total number is unknown, accounts of local draft board proceedings in states bordering Canada are filled with references to men fleeing to Canada to avoid conscription.

Civil War inductees who refused to cooperate were sent to military camps, where many were subject to starvation and torture at the hands of hostile military commanders. In 1864, President Abraham *Lincoln signed the first law offering religious resisters alternative service in hospitals or with freed slaves. Still, a core of "absolutists" refused to cooperate with the draft in any way. Eventually, the Union government exempted them from fees or service of any kind for the duration of the war.

Industrialization and World War I. After 1880, economic and labor conflicts associated with industrialization increasingly influenced the movement against war and conscription. The World War I draft law of 1917 provided exemptions from combat only for "well recognized" religious groups. Payment for substitutes was not permitted. Exempt individuals were required to report for noncombatant service in military camps, where conditions were harsh and pacifists were often treated poorly. Resisters who refused such service were sent to federal prisons, where many were chained to prison walls, sprayed with cold water from fire hoses, made to stand naked outside at night, and beaten. Some prisoners died.

Near the end of World War I, "alternative service" was made available only to members of a small group of traditional religious organizations, thereby splitting opponents of the draft into two groups: those legally qualified for exemption, who were now called *conscientious objectors* (COs), and those with no legal means of gaining exemption.

Despite harsh government repression during World War I, opposition to military conscription expanded beyond the traditional religious groups. Large numbers of political resisters appeared, including socialists and members of labor groups such as the International Workers of the World (IWW), who believed that the war primarily benefitted big business, and the United Mine Workers (UMW), who resented use of the military to break strikes. Among the political resisters, Eugene V. *Debs (of the railway workers union, the IWW, and the Socialist Party of America) was especially influential. Though imprisoned for his speeches urging opposition to the war and the draft, he ran for president while in the Atlanta Penitentiary, receiving nearly 1 million votes in the 1920 election.

Many important antiwar and antidraft organizations were founded during this period, including the *War Resisters League, the American Friends Service Committee, and the *Women's International League for Peace and Freedom, begun by Jane *Addams. The *American Civil Liberties Union (ACLU), created in 1920, grew out of the American Union Against Militarism. Roger Baldwin, ACLU director until 1950, served a year in prison for refusing induction in 1918.

Although 24 million men registered for the draft during World War I, as many as 3.5 million failed to do so, thereby successfully evading induction. Most of these were poor or working-class agricultural and industrial laborers. Among draft resisters, at least 17 were sentenced to death (none was executed) and approximately 150 received life sentences; hundreds of others received sentences ranging from 10 to 20 years. It was not until 1933 that the last World War I draft resister was released from prison, pardoned by President Roosevelt.

World War II and the 1950s. World War II was the only period in which the draft did not offer middle- and upper-class men legal means for avoiding conscription through deferments or payment of substitutes. With the draft law permitting *conscientious objection on religious grounds, approximately 5,000 men were imprisoned for draft offenses. This group included those who were denied CO deferments, as well as resisters who refused to cooperate with the draft or with alternative service.

Four important trends characterized draft resistance after World War II, culminating in the massive resistance to the *Vietnam War. First, secular resisters became more numerous than religious pacifists and, in a series of important Supreme Courts cases, gradually gained limited legal acceptance. In the most important case, the Supreme Court ruled in its *Seeger* decision (1965) that philosophical and moral—rather than religious—beliefs were sufficient to justify exemption from military service.

Second, "selective" objection to a specific war rather than to all wars became widespread, with many individuals basing claims for exemption upon the Nuremberg War Crimes Trials. To date, however, the courts have refused to permit selective objection.

Third, opposition to the draft spread to many new groups, including opponents of the testing and proliferation of *nuclear weapons. These groups wrote letters to politicians and the press, lobbied Congress, organized protests, and provided direct assistance to draft resisters and military deserters.

Fourth, opposition to the draft was predominantly a middle-class phenomenon, yet the system of channeling upper- and middle-class men into educational and occupational categories that permitted draft deferments meant that draftees were drawn primarily from among the poor and minorities.

The Vietnam War. With opponents of the Vietnam War arguing that draft resistance was a moral and civic duty, opposition to the draft reached a peak in 1964–73. Because so many Americans opposed the draft, individual avoidance of induction became a popular form of resistance. Many men publicly burned their draft cards or illegally returned them to the government; draftees either did not appear for physical exams or devised innovative ways to fail their exams; thousands refused induction. Between 30,000 and 50,000 men fled to Canada or Sweden to avoid conscription. Approximately 600,000 individuals violated the draft laws during this period; 210,000 were formally charged. During the height of prosecutions, draft cases accounted for approximately 10 percent of all cases in the federal courts. Among the hundreds of groups that advocated draft resistance were radicals such as the Resistance and *Students for a Democratic Society; liberals such as Clergy and Laity Concerned; local and regional groups such as New England Resistance; and dozens of groups on college campuses.

Despite the scope of opposition to the draft, the baby boom surplus of draft-age men meant that the Selective Service System was able to provide sufficient manpower for the military. Nevertheless, widespread draft resistance

was a significant influence upon President Nixon's decision in 1973 to end the draft, thereby eliminating one of the major reasons for protest.

In 1980, a system of compulsory registration for the draft was instituted. The major issue facing draft resisters was whether eighteen-year-olds should register with the government, as required by law. Despite the failure of several hundred thousand men to register, only a few outspoken resisters were prosecuted.

In their classic book *Nonviolence in America,* Staughton and Alice Lynd observe that draft resistance has been linked throughout American history to civil rights and labor movements. The *Quakers who refused to fight in the *French and Indian War of 1756 also opposed slavery. Labor leaders and social progressives were among the most outspoken opponents of the World War I draft. Many of the early leaders of the Congress of Racial Equality (CORE), formed in 1943, were from the pacifist *Fellowship of Reconciliation. Abraham J. *Muste, one of the signers of the influential 1964 "Declaration of Conscience" pledging support for men refusing service in Vietnam, began his activism as a labor organizer during the 1930s. The national director of the 1967 Mobilization Committee to End the War in Vietnam was James Bevel of the Southern Christian Leadership Conference, which was directed by Martin Luther King, Jr. From the long history of such links, it is clear that draft resistance and evasion in America have not only been the acts of individuals seeking to avoid military service, but have often been important expressions of broadly based movements for social change.

[*See also* Pacifism; Selective Draft Cases; Supreme Court, War, and the Military.]

• H. C. Peterson and Gilbert C. Fite, *Opponents of War, 1917–1918,* 1957. Edward Needles Wright, *Conscientious Objectors in the Civil War,* 1961. Lillian Schlissel, ed., *Conscience in America: A Documentary History of Conscientious Objection in America, 1757–1967,* 1968. Michael Ferber and Staughton Lynd, *The Resistance,* 1971. Adrian Cook, *The Armies of the Streets: The New York City Draft Riots of 1863,* 1974. Stephen M. Kohn, *Jailed for Peace: The History of American Draft Law Violators, 1658–1985,* 1986. John Whiteclay Chambers II, *To Raise an Army: The Draft Comes to Modern America,* 1987. Iver Bernstein, *The New York City Draft Riots: Their Significance for American Society and Politics in the Age of the Civil War,* 1990. Charles DeBenedetti, *An American Ordeal: The Antiwar Movement of the Vietnam Era,* 1990. James W. Tollefson, *The Strength Not to Fight: An Oral History of Conscientious Objectors of the Vietnam War,* 1993. Charles C. Moskos and John Whiteclay Chambers II, *The New Conscientious Objection: From Sacred to Secular Resistance,* 1993.
—James W. Tollefson

DREW, CHARLES (1904–1950), physician, surgeon, scientist, and educator. Drew was a pioneer in the field of blood plasma preservation. Born in Washington, D.C., he earned a B.A. from Amherst College in 1926, a medical certificate from Montreal's McGill University in 1933, and a doctorate in medical science from Columbia University in 1940. While studying at Columbia, he theorized that blood plasma could replace whole blood in transfusions because of its long shelflife. During the early days of World War II, Drew became project supervisor of a joint American *Red Cross and Blood Transfusion Betterment Association (BTBA) program to supply war-torn Great Britain with plasma. By January 1941, Drew's efforts proved so successful that Britain no longer needed American blood. Shortly thereafter, he briefly served as assistant director in a project supported by the Red Cross, the National Research Council, BTBA, and U.S. armed forces.

Previous historical accounts have considered Drew's resignation of his directorship in March 1941 as a protest by an African American against a Red Cross and military edict that ordered blood supplies be separated by race. Although evidence suggests that Drew voiced displeasure at the racial mandate, his departure was also shaped by the desire to pursue a surgical and teaching career at Howard University. Drew died in an automobile accident in 1950.

• Charles E. Wynes, *Charles Richard Drew: The Man and the Myth,* 1988. Linda O. McMurry, "Charles Richard Drew," in *The African American Encyclopedia,* ed. Michael W. Williams, 1993.

—Brian Adkins

DRUG ABUSE. *See* Substance Abuse.

DU BOIS, W. E. B. (1868–1963), civil rights leader and author. Born in Great Barrington, Massachusetts, W. E. B. Du Bois earned undergraduate degrees at Fisk University (1885) and Harvard (1890), and a doctorate in history from Harvard in 1895. Du Bois taught history and economics at Atlanta University in 1897–1910 and 1934–44. From 1910 to 1934, he served as founding editor of the *Crisis,* the official organ of the new National Association for the Advancement of Colored People (NAACP).

When his most influential book, *The Souls of Black Folk,* was published in 1903, Du Bois became the premier architect of the civil rights movement in the United States and among the first thinkers to grasp the international implications of the struggle for racial justice. The problem of the twentieth century, he wrote then, was the problem of the "color-line."

Du Bois's legacy is complex. A severe critic of racial segregation, he still enjoined other African Americans to accept, if temporarily, the segregated units and officer training facilities of the U.S. Army in 1917–18—in the hope that wartime military service would lead to full civil rights. An elitist who emphasized the leadership role of a "talented tenth" in the liberation of black people, Du Bois moved increasingly to the Left after World War II, denouncing U.S. *Cold War policies as imperialistic and espousing Communist solutions to problems of race and class. He joined the U.S. Communist Party in 1961 and spent the last two years of his life in Ghana.

[*See also* Civil Liberties and War; Race Relations and War.]

• David Levering Lewis, *W. E. B. Du Bois: Biography of a Race.* Vol. 1, 1993.

—David Levering Lewis

DULLES, ALLEN WELSH (1893–1969), lawyer, foreign service officer, and intelligence official. The grandson of one secretary of state and nephew of another, Dulles entered the foreign service in 1914. He spent World War I collecting intelligence in Bern, Switzerland, and subsequently assisted the U.S. delegation to the Versailles Conference and served in several embassies before resigning from the State Department in 1926. A Wall Street lawyer until the United States entered World War II, Dulles enlisted in the Office of Strategic Services. Returning to Bern, he earned a reputation as a master spy and covert operator, especially after his Operation Sunrise produced

the secret surrender of Germany's forces in Italy without Soviet Knowledge.

In 1947, Dulles helped to draft the section of the *National Security Act (1947) creating the *Central Intelligence Agency, and in 1951 he became its deputy director for plans, charged with covert operations and clandestine collection. These were the priorities of 1953–61, his tenure as CIA director. Encouraged by President Dwight D. *Eisenhower and supported by his brother John Foster *Dulles, the secretary of state, he presided over the overthrow of governments in Iran and Guatemala, and the initiation of *U-2 spy planes to overfly the Soviet Union. He neglected research and analysis, however, and the 1961 Bay of Pigs fiasco in Cuba culminated in a string of failures. Forced out by President Kennedy, Dulles's final government assignment was to investigate Kennedy's assassination as a member of the Warren Commission.

[*See also* Cold War: Domestic Course; Cuba, U.S. Military Involvement in.]

• John Ranelagh, *The Agency: The Rise and Fall of the CIA,* 1986. Peter Grose, *Gentleman Spy: The Life of Allen Dulles,* 1994.

—Richard H. Immerman

DULLES, JOHN FOSTER (1888–1959), lawyer, senator, diplomat, and secretary of state. Deeply influenced by his grandfather and uncle, secretaries of state under Benjamin Harrison and Woodrow *Wilson, Dulles devoted his life to foreign affairs. As a young lawyer, he was counsel to the Reparations Commission that helped draft the *Treaty of Versailles (1919). As chairman of the Federal Council of Churches' Commission to Study the Bases of a Just and Durable Peace, he presented to President Franklin D. *Roosevelt a blueprint for the postwar order.

An internationalist, the Republican Dulles frequently served in a bipartisan capacity. From the 1945 *United Nations conference, he represented Democratic president Harry S. *Truman at virtually every major international meeting. Dulles was foreign policy adviser to Republican nominee Thomas Dewey (1948), but after a brief Senate stint, he negotiated for Truman the *Japan Peace Treaty (1951) that ended the occupation while retaining U.S. military bases there.

In the 1952 U.S. election campaign, Dulles attacked the Truman administration for failing to exploit U.S. atomic supremacy in the *Cold War, insisting that liberation should replace "containment" as America's strategy toward the Soviet bloc. In 1953, he became President Dwight D. *Eisenhower's secretary of state.

Dulles did not dominate Eisenhower on foreign policy, as the conventional wisdom once held. The two were agreed on collective security and the need to build strength and cohesion among non-Communist nations. Nor was Dulles a reckless saber-rattler. He did strongly believe in what came to be called the "New Look": the threat of U.S. "massive retaliation" as the most effective means to deter Soviet expansion and aggression. Yet he understood that the threat of *nuclear weapons was not always an appropriate response, and that overseas deployment of U.S. conventional forces was both militarily and politically necessary. Indeed, by the late 1950s he was anticipating the "*flexible response" strategy associated with John F. *Kennedy's presidency. Moreover, although Dulles was a *covert operations enthusiast like his brother, Allen Welsh

*Dulles, the CIA director, he opposed direct U.S. military intervention, notably during the 1954 Indochina crisis, but he supported South Vietnam and refused to sign the *Geneva Agreement on Indochina (1954).

Dulles was largely responsible for negotiating U.S. security pacts with Middle Eastern countries and Southeast Asia. But he was usually reluctant to negotiate with the Soviets, and he thrived on crises—the last over Berlin in 1958–59 even as he battled with cancer. He died in May 1959.

[*See also* Berlin Crises.]

• Ronald W. Pruessen, *John Foster Dulles: The Road to Power*, 1982. Richard H. Immerman, ed., *John Foster Dulles and the Diplomacy of the Cold War*, 1990. Richard H. Immerman, *John Foster Dulles: Piety, Pragmatism, and Power in U.S. Foreign Policy*, 1998.

—Richard H. Immerman

E

EASTER OFFENSIVE (1972). Knowing that the United States was losing its will to continue the war in Vietnam, the North Vietnamese government in Hanoi decided in January 1972 to attack South Vietnam and thus started the war's largest battle to date. American intelligence knew Hanoi's general intentions, but was wrong on the estimates of the time and place of the offensive. On 30 March 1972—three days before Easter—the North Vietnamese Army (NVA) committed fourteen divisions backed by several hundred tanks and heavy artillery to a three-pronged assault to gain territory and possibly win the war outright.

NVA Gen. Vo Nguyen *Giap, directed spearheads toward Quang Tri and Hué in the northern provinces of South Vietnam, Kontum in the central highlands, and An Loc northwest of Saigon. Initially, South Vietnamese resistance failed, but American advisers such as John Paul Vann and Maj. Gen. James Hollingsworth helped stabilize the ground defense, supported by American airpower and naval bombardment.

Still, in early May, Gen. Creighton *Abrams, American commander in Vietnam, cabled Washington that Saigon had lost the will to fight and the war might be soon lost. The NVA had taken Quang Tri and had put Hué, Kontum, and An Loc under siege. The situation at An Loc was particularly dangerous. If it fell, there was little standing between Hanoi's forces and Saigon. President Richard M. *Nixon authorized a major buildup of American airpower, plus heavy air strikes against Hanoi and Haiphong for the first time since 1968. On 8 May, with Saigon fighting for its life, the U.S. Navy mined Haiphong Harbor to block the flow of Soviet supplies. Ultimately, the South Vietnamese, supported by American airpower, drove the NVA back from the cities and recaptured Quang Tri.

The Easter Offensive cost the NVA dearly. Americans estimated Hanoi lost 100,000 men killed and 400 tanks destroyed. The failure to end the war on the battlefield undoubtedly prodded Hanoi toward the negotiations that led to the *Paris Peace Agreements in January 1973. Three years later, forced to fight without American aid, Saigon could not duplicate its defensive victories of 1972.

During the Easter Offensive, American forces for the first time employed sizable numbers of *precision-guided munitions, "smart weapons." U.S. warplanes used wire-guided bombs to destroy North Vietnamese bridges that had withstood years of attack by conventional ordnance, and American helicopter gunships and South Vietnamese infantry employed TOW *antitank weapons with deadly effect.

[*See also* Helicopters; Missiles; Vietnam War: Military and Diplomatic Course.]

• Philip B. Davidson, *Vietnam at War: The History 1946–1975*, 1988. Jeffrey Clarke, *Advice and Support: The Final Years 1965–73*, 1988.
—Eric Bergerud

EASTMAN, CRYSTAL (1881–1928), labor lawyer, feminist, antimilitarist. Born in Marlborough, Massachusetts, the daughter of two ordained Congregationalist ministers, Eastman was raised in Glenora, New York, graduated from Vassar College, earned an M.A. in sociology at Columbia and a law degree from New York University in 1907. A labor lawyer and reformer, Eastman's first book, *Work Accidents and the Law* (1910), established her reputation and helped create workmen's compensation. A brilliant and dynamic activist, Eastman was a committed socialist, suffragist, feminist, and antimilitarist. She believed military establishments and wars defended business interests and threatened the values she most cherished. In 1914, she was one of the founders of the Woman's Peace Party (later the *Women's International League for Peace and Freedom) and became president of the radical New York branch (1914–19). She also served as executive director of the American Union Against Militarism (1915–17) and helped commit its wartime successor, the National Civil Liberties Bureau (1917–18), to the protection of *conscientious objection and free speech. After the war, she organized the First Feminist Congress in 1919, and helped found the American Civil Liberties Bureau in 1921 (renamed the American Civil Liberties Union in 1923). From 1918 to 1922, with her brother, Max Eastman, she co-owned and coedited the *Liberator*, a radical journal of politics, art, and literature. Until her death in 1928 of nephritis at forty-eight, Eastman worked tirelessly for feminism, social justice, and world peace.

[*See also* Peace and Antiwar Movements.]

• Blanche Wiesen Cook, ed., *Toward the Great Change: Crystal and Max Eastman on Feminism, Antimilitarism, and Revolution*, 1976. Blanche Wiesen Cook, ed., *Crystal Eastman on Women and Revolution*, 1978.
—Blanche Wiesen Cook

ECONOMY AND WAR. This essay offers a historical description of both the economic consequences of American wars and the manner in which the state of the economy and its mobilization sustained or hindered war's conduct. That approach reveals that war sometimes produced a prosperity that reduced the harmful economic effects of population loss, destruction of capital, disruption of trade, and financial distress.

During the seventeenth century, Native Americans posed the principal military threat to European colonists, who lived mostly in isolated frontier villages. An agricultural economy and physical dispersion left the colonists unable to maintain trained forces. Because Native Americans refused to fight in a European manner, the colonists' slim technological advantages were negated, causing poorly trained militia to adopt savage economic warfare. They attacked the Native Americans in their winter quarters, endangering families and food stocks. The Indians had to submit or starve. Economically, Indian attacks on frontier settlements meant loss of life and destruction of property. In addition to the expense of largely ineffective stockades, countering Indian raids entailed outlays for military supplies and indirect losses when extended conflict took males from farms and shops.

During the late colonial period, Great Britain began calling upon colonists to supply expeditionary forces for imperial campaigns in Canada and the Caribbean. The wartime infusion of British gold and colonial issuance of paper money to pay volunteers and buy supplies usually brought temporary prosperity, and war's death and destruction affected only small bodies of soldiers and a few frontier communities. The imperial wars left Britain deeply in debt and possessed of a vast undefended territory, which prompted its attempts to impose on the colonists the policies that led to the *Revolutionary War.

By 1775, American farmers and craftsmen could provide nearly all of the military goods for American ground forces of sufficient size to counter the army that Britain could maintain in North America. Unable to mobilize those resources, however, Congress failed to bring the Revolutionary War to a speedy conclusion, compounding the loss of life and property.

With foreign loans difficult to obtain and citizens reluctant to buy its bonds, Congress mobilized economic resources by printing bills of credit—paper money—with which to pay troops and purchase supplies. Because state governments failed to impose taxes to return those notes to Philadelphia—and instead issued fiat money of their own—military reverses caused the value on paper money to decline precipitously.

Unable to buy supplies, military commanders resorted to impressment (seizure) of food and animals, undermining civilian morale and burdening farmers nearest the troops. When a forty to one devaluation and specie loans from foreign sources failed to stem inflation the *Continental army remained ill-clothed, ill-shod, and ill-fed.

Independence, once gained, injured the economy by ending British subsidies and American access to British markets, but brought benefits by freeing Americans to sell their goods in any open port. Without access to British merchants, businessmen created new networks within the United States, and tapped a promising national market. Wartime self-sufficiency had forced Americans to manufacturing as never before—at least until postwar British dumping undermined that activity. The war's principal economic victims were the infrequently paid Continental soldiers and their families.

Although the United States lacked the ability to mobilize the necessary resources to achieve its goal of conquering Canada in the *War of 1812, the nation suffered little loss of life and—despite the burning of Washington—property destruction. Financed mostly by the sale of bonds and new excise duties, the war also created relatively few financial problems. The British blockade and prewar trade embargoes led to a revival of American manufacturing and

a postwar commitment to maintain self-sufficiency with protective tariffs.

A stronger administration and an improved economy enabled the United States in 1846 to project its military power deep into Mexico and the Pacific coast. With all but two battles fought on Mexican territory, the United States suffered little property damage during the *Mexican War. Its *casualties were light as was the financial cost of a war that increased the national domain by over a half million square miles.

To achieve its aims during the *Civil War, the Federal government relied upon bond sales, heavy taxes, minimal issue of "greenbacks," and generous contracts to mobilize its superior economy sufficiently to defeat and occupy an area roughly equal to western Europe. Despite unprecedented governmental controls over railroads, foreign trade, agriculture, and business, the Confederacy repeated Revolutionary War financial errors and failed to make effective use of its limited resources.

Along with 260,000 deaths, the Confederacy suffered virtual economic collapse. Military operations and the end of slavery devastated Southern agriculture and destroyed its rail net and nascent industry. Despite a slowdown in the growth rate of the entire nation's economy, wartime inflation created the illusion of greater growth in the Union, whose farmers, meat packers, canneries, railroads, canals, and farm implement makers made substantial profits.

The loss of over 600,000 lives and the intangibles make it difficult to assess precisely the Civil War's economic legacy. What talents fell on the battlefield? What benefits resulted from postwar investment of wartime profits? From skills businessmen acquired when filling large military contracts and distributing goods to far flung armies? From wartime legislative enactment of protective tariffs, a national banking system, a transcontinental railroad, and free homesteads? From the electoral triumph of a political party committed to using Federal power to promote economic development?

Despite the greater intensity of *World War II the parallel circumstances, policies, and consequences of both it and *World War I justify joint assessment. Particularly in World War II, an effective, if gradual, mobilization of its industrialized economy offered the United States a range of strategic options and permitted it to fight a modern, mechanized war, eventually on several global fronts, while also sustaining the military efforts of its allies.

The United States, confounded by economic downturns in 1914 and 1938, first felt the economic stimulation of war while still a neutral. By wars' end, the nation enjoyed unprecedented prosperity, a booming economy pressing on the short-term limits of its capacity, and a vast improvement in its global economic and financial position. In nominal terms, both wars doubled the gross national product. By 1916, the United States had become a creditor nation and seized many formerly European markets in Latin America. By the end of World War II, due to allied losses, America's wartime industrial expansion, and new technology resulting from scientific research and engineering development, the United States dominated its former economic competitors.

While most traditional economic sectors benefited from mobilization, World War I prompted the United States to create a chemical industry, and both wars led to vast expansions of shipbuilding and aircraft production. To meet the wars' demands and compensate for loss of workers to the armed forces, agriculture increased its mechanization and applied new technologies that boosted output. Though making limited use of government corporations, Washington gained the compliance of private producers largely through controlling scarce raw materials, banning production of inessential goods, offering lucrative contracts, subsidies, and tax breaks; patriotic appeals, and suspending antitrust laws. To win workers' cooperation, the government encouraged unionization and placed labor leaders on various government boards, while overlooking use of various devices to escape the worst effects of wage controls. By wars' end, the War Industries Board of World War I and the World War II's Office of War Mobilization sought to coordinate economy and allocate production among the armed forces, the civilian sector, and the Allies. Washington financed both world wars largely through new taxes and loans. Though applied too gradually in both cases, government management of the economy—to include rationing of consumer goods in World War II—reinforced sound war finance and helped limit wartime inflation.

Although early *Cold War programs like the *Marshall Plan had a limited stimulative effect on the economy, the four-decade confrontation with the Soviet bloc began to produce significant economic effects with the onset of the *Korean War and concurrent American rearmament, which led to sustained high levels of defense spending and the nation's first large peacetime armaments industry. Many feared this *military-industrial complex might threaten democracy or prolong Soviet-American hostility for the benefit of the military, arms manufacturers, defense workers.

When the Cold War turned "hot" in Korea, defense spending, a civilian buying spree prompted by recent memories of wartime shortages, and a delay in tax increases and governmental controls resulted in a burst of inflation. By 1951, however, a tax hike, wage and price controls, and a significant spending-induced increase in the gross national product (25 percent above the 1948 level) kept inflation below 3 percent.

Sharp limits on defense spending during the administration of President Dwight D. *Eisenhower cut that rate in half—and contributed to three recessions—until the *Vietnam War, when President Lyndon B. *Johnson sought to manage the Southeast Asian conflict and the Great Society domestic programs without resort to typical wartime economic controls. By war's end, with the economy no longer booming and the fight against inflation seemingly lost, government offered automatic cost of living adjustments for workers and government beneficiaries until, in the Cold War's final decade—the 1980s—high interest rates and limits on social programs helped tame inflation even as defense spending surged during the presidency of Ronald *Reagan. With the reduction of military spending at the end of the Cold War, many feared a major recession, but the American economy boomed throughout most of the 1990s.

[See also Agriculture and War; Finance and War; Industry and War.]

• Ralph L. Andreano, ed., The Economic Impact of the American Civil War, 1967. Robert D. Cuff, The War Industries Board: Business-Government Relations During World War I, 1973. Harold G. Vatter, The U.S. Economy in World War II, 1985. Harold G. Vatter and John F. Walker, eds., History of the U.S. Economy Since World War II, 1996. Paul A. C. Koistinen, Beating Plowshares into Swords: The Political Economy of American Warfare, 1606-1985, 1996. Paul A. C. Koistinen, Mobilizing for Modern War: The Political Economy of American Warfare, 1865-1919, 1997. Paul A. C. Koistinen, Planning War, Pursuing Peace: The Political Economy of American Warfare, 1920-1939, 1998.
—James L. Abrahamson

EDISON, THOMAS ALVA (1847–1931), prolific inventor, entrepreneur, and industrialist. A pioneer in team industrial research, Edison made significant innovations in communications technologies (telegraph, telephone, phonograph, and motion pictures) and in electric lighting and electric power systems.

Edison's laboratories in New Jersey and his worldwide acclaim as a successful inventor reinforced an aura of American industrial progress through research that fostered application of systemized research to military technology in the first half of the twentieth century. In 1915, naval secretary Josephus Daniels enlisted Edison to organize and chair a Naval Consulting Board to provide technical counsel to the navy. Edison lent his name to board activities, personally engaged in sonic research for detection of submarines, and vigorously promoted creation of a Naval Research Laboratory. His group was outflanked, however, by the National Academy of Science, representing younger, academically oriented scientists. They created a presidentially appointed National Research Council, led by the politically astute George Ellery Hale, which attained a power and influence that eclipsed the Edison group and ultimately led in World War II to establishment of Vannevar *Bush's powerful Office of Scientific Research and Development. Nevertheless, some of the Edison's companies were organized into the General Electric Company, which became a major defense contractor.

[See also Consultants; World War II: Domestic Course.]

• Reese V. Jenkins, et al., eds., Papers of Thomas Edison, 1989– . Paul Israel, Edison: A Life of Invention, 1998.
—Reese V. Jenkins

EDUCATION, MILITARY. Military *education* involves the professional preparation of officers to lead armed forces effectively in peace and war. It can be distinguished from *indoctrination* (the transmission of group values, traditions, and attitudes) and *training* (the development of concrete manual and mental skills) in that it seeks to instill an understanding of abstract principles and theory and to develop effective patterns of thought and communication.

Education has been linked closely with the growth of professionalism in the military forces of the United States since the mid-nineteenth century. Its principal purpose is to ensure the mastery of a body of specialized knowledge, one of the characteristics of any profession. Accordingly, the principal subject areas of professional military education include: the art of command (leadership); the organization and management of military forces; strategy, tactics, and logistics; military history; national security policy; the relationship of armed forces and society; and individual analytical and communication skills. The approach to these professional topics becomes broader, more complex, and more abstract at each successive level of formal military schooling.

Before World War II, the pace of peacetime garrison life or duty at sea left a good deal of time for individual professional study. Since 1945, the pace of active service and the resulting demands on an officer's time have increased tremendously, as have the breadth and complexity of the body of knowledge that must be mastered. Consequently, formal military schools now provide the principal venue for professional development.

Each of the military services has its own integrated, progressive program of formal education, which includes attendance for selected personnel at formal courses at the undergraduate, service school, staff college, and senior service college levels, as well as technical courses and courses at joint postgraduate schools. The four undergraduate national service academies (the Military Academy at West Point; the Naval Academy at Annapolis; the Air Force Academy at Colorado Springs; and the Coast Guard Academy at New London), the *ROTC programs found on many college campuses, and officer candidate schools run by each of the services prepare young men and women for initial entry to the services as commissioned officers. Basic service school courses, such as those for army infantry officers at Fort Benning, Georgia, and for Marine Corps officers at Quantico, Virginia, prepare newly commissioned junior officers for duties in operational units and aboard ship. Advanced service school courses, such as those offered by the Air Force Squadron Officers School at Maxwell Air Force Base, Alabama, and the army's Transportation School at Fort Eustis, Virginia, prepare senior company-grade officers for small unit command and staffwork through battalion level. Staff colleges—the army's Command and General Staff College at Fort Leavenworth, Kansas, for example—prepare selected mid-level career officers for service at battalion, brigade, and division level, and equivalent navy and air force echelons. Finally, the three senior service colleges—the Naval War College at Newport, Rhode Island; the Army War College at Carlisle Barracks, Pennsylvania; and the Air War College at Maxwell Air Force Base, Alabama—prepare selected senior field-grade officers for the highest command and staff positions. In addition, three joint service colleges—the Armed Forces Staff College in Norfolk, Virginia, and the National War College and the Industrial College of the Armed Forces, both in Washington, D.C.—seek to improve joint operations through interservice understanding and cooperation. A limited number of American officers are also selected to attend the military schools of other nations or the *NATO Defense College in Rome. Specialist courses, graduate degree programs at civilian universities, and training with industry complete the array of formal military schooling.

In the United States, military education has always been closely linked to developments in the civilian educational community, and military educators have often been caught up by the fads in educational theory that have swept the civilian community periodically. For example, the development in the late nineteenth century of both civilian graduate education and the military war colleges was based on German models: the seminar method of the German universities and the Prussian *Kriegsakademie*, respectively. And today the call for "back to basics" rings in the halls of military schools as loudly as in our elementary and secondary schools and colleges.

Military educators have often led the exchange of ideas with their civilian counterparts. In 1817, the U.S. Military Academy at West Point, then under the direction of Sylvanus *Thayer, established the first formal program of engineering instruction, a program later copied by civilian institutions. At the turn of the century, the army's School of the Line at Fort Leavenworth (now the U.S. Army Command and General Staff College), under the leadership of Arthur L. Wagner and Eben Swift, stressed active student learning through practical exercises in place of passive lectures. This so-called applicatory method was much admired and emulated by civilian academicians, as were the methods of standardized testing developed by the army and navy in the two world wars.

Although most civilian and military leaders agree on the ultimate goal of military education, there is considerable controversy over how that goal should be attained. One of the fundamental issues is time. Some officers (particularly in the navy) view formal schooling as a waste of time and argue that the best means of developing professional competence is on-the-job experience in active service in units and at sea. This view is reflected in all the services in the reluctance of some officers to attend formal military schools, and in lower selection and retention rates for those who "waste" too much time attending or teaching in the military educational institutions. Debate also exists over the relative value of "education" versus "training." Many critics maintain that the various military schools should train officers for their next assignment rather than educate them for greater professional contributions at some indefinite future time and place. Others insist that military education should focus on operational military matters to the exclusion of "soft" subjects such as international relations, economics, and management.

[See also Academies: Service; Schools, Postgraduate Service; Schools, Private Military; Training and Indoctrination.]

• John W. Masland and Laurence I. Radway, *Soldiers and Scholars: Military Education and National Policy*, 1957. James C. Shelburne and Kenneth J. Groves, *Education in the Armed Forces*, 1965. Lawrence J. Korb, ed., *The System for Educating Military Officers in the U.S.*, 1976. Martin van Creveld, *The Training of Officers: From Military Professionalism to Irrelevance*, 1990.

—Charles R. Shrader

EISENHOWER, DWIGHT D. (1890–1969), World War II general and thirty-fourth president of the United States. Dwight David Eisenhower was born to David and Ida Stover Eisenhower in Denison, Texas, 14 October 1890. The following year, he, his parents, and two brothers moved to Abilene, Kansas, his father's childhood home. After graduating from high school, Eisenhower received appointment to the U.S. Military Academy at West Point, and in 1915, he was commissioned second lieutenant. Following U.S. entry into World War I, he commanded the U.S. army tank corps training center at Camp Colt near Gettysburg, Pennsylvania. In the postwar years, Eisenhower held staff positions under the most accomplished and influential officers in the U.S. Army, including Generals John J. *Pershing, Fox Conner, and Douglas *MacArthur. In the process, he became a military strategist, rising slowly through the ranks from major to brigadier general. In World War II, Gen. George C. *Marshall, army chief of staff, appointed Eisenhower to command of the War Plans Division (later the Operations Division) of the Army General Staff; then to supreme command sequentially of the Allied invasions of North Africa, Sicily and Italy, and of Normandy, France, as well as being Supreme Allied Commander in Europe.

Eisenhower accepted the German unconditional surrender for the Western Allies on 8 May 1945. Returning to the United States as a five-star general (general of the army), he accepted appointment as army chief of staff. After overseeing the demobilization of the army and writing a best-selling war memoir, *Crusade in Europe*, in 1948, Eisenhower retired from the army and became president of Columbia University.

Not long after the outbreak of the *Korean War in June 1950, President Harry S. *Truman called him back to active duty as the first supreme commander of the North Atlantic Treaty Organization (*NATO), a position Eisenhower retained until May 1952, when he announced his candidacy for the Republican presidential nomination. He was elected thirty-fourth president of the United States and served two terms. His health became a problem beginning in the mid-1960s, and he died on 28 March 1969.

A man with two distinguished careers—one as a professional soldier and the other as political leader and statesman—Eisenhower was the subject of more than the usual amount of controversy, much of which was unnecessary. The first area of controversy concerned his performance as Supreme Allied Commander. American critics observed his swift rise through the ranks after the outbreak of World War II despite a lack of combat experience and erroneously attributed it mainly to "Ike's" genial manner. The British, especially Gen. Bernard Law *Montgomery, whose army had defeated the Germans and Italians at El Alamein in 1942, questioned Eisenhower's strategy for the Battle for *Germany. Instead of Eisenhower's planned broad advance, aimed at surrounding the Ruhr industrial heartland and destroying the German Army, Montgomery advocated a narrow ("pencil thrust") aimed across the northern European plain at Berlin. Eisenhower had read military history, including the works of the Prussian military intellectual Carl von *Clausewitz, and had studied the art of war under the supervision of the leading American strategists. Accordingly, he stayed with his objective and methods of attaining it. The British High Command later admitted—and American historians agree—that Eisenhower's approach was correct. Like most commanders, he had some setbacks, but his achievements were large. They included the movements that turned back the unforeseen German attacks at the Kasserine Pass in Tunisia in February 1943, and at the Ardennes—the Battle of the *Bulge in December 1944. That month, Congress bestowed on him a fifth star and the rank of general of the army.

The Eisenhower presidency, in retrospect one of the most successful of the modern era, also involved controversy, reflected by the fact that not long after he left office, historians ranked him only twenty-second in polls of presidential effectiveness. Many contemporary critics focus on his frequent relaxations, golf and trout fishing. And after his heart attack in 1955 and a slight stroke in 1957, pundits doubted his stamina. They condemned his failure publicly to repudiate the anti-Communist demagogue, Senator Joseph R. McCarthy of Wisconsin. Civil rights advocates criticized the Civil Rights Acts of 1957 and 1960 for not going far enough. Other critics incorrectly said Eisenhower turned over U.S. foreign policy to John Foster *Dulles, his secretary of state. The Soviet launching of Sputnik, the world's first artificial satellite, testing of intercontinental *missiles, and shooting down of an American U-2 reconnaissance airplane (1960) brought charges that Eisenhower had weakened American defenses, allowing an alleged "missile gap" to develop with the Soviet Union. The president, they also charged, used the *Central Intelligence Agency to put the United States on the side of right-wing dictators in Third World nations such as Iran and Guatemala.

More recently, history has been kinder to the Eisenhower presidency. Eisenhower retained many of the approaches to social, economic, and foreign policy that the American people had come to accept during the Great Depression and World War II, while at the same time altering those laws and policies that discouraged economic growth and stifled initiative. Congress, with administration prodding, strengthened and expanded Social Security, authorized the national system of interstate highways and the St. Lawrence Seaway, and brought Alaska and Hawaii into the Union. The economy flourished, the gross national product growing 70 percent to $520 billion from $365 billion. As a Republican and a conservative, Eisenhower received criticism from the liberals. But since he refused to roll back the social policies of Franklin D. *Roosevelt, he also irritated the right wing of the GOP. To the dismay of both, he refused to confront McCarthy, working instead to bring "McCarthyism" to an end by terminating executive branch cooperation with the senator's scattershot investigations. And though Eisenhower doubted the capacity of federal legislation to bring racial justice, his appointment of Earl Warren as Chief Justice of the Supreme Court and the enactment of the Civil Rights Acts of 1957 and 1960 encouraged some hope for blacks against discrimination. In his national security policies, Eisenhower obtained a negotiated armistice in Korea, increased U.S. military readiness, especially in airpower, and completed his predecessor's policy of containing Communist expansion by establishing a worldwide system of treaties and alliances. He increased U.S. assistance to South Vietnam but refused to authorize the use of U.S. combat forces there. The archival record shows that Eisenhower, not Dulles, was in active charge of U.S. foreign policy. The CIA did assist undemocratic forces in the Third World, but the allegations about a "missile gap" were without merit. The United States had a commanding lead in missile development when Eisenhower left office. By the 1980s, he had moved to ninth place in the ranking of presidential performance.

[*See also* Cold War; Commander in Chief, President as; D-Day Landing; Eisenhower Doctrine; V-2 Incident; World War I: Military and Diplomatic Course; World War II: Military and Diplomatic Course.]

• Martin Blumenson and James L. Stokesbury, *Masters of the Art of Command*, 1975. Freed I. Greenstein, *The Hidden-Hand Presidency: Eisenhower as Leader*, 1982. Stephen E. Ambrose, *Eisenhower: Soldier, General of the Army, President-Elect*, 1983. Stephen E. Ambrose, *Eisenhower: The President*, 1984. R. Alton Lee, *Dwight D. Eisenhower: A Bibliography of His Times and Presidency*, 1991. William B. Pickett, *Dwight David Eisenhower and American Power*, 1995.
—William B. Pickett

EISENHOWER DOCTRINE (1957). After the Suez Crisis of 1956, President Dwight D. *Eisenhower, citing the danger of the spread of "international Communism," told Congress on 5 January 1957 that the United States regarded "as vital to the national interest and world peace the preservation of the independence and integrity of the nations of the Middle East." He asked for authorization to develop economic and military programs, including the use of armed forces, to assist any "nation or group of nations in the general area of the Middle East desiring such assistance" to preserve their independence. After two months of acrimonious debate, Congress approved the "Eisenhower Doctrine" in a joint resolution on 9 March 1957.

The United States first invoked the Eisenhower Doctrine in the Jordanian crisis of April 1957, and again in August 1957 when a perceived Syrian-Soviet rapprochement threatened the stability of the region. But Eisenhower did not dispatch armed forces. A military coup against the pro-Western regime in Iraq on 14 July 1958 sparked the most visible manifestation of the Eisenhower Doctrine during the *Lebanon Crisis, when Lebanese president Camille Chaumon requested immediate military assistance to counter perceived Egyptian-Syrian attempts to destabilize his government. On 15 July, Eisenhower deployed the Sixth Fleet and landed nearly 15,000 U.S. troops to ensure that Lebanon could elect its own president without external interference.

Seldom mentioned after 1958, the Eisenhower Doctrine was indicative of American preoccupation with the *Cold War. Characterized by some historians as an extension of the *Truman Doctrine, Eisenhower's policy lent credence to the belief that the United States had assumed a global role in the preservation of regional stability and the promotion of its own national interests.

[See also Middle East, U.S. Military Involvement in the.]

• Dwight Eisenhower, The White House Years: Waging Peace, 1956–1961, 1965. Roger Spiller, "'Not War But Like War': The American Intervention in Lebanon." Leavenworth, Papers, 1981. Stephen E. Ambrose, Eisenhower: The President, 1984. Alan Dowty, Middle East Crisis: U.S. Decision-Making in 1958, 1970, and 1973, 1984. George Lenczowski, American Presidents and the Middle East, 1990.   —Cole C. Kingseed

ELLIS, "PETE" EARL HANCOCK (1880–1923), Marine officer and amphibious warfare specialist. Ellis was a prophetic strategist and tactician whose 1921 plan anticipated the U.S. *Navy's Central Pacific campaign of World War II. He enlisted as a private in the U.S. *Marine Corps in 1900 and was commissioned a year later. Five years' service in the Philippines and eighteen months with the Asiatic Fleet acquainted him with the Far East and with the Defense of Subic Bay. While at the Naval War College from 1911 to 1913, as student and a faculty member, Ellis developed his vision of amphibious assault operations and prepared studies for the defense of such Pacific islands as Guam, Peleliu, and Samoa. In 1914, after participating in the first advanced base exercise he reported to Guam to help plan its defense. He joined the staff of Marine Gen. John A. *Lejeune in Washington and later accompanied Lejeune to France in 1917–1918. In 1920, Maj. Ellis was assigned to USMC headquarters, under now Commandant Lejeune. There Ellis prepared his major work, a seminal report entitled "Advanced Base Operations in Micronesia," in which he prescribed amphibious assault operations to seize islands needed as advanced bases to support the naval campaign against Japan. In 1922, Lejeune granted Ellis permission for a covert mission to Micronesia to ascertain if any of the bases had been fortified. Ellis died on the trip in 1923 under mysterious circumstances. Despite rumors, no evidence exists of Japanese involvement in his death, which was instead consistent with Ellis's accelerating alcoholism.

[See also Amphibious Warfare; Marine Corps, U.S.: 1914–45.]

• Earl H. Ellis, Advanced Base Operations in Micronesia, 1921. Dirk A. Ballendorf and Merrill L. Bartlett, Pete Ellis, An Amphibious Prophet, 1880–1923, 1997.
                                    —Suzanne Borghei and Victor J. Croziat

ELLSBERG, DANIEL (1931–), military analyst, nonviolent activist. Ellsberg graduated from Harvard in 1952, served as a Marine infantry commander (1953–56), then returned to Harvard for his Ph.D. An expert on crisis decision making at the Rand Corporation think tank, he was a consultant on *nuclear weapons to the *Pentagon and Kennedy White House, notably in the *Cuban Missile Crisis. Early in the *Vietnam War (1964–65), he was special assistant to the assistant secretary of defense responsible for Vietnam policy. He spent two years in South Vietnam as a State Department adviser (1965–67), then rejoined Rand and contributed to the Pentagon's internal classified history of the war ordered by Defense Secretary Robert S. *McNamara.

In October 1969, Ellsberg tried to release the secret Pentagon history to Congress, but lawmakers refused the material. Drawn more deeply into the antiwar movement, he provided the so-called *Pentagon Papers to the New York Times and Washington Post. Its June 1971 publication revealed a history of presidential failures and deceptions and was critically important in mobilizing public opposition to the war. President Richard M. *Nixon and his national security adviser Henry *Kissinger feared further leaks by Ellsberg. To silence and slander Ellsberg and block future "leaks," they created the White House "Plumbers" unit. At Nixon's instigation, the unit conducted an illegal break-in of Ellsberg's psychiatrist's office in Los Angeles in September 1971. The same "Plumbers" unit carried out the June 1972 Watergate burglary, which led to President Nixon's resignation in August 1974. Ellsberg was tried for espionage, but because of White House tampering, the federal judge dismissed the charges. During the 1970s and 1980s, Ellsberg lectured widely and was arrested for antiwar and antinuclear civil disobedience protests.

[See also Peace and Antiwar Movements.]

• Sanford Ungar, The Papers and the Papers, 1972. Peter Schrag, Test of Loyalty: Daniel Ellsberg and the Rituals of Secret Government, 1974.
                                                        —Stewart Burns

EL SALVADOR, U.S. MILITARY INVOLVEMENT IN. Unlike most other Central American republics, El Salvador never had U.S. troops land on its territory, even during the 1932 Communist uprising. Internal security was left to various gendarmeries and the regular army, acting at the behest of a tiny planter elite. However, during the *Cold War, Salvadoran officers trained in U.S. installations and received minor amounts of military aid, and in the 1960s, the *Central Intelligence Agency helped found a rural paramilitary organization, ORDEN, birthing the "death squads" of the next two decades.

In the late 1970s, various small left-wing insurgent groups allied to "popular organizations" of peasants, students, and slum dwellers began challenging the military government. Following the 1979 Sandinista victory in Nicaragua, U.S. national security experts feared El Salvador would be the next "Cuban-Soviet proxy" on the

American mainland. From late 1979 on, the Carter administration shipped arms to weak civilian-military juntas, while death squad killings reached 1,000 per month, including 4 U.S. Catholic churchwomen and the country's archbishop, Oscar Romero, killed in March 1980 after requesting that President Jimmy *Carter cut off aid.

In October 1980, five Marxist-Leninist guerrilla organizations formed the Farabundo Marti National Liberation Front (FMLN). In January 1981, they launched a "final offensive," just before Ronald *Reagan assumed office. This attempt failed due to lack of arms and trained troops, and the guerrillas turned to consolidating their control over parts of the countryside.

Meanwhile, U.S. *counterinsurgency experts and aid flooded in, as El Salvador became the first showplace for the new "Reagan Doctrine" of stopping and rolling back Third World revolutions. Eventually, $6 billion was funneled into a country the size of Massachusetts, with a population of 5 million. U.S. advisers managed the war down to the company level, and trained ten air-mobile "hunter-killer" battalions to seek out the elusive FMLN units. For all sides, from a widespread protest movement in the United States to North American military planners to the guerrillas, it seemed a replay of Vietnam. The one signal difference was that U.S. officers at all levels, and the president himself, were deeply committed to avoiding a ground war involving U.S. troops and casualties. This was the major innovation of the so-called *Low-Intensity Conflict doctrine.

Between 1981 and 1989, the FMLN and U.S. specialists played a minuet involving all the classic elements of peasant-based insurgency and counterinsurgency. A skirmishing war or "permanent offensive" by guerrilla columns drove demoralized government forces back in 1982–84, threatening a seizure of power. It was met by an effective political charge when a pro-U.S. Christian Democrat, José Napoleon Duarte, defeated extreme rightist Roberto D'Aubuisson for president in a carefully staged 1984 election, promising peace. Meanwhile, a sophisticated air war utilizing U.S.-supplied helicopter gunships, "Puff the Magic Dragon" minigun platforms, and the heaviest bombing in the hemisphere's history punished the FMLN's "zones of control," driving out civilians and inflicting heavy losses on main force guerrilla units, which had reached a peak of more than 12,000 in 1984.

In response, the FMLN dispersed its troops throughout the country and focused on rebuilding an urban political base. Mines and constant ambushes depleted the government forces, which had quadrupled in size to 60,000 through heavy conscription. Army bases were periodically overrun, to demonstrate the guerrillas' capacity, while "solidarity organizations" in the United States and Europe supported the FMLN's civilian network. But the Left's popularity was limited by the growth of mass-based electoral politics for the first time in Salvadoran history, led by the right-wing ARENA Party, and containment of FMLN forces within thinly populated rural zones.

Growing urban unrest, the collapse of the Christian Democrats, and an increasingly professional FMLN army all led toward a massive guerrilla offensive in November 1989. In an odd valedictory for the end of the Cold War, rebel units held large parts of San Salvador for a week before retreating, their hopes for a popular uprising dashed. But the vigor of FMLN attacks, and the bankruptcy of the government forces—the U.S.-trained Atlacatl Battalion butchered prominent Jesuit priests at the offensive's height—encouraged the Bush administration to support peace negotiations with a chastened FMLN.

The negotiating process, under UN auspices, lasted from spring 1990 through New Year's Day, 1992. It was punctuated by a renewed FMLN offensive late in 1990, using surface-to-air *missiles obtained in Nicaragua, which threatened the government's air superiority. Eventually, an accord was signed that led to the retirement of most of the armed forces' senior officers, and the creation of a new civilian police incorporating members from both sides. In return, the FMLN gave up its armed struggle, and in the 1994 elections became the country's second-largest civilian political party. The bitterest military conflict in late twentieth-century Latin American history came to an end with all sides claiming a measure of victory.

[See also Guerrilla Warfare; Nicaragua, U.S. Military Involvement in.]

• Hugh Byrne, El Salvador's Civil War: A Study of Revolution, 1996. William LeoGrande, Our Own Backyard: The United States in Central America, 1998.
—Van Gosse

EMANCIPATION PROCLAMATION (1863). Abraham *Lincoln's presidency began in March 1861 with a pledge to maintain slavery by enforcing the federal fugitive slave law. By May, however, Lincoln accept a de facto "contraband" policy that permitted Union commanders to protect and employ black fugitives who came within their lines from disloyal regions. Congress suspended federal enforcement of the fugitive slave law and provided in the summer of 1862 for the confiscation and emancipation of "contraband" slaves. Gen. George B. *McClellan vehemently opposed these measures, but Lincoln soon acted as commander in chief to declare emancipation a Union war aim.

On 22 September 1862, Lincoln declared that all slaves would be freed in states or regions of states still in rebellion on the first day of the following year. After this proclamation, the prospect of pro-Southern intervention by Britain faded. The proclamation also marked a fundamental shift in Union military policy. Initially opposed to enrolling any blacks as soldiers, Lincoln authorized an aggressive recruitment campaign immediately following the issuance of the final proclamation on 1 January 1863.

The Emancipation Proclamation was Lincoln's most direct action to hasten the end of slavery. Historians have offered varied interpretations of its relative significance in the process of wartime emancipation. Louis Gerteis in From Contraband to Freedman argues that military necessity created the conditions that first prompted Congress and later required Lincoln to adopt emancipation policies. Ira Berlin and his colleagues in The Destruction of Slavery emphasize the roles played by African Americans in securing their own liberation within the conditions created by war and federal policy. In his Pulitzer Prize-winning Battle Cry of Freedom, James McPherson insists that emancipation—and the Union victory necessary to obtain it—rested fundamentally on Lincoln's leadership.

[See also: African Americans in the Military; Civil War: Domestic Course; Colored Troops, U.S.]

• Louis Gerteis, From Contraband to Freedman: Federal Policy Toward Southern Blacks, 1861–1865, 1972. Ira Berlin, Barbara J. Fields, Thavolia Glymph, Joseph P. Reidy, and Leslie S. Rowland,

Freedom: A Documentary History of Emancipation, 1861–1867, Series I, Vol. I: *The Destruction of Slavery,* 1985. James McPherson, *Battle Cry of Freedom: The Civil War Era,* 1988.

—Louis S. Gerteis

ENEMY, VIEWS OF THE. All cultures dehumanize their enemies to some degree. They do this by portraying them as aggressors or even devils, savages, torturers, rapists, or vermin. These attributes may be applied to the enemy's entire society or only to its ruler or ruling elite. Americans have typically applied this more focused view of the enemy to countries that mirror themselves racially, culturally, or ideologically. Peoples who seemed alien were more likely to be regarded all-inclusively as the enemy.

Adversaries who have most nearly resembled Americans include the British during the *Revolutionary War and the *War of 1812, the Germans of World War I and II, and of course the Northerners and Southerners of the *Civil War. In each case, the true enemy was ordinarily identified as the opponent's leadership rather than population. Thus, revolutionaries fixed most of their hostility on the British king, *George III, and his ministers, who were said to be pursuing a grand design aimed at the political enslavement of Americans. Parliament got less censure and the British public scarcely any at all. During the two world wars, the enemy was not so much the German people as "Kaiser Bill," the Prussian warlords, Adolf *Hitler, and the Nazi Party. In each case, these entities were perceived as aggressive and tyrannical. Southerners reserved most of their anger for Abraham *Lincoln, the "black Republicans," and the abolitionists. Northerners considered the common people of the South the dupes of Jefferson *Davis and the slaveholding aristocracy. The consistent common thread was a perceived threat to liberty, sometimes generalized into a threat to everything that was good, just, and holy.

This does not mean that Americans had no opinion of the soldiers who actually fought against them. In the Revolutionary era, the belief that the British government was trying to enslave them encouraged Americans to fix upon the fact that the British soldier was a professional who might receive pay but who otherwise resembled a degraded bondsman. "Hireling" was a common epithet. The fact that the British employed German mercenaries won particular opprobrium, and "hateful Hessian" was a phrase spat in anger for decades after the American Revolution. Southerners resurrected the image of the "hireling"—often extended to include the idea that Union soldiers were foreign immigrants—during the Civil War. Northerners sometimes viewed Southern soldiers as reluctant conscripts, forced into service by a planter oligarchy. German soldiers were called "Huns" or "Krauts" and were considered more prone to atrocity than Americans. In general, however, Americans tended to regard most of these enemy soldiers as honorable opponents, worthy of respect.

Much the same was true for the French, who were a major American opponent during the colonial period. One difference stemmed from the Catholicism of the French, which imparted overtones of a religious crusade to the struggle. Convinced that Catholicism represented a corruption of Christianity, many American Protestant clergymen decried the "Papists," viewed the French presence in North America as a threat to sound religion, and urged their parishioners to participate in or support expeditions against French possessions. A somewhat stronger version

of this image applied to the Catholic Spanish. Fired in part by the "Black Legend" of Spanish cruelty in South America and in part by perceptions of Spain as a civilization in decline, many Protestant Americans tended to view the Spanish as decadent and wicked. This imagery colored all American conflicts with Spain, from colonial contests to the *Spanish-American War. As an offshoot of Spain, Mexicans were seen in a similar light during both the *Mexican War and the Punitive Expedition (1916). Many North American disdained the fact that Mexicans were often of mixed Spanish and Indian heritage.

Perhaps the single most dominant American image of the enemy was that of the Indian, partly because white Americans fought Native Americans for nearly four centuries, and partly because white imagery of Native Americans would prove an important influence on subsequent images of Asian adversaries. American views of Indians were complex. On the other hand, they saw Indians as savage, cruel, and treacherous; on the other hand, many Americans perceived a noble stoicism and simplicity about them. Americans thus viewed Indians with a mixture of revulsion and admiration.

The view of the Indian as noble savage was strongest in the East; that of the Indian as just plain savage was most pronounced in frontier districts. So easterners decried the plight of the Indians while westerners called for their extermination. Nineteenth-century American Army officers often oscillated between both perspectives. Gen. Philip H. *Sheridan, for example, believed the only good Indian was a dead Indian, but also acknowledged that if he were an Indian, he would respond to the white invasion with violence, just as they did. Some officers even became involved with philanthropic projects, especially those aimed at educating Native Americans to assimilate into white society.

Most white Americans, whether animated by hatred toward Indians or a patronizing goodwill, united in the belief that Native Americans represented an inferior people. This belief grew especially pronounced in the first half of the nineteenth century, as white America became a self-consciously racist society. This is one reason that most Americans reacted with such shock to the annihilation of Gen. George Armstrong *Custer's command in 1876. It seemed impossible that Indians could utterly destroy even a heavily outnumbered force of white soldiers; some, indeed, credited rumors that the Indian battle leader had received training at West Point. The explicitly racist view of Indians extended to a heavy emphasis on sexual atrocity, something noticeably missing from earlier images of Native Americans. Although Indians had captured white women and children since colonial times, only in the nineteenth century did it become common for whites to assert that Indians raped captive females.

The dual attitude toward the Indian as a savage capable of the most wanton crimes and as an inferior human being in need of civilization was part of the dominant European attitude to nonwhite peoples during the Victorian era. It is best captured by Rudyard Kipling's poem "The White Man's Burden," which urged the reader to fight the "savage wars of peace" in order to impart by force education, technological improvement, and Western conceptions of law and order to the nonwhite peoples, "half-devil and half-child." Kipling composed the poem specifically to encourage the United States to annex the Philippine Islands after the Spanish-American War.

The American decision to annex the Philippines resulted in a prolonged pacification campaign from 1899 through 1902. Americans viewed the Filipino people as unready for self-government and saw themselves as benevolent tutors who would prepare the country for eventual independence. When Filipinos reacted with violence to this program, the United States responded harshly to them as "goo goos," an epithet that was the origin of the word *gook* of later Vietnam infamy. The degree to which American troops engaged in atrocities remains a hotly debated issue, but it is agreed that they regarded the Filipino insurgents as mere brigands and invoked the full severities available under the laws of war, including reprisals and summary executions.

Until the twentieth century, views of the enemy were disseminated principally through folklore, pamphlets, sermons, and newspapers. During World War I, however, the U.S. government played a major role in consciously shaping images and attitudes toward the enemy. The Committee of Public Information was the first governmental entity charged with this task; by World War II, propaganda was manufactured on a wide scale, using radio, film, and print media. Where the Germans were concerned, the principal emphasis was on the enemy leadership; but in the case of Japan, the entire Japanese people were characterized as inherently treacherous, vicious, and utterly inhuman. The most common image was one of vermin to be exterminated.

Implacable warfare was justified not only on the grounds that Japan deserved it for having begun the war with a "sneak" attack on *Pearl Harbor (1941), but also because the Japanese were supposedly a barbaric people bent on conquest and with no regard for human life, including their own. The kamikaze (suicide) attacks of 1944–45 reinforced this view, as did the fact that Japanese soldiers seldom surrendered. It is likely that the widespread view of the Japanese as vermin made it easier to unleash nuclear destruction in the bombings of *Hiroshima and Nagasaki in August 1945.

The wartime view of the Japanese proved readily adaptable to subsequent Asian adversaries, including the North Koreans, mainland Chinese, and North Vietnamese. The prevailing American image of the Vietnamese in particular mirrored aspects of previous U.S. encounters with nonwhite adversaries. As with the Indians and Filipinos, Americans believed they could improve the Vietnamese by fostering democratic, economic, and technological development. As with the Japanese, Americans reacted to the unexpected military prowess of this "backward" people during the *Vietnam War by endowing "Charley Cong" with superhuman determination and skill.

After World War II, however, a reaction to Nazi racism had discredited portraying the enemy in explicitly racial terms. And indeed, American views of the Koreans, Chinese, and Vietnamese, as well as the Russians, were all primarily shaped by the fact that they were Communist adversaries. Propaganda and popular perspectives during the *Cold War era portrayed the Communist adversary as faceless, godless, implacable—dedicated to nothing less than the utter destruction of the *American way of life, even at the cost of unleashing an unprovoked, full-scale nuclear strike. NSC-68, the top-secret American blueprint for military containment, portrayed the Cold War as a struggle between "the idea of freedom under a government of laws, and the idea of slavery under the grim oligarchy of the Kremlin."

Paranoia played a major role in the American image of the Communist menace. It was widely seen as a monolithic whole, with Communists everywhere pursuing a master plan orchestrated from Moscow. This view had enormous consequences. It encouraged Americans to view all Communists as a threat, so that any struggle for national liberation, if it contained a Communist presence, was viewed as a direct threat to American interests. It also rendered it difficult to perceive conflicts and cleavages between Communist countries, so that U.S. policymakers were painfully slow to recognize the hostility between, for example, the Soviet Union and China and between China and North Vietnam. It also sustained a destructive search for homegrown "Commies," of which the House UnAmerican Activies Committee and the McCarthy Hearing are just two of the best-known examples.

The 1970s ushered in yet another American enemy: the Islamic terrorist. Already angered by OPEC's threat to petroleum consumption, Americans reacted with fury to the taking of fifty-eight American hostages by Iranian revolutionaries in 1979. Islamic terrorists became the villain of choice in American films and television, and were generally portrayed as religious fanatics devoid of respect for human life. Yet the media avoided portraying the common people of the Islamic Middle East as anything much worse than backward and dirty. The U.S. government, well aware of critical economic and national security interests in the Middle East, carefully focused on specific terrorist groups or rogue dictators such as Libya's Muamar Gaddafi or Iraq's Saddam *Hussein, famously characterized by President Bush during the prelude to the *Persian Gulf War as resembling Hitler. Given a growing consciousness of cultural pluralism in the United States and an awareness of its economic interdependence on non-European countries, it is likely that future enemies will be portrayed in as focused a fashion as possible.

[*See also* Film, War and the Military in: Feature Films; Native American Wars: Wars Between Native Americans and Europeans and Euro-Americans; Philippines, U.S. Military Involvement in the; Propaganda and Public Relations, Government; World War II, U.S. Naval Operations in the Pacific.]

• Robert K. Berkhofer, Jr., *The White Man's Indian: Images of the American Indian from Columbus to the Present*, 1978. Ronald T. Takaki, *Iron Cages: Race and Culture in 19th-Century America*, 1979. Richard Slotkin, *The Fatal Environment: The Myth of the Frontier in the Age of Industrialization, 1800–1890*, 1985. John W. Dower, *War Without Mercy: Race and Power in the Pacific War*, 1986. Sam Keen, *Faces of the Enemy: Reflections of the Hostile Imagination*, 1986. Richard Slotkin, *Gunfighter Nation: The Myth of the Frontier in Twentieth-Century America*, 1992.

—Mark Grimsley

ENGINEERING, MILITARY. The U.S. Army's basic manual on what engineer troops should do in wartime defines five general tasks: mobility, countermobility, survivability, topography, and general engineering. The primary imperative is the offensive: movement. The obverse—impeding the movement of the enemy—is the engineer's second task. If the battlefield situation requires it, engineers must also provide expedient field fortifications, which will protect troops and equipment from enemy fire. Assisting the army in locating positions and understanding terrain is the engineers' fourth task. And finally, military engineers perform a variety of other duties, which change over time but are related to construction or destruction.

These five tasks, or "missions," are relatively straightforward and have defined in a general sense the responsibilities of military engineers for centuries. But the relative importance of each task has changed during the more than 200-year history of engineering in the U.S. Army.

Modern military engineering originated in seventeenth-century France under the influence of Louis XIV's great engineer, Marshal Vauban. French military engineering had a particularly strong influence on the development of engineering in the American Army. As Gen. George *Washington attempted to cobble together something approaching a respectable eighteenth-century standing army, he included on his staff a chief engineer and two assistants. Because Washington could not find Americans formally trained in military engineering, he recruited foreign, mostly French, professional military engineers.

The hallmarks of French engineers in the eighteenth century were the great bastioned *fortifications and the elaborate sieges required to capture them. In the primitive colonial environment, engineers had few opportunities for such sophisticated military engineering, but Continental army engineers made important contributions to American victory in the *Revolutionary War. They mapped terrain, designed field fortifications such as those at Saratoga, and cleared roads until they achieved preeminence in the final battle of the war. At the Battle of *Yorktown (1781), the American and French forces conducted a classic siege of the British positions and by their success ensured the independence of the American colonies.

For two decades after the Revolution, the U.S. *Army Corps of Engineers existed sporadically, for awhile in a union with the artillery. The threat of war with European powers helped revive it in 1802 when President Thomas *Jefferson and Congress reestablished the Corps at West Point, New York, where it would also "constitute a military academy" training especially military engineers. Until 1866, the Corps of Engineers ran the U.S. Military Academy and made it the first American college with a curriculum emphasizing engineering. The Corps modeled the academy on the Ecole Polytechnique and subscribed to the French view that a mathematically inclined, technical education best equipped young men to be army officers.

The Corps' French roots were demonstrated in its major activity in the early nineteenth century—designing and building brick and masonry seacoast fortifications. In a peculiarly American development born of the scarcity of native professional civilian engineers, the Corps of Engineers also became involved after 1824 in internal improvements on the rivers and harbors of the new nation. In another peculiarly American development, the army had two Corps of Engineers from 1818 to 1863: a Corps of Topographic Engineers, which devoted much attention to exploring and mapping the expanding country and to improving its rivers and harbors; and a Corps of Engineers, which concentrated on fortifications. Both groups were small and their bureaucratic domains sometimes overlapped. Both fought in the *Mexican War, and both supported the Union military effort in 1861.

Although the Corps of Engineers was reunited in 1863 and expanded during the *Civil War, most engineer troops,

like those in the rest of the *Union army, were volunteers. As in other wars, engineers mapped the theaters of operations and built bridges, but changing technology lent new urgency to some of their tasks. As rifling and breechloading increased the destructiveness of weapons, soldiers often improvised field fortifications. The war brought some grand sieges, which had been so much a part of the engineer tradition, but with ominous new dimensions. In the Confederate capture of *Fort Sumter and the Union siege of Fort Pulaski, the new artillery rapidly demolished the carefully designed battlements. These setbacks did not deter classically trained engineers, both during the war and after, from promoting the construction of more seacoast fortifications, which they attempted to protect from the growing threat of more powerful artillery. Other sieges, like the one at Petersburg, presaged the *trench warfare of the future; but Union engineers, like their peers in Europe, did not fully apprehend that new direction.

When the United States entered World War I, the great trench systems on the western front—the improvised and then improved field fortifications to protect soldiers from artillery and machine guns—were already in place. American engineers fought as infantry in the Allied assaults on the German lines and built bridges under fire, but the bulk of their work supported the enormous logistical effort required to supply the huge forces in northern France. The first engineers to France built railroads. They were followed by engineers who built roads, ports, and depots, and harvested lumber, their basic construction material. World War I made clear that engineers were critical not only in the front lines of combat but also behind those lines, where the huge logistical apparatus to support the insatiable appetites of modern industrialized warfare would require construction of all types.

On the eve of World War II, engineers could anticipate some of the growing combat and construction requirements of warfare. After the defensive deadlock of World War I, armies developed new tactics and new equipment, which emphasized movement and speed. Armored and mechanized engineer units had to keep up with the rapid movement of forces as the U.S. Army emulated the blitzkrieg warfare of the Germans. Engineers had to build bridges quickly, and these bridges had to be strong enough to carry heavy tanks. Specially equipped aviation engineer units trained to build front-line airfields quickly. No longer would combat be static and circumscribed.

Behind the front lines, the new pace of warfare and the new technology increased the demand for engineers. Dozens of highly specialized units rehabilitated ports, built petroleum pipelines, repaired and maintained equipment, supplied parts, produced highly sophisticated maps and charts, and performed a wide variety of other tasks required by the most technologically advanced army of its day. Although promoting the mobility of American forces and impeding the mobility of their enemies became the engineers' primary tasks in World War II, support for the huge military infrastructure that made that mobility possible also placed great demands on them.

Engineers had always built the military infrastructure in combat theaters, but World War II brought new responsibility for constructing the facilities required at home to mobilize and deploy American armies. Before the war, most of this task belonged to the Quartermaster Corps, but the heavy demands of wartime mobilization led the army to transfer this mission to the Corps of Engineers. The Corps had also constructed coastal defenses and kept available a large, experienced civilian workforce, which was devoted in peacetime to navigation improvements and flood control construction programs. Now this combined military and civilian group was in charge of all army and Army Air Force construction. Besides designing and supervising the construction of the *Pentagon and hundreds of mobilization facilities such as barracks, ammunition plants, and airfields, the engineers built the technologically sophisticated structures needed in the *Manhattan project to develop the atomic bomb. World War II found military engineers working around the world to perform the largest array of missions in their history.

Within five years of demobilization in 1945, engineers were fighting another war with much the same tactics and equipment used in World War II. Until the military stalemate that led to de facto peace in Korea, engineers honed their traditional skills.

A little more than a decade later, the engineers, like the rest of the U.S. Army, confronted in the *Vietnam War a conflict that was not traditional and not entirely tractable to the techniques of the two previous wars. Although the engineers built hundreds of miles of highways in South Vietnam and an elaborate logistical network that expanded beyond that typical in World War II, they struggled to best an elusive enemy that used *guerrilla warfare. Adapting to the new tactics, engineers cleared landing zones for the newly important *helicopters and cleared jungle from roadsides using massive Rome plows. Ultimately, however, their efforts accomplished little, as American troops were withdrawn from a war that bitterly divided the nation.

At home, the engineer role in prosecuting the *Cold War against the Soviet Union was more successful. After the separation of the air force from the army in 1947, the Corps of Engineers remained the primary construction agency for both services. Besides routine construction for the army, the engineers built the sophisticated facilities required by the air forces' strategic missions—airfields for heavy bombers, launch facilities for intercontinental ballistic *missiles, and *radar installations. The Corps of Engineers also built many of the facilities for the National Aeronautics and Space Administration. The Cold War kept the engineers busier with peacetime military construction than ever before in their history.

The last conflicts of the Cold War, or perhaps the first war of the post–Cold War era in the case of the *Persian Gulf War, brought the engineers like the rest of army back to their metier. Using a new generation of equipment and weapons developed during the Reagan defense buildup, the engineers assisted the Allied Coalition army in launching an air-ground blitzkrieg in the deserts of the Middle East. In a reassuring victory, which demonstrated that America could still fight a conventional war against conventional foes, the engineers maintained a secure place in an army that still needed massive logistical support and the apparatus that would allow its heavy equipment to move rapidly despite the vagaries of terrain. Though the end of the Cold War and the reduced size of the armed services lessens the need for engineer construction in the United States and abroad today, doctrine assures, as it has done since the Revolution, that engineers will have a place in the army of the future.

[See also Academies, Service: U.S. Military Academy; Education, Military.]

• William B. Parsons, *American Engineers in France*, 1920. Emanuel R. Lewis, *Fortifications of the United States: An Introductory History*, 1970. Frank N. Schubert, *Vanguard of Expansion: Army Engineers in the Exploration of the Trans-Mississippi West*, 1980. Paul K. Walker, *Engineers of Independence: A Documentary History of the Army Engineers in the American Revolution*, 1981. Dale Floyd, ed., *"Dear Friends at Home": The Letters and Diary of Thomas James Owen, Fiftieth New York Volunteer Engineer Regiment, During the Civil War*, 1985. Janice Holt Giles, *Damned Engineers*, 1985. Frank N. Schubert, ed., *The Nation Builders: A Sesquicentennial History of the Corps of Topographical Engineers, 1838–1863*, 1988. Barry W. Fowle, ed., *Builders and Fighters: U.S. Army Engineers in World War II*, 1992. Adrian Traas, *From the Golden Gate to Mexico City: The U.S. Army Topographical Engineers in the Mexican War, 1846–1848*, 1993.   —William C. Baldwin

ERICSSON, JOHN (1803–1889), engineer and inventor. Born in Sweden, Ericsson left for England in 1826 seeking sponsorship for his ideas. In 1829, his locomotive *Novelty*, with a forced-draft boiler, reached a speed of 50 miles an hour. And in 1837, his *Francis B. Ogden* successfully tested a new marine propeller. Another *Novelty* (1839) was the first propeller-driven commercial vessel. Yet Ericsson failed to interest the British Admiralty.

In 1841, Capt. Robert F. Stockton, USN, had him work for the navy designing the USS *Princeton*, the first screw-propelled naval steamer. All of its propulsion machinery was below the waterline, safe from enemy shot. Ericsson developed a stronger gun barrel using wrought iron. The *Princeton's* main battery consisted of two 12-inch wrought-iron smoothbore guns, Ericsson's "Oregon" and Stockton's similar but weaker "Peacemaker." In 1844, during a dignitary cruise, the Peacemaker exploded, killing Secretary of State Abel P. Upshur, Secretary of the Navy Thomas Gilmer, and several others.

At London's Great Exhibition in 1851, seven of his inventions on display earned him a prize medal.

Ericsson's ironclad *Monitor*, with the first revolving iron turret on a naval ship, sparked a naval ordnance revolution. It fought the CSS *Virginia* (the former USS *Merrimack*) to a draw on 9 March 1862 at the Battle of Hampton Roads and brought its inventor fame. Yet the earlier *Princeton* disaster was a factor in not using powder charges heavy enough to disable the *Virginia*.

In 1878, Ericsson's *Destroyer*, designed to fire underwater torpedoes from a 16-inch gun mounted in its bow, failed the navy's acceptance. He invented a successful shipboard depthfinder and surface condensers for marine engines, as well as pioneering solar energy. His marine steam and screw propulsion system brought the age of sail to a close.

• Ruth Morris White, *Yankee from Sweden*, 1960.

                                              —George E. Buker

ESPIONAGE AND SEDITION ACTS OF WORLD WAR I (1917, 1918) were the first forays since 1798 into federal regulation of First Amendment rights. These criminalizations of certain forms of expression, belief, and association resulted in the prosecution of over 2,000 cases, but in reaction they also produced a movement to protect the civil liberties of all Americans.

The Espionage Act (15 June 1917), enacted quickly by

Congress following the U.S. declaration of war on Germany, authorized federal officials to make summary arrests of people whose opinions "threatened national security." The measure prohibited willfully making false reports with intent to interfere with the success of the military or naval forces, inciting insubordination, disloyalty, or mutiny in the military, and obstructing recruitment or the enlistment service of the United States. Further sections authorized the Postmaster General to ban from the mails material advocating resistance to any law of the United States. This gave Post Office officials in the Wilson administration virtual dictatorial control over circulation of the nation's subsidiary press.

Realizing that the vagueness of the Espionage Act opened up opportunities for broad repression by government officials, as well as for mob violence and vigilante action, Congress augmented it with the Sedition Act on 16 May 1918. This set forth eight new criminal offenses, including uttering, printing, writing, or publishing any disloyal, profane, scurrilous, or abusive language intended to cause contempt, scorn, contumely, or disrespect for the U.S. government or the Constitution.

Before its repeal in 1921, the Sedition Act led to numerous arrests, particularly of dissident radicals, but also of important figures such as the socialist leader Eugene V. *Debs. The Espionage Act remained on the books to be invoked in the post–World War II period to charge certain controversial figures such as Julius and Ethel Rosenberg, accused of atomic espionage, with being a threat to the United States in the *Cold War.

[See also Alien and Sedition Acts; Civil Liberties and War; Schenk and Abrams Cases.]

• Harry N. Scheiber, The Wilson Administration and Civil Liberties, 1960. Paul L. Murphy, World War I and the Origin of Civil Liberties in the United States, 1979. —Paul L. Murphy

ETHNICITY AND RACE IN THE MILITARY. Ethnicity and race have been less troubling military questions for the United States than for nations where ethnic and racial competition, political power struggles, or caste systems have had a military dimension. Nonetheless, both factors have created military dilemmas for Americans from the earliest colonial settlements. Before the *Revolutionary War, many white colonists, who considered blacks biologically and culturally inferior and poor material for soldiers, were also afraid of arming slaves and free blacks and of losing their labor services. Sometimes blacks were excluded from the colonial militias, particularly in the South, but military need could overshadow racial fear, such as during the *French and Indian War. Some slaves were even granted their freedom for wartime military service.

Ethnocentrism, suspicion of loyalties, and loss of labor also militated against the military use of some non-English immigrants, but the need for frontier defense in the eighteenth century contributed to the settlement of Scotch-Irish, German, Swiss, and French Huguenot groups on the frontier to blunt Indian attacks and discourage slave rebellions. As the frontier moved westward and expeditions to distant places became the military norm, much of the actual fighting was done by recent immigrants on the fringes of the social order.

The Revolutionary War was justified as a war for liberty; but while northerners enlisted blacks, the South was opposed to arming African Americans. Diminished enlistment by whites and British offers of freedom for blacks who would desert and bear arms overcame initial attempts by southerners in the Continental Congress and the *Continental army to exclude blacks from military service. Approximately 5,000 African Americans fought with the Continental army or the militias (primarily in northern integrated units), although 1,000 joined British forces. Fighting for their freedom, many blacks were successful, although some masters sought to repossess their slaves and some blacks who fought for the British were later sold into slavery in the West Indies.

The Revolution set an enduring pattern of granting conscientious objector status to pacifist religious groups, some of whom, like the German Mennonites and Brethren, were non-English, with an obligatory commutation fee, the furnishing of a substitute, or special taxes. The war also established the principle of offering citizenship for military service, especially for enemy troops who would switch sides and to Europeans who came to join the Continental forces. The service of several European military experts in the American army during the Revolutionary War later became a source of pride to their ethnic groups in the United States. Among the most famous of these foreign officers were Marquis de *Lafayette of France, "Baron" Johann de *Kalb and "Baron" Friedrich Wilhelm von *Steuben of Germany, and Thaddeus *Kosciuszko of Poland.

Attempts to exclude immigrants and blacks from military service resurfaced after the Revolution because of decreased need for manpower in the small regular army of the early national period. An 1825 regulation banned foreigners from enlisting in the army without special permission; but the reluctance of native-born Americans to enlist in an expanding economic era, combined with a wave of immigration from Northern and Western Europe beginning in the 1830s, resulted in the foreign-born constituting a majority of the army's enlisted ranks by the 1850s, with Irish and Germans predominating. This pattern reappeared in the post–Civil War army and navy, and was beneficial for the foreign-born, who learned English and American customs, received some vocational training, and gained geographic mobility to the frontier.

Blacks were barred from army enlistment by a general order from Secretary of War John C. *Calhoun of South Carolina in 1820, although the army continued to retain black veterans and to employ black labor. The navy was not happy about recruiting African-American sailors, but its need for black labor was even greater than the army's, and black sailors were less visible to the public than black soldiers. The *War of 1812, the *Mexican War, and especially the *Civil War escalated military need for manpower. Aliens who had started the naturalization process were eligible for the draft during the Civil War, although there was a high rate of volunteering among some of the foreign-born. About 200,000 German Americans and over 170,000 Irish Americans served in the *Union army, often in highly visible ethnic units promoted and led by politically astute immigrant leaders. There was considerable draft resistance in the North, and draft riots, especially the *New York City Anti-Draft Riots in 1863, were often led by Irish and sometimes German Catholic immigrants. The Confederacy was less enthusiastic about ethnic units, although the military participation of immigrants helped to change Southern attitudes toward immigration and led to a limited recruiting campaign to encourage European migration into the South. In the North as well, suspicion and hostility toward immigrants declined, and self-conscious Americanization was furthered.

Although initial attempts were made to exclude African Americans from the Union army, the flooding of ex-slaves into Union lines, mounting *casualties, the slowing of white recruitment, as well as the growing acceptance of the abolition of slavery as a war aim, led to the ultimate enlistment of approximately 186,000 black troops, nearly 10 percent of the Union army. Blacks constituted about one-fourth of the *Union navy, and a few ships were manned almost entirely by African Americans. By 1865, desperation forced the Confederate Congress to authorize black combat troops, although the war ended before any saw service. In the North, discrimination in pay, assignments, and treatment was prevalent, and Northern appreciation for black military service soon diminished, although the temporarily favorable climate of opinion aided in the passage of the Thirteenth and Fourteenth Amendments and the Civil Rights Act of 1868.

Military need on the postbellum western frontier resulted in the retention of four black army regiments. Despite hostility by white westerners and the reluctance of some white officers to command the four black regiments, the army did make an effort to evaluate the capabilities and performance of "*Buffalo" soldiers on military rather than racial grounds, and black soldiers were military effective, with a high esprit de corps and reenlistment rate, as well as proving highly visible heroes to the black community. By the late nineteenth century, however, racial and ethnic lines were hardening in both the military and civilian worlds. New imperial roles heightened racist sentiments in the army and navy, and the "new immigration" from Southern and Eastern Europe increased ethnocentric fears. In 1894, nondeclarant aliens were banned from first enlistment in the army, and in 1906, three companies of black soldiers were dismissed without adequate investigation following a riot in Brownsville, Texas. The navy began to curtail black enlistments, segregating African Americans aboard ships and favoring Filipinos instead of blacks as stewards.

U.S. entry into World War I created a major need for manpower, met largely by the draft, and also sizable minority problems. The General Staff estimated that one-fourth of those drafted were non-English-speaking or functionally illiterate; this led to unprecedented cooperation with civilian social welfare, religious, and ethnic organizations to increase efficiency by meeting the varied needs of the immigrant soldier. "Development" battalions were created for those with insufficient knowledge of English; organized by ethnic groups, they were instructed in English. The army rejected the idea of single ethnic combat units with their own officers (Polish American leaders offered to raise a Polish legion in the United States). Ethnic National Guard units like New York City's "Fighting 69th" (Irish American) Regiment continued to exist, however. After the conclusion of the war, recruit educational center's were established to induct recent immigrants, conduct military training, teach English, and inculcate the army's version of good citizenship. Psychological tests introduced by civilians to screen mental incompetents from the army and classify inductees on the basis of intelligence were used for racist purposes after the war.

Although initially divided, the black community, like the immigrant community, ultimately supported the war effort for patriotic reasons and in hopes of bettering their condition; a number of violent racial incidents occurred, however, such as the riot in Houston, Texas, in the summer of 1917. The military initially tried to confine blacks to supporting labor roles. Ultimately, a training camp for black officers was established and two black divisions were sent to France, although one lacked divisional trains and artillery and was brigaded with the French. The Marine Corps barred the enlistment of blacks entirely, and from 1919 to 1932, the navy suspended their enlistment. The four black army regiments were retained, although the army continued to assert, based on the failure of one black regiment in France, that African American soldiers were cowardly in combat and fit only for menial labor. Discrimination and violence again awaited returning black servicemen, and race riots erupted in 1919.

After the U.S. entry into World War II, blacks were determined that there be a "Double V" campaign for victory against racism at home as well as victory abroad. Unlike World War I, blacks were underrepresented in the draft, although over million black men and women served in the armed forces, half of them overseas. The Marine Corps and the Army Air Corps admitted blacks for the first time; the army integrated its officer training schools; and during the Battle of the *Bulge (1944–45), units were integrated to the platoon level.

Ethnic issues were also more muted during the war (except for the Internment of enemy aliens, particularly Japanese and Japanese Americans). Many groups were better assimilated, there was unprecedented unity in the war effort, an emphasis on ethnic pluralism, and little ethnic discrimination in combat zones, although it persisted in civilian life at home. Military service hastened the Americanization of some groups previously outside the mainstream, creating group cohesiveness and a sense of possible upward mobility. The rate of volunteering among groups such as Native Americans and Mexican Americans, who had the largest number of Congressional Medal of Honor winners of any ethnic group, and the service of more than 33,000 Japanese Americans (the 442nd Regimental Combat Team of Nisei soldiers was the most decorated unit in the army), earned the nation's gratitude.

After the war, veterans groups, such as the G.I. Forum of Mexican Americans and Club 100 of Hawaiian Japanese Americans, were organized to promote civil rights, political participation, and group interests, and the services ultimately established personnel centers to compile computerized data on ethnic and racial groups. The military, however, was less concerned than in previous decades about the assimilation of the foreign-born, as massive immigration from Europe had ended in the 1920s and ideology began to eclipse ethnicity in the *Cold War era. Ethnicity also ceased to be a factor in *conscientious objection (CO) when the Supreme Court decreed in Welsh v. United States (1970) that religious pacifism was no longer necessary for CO exemption from military service.

Racial issues were more troublesome, although the services were finding segregation difficult in an age with increasingly specialized technological requirements, and President Harry S. *Truman, in July 1948, issued Executive Order 9981 for the racial integration of the armed forces. Integration was finally achieved during the exigencies of the *Korean War, although the *Vietnam War created new tensions. High casualty rates, especially among nonwhites, and the influence of the ethnic rights and Black Power movements, led to protests and antiwar activities within the military. Unrest—especially protest against allegedly unequal military justice—continued after the war. The military responded with seminars on race relations, basic skills, and management training programs, and affirmative action goals that led to improved racial relations. The military was the first federal body in the United States to be officially desegregated, and today it has a higher percentage of black generals and admirals than African American executives in large corporations.

Military service has also been attractive to Native Americans, whose enlistment rates during the twentieth century have been about three times as high as for non–Native Americans. Military service has revitalized the tradition of warrior societies, which performed vital military functions in preceding centuries, and service in World War II, as well as employment in war industries, brought Native Americans much more into the mainstream of American life. Veterans have provided leadership in the movement for self-determination. The Vietnam War created a generational split as many draft-age Native Americans clashed with their pro-war parents; but rejection of the war did not lessen the continuing popularity of military service.

It seems likely that the military services will continue to contain ethnic and racial minorities in excess of their percentage of the total population, and that they will serve in an environment more harmonious and welcoming than in the past. The structured and disciplined environment has always potentially enhanced the military's capacity to eliminate prejudice and discrimination, and the services seem more willing than ever before to define equality as a desirable goal.

[*See also* African Americans in the Military; Ethnicity and War; Native Americans in the Military; Race Relations and War; Vietnam Antiwar Movement; Volunteers, U.S.]

• Bruce White, "The American Military and the Melting Pot in World War I" in J. L. Granatstein and R. D. Cuff, eds. *War and Society in North America*, 1971. Jack D. Foner, *Blacks and the Military in American History*, 1974. James B. Jacobs and Leslie Anne Hayes, "Aliens in the U.S. Armed Forces: A Historico-Legal Analysis," *Armed Forces and Society* 7 (Winter 1981), pp. 187–208. Martin Binkin and Mark J. Eitelberg, *Blacks in the Military*, 1982. Bernard C. Nalty, *Strength for the Fight: A History of Black Americans in the Military*, 1986. William L. Burton, *Melting Pot Soldiers: The Union's Ethnic Regiments*, 1988. Alison R. Bernstein, *American Indians and World War II*, 1991. Nancy Gentile Ford, "War and Ethnicity: Foreign-Born Soldiers and United States Military Policy During World War I." Ph.D. dissertation, Temple University, 1994.
—Bruce White

ETHNICITY AND WAR. Throughout American history, war has often had a strong Americanizing influence on ethnic groups, increasing each group's acceptability and promoting assimilation and acculturation. Support for the war effort by the ethnic group itself has been well received by the majority. But assimilation and acculturation usually mean the erosion of the cultural and social life of the immigrant group. In addition, during wartime, pressures to conform have often become oppressive, and discrimination against immigrants—and sometimes ethnic groups—from countries with which the United States is at war has at times been appalling.

Although non-English immigrants to America during the eighteenth century helped legitimize the ideal of a composite national identity, in the succeeding century pressures for cultural conformity increased, partly as a result of America's wars. The greatest pressures on cultural diversity occurred in the late nineteenth and early twentieth centuries, when identity was most narrowly and rigidly conceived and group loyalties the most suspect. Since World War I, the United States has moved toward less rigidly defined ethnic and racial boundaries and a more inclusive sense of national identity, with the notable exceptions of the treatment of Japanese Americans during World War II and the increase of ethnic and racial tensions during the *Vietnam War.

During the colonial period, the homogeneity resulting in part from the English cultural background of most colonists and the common dangers encountered in the New World began to change by the eighteenth century. As the frontier moved westward, much of the fighting was done by recent non-English immigrants who joined expeditions or settled in frontier areas. Engagement in warfare, particularly during the *French and Indian War of 1754–63, drew many new immigrants into the political and social life of the general community. At the same time, the English language, customs, and dress became more common and new heroes, traditions, and memories were created.

The *Revolutionary War was even more significantly Americanizing. Despite a greater tendency among non-English immigrants toward loyalism or neutrality than among those of English ancestry, immigrants responded during the crisis to their immediate situation rather than to Old World loyalties or antipathies. The Revolution resulted in increased immigrant participation in the political and economic life of the new nation; it also furthered geographic mobility, and, with France as an ally, lessened anti-Catholicism. Ties with Europe were disrupted, snapping religious and cultural bonds, and leading to a further decline of European languages and the ethnic press. Although the Revolution was conceived of largely in ideological, not ethnic, terms, it did legitimize the idea of a composite national identity and gave new emphasis to the concept of America as an asylum for oppressed peoples. Group identity, however, was discouraged, and a common and effective "melting pot" was assumed.

The *Mexican War in the mid-1840s coincided with an emerging nativist movement and heightened suspicions of Roman Catholics, although the winning of the war resulted in the addition of a large Spanish-speaking Catholic minority to the United States. In the 1850s, tensions over the issue of slavery led to the decline of nativism, and immigrant groups largely reacted to the outbreak of the *Civil War in 1861 with strong sectional loyalties. In addition to patriotism, gratitude for the benefits of living in the United States, and a relative lack of local attachments, Northern immigrants responded to recruiting appeals, bounties offered, and the trade depression at the beginning of the war. Initial British hostility toward the Union cause heightened Irish support in the North for the war, and Irish American nationalists saw it as a way to further the Fenian movement to overthrow British rule in Ireland.

Strong immigrant support for the war—except for a minority of Catholic Democrats—also led to new prestige and improved status for ethnic groups in the North. Because their patriotism was often expressed collectively, many groups remained distinct and conscious of their identity and separateness. Latent hostility toward the foreign-born would again be triggered by a new wave of immigration from Southern and Eastern Europe beginning in the 1880s, but the immediate postwar period was one of relative calm. In the South, foreign-born participation in the war and a postwar need for labor led to attempts to recruit European migration to the southern states. In general, immigrants were seen as supporters of the existing order, not threats to stability.

During the *Spanish-American and *Philippine Wars, the pressure to conform was great, especially for Catholics. There was, however, a greater reluctance among ethnic groups than among the general population to support American entry into the Spanish-American War, and a greater tendency to be more critical of American imperialism, especially in the Philippines. In some instances, intraethnic issues played a role, such as the realization by the largely Irish clerical hierarchy that an appeal for unity would help to undercut the "Cahenslyite" controversy, in which non-English-language groups were seeking more autonomy within the Catholic Church. Much stronger reactions occurred among immigrants when war broke out in Europe in 1914: whatever choices the United States might make would raise strong ethnic feelings and loyalties, particularly among immigrants from the central powers and among subject groups from the Habsburg Empire.

The strength of ethnic feelings, combined with fears of the "new immigration" from Southern and Eastern Europe, and the dislocating effects of rapid industrialization and urbanization, led to a movement to "Americanize" the immigrant and thus dissipate group loyalties. Particularly unsettling, as the United States was drawn closer to the Allied cause, were anti-British sentiments and calls for *neutrality by German Americans and Irish Americans. After American entry into the war in April 1917, a wave of hysteria against all things German engulfed the nation, resulting in a permanent weakening of German culture and identity in America. Although groups not from the central powers found increased acceptability during the war by displaying "100% Americanism," this did not protect them after the armistice as a wave of antiradicalism, often targeting aliens, swept the nation; a renewed and virulent nativist movement emerged by the early 1920s.

The war strengthened the Zionist movement in the United States, and for groups such as Italian Americans, resulted in the creation of a hyphenated national identity. Such group strengthening, however, occurred within the larger context of enhanced loyalties to the American nation. The increased visibility of ethnic groups made the native-born more aware of Old World ties and of the fact that American foreign policy inevitably affected the social order. Although the Americanization campaign, which continued after the war, aimed at eradicating foreign languages and customs, it did emphasize education and vocational training to the benefit of ethnic groups. Illiteracy declined during the war years, secondary education became almost universal, and higher education also expanded after the war. The excesses of the Americanization movement led liberals largely to reject the ideal of thorough assimilation and the melting pot, and concepts of cultural relativism began to emerge.

In the late 1930s, uneasiness about the loyalties of ethnic minorities, increased as Americans reacted to the activities of the German American Bund, to a suspected "fifth column" in the United States, and to the open sympathy for Mussolini shown by many Italian Americans. Pro-Fascist sentiment was always limited, however, and almost disappeared as the horrors of Nazi Germany became better known. Most immigrants increasingly favored aid to the Allies, and the attack on *Pearl Harbor created unprecedented unity among all Americans.

World War II, was perceived primarily in ideological rather than ethnic, racial, or class terms, as reactions to the Axis powers led Americans to reemphasize a common unity based on such shared values as democracy, individual liberties, and respect for minority rights. Ethnic groups were represented on the Common Council for American Unity to foster cooperation, and even substantial tension and violence, such as the "zoot suit" riots of servicemen against Mexican Americans in Los Angeles in 1943, did not disturb a generally harmonious pattern of ethnic relations. Wartime prosperity also muted tensions.

Mobility during the war, especially into the military and to cities to join the urban labor force, brought previously isolated groups into the mainstream. Mexican Americans, for example, were drawn out of a rural agricultural and urban barrio existence. In response to an acute manpower shortage, Mexican "braceros" were recruited for agricultural labor, creating an emigration pattern that would continue after the war as large numbers migrated to cities to work in industries. Italian Americans, especially after being removed from the "enemy alien" category on Columbus Day, 1942, also moved rapidly toward assimilation. German Americans experienced much less hostility than in World War I, as they were now better assimilated and politically and economically important, and as Americans distinguished between the Nazi regime and the German people. The same distinction was not made about Japanese Americans, however, as more than 110,000, two-thirds of whom were American citizens, were removed from the West Coast and incarcerated in ten relocation centers in isolated parts of the western, mountain, and plains states. Despite such treatment, the large majority of Japanese Americans remained steadfastly loyal to the United States; a majority returned to the Pacific Coast after the war, although others located elsewhere. Fortunately, prejudice and discrimination against Japanese Americans decreased markedly in the postwar years.

The 1930s pattern of discouraging the entrance of refugees from Nazi Germany continued during and after the war; only 21,000 were admitted during the war years, about 10 percent of those eligible under existing quotas. In January 1944, President Roosevelt created the War Refugee Board, but by then it was too late to save many Jews from the Holocaust.

The ideological orientation of the war years intensified during the *Cold War, and anticommunism never stimulated a strong nativist movement. Senator Joseph McCarthy targeted the establishment rather than the foreign-born, and was even accused of being a "crypto Jew" because two of his closest aides were Jewish. Many immigrants from Eastern Europe were fervently against Soviet expansionism, thus increasing their acceptability. Richard Polenberg has argued that McCarthy's rise to power would not have been possible had it not been for the frustrations of fighting a limited war in Korea, but the *Korean War did not create anti-alien sentiments or inordinate civil tensions, in part because of its brevity.

Unlike the war in Korea, the *Vietnam War tore at the

fabric of American society and created sharp racial, ethnic, and class cleavages. Although the war most notably affected African Americans, leading to the assertion of Black Power and rejection by blacks of racism at home and imperialism abroad, it also called into the question the ideological consensus of the World War II and Cold War years, resulting in the reassertion of ethnic particularism and a promotion of the cohesiveness of the ethnic group as a model. Americans felt obliged to accept a large number of Vietnamese refugees, although attempts to disperse them throughout the country failed, and they migrated to states like California that had significant Asian communities and generous welfare benefits. The continuing turmoil in Southeast Asia after the American exodus prolonged the refugee crisis.

A general trend toward lessening ethnic pressures and tensions since the 1920s is heartening. It has been argued that, given the right conditions, hysteria and a subsequent antiradical scare such as took place in the World War I era could reoccur. It is to be hoped that the pessimists are wrong and that the nation will finally accept its increasingly multicultural nature.

[See also Economy and War; Ethnicity and Race in the Military; Holocaust, U.S. War Effort and the; Internment of Enemy Aliens; Japanese-American Internment Cases; Labor and War; Race Relations and War.]

• Richard Polenberg, One Nation Divisible: Class, Race, and Ethnicity in the United States Since 1938, 1980. Winston A. Van Horne and Thomas V. Tonnesen, eds., Ethnicity and War, 1980. John Whiteclay Chambers II, To Raise an Army: The Draft Comes to Modern America, 1987. William L. Burton, Melting Pot Soldiers: The Union's Ethnic Regiments, 1988. Maldwyn Allen Jones, American Immigration, 1960; 2nd ed. 1992.

—Bruce White

E-2. See AWACS and E3s.

EWELL, RICHARD STODDERT (1817–1872), Confederate general. Born in Georgetown, D.C., Ewell was raised in Virginia. In 1840, he graduated from West Point thirteenth in a class of forty-two and served in the cavalry during and after the *Mexican War. He joined the Confederacy in April 1861 and was promoted to brigadier general. As a major general in the *Civil War, Ewell commanded a division during "Stonewall" *Jackson's Shenandoah Valley campaign and defeated Union troops at Cross Keys in June 1862. A severe knee wound during the Battle of Groveton in August resulted in the amputation of his right leg, but he returned to duty as a lieutenant general in May 1863. After Jackson's death Ewell took over his II Corps, but his failure to attack the Union position on Cemetery Hill during the first day of the Battle of *Gettysburg led to accusations of incompetence. "Old Bald Head" subsequently fought during the *Wilderness to Petersburg Campaign, but poor health and his wife's increasing Unionist sentiments culminated in his being relieved of field command in May 1864. He commanded Richmond's defenses until captured at Sayler's Creek on 6 April 1865. Paroled in July 1865, Ewell settled at his wife's Spring Hill, Tennessee, estate; both died of pneumonia in January 1872.

• Percy Hamlin, Old Bald Head, 1940. Samuel J. Martin, The Road to Glory: Confederate General Richard S. Ewell, 1991.

—Ervin L. Jordan, Jr.

EXPANSIONISM is endemic to an unfinished world of sovereign states in which some nations possess the power and will to challenge the global distribution of land, resources, or people. Centuries of mass migrations and state-building created the modern state system without satisfying the needs and interests of all its members. The resulting instability in international life took its precise form from the existence of three worlds superimposed on one another. One consists of the economic universe of plains, valleys, rivers, harbors, and waterways—elements that determined the nature, quality, and performance of national economic activity. A second is the world of people, separated by ethnicity, language, and religion into unique cultures that seldom conform to national boundaries. The third comprises the world of nations, more artificial and malleable than the others, with boundaries created over time by natural lines of demarcation or by war.

Leaders of countries whose geographic, demographic, or political status fails to coincide with their ambition, perceived interests, and power can balance the two sets of factors in only one way: through the exertion of force. Highly dissatisfied nations may forego territorial adjustment through war by reason of prudence or morality. When states unleash force in quest of land or ethnic amalgamation, they succeed or fail according to the magnitude of the reaction. For the United States, its expansionist efforts largely preceded twentieth-century precepts of self-determination and peaceful change that rendered resorts to force immoral, and thus unacceptable. The United States, throughout its expansionist career, never faced an invincible coalition committed to blocking its expansion and defending the status quo.

American expansionism in the nineteenth century focused on bordering regions whose acquisition would enhance its security and broaden its economic base. Except for its conquest of Indian lands and its war with Mexico, the United States achieved its continental empire mainly through diplomacy. Europe's declining role in distant North America provided the United States sufficient leverage in its confrontations to assure highly beneficial boundary settlements. France, finding its claims to the vast Louisiana Territory relatively worthless, sold Louisiana to the United States in 1803 for $15 million. Spain revealed its weakening position in North America by ceding Florida and agreeing, in the Transcontinental Treaty of 1819, to a satisfactory boundary from Louisiana to the Pacific Coast Britain defined its Canadian boundary with the United States in its acceptance of the 49th parallel from the Great Lakes to the Rockies in 1818; the Maine boundary settlement in 1842; and, in 1846, the line of 49 between the Rockies and the continental shore, then continuing on to the Pacific through the Strait of Juan de Fuca. California and the Southwest were acquired in 1848, in the war with Mexico. Alaska, no longer desired by Russia, was, like Louisiana, largely a windfall.

Expansionists in the 1840s proclaimed the doctrine of "manifest destiny" to rationalize American expansion as the mere fulfillment of the country's destiny. The concept of destiny, in discounting the role of force in the country's expansion, rested on the presumed superiority and appeal of American institutions. Notions of destiny might assuage the doubts of those who abhorred force, but expansion itself required more than convictions of political and cultural superiority. Manifest destiny neglected totally questions of power or diplomacy. It embodied no need to define ends. The hand of destiny, in promoting the extension of freedom, culture, and institutions, recognized no bounds. Quite typically, journalist John L. O'Sullivan, who is credited with coining the phrase, observed in the *New York Morning News* on 27 December 1845 that it had become "our manifest destiny to occupy and to possess the whole Continent which Providence has given us...."

American expansion across the continent rested not on notions of destiny but on clearly conceived national policies, based on power and diplomacy, attached to specific territorial objectives. In the 1840s, the Polk administration pursued Texas's claims to the Rio Grande and businesses' desire for seaports on the Pacific Ocean, objectives achieved through the *Mexican War. In Oregon, the U.S. goal was the magnificent harbor of Puget Sound, with access to the Pacific through Juan de Fuca Strait. The American demand for a settlement along the 49th parallel assured access to the desired waterways. U.S. purposes in California were no less precise than those in Oregon: the harbors of San Francisco and San Diego. These objectives Polk embodied in his war aims and achieved in the Treaty of *Guadalupe-Hidalgo (1848).

American expansionism entered the vast world of the Pacific in the late nineteenth century. The region seemed to offer limitless opportunities for the expansion of Christianity and civil liberty, and also for the acquisition of new markets to complement the impressive growth of American industrial and agricultural production after the American *Civil War. What rendered the Pacific region especially inviting was the presumption that its civilizations could not resist the power, technology, and organizational skills of the Western world. Unlike other imperial powers, the United States did not create its Pacific empire by conquering previously independent peoples. Instead, it exploited opportunities for economic and territorial expansion already created by internal instabilities and weaknesses in regions regarded as strategically and economically important. Or it overthrew Spanish colonialism. After 1860, the application of American will in the Far East appeared so effortless that it ultimately led to expanded objectives, illusions of omnipotence, and wars exorbitantly expensive.

America's expansion in the Pacific advanced in spurts. By the early 1890s, it had touched China, Japan, Midway, Hawaii, Korea, and Samoa. In February 1893, the Harrison administration negotiated an annexation treaty with Hawaiian commissioners, only to have the incoming Cleveland administration reject it and condemn the previous administration's involvement in Samoa as well. The anti-imperialists demonstrated their dominance by defeating a second Hawaiian annexation treaty in 1897. It required the *Spanish-American War, in April 1898, to break the power of anti-imperialism and project the United States onto the world stage.

Shortly after the outbreak of war, fought ostensibly to free Cuba from Spain, Commodore George *Dewey's Pacific Squadron destroyed the Spanish Fleet at the Battle of *Manila Bay in the Spanish Philippines. This sudden display of naval power in the remote Pacific, and the possibil-

ities it opened for empire-building, were not lost on a group of well-placed expansionists in Washington. During June 1898, Congress annexed Hawaii by joint resolution against little opposition. Meanwhile, President William *McKinley dispatched an army to take control of Manila. On 13 August, Spanish officials surrendered the city to American forces. The decision to destroy Spanish power in the Philippines closed every easy avenue of escape. Having liberated the islands, the United States had either to restore them to Spain, free them, transfer them to another power, or retain them. Expansionists that summer clamored for their retention. On 16 September, McKinley instructed his peace commission that U.S. forces, with no thought of acquisition, had brought duties and obligations to the Filipinos that the country could not ignore. During December, the peace commission in Paris signed a treaty that conveyed the Philippines, Guam, and Puerto Rico to the United States in exchange for $20 million. The Senate, in February 1899, approved the treaty by a vote of 57 to 27, one more than the necessary two-thirds. Philippine annexation set off a bitter, costly war with Emilio *Aguinaldo's Filipino insurgents for possession of the islands. The American antiguerrilla campaign soon degenerated into a no-quarter struggle of burned villages and the deaths of innocent men, women, and children. At the end, the acquisition of the Philippines demanded a heavy price.

Still, the illusion of easy success received an even more powerful demonstration in the U.S. effort to save China from dismemberment by Russia, Britain, France, Germany, Italy, and Japan. Acceding to the American "open door" notes of 1899 and 1900, those countries accepted, in principle, China's economic, political, and administrative integrity. In the euphoria of "saving" China, the United States accepted a pervading unilateral commitment to China's independence and political integrity against Russia and Japan, whose interests in China were far greater than those of the United States. With its recent territorial accessions, the United States entered the twentieth century as the world's leading satiated power, with objectives—in China and elsewhere—anchored to the territorial status quo, but facing powers whose expansionist interests demanded further changes in the world's treaty structure, even at the price of war. For the United States, the coming century would hardly be peaceful, if no longer territorially expansionist.

[See also Native American Wars: Wars Between Native Americans and Europeans and Euro-Americans; Philippine War; Philippines, Liberation of the; Philippines, U.S. Military Involvement in the.]

• Albert K. Weinberg, *Manifest Destiny: A Study of Nationalist Expansionism in American History*, 1935. Ernest R. May, *Imperial Democracy: The Emergence of America as a Great Power*, 1961. Frederick Merk, *Manifest Destiny and Mission in American History: A Reinterpretation*, 1963. H. Wayne Morgan, *America's Road to Empire: The War with Spain and Overseas Expansion*, 1965. Norman A. Graebner, *Manifest Destiny*, 1968. David L. Anderson, *Imperialism and Idealism: American Diplomats in China, 1861–1898*, 1985. Thomas R. Hietala, *Manifest Design*, 1985.

—Norman A. Graebner

F

F-86 SABREJET. *See* Fighter Aircraft.

FAMILIES, MILITARY. "If the Army had wanted you to have a wife, it would have issued you one!" This often quoted dictum reflects a historical truth: until recently, military families have been excluded from military attention and policy, not just in the army, but in other services as well. Nonetheless, there have been American military families as long as there has been an American military establishment, and the numbers are growing. In the mid-1990s, more than 2 million military personnel (more than 60%) were married, and military families represented at least 3 percent of all U.S. households.

Military families are influenced by a unique set of circumstances. The organization that employs the breadwinner sees itself as a familylike structure, and insists that its mission must come first. Militant values such as violence and hierarchy shape the context within which family members must function, and at times the battlefield encourages stronger bonding between warriors than between family members. In addition, the military family is socially defined by the status of the soldier, and its personal life is constricted by definite rules. The military member faces more danger and a greater likelihood of death than in most other professions, and the family must either recognize or deny this reality. Whichever response it chooses has its effect. Frequent moves disrupt family life, often involve separation, and sometimes require adjustment to foreign cultures. Working hours are unpredictable.

On the other hand, there is job security, coupled with the promise of early retirement for career personnel. Although pay levels are not competitive with civilian rates, income is reliable and in recent years fringe benefits have partially balanced this disparity. A military career often provides the family with a sense of order, social solidarity, and community, as well as an unambiguous social identity based on clearcut ideals and expectations. These long-standing characteristics have varied in wartime and as the larger civilian society became more industrial, powerful, and international.

Although evidence is scant, sources claim that as many as 20,000 women were "*camp followers" during the *Revolutionary War. Most were the wives, many accompanied by their children, of the soldiers who fought the war; often they had nowhere else to go. These women nursed the sick and wounded, sewed and laundered uniforms, cooked for the troops, and struggled to follow the armies when time came to move on. Although these families were usually tolerated out of fear that the husbands would desert otherwise, only the laundresses received any official notice or recompense.

As the new nation grew, the small military's task changed to guarding ever-shifting borders, taming the West, and protecting against European incursion. Military families (both officer and enlisted) traveled with the armies, although in peacetime fewer officers were tolerant of soldiers' families, and often required permission for marriages and certification for families to accompany troop movements. In the years between 1783 and 1848, pay was low and promotion slow. Few soldiers could afford families. For those who wanted their families with them (or who had no other alternative), shelter and rations were scarce. Indian attacks, traveling mishaps, and disease, as well as death in childbirth, killed off women and children indiscriminately.

Between moves, families settled into whatever housing was possible. At some of the eastern posts, casemate housing in coastal defense forts was particularly crowded, and meals had to be taken elsewhere. Still, these brick and stone lodgings seemed luxurious compared to the sod and mud shelters in the West. Sometimes families (especially enlisted) slept in the open, in tents with the soldiers, or in caves. Laundresses, still the only women given official status, were provided with rough cabins when available. If an officer of higher rank wished, he and his family could "rank out" another family, taking over their housing if it looked more comfortable. This tradition continued at least until World War II.

Military family life was not entirely without its pleasures, particularly for officers' families. As more women followed their husbands west, the antebellum frontier posts reflected their influence. By the 1830s and 1840s, officer housing at larger posts was more spacious and weather-proofed. Flowers and vegetables appeared in gardens. Social life included dinner parties, balls, amateur theatrics, and occasional church services. For children, simple grammar schools were established, often with teachers "drafted" from the enlisted ranks. Wherever wives settled and children played, efforts to transport "civilization" from the East were not far behind.

Military family life in wartime was a different story, as the *Civil War years attest. With every war, the number of families expanded as military ranks swelled. Though many wives (both Northern and Southern) remained at home, others chose to accompany their husbands everywhere possible, or, more frequently, when they camped nearby. Sometimes wives of enlisted men had nowhere else to go. Officers' wives usually had more options, and, like Libby Custer, visited their husbands out of devotion and a desire for adventure. Wherever wives gathered, a social hierarchy based on the husband's rank soon emerged. Except for brief visits, children were left with relatives for safety from disease and wandering bullets, and thus the war precluded much normal military family life. As usual, rank had its privilege, and many senior officers enjoyed extended visits from their entire families.

After the war, resources declined and the minimal support for families available in the antebellum period decreased. Enlisted men still could not afford families. Although a minority of all military families, many more officers' wives and children went west with their husbands and fathers. Little was provided for family maintenance: minimal travel allowances, inadequate or no housing (with a few exceptions at the larger posts), scant and unhealthy food shipments, poor or nonexistent schools, and only occasional medical care by ill-trained camp doctors often unused to dealing with the health problems of women and children.

Those families without outside resources to make up for such inadequacies were at a great disadvantage, although even the poorest officer families often had the luxury of servants—either enlisted "strikers" or the wives of enlisted men. When they could afford it, officers often chose to send their older children back east (sometimes accompanied by their wives) to be educated. Younger children were often tutored in rudimentary skills by their parents or others on the post.

Yet in their frequent moves from one outpost to another, these families established a sense of community and shared experience that would be a part of professional military life until the enormous expansion of the mid-twentieth century. Most came to know each other and many were related. Their separation from civilian life, heightened by hardship and slow advancement, drew them closer. As in the antebellum period, wives worked hard to make the quarters comfortable, and to influence their environment in whatever ways were possible. Often they viewed their surroundings and "adversaries" differently from their husbands—appreciating the still untouched beauty of the plains and mountains, and empathizing with the Indians.

With the *Spanish-American War, military families found themselves facing the new challenges of empire. By 1900, wives clamored to accompany their husbands abroad, especially to the Philippines, which until the 1980s provided one of the major overseas posting for the American military and its families. Predictably, enlisted men seldom could afford to bring their wives and children with them. Once in the archipelago, however, some soldiers married Filipina women, the first of a long line of "war brides" who, along with the families of the African American "*Buffalo" Soldiers after the Civil War, would contribute to the growing heterogeneity of U.S. military families in the twentieth century. Officers, on the other hand, were sometimes allowed to bring their wives and children from the States, at their own expense. Once in the Philippines, these families struggled to find their own housing and food, fight against different diseases such as malaria and dysentery, and learn enough about the new culture to survive within it. As the American presence in the islands expanded over the next forty years, base housing became available, and military families often chose to stay within the confines of the post and try to replicate the lives they had left behind.

Between 1900 and 1941, whether their soldiers were stationed in the United States or overseas, military dependents increasingly chose to live nearby, except in wartime.

Washington still provided only the barest support: travel pay and rental allowances for officers with families, nothing for enlisted men except that granted at the mercy of individual commanders. Nonetheless, on an unofficial level, the "Old Army" continued to offer a sense of identity, order, and community derived from shared experience, common acquaintance, and a feeling of "otherness" from the civilian world.

The World War I era produced little change in military family life, and none in military policy toward families. Twenty years later, however, because of the enormous manpower needs of World War II, many more men with families joined the military. In 1942, the Dependents Allowance Act was passed by Congress—a concrete acknowledgment by the government that military families were a military responsibility. Each wife and child received an established monthly payment; and this allowance, coupled with allotments set aside by the soldiers and augmented by the government, provided some regular support to all military families.

Other conditions improved as well. Although never adequate enough to keep up with the ever-growing numbers of families, large new military bases made provision for better healthcare, shopping, schools, and housing. Since wartime contingencies forced frequent moves within the United States, and families could not accompany soldiers to most foreign postings, many families chose to stay "at home" for the duration. Others followed their soldiers whenever possible.

At war's end, the new U.S. position in the world and the advanced technology that supported it required more career military personnel with more education, who therefore were usually older. The number of military families grew exponentially. The *Pentagon gradually began to develop a more coherent military family policy. Pay rates improved and pensions encouraged long-term careers. More on-base housing was built, and in 1956 Congress passed the Dependents Medical Care Act, which provided full health benefits to families.

Since the end of World War II, life for military families in all of the services has changed. Those who accompany their spouses now are in the majority, and with the advent of the *All-Volunteer Force in the 1970s, keeping them reasonably content has increasingly been recognized as necessary to maintain satisfactory force size and efficiency.

Changes in gender attitudes throughout the society have brought changing conditions for the military. By the end of the 1950s, the traditional wife who stayed home and solved many of the special problems of the military family could no longer be counted on; instead, she often had a career of her own. Indeed, as more and more women joined the military, the spouse might be the husband. Sometimes families were "dual-service" couples. By the late 1970s, as the courts forced the services, one by one, to allow female soldiers to become mothers without discharge, such couples might be raising children. When divorce rates soared in the whole society, more single-parent families occurred in the military. To respond to these issues, the Department of *Defense generated new studies and policies, and appointed a deputy assistant secretary for personnel and family matters. Additionally, the National Military Family Association now exists, independent of the government, to highlight and respond to questions especially relevant to the military family.

A fundamental problem remains that in order to survive the stress of its special circumstances, the emotional openness that often strengthens families in other settings is sometimes suppressed in the military family. This has led to higher-than-average rates of alcoholism and other forms of dysfunction. Even in stable military families, frequent separations cause shifts in dynamics that require careful negotiation. As the U.S. armed forces move into the twenty-first century, these family dilemmas will have to be addressed.

[*See also* Bases, Military: Life On; Gender and War; Gender: Female Identity and the Military; Housing, Military; Rights in the Military, Citizens'; Women in the Military.]

• Nancy Shea, rev. Anna Perle Smith, *The Army Wife,* 1966. Patricia Y. Stallard, *Glittering Misery,* 1978. Florence W. Kaslow and Richard I. Ridenour, eds., *The Military Family,* 1984. Edward M. Coffman, *The Old Army: A Portrait of the American Army in Peacetime, 1784–1898,* 1986. Gary L. Bowen and Dennis K. Orthner, eds., *The Organization Family: Work and Family Linkages in the U.S. Military,* 1989. Betty Sowers Alt and Bonnie Domrose Stone, *Campfollowing: A History of the Military Wife,* 1991. Mary Edwards Wertsch, *Military Brats: Legacies of Childhood Inside the Fortress,* 1991.
—Carol Morris Petillo

FARRAGUT, DAVID (1801–1870), admiral in the U.S. Navy, Civil War. David Glasgow Farragut's Civil War promotions bear witness to his place in the first rank of naval heroes. Congress named him the first U.S. Navy rear admiral, vice admiral, and admiral.

Born in Tennessee in 1801, he grew up as the ward of Adm. David Dixon *Porter. By age nine, he was a midshipman; by age twelve, Porter appointed him prize master to take a captured ship into port.

After the *War of 1812, Farragut's career made slow progress through the peacetime navy's seniority system: lieutenant (1825), commander (1841), captain (1855), while working to establish the Mare Island Navy Yard in California.

He maintained a home in Norfolk, where he married, was widowed, remarried, and fathered a son, Loyall, who would be his wartime secretary and biographer. Faced with a choice of allegiance in 1861, he moved to New York. Even so, his Southern origins created suspicions, which his service in the *Union navy more than overcame.

He commanded the West Gulf Blockading Squadron, which posted ships from St. Andrew's Bay east of Pensacola westward along the Gulf Coast to the Rio Grande. Farragut gained fame by leading the expedition that was successful in the siege of *New Orleans in 1862, one of the most significant Union victories of the war. His leadership was central to the great riverine battles that secured the Mississippi and its tributaries for the Union, especially the siege of *Vicksburg. At the Battle of *Mobile Bay in 1864, his command—"Damn the torpedoes. Full speed ahead"—elevated his fame to legend.

His postwar appointment as commander of the European Squadron became a triumphal tour of "the American Nelson" through various capitals. Farragut died during a visit to the Portsmouth, New Hampshire, Navy Yard in 1870.

• Loyall Farragut, *The Life and Letters of Admiral Farragut, First Admiral of the United States Navy,* 1879. James C. Bradford, ed., *Captain of the Old Steam Navy,* 1976.
—Maxine Turner

FASHION, MILITARY INFLUENCES ON. American fashion has recruited military style again and again, recognizing the efficacy of military specifications and the charisma of heroic accomplishment. Virtually every factor of the military has been employed in civilian fashion sooner or later, including epaulets, ball buttons, khaki adapted from the British military in India, and olive drab. Special sartorial heroes have included A-2 aviators' leather jackets, navy blue as a standard of modern dress, sailors' drop-front bell-bottom trousers, pea jackets, knit sweaters of sailors and commandos, aviator glasses, and camouflage appropriated to daily use. When the late-twentieth-century fashion editor Diana Vreeland called uniforms "the sportswear of the nineteenth century," she was describing useful adaptations: examples of the cavalry to riding apparel, braid as reinforcement and decoration, plastrons and double-breasted chests as double protection for the heart, and even romantic sashes that served by necessity to carry the wounded from the battlefield.

Military fashion enters the civilian wardrobe in varied ways. With modern, nonmercenary armies, countless veterans return with favorite jackets, trousers, or other items. Paramilitary organizations, including schools and police, have modified military traditions to enforce systematic social identity in forms as varied as middie blouses for school and recreation, tartan for school identity, police outfitting, and even World War I Sam Browne belts for child safety officers.

Military traditions often enter civilian dress in ways that are only partly remembered. The regimental tartans that identified Scotland when England proscribed indigenous Highland dress to Scottish civilians have been a recurring feature of modern civilian dress, with attenuated links to Scotland and to the military source. Not only the plaid, but even the kilt and over-the-shoulder drape are of military origin. The trenchcoat, made first and continuously by Burberry of London for Boer War and World War I service for officers needing protective cloth, closings, and latched wrists and collar, has become a basic of dress for both men and women. Its origins in officers' coats are remembered in name, but many today might more readily associate the coat with glamorous espionage and Humphrey Bogart in *Casablanca,* even as contemporary fashion specifications for most trenchcoats include vestigial D-rings (designed for hand grenades) still worn by modern suburban commuter-warriors. The popular Eisenhower jacket of the 1950s emulated Gen. Dwight D. *Eisenhower's wool field jacket (M-1944), modeled after that of Field Marshal Bernard Law *Montgomery. This popularity benefitted from the "theater of war" picturing Eisenhower as Allied leader; his sartorial decisions assumed his mantle of leadership. Arguably, even exposed T-shirts are sanctioned by sailors and soldiers in World War II and romanticized by photography and such films as *South Pacific.*

Some apparel from World War II waited a generation or more to be accepted in civilian fashion. The fatigue jacket was introduced to service in 1943; the same jacket, beginning with military surplus, became popular fashion in the 1970s, ironically largely associated with militant antiestablishment advocates of Black Power and the *Vietnam Antiwar movement. The subjective but powerful value of military clothing can be demonstrated by the fact that war protesters of the 1970s frequently wore anachronistic military gear to express their opposition to the war of their time. Camouflage and desert camouflage—especially after the *Persian Gulf War—has been widely adopted in the 1980s and 1990s. In 1988, fashion designer Stephen Sprouse used Andy Warhol's red-yellow-blue camouflage for clothing that would have made any wearer stand out in a crowd.

If fashion is vested in recent wars, historical warfare also becomes transmuted for peaceful purposes. Christian Francis Roth displayed medieval inspiration in his "soft armor" outfits of 1993, resembling medieval armor in gray flannel. In 1994, Ralph Lauren created armor in silver leather accompanied by Lurex knit gowns akin to knightly mail. In 1968, the *Civil War–inspired dresses, based on Confederate officers' frock coats, by Geoffrey Beene (born in Louisiana). In 1989, Lauren emulated the tailoring of World War I uniforms. Lauren has regularly used band collars, epaulets, braid, pea coats, aviators' jumpsuits, and military tailoring as signs of crisp, effective women's attire. In the 1990s, Jean-Paul Gaultier has returned repeatedly and ironically to the sailor's middie blouse.

American democracy celebrates military officers for their perfect tailoring, but is unique in world fashion in admiring equally the quartermaster's issue to the enlisted man. Abhorring enforced homogeneity, American culture nonetheless revels in the selective possibilities of uniform. Fashion for both men and women admires alike the common soldier or seaman and the officer. Moreover, uniforms for women in the military, including the *WAVES uniforms designed in the 1940s by Mainbocher, have set a standard for orderly, smart dressing.

[See also Culture, War, and the Military; Film, War and the Military in: Feature Films; Military Uniforms.]

• Richard Martin, and Harold Koda, Swords into Ploughshares, 1995.
—Richard Martin

FELLOWSHIP OF RECONCILIATION (FOR), a religious-pacifist organization, was founded in England (1914). An American branch was established in November 1915 in Garden City, Long Island, by men and women who belonged to mainstream faiths as well as to pacifist faiths like the *Quakers.

In World War I, FOR led by Gilbert A. Beaver, Edward W. Evans, and Charles J. Rhoades, assisted conscientious objectors (COs). Afterward, it became the intellectual arm of the religious peace movement. Its popular journal, The World Tomorrow (renamed Fellowship, 1935), embodied radical Christian-motivated ideas. Membership averaged 6,000.

During the 1920s and 1930s, FOR helped establish the Committee on Militarism in Education to oppose compulsory *ROTC; it supported the Outlawry of War campaign culminating in the Kellogg-Briand Pact (1928), and cosponsored a peace mission to Nicaragua.

In the late 1930s, FOR cooperated with other peace groups in establishing the Emergency Peace Campaign, calling for strict neutrality, lower tariffs, and international organization contingent on justice. Membership increased to 10,000 during World War II as FOR aided COs, sent supplies to war relief camps in Europe, and sought release of Japanese Americans from relocation camps.

In the early years of the *Cold War, membership dropped to an all-time low of 2,000; but in the 1950s, the Fellowship promoted a nationwide campaign against *nu-

clear weapons testing and gained adherents.

During the *Vietnam War, led by David McReynolds, Allen Brick, Ron Young, Ray Gould, and Reverend William Sloane Coffin, FOR reached nearly 23,000 members, participated in numerous antiwar demonstrations, conducted draft-counseling centers, and established social service schools in South Vietnamese cities. Conflict within the national council erupted when executive secretary Al Hassler urged support for the Buddhist pacifists' "Third Force" solution, while others called for immediate unilateral U.S. troop withdrawal.

After Vietnam, FOR investigated events in Nicaragua between the Sandinistas and contras, and joined the Nuclear Freeze Campaign of the 1980s. Prior to the *Persian Gulf War, the Fellowship led a peace mission with medical supplies to refugees in Jordan and Iraq. In the mid-1990s, it instituted a Civilian Casualty Fund to aid Bosnian Muslims. FOR membership in 1998 was about 8,000—the majority from the Protestant, Catholic, or Jewish faiths.

[See also Conscientious Objection; Japanese-American Internment Cases; Pacifism.]

• Lawrence S. Witter, Rebels Against War: The American Peace Movement, 1933–1983, 2nd ed., 1984. Charles F. Howlett, "John Nevin Sayre and the American Fellowship of Reconciliation," Pennsylvania Magazine of History and Biography, 114 (July 1990), pp. 399–422. Charles F. Howlett, "The American Fellowship of Reconciliation," South of the Mountains, 37 (January–March 1993), pp. 3–14.
—Charles F. Howlett

FERMI, ENRICO (1901–1954), one of the foremost physicists of the twentieth century. Enrico Fermi was born in Rome and educated at the University of Pisa in Italy (Ph.D., 1922), and subsequently at the universities of Gottingen (Germany), Leiden (Holland), and Michigan (United States). In 1926, he made his first major discovery of quantum statistics (now known as Fermi-Dirac statistics). He accepted an appointment to Columbia University in 1939 and from there verified that nuclear fission was possible. The potential applications of this enterprise were immediately evident to the military. At the request of the U.S. government, Fermi took his research team to the University of Chicago, where in December 1942 they demonstrated the first self-sustaining chain reaction. Fermi's discoveries and his ability to apply them made him a key player in the development of the *Manhattan Project, the highly classified research that ultimately resulted in the creation and detonation of the first atomic bomb. The bombings of *Hiroshima and Nagasaki in Japan, cessation of the war in the Pacific, and the start of the Atomic Age followed. After World War II, Fermi was appointed director of what became the Enrico Fermi Institute for Nuclear Studies at the University of Chicago until his death in 1954.

[See also Atomic Scientists; Nuclear Weapons.]

• Emilio Segre, Enrico Fermi: Physicist, 1970. Laura Fermi, Atoms in the Family: My Life with Enrico Fermi, 1971.
—Peter J. McNelis

FIGHTER AIRCRAFT. Fighters are aircraft intended to win air superiority by destroying enemy aircraft. The term is generally applied to those aircraft designed to have sufficient performance to destroy enemy aircraft. However, as a result of the threat posed by strategic bombers during and after *World War II—and particularly after the development of atomic weaponry—a specialized class of fighter, called the interceptor, was developed specifically to counter the bomber threat. Most fighters are small single seat aircraft powered by one or two engines. Interceptors, however, typically have more than one crewman, and tend to be larger and heavier, with longer range. Another category of fighter is the fighter-bomber, which is capable of participating in the air superiority war, but then, when air superiority is no longer an issue, is capable of being applied as a ground attack airplane. Over time, from *World War I to the present, the fighter has gone from a 70 mph frail open-cockpit wood-and-fabric airplane to a Mach 2+ jet-propelled aircraft capable of carrying a sophisticated array of electronics and precision weapons.

Fighters, originally termed "fighting scouts," initially appeared in World War I. They were developed to counter the emergence of the reconnaissance aircraft, which, as early as 1914, had proven so valuable to ground commanders that a means had to be developed to deny one's airspace to the prying eyes of enemy airmen. Development of particular technologies to support the emergence of the fighter—specifically the synchronized forward-firing *machine gun—was swift. Indeed, from 1914 through 1918, five clear generations of fighter aircraft were produced, the latter of which were rudimentary all-metal monoplane designs by the German designer Hugo Junkers. By 1916, control of the air was a vital prerequisite for the success of any other air operations. As a rule, the Allies on the Western Front were successful in maintaining control of the air throughout the war, to the detriment of their Central Powers opponents. By 1918, the first "swing-role" air-to-air and air-to-ground fighter aircraft—the predecessors of the fighter-bombers of World War II—were in service, initially with Great Britain's Royal Flying Corps (the predecessor of today's Royal Air Force). These aircraft proved terribly destructive in attacks on enemy ground forces. In Palestine, such attacks at the battle of Wadi al Far'a were responsible for the destruction of a Turkish army and laid open the path to Damascus. Specialized doctrine was developed by leading air power teachers and practitioners during the war to govern fighter operations; notable figures include Oswald Boelcke, a great exponent of defensive air warfare, and Edward "Mick" Mannock, the most noteworthy of offensive fighter proponents. American fighter pilots, who flew British or French-designed fighters, established an excellent record for the brief time that they were in combat operations during the war. Notable American fighter pilots included "balloon buster" Frank Luke and America's Great War "Ace of aces" Eddie *Rickenbacker. An ace is an individual who has downed five aircraft in aerial combat.

In the years between World War I and the outbreak of World War II, the fighter underwent progressive refinement that matched that of aviation in general. Metal replaced wood in aircraft structures, the monoplane layout replaced the biplane, and a variety of specialized refinements were incorporated in fighter design. These included addition of radio communication, better optical gunsights, multiple guns, a streamlined design approach, internal structural bracing, refined aerodynamics including the provision of wing flaps and, in some cases, wing leading edge slats or slots, retractable landing gears, and high performance air-cooled radial piston engine or liquid-cooled inline engines enclosed within smooth cowling shapes. Such refinements first appeared—to a greater or

lesser degree—in the early 1930's on such aircraft as the Polish PZL P-7, the French Morane Saulnier MS-406, the Soviet Polikarpov I-16, the American P-35, the Japanese Nakajima Ki-27, the British Hawker Hurricane, and the German Messerschmitt Bf 109 (popularly known as the Me 109). But by 1939, many of the world's fighter forces—including that of the United States—still had a large number of biplane fighters in service. Such was particularly true for the U.S. *navy, where the slow landing speeds of such aircraft made them well-suited to the small size of prewar aircraft carriers. Interwar conflicts such as the Spanish Civil War and the Sino-Japanese War confirmed the superiority of newer aircraft technology, but also offered mixed signals that encouraged biplane designers to remain fixed in their thinking for far too long.

The fighter's influence on World War II was profound. The opening Nazi and Japanese attacks benefited greatly from fighters that seized air superiority, preventing their opponents from contesting control of the air, and allowing Axis ground movements to proceed without much threat of Allied intervention. During the Battle of Britain (1940), British fighter pilots literally saved Great Britain from destruction at the hands of Nazi Germany, the first time that a nation's fate had been determined by air warfare. Notable American fighter aircraft of World War II included the Republic P-47 Thunderbolt and the Vought F4U Corsair, both outstanding air-to-air fighters and formidable ground attackers; the North American P-51 Mustang, the finest and most refined all-around propeller-driven fighter of World War II; and the Northrop P-61 Black Widow, a specialized radar-equipped night fighter that anticipated the sophisticated interceptors of the post-1945 period. During the war, fighter speeds increased to over 400 mph, and armament went from two or four small machine guns to up to eight .50 caliber machine guns. German fighter designers, confronting the challenge of the Allies' strategic bomber offensive, emphasized heavy cannon armament, including installations of up to four 30mm cannon firing explosive shells. But Allied fighter operations swept the German air service—and Japan's as well—from the skies, rendering both Nazi Germany and Imperial Japan vulnerable to highly destructive strategic bomber attacks. Allied fighters next turned to shattering Axis ground movement through wide-ranging fighter sweeps deep into enemy territory.

The German introduction of the turbojet engine and moderate wing sweepback to improve high-speed flight performance was matched by Allied developments. Though no jet-versus-jet combat took place during the war, both Germany and Great Britain fielded jet fighters in service. The United States' first jet fighter, the Lockheed F-80 (initially P-80) Shooting Star, entered service in 1945. The first American sweptwing jet fighter, the graceful North American F-86 Sabre, followed the F-80 into service in 1948. During the *Korean War, Sabres met the Soviet Union's Mikoyan and Gurevich MiG-15 in combat over the Yalu, establishing a kill ratio of over 10-1. Korea also marked the last war in which American ground forces lost personnel from enemy air attack.

The technological developments of the 1940's and 1950's radically transformed the American fighter. The Air Force fixed on a supersonic future, with fighters becoming nuclear bomb droppers or specialized anti-bomber interceptors armed with sophisticated air-to-air radar-guided or heat-seeking missiles. As a result, virtually all of the so-called "Century series" fighters—for example the F-101, F-102, F-104, F-105, and F-106—were dedicated to missions in these roles. Only the F-100 was a true swingrole airplane for both conventional war in the tradition of the Second World War's P-47 or Corsair. For its part, the U.S. navy, shocked by its failure to develop a carrier-based fighter capable of confronting the MiG in Korea, embarked on a rigorous development program that led to the two finest fighters of mid-century: the Vought F-8 Crusader, and the McDonnell F-4 Phantom II. Both represented differing design philosophies: the F-8, a single-seat agile "dogfighter" with primarily a gun armament, and the F-4 a two-seat missile-armed fighter with a large *radar and (initially) no gun armament. The Air Force ordered the F-4 with some modifications for its own use, and it became the premier American fighter for all three fighter services—the Air Force, navy, and Marine Corps, by the mid-1960's.

Because of a lack of emphasis on teaching basic skills, the overemphasis on relatively benign missile shots at opponents, the basic limitations of early air-to-air missiles, and controversial rules of engagement, American fighter pilots in the *Vietnam War did not achieve the same level of success that their predecessors had in previous conflicts. By the late 1960's, these problems were so apparent that they had spawned two responses: greater emphasis upon fighter pilot training, and greater emphasis upon designing genuine air-superiority fighters. The former could be done relatively quickly, and the pronounced success of American pilots in air combat over North Vietnam during 1972 attests to the great success that refined training had. The latter, however, required considerably lengthier and complex efforts. However, it spawned a category of "superfighters" that still define the modern standards of fighter excellence: The Grumman F-14 Tomcat, the McDonnell-Douglas F-15 Eagle, the General Dynamics F-16 Fighting Falcon, and the McDonnell-Douglas F-18 Hornet. What made these aircraft possible were more powerful engines, advanced structural materials, improved instrumentation, and, above all, a single-minded dedication to emphasizing the ability of these aircraft to engage and defeat more numerous enemies.

The coupling of the above aircraft technologies with advances in air-to-air missile design, exemplified by the Raytheon AIM-9L Sidewinder of the late 1970's meant that, for the first time, a missile-armed fighter could engage an opponent with the expectations of success that advocates had long anticipated. This was first clearly shown in two conflicts: the Falklands War between Great Britain and Argentina, where AIM-9L-armed British Harriers dominated more numerous Argentinean opponents, preventing the destruction of the British fleet that sailed to liberate the islands; and the Israeli-Syrian war over the Bekaa Valley, where Israeli F-15 and F-16 pilots destroyed over eighty aircraft without suffering a loss in air-to-air combat.

Paralleling this improvement in air superiority fighter operations came developments in ground attack ones. The coupling of the laser-guided precision munition with an airborne laser designator, with advanced space-based navigation such as the Global Positioning System (GPS) and advanced sensor technology now meant that a precision fighter dropping a single high-explosive bomb could achieve destructive effects equivalent to many hundreds of conventional World War II bombers. During that war, to guarantee a single bomb hit on a specific 60-by-90 foot target required 108 B-17 bombers dropping 648 bombs. In the *Persian Gulf War, a single fighter bomber, dropping a single laser-guided bomb, sufficed. Precision attacks against both strategic and tactical targets paralyzed the Iraqi regime and set the stage for the destruction of Saddam *Hussein's ill-conceived occupation of Kuwait.

The emergence of airborne early warning aircraft, sophisticated *command and control, and advanced space-based navigation and communications have greatly improved the efficiency of the modern fighter. Today, beyond this, lies the incorporation of so-called "stealth" or low observable technology, sensor fusion, and advanced integration of aircraft systems. The first air combat stealth fighter—the F-22A—is under development, and expected to enter service after the turn of the century. (It is important to distinguish this aircraft from the popularly known F-117 stealth fighter which, despite the name, is really a specialized attack aircraft.) Without question, the enduring lesson of air warfare is that without air superiority, all other air operations are impossible; in the modern world, air superiority is the guarantor of success. To that end, the purpose and value of the fighter is unbroken, from Flanders in 1915 to Iraq in 1991 and beyond.

[See also Air Force Combat Organizations: Strategic Air Forces; Air Force Combat Organizations: Tactical Air Forces; Bomber Aircraft; Stealth Aircraft.]

—Richard P. Hallion

FILM, WAR AND THE MILITARY IN. *This entry consists of two articles, the first, Newsfilms and Documentaries, on how war and the military have been portrayed in newsreels and other forms of news footage as well as documentary films shown in theaters or more recently on television; and the second, Feature Films, on how the armed forces and the motion picture industry have cooperated—and sometimes failed to cooperate—in the production of dramatized feature films involving the U.S. Army, Navy, Air Force, or Marine Corps.*

Newsfilms and Documentaries
Feature Films

FILM, WAR AND THE MILITARY IN: NEWSFILMS AND DOCUMENTARIES

Visual depiction of the military has been a preoccupation of filmmakers since the first *actualités,* or nonfiction films, were shown by Louis Lumière in Paris, in 1895. Within a year, newsworthy footage was being shown by enterprising camera operators in makeshift theaters all over the world. Thomas Alva *Edison pioneered another type of newsfilm, the prize fight, as early as 1894. By the outbreak of the *Spanish-American War in April 1898, viewing "actualities"—lasting perhaps a minute or two—was already part of American leisure activity.

These early newsfilms are all documentaries, as are, in one sense, all newsreels. Every selection of subject, every change in camera angle, every decision in editing footage for a final product involves point of view. That hard-to-define word *documentary,* described by the English filmmaker John Grierson as "the creative treatment of actuality," also involves point of view. In short, there is much more to the concept of documentary than simple documented fact, as compared to, say, the official likeness recorded in a passport photograph.

Early depictions of news events made extensive use of re-creations, often amateurish, though this seems not to have provoked much comment. No camera was present at the sinking of the USS *Maine* when it was blown up in Havana Harbor, 15 February 1898; the best that Edison's operators could do was to film the half-submerged wreck and the funeral procession for the sailors who had died in the explosion. Such dull footage was replaced with more newsworthy reenactments. Two cameramen proudly recalled faking the naval Battle of *Santiago, using cardboard cutouts of U.S. and Spanish warships, pulled by threads across a container filled with water. The proclaimed "authentic" battle footage was enhanced by off-camera cigar smoke. The tension between the viewer's desire to "see" the face of battle and the camera's inability to do so was clear from the beginning, a tension that still exists.

The Boer War (1899–1902) was filmed by pioneering cameramen. W. L. Dickson could not shoot the Boer positions with an early telephoto lens in December 1899 because of poor weather conditions. To remedy the situation, fully equipped armies of mock British and Boer soldiers "fought" each other in the hills around Orange, New Jersey, site of the Edison motion picture company. It is but a short step from newsreel reenactments to soldiers fighting in some Hollywood costume drama.

The first American newsreel premiered on 8 August 1911—an American version of a French newsreel, *Pathé's Weekly.* An enthusiastic review in a trade magazine claimed that the best footage showed German soldiers on review at Potsdam near Berlin. The anonymous reviewer felt this footage allowed the viewer to see the perfection of German arms and discipline in a way possible in no other medium. Also praised in this first American newsreel was footage of an American naval vessel, the battleship *North Dakota,* undergoing repairs at the Brooklyn Navy Yard. From the start, in other words, the depiction of military might and military hardware informed the commercial newsreel in America.

Pathé, a French company that distributed in the United States, was the first of what became five American newsreel companies active until the rise of television in the mid-1950s. Hollywood's Universal Pictures newsreels did not cease operations until 1967. The newsreel was a series of short stories, lasting eight to ten minutes in total, driven by entertainment values and always meant to hold a paying audience that had come to a movie theater to see a feature-length fictional film. Military pageantry proved a favorite subject. The newsreel rarely contributed to serious debate over military policy, and almost never turned such to subjects as *women in the military, or the relationship of the military to the society from which it found its basis for support.

*War posed a special opportunity for cameramen and directors—an opportunity at first missed, thanks to censorship by governmental authorities and the inability of tradition-bound military officers to understand the potential of visual footage for making the battle front comprehensible to the home front. At first, few recognized the propaganda potential. Nor should one overlook the enormous logistical problems involved in moving cameras on tripods to the front, all too visible to soldiers from both sides.

For North Americans, the story of the Mexican guerrilla leader Francisco ("Pancho") Villa, his raid on Columbus, New Mexico, and the resulting Punitive Expedition of 1916—part of the U.S. military involvement in the *Mexican Revolution—were of intense filmic interest, an interest fueled by a unique contractual relationship between Villa and the U.S.-based Mutual Film Corporation. In an agreement signed on 3 January 1914, Villa promised to fight, whenever possible, only during daylight hours. In one important battle for the city of Ojinaga, Villa actually delayed his attack until Mutual could bring its cameras into position.

Little of Mutual's footage has survived. What has—uninteresting visually—can be seen at the Library of Congress in Washington, D.C. But extraordinary still photographs of Villa can be found in two articles by Aurelio de los Reyes, printed in the *1986* and *1987 Library of Congress Performing Arts Annual.* The Mutual contract with Villa reminds us that docudrama the combination of documentaries and feature films, is not a concept of entirely recent vintage, and that something more than newsworthiness has shaped the visual record of newsfilm.

World War I represents a turning point for nonfiction film's treatment of the military, a turning point more obvious perhaps for what British filmmakers were able to achieve than for their American competitors, who until 6 April 1917 were recording a war that seemed little more than a curiosity to most U.S. audiences. Most of the footage shot between 1914 and 1918 has long since disappeared. But much of it—the "outtakes"—was never seen by audiences of the day, and has only recently come to light. Those who unthinkingly assume that NBC's *Project XX* or CBS's *The Twentieth Century*—both pioneering television documentary series from the 1950s that are still being rerun—have included the relevant surviving footage of battle will be amazed by the existence of some 440 titles in Anouk van der Jagt and Mette Peters, *World War One on Television: An Index of Non-Fiction Programmes* (1993).

One of the more dramatic rediscoveries of recent years is a forty-minute film shot by German cameraman Oskar Messter of wartime production at a steel mill at Poldihütte (then part of Austro-Hungary) in 1916. The numerous women workers are shown manufacturing shell casings, step by step. No surviving records indicate what contemporary audiences thought of this film, or how many saw it, but its visual brilliance makes it one of the Netherlands Film Museum's outstanding pieces of wartime nonfiction footage. The skillful editing suggests that it was meant as a documentary; it survives to tell us about the role of women in wartime production, as well as to indicate state of the art steel manufacturing in a time of full-scale war.

The most important documentary to come out of World War I was Britain's *The Battle of the Somme* (1916). We know that the overwhelming majority of the British populace saw this film in the late summer and fall of 1916, and that is seemed genuinely to convey what it was like to fight in a battle that resulted in 100,000 British casualties on the first day. The unanimity of surviving contemporary opinion makes it clear that this was film propaganda that worked. The seventy-three-minute film, available on video from London's Imperial War Museum, has little impact on today's viewer, more eager to recognize the few "over-the-top" attack scenes, which were faked, than to accept the film's historical significance: the first feature-length documentary successfully to justify the meaning of total war to a home front audience.

The impact of this film was not lost on the enemy. Germany responded with a rejoinder, *With Our Heroes at the Somme* (1917), restricted in scope and unsuccessful with German viewers. Nevertheless, its title demonstrates why Adolf *Hitler and Gen. Erich *Ludendorff believed that in World War I the British were the master propagandists.

American nonfiction filmmaking in 1917–18 represents a lesser level of achievement. *The Battle of the Somme* was shown widely in the United States. The Wilson administration's Creel Committee released a seventy-minute documentary newsfilm, *Pershing's Crusaders*, in 1918, but the uninteresting footage failed to arouse enthusiasm. U.S. Army Signal Corps camera operators spent much of their time pleading with old-fashioned field officers who saw no value in film. As a result, American newsreels carried war stories based on the footage of European news cameramen, with little to show save colorful entries into towns freed from German occupation. French civilians looked appropriately joyous for the camera. The exploits of the black 369th Regiment ("Harlem Hellfighters") are shown (including a sound track with the 369th's jazz band) in William Miles's documentary, *Men of Bronze* (1977), now available on video. The best guide to American footage, curiously enough, is Roger Smither's 1994 catalogue of the film holdings of the Imperial War Museum, which includes a brief summary of every single film item relating to World War I.

Nobody has a problem locating footage for World War II. Indeed, we first recall that war from film images; few could claim never to have seen so much as a single World War II documentary. American newsreels got their battle footage through a pool system. U.S. Army, Navy, Air Force, and Marine Corps photographers shot footage at the front; after careful censorship, it was then shared with all five newsreel companies. This does not mean that every story has a dreary visual sameness, but it helps explain why there are no multiple shots of bombings of *Hiroshima and Nagasaki, for example. It is also true that the overall visual record of American battle footage is not particularly impressive, particularly when compared to the Nazi *Wochenschau*, or newsreel, now available on home video from Chicago's International Historic Films (IHF). Wartime saw no change in the entertainment-driven requirements of the American commercial newsreel. Bathing beauties appeared on screen more often than that symbol of women in the workplace, Rosie the Riveter.

Wartime documentary was official; such films must be considered as propaganda, their avowed purpose. Most were made for the government by Hollywood directors, men who had made their reputations in fictional feature production. Best known was Frank Capra, who produced for the military seven feature-length documentaries explaining the reasons why the United States was at war. The *Why We Fight* series originally included an eighth film, *War Comes to America, Part II*, which survives only as a shooting script. The Capra films (available on home video) seem strident to today's viewers, who perhaps have not thought about what they replaced—plodding, well-meaning lecturers assigned to give recruits fifteen orientation lectures, including all the facts and figures.

Capra's film unit also produced a pioneering documentary, *The Negro Soldier* (1944), describing overstated prospects for black advancement. Nevertheless, the film by its very existence and its high production values served as a threat to official segregation policy. Its radical premise could not be disguised; career advancement would mark the end of a rigidly segregated military.

The Hollywood director William Wyler directed *Memphis Belle* (1944), the finest documentary about the experience of flying on a bombing raid produced by any combatant nation. John Huston made *San Pietro* (1945), a low-key explanation about how the taking of one small Italian village from its German occupiers explains the grinding attrition of the Italian Campaign, and, by indirection, the meaning of the war to the G.I.s. Some modern viewers miss the skillful reenactments in the film, which is effective precisely because of important scenes shot just before or after the battle. Huston dealt with the problem of battle fatigue in *Let There Be Light* (1946), filmed at a hospital on Long Island. The film was denied public clearance for twenty years because Huston did not get written releases from the soldiers undergoing psychiatric treatment; for years he falsely insisted that the *Pentagon had censored his film because it was antiwar.

The most significant nonfiction footage to come out of World War II is a collective enterprise, reminding us how much the horrors of war and views of the *enemy are defined through visual media in the twentieth century. In the spring of 1945, the collective footage of skeletal figures, piles of dead bodies stacked like so much cordwood, of a bulldozer pushing countless naked bodies into a mass grave, and of such well as Dwight D. *Eisenhower and George S. *Patton walking through liberated death camps while inmates were still present, provided documentation for German crimes against humanity presented at the Nuremberg *War Crimes Trial, 1945–46. This visual record made clear in the war's aftermath that Nazi Germany had been an enemy worth fighting. Although the word *Holocaust* was not used in 1945, we must count the Holocaust footage shot by American, Russian, and British cameramen as one of the most important military uses of the medium of film.

The *Korean War was covered by newsreel cameramen; television news based its limited coverage on newsfilm shot by newsreel cameramen. It might be helpful to point out that similar footage was seen in theaters and on television, remembering that a freeze by the Federal Communications Commission restricted the total number of television stations in the United States to just 108 until mid-April 1952. Korea was an unpopular war. Millions saw Gen. Douglas *MacArthur's triumphal motorcade pass through downtown San Francisco, Chicago, and New York City after his dismissal by President Harry S. *Truman in April 1951; few found much interest in a war that soon settled into stalemate. The historian Bruce Cumings's 1990 WGBH television series has an appropriate title for Korea: *The Forgotten War.*

For Vietnam, the distinction between television news and documentary begins to erode. Americans learned of France's war in Indochina from the newsreel; the war which came to occupy American attention was covered by three national networks: NBC, CBS, and ABC, the last too weak to attract many viewers, which is worth remembering when one evaluates the impact of the conservative commentator Howard K. Smith, or such unusual ABC Vietnam television correspondents as the photographer David Douglas Duncan.

The *Vietnam War resulted in many documentaries protesting the conflict, most of which failed to find much of an audience. Peter Davis, in *The Selling of the Pentagon* (CBS, 1971), indicted the *military-industrial complex. His feature-length Technicolor *Hearts and Minds* (1974) received an Academy Award for Best Documentary. The film explains American militarism as a direct result of societal enthusiasm for Friday night high school football, and uses an editing trick to jump-cut from Gen. William C. *Westmoreland, who declares that the Oriental places little value on human life, to a Vietnamese woman weeping over the death of her child. Zina Voynow, the film's editor, told me in 1978 that she felt her work on this film to be the most important thing she had done in her life.

Quite different, in what now seems old-fashioned black and white, is Eugene Jones's *The Face of War* (1967), now available on video. The film suggests what it was like to be part of a Marine combat unit in 1966. Jones spent three months in the field with the company; his film does a remarkable job of capturing the aural presence of radio in the life of an American soldier in Vietnam. Emile de Antonio's *In the Year of the Pig* (1969) incorporated archival footage from camera operators from the former East Germany, Hanoi, and the National Liberation Front office in Prague, in a hammer-and-tongs assault on American conduct of the war.

The most important piece of newsfilm to come out of the Vietnam War was certainly the NBC color newsfilm of South Vietnamese Colonel Loan executing a Viet Cong sympathizer, 2 February 1968, on the streets of downtown Saigon, at the start of the *Tet Offensive, the turning point of the war. A three-man camera team from NBC and ABC filmed the event; Associated Press photographer Eddie Adams took a Pulitzer Prize–winning photograph of what seemed to be the instant of death. The visual microcosm of disaster suggested that America supported a government that killed innocent victims with no concern for guilt or innocence.

The Communists' Tet Offensive took the war into the cities of South Vietnam. Peter Braestrup, in *Big Story* (1977), the most comprehensive study of any foreign event ever covered by the American media, indicts both television correspondents and newspaper reporters for missing the meaning of Tet (Braestrup was *Washington Post* bureau chief in Saigon in 1968). The *Persian Gulf War, not Vietnam, was America's first "living-room war." As a general rule, television supported the war up to the fall of 1967; elite opinion in Washington—exemplified by the counsel the so-called Wise Men gave Lyndon B. *Johnson in late March 1968—turned against the war before the majority of Americans did so. Antiwar television and newspaper stories did not make American battlefield victory impossible.

The latest development in television newsfilm occurred in the 1991 Persian Gulf War. Thanks to satellite cable television, CNN's Peter Arnett was able to broadcast directly from Baghdad, and Saddam *Hussein used television to speak directly to President George *Bush and the American people. Endless media prognostications about the upcoming allied Coalition assault on Kuwait City from the sea helped mislead Hussein and his advisers as to where the attack would actually come, contributing importantly to his overwhelming defeat.

The Gulf War to date has produced no memorable documentaries. Vast amounts of television programming about that war, recorded from all over the world, can be viewed at archives at the University of Leeds in England. Yesterday's newsfilm is tomorrow's archival footage for the day-after-tomorrow's documentaries. A final word of caution may be in order: the recent enthusiasm for faked grainy newsfilm in Hollywood feature films should remind us that never has the distinction between documentary and fictional film been less clear.

[*See also* Film, War and the Military in: Feature Films; Illustration, War and the Military in; News Media, War, and the Military; Photography, War and the Military In; Propaganda and Public Relations, Government.]

• Editors of *Look, Movie Lot to Beachhead: The Motion Picture Goes to War and Prepares for the Future*, 1945. Raymond Fielding, *The American Newsreel, 1911–1967*, 1972. Erwin Leiser, *Nazi Cinema*, 1974. Peter Braestrup, *Big Story: How the American Press and Television Reported the Crisis of Tet 1968 in Vietnam and Washington*, 2 vols., 1977. Linda Dittmar and Gene Michaud, eds., *From Hanoi to Hollywood: The Vietnam War in American Film*, 1990. David Culbert, editor-in-chief, *Film and Propaganda in America: A Documentary History*, 5 vols., 1990–93. Philip M. Taylor, *War and the Media: Propaganda and Persuasion in the Gulf War*, 1992. Daan Hertogs and Nico De Klerk, *Nonfiction from the Teens: The 1994 Amsterdam Workshop*, 1994. Paolo Cherchi Usai, *Burning Passions: An Introduction to the Study of Silent Cinema*, 1994. Roger Smither, ed., *Imperial War Museum Film Catalogue I: The First World War Archive*, 1994. John Whiteclay Chambers II and David Culbert, eds., *World War II, Film, and History*, 1996.   —David Culbert

FILM, WAR AND THE MILITARY IN: FEATURE FILMS

A symbiotic relationship has existed between the United States military and the motion picture industry in the production of feature films, each institution exploiting and benefitting from the relationship with the other. The services want an attractive portrayal; the filmmakers, particularly the studios, want to use the military's equipment, personnel, and aura. Each service also seeks to build public support for its own particular needs.

During the decade before World War I, each of the services began developing its own approach to filmmakers through regulations governing assistance it might render on a particular production. The U.S. Navy, the first service to see the potential of this visual medium, sent pseudo-documentaries portraying its activities to the 1904 World's Fair in St. Louis. Later, these were used to recruit farmboys in the Middle West. By 1916, when the navy loaned Syd Chaplin, Charlie's look-alike brother, a submarine during the making of *Submarine Pirate,* the service was regularly providing men and equipment to productions it considered beneficial. On the other hand, it refused to loan a battleship during the making of Mary Pickford's *Madame Butterfly* (1915) because Secretary of the Navy Josephus Daniels felt the story did not reflect credit on the Naval Service.

The aviation branch led the army in exploring film's potential. Lt. Henry "Hap" *Arnold flew one of the first military airplanes in front of a camera in the two-reeler *Military Scout* (1911). Later, Arnold supported the Air Corps' cooperation with filmmakers in such major productions as *Wings* (1927), the first Best Picture Oscar winner, and *Air Force* (1943), a World War II epic flying film.

The Marine Corps, seeking to ensure its survival as a unique body of fighting men, cooperated with films that emphasized this, especially those featuring the rite of passage of young boys to mature men. Shortly before the

United States entered World War I, the Marine Corps allowed filmmakers to shoot *Star-Spangled Banner* at its barracks at Bremerton, Washington. After U.S. entry in April 1917, the service permitted the filmmakers to shoot the combat scenes on its base at Quantico, Virginia, providing the director with 1,000 Marines for his "over-the-top" sequence in *The Unbeliever* (1918). The service's public affairs office helped promote the film by sending news releases to newspapers in all the towns from which the Marine actors had come, explaining that the young men had now arrived in France and were helping to defeat the enemy.

As has happened after virtually every war, Hollywood lost interest in the military once hostilities ceased. Nevertheless, the connection between the two institutions remained. In trying to do for the American Revolution what he had done for the Civil War, D. W. Griffith again approached the army for assistance on *America* (1923). Secretary of War John Weeks ordered the army to give the director every reasonable help, ultimately including 1,000 cavalrymen and a military band. The army justified its cooperation by saying the filming allowed officers to study the *Revolutionary War battles with a precision never before possible.

Hollywood ultimately turned to World War I combat to portray dramatic stories of men in combat. The first of these, *The Big Parade* (1925), set the standard. Director King Vidor said that he wanted to make "an honest war picture" showing hostilities from the viewpoint of ordinary soldiers and privates. With the army's help, Vidor was able to portray the spectacle of a large-scale movement of troops and equipment to the front, "the big parade." In the picture, two of the three doughboys die and the hero loses a leg, causing many people to perceive the film as an antiwar treatise, despite its happy ending. From the military's perspective, if the ending is upbeat, even the death of one or more of the characters remains secondary to the images of men and equipment performing valiantly in the nation's cause.

During the 1920s, each of the services formalized its regulations governing cooperation with filmmakers. Once the War Department or the Navy Department, of which the Marines remained a subordinate branch, had approved a script, the local commander assumed all responsibility for providing assistance. But, the amount he gave depended on the feelings the base commander or ship captain had toward film and the production company. Only rarely did a commander object strongly enough for headquarters to rescind its approval. More often, commanders went out of their way to provide the assistance a director needed, recognizing the public relations value of the completed film.

The making of *Wings* illustrated this symbiotic relationship during the interwar years. The Army Air Corps saw the story of American fliers in France as a way to boost its branch of the army, and many of the officers at the flying facilities around San Antonio knew director William Wellman from his flying days during World War I. As a result, the service provided him with a good portion of all the airplanes it owned, as well as the troops necessary to re-create the Battle of *St. Mihiel. For its nine months of assistance, the Air Corps received a film that glorified army aviation.

Hollywood did make other combat stories featuring the U.S. military during the 1920s and 1930s, but most focused on life in the peacetime armed services. The Marines, for example, assisted on two movies portraying its aviation branch, *Flight* (1929) and *Devil Dogs of the Air* (1935).

Navy aviation, of course, reaped the reward of appearing in the film as well as several other stories set aboard *aircraft carriers. However, the submarine service faced an inherent dilemma; to make an exciting movie, the submarine had to sink, which did little to aid recruitment for the silent service. The only resolution to the problem, whether in Frank Capra's *Submarine* (1928) or later in *Gray Lady Down* (1978), was for the navy to demonstrate its salvage capability. Despite the required love interest, *Submarine D-1* (1937) became little more than a pseudo-documentary, showing how the service was preparing to deal with the sinking of *submarines.

Navy aviation faced similar problems in overcoming the dangers of flight. The service sought to explain its efforts to protect men and equipment. Consequently, in the immediate prewar years, the navy in films such as *Flight Command* (1940), which detailed efforts to improve navigation equipment, and *Dive Bomber* (1941), which portrayed the research by Navy flight doctors to overcome pilot blackout.

Hollywood failed in general to deal with the Nazi threat until late in the 1930s, but by 1940 was turning out such pro-interventionist films as *Sergeant York,* which depicted the heroic doughboy, Alvin *York, of World War I. Isolationists in Congress and across the country accused Hollywood of making propaganda films to draw the United States into the war on the side of Britain. In a Senate hearing in September 1941, the heads of all the major studios denied the charges. While acknowledging that they opposed Adolf *Hitler, they argued that they produced movies to entertain and make money.

The Japanese attack on *Pearl Harbor rendered further hearings moot and freed Hollywood to produce vehemently anti-German films as well as movies portraying the military in combat. Like the World War I-era *The Unbeliever* (1918), which showed Marines in battle before they had actually reached Europe, the initial World War II movies, such as *Bataan* (1943), *Crash Dive* (1943), and *Wing and a Prayer* (1944) contained fanciful stories, usually implausible and lacking basis in fact. *Air Force* (1943), for example, made with the blessing of "Hap" Arnold (now a general), began with the historic reality that a flight of B-17s had left San Francisco in the evening of 6 December, arriving in Hawaii in the midst of the Japanese attack on Pearl Harbor. However, the subsequent adventures of the *Mary Ann* and her crew, culminating in the almost single-handed destruction of a huge Japanese armada had no historic basis.

Sometimes, as in Wake Island (1942) and *Destination Tokyo* (1943), filmmakers combined known facts with fabrications. In reality, the last man off Wake Island before its capture had reported how a small band of Marines defended the island up to the day he left. Hollywood's portrayal of subsequent events remained at best an educated guess. An American submarine had sailed to within sight of Japan to report weather conditions for James *Doolittle's raiders. However, *Destination Tokyo* portrayed the submarine entering Tokyo Bay, landing a team of meteorologists on Japanese soil, and later sinking a Japanese aircraft carrier, none of which happened.

By 1943, however, the war had produced dramatic stories, which served as the basis for relatively accurate accounts of American experiences in combat. In particular, MGM's *Thirty Seconds Over Tokyo* (1944), directed by Mervyn LeRoy and written by Dalton Trumbo, closely followed the story of one of the pilots on the Doolittle raid. Nevertheless, for political reasons, the film did not explain that the Chinese Communists had rescued most of the fliers. Whether or not the combat films made during the war contained more fact than fantasy, they did help the war effort by showing how the military carried the war to the enemy.

Each of the armed services had more important things to do than provide men and equipment to filmmakers, even if the assistance lent an authentic ambiance to the completed movie and showed how the military was winning the war. Still, each service did cooperate with Hollywood as much as possible. Due to General Arnold's long-standing relationship with filmmakers, the Army Air Force loaned several B-17s, a fighter, and other equipment for the filming of *Air Force*. Although the navy and the Air Corps could not recreate the launch of Doolittle's planes off the deck of the USS *Hornet*, the Air Corps provided 16 B-25s for the training sequences and trundled two bombers to the MGM studio for filming shipboard sequences.

Despite the popularity of such war stories, once *victory loomed on the horizon, Hollywood began cutting back on the production of combat films, believing audiences would lose interest when the war was over. Two critically acclaimed films—*They Were Expendable* and *A Walk in the Sun*—both released in 1945 shortly after V-J Day, failed at the box office.

Only in 1948 did the small-scale *Command Decision* and *Fighter Squadron* appear in theaters. Relying on Army Air Force gun camera footage for their combat sequences, neither film enjoyed much success at the box office. However, in the next two years, four major World War II movies started a cycle of combat stories that lasted into the early 1960s. *Battleground, Sands of Iwo Jima, Task Force*, and *Twelve O'Clock High* received substantial military assistance and each presented a highly positive image of the service being portrayed.

Beyond their re-creation of World War II, two of the films became important for their portrayals of leadership. As the tough father figure, Sergeant Stryker, in *Sands of Iwo Jima* (1949), John Wayne passes his knowledge of war to the next generation of Marines and dies having accomplished his mission. Despite his inglorious death from a sniper's bullet, Wayne's performance established him as the quintessential American fightingman and role model in the eyes of most Americans. In contrast, in *Twelve O'-Clock High* (1949), General Savage, played by Gregory Peck, falls into the same trap as had the commander he replaced. After rebuilding the confidence and abilities of his bomber group through strict leadership and appropriate distance from his men, Savage begins to see them as human beings and friends. When they die in combat, Savage grieves, albeit internally, and ultimately suffers a mental breakdown. Probably the best film ever made about the U.S. Air Force, *Twelve O'Clock High* continues to be used in leadership seminars to illustrate the problems leaders face in commanding subordinates.

Most of the Pentagon's objections to scripts submitted during the 1950s focused on small matters—pilots drinking, rough treatment of recruits—and filmmakers readily acquiesced to requests for changes in order to receive the needed assistance, which gave their movies authentic military ambiance. Occasionally, however, major productions did create problems for one or another of the services that required long negotiations and compromises on both sides.

Hollywood wanted to make two popular novels, James Jones's *From Here to Eternity* and Herman Wouk's *The Caine Mutiny*, into motion pictures as quickly as possible. In the case of Jones's novel, the army did not deny the accuracy of the portrayals, but it saw little benefit in a story of an officer's abuse of power and the cruel treatment inflicted upon enlisted men in prewar Hawaii. Ultimately, the filmmakers agreed to tone down some of the brutality and have the offending officer resign rather than being promoted as in the novel; the army then allowed filming at Schofield Barracks, Hawaii, using real soldiers as extras.

Although Herman Wouk thought he had written a pronavy story based on his own experiences aboard a destroyer in World War II, the navy was opposed to the title—*The Caine Mutiny*—arguing (incorrectly) that there had never been a mutiny aboard a U.S. Navy ship. Producer Stanley Kramer refused the suggested title, *The Caine Incident*. After eighteen months of negotiation, both sides compromised on a script that put the blame for the takeover of the USS *Caine* on the civilian-appointed turned wartime officers rather than on Captain Queeg, a regular navy officer.

Ironically, one of the films that the navy thought beneficial and assisted, *The Bridges of Toko-Ri* (1954), based on James Michener's novel, contained some of Hollywood's strongest antiwar statements. The navy provided an extraordinary amount of assistance in this portrayal of carrier operations during the *Korean War. Although the film contains a strong justification for the need to fight the Communists in Korea, the closing image of the downed pilot-protagonist, shot dead in a muddy ditch by North Korean soldiers, did little to create enthusiasm for naval aviation or for war itself.

Only on very rare occasions did the Pentagon flatly refuse to provide assistance to a film during the peak of the *Cold War in the 1950s. One example was *Attack!* (1956), in which an enlisted man shoots his incompetent officer. By the end of the 1960s, the interest in World War II had about run its course. Moreover, young, independent filmmakers, not beholden to Hollywood's comfortable relationship with the military establishment, had begun to take control of the industry. Things also changed within the Pentagon as a result of the controversies surrounding the making of *The Longest Day* (1962), the film that ended the golden age of World War II movies.

The army had, of course, few problems with providing assistance to a movie about the *D-Day landing in Normandy, its greatest moment in World War II. Producer Darryl Zanuck of 20th Century Fox received help in recreating the invasion of *Normandy not only from the U.S. military but from the forces of the other three major participants in the battle, Britain, France, and Germany. But, when the American media focused attention on the amount of cooperation Zanuck was receiving, the Pentagon began reevaluating its long-standing regulations on assistance. The producer did not help the inquiry when he shot a scene of American soldiers killing German soldiers who were trying to surrender, which he had agreed not to include, and then refused to delete it despite army demands that he do so.

Although the free and easy relationship between Hollywood and the military came to an end in the 1960s, the film industry was not immediately ready to produce movies openly critical of the armed services; but filmmakers were willing to use the atomic bomb as a focus for antiwar statements. In particular, *Fail Safe* (1964), *Dr. Strangelove* (1964), and *The Bedford Incident* (1965) each argued that the Pentagon did not have the control it claimed over the use of *nuclear weapons and that an accident could lead to nuclear holocaust. The air force and navy refused to cooperate on any of these productions. And the navy would have nothing to do with *The Americanization of Emily* (1964), in which for the first time a Hollywood studio portrayed a U.S. military officer as a professed coward.

To be sure, filmmakers continued to produce traditional military stories with Pentagon assistance during the 1960s and early 1970s. These included *PT-109* (1963), *In Harm's Way* (1965), *Bridge at Remagen* (1969), *Patton* (1970), and *Tora! Tora! Tora!* (1970). Yet, even these films often contained negative images. Hollywood made one more pro-air force, pro-atomic bomb movie, *Gathering of Eagles* (1962), at the request of Curtis E. *LeMay.

John Wayne was involved in an effort to glorify the U.S. military in Vietnam, using army assistance. Unfortunately, *The Green Berets* (1968) reeked of its propaganda message about an unpopular war. It became Hollywood's sole movie on the *Vietnam War until the conflict ended in 1975. Thereafter, Hollywood set about to complete the savaging, begun by the media during the war, of the largely positive image of the U.S. military that American filmmakers had helped to create for more than seventy years.

When presented with the scripts of *Go Tell the Spartans* (1978), *Coming Home* (1978), *The Deer Hunter* (1978), and *Apocalypse Now* (1979), the Pentagon did not deny that many bad things had occurred in Vietnam. But public affairs officers in each of the services argued that the stories often lacked balance and portrayed events that simply had not occurred or had been aberrations.

In May 1975, the director Francis Ford Coppola visited the Pentagon to discuss his plans to make a film about the Vietnam War; Department of *Defense officials wanted to avoid controversy with the Oscar-winning director and they sought ways to provide him at least some assistance on *Apocalypse Now*. However, they contended that the army would never send one officer to "terminate" another officer and so could not assist on a film that used this as the springboard of its story.

In *The Deer Hunter*, director Michael Cimino turned the *My Lai Massacre into a Viet Cong atrocity. However, the film's re-creation of the American evacuation of Saigon bore no relation to historical events and the army pointed out that no American prisoners of war had ever been forced to play Russian roulette. The service declined to provide any assistance to Cimino's production.

Each service usually manifested far too much sensitivity in dealing with requests for even limited help on Vietnam War films. *Go Tell the Spartans* contained a relatively accurate portrayal of the activity of American advisers in the early 1960s. The filmmakers expressed a willingness to negotiate with the army to deal with service objections to the script, but they met with what they considered absolute intransigence from the public affairs office. Again, the Air Force refused to consider cooperation on *Rolling Thunder* (1977), claiming that there were no known cases of air force officers becoming schizophrenic "there is nothing beneficial for the Department of Defense in the dramatization of this situation."

The army flatly refused to consider assistance on *Hair* (1979), equating the *Vietnam antiwar movement message in the stage play with an entirely different screenplay. The army even refused to discuss the request with the Defense Department's public affairs office. Only after that office suggested that script contained a moral tale of one friend giving his life for another did the filmmakers receive some limited assistance from the National Guard.

The army did provide full assistance to one movie about combat during the 1970s cycle of Vietnam War movies. *Hamburger Hill* (1979) gives a highly positive portrayal of American courage in combat. Despite the heroism, however, the film contains a strongly antiwar statement: soldiers conquer an enemy-held hill at high cost and then retreat, with no explanation of the reasons for either the battle or the withdrawal.

In 1979, the first wave of Vietnam movies came to an end. Ironically, despite the negative portrayals of the American fighting experience that these films had contained, Hollywood had concurrently been rehabilitating the image of the U.S. armed forces. Not so badly tarred by the war as the other services, the navy could serve as a viable subject for filmmakers who wished to create patriotic stories of men in uniform, particularly as the United States celebrated its bicentennial in 1976.

The navy had refused to provide even limited assistance to *The Last Detail* (1973) and *Cinderella Liberty* (1973), both set in the peacetime Navy, because its public affairs office believed the films reflected anti-Vietnam War sentiment. In contrast, the navy embraced *Midway* (1976), which focused on the Battle of *Midway, the first great U.S. naval victory of World War II. The service readily ignored the insipid fictional story that overlaid the documentary-like portrayal of the famous battle, recognizing that aerial combat footage would create high drama and an appreciation of the courage of the participants.

The success of the film, perhaps due to the nation's longing for a military success following the debacle of Vietnam, encouraged Hollywood to return to the navy as a locale for other stories including *Gray Lady Down* (1978), *Raise the Titanic!* (1980), and *The Final Countdown* (1980). Each showed naval officers and men doing their jobs in a competent, highly professional manner.

Paradoxically, the navy refused to become involved with *An Officer and a Gentleman* (1982), a traditional rite-of-passage love story, not at all different from the thirties Hollywood romances for which the service regularly provided men and ships. In this case, the Navy's public affairs office objected to the language, graphic sex, and suicide of an officer who flunked out of the Naval Aviation Officer program. The service recognized its mistake after the film became a box office hit and people assumed the navy had provided the ambiance. As a result, the navy readily agreed to lend the producers of *Top Gun* (1986) an aircraft carrier and planes, and gave access to the Top Gun school of naval aviators. The top-grossing film of the year, it marked the final rehabilitation of the American military image.

Admittedly, such films as *The Great Santini* (1979) and

Private Benjamin (1980) also contributed to the more positive portrayals of the armed services. Consequently, even the second wave of Vietnam stories including Oliver Stone's *Platoon* (1986), Stanley Kubrick's *Full Metal Jacket* (1988), and Brian De Palma's *Casualties of War* (1989), despite containing some of the most vivid images, real and imagined, about the American experience in Vietnam, did not seriously affect the nation's renewed confidence in the military establishment.

At the same time, filmmakers have shown less inclination to hide the armed services' deficiencies in their contemporary stories. As a result, the military has more readily refused to provide assistance to such films as *Broken Arrow* (1996), in which an air force pilot helps steal a nuclear weapon. *The Hunt For Red October* (1990), however, which was the last film of the Cold War and the first of the "New World Order," received extensive assistance from the navy. The service did reject a request for assistance on *Crimson Tide* (1995), arguing that its portrayal of command and control of nuclear weapons aboard U.S. submarines had no basis in fact. Likewise, the army turned down a request for help on *Courage Under Fire* (1996) because this film about the *Persian Gulf War showed some U.S. soldiers being cowardly under fire and lying about their actions.

In the post–Cold War world, of course, filmmakers face the problem of deciding who poses a threat to U.S. national security. So far, Hollywood has had the armed services fight terrorists of the Irish Republican Army in *Patriot Games* (1994), Colombian drug dealers in *Clear and Present Danger* (1995), nuclear terrorists in *True Lies* (1995), and ultranationalist Russians in *Air Force One* (1997). To be sure, these enemies do not compare with the threat that Germany or Japan posed in World War II. Nevertheless, Hollywood has portrayed the cinematic sailors, soldiers, aviators, and Marines doing their jobs competently, and the armed services have willingly provided assistance as the symbiotic relationship between the film industry and the armed services continues.

[*See also* Film, War and the Military in: Newsfilms and Documentaries; News Media, War, and the Military; Photography, War and the Military in; Propaganda and Public Relations, Government.]

• Joe Morella, Edward Epstein, and John Griggs, *The Films of World War II*, 1973. Clyde Jeavons, *A Pictorial History of War Films*, 1974. Jack Shaheen, ed., *Nuclear War Films*, 1978. Lawrence Suid, *Guts & Glory*, 1978. Steven J. Rubin, *Combat Films, 1945–1970*, 1981. Lawrence Suid, ed., *Air Force* [Introduction to and script of the film], 1983. Bernard Dick, *The Star-Spangled Screen*, 1985. Jeanine Basinger, *The World War II Combat Film: Anatomy of a Genre*, 1986. Lawrence Suid, *Sailing on the Silver Screen*, 1996.

—Lawrence Suid

FIRE CONTROL SYSTEMS. *See* Detection, Observation, and Fire Control Systems.

FLAMETHROWERS. The primary effects of flame weapons are fear, blinding, choking, and asphyxiation. Germany first invented and used the modern flamethrower in World War I. Since then, all major military powers have developed and fielded both portable and vehicle-mounted versions. The United States used flamethrowers extensively in *World War II, the *Korean War, and the *Vietnam War.

The U.S. model M3 man-portable flamethrower

weighed about 65 pounds fully loaded, and projected a burning stream of semiliquid fuel about 40 yards with a duration of less than ten seconds. Its storage tanks for fuel and compressed air connected by hose to a gun and igniter held with both hands by the operator. Triggers released the jellylike fuel, propelled by air pressure and ignited as it streamed past the nozzle. The United States also fielded an armored flamethrower with greater range and duration mounted inside the Sherman tank chassis.

The U.S. Army and Marine Corps made wide use of flamethrowers in World War II, especially in the Pacific theater as part of a systematic tactical technique for attacking Japanese pillboxes, dugouts, and caves like those at Iwo Jima and Okinawa. Attackers suppressed the objective with small-arms fire, allowing flamethrower operators to get close enough to put fire into apertures and openings.

The U.S. military continued to use flamethrowers in Korea and Vietnam, but also fielded new flame weapons during the Vietnam War, including the M202 Flash, which was much lighter than the M3 and could hit point targets at over 100 yards and area targets out to 275 yards. The M202 is man-portable and weighs about 25 pounds fully loaded, with four rocket-propelled charges fired independently from the operator's shoulder.

• George Feifer, *Tennozan: The Battle of Okinawa and the Atomic Bomb*, 1992.

—George Knapp

FLEXIBLE RESPONSE. The doctrine of "flexible response" was a not entirely successful attempt to "square the circle" of *nuclear weapons strategy by suggesting ways in which nuclear weapons could be used, together with conventional weapons, in battle without invoking nuclear Armageddon. Though it remains a part of official U.S. policy in the 1990s, it has been eclipsed by increasing awareness that nuclear weapons have no utility except to deter others from using these weapons.

The phrase was widely publicized by Gen. Maxwell *Taylor in his book *The Uncertain Trumpet* (1960) published immediately after his resignation as chief of staff of the U.S. Army in protest to army budget cuts. Taylor argued that the doctrine of "massive retaliation" had been overtaken by events because of the growing Soviet nuclear capability, and that nuclear weapons, or at least strategic as distinguished from tactical nuclear weapons, by themselves did not constitute an effective response to low-level aggression. Taylor proposed a significant expansion of conventional weapons budgets and troop strength, which had been cut back during his term as chief of staff, with consequent losses to the army in its battles with the other services over the division of the military budget.

Taylor's ideas were enthusiastically adopted by the Kennedy administration, and President John F. *Kennedy appointed him a special adviser, and then chairman of the *Joint Chiefs of Staff (1962). Kennedy had already expressed the view, in a major speech on the Senate floor in 1960, that U.S. nuclear retaliatory power "cannot deter Communist aggression" and was "too limited to justify atomic war," although he did not refer to the doctrine of flexible response by name.

One of the first official acts of Secretary of Defense Robert S. *McNamara was to instruct the Joint Chiefs to revise the Single Integrated Operating Plan (SIOP) to create several options for the use of the strategic nuclear force, in place of the single option of ordering a devastating attack on Soviet society. At the same time, McNamara sought and obtained from the Congress substantial increases in funding for nonnuclear forces. These increases were designed to assure that the *NATO conventional response to a Soviet incursion across the Iron Curtain would be more than token resistance designed to trigger the employment of nuclear weapons, despite European nervousness that anything more than a conventional trigger might weaken the effectiveness of the nuclear deterrent. In a special presidential message of 28 March 1961 accompanying the major budget revisions, Kennedy asserted: "Our defense posture must be both flexible and determined ... our response ... selective, permitting deliberation and discrimination as to timing, scope and targets ..."

Reacting in part to Nikita Khrushchev's call for "wars of national liberation," the Kennedy administration made training for "sub-limited war" a key element in its flexible response policy, including special emphasis on counterinsurgency by *special operations forces such as the army's Green Beret teams.

Early theorists of nuclear strategy, like Bernard Brodie and William Kaufmann, rejecting massive retaliation except as an instrument of last resort, embraced policies that could be described as flexible response, although again they did not employ the term. Brodie for a time explored the potential of tactical nuclear weapons as offering more flexibility. Others, particularly Herman Kahn, argued that the United States could survive a major nuclear exchange, provided it undertook an extensive civil defense effort.

McNamara, applying the doctrine in practice, realized that it did not offer a ready answer to the fundamental question, How much is enough? At first he proposed, in a speech to *NATO allies later delivered in unclassified form at the University of Michigan, that strategic nuclear forces should be configured like conventional forces, "to destroy the enemy's military forces, not his civilian population." This proposal was motivated in part by the desire to constrain allied, and particularly French, nuclear forces to coordinate their war plans, in order to reduce the likelihood that uncoordinated strikes would lead rapidly to nuclear Armageddon.

McNamara later shifted his emphasis away from a counterforce strategy to base his nuclear force requirements on the capacity to inflict unacceptable damage on the enemy (i.e., Soviet) society and economy, after absorbing the most powerful first strike that could be directed against the United States. This doctrine of Mutual Assured Destruction (derisively labeled MAD by its critics) did not exclude the possibility of flexible response, including limited nuclear response to a Soviet conventional attack across the North German plain, relying on nuclear weapons to overcome an assumed Soviet conventional superiority. But MAD supporters put more faith in an assured second-strike capability than in the threat of limited nuclear weapons involvement, which could too easily escalate into an all-out nuclear exchange. President Richard M. *Nixon's substitution of "sufficiency" for "supremacy" in the vocabulary of nuclear strength made Mutual Assured Destruction more palatable.

A flexible response analysis (not under that name) had a brief revival in the 1980s when the Soviets initiated the deployment of a new nuclear-tipped missile specifically aimed at European targets, and NATO responded by beginning the deployment of two Europe-based missiles targeted on the Soviet Union, generating a major controversy in Europe and the United States over the appropriateness of the response. But Premier Mikhail Gorbachev resolved the controversy by accepting an earlier proposal by President Ronald *Reagan to terminate both deployments.

It can be argued that the shift from massive retaliation to flexible response created a more favorable climate for arms control negotiations. It seems more logical, however, to attribute both developments to the realization that eventual rough nuclear parity with the Soviets was inevitable—and rough parity was good enough to produce mutual assured destruction.

On the debit side, critics of U.S. involvement in the *Vietnam War (e.g., Brodie) argue that the idea of flexible response may have helped to lead the United States into the Vietnamese quagmire, and, as Colin Grey has observed, "Strategic concepts of flexible response and controlled escalation have ... tended to blind decision makers to the possible employment of non-military options."

• William W. Kaufmann, ed., *Military Policy and National Security,* 1956. Maxwell D. Taylor, *The Uncertain Trumpet,* 1960. William W. Kaufmann, *The McNamara Strategy,* 1964. John Newhouse, et al., *U.S. Troops in Europe,* 1971. Bernard Brodie, *War and Politics,* 1973. Colin S. Gray, *Strategic Studies and Public Policy: The American Experience,* 1982. Robert Jervis, *The Illogic of American Nuclear Strategy,* 1984. James Woolsey, ed., *Nuclear Arms: Ethics, Strategy, Politics,* 1984. Gregg Herken, *Counsels of War,* expanded ed., 1987. McGeorge Bundy, *Danger and Survival,* 1988.

—Adam Yarmolinsky

FOR. *See* Fellowship of Reconciliation.

FORD, GERALD (1913–), thirty-eighth president of the United States. Born in 1913, a decorated veteran of the Pacific theater in World War II (serving in the U.S. Navy as an ensign aboard USS *Monterey*), Ford served twelve consecutive terms in the House of Representatives before he was chosen by Richard M. *Nixon (1973) to be his vice president.

When Ford became president after Nixon's resignation in 1974, he found himself caught between two ideological camps on national security issues. Many Americans, tired of war, wanted Ford to reject any further obligations abroad. However, conservatives in both parties demanded that Ford demonstrate that the *Vietnam War had not weakened American military resolve. Himself a conservative in military affairs, who had supported the American commitment in Korea and Vietnam, Ford nevertheless wanted to win his own term as president. As a result, he followed a policy path he hoped would satisfy both camps.

In the spring of 1975, Ford did little to help either Cambodia or South Vietnam as they faced the final Communist offensives against their regimes. The fall of Saigon, which led in April to the evacuation of the U.S. Embassy there, allowed Ford to announce that "[the] war is finished as far as America is concerned," but it left him open to criticism by conservatives for abandoning an ally. They were more supportive of Ford's actions in the *Mayaguez* crisis that May, when he reacted to the seizure of an American merchant vessel by bombing the Cambodian mainland and launching a successful, though costly, rescue mission by the U.S.

Marines. Nevertheless, conservatives broke with the administration over the *SALT Treaties that they felt favored the Soviet Union, and with Ford's support of the 1975 Helsinki Accord, which acquiesced in Soviet hegemony in Eastern Europe.

While the conservatives, led by Ronald *Reagan, were unable to wrest the Republican nomination from Ford in 1976, Democratic presidential nominee Jimmy *Carter was more successful in painting Ford as showing ambiguity of purpose in the realm of military affairs.

• Gerald R. Ford, *A Time to Heal: The Autobiography of Gerald R. Ford,* 1979. John Robert Greene, *The Presidency of Gerald R. Ford,* 1995. —John Robert Greene

FORD, HENRY (1863–1947), industrialist and isolationist. Born on a Michigan farm, Ford used his skill as a machinist to develop an automobile, founding the Ford Motor Company in Detroit in 1903. Cutting production costs through an assembly line, Ford produced an inexpensive, standardized car, selling over 15 million autos between 1908 and 1928, and becoming a multimillionaire.

In 1914–15, Ford spoke out against World War I and arms races, blaming them on financiers and the military men. He personally financed an effort by pacifists to end the war through mediation by neutral nations. The "Ford Peace Ship" took a contingent of American pacifists to neutral Sweden in December 1915, and the dramatic gesture broke the previous suppression of peace news in the warring nations. Nevertheless, many newspapers derided the effort as naive, especially when Ford proclaimed that he hoped to end the war by Christmas. The Ford Neutral Conference, composed of unofficial delegations of men and women from six neutral nations, met in Stockholm in February 1916. Although Sweden and Denmark were interested in calling a conference of neutral governments, they were blocked by the belligerents.

When the United States entered World War I in 1917, Ford became a leading producer for the military, supplying airplane engines, ambulances, munitions, tanks, trucks, and submarine chasers. In the 1930s, he was a staunch supporter of *isolationism, but Ford again converted his factories to production of war material after 1941. He retired in 1945.

• Allan Nevins and Frank E. Hill, *Ford,* 3 vols., 1954–62. Barbara S. Kraft, *The Peace Ship: Henry Ford's Pacifist Adventure in the First World War,* 1978 —John Whiteclay Chambers II

FOREIGN POLICY. In the context of U.S. military history, foreign policy can be defined as "the goals the nation's officials seek to attain abroad, the values that give rise to those objectives, and the means or instruments used to pursue them." This definition has three essential elements with linkages among them. Moreover, it draws attention to the facts that U.S. foreign policy has historically exhibited change over time in each of these elements, and that their relationships with one another have also varied across different periods.

If diplomatic and military historians could reach agreement on the nature of changes in U.S. foreign policy so defined, the task of tracing this history would be relatively simple. But the challenge is difficult, because controversies over U.S. foreign policy goals, values, and instruments abound. Rather than attempting to resolve these controversies, it is more useful to clarify the three major categories within which debate has been conducted.

Goals. In the first instance, in modifying the goals of foreign policy, the major issue confronting U.S. leaders has been reconciling the advantages and disadvantages of *isolationism and *internationalism. At certain times, American leaders and public opinion have sought U.S. withdrawal from international affairs, practicing disengagement and nonentanglement in order to isolate the country from the perils of international dependence and foreign wars. At other times, American foreign policy has swung in the opposite direction, toward active engagement with other nations on the issues at the moment. In fact, U.S. foreign policy exhibits over time an ambivalent "approach-avoidance" syndrome. What is more, a cycle in these periodic oscillations between isolationism and internationalism is observable, alternating rather rhythmically every twenty to twenty-five years. As Frank Klingberg documents, an "introvert" foreign policy (isolationism) has been pronounced in the periods 1776–98, 1824–44, 1871–91, 1919–40, and 1967–86, and an "extrovert" foreign policy (internationalism) in the periods 1798–1824, 1844–71, 1891–1919, and 1940–66 (with a resurgent globalist phase underway, predictably, once again since 1986).

At its core, internationalism expresses a desire for American leadership in world affairs. It springs from the motivation for the United States to head the world, to set America apart from others, and to forge a "new world order" compatible with U.S. ideals and interests. "Unilateralism"—a self-assertive effort to be self-reliant—represents one approach to internationalism, and speaks to the quest popular at times for the United States not to act in concert with others and to avoid dependence upon them. "Globalism"—the preference to become a hegemonic world leader—is another.

At the extreme, internationalism reflects the desire for the United States to act as an agent of international reform to bring justice and order to world affairs, perhaps through imperialism and interventionism abroad, and at others more passively by serving as a model for countries to emulate. This penchant has not been without its critics. For example, John Quincy Adams counseled (4 July 1821) that a crusading, excessive U.S. involvement in world affairs dedicated to reforming the world in America's image could lead to the prostitution of the very ideals Americans hold most dear—liberty abroad and at home. Unrestrained U.S. international leadership also has been pursued as a goal, however, as seen, for example, in John F. *Kennedy's 1961 pledge that the United States would "pay any price, bear any burden, meet any hardship, support any friend, oppose any foe to assure the survival and success of liberty." This goal is sometimes termed *liberal internationalism* because it refers to what political scientist Richard Gardner calls "the intellectual and political tradition that believes in the necessity of leadership by liberal democracies in the construction of a peaceful world order."

In contrast, isolationist goals speak to the U.S. foreign policy preference to sever the country from the corrupting influences of international engagement and despotic foreign governments. George *Washington enshrined the reasoning rationalizing withdrawal when he warned the nation in his farewell address to "steer clear of entangling alliances with any portion of the foreign world." The *Monroe Doctrine (1823) stemmed from the same logic and preference, as later did the *Neutrality Acts in the 1930s. *Detachment* and *withdrawal* are also deeply instilled goals in the American diplomatic tradition, and they have periodically resurfaced as the defining characteristic of U.S. foreign policy.

Values. The push for two seemingly incompatible foreign policy goals springs from the political beliefs in which U.S. foreign policy is rooted. The values that give rise to fluctuations and alternating cycles in defining U.S. goals and postures include two quite different world views—*idealism* and *realism*—both of which at various times have dominated the thinking of U.S. leaders and shaped their foreign policies. The two value systems stem from very divergent beliefs about the ways to best reconcile the tension between ideals and interests, between principle and power, and between moral purpose and military primacy.

At the core of idealism is the belief that American foreign policy should be guided by its fundamental liberal values—what may be called the "ideology" of American foreign policy. But throughout U.S. history, Americans have often differed about the relative importance of particular liberal ideals. Still, underlying idealism has been the fundamental belief that the United States has a special mission to use power for moral purposes. Adlai Stevenson stated this "exceptionalist" version of America's international purpose, for example, when he argued that "America is much more than a geographical fact. It is a political and moral fact." Similarly, Woodrow *Wilson proclaimed that "America was established not to create wealth but to realize a vision, to realize an ideal—to discover and maintain liberty among men."

At the risk of sounding simplistic and selective, the idealist-liberal tradition may be said to stress the Enlightenment's faith in reason, progress, the essential goodness of human nature, popular sovereignty, and the benefits of equal access to opportunity. Idealism counsels the search for international cooperation through U.S. support for international law, international institutions and organizations (such as the *League of Nations and the *United Nations), a liberal trade regime, *arms control and disarmament, and the promotion of democratic governance, collective security, and multilateral approaches to international peace.

This liberal-idealist conception of a transcendent national purpose differs from the *realist* conception with which it is often juxtaposed. To this alternate frame of mind—whose roots are equally deep—*raison d'état* and national interest are, necessarily, primary goals, and in a contest between principle and power, power must be paramount. To the realist tradition, it is prudent for the United States to acquire military capabilities and use them not only for defense but also to exercise influence abroad and to compete with other states in the international struggle for power. To advocates of realpolitik, the U.S. goal should be to put the military means to American prosperity, privilege, power, and position ahead of a drive to exalt liberty or any other grand ideal.

Like internationalism and isolationism, the history of American diplomacy also can be largely written in terms of cyclical swings between idealism and realism. In general, idealist moods have been particularly dominant in the immediate aftermath of America's major war experiences and in times of optimism and prosperity, when hopes for successful American reform of international practices have

risen—for example, during and after World War I when Woodrow Wilson championed an idealist American foreign policy dedicated to building "a world safe for democracy" under a rule of law, managed by an international organization (the League of Nations). But, instructively, the idealist program was promptly repudiated, and values based on realist assumptions again prevailed in the thinking of U.S. policymakers. This reversal illustrates the general tendency for a realist mood to capture the thinking of policymakers prudently concerned more with core national interests such as defense than with ideals when war scares have been perceived to threaten U.S. security (as, for example, during the *Cold War).

Instruments. Identifying the most effective means to the ends of foreign policy (consistent with the values that inspire choices about goals) has always been a challenge. The most difficult decisions facing leaders are often not about definitions of national interests and foreign policy priorities, but about the instruments to serve them.

Whereas there are observable patterns and periodicities in the goals and values underlying U.S. foreign policy, the record with respect to choices about instruments is more erratic and episodic, depending on different leaders' perceived needs and their estimates about the probable efficacy of different tactical tools.

Salient in the U.S. experience are *military* instruments. Here a basic choice involves the desired level of military preparedness to deter an attack on the United States or to project power abroad and, potentially, to deploy U.S. military might overseas. Both military expenditures (as a percentage of the national budget) and force levels have exhibited short-term perturbations and long-term trends, as seen in the framers' rejection of a large standing army and in just that kind of massive military commitment after World War II to enforce America's contest with the Soviet Union during the Cold War. The actual U.S. use of armed force abroad has displayed more repetition and regularity. Military engagement has ranged from large-scale protracted involvements like those in World Wars I and II to frequent practice low-scale *intervention* overseas. Nearly every U.S. administration has used coercive diplomacy on numerous occasions, but especially when internationalist goals shaped by *realpolitik* have been pursued.

The "strategies" guiding military methods of foreign policy, for both deterrence and compellence, comprise a related dimension. These have been defined by the various doctrines specifying the purposes for which military might should be put. Also related to overt military instruments of foreign policy are a cluster of other, less blatant tools such as *covert operations, clandestine intelligence activities, so-called public diplomacy designed to disseminate information abroad to bolster the United States and influence public opinion, and so-called gunboat diplomacy relying on shows of force abroad to signal U.S. resolve and commitments.

A second subcategory of instruments may loosely be defined as political, inasmuch as they refer to tools on which U.S. decision makers sometimes rely to exercise influence over other nations to get them to do things they might not otherwise do. Alliances are key here, as the recruitment of allies (and prevention of states' alignment with adversaries) comprises the primary method by which leaders seek to maintain a favorable international balance of power. Foreign assistance and foreign military sales add to the arsenal of policy tools by which political influence can be exercised; for the United States, these were particularly popular during the Cold War. So, too, was the creation of international organizations, such as the *United Nations, constructed less for idealistic reasons than as mechanisms through which the United States could shape international events in directions compatible with its national interests.

A third basic subcategory of foreign policy instruments is *economic*. To serve the goal of increasing U.S. prosperity, leaders have depended on a range of divergent strategies. At one end of the philosophical spectrum are mercantilist approaches, which seek American power through trade protectionism, tariff walls, export and import controls, and, at the extreme, colonialism and imperialist *expansionism. Alexander *Hamilton's national industrialization policies to develop "infant industries" and the "open door" policies with respect to China in the 1890s reflected this approach, which sought to expand American power and territory at the expense of others; this drive is colored in realpolitik. At the other extreme, shaped heavily by liberal-idealism, are policies designed to lower barriers to free trade of the sort advocated in Woodrow Wilson's *Fourteen Points address. This approach was successfully pursued by the United States after World War II, when the United States led in the promulgation of the liberal international economic order that, through the General Agreement on Tariffs and Trade (GATT) culminated in creation of the World Trade Organization. Between these positions lie a variety of less controversial economic practices, such as embargoes and sanctions, that have been used as policy instruments to influence relations with foreign targets.

Rethinking the Concept of Foreign Policy. Scholars have disagreed about the emphasis that should be placed on pronouncement and doctrine (words) and observable behavior (deeds) as indicators of foreign policy by which changes might be measured. Beyond conceptualization, substantial disagreements exist about the best ways to characterize the goals, values, and instruments of American foreign policy. It is unlikely that consensus will crystallize, because the subject is complex and amenable to differing but equally plausible interpretations. The term *foreign policy* is elastic. Goals, values, and instruments have habitually taken new directions as global circumstances changed and American leaders sought to cope with them.

It is worth speculating that global conditions have changed so rapidly recently that traditional conceptions of foreign policy may be becoming anachronistic. With the radical expansion of international trade, travel, and communications, the international system has become perhaps unprecedentedly interdependent, and there is little prospect that this "globalization" trend will reverse direction. Borders that traditionally have divided sovereign territorial states no longer separate and buffer them from external influences as in the past. As a result, the classic distinction between "domestic" and "foreign" policy is collapsing. If this trend continues, if "domestic" policy truly becomes "foreign" policy, and vice versa, then the very meaning of foreign policy—its goals and implementations—will require reconceptualization.

[*See also* Commander in Chief, President as; Nationalism; National Security in the Nuclear Age; Peace; Peacekeeping; Strategy.]

• Lloyd C. Gardner, *Architects of Illusion: Men and Ideas in American Foreign Policy*, 1970. Edward Weisband, *The Ideology of American Foreign Policy: A Paradigm of Lockean Liberalism*, 1973. James N. Rosenau, *The Scientific Study of Foreign Policy*, 1980. Frank L. Klingberg, *Cyclical Trends in American Foreign Policy Moods: The Unfolding of Americas World Role*, 1983. Richard N. Gardner, "The Comeback of Liberal Internationalism," *Washington Quarterly*, 13 (Summer 1990), pp. 23–39. Charles W. Kegley, Jr., ed., *Controversies in International Relations Theory: Realism and the Neoliberal Challenge*, 1995. Charles W. Kegley, Jr., and Eugene R. Wittkopf, *American Foreign Policy: Pattern and Process*, 5th ed. 1996.
—Charles W. Kegley, Jr.

FORREST, NATHAN BEDFORD (1821–1877), Civil War general, slave trader, planter. Born in Bedford Country, Tennessee, Forrest received little formal education but learned to hold his own—and then some—in a violent frontier society. By ruthless drive and intelligence he made himself a planter and slave trader.

At the outset of the Civil War, Forrest raised a cavalry battalion in the Confederate army. He led his men out of Fort Donelson just before its 16 February 1862 surrender, and at the 6–7 April Battle of *Shiloh was conspicuously aggressive, being severely wounded covering the Confederate retreat. That summer he led a cavalry brigade in a spectacular raid through middle Tennessee. Promoted to brigadier general 21 July, he again raided behind Federal lines in December, helping to defeat Ulysses S. *Grant's first drive on Vicksburg.

In Alabama, in April 1863, he captured Col. Abel D. Streight's superior Union raiding force by bluff. At the Battle of *Chickamauga, 19–20 September, Forrest's troops opened the fighting. Afterward, he fell out with his army commander, Braxton *Bragg, was transferred to Mississippi, and promoted to major general on 4 December 1863.

In April 1864 his troops at the Battle of *Fort Pillow, Tennessee, stormed the fort, killing black Union soldiers as they attempted to surrender. In June, he routed a superior force under Samuel D. Sturgis at Brice's Cross Roads, Mississippi, but suffered defeat at Tupelo the following month. In November and December, Forrest commanded all the cavalry accompanying Gen. John Bell *Hood's ill-fated offensive into Tennessee, and skillfully covered the Confederate retreat.

On 28 February 1865, Forrest was promoted to lieutenant general, but he and his command were worn out, and they faced a powerful Federal mounted force under James H. Wilson driving into Alabama. Wilson defeated Forrest at Selma in April. After the war, Forrest returned to planting and served as the first grand wizard of the Ku Klux Klan.

His military usefulness in the Civil War was marred by his hot temper; he virtually required autonomy. Nevertheless, as the leader of a semi-independent mobile striking force, he has had few equals. He is also remembered for his alleged advice to commanders to "get there 'firstest' with the 'mostest.'"

[*See also* Civil War: Military and Diplomatic Course; Confederate Army.]

• Brian Steel Wills, *A Battle from the Start: The Life of Nathan Bedford Forrest*, 1992.
—Steven E. Woodworth

FORRESTAL, JAMES V. (1892–1949), investment banker, undersecretary of the navy (1940–44), secretary of the navy (1944–47), and the nation's first secretary of defense (1947–49). Forrestal was the youngest of three sons born to Irish immigrant parents in Beacon, New York. He attended Princeton University in the class of 1915, served as editor of the *Daily Princetonian*, and was voted "Most Likely to Succeed" and "The Man Nobody Knows."

After a short stint as a naval aviator in World War I, he joined the Wall Street firm of William Read & Co. (later Dillon, Read) as a bond salesman. He was elected to the partnership in 1923, became one of the "golden boys" of investment banking during the Roaring Twenties, and was made president of the firm in 1940. He married Josephine Ogden, an editor of *Vogue* magazine, in 1926.

Called to Washington by President Franklin *Roosevelt to help convert the U.S. economy to war production, Forrestal was named undersecretary of the navy (August 1940) with full authority in the area of procurement—for the design, construction, and delivery of ships to the fighting forces. Over the next three years he was the principal architect of the navy's vast World War II expansion from 1,099 to 50,759 vessels, and from 160,997 to 3,383,196 officers and men. The creation of that largest, most powerful fleet in the world was a precondition of victory.

Forrestal became secretary of the navy (in April 1944). He organized a comprehensive information effort to make the magnitude and complexity of the Pacific War—including the significance of particular naval battles and acts of heroism—more understandable to the American people. He toured the battlefronts in both the European and Pacific theaters, and went ashore at Iwo Jima on D-Day+2, "exposing himself to the dangers of warfare as no other United States official of his rank did in World War II." In August 1945, when the Japanese government expressed a readiness to surrender provided it did not "prejudice the prerogatives" of the emperor *Hirohito, President Harry S. *Truman's advisers were divided on the question whether this met the U.S. requirement for "unconditional surrender." Forrestal convinced Truman to accept the Japanese condition, but to call it "unconditional surrender" and arrange to subordinate the emperor to the U.S. Supreme Allied Commander.

Forrestal was one of the first high officials to see in the Soviet Union an ideological, political, and military threat to U.S. security and to democratic societies everywhere. He played a large, influential role in government efforts to restore a shattered postwar world, confront the new Soviet challenge, and create or restructure those agencies (*National Security Council, *Central Intelligence Agency, Department of *Defense, *Joint Chiefs of Staff, cabinet secretariat) required to handle the new, unprecedented responsibilities of the *Cold War in Europe, Asia, and the Middle East. He commissioned a Soviet expert, George F. *Kennan, to write the paper that became the famous "Mr. X" article, setting forth the "containment" doctrine that formed the definitive guideline for U.S. foreign policy throughout the Cold War.

As navy secretary, Forrestal strongly resisted President Truman's postwar plan to integrate the army, navy, and air force under a single secretary of defense. Truman's plan became law, but Forrestal succeeded in obtaining amendments that severely limited the power and authority of the new secretary: he would be essentially a presiding chairman of the board, with only "general authority" to as-

sign military roles and missions and develop a single budget for the armed forces. The secretaries of army, navy, and air force would continue to administer their own separate departments.

When Truman's first choice for the new post declined it (Robert Patterson, the outgoing Secretary of War), the president turned to Forrestal, who fatefully accepted. Almost immediately he found that the secretary of defense lacked adequate authority and staff to control an organization riven by bitter rivalries that were aggravated by a combination of expanding military technologies and sharply limited postwar military budgets. At the same time, the armed forces were charged with protecting the nation in a disordered postwar world, marked by widespread physical destruction and a dangerous new challenge from Stalinist Russia. Belatedly aware that his earlier concept had been deeply flawed, Forrestal nevertheless struggled to manage an almost unworkable organization. In the process he drove himself to exhaustion, and began a tragic descent into paranoia and self-destruction. Truman asked for his resignation in March 1949. Forrestal was hospitalized for "reactive depression"—essentially the condition of combat fatigue seen frequently during World War II. On 22 May, he committed suicide by jumping from a sixteenth-floor window of the Bethesda Naval Hospital.

• Arnold A. Rogow, *James Forrestal: A Study of Personality, Politics, and Polity*, 1963. Townsend Hoopes and Douglas Brinkley, *Driven Patriot: The Life and Times of James Forrestal*, 1992.

—Townsend Hoopes

FORTIFICATIONS, both permanent and temporary, formed an important element of American military activity as early as the colonial period and remained a highly visible aspect of national defense well into the twentieth century.

A major threat facing isolated coastal communities in colonial times was seaborne attack by European forces. The defensive works built by the colonists were mainly small, primitive attempts to replicate the European bastion-trace fortification with its prominent corner gun platforms. Most were constructed at the water's edge of port cities, using whatever local materials were available. The American Revolution triggered a revival of local construction, but with little change in either materials or design. Most fortifications built during the *Revolutionary War itself were field fortifications rather than permanent works. Classed as either *complex entrenchments* (with small, reinforced earthen and timber works often connected by ditches to serve as trenches) or *hasty entrenchments* (the normal ground configuration supplemented by minimal construction), fieldworks also followed European models. Having no indigenous military engineers, the Continental army relied mainly on French-trained officers, such as Louis La Bèque Duportail and Thaddeus *Kosciuszko, for the expertise needed to construct larger works in the field—a tradition that would continue into the nineteenth century.

The emergence of a plausible threat in the 1790s during the French Revolution led to the first of two "systems" of coastal fortifications prior to the *War of 1812. The "First System" of 1794 was the initial effort undertaken by the federal government, and it represented a continuation of past practices both in terms of design and materials and in reliance on European engineers (one of whom was Pierre

L'Enfant, the future designer of Washington, D.C.). The "Second System" emerged in 1807, also in response to a foreign threat, this time from Britain in the Napoleonic Wars. This system included works built to a novel design advocated by Jonathan Williams, first U.S.-born chief of the U.S. *Army Corps of Engineers. He endorsed the construction of works with high stone or brick walls, the guns arranged in multilevel tiers of internal chambers called *casemates*, and firing done through iron-shuttered embrasures piercing the facade. This theory, based on the ideas of a French engineer, the marquis de Montalembert, meant two or three tiers, and thus more guns and greater defensive firepower within the same ground occupied by an older-style, single-level fortification.

A handful of American fortifications designed to Williams's ideas, including Castle Williams in New York Harbor, arose before 1812; but the impact of these ideas was far greater in following decades. During the War of 1812, British coastal raids—and the burning of the national capital—persuaded national leaders to establish a board of engineers in 1816 to examine the entire coast and recommend defenses. The Bernard Board Report of 1821, named after French engineer Simon Bernard, was the first comprehensive plan for American coastal defense. It led to construction of the "Third System" of some fifty American coastal forts, almost all of them casemated works built to designs of increasing sophistication.

The leading figure of this program was Joseph G. Totten, an 1805 graduate of West Point and later chief engineer of the U.S. Army 1838–64, the longest tenure of any chief engineer. As important was Dennis Hart Mahan, a professor of engineering at West Point in 1832–71. Basing his ideas on French models, Mahan taught two generations of soldiers Americanized theories of fortification and emphasized the role of field fortifications in actual operations to steady America's partially trained troops and militia. Totten's 1851 report recommended increasing the number of projected coastal fortifications from 50 (in 1821) to 186 (with 28 for the Texas Gulf Coast and the Pacific states). Estimated cost of this increased program was $25 million, with over $20 million already expended.

Coastal fortification planning inevitably touched on naval operations, and in every report the engineers remarked, usually in passing, that the navy was the first line of defense. Since actual invasion was unlikely, the engineers stressed that the proposed fortifications were to protect cities, potential anchorages, and intracoastal navigation routes, as well as to keep blockading vessels at a distance. Confronted by choice of attacking powerful defenses head-on or landing far from their target, enemy forces might be discouraged from attacking at all. Many critics countered by asserting that fortifications alone were insufficient to protect coastal areas, suggesting various additional floating defenses or technological innovations, such as electrically detonated underwater mines demonstrated by Samuel *Colt in the 1840s.

Totten's arguments for the Third System fortifications, though, overlooked the ways the Industrial Revolution was already spawning dramatic changes in artillery and ship design. Fortifications themselves were an evolved technology. In the years shortly before the *Civil War, developments in metallurgy and ordnance design led to the production of heavy rifled and shell-firing guns of enormous power. Previous heavy naval and siege guns fired shot weighing 32 to 48 pounds, the larger guns now possible fired shot weighing up to 100 pounds, with rifled *artillery capable of accuracy at three or four times the previous ranges. During the Civil War, such guns, sited by engineer officers like Quincy Gillmore, smashed the thick brick and stone walls of Confederate-occupied forts like Sumter and Pickens into rubble in hours or days. These developments were paralleled overseas, as was the development of the armored, steam-powered, oceangoing warship.

By the end of the Civil War, it was clear that the Third System of coastal defenses was obsolete. At the same time, the rival armies learned to construct field fortifications at every opportunity. In some cases—notably the defensive works arrayed around Washington, D.C., ordered by George B. *McClellan, or the trench systems created by both sides during the Siege of *Petersburg, Virginia—these fieldworks become enormously complex. Built of earth reinforced by heavy timbers, they proved less susceptible to artillery damage than the seacoast fortifications. For more permanent defensive works, however, there was no consensus on a proper design other than returning to lower structures protected by earth. The Indian wars of the late nineteenth century did not provide an answer. The few western forts with walls of any kind generally had palisades of wood that could not resist artillery.

Toward the end of the nineteenth century, gun manufacturers, following William Armstrong in Great Britain, had successfully developed methods of compound manufacture to create increasingly powerful, long-range cannon. Steel became the predominant material, and most of these new guns were breech-loading instead of muzzle-loading, giving them higher rates of fire. Studies suggested new, slower-burning and more powerful propellants instead of traditional gunpowder. Warships increased in size, armor, and speed. Consequently, many army and navy officers urged improvements in U.S. armaments and urged a program of new coastal fortification. A persistent argument was that coastal defenses were a form of insurance against the destruction resulting from raids to major coastal cities.

In 1885, President Grover Cleveland appointed a board headed by Secretary of War William Endicott to study the issue. The report of January 1886 endorsed much the same kind of system demanded by the engineers, dismissed the idea of a full-scale invasion, and linked coastal defense to the protection of the commercial metropolises of the seacoasts. It stressed in particular the use of relatively new, and still unproved, technologies such as searchlights, steel breech-loading cannon on disappearing gun carriages, armor plate, underwater naval *mines, and auxiliary vessels, many of which did not yet exist in usable form. At the time, engineers estimated the total cost of the system at around $126 million.

The enormous cost of this effort meant that it was never entirely completed. Moreover, the original proposal underestimated the increasing power and range of artillery, and thus overestimated the number of guns needed. Eventually, some 700 heavy artillery pieces, mostly 8-, 10-, and 12-inch long-range guns, were emplaced, among them several hundred 12-inch arching-fire mortars, along with other hundreds of smaller-caliber, rapid-firing guns. The largest guns were capable of firing a 1,000-pound shell to a range of 7 or 8 miles. These were installed in fortifications that encompassed a series of connected strongpoints and batteries rather than a single, massive structure, dispersed to lessen their vulnerability to naval guns. They were low-lying, protected by thick berms of earth to absorb heavy, high-explosive shells, and built to take advantage of ground contours to make them less visible from the ocean. In some cases, older fortifications were rebuilt to accommodate the newer guns; elsewhere the newer works went up in the same general vicinity.

During the *Spanish-American War, despite unfounded fears of coastal raids by Spanish warships that triggered the emplacement of several hundred artillery pieces, no raiders attacked any U.S. cities or harbors. Still, the acquisition of overseas territories during the war, along with the realization of advancing military technology, persuaded President Theodore *Roosevelt to create another board, this one headed by Secretary of War William H. Taft, to review the coastal fortification program. Aside from suggesting the need for defenses to guard newly acquired overseas locations such as the Panama Canal, Hawaii, and Manila Bay in the Philippines, the Taft Board limited itself to modifying minor details, reestimating costs, and changing priorities slightly. It concurred with Adm. Alfred T. *Mahan (son of Dennis Mahan) that the role of a navy was offensively to seek for command of the sea, not restrict itself to direct coastal defense.

By the outbreak of World War I, moreover, battleship ordnance could once more outrange most of the guns of the shore defenses, with the plunging trajectory of naval shells making open-topped defensive works untenable. Engineers began siting defenses farther out toward the sea from the locales they defended and pushing development of more powerful 14- and 16-inch guns. Fortifications became ever simpler in design and dispersed over wider areas; 1,000 feet might separate the guns of a single battery. During the 1920s and 1930s, engineers experimented with mobile railroad- and tractor-drawn guns, utilizing wartime stocks of 8- and 14-inch guns. Employed as armament in two dozen permanent sites were newly developed 16-inch guns, which fired a 2,000-pound shell to a range of 30 miles. The new threat posed by aircraft forced planners to include antiaircraft guns, and led to a design that placed the entire battery structure under up to 30 feet of concrete and earth. The first such structure was erected outside San Francisco between 1937 and 1940, and it became the prototype for the defensive works constructed during World War II. The urgent demand for defenses early in that war could only be met by almost complete standardization into two-gun batteries, emplaced within concrete bunkers and protected by steel shields. By 1944, however, with no direct threat to American shores, construction ceased.

Field fortifications also changed during World War II, with the complex, continuous trench lines of World War I giving way to small "foxhole" emplacements for individual soldiers and weapons crews, providing greater dispersal and thus survivability from modern ordnance. In both the *Korean War and the *Vietnam War, in the absence of aerial and armor threat, fixed defenses in the field (around bases and other strongpoints) reappeared to some degree, with works protected by earth or sandbags. Structurally, these were similar to the semipermanent, complex entrenchments of the nineteenth century, albeit with electronic listening devices and mines taking the place of cruder systems of detection and forward protection.

During the *Cold War, the greater threat to American cities came from the sky, not the sea. Reliance on coastal fortifications gave way to dependence on antiaircraft guns and *missiles and early warning *radar networks against bombers and then missiles. The Reagan administration accelerated research on a satellite-based laser defense system in an attempt to protect the United States against missile attack (the *Strategic Defense Initiative). Between 1948 and 1949, nearly all the larger guns of the fortifications were scrapped, marking the end of relying on such fixed defenses for the protection of the American seaboard. In the 1960s, many of the old coastal forts were turned over to the National Park Service.

[See also Battlefields, Encampments, and Forts as Public Sites; Engineering, Military.]

• Alex Roland, Underwater Warfare in the Age of Sail, 1978. Emanuel R. Lewis, Seacoast Fortifications of the United States: An Introductory History, 1970. Robert S. Browning III, Two If by Sea: The Development of American Coastal Defense Policy, 1983. Marguerita Z. Herman, Ramparts: Fortifications from the Renaissance to West Point, 1992.
—Robert S. Browning III

FORT PILLOW, BATTLE OF (1864). By 1864, the captured Confederate earthwork Fort Pillow, located 40 miles above Memphis, Tennessee, on the Mississippi River, was garrisoned by 557 Union soldiers under Maj. Lionel F. Booth. Of these men, 262 belonged to the 11th U.S. *Colored Troops and Battery F, 4th U.S. Colored Light Artillery. On 12 April, Confederate Maj. Gen. Nathan Bedford *Forrest ordered Brig. Gen. James R. Chalmers's 1,500 men to attack the fort.

Beginning at 5:30 A.M., Confederate sharpshooters located on hills above the fort opened a devastating fire, killing many soldiers, including Booth. Forrest arrived on the field at midmorning and directed the assault that gained part of the fort for the Confederates. By 3:30 P.M., Forrest sent a surrender demand to Maj. William F. Bradford, now in command of the Union force. When Bradford delayed, Forrest attacked, quickly driving the defenders out of the fort and down the bank into a crossfire.

What happened next has served to place Fort Pillow second only in infamy in *atrocities of that war to Andersonville, the most notorious of the *Civil War *prisoner-of-war camps. At Fort Pillow, many Union soldiers tried to surrender while others continued fighting or tried to run. Forrest either ordered his men to accept no surrender or his Confederates lost control but in either case, they began to slaughter black soldiers. The casualty list confirms a massacre. Confederates suffered 14 killed and 86 wounded, while the Union force lost 231 killed and 100 wounded; only 58 of the 226 surviving Union prisoners were black soldiers.

The U.S. Congress's Committee on the Conduct of the War investigated, and after much testimony from survivors—including horrifying accounts of black soldiers being buried alive—it denounced the Confederate actions as murder and atrocity. Forrest objected, and many historians have sided with his account but Forrest's best biographer, Brian Steel Wills, concluded that the committee's findings were valid and that Forrest was responsible for the slaughter.

• Albert Castel, "The Fort Pillow Massacre: A Fresh Examination of the Evidence," Civil War History, 1958. Brian Steel Wills, A Battle from the Start: The Life of Nathan Bedford Forrest, 1992.
—Russell Duncan

FORT SUMTER, CAPTURE OF (1861). After the Republican Abraham *Lincoln won the election of 1860, seven states seceded from the Union and formed the Confederate States of America. The new president vowed in his inaugural address to "hold, occupy, and possess" federal property in the South, but by then the United States controlled only two major posts within the Confederacy: Fort Pickens, on Pensacola Bay, Florida; and Fort Sumter, in the harbor of Charleston, South Carolina. Brig. Gen. Braxton *Bragg appeared unenthusiastic about his chances of capturing Fort Pickens, and so attention centered on Fort Sumter.

On 10 April 1861, Confederate secretary of war Leroy Pope Walker ordered Gen. P. G. T. *Beauregard to demand the evacuation of the Charleston post and, if refused, to reduce it. Maj. Robert Anderson held Fort Sumter with a modest garrison and forty-eight guns, few of which could be manned. The Confederates encircled the harbor installation with thirty heavy pieces and eighteen mortars, and bombarded it from 4:30 A.M. on 12 April until early the next afternoon. Raging fires threatened the defenders and Major Anderson surrendered Fort Sumter with the honors of war. He began evacuating the post on the 14th.

[*See also* Civil War.]

• William A. Swanberg, *First Blood: The Story of Fort Sumter*, 1957. Richard N. Current, *Lincoln and the First Shot*, 1963.

—Perry D. Jamieson

FORT WAGNER, SIEGE OF (1963). Constructed on the northern end but extending completely across Morris Island, Fort (or Battery) Wagner was integral to the Confederate defensive system protecting Charleston Harbor. Along with the batteries directly across the channel at Fort Moultrie, and with Fort Sumter only a mile and a half away, Fort Wagner had to be taken before Union forces could capture Charleston. Wagner was literally built of sand, with thick sloping walls 20 feet tall lined in front with abatis (sharpened tree branches) and benefitting from high tides, when seawater narrowed the approach to the fort and filled the ditch Confederates dug just behind the abatis.

On 10 July 1863, the Federal army took control of the southern end of Morris Island. The next day Maj. Gen. Quincy A. Gillmore ordered a dawn attack against Wagner. Brig. Gen. George C. Strong with two and a half brigades dashed against the fort's 1,200 defenders under the command of William Taliaferro. Strong's force was repulsed with a loss of 339 men against 12 Confederate casualties. From Charleston, Gen. P. G. T. *Beauregard sent another 600 men to reinforce the fort.

Gillmore, who had become the Union's most renowned artillerist after he had forced the capitulation of Fort Pulaski at Savannah in April 1862, brought in heavy weaponry. On 18 July, he began a daylong bombardment with twenty six rifled guns, ten heavy mortars, and the additional firepower provided by Adm. John *Dahlgren's naval force of monitors and warships. Meanwhile, Gillmore's infantry organized for the rush everyone knew would follow.

The 54th Massachusetts Infantry Regiment of the U.S. *Colored Troops commanded by Col. Robert Gould Shaw, spearheaded General Strong's infantry assault of 5,624 men. It became quickly apparent that Gillmore's fierce bombardment had done no damage to Wagner's 1,785-man garrison. The attackers made it up past the obstacles and temporarily held a position on the fort's parapet before being repulsed. The Union suffered 246 dead, 880 wounded, and 389 missing for 1,515 total *casualties. Of these, the losses of Shaw and 272 of his 650 men were the most conspicuous. Confederates lost 36 killed, 133 wounded, and 5 missing.

With two failed infantry assaults, Gillmore began formal siege operations. He continued to hammer away with artillery; an estimated 10,000 shells struck at Wagner. On 6 September, the fifty-seventh day of the siege, Union soldiers had completed digging a series of ditches that zigzagged forward and had reached the abatis. Gillmore ordered an infantry assault for the next day, but the Confederates had slipped away during the night after Beauregard recognized the impossibility of a further defense of Wagner.

For months afterward, when reports of this encounter could get past the news about the Battle of *Gettysburg and the siege of *Vicksburg, the Northern press praised the heroic conduct of the black soldiers as proof that black men would fight and die for the Union. Confederates inadvertently contributed to the praise when in the aftermath of the 18 July battle, they threw Shaw's body into a common grave with twenty of his men. With news reported by the South that the young hero had been "buried ... with his niggers," the North had its most important martyr to the brotherhood of man since abolitionist John Brown was hanged in 1859.

The 1989 film *Glory* graphically depicts the battle at Fort Wagner.

• Luis F. Emilio, *A Brave Black Regiment: History of the Fifty-Fourth Regiment of Massachusetts Volunteer Infantry, 1863–1865*, 1894. Joseph T. Glatthaar; *Forged in Battle: The Civil War Alliance of Black Soldiers and Their White Officers*, 1990. Russell Duncan. *Blue-Eyed Child of Fortune: The Civil War Letters of Colonel Robert Gould Shaw*, 1994.

—Russell Duncan

FOURTEEN POINTS (1918). President Woodrow *Wilson's statement of January 1918 was the most important on war aims advanced during World War I. Based on his anti-imperialist "Peace without Victory" formula of the previous year, Wilson made his address owing primarily to the revolutionary upheaval that had seized Russia. By the end of 1917, Lenin and Trotsky had pulled their ravaged homeland out of the war, thus permitting Germany to transfer huge numbers of troops to the western front. They also published the Allies' secret treaties (signed by the czarist regime) for parceling out territory after victory. The Bolsheviks then summoned the soldiers of both the Allied and Central Powers to lay down their arms and repudiate plans for conquest. Because many liberal and socialist groups among the Allies had already begun to question the continuation of the carnage, it fell to Wilson to remove the suspicions hanging over their cause and explain why the conflict was any longer worth fighting.

The president argued that German militarism must be crushed, first, in order to create a new and better world. He then outlined the American peace program. Seven of the points dealt with territorial readjustments, including the "unembarrassed opportunity" for Russia to shape its own destiny. The others were characteristically Wilsonian—open covenants openly arrived at; free trade; self-determination; disarmament; impartial adjustment of colonial claims; freedom of the seas; and a league of nations.

Wilson's progressive response to the Bolshevik challenge provided the ideological cement that held the Allied coalition together for the remainder of the war. The Fourteen Points also set the public agenda for the Paris Peace Conference, but became a source of controversy when they were only partially fulfilled in the Treaty of *Versailles.

[See also League of Nations; World War I: Postwar Impact.]

• Arno J. Mayer, Political Origins of the New Diplomacy, 1959. Thomas J. Knock, To End All Wars: Woodrow Wilson and the Quest for a New World Order, 1992.   —Thomas J. Knock

FRAGGING is a term first encountered during the latter years of the *Vietnam War. It refers to the killing of officers and noncommissioned officers using fragmentation hand grenades, often thrown into a sleeping area at night. A broader definition encompasses murder by a variety of other means, including mines, shooting, and hit and run with a vehicle.

Instances of leaders being killed by subordinates have occurred in American forces since the *Revolutionary War. Often the cause appeared to be concern for survival in a combat environment made more hazardous by a leader perceived to be incompetent or unconcerned with soldier welfare. Although records are incomplete, the rate of such incidents was relatively low until the Vietnam War, when fragging increased dramatically. The highest incidence in Vietnam occurred between 1968 and 1972. Most episodes were in the army and Marine Corps, especially among support and rear area units. There were approximately 830 actual and suspected fraggings in Vietnam, with the annual number peaking at 333 in 1971. Fragging declined significantly in 1972 as American troops were withdrawn.

The explanation for the fragging epidemic can be found in the interaction of two broad factors, one societal and the other organizational. Widespread and severe change and conflict emerged in American society during the period. This combined with unfortunate organizational policies and a demoralizing military strategy to produce an unprecedented internal crisis within U.S. forces, characterized by poor leadership and unit performance. An individual replacement system that rotated soldiers back to the U.S. after twelve months along with frequent reassignments within Vietnam had a strongly corrosive effect on unit-leader bonding. In Vietnam, erosion of effective leadership, and the unraveling of unit cohesion exposed the forces in Southeast Asia to the full impact of drug abuse, racial conflict, and antiwar activism then rampant in the United States. Fragging was an unfortunate symptom of the internal crisis experienced by the U.S. military in Vietnam during this period.

[See also Morale, Troop.]

• Eugene Linden, "The Demoralization of an Army; Fragging and Other Withdrawal Symptoms," Saturday Review (January 1972). Guenter Lewy, American in Vietnam, 1978. W. D. Henderson, Cohesion: The Human Element in Combat, 1985.
                    —William Darryl Henderson

FRANCE, LIBERATION OF (1944–45). Following the invasion of *Normandy, the breakout by Omar N. *Bradley's U.S. First Army created conditions for mobile warfare that permitted the World War II Allied armies to liberate France by the late summer of 1944. In the aftermath of the American breakthrough of German lines, George S. *Patton's newly activated U.S. Third Army swept west through the Brittany peninsula. Meanwhile, British and Canadian armies under Bernard Law *Montgomery pushed further into Northern France. On 6 August, the Germans launched a large counterattack at Mortain to defeat the Americans and push them back into the English Channel. But the fighting ability of U.S. ground and air forces, advised of Berlin's plans by *ULTRA intelligence, resulted in the German's defeat after two days of fighting.

On 8 August, in bold disregard of the recent threat at Mortain, Bradley devised a plan to cut off the German Army before it could withdraw to the Seine River. He ordered Patton to swing around the German left and cut off the enemy escape route by capturing Argentan. Meanwhile, the Canadian First Army under Henry Crerar was to close the trap from the north by seizing Falaise. Patton's troops moved aggressively, capturing Argentan on 13 August, while the Canadians pressed toward Falaise against stiff German resistance. However, concerns that an unexpected encounter between U.S. and Canadian troops might result in numerous friendly *casualties caused a halt in Allied operations and left the pincers' jaws open. The Germans now had an escape route through the Falaise-Argentan gap. Allied airpower savaged the German ranks, but a considerable portion of the enemy escaped. Still, German losses in the Falaise-Argentan pocket included 10,000 killed and 50,000 captured. The failure of Allied generals to close the Falaise-Argentan gap remains one of the great controversies of the war in Western Europe.

On 19 August, Supreme Allied Commander Dwight D. *Eisenhower modified his pre-invasion plans. He had originally planned to halt his armies along the Seine River to reorganize and resupply, but the deteriorating enemy situation prompted him to order exploitation to the Seine and beyond. Montgomery now urged the encirclement of the remnants of the German Army. The Allies attempted another large pincer movement south of the Seine, but most of the German infantry escaped and made it over the river. The Allied approach toward Paris caused Free French uprisings on 19 August that soon needed assistance. The U.S. V Corps took Paris on 25 August with the honor of the triumphal entry going to the French 2nd Armored Division. French Gen. Charles de Gaulle entered Paris the same day and installed his government in the French capital.

As the Allies advanced toward the Seine River, a second Allied coalition force landed in southern France. On 15 August, U.S. Gen. Jacob Dever's Sixth Army Group, consisting of the U.S. Seventh and French First Armies, landed in southern France in Operation Dragoon, captured the key port at Marseilles, and began an offensive up the Rhône River valley. The Germans successfully withdrew more than half of their forces from southern France before the Allied armies effected a juncture on 11 September. Dever's army group was then ordered to protect the Allied southern flank during the drive into Germany. Meanwhile, U.S. efforts in clearing the Brittany peninsula to the west came to naught. After a stubborn fight, the Germans finally surrendered Brest on 25 August, but not before destroying nearly all of the port facilities. With the opening of Marseilles in the South, of Cherbourg, and with the imminent capture of other Channel ports, logisticians saw little need for capturing additional harbor facilities in Brittany.

Flushed by the past month's tremendous successes, Montgomery and Bradley argued for a single, bold thrust into Germany launched from their respective sectors. But Eisenhower, concerned that a single drive might be too vulnerable to counterattack, ordered his armies to advance simultaneously on a broad front. To implement the "broad front" strategy, Eisenhower directed that Montgomery's continued attacks in the north be supported by Courtney Hodges's U.S. First Army. Patton's Third Army was to advance only as supplies permitted.

As the Allied armies moved beyond the Seine, logistics began to govern operations. The beach unloading facilities in Normandy were unable to accommodate the large amounts of gasoline, munitions, and other supplies the armies required, and in some cases, advance units were more than 300 miles from the beaches. Despite expedients such as airdrops and the implementation of a truck convoy system called the "Red Ball Express," supply levels remained inadequate.

To ease the logistics crisis, Eisenhower gave priority of supplies to Montgomery and ordered him to capture the port facilities at Antwerp in Belgium. The British moved rapidly, capturing Brussels on 3 September. Antwerp fell the next day, though continued German resistance did not permit the port's use until late November. Meanwhile, American progress slowed considerably due to lack of gasoline. Patton's Third Army crossed the Meuse River on 30 August but had to halt for lack of fuel. Hodge's First Army captured a large number of Germans near Mons on 3 September, but the advance then ground to a halt. Finally, on 14 September, troops from Hodges's army became the first Allied soldiers to set foot on German soil. Days later, Patton's supply situation improved, and Third Army moved westward to complete the liberation of France.

Adolf *Hitler brought in Field Marshal Gerd von Rundstedt on 5 September to take charge of the German Army in the West. In the face of the Allied advance, Rundstedt consolidated his forces and stabilized a defensive line. A key element of the defense was the West Wall, a dense line of small, mutually supporting pillboxes that stretched the length of the German border. In an abortive effort to outflank the West Wall by capturing a bridgehead across the lower Rhine River at the Dutch town of Arnhem near the German border, Field Marshal Montgomery planned operation "Market-Garden." On 17 September 1944, the 82nd and 101st U.S. Airborne Divisions and 1st British Airborne Division (16,500 paratroopers and 3,500 troopers in gliders), dropped near the Rhine bridges. However, many were blocked by two SS Panzer divisions, whose recent move into the area had been ignored. The British armored column coming by land was delayed by stiff German resistance and bad weather, and eventually prevented from reaching Arnhem, thus losing 6,000 British paratroopers as prisoners of war. The two U.S. airborne divisions held their ground and suffered 3,500 casualties. "Market-Garden" failed to gain a major bridgehead across the lower Rhine and by diverting sizable forces produced major delays in defeating Germans in the estuaries to open the vital port of Antwerp.

Between 6 June and 14 September, the Allies put 2.1 million soldiers on French soil, severely punished the German Army in the west, liberated the French people, and advanced to the German frontier. Despite the huge, sweeping success, Allied losses were heavy: 40,000 killed, 165,000 wounded, and 20,000 missing. In all, German forces suffered nearly 700,000 casualties. Still, the German Army remained intact, and larger battles loomed on the horizon as Allied forces began the Battle for *Germany.

• Martin Blumenson, Breakout and Pursuit, 1961; repr. 1977. Cornelius Ryan, A Bridge Too Far, 1974. Russell Weigley, Eisenhower's Lieutenants, 1981. Martin Blumenson, The Battle of the Generals, 1993. Michael D. Doubler, Closing with the Enemy: How GIs Fought the War in Europe, 1944–1945, 1994.

—Michael D. Doubler

FRANCE, UNDECLARED NAVAL WAR WITH

FRANCE, UNDECLARED NAVAL WAR WITH (1798–1800). In the 1778 treaty that created the *Franco-American Alliance, the two countries agreed to mutual defense and accepted the doctrine that neutral ships carried neutral cargoes. But under President George *Washington, the United States retained its neutrality when England and Revolutionary France went to war in 1793; and in 1794, John Jay negotiated a treaty conceding both favored status in trade and a broad definition of contraband to England—in effect, agreeing to limit trade with France. French privateers responded by seizing nearly $200,000 worth of American shipping during 1796–97.

President John *Adams wanted to send either Vice President Thomas *Jefferson or Congressman James *Madison to France. Both were Republicans, more favorably disposed to France than Federalists like Washington and Adams, but neither man would go, and Adams's Federalist cabinet refused to grant the opposition so prominent a role. When Adams learned in May that France had authorized seaborne *privateering to seize neutral American ships carrying British goods, he called Congress into special session. To start negotiations, he dispatched two Federalists, Charles Cotesworth Pinckney and John Marshall, and a moderate Republican, Elbridge Gerry, to France, but he also started military preparations. Three frigates begun in 1793—the United States, the Constellation, and the Constitution—were to be completed as quickly as possible; 80,000 militiamen were to be armed and trained; harbor defenses built; and $800,000 borrowed to pay for an undeclared "Quasi-War" with France.

France's foreign minister, the comte de Talleyrand, declined to receive the U.S. commissioners formally, but made subsequent contact through agents who insisted that the United States loan France $6 million and provide $250,000 in presents. Pinckney's famous response "[N]ot no; not a sixpence"—came just as Napoleon Bonaparte's army defeated the Austrians in Italy. Contemplating France's control of Western Europe, John Marshall commented that "the Atlantic only can save us."

In March 1798, President Adams reported to Congress, substituting "W, X, Y, and Z" for the names of the French agents (hence the "XYZ Affair"). He vowed never to send another minister to France unless he would be "received, respected, and honored" as representing "a great, free, powerful, and independent nation." Congress commissioned 1,000 privateers to capture or repel French vessels, established the Department of the Navy (30 April), levied $2 million in taxes, and passed the *Alien and Sedition Acts to restrict domestic dissent. Pinckney and Marshall returned as heroes (Gerry, less obnoxious to the French, stayed in Paris), and "Millions for defense, but not one cent for tribute" became a Federalist slogan.

By May 1798, the U.S. war sloop Ganges was guarding

the coast between Long Island and the Chesapeake, joined in June by the *Constellation* and the *United States*. In July 1798, Stephen *Decatur, on the sloop *Delaware,* captured the French schooner *Croyable* off New Jersey. After the British navy defeated French forces in the Battle of the Nile (1 August 1798), the U.S. Navy drove the French away from the U.S. coast to the Caribbean. Ten important naval engagements ensued, six of them in February and March 1799. The Americans lost only once: the *Retaliation* (formerly the *Croyable*) was captured in November 1798. In February 1799, the *Constellation* captured the frigate *L'Insurgente.* The French captain blamed U.S. Capt. Thomas Truxtun for provoking war between the United States and France.

Despite ship-to-ship actions and U.S. support for former slave Toussaint Louverture's independence movement on Haiti, neither side declared war. Adams resisted Federalist pressure for war; while congressional Federalists created a provisional army with Washington as commander in chief and Alexander *Hamilton as second in command, Adams favored a strong navy to make the United States independent of both England and France. The French Army, he told Hamilton, was more likely to invade heaven than the United States.

Napoleon's *coup d' état* on 9 November 1799 changed French politics and policy. Needing the support of neutral Denmark and Sweden, he returned in December 1799 to the principle that neutral ships make neutral goods. American diplomats at the Hague (William Vans Murray) and Berlin (John Quincy Adams) sent word that France wanted to negotiate. In November 1799, Adams dispatched official envoys to France.

On 7 March 1800, the American diplomats—William Vans Murray, Chief Justice Oliver Ellsworth, and Governor William Davie of North Carolina—met with Napoleon. In September, the Americans and French completed a convention that restored amity and deferred to future consideration the vexing issues of indemnities for seized property and the status of the 1778 treaty. The peace mission cost Adams much Federalist support. In 1800, Hamilton backed Pinckney instead of Adams for president, a split that resulted in Jefferson's election.

• Alexander DeConde, *The Quasi-War: The Politics and Diplomacy of the Undeclared War with France 1797–1801,* 1966.

—Robert J. Allison

FRANCO-AMERICAN ALLIANCE (1778–1800).

In 1778, Benjamin Franklin and France's foreign minister, the comte de Vergennes, signed two documents—a Treaty of Amity and Commerce, and a Treaty of Alliance—midway through the American *Revolutionary War. They expressed realpolitik for both parties. Vergennes hoped to weaken the British, make France the Americans' primary trade partner, and contain U.S. expansion. American leaders had hoped to achieve independence without a binding military alliance, but after the battlefield setbacks in 1776, they saw the treaty as the only way to overcome the British forces. Britain's willingness to negotiate after the American victory at the Battles of *Saratoga in October 1777 convinced Vergennes that only a "permanent" alliance could prevent American-British rapprochement. Hence, he proposed preferential Franco-American commercial ties, French recognition of U.S. independence, renunciation of any French claims to Canada, military cooperation against

Britain, and a U.S. guarantee of France's Caribbean holdings. French recognition helped legitimize the American Declaration of Independence, and French military and financial aid contributed decisively to U.S. military victory, particularly in the decisive Battle of *Yorktown (1781).

As peace approached, American leaders lost interest in the alliance. In 1782, Franklin, John *Adams, and John Jay began peace negotiations with Britain, without consulting the French. After independence in 1783, many Americans increasingly viewed the French alliance as a dangerous foreign entanglement, particularly after the French Revolution led to a new Anglo-French war in 1793. President George *Washington declared America's *neutrality despite the alliance and even allowed Jay to sign a favorable commercial treaty with Britain in 1794. French efforts to bring a more friendly American government to power led Washington to warn against "entangling Alliances" in his farewell address (1796)—words that became the cornerstone of U.S. foreign policy until the twentieth century. The alliance proved an embarrassment in the Undeclared Naval War with *France (1798–1800) and was ended with the 1800 Convention of Morfontaine, when Napoleon Bonaparte's government signed it away in return for economic concessions. The United States would not sign another peacetime military alliance until the *NATO pact of 1949.

• Ronald Hoffman and Peter J. Albert, eds., *Diplomacy and Revolution: The Franco-American Alliance of 1778,* 1981. Lawrence S. Kaplan, *Entangling Alliances with None: American Foreign Policy in the Age of Jefferson,* 1987.

—Jeffrey G. Giauque

FRANKLIN, BATTLE OF (1864).

After Union General William Tecumseh *Sherman had captured the capital of Georgia in the Battle of *Atlanta, he cut loose from his supply lines and set out with 62,000 of his troops in mid-November 1864 on *Sherman's march to the sea to cripple southern resources and demonstrate the hopelessness of the Confederate cause. But, while Sherman headed east, Confederate Gen. John B. *Hood headed into Tennessee behind Sherman.

To guard against this move, Sherman had left George H. *Thomas in Tennessee. Once Thomas could gather the numerous garrison troops there, he would have an army of ample size to deal with Hood. Meanwhile, Thomas assigned Gen. John M. Schofield with 34,000 men to watch Hood. Hood advanced rapidly from northern Alabama, outmaneuvered Schofield, and nearly captured his force at Spring Hill, Tennessee, 29 November 1864. Something went wrong—just what did remains controversial—in the Confederate army's command structure, and Schofield's army was able to escape from the trap.

The next morning, an enraged Hood put his army in pursuit. He caught Schofield at Franklin, Tennessee. The Federals' backs were to the unbridged Harpeth River, but in front of them were powerful entrenchments and an open plain two miles wide. Though two of his divisions and nearly all his artillery had not yet arrived, Hood hurled his 30,000 available men against the Union fortifications in a series of bloody and futile charges. Six of Hood's generals were killed, and 6,245 other Confederates became casualties. Union casualties numbered only 2,326.

After the battle, Schofield withdrew at his leisure, joining Thomas in Nashville. Hood followed. The slaughter at

Franklin substantially weakened Hood's army and made easier and more complete Thomas's devastating victory at the Battle of *Nashville a fortnight later.

• Richard M. McMurry, *John Bell Hood and the War for Southern Independence*, 1982. James Lee McDonough and Thomas L. Connelly, *Five Tragic Hours: The Battle of Franklin*, 1983.

—Steven E. Woodworth

FREDERICKSBURG, BATTLE OF (1862). After repelling the Confederates at the battles of *Antietam, *Perryville, and Corinth, the Union forces in the fall of 1862 renewed their offensives against Richmond, Chattanooga, and Vicksburg. President Abraham *Lincoln replaced Gen. George B. *McClellan with Gen. Ambrose *Burnside in November 1862 in command of the Army of the Potomac. Burnside proposed to move toward Fredericksburg, Virginia, as a preliminary to an offensive against Richmond. Moving quickly, his army covered 40 miles in two days, leaving Confederate Gen. Robert E. *Lee guessing as to its destination, but confused orders and bureaucratic bungling delayed the arrival of pontoons for bridging the Rappahannock River for a week. These delays and Burnside's own indecisiveness allowed Lee to concentrate his forces and establish strong defensive positions on the hills behind Fredericksburg.

In the early morning of 11 December, Burnside's engineers began laying pontoon bridges. A heavy *artillery bombardment and a crossing on the upper bridges by a Union brigade drove out the Confederate defenders. On the evening of 11 December and throughout 12 December, Federal troops moved into position in Fredericksburg. For the next several days, the soldiers thoroughly sacked the city.

On 13 December, Burnside ordered William B. Franklin to attack the Confederate right. However, carelessly drafted orders and Franklin's own lack of initiative led to delay and a weak assault with only one division. Despite these problems, however, George Gordon *Meade's men poured through a gap in Gen. Thomas *Jackson's line. A vigorous Confederate counterattack drove Meade's unsupported division back, and twilight ended the fighting on this part of the field.

While waiting impatiently for news of Franklin's attack, Burnside ordered Edwin Summer to take Marye's Heights in the rear of Fredericksburg. Around noon, William French's division moved through the streets toward a sunken road and stone wall at the base of Marye's Heights. French's brigades were thrown back by well-placed Confederate artillery fire and what many participants described as a "sheet of flame" from Georgia and North Carolina infantry stationed behind a stone wall. Assaults by parts of five more Union divisions proved equally disastrous. Several generals talked Burnside out of leading the Ninth Corps in a desperate attack the following day, and by 16 December the Army of the Potomac had been withdrawn from Fredericksburg.

Although the battle had cost the Confederates over 5,000 *casualties, the Federals had lost nearly 13,000. Historians have long criticized Burnside for both rashness and indecisiveness, yet the Union general was badly served by several subordinates. Some believe his battle plan stood a reasonable chance of success if properly executed. Whatever the merits of this argument, the results of the battle in the North were demoralization and political recrimination. For the Confederates, a relatively easy victory added to public confidence while producing fresh rumors of foreign mediation and peace negotiations.

[*See also* Civil War: Military and Diplomatic Course.]

• Frank A. O'Reilly, *"Stonewall" Jackson at Fredericksburg: The Battle of Prospect Hill*, 1993. Gary W. Gallagher, ed., *Decision on the Rappahannock: Causes and Consequences of the Fredericksburg Campaign*, 1995.

—George C. Rable

FRÉMONT, JOHN C. (1813–1890), explorer, Civil War general, U.S. senator, and first Republican candidate for president. Born in Georgia, Frémont briefly attended the College of Charleston. He began his military career in 1833, teaching mathematics to shipborne cadets aboard the sloop-of-war *Natchez*. Five years later, he was appointed a second lieutenant in the army's Topographical Engineers.

In 1846, on the eve of the *Mexican War, Frémont, sometimes called "the Pathfinder," was leading his third exploring expedition in the Far West. Although he led only part of the U.S. conquest of California, Frémont denied that his scientific expedition there was a mere pretext—one in fact encouraged by his powerful father-in-law, Senator Thomas Hart Benton, and by President James K. *Polk.

Before the Mexican War began, Frémont encouraged a band of disgruntled U.S. settlers near Sonoma, California, to oppose Mexican soldiers and form an independent "Bear Flag Republic." After war broke out, he reorganized his Topographical Engineers into the "California Battalion." Appointed by Commodore Robert F. Stockton as naval commander of U.S. forces in California, Frémont was later court-martialed for insubordination. Although President Polk commuted the sentence, Frémont resigned his commission and returned to civilian life.

Failing in his Republican presidential bid in 1856, Frémont reentered the army upon the outbreak of the Civil War as a major general. Commander of the Department of the West, he made the mistake of issuing an emancipation proclamation without presidential authorization. Consequently, he was transferred to the Shenandoah Valley, where he encountered the Confederate forces of Thomas "Stonewall" *Jackson. Frémont's controversial military career came to an ignominious end when his defeat at Cross Keys caused Lincoln to relieve him from command. On 12 August 1863, Frémont once again resigned his commission, his military career over.

• Allan Nevins, *Frémont, Pathfinder of the West*, 1955. Andrew Rolle, *John Charles Frémont: Character as Destiny*, 1991.

—Andrew Rolle

FRENCH AND INDIAN WAR (1754–63). Three longstanding contests came together again in the Seven Years' War, which British colonial Americans called the French and Indian War. The ancient Anglo-French rivalry, which predated their colonization of America, became truly global, including unprecedented martial commitments to North America. Secondly, the war continued an equally epic battle between Indians and Europeans, a struggle that Indians could sustain best as allies of one European supplier and enemies of another. The third enduring contest pitted the North American colonists of Britain against those of France in a frequently brutal 150-year-old struggle for trade and land.

An intercolonial boundary dispute between British and French colonies sparked a war that became imperial as well as Indian. The Upper Ohio Valley had been an underpopulated borderland that, by 1748, had become home to Delaware, Shawnee, and Mingo migrants from east of the Appalachians. Although long since denuded of valuable furs and peripheral to Canadian trade routes, this area gained strategic value with the arrival of Pennsylvania traders and Virginia land speculators. The government of New France responded with diplomacy; raids against British American traders and their protectors; and the building (1753) of three forts between Lake Erie and the forks of the Ohio River. Virginia's governor sent Col. George *Washington on a futile mission to order the French out, and obtained formal British permission to use force to expel the French Canadians.

Fighting began when, on 28 May 1754, Washington's Virginia troops ambushed a Canadian reconnaissance party, killing ten and taking twenty-one prisoners. Retaliation led to Washington's surrender of hastily fortified and aptly named Fort Necessity on 3 July. The French marked their victory by turning another unfinished Virginian fort into Fort Duquesne.

British government response to Washington's defeat proved uncharacteristically strong. While claiming to preserve the peace, the ministry sent two regular regiments to America under Gen. Edward *Braddock with instructions to remove French "encroachments" from British-claimed territory. What was to have been a series of attacks by a single army became, because of enthusiastic New England preparations, four simultaneous British and colonial expeditions against Forts Duquesne, Niagara, Ste. Frédéric, and Beauséjour in 1755. The British attack on Fort Duquesne ended in *Braddock's defeat at the Monongahela River, nine miles from his destination, when Indians and Canadian irregulars exploited flanking woods and poor British scouting to surprise and slaughter much of his column. Another army under Governor William Shirley of Massachusetts failed to reach Fort Niagara. William Johnson led the British colonial army that failed to reach Fort Ste. Frédéric, but won a defensive victory at the Battle of Lake George. The only clear British success was by New Englanders, led by British colonel Robert Monckton, who easily took Forts Beauséjour and Gaspereau in Canada, and then expelled 6,000 French Acadian neutrals. The British sent more regulars to avenge Braddock and gave Commanders in Chief Shirley (1756) and John Campbell, earl of Loudoun (1756–58), powers that centralized the war effort and antagonized the colonies.

New France, United under Governor Pierre-François de Rigaud, marquis de Vaudreuil (1755–60), seized the military initiative. Indian raids launched from Fort Duquesne terrorized the Pennsylvania and Virginia frontiers, while other raiders destroyed New York outposts. General Louis-Joseph, marquis de Montcalm, led well-coordinated forces of French regulars, Canadians, and Indians to conquer Fort Oswego in August 1756 and Fort William Henry a year later.

The British recovered the offensive in 1758, as the eloquent and efficient secretary of state, William Pitt, took control of the war effort. Pitt reassured British voters and creditors while spending massively on war in both Europe and America. He cut the power of his new commander in chief and negotiated a "subsidy plan" with colonial governments that was generous enough to promote unprecedented levels of imperial cooperation in supply, transport, and recruitment. British regulars, recruited in Europe and America, now constituted a majority of the much larger forces available. Britain's North American initiatives for 1758, against fortress Louisbourg and Forts Carillon, Frontenac, and Duquesne, paralleled the strategy of 1755, but met with more success. In July, 13,000 British regulars under Maj. Gen. Jeffrey *Amherst besieged and captured Louisbourg. Gen. James Abercromby's hurried assault against Montcalm's entrenched defenders at Ticonderoga (Carillon) failed disastrously, increasing Montcalm's influence over military strategy for New France. Abercromby then authorized an expedition by 3,600 colonial volunteers that took Fort Frontenac. Seven thousand men under Brig. Gen. John Forbes constructed a military road across Pennsylvania to Fort Duquesne, which the French destroyed and evacuated on 25 November 1758.

British intent to capture the core of New France in 1759 met such determined French and Canadian resistance that Amherst countered cautiously, and met shifts in Indian diplomacy that proved diversionary. By early 1759, the Delaware and Shawnee had made peace overtures, and the Six Nations of the Iroquois Confederation were reconsidering their uneasy neutrality. The siege of increasingly isolated Fort Niagara in July 1759 reflected Amherst's caution, impressed the Six Nations by clearing the French from their territory, and afforded some Ohio Indians an opportunity to change sides decisively. While these Indians strengthened the British side, the Cherokee in the South moved from their traditional alliance to open war with the British colonies between 1759 and 1761. Annual punitive expeditions, the first by South Carolina volunteers and the other two by British regulars, burned abandoned Cherokee towns, provoked retaliation, and may have helped bring a negotiated peace by the end of 1761.

Conquest of New France was not completed in 1759, but the capture of Fort Niagara and the French evacuation of Fort Ste. Frédéric and reoccupied Fort Frontenac represented British success on two of the three prongs of that attack. The third prong, a nearly three-month amphibious campaign led by Brig. Gen. James Wolfe against the walled city of Québec, stalled until a well-exploited gamble in the Battle of *Québec gave the British victory on 13 September 1759, and control of the city four days later. Control of these areas remained precarious during a successful French counteroffensive that ended only with the arrival of British warships in May 1760. On 8 September, with 17,000 British and American soldiers surrounding Montréal, which was defended by some 3,000 French, Governor Vaudreuil surrendered New France. British and American colonial troops reported the conquest to the interior posts without meeting resistance and mounted major campaigns in the French West Indies that captured Guadeloupe (1759) and Martinique (1762). The Peace of Paris ended the war 10 February 1763, confirmed the conquest of New France, and ceded to the British all lands east of the Mississippi.

The war decided only one of the three long-standing contests. The Anglo-French duel would resume regularly for another half century, and the equally long-lived military struggle between Indians and Europeans reopened immediately with *Pontiac's Rebellion. However, the struggle between the British and French North American colonies had been decided. Some Americans opposed the way Britain integrated both New France and "Indian country" into its empire; many more resisted imperial taxation imposed to help pay for the war and for the regular army garrisons of the peace. The war that had unified the British Atlantic empire to an unprecendented degree thus, not surprisingly, helped produce the American *Revolutionary War for Independence a decade later.

[See also Native American Wars: Wars Between Native Americans and Europeans and Euro-Americans; Québec, Battle of; Revolutionary War: Causes.]

• Lawrence H. Gipson, *The British Empire Before the American Revolution*, 15 vols., 1936–70, Vols. 2–9. Fred Anderson, *A People's Army: Massachusetts Soldiers and Society in the Seven Years' War*, 1984. Richard Middleton, *The Bells of Victory: The Pitt-Newcastle Ministry and the Conduct of the Seven Years' War, 1757–1762*, 1985. W. J. Eccles, *Essays on New France*, 1987. Francis Jennings, *Empire of Fortune: Crowns, Colonies and Tribes in the Seven Years' War in America*, 1988. Ian K. Steele, *Betrayals: Fort William Henry and the "Massacre,"* 1990.   —Ian K. Steele

FRIENDLY FIRE. So-called friendly fire, sometimes termed *fratricide* or *amicicide*, is officially defined by the U.S. Army as "the employment of friendly weapons … which results in unforeseen and unintentional death or injury to friendly personnel." Intentional firing on friendly troops and true accidents are properly excluded from the definition.

The difficulties posed by terrain, poor visibility, and the type and size of operations all contribute to friendly fire. The immediate causes include mechanical defects, simple carelessness, poor spatial orientation, misidentification of the target, and miscalculation of firing data. Poor coordination of the movement of forces on the battlefield, lack of training, and poor discipline also play a role; but the fear, uncertainty, and excitement of the combat environment are perhaps the most important factors.

The statistical dimensions of the friendly fire problem have yet to be defined; reliable data are simply not available in most cases. Operational and medical reports suggest, however, that the relationship of friendly fire casualties to overall friendly casualties is between 2 percent and 25 percent. In the *Persian Gulf War of 1991, there were 615 American casualties; 23 percent of the personnel (35 killed and 72 wounded) and 77 percent of the combat vehicle losses were attributable to friendly fire.

Whatever the statistical reality, friendly fire is known to have occurred in all of America's wars, and the victims have ranged from the rawest recruits to very senior officers. The Confederate general "Stonewall" *Jackson died after being mistakenly shot by one of his own soldiers at Chancellorsville in 1863. In World War II, Lieut. Gen. Lesley J. McNair and 813 other Americans were killed or wounded near St. Lô in Normandy in one of the most costly incidents of friendly fire ever to occur. The use of American medium and heavy bombers to provide close support for ground troops in Operation Cobra, the breakout of Allied forces from Normandy, resulted in mistaken

bombing of American positions on two successive days, 24–25 July 1944. The planned ground attack was delayed but ultimately succeeded despite the frightful toll.

Earlier, in July 1943, nervous American naval and ground troops Gela, Sicily, fired on aircraft carrying paratroopers of the 82nd Airborne Division and caused 319 casualties (88 dead, 162 wounded, and 69 missing) plus 80 aircraft destroyed or badly damaged. In the Pacific, a month later, 15–16 August, 28 Americans and Canadians were killed and 55 wounded during the invasion of Kiska in the Aleutian Islands. There were no enemy troops on the island; all of the casualties were from friendly fire.

As weapons have become more complicated and more deadly, the ability of human beings to control them has been stretched to its limits, and both the number and the severity of friendly fire incidents have increased. Modern armies search earnestly for ways to reduce or eliminate friendly fire. Improved training and sophisticated electronic devices are sure to have a positive effect, yet it is equally certain that the problem cannot be eradicated altogether. As long as men make war, friendly fire will continue to occur.

[See also Casualties.]

• Charles R. Shrader, *Amicicide: The Problem of Friendly Fire in Modern War*, 1982. Charles R. Shrader, "Friendly Fire: The Inevitable Price," *Parameters: The Journal of the U.S. Army War College*, 22, no. 3 (Autumn 1992), pp. 29–44. Kenneth K. Steinweg, "Dealing Realistically with Fratricide," *Parameters: The Journal of the U.S. Army War College*, 25, no. 1 (Spring 1995), pp. 4–29.
                                          —Charles R. Shrader

FULTON, ROBERT (1765–1815), inventor. Best known for his development of the first commercially successful steamboat in 1807, Fulton also made important contributions in portrait painting, canal engineering, and naval warfare. Born in Pennsylvania, he lived most of his adult life in Europe. His first naval project was the *submarine *Nautilus*, manually driven underwater and tested successfully in French waters in 1800. Shifting to mine warfare, Fulton successfully blew up two brigs with floating mines in tests off Dover, England, in 1805 and New York in 1807. His grand vision was to promote freedom of the seas and free trade, using naval weapons to prevent war. He offered these weapons alternately to Napoleon and the British with little success. Returning to America, Fulton continued developing steamboats and naval weapons until his death. His American-developed weapons concepts stressed harbor defense, and included the moored mine, the submarine gun, use of the steamboat for troop transport in the *War of 1812, and the construction of the first steam warship in history, USS *Fulton the First*. His *Nautilus* was the first cigar-shaped submarine, and he was the first to conceive of the moored mine. Fulton's emphasis on the submarine, on mines, and on the deterrent effect have particular relevance for the modern era.

• Alex Roland, *Underwater Warfare in the Age of Sail*, 1978. Wallace S. Hutcheon, Jr., *Robert Fulton: Pioneer of Undersea Warfare*, 1981. Cynthia Owen Philip, *Robert Fulton: A Biography*, 1985.
                                          —Wallace S. Hutcheon, Jr.

G

GAGE, THOMAS (1721–1787), British general and royal governor of Massachusetts. In the *French and Indian War, Gage demonstrated personal courage on the battlefield, but little talent for command. His real skill was as an administrator, and he fully proved it as the military governor of Montréal from 1761 to 1763. For more than a decade after succeeding Jeffrey *Amherst as commander in chief of British North America in 1763, Gage confronted the legacies of the French and Indian War. After suppressing *Pontiac's Rebellion, he struggled to keep land-hungry colonists from new conflicts with the Indians. Following the Stamp Act upheavals, he tried to keep smugglers and other scofflaws from flouting Parliament's authority. Gage's mission soon shifted from protecting American colonists to controlling them. In 1774, Gage, newly appointed governor in chief of Massachusetts, enforced the Coercive Acts by closing the port of Boston and suspending representative government in the colony. In the ensuing crisis, he sent British troops to seize patriot supplies in the battles of Lexington and Concord (19 April 1775), triggering the *Revolutionary War. Following the Battle of *Bunker Hill (17 June 1775), he was recalled to England and blamed for allowing the American colonies to rebel.

• John R. Alden, *General Gage in America*, 1948. George Athan Billias, *George Washington's Opponents*, 1969.

—Jon T. Coleman

GAME THEORY. Within national security analysis, *Game theory* deals with parties making choices that influence each other's interests, where they all know that they are making such choices. Using mathematics, it analyzes the think/doublethink logic of how each adversary sees the other, sees the other's view of it, and so on. Unlike *war gaming*, where real players assume roles, it involves only mathematical calculations.

John von *Neumann and Oskar Morgenstern laid the foundation of game theory in the 1940s. Its application to military problems has been limited but interesting. One World War II example involved *submarine warfare. A submarine is passing through a corridor patrolled by submarine-hunting planes. The submarine must spend some time traveling on the surface to recharge its batteries. The corridor widens and narrows, and the submarine is easier to detect in the narrower parts, with less sea for the hunters to scan. Where should the submarine surface? Where should the hunters focus their effort? The premise that the wide part is the one logical place is self-refuting. If it were true, the hunters would deduce that, would head there and leave the narrower part alone, making the narrower part better. Choosing the narrow part likewise leads to a contradiction. Game theory advises a "mixed" strategy—do one or the other unpredictably, using exact probabilities calculated from the ease of detection in each section.

Other applications have addressed the problems of when an interceptor aircraft closing on a bomber should open fire, how to allocate antimissile defenses to targets of varying value, and when to fire intercontinental *missiles to avoid Soviet nuclear explosions in the stratosphere.

These problems involved specific wartime encounters. Another area is broad strategy. A prevalent misconception is that game theory set the principles of nuclear strategy. In the 1940s, planners hoped that the new mathematics would do this, but strategic problems proved too complex. It was hard even to specify each side's goals. Game theory has not given exact strategic advice, but it has clarified general principles. In a model of crisis confrontation, for example, one side wants to show the adversary that it values winning very highly, to induce the other side to back down. It uses the tactic of sacrifice-to-show-resolve—make some costly military deployment so the adversary will conclude that only a determined government would pay such a cost to prove its determination. The model precisely illustrates the skeletal structure of strategic concepts such as showing resolve or enhancing credibility. By the 1990s, a sophisticated body of academic work had addressed *deterrence, escalation, war alliances, and the verification of arms treaties.

[*See also* Disciplinary Views of War: Political Science and International Relations; Operations Research; Strategy; War Plans.]

• Melvin Dresher, *Games of Strategy: Theory and Applications*, 1961. Barry O'Neill, "A Survey of Game Theory Studies of Peace and War," in Robert Aumann and Sergiu Hart, eds., *Handbook of Game Theory*, 1994.

—Barry O'Neill

GARRISON, WILLIAM LLOYD (1805–1879), abolitionist, nonresistant, and feminist. With the publication of the first issue of the *Liberator* on 1 January 1831, William Lloyd Garrison became the undisputed leader of the U.S. abolitionist movement. Garrison called for the "immediate" and "complete" emancipation of slaves. Yet he was also a confirmed advocate of nonviolence. In 1838, he and other abolitionists formed the New England Non-Resistance Society. In its "Declaration of Sentiments," Garrison pledged its members to oppose all preparation and exercise of war and all cooperation with institutions of war.

Although nonviolence was his key stance, Garrison and his abolitionist wife, Helen Eliza Benson, openly supported the *Civil War once it had begun since it brought about the end of slavery. Their eldest son, George Thompson, fought with the 55th Massachusetts (Colored) Regiment. Their other sons (William Lloyd Junior, Wendell Phillips, and teenager Francis Jackson) took philosophically *conscientious objection stances, as did their daughter, Helen Frances (Fanny). Garrison's legacy is most visible in the pacifist-feminist-antiracist lives of succeeding generations of the family who participated in post–Civil War freedmen's associations, the 1898 anti-imperialist impetus, the *peace and antiwar movements from 1915 to today, the founding of the National Association for the Advancement of Colored People, and the antinuclear and environmental movements.

[*See also* Pacifism; Villard, Oswald and Fanny Garrison.]

• Walter M. Merrill, *Against Wind and Tide: A Biography of William Lloyd Garrison*, 1963. James Brewer Stewart, *William Lloyd Garrison and the Challenge of Emancipation*, 1992. Henry Mayer, *All on Fire: William Lloyd Garrison and the Abolition of Slavery*, 1998.

—Harriet Hyman Alonso

GATES, HORATIO (1727/8–1806), Revolutionary War general. Born in Old Malden, Surrey, to an unlettered English customs official and the housekeeper of the duke of Bolton's mistress, Gates was commissioned a British army lieutenant in 1745, through Bolton's influence. In the *French and Indian War, after being wounded at Monongahela in 1755, he rose to the rank of major, but eventually barred from further advancement, he retired in 1769. Living in Virginia at the outbreak of the *Revolutionary War, Gates was appointed adjutant general by the Continental Congress, and he helped George *Washington organize the Continental army. Popular with New Englanders, he replaced Philip Schuyler as commander of the northern army after the loss of Fort Ticonderoga. At the two battles of *Saratoga, he employed his numerical superiority to force the surrender of British Gen. John *Burgoyne's entire army on 17 October 1777.

Gates planned to follow up by invading Canada, but Washington blocked the expedition. A hero after Saratoga, Gates became Washington's rival, but in 1778 was discredited on the spurious charge that he had plotted with the "Conway cabal" to elevate himself over Washington. Assigned to command the Continentals in South Carolina in 1780, he undertook a rash offensive with ill-prepared troops and was disastrously defeated at the Battle of Camden by Gen. Charles *Cornwallis. In 1783, he was associated with, but took no active part in, the officers' aborted *Newburgh "conspiracy" to coerce Congress into giving them backpay. A novel combination of professional and populist, Gates managed short-term militia unusually well, and was a generally competent, if ultimately flawed, commander.

• Paul David Nelson, *General Horatio Gates*, 1976. Max M. Mintz, *The Generals of Saratoga: John Burgoyne and Horatio Gates*, 1990.

—Max. M. Mintz

GATES, THOMAS (1906–1983), secretary of defense (1959–61). Gates was born in Philadelphia and became an investment banker, serving in the navy in World War II. In the Eisenhower administration, he was successively undersecretary (1953–57) and secretary of the navy (1957–59) and deputy secretary of defense before succeeding Neil *McElroy as secretary on 2 December 1959.

Gates moved quickly to establish close relations with the *Joint Chiefs of Staff, meeting with them regularly to force decisions on disputed issues. Gates's principal contribution to defense planning was his institution of the Single Integrated Operating Plan (SIOP), which unified the targeting of all strategic *nuclear weapons in general war. In doing so, he overrode strong opposition from the navy, with its traditional hostility to centralized defense organization.

While supporting President Dwight D. *Eisenhower's effort to hold down defense spending, Gates recognized the need for a modest increase to meet growing Soviet power. He firmly and accurately denied the existence of a "missile gap"—an advantage in *missiles favoring the Soviet Union. In 1969, President Richard M. *Nixon appointed Gates to head a commission that successfully recommended replacing the *conscription with an *All-Volunteer Force.

[*See also* Defense, Department of; McNamara, Robert S.]

• James M. Roherty, *Decisions of Robert S. McNamara: A Study of the Role of the Secretary of Defense*, 1970. Roger R. Trask, *The Secretaries of Defense: A Brief History, 1947–1985*, 1985. Robert J. Watson, *History of the Office of the Secretary of Defense*, Vol. 4, 1998.

—Robert J. Watson

GATLING GUN. The precursor of the modern machine gun was invented in 1862 by Richard J. Gatling. Born in North Carolina, Gatling had moved to St. Louis, Missouri, where he invented and manufactured agricultural machines. Previous attempts at designing an automatically reloading multishot gun were stymied by the loading and ignition techniques of the mid-nineteenth century: bullet and gunpowder had to be loaded separately, and the powder ignited via an external percussion cap. The introduction of metal-jacketed cartridges containing a percussive, explosive charge and a bullet in a single unit enabled Gatling to invent a self-loading primitive machine gun.

The Gatling gun featured a circle of ten barrels attached to a rotating shaft turned by a hand-operated crank, which drove the entire device. As the barrels revolved, they passed by a firing hammer that discharged the cartridge, which was automatically ejected and replaced by a new breech-loaded cartridge from a gravity-fed hopper. The gun could be fired continuously as long as the crank was turned; externally powered Gatling guns could fire up to 3,000 rounds a minute.

Despite their obvious potential against infantry attacks, Gatling guns were infrequently used during the *Civil War. Gen. James W. Ripley, the *Union army's chief of ordnance, opposed their development, due to suspicion of Gatling's Southern birth and concern about the weapon's reliability and the enormous supply of munitions such guns would require. The U.S. Army eventually adopted the Gatling gun, assigning the large wheeled, horse-drawn weapons and their munitions limbers, to artillery units that used them in the *Plains Indians Wars and in the *Spanish-American War. The U.S. Army replaced these with smaller, lighter, and recoil-powered modern *machine guns in the twentieth century.

• Joseph Berk, *The Gatling Gun: 19th Century Machine Gun to 21st Century Vulcan*, 1991.

—T. R. Brereton

GAY MEN AND LESBIANS IN THE MILITARY. Homosexuality is one of many categories that people use to think about, define, and organize their sexual identities and behaviors. Although the term *homosexuality* refers to loving or desiring or having sex with someone of the same sex, there is no straightforward, agreed-upon definition of homosexuality, and no clear relationship between the types of sexual acts that people perform and whether they define themselves as gay or lesbian. Eve Sedgwick, a prominent cultural theorist, refers to homosexuality as a space of overlapping, contradictory, and conflictual meanings. In addition, Sedgwick argues that notwithstanding evidence of same-sex love and desire throughout history, modern understandings of homosexuality may be different from previous arrangements of same-sex relations.

The history of same-sex desire in the military dates back to the earliest days of the military. In the United States, Gen. Friedrich Wilhelm von *Steuben, who trained the *Continental army at Valley Forge, is believed by some to have had male lovers, and Lt. Gotthold Frederick Enslin became the first soldier drummed out of the Continental army for sodomy on 11 March 1778. The military's first known lesbian soldiers apparently disguised themselves as men and fought in the 15th Missouri Regiment during the *Civil War. Indeed, gay men and lesbians have served in every sector of the military, including the Navy SEALs, Green Berets, and the cockpit of Air Force One. According to the journalist Randy Shilts, they have included army and marine four-star generals, a lesbian admiral, and a member of the *Joint Chiefs of Staff.

Military understandings of homosexuality have reflected larger societal understandings even as actions taken by the military have in turn influenced society. As the United States mobilized for World War II, military officials who believed that homosexuals were not fit for combat used new screening procedures to attempt to identify homosexual men. For the first time, regulations focused on whether recruits and soldiers had gay identities, not just whether they committed sodomy. Of 18 million men examined during the war, the military rejected 4,000–5,000 for homosexuality. After the war, 9,000 gays and lesbians who did serve were disqualified from obtaining G.I. benefits when they received section eight or "blue" discharges for undesirable habits or character traits. Many returned to port cities where they formed the nuclei of emerging gay communities. Historian Alan Bérubé argues that by identifying and managing people as homosexual persons rather than focusing narrowly on the act of sodomy, the military encouraged gays and lesbians to assume a stronger identity.

In 1950, Congress enacted the Uniform Code of Military Justice, which subjected any persons who engaged in oral or anal sex to court-martial and five years' incarceration. To enforce regulations, military investigators sought to identify gays and lesbians by detaining suspects and forcing them to specify their peers' sexual orientation. During witch-hunts, it was not uncommon for investigators to extract confessions by threatening incarceration. Between 1941 and 1996, the military discharged about 100,000 gays and lesbians, an average of roughly 2,000 per year; the 1996 discharge figure was 850. The navy tends to account for the highest percentage of discharges and women are discharged at a proportionally higher rate than men.

Discharges tend to decrease during wartime when the need for personnel increases. The navy discharged only 483 gays and lesbians (about half its annual average) in 1950 during the *Korean War and 461 in 1970 during the *Vietnam War. In 1942, during World War II, the commander at Moffett Field, California, canceled the dishonorable discharges of seven gay men so they could be reassigned after their prison sentences. Many gay men and lesbians have been separated under less than honorable conditions. Of 1,648 enlisted personnel ousted in 1985 for homosexuality, for example, over 600 were denied honorable discharges. In addition, prison sentences for same-sex sodomy were common until the late 1980s. Although prohibited by military law, sodomy between men and women rarely has invited court-martial or incarceration.

Despite the threat of punishment, enforcement of antigay regulations has varied considerably among units and service branches and has depended on the discretion of individual commanders. As a result, while some gay and lesbian service members do not reveal their sexual orientation, others have served openly. Gay military networks that emerged in World War II developed into vast subcultures by the 1970s, and by the late 1980s, much of the military's gay subculture was barely hidden.

In 1973, gays and lesbians began to use courts to challenge the substantive constitutionality of antigay regulations and to question the rationale for retaining some soldiers while discharging others. The Department of *Defense responded in 1981 by promulgating Directive 1332.14, which made the discharge of gay and lesbian soldiers more clearly mandatory. President Bill *Clinton attempted to overturn this policy in 1993 by proposing to allow gay and lesbian soldiers to serve openly. In response, advocates of antigay regulations who invoked mental illness, unfitness for duty, and vulnerability to blackmail to justify discriminations during the *Cold War contended that unit cohesion would suffer if the military allowed gays and lesbians to be open about their sexuality.

Some scholars responded that gays and lesbians do serve openly in the United States and foreign militaries and in American police and fire departments without jeopardizing cohesion. In addition, they noted that racial integration did not undermine cohesion, although 1948 polls indicated that 63 percent of the public favored segregation in the military. Finally, they pointed to organizational theory that indicates that performance depends on task cohesion (shared commitment to group objectives) but not social cohesion (emotional bonds).

The subsequent compromise between pro- and antigay advocates is known as "Don't Ask, Don't Tell, Don't Pursue." The policy prohibits asking recruits about their sexual orientation, although the military has breached regulations 1,632 times since 1994 according to the Servicemembers Legal Defense Network. Under this new policy, homosexual but not heterosexual status passes as evidence that a service member has violated antisodomy laws. Federal courts ruled both ways on the "Don't Ask, Don't Tell" policy, but the Supreme Court has declined to rule on the policy's constitutionality.

Antigay regulations have important negative consequences. Regulations can compromise unit cohesion when soldiers are encouraged to turn against each other. They can lead to suicides and also deter rape victims from reporting assaults when rapists threaten to accuse victims of homosexuality. Regulations enable commanders to question the sexual orientation of service members who report antigay death threats. Because investigators require only rumors to discharge service members for homosexuality, threatening to label a women as a lesbian probably is the most prevalent form of *sexual harassment in the military. Antigay regulations also have economic consequences. According to the Servicemembers Legal Defense Network, between 1980 and 1995 the government spent more than $600 million on training those subsequently discharged as homosexuals. In January 1999, the Pentagon reported that the four services had discharged 1,145 gay men and lesbians in fiscal year 1998, a 13 percent increase from 1997 and nearly double the number in 1993, the year before the "Don't Ask, Don't Tell" policy went into effect.

• Lawrence R. Murphy, *Perverts by Official Order: The Campaign Against Homosexuals by the United States Navy,* 1986. Allan Bérubé, *Coming Out Under Fire: The History of Gay Men and Women in World War Two,* 1990. Eve Kosofsky Sedgwick, *Epistemology of the Closet,* 1990. Kate Dyer, ed., *Gays in Uniform: The Pentagon's Secret Reports,* 1990. Committee on Armed Services, U.S. Senate, *Policy Concerning Homosexuality in the Armed Forces,* 1993. National Defense Research Institute, RAND, *Sexual Orientation and U.S. Military Personnel Policy: Options and Assessment,* 1993. Randy Shilts, *Conduct Unbecoming: Gays and Lesbians in the U.S. Military,* 1993. Winni S. Webber, *Lesbians in the Military Speak Out,* 1993. Janet Halley, "The Status/Conduct Distinction in the 1993 Revisions to Military Anti-Gay Policy," *GLQ,* 3 (1996), pp. 159–252. Steven Zeeland, *The Masculine Marine: Homoeroticism in the U.S. Marine Corps,* 1996. Elizabeth Kier, "Homosexuals in the U.S. Military: Open Integration and Combat Effectiveness," *International Security,* vol. 23, no. 2 (Fall 1998), pp. 5–39.   —Aaron Belkin

GENDER. *This entry consists of two articles, each of which deals with the issue of gender and the military from a different perspective. The first,* Male Identity and the Military, *examines the concept of men as warriors and protectors. The second,* Female Identity and the Military, *emphasizes the relationship that women have had to war and the military.*
For more detailed related discussions, see Combat Effectiveness, Gays and Lesbians in the Military, Gender and War, Military Ideals, Sex and the Military, Sexual Harassment, Women in the Military.

Male Identity and the Military
Female Identity and the Military

GENDER: MALE IDENTITY AND THE MILITARY

Male identity in the United States, except in certain pacifist groups, has generally been closely tied to the socially defined role of warrior and protector. Throughout American military history, the manipulation and exploitation of this gender identity has been among the most important means of persuading men to join the service or informally coercing them to participate. This process has served three major purposes: first, it draws huge numbers of men into uniform without having to resort to widespread physical coercion by the state; second, it serves a military useful role by defining behavioral standards that make for effective combatants and contribute to post-service reintegration; and third, the gender roles fostered by the military bolster and legitimize gender roles in society as a whole. The agents of this manipulation have been as diverse and pervasive as their message, including politicians, military leaders, commercial interests, and religious and educational institutions.

The creation of male gender identity has been tied explicitly to a warrior role and military service for the local community and the *state. That this was a product of the natural order went virtually unchallenged throughout the colonial and early national periods, and military service for men was explicitly tied to rights and obligations of citizenship. By the end of the nineteenth century, however, with the rise of industrialization and urbanization, the closing of the frontier, slowly expanding roles for women, and the influence of social Darwinism, this assumption came into question. To reaffirm it, some Americans like Theodore *Roosevelt openly embraced war with Spain in 1898 in part to restore the individual and collective masculine virtues apparently eroded by modern, materialistic, urban society.

The twentieth century has witnessed a dynamic of ever stronger attacks on traditional, polarized gender identities, and increasingly extreme retrenchments of the male warrior identity. As women's roles in the workplace and the military expanded with national *mobilization in two world wars, they directly challenged the underlying assumptions of male-warrior exclusivity. If women were allowed to step into uniform, as temporary auxiliaries in 1917, in segregated branches of the armed forces in 1943, and integrated into the force beginning in 1978, their specialties and geographic assignments were still carefully circumscribed away from combat in efforts to protect the male-warrior status.

As the reserved male domains shrank, definitions and defense of those domains became more polarized. When the military as a whole was an exclusively male sphere, there was no need to draw gendered distinctions within it, but as women entered the military, gendered distinctions sharpened between the warriors and supporting personnel. This also marked the rise of concern over sexual orientation, which threatened further to subvert the traditional male identity. In *training and indoctrination of male recruits, gendered behavior emphasized boundaries and fostered extreme behavioral standards. The hypermasculine ideals espoused and often embodied by drill instructors and unit leaders fostered effective battlefield performance, especially among various airborne, amphibious, and aviation elite forces. But while such indoctrination served short-term institutional needs and provided individual affirmation of male gender values, it also promoted behavior increasingly incompatible with gender relations in society as a whole. This has been seen in dramatic fashion in the last twenty years with the integration of the services and the incremental lifting of many restrictions on women serving in combat.

The integration of women in the military has exposed the false premise of the traditional male gender identity, which insists that the role of warrior and protector must be an exclusive province of men. The myths that have long underpinned this identity are deeply interwoven into the fabric of American society, and efforts to redefine gender roles have encountered widespread resistance from many sources. If men are no longer to hold exclusive control of sanctioned organized *aggression and violence, then the basis for individual and collective roles and behavioral standards will require fundamental change, such change is unlikely to come about without intense and protracted conflict.

• Morris Janowitz and Roger Little, *Sociology and the Military Establishment,* 1959; 3rd ed. 1974. Jean Bethke Elshtain, *Women and War,* 1987. Judith Hicks Stiehm, *Arms and the Enlisted Woman,*

1989. Elisabetta Addis, Valeria E. Russo, and Lorenza Sebesta, eds., *Women Soldiers: Images and Reality,* 1994. Linda Bird Francke, *Ground Zero: The Gender War in the Military,* 1997. Melissa S. Herbert, *Camouflage Isn't Only for Combat: Gender, Sexuality, and Women in the Military,* 1998. —Craig M. Cameron

GENDER: FEMALE IDENTITY AND THE MILITARY

Gender—male and female identity—has both "always" and "never" been relevant to the American military. All societies make distinctions between women and men. Across societies, though, there is enormous variation between what men do and what women do except with regard to two activities. Everywhere, weapons belong mainly to men and care of the very young mainly to women. Warfare and child care have traditionally been reserved roles. However, there is an asymmetry in this specialization. Women's special role has a biological underpinning. Men cannot give birth to or physically nurse children. Women therefore do not have to defend or protect their special reserved activity. In contrast, women can fight, can wage war, and in fact their help in doing this is periodically sought. They then do have the capacity to do men's special work. This has meant that in this area men have a continuing need to defend, to separate, or to distinguish what they do from what women do. They have to prohibit—to bar—women, since "nature" does not.

The special task of the military is to fight. Fighters require a lot of support, which in the early years of the American military was provided by civilians, civilians who often included women who did laundry, sewing, cooking, and other tasks for the soldiers. Thus, some women have always been involved with the military. Some have unofficially fought in the military (in the early years disguised as men), others have officially helped support the military. Indeed, when the military did not have enough men to perform the required support tasks, it either employed civilians or recruited women who accepted these tasks, such as the temporary auxiliaries who served in uniform as military telephone operators or clerks in World War I.

Even before World War I, nurses were the military women's vanguard, the first group to crack the military's gender barrier. At the same time, they unequivocally maintained their female identity. It was only in the Civil War, in the North, that women began to work as nurses regularly in military hospitals. First brought into the military because of need, they served as auxiliaries with different rules, benefits, and compensation from men. For their performance, they were later rewarded with more "regular" status. But they were also kept in sex-segregated units until long after World War II. This was a pattern replicated for other women as they entered the U.S. military.

In the second half of the twentieth century, *guerrilla warfare and the threat of nuclear war made it clear that women could not be protected simply by keeping them out of uniform. Furthermore, once the draft ended in 1972, the military again needed women to help fill its ranks. This need coincided with a push by feminists for an end to all discrimination, all prohibitions, based on sex. Although men's reserved role shrank and its boundaries became somewhat ambiguous, in principle, the warrior role remained men's.

Equity arguments against exclusion continued in court and in public, but although many continued to argue against allowing women in combat roles, their argument was diminished by the fact that modern war claims as many or more civilian casualties as military *casualties. Women could not be kept safe. The physical strength argument was diminished by the achievements of women athletes and by the reduced role of physical strength in technological combat such as is common in the air force and the navy. Indeed, the combat restriction was removed under President Bill *Clinton for aviation and naval ships, a result in part of the navy's embarrassment over the *sexual harassment of women at its aviators' Tailhook Convention. The change was also supported by the public acclaim for the professional behavior of Maj. Rhonda Cornum as a prisoner of war during the *Persian Gulf War, and the public's acceptance of American women casualties in that war.

Still, women at the end of the twentieth century remained excluded from ground combat. Much of the argument for maintaining this area of combat exclusion ultimately focused on *combat effectiveness arguments related to group cohesion and individual performance—contentions that emphasized the need for male bonding and men's alleged inability to perform professionally in women's presence (arguments that were once applied to African Americans and that continue to be applied to homosexuals).

Some have argued that citizenship is linked to military service, and for men this has been true. But the United States was also founded in part on the argument that citizenship is linked to paying taxes (that taxation requires representation). Thus, it could be argued that women's early limited citizenship was associated not with their failure to perform military service but with their sparse property rights and consequent lack of status as taxpayers. Since the U.S. military is so clearly accountable to elected civilians, the resistance to women's full participation in the military probably lies not with the desire to restrict women's citizenship, but with the desire to maintain the role of the warrior as one still reserved for men.

• Cynthia H. Enloe, *Does Khaki Become You?: The Militarization of Women's Lives,* 1983. Eva Isaksson, ed., *Women and the Military System: Proceedings of a Symposium Arranged by the International Peace Bureau and Peace Union of Finland,* 1988. Susan Jeffords, *The Remasculization of America: Gender and the Vietnam War,* 1989. Judith Stiehm, *Arms and the Enlisted Woman,* 1989. Rhonda Cornum and Peter Copeland, *She Went to War: The Rhonda Cornum Story,* 1992. Jeanne Holm, *Women in the Military: An Unfinished Revolution,* 1992. Miriam Cook and Angela Woollacott, eds., *Gendering War Talk,* 1993. Judith Stiehm, ed., *It's Our Military, Too!: Woman and the U.S. Military,* 1996. —Judith Hicks Stiehm

GENDER AND WAR. War is a gendered phenomenon, one with meaning for the relative status of men and women within American society. Times of national emergency create enormous possibilities for change, and often threaten foundational social hierarchies, such as gender, race, and class relations. Yet many of the new opportunities for traditionally marginalized groups have historically been circumscribed by powerful ideological constructions of the meanings of *war. These social myths define war itself as a masculine undertaking and delineate the differential duties prescribed for men and women during wartime. White men (and by the late twentieth century, all men) were expected to *protect* "their" figurative women, homes, and families, especially through military service. Women's ostensibly passive role as *protectees* during war highlights their efforts to maintain these same homes and families, thereby supporting their men, and waiting for them to return. The actual experience of men and women during American wars belies this easy dichotomy; many men did not serve in the military and many military men never saw combat. Similarly, many women, particularly when wars were fought on American soil, achieved wartime access to political, economic, and social means of power to which they were barred in peacetime. Yet such activities were contained, often through deliberate propaganda, within a cultural framework that allowed for elasticity in gender behavior during wartime, but did not sanction such activities as appropriate in *peace.

One of the most frequently employed models for analyzing the topic of gender and war has been the "watershed" approach. This assesses whether the impact of war on gender relations proves a "watershed" that results in long-term change, or whether traditional gender systems were successfully reinstituted after the war to minimize wartime gains by marginalized groups. The *Revolutionary War, for instance, provided a vehicle through which some women challenged their exclusion from the definitions of republican citizenship as the province of free, white, propertied men. During the Revolutionary era, free white women were central to the success of boycotts of imported products, and subsequently to the production of household manufactures, that were so critical to the Revolution's success. Their activities politicized the domestic sphere itself: the daily female tasks of shopping and home production. However, these activities were consistent with white propertied women's prescribed identification with home and family. Caricatured as domineering and masculine by the British in an attempt to shame patriot men, many American white women nevertheless continued their increasingly public political actions. In the same period, moreover, some northern enslaved African women employed the rhetoric of the Revolution in successful attempts to free themselves and their families via the colonial and early state court systems.

The resulting gender system, a product of contestation and negotiation during the Revolution, provided a limited space within which some women might assert themselves as political actors. In particular, the question of how female citizenship would be defined in the new nation was answered by extending the politicization of domestic duties during the Revolution into the postwar republic—in other words, endowing domesticity itself with political meaning. Embodied in the role of the "Republican mother," such politicization included the presumption that white, propertied women would educate their children at home to be good republican citizens. The increased ideological importance assigned to women as educators—especially of male children—linked white, educated, propertied women to the newly created nation, and gave them some degree of power over its future. Since their duty to the state was to reproduce a virtuous citizenry, elite and educated women had to be able to write as well as to read. They had to be schooled in matters of government in order to develop in themselves the political virtue necessary to reproduce these values in their children. In the years following the Revolution, white, propertied northern women would expand upon this strategy as a means of enlarging their roles as political actors outside the domestic realm.

Like the Revolutionary War, the *Civil War is distinguished by the fact that the entire conflict was a domestic one. The Civil War was further marked by the direct impact of military action on civilian populations as targets of military violence. Most of the campaigns that led to violence against civilian populations and their property took place within the American South. As distinctions between "home front" and "battle front" blurred, so too did the asymmetrical relationship between men as "protectors" and women as "protected" that undergirded the southern gender system. The *Union army's wartime occupation of many southern towns and cities, for instance, undercut the ability of white southern men to come to the aid of their families, and forced elite and educated white southern women to devise strategies in their own defense. Moreover, Union Gen. William Tecumseh *Sherman's March to the Sea through Georgia and the Carolinas late in the war not only demonstrated the vulnerability of "unprotected" southern women but attacked the manhood of southern men who failed as "protectors." In response, southern elite and middle-class white women directed their anger not just at Yankee soldiers and officers but also at Confederate men and the Confederate government. As many noted in their diaries, their encounter with the enemy ruined forever their trust in men as protectors. Thus, the southern framework of protection was undercut by a more powerful axiom of warfare illustrating the white southerners' defeat by demonstrating their inability to protect "their" women.

The two world wars of the twentieth century were distinguished from past conflicts by the massive mobilization of all parts of the civilian population to support war efforts, the *conscription of huge armies to wage the war, and especially during World War II the *bombing of civilians. U.S. *mobilization for both world wars catalyzed popular concerns that mobilizing large portions of the populace might undermine the established gender and sexual order. To offset this potential threat, during World War II federal government and media propaganda created the image of "Rosie the Riveter." This image depicted a first-time female worker who enters the labor force, not for the extra income such employment might bring into her home, but rather for solely patriotic reasons to "support the war effort." Rosie the Riveter was also characterized by wartime propaganda as a temporary worker, completely "feminine," and perfectly willing to "give up" her job and return to her role as wife and mother as soon as the war concluded. On the one hand, Rosie the Riveter was used by federal and private agencies as a recruiting device to encourage women to enter the paid labor force. On the other hand, by portraying Rosie's service as "for the duration only," the propaganda highlighted female workforce participation as motivated by wartime necessity, and made invisible the thousands of women who had worked outside their homes prior to the war. Thus, the symbol of Rosie the Riveter contained within it the ideological means to push women out of the labor force, or out of higher-paying jobs, once the war concluded.

During both world wars, moreover, the fact that the vast majority of the conflict was not fought on American soil maintained the distinctions between home front and battle front and thus between male "protectors" fighting and the women they "protected." The lack of tangible evidence of the need for immediate protection, however, necessitated propagandistic representations of the potential dangers an enemy victory would pose to American women and the potential rewards protectors might expect to reap for their role as guardians of the American home front. Scholars have argued, for instance, that during World War II, "pinups" visible in soldiers/officers' footlockers, bunks, and barracks, as well as bombers and *tanks named after female movie stars, models, and sweethearts, functioned as symbols of the private obligations for which men were fighting and as surrogate objects of sexual desire—the potential "bounty" servicemen and officers might claim if they successfully defended the home front. A counterpoint to the "'good woman' as spoils" image was the threat throughout the war of American women being raped. During World War II, for instance, the U.S. government *Who Is the Enemy?* series of films presented the "enemy" as a soldier (Japanese or German) or male leader (often Hitler), who would rape and murder "our" women if the enemy were not defeated. Both "pinups" and representations of posited dangers for American women maintained and reinforced the gender system and the unequal distribution of power contained within it.

What these propagandistic attempts to contain any threats to the gender order concealed, however, were the many ways in which women's activities in support of both wars *did* represent new possibilities and roles for women and result in challenges to prevailing notions of the proper identities of women and men. While American women's participation in the World War I war effort was far less than that of their European counterparts, for instance, American feminists and suffrage leaders nonetheless argued that women's war work demanded that they be accepted fully as citizens. In fact, the Nineteenth Amendment, giving American women the right to vote, was finally supported by President Woodrow *Wilson in 1918, before the end of the war, and was adopted as law in 1920. Moreover, the escalation of women's participation in the paid labor force during World War II resulted in what some historians have termed a "change in consciousness" that set the stage for the modern women's movement twenty years later. Although World War II was followed by the reinstitution of fairly rigid gender norms and a reemphasis on conformity, some scholars have contended that the abrupt withdrawal of wartime options for some women was one of the major catalysts to the feminist movement of the 1960s.

Another prominent gender legacy of World War II was what some scholars have characterized as a new politicization of nuclear families. As in the Revolution, women were deemed during the *Cold War to be essential to the "family's" and the nation's survival and stability. The significance of the nuclear family was particularly emphasized in the 1950s as women's prescriptive roles as wives and mothers were ideologically joined to the stability of the nation, national defense, and the superiority of the American over the Soviet model of government and society. Epitomized in the "kitchen debates" between Vice President Richard M. *Nixon and Soviet premier Nikita Khrushchev in 1959 in Moscow, the American system was symbolized by the contrast between the U.S. housewife who was allegedly "free" not to work (at least outside her home) and the Soviet woman who was "forced" to work outside her home. Thus, Soviet women were depicted as unprotected within a coercive system that provided endless drudgery, while the protected American housewife was a consumer, with both "choices" and access to "labor-saving" household devices.

In the 1960s and 1970s, the civil rights, antiwar, student, and feminist movements coinciding with U.S. involvement in the *Vietnam War made the period paradoxically one of the most violent and hopeful in American history. Questions of racial justice, class disparities, gender equity, and the meanings of "manhood" and "womanhood" were actively debated amid the backdrop of nightly news coverage of American military involvement in Vietnam. As for women during World War I, the franchise as a right of citizens was again raised—this time by young men, drafted or volunteering for military service in Vietnam, whose age (below twenty-one) made them eligible to fight and die for their country but not to vote. The voting age was reduced to 18. Many young men during the 1960s engaged in serious debate about definitions of "manhood" and constructions of the duties and rights of male citizens. Those involved in the *Vietnam antiwar movement protested what they believed was an illegitimate war, and in so doing disrupted the historic link between male citizenship, American manhood, and military service.

*Conscientious objection to *conscription, draft card burnings, draft evasion, and participation in massive antiwar demonstrations, which marked a new definition of "manhood" for some American men, were met by accusations of cowardice, characterized as Communist sympathy, and decried by many in both Congress and the broader civilian population. This contestation over the meaning of American "manhood" and the obligations of male citizens was heightened by male veterans' creation of Vietnam Veterans Against the War. Some veterans decorated for valor literally threw away their medals to symbolize their rejection of those symbols conflating courage, manhood, and obligatory military service. A popular antiwar slogan, "Women say Yes to Men who say No," however, reinforced the conventional system of gender relations by placing women once again in the position of "bounty"—this time not for those who served but for those who did not.

The legacy of the Vietnam War was also gendered, as the first U.S. military "loss," and the first war in which a significant minority of American sons resisted the rite of passage to manhood that military service during wartime had historically provided to their fathers and grandfathers. It was also the first American war in which some veterans' return was an occasion for shaming—by both civilians and male veterans of "successful" American wars. This legacy would not be erased until the 1980s, first through Hollywood films portraying the "remasculinization" of America, such as the *Rambo* films in which a hypermasculine John Rambo "returned" to Vietnam, this time to "win" and, at least symbolically, restore the masculinity of those who had fought and lost. The most significant erasure of the Vietnam legacy, however, came in the shape of new conflicts (Grenada and Panama) and finally a new war that the United States could and did convincingly win: the *Persian Gulf War of 1991. The Gulf War, in all its glory, put to rest the memory of resistant sons and the broader antiwar discourse highlighted during the Vietnam conflict. Yet the Gulf War also made explicit new questions about the gendered nature of warfare, including renewed scrutiny of the "proper" roles of men and women during times of war in the context of the gender-integrated military.

[*See also* Disciplinary Views of War: Feminist and Gender Studies; Gender; Propaganda and Public Relations; Race Relations and War; Veterans; Vietnam War; Women in the Military.]

• Eric Leed, *No Man's Land: Combat and Identity in World War I*, 1979. Cynthia Enloe, *Does Khaki Become You?: The Militarization of Women's Lives*, 2nd ed. 1987. Margaret Randolph Higonnet, Jane Jenson, Sonya Michel, and Margaret Collins Wietz, eds., *Behind the Lines: Gender and the Two World Wars*, 1987. Elaine Tyler May, *Homeward Bound: American Families in the Cold War Era*, 1988. Susan Jeffords, *The Remasculinization of America: Gender and the Vietnam War*, 1989. Jean Bethke Elshtain, ed., *Women, Militarism, and War: Essays in History, Politics, and Social Theory*, 1990. Robert B. Westbrook, "'I Want a Girl, Just Like the Girl That Married Harry James': American Women and the Problem of Political Obligation in World War II," *American Quarterly*, 42, no. 4 (December 1990), pp. 587–616. Allan Bérubé, *Coming Out Under Fire: The History of Gay Men and Women During World War II*, 1991. Marilyn Young, *The Vietnam Wars: 1945–1990*, 1991. Catherine Clinton and Nina Silber, eds., *Divided Houses: Gender and the Civil War*, 1992. Miriam Cooke and Angela Woollacott, eds., *Gendering War Talk*, 1993.   —Leisa D. Meyer

GENERAL STAFF ACT (1903). The General Staff Act of 1903 culminated the reforms initiated by Secretary of War Elihu *Root and provided the U.S. Army with a central planning body. The immediate impetus for creating such an agency was the chaotic mobilization for the *Spanish-American War (1898). Since the Franco-Prussian War of 1870–71, 11 major powers had been creating some variant of the German General Staff. Root shepherded the legislation through Congress, but ran into opposition from congressional antimilitarists and Lieut. Gen. Nelson Miles, the commanding general of the army.

Miles helped to kill an ambitious general staff bill in 1902. A narrower law in 1903 provided for a small General Staff Corps, limited to forty-five officers and assigned to the War Department. It also sanctioned the Army War College, a planning entity that Root had created in 1900. The legislation replaced the commanding general with an army chief of staff, who supervised the staff corps and served as principal military adviser to the secretary of war. Congress required that the chief of staff serve for no more than four years and that the staff officers rotate out of Washington and into the field. The chiefs of existing bureaus such as the Quartermaster and Ordnance departments, and especially the Adjutant General's office, remained powerfully allied with Congress and worked to marginalize the general staff until U.S. entry into World War I.

• James E. Hewes, Jr., *From Root to McNamara: Army Organization and Administration 1900–1963*, 1975.   —Matthew Oyos

GENEVA AGREEMENT ON INDOCHINA (1954). The "Agreement on the Cessation of Hostilities in Viet-Nam" ended the eight-year war over the decolonization of Indochina between France and the Communist forces under the command of the leader of the League for Vietnamese Independence, *Ho Chi Minh. It was the result of an international conference held in Geneva between 8 May and 20 July 1954, following the fall of the French-held fortress at Dien Bien Phu and the collapse of the French military effort to retain control over their colonial empire in Southeast Asia.

The agreement provided for a cease-fire, established a provisional military demarcation line at the 17th parallel, empowered the two Vietnamese "parties" (later to be called North and South Vietnam) to administer their zones of control, and called for "general elections which will bring about the unification of Viet-Nam" in July 1956. The representatives of the United States and of the state of Vietnam (which was to become South Vietnam) refused to sign the agreement. Three other agreements were issued, providing for cease-fires in Laos and Cambodia and relating to international inspection arrangements. Conference participants also made seven declarations about intended compliance with the agreement.

The outcome at Geneva was a product largely of secret negotiations between China's foreign minister Zhou Enlai and Pierre Mendès-France, the new prime minister of France. Mendès-France had publicly denounced the war for some time; on taking office in June, he staked his prime ministership on achieving a "satisfactory solution" within four weeks.

The outcome, however, sowed the seeds of future war and ultimate intervention by U.S. military forces. The People's Republic of China used the threat of withholding future aid to the new Vietnamese Communist state to force the leaders in Hanoi to reach a settlement that ceded authority over much less than Ho Chi Minh's forces had actually won on the battlefield. Zhou thought he had written into the agreement a process leading to the eventual unification of the two Vietnams and the consolidation of Communist political control that would deny the United States any future pretext to intervene in Indochina, where its forces could then threaten China.

The final declaration of the conference, 21 July 1954, called for a prohibition on "the introduction into Viet-Nam of foreign troops and military personnel as well as of all kinds of arms and munitions." This provision was aimed at preventing U.S. aid from shoring up what was perceived to be a weak and also temporary government in the South. In fact, President Dwight D. *Eisenhower began to provide military aid in October 1954, and U.S. military advisers to train South Vietnamese forces began arriving in February 1955.

Eisenhower, who rejected French requests for U.S. air support when they were under siege at Dien Bien Phu, responded much more positively to the request from the new South Vietnamese government under Prime Minister Ngo Dinh Diem for help, and was persuaded by his secretary of state, John Foster *Dulles, that it was important for South Vietnam to serve as bulwark against communism in Asia. Dulles was also against holding the prescribed plebiscite called for in the agreement on grounds that the elections in the North would not be conducted fairly and that the communists would win an overwhelming political victory.

By 1957, the Soviet Union, in part to weaken China's influence in Southeast Asia, proposed that the *United Nations admit Vietnam as "two separate states ... which differ from one another in political and economic structure." The United States rejected this proposal, refusing to recognize any Communist country.

The negotiations surrounding the Geneva Agreement also prompted the United States to take the lead in forming a regional collective security pact "to deter and if necessary combat Communist aggression." The Southeast Asia Treaty Organization (SEATO) was organized in Manila in September 1954, and placed South Vietnam under its protection. A month earlier, the *SEATO Treaty was debated in the U.S. National Security Council, where Secretary of State Dulles explained that a "line against aggression" needed to be drawn "to include Laos, Cambodia, and South Vietnam on our side."

[*See also* Vietnam War: Causes.]

• R. B. Smith, *An International History of the Vietnam War*, Vol. I: *Revolution versus Containment, 1955–1961*, 1983. William J. Duiker, *U.S. Containment Policy and the Conflict in Indochina*, 1994.   —Allan E. Goodman

GENEVA AGREEMENT ON LAOS (1962). In Southeast Asia, Laos had descended by 1961 into a threeway civil war that was becoming internationalized as part of the *Cold War. Struggling to control the country were Pathet Lao Communists, backed by North Vietnam and the Soviet Union; Souvanna Phouma's neutralist Laotian government, which at times enjoyed the favor of the Soviet Union, the People's Republic of China (PRC), and the United States; and a revolutionary committee headed by Gen. Phoumi Nosavan, which received covert support from the U.S. *Central Intelligence Agency (CIA).

The administration of President John F. *Kennedy believed that geography made Laos a poor place to use military force to stop the spread of communism in Southeast Asia. Pathet Lao advances, however, suggested that covert U.S. support would be insufficient to save General Nosavan or prevent Souvanna Pouma from falling under the sway of the Communists. Several military actions were considered to stem a Pathet Lao victory; the most drastic proposal called for 60,000 American soldiers to occupy southern Laos.

On 11 May 1961, Soviet and British officials defused the impending crisis in Laos by orchestrating a truce and by reactivating the International Control Commission (associated with the 1954 *Geneva Agreement on Indochina that led to the division of Vietnam). Five days later, a second Geneva conference was convened by the PRC, Cambodia, France, Laos, the Soviet Union, Great Britain, the United States, South Vietnam, North Vietnam, India, Canada, Poland, Burma, and Thailand. The negotiations led to the 23 July 1962 Declaration and Protocol on the Neutrality of Laos. These second Geneva accords called for a peaceful, neutral, independent, and democratic Laos, and for the removal of foreign military units from Laotian soil.

Hope faded quickly that the accords would lead to real neutralization, although the agreement reflected a tacit understanding that conflict in Laos would remain limited. The North Vietnamese preferred to use the country to infiltrate soldiers and material into South Vietnam. The United States, which concentrated its efforts in Vietnam, used a CIA-led army of Laotian Hmong tribesmen to harass North Vietnamese infiltrators in Laos. The Geneva accords helped turn Laos into a sideshow to the Vietnam War, but they did not save the Laotian people from years of bloodshed.

[*See also* Vietnam War.]

• Timothy N. Castle, *At War in the Shadow of Vietnam: U.S. Military Aid to the Royal Lao Government 1955–1975*, 1993.
                                                          —James J. Wirtz

GENEVA CONVENTIONS (1864). The Geneva Convention of 22 August 1864 was the world's first multilateral humanitarian treaty. Sixteen nations were present, responding to public concern about the sufferings of sick and wounded soldiers, well publicized by the labors of Flo-

rence Nightingale in the Crimean War, Clara *Barton and the U.S. *Sanitary Commission in the American *Civil War, and the dramatic book *The Memory of Solferino* (1862) by Henry Dunant, a Swiss, about the casualties at the Battle of Solferino in 1859. Dunant and four other Genevan philanthropists had already launched, in October 1863, what would become the international Red Cross movement. Now the twelve initial signatories bound their armies to respect and protect the lives and workplaces of each other's ambulance and medical personnel; to incorporate volunteer auxiliaries into their medical corps; and to signify their virtual neutrality by a protective emblem, "a red cross on a white ground." The United States acceded to the convention in 1882.

Its consequences were mixed. The popularity of national Red Cross societies actually facilitated social mobilization for war purposes. On the other hand, the convention set a valuable humanitarian precedent, of which the most obvious sequels were its successively extended versions of 1906, 1929, 1949, and 1977.

[*See also* Laws of War; Red Cross, American.]

• Dietrich Schindler and Jiri Toman, eds., *The Laws of Armed Conflicts: A Collection of Conventions, Resolutions and Other' Documents*, 1973; 2nd ed. 1981. John F. Hutchinson, *Champions of Charity: The Red Cross and the Great Powers*, 1995.
                                                          —Geoffrey Best

GENEVA PROTOCOL ON CHEMICAL WARFARE (1925). Widespread revulsion against the World War I use of poison gas led to the Geneva Protocol in 1925, restricting chemical warfare. The agreement, ratified by most powers, was rejected by Japan and by the U.S. Senate.

Senators blocked it despite popular belief that gas warfare was immoral and military skepticism of its value. Supporters of stockpiling chemical weapons, including the U.S. Army's Chemical Warfare Service, argued that any ban was ineffective and that possession of such weapons was the best deterrent. Still, U.S. presidents abided by the protocol, and the military did not obtain any toxins between 1922 and 1937.

At the outset of World War II, the allies announced adherence to the Geneva Protocol, but reserved the right to retaliate, a conditional pledge based on mutual restraint. In 1942, the British and Americans changed explicitly to deterrence, threatening massive retaliation if the Axis initiated chemical warfare. (The Nazis used gas to murder millions of Jews and other civilians during World War II, but Allied leaders did not consider that to be chemical warfare.)

The Geneva Protocol was subsequently weakened by its own ambiguous language, and by Soviet and American stockpiling of large quantities of chemical weapons during the Cold War. One of the main problems of enforcing a ban was how to prevent clandestine conversion of commercial pesticide plants to military use. In the 1990s, the Russians finally agreed to U.S. demands for short notice, on-site inspections, but by then chemical weapons were being stockpiled by fifteen to twenty other nations (Iraq, for example, used them against Iran).

A new Chemical Weapons Convention, prohibiting the production, storage, and use of poison gas, and providing for monitoring of the civilian chemical industry with systematic and also surprise inspections, was signed by President George *Bush in January 1993 after ten years of negotiations. Pressed by President Bill *Clinton and Senator Major Leader Trent Lott (Rep.-Miss.), the U.S. Senate overrode concerns from the chemical industry and from conservatives worried about North Korea, Iran, Iraq, and Syria, and ratified the treaty 74–26 on 24 April 1997. With seventy-five nations ratifying the treaty, it went into effect on 29 April 1997.

[*See also* Chemical and Biological Weapons and Warfare.]

• Frederick J. Brown, *United States Chemical Warfare Policy, 1919–1945: A Study of Restraints,* 1967. Stockholm International Peace Research Institute, *The Problem of Chemical and Biological Warfare: A Study of the Historical, Technical, Military, Legal and Political Aspects of CBW and Possible Disarmament Measures,* 6 vols., 1971–75.
—John Whiteclay Chambers II

GENOCIDE. The UN Genocide Convention, passed on 9 December 1948, defined genocide as "acts committed with intent to destroy in whole or in part, a national, ethnical, racial or religious group...." Although political groups were not included—due to objections by the Soviet Union and other nations—most students of genocide consider such acts against political groups as genocide. UN conventions and statements of principles have created a body of "international law," but enforcement mechanisms have been nonexistent, highly limited, or ad hoc, like the tribunals created to try perpetrators in Bosnia and Rwanda, and usually ineffective.

Perpetrators of genocide tend to offer justifications, such as destructive actions or intentions by the victims. Usually, these justifications are unfounded or greatly exaggerated; moreover, since old and young, women and children are killed, genocidal violence, even if partially defensive, is never morally justifiable. To understand the origins of genocide, it is necessary to consider societal conditions, the political system (genocide is less likely in a pluralistic, democratic society), cultural characteristics, the psychology of perpetrators and of internal bystanders (members of the society in which genocide takes place who are not themselves perpetrators), and the role of external bystanders (especially other nations).

Difficult social conditions are frequently the starting point for genocide. These are created by intense economic problems; by intense political conflict within a society—which can take varied forms, one of which is conflict between a dominant group and a subordinate group that is poor and has limited rights; or by very great and rapid social changes; or a combination of all these factors.

Under such conditions, people often scapegoat a subgroup of society for their problems, or create an ideology that promises a better life but identifies an enemy that stands in the way of its fulfillment. As the group or its members begin to harm the scapegoat or ideological enemy, they begin to change. Individuals and groups "learn by doing," changing as the result of their own actions. Perpetrators further devalue their victims, exclude them from the human and moral realm, and create institutions to harm and kill them. An evolution of increasing violence leads to genocide.

All this is more likely to happen in cultures with certain characteristics. One of these is a history of devaluation of the group that becomes the victim. Cultural devaluation is usually deeply set and becomes influential when conditions are difficult, as was the case with anti-Semitism in Nazi Germany in the 1930s. At times instead of devaluation by one group of another there is a history of conflict and violence between two groups, and intense mutual antagonism, as was the case in both Rwanda and Bosnia, in the 1990s. Other characteristics of culture that make the genocidal process probable include a strong respect for authority, a monolithic rather than pluralistic society, certain ways members of a group see their group, and a history of violence in dealing with conflict.

The evolution toward genocide is usually made possible by the passivity of both internal and external bystanders. Their passivity affirms the perpetrators. Early strong reactions by bystanders, such as protests, boycotts, and sanctions, occurring before the perpetrators have developed strong commitment to their ideology and murderous course, could inhibit this evolution.

There is a history of passivity. While internal enemies and the Jews were increasingly persecuted in Nazi Germany, all nations went to Berlin to participate in the 1936 Olympics. At the same time, U.S. corporations did business in Germany. Jews were kept out of the United States—only about one-tenth of the legal quota of Jewish immigrants was filled. During World War II, the Allies refused to bomb Auschwitz or the railroad leading to it. At the time of the genocide of the Armenians by the Turks in World War I, the United States had limited influence over Turkey, but Germany, Turkey's supporter and ally, did nothing. In Cambodia in the 1970s, U.S. actions destabilized the country. Once the Communist Khmer Rouge took over, the United States had little influence over Pol Pot's genocidal regime. However, after Vietnam invaded Cambodia and stopped the genocide, the United States showed strong hostility toward Vietnam and joined with China to insist that the Khmer Rouge government was the legitimate representative of Cambodia in the *United Nations. In the 1980s, the United States supported Iraq against Iran, even though it was using chemical weapons against its Kurdish citizens. Washington turned against Iraq only after it invaded Kuwait.

Early nonviolent actions by the community of nations might have inhibited the evolution and continuation of violence in the former Yugoslavia. However, the bombing of Serb positions in Bosnia, and the subsequent peacekeeping role of *NATO and the United States, set a positive precedent.

The influences that give rise to genocide create other forms of violence between groups as well, including mass killings, and, at times, war. In the course of the evolution described above the targets of violence may expand, to other groups within a country, or to other countries. In Argentina, the murder of dissenters in the late 1970s was followed by the Falklands War. At times war provides a cover for genocide, or its violence makes genocide easier to commit, as it did in Nazi Germany, 1939–45, and in Turkey, 1915–16.

Cultural characteristics and political organization in the United States now make genocide unlikely, yet the history of exclusion of Native Americans and African Americans from the public domain rendered violence against them probable. The violence in the United States against Native Americans is perhaps best described not as genocide but as group violence, including mass killings. However, genocide and mass killing have fuzzy boundaries. Intense devaluation, self-interest in gaining territory, conflict and mutual antagonism, and learning-by-doing probably all shared roles in the violence against Native Americans.

[See also Atrocities; Bosnian Crisis; Holocaust, U.S. War Effort and the; Native American Wars: Wars Between Native Americans and Europeans and Euro-Americans; War Crimes.]

• Bernard W. Sheehan, Seeds of Extinction, 1973. David S. Wyman, The Abandonment of Jew: America and the Holocaust, 1941–1945, 1984. Ervin Staub, The Roots of Evil: The Origins of Genocide and Other Group Violence, 1989. Helen Fein, Genocide: A Sociological Perspective, 1993.   —Ervin Staub

GEORGE III (1738–1820), king of Great Britain. George III ascended the throne in 1760 upon the sudden death of his grandfather, George II, with whom he was politically at odds. He was a member of the House of Hanover, an ethnic German family that succeeded to the British throne in 1714. The new king tended to defer to his ministers' advice, especially in colonial matters. He was not averse to conciliation, provided that it did not diminish the authority of king and Parliament. In 1766, he backed the repeal of the Stamp Act. After the Boston Tea Party in 1774, however, his willingness to compromise vanished. The king supported the Coercive Acts of that year and adamantly rejected the colonists' argument that they could disobey Parliament while remaining loyal to the king.

George III became a fervent advocate of the war against the Americans. He participated minimally in the war's actual planning and management, but he used his influence to commit his government and his people to enforcing the colonies' obedience. During the Revolutionary War, the king never wavered in his support of Lord North, his chief minister (1770–1782), and his backing delayed the emergence of an opposition party strong enough to bring down North's ministry and foster a compromise.

Perhaps George III's most significant contribution to the American Revolution was his presence as a symbol of British sovereignty—and, ultimately, tyranny. The patriot leaders always insisted, down to 1776, on their loyalty to the crown, as the only legitimate link between America and Great Britain. Hence the Declaration of Independence indicted the king, rather than Parliament, for Britain's misdeeds. George III's rhetorical transformation from symbol of monarchical benevolence to tyrant provided the ultimate justification for revolution. After 1784, George III largely retired from an active role in government. He suffered a nervous breakdown in 1788–89; when he was declared insane in 1810, his son was appointed regent.

• Stanley Ayling, George III, 1972.   —Jon T. Coleman

GERMANY, BATTLE FOR (1945). During the 1945 battle for Germany, the Americans effectively led the World War II Allied effort in the West; but in accommodating the Soviets, whose Red Army was invading from the East, they won military victory at a great geopolitical cost.

As their armies recovered from the temporary reverses suffered in late 1944 during the liberation of *France and the Battle of the *Bulge, the American, British, Canadian, and other generals agreed upon certain key objectives of the forthcoming campaign for Germany. By late January 1945, the Anglo-American armies had 4 million men, two-thirds of them American; the Soviet armies numbered nearly 7 million. The Western Allies were preparing to

seize the Ruhr, home of much of the German armaments industry. The North German plain with its Baltic ports was also a major target. The Allies further desired to strike at other points along the Rhenish front so as to envelop the Wehrmacht. After achieving their initial aims, they would then race through the heart of Germany, perhaps effecting a junction with the Soviet forces but certainly bringing about an end to the European War.

And yet considerable discord existed. British Field Marshal Bernard Law *Montgomery expressed contempt for Supreme Allied Commander Dwight D. *Eisenhower's deliberate, "broad front" tactics. Montgomery insisted that he should command not only the British and Canadian troops but two U.S. armies and make what he predicted would be a rapid, concentrated thrust through the Rhine Valley north of the Ruhr and eventually on to Berlin itself. He and fellow British generals—joined by some postwar British historians—believed "Ike" to have been vacillating and unreliable. But the American generals as well as their troops disliked Montgomery and did not want to serve under him. To them, "too-tidy Monty" wasted too much time in campaign preparation and sometimes failed to carry through. And they resented his attitude toward Eisenhower.

As most historians have concluded, Eisenhower tactfully but decisively exercised a firm command. He resolved disputes among contentious generals while maintaining tight discipline. Throughout the battle for Germany, Ike listened to advice but made his own choices.

Although both American and British units had entered Germany as early as 12 September 1944, the first massive crossings of the Rhine occurred in March 1945. After capturing 250,000 prisoners and inflicting 60,000 German casualties while on the west bank, the Allies searched for bridgeheads over the river. On 7 March elements of the U.S. Ninth Army found a lightly defended span at Remagen, and within a day 8,000 Americans stood on the eastern shore of the Rhine. Within several more days, not only the Remagen bridgehead but also many others made possible the crossing of all 7 Allied armies, primarily because 62 bridges were constructed by 75,000 men of the U.S. *Army Corps of Engineers. By 25 March the greatest aggregation of armor ever assembled in Western Europe was bearing down upon the Reich.

The double envelope of the Ruhr then proceeded with brilliant success. Courtney Hodges's First U.S. Army and William Simpson's Ninth caught the Reichswehr forces inside a circle of 80 miles diameter. With tremendous air, artillery, and naval support, the fast-moving Allied armored columns forced 400,000 German troops to surrender. By early April 1945 German resistance was futile, and Adolf *Hitler had neither the materiel nor the personnel to block the Allied armies from the West or the Soviets from the East.

While British and Canadian troops advanced through North Germany after sealing off Holland and Denmark, and French soldiers moved through the south, the Ninth U.S. Army stormed to within 63 miles of Berlin by 21 April. Further south, George S. *Patton's Third Army achieved even more spectacular results, sometimes covering 100 miles a day, as it took Frankfurt on 27 March and raged through Czechoslovakia, Bavaria, and Austria during April. The U.S. Seventh Army headed south, and in early May, at the Brenner Pass, linked with American troops from the former Italian theater of war. On 25 April, the historic meeting of Soviet patrols with advance units of the American Ninth Army occurred at Torgau on the Elbe River, the prearranged meeting place.

Overwhelming power and logistic skill were primarily responsible for the American success. The U.S. Army had enormous numerical advantages in manpower, tanks, and artillery, and the supportive air forces commanding the skies could disrupt German industry, troop movements, and supplies. The Army Corps of Engineers used their bridging equipment effectively, and the Army Air Force—with more than 1,600 "flying boxcars" and other aircraft—transported 60,000 tons of supplies, including 10 million gallons of gasoline, to the rapidly advancing front during April 1945.

Unwilling to risk American and other Allied lives in an attack upon Berlin since the Soviets had been promised a postwar occupation zone, Eisenhower, under orders from Washington, restrained the Allied armies at the Elbe River, thus allowing the Red Army to seize Berlin, East Germany, and additional territory in Central Europe.

The invasion of Germany also led to the liberation of the German concentration and death camps. Generals Eisenhower and Omar N. *Bradley personally visited Ohrdruf on 12 April, and soon Buchenwald, Dachau, and several others were liberated. To the world, the Americans exposed these ghastly horrors of Nazi cruelty, causing shock and revulsion.

For Germany, there was only complete and humiliating defeat. As the Red Army battled into Berlin, Hitler committed suicide there on 30 April 1945. At the command of his successor, Grand Admiral Karl Doenitz, Field Marshal Alfred Jodl went to Eisenhower's forward headquarters in Reims, France, and signed an unconditional surrender of 7 May. Josef *Stalin demanded a second signing in Berlin on 8 May, which was hailed as V-E Day—Victory in Europe Day—marking the formal end of the war in Europe. On 5 June 1945, Germany was placed under an Allied Control Council and divided into four occupation zones.

[See also Germany, U.S. Military Involvement in; Holocaust, U.S. War Effort and the; World War II: Military and Diplomatic Course; World War II: U.S. Air Operations in: The Air War in Europe.]

• John Toland, The Last 100 Days: The Final Fighting in Europe, 1966. Hubert Essame, The Battle for Germany, 1969. Alfred D. Chandler, ed., The Papers of Dwight David Eisenhower, Vol. Vı The War Years, 1970. Russell F. Weigley, Eisenhower's Lieutenants: The Campaign for France and Germany, 1944–1945, 1981. Stephen E. Ambrose, Eisenhower, 1983. Gerhard L. Weinberg, A World at Arms, 1994.
—Richard Anderson

GERMANY, U.S. MILITARY INVOLVEMENT IN. American military involvement in or with Germany has followed a mixed course over the past two centuries. Initial American sympathy for German unification in 1871 in appreciation of German support for the Union in the *Civil War was transformed as Germany evolved into an autocratic and militaristic state, dominated by a blustering kaiser, *Wilhelm II. Imperial Germany soon became a rival of the United States as both nations embarked on rapid industrialization and expansion of their world trade, built large navies, and began to engage in overseas expansion. Although the Americans were concerned with competitive German ambitions in Latin America, Asia, and the Pacific, the primary threat was seen as potential German hegemony that would upset the balance of power in Europe.

When World War I broke out in 1914, Americans were divided, and President Woodrow *Wilson declared *neutrality. Though the United States remained legally neutral until 1917, its trade and financial support with the Allies grew dramatically. Eventually, Berlin's decision for unrestricted *submarine warfare brought the United States into the war in April 1917 to prevent German hegemony and to establish a stable world order. The arrival of masses of fresh American troops in 1918 helped halt the German's spring offensive and fuel the Allies' counteroffensive, which led German military commanders to ask Berlin to obtain an armistice. Wilson refused to deal with the monarchy and a republic was established before the armistice was concluded 11 November 1918. U.S. troops participated in the temporary occupation of the Rhineland, 1918–23.

Although Wilson wanted some leniency for Germany because he supported the new Weimar Republic and because he feared Communist expansion from Eastern to Central Europe, the Allies imposed harsh terms in the Treaty of *Versailles in 1919. Weimar had to accept them, but it then sought American help in the 1920s to ameliorate them. The U.S. Senate rejected the treaty because of provisions for the *League of Nations, but made a separate peace with Germany. Politically isolationist in the 1920s, the United States aided Weimar economically by giving it most-favored-nation status and reducing its reparations payments, especially through the Dawes Plan of 1924; and American investments helped to stimulate the German economy, but this ended with the stock market crash of 1929 and the Great Depression.

The end of the Weimar Republic and the establishment of Adolf *Hitler's Nazi dictatorship in 1933 rekindled American concern about the geostrategic and moral threat posed by an aggressively expansionist, antidemocratic Germany, Hitler's Third Reich (Third Empire). Nevertheless, antiwar sentiment led an isolationist Congress to adopt legislation emphasizing U.S. *neutrality in 1935, 1936, and 1937.

After the outbreak of World War II in 1939, President Franklin D. *Roosevelt followed an anti-German course. The United States became the "great arsenal of democracy," supplying the Allies, occupying Greenland and Iceland, and patrolling the North Atlantic, even engaging in actions with German submarines. On 11 December 1941, four days after the attack on *Pearl Harbor, Hitler declared war on the United States. Unlike World War I, the United States fully joined the Allies against Germany and gradually took the lead in directing Western military operations. To avoid a resurgent militarized Germany and to reassure the Soviet Union, which bore the brunt of the land war, the Allies insisted on unconditional surrender. Roosevelt considered postwar dismemberment and deindustrialization of Germany (the Morgenthau Plan of 1944), but abandoned the idea as creating a power vacuum in Central Europe.

After the Battle for *Germany and Berlin's surrender in May 1945, Allied policies included occupation, denazification, and demilitarization in order to eliminate the threat of a resurgent aggressive Germany. Gen. Lucius *Clay was the U.S. military occupation commander. *Cold War conflict with the Soviet Union led the United States to seek German economic revival and press the Western Allies to merge their occupation zones. Soviet resistance through a blockade of divided Berlin in the Russian zone in 1948 was overcome by the *Berlin Airlift (1948–1949).

In May 1949, the Federal Republic of Germany (West Germany) was established as much as possible in the political image of the American republic. Initially, West Germany had limited domestic and foreign authority, and the Allies retained supervision and military bases. Under Konrad Adenauer (chancellor, 1949–63), West Germany received massive *Marshall Plan aid, was rearmed, and was made a member of the North Atlantic Treaty Organization (*NATO) in 1955; U.S. policy was to integrate Germany into Europe as a bastion against the expansion of Soviet influence and control. The Soviets converted their zone into the German Democratic Republic (GDR) in 1949 and made it part of the *Warsaw Pact in 1955.

Beginning in the 1950s, as part of the U.S. commitment to NATO, large numbers of American troops and weapons were stationed in Germany. These included *nuclear weapons by the mid-1950s. In the *Berlin Crises (1958, 1962) President John F. *Kennedy protested but acquiesced when the Russians built a wall around Berlin in 1961. With the growth of U.S. and Soviet nuclear ICBM arsenals in the 1960s, the American troops in West Germany took on the added role of guarantor of the U.S. commitment to Central European defense, with the partnership between the United States and West Germany becoming the military core of NATO after France withdrew in 1966. That partnership became strained in the early 1980s when the USSR and the United States deployed a new generation of intermediate-range nuclear *missiles in the two Germanies.

The fall of the Berlin Wall in November 1989, and the reunification of Germany with the consent of the four former occupying powers, accompanied the collapse of the Soviet empire and the end of the Cold War. As the United States reduced its military prescence in Germany, NATO expanded its original political purpose of linking the United States to Europe and Germany to the West by expanding that linkage beyond Germany into newly democratizing states in Eastern Europe.

• John Gimbel, *The American Occupation of Germany: Politics and the Military, 1945–1949*, 1968. Keith L. Nelson, *Victors Divided: America and the Allies in Germany, 1989–1923*, 1975. David Calleo, *The German Problem Reconsidered: Germany and the World Order, 1870 to the Present*, 1978. Hans W. Gatzke, *Germany and the United States: A "Special Relationship"?*, 1980. Manfred Jonas, *The United States and Germany: A Diplomatic History*, 1984. Wolfram F. Hanrieder, *Germany, America, Europe: Forty Years of German Foreign Policy*, 1989, 2nd ed. 1991. Frank Ninkovich, *Germany and the United States: The Transformation of the German Question Since 1945*, 1995.
—Manfred Jonas

GERONIMO (1823?–1909), Apache Indian leader. To North Americans and Mexicans of the 1870s and 1880s, Geronimo personalized the horrors of Apache warfare. Never a chief, and despised by many of his people, he nonetheless attained leadership through mastery of the partisan fighting style that baffled U.S. and Mexican troops. In cunning, stealth, endurance, perseverance, ruthlessness, fortitude, fighting skill, and command of the harsh conditions of his homeland, he excelled. With small followings, he alternated between reservation life in Arizona and raids from Mexico's Sierra Madre. In 1882, Brig. Gen. George Crook, relying heavily on Apache scouts and pack mules, penetrated the Sierra Madre and obtained

Geronimo's surrender. In 1885, however, Geronimo again took refuge in Mexico. Again Crook and his scouts pursued, and again Geronimo surrendered. But he had second thoughts, and fled to the mountains.

Crook, his methods under fire from Washington, asked to be relieved. Brig. Gen. Nelson A. Miles took his place, but eventually had to adopt Crook's unorthodox approach. Geronimo surrendered to Miles at Skeleton Canyon, Arizona, on 4 September 1886. Confined in Florida, Alabama, and finally near Fort Sill in present-day Oklahoma, he became a celebrity in parades and expositions. Pneumonia took his life in his eighty-sixth year.

• Angie Debo, *Geronimo: The Man, His Time, His Place*, 1976.
—Robert M. Utley

GETTYSBURG, BATTLE OF (1863). One of the most decisive battles of the *Civil War raged from July 1–3 1863 at Gettysburg, Pennsylvania. General Robert E. *Lee decided to invade Pennsylvania and threaten Harrisburg, Baltimore, and Washington, not only to carry the war to the enemy but also to relieve the pressure on the siege of *Vicksburg. The *Confederate Army of Northern Virginia, 75,000 strong, crossed the Potomac in June and the *Union Army of the Potomac, 88,000 strong, moved to stay between the Rebels and Washington. Command of the Union army had been given to Gen. George Gordon *Meade on June 28 and he determined to find and fight Lee.

Union and Confederate troops met each other near Gettysburg. Rebels were looking for shoes and other supplies; Yanks were looking for Rebs. Fighting erupted near Gettysburg early on 1 July as outnumbered Union cavalry under John Buford skirmished with Rebel infantry. Reinforcements came to both sides, but by afternoon, Union Maj. Gen. John Reynolds had been killed and Federal troops retired southeastward from the town to Cemetery Hill and Cemetery Ridge. Lee arrived and vainly urged Lt. Gen. Richard S. *Ewell to attack Cemetery Hill. This wasted chance gave Meade time to get his army set in a fish-hook line, with his right anchored on Culp's Hill, the center on Cemetery Ridge and the left on a hill later called Little Round Top. Lee's men deployed during the night along the lower Seminary Ridge to the west. The first day went to the Rebels, but at high human cost.

Daylight on 2 July showed the two armies formed, with open country yawning between the lines. The initiative was with Lee, who ordered Lieutenant General James *Longstreet's Corps to attack the Union left while Ewell's corps struck the Union right at Culp's Hill and Cemetery Ridge.

Lee's orders were delayed and compliance lagged (the source of much controversy later); Longstreet, Lee's "Warhorse," opposed the plan (he thought the Confederate army should move south, get between Meade and Washington, pick a good defensive spot and receive attack); troops were shifted, time passed.

While the Confederates were shuffling their plans, Union III Corps commander Maj. Gen. Dan *Sickles, worried about being flanked, initiated an advance into the Peace Orchard, Devil's Den, almost to the Emmitsburg Road between the two forces—and, hence, offered a weak salient to the enemy.

The whole Union line depended on the left flank position at Little Round Top—a fact noticed by Meade's chief engineer, Maj. Gen. G. K. Warren, who was horrified to see that hill unoccupied. Warren saved the day by pulling in brigades and batteries just as Longstreet's men charged Little and Big Round Top and nearly took the high ground. The Twentieth Maine, under Col. Joshua Chamberlain, held out against furious Confederate attacks and saved the flank. Longstreet's efforts against the Peach Orchard, the Wheatfield, Devil's Den, the lower slopes of the Round Tops and on to the Emmitsburg road were successful and Sickles finally retreated to Cemetery Ridge.

About dusk, too late to help Longstreet, Maj. Gen. Jubal A. Early, of Ewell's corps, fiercely attacked the Union right at East Cemetery Hill and nearly took the crest. No help came to Early and he abandoned the hill at about 10 P.M. A similar fate, at roughly the same time, met Maj. Gen. Edward Johnson's energetic divisional drive against Yankee positions on Culp's Hill.

Fighting on 2 July went to neither side but casualties were high and controversies were brewing: Longstreet's efforts were slow, Lee's attacks uncoordinated; Sickles had blundered and the Union high command had nearly missed the importance of Little Round Top.

Meade, steady in crisis, suffered uncertainty as night fell on 2 July. His left and right had held. Would Lee try them again or switch to the center? Or would the wily Rebel leader simply slip away and appear somewhere closer to Harrisburg or Washington? Calling his corps commanders together after midnight, Meade discussed possibilities. Unlike his predecessors, Meade did not urge retreat; instead he decided to wait for Lee's next move. He expected a strong Rebel attack on his center and ordered men and artillery there from the flanks. Union morale remained high.

Lee was not well. Stomach trouble plagued him and he had chest problems. Illness, and Gen. J.E.B. ("Jeb") *Stuart's absence on a wagon hunting raid with most of the cavalry, edged Lee's temper and subordinates noted him unusually touchy that night. By morning his temper was shorter. He had decided to test the Union center, since the flanks were strong. This decision irked Longstreet, who felt the center would be tougher than the rest of the line. Why hit the one untouched Union position on the field? Why a frontal attack against so many visible enemy guns? Unmoved, Lee ordered Maj. Gen. George Pickett's division of Longstreet's corps, with some of Gen. A. P. *Hill's units, to attack on 3 July.

On the third day, Confederates who participated in "Pickett's Charge" and lived to tell about it, recalled that 143 Southern guns bristled in the lines and that the sun etched things sharply. It was a strange kind of day, one fragmented by small memories. Men noted the flights of birds, some listened to a band, many lay on soft ground and waited as Federal shells probed the trees on Seminary Ridge, and many of them died. One, a sergeant in Company A, 14th Tennessee, could hear, years later, the things he said to himself. June Kimble was his name, his was a center regiment, and he was curious. In a lull after a morning shelling he walked to the fringe of the woods and looked at the place his men would go. Guns crowning the Federal hills, the little clump of trees that fixed so many an eye that day, the low stone wall thronging with bluecoats—the whole position lay shimmering far away across almost a mile of open, rolling land. There, up there, into that line of black guns behind the low stone wall, there his men would go. Kimble was scared, almost sick at the sight, and

began mumbling to himself: "June Kimble, are you going to do your duty today?" And he answered, "I'll do it, so help me God."

Confederate artillery started a thunderous and wasteful artillery duel in the early afternoon that lasted almost two hours. Union fire slacked off—both to conserve shells and to fool the Rebels into thinking that the Southern guns commanded the field. During a lull in the bombardment a grandly mounted General Pickett scratched a brief note to his fiancee, talked briefly to Longstreet, then rode to one of gallantry's last great gestures.

Confederates came out of the woods at about 3:15 P.M. Yankees counted many battle flags; and noted the formation was trim as the enemy march began slowly, to allow for distance and rising ground. Some direction changes were accomplished by the 12,000 to 15,000 Southerners marching. Silence. Union gunners waited. Steadily the "Johnny Rebs" marched, lines dressed and closing. Across a small stream they went, through a fence, then straight up the hill toward the trees, the guns, the infantry. Men remembered how it was on the way; to some the silence crowned the world, then broke in a clap so awful it was more than sound, in a roar so angry it was tangible, in an endless crack of doom. Union shells raked lines, cut gaps in ranks; the gaps closed, the lines moved on, faster; men leaned forward against some great wind that winnowed them, bunching as Yankee batteries ate away the flanks. Then they ran, crouched, flags waving as they began their "Rebel yell." Some stopped to fire near the wall at the little clump of trees, took a withering volley right in the face, recoiled, went on and carried the wall. Then the charge faded in carnage. "Men fire into each other's faces," a witness wrote. "There are bayonet-thrusts, sabre-strokes, pistol shots; ... men ... spinning around like tops, throwing out their arms, gulping up blood, falling, legless, armless, headless ... ghastly heaps of dead men...." A handful, maybe 300, rode the Southern tide to its height; most of them died in an angle by the clump of trees, including Confederate Gen. Lewis A. Armistead.

Back down the slope scarcely 5,000 survivors fled, razed and raked and maimed again. Many heard Lee greet them. "All this is my fault. Too bad! Too bad! Oh, TOO BAD!"

Meade wasted a chance to counterattack, and two days later on a rainy night, Lee began a woeful journey back to Virginia with a wounded column seven miles long.

An incredulous President Abraham *Lincoln fumed that Lee's army had escaped. "We had them within our grasp," he lamented. "We had only to stretch forth our hands and they were ours." He blamed Meade's excessive caution. Although Meade had a fresh corps available for pursuit, his caution came from his own casualties as well as appreciation of local conditions. More than 3,155 bluecoats were dead, 14,529 wounded and 5,365 missing—a total of 23,049, about a quarter of Meade's force. More than 2,500 Rebels were dead, nearly 13,000 wounded and almost 5,500 missing—some 21,000, or nearly a third of Lee's army, along with 25,000 weapons. Lee's men reached Virginia on 13 July.

Lincoln's anguish was understandable. Vicksburg, the main Rebel bastion on the Mississippi, fell on 4 July, and had Meade destroyed Lee's army, the twin victories might have ended the war.

Gettysburg nonetheless stands as America's greatest battle; it stopped further Confederate invasions, and the

South could never make up the losses in men and equipment. The tide of the war had changed.

[See also Civil War: Military and Diplomatic Course; Gettysburg National Military Park.]

• George R. Stewart, *Pickett's Charge: A Microhistory of the Final Attack at Gettysburg, July 3, 1863,* 1959. Edwin B. Coddington, *The Gettysburg Campaign: A Study in Command,* 1968. Michael Shaara, *The Killer Angels: A Novel,* 1974. Harry W. Pfanz, *Gettysburg: The Second Day,* 1987. Alice Rains Trulock, *In the Hands of Providence: Joshua L. Chamberlain and the American Civil War,* 1992. Harry W. Pfanz, *Gettysburg: Culp's Hill and Cemetery Hill,* 1993. Richard Rollins, ed., *Picketts Charge: Eyewitness Accounts,* 1994. Carol Reardon, *Pickett's Charge in History and Memory,* 1997. Gabor S. Boritt, ed., *The Gettysburg Nobody Knows,* 1997.

—Frank E. Vandiver

GETTYSBURG NATIONAL MILITARY PARK. The nucleus for the park began shortly after the Battle of *Gettysburg, when the state-sponsored Gettysburg Battlefield Memorial Association sought to raise private funds for a permanent Soldier's National Cemetery there. In October 1863, the association began exhuming 3,354 bodies of Union soldiers for permanent burial on a site at the edge of the battlefield. In November 1864, at the dedication ceremonies for the cemetery, President Abraham *Lincoln delivered what later became known as the "Gettysburg Address," a brief address in which he defined American democracy and sanctified the war for the Union.

In 1895, in order to forestall railroad lines being built through the battlefield, Congress established the Gettysburg National Military Park. The National Park Service succeeded the War Department in administering the site in 1933. In 1972, a controversial privately owned observation tower was constructed. Many preservationists and Civil War organizations continue to express alarm over the commercialization of parts of the battlefield not under federal control.

Despite its national symbolism, the battlefield retained strong regional and local ties. State governments and veterans' groups, on both sides, erected commemorative statues, markers, and other memorials. For decades, *Civil War *veterans gathered at Gettysburg for reunions, which by the 1890s often included ex-Confederates. In recent years, reenactments have taken place outside the park boundaries, except for the motion picture *Gettysburg* (1993), which was filmed inside the park.

[See also Battlefields, Encampments, and Forts as Public Sites; Cemeteries, Military Commemoration and Public Ritual.]

• John S. Patterson, "A Patriotic Landscape: Gettysburg, 1863–1913," *Prospects,* 7 (1982), pp. 315–33. Edward Tabor Linenthal, *Sacred Ground: Americans and Their Battlefields,* 1991. Garry Wills, *Lincoln at Gettysburg,* 1992.

—G. Kurt Piehler

GIAP, VO NGUYEN (1910–), North Vietnamese general and government minister. Born into a family of small landowners in Quang Binh, Central Vietnam, Giap had an early education in Chinese, followed by one in French. Involved in student political disturbances of 1926, he was expelled from school. Thereafter, he joined the New Vietnam Revolutionary party advocating independence from French rule. In the 1930s, he was a political prisoner for two years and became a member of the Indochinese Communist Party. He also became a history teacher and a journalist who campaigned for press freedom and the diffusion of the national language. In 1939, he wrote a book on the military situation in China and co-authored another about Vietnamese peasants. Two years later, he joined *Ho Chi Minh in China and learned more about *guerrilla warfare.

Back in Vietnam by 1944, Giap helped to organize the Viet Minh forces, the nucleus of the Vietnam People's Army (VPA), in order to oust the Japanese and, after World War II, the French. After the August 1945 revolution, he held a number of posts in the Democratic Republic of Vietnam, including minister for defense and commander in chief of the VPA. In 1954, he overrode Chinese tactical advice and decisively defeated the French in the battle for Dien Bien Phu. From 1958, Giap as vice premier (1955) envisaged development of the Ho Chi Minh Trail to supply South Vietnamese insurgents. An authority on guerrilla warfare, General Giap had a major influence on strategy in the war against American and/south Vietnamese forces. His many books include *People's War People's Army* (1961), and *The Military Art of People's War* (1970).

He began to shed his military posts in 1976, and became minister for science and technology. During an interview he gave Greg Lockhart in Hanoi in 1989, he stated that he had become "a general of peace."

[See also Vietnam War.]

• R. J. O'Neill, *General Giap,* 1969. Peter MacDonald, *Giap: Victor in Vietnam,* 1994.

—Greg Lockhart

The **G.I. BILL** (1944) was a series of benefits for World War II *veterans granted by the U.S. Congress under the Servicemen's Readjustment Act of 1944 and extended by later legislation. Administrated by the *Veterans Administration, these benefits included educational grants for higher education or vocational training, mortgage loan guarantees for home buyers, and cash payments for those unemployed after discharge.

Initially, President Franklin D. *Roosevelt favored a comprehensive approach to dealing with postwar *demobilization, especially in the areas of job retraining and vocational rehabilitation. However, faced with significant opposition in Congress and among veterans' organizations to such broad-based plans, he bowed to political realities and supported narrower legislation aimed at veterans. Substantial public pressure developed in 1943 and 1944, led by the *Veterans of Foreign Wars and the Hearst newspaper syndicate, to provide a bonus and other benefits to discharged service men and women. The *American Legion, eager to attract World War II veterans to its organization, played a pivotal role in drafting and lobbying for the so-called G.I. Bill.

The bill's emphasis on aiding able-bodied veterans established important precedents that stemmed in part from fears of massive unemployment caused by demobilization and the return of millions of ex-service men and women.

Between 1944 and 1949, nearly 9 million veterans received a total of $4 billion from the G.I. Bill's compensation program. Although unemployment increased after V-J Day, the provisions of the bill, the unemployment insurance popularly known as the "52-20 club," played an instrumental role in ensuring that the United States avoided a postwar depression similar to that after World War I. In addition, over 3.5 million mortgages would be partially guaranteed under the homeowners' loan provisions of the bill, and this was instrumental in encouraging rapid growth of suburbia after 1945. At the peak, in 1947, slightly over 40 percent of all housing starts in the nation would be funded by the guarantee.

The G.I. Bill's education and training programs reached slightly over half of the nearly 16 million eligible veterans in 1945–56. College enrollments increased by 70 percent over prewar levels. Ex-service men dominated student bodies at American colleges in the late 1940s; in 1947, close to half the college students had served in the military. G.I. Bill recipients as a group tended to outperform traditional nonveteran students.

Benefits similar to the G.I. Bill would be extended to veterans of the *Korean War. Subsequently, the Veterans' Readjustment Benefits Act of 1966 extended such provisions to all who serve in the armed forces, even in peacetime. The precedents established by the G.I. Bill for federal aid to higher education would expand over the course of the *Cold War. Totaling over $14 billion, the bill was crucial to the expansion of the middle class.

[*See also* Veterans: World War II.]

• Davis R. B. Ross, *Preparing for Ulysses: Politics and Veterans During World War II*, 1969. Keith W. Olson, *The G.I. Bill, the Veterans, and the Colleges*, 1974. Michael J. Bennett, *When Dreams Came True: The G.I. Bill and the Making of Modern America*, 1996.

—G. Kurt Piehler

GOETHALS, GEORGE W. (1858–1928), U.S. *Army engineer and builder of the Panama Canal. Born in Brooklyn on 29 June 1858, Goethals graduated second in his West Point class in 1880, and went on to achieve what William Tecumseh *Sherman predicted would be a "brilliant future." Early in his career with the U.S. *Army Corps of Engineers, he worked on lock and dam projects that later served him well in Panama. More engineer than soldier, Goethals viewed the military simply as a vehicle through which he could express his talent.

On President Theodore *Roosevelt's order, Goethals was appointed chief engineer of the Panama Canal in 1907 when John F. Stevens resigned because of the difficulties in the first three years of construction. Goethals supervised nearly all major excavation and all construction. He vastly expanded the proposed canal's size, taking into account U.S. *Navy preferences for access, passage, and defense. To oversee the building of immense locks and dams, Goethals brought in army and civilian engineers who had distinguished themselves in similar work. He then set the two groups to work on opposite sides of the canal, expectant that professional rivalry would encourage speed and excellence.

Goethals's responsibilities at Panama extended well beyond construction. He organized a strictly regimented social order, with engineers and designers at the top and workers at the bottom. Each lived in separate communities with separate amenities, with a court system adjudicated by Goethals himself. Goethals had the ability to manage an incredibly diverse number of workers. He completed the canal in 1914, having done the job under budget and ahead of schedule, and still operating with most of the original construction equipment. General Goethals served as governor of the Canal Zone (1914–16) and then with the War Department's supply agencies in World War I.

• Joseph B. Bishop, *Goethals, Genius of the Panama Canal: A Biography*, 1930.

—T. R. Brereton

GOLDWATER-NICHOLS ACT (1986). The Goldwater-Nichols Department of Defense (DoD) Reorganization Act of 1986, sponsored by Senator Barry Goldwater and Representative Bill Nichols, was enacted primarily to improve the ability of U.S. armed forces to conduct joint (interservice) and combined (interallied) operations in the field, and secondarily to improve the DoD budget process. The act contained three major changes: it greatly strengthened the influence and staff of the *Joint Chiefs of Staff (JCS) chairman, compared to those of the service chiefs and military departments; it increased the authority and influence of the unified combatant commands that control U.S. forces in the United States and around the world; and it created a "joint officer specialization" within each service to improve the quality of officers assigned to the Joint Staff.

The act's supporters felt that U.S. military operations since World War II had suffered from conflict and inadequate coordination among the services. They believed that individual service programs and priorities, rather than the needs of actual joint military operations—the ultimate purpose for which the armed forces were maintained—dominated DoD. Enough retired senior officers, former civilian DoD officials, and private analysts and commentators, as well as members of Congress, agreed with these views to make it possible for the act to be enacted over the objections of the uniformed military leadership.

The intensity of objection was much greater in the navy and Marine Corps, as had been the case for all disagreements about service unification since the end of World War II. In general, those who objected to the act felt that DoD operational and budgetary problems in the post–World War II era resulted from lack of political will, inadequate defense budgets, excessive civilian "micromanagement" of military operations and defense budgets, and the inevitable chaos and friction attendant on war or the operations of any large organization. They were also skeptical of "jointness," believing that service-unique assets and views needed to be nurtured, not submerged; and that increased requirements for joint and central organizations created unnecessary bureaucracy, subsuming service assets and doctrine into less than optimal joint doctrines or systems.

The act has been accepted by most officers and civilian analysts, but certain issues remain: Is the increased authority of the JCS chairman compatible with an appropriate degree of civilian control of the military, or does it threaten that control, as some—for example, military historians Richard Kohn and Russell F. Weigley—have charged? Has pressure for more joint operations added unnecessary layers of command and awkward "marriages of convenience" among the services, or has it been material in various military victories since 1989? (Many analysts regard the act as instrumental in ensuring the success of U.S. combat operations in Panama in 1989–90, and in the *Persian Gulf War of 1991, although it proved no substitute for clear political guidance during the U.S. military operations in Somalia in 1992–94.) Is increased Joint Staff involvement in weapons system procurement a long-overdue step toward effective management of DoD acquisition, or does it remove service-unique perspectives where needed?

[*See also* Civil-Military Relations; Civilian Control of the Military; Command and Control; Defense, Department of.]

• Vincent Davis, "Defense Reorganization and National Security," *Annals of the American Academy of Political and Social Sciences,* 517 (September 1991), pp. 157–73. Russell F. Weigley, "The American Military and the Principle of Civilian Control from McClellan to Powell," *Journal of Military History,* 57, no. 5 (Special Issue, October 1993), pp. 27–58. Edward N. Luttwak, "Washington's Biggest Scandal," *Commentary,* 97, no. 5 (May 1994), pp. 29–33. Richard H. Kohn, "Out of Control: The Crisis in Civil-Military Relations," *The National Interest,* no. 35 (Spring 1994), pp. 3–17.

—Robert L. Goldich

GORGAS, WILLIAM C. (1854–1920), military physician, sanitarian expert, and surgeon general. Born in Alabama, the son of a West Pointer who had been the Confederacy's chief ordnance officer, Gorgas received a medical degree from New York's Bellevue Hospital Medical College in 1876 and joined the U.S. Army Medical Corps in 1880. When army surgeon Walter *Reed proved mosquitoes were the transmitters of the yellow fever virus, Gorgas, as the army's chief health officer in Havana, Cuba, during the U. S. occupation (1889–1902), initiated sanitation countermeasures that eradicated the disease in Cuba by eliminating the mosquito-breeding areas and segregating stricken patients. During 1904–13, he served in Panama, duplicating his successes and greatly contributing to the completion of the canal by reducing malaria outbreaks among laborers. He later applied his sanitary measures in other parts of the world, including Ecuador and South Africa. In 1914, he was promoted to major general and appointed surgeon general of the U. S. Army. Gorgas served from 1914 to 1919, skillfully administering the Medical Corps during World War I. He died in London of a stroke. After a military funeral, his body was returned for burial in Arlington National Cemetery.

• Marie D. Gorgas and Burton J. Hendrick, *William Crawford Gorgas: His Life and Work,* 1924. Edward F. Dolan, Jr. and H.T. Silver, *William Crawford Gorgas: Warrior In White,* 1968.

—Ervin L. Jordan, Jr.

GRAND ARMY OF THE REPUBLIC. The Grand Army of the Republic (GAR) was the largest and most powerful organization of *Union army and navy veterans. Founded on 6 April 1866 at Decatur, Illinois, by former army surgeon Benjamin Franklin Stephenson, its proclaimed objects were "Fraternity, Charity, and Loyalty." Its basic unit was the local post, with membership open to any honorably discharged Union veteran. The social composition of GAR membership was cross-class, and to some extent cross-racial, though black veterans usually were relegated to segregated posts.

Between 1866 and 1872, the GAR operated as a virtual wing of the Republican Party, boosting the careers of soldier-politicians such as Sen. John *Logan of Illinois. After 1872, it entered a steep decline, reaching a low of 26,899 members in 1876. In the 1880s, the GAR revived as a fraternal order, emphasizing its secret initiation ritual and the provision of charity to needy veterans. It soon became an active and powerful national pension lobby, and the custodian of a conservative version of American *nationalism, stressing the ideals of the independent producer and the volunteer *citizen-soldier. At its peak membership of 409,489 in 1890, the Grand Army enrolled about 40 percent of eligible Union veterans. The GAR declined in influence after 1900, acting largely as the keeper of Memorial Day, which Commander in Chief Logan had first proclaimed as gravesite Decoration Day in 1868. It held its last national encampment at Indianapolis in 1949. The GAR never became a hereditary order or admitted veterans of later wars; thus it disappeared with the death of its last member in 1956.

[*See also* Veterans: Civil War.]

• Mary R. Dearing, *Veterans in Politics: The Story of the G.A.R.,* 1952. Stuart McConnell, *Glorious Contentment: The Grand Army of the Republic, 1866–1900,* 1992. —Stuart McConnell

GRANT, ULYSSES S. (1822–1885), Civil War general and eighteenth president of the United States. Born at Point Pleasant, Ohio, on 27 April 1822, and named Hiram Ulysses, young Ulysses (as his father called him) grew up in nearby Georgetown, across the street from his father's tannery, and acquired an intense aversion to the stench of death. He attended local schools, did farm chores, and demonstrated unusual skill with horses. Appointed to the U.S. Military Academy at West Point, he was mistakenly registered as Ulysses S., which he eventually accepted, though insisting that his middle initial stood for nothing.

Graduating in 1843, he was assigned to Jefferson Barracks in St. Louis County. In the *Mexican War, 1846–48, Grant displayed commendable gallantry under Zachary *Taylor, but chafed at assignments as quartermaster and commissary in the army of Winfield *Scott until the final approach to Mexico City provided opportunity to earn brevet (temporary) promotion to captain. Grant encountered different styles of command and management, maintained an aversion to military protocol, and believed that the war represented aggression against Mexico.

In 1848, Grant married Julia Dent, daughter of a Missouri slaveholder, and in 1850 they had a son. Grant was soon separated from his family when the army assigned him to the Pacific Coast. Paid too little to reunite the family in California, he was miserably unhappy; nonetheless, tales of his heavy drinking then and later are unsupported. He resigned in 1854 to begin farming on his father-in-law's estate in St. Louis County. When his farm failed in the Panic of 1857, he could not find employment in St. Louis. By 1860, necessity forced him to his father's leather goods store in Galena, Illinois.

When the *Civil War began, Grant, impelled by a sense of patriotic obligation, reluctantly left his wife and four children. He served Governor Richard Yates of Illinois temporarily as aide and mustering officer but failed to find an appropriate command in the frenzied pursuit of officerships for units of U.S. *Volunteers. Yates eventually gave him a regiment, and Grant quickly established discipline and marched the 21st Illinois to Missouri. Before he engaged the enemy, he acquired promotion to brigadier general chiefly because an Illinois congressman had no superior candidate in his home district. Chance placed Grant in command at Cairo, Illinois, just as the Confederates occupied Columbus and Hickman on the Mississippi River in previously neutral Kentucky. Grant then boldly occupied Paducah and Smithland at the mouths of the Tennessee and Cumberland Rivers. On 7 November 1861, he led 3,000 troops from Cairo to Belmont, Missouri. Initially successful in overrunning a Confederate camp, Grant was unprepared for the counterattack that drove his men back to their transports in disarray. Because Grant had displayed aggressiveness and suffered no greater casualties than he had inflicted, this indecisive encounter provided experience without damaging his prospects.

In January 1862, Grant wrung permission from his conservative superior, Maj. Gen. Henry W. Halleck, to attack Fort Henry on the Tennessee River. Union gunboats compelled the fort's surrender (6 February) before the arrival of all Grant's forces, and much of the garrison fled to Fort Donelson on the Cumberland River. Grant followed, sending gunboats to the Cumberland and troops overland. Rather than await expected reinforcements, Grant then besieged the 21,000 Confederates with his own army of 15,000. On 14 February, the gunboats attacked unsuccessfully. The next day, while Grant visited the wounded naval commander on shipboard, a surprise Confederate attack rolled up the Union right and opened the road for escape. As the Confederate commander dawdled, Grant returned and launched a counterattack that removed all options save "unconditional surrender"—Grant's phrase that matched his initials and provided a popular nickname. Grant captured about 15,000 men and compelled the Confederates to fall back from Kentucky and much of middle Tennessee. The first major Union victory of the war won Grant promotion to major general.

Advancing up the Tennessee River to attack Corinth, Mississippi, Grant assembled troops at Pittsburgh Landing, Tennessee, where Confederates unexpectedly attacked at Shiloh Church (6 April) in the Battle of *Shiloh. Pushed to the edge of destruction on the riverbank after a frightful encounter, Grant used reinforcements for a second day of fighting that recaptured the field. Grant's resilience and indomitability won acclaim, but heavy casualties and rumors raised questions that temporarily cost him his command. Not until Halleck left for Washington as general in chief did Grant resume leadership.

His campaign in the siege of *Vicksburg, Mississippi, began in late 1862 with setbacks. Confederate cavalry captured Grant's supply base at Holly Springs and William Tecumsch *Sherman's premature assault on Vicksburg failed. After a winter of frustration, Grant's supporting fleet ran past the batteries and landed troops south of Vicksburg. Grant then unexpectedly struck at Jackson, Mississippi, before turning toward Vicksburg. His lightning moves prevented the cooperation of two Confederate armies in Mississippi and led to eventual surrender of the besieged citadel of Vicksburg in July 1863. Grant's military masterpiece virtually opened the river and bisected the Confederacy. A smashing victory against Gen. Braxton Bragg at Chattanooga in November 1863 firmly established his reputation as the Union's finest commander.

Promoted to lieutenant general and given command of all Union forces in March 1864, Grant left Halleck in Washington as chief of staff while he accompanied the Army of the Potomac in Virginia. He planned a coordinated campaign with two western armies converging on Atlanta and three eastern armies aimed at Richmond. In spring 1864, Grant faced Robert E. *Lee in a bloody series of encounters, including at the Battle of the *Wilderness (5–6 May), fighting at Spotsylvania (7–19 May), North Anna (23–26 May), and Cold Harbor (1–3 June) in the *Wilderness to Petersburg Campaign. Shocking Union casualties accompanied Grant's approach to Richmond, but a brilliant crossing of the James River then brought his armies to thinly defended Petersburg, Virginia, where subordinates immediately bungled a dazzling opportunity to end the war. Grant settled uncomfortably into siege. Four of five armies had failed to achieve their missions; only Sherman's victory in the Battle of *Atlanta (2 September) redeemed his strategy.

Grant maintained pressure on Lee as *Sherman's march to the sea again divided the Confederacy. In late March 1865, Grant launched another lightning campaign that drove Lee from Richmond and to surrender at Appomattox Courthouse (9 April). President Andrew *Johnson tried to harness Grant's popularity in an effort to restore Southern statehood at the expense of the freed slaves. Grant's refusal to abandon his soldiers or his black veterans frustrated Johnson's attempt to replace Secretary of War Edwin M. *Stanton with Grant and drove him to support the Republican Party. Grant's reputation as a wartime commander carried him on to two terms as president (1869–77). Contrast between expectation and fulfillment in the political arena dimmed Grant's fame, which revived shortly after his death with posthumous publication of his Memoirs—a splendid military autobiography written with fairness, candor, and surprising humor.

Grant's popular reputation as an impassive "butcher" whose victories depended on luck and larger armies arose amid strivings for sectional reconciliation. Military analysis by the English soldier-scholar J. F. C. Fuller and later by American military historians T. Harry Williams and Bruce Catton promoted reappraisal. Lincoln's understanding that Grant deplored politics but valued freedom in military matters formed the cornerstone of their effective partnership. Sherman, who also deferred to Grant's military mastery, became his ideal lieutenant. Grant's resilience, unpredictability, and strategic grasp continue to challenge scholars, as does Grant's meteoric rise from provincial clerk to military eminence. "The laws of successful war in one generation would insure defeat in another," he wrote, but arguments that his innovations foreshadowed modern total warfare lack historical perspective.

[See also Civil War: Military and Diplomatic Course; Commander in Chief, President as; Reconstruction.]

• U.S. Grant, *Personal Memoirs of U. S. Grant*, 2 vols., 1885–86. Horace Porter, *Campaigning with Grant*, 1897. J. F. C. Fuller, *Grant and Lee: A Study in Personality and Generalship*, 1933. T. Harry Williams, *Lincoln and His Generals*, 1952. Bruce Catton, *Grant Moves South*, 1960. John Y. Simon, ed., *The Papers of Ulysses S. Grant*, 20 vols. to date, 1967– . Bruce Catton, *Grant Takes Command*, 1969. William S. McFeely, *Grant: A Biography*, 1981. Brooks D. Simpson, *Let Us Have Peace: Ulysses S. Grant and the Politics of War and Reconstruction, 1861–1868*, 1991. John Y. Simon, "Grant, Lincoln, and Unconditional Surrender," in Gabor S. Boritt, ed., *Lincoln's Generals*, 1994.

—John Y. Simon

GREAT BRITAIN. *See* United Kingdom, U.S. Military Involvement in.

GREEN BERETS. *See* Special Operations Forces: Army Special Forces.

GREENE, NATHANAEL (1742–1786), Continental army general. Nathanael Greene was born into a Warwick, Rhode Island, family of anchorsmiths and millowners. Raised a *Quaker, Greene nevertheless developed a youthful fascination for military history. In 1775 Private Greene joined patriots besieging Boston. His intelligence, knowledge of military affairs, and managerial skills, led Congress to appoint him a brigadier general and placed him in charge of Boston when the British left.

Greene was one of George *Washington's favorite lieutenants. An amateur, Greene initially made by-the-book mistakes; learning war through war, however, he grew as a leader. Promoted to major-general, Greene fought the Battles of *Trenton and Princeton (1776–77), Brandywine (1777), Germantown (1777), Monmouth (1778), and Newport (1778), and often commanded in Washington's absence. Appointed quartermaster general (1778), his business experience aided him immeasurably. Resuming field duty, Greene fought at Springfield (1780) before accepting command of the Southern Department in December 1780.

In the South, Greene's position appeared hopeless. Georgia and South Carolina had fallen, North Carolina and Virginia lay exposed to British invasion, and his small detachment of the *Continental army was ill-clothed, starving, and demoralized. Greene quickly restored discipline and morale. Next, he boldly divided his force, detaching Daniel *Morgan into South Carolina's backcountry and Henry *Lee's cavalry to join Francis *Marion's coastal guerrillas. It was a stroke of genius. With one order, Greene recaptured the strategic initiative. After Morgan's victory at the Battle of *Cowpens (1781), Greene concentrated his forces and led British Gen. Charles *Cornwallis deep into North Carolina. At the Battle of *Guilford Courthouse (1781) they fought a bitter engagement, with Cornwallis winning a Pyrrhic victory. Lord Cornwallis retired to Virginia to meet ultimate defeat by Washington at the Battle of *Yorktown.

Greene returned south. Combining guerrillas, militia, and regulars as integral parts of his operational strategy, he fought several battles (Ninety-Six, Hobkirk's Hill, Eutaw Springs). The British won all of them, but at high cost. By October 1781, except for Charleston and Savannah, the South was under American control. A brilliant, innovative leader practicing in *guerrilla warfare, Greene left the army in 1783. Soon after (1786), he died of sunstroke in Georgia.

[See also Revolutionary War: Military and Diplomatic Course; Yorktown, Battle of.]

• Theodore Thayer, Nathanael Greene: Strategist of the Revolution, 1960. Morgan Dederer, Making Bricks Without Straw: Nathanael Greene's Southern Campaigns and Mao Tse-Tung's Mobile War, 1983.   —John Morgan Dederer

GRENADA, U.S. INTERVENTION IN (1983). Grenada first attracted the military interest of the United States in 1979. A Marxist-Leninist coup that year, led by Maurice Bishop and the New Jewel movement, overthrew the government; the Communists also began construction of a 9,800-foot airstrip. A second and more violent coup in 1983 left Bishop and more than 100 other Grenadians dead and Deputy Prime Minister Bernard Coard and Gen. Hudson Austin in charge. In response to this violence and disorder, Grenada's governor general, Sir Paul Scoon, secretly asked the Organization of Eastern Caribbean States (OECS) for assistance in restoring order. The OECS, in turn, requested help from the United States.

To the strongly anti-Communist U.S. president, Ronald *Reagan, the possibility of a Soviet client-state in such a strategic location was unacceptable. The airstrip was seen as a threat to vital Caribbean sealanes and the Panama Canal, and it could have been used for staging Cuban and Soviet military flights to Africa and Nicaragua. U.S. officials also expressed their concern for the safety of approximately 1,000 Americans, mostly medical students, living in Grenada. The day after Bishop was murdered, a U.S. Navy task force, with Marines, was ordered to Grenada.

U.S. military intervention in Grenada in 1983, code-named "Urgent Fury," was hastily planned but overwhelming. The invasion force included the *Independence* Carrier Battle Group; the helicopter carrier *Guam* and Amphibious Squadron Four; 1,700 Marines of the 22nd Marine Amphibious Unit; two army ranger battalions; a ready brigade of the 82nd Airborne Division; various special operations units; and token forces from the OECS. It turned out that the island was defended by only about 500 to 600 Grenadian troops; 2,000 to 2,500 militiamen; and 750 to 800 Cubans, mostly military construction workers.

U.S. forces began landing on Grenada on 25 October. Their objectives were to seize the airports, destroy Radio Free Grenada, and ensure the safety of resident U.S. citizens. By 28 October, Grenada was firmly under the control of U.S. and OECS forces. Although ultimately successful, there were a number of serious problems with Urgent Fury, among them inadequate and poorly disseminated intelligence information and failures of communications and coordination failure among army, navy, and Marine units. The brief battle for Grenada cost the lives of 18 U.S. servicemen, including eleven soldiers, 3 Marines, and 4 Navy SEALS; another 116 U.S. servicemen were wounded. Cuban casualties were 25 dead and 59 wounded; Grenadian casualties 45 dead and 350 wounded.

[See also Caribbean and Latin America, U.S. Military Involvement in the.]

• William C. Gilmore, The Grenada Intervention: Analysis and Documentation, 1984. Paul Seabury and Walter A. McDougall, eds., The Grenada Papers, 1984.   —Craig Swanson

GRENADES AND GRENADE LAUNCHERS. Essentially small bombs, grenades contain two basic parts: a body and a fuse. A hollow container holds the explosive charge and provides the piercing shards of metal. Screwed into the grenade's body is a fuse that burns at a controlled rate, allowing the weapon time to reach its target before exploding. Besides such fragmentation grenades, smoke, chemical, and incendiary types are also produced. To increase range, the World War II service rifle was fitted with an adapter to fire grenades, but it proved unpopular because of recoil and the special blank cartridge required. After 1945, hand grenades were improved by making the body from sheet metal, but wrapping the explosive charge with pre-notched wire, increasing the amount of fragmentation. During the *Vietnam War, special grenade launchers resembled large, single-barred shotguns that propelled a grenade almost 1,500 feet. Additionally, modifications were made to the service rifle's muzzle to accept a rifle-projected grenade propelled by ball ammunition caught in a "bullet trap."

[See also Weaponry, Army.]

• S. L. A. Marshall, Infantry Weapons & Usage in Korea, 1952; rpt. 1988. The Diagram Group, Weapons: An International Encyclopedia from 5000 B.C. to 2000 A.D.., 1990.   —William F. Atwater

GROUND ATTACK AIRCRAFT. World War I established the requirements for ground attack airplanes: armored aircraft, capable of high speed but also maneuverable and agile at low speeds and altitudes, equipped with multiple *machine guns and bomb delivery capability. In World War II, the German Ju-87 "Stuka" dive-bomber spearheaded the early success of blitzkrieg operations and triggered increased interest in ground attack aircraft. Improved air defense capabilities and changes in battlefield doctrine created a less permissive operating environment, making the advantages of designated ground attack aircraft less obvious as World War II progressed. The *Korean War revived the controversy over fast versus slow air speeds, high- versus low-altitude strikes, air-ground communication, and air control links.

In recent years, the U.S. Air Force has preferred to build air-ground capabilities into its general purpose fighter and medium bomber aircraft, like the F-111 and the F-16. Still, its fixed-wing gunships (the AC-47 and the AC-130) played an important role in the *Vietnam War, and the A-10 Thunderbolt attack aircraft did yeoman's duty in the *Persian Gulf War. The army has developed the AH-64 "Apache" attack helicopter and other rotary-wing aircraft; the Marine Corps has acquired both fixed-wing ground attack aircraft, including the AV-8B "Harrier," and attack *helicopters such as the AH-1 "Cobra."

Airmen and soldiers agree on the potentially decisive nature of air-ground attack, but have reached no consensus on the best platform for delivering such firepower. The increasing lethality of the modern battlefield for all aircraft in the era of *heat-seeking technology and laser-guided *missiles keeps the debate over air-ground aviation alive.

[See also Air Force Combat Organizations: Tactical Air Forces; Air Warfare.]

• Richard P. Hallion, Strike from the Sky: The History of Battlefield Air Attack, 1911–1945, 1989. Benjamin Franklin Cooling, ed., Case Studies in the Development of Close Air Support, 1990.

—Caroline F. Ziemke

GUADALCANAL, BATTLE OF (1942–43). The Guadalcanal campaign, unexcelled for sustained violence on land, sea, and in the air in World War II, lasted for six months: August 1942 to February 1943. The struggle arose because Adm. Ernest J. *King countered a planned Japanese thrust down through the South Pacific to isolate Australia by initiating an offensive following the U.S. naval victory at the Battle of *Midway. King targeted Guadalcanal, a jungle-entangled island ninety miles long and twenty-five miles wide in the Solomon Islands in the southern Pacific. Radio intelligence showed the Japanese planned to prepare an airfield there to intercept U.S. convoys to Australia. The landing by the 1st Marine Division achieved tactical and strategic surprise and seized the nearly completed airfield. Immediately thereafter, in the first of a series of dramatic reversals, a Japanese task force defeated Allied warships off Savo Island and forced the withdrawal of the transports. The Marines were left isolated.

The airfield, renamed Henderson Field and located in the northwest corner of Guadalcanal, proved a key to the campaign. From its runway, a conglomerate of Marine, navy, and army squadrons defended the local air space, eventually permitting resupply and reinforcement. Air attacks denied the Japanese daylight access to the island, and compelled them to resort to night runs by destroyers—

dubbed the "Tokyo Express"—to reinforce and maintain their forces. Over the next three months, the Japanese sought to recapture Henderson Field with successive counterattacks. Each time, they were repulsed. Four U.S. divisions, two Marine and two army, successfully defeated the Japanese in bloody fighting.

The ultimate decision in the campaign came at sea. The Americans won a carrier clash at Eastern Solomons in August, and a night encounter in October at Cape Esperance. When the South Pacific theater commander, Vice Adm. Robert L. Ghormley, faltered, Pacific naval commander Adm. Chester *Nimitz replaced him with the dynamic Vice Adm. William F. *Halsey. But "Bull" Halsey's positive impact on morale was initially balanced by a defeat in carrier battle at Santa Cruz. In a wild series of air and sea battles between 12 and 15 November, Halsey threw in everything he had. American arms prevailed—barely—at a fearful cost.

The Japanese would win another night sea action at Tassafaronga, but they decided to evacuate their surviving troops. This they did successfully in the last week of the campaign in the face of local Allied air and sea superiority, and under pressure of an American ground offensive. The campaign cost the Japanese over 680 aircraft and 24 warships; American losses were 615 planes and 25 ships. The United States lost an estimated 5,000 sailors and about 2,500 soldiers, Marines, and airmen killed in action; the Japanese lost about 30,000 men.

The lasting importance of the U.S. victory at Guadalcanal rested in its vindication of American will and morale; in the severe attrition it inflicted on the Japanese, especially on experienced pilots; and in the American destruction of the myth of Japanese invincibility.

[See also Marine Corps, U.S.: 1914–1945; World War II, U.S. Naval Operations in: The Pacific.]

• Richard B. Frank, Guadalcanal, 1990. John B. Lundstrom, The First Team and the Guadalcanal Campaign, 1994.

—Richard B. Frank

GUADALUPE-HIDALGO, TREATY OF (1848). The treaty that ended the *Mexican War with the United States was signed in Guadalupe-Hidalgo, a suburb of Mexico City, on 2 February 1848. President James K. *Polk had already discharged negotiator Nicholas P. Trist, but the U.S. envoy used his imminent departure to persuade a fragile Mexican provisional government to consent to a substantial loss of territory rather than continuing a disastrous war or risking a more draconian peace. U.S. forces already controlled the capital, the major ports, and the northern half of Mexico. Polk, facing a fractious Congress and fearing the costs of an open-ended occupation, reluctantly accepted Trist's handiwork.

The U.S. agreed to pay Mexico $15 million and assume adjusted claims of U.S. citizens of $3 million. The territorial settlement—a Río Grande boundary for Texas, and the annexation by the United States of Mexico's northern provinces—New Mexico and Alta California—was the most important and durable legacy of the treaty. The pact's most controversial provisions were those that assured political and religious liberty and the security of property to Mexicans who remained in the transferred territories. During the ratification process, the U.S. Senate modified Article IX, which had originally promised U.S. citizenship to these people "as soon as possible," and struck out entirely Article X, which had guaranteed Mexican land grants in all of its former territories, including Texas. The U.S. Senate ratified the treaty (38 to 14) on 10 March 1848.

Although U.S. emissaries sought to reassure Mexico through the "Protocol of Querétaro"—signed in that city when the two countries exchanged ratifications of the treaty in May 1848—that civil and property rights were not threatened by the Senate's modifications, these presumed privileges were in fact sharply circumscribed in the decades following the war.

[*See also* Mexican War.]

• David M. Pletcher, *The Diplomacy of Annexation: Texas, Oregon, and the Mexican War,* 1973. Richard Griswold del Castillo, *The Treaty of Guadalupe Hidalgo: A Legacy of Conflict,* 1990.

—James E. Crisp

The term **GUERRE DE COURSE** describes a form of maritime warfare aimed at disrupting seaborne commerce. Derived from the French word for "privateer" (*course*), it is usually rendered as "commerce raiding" in English. Operationally, *guerre de course* resembles *blockades in that it is primarily a form of economic warfare, in which combat with enemy warships is at best a secondary consideration. Tactically, however, its methods differ from those of a blockade. Blockades seek to apply continuous pressure, either along the entire coastline of the enemy or at key chokepoints through which ships must pass on their way to the open sea. Blockades succeed less by sinking or seizing enemy vessels than by discouraging them from embarking in the first place. If a blockade is to endure for any length of time, it always requires the deployment of forces markedly superior to those of one's adversary.

Guerre de course, in contrast, is usually adopted by countries too weak to attempt such continuous, large-scale operations; or unwilling to risk the kind of fleet action that may be necessary to impose or break a blockade. It is conducted by individual ships (naval warships or privately owned ships armed with guns and authorized by government letters of marque to engage in legal privateering) or small squadrons. These operate in hit-and-run fashion along oceanic shipping lanes, or in coastal or archipelagic waters, where geography affords some means of escape should superior naval forces appear. Strategically, *guerre de course* represents an alternative to operations directed against the main naval forces of the enemy. *Guerre de course* in the form of privateering was widely employed by Americans in the *Revolutionary War and the *War of 1812.

Fundamentally attritional in nature, *guerre de course* aims to erode the enemy's warmaking capacity by depriving it of materiel, financial assistance, or military support from overseas; to undermine public morale by inflicting economic losses and depriving the population of necessary or familiar goods; and to divert a disproportionate share of the enemy's naval strength, which might otherwise be employed in more aggressive operations. It normally requires several warships, and sometimes a great many, to find and sink a single commerce raider—an imbalance that arises regardless of whether one seeks to hunt down the raiders or simply to fend them off by means of convoys. In theory, defense against a vigorously conducted *guerre de course* might stretch the resources of a superior navy to the point where it could not conduct offensive operations of its own.

In practice, it at least affords a cost-effective means of harassment, one whose psychological impact usually exceeds whatever material results are achieved.

Guerre de course is most frequently attempted as a counter to an enemy-imposed blockade. During the *Civil War, Confederate privateers conducted long-range sweeps against Union shipping around the world, in order to disrupt northern trade and draw off Union warships that might otherwise have contributed to the blockade of southern ports. The exploits of the Confederate raiders became legendary. The most famous was the British-built *Alabama,* an eight-gun Barkentine-rigged, sail and steamship that roamed the high seas for 22 months, seizing or sinking nearly 70 Union merchantmen along the way until it was sunk by the USS *Kearsarge* in June 1864. By the end of the war, more than a third of all northern seaborne trade had been shifted to neutral-flag vessels, a tribute to the predatory brilliance of men like Raphael Semmes, the *Alabama*'s captain. (After the war, in the *Alabama* claims, an arbitration panel awarded the United States $15 million for merchant ships sunk by Confederate raiders built in British shipyards.)

Like Sir Francis Drake, Semmes was a private individual sailing what amounted to an armed merchantman (albeit under the Confederate flag) rather than a commissioned officer commanding a naval warship. To that extent, he was a figure of the past. The peace settlement that ended the Crimean War in 1856 included a declaration outlawing commerce raiding by irregular forces or privateers—a declaration the United States had refused to ratify because it believed efforts to codify the *guerre de course* favored the large professional navies of Europe over the American privateering tradition.

From the outset of the Industrial Revolution, however, it had been clear that the rising value of world maritime trade would make it an increasingly important target for regular navies; and also that such attacks would come in for an increasing share of legal scrutiny. The Declaration of 1856 was but the first in a series of attempts (including at the *Hague Peace Conferences of 1899 and 1907, and the London Naval Conference in 1908) to make explicit the rights and obligations of all those caught up in a form of warfare that was, by definition, directed against unarmed ships crewed by civilians.

These matters were rendered vastly more weighty in the twentieth century by the advent of torpedo-armed *submarines, which brought to the *guerre de course* a ferocity and decisiveness it had not previously possessed. A surface cruiser operating under the rules of engagement accepted by nineteenth-century navies was expected to board a prospective target, determine if its nationality and cargo made it a legal prize, and see to the safety of the crew before taking further action. However, the early months of World War I revealed that similar conduct by German submarines exposed them to enormous risks, and reduced their tactical effectiveness far below what was possible if such scruples were set aside. *Guerre de course* accordingly lost its traditional character as a relatively bloodless and vaguely romantic sort of peripheral operation, and became a desperate and murderous struggle capable of deciding a major war.

This trend culminated in the devastating campaign against Japanese commerce conducted by American submarines (and to a lesser extent by carrier-based aircraft) during World War II—a rare example of *guerre de course* waged by the stronger side, but also suggestive of the degree to which the tactic was now losing its distinctiveness, and its historic rationale. By 1945, *guerre de course* had become little more than one of the modalities of total war, and scarcely the most efficient, given the capabilities of modern airpower. No first-class navy today regards the maritime trade of its adversary as an important target, and no second-class navy, facing a strong opponent, would consider it a feasible or fruitful one. If the spirit of Drake and Semmes survives, it does so in the small diesel submarines and fast, well-armed patrol boats that increasingly populate the littoral regions of the world—vessels whose targets, in all probability, will be not the commerce but the capital ships of their foe.

[*See also* Confederate Navy; Privateering; World War II: U.S. Naval Operations in: The Pacific.]

• Stuart L. Bernath, *Squall Across the Atlantic*, 1970. Ernest Andrade, Jr., "Submarine Policy in the United States Navy, 1919–1941," *Military Affairs* 35/2 (April 1971). D. P. O'Connell, *The Influence of Law on Sea Power*, 1975. William M. Robinson, Jr., *The Confederate Privateers*, 1990.
—Daniel Moran

GUERRILLA WARFARE. Guerrilla warfare (the word guerrilla comes from the Spanish meaning "little war") is often the means used by weaker nations or military organizations against a larger, stronger foe. Fought largely by independent, irregular bands, sometimes linked to regular forces, it is a warfare of harassment through surprise. It features the use of ambushes, hit-and-run raids, sabotage, and, on occasion, terrorism to wear down the enemy. Typically, a small guerrilla force seeks to concentrate its strength against the weaker portions of the enemy's forces, such as outposts or lines of communication and logistics, to strike suddenly, and then to disappear into the surrounding countryside. In the American experience, this type of warfare has been used since the *French and Indian War (1754–63), when colonists adopted American Indian tactics to strike back against French forces and their Indian allies. Maj. Robert Rogers of Connecticut, considered a founder of the guerrilla tradition in America, organized Rogers's Royal American Rangers in 1756 and trained them to carry the war deep into enemy territory. His doctrine, published as *Rogers' Rules for Ranging* (1757), is considered a classic and is still issued to all soldiers attending the school for U.S. Army *Rangers (Fort Benning, Georgia).

During the *Revolutionary War, the guerrilla legacy was reflected in Col. Ethan *Allen's capture of Ticonderoga (1775); Col. Francis *Marion's operations against Col. Bonastre Tarleton's cavalry (1780); and Brig. Gen. Daniel *Morgan's victory at the Battle of *Cowpens (1781). Gen. Nathanael *Greene even developed principles of guerrilla warfare in his successful campaign against the British in the South (1780–81). During the *Civil War, the outnumbered Confederate forces featured several guerrilla leaders, including Col. John Singleton Mosby and Gen. Nathan Bedford *Forrest. A particularly fierce guerrilla war was waged in the border states of Kansas and Missouri, where Southern sympathizers organized into partisan bands that attacked Federal supply trains and harassed Union sympathizers. The more prominent partisan leaders were William Quantrill and William "Bloody Bill" Anderson. The former is best known for his daylight raid and destruction of the city of Lawrence, Kansas (1863), and the fact that his followers included Frank and Jesse James and the Younger brothers, destined to become prominent outlaws in the postwar years.

After the Civil War, the much-reduced regular army was fully engaged in supporting the westward expansion of the United States, a mission that entailed years of fighting against American Indian tribes that opposed encroachment. Considered one of the premier practitioners of guerrilla warfare, the American Indian proved a formidable and elusive foe. Before being ultimately defeated, the Indians occasionally inflicted stunning reverses on units of the regular army—in the Fetterman fight (1866) for example, and the defeat of Custer's 7th Cavalry at the Battle of the *Little Bighorn (1876). Those army officers who were most successful at countering the Indians did so primarily through their adoption of unconventional tactics. Among these innovators were Gen. George Crook, who pioneered the use of pack mules to enhance the mobility of his columns and employed Apache Indian scouts against hostile Apache clans led by Geronimo; and Gen. Nelson Miles, who struck at hostile tribes during the winter months when the warriors' mobility was restricted by deep snows and lack of forage for their ponies. Significantly, although the *Plains Indians Wars lasted well over thirty years, the army regarded this sort of warfare as a temporary condition and never developed a coherent doctrine for countering a guerrilla foe. Even protracted operations against Philippine *insurrectos* in the *Philippine War (1899–1902) and Mexican general Francisco "Pancho" Villa's irregular forces (1915–16) failed to engage the interest of army theorists.

It was the U.S. Marine Corps, engaged in a number of expeditionary missions in Asia and Latin America during the late nineteenth and early twentieth centuries, that began to codify the techniques, tactics, and procedures necessary for conducting counterguerrilla operations. The Marine's efforts culminated in the publication of the *Small Wars Manual* (1940), a work that is still issued to Marine officers.

In World War II, some U.S. servicemen in the Philippines retreated into the hills after the Japanese conquest, set up guerrilla organizations, and continued to harass the enemy throughout the occupation. At the same time, the army and Marine Corps began to form and train units for irregular or guerrilla war operations, most notably Brig. Gen. Frank Merrill's "Marauders" and Col. William "Wild Bill" Donovan's Office of Strategic Services. The latter fielded a number of three-man "Jedburgh Teams" (contrary to more romantic theories, "Jedburgh" was selected from a series of randomly generated code names), who were inserted behind Axis lines in Asia and Europe to perform *covert operations, organize and advise resistance groups, conduct acts of sabotage, and collect military and political intelligence.

After World War II, the American military gave little thought to guerrilla war theory, despite the examples of the French in Indochina and Algeria, the British in Malaya, and the defeat of the Huks in the Philippines. Even the brief involvement of U.S. military advisers from the fledgling *Special Operations Forces (formed by direction of President Eisenhower in June 1952) in the Greek civil war made little impression on American military thought. It was not until the United States had become engaged in

Southeast Asia that military planners began grappling seriously with the problem of guerrilla warfare and counterinsurgency. The immediate result was President John F. *Kennedy's decision to expand the U.S. Special Forces (1961). Called "Green Berets" because of their distinctive headgear, these are carefully selected and highly trained troops organized into ten-man operational "A-Teams" (logistics and other support activities being handled by larger "B-Teams"). Each soldier was required to be an accomplished parachutist and capable of speaking at least one foreign language. Additionally, each team member was cross-trained in two military occupational specialties (e.g., a radio operator might also be certified as a demolitions expert). Special Forces operational teams were organized and trained to act as advisers and planners for indigenous guerrilla units and achieved some measure of success, especially among the Hmong and Montagnard tribesmen of the Vietnamese highlands. These minor successes were not enough to turn the tide of battle, and with the end of the *Vietnam War (1975), the Special Forces were relegated to a secondary status in the armed forces.

In the 1980s, in response to increased guerrilla activity in Central and South America, the U.S. military experienced a resurgence of interest in the problem of guerrilla warfare, now under the rubric of *Low-Intensity Conflict (LIC)—in turn superseded by Operations Other Than War (OOTW), and then by Military Operations Other Than War (MOOTW), encompassing *peacekeeping, peace enforcement and humanitarian assistance, or stability and support operations—which resulted in the formation of a separate Special Operations Command (SOCOM), and the establishment of a separate source of funding to support special operations missions, training, and equipment.

[See also Caribbean and Latin America. U.S. Military Involvement in the; Counterinsurgency; Covert Operations; Terrorism and Counterterrorism.]

• NAVMC 2890, Small Wars Manual, 1940. Robert Utley, Frontier Regulars, 1973. Robert Asprey, War in the Shadows, 1975. U.S. Army Field Manual 90-8, Counterguerilla Operations, 1986. U.S. Army Field Manual 100-20, Low-Intensity Conflict, 1990. Joint Publication 3-0, Joint Operations, 1994. Joint Publication 3-7, Military Operations Other Than War, 1995. U.S. Army Field Manual 100-5 (Draft), Stability and Support Operations, 1997.

—Frederick J. Chiaventone

GUILFORD COURTHOUSE, BATTLE OF (1781). A pivotal *Revolutionary War battle, the engagement at Guilford Courthouse, North Carolina, strategically altered the war's course and ultimately led to victory in the South and at the Battle of *Yorktown.

Stymied in the North, England in 1780 initiated a "Southern strategy," the state-by-state reinstallation of loyalist governments. Georgia and South Carolina fell, and North Carolina and Virginia awaited invasion by Gen. Charles *Cornwallis. In December 1780, Maj. Gen. Nathanael *Greene assumed command of a tiny, demoralized segment of the Continental Army in the South. Brilliant and innovative, Greene restored discipline and morale, then divided his small force and took the strategic initiative. Following the U.S. victory at the Battle of *Cowpens (January 1781), Cornwallis cut communications and launched a pursuit. Greene concentrated his detachments and in a punishing, epic march led the enemy deep into North Carolina.

At Guilford Courthouse on 15 March, Greene sought battle. He copied Daniel *Morgan's successful Cowpens tactics—militia backed by Continentals with cavalry in reserve—but without Morgan, who was ill. Cornwallis launched a frontal assault. The militia bolted, but Greene's staunch Maryland and Delaware Continentals held. Desperate, Cornwallis's artillery fired into the melee, killing friend and foe alike. Greene withdrew, leaving Cornwallis a hollow victory (American casualties numbered 261; British 532). Cornwallis left for Virginia, and Greene returned south. In six months, he had liberated the entire region, confining the British to two seacoast strongholds, Savannah and Charleston.

[See also Revolutionary War: Military and Diplomatic Course.]

• M. L. Treacy, Prelude to Yorktown: The Southern Campaigns of Nathanael Greene, 1780–1781, 1963. Franklin and Mary Wickwire, Cornwallis: The American Adventure, 1970. John Buchanan, The Road to Guilford Courthouse: The American Revolution in the Carolinas, 1997.

—John Morgan Dederer

GULF OF TONKIN INCIDENTS (1964). In 1964, under OPLAN (Operations Plan) 34A, the United States was sending small vessels with Vietnamese crews into the Gulf of Tonkin on convert raids against the North Vietnamese coast. On the afternoon of 2 August, the U.S. Navy destroyer Maddox, on what was called a DeSoto patrol, was gathering various information, including electronics intelligence (elint) about the coastal radar defenses, and signals intelligence (sigint) from intercepted radio messages. North Vietnamese *torpedo boats attacked the Maddox, unsuccessfully, near an island that had been shelled in an OPLAN 34A raid three nights before. U.S. aircraft briefly pursued the retreating torpedo boats attempting to sink them, but otherwise there was no retaliation.

A second incident was reported on the night of 4 August. The men on the destroyers Maddox and Turner Joy who described torpedo boats attacking them certainly believed this at the time. Many later decided they had been shooting at ghost images on their radar. Many others who were there, and some later historians like Marolda and Fitzgerald, believe there was a genuine attack. The preponderance of the available evidence indicates there was no attack.

In retaliation for the supposed second attack, U.S. aircraft attacked North Vietnamese naval vessels at several locations along the coast 5 August, plus a fuel storage facility at Vinh. On 7 August, the House of Representatives passed 416–0, and the Senate 98–2, the so-called Tonkin Gulf Resolution, giving the President Lyndon B. *Johnson a blank check for further military action in Vietnam.

[See also Commander in Chief, President as; Vietnam War, U.S. Naval Operations in the; Vietnam War: Causes.]

• Edward Marolda and Oscar Fitzgerald, From Military Assistance to Combat, 1959–1965, 1986. Edwin Moise, Tonkin Gulf and the Escalation of the Vietnam War (1996).

—Edwin E. Moise

GULF WAR. See Persian Gulf War (1991).

GUNS. See Browning Automatic Rifle; Gatling Gun; M-1 Rifle; M-16 Rifle; Machine Guns; Naval Guns; Rifled Musket; Side Arms, Standard Infantry; Springfield Model 1903.

H

HABEAS CORPUS ACT (1863). In the early months of the *Civil War, President Abraham *Lincoln suspended the privilege of the writ of habeas corpus in the border states and subsequently throughout the North. A writ of habeas corpus orders a person detaining another, the petitioner, to bring that person before a judge, who can determine the lawfulness of the detention. The suspension of this privilege allowed the government to take into custody persons suspected of disloyal activities and hold them until they no longer posed a threat to the Union. In response to complaints about arbitrary arrests and doubts about the president's authority to suspend the writ, Congress enacted the Habeas Corpus Act in March 1863. The act legitimized Lincoln's suspensions of habeas corpus and approved future suspensions for the duration of the war. It also sharply limited the time a prisoner could be held without trial by requiring that civilians arrested and detained by the military be released if grand juries failed to indict them. Finally, the act afforded protection to federal officials who were sued in state court for arresting and detaining civilians and for acts performed while enforcing federal *conscription and emancipation policies. It authorized removal of these suits to federal courts (where defendants were less likely to face hostile judges and juries) and stipulated that any order made under authority of the president was a defense against such suits.

[*See also* Civil Liberties and War; Commander in Chief, President as; *Merryman, Ex Parte; Milligan, Ex Parte.*]

• James G. Randall, *Constitutional Problems Under Lincoln,* 1926. Harold M. Hyman and William M. Wiecek, *Equal Justice Under Law: Constitutional Development, 1835–1875,* 1982.

—Mary J. Farmer

HAGUE PEACE CONFERENCES (1899, 1907) were the largest diplomatic conferences between the Congress of Vienna and the outbreak of World War I. Czar Nicholas II of Russia, calling for limitation of armaments, proposed the first conference (1899) at the Dutch seat of government. Representatives of twenty-six governments attended. President Theodore *Roosevelt, responding to wishes of peace movement leaders, in 1904 proposed a second conference, and the czar officially called the 1907 conference. Forty-four governments attended.

The Russians originally proposed discussion only of limitation of armaments at the 1899 conference, but expanded the agenda to include the laws of war on land; extension of the 1864 *Geneva Conventions to the sea; and international arbitration. These topics made the conference acceptable to governments determined to oppose arms limitation. At the same time, peace movement leaders and some journalists, who labeled the proposed meeting a "Peace Conference," welcomed addition of arbitration to the agenda. The 1899 conference accomplished little in regards to armaments. The German delegates opposed limits on armies; the British on navies. U.S. naval delegate Capt. Alfred T. *Mahan, famed historian of seapower, made clear his opposition to limiting armaments. The Russians proposed bans on new firearms, *submarines, and ships with rams, and prohibitions against throwing projectiles or explosives from balloons or "similar means." The conference did nothing about new firearms or submarines but negotiated declarations against expanding ("dumdum") bullets, poison gas, and the aerial use of explosives from balloons. Renewal of the balloon declaration was the only arms limitation of the 1907 conference. German opposition convinced the Russians that limitation should not appear on the 1907 program; an Anglo-American resolution recognizing the seriousness of the *arms race was only a gesture.

The Hague conferences made important advances in codification of the laws of *land warfare. General Orders No. 100, The Union army code announced in 1863 strongly influenced the unratified Declaration of Brussels (1874). The 1899 conference concluded a comprehensive convention based on that declaration, which proved its worth during the Boer and Russo-Japanese Wars. The 1907 conference revised that convention and concluded two related conventions: one concerned neutral rights and duties on land; the other required formal declarations before beginning hostilities. Angry over the surprise Japanese attack on Port Arthur, Manchuria, in 1904, the Russians urged agreement on this convention. Generally respected during World War I, this convention was often disregarded thereafter, notably by the Japanese when they attacked on *Pearl Harbor in 1941. The 1899 conference achieved little for the laws of war at sea. The Russian program called for extension of the 1864 Geneva convention which protected victims of war on land to the sea, and this was done; but there was little discussion of larger matters. An American proposal that the conference consider immunity of private property at sea from capture—a traditional U.S. principle—was blocked by the British.

The 1907 conference, however, dealt seriously with war at sea, for the Russo-Japanese War had presented neutrals with numerous maritime problems. The conference concluded a new convention about the Geneva rules at sea and conventions about the status of merchant ships at the beginning of hostilities, conversion of such vessels into warships, submarine mines, and the maritime rights and duties of neutrals. British, German, and American delegates obtained Convention XII, which provided for an international prize court, but there was general recognition that the restrictions on capture in Convention XI were inadequate for decisions by the proposed court. The British called a special conference to consider *blockades and contraband. The result was the Declaration of London (1909), a careful statement of prize law; but when the British House of Lords blocked ratification, other governments also delayed action. During the first months of World War I, American efforts to secure the adherence of the belligerents failed, largely because of British objections. The project for an international prize court was soon forgotten.

International arbitration agreements were major achievements of the Hague conferences. The 1899 conference framed a convention setting forth principles and procedures. British and American proposals resulted in the Permanent Court of Arbitration—a list of judges named by signatory powers from which parties to an arbitration could select a panel of judges. U.S. delegates at the 1907 conference called for a worldwide agreement to make arbitration obligatory in a very limited sense and a Court of Arbitral Justice that would have had a few judges sitting continuously. The Germans defeated agreement on obligatory arbitration; several small nations, particularly in Latin America, defeated the court proposal by insisting upon equal representation for all member governments. The United States, however, secured a convention requiring that no nation use force to collect debts unless arbitration had been offered and refused.

The 1907 conference called for a third conference in 1915, but the outbreak of war in 1914 prevented that meeting. Much of the work of the Hague conferences survived. The *League of Nations in 1920 adopted a world court statute based on the 1907 court project. The United States never adhered to that statute but in 1945 accepted the *United Nations version. The Hague conventions on warfare were of large importance during the two world wars and other wars. Since World War I, the Hague idea of limiting armaments through multilateral negotiations has often inspired the calling of large international conferences.

[See also Arms Control and Disarmament; Internationalism; Neutrality; Peace and Antiwar Movements.]

• Merze Tate, *The Disarmament Illusion: The Movement for a Limitation of Armaments to 1907*, 1930. Calvin D. Davis, *The United States and the First Hague Peace Conference*, 1962. Warren F. Kuehl, *Seeking World Order: The United States and International Organization to 1920*, 1969. Calvin D. Davis, *The United States and the Second Hague Peace Conference: American Diplomacy and International Organization 1899–1914*, 1976.   —Calvin D. Davis

HAIG, ALEXANDER MEIGS (1924–), U.S. Army officer, secretary of state, business executive. Born near Philadelphia, Haig attended Notre Dame University and then graduated from West Point in 1947. He soon joined the staff of Gen. Douglas *MacArthur in Japan and served under him in the *Korean War. Subsequently, Haig taught at West Point, held a succession of line, staff, and school assignments in the United States and Europe, and earned an M.A. in international relations from Georgetown University. In 1966–67, he served as a battalion and then brigade commander during the *Vietnam War, returning to West Point as deputy commandant.

Between 1969 and 1974, already known as an able officer knowledgeable about the polical-diplomatic aspects of

military affairs, Haig served in the Nixon White House as an assistant to national security adviser Henry *Kissinger. He had an important role in the 1972–73 negotiations culminating in the *Paris Peace Agreements. Appointed a four-star general, Haig served as Richard M. *Nixon's chief of staff, 1973–74. After Nixon's resignation, Haig was appointed commander of *NATO forces. Retiring from the army in 1979, he became president and CEO (1979–81) of United Technologies, a major defense contractor.

Under President Ronald *Reagan, Haig served as secretary of state, 1981–82, taking a hard line toward the Soviet Union and insurgencies in Central America. In 1982, he supported Britain during the Falklands/Malvinas War and Israel in its invasion of Lebanon. Disputes with Defense Secretary Caspar *Weinberger and national security adviser William Clark led to Haig's resignation. Afterward, he served on a number of corporate boards and was briefly a Republican candidate for president in 1988.

• Roger Morris, *HAIG! The General's Progress*, 1984. Alexander M. Haig, *Caveat: Realism, Reagan and Foreign Policy*, 1984. Alexander M. Haig, *Inner Circle: How America Changed the World: A Memoir*, 1992.   —John Whiteclay Chambers II

HAITI, U.S. MILITARY INVOLVEMENT IN. Given Haiti's location and the growing U.S. role in the Caribbean, Washington at the end of the nineteenth century paid increased attention to the island republic. By 1890, Americans provided half its imports and dominated its banks and railroads. When dictator Guillaume Sam was hacked to death in an uprising in 1915, President Woodrow *Wilson, concerned about U.S. investments as well as possible German seizure of the island, directed Rear Adm. William B. Caperton to land Marines and sailors from the USS *Washington* to protect lives and property. They were followed by a brigade of Marines.

Real authority in Haiti then rested with the Americans, although they permitted the election of President Philippe S. Dartiguenave. Normally, the cacos (rebel bandits) would have faded back into the hills; but angered by white American occupation, they lashed out, particularly in northern Haiti. The Marines quelled sporadic violence for over a year. In 1916–18, U.S. occupation forces attempted to win over the peasantry and implement construction programs, but they remained unpopular. The resident U.S. naval commander dissolved the Haitian Congress and dictated a new constitution. By 1918, opposition leader Charlemagne Peralte mounted a rebellion in the north, while his lieutenant, Benoit Batraville, led a revolt in central Haiti. The Gendarmerie (local constabulary trained and officered by Marines), supported by the Marine brigade, tracked down and killed Peralte (1919) and Batraville (1920).

During the depression, President Herbert *Hoover appointed the Forbes Commission, which concluded that the occupation, failing to respond to Haiti's problems, should be abolished. U.S. troops began to transfer responsibilities to Haitian nationals. The last Marines left Haiti under President Franklin D. *Roosevelt's order in 1934, although U.S. fiscal control remained until 1947.

The United States took a renewed interest in Haiti during the *Cold War. Washington reluctantly backed a series of military strongmen, including François ("Papa Doc") Duvalier, a disarmingly simple country doctor without apparent military connections who was elected president in

1957. In 1958, Duvalier asked that Marines retrain and reorganize the Haitian Army, and again the Marines handled public works as well as police functions while trying to develop an army that would resist communism. Duvalier became increasingly dictatorial, using a paramilitary secret police to impose terror. Although the United States government was reluctant to cut off aid to Haiti after Cuba became Communist in 1959, it withdrew its military mission and virtually shut down its embassy. "Papa Doc" died in 1971; he was succeeded by his son, Jean Claude ("Baby Doc") Duvalier.

Unprecedented famine and terrorism in the 1970s and 1980s drove desperate peasants to flee to the United States. Duvalier responded to the Carter administration's outrage with inconsequential reforms. In 1983, Pope John Paul II visited Haiti. His attention to human rights emboldened Haiti's Catholic clergy to call for improvements in social conditions and a grassroots movement responded.

The Reagan administration distanced itself from Duvalier, now clearly weakened by internal unrest, and the United States orchestrated his departure in 1986. A National Council of Government took over, but showed little interest in reform. The growing liberation theology began to coalesce around Father Jean-Bertrand Aristide, who was elected president in December 1990, in Haiti's first free election. Overthrown in September 1991 by a military coup, Aristide fled to the United States.

In 1994, the Clinton administration, confronted with a continuing exodus of seaborne Haitians seeking refuge in the United States, obtained economic sanctions and then authorization from the *United Nations for military force to remove the junta. With a U.S. military and naval force offshore, and paratroopers en route to the island, a last-minute mission headed by former president Jimmy *Carter achieved an agreement with the junta on 18 September for its resignation. U.S. troops came ashore without opposition. Aristide returned 15 October. A U.S. intervention force of 20,000 remained in Haiti from September 1994 to March 1995, when it was replaced by a UN *peacekeeping force of 6,000, including 2,400 U.S. troops. The poorest nation in the hemisphere, Haiti remained impoverished and plagued by periodic strikes and violence, but it had a democratically elected government at last.

[See also Caribbean and Latin America, U.S. Military Involvement in the.]

• James H. McCrockin, *Garde d'Haiti, 1915–1934,* 1956. Dana G. Munro, "The American Withdrawal from Haiti, 1929–1934," *Hispanic American Historical Review,* 49 (February 1969), pp. 1–26. Hans Schmidt, *The United States Occupation of Haiti, 1915–1934,* 1971. Robert D. and Nancy G. Heinl, *Written in Blood,* 1978. James Ferguson, *Papa Doc, Baby Doc. Haiti and the Duvaliers,* 1987.
—Anne Cipriano Venzon

HALSEY, WILLIAM F. (1882–1959) fleet admiral, U.S. Navy, World War II. Born in Elizabeth, New Jersey, Halsey graduated from the Naval Academy in 1904. In the 1930s, he learned to fly and became a leading advocate of *carrier warfare. During the Japanese attack on *Pearl Harbor, he was at sea, commanding the carrier *Enterprise.* In the spring of 1942, he helped orchestrate a series of carrier raids in the Pacific against enemy strongholds, including the famous James *Doolittle bomber attack on Tokyo. Later, as commander of the South Pacific theater in 1942–44, he directed forces that captured Guadalcanal, Bougainville, and several other key islands in the Solomons.

During and after the Battle of *Leyte Gulf (October 1944), Halsey was criticized for sailing his fleet northward in pursuit of enemy decoy carriers and leaving the San Bernardino Straits open to defended attack by a main enemy force. Later that year, he was again questioned for heading into a typhoon and losing three ships. By war's end, however, the agressive commander, known as "Bull" Halsey, was hailed as a popular hero, awarded a fifth star, and promoted to the rank of fleet admiral.

In retirement, Halsey often defended his Leyte Gulf decision, claiming that under the circumstances it was the best of all options. Above all, he was an energetic and demanding leader, who had the ability to invigorate the U.S. Navy's fighting spirit when most required.

[See also Guadalcanal, Battle of; Navy, U.S.: 1899–1945; Navy Combat Branches: Surface Forces; World War II, U.S. Naval Operations in: The Pacific.]

• E. B. Potter, *Bull Halsey,* 1985.
—Donald D. Chipman

HAMBURGER HILL, BATTLE OF (1969). For ten days in May 1969 during the Vietnam War, units of the 101st U.S. Airborne Division and the Army of the Republic of Vietnam (ARV) attacked North Vietnamese Army units dug in on a mountain called Dong Ap Bia, in A Shau Valley, Thua Thien Province—part of I Corps Tactical Zone in northernmost South Vietnam. Heavy losses among all combatants gave the mountain a new name: Hamburger Hill.

Long the scene of fierce battles between U.S. and their South Vietnamese allies and North Vietnamese forces, the A Shau closely parallels the Vietnam-Laos border. This made it easy for North Vietnamese units to cross from their Laotian sanctuary, lure allied units into battle, inflict heavy casualties, then vanish into sanctuary. On Hamburger Hill, the North Vietnamese strategy was again effective: 56 Americans died, and 420 were wounded; South Vietnamese losses were also high. An estimated 600 North Vietnamese soldiers died and many more were wounded. Over 270 close air support sorties and 22,000 rounds of *artillery were delivered to support a poorly coordinated piecemeal ground assault by about ten battalions—four of them U.S. Both sides abandoned the fight—and the hill.

The newly installed Nixon administration was severely criticized for announcing the beginning of "Vietnamization" a policy of turning the war over to the South Vietnamese, then wasting U.S. lives attacking an entrenched enemy on what appeared useless terrain. The controversy seemed to stiffen President Richard M. *Nixon's determination to remove U.S. forces from Vietnam quickly.

[See also Vietnam War: Military and Diplomatic Course.]

• Guenter Lewy, *America in Vietnam,* 1978. Phillip B. Davidson, *Vietnam at War,* 1988.
—Donn A. Starry

HAMILTON, ALEXANDER (1755–1804), Revolutionary soldier and statesman. Born in Nevis, Hamilton migrated to New York in 1772, where he studied at King's College until lured into the Revolutionary War. Hamilton caught Gen. George *Washington's eye, and in 1777 became his aide-de-camp. In 1781, Hamilton led an infantry regiment to victory against a British redoubt at the Battle of *Yorktown.

Hamilton's wartime experiences convinced him that only a strong central government led by a natural aristocracy could preserve American liberty. In 1782, he entered the Confederation Congress, a body he worked to invigorate; Hamilton's Annapolis Convention report (1786) summoned the 1787 Constitutional Convention. At the Philadelphia meeting, he pushed a powerful national government; thereafter he wrote fifty-one of the celebrated *Federalist Papers*.

As the first Treasury secretary (1789–95), Hamilton issued three brilliant, controversial reports to Congress, aimed at strengthening the national government. The first, favoring funding of the federal deficit at par and assuming state debts, helped establish national credit; the second proposed a national bank; the third (never enacted) advocated bounties and subsidies to boost manufacturing. Taken as a whole, Hamilton designed his program to win the public creditors to the government's support and to help the nation develop economically. His financial and diplomatic policies inspired the formation of the Republican opposition.

Hamilton's vision for national grandeur included a military establishment. Through a series of crises—including the *Whiskey Rebellion, which Hamilton personally helped quell—the Federalists built a professional force despite the public's fear of standing armies. Appointed Inspector General in 1798 under Washington, Hamilton broke with John *Adams when the president negotiated America's differences with France instead of waging war. In 1804, fearing a secessionist conspiracy, Hamilton opposed Aaron Burr's bid to become New York's governor. After his defeat, Burr challenged Hamilton to a duel, wounding him mortally at Weehawken, New Jersey.

[*See also* Jefferson, Thomas; Madison, James; Revolutionary War: Military and Diplomatic Course.]

• Forrest McDonald, *Alexander Hamilton, a Biography*, 1979. Jacob Cooke, *Alexander Hamilton, a Biography*, 1982.

—Stuart Leibiger

HAMPTON ROADS, BATTLE OF (1862). Confederate Secretary of the Navy Stephen R. Mallory believed ironclads could break the Civil War blockade by the Union navy. On 11 July 1861, he ordered the conversion of the captured USS *Merrimack* into the ironclad CSS *Virginia*. His Federal counterpart, Gideon *Welles, on 4 October 1861 directed John *Ericsson to build the ironclad USS *Monitor*. Although the Europeans had started to build iron ships, the battle between these two vessels on 9 March 1862 in Hampton Roads, Virginia, near Norfolk, was the world's first combat between armored warships.

The two vessels incorporated the latest naval advances: steam-powered, screw-propelled, and ironclad-hull. The *Virginia* (*Merrimack*) carried ten major guns (four in each broadside, one bow and one stern gun) and an iron ram. The low-silhouetted *Monitor* resembled a "cheesebox on a raft" with its rotating centerline gun-turret, housing two 11-inch guns.

On 8 March 1862, the *Virginia* sortied against the Union navy's blockade. It sank the USS *Cumberland* with its ram, burned the *Congress* with incendiary shells, but it disengaged when it could not approach the grounded *Minnesota*. The next day, Lt. Catesby ap Rogers Jones succeeded the wounded captain in command of the *Virginia* and found the waiting *Monitor*, which had just arrived with Lt. John L. Worden in command.

For four hours the two ironclads pounded each other at close range (at times only 15 yards apart). The larger *Virginia* tried without success to ram the *Monitor* and to board. Neither ship could sink the other, nor pierce the armor plate, but the *Virginia*, taking on water from hull damage, withdrew. Although the engagement between the two ships was inconclusive, the withdrawal of the *Virginia* for substantial repairs left the blockade in place and was proclaimed a victory by the Union. The "battles of the ironclads" presaged an eventual revolution in naval warfare. When the Confederates abandoned Norfolk in May, they destroyed the *Virginia;* the *Monitor* foundered off the Carolina capes later in 1862.

[*See also* Civil War: Military and Diplomatic Course; Confederate Navy; Union Navy; U.S. Navy: 1783–1865.]

• James P. Baxter III, *The Introduction of the Ironclad Warship*, 1933; Robert W. Daly, *How the Merrimac Won*, 1957; William C. Davis, *Duel Between the First Ironclads*, 1975.   —George E. Buker

HEAT-SEEKING TECHNOLOGY is most commonly associated with the detection of infrared radiation. All objects with a temperature greater than absolute zero emit infrared energy, the most common characteristic of which is heat. Detection of this heat can be utilized for many purposes.

Military adaptations of infrared technology began during World War II. A device called the Sniperscope was developed by the Allies, enabling the soldiers to see and shoot at night by distinguishing the heat differentials of the terrain. In addition to the Sniperscope and other night-vision devices, the potential of this technology for guidance purposes began to be realized. An infrared detector could be added to a missile, allowing the missile to seek out and follow the heat given off by the target. The U.S. military has since developed a number of such *missiles, beginning with the Sidewinder, an antiaircraft missile successfully tested in 1953 and deployed in 1956. This new missile was quickly adapted for use by the other service branches, especially the air force. Since that time, missiles equipped with infrared seekers, including the Sidewinder and the Maverick, have been responsible for the destruction of aviation, maritime, and ground targets. Heat-seeking missiles have been used in every major U.S. military conflict since the *Vietnam War.

*Satellites equipped with infrared sensors use heat-seeking technology for reconnaissance. The infrared sensors can aid in standard intelligence-gathering purposes or to provide early warning of the launch of an attacking missile. This real-time technology was utilized during the *Persian Gulf War (1991), when satellites equipped with forward-looking infrared sensors detected the launch of Iraqi Scud missiles.

Infrared seekers offer a number of advantages over other guidance systems (such as *radar). First, infrared sensors cost less per unit; second, heat-seeking sensors operate well by day or night, in good weather and bad. In addition, they are effective despite electronic countermeasures. Finally, infrared seekers improve the safety of the pilots whose planes bear the missiles through the use of "fire-and-forget" capabilities. After releasing the missile, the pilot can leave the area while the missile guides itself to the target.

These sensors do not provide a perfect system. One disadvantage is that objects that emit little heat are difficult to detect: the Tomahawk cruise missile, for example, is therefore difficult to detect with an infrared sensor. Second problem is that heat sensors are sensitive to shock and can be thrown off course during flight by a nearby explosion or disturbance. Nevertheless, heat-seeking technology continues to play an important role in the observation and guidance systems of the U.S. military.

[See also Missiles.]

• John Lester Miller, *Principles of Infrared Technology*, 1994.
—Michelle L. Nelson

HELICOPTERS. With its ability to hover, take off and land rapidly, and fly close to the world's land and seas, the helicopter has extended the efficacy of air power by bringing it down to earth. In contrast to many other aviation developments which seemed focused on creating an independent role for airpower, for most of its existence helicopter aviation has concentrated on intimate involvement with land and sea forces.

The first complete helicopter ("gyroplane") performance was accomplished by Louis-Charles Breguet in 1935. Four years later, Igor Sikorsky captured the imagination of the military with several demonstrations of his VS-300, XR-4, and XR-6 helicopters before high-ranking officials of various U.S. and British defense units. After developing Sikorsky's ideas, the U.S. military put helicopters into service at the end of *World War II, primarily for air rescue. In the *Korean War, the United States expanded on tactics developed by the French during their involvement in Algeria, and began experimentally to arm its helicopters. These innovations, along the with deployment of troops by U.S. Marine Corps helicopters, and medical evacuations (medevacs) were key developments in helicopter applications. Helicopters were also used for resupply and observation; and the potential for *command and control from above became clearer. The introduction of the helicopter into the battlefield gave the United States a valuable new offensive weapon.

The experiences with helicopters in the Korean War provided impetus for postwar experimentation. Several attempts were made to integrate offensive armaments with other helicopter systems. The U.S. Army, in particular, led by Brig. Gen. Carl I. Hutton, Commandant of the Army Aviation School at Fort Rucker, Alabama, aided by Col. J. D. Vanderpool, sought to construct and employ helicopters which could perform in the traditional cavalry roles, including reconnaissance, flank security, and shock as well as transportation of ground troops.

There was great resistance in political and military circles towards the development of a large, sophisticated, or autonomous army aviation element. One of the main sources of this antipathy was the feeling that all air operations belonged to the air force. Many in the army feared the consequences of a bitter schism similar to that which occurred when the air force itself became autonomous from the army in the previous decade. Proponents, however, argued that army aviation was necessary to fulfill the close air support mission; there was a pervasive feeling, felt most strongly in the army, that the air force was simply not interested in supporting small ground units in close combat.

The development of the UH-1 "Huey" helicopter gave

proponents of an airmobile division the craft, which ultimately persuaded policymakers that such an organization, within the Army, could flourish. Originally planned as an air ambulance, the Huey was later rigged as a gun ship and a troop carrier. The presence of the Huey in all of its multiple roles allowed the army to ask for a division-sized airmobile unit and to press for the infusion of helicopters into already existing ground units.

Within the army hierarchy individuals such as former paratroop commander Gen. James Gavin were advocates of an increasing role for army aviation. One of Gavin's proteges, Gen. Hamilton Howze, was a Director of Army Aviation and the chief of the Army Tactical Mobility Requirements Board, which during the Kennedy administration advocated an Airmobile Division. Tests for a new 11th Air Assault Division, which largely used UH-1 Hueys, under Gen. Harry Kinnard began in earnest with a key evaluator being an ardent army aviation supporter, Gen. Robert R. Williams.

In 1965, the army and the air force reached an understanding in which responsibility for helicopter operations were assigned to the army. At approximately the same time the 11th Air Assault Division was redesignated the 1st Cavalry Division (Airmobile), and with its 16,000 troops and more than 400 helicopters was assigned to Vietnam. A second Army division (101st Airborne) became airmobile and aviation assets were assigned to other army and Marine units in large numbers. In many respects the *Vietnam War was a "helicopter war" and by 1970 the U.S. Army operated about 12,000 aircraft, the overwhelming majority of which were helicopters.

Helicopters provided American commanders in Vietnam a great deal of flexibility in their operations. They enabled the quick evacuation of wounded troops from the battlefield and saved thousands of lives, thereby holding the politically important death statistics down. Paradoxically, helicopters enabled U.S. troops to engage in combat in areas that otherwise would be inaccessible. The ability to land helicopters in any area with a small cleared space enabled the United States to establish bases known as LZs (landing zones), which produced a battlefield which distinctly lacked a clear demarcation between the friendly and enemy lines. The airmobile capability of helicopters created a more effective fighting force for Vietnam, but it also limited the imagination of tacticians who used this asset in cases where helicopters may not have been the wisest choice to employ. Nevertheless, the sound of helicopters became associated with the Vietnam War in the nightly news and motion pictures.

In 1983, army aviation became a separate branch within the United States army. This was a step along the way toward demand for greater autonomy for army aviators. The Marine Corps organizational structure also promotes considerable autonomy for their aviation forces. Following Vietnam, the army acquired an advanced attack helicopter, the AH-64 Apache, a modern multi-purpose craft, the UH-60 Black Hawk, and an armed reconnaissance craft, the OH-58D Kiowa Warrior. Other services use, among other helicopters, variants of these craft.

Operation Desert Storm, the American-led assault to evict Iraqi forces from Kuwait, was initiated in early 1991 by Apache attacks on Iraqi long range radar. The *Persian Gulf War presented army aviation with the opportunity to use airmobile tactics to the fullest. The strategic scheme of maneuver for the final assault on Iraqi troops in both Kuwait and Iraq was a flanking attack from the west, known as the "left hook." The execution of the "left hook," deep into Iraq, confirmed the faith of military planners who believed in the centrality of helicopters for cavalry and logistical missions.

Over the years the primary criticism of helicopters has been their vulnerability to ground fire. This vulnerability was made clear, once again, when two Black Hawks were shot down in Mogadishu, Somalia almost three years after the Persian Gulf War. Though helicopters may be somewhat vulnerable to ground fire, they are still feared by opposition forces because their ability to fly along the nap of the earth makes them difficult to track via electronic methods. The enemy's frequent inability precisely to locate a helicopter via electronic means contributes to the helicopter's effectiveness and the ground troops' terror. For example, the fear of U.S. helicopters by opposition forces has been noted by implementation force (IFOR) peacekeeping soldiers who served during the *Bosnian Crisis in the late 1990s.

[See also Rivalry, Interservice; Vietnam War, U.S. Air Operations in.]

• Frederic A. Bergerson, The Army Gets an Airforce: Tactics of Insurgent Bureaucratic Politics, 1980. Eugene H. Grayson. "Where do we go from here?" U.S. Army Aviation Digest, March/April 1992, pp. 44–47. James L. Cox, "The Decline of Marine Helicopter Aviation," Marine Corps Gazette, December 1994, pp. 47–48. David S. Harvey, "The Choppy World of Army Aviation," Air Force Magazine, January 1994, pp. 56–60. Marvin Leibstone, "U.S. Military Helicopter Programmes," Military Technology, June 1994, pp. 53–57.
—Frederic A. Bergerson and Jason E. Trumpler

HELSINKI AGREEMENTS. See Conference on Security and Cooperation in Europe.

HELSINKI WATCH (1978), a division of the U.S.-based nongovernmental organization Human Rights Watch, was founded to monitor and promote the human rights provisions of the 1975 Helsinki Accords. Those accords focused primarily on the security and economic dimensions of East–West Cold War relations, confirming, among other things, the Soviet Union's post–World War II borders. But the agreements also made economic and security cooperation dependent on the human rights practices of signatory countries. Activists throughout the Eastern bloc seized on these provisions to demand greater political freedoms, and established local committees to fight for government compliance. The groups were harshly repressed by incumbent Communist regimes. The first arrests of human rights monitors were carried out by Soviet authorities in early 1977. Helsinki Watch was organized to campaign internationally on behalf of the imprisoned monitors in the Soviet Union and Eastern Europe, spearheading efforts to free such leading figures as Yuri Orlov in the Soviet Union, Vaclav Havel in Czechoslovakia, and Adam Michnik in Poland. The group lobbied Western and neutral governments meeting at periodic Helsinki review conferences to pressure Eastern bloc signatories to live up to their human rights commitments under the accords.

During heightened Cold War tensions in the 1980s, Helsinki Watch worked closely with U.S. government officials, whose strategic agenda included the promotion of civil and political freedoms in the Soviet Union and East-

ern Europe. Relations with official Washington became more distant after the end of the Cold War, as the United States stressed economic development and political stability over human rights concerns, or was simply unwilling to become involved in outbreaks of ethnic or communal violence in former Communist states. Since the eruption of wars in Bosnia and Chechnya, Helsinki Watch has focused its efforts on promoting respect for the *laws of war, including the treatment of civilian noncombatants in conflict areas, conditions in prison camps, and the use of rape as a weapon of political terror.

[See also Bosnian Crisis; Cold War: External Course; Cold War: Changing Interpretations.]

—Cynthia J. Arnson

HILL, A. P. (1825–1865), Confederate general. Born in Culpeper County, Virginia, Hill graduated from West Point in 1847, fifteenth in a class of thirty-eight. While still a cadet he contracted gonorrhea, which caused recurrent prostatitis that afflicted him physically and psychosomatically for life. Hill served in the *Mexican War and the Seminole Wars; his 1859 marriage to Kitty Morgan was a happy one that produced four daughters. After Virginia seceded in 1861, Hill resigned; he was appointed Confederate colonel of the 13th Virginia Infantry and fought at First Manassas. Promoted to brigadier general in February 1862, and major general in May 1862, Hill's Light Division became deservedly renowned during the Civil War for its fighting abilities; his energetic leadership distinguished him at the *Seven Days' Battle, as well as the Battle of *Fredericksburg, and the Battle of *Antietam, where his timely arrival saved Robert E. *Lee's right flank. In May 1863, he was promoted lieutenant general after "Stonewall" *Jackson's death at Chancellorsville, assigned command of the Army of Northern Virginia's new III Corps, and led it from Gettysburg to the Wilderness. After 1863, repeated illnesses and quarrels with superiors marred Hill's temperamental leadership, especially during the 1864–65 *Wilderness to Petersburg Campaign. Shortly after returning from sick leave, he was killed on 2 April 1865 at Petersburg by a Union infantryman while attempting to reconnoiter lines and rally his troops.

[See also Civil War: Military and Diplomatic Course.]

• William W. Hassler, A. P. Hill: Lee's Forgotten General, 1979. James I. Robertson, Jr., General A. P. Hill: The Story of A Confederate Warrior, 1987.
—Ervin L. Jordan, Jr.

HINDENBURG, PAUL VON (1847–1934), German field marshal and president. Member of an aristocratic Prussian family, Hindenburg saw action as a junior officer in 1866 and 1870–71 and retired in 1922 as a corps commander. After the victory at Tannenberg in August 1914, Hindenburg became a national symbol. The mystique of the "wooden titan" increased during 1915 and 1916, less for his own achievements than through the continued discrediting of rival symbols: Chief of Staff Erich von Falkenhayn, Chancellor Theobald von Bethmann Hollweg, and not least Kaiser Wilhelm himself.

Appointed chief of the General Staff in August 1916, Hindenburg was over his head as the supreme commander of a total war effort in a state already stumbling from exhaustion. He lent his name and prestige to a series of fumbling, even disastrous, policies. He supported the increasingly unrealistic war aims of the militarists and nationalists. Yet, at the end, he did facilitate acceptance of the kaiser's abdication, the establishment of the Weimar Republic, and the armistice, and he remained a hero. Elected president of the Weimar Republic in 1925 by a coalition of conservatives and nationalists, Hindenburg initially performed his limited duties loyally and with the same success. The Great Depression, the rise of National Socialism, and his own advancing age, however, reduced his effectiveness. Reelected in 1932 and fearing civil war, the nearly senile president appointed Adolf *Hitler as chancellor in January 1933, and thereafter remained a figurehead until his death in 1934.

[See also Ludendorff, Erich; World War I: Causes.]

• Andreas Dorpalen, *Hindenburg and the Weimar Republic*, 1964. Martin Kitchen, *The Silent Dictatorship: The Politics of the High Command under Hindenburg and Ludendorff, 1916–1918*, 1976.

—Dennis E. Showalter

HIROHITO (1901–1989), emperor of Japan from December 1926 until his death in January 1989. A timid man, preferring marine biology to affairs of state, Hirohito reigned over but did not directly rule Japan; from early in his reign, the military increasingly held sway and committed Japan to war in his name. Hirohito unwittingly contributed to this outcome: as a constitutional monarch he always felt obliged formally to sanction the government's aggressive policies, however much he disagreed with them.

Hirohito privately but unsuccessfully opposed Japan's undeclared war with China, beginning in July 1937, and Japan's entry into the Tripartite Pact with Germany and Italy in September 1940, fearing that this would lead Japan into an unwanted war with the United States and Great Britain. However, he was a nationalist, not the pacifist some accounts imply, and when the United States ended oil exports to Japan on 1 August 1941 in retaliation for Japan's military occupation of French Indochina, Hirohito eventually accepted that war was inevitable. That Japan formally declared war on the United States only after it attacked the U.S. naval base at Pearl Harbor on 7 December 1941 had not been his intention.

During the Pacific War, even as he publicly exhorted his countrymen to sacrifice their lives for victory, Hirohito instructed Prime Minister *Tōjō Hideki to work for peace. Ironically, Hirohito may have prolonged the war, first by protecting the die-hard Tōjō, upon whom he relied politically, from critics until Tōjō finally resigned in July 1944 following the fall of Saipan; and second, by advocating the last "decisive" Battle of *Okinawa, which he hoped would strengthen Japan's position in any forthcoming peace negotiations.

Ultimately, when the war was clearly lost, but with the government deadlocked over whether to accept the Allies' Potsdam Proclamation (26 July 1945) calling for Japan's "unconditional surrender," Hirohito personally intervened and Japan capitulated 15 August 1945. In September, when he first met Gen. Douglas *MacArthur, Supreme Allied Commander in Japan, Hirohito offered to take responsibility for the war. However, he was exempted from standing trial as a war criminal and retained on the throne so that the occupation could use his authority in the demilitarization and democratization of Japan. The new 1947 Constitution stripped him of all prerogatives, leaving a purely ceremonial role.

Despite Hirohito's formal apology for the war, made years later (1975) during a state visit to the United States, many Americans regard him as a controversial figure. However, there is no evidence that Hirohito knew in advance of, or sanctioned, the great many *atrocities committed by Japanese forces during the Pacific War.

[See also Japan, Peace Treaty with; Pearl Harbor, Attack on; Potsdam Conference; World War II, U.S. Air Operations in: The Air War Against Japan; World War II, U.S. Naval Operations in: The Pacific.]

• Toshiaki Kawahara, *Hirohito and His Times: A Japanese Perspective*, 1990. Stephen S. Large, *Emperor Hirohito and Shōwa Japan: A Political Biography*, 1992.

—Stephen S. Large

HIROSHIMA AND NAGASAKI, BOMBINGS OF (1945). The U.S. Army Air Forces' (USAAF) mission to use atomic bombs began in mid-1944 when Gen. "Hap" *Arnold, USAAF commander, initiated a special force to deliver a new "heavy and bulky" superweapon. He appointed Col. Paul W. Tibbets, a veteran of the first B-17 mission over Europe, to command the 509th Composite Group, built around the 393rd Bombardment Squadron, commanded by Maj. Charles W. Sweeney. To accommodate the bomb, Tibbets had his B-29s stripped of most defensive armaments. Most crew training took place at Wendover Field, Utah. The lead aircraft, flown by Tibbets, was a new B-29, which he named the *Enola Gay* after his mother.

By mid-1945, *Manhattan Project scientists produced two kinds of atomic bombs: a *gun type*, detonated by firing one mass of uranium down a cylinder into another mass to create a self-sustaining chain reaction; and an *implosion bomb*, which detonated when a volatile outer shell drove a layer of plutonium inward to collapse into a plutonium core and form a critical mass.

On 16 July 1945, as President Harry S. *Truman began meeting with Soviet leader Josef *Stalin and British prime minister Winston S. *Churchill at the *Potsdam Conference, Manhattan Project officials oversaw the first successful test of a nuclear weapon at Trinity Site, Alamogordo, New Mexico. Debate had already begun as to the wisdom and morality of using the bomb. It came to a choice between demonstrating the bomb (e.g., by destroying an island in Tokyo Bay), or obliterating an actual city. A panel of scientists concluded that saving American lives outweighed all other considerations and that no effective demonstration was feasible.

During the Potsdam Conference, Arnold argued that USAAF raids over Japan could end the war. Army Chief of Staff Gen. George C. *Marshall worried that conventional bombing could not defeat such a determined enemy and would require an invasion of Japan. Marshall's view reinforced Secretary of War Henry L. *Stimson's view and Truman's own belief that the bomb should be dropped before the U.S. invasion, scheduled for November 1945.

After informing Churchill and providing a vague reference about the weapon to Stalin, Truman issued a warning to Japan to surrender. Tokyo did not respond to the offer because the Japanese leaders were deeply divided. Some saw no alternative to surrender, while others wanted peace but feared for Emperor *Hirohito's safety. A small faction advocated fighting to the death. There were deluded hopes that the Soviet Union might mediate for Japan. These notions created official paralysis. On 30 July, Truman approved the use of the atomic bomb.

On 3 August 1945, orders were issued to drop the first bomb when weather permitted. Operations began at 2:45 A.M., 6 August, as the *Enola Gay* and two observation B-29s launched from Tinian. The primary target was Hiroshima, an industrial city that had seldom been attacked. Of little military significance, the city of 250,000 provided a good test of the bomb's destructiveness.

At 8:15 A.M. local time, the *Enola Gay* dropped the gun-type uranium device, nicknamed "Little Boy," from 31,600 feet. It detonated in the center of the city fifty seconds later. A 20,000-foot mushroom cloud of smoke and debris whirled upward. At its base, a combination of blast, fire, and lethal radiation killed at least 60,000 civilians and several thousand military personnel; subsequently another 60,000 fatalities resulted from injuries or radiation poisoning. It also destroyed 81 percent of the city's structures.

When the Japanese government remained deadlocked, U.S. officials authorized the use of a second bomb. The primary target for the plutonium, implosion bomb, nicknamed "Fat Man," was Kokura, a steel manufacturing center. Major Sweeney, who had flown his observation B-29, *The Great Artiste*, during the Hiroshima raid, led the second mission. Without time to restore his plane to a bombing configuration, Sweeney switched planes with Capt. Frederick C. Bock, taking off in *Bock's Car* around 3:30 A.M. on 9 August. Sweeney found Kokura obscured by clouds and turned to a secondary target, Nagasaki, a seaport. At 10:58 A.M. local time, the bomb was dropped from 28,900 feet. It exploded two miles wide of the target because of the bombardier's reliance on *radar until, when the clouds broke at the last minute, he returned to visual aiming. Because Nagasaki lay among hills surrounding the bay, whereas Hiroshima sat on a plain, parts of the city of 200,000 were sheltered from the blast. Still, at least 35,000 persons were killed. Afterwards, 40,000 more died from radiation and other injuries. Nearly half of the city's buildings were destroyed.

On 8 August, Soviet forces had overrun Japanese defenses in Manchuria, and with this and the atomic bombing, Emperor Hirohito concluded that the situation was hopeless. While still uncertain of his future, he chose to seek peace, thus invoking the moral authority of his office and defying the tradition that made the emperor a spokesman for his ministers rather than a ruler. After resistance by a few obsessed by the humiliation of surrender, he prevailed. This debate took time, and U.S. officials believed progress toward peace had failed. Truman ordered the resumption of conventional bombing on 14 August, with more than 1,000 B-29s attacking Japan. As the B-29s returned, Truman announced that the war was over. That same evening, Japan surrendered unconditionally, with official ceremonies held aboard the USS *Missouri* on 2 September, in Tokyo Bay.

The controversy over the use of the atomic bombs emerged during the *Cold War as the world agonized over the possibility of a nuclear holocaust. In 1994–95, the debate focused on the nature of a planned exhibit of the *Enola Gay* at the Smithsonian Institution's Air and Space Museum in connection with the fiftieth anniversary of the bombing.

The atomic bomb has had a profound effect, ushering in the Cold War and the proliferation of *nuclear weapons.

Thus far, the era has also shown ostensibly that there is a point beyond which mankind will not go. Today, civilization's greatest challenge is to make sure that the atomic bombings of Hiroshima and Nagasaki remain singular events.

[*See also* Atomic Scientists; World War II: Military and Diplomatic Course; World War II: Postwar Impact; World War II: Changing Interpretations; World War II, U.S. Air Operations in: The Air War Against Japan.]

• Herbert Feis, *The Atomic Bomb and the End of World War II*, 1966. Martin Sherwin, *A World Destroyed: Hiroshima and the Origins of the Arms Race*, 1973; rev. ed. 1987. Paul W. Tibbets, with Clair Stebbins and Harry Franken, *The Tibbets Story*, 1978. Wesley Frank Craven and James Lea Cate, eds., *The Army Air Forces in World War II*, Vol. V: *The Pacific: Matterhorn to Nagasaki, June 1944 to August 1945*, 1983. Bernard C. Nalty, John F. Shiner, and George M. Watson, *With Courage: The U.S. Army Air Forces in World War II*, 1994. Barton J. Bernstein, "The Atomic Bombings Reconsidered," *Foreign Affairs* (January/February 1995); pp. 135–52. Ralph J. Capio, "The Atomic Bombings of Japan: A 50-Year Retrospective," *Air Power Journal* (Summer 1995); pp. 65–73. Charles G. Hibbard, "Training the Atomic Bomb Group," *Air Power History* (Fall 1995); pp. 25–33. Robert P. Newman, *Truman and the Hiroshima Cult*, 1995. Edward T. Linenthal and Tom Engelhardt, eds., *History Wars: The Enola Gay and Other Battles for the American Past*, 1996. Dennis D. Wainstock, *The Decision to Drop the Atomic Bomb*, 1996.

—William Head

HISTORY, MILITARY USE OF. The armed forces have periodically emphasized or de-emphasized the study of history. Their approach, generally, has been one of "lessons learned," to study the past so as to avoid mistakes in the future. To accomplish this goal, the analysis of history has ranged from individual study requirements to inclusion in professional military *education and training courses, the establishment of history offices at service headquarters levels, and other centers to analyze experience.

For decades, all the services have included the study of *war and battle in officer cadet and professional schooling. After the *Korean War, for example, Army Reserve Officer Training Corps (*ROTC) cadets studied every major battle and campaign of the U.S. *Army, from before the *Revolutionary War to the *Korean War; the text: an army-produced manual, ROTCM 145-20, *American Military History, 1607–1958* (1959). Newly commissioned officers in their initial training also have received service, and now joint-oriented, history. A renewed emphasis and more in-depth study of history has occurred in the late twentieth century in all the professional military education schools. But this is not new; the Naval War College in the years between the world wars analyzed the 1916 Naval Battle of Jutland, while in the 1930s the Marine Corps Schools at Quantico, Virginia, studied the failed Gallipoli campaign of 1915—and the analysis contributed to the development of *amphibious warfare doctrine.

Historical examples of campaigns and battles have always been used in officer education, with the *Civil War a constant, and others studied from the experience of American and foreign armies. Such study ranges from detailed analysis of campaigns and battles to lead-in examples for contemporary exercises. An extension of this are the "staff rides," which date from 1906. In these, military personnel visit the sites of battles or campaigns; in the ensuing "staff ride" (originally on horseback), extensive analysis is conducted through discussion and interaction. The U.S. Army pioneered this approach, and the Marine Corps and air force have included such "rides" in their professional educational programs.

All four armed services, plus the *Joint Chiefs of Staff (JCS) and the Department of *Defense, have established history offices. These have multiple missions, from recording the history of the services and events in which they have participated to responding to inquiries from the heads of services and their supporting staffs to answering public inquiries and assisting in official and unofficial research. The U.S. Army's Center of Military History is a prime example: it has published works spanning the spectrum from unit lineages to its monumental 78-volume history of the U.S. Army in World War II. The sister services have similar agencies, and all also have historical museum programs for preservation of artifacts and display for specific service and public education.

The armed forces also established programs for individual education. For example, during the commandancy of Gen. Alfred Gray (1987–1991), the U.S. Marine Corps set up a reading program for all Marines, from privates to generals. Most of this is rooted in history. The list is revised periodically, most recently in 1996. The other services, in various forms, have their own programs; for example, in 1995, students attending the U.S. Air Force's Air Command and Staff College received a reading list, history-based, of 95 books.

However, a word of caution. Many professionals study history to "learn lessons." Thucydides, still studied by the military, pioneered this approach in his history of the Peloponnesian War. But there is an inherent temptation here to use the past to prove a point or theory. This dilemma was addressed decades ago, when the Prussian general Paul Bronsart von Schellendorf commented: "It is well known that military history, when superficially studied, will furnish arguments in support of any theory or opinion."

Another aspect of the study of military history has been the attempt to determine "principles." A listing of *principles of war first appeared in 1921 in a U.S. Army training regulation, and in the ensuing decades has appeared in various forms in *FM 100-5, Military Operations*. These still appear in all contemporary doctrinal publications, as well as those promulgating joint doctrine (for example, *Joint Pub 1: Joint Warfare of the Armed Forces of the United States*, 1995, and *Joint Pub 3-0: Doctrine for Joint Operations*, 1995). Too much focus on or adherence to the "principles" of war, however, can be a liability. Gen. Ulysses S. *Grant cautioned that "If men make war in slavish obedience to rules, they will fail."

How can the misuses of history be avoided? Today, within armed forces professional military education institutions, academically educated historians—both civilian and uniformed—are faculty members. Integrated into both course development and teaching, they bring their education, standards, and approaches to the evaluative process. Whether in separate organizations (the Combat Studies Institute at the U.S. Army's Command and General Staff College), or within academic departments (the Air University and Naval War College), or paired with uniformed colleagues into faculty advisory teams (the Marine Corps Command and Staff College), they help ensure perspective and contribute to the broader training and experience of their students.

The armed forces believe in the value of history. There are three main reasons for this. Conceptually, most problems personnel will face as commanders or staff officers have been confronted by their predecessors in the profession of arms. History provides an opportunity to learn from the experience of others. And a study of history can reveal what succeeded and failed in the past, as well as the reasons why. This military faith in the study of history is expressed in the Marine Corps publication on *Warfighting* (1997): "The military is a thinking profession. Every Marine is expected to be a student of the art and science of war. Officers especially are expected to have a solid foundation in military theory and a knowledge of military history and the timeless lessons to be gained from it."

The armed forces have faith in the lessons of history. The key is asking the right questions of the past—with the ensuing analysis, interpretation, and conclusions. As Professor Jay Luvaas, formerly of the U.S. Army War College, has so often counseled professional military officers: "No source can answer an unasked question"; and then the important follow-on: "Ask not just what, but why."

[*See also* Disciplinary Views of War: Military History; Museums, Military History.]

• Michael Howard, "The Use and Abuse of Military History," *Journal of the Royal United Services Institution*, 107 (February 1962); pp. 4–10. Allan R. Millett, *Military Professionalism and Officership in America*, 1977. John E. Jessup and Robert W. Coakley, *A Guide to the Study of Military History*, 1979. William G. Robertson, *The Staff Ride*, 1987. Carol Reardon, *Soldiers and Scholars: The U.S. Army and the Uses of Military History, 1865–1920*, 1990. Ronald H. Spector, "Military History and the Academic World," *Army Historian: The Professional Bulletin of Army History*, 19 (Summer 1991), pp. 1–7. David A. Charters, Marc Milner, J. Brent Wilson, eds., *Military History and the Military Profession*, 1992. E. H. Simmons, "Why You Should Study Military History," *Fortitudine: Bulletin of the Marine Corps Historical Program*, 25 (Fall 1995), pp. 3–8. Marvin T. Hopgood, Jr., "The Professional Reading Program," with insert "The Commandant's Reading List," *Marine Corps Gazette*, 80 (July 1996), p. 44. U.S. Marine Corps, *MCRP 6-11A. A Book on Books* (14 April 1997).

—Donald F. Bittner

HITLER, ADOLF (1889–1945), German leader, Führer (leader) of the Nazi empire. Born in Austria, Hitler fought in the German Army as a corporal in World War I. Self-styled *Führer* (leader) of the Nazi Party (NSDAP, or National Socialist German Workers' Party) after 1921, he was briefly imprisoned by the Weimar Republic following a failed coup d'état in Munich in 1923, during which time he wrote *Mein Kampf* (*My Struggle*, 1924). The book sketched out Hitler's belief that the noble "Aryan" or Germanic race was engaged in a life-and-death battle with other inferior races, of which the Jews were the most insidious and dangerous. It called for the creation of a racially pure *Reich* (empire), ruled by a dictatorship, which would impose the German "master race" over the rest of "subhumanity." In the wake of the Great Depression, the NSDAP became the largest party in Germany in 1932. Appointed Reich chancellor in 1933, Hitler soon assumed dictatorial powers, dismantled all other political parties, introduced conscription, and promulgated the racial "Nuremberg Laws" of 1935. Meeting little international or domestic opposition, Hitler reoccupied the demilitarized Rhineland, annexed Austria and the Czech Sudetenland, purged the leadership of the German Army, and set loose a widespread anti-Jewish pogrom in 1938.

Having signed a nonaggression treaty with the Soviet Union, Hitler invaded Poland on 1 September 1939, conquered Western Europe in spring 1940, occupied southeastern Europe, and attacked Russia in the summer of 1941. The fighting was accompanied by untold *atrocities against enemy soldiers and civilians, and the Nazi regime simultaneously implemented the "Final Solution," the genocide of European Jewry. Yet the reverses of the so-called Third Reich multiplied with the Soviet counteroffensive and the entry of the United States into the war in December 1941, the German debacles at Stalingrad and El Alamein the following winter, the Allied invasion of Italy in summer 1943, and the invasion of *Normandy, France, in June 1944. A failed assassination attempt on Hitler's life in July 1944 led to a widespread purge of the plotters; but as American and Soviet troops met on the Elbe River on 25 April 1945 and the Red Army entered Berlin, he committed suicide on 30 April, only days before Germany capitulated on 7–9 May 1945.

Historians debate the extent to which Hitler forged Germany's fate during his twelve-year dictatorship. Some, like Eberhard Jäckel, argue that his totalitarian regime held Germany under complete control, and that Hitler personally had set his goals and decided as early as the 1920s on the means to achieve those goals. Others, such as Martin Broszat, assert that Hitler had far less control over events, that his regime was based on a chaotic struggle of power between competing agencies, and that his policies were largely the function of circumstances rather than careful, farsighted planning. Nevertheless, most historians agree that Hitler strove to achieve two major goals: the winning of additional "living space" for the German people, mainly in the East; and the destruction of the Jews. There is little doubt that he was obsessed with questions of race and social Darwinian "struggle for existence." What is still unclear is how much of the population shared his ideas, and whether the main engine for the implementation of the war of expansion and extermination that Germany unleashed in 1939 was only his personal obsession or the outcome of much more widespread prejudices, phobias, and aspirations at least among the German political, economic, and military elites.

There is also some debate on Hitler's role in the conduct of military operations. Though German generals subsequently claimed they were only following Hitler's orders and that he had a detrimental effect on operations, evidence shows that they shared his urge for conquest and subjugation, and utilized his popularity among the soldiers to boost the troops' morale and motivate them in fighting. This applies also to the popular view that Hitler was a raving madman who somehow seized control of a civilized nation that could liberate itself from his hold only with the assistance of others. As historians such as Ian Kershaw have shown, the "Hitler myth" was a potent political force during much of the regime. Whether or not Hitler was insane, for a long time he seems to have been supported by much of the population of Germany.

[*See also* Holocaust; U.S. War Effort and the; World War II: Military and Diplomatic Course.]

• Joachim C. Fest, *Hitler*, trans. Richard and Clara Winston, 1974. Martin Broszat, *The Hitler State: The Foundation and Development of the Internal Structure of the Third Reich*, trans. John W. Hiden, 1981. Eberhard Jäckel, *Hitler's World View: A Blueprint for Power*, trans. Herbert Arnold, 1981. Ian Kershaw, *The "Hitler Myth": Image and Reality in the Third Reich*, 1987. Ian Kershaw, *Hitler: 1889–1936: Hubris*, 1999.
—Omer Bartov

HOBBY, OVETA CULP (1905–1995), public official and newspaper publisher. Born and raised in Killeen, Texas, Oveta Culp accompanied her father, a lawyer-politician, to Austin when he was elected to the state House of Representatives. She served as parliamentarian of the house (1925–31, 1939–41). In 1931, she married William P. Hobby, former governor of Texas and publisher of the *Houston Post*, on which she later held several positions. In World War II, when Congress created the Women's Auxiliary Army Corps (WAACs), she was appointed first director of the WAACs in 1942, and first director of its successor, the Women's Army Corps (*WACs), established in 1943 as a branch of the U.S. *Army.

Despite the important roles of the WAACs and WACs, many military commanders resented the idea of women undertaking military jobs, and many male soldiers shared this misogyny, which resulted in vicious rumor campaigns against the female soldiers. Hobby and her supporters withstood extremists' accusations of undermining American womanhood and undermining the sanctity of home and the family. Despite the valuable service of the women in uniform, Hobby's rank was limited to colonel, even though the WACs eventually numbered more than 100,000 female soldiers. She remained director of the WACs until 1945 and was awarded the Distinguished Service Medal.

In 1953, President Dwight D. *Eisenhower appointed her first secretary of the newly created Department of Health, Education and Welfare. She thus became the second woman (after former Secretary of Labor Frances Perkins) to hold a cabinet post. In 1955, she resigned to succeed her ailing husband as editor of the *Houston Post*; she became chair of the newspaper's board of directors in 1965.

[*See also* Women in the Military.]
—RitaVictoria Gomez

HO CHI MINH (1890?–1969), international Communist and president of the Democratic Republic of Vietnam (DRV). The son of a scholar-official, Ho was born in Nghe An, central Vietnam, and went to a Franco-Vietnamese school. He moved to France in 1911 and thereafter used over 100 aliases.

A sailor for two years, Ho worked between Le Havre, London, and New York. During World War I, he lived in London, working as a domestic. Back in France, he became a founding member of the French Communist Party in 1920, and, in Moscow from 1923, a Comintern (Communist International) expert on colonial and Asian questions. During long periods in China Ho was instrumental in forming the proto-Communist Vietnamese Youth League in Canton (1925) and the Indochinese Communist Party in Hong Kong (1930).

Ho returned to Vietnam in 1941 and emerged at the head of the Vietnamese Independence League (Viet Minh). Using the code name "Lucius," he supplied anti-Japanese intelligence to American authorities in Kunming, China, in 1944–45. As he led the Viet Minh to power in Vietnam in the August 1945 revolution, Ho's attempts to gain American support against a resumption of French rule continued, but failed. During the thirty-year war for independence against French rule and American intervention, he remained president of the DRV until his death. Although he wanted to be cremated, the myth of the "Uncle-President" became so central to Vietnamese political culture that Ho's body was embalmed and placed in a mausoleum.

[See also Vietnam War: Causes; Vietnam War: Military and Diplomatic Course.]

• Jean Lacouture, Ho Chi Minh, A Political Biography, 1968. Charles Fenn, Ho Chi Minh: A Biographical Introduction, 1973.

—Greg Lockhart

HOLLAND, JOHN (1841–1914). America's preeminent submarine pioneer was born at Liscannor, County Clare, Ireland, and educated by the Christian Brothers, who recognized his drafting skill and mechanical aptitude. As a parochial schoolteacher, Holland studied earlier efforts by William Bourne, David Bushnell, and Robert *Fulton to construct underwater boats. Emigrating from famine-ravaged Ireland in 1873, he secured teaching employment in Paterson, New Jersey, and won support from the Irish Revolutionary Brotherhood to construct his first submersible, tested on the Passaic River in 1878. Similarly funded, he successfully demonstrated his Fenian Ram at New York in 1881. Gaining only limited official attention, not until 1895 did he win a contract to construct the navy's steam-powered submersible Plunger.

Holland's advanced ideas on armament, hull form, and electric underwater propulsion were embodied in his Holland VI, the first modern submarine, constructed at Elizabethport, New Jersey, in 1897 and commissioned by the U.S. Navy as SS-1 in 1900. Holland's Electric Boat Company secured navy contracts for five additional submersibles, followed by orders from Great Britain, Russia, and Japan. Simon Lake, Holland's principal design rival, entered mounting international competition with contracts for Russia, Austria, Germany, and in 1911 with the United States. Shuffled aside by Electric Boat management, Holland, father of the American and the British submarine, devoted his final years to aeronautical research.

[See also Submarines.]

• Frank T. Cable, The Birth and Development of the American Submarine, 1924. Richard K. Morris, John Holland, 1841–1914: Inventor of the Modern Submarine, 1966.

—Philip K. Lundeberg

HOLOCAUST, U.S. WAR EFFORT AND THE. The Holocaust, Nazi Germany's systematic destruction of the European Jews, began in June 1941 and ended with the defeat of Germany in May 1945. The U.S. government was aware of Germany's program of extermination by November 1942, but for fourteen months thereafter the State Department, with the knowledge and acquiescence of President Franklin D. *Roosevelt, made virtually no attempt to rescue Jews. Only in January 1944 did Roosevelt act, and then only when confronted with pressure from many members of Congress, as well as documentation presented by the Treasure Department proving that the State Department had for the most part been following a policy of active obstruction of rescue. Faced with incipient scandal, the president established a government rescue agency called the War Refugee Board. It ultimately helped to save the lives of

about 200,000 European Jews. The British government, whose policy on the Holocaust had paralleled that of the State Department, declined to form a rescue agency and never altered its program of inaction.

Throughout World War II, the U.S. military considered proposals to rescue Jews as outside the scope of its mission. As early as April 1943, responding to inquiries from the Anglo-American Bermuda Conference on Refugees, the War Department made clear its unwillingness to support even minor rescue efforts. The *Joint Chiefs of Staff (JCS) urged rejection of a proposal to move 3,000 Jewish refugees from danger in Spain to safety in North Africa, pointing to the shortage of shipping, the added administrative burden the refugees would put on the military government in North Africa, and the possibility that Arab resentment might require military action to keep order.

In December 1943, the JCS refused a State Department request for military help in moving 4,000 Jews to southern Italy from the Adriatic island of Rab before the Germans seized the island. The chiefs explained that Allied forces in Italy were already overloaded with refugees (mostly non-Jewish Yugoslavs) and action to help those on Rab "might create a precedent which would lead to other demands and an influx of additional refugees." Edward R. Stettinius, Jr., recently appointed undersecretary of state and one of the very few State Department officials interested in rescuing Jews, declared that if this response accurately reflected military policy, the United States might as well "shut up shop" on its efforts to rescue any more refugees from Axis Europe. Stettinius recommended that President Roosevelt inform the military that rescue was "extremely important … in fact sufficiently important to require unusual effort on their part and to be set aside only for important military operational reasons." Nothing came of his suggestion.

The military's noninvolvement in rescue might have changed in early 1944 when Roosevelt formed the War Refugee Board. The president's executive order specified that the State, Treasury, and War Departments each had a special responsibility to help the new agency in its rescue endeavors. War Department officials, concerned that this could mean military forces might be diverted to rescue missions, decided, secretly, in February 1944 not to participate in rescue operations despite the executive order.

By late spring 1944, the massive killing operations at Auschwitz, in Poland, were known to the Allied governments, and Allied air forces had the range to strike the gas chambers as well as the railroads leading to them. Yet no effort was made to bomb those locations, despite several requests for action. Such proposals began to reach the United States from occupied Europe in June 1944, as the deportation of the 760,000 Jews in Hungary went forward.

The first request was turned down by the War Department in late June on the ground that "it could be executed only by diversion of considerable air support essential to the success of our forces now engaged in decisive operations." In reality, the decision was not based on any analysis of air force operations. The War Department did not consult the commanders of the Italy-based U.S. 15th Air Force, which was in the best position to conduct the proposed strikes. Instead, when the War Refugee Board forwarded the initial bombing request to them, War Department officials measured it against their February 1944 policy of noninvolvement. On that basis they decided against the proposal, without investigating its feasibility.

Obviously, they could not inform the board of the real reason for rejection. Instead, they used the best argument available: that the operation would divert considerable military power from essential war plans. With this, the pattern was set. All succeeding requests were rejected on the same grounds as the first.

In fact, bombing the gas chambers at Auschwitz could have been accomplished with little diversion of airpower. Because the complex included a major industrial area adjacent to the camp, Auschwitz itself was a military target—the primary objective a synthetic oil refinery. The Germans has seven other synthetic oil plants in the region, all based on the coal resources of Upper Silesia and all within forty-five miles of Auschwitz. From July through November 1944, more than 2,800 American heavy bombers pounded the eight oil installations. En route to their targets, all of these aircraft flew along or over key deportation railways. On two occasions (20 August and 13 September) large fleets of American heavy bombers struck the industrial area at Auschwitz itself, less than five miles from the four large gas chambers. Yet the War Department stated in a letter of 14 August 1944 that the bombing was not possible because such actions "could be executed only by the diversion of considerable air support essential to the success of our forces now engaged in decisive operations elsewhere."

The last of the attempts to persuade the War Department to bomb Auschwitz came in November 1944. War Refugee Board director John Pehle wrote a strong letter urging destruction of the gas chambers and pointing out the military advantages in simultaneously bombing industrial sites at Auschwitz (the board was not aware of the earlier raids on Auschwitz industries). Once again Pehle's appeal was rejected on grounds that airpower should not be diverted from vital "industrial target systems."

In late November 1944, SS chief Heinrich Himmler ordered the killing machinery at Auschwitz destroyed. On 18 and 26 December 1944, American bombers again pounded the Auschwitz industries. The Soviet army captured the camp 27 January 1945.

As Red Army forces advanced across Eastern Europe in 1944 and 1945, they overran several Nazi concentration camps, including those at Lublin and Auschwitz. In April and May 1945, American and British soldiers came upon the concentration camps in Western Europe—Dachau, Bergen-Belsen, Buchenwald, and others. The liberation of these camps has been cited as proof of the Allied governments' and the armies' concern for the helpless Jews and other victims trapped there.

It is important to keep in mind that these liberations were completely unintentional—an unexpected byproduct of military advances, not the result of military planning. The camps were not assigned as objectives; in reality, the Allied troops came upon them entirely by chance. These facts are clearly reflected in two aspects of the responses to the camps by the American and British armies. First, the officers and men were totally surprised at what they found. There was also shock at the extent of the Nazi depravity. To make certain the Germans could never claim doubt about what had been found, the troops forced local civilians to view the camps and help bury the dead. Second, the armies came without provisions or emergency equipment appropriate to the acute needs of concentration camp survivors. The troops' efforts to help were indeed compassionate, but their attempts to keep the surviving inmates alive had to be improvised. About one-third of those found in the camps died within a month.

The U.S. military's final connection with the Holocaust came about after the defeat of Germany. One result of World War II was that more than 8 million displaced persons (DPs) were stranded in Germany and Austria when the war ended, including former slave laborers and concentration camp inmates, prisoners of war, Eastern Europeans fleeing the Russians, and others. The Allied military forces, in a highly successful operation, managed to repatriate about 7 million DPs by September 1945. Of the more than 1 million who remained, about 100,000 were Jewish survivors of the Holocaust.

Nonrepatriable DPs were to have been cared for jointly by the *United Nations Relief and Rehabilitation Administration (UNRRA) and the Allied military forces. As it turned out, UNRRA was unable to meet its responsibilities, so the military had to fill the vacuum in an assignment for which it had not been trained. The consequence was a continuing disaster for the Jewish survivors. The U.S. Army had very little sympathy for or understanding of the difficult problems of these people, who had been most damaged by the Nazis. Most were kept in inadequate camps (some were former concentration camps) and provided with rations similar to those they had received from the Nazis.

In July 1945, responding to pressure from American Jewish leaders, President Harry S. *Truman agreed to send Earl G. Harrison, former U.S. commissioner of immigration and dean of the University of Pennsylvania Law School, to investigate the situation in the DP camps. Harrison found the plight of the Jews to be "far worse than that of other groups." He denounced "the continuance of barbed-wire fences, armed guards, and prohibition against leaving the camp except by passes," and declared that "as matters now stand, we appear to be treating the Jews as the Nazis treated them except that we do not exterminate them." In early August 1945, the War Department instructed General Dwight D. *Eisenhower, Supreme Allied Commander in Europe, to do everything possible to improve the situation. Eisenhower issued several directives, and by late 1945 conditions for Jewish DPs were generally better, although many military officials in the field continued to show little inclination to implement the new policy adequately.

[*See also* Genocide; Hitler, Adolf; World War II: Military and Diplomatic Course.]

• Martin Gilbert, *Auschwitz and the Allies*, 1981. Leonard Dinnerstein, *America and the Survivors of the Holocaust*, 1982. David S. Wyman, *The Abandonment of the Jews: America and the Holocaust 1941–1945*, 1984. Robert H. Abzug, *Inside the Vicious Heart: Americans and the Liberation of Nazi Concentration Camps*, 1985. David S. Wyman, ed., *Bombing Auschwitz and the Auschwitz Escapees' Report*, Vol. 12 in the series *America and the Holocaust*, 1990. Kai Bird, *The Chairman: John J. McCloy*, 1992.   —David S. Wyman

HOMOSEXUALS IN THE MILITARY. *See* Gay Men and Lesbians in the Military.

HONORS, MILITARY. *See* Awards, Decorations, and Honors.

HOOD, JOHN BELL (1831–1879), Civil War general. Hood graduated from West Point in 1853 and served on the frontier before resigning to join the Confederacy.

Rising rapidly in rank, he won glory at the head of "Hood's Texas Brigade" in the *Seven Days' Battle, Second Bull Run, Antietam, and Fredericksburg, being promoted to major general in October 1862.

At the Battle of *Gettysburg he was severely wounded, permanently crippling his left arm. Returning to duty, he accompanied his division to Georgia, where at Chickamauga troops under his command made a key breakthrough. Again wounded, Hood lost his right leg.

Promoted to lieutenant general and assigned to command one of Joseph E. *Johnston's corps in Georgia the following spring, Hood undermined his commander with a stream of critical letters to President Jefferson *Davis. On 17 July 1864, Davis replaced Johnston with Hood. Backed into the outskirts of Atlanta by Johnston's retreat, Hood had no choice but to fight. In eight days, he fought three battles. The Confederates lost because they were outnumbered, because Hood's physical impairment prevented his supervising operations personally, and because William J. Hardee, upon whom he depended, was resentful and uncooperative after being passed over in Hood's favor.

Union general William Tecumseh *Sherman cut the Confederate supply line at Jonesboro, forcing Hood to evacuate Atlanta 1 September. Hood then tried threatening Sherman's supply lines in northern Georgia, with moderate success, but in November, when Sherman set out on his march to the sea, Hood invaded Tennessee. He outmaneuvered a Federal force under John M. Schofield near Spring Hill and might have destroyed it except that inexplicably the army's command system again failed. Schofield's force escaped, and at the Battle of *Franklin on 30 November, Hood, beside himself with rage, hurled his army at Schofield's entrenched soldiers with devastating *casualties for the Confederates. Incredibly, after this slaughter, Hood followed Schofield to Nashville, where the Federals became part of a huge Union army under George H. *Thomas. In two days of fighting, 15–16 December 1864, Thomas virtually eliminated Hood's army as an effective fighting force. Relieved at his own request, Hood held no other important command.

[*See also* Civil War: Military and Diplomatic Course; Confederate Army.]

• Thomas Lawrence Connelly, *Autumn of Glory: The Army of Tennessee, 1862–1865,* 1971. Richard M. McMurry, *John Bell Hood and the War for Southern Independence,* 1982.

—Steven E. Woodworth

HOOKER, JOSEPH (1814–1879), Civil War general.

Graduating twenty-ninth of a class of fifty at the U.S. Military Academy, Hooker won three brevets in the *Mexican War, but angered Winfield *Scott by testifying against him in a court of inquiry. While a civilian colonel in the California militia in the 1850s, he had a major disagreement with Henry W. Halleck. During the Civil War, he advanced his way up the promotion ladder as a Union leader, often denigrating other officers, until he found himself commanding the Army of the Potomac to its disastrous defeat at the Battle of *Chancellorsville. He served under William Tecumseh *Sherman as a corps commander but demanded reassignment when he failed to receive command of the Army of the Tennessee. From 1 October 1864 to his retirement in 1868, he held inconspicuous assignments.

Hooker had the reputation for being a drinker and a womanizer and is often erroneously cited as the inspiration for prostitutes being called "hookers." He gained the nickname "Fighting Joe" when the newspaper headline "Fighting—Joe Hooker" was in error printed as "Fighting Joe Hooker." His is the tale of a military man of limited ability, reaching command beyond his talents and paying the awful price of *casualties to his men and ruin to his reputation.

[*See also* Civil War: Military and Diplomatic Course; Union Army.]

• Walter H. Herbert, *Fighting Joe Hooker,* 1944. Ernest B. Furgurson, *Chancellorsville 1863: The Souls of the Brave,* 1992.

—John F. Marszalek

HOOVER, HERBERT C. (1874–1964), U.S. president.

Born in West Branch, Iowa, son of a Quaker blacksmith, Hoover was orphaned, then raised by relatives in Oregon. Graduating from Stanford University in 1895, he soon became a millionaire as a global metallurgical engineer.

His humanitarian reputation stemmed from his direction of food relief for occupied Belgium, 1914–17. As head of the U.S. Food Administration (1917–18) under Democratic president Woodrow *Wilson, and as secretary of commerce under Republican presidents Harding and Coolidge (1921–28), Hoover also established a reputation for efficient administration. Defeating Al Smith, he became president, 1929–33.

Although a progressive Republican, Hoover's popularity was undermined by the onset of the depression. In his foreign policy, he struck a balance between *internationalism and traditional U.S. unilateralism, supporting open trade, but accepting a congressional high tariff. Thinking in terms of economic self-sufficiency for the western hemisphere, he repudiated Theodore *Roosevelt's interventionism and withdrew the Marines from Nicaragua.

Hoover emphasized arms reduction and nonmilitary strategies. He obtained some success in the London Naval Disarmament Treaty (1930), extending the 1922 battleship limitation to *cruisers and *submarines. His *pacifism appeared most clearly after Japan's conquest of Manchuria in 1931. When the *League of Nations failed to act, Hoover eschewed economic sanctions, which he thought might lead to war in an area not vital to the United States. Instead, he had Secretary of State Henry L. *Stimson respond with the doctrine of nonrecognition of the illegal conquest.

Hoover's fear of an expansionist Soviet Union led him to oppose U.S. intervention in Europe on the Pacific before 7 December 1941, because although he abhorred the German and Japanese regimes, he feared Josef *Stalin more. In 1942, he co-authored *The Problems of Lasting Peace,* emphasizing that military success alone would not ensure peace, and urging a new postwar international organization to settle disputes peacefully; gradual disarmament; and a ban on military alliances. Hoover coordinated European food relief again in 1945–47. During the *Cold War, he advocated U.S. naval and air defense of the western hemisphere and island bastions from Britain to Japan, Taiwan, and the Philippines. Against commitment of U.S. ground troops overseas, he opposed *NATO and the *Korean War, and supported President Eisenhower's increased reliance upon airpower.

[*See also* Nicaragua, U.S. Military Involvement in; World War I: Causes; World War I: Postwar Impact; World War II: Postwar Impact.]

• David Burner, *Herbert Hoover: A Public Life,* 1979. Gary Dean Best, *Herbert Hoover: The Postpresidential Years,* 2 vols., 1983. Richard Norton Smith, *An Uncommon Man: The Triumph of Herbert Hoover,* 1984.   —Gary Dean Best

HOPKINS, HARRY (1890–1946), social reformer, statesman. Beginning in 1940, this Iowa-born social worker and New Deal relief administrator became President Franklin D. *Roosevelt's surrogate in matters of international security. Residing in the White House and heading a staff that oversaw interagency preparation for American participation in World War II, Hopkins visited England to accelerate assistance against Nazi Germany and became Lend-Lease coordinator in March 1941. Following Germany's attack on the Soviet Union in June, Hopkins flew to Moscow and recommended immediate Lend-Lease to the Russians. In London, he accompanied Prime Minister Winston S. *Churchill to his Atlantic Charter meeting with FDR in August 1941. Hopkins then expedited military aid to Allies ahead of America's own rearmament in the remaining months before the attack on *Pearl Harbor.

At wartime conferences, Hopkins supported Roosevelt's "grand design" for a liberal postwar international order shaped and supervised by the Big Three. With a naval-oriented president, Hopkins, who emphasized the goal of defeating Nazi Germany in Europe, proved a "Godsend" to Gen. George C. *Marshall and Secretary of War Henry L. *Stimson; at the Teheran conference in 1943, he vigorously opposed Churchill's proposed Balkan invasion. At Yalta, early 1945, he optimistically viewed the compromise agreements as "the first great victory of the peace." Hopkins served as President Harry S. *Truman's special envoy to Josef *Stalin in June 1945; he died of stomach cancer six months later.

[*See also* Lend-Lease Act and Agreements; World War II: Military and Diplomatic Course; World War II: Postwar Impact.]

• Robert E. Sherwood, *Roosevelt and Hopkins,* 1948. George McJimsey, *Harry Hopkins,* 1988.   —J. Garry Clifford

HOUSING, MILITARY. The U.S. Constitution specifically prohibited the European practice of quartering soldiers in private homes. The Quartermaster Corps, founded June 1775, was responsible for the construction of training cantonments and more permanent structured camps. During the *Revolutionary War, tents were issued to soldiers in the campaign season, providing shelter for up to six men. Lack of textiles caused tent shortages—a trend that would continue through American history. For winter quarters, lumber, brick, or stone and related supplies were issued for more substantial structures.

In the *War of 1812, the Quartermaster Corps again struggled to provide sufficient quantities of tentage. Afterwards, the War Department decreed that the *Army Corps of Engineers would be responsible for constructing barracks; the Quartermaster Corps would focus primarily on field military housing. The role of the Engineers Corps eventually evolved into the construction of more permanent military housing for soldiers and their families.

During the years that preceded the *Mexican War of 1846–48, the Quartermaster Corps had difficulty obtaining proper materials for tents. Cotton canvas was procured in lieu of imported hemp canvas, which was more suitable for the hardships of extended military campaigning. Soldiers in the field were dissatisfied with the cotton tents issued to them—when they could get them. Common complaints ranged from tents tearing too easily to inadequate protection against rain.

In the American *Civil War, textile shortages again hampered the Quartermaster Department's efforts to procure tentage. The supply of tents was exhausted at the Philadelphia depot as early as 1861. With the exception of field hospitals, large tents were practically nonexistent. To protect troops in the field, the Quartermaster Department obtained tents manufactured on the pattern of the French *d'Abri* tent; thus the shelter-half, so familiar to soldiers in the Civil War, was introduced. Field soldiers of this period affectionately referred to their new shelter as a "pup" tent. The term remains a part of military jargon to this day, along with the standard issue shelter-half tent.

During the Indian campaigns, scattered frontier posts were erected mostly with troop labor, using lumber from nearby forests or transporting it to the Great Plains. The *Spanish-American War of 1898, and burgeoning overseas territories, put further strain on the Quartermaster Department's resources to erect increasing numbers of barracks, hospitals, and post accommodations.

In World War I, larger canvas tents were used to house American Expeditionary Force members in field hospitals. American *Red Cross recreation tents in rear areas provided a respite from the harsh *trench warfare. The Corps of Engineers built wooden structured training facilities, then called *cantonments,* throughout the United States.

The interwar period featured a retrenchment in housing construction as the military was reduced in size. During the Great Depression, the army's housing program was supplemented by the Works Progress Administration. With the defense mobilization beginning in 1940, responsibility for military housing was formally transferred to the Corps of Engineers which constructed bases in the United States and abroad. The Quartermaster Corps continued to retain responsibility for tentage. Troops in the field during World War II, again suffered from tent shortages as the textile industry was hardpressed to keep up with demand.

During the *Korean War and the *Vietnam War, a half-moon-shaped structure, constructed with a thin layer of corrugated steel or aluminum—known as the *Quonset hut*—dotted the landscape. These semipermanent structures offered adequate protection from the elements, and were relatively easy to build and tear down quickly. Soldiers "in the bush" still shared the shelter-half, as their predecessors had done since the Civil War. The Corps of Engineers built military housing in base camps.

Base family housing construction during the Cold War era increased in the United States and in Western Europe—where large numbers of uniformed service members were stationed. The Army Corps of Engineers built housing (as well as airfields) for the air force after 1947. The U.S. Navy began to provide increased amounts of shore-based housing for sailors and Marines in the 1950s and thereafter.

When the *All-Volunteer Force was instigated in the 1970s, apartment-style quarters began to replace the traditional "open bay"–type barracks, which had wide-open rooms that typically housed up to 100 men on one level, along with a common-use latrine. Many of the newer barracks featured two-person rooms equipped with a private bathroom.

In Operation Desert Shield/Desert Storm during the *Persian Gulf War (1991), elaborate portable shelters provided some fortunate service members with a self-enclosed home that not only housed them but also met their messing, laundry, and bath needs—all under a central air-conditioned/heated canvas unit. However, as in the past, not enough of these facilities were available to match mission needs. Soldiers in the front lines in the 1990s still shared the warmth of the familiar "pup" tent as soldiers had done long before them.

[See also Bases, Military: Development of; Bases, Military: Life on; Families, Military.]

• James A. Huston, *The Sinews of War: Army Logistics—1775–1953,* 1966. Erna Risch, *Quartermaster Support of the Army—1775–1939,* 1989.
—Ralph Nichols

HOWARD, O. O. (1830–1909), Union army general and educator. A native of Maine and a graduate of West Point in 1854, Howard entered the U.S. Volunteers during the Civil War as a colonel in June 1861. Promoted brigadier general after the First Battle of *Bull Run, he lost an arm at Seven Pines, but recovered quickly and attained division command at the battles of Antietam and Fredericksburg. After promotion to major general, he took over XI Corps in April 1863, overseeing a disastrous defeat at Chancellorsville the following month. As ranking officer on the afternoon of 1 July 1863 at the Battle of *Gettysburg, he briefly commanded all Federal forces on the field.

Transferring to the western theater, Howard commanded the reorganized IV Corps during the Atlanta campaign of 1864, where he again suffered defeat at Pickett's Mill. Given the Army of Tennessee, Howard commanded without particular distinction during William Tecumseh *Sherman's march to the sea and the Carolinas campaign. An extremely pious and moralistic officer, he led the Freedmen's Bureau during Reconstruction. On the Indian frontier, he accepted the surrender of Chief *Joseph's Nez Percé band in 1877. A lifelong advocate of minority rights, Howard was instrumental in founding Howard University and Lincoln Memorial University before his death in 1909.

[See also Civil War: Military and Diplomatic Course; Union Army.]

• John A. Carpenter, *Sword and Olive Branch: Oliver Otis Howard,* 1964. William S. McFeely, *Yankee Stepfather: General O. O. Howard and the Freedmen,* 1968.
—William Glenn Robertson

HOWE, SIR WILLIAM (1729–1814), British general. The youngest of the second Viscount Howe's three sons, all of whom served in America, William Howe joined the British army in 1746. During the *French and Indian War he served at the *Louisbourg Siege and the Battle of *Québec. Howe returned to America in 1775 to reinforce Gen. Thomas *Gage in the Revolutionary War, arriving in time to command British forces at the Battle of *Bunker Hill. Howe won that battle (losing nearly 40% of his attack force) and succeeded Gage as commander in chief October 1775. During the campaign of 1776, Howe defeated the *Continental army at Long Island, New York City, and White Plains. In 1777, hoping to capture the Congress,

he invaded Pennsylvania, but had to settle for occupying Philadelphia, while the northern Continentals and militia defeated Gen. John *Burgoyne's invading army in New York at the Battles of *Saratoga. Upon Burgoyne's surrender, Howe resigned his command, leaving for England in 1778.

During his three years as commander in chief, Howe consistently stopped short of destroying his enemy when the opportunity arose—perhaps from a sensible estimate of the dangers of pursuit, or from Howe's contradictory roles. As peace commissioner, he was required to negotiate a peace that would bring the colonies voluntarily back into the empire. Howe squandered the British army's numerical superiority by refusing to unleash its full force on the Americans.

[See also Cornwallis, Charles; Clinton, Henry; Revolutionary War: Military and Diplomatic Course.]

• Ira Gruber, *The Howe Brothers and the American Revolution,* 1972.
—Jon T. Coleman

HUSSEIN, SADDAM (1937–), Iraqi dictator. From the provincial town of Tikrit, Saddam rose in the national-socialist Ba'ath Party, becoming Iraq's vice president in July 1968 when Ba'athists seized power. After a decade of ruthless elimination of civilian officials and military officers, he forced out his predecessor and benefactor, Gen. Ahmad Hasan al-Bakr, became president in July 1979, and killed most of his opponents, establishing himself as dictator. Using Iraq's growing oil wealth to support development, grandiose public works, and massive arms purchases, Saddam invaded Iran, whose militant Islamic regime he considered a threat. After the death of 1 million Iranians and Iraqis, the war ended in a stalemate in August 1988. Hussein's forces then killed tens of thousands of Iraq's Kurdish minority, which had rebelled or supported Iran during the war.

With Iraq nearly bankrupt, despite loans of $80 billion (nearly half from Saudi Arabia and Kuwait), Hussein sought to bully Kuwait into bailing him out. Then, on 2 August 1990, he invaded and conquered the emirate. Hussein was accustomed to taking calculated risks, but he had overreached and found himself confronted by almost unified opposition from the West and the rest of the Arab world. In January–February 1991, a U.S.-led Coalition army liberated Kuwait in the *Persian Gulf War.

Since the international coalition did not attempt to topple Saddam and even refrained from supporting Iraqi uprisings, his regime continued, brutally suppressing Kurds and Shiites. Although Saddam survived attempted coups in 1992 and 1993, and a major defection in 1995, UN sanctions hurt Iraq and prevented its resurgence as a major military threat in the Gulf.

[See also Bush, George; Middle East, U.S. Military Involvement in the; United Nations.]

• Efraim Karsh and Inari Rautsi, *Saddam Hussein: A Political Biography,* 1991. Samir al-Khalil, *Republic of Fear,* 1991. Anthony H. Cordesman, *Iran and Iraq: The Threat from the Northern Gulf,* 1994.
—Efraim Karsh

HYDROGEN BOMB. See Nuclear Weapons.

IA DRANG VALLEY, BATTLE OF THE (1965). One of the most significant battles of the Vietnam War, the 14–16 November 1965 battle in the Ia Drang Valley in South Vietnam's central highlands between the U.S. Army's 1st Cavalry Division (Airmobile) and the 33rd and 66th Regiments of the North Vietnamese Army (NVA) marked a watershed change in the military strategies of both sides. For the NVA, it was a shift from reliance solely on Viet Cong guerrilla forces to the use of conventional military forces in order to achieve victory. For the United States, it marked the beginning of direct massive involvement in ground combat operations, as well as a test of the heliborne air mobility tactics that were to become the hallmark of the war.

Thwarting an NVA plan to cut South Vietnam in two by attacking eastward across the central highlands to the South China Sea, the 1st Cavalry Division's 1st Battalion, 7th Cavalry Regiment, made a heliborne combat assault directly into the enemy assembly area. Supported by massive air and *artillery fires, including strikes by B-52 bombers, the NVA were routed and forced to retreat back into their Cambodian sanctuaries. The victory was marred, however, by the ambush of the 2nd Battalion, 7th Cavalry, by remnants of the NVA force as it withdrew from the battle area. *Casualties totaled 234 killed in action during the landing zone X-Ray and Albany actions.

[*See also* Guerrilla Warfare; Helicopters; Vietnam War: Military and Diplomatic Course.]

• Harry G. Summers, Jr., "The Bitter Triumph of the Ia Drang," *American Heritage* (February 1984). Harold G. Moore and Joseph L. Galloway, *We Were Soldiers Once ... And Young,* 1992.

—Harry G. Summers, Jr.

IDEALS, MILITARY. No single authoritative document sets forth America's military ideals. However, we may note three groupings that appear to be valid subsets of military ideals, recognizing that discussion cannot always accommodate compartmentalization along such analytic lines: ethical ideals, establishing standards of professional conduct; ideals in operational matters, that is, in the conduct of war itself; and ideals of military leadership.

Ethical Ideals. The early provenance of American military ideals lies in the history of war itself, predating by centuries the emergence of military professionalism among American officers in the nineteenth century. The British code of military honor as it existed in the later eighteenth century, distinctly aristocratic in tone, served as a model for George *Washington's Revolutionary forces, though it was substantially revised to fit social and political conditions in America. Itself an evolved adaptation of the code of chivalry from feudal times, the British "code" was in fact an amorphous array of principles, values, and traditions that collectively served to encompass the British officer's concept of honor. Morris Janowitz has abstracted the four basic elements of the code: (1) officers fought for traditional military glory; (2) officers were gentlemen; (3) officers owed personal loyalty to their commander; and (4) officers were members of a cohesive, self-regulating brotherhood.

So far as military glory is concerned, modern vestiges of chivalric forms—medals and ribbons for heroism, unit patches on uniforms, unit mottoes and histories, and the celebration of individual and unit heroics in service lore—bespeak a continuing preoccupation with courage under fire and the justified pride and reputation that attends such courage. As to the tradition of officer-as-gentleman, Washington's embrace of that view, in combination with the fact that he became and remains the ideal of the American officer-gentleman to this day, has been a major factor in the persistence of the notion that officers are, first of all, gentlemen. This formulation survives today in Article 133 of the Uniform Code of Military Justice: "Any officer, cadet, or midshipman who is convicted of conduct unbecoming an officer and a gentleman shall be punished as a court-martial may direct." Edwin Cady isolated three persisting traits of the American gentleman that pertain to the realm of ideals: character, courtesy, and cultivation. Character in turn includes the entire range of patrician virtues, a central one being the habit of truthfulness. Out of such a mix emerged the principle that comes close to defining the ethical nucleus of the officer's code of honor: "A gentleman's word is his bond."

The British concept of personalized loyalty to one's commander underwent radical transformation in the American military, owing to constitutional strictures. Loyalty to one's immediate superiors in the military chain of command remains a strongly felt ideal—indeed, loyalty and obedience are the supreme military virtues—but it is always understood, both legally and professionally, that the loyalty owed is to the office, not to particular incumbent individuals. Under the American constitutional system, the loyalty, allegiance, and obedience owed by officers to the military chain of command, including the commander in chief, are subordinated to their allegiance to the Constitution and to the laws that flow therefrom. The primacy of the Constitution in establishing the officer's loyalties derives from the officer's oath of office, the current version having been set down by Congress in 1884. For orders issued by officers in the chain of command to be legally enforceable, including those issued by the commander in chief, they must be lawful. This requirement is spelled out in the officer's commission and is given legal force by Articles 90 and 92 of the Uniform Code of Military Justice.

The fact that within the chain of command, even at the topmost rung, loyalty extended to the office instead of the occupant was a prominent factor in the gradual emergence before the turn of the century of the ideal that officers were "above politics." The ideal of remaining above politics grew finally to embrace the notion that regulars should refrain from affiliating with particular political parties and even refrain from voting. The rationale was that the professional military must loyally serve the nation, regardless of whom political vicissitudes bring to the presidency or Congress, and that political involvement could be seen as compromising the impartiality of professional military advice. Since the 1960s, the strength of this ideal has waned, with the services now actively promoting voting by members through absentee ballots. However, the ideal of the apolitical officer who serves loyally and impartially, regardless of the party in power, remains. A corollary to the officer's allegiance to the Constitution, and closely related to his aim to remain aloof from politics, is the ideal of civilian control of the military. The professional military accepts the ideal of civilian control absolutely without question.

With respect to officers as members of an exclusive brotherhood, the connection between brotherhood and honor becomes clearer when we consider that soldiers, sailors, Marines, and airmen—enlisted members as well as officers—successfully confront the rigors of war only as members of teams, not as individuals. It is to the team that one looks for survival. It is only through the team that the mission is accomplished. To show cowardice and let down one's comrades is thus the ultimate martial sin, the worst form of dishonor.

The American officer's "code of honor," as abstracted and construed by Janowitz but never codified, is not to be confused with the widely noted cadet honor codes of the U.S. service *academies, for example, the honor code of the U.S. Air Force Academy: "We will not lie, steal or cheat, nor tolerate among us anyone who does." Such cadet codes neither pretend nor intend to be a complete description of honorable behavior on the part of military professionals. For cadets who graduate and are commissioned in the corps of officers, their academy honor codes, while remaining a strong force in their professional lives, must accommodate to the professional military ethic itself (i.e., the grand corpus of ethical prescriptions having claim to compliance by service members), which subsumes the codes and extends them so as to confront the ever-growing ethical complexities of today's professional *careers in the military.

None of the individual armed services has thus far elected to codify and officially promulgate a professional ethic in the sense of a comprehensive prescription for ethical behavior along the lines of the American Bar Association's *Model Rules of Professional Conduct* or the American Medical Association's *Principles of Medical Ethics*. A major task of winnowing confronts any officer who would seriously attempt to distill that core of ethical principles having the strongest claim upon his or her professional conscience. We can record here only the most salient elements: the West Point motto, adjuring all service members to accept as their highest values Duty, Honor, Country; the tradition implicit in that motto of always accomplishing the assigned mission, regardless of obstacles; the preeminence of the Constitution in the officer's hierarchy of allegiances; loyalty and obedience as the supreme military virtues, with

the precondition that orders be lawful; the imperative that officers be and act as gentlemen, the essential trait of which is strong character; the precept that an officer's word is his or her bond; *patriotism, valor, fidelity, and professional competence, as enjoined by the officer's commission; the injunction to remain above politics in all professional activity; the principle of civilian control of the military; the principle that one's acts in war itself are subject to constraints laid down in law and that one remains no less an ethical agent in the most desperate straits of battle; the principle that law and ethical obligation follow the service member even after capture by the enemy; and the principle that officers must avoid conflicts between their private interests and official duties, and that this obligation remains after retirement or separation.

Operational Ideals. Such ideals are not to be confused with actual tactical, theater, or strategic principles, or with the principles of war themselves, all of which are subsumed under that universal body of disciplinary knowledge and theory associated with the art and science of war. Rather, there are overarching operational ideals that are peculiarly American, a product of the United States's unique economic, political, social, and geostrategic identity at the dawn of the twenty-first century. These include the following:

(1) U.S. forces are imbued with the spirit of the offensive, characterized by an indomitable will to win and an aggressive determination to carry the battle to the enemy. Their aim is to inflict on the enemy an early and decisive defeat.

(2) Concern for minimizing *casualties to U.S. forces has come to be a principal if not overriding factor in a commander's war-fighting deliberations, though there is no consensus on the best means to minimize friendly casualties (casualties among one's *own* forces) and still accomplish the mission.

(3) Doctrinally, U.S. forces cling to the ideal of maneuver warfare, which entails the rapid, decentralized movement of forces relative to the enemy, with the aim of outpacing the reactive capabilities of his command and control structures and achieving a prohibitive positional advantage. In theory, maneuver warfare is less costly in terms of lives, equipment, and munitions expended because it is indirect, targeting the enemy's will rather than his force. In modern practice, the maneuver ideal has been qualified by a tendency to append industrial-style variations—the habitual use of massive preparatory and concurrent supporting fires as adjuncts to, and in some cases substitutes for, purposeful and rapid movement.

(4) U.S. forces preferably wage war as part of a multinational force, one having the widest possible national representation. The object is not simply to gain additional power but to enhance legitimacy.

(5) War is waged with forces jointly organized and directed. The joint (i.e., multiservice) ideal has been imposed by Congress and the Department of *Defense, and is not yet fully assimilated by the services, though it is embodied in their doctrine. The army, lacking organic means to move its forces to the theater of war and lacking heavy air support, is perforce the most joint-minded of the services; the navy, with its own organic air arm and having the Marines as a land force, finds itself least prompted toward the joint ideal.

(6) U.S. forces seek always to capitalize upon modern

technology. A technological edge offers the advantages both of replacing humans with machines on the battlefield in many cases, thus reducing casualties, and of increasing the capabilities of logistics, transport, communications, intelligence, and fires beyond any level the enemy can match. Advanced computer technology is particularly exploited.

(7) War is waged in ways that minimize collateral damage to areas and structures that are not military targets and that minimize casualties among the enemy civilian population, even though such humanitarian concerns may reduce mission effectiveness.

(8) U.S. forces undertake a spectrum of ancillary missions, such as *peacekeeping and disaster relief, unparalleled in modern arms.

(9) Troops in the battle area are maintained and provisioned in the most unsparing manner possible consistent with the rigors of war. Such comparative plenitude of creature comforts is made possible by the vaunted responsiveness of the American military's logistical system.

Ideals of Military Leadership. The peculiar genius of the American people, among whom liberty and equality remain touchstone values, has predisposed those in uniform to respond better to certain broad leadership approaches than to others. Though such values as liberty and equality obviously cannot receive full or even substantial expression in military service, they do instill expectations in the minds of service members that military leaders ignore at their peril. These expectations have generated two transcendent leadership ideals within the American military tradition. First, regardless of the particular leadership style selected, leaders must always respect the innate human dignity of each of those being led. Second, leaders must recognize the status of American service members as thinking individuals rather than mindless automatons, giving them opportunity wherever feasible to exercise initiative, shoulder responsibility, and employ their native ingenuity in accomplishing assigned tasks.

These ideals, at least in rudimentary form, have always been present in the army, going back to the days of the *Revolutionary War. For the navy, faced with the unique disciplinary demands of harsh duty on the high seas, such ideals did not begin to emerge until after the abolition of flogging in 1850. In the services today, an enlightened philosophy of leadership based upon scientifically derived principles of human motivation has come to take hold. Among the five services, the air force, which did not gain full independence until 1947, is least afflicted by vestiges of rigidly authoritarian leadership, a fact largely attributable to the high educational standards of the enlisted component and the [intimate working relationship officer air crews and enlisted aircraft maintenance personnel], which tend to dilute the formalities of rank and station.

The entire spectrum of American military ideals—from the U.S. *Coast Guard motto *Semper paratus* (Always prepared) to the Marine Corps motto *Semper fidelis* (Always faithful), reflects the earnest idealism that continues to animate the professional conduct of the men and women who don military uniform to defend America. Such idealism in the military is both fitting and necessary. For, of all professionals, it is the soldier, sailor, Marine, and airman alone who must be prepared to face the ultimate trial and rigor of killing—and being killed—in service to their country.

[*See also* Commemoration and Public Ritual; Disciplinary Views of War: Military History; Doctrine, Military; Leadership, Concepts of Military.]

• Edwin Cady, *The Gentleman in America;* 1949. Samuel P. Huntington, *The Soldier and the State,* 1957. Malcom E. Wolfe, et al., *Naval Leadership,* 1949; 2nd ed., 1959. Morris Janowitz, *The Professional Soldier,* 1960. Charles Royster, *A Revolutionary People at War: The Continental Army and American Character, 1775–1783,* 1979. James E. Valle, *Rock and Shoals: Order and Discipline in the Old Navy, 1800–1861,* 1980. Peter L. Stromberg, Malham Wakin, and Daniel Callahan, eds., *The Teaching of Ethics in the Military,* 1982. Department of Defense, *The Armed Forces Officer,* 1988. Anthony E. Hartle, *Moral Issues in Military Decisionmaking,* 1989. Fleet Marine Force Manual 1 (U.S. Marine Corps), *Warfighting,* 1989. Field Manual 100-5 (U.S. Army), *Operations,* 1993.

—Lloyd J. Matthews

ILLUSTRATION, WAR AND THE MILITARY IN. What distinguishes art from illustration has long been a vexing problem, but it is less a judgment of relative quality than ultimate purpose. As the famous American illustrator Norman Rockwell pointed out, "The illustrator has, unlike the painter, a primary interest in telling a story." Illustration in addition is almost always commissioned, and its ultimate purpose is reproduction and dissemination.

War and the military have long been subjects for both artists and illustrators. In the Revolutionary era, Paul Revere's widely disseminated engraving of the *Boston Massacre of 1770 helped inflame public opinion. In 1775, Amos Doolittle (1754–1832) issued contemporary engravings on the battles of *Lexington and Concord; Bernard Romans did the same for the Battle of *Bunker Hill. During the Revolution, the *Continental army used illustrations on recruiting posters (usually showing sharply dressed professional soldiers going through the manual of arms).

By the *War of 1812, hand-colored engravings publicized U.S. naval victories in the Atlantic and on Lakes Erie and Champlain, the burning of the nation's capital, the successful resistance of Fort McHenry in Baltimore Harbor, and Andrew *Jackson's victory in New Orleans.

In the early nineteenth century, wood-block engraving was increasingly displaced for producing inexpensive "news" and "history" prints for the general public by lithography, a process in which the illustration was drawn in reverse with crayon on a porous stone plate, which produced much finer gradations and values than sharp-line wood-block engraving. The most noted firm, Currier & Ives (initiated by Nathaniel Currier in 1834 and joined by James Ives in 1852), issued "news" prints of American military conflicts from the *Mexican War to the *Spanish-American War. They issued thousands of copies of some 100 different prints of *Civil War battles. Since the firm never sent any artists into the field, but relied upon newspaper accounts for their research, the prints have little value as firsthand visual accounts of particular battles. However, they did have considerable impact upon large numbers of Northerners as Union propaganda; the legends described every battle as a Union victory, regardless of the true outcome.

By the mid-nineteenth century, photography began to emerge as a competitor in disseminating to the public scenes of war and the military (for example, the Civil War photographs of the teams headed by Mathew Brady and Alexander Gardner). But the slow exposure time for photographic plates of the period made it impossible for cameras to capture action except as a blur.

It was artist-illustrators as well as photographers who made the Civil War the most visually documented war up to that time. Developments in printing had led to new weekly and monthly illustrated magazines such as *Harper's, Frank Leslie's,* and *Century,* which sent teams of "visual reporters" to accompany the *Union army on its campaigns. Among those sending back on-the-spot drawings of camp life and combat to the Northern magazines and weekly newspapers were Winslow Homer (1836–1910), Edwin Forbes (1839–1895), James E. Taylor (1839–1901), and Alfred R. Waud (1828–1891). Conrad Wise Chapman (1842–1910) was one of the well-regarded illustrators on the Confederate side. In the 1880s, as nostalgia set in, there was another outpouring of Civil War battle illustrations, such as the famous Kurz and Allison thirty-six–print set Battles of the Civil War and in the heavily illustrated four-volume series *Battles and Leaders of the Civil War.*

Beginning in the late 1890s, the new photomechanical process of halftone printing contributed to an astounding growth of illustrated mass-market newspapers and magazines. Sensationalist New York newspapers such as William Randolph Hearst's *Journal* and Joseph Pulitzer's *World* sent artist-illustrators to Cuba to cover the Spanish-American War, among them Frederic Remington (1861–1909), William Glackens (1870–1938), and the noted marine artist and naval officer, Henry Reuterdahl (1871–1925).

It was World War I, however, that expanded the wartime role of American illustrators, particularly via the medium of the poster. Emerging in France in the 1890s as a major commercial force through the combination of art and lithography, the large-scale poster became widely used as a means for informing and persuading the urban masses. During World War I, all the belligerents employed posters for mobilization, not simply to recruit for the armed forces but also to encourage the public to buy war bonds, increase munitions production, conserve food, hate the enemy, and support the war effort. To mobilize public opinion when the United States entered the war in 1917, the Wilson administration created a Committee on Public Information, which in turn formed a Division of Pictorial Publicity headed by noted artist Charles Dana Gibson (1867–1944), president of the Society of Illustrators. Gibson obtained the services of some of the most famous illustrators, who worked almost exclusively in hand-prepared, full color commercial lithography. Among them were Howard Chandler Christy (1873–1952), Joseph Christian Leyendecker (1874–1951), Joseph Pennell (1860–1926), Edward Penfield (1866–1925), and James Montgomery Flagg (1877–1960), whose self-image as "Uncle Sam" pointedly declaring: "I Want You for U.S. Army" is perhaps the best-known poster in American history. The armed services also commissioned combat artists to record the war.

By World War II, motion picture and still photographers had taken over production of most of the visual record of war and the military for newspapers, magazines, and movie theaters. Nevertheless, well-known artist-illustrators continued to work in the field, including Flagg, Reuterdahl, and Leyendecker, who had produced such notable posters in World War I. Others like Norman Rockwell (1894–1978) produced both posters, such as his famous *Four Freedoms* series, and magazine illustrations, such as his well-known *Saturday Evening Post* cover of "Rosie the Riveter." Mead Schaeffer (1898–1980) did a series of action covers for that magazine to characterize personnel from the particular branches of the armed services; Noel Nickles (1911–1982) did a similar series for *Life* magazine. Walt Disney (1901–1966) contributed his artists' efforts in many ways, including the design of some 1,200 unit insignias. The armed forces also had combat artists, but the most widely reproduced battlefield illustrations were undoubtedly those of the bedraggled foxhole denizens "Willie" and "Joe," in Bill *Mauldin's cartoons for the army's overseas newspaper, *Stars and Stripes.*

With the extension of photographic and television coverage of war, illustrators participated to a much lesser extent in American conflicts after World War II. Political cartoonists drew caricatures in the *Cold War and the "hot" wars of the period. The armed forces commissioned illustrators to record the *Korean War, among them John Pike (1911–1979), Steve Kidd (b. 1911), Clayton Knight (1891–1969), William A. Smith (b. 1918), and Ward Brackett (b. 1914). The antinuclear organizations' *peace and antiwar movements of the *Vietnam War also used cartoons and posters. Robert T. McCall (b. 1919) and Robert Benney (b. 1904) recorded everyday military life in Vietnam, and Charles Waterhouse provided more than 500 combat drawings of the navy and Marines in Southeast Asia. By the end of the twentieth century, illustrators had been largely replaced by still and motion picture photographers in the on-the-scene portrayal of war and the military.

[*See also* Commemoration and Public Ritual; Culture, War, and the Military; Nuclear Weapons and War, Popular Images of; Propaganda and Public Relations, Government.]

• Henry C. Pitz, *200 Years of American Illustration,* 1977. Walton H. Rawls, *The Great Book of Currier & Ives America,* 1979. Marshall B. Davidson, *The Drawing of America,* 1983. Walt and Roger Reed, *The Illustrator in America, 1880–1980,* 1984. Walton H. Rawls, *Great Civil War Heroes and Their Battles,* 1985. Gloria Gilda Deák, *Picturing America, 1494–1899,* 2 vols., 1988. Walton H. Rawls, *Wake Up, America! World War I and the American Poster,* 1988. Walton H. Rawls, *Disney Dons Dogtags,* 1992. Peter Paret, Beth Irwin Lewis, and Paul Paret, *Persuasive Images: Posters of War and Revolution,* 1992. Bill Mauldin, *Up Front (50th Anniversary Edition),* 1995.
—Walton H. Rawls

IMPERIAL WARS. Although North America was peripheral to Western European rivalries in trade, revenue, and power, imperial wars strongly shaped modern North American history. Conflicts between Europeans and Indian communities were also imperial, but conflicts between European settlements and between European forces in America extended European military competition more directly. Generally, these wars reflected rather than affected European power. Their phases correspond to the dominance of Spain, the Netherlands, France, and Britain.

Spain's initial adventures in America roused little rivalry beyond the English-sponsored explorations of John Cabot and the Portuguese voyages of the Corte-Réal brothers. Although Portugal had fought Spain for the Canary Islands, the Portuguese crown quickly gained so much in the Far East that it seemed sensible to respect the 1494 Treaty of Tordesillas with Spain, a hemispheric apportionment of all the worlds that Iberians might discover. Other European courts made no forceful objections to Spain's modest initial colonies on Haiti and Cuba. The conquest of Mexico in 1521, however, soon changed everything.

The silver and gold of Central and South America were by far the greatest prizes any European power derived from the Americas, translating immediately into pay for armies and fleets, funds for dissidents in neighboring European countries, and collateral for a scale of borrowing that transformed European warfare. The year Mexico was conquered, rivalry between Habsburg emperor Charles V (1500–1558), who was also king of Spain, and French king Francis I (1494–1547) launched nearly forty years of Habsburg-Valois wars in Europe (1521–1559). French privateers captured their first Mexican treasure in 1523, initiating one strategy against Spain's American-supported power. Efforts to find riches equivalent to those of the Aztecs, Mayans, and Incas inspired French voyages by Giovanni da Verrazzano (1524) and Jacques Cartier (1534, 1535–36, 1542–43). They failed to find either North American wealth or a passage to the Orient, but Spain's rivals retained the option of stealing what Spain was taking from the New World. As Spain invested more in convoys for its American bullion fleets, French privateers attacked Spanish Caribbean ports, in the hope of diverting Spanish men-of-war from their primary task. When these Franco-Spanish wars ended in 1559, the two courts informally agreed that depradations occurring west of the Canary Islands would not disturb the peace of Europe. There was to be "no peace beyond the Line."

For the next half century, North America served primarily as a *privateering base for Spain's Protestant rivals. As France collapsed in religiously inspired civil war (1559–89), French Huguenots established a refuge and privateering base at Fort Caroline (Jacksonville, Florida) in 1564. The Spanish responded decisively the following year, capturing the fort, executing most of the prisoners, and establishing St. Augustine, the first permanent European settlement in North America. English illegal traders in the Caribbean, led by John Hawkins, were succeeded by pirates, led by Francis Drake. Elizabethan colonizing ventures in North America failed, under Humphrey Gilbert in Newfoundland (1582) and Walter Raleigh at Roanoke Island (1584–87); both had been intended as bases for raiding Spanish American shipping. During the Anglo-Spanish War (1585–1604), English privateers built fleets and gained navigational knowledge of the Americas, but failed to capture the treasure fleets.

Peace between European maritime powers allowed the English, French, and Dutch to establish permanent North American colonies. Spain took no military action against them, but the English Virginia Company destroyed French settlements at Mount Desert Island, the St. Croix River, and Port Royal (Annapolis Royal, Nova Scotia) in 1613. During the Anglo-French War of 1627–29, English privateers captured French fishing and trading fleets in the Gulf of St. Lawrence, and seized settlements at Tadoussac and Québec.

The Dutch, emerging from their long war for independence from Spain (1572–1648), became Europe's next dominant maritime power. The only mariners ever to capture an entire Spanish treasure fleet (1628), the Dutch forced Spain to extend Europe's peace "beyond the Line" in self-defense. The Dutch built their imperial success on efficient shipping and a global network of trade in exotic commodities for expanding European consumption. For example, Dutch traders provided capital, expertise, shipping, and markets for sugar production on English and French Caribbean Islands in the 1640s, stimulating the growth of trade in both African slaves and North American provisions, lumber, and horses. Unable to compete with the Dutch, French and English competitors sought government support for exclusionary mercantilist trade laws, and for the maritime wars to enforce them.

Three Anglo-Dutch Wars (1652–54, 1665–67, 1672–74) reduced Dutch trading advantages by escalating their costs for battle fleets, convoys, forts, and marine insurance. Over 1,000 Dutch merchant vessels captured in the first war gave England enough ships to transport colonial commodities that the new Navigation Laws insisted must be carried in English or colonial-owned ships. Little fighting occurred in North America during this war, but the English capture of New York in 1664 helped provoke the Second Anglo-Dutch War. The Dutch readily recaptured New York in 1673 but, severely tested at home by the massive military power of Louis XIV's France, returned the colony to England a year later.

By the 1680s, France had become the paramount power in Western Europe, whether measured by population, tax revenues, or standing armies. Although Jean-Baptiste Colbert (1619–1683) developed impressive naval power and mercantilist colonial policies, America was less necessary to France than it had been to Spain or the Netherlands; maritime war could never cripple a French economy based primarily upon internal markets.

The Anglo-French struggle for North America involved four wars over a period of seventy-five years (1689–1763). Although the British colonists persistently outnumbered their French counterparts by at least twenty to one, the manpower advantage was offset by decentralized and disunited British colonial governments. Many Indians, using intercolonial wars to gain supplies for their resistance against encroaching European settlement, helped prolong the contest by supporting the Canadians. European navies helped insulate the American contests. European courts declared each war and proclaimed each peace, but were slow to undertake serious fighting in North America.

The shared pattern of the first three Anglo-French wars helps explain their inconclusiveness. British Americans rather optimistically named them after their monarchs: King William's War (1689–97), Queen Anne's War (1702–14), and King George's War (1744–48). Monarchs declared war, then hurried the news to the West Indies to snatch a rival's unsuspecting sugar colony. In North America, it was the Canadian governors who invariably initiated serious belligerence, putting stronger enemies on the defensive and consolidating Indian alliances. The first devastating blows in 1690 fell on Schenectady, New York; Salmon Falls, New Hampshire; and Forts Casco and Loyal in Maine. These were paralleled in 1703–04 by attacks on Wells, York, Saco, Winter Harbor, Casco, and Deerfield, and in 1744, by the capture of Canso.

The northern British colonies responded, in each case, with a major siege in Acadia as preliminary to a two-pronged attack on Québec. This type of offensive suited provincial armies recruited on eight-month contracts, trained for only a few weeks, and reliant on shipborne cannon. Such campaigns could promise to "extirpate" an otherwise elusive enemy at predictable costs. William Phips led New England volunteers who profitably captured Port

Royal in 1690, then formed a larger expedition that failed to take Québec. Meanwhile, New York and Connecticut volunteers joined Mohawk and Mohegan warriors in the overland force, stalling at Lake Champlain and sending a small raiding party that attacked La Prairie too early to divert Canadian forces from Québec. In the next war, New Englanders twice failed to take Port Royal in 1707. They awaited British assistance before capturing that base again in 1710, then became junior partners in the British Walker expedition that failed to reach Québec the following year. In King George's War, the New England provinces responded to the capture of Canso by conquering Louisbourg. Plans for an attack on Québec in 1746 collapsed when Britain diverted the intended battle fleet to Portugal, but the British government showed growing commitment when it reimbursed colonial expenses.

In all three wars, the failure of a massive British-American endeavor against Québec heralded reduced colonial effort on both sides, as though a balance of usable force had been confirmed. Profitable raiding, of Hudson Bay fur posts and Newfoundland fishing stations, continued, and colonists claimed to be pursuing the imperial war while "settling with" their Indian enemies as the wars ended. In 1697, the New Englanders fought the Abenaki while New France fought the Iroquois. After 1711 the Carolinas were embroiled in war, first with the Tuscarora, then with the Yamasee. British and French colonials struggled to control the Indians of the Upper Ohio Valley from 1747 in a contest that would defy the peace of 1748 and start a new imperial war six years later.

Whenever European governments contemplated peace negotiations, they became more willing to divert martial resources to America. Captured forts and colonies were useful bargaining items at the peace talks. Thus the French captured English St. John's, Newfoundland, in 1696, but it was retaken the following year while the French captured Spanish Cartagena. Peace negotiations had begun in the second war before the Walker expedition sailed to Québec. As the War of the Austrian Succession seemed decided in Europe, a massive French fleet set off on its disastrous attempt to retake Louisbourg in 1746.

This pattern of intercolonial warfare was broken in 1754, when Virginia troops clashed with Canadians and Indians near the forks of the Ohio River, launching the *French and Indian War two years before the European courts declared what would be known as the Seven Years' War (1756–63). Both Britain and France committed regular ground troops to North America from 1755, and this increased regular army and navy commitment reinforced unprecedented colonial military and financial efforts. French, Canadian, and Indian successes marked the first five years of the war, from the defeat of Virginians under Col. George *Washington (1754) and British regulars under Gen. Edward *Braddock (1755) through the capture of Fort Oswego (1756) and Fort William Henry (1757), to the defense of Fort Carillon (Ticonderoga, 1758). A comparatively unified command gave France advantages not matched until William Pitt inaugurated a subsidy system to encourage colonial participation and end a crippling series of disputes between colonial assemblies and military commanders. British and American victories followed: the recapture of Louisbourg and the taking of Fort Duquesne (1759); successful sieges of Fort Niagara and Québec (1759); and the surrender of Montréal (1760).

Spain belatedly joined its French ally in 1761, marking the fourth time the British and Spanish had been at war since 1717. The wars of 1717–18 and 1727–28 had been brief maritime confrontations, though South Carolina forces and their Indian allies besieged St. Augustine unsuccessfully in 1728. The British and British colonials enthusiastically undertook the War of Jenkins' Ear (1739–44), only to fail at St. Augustine (1740) and more miserably at Cartagena (1741). Spanish entry into the Seven Years' War proved less fortunate, for British forces supplemented by American volunteers captured Havana, which would be exchanged for Florida at the Peace of Paris (1763).

The protracted Anglo-French struggle had fulfilled Indian and Canadian objectives by limiting the expansion of British American settlement and trade. These wars climaxed in a ruinously expensive contest after which the victorious British government felt compelled to reduce North American expenses drastically. Indians were soon at war with a government that eliminated traditional gifts. American colonists, expecting the benefits of peace, soon replaced their celebration of imperial victory with resistance to new imperial taxation, a resistance that could be more confident because French power had been eliminated from the continent.

[See also Braddock's Defeat; Louisbourg Siege; Native Americans: U.S. Military Relations with; Native American Wars: Wars Between Native Americans and Europeans and Euro-Americans.]

• J. H. Elliott, *Imperial Spain, 1469–1716*, 1963. J. H. Elliott, *The Old World and the New 1492–1650*, 1970. Douglas Edward Leach, *Arms for Empire: A Military History of the British Colonies in North America, 1607–1763*, 1973. Fred Anderson, *A People's Army: Massachusetts Soldiers and Society in the Seven Years' War*, 1984. Geoffrey Parker, *The Military Revolution: Military Innovation and the Rise of the West, 1500–1800*, 1988. G. V. Scammell, *The First Imperial Age: European Overseas Expansion c. 1400–1715*, 1989. William John Eccles, *France in America*, 1972; 2nd ed. 1990. Ian K. Steele, *Warpaths: Invasions of North America*, 1994.   —Ian K. Steele

INCHON LANDING (1950). During the Korean War, in the summer of 1950 *United Nations forces were pushed back to the Pusan perimeter. In spite of this calamitous situation, Gen. Douglas *MacArthur, as early as July, had conceived of a great amphibious operation that would land at Inchon, South Korea's principal west coast port, and drive inland to liberate Seoul, South Korea's capital. He envisaged a huge turning movement that would cut the enemy's major lines of communication and force the North Korean Army, already overextended, to face around and defend on a new front.

Naval commanders saw horrendous problems in assembling the necessary amphibious shipping and negotiating the treacherous sea approaches to Inchon. The tides, up to 30 feet, were among the highest in the world. Low tide left vast mudflats across which landing ships and *landing craft could not beach and amphibian tractors could not crawl. Hydrographers stipulated that the best date for the landing would be 15 September, when the morning high tide would be at 6:59 A.M. and the evening high tide at 7:19 P.M.

The landing force, which MacArthur designated X Corps, would have to be gathered from parts scattered around the world. In the assault would be the hastily assembled 1st Marine Division. In reserve would be the 7th U.S. Infantry Division, weakest of the four divisions that had made up the occupation force in Japan and with untrained South Korean conscripts as half its rifle strength.

At daybreak on 15 September, a Marine battalion landed on Wolmi-do, an island forming the northern arm of the channel. That evening, two Marine regiments made the main landing against Inchon itself, going over sea walls that were themselves formidable barriers. The assault, with a five-to-one strength advantage, easily overcame the 2,200 second-rate North Korean troops defending the city.

The march to Seoul, against thickening defenses, began the next morning. After heavy fighting, Seoul was declared "secured" on 28 September. The next day, MacArthur escorted President Syngman Rhee in a triumphal reentry into his capital city.

[*See also* Korea, U.S. Military Involvement in; Korean War.]

• Lynn Montross and Nicholas A. Canzona, *The Inchon-Seoul Operation,* 1955. Robert D. Heinl, *Victory at High Tide,* 1968.

—Edwin Howard Simmons

INCIDENTS-AT-SEA TREATY, U.S.–SOVIET (1972). This treaty, signed in Moscow 25 May 1972, prescribed measures to prevent incidents at sea and in the air space over it between the ships and aircraft of the U.S. and Soviet navies. Agreed procedures were necessary for ships and aircraft operating in close proximity to diminish chances of dangerous accidents. It was also agreed that there should be no simulated attacks upon each other's ships, such as aiming guns, missile launchers, torpedo tubes, and other weapons, or illuminating each other with searchlights. At U.S. insistence, this treaty did not provide rules for submarine-versus-submarine operations.

The rapid expansion of the Soviet Navy in the mid-1960s brought their fleet from a coastal force to one with worldwide capability, sailing to troublespots where U.S. ships operated. After two serious collisions between Soviet warships and U.S. destroyers in April 1970 and October 1971, it was obvious something had to be done.

In 1968, the United States invited the Soviets for discussions to reduce incidents, and in 1970 the Soviets accepted this invitation. The first negotiating session was held in Moscow in late 1971 and the second just prior to signing in 1972. This treaty, still in effect, was negotiated in only two nine-day sessions because it was a practical discussion conducted by naval staffs and successfully kept out of the political limelight.

The formal signing was conducted by Admiral of the Fleet Sergei G. Gorshkov and Secretary of the Navy John Warner during a historic visit to the Soviet Union by President Richard M. *Nixon.

• "Incidents-at-Sea Treaty, U.S.-Soviet" (full text), reprinted from the *New York Times,* 26 May 1972, p. 4.   —William D. Smith

INDEPENDENCE, WAR OF. *See* Revolutionary War (1775–1783).

INDIANS. *See* Native Americans in the Military; Native Americans, U.S. Military Relations with; Native American Wars.

INDIAN TREATIES AND CONGRESSES. Treaties, although often broken and usually seen as expeditious and economical methods of relieving Native Americans of

their lands, nevertheless have historically served as the foundations of tribal relations with the federal government. Hundreds of treaties were signed, but scholars disagree on the exact number and, significantly, on what an Indian treaty really means. There were probably more than 200 treaties concluded during the colonial period alone. The U.S. Senate ratified at least 367 treaties and perhaps, according to some scholars, as many as 5 to 8 more. Treaties negotiated but never ratified numbered over 150. States and citizens worked out treatylike agreements with several tribes, and individual communities also reached contractual agreements with Native American groups. The Confederate government made twelve treaties with Indian nations during the *Civil War, and by the early 1870s federally appointed intermediaries negotiated well over 100 intertribal treaties. U.S. Army officers serving in the field may have worked out as many as 50 unratified agreements with tribal leaders in the years between 1790 and 1890. Even after Congress officially ended the policy of making treaties with Indian tribes, the federal government negotiated close to 75 additional "agreements," the last in 1911 or 1914, depending on the authority.

To the Western Europeans who came to the New World, treaties were documents that essentially codified agreements made between two or more sovereignties. They could be made to end wars and reestablish peaceful relationships, define commercial interactions, create political and military alliances, or transfer territory from one nation to another.

The European discovery of the Americas created serious moral, legal, and cultural doubts about how to deal with Native Americans. Advocates of out-and-out conquest argued that Indians were either subhumans or heathens and were therefore incapable of having dominion over themselves or over property. In the 1530s, Francisco de Vitoria, who held the *prima* chair of theology at Salamanca University, wrote a series of discourses known as the *Relectios* in answer to the Spanish emperor's inquiries regarding the status of Native Americans under human, church, and natural laws. Victoria argued effectively that Indians were indeed human, had a religion, were politically organized, and held rights to property. He concluded that Indian land could not be taken by right of discovery, or by right of conquest in the absence of a just war. It had to be secured by purchase from the legitimate rulers of the tribes. The Spanish were thus legally obliged to treat with indigenous tribes as sovereign nations.

Every other European empire in the Americas more or less followed suit. In several cases, Indian groups were more powerful than the colonists militarily and the whites were forced to deal with them as equal, sovereign polities. Treaty negotiations with Native American nations became customary to establish boundaries, obtain land cessions, end wars, and gain trade concessions. Native Americans too had a long history of extratribal relations and numerous customs that helped manage affairs between nations.

By the time the American colonies gained independence, the treaty-making process was well established and had become a ritual of no small consequence. Of course the Americans, who emphasized due process and documentation, always focused on the final wording of the treaties themselves. Tribal leaders, coming from societies that relied on the power of ceremony and the spoken word, probably paid more attention to the rituals of, and the speeches made during, the formal negotiations. Whatever the case, the councils and congresses called for the purposes of making treaties were often many-sided exhibitions of generosity, oratory, and military might. Following tribal customs, gifts were always exchanged. The federal government had special silver peace medals struck for presentation to tribal leaders. Federal negotiators, in turn, received wampum, pipes, and sometimes weapons. Few councils occurred without a military presence, the officers and troops always at their parade-ready best. The tribes, too, put on military displays of no mean quality. Witnesses have described hundreds of tribal horsemen appearing at treaty councils heavily armed and dressed in their finest apparel.

Since 1776, more than 1,000 treaty councils or meetings have been conducted to reach formal agreements between various tribes and the federal government. Many occurred at frontier *fortifications; numerous others took place on tribal grounds. In the obvious attempt to impress upon the tribes the power of the federal government and the size of the white population, Indian leaders were invited to attend treaty councils in major cities. No fewer than twenty-four ratified treaties were signed in St. Louis and at least sixty-nine were negotiated in Washington, D.C. On hundreds of occasions tribes were asked to send delegations to tribal congresses at the Capitol to discuss problems and to reaffirm the relationship between the tribes and the federal government. President Bill *Clinton called one such congress in 1994. The ceremonial side of treaty making—the desire to influence and awe the tribes—attested to the apparent seriousness the federal government attached to dealing with Native Americans. The tribes, in turn, placed equal and, as the United States became more powerful, even more weight on the process of treaty making to secure their sovereign rights. Native Americans in general felt betrayed when the federal government decided that it could not only end the process entirely but unilaterally abrogate specific provisions of Indian treaties.

The flaw in American Indian treaties that led to the betrayal of the tribes was built into the U.S. Constitution itself. Article VI clearly states that treaties, along with the Constitution itself and the laws of the United States, "shall be the supreme Law of the Land." This stipulation followed customary practices in international relations, which construed treaties as commitments between two or more sovereigns that could not be abrogated without grave consequences. Once signed and ratified by the Senate, treaties were to carry the full weight of the Constitution and should not be violated even by federal statute. All lower levels of government and individual citizens were of course legally obligated to obey treaty provisions.

On the other hand, Article I, section 8, gave Congress the power "To regulate Commerce with foreign Nations, and among the several States, and with the Indian tribes." The word *Commerce* when used in regard to Indians was quickly assumed to have the same connotation as the term *affairs*. This clause also set Indian tribes apart from states and foreign nations, a distinction the Supreme Court would later use to decide that Indian treaties could be judged according to a very different set of rules.

In the Supreme Court cases *Marbury* v. *Madison* (1803) and *McCulloch* v. *Maryland* (1819), Chief Justice John Marshall established the precedent of judicial review, which empowered the federal judiciary to decide whether or not a statute was unconstitutional and thus null and void. Judicial review allowed the federal court system to decide which article of the Constitution, III or VI, actually governed Indian relations. The first inkling that the Supreme Court was leaning toward the commerce clause interpretation of Indian affairs came in a 1831 case, *Cherokee Nation* v. *Georgia*. Chief Justice Marshall, still on the bench after thirty years, ruled that the tribes acknowledged in treaties that they were under the protection of the United States and that "The Indian territory is admitted to compose a part of the United States." Therefore, Marshall held, Indian tribes were not foreign but "domestic dependent" nations, and Article I, section 8, of the Constitution refers to Indian tribes by a "distinct appellation." Although he used this argument to throw the Cherokee case out of court, Marshall nevertheless set the precedent of utilizing the commerce clause to define Indians and interpret the status of Indian tribes and treaties, under constitutional law.

In December 1870, the Supreme Court under Chief Justice Salmon P. Chase delivered one of the more perplexing rulings yet made in regard to Indian treaties. Two years before, Congress had imposed a tax on tobacco products and two Cherokee tobacco manufacturers, Elias C. Boudinot and Stand Watie, had refused to pay it, maintaining that the Cherokee treaty of 1866 exempted the Cherokees from any such levy. Quoting the supremacy clause of the Constitution, the Court reasoned in the *Cherokee Tobacco* Case that the Constitution really did *not* settle the problems that might arise when treaties conflicted with acts of Congress. The Court ruled that a "treaty may supersede a prior act of Congress, and an act of Congress may supersede a prior treaty," placing treaties on an equal basis with ordinary legislation and weakening the supremacy clause considerably. This subjected the Cherokee treaty, and by extension all other Indian treaties, to unilateral congressional action.

Within three months, on 3 March 1871, Congress abolished treaty making with the tribes altogether. The act was as much the result of murky congressional politics as of the widespread belief that Indian tribes were really not worthy of being treated as sovereign states. For several years, the federal government had been subsidizing the railroad industry with land grants taken from the territorial concessions made in Indian treaties. The executive branch negotiated the treaties and the Senate ratified them. The lands obtained from the tribes were not really placed in the public domain. Members of the House of Representatives felt that their collective authority, as protectors of the electorate's interest in the public domain, had been usurped. The House used the power of the purse to halt allocations to the Indian Office and finally attached the rider abolishing treaty making to the Indian Appropriations Act. A major policy decision had thus been made within the framework of a relatively minor piece of legislation.

The act did not abrogate prior treaties, nor did it end the process of treaty making entirely. Because the treaties were still in effect, the only way to change or alter them was to make another treaty. Since Congress had abolished treaty making, however, the federal government instituted negotiating "agreements" with the tribes in 1872.

The most severe judicial blow made against Indian treaties came in the 1903 case, *Lone Wolf* v. *Hitchcock*. In 1867, the Kiowas and Comanches signed the Treaty of Medicine Lodge. Among other things, the treaty stipulated that no part of the Kiowa-Comanche reservation in the Indian Territory could be ceded without the consent of a three-fourths majority of the tribes' adult males. In the 1890s, Congress began the process of surveying and allotting tribal lands to individual Kiowas and Comanches in an effort to force them to become farmers and ranchers and enter mainstream American society. Surplus lands were to be sold to non-Indians. Arguing that the sale violated the three-fourths majority stipulation in the Medicine Lodge treaty, the lawyers for the Kiowa leader Lone Wolf took the case to the Supreme Court. The Court, however, found that Congress had the power to abrogate Indian treaties "from the beginning," and thus had plenary authority over the tribes. In effect, Indian treaties were relegated to a lower level of law.

Since 1903, Indian treaties have been viewed in a somewhat different light. Treaties serve as the basis for the trust and the direct "government-to-government" relationships between the United States and the tribes. As a result of a number of legal precedents, Indian tribes now enjoy certain reserved rights that have not been specifically stripped away by congressional action. In short, a number of tribes have retained at least some sovereign rights recognized by treaty.

[See also Native Americans, U.S. Military Relations with.]

• Felix S. Cohen, Handbook of Federal Indian Law, 1942. Douglas C. Jones, The Treaty of Medicine Lodge, 1966. Wilcolm E. Washburn, Red Man's Land, White Man's Law, 1971. Vine Deloria, Jr., comp., A Chronological List of Treaties and Agreements Made by Indian Tribes with the United States, 1973. Francis Paul Prucha, ed., Documents of Federal Indian Policy, 1975. Vine Deloria, Jr. and Clifford M. Lytle, American Indians, American Justice, 1983. Monroe E. Price and Robert N. Clinton, Law and the American Indian, 1983. David H. Getches, Charles F. Wilkinson, and Robert A. Williams, Jr., Federal Indian Law, 1993. Francis Paul Prucha, American Indian Treaties, 1994.   —Tom Holm

INDOCTRINATION. See Training and Indoctrination.

INDUSTRY AND WAR. The impact of America's wars on industrial production has varied dramatically, depending on the particular war and the stage of industrial development.

The key economic fact about the American *Revolutionary War is how little it affected industrial production. Since the *Continental army never exceeded 20,000 men, its material demands were comparatively small. Because a majority of Americans had no strong preference as to the outcome, major sacrifices were not to be expected, and little time was spent in actual combat. The southern plantation economy was of course disrupted, but exports still remained substantial. Although the government built armories, nevertheless, about 60 percent of U.S. gunpowder was imported. The Revolutionary War did retard the development of the iron industry, and the gross domestic product (GDP)—which at this time can only be very crudely estimated—probably declined somewhat during and immediately following that war.

Of somewhat greater significance was the impact of the *War of 1812. British *blockades of U.S. ports almost dried up American exports. This also meant that foreigners could not trade with the United States—hence encouraging import substitutes, especially textiles. Some see this development as the first faint beginnings of industrialization in America.

The impact of the *Civil War on industrial growth has been much studied. Traditionally (that is, in major studies of the topic from the 1920s to the 1950s), the Civil War was seen as a spur to industrialization. Charles and Mary Beard as well as Louis Hacker took this position, arguing that by destroying the Southern slaveocracy, the Civil War shifted the balance of political power to the industrial North, and the Northern Republicans passed laws that stimulated industrialization. In a classic article in 1961, Thomas Cochran argued that the rate of real growth in value added in U.S. manufacturing actually slowed during the Civil War decade. Pig iron and bituminous coal production—key elements in the manufacturing process—also declined or showed little growth during the war years. Railroad track growth rates were retarded, immigration declined, bank loans dropped, construction slowed. Nor did freeing the slaves help industrialization because former slaves largely became sharecroppers.

Other writers have emphasized the continuity of industrial development prior to and after the Civil War. Factory building and mechanized *transportation were continuous and rapid, both before the war and after. Industrial "takeoff" was well underway before the war started, Walt Rostow has argued, and industrial profits during the war largely lagged behind price increases. Real wages fell about 20 percent during the war. Government borrowing certainly drove up interest rates, as public debt rose from $65 million in 1860 to $2,678 million in 1865. In short, Cochran's position that the Civil War actually retarded industrial growth has become the dominant one, but it needs to be modified by the less quantifiable view that changes wrought by the rise of the Republican Party probably did enhance the "capitalist spirit," and certainly a host of Supreme Court decisions over the next three decades favored industrialists over labor and farmers and legitimized a high protective tariff.

World War I marked the transfer of world economic leadership from Europe, and especially Great Britain, to the United States, and quickly proved a boon to U.S. industrial economy. Early on, America became the arsenal as well as the granary for the Allied powers. To achieve this end, the government quickly seized control of the economy and passed laws to fix prices, shifted plants to war needs, established minimum wages and maximum hours, and imposed controls on foreign commerce. By 1918, the government had absolute control over industrial raw materials, the railway system had been nationalized, and marginal mines had been brought into production. Estimates of the growth of GDP during wartime are controversial, ranging from 5 to 18 percent, but by 1920 the high levels of wartime employment in manufacturing had been reached again, thus preparing the nation for a period of prosperity. Finally, World War I changed America's role in the world economy from a debtor nation to a creditor nation, and clearly established the United States as the foremost industrial nation in the world.

World War II solved the problem of the Great Depression, the greatest economic calamity America has ever faced. Even before the attack on *Pearl Harbor, unemployment and industrial sluggishness had almost vanished in the wave of increased defense spending, and by 1945 the real GDP per capita had almost doubled from its prewar base. Expenditures of the War Department rose from $2 billion in 1939 to $80 billion in 1945. The impact of industrial war spending was most dramatic in the Far West, and especially California, which became the fulcrum for the naval war against Japan. By the end of the war, California was the center of the aircraft industry and Los Angeles had risen from a film industry city to a center of shipyards and aircraft plants. In fact, World War II really set the stage for the West to become the fastest-growing region in America since 1945. Overall, by 1944 the United States had indeed become the "arsenal of democracy," outproducing both Germany and Japan almost twofold, boasting the world's largest navy and air force and one of the world's largest armies.

The War Production Board controlled all raw materials and finished goods, both military and civilian, and the Office of War Mobilization and Reconversion served as an umpire over conflicting claims of government agencies. Under their guidance unemployment fell to 1 percent by 1944; industrial employment for blacks and other minorities jumped dramatically; and about half of all new civilian jobs were filled by women. Almost half of all men over the age of sixty-five were in the workforce during that war, compared to 2 percent in the 1990s. The war also saw a tremendous increase in union membership, but union leaders had to accept modest wage increases and agree to a "no-strike" pledge. A government freeze on prices, wages, salaries, and rents made inflation less of a problem than in World War I, but these controls were widely resented and a black market of troubling proportions emerged.

Great advances in technology and scientific research were achieved through war expenditures—most notably jet engines, rocket propulsion, plastics and other synthetics, and television and *radar. Many if not all of these products would have come about anyway, but World War II certainly speeded their development. Medical breakthroughs, including sulfa drugs, penicillin, and quinine, were also a consequence of the war. Most obviously, nuclear energy, with all its positive and negative consequences, was a direct result of the development of the atomic bomb.

World War II industrial mobilization was paid for by taxes and borrowing in about equal proportions. The national debt rose from $41 billion in 1941 to $271 billion in 1946, or 114 percent of GDP. It has never been paid off, although it has been paid down to 52 percent of GDP (which includes nonwar debt as well). Few have questioned the value of this investment. The war also altered fundamentally our attitude toward government, making Keynesian fiscal policy the preferred approach to industrial development. With the passage of the Employment Act (1946), the federal government became responsible for maximum industrial development, employment, and purchasing power. Consequently, the public has come to expect full employment and an ever-growing economy.

The cost and consequences of the *Cold War, including the Korean and Vietnam conflicts, for industrial development have been substantial. Defense purchases as a percent of GDP reached 14 percent at the peak of the *Korean War and 10 percent during the *Vietnam War. During the Reagan defense buildup of the 1980s, military purchases peaked at 7 percent, and by the mid-1990s they were still in the 4 percent range. In the 1950s and 1960s, defense spending represented about one-half of all federal government outlays; in the 1970s and 1980s, it fell to about 25 percent; and by the mid-1990s, the figure had fallen to about 15 percent, not because defense expenditures plummeted but because social spending rose dramatically. This military spending created powerful vested interest groups, sometimes referred to as the *military-industrial complex. Aerospace, electronics, shipbuilding, and computer industries benefited substantially from defense spending during these years, as did the interstate highway system and higher education. The great majority of America's largest corporations, however, derived only a small portion of their revenues from defense spending in this period, and the so-called "military-industrial complex" was and is only one of numerous and powerful interest groups with conflicting goals in the American system. Nor has defense spending had much influence on the stock market, which in recent years has boomed as defense has declined relative to other outlays.

Defense infusions into the American industrial base since 1950 correlate closely with the prevalence of fear of an external threat to U.S. security, principally from the former Soviet Union. Looking back, the level of fear was not irrational, and careful studies of congressional voting patterns in heavily defense-oriented districts show that the representatives in these districts were not more hawkish than those with little defense spending. On the contrary, big spenders in both parties tended to be those who were in Congress the longest.

During the 1990s, defense spending has tended to be highly concentrated by industry, with major impacts in ordnance, aircraft, and shipbuilding. Less than 100 companies dominated the market, most of them middle-sized corporations, and there has been little turnover and few failures for these businesses. Nor has there been much spillover to the private economy. The geographic impact industrially has tended to concentrate in a handful of states, notably California, Texas, and Massachusetts. At its last peak, in 1967, defense spending represented about 10 percent of U.S. industrial output and employed about 7.5 million workers. At that time, about one in every five scientists and engineers in private industry were employed in defense industries. By 1995, defense outlays amounted to $272 billion, which was 18 percent of federal expenditures and 3.9 percent of GDP. Of this, about $110 billion was in military prime contracts to industry, employing 800,000 civilians, about half of whom lived in the South.

[See also Defense, Department of; Labor and War; World War I: Postwar Impact; World War II: Domestic Course; World War II: Postwar Impact.]

• Charles and Mary Beard, The Rise of American Civilization, 1927. Louis Hacker, The Triumph of American Capitalism, 1940. Chester W. Wright, "The More Enduring Economic Consequences of America's Wars," Journal of Economic History, Supp. 3 (1943). Walter Rostow, The Stages of Economic Growth, 1960. Thomas C. Cochran, "Did the Civil War Retard Industrialization?" Mississippi Valley Historical Review, 1961. James L. Clayton, ed., The Economic Impact of the Cold War, 1970. Adam Yarmolinsky, The Military Establishment, 1971. Steven Rosen, ed. Testing the Theory of the Military-Industrial Complex, 1973. Murray Weidenbaum, Military Spending and the Myth of Global Overstretch, 1989. Glen Pascall and Robert Lamson, Beyond Guns and Butter, 1991. Jeremy Atack and Peter Passell, "The Economics of the Civil War," in An Economic View of American History for Colonial Times to 1940, eds. Susan P. Lee and Peter Passell, 1979; 2nd ed., 1994. —James L. Clayton

INFANTRY. See Army Combat Branches: Infantry.

INF TREATY (1987). Signed by U.S. president Ronald *Reagan and Soviet general secretary Mikhail Gorbachev on 7 December 1987, the treaty on the elimination of U.S. and Soviet intermediate- and shorter-range *missiles was the first arms control agreement to eliminate—not simply set limits on—nuclear missile systems. Informally known as the INF Treaty (or Intermediate-range Nuclear Forces Treaty), it required the destruction of all U.S. and Soviet ground-launched ballistic and cruise missiles with ranges between 500 and 5,500 kilometers and of the missiles' essential infrastructure. The treaty resulted in the elimination within three years of 846 U.S. longer- and shorter-range INF missile systems and 1,846 similar Soviet systems, and it banned such systems in the future.

In the mid-1970s, the Soviets deployed new, highly accurate, intermediate-range mobile Soviet SS-20 missile systems, targeted on Europe. A 1979 *NATO "dual-track" response to pursue arms control talks while proceeding with counterdeployments of new, modernized U.S. intermediate missile systems in Europe led to the INF negotiations, which began in Geneva on 30 November 1981. The talks were briefly terminated by the Soviet Union on 23 November 1983 as deployments of the new U.S. systems began, but resumed in Geneva in March 1985 as part of broader discussions on nuclear and space issues.

To ensure compliance, the INF Treaty contains the most extensive verification structure achieved to that time, including a comprehensive regimen of on-site inspections and a provision for continuous monitoring of the former INF missile production plants at Votkinsk, Russia, and Magna, Utah, in the United States to confirm the treaty's production ban. The treaty's pioneering verification process has served as the model for all subsequent arms control agreements. In addition, it led to the creation of the U.S. *On-Site Inspection Agency and other permanent arms control bodies since used to implement arms control treaties.

[*See also* Arms Control and Disarmament: Nuclear; Arms Control and Disarmament: Nonnuclear; Arms Race: Nuclear Arms Race; CFE Treaty; Cold War: External Course; SALT Treaties.]

• Joseph P. Harahan, *On-Site Inspections Under the INF Treaty,* 1993. George L. Rueckert, *Global Double Zero: The INF Treaty from Its Origins to Implementation,* 1993. —George L. Rueckert

INSIGNIA. Special identification for soldiers and their instruments of war predates recorded history, going back to specially carved prehistoric clubs, and including such well-known examples as Egyptian chariots, Israelite tribal symbols, Roman standards, Zulu regalia, and American Indian warpaint. Anthropologists and psychologists have suggested a warrior's need to identify with a proud unit, or to personalize, trust, and feel affection for those implements that deliver the warrior from or to destruction.

During the Crusades, at the siege of Antioch in 1097, since suits of armor were somewhat anonymous, the Crusaders painted their shields to help them recognize each other in the heat of battle. These later evolved into official coats of arms, representing families and clans. The spirit of knighthood quickly transferred such symbols into elaborate robes, medals, and rings, which became the forerunners of modern metal military insignia.

As weaponry began to render *body armor obsolete, coats of arms were scaled down and used on tunics and caps, still in the form of the escutcheon or shield. In 1484, Richard III of England founded the Herald's College or College of Arms to determine who would wear certain coats of arms and what the symbols would look like. From this arose the term *heraldry,* an art form that, in the modern military services, remains basically unchanged from Richard's original intent. To avoid duplication and confusion, unit members who wish to create or change their primary emblem must still submit a preliminary piece of artwork to their service heraldry organization and have it officially approved.

As regular standing armies emerged in America in the seventeenth and eighteenth centuries, unit insignia became standardized. Men of common ancestry could now wear the colors of famous units on their uniforms, enhancing both esprit de corps and fighting *troop morale. When George *Washington took command of the *Continental army in 1775, he ordered his officers to wear colored rosettes on their hats as symbols of rank, beginning a long tradition of American military insignia that followed the European style. From these emblems of rank evolved the current use of shoulder or sleeve stripes and metal pins or embroidery as rank insignia. The pride and sense of history generated by such insignia remains a significant part of the military mystique.

Some weapons systems were also identified with official and sometimes unofficial identification symbols. In the twentieth century, the airplane provided the ultimate evolution of the medieval steed carrying a knight's colors into battle. Aircraft nose art—the most popular form of aircraft insignia—was created almost as soon as there were military aircraft. Italy was the first country to use the aircraft in war, deploying several planes to Tripoli in 1912. By 1913, a number of squadrons were using unit and identification markings, since, as the knights of old had discovered, friend and foe were anonymous in battle without some form of decoration. A Nieuport-Macchi of the Italian Navy was painted like a sea monster, with a face, teeth, eyes, and large ears, and the number 20 in large black numerals. In addition, the Italians marked the aircraft with 1-inch by 5-inch white wound stripes for each bullet hole received in combat.

At the start of World War I, the first additions of color to warplanes centered on national and squadron markings; on the ground, French motor transport units were the first to use a form of stylized identification, painted on the sides of their vans. Later, a young, idealistic American ambulance driver and fledgling artist named Walt Disney painted his own vehicle's canvas sides. These insignia, particularly on ambulances, were so graphic in depicting nurses, Indian heads, cartoon characters, and animals that French aircraft squadrons quickly applied similar motifs.

Though the British Royal Flying Corps (RFC) was the first to introduce numbers and letters on their aircraft, it was the Belgians, French, Italians, and Russians who used unit symbols as a departure to embellish their planes with a colorful variety of emblems. At this point, individual pieces of art began to appear, unique to the pilot. The British were the first to name individual aircraft. No. 10 (Naval) Squadron's "Black Flight" of black-painted Sopwith Triplanes became famous when its core of five Canadians painted names on their machines.

In late 1916, Allied pilots started reporting brightly

colored, outlandish, even fantastic German fighters, using every color of the rainbow. The *Jagdstaffein*, on an incredible victory streak that peaked during what the RFC remembered as "Bloody April" 1917, were allowing their pilots to paint their fighters in any combination of colors they wanted.

The trend was initiated by German ace Oswald Boelcke, who painted his Halberstadt blue; it was then imitated by Manfred von Richthofen, known as the "Red Baron" for his red Albatros D III. Before long, the Red Baron's *Jasta* 11 pilots were using some form of red on their aircraft, with the understanding that only the Red Baron's would remain entirely red. Other *Jagdstaffein* followed with what became known as the "Flying Circus" rainbow of colors, as well as individual art painted on the aircraft at the pilot's request. Belgian, French, Russian, Polish, and finally American Nieuports, and then Spads, began to sport their pilots' heraldry, reviving a medieval tradition as "Knights of the Air."

With World War II came the golden age of aircraft insignia. Though other nations identified and to some extent decorated their aircraft, the Americans made individual nose insignia an art form, plastering them on almost anything that flew, and even on tanks and ships. Listening to some of the crews who fought that war in the air, one would not be hard-pressed to conclude that the American pinup, and the field art it inspired, helped win the war. Though there were almost as many examples of nose art without them, women, usually in pinups, served as the prime movers for this phenomenon of flying personalized aircraft into combat. Americans defined much of what has come to be accepted as aircraft insignia, influencing the history profoundly.

Since World War II, American military insignia—in the air, at sea, and on the ground—have for the most part been muted by the generals and admirals for camouflage reasons. Anything that glinted or was colorful was given earth, sea, or sky tones to match its surroundings. But invariably the colors break out, enhancing morale and spirit. Military insignia, particularly the variety created by Americans, will always represent pride and color in a very dangerous profession.

[See also Air Warfare; Awards, Decorations, and Honors.]

• Jeffrey L. Ethell and Clarence Simonsen, *The History of Aircraft Nose Art: World War I to Today*, 1991.
                                                —Jeffrey L. Ethell

INTELLIGENCE, MILITARY AND POLITICAL. Intelligence is often referred to as the "second oldest profession," but for the United States, intelligence is still a relative newcomer as an accepted government function. The United States has been largely free of proximate security threats for much of its history. This fact, and the ongoing lessons from the founders about the dangers of large standing armies, meant that intelligence activities played little role in U.S. history until the mid-twentieth century.

The term *intelligence*, as used here, means two significant functions, one large and one small. The large function is the collection, analysis, and dissemination of relevant national security information. The smaller function is covert activities—a broad range of actions intended to influence events overseas with the role of the United States either unknown or at least plausibly denied. This is a very small part of intelligence in terms of manpower and budget, although it proved extremely important politically during the Cold War.

Prehistory: The Eighteenth and Nineteenth Centuries. The founders were not unaware of the uses and practice of intelligence. The European state system of which they had been an imperial appendage had a long history of secret agents and spies by the time the American Revolution began. Many of these practices had been carried over to the New World. Indeed, George *Washington's famous mission into the Ohio wilderness as a young officer in 1754 was both a diplomatic and a reconnaissance expedition.

The *Revolutionary War benefited from a number of intelligence practices. Washington, as a commander, understood the utility of espionage and employed spies. As is always the case, their success and veracity varied widely. (The most famous and unfortunate American spy, Nathan Hale, was a poor collector of accurate intelligence.) The Continental Congress had a Committee of Secret Correspondence to maintain communications with those in Europe (including some in Britain) who might be friendly to the American cause. Finally, prior to official diplomatic recognition in 1778, France clandestinely supplied crucial arms via what would be called today a "front company."

As with much else, President Washington established important precedents for U.S. intelligence. At his request, Congress supported what became known as the Secret Service Fund, which at one point amounted to 12 percent of the federal budget. Presidents had to certify the amounts they spent, but did not have to state the purposes, which were widely acknowledged to be intelligence-related.

During the nineteenth century, what little U.S. intelligence activity occurred largely meant wartime tactical reconnaissance. Intelligence played little role beyond that during the *War of 1812 or the *Mexican War. During the *Civil War, both sides employed spies, to little effect. The Union achieved one short-lived technological breakthrough: airborne reconnaissance via balloons. Although these had some success in increasing the range of the commander's vision, the experiment was abandoned mid-war. The Army of the Potomac created a Bureau of Military Intelligence in 1863, which the historian Christopher Andrews credits with having made some contribution to Union victory by its ability to give accurate information as to the Confederate forces' strength and movement.

The first U.S. military attaché—an officer accredited abroad to collect information overtly—was a naval officer posted overseas in 1872. The first standing U.S. intelligence components were created in the 1880s: the Office of Naval Intelligence (ONI) in 1882 and the army's Military Intelligence Division (MID) in 1885. Both were small and largely devoted to collecting data that might be relevant in time of war. These can also be seen as part of a larger military trend then prevalent in Europe, the growing appreciation of the value of a more coherent military staff that was highlighted by Prussia's recent victories.

The prehistory of U.S. intelligence ended with the successful covert action (a not overly indigenous revolution) that created an independent Panama in 1903: the province successfully broke away from Colombia under the auspices of President Theodore *Roosevelt, so that the United States could obtain what became the Canal Zone.

The Early Twentieth Century: 1903–40. In the early part of World War I, the United States—the most influential neutral power—was essentially an intelligence target of both Britain and Germany. A British intelligence success helped shift much U.S. opinion away from cherished *neutrality. British codebreakers intercepted and deciphered Germany's offer of support and territorial spoils to Mexico should Mexico go to war with the United States, the famous Zimmermann telegram.

Once the United States entered the war, its predominant intelligence concerns were related to supporting eventual combat operations in France. There were two notable precedents: the beginning of U.S.-British intelligence cooperation, the famous "special relationship" and the beginning of U.S. signals intelligence (SIGINT), with the creation of a code and cipher unit in 1917 under the legendary Herbert Yardley.

The postwar period also saw two important developments. First, despite the usual *demobilization, Yardley's interception and codebreaking efforts survived as the Cipher Bureau—more familiarly called the "Black Chamber"—funded jointly by the State and War Departments. Second, the infamous Red Scare led to the creation of a General Intelligence Division within the Justice Department's Bureau of Investigation, the forerunner of the Federal Bureau of Investigation (FBI), which was created in 1935.

The Black Chamber contributed to a major U.S. diplomatic, rather than military, success. Having broken Japanese diplomatic codes, Yardley gave the U.S. delegation at the Washington Naval Conference (1921–22) the details of Japan's naval limits negotiating position, a striking coup. However, as U.S. interest in international issues waned, so did support for the Black Chamber. In 1929, Secretary of State Henry L. *Stimson shut it down (with the probably apocryphal comment: "Gentlemen do not read each other's mail"). Army codebreaking efforts continued, and were enlarged and consolidated with the Signal Intelligence Service (SIS), created in 1930.

Codebreaking remained the mainstay of pre–World War II intelligence efforts. SIS cracked Japan's diplomatic PURPLE code in 1940; the resulting decoded messages were called *MAGIC. The army and navy also continued to use attachés abroad, but these officers were often chosen more for their social skills than for their acuity as intelligence collectors.

World War II. The outbreak of war in Europe in 1939 (preceded by undeclared war in Asia in 1937) revealed once again the paucity of U.S. intelligence. President Franklin D. *Roosevelt relied on his own network of well-traveled friends, including attorney William Donovan, for international information. Under British tutelage, Donovan became convinced of the need for a central intelligence organization to handle collection, analysis, and operations. Roosevelt was more cautious, designating Donovan Coordinator of Information (COI), with the vague charter to collect and analyze information bearing on national security. Donovan ambitiously made the most of this, but faced rival organizations, predominantly in the military.

Pearl Harbor has become synonymous with the often overused but in this case apt phrase "intelligence failure." U.S. intelligence efforts were too disparate and disunited across the government, making it impossible to derive a coherent picture; analysts falsely "mirror-imaged" Japanese behavior and underestimated their capabilities; intelligence dissemination was deeply flawed. Anticipating blows in Southeast Asia, Washington was caught completely by surprise with the actual attack on *Pearl Harbor.

The sudden advent of war saw a new intelligence turf battle. The military rapidly built up all functions, including intelligence. This imperiled the COI, but Donovan was a bureaucratic survivor. In 1942, his office became the Office of Strategic Services (OSS), which retained the collection and analysis functions and gained the task of planning and conducting "special services"—i.e., *covert operations. The military remained opposed to a separate intelligence entity and had OSS placed under the jurisdiction of the newly formed *Joint Chiefs of Staff (JCS). The OSS-JCS relationship remained difficult throughout the war. Interestingly, OSS emerged from the war with a legendary reputation for operational prowess, although these operations had little effect on the war's outcome. OSS's analytical efforts were also modest contributors, competing with both military intelligence and the FBI. Still, the OSS served one important intelligence function as the training academy for many who shaped the postwar intelligence community.

SIGINT played a much greater role in the Allied victory. MAGIC, once the Japanese naval codes were broken in 1942, was central to U.S. victories at the Battle of *Midway and elsewhere in the Pacific, just as Britain's *ULTRA, the deciphering of German military codes—shared with the United States—helped to defeat Germany in the Atlantic, North Africa, and in Europe.

The Modern Intelligence Community. President Harry S. *Truman disbanded OSS one month after Japan surrendered, dispersing analysis to the State Department and some operations to the army. The future of U.S. intelligence became part of the larger debate over the entire national security apparatus, largely prompted by wartime studies to unite the military departments.

Truman became increasingly unhappy with intelligence reporting, finding it difficult to make sense of conflicting reports and analyses. In 1946, he created a Central Intelligence Group under a Director of Central Intelligence (DCI) to improve coordination among the disparate reports. Devoid of any institutional base, however, the DCI found this hard to do.

In 1947, the *National Security Act became law. This established a *National Security Council (NSC), to coordinate civilian and military policy; placed the DCI under the NSC, and replaced the CIG with a *Central Intelligence Agency (CIA) under the DCI to coordinate intelligence. The military was adamant, however, that each service maintain its own individual intelligence office despite the creation of the new CIA. (The military services also held to this position in 1961, when Secretary of Defense Robert S. *McNamara created the *Defense Intelligence Agency, hoping to consolidate defense intelligence activities. The service's resistance limited the extent of this consolidation.)

Truman envisioned the CIA as a coordinator, not a new intelligence producer or operator. But the CIA's legislative charter was vague, including the mandate to perform "such other functions and duties related to intelligence" as required by the NSC. A combination of unwillingness by other agencies to undertake broader analyses (rather than that written for one department only) or operations of any sort, coupled with a more bureaucratically aggressive CIA leadership willing to fill these gaps, quickly broadened the CIA's role.

Policymaker demands for current intelligence reports

and longer-range estimates gave CIA entree into analysis. Operations—i.e., covert action—began as a means of resisting Soviet advances in Europe. Gen. Walter Bedell Smith, Gen. Dwight D. *Eisenhower's wartime chief of staff, became DCI in 1950, shortly after the surprise outbreak of war in Korea. Smith capitalized on these trends in analysis and operations, solidifying the CIA into the agency familiar throughout the Cold War.

In 1952, Truman created the *National Security Agency (NSA) via a secret directive. NSA was charged with the protection of U.S. encoded communications and the interception and breaking of foreign ones, the lineal descendant of Yardley's early SIGINT efforts.

It is likely that, given the United States's postwar global responsibilities, an intelligence community of some sort would have been created. It is less debatable, however, that the Cold War greatly gave shape and form to U.S. intelligence.

Having opposed creation of the CIA, the military now found it useful, despite lingering rivalries. Military services warning of growing Soviet strength could appear self-serving; a national estimate from the CIA raising a similar concern had the advantage of appearing bureaucratically neutral.

But bureaucratic neutrality did not translate into political neutrality. Politicians in both parties used intelligence (or their version of it) about alleged Soviet strength for partisan means. The late 1940s and early 1950s saw the "bomber gap" debate. More illustrative and strikingly similar were the next two "gap" debates. In the early 1960s, Democrats—then out of power—charged that the United States suffered from a "missile gap." In the late 1970s and early 1980s, Republicans—also out of power—warned about a strategic "window of vulnerability." These were seen as legitimate issues in the presidential elections of 1960 and 1980. In both elections, interestingly, those raising the alarms won, only to declare the problem solved once they took office.

These repeated debates led some critics to conclude that the intelligence community (read CIA) was an intellectual pawn of the military, creating false alarms to justify larger defense budgets. This view was unrealistic, at least bureaucratically, since the CIA was a competitor with the *Department of Defense for national security dollars. Still, the legend remained—even among some senior officials, such as Secretary of Defense McNamara.

The tremendous growth of intelligence-related technology was a boon for both intelligence and the military. SIGINT and photoimage intelligence (IMINT) first by *U-2 spy planes and then by *satellites, not only greatly improved strategic warning, but helped give a better—albeit always incomplete—view of Soviet capabilities. One goal of U.S. Cold War diplomacy—often successful—was placing intelligence technical collection sites in nations bordering the USSR, just as orbiting improved intelligence collection satellites was a major goal of the U.S. space program.

Increased use of covert action was another Cold War intelligence feature. Proponents of covert action customarily defend this option as a necessary choice between doing nothing and using armed force. But covert action has proved to be a difficult instrument to use. In general, the closer the covert action supported a very specific overt policy goal and the more tightly focused were the operation's goals, the more likely the operation would be successful.

U.S.-abetted coups in Guatemala and Iran were successful—at least in the near to medium term (as much as twenty-five years). But large-scale paramilitary operations such as the abortive Bay of Pigs or the contra effort in Nicaragua were not. These operations tended to be extremely difficult to keep covert, given their scope; extremely difficult for the United States to claim "plausible deniability," and difficult to sustain politically if they dragged on too long. Paramilitary operations also raised issues for the CIA. Was the CIA competent to undertake such efforts or would it be of greater propriety or legality for the Defense Department to do so? Could CIA analysts provide unbiased assessments of situations in which the CIA was also supporting one faction via paramilitary operations?

Vietnam became the Cold War crucible for the entire national security community. Frustration over the inability to bring the *Vietnam War to a successful conclusion led to fissures between intelligence providers and policy customers. The infamous "order of battle" dispute—in which Defense analysts took issue with CIA estimates showing higher numbers of enemy troops, as these undercut claims of operational success in the field—typified both the overquantification of the war and the inapplicability of U.S. military resources.

Vietnam undermined the Cold War national security political consensus. The end of the war in 1975 was quickly followed by a series of revelations about and investigations of the intelligence community, detailing how agencies (CIA, NSA, FBI) had violated the limits of their charters, engaged in questionable activities at home and abroad, and had had insufficient executive and congressional oversight. From then on, the intelligence community could never return to its cloak of relative obscurity. Indeed, new intelligence-related revelations or scandals became a recurrent feature.

The Cold War continued for another fifteen years. President Ronald *Reagan espoused a never fully defined Reagan Doctrine that sought to reverse the Cold War pattern, making the Soviets and their allies pay the price of overseas involvement against *guerrilla warfare supported by U.S. intelligence operations. This policy was successful in Afghanistan, important in Angola, but inconclusive and very costly politically in the case of the contras in Nicaragua.

The vagueness at the core of the Cold War—a dogged and deadly serious competition that never erupted into outright, direct hostilities—makes it difficult to assess the factors that contributed to the U.S. victory, including the role played by intelligence. The key issue for many is the degree to which the intelligence community predicted or failed to predict the collapse of the Soviet Union. Critics observe that the very ability to track Soviet military in detail ultimately gave a false picture of Soviet strength obscuring the underlying economic and social weakness. Others note, more favorably, that intelligence had increasing knowledge of the systemic Soviet failure and the restiveness of nominal allies. But these warnings were not the same as a bold prediction that a positive end to the Cold War was in sight—although this may not have been predictable, even to the Soviet leadership.

The end of the Cold War also gave rise to familiar demands for a decrease in national security spending. Cuts in military and intelligence spending began even as political leaders came to appreciate that the post–Cold War world was less threatening but perhaps more complex than the old bipolar struggle had been.

The *Persian Gulf War created new strains for intelligence and for its relationship with the military. Critics charged that U.S. surprise at Iraq's invasion of Kuwait was another "intelligence failure." Successful prosecution of Operation Desert Storm in 1991 revealed a number of new intelligence-related contributions: precise targeting information allowed the use of "smart" weapons that increase the likelihood of a "kill" while minimizing collateral damage; and "information warfare," the ability to attack important technological nodes—finance, utilities, communications, security—via computers, thus disrupting enemy efforts silently at their centers. Military intelligence professionals describe this as a major shift: they have gone from combat support to combatant. There were also intelligence problems: the "battle damage assessment" debate between the field command and Washington-based analysts; difficulties (largely technical in nature) in disseminating the right intelligence information to the right user when needed; and, in a debate that continued for years after the war, whether the CIA was explicit enough in detailing the location of Iraqi chemical weapons sites to U.S. troops sent to destroy them, perhaps resulting in chemical exposure and "Gulf War syndrome."

On the verge of the twenty-first century, intelligence is being asked to contribute to a new—and still debated—military doctrine: "dominant battlefield awareness." Proponents argue that technology now allows commanders to have intelligence about the battlefield in such depth and detail as greatly to reduce the size of forces and likely *casualties. Critics wonder whether this degree of knowledge is realistically attainable, what effect it will have on competing demands for intelligence resources both within the military and with nonmilitary national security users, and whether it is necessary. At one level, the debate is part of an ongoing evolutionary relationship; at another, it reflects how intelligence technology is once again sparking potential changes in combat doctrine.

[See also Chemical and Biological Weapons and Warfare; Cold War: External Course; Cold War: Domestic Course; Counterintelligence; Nicaragua, U.S. Military Involvement in; Panama, U.S. Military Involvement in.]

• Herbert O. Yardley, The American Black Chamber, 1931. U.S. Army Intelligence Center and School, Fort Huachuca, Evolution of American Intelligence, 1973. Jeffrey M. Dorwart, The Office of Naval Intelligence, 1865–1918, 1979. Thomas F. Troy, Donovan and the CIA: A History of the Establishment of the Central Intelligence Agency, 1981. James Bamford, The Puzzle Palace: A Report on America's Most Secret Agency, 1982. Bruce Bidwell, History of the Military Intelligence Division, Department of the Army General Staff, 1986. William E. Burrows, Deep Black: Space Espionage and National Security, 1986. John Ranelagh, The Agency: The Rise and Decline of the CIA, 1987. Bruce W. Watson, Susan M. Watson, and Gerald W. Hopple, eds., United States Intelligence: An Encyclopedia, 1990. Mark M. Lowenthal, U.S. Intelligence: Evolution and Anatomy, 1984; 2nd ed. 1992. Christopher Andrews, For the President's Eyes Only, 1995.
—Mark M. Lowenthal

INTER-AMERICAN TREATY OF RECIPROCAL ASSISTANCE (1947). The United States signed the Inter-American Treaty of Reciprocal Assistance—popularly known as the Rio Treaty—with the twenty Latin American nations in 1947 in Brazil. This regional security pact, permitted under Article 51 of the *United Nations Charter, incorporated the principle that an attack against one was to be considered an attack against all. Signatories would decide by a two-thirds majority what kind of collective action might be taken against aggression. No nation would be required, however, to use force without its consent. The treaty continued the military cooperation that had characterized inter-American relations during World War II. The Rio Treaty was also a *Cold War pact aimed at the Soviet Union.

In practice, the treaty has been largely invoked, in conjunction with the consultative organs of the Organization of the American States (1948), to resolve intrahemispheric controversies, such as the dispute between Costa Rica and Nicaragua in 1955 or the Dominican Republic's attack on Venezuelan president Rómulo Betancourt in 1960. President John F. *Kennedy did cite the Rio Treaty in justifying his quarantine order during the *Cuban Missile Crisis of 1962. But usually when the United States decided that the Soviet Union threatened its hemispheric interests, Washington bypassed the treaty and acted unilaterally, as in Guatemala (1954), Cuba (1961), the Dominican Republic (1965), Chile (1970–73), and Nicaragua (1980s). The United States also refused the request of Latin American nations to invoke the Rio Treaty against Great Britain during the 1982 Anglo-Argentine war over the Falkland Islands.

[See also Caribbean and Latin America, U.S. Military Involvement in the.]

• J. Lloyd Mecham, The United States and Inter-American Security, 1889–1960, 1961. Gordon Connell-Smith, The Inter-American System, 1966.
—Stephen G. Rabe

INTERNATIONALISM. Internationalism emerged early in the twentieth century to challenge isolationism as a proper American approach to international affairs. In the balance between them lay competing perceptions of the role of external conditions in the country's remarkable security and well-being.

For some Americans, the country's favored position rested on elements of international stability whose permanence required the nation's attention. At the turn of the twentieth century, writers such as Alfred T. *Mahan, supported by members of the eastern Anglo-Saxon elite, argued that the rise of potentially expansionist Germany and Japan demanded closer ties to Britain. Other internationalists discovered the surest guarantee of universal peace, and with it the perpetuation of a world that served U.S. interests admirably, not in superior force but in the international acceptance of non-power devices, such as arbitration and conciliation, for the settlement of international disputes. For such legalists as William Howard Taft and Elihu *Root, the final guarantee of world peace lay in a world court that would command the absolute confidence of the entire world. American internationalism scored its initial triumph in response to the horrors of the Great War of 1914. Pressed by President Woodrow *Wilson, the Versailles Conference in 1919 adopted the American program for institutionalized peace in the form of the *League of Nations and the World Court.

If the Senate's rejection of the Treaty of *Versailles marked a powerful resurgence of American isolationism, it did not quell the determination of the country's internationalists to fulfill Wilson's admonition that the United States actively pursue the cause of peace. In the vanguard of the country's postwar internationalism were academics and students of international law, such as the University of Chicago's Quincy Wright and Columbia's James T. Shotwell. Members of the eastern establishment of international bankers and lawyers entered the internationalist ranks through membership in the recently founded New York Council on Foreign Relations. Internationalists comprised largely the country's pro-League forces, who predicted endless triumphs for peace from a League of Nations morally enhanced by American membership.

In practice, the internationalists, no less than the isolationists, ignored the persistent role of power in affairs among nations. For them the goal of universal peace, rendered essential by the recent experience of war, was sufficiently overwhelming to eliminate the problem of means. Internationalists denied that the United States need be concerned with any specific configuration of political or military power in Europe or Asia. Whereas isolationism insisted that the United States had no external interests that merited resorts to force, internationalism declared that American interests existed wherever governments challenged peace or human rights. It presumed, however, that the universal acceptance of the principle that change, to be legitimate, needed also to be peaceful would control undesirable international behavior. Every program fostered by American internationalists during the 1920s—membership in the League of Nations and the World Court, the employment of arbitration conventions, the resort to consultation in the event of crises, collective security, naval disarmament, or the outlawry of war as embodied in the Kellogg-Briand Peace Pact of 1928—denied the requirement of any precise definition of ends and means in external policy, and anchored the effectiveness of any moral condemnation of aggressors to the power of an aroused world opinion.

Consigned by adverse opinion to failure on the League issue, internationalists seized World Court membership as the alternative approach to effective international cooperation. Eventually the court battle comprised the most determined internationalist counterattack of the decade. When in May 1922 the court officially opened, a noted American authority on international law, John Bassett Moore, was among its eleven judges. Under internationalist pressure, President Warren G. Harding, in February 1923, submitted the question of court membership to the Senate. To satisfy congressional isolationists, Harding recommended four reservations that would absolve the United States of all commitments to the League but would retain for the country all powers on the court enjoyed by members of the League. Isolationists killed the measure as an overcommitment of American power and prestige.

Not until December 1925, when the issue of membership had won the support of peace groups, women's clubs, pro-League forces, countless mass meetings, and much of the press, did the Senate agree to act. It approved membership, 76–17, in early 1926. But Senator Claude A. Swanson of Virginia introduced a fifth reservation that denied the court the right to render an advisory opinion on any question touching the interests of the United States. That reservation the court rejected; by the end of 1926, U.S. membership in the court had become a dead issue. Yet such

membership would have entailed no commitment for the United States beyond paying its share of the court's expenses. Internationalists agreed that neither the League nor the World Court had confronted any major challenges, nor had either institution demonstrated any capacity to restrain a major power.

Despite its limited prospects, the internationalist faith in such institutions continued into the following decade. However, its central assumption that world opinion was the ultimate arbiter in world affairs denied its adherents any answer to the troubling aggressions of the 1930s. As late as 1939, internationalists looked to the League as the world's primary hope for peace. In their general unconcern for military preparedness, they had done little in previous years to provide the League with either the sanctions or the means required for effective collective security. But internationalism, as embodied in the ideals of the League of Nations, failed not only in its unwillingness to provide a defense against *aggression and violence but also in its refusal to seek some accommodation with change as the only long-term alternative to war. Any system of collective security would seek order rather than change.

For the British historian Edward Hallett Carr, in his noted book *The Twenty Years' Crisis* (1939), collective security, like American internationalism, expressed the concern of status quo powers to prevent unwanted change in the international system. Thus peace became the vested interest of the predominant powers. With no single country strong enough to exercise a *pax Romana* or a *pax Britannica*, slogans such as "collective security" and "resistance to aggression" proclaimed the identity of interest between the dominant, satisfied group of nations and the world as a whole in the maintenance of peace. Throughout the interwar years American internationalism, despite its persistent effort to engage the United States in world affairs, remained essentially an effort to sustain the status quo without accepting the price, either in military preparations or in concessions, that international peace demanded.

The attack on *Pearl Harbor destroyed the illusion that the United States could have the world of its choice without cost. That event not only diminished the power of isolationism in Congress and the nation but also reinvented American internationalism. The realization that war had come unexpectedly and over vast distances recommended, at least to the country's military leaders, that the United States never again entrust its peace to world opinion or the oceans. Rather, its continuing interest in international stability required a military structure of sufficient magnitude to discourage aggression everywhere. The wartime decisions designed to engage the nation heavily in the postwar world included commitments to the *United Nations, the International Monetary Fund, the *World Bank, and other postwar international institutions. These decisions to assure postwar peace and stability received the support of an overwhelming national consensus. Internationalism emerged from the war firmly in the saddle.

What ultimately converted internationalism into an unprecedented body of worldwide economic and security commitments was the assumption that Soviet *expansionism, rendered global and unlimited by the Kremlin's alleged control of international communism, endangered American and world security. Such fears led to a system of global military containment, including *NATO and eventually treaties of alliance with dozens of countries throughout the world. More limited, yet more pervading, internationalists embraced the *Marshall Plan to rebuild the economies of Europe. Acting through international agencies of trade and monetary stabilization, the plan contributed heavily to the world's unprecedented prosperity. Through forty years of *Cold War, the USSR, as a perceived global danger, enabled the United States, with its abundance of economic and military power, to maintain a worldwide influence without precedent in modern history.

After 1990, the passing of the Cold War, in denying the United States its special role as the world's self-appointed defender against communism, again compelled the country to redefine the meaning of its internationalism. Internationalists quickly detected new foreign challenges in the form of resurgent nationalism, ethnic strife, border disputes, economic chaos, and civil war. Confronting them in their demands for national action, moderates cited the potentially heavy costs of involvement in the world's domestic turmoil, especially when contrasted to the minimal U.S. interests at risk. Internationalism, as the past had demonstrated, was never an absolute good in itself; its utility hinged on its success in advancing the interests of the nation and its citizens.

[See also Isolationism.]

• Edward Hallett Carr, The Twenty Years' Crisis, 1939. Akira Iriye, From Nationalism to Internationalism: United States Foreign Policy to 1914, 1977. Michael S. Sherry, Preparing for the Next War: American Plans for Postwar Defense, 1941–45, 1977. Norman A. Graebner, America as a World Power: A Realist Appraisal from Wilson to Reagan, 1984. Robert D. Schulzinger, The Wise Men of Foreign Affairs: The History of the Council on Foreign Relations, 1984. Lloyd E. Ambrosius, Wilson's Statecraft: Theory and Practice of Liberal Internationalism During World War I, 1991. Jeremy Aynsley, Nationalism and Internationalism, 1993. Kjell Goldmann, The Logic of Internationalism: Coercion and Accommodation, 1994.

—Norman A. Graebner

INTERNMENT OF ENEMY ALIENS. Inevitably in time of war, American expectations of due process and protection of civil liberties have been reshaped into a peculiar synthesis of principle and expediency. Too frequently, expediency has triumphed over principle, and while the lapses in American commitment to these liberties has always been characterized by its perpetrators as temporary, and resulting from emergency conditions, it may be appropriate to ask: if such vital legal protections are disregarded when they are most needed, how deeply do they reflect American devotion to them?

Although internment of enemy aliens during the *Civil War was of minimal importance, given the internal nature of the conflict, in both world wars the practice was much more common. It had deep roots in American history, beginning with the Alien Enemies Act of 1792. Part of the notorious series of statutes known as the *Alien and Sedition Acts, this act somehow had escaped repeal—and President Woodrow *Wilson invoked its provisions in April 1917 shortly after the United States entered World War I. By the time of the armistice, more than 6,300 German aliens had been detained, while others who had not been arrested were forced to register with federal authorities and barred from moving without official sanction. Moreover, authorities frequently found it convenient to label labor-organizing activities as conduct by enemy aliens. Indeed,

the infamous Red Scare took place well over a year after the armistice, and resulted in the internment of more than 4,000 individuals—arrested and imprisoned without either warrants or trials.

Americans fought in World War II with much less antiforeign hysteria than in 1917–19, yet one episode involving enemy aliens remains a terrible blot on the American tradition of civil liberties. The internment of Japanese Americans was in fact what the constitutional scholar Edward Corwin called "the most dramatic invasion of the rights [of U.S. citizens] by their own government that had thus far occurred in the history of our nation." Although no specific evidence of sabotage by Japanese Americans was produced, in the wake of the attack on *Pearl Harbor neither the Justice Department nor the U.S. Attorney General was willing to confront the military on what it claimed to be a matter of "military necessity." Nor, were the executive and judicial branches of federal government. President Franklin D. *Roosevelt signed the evacuation and internment order without any discussion with his cabinet, followed by the supine acceptance of this action by the U.S. Supreme Court.

Solely because of their racial heritage, rather than their conduct, Japanese Americans on the West Coast suffered severe personal stress and loss. They were forced, often overnight, to sell their property—including "land, stores, homes," and personal possessions—before being forcibly relocated to confinement camps. The fact that Congress apologized for the internment many years after the war, and awarded some financial restitution to its survivors, only indicates the sense of national guilt over this episode, guilt that was fully warranted. The internment of Japanese Americans as enemy aliens, classified as such for reasons of expediency rather than evidence, remains an unnecessary blemish on the American heritage of equal protection under the law.

[See also Japanese-American Internment Cases.]

• Martin Grodzins, Americans Betrayed: Politics and the Japanese Evacuation, 1949. Paul L. Murphy, The Constitution in Crisis Times, 1918–1969, 1972.

—Jonathan Lurie

INTERSERVICE AGREEMENT. See Key West Agreement (1948).

IRAN, U.S. MILITARY INVOLVEMENT IN. The American military first assumed a role in Iran in 1942. The shift of the lend-lease supply route to the Soviet Union from Murmansk to the Persian corridor brought American military personnel to Iran. They came for two reasons: to move supplies across Iran and to shore up the Iranian government headed by Mohammed Reza Shah Pahlevi. The Americans organized a series of advisory missions to stabilize Iran, including one to reform its army and another to reorganize the gendarmerie (state police). The first adviser, Gen. John Greely, set out to improve the army's fighting quality, but lacked authorization or resources. His successor, Gen. Clarence Ridley, followed War Department guidelines to evaluate a military assistance program and reorganize the Iranian military supply system. Col. H. Norman Schwarzkopf (father of the leader of Desert Storm) headed the gendarmerie mission. By 1943, some 30,000 troops of the Persian Gulf Service Command (PGC) under Gen. Donald Connolly had begun rebuilding roads the railroad to move Lend-Lease supplies from the gulf to the Soviet Union.

Immediately after the war ended, the United States dismantled the PGC. President Harry S. *Truman, at State Department urging, exempted the advisory missions from his order to remove all American troops.

The American military played no significant role during the Soviet-American crisis over Iran between November 1945 and April 1946. The *Joint Chiefs of Staff did warn that in any armed conflict, logistical difficulties prevented an effective military response. They later supported a *National Security Council finding that Iran had become "a major strategic interest to the United States." The region's oil was vital to postwar energy policy. Iran also shared with the Soviet Union a 1,300-mile border and blocked the traditional Russian aspiration for a warm-water gulf port. Both factors created long-term American concern with Iran's stability and independence.

Over the next two decades the Department of *Defense (DoD) resisted the Shah's requests for help in building Iran's military forces. Military advisers remained until the 1979 revolution, organized after 1950 as ARMISH-MAAG and GENMISH. They supported the American policy to contain Soviet ambitions in Iran, but played no significant role in the *Central Intelligence Agency operation that overthrew Mohammed Mossadeq in 1953. The Eisenhower and Kennedy administrations both stressed economic development and social reform rather than military strength as the key to Iran's future security. In case of conflict, the *Pentagon planned to use American forces to stop the Russians. The primary threat in the late 1950s came from Soviet arms shipments to Iraq. In 1964, the United States extracted a Status of Forces Agreement that exempted American military advisers from Iranian law. As a reward, the Shah received $200 million in loans and credits to buy arms. That agreement angered conservative Islamic opponents of the Shah, especially Ayatollah Rouhallah Khomeini.

By 1970, some 778 Defense personnel were in Iran. In May 1972, over Defense objections, President Richard M. *Nixon and NSC adviser Henry *Kissinger granted the Shah unlimited access to the most advanced American weapons, including F-14 and F-15 aircraft. In 1972–77, American arms sales totaled $16.2 billion as Iran's defense budget rose 680 percent. Nixon and Kissinger justified this policy under the *Nixon Doctrine, which shifted the burden of regional defense to key allies. The buildup brought 30,000 Americans to Iran and increased the nationalist resentment of the Shah, ultimately triggering the revolution of 1978. On 24 April 1980, the military launched Operation Eagle Claw, a disastrous mission to rescue fifty-two Americans held hostage by Iranian militants. Eight *helicopters from the carrier Nimitz flew 600 miles to a site called Desert One to rendezvous with C-130 transport planes. A combination of bad weather and mechanical failure aborted the mission, leaving eight American Marines dead.

In response to Iran's revolution, President Jimmy *Carter on 23 January 1980 enunciated the *Carter Doctrine: the United States would use military force if necessary to defend its "vital interests" in the Persian Gulf region. A major buildup of American naval forces and the development of the Rapid Deployment force and CENT-, its command structure, continued under Ronald

*Reagan. After the outbreak of the Iran-Iraq War in September 1980, both sides attacked tankers and oil facilities critical to the West.

In 1986, Iran focused its attack on Kuwait and Kuwaiti-bound ships in the gulf. American policy by then had tilted toward an Iraqi victory. The *Iran-Contra Affair of 1986 confused the issue as the Reagan administration, which publicly condemned Iran, privately shipped arms to Teheran. To protect the flow of oil from Iranian attacks, the U.S. Navy began to escort American and "reflagged" Kuwaiti tankers. In May 1987, an Iraqi Mirage F-1 fighter in error fired two Exocet missiles that killed thirty-seven sailors aboard the American destroyer USS Stark.

By late 1987, the United States had some thirteen naval ships in the gulf, supported by another twelve in the Gulf of Oman and a substantial allied force. American forces several times attacked small Irani ships. Iranian-laid naval *mines posed the gravest threat to gulf shipping. On 18 April 1988, in retaliation for a mine attack on the frigate Samuel B. Roberts, the navy fought its largest surface action since World War II. Operation Praying Mantis destroyed two armed oil platforms, a frigate, a fast attack craft, and two armed speed boats. As a war-weary Iran moved toward peace, the cruiser Vincennes on 3 July 1988 mistakenly shot down a civilian Iranian airliner with the loss of 290 lives.

After the Iran-Iraq War ended in July 1988, overt hostility between the United States and Iran ceased. Iran remained neutral during the *Persian Gulf War in 1991 and figured prominently only when over 100 Iraqi fighter planes fled there to avoid destruction from Operation Desert Storm. Friction with the United States persisted through 1995, primarily from Iran's support for international *terrorism and its program to build *nuclear weapons. Friction with the United States persisted into 1999, but the rise of more moderate leaders and Iran's continuing role as a counter-weight to Saddam Hussein in Iraq gave hints that tensions might ease.

[See also Iran, U.S. Military Involvement in; Middle East, U.S. Military Involvement in the.]

• Ervand Abrahamian, Iran: Between Two Revolutions, 1982. Mark H. Lytle, The Origins of the Iranian-American Alliance, 1941–1953, 1987. James Bill, The Eagle and the Lion: The Tragedy of American-Iranian Relations, 1988. Dilip Hiro, Desert Storm to Desert Shield: The Second Gulf War, 1992. Michael A. Palmer, Guardians of the Gulf: A History of America's Expanding Role in the Persian Gulf, 1833–1992, 1992.
—Mark H. Lytle

IRAN-CONTRA AFFAIR (1986) represented the confluence of two politically controversial and arguably illegal foreign policies conducted by the Reagan administration: the arming of Nicaraguan counterrevolutionaries (the Contras) after Congress had banned such aid, and the selling of weapons to the government of Iran in order to secure the release of U.S. citizens held hostage in Lebanon. Both policies became publicly linked following press reports on the Iranian operation in November 1986, when a Justice Department review turned up evidence that millions of dollars in profits from the sale of arms to Iran had been diverted to fund the Contra rebels.

The revelations mushroomed into the greatest U.S. political scandal since Watergate, raising constitutional, legal, and ethical issues concerning the congressional role in foreign policy and the conduct of administration officials. Investigations by a presidentially appointed panel and a joint committee of Congress focused on whether or not President Ronald *Reagan knew about or had authorized the diversion—an act that could have constituted an impeachable offense—and whether Congress's constitutional foreign policy and budget prerogatives as well as U.S. laws had been violated. An independent counsel investigated the legality of third-country fund-raising for projects banned by Congress, as well as the obstruction of justice by administration officials. Congress ultimately found that the common ingredients of the Iran and Contra policies were "secrecy, deception, and disdain for the law." And while blaming President Reagan for allowing a "cabal of the zealots" to take charge of foreign policy, it backed away from accusing him directly of illegal acts. The parallel investigation by Independent Counsel Lawrence Walsh secured criminal convictions of nearly a dozen senior administration officials and private citizens for acts such as perjury, conspiracy, fraud, and the destruction of evidence. Walsh's efforts were compromised by congressional grants of immunity to key U.S. officials during several months of televised hearings. All convicted U.S. officials and those awaiting trial, including Secretary of Defense Caspar *Weinberger, were pardoned by President George *Bush on 24 December 1992 following his defeat for reelection.

The roots of the scandal involving the Contras lay in the Reagan administration's decision in 1981 to conduct covert political and paramilitary operations aimed at "the Cuban presence and Cuban-Sandinista support structure in Nicaragua and elsewhere in Central America." Following a series of controversies, including that over the participation of the *Central Intelligence Agency in the mining of Nicaragua's harbors in 1983 and 1984, Congress enacted 1984 legislation known as the Boland amendment, which banned any U.S. agency involved in intelligence activities from supporting military and paramilitary operations in Nicaragua.

Notwithstanding the law, President Reagan instructed subordinates to keep the Contras together "body and soul." Operational control of the Contra program shifted from the *Central Intelligence Agency (CIA) to the *National Security Council. Both prior to and after the passage of the Boland amendment, senior U.S. officials, including the president himself, solicited Contra military aid from private individuals and third countries, including South Africa, Saudi Arabia, Taiwan, and Brunei. National Security Council aide Marine Lt. Col. Oliver North coordinated the resupply operation, which had its own pilots, planes, secure communications, and secret Swiss bank accounts. With the support of his superiors, national security advisers Robert McFarlane and John Poindexter, and, apparently, CIA director William Casey, North directed a network of former military and intelligence officials and businesspeople, code-named "the Enterprise," in effect creating a private *covert operations capability outside normal channels of oversight and accountability. All the while, the administration insisted publicly that the Contras were in desperate straits due to the congressional cutoff; it also spent federal funds for prohibited *propaganda operations aimed at influencing future congressional votes.

U.S. policy toward Iran was developed independently of Nicaragua, but shared many of the same operatives as well as covert practice. After the seizure of the U.S. Embassy in Teheran by Islamic militants in November 1979, the Carter administration had embargoed trade and financial trans-actions, including arms shipments, to the Iranian regime. The Reagan administration sought to tighten the embargo by enlisting the cooperation of European and other governments, designating Iran as a sponsor of international *terrorism.

Despite the public policy of isolation, when U.S. hostages were seized in Lebanon by militants with apparent ties to Iran, the administration undertook covert "arms-for-hostage" sales of weapons to the Iranian government in 1985–86. President Reagan did not issue the legally required intelligence "findings" before initiating the covert sales of antitank and antiaircraft *missiles, and Congress was not notified of them. The sales also appeared to have violated U.S. arms export laws. The secret arms sales occurred against a backdrop of public statements by President Reagan that the United States would make no deals with terrorists. Although three hostages were released as a result of U.S. efforts, three new ones were taken during the same period.

In the wake of the Iran-Contra Affair, Congress and President Bush skirmished over reforms to the Intelligence Oversight Act. Bush refused to sign the bill in 1990, although a compromise was enacted in 1991.

[See also Civil-Military Relations; Iran, U.S. Military Involvement in; Nicaragua, U.S. Military Involvement in.]

• House Select Committee to Investigate Covert Arms Transactions with Iran and Senate Select Committee on Secret Military Assistance to Iran and the Nicaraguan Opposition, *Iran-Contra Affair,* 13 November 1987, 100th Cong., 1st Sess., 1987. Oliver L. North, *Taking the Stand: The Testimony of Lieutenant Colonel Oliver L. North,* 1987. Tower Commission Report: *The Full Text of the President's Special Review Board,* 1987. Theodore Draper, *A Very Thin Line: The Iran-Contra Affairs,* 1991. Cynthia J. Arnson, *Crossroads: Congress, the President, and Central America, 1976–1993,* 1993. Lawrence E. Walsh, *Firewall: The Iran-Contra Conspiracy and Cover-up,* 1997.
—Cynthia J. Arnson

ISOLATIONISM as a historic attitude in the United States can best be defined as opposition to intervention in war outside the western hemisphere, particularly in Europe; to involvement in permanent military alliances; and to participation in organizations of collective security. Above all, isolationists seek to preserve the United States's freedom of action. Isolationists often differ from pacifists, those who refuse to sanction any conflict and absolutely renounce any war, for isolationists often favor unilateral military action, what some call the doctrine of the "free hand." Indeed, an isolationist can be stridently nationalistic, endorse military preparations, sanction certain forms of imperialism, and engage in outright war, particularly in Latin America or the Pacific. At no time did most isolationists seek literally to "isolate" the United States from either the world's culture or its commerce.

By the above definition, American policy has been isolationist until the twentieth century. Thomas Paine's *Common Sense* (1776) combined calls for an independent foreign policy with a plea for commercial supremacy. John *Adams's Model Treaty of 1776 envisioned a purely commercial treaty with the French, not a binding military alliance. George *Washington's farewell address of 1796 advised his countrymen "to steer clear of permanent Alliances," a reference to the Franco-American Alliance of 1778–1800. Thomas *Jefferson's first inaugural of 1801 sought "peace, commerce and honest friendship with all nations, entangling alliances with none." When in 1823 President James *Monroe advanced what later became known as the *Monroe Doctrine, he said: "In the wars of the European powers in matters relating to themselves we have never taken part, nor does it comport with our policy to do so."

Of course, a nation may pursue an isolationist foreign policy while involving itself extensively in political and military matters outside its borders. In 1812, the United States fought Britain; in 1846, Mexico; and in 1898, Spain. All such engagements were unilateral decisions by the United States and hence did not violate the classic isolationism espoused in the eighteenth century. During the nineteenth century, the United States encouraged the revolts of Latin American nations against Spain, vied with the British to control the Oregon Territory, and sympathized with the European revolutions of 1830 and 1948. It entered into only one agreement involving joint action with another power, the Clayton-Bulwer Treaty of 1850 with Britain, which limited U.S. action in building a transisthmian canal. Toward the end of the century, the United States possessed its own colonies and played a decisive role in reshaping a new military balance in the world. Yet just three months before the outbreak of World War I, President Woodrow *Wilson insisted that "we need not and we should not form alliances with any nation in the world."

Once, however, Wilson sought U.S. entry into the *League of Nations—a full-fledged system of collective security—isolationism emerged as a distinctive political position. Such opponents of the League as Republican senators Henry Cabot Lodge (Mass.), William E. Borah (Idaho), and Hiram Johnson (Calif.) successfully fought U.S. membership, thereby reasserting the traditional policy of isolationism in the face of its first real challenge.

Only in the 1930s was the general isolationist consensus threatened, for President Franklin D. *Roosevelt sought discretionary power to aid victims of aggression. Opponents of such policies fought back so successfully that the years 1934–37 marked the high tide of isolationist legislation. In 1934, Congress adopted the Johnson Act, which prohibited private loans to nations in default of obligations. In 1935, it voted down U.S. membership in the World Court. From 1934 to 1936, the Senate sponsored an investigation, led by Republican Gerald P. *Nye, of the munitions industry. From 1935 to 1937, a battery of *neutrality legislation was passed, including a ban on loans and credits to belligerents; a mandatory embargo on direct or indirect shipments of arms or munitions; presidential discretion to require payment or transfer of title before exporting any goods to a belligerent; prohibiting American citizens from traveling on ships of belligerents; and enjoining the arming of American merchant ships. Much of this legislation was passed in the belief that lack of such safeguards had led the United States into full-scale belligerency in World War I. By the 1930s, however, there was enough *internationalism in the United States, rooted in the desire for collective action against the rising dictatorships, that isolationism became a distinctive political position and one that was increasingly contested. The word itself became increasingly pejorative, and isolationists preferred such terms as *anti-interventionist, noninterventionist,* and *nationalist.*

In 1938, the isolationists met with their first failure, for they lacked sufficient support in the House of Representa-

tives to pass the Ludlow amendment to the Constitution, a proposal that would have prohibited Congress from declaring war until confirmed by majority vote in a national referendum. Once war again broke out in Europe in 1939, the ranks of isolationists thinned and Roosevelt increasingly aided the Allies. His legislative triumphs included military aid to France and Britain on a cash-and-carry basis in November 1939; military *conscription in September 1940; Lend-Lease aid to all nations fighting the Axis in March 1941; extending the terms of army service for draftees in August 1941; and authorizing the arming of U.S. merchant vessels and permitting them to carry cargoes to belligerent ports in November 1941. Acting on his own authority, the president ordered the military occupation of Greenland (April 1941) and Iceland (July 1940); froze Japanese assets (July 1941), thereby bringing all U.S. trade with Japan to a halt; issued a set of postwar aims with Britain called the Atlantic Charter (August 1941); extended aid to the Soviet Union (October 1941); and entered into a undeclared naval war with Germany (fall 1941).

All these moves the isolationists fought bitterly. Isolationist sentiment was increasingly concentrated in the America First Committee (AFC), organized in September 1940 as the major anti-interventionist group fighting Roosevelt's policies. The AFC was founded by Yale law student R. Douglas Stuart, chaired by Sears, Roebuck executive Gen. Robert E. Wood, and included in its ranks such figures as journalist John T. Flynn, diplomat William R. Castle, former New Dealer Gen. Hugh Johnson, advertising executive Chester Bowles, and aviator Charles *Lindbergh. At its peak it had 450 chapters, a membership of 850,000, and an income of $370,000 donated by 25,000 contributors. Huge AFC rallies often featured such speakers as Nye, Lindbergh, Flynn, Democratic senator Burton K. Wheeler (Mont.), and Representative Hamilton Fish. The AFC was unable to defeat any of Roosevelt's legislative proposals, though it undoubtedly caused the president to be more circumspect on such matters as extending terms for draftees and convoying British vessels. The president's specific legislative policies were always supported in the polls, while the AFC stressed that nearly 80 percent of the American people, expressing themselves in the same polls, opposed a declaration of war on the Axis powers.

Although several leading isolationists endorsed *conscription for hemispheric defense, many more saw little need for a mass army. In isolationist eyes, a new American Expeditionary Force would simply prolong the struggle overseas and cost over 1 million U.S. lives. Furthermore, it would work against needed negotiation between England and Germany and ensure Soviet domination of Europe. Isolationists claimed that Hitler's blitzkrieg tactics had shown that mass armies were obsolete, and they called for small, highly mobile volunteer forces.

Isolationists differed among themselves as to the efficacy of large naval fleets, while strongly stressing airpower. Airpower, they claimed, was the most cost effective way of defending the United States. They argued that while no foreign power was able to conduct continuous bombardment of the nation, the United States could easily pick off any attacking planes. Moreover, a strong air arm was not dependent upon untrained conscripts.

The Japanese attack on *Pearl Harbor put an end to classic isolationism. The AFC promptly disbanded. In

1945, the United States became a charter member of the *United Nations, occupying a seat on its powerful Security Council. In 1949, it entered its first binding military alliance, the North Atlantic Treaty Organization (*NATO). In 1950, it was fighting in Korea under UN auspices, and in 1965 U.S. ground troops were committed to overt fighting in Vietnam.

During the *Cold War, many former isolationists became "Asia Firsters," warning against involvements in Europe while supporting increased action against communism in Asia. The 1948 and 1952 presidential bids of the isolationist-leaning Senator Robert A. Taft failed. Anti-Roosevelt works by such isolationist historians as Charles A. Beard, Charles Callan Tansill, and Harry Elmer Barnes did not receive scholarly acceptance. In 1953 and 1954, Ohio Republican senator John Bricker proposed a constitutional amendment limiting presidential treaty-making power, but it was opposed by President Dwight D. *Eisenhower and defeated in the Senate. A military alternative to NATO, victory over the Soviet Union through airpower alone, was espoused by former isolationist Gen. Bonner Fellers, but lacked widespread support.

In the wake of the *Vietnam War, some commentators—such as Democratic senator J. William Fulbright and political scientist Earl C. Ravenal—were dubbed "neo-isolationists" as they sought drastically reduced American commitments. Yet they differed significantly among themselves, and seldom in principle totally repudiated membership in international organizations, military aid overseas, economic sanctions, and even combat forces.

[See also Lend-Lease Act and Agreements; Nationalism.]

• John Milton Cooper, Jr., *The Vanity of Power: American Isolationism and World War I, 1914–1917,* 1969. Wayne S. Cole, *America First: The Battle Against Intervention, 1940–1941,* 1953. Manfred Jonas, *Isolationism in America, 1935–1941,* 1966. Manfred Jonas, "Isolationism," in Alexander DeConde, ed., *Encyclopedia of American Foreign Policy,* 1978. Justus D. Doenecke, *Not to the Swift: The Old Isolationists in the Cold War Era,* 1979. Wayne S. Cole, *Roosevelt and the Isolationists, 1932–45,* 1983. Justus D. Doenecke, *Anti-Intervention: A Bibliographical Introduction to Isolationism and Pacifism from World War I to the Early Cold War,* 1987. Justus D. Doenecke, ed., *In Danger Undaunted: The Anti-Interventionist Movement as Revealed in the Papers of the America First Committee,* 1990. Wayne S. Cole, "United States Isolationism in the 1990s?" *International Journal,* 48 (Winter 1992–93).   —Justus D. Doenecke

ITALY, INVASION AND CONQUEST OF (1943–45). After Italy surrendered to the Allies in July 1943 at the height of World War II, Josef *Stalin continued to demand that the Allies open a second front in the west. The inability of the two Western Allies to mount a cross-Channel invasion into Northwest France until the late spring of 1944 made the invasion of Italy an attractive alternative to the British, who insisted that military operations continue in the Mediterranean. Allied strategy was always vague but was generally to tie up large numbers of German troops in Italy who would otherwise be dispersed to France or the eastern front.

Opposing the Allies was a German army group commanded by Field Marshal Albert Kesselring, who persuaded Adolf *Hitler to defend Italy south of Rome instead of in the Apennine Mountains of northern Italy.

The invasion of Salerno by elements of Lt. Gen. Mark *Clark's U.S. Fifth Army on 9 September 1943 was the first major battle in the longest and bloodiest European campaign fought by the Western Allies. The landings were bitterly resisted by the German Tenth Army and nearly failed. When the Germans exhausted their resources in unsuccessful counterattacks, Kesselring ordered a fighting withdrawal north to the new Gustav Line, and anchored on Cassino.

The Allied High Command erroneously believed Rome would fall by the end of October 1943. However, without a second amphibious landing north of Salerno, the Allies were compelled to advance through the great chain of mountains that bisects central Italy, where freezing winter weather and numerous rivers proved the worst imaginable place to fight a large-scale military campaign. By December 1943, the Allies had failed to break the Gustav Line and the Italian campaign was stalemated.

On 22 January 1944, the Allied ground commander in chief, Gen. Sir Harold Alexander, launched an amphibious end run behind the German lines at Anzio, thirty-five miles southwest of Rome. Alexander believed the Anzio landings would force Kesselring to abandon the Gustav Line and retreat to the Apennines. However, an assault of the Rapido River by the U.S. 36th Division two days earlier was one of the bloodiest failures of the war and enabled Kesselring to reinforce Anzio with troops from the Cassino front—and from outside Italy.

Kesselring quickly contained the Allied threat, and in mid-February 1944 he attempted to carry out Hitler's directive to "lance the abscess south of Rome" by launching a powerful counteroffensive to destroy the Anzio beachhead. Ferocious German infantry attacks cracked but ultimately failed to break the Allied defenses.

Nevertheless, this was a decisive moment in the war in Italy: Anzio became a colossal liability for the Allies, who were obliged to rush reinforcements from the south to meet the threat of the massive German buildup. Instead of a stalemate on one front, the Allies were now deadlocked on *two* widely dispersed fronts.

Earlier in February, the Allies had failed to capture either the town of Cassino or one of the holiest shrines of Roman Catholicism, the abbey of Monte Cassino. Its needless destruction by Allied bombers on February 15 remains one of the most hotly debated incidents of the war and the most visible example of the failure of Allied *strategy in Italy in 1944.

The stalemate dragged on into the spring of 1944, with neither belligerent posing a serious threat to the other until overwhelming Allied offensives at Cassino and Anzio in May finally resulted in the collapse of the Gustav Line and a full-scale German retreat into northern Italy.

Rome was occupied 4 June 1944, but during their fighting withdrawal to the north the Germans inflicted 34,000 *casualties upon the pursuing Allied forces. The Gothic Line north of Florence was a defensive barrier where Kesselring successfully obstructed the Allied advance in the autumn of 1944, thereby continuing the war in Italy into 1945. The final Allied offensive that spring resulted in the surrender of all German forces on 2 May 1945.

The Italian campaign lasted 602 days. Overall Allied casualties were 312,000, of which 189,000 (60%) were sustained by the Fifth U.S. Army. Of these, 31,886 men were killed in action. Most were American (19,475 killed of 109,642 total U.S. casualties). German losses have been estimated at 434,646, including 48,067 killed in action, with another 214,048 reported missing.

Allied grand strategy was less to win than to prolong the campaign and thus prevent the dispersal of German formations to other fronts, particularly France, where it was correctly feared their presence might well have made a decisive difference between success and failure when the Allies invaded Northwest France in the *D-Day landing, 6 June 1944.

[See also Anzio, Battle of; Bombing, Ethics of; World War II: Military and Diplomatic Course; World War II, U.S. Naval Operations in: The North Atlantic.]

• Mark Clark, Calculated Risk, 1951. Raleigh Trevelyan, Rome '44: The Battle for the Eternal City, 1981. John Ellis, Cassino: The Hollow Victory, 1984. Ernest F. Fisher, Jr., Cassino to the Alps, 1984. Dominick Graham and Shelford Bidwell, Tug of War: The Battle for Italy, 1943–45, 1986. Carlo D'Este, Fatal Decision: Anzio and the Battle for Rome, 1991.   —Carlo D'Este

IWO JIMA, BATTLE OF (1945). When the *Joint Chiefs of Staff directed the Pacific Fleet commander, Adm. Chester *Nimitz, to occupy an island in the Bonin volcano group during the western Pacific campaign in World War II, the only island of significance was Iwo Jima. Early in 1945, Japanese fighter aircraft from there were harassing the B-29s, which had begun their raids from the Marianas against Japan. Also, an emergency recovery airfield was needed for B-29s returning damaged or short on fuel.

Mt. Suribachi, at 556 feet, is the most prominent landmark of the seven-mile long, pork chop–shaped island, where Lt. Gen. Tadamichi Kuribayashi had 21,000 men and 1,000 guns. Forsaking the Japan doctrine of defending at the water's edge, he decided instead to defend from an elaborate system of caves and tunnels.

On the American side, Vice Adm. Richmond K. Turner commanded the Joint Expeditionary Force with Lt. Gen. Holland M. Smith as commander of the Joint Expeditionary Troops, while Maj. Gen. Harry Schmidt commanded the Marine V Amphibious Corps, consisting of the 3rd (Maj. Gen. Graves B. Erskine), 4th (Maj. Gen. Clifton B. Cates), and 5th (Maj. Gen. Keller E. Rockey) Marine Divisions. At 0930 on 19 February 1945, the first wave of armored amphibian tractors touched down, 5th Division on the left and 4th Division on the right. On the left, the 28th Marines, an infantry regiment, turned south toward Suribachi, and after four days of fighting gained the top of the mountain. A patrol reached the crest and tied a small American flag to a piece of pipe. Three hours later, a larger flag was brought up—one that could be seen from all over the island. Joe Rosenthal, an Associated Press photographer, took a picture of its raising that was published around the world.

The main effort was a slow advance to the north, with the 5th Division on the left and the 4th Division on the right. The 3rd Division was fed into the center of the line and the attack shouldered forward. After days of heavy fighting, the island was secured on 26 March. Altogether, 71,245 Marines had been put ashore; of these, 5,931 were killed in action, and 17,372 wounded. Twenty-two Marines, four navy hospital corpsmen, and one navy *landing craft commander were awarded the Medal of Honor, half of them posthumous awards. The number of Japanese killed has never been determined exactly, but only 216 prisoners were taken, most of them Korean conscript laborers. The terrible cost to Americans was somewhat balanced by another statistic: by war's end, 2,251 heavy bombers, with crews totaling 24,761, had made emergency landings on Iwo.

[See also Awards, Decorations, and Honors; World War II, U.S. Air Operations in: The Air War Against Japan; World War II, U.S. Naval Operations in: The Pacific.]

• Joseph H. Alexander, Closing In: Marines in the Seizure of Iwo Jima, 1995. George C. Garand and Truman R. Strobridge, History of U.S. Marine Corps Operations in World War II: Vol. IV, Western Pacific Operations, 1971.   —Benis M. Frank

J

JACKSON, ANDREW (1767–1845), *War of 1812 general and seventh president of the United States. Jackson first experienced war at thirteen, fighting in the Battle of Hanging Rock, South Carolina (6 August 1780). Subsequently captured, he remained uncooperative and was slashed by a British officer, creating an antipathy as permanent as the scar on his face. Jackson's entire family perished in the *Revolutionary War.

In 1788, Jackson moved to western North Carolina (now Tennessee), where he served as a field-grade officer in the Tennessee militia and was elected, 1802, as major general—a post considered second only to that of the governor. In 1813, he commanded the Tennessee troops sent to subdue the Creeks in present-day Alabama. After several minor victories that significantly weakened the Indians, Jackson delivered a devastating blow at the Battle of Horseshoe Bend, 27–28 March 1814.

Thereafter, Jackson was given a major generalship in the U.S. Army and put in charge of the Gulf Coast region. He seized Spanish Pensacola in the fall of 1814 and then marched to New Orleans to counter a British invasion. After a series of largely successful preliminary engagements, on 8 January 1815 he and his troops won the main Battle of *New Orleans, one of the severest defeats ever suffered by a British army. Jackson emerged a national hero.

Retaining his major generalship after the war, Jackson in 1818 pursued Indians into Spanish Florida and again occupied Pensacola. The Monroe administration reluctantly supported him, using the conquest to force Spain to sell the Floridas to the United States. Jackson resigned his commission in 1821. Except while acting as commander in chief during his presidency, he never held another command.

Jackson was a superb general. Although unschooled in theory, he was a competent tactician and strategist. He thoroughly prepared for battle and acted quickly and resourcefully to take the war to the enemy and to catch him by surprise. Among his greatest assets as a leader was an indomitable will, which earned him the nickname "Old Hickory" in 1813 when he continued to campaign despite a nearly crippling case of dysentery. He expected the same devotion to duty from others. During the War of 1812, he sanctioned the hanging of seven militiamen for disobedience or desertion, and jailed several New Orleans officials (including a federal judge) who challenged his decision to continue martial law after the British had left. Jackson often inspired fierce loyalty in officers and enlisted men alike; even his critics followed him into battle, if only because they feared him more than the enemy.

Jackson was the first westerner to become a national military hero. Like few of his contemporaries, he demonstrated a talent for commanding militia and volunteers no less than regulars, and showed equal skill in conducting conventional operations against European regulars and unconventional warfare against Indians.

[See also Commander in Chief, President as; Native American Wars: Wars Between Native Americans and Europeans and Euro-Americans; Seminole Wars.]

• Robert V. Remini, *Andrew Jackson,* 3 vols., 1977–84.

—Donald R. Hickey

JACKSON, "SCOOP" [HENRY] (1912–1983), U.S. senator. Born in Everett, Washington, Jackson was the son of working-class Norwegian immigrants. As a young boy he sold newspapers, the source of his lifelong nickname, "Scoop." After becoming a lawyer and county prosecutor, Jackson won election to the House of Representatives in 1940 as a Democrat, serving six terms before winning a Senate seat in 1952.

Between 1952 and his death of a heart attack in 1983, Jackson became one of the Senate's major champions of a strong military defense. In the late 1950s, he criticized the Eisenhower administration for neglecting defense and supported controversial claims of a "missile gap" with the Soviet Union. Deeply suspicious of the Soviets, Jackson opposed arms limitations, arguing against President John F. Kennedy's creation of the Arms Control and Disarmament Agency and voting reluctantly for the *Limited Test Ban Treaty in 1963. Later, he opposed the Anti-Ballistic Missile Treaty, and he extracted major concessions from the Nixon administration on the SALT arms control agreement. He opposed SALT II.

Jackson vigorously supported U.S. military involvement in Southeast Asia, beginning with Laos in 1962, and more particularly in Vietnam. He only reluctantly voted against President Gerald *Ford's 1975 request for aid to South Vietnam, claiming the United States had been correct in entering the *Vietnam War.

A ranking member of the Senate Armed Services Committee when he died, Jackson was known as a centrist Democrat, a lifetime liberal in civil rights and organized labor, a strong backer of Israel and Jewish immigration from the USSR, and a major supporter of the Boeing Aircraft Corporation, one of the largest employers in his state.

[See also Arms Control and Disarmament: Nuclear; SALT Treaties.]

• Peter J. Ognibene, *Scoop: The Life and Politics of Henry Jackson,* 1975.

—John Whiteclay Chambers II

JACKSON, "STONEWALL" [THOMAS] (1824–1863), Confederate army general. Born in what is now West

Virginia, Jackson was orphaned at an early age and raised by paternal relatives. Although he had little formal education, he was appointed to West Point and by diligent study graduated in 1846. He distinguished himself as an artilleryman in the *Mexican War, serving under Winfield *Scott and winning brevets to major. After the war, as a lieutenant, he served in Florida, where he quarreled with his commanding officer, Capt. (later Union Maj. Gen.) William French, whom he did his best to have court-martialed. In 1852, when opportunity offered, Jackson resigned his commission in the U.S. Army to accept a position as a professor at the Virginia Military Institute at Lexington. Although a poor teacher, he remained there until the beginning of the Civil War.

In 1861, when Virginia seceded from the Union, Jackson was commissioned a colonel in the Confederate army and put in charge of the defense of Harpers Ferry. Although superseded there by Gen. Joseph E. *Johnston, he was soon promoted to brigadier general. He earned the enmity of his men, even many of his most senior officers, by pushing them through a punishing, futile midwinter campaign; but he distinguished himself in the First Battle of *Bull Run, winning the sobriquet of "Stonewall" when Gen. Barnard E. Bee called out to his troops, "There is Jackson standing like a stone wall! Rally behind the Virginians!"—or words to that effect. The name stuck, though it seems inappropriate when applied to a man who proved one of the South's most aggressive generals.

In spring 1862, Jackson fought the brilliant Shenandoah Valley Campaign that brought him his greatest fame, for he performed best as an independent commander. Here he proved himself a brilliant strategist, and his attack upon Front Royal and Winchester drove the *Union army of Gen. Nathaniel Banks across the Potomac and out of Virginia. Although he pressed his men relentlessly, he earned their respect, for troops will endure much for generals who provide victories.

Serving directly under Gen. Robert E. *Lee in the Army of Northern Virginia, Jackson took part in the *Seven Days' Battle, where he was less than his best, his judgment and mettle blunted by fatigue and above all by an overpowering need for sleep, which even his iron will could not overcome.

In August 1862, he advanced against Union Gen. John Pope, capturing and destroying the Union army's principal supply depot in Virginia at Manassas and driving Pope's forces north. He played a notable part in the Second Battle of *Bull Run and defeated the Union forces at Chantilly. He commanded a corps in the invasion of Maryland, and it was he who captured some 12,000 Union troops at Harpers Ferry.

At the Battle of *Antietam, Jackson ably commanded a corps on the left of the Confederate line; at Fredericksburg, he held fast on the right of Lee's line. At the Battle of *Chancellorsville, he attacked with great élan the right of the line of Gen. Joseph *Hooker, resulting in one of the most remarkable victories of inferior over numerically superior forces in the history of warfare. But there, on the night of 2 May 1863, while making a personal reconnaissance in front of the lines with a few other officers, his returning knot of horsemen was mistaken for enemy cavalry and Jackson was shot by Confederate pickets. His shattered arm was amputated, but he died eight days later of complications of pneumonia.

Like Lee, Jackson was a bold, aggressive soldier. Unlike most Civil War generals, he did not try to aggrandize himself, and he was so secretive that he refused to reveal his plans even to key members of his staff—a policy that would have proved disastrous had he succeeded to a higher command. A stern disciplinarian, he held his officers to exacting standards, and no general North or South court-martialed or tried to cashier so many subordinates.

An austere man, deeply religious, Jackson did not drink, gamble, or smoke, and his years as an artilleryman had left him partially deaf, a severe handicap to a lively social life. He was by nature a reserved man but not a cold one. His few intimates found him a warm friend, and he was a loving, even playful husband to two successive wives, both daughters of Presbyterian ministers who were college presidents.

He died at an early age, not yet forty, at the pinnacle of his reputation, which has proved enduring.

[See also Civil War: Military and Diplomatic Course.]

• R. L. Dabney, Life and Campaigns of Lieut.-Gen. Thomas J. Jackson, 1885. Byron Farwell, Stonewall: A Biography of General, 1992. James I. Robertson, Jr., Stonewall Jackson: The Man, the Soldier, the Legend, 1997.
—Byron Farwell

JAPAN, PEACE TREATY WITH (1952). With the advent of the *Cold War, and more especially the Sino-Soviet alliance and the *Korean War, the U.S. and Japanese governments moved toward an agreement concerning the role of Japan in the struggle against communism in Asia. Earlier, Tokyo had sought to exclude U.S. bases from Japan (although not Okinawa) when the occupation of Japan ended. But by 1950, Prime Minister Yoshida Shigeru was driven to accept U.S. bases even on the home islands by increasing Communist threat not only in the USSR, China, and Korea, but within Japan in the form of a larger, more militant Communist Party.

Negotiating in 1951 with President Harry S. *Truman's envoy, John Foster *Dulles, Yoshida agreed to the U.S. bases in return for American protection, but refused U.S. pressure for Japan itself to rearm. The result was two treaties. A multinational peace treaty, signed in San Francisco 8 September 1951 (with the Communist nations abstaining), was extraordinarily generous, providing for an end to the occupation, recognizing Japan's "full sovereignty," and mandating no Japanese reparations to its wartime victims. The same day, the United States and Japan signed a bilateral agreement for U.S. troops to remain indefinitely, even allowing their use against domestic disturbances. On 8 February 1952, both parties signed another treaty authorizing the United States to maintain military bases in Japan and Okinawa.

Tensions led to a new U.S.-Japan security agreement in 1960 providing for more mutual consultation on defense, but many Japanese still feared that Washington's policies might drag Japan into an unwanted war.

[See also Japan, U.S. Military Involvement in; World War II: Military and Diplomatic Course.]

• Michael Schaller, The American Occupation of Japan: The Origins of the Cold War in Asia, 1985. Roger Buckley, U.S.-Japan Alliance Diplomacy, 1945–1990, 1992. Michael Barnhart, Japan and the World Since 1868, 1995.
—Michael Barnhart

JAPAN, U.S. MILITARY INVOLVEMENT IN. Initial U.S. military involvement with Japan occurred in 1853, when Comm. Matthew C. Perry led a naval expedition there. Perry sought to compel the ruling Tokugawa Shogun to open Japan to foreign commerce on American terms. In the face of superior technology, the Japanese acceded to Perry's demand in 1854. In the early twentieth century, despite disputes over immigration restriction and mistreatment of Japanese residents in the United States, the two Pacific nations became major trading partners and cooperated in creating a balance of power in the Asia-Pacific region. The collapse of world trade after 1929, however, prompted Japanese militarists and nationalist politicians to abandon the framework of cooperation established with the West under the *League of Nations (1919) and *Washington Naval Arms Limitation Treaty (1922) and to seek creation of a self-supporting Japanese empire. In 1931, the Japanese Army seized Manchuria, and in 1937 it invaded China proper.

Japan's cooperation with Nazi Germany from 1936 on, as well as its threat to the American and European colonies in Asia, prompted the Roosevelt administration to begin aiding China in 1938. By July 1941, Japan's occupation of French Indochina prompted President Franklin D. *Roosevelt to embargo all sales to Japan and boost military aid to China. Months of fruitless negotiations culminated in the attack on *Pearl Harbor, 7 December 1941.

In the three months following the outbreak of war, Japanese air, sea, and land forces swept over colonial Southeast Asia and the western Pacific, including the Philippines. Although Roosevelt and his military advisers adopted a "Europe-first" strategy, they were able to send sizable military and naval resources to the Pacific before Germany's defeat. U.S. intelligence also broke important Japanese naval codes. By the end of 1942, the Japanese lost the initiative in the Pacific. American forces then embarked on the long push to Tokyo.

In the spring of 1945, the Army Air Force began massive raids on Japanese cities. At about the same time, after incredibly bloody fighting, U.S. forces seized two strategic islands, part of Japan's inner defense ring, in the battles of *Iwo Jima and *Okinawa. In June, President Harry S. *Truman authorized plans for the invasion of Japan, tentatively scheduled for November. The successful testing of the atomic bomb that July provided the United States an alternative to invading the home islands. The shock of the new weapon, U.S. strategists hoped, would convince deadlocked Japanese decision makers to surrender quickly. Besides saving lives on all sides, an early surrender might keep Soviet troops from occupying China and gaining a foothold in Japan.

The air force dropped the first atomic bomb on Hiroshima on 6 August 1945, the second against Nagasaki 9 August. The combined shock of the atomic bombs and the Soviet entry into the war prompted Japanese emperor *Hirohito to break the deadlock among his advisers in favor of agreeing to U.S. surrender terms. President Truman accepted the surrender 15 August 1945, and the Japanese signed surrender documents at a ceremony aboard the battleship *Missouri* in Tokyo Bay 2 September. Over 2 million Japanese (including some 400,000 civilians) and 100,000 Americans died in the Pacific War.

The American military occupation of Japan lasted from August 1945 through April 1952. Gen. Douglas *Mac-

Arthur served as Supreme Commander of the Allied Powers until his removal in April 1951. Gen. Matthew B. *Ridgway succeeded him. Among the many liberal reforms instituted by the Americans was Article 9 of the new Japanese Constitution barring the establishment of armed forces or the right to conduct war, a clause regretted by U.S. policymakers in the *Cold War. When the *Korean War broke out in June 1950, the United States ordered Japan to create a small "national police reserve" that assumed the defense duties of American forces shifted to Korea. Gradually, this evolved into Japan's Self-Defense Forces.

In September 1951, when the United States and its allies signed a peace treaty with Japan, it compelled Tokyo to sign a bilateral security treaty with Washington that permitted sizable American forces to use military bases in Japan indefinitely. The arrangement, which many Japanese saw as a demeaning continuation of the occupation, was extremely unpopular. However, it was understood as the price that must be paid to regain sovereignty. The treaty was revised in 1960 to make it more equitable.

During the *Korean and War the *Vietnam War and in Cold War *strategy, military base and logistic facilities in Japan were vital for U.S. military operations. In the late 1990s, sizable American military units remained stationed on Okinawa and Japan proper. Since the early 1950s, the United States has encouraged Japanese rearmament and urged Tokyo to take a more active role in Asian security matters. Public opinion in Japan has resisted expanding the limited role of the Self-Defense Forces, but the Japanese government appeared ready by the late 1990s to play a more active role both in regional military defense and in international *peacekeeping operations.

[See also Hiroshima and Nagasaki, Bombings of; Japan, Peace Treaty with; MAGIC; World War II: Military and Diplomatic Course; World War II, U.S. Air Operations in: The Air War Against Japan; World War II, U.S. Naval Operations in: The Pacific.]

• Michael Schaller, *The American Occupation of Japan: The Origins of the Cold War in Asia*, 1985. Ronald H. Spector, *Eagle Against the Sun: The American War with Japan*, 1985. John Dower, *War Without Mercy: Race and Power in the Pacific War*, 1986. Michael Barnhart, *Japan and the World since 1868*, 1995. Walter La Feber, *The Clash: U.S.-Japanese Relations Throughout History*, 1997. Michael Schaller, *Altered States: The U.S. and Japan Since the Occupation*, 1997.
—Michael Schaller

JAPANESE-AMERICAN INTERNMENT CASES. During World War II, the U.S. Army, acting under Executive Order 9066 signed by President Franklin D. *Roosevelt on 19 February 1942 (and ratified by Congress a month later), ordered nearly 120,000 Japanese nationals and Japanese Americans from the West Coast where the majority of them lived to move to prisonlike "relocation" camps in the interior of the United States. In the case of U.S. citizens, such action was taken only against those of Japanese ancestry, not against German Americans or Italian Americans. As a November 1941 civilian report stressed the loyalty of most Japanese Americans to the United States, and the FBI and U.S. military intelligence had planned only to detain potential spies or saboteurs, Roosevelt's claim of "military necessity" appears to have been a legal cover for the administration's concession to anti–Japanese-American groups. These included economic competitors, racists, and politicians appealing to a public frightened after the attack on

*Pearl Harbor. Gen. John L. De Witt, army chief of the Western Defense Command, declared that racial ties made all ethnic Japanese potentially disloyal, and directed their immediate removal from their homes on the West Coast. Most internees remained in the camps until 1944; they were not closed until late 1945.

The Japanese-American Internment Cases resulted from legal claims by Japanese Americans that these actions violated their rights as U.S. citizens. Gordon Kyoshi Hirabayashi was born in Seattle in 1918 and was a senior at the University of Washington when he was arrested in 1942 for failing to register for evacuation and for violating the curfew imposed on all ethnic Japanese. In *Hirabayashi* v. *U.S.* (20 U.S. 81) in 1943, the U.S. Supreme Court unanimously upheld the military curfew regulations under the war powers, and thus his conviction, but declined to consider the issue of Japanese exclusion from the area. The Court similarly upheld the curfew conviction of Minoru Yasui, born in Oregon in 1916, who was a lawyer and a second lieutenant in the U.S. Army Reserve.

In December 1944, the Supreme Court upheld the legality of the forced evacuation of U.S. citizens of Japanese ancestry in *Korematsu* v. *U.S.* (323 U.S. 214). But three justices, Robert Jackson, Frank Murphy, and Owen J. Roberts, dissented, claiming the relocation program was unconstitutional. Fred Toyosaburo Korematsu, born in Oakland, California, in 1919, had been arrested in 1942 for refusing to comply with the military's exclusion order. In a gesture to the dissenters, in *Ex parte Endo* (323 U.S. 283), the Supreme Court held in 1944 that the War Relocation Authority, which oversaw the relocation program, could not detain a person whose loyalty had been established.

Thus, the Supreme Court largely upheld the government during the war, limiting the Constitution's guarantees of equal protection under the law, and allowing the supremacy of military over civil judgment and authority on the basis of claims of "military necessity."

In 1983, a team of attorneys reopened the internment cases based on documentary findings that in their original presentation to the Supreme Court, the government's lawyers had suppressed evidence and made false statements. Lower courts vacated the wartime convictions of Hirabayashi and Korematsu, but refused to hear Yasui's petition, and the government chose to end the litigation by not appealing those decisions to the Supreme Court, the sole court with the authority to reverse its own rulings. In 1988, Congress provided for partial restitution payments of $20,000 to each of the 60,000 surviving internees from the camps.

[*See also* Civil Liberties and War; Internment of Enemy Aliens; Supreme Court, War, and the Military.]

• Peter Irons, *Justice at War: The Story of the Japanese American Internment Cases*, 1983. Peter Irons, *Justice Delayed: The Record of the Japanese American Internment Cases*, 1989. *Personal Justice Denied. Report of the Commission on Wartime Relocation and Internment of Civilians*, 1997.　　　　　　　　　　—Gary Y. Okihiro

JAPANESE-AMERICAN RELOCATION AND INTERNMENT. *See* Internment of Enemy Aliens; Japanese-American Internment Cases.

JAVITS ACTS. *See* War Powers Resolution (1973).

JEFFERSON, THOMAS (1743–1826), secretary of state, vice president, and third president of the United States. Thomas Jefferson believed that a large military establishment would both increase the nation's debt and threaten American liberty. As the first secretary of state (1789–93), he urged *neutrality in the war between England and France; as president (1801–09), he pursued a policy of "peace, commerce, and honest friendship" with all nations, but "entangling alliances with none." Jefferson's administration cut military spending drastically, from over $3 million annually to $1.9 million, although his administration also founded the U.S. Military Academy, first proposed by Washington, at West Point, New York, in 1802. Neutrality, though, was not isolation: Jefferson sent the U.S. Fleet to the Mediterranean in 1801, and cooperated with Sweden, Portugal, Naples, and other neutral powers in a multinational alliance against Tripoli. To replace the expensive frigates built by the Federalist administrations, Jefferson built 180 gunboats, 50 feet long, with crews of 20 and cannon mounted in bow and stern, primarily to defend American harbors. Instead of military force, the United States would use economic pressure in international affairs. The Europeans, he reasoned, depended on American grain and fish to feed their large armies and overtaxed populations. When both France and England attacked American commercial policy in 1807, Jefferson closed U.S. ports, depriving the belligerent Europeans of American goods. Though the embargo of 1808–09 did not force France or England to negotiate, Jefferson did not lose faith in economic power as the most potent weapon in the American arsenal.

[*See also* Academies, Service: U.S. Military Academy; Economy and War; Hamilton, Alexander; Tripolitan War.]

• Merrill Peterson, *Thomas Jefferson and the New Nation*, 1970. Reginald C. Stuart, *The Half-Way Pacifist: Thomas Jefferson's View of War*, 1978. Drew R. McCoy, *The Elusive Republic: Political Economy in Jeffersonian America*, 1980. Robert W. Tucker and David C. Hendrickson, *Empire of Liberty: The Statecraft of Thomas Jefferson*, 1990.　　　　　　　　　　—Robert J. Allison

JOHNSON, ANDREW (1808–1875), vice president, seventeenth president of the United States. As a Tennessee congressman in 1843–53 and senator in 1857–62, Johnson provided mixed signals on military issues. In 1850, he remarked that he might like to have one of his sons in the navy, and he worked to get Tennessee boys into West Point and the U.S. Naval Academy. Yet Johnson was at heart a small government Democrat, with special concerns about money and class privilege. Thus in a speech on appropriations in August 1852 he derided the "imbecile" congressional sons who got preference; proposed to close both academies; attacked the wasteful War and Navy Department bureaucracies; and called the army and navy expensive and oppressive in the European style.

Johnson was a strong nationalist, who favored expansion and strongly supported the administration during the *Mexican War, even though he and President James K. *Polk openly despised each other. During the secession crisis, Johnson remained firmly loyal to the Union. Abraham *Lincoln, needing a strong-willed figure to begin *Reconstruction in Tennessee, appointed Johnson military governor in 1862. This was an anomalous position in American law, and one that the fortunes of war and necessities of politics made frustrating. Johnson's relations with Union generals were often strained.

Upon Lincoln's death (1865), Johnson succeeded to the assassination presidency. In implementing Reconstruction policy the army played a central role in the institutional struggle between Congress and the president in 1866–67. Johnson's efforts to bring Ulysses S. *Grant into his political circle led to a public breach with the popular general. Johnson did have friendly relations with William Tecumseh *Sherman, who nonetheless refused a political role. Impeachment proceedings in 1868 were on an asserted violation of the Tenure of Office Act, arising out of the removal of Secretary of War Edwin M. *Stanton—a step Johnson justified both on his general executive authority under the Constitution and his specific function as commander in chief.

[See also Civil War: Postwar Impact; Commander in Chief, President as; Expansionism.]

• James E. Sefton, *Andrew Johnson and the Uses of Constitutional Power*, 1980. Hans L. Trefousse, *Andrew Johnson: A Biography*, 1989.
—James E. Sefton

JOHNSON, LOUIS (1891–1966), secretary of defense. As defense secretary from 28 March 1949 to 19 September 1950, Louis Johnson was best known for his controversial money-saving measures. The most contentious was his decision in April 1949 to cancel the navy's experimental flush-deck "supercarrier," the *United States*, which was in the initial stages of construction. Johnson thought the supercarrier would duplicate strategic bombing functions performed by the air force, but his cancelation order outraged the navy and its partisans and provoked a congressional investigation. Johnson insisted he was only complying with President Harry S. *Truman's instructions to hold down defense spending. He was absolved of any wrongdoing, but some critics felt his economy drive went too far and weakened the armed forces.

Johnson's tempestuous tenure as secretary of defense came in the wake of earlier controversy surrounding his actions as assistant secretary of war (1937–40). At that time, Johnson had pressed vigorously for U.S. rearmament as war clouds gathered over Europe and the Far East, even though U.S. policy stressed *neutrality and noninvolvement. During World War II, Johnson served briefly as U.S. representative to India.

As secretary of defense, Johnson favored a defense posture resting on strategic nuclear airpower, while his rival, Secretary of State Dean *Acheson, wanted a more broadly based military that would allow greater diplomatic flexibility. Their differences came to a head in the spring of 1950 during deliberations over a paper (NSC 68) recommending a U.S. military buildup to counter recent increases in Soviet military power. President Truman sided with Acheson and decided to fire Johnson in the light of early U.S. reverses in the *Korean War. Though Johnson had once aspired to the presidency, he felt disgraced and quietly returned to his West Virginia law practice.

[See also Carrier Warfare; Defense, Department of.]

• Carl W. Borklund, *Men of the Pentagon: From Forrestal to McNamara*, 1966. Steven L. Rearden, *History of the Office of the Secretary of Defense: The Formative Years, 1947–1950*, 1984. Roger R. Trask, *The Secretaries of Defense: A Brief History, 1947–1985*, 1985.
—Steven L. Rearden

JOHNSON, LYNDON B. (1908–1973), thirty-sixth president of the United States. Johnson was born on 27 August 1908 in the Hill Country of central Texas. His father was a Democratic politician from whom Lyndon inherited his lifelong passion for politics. He was educated in nearby schools and Southwest Texas State Teachers College in San Marcos. He then taught in Cotulla and Houston.

In the thirties, Johnson went to Washington and became an ardent admirer of FDR and his New Deal. In 1938, he captured his first elective office for the Tenth Congressional District, including the Hill Country and Austin, and was reelected several times. In 1948, he "won" an extremely close and tainted election to the Senate. He became minority leader of the Senate (1953), where he was a master congressional politician and emerged as a candidate for president.

The 1960 election was Johnson's big chance. But he believed it hopeless because he came from the South and the convention would be dominated by northern Democrats. He entered no primaries and made virtually no campaign, thereby ceding the nomination to John F. *Kennedy on the first ballot. But Kennedy, concerned that his Catholicism would bring defeat in the South, offered Johnson the second place, and he accepted. Johnson's powerful campaign in the South made victory possible by a thin margin. Thus, for almost three years he served in the meaningless job of vice president, loyal, to be sure, but bored and frustrated. On 22 November 1963, Lee Harvey Oswald's bullet catapulted him into the presidency.

Johnson, with his exceptional intelligence, his feel for the legislative process, and his experience on Capitol Hill, was superbly qualified in domestic policy; he was less experienced in international affairs. Among the most aggressive cold warriors, Johnson determined to halt Soviet and Chinese expansion. His key advisers, Secretary of Defense Robert S. *McNamara and national security adviser McGeorge Bundy, both holdovers from the Kennedy administration, shared these views.

The Eisenhower and Kennedy administrations were baffled by the problem of Communist-Nationalist influence in Vietnam. Kennedy had increased the number of U.S. advisers and introduced "Green Beret" *counterinsurgency combat advisers. He had supported Ngo No Dingh Diem in South Vietnam. But Diem and his family were brutal and corrupt; the Viet Cong controlled much of the country; there was bitter Catholic-Buddhist conflict; the Soviets and the Chinese supplied *Ho Chi Minh in the North. The assassination of Diem and his brother with U.S. assent was followed by a revolving door of "governments" that quickly collapsed. There seemed no way to save South Vietnam from the Communists. A military venture appeared reckless, but the United States refused to accept Communist control of the South. The result was a limited commitment: financial support; U.S. military supplies and *covert operations; and training the Vietnamese forces. This was the situation Johnson inherited.

As an accidental president obligated to complete Kennedy's legacy, he was not ready for war in 1964. He needed to legitimize his own presidency, which he achieved in November with his landslide electoral victory against Barry Goldwater.

Johnson's primary advisers concluded that South Vietnam was the linchpin of the *Cold War. If it fell, the

Communists would take over Southeast Asia, perhaps followed by South Korea, Taiwan, India, and Iran. This was Eisenhower's "domino theory" writ large. South Vietnam was so weak that the United States had no bargaining power with the North. To achieve peace, therefore, the United States must smash North Vietnam by bombing. The advisers did not mention a land war, but that was the only alternative if bombing failed.

This made no sense. The Communist world was divided and South Vietnam was in reality no linchpin at all. Air bombardment was little threat to an agricultural nation supplied by the Soviets. If the United States moved to a land war, Ho Chi Minh held the winning cards because it would mean *guerrilla warfare. Dissenters, Undersecretary of State George *Ball, Senate majority leader Mike Mansfield, as well as French president Charles de Gaulle, all made these arguments, but Johnson would not heed them.

Early in 1965, Johnson started air attacks with Operation Flaming Dart, which soon widened into Rolling Thunder. In March, the Marines splashed ashore to establish a base at Danang. On 6 April, Johnson signed National Security Action Memorandum No. 328, which authorized the use of American combat troops.

Gen. William C. *Westmoreland, the U.S. commander in Vietnam, made enormous demands for troops; the president gave him part of what he asked. By mid-1966, Westmoreland had 600,000 American troops with immense firepower, a huge air force, and a giant infrastructure. Johnson controlled their use, particularly the air war. The bombing had little military effect. Westmoreland waited for major battles where his firepower would prevail, but they seldom took place. Meantime the North Vietnamese and the Viet Cong imposed a heavy toll in U.S. and South Vietnamese *casualties.

Support for the war at home, strong at the outset, eroded steadily. Mounting casualties, lack of victory, and increasingly skeptical television coverage fed opposition. Opponents of the war staged massive demonstrations, and the Johnson administration started to crack internally.

The *Tet Offensive, launched by the Viet Cong at the end of January 1968, caught Westmoreland by surprise. There were attacks on cities and towns throughout the country with many initial successes. Though American forces recaptured these places, it was at heavy cost to both sides.

Tet convinced the American people that the war could go on for years and might never be won. The Johnson administration was shredded, the *peace and antiwar movements grew dramatically, conservatives in Congress ran roughshod over the Great Society, and the Democratic Party split. Johnson withdrew from the presidential race in 1968; Bobby Kennedy and Martin Luther King, Jr., were assassinated; and there were riots at the Democratic National Convention in Chicago. Richard M. *Nixon prevailed over Johnson's vice president, Hubert Humphrey, in the 1968 election, with a promise to end the war with honor.

In 1969, Lyndon Johnson returned to his ranch to spend his few remaining years with his memories. He had been a bold president on domestic issues and a misguided one on the Vietnam War.

[See also Bombing, Ethics of; Bombing of Civilians; Vietnam Antiwar Movement; Vietnam War: Causes; Vietnam War: Military and Diplomatic Course; Vietnam War: Domestic Course.]

• Lyndon Baines Johnson, The Vantage Point, 1971. The Pentagon Papers, Senator Gravel, ed., 4 vols., 1971. Stanley Karnow, Vietnam, A History, 1983. Clark Clifford, Counsel to the President, 1991. Robert S. McNamara, In Retrospect, 1995. Irving Bernstein, Guns or Butter, 1996.
—Irving Bernstein

JOHNSTON, JOSEPH E. (1807–1891), *Confederate army general. Born near Farmville, Virginia, Johnston attended Abingdon Academy and graduated from West Point in 1829. He fought in the *Seminole and *Mexican Wars, was often breveted for gallantry, and became quartermaster general (with staff rank of brigadier general) of the U.S. Army in June 1860.

Johnston joined the Confederacy as a brigadier in May and became a full general in August 1861. He stood fourth in general's rank, and that led to a caustic breach with President Jefferson *Davis that affected Johnston's, and the Confederacy's, career.

First assigned to the Shenandoah Valley, he eluded a Union force and marched his troops to aid Gen. P.G.T. *Beauregard at First Manassas. In 1862, Johnston, in command of the army, moved his force south to oppose Gen. George B. *McClellan's advance toward Richmond. He attacked at Seven Pines on the York peninsula in May 1862, failed to achieve a decisive victory, was severely wounded, and was replaced by Robert E. *Lee.

In November 1862, Davis, overcoming doubt and dislike, gave Johnston one of the great opportunities of the war as commander of the new Department of the West. Failing to understand a unique experiment in theater command or that he had been handed a satrap's wide powers, Johnston missed his chance to combine the military, social, and economic resources of a vast area against various enemy armies in a grand scheme to save the western flank of the Confederacy. He lapsed, instead, into the role of a local army commander in trying to relieve the siege of *Vicksburg. Understanding the crisis there, he worked earnestly to build an army with which to attack Ulysses S. *Grant's siege lines from behind. But he could not gather enough men or supplies quickly enough to save that important Mississippi River bastion.

In November 1863, Johnston took command of the Army of Tennessee, which languished in the doldrums after the loss of Chattanooga, Tennessee. His masterly strategic retreat down the Western & Atlantic Railroad from Dalton to Atlanta, Georgia, ahead of William Tecumseh *Sherman's larger army ranks as a model strategic retreat. His withdrawal into Atlanta's defenses displeased Davis, however, who replaced him with the more aggressive Gen. John B. *Hood in July 1864. Recalled to duty in February 1865 to command the remnants of his old army, after Hood's shattering defeats, he could not halt Sherman's march. Johnston surrendered at Durham Station, North Carolina, 26 April 1865.

In 1874, Johnston published Narrative of Military Operations. Subsequently a congressman from Virginia (1879–81), he became U.S. Commissioner of Railroads, 1885–91. He died in Washington, D.C., in March 1891 from a cold apparently caught while marching bareheaded in General Sherman's funeral procession.

Was Johnston a defensive genius or a nonfighter? The question persists. His quarrel with Davis limited his usefulness, but his Atlanta campaign shows him to have been a brilliant defensive tactician. Critics say he lacked aggressiveness and brand him too harshly as "Retreating Joe." Audacity is often urged on the weaker side, but Johnston's method of staging fighting retreats, which inflicted more *casualties than he took, might have prolonged the Confederacy's existence.

[See also Civil War: Military and Diplomatic Course.]

• Gilbert E. Govan and James W. Livingood, A Different Valor: The Story of General Joseph E. Johnston, 1956. Joseph E. Johnston, Narrative of Military Operations, Directed, During the Late War Between the States, 1874; repr. 1959. Craig L. Symonds, Joseph E. Johnston, 1992.
—Frank E. Vandiver

The **JOINT CHIEFS OF STAFF** (JCS), who consist of the head, or chief of staff, of each military service and an additional high-ranking officer from one of the services who serves as chair, function as the virtual high command of the U.S. armed forces, the key planning organization for and coordinating link between the services, and the foremost military advisers to the president, secretary of defense, *National Security Council, and Congress. The organization was established informally during World War II and institutionalized by an act of Congress in 1947. It has been altered on numerous occasions since then, with the emergence of a powerful chairman and joint staff the most notable change.

The roots of the JCS date back to turn-of-the-century managerial revolution in warfare that resulted in the establishment throughout the world of general staffs headed by chiefs of staff to plan for and command national military establishments. Although the United States lagged behind many of its European counterparts in this development, in the first two decades of the twentieth century it did create army and navy staffs headed by service chiefs, as well as a Joint Army-Navy Board composed of these chiefs and their key strategic planners. However, widespread fears of militarism, as well as intense interservice rivalries and bureaucratic political conflicts, for many years precluded the chiefs from exercising any real power or influence.

President Franklin D. *Roosevelt altered this situation in 1939 by personally selecting and directly consulting with Gen. George C. *Marshall and Adm. Harold E. Stark as the army and navy chiefs, and by placing the Joint Board into the newly created executive office of the president. In doing so, he bypassed the secretaries of war and navy, established a direct link between the chiefs and the White House, made those chiefs his foremost military advisers, and altered and expanded their powers. Nevertheless, the Joint Board continued to exhibit severe problems and limitations between the outbreak of World War II in 1939 and U.S. entry in late 1941 in terms of both interservice coordination and civil-military coordination, and by early 1942 it was apparent that the organization was simply inadequate for the conduct of global war.

At that time the JCS came into existence and replaced the Joint Board. This occurred during and immediately after the Anglo-American Arcadia Conference of December–January 1941–42, which established the Anglo-American Combined Chiefs of Staff to plan global strategy. The British section of this organization was to be composed of the already existing British Chiefs of Staff Committee; the U.S. Joint Chiefs of Staff was formed along roughly parallel lines to ensure effective Anglo-American, as well as U.S. Army-Navy and civil-military, coordination. In its original form, the U.S. organization consisted of army chief General Marshall; naval chief Admiral Stark; Army Air Forces Commanding Gen. "Hap" *Arnold; and Commander in Chief of the U.S. Fleet Adm. Ernest J. *King.

This was not an exact duplication of the British organization, which consisted of independent army, navy, and air chiefs along with a special officer to represent the defense minister and Prime Minister Winston S. *Churchill. Roosevelt at first opposed the appointment of such a special officer within the U.S. organization as an infringement upon his powers. Furthermore, unlike its British counterpart, the American air force was a part of the army rather than independent, and the inclusion of Arnold on the JCS so as to parallel the British chiefs of staff thus aroused naval fears of being outvoted. This problem, and the one caused by the still limited powers of the U.S. chief of naval operations, were temporarily resolved by including King in the new organization as a second admiral.

Two alterations were made in the membership of the JCS between March and July 1942. In March, Stark left for England to head U.S. naval forces in Europe and King assumed the title of chief of naval operations while retaining his previous one of commander in chief of the fleet. Then, in July, Marshall succeeded in convincing the president to appoint the former chief of naval operations and Roosevelt's close confidant Adm. William D. Leahy as chief of staff to the commander in chief. This reestablished an army-navy balance on the JCS, provided a direct link to the president, and stabilized the organization's membership: Marshall, King, Arnold, and Leahy would constitute the JCS for the duration of the war. Roosevelt, however, refused to allow Leahy to assume the functions Marshall had desired for him as chairman of and representative to the president. Leahy did preside over JCS meetings, but essentially remained merely Roosevelt's "leg man" to the chiefs, while Marshall himself gradually and informally assumed the leadership role within the organization as "first among equals."

The U.S. JCS, the British chiefs, and the Combined Chiefs of Staff all proved to be highly effective organizations in the strategic direction of global war. By agreements reached at the Arcadia Conference and soon thereafter, the combined chiefs would meet in continuous session, in person when Churchill and Roosevelt met, and via deputies in Washington at other times. They were charged with planning for and directing all Anglo-American land, naval, and air forces, which would be commanded in each theater by a single officer under the principle of unity of command. This critical decision made possible the effective integration of British and American forces as well as, for the first time, all U.S. Army and Navy forces. Within this system, the combined chiefs as a whole were responsible for the European-Mediterranean theater of operations. Responsibility for the other theaters was divided between the British and the U.S. chiefs, with the British in charge of the Indian Ocean/Middle East theater and the Americans in charge of the Pacific theater (Southwest Pacific under Gen. Douglas *MacArthur and Pacific Ocean Areas under Adm. Chester *Nimitz). As the war progressed, the JCS developed an extensive structure of joint army-navy planning committees staffed by officers from each service, who also served on an equally extensive series of Anglo-American Combined Chiefs of Staff committees.

Numerous strategic conflicts arose both within the U.S.

chiefs and between them and the British on the Combined Chiefs of Staff, most notably over cross-Channel vs. Mediterranean operations and Europe vs. Asia/Pacific priorities. Overall, however, these organizations succeeded in compromising interservice and national differences, in working with their political superiors, and in developing and implementing an effective global *strategy to defeat the Axis powers. Indeed, both U.S. Army-Navy and Anglo-American military cooperation and coordination during World War II reached unprecedented levels and played a major role in Allied victory. Consequently, there was fundamental agreement at war's end that some form of continued interservice coordination and control at the chiefs' level would be mandatory. The form eventually selected was essentially a retention of the World War II system into the postwar era.

Throughout World War II, the JCS had existed solely at presidential discretion. Two years after Allied victory, however, Congress formalized the institution as the centerpiece of the postwar U.S. military establishment in the *National Security Act of 1947. This formalization, and the other components of the National Security Act, were the end result of an extensive debate between the services and their congressional allies over the proper shape of the postwar armed forces. American Air Force officers pressed for independence as a third branch of service, and—together with army officers—for full unification of the three services under a single military staff, a single chief, and a single cabinet secretary. Naval officers remained fearful of being outvoted and overwhelmed in such a unification and proposed instead continuation of the World War II system whereby the separate service chiefs would retain their individual powers while serving as members of the JCS. The final act was largely a naval victory, which preserved this "federal" or "dual-hat" system of World War II, whereby the JCS represented both their individual services and the armed forces as a whole, rather than creating any true unification. Instead of a single general staff under one chief, the U.S. armed forces would include separate army, navy, and air staffs as well as separate civilian departments for the army, navy, and air force. The chiefs of the three military staffs would retain full powers within their services and meet as independent equals (along with the chief of staff to the commander in chief) within the JCS, where they would negotiate their differences as they had during World War II. Similarly, army, navy, and air force staff planners would meet and negotiate in a series of joint staff committees. In 1953, the commandant of the Marine Corps was added to the JCS when it considered matters of direct concern to the Marines, and in 1978 the commandant became a full member.

Continued and extensive interservice conflict, illustrated by the so-called "Revolt of the Admirals" in 1949, led Congress to amend the National Security Act in 1949 so as to create a single Department of *Defense and an official chairman of the JCS, who would not, however, have a vote on issues dividing the chiefs. Although far from the single chief of staff originally envisioned by army and air force planners, that individual did become the principal military adviser to the president and the secretary of defense. Despite his lack of an official vote, he was also able to exercise some leadership over the JCS, speak for them, and clarify their authority over all theater commanders—most notably in the Truman-MacArthur controversy of 1951 during the *Korean War when Gen. Omar N. *Bradley held the post of chairman.

From that time onward, the power of the chairman of the JCS has gradually increased, though haltingly, amid continued buraucratic and political conflict, and never to the extent of creating a single chief of a general staff as reformers desired. In 1953, the chairman was given control over an enlarged joint staff and in 1958 a vote on the JCS. The most far-reaching increase in his power, and reform of the entire joint chiefs system, took place in 1986 with the passage of the *Goldwater-Nichols Act. This Department of Defense reorganization act made the chairman the principal military adviser within the executive branch, enabled him to speak independently of the service chiefs, enlarged his joint staff, and gave the joint staff additional autonomy and responsibility. A few years later Gen. Colin *Powell would vividly illustrate just how powerful and important the chairman had become. The service chiefs still retained enormous powers, however, and by no means did the act create a general staff with a single chief. Although reformers continue to argue that such a staff and chief are necessary to create true interservice coordination and halt service parochialism, such parochialism has combined with a continued, traditional American fear of centralized military authority to preclude the replacement of the JCS with such a system.

In September 1998, the JCS warned that the combat readiness of the armed forces was being endangered by chronic problems, from replacing aging equipment to recruiting and retaining qualified service people, particularly pilots. Gen. Henry Shelton, JCS chairman, urged fixing the military's retirement system and closing the pay gap between military personnel and civilians with similar training, recommending an additional $40 billion over five years to a Pentagon budget that was $271 for fiscal year 1998–99.

In effect, the JCS organization, from its World War II inception down to the present day, has attempted to provide the nation with the advantages of full interservice coordination and control, but without a loss of service identity or the creation of an all-powerful and threatening central military command. In so doing it has created a military version of the constitutional system of checks and balances, albeit between the services rather than between the different branches of government. And as a combination of external threats and internal problems led the executive branch during the twentieth century to expand enormously its powers within this system of government, so a combination of external threats and internal inefficiencies within the JCS system has led to the rise of a chairman within that body and a continual increase in his powers—though never to the extent reformers have desired.

[See also Jones, David; World War II: Military and Diplomatic Course; World War II: Domestic Course; World War II: Postwar Impact.]

• Grace Person Hayes, The History of the Joint Chiefs of Staff in World War II: The War Against Japan, 1982. Historical Division, Joint Secretariat, The History of the Joint Chiefs of Staff in World War II: The War Against Germany (undated). Vernon E. Davis, The History of the Joint Chiefs of Staff in World War II: Organizational Development, 2 vols., 1972. Lawrence J. Korb, The Joint Chiefs of Staff: The First Twenty-five Years, 1976. Richard K., Betts, Soldiers, Statesmen, and Cold War Crises, 1977. Robert J. Watson, "The Evolving Role of the Joint Chiefs of Staff in the National Security Structure,"

in *Evolution of the American Military Establishment Since World War II*, ed. Paul R. Schratz, 1978. Historical Division, Joint Secretariat, *The History of the Joint Chiefs of Staff: The Joint Chiefs of Staff and National Policy, 1945–1956*, 6 vols., 1979– . Historical Division, Joint Secretariat, *History of the Joint Chiefs of Staff: The Joint Chiefs of Staff and the War in Vietnam, History of the Indochina Incident, 1940–1954*, Vol. 1, 1982. D. Clayton James, *A Time for Giants: The Politics of the American High Command in World War II*, 1987. Eric Larrabee, *Commander in Chief: Franklin Delano Roosevelt, His Lieutenants, and Their War*, 1987. Robert J. Watson, *History of the Joint Chiefs of Staff, 5: The Joint Chiefs of Staff and National Policy, 1953–1954*, 1986. Kenneth W. Condit, *History of the Joint Chiefs of Staff, 6: the Joint Chiefs of Staff and National Policy, 1955–1956* 1992. Mark A. Stoler, *Allies, Adversaries and Interests: The Joint Chiefs of Staff, the Grand Alliance, and American Strategy in World War II*, 2000.
—Mark A. Stoler

JOMINI, ANTOINE-HENRI (1779–1869), authority on the art of war. A Swiss citizen in Napoleon's service, Jomini wrote profusely while becoming a general officer and chief of staff to Marshal Michel Ney and then had a long career in the Russian Army.

In his histories of the campaigns of Frederick the Great, the French Revolution, and Napoleon, Jomini expounded what he saw as the essence of the offensive strategy of *Napoleonic warfare. In this, he assumed dispersed armies and advocated the use of interior lines of communication and supply, concentration against the center of a too-dispersed adversary, and turning the flank of an opponent who was too concentrated. Napoleon's victories at Marengo, Ulm, and Jena illustrated this turning movement. Jomini summarized these ideas in his influential *Précis de l'art de guerre* (1837). Jomini had many expositors who helped educate English-speaking soldiers in the British empire and the United States.

Beginning in the 1950s, some American military historians incorrectly attributed to Jomini an immense influence on the generals of the U.S. *Civil War, who were, of course, influenced by Napoleon.

[*See also* Clausewitz, Carl von; Strategy: Fundamentals.]

• Richard E. Beringer, et al., *Why the South Lost the Civil War*, 1986. John Shy, "Jomini," in *Makers of Modern Strategy*, ed. Peter Paret, 1986.
—Archer Jones

JONES, DAVID (1921–), air force chief of staff and chairman of the *Joint Chiefs of Staff (JCS). Jones was born in South Dakota and grew up in North Dakota. He received a commission in the Army Air Forces in 1943 and followed a career as a bomber pilot. He led a squadron during the *Korean War, and later commanded the U.S. Air Forces in Europe. Becoming air force chief of staff in 1974, he made substantial reductions in headquarters staff and reorganized the air force hierarchy. Support for the Panama Canal Treaties and cancellation of the B-1 bomber earned him congressional criticism.

President Jimmy *Carter appointed Jones the ninth chairman of the JCS in 1978. Jones's support for the SALT II agreement in 1979 and the failed Iranian hostage rescue in 1980 brought further congressional hostility and some initial opposition to his reappointment as chairman in 1980. After eight years as a JCS member, Jones recommended major changes in the joint system in 1982. He found JCS advice to the president untimely and diluted by interservice compromise, and he criticized the chairman's lack of authority. He proposed making the chairman the principal military adviser to the president instead of the corporate JCS, placing the chairman alone in the chain between the secretary of defense and the major commanders, and giving the chairman a four-star deputy. Neither the Reagan administration nor the other chiefs proved receptive, and no immediate action resulted. In 1986, however, the *Goldwater-Nichols Act included all of Jones's recommendations.

[*See also* Defense, Department of; SALT Treaties.]

• U.S. Air Force Biography, *General David C. Jones*, 1978. Willard J. Webb and Ronald H. Cole, *The Chairmen of the Joint Chiefs of Staff*, 1989.
—Willard J. Webb

JONES, JOHN PAUL (1747–1792), *Continental navy officer. Born in Scotland, John Paul Jones signed on as a British merchantman at the age of thirteen. After sailing on several vessels in the West Indian trade, he became a captain in 1768. Discipline problems plagued his command. In 1770, one of his men died after a flogging, and he later killed another sailor during a mutiny. Fearing that he would be charged with murder, Jones fled to Virginia in 1774.

The American *Revolutionary War offered him a second chance at command. Appointed first lieutenant in the Continental navy in 1775, Jones received the command of the eighteen-gun sloop *Ranger* in 1777. Based in France, Jones captured the twenty-gun HMS *Drake* and attacked the northern British port of Whitehaven during a cruise in 1778. The next year, he took command of the forty-gun converted merchantman *Bonhomme Richard*. In September, he led the American assault on a British merchant squadron escorted by HMS *Serapis*. Jones's crew suffered heavy losses, but when the commander of the *Serapis* asked if he would surrender, he replied, "I have not yet begun to fight." After a grenade caused a massive explosion aboard the *Serapis*, the British captain surrendered. The fight transformed Jones into America's first naval hero. It was to be his last action. Returning to the United States as commander of the captured British sloop *Ariel*, he was assigned to command the seventy-four-gun *America*, but it was not finished until the end of the war, and was then presented as a gift to France.

[*See also* Navy, U.S.: Overview.]

• Samuel Eliot Morison, *John Paul Jones: A Sailor's Biography*, 1959. James C. Bradford, "John Paul Jones: Honor and Professionalism," in *Command Under Sail: Makers of the American Naval Tradition, 1775–1850*, ed. James C. Bradford, 1985.
—Jon T. Coleman

JOSEPH, CHIEF (1840–1904), Nez Percé Indian chief, leader of a band living in the Wallowa Valley of eastern Oregon. Neither father nor son had subscribed to the treaties that established and then reduced the Nez Perce Reservation in Idaho. When the federal government ordered all Nez Percés to settle on the reservation, Joseph complied, but en route some young men committed depredations that set off the Nez Percé War of 1877. In subsequent battles with the U.S. Army, and in the famed trek of 800 Nez Percés in a desperate bid for a Canadian refuge, Chief Joseph was one of several chiefs. Others, war chiefs, played a larger military role. However, in the final battle at Bear Paw Mountain, with other leading chiefs dead or escaping to Canada, Chief Joseph surrendered with the famous speech ending, "From where the sun now stands, I will fight no more forever." Thus in white perceptions Chief Joseph became the "Red Napoleon" who had repeatedly outwitted American generals and conducted a humane war. Confined with his people in the Indian Territory (later Oklahoma), he endeared himself to Americans and in 1885 was allowed to move to a reservation in Washington, where he passed his remaining years.

[See also Native American Wars: Wars Between Native American and Europeans and Euro-Americans.]

• Alvin M. Josephy, Jr., The Nez Perce Indians and the Opening of the Northwest, 1965.   —Robert M. Utley

JUNGLE WARFARE. War in the jungle is the province of the infantry. In a tropical or semitropical environment of triple canopy forests, swamps, marshes, or densely forested mountains, tanks, aircraft, and even *artillery are of little use. The dense vegetation and general lack of infrastructure, along with reduced visibility and engagement ranges, make it extremely difficult to locate and engage enemy forces. These factors also tend to militate against the use of armored and mechanized forces and reduce the effectiveness of aircraft designed to provide intelligence and close air support to ground combat units. Further, the environment of extreme heat, virulent diseases, and frequently dangerous flora and fauna requires that units are carefully trained, equipped, and acclimated before deployment. Today, a typical operation employs *Special Operations Forces conducting long-range reconnaissance to locate concentrations of enemy forces and critical targets. Light infantry or air-mobile units then "fix" the enemy in position while air and artillery are used to complete the destruction of the hostile force.

The American military's expertise in jungle warfare has been hard won. First exposed to the phenomenon in the *Spanish-American War (1898) and the subsequent *Philippine War (1899–1902), the U.S. Army was slow to develop a doctrine for such operations. But the U.S. Marine Corps began compiling data from after-action reports of its operations in Central America and the Caribbean in the 1920s and incorporated lessons learned into its Small Wars Manual (1940). During World War II, both the army and the Marine Corps main forces fought a series of fierce battles in the jungles of Guadalcanal, New Guinea, and the Philippines. These main forces were augmented in the *China-Burma-India theater with smaller, fast-moving organizations. The army's "Merrill's Marauders" and the Marines' "Carlson's Raiders," along with OSS (Office of Strategic Services) Detachment 101, were specially trained in irregular warfare and employed in jungle operations deep in Japanese-held territory. Other specially trained and equipped forces such as the navy's Seabees (derived from the designation "CB" for Construction Battalion) were organized to prepare and improve beach landing sites and, later, cut airstrips out of the jungles. The medical services, faced with a bewildering array of exotic tropical maladies, were especially challenged by jungle operations.

During the 1960s and early 1970s, the United States had to relearn the lessons of jungle warfare in Vietnam. The army especially, trained and equipped for a conventional, mechanized war in Europe, was almost wholly unprepared for *guerrilla warfare in Vietnam's jungles. For a consider-

able portion of the war the American military employed large mechanized and air-mobile formations in "search and destroy" operations, hoping to force the enemy into a setpiece battle. To this end, much of the war was conducted in a fairly conventional manner but using newly developed technology and techniques such as ground surveillance *radar and remote sensors to locate enemy forces, and defoliants and napalm (jellied gasoline munitions) to expose and destroy those forces. North Vietnamese Army (NVA) regular forces occasionally committed to conventional battle, but in accepting battle on U.S. terms almost invariably fared badly. Thus the bulk of the conflict was characterized by ambuscades and hit-and-run assaults by small units of Viet Cong irregulars, and it was not until the period of "Vietnamization" and the withdrawal of U.S. main forces that the NVA regular forces began to reappear in strength. Throughout the conflict, U.S. Army Special Forces detachments worked at raising, equipping, training, and advising Vietnamese auxiliary troops composed of the Hmong and Montagnard tribes of the highlands. These native forces were later abandoned, but many carried on the war for years after the withdrawal of U.S. forces. The U.S. Marine Corps, having experienced some significant successes with their CORDS (Civil Operations and Revolutionary Development Support) program, which assigned small units to patrol and administer specific villages and environs, abandoned that program after the *Tet Offensive (1968) and embraced a policy almost indistinguishable from the army's.

Jungle warfare techniques, informed by the Vietnam experience, were being taught in the 1990s at the U.S. Army's John F. Kennedy Special Warfare Center and School (Fort Bragg, North Carolina) and Ranger School (Fort Benning, Georgia). It should be noted that the Vietnam War proved such a traumatic experience for the U.S. Army that until the 1980s virtually no aspect of that war was addressed in its formal schooling programs (i.e., at the Basic and Advanced Officer Training Courses and at the Command and General Staff and War Colleges).

[See also Caribbean and Latin America, U.S. Military Involvement in the; Disease, Tropical; Low-Intensity Conflict; Vietnam War: Military and Diplomatic Course; World War II, U.S. Air Operations in: The Air War Against Japan; World War II, U.S. Naval Operations in: The Pacific.]

• U.S. Marine Corps, Small Wars Manual, 1940. Bryan Perret, Canopy of War, 1990.   —Frederick J. Chiaventone

JUSTICE, MILITARY. This entry consists of a seven-part examination of the system of military law and justice, the system established by Congress for the government of persons in the armed forces. The organization is topical and then chronological within each article. The entries are:

Articles of War (1775–1950)
Uniform Code of Military Justice (1950–Present)
Military Crimes
Military Police
Military Courts
Military Punishment
Military Prisons

For related entries involving military or war crimes, see Atrocities; Desertion; Genocide; Laws of War; Martial Law;

Mutiny; Rights in the Military, Citizens'; Rape by Military Personnel; Treason; War Crimes.

JUSTICE, MILITARY: ARTICLES OF WAR (1775–1950)

Articles of War was the term used to describe the statutes governing military discipline and justice in the American armed services from 1775 to 1950, when they were replaced by the Uniform Code of Military Justice.

With the outbreak of the *Revolutionary War, the Continental Congress in 1775 adopted two codes of military law: the "Rules for the Regulation of the Navy of the United Colonies" and the "American Articles of War" (the latter revised in 1776). Both were written by John *Adams—then an attorney, representative from Massachusetts, and chair of the Naval Committee—and both were drawn largely from the codes governing the Royal Navy and the British army.

After the adoption of the Constitution and the establishment of the federal government, the first Congress merely stated that the provisions from the earlier period would continue to apply. The U.S. Navy was expanded in the late 1790s, and in 1799, Congress adopted an Act for Government of the Navy, revising the Continental Rules. These also applied to the Marine Corps, as part of the navy. A year later, Congress passed the Articles for the Government of the Navy (1800). Within the navy, this governing statute was nicknamed "Rocks and Shoals" because that phrase was included in the provision authorizing punishment for those responsible for damage to ships due to improper navigation. The statute was amended periodically to reflect changes in the service. In one important reform of discipline, flogging (the whipping of sailors with a lash) was abolished as a punishment in 1850. An amendment in 1855 authorized summary courts-martial, with a single officer sitting as the military tribunal. During the dramatic, if temporary, expansion of the navy in the *Civil War, the Articles for the Government of the Navy were recompiled, and this compilation, as amended, remained in effect through World War II. The navy's ambitious plans to rewrite the articles after 1945 were overtaken by the drive for "unification" of the armed services and by the passage of the Uniform Code of Military Justice, which was modeled largely after the army's Articles of War.

The Articles of War governing discipline and justice in the army, first formulated in 1775 and revised in 1776, underwent minor revisions in 1806 by John Quincy Adams, son of the original drafter. The basic Articles of War remained in effect for 111 years, from 1776 to 1917. During that period, there were a number of important changes: one in 1830 regarding the appointment of courts-martial; and several during the Civil War, primarily intended to extend courts' jurisdiction over crimes and persons. Some articles of the code were deleted, such as those relating to irreverent or indecent behavior at worship services, or the use of oaths or other offensive utterances.

The Articles of War were substantially revised to deal with the mass army of *citizen-soldiers in World War I. At the instigation of Enoch Crowder, judge advocate general of the U.S. Army, Congress passed a complete revision in March 1917. There were major problems with this revision, however. For example, in November 1917, under its wartime provisions, thirteen black enlisted men were too hastily executed after a court-martial following a race riot

in Houston. Secretary of War Newton D. *Baker prohibited any further executions without express approval from Washington. During World War I, a number of other citizen-soldiers were sentenced to long prison terms or even to death for breaches of military discipline, although these sentences were subsequently modified. Widespread complaints in the press and Congress against such mistreatment led to Senate hearings in 1919, which contributed to a revision of the Articles of War in 1920, although the liberal reforms proposed by Samuel T. Ansell, acting judge advocate general while Crowder had been provost marshal general in charge of the draft, were rejected after a heated public debate.

Similar complaints of the harshness of military discipline during and after World War II led Congress to adopt the Elston Act of 1948, modifying the code of conduct for the army and the newly independent air force. In 1950, as part of the movement toward unification as well as modernization of the postwar armed forces, Congress made the name Articles of War obsolete when it adopted the Uniform Code of Military Justice.

During the period 1775–1950 in which the army and navy Articles of War were in effect, they were supplemented by a number of various publications. General Orders issued by the commanding general of the army or his subordinates, particularly during the Civil War, set maximum punishments, established court-martial procedures, and formally supplemented the Articles of War. The *general regulations* for the navy and Marine Corps, first published in 1841, contained provisions relating to courts-martial. The army published its first *Manual for Courts-Martial* in 1917, an amended version in 1921, and another in 1928; the last remained in effect through World War II. The navy's counterpart to the army's *Manual* was *Naval Courts and Boards,* the 1937 edition of which was used throughout World War II. These manuals provided details for the implementation in all services of the military laws designed to maintain discipline and secure justice in the armed forces.

• William Winthrop, *Military Law and Precedents,* 1886; 2nd ed., 1920. Robert Pasley and Felix E. Larkin, "The Navy Court-Martial: Proposals for Its Reform," *Cornell Law Quarterly,* 33 (1947), pp. 195–234. Frederick B. Weiner, "Courts-Martial and the Bill of Rights: The Original Practice," *Harvard Law Review,* 72 (1958–59), pp. 1–304. Frederick B. Weiner, "American Military Law in the Light of the First Mutiny Act's Tricentennial," *Military Law Review,* 126 (1989), pp. 1–88. John M. Lindley, *A Soldier Is Also a Citizen: The Controversy over Military Justice in the U.S. Army, 1917–1920,* 1990. Jonathan Lurie, *Arming Military Justice: The Origins of the United States Court of Appeals, 1775–1950,* 1992. Jonathan Lurie, *Pursuing Military Justice: The History of the United States Court of Appeals for the Armed Forces, 1951–1980,* 1998.   —Michael Noone

JUSTICE, MILITARY: UNIFORM CODE OF MILITARY JUSTICE (1950–PRESENT)

The Uniform Code of Military Justice (UCMJ) is a comprehensive federal statute that established essential procedures, policies, and penalties for the military justice system. Enacted by Congress in 1950, the UCMJ continues in effect to the present with few alterations since its passage.

The UCMJ actually resulted from the confluence of factors. First was underlying dissatisfaction with some existing practices of military justice, especially as rel courts-martial appeals. Second was the unification of the armed forces into one Department of *Defense "establishment" in 1947–48. This step rendered retention of traditional systems such as the army's Articles of War and the navy's Articles for the Government of the Navy impractical and unnecessary.

The UCMJ was essentially the work of civilian committee selected by Secretary of Defense James V. *Forrestal. It included the three undersecretaries of the army, navy, and air force, with a well-known professor of evidence from Harvard Law School, Edmund Morgan, as its chair. This committee was assisted by a "working group" that consisted of several military lawyers, as well as some civilian attorneys from the newly established Defense Department. Although the military was well represented on the working group, which undertook the initial drafting of most articles in the new code, in general the UCMJ was a civilian effort. Indeed, Forrestal made it clear that where the Morgan Committee could not agree, he would ultimately decide, and that once the proposed code was submitted to Congress, the military's role was over. Unlike earlier attempts to reform military justice, in the case of the UCMJ, although the military might discuss and even debate, it was unable to derail.

Nevertheless, Morgan's committee recognized that the two basic sources of military discipline that had effectively guided the armed services since the Revolutionary era had to be considered and to a great extent integrated into the new legislation. Indeed, its great challenge was to synthesize key provisions from both army and navy regulations into a uniform, workable system, as well as to introduce new innovations now deemed necessary. Thus, it retained—and still retains—some traditional prohibitions that had existed for almost two centuries such as the bans against "conduct unbecoming an officer and a gentlemen," "dueling," and "improper use of a countersign."

Based upon plenary congressional authority to enact rules and regulations for the military, the UCMJ ranks just below the Constitution as the basis for federal military regulation. Indeed, on several occasions its provisions have been held to supersede those found in the *Manual for Courts-Martial*, the detailed book of regulations supposedly issued by the president in his capacity as commander in chief, but in fact drafted largely by the military. The court that made these rulings may be the best example of innovative change produced by the UCMJ.

Creation of an appeals court within the military had been proposed during World War I by acting Judge Advocate General (JAG) officer Samuel Ansell, but strong opposition from the army doomed both Ansell's efforts and his continued military career. He was still alive, however, in 1951 when the UCMJ, replete with not one but two levels of appellate review, became law. As submitted to Congress, the UCMJ included two separate appellate systems: an intermediate court, administered within the military; and an appellate tribunal, to consist of three judges drawn from "civilian life." Morgan had intended the new court to have the same perquisites and benefits as other federal Courts of Appeals, including life tenure; and indeed, as passed by the House in 1949, the UCMJ so provided. But the final Congressional product rejected life tenure, and substituted fixed terms of fifteen, ten, and five years. To this day, emphasizing that its highest court for military appeals no different from other federal appellate tribunals

in terms of salary, Congress has consistently declined to give its judges life tenure.

Although justifiably described a civilian effort, the UCMJ was heavily influenced by the military viewpoint. Thus, commanders retained (and still do) authority to select members of a court-martial. The intermediate appellate courts, controlled by the military, received greater authority than Morgan had originally intended. Moreover, the code failed to set out a clear demarcation between the JAGs and the new court concerning supervision over military justice. In spite of these possible weaknesses, the basic premises of the UCMJ—that a single military justice system can be applicable to all branches of the American military, and that its "uniformity" would not undercut its effectiveness in time of armed conflict—have been vindicated since 1951.

• Homer F. Moyer, Jr., *Justice and the Military*, 1972. Jonathan Lurie, *Arming Military Justice*. Vol. 1 of *Origins of the United States Court of Appeals for the Armed Forces 1775–1950*, 1992. Jonathan Lurie, *Pursuing Military Justice*. Vol. 2 of *History of the United States Court of Appeals for the Armed Forces, 1951–1980*, 1998.

—Jonathan Lurie

JUSTICE, MILITARY: MILITARY CRIMES

The Articles of War adopted by the Continental Congress in 1775 and based largely on those of the British army specified military offenses ranging from mutiny to misbehavior before the enemy. However, there was no American counterpart to a British provision which, if the offenses occurred where there were no civil courts, granted jurisdiction over soldiers who committed common law crimes (murder, theft, robbery, and rape) to courts-martial. Congress assumed that these crimes, if committed by soldiers, would be punished by U.S. civilian courts. The navy and Marine Corps were, of course, permitted to try their overseas and afloat offenders according to naval custom. A congressional act of 1863 first gave the army concurrent jurisdiction over common law crimes, if they occurred where the civil courts were functioning; otherwise, the military had exclusive jurisdiction. Thus, any history of military crimes must distinguish between the land and sea services and between military offenses and civil offenses, while recognizing that some military offenses, such as theft of government property, will have a civil analog.

The military crimes specified in the present Uniform Code of Military Justice can be found in the 1775 articles: absence offenses, disrespect and disobedience, offenses involving military property, misbehavior (*mutiny, malingering, provoking speech or gestures). The articles followed British practice and provided for the discharge of any officer convicted of "behaving in a scandalous, infamous manner, such as is unbecoming the character of an officer and a gentleman."

In 1776, when the articles were revised, Congress added a provision that had, in various forms, been in the British code since 1686 and that prohibited "[a] ll Crimes not Capital and all Disorders and Neglects, which Officers and soldiers may be guilty of to the Prejudice of good Order and Military Discipline, though not mentioned in the above Articles of War." The "conduct unbecoming" provision was amended in 1806 by deletion of the phrasing "scandalous and infamous," although the words were retained in the Naval Code. Nineteenth- and early-twentieth-century military law treaties listed the kinds of behavior that usually involved lying or dishonorable failure to meet financial obligations but also applied to public drunkenness, bigamy, wife abuse, association with prostitutes, and mistreatment of, or undue fraternization with, enlisted men. The 1951 *Manual for Courts-Martial* discussion of Article 133, where the provision is now found, acknowledged the presence of women in forces by providing that they should be held to the standards of a "gentlewoman." In recent years, however, officer misconduct is usually charged under Article 134, as conduct prejudicial to good order and discipline.

Article 134 serves as the legal basis for charging three classes of offenses, two found in the 1776 articles: crimes and offenses not capital, and conduct prejudicial to good order and discipline; while the third, conduct of a nature to bring discredit upon the military service, was added after World War I. The "crimes and offenses" provisions incorporate all federal crimes that are not punishable by another article. Thus, a military counterfeiter of U.S. currency would be charged under this provision. If there were a violation of a state law that had no federal counterpart, the offender could only be charged under Article 134 if the conduct was service-discrediting. Officers who failed to pay their debts were often charged under this provision which, unlike the "conduct unbecoming" article, did not require dismissal on conviction. Gen. Billy *Mitchell was court-martialed in 1925 for service-discrediting behavior after issuing a press release accusing the War and Naval Departments of "incompetency, criminal negligence, and almost treasonable administration of the National Defense."

Of the three provisions, that relating to conduct prejudicial to good order and discipline is the most comprehensive and potentially the most subject to abuse; hence its traditional British nickname, "the Devil's Article." The 1928 *Manual for Courts-Martial* listed typical offenses ranging from abuse of a public animal to self-maiming. The list was not intended to be exclusive: adultery was added in the 1951 *Manual*, but there had been prosecutions for adultery during and immediately after World War II. Fraternization—undue familiarity between individuals of different rank—is considered to be prejudicial to good order and discipline. However, a 1985 decision by the Court of Military Appeals, *Johanns v. United States,* concluded that a male officer's sexual relationship with three enlisted women in his unit was not prejudicial in the absence of an explicit prohibition in service regulations. Subsequently the services issued regulations intended to define fraternization.

Crimes that have no counterpart in civilian life—mutiny, *desertion, misbehavior before the enemy—have been the subject of numerous monographs, as have *war crimes. The term *war crime* has no legal meaning, but it is used to describe deviations from accepted standards of what used to be called the law of war and now is called international humanitarian law. General Order 100 (1863), "Instructions for the Government of Armies of the United States in the Field," prepared by Professor Francis Lieber of Columbia College, was the first codification of these standards. War crimes encompass both offenses against a belligerent's armed forces and against the civilian population in the war zone.

Crimes committed overseas by visiting forces create particular problems because international law gives the local country the right to prosecute. When U.S. troops were first deployed overseas to France and England during World War I, Washington agreed to a distribution of jurisdiction based on the nature of the offense. Similar agreements were entered into during World War II and became formalized as Status of Forces Treaties when *Cold War requirements mandated a continued U.S. troop presence in Europe and the Far East. The treaties established three categories. Behavior that was a crime in the sending state but not in the receiving state would be tried by the sender. Behavior that was a crime in the receiving state but not in the sending state would be tried by the receiver. When behavior violated both countries' laws, the receiving state had primary claim but was expected to give "sympathetic consideration" to the sender's request to try the offender. Host country waivers of jurisdiction, permitting the United States to try military rapists and murderers of local citizens, were, and continue to be, a persistent source of controversy.

• George Davis, *A Treatise on the Military Law of the United States,* 1915. Richard C. Knopf, "Crime and Punishment in the Legion, 1792–1793," *Bulletin of the Historical and Philosophical Society of Ohio* (July 1956), pp. 232–38. Clifton D. Bryant, *Khaki-Collar Crime,* 1979. Lawrence J. Morris, "Our Mission, No Future: The Case for Closing the United States Army Disciplinary Barracks," *Kansas Journal of Law and Public Policy,* 6 (Fall 1996), pp. 77–98. Gary Solis, *Son Thang, an American War Crime,* 1997.

—Michael Noone

JUSTICE, MILITARY: MILITARY POLICE

Military forces have always assigned some personnel to ensure that order was maintained, stragglers or deserters were brought under control, and prisoners of war taken into custody. In the *Revolutionary War, the *Continental army in 1778 adopted British practice by creating a provost unit, but calling it by the French name, the *Marechaussée* Corps. From 1783 to 1861, however, the U.S. Army simply detailed regular troops to perform military police functions when necessary.

The *Civil War led to the creation of a massive if temporary system of provost marshals. The huge armies of citizen-soldiers proved unruly in camp and field. Consequently, in 1861, the *Union army established regimental provost marshals assisted by designated enlisted personnel to serve as a permanent police force, with the duties of preventing riotous conduct, controlling stragglers, and preventing looting and personal violence against civilians as the army advanced into the South. In March 1863, the army created a Provost Marshal Department, which, with congressional authorization, extended the role of the provost marshals from controlling undisciplined Union troops and guarding Confederate prisoners of war to including operation of the system of *conscription even at the local level, as well as control of local government in occupied Southern states.

In World War I, a temporary Military Police Corps was created, with assigned soldiers wearing "MP" armbands. It garnered soldiers absent without leave (AWOL), guarded prisoners of war in France, and investigated *desertion, draft evasion, and related military offenses, as well as policing military prisons and prisoner-of-war camps in the United States. In 1920, Congress refused a permanent MP corps, but authorized reserve MP units.

Similarly, for most of its history, the navy relied primarily upon temporary assignment of regular personnel to maintain order and discipline. The navy assigns sailors to duty as a shore patrol (with "SP" armbands) to prevent disorder between crew members on liberty and local civilians. Longer-term security is provided by naval masters-at-arms or by Marines, who are assigned to guard naval "brigs" aboard ship or ashore.

With the United States *mobilization for World War II, Secretary of War Henry L. *Stimson, on 26 September 1941 authorized a Military Police Corps, and it has remained a permanent part of the U.S. Army ever since. Nearly 210,000 officers and enlisted personnel served in the army's MP Corps in 1941–45, and an MP school was established, first in Arlington, Virginia, and after the war in Fort McClellan, Alabama. During World War II and the wars in Korea, Vietnam, and the Persian Gulf, MPs secured movement in and out of theaters of operation, processed and guarded thousands of prisoners of war, and in war and peace provided protection for military facilities.

During the guerrilla-style *Vietnam War, MP units sometimes engaged directly with the enemy, securing lines of communication by preventing Viet Cong roadblocks, ambushes, and attacks on U.S. facilities. Such active participation in tactical operations led to the redesignation of the Military Police Corps as an arm and a service with a primary mission of combat support. In Kuwait during the *Persian Gulf War, the MPs processed and secured nearly 70,000 Iraqi prisoners of war.

[See also Prisoners of War: Enemy POWs.]

• Brent L. Richens and Russell B. Shor, "18th Military Police Brigade, Three Years in Vietnam," Military Police Journal, 19 (September 1969); p. 5. Mary R. Hines, "Military Police Duties in the Federal Army," Military Police Journal, 11 (Summer 1984), p. 20. Thomas J. Johnson and Mary R. Himes, "The Battle of the American Embassy," Military Police Journal, 11 (Summer 1984), p. 6. U.S. Army Military Police School, Military Police Corps Regimental History, 1986.
—John Whiteclay Chambers II

JUSTICE, MILITARY: MILITARY COURTS

Military courts can be classified by the persons over whom they exercise their jurisdiction. Courts-martial and military courts of inquiry are concerned with members of the armed forces. Military commissions and provost courts (operated by officers of the provost marshal general) exercise their power over civilians who, although not affiliated with the military, may face a military court in time of war or rebellion. In the early days of the republic, the distinction was not as clearly drawn. Winthrop's Military Law and Precedents remarks on the courts-martial of civilians for collaboration with the traitor Benedict *Arnold in 1780, for spying on New Orleans in 1815, and for inciting and supplying the Creek Indians in Florida in 1818.

The same confusion attended courts of inquiry, authorized by the Articles of War, and considered to be quasi-judicial boards of investigation; yet it was such a court, convened by Gen. George *Washington, which recommended that Maj. John André of the British army be treated as a spy and executed. Courts of inquiry were common in the 19th century, when one was used to inquire into the conduct of Major Reno at the 1876 Battle of the *Little Bighorn. However, they came to be replaced by less formal administrative boards. Still authorized by the Uniform Code of Military Justice, they have in recent years only been utilized by the U.S. Navy, for example, to deal with the losses of vessels such as the USS Scorpion, and in the Pueblo incident (1968).

Similarly, military commissions (established to try civilians for criminal offenses) and provost courts (intended to resolve civil disputes) are still authorized by the Uniform Code. When established in occupied territory and utilized to try cases involving local residents, these courts derive their authority from international law. Their authority over U.S. citizens was challenged in Ex parte *Milligan (1866) and Duncan v. Kahanamoku (1946), in which majorities of the Supreme Court held that jurisdiction could not be exercised in areas where U.S. civil courts were open and functioning. However, in Ex parte Quirin (1942), a case involving Nazi saboteurs, a majority of the Court approved of a commission that tried alien enemies found in the United States. The Court similarly approved their use to try *war crimes overseas, for example, in In re Yamashita (1946), which led to the execution of the Japanese general in charge of Manila in 1945.

Courts-martial are the best known military courts. The 1775 Articles of War, following British practice, established three categories of such courts for the army: general, for the most serious offenses and for cases involving officers; regimental; and detachment or garrison courts. The so-called inferior courts were limited in their jurisdiction to noncapital offenses, to offenders who were enlisted men (and, in the case of regimental courts, to enlisted personnel who were members of that unit), and by the kinds of punishment they could impose. The Naval Rules made no such distinction and relied on naval custom. Military law treatises uniformly state that courts-martial were always composed of officers; had to consist of at least three members; and that there was no American equivalent of the English "Drum Head" court-martial, where punishment was summarily imposed. However, Stephen Ambrose's account, in Undaunted Courage (1996), of the *Lewis and Clark Expedition (1804–06) reports instances where enlisted men were appointed as the court-martial to decide what punishment should be imposed on a fellow soldier, and one case in which the joint commanders appointed themselves as the court. The punishments imposed (typically flogging) were within statutory limits. The history of such informal courts remains to be written, as does the use of these courts to try prisoners of war (POWs). During World War II, seven German POWS in the United States were convicted of murder of fellow prisoners and were executed at the U.S. Disciplinary Barracks at Fort Leavenworth.

Nonjudicial punishment, permitted by naval custom (called in the navy, "Captain's Mast," and in the Marine Corps, "Office Hours"), was prohibited in the army, whose statutes and regulations required a court-martial composed of at least three officers. During the *Civil War, single officer field officer's courts were permitted but ceased at the war's end. In 1890, the first single army summary courts were established by regulation; it was not until World War I and congressional passage of Article 104 that army commanders were permitted to impose minor punishments without trial. Even as army commanders' authority was thus enhanced, it was also curtailed by legislation which required that courts-martial convictions be scrutinized by Boards of Review. With the passage of the Uniform Code of Military Justice (1950) that practice was extended to the air force, Coast Guard, the navy, and the Marine Corps. Board decisions could be reviewed by the Court of Military Appeals, subsequently renamed the U.S. Court of Appeals for the Armed Forces, as the boards became known as Military Courts of Appeal. Thus, for the past half century, the organization of courts-martial has remained unchanged.

• William C. Dehart, *Observations on Military Law, and the Practice of Courts-Martial, with a Summary of the Laws of Evidence, as Applicable to Military Trials; Adapted to the Laws, Regulations and Customs of the Army and Navy of the United States*, 1846, reprinted in Vol. XVIII, *Classics in Legal History*, ed. Roy M. Mersky and J. Myron Jacobstein, 1973. Edward M. Byrne, *Military Law: A Handbook for the Navy and Marine Corps*, 1970. Richard Whittingham, *Martial Justice: The Last Mass Execution in the United States*, 1988; repr. 1997. David J. Danecski, "The Saboteurs Case," *Journal of Supreme Court History* (1996), pp. 61–82. *The Army Lawyer: A History of the Judge Advocate General's Corps*, 1993.   —Michael Noone

JUSTICE, MILITARY: MILITARY PUNISHMENT

Few punishments were specified in the American Articles of War of 1775. The death penalty was limited to specified offenses—"nor shall any punishment be inflicted at the discretion of a court-martial, other than degrading, cashiering, drumming out of the army, whipping not exceeding thirty-nine lashes, fine not exceeding two months pay of the offender, imprisonment not exceeding one month." The articles' naval counterpart similarly relied on custom rather than specifying punishments. The most noticeable characteristic of the "old" (pre–Civil War) army and navy is the fact that deterrence seems to have been punishment's only goal. This policy is exemplified by the navy's practice of summarily executing seamen who left their posts in battle. Because a jailed soldier or sailor was considered to be evading the hardships of military life, commanders relied on flogging as the punishment. The maximum number of lashes allowed to army courts-martial was increased to 100 in the 1776 articles and then curtailed to 50 in 1806. In 1812, Congress eliminated flogging as a permitted punishment in the army, reinstated it for *desertion in 1833, and finally abolished it in 1861.

Flogging and "colting" (striking with a rope end) were the main punishments used in the navy. Naval regulations permitted up to 12 lashes as nonjudicial punishment; naval courts-martial awarded 100 lashes for drunkenness and mutinous behavior. Branding with a hot iron or tattooing was permitted until Congress forbade the practice in 1872. Army records confirm the wearing of irons, placarding, gagging, standing on or wearing a barrel, and tarring and feathering. The navy imposed similar punishments after flogging was abolished by Congress in 1850 following a campaign waged by the author Herman Melville, who had served on the "hell ship" *United States*. Sweatboxes, dousing with bilge water, tricing to the rigging, or hanging from a boom were other naval punishments. Not all punishments were, to modern eyes, barbaric: dismissal or dishonorable discharge; demotion, fines, or forfeitures (the last from pay prospectively due); confinement; and, for officers, suspension from command or active command or active service were also permitted.

The military courts' discretion, in noncapital cases, to impose punishment was gradually curtailed. In 1855, when Congress established naval summary courts-martial, limits on minor punishments—confinement and reduced rations—were included in the statute. In 1862, President Abraham *Lincoln issued a list of maximum punishments that could be imposed for various offenses, and in 1890, Congress ordered that, where an article provided

that punishment would be left to the discretion of the court, the punishment could not exceed that directed by the president.

The army and navy codes limited the death penalty to specified offenses, or those made capital by local state law, and required a higher percentage of the court members to agree on the sentence than was required for lesser punishments. Statutes required presidential approval of the penalty if it had been imposed by a court-martial within the United States; when, in 1849, Commodore Thomas Jones of the Pacific Squadron permitted the hanging of two mutineers in California, he was court-martialed and received five years' suspension from duty. Nineteenth-century army tradition dictated that capital military offenses, with the exception of desertion, be punished by shooting, while hanging was dictated for civilian capital crimes, or for desertion or spying. Naval tradition called for hanging from the fore yardarm of the vessel. The 1917 Texas *Mutiny Cases, in which black American soldiers were hastily hanged after their court-martial, led to a revision of the 1916 Articles of War, as the World War II execution of Private Eddy Slovik after the Battle of the *Bulge led to postwar reform efforts, although the death penalty is still permitted by the Uniform Code of Military Justice.

After 1916, the army articles, unlike those of the navy, required a Board of Review if the sentence included the death penalty or dismissal of an officer (which required presidential approval in the navy) or dishonorable discharge (there was no similar provision in the navy). However, in the post–World War II period, when manpower requirements exceeded enlistments, prisoner rehabilitation units were established in each of the armed services. With the advent of the *All-Volunteer Force in 1973 and its higher standards of pay and performance, such units were disbanded.

• John S. Hare, "Military Punishments in the War of 1812," *Journal of American Military History*, 4 (Winter 1940), pp. 225–29. Leo F.S. Horan, "Flogging in the United States Navy, Unfamiliar Facts Regarding Its Origins and Abolition," *United States Naval Institute Proceedings*, 76 (1950), pp. 969–75. Frederick B. Wiener, "Crime and Justice in the Days of Empire," *History, Numbers, and War*, 2 (1980), pp. 23–28. Robert I. Alotta, *Civil War Justice, Union Army Executions Under Lincoln*, 1989. Mark A. Vargas, "The Military Justice System and the Use of Illegal Punishments as Causes of Desertion in the U.S. Army, 1821–1835," *Journal of Military History*, vol. 55, no. 1 (1991), pp. 1–19.   —Michael Noone

JUSTICE, MILITARY: MILITARY PRISONS

For short-term confinement for purposes of discipline or criminal proceedings involving their own military personnel (*prisoners of war fall into a separate category), the armed forces have used various temporary and long-term facilities. Temporary arrangements range from the U.S. Navy's brigs (restraining cells aboard ship or guardhouses ashore) to the U.S. Army's stockades at particular posts or camps or holding cells in nineteenth-century fortresses. Some of the short-term facilities were subsequently expanded for long-term use. The navy established prison at Portsmouth, New Hampshire, and later on Treasure Island near San Francisco. The army long maintained a prison at Fortress Monroe, Virginia. Most famously, the army created a prison on Alcatraz Island in San Francisco, where a wooden stockade added to the fort then being built was replaced by a modern concrete cell block

1934, the military prison on Alcatraz became a federal civil penitentiary (nicknamed "the Rock"), which it remained until closed in 1963.

The first federal military prison was the U.S. Military Prison, established at Fort Leavenworth, Kansas, in 1875, in response to complaints of varied and often harsh treatment of military prisoners at post stockades and state penitentiaries. In 1873, Congress had approved a military prison, but directed that it be constructed near the federal arsenal at Rock Island, Illinois, to employ prison labor. After the Ordnance Department and the secretary of war protested that prisoners could not be trusted to work with munitions, Congress passed an 1874 amendment to locate the prison at Fort Leavenworth, a military post dating from 1827.

The Leavenworth facility, about twenty miles from Kansas City, later also served as a federal prison for civil offenders. In 1895, it was transferred to the U.S. Department of Justice, but returned in 1906 to the army and renamed in 1915, the U.S. Disciplinary Barracks. During World War I, a number of conscientious objectors were confined there along with uniformed personnel. In 1929, the facility was again transferred to the Department of Justice and designated the Leavenworth Penitentiary Branch.

In November 1940, it was returned to the army and redesignated the U.S. Disciplinary Barracks. Since then, it has been operated by the army. Today, it is the only long-term maximum security facility operated by the Department of *Defense, and includes inmates from each of the armed services.

Although the maximum housing capacity is 1,500, the average population in the 1990s was 1,350 inmates. These men and women, officers and enlisted personnel, were serving terms from a few years to life imprisonment; half a dozen were serving death sentences. The average sentence length is fourteen years; most inmates were first-time offenders.

In the 1990s, approximately three-quarters of the inmates at the U.S. Disciplinary Barracks were confined for crimes against persons—from assault to murder. Nearly half were convicted of sexually related offenses. Slightly more than 10 percent also involved drug-related offenses. Another 10 percent had committed property crimes. In the 1990s, only 1 percent of inmates were confined for strictly military-related offenses. Nearly 96 percent were sentenced to punitive discharge. In addition to the military prison, a civil prison, the U.S. Penitentiary, Leavenworth, is also located on the grounds of Fort Leavenworth.

[See also Conscientious Objection; Justice, Military: Military Crimes; Justice, Military: Military Police.]

• United States Disciplinary Barracks: Fort Leavenworth, Kansas, n.d.
—John Whiteclay Chambers II

JUST WAR THEORY. The term *just war* in its fullest sense refers to the broad tradition of interrelated theory and practice that defines for Western culture when the use of armed force for political purposes is justified and what limits or restraints ought to be observed in the employment of such force. Reflecting both the practical experience of war and normative thought on the place of force in society, just war tradition first coalesced during the Middle Ages as a cultural consensus drawing on canon law, the Augustinian theology and political theory, inherited Roman concepts of *jus gentium* and *jus naturale*, existing customs and practices of statecraft, and the code of chivalry. The roots of this tradition reach back through theology and law to classical Rome and Greece and to biblical Israel, and through chivalry to earlier Germanic conceptions of war and the soldier. The classical and biblical heritage was principally mediated to the Middle Ages by Augustine, who took the phrase "just war" itself (*bellum justum*) and a number of associated concepts from late Roman theory and practice, wedding them to a Christian ethic of intention based on love of neighbor and a concept of divinely instituted justice drawn from the Old Testament. Other elements of the medieval just war consensus traveled other routes. The result exceeded the sum of its parts both in content and in the breadth of its implications: a collection of restraints on war shaped by legal, moral, and practical concerns, and molded by the experience of war and statecraft.

This conception of just war sought to deal with two main concerns: the justification and limitation of the resort to armed force (in traditional terms, the *jus ad bellum*) and restraints on the actual employment of force (in traditional terms, the *jus in bello*). In its fullest and classic form, reached by the end of the medieval period, the *jus ad bellum* was defined by seven distinct requirements: just cause (defense, retaking something wrongly taken, punishment of evil); right authority (temporal rulers with no superior); right intention (no hatred of the enemy, desire for vainglory or power, bullying, etc.); the goal of peace; a reasonable hope of success; and the two conditions that the use of force in question achieve more good than harm and that the use of force be a last resort. The *jus in bello* took shape around two further requirements: that the force employed not cause more destruction than necessary, and the concept of immunity from harm for noncombatants, persons not directly involved in the waging of war.

In such form, just war tradition carried into the early modern period. Theorists like Vitoria, Suarez, Gentili, and Grotius assumed this concept of just war. Shakespeare displayed a remarkably complete knowledge of the conditions for just war in *Henry V*. Apologists on both sides of the post-Reformation wars of religion employed just war criteria to argue the rightness of their respective causes. The early codes of military discipline which appeared in this period similarly reflected the influence of the inherited just war synthesis.

Yet while the tendencies of the Middle Ages were centripetal, those of the modern era have been centrifugal. Just war tradition in the modern period has been carried and developed not as a single entity but in the form of various distinct streams of thought and practice, sometimes in relation to one another, but more often moving according to their own logic.

One of the major streams of development of just war tradition through most of the modern period has been international law, from naturalists like Vitoria and Grotius through the juristic theorists to present customary and positive law. Contemporary positive international law on war includes a detailed *jus in bello* defined by the *Geneva Conventions, the Hague Rules, various international efforts to limit or forbid use of certain weapons, and the findings of the Nuremberg and Tokyo war crimes trials, as well as a somewhat truncated *jus ad bellum* focused on the right of defense as defined in the *United Nations Charter.

The development of military codes of conduct, theories and practice of limited war, and the persistence of the idea of chivalry in some form together make up a second major stream of just war tradition in the modern era. A landmark among the military regulations is the U.S. Army's *General Orders No. 100 of 1863*, a comprehensive code for conduct during war that strongly influenced both subsequent military codes and later positive international law on war. The limited war idea, operationalized in the "sovereigns' wars" of the eighteenth century, has emerged into new prominence in post–World War II military thought.

Within the sphere of religion, just war tradition remained acknowledged but without much attention or development through most of the modern period. In the last half of the twentieth century, however, led by American thought, a highly creative recovery of religiously based just war reasoning has taken place, responding to the strategic bombing of cities by both Axis and Allied powers during World War II, the development of *nuclear weapons and strategic targeting doctrine, and the *Vietnam War. This development within religious thought has in turn stimulated both the emergence of philosophical just war analysis and efforts to recover and understand historical just war tradition.

The recovery of just war thought in the religious sphere was largely initiated by the Protestant theologian Paul Ramsey, who in influential books and articles written mostly during the 1960s argued after the manner of Augustine for a conception of just war based in Christian love. Ramsey's historical context was the developing debates over strategic nuclear targeting and the initial stages of American involvement in Vietnam. Taking on various sorts of pacifists and others who argued that no contemporary war can be just because of the destructiveness of nuclear and other weapons, Ramsey insisted that there remains a place for responsible use of force by nations. Such a use, as he described it, would both serve justice and reflect the concerns of political prudence, traditional just war aims. The major focus of his work, though, was the just conduct of war. Hence he stressed the importance of discrimination (noncombatant immunity), which he understood as a direct requirement of Christian love, and the requirement of proportionality of means, an expression of political prudence.

Ramsey's importance for contemporary just war thought follows both from what he argued and from the partners he engaged in dialogue on just war terms: Protestant and secular pacifists; Catholic thinkers through detailed comments on papal and Vatican II statements on nuclear war; the secular policy community through debate with figures like Herman Kahn, Thomas Schelling, Robert W. Tucker, and many others; philosophers and theologians in America and other countries like Elizabeth Anscombe and Walter Stein in England. Though not himself a historian, he also encouraged historical efforts like those of James Turner Johnson to recover just war tradition as it existed and was applied to war in the past.

Use of just war categories and the effort to engage the policy community also characterize prominent recent church statements on ethics and war, such as the pastoral letters of the American Catholic bishops (1983) and the United Methodist bishops (1986). Both these documents, however, also nod significantly toward *pacifism. The Catholic pastoral, for example, grounds just war thought in a presumption against war, while the Methodist document explicitly rejects war as incompatible with Christ's teachings and example. Both these concepts are at odds with the traditional Christian derivation of just war from the moral obligation to seek justice and protect the innocent.

In the philosophical sphere, the most important and most comprehensive recent treatment of just war ideas is Michael Walzer's *Just and Unjust Wars*. Aiming explicitly at recapturing just war reasoning for political and moral theory, this book develops the major traditional just war criteria through a mix of thematic analysis, utilitarian reasoning, and historical examples out of which the various just war principles arise as responses to evil in one or another concrete form. Like other modern just war thought, Walzer's analysis dwells heavily on the problem of ethical conduct during war; like positive international law, he treats the question of justification for use of force in the truncated terms of aggression and defense. Some of his most creative thought presses hard cases: whether the strategic bombing of German cities during World War II was justified by "supreme emergency," for example. But on most matters Walzer concludes in or near the mainstream of the tradition, connecting especially strongly with developments in international law.

Recent military thought has also proved a fertile ground for recovery and development of just war thinking. Examples abound: Walzer's book has served as a text at the U.S. Military Academy; the service academies, the war colleges, and the National Defense University have sponsored various conferences and lectures examining or seeking to apply just war reasoning; a joint service committee on professional ethics provides a regular forum for consideration of just war and other ethical concepts related to the use of military force; revisions of the air force and army manuals on the law of war in the 1980s took close account of developments in international law on war and traditional principles like chivalry; the "Weinberger doctrine" of 1986 specifying conditions for commitment of American military forces closely correlates with the structure and elements of the content of traditional just war theory; and the formal justifications of the largest American military commitment since Vietnam, the *Persian Gulf War, closely followed the form of just war tradition as found in international law, while the conduct of that war in numerous ways reflected the debate over ethical conduct in war developed in just war terms over the previous three decades.

Contemporary just war thinking is challenged in three major ways: by the growth of pacifist rejection of all war; by the question of how to relate historical just war tradition to contemporary international politics and war; and by the growing problem of cultural relativism, which challenges the universality of just war principles and sets up alternative traditions as guides for international conduct in the use of force.

Yet, as the above religious, philosophical, military, and legal examples show, just war tradition is deeply embedded in Western culture and is particularly vigorous in recent American debate over the proper role, structure, and use of armed force. Contemporary American discourse on wa reflects both the traditional just war categories and t content of those categories, mediated through the strea of modern thought that have carried this tradition merging these streams in a common debate, moreov cent American just war thought has tended to rees their relationship as elements of a broader tradition, restoring a synthesis approach to just war long absent in Western thought.

[*See also* Aggression and Violence; Academies, Service; Bombing, Ethics of; Bombing of Civilians; Disciplinary Views of War; Laws of War; Religion and War; Rules of Engagement; War: Nature of War.]

• Paul Ramsey, *War and the Christian Conscience,* 1961. Paul Ramsey, *The Just War,* 1968. Frederick H. Russell, *The Just War in the Middle Ages,* 1975. Michael Walzer, *Just and Unjust Wars,* 1977, rev. ed. 1992. Stanley Hoffman, *Duties Beyond Borders,* 1981. James Turner Johnson, *Just War Tradition and the Restraint of War,* 1981. William V. O'Brien, *The Conduct of Just and Limited War,* 1981. National Conference of Catholic Bishops, *The Challenge of Peace,* 1983. James Turner Johnson, *Can Modern War Be Just?,* 1984. James Turner Johnson, *Moral Issues in Contemporary War,* 1999.

—James Turner Johnson

KALB, JOHANN [BARON DE] (1721–1780), Revolutionary War general. Johann Kalb grew up a peasant's son in the Bavarian town of Hüttendorf. Despite humble origins, he became a military officer, a French Army veteran with service under maréchal de Saxe, and a protégé of the militarily influential Broglie family. He first traveled to North America in 1768 to assess the growing Anglo-American split, and with the outbreak of war returned to seek a command in the *Continental army.

Kalb's skill and credentials, coupled with the Marquis de *Lafayette's influence and devotion to the Revolution's principles, overcame Congress's suspicion of foreign adventurers and earned a major general's commission. Despite the appointment, Kalb found battle elusive. Congress made him second in command for a proposed invasion of Canada in 1778, then canceled the operation. Washington subsequently ordered him to relieve the Continentals at the siege of *Charleston, South Carolina, but the city fell before Kalb's arrival. He reorganized the Southern Department's remaining forces, only to have Congress place Horatio *Gates at their head. On 16 August 1780, Kalb led a Continental regiment at the disastrous Battle of Camden, where he received numerous bayonet wounds. He died three days later.

[*See also* Revolutionary War: Military and Diplomatic Course.]

• Adolf E. Zucker, *General de Kalb: Lafayette's Mentor,* 1966.
—J. Mark Thompson

KEARNY, STEPHEN WATTS (1794–1848), frontier army commander, conqueror of New Mexico, governor of California. Born in Newark to a prominent New Jersey family, Kearny became a regular army lieutenant in the *War of 1812. He served with distinction at the Battle of Queenston Heights on the Niagara frontier. Promoted in the postwar period, he served in several expeditions and posts on the western frontier and molded the dragoons into one of the U.S. Army's crack units.

During the *Mexican War, Colonel Kearny received orders to organize an expedition of dragoons and Missouri Volunteers and seize Sante Fe, the provincial capital of New Mexico. Commanding the Army of the West, Kearny led 1,800 men 700 miles from Fort Leavenworth, Kansas, on 30 June 1846, arriving at Santa Fe on 18 August. As a brigadier general, he established a U.S. civil government and a territorial constitution there, then left on 25 September with 700 men for his second objective, the seizure of California. Learning that Commodore Robert F. Stockton had already conquered California, Kearny sent half his command back to Sante Fe and proceeded with 300 troops overland to California.

In December, he arrived near Los Angeles, which had been retaken by Mexican Californians. On 6 December, at San Pascual, Kearny defeated a Mexican detachment. After reprovisioning in San Diego, Kearny's soldiers and Stockton's sailors and Marines defeated 600 Mexicans at San Gabriel and retook Los Angeles. A feud between Kearny and Stockton, the latter supported by John C. *Fremont, over who was in charge in California led to Kearny's recognition as the military governor and ultimately to Fremont's court-martial for insubordination. Kearny died from yellow fever.

• Dwight L. Clarke, *Stephen Watts Kearny: Soldier of the West,* 1961.
—John M. Hart

KENNAN, GEORGE F. (1904–), diplomat, historian, foreign policy critic. Born in Milwaukee, Wisconsin, in 1904, Kennan attended Princeton University and joined the foreign service in 1926. Over the next two decades he labored as a diplomat in relative obscurity at postings in Riga, Moscow, Vienna, Prague, and Berlin, and earned some reputation for expertise on the Soviet Union. His obscurity ended with the dispatch from Moscow of his Long Telegram in February 1946 and especially with the publication of his 1947 article, "The Source of Soviet Conduct," in *Foreign Affairs.* He was accorded authorship of "containment" doctrine and deemed a principal architect of America's Cold War strategy.

As director of Policy Planning Staff in the State Department from 1947 to 1950 Kennan principally advocated political and economic measures, such as the *Marshall Plan, to implement containment. He objected to what he considered the overmilitarization of containment as evidenced by *NATO, the hydrogen bomb, and NSC 68. Although he supported U.S. entry into the *Korean War, he unsuccessfully opposed crossing the 38th parallel there. Kennan left the State Department in 1950 in dissent from the expansive national security strategy favored by Dean *Acheson. His direct influence on U.S. foreign policy ended then.

While pursuing a distinguished career as a historian at the Institute for Advanced Studies, Kennan also engaged in commentary on foreign policy matters. He contributed significantly to the realist approach to international relations characterized by a fundamental concern to root foreign policy in calculations of national interest. In 1950s, he argued for the reunification of Germany and withdrawal of American troops from Europe. Later, he posed U.S. involvement in the *Vietnam War, offered structurally critical support to the Nixon-Kissinger detente with the Soviet Union, and passionately the resumed nuclear *arms race that characteri

Carter and early Reagan presidencies. With the end of the Cold War, Kennan continued to emphasize the limits of American power and the need for restraint in the exercise of it.

[See also Cold War: External Course; Cold War: Domestic Course; Cold War: Changing Interpretations.]

• David Mayers, George Kennan and the Dilemmas of U.S. Foreign Policy, 1988. Wilson D. Miscamble, George F. Kennan and the Making of American Foreign Policy, 1947–1950, 1992.

—Wilson D. Miscamble

KENNEDY, JOHN F. (1917–1963), thirty-fifth U.S. president. Born in Brookline, Massachusetts, to a large, wealthy, politically active Irish American family, "Jack" Kennedy graduated from Harvard in 1940 when his financier father, Joseph Kennedy, was U.S. Ambassador to Britain. In the navy (1941–45), John Kennedy commanded a torpedo boat in the Pacific. He was hailed a hero when he helped rescue crew members after a Japanese destroyer sank PT-109 in 1943.

As a *Cold War Democrat from Massachusetts, Kennedy served in the House of Representatives (1947–53) and U.S. Senate (1953–61), calling for increased military spending and the vigorous containment of communism, particularly in the Third World.

In 1960, Kennedy defeated Vice President Richard M. *Nixon to become the first Catholic and the youngest man (at forty-three) to become president. In the campaign, Kennedy had incorrectly charged that the Eisenhower administration allowed a "missile gap" to develop in the Soviet Union's favor. Kennedy's failure during the CIA-sponsored invasion of the Bay of Pigs by Cuban exiles in April 1961 may have emboldened him to be assertive elsewhere. Kennedy and Secretary of Defense Robert S. *McNamara dramatically expanded the defense budget, increasing nuclear *missiles (from 63 to 424 ICMBs, 1961–63) and conventional forces (including the elite *counterinsurgency *Special Forces) under the concept of "flexible response." Kennedy also instituted *covert operations to depose Cuba's Fidel Castro, and mobilized military reservists in the Berlin Crisis of 1961. During the *Cuban Missile Crisis of October 1962, Kennedy directly challenged Soviet deployment of medium-range missiles in Cuba, even risking nuclear war before the Soviets backed down. Afterwards, Kennedy obtained a *Limited Nuclear Test Ban Treaty (1963), but continued the arms buildup. *NATO allies, meanwhile, began to complain that the United States too seldom consulted them.

To combat suspected communism in the Third World, Kennedy developed the Peace Corps and the Food for Peace program, but he also used military force. Responding to Communist *guerrilla warfare in Southeast Asia, Kennedy accepted neutralization of Laos, but he committed American military assistance to South Vietnam, increasing the number of U.S. military "advisers" attached to the South Vietnamese Army from 685 to 16,732. By the end of 1963, 120 Americans had died in combat there. The administration later tacitly authorized the Vietnamese generals' coup against the unpopular Ngo Dinh Diem, although not his murder on 1 November 1963. Kennedy himself was assassinated three weeks later in Dallas, Texas. The debate over what Kennedy would have done had he continues. He offered some statements favorable to others to doves. His actions, however, dramatically increased the U.S. military role in Vietnam and emphasized it as the test case against Communist wars of "national liberation." At the end, ambiguity marked his presidency, as mystery shrouded his assassination.

[See also Berlin Crises; Central Intelligence Agency; Vietnam War: Causes.]

• Arthur M. Schlesinger, Jr., A Thousand Days: John F. Kennedy in the White House, 1965. Thomas G. Paterson, ed., Kennedy's Quest for Victory: American Foreign Policy, 1961–1963, 1989. Michael R. Beschloss, The Crisis Years: Kennedy and Khrushchev, 1960–1963, 1991. James N. Giglio, The Presidency of John F. Kennedy, 1991. Diane B. Kunz, ed., The Diplomacy of the Crucial Decade: American Foreign Relations During the 1960s, 1994.

—Thomas G. Paterson

KETTLE HILL, BATTLE OF. See San Juan Hill, Battle of (1898).

The **KEY WEST AGREEMENT** (1948) was a major step toward composing differences between the military services over their respective roles and missions. The immediate purpose was to reconcile the inconsistent treatment of service functions in the *National Security Act of 1947, which had unified the armed forces under the National Military Establishment (later the Department of *Defense), and its companion Executive Order 9877. Two issues were uppermost: in regard to air power, whether the air force should share its strategic nuclear bombing function with the navy's carrier-based aircraft; and in regard to ground forces, whether limitations urged by the army should be imposed on the size and capabilities of the Marine Corps.

Growing interservice friction over these issues prompted Secretary of Defense James V. *Forrestal to meet privately with the *Joint Chiefs of Staff at Key West, Florida, 11–14 March 1948, where he brokered a compromise. Although primary service functions—air, land, and sea warfare—remained unchanged, each service received a secondary, or collateral, assignment. These were summarized in a paper entitled "Functions of the Armed Forces and the Joint Chiefs of Staff," which replaced the executive order. Forrestal hoped that this agreement would encourage more interservice collaboration—between the air force and the navy in planning nuclear warfare, and between the army and Marine Corps in amphibious operations.

Although the Key West Agreement provided a framework for resolving disagreements over service functions, it did little to eliminate the underlying sources of interservice rivalry. Money remained tight up to the outbreak of the *Korean War in June 1950, and until then, no service would readily part with or share responsibilities on which its budget claims rested. The Key West Agreement stood as the official statement of service functions until an updated directive replaced it in March 1954.

[See also Rivalry, Interservice.]

• Alice C. Cole, et al., eds., The Department of Defense: Documents on Establishment and Organization, 1944–1978, 1978. Steven L. Rearden, History of the Office of the Secretary of Defense: The Formative Years, 1947–1950, 1984.

—Steven L. Rearden

KHE SANH, SIEGE OF (1968). Among key engagements of the Vietnam War, the siege of Khe Sanh also marked one of the largest setpiece battles of that conflict. The relationship between Khe Sanh and the *Tet Offensive of 1968 continues to be the most controversial aspect of the siege. In fighting prior to the offensive, U.S. commander Gen. William C. *Westmoreland became convinced that this base at the northwestern corner of South Vietnam would be the major objective for North Vietnamese forces in the attack he expected. Instead, the forces directed by Gen. V. Nguyen *Giap struck cities and towns throughout South Vietnam. Whether or not Hanoi mounted a deliberate deception remains at issue. In any case, Westmoreland's focus on Khe Sanh helped Hanoi gain position for its assaults at Tet.

In the prelude to the Khe Sanh siege, increasing numbers of Hanoi's troops were detected in the vicinity of the combat base, which had been a military post or Special Forces camp since July 1962. That Special Forces camp was first hit by mortar bombardment in January 1966; in May 1967, after the facility moved to nearby Lang Vei, it received a ground attack. U.S. Marines began operating in the area, establishing and improving the Khe Sanh combat base and gradually reinforcing it as the suspected North Vietnamese presence grew to an estimated 25,000–40,000 men. By January 1968, the combat base was manned by 6,806 American troops (including 5,905 Marines) under Col. David E. Lownds. There were also about 360 Americans and indigenous soldiers at Lang Vei Special Forces camp and another 175 troops in and around Khe Sanh village.

The events of the seventy-eight day siege began with an attack on an outlying position (Hill 861) on 20/21 January 1968, coupled with a bombardment of the main base that destroyed much of the Marines' reserve ammunition. The force at Khe Sanh village withstood an attack the next night but was then withdrawn. There were several pitched battles for outposts but no more than probes at the combat base. These included the battles at Hill 861A (5 February), Lang Vei (7 February), and Hill 64 (8 February). All the posts except Lang Vei were successfully defended. On 21 February, there was a probe against South Vietnamese Ranger positions in the main base. The base and its outposts were heavily supported throughout the siege by U.S. airpower and artillery fire in an exceptional effort that General Westmoreland called Operation Niagara. It remains unclear whether the lack of a big North Vietnamese attack was intentional or resulted from losses inflicted by this firepower. Khe Sanh was relieved by an overland attack, Operation Pegasus, involving some 30,000 troops, that made contact with the isolated base on 7 April 1968. After a period of mobile action, the United States withdrew from Khe Sanh on 6 July.

Official U.S. figures for *casualties, which exclude several sources of losses, amount to 205 killed and 816 wounded who were evacuated; a more detailed assessment indicates about 730 battle deaths, 2,598 wounded, and 7 missing. Losses during the period of mobile operations in the surrounding zone include another 326 killed, 1,888 wounded, and 3 missing. North Vietnamese losses have been estimated by Americans at between 10,000 and 15,000 in dead alone.

[See also Vietnam War: Military and Diplomatic Course.]

• Robert Pisor, The End of the Line: The Siege of Khe Sanh, 1982. Eric Hammel, Khe Sanh: Siege in the Clouds, an Oral History, 1989. John Prados and Ray W. Stubbe, Valley of Decision: The Siege of Khe Sanh, 1991.
—John Prados

KING, ERNEST J. (1878–1956), American admiral; chief of U.S. naval forces in World War II. Born in Lorain, Ohio, King graduated from the U.S. Naval Academy in 1901. King's first command was with destroyers. But during World War I, he served as assistant chief of staff to Adm. Henry Mayo, commander of the Atlantic Fleet, joining him at conferences in England. After the war, Captain King studied and took leadership roles in two of the navy's new branches, submarines and aviation, in 1930 being given command of the aircraft carrier, Lexington. In 1933, when Chief of the Bureau of Aeronautics, Rear Adm. William A. *Moffett, died in a crash, King, his former assistant and now a rear admiral, succeeded him as the navy's aviation chief. In 1938, he commanded the navy's aircraft carrier force in the Pacific. King had hoped to become chief of naval operations (CNO), the navy's service chief, but in 1939 that position went to Adm. Harold Stark.

It was King not Stark, however, who would command the navy during World War II. In January 1941, as vice admiral and soon a full admiral, King with a reputation as knowledgeable, tough and dedicated officer, was appointed commander of the Atlantic Fleet with the mission of protecting vital supplies being sent to the Allies. In December 1941, after the Japanese attack on *Pearl Harbor and the U.S. declaration of war, President Franklin D. *Roosevelt created a new position and appointed King, commander in chief, U.S. Fleet, as head of all naval operating forces. Conflict between King and Stark led Roosevelt in March 1942 to appoint King also as chief of naval operations and send Stark to London as commander of U.S. naval forces in Europe. Holding these two positions as well as a seat on the *Joint Chiefs of Staff for the rest of the war, King had unprecedented authority over all aspects of the navy and its operations as well as joint planning. As his personal adviser, however, Roosevelt appointed Adm. William Leahy, a trusted friend and former CNO, as chief of staff to the president.

During World War II, King accepted the decision that Germany should be defeated first, but with the U.S. Navy's major combat role against the Japanese navy, he insisted that as many resources as possible be sent to the Pacific. His continued insistence led to disagreements with Gen. Dwight D. *Eisenhower, the U.S. military commander in Europe. King also clashed with Gen. Douglas *MacArthur, senior army commander in the Pacific over priorities in the region, leading Roosevelt to divide the area between MacArthur and Adm. Chester *Nimitz. In the summer of 1943, as MacArthur drove through the Southwest Pacific, King and Gen. H. H. ("Hap") *Arnold, chief of the Army Air Forces, pressed for a major drive by Nimitz through the Central Pacific. Roosevelt controversially accepted both campaigns, but in 1944, the president sided with MacArthur in favor of liberating the Philippines rather than bypassing them and taking Taiwan as the navy recommended.

In December 1944, King was given the five-star rank of fleet admiral. When Japan surrendered in September 1945, King recommended abolition of the position of commander in chief, U.S. fleet. He remained CNO until his retirement from the navy in December 1945.

[See also: Navy, U.S., 1899–1945.]

• Ernest J. King and W.M. Whitehill, Fleet Admiral King: A Record, 1952; Thomas B. Buell, Master of Seapower: A Biography of Fleet Admiral Ernest J. King, 1980; Robert William L

The Chiefs of Naval Operation, 1980; Eric Larrabee, Commander in Chief: Franklin Delano Roosevelt, His Lieutenants and Their War, 1987.

—John Whiteclay Chambers II

KING, MARTIN LUTHER, JR. (1929–1968), religious and protest leader and recipient of the 1964 Nobel Prize for Peace. King gained national prominence as a black civil rights leader and, during his final years, as a critic of American military involvement in Vietnam. In his memoir, Stride Toward Freedom (1958), King recalled that when initially exposed to *pacifism, he concluded that war "could serve as a negative good in the sense of preventing the spread and growth of an evil force." Only after becoming familiar with Gandhian notions of nonviolent resistance was he convinced that "the love ethic of Jesus" could be "a potent instrument for social and collective transformation." As the president of the Southern Christian Leadership Conference (SCLC), King became a nationally known advocate of civil disobedience. He led protest movements in Montgomery (1955–56), Birmingham (1963), and Selma (1965), Alabama, that demonstrated the effectiveness of nonviolent tactics in spurring passage of the 1964 Civil Rights Act and the 1965 Voting Rights Act.

Although King was reluctant to risk his prestige as a civil rights leader by opposing the *Vietnam War, he eventually publicly criticized President Lyndon B. *Johnson's war policies as immoral and a harmful diversion of funds from antipoverty programs. On 4 April 1967, in his first major public statement against the war, King explained at New York's Riverside Church that "if we are to get on the right side of the world revolution, we as a nation must undergo a radical revolution of values." King's advocacy of *conscientious objection to military service and his call for a unilateral cease-fire in Vietnam hurt his popularity and ability to influence domestic policies; nonetheless he remained an internationally recognized advocate of world peace and militant *nonviolence until his assassination on 4 April 1968.

[See also Civil Liberties and War; Peace and Antiwar Movements; Vietnam Antiwar Movement.]

• James M. Washington, ed., The Essential Writings and Speeches of Martin Luther King, Jr., 1986. David J. Garrow, Bearing the Cross: Martin Luther King, Jr. and the Southern Christian Leadership Conference, 1988. Clayborne Carson, et al., eds. The Papers of Martin Luther King, Jr., 14 vols., 1992– . Clayborne Carson, ed., The Autobiography of Martin Luther King, Jr., 1998.

—Clayborne Carson

KING PHILIP'S WAR (1675–77). The first large-scale military action in the American colonies, King Philip's War pitted bands from various tribes against the New England colonists and their Indian allies. The causes of the war were rooted in the frictions between an expanding, assertive culture and a threatened, increasingly dependent one. Native Americans, whose currency (wampum) was losing value, had to sell land to acquire trade goods. Tribal leaders so resented the imposition of European authority and decline of their own power. Indians had other grievances as well.

The war began in Plymouth Colony in 1675, then spread throughout New England. Although colonists blamed "Philip," principal sachem of the Wampanoags, for hostilities, his warriors probably acted independently, not as part of an intertribal conspiracy. The colonists' clumsy reaction to a local uprising soon produced a major rebellion. Nipmucks, Pocumtucks, Abenakis, and other resisting groups either cooperated with Philip's few hundred Wampanoags or conducted their own operations. A preemptive campaign by Josiah Winslow's 1,000-man army against the menacing but officially neutral Narragansetts resulted in the fiery destruction of the tribe's fort and the killing of hundreds of men, women, and children. But colonists' victories were rare in the first half of a war that saw more than a dozen towns burned and entire companies ambushed by Indian marksmen firing flintlock muskets. Had warriors not been reluctant to assault garrison houses, colonial losses would have been even higher.

Distrust of Indian auxiliaries handicapped militia units for crucial months. Europeans who trained to fire volleys on open battlefields were unprepared for fights with warriors who aimed at individuals from behind trees and used stealth, surprise, and mobility. Eventually, resourceful officers put Native Americans to work as scouts, fighters, and informants. Adopting Indian raid and ambush techniques, companies hunted down their starving enemies. Philip fell in 1676, shot by an Indian in Benjamin *Church's mixed force. The Mohawks in New York also contributed to the defeat of the insurgents by preventing outside assistance or escape.

Resistance finally ended in 1677. Thousands had perished, including approximately 500 colonial soldiers. It took years to rebuild frontier towns. The war caused higher taxes and damaged the economy, particularly the fur trade. All the southern New England tribes lost cultural autonomy and political and military influence. Nevertheless, the tactical lessons learned from Indians in this costly war had a lasting impact on American military *doctrine.

[See also Native Americans: U.S. Military Relations with; Native American Wars: Wars Between Native Americans and Europeans and Euro-Americans.]

• Douglas E. Leach, Flintock and Tomahawk, 1958. Russell Bourne, The Red King's Rebellion, 1990. Patrick M. Malone, The Skulking War of War, 1991. Jill Lepore, The Name of War: King Philip's War and the Origins of American Identity, 1998.

—Patrick M. Malone

KINGS MOUNTAIN, BATTLE OF (1780). The defeat of Maj. Patrick Ferguson's loyalist force at Kings Mountain in northwest South Carolina by a coalition of frontiersmen on 7 October 1780 marked the start of the American recovery in the South during the Revolutionary War and the beginning of the end for Britain's hopes of using loyalists to suppress the southern countryside. Following British victories at the siege of *Charleston and the Battle of Camden in May and August 1780, strong British and loyalist forces roamed the backcountry, intimidating rebels and heartening those who favored royal government. Settlers on the North Carolina and Virginia frontier—mostly Scots-Irish—feared that the British would unleash Indian attacks on their communities. On 26 September, a nucleus of "over-the-mountain men" gathered at Sycamore Shoals, near present-day Johnson City, Tennessee, and resolved to defend their families and farms.

By the time they ran Ferguson's 1,100-man army to ground at Kings Mountain, the frontier militia numbered between 1,500 and 1,800, most armed with "longrifles." Leaders of individual groups regarded William Campbell of Virginia as their commander, but the force really consisted of independent men who shared a common purpose. Ferguson's loyalist militiamen waited atop the wooded King's Mountain ridge, treeless at the summit, for the climactic battle of the backcountry civil war. Ferguson, an urbane man with a flair for tactics and invention, had chosen a position that allowed his opponents to use their rifles to inflict maximum damage on his force. Campbell's men surrounded the loyalists late in the afternoon of 7 October, and kept up such an accurate and deadly fire that Ferguson's worn-down force surrendered an hour later, its leader dead from multiple gunshot wounds. Having accomplished their objective, the winners dispersed to their homes, stopping long enough to execute nine of the captured loyalists.

King's Mountain was the turning point of the South's bitter civil war. Potential loyalists would thereafter sit on the fence until Britain could reestablish its military domination, something the British lacked the resources to accomplish.

[See also Citizen-Soldier; Revolutionary War: Military and Diplomatic Course.]

• Lyman C. Draper, *King's Mountain and its Heroes*, 1881. Wilma Dykeman, *With Fire and Sword*, 1991.   —Harold E. Selesky

KINKAID, THOMAS C. (1888–1972), career naval officer and commander during World War II. Promoted to rear admiral on the eve of World War II, Thomas C. Kinkaid developed a reputation for completing assignments successfully. During 1942, Admiral Kinkaid commanded cruiser divisions in the battle of the *Coral Sea (May) and at Midway (June), and then carrier task forces in engagements around the island of Guadalcanal (August–November). In December 1942, Kinkaid took command of the North Pacific Force, a joint navy, army, and Army Air Force command in Alaska. His troops ejected the Japanese from Attu in May 1943 and forced their retreat from Kiska in July. For his accomplishments, Kinkaid received a third Distinguished Service Medal and promotion to vice admiral.

Successful at joint operations, in November 1943 the admiral transferred to the Southwest Pacific Area to serve under Gen. Douglas *MacArthur. Here he commanded all Allied naval forces, including the U. S. Seventh Fleet. In October 1944, Kinkaid's Seventh Fleet landed MacArthur's forces at Leyte Gulf in the Philippines. Japanese attempts to drive the Americans from the island failed in the decisive Battle for *Leyte Gulf, 23–24 October 1944. Following this great naval victory, in January 1945 Kinkaid's Seventh Fleet landed MacArthur's troops on Luzon at Lingayen Gulf. With Luzon secured, Kinkaid became a full admiral. Known as a "fighting admiral," with a deserved reputation for outstanding interservice operations, Kinkaid is honored in American naval history.

[See also Navy, U.S.: 1899–1945; World War II, U.S. Naval Operations in: The Pacific.]

• Gerald E. Wheeler, "Thomas C. Kinkaid: MacArthur's Master of Naval Warfare," in William M. Leary, ed., *We Shall Return! MacArthur's Commanders and the Defeat of Japan*, 1988. Gerald E. Wheeler, *Kinkaid of the Seventh Fleet: A Biography of Admiral Thomas C. Kinkaid*, U. S. Navy, 1995.   —Gerald E. Wheeler

KISSINGER, HENRY (1923–), Statesman. Kissinger's family emigrated from Fuerth, Germany, to escape Nazi persecution in 1938. After U.S. Army service during World War II and with the occupation forces in Germany, Kissinger compiled a superlative record as an undergraduate and graduate student at Harvard University. He then became a prominent academic specialist in international relations and nuclear *strategy. While a professor of government at Harvard (1955–68), he wrote widely on international relations and *nuclear weapons, arguing that the possession of nuclear weapons by the United States and the Soviet Union had not fundamentally altered the balance of power. States still pursued basic interests, nuclear weapons were a tool of influence, and the nuclear powers could manage to contain a destructive *arms race.

Kissinger advised New York governor Nelson Rockefeller, Republican presidents, and their senior foreign policy subordinates. During the 1960s, he tried to fashion *NATO's nuclear strategy in light of France's withdrawal, urging understanding of French and German pride. As the *Vietnam War intensified after 1965, Kissinger was drawn deeply into efforts to end it. He undertook an important diplomatic mission for President Lyndon B. *Johnson (1967), but his attempt to arrange a cease-fire faltered when the U.S. government refused to promise an unconditional halt to bombing of all North Vietnam.

President Richard M. *Nixon named him national security adviser in 1969; in September 1973, Kissinger was also confirmed as secretary of state, a position he held concurrently until November 1975, when President Gerald R. *Ford appointed Brent Scowcroft national security adviser; Kissinger remained secretary of state until the end of Ford's administration.

During these eight years, Kissinger helped craft the policy of detente with the Soviet Union and to end U.S. involvement in Vietnam. Under his direction, the United States and the Soviet Union made significant progress toward arms control, with the Interim Agreement of Limitations of Strategic Armaments (SALT I, 1972), the *Anti-Ballistic Missile Treaty (1972), and the Vladivostok Agreement (1974). These efforts provoked opposition from conservatives both Democratic and Republican who incorrectly accused Kissinger of drafting agreements that gave the Soviet Union a military advantage over the United States.

Kissinger worked with Nixon to reduce U.S. involvement in Vietnam, concluding the *Paris Peace Agreements establishing a cease-fire in January 1973. The peace proved remarkably short-lived: both North and South Vietnam repeatedly violated the cease-fire. Kissinger argued strenuously for additional aid to South Vietnam, but by 1975 U.S. public opinion had turned sharply against any additional involvement.

Kissinger's accomplishments before 1974 won him wide public praise; he earned the Nobel Peace Prize for arranging the cease-fire in Vietnam. After 1975, however, his reputation diminished. His diplomatic triumphs were based on illusion and manipulation. Believing that only power mattered in international affairs, Kissinger and Nixon often expressed contempt for democratic processes of foreign policy. Furthermore, he appeared arrogant and showed little desire to uphold traditional U.S. standards of human rights in other countries.

[See also SALT Treaties.]

• Henry Kissinger, *Nuclear Weapons and Foreign Policy*, 1958. Robert D. Schulzinger, *Henry Kissinger: Doctor of Diplomacy*, 1989. Walter Isaacson, *Kissinger: A Biography*, 1992. Henry Kissinger, *Diplomacy*, 1994.
—Robert D. Schulzinger

KNOX, HENRY (1750–1806), *Revolutionary War general, secretary of war. As a twenty-five-year-old Boston bookseller, Knox became a colonel and head of the *Continental army's artillery regiment in November 1775. In the prewar period he had served in a local militia unit, observed British regulars, and read extensively in military works. Thirteen months later, Congress made him a brigadier general and the chief of a growing *artillery corps.

Knox's corps distinguished itself in sieges, most notably at Boston and Yorktown, and also in open field engagements, like those at Trenton and Monmouth, where he made mobile and effective use of his cannon.

In the postwar period, Knox headed the War Department (1874–94). During his tenure as secretary of war, he oversaw an extensive coast artillery construction program. He also faced the difficult task of reconciling the country's security needs with an anti–standing army bias, financial limitations, and embryonic political structure. A strong nationalist, Knox proposed a small regular army, an academy to train officers, and a nationalized militia of adult male citizens. Though not fully accepted before his retirement in 1794, Knox's ideas helped lay the foundations of American military policy for the next century.

[See also Coast Guard, U.S.; Citizen-Soldier; Fortifications; Monmouth, Battle of; Yorktown, Battle of.]

• North Callahan, *Henry Knox: General Washington's General*, 1958. Richard H. Kohn, *Eagle and Sword: The Federalists and the Creation of the Military Establishment in America, 1783–1802*, 1975.
—J. Mark Thompson

KOREA, U.S. MILITARY INVOLVEMENT IN. U.S. military involvement began almost from the outset as the United States sought in the mid-nineteenth century to establish commercial and diplomatic relations with the so-called "Hermit Kingdom." After a number of Korean attacks on American merchant ships trying to penetrate the peninsula, a U.S. naval squadron of launched an unsuccessful punitive assault near Seoul (1871). China soon gained control of Korea and opened it to other countries, beginning in 1882 with the United States. In the Sino-Japanese War (1894–95) and the Russo-Japanese War (1904–05), Tokyo increasingly took over Korea, which became part of the Japanese empire, 1905–45.

With the defeat of Japan in 1945, the United States and the Soviet Union shared a trusteeship over the Korean peninsula, the Red Army occupying the area north of the 38th parallel and the U.S. Army under Gen. John R. Hodge ʜe South. That division, meant to have been temporary, ᵃame permanent with the hardening of the Cold War.

ᴬ 1948, after Moscow rejected a *United Nations plan ᵉe elections throughout Korea, elections in the South ᵗhe Republic of Korea; a former exile from the States, Syngman Rhee, served as president In response, Moscow created the Democratic ᵖublic of Korea in the North, headed by Com- Kim Il Sung (1948–94).

ᵉ Republic of Korea initially received some ᵉhe *Joint Chiefs of Staff advised President

Harry S. *Truman that the United States had little strategic interest in maintaining American troops and bases there. In June 1949, the troops were withdrawn; Soviet troops also withdrew that year. In January 1950, Secretary of State Dean *Acheson publicly defined the U.S. defense perimeter as including Japan and Taiwan but not Korea. Six months later, after a series of border clashes, Soviet-backed North Korean forces invaded and conquered much of the South. The Truman administration reevaluated its position and led a UN-authorized military coalition to repel the Communist aggression.

The *Korean War (1950–53), in which the U.S. military suffered 196,000 *casualties, including 54,000 dead, in a war against North Korea and ultimately also "volunteers" from the People's Republic of China, ended in a truce signed in Panmunjon by military representatives from the United States and North Korea but not South Korea. Rhee's resistance was softened, however, by guarantees of increased military assistance, continued U.S. troops, and a mutual security treaty with the United States.

As a symbolic bastion of containment policy during the Cold War, Korea remained an area of major U.S. military commitment and periodic incidents, particularly along the fortified demilitarized zone (DMZ) between North and South. Under Gen. Park Chung Hee (president, 1961–79), South Korea sent troops to fight alongside U.S. forces in South Vietnam. In 1968, North Korea curtailed U.S. seaborne electronic intelligence gathering off its coast by capturing the USS *Pueblo* and its crew. In the early 1970s, the Nixon administration's Asian self-defense policy led to the removal of one U.S. division from Korea, but an attempt by the Carter administration to reduce U.S. forces there was thwarted. When Park's successor, Gen. Chun Doo Hwan, used the South Korean Army to crush a May 1980 insurrection in Kwangju, there were allegations of U.S. complicity.

The collapse of the Soviet empire in 1989–90 rendered Communist North Korea increasingly isolated and impoverished, while the South Korean government flourished with the resumption of popularly elected government in 1987. The North Korean nuclear program, which may have included nuclear weapons, led to a major international crisis in 1994, when Pyongyang initially rejected UN monitoring. The Clinton administration threatened an economic blockade and there was speculation about possible U.S. air strikes. However, the crisis was defused with the help of former President Jimmy *Carter. The United States and the two Koreas began talks, which continued in the late 1990s despite the death of Kim Il Sung (1994) and periodic North Korean incidents such as the shooting down (1994) of a U.S. Army helicopter that had strayed into the DMZ, and the foiled attempt (1996) to stage commando raids from a submarine off South Korea. With North Korea facing economic collapse that might lead to military action, the United States retained some 36,000 military personnel in Korea, its third-largest permanent overseas contingent in the 1990s.

[See also Civil–Military Relations: Military Governments and Occupation; Cold War: Causes; Cold War: External Course; Cold War: Changing Interpretations; Korean War.]

• E. Grant Meade, *American Military Government in Korea*, 1951. Robert K. Sawyer, *Military Advisers in Korea: KMAG in War and Peace*, 1962. Ralph N. Clough, *Embattled Korea*, 1987. Edward A.

Olsen, *U.S. Policy and the Two Koreas*, 1988. Bruce Cumings, *The Origins of the Korean War*, 2 vols., 1990. Doug Bandow and Ted Galen Carpenter, eds., *The U.S.-South Korean Alliance: Time for a Change*, 1992. William Stueck, *The Korean War: An International History*, 1995.   —John Whiteclay Chambers II

KOREAN WAR (1950–1953). War came to Korea in 1950–53 as both a civil war on the Korean peninsula and the first military clash of the *Cold War between forces of the Soviet Union and its Communist clients and the United States and its allies. It was, therefore, potentially the most dangerous war in world history.

Even before the war against Germany and Japan drew to a close in 1945, the United States and the Soviet Union assumed competing roles in shaping the postwar world. As the two undisputed victorious powers, they influenced the course of every political problem emerging from the debris of war. Unfortunately, hostility between the two powers increased at the same time and threatened the outbreak of another war, which after 1949 risked the use of atomic weapons.

The conservative forces eventually coalesced in the Republic of Korea under the leadership of President Syngman Rhee. A North Korean state, The Democratic People's Republic created by the Soviet Union and headed by Premier Kim Il-sung, adopted a policy of opposition to Rhee's government and for unification of the Korean peninsula by armed force.

North Korean ground forces crossed the 38th Parallel into South Korea about 4:30 A.M. on 25 June 1950 (24 June Washington time). The main attack, led by two divisions and a tank brigade, aimed at Uijongbu and Seoul. In the central mountains, two North Korean divisions drove toward Yoju and Wonju and on the east coast, a reinforced division headed for Samchok.

In an emergency session on Sunday, 25 June, the UN Security Council (with the USSR boycotting because of the refusal to admit the People's Republic of China) adopted an U.S.-sponsored resolution branding the North Korean attack a breach of the peace and calling on the North Korean government to cease hostilities and withdraw. The North Koreans did not respond to the UN resolution, so on the following Tuesday, the United States offered a follow-up proposal that "the members of the United Nations furnish such assistance to the Republic of Korea as may be necessary to repel the armed attack and to restore international peace and security in the area." Subsequently, the UN Security Council designated the president of the United States as its executive agent for the war in Korea. President Truman, in turn, appointed Gen. Douglas *MacArthur as the Commander in Chief, United Nations Command (CICUNC). The military organization to wage war was in place.

Saving South Korea was certainly the most urgent UN war aim, but President Harry S. *Truman also believed that the Soviet Union was the most dangerous threat to the western allies. The UN Command had to stop the North Koreans and eject them from South Korea by military means, no small task with the North Korean army rolling south and no UN troops on the ground. Moreover, while accomplishing this, the UN coalition had to avoid expanding the war into Asia and to Europe by provoking China or the Soviet Union to enter the struggle. So the Truman administration adopted additional, unilateral war aims designed to keep the violence confined to the Korean Peninsula, to keep the Soviets out of the war, to maintain a strongly committed UN (and *NATO) coalition, and to buy time to rearm the United States and its allies.

At first, MacArthur had little choice in how to fight the North Koreans. Somehow he had to slow down their offensive sufficiently to give him time to mount a counterattack against their flanks or rear. His forces consisted of four undermanned and partially trained U.S. Army divisions comprising Gen. Walton Walker's Eighth Army, the South Korean army, then falling back in front of the enemy, an ill-equipped U.S. air force, and growing naval U.S. strength. When the President ordered use of American troops, the *Joint Chiefs of Staff (JCS) immediately sent additional army forces, marines, and air and naval forces to strengthen MacArthur's command. As these units began to deploy, MacArthur requested more reinforcements that included between four and five additional divisions.

In all, fifty-three UN member nations promised troops to assist South Korea. Of all, the nations of the British Commonwealth were most ready to fight when war broke out. Great Britain, Australia, New Zealand and Canada were the first to send air, sea, and ground forces. Eventually UN allies sent over 19,000 troops to Korea. All were assigned to the U.S. Eighth Army.

MacArthur's first task was to block what appeared to be the enemy's main attack leading to the port of Pusan in the south. Rushing American ground and air forces from Japan to Korea, he hoped to delay the enemy column and force it to deploy, then withdraw UN forces to new delaying positions and repeat the process. With any luck, he could gain enough time to muster an effective force on the ground. For this task he ordered General Walker to send units to confront the enemy on the road to Pusan. Walker sent a small infantry force—Task Force Smith—to lead the way. While reinforcements were moving to Korea, MacArthur pushed the rest of Walker's Eighth Army (less the 7th Infantry Division) into Korea to build up resistance on the enemy's main axis of advance. With these forces and the South Koreans, Walker hoped to delay the enemy north and west of a line following the Naktong River, to the north, then east to Yongdok on the Sea of Japan. If forced to withdraw farther, he proposed to occupy the Naktong River line as the primary position from which Eighth Army would defend the port of Pusan.

With the main enemy force applying heavy pressure along the primary axis aimed at Pusan, Walker had to fight off two North Korean divisions, advancing around the west flank deep into southwest Korea. From there they could turn east and strike directly at Pusan. To head off this threat, Walker sent the 25th Infantry Division to meet the North Koreans west of Masan and stop them. In savage battle, the 25th slowed the North Koreans, and Walker pulled the Eighth Army and Republic of Korea Army (ROKA) behind the Naktong River line to defend Pusan.

Walker's retirement into the Pusan Perimeter MacArthur's plans perfectly. Now he could exercise control over both the battle on the peninsula and pr tions for an amphibious counterstroke, now plan mid-September. As reinforcements poured into P combat strength began to favor Walker, MacArt to shunt units, equipment, and individual repl Japan to rebuild a corps for use in the amph tion. With complete superiority of air pow strength in tanks, artillery, and infantry, MacArthur believed that Eighth Army and the ROKA could hold Pusan.

North Koreans launched violent, piecemeal attacks against the perimeter beginning on 5 August. By the end of August, the defenders had thrown back the first barrage of attacks, but a new onslaught began on the night of 31 August. This time the enemy hit simultaneously and even more savagely. American reinforcements had, however, greatly increased the combat power of the allies, and by 12 September the North Korean offensive had spent itself on all fronts against Walkers' skillful defense.

While the Eighth Army fought to hold Pusan, MacArthur readied the forces he had assembled in Japan to eject the North Koreans from Korea. He selected the port of Inchon near Seoul as the objective in spite of undesirable hydrographic characteristics. High tides, swift currents, and broad mud flats threatened the safety of an amphibious assault force. But Inchon also had some features that convinced MacArthur that the prize was worth the risk. The North Koreans, concentrated around Pusan in the south, would be vulnerable to an attack so far to the north, and the capture of Inchon would lead directly to the fall of Seoul. Because Seoul, the capital of South Korea, was the intersection of most of the major roads and railroads in South Korea, its capture would trap the North Koreans and force them to surrender or escape to the mountains, abandoning all their heavy equipment. MacArthur believed he could defeat the North Koreans in one decisive battle—the *Inchon Landing.

Early in September, naval air forces struck targets up and down the west coast of Korea. As D-day for Inchon approached, surface gunfire support ships began to add their weight. On 15 September, U.S. Marines of the newly formed X Corps successfully assaulted the port, paving the way for army troops that followed. In the ensuing campaign, North Korea forces fought bitterly to hold the capital. On September 28, Seoul fell, and by October 1, Marines held a line close to the 38th Parallel, blocking all roads and passes leading to Seoul and its port at Inchon.

Weakened by the heavy fighting of July and August, the Eighth Army could not at first break out of the Pusan perimeter. Finally, a week after X Corps landed at Inchon, the North Koreans began to waver. On 23 September they began a general withdrawal, and Eighth Army units advanced to link up with X Corps. MacArthur had won his battle and the UN was poised to exploit his success.

In retrospect, the turning point in the Korean War was the decision now made to cross the 38th Parallel and pursue the retreating enemy into North Korea. At President Truman's direction, the *National Security Council (NSC) staff had studied the question and recommended against crossing the 38th because ejecting the North Koreans from South Korea was a sufficient victory. To this, the JCS objected. MacArthur, they argued, must destroy the North ῀orean army to prevent a renewal of the aggression. On 11 ῀tember—four days before the Inchon Landing—the ῀ident adopted the arguments of the JCS. Most impor-῀, Truman changed the national objective from saving ῀Korea to unifying the peninsula. After the UN As-῀assed a resolution on 7 October 1950 calling for ῀n of Korea, MacArthur was free to send forces ῀Korea.

῀ur's attack on North Korea never achieved the ῀ earlier operations. Beginning 7 October, he

sent the weakened Eighth Army in the main attack against the North Korean capital of P'yongyang without adequate combat support. As the supporting attack, he planned another powerful amphibious assault by X Corps to strike the east coast port of Wonsan on 20 October. Although the Eighth Army advanced rapidly toward P'yongyang against light resistance, the amphibious attack by X Corps was six days late landing in its objective area because mine sweepers had to clear an elaborate minefield. On 11 October, Wonsan fell to a South Korean corps, almost two weeks before the marines could land. P'yongyang fell on the 19 October.

After the capture of P'yongyang and Wonsan, allied troops streamed north virtually unopposed. Truman worried about possible Chinese intervention, but at a conference at Wake Island on 15 October, MacArthur belittled this possibility and was optimistic about an early victory. There was, however, little time to enjoy the successes of mid-October. Beginning on the 25 October, a reinvigorated enemy struck the Eighth Army in a brief but furious counterattack. By 2 November intelligence officers had accumulated undeniable evidence from across the front that Chinese forces had intervened, and the Eighth Army had to stop its advance.

Chinese leaders had tried to ward off a direct confrontation with the Americans by warning the UN not to cross the 38th Parallel. American leaders interpreted these statements as bluff rather than policy. But they were wrong; Josef *Stalin, the Soviet premier, asked Mao Zedong, the Chinese premier, to send Chinese forces to the aid of his clients, the North Koreans. After much deliberation, Mao decided to intervene. On 19 October Chinese Peoples Volunteers (CPV) crossed the Yalu River and massed some 260,000 troops in front of the UN Command.

After replenishing supplies, MacArthur's forces were ready. On 24 November the troops of the Eighth Army, unaware of the presence of massed Chinese forces, crossed their lines of departure. Within twenty-four hours after the Eighth Army jumped off, the Chinese struck back, aiming their main attack at the South Korean ROKA II Corps on the army's right flank. Two days later the CPV hit U.S. X Corps as it advanced into the mountains of eastern Korea. Stunned and outnumbered, American and South Korean units recoiled, beginning a long retreat that ended in January 1951, only after the UN forces fell back south of the 38th Parallel and once again gave up the city of Seoul. X Corps fought its way back to the port of Hungnam on the east coast and then rejoined Eighth Army in the south.

During the first week of December 1950 when reports from the front were incomplete and most grim, President Truman met in Washington with Prime Minister Clement Attlee of the United Kingdom. Though initially far apart, Truman and Attlee, after four days of intense discussion, reached a compromise solution on Korea. They would continue to fight side-by-side, find a line and hold it, and wait for an opportunity to negotiate an end to the fighting from a position of military strength. Moreover, they reaffirmed their commitment to "Europe first" in the face of Soviet hostility toward NATO. In this way, the decision to unify Korea was abrogated and a new war aim adopted.

The most immediate military effect of the talks was to prevent MacArthur from exacting revenge for his humiliating defeat. The JCS limited his reinforcements to replacements, shifted the priority of military production to strengthening NATO forces, and wrote a new directive for MacArthur requiring him to defend in Korea as far to the north as possible. MacArthur disagreed with giving priority to Europe at the expense of the shooting war in Korea. He was outraged at the thought of going on the strategic defensive and fought against his new directive with all his might. Nevertheless, on 12 January 1951, the JCS sent him the final version of the directive, and the UN coalition had a new war aim designed to bring about a negotiated settlement.

Just two days before Christmas 1950, the command of the Eighth Army passed to Lt. Gen. Matthew B. *Ridgway after Gen. Walker died in a truck accident. From his position on the Department of the Army staff in Washington, Ridgway came to the Eighth Army well informed of the strategic situation in Korea. He arrived at his new headquarters determined to attack north as soon as possible. Somehow he had to stop the retreat and turn the army around; until then the Eighth Army continued to withdraw. In early January 1951 UN forces gave up Seoul.

Finally, Ridgway's front line units began reporting light contact with the enemy. Sensing the opportunity to turn on the Chinese, Ridgway stopped the army on a line from P'yongt'aek in the west, through Wonju in the center, to Samch'ok on the east coast. When American divisions, withdrawn with X Corps, moved up to thicken the line in the lightly held center, Ridgway ordered his forces to patrol north and find the enemy. In a series of increasingly powerful offensives, he then sent the Eighth Army north: Operation Thunderbolt jumped off in January, Roundup in February (though a tactical setback), Killer in late February, Ripper in March, and Rugged in April. By this time, Ridgway's army had once again crossed the 38th Parallel where its forward units dug into strong defensive ground in anticipation of an enemy counteroffensive. Surprisingly, the shock came, not from the enemy as Ridgway expected, but from Washington, when MacArthur was dismissed by President Truman.

MacArthur's dismissal resulted from his rejection of Truman's policy. As Ridgway neared the 38th again, the position of military strength envisioned in the Truman-Attlee conference had seemed near at hand. Truman took advantage of Ridgway's success to invite the Communists to negotiate a cease fire. After reading the text of Truman's proposed message, MacArthur broadcast a bellicose ultimatum to the enemy commander that undermined the president's plan. Truman was furious. MacArthur had preempted presidential prerogative, confused friends and enemies alike about who was directing the war, and directly challenged the president's authority as *Commander in Chief. As Truman pondered how to handle the problem, Congressman Joseph W. Martin, Minority (Republican) Leader of the House of Representatives, released the contents of a letter from MacArthur in which the general repeated his criticism of the administration. The next day Truman began the process that was to end with MacArthur's being relieved from command on 11 April 1951.

After MacArthur's dismissal, Ridgway took his place as Commander in Chief, Far East and CINCUNC. Lt. Gen. James A. Van Fleet, an experienced and successful World War II combat leader, took command of the Eighth Army. On 22 April, as Van Fleet's Eighth army edged north, the CPV opened the expected general offensive, aiming their main attack toward Seoul in the west. The Chinese, num-

bering almost a half million men, drove Van Fleet once again below the 38th Parallel. On 10 May, the Chinese jumped off again after shifting seven armies to their main effort against the eastern half of the UN line. Taking advantage of the Chinese concentration in the east, Van Fleet attacked suddenly in the west, north of Seoul. The effect was dramatic; surprised CPV units pulled back, suffering their heaviest *casualties of the war, and by the end of May found themselves retreating into North Korea. By mid-June, UN forces had regained a line, for the most part, north of the 38th Parallel.

Regardless of UN success on the battlefield, ending the war turned out to be a maddeningly long process. U.S. planners knew that the Truman-Attlee agreement made it unlikely that the war would end in a conventional victory. The UN allies had even adopted negotiating an armistice as a war aim. The time seemed right for the Chinese and North Koreans as well since they needed a respite from the heavy casualties suffered in the UN offensive. They agreed to meet with UN representatives when in late June 1951, the Soviets proposed a conference among the belligerents.

Negotiations were initially hampered by silly haggling over matters of protocol and the selection of a truly neutral negotiating site. Even so, on 26 July 1951 the two sides finally reached an agreement on an agenda containing four major points: selection of a demarcation line and demilitarized zone, supervision of the truce, arrangements for *prisoners of war (POWs), and recommendations to the governments involved in the war. With an agreed agenda in hand, and Panmunjom—a town between opposing lines, suitable to hold talks—the negotiators began the lengthy process of debating each item. Handling POWs proved to be the most difficult problem on the agenda, but fixing the demarcation line was the most damaging. By dealing with the final position of the armies *first*, the UN negotiators blundered into an agreement that permitted the Communists to stalemate the battlefield and to wage a two-year political war at the negotiating table.

At issue was a U.S. scheme seeking quick agreement on a demarcation line. On 17 November the UN delegation proposed the current line of contact as the demarcation line providing that all remaining agenda items were resolved within thirty days. The communists accepted the proposal on 27 November debated the remaining agenda items for thirty days, and then failed to reach agreement. They used the thirty days to create a tactical defense so deeply dug in that both sides had to accept a stalemate.

From that moment on, the battlefield changed to a static kind of war, more reminiscent of World War I than anything that had happened since. Beginning in the winter of 1951–1952, the war came to be defined by elevated sites named Porkchop Hill, Sniper's Ridge, Old Baldy, T-Bone, Whitehorse, Punchbowl and a hundred other hilltops between the two armies. There followed a seemingly endless succession of violent fire fights, most of them at night gain or maintain control of hills that were a little hi and ridges that were a bit straighter. All of them, no r how large the forces engaged, were deadly encount signed to provide leverage for one side or the oth protracted political battle going on at Panmunj historical age when technology enabled great than at any other time, tactical warfare in through a regression that can only be explair its close relationship to the negotiations. Constant pressure was its purpose, not decisive victory.

In Panmunjom negotiators plodded through the remaining agenda items. Supervising the armistice agreement was an extremely complex issue, but a compromise emerged that permitted rotation of 35,000 UN troops and supplies each month through specified ports of entry. In addition, both sides accepted Swedish, Swiss, Polish, and Czech membership on an armistice commission. Political recommendations to the belligerents were agreed in the astonishingly short period of eleven days. Both sides called for a conference to convene three months after a cease fire. At that time all political issues that had not been settled during the negotiations would be discussed.

What to do about prisoners of war was the major obstacle to final agreement. The UN Command wanted prisoners to decide for themselves whether or not they would return home. The Communists insisted on forced repatriation. To restore movement to the talks, the International Red Cross polled prisoners as to where they wanted to go. The results, announced early in April 1952, surprised everyone. Of 132,000 Chinese and North Korean POWs screened, only 54,000 North Koreans and 5,100 Chinese wanted to go home. The communist delegation was incredulous and accused the United Nations of influencing the poll. From that moment on, negotiations bogged down on the POW issue.

At about this time, May 1952, General Ridgway left Tokyo to become Supreme Allied Commander, Europe. Gen. Mark *Clark, who had made his reputation during World War II in Italy, replaced Ridgway as CINCUNC and inherited a difficult situation. Unable to carry the war to the enemy in a decisive way and stalemated in the armistice talks, Clark—with the approval of the administration—finally ordered the UN delegation to walk out of Panmunjom on 8 October. With no one to talk to, the Communists hammered away at UN treatment of POWs and alleged UN violations of the neutral zones surrounding the negotiating site.

Over the fall and winter of 1952–53, three events broke the impasse. In November, Dwight D. *Eisenhower won the election for the presidency, ushering in a new style of toughness toward the Communists—including discussion of using atomic weapons. In December, Clark read about an International Red Cross resolution calling for the exchange of sick and wounded POWs. In February 1953 Clark sent letters to the Chinese and North Korean leaders proposing that they exchange the sick and wounded. Before the Communists could respond, the third and perhaps most important event occurred: Josef *Stalin died on 5 March 1953.

So achieving a cease-fire was the result of a complex set of circumstances and interwoven pressures. Eisenhower's toughness increased the pressure on the battlefield. He believed that the Truman strategy was the only practical one, but still something ought to be done to give the Communists an incentive to reach agreement. He permitted Clark's ⸜raft to bomb dams in North Korea, flooding the coun-⸜de. He instructed the JCS to prepare plans for more ⸜ive maneuver—even atomic warfare—should nego-⸜break down. He authorized movement of atomic ⸜aircraft to the Far East and initiated training for ⸜ttack with atomic bombs. And he sent John Fos-⸜his Secretary of State, to India in April to let it

be known that the United States was prepared to renew the war at a higher level unless progress was made at Panmunjom.

Clearly, Chinese leaders carefully considered these news signals, but it is conjectural to connect Ike's toughness and Stalin's death directly to the Communist agreement to end the war. Still, we do know that Stalin's death resulted in a deadly power struggle in the Kremlin that probably focused Soviet leaders on settling their internal problems rather than supporting a prolonged war. Moreover, East European states needed to be kept in line after Stalin's death, and something had to be done to restore deteriorating relations with the governments of China and North Korea, both of which had lost confidence in the Soviet government for not taking a more active part in the war.

On 26 April, negotiating sessions resumed at Panmunjom where a final solution to handling the remaining POWs took shape in the months that followed. Those who chose not to go home were to be turned over to a neutral repatriation commission. If they still did not want to go home, the neutral commission would release them to whichever government they chose. As the delegations wrapped up the details, it seemed that a cease-fire was not far off.

While the UN worked diligently toward an armistice, South Korean President Syngman Rhee became obstructive. Rhee saw the rush toward an armistice as contrary to South Korea's best interest, and he did not trust the Communists should the UN Command pull out. So on the night of 18 June, Rhee ordered his guards on the POW compounds to release some 25,000 friendly North Koreans. The Communists cried "foul." Eisenhower, feeling betrayed, was outraged. But in order to save the cease-fire, he negotiated with the South Korean president, pledging a mutual security pact after the cease-fire, long term economic aid, expansion of the South Korean armed forces, and coordination of U.S. and ROK objectives at the political conference. Though costly for the United States, the agreement secured Rhee's cooperation and cleared the way for an armistice.

While negotiating the final details of a truce, the Chinese communists sought one last military advantage. They mounted a limited offensive that was designed to push UN negotiators toward a settlement more agreeable to the Communist side; managed carefully, the offensive might also create the illusion of a peaceful settlement following a Communist victory. The attacks began on 10 June 1951 and by 16 June the UN line had been pushed back some 4,000 yards. Although some ground was recovered, fighting slackened as commanders of contending armies prepared to sign the truce. At 10 A.M. 27 July 1953, the darkest moment in Mark Clark's life, he signed the armistice documents to end the Korean War.

For a war intended to be limited, the human toll was staggering. Although Chinese and North Korean casualties are unknown, estimates of total losses amounted to almost two million, plus perhaps a million civilians. The UN Command suffered a total of 88,000 killed, of which 23,300 were American. Total casualties for the UN (killed, wounded, missing) were 459,360, 300,000 of whom were South Korean.

Nevertheless, limiting the war in Korea made a significant contribution to the history of the art of war. First, the Korean War demonstrated alternative strategies designed to gain national objectives without resorting to atomic war. For this reason, the Korean War is less about tactical evolution than about political goals, the strategy to achieve those goals, and the operational art designed to make the strategy succeed. Second, the war caused the U.S. government to arm the nation and its allies on a permanent basis and to bring its military force to a high state of combat readiness, prepared to respond quickly to any threat to national or alliance security. Never again would the United States find itself as ill-prepared as it had been when the Korean War began.

[See also Korea, U.S. Military Involvement in; Korean War, U.S. Air Operations in; Korean War, U.S. Naval Operations in.]

• Mark W. Clark, From the Danube to the Yalu, 1954. Roy E. Appleman, South to the Naktong, North to the Yalu, June-November 1950, 1961. Walter G. Hermes, Truce Tent and Fighting Front, 1966. Matthew B. Ridgway, The Korean War, 1967. J. Lawton Collins, War in Peacetime, 1969. James E. Schnabel, Policy and Direction, the First Year, 1972. Joseph C. Goulden, Korea: the Untold Story of the War, 1982. D. Clayton James, The Years of MacArthur: Triumph and Disaster, 1945–1964, 1995. Burton I. Kaufman, The Korean War: Challenges in Crisis, Credibility and Command, 1986. Rosemary Foot, A Substitute for Victory: The Policy of Peacemaking at the Korean Armistice Talks, 1990. Shu Guang Zhang, Deterrence and Strategic Culture: Chinese American Confrontations, 1949–1958, 1992.
—Roy K. Flint

KOREAN WAR, U.S. AIR OPERATIONS IN THE. Aerial operations controlled and conducted by the U.S. Air Force (USAF) played a major part in the prosecution of the Korean War by the *United Nations Command. These operations fell into several categories: the campaign to gain and retain aerial superiority over the North Korean and later the Chinese Communist air forces; the bombing campaign against military and industrial targets in North Korea; close air support to the ground forces of the United Nations; airlift operations, both intratheater and intertheater; coordination of air assets provided not only by the USAF but the U.S. Navy and Marine Corps and a half dozen other UN air forces. In addition, there were many other duties, such as search and rescue operations, aeromedical evacuation, aerial reconnaissance, and air defense operations over the Korean peninsula and Japan.

The Far East Air Force (FEAF) controlled and coordinated all operations from its headquarters in Japan through four subordinate commands: the Fifth Air Force (responsible for close air support, interdiction, and reconnaissance); Bomber Command (responsible for strategic bombing); Combat Cargo Command; and the Japan Air Defense Force. In practice, however, the U.S. Navy and the U.S. Marine Corps were semiautonomous in their air operations.

During the opening weeks of the war in July and August 1950, the close air support provided by the FEAF was often responsible for the survival of the ground forces, and throughout the war, it was often the decisive factor in ground combat. This critical support came at a price, however. The USAF had considered close air support obsolescent after World War II and had virtually abandoned it, closing down the Tactical Air Command responsible for the mission. As a result, the FEAF had neither equipment nor trained personnel, and had to resort to inappropriate aircraft, including strategic bombers and high-speed jet aircraft, for bombing missions supporting ground forces. *Friendly fire casualties were common among ground troops. The Marine Corps, by contrast, had emphasized close air support in the postwar years, and its pilots were trained and had the planes to deliver accurate ordnance in support of ground troops. Throughout the war, Marine aircraft were the supporting weapon of choice among ground troops of all services.

The Korean War occurred as all air forces were making the transition from propeller-driven craft to jets. The Chinese forces had the best jet fighter early in the war in the Soviet-supplied MiG-15, until the USAF F-86 Sabrejet arrived, late in 1950. The Sabrejets quickly became the "MiG killers"; by the end of the war, FEAF had downed more than 950 enemy aircraft, while losing only 147 in air-to-air combat.

The Strategic Bombing Survey ordered after World War II had convinced aerial planners that it was critical to concentrate on one key component of an opponent's assets for victory in a bombing campaign. In the little-industrialized country of North Korea, such strategic targets were sparse; FEAF settled on the electrical power grid—particularly the large dams that generated hydroelectric power near the Chinese border—and in the waning months of the war on agricultural irrigation dams. Both campaigns were largely successful in achieving their goals of destruction, but their effect on shortening the war is debatable.

The political aim of avoiding a wider war prohibited bombing outside North Korea's borders. This provided a sanctuary for enemy aircraft in Manchuria, a bitter frustration for U.S. airmen throughout the war. Often forgotten, however, is that by tacit agreement Chinese aircraft did not bomb FEAF bases in Japan or South Korea, providing the United Nations a sanctuary as well.

Airpower achieved several important innovations during the Korean War. Delivery of personnel and supplies was much improved, particularly using the C-119 "Flying Boxcar." Given the primitive road network on the Korean peninsula, delivery by parachute was often the only way of getting supplies to isolated areas. Parachute delivery of bombs allowed bombers to fly much lower and to drop with far greater accuracy on such targets as bridges.

Helicopter operations became routine, foreshadowing their role in the *Vietnam War. *Helicopters were used for search and rescue of downed aviators on land and sea; for medical evacuation from the battlefield; for tactical reconnaissance and staff transport; and, to a limited degree, for moving troops on the battlefield.

In the aftermath of the war, advocates of airpower maintained an exaggerated primacy for aerial weapons in bringing it to a close, not unlike the arguments that would be used after the *Persian Gulf War.

[See also Bomber Aircraft; Bombs; Fighter Aircraft; Korean War; Korean War: U.S. Air Operations in the; Strategy: Air Warfare Strategy; Tactics: Air Warfare Tactics.]

• Robert F. Futrell, The United States Air Force in Korea 1950–195? 1983. Richard P. Hallion, The Naval Air War in Korea, 1986.
—Kenneth E. Hamb?

KOREAN WAR, U.S. NAVAL OPERATIONS IN ? addition to the role of the U.S. *Marine Corps, ? and planes of the U.S. *Navy played a vital role i? rean War (1950–1953). When President Harr?

ordered U.S. forces to try to block the North Korean invasion of South Korea, the first units deployed were aircraft from the navy and the air force. U.S. naval forces in the western Pacific in 1950 included Vice Admiral C. Turner Joy's force in Japan consisting of a light cruiser and four destroyers and the Seventh Fleet in the Philippines under Vice Admiral Arthur D. Struble, comprising the carrier *Valley Forge*, a heavy cruiser, and several destroyers and submarines. Since the North Korean navy consisted only of 45 small craft, these U.S. naval vessels eventually joined by the British light carrier *Triumph* and a some other warships, took command of the seas around the Korean peninsula. Naval and air force planes also quickly destroyed the small North Korean air force. This allowed the forces of the *United Nations to move and be supplied unimpeded and it enabled carrier-based planes and sometimes surface ships to bombard the enemy forces and supply lines.

The navy's most dramatic exploit was the *Inchon Landing (1950), a daring amphibious envelopment planned by Gen. Douglas *MacArthur, Commander in Chief Far East, to capture the South Korean capital of Seoul and its port, Inchon, then deep behind North Korean lines. The difficulties were enormous, for Inchon lay behind miles of islands, shoals, and mud flats, approachable from the sea only through two narrow, winding channels. These could be easily mined and if an attacking ship were disabled by mine, bomb, or a shell from the guarding fortified island it would trap those ahead and block those behind. Nevertheless, Admiral Forrest *Sherman, chief of naval operations, agreed, and an international fleet of 230 ships carried the more than 70,000 soldiers and Marines to the successful Inchon landing, catching the defenders, who had not mined the harbor, largely by surprise.

Later, when the Chinese intervened and the war turned against the U.N. forces again, the navy evacuated 100,000 army and Marine forces from the northeast coast. Despite the Chinese advances, air strikes from land- and ship-based planes destroyed bridges and interdicted roads and railroads by day. Truman rejected MacArthur's proposal to widen the war by bombing the Peoples Republic of China and using the Seventh Fleet to blockade its coasts and transport Nationalist Chinese troops from Taiwan to fight in Korea or mainland China. But the communist forces were soon halted in 1951 and agreed to truce talks.

Naval success in the Korean War, in particular the Inchon landing and the continual employment of carrier-based air attacks, won congressional support for an expanded navy, including supercarriers, to implement the navy's forward maritime strategy in the Cold War.

[See also Korean War: U.S. Air Operations in the; Navy, U.S.: Since 1946.]

• James A. Field, Jr., *United States Naval Operations, Korea*, 1962; Richard P. Hallion, *The Naval Air War in Korea*, 1986; Allan R. Millett, "Korea, 1950–1953," in Benjamin Franklin Cooling, ed., *Case Studies in the Development of Close Air Support*, 1990.

—John Whiteclay Chambers II

SCIUSZKO, THADDEUS (1746–17), Polish patriot, lutionary War general. Revered for his role in Poland's al struggles, Thaddeus Kosciuszko was also a significure in the Revolutionary War, principally for his ex-s a military engineer. Born in the province of sciuszko was educated in Poland's finer schools,

and enlisted in its Corps of Cadets before departing for advanced training in *artillery and engineering at Paris. Returning to Poland in 1774, he found his country divided, his family finances in disarray, and opportunities in North America appealing. In mid-1776, he sought a *Continental army commission.

The Polish captain stood out in an army bereft of military engineers, a shortage of immense concern to Washington and Congress. On 18 October 1776, Congress commissioned Kosciuszko a colonel and later authorized an *Army Corps of Engineers, long delayed by the dearth of qualified candidates. The arrival of Louis Le Bègue de Presie Duportail with a coterie of French veterans hastened the Corps' formation but slowed Kosciuszko's ascent, for the two men distrusted one another. Nevertheless, Kosciuszko served with distinction throughout the war, most notably in laying out West Point's defenses, fatally slowing Gen. John *Burgoyne's 1777 expedition below Ticonderoga, and selecting the battlefield for the American victory at Bemis Heights.

[See also Engineering, Military; Revolutionary War: Military and Diplomatic Course.]

• Miecislaus Haiman, *Kosciuszko in the American Revolution*, 1972.

—J. Mark Thompson

KOSOVO CRISIS (1999). In spring 1999, a major crisis erupted over Kosovo, the southernmost province of the Federal Republic of Yugoslavia, with the forces of Yugoslavian president Slobodan Milosevic escalating a terrorist campaign to drive out the ethnic Albanian Muslim majority and ensure dominance of the historic region by the Serbian Orthodox Christian minority. When Milosevic had earlier revoked the province's semi-autonomous status and begun the persecution, ethnic Albanians had protested, then formed a rebel terrorist group, the Kosovo Liberation Army, seeking independence. In early 1999, *NATO sponsored talks between Kosovo Albanians and Serbs in Rambouillet, France, but although the Kosovo Albanians grudgingly accepted a proposed settlement for broad autonomy for the province for three years (with possible independence afterwards) and 28,000 NATO troops in Kosovo and Serbia to enforce it, the Serbs rejected it.

Milosevic increased his forces in Kosovo and began mass terrorism of the ethnic Albanian population, killing some inhabitants to frighten the rest and burning entire villages. NATO had already authorized the use of force, and on 23 March 1999, President Bill *Clinton declared that military means were necessary to halt the Serbian aggression. The next day, NATO forces began an extensive air assault on targets in Serbia, Montenegro, and Kosovo, the majority of cruise missiles and bombs delivered from American planes and ships. It was the biggest allied military assault in Europe since World War II and NATO's first actual combat, but Serbian forces quickly continued to drive ethnic Albanian refugees—ultimately a million of them—from their homes into neighboring Macedonia, Montenegro, and Albania, as the Kosovo Crisis threatened to spread throughout the Balkans.

In the next ten weeks, NATO waged an escalating air war against military and other targets in Serbia and Kosovo, flying 35,000 missions, including 10,000 in which 23,000 bombs or missiles were dropped. Hampered by bad weather and political fears in the alliance, the air campaign started slowly and ineffectively, but over time, more aggressive bombing and the use of *precision-guided munitions enabled NATO to destroy numerous military targets as well as targets in the urban infrastructure, including ultimately electricity grids and water supplies. NATO estimated that at least 5,000 Yugoslavian soldiers and police were killed (Serbia said 600); in addition, perhaps 1,200 civilians died as a result of mistaken bombings of trains, hospitals, and most prominently, the Chinese embassy in Belgrade. NATO lost only two aircraft, one of them a Stealth fighter, but both American pilots were rescued. By the end of May, a ground offensive along the Kosovo borders by the rebel Kosovo Liberation Army dislodged many Serbian forces out of their hiding places, allowing NATO aircraft to destroy them. The civilian population in the Serbian cities was suffering deprivation from the bombings. Although the British government pressed for a ground attack, political opposition to the war grew within Italy, Greece, and Germany, and the resolve of the NATO alliance showed signs of weakening.

On 3 June 1999, responding to the deteriorating situation and pressed by Russian and Finnish envoys, Milosevic declared that he accepted an international peace plan aimed at ending the Kosovo conflict and allowing the ethnic Albanian refugees to return to what remained of their homes in Kosovo. Under its terms, all of the 40,000 Serbian military and police forces would withdraw rapidly from Kosovo which they did beginning 10 June, following another week of bombing, and some 50,000 foreign troops all under a *United Nations flag—many of them, including an estimated 7,000 U.S. forces, from NATO and under NATO command—would move in to police the province. Independence for Kosovo was not part of the new proposal, instead there would be "substantial autonomy" to be decided by the UN Security Council. The sixteen-member NATO alliance had held together long enough to force Milosevic to let the Kosovar refugees return, but what remained uncertain was the ultimate future of Kosovo as well as the long-term use of NATO military forces in such wars and *peacekeeping operations in the twenty-first century.

[See also Bosnian Crisis.]

• Traian Stoianovich, Balkan Worlds: The First and Last Europe, 1994. Susan L. Woodward, Balkan Tragedy: Chaos and Dissolution after the Cold War, 1995. Miranda Vickers, Between Serb and Albanian: A History of Kosovo, 1998. Greg Campell, The Road to Kosovo: A Balkan Diary, 1999.

—John Whiteclay Chambers II

KOSZKIOWSKO, TADEUSZ. See Kosciuszko, Thaddeus.

L

LABOR AND WAR. The relationship between the paid labor force (union and nonunion workers) and the government at war is twofold. First, any country engaged in hostilities needs the ability to employ an ever-increasing proportion of the general population in both military service and defense industries. In the twentieth century, demands for wartime labor increased dramatically from earlier centuries. Labor shortages were among the greatest obstacles to steady production of armaments and war materiel and the mobilization of mass armies. Need for labor increased its value, necessitating serious consideration of workers' demands. As a result, the major wars of the twentieth century witnessed record levels of union growth and labor militancy. Such militancy was further spurred by inflation and food and housing shortages. At the same time, political pressure to produce materiel and to reduce social conflict provided the context for the suppression of civil liberties and the right to organize and collectively bargain with employers. Both world wars were followed by prolonged civil conflict, political repression—especially on the basis of class politics—and widespread antiunion sentiment. The Red Scare of 1919, McCarthyism in the 1950s, and the *Cold War had detrimental effects on organized labor and workers' welfare in general, leading to antiunion activism, labor legislation that undermined union legitimacy, and declines in membership.

The *Revolutionary War and the *Civil War, while massive in their social impact, were little affected by battles over labor. In the both cases, domestic military conflict and its drain on labor power were confined to local areas, undercut by the widespread use of mercenaries in the Revolution and by military bounties and paid substitutes for those conscripted in the Civil War. In the Civil War, military forces in excess of 1 million men exacted far greater strain on the Southern economy than on the Northern. Wartime laborers seemed to acquire few gains from participation either as soldiers or as workers in defense industry. The production of armaments and supplies expanded, but the demands on the labor force were comparably light. Hundreds of thousands of workers volunteered or served as conscripts in the armed forces, but millions more were able to continue regular lives. Resistance to the draft in New York City, and in outlying regions such as the anthracite country of Pennsylvania, did have a class character, as workers were little able to afford the costs of substitutes and draft quotas appeared to be rigged to weed out political rivals and labor militants. Some workers abandoned their occupations and fledgling unions to join the "Christian Soldiers" of the republic. Under the banner of free labor, Northern workingmen fought the war as a crusade. Southern urban workingmen, far less organized or numerous, nonetheless went to battle, oftentimes to defend states' rights, or (some have argued) to prevent the use of slaves in industry.

Few labor unions survived the Civil War. What did remain was a loose confederation of local unions. Fearing prosecution for conspiracy and blacklisting in the workplace, workers often formed secret associations (such as the Molly Maguires) to elude political and economic repercussions; and they echoed fraternal and military orders in their organization. Such precautions were necessary, given the widespread use of troops in labor conflict. Yet the activists of the 1870s and 1880s often were *veterans of the Civil War and members of the *Grand Army of the Republic. By the 1880s, they publicly acknowledged both their veteran status and their status as "workingmen" in political campaigns. Much labor protest of the period was framed in the language of the *citizen-soldier, who had sacrificed his country and deserved his share of prosperity.

At the end of the century, the labor movement found its strongest expression in the American Federation of Labor (AFL), a conservative trade union organization. Labor employed military metaphor to describe both conflict and solidarity, sharing much with the political language of the time. As a further consequence, the AFL shared republican suspicion of *expansionism and contributed to the debate over U.S. entry into the *Spanish-American War. Small in scale and short in duration, that war required little additional armament production; volunteer soldiers provided its military labor force. Labor's gains and losses were few. Still, as the United States debated territorial acquisitions from Spain and its new status as a world power, the U.S. labor movement made itself heard in opposition to annexation of colonies.

European colonial expansion, an escalating *arms race, and increasing ethnic and nationalist tensions laid the preconditions for World War I. The onset of war in Europe and later entry of the United States presented labor with its first major political crisis of the twentieth century. Labor leaders, socialist advocates, and rank-and-file unionists were deeply divided over the role the United States should play, their support for both military preparedness and the draft, and their response to the final Treaty of *Versailles. While the Socialist Party and the Industrial Workers of the World opposed U.S. participation and its policy of military *conscription, the AFL and the Railway Brotherhoods (which constituted the great bulk of organized labor) supported the Wilson administration's decisions. The AFL voluntarily offered a "no-strike" pledge, and its leaders participated in many governmental bodies that regulated defense industries. Labor leaders sought to parlay bargaining power from the convergence of labor shortages and the new position of organized labor in government. Nearly 5 million soldiers, the majority draftees, entered the wartime army. Their absence created a great void in domestic industrial production and service. For the first time, large numbers of women workers replaced men in defense industries.

Wartime inflation and the context of fighting a "war for democracy" (and, by extension, for industrial democracy) encouraged the rapid growth of unions and labor militancy, even in such nonunion strongholds as mass production industries (textiles, steel, meatpacking) and clerical and service sectors (including police, telephone operators, and transport workers). Government administration of the railroads created the first Federal Mediation Board for labor disputes. Union membership was phenomenal, the numbers rising from 3 million (1916) to 5 million after the war. In 1919 huge strikes, such as those in the steel industry and meatpacking, mobilized 1 million workers to strike for better wages, working conditions, and the right to bargain collectively. A postwar Red Scare involving the imprisonment and deportation of radicals, the use of troops to suppress strikes, and the depression soon quelled labor militancy. The termination of wartime agencies also removed organized labor from government.

A decade of depression coincided with the resurrection of the labor movement during the 1930s. By the end of the decade, organized labor had the nominal support of the new National Labor Relations Board, millions of new union members, and considerable influence in Democratic Party politics. When the United States started to rearm and mobilize its army in 1940 in response to fascism in Europe and the expansion of Japan in Asia, the labor movement was in the best bargaining position in its history.

During World War II, the massive efforts of the United States in war production and the addition of over 16 million men and women to the armed forces led to an unprecedented drain on labor power and to new government intervention in employment. Several agencies were created to facilitate and regulate hiring (the War Manpower Commission and the U.S. Employment Agency), to set production goals (the War Production Board), and to intervene in labor relations (the War Labor Board). In each, leaders from organized labor played a major role. Wartime policy sought to prevent the pirating of skilled labor in vital defense industries—shipbuilding, aircraft, and armaments. At the same time, political pressure—from both labor and civil rights organizations—strove to maintain labor standards (wages and hours) during the war, and to make some inroads against race and sex discrimination (Executive Order 8802 established the Committee on Fair Employment Practices).

Organized labor, in the form of the Congress of Industrial Organizations (CIO) and the AFL offered the cooperation and support of unions, an offer that culminated in the CIO's no-strike pledge. In return, major industrial unions received guarantees on wages and union membership. Dues were no longer collected individually but through the "dues check-off" from paychecks in unionized firms. Unions pushed for—and often received—the guarantee that the job, if not the worker, would remain unionized. High demand for labor, guaranteed profits in defense industries, and the War Labor Board's favorable policies resulted in a membership increase of nearly 50 percent, from 9 million to 14.5 million.

Yet workers in defense industries were not entirely cooperative. Wartime inflation, increased pressures in production industry, tight control of the workplace, and the no-strike pledge opened the door to "wildcat" strikes (work stoppages unsanctioned by unions). Further complications arose with the increase in the paid labor force of African American and Latino workers and women as well. Minority workers occasionally met with conflict, and in certain factories, white workers conducted hate strikes. Women workers were trained but not always placed in defense production jobs. When they arrived on the shop floor, veteran workingmen, who viewed women as temporary replacements at best, were sometimes hostile. Both during and after the war, mass production in steel, mining, aircraft, and other defense industries was the target of a new, broad-based militancy. Mobilization reached its peak after the war, in 1946, when the greatest number of workers in U.S. history went on strike.

In the postwar world, the United States entered into a long-standing conflict with the Soviet Union, a Cold War fought in economic, ideological, even military terms. Though the two nations never fought one another on the battlefield, each was involved in small "hot" wars—especially in regions recently emerged from colonialism. Domestically, these developments found expression in McCarthyism, and organized labor was one of its targets. At the same time, the escalating *arms race between the United States and the USSR led to an expansion of defense industries and a continued high wage economy in this highly unionized sector. The labor movement supported U.S. foreign policy and the military interventions around the globe that came under the rubric of "containment." Unions on the home front even voluntarily purged members who refused to sign anti-Communist affidavits required by the Taft-Hartley labor law.

The *Vietnam War, the major military action stemming from containment policy, lost the long-standing support of mainstream labor. Initial union support for U.S. intervention in Vietnam was followed, in the late sixties and seventies, by individual and later organizational opposition to the war. The United Auto Workers were among the first publicly to oppose U.S. policy under the Johnson and Nixon administrations. Newspapers reported confrontations between "hard-hat workers" and war protesters, yet the actual stance of workers and their union organizations was far more complex. Working-class disillusionment with U.S. foreign policy, and, in particular, the growing belief in unequal sacrifice—"a rich man's war and a poor man's fight"—led to growing opposition to the war.

Overall, the contemporary labor movement has followed an increasingly autonomous path in foreign policy. In one prominent case, labor joined in domestic opposition to U.S. military aid to governments in Central American conflicts. Though such efforts express an incipient *internationalism, organized labor remains primarily a national movement, combining a strong voice for workers' rights with working-class patriotism, and a history of labor militancy with an equally militant history of working-class support for the nation in time of war.

[See also Agriculture and War; Class and War; Industry and War; Vietnam Antiwar Movement; War: Effects of War on the Economy.]

• Alexander M. Bing, *Wartime Strikes and Their Adjustment*, 1921. Joel Seidman, *American Labor from Defense to Reconversion*, 1953. David Montgomery, *Beyond Equality*, 1967. Ronald Radosh,

American Labor and U.S. Foreign Policy, 1969. Frank Grubbs, *Gompers and the Great War,* 1982. Nelson Lichtenstein, *Labor's War at Home,* 1983. Ruth Milkman, *Gender at Work,* 1986. Philip Foner, *U.S. Labor and the Vietnam War,* 1989. Peter Levy, *The New Left and Labor in the 1960s,* 1994.

—Elizabeth Faue

LAFAYETTE, MARQUIS DE (1757–1834), French statesman and *Revolutionary War general. The marquis de Lafayette was the most influential Frenchman in the early American republic. The prospect of military advancement and an affinity for republican principles drew the young cavalry captain to join the *Continental army during the Revolutionary War. Americans appreciated his powerful court connections, unwavering enthusiasm for their cause, and offer to serve without pay. Despite Congress's growing irritation with troublesome foreign adventurers, the nineteen-year-old nobleman acquired, on 31 July 1777, a major general's commission in the army, albeit without pay or a command.

Lafayette's notable services, first at the Battle of Brandywine in September 1777, eventually won him his own troops. In 1778, Congress designated him to head the proposed invasion of Canada, a plan eventually canceled; then George *Washington gave him a division to strike the British near Monmouth, an assignment that Charles *Lee ultimately claimed on the basis of higher rank. Lafayette finally led six light infantry battalions in 1780 and a Light Corps in 1781, moving to the Southern Department, where his troops help confine Charles *Cornwallis's army to the Virginia coast and set up the decisive siege of Yorktown.

Lafayette remained a supporter of the United States during the French Revolution, despite considerable risk to himself and his family. In 1824–25, he returned to the United States for a triumphal tour that symbolized the passing of the revolutionary generation.

[*See also* Revolutionary War: Military and Diplomatic Course; Yorktown, Battle of.]

• Louis Gottschalk, *Lafayette Joins the American Army,* 1937. Louis Gottschalk, *Lafayette and the Close of the American Revolution,* 1942. Stanley J. Idzerda, ed., *Lafayette in the Age of the American Revolution: Selected Letters and Papers, 1776–1790,* 1977– .

—J. Mark Thompson

LAIRD, MELVIN R. (1922–), secretary of defense, 1969–73. Laird began his political career in the Republican Party after military service in World War II, serving in the Wisconsin State Senate (1946–52) and then in the U.S. House of Representatives (1953–69). President Richard M. *Nixon appointed him secretary of defense in 1969.

Under Laird's leadership, the *Pentagon experienced cuts in military spending, the closing of military installations, and withdrawal of forces in the *Vietnam War. However, he pleased the services by ending many procurement policies of Secretary of Defense Robert S. *McNamara. During Laird's tenure, the United States under the *Nixon Doctrine urged its allies to do more for their common defense via emphasis on regional alliances and increases in their defense budgets.

Besides focusing on Vietnam, Laird also dealt with arms control issues and changes in the military draft. In 1972, the United States and USSR agreed to a treaty limiting each country to two antiballistic missile sites of 100 missiles each. In response to controversy over inequities in *conscription, Laird helped move to "zero draft calls" and an *All-Volunteer Force by 1972.

—Mark R. Polelle

LAND WARFARE. By definition, warfare involves military operations to defeat an adversary to attain political, economic, or social ends. It is conducted on behalf of a nation-state, international coalition, or other political entity, usually, or at least initially, in accordance with a strategy formulated to achieve specific ends. Actual warfare, however, may not be necessary to compel or deter an adversary's behavior; the threat of military force may be sufficient.

Though conducted on land, modern land warfare doctrine incorporates the combined capabilities of landpower, seapower, and airpower to achieve operational objectives. Land warfare integrates maneuver of forces and firepower, in coordination with air and naval support, to take advantage of an adversary's weaknesses, avoid his strengths, and defeat him in the accomplishment of assigned campaign objectives with minimum expenditure of resources. Complete victory over an adversary is assured only through land force dominance.

Technology has played a central role in defining how armies fight to win wars. Historically, the application of technology to weaponry, beginning with the bow and later the musket, has allowed combatants to fight at ever-increasing ranges and with greater lethality. Today, enemy targets can be engaged at ranges where they are seen on an electronic device solely as an item of electromagnetic, infrared, or acoustic data.

Ancient Roots. Land warfare originated in the conflicts of ancient tribes, villages, and city-states. Early combatants on foot engaged in brutal hand-to-hand combat using bare hands and objects within reach, such as stones, to subdue an adversary. To gain some protection by distancing themselves from the dangers of close combat, early fighters used throwing weapons—slings, bows, javelins, and spears. Thus began the cycle of using advancing technology to improve the weapons of war to gain advantage over an enemy.

The Assyrians left one of the earliest records (1000 B.C.) of weaponry, tactics, and battlefield engagements. They were adept at maneuvering military formations to their advantage. Soldiers were armed with bow and arrows, spears and slings; they fought on foot, on horseback, or on horse-drawn chariots. The military capabilities of the Assyrians were enhanced by the combined effect of firepower and maneuver of forces to overwhelm an adversary and ultimately his will to fight. This approach remains the cornerstone of modern military *doctrine.

The Persians further refined the execution of massed firepower and maneuver. In response, the Greeks made use of large formations of well-disciplined infantry; each soldier in the phalanx was protected by a helmet and a large shield and armed with a lengthy spear. The Greeks used the heavily protected formation to reduce the effects of Persian massed fire. The Romans further improved on the use of combat formations by making them more flexible in size and spaced so that spears could be thrown by soldiers while bearing a large shield for protection. Short swords proved highly effective in hand-to-hand combat.

Ancient civilizations have contributed strategists, generals, and great captains who have had lasting effects on the art and science of warfare. Their contributions remain relevant to modern land warfare doctrine, often articulated in principles of war and their application in battle. Current U.S. Army doctrine recognizes nine principles: objective, offensive, mass, economy of force, maneuver, unity of command, security, surprise, and simplicity.

Ancient military thinkers and generals included China's Sun Tzu (ca. 500 B.C.), who defined the fundamentals that underlie modern-day principles of war; Alexander the Great (ca. 300 B.C.) of Greece, who conquered Persia, Egypt, and India, adapting firepower, movement, and organization to the nuances of his enemies; Hannibal (ca. 200 B.C.), the Carthaginian, who crossed the Alps into Italy, avoiding Rome's major forces, then marched through foreboding terrain to surprise and defeat other Roman legions; and Julius Caesar (ca. 50 B.C.), the Roman who adapted the tactics of the legion to the terrain and enemy, maintained the discipline of soldiers in battle, and attacked at the decisive time and place to defeat tribes of Gaul (France). Other great captains have included Gustavus Adolphus of Sweden (seventeenth century); Marlborough of England and the Prussian Frederick the Great (both eighteenth century); and France's Napoleon Bonaparte (nineteenth century). Historians debate who are the great captains of the twentieth century.

Evolution of Land Warfare. The weapons of ancient land warfare that brought about significant changes included the short bow, sling, and javelin. Chariots gave soldiers a mobile, stable platform from which to employ weapons. The soldier wore helmet, breastplate, and shin guards; protection also came from a shield. He was armed with a spear, ax, or sword. City-states were defended by works of earth and stone. They were besieged by opposing armies using towers, battering rams, catapults, and flame weapons.

In the first millennium A.D., the soldier on horseback used a saddle and stirrup to provide a stable platform and leverage to employ his weapons. The individual mounted soldier replaced the two-horsed chariot with driver and archer. This saved resources by reducing the number of soldiers per horse and also forage. The long bow and the cross-bow were used on the battlefield at the start of the second millennium.

The battlefield of the 1400s saw the introduction of gunpowder, cannon, and musket—missile weapons. This gave armies the ability to inflict significant *casualties on opposing forces at a distance. The musket also ended the dominance of the armored knights on horseback. During the next four centuries, the increasing improvements and variety of cannon, *artillery, and firearms further revolutionized the battlefield. The bullet, more lethal explosives, improved powders, fuse, shrapnel, the accuracy of rifled weapons, artillery that could be breech-loaded, the repeating rifle, and *machine guns beginning in the late nineteenth century increased rates of fire, range, and casualties. With the Industrial Revolution came the means to mass-produce weapons. Mobility was enhanced first by the locomotive and then by the internal combustion engine. The telegraph gave commanders the ability to control operations from great distances, and the political hierarchy a means to keep rein on field commanders.

More lethal weapons meant ever greater casualties, particularly among the mass *conscription armies of the nine-teenth and early twentieth centuries. This was evident in the era of Napoleon, the American *Civil War, the Russo-Japanese War, and in *World War I, the last with the extensive use of artillery, the machine gun, and chemical weapons.

The airplane and armored tank were introduced in World War I to overcome the stagnation and attrition of *trench warfare. The two systems became the centerpieces of war fighting in World War II and remain so to this day. The breadth and depth of military operations were greatly expanded by these systems; warfare could be extended to the industrial capabilities of the enemy and their civilian populations. *Radar, advanced communications, and encryption were added to *World War II capabilities.

The mobility inherent in World War II mechanized forces, with their improved firepower, supporting close air support, and artillery preparations, allowed attacking forces to engage an opposing force at its point of greatest vulnerability while avoiding its strengths. This combined arms approach, used initially with great success by the Germans in World War II, was adopted by the Allies and has provided the framework for the weapons, tactics, and doctrine of land armies throughout the *Cold War era.

Modern Land Warfare. The information revolution of the post–Cold War period, exemplified by the modern computer and coupled with rapidly expanding technological innovations in materials, propellants, and electronics, is revolutionizing land warfare.

Traditional land war systems now have microminiaturized components. Near real-time dissemination of information, ground positioning systems, satellites, laser designation of targets, increased lethality and accuracy of laser-guided warheads, and improved armor protection all are examples of the new generations of technological adaptations, occurring every few years, that define the core process of emerging modern warfare. The twenty-first century will include information warfare, making the field commander aware of the friendly and enemy situations in real time while thwarting the enemy's attempts to do the same.

The accelerated pace of improvements can be seen in the modern-day U.S. battle tank. The operational readiness of the U.S. Army M1A1 Main Battle Tank in the *Persian Gulf War with Iraq (1991) exceeded 90 percent, even after four days of almost continuous operation. In a night movement across open desert, all tanks—more than 300 of them—arrived at their destinations, demonstrating their excellent reliability. M1A1 tanks that received frontal hits from antitank rounds sustained little or no damage. The special armor was made of depleted uranium. The thermal night sight gave crews the ability to see through smoke; the laser range finder, with gun stabilization on the move, allowed crews to destroy targets at ranges that exceeded 3 kilometers. The 120mm antitank round, using a depleted uranium core, penetrated the earthen berms protectin enemy tanks and destroyed them.

An individual soldier with night-vision equipment see at night. The combat soldier can designate targets *lasers for engagement by artillery and armed *helic fire antitank "smart" rounds, and use a should heat-seeking antiaircraft missile system again close air support aircraft and helicopters. He ca position within a few feet with a hand-held gl device that receives the information from reconnaissance *satellites.

Fire support for the soldier includes artillery weapons that fire smart rounds to seek out and destroy tanks from overhead. Artillery projectiles also scatter antipersonnel and antitank mines over terrain the enemy might use. A counterbattery radar system can backtrack the path of enemy projectiles to the launch site and automatically provide location information, telling friendly forces where to fire. Modern ground forces use aircraft in traditional close air support roles. Add to this capability the missile-armed helicopter, which can maneuver against and engage enemy tanks by day or night; during periods of reduced visibility, using *missiles that can hit targets designated by a laser or emitting infrared emissions, it can hit targets otherwise invisible to the naked eye.

Twenty-first–Century Land Warfare. Since the Gulf War, the international arena has seen few purely military operations; most efforts are humanitarian or for *peacekeeping. The United States, with the strategic capabilities to respond promptly, has supported numerous operations, including those in Somalia, Rwanda, Haiti, Bosnia, and Macedonia.

Weapons of mass destruction, including chemical, biological, and even *nuclear weapons, particularly under the control of rogue states and terrorists, pose an additional destructive dimension in land warfare. Compounding this situation, several states are gaining ballistic missile capabilities that can launch these terrifying weapons on the battlefield and elsewhere as terrorist weapons. The challenge is preparing for this diverse, unpredictable future, which will be further complicated by the availability on the world market of relatively inexpensive advanced weapons systems to lesser powers.

Technology will continue to expand and provide exponential improvements to traditional weapons systems. The success of this revolution in land warfare depends on the ability of individuals to use the systems under extreme conditions on the battlefield. Balances of automation, robotics, and the ability to process selective information in order to make good decisions—by the tank gunner to fire at a target or the corps commander to launch a combined arms attack at the right time and place—will have to be continually assessed. Warfare, ancient and modern, still depends on the initiative, tenacity, and competence of the soldiers and generals who do the fighting.

[See also Army, U.S.; Strategy; Land Warfare Strategy; Tactics: Land Warfare Tactics; War.]

• Carl von Clausewitz, On War, 1833; repr. 1976. Basil H. Liddell Hart. The Strategy of Indirect Approach, 1941; repr. 1974. K. Macksey, The Guinness History of Land Warfare, 1973. Chris Bellamy, The Future of Land Warfare, 1987. Archer Jones, The Art of War in the Western World, 1987. R. A. Gabriel, The Culture of War: Invention and Early Development, 1990. Victor Davis Hansen, The Western Way of War, 1990. John Keegan, A History of Warfare, 1993.

—James D. Blundell

LANGUAGE, MILITARY: OFFICIAL TERMINOLOGY.
[Officia]l military terminology takes a wide range of forms, [some int]ended purely for internal use, others meant to rep[resent the] military to the outside. At its most basic level, of[ficial termi]nology functions to narrow the potential mean[ing of parti]cular words. In casual speech, there is often [much a]mbiguity in the way a given word is used.

There can therefore be a wide range of possible interpretations. This is tolerable in informal conversation, where a misunderstanding can usually be rectified; but military organizations must be prepared to operate under great stress, in situations where misunderstanding can lead to catastrophe. Thus, official terminology for internal use attempts to foreclose as many interpretive options as possible in order to reduce the likelihood of error or misjudgment.

As with most specialized language forms, focusing on the function that language plays within an organization is not sufficient. All use of language bears an implicit logic about the world that can provide insight into the organization responsible for that language. Put more broadly, whenever a specialized language exists for the use of a particular group, that language can provide evidence useful in understanding the way the group views itself, its role in the larger world, and the world as a whole. Language use carries with it implicit arguments, which can be made explicit through careful analysis in order better to assess the world view the language helps to create and sustain. The use of language always has embedded within it these implicit arguments. A statement as simple as, "Forward presence is a vital naval mission," contains a variety of assumptions about the likelihood of future conflict, the likely locations of future conflicts, the probability that future conflicts will involve national interests, and the way military power can be manipulated to affect the chance of conflict starting. Language, then, constructs a social reality.

Official military language has at least three characteristics that are revealed through linguistic analysis. It tends to be a sanitized form of language; it emphasizes the expertise of those who use it; and it contains a specific notion of hierarchy.

The language of expertise marks any professional community. Indeed, the ability to use and understand specific technical language is a large part of what determines membership in professional communities. This aspect of technical and professional language is even more marked when the language is in large part characterized by acronyms and jargon that in effect create another language altogether. Technical language of this type emphasizes the expertise necessary for participation and therefore implicitly makes the argument that knowledge of the language serves in effect as a threshold for participation: If you cannot understand and use the language, you mark yourself as being unqualified to participate in the technical debates taking place. This is no less true of official documents emanating from the Department of *Defense (which are likely to make arcane statements such as "SECDEF authorized CINCENT's use of two JSTARS") than those written by doctors, lawyers, or engineers.

Euphemistic language can serve to mask and deemphasize what it is that the words are actually referring to. It is easier to refer to "surgical strikes" and "collateral damage" than to bombing attacks in which civilians are killed. Such indirect language is especially notable in military discussions about the use of *nuclear weapons: phrases like "first," "second," or "preemptive" strikes, or "ride out" and "assured destruction" are preferred over those connoting apocalyptic levels of destruction.

By the same token, this creation of what is virtually another language not only builds a wall between the insider and the outsider but simultaneously reinforces the connection between those who are masters of the form. The ability to control and manipulate an insider linguistic form identifies one as a member of the institution, forging an automatic link between people who have the same ability, while reinforcing the distinction between these insiders and outsiders. Indeed, military service has its own jargon, acronyms, phrases. Not only do different services use different terms; sometimes the same word can mean different things to different services.

Yet another form of official language is used when the military communicates with those on the outside. During conflict, for example, official rhetoric can emphasize the humanitarian concerns with which we go to war, or can distract attention from the costs that are inevitably involved in the use of military power. Descriptions center on the technology that has been destroyed, so that there are reports of the number of sorties successfully completed, the number of aircraft or *tanks destroyed. This permits a focus on the objects, the things, and away from the people close to or within the objects destroyed.

• Peter Berger and Thomas Luckmann, *The Social Construction of Reality*, 1967. George Lakoff and Mark Johnson, *Metaphors We Live By*, 1980. Edward Tabor Linenthal, *Symbolic Defense: The Cultural Significance of the Strategic Defense Initiative*, 1989. Cori Dauber, "Negotiating from Strength: Arms Control and the Rhetoric of Denial," *Political Communication and Persuasion*, 7 (1990), pp. 97–115. Paul Chilton, *Security Metaphors*, 1996.

—Cori Dauber

LANGUAGE, MILITARY: INFORMAL SPEECH. Through language, groups of individuals form what can be termed *discourse communities*. By using slang and jargon unknown to the outsider, individual members of specific groups form bonds of identification with one another. The language used within a given community serves both to construct a vision of the world into which initiates are socialized and to draw a line between those in the group and those on the outside. In official language, this occurs through the use of technical terms—acronyms and jargon. In informal language, it is accomplished by knowledge of terms whose meanings are not available except through direct participation in the group—meanings that appear in no formal glossary.

Informal military language reinforces a service member's primary identity as being part of the group, along with those who share his or her language. Beyond that, informal language constructs a vision of the world that becomes the defining characteristic of group membership. This is done most directly through *naming*. The names we give to things are of vital importance in understanding the view of the world the namers participate in and is an important part of all language use. Names of objects, perhaps more than any other words, constitute implicit arguments. In informal language, names are often metaphors. Sometimes, these metaphors are obscure. When naval officers associated with aviation refer to the surface fleet surrounding and supporting the carriers as "greyhounds," they use language that seems positive, implying an image of sleekness and speed. However, the relationship drawn on is that between dog and master. The argument, in other words, is that the rest of the surface fleet is useful insofar as it serves the needs dictated by the carriers. Similarly, members of the U.S. military who handle *nuclear weapons informally use metaphors, naming places where U.S. nuclear bombs are aimed as "home addresses" and referring to nuclear

missiles on board U.S. *submarines as "Christmas trees." These homey and domestic metaphors convey the meaning that U.S. nuclear weapons, although extraordinarily destructive, are safe for the U.S. military to handle.

Such examples point to another important function of language. The arguments that are implicit in the words we use, particularly the names, often are those that construct hierarchies. Discourse communities use language that possesses its own internal symbolic logic, and this places the members of the community in a hierarchical relationship with those of other communities. Language not only bonds the membership; it also helps construct a world view in which that membership can be secure in the superiority of its knowledge. Because language is never value-neutral but always contains embedded arguments, it is always taking a position on whether that which is named is "good" or "bad." Thus, homey metaphors such as the one about "Christmas trees" bond members of the military community and place a positive value on their work.

This function of informal language will generate terms and labels that differ from official usage in several ways. Such terms may be less euphemistic. This is in part because official terminology is intended as an aid to the institution as it represents itself to outsiders, while informal language is designed to emphasize the insider status of participants. Further, informal language is likely to create a bond between the members of the community even if that bond is created by highlighting divisions between the individuals and the institutions they represent that would not be acceptable in formal use.

In the U.S. military, a proportion of informal language is used to reinforce a worldview that emphasizes the importance of a given service or warfare community versus others. All are members of the military, officially a single institution with the same mission and perspective. Unofficially, informal language creates connections and identity particularly through defining the group in terms of what it is *not*: the navy, then, defines itself in part as being *not* the army or air force. Naval personnel who do not serve on submarines will say that there are two kinds of ships: "submarines and targets." Air force personnel refer to anyone in naval uniform as a "squid." Such distinctions can be achieved through joking and narratives as well. Army personnel will say that "the difference between the Army and the Marines is that the Army will call in air strikes and then take the hill, while the Marines will take the hill and then call in air strikes."

Informal language can also serve, particularly during times of war, to dehumanize the enemy. This can be accomplished, as in official terminology, through the naming of enemy combatants in a sterile or neutral way, in order to elide the fact that combat involves the killing of human beings. But it is more likely to function by referents implying that enemy personnel are inferior, that they are "gooks" or "camel jockeys."

Because of the extensive media coverage of most military operations, many military terms have entered into the civilian lexicon. Indeed, a feedback loop of sorts operates, wherein military terms enter civilian usage as metaphors while linguistic terms from civilian life simultaneously enter military usage. In many civilian communities, militarized language denotes a level of seriousness that could not be conveyed as effectively in other ways. Thus, the Clinton headquarters in the 1992 presidential campaign was th

"War Room"; Arkansas's system of substitutions in college basketball is known as "platooning"; team leaders are "floor generals"; and business schools assign Sun Tzu and the U.S. Marine Corps doctrinal manuals about tactics and strategy. At the same time, language and metaphors from civilian life cycle into military usage, downplaying the level of seriousness involved. Particularly prevalent is the language of sports and games, so that the now famous "Left Hook" in the Saudi Desert was the "Hail Mary pass" and the war began with a "kickoff" or a "tip-off."

All of these linguistic tools facilitate the use of language itself as both a source for, and mechanism to sustain, a given community, while simultaneously serving to define the community in positive ways by the use of arguments implicit in the words chosen.

• Kenneth Burke, *Language as Symbolic Action,* 1966. Carol Cohn, "Slick'ems, Glick'ems, Christmas Trees and Cookie Cutters: Nuclear Language and How We Learned to Pat the Bomb," *Bulletin of Atomic Scientists,* Vol. 43 (1987), pp. 17–24. Michael Shapiro, "Representing World Politics: The Sport/War Intertext," in James Der Derian and Michael Shapiro, eds., *International/Intertextual Relations: Postmodern Readings of World Politics,* 1989. Daniel Hallin, "TV's Clean Little War," *Bulletin of the Atomic Scientists,* 47 (1991), pp. 17–24.

—Cori Dauber

LANSDALE, EDWARD G. (1908–1987), U.S. intelligence officer and general. Born in Detroit, Michigan, Lansdale attended UCLA and then became an advertising executive. He served with the Office of Strategic Services (OSS) in World War II, but achieved fame during the *Cold War as one of the most celebrated U.S. intelligence officers. While he was never an employee of the *Central Intelligence Agency (CIA), he often worked on behalf of the CIA using the cover of an Air Force officer.

Technically a mid-level operative, Lansdale became legendary for identifying and funding effective non-communist alternative leaders, becoming known in the 1950s as "our man in Asia." In the Philippines, he played a controversial but important role in helping President Ramon Magsaysay gain power and defeat communist insurgents. Later, in Vietnam, he engineered psychological warfare operations in North Vietnam in 1954–55 and channeled U.S. support to the newly created Republic of South Vietnam and its president, Ngo Dinh Diem. Under President John F. *Kennedy, Lansdale was put in charge of Operation Mongoose, which involved a series of attempts to eliminate Fidel Castro and disrupt the economy of communist Cuba.

Seen by many during the Cold War as "America's Number One Spy Master," Lansdale was famously reviled in *The Quiet American* (1955) an attack on U.S. foreign policy by British novelist Graham Greene (despite the fact that both Lansdale and Greene denied the connection). But the 1958 Hollywood film version reversed Greene's judgment by portraying the Lansdale-type character as a true hero. By the 1960s, Lansdale's public persona had overshadowed the real actions, and he had become a legend of American success in the Cold War.

[*See also* Cuba, U.S. Military Involvement in; Philippines, U.S. Military Involvement in; Vietnam War.]

• Edward G. Lansdale, *In the Midst of Wars: An American's Mission ot Southeast Asia,* 1972; Cecil B. Currey, *Edward Lansdale, The Unquiet American,* 1988.

—Jonathan Nashel

LA ROCQUE, GENE (1918–), naval officer, founder of the Center for Defense Information. Born in Kankakee, Illinois, commissioned in the naval reserve (1940), La Rocque served thirty-one years on active duty, participating in thirteen major battles in the Pacific during World War II. His postwar career included a variety of ship commands and seven years in the Strategic Plans Directorate of the *Joint Chiefs of Staff (JCS).

Retiring in 1972 and disillusioned over the *Vietnam War, La Rocque established the Center for Defense Information as source of critical information on military spending and policies. Staffed by retired military officers, the center opposes excessive spending and encourages efforts to prevent nuclear war, believing that social, economic, political, and military structures contribute equally to national security. It also publishes *The Defense Monitor,* founded in 1972.

La Rocque and his colleagues testified before Congress, appeared frequently in the media, and consulted many national and international political leaders. In the 1980s, La Rocque founded a weekly public affairs television program, *America's Defense Monitor.*

La Rocque's stature as a "peace admiral" won him praise from peace leaders and hostility from military ones. In August 1983, 575 retired admirals, led by former chairman of the JCS Thomas *Moorer, placed an advertisement in *The Washington Times* criticizing La Rocque for appearing on Soviet television. La Rocque refused to yield to *Cold War animosities, however, and organized ground-breaking meetings between retired military officers in the United States and the Soviet Union. In August 1985, he was credited with playing a significant role in persuading Mikhail Gorbachev, to declare a moratorium on nuclear testing. La Rocque retired from the center in 1993.

[*See also* Nuclear War, Prevention of Accidental.]

• Michael N. Harbottle, Introduction, *Generals for Peace and Disarmament: A Challenge to U.S./NATO Strategy,* 1984. Herbert Mitgang, "Sentinel: Gene Robert La Rocque," *The New Yorker,* 6 October 1986, pp. 88–103.

—David Cortright

LASERS. *Laser* is an acronym for *l*ight *a*mplification by *s*timulated *e*mission of *r*adiation. External energy pumped into the atoms of the lasing medium excites electrons to higher energy states; returning to their base state, they emit photons. Cascading photons produce a narrow, tightly focused beam of intense, coherent, monochromatic light.

The special properties of laser beams—intensity, coherence, directionality—held obvious promise for military purposes. Beginning promptly with the 1961 invention, mission-oriented laser research and development centered on such practical applications as range finding and guidance.

Operational range finders began seeing field service during the *Vietnam War by the mid-1960s. Incorporated in fire control systems, they especially suited direct fire weapons like tank guns; such units for the M-60 tank began service in 1968. Immediately successful, laser range-finding and fire control systems rapidly became standard equipment. Laser simulators have also sharply enhanced training realism for tank gunners and infantry small arms.

Laser guidance, teaming ground-based or airborne target designators with projectile-borne sensors, was one of the precision methods that began revolutionizing air attack on surface targets from the late 1960s onward. The designator directs a laser beam at the target, the laser seeker picks up the reflected light, and the bomb or missile homes in on the illuminated target.

Laser-guided bombs made their first appearance under the U.S. Air Force's Paveway program. Field modification kits for several standard bomb models began reaching Vietnam in 1971. Each included a laser seeker, guidance unit, and control canards bolted to the bomb's nose, enlarged tail fins bolted to the rear. This first Paveway generation met outstanding success in 1972 attacks on North Vietnamese bridges. Paveway II arrived in 1980, Paveway III in 1987, each kit more sophisticated and costly than its predecessor.

Augmented with an off-the-shelf rocket motor, Paveway II also became the basis for the navy's Skipper II air-to-surface missile. It entered service in 1985 as a low-cost (though less capable) alternative to the Maverick, a 1977 version of which was the first U.S. laser-guided missile. Superseded in 1983 by an upgraded model with a better laser seeker and larger warhead, the Maverick now largely serves a Marine close air support role.

The army fielded its first laser-guided missile, the Hellfire, in the early 1980s. Developed specifically as an antitank missile for Apache attack *helicopters, it could acquire its target after launch. Outstanding capabilities and performance led the army to adapt Hellfire for other aircraft and make it the focus of antitank tactics.

Less successful was the Copperhead cannon-launched guided projectile, also intended as a tank killer. Production began in 1981, but persistent technical difficulties and escalating costs ended its procurement in 1990.

From the beginning, the laser's potential as a weapon excited military interest, peaking in the proposed missile defense system called the *Strategic Defense Initiative. Other potential military roles for lasers, more or less speculative in the early 1990s, include laser equivalents of *radar (LADAR), beam-riding missiles, and communication systems.

[See also Antitank Weapons; Missiles.]

• Bengt Anderberg and Myron L. Wolbarsht, *Laser Weapons: The Dawn of a New Military Age,* 1992. Guy Hartcup, *The Silent Revolution: Development of Conventional Weapons, 1945–85,* 1993.

—Barton C. Hacker

LAWS OF WAR. The idea of laws of war is ancient and ubiquitous; fragmentary indications appear in the records of most known civilizations and cultures. The international laws of war as known today, however, are of relatively modern and regional origin. The Roman concept of a law of nations (*jus gentium*), persisting through Europe's medieval centuries and ingesting elements of Christian "just war" doctrine, chivalric honor, military professionalism, and commercial prudence, produced by the sixteenth century a body of customary principles and rules purporting to show how to judge whether a war was justified (*jus ad bellum*) and how wars should ideally be conducted (*jus in bello*). Reality, always falling short of the ideal, became so horrific in the Thirty Years' War that the Dutch Christian-humanist-diplomat Hugo Grotius (1583–1645) was prompted to publish in 1625 *De jure belli ac pacis* (*Concerning the Law of War and Peace*), usually considered the first definitive text on international law. Accepting war as a legitimate political institution, he maintained the just war thesis that it should not be begun without good cause, and argued with moral fervor that war could, indeed should, be conducted with more moderation than was usually the case. When, in the later nineteenth century, modern international law crystallized and the customary laws of war began to be codified, Grotius's visions of international community and universal standards renewed the respect for him that persists today.

The temporary eclipse of *jus ad bellum* did not mean that *jus in bello* was neglected. Men of honor took it seriously. Self-respecting commanders of opposing forces made local agreements ("conventions") to facilitate exchanges of prisoners and protect medical units. Recurrent disputes about particular incidents testified to the persistence of the ideas that there must be standards for governing the conduct of military operations, and that civilized states should wish their armed forces to observe them. So demanding had these ideas become by mid-nineteenth century that they issued in four epochmaking and trailblazing events: the Paris Declaration of 1856, regulating the relations of belligerents and neutrals in maritime war; the *Geneva Conventions of 1864; General Order No. 100 of the U. S. Army of 1864, Instructions for the Government of [Its] Armies in the Field—often known, after its principal author, as "the Lieber code"; and the St. Petersburg Declaration of 1868, a prohibition of an "atrocious" new weapon (explosive bullets).

From those close-bunched beginnings, the laws of war developed along two main lines. "Geneva law" aimed to protect victims and innocents: the 1929 revision added to the existing conventions (for sick and wounded combatants on land and sea), a third regarding prisoners of war; in 1949, a fourth aimed to protect civilians who fell into enemy hands at the outbreak of hostilities or because of military occupation. The other line, law regarding the conduct of hostilities, of which Francis Lieber's code was for long the most famous and complete national example, became known as "Hague law" after the international standard setting in 1899 (reaffirmed by the Fourth Hague Convention of 1907) of the Hague Regulations Respecting the Laws and Customs of War on Land. Supplemented since 1977 by the First Protocol Additional to the Geneva Conventions (in fact, a convergence of Geneva and Hague law, to which most states by now have acceded), the Hague Regulations have ever been, and still are, fundamental to the laws of land war. Along with the Geneva Conventions, they formed the basis for the war crimes trials after World War II; most of which had to do with the behavior of armed forces in (contested) occupation of alien territories, and with the treatment of prisoners.

Standards for the conduct of war by air and sea have not been so easily reached. In these fields especially, military applications of science and technology have posed problems defying simple solution. New inventions promising military advantage have often at first been denounced as dishonorable or inhumane, but a few have ultimately been added to the list of weapons (e.g., *chemical and biological weapons) covered by multilateral treaty prohibitions (1' and 1972, respectively). It remains to be seen how effe will be the 1981 prohibitions or restrictions on the certain conventional weapons (mainly land *mines, boobytraps, and incendiary weapons). Efforts were made between 1919 and 1939 to restrict submarine and aerial warfare, but they proved useless during World War II. *Submarines were so vulnerable on the surface that, having to stay submerged, they could not observe the classic distinction between civilian and military; together with mines, they revolutionized war at sea by making possible *blockades more total than ever before. Bombers dared not fly so low or slow that they could guarantee to hit only military objectives; at the same time, the passions of prolonged total war tended to encourage the indiscriminate and terroristic *bombing of civilians. Both sides having waged air and sea war in these extreme and disproportionate ways, they figured hardly at all in the Nuremberg and Tokyo International Military Tribunals and the many nationally run war crimes trials. Not until 1977 were these specific problems addressed. Among the more valuable achievements of the First Additional Protocol is civilian-protecting definition of military objectives, and, associated with it, rules of proportionality aimed at reducing to the realistic minimum the incidental risks to nonmilitary persons and places.

The laws of war are incapable of perfect observance. Beyond the fact that law like all other elements of war is subject to the erosions of confusion, error, and chance, observance is likely to be highest when states wish a war to remain limited, when neutrals are critically watchful, and when well-disciplined armed forces fight one another in a relatively civilian-free environment. The "desert war" in North Africa (1940–43), and the brief Falklands War in the South Atlantic between Britain and Argentina (1982) are exceptional. Circumstances are rarely so favorable. Wars between states are more likely to be all-out than limited; nor are they often simply between states. The laws of war make some room for "noninternational armed conflict," but nonstate parties may not wish or be able to conduct hostilities in a style consistent with the law, while states combating them may not like to regard them as if they were lawful belligerents. Civilians tend to be difficult to distinguish from combatants in *guerrilla warfare, or revolutionary and people's wars; in such situations, all parties are tempted to turn to terror. And through it all runs the problem that has forever dogged the laws of war, and whose handling reveals the quality of the culture and the politics of which the warrior is the armed representative: how to distinguish what may be militarily necessary from what is merely convenient, and how to judge when enough violence is enough. Important to all, the laws of war are not a matter of concern solely to the military.

[See also Geneva Protocol on Chemical Warfare; Hague Peace Conferences: Just War Theory; War: Nature of War; War Crimes.]

• Oppenheim's International Law, Vol. 2: Disputes, War and Neutrality, 1905; 7th ed., ed. Hersch Lauterpacht, 1952. Daniel O'Connell, The Influence of Law on Sea Power, 1975. David Forsythe, Humanitarian Politics: The International Committee of the Red Cross, 1977. Philip R. Piccigallo, The Japanese on Trial. Allied War Crimes Operations in the East, 1945–1951, 1979. Adam Roberts and Richard ⸻elff, eds., Documents on the Laws of War, 1982; 2nd ed. 1989. W. ⸻vs Parks, "Air Law and the Law of War," Air Force Law Review, ⸻32, no. 1 (1990), pp. 1–225. Telford Taylor, The Anatomy of the ⸻nberg Trials, 1993. Geoffrey Best, War and Law Since 1945, ⸻lichael Howard, George J. Andreopoulos, and Mark R. Shul- man, eds., The Laws of War: Constraints on Warfare in the Western World, 1994.
—Geoffrey Best

LEADERSHIP, CONCEPTS OF MILITARY. Within the U.S. military, leadership is generally considered something of a given. It is a fundamental ingredient of warfare, without which the outcome of a combat operation cannot be assured. The leader is the brain, the motive power of command, upon whom subordinates rely for guidance and wisdom, and depend upon for good judgment. The leader must be determined, unflappable and charismatic; confident in delegation of authority; able to combine the various strands of command into a common thread; seasoned, intelligent, and thoughtful.

When judging the qualities of leadership, there is a tendency to think of the gifted, or natural leader, involving some expectation that leadership is an inherent personality quality that some have, and others have not. Military history is full of "born leaders," suggesting that "inspired leadership" is the only true measure of the trait. For a very long time the American people relied on the emergence of just such an individual when necessity demanded it, and fortunately the country has been well-served in this respect. Much of this has been due to American military egalitarianism, which presumed that any individual, regardless of background, could lead a body of troops in combat as long as the leader had the requisite ability. An obvious case in point is the *Civil War, which gave rise to a number of gifted commanders—Joshua Chamberlain, Nathan Bedford *Forrest, John *Logan, and Nelson A. Miles, to name but a few—who yet had little, if any, military training. So great was the renown of such natural leaders that a veritable school of military command grew up around them, declaring that genius alone was the true sign of leadership, and that leaders were born, not made.

As the army matured and professionalized after the Civil War, these sorts of arguments met the resistance of educational reformers who argued that certain principles of leadership could be taught, given the proper lessons from military history. Beginning in the 1880s, the army and navy both sought to teach certain principles of leadership, although they were not so-called at the time, through the Infantry and Cavalry School, the U.S. Army Staff College, and the Naval War College. Historical examples of military success and failure featured prominently in their curricula, on the assumption that trial-and-error under combat conditions was a poor method of inculcating leadership skills. Lessons learned in the classroom were then effected in map and field exercises. The expectation was, and still is, that non-combat training would provide a fund of practical knowledge upon which a commander could use as a point of departure under battlefield conditions.

For the educational reformers, emulation was key, although they admitted that talent was also valuable. Raw talent, however, was no substitute for its disciplined application. Considering the growing complexity and lethality of war, education was regarded as the surest means of directing talent toward the desired end. Yet the question of native ability remained; could those without it become effective leaders? A problem reformers grappled with was the difference between leadership and command; they are not the same thing, for not all commanders are good leaders, and not all leaders are good commanders. During the Civil War, Gen. George *McClellan, for example, was a truly inspirational leader who won the total devotion of his troops, yet consistently failed to achieve decisive *victory in battle. Gen. Ulysses S. *Grant, on the other hand, was an excellent commander, to whom few would attribute any great affection by the soldiers of his command at the time. Gen. Robert E. *Lee would seem to encompass the best qualities of both.

The essence of military leadership is not, of course, embodied in how much devotion a commander may inspire among the troops. While the ability to command is tied to a leader's general competence—the commander's ability to make correct decisions based on a given situation—the ability to lead remains more ethereal. Because of the intrinsic individuality of leadership, the military encourages the adoption of a particular "style" suited to the personality of the leader or to the situation at hand. One may be a director, a participant, or a delegator, but the centrality of the leader remains unquestioned. Whichever style is used, the expectation is that a positive result will emerge.

Because there seems to be no precise definition of what leadership is, the use of historical example (lessons learned, in current military jargon) has generally been the method through which qualities of leadership have been ascertained. Just as important are examples of bad leadership, which is apt to get troops killed. The balance between the two provides the would-be leader with patterns to avoid and copy.

Definitions of military leadership generally describe what a good leader *does,* not necessarily what leadership *is.* According to current U.S. Army doctrine, "leadership is the process of influencing others to accomplish the mission by providing purpose, direction, and motivation." Traditionally, applying those skills competently has been achieved through intensive theoretical and practical training.

The learning-by-example method might thus be described as a means of augmenting the capabilities of those who, for whatever reason, show promise of true leadership skill, while eliminating those who have no aptitude. Testing and promotion review replace the combat situation, while leadership itself becomes genuine military doctrine. The guiding assumption of leadership doctrine is that incapable practitioners will be winnowed out before their mediocrity costs lives in battle.

Battle represents the severest test of a commander's mastery of leadership doctrine, for the commander must stimulate subordinates to do things that would imperil their health, even cost them their lives. It is here that the leadership role diverges from the command role. Command merely vests the leader with authority to define and order the accomplishment of an objective. Achieving it requires the additional influence of leadership. Ideally, the leader sets the standard for command through personal example and shared sacrifice. He must, therefore, demonstrate confidence in the troops and in his own abilities, while acknowledging the risks his decisions may entail. If subordinates trust the leader's judgment and abilities, and believe that he would not unnecessarily expose them to danger, his authority and decisions will not be questioned. Under the stress of combat, however, a leader cannot assume instant obedience. Fear and the instinct for self-preservation are powerful disincentives to any dangerous enterprise, and the commander cannot simply will them away. He must, therefore, anticipate their appearance while limiting their effect through assiduous training, prepara-

tion, and the promotion of team spirit and identification.

Military leadership is thus a continuous process that extends well beyond the battlefield. Its application and cultivation are as important in times of peace as in war. While the essence of leadership remains beyond easy or precise definition, its fruits are readily apparent. The concepts on which leadership is built—courage, intelligence, experience, discipline and decisiveness, among a score of other virtues—combine to produce an idea of what leadership is, and how it may be achieved.   —T. R. Brereton

The **LEAGUE OF NATIONS** (1919–46) *peacekeeping organization began when Woodrow *Wilson secured the inclusion of its charter in the Treaty of *Versailles (1919). The League's "Covenant" represented the work of many internationalists on both sides of the Atlantic. It contained provisions for the arbitration of international disputes, the reduction of armaments, and for the imposition of collective military and economic sanctions against any nation that violated the political independence and territorial integrity of another (Article X).

The Covenant, like all constitutions, was subject to interpretation. Two competing tendencies existed in the American internationalist movement, both born of the politics of *neutrality and preparedness of 1915–16. "Progressive internationalists" considered peace essential to the cause of domestic reform. Like Wilson, they saw European *imperialism, *militarism, and balance-of-power politics as the root causes of the war; in their stead, they promoted the idea of a "community of nations," to be sustained by a league.

Conservative internationalists, led by William Howard Taft and the League to Enforce Peace, also advocated a world parliament; but, while more or less endorsing the principle of collective security, most of them believed that the United States should expand its army and navy and reserve the right to exercise force independently. Disarmament and self-determination were not among their concerns. Progressive internationalists viewed their conservative rivals as enemies of reform and as advocates of militarism. The two sides disagreed over domestic politics and foreign policy alike.

Had a national referendum been held in July 1919, the United States almost certainly would have joined the League. Two main factors, however, compounded the problem of ratifying the treaty. First, the Republicans, having captured majority control of Congress in the 1918 midterm elections, launched a fierce attack on Wilson's overall program. Second, large numbers of progressive internationalists had begun to abandon Wilson because the peace settlement had fallen short of the promised *Fourteen Points; moreover, his acquiescence in the wartime suppression of civil liberties had further eroded his support among progressives.

As for the Senate itself, the preponderance of opposition was grounded in both partisanship and ideological principle, though only a few of the League's critics were irreconcilable isolationists. In part to preserve America's freedom of action, the Republicans, led by Henry Cabot *Lodge, drew up fourteen reservations as conditions for ratification. Some of these reservations would have undermined the League's ability to arbitrate disputes, to supervise a reduction of armaments, and to impose sanctions embodied in Article X. In September, Wilson embarked upon a strenuous speaking tour on behalf of unqualified American membership. His exertions brought on a nearly fatal, paralytic stroke that rendered him a recluse. Political gridlock then ensued.

The Senate roll was called three times, in November 1919 and March 1920; but whether on a motion to ratify unconditionally or with the Lodge reservations, the necessary two-thirds majority could never be mustered. In November 1920, the Republican Warren G. Harding won a landslide victory over Democrat James M. Cox. Alluding to Wilson's erstwhile wish that the election might take the form of a referendum, Lodge now declared, "that League is dead."

Some historians have argued that Wilson's stroke prevented him from striving for the middle ground on the question of reservations. Other historians maintain that even a healthy Wilson would have refused to compromise, owing to his personality. Still others have stressed that the ideological gulf that separated the two branches of American *internationalism, along with the president's failure to rekindle his own progressive coalition just as the parliamentary struggle began, sealed the fate of a Wilsonian league.

At least in part because of the absence of the United States, the fledgling organization boasted few achievements in the interwar period. Republican administrations assiduously avoided all formal association with it throughout the 1920s, even, for example, when promulgating the Dawes Plan of 1924, the effort to compose Europe's reparations–war debt tangle. Yet, in this endeavor, the League undoubtedly facilitated Secretary of State Charles Evans Hughes's labors. Then, too, Hughes staunchly (if ineffectively) advocated American membership in the World Court. The United States further underscored its ambivalence in the salutary achievement of the Washington Naval Conference of 1921–22 as well as in the innocuous Kellogg-Briand Pact of 1928; in both instances of internationalist foreign policy, the Americans conspicuously ignored the League. Perhaps the final blow came during the Manchurian incident of 1931–32. While condemning Japanese aggression there, the League proved utterly powerless to undertake effective sanctions; the United States merely refused to recognize Japan's puppet state, Manchukuo. During the 1930s, the League receded further into impotence as mounting crises led to renewed international conflict.

By 1944–45, many Americans had concluded that World War II might have been averted had they followed Wilson's counsel. Franklin D. *Roosevelt successfully championed a new international organization, the *United Nations, whose Charter incorporated many of the reservations prescribed by the Republicans in 1919. Although the United States took the lead in founding the United Nations in 1945, American foreign policy makers deemed it an inadequate instrument and they created regional alliances, particularly *NATO, as the means of collective security.

[See also Isolationism; Washington Naval Arms Limitation Treaty; World War II: Causes.]

• Thomas A. Bailey, *Woodrow Wilson and the Great Betrayal*, 1945. Alexander L. George and Juliette L. George, *Woodrow Wilson and Colonel House*, 1956. Arthur S. Link, *Woodrow Wilson, Revolution, War and Peace*, 1979. William C. Widenor, *Henry Cabot Lodge and the Search for an American Foreign Policy*, 1980. Lloyd E. Ambrosius, *Woodrow Wilson and the American Diplomatic Tradition, The Treaty Fight in Perspective*, 1987. Thomas J. Knock, *To End All Wars: Woodrow Wilson and the Quest for a New World Order*, 1992.
—Thomas J. Knock

LEAVES AND FURLOUGHS, long a benefit reserved for officers, were not a right for enlisted men until the mid-twentieth century, when some of the links between rank and privilege slowly dissolved in the American military. After the *Revolutionary War, the American military incorporated British principles on leaves into the Articles of War. A commanding officer exercised wide discretion over how to maintain discipline within his command, ranging from the reward of a leave to punishment with a court-martial. The only restrictions placed on officers granting furloughs limited leaves to no more than thirty days for 5 percent of the unit at one time. The statute authorizing *conscription during the *Civil War reiterated this principle. By 1890, however, the continually high *desertion rate in the regular army led to calls for a new approach in using leaves to improve *morale among enlisted troops. Over a period of seven years, an enlisted man was entitled to a three-month annual furlough after serving three years of his five-year enlistment. Officers' complaints about constant unit disruption caused Congress to end this experiment in 1897. A simultaneous reform impulse was evident among naval officers who argued that punishing sailors by restricting liberty caused, rather than prevented, desertion. It remained up to the naval commander, whether or not to give half the crew liberty during a port call (three-quarters if anchored in a navy yard).

In marked contrast to the enlisted man or sailor, officers enjoyed a legal right to request and take paid leaves and furloughs. In 1835, the secretary of the navy lost his ability to save money by furloughing officers waiting for a new posting. Naval officers could still request a paid three-month leave to attend to domestic business or an indefinite furlough to leave the nation's borders. Army officers took advantage of their more extensive privileges to work for civilian engineering companies, lobby in Washington on their unit's behalf, or enjoy eastern urban attractions. In addition to the possibility of a personal leave of up to eighteen months, a doctor's certificate was all an army officer needed for a year of sick leave in the nineteenth century.

The creation of a conscripted army of citizen-soldiers during World War I brought the nation's attention to the problem of fighting a war for democracy with an army that maintained a sharp distinction between the privileges enjoyed by commissioned officers and enlisted troops. After World War II, Congress reacted to a similar public outcry by giving enlisted men the legal right to a paid thirty-day leave each year. The Armed Forces Leave Act of 1946 continued to democratize military leaves by giving officers and troops equal amounts of annual leave and paying them for up to sixty days' accumulated leave when their term of service ended. in 1975, Congress rejected a General Accounting Office proposal to eliminate the financial incentive this second benefit gave to save rather than take leave after the Department of *Defense argued that servicemen would lose an advantage still enjoyed by civilian federal employees.

[See also Army, U.S.; Citizen-Soldier; Class and the Military; Navy, U.S.]
—Jennifer D. Keene

LEBANON, U.S. MILITARY INVOLVEMENT IN. Lebanon, a multi-ethnic, multi-religious nation situated between Syria and Israel on the eastern edge of the Mediterranean Ocean, became of particular importance to America in 1957 when President Dwight D. *Eisenhower issued the *Eisenhower Doctrine declaring the Middle East vital to U.S. national security interests. Subsequently, fighting and political disputes in the *Lebanon Crisis (1958) caused three U.S. military incursions, actions that proved only marginally successful in producing stable solutions favorable to America's Middle Eastern policies.

Following Eisenhower's announcement, the U.S. Sixth Fleet, patrolling the eastern Mediterranean, became a visible symbol of U.S. interest and power in the region. However, such a display of force failed to stymie the onrush of events that challenged American aims. The creation of the United Arab Republic, an anti-U.S. union of Syria and Egypt in early 1958; the outbreak of civil war in Lebanon in May 1958; and finally, the overthrow of a pro-Western regime in Iraq in early July, all provoked Eisenhower to order three U.S. Marine Corps battalion landing teams ashore in Lebanon on 15–16 July 1958. U.S. Army airborne forces were flown in from Germany on 19 July. By August, the American military contingent in the country consisted of over 15,000 troops. An uneasy truce came about in September, and when elections were announced, U.S. forces were withdrawn in October 1958.

The 1958 American incursion in Lebanon was practically casualty-free, but the 1982–84 involvement was wholly different. When Israeli forces invaded Lebanon in an attack on anti-Israeli forces in June 1982, the administration of President Ronald *Reagan became concerned over the region's instability and opted to land Marines at Beirut in August to help restore stability in the divided country. The 800-man unit, the 32nd Marine Amphibious Unit, was withdrawn in 15 days. Negotiating with its Western allies, the United States participated in a multinational stability effort later that fall. Two U.S. military missions were established. First, Army Special Forces units were deployed to Beirut with the task of training pro-Western Lebanese forces; second, U.S. Marines were once again landed with the assignment to protect the Beirut airport. The Marines went ashore amid lavish press coverage and promptly became targets of snipers and occasional artillery fire. Attempts to quell these attacks by U.S. naval gunfire and air strikes failed to stop the harassment. Special Forces troopers kept a low profile in Lebanon, dodging the press and melding in with their Lebanese trainees.

In mid-April 1983, a truck bomb exploded near the U.S. Embassy in Beirut, killing more than 60 people, including 17 Americans. Despite this episode, on 23 October 1983, a terrorist was able to drive a truck loaded with explosives past Marine guards and into the Marine headquarters. The terrorist detonated the load, killing himself and 241 of the 300 Marines asleep in the building. The Marines were withdrawn from Lebanon on 26 February 1984; in March, the United States announced its abandonment of the multinational security effort. Army Special Forces elements remained in Lebanon and continued their mission for a few more months without incident. Fighting in Lebanon continued through most of the 1980s.

[See also Middle East, U.S. Military Involvement in the; Peacekeeping.]

• Roger J. Spiller, "Not War But Like War": The American Intervention in Lebanon, 1981. Eric M. Hammel, The Root: The Marines in Beirut, August 1982–February 1984, 1985.   —Rod Paschall

LEBANON CRISIS (1958). The underlying cause of the 1958 Lebanon crisis was the instability of the country's Christian-Muslim political coalition under pressure from the *Cold War Pan-Arab nationalism of Egypt's Gamal Abdel Nasser. Following creation of a pro-Soviet United Arab Republic by Egypt and Syria in February 1958, severe rioting broke out against the pro-Western Lebanese government of President Camille Chamoun, a Christian. The crisis came to a head on 14 July, when an Arab nationalist coup in Iraq overthrew King Faisal and similar coup attempts in Jordan and Lebanon appeared likely. Invoking the *Eisenhower Doctrine, Chamoun immediately requested U.S. troops.

At Eisenhower's orders the first of the three Marine battalions located in the Mediterranean landed to take control of the Beirut airport on 15 July. The other two were ashore by 18 July, plus a fourth battalion airlifted from the United States. Opposition to the Marine presence was limited to snipers and small groups of "rebels" who probed Marine positions but did not attack. An understanding with the initially hostile Lebanese Army resulted in provision of liaison officers and some joint operations.

A U.S. Army airborne battle group from Germany landed at Beirut airport on 19 July. More units followed by sea and air until a maximum of 14,357 troops (8,515 army, 5,842 Marine) was reached on 8 August. An orderly presidential election was held in Lebanon on 31 July; American troop withdrawals began in late August and were completed by 15 October.

The United States's first intervention in the Middle East was also the first time *NATO-committed troops were withdrawn for out-of-area operations. Although the planning and initial operations suffered from important American misconceptions about Lebanon and lack of joint service doctrine, the intervention helped stabilize Lebanon for another twenty-four years.

[See also Lebanon, U.S. Military Involvement in.]

• Jack Shulimson, Marines in Lebanon 1958, 1966. Roger J. Spiller, "Not War But Like War": The American Intervention in Lebanon, 1981.   —Gerald C. Thomas, Jr.

LEE, CHARLES (1731–1782), British army officer, Revolutionary War general. Born in Cheshire, England, Lee fought in the *French and Indian War, serving from Edward *Braddock's ill-fated campaign against Fort Duquesne to the 1760 conquest of Montréal.

Siding with America's revolutionaries, the politically radical Lee became the *Continental army's third-ranking general in 1775. He improved coastal *fortifications and helped George *Washington's army escape from a precarious position on Manhattan. A student of war and society, Lee advocated a mass guerrilla conflict because he believed that Americans, accustomed to liberty, lacked the discipline necessary to defeat professional soldiers in conventional battle.

Late in 1776, Lee's career began to deteriorate. Having lost faith in Washington and hoping to sustain popular resistance in New Jersey, he defied the commander in chief's orders to move his detachment west of the Delaware River

Captured and imprisoned, he submitted military plans to the British that could be construed as treasonous. Exchanged in April 1778, he commanded 5,000 Continentals at the Battle of *Monmouth, where his decision to order a retreat resulted in an angry exchange with Washington. Lee demanded a court-martial. Found guilty of disobedience, disrespect, and misbehavior before the enemy, he was suspended from the army for a year, then dismissed. His outspoken opposition to Washington, not incompetence or disloyalty, caused his downfall.

[See also Braddock's Defeat; Revolutionary War: Military and Diplomatic Course; Treason.]

• John Richard Alden, *General Charles Lee, Traitor or Patriot?*, 1951. John Shy, "Charles Lee and the Radical Alternative," in Shy, *A People Numerous and Armed*, 1976.　　　　　—Stuart Leibiger

LEE, HENRY (1756–1818), Revolutionary War officer and early national statesman. Born in Prince William County, Virginia, Lee graduated from the College of New Jersey in 1773. An exceptional cavalryman, he rose to lieutenant colonel in the *Continental army, where he commanded "Lee's Legion" and was known as "Light-Horse Harry" Lee. In 1779, he captured a British force at Paulus Hook, New Jersey, and performed with distinction during the 1780–81 southern campaign.

Lee's military experience convinced him that American liberty depended on a strong central government led by proven patriots. He was a friend and supporter of George *Washington, whom he eulogized as "first in war, first in peace and first in the hearts of his countrymen." A staunch Federalist, Lee defended the Constitution at the 1788 Virginia ratifying convention and while serving as governor of Virginia commanded the 1794 Federal expedition against the *Whiskey Rebellion.

In private life, Lee fared poorly. Failed speculations landed him in debtor's prison in 1808. Four years later, a Baltimore mob injured him after he attempted to defend the office of an unpopular newspaper. In 1813–18, he convalesced in the West Indies, but never recovered; he returned to die at the Georgia home of his late comrade, Nathanael *Greene. One of his sons, Robert E. *Lee, would become the leading general of the Confederacy.

[See also Revolutionary War: Military and Diplomatic Course.]

• Thomas Boyd, *Light-horse Harry Lee*, 1931. Charles Royster, *Light-Horse Harry Lee and the Legacy of the American Revolution*, 1981.
　　　　　—Stuart Leibiger

LEE, ROBERT E. (1807–1870), Confederate Civil War general. Born at Stratford, a family plantation in Virginia, Robert E. Lee was the son of Henry *Lee ("Light-Horse Harry") of the *Revolutionary War. He graduated with great distinction from West Point in 1829, and in 1831 he married Mary Custis, daughter of Martha Washington's grandson, George Washington Parke Custis, who was also George *Washington's adopted son. The Lees made their home at Arlington, the Custis mansion overlooking Washington, D.C. The marriage produced four daughters and three sons. The sons—George Washington Custis Lee, William Henry Fitzhugh Lee, and Robert E. Lee, Jr.—all served as officers in the *Confederate army.

Lee's continuous and distinguished service in the U.S. Army before the Civil War included highly acclaimed action in the *Mexican War, the superintendency at West Point from September 1852 to March 1855, and western Indian fighting. Lee was a protégé of Gen. Winfield Scott, general-in-chief of the U.S. Army at the outbreak of the Civil War. When Virginia seceded, Colonel Lee resigned his commission in the U.S. Army (he had previously been offered high Federal command, but rejected it) and accepted command of his state's military forces. After service that included a position as military adviser to Confederate president Jefferson *Davis, Lee in June 1862 succeeded Joseph E. *Johnston as commanding general of the Army of Northern Virginia. Three years later, in February 1865, he was also appointed general-in-chief of the Confederate forces. In April 1865, having been besieged in the Richmond defenses, he surrendered the Army of Northern Virginia to Gen. Ulysses S. *Grant at Appomattox, Virginia. Lee and his soldiers were paroled by Grant to go home.

After the war, Lee rejected lucrative business opportunities and accepted the presidency of Washington College at Lexington, Virginia. An excellent educational administrator, Lee's leadership was marked by curriculum development in advance of the times. He died there in 1870 and is buried on the campus of the college, subsequently known as Washington and Lee University.

Lee was a man of high personal character and intelligence, charismatic and charming, a natural leader. As a leading actor in the Civil War legend of martial glory, he has become a legendary figure, an American hero of exceptional nobility. The legend rationalizes or rejects characteristics of the man that might lessen his appeal.

Lee's fame rests principally on his leadership of the Army of Northern Virginia. Having driven a numerically superior Federal army from the Virginia Peninsula near Richmond in 1862, Lee, ably supported by "Stonewall" *Jackson, won a series of brilliant tactical victories in 1862 and 1863 at the Second Battle of *Bull Run, and the Battles of *Fredericksburg and *Chancellorsville, and he fought George B. *McClellan to a standstill at the Battle of *Antietam. These battles were followed, however, by defeat at the Battle of *Gettysburg in 1863. Subsequently, Lee conducted a skillful, costly defense against Grant's Overland Campaign in Virginia in 1864–65, but in this he eventually failed.

Questions have been raised about Lee's leadership. In strategic terms, Lee believed that the South had to defeat the North militarily, that is, by actual combat in the field as distinguished from conducting the contest so that the North would give it up as too costly in blood and treasure. Thus, in a letter to President Davis on 6 July 1864 he wrote that it was necessary for the Confederacy to "defeat or drive the armies of the enemy from the field." Accordingly, before being besieged, Lee took the offensive whenever possible. Critics argue that in view of the South's manpower and materiel disadvantages, it could not defeat the North militarily. Lee's strategic and tactical aggressiveness produced unnecessarily large and disproportionate Confederate *casualties, which the outnumbered South was unable to replace. These casualties significantly reduced the number of troops, increasing the South's disadvantage. This, in turn, deprived his army of mobility and ultimately led to its being caught in the fatal siege.

Lee's defenders reply that a desperate situation required desperate gambles, and that his battlefield successes were perhaps the principal encouragement to the continued

Confederate resistance. Whatever his shortcomings, Lee became the white South's greatest hero, and many northern and foreign commentators have praised both the man and the general.

[See also Civil War: Military and Diplomatic Course; Civil War: Changing Interpretations; Petersburg, Siege of; Wilderness to Petersburg Campaign.]

• Douglas Southall Freeman, R. E. Lee, 4 vols. 1934–35. J. F. C. Fuller, Grant & Lee: A Study in Personality and Generalship, repr. 1957; 1982. Thomas L. Connelly, The Marble Man: Robert E. Lee and His Image in American Society, 1977. Alan T. Nolan, Lee Considered: General Robert E. Lee and Civil War History, 1991. Emory H. Thomas, Robert E. Lee, 1995. Joseph L. Harsh, Confederate Tide Rising: Robert E. Lee and the Making of Southern Strategy, 1861–1862, 1997.
—Alan T. Nolan

LEJEUNE, JOHN A. (1867–1942). Major general, commandant of the Marine Corps (1920–29), reformer, and champion of *amphibious warfare. An 1890 Annapolis graduate who spent twenty-seven years in shipboard service and expeditionary duty in the Caribbean, Lejeune, a tough-minded Louisianan with sharp political skills, emerged from divisional command in Europe in World War I with a reputation second only to George Barnett and Smedley *Butler as a Marine Corps leader. Replacing Barnett as commandant amid controversy about the Corps' future functions, Lejeune stressed a single reason for Corps' existence: wartime seizure and defense of advanced naval bases in a Pacific war against Japan. In July 1921, Lejeune endorsed a study of Pacific Ocean offensive amphibious operations by Maj. "Pete" *Ellis and announced that henceforth Marine Corps officer education, troop training, major exercises, and equipment development would focus on amphibious landings. He also stressed that Marine aviation belonged within the assault force. He sponsored expeditionary force exercises in 1924 and 1925, but the undermanned Corps lost its landing forces to interventions in China and Nicaragua until 1934. Nevertheless, Lejeune set the Corps on its most important and persistent mission. After retirement in 1929, he served as president of Virginia Military Institute until 1937.

[See also Marine Corps, U.S.: 1914–45; Marine Corps Combat Branches: Ground Forces; Marine Corps Combat Branches: Aviation Forces.]

• John A. Lejeune, The Reminiscences of a Marine, 1930. Merrill L. Bartlett, Lejeune: A Marine's Life, 1991.
—Allan R. Millett

LEMAY, CURTIS E. (1906–1990), air tactician and *World War II general. Lemay began his career in 1929 as a fighter pilot and transferred to bombers in 1937. In May 1942, he took command of the 305th Bomb Grooup. He trained the group and took it to England. LeMay increased bombing accuracy by discontinuing evasive action during bombing and substituted straight, level approaches, resulting in no increase in *casualties. By June 1944, he commanded almost 500 heavy bombers. After transferring to the *China-Burma-India Theater in August 1944, he next transferred to Twenty-First Bomber Command in Guam. In March 1945, he abandoned daylight attacks, stripped his B-29s of unnecessary weight, and began a campaign of night fire bombing that damaged numerous Japanese cities. This campaign was a decisive factor in Japan's defeat.

In October 1947, LeMay became the commander of the newly created U.S. Air *Force (USAF) in Europe. He organized the Berlin Airlift before returning to the United States to take over the Strategic Air Command (SAC) in October 1948, where he changed a dispirited force into an elite unit. His nine-year tenure (unheard of in the U.S. military) enabled him to apply consistent management practices and his remake of the organization was his most important achievement. SAC became an all-jet bomber force, developed in-flight refueling, and increased readiness to unprecedented heights. It served as the linchpin of the *Eisenhower administration's military/diplomatic philosophy of massive nuclear retaliation. In 1957, LeMay became the Vice Chief of Staff, USAF—the man responsible for the day-to-day operations of the service—and in 1961, he became Chief of Staff. He found himself in the invidious position of opposing the strategic and tactical philosophies of the *Kennedy and *Johnson administrations with their emphasis on conventional warfare and *tactics, especially in Southeast Asia. LeMay further objected to the analytical management style of Secretary of Defense Robert S. *McNamara. LeMay retired in 1965.

• LeMay, Curtis, E., with MacKinlay Kantor, Mission With LeMay, 1965.
—Richard G. Davis

LEMNITZER, LYMAN (1899–1988), World War II planner and negotiator; Chairman, *Joint Chiefs of Staff (JCS); NATO *Supreme Allied Commander, Europe. Lemnitzer was educated at West Point and served in the U.S. Army. In 1942, he was chosen as air-land planner for the *North Africa campaign, and later, as a planner for Gen. George S. *Patton, he helped plan the Allied invasion of Sicily. Along with Allen Welsh *Dulles he was selected in April 1945 as an Allied negotiator for the German surrender.

From 1945 to 1950, Lemnitzer was a military representative in diplomatic negotiations leading to the signing of the North Atlantic Treaty creating NATO and headed the U.S. program providing military assistance to Europe (MDAP).

During the 1950s, Lemnitzer served as CINCFE (Commander in Chief—Far East), became army representative to the JCS, and was promoted to chairman of the JCS in 1960 under the Eisenhower administration. As chairman, he was cognizant of the decision to launch the ill-fated Bay of Pigs invasion (April 1961), although he later maintained that the joint chiefs were asked only to evaluate the feasibility of the plan and did not approve it as finally executed. Despite harsh criticism of his tenure, the JCS's involvement in this debacle, and at one juncture his threatened removal, in July 1962 he was appointed as NATO's Supreme Allied Commander in Europe, the highest military position in the organization. In his six-and-a-half-year tenure, he dealt with the French withdrawal from NATO (1966), the relocation of NATO headquarters from Paris to Brussels, and the crisis in Cyprus. He retired at the rank of four-star general in July 1969 after fifty-one years of service.

[See also Cuba, U.S. Military Involvement in.]

• Lawrence S. Kaplan, A Community of Interests: NATO and the Military Assistance Program, 1948–1951, 1980. Lawrence S. Kaplan and Kathleen Kellner, "Lemnitzer: Surviving the French Military Withdrawal," in Robert S. Jordan., ed., General in International Politics: NATO's Supreme Allied Commander, Europe, 1987.
—Kathleen F. Kellner

LEND-LEASE ACT AND AGREEMENTS (1941). When the British could no longer pay cash for arms and munitions in December 1940, after the presidential election Franklin D. *Roosevelt suggested leasing or lending war supplies to those fighting the Axis. He likened it to lending a garden hose to a neighbor whose house was burning. Once the fire was out, said FDR, "he gives it back to me and thanks me very much," or, if damaged, he replaced it. For three months Americans debated the Lend-Lease bill in Congress. Isolationists condemned it as leading America into another European war, as in World War I. But many Americans saw the need to aid Britain and China against Germany and Japan. Numbering the bill H.R. 1776 gave it a patriotic aura, and Lend-Lease eventually passed by a 60–31 vote in the Senate and 317–71 in the House.

Signed into law on 11 March 1941, Lend-Lease permitted the president to "sell, transfer title to, exchange, lease, lend, or otherwise dispose of" defense articles to "any country whose defense the President deems vital to the defense of the United States." Congress initially appropriated $7 billion, with a total expenditure of more than $50 billion by the end of World War II. The British received the lion's share, $31.6 billion in Lend-Lease aid. After the German invasion of the Soviet Union in June 1941, Roosevelt provided Lend-Lease to the USSR, $11 billion, without which "the war would have been lost," as Josef *Stalin admitted. That "most unsordid act," as Winston S. *Churchill called Lend-Lease, turned the United States into the "arsenal of democracy" that forged victory in World War II.

[*See also* Isolationism; World War II: Military and Diplomatic Course.]

• Warren F. Kimball, *The Most Unsordid Act: Lend-Lease, 1939–1941,* 1969.
—J. Garry Clifford

LESBIANS IN THE MILITARY. *See* Gay Men and Lesbians in the Military.

LEWIS AND CLARK EXPEDITION (1804–06). In 1803, Thomas *Jefferson commissioned Capt. Meriwether Lewis and Lt. William Clark to explore what is now the northwest United States. The Louisiana Purchase later the same year altered the character of the planned expedition from an exploration of French territory to a first glimpse of lands that, in the view of many contemporaries, were essential to maintaining the agrarian, republican character of the nation.

The party of nearly thirty men—including Lewis and Clark, three sergeants, twenty-two enlisted men, volunteers, interpreters, and Clark's slave—departed St. Louis in May 1804 heading up the Missouri River. They wintered at the present site of Bismarck, North Dakota, where they acquired a guide and translator, the Shoshone woman Sacagawea. In spring 1805, they continued to the headwaters of the Missouri River, struggled across the Continental Divide, and headed west along the Salmon, Snake, and Columbia Rivers to the Pacific. They returned to St. Louis the following year.

Their exploration revealed both the absence of a transcontinental water route and a wealth of information, including detailed maps of their route, the earliest descriptions of Plains Indian culture, and observations of the

environment. Until the development of the railroad and steamboat, however, the region they had explored remained a fur-trapping ground and repository for removed Indians.

[*See also* Native Americans, U.S. Military Relations with.]

• James P. Ronda, *Lewis and Clark Among the Indians,* 1984. Stephen E. Ambrose, *Undaunted Courage: Meriwether Lewis, Thomas Jefferson, and the Opening of the American West,* 1996.
—James D. Drake

LEXINGTON AND CONCORD, BATTLES OF (1775). The political dispute between Britain and its American colonies flared into open conflict on 19 April 1775 at two towns outside Boston, Massachusetts. Maj. Gen. Thomas *Gage, commander in chief and governor of Massachusetts, dispatched some 800 soldiers to confiscate provincial military supplies stockpiled at Concord, about twenty miles inland. Six months earlier, colonial leaders, anticipating British action, had formed a quarter of the militia into a force ready to repel any attack on short notice. Warned of the British expedition by several dispatch riders, including Paul Revere, these "minutemen" gathered in the path of the advancing British force.

As dawn broke on the 19th, the British advance guard, roughly 250 men under Maj. John Pitcairn, approached Lexington, where the militia company, perhaps 70 men under Capt. John Parker, was assembling on the green. Pitcairn, seeing armed men on his right flank, deployed part of his command. Suddenly, nearby, a gun fired—perhaps accidentally. The British soldiers, thinking they were under attack, fired on Parker's company. By the time Pitcairn restrained them, eight colonists lay dead or dying on Lexington green.

When the raiders reached Concord, they found that the colonists had removed the stores, and that groups of armed men were converging on their line of march. In a firefight at the North Bridge over the Concord River, the militiamen demonstrated that they were capable of resisting by force of arms the passage of British regulars through the countryside.

Although it lacked central direction, resistance to the raiders mounted as they marched back to Boston. Pecked at by several thousand colonists, mostly firing from behind the stone walls that lined the route, the column was saved from destruction only by a force sent by Gage to ensure its safe return. The British retreat to Boston was the high-water mark for American militiamen during the war. Operating in small groups on home ground against an outnumbered enemy, they used their skills to best advantage. The colonists would have to create more permanent forms of military organization, however, to bring their rebellion to a successful conclusion.

[*See also* Citizen-Soldier; Revolutionary War: Causes; Revolutionary War: Military and Diplomatic Course.]

• Allen French, *The First Year of the American Revolution,* 1934. David Hackett Fischer, *Paul Revere's Ride,* 1994.
—Harold E. Selesky

LEYTE GULF, BATTLE OF (1944). Leyte Gulf—23–25 October 1944—the largest naval battle in history, was precipitated by the U.S. invasion of the Philippines during

World War II. Carrying out the landings at Leyte were the amphibious ships of the Seventh Fleet commanded by Vice Adm. Thomas C. *Kinkaid; providing cover against the Japanese Imperial Navy were the fast carriers and *battle-ships of the Third Fleet under Adm. William F. *Halsey. This divided American command, with no common superior nearer than Washington, afforded the weaker Imperial Fleet an opportunity.

Operation Sho-I, a typically complex Japanese plan, called for closely coordinated movements by four separate forces. To lure Halsey's Third Fleet away, the Japanese dangled far to the north four *aircraft carriers, which had lost most of their planes in June during the earlier Battle of the *Philippine Sea. Meanwhile, Vice Adm. Takeo Kurita's central force, composed of the strongest gun ships, including the giant battleships *Yamato* and *Musashi*, was to pass through San Bernardino Strait and fall upon Kinkaid's transports and supply ships from the east. The Japanese southern force, composed of two weaker groups of gun ships, would advance through Surigao Strait and assail the American landing from the south.

The battle started badly for the Japanese when their central force was ambushed on 23 October by *submarines, which sounded the alarm and sank two *cruisers. Alerted to the approach of Kurita, Halsey's aviators concentrated on the *Musashi*, sinking that battleship and compelling the central force to reverse course. Halsey next sighted the Japanese carriers, and thinking that Kurita was in retreat, headed north with his entire force. Unobserved, Kurita soon doubled back and slipped through San Bernardino Strait.

Simultaneously, the Japanese gun ships making up the southern force approached Surigao Strait. They ran headlong into Kinkaid's warships: destroyers, cruisers, and six old battleships, five of which were veterans of the attack on *Pearl Harbor. In history's last clash between battleships, the Japanese were routed early on 25 October at trifling cost to the Americans.

But at sunrise the same morning, the larger Japanese gamble seemed to have paid off. Kurita's ships fell on the few American vessels steaming to the east of Leyte Gulf: six small escort carriers with their spare destroyer screen. Tailored to the support of ground troops, these American vessels were ill-prepared to deal with the largest ships in the Imperial Fleet. Yet off the island of Samar, American sailors fought for over two hours with such skill and bravery that Kurita, after losing three heavy cruisers to *torpedoes, and believing he confronted Halsey's Third Fleet, ordered withdrawal. Having sunk only the escort carrier *Gambier Bay* and three smaller ships, Kurita limped back through San Bernardino Strait leaving untouched the vital American transports and landing craft at Leyte.

Overall, the American triumph was not unalloyed. Kurita's appearance off Leyte had compelled Halsey to break off his pursuit of the remainder of the Japanese northern force, although not before his aviators had sunk all four of the enemy carriers. The Japanese also won some successes with their land-based aircraft. On 24 October, a dive-bomber hit the torpedo storage area of the light carrier *Princeton,* setting off explosions that sank the ship. The next day, the first kamikazes of the war damaged five escort carriers and sank a sixth, the *St. Lô.*

Still, the battle was an overwhelming defeat for the Imperial Fleet. Of the 282 warships engaged (216 American, 2 Australian, and 64 Japanese), the Japanese lost 4 carriers, 3 battleships, 10 cruisers, and 11 destroyers. American losses totaled one light carrier, two escort carriers, and three destroyers. For all practical purposes, the Japanese navy had ceased to exist as an organized fighting force.

[*See also* Navy, U.S.: 1899–1945; World War II: Military and Diplomatic Course; World War II: U.S. Naval Operations in: The Pacific.]

• C. Vann Woodward, *The Battle for Leyte Gulf,* 1947. Samuel E. Morison, *History of United States Naval Operations in World War II,* Vol. 12: *Leyte: June 1944–January 1945,* 1963. Edwin Hoyt, *The Battle for Leyte Gulf,* 1972. Thomas J. Cutler, *The Battle of Leyte Gulf, 23–26 October 1944,* 1994.   —Malcolm Muir, Jr.

LIDDELL HART, BASIL H. (1895–1970), English military writer and theorist. Liddell Hart, Cambridge-educated, served as an infantry officer on the western front in World War I (twice wounded) and retired from the army as a captain (1924) for health reasons. He was a lifelong student and critic of war and generalship, though never a pacifist. He became military correspondent for the *Daily Telegraph* (1925–35) and *The Times* (1935–39), reaching the peak of his influence as an innovative thinker on army reform. His tactical ideas (the "expanding torrent" of attack, based on the German World War I offensive of spring 1918), spread to the strategic sphere, and ultimately to grand strategy and national policy (the "British Way in Warfare," based on naval power and economic blockade, and "limited liability" with regard to a British army commitment on the Continent). In the United States he was probably best known for his biography, *Sherman* (1929). Above all, with Maj. Gen. J. F. C. Fuller, Liddell Hart became internationally famous as the proponent of mechanization and armored warfare by highly trained professional forces. He fostered a remarkable number of influential contacts in the British army, and also in Weimar and Nazi Germany, though he was probably not as influential there as he and others were to claim after 1945. Emphasizing the importance of air support to *tanks, as well as the need for mechanized infantry, he argued that such forces would restore mobility and decisiveness to warfare.

Liddell Hart opposed sending the British army to Europe in 1939, and then argued against Winston S. *Churchill's policy of Total War, including *conscription, strategic bombing, and a goal of "Unconditional Surrender." After the war, his reputation as a military theorist revived, Liddell Hart published his interviews with German generals and edited Erwin *Rommel's papers. Among the first to argue that nuclear weapons could deter all-out conflict between nations but not prevent conventional warfare, his advocacy of restraint and avoidance of showdowns seemed more acceptable by the nuclear age than in the dark days of Nazi ascendancy. His final book about contemporary strategic issues, *Deterrent or Defence* (1961), was well received; he was knighted in 1966. His reputation is now being reassessed, but Liddell Hart will figure prominently in any account of twentieth-century military history and strategic thought.

[*See also* Deterrence; Strategy; Tactics.]

• Basil H. Liddell Hart, *Memoirs*, 2 vols., 1965. John J. Mearsheimer, *Liddell Hart and the Weight of History*, 1988. Brian Bond, *Liddell Hart: A Study of His Military Thought*, 1991.   —Brian Bond

The **LIMITED TEST BAN TREATY** (1963) prohibits all but underground nuclear weapons tests. It has been joined by most countries of the world.

Support for a treaty to ban nuclear weapons tests ballooned in 1954 during the *Cold War, when radioactive fallout from U.S. nuclear tests above the South Pacific fell on a Japanese fishing boat, the *Lucky Dragon*, after it entered a zone that ships had been asked to avoid during testing. The fallout was thought to have caused the death of one fisherman and sickness for several others. India's Prime Minister Jawaharlal Nehru spoke for many when he called for a ban on all further testing.

President Dwight D. *Eisenhower and Soviet premier Nikita Khrushchev authorized talks that came close to producing a treaty banning tests and did produce a temporary suspension of testing from 1958 to 1961. But the United States insisted on on-site inspections to verify that the Soviet Union was not testing, and the Soviet Union rejected such inspections as a form of espionage. Finally, after coming close to a nuclear exchange in the *Cuban Missile Crisis of 1962, Khrushchev and President John F. *Kennedy compromised in 1963 on a treaty that banned all but underground tests. Onsite inspections were most important for these tests; by not including underground tests in the treaty, the inspection issue went away. The treaty did not deal with the nuclear *missiles of the Cuban crisis but it symbolized the two leaders' desire to reduce tensions through negotiations to limit nuclear weapons.

Though the treaty was opposed by some responsible for designing nuclear weapons, it was welcomed around the world. Efforts since 1963 to extend its ban to underground tests produced 1996 agreement on a Comprehensive Test Ban Treaty. India, whose prime minister first called for an end to testing, refused to sign the treaty and set off underground nuclear weapon tests in May of 1998. Pakistan followed suit. The condemnation of both countries that followed was world-wide; economic sanctions were imposed by the United States and a few others. While most countries of the world had signed the treaty, many delayed their ratification. India and Pakistan indicated they would sign the new treaty if sanctions were lifted and other demands were met. But, by the end of 1998, they had not signed and the new treaty could not go into effect without them or without several other countries that had signed but not ratified, including China, Russia, and the United States.

[*See also* Arms Control and Disarmament: Nuclear Arms Race; Nonproliferation of Nuclear Weapons, Treaty on the.]

• Glenn T. Seaborg with Benjamin Loeb, *Kennedy, Krushchev and the Test Ban*, 1981. George Bunn, *Arms Control by Committee: Managing Negotiations with the Russians*, chaps. 2 and 3, 1992. Rebecca Johnson, *A Comprehensive Test Ban Treaty: Signed but not Sealed*, Acronym No. 10, 1997.   —George Bunn

LIMITED WAR, JOINT CHIEFS OF STAFF AND. During the *Cold War, the American military became involved in two major if limited wars or police actions: Korea (1950–53) and Vietnam (1964–72). Before the large-scale commitment of American military forces to these Asian nations, the military leadership, the *Joint Chiefs of Staff (JCS), was conservative in estimating the strategic importance of both areas, hesitant about U.S. involvement, and disagreed over the form of involvement. The impetus came from other agencies such as the State Department, and JCS endorsement was based upon psychological rather than military grounds. However, after the introduction of American forces in each case, military leverage on the policymakers increased; and as the wars dragged on, JCS identification with the policy became closer.

In the *Korean War, the JCS supported a policy labeled as "no win" by the field commander, Gen. Douglas *MacArthur, many congressmen, and a significant part of the public. In the *Vietnam War, the JCS advocated a policy that continually raised the stakes in a desperate attempt to achieve some form of victory. During Korea, President Harry S. *Truman fired the recalcitrant field commander and relied heavily on the JCS. During Vietnam, President Lyndon B. *Johnson fired Secretary of Defense Robert S. *McNamara "when he became soft," and again began to depend heavily on the JCS.

The joint chiefs played a role in keeping with the American tradition of civil-military relations. In Korea, the JCS took part in every major decision from the first involvement to the dismissal of MacArthur and the move toward a negotiated settlement. Both Truman and Secretary of State Dean *Acheson in their memoirs have nothing but praise for the JCS's conduct during the conflict.

JCS advice was solicited throughout the American involvement in Southeast Asia. The battlefield tactics of Gen. William C. *Westmoreland, Vietnam commander 1964–68, may have been questionable, but his support for administration objectives was never doubted. His successor, Gen. Creighton *Abrams, also loyally supported Washington policy.

The JCS did become involved in bureaucratic struggles with the Kennedy and Johnson administrations. Throughout, the joint chiefs always wanted to expand the war in Vietnam and make it more extensive than did most of their civilian counterparts. The resultant infighting led to actions by both sides that could have upset the civil-military balance. Initially, no member of the JCS was summoned to President Johnson's Tuesday White House lunches where U.S. bombing policy was established. After negative reaction in Congress and the press, Gen. Earle G. *Wheeler, chairman of the JCS, was invited.

The JCS recommended and supported the U.S. military withdrawal from Korea (1949) that helped precipitate the Communist invasion. In 1950, the chiefs urged the president to allow MacArthur to cross the 38th parallel, then refused to curb the field commander's provocative tactics, which ultimately led to massive Chinese intervention and near annihilation of American forces. Beginning in 1961, the JCS, accepting the ill-conceived domino theory, urged the commitment of significant numbers of American ground troops into Vietnam. Early in the Johnson administration, the JCS importuned the chief executive to bomb North Vietnam and recommended a strategy of provocation. Once troops had been committed and the bombing begun, the JCS urged the introduction of more troops and heavier bombing despite evidence that both were ineffective in getting the North Vietnamese to accept American war aims.

Responsibility is a two-edged sword. The joint chiefs

can claim credit for some of the successes of both wars. The decision of the Truman administration to seek a negotiated settlement in Korea rather than attempt a military victory over the Chinese was aided by JCS support. Likewise, the actions that apparently helped convince the North Vietnamese to accept a negotiated settlement—the mining of Haiphong Harbor in May 1972 and the massive bombing of Hanoi in December 1972—were originally conceived by the JCS.

[See also Civil-Military Relations: Civilian Control of the Military; National Security Act (1947).]

• Harry S. Truman, Years of Trial and Hope, 1956. Matthew Ridgway, The Korean War, 1956. Townsend Hoopes, The Limits of Intervention, 1969. Dean Acheson, The Korean War, 1971. Lyndon B. Johnson, The Vantage Point, Perspective of the Presidency, 1963–1969, 1971. David Halberstam, The Best and the Brightest, 1972. Maxwell Taylor, Swords and Plowshares, 1972. Richard Nixon, The Memoirs of Richard Nixon, 1978.   —Lawrence J. Korb

LINCOLN, ABRAHAM (1809–1865), sixteenth president of the United States. Born into a poor family in Hardin County, Kentucky, Lincoln moved with his family to Indiana in 1816 and to Illinois in 1830. In 1831, he settled in New Salem, near Springfield; in 1842, he married Mary Todd, daughter of a prominent family. Lincoln pursued the law and politics, both successfully. As a Whig he served in the state legislature (1834–41) and in the House of Representatives (1847–49), where he criticized the *Mexican War. The slavery expansion controversy prompted his reentry into public life in 1854, now in the new Republican Party. His national stature was enhanced when he challenged and lost to Stephen A. Douglas for the U.S. Senate in 1858.

In 1860, Lincoln won the Republican presidential nomination because of his reputation for public honesty, his availability, and because his rivals had too many political enemies. Winning popular votes only in the North, Lincoln carried the electoral vote against three opponents (including Douglas) and took office on 4 March 1861. The country was divided by the secession of seven Southern states, whose white population believed that Lincoln's election portended the death of slavery. In his inaugural address, Lincoln tried to reassure his "dissatisfied fellow countrymen" that he would not attack slavery where it existed, but neither would he allow the Union to be destroyed. The Southern capture of *Fort Sumter in April 1861 did lead to war, to the secession of additional Southern states, and ultimately to the end of slavery.

Thus, Abraham Lincoln addressed two mortal public issues: war and freedom. He addressed them with a political skill never before demanded of a U.S. president and never matched thereafter. Lincoln understood his limitations and his strengths, at once willing to defer to men of demonstrably greater knowledge or ability yet willing to impose his authority over them. As commander in chief, Lincoln understood that mobilizing an effective military force was similar to forming a political coalition, that political goals were akin to grand strategy. He also promoted professional soldiers, usually West Pointers, to significant commands, but he was chided too for appointing "political generals," which he believed necessary in order to gain popular support for the war. Some of the most egregious tactical blunders on both sides—from Malvern Hill to Cold Harbor to Franklin—occurred under the command of West Pointers.

During 1862–63, when Lincoln effectively acted as general in chief, he tried to impress upon his generals the need for precise aims and energetic execution of plans. Most notable was his frustration with George B. *McClellan, a general of ability who seemed reluctant to engage the enemy even when he held a military advantage, which he always did. When McClellan refused to press Robert E. *Lee after the Battle of *Antietam, Lincoln removed him from command. He also removed another general given to inertia, Don Carlos Buell, Union commander in Kentucky. Only days later, Lincoln wondered if the problem was "in our case" and not in the generals. Their successors (Ambrose *Burnside and William S. *Rosecrans) could do no better. Hard facts of terrain, distance, and a determined enemy would dictate military progress or the lack of it.

The *Union army did know success, however, notably in the major Battle of *Gettysburg (July 1863) and the siege of *Vicksburg (which ended with Vicksburg's surrender on 4 July 1863). Yet there was no decisive, or Napoleonic victory, nor could there be, as Lincoln came to understand; there would be only a remorseless and bloody struggle until the *Confederate army and the Southern will were broken, as they finally were in 1864–65. Victories in Virginia and Georgia were achieved by veteran armies led by redoubtable soldiers, Grant and Sherman, men of ability and determination, educated by their victories and their defeats. In order to overcome criticism of his wartime policies—the *Habeas Corpus Act, the establishment of martial law, censorship of opposition newspapers, and arrests of vocal opponents of the war—and to gain the support of War Democrats, Lincoln led a Union Party in 1864 and named Andrew *Johnson of Tennessee as his vice president. The Democrats nominated George B. McClellan, but military success, especially after the Battle of *Atlanta in September 1864, assured Lincoln's reelection.

Emancipation is the event most associated with Lincoln next to the preservation of the Union. His enemies, North and South, resisted freedom for the slaves during the *Civil War; his public friends thought that he was a reluctant emancipator, too calculating in advancing the great cause. A politician of Lincoln's time and place could not be unaware of the depths of racial animosity in the North, a social bias offset only by an intensity of feeling for the Union; yet this should not obscure the time and thought Lincoln gave to emancipation. He commented favorably on various options: colonization; gradual and compensated emancipation; and in 1862, he proposed an amendment to the Constitution that would abolish slavery. On 22 September 1862, after Antietam, he announced the *Emancipation Proclamation, a war measure grounded in his constitutional mandate as commander in chief, to take effect on 1 January 1863. Lincoln's eloquence of advocacy thereafter elevated political rhetoric to levels unequaled before or since. The Union could be saved only through military force, he said, and emancipation was a necessary corollary to military action. Thus were joined the great issues of war and freedom. Lincoln had effected a revolution and said as much in his immortal speech at Gettysburg.

In his second inaugural address, Lincoln suggested that the Civil War was God's punishment for the great sin of slavery, and that even if it continued "until every drop of blood drawn with the lash, shall be paid by another with the sword, as was said three thousand years ago, so still it must be said, 'the judgments of the Lord are true and righteous altogether,'" Five days after the war ended, Lincoln was shot by John Wilkes Booth while watching a play at Ford's Theatre. He died on Good Friday, 15 April 1865.

[*See also* Civil War: Military and Diplomatic Course; Civil War: Domestic Course; Commander in Chief, President as.]

• Godfrey R. B. Charnwood, *Abraham Lincoln*, 1916. John G. Nicolay and John Hay, *Abraham Lincoln: A History*, 1890; rev. ed. 1917. James G. Randall, *Lincoln the President*, 4 vols., 1945–55. Roy P. Basler, ed., *Abraham Lincoln: Collected Works*, 9 vols., 1953–55. Mark E. Neely, *Abraham Lincoln and the Promise of America*, 1993. David Herbert Donald, *Lincoln*, 1995. James A. Rawley, *Abraham Lincoln and a Nation Worth Fighting For*, 1996.
—John T. Hubbell

LINDBERGH, CHARLES (1902–1974), U.S. flier, aviation consultant, author, and conservationist. An army-trained pilot who also flew the mail, Lindbergh achieved world fame in 1927 for his New York–to–Paris flight, the first solo transatlantic air crossing. The hero was awarded the Distinguished Flying Cross, the Medal of Honor, and promoted to colonel in the Air Corps Reserve.

While in Europe in the 1930s, Lindbergh made several visits to Germany and was credited with obtaining valuable air intelligence for the United States. In 1938, the U.S. ambassador in London, Joseph Kennedy, asked Lindbergh to assess the military situation in Europe. Lindbergh argued against fighting Germany because he believed German airpower would be overwhelming.

Upon returning home in 1939, Lindbergh advised the Air Corps on its expansion. When war came in Europe, he spoke out against U.S. involvement and eventually joined the isolationist America First Committee. Denounced by President Franklin D. *Roosevelt for his stand, he resigned his reserve commission. In a Des Moines speech (1941), he singled out the Roosevelt administration, the British, and the Jews as "war agitators." The speech caused a furor in which Lindbergh was widely attacked as an anti-Semite.

After the attack on *Pearl Harbor, Roosevelt blocked Lindbergh from serving in uniform. Nonetheless, Lindbergh joined the war effort. He became a consultant at the Willow Run bomber plant, and evaluated the F4U Corsair fighter for United Aircraft. Although a civilian, Lindbergh made his way to the Pacific and persuaded local commanders to allow him to fly in combat. He completed fifty missions and was credited with downing one Japanese plane.

Lindbergh traveled to Europe after V-E Day to study German jets and rockets. As an air force adviser he inspected military units, helped select the Air Force Academy site in Colorado, and served six years on the Scientific Advisory Committee of the Department of *Defense. In 1960, he retired as a reserve brigadier general, having been appointed to that rank in 1954.

[*See also* Academies, Service: U.S. Air Force Academy; Isolationism; World War II, U.S. Air Operations in: The Air War Against Japan.]

• Charles A. Lindbergh, *The Wartime Journals*, 1970. Wayne S. Cole, *Charles A. Lindbergh and the Battle Against American Intervention in World War II*, 1974.
—Raymond H. Fredette

LISBON AGREEMENT ON NATO FORCE LEVELS (1952). The Lisbon force goals, which were adopted by the North Atlantic Council (NAC) in February 1952, represented the high point of *NATO's attempt to build up the conventional forces defending Western Europe following the outbreak of the Korean War. They were based on the recommendations of the Temporary Council Committee (TCC), an ad hoc body established by the NAC the previous September to reconcile NATO's military requirements with the political and economic constraints that were already causing the initial rearmament efforts of the European members to falter. In December, the TCC presented a detailed program that called for the creation by the end of 1954 of a total of forty-two ready divisions and forty-five (increased to forty-eight by the NAC) reserve divisions mobilizable within thirty days. Soon after these goals were adopted, however, it became clear that they could not be achieved, primarily because the economic assumptions on which they were based were overoptimistic. The NATO force goals for the end of 1952 adopted at Lisbon were twenty-five ready divisions and twenty-eight and two-thirds reserve divisions mobilizable within thirty days. Actual forces in existence at the end of 1952 were twenty-five ready divisions and twenty reserve divisions. Although the goals for 1952 were largely met by the end of the year, further significant increases, especially in mobilizable divisions, seemed doubtful. Force goals for the end of 1953 were thirty-six and two-thirds ready divisions and thirty-five and two-thirds reserve divisions; in April 1953, however, the NAC revised these goals downward to thirty and one-third ready divisions and twenty-six and one-third reserve divisions.

[*See also* Korean War.]
—John S. Duffield

LITERATURE, WAR AND THE MILITARY IN. Fascination with war continues in the twentieth century, and no less fascinating is the literature that war has spawned. In novels, poems, memoirs, and plays, the subject finds an immense readership. Half a century after the end of World War II, books continue to issue from major publishers. Manuscript memoirs circulate widely among former warriors. Diaries and journals (kept secretly during wartime service, and subject to court-martial if discovered) surface every day to find their way into print. As the literature of war grows, readership grows too among combat veterans, professional historians, and students of the matrix of twentieth-century military life who yearn for the intimate details of war told by those who experienced it.

War fiction—short stories and novels—has had a major impact on readers in this century. For the most part, the significant war fiction finds its roots in the classic tales of earlier centuries. Writers on war often cite Leo Tolstoy's *War and Peace* and Stephen Crane's *Red Badge of Courage* as inspiration. At the core of Crane's small masterpiece lies a preeminent theme: the rapid, tragic maturation of youth. This theme is also included in Erich Maria Remarque's classic, *All Quiet on the Western Front*, the tale of a naive and idealistic German lad who slowly loses his idealism as *trench warfare inexorably destroys his comrades and, eventually, himself. No novel of World War I more poignantly captures the utter futility of war and of an epoch.

Much of this nihilistic attitude is also found in William March's *Company K* and Ernest Hemingway's *A Farewell to Arms* and *The Sun Also Rises*. Although the last cannot be categorized as a novel of World War I in the sense that it is a chronicle of combat, it does speak of the aftermath of that war and the symbolic emasculation of all its participants. The Australian novelist Frederic Manning addresses this same futility in *The Middle Parts of Fortune,* first published anonymously in 1929 and a year later in an expurgated version, as *Her Privates We.*

The poetry of World War I continues to reach as wide an audience as did the fiction of that war. Thematically, this verse differed little from the novels: loss of innocence, idealism, and patriotism; the shock of combat and its aftermath; the wanton destruction of the natural world. Wilfred Owen (the best of the poets), Rupert Brooke, Julian Grenfell, Isaac Rosenberg, Edward Thomas, and the American soldier-poet Joyce Kilmer, all died in the Great War, leaving behind them a considerable body of small masterpieces. Others—Edmund Blunden, Herbert Asquith (son of the British prime minister), Robert Graves, A. P. Herbert, Herbert Read, and Siegfried Sassoon—survived the war, but each in his own way was indelibly marked by it. They expressed their psychic wounds in a number of memorable poems, all speaking to the same theme: the intense violence of battle, the long reflection after combat, and the anguish suffered over lost comrades. The war's greatest verse is marked by these themes.

Much of the literature evinces language that war itself engenders. Warriors tend to be word merchants. They manufacture words and phrases that seem appropriate to themselves and to their plights. In every war—and surely most obvious in World War II—warriors created a vocabulary that proved to have remarkable staying power. Few military men or women speak a genteel language, for the very magnitude of what they do and the traumas they undergo spawn a vocabulary that fits their moods, actions, thoughts, and ideals. The ubiquitous word *fuck* (used with great frequency for every situation and as practically every part of speech) began to appear in print soon after the end of World War II. (In World War I, the British *bloody* served a similar function.) Hemingway's *Across the River and into the Trees* appeared first in *Cosmopolitan* magazine. His Colonel Cantwell's "f- - -" was considered a breakthrough in the era's publishing censorship; but in Norman Mailer's *The Naked and the Dead, fuggin* became for the general reading public what all veterans of World War II (and other wars) understood: The warriors' curse. The ingenuity of their cursing became the subject of some mirth and eventually found its way into a great deal of the literature of the twentieth century. Some language was simply dusted off from earlier wars: *K.P.* and *AWOL* date from the American *Civil War. But the scope, mechanization, and immensity of World War II gave rise to an entirely new and highly imaginative language. The acronyms *WAVE, WACK, and SNAFU, along with words and phrases like "TS cards," "flak," "chickenshit," "K rations," "jerry cans," "gremlins," "sky pilot," and the ubiquitous "Kilroy Was Here," all attest to the fanciful coinages of war. Thus no novel, poem, or short story needed a gloss to help readers define terms or fathom dialogue. And years after that war, many such words and phrases (for veteran and civilian alike) remain in our vocabulary. The wars in Korea and Vietnam have added to, and in some cases enriched, the language. The flexibility and breadth of English in great measure account for this phenomenon.

The huge differences between World Wars I and II ac-count in some ways for the quality and scope of their literature. World War I, as historians and literary critics have noted for years, was a relatively contained war; that is, the major battles were fought in the trenches and bunkers of Western Europe. Day after day, week after week, stalemated armies fought and died over a few yards of mud and rubble. There were no great decisive sea battles in World War I—battles involving massive task forces, submarines, and thousands of aircraft. The daily horrors of trench warfare, then, became the metaphors of the war and found their way into impressive works of literature. World War II was a vastly different war. It covered a huge geographic area, involved far more combatants and civilians, and resulted in far greater *casualties. It also involved massive amounts of highly sophisticated and deadly efficient weapons (*radar, aircraft, *tanks, and the like) and at times moved with blinding speed across the terrain. Unlike World War I, when battles like the Somme and Verdun symbolized the entire war experience, World War II was marked by many battles sprawled across vast areas, each one a tragic symbol of the era. Guadalcanal, Midway, Iwo Jima, Kasserine Pass, Anzio, Leyte Gulf, Okinawa, the bomber campaign over Germany, the invasion of *Normandy, the Battle of the *Bulge—all represented separate and distinct facets of the World War II experience.

Just as American novelists from the World War I era strove to share their stories soon after the armistice was signed (William Boyd's *Through the Wheat* and William March's *Company K*), novels of World War II began to appear as early as the mid-forties and into the early fifties. First, in 1944, was John Hersey's *A Bell for Adano.* In 1946, Thomas Heggen's *Mr. Roberts* was published. John Horne Burns's *The Gallery* and James Michener's *Tales of the South Pacific* appeared in 1947; and a year later came James Gould Cozzens's *Guard of Honor.* Irwin Shaw's *The Young Lions* and Norman Mailer's *The Naked and the Dead* were both published in 1948. James Jones's *From Here to Eternity* appeared in 1951, as did Herman Wouk's *The Caine Mutiny.* All were critically acclaimed; several became successful films; Hersey, Cozzens, and Michener won Pulitzer Prizes.

American dramatists soon followed suit. In 1947, Arthur Miller's *All My Sons* was staged. In one sense, Miller's drama was a more political statement than the famous World War I play by Maxwell Anderson and Laurence Stallings, *What Price Glory?* A chronicle of wartime profiteering, *All My Sons* dwelt on many of the same themes employed by the fiction writers of the period: human waste, Pyrrhic victories, and self-aggrandizement in both military and civilian life. Since then, Vietnam (far more than Korea) has become a metaphor for American involvement in foreign wars—as well as the basis for a literature of angst that has dominated the contemporary creative imagination.

England's role in World War II has been captured in a number of significant novels, many of them masterpieces of the genre. Alexander Baron's *From the City, from the Plough,* written soon after the novelist's return from six years as a combat infantryman in the British army, is a graphic account of a rifleman's life given in a tone that belies its content. No better novel of the war at sea has been written than Nicholas Monsarrat's *The Cruel Sea;* and few novels of World War II—or any war—captured the degradation and pain suffered in prisoner-of-war camps better than Pierre Boulle's *Bridge on the River Kwai*, based on the story of the Burma-Thailand rail line built by British POWs and impressed native laborers.

Now, more than half a century from the end of World War II, personal memories dominate the English and American literary scene. In recent decades, the works of both professional and amateur writers have flooded the market; many have received high praise, and rightly so. Joseph Heller's *Catch-22* is both a comic novel and a bitter indictment of war. The book quickly became a cult favorite, and the title has become part of contemporary vocabulary. War in the air has been graphically portrayed by Samuel Hynes's *Flights of Passage*, Elmer Bendiner's *Fall of Fortresses*, and Richard Hillary's *The Last Enemy. Last Letters from Stalingrad*, edited by Franz Schneider, reveals the full horrors of Adolf *Hitler's military and political madness in throwing German youth against Russia's might and its winter ally. Guy Sajer compounds those horrors in *The Forgotten Soldier*, the best German warrior's memoir of the eastern front. Harold Bond's *Return to Cassino* and Farley Mowat's *And No Birds Sang* are gripping accounts of the Allied campaign in Italy. John Hersey's *Into the Valley*, Richard Tregaskis's *Guadalcanal Diary*, and Eugene Sledge's *With the Old Breed on Peliliu and Okinawa* deal with Pacific *jungle warfare in all its Goyaesque images. Few prisoner-of-war chronicles achieve such power and poignancy as Manny Lawton's *Some Survived*. Donald Burgett's *Currahee*, told with chilling fidelity to detail, is the only first-person account of the invasion of Normandy by an American paratrooper. *D-Day*, a collection of memoirs by participants in the greatest seaborne invasion in history, has been edited by Stephen Ambrose.

In all of these memoirs, themes found in World War II fiction are evident; and all speak of the sense that each participant in war is aware in some vague way that he or she is involved in a monumental undertaking—but that the full scope and significance of that participation can never be fully fathomed. Personal memoirs of war also focus on the demeaning nature of man in battle, the atavistic nature of combat, and the agony experienced by boyish warriors assigned tasks they never believed they would experience. The most memorable memoirs all ring with war's bitter truth spoken by Walt Whitman: "I was the man, I suffered, I was there."

World War II memoir writers pay homage to their predecessors, especially the artists of World War I. English participants in the Great War wrote a remarkable number of evocative memoirs. The tone of most is modest and straightforward, but beneath their surface lies a deep vein of anger, fear, and chaos engendered by the daily brutality of trench warfare. Among the genuine classics in this genre is Siegfried Sassoon's trilogy, *Memoirs of a Fox-Hunting Man, Memoirs of an Infantry Officer*, and *Sherston's Progress*. Assuming the persona of George Sherston, Sassoon relates his wartime experiences, the Edwardian world he grew up in, and his growing bitterness at the graft, political maneuvering, and civilian indifference to the meaningless slaughter on the western front. No writer of his generation was more responsible for the widespread antiwar movement in England in the years following the war.

War correspondents—men and women who sketched, painted, photographed, and wrote about war from frontline positions or as part of vast sea and air armadas—achieved some considerable measure of distinction through the quality and quantity of their work. Their collected dispatches have now become a distinct genre in the literature of war and deserve high praise. Among the best journalistic writings to emerge from World War II are those of Ernie Pyle—*Brave Men;* Bill *Mauldin—Up Front;* and Homer Biggart—*Forward Positions*. Biggart's fierce competitor and colleague, Marguerite "Maggie" Higgins, reported brilliantly from Korea. Her dispatches are among the finest from that war.

Stanley Karnow's *Vietnam: A History* is the definitive work on the period and the war, while Michael Herr's *Dispatches* is among the best work by a correspondent who covered the jungle battles. A gripping, fanciful novel on Vietnam is Tim O'Brien's *Going After Cacciato*. Ron Kovic's *Born on the Fourth of July* is among the finest of the personal accounts of war and the nation's attitude towards its returning veterans. Nathaniel Tripp's *Father, Soldier, Son* is a brilliant memoir of Vietnam; the work alternates between the Vietnam years and Tripp's father's emotional struggles in World War II.

To many, verse is not an art form that lends itself to a depiction of war. Yet the shock of combat and the chaos of the battlefield became a muse for a number of American and British warrior-poets of World War II. The best of these poets seemed to find that only verse could capture the immensity of what they had experienced—that only verse could speak the unspeakable. World War I verse disproves William Butler Yeats's maxim that "passive suffering is not a theme for poetry." Compared with the quality and quantity of poetry of the Great War, however, little verse from World War II measured up. The lengthy immersion in war by British soldiers on the western front from 1914 to 1918 supplied them with the subject matter of the loss of all illusions and death in its most horrible forms. At the same time, there seemed to develop among these poets a particular sensibility and ironic feeling that in the beauty of verse lay the vehicle to express that what they were doing and seeing. During and after World War II, no American poet captured the vision or intensity of an Owen or a Sassoon. But a handful of American poems stand out. Among them are Randall Jarrell's "Death of the Ball Turret Gunner," Richard Eberhart's "The Fury of Aerial Bombardment," and Louis Simpson's "The Runner." In England, Henry Reed's collection, *Lessons of War*, represents one powerful voice to emerge from the era.

From the ancient historian Thucydides to those writing in the waning decades of this century, men and women continue to strive for words to articulate their war experiences and to share them with others. One thing is certain, however. Thomas Hardy, too old to serve in World War I but caught up in the hideous drama unfolding before him, wrote that one day "war's annals will fade into night." Judging from the continuing flow of war literature in our time, it appears that "war's annals" are far from that. Rather, they lie at the dawn of the memories and imaginations of creative artists.

[See also Korean War; Vietnam War: Postwar Impact; World War I: Postwar Impact; World War II: Military and Diplomatic Course; World War II: Postwar Impact.]

• John H. Johnson, *English Poetry of the First World War*, 1964. Stanley Cooperman, *World War I and the American Novel*, 1967. George G. Panichas, ed., *Promise of Greatness*, 1968. Peter Aichinger, *The American Soldier in Fiction, 1880–1963*, 1975. Paul Fussell, *The Great War and Modern Memory*, 1975. Jean Morton Cru, *War*

Books, 1976. Peter G. Jones, *War and the Novelist*, 1976. Jon Stallworthy, ed., *The Oxford Book of War Poetry*, 1984. Margaret Higonnet, et al., eds., *Behind the Lines: Gender and the Two World Wars*, 1987. Helen Cooper, Adrienne Munich, and Susan Squier, *Arms and the Woman: War, Gender and Literary Representation*, 1989. Jon Glover and Jon Silkin, eds., *The Penguin Book of First World War Prose*, 1989. Paul Fussell, ed., *The Norton Book of Modern War*, 1991. Samuel Hynes, *A War Imagined: The First World War and English Culture*, 1991.   —Alexander Medlicott, Jr.

LITTLE BIGHORN, BATTLE OF THE (1876). This clash between U.S. cavalry and Sioux and Cheyenne Indians has gained renown in both history and legend. Although a triumph for the Indians, the disaster celebrated as "Custer's Last Stand" so outraged the American people that the army launched a counteroffensive that ended warfare on the northern plains.

The Sioux War of 1876 originated in the Treaty of 1868, which established the Great Sioux Reservation in Dakota Territory. Part of the seven tribes of Lakota Sioux and their Cheyenne allies settled on the reservation, while the rest gathered with *Sitting Bull, *Crazy Horse, and other "nontreaties" in the "unceded" Powder River country to the west. After discovery of gold in the Black Hills in 1874, the government sought to buy the hills from the reservation chiefs. The attempt failed in large part because of the opposition of the nontreaty chiefs. To destroy their independence, the government ordered all Indians to their agencies by 31 January 1876 or face military action. The nontreaties did not comply.

Lt. Col. George Armstrong *Custer's Seventh Cavalry marched with one of three columns that converged on the unceded territory. Battlefield reverses turned back Gen. George Crook, but Gen. Alfred H. Terry and Col. John Gibbon united on the Yellowstone River at the mouth of the Rosebud Creek and formed plans to strike the Indians, thought to be in the Little Bighorn Valley. Custer would march up the Rosebud and hit from the south, while Terry and Gibbon would ascend the Yellowstone and Bighorn and position themselves to head off any Indians flushed by Custer.

On 25 June, before Terry and Gibbon were in position, Custer found and attacked the Indian village on the Little Bighorn. It contained about 7,000 people, 2,000 fighting men. Custer's regiment numbered about 600, which he divided into three battalions, one under Maj. Marcus A. Reno, one under Capt. Frederick W. Benteen, and one under his personal command. Benteen departed on a mission to ensure that no Indians camped in the valley above the main village. Custer and Reno approached the village itself, which Custer apparently intended to strike from two directions. While Custer and five companies rode downstream behind masking bluffs, Reno and three companies charged the upper end of the village.

Although surprised, the warriors rallied and threw Reno's small command back across the river with heavy *casualties. Reno's retreat freed the Indians to concentrate on Custer at the other end of the village. They caught him in broken terrain east of the river. Within an hour, all five companies, 210 men, had been wiped out. No man survived. Joined by Benteen, Reno held hilltop positions four miles to the south through the next day, when the Indians, discovering Terry's approach from the north, pulled off to the south.

The disaster promptly set off a controversy that still rages. Whether a reckless glory hunter or a capable field commander victimized by bad luck, in defeat Custer gained an immortality that no victory could have conferred.

[*See also* Plains Indians Wars; Army, U.S.: 1866–99.]

• John S. Gray, *Centennial Campaign: The Sioux War of 1876*, 1976. John S. Gray, *Mitch Boyer and the Little Bighorn Reconstructed*, 1991. Paul Andrew Hutton, ed., *The Custer Reader*, 1992.
                                        —Robert M. Utley

LOBBIES, MILITARY. Curiously absent in discussions of American *civil-military relations is any mention of the lobbying organizations that do the daily work of politics. Yet the defense arena features organizations very similar in form and action to those that permeate the political system. Although not as well known as the veterans' organizations, organizations such as the Association of the United States Army (AUSA) and the American Defense Preparedness Association play active political roles. While not all "lobby" in the legal sense, all seek to influence government decisions by mobilizing attention, money, and votes.

The history of these organizations reflects the history of the American political system and the American military. The late nineteenth century saw the first foundings of military professional and political organizations. For example, the National Guard Association of the United States (NGAUS) was formed in 1878 for "practical reform which would make the Militia a more effective instrument ... of National Defense." Today, some of these organizations are narrowly professional; others have evolved into politically active organizations.

The history of two organizations of this era, the Navy League and the Marine Corps Association, however, illustrates the difficulty of separating the professional from the political. The Navy League, sponsored by Theodore *Roosevelt, was founded in 1902, "not to formulate specific needs for Navy ... but rather to educate the people on the importance of sea power." Education about the navy was in fact education about Theodore Roosevelt's expansionist policy. The Marine Corps Association was founded in 1911, born in the heat of politics as a response to an effort to reduce the role of the *Marine Corps. It succeeded in sustaining the Corps in part because of the political connections of its members.

Several organizations were founded after World War I, including the Reserve Officers Association (ROA) and the Fleet Reserve Association. There was a second surge of foundings between 1946 and 1955; many of these were industrial organizations, like the American Defense Preparedness Association. Organizations founded in the 1960s through the 1980s were more specialized (the Army Warrant Officers Association) or focused on enlisted members and families (the Non-Commissioned Officers Association and the National Military Family Association). Today, fifty to sixty organizations claim to represent the views of military members or their families.

Lobbying organizations fall into three main types. First are the industry-based educational associations, such as Armed Forces Communications and Electronics Association (AFCEA, with 25,000 individual members and 12,000 corporate sponsors), which operate under sections of the Internal Revenue Code that restrict explicit lobbying and political activity. They do not employ registered lobbyists or undertake explicit political efforts. They do sponsor educational activities on general issues, such as the health of the military's industrial base, and develop policy agendas. Their budgets may be substantial, in the $1–$7 million range.

Other organizations, such as The Retired Officers Association (TROA) and the National Association for Uniformed Services (NAUS), specialize in personnel issues and have memberships of 100,000 or more; ROA is the largest at 400,000, with an $11 million annual budget. These organizations may employ registered lobbyists, and NAUS has its own political action committee, a rarity. To sustain their membership base, they feature extensive membership packages ranging from credit cards to health insurance.

The third major type is the "peak organization," as in the AUSA and the Navy League. Though they receive Department of *Defense (DoD) support for annual meetings, they are independent organizations, have corporate members and individual memberships of 50,000–170,000 people, and budgets of $3.5–$13 million. Several have registered lobbyists, and all undertake extensive political activity, in the broadest sense. The ROA, for example, publishes a legislative agenda and organizes "meet your congressman" breakfasts.

All of these organizations monitor governmental activity, seek to shape public opinion, and intervene in the policy process. They are not direct channels of campaign contributions. Rather, they gain influence either through their voting strength (military personnel groups represent 3.75 million voters) or personal contacts (most organizations employ veterans from the executive branch or Capitol Hill).

How much impact do these organizations have? Personnel issues have shown where they are most influential. Since the 1970s, the organizations have won improvements in pay and personnel support. They have been relatively effective, though not triumphant, in mitigating efforts to reduce military and retiree benefits. They also have had impact on actions within the DoD. For example, the DoD comptroller once got 7,000 letters prompted by lobbying groups when he proposed cutting commissary benefits; he reversed his course.

These organizations serve a classic political function: the representation of citizens before their government. Though they frequently support articulated DoD positions, they are not mere mouthpieces. For example, NGAUS and ROA have provided active voices for the reserve components, sometimes in quiet opposition to DoD and occasionally in active battle with DoD and each other. Study of the "losses" of these organizations is also instructive. The Air Force Association undertook an effort to fund additional B-2 bombers. This effort was contrary to DoD policy, but featured several recently retired generals pressing the case. The effort died; absent administration support, it was not able to develop congressional support. Lobbying organizations have also failed in the effort to gain greater access to the military commissary system for reservists.

Some of the issues that activate these organizations have nothing to do with pay or procurement. The Air Force Association started the controversy in 1995 over the Smithsonian Institution's *Enola Gay* exhibit. The association's membership was very active in the campaign to change the exhibit, in coalition with veterans' groups. For the Air Force Sergeants' Association, one of the biggest nonbenefits issues has been its opposition to gays in the military. Lobbying organizations have also been active at the state level: the California department of the ROA has been an opponent of efforts to remove *ROTC from state colleges.

Military lobbying groups have a long history. Though their policy positions differ from the Sierra Club, say, they perform a similar function and use similar techniques. But declining defense budgets, aging memberships, smaller armed forces, and the decline in military experience in Congress all signal a potential for more limited effectiveness.

[*See also* Families, Military; Gay Men and Lesbians in the Military; Veterans Administration.]

• Gordon Adams, *The Politics of Defense Contracting: The Iron Triangle*, 1982. John T. Carlton and John F. Slinkman, *The ROA Story: A History of the Reserve Officers Association of the United States*, 1982. Bruce C. Wolpe and Bertram J. Levine, *Lobbying Congress: How the System Works*, 1990; 2nd ed., 1996. Jack L. Walker, *Mobilizing Interest Groups in America: Patrons, Professions and Social Movements*, 1991. Ronald J. Hrebenar, *Interest Group Politics in America*, 3rd ed., 1997. Frank R. Baumgartner and Beth L. Leech, *Basic Interests: The Importance of Groups in Politics and in Political Science*, 1998. William Paul Brown, *Groups, Interests and U.S. Public Policy*, 1998.

—Dana Eyre

LODGE, HENRY CABOT (1902–1985), senator and diplomat. Born in Massachusetts, Lodge was the grandson of the Massachusetts senator for whom he was named. Elected to the U.S. Senate in 1936 and 1942, he resigned in 1944 to go on active duty in Europe with the Second Armored Division. Lieutenant Colonel Lodge received several combat decorations. Reelected to the Senate in 1946, he lost his seat to John F. *Kennedy in 1952. Lodge served from 1953 to 1960 as U.S. ambassador to the *United Nations and was the Republican nominee for vice president in 1960.

President Kennedy named Lodge ambassador to South Vietnam. When Lodge arrived in Saigon in August 1963, members of South Vietnam's armed forces were plotting the overthrow of President Ngo Dinh Diem. Lodge tried unsuccessfully to get Diem to remove his unpopular brother, Ngo Dinh Nhu, from the government, and the ambassador concluded that Diem was politically doomed. On 1 November 1963, a coup toppled Diem's government and led to the murders of Diem and Nhu. Lodge emphatically denied subsequent allegations in *The Pentagon Papers* (1971) and other accounts that he authorized or encouraged the coup on instructions from Washington. The embassy had knowledge of the plot, he admitted, but not of its timing and details, especially the murders.

Lodge resigned as ambassador in June 1964 to participate in the Republican presidential nomination process, but he returned to head the U.S. Embassy in Saigon July 1965–April 1967. From June to December 1966, he engaged in Project Marigold—secret but futile talks through Polish intermediaries to explore a negotiated settlement with North Vietnam. In March 1968, Lodge was part of the group of elder statesmen, the Wise Men, who advised Lyndon B. *Johnson not to send more troops to Vietnam. He was a delegate to the Vietnam peace talks in Paris in 1969 and served as ambassador to Bonn and the Vatican before retiring in 1977.

[See also Pentagon Papers; Vietnam War: Military and Diplomatic Course.]

• Henry Cabot Lodge, The Storm Has Many Eyes, 1973. Ellen J. Hammer, A Death in November: America in Vietnam, 1963, 1987.
—David L. Anderson

LOGAN, JOHN (1826–1886), *Civil War general, politician, author. Logan abandoned his political career in 1861 to raise an Illinois volunteer regiment for the Union during the Civil War. "Black Jack" Logan served in the western theater, where he won a major generalcy by 1863. Following division and corps commands, he temporarily led the Army of the Tennessee in the 1864 Atlanta campaign.

Subsequently, Logan chaired the Military Affairs Committees during his years in the House and Senate (1866–86); he founded and was three-time president of the *Grand Army of the Republic, 1869 through 1871. In both roles, he extolled the volunteer *citizen-soldier and excoriated the dominance of military high command by "aristocratic" army officers. Logan's ponderous The Volunteer Soldier of America (1887) reiterated these themes.

Logan's attacks on the regular army represented in part resentment following Gen. William Tecumseh *Sherman's selection (1864) of a West Pointer to permanent command of the Army of the Tennessee. Logan was more than the mere political hack and unthinking military critic some scholars have depicted. Recognized as the one of best of the "political" volunteer generals, his ideas for training citizen-soldiers and opening high command opportunities for them were not mindless. The hyperbole of Logan's rhetoric, however, gravely weakened his assessment of postwar military policy.

[See also Atlanta, Battle of; Civil War: Military and Diplomatic Course; Union Army.]

• Russell F. Weigley, "John A. Logan: The Rebuttal for a Citizen Army," in Weigley, ed., Towards an American Army: Military Thought from Washington to Marshall, 1962. James P. Jones, "Black Jack": John A. Logan and Southern Illinois in the Civil War Era, 1967. James P. Jones, John A. Logan: Stalwart Republican from Illinois, 1982.
—Jerry Cooper

LOGISTICS. Early in the twentieth century, Secretary of War Elihu *Root observed that for Americans the difficulties of making war lay not in the raising of soldiers, but in equipping, supplying, and transporting them. The evolution of modern warfare since 1898 amply demonstrates the truth of Root's observation. The scale and scope of modern wars, rapidly changing technology, and new military doctrines involving the rapid movement of large forces over great distances have made logistics the key to modern warfare.

The Definition of Logistics. The word *logistics* comes from the Greek *logistikos*, meaning one expert in enumeration. First used in the eighteenth century, the word in its current meaning became popular during World War II. In 1949, the army's *Field Service Regulations* defined logistics as "that branch of administration which embraces the management and provision of supplies, evacuation and hospitalization, transportation, and services. It envisages getting the right people and the appropriate supplies to the right place at the right time and in the proper condition." In his 1966 history of army logistics, James A. Huston points out that logistics is the application of time and space factors to war and consists of "the three big M's of warfare—*matériel, movement,* and *maintenance.*"

Narrowly construed, logistics encompasses the four main activities noted in the 1949 *Field Service Regulations:* supply, transportation, evacuation and hospitalization, and services (maintenance being the most prominent). A broader understanding might encompass all measures taken by a state to raise, arm, equip, feed, move, maintain, and otherwise care for its armies in the field. In its broadest construction, logistics also properly includes the mobilization of industry and manpower, research and development, procurement, construction of facilities, personnel management, and allied tasks.

Logistical Functions. Each of the armed services maintains its own logistical system. Despite obvious differences in equipment and certain specialized activities, such as underway replenishment of ships at sea and the aerial refueling of aircraft, each of these systems performs essentially the same five functions: the determination of requirements; acquisition; distribution; maintenance; and disposal. The determination of requirements involves the statement of needs and the definition of the resources required to meet those needs. Acquisition encompasses research and development, design, testing, production, and purchase of ships, aircraft, weapons, vehicles, ammunition, fuel, rations, clothing, and other equipment and supplies. Distribution includes the *transportation, receipt, storage, and issue of materiel of all kinds. Maintenance involves the inspection, service, lubrication, and adjustment of equipment, and its calibration, repair, or refurbishment. The final logistical function is the disposal of worn, damaged, or surplus supplies and equipment.

Principles of Logistics. Although logistical organization and procedures vary among the services, the logistical systems of the army, navy, Marine Corps, and air force all respond to the same set of logistical principles. Most students of military affairs are familiar with the nine "Principles of War"—Mass, Objective, Simplicity, Unity of Command, Maneuver, Offensive, Surprise, Security, and Economy of Force—developed to serve as guides to the conduct of *strategy and *tactics. The principles governing the conduct of logistics are less well known but no less important.

Many commentators have tried to formulate the "principles of logistics." Huston, for example, proposes fourteen principles based on the American experiences in war, and the army officially adheres to the nine set forth in chapter 3 of *Army Regulation 11-8: Principles and Policies of the Army Logistics System* (1976). Both are too long and complex for practical purposes, but can conveniently be summarized under five headings: *Concentration, Austerity, Visibility, Mobility,* and *Flexibility.* Concentration is the key, and its accomplishment involves the positioning of superior combat power at the decisive time and place. Allied successes in World War II, and more recently during the *Persian Gulf War in Operation Desert Storm, were due to observing just this principle. Resources are always limited, and thus logisticians must always observe the principle of Austerity, which has two aspects. The first is economy—the conservation of available resources before battle and the economical distribution of materiel to other, less vital, areas. Economy involves avoiding both excessive expenditure and unnecessary duplication of resources. The second is Simplicity. Simplicity of doctrine, organization, equipment and plans is essential to the successful logistical support of combat operations. The third principle is that of Visibility. Because the inability to locate a critical item is tantamount to not having it at all, the successful commander or logistician must always know what he or she has and where it is. Mobility is the fourth principle. Insofar as mobile troops are essential to success on the modern battlefield, adequate transportation must be provided for all military operations, and all military equipment must be designed for agility and transportability. The final principle is Flexibility, or the capacity to accommodate the unforeseen. This can be accomplished by flexibility of organization, plans, and materiel, and, above all, by flexibility of mind.

Periods in the History of American Military Logistics. The history of American military logistics can be divided into four grand periods, each of which has posed new challenges for American logisticians. The period from 1775 to 1845 was an Era of Creation, in which civilian and military leaders struggled to establish effective mechanisms for supporting the armed forces just as the nation searched for effective mechanisms of political and social organization. The challenges of creating effective logistical systems were ultimately met, but not without significant delays, setbacks, and near disasters. The second period ran roughly from the *Mexican War (1846–48) to the *Spanish-American War (1989). In this Era of Professionalization, primitive logistical organizations and procedures were placed on a regular and continuous basis, and the practitioners of logistics developed standards of training and performance suitable for a well-established organization. The development of modern technology and the necessity of worldwide operations after 1898 thrust logisticians into a new Era of Specialization, which lasted roughly until the end of World War II. The relatively simple logistical tasks and organizations that had met the needs of earlier times became much more complex, requiring more and better trained personnel, larger and more diverse logistical organizations, and greater management and control. The Era of Specialization overlapped the fourth phase, the Era of Integration, which began before World War II and continues today. This most recent period is characterized by an emphasis on centralized direction of logistical activities, organization along functional lines, and joint and combined operations employing a variety of advanced technologies.

Themes in American Military Logistics. A chronological account alone cannot fully explain the uneven history of logistical organization and doctrine, in which many key concepts cannot be pigeonholed, and prominent themes cross the boundaries of the four periods. Fortunately, although the history of military logistics in America is complex, its nine salient themes can be concisely stated.

1. *Increasing importance of logistics vs. strategy and tactics.* Since 1898, logistical considerations have increasingly dominated the formulation and execution of both strategy and tactics; yet obvious as it may seem, in practice many military leaders continue to ignore the importance of logistics. At best, logistical considerations and logisticians are seen as unwelcome, if necessary, adjuncts to strategic planning and the management of "important" problems such as tactical doctrine. Nevertheless, logistics is the primary consideration in all modern military operations. World War II provides an excellent example. Allied victory depended in large part on America's ability to organize and to project its industrial might. Indeed, the great demand for logistical support engendered in World War II had a basic and profound effect on the organization of forces and the strategies adopted. The basic American strategic decision of the war—to defeat "Germany First"—and its corollary—the abandonment of U.S. forces in the Philippines—were dictated mainly by logistical considerations. So too were such key strategic decisions as the timing of the invasion of Europe and the pace of the attack across France in 1944. Many military leaders have failed to understand the significance of this trend, and exclude logisticians and logistical considerations from planning.

2. *Increasing complexity and scale.* The United States has been a major power with global responsibilities since the Spanish-American War. As the armed forces have become larger, used more sophisticated weapons, and operated further from home in a variety of climates and terrain, their supply and movement have become increasingly complex. At the same time, technology has evolved at a heady pace, and the tactical doctrines and organizations required to incorporate new technology have demanded correspondingly new and complex logistical doctrines and organizations.

3. *Increasing proportion of manpower required in the logistical "tail."* The increasingly logistical demands of modern warfare have required that an ever-increasing proportion of total manpower be dedicated to the task of supporting combat forces. Indeed, the adequacy of logistical support has proven critical to the success of combat operations, and a nation's ability to mobilize and support its combat forces has become equal in importance to the actual performance of such forces on the battlefield. Many American commanders have fought to keep their military forces lean and simple, with a very high proportion of combat troops. World War II proved such thinking to be shortsighted by demonstrating that modern, complex, mechanized, and technically sophisticated armies, operating worldwide and often in conjunction with allies, require that much if not most of the total force be dedicated to supporting those few who actually do the fighting. The bigger "tail" and fewer "teeth" of today's army may be a function of modern warfare rather than the perversion of military organization that critics often proclaim it to be.

4. *Specialization.* The same stimuli that influence the structure of combat forces—changes in organization, doctrine, and technology—also shape logistical organizations, which respond with special sensitivity to technological developments and the widening scope and scale of modern war. As warfare in the last two centuries has become more mechanized, the demand for specialized personnel to sustain the equipment of war has increased dramatically. This is particularly true for American armed forces, which have traditionally relied on advanced technology rather than mass manpower to achieve victory. Since 1775, the increasing size and diversity of American military forces, and the wide variety of geographic and climatic conditions under which they have operated, have also had a significant impact on the size and composition of logistical forces. Modern, mechanized, total war, conducted with allies on a global scale, has demanded the creation of ever greater numbers and types of logistical units, staffed with highly trained soldier specialists. This trend is not unique to military affairs. Since the Industrial Revolution in the late eighteenth century, there has been an increasing drive toward specialization and division of labor in all human activities.

5. *Rationalization.* The trend toward specialization has been accompanied by increasing centralization of control over logistical planning and operations focused at the highest, Department of *Defense (DoD) level, and by a parallel effort to increase efficiency by organizing logistical tasks along functional rather than commodity-related lines. These efforts have involved the increased application of modern business management techniques to achieve a "rational," and thus more efficient, system. For the army, this process began with the reforms carried out by Secretary of War Root in 1903 in response to problems uncovered during the Spanish-American War and issues that emerged from the creation of a General Staff. Root described the army as a "big business," which could best be managed by commercial methods. Later, army depots and navy shipyards experimented with Frederick W. Taylor's "time and motion" prescriptions, and World War I brought to the services the concept of statistical controls. World War II saw increased use of statistics, as well as the advent of "operations research" and "systems analysis." Since World War II, the independent service logistical systems have been linked by the consolidation of selected logistical functions (e.g., the acquisition of food, fuel, and housekeeping supplies) at DoD level for greater managerial efficiency and economy of scale. This rationalization process intensified in the 1960s under the administration of Secretary of Defense Robert S. *McNamara. McNamara and his so-called Whiz Kids employed techniques derived from the business world to transform military logistics. The military forces have benefited in many ways from the utilization of civilian experts and civilian techniques for the management of logistics; but there have been serious adverse effects as well, of which the "body count" and "cost-effectiveness analysis" are prominent examples.

6. *Changing the civilian-military mix.* Finding the manpower needed to provide adequate logistical support to the combat forces has been a continuing problem, and traditionally American military leaders have relied heavily on civilians to perform logistical tasks. Overseas operations and the drive toward specialization in the first half of this century led to an increased emphasis on uniformed, disciplined logistical personnel. Nevertheless, the overall trend has been toward increasing "civilianization" of military logistics, particularly at higher management levels.

7. *Cyclical attention.* Historically, American military leaders have tended to neglect logistical activities in peacetime and to expand and improve them hastily once a conflict has broken out. Politicians and generals have proclaimed at the end of every war that the nation will never be caught unprepared again; but inevitably the nation has been unprepared for the next conflict and has only been saved by its enormous resources of human and material capital. The nineteenth-century military critic Emory Upton was among the first to decry this "chronic unpreparedness." Since World War II, the demands of a constant state of "near war" have demonstrated that the United States can no longer afford a cavalier attitude toward military readiness; although specific instances continue to arise, the trend appears to have been broken since the *Vietnam War.

8. *Primacy of logistical mobilization.* Given a tradition of cyclical attention to things military and a myopic focus on combat forces, it is not surprising that logistical support forces have been the first to be demobilized at the end of one war and the last to be formed once a new war has be-

gun. It takes comparatively little time to assemble men and begin their military training, but the lead time for housing, clothing, feeding, and equipping them is much longer, a fact that *mobilization planners tend to forget. The results have been all too obvious: troops guarding the Capitol in 1861 without trousers and soldiers in 1941 training with wooden "guns," stovepipe "artillery," and cardboard "tanks." Yet Americans have thus far escaped the consequences of such faulty planning. Until now, the United States has always had the time needed to correct the worst problems, and in the end an enormous industrial capacity has allowed the nation to compensate for many mistakes.

9. *Coalition logistics.* American warmaking in the twentieth century has been largely a coalition activity, and since World War I, the United States has been forced to provide support to its allies or, in some cases, to receive logistical support from them. This trend has introduced further complexities into the problem of providing adequate logistical support for forces in the field, and on occasion America's productive capacity has been severely challenged by the competing demands of supporting both American and allied forces. Although cooperative logistical arrangements have worked effectively in most instances, national preferences and prejudices make the logistician's job more difficult by expanding the number and types of items that have to be supplied. Recently, in an effort to do more with less and to reduce costs, American military leaders have turned increasingly to "host nation support" and "burden sharing" with their allies as means of providing their combat troops with the necessary logistical support.

Modern war requires nations to commit their total resources and victory is determined less by the brilliance of a nation's strategic and tactical thought, and even the valor and skill of its soldiers and leaders, than by its ability to organize and direct the vast machinery needed to project combat power onto the battlefield. From the establishment of the U.S. armed forces in 1775, American military leaders have had to wrestle with the problem of providing adequate logistical support to the combat forces in the field and at sea, in garrison, in port, and in the air. Finding the necessary resources, creating efficient organizations and efficient military *doctrine, and achieving a proper balance between fighting and supporting forces has never been easy. Only the quality of the men and women who provide support to the combat forces has remained constant. Without their dedication, skill, and endurance, military success remains uncertain, regardless of the number of machines and the sophistication of the doctrines employed.

[*See also* Combat Effectiveness; Combat Support; War: Nature of War.]

• George Cyrus Thorpe, *Pure Logistics: The Science of War Preparation,* 1917. George C. Shaw, *Supply in Modern War,* 1939. John D. Millett, "Logistics and Modern War," *Military Affairs,* 9, no. 3 (Fall 1945), pp. 193–207. Daniel Hawthorne, *For Want of a Nail: The Influence of Logistics on War,* 1948. United States Army Service Forces, *Logistics in World War II: Final Report of the Army Service Forces,* 1948. Marvin A. Kreidberg and Merton G. Henry, *History of Military Mobilization in the United States Army, 1775–1945,* 1955. George C. Dyer, *Modern Air Logistics,* 1956. Henry Effingham Eccles, *Logistics in the National Defense,* 1959. George C. Dyer, *Naval Logistics,* 1960. James A. Huston, *The Sinews of War: Army Logistics, 1775–1953,* 1966. James E. Hewes, Jr., *From Root to McNamara: Army Organization and Administration, 1900–1963,* 1975. Richard L. Kelley, "Applying Logistics Principles," *Military Review,* 57, no. 9

(September 1977), pp. 57–63. David C. Rutenberg and Jane S. Allen, eds., *The Logistics of Waging War: American Logistics, 1774–1985, Emphasizing the Development of Airpower,* 1986.

—Charles R. Shrader

LONGSTREET, JAMES (1821–1904), Civil War general. Born in South Carolina, Longstreet grew up in Gainesville and Augusta, Georgia. Graduating from West Point in 1842, he served in the *Mexican War and was a major when, in June 1861, he resigned, offering his services to the Confederacy.

Longstreet was commissioned brigadier general in June 1861, major general in October 1861, and lieutenant general in October 1862. Except for medical leave when wounded in the *Wilderness to Petersburg Campaign, he led the First Corps of the Army of Northern Virginia from its establishment in 1862 to the surrender at Appomattox in 1865. He fought in every major battle in the East except Chancellorsville, and took the First Corps west on detached service to participate in the Confederate victory at the Battle of *Chickamauga in September 1863.

Robert E. *Lee selected Longstreet as his second in command, and although authorities differ, it can be agreed that Longstreet, not "Stonewall" *Jackson, was Lee's most trusted and perhaps most talented subordinate. Outstanding in combat, Longstreet was an excellent corps-level commander and one of the most modern soldiers of his day. He helped to popularize the use of extensive field *fortifications and foreshadowed later Prussian doctrine by favoring the use of maneuver to compel the enemy to attack at a disadvantage. He argued that Northern civilian morale should be the true target of overall Confederate strategy. Longstreet was immensely popular with his men, who called him "the Old Bulldog."

During *Reconstruction, Longstreet settled in New Orleans and joined the Republican Party. He held a variety of political patronage positions until his death in 1904. Viewing him as a traitor to the white South, many former comrades turned against him and attacked his military record. His enemies' lies and fabrications, particularly in relation to the Battle of *Gettysburg, where he was unfairly accused of deliberately delaying the attack on the second day, were accepted uncritically by later historians, such as Douglas Southall Freeman, who misrepresented both Longstreet's personality and his record.

[*See also* Civil War: Military and Diplomatic Course; Confederate Army.]

• William Garrett Piston, *Lee's Tarnished Lieutenant: James Longstreet and His Place in Southern History,* 1987. Jeffry D. Wert, *General James Longstreet: The Confederacy's Most Controversial Soldier,* 1993.

—William Garrett Piston

LOUISBOURG SIEGE (1745). The French commander of Louisbourg fortress at the entrance to the St. Lawrence River launched the renewed Anglo-French war in 1744 by capturing Canso, besieging Annapolis (Nova Scotia), and encouraging raids on New England shipping. New England responded by besieging Louisbourg with 4,000 volunteers, led by William Pepperrell and supported by Commodore Peter Warren's British naval squadron. With French aid intercepted, and the fortress bombarded by both field cannon and those of its own captured Grand Battery, Louisbourg's 600-man garrison surrendered after a 39-day siege in which 101 attackers and 53 defenders were killed.

Louisbourg's fall had wide-ranging consequences. Cancellation of Britain's planned invasion of Canada in 1746 allowed relieved Canadian defenders to capture both Fort Massachusetts and Saratoga. France's Indian allies in the Ohio Valley, deprived of supplies by the siege of Louisbourg, formed a pro-British "Indian Conspiracy." France sent a massive sixty-four-vessel armada to Louisbourg, only to have it disrupted en route by storms, calms, and disease. Naval escalation strained British colonial resources, necessitating imperial assistance and causing the frictions that provoked a three-day impressment riot in Boston late in 1747. New Englanders felt betrayed when Britain returned Louisbourg to the French at the Peace of Aix-la-Chapelle (1748).

[*See also* Canada, U.S. Military Involvement in.]

• G. A. Rawlyk, *Yankees at Louisbourg,* 1967.   —Ian K. Steele

LOW-INTENSITY CONFLICT (LIC is the *Pentagon acronym) refers to a level of hostilities or use of military power that falls short of a full-scale conventional or general war. It includes *peacekeeping, antiterrorism, assistance to foreign countries for internal defense, fulfillment of international treaty obligations, assistance to foreign law enforcement agencies, and commando operations.

Interest in LIC began in the years after the *Vietnam War. In the immediate post-Vietnam era, events overseas made it very clear that U.S. military power remained essential diplomatic currency. Major regional wars in Central Asia and the Mideast served as grim reminders that diplomacy alone could not stop potentially dangerous conflicts. The Arab oil embargo of 1973 emphasized the importance of the Persian Gulf to the economic existence of the industrial West. Washington watched with anxiety as Cuban troops moved into Angola and Mozambique, raising the possibility of major conflict between Soviet-backed Havana and Pretoria. The dramatic rise in terrorism during the 1970s, much of it supported by hostile nations, posed a new challenge to the United States.

As these events unfolded, the Pentagon, regardless of the lingering effects of the Vietnam trauma, realized it was very likely that a limited use of military power would again be needed to support American foreign policy objectives.

In the late 1970s, when defense budgets began to climb again, much thought and planning inside the military was devoted to low-intensity conflict. The military also altered its force structure to meet the demands of LIC. Some army divisions shed heavy equipment so they could be moved rapidly to areas facing limited threat. Because speed in LIC operations was considered paramount, the Pentagon invested substantial resources in flexible air deployment of ground forces. Sophisticated "smart" weapons, such as cruise *missiles, although originally designed for general war with the nations of the *Warsaw Pact, also proved ideal for a "surgical strike" against a lesser foe. The navy pointed to *aircraft carriers, with their ability to "show the flag" or project airpower quickly, as excellent weapons for low-intensity conflict. Sophisticated communications allowed tight control of complex operations anywhere in the world. LIC also required a high degree of interservice cooperation, accelerating the trend toward operational integration within the armed forces.

There were several examples of LIC during the Reagan and Bush administrations. The first was an inauspicious beginning for the return of the U.S. military to the world stage. In 1982, Israel invaded Lebanon and surrounded Beirut. President Ronald *Reagan and Secretary of State George Shultz agreed to send a Marine contingent to Beirut as part of an international force to escort elements of the Palestine Liberation Organization out of the city. That objective was completed quickly. However, despite strenuous objections from the Pentagon and Secretary of Defense Caspar *Weinberger, the United States soon became involved in the Lebanese civil war itself. In October 1983, a suicide attacker drove a car bomb into the Marine headquarters and killed 241 Marines and 50 French troops. Lebanon, in the Pentagon's eyes, was developing into exactly the kind of situation they feared the most: an open-ended struggle with no clear objective. Despite the humiliation (more Marines died in the bomb attack than were lost later by the entire U.S. force during Desert Storm), Reagan was wise enough to withdraw the Marine contingent.

The setback in Lebanon did not seriously concern Reagan nor did it harm his resilient popularity. The Caribbean and Central America were particular points of attention. In the late 1970s, the Sandinista regime in Nicaragua had taken a sharp turn to the left. Marxist insurgencies were building in both Guatemala and El Salvador. A pro-Marxist government was in power on the small island of Grenada. Reagan believed, with some reason, that Fidel Castro and the Soviet Union were involved in all of these problems. When an extremist Marxist faction violently overthrew the government in Grenada, Reagan sent in the troops. In October 1983, two weeks after the suicide bombing in Beirut, American forces quickly occupied Grenada. In marked contrast to Lebanon, the Americans were treated like liberators by the local population. During the U.S. intervention in *Grenada, the military put on a major show of force in Central America. The army airlifted men to Honduras and a large naval task force staged a maneuver off the coast of Nicaragua.

Both Congress and the Pentagon were very uneasy about a direct American military involvement in Central America. American participation in the conflict remained deep as Reagan sent economic aid to anti-Communist governments in the region. The Pentagon stayed in the background, however. Except for a small team of military advisers sent to El Salvador, military training for Central American officers was done in the United States. The United States did funnel aid to anti-Sandinista guerrilla forces, nicknamed the "Contras," but this project was run by the *Central Intelligence Agency and individuals inside the White House. The same was true of American aid sent to back up *guerrilla warfare opposing Cuban-aided Marxist governments in Africa. Later, George *Bush extended covert aid to Afghan forces fighting the Russians.

In the 1980s, the American military became involved in some unfamiliar territory. Because the United States was Israel's strongest supporter, American civilians had become frequent targets for Arab terrorism. Unfortunately, it was very clear that many terrorists were receiving direct support from several governments—including Iran, Syria, Iraq, and Libya. On 15 April 1986, the United States launched a heavy air strike against several targets in Libya. Since that time the Pentagon has developed extensive contingency plans for dealing with a serious terrorist threat in the United States or abroad. Indeed, many officials believe that a terrorist group procuring *nuclear weapons raises one of the most serious threats facing the United States today.

The Pentagon also became entangled in the "war" against the illegal drug traffic first announced by Reagan and endorsed by all subsequent administrations. This is another area where the military has preferred to stay in the background. Nevertheless, military advisers have helped governments in Latin America operate various drug interdiction and drug eradication programs. Although the military views drug interdiction as a law enforcement problem, the Pentagon continues to play a role in this politically sensitive issue.

The stunning collapse of the Warsaw Pact and the Soviet Union in 1991 caused a difficult reappraisal of the essential mission of U.S. armed forces. Fighting a massive conventional war with the old Warsaw Pact nations was no longer a realistic possibility. A nuclear threat remained, but the direct military confrontation that would trigger an exchange of strategic weapons became far less likely. The fall of the Soviet Union raised the possibility of ethnic conflict and political breakdown throughout the Eurasian landmass. The United States, by default, found itself the only major military power in a dangerous and disorderly world. Consequently, LIC became, outside the nuclear realm, the principal mission of the American military. Although it is impossible to foresee events, the Pentagon believes that LIC will continue to be crucial in the decades to come.

[See also Caribbean and Latin America, U.S. Military Involvement in the; Counterinsurgency; El Salvador, U.S. Military Involvement in; Middle East, U.S. Military Involvement in the; Nicaragua, U.S. Military Involvement in; Terrorism and Counterterrorism.]

• Patrick Brogan, The Fighting Never Stopped: A Comprehensive Guide to World Conflict Since 1945, 1990. Martin Walker, The Cold War, 1994. Samuel Huntington, The Clash of Civilizations and the Remaking of the World Order, 1996. Lawrence E. Walsh, Firewall: The Iran-Contra Conspiracy and Cover-Up, 1997.

—Eric Bergerud

LUCE, STEPHEN B. (1827–1917), naval officer, reformer, and founder of the Naval War College. Born in Albany, New York, Stephen Luce became a naval midshipman in 1841 and spent six years at sea, before being appointed to the Naval Academy at Annapolis. Graduating in 1849, Luce's experience caused him to think about improving naval training and education, and he became an instructor of seamanship and gunnery at Annapolis in 1860. During the *Civil War, Luce alternated between the academy and participating in the Union blockade of the Confederacy.

After the war, Luce experimented with training reforms, corresponding with Gen. Emory *Upton and observing Gen. William Tecumseh *Sherman's efforts to establish an army postgraduate school system. Luce's efforts resulted in the establishment of the Naval War College at Newport in 1884. He was its president from 1884 to 1886, when, promoted rear admiral, he turned the college over to his friend and protégé, Capt. Alfred T. *Mahan, and took command of the North Atlantic Station until his retirement in 1889. Luce continued to write, served as president of the Naval Institute, and later rejoined the Naval War College staff.

While not as intellectual as Mahan, Luce was a reformer and a practical sailor, who saw education as a way to harness technology. Luce influenced a generation of officers and played a crucial role in American military *education.

• Albert Gleaves, *Life and Letters of Stephen B. Luce: Rear Admiral, U.S.N., Founder of the Naval War College,* 1925. Ronald Spector, *Professor of War: The Naval War College and the Development of the Naval Profession,* 1977. James L. Abrahamson, *America Arms for a New Century,* 1981.   —Steven C. Gravlin

LUDENDORFF, ERICH (1865–1937), German general. Ludendorff embodied two of the twentieth century's shaping events: German *imperialism and total war. As a young General Staff officer his outspoken advocacy of engaging the army earned him a punitive transfer. On the outbreak of World War I, he was the architect of the victory over the Russians at Tannenberg (August 1914), while serving as chief of staff to Paul von *Hindenburg. Through political intrigue and battlefield victories the ambitious, mercurial Ludendorff sought to become chief of staff of the German Army. When Erich von Falkenhayn was dismissed in 1916, Hindenburg became supreme military commander and Ludendorff his deputy—reflecting the doubts about Ludendorff's character that permeated the German hierarchy.

Ludendorff galvanized what remained of Germany's human and material resources behind the war effort. He also overhauled the army's tactical doctrines. In domestic politics, he orchestrated the dismissal (July 1917) of Chancellor Bethmann Hollweg and dominated his successors. With the collapse of Russia, Ludendorff extended German power far eastward in the vindictive Peace of Brest-Litovsk. But his deficiencies as a general brought about his downfall. Ludendorff's spring 1918 offensives in the west lacked strategic objective and exhausted Germany's fighting power. With the Allies on the offensive, Ludendorff in September demanded an armistice. He was dismissed by the new government. In the Weimar Republic, he took part in two unsuccessful rightist putsches—by Friedrich Kapp (1920) and Adolf *Hitler (1923)—and became an outspoken "Aryan" racist.

[*See also* World War I: Military and Diplomatic Course.]

• Covelli Barnett, *The Swordbearers: Studies in Supreme Command*

in the First World War, 1963. Norman Stone, "Ludendorff," in *The War Lords: Military Commanders of the Twentieth Century,* ed. M. Carver, 1976, pp. 73–83.   —Dennis E. Showalter

LUSITANIA, SINKING OF THE (1915). On 3 November 1914, Great Britain began mining the North Sea as part of a blockade of Germany, during World War I, ultimately including foodstuffs. German proclaimed a "war zone" around the British Isles (4 February 1915), advising merchant shipping that it must anticipate attack without warning. Berlin cited the submarine's vulnerability to justify abandoning rules of cruiser warfare, which called for warnings and then visit-and-search of merchant ships suspected of transporting contraband. If contraband were discovered, the belligerent must ensure the crew's safety before seizing or destroying the vessel. Britain deemed the war zone an illegal blockade, armed its merchant ships, and ordered them to attack surfaced *submarines. The United States, not yet in the war, announced it would hold Germany to "strict accountability" for loss of American lives and property.

On 7 May 1915, the German submarine *U-20* sank the unprotected British liner *Lusitania* without warning in its approach to the Irish Sea. The giant Cunard Vessel sank in twenty minutes. Of 1,959 passengers and crew, 1,128 perished—128 of them Americans. Although the *Lusitania* was carrying 4,200 cases of contraband ammunition, the reasons why it sank so quickly are still debated.

Attack without warning defied American support of neutral/noncombatant rights. On 13 May, President Woodrow *Wilson asked Germany to disavow its action but avoided a diplomatic break, having noted that a people could be "too proud to fight." When Germany delayed, Wilson moved to preserve national honor, rights, and prestige, insisting on visit-and-search, indemnity, and no further attacks on liners. Secretary of State William Jennings *Bryan resigned in protest. Eventually, Germany suspended unrestricted attacks, and in February 1916 it apologized and offered indemnity without acknowledging illegality. But the incident strengthened America's perception of Germany as a ruthless and lawless nation.

[*See also* Blockades.]

• Thomas M. Bailey and Paul B. Ryan, *The Lusitania Disaster: An Episode in Modern Warfare and Diplomacy,* 1975.

—David F. Trask

The **M-1 RIFLE** was the standard small-arms weapon of the U.S. Army in World War II and the *Korean War. Its inventor, Canadian-born John Cantius Garand, developed the gas-operated semiautomatic rifle at the Springfield Armory during the 1920s. Gen. Douglas *MacArthur ordered Garand's original .276-caliber changed to .30-06 (.30 caliber cartridge developed in 1906) as the army retained vast stocks of such cartridges from World War I. In 1936 the army officially adapted the M-1 Garand rifle. Officers were assigned M-1 carbines, smaller and lighter. The rifle weighed 11.25 pounds with an eight-round clip and had a maximum range of 460 meters. The weapon could be fitted with a knife bayonet.

The Marine Corps favored its own semiautomatic rifle, designed by Marine Corps Officer Melvin Johnson, but Congress opted for the M-1. World War I veterans preferred the 1903 Springfield bolt action and were concerned about the M-1 semiautomatic's reliability and accuracy in combat situations. Those questions were emphatically vindicated in World War II. In that war, most other armies still used bolt-action rifles. Although both the Germans and the Russians fielded small numbers of semiautomatic rifles, the United States was the only nation to fight the war armed primarily with a semiautomatic rifle. The Garand M-14 model was eventually replaced by the *M-16 rifle in the 1960s.

[*See also* Springfield Model 1903; Weaponry, Army; Weaponry, Marine Corps.]

• Bruce N. Canfield, *The M-1 Garand and the M-1 Carbine*, 1988.

—Thomas Christianson

M-16 RIFLE. The prototype for the M-16 rifle was developed by Armalik Division of Fairchild Corporation in the late 1950s. In 1959, Colt purchased the right to manufacture the rifles. This rifle could fire in either semiautomatic or automatic mode. The South Vietnamese, who favored a light, almost recoilless rifle, field-tested the weapon in 1962 and found it ideally suited to mobile combat *counterinsurgency operations. The M-16 rifle along with 120 rounds of ammunition weighed only 11.1 pounds compared to the M-14's 18.75 pounds. The M-16, with its twenty-round magazine, had an effective range of 460 meters and a high rate of fire. In 1965, Gen. William C. *Westmoreland ordered 100,000 M-16 rifles for the U.S. Army and Marines in Vietnam, and in 1969 the M-16 officially replaced the M-14 Garand as the standard small arm.

Controversy erupted immediately and continued for years. Reports from Vietnam of jamming led to questions of reliability. Investigation proved jams resulted from not cleaning the rifle, and that it was not a self-cleaning weapon as manufacturers claimed. Some complaints indicated that the small 5.56-caliber 55-grain bullet lacked adequate impact. Conversely, others charged the ultrafast munition caused inhumane internal damage to its victims. Soldiers eventually adapted to the M-16 and accepted its capabilities along with its shortcomings.

In the 1990s, the model M-16A2 was still the standard small arm for the United States. The 7.78-pound rifle is equipped with a 30-round magazine and fires a 62-grain bullet with an effective range of 550 meters.

[*See also* M-1 Rifle; Vietnam War: Military and Diplomatic Course; Weaponry, Army; Weaponry, Marine Corps.]

• Ivan V. Hogg, *Military Small Arms of the 20th Century*, 1981.

—Thomas Christianson

MACARTHUR, DOUGLAS (1880–1964), American general in World War II and the Korean War. Born in Little Rock, Arkansas, and raised on army posts by his father, Gen. Arthur MacArthur, and mother, Mary, Douglas MacArthur graduated from West Point in 1903. An engineering officer, he served in the Philippines and Panama. In 1913–17, he was assigned to the army's General Staff. During World War I, he was chief of staff of the 42nd (Rainbow) Division in France and subsequently commanded the 84th Infantry Brigade as a brigadier general. In 1919–22, he was superintendent of West Point, then served two tours of duty in the Philippines. As army chief of staff (1930–35), MacArthur evoked much criticism by using military force in 1932 to disperse encampments in Washington, D.C., of unemployed veterans, "Bonus Marchers," seeking their pensions. In 1935, President Franklin D. *Roosevelt appointed MacArthur military adviser to the U.S. colony of the Philippines, and the general spent the next six years training the Filipino Army.

In July 1941, MacArthur was appointed to command all U.S. forces in East Asia, but when Japanese planes attacked American bases near Manila several hours after their attack on *Pearl Harbor, they destroyed most of the American warplanes on the ground. For three months, MacArthur led the defense of the Philippines; but in March 1942, Roosevelt ordered him to Australia to command the Southwest Pacific Area theater. MacArthur vowed: "I shall return."

While the U.S. Navy pushed through the Central Pacific, MacArthur, with American reinforcements, launched an offensive from Australia against Japanese forces on the coastline of New Guinea, using highly successful "leapfrogging" flanking envelopments with combined air, land, and sea forces. The high point of MacArthur's campaign came in October 1944, when despite the reluctance of the *Joint Chiefs of Staff (JCS), he convinced Roosevelt to allow him to liberate the Philippines rather than bypass the archipelago. The image of MacArthur with his crushed officer's hat, aviator sunglasses, and corncob pipe was familiar to Americans. Most famously, photographers showed him wading ashore at Leyte in the Philippines as he launched the liberation that continued through July 1945. In December 1944, he was promoted to the new rank of general of the army (five stars). He accepted the Japanese surrender on the USS *Missouri* on 2 September 1945.

Appointed by President Harry S. *Truman as Supreme Allied Powers Commander, MacArthur directed the occupation of Japan (1945–50), implementing generally liberal economic, social, and political reforms, but delaying rebuilding of Japan's industrial economy until ordered by Truman in 1948. As a conservative Republican, MacArthur was seriously considered for the GOP presidential nomination in 1948, but he was defeated in the early primaries.

With the outbreak of the Korean War in June 1950, Truman also named MacArthur commander of the U.S. and *United Nations forces there. The general persuaded the JCS to authorize an amphibious flanking envelopment at Inchon in September, and by October, South Korea had been liberated. Truman, with MacArthur's concurrence, then expanded the war aims to unify the peninsula. When UN forces crossed the 38th parallel and advanced toward the Yalu River, the border with China, despite warnings from Beijing, MacArthur met with Truman on Wake Island, dismissing the danger of Chinese intervention and predicting quick victory.

China intervened massively in late November, pushing the UN forces back to the 38th parallel and beyond. MacArthur then clashed with the JCS and the White House, blaming them for forcing him to fight a limited war. Arguing that there was "no substitute for victory," MacArthur sought permission to expand the war to China by bombing bases in Manchuria, perhaps with *nuclear weapons, and by assisting Chinese Nationalist troops from Taiwan to invade the mainland. However, as the JCS discovered early in 1951, MacArthur exaggerated the Communist Chinese threat to overrun South Korea. Battle lines stabilized in March 1951 when a new field commander, Gen. Matthew B. *Ridgway, rallied the U.S. and UN forces.

Truman proposed a cease-fire that month, but MacArthur sabotaged the plan. When the press printed a letter from the general to Republican congressman Joseph Martin condemning Truman's policy in Korea as appeasement, an outraged president, supported by the JCS, removed MacArthur from all his commands on 11 April 1951. Two weeks later, after returning to a hero's welcome, MacArthur addressed a joint session of Congress and appealed for public support for his strategy. But although Americans were frustrated with the stalemated war, Senate hearings into MacArthur's accusations revealed that most military and diplomatic experts opposed his plan at a time when the Soviet Union in Europe was seen as the main threat to U.S. interests. Few Americans wanted an expanded war with China.

After fifty-two years of active service, the general with his flare for the dramatic gesture and his penchant for political controversy retired from the army and became an officer of a large business corporation. Another effort to nominate him for president failed in 1952 when the GOP chose a far more genial and less controversial general, Dwight D. *Eisenhower.

[See also Inchon Landing; Korean War; Korean War: U.S. Naval Operations in; Philippines, U.S. Involvement in the; World War II, U.S. Naval Operations in: The Pacific.]

• D. Clayton James, *The Years of MacArthur*, 3 vols., 1970–85. Carol Petillo, *Douglas MacArthur: The Philippine Years*, 1981. Michael Schaller, *Douglas MacArthur: The Far Eastern General*, 1989.

—Michael Schaller

MACHINE GUNS are repeating firearms that when triggered will load and fire automatically until their ammunition is exhausted. In 1861, the U.S. Army was offered its first machine gun: Wilson Ager's single-barrel, hand-cranked weapon, often called the "coffee mill" gun due to its resemblance to a coffee grinder. At the order of President Lincoln, a few Ager guns were purchased; however, mechanical problems and the opposition of chief of ordnance, Brig. Gen. James W. Ripley, blocked adoption of the gun.

Patented in November 1862 by Dr. Richard J. Gatling, early versions of the *Gatling gun were rejected by the conservative Union Ordnance Department. Purchased in 1866, improved .50-caliber and 1-inch versions of Gatling's hand-cranked, multibarred machine gun were intended for use in the close-in defenses of coastal *fortifications, frontier forts, and aboard ship. The .50-caliber version of the gun weighed 224 pounds and the 1-inch version 1,008 pounds; later rifle-caliber Gatlings weighed from 135 to 200 pounds.

Because he feared the weapons might hamper his column's movement through the rugged valley of the Little Bighorn River, Lt. Col. George Armstrong *Custer declined an offer of Gatling guns. Complex, heavy, and difficult to transport and supply, early machine guns saw little use during the *Civil War and in the Indian wars. For almost four decades the Ordnance Department procured a small number of Gatlings. Interest in the weapon lagged, however, and doctrine for its use and a unit to use it were neglected.

The perfection of smokeless powder in 1886 and the final development of small-caliber, high-velocity rifle ammunition made the development of fully automatic machine guns practical. In 1898, American expeditionary forces in Cuba included an improvised machine-gun unit with Gatling guns manned by infantrymen. Commanded by Lt. John Henry Parker, the Gatlings provided decisive support for the attack during the Battle of *San Juan Hill. In 1900, the army tested replacements for the Gatling gun. Among the competitors were two American designs: a recoil-operated gun patented by Hiram *Maxim in 1885, and the gas-operated Colt machine gun patented by John M. Browning in 1895. Adopted in 1904, the heavy and complex Maxim gun (gun, tripod, and full water jacket weighed 153.5 pounds) was replaced in 1909 by the French-designed Benét-Mercié, an air-cooled weapon weighing 27 pounds. However, the fragile Benét-Mercié also failed to meet army needs, and in 1916 it was replaced by a new weapon, the water-cooled, British Vickers machine gun (gun, tripod, and full water jacket weighed 75.5 pounds).

Despite domination of World War I battlefields by machine guns and *artillery, each U.S. infantry regiment in 1917 had only six machine guns, and the army possessed a total of fewer than 1,500. The first twelve American divisions sent to France were equipped with French Hotchkiss machine guns. By July 1918, embarking American units were issued the new water-cooled, .30-caliber Browning machine gun (gun, tripod, and full water jacket weighed 74 pounds) and the *Browning Automatic Rifle (BAR; 19.4 pounds), developed to provide an air-cooled, light machine gun carried and operated by a single infantryman. From 50 machine guns in early 1917, U.S. infantry divisions ended the war with 260 machine guns and 768 BARs per division.

In the 1930s, the army adopted the air-cooled .30-caliber Browning M-1919A4 (gun and tripod weighed 45.5 pounds) and the more powerful, air-cooled, .50-caliber Browning M-2, heavy machine gun (gun and tripod weighed 128 pounds). During World War II, the number of machine guns multiplied in the increasingly mechanized American forces. In 1943, each American infantry division was issued 157 .30-caliber and 236 .50-caliber Browning machine guns. In addition, Browning .50-caliber guns were standard on most American aircraft; they also saw widespread use as antiaircraft weapons.

In 1957, the .30-caliber Browning was replaced by the 7.62-millimeter, air-cooled M-60 machine gun, weighing 23 pounds; the BAR was replaced by a version of the M-14 service rifle. The .50-caliber M-2, however, remained the standard American heavy machine gun. During the 1990s, American forces were equipped with a variety of air-cooled machine guns—the 5.56-millimeter, M-249 squad automatic weapon, which performed a function similar to the BAR (gun and 200 rounds of ammunition weigh 22 pounds); the M-60, and the 7.62-millimeter, air-cooled, M-240C coaxial machine gun mounted in tanks and armored fighting vehicles; as well as the .50-caliber Browning M-2.

Adoption and use of machine guns has been affected primarily by mechanical problems such as overheating, by their size and weight, and by problems of transport and ammunition supply. Development of metallic cartridges and smokeless powder and design improvement—recoil and gas-operated guns and reliable, air-cooled weapons—gradually produced lightweight machine guns suitable for widespread combat use. Mechanization of American forces overcame logistical constraints and by mid-twentieth century the machine gun was fully integrated into the armory of the American military.

[See also Caribbean and Latin America, U.S. Military Involvement in the; Cuba, U.S. Military Involvement in; Weaponry, Army; Weaponry, Marine Corps.]

• Graham Seton Hutchinson, *Machine Guns: Their History and Tactical Employment*, 1938. George M. Chinn, *The Machine Gun*, Vol. 1, 1951. Konrad F. Schreier, Jr., *Guide to United States Machine Guns*, 1971. David A. Armstrong, *Bullets and Bureaucrats, The Machine Gun and the United States Army, 1861–1961*, 1982.

—David A. Armstrong

MADISON, JAMES (1751–1836), statesman, fourth U.S. president. After growing up at his lifelong home, Montpelier, in Orange County, Virginia, and graduating from the College of New Jersey in 1771, Madison entered politics. As a Confederation congressman (1780–83 and 1787–89), he favored strengthening the national union but never endorsed Robert *Morris's fiscal agenda. Service in the Virginia legislature (1784–86) convinced him that individual liberties needed protection from majority tyranny.

Having studied ancient and modern confederacies (thereby becoming the best-prepared delegate at the 1787 Constitutional Convention), Madison concluded that republics would endure without strong central governments. To help achieve ratification, he penned twenty-nine of the celebrated *Federalist Papers*. No. 10, his most famous essay, argued that large republics, if properly constructed, could endure best because conflicting factions would make majority tyranny unlikely. During the first Federal Congress, Madison drafted the Bill of Rights. In the 1790s, he resisted Federalist financial and diplomatic policies in favor of perpetuating an agricultural republic friendly to France. His opposition culminated in his authorship of the 1798 Virginia Resolutions, which called for repeal of the *Alien and Sedition Acts.

As Thomas *Jefferson's secretary of state (1801–09), Madison tried to force Great Britain to grant neutral rights through economic coercion. When this policy failed, Madison as president obtained a declaration of war in 1812. Blame for the military disasters that ensued—including botched invasions of Canada and the burning of Washington, D.C.—belong to Madison. He failed to prepare the country for hostilities, tolerated incompetent generals, and proved a weak commander in chief. These shortcomings resulted from his inveterate determination to allow neither war nor the threat of war to endanger republicanism or personal rights.

[See also Canada, U.S. Military Involvement in; Civil Liberties and War; Commander in Chief, President as; War of 1812.]

• Ralph Ketcham, *James Madison, A Biography*, 1971. John Stagg, *Mr. Madison's War*, 1983. Lance Banning, *The Sacred Fire of Liberty: James Madison and the Founding of the Federal Republic*, 1995.

—Stuart Leibiger

MAGIC. By the late summer of 1940, American cryptanalysts managed to break some of Japan's most secret diplomatic codes. This remarkable achievement was designated MAGIC. Although American officials frequently used the same cover name referring to later successes against Japanese military and naval codes, which were called *ULTRA, the MAGIC operation dealt primarily with Japanese diplomatic communications. The road to the major breakthrough, however, was long and uneven.

In the mid-1930s, the U.S. *Navy concentrated on Japanese naval cryptographic systems while the U.S. Army Signal Intelligence Service (SIS), under the direction of William F. Friedman, tackled Japanese diplomatic codes. By 1935, the SIS managed to crack Japanese diplomatic messages encrypted by the sophisticated "Red Machine," which was put into use in the early 1930s. The accomplishments of Friedman and his team were short-lived because in late 1938, the Japanese foreign ministry introduced a new and more secure cipher machine, the "Purple Machine," for its top-secret messages. By the spring of 1939, the new Purple Machine replaced much of the Red Machine traffic. As a result, the SIS found that its vital source of intelligence on Japanese intentions and developments dried up completely. Immediately, Friedman and a group of SIS colleagues focused their attention on unraveling this setback. Friedman benefited immensely from the input of his team, including mathematicians, cryptanalysts, and linguists. They worked laboriously for the next eighteen months to solve Purple and also to construct a Purple Machine.

The breaking of Purple was such a daunting and seemingly unachievable endeavor that Brig. Gen. Joseph O. Mauborgne, chief signal officer, referred to the cryptanalysts as "magicians" and to their results as "magic." From then onward, the codeword MAGIC was given to the solution of Japanese diplomatic messages that were encrypted by the Purple Machine.

After the initial breakthrough in the fall of 1940, the Americans swiftly found that they had access to a huge volume of radio traffic between Tokyo and its diplomatic representatives throughout the world. Cryptanalysts were soon processing fifty to seventy-five Japanese messages a day. The increase in workload strained the resources of the understaffed SIS. Consequently, the U.S. Army and the U.S. Navy made an agreement to share responsibility for MAGIC whereby the army was in charge of decrypting and translating materials on odd days while the navy was given even days. This arrangement between both services continued until early 1942.

The United States realized that MAGIC provided invaluable insights into the inner workings of the foreign ministry in Tokyo. In order to protect this secret source of intelligence, American authorities adopted stringent security measures for the dissemination of MAGIC reports. Distribution of the highly sensitive materials was intentionally limited to a select group of the highest-ranking officials. Neither the secretary of state nor President Franklin D. *Roosevelt was permitted to retain copies of MAGIC. The army, and the navy later, even took President Roosevelt off the list of authorized personnel for a short time when it was discovered that a copy of MAGIC found its way into the wastebasket of a senior official at the White House.

In early 1941, Friedman and his group managed to recreate several duplicate copies of the machine that enciphered Purple. By the end of the year, eight of these machines had been built. Four remained in Washington (two each for the army and navy), three were given to the British, and one was sent to intelligence headquarters of Gen. Douglas *MacArthur on Corregidor Island in the Philippines.

A staggering amount of Japanese messages became available to American intelligence agencies by 1941 because MAGIC included diplomatic communications between Tokyo and all its consular and embassy representatives throughout the world. Given the limited number of personnel, especially experienced linguists, working on this secret program, Washington had to make a choice from among the flood of despatches that were being intercepted. Since crucial negotiations between the United States and Japan were taking place in 1941, priority was given to the Tokyo/Washington circuit. Working under pressure and tight schedules, the MAGIC team of codebreakers made outstanding progress. As the historian David Kahn, a leading authority on code and codebreaking, has noted, from March until December 1941, only 4 messages out of 227 relating to the talks between Secretary of State Cordell Hull and Ambassador Kichisaburo Nomura failed to be picked up by the United States.

MAGIC revealed only what the foreign ministry discussed with its diplomats and what these representatives reported back to Tokyo. Accordingly, the U.S. government did not obtain a complete picture of Japanese military planning, which was often not passed along to their diplomats until matters had proceeded well along course. In fact, the United States had been unable to break high-level Japanese Army and naval codes until after the attack on *Pearl Harbor, especially since each Japanese agency utilized systems entirely different systems from the foreign ministry.

Unexpectedly, MAGIC turned out to be an excellent source of military and diplomatic intelligence on the war in Europe, especially on German plans and intentions. While serving his second tour as Japanese ambassador to Germany from February 1941 to May 1945, Hiroshi Oshima, who had direct access to Adolf *Hitler and his closest advisers, sent to Tokyo detailed reports on his conversations with German officials and also his observations while touring the German front lines. Even Gen. George C. *Marshall, U.S. army chief of staff, acknowledged privately in 1944 that Oshima's despatches were one of the most important sources of intelligence on Germany during World War II. The United States had forewarning and details of Hitler's planned invasion of the Soviet Union in spring 1941 because of reports from Oshima. Another vital piece of intelligence surfaced in May 1944, when the Japanese ambassador informed Tokyo that Hitler remained convinced that the main Allied invasion of France would take place near Calais and that operations against Normandy were diversionary.

Despite strenuous measures to conceal MAGIC, certain aspects of the operation became public knowledge in late 1945 during the joint congressional investigations into the Pearl Harbor attack. In response to a determined national quest to find blame for one of America's worst military and naval disasters, President Harry S. *Truman reluctantly reversed his initial decision and authorized the release of limited MAGIC messages dealing with U.S.-Japan relations prior to 7 December 1941. The revelation immediately generated sensational headlines and commentaries. No further materials on MAGIC were released until 1977, when the Department of *Defense published a five-volume history of communication intelligence and the Pearl Harbor attack. Since then, the U.S. government has periodically declassified its records on MAGIC and continues to do so.

Ever since MAGIC was made public, historians have drawn upon the vast collection of translated messages to reevaluate certain aspects of American history between 1940 and 1945. These despatches have provided fuel for both proponents and opponents of the theory that the United States had prior warning of the bombing of Pearl Harbor. To this day, no specific evidence shows that there were definite indications within the messages that referred to the Japanese plans for the attack. However, a careful and thorough analysis could have shown that Japan in late 1941 was determined to confront the United States and that plans for an attack on U.S. forces somewhere in the Pacific were underway.

The MAGIC materials have also been used to justify or deny the successful efforts by Japanese Americans during the 1980s to obtain redress from the U.S. government for the wartime internment of Americans of Japanese ancestry. Opponents pointed out that several communications from the West Coast Japanese consulates and the embassy in Washington in 1941 reported that they were attempting to recruit second-generation Japanese Americans for propaganda and espionage purposes. On the other hand,

Japanese Americans have argued that there has never been a documented case of any disloyalty among them.

In recent years, MAGIC intercepts helped fuel the heated controversy over the American decision to order the atomic bombings of *Hiroshima and Nagasaki. Indeed, intercepted messages confirmed that the Japanese government was deeply divided over whether to accept the Allied ultimatum for an unconditional surrender. Critics of the bombing emphasized that in 1945, strong elements within the government of Japan desperately sought the mediation of the Soviet Union so that the war could be ended without the termination of the emperor system and the imperial household. Proponents of the atomic bomb, however, suggested that these MAGIC messages indicated that Japan would not have agreed to the unconditional surrender if *nuclear weapons had not been used.

In the final analysis, contrary to popular belief, MAGIC did not provide any specific indications of Japan's surprise air attack on Pearl Harbor, nor—unlike the breaking of the Japanese Navy and Army codes in 1942 through ULTRA— did it have any significant impact on operations during the Pacific War.

[See also Coding and Decoding; Intelligence, Military and Political; Japanese-American Internment Cases; World War II: Military and Diplomatic Course; World War II: Changing Interpretations.]

• Roberta Wohlstetter, Pearl Harbor: Warning and Decision, 1962. Ronald W. Clark, The Man Who Broke Purple: The Life of Colonel William F. Friedman, Who Deciphered the Japanese Code in World War II, 1977. U.S. Department of Defense, The "Magic" Background of Pearl Harbor, 1977–78. Ronald Lewin, The American Magic: Codes, Ciphers and the Defeat of Japan, 1982. Carl Boyd, Hitler's Japanese Confidant: General Oshima Hiroshi and MAGIC Intelligence, 1941–1945, 1993. David Kahn, The Codebreakers: The Comprehensive History of Secret Communication from Ancient Times to the Internet, 1996.   —Pedro Loureiro

MAHAN, ALFRED T. (1840–1914), naval officer and theorist. Born to Mary Okill and Dennis Hart Mahan, the latter a professor of civil and military engineering at West Point, Mahan became a career naval officer. He also became a historian and strategic analyst upon his appointment to the new Naval War College in Newport, Rhode Island, in 1885. Over the following quarter century, he wrote some of the most influential works on history and strategy ever produced.

Mahan's studies range widely, incorporating innovative and resourceful historical research and analysis with the perceived strategic and political needs of his day. Though his writings were long ago distilled into dogma from which U.S. naval doctrine has frequently been derived, Mahan himself aimed for accuracy and insight as much as for political or strategic influence. In fact, by the 1906 all-big-gun battleship controversies, Mahan had already been outpaced by enthusiasts willing to go even further in defense of these behemoths of concentrated fire.

Much of Mahan's forty-year naval career passed with barely a hint of his future influence. Prickly young Mahan completed two years at Columbia College before entering the U.S. Naval Academy's Class of 1859. His *Civil War service was limited to blockade duty except for a few hours of combat during the assault on Port Royal. In successive postwar assignments, he rose slowly through the ranks without distinction. Most of his cruises were on the remote Pacific or Asiatic Squadrons, reinforcing his alienated nature and encouraging his chauvinistic views toward the peoples of the Pacific Basin. His High Church Episcopal beliefs aggravated the disdain he felt for most people— naval officers, sailors, and foreigners alike.

Mahan's most famous and important work—The Influence of Sea Power upon History, 1660–1783—first published in 1890, suggests the main thrust of his historical efforts. From 1885 to 1893 he was assigned to the Naval War College, briefly as a professor and soon as president of the fledgling institution. In the years before his retirement in 1896, he prepared his most influential studies. Originally, these were designed for his midlevel officer students. They quickly lost their heuristic value, becoming instead primers of international relations, force, and diplomacy. Over the course of a long second career, Mahan produced twenty-one books, including eleven collections of essays, two naval biographies, two memoirs, and the famous Influence series that examined international history from 1660 to 1815. His histories emphasized the persistent nature of international conflict, particularly between great powers competing for access to trade and resources. His religion, research, and theorizing, as well as his experiences at the First Hague Conference for limiting warfare (1899), led him to believe that diplomacy was best engaged in after successful conclusion of the battle. For Mahan, international relations hinged on power projection. In the modern era, this was best exercised by navies.

Mahan identified three critical elements of seapower: (1) weapons of war, primarily *battleships and their supply bases; (2) a near monopoly of seaborne commerce from which to draw wealth, manpower, and supplies; and (3) a string of colonies to support both of the above. His theories, however, rested on two serious fallacies. First, his overreliance upon the notion of concentrating forces falsely denied the importance of coastal defense, and undervalued commerce raiding. These assumptions forced strategists to search for a decisive, war-winning battle, often in vain. Second, he overstated the strategic benefits of controlling seaborne commerce and colonies. Whereas in peacetime these components of empire frequently contributed to wealth and consequently to long-term strength, in war they often proved to be liabilities. Mahan's timeless principles, as enacted along the lines of late-nineteenth-century navalism, had the effect of turning America's strategic vision of itself on its side; instead of remaining an unassailable continental power with maritime reach, it became an overstretched maritime power with global vulnerabilities.

From 1896 until his death, Mahan lived in New York City and at Quogue on Long Island with his wife and unmarried daughters. Though the value of his writings continues to be debated, of their influence on the navies of the United States and other countries there can be no doubt.

[See also Doctrine, Military; Sea Warfare; Strategy: Naval Warfare Strategy; Tactics: Naval Warfare Tactics.]

• Robert Seager II and Doris Maguire, The Letters and Papers of Alfred Thayer Mahan, 3 vols., 1975. Robert Seager II, Alfred Thayer Mahan: The Man and His Letters, 1977. John B. Hattendorf and Lynn C. Hattendorf, A Bibliography of the Works of Alfred Thayer Mahan, 1986. Kenneth J. Hagan, This People's Navy, 1991. Mark Russell Shulman, Navalism and the Emergence of American Sea Power, 1882–1893, 1995.   —Mark R. Shulman

MAINE, SINKING OF THE USS (1898). In January 1898, Spain was winning its war against Cuban insurrectionists, but faced pressure from U.S. president William *McKinley to make concessions. When in response to reforms from Madrid, Spanish officers and Cuban loyalists rioted in Havana, U.S. consul Fitzhugh Lee requested a warship to protect American lives and property. There was also concern about rumored Spanish intentions to turn Cuba over to Germany. These circumstances induced McKinley to dispatch the USS *Maine* a second-class battleship (its keel was laid in 1888, but it was not commissioned until 1895) to Havana.

The *Maine* arrived off Havana on 25 January; Spanish authorities reluctantly allowed her entry to the harbor and assigned an anchorage. On the night of 15 February, an explosion ripped the ship's hull open, and she sank with over 260 men (two-thirds of her complement) killed. Encouraged by sensationalist newspapers, many Americans believed the explosion resulted from an external mine set off by the Spaniards. On 21 March 1898, a U.S. Naval Court of Inquiry concluded that an external explosion caused by unknown persons had detonated one of the *Maine*'s forward ammunition magazines. The court rejected an alternative explanation, that spontaneous combustion in a coal bunker set off nearby ammunition. So did a second inquiry held in 1911, when the *Maine*'s half-submerged hulk was raised and examined before being disposed of at sea. In 1975, another inquiry, headed by Adm. Hyman *Rickover, reassessed the 1911 photographs of the wreckage, and concluded that the *Maine* was the victim of an internal explosion from spontaneous combustion in an inadequately ventilated bituminous coal bunker, which then exploded adjoining magazines. But the explosion's true cause remains a mystery.

Many regard the sinking of the *Maine* as the cause of the Spanish-American War. This simplistic explanation ignores the fact that McKinley tried to avoid war for a month after the court finding. A combination of events led to war in April 1898.

[*See also* Spanish-American War.]

• Hyman G. Rickover, *How the Battleship Maine Was Destroyed*, 1976. David F. Trask, *The War with Spain in 1898*, 1981. Albert A. Nofi, *The Spanish-American War, 1898*, 1996.

—Steven C. Gravlin

MAINTENANCE is an important aspect of military *logistics and includes those activities needed to keep weapons, vehicles, and other materiel in an operable condition; to restore them to a serviceable condition when necessary; or to improve their usefulness through modifications. Such maintenance activities include inspection, testing, classification as to serviceability, adjustment, servicing, recovery, evacuation, repair, overhaul, and modification. Salvage and disposal are related functions.

Modern military equipment is complex and expensive and must be designed with reliability, durability, and ease of maintenance in mind. Thus, maintenance requirements, the potential usage of repair parts, and the tools and equipment needed to effect repairs are determined during the equipment development process, and operational capabilities must sometimes be sacrificed for greater reliability or ease of maintenance. Life cycle maintenance costs are also an important consideration inasmuch as the lifetime maintenance costs usually exceed an item's initial acquisition cost.

Traditionally, maintenance support has been divided into five levels, or *echelons*. *User* (first echelon) maintenance includes inspection, cleaning, tightening, lubrication, and minor adjustments performed by the equipment operator. *Organizational* (second echelon) maintenance is performed by unit maintenance personnel and involves recovery, evacuation, inspection, troubleshooting, and some replacement of parts and assemblies. *Direct support* (third echelon) maintenance is carried out by specialized maintenance units in fixed or semimobile maintenance facilities—or by mobile teams—and involves recovery, evacuation, inspection, replacement of major parts and assemblies, and the repair of some assemblies. Items repaired at the direct support level are normally returned to the using unit. *General support* (fourth echelon) maintenance involves the systematic repair and rebuilding of equipment and is generally performed by highly specialized maintenance units in fixed general support technical centers, each of which specializes in a particular type of equipment (e.g., combat vehicles or *missiles). Items repaired or rebuilt at the general support level are returned to general stocks rather than to the using unit. *Depot* (fifth echelon) maintenance is also carried out by highly specialized maintenance personnel in fixed facilities; it involves the complete rebuilding of entire items and the renovation of major assemblies (such as motors or transmissions) for return to general stocks.

In recent years, the armed services have streamlined the maintenance process and now recognize only three echelons: *user/direct support, intermediate/general support,* and *wholesale*. In practice, the type and amount of work to be accomplished at each level is determined by the missions of the units involved, the probable operational situation, and the most cost-effective use of available maintenance resources. The thrust of modern maintenance doctrine is to perform maintenance functions as far forward on the battlefield as possible by employing mobile repair teams, rapid battlefield recovery, and cannibalization (the reuse of serviceable parts taken from an otherwise unrepairable item). In general, it is easier and quicker to maintain a piece of equipment in a fully equipped fixed maintenance shop rather than in the field, but by maintaining equipment as far forward as possible, evacuation and repair time is minimized. Thus, the time an item is available to perform its combat function is increased.

Although some common maintenance support is provided by the General Services Administration and the Defense Logistics Agency, each of the armed services has its own system to provide every level of maintenance support. Army wholesale maintenance activities are overseen by the U.S. Army Materiel Command, which controls seven commodity-oriented subordinate commands, each of which specializes in a particular type of materiel (e.g., wheeled vehicles or communications-electronics equipment). Most army units, including maintenance units themselves, are organized with organic maintenance personnel and equipment. Thus, an infantry company normally has an organic maintenance section and an infantry division has an organic direct support maintenance battalion. Intermediate/general support maintenance activities are usually controlled by combat service support commands (e.g., a corps support command or a theater army area command).

The U.S. *Marine Corps operates two distinct maintenance systems of its own, although the navy provides aviation and medical supply and maintenance support. Marine Corps base maintenance activities provide all levels of support for commercial-type equipment or contract out what is beyond their capability. Fleet Marine Force units are supported by a system similar to that of army field forces, with organic maintenance units backed by specialized direct and general support maintenance units. Wholesale maintenance activities are carried out at Marine Corps logistics bases in Georgia and California.

Responsibility for navy maintenance activities is assigned to the Navy Systems Command, which oversees a number of specialized commodity-oriented commands (e.g., the Naval Air Systems Command for naval aviation repair and the Naval Sea Systems Command for shipyards and ship repair facilities). User/direct support–level maintenance is performed by the using ship or air squadron. Intermediate/general support–level maintenance is performed in local repair facilities, which include combat logistics force ships and overseas bases. Wholesale-level maintenance is performed in navy or commercial facilities in the continental United States.

Air force maintenance activities are the responsibility of the Air Force Logistics Command, which monitors the operation of five Air Logistics Centers. These centers, located in Georgia, Oklahoma, Texas, Utah, and California, are centralized wholesale repair facilities. Retail aircraft maintenance is performed at air base level. For nontactical (transport and utility) aircraft, a centralized concept is employed, and the work is normally performed in fixed base maintenance facilities by air force maintenance squadrons. Tactical aircraft are also maintained by air force maintenance squadrons, using a more decentralized concept designed to produce the maximum number of combat sorties.

Effective and cost-efficient maintenance systems are essential to the success of military forces on land, at sea, and in the air. The complexity of modern weapons systems and the large number of such systems deployed in all types of climatic and terrain require extraordinarily good design and effective maintenance procedures and personnel if they are to perform their intended functions. The ability to ensure that weapons, vehicles, and other equipment are available and function properly gives a military force a decided advantage over an opponent who does not have that ability.

[See also Weaponry.]

• Headquarters, Department of the Army, *The Department of the Army*, 1977. Headquarters, Department of the Army, *Field Manual 54-10: Logistics—An Overview of the Total System*, 1977. United States Army War College, Department of Military Strategy, Planning, and Operations, *Materiel Logistics—Service Logistics: Concepts, Organization, and Planning*, 1991.

—Charles R. Shrader

MANASSAS, BATTLES OF. *See* Bull Run, First Battle of (1861); Bull Run, Second Battle of (1862).

MANHATTAN PROJECT, the U.S. effort in World War II that developed the atomic bomb. The possibility of developing an atomic bomb became evident late in 1938 when scientists in Germany successfully split a uranium atom by bombarding it with neutrons. In the United States, Leo *Szilard, a physicist at the University of Chicago, recognized that as a result of such nuclear fission, a critical mass of uranium could produce enough neutrons to generate a chain reaction of radioactive material culminating in an enormous nuclear explosion. Prodded by Szilard, Albert Einstein, world-renowned German physicist who had fled to the United States, wrote to President Franklin D. *Roosevelt on 2 August 1939 warning that the Nazis might develop an atomic bomb.

Roosevelt formed a committee of scientists headed first by Enrico *Fermi and subsequently by Vannevar *Bush (renamed the National Defense Research Committee) to study the feasibility of building such a weapon. In October 1941, this was merged into the new Office of Scientific Research and Development. In spring 1942, Ernest Lawrence of the University of California, Berkeley, demonstrated that in addition to the scarce uranium isotope U-235, the more available U-238 could be converted into a new element, plutonium, which was also fissionable. After the United States entered the war, Roosevelt gave the development of nuclear weapons top priority, and in August 1942 he assigned the top-secret project to the U.S. *Army Corps of Engineers. Its code name, the "Manhattan Project," derived from the Manhattan Engineer District established to supervise the weapon's construction. The commanding officer, Maj. (later Brig. Gen.) Leslie R. Groves, spent $2 billion to develop the atomic bomb.

The Manhattan Project had four main facilities. In the basement of the unused football stadium of the University of Chicago, scientists Enrico Fermi and Arthur Compton built an atomic pile and in December 1942 produced the first chain reaction in uranium. At Hanford, Washington, a plant produced plutonium-239 from uranium-238. The Clinton Engineer Works at Oak Ridge, Tennessee, separated uranium-235 from uranium-238 through gaseous diffusion. A secret new laboratory, headed by physicist J. Robert *Oppenheimer, was built in 1943 on a secluded mesa at Los Alamos, New Mexico, to design and build atomic bombs.

Secrecy was an obsession with Groves, and only a handful of the 125,000 people at the Project's four facilities understood the purpose of their work. Just a few military and congressional leaders knew the reason for the project's huge expenditures, which were concealed within War Department appropriations.

Since scientists in Britain had been working toward a bomb since 1940 and discovered the new element called "plutonium," Roosevelt and British prime minister Winston S. *Churchill cooperated in the research. However, in September 1944, the two leaders decided not to share their information with the Soviet Union. Russia initiated an intense espionage effort in Britain and the United States to aid its own program, headed by physicist Igor Kurchatov.

Soviet leader Josef *Stalin learned details of the bomb's progress from Communist sympathizers, among them atomic scientist Klaus Fuchs in Britain, and David Greenglass, an American soldier stationed near Los Alamos. In a controversial trial in 1950, following Fuchs's postwar confession, Greenglass testified that his brother-in-law, Julius Rosenberg, and Rosenberg's wife, Ethel, had passed to the Russians atomic secrets he had obtained. The Rosenbergs were executed in 1953. (The Nazi regime did not race to build an atomic bomb, although whether this was due to pessimistic miscalculations by its leading physicist, Werner

Heisenberg, or to his moral opposition to such a weapon, remains unclear.)

Following Roosevelt's death on 12 April 1945, President Harry S. *Truman was told about the atomic bomb (code-named "S-1") twelve days later. With Germany nearing surrender and the construction of a test device only three months away, Truman created an Interim Committee to study the use of atomic bombs against Japan.

On 31 May 1945, the Interim Committee, composed of Secretary of War Henry L. *Stimson, Secretary of State designate James Byrnes, Harvard president James Conant, physicist and educator Karl Compton, Vannevar Bush, and a few others, listened to Oppenheimer predict the bomb would be equal to 2,000 to 20,000 tons of TNT and with its blast and radiation would kill perhaps 20,000 Japanese. After consulting other scientists and the *Joint Chiefs of Staff, the committee agreed on 1 June 1945 that for maximum psychological effect, the atomic bomb should be used without warning against a Japanese city containing a military facility.

Not all the scientists working on the Manhattan Project agreed with this. Szilard, James Franck, and a majority of the scientists at the Chicago laboratory asserted that military use against a Japanese city was unnecessary and immoral and would start a postwar nuclear *arms race. In response to their petition for a test demonstration and warning for Japan, a special scientific advisory committee—composed of Fermi, Lawrence, Oppenheimer, and Arthur Compton—met on 16 June but rejected the idea of a noncombat demonstration (the bomb might not explode, and even if it did, its lethality would not be adequately demonstrated).

On 16 July 1945, the first atomic weapon test, code-named "Trinity," was held on a desert bombing range at Alamogordo, New Mexico, 200 miles south of Los Alamos. Mounted on a metal tower, the test device—13.5 pounds of plutonium inside 2.5 tons of explosives—was exploded at 5:29 A.M. as Groves, Oppenheimer, Bush, and others watched in awe. The blast equaled 15,000–20,000 tons of TNT and generated a fireball visible for 60 miles.

Truman learned of the successful test while at the *Potsdam Conference in Germany. After mentioning cryptically to Stalin that the United States had a new weapon, Truman on 24 July ordered preparations for use against Japan. On the 26th, he issued the Potsdam Declaration, a vague modification of unconditional surrender. When Tokyo declined to consider the offer because it did not guarantee retention of the emperor, Truman, on 30 July, ordered the Army Air Forces to use America's two atomic bombs—one uranium-cored, the other plutonium-cored—against Japan. On 6 and 9 August, solitary American B-29s carried out the atomic bombings of *Hiroshima and Nagasaki. The bombings, combined with the Soviet Union's declaration of war against Japan on 8 August, led Tokyo to surrender on 14 August 1945. World War II ended; the atomic age had begun.

[See also Atomic Scientists; Nuclear Weapons; Science, Technology, War, and the Military; World War II: Military and Diplomatic Course; World War II: Domestic Course; World War II: Postwar Impact; World War II: Changing Interpretations.]

• Martin Sherwin, A World Destroyed: Hiroshima and the Origins of the Arms Race, 1973; rev. ed. 1987. Leslie R. Groves, Now It Can Be Told: The Story of the Manhattan Project, 1975. Richard Rhodes, The Making of the Atomic Bomb, 1986. James G. Hershberg, James B. Conant: Harvard to Hiroshima and the Making of the Nuclear Age, 1993. Gar Alperovitz, The Decision to Use the Atomic Bomb—and the Architecture of an American Myth, 1995. Barton J. Bernstein, "The Atomic Bombings Reconsidered," Foreign Affairs (January–February 1995), pp. 135–52. Robert P. Newman, Truman and the Hiroshima Cult, 1995. Dennis D. Wainstock, The Decision to Drop the Atomic Bomb, 1996.　—Dennis D. Wainstock

MANILA BAY, BATTLE OF (1898). As tensions between Spain and the United States over Cuba increased during 1896 and 1897, naval officers in the Office of Naval Intelligence and the Naval War College began to develop plans for a conflict with Spain. As finally adopted in the spring of 1897, these plans included an attack on the Spanish Philippines as a diversion from the Cuban theater, and as a way of improving the U.S. position in peace negotiations.

After the outbreak of war in April 1898, the commander of the Asiatic Squadron, Commodore George *Dewey, who had already been alerted to the imminence of war by Navy assistant secretary Theodore *Roosevelt, received orders from President William *McKinley to "capture or destroy" the Spanish naval squadron in the Philippines.

Dewey's six modern warships, some armed with guns as large as 8-inch caliber, completely outclassed Adm. Patricio Montojo's Spanish squadron at Manila, which consisted of seven antiquated *cruisers and gunboats; the harbor defenses were in disarray. Armed with timely reports of this by the American consul in Manila, Dewey decided from Hong Kong to attack immediately. In a few hours, on 1 May 1898, his squadron annihilated the Spanish fleet without the loss of a single American life, and blockaded Manila. This dramatic victory made Dewey a popular hero and began a chain of events that led to the U.S. annexation of the Philippines.

[See also Navy, U.S.: 1866–98; Philippines, U.S. Military Involvement in the.]　—Ronald H. Spector

MARCH, PEYTON C. (1864–1955), army chief of staff in World War I. A West Pointer (Class of 1888) and *artillery officer, March won distinction in combat during the *Spanish-American War and the *Philippine War. Later, he enhanced his reputation as a troop leader in battery and regimental commands and as an efficient staff officer through his service on the first General Staff and in the Adjutant General's Office. During World War I, after serving as chief of artillery in the American Expeditionary Force, he returned to become the army's chief of staff in the spring of 1918. His hard, coldly efficient dynamism galvanized army *logistics during the remaining months of the war.

March's major achievement was the shipment of 1.75 million men to France in time to turn the tide to victory. In his remaining years in office, until 1921, he supervised the *demobilization of the wartime army and the reorganization of the postwar army. As the nation's first strong wartime chief of staff, he developed a tense relationship with field commander Gen. John J. *Pershing, but he laid the foundation for the future power of that office. In 1932, March published The Nation at War, an account of his and the General Staff's contributions in World War I.

[See also World War I: Military and Diplomatic Course; World War I: Postwar Impact.]

• Edward M. Coffman, The Hilt of the Sword: The Career of Peyton C. March, 1966.　—Edward M. Coffman

MARINE CORPS, U.S.

Overview
Marine Corps, U.S., 1775–1865
Marine Corps, U.S., 1865–1914
Marine Corps, U.S., 1914–45
Marine Corps, U.S., Since 1945

MARINE CORPS, U.S.: OVERVIEW

The U.S. Marine Corps is a separate service within the Department of the Navy. The Commandant of the Marine Corps is a member of the *Joint Chiefs of Staff (JCS). The Marines changed their traditional roles of providing guards of ships and naval installations and light infantry for colonial interventions by developing in the twentieth century into an amphibious force that conducts land operations essential to a naval campaign or participates in other expeditionary operations. The Corps receives much of its support from the U.S. *Navy. Particularly in the twentieth century, the U.S. Marine Corps has emphasized physical fitness, intensive individual training for combat, and *esprit de corps.*

Although it claims lineage to the Continental Marines of the *Revolutionary War, the Marine Corps began its continued existence with a congressional authorization of 11 July 1798 that established a "corps of Marines" (originally some 350 officers and enlisted personnel) headed by a Commandant, for service aboard the warships of the navy then being expanded for the Undeclared Naval War with *France (1798–99). Like the British Marines, after which they were modeled, the first American Marines functioned as ships' guards and the nucleus of ships' landing parties for raids on harbors and other coastal sites.

Two centuries after its founding, the U.S. Marine Corps, with 172,200 officers and enlisted personnel in 1998, has no counterpart of comparable size and diversity among the world's armed forces. Its Fleet Marine Forces of three divisions and aircraft wings, plus other special operational units, can provide air-ground expeditionary forces especially trained for operations from the sea, including capturing littoral objectives with amphibious assaults by surface vehicles and watercraft or *helicopters. The modern Marine Corps is larger and more capable than many armies, and its aviation component, with more than 800 fighter-attack aircraft and helicopters, is among the ten largest in the world. Although there are functional reasons for a maritime power like the United States to have such a force, the continued existence of the U.S. Marine Corps as a separate service is also a monument to the power of image, the persistence of popular and congressional support, and the unflagging belief of Marines in themselves.

The U.S. Marine Corps enjoyed no special permanence, despite its wartime origins in 1775. After the Revolution, the Continental Marines disbanded in 1783. Despite its establishment in 1798, the U.S. Marine Corps seldom exceeded 5,000 officers and men for the next 100 years. Between 1798 and 1865, its best service came as shipborne infantry and emergency cannoneers aboard American warships. When not at sea, Marines lived in barracks in navy yards to provide a guard force, sometimes joining in regional defense. The Marine Corps Act of 1834 made the Corps a distinct service within the Navy Department.

The Commandants of the Marine Corps understood that sea service had its limitations, so they stressed the readiness of barracks Marines "for such duties as the Presi-

dent shall direct." These included fighting Native Americans in the *Seminole Wars, quelling urban riots and small rebellions (such as John Brown's attack on the Harpers Ferry arsenal), and adding token battalions to field armies, as in the U.S. *Army's capture of Veracruz and Mexico City during the *Mexican War. In the Civil War, Congress considered amalgamating the Marines into the Army, but decided against it. After the war, some navy officers sought to eliminate the ships' guards and, perhaps, the entire Marine Corps. Other naval officers saw new missions for Marines in a modernized navy, including the seizure of advanced bases in the Caribbean.

U.S. expansion in the wake of the *Spanish-American War (1898) brought a new era to the Corps' development. The Marines added two new missions: the wartime task of defending advanced U.S. naval bases in the Caribbean and the Pacific; and putting small but highly trained light infantry forces behind U.S. interventions and occupations in the Caribbean, Central America, and Asia. Serving as colonial infantry in China, the Dominican Republic, Haiti, Nicaragua, Panama, and elsewhere gave the Marine Corps, which ranged between 10,000 and 18,000, a popular image of toughness, daring, and *esprit de corps.*

In *World War I, the Marine brigade in the American Expeditionary Forces gained combat experience and new public praise. The Corps grew to 75,000. At the Battle of *Belleau Wood and subsequent engagements it suffered 11,500 casualties. Marines also began to use heavy artillery and airplanes in combat.

With the decline of its role as colonial infantry, the Marine Corps turned its attention in the interwar period to creating a combined arms amphibious assault force with a central wartime mission: the seizure and defense of bases in the anticipated naval campaign against Japan in the Pacific. The Fleet Marine Force was formed in 1933 as the operational arm of the Corps, supported by Marine aviation.

During *World War II, the successful war against Japan (1941–45) gave the Marine Corps a favored position in the U.S. defense establishment. The Fleet Marine Force battled its way from Guadalcanal to Okinawa, solidifying in the public mind the image of the Marine as the ultimate American warrior, thus providing the Corps with the ability to survive interservice challenges, particularly from the U.S. Army. Marines paid for the glory with some 90,000 casualties, including 19,700 killed in combat. With little administrative and logistical personnel of their own, the Marines were primarily a fighting force. Almost all Marines of World War II (a total of 669,000 men and women) served overseas. Only five percent of the U.S. armed forces, the Marine Corps suffered ten percent of all American battlefield casualties. The Marines played a vital role in the defeat of Japan, and indirectly, through creating the doctrine for amphibious landings, contributed to the defeat of Germany as well.

During the *Cold War, the Marine Corps maintained its amphibious assault mission (confirmed by congressional legislation in 1947 and 1952) and added another function, the deployment to regional trouble spots of air-ground task forces. In addition, the Corps participated in the *Korean War (1950–53) and the *Vietnam War (1961–75). In Korea, the Marines played pivotal roles, particularly in the 1950 *Inchon landing and in the 1951 campaign that drove the Chinese from South Korea. Marines suffered 30,000 casualties in heavy fighting. As a result of the Corps' proven competence, it was authorized to double its permanent size to approximately 190,000 and to maintain three divisions and aircraft wings.

The Vietnam War showed the Marines could fight well in another extended land campaign, but at great cost. More Marines served (794,000) and more became casualties (103,000) in the Vietnam War than in World War II, in what proved to be a losing cause. By 1969, the Corps had grown to 315,000. Maintaining a Marine expeditionary force of more than two divisions and one aircraft wing in the northern five provinces of the Republic of Vietnam stretched the Corps to its limit, and traditional standards of discipline, morale, and field performance suffered.

In the post-Vietnam era, internal reform helped restore public and congressional confidence in the Corps. A terrorist truck-bombing in Lebanon killed 241 U.S. servicemen, including 220 U.S. Marines in their barracks in 1983. Participation in the intervention in Grenada (1983) and Panama (1989), the Marine Corps performed an important role in the Persian Gulf War (1991). A Marine Expeditionary Force of some 93,000 troops fought in Kuwait or held some six division of Iraqi soldiers in place along the Kuwait coast while the Allied coalition forces began their major flanking attack. Two Marine divisions breached the Kuwait border fortifications, freed the capital, and took 20,000 prisoners. Although the Marine Corps was reduced from 194,000 in 1991 to 172,200 by 1998 in the contraction of the U.S. armed forces, the Corps fended off attempts to reduce its role in the post–Cold War world. It remains the nation's principal "force in readiness."

[See also Marine Corps, U.S.; Marine Corps Combat Branches.]

• Robert D. Heinl, Jr., *Soldiers of the Sea: The United States Marine Corps, 1775–1962*, 1962. Peter B. Mersky, *U.S. Marine Corps Aviation, 1912 to the Present*, 1983. Allan R. Millett, *Semper Fidelis: The History of the United States Marine Corps*, rev. ed., 1991. Karl Schuon, comp., *U.S. Marine Corps Biographical Dictionary*, 1963. Edwin H. Simmons, *The United States Marines*. rev. ed., 1998.
—Allan R. Millett

MARINE CORPS, U.S.: 1775–1865

America's Marines date back to the *Revolutionary War, when, on 10 November 1775, the Second Continental Congress authorized two battalions for expeditionary service. Functioning as ships' guards and maritime infantry, the Continental Marines resembled the British Navy's marines. In their green uniforms, Continental Marines took part in a number of naval raids and at the Battle of Princeton.

Disbanded after the Revolution, the Marines were re-created by Congress on 11 July 1798 as the United States Marine Corps, under a lieutenant colonel. Authority was ambiguously divided, for they were subject to navy regulations at sea and the army's Articles of War on land. Furthermore, their *uniforms (blue with red facing), muskets, and other equipment were furnished by the War Department. More than 300 Marines served aboard warship in the Undeclared Naval War with *France (1798–99), and fought in several ship-to-ship battles.

In the first half of the nineteenth century, Marines accompanied the navy in expeditions in the *Tripolitan War (1801–05), against the Barbary pirates in Libya and in the *War of 1812 in actions in the Atlantic and Lake Erie. Ashore in 1814–15, they helped protect the Baltimore and Norfolk naval yards and participated in the defense of New Orleans.

Under Archibald Henderson (Commandant, 1820–59),

the Corps used opportunities in the second of the *Seminole Wars and the *Mexican War to build a public reputation as effective infantry while convincing the admirals that they were necessary to guard ships and naval yards. In the Marine Corps Act of 1834, Congress ended previous confusion over the Marine's status by making the Marine Corps a service within the Navy Department, subject to naval regulations at sea and ashore. The Corps was increased to 1,500 during the second Seminole War (1835–42). During the Mexican War, some 1,800 Marines engaged in a several effective landings in California, Mexico's east coast, and the Gulf of Mexico. A small Marine battalion participated in the Battle of *Chapultepec and the capture of Mexico City (1847).

During the *Civil War, with the dramatic expansion of the *Union navy, the U.S. Marine Corps increased to only 3,800 men. In 1861, one-third of the Marine officers joined the secession and helped establish a small Confederate Marine Corps. The U.S. Marines served mainly as guards for ships and navy yards as well as gun crews aboard ships of the Union navy. Marines took part in a number of small landing parties, but the Corps eschewed larger-scale land operations, partly out of fear that a large land role might lead to amalgamation with the army, an action considered by Congress in 1863 and 1864.

[See also Marine Corps, U.S.: Overview; Marine Corps Combat Branches: Ground Forces.]

• Karl Schuon, comp., *U.S. Marine Corps Biographical Dictionary*, 1963. K. Jack Bauer, *Surf Boats and Horse Marines*, 1969. Charles R. Smith, *Marines in the Revolution: A History of the Continental Marines in the American Revolution, 1775–1783*, 1975. Allan R. Millett, *Semper Fidelis: The History of the United States Marine Corps*, rev. ed. 1991.
—John Whiteclay Chambers II

MARINE CORPS, U.S.: 1865–1914

Following the *Civil War, the Marine Corps survived a period of relative doldrums, including downsizing and even attempts by naval officers to disband the Marines, whose major role was as guards of ships and naval yards. By 1876, Congress had reduced the Corps from 3,000 to under 2,000 men. As commandant in 1864–76, Jacob Zeilin adopted the army's new system of infantry tactics, rearmed the Marines with breech-loading rifles, and gave them a new emblem, the Eagle, Globe, and Anchor, and the motto *Semper fidelis* ("Always Faithful"). The Marine Band also began to play a new marching song, "From the Halls of Montezuma to the Shores of Tripoli," based on lyrics written sometime after the *Mexican War. In 1880, John Philip Sousa became leader of the Marine Band. A major change in officer commissioning in 1882 limited new Marine officers to graduates of the U.S. Naval Academy.

The Marine Corps was transformed at the turn of the century by the acquisition of a U.S. insular empire following the *Spanish-American War. On 10 June 1898, a Marine battalion landed at Guantanamo Bay, Cuba, and secured an advanced coaling base from which the U.S. *Navy could blockade Santiago. Following the war, with U.S. commitment to overseas expansion in the Caribbean, Central America, the Pacific, and East Asia, naval strategists emphasized the need for a mobile force to establish advanced fueling and repair bases for the fleet. In October 1900, the navy's General Board recommended a Marine advanced base force; and in 1901, a regiment of 700 Marines landed on Culebra Island near Puerto Rico as part of the fleet maneuvers in the Caribbean. In 1913, the Marine Advance Base Force, forerunner of the Fleet Marine Forces, was established at the Philadelphia Navy Yard; it consisted of two small regiments and two seaplanes. Marine aviation dates from 22 May 1912, when the first Marine aviator, Lt. Alfred A. Cunningham, reported to naval aviation camp at Annapolis.

During the early twentieth century, the Marines were particularly active in a new role as colonial infantry in America's expanding empire. Marines landed and helped protect U.S. citizens and their property in China (the *China Relief Expedition of 1900); in the Philippines; and in Panama in 1903 and 1904, in Nicaragua in 1912, and eight landings in Cuba between 1907 and 1912. The Corps increased from 2,000 in 1896 to 9,000 by 1908, remaining at approximately that level until World War I.

While debate over the use of Marine guards on shipboard would occasionally continue to ruffle relations between the navy and the Marines, a consensus soon developed on the importance of the advance base and expeditionary roles of the U.S. Marine Corps.

[See also Caribbean, U.S. Military Involvement in; Marine Corps, U.S.: Overview; Marine Corps Combat Branches.]

• Merrill L. Bartlett, ed., Assault from the Sea: Essays on the History of Amphibious Warfare, 1983. Allan R. Millett, Semper Fidelis: The History of the United States Marine Corps, rev. ed. 1991. Jack Shulimson, The Marines Search for a Mission, 1880–1898, 1993.

—Jack Shulimson

MARINE CORPS, U.S.: 1914–45

In 1914, the Marine Corps stood on the threshold of revolutionary change in its traditional mission of providing guards for ships and navy yards. During U.S. participation in *World War I (1917–18), the Marines' numbers expanded from 10,000 to 73,000, one-third of whom fought in France. As part of the U.S. *Army's Second Division, the Marine Fourth Brigade distinguished itself against the German Army at the Battle of *Belleau Wood, at Soissons, at Mont Blanc, and in the *Meuse-Argonne offensive. Some Marine leaders, such as Maj. Gen. John A. *Lejeune, who was given command of the Second Division, subsequently saw the Corps' future moving away from sustained land operations.

In the decade after 1914, the Marines also developed their role as colonial infantry, imposing order and protecting U.S. interests overseas. In 1914, Marine units helped occupy the Mexican port of Veracruz and went ashore on three occasions in Haiti. In 1915, in the wake of bloody uprising, 2,000 Marines landed in Haiti with President Woodrow *Wilson's goal of restoring order and reforming that troubled nation. One of them, Smedley *Butler, took the rank of Haitian major general and organized a new national constabulary. The last of the Marines left in 1934. From 1916 to 1926, a Marine force occupied the Dominican Republic. In Nicaragua, Marines manned a legation guard, 1912–24, intervened in force in 1926, and returned in 1927 and remained until 1934. Marines also guarded the legation in Peking (Beijing), China, and kept at least one regiment in Shanghai from 1927 to 1941. In these actions, the Marines' fledgling air arm was shaped for direct support of ground operations.

The role of colonial infantry declined in the 1930s as the United States reduced the use of force in Latin America. But the diminishment of that role coincided with the expansion of a new mission: seizing and defending advanced naval bases in the Pacific. In the 1920s, with the U.S. *Navy developing contingency plans for war with Japan, the Corps cut back to 20,000, and the Marines started to develop the doctrine of *amphibious warfare. In 1921, Gen. Lejeune (commandant, 1920–29) approved a study by Maj. "Pete" *Ellis to seize Japanese fortified islands in a future war as the U.S. Fleet battled its way across the western Pacific. Some exercises were conducted through 1926, but Marine attention was diverted to China and the Caribbean. During the depression, an attempt in 1931 by the U.S. Army to drastically curtail the Marines led the Corps and the navy to refocus on amphibious operations.

The Corps created the Fleet Marine Force in 1933, published its Tentative Manual for Landing Operations in 1934, and began new landing exercises with the navy. Technology lagged, however. Not until the late 1930s was a suitable landing craft developed.

In World War II, the Marine Corps, headed by Gen. Thomas Holcomb (commandant, 1936–44), fought the Japanese in the Pacific. Early in the war, ground and air Marines reinforced their reputations as tough fighters in desperate battles to defend the islands of Wake, Midway, and the Philippines. In mid-1942, they shifted to their base-seizure mission in the air-land-sea campaign against an expanded Japanese empire. The First Marine Division opened the Allied ground offensive in the Pacific in August 1942 in the Battle of *Guadalcanal in the Solomons. It was a Marine and army campaign lasting through February 1943. The commander, Maj. Gen. Alexander A. Vandegrift, became Marine commandant in January 1944. The first real test of the Marines' amphibious doctrine against a hostile shore came on 20–23 November 1943 at the Battle of *Tarawa in the Gilbert Islands, where, despite severe losses, the Marines proved that they could seize heavily fortified islands. In 1944–45, improved equipment and tactics and better coordination helped the Marines, sometimes accompanied by army units, succeed against increasingly sophisticated Japanese defenses on New Britain, the central and northern Solomons, and Roi-Namur, Kwajalein, Eniwetok, Saipan, Tinian, Guam, Peleliu, Okinawa, and most famously Iwo Jima. Marine air also helped to liberate the Philippines.

During World War II, the Marine Corps expanded from 19,000 in 1939 to a peak strength of 475,000 men and women in 1945. The force structure had grown to two amphibious corps each composed of divisions and supporting units, plus five aircraft wings. The secretary of the navy declared that the historic flag-raising over Iwo Jima meant that "there will be a Marine Corps for the next 500 years."

[See also Iwo Jima, Battle of; Marine Corps, U.S.: Overview; Marine Corps Combat Branches; World War II, U.S. Naval Operations in: The Pacific.]

• History of the U.S. Marine Corps Operations in World War II, 5 vols., 1958–68. Robert B. Asprey, At Belleau Wood, 1965. Eugene B. Sledge, With the Old Breed at Peleliu and Okinawa, 1981. Allan R. Millett, Semper Fidelis: The History of the United States Marine Corps, rev. ed., 1991. Jon T. Hoffman, Once a Legend: "Red Mike" Edson of the Marine Raiders, 1994.

—Jon T. Hoffman

MARINE CORPS, U.S.: SINCE 1945

Immediately after World War II, the U.S. Marine Corps, despite its battlefield successes, found itself fighting for its existence under the pressures of *demobilization, the "unification" struggle, and contentions that the atomic bomb had made obsolete the Marine Corps' specialty of amphibious assault.

The Marine Corps reorganized its shrunken operating forces symmetrically into a Fleet Marine Force, Pacific, and Fleet Marine Force, Atlantic, each with a division and an aircraft wing.

Personnel strengths dropped from a World War II peak of 465,053 to 74,279 by the summer of 1950. Peacetime manning of the divisions and wings was at less than 50 percent. To provide a brigade for the critical defense of Korea's Pusan Perimeter in August, virtually all of the 1st Marine Division was required. To flesh out the division for the *Inchon landing in September, the Marine Corps Reserve had to be called up and the Second Marine Division stripped of its battalions.

Partial *mobilization eased the personnel situation. The Third Marine Division and 3rd Marine Aircraft Wing were reactivated. Legislation in 1952 fixed the minimum force structure of the active duty Marine Corps at three divisions and three wings, with a fourth division and wing in the Organized Reserve. Marine strength climbed to nearly 250,000 in 1953.

In experimenting on how to achieve the dispersion of an amphibious task force in light of possible use of nuclear weapons, the Marine Corps decided that *helicopters with specially configured landing ships to act as their carriers offered a solution to the critical ship-to-shore movement.

Presaging what would become an increasing involvement in the Middle East, a brigade-size Marine force was landed in Lebanon in 1958 as a *peacekeeping presence.

The civil war, and particularly the assassination of President Ngo Dinh Diem in 1963, caused an increasing involvement in Vietnam of Marine forces, initially as advisers and helicopter support. The landing of the 9th Marine Expeditionary Brigade at Danang in March 1965 was the first significant introduction of U.S. ground combat elements into South Vietnam.

The Marine Corps employed the term *Marine Air-Ground Task Force* (*MAGTF*) to designate tactical groupings that, with an occasional exception, came in three sizes: A Marine Expeditionary Unit (MEU) combined a battalion landing team with a reinforced helicopter squadron. A Marine Expeditionary Brigade (MEB) usually had a regimental landing team and a composite aircraft group. A Marine Expeditionary Force (MEF) was organized around a division and an aircraft wing.

The Dominican intervention of 1965 saw the employment initially of the 6th Marine Expeditionary Unit and a buildup to the 4th Marine Expeditionary Brigade.

During the *Vietnam War, the 9th MEB grew with successive deployments into the III Marine Expeditionary (alternately called Amphibious) Force. The strength of the III Marine Amphibious Force reached 85,755 in 1968, more Marines than had been ashore at Iwo Jima or Okinawa.

In size the Corps grew from a 1965 strength of 190,213 to a peak of 314,917 in 1969. With the withdrawal from Vietnam, it slipped back quickly to a plateau of just under 200,000.

In August 1982, the 32nd Marine Amphibious Unit (MAU) landed at Beirut, Lebanon, as part of a multinational peacekeeping force. The Marine Corps "presence" in Lebanon continued, one MAU relieving another at roughly four-month intervals. Early Sunday morning, 23 October,

a truck bomb detonated under the building housing the Marine Corps headquarters on the airfield, killing 241 American servicemen, 220 of them Marines.

Almost simultaneously with the Beirut barracks tragedy, the 22nd Marine Amphibious Unit landed on the northeast corner of Grenada in a near-bloodless operation.

In the absence of sufficient amphibious shipping, a new program called the *Maritime Prepositioned Force (MPF)* came into being in the 1980s. Three squadrons of cargo ships, each squadron loaded with most of an MEB's combat equipment and about thirty days of supply, were positioned strategically around the globe.

At the outset of Operation Desert Shield, the buildup for the *Persian Gulf War, in August 1990, the airlifted 1st and 7th Marine Expeditionary Brigades were met at Saudi Arabia's ports by MPF squadrons. On 2 September, the I Marine Expeditionary Force was formed by "compositing" the two MEBs. Meanwhile, the 4th Marine Expeditionary Brigade, fully equipped and embarked in amphibious shipping, was en route. On 13 November, the involuntary call-up of Selected Marine Corps Reserve units began. The 5th Marine Expeditionary Brigade sailed from San Diego in amphibious ships on 1 December. Most of the East Coast–based II Marine Expeditionary Force—numbering some 30,000 Marines and sailors, and including the Second Marine Division—started its move to the gulf on 9 December.

When actual hostilities began on 16 January 1991, the I Marine Expeditionary Force had two divisions, a very large wing, and a substantial service support command ashore. In addition, there were two Marine expeditionary brigades and a Marine expeditionary unit afloat.

When the shooting stopped on 28 February, I MEF and Marine forces afloat had a strength of 92,990 (of the 540,000 total U.S. force), making Desert Storm by far the largest Marine Corps operation in history.

Subsequent to the Persian Gulf, there was almost continuous employment of Marine air-ground task forces in peacekeeping and humanitarian missions. The I Marine Expeditionary Force deployed to Somalia in 1992. A MAU-size Special Purpose MAGTF swiftly occupied Cap Haitien, Haiti, in September 1994.

Downsizing incident to President Bill *Clinton's "bottom-up" review of the armed services took the Corps from an active strength of 193,735 in 1991 to 173,031 in 1998.

[*See also* Amphibious Warfare; Marine Corps, U.S.: Overview; Marine Corps Combat Branches.]

• Allan R. Millett, *Semper Fidelis*, 1991. J. Robert Moskin, *The U.S. Marine Corps Story*, 1992. Joseph H. Alexander, *A Fellowship of Valor*, 1997. Edwin H. Simmons, *The United States Marines: A History*, 1998.
                                                —Edwin Howard Simmons

MARINE CORPS COMBAT BRANCHES

Ground Forces
Aviation Forces

For related articles, see the chronologically organized essays in the entry, Marine Corps, U.S.

MARINE CORPS COMBAT BRANCHES: GROUND FORCES

The U. S. Marine Corps, the smaller of the naval services, traces its origins to the American *Revolutionary War. Like the navy, it was re-created in 1798 during the Undeclared

War with *France. For much of the nineteenth century, the Marine Corps served as a lightly-armed constabulary at sea, mostly to enforce order and discipline aboard ship and to man small landing parties for infrequent forays ashore. In addition to their normal duties in support of the navy, Marines also served with the army in suppressing a rebellion by the Seminoles in Florida and in the *Mexican War.

Between the *Civil War and the *Spanish-American War, various commandants of the Corps instituted reform measures. In 1870, the muster rolls listed barely 2,000 "Leathernecks" (as they were sometimes called), but one-fourth were deserters. Reformist efforts focused on the quality of the Marines. Beginning in 1883, all Marine junior officers came from the U. S. Naval Academy. A reformist element within the navy wanted to deploy Marines in battalions, readily available to the various fleet commanders. Such usage had already been demonstrated during an incursion into Panama in 1885, and again with the expeditionary force that landed at Guantanamo Bay, Cuba, in 1898. Some senior officers in the Navy argued that the manning for these "ready battalions" could be accomplished by eliminating Marines from their traditional duties aboard ship, a proposal viewed with disdain by the Marines.

Then, with the era of neocolonialism that followed the Spanish-American War, the Marine Corps was used to provide the constabulary for colonial infantry duties as part of the U. S. military involvement in the Caribbean well into the interwar era. Marines served also in a variety of overseas capacities in Latin America and East Asia. The Marine Corps also served during World War I with the American Expeditionary Forces in France.

A new justification for the Marine Corps became codified in 1927 when the Joint-Army Navy Board gave it the mission of amphibious assault in support of naval operations. It assumed that, in the event of war with Japan, the Marines would be responsible for seizing Japanese-held islands in the Pacific. The Corps developed a doctrine of *amphibious warfare, which appeared as *The Tentative Manual for Landing Operations* in 1934. During *World War II, Marines, sometimes in conjunction with the army, won a number of bloody battles on islands whose names would go down in history. Between 1941 and 1945, the Marine Corps expanded from 1,556 to 37,664 officers and 26,369 to 447,389 enlisted men. Nearly 90,000 Marines were killed or wounded during World War II; eighty Marines earned Medals of Honor.

Although a small number of women had been accepted briefly during the World War I era (known pejoratively as "Marinettes"), more than 18,000 women Marines served in World War II, and many chose to remain in uniform after the war. Some African Americans gained entry into the traditionally all-white ranks, but they were relegated to support duties. It was not until 1948 that a black American received a Marine Corps officer's commission.

A postwar effort to reduce the size and limit the mission of the Marine Corps was thwarted. Nonetheless, on the eve of the *Korean War, the Marine Corps numbered barely more than 70,000. Although used initially to buttress the collapsing forces of the Republic of Korea, an under-strength division of Marines staged a successful amphibious landing behind enemy lines at Inchon in September 1950 that paved the way for the liberation of Seoul and helped break the back of the North Korean incursion into the south.

Between the end of the Korean War and the *Vietnam War, the Marine Corps embraced the concept of vertical envelopment using *helicopters to move troops beyond the beachhead. Early in 1965, Marine units were among the first U. S. combat units deployed to South Vietnam. Ultimately, two Marine divisions and an air wing, as well as support elements and the headquarters of the III Marine Amphibious Force, served in Vietnam. The lengthy deployment taxed the capabilities of the small armed service to provide replacements and maintain its professionalism. The Marine Corps lost 12,926 men killed and 88,542 suffered wounds.

For a decade after the end of the war in 1973, the ills plaguing American society as a whole impacted upon Marine ranks: social unrest, exacerbated by racial tensions; substance abuse; and recruiting difficulties resulting from public disenchantment with the Vietnam conflict. By the early 1990s, however, the Marine Corps had coped successfully with its problems all the while enhancing its amphibious capabilities. During the *Persian Gulf War of 1991, amphibious units maneuvered and demonstrated to convince the Iraqi leadership that an amphibious invasion of Kuwait was imminent, and an entire Marine Amphibious Force (two divisions, supported by an air wing and two force service support groups) stormed north from Saudi Arabia to help breach Iraqi defenses in Kuwait.

[*See also* Marine Corps, U.S.]

• Robert D. Heinl, Jr., *Soldiers of the Sea: The United States Marine Corps, 1775–1962*, 1962. Edwin H. Simmons, *The United States Marines, 1775–1975*, 1976; 3rd ed., 1998. J. Robert Moskin, *The U.S. Marine Corps Story*, 1977. Allan R. Millett, *Semper Fidelis: The History of the United States Marine Corps*, 1980. Merrill L. Bartlett, *Lejeune: A Marine's Life, 1867–1942*, 1991. Jack Shulimson, *The Marine Corps' Search for a Mission, 1880–1898*, 1993. Joseph H. Alexander and Merrill L. Bartlett, *Sea Soldiers in the Cold War*, 1995. Dirk Anthony Ballendorf and Merrill L. Bartlett, *Pete Ellis: An Amphibious Warfare Prophet, 1880–1923*, 1997. Joseph H. Alexander, *A Fellowship of Valor: The Battle History of the United States Marine Corps*, 1997.

—Merrill L. Bartlett

MARINE CORPS COMBAT BRANCHES: AVIATION FORCES

Since its beginning in 1912, Marine Corps Aviation has defined an enduring relationship to Marine ground units and to aerial components of the U.S. *Navy, *Army, and, after 1947, to the U.S. *Air Force.

During World War I (1917–18), the Marine aviators flew their missions far from the Marine brigade fighting alongside the army in France, either bombing targets in Belgium or patrolling from the Azores for German *submarines. After the war, in the course of expeditionary duty in Haiti (1920–34) and in Nicaragua (1927–32), Marine airmen began specializing in the support of ground forces—conducting reconnaissance, strafing, dive-bombing, delivering supplies, and evacuating *casualties. By the time the United States entered World War II in 1941, aviation formed an integral part of the Fleet Marine Force, organized in 1933 for expeditionary service and operated from the navy's *aircraft carriers.

During *World War II, Marine aviation supported amphibious, ground, and sea operations against the Japanese. In 1945 on Luzon during the liberation of the *Philippines, Marine dive-bombers protected the flank of an army division. Ground support, however, was overshadowed by aerial combat; Marine fighter pilots downed 2,300 Japanese aircraft.

By the *Korean War (1950–53), the Marine Corps embraced the concept of the air-ground team, normally pairing an aircraft wing with a ground division. Although Marine pilots scored a few aerial victories in Korea, they concentrated on supporting Marine ground forces.

In the *Vietnam War (1965–73), since the objective of an air-ground team under Marine control clashed with U.S. Air Force doctrine, which centralized all land-based combat aviation under air force control—overcoming intense objections—the Air Force in March 1968 obtained operational control over all Marine Corps aircraft in Southeast Asia, except for transports, reconnaissance craft, and *helicopters. In practice, such centralization proved too cumbersome, and within six months the air force headquarters in the theater began releasing blocks of sorties for the Marines to use in support of their own ground forces.

After Vietnam, Marine Corps Aviation evolved into a force—roughly 60 percent fixed-wing aircraft and 40 percent helicopters—designed to operate from small aircraft carriers in support of amphibious operations but also capable of sustained activity from airfields ashore. During the *Persian Gulf War (1991), the 3rd Marine Aircraft Wing operated against Iraqi troops opposing two Marine divisions. Because the coalition dominated the air, centralization proved unnecessary and the Marines used their sorties as they chose.

• Robert Sherrod, *History of Marine Corps Aviation in World War II*, 1952; repr. 1987. Peter B. Mersky, *Marine Corps Aviation, 1912 to the Present*, 1983.

—Bernard C. Nalty

The **MARINE CORPS RESERVE**, established by the Naval Appropriations Act (1916), provided for the wartime expansion of the Corps without changing its statutory regular strength. The initial legislation focused on establishing the mobilization status of individuals, not units. In World War I, 7,500 Marines (including 277 women) were reservists.

Aware that its war plans required two to three times as many Marines as it could maintain on active duty, Headquarters Marine Corps gave its reserve program greater attention in the interwar period, especially training junior officers. Of the 600,000 men and women who served in the Marine Corps in World War II, about two-thirds fell into some reserve category that provided for the service of retirees, wartime volunteers and draftees, college students, volunteers below draft age, specialists, limited service personnel, and women.

The *Cold War military establishment required a higher level of reserve training readiness as well as more reservists. The Reserve Forces Act (1948) finally provided regularized pay for drills and active duty training as well as a retirement system. The Marine Corps divided its members into an Organized Marine Corps Reserve (OMCR) (drill pay units); Volunteer Training Units (no pay, but retirement credit points); and the Volunteer Reserve (a pool of veterans with no training obligations, but some active duty training opportunities). The last group became known as the Individual Ready Reserve (IRR). In 1950, the Marine Corps Reserve numbered almost 40,000 members

of the OMCR and 88,000 members in other categories. Over 95 percent of these Marines came on active duty during the *Korean War.

Reserve reform acts in 1952, 1955, and 1957 did much to improve the preactivation readiness of Marine reserves. The most important provision (1955) was that all Marine reservists complete at least six months of initial active duty training before joining an Organized Marine Corps Reserve unit. The requirements for reserve officers were even more stringent—two or more years of active duty. The requirements for training increased. Summer camps expanded to two weeks, and drills shifted from one night a week to one or more weekends a month. The Ready Reservists numbered around 45,000 in drill pay units and 80,000 in the Individual Ready Reserve.

In the early 1960s, the Organized (or Select) Marine Corps Reserve became a regular part of the Fleet Marine Force: the 4th Marine Division, the 4th Marine Aircraft Wing, and the 4th Force Service Support Group. Unlike the army, the active duty Marine Corps (around 190,000 before and after the *Vietnam War) remained four times as large as the organized reserves. Marine Corps reserve units did not mobilize for the war, but countless thousands of reservists volunteered as individuals for active duty in Southeast Asia.

After a troubled transition to an *All-Volunteer Force system in the 1970s, the Marine Corps Reserve rebuilt itself into a force of 40,000 members of the Select Reserve and 68,000 members of the Individual Ready Reserve. Around 28,000 members of this force came on active duty by volunteering or by federal activation to serve in the *Persian Gulf War (1991). Operation Desert Storm showed that the policy of extensive active duty training and a generous commitment of regulars and full-time reservists to reserve training and administration paid dividends in readiness.

[*See also* Marine Corps, U.S.; Marine Corps Women's Reserve; ROTC.]

• Public Affairs Unit 4-1, USMCR, *The Marine Corps Reserve: A History*, 1966. Allan R. Millett, *Semper Fidelis: The History of the United States Marine Corps*, 1980; rev. ed. 1991.

—Allan R. Millett

MARINE CORPS WOMEN'S RESERVE, U.S. The Marine Corps Women's Reserve (MCWR) was authorized by Congress in July 1942 to relieve male Marines for combat duty in World War II. However, Maj. Gen. Comm. Thomas Holcomb delayed until October, when mounting losses, an order to add 164,273 Marines, and a plan to include draftees (viewed as a threat to the Corps' elite volunteer image) forced him to consider joining the other services in accepting women in uniform.

In January 1943, the MCWR swore in its first director, Maj. Ruth Cheney Streeter, forty-seven, wife of an attorney and mother of four. The MCWR officially began on 13 February 1943. In March, the first 71 officer candidates arrived at the U.S. Midshipmen School at Mount Holyoke College; 722 enlisted women entered boot camp at Hunter College in New York City.

Although the public wanted an acronym like the *WACs and *WAVES, the commandant refused any catchy name for Marines. The formal title remained, but informally they were called Women Reservists, shortened to WRs.

More than half of the WRs performed clerical work; the

others were assigned various duties, including radio operator, photographer, parachute rigger, motor transport driver, aerial gunnery instructor, link trainer instructor, control tower operator, automotive mechanic, teletype operator, cryptographer, laundry manager, and assembly and repair mechanic. At the end of the war, the MCWR had 820 officers and 17,640 enlisted women. They worked in 225 specialties, filling 85 percent of the enlisted jobs at Marine Corps Headquarters and comprising nearly two-thirds of the permanent personnel at all large posts and stations.

*Demobilization began in June 1945, and the office of the wartime MCWR closed June 1946. However, the need for clerks to process separation orders and transportation, and settle the accounts of thousands of combat Marines, plus a growing sense of the inevitability of a permanent women's military organization, prevented total disbandment. Several hundred WRs were retained at headquarters until June 1948, when President Harry S. *Truman signed the Women's Armed Services Integration Act giving equal status to women in uniform. Women then became part of the regular Marine Corps.

[See also Marine Corps, U.S.; Women in the Military.]

• Jeanne J. Holm, Women in the Military, 1982. Mary V. Stremlow, Free a Marine to Fight: Women Marines in World War II, 1994.
—Mary V. Stremlow

MARION, FRANCIS (1732–1795), the "Swamp Fox," Revolutionary War partisan leader. Marion looked frail and unmilitary, but he served brilliantly as a provincial lieutenant in the Cherokee War (1761), as a major defending Sullivan's Island (1776), and as a regimental commander in comte d'Estaing's attack on Savannah (1779). Escaping the British siege of *Charleston in May 1780, he raised a partisan militia to oppose the occupation of his native South Carolina. His first operation (20 August) became his trademark: surprise night attack on a larger British-loyalist force and then a skillful withdrawal. In this case he liberated 147 American prisoners. In December he became a brigadier general, commanding the militia of eastern South Carolina. He followed directives from theater commander Nathanael *Greene but opposed cooperation with fellow partisan Thomas Sumter, whom he considered a plunderer.

Marion's perseverance, leadership, and cunning kept his force alive and earned him the sobriquet, the "Swamp Fox." The partisans denied the British a secure base, terrorized the loyalists, decimated their militia, and forced British regulars to become constables instead of concentrating against Greene's army. During 1781, Marion's brigade fought twenty-five engagements, captured Fort Watson, Fort Motte, and Georgetown, and led Greene's attack at Eutaw Springs. In the postwar period, Marion campaigned in the state assembly to restore former loyalists to society.

[See also Revolutionary War: Military and Diplomatic Course.]

• Hugh F. Rankin, Francis Marion: The Swamp Fox, 1973. Clyde R. Ferguson, "Functions of the Partisan Militia in the South During the American Revolution: An Interpretation," in W. Robert Higgins, ed., The Revolutionary War in the South: Power, Conflict, and Leadership, 1979.
—Louis D. F. Frasché

MARNE, SECOND BATTLE OF THE (1918). Marne was the area west of Reims, France, in which the Germans made their greatest gains in World War I since the battle in the same area in 1914. On 15 June 1918, fourteen German divisions forced the Marne River against French and British armies. A French division and two Italian divisions folded. Earlier, at Cantigny, the U.S. 1st Division had halted the Germans, and the 2nd Division helped recapture Belleau Wood and Vaux. The U.S. 3rd Division, hastily committed against the point of the German drive, stopped the advance, in bloody, hand-to-hand fighting, although the Americans were beset on three sides. The German drive continued around the Americans, establishing a sizable bridgehead across the Marne. British divisions from the north arrived and blunted the German offensive, as they and the French reconstituted defenses on the river line, building on the 3rd Division's positions. Through the ranks of the German assault troops ran the rumor, "The Americans are killing everyone."

Allied *artillery and aircraft, striking beyond the salient, destroyed the Marne bridges, disrupting German reinforcement and resupply. With the French line holding from Soissons to Reims, the German offensive was halted. By 17 July, it was apparent to the German High Command that the offensive had run its course. American forces were arriving in France at the rate of 300,000 a month. Although Gen. Erich *Ludendorff, commander of the German forces, planned another offensive in Flanders, the offensive in the Champagne-Marne marked the last westward movement of the German Army in World War I.

American forces had been "bloodied" in two scorching hot days of close combat; they had proven themselves brave, even aggressive, though still "green" in battle. The Third Division's steadfast defense, especially that of the 38th Infantry Regiment, earned it the title "The Rock of the Marne."

[See also Army, U.S.: 1900–41; Belleau Wood, Battle of; World War I: Military and Diplomatic Course.]

• Edward M. Coffman, The War to End All Wars: The American Military Experience in World War I, 1968. Paul F. Braim, The Test of Battle: The American Expeditionary Forces in the Meuse-Argonne Campaign, 1987; rev. ed. 1997.
—Paul F. Braim

MARSHALL, GEORGE C. (1880–1959), World War II army chief of staff; secretary of state, 1947–49; *Korean War secretary of defense. Marshall is considered the creator of the World War II U.S. Army, the organizer of Allied victory, and the architect of key U.S. *Cold War policies. In 1953, he received the Nobel Peace Prize for the European Recovery Program (*Marshall Plan) that bears his name. He is the first professional soldier to be so honored.

Born in Uniontown, Pennsylvania, Marshall graduated from the Virginia Military Institute in 1901 and in 1902 was commissioned a second lieutenant. Throughout his early military career, he exhibited extraordinary ability as a staff officer. Consequently, he was given responsibilities far beyond his rank and deeply impressed his superiors—most notably Gen. John J. *Pershing, who assigned Marshall to his World War I staff and became his mentor and supporter. Marshall played a major role in planning the St. Mihiel and *Meuse-Argonne offensives, and developed an exceptional reputation for organizing and operating within Allied commands. During the interwar years, he developed a similar reputation for working with civilians. As head of the Infantry School at Fort Benning (1927–32) he also trained what would become the U.S. High Command in World War II. Promotion during this time was slow, however, and only in 1936 did he obtain his first general's star. Yet in 1939 President Franklin D. *Roosevelt selected him over numerous senior officers to be the new army chief of staff.

In 1939–41, Marshall focused his energies on the creation of a large, modern army to meet the threat posed by Axis military victories. In the process he developed an extraordinary reputation with Congress for honesty as well as military expertise, and he became the administration's most convincing military advocate on Capitol Hill. Largely as a result of his efforts, the army expanded from 175,000 in 1939 to 1.4 million in 1941. Plans were also completed for additional expansion to 8 million and for a global strategy of alliance with Britain to defeat Germany before Japan, if and when the United States officially entered the war. Marshall was far less successful in halting Roosevelt's proclivity to overcommitment, however, particularly in the Far East, and over whether scarce resources should be allocated to the U.S. Army or to potential allies under the *Lend-Lease Act and Agreements.

After the attack on *Pearl Harbor, Marshall became the leading figure in the newly formed U.S. Joint and Anglo-American Combined Chiefs of Staff and gradually emerged as Roosevelt's chief military adviser. He attended all Allied wartime summit conferences and played a major role in the creation of the joint and combined chiefs and in the application of the unity of command principle to all U.S. and British ground, naval, and air forces. He also strongly promoted a cross-Channel invasion over British-supported Mediterranean operations, but he lost that debate and was forced to acquiesce in the 1942–43 *North Africa Campaign and the 1943 invasion and conquest of *Sicily and *Italy. In return, Marshall won presidential and British support for the 1944 cross-Channel assault that would culminate in the decisive invasion of *Normandy. Although it was expected he would command that operation, Marshall was not selected because he had become indispensable in Washington and because he refused to request the position. For such self-denial as well as for his accomplishments, Marshall was selected *Time* magazine's "Man of the Year" in 1944, and Congress awarded him a fifth star and the title "General of the Army."

After World War II, Marshall served as special presidential emissary to China in an unsuccessful effort to avert civil war, and then as Truman's secretary of state from 1947 to 1949. In this position he played a major role in defining, implementing, and winning bipartisan support for an activist Cold War policy of containing Soviet *expansionism, most notably in the European Recovery Program (*Marshall Plan), and won a second "Man of the Year" award as well as a Nobel Prize. He played a major role, too, in the formation of West Germany and *NATO. As secretary of defense (1950–51), he rebuilt U.S. military forces during the Korean War and took a key part in the controversial relief of Gen. Douglas MacArthur. For this, as well as his Asian policies while secretary of state, he became a target of attacks by Senator Joseph McCarthy and his associates.

Despite those attacks, Marshall's reputation continued to grow after his death in 1959. In addition to his extraordinary accomplishments, he was one of the foremost defenders of civilian control of the military, a key definer of the army's proper role in a democratic society, and a model of both personal integrity and selfless public service. For all of this he is widely considered one of the world's greatest soldier-statesmen.

[See also Civil-Military Relations: Civil Control of the Military; World War II: Military and Diplomatic Course; Joint Chiefs of Staff.]

• Forrest C. Pogue, *George C. Marshall*, 4 vols., 1963–87. Larry I. Bland, ed., *The Papers of George Catlett Marshall*, 3 of 6 vols., 1981–91. Thomas Parrish, *Roosevelt and Marshall: Partners in Politics and War*, 1989. Mark A. Stoler, *George C. Marshall: Soldier-Statesman of the American Century*, 1989. Edward Cray, *General of the Army: George C. Marshall, Soldier and Statesman*, 1990. Larry I. Bland, ed., *George C. Marshall: Interviews and Reminiscences for Forrest C. Pogue*, 1991.

—Mark A. Stoler

MARSHALL, S. L. A. (1900–1977), military writer, journalist, army officer, pioneer of combat history techniques in World War II. Born in Catskill, New York, Samuel A. Marshall grew up in El Paso, Texas, enlisted in the army in 1917, and won a lieutenant's commission in France. He subsequently joined the National Guard. Marshall became a journalist in El Paso in 1923, but moved in 1927 to the *Detroit News,* from which, except during tours of army duty, he covered wars for forty years. Through his syndicated column and other publications, "SLAM" Marshall became one of America's best-known military writers.

In writing battlefield history, Marshall's technique was to interview survivors, particularly enlisted men and junior officers, individually and in groups, soon after an encounter. He elicited and compared details and wrote up his findings almost immediately in a highly readable, anecdotal narrative style.

Two books (1940 and 1941) by Marshall on Germany's mobile warfare led to his appointment in 1942 as a major in charge of army orientation. In 1943, he helped found the army's Historical Branch and followed American troops through the Gilbert and Marshall Islands, where he conducted his first after action interviews. In 1944–45, he covered the Allied invasion of Western Europe, spending considerable time interviewing under fire.

Afterward, resuming his journalistic career, Marshall wrote a number of books on World War II battles. Most influential was *Men Against Fire* (1947). His assertion that only 25 to 30 percent of front-line American soldiers fired their weapons, even when under attack, provoked considerable controversy. *Infantry Journal* contained articles by professional officers challenging his figures. Despite this skepticism, Marshall's findings contributed to changes in army training doctrine.

(Marshall said his evidence came from his interviews with combat soldiers, but after his death, when no notes of such interviews were found in his papers, a new debate emerged in 1989 over the authenticity of these findings. Roger J. Spiller of the army's Combat Studies Institute challenged the evidence, but Marshall's grandson, John Douglas Marshall—who had broken with his grandfather by resigning his commission as a conscientious objector during the *Vietnam War—defended him.)

During the *Korean War, Marshall was promoted to brigadier general in 1951 and assigned to the Eighth Army. Afterward, he wrote *Pork Chop Hill* (1956), later a Hollywood film. Having accompanied the Israeli Army in 1956, he wrote *Sinai Victory* (1958).

The army sent Marshall to Vietnam in 1967. He defended U.S. military action there, criticized the press, and later opposed the withdrawal of American troops.

As a syndicated columnist, military historian, and author of more than thirty books, Marshall had a significant influence—especially in the 1940s and 1950s—on the way combat was perceived by the public and by many in the military.

[See also Combat Effectiveness; Training and Indoctrination.]

• S. L. A. Marshall, *Island Victory*, 1944. S. L. A. Marshall, *Men Against Fire: The Problem of Command in Future War*, 1947. S. L. A. Marshall, *Pork Chop Hill: The American Fighting Man in Action*, 1956. S. L. A. Marshall, *Battles in the Monsoon*, 1976. S. L. A. Marshall, *Bringing Up the Rear*, ed. Cate Marshall, 1980. Roger J. Spiller, "S. L. A. Marshall and the Ratio of Fire," *RUSI Journal*, vol. 133, no. 4 (1988), pp. 63–71. F. D. G. Williams, *SLAM: The Influence of S. L. A. Marshall on the United States Army*, 1990. John Douglas Marshall, *Reconciliation Road: A Family Odyssey of War and Honor*, 1993.   —John Whiteclay Chambers II

The **MARSHALL PLAN** (1948–52) was the largest and most successful program of foreign assistance ever undertaken by the U.S. government. The harsh winter of 1946–47 underlined the inability of European countries to achieve a sustained economic recovery from the dislocations and destruction of World War II. Following the proclamation of the *Truman Doctrine in March 1947, and the failure of the Moscow Conference that April to reach agreement on German reparations, Secretary of State George C. *Marshall came to believe that "The patient is sinking while the doctors deliberate." American leaders feared that poverty and hunger would make Western European countries vulnerable to Communist appeals. Marshall's speech at Harvard University's commencement in June offered American funding for a cooperative European recovery program, including Germany. Marshall even invited the Soviet Union to participate, arguing that "our policy is directed not against any country or doctrine but against hunger, poverty, desperation, and chaos." The Soviet Union, however, refused, since Josef *Stalin feared that the Americans intended to use their economic strength to undermine Soviet control in Eastern Europe. The Soviet Union responded to the plan by further tightening its control over Eastern Europe, a reaction that encouraged Western European countries to seek a formal political and military alliance with the United States. The Marshall Plan, with its huge commitment of American prestige and treasure in Western Europe, laid the foundations for *NATO and the Atlantic alliance.

Between 1948 and 1951, the Congress authorized more than $13 billion for the European Recovery Program, approximately 10 percent of the annual federal budget. Although some contemporaries may have exaggerated the importance of Marshall Plan assistance in Europe's reconstruction, there is little question that the aid helped overcome bottlenecks within the European economy and created a basis for rapid economic growth. Western European production rose rapidly, and by 1950 it had topped the prewar level by 25 percent.

Although the Marshall Plan was presented as part of the "containment" of Soviet *expansionism, Congress initially prohibited the use of Marshall Plan assistance for military supplies. (This did not prevent colonial powers such as the French from indirect use of such assistance to continue their war in Indochina.) After the outbreak of the *Korean War in June 1950, the United States reversed this policy and encouraged the use of Marshall Plan assistance to provide for the rearmament of Western Europe within the NATO alliance. At the end of 1951, this change in emphasis became official when the Economic Cooperation Administration was renamed the Mutual Security Administration.

[See also Cold War: External Course; Cold War: Domestic Course.]

• Michael J. Hogan, *The Marshall Plan: America, Britain, and the Reconstruction of Western Europe*, 1987. Charles S. Maier and Günter Bischof, eds., *The Marshall Plan and Germany*, 1991.
                                   —Thomas A. Schwartz

MARTIAL LAW, sometimes defined as merely the will of the commanding general or whatever is necessary to preserve governmental authority, is the temporary control by military authorities of the civilian population in a particular area. Its application is generally to battle zones during war or areas of great or potentially great public disturbance in peacetime.

Americans rejected martial law in the Declaration of Independence, indicting George III for having put colonial Massachusetts under control of the British army. The U.S. Constitution limited the federal government's application of martial law by the provision in Article I, section 9, concerning the right of habeas corpus.

After 1798, the new government differentiated between military law and martial law. The former are the rules that govern members of the armed forces. The latter is the mechanism under which the military governs civilians. Martial law by federal authorities was viewed as permissible only under extraordinary circumstances which, as with suspension of habeas corpus, presumed congressional authorization.

Martial law was imposed by U.S. forces briefly on New Orleans during the *War of 1812 and on areas of Mexico occupied by the U.S. Army during the *Mexican War. But it became a major issue in the *Civil War, when President Abraham *Lincoln and the *Union army used it in various states to restrain behavior by civilians both in the war zones and eventually in areas far removed from battle such as Ohio and Indiana. This virtual independence of military courts from supervision by civilian courts raised troubling questions; after the war, the U.S. Supreme Court in *Ex Parte *Milligan* (1866) severely limited its application by the federal government and precluded it where civil courts functioned. Although martial law has been declared by state governors for areas hit by natural disasters or extensive violence, the federal government, with the exception of the treatment of the Japanese Americans on the West Coast in World War II, has seldom used martial law in the United States in the twentieth century.

[See also Civil-Military Relations: Civilian Control of the Military; Civil-Military Relations: Military Government and Occupation; Japanese-American Internment Cases; Justice, Military: Military Courts; *Merryman, Ex Parte*; Supreme Court; War, and the Military.]

• James E. Sefton, *The U.S. Army and Reconstruction*, 1967. Robin Higham, ed., *Bayonets in the Streets: The Use of Troops in Civil Disturbances*, 1969. Robert W. Coakley, *The Role of Federal Military Forces in Domestic Disorders, 1789–1878*, 1988. Paul L. Murphy, ed., *The Bill of Rights and American Legal History*, 1990. Mark E. Neely,

Jr., *The Fate of Liberty: Abraham Lincoln and Civil Liberties*, 1991. Clayton D. Laurie, *The Role of Federal Military Forces in Domestic Disorders, 1879–1945*, 1993.
—Paul L. Murphy

MAULDIN, BILL [WILLIAM] (1921–), trained through correspondence classes as well as a year spent at the Chicago Academy of Art, American editorial cartoonist of World War II. Mauldin was unable to gain steady employment as a newspaper cartoonist, so the New Mexican native enlisted in 1940 in the Arizona National Guard. Mauldin's talents were first recognized during his assignment to the 45th Division's newspaper staff. Still he served as an infantryman once the United States entered the war.

In 1944, Mauldin joined *Stars and Stripes* and developed the distinctive characters of "Willie" and "Joe" to depict the drudgery and misery faced by the average G.I. in the European theater. Filthy, aged beyond their years, irreverent in their attitudes toward officers and rear echelon personnel, Willie and Joe became among the most widely recognized symbols of the American combat infantryman. Mauldin was awarded the Pulitzer Prize in 1945, and the United Features Syndicate distributed his cartoons to hundreds of newspapers. In his book *Up Front* (1945), an instant bestseller, Mauldin interpreted his cartoons and the experiences of the average soldier.

After the war, Mauldin continued his career as a cartoonist, satirizing a variety of political and social topics. During the *Korean War, he visited the front and described his experiences in *Bill Mauldin in Korea* (1952). Mauldin spent much of his postwar career with the *Chicago Sun-Times*.

[*See also* Culture, War, and the Military; Illustration, War and the Military in.]

• Frederick S. Voss, *Reporting the War: The Journalistic Coverage of World War II*, 1994.
—G. Kurt Piehler

MAXIM, HIRAM (1840–1916), self-taught engineer and inventor of the first automatic machine gun. Born in Maine, Maxim's early work focused on electrical design and the incandescent light bulb. In the early 1880s, he moved to London as representative of the U.S. Electric Lighting Company. As a sideline, he experimented with early *machine guns. In 1885, Maxim developed a single-barrel weapon that could fire 500 rounds of ammunition a minute. Although not the first machine gun, the Maxim gun, as it was called, remained vastly superior to the earlier multibarreled hand-cranked *Gatling gun (1862) and the Nordenfelt gun (1877). An avid promoter, Maxim effectively cultivated support from the British royal family and other influential Britons, which helped promote the adoption of the Maxim gun by the British army (1889) and the Royal Navy (1892). His company was consolidated with the Vickers Company in 1896. He became a British subject in 1900 and was knighted in 1901. His brother, Hudson Maxim (1853–1927), remained in the United States and developed a high explosive (Maximite). Despite the technical superiority of the Maxim gun, the U.S. Army resisted using it until 1904.

Neither Maxim nor most military men initially recognized the revolutionary impact the Maxim gun would have on the nature of battle. Although the machine gun would be used with deadly effectiveness by British imperial forces in suppressing colonial insurrections in Africa, few anticipated its extensive use in European warfare beginning in World War I.

• Hiram S. Maxim, *My Life*, 1915. John Ellis, *The Social History of the Machine Gun*, 1975.
—G. Kurt Piehler

MAYAGUEZ INCIDENT (1975). On 12 May 1975, Cambodian gunboats seized the U.S. merchant ship *Mayaguez* near Cambodia's Koh Tang Island. Claiming the ship was spying, Cambodia's Khmer Rouge government imprisoned the forty-member crew. President Gerald *Ford labeled the action piracy. After the fall of Saigon that year and the unsuccessful end of the *Vietnam War, Ford and Secretary of State Henry *Kissinger believed that only forceful response to the *Mayaguez* provocation could bolster damaged U.S. credibility. Also, memories of North Korea's 1968 capture of the USS *Pueblo*, an intelligence-gathering ship, and the year-long incarceration of its crew, prompted quick action. Lacking diplomatic relations with Phnom Penh, Washington attempted to communicate demands for release of the crew through Beijing and the *United Nations, but received no clear response from the Cambodians.

On 14 May, 179 U.S. Marines used *helicopters to assault Koh Tang Island while a Marine boarding party retook the empty *Mayaguez*; U.S. aircraft bombed nearby military targets. The crew was not on the island, but the Cambodians on their own released the crew from the mainland as the operation began. The Marines on the island encountered strong resistance and could not be extracted until the 15th. U.S. *casualties were fifteen killed in action, three missing, fifty wounded, and twenty-three killed in a helicopter crash.

Heeding the *War Powers Resolution of 1973, the Ford administration had notified Congress as it issued its military orders. Some legislators charged that the president had abused the law, and some historians have characterized Ford's use of force as precipitous and excessive. Ford insisted that the operation helped restore America's self-confidence. Many editorial writers agreed, and the president's public approval rating surged 11 percent.

[*See also* Commander in Chief, President as; Korea, U.S. Military Involvement in.]

• Roy Rowan, *The Four Days of Mayaguez*, 1975. David L. Anderson, "Gerald R. Ford and the Presidents' War in Vietnam," in Anderson, ed., *Shadow on the White House*, 1993.

—David L. Anderson

The **McCARRAN INTERNAL SECURITY ACT** (1950) was enacted during the early Cold War years and shortly after U.S. intervention in the *Korean War in response to growing domestic anti-Communist fears. In the wake of Republican accusations that the Truman administration was not diligent enough against Communists and Communist sympathizers in the United States, a coalition of conservative Democrats and Republicans adopted the measure.

The act, named after Democratic senator Patrick A. McCarran of Nevada, required "communist-action" and "communist front" organizations to register with the Justice Department. It also increased the statute of limitations, required registration of individuals trained in espionage, authorized the exclusion and deportation of Communists and other "subversives," and provided for the detention of potential espionage agents and subversives whenever the president proclaimed an "internal security emergency." President Harry S. *Truman vetoed the bill, which was criticized as an abridgment of civil liberties; but the measure became law on 23 September 1950 after Congress overrode his veto. The registration measures were challenged in the courts and declared unconstitutional in the 1960s. The emergency detention provisions were repealed by Congress in 1971 during the presidency of Richard M. *Nixon and the controversial *Vietnam Antiwar Movement.

[See also Civil Liberties and War; Cold War: Domestic Course; Supreme Court, War, and the Military; Vietnam War: Postwar Impact.]

• Earl Lathan, The Communist Controversy in Washington, 1966. William R. Tanner and Robert Griffith, "Legislative Politics and 'McCarthyism': The Internal Security Act of 1950," in The Spectator, eds. Robert Griffith and Athan Theoharis, 1974.

—William R. Tanner

McCAULEY, MARY LUDWIG HAYS. See Pitcher, Molly.

McCLELLAN, GEORGE B. (1826–1885), Civil War general. McClellan was born to a wealthy family in Philadelphia; at the age of fifteen, he entered West Point and eventually graduated second in his class. During the *Mexican War, he won two promotions on the field for distinguished conduct under fire, but he resigned his commission (1857), becoming chief engineer and then president of railroad companies in Illinois and Ohio.

When the Civil War broke out, McClellan received an appointment as major-general and commanded Union forces that drove the Confederates out of western Virginia in July 1861. After the Union disaster at the First Battle of *Bull Run, President Abraham *Lincoln brought him east to reorganize and command the Army of the Potomac. McClellan was greeted with widespread public enthusiasm as "the Young Napoleon" who would produce a swift and decisive victory over the Confederacy. Unfortunately, these expectations—partly of his own making but mostly a reflection of a conviction early in the war that "hard fighting" would lead to a quick and relatively painless victory—would haunt McClellan's tenure as a Union general as well as his historical reputation.

In the late summer and fall of 1861, McClellan set out methodically to rebuild the Army of the Potomac. Despite public pressure for an immediate attack, McClellan prepared for an assault in the spring of 1862. His meticulous plans for one big offensive to seize Richmond, Virginia, the Confederate capital, resulted in the Peninsula Campaign from March to July 1862, in which the Army of the Potomac came within five miles of the city, but was thrown back by Robert E. *Lee in the *Seven Days' Battle (25 June–1 July 1862). Disillusioned by McClellan's apparent lack of progress and demands for additional manpower, Lincoln withdrew McClellan and his army from the peninsula, and placed John Pope in charge of Union forces in northern Virginia.

However, after humiliating Pope at the Second Battle of *Bull Run, Lee invaded Maryland, and Lincoln recalled McClellan to lead the Army of the Potomac once again. "Little Mac" brought together the disorganized and dispirited *Union army, and after Union troops discovered the

"lost" plans to Lee's invasion, he moved rapidly to track Lee down. McClellan cornered Lee's forces near Sharpsburg in western Maryland: at the Battle of *Antietam (17 September 1862), the two armies fought the bloodiest one-day conflict of the war. Lee was forced to retreat back into Virginia. The battle has been described as a tactical draw, but a strategic victory. McClellan has been criticized by some historians for failure to commit his reserves at the end of the day to destroy the Rebels. Under substantial pressure himself, Lincoln once again relieved McClellan of command in November 1862.

Although he understood that the Confederacy had to be defeated, McClellan, a member of the Democratic Party, advocated military conduct under "the highest principles known to Christian civilization" and was generally conservative on slavery. Hence, he was never in favor with Radical Republicans, who demanded the immediate abolition of slavery and regarded McClellan as "soft" on military measures. McClellan's supposed moderation became a central issue when he ran for president in 1864. Although he strongly advocated continuing the war until victory was achieved, some historians have suggested that if McClellan had defeated the Republican Lincoln, the peace faction within the Democratic Party would have insisted that the war effort be suspended, and the Confederacy would thereby have achieved independence. Such assessments, however, are speculative.

McClellan was a brilliant organizer, who inspired devotion from the common infantryman. He could also be contemptuous of politicians, which has led some historians to describe him as vain, arrogant, and paranoid. A tragic failure, he had a Cassandra-like quality in correctly warning that it would take substantial resources and repeated attempts to capture Richmond. For the first two years of the war, each time Lincoln replaced McClellan, the Union army, in less capable hands, went on humiliating debacles. George B. McClellan proved, and will probably remain, one of the most controversial generals of the American Civil War.

[See also Civil War: Military and Diplomatic Course; Civil War: Changing Interpretations.]

• Warren W. Hassler, Jr., General George B. McClellan: Shield of the Union, 1957. Joseph L. Harsh, "On the McClellan-Go-Round," Civil War History, 19 (1973), pp. 101–18. Stephen W. Sears, George B. McClellan: The Young Napoleon, 1988. Eric T. Dean, Jr., "Rethinking the Civil War: Beyond 'Revolutions,' 'Reconstructions,' and the 'New Social History,'" Southern Historian, 15 (Spring 1994), pp. 28–50. Thomas J. Rowland, "In the Shadows of Grant and Sherman: George B. McClellan Revisited," Civil War History, 40(3) (September 1994), pp. 202–25.

—Eric T. Dean, Jr.

McCLOY, JOHN J. (1895–1989), advocate of national security in the *Cold War era. Born in Philadelphia, McCloy was educated at Amherst College and Harvard Law School. After attending the Plattsburgh military training camps for civilians in 1915–16, McCloy developed a lifelong interest in the military. He joined the American Expeditionary Force in World War I, and later became a Wall Street lawyer, best known for his success in pursuing the "Black Tom" sabotage case against Germany in the 1930s. During World War II, McCloy was assistant secretary of war, handling the political dimension of military problems. He advocated the racial integration of the U.S. military on grounds of increased "efficiency." However, McCloy also was a central figure in the controversial decisions to intern Japanese Americans and not to bomb the Nazi extermination camp at Auschwitz. Along with Secretary of War Henry L. *Stimson, McCloy helped defeat the Morgenthau Plan to deindustrialize Germany, and he advocated an international tribunal to investigate German *war crimes. His willingness to countenance a significant increase in the power and secrecy of the national government places him as one of the founders of the so-called national security state. After the war, McCloy served as president of the *World Bank (1947–49) and as high commissioner to Germany (1949–52), strongly supporting the rearmament of West Germany and its entry into the *NATO alliance.

Although his position as high commissioner was his most significant public office, McCloy played a continuing role in formation of U.S. policy on *national security in the nuclear age. He was John F. *Kennedy's adviser on disarmament, and served Lyndon B. *Johnson in the Trilateral Negotiations of 1966–67, which readjusted NATO's financial burdens after the withdrawal of France. An unapologetic advocate of a Pax Americana, McCloy never wavered in his view of America's international responsibilities and the need for a strong military to exercise global leadership.

[See also Germany, U.S. Military Involvement in; Holocaust, U.S. War Effort and the; Japanese-American Internment Cases; Morgenthau, Henry.]

• Thomas Alan Schwartz, *America's Germany: John J. McCloy and the Federal Republic of Germany*, 1991. Kai Bird, *The Chairman: John J. McCloy*, 1992.   —Thomas A. Schwartz

McELROY, NEIL (1904–1972), secretary of defense (1957–59). McElroy was born in Berea, Ohio, and graduated from Harvard in 1925. He was employed by Procter & Gamble, rising to the presidency in 1948. Chairmanship of a White House conference on education (1955–56) brought him to the attention of President Dwight D. *Eisenhower, who appointed him secretary of defense effective 9 October 1957.

McElroy's accession followed by a few days the launching of the first global-orbiting satellite (Sputnik) by the Soviet Union, which ushered in the age of long-range rocketry and space exploration. During McElroy's tenure, major U.S. missile projects begun several years earlier came to fruition. McElroy ordered production of two intermediate-range (1,500-mile) *missiles, Jupiter and Thor, developed by the army and air force respectively. He accelerated development of the air force intercontinental missiles, Atlas and Titan, and of the navy's Polaris (submarine) system. He also authorized development of the improved Minuteman missile by the air force and established the Advanced Research Projects Agency to supervise the development of new weapons.

McElroy presided over a comprehensive reorganization of the Department of *Defense in 1958. Initiative for this came from President Eisenhower, but McElroy appointed the committee that worked out the details and transmitted its conclusions to Eisenhower. The reorganization enhanced the position of the secretary of defense, making him virtual deputy commander in chief.

After leaving office on 1 December 1959, McElroy rejoined Procter & Gamble.

[See also Defense Reorganization Acts; Satellites, Reconnaissance.]

• Roger R. Trask, *The Secretaries of Defense: A Brief History*, 1985. Robert J. Watson, *Into the Missile Age, 1956–1960*, 1997.
                                                         —Robert J. Watson

McKINLEY, WILLIAM (1843–1901), *Civil War veteran and twenty-fifth president of the United States. Born and raised in Ohio, McKinley enlisted in 1861 as a private in the 23rd Ohio Volunteer Regiment. A commissary sergeant at the Battle of *Antietam (1862), he was later promoted to captain and ended his military service as brevet major. His career in law and Republican politics included terms as congressman, senator, and two-term governor of Ohio before his election as president in 1896.

The president's own military experience and the opposition of big business made him reluctant to lead the nation into war, so he pressed the Spanish government to control a rebellion that had begun in Cuba in 1895. An astute politician, McKinley was aware of his countrymen's growing impatience as the conflict persisted, particularly after the sinking of the USS *Maine in Havana Harbor. When the Spanish government proved unable to end the war, he asked Congress for a war declaration in April 1898.

As commander in chief in the Spanish-American War, McKinley monitored all phases of the conflict. He also stepped in to run the War Department when Secretary of War Russell Alger proved incapable of the demands of managing a 27,000-man regular army and thousands of volunteers. Fortunately, the Spanish were war-weary and poorly supplied, and the U.S. Navy was newly outfitted. Only 379 Americans lost their lives in combat.

McKinley gave subordinates such as Commodore George *Dewey in the Philippines and Gen. Rufus Shafter in Cuba considerable latitude, though he approved all key decisions, such as sending ground forces to support Dewey's tenuous naval control. (He welcomed Shafter's negotiation of a peaceful occupation of Santiago de Cuba after that city had fallen under U.S. siege.)

The president controlled the diplomatic agenda as well. He supported the *Teller Amendment to the war declaration that ruled out annexation of Cuba, but refused to extend recognition to the rebel governments in Cuba or in the Philippines. The occupation government that Gen. Leonard *Wood established in Cuba was removed only when the Cubans approved the *Platt Amendment (1901) that effectively made their island a U.S. protectorate. McKinley demanded that Spain relinquish control of the Philippines to the United States in the peace treaty signed in Paris 10 December 1898, and he authorized the use of U.S. troops to put down a bloody guerrilla war against U.S. occupation of the Philippines.

[See also Cuba, U.S. Military Involvement in; Philippine War; Philippines, U.S. Military Involvement in the; Spanish-American War.]

• Lewis L. Gould, *The Presidency of William McKinley*, 1982. John Dobson, *Reticent Expansionism*, 1988.   —John M. Dobson

McNAMARA, ROBERT S. (1916–), secretary of defense and president of the World Bank. Born in San Francisco into a family of humble means, McNamara graduated from the University of California, Berkeley, with an economics degree in 1937, and earned an MBA from Harvard

Business School in 1939, where he also joined the faculty, teaching financial management systems based on statistical controls. During World War II, the Army Air Forces appointed McNamara and several of his colleagues as officers to develop methods of statistical control for managing the strategic bombing campaign against Germany.

Hailed for their brilliance in applying statistical methods to large-scale organization in this pre-computer age, McNamara and several other "stat control" officers were hired by the Ford Motor Company in 1946 to rejuvenate the flagging auto giant. The "whiz kids" introduced new managerial and product changes and built Ford into a success. Six of the men eventually became Ford executives.

Shortly after becoming company president in late 1960, McNamara resigned to become John F. *Kennedy's secretary of defense, a position he held from 1961 to 1968. Kennedy's respect for McNamara's liberal Harvard connections, youthful vigor, and reputation for efficiency and success were key factors behind his appointment. With his confidence in civilianized, centralized defense decision making, McNamara appointed a team of civilian analysts—"defense intellectuals"—to apply quantitative systems analysis for "cost effectiveness" (capability as a return on investment) over procurement and other decisions of the military. The McNamara "revolution" at the Department of *Defense (DoD) included program budgeting, evaluation of systems-wide costs, five-year plans linking defense spending with missions, and efforts at reducing *interservice rivalry and redundancy and increasing coordination and efficiency. Although a number of the McNamara reforms proved successful and were permanently accepted by the *Pentagon, others put him continually at odds with the top brass.

While reforming Pentagon practices, McNamara also engaged in the military buildup of the early years of the Kennedy administration. He improved the strategic nuclear forces, increasing the number of intercontinental ballistic missiles and submarine-launched ballistic missiles (while reducing the number of manned bombers) and bolstering the capability of U.S. nuclear forces to survive a nuclear attack and thus mount a retaliatory "second strike." After briefly supporting a "counterforce" policy of targeting only Soviet missiles, not cities, McNamara reluctantly returned to a deterrence policy of "Mutual Assured Destruction." Endorsing the doctrine of *Flexible Response, which envisioned U.S. capability of responding to a variety of levels of threat, McNamara also expanded U.S. conventional forces.

McNamara's influence on policymaking stemmed from his overwhelming use of quantitative analysis, his reputation for success, and his personal friendship with John Kennedy and later Lyndon B. *Johnson. In the *Cuban Missile Crisis of 1962, McNamara proposed the selective naval blockade which successfully sealed off the island.

During the *Vietnam War (1960–75), McNamara supported the policies of Presidents Kennedy and Johnson to prevent the victory of Communist-led insurgents, later joined by North Vietnamese regular forces, to overthrow the U.S.-backed government of South Vietnam. This included expanding U.S. military advisers' roles under Kennedy, and then under Johnson a policy of graduated escalation that sought to maintain the Saigon government with increasing use of U.S. ground, air, and naval forces while not disrupting Johnson's domestic reforms in the United States. Years later, McNamara said that the United States could have disengaged after Kennedy's death in 1963; but at the time, he supported Johnson's decision to remain committed. Linked to Johnson's conduct of the war, McNamara was attacked by *peace and antiwar movements for continuing the war and by the political Right for restricting U.S. military force. By 1967, he privately advised the president to end the war through negotiations.

In February 1968 McNamara left the Pentagon to become president of the *World Bank. He served as its head from 1968 to 1981, focusing on the Third World. In later years, he became a prolific author and lecturer suggesting in books such as *Blundering into Disaster* (1986) drastic limitations on *nuclear weapons. McNamara's principal role during Vietnam, however, has continued to haunt him. His controversial memoir, *In Retrospect: The Tragedy and Lessons of Vietnam* (1995)—where the aging former secretary of defense called the war "terribly wrong"—outraged both supporters and critics of the war, and highlighted the deep divisions that still surrounded America's involvement in Vietnam.

[*See also* Civil-Military Relations: Civilian Control of the Military; Joint Chiefs of Staff; Strategy: Nuclear Warfare Strategy and War Plans.]

• David M. Barrett, *Uncertain Warriors: Lyndon Johnson and His Vietnam Advisors*, 1993. Deborah Shapley, *Promise and Power: The Life and Times of Robert McNamara*, 1993. Paul Hendrickson, *The Living and the Dead: Robert McNamara and the Five Lives of a Lost War*, 1996. H. R. McMaster, *Dereliction of Duty: Lyndon Johnson, Robert McNamara, the Joint Chiefs of Staff, and the Lies That Led to Vietnam*, 1997.

—John Whiteclay Chambers II *and* Brian Adkins

MEADE, GEORGE GORDON (1815–1872), Union Civil War general. Born in Cadiz, Spain, Meade, the son of an American naval agent, graduated from the U.S. Military Academy in 1835 and served in the Second Seminole War and the *Mexican War.

Appointed brigadier general of U.S. *Volunteers when the *Civil War began, Meade fought in most of the Army of the Potomac's main battles. Daring at the Battle of *Fredericksburg won him a corps command. When Gen. Robert E. *Lee moved his Army of Northern Virginia north in June 1863, President Abraham *Lincoln gave Meade command of the Army of the Potomac (nearly 88,000 men) with orders to stop the Confederates. Three days into his new assignment, Meade faced Lee's army of some 75,000 near Gettysburg, Pennsylvania. A three-day, nearly decisive, battle began on July 1. Meade's steady command contributed greatly to a vital Union victory. Although criticized for permitting Lee's retreat to Virginia, Meade kept his command of the Army of the Potomac.

Gen. Ulysses S. *Grant, appointed to head all Union armies in March 1864, put his headquarters near Meade's. Both generals handled this potentially awkward command situation tactfully and cooperated well to war's end. Meade correctly tried to stop Grant's front assaults in the *Wilderness campaign.

After the war, Meade's outspokenness hurt his reputation, and he sank into undeserved obscurity. He died in Philadelphia, Pennsylvania.

[*See also* Gettysburg, Battle of; Union Army.]

• Freeman Cleaves, *Meade of Gettysburg,* 1960. Herman Hattaway and Archer P. Jones, *Why the North Won the Civil War,* 1983. Joseph T. Glatthaar, *Partners in Command: The Relationship Between Leaders in the Civil War,* 1994. Charles F. Ritter and Jon Wakelyn, eds., *Leaders of the American Civil War,* 1998.   —Frank E. Vandiver

MEDALS. *See* Awards, Decorations, and Honors.

MEDIA. *See* Film; News Media, War, and the Military; Photography, War and the Military in.

MEDICAL PRACTICE IN THE MILITARY. Military medicine in the United States has both led and followed overall American medical practice. Military medicine has been responsible for some of the most dramatic worldwide advances in health care science; at the same time, it has greatly benefited from the civilian sector's progress. Not surprisingly, military medicine has been in the forefront of mass casualty treatment and trauma care. On occasion, U.S. military surgeons and physicians have also extended the capabilities of international science in diagnosing and defeating some of humanity's most powerful killers, such as malaria. Military medicine has contributed too in the field of prevention.

Colonial and Revolutionary War Practice. For the first three centuries of American history, New World military medical practices differed little from, and often trailed, European practices. In the late eighteenth century, however, at the time of the *Revolutionary War, the social standing of American medical doctors began to rise in comparison to their Old World counterparts.

Before the Revolution, following British practice, American colonial militia organizations usually provided for a surgeon to accompany a regimental-size force on campaign. In this setting, with an officer class that was heavily oriented to an aristocratic hierarchy, the decidedly middle-class medical profession was in the lower reaches of influence. Additionally, although there was considerable knowledge of anatomy, a doctor's ability to heal was extremely limited. Surgeons were not commissioned. They were regarded as contract personnel, necessary for military operations, but little more than the tradesmen and teamsters who also accompanied a military column. Military doctors were expected to be both physicians (healing primarily by medicine) and surgeons (healing by manual or instrumental operations). In the English hierarchy, the doctor was only one step above a barber.

Several prewar militia surgeons participated in the opening years of Revolutionary War. John Warren of Boston, who had studied medicine as an apprentice, served with Massachusetts units besieging the British in Boston in 1776 and performed smallpox inoculations. He accompanied Gen. Nathanael *Greene's column when the war moved to Long Island, New York, and was appointed surgeon to the *Continental army's hospital in Boston.

During the Revolutionary War, American military medical practice did not differ from European in the treatment of wounds and diseases. Such treatment had remained essentially unchanged for two centuries and would see little improvement in the first fifty years of U.S. history. University-trained physicians were rarely found in British or British colonial military organizations. A military surgeon was likely to be only modestly qualified and had simply taken the title after a period understudying another doctor. Bleeding, based on the theory that purges rid the system of impurities, and the use of mineral drugs—especially heavy metal compounds of mercury, antimony, and arsenic—were common practices. Opium was occasionally used, but alcohol was the more common analgesic. Literature on the subject of military medicine was largely limited to Richard Brocklesby's *Economical and Medical Observations on Military Hospitals* (1764) and to Philadelphian Benjamin Rush's *Directions for Preserving the Health of Soldiers,* published during the Revolution. It was not necessarily true that those claiming to be doctors were familiar with even the most fundamental medical texts. The lack of standards on licensing allowed almost anyone to claim expertise in healing.

British physicians went mostly unnoticed during the war, but Rush and four other American medical doctors were signers of the Declaration of Independence. These men and others used their prominence successfully to impress on the Congress and Gen. George *Washington the need to create hospitals, stockpile medical supplies, and institute smallpox inoculation for U.S. military forces. Smallpox inoculation—considered a novel and advanced practice for the period—is credited with preserving the Continental army at a critical juncture. Revolutionary War military medicine left its mark on the profession when John Warren's (1753–1815) Boston Army Hospital course on surgical anatomy for young physicians provided the basis for Harvard College's new medical education department. The absence of a rigid social hierarchy in America contributed to the elevation of surgeons and physicians in the New World, rendering their advice in the young nation's governing circles more weighty than in an English setting.

American naval medical practice differed substantially from the army. Naval health care was limited to the use of contract surgeons, who signed on to a ship for a single cruise during the War for Independence. This continued after the war, but in 1801, Congress authorized half-pay for naval surgeons between cruises, thereby ensuring stability in the navy's medical ranks. The most prominent U.S. naval physician of this era was Edward Cutbush, a militia surgeon during the 1794 *Whiskey Rebellion, who worked aboard the frigate *United States* in 1799. Cutbush produced a widely used text on naval medicine in 1808 that stressed the importance of hygiene and proper diet.

Pre–Civil War Practice. The pre–*Civil War era was marked by the achievement of badly needed military medical organizational and pay changes along with welcome advances in healing. In 1818, Secretary of War John C. *Calhoun brought about a permanent medical department to administer health care for the army. His choice to head the department was Dr. Joseph Lovell, an energetic physician who began the systematic collection of medical data and standardization of entrance examinations for aspiring military surgeons. In 1834, Lovell finally persuaded Congress to tie the pay of army surgeons to a major's salary. During the *Seminole Wars in Florida, army physicians conducted experiments on malaria victims, and in contradiction to prevalent practice, discovered that large doses of quinine were effective in saving lives. The army's treatment quickly entered civilian practice and this powerful age-old killer began to be tamed. In 1847, Congress gave army medical officers commissioned rank; for the first time, they began to use military titles. Later, the navy followed suit.

While American military medicine was improving in organization, system, and prestige, it was making little headway against the appalling loss of life in military campaigns—save for the experience with malaria. During the *Mexican War, the approximately 100,000-strong U.S. expeditionary forces lost about 1,500 men in battle, but more than 10,000 to disease. Much of this loss was due to unsanitary conditions in the camps, shallow latrines, ill-sited drinking water and wash areas, and the lack of sufficient ambulance wagons. Failing to cover body wastes in open latrines promoted the spread of disease by flies. Cooks who handled food with dirty hands and washing areas sited upstream of watering areas were common practices that contributed to long sick lists. These errors and unnecessary losses, chiefly due to the chaos caused by the rapid *mobilization of an untrained, ill-experienced officer corps, were repeated at the beginning of the *Civil War.

The Civil War and Post–Civil War Eras. Shocked by the large numbers of camp deaths during 1861 and the early months of 1862, regular *Union army surgeons moved quickly to preserve lives. The Army of the Potomac's medical directors, Charles Tripler and Jonathan Letterman, created a large ambulance service to evacuate the sick and wounded, ordered vaccination against smallpox, and supervised quinine prophylaxis for malaria. These two officers also established a network of supporting hospitals and impressed on Northern officers their duties to constantly stress sound field sanitation practices. By the Battle of *Fredericksburg in December 1862, Federal forces enjoyed a decided medical advantage over their less well equipped and less well medically staffed Confederate opponents. This advantage contributed to the all-important battlefield numerical superiority of Union forces.

Neither Confederate nor Union surgeons were capable of reducing the chances of death due to gunshot wounds. Penetrating wounds by minié balls were usually fatal. A mortality rate of more than 62 percent occurred with a chest penetration, and only 11 percent of the soldiers who received a stomach wound survived.

Although the post–Civil War era, 1866–98, saw little serious American military action, it was a period of progressive change and innovation that produced the golden age of American military medicine. Army and navy surgeons embraced the best of European medical science: Louis Pasteur's germ theory of disease during the late 1860s and Joseph Lister's techniques of antiseptic surgery. Physicians in both services increasingly found themselves giving care to service members' wives and children. This change corresponded with growth in the scope and frequency of medical care for the general population of the United States. In 1884, Congress formally authorized what had been common practice for some time, health care for military dependents. Additionally, the American military, along with the rest of American society, learned about the purification of water supplies and the sanitary control of sewage.

The foundation for U.S. military medicine's claim to nineteenth-century world renown was brought about by a former Civil War surgeon, George Miller Sternberg. Sternberg, a yellow fever victim in 1875, was detailed to the National Board of Health in 1879 with the Havana Yellow Fever Commission after his recovery and began working at Johns Hopkins University in conjunction with an army assignment a few years later. Sternberg traveled to Europe and learned the best science of bacteriology of the time; he published a book on malaria. This was followed in 1892 by the first American textbook on bacteriology. Established as the premier bacteriologist in the United States, Sternberg was appointed surgeon general of the U.S. Army by President Grover Cleveland in 1893. Using his authority and prestige, Sternberg convinced Congress to found the Army Medical School and recruited such promising young medical officers as Capt. Walter *Reed.

The *Spanish-American War of 1898 provided the opportunity for Sternberg, Reed, and others to use their knowledge in the fight against disease. As in the case of the Mexican and Civil Wars, "camp fevers" were rife, especially in the southern U.S. mobilization centers. Of the 6,400 men who died between 1 May 1898 and 30 April 1899, fully 5,400 or 84 percent died of disease. The "fevers" were variously diagnosed as typhoid, malaria, yellow fever, and typhomalaria. Reed, using microscopic examination of blood smears, discovered that the chief culprit was typhoid, a disease that could be halted by well-known camp sanitation practices. Unfortunately, the rapidly mobilized, mostly volunteer force had a predominantly politically appointed officer corps that was almost wholly ignorant of military affairs and proper field sanitation practices.

Twentieth-Century Medical Practice. After the war, The United States had acquired a tropical colonial empire and desired to build a canal linking the Pacific and Atlantic Oceans in Central America. It therefore had great need of experienced military physicians—for both research and teaching. Reed headed the Yellow Fever Commission in 1900–01. The commission proved beyond doubt that the previously established mosquito transmission theory for the disease was correct. Another army surgeon, William C. *Gorgas, quickly used his authority as sanitation officer in Havana, Cuba, to eliminate mosquito breeding places; he demonstrated a dramatic decline in that city's normal yellow fever and malaria sickness and mortality rates. Sent to Panama for the canal project, Gorgas brought the malaria morbidity rate down by 90 percent in 1913. The Panama Canal was made possible by the work of Reed, Gorgas, and their fellow army medical workers.

The U.S. Navy began improving its medical practices during the Spanish-American War and enhanced the prestige of its medical personnel shortly thereafter. A medical corps had been created in 1898, and while fighting was still in progress several merchantmen (commercial cargo ships) were converted into hospital ships. The next year, medical officers were given commissioned rank. Later, medical officers were given command authority over the hospital ships and crews, a controversial decision that was ultimately resolved in favor of the nautical surgeons by the commander in chief, Theodore *Roosevelt.

In 1908, the army created the Medical Reserve Corps, an augmentation organization that was separate from the National Guard. A veterinary corps was added to the medical department. Not only were veterinarians highly useful in promoting the health and utility of horses and mules, they were essential in the inspection of meat for troop consumption. Provisions were made with the *American Red Cross to supply nurses in time of emergency. The prestige of army doctors rose when Gen. Leonard *Wood, a Harvard Medical School graduate and former army physician, became chief of staff of the army in 1910.

These innovations and changes were needed when the United States became involved in World War I in April

1917, joining the Allies in opposition to the Axis powers. Some of the first medical problems faced by the rapidly expanding military medical organization centered on combat aviation. Early in U.S. operations, it was discovered that 300 percent more pilots were dying from accidents than from enemy action. Army medical officers learned that aviators were flying to the point of exhaustion. Flight surgeons were created, and these specialists impressed on commanders the need for sufficient rest between missions. Chemical warfare required the creation of mobile degassing units—organizations that operated under medical supervision and provided showers and new clothing for units that had been exposed to chemical weapons. With the aid of British researchers, the U.S. Army and Navy had adopted a typhoid fever vaccine in 1911, a practice that saved the lives of large numbers of American youth. Compared with 1898, the typhoid death rate in 1917–18 was reduced 185 times. Additionally, an antitetanus serum introduced at the turn of the century greatly reduced the incidence of wounded men succumbing to lockjaw. In France, the Allies instituted a disciplined triage system. *Casualties were sorted to facilitate life-saving priority treatment according to chances of survival. The practice of attaching laboratories to hospitals contributed to rapid diagnosis, and X-ray machines found their way into military hospitals in France. However, the greatest single improvement was undoubtedly the introduction of blood transfusion to reduce the deadly effects of shock among wounded soldiers.

Between the world wars, military medicine in the United States was influenced by socioeconomic changes and by the burgeoning technological innovations associated with increasingly complex methods of waging war. The growth in specializations within civilian medicine also affected military practice. Increasingly—especially in the navy—officers were selected for postgraduate specialty training in such fields as neurology. As greater percentages of American women chose hospital deliveries, the military services sought out training in obstetrics and gynecology from civilian medical colleges and universities so as to provide military dependents with the modern procedures that all U.S. citizens had grown to expect.

In the 1920s, the income of physicians grew faster than American society in general and service recruiting of medical practioners became more difficult. The *Veterans Administration was divorced from the military departments, but it had the indirect effect of assisting in service recruitment by providing an added, postcareer benefit, medical care for those who incur health problems during military service. Both the army and the navy established aviation medical research facilities that developed equipment to allow aircrews to cope with high altitudes and extreme cold. At Wright Field, Ohio, Capt. Harry G. Armstrong of the Army Air Corps studied embolism in pilots and determined that the governing factor was the formation of nitrogen bubbles in the body at high altitudes. The navy also established a submarine medicine program at New London, Connecticut, which produced specially trained corpsmen for *submarines and assisted in the development of underwater breathing equipment for use in escape techniques.

During World War II, American military medicine benefited greatly from technological advances. German-developed atabrine of the 1930s produced a superior prophy-

laxis against malaria; and the development of penicillin by the pharmaceutical industry vastly improved the chances that a wound victim would overcome infection. Experience with "shell shock" in World War I had stimulated the field of military neuropsychiatry to improve the treatment and handling of World War II soldiers who experienced "battle fatigue." During that war, psychiatrists discovered that greater recovery rates were often possible if a shaken soldier was returned to his unit and resumed friendships and customary relationships than if he was retained in an unfamiliar mental treatment setting.

Further advances in life-saving techniques came about through the navy's modification of LSTs (Landing Ship Tanks) into floating evacuation hospitals and the army's creation of Portable Surgical Hospitals. The wide-scale use of DDT controlled a serious outbreak of typhus in Italy. Defeating typhus, a debilitating, sometimes deadly disease caused by several types of *Rickettsia* microorganisms, was critical to the Allied cause. Carried by fleas and lice, these microorganisms spread from the civilian to the military populations quickly. The menace was only quelled by a massive overall "dusting" with DDT insecticide. Finally, the scale of American military medicine in World War II explained much of its success. In 1942–45, 40 percent of the country's physicians and health care givers served the military, a population that comprised only 8 percent of U.S. society.

In the three-decade-long Cold War era, 1957–89, military medicine continued to adapt to civilian standards, adjusting for the continued diminishment of monetary incentives for doctors choosing a military career while adding to the record of significant advances for the medical profession. Both the army and the navy established residency programs in military hospitals that were designed to meet civilian specialty requirements. Dependent care burdens were partially eased by the 1956 Dependents Medical Care Program, which permitted the use of and compensation for civilian medical care when military facilities were not available. Recruiting difficulties were somewhat ameliorated by the 1972 Health Profession Scholarship Program, which provided medical college tuition and stipends in return for a period of uniformed service. And members of the Army and Navy *Nurse Corps, given temporary commissions during World War II, were established as a regular branch and awarded permanent commissioned status.

Cold War medical professionals achieved improvement on the World War II record in saving the lives of American battle casualties. Partially due to the transport of the wounded by *helicopters, the rate of those who died from wounds was halved during the *Korean War (1950–53) over that of the 1940s. Long-range air transportation of patients, a World War II innovation, was extended so that almost 30 percent of evacuations were accomplished by this means. The technique of using helicopters and long-range evacuation continued during the *Vietnam War in the 1960s.

Medical advances by military officers in this era included the breakthrough achievements of Navy Capt. Robert Phillips's work on carefully balanced fluids and electrolytes in the treatment of another ancient and worldwide killer, cholera. Army Capt. Edwin J. Pulaski's pioneering work on burn victims in 1947, the establishment of the burn research unit at Brooke Army Medical Center in San

Antonio, Texas, and the skin graft innovations of Col. Curtis Artz that followed all contributed to wholly new methods in treating burns throughout the world.

Conclusion. American military medical experience in the initial years of the post–Cold War era provided every reason to expect a continuing story of successful adaptation to changing environments. By 1991 and the *Persian Gulf War, the military establishment had adjusted to its scarcity of doctors by producing an elaborate organization of helpers, technicians, and specialists, who worked under the supervision of doctors. Of the more than 24,000 U.S. Army medical personnel sent to Saudi Arabia, just over 3,000 were medical doctors or dentists. The rest—nurses, assistants, technicians, and specialists—carried on the bulk of health care tasks. Combat casualties in this war were thankfully few, but there was no reason to expect that this new structure could not have performed well in more traumatic circumstances. It had adapted successfully to changing conditions—an established and centuries-old hallmark of American military medicine.

[*See also* Combat Trauma; Demography and War; Disease, Tropical; Diseases, Sexually Transmitted; Toxic Agents.]

• Surgeon General of the Navy, ed., *The History of the Medical Department of the United States Navy in World War II.* 3 vols., 1950–53. M. M. Link and H. A. Coleman, *Medical Support of the Army Air Forces in World War II,* 1955. Bureau of Medicine and Surgery, *The History of the Medical Department of the United States Navy, 1945–1955,* 1957. S. Bane-Jones, *The Evolution of Preventive Medicine in the United States Army, 1607–1939,* 1968. S. Neel, *Medical Support of the U.S. Army in Vietnam, 1965–1970,* 1973. D. H. Robinson, *The Dangerous Sky: A History of Aerospace Medicine,* 1973. R. C. Engelman and Robert J. T. Joy, *Two Hundred Years of Military Medicine,* 1975. Albert E. Cowdrey, *The Medic's War: Korea,* 1987. Graham A. Cosmas and Albert E. Cowdrey, *Medical Service in the European Theater of Operations,* 1992.

—Rod Paschall

MEIGS, MONTGOMERY (1816–1892), military engineer and quartermaster general of the U.S. Army. Born into a distinguished family, Meigs graduated near the top of his West Point class in 1836 and was appointed to the U.S. *Army Corps of Engineers. Though only a lieutenant, Meigs's natural ability won him sufficient notice to become chief engineer for the expansion of the U.S. Capitol and construction of its dome. More important was his brilliant work on the twelve-mile-long Washington aqueduct. Part of this structure, the Cabin John Bridge, remained the longest masonry arch in the world until the twentieth century. To both these projects Meigs brought speed, efficiency, and frugality. Indeed, his unwillingness to tolerate political appointees on the aqueduct's construction led to his brief "administrative exile" to positions in the Dry Tortugas, in the Florida keys.

When the Civil War began, Meigs was initially appointed to a field command, for which he was not suited. In May 1861, he accepted a more appropriate commission as quartermaster general, a post he held until 1882. Meigs was responsible for supplying the *Union army's entire war effort—a gargantuan task to which he successfully applied his considerable organizational talent. Not one to hold the reins of authority too tightly, Meigs divided his department into nine semiautonomous divisions in order to achieve both efficiency and cost-effectiveness. In conjunction with Herman Haupt, head of the U.S. Military Railroad, Meigs saw to it that Union soldiers were never far from a supply depot and always well provisioned. His marshaling of the North's vast economic potential toward a single end was a major reason for Union victory. Meigs's example of wartime bureaucratic efficiency helped govern the economic expansion that followed, which was to turn the United States into a global industrial giant.

[*See also* Civil War: Military and Diplomatic Course.]

• Russell F. Weigley, *Quartermaster General of the Union Army: A Biography of M. C. Meigs,* 1959.

—T. R. Brereton

MEMORIALS, WAR. Wars are commemorated by an immense variety of devices—obelisks, monoliths, marble temples, battlefields and battle markers, statues, cemeteries, tombs, memorial chapels and parks, plaques and walls bearing the names of the dead, place names, and "living memorials"—including hospitals, stadiums, and highways. War memorials are designed to consecrate great struggles that protect the nation's interests and preserve its existence.

Two aspects of every war affect the way memorials represent it: (1) whether it ended in victory or defeat; and (2) whether it was believed necessary or unnecessary, morally just or wrong. To four kinds of war—victories and defeats in good causes and bad—correspond four sets of memorials. The symbolic qualities of these memorials overlap, however, because they are determined by more than the wars they represent. Memorials adapt the realities of wars to the needs and concerns of the generation that commemorates them.

The *Revolutionary War, first of America's just victories, was not widely commemorated by the generation that fought it. Throughout the late eighteenth and early nineteenth centuries, many communities devised objects to mark the war, but almost all were obscure, and even the most notable—the Bunker Hill obelisk—was meagerly ornamented and conveyed no sense of the cause it symbolized. Commemorative restraint reflected a political culture that was antiauthoritarian, suspicious of standing armies, and associated military monuments with centralized state power. Most of the monuments that presently commemorate the Revolution were erected at the turn of twentieth century.

*Civil War commemorations began as soon as the fighting stopped, but their scale was again limited. In the South, memories of a lost but noble cause took root, but a shattered economy and social system precluded extensive monument making. In the North, local cemeteries were embellished, bodies were exhumed to fill new military *cemeteries, and many monuments appeared. However, the most familiar memorials—statues of anonymous soldiers—were erected on town squares and outside city halls during the late nineteenth and early twentieth centuries. By that time the last of the Civil War generation, along with its many resentments, was dying off and the memorials assumed new meaning. Northerners and Southerners respected each other's conception of the war as a just cause; each side embraced the other as it erected similar monuments to itself. The North's largest commemorative center, *Gettysburg National Military Park, incorporated monuments to Southern soldiers; Southern cemeteries included honored places for

Northern soldiers. The ideal of regional reconciliation was made visible and tangible in monuments to the Civil War dead.

World War I cost the United States less in life and treasure than did the Civil War, but its proclaimed achievement, saving the world for democracy, was greater, and so was its monument production. Massive numbers of monuments emerged right after the armistice, ranging all the way from plaques to statues of "doughboys" (common soldiers) at city halls and town squares to massive commemorative centers. America's fatalities—117,000—were relatively light, but its memorials were grand and somber.

Early twentieth-century monument production in America was accelerated by a City Beautiful movement that used the Industrial Revolution's wealth to clear away its debris. Of the many objects chosen to beautify the city, war memorials were best suited because they symbolized the expanding power and reach of the state and the great wave of "Americanism" that inundated the society during the first quarter of the twentieth century. Nowhere is this confluence of statism and democratization better exemplified than in Newark, New Jersey's, *Wars of America* (1926)—a massive sculpture of forty-two figures representing all wars from the Revolution to World War I. What distinguishes this monument is not its size and scope, but its depiction of young men being embraced by their mothers and fathers, wives and children, as they go off to fight. In *Wars of America*, civilians and soldiers are commemorated together. This same theme, the continuity of civil and military institutions, is manifested in the Tomb of the Unknown Soldier. Dedicated in 1921 as a monument to World War I's common soldier, the Tomb ennobles the common people of a democratic society.

The Tomb of the Unknown Soldier is located in Arlington, Virginia, Military Cemetery. Military cemeteries are the most moving of all memorial forms because they embody the culture of modern democracy. Before the Civil War, soldiers were buried together in unmarked graves near the field on which they fell. During the Civil War, state governments built military cemeteries to provide the dead with "decent" (individual) resting places. However, only one of these cemeteries, Gettysburg's, became a prominent memorial site during the war; most, including thirteen federal cemeteries, were established too late to accommodate the great number killed. Not until World War I did field graves become the exception rather than the rule. Seventy percent of the World War I dead were returned directly to their families for private burial; the remainder were buried in overseas cemeteries. Almost half of these—some 14,000 men—rest in the Meuse-Argonne cemetery's separately marked but identical graves, laid out without regard to rank in rectangular equality—a perfect democracy of the dead.

World War I's techniques did not all transfer to World War II; in fact, World War II was undramatically commemorated. Arlington's Iwo Jima Memorial is probably the war's best-known and most popular memorial in the United States, but it is atypical. The typical monument is utilitarian, created by attaching the adjective "memorial" to the names of auditoriums, schools, hospitals, community centers, sports arenas, highways, and other public places. The concept of the "living memorial" proved compatible with the muted idealism and restrained nationalism of the late 1940s and 1950s. Living memorials, indeed, desanctify war by melding memory of the hallowed dead with secular pursuits of everyday life.

Overseas, however, U.S. World War II commemorations outdid the traditional World War I pattern. Most of the American dead, as before, were returned to their families; but not all. More than 10,000 were interred in the Lorraine cemetery; 9,000, in the Normandy cemetery; and more than 7,000, in the Sicily-Rome cemetery. At each place, marble walls were built in memory of the missing. At the National Memorial Cemetery of the Pacific in Honolulu lie the remains of 13,000 soldiers who died throughout the Pacific theater of war. The cemetery wall's 18,000 names include both the missing and the dead. The United States maintains twenty-four cemeteries on foreign soil. Most of these are imposing in size and adorned with great monuments and statuary, but their most conspicuous feature is their immaculateness—itself an aspect of democratic culture. The impressively landscaped ground with its perfectly kept graves and regularly scrubbed stones dignifies the common soldier as it legitimates his death.

America's "bad victories," unlike its good ones, were controversial at the time they were achieved and are ambivalently remembered. The Perry Peace Memorial on Lake Erie, Andrew *Jackson's statue across from the White House in Lafayette Park, and the Battle of *New Orleans site in Chalmette National Historical Park symbolize the *War of 1812's high points, but are dissociated from its controversies and humiliating defeats. Baltimore's Battle Monument for the War of 1812—one of the nation's oldest war memorials—is far less notable than Fort McHenry, commemorated as the site that inspired "The Star-Spangled Banner." To the west, impressive monuments (including the Alamo and the San Jacinto Monument), are almost forgotten today. "Hiker" and "Rough Rider" statues and the memorial commemorating the sinking of the USS *Maine* (1898) in Havana, Cuba, were erected in the early decades of the twentieth century, but few Americans are familiar with these monuments or find them stirring.

One of America's several so-called bad wars, the *Vietnam War, ended in defeat; but defeat alone does not account for the new forms its memorials assumed. The most prominent, the Vietnam Veterans Memorial in Washington, D.C., lists on its black marble walls all 58,000 war dead. It is the first national monument to elevate the individual above the cause. Later, public pressure forced the U.S. Commission of Fine Arts to identify the war on the monument's wall and to place on a nearby site a statue of soldiers with the American flag.

The new Vietnam monuments expressly affirm the ideal of gender and racial equality. The inclusion of a black soldier in the Vietnam Veterans Memorial statue symbolizes the many African-American men who died, while the inclusion of a black nurse in a nearby Vietnam Women's Memorial statue represents the many African-American women who served. Elsewhere in Washington stands the African-American Civil War War Memorial commemorating black soldiers who fought to secure the Union. Across the Potomac River, in Arlington Cemetery, is the Memorial to Women in Military Service to America.

Nowhere are minorities more vividly recognized, however, than in the many memorials dedicated to the *Korean War between the mid-1980s and mid-1990s. The Korean War Veterans Memorial on the Mall in Washington includes 19 stainless-steel statues of white and black combat troops in action, and a 164-foot wall of polished black granite with 2,400 faces of male and female, black and white support personnel. This structure, along with its local variants, is at once a return to and departure from the traditional genre. Its life-size statues, all armed, repudiate the pacifist bias of many Vietnam War memorials, while it greatly extends the recognition of the nation's minorities. The will to commemorate the "forgotten war"—as the Korean War is popularly known—and broader efforts to incorporate forgotten people into the mainstream of American society are both manifestations of a late twentieth-century culture of inclusion.

At the turn of the twenty-first century, the war memorial remains part of the symbolism of political order, its visitation part of the liturgy of public commitment. As much as any other form of commemoration, it is the vehicle by which the nation's legacy is sustained.

• Jan C. Scruggs and Joel L. Swerdlow, *To Heal a Nation: The Vietnam Veterans Memorial*, 1985. James M. Mayo, *War Memorials as Political Landscape*, 1988. Wilbur Zelinsky, *Nation into State*, 1988. George L. Mosse, *Fallen Soldiers*, 1990. Edward T. Linenthal, *Sacred Ground: Americans and Their Battlefields*, 1991. Dean W. Holt, *American Military Cemeteries*, 1992. John R. Gillis, ed., *Commemorations: The Politics of National Identity*, 1994. G. Kurt Piehler, *Remembering War the American Way*, 1995. Lorett Treese, *Valley Forge: Making and Remaking a National Symbol*, 1995.

—Barry Schwartz

MERRYMAN, EX PARTE. The *Merryman* case, 17 Federal Cases 144 (Circuit Court Md. 1861) (No. 9487), raised fundamental questions regarding military authority over civilians and the president's emergency powers in wartime. Upon his arrest and detention during the *Civil War by Union military officials in May 1861, John Merryman, a civilian Confederate sympathizer in Maryland, petitioned for a writ of habeas corpus. U.S. Chief Justice Roger Taney issued the writ, challenging President Abraham *Lincoln's suspension of the privilege of the writ of habeas corpus. Following the president's order, the commanding officer refused to bring Merryman before a civil court. Outraged, Taney issued a forceful opinion denying the president's power to suspend the privilege and insisting that Article I of the U.S. Constitution granted the power to suspend habeas corpus to Congress alone. Lincoln, however, ordered the army not to obey Taney's writ, later asserting that the president and Congress shared the power to suspend habeas corpus.

[*See also* Civil-Military Relations: Civilian Control of the Military; Commander in Chief, President as; Habeas Corpus Act (1863); Martial Law; *Milligan, Ex Parte.*]

• James G. Randall, *Constitutional Problems Under Lincoln*, 1926. Mark E. Neely, Jr., *The Fate of Liberty: Abraham Lincoln and Civil Liberties*, 1991.

—Mary J. Farmer

METACOMET. *See* Philip.

The **MEUSE-ARGONNE OFFENSIVE** (1918) was the final and most important campaign for the American Expeditionary Forces (AEF), commanded by Gen. John J. *Pershing. This offensive was the eastern pincer of the grand Allied offensive of 1918 at the end of World War I. The American zone extended from the middle of the Argonne Forest east to the Meuse River. Although the Ameri-

can First Army of 600,000 troops deployed to begin the attack outnumbered the five German divisions defending the area, the nine forward divisions of the AEF were ill-trained and untested, and most lacked their own support. More than half of the *artillery support was provided by the French, as were the 189 *tanks (most manned by Americans) and 840 aircraft (604 piloted by Americans). After a three-hour artillery barrage, 140,000 men of the American First Army attacked on 26 September, driving north—three corps (nine divisions) abreast—in fog and light rain.

Their initial advance was rapid, with only light contact ahead of the first German line. At about 9:30 A.M., German fire from strong defenses struck the Americans. Most of the men dove for low ground, which, unknown to the Americans, had been pretargeted by German artillery. The American advance was halted in this "killing zone." However, in hard and bloody fighting, the Americans broke the German line on the second day. First Army seized the key hill mass of Montfauçon, advancing six miles. But *casualties were high, and the attacking units were disorganized, out of support and sustenance. AEF headquarters moved veteran divisions from St. Mihiel into the battle.

On 4 October, First Army resumed its offensive against the main line of the German defenses—with reinforcements, and, more wisely, somewhat more experienced leaders. The troops immediately made heavy contact with the enemy all along the front. Fighting their way up the Cunel-Romagne Heights, the Americans also drove Germans from the Argonne Forest in bitter fighting. With the Americans holding the high ground, their artillery could strike the railroad at Sedan. But the First Army was again losing *combat effectiveness. Casualties rose to over 100,000, many stricken by influenza.

The army went into a defensive posture again on 11 October. Pershing reorganized, appointing Maj. Gen. Hunter Liggett as commander of First Army, creating a Second Army, and taking himself out of direct combat command. First Army was ordered to continue to attack north in its zone to seize the line of the Meuse River and the heights south of Sedan. Second Army, under Maj. Gen. Robert Bullard, was given the mission to attack east of the Meuse into the Woevre Plain.

At 3:30 A.M. on 1 November 1918, the last American barrage of the war struck the enemy positions, and the infantry assault broke the German defenses, the defenders fleeing northward. By 4 November, the Germans began a general withdrawal to a new line north of the Meuse. The Americans continued their pursuit. The Second Army drove east into the Woevre Plain, while the First Army attacked and seized the heights over Sedan. Both armies were preparing for further offensives north and east when the armistice went into effect on 11 November.

The Meuse-Argonne campaign lasted forty-seven days. A total of 1.2 million Americans were engaged in the campaign, of whom 117,000 were killed or wounded—about half of the total AEF casualties for the war. The AEF claimed to have inflicted 100,000 enemy casualties. In combination with British and French advances, the Meuse-Argonne Offensive helped drive the German Army out of strong defenses in France and led Berlin to accept an armistice.

[*See also* World War I: Military and Diplomatic Course.]

• John J. Pershing, *My Experiences in the World War*, 1931. George C. Marshall, *Memoirs of My Services in the World War, 1917, 1918*, 1976. Barry Gregory, *Argonne*, 1982. Donald Smythe, *Pershing: General of the Armies*, 1986. Paul F. Braim, *The Test of Battle: The American Expeditionary Forces in the Meuse-Argonne Campaign*, 1987.
                                                              —Paul F. Braim

MEXICAN PUNITIVE EXPEDITION. *See* Mexican Revolution, U.S. Military Involvement in the.

MEXICAN REVOLUTION, U.S. MILITARY INVOLVEMENT IN THE. Woodrow *Wilson ordered two U.S. military interventions into Mexico during the Mexican Revolution. In the first, at Veracruz in 1914, the president sought to influence the conflict by controlling the flow of foreign military supplies to Mexico through its chief port. In the second, the 1916 *Punitive Expedition headed by Gen. John J. *Pershing, Wilson tried to eliminate the "problem" of Francisco "Pancho" Villa and satisfy public outrage in the United States against a Villista raid on Columbus, New Mexico.

At Veracruz, despite serious reservations, Wilson yielded to pressures for intervention from U.S. business interests, cabinet members, newspapers, and representatives of the Southwest. In January 1914, the president and his cabinet agreed to prepare the U.S. armed forces for an invasion of the Mexican port. Wilson ordered Secretary of War Lindley Garrison and Secretary of the Navy Josephus Daniels to make the preparations, saying that it was "only a question of an opportune time and sufficient arrangements."

The president ordered the invasion of Veracruz on 23 April 1914. His decision followed a minor episode at nearby Tampico that revealed a U.S. admiral's readiness to fight, if nothing else. The pretext for the invasion was a so-called German ship, the *Ypiranga*, destined for Veracruz and carrying supplies for the Mexican armed forces. Actually the *Ypiranga* was at least one-half American-owned. It had received clearance for its cargo from Wilson himself well in advance of its departure for Mexico. If U.S. authorities had wanted to stop the ship, it could have been boarded at sea. When Veracruz was seized, the *Ypiranga* discharged its cargo at Puerto Mexico.

In reality, the intervention intended to depose the government of Gen. Victoriano Huerta by seizing and blockading Veracruz, the most important entrepôt for arms flowing to Mexico. By occupying the port city, Wilson could curtail the Mexican Army's access to military supplies and could dictate the flow of arms to the next government of Mexico. In Wilson's view, President Huerta had two major failings. First, the Mexican president could not maintain order and protect U.S. private and public interests—including the strategically important production of oil and rubber; and second, Huerta was a dictator who had imposed himself on the Mexican republic after murdering his democratically elected predecessor, Francisco Madero.

The U.S. attack on Veracruz turned into a tragedy when the Mexican civilian populace decided to resist. The recently upgraded guns of the U.S. warships took a terrible toll on the city. The Mexican casualty estimates vary so widely between the official U.S. figure and that of the *cronista de la ciudad de Veracruz* that accurate figures cannot be determined; but the U.S. forces lost nineteen dead and forty-seven wounded. American troops stayed on after the

fall of Huerta. During the summer of 1914, U.S. military officers worked with the constitutionalist faction among the Mexican revolutionary forces in Veracruz, establishing a joint administration of the customshouse and warehouse area. Between 19 and 23 November, as the first U.S. troops were leaving, U.S. officers supervised the unloading from five ships of military materials, which filled the warehouses and piers. In their last act the U.S. officers turned over the keys to the warehouses to the constitutionalist leaders two months later, the forces of Venustiano Carranza marched out of Veracruz to defeat the other revolutionary factions; they carried a wide array of U.S.-supplied arms.

In 1916, President Wilson reacted to the attack of a defeated and embittered Mexican presidential Francisco Villa, on the hopeful border town of Columbus by launching a major punitive expedition to Mexico under the command of General Pershing. The U.S. president hoped to strengthen his position in acrimonious negotiations with Acting President Carranza and to eliminate the threat Villa's forces posed along the border. The Mexican government was increasingly nationalistic, and U.S. public and press opinion demanded security. The U.S. forces, 12,000 strong, brought a full complement of cavalry trucks and even observation aircraft with them. They marched as far as Parral, 419 miles inside Mexico, incurring serious resistance only a few times. The most notable battle was fought at El Carrizal between the U.S. detachment and Carranza's federal forces. The Mexicans surprised the U.S. commander by their resolve to fight and justified their claims of a tactical victory.

One of Pershing's contingency plans included the establishment of his headquarters at Parral just north of a line extending from Mazatlán to Tampico. That possibility must have occurred to the Mexican government because of the inordinate size of the U.S. force. At the onset of the U.S. invasion, Villa had lost popularity and could concentrate only slightly more than 500 combatants. Instead of being eliminated by the Punitive Expedition, Villa's forces grew until they reached 5,000, and Carranza found his government threatened by a loss of public support for its failure to halt the U.S. invasion. The Mexican public and government expressed deepening resentment toward the invading U.S. troops.

U.S. interventions affected the welfare of the approximately 50,000 North Americans living in Mexico even more than those at home. In the wake of the Veracruz invasion, anti North American riots broke out in diverse parts of Mexico. The U.S. government set up stations at New Orleans, Texas City, and San Diego for the handling of North American refugees, many of whom lost virtually everything they owned in Mexico.

The U.S. government grew less belligerent toward Mexico as tensions with Germany deepened and the Carranza government, demonstrating increasing stability, prepared to promulgate a new constitution. On 27 January 1917, President Wilson ordered the U.S. troops withdrawn from Mexico. A new Mexican Constitution was proclaimed on 5 February 1917; Carranza was elected president on 11 March for a regular term, and the Wilson administration formally recognized the new Mexican government.

[*See also* Mexican War.]

• Friedrich Katz, *The Secret War in Mexico: Europe, the United States and the Mexican Revolution*, 1981. Alan Knight, *The Mexican Revolution*, 2 vols., 1986. John Mason Hart, *Revolutionary Mexico: The*

Coming and Process of the Mexican Revolution, 1998. Friedrich Katz, *The Life and Times of Pancho Villa,* 1998.　　—John M. Hart

MEXICAN WAR (1846–48). After weeks of fruitless diplomacy, the United States and the republic of Mexico declared war on each other in the spring of 1846. By the 1840s, many Americans held the view that the United States should reach from the Atlantic all the way to the Pacific Ocean. In 1844, Democrat James K. *Polk of Tennessee ran for the presidency and won on a platform of *expansionism, embracing the popular concept of "manifest destiny"—that God approved U.S. expansion throughout the continent. Polk opened diplomacy designed to redeem his campaign pledges to purchase California and other Mexican lands as well as to obtain the Oregon country from Britain. Considered in grand strategic terms, Polk intended to make the United States the undisputed national power on the North American continent and to obtain West Coast ports. The British agreed to an equitable treaty dividing Oregon, but no self-respecting patriotic Mexican leader would be satisfied with any amount of money for California.

U.S. annexation of Texas sparked the war. The Texas Revolution of 1836 had won independence for the republic of Texas, but Mexico never officially recognized the loss of the province. Polk's predecessor, John Tyler, arranged the annexation of Texas into the United States in 1845 by a joint resolution of both Houses of Congress before Polk was sworn in. According to Mexico, the United States had torn away one of its provinces. The Mexican government rejected Polk's final offer of $35 million for California and other lands and dispatched military forces to the Rio Grande. It also rejected Texas and U.S. claims that the border extended south to the Rio Grande instead of the Nueces River.

On 23 April 1846, President Mariano Paredes announced that a state of "defensive" war existed between Mexico and the United States, in response to the violation of the Texas border by U.S. soldiers under Gen. Zachary *Taylor, who marched under Polk's orders from Louisiana through Texas up to the Nueces River. On 25 April, Mexican and U.S. forces fought a skirmish between the Nueces and the Rio Grande. Eleven U.S. dragons were killed, five wounded and forty-seven captured. It took several days for word of the skirmish to reach President Polk, who had previously decided on war even before Paredes's announcement. On 11 May, he asked Congress to acknowledge the state of war that Mexico had already announced, but did so with a resounding and controversial call: "American blood has been shed on American soil." On 13 May, Congress strongly endorsed Polk's request, 174–14 in the House of Representatives and 40–2 in the Senate. Critics, mostly northern Whigs, condemned the president's action, asserting that he sought war to acquire more slave territory and denying that the disputed border area belonged to the United States.

Northern Mexico included two commercial centers, Santa Fe, New Mexico, and San Francisco, California. Lightly populated and distant from Mexico City, both provinces were difficult to defend. Polk met with his cabinet and formulated a remarkably ambitious strategy. He ordered U.S. soldiers to invade New Mexico, capture Santa Fe, then proceed to conquer California, where a naval squadron would assist them in securing the province.

Meanwhile, General Taylor with less than 3,000 regulars would drive Mexican forces south of the Rio Grande, which the United States claimed as the international boundary. Polk assumed that if U.S. forces occupied the Rio Grande as well as key spots in New Mexico and California, Mexico would have no choice but to concede the fait accompli, and the United States would have won the war.

For their part, however, the Mexicans stood ready to fight, both for the defense of their territory and the future of their fledgling nation, which only twenty-four years earlier had won its independence from Spain. Mexico possessed a tiny naval coast guard and on paper had a national army of more than 30,000 soldiers, over three times the U.S. Army's size at 8,500 officers and men. Numbers masked contrasts between the two armies, however. The Mexican Army was indifferently trained and unevenly equipped. Some units had enthusiastic officers, good weapons, and adequate supplies; others were deficient in all respects. Many Mexican officers held honorific commissions but knew little about military matters. The army had been involved with intrigues in the national capital, where commanders went in and out of favor with the political winds. Thus, the Mexican Army had more weaknesses than strengths. In contrast, the United States possessed an excellent navy, which could dominate the Gulf of Mexico and the California coast. The U.S. Army had competent officers, excellent weapons, good training, and the advantage of a uniform supply system. Many of its company officers (captains and lieutenants) were graduates of the U.S. Military Academy at West Point, where they received training and education in weaponry and engineering. Many Mexican officers lacked these fundamentals and had no common base of education. U.S. *artillery units were particularly noted for their high quality. Although it was smaller, the U.S. Army was superior to the Mexican Army.

But the regular U.S. Army would have to be supplemented by state volunteer units. President Polk asked Congress to approve a call for thousands of volunteers, prompting an initial positive response across the country. Dozens of state volunteer regiments were recruited for federal service, giving the United States the minimum manpower it needed to fight a war over a broad expanse of territory. Approximately 73,500 volunteers served in 1846–48.

While Congress considered the issue of war, soldiers fought the first major battle above the Rio Grande at a spot called Palo Alto (near Brownsville, Texas). Leading the U.S. forces, Zachary Taylor, a professional soldier since 1808, was an intuitive commander who had seen combat against Indian tribes. Taylor's force encountered the Mexican Army of the North, with about 6,000 soldiers, under Gen. Mariano Arista on 8 May 1846. The four-hour combat was intense and indicated the bravery and dedication of the men on both sides, with each fielding some of the best regular units of their respective armies. Several times the Mexicans delivered strong charges into well-directed U.S. artillery fire. The Americans repulsed the attacks and Arista elected to retreat. The next day, Taylor advanced his force to locate and fight the Mexicans, who had chosen defensive positions along an old path of the Rio Grande, the Resaca de la Palma. Taylor directed an assault that broke the Mexican line. Panic gripped some Mexican units and Arista and his officers could not prevent a rout. The U.S. victory inflicted serious casualties on some of the most well-equipped Mexican Army units, which threw away arms and supplies in their hasty withdrawal. During the two days of combat, Taylor's army suffered less than 200 killed and wounded, but the Mexicans suffered more than 600 casualties. Arista retreated again, this time south of the Rio Grande.

In the weeks to come Taylor moved his army southward, occupying Matamoros, Mexico, on 17 May and Camargo on 14 July. Pressing deeper into Mexico, he fought a battle at Monterrey in late September, captured the city, then marched on to occupy Saltillo in November. The initial phase of the war had gone just as President Polk wanted. It had also made a national hero of General Taylor, who became a likely presidential nominee for the Whig Party.

Occurring simultaneously with part of Taylor's northern Mexico campaign was the U.S. invasion of New Mexico and California. The movement of multiple U.S. units threatened the Mexicans with a cordon offensive; that is, the U.S. forces put more than one offensive action into motion at almost the same time, not allowing the Mexicans to focus only on a single campaign.

Under orders from President Polk, Col. Stephen Watts *Kearny mounted the campaign against Santa Fe from a training base at Fort Leavenworth (Kansas). Kearny led a mixed force of 1,600 soldiers (including 500 regulars), departing Leavenworth on 5 June and arriving at Santa Fe on 18 August after a grueling overland march. The Mexican authorities could neither raise nor send adequate military forces to resist Kearny, who entered the city unopposed. In only a few weeks, 1,000 more volunteers were expected to arrive, allowing Kearny to take the regulars in another overland march from Santa Fe to California, while 1,200 volunteers under Alexander *Doniphan, a colonel of the Missouri volunteers, moved on El Paso del Norte (modern Juarez, Mexico).

The U.S. forces completed Polk's initial plan for the war without losing a battle. Kearny arrived in California in early December 1846. By that time U.S. sympathizers had declared the "Bear Flag Republic" on 4 July. U.S. naval forces under Commodore John D. Sloat had disembarked at Monterey 7 July, and another force under Commodore Robert Stockton had occupied Los Angeles 12 August. Meeting scattered resistance, the U.S. military forces appeared to have plucked California from Mexico like a bunch of grapes. Refusing to go down without a fight, Mexicans rose against the U.S. occupation in September and fought several skirmishes, the most important of which were at San Pasqual (northeast of San Diego) on 6 December 1846, and at San Gabriel on 8 January 1847. Following that U.S. victory, however, the province was effectively in North American hands.

In the meantime, on 25 December 1846, Doniphan's men defeated a Mexican force twice their size north of El Paso. Occupying El Paso, Doniphan waited for reinforcing artillery and then marched across inhospitably dry terrain toward Chihuahua. Outside the city, a hastily trained, inadequately equipped army opposed him. Deep in enemy territory with little prospect of support, Doniphan decided to attack the Mexican Army, although his men were again outnumbered more than two to one. The battle of 28 February 1847 sent the Mexicans into headlong retreat and allowed Doniphan to occupy Chihuahua.

North Americans had invaded Mexican territory in several places and been victorious in all of the war's opening campaigns. Yet the Mexican government refused to acknowledge defeat. Until a treaty confirmed Mexico's loss of California and New Mexico, the United States could not officially claim those vast territories.

Even before word of all the North American successes in California and the Southwest had reached Washington, President Polk and Winfield *Scott, general in chief of the U.S. Army, had decided to open a new phase of the war. This would require another invasion of Mexico, intended to capture Mexico City itself. If Mexico's government would not concede defeat, then Polk intended to demand concessions at bayonet point in the enemy capital. Polk ordered Scott to assemble a strong expeditionary force by taking most of Taylor's regulars and supplementing them with several thousand volunteers and a few hundred U.S. Marines. The transfer of Taylor's regulars began 3 January 1847. Eased out of the war's climactic campaign, Taylor's temper flared at Polk as well as Scott. Brilliant, and something of a perfectionist, Scott plunged into plans for the expedition, including having special wooden landing boats built to carry his soldiers from ships offshore to the Mexican beaches. The Mexican port city of Veracruz on the Gulf of Mexico was selected as the U.S. base of operations, which meant that the port would have to be taken as the first step of the campaign. Scott prepared to launch his invasion in early March.

The Mexicans were not standing idle during the U.S. preparations. Their new and controversial president, Gen. Antonio Lopez de *Santa Anna, envisioned a daring gamble that might yet turn the tide of the war. Demonstrating his inspirational leadership, Santa Anna created a new field army of 25,000 soldiers though the Mexican treasury was all but empty. Several of the units were brand-new. A number had inadequate equipment and supplies, but there was a remarkable patriotic fervor as recruits and veterans marched north to carry out their president's risky design. A captured letter informed Santa Anna of Scott's campaign plan. Therefore, Santa Anna intended to defeat Taylor's reduced army (numbering less than 5,000), encamped near Buena Vista ranch, not far from Saltillo, then return to his capital and blunt the new American threat to the heart of Mexico. To reach Buena Vista, Santa Anna sent his men over 400 miles of rough terrain in the winter. This audacious plan missed succeeding by only a narrow margin.

On 22 February 1847, Santa Anna's army attacked Taylor's near Buena Vista in a series of piecemeal assaults turned back by blistering U.S. artillery fire. The next day, the Mexicans seemed on the verge of breaking through the U.S. line when they were met by a sharp counterattack led by Col. Jefferson *Davis and his Mississippi volunteers. Relying on personal inspiration, Santa Anna persuaded his men to attack again, but again the North Americans repulsed them. The two armies glared at each other on the 23rd, and that night Santa Anna decided to retreat. The road south to Mexico City was littered with discarded weapons and wounded men. Santa Anna had lost almost 40 percent of his army killed, wounded, and missing. Taylor suffered around 700 killed and wounded some 15 percent of his army.

Upon his return to Mexico City, Santa Anna appealed to patriotism and used conscription. Drawing upon new taxes and extraordinary funds taken from the Catholic Church, he formed and began training another army. Meanwhile, Scott's expedition had landed below Veracruz on 9 March, laid siege to the city, and forced its garrison to surrender twenty days later. The North Americans organized the port as their base of operations and on 8 April Scott set out on the National Road to the capital.

Santa Anna hoped to bleed Scott's army (only about 14,000 at its strongest point) as it marched inland, forcing it to fight at roadblocks and weakening it to such an extent that it would either retreat or be vulnerable to a showdown battle. On 12 April at Cerro Gordo, about fifty miles from Veracruz, Santa Anna deployed 11,000 soldiers on a natural defensive position. Scott, however, had no intention of playing to Santa Anna's strengths. Using information brought by skilled staff officers—including Robert E. *Lee, P. G. T. *Beauregard, and George B. *McClellan—Scott maneuvered his units in such a way as to outflank the Mexican defenses, dislodging Santa Anna and pushing him back on 18 April. U.S. *Casualties were about 425 killed and wounded; Mexican losses were 1,000 killed and wounded and 3,000 taken prisoner.

Although he won the first encounter with Santa Anna, Scott had numerous problems. Diseases wracked his army. One thousand North Americans lay ill in hospitals in Veracruz, and another 1,000 were ill in Jalapa, a few miles west of Cerro Gordo. Moreover, the enlistment of thousands of volunteers expired in June. Scott held up his advance at Puebla on 15 May, sending the veterans home, awaiting the arrival of reinforcements, and buying provisions for his men. His army's enrollment stood at only around 7,000. The general determined that he could not garrison a string of depots or forts along the National Road and decided to cut himself off from his supply base (Veracruz) and live off the land, rendering his army even more vulnerable than before. However, using generous terms with local mayors and townsfolk, Scott maintained unusually good relations with the Mexican populace. Some guerrillas picked at the edges of his camps and line of march, but did not weaken him appreciably.

Commanding about 10,000 soldiers, Scott proceeded to the outskirts of Mexico City. Arriving near the capital in mid-August 1847, the general relied on his staff officers for reliable information about terrain and enemy strengths and weaknesses. Santa Anna had mustered nearly 25,000 men, mostly new recruits and national militia leavened with only a few thousand regulars, spread all around the city. Scott chose to approach from the south, crossing terrain that Santa Anna and his subordinates considered impassable, thus creating a measure of tactical surprise that gave him an advantage. The U.S. forces launched attacks against selected Mexican strongpoints, knowing that if they suffered serious losses they might yet be overwhelmed, just as Santa Anna envisioned. In a series of major battles between mid-August and mid-September, Scott's soldiers fought admirably, outflanking or breaking through well-placed and often determined Mexican defenses, such as that conducted at the Battle of *Chapultepec by regulars and cadets of the Mexican military academy. Scott's army suffered more than 3,000 killed, wounded, and lost to disease during the battles for the capital. On 14 September, the victorious U.S. forces entered the plaza of downtown Mexico City, ending a remarkable military campaign. Great Britain's duke of Wellington, who had declared the expedition lost when it cut loose from its supply line, now landed Scott's achievement.

Reinforced during the weeks to come, Scott's army occupied the capital for several months, employing an effective military government while diplomatic negotiations brought the war to an official end. Other army officers also provided governmental leadership for the territory of California from 1848 to 1850. No Mexican politicians wanted to affix their names to the treaty that would give up half of their country's territory to the United States. Finally, on 2 February 1848, the diplomats agreed to the terms of the Treaty of *Guadalupe-Hidalgo. The U.S. Senate ratified the treaty on 17 March. Both sides confirmed the agreement 30 May. The United States gained all of the vast lands Polk had sought at the beginning of the war—later to become the states of California, New Mexico, Arizona, Nevada, Colorado, and Utah—taking about half of the land of Mexico but only about 1 percent of its population. The Rio Grande would form part of the boundary between Texas and Mexico. In return, the United States agreed to pay Mexico $15 million and assume all claims of American citizens against the Mexican government, about another $3 million.

In addition to the territories lost by Mexico and gained by the United States, the war produced several other important results. After expending $100 million and losing more than 10,000 military personnel (killed or died of disease), the United States became a truly continental power, stretching from the Atlantic to the Pacific, and had a vast potential for the future. Only a few months after the war, gold was discovered in California, prompting a frantic rush of settlers from all parts of the world and making California eligible for statehood in 1850, ahead of expectations. Most of the West Point graduates had acquitted themselves with distinction during the war, confirming the place of the academy in American life. The U.S. Army had fought its first overseas war and its services of supply and recruitment had worked satisfactorily enough to give the nation a victory. Scott's campaign to capture Mexico City provided notable operations for U.S. military officers to study in the future. Although only a few U.S. Marines participated in that campaign their role received favorable publicity, helping to gain continued congressional support for the Marine Corps.

Moreover, the war produced notable political consequences. By his audacious decisions and detailed direction of the war, James K. Polk broadened the powers of the president as *commander in chief. The Whigs nominated Zachary Taylor and he won the presidential election of 1848. In 1852, the Whigs nominated Winfield Scott, but he lost to his former subordinate, volunteer general and New Hampshire politician Franklin Pierce, the Democratic nominee. Debates intensified over the status of slavery in the new territories, leading most immediately to the Compromise of 1850. That measure admitted California as a free state but allowed slaveowners to bring slaves into the western territories captured from Mexico. Other provisions ended the slave trade in Washington, D.C., and provided a new Fugitive Slave Law. Thus, the successful war that expanded the United States to the Pacific also further intensified the debate over issues relating to slavery and led toward the sectional crisis of 1860, secession, and the U.S. Civil War.

[See also Academics, Service: U.S. Military Academy; Army, U.S.: 1783–1865; Civil War: Causes; Marine Corps, U.S.: 1775–1865; Mexican Revolution, U.S. Military Involvement in the; Texas War of Independence.]

• Ramon Alcaraz, *The Other Side*, trans. Albert C. Ramsey, 1850. Justin H. Smith, *The War with Mexico*, 2 vols., 1919. Robert S.

Henry, *The Mexican War*, 1950. Otis A. Singletary, *The Mexican War*, 1960. George W. Smith and Charles Judah, eds., *Chronicles of the Gringos: The U.S. Army in the Mexican War*, 1968. David M. Pletcher, *The Diplomacy of Annexation: Texas, Oregon, and the Mexican War*, 1973. K. Jack Bauer, *The Mexican War*, 1974. John E. Weems, *To Conquer a Peace*, 1974. Robert W. Johannsen, *To the Halls of the Montezumas*, 1985.   —Joseph G. Dawson III

MIDDLE EAST, U.S. MILITARY INVOLVEMENT IN THE. The Middle East—defined here as the area stretching from the Persian Gulf to North Africa—has witnessed sporadic U.S. military intervention since 1801, when Thomas *Jefferson dispatched a flotilla of warships to the shores of Tripoli to protect American commerce from raids by the Barbary pirates. The U.S. Navy periodically patrolled the Mediterranean during the nineteenth century from bases in Minorca and Sicily, and American troops fought their first major engagement of World War II—Operation Torch—in Algeria.

America's sustained military involvement in the Middle East, however, dates from the late 1940s, a time of growing Cold War rivalry with the Kremlin, deepening Western dependence on Persian Gulf oil, and mounting tensions between Arabs and Israelis. After an impromptu naval show of force helped reduce Soviet diplomatic pressure on Turkey in 1946, the Truman administration projected American power into the eastern Mediterranean on a permanent basis by establishing the U.S. Sixth Fleet, based in Naples. Some in Washington worried that the partition of Palestine in November 1947 and U.S. recognition of the state of Israel six months later might necessitate armed intervention to prevent Soviet meddling and to protect the Jewish state.

By early 1949, however, the Israelis had won a stunning victory, and the United States spent the next two decades seeking to preserve a fragile military balance between Israel and its Arab neighbors. To this end, the Truman administration took the lead in drafting the Tripartite Declaration of May 1950, which placed strict limits on the flow of American, British, and French arms into the Middle East. And when the Israelis, supported by British and French, attacked Egypt during the 1956 Suez Crisis, the Eisenhower administration used diplomatic and economic leverage to force them to withdraw. After the Arabs began to receive large amounts of Soviet arms during the late 1950s, America moved to ensure Israeli security by providing Tel Aviv with recoilless rifles in 1958, antiaircraft *missiles in 1962, battle *tanks in 1965, and jet fighters in 1966.

In May 1967, Egypt's Gamal Abdel Nasser closed the Strait of Tiran at the mouth of the Gulf of Aqaba to Israeli shipping and expelled *United Nations *peacekeeping forces from the Sinai Desert, moves that Israel regarded as acts of war. The Johnson administration hoped to ease tensions and prevent the outbreak of hostilities by attempting to organize a multinational naval force to patrol the disputed waters. On 5 June 1967, however, Israel in a preemptive strike attacked Egypt and Jordan, which had allied itself with the Nasser regime, and occupied the Sinai and the West Bank. Five days later, Israel invaded Syria and seized the Golan Heights. When Moscow threatened to intervene during the final hours of the Six-Day War to prevent the defeat of its Arab clients, Washington sent the U.S. Sixth Fleet into the eastern Mediterranean to discourage Soviet adventurism.

Anwar Sadat, who had become president of Egypt after Nasser's death in September 1970, and Syria's Hafaz al Assad decided to use force to recapture the territory lost to Israel in 1967. In October 1973, they launched a surprise attack on Israel during the Yom Kippur holiday. In the first days of the fighting, Egyptian troops recaptured part of the Sinai, and Syrian tanks nearly overran Israeli positions in the Golan Heights. The tide began to turn rapidly in Israel's favor, however, as the Nixon administration agreed to airlift badly needed war material to Tel Aviv. With the Israeli troops within striking distance of Cairo and Damascus, the Soviet Union, as it had done six years earlier, threatened to intervene militarily. After deterring the Kremlin by briefly placing U.S. strategic forces at the highest level of readiness, the White House brokered a cease-fire in late October and Henry *Kissinger undertook a lengthy process of shuttle diplomacy that brought about military disengagement between Israel and Egypt in 1974 and between Israel and Syria a year later. As part of the September 1978 *Camp David Accords that led to the signing of a comprehensive Egyptian-Israeli peace treaty in March 1979, the United States agreed to station several hundred U.S. troops in the Sinai Desert, where they served as peacekeepers throughout the 1980s.

Although the United States managed for the most part to avoid becoming militarily involved in the Arab-Israeli conflict during the half century after World War II, persistent political instability in the Muslim world triggered armed American intervention in the Middle East with increasing frequency after the late 1950s. On 15 July 1958, Dwight D. *Eisenhower dispatched 15,000 American Marines to Lebanon following a bloody left-wing coup d'état in Iraq that threatened Lebanese president Camille Chamoun and raised fears in Washington that events in Beirut were about to parallel those in Baghdad. During their four-month tour of duty in Lebanon, U.S. troops helped restore order, enabling American diplomats to arrange a truce between warring Christian and Muslim factions. The Marines pulled out of Beirut on 25 October 1958 without having suffered any casualties.

During the mid-1960s, the United States intervened briefly in Saudi Arabia, where the *Pentagon had obtained rights to a small air base at Dhahran at the end of World War II. In October 1962, radical Arab nationalists staged a coup against the house of Saud's royalist neighbors next door in Yemen, prompting Nasser to send 70,000 troops to assist the Yemeni revolutionaries. Eager to reassure the jittery Saudis, who feared that Egypt would use Yemen as a springboard for further adventures in the Arabian peninsula, John F. *Kennedy agreed in March 1963 to station a squadron of U.S. jet fighters in Dhahran. There they played a high-altitude game of "cat and mouse" with Egyptians MiGs along the Saudi-Yemeni frontier until Lyndon B. *Johnson terminated "Operation Hard Surface" in early 1964.

American military involvement in the Middle East increased during the 1970s following a series of sudden shifts in the regional balance of power. In 1971, Great Britain pulled its armed forces out of the Persian Gulf. In early 1979, Islamic revolutionaries inspired by the Ayatollah Rouhallah Khomeini toppled the shah of Iran, then took fifty-three U.S. diplomats hostage in November. One month later, Russian troops invaded Afghanistan to prop up the pro-Soviet government in Kabul.

President Jimmy *Carter responded by promulgating the *Carter Doctrine in January 1980, promising to protect American interests in the Persian Gulf. He moved quickly to acquire a string of strategic bases stretching from Kenya to Diego Garcia, and announced plans for a new "rapid deployment force" of 85,000 U.S. troops. In April 1980, however, a U.S. military attempt to free the Americans held hostage in Iran failed spectacularly when two American *helicopters collided at a secret desert airstrip just outside Teheran, killing eight crewmen.

Although the hostages were released at the outset of his presidency, Carter's successor, Ronald *Reagan, fared little better. Determined to combat state-sponsored terrorism in the Middle East, the Reagan administration did succeed in reining in Libya's Muamar Gaddafi by staging two U.S. air raids against Libyan targets, first in August 1981 and again in April 1986. But when Reagan agreed to send 800 American troops to Beirut as part of a multinational peacekeeping force in the aftermath of Israel's invasion of Lebanon in June 1982, disaster ensued. In October 1983, Iranian-backed terrorists detonated a huge truck bomb at the Beirut airport housing the Manne ground-force headquarters, killing 241 U.S. Marines. Four years later, there was more trouble after the Reagan administration moved to contain the Iran-Iraq War, which had been raging since September 1980. Hoping to prevent the conflict from disrupting the flow of Middle East oil to Western consumers, Washington reflagged Kuwaiti tankers in early 1987 and then sent the U.S. Navy into the Persian Gulf to escort them through the war zone. In April, an Iraqi jet hit an American frigate, the USS *Stark*, with an Exocet missile, killing thirty-seven sailors. Fifteen months later, in July 1988, an American guided missile cruiser, the USS *Vincennes*, accidentally downed an Iranian airbus, killing all 290 aboard.

The Iraqi invasion of Kuwait on 2 August 1990 triggered a dramatic escalation of the U.S. military presence in the Persian Gulf. Fearful that Saddam *Hussein might attack Saudi Arabia next, President George *Bush sent 200,000 American troops to the Persian Gulf as part of Operation Desert Shield in late August. Determined to force Saddam to pull out of Kuwait, Bush increased the number of U.S. soldiers and sailors in the gulf to 541,000 by the end of the year and put together a broad anti-Iraqi military coalition that included America's *NATO allies and several Arab states, among them Egypt, Syria, and Saudi Arabia. On 16 January 1991, Bush unleashed Operation Desert Storm, which saw a monthlong U.S. aerial bombardment of Iraq followed by a swift flanking attack on Saddam's troops, who fled Kuwait in disarray in late February. American *casualties during the *Persian Gulf War totaled 146 dead, while estimates for Iraqi troops killed in action range from as few as 6,000 to as many as 100,000. In the aftermath of Operation Desert Storm, the United States stationed 24,000 troops and 26 warships in the Persian Gulf on a long-term basis to ensure continued access to Middle East oil and to promote regional security and stability—objectives first articulated by the Truman administration a half century earlier. In 1998–99, Saddam Hussein hampered UN weapons inspectors and challenged U.S. air surveillance. Consequently, President Bill *Clinton in Operation Desert Fox increased American military presence in the Persian Gulf to 33,000 service people and American and British aircraft began sporadic air attacks on Iraqi military

targets. In October 1998, President Clinton brokered the so-called Wye Accord between the Palestinians and the Israelis in which the Palestinians received more land on the West Bank and security control over it and in turn accepted monitoring by the U.S. *Central Intelligence Agency to ensure active efforts to control terrorists.

[*See also* Cold War: Causes; Eisenhower Doctrine; Lebanon, U.S. Military Involvement in; Lebanon Crisis; Navy, U.S.: Since 1946; Terrorism and Counterterrorism.]

• Seth P. Tillman, *The United States in the Middle East: Interests and Obstacles*, 1982. L. Carl Brown, *International Politics and the Middle East: Old Rules, Dangerous Game*, 1984. Wm. Roger Louis, *The British Empire in the Middle East 1945–1951: Arab Nationalism, the United States, and Postwar Imperialism*, 1984. David Painter, *Oil and the American Century: The Political Economy of U.S. Foreign Oil Policy, 1941–1954*, 1986. James A. Bill, *The Eagle and the Lion: The Tragedy of American-Iranian Relations*, 1988. Lawrence Freedman and Efraim Karsh, *The Gulf Conflict, 1990–91: Diplomacy and War in the New World Order*, 1993. William Quandt, *Peace Process: American Diplomacy and the Arab-Israeli Conflict since 1967*, 1993. David Schoenbaum, *The United States and the State of Israel*, 1993. Burton Kaufman, *The Arab Middle East and the United States: Inter-Arab Rivalry and Superpower Diplomacy*, 1995.   —Douglas Little

MIDWAY, BATTLE OF (1942). Within a month of the Imperial Japanese Navy's surprise attack on the U.S. Pacific Fleet in Pearl Harbor on 7 December 1941, Adm. Isoroku *Yamamoto, commander in chief of Japan's Combined Fleet, realized that the Hawaii attack had not achieved its main purpose, the complete destruction of the U.S. Pacific Fleet, including *aircraft carriers. On 14 January 1942, Yamamoto's staff recommended an attack on Midway, a defended American atoll 1,100 miles northwest of Pearl Harbor. Japanese planners assumed the U.S. Pacific Fleet would rush to the outpost's aid, whereupon the more powerful Combined Fleet would engage and destroy it. Such a victory could open the prospect of invading Hawaii, thus extending the Japanese defensive perimeter eastward. With the loss of their fleet and the bare essentials to their success against Japan, the Americans might accept a negotiated end to war.

Fearful that Hawaii was unobtainable and that, without it, possession of Midway would become a liability, the Naval General Staff in Tokyo fought the plan, presented on 2 April 1942; but by the 5th, Yamamoto had triumphed. Later, Yamamoto added a diversionary air raid on the small American air base at Dutch Harbor, Unalaska, and seizure of Attu and Kiska at the western end of the Aleutian chain. The main assault would be against Midway far south, with a naval air attack on 4 June and invasion 6 June. Late in May the Combined Fleet headed east.

In the meantime Adm. Chester *Nimitz, commander in chief of the U.S. Pacific Fleet, heeded warnings of an imminent assault upon Midway from Lt. Comm. Joseph J. Rochefort, whose cryptanalysts, using *MAGIC, had entered the Japanese Navy's radio communication system. Knowing the Aleutians were a feint, Nimitz concentrated his three carriers where needed, misinformed the Japanese as to their location, and until the last minute denied the enemy accurate information about them. At the same time, first his cryptanalysts and then his patrol planes from Midway kept Nimitz and his tactical commanders at sea— Rear Admirals Frank Jack Fletcher and Raymond A. *Spruance—informed of the progress of the enemy fleet.

Early on 4 June, Vice Adm. Chuichi Nagumo, commanding four of Japan's most powerful carriers, launched his attack upon Midway. Simultaneously, Midway-based U.S. aircraft attacked his ships, but none gained a hit and most were shot down. Then, in quick succession, a Japanese scout plane reported the presence of an American carrier; U.S. carrier-based torpedo planes began to attack Nagumo's carriers (almost all were shot down without getting a single hit); the Japanese aircraft that had attacked Midway returned, needing to land on deck; and three U.S. dive-bomber squadrons, one from the *Yorktown* and two from the *Enterprise,* arrived over the Japanese Fleet. The dive-bombers destroyed three of Nagumo's carriers: the *Kaga, Akagi,* and *Soryu.* The *Hiryu* survived long enough for her planes to hit the *Yorktown,* then she too sank under air attack from *Yorktown* and *Enterprise.* Defeated, Yamamoto turned his fleet homeward. On 6 June, aircraft from the *Enterprise* and *Hornet* sank a Japanese cruiser, while the Japanese submarine *I-168* finished off the damaged *Yorktown.*

Japan had gained possession of two barren islands in the Aleutians. It had lost four irreplaceable carriers and many equally irreplaceable aviators. The United States had also lost aviators, but only one carrier. The Japanese Combined Fleet no longer had an appreciable edge over the U.S. Pacific Fleet. The United States had saved Midway and perhaps Hawaii, gaining the opportunity to go on the offensive two months hence at Guadalcanal. In Admiral Spruance, it had found one of the Pacific War's most effective tactical naval commanders. And in retrospect, Midway proved to be the turning point of the naval war in the Pacific. The United States now seized the offensive.

[*See also* Guadalcanal, Battle of (1942–1943), Navy, U.S. 1899–1945; Pearl Harbor, Attack on; Sea Warfare; World War II, U.S. Naval Operations in: The Pacific.]

• John B. Lundstrom, *The First South Pacific Campaign: Pacific Fleet Strategy, December 1941–June 1942,* 1976. Hiroyuki Agawa, *The Reluctant Admiral: Yamamoto and the Imperial Navy,* trans. John Bester, 1979. George W. Prange, Donald M. Goldstein, and Katherine V. Dillon, *Miracle at Midway,* 1982. John J. Stephan, *Hawaii Under the Rising Sun: Japan's Plans for Conquest After Pearl Harbor,* 1984. Donald M. Goldstein and Katherine V. Dillon, eds. *Fading Victory: The Diary of Admiral Matome Ugaki, 1941–1945,* trans. Masatake Chihaya, 1991.
—Frank Uhlig, Jr.

MILITARISM AND ANTIMILITARISM. The term *militarism* describes a society in which war, or preparation for war, dominates politics and foreign policy. Soldiers and military-minded civilians become a governing elite dedicated to expanding the military establishment and inculcating martial values. *Antimilitarism*—militarism's opposite—is not the same as a pacifist resistance to all war. But, like pacifists, antimilitarists are hostile to the military and believe that, in the words of Alexis de Tocqueville, "a large army in the midst of a democratic people will always be a source of great danger."

Beginning with the colonists' aggression against the native Indians, Americans have frequently gone to war. But, if not historically a peace-loving people, they have traditionally distrusted militarism. In accord with the English radical Whig tradition, they preferred an informal militia to a standing army. Thus, the Declaration of Independence asserted that *George III "has kept among us, in times of peace, Standing Armies without the Consent of our legisla-

tures. He has affected to render the Military independent of and superior to the Civil Power."

The *Revolutionary War did not diminish American aversion to militarism. George *Washington gracefully relinquished his command, while the new state and federal constitutions affirmed the supremacy of civil over military authority. Military power was divided between Congress, which had the sole power to declare war, and the civilian president as *commander in chief of the armed forces. In the *Civil War, although Abraham *Lincoln assumed some aspects of military rule, the Union was preserved without a military dictatorship. Isolated from the strife of Europe, the United States during the nineteenth century enjoyed free, or near-free national security, with a minuscule regular army and a small navy. Through the early twentieth century, America was celebrated as a haven of refuge for young men fleeing the wars and military *conscription of the Old World.

The first major break in the liberal antimilitarist tradition of the American republic followed the *Spanish-American War. Under the new imperialistically minded leadership of Theodore *Roosevelt as president, and Secretary of War Elihu *Root, the army, with a General Staff and National Guard, was reorganized along the lines of the major military powers of Europe. Selective Service in World Wars I and II completed federal control; but conscription, though democratic in its rough equality of obligatory service, was opposed in peacetime as a bulwark of militarism.

By the second half of the twentieth century, the *Cold War's Pax Americana, along with the enormous technological achievements of modern *nuclear weapons, made possible a new type of militarism unrecognizable to those who looked for its historic characteristics. Militarism might now be clothed in a civilian uniform and imposed upon a people who accepted a permanent warfare economy as no more than a way to full employment and a welfare state.

Historically, Americans have preferred that the soldiers they have chosen as presidents exemplify civilian virtues. Thus, Dwight D. *Eisenhower, a career army officer for most of his life, nevertheless in his farewell presidential address in January 1961 warned that America could be menaced by the rise of a *military-industrial complex. "We must never," he declared, "let the weight of this combination endanger our liberties or democratic processes.... Only an alert and knowledgeable citizenry can compel the proper meshing of the huge industrial and military machinery of defense with our peaceful methods and goals so that security and liberty may prosper together."

[*See also* Civil-Military Relations: Civilian Control of the Military; Militia and National Guard; Pacifism; Peace and Antiwar Movements; War: Nature of War.]

• Arthur A. Ekirch, Jr., *The Civilian and the Military: A History of the American Antimilitarist Tradition,* 1956; repr. 1972. Marcus Cunliffe, *Soldiers and Civilians: The Martial Spirit in America, 1775–1865,* 1968; repr. 1993. Michael S. Sherry, *In the Shadow of War: The United States Since the 1930s,* 1995.
—Arthur A. Ekirch, Jr.

MILITARY HISTORY. *See* Disciplinary Views of War: Military History.

The term **MILITARY-INDUSTRIAL COMPLEX** has a clearly defined history. It was first used by President Dwight D. *Eisenhower in his farewell address in January

1961, when he warned that "In the councils of government, we must guard against the acquisition of unwarranted influence, whether sought or unsought, by the military-industrial complex. The potential for the disastrous rise of misplaced power exists and will persist."

The term soon came into widespread use because it seemed to fit and explain some of the new military realities of the time: the persistent high military spending in peacetime, which was unprecedented in American history; the persistent and costly *arms race between the United States and the Soviet Union; and the persistent and seemingly pointless U.S. military involvement in Vietnam. The 1960s–1970s saw a flood of writings about the military-industrial complex, a flood that crested during the last years of the *Vietnam War. By the mid-1980s, however, the term had largely fallen out of public discussion.

Whatever the ebb and flow of language, the concept reflects an enduring reality. Since the beginning of the Industrial Revolution in the late eighteenth century, every great power has demonstrated a close connection between its military and its industry. Industrial development led to military advantage (e.g., the British steel industry and the Royal Navy) and military needs led to industrial development (e.g., the German Army and the German steel industry).

This military-industrial connection existed even in the commercial United States. Eli *Whitney developed the mass-production process in 1798 while seeking a better way to manufacture U.S. Army muskets. For a century and a half thereafter, the U.S. government arsenal system was a military-industrial complex of the clearest and simplest sort.

The arsenal system was not the most common pattern of military-industrial relations in the United States, however. Normally, commercial demands first called an industry into being, and then the U.S. military, following the lead of the militaries of other great powers, applied the products of the new industry to military purposes. The expanding American steel industry after the *Civil War soon found a market in the new steel-hulled U.S. Navy, but its major markets remained civilian. The next waves of American industry—successively the chemical, electrical, and automobile industries—also developed because of civilian, not military, demand.

Beginning in the 1930s and continuing through World War II and the *Cold War, this pattern of civilian production leading military production was reversed. The next waves of American industry—aviation (later aerospace), computers, and semiconductors—were brought into being by military demand, and their products only later found civilian applications.

Two world wars reinforced the connection between the military and industry. In both wars, the largest defense contractors were the largest industrial corporations (in World War II, these included U.S. Steel, Bethlehem Steel, Dupont, General Electric, Westinghouse, General Motors, and Ford). However, when these wars were over (as after all previous U.S. wars), these American corporations quickly converted from production for military purposes back to production for commercial markets. With the minor exceptions of the U.S. government arsenals and shipyards, the military-industrial complex in the United States was a reality only in wartime.

A new kind of military-industrial complex came into being in the 1950s. The comprehensive national strategy presented in *National Security Council memorandum No. 68, a call for Cold War, rearmament, seemed to legitimate, and the experience of the *Korean War seemed to necessitate, a permanent military-industrial establishment, in peacetime as well as in wartime or at least in cold as well as hot war. After the Korean War, the Eisenhower administration did not undertake drastic reductions in military spending like the reductions after previous wars but rather maintained military spending at the level of about 10 percent of GNP. Much of this spending went for the procurement of weapons systems, especially aircraft and *missiles. Moreover, several large corporations, particularly those in the aerospace industry, became completely dependent upon military contracts (e.g., Lockheed, General Dynamics, North American, McDonnell, and Grumman). Eisenhower himself presided over the institutionalization of the military-industrial complex that he would later warn against.

Many of the major military contractors were clustered in California and Texas. This concentration within particular states and congressional districts meant that their representatives in Congress became representatives of the contractors and of the military-industrial complex more generally. These representatives often became members of the House and Senate armed services committees, where they heavily influenced military procurement. The military-industrial complex thus developed into the "iron triangle," composed of congressional committees, military services, and military contractors.

During the two decades of the greatest public discussion about the military-industrial complex in 1960–80, several arguments were put forward about its consequences for public policy:

Military Keynesianism. Some analysts argued that the military-industrial complex promoted military spending as the way to use fiscal policy to manage the national economy, a military version of the macroeconomic prescriptions of John Maynard Keynes. This led to persistent and massive federal budget deficits.

The Depleted Society. A related argument was that the military-industrial complex diverted resources from investment in long-run economic and social development into spending on nonproductive military weapons, depleting society instead of developing it. In particular, there were too many engineers devoted to developing military products and not enough developing commercial ones. This seemed to explain why Japan and Germany, which had much lower military spending per capita than the United States, were more successful in international commercial markets. This led to persistent and massive U.S. trade deficits.

The Follow-on System. It was also argued that, in order to preserve particular military contractors and their production facilities, the military-industrial complex promoted weapons systems that were merely new variations or "follow-ons" of previous systems from a particular production line. This led to a sort of technological stagnation.

The Gold-plating Syndrome. A related argument was that, in order to maintain the profits of military contractors, the military-industrial complex promoted excessive spending on superfluous features of weapons systems, often referred to as "waste, fraud, and abuse." This led to fewer numbers of more expensive weapons.

Each of these arguments was highly controversial when first made. This is not surprising, given the high stakes in military expenditures that were involved. By now, however, most analysts of military procurement agree that there is substantial evidence supporting each as they apply to much of the period from the 1960s to the 1980s.

It was also argued, especially at the height of the Vietnam War, that the military-industrial complex put strong and persistent pressure on U.S. leaders to undertake military interventions and an adventurous foreign policy. Yet the evidence is largely against this argument. The U.S. military services, at least the army and the Marines, have consistently been reluctant to undertake military interventions. The military services generally have been in favor of the procurement of new weapons, but not the employment of them.

Whatever the power of arguments about the influence of the military-industrial complex on weapons procurement during the Cold War, they are much less relevant to the current era. The end of the Cold War and the fiscal constraints imposed by federal budget deficits brought an end to military Keynesianism. American society is certainly depleted in many ways, but its current problems do not include too little investment and too few engineers for commercial products. The follow-on system is less evident, since a major defense contractor (Grumman) was allowed to go out of business, and other production lines have shrunk greatly. There is still ample gold-plating—waste, fraud, and abuse—but it can now be seen as a sort of welfare system (like public works during the Great Depression) for a limited number of distressed localities.

A military-industrial complex still exists, but it is now a much smaller part of the U.S. economy than it was during most of the Cold War (military spending in the late 1990s is less than 3% of GNP). Because of this relatively small size, the military-industrial complex no longer seems to have consequences that are really damaging to American interests. The major problems now seem to arise from other complexes—perhaps the financial, medical, educational, or entertainment complexes—and from the complexity of America itself.

[See also Consultants; Economy and War; Industry and War; Procurement; Weaponry.]

• Mary Kaldor, The Baroque Arsenal, 1981. Thomas L. McNaugher, New Weapons: Old Politics: America's Military Procurement Muddle, 1989. Gregory Michael Hooks, Forging the Military-Industrial Complex World War II's Battle of the Potomac, 1991. Ann Markusen et al., The Rise of the Gunbelt: The Military Remapping of Industrial America, 1991. Jacob A. Vander Meulen, The Politics of Aircraft: Building an American Military Industry, 1991. Ethan B. Kapstein, The Political Economy of National Security: A Global Perspective, 1992. Ann Markusen and Joel Yudken, Dismantling the Cold War Economy, 1992. Raymond Vernon and Ethan B. Kapstein, editors, Defense and Dependence in a Global Economy, 1992. John L. Bois, Buying for Armageddon: Business, Society, and Military Spending since the Cuban Missile Crisis, 1994.   —James Kurth

MILITARY POLICE. See Justice, Military: Military Police.

MILITIA ACTS. From 1792 through 1916, Congress struggled to devise a policy to make the state citizen soldiery an effective reserve to augment the U.S. Army in national emergencies and yet preserve the militia's prerogatives as guaranteed in the Constitution. The Militia Act of 1792 left the militia, all able-bodied men between eighteen and forty-five, wholly under the control of the states. Although Congress approved a law in 1808 providing $200,000 worth of weapons to be shared among the states, and doubled the amount in 1887, the act left the nation with no reserve and dependent on untrained wartime volunteers.

The Militia Act of 1903, as amended in 1906 and 1908, increased federal aid to $4 million annually and recognized the National Guard as the "Organized Militia." The amended 1903 act deemed state units the first reserve to be called in any war. It limited federal control, however, and in the *National Defense Act of 1916, Congress gave the army extensive control over National Guard officers and units, made state forces available for service overseas, and greatly increased financial support. As amended in 1920, provisions of the 1916 law essentially have governed federal-state military relations to the present.

[See also Citizen-Soldier; Militia and National Guard.]

• Richard H. Kohn, ed., Military Laws of the United States from the Civil War Through the War Powers Act of 1973, 1979. John K. Mahon, History of the Militia and the National Guard, 1983.

—Jerry Cooper

MILITIA AND NATIONAL GUARD. Colonial and subsequently state militia systems have played a central role in military affairs for much of America's history. From the first Indian wars of the seventeenth century through the *Spanish-American War in 1898, colonial and state militias raised the majority of soldiers who fought these conflicts. Colonies largely waged war as individual efforts until the 1690s. Thereafter, the colonies provided troops to assist the crown and the states did the same for the United States. Provincial and state units serving with the British army, the *Continental army, or the U.S. Army resisted regular military discipline and earned in return the contempt of professional officers. The combination of militia troops and regular forces from America's earliest history engendered what Russell F. Weigley identifies as an American "dual army tradition."

The militia took root in the British colonies when most European nations abandoned the feudal levy and organized standing armies. Because the private groups that founded the early settlements received no military assistance from the crown, they adopted the fading English militia practice to defend themselves. Virginia, Plymouth Colony, and Massachusetts approved laws that in their general provisions came to prevail throughout the colonies, except Pennsylvania. (There the *pacifism of the elite *Quakers prevented the organization of a militia until the 1750s.)

Colonial laws levied a military obligation on all able-bodied white men, the ages of obligation varying from colony to colony. The laws exempted some men due to their occupations or religious beliefs, and usually excluded indentured servants and slaves. However, in times of crisis colonies ignored race or condition of servitude. Obligated militiamen were required to arm and equip themselves, and take part in occasional musters and training sessions. Training in the colonial era was usually perfunctory. Officers inspected weapons and equipment, led their men in close order drill, and sometimes permitted volley firing or individual marksmanship contests.

Informality and inefficiency marked the colonial militia. By nature the institution was intensely local. Militiamen often elected their own officers, defied the decisions of courts-martial, and ignored orders from colonial capitals. A geographically dispersed farming population produced few men with the time, money, or inclination to make themselves efficient soldiers. Even the ardent were not likely to become skilled with only a few days' annual training. As the colonies matured and immediate Indian threats disappeared, the militia lost much of the military effectiveness it initially developed; yet it persisted because it served important social, political, and community functions.

The very fact that the colonies succeeded illustrates that for all its weaknesses the militia ensured colonial survival and expansion. After the early struggles, however, the militia rarely functioned as a community-in-arms. Conquest of Indian territory required offensive operations—a function to which the obligated militia was unsuited. From the late seventeenth century, therefore, the colonies used the system to mobilize provincial soldiers to man expeditionary forces, to maintain frontier garrisons, and to support slave patrols. Colonies used various methods to recruit men: appeals for volunteers, offers of cash or land bounties, and if necessary, *conscription. Men normally excluded from the militia, including slaves and Indians, often served in provincial forces.

The *Revolutionary War tested the militia as no previous conflict had done. Americans confronted a great imperial power with neither a central government nor a standing army of their own. Although leaders extolled the militiaman as an idealized republican *citizen-soldier whose virtue and zeal could beat the British army, after 1775 state militias generally failed to fight effectively, or to recruit enough men to meet the demands of the Continental army. Militia units called to temporary duty to assist the Continentals often performed poorly, earning the condemnation of Gen. George *Washington and his fellow officers, and providing the basis for an antimilitia prejudice that persisted within the army into the twentieth century. Even so, the revolutionary militias served the country well. The Continental Congress lacked the money, bureaucracy, and political legitimacy to raise troops on its own. Without militias to organize men and supplies within the states, there would have been no Continental army.

The militia remained the source of troops for Congress after the Peace of Paris (1783). The ratification of the U.S. Constitution in 1788 gave the federal government the authority to raise an army, while the Second Amendment (1791) guaranteed the states the right to keep their militias. The Federalist administration of President George Washington established a regular army in the early 1790s, but failed to assert federal control over the militia. Congress perpetuated colonial militia practice when it approved the Militia Act of 1792.

Although new states entering the Union enshrined the militia in their constitutions and statutes, over the next three decades the obligated militia faded into insignificance. Few men enrolled in militia formations and few states made efforts to organize the system. Reform groups pressured state legislatures to repeal militia fines and abolish compulsory musters and training; ultimately state adjutants general merely estimated the size of the obligated population. Although Congress approved an innocuous law in 1808 providing $200,000 worth of weapons to be distributed annually to states and territories, it made no effort to reform the state forces after 1792.

Despite the disintegration of the obligated militia, the state soldiery remained central to military affairs. President James *Madison's administration called on the militia repeatedly during the *War of 1812, when its woeful performance added to its miserable reputation within the regular army. After the War of 1812, the army assumed the central role in protecting the frontier and forming the core around which war armies were built. The regulars, however, could fight neither extended Indian wars nor conventional conflicts without reinforcement by citizen-soldiers.

With the obligated militia moribund, states called for volunteers when assigned manpower quotas by the federal government—a practice with colonial precedents that survived to the end of the nineteenth century. Colonial practice persisted as well when Congress permitted the states to select officers according to local preference, which usually meant by election. Although adjutants general and other part-time staff officers assumed important *mobilization responsibilities, states generally turned to regimental and company officers at the county and municipal level to organized volunteer troops. The call for volunteers thus invariably animated a system that seemed otherwise defunct and perpetuated the militia as a mobilization system.

State soldiers assisted the army in the *Black Hawk War (1832) and the second of the *Seminole Wars (1836–42). States organized 40,000 volunteers for the *Mexican War and approximately 175,000 for the *Spanish-American War. Though both the Union and the Confederacy utilized conscription during the *Civil War, 96 percent of the *Union army and 80 percent of *Confederate army troops entered service as state volunteers. Volunteer soldiers came to military duty no better armed, equipped, or trained than had their earlier militia counterparts. Yet as the Mexican and Civil Wars demonstrated, time and training made them creditable soldiers. Nonetheless, army officers lambasted the volunteers for their lack of discipline and military effectiveness. Deep dismay with the inefficiency he saw in the Civil War led Emory *Upton to write *Military Policy of the United States* (1904), a polemic against reliance on state militia and volunteers that became a favorite text among army officers in ensuing decades.

State mobilization explains in part why the militia persisted, but it served other functions as well. Until the obligated militia disappeared, states called on it to meet local Indian uprisings; militia also served to suppress urban disorders and real, or threatened, slave insurrections. More important, even as the old obligatory system shriveled, one element—the uniformed militia—expanded.

Uniformed militia could be found as elite *artillery, cavalry, and "cadet" units in colonial America and the early republic, but did not become widespread until after the War of 1812. Men with avocational interests in military affairs organized uniformed militia units, voluntarily meeting to train and purchasing their own *uniforms. Many voluntary units lasted only a short time, but some became permanent elements of their state militias. A few voluntary companies reflected an elite tinge with their expensive uniforms, high company dues, and costly armory expenses. They sponsored dinners, theatricals, and balls that attracted the socially active in their communities.

The years from 1830 to 1860 were the heyday of the uniformed militia, as middle-class men—especially, after the 1840s, in towns and cities with an Irish or German ethnic element—became active in forming units. There was much to mock in the activities of these part-time citizen-soldiers. Their self-designed uniforms featured a good deal of gold braid, bearskin hats, and bright colors. They spent most of their money and time on social activities rather than training. Military activities centered on close order drill competitions and marksmanship contests, with an occasional foray into camp to hold sham battles.

On the other hand, by the late 1850s, some 75,000 men demonstrated enough interest in military matters to join a company, support it financially, and gain limited military training. The uniformed militia aided municipalities and states when public disorders or natural disasters required a show of public force. Except for Connecticut, Massachusetts, and New York, states neither aided these organizations financially nor supervised their activities. Answerable only to themselves, the uniformed militia nonetheless provided the only martial experience for thousands of otherwise untutored citizen-soldiers who would volunteer for the next war.

The Civil War swallowed up the uniformed militia. In the decade following the war, however, state voluntary units revived to become the National Guard. Guard units differed from uniformed militia in that state governments gave them financial support. Governors and legislatures also imposed centralized control over local companies and established minimum standards to qualify for state subsidies. Money was forthcoming in part because Guardsmen lobbied for it, but more so because states sought a constabulary force to control urban and industrial disorders. Although a state military revival was underway before 1877, the destructive railroad disorders of that year spurred new interest in the Guard.

In training, arms, equipment, and numbers, the National Guard represented a vast improvement over the uniformed militia. By the 1890s, over 100,000 men in Guard regiments regularly attended summer training camps. Most states made their adjutants general full-time employees to supervise and administer their citizen-soldiers. The Guard, however, continued to resemble the uniformed militia in many ways. It still elected its officers, sponsored social and athletic events, and except in some northeastern states, remained largely self-supporting. The Guard's military efficiency left much to be desired, even in suppressing civil disorder.

Many Guardsmen disliked the constabulary role and presented themselves as an organized volunteer reserve. The National Guard Association, founded in 1879, initiated a campaign to win increased federal aid in recognition of that reserve function. Congress remained unmoved until the calamities of the Spanish-American War fostered wide-ranging military reform. Although the Guard had volunteered willingly in 1898, the war demonstrated that it was poorly prepared to fight. Over the next five years, Congress increased federal aid to the states and granted the National Guard a limited reserve role in the Militia Act of 1903.

Although the act gave the state soldiery a legal recognition never granted before, during the ensuing fifteen years it lost its centrality in military affairs. Military reform also created a general staff manned by professional soldiers intent on creating a military policy fully under their control. Army reformers failed to replace the Guard with a federal volunteer reserve but nonetheless gained significant control in the National Defense Act of 1916. Although the

National Guard survived the army challenge, use of conscription to meet the manpower demands of World War I drastically reduced the percentage of state-recruited soldiers serving in the war army. Of these nearly 4 million men, only 10 percent were Guardsmen. The 400,000 called in 1917, however, represent the largest state effort in the twentieth century. For the next fifty years national draftees, not state soldiers, would represent the nation's citizen-soldiers.

Despite another regular army effort to eliminate it, the Guard survived under the National Defense Act of 1920. The law continued the state reserve role, but placed the Guard under close federal control and limited its forces to 400,000 men. In fact, the Guard never exceeded 200,000 during the interwar years, and poor funding prevented implementation of policy outlined in 1920. A shortage of equipment and an understrength regular force limited National Guard training, and the army displayed little enthusiasm for instructing the state troops. Consequently, when the Guard was mobilized in 1940, it fell well short of combat readiness. Just under 300,000 Guardsmen served in World War II, but their service was vital to the effort. Guard divisions provided the cadre and units that trained millions of draftees, and represented seven of the eleven combat divisions sent overseas in 1942.

In the fifty years since the end of World War II, the National Guard has remained a reserve component to the army and gained a similar function with the air force as well. Federal funding came to total 95 percent of support for the Army and Air National Guard. Despite that support, however, the Guard's part in war has diminished since 1945. The demands of the *Cold War led to a much larger regular army that drew its manpower from the Selective Service, men who then met their reserve obligation in the Army Reserve. In the four significant mobilizations since 1945—the *Korean War, the 1961 Berlin call-up, the *Vietnam War, and the *Persian Gulf War—the *Department of Defense mobilized more reservists than Guardsmen except in the very limited Vietnam activation of Air National Guard units.

The army struggled to develop a rational reserve policy after 1945. It had none for the Korean War and out of desperation called thousands of individual reservists rather than mobilize understrength Guard units that were poorly trained and equipped. Reserve policy began to make sense only in the early 1960s. Policies adopted since then have followed a logical trend: reduce the number of reservists and provide sufficient funding to create fully manned, fully equipped, properly trained units that were genuinely combat ready. During the Vietnam War, the army relied on draftees rather than reservists, but the decision not to call the Guard and Army Reserve represented a political, not a military, choice.

Even as the National Guard assumed a more rigorous combat training program in the 1960s, its state constabulary function engulfed it with demands for which it was unprepared. Armed, equipped, and trained for combat, Guardsmen called to suppress urban ghetto riots and campus protests displayed limited knowledge of the legal requirements in aiding civil authorities, and relied too often on firepower. More than once, as during the 1967 Detroit riot, the failure of the Guard to suppress violence led state officials to request federal military aid. Riots following the assassination of Martin Luther *King, Jr., in April 1968 brought out 40,000 Guardsmen in 14 states. That year the army directed to the Guard to conduct thirty-two hours of riot control training each year. Use of the National Guard to control war protests engendered irony for many young men who joined reserve components to avoid combat duty in Vietnam.

In the aftermath of Vietnam, the army adopted a Total Force policy that allowed it to maintain a large number of combat units by assigning key combat and service support roles to the National Guard and Army Reserve. The end of Selective Service and budget cuts that seriously reduced the active army led to the policy. Under Total Force, the army could not fight a war without mobilizing reserve components. The Gulf War tested that assumption and it seemed to work. One aspect of Total Force, however, apparently failed in 1990–91: three Guard combat brigades were mobilized but not deployed because they fell short of combat readiness.

The decision not to deploy the Guard brigades initiated a dispute that echoed the complaints of George Washington, Emory Upton, and early twentieth-century General Staff reformers. Army leaders did not want to commit poorly prepared state forces to battle led by improperly trained officers. The army complaint implied that no unit not fully under its control could be ready for combat. This recapitulation of an argument as old as the republic raises the question of why the ancient institution of the militia endures in the guise of the National Guard. The state soldiery persisted because it exemplified strains in the American experience that honored the self-taught amateur, the citizen-soldier, and localism, enshrined in the Constitution through federalism. Militiamen were citizens first but effective soldiers as well who, unlike regulars, did not threaten community freedom. A significant gap often existed between the theoretical martial qualities of the militiaman and the realities of his wartime performance. Nonetheless, the state citizen-soldiery with its historically established combat record has endured.

[See also Army Reserves and National Guard; Civil-Military Relations: Civilian Control of the Military; Disciplinary Views of War: Military History; Militia Acts; National Defense Acts; Native Americans: Wars Between Native Americans and Europeans and Euro-Americans; Volunteers, U.S.]

• William H. Riker, Soldiers of the States: The Role of the National Guard in American Democracy, 1957; repr. 1979. John K. Mahon, The American Militia: Decade of Decision, 1789–1800, 1960. Russell F. Weigley, Towards an American Army, 1962. Jim Dan Hill, The Minute Man in Peace and War: A History of the National Guard, 1964. Martha Derthick, The National Guard in Politics (1965). Marcus Cunliffe, Soldiers and Civilians: The Martial Spirit in America, 1775–1865, 1968; ed. 1973. Lawrence D. Cress, Citizens in Arms: The Army and the Militia in American Society to the War of 1812, 1982. John K. Mahon, History of the Militia and the National Guard, 1983. Fred Anderson, A People's Army: Massachusetts Soldiers and Society in the Seven Years War, 1984. Martin Binkin and William W. Kaufman, U.S. Army Guard and Reserve: Rhetoric, Realities, Risks, 1989. Charles Johnson, Jr., African American Soldiers in the National Guard: Recruitment and Deployment During Peacetime and War, 1992. Jerry Cooper, The Militia and the National Guard in America Since Colonial Times, 1993.   —Jerry Cooper

MILLIGAN, EX PARTE (1866). The case, Milligan 71 U.S. 2 (1866), brought to the U.S. Supreme Court fundamental questions regarding military authority over civilians. In 1864, a military commission in Indiana during the *Civil War convicted Lambdin P. Milligan on charges of conspiracy for his part in an alleged plot to release and arm Confederate prisoners in Northern prison camps and sentenced him to death. Milligan appealed to the civil courts, challenging the military tribunal's jurisdiction over his case. When the case reached the Supreme Court in 1866, the justices unanimously ordered Milligan's release. In the majority opinion for the Court, Justice David Davis held that the Constitution prohibited military trials of civilians where civil courts remained open. Martial law was only permissible, he insisted, in "the theater of active military operations," where civil courts could no longer function. In a concurring opinion joined by three other justices, Chief Justice Salmon P. Chase argued that Congress intended to ensure civil trials to civilians when it adopted the *Habeas Corpus Act of 1863, and therefore Milligan had been wrongly tried. However, unlike Davis, Chase insisted that Congress under its war powers had the authority to enact *martial law, even in areas removed from the theater of war.

Milligan promptly provoked criticism from those who feared that it compromised Republican *Reconstruction plans for the South by restricting military authority over civilians. Although in the twentieth century the Supreme Court has been reluctant to endorse *Milligan's* wholesale ban on martial law outside the theater of war, the case has never been reversed and scholars continue to hail it as a landmark constitutional protection of civil rights.

[See also Civil Liberties and War; Civil-Military Relations: Civilian Control of the Military; Merryman, Ex Parte; Supreme Court, War, and the Military.]

• Harold M. Hyman and William M. Wiecek, Equal Justice Under Law: Constitutional Development, 1835–1875, 1982. Mark E. Neely, Jr., The Fate of Liberty: Abraham Lincoln and Civil Liberties, 1991.

—Mary J. Farmer

MINES, LAND. Originally mine warfare consisted of tunneling beneath enemy positions and destroying them with explosives. In the *Civil War, Union troops successfully detonated a mine containing 4 tons of gunpowder under a Confederate position near Petersburg, Virginia, on 30 July 1864. Modern land mines may be an encased charge of explosive or may contain a chemical agent or incendiary device. They can be detonated in numerous ways: pressure (stepping or driving over it), pull (using a trip-wire), tension release (cutting a trip wire), pressure release (removing a weight), or by electrical means (command detonation). More exotic ways are through magnetic induction (driving near the mine in a vehicle), frequency induction (using a radio nearby), audio frequency (any loud noise), and infrared (large heat sources). Mines can come in different sizes and shapes and can weigh as much as 20 pounds, with the capacity of destroying a tank, down to 4 ounces, enough to mangle a foot.

The purpose of mines is to deny ground to the enemy, forcing him either to breach or to circumvent the mine barrier. In either case, the enemy's movement is restricted and he is forced to concentrate in areas that can be covered by direct or indirect fire. Mines are normally emplaced by burial in the ground or scattered upon the surface, where they pose a two-edged weapon against both enemy and friendly forces. Modern mines can be controlled electronically and can turn themselves on and off at the whim of the dispenser. Though the most common type requires direct pressure to activate, command-detonated mines are frequently employed in prepared defensive positions or ambushes. This type is also called a *directional* mine because 80 percent of the fragments are propelled outward in a 60-degree arc. The effect is lethal up to 50 meters and can cause wounds out to 100 meters.

Another antipersonnel mine is the *bounding* type. Upon activation, a small expelling charge in the base of the mine propels the main charge about 1 meter into the air, where it explodes. Antitank mines can attack armored vehicles through shaped charges aimed at the underside of the vehicle, blast effects to blow off a tire or track, or using advanced technology with *off-route* types. Off-route methods involve using acoustic, seismic, and passive infrared sensors to identify a target and then firing a missile down the weapon's line of sight.

Future development of mines will be closely tied to the development of electronic sensors in such areas as identification friend or foe (IFF) technology and methods of deploying mines either mechanically or by remote delivery by aircraft, gun, or rocket systems. Mine warfare is a complicated and wasteful form of engineer combat. Unfortunately, as the size of military units shrink, its appeal will increase as armies seek ways to offset their numerical weaknesses. The widespread use of relatively inexpensive land mines in Third World countries led to numerous civilian casualties long after the end of the conflicts for which the mines were originally placed. So far the United States has not signed an international treaty banning the use of mines because of its obligations to defend large land areas in such far-flung places as Korea and Guantanamo, Cuba.

[*See also* Weapons, Army.]

• Christopher Chant, ed., *How Weapons Work*, 1976. The Diagram Group, *Weapons: An International Encyclopedia from 5000 B.C. to 2000 A.D.*, 1990.

—William F. Atwater

MINES, NAVAL. Underwater explosive devices are designed to sink ships, submarines, or other seaborne craft or by such threat to prevent them from using an area. Their firing mechanisms are either the traditional pressure points which detonate the explosive on contact or the modern influence devices which are triggered through magnetic or electronic sensors merely by the approach of a vessel. Most mines are automatic, but some harbor mines, controlled electrically by cable from shore, can be turned off to allow transit of friendly vessels. Moored mines are tethered to sinkers, and they float at predetermined depths generally to cut off particular areas. Traditionally they have been contact mines floating just below the water to damage surface ships that touch them, but more recently moored mines can serve as influence mines at depths of 3,000 feet or more against submarines. Ground or bottom mines are settled on the bottom in shallow waters such as rivers, harbors, and tidal areas to block their use, especially against amphibious invasion. In contrast to these stationary mines, a broad group of moving mines includes drifting and homing mines and deep-water mobile and rising mines. Mines are small, relatively inexpensive, easily laid down, and require little maintenance. Yet they have the explosive ability to sink or badly damage even large vessels by blowing open their hull below the waterline. Conse-

quently, smaller naval powers have often used them to impede the larger fleets of major powers.

Naval mines originated in the sixteenth century, but their use in naval combat began in the American *Revolutionary War by David Bushnell, who placed such devices under the hulls of British ships in New York harbor using a small one-man, wooden *submarine he invented. During the *Civil War, the *Confederate Navy protected its harbors and sank a number of *Union Navy ships using moored and mobile contact or electrically controlled mines (mislabeled "torpedoes"). Major use of underwater mines began in World War I with the British and later Americans planting tens of thousands of mines to contain the German surface and submarine fleets, and the Germans laying mines in British coastal waters. The Allies lost 586 ships and the Germans lost 150 warships and 40 submarines. In World War II, nearly 700,000 naval mines were laid, accounting for more ships sunk or damaged than any other weapon (the Allies lost 650 ships to mines, the Axis lost around 1,100).

Mining operations and countermining operations have been part of America's wars since World War II. Although the North Koreans did not use mines to try to prevent the *Inchon Landing (1950), in the *Korean War, they subsequently planted 3,500 Soviet magnetic mines at Wonsan, which took U.S. minesweepers a week to clear before the landing of *United Nations forces there. In the *Vietnam War, the U.S. Navy cleared mines so it could operate off the coast of North Vietnam, and in 1972 it mined Haiphong harbor, thereby blocking the influx of Soviet supplies. In the *Persian Gulf War (1991), Iraq laid mines to block oil shipments and impede seaborne assault by the forces of the U.S.-led coalition, but helicopter air sweeps, surface minesweeper ships, and underwater demolition teams cleared the sea lanes and access routes. Development of detection and countermeasures are becoming increasingly important since terrorists, such as those who planted mines in the Red Sea and the Persian Gulf in the 1980s, have begun to use this inexpensive stealthful weapon for its military, economic and considerable psychological effect.

[*See also* Anti-Submarine Warfare Systems; Blockade; Mines, Land.]

• Louis Gerken, *Mine Warfare Technology*, 1989; Tamara Moser Melia, *Damn the Torpedoes: A Short History of U.S. Naval Mine Countermeasures, 1777–1991*, 1991; Howard S. Levie, *Mine Warfare at Sea*, 1992; Samuel Loring Morison, *Guide to Naval Mine Warfare*, 1995.

—John Whiteclay Chambers II

MINUTE MEN. *See* Militia and National Guard; Citizen-Soldier; Lexington and Concord, Battles of (1775).

MIRV (MULTIPLE INDEPENDENTLY TARGETED REENTRY VEHICLE). *See* SALT Treaties (1972, 1979).

MISSILES. Airborne missiles were experimented with in World War I and used extensively in World War II. Since then a wide variety of airborne missiles have been tested in combat many times. Their performance has continuously improved because of technological advances in aerodynamics, guidance, propulsion, and warheads.

Air-to-Air Missiles. The very first air-to-air missile was an aircraft rocket designed primarily for antiballoon or anti-Zeppelin work. Invented by Lt. Y. P. G. Le Prieur of the

French Naval Air Service, the rocket came into use in 1916 by both the French and British air forces. Four or five projectiles, each with a Congreve rocket-like stick for stability, were connected to interplane struts on either side of biplane fighters. Salvoed by electric ignition, the unguided rockets were most effective against larger targets such as observation balloons, but successes were also scored against other aircraft.

World War II brought about the widespread use of aerial rockets, primarily as an air-to-ground weapon against armor. Early in the war, the Germans used fighters to lob a rather primitive conversion of their 21cm mortar shells to break up bomber formations. Later, twenty-four to forty-eight R4M rockets were carried under the wings of a Messerschmitt Me 262 jet fighter. Salvo-fired, they dispersed to cover an area about the size of a football field; a single hit was deadly.

During World War II, the Germans developed radio-controlled and wire-guided versions of the Henschel Hs 298, and the supersonic wire-guided X-4, designed by Dr. Max Kramer in 1943. Both missiles were intended to have proximity fuses, with the X-4 testing an acoustic version. Their most important legacy was probably in proving the feasibility of wire guidance, which has been so widely used on antiarmor rocket weapons.

The *Cold War requirement to shoot down incoming nuclear bomb–laden enemy *bomber aircraft created a demand within the U.S. Air Force for air-to-air missiles for its interceptors. The Lockheed F-94 Starfighter and Northrop F-89 Scorpion were initially armed with 2.75-inch-diameter unguided aerial rockets. These were supplemented by the Hughes GAR (later AIM) Falcon and the McDonnell-Douglas MB-1 (AIR-2A) Genie. The latter was an unguided rocket with a speed of Mach 3, a range of 6 miles, and a 1.5-kiloton warhead intended to break up formations of incoming bombers. Aircraft carrying the Genie were routinely parked at civil airports during the years of the Air Defense Command dispersal program, a practice that might have disturbed modern environmentalist sensibilities.

The long-lived Hughes Falcon was a short- to medium-range missile capable of Mach 4 speed and a range of about 7 miles. Guidance was by a Hughes-developed semiactive *radar homing system.

Missile design improved rapidly as better propellants, miniaturized circuitry, and improved systems came into being. A series of American missiles appeared that would continue in service for decades and be used in air forces around the world. Foreign industries arrived at similar solutions, and their designs were similarly long-lived and widely used.

The heat-seeking AIM-9 Sidewinder first flew in September 1953, and continues in use today, after more than 110,000 have been produced. The successful and widely used Soviet AA-2A Atoll was developed directly from captured Sidewinders. Missiles similar in principle and performance to the Sidewinder have also been built in China, France, Germany, Italy, Israel, and South Africa.

The 186-pound AIM-9 has been produced in many variants, but may be described in general as a solid fuel rocket with a Mach 2 speed and a range of 10 miles. The infrared homing device detects a target's heat source (e.g., a jet aircraft's tailpipe) and homes in on it. Raytheon and Loral are the primary contractors.

A second long-lived air-to-air missile is the AIM-7 Sparrow, a semiactive Döppler radar-guided medium-range missile that was first flown in 1952 and came into operational use in 1958. It has a maximum speed of Mach 3.5 and a range of 25 miles. More than 40,000 had been built when production ended in 1990. Principal contractors include Raytheon and Hughes Missile Systems. The Sparrow was effective during the *Persian Gulf War in Operation Desert Storm, shooting down twenty-three aircraft.

The 510-pound Sparrow carries an 86-pound warhead. The target is first acquired by the carrier's radar; after launch, a radar in the missile's nose, tuned to the fighter's radar signals, picks up the radiation reflected from the target and steers the missile to it.

Intended for use against bombers, air-to-air missiles were disappointing in combat against fighter *aircraft. In the *Vietnam War, the Sparrow had a probability of kill (PK) of only about 9 percent, while the Sidewinder had a PK of about 15 percent, both exceedingly low figures when one considers the time and money expended on them and the expectations they had evoked. Later variants offered more discriminating seekers and better reliability.

For many years the most sophisticated air-to-air missile in the world, the U.S. Navy's long-range AIM-54 Phoenix is used by the Northrop/Grumman F-14 Tomcat and incorporates the Hughes AWG-9 or AWG-17 radar/fire control system. A large weapon weighing about 1,000 pounds, the Phoenix carries a 135-pound warhead, and can reach a speed of Mach 5. The F-14's Phoenix missile weapon system permits the tracking of up to twenty-four targets and a choice of up to six simultaneous interceptions, over a range in excess of 125 miles.

Designed to replace the AIM-7, the AIM-120A Advanced Medium-Range Air-to-Air Missile (AMRAAM) was developed jointly by the U.S. Air Force and the U.S. Navy, and entered service in 1992. Like the Phoenix, a "beyond visual range" (BVR) missile, it is intended for use on the F-15, F-16, F/A F-18, and Tornado aircraft. The AIM-120A is slightly smaller than the Sparrow, weighing only 345 pounds, and has a speed of about Mach 4, a range of 30 miles, with a 48-pound warhead. The AIM-120A has a high kill probability stemming from its being able to launch at any aircraft speed or target angle and from its "look-down, shoot-down" capability, meaning its ability to discern and hit a target against any background. Hughes Missile Systems and Raytheon are the principal contractors.

The Soviet Union, and its principal successor state, Russia, maintained a missile development program that closely matched that of the United States. The latest versions of the AA-10 Alamo missile and the AA-12 Adder have many of the characteristics of the AMRAAM. Other nations tend to create niche market air-to-air missiles tailored to their industrial capability and particular defense needs.

Air-to-Surface Missiles. World War II saw the development of several air-to-surface tactical missiles, which ranged from the relatively simple 2.75-inch-diameter high-velocity aerial rockets (HVAR) to forerunners of today's cruise missiles such as the Japanese Ohka kamikaze aircraft launched from Mitsubishi G4M "Betty" bombers.

The first major U.S. air-to-surface missile was the AGM-12B Bullpup, developed for the U.S. Navy during the *Korean War, but later adopted by the U.S. Air Force and many foreign air forces. The Bullpup was essentially a rocket-propelled bomb guided by radio from the launch aircraft. Very inexpensive (at one point having a unit cost of only $5,000), the Bullpup was built by the tens of thousands and used by aircraft of many countries. It was continually improved over time, and a laser-guided version was built for the U.S. Marine Corps.

First produced in 1971, the Hughes AGM-65 Maverick represented a giant step forward technologically. The "launch and leave" Maverick depicts a target on a cockpit television screen; when launched, it homes automatically to its target. Later Mavericks had improved optics or an imaging-infrared seeker. In the Gulf War, about 100 Mavericks a day were fired, about 90 percent by Fairchild A-10 close air support aircraft.

The development of powerful Soviet defenses against air attack made air-launched missiles attractive to the U.S. Air Force. The 30-foot-long, 13,000-pound Bell XB-63 Rascal was a supersonic missile attached like an enormous goiter to the side of Boeing DB-47E carrier aircraft. After a troubled development, it entered service in October 1957. It was followed by the GAM-72 Quail, a decoy missile intended to confuse enemy radar as to the strength and direction of attacking Boeing B-52s.

Missiles soon acquired a strategic capability. The North American AGM-28A Hound Dog was an impressive Mach 2.1 delta-wing aircraft that would today be termed a cruise missile. It could fly at any altitude from tree-top level to more than 50,000 feet, with a maximum range of 710 miles; later models carried terrain avoidance and electronic warfare equipment. The Hound Dog carried a thermonuclear warhead of up to 4 megatons, and would have been used to blast a way for the carrier aircraft to reach its targets. B-52 G and H models could carry two Hound Dogs whose 7,500-pound-thrust Pratt & Whitney J52 engines could be used to augment takeoff power. Over 590 Hound Dogs were delivered to the Strategic Air Command, serving from 1961 to 1976.

Advances in computers and microcircuitry led to the development of the Boeing AGM-69A SRAM (short-range attack missile), only 14 feet long and weighing but 2,320 pounds. Eight SRAMs could be fitted into each of the rotary launchers installed in a B-52 bomb bay. Additional SRAMs could be carried on the wing pylons formerly used for Hound Dog missiles, so that a B-52 might carry as many as twenty missiles to cover a wide array of targets. The FB-111 and B-1 were also designed to accommodate SRAMs. The SRAM had a range of 35 to 105 miles, depending upon its launch altitude, at speeds up to Mach 3.5. The 170-kiloton nuclear warhead made the SRAM a true force multiplier; but unexpected difficulties with propellant storage led to an earlier than planned removal from the fleet.

The SRAM was followed by a political football, the Air-Launched Cruise Missile (ALCM). Originally designed as the AGM-86 SCAD (Subsonic Cruise Armed Decoy) and intended as a more potent version of the Quail decoy, the missile was upgraded to ALCM status to be used as a bargaining chip in disarmament talks. President Jimmy *Carter presented the ALCM as an inexpensive new idea that justified canceling the Rockwell B-1 bomber.

The AGM-86B ALCM is a small, unmanned, winged subsonic vehicle with an approximate speed of 500 mph and a range of 1,555 miles. The ALCM uses a terrain contour matching system (TERCOM) to update its inertial guidance system to achieve pinpoint navigational accuracy. B-52s typically carry twelve ALCMs externally and eight more in the bomb bay. The longest combat mission in history took place when seven B-52Gs took off from Barksdale Air Force Base, Louisiana, and opened the 17 January 1991 Desert Storm air offensive with a barrage of thirty-five AGM-86Cs with conventional high-explosive warheads.

The most modern cruise missile in service is the AGM-129 Advanced Cruise Missile, manufactured in the early 1990s by General Dynamics. The AGM-129 has stealth characteristics coupled with a 2,000-mile range and Mach .9 speed. A total procurement of 2,000 missiles was planned, but the breakup of the Soviet Union and some program delays resulted in termination of the program after 461 missiles were delivered.

The AGM-84E-1 standoff land-attack missile (SLAM) is a derivative of the Harpoon (described below) and has similar physical characteristics and performance. It was created by combining the basic Harpoon with components of other systems, including the Maverick infrared seeker, a Global Positioning System, and a Walleye data link.

The former Soviet Union developed a parallel series of cruise and attack missiles, the most important of which was the AS-15 "Kent." The Kent corresponds to the ALCM and could be launched by air, land, or sea. It has an estimated range of 1,800 miles.

Antiradar Missiles. The appearance of Soviet surface-to-air missiles forced the development of the first antiradar missile, the AGM-45 Shrike. A development of the AIM-7 Sparrow, the Shrike was first used in combat in 1966. With a Mach 2 speed and a range of up to 25 nautical miles, the Shrike weighs about 390 pounds, with a 145-pound warhead. The Shrike is a joint product of Texas Instruments, Sperry-Rand, and Univac.

The Shrike was succeeded first by the General Dynamics "Standard Arm," the AGM-78 Standard Antiradar Missile, which could continue homing in on the radar even after it had shut down. Like the Shrike, it was used in Vietnam and by the Israeli Air Force. Weighing 1,799 pounds, with a 215-pound warhead, the AGM-78 has a speed of Mach 2.5 and a maximum range of 30 nautical miles.

The current antiradar missile is the AGM-88 High Speed Anti-radiation Missile (HARM), developed jointly by the Naval Weapons Center at China Lake, California, and Texas Instruments. The Mach 2+ HARM has a much greater capability to lock on to enemy radar than its predecessors. It can be fired as a long-range standoff missile, or its all-aspect passive radar homing seeker can be used to detect and attack targets of opportunity. It demonstrated its prowess in the 1986 U.S. naval air strikes against Libya, and in the Gulf War, where more than 1,000 HARMs were fired. The AGM-78 weighs about 800 pounds; its 145-pound high-explosive warhead is designed specifically for damaging radar antenna. The sophisticated British ALARM antiradar weapon also did well in the Gulf War.

Antiship Missiles. The vulnerability of ships to missiles was first demonstrated in World War II, when a Luftwaffe Dornier Do 217 sank the Italian battleship *Roma* with two Fritz-X missiles. In the 1982 Falklands War, Argentine Naval Air Force Super Entendard fighters launched Aerospatiale MM 38 Exocet missiles to sink the Royal Navy destroyer HMS *Sheffield* and the aviation supply ship HMS *Atlantic Conveyor*.

The principal U.S. antiship missile is the McDonnell-Douglas AGM-84 Harpoon, a long-range, sea-skimming "fire-and-forget" weapon manufactured in a variety of models. Its wings and control surfaces fold for storage, popping out after launch. About 13 feet long and weighing 1,170 pounds, the Harpoon is powered by a 600-pound static-thrust Teledyne Continental turbojet engine and cruises at Mach .85.

The Chinese have been especially active in building and selling antiship missiles like the HY-4, designated "Silkworm" by *NATO. While derivative of the early Soviet SS-N-2 "Styx," the Silkworm's Mach 1.2 speed and 20-mile range make it a formidable weapon. Other nations, including the former Soviet Union, France, Germany, Italy, Norway, and Sweden, have all developed specialized antishipping missiles, which have in turn led to the development of extraordinarily expensive defensive systems.

Airborne Antitank Guided Missiles. Beginning with the World War II American "Bazooka" and the German *Panzerfaust*, antiarmor missiles became common, for they provide infantry with an inexpensive, flexible, and effective means to defeat opposing armor. The improvements in the guidance, propulsion, and warheads of *antitank weapons have exceeded the ability of tank designers to defend against them.

The proliferation of antitank missiles can be traced to the French Nord SS-10 guided missiles. Used by French helicopters in Algeria (the first combat role for helicopters), the SS-10 has been called the "smallest, cheapest and most significant" missile since 1945 in that it expanded on German World War II practice and was exported to many foreign countries. A host of wire-guided missiles followed, most line-of-sight missiles with manual control systems and an effective range of just over 1 mile. The second generation of weapons used computer technology to allow the gunner to "fly" the missile to the target by keeping it centered in his sights. The subsequent generation will be almost fully automatic, making full use of computers, television, fiber optics, guidance by *lasers, and other technological advances.

The most important U.S. airborne antitank guided missile is the Rockwell International AGM-114 Hellfire (the name deriving from "helicopter fire and forget"). Initially fielded as a laser-guided weapon, the Hellfire accepts other guidance packages, including imaging-infrared, radio frequency, and millimeter wavelength seekers.

The Hellfire is deployed on a wide variety of U.S. Army and Marine and Israeli Air Force helicopters. U.S. Army Bell "Apache" helicopters used it with effect in Operation Just Cause in Panama and in the Persian Gulf War. There it opened the war with a long-distance raid on Iraqi early warning radar sites, scoring fifteen hits in two minutes. The Hellfire is a small, 100-pound weapon with a wingspan of just over 1 foot, a speed of Mach 2.2, and a range of about 4 miles.

The first and most widely used U.S. antitank guided missile is the Hughes BGM-71 TOW (*t*ube-launched, *o*ptically tracked, *w*ired-guided) weapon, which is fired from helicopters as well from a variety of ground installations. First used in Vietnam in May, 1972, the TOW had a sensational 80 percent hit record. With tens of thousands of TOWs in the field in armies around the world, the weapon has been used with effect in wars in Israel, Lebanon, Morocco, Iran, Pakistan, and Iraq. Weighing about 42 pounds,

with a shaped, charged, high-explosive armor-piercing warhead, the TOW is effective at ranges up to about 3 miles. The TOW has been complemented by the formidable FIM-92A Stinger, used by rebels with such devastating effect against the Soviet Union in Afghanistan, and adapted for current American *helicopters. Hughes is the principal contractor but the vast quantities required called for a second source, Raytheon.

The Stinger is a "fire-and-forget" missile, weighing 22 pounds and with a speed of Mach 1. Designed for close-in fighting, over ranges of less than 3 miles, the Stinger uses an all-aspect automatic passive infrared homing device.

Helicopter warfare also requires an antiradar missile. The Motorola AGM-122 Sidearm is essentially an AIM-9C Sidewinder modified to have a broad band passive radar homing sensor. The missile is used primarily by the U.S. Marine Corps on both helicopters and fixed-wing aircraft.

The role of the airborne missile can be expected to grow in the future; it waits in the wings as an antisatellite device, and will undoubtedly be employed in the next century by unmanned remote-piloted vehicles in futuristic dogfights.

[*See also* Heat-Seeking Technology; Marine Corps, U.S.: Since 1945; Panama, U.S. Military Involvement in; Weaponry.]

• Bill Gunston, *Rockets and Missiles*, 1979. Michael J. H. Taylor, *Missiles of the World*, 1980; 3rd ed. 1980. Charles A. Sorrels, *U.S. Cruise Missile Programs*, 1983. Kenneth P. Werrell, *The Evolution of the Cruise Missile*, 1985. Lon O. Nordeen, *Air Warfare in the Missile Age*, 1985. Christopher Chant, *Compendium of Armaments and Military Hardware*, 1987. R. G. Lee, et al., *Guided Weapons*, 1988. Michael Del Papa, *From SNARK to Peacekeeper*, 1990. Trevor N. Dupuy, editor in chief, *International Military Defense Encyclopedia*, Vol. 4, 1993.

—Walter J. Boyne

MISSIONARY RIDGE, BATTLE OF (1863). After the Battle of *Chickamauga (September 1863), the defeated *Union army retreated into Chattanooga, Tennessee. The victorious *Confederate army virtually besieged it there by occupying high ground west, south, and east of the city, practically cutting off Union supplies.

The federal government reacted by sending reinforcements—Gen. Joseph *Hooker and 10,000 men from Virginia, and William Tecumseh *Sherman and 20,000 men from Mississippi. More important, it sent a new commander: Ulysses S. *Grant. Grant opened an adequate supply line and prepared his combined armies for battle. Meanwhile, Confederate commander Braxton *Bragg was plagued by backbiting and noncooperation from his subordinates.

By late November, Grant was ready. His plan was that Hooker should threaten the Confederate left on Lookout Mountain to the southwest of the city and George H. *Thomas the Confederate center along Missionary Ridge to the east, while Sherman broke the Confederate right on Tunnel Hill. On 24 November, Hooker actually drove the Confederates off Lookout Mountain; but the terrain around Tunnel Hill proved deceptively difficult, the Confederate defense skillful and stubborn. Sherman's 25 November attacks got nowhere. To ease pressure on Sherman, Grant ordered Thomas to take a line of Confederate rifle pits at the base of Missionary Ridge. Confusion regarding orders and the impossibility of remaining at the base of the ridge under fire from the Confederates on the crest led Thomas's troops to continue their charge and—

astoundingly—take the ridge. Why? First, ravines on the slope covered the attackers. Second, the confederate defensive line was poorly sited. Third, the Confederate troops' *morale was low since they had lost confidence in Bragg. And fourth, Thomas's Federals were unusually aggressive, determined to blot out the shame of their recent debacle at Chickamauga. In all, 56,000 Federals engaged 46,000 Confederates on Missionary Ridge. *Casualties were 5,824 Union men to 6,667 Confederates.

As a result of the battle, Bragg was removed from command. His army retreated to Dalton, Georgia, and the stage was set for the start of Sherman's Atlanta campaign the following spring.

[See also Civil War: Military and Diplomatic Course.]

• James L. McDonough, Chattanooga—A Death Grip on the Confederacy, 1984. Peter Cozzens, The Shipwreck of Their Hopes: The Battles for Chattanooga, 1994. Steven E. Woodworth, Six Armies in Tennessee: The Chickamauga and Chattanooga Campaigns, 1998.
—Steven E. Woodworth

MITCHELL, BILLY [WILLIAM] (1879–1936), army officer, airpower theorist. Scion of a Wisconsin railroad and banking family, Mitchell was born in Nice, France, where his parents were vacationing. Enlisting as a private in the *Spanish-American War, nineteen-year-old Billy was promoted to lieutenant as a result of an appeal by his father, John Mitchell, a U.S. senator. In 1901, he became a regular army lieutenant in the Signal Corps. Promoted to major, he was appointed chief of the Signal Corps' new aviation section in 1916.

In World War I, as a brigadier general, Mitchell organized and ably led the U.S. Army's fledgling Air Service in France. In addition to aerial pursuit, reconnaissance, and ground support, he experimented with mass bombing of enemy military formations and installations in the war zone. From this experience and his discussions with Sir Hugh Trenchard, head of the Royal Flying Corps, Mitchell became a champion of airpower.

In the early 1920s, as a war hero and assistant chief of the army's Air Service with headquarters in Washington, D.C., Mitchell campaigned for a large, independent air force. He used the new mass media, including motion pictures, to advance his program against the opposition of senior army and navy officers as well as cost-cutting Republican administrations and Congress. Mitchell's planes dramatically sank captured naval warships in prearranged tests off the Virginia Capes in 1921–22, but his constant criticism led to his reassignment to Texas.

Even more outspoken in 1925, Mitchell was tried by a court-martial for calling army and navy leaders criminally negligent and responsible for the deaths of aviators in outmoded aircraft. His trial, portrayed by the media as the martyrdom of a prophet standing alone against entrenched bureaucracy, was one of the most sensational of the decade. Found guilty, Mitchell was suspended from active duty for five years; instead, he resigned from the army in 1926.

As a civilian, Mitchell became even more strident in interviews, articles, and books. Much like Trenchard and the Italian airpower theorist Giulio *Douhet, Mitchell claimed that strategic bombing would be decisive in future wars, and as a deterrent to war, because it could bypass enemy fleets and armies to strike directly at the industrial and population centers of hostile nations. Mitchell died of a heart attack in 1936, but since the adoption of many of his ideas in World War II, he has been eulogized by the air force.

[See also Air Force, Predecessors of: 1907–46; Air Warfare.]

• Alfred F. Hurley, Billy Mitchell: Crusader for Air Power, 1964. Burke Davis, The Billy Mitchell Affair, 1967.   —Michael L. Grumelli

MOBILE BAY, BATTLE OF (1864). Confederate Mobile, Alabama, was a major port, ranking second to New Orleans on the gulf. After New Orleans and the mouth of the Mississippi fell to the Union in 1862, Adm. David *Farragut moved into Mobile Bay early in August 1864, countering the most serious threat from that quarter, the formidable Confederate ironclad Tennessee.

Three wooden gunboats completed the Confederate squadron, which patrolled more than twenty miles from Mobile south to Fort Gaines on the eastern tip of Dauphin Island and Fort Morgan on the western end of Mobile Point. They guarded a three-mile passage into the bay, which had been narrowed with pilings and a minefield to force approaching ships toward Fort Morgan.

Farragut sent 1,500 soldiers to engage Fort Gaines on the night of 4/5 August. At 5:30 A.M., a floodtide helped propel eighteen Union ships along a west-east course toward Fort Morgan. The first rank of four turreted monitors could fire head-on; then seven warships could fire broadside at the fort as they steered sharply to port into the bay. Lashed to the port side of each warship was a smaller gunboat with guns trained west on Fort Gaines.

Tecumseh, the lead U.S. monitor, hit a mine and sank while steaming toward the Tennessee. The lead ship Brooklin deployed nets to sweep for floating mines (then called "torpedoes"), but her commander hesitated, prompting Farragut to order his flagship Hartford forward with his legendary "Damn the torpedoes! Full speed ahead!"

By 10. A.M., the Union force had captured the Tennessee and routed the wooden defenders. Farragut's effort sealed off the port, and the naval victory, together with Gen. William Tecumseh *Sherman's capturing of Atlanta a week later, contributed to the reelection of President Abraham *Lincoln.

[See also Civil War: Military and Diplomatic Course; Confederate Navy; Mines, Naval; New Orleans, Siege of (1862); Union Navy.]

• Emory M. Thomas, "'Damn the Topedoes': The Battle of Mobile Bay," Civil War Times Illustrated, vol. 16, no. 1 (1977), pp. 5–9; Ivan Musicant, Divided Waters: The Naval History of the Civil War, 1995.
—Maxine T. Turner

MOBILIZATION is the process of assembling and organizing troops, materiel, and equipment for active military service in time of war or national emergency. As such, it brings together the military and civilian sectors of society to harness the total power of the nation. It is the mechanism that facilitates the successful prosecution of any conflict.

The modern process of preparing armies for war originated in the mid-nineteenth century. Inherent in the modern usage of the term is the concept of a large national force, as opposed to the smaller professional forces of earlier times—armies that depended upon a warrior class maintained in almost perpetual readiness. As they developed generally, and in response to the Napoleonic Wars, European nations shifted to marshaling the entire nation-state for war, and building large national armies. The term *mobilization* was first used in the 1850s to describe the preparation of the Prussian Army for deployment. Since then, it has become commonplace for governments, or states, to raise *volunteers and employ *conscription to create mass forces. Mobilization of the state harnesses the national economy to the military machine in order to conduct war.

For the United States, the *Civil War brought the draft, mass armies, and massive economic changes. With full public support, both Northern and Southern governments raised volunteers, and within a year or two turned to conscription to help field national armies. Both governments tied their militaries to their respective economic bases to sustain the war effort for a prolonged period.

In the years following, America industrialized, expanding markets and interests beyond its own borders. International presence and wartime experience in Cuba and the Philippines kept military issues at the forefront of American policy. Although the armed forces were maintained at a relatively low level, reorganization in 1903 brought a General Staff to oversee the U.S. *Army; planning and mobilization became regular missions.

In May 1917, President Woodrow *Wilson approved the Selective Service System, which remained an instrument for raising armies in war and the *Cold War until 1973. That solved the problem of recruiting and maintaining large national armies, but did not address the other half of the mobilization process. Producing equipment, supplies, and facilities turned out to be a far greater challenge. By sheer economic strength, at the end of World War I, the United States had built an army over 3.5 million strong with equally huge equipment surpluses.

The United States took some lessons from the staging and conducting of World War I. The warmaking had been so massive that an effort was made to standardize at least some of the procedures. The National Defense Act of June 1920 gave the assistant secretary of war responsibility for planning for industrial mobilization and for procurement through the War Department. Planning was done in the War Plans Division of the General Staff. Two initiatives were significant. One was the establishment of the Joint Army and Navy Munitions Board in 1922, which brought the two services together to formulate joint *strategy. The second was the creation of the Army Industrial College, which gave officers the opportunity to examine mobilization. Plans and studies followed. In these, availability of supplies and equipment determined the rate at which troops could be absorbed. However, they assumed that production would adjust to strategic plans—expanding and contracting as necessary—and that only one mobilization plan would cover a variety of possible contingencies. Gradual changes in preparedness or a measured transition to a mobilized state did not exist. Manpower and materiel were considered separately.

By the end of the 1930s, plans went beyond the role of the army to examine how the nation should organize the control of industry in war. In 1936, the War Resources Administration was designated responsible for control of wartime finance, trade, labor, and price control. By 1939, industrial mobilization plans stipulated that the War Resources Administration be established as soon as it became practical to do so. Economic mobilization was no longer tied to the outbreak of hostilities.

The army began developing defensive plans in the mid-1930s, addressing the size and composition of an initial defense force and its support. They sought to mesh production schedules and to bring together rates of troop and materiel mobilization. They also provided for a small, well-equipped emergency force to ensure security during general mobilization. That was sound enough to become the permanent basis for mobilization. The plans provided for detailed unit and individual training programs, as well as manuals and associated training materials. They established a system for mobilizing men and equipment already available.

The United States began mobilizing for World War II by the end of 1939, despite the American public's alienation from military participation in world affairs. The depression had produced much idle and obsolete industrial capacity. The Roosevelt administration encouraged private expansion of facilities for war production through accelerated depreciation and government financing. Lend-Lease also helped stimulate production. Mobilization sped up in 1941, expanded dramatically in 1942, and peaked in 1943.

Although the United States has historically relied on mobilization to meet its wartime needs, with the start of the Cold War it began to maintain higher levels of military forces in peacetime and to deploy them in close proximity to potential enemies. American strategy assumed a short warning time to respond to its major threat, the Soviet Union. The ebb and flow of the Cold War was such that public consensus allowed the military to maintain a large active force in high state of readiness, with sizable stocks of supplies for *logistics support.

The *National Security Act of 1947 instituted governmentwide planning by establishing the organizational machinery to implement mobilization and deployment strategy. Management structures include the Department of *Defense (DoD), the Office of the Secretary of Defense, the Office of the *Joint Chiefs of Staff (JCS), and the Federal Emergency Management Agency. The nation's commitment to readiness, in great part, was enabled by the Defense Production Act of 1950, which has since been extended or amended over forty times.

Success in mobilization depends upon the health of the national industrial base, the availability of manpower, the state of international trade, and the condition of the nation's foreign relations. In time of war or urgent national need, it is assumed that the marketplace will provide adequate industrial capacity.

Historically, the National Guard and Organized reserves have been the assets that supported national defense. Currently, America's reserve forces consist of two National Guard components, the army and air guard; and five reserve components, the army, navy, air force, Marine Corps, and Coast Guard Reserves. The Guard and organized reserves form the basis for expanding the active component in a military emergency. The National Guard and reserves are similar in that during wartime both are federal forces serving under the president. During peacetime, however, while the reserve is a federal force subordinate to the president, the Guard remains subordinate to the governor of each state, unless federalized by the president.

Mobilization levels depend upon the existence of

forward bases, the level of industrial infrastructure, prepositioned equipment, industrial preparedness, preparedness planning, and public and congressional support. Ideally, high levels of any or all of those factors ease the entire process. Naturally, all are influenced by perceived threat. Generally, the higher the level of perceived threat, the higher the corresponding levels of support.

There are currently five levels of mobilization, governed by Title 10 of the U.S. code: selective, presidential selected reserve call-up, partial, full, and total. These levels are not necessarily sequential. One level may precede another, but may not; they need not build upon one another. Certain policies and programs that immediately increase unit resources and readiness are available only when the president and Congress mobilize the reserve components of the armed forces. Conscription supports the expanding force structure, as determined by Congress and the president, but is not tied to any level of mobilization.

Selective mobilization is the expansion of the active forces by activating units and individuals of the selected reserve to protect life, federal property, and functions, or to prevent disruption of federal activities. This includes the call-up of the National Guard, which can be done only for a specific purpose, such as the suppression of insurrection or conspiracy, prevention of unlawful obstructions or rebellions or abridgments of civil rights, to repel an invasion, or to execute the laws under legal authorities.

Presidential selected reserve call-up gives the president authority to augment the active force with up to 200,000 members of the reserve component for up to 90 days, with an extension of a further 90 days. It does not require a declaration of national emergency, but does require a report to Congress within twenty-four hours.

Partial mobilization requires presidential or congressional declaration of national emergency. The total force level could be as high as 1 million members of all services for up to twenty-four months or less by presidential authority. If the presidential selected reserve call-up already is in effect, the levels are cumulative; the ceiling is 1 million. A partial mobilization allows all selected reserve units and individuals (individual ready reserve, standby, and retired reserve) to be ordered to active duty.

Full mobilization is the state that exists when all units in the current force structure are called to active duty, fully equipped, fully manned, and sustained. Assumptions are that presidential selected reserve call-up and partial mobilization have been completed and Congress has declared war or a state of national emergency. All reserve components are ordered to active duty for the duration of the war or emergency plus six months; industrial mobilization is initiated; allies are called on for support according to their treaty commitments.

Total mobilization is the expansion of the active armed force and the activation of additional units beyond the approved force structure. All additional resources, including production facilities, may be mobilized to support and sustain the active forces.

Overall, mobilization reflects American national and military history. As the nation has grown, physically and economically, so has its standing in the international community. Given the size of the armed forces today, their technological level and equipment requirements, and the diversity of threat and mission, the process of mobilization has become both more complex and more significant to the eventual success of the military force.

[*See also* Demobilization; Militia and National Guard; National Defense Acts; Reserve Forces Act; War Plans.]

• Jacques S. Gansler, *The Defense Industry*, 1980. Joint Chiefs of Staff, *Mobilization*, JCS no. 21, 1983. Robert L. Pfaltzgraff, Jr., and Uri Ra'anan, eds., *The U.S. Defense Mobilization Infrastructure*, 1983. Roderick L. Vawter, *Industrial Mobilization*, 1983. Hardy L. Merritt and Luther F. Carter, eds., *Mobilization and the National Defense*, 1985.
—Susan Canedy

MOFFETT, WILLIAM A. (1869–1933), U.S. naval officer, aviation pioneer. An 1890 graduate of the U.S. Naval Academy, Moffett saw action in the *Spanish-American War and the Veracruz expedition of 1914. He became director of naval aviation in March 1921 after successfully using small aircraft to spot the gunfire of the battleship *Mississippi*, which he commanded.

In July 1921 Moffett was appointed chief of the navy's newly created Bureau of Aeronautics, and served three successive terms in this position with the rank of rear admiral. He lobbied effectively for acceptance of aviation with the navy, in the halls of Congress, and in the public arena. Moffett's skills at low-keyed political maneuvering helped to counter naval aviation's most flamboyant critic, Gen. Billy *Mitchell of the Army Air Service. Moffett participated in the Washington and London naval arms limitation conferences (leading to their respective treaties); in 1922 he also qualified as a naval aviation observer.

Within the bureau and the fleet, Moffett concentrated on the development of patrol and scouting seaplanes and dirigibles, airplane technology and *logistics, *aircraft carriers, and naval air stations. His genius as manager and advocate led to success in virtually all categories—except airships. In 1933, he was aboard the navy dirigible *Akron* and died when it crashed into the sea during a storm, virtually ending the airship program. Moffett nevertheless had skillfully laid the foundations for the aviation-dominated navy that would emerge in World War II.

[*See also* Airborne Warfare; Navy, U.S.: 1899–1945; Navy Combat Branches: Naval Air Forces; Sea Warfare; Washington Naval Arms Limitation Treaty.]

• Clark G. Reynolds, "William A. Moffett: Steward of the Air Revolution," in James C. Bradford, ed., *Admirals of the New Steel Navy*, 1990. William F. Trimble, *Admiral William A. Moffett: Architect of Naval Aviation*, 1994.
—Clark G. Reynolds

MONMOUTH, BATTLE OF (1778). By the spring of 1778, George *Washington's ambition to make the *Continental army a force proficient in linear European tactics seemed—thanks largely to the efforts of Friedrich Wilhelm von *Steuben—to be near realization. When Henry *Clinton, the British commander in chief, abandoned Philadelphia and marched for New York City, Washington decided to force a battle in the open field. On 28 June 1778, he ordered a 5,000-man advance force under his second in command, Charles *Lee, to attack the British rear guard.

Lee found Clinton's force near Monmouth in the hills of northern New Jersey, about twenty miles from Sandy Hook where the Royal Navy waited to transport the army to New York. Clinton's 2,000-man rear guard initiated a piecemeal engagement into which he eventually fed 6,000 men of his 10,000-man army. As the clear summer day wore on in heat that may have reached 100 degrees Fahrenheit, the Americans proved their mettle in open battle. Yet, it was easier to train the soldiers how to fight than to find competent general officers to lead them. In blazing heat and broken terrain, Lee lost touch with the flow of the battle. When Washington arrived with the 6,000-man main army and found many American soldiers retreating, he severely reprimanded Lee, who was later court-martialed and removed from the army.

Washington's frustration was understandable. For the first—and what would turn out to be the only—time during the war, he thought he had the enemy at a disadvantage in a fight his army stood a chance of winning. He stabilized the American position, but Clinton won the larger contest. On the night of the 28th, the British army slipped away from the battlefield, and guarding its 1,500-wagon supply train, reached Sandy Hook on the 30th. Monmouth, the longest continuous battle of the war, settled nothing, but displayed the growing ability and professionalism of the Continental army.

[See also Revolutionary War: Military and Diplomatic Course.]

• Christopher Ward, *The War of the Revolution*, 1952. Samuel S. Smith, *The Battle of Monmouth*, 1964.   —Harold E. Selesky

MONROE, JAMES (1758–1831), senator, diplomat, secretary of state, secretary of war, and fifth president of the United States. While at William and Mary in 1776, Monroe was commissioned an infantry lieutenant in the 3rd Virginia Regiment. He subsequently rose to lieutenant colonel, serving with the *Continental army in the battles of Long Island, New York; Trenton (where he was severely wounded); Brandywine; and the Battle of *Monmouth.

In 1782, Monroe entered the Virginia House of Delegates; later he held positions in the Continental Congress (1783–86) and U.S. Senate (1790–93), and as governor of Virginia (1799–1802 and 1811). In 1793–96, he was U.S. minister to France, returning there in 1803 to help negotiate the Louisiana Purchase. Thereafter he served as minister in London and Madrid until 1807.

Monroe became secretary of state and a leading advocate for the diplomatic and military policies of James *Madison's administration in 1811. As acting secretary of war during the winter of 1812–13 and secretary of war, October 1814–March 1815, he shaped U.S. manpower policies during the *War of 1812.

Monroe's presidency (1817–25) contributed significantly to national defense and security. The 1819 *Adams-Onís Treaty (or Transcontinental Treaty) acquired the Floridas, established clear boundaries for the Louisiana Purchase, and extended U.S. territory to the Pacific. His annual message of 1823, subsequently known as the *Monroe Doctrine, laid the foundation for U.S. diplomatic hegemony in the Americas. His administrations improved the efficiency of the army and began the professionalization of its officer corps. In 1825, Monroe retired to New York City; he died on 4 July 1831.

[See also Army, U.S.: 1783–1865; Commander in Chief, President as; Revolutionary War: Military and Diplomatic Course.]

• William P. Cresson, *James Monroe*, 1946. Harry Ammon, *James Monroe: The Quest for National Identity*, 1971.

—J. C. A. Stagg

MONROE DOCTRINE. In his message of 2 December 1823, President James *Monroe articulated two principles that by the 1850s were regarded as the basis for the so-called Monroe Doctrine. The first stipulated that the "American Continents, by the free and independent condition which they have assumed and maintain, are henceforth not to be considered as subjects for future colonization by any European Power." The second embodied Monroe's support for the newly independent Latin American republics by stating that the American and European political systems were "essentially different," and that the United States would consider efforts by European nations "to extend their system to any portion of this hemisphere as dangerous to our peace and safety."

James K. *Polk, in the 1840s, was the first president to invoke Monroe's message as a form of policy justification, but his conduct did not immediately set a precedent. For much of the nineteenth century the Monroe Doctrine was ignored or violated far more than it was observed. U.S. acquiescence in such developments as the British occupation of the Falkland Islands (1833), British activities in the Central American isthmus throughout the 1850s, Spain's reannexation of Santo Domingo in 1861, and France's installation of a Bourbon monarch in Mexico in the 1860s were hardly in accord with the principles of 1823.

In the last quarter of the nineteenth century, in response to rising concerns about European *imperialism coupled with a more assertive sense of American *nationalism, the United States began to invoke the Monroe Doctrine more consistently. This was particularly so in 1895, when the Cleveland administration insisted, successfully, that Great Britain submit to arbitration a long-standing boundary dispute between Venezuela and British Guiana. On that occasion Secretary of State Richard Olney formulated the first major corollary to the 1823 message by asserting that "the United States is practically sovereign on this continent, and its fiat is law upon the subjects to which it confines its interposition."

After the turn of the century, the United States redefined the Monroe Doctrine in ways that were also intended to justify greater U.S. activity in the Americas. In 1904, President Theodore *Roosevelt, anxious that financial malfeasance in the nations of Central America and the Caribbean might provoke intervention by European creditor nations, announced a second major corollary to the Monroe Doctrine to the effect that no American nation could use the doctrine "as a shield to protect it from the consequences of its own misdeeds against foreign nations." In effect, this required the United States to intervene in the affairs of other American nations. Acting on this basis, the United States took over the management of the finances of the Dominican Republic (in 1907) and of Nicaragua (in 1911), and in 1915 it actually occupied the republic of Haiti.

The assumptions behind the "Roosevelt corollary," although repudiated in the 1930s in favor of Franklin D. *Roosevelt's "Good Neighbor" policy, continued to influence U.S. policy in the Americas through the 1980s. Beginning with Woodrow *Wilson, U.S. presidents have sought to reconcile the regional principles of the doctrine with the increasingly global reach of their foreign policies. Worried about aggression from Nazi Germany, Franklin Roosevelt even expanded the doctrine to include both Canada and Greenland.

In the early years of the *Cold War after 1945, the United States internationalized the democratic and noninterventionist principles of the Monroe Doctrine in the *Truman Doctrine of 1947, while at the same time it preserved its regional hegemony in the Americas through the framework of the Rio Pact (1947) and the Organization of American States (1948). The concern to keep communism out of the Americas subsequently led to U.S. intervention in various forms in Guatemala (1954), Cuba (1961), the Dominican Republic (1965), Chile (1973), and Grenada (1983), as well as to active involvement in the insurgencies in El Salvador and Nicaragua in the 1980s. In each case the United States either overthrew, or attempted to overthrow, left-wing regimes in order to replace them with dictatorial governments whose members supported U.S. priorities. Critics argued that these repressive governments violated the principles that Monroe had proclaimed in 1823.

The most serious crisis of the Monroe Doctrine occurred in Communist Cuba in 1962. As early as 1960, Soviet premier Nikita Khrushchev openly proclaimed that the Monroe Doctrine was dead. Two years later, Khrushchev installed intermediate-range *missiles on the island to protect Fidel Castro's regime. Throughout the ensuing *Cuban Missile Crisis, which was eventually resolved by the removal of the missiles, President John F. *Kennedy did not invoke the Monroe Doctrine in defense of his actions, but concern for its traditions was never far from his mind.

With the end of the Cold War in 1991 and the disappearance of any regional threats to the security of the United States in the western hemisphere, the Monroe Doctrine might be fairly regarded as moribund, if not entirely dead. The doctrine was never accepted as valid international law by any European nation, and it would be inaccurate to say that it saved Latin America from any form of recolonization. Nor did the doctrine ever receive much support in Latin America; indeed, to the extent that the United States invoked it in the twentieth century, it became increasingly unpopular there as a symbol of an overbearing Yankee supremacy. The true significance of the Monroe Doctrine, however, has always depended on circumstances.

[See also Caribbean and Latin America, U.S. Military Involvement in the; Dominican Republic, U.S. Military Involvement in the; El Salvador, U.S. Military Involvement in; Nicaragua, U.S. Military Involvement in.]

• Dexter Perkins, A History of the Monroe Doctrine, 1941; rev. ed. 1955. Gaddis Smith, The Last Years of the Monroe Doctrine 1945–1993, 1994.
—J. C. A. Stagg

MONTGOMERY, BERNARD LAW (1887–1976). British field marshal. One of the best-known and controversial commanders of World War II, Montgomery—or Monty as he was better known—commanded Allied armies in two of the decisive battles of the war, El Alamein and Normandy. A Sandhurst graduate, he entered the British army in 1908, and served with distinction in World War I. Between the wars Montgomery was among the few army officers who grasped the need for new ideas, new equipment and new techniques. He was an unorthodox individualist.

In August 1942, with the legendary Gen. Erwin *Rommel almost at the gates of Cairo and the oil fields of the Middle East, the almost unknown Montgomery took command of the British Eighth Army and defeated the Axis forces at the Battle of El Alamein, the foundation of Monty's fame, October 23-November 4, 1942.

A small, wiry man with hawk-like features, a neatly-trimmed moustache, and a jaunty black beret, he was boastful and blunt. Critics have called him an egomaniac, overrated, and worse. His "finest hour" came both before and during the invasion of *Normandy in which he commanded all Allied ground forces from June to August 1944. He became the lightning rod for criticism when temporary stalemate followed *D-Day. Relations with Supreme Allied Commander Gen. Dwight D. *Eisenhower soured; exuding infallibility, Montgomery was his own worst enemy, and the myth took root that he had failed in Normandy. In practice, his generalship displayed far greater flexibility than he ever acknowledged. Original intention or not, Montgomery succeeded in keeping German armored divisions tied down on the British and Canadian front, thus assisting the American breakout on the right flank in July.

Differences continued to mar Monty's relationship with Ike following the Allied victory in Normandy, with the newly created field marshal advocating a single, concentrated blow to end the war in 1944, and the Supreme Commander's decision to adopt a broad-broad strategy. In September 1944, Montgomery launched Operation Market-Garden, the largest airborne and glider operation in history. The attempt to seize a bridgehead over the Rhine at Arnhem failed.

In the Battle of the *Bulge, Eisenhower placed all American troops north of the German thrust under Montgomery's command, a courageous decision that was contrary to the advice of Gen. Omar N. *Bradley. Fighting desperately to stop the German counteroffensive, subordinate American commanders welcomed Montgomery's arrival. At a press conference after the battle, Monty praised the fighting qualities of the American soldier, but left the impression he had saved the American high command from disaster. He noted in his Memoirs, "I should have held my tongue." Britain hailed Montgomery as another Wellington and he was made viscount of Alamein in 1946. He served as deputy commander of *NATO forces, 1951–58.

[See also France, Liberation of; Germany, Battle for; Italy, Invasion and Conquest of; Sicily, Invasion of; World War II: Military and Diplomatic Course.]

• Nigel Hamilton, Monty, 3 vols., 1981–86. Carlo D'Este, Decision in Normandy, 1983. Richard Overy, Why The Allies Won, 1996.
—Colin F. Baxter

MOORER, THOMAS (1912–), *Cold War U.S. naval leader; chairman of the *Joint Chiefs of Staff (JCS), 1970–74. A blunt but affable Alabaman, Moorer was a graduate of the U.S. Naval Academy and saw combat as a naval aviator early in World War II and participated in the postwar Strategic Bombing Survey. Later he commanded the Pacific Fleet (during the Tonkin Gulf incident and the air campaign over Vietnam), and the Atlantic Fleet (during the Dominican Republic intervention). Moorer served as *NATO's Atlantic commander (during France's pullout from NATO commands) and commander in chief of the U.S. unified Atlantic Command. Chief of Naval Operations in 1967, his term saw intensive operations in the *Vietnam War, the *Pueblo incident in Korea (1968), increased public antipathy toward the military, Soviet challenges to U.S. naval dominance, and decline of U.S. naval strength.

As chairman of the JCS (1970–74), Moorer served President Nixon and defense secretaries Laird, Richardson, and

Schlesinger. Bombing and mining campaigns against North Vietnam (which he championed), "Vietnamization," strategic arms limitation talks, conventional force cuts, the end of *Conscription, and two Middle East crises highlighted his term.

Following retirement, Moorer remained active in research and industry, notably as senior adviser at the Center for Strategic and International Studies.

[See also Dominican Republic, U.S. Military Involvement in; Middle East, U.S. Military Involvement in the; Navy, U.S.: Since 1946, SALT Treaties.]

• J. Kenneth McDonald, "Thomas Hinman Moorer," in Robert William Love, Jr., ed., The Chiefs of Naval Operations, 1980. Willard J. Webb and Ronald H. Cole, The Chairmen of the Joint Chiefs of Staff, 1989.
                                                        —Peter M. Swartz

MORALE, TROOP. Morale, generally defined, is a state of mind that either encourages or impedes action. The greatest combat commanders have always understood that morale reflects the mental, moral, and physical condition of their troops. These conditions, in turn, directly relate to the troops' courage, confidence, discipline, enthusiasm, and willingness to endure the sacrifices and hardships of military duty. Troops with high morale can operate, even succeed against high odds, in all kinds of conditions. Poor morale can lead to failure, even when odds favor victory. At a basic level, good morale allows soldiers to overcome fear.

Troop morale has been studied since ancient times, and early modern military leaders like Frederick the Great understood such notions thoroughly; defeat, he observed, resulted more from discouragement than *casualties. Napoleon's famous aphorism, "in war the moral is to the physical as three is to one," brings into focus the pivotal importance of troop morale, and he frequently tried to motivate his troops by rewards, medals, or promotion. His views, along with those of the other "great captains," underscore the complex relationship between morale and success in combat.

Prior to the twentieth century, commanders attentive to their soldiers' morale mainly attended to their physical well-being. As long as an army was reasonably well fed, had adequate clothing and shelter, and could expect to be paid more or less regularly, its morale might be considered adequate to the task at hand. Belief in a "cause" was thought less important than strong affection for a leader, or the promise of glory or loot. During eras when armies faced each other across open fields, the outcome of battles often hung on the state of morale. An intuitive desire for safety or instinct for survival could lead soldiers to abandon their duty and dissolve into rabble, while those suddenly inspired might snatch victory from defeat.

Modern notions of troop morale arose out of the horrific casualties generated by the *trench warfare of World War I. Some military historians suggest that stress-related casualties were almost unknown earlier. Evolution of *weapons technology, mass armies, and General Staff leadership increased the scale and magnified the intensity of warfare, levying terrific burdens on a soldier's mental fitness. Accordingly, troop morale attracted the detailed attention of military and medical authorities. In general terms, researchers understood that men subjected to severe combat conditions for prolonged periods would have to be relieved at regular intervals. Men unable to continue in combat were either deemed cowards or thought to be victims of a debilitating physical condition, "shell shock."

Lord Charles Moran, a former World War I medical officer, wrote the first systematic explanation of troop morale. Anatomy of Courage, first published in 1945, postulated an explanation for troop morale and explained how it might be managed. Moran argued that courage had measurable limits and could be expended as easily as water can be poured from a beaker. Commanders had to determine how much bravery soldiers possessed and not allow them to exceed those limits without replenishment. Moran also believed courage was largely a function of a man's character. Cowards simply lacked moral strength.

Events of World War II only partially supported Moran's notions. By then, psychiatrists and psychologists had more fully investigated the components of morale, and come to recognize that all troops, not just the weak or morally flawed, were subject to the effects of unrelenting fear and anxiety. Only a sense of duty allowed men to overcome their fears; thus duty—devotion to a cause or to comrades—joined the traditional factors—food, clothing, training, discipline, and leadership—as a defining component of morale. Research conducted during the war, especially that of S. L. A. *Marshall, argued that troop morale rose and fell principally as a result of a shared sense of danger. According to Marshall's book, Men Against Fire, (1947), small group dynamics were more important to success in battle than any other factor.

Despite critics' charges of sloppiness and lack of genuine support data, Marshall's main point is hard to ignore. Subsequent research, carried out by experts like Samuel Stouffer, E. A. Shils, and Morris Janowitz, clearly demonstrated the connection between small unit cohesion, morale, and combat capability. By investigating the German army of the Nazi era, Shils and Janowitz showed that the Wehrmacht's ability to fight so effectively, and survive for so long, resulted partly from the German focus on group leadership, human dynamics, and troop morale. Later research by Trevor Dupuy and Martin van Creveld underscored these conclusions. Moreover, Dupuy argued that German effectiveness at the tactical and operational level exceeded that of its opponents. Even when in retreat or significantly outnumbered, the Wehrmacht managed more tactical victories and inflicted more casualties man-for-man than did its enemies.

It seems clear that troop morale in the post–*Cold War era will remain no less important than before in influencing the outcome of combat. Small professional armies, even when extraordinarily well led, trained, and disciplined, will nevertheless be subject to the same rigors as their ancestors; indeed, the exponential advances in military weapons technology, the increasing impact of artificial intelligence, and the exploitation of the electromagnetic spectrum will only increase the scope and lethality of battle, and magnify the pressure on combatants to survive and function effectively. It will also mandate the continued efforts of senior leadership and medical officers to understand and sustain morale, which is sure to remain crucial to measuring the critical interval between victory and defeat.

[See also Awards, Decorations, and Honors; Combat Effectiveness; Combat Trauma; Leadership, Concepts of Military; Leaves and Furloughs; Religion and the Military.]

• Lord Charles Moran, *Anatomy of Courage*, 1945; repr. 1987. S. L. A. Marshall, *Men Against Fire: The Problem of Battle Command in Future War*, 1947; repr. 1978. E. A. Shils and Morris Janowitz, "Cohesion and Disintegration in the Wehrmacht in World War II," *Public Opinion Quarterly*, 12 (1948), pp. 280–315. Samuel Stouffer, et al., *Studies in Social Psychology in World War Two*, 2 vols., 1949. J. Glenn Gray, *The Warriors: Reflections of Men in Battle*, 1959. Trevor N. Dupuy, *A Genius for War: The German Army and General Staff, 1807–1945, 1977*. F. M. Richardson, *Fighting Spirit: Psychological Factors in War*, 1978. Martin van Creveld, *Fighting Power: German and U.S. Army Performance, 1939–1945*, 1983. Richard Holmes, *Acts of War: The Behavior of Men in Battle*, 1985.

—Mark K. Wells

MORGAN, DANIEL (c. 1735–1802), Revolutionary War general and Federalist Party leader. The son of Welsh farmers, Morgan grew up along the Pennsylvania–New Jersey border before settling in the Virginia backcountry in the 1750s. A teamster with the Braddock expedition, he then became a provincial ranger. Later he fought the Shawnee in Lord Dunmore's War. Given to brawling and drinking, he settled down, taking a common-law wife and fathering two daughters.

At the outbreak of the Revolutionary War, Morgan received command of a rifle company raised by the Continental Congress and performed heroically in Benedict *Arnold's ill-fated Québec expedition. An authority on guerrilla tactics, Morgan commanded a ranger regiment that helped defeat Gen. John *Burgoyne in the Battles of *Saratoga (1777). After serving under George *Washington in the Middle States in 1778–79, Morgan transferred to the American Southern Army. In January 1781, at the Battle of *Cowpens in South Carolina, his forces destroyed Banastre Tarleton's Tory Legion; Morgan's double envelopment was the tactical masterpiece of the war. Becoming ill, he returned home, but not before providing Gen. Nathanael *Greene with a useful battle plan against Cornwallis at the Battle of *Guilford Courthouse (1781).

After the war, Morgan headed part of the militia army that put down the *Whiskey Rebellion in 1794–95; he served a single term (1797–99) as a Federalist in the House of Representatives.

[*See also* Braddock's Defeat; Revolutionary War: Military and Diplomatic Course.]

• Don Higginbotham, *Daniel Morgan: Revolutionary Rifleman*, 1961.

—Don Higginbotham

MORGENTHAU, HENRY, JR. (1891–1967), secretary of the treasury, 1934–45. This former Dutchess County gentleman farmer and member of a prominent New York German Jewish family was a close personal friend and political confidant of President Franklin D. *Roosevelt. Morgenthau was an important figure in the Roosevelt administration.

Responsible for U.S. financing of World War II, Morgenthau, as head of the Treasury Department, advocated relying on increases in the income tax to dampen inflationary pressures while raising revenue. Although he prevented a regressive national sales tax advocated by conservatives, Morgenthau faced a series of defeats in Congress over fiscal policies, especially on the income tax. He did, however, organize several highly publicized bond drives.

When the Roosevelt administration, especially the State Department, proved unresponsive to reports of systematic extermination of European Jewry by the Nazi regime of Adolf *Hitler in 1940–43, Morgenthau and the Treasury Department proved to be one of the few federal agencies pressing for the United States to take decisive action against the Holocaust. On 16 January 1944, Morgenthau directly confronted Roosevelt with evidence of the Holocaust as well as the reluctance of the State Department to provide visas to Jewish refugees or facilitate rescue efforts by Jewish organizations in Europe. Shortly after this meeting, Roosevelt established the U.S. War Refugee Board by executive order. This body, with Morgenthau an active member, undertook a series of relief efforts, albeit limited, to aid Jewish refugees.

In 1944, Morgenthau—over the objections of the State and War Departments—forcefully advocated a harsh peace settlement. His plan called for stripping Germany of all heavy industry and partitioning the country into a series of demilitarized agricultural states. Attending the Quebec Conference in September 1944, Morgenthau prodded Roosevelt and Prime Minister Winston S. *Churchill to initial a memorandum of agreement supporting his plan. This was later reversed by Roosevelt and his successor, Harry S. *Truman, after intense lobbying by the State and War Departments, which denounced the plan as both unrealistic and detrimental to U.S. interests, given the need for a European counterweight to the expanded power of the Soviet Union.

Morgenthau proved more successful in shaping the postwar international monetary system. Relying heavily on expertise of Assistant Secretary of the Treasury Harry Dexter White, Morgenthau organized the Bretton Woods Conference of June–July 1944, which established the International Monetary Fund (IMF) and the International Bank for Reconstruction and Development.

Shortly after Truman assumed the presidency in April 1945, Morgenthau resigned as Treasury secretary. In retirement, he became an ardent supporter of the state of Israel and active in a number of Jewish philanthropic causes.

[*See also* Holocaust, U.S. War Effort and the; Public Financing and Budgeting for War; World War II: Domestic Course.]

• John Morton Blum, *From the Morgenthau Diaries*, 3 vols., 1959–67, David S. Wyman, *The Abandonment of the Jews: America and the Holocaust, 1941–1945*, 1984. Henry Morgenthau III, *Mostly Morgenthaus: A Family History*, 1991.

—G. Kurt Piehler

MORMON "WAR" (1857–58). Federal administrators assigned in the 1850s to Utah Territory, after it had been acquired from Mexico in 1848, frequently complained of harassment and abuse at the hands of the Latter-day Saints (Mormons). Some contended the Mormons were essentially in a state of rebellion against the United States. By 1857, the cry for a settlement of the "Mormon Question" reached critical proportions. President James Buchanan appointed Alfred Cumming of Georgia, a non-Mormon, to replace Mormon leader Brigham Young as governor of Utah. Expecting the Mormons to resist, Buchanan ordered an expeditionary force of 2,500 soldiers to the territory. Under the command of Gen. William S. Harney, the 5th Infantry Regiment, elements of the 10th Regiment, the 2nd Dragoons, and two *artillery batteries marched from Fort Leavenworth, Kansas, on 18 July 1857, hoping to occupy

Utah by fall. Gen. Albert Sidney Johnston succeeded Harney as commander of the expedition, 11 September.

Viewing the army as a hostile invasion force, Governor Young mobilized the Utah Militia and began preparations for a guerrilla war. Although the campaign—the so-called Mormon War—was bloodless, Mormon militiamen were successful in impeding the progress of U.S. forces, which were forced into winter encampment near Fort Bridger in the fall of 1857.

Peace commissioners authorized by President Buchanan arrived in Utah in June 1858, and a settlement was reached. Young resigned as governor; the Mormons were pardoned for acts of rebellion; and U.S. forces established Camp Floyd (later Fort Crittenden) forty miles southwest of Salt Lake City. The camp was abandoned in 1861 with the outbreak of the *Civil War.
[See also Army, U.S.: 1783–1865.]

• Norman F. Furniss, The Mormon Conflict, 1850–1859, 1960. Clifford L. Stott, Search for Sanctuary, Brigham Young and the White Mountain Expedition, 1984.   —Clifford L. Stott

MORRIS, ROBERT (1734–1806), signer of the Declaration of Independence, Articles of Confederation, and U.S. Constitution; "financier of the Revolution." Born in Liverpool, Morris came to America in 1747. As active partner of the trading firm of Willing, Morris & Co. of Philadelphia, Morris integrated his European and West Indian commercial network into the *Revolutionary War effort in 1775.

A shrewd entrepreneur and energetic administrator, Morris became vice president of Pennsylvania's revolutionary governing body, the Council of Safety, in 1775, and organized the state's defenses. After election to the Second Continental Congress in November 1775, he became chairman of the Secret Committee of Trade and managed international procurement and naval affairs. He also participated in supply contracts and often disguised public ventures as private ones to facilitate secrecy and economy. The potential conflict of interest produced much controversy.

Morris retired from Congress in 1778, becoming an agent for supplying French forces in the United States and greatly augmenting his wealth and credit. When Congress was faced with financial and military collapse in 1781, it turned to Morris, by now the most prominent merchant in America, for help. As superintendent of finance, from February 1781 to November 1784, he raised money and supplies for the Yorktown campaign, then struggled to reestablish public credit by measures that included controlling the budget, founding the nation's first bank, settling the public debt, advocating a funding plan and mint, administering foreign loans, and replacing staff departments with military contracts. His administrative and financial skills are considered to have been indispensable to military success in the Revolutionary War.
[See also Revolutionary War: Domestic Course.]

• Clarence L. Ver Steeg, Robert Morris, Revolutionary Financier, 1954; repr. 1972. E. James Ferguson, et al., eds., The Papers of Robert Morris, 1781–1784, 9 vols., 1973–99.   —Elizabeth Nuxoll

MORTARS. The mortar is a very simple piece of *artillery, essentially a firing tube, that fires a high arc and imparts its main recoil force directly into the ground through a base plate. The lack of a recoil system distinguishes this weapon from other pieces of artillery. Dating back to at least the fifteenth century, mortars became most common in World War I. With opposing forces dug in at close ranges, a simple weapon capable of high-angle fire was needed to drop rounds in the enemies' trenches. In Britain in 1915, Sir Wilfred Stokes produced the prototype that has become the world's standard, consisting of a tube with a fixed firing pin at the breech attached to a base plate and supported at the muzzle end by a bipod. It can be adjusted in both azimuth and elevation by a screw mechanism. To fire the weapon a projectile containing the propellant and explosive is dropped into the muzzle.

After World War I, mortars passed into the hands of infantry units, while very heavy pieces remained with the artillery. The U.S. Army classifies mortars as light (60mm), medium (81mm), and heavy (120mm and above). All light and medium mortars are carried by infantrymen. They are inexpensive and easy to maintain, and can achieve a very high rate of fire. An 81mm mortar platoon can fire 196 rounds in a minute—a far greater weight of ammunition on a target than can be achieved by a field artillery battery, but one that can only be sustained over a short period of time. Concealment is easy and fire control is straightforward. With the advent of global satellite positioning systems, accuracy has been improved. The high-angle fire associated with this weapon allows it to engage targets concealed behind cover.
[See also Weaponry, Army; World War I: Military and Diplomatic Course.]

• The Diagram Group, Weapons: An International Encyclopedia from 5000 B.C. to 2000 A.D., 1990. Timothy M. Laur and Steven L. Llanso, Encyclopedia of Modern U.S. Weapons, 1995.
                                              —William F. Atwater

MOURNING WARS. See Native American Wars: Warfare in Native-American Societies; Native American Wars: Wars among Native Americans.

MURPHY, AUDIE (1924–1971), World War II war hero. Audie Murphy was the most highly decorated American soldier of World War II. Diminutive, self-reliant, and ambitious to escape his hardscrabble Texas origins, Murphy joined the army in 1942 at the age of seventeen. He soon proved himself more than equal to the demands of combat soldiering, fighting his way unwounded through Sicily and Italy. By 1944, Murphy had won several medals and the offer of a battlefield commission, which at first he refused.

During the invasion of southern France in June 1944, Sergeant Murphy won the Distinguished Service Cross for destroying several enemy *machine guns in the course of a few minutes' action. Wounded a few weeks later, Murphy returned to combat as a lieutenant and resumed his near-suicidal habits. These habits were in evidence in January 1945, when virtually alone he wrecked a German counterattack by 6 *tanks and 250 infantrymen in the Colmar Pocket. For this action he won the Congressional Medal of Honor.

Murphy returned to America and genuine celebrity in the summer of 1945, when his photo appeared on the cover of Life magazine. A successful postwar acting career in films kept him in the public eye. With a friend's help, Murphy wrote a best-selling memoir, To Hell and Back, and starred in the motion picture version (1955) as well.

Murphy's star faded by the 1960s. He was attempting to retrieve his fortunes when he died in a plane crash in 1971.

[*See also* Awards, Decorations, and Honors; France, Liberation of; Germany; Italy, Invasion of; Sicily, Invasion of; World War II: Military and Diplomatic Course.]

• Harold Simpson, *Audie Murphy: American Hero*, 1982. Don Graham, *No Name on the Bullet: A Biography of Audie Murphy*, 1990.

—Roger Spiller

MUSEUMS, MILITARY HISTORY. The essential mission of military museums in the United States remains teaching through the study and interpretation of historical artifacts, first exemplified at America's oldest armed forces museum, the Musée d'Artillerie (1843) at West Point. Unlike centralized war museums found in many European capitals, American military museums and sites are located throughout the nation, frequently at battlefields, seaports, forts, or *military bases that provide added ambiance. Scores of specialized facilities in the U.S. Army, Navy, Air Force, Marine Corps, and Coast Guard museum systems serve primarily for the instruction and inspiration of military personnel. Yet, like many nonservice museums—including those of the National Park Service, Smithsonian Institution, state governments, and private associations—service museums possess a widespread public constituency, at whose care is the *veterans' community.

Reflecting broader historical perspective, American military museums currently build collections documenting both military material and the experience of all ranks in the services, envisioned in relation to national social, political, and economic development. Exhibit policies are founded upon major collections of militaria that emerged during the nineteenth century, beginning with ranks of British field guns, surrendered at the Battles of *Saratoga in 1777, that provided the initial artifactual core at West Point. Under Congressional authorization (1814), trophy flags taken during the *War of 1812, *Mexican War, and *Civil War were deposited at West Point and the Naval Academy Lyceum (1845) at Annapolis, Maryland. Construction of the nation's first system of coastal *fortifications (1815–53), the founding of armories at Springfield (1794) and Harpers Ferry (1796), and establishment of arsenals at Watervliet (1813) and Rock Island (1862) provided an enduring material heritage, presently evoked in museums at Springfield, Harpers Ferry, Rock Island, Fort McHenry, Fort Monroe, Fort Adams, and Fort Point. The Quartermaster Corps Collection, begun in 1832 at Schuylkill Arsenal, Philadelphia, provided the basis for the army's extensive collections of *uniforms, transferred in 1919 to the Smithsonian Institution. That congressionally mandated institution, whose first scientific collections were provided by the U.S. Exploring (Wilkes) Expedition of (1838–42), would emerge after World War I as a major repository of American army *weaponry and biographical militaria, ultimately exhibited in the National Museum of American History (1961).

The Centennial of the American Revolution (1876) provided powerful impetus for establishment of national battlefield parks from that war and the *Civil War, many eventually including museums with particularly evocative appeal—notably at Saratoga, Yorktown, Gettysburg, Chickamauga, and Vicksburg. The advent of the modern steel navy, heralded at the Columbian Exposition in 1893, launched the navy's renowned warship model program, whose technical apogee was attained in the detailed models of *battleship models constructed during World War II. Consisting of some 1,900 models, this collection is generously represented at the Naval Academy Museum at Annapolis, Maryland, the Navy Museum at Washington Navy Yard in Washington, D.C., and the Smithsonian's National Museum of American History. Notwithstanding congressional proposals (1889) to establish a "national military and naval museum" in Washington, D.C., major efforts after two world wars for a national armed forces museum proved fruitless, most recently falling victim to antimilitary sentiment during the *Vietnam War. In an era of rogue terrorism, the wide dispersal of military museums curiously bodes well for survival of the nation's military heritage.

The Army Museum System, including forty-three accredited facilities in 1998, is located at West Point, New York, and at numerous training establishments in the South and Southwest, all of whose artifacts are recorded in the Center of Military History in Washington, D. C. Structured, like the maturely conceived West Point Museum, to serve an educational mission, the army's branch and service corps museums preserve and interpret specialized military collections. Notable branch museums range from the Ordnance Museum in Aberdeen, Maryland; the Medical Museum in Washington D.C.; the Infantry Museum at Fort Benning, Georgia; to the Special Warfare Museum at Fort Bragg North Carolina; the Cavalry Museum at Fort Riley, Kansas; and the Field Artillery Museum at Fort Sill, Oklahoma. Army service corps establishments include the Transportation Corps Museum at Fort Eustis, Army Women's Museum at Fort Lee, Virginia, and the Signal Corps Museum at Fort Gordon, Georgia. Among historic army posts, Fort Snelling at Minneapolis, Minnesota, and the Frontier Army Museum at Fort Leavenworth, Kansas, interpret the regular army's role in settlement of the West.

Similarly troop-oriented are the seven facilities of the Marine Corps Museum System, including the U.S. Marine Corps Museum at Washington Navy Yard, the Marine Air-Ground Museum at Quantico, Virginia, and the Parris Island Museum in South Carolina. The evolution of the oldest sea service is traced at the U.S. Coast Guard Museum at New London, Connecticut, and the Coast Guard Museum of the Northwest in Seattle, Washington. Evocative of America's role in the history of seapower are eleven elements of the Navy Museum System, particularly the Naval War College Museum at Newport, Rhode Island; the U.S. Navy Museum at Washington Navy Yard; Hampton Roads Museum at Norfolk, Virginia; and the Naval Academy Museum. The evolution of undersea warfare is recounted at the Submarine Force Museum at Groton, Connecticut, and the Naval Undersea Museum at Keyport. Necessarily more modern in orientation are the National Museum of Naval Aviation at Pensacola, Florida, and the Seabee Museum at Port Hueneme, Georgia. Monuments of American naval architecture are preserved in USS *Constitution* (still in commission) at Boston, Dewey's flagship *Olympia* at Philadelphia, and surviving World War II battleships, *aircraft carriers, *cruisers, *destroyers, and *submarines.

According to the Historic Naval Ships Association, in 1998 there were fifty-six historic military vessels from World War II on exhibit in the United States. These included forty-six U.S. warships, four armed merchant ships, and six Axis submarines (all midget subs except for the *U-505* at Chicago, Illinois). Of the U.S. warships, 15 were submarines. The rest included the battleships *Alabama* at Mobile, Alabama; *Arizona* and *Missouri* at Pearl Harbor, Hawaii; *North Carolina* at Wilmington, North Carolina; and *Texas* at LaPorte, Texas. In 1998, groups were still seeking to acquire and exhibit *Iowa, New Jersey,* and *Wisconsin.* Also on display were the aircraft carriers *Hornet* at Alameda, California; *Intrepid* at New York, New York; *Lexington* at Corpus Christi, Texas; and *Yorktown* at Mt. Pleasant, South Carolina (with a group seeking to acquire the *Midway* for San Diego, California). The Association includes World War II era warships on display abroad, notably the cruiser H.M.S. *Belfast* at London.

The development of American military aviation is emphasized in twenty-six installations of the U.S. Air Force Museum System, including the Air Force Armament Museum at Eglin AFB, Pensacola, Florida; the Air Force Space Museum at Cape Canaveral, Florida; and the extensive collection at the U.S. Air Force Museum, operated under the Air Force Logistics Command at Wright-Patterson Air Force Base near Dayton, Ohio. This is the oldest and largest aviation museum in the world, with more than 200 aircraft and large *missiles, as well as over 20,000 aircraft components, personal effects, and photographs. Also technically oriented, the Smithsonian's National Air and Space Museum includes vignettes of naval and military air service during the two world wars.

American military and naval history is explored in numerous private and state-owned museums, reflecting widespread public appreciation of the armed forces' role in national development. Notable examples include the Museum of the Confederacy at Richmond, Virginia; the War Memorial Museum and Mariners' Museum at Newport News, Virginia; the Liberty Memorial Museum in Kansas City; and the Wisconsin Veterans' Museum in Madison. Exceptional insight into World War II strategy is afforded at President Franklin D. *Roosevelt's estate at Hyde Park, New York; the Marshall Library and Museum at Lexington, Virginia; the MacArthur Memorial at Norfolk, Virginia; the Nimitz Historic Park at Fredericksburg, Virginia; and the Eisenhower Library and Museum in Abilene, Kansas.

Often highly popular not just with veterans and their families but with much of the general public, military museums in the United States perform important functions for the military and for the public, reminding them of the significant role the military has played in the nation's heritage.

[*See also* Academies, Service; Memorials, War.]

• James V. Murfin, *National Park Service Guide to the Historic Places of the American Revolution,* 1974. Richard E. Kuehne and Michael E. Moss, *The West Point Museum: A Guide to the Collections,* 1987. Bryce D. Thompson, *The U.S. Military Museums, Historic Sites, and Exhibits,* 1989. Joseph M. Stanford, ed., *Sea History's Guide to American and Canadian Maritime Museums,* 1990. R. Cody Phillips, *A Guide to U.S. Army Museums,* 1992. Philip K. Lundeberg, "Military Museums," in John E. Jessup, Jr., and Louise B. Ketz, eds., *Encyclopedia of the American Military,* 3 vols., 1994, Vol. III, pp. 2133–57.
                                                —Philip Karl Lundeberg

MUSIC, WAR AND THE MILITARY IN. From the earliest major American wars to the *Persian Gulf War, music has played an active role in wartime activities of both military and civilian populations. Soldiers wrote their own lyrics,

and occasionally even the songs themselves, which they sang and played to pass the time or while marching into war. Civilians at home wrote and sang popular songs to support or oppose the war effort, and composers wrote more involved instrumental or vocal works dealing with the subject of war, often long after a war was over. In this century as well, composers have created music to be part of films and television shows dealing with war. Music and war have clearly had a strong relationship in America since the mid-eighteenth century.

During the *Revolutionary War, several *Continental army regiments had small bands, but it was two decades after the war that Congress authorized a Marine band, in 1798. It consisted of thirty-two members, playing exclusively drums and fifes. Most active during the Revolutionary War were the soldiers who sang ballads and strophic songs, the majority of which were usually set to British tunes since there were few composers in America. For many of those songs the music has been lost; only the lyrics were published in papers at the time. But some of the music is known. The most popular songs during the war were "Yankee Doodle," "The Battle of the Kegs," and "Volunteer Boys." William Billings, the most significant American composer of this era, also wrote important songs dealing with the war, such as "Chester," "Lamentation Over Boston," "Retrospect," and "Victory."

Other genres appeared somewhat later, specifically battle pieces, which were popular in Europe and America in the late eighteenth and early nineteenth centuries. These battle pieces were sectionalized, programmatic keyboard works that attempted musically to reenact battle situations, and often incorporated national airs or military songs. One of the earliest American examples was James Hewitt's *Battle of Trenton,* written in 1792. Hewitt dedicated the piece to George Washington, composed a detailed program indicating how the general's army marched, crossed the Delaware, and defeated the Hessians, and included popular tunes such as "Yankee Doodle" and "Roslin Castle."

The relationship of music and war during the early nineteenth-century American wars was similar to that in the Revolution, chiefly patriotic songs and programmatic piano battle pieces. Benjamin Carr wrote one of the most difficult early pieces in his *Siege of Tripoli* (1801), concluding again with "Yankee Doodle." Other works glorified America's victories, such as Denis-Germain Etienne's *Battle of New Orleans* (1816), with a programmatic journey including "Hail Columbia" and "Yankee Doodle." The most important song to be written during the War of 1812 was certainly Francis Scott Key's poem "The Star-Spangled Banner" (1814), set to John Stafford Smith's song, "To Anacreon in Heaven." Not until 1931 did it become America's official national anthem.

Although war-related music in Europe changed during the mid-nineteenth century with more sincere forays into seriousness of purpose (particularly in the music of Franz Liszt, Giuseppi Verdi, and Pyotr Tchaikovsky), American music devoted to war remained limited in its focus and quality. However, these pianistic battle pieces and salon works for voice and piano remained popular during the Mexican War. In 1846 and 1847, Charles Grobe composed two piano works, *The Battle of Buena Vista* and *The Battle of Palo Alto and Resaca de la Palma,* dedicated respectively to Gen. Zachary *Taylor, "who never lost a battle," and to the men of the U.S. Army. In 1847, William Cumming composed a simple piano work, *Santa Anna's Retreat from Cerro Cordo*, in which the composer indicates at specific moments in the score how Antonio López de *Santa Anna lost his wooden leg and later his Mexican hat. The most popular war songs during this time were T. A. Durriage's "Remember the Alamo," sung to the tune of "Bruce's Address," and Park Benjamin's "To Arms."

The *Civil War was a turning point in song writing. America was sufficiently established to have composers writing both the lyrics and the tunes, unlike the popular songs of the earlier wars that were chiefly set to preexisting tunes. George F. Root was the most gifted of the Union song writers and his "Tramp, Tramp, Tramp, the Boys are Marching," "The Battle-Cry of Freedom," and "Just Before the Battle, Mother," were among the most popular songs. Other particularly noteworthy songs of the North were Julia Ward Howe's "Battle Hymn of the Republic" and Henry C. Work's "Marching Through Georgia." Some of the most famous songs sung in the South were Daniel Emmett's "Dixie," Harry Macarthy's "The Bonnie Blue Flag," James R. Randall's "Maryland, My Maryland," and "Marie Ravenal de la Coste" and John Hill Hewitt's "Somebody's Darling." Many songs, however, crossed battle lines with different texts to the same tunes often parodying the originals. Emmett composed "Dixie," the most famous song of the war, in 1859 as a minstrel song, but it soon was adopted by both the Union and Confederate states. For the Confederacy, it became an unofficial national anthem; President Lincoln liked it and had a White House band perform it as well.

Pianistic battle pieces continued, as seen in the blind slave Thomas Bethune's *Battle of Manassas* (1866), which quotes "Dixie," "The Star-Spangled Banner," and "Yankee Doodle," and uses clusters to imitate cannon shots in the lower part of the keyboard. The most serious composer of keyboard music in America during the mid-nineteenth century, however, was Louis Moreau Gottschalk. He wrote several piano works that significantly elevated both the virtuosity and the quality of battle-like pieces for the instrument. His *L'Union* (1862), for which Samuel Adler made an arrangement for piano and orchestra in 1972, is a brilliant showpiece for the pianist, with interlocking offices, rapid figurations, and cannon imitations. By the Civil War period, military brass bands were prevalent, having significantly replaced the drum and fife bands by 1834. During the war, several of these bands chiefly the Stonewall Brigade Band, the Spring Garden Band, and the Fencible Band—became well-known, playing concerts and assisting with recruitment.

The Civil War has remained vivid in the American consciousness to the present day, as is evident in the large number of works composed about it in this century—an inspiration due in part to the excellent poetry and prose that emerged about the war from Abraham Lincoln, Stephen Crane, Herman Melville, and Walt Whitman.

The most important setting of Crane's "War Is Kind" is Ulysses Kay's *Stephen Crane Set* (1967) and the best settings of Melville include Joseph Baber's *Shiloh and Other Songs from Herman Melville's "Battle Pieces"* (1991) and Gordon Binkerd's *Requiem for Soldiers Lost in Ocean Transports* (1984). David Diamond composed his *Epitaph (On the Grave of a Young Cavalry Officer Killed in the Valley of Virginia)* in 1945.

The poet most frequently set to music is Walt Whitman. Paul Hindemith (1946) and Roger Sessions (1964–70) both wrote outstanding large-scale works on "When Lilacs Last in the Dooryard Bloom'd." Other noteworthy Whitman settings include Howard Hanson's *Drum Taps* (1935), Norman Dello Joio's *Songs of Walt Whitman* (1966), Thomas Pasatieri's *Dirge for Two Veterans* (1973), Ned Rorem's *Whitman Cantata* (1983), and John Adams's *The Wound Dresser* (1989).

Numerous composers have also set Lincoln's Gettysburg Address to music. Other works, such as Rubin Goldmark's *Requiem* (1919) and Ernest Bloch's *America* (1926), include portions of the address or are based on Lincoln's life. Perhaps the most famous and most frequently performed work about Lincoln is Aaron Copland's *A Lincoln Portrait* (1942), which uses a portion of the Gettysburg Address. Roy Harris based his four-movement Symphony No. 6 ("Gettysburg") (1943–44) on the address and composed his Symphony No. 10 ("Abraham Lincoln") (1965) in honor of Lincoln. Warner Hutchison wrote an experimental *Mass: For Abraham Lincoln* (1974), and Vincent Persichetti set Lincoln's second inaugural address in *A Lincoln Address* (1973).

Very few works emerged from the *Spanish-American War, although some popular songs such as Charles K. Harris's "Just Break the News to Mother," "Good-bye, Dolly Gray," and Joe Hayden and Theodore Mertz's popular "There'll be a Hot Time in the Old Town Tonight"—which became the official song of Theodore *Roosevelt's Rough Riders—were well established. It was finally during the Spanish-American War that piano battle pieces reached their demise after having dominated American war music during the nineteenth century. In their place, for the first time in America, composers created serious large-scale compositions dealing with war for chorus and orchestra, such as Walter Damrosch's *Manila Te Deum* (1898).

In the last quarter of the nineteenth century and the first quarter of the twentieth, John Philip Sousa composed about 140 marches for military band that represented the glorification of the martial, patriotic, and expansionistic spirit of the turn of the century. His most significant marches include "Stars and Stripes Forever!" (1896), "Washington Post March" (1889), "King Cotton" (1895), and "U.S. Field Artillery" (1917). Many other patriotic tunes related to the military emerged from this era as well, including Alfred Miles and Charles Zimmerman's "Anchors Aweigh" (1906) and Edmund Gruber's "The Caissons Go Rolling Along" (1907).

Charles Ives was the composer most interested in writing serious music for *World War I. He composed two songs in 1917—"He is There!", later expanded to *They Are There: A War Song March*, and "In Flanders Fields." Ives dedicated the *Second Orchestral Set "From Hanover Square North at the End of a Tragic Day the People Again Arose"* (1915) to the victims of the sinking of the *Lusitania*. Few American works were written during the war; however, a number of pieces appeared after the war, such as Frederick Converse's *The Answer of the Stars* (1919) and Ernest Schelling's *A Victory Ball* (1922). American composers also wrote pieces lamenting those lost in the war, as did their European counterparts during this time. Arthur Foote composed *Three Songs 1914–1918* (1919), and Horatio Parker A.D. *1919* for chorus and piano (1919) in memory of the Yale graduates who lost their lives in the war. The

American G.I.s enthusiastically adopted British songs, chiefly Harry Williams's or Jack Judge's "It's a Long Way to Tipperary," and Ivor Novello's "Keep the Home Fires Burning." George M. Cohan's "Over There" and "Johnny, Get Your Gun" were two of the most famous popular war songs in the United States.

*World War II witnessed the greatest outpouring of war music ever in America. By the midpoint in the war, the American government and other civic organizations were commissioning music for war bonds, films, education, recruitment, and patriotic fanfares. The government supplied 12-inch, 78 rpm V-Discs to servicemen abroad (chiefly popular and light classical music), and the Department of Public Instruction in Indiana published a book, *Music and Morale in Wartime*, for civilians to sing in support of the war effort. The War Production Drive Headquarters even produced a study of the effect of music in armament factories, Wheeler Beckett's *Music in War Plants* (1943). Otto M. Helbig focused on the therapeutic importance of music in his *History of Music in the U.S. Armed Forces During World War II* (1966). Eugene Goossens and the Cincinnati Symphony Orchestra invited composers to create short fanfares that opened their concerts, and the League of Composers commissioned short pieces, based on a war-associated theme, which the New York Philharmonic premiered between 1943 and 1945. Aaron Copland's *A Fanfare for the Common Man* was the most important of these, and Copland later incorporated the work into his optimistic postwar Symphony No. 3 (1946).

Many composers dedicated these works to the war effort. Morton Gould dedicated his Symphony No. 1 (1943) to his three brothers in the service and to their fellow fighters; Marc Blitzstein wrote *Freedom Morning* (1943) for the black troops of the U.S. Army; Paul Hindemith dedicated his *When Lilacs Last in the Door-yard Bloom'd: A Requiem for Those We Love* (1946) to the memory of President Franklin D. *Roosevelt and to the American soldiers killed during World War II; Dai Keong Lee offered his *Pacific Prayer* (1943) to the fighting men in the Pacific; and Roy Harris originally dedicated his Fifth Symphony (1942) to the USSR before later removing the dedication.

Other composers wrote laments for the soldiers who had died: Bernard Herrmann's *For the Fallen* (1943); Douglas Moore's *In Memoriam* (1943); and William Grant Still's *In Memoriam: The Colored Soldiers Who Died for Democracy* (1943). A large number of popular songs, such as "Comin' in on a Wing and a Prayer," "Der Fuehrer's Face," and Frank Loesser's "Praise the Lord and Pass the Ammunition" placed high on the popular charts of the era. Among the most popular of all the music composed about World War II was Richard Rodgers's incidental music to *Victory at Sea* in 1952.

Some of the most intense works deal with the Holocaust. Both Part III: "Night" of Morton Subotnick's *Jacob's Room* (1985–86) and the second movement of Steve Reich's *Different Trains* (1988) tragically depict a train journey to the concentration camps. Lukas Foss wrote an *Elegy for Anne Frank* (1989), which he later incorporated into his Symphony No. 3 ("Symphony of Sorrows") (1991). Morton Gould extracted a *Holocaust Suite* (1978) from his music for a television docudrama about the Holocaust.

The *Korean War produced very few compositions. Only two Americans composed serious works dealing with the war and only one during the actual conflict—Lowndes Maury wrote his *Sonata in Memory of the Korean War Dead* for violin and piano in 1952, and Donald Erb composed his *God Love You Now* in 1971.

The Vietnam War, however, marked a significant change. Its art and popular music mirrored youthful perceptions of the war. Early on, Sgt. Barry Sadler's "Ballad of the Green Beret" paid tribute to these extraordinary new special forces. Later, as young men and women vocalized forceful opposition to the war, their music reflected that protest. Compositions such as William Mayer's *Letters Home* (1968), Gail Kubik's *A Record of Our Time* (1970), or Lou Harrison's *Peace Pieces* (1968) were clearly antiwar works, as were many songs by the popular songwriters, such as Joan Baez, Bob Dylan ("Blowin' in the Wind," "A hard rain's a-gonna fall," and "Masters of War"), and Phil Ochs ("Talking Vietnam" and "Draft Dodger Rag"). Dylan, following in the protest tradition of Woody Guthrie, became the spokesman for the Vietnam era and many musicians sang his songs, including Baez and Peter, Paul, and Mary. Joe MacDonald's "I-Feel-Like-I'm-Fixin'-to-Die" makes fun of the soldiers and their willingness to die at any cost.

Furthermore, the cynicism found in the novels and films of the early sixties is active in war-related compositions of the time. Donald Martirano's *L'sGA* (1968) includes a speaker who cites the Gettysburg Address while inhaling helium gas. Arnold Rosner's *A Mylai Elegy* (1971), Dai-Keong Lee's *Canticle of the Pacific* (1968), and Donald Lybbert's *Lines for the Fallen* (1971) were all laments for those who died in the war; there were few optimistic compositions. But perhaps the most significant work related to the Vietnam War is George Crumb's *Black Angels* (1970) for electrified string quartet. The soldiers in the war continued their output of lyrics to preexisting melodies. Joseph F. Tuso's *Singing the Vietnam Blues: Songs of the Air Force in Southeast Asia* (1990) contains 148 songs written solely by U.S. Air Force combat flyers during the Vietnam War.

The *Persian Gulf War, in contrast, was a popular war and the majority of songs supported the war effort. A new outpouring of patriotism could be seen in Whitney Houston's performance of "The Star-Spangled Banner" and Lee Greenwood's "God Bless the U.S.A." which were regularly heard during the conflict. Most recently, Aaron Jay Kernis premiered *Colored Fields* (1996), a three-movement concerto for English horn that deals with the fighting in Bosnia.

[*See also* Bosnian Crisis; Culture, War, and the Military; Vietnam Antiwar Movement; World War I: Military and Diplomatic Course; World War II: Military and Diplomatic Course.]

• Edward A. Dolph, ed., *"Sound Off!": Soldier Songs from the Revolution to World War II*, 1942. Richard B. Harwell, *Confederate Music*, 1950. Willard A. and Porter W. Heaps, *The Singing Sixties: The Spirit of the Civil War Days Drawn from the Music of the Times*, 1960. Irwin Silber, ed., *Songs of the Civil War*, 1960. Kenneth A. Bernard, *Lincoln and the Music of the Civil War*, 1966. Francis A. Lord and Arthur Wise, *Bands and Drummer Boys of the Civil War*, 1966. Paul Glass and Louis C. Singer, *Singing Soldiers: The Spirit of the Sixties*, 1968. Barbara Dan and Irwin Silber, eds., *The Vietnam Songbook*, 1969. Carolyn Rabson, *Songbook of the American Revolution*, 1974. Raoul F. Camus, *Military Music of the American Revolution*, 1976. Kenneth E. Olson, *Music and Musket: Bands and Bandsmen of the American Civil War*, 1981. Kent A. Bowman, *Voices of*

Combat: A Century of Liberty and War Songs, 1965–1865, 1987. Ben Arnold, *Music and War: A Research and Information Guide,* 1993. Les Cleveland, *Dark Laughter: War in Song and Popular Culture,* 1994.

—Ben Arnold

The rifled **MUSKET,** adopted by the U.S. Army in 1858, represented a significant departure from previous weapons technology. In contrast to the notoriously inaccurate and short-ranged smoothbore musket, the rifled musket featured helical grooves running the length of the barrel that caused a bullet to spin as it left the muzzle. The spinning projectile was less susceptible to air resistance and drop, and hence had a longer, flatter trajectory. Integral to the rifled musket's design was a conoidal-cylindrical bullet, invented by French infantry captain Claude Minié (hence the Americanized name, *minie ball*). When fired, the exploding powder in the rifle's breech caused a shallow concavity in the bullet's butt end to expand, grip the rifling, and create spin.

During the *Civil War, both sides used rifles with close order infantry tactics designed around smoothbores, which emphasized volume of fire rather than accuracy or distance. Rifles, however, greatly increased the range at which an opponent could be brought under effective fire, and magnified the length of time spent under that fire. Consequently, *casualties—and the natural power of the defense—increased dramatically. Some Civil War generals recognized the problem and began experimenting with disordered attack formations that spread soldiers out in a more open, less vulnerable configuration. Most commanders, however, persisted in traditional tactics, and disordered attacks were not accepted as official army doctrine until after the war. The rifled musket itself was the last evolutionary step in muzzle-loaded small arms, and was quickly superseded by breech-loading rifles that fired jacketed, metal cartridge bullets.

[*See also* Army, U.S.: 1866–99; Tactics, Fundamentals.]

• Robert M. Reilly, *United States Military Small Arms, 1816–1865: the Federal Firearms of the Civil War,* 1970.

—T. R. Brereton

MUSTE, ABRAHAM J. (1885–1967), minister, labor organizer, antiwar activist. Born in the Netherlands, Muste studied at theological seminaries in the United States and became a minister in the Dutch Reformed Church (1909–14), the Congregational Church (1914–18), and the Society of Friends (1918–26).

Muste opposed World War I through the *Fellowship of Reconciliation (FOR). During the 1920s and 1930s, he worked in support of industrial unionism through FOR and more radical secular groups. In the early 1930s, his labor activities led him to become a full-fledged Marxist revolutionary, but by 1936 he became once again a Christian pacifist, urging workers to use *nonviolence.

During World War II, as executive secretary of FOR, Muste maintained that military action against fascism only encouraged the forces of hatred and brutality that had created it. He supported *conscientious objection and *draft resistance and evasion. He also urged U.S. assistance to Jewish and other victims of Nazi persecution in Europe. To avert future wars, he recommended more equitable distribution of the world's resources.

In the *Cold War, a more radical Muste opposed the nuclear *arms race through the *War Resisters League and the Committee for Nonviolent Action. He also encouraged nonviolent direct action in civil rights and the *Vietnam Antiwar movement. Muste's activism made him one of the intellectual leaders of the American movement for peace and social justice.

[*See also* Pacifism.]

• A. J. Muste, *Nonviolence in an Aggressive World,* 1940. A. J. Muste, *Not by Might,* 1947. Jo Ann O. Robinson, *Abraham Went Out: A Biography of A. J. Muste,* 1982.

—John Whiteclay Chambers II

MUTINY. Despite its emotional connotation, *mutiny* is simply defined as collective military insubordination; it is the antithesis of discipline, which is itself the basis of military behavior. As a phenomenon, it is probably as old as armies and navies; in the case of the American armed forces, it dates back to the *Revolutionary War. In the American services, as elsewhere, mutiny is nowadays a relatively rare occurrence.

Mutiny can be active or passive; conducted with or without arms, with or without violence. It can take place in peace or war, on ship or on shore, at the front or in the rear. It is the collective aspect of mutiny that presents such a challenge to the stability of the particular military organization, or, when it exists on a very large scale, to the state itself. That, and the disgrace to the affected unit, accounts for the secrecy and lack of candor that is usually associated with mutinous incidents. Thus, actions that are, in fact, mutinies, are often cloaked in euphemisms: during the *Vietnam War, the U.S. Army referred to its mutinies as "battlefield refusals," a rhetorical invention without any basis in military law.

Historically, the main sources of mutiny have been rooted in a perception of unfairness on the part of the troops, of burdens inequitably shared vis-à-vis their military colleagues or their parent society. In the American military, this sense of relative deprivation has most often occurred as the result of perceived or actual racial discrimination. World War II saw several major mutinies by black soldiers and sailors in which the issues were discriminatory treatment: Bamber Bridge, England (1943); Port Chicago, California (1945); Guam (1944); Port Hueneme, California (1945). During the Vietnam War, in addition to some small unit incidents in the war zone, a major racially motivated mutiny involving over 100 sailors took place on board the USS *Constellation* (1972).

The notion of unfairness has also resulted from the demands of the military for service beyond an agreed or implied enlistment period. The mutiny of the Pennsylvania Line in June 1783 had as its central grievance the extension of duty beyond the original enlistment term; there were similar cases in the Civil War. In January 1946, in the immediate aftermath of World War II, mutinous outbreaks took place in several overseas garrisons—notably at Manila in the Philippines—in which the troops protested their retention in service following the termination of actual hostilities.

The twentieth century has seen another fundamental source of discontent take root in American and foreign military organizations: the reluctance to serve for ethical, political, or moral reasons. U.S. Army troops questioned the legitimacy of their service in North Russia in 1919; in Vietnam there were many small unit mutinies in which the essential issue centered on the why rather than the how of service.

The process of most American mutinies has followed the pattern of mutinies in general: they tend to be passive refusals to participate rather than acts of violence; of short duration, usually measured in hours rather than days; and spontaneous rather than premeditated.

In spite of the gravity of the offense, the penalties for mutiny in the American military have been minimal. Reluctance even to use the term *mutiny* has resulted in troops being court-martialed, if at all, for lesser offenses. The acceptance of the industrial strike as a legitimate expression of collective protest in twentieth-century civil society has fostered a more lenient view of what was classically considered the most serious of military crimes.

[*See also* Ethnicity and War; Morale, Troop; Philippines, U.S. Military Involvement in the; Vietnam Antiwar Movement.]

• Robert I. Allen, *The Port Chicago Mutiny,* 1989. Leonard F. Guttridge, *Mutiny,* 1992.   —Elihu Rose

MUTUAL DEFENSE ASSISTANCE ACT (1949).

Signed by President Harry S. *Truman on 6 October 1949, the Mutual Defense Assistance Act (MDAA) was the first global U.S. military assistance legislation of the *Cold War. Military officials began calling for the introduction of such legislation two years earlier, arguing that depleted inventories of surplus armaments, piecemeal planning, and restrictions on presidential authority threatened current and future efforts to arm foreign nations. New legislation became a necessity by mid-1948 because of plans to negotiate a North Atlantic defense treaty and furnish arms aid to strengthen the connectional defenses and the will to resist Communist expansion of the signatories.

Truman sent the bill to Congress on 25 July 1949, the day he ratified the North Atlantic Treaty. Opposition from Senator Arthur H. Vandenberg (R-Mich.) to the bill's broad executive powers forced submission of new legislation, which specified the recipients and the amounts of assistance. Controversy also arose over the omission of China, resulting in an unvouchered fund for the "general area" of China. Overall, the MDAA authorized $1.314 billion: $1 billion for *NATO countries; $211.4 for Greece and Turkey; $27.6 million for Iran, the Philippines, and South Korea; and $75 million for the "general area" of China. Administration planners believed the MDAA's immediate effects were to raise the morale of friendly nations and prove U.S. reliability and resolve to meet Communist threats. The MDAA also institutionalized the military aid program, a result ensured by enactment of similar legislation in 1950 and an increase in annual spending on military aid to $5.222 billion after the outbreak of the *Korean War.

• Lawrence S. Kaplan, *A Community of Interests: NATO and the Military Assistance Program, 1948–1951,* 1980. Chester J. Pach, Jr., *Arming the Free World: The Origins of the United States Military Assistance Program, 1945–1950,* 1991.   —Chester J. Pach, Jr.

MUTUAL SECURITY ACT (1951).

Successor to the *Mutual Defense Assistance Act and the Economic Cooperation Act, the Mutual Security Act became law on 10 October 1951. It created a new, independent agency, the Mutual Security Administration, to supervise all foreign aid programs including military assistance and economic programs that bolstered the defense capability of U.S. allies.

Submitted on 24 May 1951, President Harry S. *Truman's omnibus foreign aid bill got a hostile reception on Capitol Hill. Rapid expansion of national security expenditures during the *Korean War had produced alarm over high taxes, large deficits, government controls, and a possible "garrison state" among such prominent conservatives as Senator Robert *Taft (R-Ohio). Truman's decision to send U.S. troops to Europe as part of a standing *NATO force further antagonized congressional conservatives and exacerbated their fears that European nations were not doing enough for their own defense. Congress thus reduced the administration's request for Mutual Security funds by 15 percent and authorized $5.998 billion and $1.486 billion, respectively, for military and economic assistance. The deepest cuts were in economic aid, thus ensuring its subordination to military assistance as "defense support." Renewed each year until 1961 (on the reorganization of the program under new legislation), the Mutual Security Act produced annual struggles over the size of the foreign aid budget and the balance between military and economic aid.

[*See also* Isolationism; Marshall Plan.]

• Michael J. Hogan, *The Marshall Plan: America, Britain, and the Reconstruction of Western Europe, 1947–1952,* 1987. Alfred Goldberg, ed., *History of the Office of the Secretary of Defense,* Vol. 2: Doris M. Condit, *The Test of War, 1950–1953,* 1988.

                                                —Chester J. Pach, Jr.

MY LAI MASSACRE (1968).

In South Vietnam on 16 March 1968, American soldiers of Company C (Charlie) of Task Force Barker, Americal Division, assaulted the hamlet of My Lai (4), part of the village of Son My in Quang Ngai province. The entire Son My area was a stronghold of the Viet Cong and American units there had taken repeated *casualties from snipers, land *mines, and booby traps, without making any significant contact with the enemy. During a briefing prior to the assault, the commander of Charlie Company, Capt. Ernest L. Medina, had ordered his men to burn and destroy the hamlet of My Lai (4), which was said to be fortified and held by the 48th Viet Cong Battalion.

Contrary to expectations, no enemy forces were encountered during the assault on My Lai (4), yet the men of Charlie Company swept through the hamlet and systematically killed all the inhabitants—almost exclusively old men, women, and children. There were several rape killings and at least one gang rape. The total number of Vietnamese civilians killed could not be determined: it was at least 175 and may have exceeded 400.

The massacre at My Lai was successfully concealed within all command levels of the Americal Division for more than a year. In 1969, a letter sent by a serviceman not connected with the division, who had heard stories of a massacre, brought the incident to the attention of the secretary of defense and other government officials. A commission of inquiry, appointed by the secretary of the army and headed by Lt. Gen. W. R. Peers, eventually listed thirty individuals as implicated in various "commissions and omissions" related to the Son My operation. Criminal charges were preferred against sixteen of these. Five were tried by court-martial, but only one individual, 1st Lt. William L. Calley, was found guilty.

On 29, March 1971, after a court-martial of over four months, Calley was convicted of three counts of premeditated murder of not less than twenty-two Vietnamese; he was sentenced to life imprisonment at hard labor. During several stages of review, Calley's life sentence was reduced to ten years' imprisonment; he was granted parole effective 19 November 1974. Captain Medina, Calley's company commander, was charged with involuntary manslaughter—failure to exercise proper control over his men engaged in unlawful homicide of at least 100 unidentified Vietnamese. He was acquitted because of the military judge's faulty instructions on the issue of command responsibility. Altogether, the legal consequences of the My Lai incident left much to be desired. General Peers on 2 December 1974 called it a "horrible thing, and we find we have only one man finally convicted and he's set free after doing a relatively small part of his sentence."

Many Americans disagreed with this conclusion. President Nixon had been deluged with letters protesting Calley's conviction. The young lieutenant and his men, it was argued, had acted out of frustration and hatred of the Vietnamese who had killed and wounded their comrades. Calley's supporters on the right wing of the American political spectrum were sometimes joined by those in the *Vietnam antiwar movement who regarded My Lai as merely a particularly horrible example of everyday American military tactics.

The environment of *guerrilla warfare, a war without fronts, undoubtedly created a setting conducive to *atrocities. Some apparent civilians were actually combatants who tossed grenades or planted booby traps. Yet these facts cannot provide legal exculpation for the cold-blooded slaughter of old men, women, and children. Despite pressure for a high enemy casualty toll, most U.S. sol-

diers in Vietnam did not intentionally shoot unarmed villagers. Indeed, some U.S. soldiers tried to stop the slaughter at My Lai, notably the helicopter pilot Hugh Thompson. The My Lai massacre was not a typical occurrence. The openness of the fighting in Vietnam to journalistic coverage and the encouragement which the My Lai affair gave to other service people to come forward with reports of atrocities made it quite unlikely that any other massacre could escape attention. True, villagers were regularly killed in combat assaults on defended hamlets; but the rounding up and shooting of civilians was an unusual event, and the men involved in the massacre at My Lai knew it.

The final report of the Peers Commission listed perfunctory instruction in the laws of war in U.S. Army training as a contributory cause of the My Lai massacre. Since then, this aspect of training has been thoroughly revised. Servicepeople are instructed that acting under superior orders is no defense to a charge of murder or other *war crimes. New channels have been set up for the reporting of violations of the laws of war. It is to be hoped that these changes will prevent a recurrence of a dark chapter in the history of the U.S. Army.

[See also Army, U.S.: Since 1941; Leadership, Concepts of Military; Morale, Troop; Training and Indoctrination; Vietnam War: Military and Domestic Course; Vietnam War: Changing Interpretations.]

• Joseph Goldstein, et al., eds., *The My Lai Massacre and Its Coverup: The Peers Commission Report with a Supplement and Introductory Essay on the Limits of Law*, 1976. Guenter Lewy, *America in Vietnam*, 1978.
                                                          —Guenter Lewy

NAPOLEONIC WARFARE. For most of the years from 1799 to 1815, Napoleon Bonaparte led the armies of France to victory over successive hostile coalitions. Despite his ultimate defeat and his mobile and offensive way of war, his personal leadership and strategic approach were widely admired in his day and are still studied.

Napoleon's achievements did not rest on superior armament or totally new *tactics. His army's *weapons differed little from those of his opponents, and his tactics were adapted from those practiced by the mass conscript forces of the French Revolution. What made Napoleon so formidable was the combination of his genius and a large, offensive-minded army led by young and ambitious officers. A charismatic leader, he inspired his troops, Frenchmen and foreigners, with fierce loyalty and devotion. His greatest shortcoming was his refusal to train his senior subordinates for independent command; consequently, their performance often was faulty.

Between 1801 and 1805, Napoleon reorganized the French forces, creating what was called the *Grande Armée*. The permanent institution of the corps system perhaps was most important. Normally commanded by a marshal, a corps consisted of two to four infantry divisions, some cavalry, *artillery, and support troops, strong enough to defeat equal numbers and hold against superior forces until reinforced. Some formations Napoleon kept under his own control: the Army Artillery Reserve, the Army Cavalry Reserve, and the Imperial Guard.

Napoleon always preferred to fight on the offensive, and acting as his own operations officer, made all major decisions. He had the unique talent to conceive a campaign as a complete sequence leading to his main objective: the destruction of the enemy's army or will to fight in one great decisive battle, followed by vigorous pursuit. Careful planning, combining deception and rapid movement, was designed to compel the enemy to fight this battle at a disadvantage. In the Italian campaign of 1796, Napoleon's small army of 35,000 men won victories over the stronger Austrians and Piedmontese by bringing superior strength to bear against each individual enemy force, defeating them in succession. Greater numbers and the corps system enabled Napoleon to develop new strategic sequences. Normally a campaign started with the corps marching widely dispersed along separate routes. Once the enemy's main force was located, the corps pulled closer together, advancing in a diamond-shaped formation. The first corps to contact the enemy engaged him at once while the other corps came into action along the flanks and the rearmost corps remained reserve. A variant of this strategic movement was Napoleon's famous maneuver in the rear. The enemy would be pinned by what he believed was Napoleon's main force, while the bulk of the French Army swept around to cut his communications and compel him to turn and fight at a disadvantage or to surrender. The 1805 Ulm campaign and the Battle of Austerlitz are the most successful examples.

In battle, Napoleon favored the offensive and stood on the defensive only three times, at Leipzig (1813) and at La Rothière and Arcis (1814). Each time he assumed the defensive only after his initial attack had failed. Basically, his battle tactics stressed offensive movement supported by massive fire, though he tried to retain an element of surprise. He usually sought to direct his main blow against an enemy flank while occupying his front with simultaneous attacks, often infantry combined with cavalry. A second variant was the frontal attack while a flanking maneuver was launched. In both cases, the enemy was gradually weakened, and then, with a superb sense of timing, Napoleon would release his reserve for the smashing blow. Infantry attack columns supported by cavalry and horse artillery moved to breach the enemy's front or flank, while light cavalry would be launched to turn retreat into rout. From Marengo (1800) to Wagram (1809), Napoleon's talent to seize the right moment, together with the overall superior quality of his army, assured victory. But as time passed, he no longer was at his peak, and the quality of his troops declined, while his enemies had learned their lessons.

Besides improving their forces, Napoleon's opponents adopted the corps system that made it impossible to destroy an entire army in one battle. Ultimately, Napoleon's attempt to exploit the central position failed because of British-Prussian strategic cooperation at Waterloo (1815).

Nonetheless, the pattern of Napoleonic warfare continued to be studied and many of his innovations, especially the corps system, were retained. His strategic concepts—in particular, the central position and the maneuver on the rear—remained models for future commanders and were studied even in the fledgling U.S. *Army. Napoleonic warfare as expounded in the writings of Baron Antoine Henri *Jomini was transmitted to American officers by the teaching at the recently founded Military Academy at West Point and came to influence the generals of the Civil War.

Jomini's writings provided a schematic and prescriptive interpretation of Napoleonic operations, an approach well suited to West Point's engineering emphasis. They provided the basis for the teachings of Dennis Hart Mahan, professor of civil engineering and the science of war from 1832 to 1871. Over time, Mahan came to stress the more offensive aspects of Jomini, while Mahan's most brilliant student, Henry W. Halleck, published his *Elements of Military Art and Science* in 1846—an influential work presenting a more defensive-minded view of Jomini's principles.

American operations in Mexico in 1846, offensive though hardly Napoleonic, provided additional impetus for strategic studies, and in 1848 officers at West Point founded a Napoleonic Club, chaired by Mahan, to discuss Napoleonic campaigns. Participants included Robert E. *Lee and George B. *McClellan.

If a clear consensus on the thrust of Jomini's work did not emerge, his influence on the commanders in the Civil War was great. It has been said that they went to war with the sword in one hand and a copy of Jomini in the other. But the results were unclear. Jomini's influence may have made McClellan and Halleck too cautious, while Lee's use of the central position and his turning maneuver at the Second Battle of *Bull Run (1862) and at the Battle of *Chancellorsville (1863) showed a Napoleonic touch. In the end, of course, the new rifled weapons, extended frontages, and rapid rail movements, which negated much of the advantage of the central position, required a quite different approach. The Civil War victory was devised by Ulysses S. *Grant, who claimed that he had never paid much attention to Jomini, and echoing a statement attributed also to Napoleon, declared that the art of war was simple enough: find your enemy and hit him as hard as you can.

[See also Academies, Service: U.S. Military Academy; Civil War: Military and Diplomatic Course; Strategy: Fundamentals; Strategy: Historical Development.]

• David Chandler, The Campaigns of Napoleon, 1966. James Marshall-Cornwall, Napoleon as Military Commander, 1967. Gunther E. Rothenberg, The Art of Warfare in the Age of Napoleon, 1977. Owen Connelly, Blundering to Glory: Napoleon's Military Campaigns, 1988.   —Gunther E. Rothenberg

NASHVILLE, BATTLE OF (1864). After losing the Battle of *Atlanta, John B. *Hood in November 1864 took the Confederacy's chief western army into Tennessee in a quixotic campaign to reverse the situation. Opposing him was George H. *Thomas, who would have a very substantial force once he gathered the various Union garrisons in Tennessee.

Hood started well, nearly catching a Federal delaying force under John M. Schofield at Spring Hill, Tennessee. When a *Confederate army command error allowed Schofield to escape, Hood became enraged, and the next day recklessly sacrificed much of his army against Schofield's entrenchments at Franklin, Tennessee. After Schofield retired at his leisure to join Thomas at Nashville, Hood followed.

Though he was now outnumbered two to one, Hood took a position outside Nashville and waited for something to turn up. Both Abraham *Lincoln, in Washington, and Ulysses S. *Grant, near Petersburg, were very anxious for Thomas to get on with the business of smashing Hood; but Thomas was not to be hurried. Sleet, snow, and ice made conditions difficult. On 15 December 1864, Thomas attacked, with 55,000 men to perhaps 28,000 for Hood. The Confederates were driven back to a line of hills about a mile to the rear, but still maintained their cohesion. The next day, Thomas renewed the assault, and that afternoon Hood's army collapsed. Federal cavalry pursued the remnants southward toward Alabama. *Union army *casualties were 3,061; Confederate were about 6,000, of whom three-fourths were captured.

One of the most complete victories of the Civil War, the Battle of Nashville was also the last major battle west of the Appalachians.

[See also Civil War: Military and Diplomatic Course.]

• Stanley Horn, The Decisive Battle of Nashville, 1956. Wiley Sword, The Confederacy's Last Hurrah: Spring Hill, Franklin, and Nashville, 1993.

—Steven E. Woodworth

NATIONAL COMMITTEE FOR A SANE NUCLEAR POLICY. In June 1957, twenty-seven prominent citizens concerned with the direct and indirect hazards of nuclear fallout (e.g., strontium 90 found in cow's milk) met in New York City and formed the Provisional Committee to Stop Nuclear Tests. In the fall, they adopted the name National Committee for a Sane Nuclear Policy, commonly known as SANE, and placed a full-page advertisement in the New York Times that read: "We Are Facing a Danger Unlike Any Danger That Has Ever Existed." SANE quickly became the largest and most influential nuclear disarmament organization in the United States. By the summer of 1958, it had about 130 chapters representing approximately 25,000 Americans.

For over three decades, men and women prominently associated with SANE, such as Norman Cousins, Clarence Pickett, Lenore Marshall, Norman Thomas, Dr. Benjamin Spock, H. Stuart Hughes, Sanford Gottlieb, and Rev. William Sloane Coffin, Jr., published full-page advertisements, wrote letters, signed petitions, staged impressive rallies, and took to the streets to pressure U.S. leaders to stop testing, to lessen the risk of nuclear war, and to move toward peace with justice. From the first large American antinuclear rallies of the late 1950s and early 1960s, through the organizing of the largest yet demonstration of the *Vietnam antiwar movement in November 1965, to helping bring about the massive June 1982 disarmament march and rally in New York City, SANE was at the forefront of liberal *nuclear protest movements. The organization's greatest achievement was the *Limited Test Ban Treaty of 1963, halting atmospheric nuclear tests.

In the 1980s, SANE activists played a leading role in the campaign to "freeze" *nuclear weapons (to prevent proposed escalation of the *arms race). In 1987, the two largest peace organizations in the country merged into SANE/FREEZE: Campaign for Global Security, an organization of over 240 local groups, 24 state affiliates, and 170,000 members. The goals of SANE/FREEZE remained a comprehensive ban on nuclear testing as the first step toward complete disarmament and a redirection of military spending to social programs. Reverend Coffin served as president until the end of the *Cold War in 1989. In 1993, SANE/FREEZE adopted a new name, Peace Action.

[See also Arms Control and Disarmament: Nuclear; Peace and Antiwar Movements.]

• Milton S. Katz, Ban the Bomb: A History of SANE, the Committee for a Sane Nuclear Policy, 1986. Robert Kleidman, Organizing for Peace: Neutrality, the Test Ban, and the Freeze, 1993.

—Milton S. Katz

NATIONAL DEFENSE ACTS (1916, 1920). These statutes provided major restructuring of the U.S. Army. The 1916 act resulted from the "Preparedness" movement to ready the United States for modern war. It authorized nearly doubling the regular army, to 175,000 (and 286,000 in war), but failed to eliminate state militias as nationalists and regulars desired. Instead, Congress designated the National Guard the primary trained reserve, increased its funding and regulation, and authorized its expansion to 450,000. The law required Guard members to take a dual oath to the nation and their state, enabling the president to "federalize" them and even send them overseas. To prepare reserve army and National Guard officers, Congress established a campus-based Reserve Officers Training Corps (*ROTC) and provided federal funds for summertime officers' training camps for business and professional men. It also authorized steps toward industrial *mobilization that led to a Council of National Defense. When the United States entered World War I in 1917, the regular army expanded, the president federalized the National Guard, and Congress authorized temporary wartime selective *conscription.

The National Defense Act of 1920 expanded the 1916 legislation and provided for postwar reorganization of the army. The 1920 law governed organization and regulation for three decades—until the *Army Reorganization Act (1950)—codifying the three-component army: regular, National Guard, and Army Reserve. Rejecting peacetime conscription, the lawmakers relied on voluntarism; denying the General Staff's proposal for a 500,000-man standing army, Congress authorized a regular army of 280,000, a National Guard of 430,000, a skeletal Army Reserve, to be filled with veterans, and expanded programs for commissioning reserve officers. The legislators made permanent some wartime organizational additions: the Financial Department, the Chemical Warfare Service, and the Air Service, which was separated from the Signal Corps. It also rescinded some changes: the Tank Corps was put back in the infantry. Furthering the Elihu *Root reforms, the legislation enlarged the General Staff, giving it responsibility for overall military planning. It also authorized an assistant secretary of war for planning business and industrial mobilization. The General Staff's importance in planning and combined operations would become evident in World War II.

[See also Army, U.S.: 1900–41; World War I: Military and Diplomatic Course.]

• Marvin A. Kreidberg and Merton G. Henry, *History of Military Mobilization of the United States Army, 1775–1945,* 1955. I. B. Holley, *General John M. Palmer, Citizen Soldiers, and the Army of a Democracy,* 1982. Russell F. Weigley, *History of the United States Army,* 1984. John Whiteclay Chambers II, *To Raise an Army: The Draft Comes to Modern America,* 1987.

—John Whiteclay Chambers II

NATIONAL GUARD. *See* Militia and National Guard; Army Reserves and National Guard.

NATIONALISM is a loyalty to an "imagined community." It creates a sense of common identity even among people who have never met one another and probably never will. In large part, that is its function. We speak of American or German nationalism, but not the national identity of Luxembourg or Liechtenstein, where a far higher percentage of the people do in fact know one another. Even in large nations, the issues of who is imagined to be part of the community and who is entitled to do the imagining have often been fiercely contested. Beginning with the *Revolutionary

War, African Americans have tried to use their participation in major wars to win acceptance of their membership in the national community, while those who founded and sustained that community have tried to exclude them or restrict their participation. By contrast, some white reformers were trying to turn Indians into American citizens at a time when most Indians preferred to be left alone as distinct peoples on enough land to sustain their ancestral ways. The American quest for national identity has shown a pattern toward greater inclusiveness over time, but the stages of that struggle have been marked by some of the most violent confrontations in the history of the country.

In the great age of European nationalism from the French Revolution to World War II, peoples who spoke the same language or shared a common ethnicity fought to build their own nation-states. The unification of Germany and Italy, and later the achievement of independence by Poland and other East European states, also meant the weakening and eventual destruction of the polyglot Habsburg and Ottoman empires. German nationalism took shape in sharp reaction against Napoleonic France, while Italian unity required the repudiation of rule from Vienna. Most historians—always with a nervous glance at Germany from the 1860s to 1945—have assumed that the stronger the nationalism, the greater its ability to prevail.

These nineteenth-century European models do not help much in trying to understand nationalism in the Americas. The thirteen colonies won independence from Britain without claiming a preexisting common identity distinct from that of the mother country. They certainly had no quarrel with the English language. That pattern recurred a generation later in the Latin American struggles for independence. The Latin revolutionaries, like those in North America, accepted most of the geographical boundaries that had been laid out by the imperial states of Spain and Portugal and continued to use the old imperial languages after independence. In North America in the nineteenth century, only one major nationalist movement failed: the attempt to establish the Confederate States of America. Ironically, at least by European norms, the Confederacy was the most militantly nationalist movement to appear in the Americas. In North America, unlike Europe, the gentler and weaker nationalisms of the United States and Canada have survived, but the Confederacy was crushed.

The United States of America emerged as a separate nation before its citizens had any firm sense of a distinct national identity. In England's mainland colonies in the seventeenth century, most settlers assumed that they belonged to the English "nation," the first European society to define itself in these terms. An Englishman's identity involved a strong commitment to liberty, property, and "no popery," although the English quarreled fiercely and sometimes violently over how Protestant, or Puritan, England should be. These quarrels crossed the ocean, but the rival positions tended to take hold in different colonies, which were also founded for different purposes. Moderate Anglicans always controlled Virginia, and over time these values took hold throughout the southern colonies, where the pursuit of wealth energized the settlers far more than the demands of piety. By contrast, Puritanism largely defined what was most distinctive about the New England colonies. In the middle colonies, the competition among denominations in New York and New Jersey, and the

*Quakers' idealism in Pennsylvania, together guaranteed a regional victory for religious liberty by about 1720. But in this region ethnic and religious pluralism made even a sense of English identity problematic.

Many seventeenth-century colonists believed that they could create overseas a better society than England was ever likely to become. Then England's Glorious Revolution of 1688 guaranteed a Protestant succession to the throne, annual meetings of Parliament, and toleration for Protestant dissenters. Over the next twenty-five years, England (which united with Scotland to form the kingdom of Great Britain in 1707) emerged quite unexpectedly as one of Europe's great powers, the one usually best positioned to prevent France, or any other power, from establishing hegemony over the rest. Britons began to celebrate their "mixed and balanced constitution" of king, Lords, and Commons as the great wonder of the age, the foundation for the liberty, property, and Protestantism that made the nation distinct. Colonists joined in this celebration, and in the process of embracing a British national identity also seemed quietly to abandon any ambitions of creating a more just society than Britain's. This trend became most visible during Britain's mid-eighteenth-century wars with Catholic Spain and France. Colonial spokesmen proudly proclaimed their loyalty to the world's most successful empire, which by 1763 had expelled France from Canada and Spain from Florida and had taken control of everything east of the Mississippi River except New Orleans.

In one of history's most astonishing reversals, triumphant Britain then alienated the colonists so totally over the next twelve years that war broke out between the two sides in April 1775. Britain's policies included two major attempts to tax the settlers without their consent—the Sugar and Stamp Acts of 1764–65, and the Townshend Revenue Act of 1767. At first the revenue was to be used only to pay part of the costs of North America's military establishment; but by 1767, some of it was designed to make royal governors and judges independent of the financial support of the colonies' elective assemblies. To North American settlers, the insistence on "no taxation without representation" marked a demand for traditional English property rights, not a quest for something distinctively "American."

For decades British spokesmen had predicted that eventually the American colonies would be strong enough to throw off all subjection to Britain. The reforms of 1763–67 were designed, at least in part, to postpone that terrible day. Colonists found this fear misconceived and even dangerous. Acutely aware of how different the colonies were from one another, they repeatedly affirmed their loyalty to Britain and their admiration for the British constitution. They denied that they harbored any desire for independence, and many of them doubted that any viable union of such disparate colonies was even possible. In short, "America" began as Britain's idea. Into the 1770s, almost nobody on either side of the Atlantic actively favored the creation of a separate American nation.

Fifteen months of terrible warfare, beginning at Lexington in April 1775, changed these sensibilities. The Second Continental Congress long insisted that it was fighting only to restore English rights to the settlers under the traditional government of the empire. But when *George III refused even to receive Congress's very moderate Olive Branch Petition and instead proclaimed the colonists rebels in August 1775, sentiment began to shift, more obviously at first in private correspondence than in public statements. In January 1776, Thomas Paine published *Common Sense*, a call for both independence and American union. An English immigrant who had been in Philadelphia for only fourteen months, Paine saw an "American" nation around him, where other settlers were able to perceive only separate colonies. His eloquence was infectious, however, and *Common Sense* persuaded many colonists that both independence and union were attainable. In July 1776 Congress concluded that independence was necessary, but union remained another matter.

Many things seemed self-evident to the patriots of 1776, but the benefits of a unified nation-state were not among them. John Dickinson of Pennsylvania believed that the colonies were strong enough to resist even Britain's military might, but the prospect of success terrified him. Where "shall we find another Britain, to supply our loss?" he asked. "Torn from the body to which we are united by religion, liberty, laws, affections, relation, language, and commerce, we must bleed at every vein." Even though he refused to sign the Declaration of Independence, he did become the principal draftsman of the Articles of Confederation, which Congress did not send to the states until late 1777, and which failed to win ratification by all thirteen states until March 1781. Charles Thomson, secretary to Congress from 1774 until 1789, doubted that the American Union could long outlast the war. Even though Congress prevailed in the long struggle for independence, scored two diplomatic triumphs in the French alliance of 1778 and the Peace of Paris in 1783, and designed an imaginative and expansionist western policy culminating in the Northwest Ordinance of 1787, it provided little focus for popular loyalty and won little respect, even among its own members. By 1786–87, with Daniel Shays's Rebellion disrupting rural Massachusetts and with Congress itself ominously divided over the proposed Jay-Gardoquí Treaty, which would have surrendered the navigation of the Mississippi for twenty-five years in exchange for commercial privileges within the Spanish empire, talk of disunion became serious and even erupted into the newspapers. Southern states blocked the treaty because it would have privileged northeastern merchants at the expense of southern planters.

In May 1787, the Constitutional Convention met in Philadelphia and, by September, produced a charter for a radically new form of federal government, one that lodged sovereignty in the people themselves while permitting them to delegate sovereign powers to both their state and national governments. One of the most thoughtful delegates, James Wilson of Pennsylvania, declared that the United States was not yet a nation, but that the Constitution would create a framework to make that transition possible. "As we shall become a nation, I trust that we shall also form a national character; and that this character will be adapted to the principles and genius of our system of government." He based that expectation, not upon the shared memories of a largely mythical past (the kind of thing that shaped English nationalism), but upon popular expectations for a glorious and prosperous future in a vast continent with enormous resources.

Without the Constitution, the Union would probably not have survived the tumultuous years of the French Revolution and the Napoleonic wars. American national identity would have died in infancy. But the Constitution by itself could not guarantee the success of the Union, or even define the form that American political culture would assume.

The struggles between the Federalists and the Democratic-Republicans after 1790 reshaped American political culture and, indeed, American identity. "A nation without a national government is, in my view, an awful spectacle," proclaimed Alexander *Hamilton in the last of *The Federalist Papers*. He and other Federalists believed that creating a national government capable of holding its own against the great powers of the Atlantic world required funding the Revolutionary War debt at par, collecting sufficient revenue to meet other national objectives, empowering a vigorous executive, creating an efficient army and navy, and establishing an activist federal court system—measures that made the United States resemble a transplanted Britain, lacking only a royal court and an hereditary aristocracy. His opponents insisted that Americans had fought Britain to become something quite different. Once they captured power in 1801, they began to define what such a nation could become.

Jeffersonians set out to pay off the national debt as soon as possible, reduced the army and navy to token forces, repealed all internal taxes, and did their best to tame the federal judiciary. Especially after the Louisiana Purchase of 1803, they began to seek a combination of goals that no other movement or nation, anywhere else in the world, had yet put together. Under their leadership, the United States would repudiate the balance-of-power politics that prevailed in Europe. Within the Atlantic world, Jeffersonians favored trade with all of Europe's maritime powers but alliances with none. They believed that American commerce was so important that a mere threat of withholding it could force the great powers to respect American rights without resort to war, a policy that revealed its limitations when the United States finally declared war on Britain in the *War of 1812. But on this side of the ocean, the new republic would achieve hegemony within the western hemisphere—that is, it would be stronger than any combination of enemies that could be aligned against it—*without* the need to create standing armies or impose heavy taxes. The energy of the people, especially their determination to settle ever more western lands, would achieve this hegemonic goal with little more than mild supervision from Washington, while avoiding the class conflicts of Europe. The Jacksonian era saw this process become the ideology of "manifest destiny," whose apologists saw almost no limit to how large the United States might become (some even favored the annexation of Ireland!), provided that most governmental activities remained decentralized to the state level.

Liberty and empire remained compatible so long as the free and slave states could agree on how to share the spoils of western lands. By the 1830s, the Jeffersonian formula for hemispheric hegemony had won wide acceptance. As Abraham *Lincoln argued in one of his earliest speeches, "All the armies of Europe, Asia and Africa combined ... could not by force, take a drink from the Ohio, or make a track on the Blue Ridge, in a trial of a thousand years." Any threat to the Union, he insisted in 1838, "cannot come from abroad. If destruction be our lot, we must ourselves be its author and finisher. As a nation of freemen, we must live through all time, or die by suicide."

When Lincoln wrote, the "imagined community" of the United States was still restricted to white men. Its success depended on the republic's ability to deprive Indians of nearly all of their land, usually without significant compensation or any willingness to incorporate Indians into the polity. Enslaved African Americans were not part of the polity either. During the Revolution, most blacks south of New England in a position to choose sided with the British, not the American republic. Partly because Federalists pushed harder for abolition in northern states than did their opponents, the Jeffersonian triumph magnified these trends. In 1807, when the Democratic-Republicans took control of New Jersey (the only state that permitted some women to vote), they righteously disfranchised women, Indians, and free blacks, thus announcing to the world that their brand of democracy applied to white men only.

The early 1830s largely defined the extremes that would shape American politics and national identity for the next three decades. Northern evangelical Protestants launched a vigorous abolitionist movement that increasingly alarmed the South. South Carolina nullified the tariff in 1832 and threatened secession if President Andrew *Jackson resorted to force. Jackson pushed a "Force Act" through Congress but also agreed with Congress's decision to lower the tariff by stages over the next decade. Disillusioned nullifiers began to envision an independent southern nation taking shape, united in the defense of slavery. Jackson's supporters, for the first time in the history of the republic, insisted that the Constitution had created a "perpetual union," one that could not be destroyed. Many of Jackson's northern opponents agreed. As Daniel Webster put it in 1830, "Liberty and Union, now and forever, one and inseparable." But after the *Mexican War, North and South could not agree on how to digest America's enormous conquest, nor even on how to divide between them the remaining unsettled portion of the Louisiana Purchase. *Expansionism, instead of solving the nation's problems, was tearing it apart. The two ideas, of a southern nation and an indestructible union, finally clashed when the *Civil War erupted in April 1861.

Both sides did their best to appropriate the principles of 1776. Confederate apologists insisted that they were the true heirs of the Revolution, much as the patriots of that era had claimed to be defending English liberty against a government bent on destroying it. Lincoln insisted well into 1862 that he was fighting only to preserve the Union that the founding fathers had created.

Despite these similarities between the Revolution and the Civil War, the differences are even more compelling. In 1775–76, the colonists went to war and fought for fifteen months before Congress finally proclaimed American independence. In 1860–61, seven Southern states seceded from the Union, created the Confederate States of America and then began a war against the United States by firing upon *Fort Sumter. When President Lincoln responded with a summons to arms, four more states seceded and joined the Confederacy. In other words, the Revolutionary War preceded the creation of an American nation, but the Confederate nation preceded the Civil War. Some "fire-eaters" had been agitating for a southern nation for nearly three decades by then, a movement without parallel in the colonies before 1776. The Confederacy was, in short, very much the product of an active and aggressive nationalism in a way that the original American Union had not been.

At first, both sides tried not to interfere with the constricted sense of American identity that Jeffersonians had bequeathed to them. But the *Emancipation Proclamation, followed by the Thirteenth, Fourteenth, and Fifteenth Amendments to the Constitution, boldly offered freedom, citizenship, the duty to bear arms, and suffrage to black males while ignoring the demands of the early women's suffrage movement. This mobilization of blacks contributed immensely to Union victory by 1865. But the failure of Radical *Reconstruction and the imposition of Jim Crow legislation throughout the former Confederate and border states deprived nearly all black men of the ability to vote by the early twentieth century. Blacks were free but not equal. The warring sections of the republic achieved reconciliation around principles of liberty, union—and white supremacy. While disfranchising blacks, they enfranchised white women, beginning in several western states near the end of the nineteenth century and culminating in the Nineteenth Amendment to the Constitution during World War I.

World War II marked the next watershed. The Pacific War became a merciless contest between two racial ideologies—Japan's determination to make the divine Yamato race prevail throughout Asia and the Pacific versus the white supremacy of the Western powers, led by the United States. By contrast, the United States fought to destroy Nazi racism in the European theater; and in the aftermath of the war and during the onset of the *Cold War, the attack on racism became a major force in domestic politics as well. President Harry S. *Truman began the desegregation of American armed forces on the eve of the *Korean War. Over the next two decades, the American defense establishment (along with the world of professional and intercollegiate sports) led all other sectors of American society in the quest for equal opportunity regardless of race. Ironically, while the rest of the world largely condemned American intervention in Vietnam as a ruthless manifestation of arrogant racial supremacy, the United States fought the *Vietnam War with the most completely integrated military establishment the nation had ever possessed. Colin *Powell, an African American who fought in Vietnam as a junior officer, would become by the 1990s the most powerful military officer in the land, chairman of the *Joint Chiefs of Staff. By then, women had also won far broader opportunities for military careers than had ever been available to them before.

What it means to belong to the American nation is still hotly contested, but at the end of the twentieth century that identity has become far more inclusive than ever before.

[See also Culture, War, and the Military; Internationalism; Militarism and Antimilitarism; Patriotism; Religion and War; Women in the Military.]

• Frederick Merk, *Manifest Destiny and Mission in American History*, 1963. David M. Potter, "The Historian's Use of Nationalism and Vice Versa," in his *The South and the Sectional Conflict*, 1968, pp. 34–83. Lance Banning, "Republican Ideology and the Triumph of the Constitution, 1789 to 1793," *The William and Mary Quarterly*, 3d ser., 31 (1974), pp. 167–88. J. M. Bumsted, "'Things in the Womb of Time': Ideas of American Independence, 1633 to 1763," *The William and Mary Quarterly*, 3d ser., 31 (1974), pp. 533–64. Paul D. Escott, *After Secession: Jefferson Davis and the Failure of Confederate Nationalism*, 1978. Kenneth M. Stampp, "The Concept of a Perpetual Union," in his *The Imperiled Union: Essays on the Background of the Civil War*, 1980, pp. 3–36. John M. Murrin, "A Roof Without Walls: The Dilemma of American National Identity," in Richard Beeman, Stephen Botein, and Edward C. Carter II, eds., *Beyond Confederation: Origins of the Constitution and American National Identity*, 1987, pp. 333–48. Benedict Anderson, *Imagined Communities: Reflections on the Origins and Spread of Nationalism*, rev. ed., 1991. Liah Greenfeld, *Nationalism: Five Roads to Modernity*, 1992. Linda Colley, *Britons: Forging the Nation, 1707–1837*, 1992. David Waldstreicher, *In the Midst of Perpetual Fetes: The Making of American Nationalism, 1776–1820*, 1997. Gary W. Gallagher, *The Confederate War*, 1997.
—John M. Murrin

NATIONAL LABORATORIES. Since the mid-twentieth century, the U.S. government has supported hundreds of science and technology laboratories, many for military purposes. Those designated *national* laboratories combine wide-ranging research and development programs with administration by the Department of Energy (1977) as government-owned, contractor-operated facilities. Although the national laboratory system traces its roots to World War II's atomic bomb project, only three have maintained significant roles in designing, developing, and engineering *nuclear weapons: Los Alamos (1943), Sandia (1948), and Lawrence Livermore (1952). The two other major wartime laboratories, Oak Ridge National Laboratory and Argonne National Laboratory, abandoned military-related work. An additional three national laboratories created subsequently—Brookhaven National Laboratory, Fermi National Accelerator Laboratory, and Idaho National Engineering Laboratory—rarely performed any.

Until the early twentieth century, new military technology normally originated outside the military establishment. Although individual soldiers might have a hand in invention, manufacturing rather than innovation tended to characterize the century-old network of army arsenals and navy shipyards. In 1915, however, the creation of the National Advisory Committee for Aeronautics (NACA) inaugurated a new era.

Advisory to be sure, NACA (1915–58) also directed a premier research facility, Langley Aeronautical Laboratory in Virginia. Not only did NACA become an interwar byword for cutting-edge military (and civilian) aeronautical research, it also provided the Office of Scientific Research and Development with a model for organizing American science in World War II. Government contracts with well-established academic and industrial organizations became the normal route for military research and development during the war and after.

Ultimately, the most renowned instance of this new partnership was the *Manhattan Project. To produce a totally new weapon, the atomic bomb, the army's wartime Manhattan Engineer District contracted with universities and corporations for the necessary applied scientific research, engineering development, proof testing, and manufacturing. Facilities created to further the project included what would become the national laboratories, all inherited by the Atomic Energy Commission (1947–75) when it succeeded the army team.

When the war ended, only Los Alamos, the New Mexico laboratory managed by the University of California, remained in the weapons business, though it soon had company. The laboratory's weaponization group (responsible for converting designs to functional weapons) moved to Albuquerque, changed its name to Sandia, and became an independent engineering laboratory in 1948. The following year, its management passed from the university to Bell Telephone, succeeded in its turn by Martin Marietta in 1995.

Concerns about the development of thermonuclear weapons underlay the 1952 establishment of the third nuclear weapons laboratory at Livermore, California. Originally a branch of the University of California Radiation Laboratory (now Lawrence Berkeley Laboratory), Lawrence Livermore became independent in 1971, though still under university management. To provide weaponization support for the new laboratory, Sandia in 1956 opened its own branch laboratory in Livermore.

Los Alamos, Lawrence Livermore, and Sandia were responsible for designing and developing every warhead in America's entire nuclear arsenal. And although the research, development, and testing of nuclear weapons remains their core concern, they expanded their scope far beyond any narrow military requirements into such areas as computers, *lasers, and biomedical technology.

[See also Atomic Scientists.]

• Richard G. Hewlett, et al., *A History of the United States Atomic Energy Commission,* 3 vols., 1962–89. Thomas E. Cochran, et al., *Nuclear Weapons Databook,* Vol. 3: *U.S. Nuclear Warhead Facility Profiles,* 1987.   —Barton C. Hacker

NATIONAL SECURITY ACT (1947). The conditions leading to the entry of the United States into World War II in 1941 revealed a number of deficiencies in how its national security apparatus was organized. There were inadequacies in civil-military policy coordination, in interservice coordination, and in intelligence. During the latter part of the war, debate arose over the possibility of merging the U.S. Army (and its subordinate air force) and the U.S. Navy into a single department. The army largely favored the concept; the air force saw it as the means to its independence; the navy was opposed.

It became apparent to Navy Secretary James V. *Forrestal in 1945 that, given congressional interest, outright opposition was doomed. He decided it was best to come up with an alternative that he could support. He asked his former business colleague Ferdinand Eberstadt to review the issue.

Once immersed, Eberstadt realized that military coordination and unification was far from the entire problem. Indeed, in a very logical order, Eberstadt saw that each proposed solution led to the need for further change. If there was going to be a unified military, civil-military coordination also had to be improved. Further, improved policy coordination also required more coherent intelligence support.

The idea of improved civil-military coordination was not new. Various types of structures had been tried since at least Woodrow *Wilson's administration, all with little effect. But the combination of evident problems at the outset of World War II, coupled with the growing demands of the postwar world and nascent *Cold War, created a political consensus for some kind of action hitherto lacking. Even so, the unification struggle was in a long congressional debate (1945–47) that required the intervention of President Harry S. *Truman for its completion.

The National Security Act signed into law on 26 July 1947 created a number of enduring structures: a *National Security Council (NSC) to coordinate policy, consisting of the president, vice president, secretary of state, and the newly created secretary of defense (which went to Forrestal); a Department of *Defense (actually created in a 1949 amendment, initially called a National Military Establishment), including a statutory *Joint Chiefs of Staff (JCS); and a *Central Intelligence Agency (CIA). The U.S. *Air Force was recognized as an independent service from the army, but the navy retained its own aviation force and prevented the marines from being absorbed by the army.

The controversies in the prolonged congressional debate over the act centered on four main areas. The new defense structure raised concerns about the distinct roles and missions of the services, a vital issue in terms of doctrine, force structure, and budgets. It is also a continuing issue. Some in Congress worried about the role and powers of the JCS, fearing that it might become a "Prussian General Staff," threatening the concept of civilian control. Limits were placed, therefore, on the size of the JCS's joint staff and the powers of the chairman. A disproportionate amount of time was spent on the propriety of allowing the director of Central Intelligence to be an active duty military officer. Finally, there were concerns about the CIA becoming a "Gestapo." Therefore, provisions were included denying the CIA police or subpoena powers or any internal security role.

Of equal interest are the issues that did not arise. The NSC, which proved to be a crucial policy vehicle for successive presidents (through the unforeseen and still not statutory position of national security adviser), raised little interest. Nor did the clause tasking the CIA with "other functions and duties related to intelligence," which became the legal basis for *covert operations.

The National Security Act was a central document in U.S. Cold War policy and in the acceptance by the nation of its position as world leader. Although the act did not actually unify the armed services, it did increase the coordination of the national security establishment. This went from a very ramshackle ad hoc structure to a much more coherent and more centralized one—via the president through the NSC, the increasing power of the secretary of defense, and the role of the CIA in intelligence.

One of the most striking features of the act has been its relative stability. Although all have been strengthened, the NSC, Defense Department, and CIA continue on in basic roles not very far from those envisioned by Eberstadt. There have been necessary adjustments to the act: the 1949 amendments creating a stronger central control in the office of the secretary of defense; improved congressional oversight of the CIA; and the *Goldwater-Nichols Act (1946) increasing the JCS structure and role. But the essentials remain largely the same.

[See also Civil-Military Relations: Civilian Control of the Military; Commander in Chief, President as.]

—Mark M. Lowenthal

The **NATIONAL SECURITY AGENCY** (NSA) is the lineal successor to a number of U.S. code-breaking organizations and projects before and during World War II—Herbert Yardley's "Black Chamber," *MAGIC, and *ULTRA.

Created by President Harry S. *Truman in a secret directive in 1952, NSA is responsible for the protection of U.S. coded communications and for intercepting and breaking foreign communications—customarily referred to as *signals intelligence* (SIGINT). SIGINT is one of four major intelligence collection branches; it is highly prized by intelligence analysts and policy customers as SIGINT often reveals plans and intentions.

A three-star flag officer heads NSA, rotating among the services. Budget and personnel figures are classified, although NSA is widely acknowledged to be the largest of the intelligence agencies. James Bamford in 1982 estimated a budget of over $1 billion and 80,000–120,000 employees. NSA's major components are regional operational groups: the former Soviet Union and allies; communist Asian nations; Third World and others.

Like all other intelligence agencies, NSA came under post–*Cold War pressure to reduce size and costs while maintaining production and modernizing its workforce skills. A longtime leader in computer technology, NSA in the 1990s has been involved in a debate over a data encryption standard, which would allow enciphering nongovernmental data and which NSA opposed. It is assumed that NSA will play a role in "information warfare" (computer attacks on *communications, financial, and other nodes) as this becomes both a new capability and a growing defensive concern.

[*See also* Intelligence, Military and Political.]

• George A. Brownell, *The Origin and Development of the National Security Agency,* 1981. James Bamford, *The Puzzle Palace: A Report on America's Most Secret Agency,* 1982.

—Mark M. Lowenthal

NATIONAL SECURITY COUNCIL. Since its origins in 1947, the interagency, cabinet-level National Security Council (NSC) has played major roles, ranging from advising the president and coordinating various strands of policy to formulating and ratifying policy decisions. Because it is primarily an instrument of presidential power, each president has employed the NSC as he has seen fit. Since the 1960s, however, presidents have made sporadic use of the council itself but have assigned its White House–based staff important roles in policymaking not anticipated by the NSC's inventors. Moreover, the president's national security adviser, a position unforeseen in 1947, has become central to national policymaking.

The NSC was part of a compromise, fashioned in 1947, in postwar decisions over armed services unification. The council as a mechanism to coordinate foreign and military policy was first proposed in the Eberstadt Report (1946), sponsored by Navy Secretary James V. *Forrestal. Seeking an American version of the British Committee of Imperial Defence, Forrestal saw an NSC as a way to ensure timely and unified action in time of crisis, avoid the organizational confusion of World War II, and check the authority of a president—Harry S. *Truman—in whom he had little confidence. In particular, Forrestal and the navy saw the council as an alternative to the strong secretary of defense favored by proponents of unification because it would provide a decentralized military structure and preserve the navy's autonomy. Though the navy could not stop the plan for a secretary of defense, its proposal for an NSC endured, if in watered-down form; Truman's advisers altered early proposals granting the council statutory authority and ensured that the legislative language provided for advisory functions.

In the 1947 *National Security Act, Congress declared that the NSC's purpose would be to "advise the President

with respect to the integration of domestic, foreign, and military policies" so as to ensure more effective cooperation in national security policy. Moreover, the council would supervise the *Central Intelligence Agency (CIA). The council's members would be the president, the secretary of defense, the secretary of state, the three service secretaries, the chairman of the National Security Resources Board, and other such officials as the president chose to designate. The director of Central Intelligence would be an adviser, not a member. In a 1949 amendment, Congress removed the service secretaries and the National Security Resources Board, added the vice president, and designated the director of Central Intelligence and the chairman of the *Joint Chiefs of Staff as statutory advisers. The amendment also provided for a small staff with an executive secretary.

During the first few years of the council's existence, in order to preserve his freedom of action and avoid pressure to make decisions on the spot, Truman seldom attended meetings. Nevertheless, he approved a number of policy papers that the council had generated to provide guidance to the agencies. After the *Korean War broke out, Truman raised the council's status by routinely presiding over its meetings. In 1950, he also designated an NSC senior staff, under the direction of the council's executive secretary, and enhanced the council by integrating it into the executive office of the president. The senior staff met frequently for policy coordination purposes but had little impact on NSC policy papers, which were generated primarily by the State Department and the Department of *Defense. Although Truman had resisted suggestions that he appoint a national security assistant to help him coordinate policy, in 1950 he partially conceded by designating W. Averell Harriman as a special assistant, charged with monitoring the implementation of national security policy.

Of all Cold War presidents, Dwight D. *Eisenhower made the fullest use of the NSC, often meeting with its members on a weekly basis throughout his eight years in office. Those meetings provided agency chiefs with a forum to debate the issues and a means for them to ascertain presidential thinking. Significantly, Eisenhower tapped Robert Cutler, Dillon Anderson, and Gordon Gray to serve, at various times, as special assistant to the president for national security affairs, a position not specified in the National Security Act. He made great use of the assistant to keep abreast of current problems, to plan meetings, and to follow up decisions. He also authorized auxiliary NSC planning and coordinating boards, based upon agency representation, for policy coordination and for developing the position papers that provided guidelines for official policy on many issues. Although some Democratic critics charged Eisenhower with constructing a cumbersome decision-making process, he seldom relied on the NSC structure for decisions during crises; those he reserved for the flexibility of smaller meetings in his private office.

After Eisenhower, the council fell into relative eclipse as a means for policy guidance. Under President John F. *Kennedy, Eisenhower's elaborate NSC structure was torn down and the council met infrequently. Moreover, Kennedy's national security assistant, McGeorge *Bundy, became an adviser as well as a policy coordinator. Dissatisfied with advice from the State Department, Kennedy encouraged Bundy to turn the NSC staff into an instrument that could work quickly and secretly at the president's command and develop a "White House" perspective that was not restricted by the bureaucracy's recommendations. Lyndon B. *Johnson followed suit; he virtually did away with council meetings, developing his own mechanisms, primarily the "Tuesday lunch," for policy discussion and coordination.

The council as a forum for policy discussion and advice continued its decline during the Nixon-Ford period, while the council's staff and the national security adviser acquired an unprecedented level of prestige and prominence. Richard M. *Nixon declared that he was restoring the Eisenhower system, but his deep suspicion of the State Department and his desire to centralize command over policy worked against that purpose. To strengthen presidential control, Nixon and his ambitious national security adviser, Henry *Kissinger, created new advisory and decision-making mechanisms such as the Washington Special Action Group. Moreover, circumventing the State Department, Nixon and Kissinger established secret communications ("backchannels") with key allies and adversaries, e.g., with the Soviet Union, for arms control talks, and with the People's Republic of China, for normalizing relations. The unparalleled secret bombing of Cambodia during the *Vietnam War symbolized the extent to which Kissinger and the NSC staff had developed operational control over national security policy in this period.

Kissinger's use of "backchannels" and secret missions had mixed results—by leaving agency heads out of the picture and by confusing negotiators working in regular channels, an outcome that Jimmy *Carter criticized during his 1976 campaign. But like Nixon and Ford, President Carter established specific structures for policy advice and coordination as well as for crisis management. Moreover, Carter's national security adviser, Zbigniew Brzezinski, and the NSC staff played central roles in offering policy advice, sometimes to the discomfort of agency heads, especially Secretary of State Cyrus Vance. Although Brzezinski operated in a less Byzantine fashion than his predecessor, Carter sustained the trend toward a strong national security adviser and prominent NSC staff. This development led to an inconclusive debate over whether the president's choice for national security adviser should require the Senate's consent.

When Ronald *Reagan came to power, he pledged that cabinet members, not national security advisers, would have a dominant role in policymaking, a procedure that was consistent with his lack of interest in the details of foreign policy. Though the council met more frequently, Reagan followed his predecessors by approving new structures for discussion and decision making. No powerful national security adviser emerged, but activism in policymaking and implementation at the NSC staff level reached its apogee in the "Iran-Contra" activities of national security advisers Robert McFarlane and John Poindexter and their assistant, Lt. Col. Oliver North. Ignoring congressional restrictions, they secretly provided aid to the anti-Sandinista Contras with funds raised through arms sales to Iran and other sources. When the scandal broke in late 1986, Reagan claimed that his management style had precluded tight control over the NSC staff. But declassified documents and his own public statements suggest that Reagan provided overall direction, and that several of the *covert operations had his approval, if not the wholehearted support of some cabinet members.

Since the *Iran-Contra Affair, presidents have avoided the excesses of the Reagan system but have continued to supplant the council with other advisory and decision-making mechanisms. For example, President George *Bush made modest use of the council, relying instead on regular meetings of deputies' committees for policy development. The national security adviser and NSC staff have remained central for coordinating the strands of diplomatic, military, economic, and intelligence policy; for serving as sources of policy advice; and for managing important initiatives.

[See also Cold War: Domestic Course; Commander in Chief, President as; National Security Council Memoranda.]

• Mark M. Lowenthal, The National Security Council: Organizational History, 1978. Anna K. Nelson, "President Truman and the Evolution of the National Security Council," Journal of American History, 71 (September 1985), pp. 360–78. John Prados, Keepers of the Keys: A History of the National Security Council from Truman to Bush, 1991. Christopher Shoemaker, The NSC Staff: Counseling the President, 1991. Anna K. Nelson, "The Importance of Foreign Policy Process: Eisenhower and the National Security Council," in Gunter Bischof and Stephen Ambrose, eds., Eisenhower: A Centenary Assessment, 1995.
—William Burr

NATIONAL SECURITY COUNCIL MEMORANDA. Soon after President Harry S. *Truman established the *National Security Council (NSC), its participants developed an extended series of memoranda recording basic policy on diplomatic, intelligence, and military issues. Most comprehensive and ambitious was NSC 68, 14 April 1950, "United States Objectives and Programs for National Security," which called for massive increases in military spending to support the U.S. position in Europe and East Asia. Besides the policy papers, Truman's NSC institutionalized National Security Intelligence Directives (NSIDs) that specified tasks for the intelligence establishment. For the most part, NSC memoranda had high security classifications—often top secret—a practice that Truman's successors carefully followed.

President Dwight D. *Eisenhower's NSC apparatus continued Truman's precedent. Among important papers issued were annual statements on basic national security policy that delineated foreign and military policy objectives, strategic concepts, and requirements for foreign aid and military capabilities. Like Truman's policy papers, Eisenhower's documents created a framework for policymaking, seldom recording particular decisions.

When President John F. *Kennedy came to power, he abolished the NSC policy paper and institutionalized more informal arrangements through National Security Action Memoranda (NSAMs). Kennedy and his national security adviser McGeorge *Bundy used NSAMs for a variety of purposes—to communicate a policy decision, request specific information, or ask for studies on a particular issue. President Lyndon B. *Johnson continued this format, although less frequently than his predecessor.

After President Richard M. *Nixon appointed Henry *Kissinger as his national security adviser, a more formal system of National Security Study Memoranda (NSSMs) and National Security Decision Memoranda (NSDMs) appeared. NSSMs were White House requests for studies by the agencies, while NSDMs represented a presidential decision made after an NSC Senior Review Group, NSC members, and the president had completed the study and review process. Some have claimed that Kissinger used this process to distract the bureaucracy, but others have argued that it gave White House decision makers a better sense of the available options. For example, NSC agencies produced important studies on strategic arms control that led to NSDMs on negotiating positions for the *SALT Treaties. Nevertheless, the NSDMs only reflected part of the diplomatic process; Nixon and Kissinger never incorporated positions discussed in secret "backchannel" negotiations.

President Gerald *Ford continued the NSSM/NSDM process, and subsequent presidents adopted the same routine although using different terminology. Under President Jimmy *Carter, there were Presidential Directives (PDs) and Presidential Review Memoranda (PRMs), while under President Ronald *Reagan the national security system produced National Security Study Directives (NSSDs) and National Security Decision Directives (NSDDs). During the Reagan and Bush administrations, congressional investigators tried to get information about the scope and content of presidential directives; however, both administrations refused to cooperate because they considered them too important and too sensitive to divulge. Although giving new nomenclature to his NSC memoranda, the first post–Cold War president, Bill *Clinton, continued the practice of shrouding most of them in secrecy.

[See also Arms Control and Disarmament: Nuclear; Commander in Chief, President as; Intelligence, Military and Political.]

• John Prados, *Keepers of the Keys: A History of the National Security Council from Truman to Bush*, 1991. Jeffrey Richelson, ed., *Presidential Directives on National Security from Truman to Clinton*, 1994.

—William Burr

NATIONAL SECURITY IN THE NUCLEAR AGE. The concept of national security in the nuclear age is a product of the World War II experience that found intellectual and organizational expression during the *Cold War. Before 1942, the Departments of State, War, and Treasury—the three departments with foreign responsibilities—consulted with one another but developed compartmentalized approaches to diplomatic, military, and economic problems. National security was intended to provide organizing principles for a more coherent and integrated response to the problems of the postwar world. The *National Security Act (1947) created the *National Security Council and gave it overall responsibility for guidance and coordination of foreign and defense policies. The same act established the *Central Intelligence Agency (CIA) and the Department of *Defense, and made the three military services subservient to the latter.

For most of the Cold War, national security policy rested on the twin pillars of containment and *deterrence. Containment, the theme of George F. *Kennan's famous "X" article in *Foreign Affairs* (1947), looked forward to a time when the Soviet Union might become a less aggressive and more "normal" state. In the interim, the United States could protect itself, and hasten the transformation of the Soviet Union, by helping to rebuild the economies of key industrial regions (i.e., Western Europe and Japan) along the Soviet periphery and by strengthening the political will of their peoples to maintain their independence.

Deterrence is a strategy of conflict management that relies on threats of punishment to prevent a specified behavior. Successful threats need to be sufficient and credible.

They must hold out the prospect of enough loss to convince their target that restraint is in its self-interest. Implementation must also appear certain, or at least very probable, in the absence of compliance. The United States employed deterrence to restrain the Soviet Union and China militarily, and more specifically, to prevent an invasion of Western Europe or Japan. Washington threatened both countries with nuclear annihilation.

Deterrence became the military arm of containment. Kennan had conceived of containment as primarily a political-economic strategy, but NSC 68 and the *Korean War encouraged greater emphasis on military means of opposing communism. By the mid-1950s, the Communist threat was also regarded as largely military. Successive State and Defense Department annual reports described deterrence as the "foundation" of national security policy.

Deterrence was attractive to the American national security establishment for military, political, and economic reasons. Wars between nuclear powers were too costly to fight, and the strategy of deterrence was specifically designed to prevent them. Deterrence, and the related strategy of compellence, also appeared to provide a mechanism by which the United States could exploit its strategic superiority for political ends. Nuclear retaliation was also much cheaper than any attempt to match Soviet conventional capabilities. President Dwight D. *Eisenhower—and Premier Nikita Khrushchev—invoked the security conferred by nuclear deterrence to justify cuts in conventional force levels.

The implementation of threats usually involves costs for threat makers, too, and credibility is difficult to establish in proportion to these costs. In the opinion of many strategists, within and without the government, the credibility of the American commitment to attack the Soviet Union with *nuclear weapons in response to an invasion of Western Europe became increasingly problematic once the Soviet Union developed the capability to attack the United States with its own nuclear weapons. From the early 1960s on, successive American administrations grappled with this dilemma. Through a combination of arms buildups and deployments, nuclear doctrines and targeting, and rhetorical commitment, they sought to convey resolve to the Soviet Union and reassure the European allies without unduly frightening them.

Controversies. The role of nuclear weapons in Soviet-American relations was and remains controversial. The debate centers on four questions. First and foremost is the contribution nuclear deterrence made to the prevention of World War III. The conventional wisdom regards deterrence as the principal pillar of the postwar peace between the superpowers. Critics charge that deterrence was beside the point or a threat to the peace.

The second question, of interest to those who believe that deterrence worked, is why and how it works. Some insist that it forestalled Soviet aggression; in its absence, Moscow would have attacked Western Europe and possibly sent forces to the Middle East. More reserved supporters credit the reality of nuclear deterrence with moderating the foreign policies of both superpowers.

The third question concerns the military requirements of deterrence. In the 1960s, Defense Secretary Robert S. *McNamara adopted Mutual Assured Destruction (MAD) as the official American strategic doctrine. McNamara contended that the Soviet Union could be deterred by the

American capability to destroy 50 percent of its population and industry in a retaliatory strike. He welcomed the effort by the Soviet Union to develop a similar capability in the expectation that secure retaliatory capabilities on both sides would foster stability.

Many military officers and civilian strategists rejected MAD on the grounds that it was not credible to Moscow. To deter the Soviet Union, the United States needed to be able to prevail at any level of conflict. This required a much larger nuclear arsenal and highly accurate *missiles necessary to destroy Soviet missiles in their silos and the underground bunkers where the political and military elite would take refuge in any conflict. Nuclear "war fighting" supplanted MAD as the official strategic doctrine during the presidency of Jimmy *Carter. The Reagan administration spent vast sums of money to augment conventional forces and to buy the strategic weapons and command and control networks that *Pentagon planners considered essential to nuclear war fighting.

An alternate approach to nuclear weapons, "finite deterrence," maintained that Soviet leaders were as cautious as their Western counterparts and just as frightened by the prospects of nuclear war. Nuclear deterrence was far more robust than proponents of either MAD or war fighting acknowledged and required only limited capabilities—several hundred nuclear weapons would probably suffice. The doctrine of finite deterrence never had visible support within the American government.

The fourth question concerns the broader political value of nuclear weapons. War fighters maintained that strategic superiority was politically useful and conferred bargaining leverage on a wide range of issues. Most supporters of MAD contended that strategic advantages could only be translated into political influence in confrontations like the *Cuban Missile Crisis (1962–63), where vital interests were at stake. Other supporters of MAD, and all advocates of finite deterrence, denied that nuclear weapons could serve any purpose beyond deterrence.

Nuclear Deterrence in Retrospect. Evidence in the 1990s from recently declassified Soviet and American documents, memoirs, and interviews with former policymakers of both superpowers has allowed scholars to reconstruct some of the critical events of the Cold War. These histories, and the evidence on which they are based, permit some answers to the four questions that have been posed, although such answers must remain tentative until additional evidence becomes available about the role of nuclear weapons in other critical Soviet-American confrontations, and in Sino-American and Sino-Soviet relations.

1. *Leaders who try to exploit real or imagined nuclear advantages for political gain are not likely to succeed.* Khrushchev and Kennedy tried and failed to intimidate one another with claims of strategic superiority in the late 1950s and early 1960s. Khrushchev's threats and boasts strengthened Western resolve not to yield in Berlin and provoked Kennedy to order a major strategic buildup. Kennedy's threats against Cuba, his administration's assertions of strategic superiority, and the deployment of Jupiter missiles in Turkey—all intended to dissuade Khrushchev from challenging the West in Berlin—led directly to the Soviet decision to send missiles to Cuba. Both leaders were willing to assume the risks of a serious confrontation to avoid creating the impression of weakness or irresolution.

2. *Credible nuclear threats are very difficult to make.* The destructiveness of nuclear weapons makes nuclear threats more frightening but less credible. It is especially difficult to make nuclear threats credible when they are directed against nuclear adversaries who have the capability to retaliate in kind. Many Soviets worried about nuclear war during the Cuban Missile Crisis, but Khrushchev judged correctly that Kennedy would not initiate a nuclear war in response to the deployment of Soviet missiles. Khrushchev's principal concerns were that the president would be pushed into attacking Cuba, and that armed clashes between the invading Americans and the Soviet forces on the island committed to Cuba's defense would escalate into a wider and perhaps uncontrollable war.

In 1973 during the Yom Kippur War, the American alert had even less influence on the Soviet leadership. It was inconceivable to Leonid Brezhnev and his colleagues that the United States would attack the Soviet Union with nuclear weapons. They did not believe that the interests at stake for either the United States or the Soviet Union justified war. The American nuclear threat was therefore incredible. The Politburo assumed that it was directed against President Nixon's domestic opponents.

3. *Nuclear threats are fraught with risk.* In both 1962 and 1973, American leaders were uninformed about the consequences and implications of strategic alerts. In 1973, they did not understand the technical meaning or the operational consequences of the DEFCON III alert (U.S. forces were normally kept at DEFCON IV) and chose the alert in full confidence that it entailed no risks. During the 1962 missile crisis, when conventional and nuclear forces were moved to an even higher level of alert (DEFCON II), it was very difficult to control alerted forces. Military routines and insubordination posed a serious threat to the resolution of the crisis.

Evidence from these two cases suggests that there are stark trade-offs between the political leverage that military preparations are expected to confer and the risks of inadvertent escalation they entail. American leaders had a poor understanding of these trade-offs: they significantly overvalued the political value of nuclear alerts and were relatively insensitive to their risks.

4. *Strategic buildups are more likely to provoke than to restrain adversaries because of their impact on the domestic balance of political power in the target state.* Josef *Stalin, Khrushchev, and Brezhnev all believed that strategic advantage would restrain adversaries. Khrushchev believed that the West behaved cautiously in the 1950s because of a growing respect for the economic as well as the military power of the socialist camp. He was convinced that the visible demonstration of Soviet power—through nuclear threats and the deployment of missiles in Cuba—would strengthen the hands of "sober realists" in Washington who favored accommodation with the Soviet Union. Khrushchev's actions had the opposite impact: they strengthened anti-Soviet militants by intensifying American fears of Soviet intentions and capabilities. Kennedy's warnings to Khrushchev not to deploy missiles in Cuba, and his subsequent blockade, were in large part a response to the growing domestic political pressures to act decisively against the Soviet Union and its Cuban ally.

Brezhnev's strategic buildup was a continuation of Khrushchev's program. American officials considered that the Soviet buildup continued after parity had been achieved. Soviet strategic spending appeared to confirm the predictions of militants in Washington that Moscow's goal was strategic superiority, even a first-strike capability. Brezhnev, on the other hand, expected Soviet nuclear capabilities to prevent the United States from engaging in "nuclear blackmail." Instead, it gave Republicans ammunition to use against President Carter and the SALT II agreement. The Soviet arms buildup and invasion of Afghanistan contributed to Ronald *Reagan's landslide victory in 1980 and provided the justification for his administration's massive arms spending. American attempts to put pressure on the Soviet Union through arms buildups were equally counterproductive.

5. *Nuclear deterrence is robust when leaders on both sides fear war and are aware of each other's fears.* War fighting, MAD, and finite deterrence all mistakenly equate stability with specific arms configurations. More important than the distribution of nuclear capabilities, or leaders' estimates of relative nuclear advantage, is their judgment of an adversary's intentions. The Cuban Missile Crisis was a critical turning point in Soviet-American relations because it convinced Kennedy and Khrushchev, and some of their most important advisers as well, that their adversary was as committed as they were to avoiding nuclear war. This mutually acknowledged fear of war made the other side's nuclear capabilities less threatening and paved the way for the first arms control agreements.

Not all American and Soviet leaders shared this interpretation. Large segments of the national security elites of both superpowers continued to regard their adversary as implacably hostile and willing to use nuclear weapons. Even when Brezhnev and Nixon acknowledged the other's fear of war, they used the umbrella of nuclear *deterrence to compete vigorously for unilateral gain. Western militants did not begin to change their estimate of Soviet intentions until Mikhail Gorbachev made clear his commitment to ending the arms race and the Cold War.

Deterrence and the Cold War. The Cold War was the result of Soviet-American competition in Central Europe in the aftermath of Germany's defeat. Once recognized spheres of influence were established, confrontations between the superpowers in the heart of Europe diminished. Only Berlin continued to be a flashpoint until the superpowers reached an understanding about the two Germanies.

The conventional and nuclear arms buildup that followed in the wake of the crises of the early Cold War was a reaction to the mutual insecurities they generated. By the 1970s, the growing arsenal and increasingly accurate weapons of mass destruction that each superpower aimed at the other had become the primary source of mutual insecurity and tension. Moscow and Washington no longer argued about the status quo in Europe but about the new weapons systems each deployed to threaten the other. Each thought that deterrence was far less robust than it was. Their search for deterrence reversed cause and effect and prolonged the Cold War.

The history of the Cold War provides compelling evidence of the pernicious effects of the open-ended quest for nuclear deterrence. But nuclear weapons also moderated superpower behavior, once leaders in Moscow and Washington recognized and acknowledged to the other that a nuclear war between them would almost certainly lead to their mutual destruction.

After the late 1960s, when the Soviet Union developed an effective retaliatory capability, both superpowers had to live with nuclear vulnerability. There were always advocates of preemption, ballistic missile defense, or other illusory visions of security in a nuclear world. But nuclear vulnerability could not be eliminated. Mutual Assured Destruction was a reality from which there was no escape short of the most far-reaching arms control. Even after the dissolution of the Soviet Union in 1991 and the proposed deep cuts in nuclear weapons, Russia and the United States still possess enough nuclear weapons to destroy each other several times over.

Nuclear vulnerability distinguished the Soviet-American conflict from conventional conflicts of the past or present. In conventional conflicts, leaders could believe that war might benefit their country. Leaders have often gone to war with this expectation, although more often than not they have been proven wrong. The consequences of war turned out very differently than leaders in Iraq in 1980, Argentina in 1982, and Israel in 1982 expected.

Fear of the consequences of nuclear war not only made it exceedingly improbable that either superpower would deliberately seek a military confrontation with the other; it made their leaders extremely reluctant to take any action that they considered would seriously raise the risk of war. Over the years they developed a much better appreciation of each other's interests. In the last years of the Soviet-American conflict, leaders on both sides acknowledged and refrained from any challenge of the other's vital interests.

The ultimate irony of nuclear deterrence may be the way in which the strategy of deterrence undercut much of the political stability the reality of deterrence should have created. The arms buildups, threatened military deployments, and confrontational rhetoric that characterized the strategy of deterrence effectively obscured deep-seated, mutual fears of war. Fear of nuclear war made leaders inwardly cautious, but their public posturing convinced their adversaries that they were aggressive, risk-prone, and even irrational.

This kind of behavior was consistent with the strategy of deterrence. Leaders on both sides recognized that only a madman would use nuclear weapons against a nuclear adversary. To reinforce deterrence, they therefore tried, and to a disturbing degree succeeded, in convincing the other that they might be irrational enough or sufficiently out of control to implement their threats. Each consequently became less secure, more threatened, and less confident of the robust reality of deterrence. The strategy of deterrence was self-defeating: it provoked the kind of behavior it was designed to prevent.

The history of the Cold War suggests that nuclear deterrence should be viewed as a powerful but very dangerous medicine. Arsenic, formerly used to treat syphilis and schistosomiasis, or chemotherapy, routinely used to treat cancer, can kill or cure a patient. The outcome depends on the virulence of the disease, how early the disease is detected, the amount of drugs administered, and the resistance of the patient to both the disease and the cure. So it is with nuclear deterrence. Finite deterrence can be stabilizing when it prompts mutual caution. Too much deterrence, or deterrence applied inappropriately to a frightened and vulnerable adversary, can fuel an arms race that makes both sides less rather than more secure and provokes the very aggression it is designed to prevent. As with any medicine, the key to successful deterrence is to administer correctly the proper dosage.

[See also Arms Control and Disarmament, Berlin Crises; Carter Doctrine; National Security Council Memoranda; SALT Treaties; Strategic Defense Initiative; Strategy: Nuclear Warfare Strategy; World War II: Military and Diplomatic Course.]

• George F. Kennan, "The Sources of Soviet Conduct," Foreign Affairs, 25 (July 1947), pp. 566–82. Lawrence Freedman, The Evolution of Nuclear Strategy, 1981. John Lewis Gaddis, Strategies of Containment, 1982. I. M. Destler, Leslie H. Gelb, and Anthony Lake, Our Own Worst Enemy: The Unmaking of American Foreign Policy, 1984. McGeorge Bundy, Danger and Survival: Choices About the Bomb in the First Fifty Years, 1988. Karl F. Inderfurth and Lock K. Johnson, eds., Decisions of the Highest Order: Perspectives on the National Security Council, 1988. Robert Jervis, The Meaning of the Nuclear Revolution: Statecraft and the Prospect of Armageddon, 1989. Ted Hopf, Peripheral Visions: Deterrence Theory and American Foreign Policy in the Third World, 1965–1990, 1994. Richard Ned Lebow and Janice Gross Stein, We All Lost the Cold War, 1994.
—Richard Ned Lebow

NATIONAL SERVICE in the United States conventionally refers to the performance of full-time civilian service on the part of youth. The concept is usually traced back to William James's essay, "The Moral Equivalent of War" (1910). James coined the concept to contrast the noble human qualities evoked by war with the destructive purposes they served. Ever since James there has been a marked tendency to think of military and civilian service as alternate, if not opposing, ideals.

The Great Depression of the 1930s placed national service on center stage. Two of the most successful initiatives of the New Deal were national programs for youth: the Civilian Conservation Corps (CCC) and the National Youth Administration (NYA). President Franklin D. *Roosevelt gave some thought to putting national service on a more permanent footing after World War II, but his death intervened.

The 1950s were the doldrums for the idea of civilian national service, but the climate changed when President John F. *Kennedy in 1961 set up the Peace Corps, an overseas youth corps to serve primarily in Third World countries. Participants received a subsistence allowance plus free health insurance. Despite changes of fortune, the Peace Corps has proved remarkably durable. Some 150,000 volunteers have served in 92 countries.

The early success of the Peace Corps made a domestic equivalent seem a natural sequel. In 1964, VISTA (Volunteers in Service to America) was established as part of President Lyndon B. *Johnson's Great Society program. Though it never gained the popularity of the Peace Corps, VISTA has shown durability as well.

In 1988, the Democratic Leadership Council (DLC), an organization of centrist Democrats, proposed its own national service program. Senator Sam *Nunn of Geoᵊgia and Congressman Dave McCurdy of Oklahoma introduced a bill in 1989 that called for the establishment of a Citizen Corps for two years service in a civilian or military capacity. The conceptual breakthrough was the linkage of military and civilian service under the broader heading of national service. The policy breakthrough was the broadening of postservice educational benefits, e.g., the

*G.I. Bill principle, to include civilian as well as military service to the nation.

Although the Nunn-McCurdy bill did not move far in Congress, it set the stage for a public debate on national service. During the 1992 presidential campaign, candidate Bill *Clinton made national service one of his key campaign planks, part of his "New Democrat" image. In September 1993, President Clinton signed the National and Community Service Trust Act setting up a corporation to oversee the management and funding of an AmeriCorps program. Enrollees would work in nonprofit agencies, community centers, parks, government agencies, and public hospitals.

Since 1994, the annual budget of AmeriCorps has been around $300 million annually. Enrollment averaged between thirty and forty thousand a year. A major threshold was crossed in 1997 when AmeriCorps members could also perform service in faith-based organizations. In October 1998, a milestone was reached when the 100,000th member of AmeriCorps was enrolled.

The basic term of service in AmeriCorps was one or two years of full-time duty. Enrollees were paid 85 percent of the minimum wage, about $7,500 a year. In addition, for each year of service, a participant would receive an educational voucher worth $4,725 to be used for vocational education, college, graduate school, or to pay off a college loan. AmeriCorps set a notable precedent: a recognizable civilian variant of the G.I. Bill was codified into law.

The contemporary debate on national service reflects certain ongoing realities. One is that federally run programs have much more national visibility than decentralized programs. Even though AmeriCorps's first-year membership of 20,000 members was greater than that of the Peace Corps at any time, AmeriCorps's did not achieve the name recognition of the Peace Corps. Even more striking, the aura of the highly centralized and army-run CCC remains strong in the national consciousness, even though it expired a half century ago, while its larger decentralized and fully civilian counterpart, the NYA, is all but forgotten. A second reality was the continuing tension between proponents of national service who variously emphasized the good done for the server or the value of the work being delivered.

When the Republicans became the new Congressional majority in 1994, it appeared that national service would be placed on the budgetary chopping block. By 1998, however, AmeriCorps had gained more bipartisan support and its future seemed somewhat secure. Indeed, national service for youth was becoming increasingly popular in the United States as the century came to a close. In the late 1990s, AmeriCorps had four applicants for each available opening.

• Richard Danzig and Peter Szanton, National Service: What Would It Mean?, 1986. Alvin From and Will Marshall, Citizenship and National Service, 1988. Donald J. Eberly, National Service: A Promise to Keep, 1989. Williamson M. Evers, ed., National Service: Pro and Con, 1990. Steven Waldman, The Bill, 1995. Charles Moskos, A Call to Civic Service: National Service for Country and Community, 1998.
—Charles Moskos

NATIVE AMERICANS, U.S. MILITARY RELATIONS WITH. American military history twists around and through Native American lives like a corkscrew. Of all the direct relationships that developed between Native Americans and the various offices, agencies, and branches of the federal government, none has been more ambiguous than that which evolved between the tribes and the U.S. *Army. As an agent of conquest, the army undeniably used violence and terror to subjugate the tribes. But the violence was arbitrary and sporadic rather than methodical and unremitting. The army also performed numerous administrative tasks connected with Indian affairs, played an important diplomatic and ceremonial role in treaty negotiations, served as a constabulary on the reservations, sometimes provided tribes with rudimentary health care, distributed rations and annuities, and often acted as an intermediary between different tribes as well as between local whites and tribal leaders. The army recruited native males for military service, and numerous Indians developed strong bonds with the U.S. military as allies, auxiliaries, or scouts in conflicts with other tribal groups or foreign enemies. In short, the Native American–military relationship was a strange mixture of extreme emotions and behaviors: violence and compassion, hatred and comradeship, deceit and sincerity, moderation and excess.

The post–Revolutionary War United States made a national policy of expansion, despite the fact that the government lacked the military and financial strength to wage large-scale wars of conquest against the tribes. Tribal land cessions and peace and friendship treaties between the tribes and Congress failed to halt white encroachments on Indian lands. Warfare erupted along the frontier. When Congress established the War Department in 1789, it allocated Indian affairs to the secretary of war, defining the "Indian problem" as one to be solved by military means.

Secretary of War Henry *Knox, however, recognized that a military solution to the problem on the frontier would cost far too much blood and treasure. Several tribes, especially the Cherokees and Creeks in the South and the Shawnees, Kickapoos, Miamis, and others north of the Ohio River, held substantial military power. Knox's misgivings proved well founded in 1790 and again in 1791, when two military expeditions into the country north of the Ohio met with disaster at the hands of an Indian confederacy under the Miami war leader Little Turtle.

Knox and George *Washington therefore designed an Indian policy to carry forward expansion in a more orderly fashion. This policy provided for an impartial dispensation of justice, a method of purchasing (rather than simply taking) Indian lands, the regulation of commerce with a view to ending the liquor trade, the punishment of those who infringed on tribal rights, and the promotion of "civilization," or the propagation of economic techniques that would enable tribes to survive on greatly diminished landholdings. These ideas were incorporated into the Trade and Intercourse Acts between 1790 and 1834, and the army was authorized to police the frontier and implement the new policy. The War Department retained administrative control over Indian affairs until 1849, when the Indian Office was transferred to the new Department of the Interior.

From the 1790s on, the army functioned in the dichotomous role of trained fighting force and diplomatic representative. As Americans extended their frontiers, the army erected forts on the boundaries of Indian lands. These *fortifications could be sallying points for punitive expeditions against the tribes, but were also trading posts, meeting places for treaty negotiations, depots for issuing rations, and temporary jails for rounded-up whites who violated Indian territorial rights. Indians often came to the forts to complain of maltreatment or encroaching white settlers. A few treaties required army surgeons to provide health care for the tribes. A number of officers served as Indian agents and often used the forts as their administrative headquarters.

In the 1830s, the army acquired the onerous task of removal. The Indian Removal Act (1830) decreed that the eastern tribes were to be relocated west of the Mississippi. The army was assigned to round up tribal members, place them in stockades, and transport them to the Indian Territory (Oklahoma), which Congress created in 1834. Removal was neither war nor an effort to protect human rights, and officers not infrequently questioned the ultimate goals of their missions. Cherokee removal particularly galled the officer corps. Major W. G. Davis, who assessed the Cherokee improvements on their lands, protested to the secretary of war that the Cherokee removal treaty was fraudulent and that the removal itself stained the army's reputation. Both Brig. Gen. R. G. Dunlap and the overall federal commander Gen. John Ellis Wool looked upon the whites waiting to move onto Cherokee property with disdain and asked to be relieved of their commands.

Until the *Civil War, the army was primarily a small frontier force that mapped new regions, built roads, and implemented Indian policies. Except during major wars, such as the *War of 1812, the second of the *Seminole Wars, and the *Mexican War, regular army strength never exceeded 10,000 soldiers and officers. The Civil War's phenomenal increase of regular and volunteer regiments helped to militarize public attitudes and produced a series of ruthless and sanguinary wars against the western Indians. The long Apache Wars, the bloody Santee Sioux War in Minnesota, and the massacres of the Navajos at Canyon de Chelly, the Cheyennes at Sand Creek, and the Aravaipa Apaches at Camp Grant can all be traced directly to the actions of volunteer militia, overzealous and inexperienced junior officers, and armed citizens' groups.

After the Civil War, the army was reduced in size and once more became basically a frontier force. Between 1867 and 1876, army manpower fell from 57,000 to about 25,000, where it remained until the outbreak of the *Spanish-American War. It was not, however, the same kind of army as it had been prior to the great conflict of 1861 to 1865. The warfare between the tribes of the Far West and the whites was a nightmare of violence, and the army seemed a potential agency to control the situation; there was even a movement to transfer the Indian Office back to the War Department. It was thought that regular army officers were better educated, had no local political axes to grind, and could look upon Indian affairs from a purely professional standpoint.

Christian missionary influences prevented the transfer of the Indian Office, but William Tecumseh *Sherman, Philip H. *Sheridan, Nelson A. Miles, George Crook, and other veterans of Civil War service made efficient and merciless war on the tribes, regardless of the army's subordination to civilian Indian agencies. The army destroyed tribal horse herds, burned homes and food caches, chased Indians who had left their reservations, quelled internal disturbances, and generally made total war on recalcitrant native people until the 1890s. The outbreaks of warfare were unceasing, and the ruthlessness of these campaigns left a legacy of animosity toward the army that has lasted among some native people to this day.

Although the army made relentless war on Native Americans, the tribes did not break easily. On several occasions they foiled and defeated army units by better tactics and greater mobility. Badly needing personnel knowledgeable of Indian tactics and of western terrain, in 1866 the army formed the Indian Scouting Service. Thereafter, Native American men were recruited and paid regular army wages to track down and fight their traditional enemies or, most notably in the Apache outbreaks, their own people. The Indian Scouting Service was disbanded in 1943, after achieving a record of bravery in action unequaled in American military history.

By the time the Scouting Service had been formed, many whites had already formed the opinion that Indians were naturally adept at making war and would make excellent soldiers. In 1890, Secretary of War Redfield Proctor authorized raising several all-Indian infantry and cavalry units in order to capitalize on the presumed Indian proclivity for war and to legitimize Indians as American citizens. For a variety of reasons, these units were disbanded after seven years; but the active recruitment of Native Americans for military service has continued. Native Americans have served in every American war of the twentieth century in numbers greatly exceeding their proportional population. This, too, is a legacy of the long, stormy relationship between Indians and the U.S. military.

[See also Indian Treaties and Congresses; Native Americans in the Military; Native American Wars.]

• Francis Paul Prucha, *American Indian Policy in the Formative Years*, 1962. Don Rickey, Jr., *Forty Miles a Day on Beans and Hay*, 1963. Francis Paul Prucha, *The Sword of the Republic*, 1969. Fairfax Downey and Jacques Noel Jacobsen, Jr., *The Red Bluecoats*, 1973. Robert M. Utley, *Frontier Regulars*, 1973. Robert M. Utley and Wilcomb E. Washburn, *Indian Wars*, 1977. Thomas W. Dunlay, *Wolves for the Blue Soldiers: Indian Scouts and Auxiliaries with the United States Army, 1860–90*, 1982. Tom Holm, "Stereotypes, State Elites and the Military Use of American Indian Troops," *Plural Societies*, 15, 1984, pp. 265–82. Maurice Matloff, ed., *American Military History*, 1985.   —Tom Holm

NATIVE AMERICANS IN THE MILITARY. From the *Revolutionary War to the present, American Indians have served in the U.S. military in a variety of roles. During the Revolutionary War, Native Americans sought initially to remain neutral, but eventually most sided with the British, who seemed less expansionist. Nevertheless, Indians in south and central New England ultimately rallied to the American cause against the British and their Tory allies. Primarily these were alliances, but sometimes Indians, particularly religiously converted Indians, served as individuals in the American forces. Indians also fought on both sides in the *War of 1812; in the South, the Choctaw and Cherokee fought alongside Andrew *Jackson, while the Creek divided their allegiance.

During the *Civil War, Indians were first recruited by the Confederacy, which in 1861 raised four regiments from among the Cherokee, Chickasaw, Choctaw, Creek, and Seminole in the Indian Territory (Oklahoma) to drive neutrals across the border into Kansas. The most famous Confederate Indian, Col. Stand Watie, led his Cherokee Mounted Rifles in capturing *Union army *artillery batteries in the Battle of *Pea Ridge, Arkansas, in 1862. However, hundreds of these Indians eventually went over to the Union side, and an all-Indian brigade was organized in the Indian Territory. Aside from these Indian units with their

Indian officers, the most famous Indian to serve in the war was the Seneca Ely S. Parker, who rose to the rank of general and served as secretary to Gen. Ulysses S. *Grant.

In the thirty years of *Plains Indians Wars across the Great Plains from 1860 to 1890, members of certain tribes, especially the Crow and Pawnee, fought alongside regular army soldiers, black and white, against their traditional tribal enemies, especially the Lakota Sioux, helping the army wipe out tribal resistance to the encroaching settlement. During the postwar reorganization of the U.S. Army in 1866, Congress authorized the enlistment of up to 1,000 Indians as "scouts," making permanent a previously informal policy. The Indian Scouts, who may have reached as many as 1,500 in some decades, won high praise from generals like George Crook and Nelson A. Miles for their horsemanship, tracking, and fighting ability. An experiment begun in 1890 by Secretary of War Redfield Proctor and Gen. John Schofield to add all-Indian companies, under white officers, in each of the western regiments, was abandoned by 1897.

In the twentieth century, Indians, who participated in all the major U.S. military conflicts, would serve as individuals, not in Native American units. In World War I, perhaps as many as one-half of the Native American population were not U.S. citizens and were not eligible for the draft. Volunteer service was rewarded with U.S. citizenship. Including draftees and volunteers, some 10,000 Indians served in World War I. The service of these Indians contributed to the decision of Congress in 1924 to grant U.S. citizenship to all Native Americans.

In World War II, some 25,000 Indians served in the military, up from the 4,000 who had been in the military in 1940 before wartime *mobilization. Their participation marked a turning point in the relations of Indians with the larger American society. It produced the largest single exodus of Indian males from the reservations and allowed them to compete in an arena where the fighting ability of those from tribes with strong warrior traditions inspired respect among the whites with whom they served. (Indians did not usually serve in racially segregated units as did African Americans.)

Though the number of Indians in the Marine Corps never exceeded 800, their experience certainly obtained the most publicity but in many ways also reflected Indian experiences in other services. One exception to integration was the Navajo Code Talkers communication units, which worked behind enemy lines in the Pacific Theater and sent radio messages on enemy troop maneuvers in Navajo language, thus avoiding the need for mechanical decoding equipment while baffling the Japanese. From these units came several postwar tribal and national Indian leaders such as chairman of the Navajo Tribal Council Peter MacDonald.

It was an Indian Marine, Ira Hayes, a full-blooded member of the small Pima tribe in Arizona, who emerged as the most famous Indian of the war. One of the six Marines and Navy Corpsmen who were photographed raising the flag atop Mt. Suribachi after the Battle of *Iwo Jima, Hayes became a special celebrity used to demonstrate wartime unity. He struggled for the rest of his life with that notoriety, and finally died, destitute and suffering from alcoholism, at the age of thirty-three in 1955.

Military service during World War II did more than provide an arena where Indians could perform as equals. For the first time, thousands of young Indian men and women earned a decent wage. The average Indian's income increased two and a half times, to $2,500, between 1940 and 1944. Thousands married non-Indians, converted to Christianity, and relocated off the reservations after the war.

In the immediate postwar years, many of the Indian veterans benefitted from the *G.I. Bill. Some took a lead in battling for full civil rights and a better life. In 1947, they led a successful campaign for the vote in Arizona and New Mexico. Joseph Garry, an ex-Marine, chair of the Coeur d'Alene Tribal Council in Idaho and of the National Congress of American Indians, headed a fight in the early 1950s against assimilationist federal efforts to liquidate reservations and divide tribal assets.

Although no firm figures exist, estimates are that between 10,000 and 15,000 Native Americans served in the *Korean War and more then 42,000 served in the *Vietnam War. The conflict in Southeast Asia led many Indian Vietnam *veterans to begin to reexamine their situation in American society. Consequently, many joined with the most traditional tribal elders in attempts to revitalize indigenous warrior societies. Moreover, a number of disillusioned veterans became leaders of militant Indian rights organizations, such as the American Indian Movement (AIM) in the mid-1970s.

In the 1990s, about 10,000 Indians were serving in the *All-Volunteer Army, which revised many of its policies to accommodate Indian traditions and religious customs. Estimates from the *Veterans Administration and the Census Bureau suggest that in the 1990s there were 160,000 living Indian veterans. This represented nearly 10 percent of all living Indians—a proportion triple that of the non-Indian population—and confirms once again that Native Americans play an important role in the U.S. military.

[See also Native Americans, U.S. Military Relations with; Native American Wars: Wars Among Native Americans; World War I: Military and Diplomatic Course; World War II: Military and Diplomatic Course.]

• Thomas W. Dunlay, *Wolves for the Blue Soldiers: Indian Scouts and Auxiliaries with the United States Army, 1860–90,* 1982. Robert Wooster, *The Military and United States Indian Policy,* 1988. Alison R. Bernstein, *American Indians and World War Two: Towards a New Era in Indian Affairs,* 1991. Annie Heloise Abel, *The American Indian in the Civil War, 1862–1865,* 1992. Colin G. Calloway, *The American Revolution in Indian Country: Crisis and Diversity in Native American Communities,* 1995.　　　—Alison R. Bernstein

NATIVE AMERICAN WARS. *This essay consists of three articles that examine different aspects of Native American wars and warfare.* Warfare in Native American Societies *discusses the changing nature of organized armed conflict in disparate Native American societies.* Wars Among Native Americans *examines warfare between different Indian nations before and after contact with Euro-Americans.* Wars Between Native Americans and Europeans and Euro-Americans *traces the history of warfare between Indians and European nations, American colonies and states, and the United States.*

NATIVE AMERICAN WARS:
WARFARE IN NATIVE AMERICAN SOCIETIES

The significance of warfare varied tremendously among the hundreds of pre-Columbian Native American societies, and its meanings and implications changed dramatically for all of them after European contact. Among the more densely populated Eastern Woodland cultures, warfare often served as a means of coping with grief and depopulation. Such conflict, commonly known as a "mourning war," usually began at the behest of women who had lost a son or husband and desired the group's male warriors to capture individuals from other groups who could replace those they had lost. Captives might help maintain a stable population or appease the grief of bereaved relatives: if the women of the tribe so demanded, captives would be ritually tortured, sometimes to death if the captive was deemed unfit for adoption into the tribe. Because the aim in warfare was to acquire captives, quick raids, as opposed to pitched battles, predominated. Warfare in Eastern Woodland cultures also allowed young males to acquire prestige or status through the demonstration of martial skill and courage. Conflicts among these groups thus stemmed as much from internal social reasons as from external relations with neighbors. Territory and commerce provided little impetus to fight.

Trade contacts with Europeans changed this situation by creating economic motives to fight, as Indians sought European goods. The arrival of Europeans also dramatically intensified mourning warfare as it ushered in an era of depopulation stemming from colonization, intertribal warfare, and epidemic disease. In the seventeenth century, Algonquian and Iroquoian groups fought a series of "beaver wars" to control access to pelts, which could be traded for iron tools and firearms from Europe. Casualties and losses from disease ignited more mourning wars in a vicious cycle that threatened the viability of many Eastern Woodland cultures.

On the Western Plains, pre-Columbian warfare—before the introduction of horses and guns—pitted tribes against one another for control of territory and its resources, as well as for captives and honor. Indian forces marched on foot to attack rival tribes who sometimes resided in palisaded villages. Before the arrival of the horse and gun, battles could last days, and casualties could number in the hundreds; thereafter, both Plains Indian culture and the character and meaning of war changed dramatically. The horse facilitated quick, long-distance raids to acquire goods. Warfare became more individualistic and less bloody: an opportunity for adolescent males to acquire prestige through demonstrations of courage. It became more honorable for a warrior to touch his enemy (to count "coup") or steal his horse than to kill him.

Although the arrival of the horse may have moderated Plains warfare, its stakes remained high. Bands of Lakota Sioux moved westward from the Eastern Woodlands and waged war against Plains residents to secure access to buffalo for subsistence and trade with Euro-Americans. Lakota Sioux populations, unlike most Indian groups, increased in the eighteenth and early nineteenth centuries; this expansion required greater access to buffalo and thus more territory.

Unlike the Plains and the Eastern Woodlands, pre-Columbian warfare was almost negligible west of the Rockies. Northwest Coast, Columbia Plateau, and Arctic peoples tended to express violence at a personal level rather than between more elaborate political entities. Ceremonies often resolved conflicts between groups; rituals such as ceremonial gaming and the potlatch—a gathering at which the host acquired honor and privilege through the distribution of goods—allowed individuals peaceably to acquire prestige and leaders to compete for the allegiance of followers, and minimized warfare in the northwestern quadrant before the arrival of Europeans.

As always, European contact ushered in an era of greater warfare by intensifying competition for resources. Mounted Lakota Sioux warriors pushed such Plains nations as the Blackfeet and the Crow westward, into contact with Plateau Indians, precipitating violence between groups that shared little common cultural ground by which to mediate disputes. Some Plateau groups, such as the Nez Percé, adapted culturally, closely approximating Plains horse culture, including its martial components. Similarly, European traders, who approached trade as a competitive endeavor instead of one of reciprocity that created ties of mutual obligation, provoked disputes and sporadic violence in the eighteenth and nineteenth centuries. The European settlement that followed more distant trade relationships led to many wars for the control of land, some of which promoted united, pan-Indian resistance.

Despite the diversity of Indian cultures in North America, patterns of resistance to Euro-American conquest followed certain rules: sedentary groups tended to capitulate more quickly than their nomadic counterparts, because nomads faced more drastic changes in lifestyle if they surrendered to European domination, and because they could capitalize on their mobility to resist Euro-Americans militarily. Semisedentary and sedentary groups, lacking the means to carry out *guerrilla warfare, found it more feasible to accept reservation life and European-style agriculture.

• Frank Raymond Secoy, *Changing Military Patterns on the Great Plains*, 1953. Richard White, "The Winning of the West: The Expansion of the Western Sioux in the Eighteenth and Nineteenth Centuries," *Journal of American History*, 65 (September 1978), pp. 319–43. Patrick M. Malone, *The Skulking Way of War: Technology and Tactics Among the New England Indians*, 1991. Richard White, *The Middle Ground: Indians, Empires, and Republics in the Great Lakes Region, 1650–1815*, 1991. Daniel K. Richter, *The Ordeal of the Longhouse: The Peoples of the Iroquois League in the Era of European Colonization*, 1992. Stan Hoig, *Tribal Wars of the Southern Plains*, 1993.

—James D. Drake

NATIVE AMERICAN WARS: WARS AMONG NATIVE AMERICANS

Among most Indian groups east of Mississippi River on the eve of European contact—including the Iroquois and Cherokee—warfare served both social-psychological and demographic functions. Indians waged war against one another to help members of their group cope with the grief experienced at the loss of a loved one or to avenge the death of a relative. Known as "mourning wars," these conflicts were intended to acquire captives who would in turn either be ceremonially tortured to death or adopted into the group. Although men had responsibility for waging war and conducting the raids for captives, women often decided to initiate wars and typically chose between killing and adopting captives. Because taking captives rather than acquiring territory or economic goods was the primary impetus to fight, most wars before the arrival of Europeans were sporadic and consisted of relatively quick raids with little bloodshed.

Contact with Europeans spread trade goods and new diseases throughout the Eastern Woodlands, changing and intensifying wars between Indian groups. In the Northeast,

for example, Iroquoian peoples dependent on European firearms and iron tools expanded militarily to acquire the beaver pelts Europeans sought in exchange for their goods. The result, a protracted series of "beaver wars" between Iroquoian and Algonquian groups near the Great Lakes from the 1640s to 1680s, had both economic and demographic motives. Having lost many members to European diseases, the Iroquois waged mourning wars in a desperate effort to maintain their populations; meanwhile, having hunted out the local beaver supply, they expanded their hunting grounds, creating conflict with neighboring groups. The attendant warfare led to further depopulation, and, in a dangerous cycle, escalated mourning wars.

Beginning in the 1680s, wars among the Eastern Woodland Indians became entangled with the European wars for control of the continent and the Atlantic trade. King William's War (1689–97), Queen Anne's War (1702–13), King George's War (1744–48), and the *French and Indian War (1754–63), all pitted Indians against one another as allies of European powers. Incentives for Indians in these wars were both economic and demographic. Indians used European allies to further their interests in wars for captives and control of economic resources.

Indian rebellions against colonial domination also tended to become wars among Indian groups. In *King Philip's War (1675–76), for example, Indian groups including the Mohawks helped the New England colonies put down a great Wampanoag-Narragansett-Abenaki uprising. These actions reflected old rivalries among New England's Indians, as well as the view of some who preferred a strategy of accommodation toward the English over violent resistance. Similarly, in the Yamasee War (1715), Cherokees seeking English trade goods helped white Carolinians suppress the Yamasee and Creek Indians who resisted European military encroachments.

Wars on the Plains and in the Southwest differed from those in the Eastern Woodlands in that these primarily broke out between peoples pursuing two distinct lifestyles—nomadic and horticulturist. While such groups often forged symbiotic relationships, e.g., exchanging crops for buffalo meat, these contacts sometimes degenerated into nomadic raids on villages. The arrival of Europeans and the spread of the horse heightened distinctions between nomads and villagers. Most horticulturists, like the Pueblos, Pawnees, Navajos, Omahas, and Arikaras, remained sedentary once they acquired the horse; but others, such as the Cheyennes and Crows, abandoned horticulture for nomadism. Yet other groups, such as the Lakota Sioux and Blackfeet, moved onto the Plains from the east to take advantage of the buffalo supply and became nomads in the process. Those Plains and southwestern groups that had practiced nomadism before European contact usually continued after the arrival of the horse. The horse enabled nomads to hunt more efficiently, but did not end their reliance on agricultural peoples for many goods; trade between nomads and villagers became rarer, however, as raids largely supplanted trading as a means of procuring agricultural products.

The development of horse culture shifted the military balance of power on the Plains in favor of nomads. The Comanches came to dominate the southern Plains in the first half of the eighteenth century at the expense of Pueblos, Plains Apaches, and Navajos. Early in the eighteenth century, for example, the Navajos lived north of Santa Fe;

pressures from northern raiders gradually drove them westward, until by 1750 they inhabited what is now Arizona and western New Mexico.

In the second half of the eighteenth century, the Lakota Sioux did to northern and central Plains Indians what the Comanches had done to the Navajos. Originally residents of the Eastern Woodlands, the Sioux became the dominant power of the northern and central Plains through their willingness to use the horse as a tool of conquest against the horticulturists of the upper Missouri River. From Minnesota, they ranged westward to the Rocky Mountains and southward to the Platte River, finding allies in the Arapahos and Cheyennes, who helped devastate the Pawnees, Arikaras, and other groups by the mid-nineteenth century. The rise of the Lakota Sioux at the expense of sedentary tribes explains why the latter behaved as they did after the arrival of the United States on the Plains in the 1840s. Horticultural groups saw a greater threat in the expanding Lakota Sioux than the United States. They felt that a military alliance with the United States against the Lakota Sioux offered their best hope for survival.

• Frank Raymond Secoy, *Changing Military Patterns on the Great Plains*, 1953. Richard White, "The Winning of the West: The Expansion of the Western Sioux in the Eighteenth and Nineteenth Centuries," *Journal of American History*, 65 (September 1978), pp. 319–43. Thomas D. Hall, *Social Change in the Southwest, 1350–1880*, 1989. Richard White, *The Middle Ground: Indians, Empires, and Republics in the Great Lakes Region, 1650–1815*, 1991. Daniel K. Richter, *The Ordeal of the Longhouse: The Peoples of the Iroquois League in the Era of European Colonization*, 1992. Stan Hoig, *Tribal Wars of the Southern Plains*, 1993.

—James D. Drake

NATIVE AMERICAN WARS:
WARS BETWEEN NATIVE AMERICANS AND
EUROPEANS AND EURO-AMERICANS

Despite the diversity of Euro-American and American Indian societies, wars between the two have shared certain features. In most eras of conflict, Euro-Americans had Indian allies; Euro-American citizen soldiers tended toward greater brutality and less military discipline than professional soldiers; nomadic groups of Indians usually waged war more tenaciously than the more sedentary ones; and the eruption and expansion of war usually stemmed from a Euro-American drive to acquire Indian land.

During the sixteenth and seventeenth centuries, European powers established military presences in North America from which they could make and defend claims— by right of discovery, settlement, or conquest—to vast portions of a continent already inhabited by Indians. In response, many Native Americans waged wars to resist European colonial domination. In the seventeenth century, the Powhatan Confederacy threatened the existence of the Virginia Colony with attacks in 1622 and 1644. Four decades after their devastation of the Pequots in the Pequot War (1636–37); New England colonists faced a massive uprising among the Algonquians living within their borders in *King Philip's War (1675–76). The Pueblo Revolt (1680) drove the Spanish out of New Mexico for thirteen years. In the eighteenth century, colonists in Virginia and the Carolinas forcibly acquired land from Tuscaroras, Yamasees, and Cherokees, while the French put down the armed resistance of the Natchez, Chickasaw, and Fox.

In these wars and others, many groups of Indians flirted with a united pan-Indian alliance against colonists, but such alliances usually failed to reach fruition. With the French defeat in the *French and Indian War (1754–63), Indians west of the Appalachians found their survival threatened because they could no longer play off the French against the English. Aware that the presence of only one European power in their vicinity meant that the old trade system had broken down, in 1763 the Ottawa Chief *Pontiac rallied many groups formerly allied with the French in an effort to oust the English from the Ohio Valley. *Pontiac's Rebellion (1763–66), although relatively successful in cementing a pan-Indian alliance, ultimately failed. The English government tried to achieve peace in 1763 by a royal proclamation separating Indians and English settlers at the crest of the Appalachian Mountains. While the proclamation's promise that all land west of he Appalachians would be reserved for the Indians weakened Pontiac's alliance, it did nothing to lessen Euro-American pressures on Indian land, as American traders, squatters, and speculators flowed unchecked into the Ohio Valley.

Throughout the colonial era, European imperial rivalries overlaid warfare between Europeans and Native Americans. For example, during King William's (1689–97), Queen Anne's (1702–13), and King George's (1744–48) Wars, the French supported Algonquian raids against the English colonies, while New England's domesticated Indians and certain Iroquoian allies aided the English. In the French and Indian War, the French and their mostly Algonquian allies initially made impressive strides toward controlling the Ohio Valley, beginning with *Braddock's Defeat (1755), only to be overcome by the more numerous English and their Iroquoian supporters. Indians fought as European allies in these wars to advance their own perceived interests in acquiring weapons and other trade goods and captives for adoption, status, or revenge. Until the end of the French and Indian War, Indians succeeded in using these imperial contests to preserve their freedom of action.

The *Revolutionary War, however, forced the Indians of the Eastern Woodlands to deal with a United States that by the Treaty of *Paris (1783) had acquired all British claims south of the Great Lakes and east of the Mississippi. The United States encouraged settlement in its newly acquired lands, and the resulting Euro-American pressures for Indian land generated sporadic fighting in the Old Northwest. In the late 1780s, Shawnees and other Indians launched attacks that swept across Indiana, Ohio, and western Pennsylvania, and soundly defeated contingents of the U.S. *Army in 1790 ("Harmar's Defeat") and 1791 ("St. Clair's Defeat," which inflicted 900 *casualties on the 1,400 Americans under Arthur St. Clair). It took until 1794 for U.S. troops to quell the Indian warriors in the Battle of Fallen Timbers, in which Gen. Anthony *Wayne decisively defeated the Indians, securing the Old Northwest—for the time being—to Euro-American control.

Following their defeat in 1794 and the Treaty of Greenville (1795), the Indian land base continued to shrink until 1809, when the Shawnee brothers *Tecumseh and Tenskwatawa fostered a message of Indian unity and nativism among the tribes of the Old Northwest. Tensions in the region climaxed when Indians capitalized on the *War of 1812 between the United States and England to wage their own war. Despite several initial battlefield victories, these Indian efforts failed to do more than briefly delay the completion of American dominion in the Old Northwest. A final Indian attempt failed in the *Black Hawk War (1832).

To the south, diverse Creek leaders united to challenge white encroachment. Although some Creeks advocated accommodation, their voices went unheard as whites from Georgia, Alabama, Kentucky, and Tennessee, the last under the leadership of Andrew *Jackson, sought land and retribution for alleged Creek atrocities. The resulting Creek War (1811–14) ended with the Battle of Horseshoe Bend, in Alabama, in which 800 Indians died, the greatest Indian battle loss in U.S. history. The Cherokees were driven west in the *Trail of Tears (1838–39). Most of the Florida Indians were conquered and forced west in the *Seminole Wars (1818; 1835–42; 1855–58). Like the Indians in the Old Northwest, the Indians of the South had succumbed to U.S. expansion.

Peace, interrupted by only periodic armed resistance to removal policies, lasted until the end of the *Mexican War in 1848. After that conflict, the U.S. government and Indians west of the Mississipi River confronted a new burst of westward migration propelled by gold discoveries in California. The populous yet atomized Indians of California faced local posses and militias rather than federal troops. The result was devastating; if Euro-Americans committed genocide anywhere on the continent against Native Americans, it was in California. Between 1850 and 1860, war, disease, and starvation reduced the population of California Indians from 150,000 to 35,000. When prospectors found gold in the Pacific Northwest, warfare erupted in that region. The U.S. *Army engaged in the Rogue River (1855–56), Yakima (1855–56), and Spokane (1858) Wars to force a number of tribes onto reservations in the eastern portions of Oregon and Washington.

The Modocs and Nez Percé mounted the most determined resistance in the Pacific Northwest. The former, under the leadership of Keintpoos, holed up in a ten-square-mile area of lava deposits rife with caves and trenches. From this advantageous position, 60 Modoc warriors held off 1,000 federal troops for seven months in 1873. When the Modoc finally surrendered, the United States executed four of their leaders and sent the remainder to the Indian Territory. The Nez Percé, under the leadership of Chief *Joseph, led the army through more than 1,500 miles of rugged territory in Idaho, Wyoming, and Montana, until most were captured shortly before attempting to cross the Canadian border in 1877.

Initially, the United States sought to protect the overland trails leading to the West Coast from possible Indian attacks. While these attacks were minimal in the 1840s, Indians felt the presence of the migrants early as they brought disease and depleted game along the routes. Such repercussions escalated tensions. The Treaty of Fort Laramie, sponsored by the United States in 1851, sought to preserve peace on the plains by restricting tribes to designated lands. Yet fighting erupted as the parties largely ignored the treaty's terms and American migration continued to have detrimental effects on the buffalo herds on which Plains Indians relied for subsistence. Although Americans' westward migration temporarily abated during the *Civil War, tensions between Indians and settlers remained high. In Minnesota, groups of Eastern Sioux raided American settlements in 1862, only to face retalia-

tion from American troops who pushed many of them onto the plains. These Sioux faced relatively disciplined American troops and fared much better than the Cheyennes and Arapahos did at the hands of a volunteer Colorado militia. Sporadic Indian raids on Santa Fe Trail travelers led to fears in Colorado of a widespread Indian war. Hoping to make a preemptive strike, John Chivington led volunteers from Denver in the slaughter of most of Black Kettle's Cheyenne band, together with some southern Arapahos near Sand Creek—a location in southeastern Colorado where the U.S. government had promised them safety. The *Sand Creek Massacre (1864) precipitated Cheyenne and Arapaho revenge as they joined the Sioux in what would be a sporadic twenty-year war against the United States. In the *Plains Indians Wars (1854–90), U.S. soldiers waged war to open the plains to safe travel and settlement by confining Indians to reservations; Plains Indian warriors sought increased individual status through wartime acts of bravery and preservation of their way of life. Plains Indians now faced vast numbers of Euro-Americans, because the development of the railroad provided white soldiers and settlers efficient and economical *transportation to the contested territory. In the end, U.S. destruction of the Indians' main food source—the buffalo—combined with persistent attacks on Indian villages subdued the Indians on the plains.

Nevertheless, Plains Indians mounted a spirited resistance. In the north, the Oglala Chief Red Cloud's warriors stopped the building of the Bozeman Trail between Fort Laramie and western Montana (1866–67). In 1868, the Sioux received U.S. treaty guarantees to their territory, including the Black Hills of South Dakota. Yet in the northern plains, these victories proved short-lived. The discovery of gold in the Black Hills in the 1870s led to new white pressures for Sioux land, as the United States failed to live up to the terms of the 1868 Fort Laramie Treaty. Crow and Shoshone warriors assisted American soldiers in their effort to conquer and pacify Sioux country. Determined to avenge the annihilation of George Armstrong *Custer and much of the Seventh Cavalry in the Battle of the *Little Bighorn in 1876, the army persisted until the last of the northern Plains Indians surrendered. By 1877, Sioux armed resistance came to a virtual end when Chief *Sitting Bull fled to Canada and *Crazy Horse surrendered.

On the southern plains, Kiowas, Comanches, and southern Cheyennes faced a similar fate. Hemmed in by Texans to the south and settlers along the Platte River to the north, at the Treaty of Medicine Lodge in 1867, these Indians agreed to live on reservations in exchange for the protection and supplies of the federal government. When the federal government failed to provide the promised supplies, Indian men left the reservations to hunt and conduct raids. Gen. Philip H. *Sheridan and other officers retaliated with winter campaigns against Indian villages in the region beginning in 1868. Warfare lasted until 1875, by which time nearly all southern Plains Indians had submitted to life on reservations. The final denouement came in the tragedy known as the Battle of *Wounded Knee (1890).

In the American Southwest, the last region of the United States to face intense Euro-American pressure for land, various bands of Apaches under such prominent leaders as Cochise, Victorio, and *Geronimo mounted perhaps the most protracted military resistance of Indians to Euro-American expansion. Unlike the nearby Navajo, whose more sedentary existence had helped compel them to surrender in the 1860s, the prospect of surrender to American troops confronted the Apache with a catastrophic lifestyle change. Moreover, the Apache resided on more rugged territory than the Navajo, and their more nomadic existence facilitated their crossing and recrossing the Mexican border as they fled U.S. troops. Apache resistance came to an end in 1886 only after the army committed thousands of troop to the region and allowed them to cross the Mexican border in pursuit of the Apache.

• Francis Paul Prucha, *The Sword of the Republic: The United States Army on the Frontier, 1783–1846,* 1969; repr. 1977. Robert M. Utley, *Frontier Regulars: The United States Army and the Indian, 1866–1890,* 1973. Russell Thornton, *American Indian Holocaust and Survival: A Population History Since 1492,* 1987. David J. Weber, *The Spanish Frontier in North America,* 1992. Stan Hoig, *Tribal Wars of the Southern Plains,* 1993. Ian K. Steele, *Warpaths: Invasions of North America,* 1994. Colin G. Calloway, ed., *Our Hearts Fell to the Ground: Plains Indian Views of How the West Was Lost,* 1996. Jill Lepore, *The Name of War: King Philip's War and the Origins of American Identity,* 1998. —James D. Drake

NATO—the North Atlantic Treaty Organization—was originally created by representatives of twelve Western powers: Belgium, Canada, Denmark, France, Iceland, Italy, Luxembourg, the Netherlands, Norway, Portugal, the United Kingdom, and the United States, in 1949, as a military security alliance to deter the Union of Soviet Socialist Republics' (USSR) expansion on the European Continent. From 1945 to 1949, to widen the Communist sphere of influence, the USSR had annexed Czechoslovakia, East Prussia, Estonia, Latvia, Lithuania, Poland, Romania, and sections of Finland, and had penetrated into the governments of Albania, Bulgaria, and Hungary.

The foundation for NATO had been set in Brussels, Belgium, in March 1948, when representatives of Belgium, France, Luxembourg, the Netherlands, and the United Kingdom met to forge a mutual assistance treaty to provide a common defense system. The Brussels Treaty stipulated that should any of the five signatories be the target of "armed aggression in Europe," the other treaty parties would provide the party attacked "all the military aid and assistance in their power." In June 1948, after a losing battle by isolationists, the U.S. Congress adopted a resolution recommending that the United States join in a defensive pact for the North Atlantic area. President Harry S. *Truman urged U.S. participation in NATO as a critical part of his policy of containment of Soviet expansion. Containment had begun with the *Truman Doctrine of 1947 with military assistance to Greece and Turkey to resist Communist subversion. The North Atlantic Treaty was signed on 4 April 1949 in Washington, D.C. It formally committed the European signatories and the United States and Canada to the defense of Western Europe. The U.S. Senate ratified the treaty, 82 to 13. This treaty marked a fundamental departure with tradition of the United States because it was Washington's first peacetime military alliance since the Franco-American Alliance of 1778. In October 1949, in the *Mutual Defense Assistance Act, Congress authorized $1.3 billion in military aid for NATO. Greece and Turkey joined NATO in 1952. The Federal Republic of Germany joined in 1955 following an agreement on the termination of the Allies' postwar occupation of West Germany and an understanding that the country would maintain foreign forces on its soil. A rearmed Germany became a major component of NATO.

The USSR strongly opposed the NATO alliance. The Berlin Blockade in 1947–48 and the threat of war had in fact given impetus to the creation of NATO. Following the outbreak of the *Korean War in June 1950, fearing the possibility of a Soviet invasion of Western Europe as a result of a miscalculation by Moscow, NATO countries expanded their military forces in Europe. Allied forces in Western Europe numbered twelve divisions to deter a Soviet threat of eighty divisions. The sending of several U.S. divisions to Europe was strongly debated in the U.S. Congress. Proponents of *isolationism, including former President Herbert *Hoover and Senator Robert *Taft, opposed the assignment of ground troops to Europe. Others, including retired Gen. Dwight D. *Eisenhower, supported an increase in the U.S. commitment to the *Cold War and urged expansion of NATO forces. The isolationists lost, and Truman in 1951 added four more to the two divisions already in Germany to bring the Seventh U.S. Army to six divisions. Truman also brought Eisenhower out of retirement to become Supreme Allied Commander in Europe (SACEUR), following the creation of Supreme Headquarters Allied Powers Europe (SHAPE) in 1951. NATO ministers, in the *Lisbon Agreement on NATO Force Levels of February 1952, set new force goals for 1954 consisting of 10,000 aircraft and 89 divisions, half of them combat-ready. These were unrealistic; but by 1953, NATO had fielded 25 active divisions, 15 in Central Europe, and 5,200 aircraft, making it at least equal to Soviet forces in East Germany. In 1955, Moscow created the *Warsaw Pact, a military alliance composed of Albania, Bulgaria, Czechoslovakia, the German Democratic Republic (GDR), Hungary, Poland, and Romania.

East-West relations were further strained by Nikita Khrushchev, who emerged as the Soviet leader after Josef *Stalin's death in 1953. Although he had criticized Stalin's dictatorship and had accused his predecessor of escalating international tensions, Khrushchev ordered a Soviet force into Hungary to suppress a rebellion and maintain Communist rule in 1956. In 1957, the USSR's launching of Sputnik, the first of the space *satellites, indicated that the Soviet Union was developing long-range nuclear *missiles. NATO had planned in 1954 to use *nuclear weapons in case of a massive Soviet invasion. In 1957, it planned to make the thirty NATO divisions and its tactical aircraft nuclear-capable. By 1960, NATO's commander, SACEUR, probably had some 7,000 nuclear weapons; but two SACEURs, Gen. Alfred Gruenther and Gen. Lauris Norstad, warned of NATO's declining conventional capabilities as a result of reductions or redeployments in British and French forces.

During the 1960s, French president Charles de Gaulle rejected the lead of the United States and Britain in Europe and pushed for a larger diplomatic role for France. The French developed their own nuclear capacity; then, in 1966, while still remaining a part of the NATO community, France withdrew its troops from the alliance and requested that NATO's headquarters and all allied units and installations not under the control of French authorities be removed from French soil. NATO headquarters officially opened in October 1967, in Brussels, where it has remained. East and West efforts to achieve peaceful coexistence decreased a year later when the Soviet Union and four of its satellite nations invaded Czechoslovakia.

In an effort to reach an era of detente, a relaxation of tensions reached through reciprocal beneficial relations between East and West, the Nixon administration took the lead with the Leonid Brezhnev government in Moscow, and NATO members and Warsaw Pact members opened the Strategic Arms Limitation Talks (SALT) in November 1969. In May 1972, the first series of *SALT Treaties was signed. The following year a SALT II agreement was reached, although it was never ratified by the United States. Further efforts during the 1970s for East-West balanced force reductions proved unsuccessful. The Arab-Israeli War did little to ease world tensions when it erupted on 6 October 1973, after which the Soviets implied that they might intervene in the crisis due to the strategic importance of oil reserves in that part of the world. A year later, Brezhnev accused NATO of creating a multinational nuclear force and called for cancelation of the alliance as a first step toward world peace. In 1979, the USSR invaded Afghanistan and that ongoing conflict caused the suspension of negotiations between the United States and the USSR on reductions in intermediate-range nuclear forces (INF) that had opened in 1981. Talks resumed in 1984 primarily to prevent the militarization of outer space and then led to negotiations on *arms control and disarmament. Reformer Mikhail Gorbachev came to power in the USSR in March 1985, and that October he met President Ronald *Reagan in Reykjavik, Iceland, to discuss ceilings of 100 nuclear missile warheads for each side (none of which would remain in Europe) and 100 residual warheads to remain in Soviet Asia and on U.S. territories in the Pacific. Verification arrangements were also agreed upon for the first time.

By the end of the 1980s, dramatic changes had occurred in the Warsaw Pact countries. In November 1989, the Berlin Wall was opened, which led the way to a unified Germany ten months later. Bulgaria, Czechoslovakia, and Romania took steps toward breaking from Soviet domination. When Russian troops were withdrawn from Eastern Europe in 1990, the Warsaw Pact was dissolved. In response to these events, NATO members at a summit conference in London in July 1990 declared that they no longer considered the Soviets to be an adversary and laid plans for a new strategic concept that was adopted in 1991 in Rome. The concept reaffirmed the significance of collective defense to meet evolving security threats—particularly from civil wars and massive refugee problems—and established the basis for *peacekeeping operations, as well as coalition crisis management both inside and outside the NATO area. It also stressed cooperation and partnership with the emerging democracies of the former Warsaw Pact.

The North Atlantic Cooperation Council (NACC) was created in 1991 to draw former Soviet republics, as well as the Baltic states and Albania, into a closer relationship with NATO countries. The same year, the Soviet Union established diplomatic links with NATO and joined the NACC on a foreign ministerial level. Hungary and Romania entered a twenty-five-nation Partnership for Peace (PFP), an arm of NATO created in 1994. The PFP administers exercises, exchanges, and other military contacts to encourage military reform. The partnership also provides for peacekeeping, humanitarian, and rescue operations. Hungary, Romania, Slovakia, Poland, and the Czech Republic aspired to become full members of NATO, and debate opened on a second-tier Russian NATO membership allowing for political, but not military, integration for the former Soviet Union. In June 1994, Russian leader Boris Yeltsin announced that the Russians would join the PFP, but Russian fears of an eastward expansion of NATO remained a contentious issue.

In 1992, due to the escalation of the *Bosnian Crisis, and Serbia's armed support of the Bosnian Serbs against Muslims and Croats, NATO's mission was expanded to include peacekeeping operations in support of *United Nations (UN) efforts to restrain the fighting and find a solution to the conflict. In July 1992, NATO ships and aircraft commenced monitoring operations in support of the UN arms embargoes on Serbia and Bosnia from the former Yugoslavia. In April 1993, NATO aircraft began patrolling the skies over Bosnia to monitor and enforce the UN ban on Serbian military aircraft. In November 1995, following U.S.-sponsored peace talks in Dayton, Ohio, a peace agreement was signed in Paris in December calling for a Muslim-Croat federation and a Serb entity in Bosnia. During 1996, fourteen non-NATO countries (Austria, Czech Republic, Estonia, Finland, Hungary, Latvia, Lithuania, Pakistan, Poland, Romania, Russia, Slovakia, Sweden, and Ukraine) were invited to contribute to the NATO-led Implementation Force (IFOR). All the NATO countries with armed forces (Belgium, Canada, Denmark, France, Germany, Greece, Italy, Luxembourg, the Netherlands, Norway, Portugal, Spain, Turkey, United Kingdom, and the United States) pledged to contribute military forces to the operation, and Iceland provided medical personnel. With 60,000 troops, 20,000 of them from the U.S. forces, IFOR was the largest military operation ever undertaken by NATO. It was the first ground force operation, the first deployment "out of area," and the first joint operation with NATO's PFP partners and other non-NATO countries. NATO's IFOR halted the pitched battles and urban sieges that ravaged Bosnia during the four-year war. National elections were held in September 1996, and plans were made for a reduced IFOR force.

The collapse of Communism in Europe led NATO to search for new roles beyond that of a mutual defense pact. One was to bolster democracy and national security in former Warsaw bloc nations; consequently in March 1999, the Czech Republic, Hungary, and Poland were made members of NATO. The other new role for NATO was as a regional policeman seeking to restrict ethnic wars, terrorism, and the generation of massive flows of refugees through genocidal violence. Consequently, as a result of military and paramilitary actions by Serbian president Slobodan Milosevic against hundreds of thousands of ethnic Albanians in the Serbian province of Kosovo, NATO in late March 1999 began a military offensive against Serbian forces and installations By April 1999, when the 50th anniversary of the establishment of NATO was observed, NATO forces in the *Kosovo Crisis were engaged in the largest military assault in Europe since World War II. The NATO air offensive ended successfully with the Serbian forces withdrawal from Kosovo in June and the establishment of a UN administered and NATO implemented peacekeeping force there. With the end of the Cold War (and NATO's first war), a new era for NATO had clearly emerged.

[*See also* Berlin Crises; Collective Security.]

• NATO Information Service, *NATO Today,* 1987. NATO Information Service, *The North Atlantic Treaty Organization Facts and*

Figures, 11th ed., 1989. Lawrence S. Kaplan, *NATO & the US: The Enduring Alliance,* 1994. NATO Office of Information and Press, *NATO Handbook,* 1995. Department of Defense, Office of International Security Affairs, *U.S. Security for Europe and NATO* (June 1995). S. Nelson Drew, *NATO from Berlin to Bosnia: Trans-Atlantic Security in Transition,* 1995. William Thomas Johnsen, *NATO Strategy in the 1990s: Reaping the Peace Dividend or the Whirlwind?,* 1995.
—Trudie Eklund

NAVAL GUNS. Large-caliber tube weapons firing projectiles propelled by chemical explosives, naval guns dominated the conduct of war at sea from the seventeenth to the early twentieth century.

Even in their earliest applications, naval guns were part of what would today be termed a *weapons system,* and their use was closely connected with other elements of ship design. The first guns were smoothbore cannon mounted in a ship's "castles," where they could be fired down at the enemy deck. As improved metallurgy made heavier guns possible, however, it became necessary for balance to carry them closer to the waterline, a development that led to the cutting of gun ports into the sides of ships. Wheeled gun carriages followed, allowing the muzzle to be drawn back for reloading. Lowering the gun mountings to, and then below, the weather deck in turn made the ships themselves, rather than their crews, the immediate targets of gunfire—though experience soon showed it was not easy to sink a heavily timbered ship by fire with solid shot.

Throughout the age of *sailing warships, naval guns did their work primarily by killing enemy sailors in a hail of splinters, and by disabling the opposing ship's rigging. More combats ended by boarding than by sinking, a process made easier because all guns of this era were so inaccurate that effective fire was impossible beyond a few hundred yards. Gun laying (aiming the guns) was a matter of ship handling. Tactics evolved accordingly, most fruitfully in the practice of sailing in "line ahead," to allow multiple ships to concentrate their broadside fire against a single target.

The history of naval guns in the preindustrial era is thus a tale of evolving consensus, driven by the well-understood characteristics of weapons whose superiority was unquestioned, and which changed only very slowly over several centuries. From the middle decades of the nineteenth century onward, this consensus—embodied in the long careers of ships like the USS *Constitution,* a forty-four-gun frigate laid down in 1797, and still a plausible choice as flagship of the Pacific Squadron in 1839—would be shattered by rapid technological innovation.

The Industrial Revolution introduced two basic changes in the character of naval guns. Improved gun founding (casting) and precision machining allowed the production of ever larger guns, strong enough to stand rifling, breechloading, and vast increases in tube pressures. At the same time, advances in chemistry and industrial design made it possible to replace solid shot with exploding shells. These developments necessitated fundamental changes in ship design. Rifled weapons were more accurate at longer distances than their smoothbore predecessors, characteristics that combined with the superior maneuverability of ships afforded by steam propulsion to increase the range of effective fire from a few hundred to a few thousand yards. The practice of mounting a ship's main batteries of guns in turrets on the center line by the end of the century was also linked to the characteristics of steam propulsion: the advantages of tactical movement in any direction could only be realized by ships that could also fire in any direction. Center-line turrets also allowed much larger guns to be mounted safely.

The rifled shell gun placed a great premium upon the protective qualities of armor plate. The inconclusive four-hour duel in the *Civil War between the USS *Monitor* and the CSS *Virginia* (formerly the USS *Merrimack*) off Hampton Roads, Virginia, in March 1862 introduced the world to the spectacle of ironclad warships in action; but it was scarcely typical of what the future would hold, because both ships fired only solid shot. Their encounter confirmed initial impressions that the use of armor would increase a ship's defensive staying power. Early steam-powered ironclads were routinely fitted with rams to make up for any possible deficiency in offensive capability. Once large-caliber explosive shells become the norm in the 1880s and 1890s, however, it was rare for the resistive power of a ship's armor to equal the penetrative power of its biggest guns. At the same time, it became increasingly clear that against heavily armored ships, it was only the biggest guns that mattered, a principle that culminated in the all-big-gun design of the HMS *Dreadnought* (1905), the type for all subsequent battleships.

The aggregate effect of all these changes from the 1880s onward brought an almost unmanageable increase in naval firepower, which in the nineteenth century was calculated in terms of "broadside muzzle energy": the total kinetic energy generated by the maximum number of guns on a ship capable of firing in a single direction. In 1860, the best ironclad warships disposed of just under 30,000 foot-tons of muzzle energy. For capital ships laid down on the eve of World War I, the figure was about 600,000 foot-tons—a comparison that does not take account of the fact that it took at least four or five minutes (often much longer) to reload a large naval gun in 1860, and less than one minute fifty years later.

Neither, however, does this comparison take account of the difficulty of actually hitting anything with these formidable weapons. At the start of the twentieth century, naval guns were still direct-fire weapons in the strictest sense: they could be fired only at targets the operators could see, and effectively only at distances close enough to allow the gun to be laid horizontally (without regard to range). Even then, results could be disheartening: in the *Spanish-American War, the American squadron that sank four Spanish cruisers off Santiago, Cuba, in 1898, fired its guns at ranges closing to 1,000 yards, and still managed a hit rate of only 4 percent—with no hits at all by the main 13-inch batteries. It was not until World War I that improved range keeping and fire control equipment permitted ships to employ indirect plunging fire at longer distances; and not until World War II that *radar allowed guns to acquire targets beyond visual range.

By the 1940s, however, naval guns were losing their preeminence as the arbiters of combat at sea, first to airplanes, and most recently and more decisively, to guided missiles. Naval guns survive today only in vestigial form, as weapons for close-in defense and as instruments of communication: despite far-reaching technological change, there remains no substitute in naval communication for a shot fired across the bow.

[*See also* Battleships; Dahlgren, John; Precision-Guided Munitions; Rodman, Thomas; Weaponry, Naval.]

• James P. Baxter, *The Introduction of the Ironclad Warship*, 1933. Bernard Brodie, *Sea Power in the Machine Age*, 1944. John D. Alden, *The American Steel Navy*, 1972. Stanley Sandler, *The Emergence of the Modern Capital Ship*, 1979. Andrew Lambert, *Battleships in Transition*, 1984.   —Daniel Moran

NAVAL MILITIA. A late nineteenth-century offspring of the National Guard and "New Navy" movements, the naval militia championed a place for the citizen-sailor in national defense. The resurgence of the National Guard ensured a positive reception in coastal and Great Lake state legislatures to the idea of training a citizen-based naval reserve. Massachusetts formed the first state Naval Battalion in 1890. By the *Spanish-American War, fifteen states had naval militia to quell waterfront strikes and defend coastal areas. Interest in developing a world-class New Navy also contributed to the popularity of the naval militia concept. Accordingly, the navy, beginning in 1891, provided funds and equipment for training and did not hesitate to call upon these forces when war came with Spain in 1898. Four thousand militiamen served on auxiliary *cruisers performing scouting and blockade missions—which included providing cover for the Marine landing at Guantanamo Bay, Cuba—or manned stateside coastal signal stations.

In 1914, the naval militia received federal recognition as an official reserve force comparable in status to the National Guard. During World War I, however, naval militia units lost their state designation when members were assigned indiscriminately to U.S. Navy ships. The Naval Reserve Act of 1938 permanently federalized the naval militia as a training unit for the U.S. *Naval Reserves. Unlike National Guardsmen, naval militiamen now volunteered to serve first in the reserves, then the militia. Reflecting the trend toward federal supervision and the emphasis on billet over unit training, only three states continued their naval militia units by 1960.

[*See also* Militia and National Guard; Navy, U.S.: 1866–1898; Navy, U.S.: 1899–1945.]

• Jim Dan Hill, *The Minute Man in Peace and War*, 1964. Kevin R. Hart, "Towards a Citizen Sailor: The History of the Naval Militia Movement, 1888–1898," *American Neptune*, 33 (October 1973), pp. 258–79.   —Jennifer D. Keene

The U.S. **NAVAL RESERVE** was created by several statutes enacted in the period 1915–18 as the successor to the *"naval militia"—naval versions of the National Guard—of several states. The naval militia, as was the case with their army counterparts, was established in the late nineteenth century as part of a general attempt by state military forces to seek higher status and readiness and obtain more federal recognition.

The Naval Reserve did not become a force of federally controlled "citizen-sailors," who underwent periodic peacetime training, until the 1920s and 1930s. During those decades, the reserve provided core crews for ships not in commission and personnel to augment crews of both active U.S. Navy ships and the navy shore establishment upon *mobilization for war. (In addition to these organized reserves, many people who served on active duty in World Wars I and II, the *Korean War, and the *Vietnam War, or the peacetime navy, were designated naval re-

servists, although they were not members of an organized reserve unit called to active duty in time of crisis.) Between the end of the Korean War in mid-1953 and March 1995, Naval Reserve strength has fluctuated from a low of 82,800 in 1978 to a high of 152,800 in 1990. Planned strength for the post–*Cold War era is about 94,000.

Most Naval Reserve units have not mobilized and deployed to a theater of war as units. Rather, individuals and small groups have been used to augment units of the active navy. Reasons for this include the requirements of highly complicated vessels and aircraft for full-time manpower, which limits the extent to which a reserve ship or aircraft squadron can be manned by reservists (a Naval Reserve frigate, for example, actually has a crew of 72 percent active navy and 28 percent reserve sailors). In addition, the need for a large overseas naval presence in peacetime requires the navy and Marine Corps to maintain more of their total force structure—active and reserve—in the active component than do the other services.

Until recently, the "service culture" of the U.S. Navy has probably reflected somewhat more disdain in its attitude toward its reserve component than have the other services' active components. Some of this probably results from the factors noted above, which do limit the extent to which the active navy can rely on reserves. It may also be driven by what was, until recently, a much more inbred hierarchy and socially conservative milieu than the other services (Naval Academy graduates, for example, form a much greater proportion of admirals than do service academy graduates in the army and air force).

This attitude has changed considerably in the late 1990s—out of necessity. Austere defense budgets have forced the navy to rely increasingly on the Naval Reserve to meet its peacetime commitments as well as to provide mobilization assets. Naval Reserve ships, aircraft, and shore units operate with active navy units around the world; individual naval reservists spend tours of duty varying from a few days to many months as integral parts of active navy or joint operations. Finally, the activation of over 21,000 naval reservists (out of a total of about 250,000 reservists from all five military services) for the victorious *Persian Gulf War has given immense legitimacy to this military institution.

[*See also* Navy, U.S.: 1899–1945; Navy, U.S.: Since 1946.]

• Office of the Assistant Secretary of Defense for Reserve Affairs, *The Reserve Components of the United States Armed Forces* (June 1994; updated and reissued periodically). Sol Gordon, Gary L. Smith, and Debra M. Gordon, *1996 Reserve Forces Almanac*, 1996.   —Robert L. Goldich

NAVY, U.S.

Overview
1783–1865
1866–1898
1899–1945
Since 1946

NAVY, U.S.: OVERVIEW

In the summer of 1775, the Continental Congress authorized the first ships of what became the U.S. Navy. Through the course of the *Revolutionary War, each ship and each commission was made to fit an ad hoc need: to defend ports, to interrupt the flow of British personnel and goods, or to fight the enemy's warships at sea. Each of these—along with admirable cooperation from privateers and from the French and Spanish fleets—contributed to Britain's defeat. These operations and John Paul *Jones's raids on British coastal communities gave the fledgling service a reputation for valor.

Like the *Continental Army, the *Continental Navy was all but dissolved after the war. The global wars of the French Revolution and British empire quickly showed the United States the importance of maintaining a navy, if only to protect a neutral's rights at sea. In 1794, Congress recognized this need, authorizing the first heavily armed frigates designed to deter depredations by European nations as well as those of the Barbary pirates. In 1798, it established a Navy Department to administer, procure, train, and direct the new fleet. President Thomas *Jefferson had hoped that small coastal defense gunboats would take the place of a blue water navy, but these lacked sufficient deterrence value. By 1812, *deterrence failed and war with Britain brought humiliating military defeats in Canada and the United States. Nonetheless, the navy's heroic deeds—particularly those of Oliver Hazard *Perry and James Lawrence—ensured its survival for another generation.

Organized by bureaus and rapidly supplemented from the huge merchant marine community and unprecedented expenditures, the U.S. Navy thrived during the *Civil War. It developed new gun and steam propulsion technology that made it one of the most modern and effective forces in the world. Critical to the Union strategy, a naval blockade cut off the rebellious states from life-sustaining trade. Control of the littoral also provided the necessary platform for amphibious assaults of Confederate harbors and eventually for the riverine operations that split the Confederacy. Like the *Mexican War, the Civil War saw extensive joint army-navy operations.

After Appomattox, the navy reduced its vessels from over 700 to 200 mostly hybrid steam/sail frigates that aged quickly in an era of rapid technological change. With an aging, pre–Civil War officer class, relatively unskilled sailors, and increasingly decrepit ships, the navy barely performed its peacetime functions of policing American interests on far-flung stations and undertaking occasional diplomatic or scientific missions. Between 1882 and 1916, navalists (such as Alfred T. *Mahan and Theodore *Roosevelt) revolutionized the service, constructing many first-class steel *battleships, training competent sailors, and educating first-class officers. Against the decrepit Spanish fleet in 1898, the "New Navy" appeared to vindicate itself, winning dramatic victories at Manila and Santiago Bays.

In 1917, the U.S. Navy entered a war for which its battleship-heavy fleet was ludicrously ill-suited. Fortunately, in the process of building a large navy, the nation had also created the bureaucracy, education and training systems, and industrial capacity sufficient to adapt successfully to the challenges of convoys, troop transport, and *antisubmarine warfare systems. Before it was over, the nation had joined with the Royal Navy to escort over 2 million men and supplies that aided the Allies to victory.

Following World War I, the Republican Party, blaming international naval competition, financial obligations, and Woodrow *Wilson's idealism for America's participation in the war, managed a global political and military withdrawal now called *isolationism. Successive administrations negotiated arms limitations treaties while Congress consistently kept the fleet below even permitted strength. This pruning proved healthy, as the smaller navy learned to adapt new technologies to enhance capabilities. While the U.S. *Marine Corps developed a forward base concept and *amphibious warfare capabilities, the navy concentrated on improving gunfire, *submarine warfare, and—increasingly—carrier-based aviation.

In the Depression of the 1930s, President Franklin D. *Roosevelt and Congress began building ships to restart the economy as well as to counter the growing militaristic menaces in Germany and Japan. Most critically, Washington started the fast attack carriers that fortuitously avoided the December 1941 raid on the battle fleet at Pearl Harbor. From America's entry into World War II, the armed forces recognized the need for combined and joint operations. Adm. Chester *Nimitz divided responsibility for the Pacific with Gen. Douglas *MacArthur. Admiral Ernest J. *King and Adm. Royal E. Ingersoll shared the Atlantic with the Royal Navy, combatting the U-boat threat and securing the astonishing flow of goods, personnel, and supplies to Britain and the Soviet Union. The amphibious operations in North Africa, Italy, Normandy, and across the Pacific offered the navy and its sister services some of their most daunting military challenges. American *submarines established a deadly blockade of Japan. Again, battleships only supported the critical action. Two of the greatest naval battles ever—at Midway and the Philippine Sea—were fought by naval aviation, between commanders who could not see one another.

After World War II, U.S. blue water naval supremacy would remain virtually unchallenged, although the Soviet bloc did pose considerable threats across the globe. During the *Cold War, the navy's role in national defense waned and waxed, vacillating with the intensity of operations and the current state of technology. An early bid for nuclear capabilities—the atomic-bomb-launching supercarrier—was canceled in 1949. Only with the advent of the Polaris missile-launching submarine in 1960 did naval ships join the bombers and intercontinental ballistic missiles as one leg of a nuclear triad. The surface navy remained centered on the *aircraft carriers. During the *Vietnam War, carrier task forces were supplemented by river gunboats for some of the most dangerous operations of the war.

In the decades following the fall of Saigon, the navy continued to move to a high-low mix. Still, the carrier groups dominated the fleet, particularly after the 1985 introduction of a "maritime strategy"—a forward-oriented, carrier-based plan to bring a nonnuclear war to the Soviets. The collapse of the Soviet Union left the U.S. Navy without a credible strategic rival. Nonetheless, the carriers and amphibious capabilities developed in the late eighties were refocused for the expeditions and police actions the United States faced as the only superpower and the only sea power.

[See also Midway, Battle of; Philippine Sea, Battle of the; World War II, Naval Operations in: The North Atlantic; World War II, Naval Operations in: The Pacific.]

• Peter Karsten, Naval Aristocracy: The Golden of Age of Annapolis and the Emergence of Modern American Navalism, 1972. Ronald Spector, Eagle Against the Sun: The American War with Japan, 1985. David Long, Gold Braid and Foreign Relations: Diplomatic Activities of U.S. Naval Officers, 1798–1883, 1988. Kenneth Hagan, This People's Navy: The Making of American Sea Power, 1991. Christopher McKee, A Gentlemanly and Honorable Profession: The Creation of the U.S. Naval Officer Corps, 1794–1815, 1991. George Baer, One Hundred Years of Sea Power: The U.S. Navy, 1890–1990, 1994. Edward J. Marolda, By Sea, Air, and Land: An Illustrated History of the United States Navy and the War in Southeast Asia, 1994. Mark Shulman, Navalism and the Emergence of American Sea Power, 1882–1893, 1995.   —Mark R. Shulman

NAVY, U.S.: 1783–1865

At the end of the *Revolutionary War Americans had yet to form a political consensus for a strong nation and saw little need for an expensive and unnecessary navy. In 1785 the Confederation Congress sold off the frigate Alliance, the last ship of the *Continental navy.

In the late 1780s, when Barbary corsairs preyed upon Yankee ships, Americans discovered that their vision of a new world order dominated by concepts of limited government and free trade was not universally shared. The Confederation Congress, without the power to tax, lacked the money to pay the tribute demanded by the Barbary states and lacked the ships to respond to force with force. This powerlessness contributed to a movement for a stronger national government and the ratification of the federal constitution in 1789.

When new Barbary troubles arose in the 1790s, the new U.S. government possessed options, and Congress and President George *Washington responded in classic fashion, following the Roman maxim "if you wish peace, prepare for war." Congress negotiated, but simultaneously passed the Naval Act of March 1794 calling for the construction of six large frigates. The Algerians signed a treaty in 1796.

American determination failed to deter the new French Republic, which angered by the Anglo-American Jay Treaty of 1795, unleashed a war against U.S. commerce in 1797. When the French rebuffed the negotiators sent to Paris, the Federalist-dominated Congress, with a core of six frigates built or being built (including the USS Constitution, completed in 1797), voted to expand the navy to a force of over thirty ships. To oversee the expansion, Congress established a separate Department of the Navy on 30 April 1798.

Between the spring of 1798 and 1801 the navy waged an undeclared naval war with *France—the so-called Quasi-War. Benjamin Stoddert, the navy's first secretary, headed a minuscule administration that oversaw operations centered in the West Indies. Stoddert adopted an aggressive, offensive strategy, successfully carrying the war to the French bases in the Caribbean. The new American navy mostly patrolled the shipping lanes and escorted hundreds of merchantmen clear of danger, although there were a few battles of note. In February 1799 Captain Thomas Truxtun, commanding the thirty-eight-gun frigate Constellation, captured the French forty-gun frigate l'Insurgente near Nevis.

For the navy, the Quasi-War was a formative experience. The disappointments of the Continental navy were forgotten. The new American marine force emerged from the war with an excellent reputation, a core of powerful frigates, and a cadre of young officers including Edward Preble and Stephen *Decatur.

Despite the efforts of Stoddert and other navalists, the United States did not emerge from the war with a big-ship navy. Construction of a squadron of seventy-four-gun *battleships began in 1799, but none was completed. The

nation possessed the means to build such ships, and could have made good use of them in 1812. But for a navy that was usually 10 to 15 percent understrength, manning might have been a practical and political impossibility in a nation unwilling to resort to the press gang.

The electoral victor of President Thomas *Jefferson's Democratic-Republicans in 1800 terminated the building of the program. In Jefferson's scheme, army fortifications and an army and navy militia bore primary responsibility for national defense. The navy played a subsidiary role, protecting commerce and supporting coastal defense efforts with a fleet of small harbor gunboats. Jefferson's was in many ways a sensible policy, though he could have spared the nation the cost of the gunboat fleet.

Jefferson considered economic sanctions the chief weapon in his arsenal, a weapon he and his successors employed against Britain between 1807 and 1812 to no avail. Republican embargoes sent the American economy into a depression from which the commercial sector did not fully recover until the 1830s. James *Madison and a frustrated Republican Congress declared war in 1812.

In the *War of 1812, the nation's small navy achieved some notable successes, capturing three Royal Navy frigates in the first months of the war. But the navy could not prevent the British from blockading and raiding the coast. At Baltimore and New Orleans, Republican defense policies succeeded; but the British marched into Washington and burned the "President's Mansion." Along the frontier with Canada, the navy achieved mixed success, winning significant battles on Lakes Erie and Champlain, but not on the most important of the lakes—Ontario. For the navy, war ended none to soon.

After 1815, the Democratic-Republicans (soon to be simply Democrats) embraced many Federalist naval policies. They built more and larger ships, just in time for the "era of free security." Many of the big ships were soon laid up, while the smaller vessels operated globally in support of American commerce, suppressing piracy in the Caribbean and conducting anti-slavery patrols off the African coast. In 1854, Commodore Matthew *Perry opened Japan to American trade. The navy also undertook scientific and geographic missions. Matthew Fontaine Maury broke ground in ocean science; William Lynch explored the Dead Sea, and Charles Wilkes the Pacific.

The post-1815 era was also one of administrative reform and technological advance. Congress established the Board of Navy Commissioners (1815), the Navy Bureau system (1842), and the U.S. Naval Academy at Annapolis (1845). Other reforms included the prohibition of dueling (1857) and flogging (1850), and (unsuccessful) attempts to limit the spirit ration. The navy experimented with and embraced myriad new technologies—shell-firing cannon, heavy guns, armor plating, steam power, and screw propulsion.

During the *Mexican War (1846–48) the navy played a subsidiary, but important, role. The few American warships executed a big-navy strategy—blockading the Mexican coasts, helping defeat the Mexicans in California, and transporting Gen. Winfield *Scott's army to Vera Cruz in an amphibious operation that ultimately brought the war to a successful conclusion.

At the start of the *Civil War, the U.S. Navy's officer corps suffered fewer defections than that of the U.S. Army. Employing many new technologies, the Union navy performed well, blockading the Confederate coast, supporting amphibious operations around the Confederate periphery, and conducting critically important riverine operations in the west. The navy did have a difficult time tracking down the handful of Confederate naval commerce raiders, although the Union cruiser *Kearsarge* destroyed the *Alabama* off Cherbourg, France, in 1864.

By 1865 the navy had reached a peak of efficiency and was one of the largest in the world. But many of its ships were hastily built or poorly suited for service beyond American coastal waters. Moreover, the immediate postwar decades were years of national reconstruction and introspection during which American naval policy atrophied.

The years 1783–1865 marked a formative period for the U.S. navy. The service's roles and missions were limited, in that the government assigned the navy the roles of safeguarding overseas commercial and diplomatic interests, and not the defending the nation itself. Nevertheless, the navy performed well and earned a reputation for excellence, despite its diminutive size. Over the decades American naval officers gained experience in all the corners of the globe and through their efforts, and those of a handful of competent civilian secretaries, laid the foundation for the establishment of a larger, more powerful, truly national navy in the 1880s and 1890s.

[*See also* Continental Navy.]

• Theodore Roosevelt, *The Naval War of 1812,* 1882. Alfred T. Mahan, *Admiral Farragut,* 1892. Craig L. Symonds, *Navalists and Antinavalists: The Naval Debate in the United States, 1785–1827,* 1980. John Schroeder, *Shaping a Maritime Empire: The Commercial and Diplomatic Role of the American Navy, 1829–1861,* 1985. Michael A. Palmer, *Stoddert's War: Naval Operations during the Quasi-War with France, 1798–1801,* 1987. David F. Long, *Gold Braid and Foreign Relations: Diplomatic Activities of American Naval Officers, 1798–1833,* 1988.   —Michael A. Palmer

NAVY, U.S.: 1866–1898

Following the *Civil War, the U.S. Navy suffered a sharp decline for over a decade. American commerce was in a shrunken state, and the country, with little foreign menace, was preoccupied with domestic matters. But in the 1880s a resurgence of "manifest destiny," increased involvement in foreign affairs, and heightened professionalism within the service brought a naval renaissance that culminated in the navy's overwhelming victories during the *Spanish-American War of 1898.

In 1865, the U.S. Navy, with 471 warships on its roster, ranked as one of the world's largest in numbers, but it was strongly oriented toward coastal and riverine operations. With peace, Congress quickly ended funding for new construction and laid up or sold off the bulk of the Civil War fleet. The principal remaining mission for the navy was to show the flag on foreign stations; its active *sailing warships, mostly wooden vessels, were prized more for their economy and cruising radius than for their military qualities. The few ironclad monitors retained were overhauled for lengthy periods at great expense, essentially with an eye to keeping the dockyards in existence rather than to strengthening the force. In personnel, the service grew topheavy with officers (one for every four enlisted men in 1882), and promotion, based entirely on seniority, came to a virtual standstill. As late as 1896, some lieutenants dated their ranks to the Civil War. Enlisted life was so unattrac-

tive that in the late 1870s, the navy averaged 1,000 desertions yearly out its authorized strength of 8,000 men. At the top, the navy was run by a series of political secretaries, some of whom were incompetent or corrupt. Abroad, its reputation so declined that an Oscar Wilde character who lamented that the United States had neither ruins nor curiosities was contradicted by reference to its navy.

Behind this facade of stagnation, the navy made some important advances. The quasi-official U.S. Naval Institute, organized in 1873, initiated the next year the publication of a journal of professional opinion, the *Proceedings.* The pace of reform accelerated in the next decade. In 1882, the Office of Naval Intelligence was established. Two years later, the Naval War College at Newport, Rhode Island, began instruction under its first president, Rear Adm. Stephen B. Luce. One of its early luminaries was Alfred T. *Mahan, president in 1886–89 and 1892–93, whose stress on *war games highlighted for the navy the importance of such disparate items as oil fuel, an isthmian canal, and bases in Hawaii. Mahan's cardinal book, *The Influence of Sea Power Upon History, 1660–1783,* published in 1890 and soon translated into six major languages, established him as the world's foremost naval thinker.

In force structure, the navy began in 1883 to match these quickening steps toward modernization when Congress provided funds for three new steel *cruisers. This modest program was augmented later in the decade with the authorization of twelve more cruisers and the navy's first big-gun ships, the *Maine* and *Texas.* Early in the 1890s, four *battleships and three large cruisers followed. The military characteristics of these new steam-powered ships reflected the essentially defensive mission of the service. The battleships were of low freeboard and thus best suited for coastal defense; the cruisers, such as the *Columbia,* possessed high speed and were designed as commerce raiders to hunt down fast passenger liners. The navy also experimented with smaller craft, such as *torpedo boats and the ram *Katahdin.*

This expansion was stoked in part by a war scare with Chile in 1891, by the resurrection of the American merchant marine, and by rising imperial ambitions. Also, Mahan argued forcefully for the construction of a battle fleet and influenced civilian policymakers such as Secretaries of the Navy Benjamin F. Tracy (1869–93) and Hilary A. Herbert (1893–97). Congress in 1895 and 1896 funded five additional battleships.

Before these could be completed, the steel navy was tested in war with Spain in 1898. Competent prewar preparations by Secretary of the Navy John Davis Long and his assistant Theodore *Roosevelt paid dividends at the outset, when Commodore George *Dewey moved quickly to defeat the Spanish fleet at the Battle of *Manila Bay. Off Cuba, the fleet of Rear Adm. William *Sampson won an easy naval victory at Santiago Bay. Materially, the new ships of the navy performed well, with the battleship *Oregon* steaming from the West Coast around Cape Horn to the Caribbean in seventy-one days, arriving in time to play a key role during the Santiago engagement. The Marines impressed observers with their élan and professionalism at Guantanamo Bay, earning the sobriquet from reporters of "first to fight."

The navy's victories in 1898 helped lead to far-flung bases and vast new commitments; the successes also garnered public acclaim, which translated into congressional support for ambitious construction programs that moved the navy rapidly into the first ranks of the world's powers. The contrast with the demoralized and decrepit service of only two decades earlier was marked indeed.

[*See also* Academies, Service: U.S. Naval Academy; Luce, Stephen B.; Marine Corps, U.S.: 1865–1914.]

• Harold and Margaret Sprout, *The Rise of American Naval Power, 1776–1918,* 1939. Walter R. Herrick, Jr., *The American Naval Revolution,* 1966. Robert Seager II, *Alfred Thayer Mahan,* 1975. James C. Bradford, ed., *Admirals of the New Steel Navy,* 1990. Robert W. Love, Jr., *History of the U.S. Navy,* Vol. 1: *1775–1941,* 1992.

—Malcolm Muir, Jr.

NAVY, U.S.: 1899–1945

The U.S. Navy matured from a respectable and growing fleet in 1899 to a navy that was incontestably the greatest in the world by the end of World War II. Built initially around the big-gun ship, the navy during World War II shifted its primary focus to aerial warfare and also waged a submarine campaign of unparalleled effectiveness.

Emerging triumphant from the *Spanish-American War (1898), the navy enjoyed generous support early in the century from presidents and the Congress, which yearly funded battleship construction. By 1902, the U.S. Navy ranked third in the world in battle line strength. Its new ships were tested and America's naval might flexed with the cruise of the Great White Fleet of 1907–09. The navy's personnel expanded correspondingly, from 16,000 in 1899 to 60,000 by 1916. With its emphasis on *battleships, the navy paid less attention to smaller craft, arguing that those could be built quickly in an emergency. Nonetheless, the service did commission its first submarine in 1900 and led the world in experiments with naval aviation, conducting the first flight from a ship in 1910.

To provide leadership for the growing force, the Naval Academy was completely rebuilt, and the system of officer promotion by seniority was replaced by merit. At the top, the Naval General Board was established in 1900 as an advisory planning body to link the navy's strategy with its force structure. In 1915, Congress established the office of the chief of naval operations to oversee fleet readiness and employment. The next year, Congress authorized the construction of sixteen warships of unprecedented size to give the nation a "navy second to none."

Work on this ambitious program was hardly under way when the United States entered *World War I. Because German U-boats posed the principal menace, the navy, needing *destroyers desperately, suspended the 1916 construction program. During the war, American warships sank few *submarines, but the navy did make significant contributions to the Allied victory by advocating the adoption of the convoy system and by escorting over 2 million army and Marine troops to France without the loss of a single sailor.

Following the armistice, the navy reverted to its emphasis on the big gun, but soon found its building plans stymied when the *Washington Naval Arms Limitation Treaty of 1922 mandated a ten-year moratorium on battleship construction. Despite this setback, the navy worked hard on its long-range gunnery in planning to fight in the Pacific. To that end, it placed great emphasis on aviation, which could provide the necessary spotting and air control. In 1921, the navy created a separate Bureau of Aeronautics, and in 1927 commissioned powerful *aircraft carriers of the *Lexington* class. With almost 100 planes each, these ships possessed great striking power, and under the leadership of such air-minded officers as Joseph M. Reeves, William A. *Moffett, John H. Towers, and Ernest J. *King, they became a potent force in their own right. Conversely, the threat of hostile aircraft caused such concern that navy planners made determined efforts to develop efficient antiaircraft defenses during the 1930s. The navy also experimented with *radar for early warning and aircraft control, with dirigibles and seaplanes for long-range scouting, and with at-sea refueling and replenishment. Given its Pacific focus, the navy built fast long-range submarines armed with an advanced torpedo, although lack of funding prevented adequate testing of this weapon. The Marines, studying the problem of seizing forward bases, focused on *amphibious warfare, a mission that many military analysts deemed impossible.

Increasing tensions of the late 1930s and the outbreak of *World War II in 1939 led to renewed warship construction; following Germany's defeat of France in 1940, the U.S. Navy won funds for essentially unlimited expansion. Before the new vessels entered the fleet, active belligerency brought crises in both the Atlantic and Pacific oceans. The destruction of the battleships at the attack on *Pearl Harbor forced the navy to scrap its plans for an advance with the battle line across the central Pacific; a German submarine offensive along the eastern coast of the United States caught the navy unprepared. But the emergency moved to the fore officers who would guide the fleet to *victory: Ernest J. *King as chief of naval operations, Chester *Nimitz to head the Pacific Fleet, and William F. *Halsey and Raymond A. *Spruance as commanders of fast carrier task forces.

After a slow start, the navy helped win the Battle of the Atlantic against the U-boats with long-range aircraft and blimps, large numbers of specialized antisubmarine ships such as escort carriers and destroyer escorts, *radar in both ships and planes, and code-breaking successes. The navy's victory in this vitally important campaign enabled the U.S. Army and air forces to bring their weight to bear in the European theater with the strategic bombing campaign against Germany and the landings in North Africa, Italy, and France.

In the Pacific theater, the navy recovered rapidly from the Pearl Harbor defeat. Relying of necessity on *aircraft carriers, the navy struck back with raids on Japanese-held territories and on the home islands themselves. Then, in the first carrier battles of the war, the navy fought the Japanese to a draw at the Battle of the *Coral Sea and won a stunning victory at the Battle of *Midway. Quickly going over to the offensive, the navy with its Marine component began at Guadalcanal in August 1942 a series of amphibious operations against a skillful and dedicated enemy defending terrain from jungle to atoll and from the Aleutians to New Guinea. Despite some heavy *casualties, not a single American landing over the next three years was repulsed. Simultaneously, U.S. *submarines were cutting Japanese lifelines. Once their formerly faulty *torpedoes became effective, the submarines inflicted lethal damage on the Japanese war machine by sinking 56 percent of its merchant marine and numerous imperial warships.

In 1944, the navy crushed the Japanese Imperial Fleet in two of the greatest naval battles in history: Philippine Sea and Leyte Gulf. Closing in on Japan, the navy and Marines secured bases in the Marianas and at Iwo Jima and Okinawa, thereby making possible the B-29 aerial offensive. Despite grievous losses in men and ships to kamikaze aircraft late in the war, the U.S. Navy's triumph was complete. By the end of the conflict, its foes in both oceans had been utterly crushed, and it was bigger than all the rest of the navies in the world combined.

[See also Academies, Service: U.S. Naval Academy; Battle of Leyte Gulf; Philippine Sea, Battle of the; World War I, U.S. Naval Operations in; World War II, U.S. Naval Operations in: The North Atlantic; World War II, U.S. Naval Operation in: The Pacific.]

• William S. Sims, The Victory at Sea, 1920. Ernest J. King and Walter M. Whitehall, Fleet Admiral King, 1952. Samuel E. Morison, The Two-Ocean War, 1963. Patrick Abbazia, Mr. Roosevelt's Navy, 1975. Robert W. Love, Jr., The Chiefs of Naval Operations, 1980. Clark G. Reynolds, The Fast Carriers: The Forging of an Air Navy, 1992.

—Malcolm Muir, Jr.

NAVY, U.S.: SINCE 1946

On V-J Day, 1945, the U.S. Navy—the world's largest—had 105 aircraft carriers, 5,000 ships and submarines, and 82,000 vessels and landing craft deployed around the world, manned by experienced citizen-sailors and led by aggressive and seasoned admirals. Arguably the most glamorous, tradition-bound, and elitist of the American armed services, the navy had been given pride of place by President Franklin D. *Roosevelt. Now with no potentially threatening navy in existence, a new president, Harry S. *Truman, who disliked the navy, endorsed the War Department's recommendation for centralization and reduction of the armed forces and ordered the process begun. Thus commenced the most bitter internal political struggle experienced by the U.S. government since the Civil War. On one side were the navy and Marine Corps and their congressional allies, and on the other the Truman White House, the army and the army air force, and their congressional allies. The army wanted the navy under the War Department and the marines integrated into the army. The air force wanted independence from the army and naval aviation put under the air force.

The battle for complete independence was lost by the Navy Department, which was moved under a new Defense Department. The air force gained independence from the army, but failed to obtain control of naval aviation, and the army failed to get the Marines. Largely through the leadership of Navy Secretary James V. *Forrestal, the navy retained much autonomy and most of its roles and missions. To obtain the compromise, Forrestal was named the first Secretary of Defense. After Forrestal's suicide, he was succeeded by Louis *Johnson, who set about reducing the navy with a vengeance. The triumphant 5,000-ship fleet was retired wholesale, the 105 carriers were reduced to six, and the first supercarrier, the USS United States under construction at Newport News, was scrapped. That triggered the immediate resignation of Navy Secretary John Sullivan and the public protest in 1949 known as the "Revolt of the Admirals." The lead role in the new nuclear strategy was taken from the navy and its carriers and given to the new air force and its B-36 bomber.

The *Korean War reversed the decline of the navy. Its reactivated carriers provided the bulk of allied air power after all land bases were captured or destroyed in the initial Communist attack. The dramatically successful amphibious flanking attack at *Inchon renewed the important navy-marine mission of "amphibious assault."

Naval planning and procurement were centered for the next twenty years on the mission of projecting power ashore. Supercarriers were built and new aircraft procured to strike deep into the Soviet heartland from the sea around its periphery. The surge of the *Cold War and adoption of the "containment strategy" launched the navy into a new (and classic) naval mission of "presence."

By the mid-1950s *battleships and carriers were being kept permanently on station in the Mediterranean and were being deployed to trouble spots around the world. A small naval force was now kept permanently in the Persian Gulf in recognition of the new strategic value of oil in a region of volatile politics. Between 1946 and 1996, the navy was deployed in crises short of war 270 times. Crisis deterrence and crisis management have proved to be the most consistent and enduring naval mission throughout the last fifty years.

In pursuit of containment the direct U.S. combat involvement in the *Vietnam War in 1964 began an intense decade of naval combat using virtually every dimension of naval warfare. SEAL team commandos and riverine gunboats engaged in bloody counter-insurgent operations; *destroyers, *cruisers, and for a short time the battleship USS New Jersey provided massive naval gunfire supporting land forces; patrol aircraft and surface ships tried to prevent supply of the Communists by sea.

The overwhelming naval task, however, was the use of carrier aircraft to provide air support to land operations in South Vietnam, interdict supply routes to the south, and engage in strategic bombing in North Vietnam. The air war had an enormous impact on the naval service. All other naval missions were subordinated worldwide. Because the U.S. government wished to avoid "wartime" budgets, the navy consumed its capital, forgoing necessary maintenance of ships and equipment, much research and development, and quality-of-life expenditures. When combat operations ended in 1973, the navy was in very poor condition. Morale was corrosive, with mutinies breaking out on three capital ships, and the officer corps cynical about the constraints under which they had fought. Ships and aircraft were in disastrous condition after deferred repairs.

Chief of Naval Operations (CNO) Elmo *Zumwalt and his successor James Holloway carried out a program of dramatic reforms to rebuild the navy for the post–Vietnam War era. Planning focus was shifted away from projecting power ashore to dealing with the enormous new Soviet blue water fleet that had taken shape during the 1960s under the forceful Soviet Adm. Sergei Gorshkov, who was intent on achieving maritime superiority over the United States and *NATO. The post–Vietnam, post-Watergate defense cuts made rebuilding the U.S. Navy a difficult challenge. Zumwalt decided to retire some 500 ships to save the huge deferred cost of maintaining them, and directed funding instead to new ships and weapons to regain sea-control credibility. Zumwalt later expressed the considered judgment that had war with the Soviets broken out during this period, the United States would have been defeated at sea. The arrival of the administration of President Jimmy *Carter further slowed the renewal effort, with adoption of a security policy, PRM 10, that relegated the navy to a secondary role.

Modernization was cut back, pay frozen, and in 1979

the president vetoed the defense bill because Congress had authorized a new nuclear aircraft carrier. There was very nearly a repeat of the "Revolt of the Admirals," when the CNO, Adm. James Holloway, refused to testify that the navy could continue to do its mission.

President Ronald *Reagan had campaigned on a promise to build a "600-ship navy," to restore "maritime supremacy." Immediately after his inauguration naval shipbuilding and aircraft procurement were nearly doubled, pay was substantially increased, and weapons modernization was intensified. Navy Secretary John Lehman and CNO James Watkins led the development of an assertive new forward naval strategy to put the Soviet navy on the defensive and convince the Soviets they would lose a naval war decisively. Massive annual naval exercises were held annually in sea areas close to the Soviet Union. By 1987 the U.S. Navy had ordered more than 200 new combatants including 5 nuclear carriers and had 592 ships in commission, including 4 recommissioned battleships. During this period the navy was engaged in sustained operations in the Persian Gulf, the Mediterranean, Lebanon, and Grenada. Three confrontations off Libya including the shooting down of four Libyan aircraft, and air strikes against Tripoli and Benghazi and the dramatic air intercept of the "Achille Lauro" terrorists. The culmination of this naval renaissance was reached with the unexpected collapse of Soviet communism, and the disintegration of the 1700-ship Soviet fleet.

The aftermath of the Cold War victory once again brought difficult times for the navy. The disruptions of integrating women into combat roles, sharply reduced budgets, and leadership turmoil (from 1987 to 1995, five new secretaries of the navy were named and fourteen admirals were fired) made the navy a whipping boy for the media and Congress. Despite the political trauma, the navy played a vital role in shielding Saudi Arabia after Iraq invaded Kuwait, transporting the massive Desert Shield buildup and then conducting surface, submarine, and air operations during Desert Storm in the *Persian Gulf War.

A new post–Cold War strategy was also developed that focused planning once again on projecting power ashore. The innovations were applied in peacekeeping operations in Somalia in 1993, Haiti in 1994, Bosnia in 1995, and Yugoslavia in 1999.

[See also Korean War, U.S. Naval Operations in the; Vietnam War, U.S. Naval Operations in.]

• Elmo Zumwalt, On Watch, 1976. Norman Polmar and Thomas Allen, Rickover, 1981. Edward J. Marolda and G. Wesley Pryce III, A Short History of the U.S. Navy and the Southeast Asia Conflict, 1984. John F. Lehman, Jr., Command of the Seas, 1988. Robert W. Love, Jr., History of the U.S. Navy, Vol. II, 1942–1991, 1992.

—John Lehman

NAVY COMBAT BRANCHES

Surface Forces
Submarine Forces
Naval Air Forces

NAVY COMBAT BRANCHES: SURFACE FORCES

Until the twentieth century, surface warfare was naturally the focus of the U.S. Navy. The navy's force structure was built around major surface warships: the frigates of the 1794 program, the ships of the line after the *War of 1812,

the monitors of the *Civil War era, and, beginning in the 1880s, the *cruisers and the *battleships. Missions for these naval vessels included commerce raiding, trade protection, coast defense, and sea control. In the 1890s, a smaller type, the destroyer, emerged to shield larger vessels from enemy *torpedo boats; it soon undertook myriad other tasks.

Following the turn of the century, radical technological advances embodied in the aircraft and *submarine began to challenge the primacy of the surface combatant. Although the navy incorporated both innovations into its fleet structure by the end of *World War I, the battleship remained the "backbone of the fleet." For able officers, the swiftest path to advancement remained duty aboard large surface warships. Top midshipmen at the U.S. Naval Academy took seriously the aphorism, "Get behind the big guns and stay there."

*World War II overturned this long-standing system. The successes of submarine forces, while serious enough, paled in comparison with the rising challenge of the aircraft, whether sea- or land-based. The navy's building programs, initially centered around the battleship and cruiser, were redirected in mid-course to emphasize *aircraft carriers. Although surface warships still proved quite useful, both in sea control and in a variety of subsidiary roles, the carrier by 1944 was unquestionably the single most important type of combatant. Many ambitious junior officers of the surface line put in for flight training.

The drawdown following V-J Day reflected these changing priorities, with most of the battleships and cruisers going to the breakers or into "mothball" storage; destroyers remained operational in substantial numbers, principally for their utility in the antisubmarine mission. For the next decades, the carrier ruled supreme within the navy, although the Korean War showed again the indispensability of surface warships for shore bombardment and blockade work. Surface warriors also found a champion in Arleigh *Burke, Chief of Naval Operations (CNO) from 1955 to 1961. Burke, a former destroyer officer, advanced an ambitious program to update the surface navy by a large building program of new ships equipped variously with antiaircraft *missiles for the defense of carriers, with *helicopters for anti-submarine work, and with nuclear powerplants for propulsion.

Despite these gains, the 1960s dealt harshly with the surface navy. Early troubles with this costly new technology rendered the new combatants of questionable worth; at the same time, Vietnam deployments wore out older warships and deprived the fleet of funding for replacements. More ominous, the lethality of Soviet antiship missile, as demonstrated by proxy in the 1967 six-day Arab-Israeli conflict, threatened—as had *torpedoes and the aircraft in earlier decades—the very survival of surface warships.

In 1970, another surface warfare officer, Elmo *Zumwalt, Jr., became CNO. Zumwalt began or accelerated a number of initiatives: innovative warships propelled by gas turbine engines; the Harpoon and Tomahawk missiles to give cruisers and destroyers extended reach against sea and shore targets; and advanced air defense capabilities (such as the Standard air defense missile, the Phalanx point-defense gun, and the computerized Aegis weapons control system).

Mirroring the renaissance of surface warfare in the 1970s was the creation of a distinctive branch insignia and an organizational restructuring within the Navy Department to give surface forces an institutional voice equal to those of the aviation and submarine branches. Additionally, the navy's mine, amphibious, and service elements were fused with the cruiser/destroyer/frigate forces; the establishment of the Surface Warfare Officer School at Newport, Rhode Island, enhanced professionalism.

The surface navy continued to prosper during the Reagan and Bush years. Returned to active duty were the four Iowa-class battleships armed with cruise missiles. New cruisers and destroyers of the Yorktown- and Arleigh Burke-classes went to sea equipped with the Aegis system. During the *Persian Gulf War, surface warships demonstrated their versatility by conducting long-range missile strikes, shore bombardment, and blockade duties. In 1999, the surface navy launched missiles from the Adriatic Sea as part of *NATO measures against Yugoslavia during the *Kosovo Crisis.

At the close of the century, surface warfare, lost for much of the century in the shadows of the air and subsurface specialties, had been rejuvenated. With the navy's new emphasis on littoral warfare, surface warships promise to remain an essential and viable component for the foreseeable future. Thus, the oldest branch of the navy has learned to cope with a host of threats; its motto, "Up, Out, and Down," succinctly describes the capabilities that surface forces continue to offer the nation.

• Vincent Davis, *The Admirals Lobby*, 1967. Norman Friedman, *The Postwar Naval Revolution*, 1986. Frederick H. Hartmann, *Naval Renaissance: The U.S. Navy in the 1980s*, 1990. George W. Bear, *One Hundred Years of Sea Power: The U.S. Navy, 1890–1990*, 1993. Malcolm Muir, Jr., *Black Shoes and Blue Water: Surface Warfare in the United States Navy, 1945–1975*, 1996.

—Malcolm Muir, Jr.

NAVY COMBAT BRANCHES: SUBMARINE FORCES

The modern U.S. Navy's first submarine, named in honor of its designer, the Irish-American inventor John P. Holland, was commissioned on 12 October 1900. The 54-foot *Holland* and the succeeding thirty-one submarines completed through early 1915 were capable of carrying only a handful of *torpedoes, had limited endurance on the surface (and even less when running submerged on their batteries), and were considered fit only for harbor defense duties. They played little part in the doctrine or strategy of a U.S. Navy focused on the great power theories of Alfred T. *Mahan. Most of the tiny, dangerous submarines, under the command of junior officers, were exiled to the Philippines and Panama.

Of the twenty-three U.S. Navy submarines sent to European waters during World War I, none had the opportunity to attack an enemy vessel. The war ended with a large number of still primitive submarines under construction, and their sheer numbers meant that few new submarines would be built in the 1920s—an era of treaty-mandated force reductions and in a climate where submarine attacks, especially against merchant ships, were unpalatable. Nonetheless, the U.S. Navy studied German submarine designs and attempted to adapt the superior German diesel engines to a series of unsuccessful large experimental "boats" that were intended to act in concert with the battle fleet.

Unreliable diesel engines remained a problem until the late 1930s, when railroad diesel engine designs were adapted to submarine propulsion, providing the reliability

and endurance that later allowed submarines operating from Hawaii, Australia, and the Aleutians to stay for extended periods in Japanese home waters. Problems with torpedo exploders, however, took longer to be recognized and corrected, and it was not until well into 1943 that submariners could expect their weapons to detonate reliably.

The trial-and-error experiences of the first four decades of submarine operations nonetheless paid off handsomely in the war against Japan: for a loss of 52 submarines (and 3,506 personnel), U.S. Navy submarines sank a confirmed 1,314 Japanese ships totaling some 5.3 million tons; among these were 1 battleship, 8 *aircraft carriers, and 11 *cruisers. In the Atlantic, however, only 113 war patrols were made, and no enemy ships were sunk or damaged.

The Cold War era initially saw innovative attempts to adapt German concepts such as the snorkel (which permitted submerged operations on the diesels while charging the batteries); improved hull forms; and better batteries, sensors, and homing torpedoes to the large numbers of "fleet boat" submarines left over from wartime construction. The growing Soviet submarine force became the prime prospective target of its U.S. counterpart, and operations against surface targets gradually became secondary.

Diesel-electric submarines, however, were still limited in submerged endurance, and when running on their diesels were subject to detection by increasingly sophisticated anti-submarine sensors. The solution, forcefully advocated by Hyman *Rickover, was the development of nuclear power for submarines, giving endurance limited only by the submarine's food supplies (oxygen could be regenerated by the electrical power available from the nuclear reactors) and sustained speeds rivaling those of the fastest surface ships. Rickover's creation, the USS *Nautilus* (SSBN 571) was commissioned on 30 September 1954, and some 195 additional nuclear-powered submarines have since been ordered. The last diesel combatant submarine was retired in 1990.

Experiments with adaptations of the German V-1 cruise missile led to the deployment of a limited number of Regulus-I strategic *missiles on navy submarines in the late 1950s, but it was the synthesis of the nuclear-powered submarine and the submerged-launched Polaris ballistic missile that gave the submarine force an entirely new strategic mission as one leg of the nation's nuclear *deterrence triad; USS *George Washington* (SSBN 598) completed the first Polaris missile patrol on 21 January 1961. Later, the longer-ranged Poseidon replaced Polaris, and USS *Ohio* (SSBN 726) completed the first multiwarhead Trident missile patrol on 10 December 1982.

The submarine force at the turn of the century faces fiscal constraints and a crisis of vision. The vastly increased costs of building, operating, and maintaining nuclear-powered submarines, balanced against the drastic reduction in the Russian submarine fleet, have inspired the U.S. submarine "community" to investigate new missions and capabilities for its smaller fleet of the future.

[See also Cold War: External Course; Submarines.]

• Clay Blair, Jr., *Silent Victory*, 1974. Francis Duncan, *Rickover and the Nuclear Navy*, 1989. Steve and Yogi Kaufman, *Sharks of Steel*, 1993. Norman Friedman, *U.S. Submarines Since 1945*, 1994. Theodore Rockwell, *The Rickover Effect*, 1994. Norman Friedman, *U.S. Submarines Through 1945*, 1995.

—Arthur D. Baker III

NAVY COMBAT BRANCHES: NAVAL AIR FORCES

Naval aviation has been an integral component of the U.S. Navy's administrative and operational structure because the fleet's aircraft have been long-range extensions of the traditional naval gun and scouting ship. Eventually, the navy's air forces dominated policy, strategy, and force structures as they extended their direct influence throughout the service—personnel, training, ordnance, *logistics, shipbuilding and maintenance, medicine, navigation, *submarine warfare, and the *Marine Corps. This ascendancy generated stresses within the U.S. Navy—and controversy with the army's air forces and later the U.S. Air Force—over strategic roles and missions and the competition for funding.

Initially, in 1910–16, a director of aviation activities, a captain, supervised the few dozen navy planes and pilots until America's entry into World War I. The need to patrol the coastal waters of Europe and North America against Germany's U-boats and to bomb their bases led to a strengthened directorship in 1917. The director wielded immense authority over naval aviation's wartime expansion to 2,107 aircraft; 15 dirigibles; 205 kite and free balloons; 6,998 officers, mostly pilots; 32,882 enlisted men, some pilots; 31 air stations in Europe and 24 in the United States. The navy's aviation proved so essential to victory that postwar personnel strength was set at 500 officers and 5,000 enlisted men. Patrol seaplanes and dirigibles were employed in reconnaissance roles; land-based planes assigned to *battleships to scout and spot gunfire; and an experimental aircraft carrier commissioned. Major recognition came with the creation of the Bureau of Aeronautics, headed by a rear admiral, in 1921.

Under the inspired leadership of the first chief of the Bureau of Aeronautics, Adm. William A. *Moffett (1921–33), the navy's air forces were integrated into fleet operations in anticipation of war with Japan. The two major aviation components became the carriers and land-based and amphibian patrol-bombers. Depression-era budgetary constraints did not deter Moffett and his successors from forging a qualitatively advanced naval air force centered on seven aircraft *carriers and five patrol wings during the interwar period. A civilian assistant secretary of the navy for aeronautics facilitated progress in 1926–32, and again after 1941.

The immense expansion of fleet aviation for World War II was brilliantly managed by Adm. John H. Towers (chief of bureau, 1939–42). It attained an eventual strength of over 36 attack carriers, 84 escort carriers, dozens of seaplane tenders, numerous training bases and air stations; 40,912 aircraft, 139 blimps, and 27 *helicopters; 60,095 pilots (navy and Marine), 33,044 nonflying officers, and 337,718 nonflying enlisted sailors. Such growth led in 1943 to the new post of deputy chief of naval operations (Air), held by a vice admiral. The primary role of naval aviation in the destruction of Japan's Imperial Fleet and Germany's U-boats established it at the center of the postwar navy.

During and after the *Cold War, aviators occupied the post of chief of naval operations (CNO) and were commanders or deputy commanders of the Atlantic and Pacific Fleets. The deputy CNO (Air Warfare, after 1971) remained the highest aviation billet. At the technical and logistical level, the Bureau of Aeronautics merged with the Bureau of Ordnance to become the Bureau of Weapons in 1959; its chief was a naval aviator. Simultaneously, the office of assistant secretary (Air) was discontinued. In the Navy Department reorganization of 1966, the Naval Air Systems Command superseded the Bureau of Weapons. With the aircraft carrier as the focus of its strategy, the Cold War navy countered the Soviet navy and projected its power over land and sea during limited wars and confrontations in Korea, Vietnam, and the Middle East. Attack carrier strength varied between twelve and fifteen, augmented by land-based patrol planes and antisubmarine and helicopter carriers. The 1980 overall naval-Marine aviation personnel strength was typical for the post–Vietnam period: 160,675, of whom 12,774 were pilots. The navy's air forces have remained a major component of the nation's global *peacekeeping forces since the end of the Cold War.

[See also Air Warfare; Tactics: Air Warfare Tactics.]

• Archibald D. Turnbull and Clifford L. Lord, History of United States Naval Aviation, 1949. Robert Sherrod, U.S. Marine Corps Aviation in World War II, 1952. George van Deurs, Wings of the Fleet: A Narrative of Naval Aviation's Early Development, 1910–1916, 1966. Gordon Swanborough and Peter M. Bowers, United States Naval Aircraft Since 1911, 1968; 3rd ed. 1990. Clark G. Reynolds, Admiral John H. Towers: The Struggle for Naval Air Supremacy, 1991. E. T. Wooldridge, ed., Into the Jet Age: Conflict and Change in Naval Aviation, 1945–1975, 1995.

—Clark G. Reynolds

NAVY SEALS. See Special Operations Forces: U.S. Navy Seals.

NEUMANN, JOHN VON (1903–1957), pioneer of computation; founder of *game theory. Von Neumann's wide-ranging genius shaped more scientific and technological fields than probably anyone of the century. Born in Budapest, he made basic discoveries in set theory, algebra, and quantum mechanics. In 1930, he moved to Princeton University and, as war loomed, turned to *weaponry, studying the mechanics of shock waves for the optimal height of explosion attacking a structure. For the *Manhattan Project, he researched the implosion trigger for an atomic bomb.

Von Neumann's pervading contribution was promoting computers for military and scientific research. As the United States entered World War II, computers were primitive. Typically used to calculate mathematical tables, they required operators manually to plug in connector cables for each task. Von Neumann's group put the commands controlling the computer's action sequence into its electronic memory, making it fast and flexible. In 1951, a computer simulated the triggering of the first thermonuclear explosion. Von Neumann pioneered the abstract study of computation, with his British student Alan Turing, and founded game theory, used to analyze *deterrence and escalation.

His postwar military work was driven by an abhorrence of communism, but he avoided the excesses of McCarthyism, testifying in support of J. Robert *Oppenheimer. Under President Dwight D. *Eisenhower, he oversaw the development of the first U.S. intercontinental *missiles. Von Neumann preferred behind-the-scenes influence to the popular celebrity of an Albert Einstein or an Edward *Teller, and his wide grasp of science and technology made him adept in that role.

[See also Consultants to the Military; Disciplinary Views of War: History of Science and Technology; Operations Research; Science, Technology, War, and the Military.]

• Steve Heims, *John von Neumann and Norbert Weiner: From Mathematics to the Technologies of Life and Death*, 1980. William Aspray, *John von Neumann and the Origins of Modern Computing*, 1990.
—Barry O'Neill

NEUTRALITY was among the predominant principles of U.S. foreign policy from the *Revolutionary War until 1941, reflecting a national determination to avoid involvement in other nations' wars. In the twentieth century, and particularly since U.S. entry into World War II, rigid neutrality has been seen as bad, even "immoral," as the United States has sought to exercise world leadership. The definitions of neutrality have varied as the United States has sought to integrate it with other policies.

The first English settlers in North America found themselves constantly at war under the doctrine of "no peace beyond the line," a diplomatic principle that allowed European states to remain at peace to the east of a north-south line 370 leagues west of the Cape Verde Islands, while placing no restrictions on military action to the west of that boundary. Those engaged in Spanish, French, and Dutch *privateering held that the English colonies were fair game even when their nations were officially at peace. When King William's War began in 1689, many colonists were indifferent to whether William III or James II ruled England, but reciprocal raids made neutrality difficult. There were local live-and-let-live agreements, the most successful between New York and Canada during Queen Anne's and King George's Wars. Generally, however, the colonists rallied to king and country as war followed war in Europe from 1689 to 1763.

Benjamin Franklin was among the first to note that the British North American colonies had developed common interests distinct from those of London. The colonists hardly objected to fighting: when the Seven Years War began officially in Europe in 1756 it had been going on for two years in the Ohio Valley. But Americans, who saw every reason to destroy the French empire in America, saw no reason to fight so that Prussia could rule Saxony in Europe.

Thus, a decade before independence, the colonists had developed a concept of neutrality in regard to European wars. This idea had many roots: a realpolitik definition of national interest; a commitment to trade; a notion of American exceptionalism; a legalist view of the rule of law among nations. Yet these emerged from the central idea that Americans, while ready to fight in causes that concerned them, should recognize that most world disputes did not. Instead, America would benefit by detachment from such conflicts while trading under a broad definition of neutral shipping rights.

By 1775, neutrality was a fundamental assumption of revolutionary ideology. The Continental Congress's Model Treaty of 1776 called for commerce and neutral rights without political commitments. Congress abandoned this ideal to sign an alliance with France in 1778, but the goal of isolation from European conflicts remained. When Russia organized an "armed neutrality" in 1780, the United States failed to join only because a belligerent, by definition, would not join a league of neutrals.

International recognition of U.S. independence in 1783 after the Revolutionary War left the new nation with contradictory commitments to neutrality and to France. This contradiction became critical in 1793, when Europe again went to war. On 22 April, President George *Washington proclaimed neutrality, then set out to define it. Secretary of the Treasury Alexander *Hamilton favored restricting neutral rights to ease relations with Britain, while Secretary of State Thomas *Jefferson favored strict enforcement of neutral rights, which would aid France.

Washington tried to navigate between belligerents, publicly claiming to honor the French alliance while violating its definitions of neutrality by concluding Jay's Treaty in 1795. He insisted that the United States had a right to noncontraband trade despite friction with Britain. In his farewell address of 1796, Washington argued that Europeans had interests distinct from those of the United States: the proper policy of which was to trade widely, have as little political connection to Europe as possible, and grow strong by avoiding Europe's inevitable quarrels.

Washington's advice guided his successors. John *Adams fought the Undeclared Naval War with *France; Thomas Jefferson conducted economic warfare while warning against "entangling alliances"; and James *Madison fought the *War of 1812. Each showed tactical flexibility, but upheld the principle of neutrality. Adams allowed British and American warships to cooperate, but rejected high Federalist demands for an Anglo-American alliance to conquer a Caribbean Empire. Jefferson threatened a British alliance, but purchased Louisiana instead. Madison went to war with Britain, but refused alliance with Napoleon. Even when they used force, they did so to defend American neutrality.

James *Monroe redefined this policy in 1823 with a doctrine that divided the world into an eastern hemisphere, where European rules would apply, and a western hemisphere, where American rules would prevail. America's rules included an end to European colonization and interference. The United States welcomed trade with the Old World, but not political ties with it. In Europe's conflicts the United States would remain neutral, trading with all according to its broad definition of neutral rights.

The American *Civil War caused some rethinking for a United States concerned not with avoiding involvement in the wars of other nations but rather with preventing European intervention in its own internal conflict. President Abraham *Lincoln initiated a blockade of the South that disregarded a century of maritime rights precedents. The success of the blockade played a major role in preservation of the Union.

The end of the Civil War left the United States reunited, still committed to neutrality in the abstract, and eager to forget its recent enforcement of broad belligerent rights. The nation maintained its neutrality through Europe's late-nineteenth-century wars, but found itself drawn into great power rivalries in East Asia as its economic interest in China conflicted with its determination to avoid political entanglements. Annexation of Hawaii and the Philippines in 1898 carried the American flag across the Pacific, and Secretary of State John Hay's "open door" notes of 1899 and 1900 reaffirmed U.S. policies of commerce with all, political involvement with none. But with U.S. troops helping Europeans and the Japanese to suppress the Boxer Rebellion in China, the strains between neutrality and reality were obvious.

These strains became even more evident under President Theodore *Roosevelt. His definition of U.S. neutrality during the Russo-Japanese War favored Japan. His personal intervention with German Kaiser *Wilhelm II helped to determine the outcome of the 1906 Moroccan crisis in favor of France. Roosevelt talked of neutrality but believed a balance of power in Europe and Asia served the national interest, and he acted on that belief even when it violated traditional policies.

This pattern of neutral rhetoric but unneutral action continued under President Woodrow *Wilson. Though he proclaimed U.S. neutrality in August 1914, Wilson's policies favored Britain over Germany in World War I, allowing sales of munitions, credits to belligerents, and travel on belligerent ships, but restricting German submarine warfare. Wilson protested but did not take similar action against British violations of U.S. neutral rights, such as the illegal seizure of food, cotton, and other American exports to the central powers and European neutrals. By recognizing the British *blockades but not those of Germany, Wilson placed the United States from 1914 to April 1917 in legal limbo, as a non-neutral nonbelligerent.

World War I left the United States caught between two visions of the world. One was its traditional policy: trade with all but political entanglement with none outside the Americas. Wilson presented another: the United States must lead a new international order in which neutrality would be inconceivable. The heart of this order would be the *League of Nations, which Wilson wrote into the Treaty of *Versailles in 1919.

The American people received the League's covenant with deep ambivalence. Many were simply confused. The popular groundswell the administration counted on to push the treaty through a partisan Senate never developed. Wilson himself killed any compromise. The Senate defeated the treaty and the people sealed its defeat in the 1920 election.

The Republican administrations of 1921–33 publicly reaffirmed their commitment to neutrality, repudiating the League in favor of a policy of commercial expansion and political nonintervention. Yet they found themselves caught in a web of existing commitments. Commerce and politics were not so easily separated in an increasingly interdependent global economy.

While the difficulties of returning to neutrality were becoming evident to American statesmen, the demand for such a return was growing among the American people. By the 1930s, many Americans believed that participation in World War I had been a mistake. To avoid a repetition, many supported congressional passage of neutrality laws. Wars in Spain, Ethiopia, and the Far East raised moral questions about U.S. neutrality, however, and disagreement between those who favored a return to traditional definitions of neutral rights and those who favored abandonment of neutrality altogether divided the movement, allowing President Franklin D. *Roosevelt to eliminate many objectionable provisions. But the *Neutrality Acts of 1935, 1936, and 1937 nevertheless represented a repudiation of Wilsonianism.

Although Roosevelt publicly supported these acts, he complained privately that they limited his authority. In November 1939 he secured passage of a modified Neutrality Act, which allowed him to begin supplying arms to nations fighting Germany and Japan in World War II. Over the next two years he eroded neutrality by trading surplus destroyers to the British, providing massive amounts of equipment under the Lend-Lease *Destroyers-for-Bases Agreement, and using the U.S. Navy to convoy Allied ships

in the North Atlantic. By 1940, U.S. policy was again in a legal limbo, neither belligerent nor neutral.

World War II saw the end of neutrality as a principle of U.S. foreign policy. President Roosevelt forged a bipartisan coalition behind U.S. membership in the *United Nations. Under the UN charter, the major powers have an obligation to maintain or restore peace, by collective force if necessary. In the postwar world, the United States emerged as the major economic and military power. During the *Cold War confrontation with communism, particularly in the Soviet Union and China, the U.S. government abandoned neutrality for an active policy of containment. In pursuit of that policy, it ended the century-old policy of avoiding prewar military alliances by organizing the North Atlantic Treaty Organization (*NATO) and pledging U.S. military forces to defend Western Europe and, through other commitments, numerous regions of the globe in defense of U.S. *national security in the nuclear age.

[See also Isolationism; Truman Doctrine.]

• John Bassett Moore, *A Digest of International Law*, 8 vols., 1906. Philip C. Jessup, ed., *Neutrality*, 4 vols., 1935–36. Ernest R. May, *The World War and American Isolation, 1914–1917*, 1959. Max Savelle, *The Origins of American Diplomacy*, 1967. Stephen E. Ambrose, *Rise to Globalism: American Foreign Policy Since 1938*, 1971; 7th rev. ed., 1993. Charles DeBenedetti, *The Peace Reform in American History*, 1980. John W. Coogan, *The End of Neutrality*, 1981. Lawrence S. Kaplan, *Entangling Alliances with None*, 1987. J. M. Gabriel, *The American Conception of Neutrality After 1941*, 1989.

—John W. Coogan

The **NEUTRALITY ACTS** were laws passed in 1935, 1936, 1937, and 1939 to limit U.S. involvement in future wars. They were based on the widespread disillusionment with World War I in the early 1930s and the belief that the United States had been drawn into the war through loans and trade with the Allies. *Isolationism was particularly strong in the Midwest.

Congressional proponents of neutrality legislation sought to prevent similar mistakes. The 1935 act banned munitions exports to belligerents and restricted American travel on belligerent ships. The 1936 act banned loans to belligerents. The 1937 act extended these provisions to civil wars and gave the president discretionary authority to restrict nonmunitions sales to a "cash-and-carry" basis (belligerents had to pay in advance then export goods in their own ships). (These bills were signed and publicly applauded by President Franklin D. *Roosevelt, although he complained privately that they limited presidential authority.) The 1939 act, passed with President Roosevelt's active support in November under the shadow of the European war, banned U.S. ships from carrying goods or passengers to belligerent ports but allowed the United States to sell munitions, although on a "cash-and-carry" basis. Roosevelt further eroded neutrality over the next two years, trading surplus U.S. *destroyers to Britain for access to naval and air bases and providing U.S. military equipment to enemies of Germany and Japan under the *Lend-Lease Act. Congress repealed the Neutrality Acts on 13 November 1941.

Although seen as the high tide of interwar isolationism, the neutrality legislation of 1935–37 had minimal impact on U.S. defense planning. The 1939 act encouraged combat testing of U.S. equipment by Allied forces, but also created shortages as U.S. production initially was unable to meet requirements of both Allies and expanding U.S. forces.

[*See also* Destroyers-For-Bases Agreement (1940); Neutrality; Nye, Gerald.]

• Robert Dallek, *Franklin D. Roosevelt and American Foreign Policy, 1932–1945*, 1979. Wayne S. Cole, *Roosevelt and the Isolationists, 1932–1945*, 1983.
—John W. Coogan

NEWBURGH "CONSPIRACY" (1783). Following victory at the Battle of *Yorktown in October 1781, George *Washington's army returned to the Hudson Highlands to stand watch over the British garrison at New York City, forty-five miles downriver. The Revolutionary War now entered a new phase in which the army seemed to Congress to absorb scarce money and supplies for no immediate purpose. Moreover, some Americans worried that an idle standing army might overthrow civilian control and sought to keep it under tight supervision. Increasingly marginalized, the army's officers brooded about their lack of pay, food, clothing, pensions, and respect from the public.

The crisis in civil-military relations came in early March 1783 when an anonymous address circulated at army headquarters at Newburgh, eight miles north of West Point, threatening that the army would not disband at the end of the war if its financial demands were not met or that it would refuse to fight if the war continued. The address called for a meeting of officers on 11 March; Washington, who knew the officers' concerns were legitimate but who also understood the need to maintain order and discipline, issued his own call for a meeting for 15 March, transforming an irregular proceeding into an official airing of grievances.

At that meeting, Washington entreated his officers not to "lessen the dignity and sully the glory you have hitherto maintained" and produced a letter from a Virginia congressman that attempted to explain Congress's problems in meeting the army's financial demands. Beginning to read, he stumbled over the tightly written words, and drawing out his eyeglasses, reportedly "begged the indulgence of his audience," observing that "he had grown gray in their service, and now found himself growing blind." No other words could have reminded the officers so effectively that, if anyone had a right to be frustrated with Congress, it was Washington. If he was willing to trust Congress's goodwill, so should they. The so-called conspiracy collapsed immediately.

There is reason to doubt the seriousness of the officers' threat to civilian control of the military. While they had cause to complain about a dilatory and pusillanimous Congress, they were members of the same society, with no real prospects but a return to their homes and former employments when the war ended. There is, however, no reason to doubt the power of Washington's leadership. At Newburgh, he reasserted the principle that Congress controls the army, the cornerstone of the American military tradition.

[*See also* Civil-Military Relations: Civilian Control of the Military; Continental Army; Revolutionary War: Military and Diplomatic Course.]

• Richard H. Kohn, "The Inside History of the Newburgh Conspiracy," *William and Mary Quarterly,* 3rd ser., vol. 27 (April 1970), pp. 187–220. Paul D. Nelson, "Horatio Gates at Newburgh," *William and Mary Quarterly,* 3rd ser., vol. 29 (January 1972), pp. 143–58.
—Harold E. Selesky

NEW GUINEA CAMPAIGN (1942–44). Probably few of the 685,407 Americans sent to the Southwest Pacific Area (SWPA) through 1944 knew much about New Guinea prior to Japan's attack on *Pearl Harbor—initiating the American entrance into World War II. Nevertheless, the New Guinea campaign began in summer 1942 when Japan attempted to isolate Australia through an overland attack from Buna to Port Moresby. This attack resulted in the first American action on that mountainous and jungle-covered island. After the Australians successfully defended Port Moresby along the Kokoda Trail, U.S. forces launched an unsuccessful strike against the Japanese at Buna on the island's northern coast. Impatient with the lack of progress, Gen. Douglas *MacArthur, chief of SWPA, replaced the commander, Maj. Gen. Edwin Forrest Harding, with Lt. Gen. Robert L. Eichelberger, who initially fared no better. However, MacArthur pushed Eichelberger onward, and the enemy force was finally defeated on 22 January 1943 through a grueling battle of attrition.

After the Buna campaign, MacArthur created the Sixth U.S. Army under the command of Lt. Gen. Walter Krueger. Although historians have largely overlooked Krueger's overall role in New Guinea, he coordinated the various services and developed operational plans that made MacArthur's strategy a success.

Krueger's first order was an attack on Saidor in January 1944 as part of an effort to seize the Vitiaz Strait. Next, MacArthur wanted Hansa Bay, but intercepted and decrypted Japanese Army messages (through *ULTRA) tipped off SWPA leaders that the Japanese were expecting a landing there. So, he directed Krueger to seize Hollandia in April 1944. Thus began a string of amphibious assaults along the northern coast of New Guinea. Following Hollandia came Wakde and Biak in May 1944, and Noemfoor and Sansapor in July 1944. By the fall of 1944, the Sixth Army had secured New Guinea sufficiently to invade the Philippines.

Both sides invested heavily in the campaign. The Japanese committed 180,000 men, while the Allies employed five Australian divisions and six American divisions. The Americans suffered approximately 16,850 *casualties and the Australians over 17,000. The Japanese lost the most, with 123,000 killed.

The New Guinea campaign was important for several reasons. It protected Australia and provided a stepladder for the liberation of the Philippines; it demonstrated the valuable role of Krueger; it illustrated the American strategy of leapfrogging, one that emphasized bypassing Japanese strongholds while capturing less defended areas; and it reflected MacArthur's obsessive desire to return to the Philippines as quickly as possible.

[*See also* Philippines, Liberation of the; World War II, U.S. Naval Operations in: The Pacific.]

• Robert Ross Smith, *The Approach to the Philippines,* 1953. Samuel Eliot Morison, *History of United States Naval Operations in World War II.* Vol. 8: *New Guinea and the Marianas, March 1944–August 1944,* 1962. Ronald H. Spector, *Eagle Against the Sun: The American War with Japan,* 1985. Edward J. Drea, *MacArthur's ULTRA: Codebreaking and the War Against Japan, 1942–1945,* 1992. Kevin C. Holzimmer, "Walter Krueger, Douglas MacArthur, and the Pacific War: The Wakde-Sarmi Campaign as a Case Study," *Journal of Military History,* 59 (October 1995), pp. 661–85. Stephen R. Taaffe, *MacArthur's Jungle War: The 1944 New Guinea Campaign,* 1998.
—Kevin C. Holzimmer

NEW ORLEANS, BATTLE OF (1815). This encounter concluded the *War of 1812 against the British. Approximately 5,300 British regulars under Maj. Gen. Sir Edward Pakenham, accompanied by naval forces under Vice Adm. Sir Alexander Cochrane, attacked New Orleans to relieve American military pressure on Canada and improve Great Britain's position in peace negotiations. Major Gen. Andrew *Jackson opposed them with a force of about 4,700 drawn from the U.S. Army, the free colored population of New Orleans, the militias of Kentucky, Louisiana, and Tennessee, and the pirates of Barataria.

Three lesser engagements preceded the battle. On 23 December 1814, Jackson attempted to drive the British off, and on 28 December and New Year's Day, Pakenham probed Jackson's defenses with a reconnaissance in force and an *artillery attack. On 8 January 1815, Pakenham assaulted Jackson's line on the east bank of the Mississippi, making a secondary attack on his position on the west bank. The latter succeeded, but the main attack failed as Jackson's artillery fired grapeshot and canister shot into the advancing British line. British losses amounted to 2,400 *casualties and prisoners; the Americans lost about 70 men.

Since the Treaty of Ghent, ending the war, had been signed on 24 December 1814, the battle's impact was symbolic, but nevertheless significant. It reinforced the legend of the volunteer American *citizen-soldier, made Jackson a national hero, and contributed eventually to his election as president in 1828.

[See also Army, U.S.: 1783–1865; Militia and National Guard.]

• Charles B. Brooks, The Siege of New Orleans, 1961. Wilburt S. Brown, The Amphibious Campaign for West Florida and Louisiana, 1814–1815: A Critical Review of Strategy and Tactics at New Orleans, 1969.
—J. C. A. Stagg

NEW ORLEANS, SIEGE OF (1862). Anxious to control the Mississippi River early in the Civil War, the Lincoln administration sent an expedition to the Gulf of Mexico after efforts to descend that waterway failed. Capt. David *Farragut commanded the Union naval contingent, Maj. Gen. Benjamin F. *Butler the army. Their concentration at Ship Island caused Confederate authorities mistakenly to believe their objective was Mobile or Pensacola. Thousands of troops were withdrawn from New Orleans, leaving less than 5,000 militia when Farragut entered the Mississippi.

On 8 April, Farragut assembled his fleet of 24 wooden vessels, mounting about 200 cannon, and 19 mortar schooners. Blocking Farragut's path were 500 Confederates and 80 cannon in Forts Jackson and St. Philip; a chain barricade across the river; and naval vessels. This fleet consisted of three ironclads (the ram Manassas, the underpowered Louisiana, and the unfinished Mississippi), twelve armed wooden vessels, seven tugs, and some fire rafts.

On 18 April, Union mortars began bombarding the forts. Disregarding orders to wait until the forts were silenced, Farragut got under way at 2:00 A.M. on the 24th. Twenty-one vessels cleared the gauntlet. In a wild melee, they destroyed the Confederate fleet, losing only 1 vessel and 171 sailors killed or wounded. Confederates ashore suffered fewer than 50 *casualties.

After detaching two vessels to support Butler's movement ashore, Farragut proceeded upriver and captured New Orleans on the 25th. Confederate Maj. Gen. Mansfield Lovell evacuated the city to prevent its destruction and civilian authorities formally surrendered the city on the 28th. A mutiny in the forts forced Brig. Gen. Johnson

K. Duncan to surrender them the same day. On 1 May, Butler's troops occupied New Orleans.

Farragut's victory gave the Union control of the lower Mississippi. A court of inquiry cleared Lovell; it blamed the disaster on the Davis administration for reducing the garrison and failing to unite all naval forces under Lovell.

[See also Civil War: Military and Diplomatic Course; Confederate Army; Confederate Navy; Union Navy.]

• Charles L. Dufour, The Night the War Was Lost, 1960. Arthur W. Bergeron, Jr., "Mansfield Lovell," in Roman J. Heleniak and Lawrence L. Hewitt, eds., The 1989 Deep Delta Civil War Symposium: Leadership During the Civil War, 1991.
—Lawrence L. Hewitt

NEWS MEDIA, WAR, AND THE MILITARY. From the earliest days of the republic, American leaders encountered difficulties trying to balance the need for secrecy in diplomatic and military affairs with America's tradition of a free and independent press. As early as 1792, Secretary of State Thomas *Jefferson wrote to President George *Washington that "No government ought to be without censors and where the press is free, no one ever will." Yet, only three years earlier, Congress passed a statute requiring each department to establish regulations for the custody, use, and preservation of official documents. That seemingly innocuous statute implicitly included rules for classification and censorship. The imposition of such rules has been especially important during periods of international crisis and war when citizens have been asked by presidents, who controlled the flow of government information, to surrender their lives and treasure to defend national security. Looking over America's military past, many observers would agree with Senator Hiram Johnson (R-Calif.) who said in 1917 that "The first casualty when war comes is truth."

Obviously, few citizens in any nation approve the publication in wartime of information about troop movements and military strategies that would help their enemies defeat their fighting men and women. Not all citizens agree about the necessity of government suppression or censorship of journalists or those opposed to war who allegedly give aid and comfort to the enemy by criticizing presidents or generals or organizing antiwar groups.

This was the case with the first major assault against free speech and the free press in the United States, the Federalists' controversial Sedition Act of 1798, which made it a crime to write or speak against the president or Congress in a defamatory way during the Undeclared Naval War with *France. However, during that "Quasi-War" and subsequently the *War of 1812, commodores and generals did not have to worry about war correspondents. Military officials controlled the channels of communication in the combat theaters. Whatever appeared in newspapers— sometimes weeks or even months after the events—was little more than the sort of propagandistic official war dispatches that had recently been perfected in France by Napoleon, although Andrew *Jackson did institute censorship for a brief period early in 1815 after he occupied New Orleans. It was not until the *Mexican War that the wartime relationship between journalists and the government began to assume its contemporary shape.

Because of the development of high-speed printing presses in the 1840s, the "penny press" could be produced rapidly and cheaply in large numbers. Newspapers like the New York Morning News and the New York Herald competed with one another for jingoistic readers and thus contributed to the spirit of "manifest destiny"—a slogan coined by the *Morning News*'s John L. O'Sullivan—that swept over the nation.

The development of the telegraph and other improvements in land and sea *transportation soon made it easier to bring news from afar to major urban areas. Nonetheless, because telegraph lines did not reach south of Richmond during the 1840s, it still took as much as three weeks or more for news from Mexico to arrive in Washington and New York, via New Orleans and the sea. All the same, the war in Mexico was the best-covered war to date as journalists like the dashing George V. Kendall did not have to put up with censorship and often fought in battle alongside the men about whom they were writing.

For the emerging profession of war correspondent, the war was just a warmup for the Crimean War and the *Civil War, where modern problems of censorship on the battlefield first appeared. At the start of the Civil War, Abraham *Lincoln placed the telegraph lines in Washington under federal control, but allowed journalists free rein elsewhere. Because of major divisions in the North, the policy changed in February 1862 when Lincoln took control of all telegraph lines and ordered the U.S. Postmaster General to deny the use of mail service to disloyal newspapers. Operating under that order, Lincoln's agents completely suppressed several Democratic newspapers and imprisoned editors.

Northern newspapers and illustrated magazines sent 500 correspondents and a few illustrators into the field, almost all of whom supported the Union cause. The same could be said for their 100 Southern counterparts, most of whom did double duty in the *Confederate army. Due to self-censorship as well as official censorship, reporters underestimated *casualties and reported uncritically about strategic and tactical blunders. This was the first American war in which the media played an important role in intelligence. Despite the censorship, both Robert E. *Lee and William Tecumseh *Sherman, among other generals, claimed to have discovered valuable information about troop movements and future battle plans from newspapers.

The public's demand for war news proved insatiable. The more colorful and breathless the story, the more newspapers were sold. As in later wars, reporters sometimes made up "eyewitness" accounts of battles hundreds of miles from their positions. In 1864, Secretary of War Edwin M. *Stanton began issuing daily war bulletins, a practice that made it easier for journalists to write their reports and easier for Washington to control the news.

The press played a more important role prior to the next war, the *Spanish-American War, than during it. From the beginning of the Cuban insurrection against Spain in 1895, the new sensationalist "yellow press," exemplified by William Randolph Hearst's *New York Journal* and Joseph Pulitzer's *New York World,* increased circulation exponentially as it called for American intervention against the Spanish, who were accused of committing some real and many imagined crimes against humanity. On the other hand, as the United States prepared to enter the war, President William *McKinley masterfully manipulated the news so that skeptics would ultimately support his call to arms.

The U.S. government centralized the release of war information from Washington, took control of telegraph facilities at Key West, Florida, and censored dispatches that arrived in New York City. Nonetheless, embarrassing stories did manage to leak out concerning gross mismanagement and scandals in the food and supply lines. Two hundred correspondents, including the novelist Stephen Crane and the flamboyant Richard Harding Davis, covered the Caribbean campaign, while fledgling motion picture companies made reenacted newsreels they sold as authentic to a public thrilled with this "splendid little war."

Military censorship in Manila posed greater difficulties for journalists covering the less popular follow-up *Philippine War against Filipino insurrectionists. But material did appear in the press that highlighted torture and *atrocities committed by American soldiers in a dirty, counterrevolutionary war and encouraged a potent anti-imperialist movement.

After the United States entered World War I in April 1917, the War Department, following the policies of the European nations, established its first formal accrediting procedure for war correspondents. A journalist had to agree in writing to submit dispatches to military censors and to behave "like a gentleman of the press." In addition, back in Washington, Woodrow *Wilson established the controversial Committee on Public Information, which was not only in charge of censorship but also ran an elaborate propaganda campaign at home and abroad. For example, the committee employed 75,000 speakers who delivered 750,000 four-minute pep talks, often in movie theaters, in 5,000 cities and towns in support of the war.

The administration also obtained from Congress the *Espionage and Sedition Acts of World War I. The former permitted the Postmaster General to refuse to mail magazines or other publications detrimental to the war effort; the latter prohibited speech that did not support that effort. Under such laws, Socialist Party presidential nominee Eugene V. *Debs was sent to jail, as was a movie producer for making a film about the *Revolutionary War in which the British appeared as villains.

During World War II, military authorities again imposed strict censorship at the source for correspondents who numbered as many as 1,000 in Europe alone. Among other matters deemed threatening to national security were stories and, especially, pictures that portrayed too graphically G.I. injuries and death, or reported incidents of cowardice, as was the case during the Battle of the *Bulge, or revealed information embarrassing to the United States and its Allies. And as in previous wars, once they learned the rules, correspondents practiced self-censorship so that they would not have to rewrite their articles completely after censors got through with them.

Back home, the government issued a voluntary code of wartime practices for the media, to which, in most cases, the mainstream press adhered. The *Chicago Tribune* was a notable exception when it revealed *mobilization plans on the eve of the attack on *Pearl Harbor, and later ran a story about the breaking of Japanese codes. Although the Office of Censorship did intercept and read letters and cablegrams and tap phone calls, most Americans accepted the abridgment of their First Amendment rights during the global crisis.

The Office of War Information (OWI), headed by radio commentator Elmer Davis, coordinated propaganda activities. Somewhat more sophisticated than the Creel Committee of World War I, OWI staffers met regularly with the media, including the heads of Hollywood studios, to suggest political themes they wanted to promote.

No such elaborate activities were needed during the limited *Korean War. From June through December 1950, journalists at the front adhered to a voluntary code of self-censorship. But when South Korean leaders began complaining about articles critical of their repressive actions, Washington imposed full military censorship. Few Americans ever learned the truth about the nature of their ally or of the devastating American *bombing of civilians in North Korea that resulted in hundreds of thousands of deaths.

Such was not the case in the *Vietnam War—the most controversial war in American history in many ways, including the relationship between the media and the military. According to critics of press performance, journalists in the combat theater, not subject to censorship, wrote stories and shot television footage that distorted and hurt the war effort—most controversially, media coverage of the *Tet Offensive of early 1968. That charge dramatically influenced the way the government subsequently limited journalists' access during the 1983 U.S. intervention in *Grenada, the 1989 Panama intervention, and, above all, the 1991 *Persian Gulf War.

But the charge that the media "lost the war" in Vietnam was a myth. Except for a brief period during the Kennedy administration when several young journalists who supported the war criticized military tactics and the venality of the Saigon regime, most of the coverage favored administration policies, at least until 1968. Even during that earlier period, the government in Saigon expelled American journalists, and Washington influenced publishers to alter their coverage. To be sure, in several celebrated cases—notably Morley Safer's 1965 account on CBS of Marines burning hooches, and his later coverage of the Tet Offensive—the media apparently contributed to the growth of antiwar sentiments, but no more so than the American rates of casualties. But the fact that reporters shared the national *Cold War consensus and that the tenets of so-called objective journalism demanded that they report official briefings (the "Five O'clock Follies"), often uncritically, guaranteed a relatively favorable press until almost the end. The Johnson administration did not institute full censorship because it wanted to play down the importance of this undeclared war.

Another view suggests that the Vietnam War was the first televised live or "living-room war." But it was not projected live into viewers' homes. In this era before the development of satellite hookup, the news film for stories emanating either from Saigon or Japan was flown by air to New York, then edited and broadcast. As in World War II, those in charge of deciding what to air generally eliminated pictures of bloodied soldiers and the other worst horrors of war.

The situation was different during the Persian Gulf War in 1991, with strict censorship and "pool" reporting for the more than 1,000 journalists who covered the fighting in real time—primarily from hotels in Saudi Arabia. Military authorities banned several magazines from the combat theater and arrested at least eight American correspondents for violating aspects of the censorship rules. Aside from reports from the Cable News Network's (CNN) Peter Arnett in Baghdad, which were themselves censored by the Iraqis, most of what Americans saw on television was exactly what the military wanted Americans—and anyone else tuning in—to see.

Beginning in the 1980s, worldwide television news services, led by CNN, began to play an increasingly important role in crises and wars. Before the Gulf War broke out, Saddam *Hussein, the Iraqi leader, was encouraged by strong congressional opposition to President George *Bush's policies, broadcast by satellite to Iraq. Later, coalition commander Gen. H. Norman Schwarzkopf tailored his televised briefings for those in Baghdad who were watching. In 1991, Haitian dictator Gen. Raoul Cédras's viewing of congressional and other opposition to American policies, brought to him by the ubiquitous CNN, may have contributed to his recalcitrance.

As nations become even more completely electronically connected to one another in years to come, the problems inherent in maintaining a free press during times of international crisis may become even more severe.

[See also Intelligence, Military and Political; Panama, U.S. Military Involvement in; Peace and Antiwar Movements; Propaganda and Public Relations, Government.]

• Joseph J. Mathews, *Reporting the Wars,* 1957. John Hohenberg, *Foreign Correspondence: The Great Reporters and Their Times,* 1964. Doris A. Graber, *Public Opinion, the President, and Foreign Policy: Four Case Studies from the Formative Years,* 1968. Philip Knightly, *The First Casualty: From the Crimea to Vietnam: The War Correspondent as Hero, Propagandist, and Myth Maker,* 1975. Allan M. Winkler, *The Politics of Propaganda: The Office of War Information, 1942–1945,* 1975. Stephen Vaughn, *Holding Fast the Inner Lines: Democracy, Nationalism, and the Committee on Public Information,* 1980. Daniel C. Hallin, *The "Uncensored War": The Media and Vietnam,* 1986. Robert E. Denton Jr., ed., *The Media and the Persian Gulf War,* 1993. Clarence R. Wyatt, *Paper Soldiers: The American Press and the Vietnam War,* 1993.

—Melvin Small

NEW YORK, BATTLE OF (1776). When the British evacuated Boston in March 1776 early in the Revolutionary War, no royal government remained between New Hampshire and Georgia. New York, with its central location and superb harbor, was the logical place to reassert British authority. Congress—hoping to prevent such a reassertion and forestall the loss of overland communication between New England and the other colonies—urged Gen. George *Washington to undertake the almost hopeless task of defending New York. Without a navy, Washington hoped that shore batteries would protect his army from defeat. With perhaps 19,000 men, many of them poorly trained militia, he faced the largest force Britain had yet sent overseas, over 40,000 soldiers and sailors under the command of the brothers Gen. William *Howe and Adm. Richard Howe.

The British landed on undefended Staten Island on 2 July, and after seven weeks of careful preparation, launched a campaign based on turning the Americans out of their earthworks, as he had planned to do at the Battle of *Bunker Hill in June 1775. This cautious plan made effective use of British resources and envisioned a negotiated settlement after the American army had been beaten but not martyred.

In retrospect, the Howes were overly cautious in not exploiting their naval strength, but their initial successes on land were spectacular. Crossing the Narrows to Long Island on 22 August, William Howe five days later implemented the plan that had gone awry at Bunker Hill: pin down the Americans' right flank and send a strong force around their left. Brilliantly executed by 10,000 men under Howe's personal command, the attack routed the Americans from advanced positions on the Heights of Guan.

Although many American units fought well, the army retreated several miles to entrenchments on Brooklyn Heights. Expecting a renewed British attack in the morning, Washington on the night of 29–30 August evacuated his exhausted men to Manhattan Island.

Howe waited until 15 September before picking Kip's Bay on the east side of Manhattan as the site of his next turning movement; only Howe's failure to move west to the Hudson River allowed the Americans to escape. Howe pushed Washington north into Westchester County by late October, then retired to consolidate his gains. The last American position on Manhattan, Fort Washington, fell to assault on 16 November. Four days later, Howe began a slow pursuit of the battered remnants of the American army across northern New Jersey.

Washington made serious mistakes at New York, especially by attempting to defend everything rather than deny Howe New York for as long as possible without losing his own army. Although it lost over 5,000 men—killed, wounded, and captured, Washington's army performed creditably in its first campaign of maneuver. Outnumbered, incompletely trained, crippled by inexperienced general officers, and forced to defend an impossible position, it survived because of the determination, courage, and leadership of a core of officers and soldiers, foremost among whom was George Washington. Howe's failure to destroy Washington's army cost the British their best chance of ending the rebellion.

[*See also* Militia and National Guard; Revolutionary War: Military and Diplomatic Course.]

• Henry P. Johnston, *The Campaign of 1776 Around New York and Brooklyn*, 1878. Douglas S. Freeman, *George Washington, Leader of the Revolution*, Chaps. 4–14, 1951. Ira D. Gruber, *The Howe Brothers and the American Revolution*, 1972.   —Harold E. Selesky

The **NEW YORK CITY ANTI-DRAFT RIOTS** (1863) constituted the largest domestic uprising in the North during the Civil War. Caused by a newly enacted draft law, which fell heavily upon the poor because of the clause offering an exemption to anyone furnishing a substitute or paying a $300 fee, the riot started on 13 July 1863, and lasted until 17 July, when newly arrived troops brought it under control.

New York City had long been seething with discontent. A Democratic community in an often Republican state, it contained many immigrants, especially Irish Catholics, who feared black competition and were enraged by the *Emancipation Proclamation. Fueled by the exasperation of the badly exploited poor and the increasingly difficult situation of many workingmen, on Monday, 13 July, a large group of disaffected volunteer firemen and laborers converged upon the district office of the Provost Marshal responsible for implementing *conscription, stormed and wrecked the building, and stopped the draft process. Superintendent of Police John A. Kennedy was badly beaten; trolley tracks and telegraph wires were torn up, and many shops and factories closed.

Soon the rioters began indiscriminate attacks on black residents, many of whom were killed. The crowd also vented its anger upon the Republican press, attempting to storm the building of the *New York Tribune*, from which editor Horace Greeley escaped only with difficulty. In the afternoon, rioters attacked and burned the black orphan

asylum on Fifth Avenue, attempted to secure guns at a gun factory, and gutted a number of police stations. The rioting continued for four more days; Col. Henry O'Brien of the 11th New York Regiment was murdered, and general looting of stores, hotels, and the homes of the rich made the city unsafe.

In the meantime, Gen. Harvey Brown had taken over command of the troops in the city and, cooperating with the police, managed to beat back a number of attacks. Democratic governor Horatio Seymour, vacationing on the New Jersey coast, came back on Tuesday and addressed the crowd at City Hall, allegedly calling them "My Friends" and exhorting them to return to their homes. He also sought a suspension of the draft, of which he thoroughly disapproved. It was not until Thursday, 16 July, that federal troops, some of them summoned from Gettysburg, were able to assist in ending the rioting. On 17 July, the Roman Catholic archbishop John Hughes cooperated with Mayor George Opdyke in pacifying the crowd, and order was restored.

The result of the riot was that the draft in New York was suspended until August, while the city and county raised a fund to help pay exemption fees for those unable to afford them. The national administration did not impose martial law, as had been requested, but it did put conservative Gen. John A. Dix in charge of the Department of the East. Estimates of effects of the riots are usually set at over $1 million in property damage and perhaps 120 people killed and more than 120 wounded. The Tammany wing of the Democratic Party under William M. Tweed took over the city's affairs and continued in power until 1871. In the long run, recruitment continued undisturbed.

[*See also* Civil War: Domestic Course; Draft Resistance and Evasion.]

• James McCague, *The Second Rebellion*, 1968. Adrian Cook, *The Armies of the Streets: The New York City Draft Riots of 1863*, 1974. Iver Bernstein, *The New York City Draft Riots*, 1990.

                                                        —Hans L. Trefousse

***NEW YORK TIMES* v. U.S.** (1971). *See* Pentagon Papers (1971).

NICARAGUA, U.S. MILITARY INVOLVEMENT IN. The United States has directly intervened militarily in Nicaragua three times, 1909–10, 1912–25, and 1926–33, and once indirectly, 1981–89. The direct interventions were extensions of the 1904 *Roosevelt Corollary to the Monroe Doctrine, in which President Theodore *Roosevelt proclaimed the right of U.S. intervention to preclude European intervention in the Caribbean.

Nicaragua first gained importance to the United States as a potential canal route through Central America. With the construction of the Panama Canal, that importance shifted to economic and security concerns. Instability or a government unfriendly to the United States were seen as threats to the Panama Canal. It was just such conditions that prompted the first intervention and led to the establishment of what was in effect an American protectorate over Nicaragua until 1933.

In 1909, President José Zelaya's government executed two Americans who had joined a revolutionary force opposing his rule. The United States broke relations with the government in Managua, and the U.S. Navy was used to aid the rebels in a decisive battle against Zelaya's forces. The victorious revolutionaries, under the leadership of Adolfo Díaz, negotiated a treaty establishing U.S. control over Nicaragua's customs—the exporting nation's main source of revenue. American forces were removed in 1910, but over 2,000 U.S. Marines were sent back in 1912 to help protect the Díaz government against a new uprising. After the defeat of the rebellion, most Marines were withdrawn, but 100 remained to ensure stability. This arrangement was ratified in the 1916 Bryan-Chamorro Treaty, which extended American financial aid to Nicaragua and granted the United States sole rights for any future canal built there.

By 1925, the Coolidge administration concluded that Nicaragua was stable enough for U.S. forces to depart. The outbreak of civil war in late 1926, however, brought a third round of American intervention. Secretary of State Frank Kellogg justified military intervention because Communists were fighting the government. Actually, liberal forces were contesting Díaz's taking of the presidency from Gen. Emiliano Chamorro Vargas. Washington quickly recognized Díaz and sent lawyer-diplomat Henry L. *Stimson to Nicaragua to supervise elections and establish a National Guard (*Guardia Nacional*) to be trained by the Marines. All the liberal forces agreed to the settlement imposed by Stimson except for Augusto Sandino, who vowed to fight until U.S. forces were withdrawn.

Stimson, appointed secretary of state by Herbert C. *Hoover, concluded that the *Guardia Nacional* was ready to handle the problem of Sandino and maintain order in Nicaragua. The last of the Marines departed in 1933, and the *Guardia Nacional* under Anastasio Somoza became the most powerful military force in Nicaragua. Sandino ended his fighting as promised, but was killed in 1934 by the *Guardia Nacional*. In 1936, Somoza formally took over all power in Nicaragua. He and his two sons would rule with American support until 1979, when the Somoza dictatorship was overthrown by the Sandinista National Liberation Front.

In the 1980s, tensions developed quickly between the leftist Sandinistas and the U.S. government. When promised U.S. economic aid was delayed by Congress, the new revolutionary government turned to other nations, particularly Cuba, for advisers and technicians, and produced scathing criticisms of American foreign policy in Latin America. As it left office, the Carter administration suspended the belated economic assistance on the grounds that the Sandinistas were aiding leftist rebels in neighboring El Salvador. In 1981, the Reagan administration came to office determined to oust the Sandinistas. To do so, the United States applied a wide range of political and economic pressure to undermine the Nicaraguan government. Most important, Reagan provided $19 million to the *Central Intelligence Agency in November 1981 to begin training a counterrevolutionary army known as the Contras. Led by former *Guardia Nacional* officers, the Contras by 1986 consisted of over 15,000 soldiers supported by the United States. During the period when a Democratic majority in Congress banned aid to the rebels, the administration used a variety of means to funnel funds to them illegally. In what became known as the *Iran-Contra Affair (1986), one scheme diverted money from secret arms sales to Iran to the Contras. Even with U.S. aid and bases in Honduras, the Contras were unable to unseat the Sandinistas. The war ended after a negotiated settlement sponsored by other Latin American nations led to free elections in 1989 and the victory of the anti-Sandinista coalition.

[*See also* Caribbean and Latin America, U.S. Military Involvement in the; Marine Corps, U.S.: 1865–1914; Marine Corps, U.S.: 1914–1945.]

• Neill Macaulay, *The Sandino Affair*, 1967. William Kammen, *A Search for Stability: United States Diplomacy Toward Nicaragua, 1925–1933*, 1968. Richard Millett, *Guardians of the Dynasty: A History of the U.S.-Created Guardia Nacional de Nicaragua and the Somoza Family*, 1977. Robert Pastor, *Condemned to Repetition: The United States and Nicaragua*, 1987. Cynthia J. Arnson, *Crossroads: Congress, the President, and Central America, 1976–1993*, 1993. Robert Kagan, *A Twilight Struggle: America Power and Nicaragua, 1977–1990*, 1995. Walter LaFeber, *Inevitable Revolutions: The United States in Central America*, 2nd rev. ed. 1993.

—David F. Schmitz

NIMITZ, CHESTER (1885–1966), World War II Commander in Chief of the U.S. Pacific Fleet. Born in Fredericksburg, Texas, on 24 February 1885, Nimitz graduated from the U.S. Naval Academy in 1905, and served in the Pacific successively in a battleship and as commanding officer of a gunboat and of a destroyer. In 1909, transferred to the Atlantic for submarine duty, he made himself an expert in submarine diesel engines. In 1913, sent by the navy to Germany to perfect his knowledge of such engines, he returned and supervised construction of diesels in a new oiler. In *World War I, Nimitz served as engineering aide and chief of staff to the commander of the U.S. Atlantic submarine flotilla.

Nimitz, recognizing his main talent, now shifted the direction of his career from operating machinery to directing people, a new emphasis put severely to the test in 1920 when he oversaw the building of a submarine base at Pearl Harbor. In 1922–23, Commander Nimitz attended the Naval War College. Thereafter, in a series of promotions, he rose in rank and command. In 1933, as captain, he commanded a heavy cruiser. In 1938, as rear admiral, he assumed command of Battleship Division One. The following year he went ashore as a bureau chief with the function of assembling and training officers and enlisted men for naval expansion in the impending *World War II.

President Franklin D. *Roosevelt, following the December 1941 Japanese attack on *Pearl Harbor, appointed Nimitz commander in chief of the Pacific Fleet and subsequently of the Pacific Ocean Areas, entrusting to his command all American and Allied sea, land, and air forces in the north, central, and south Pacific. From his Pearl Harbor headquarters, Nimitz directed growing American forces in the 1942 carrier battles of the *Coral Sea and *Midway and in the reconquest of *Guadalcanal, victories that brought the southern and eastern advance of the Japanese to a halt and turned the tide of war.

In 1943, forces under Nimitz ousted the Japanese from the Aleutians and collaborated with Gen. Douglas *MacArthur's southwest Pacific forces in reconquering the Solomons and eastern *New Guinea. In 1944, the two commanders cooperated in a drive to the Philippines, MacArthur by amphibious advances along the New Guinea north coast, Nimitz by conquest of the Gilbert, Marshall, and Mariana islands and the Battle of the *Philippine Sea and the Battle of *Leyte Gulf, sea fights that virtually eliminated the Japanese fleet.

In 1945, Nimitz, wearing the five stars of his new rank

of fleet admiral, directed the invasions of *Iwo Jima and *Okinawa from his advanced headquarters on Guam and ordered the bombings and bombardments of Japan that preceded the Japanese capitulation. On the deck of the battleship *Missouri* he and General MacArthur signed the instrument of surrender on behalf of the United States.

Following the war, Nimitz served two years as chief of naval operations, then settled at Berkeley, California. He limited his public activities to making an occasional speech on behalf of the United Nations and serving as regent of the University of California. His health declining, the navy transferred him to more comfortable quarters on Yerba Buena Island in San Francisco Bay. Here he died 20 February 1966.

[*See also* World War II, U.S. Naval Operations in: The Pacific.]

• E. B. Potter, *Nimitz*, 1976.
—E. B. Potter

NITZE, PAUL H. (1907–). U.S. government official, author, educator. Early in 1950, as director of the State Department's Policy Planning Staff, Paul H. Nitze oversaw the drafting of a report, NSC 68, to President Harry S. *Truman urging a general strengthening of U.S. armed forces to counter the threat of Soviet aggression. The outbreak of the *Korean War in June 1950 convinced many policymakers, including Truman, that the report had merit. It thus became for all practical purposes the basic blueprint for the ensuing Cold War military buildup.

Nitze's role in NSC 68 was only one of the many crucial decisions in which he participated during a public career spanning fifty years. Despite the Great Depression, Nitze prospered as a Wall Street bond trader in the 1930s, but came to Washington in 1940 at the request of his business partner, James V. *Forrestal, to work part-time on the mobilization effort. In World War II Nitze served with the Board of Economic Warfare and as a director of the U.S. Strategic Bombing Survey. After the war, he joined the State Department and helped draft the 1948 *Marshall Plan legislation to rebuild war-torn Europe. Nitze left government in 1953, but returned with the Kennedy administration as assistant secretary of defense for international security affairs to become a key figure in U.S. policy during the Berlin Wall Crisis (1961) and the *Cuban Missile Crisis (1962). Though regarded as a "hawk" on most defense matters, he was a "dove" on Vietnam and regretted U.S. involvement in the *Vietnam War during the 1960s because it drained American resources and diverted attention from the growing problem of Soviet strategic nuclear power.

In the 1970s and 1980s Nitze turned his attention to nuclear *arms control and disarmament, first as a member of the U.S. delegation to the Strategic Arms Limitation Talks (SALT) between Washington and Moscow. Though instrumental in negotiating the 1972 Anti-Ballistic Missile Treaty, he lobbied against Senate ratification of the 1979 SALT II Treaty limiting offensive strategic launchers because he felt it made too many concessions to the Russians. Under President Ronald *Reagan, however, he helped negotiate the 1987 ban on U.S. and Soviet intermediate range nuclear *missiles and participated in laying the groundwork for the 1991 Strategic Arms Reduction Treaty.

When not serving in government, Nitze was a highly successful businessman and a prolific writer on arms control, foreign policy, and strategic theory. He encouraged closer ties between government and academia and was one of the founders in 1944 of what became the Johns Hopkins University School of Advanced International Studies, which now bears his name.

[*See also* Berlin Crises; Cold War: External Course; Cold War: Domestic Course; National Council Memoranda; National Security in the Nuclear Age; SALT Treaties.]

• Steven L. Rearden, *The Evolution of American Strategic Doctrine: Paul H. Nitze and the Soviet Challenge*, 1984. Strobe Talbott, *The Master of the Game: Paul Nitze and the Nuclear Peace*, 1988. Paul H. Nitze, *From Hiroshima to Glasnost: At the Center of Decision—A Memoir*, 1989. David Callahan, *Dangerous Capabilities: Paul Nitze and the Cold War*, 1990.
—Steven L. Rearden

NIXON, RICHARD M. (1913–1994), congressman, vice president, thirty-seventh president of the United States. Richard Nixon became president in January 1969, when the era of American strategic superiority was waning and rising domestic discontent with the pace of reform and the U.S. involvement in Vietnam was fueling a political backlash. Nixon, working closely with his national security adviser, Henry *Kissinger, appreciated that the United States did not have unlimited resources or unlimited interests, and sought to redefine America's role in the world through a retrenchment of its global commitments. Nixon's accomplishments and reputation as a strategist are overshadowed by his resignation in 1974 over the Watergate scandal.

The centerpiece of Nixon's international strategy was to manage the Soviet threat by inducing Moscow to moderate its behavior in the world arena. To achieve this, he endeavored to engage the Soviet Union in a web of relations that would furnish Moscow with incentives to seek accommodation with the United States. Vital to this were the Strategic Arms Limitation Talks (SALT), which in 1972 resulted in an agreement to limit the deployment of strategic offensive *missiles and antiballistic missile systems. Although the interim agreement on ballistic missiles arguably was flawed, the *SALT Treaties paved the way for subsequent superpower nuclear *arms control and disarmament agreements.

Another cornerstone of Nixon's policy was his historic opening to Communist China. Nixon correctly perceived, where others did not, that for strategic reasons China would welcome an approach from the United States, and Nixon, the staunch anti-Communist, was comparatively invulnerable to partisan attacks of being "soft on communism." The president recognized that a rapprochement with the People's Republic of China would help to isolate North Vietnam—which the United States was attempting to force into a settlement of the *Vietnam War—and would confront the Soviet Union with the prospect of cooperation between its two greatest enemies, the United States and China.

Nixon's triumphant summit meeting in Beijing in 1972 and his visit to Moscow to sign the SALT Treaties a few weeks later marked the beginning of a period of detente ("easing of tensions"), in which Washington and Moscow sought to achieve accommodation and reduce the danger of nuclear war. Detente did not last, in part, critics have argued, because Nixon's policy lacked forceful disincentives to discipline Soviet misbehavior.

Nixon's principal electoral mandate was to end the war in Vietnam. He authorized the gradual withdrawal of the

500,000 American troops from South Vietnam and sought to negotiate a settlement that would not harm U.S. interests or credibility. U.S. draft calls and *casualties declined, but the war continued. To increase U.S. leverage, Nixon ordered the incursion into Cambodia in 1970, the massive bombing of Hanoi, and the mining of Haiphong Harbor to cut off Soviet aid. These actions were domestically unpopular and are extremely contentious, even though Nixon claimed that they were instrumental to reaching the settlement by which all American combat forces were withdrawn and all known prisoners of war freed by March 1973. Fulfilling a campaign promise, Nixon ended *conscription in 1973, transforming the U.S. military into an *All-Volunteer Force.

Nixon's Vietnam policy was and remains controversial. Some assert that he sold out the South Vietnamese government. Others argue that his attempt to negotiate conditions advantageous to U.S. objectives needlessly prolonged the war, for these were never attained, and the settlement eventually negotiated had been obtainable much earlier.

[See also Cold War: External Course; Cold War: Domestic Course; Nixon Doctrine.]

• Stephen E. Ambrose, *Nixon*, 3 vols., 1987–91. Herbert S. Parmet, *Richard Nixon and His America*, 1996.   —Terry Terriff

The **NIXON DOCTRINE** (1969) was first introduced by President Richard M. *Nixon at an informal background press conference in Guam on 25 July. After more than four years of U.S. military intervention, beginning with President Lyndon B. *Johnson's extension of bombing into North Vietnam, Nixon proclaimed an ostensible reduction in Washington's future role in the former Indochina. According to the new approach advanced by Secretary of State Henry *Kissinger and the president, future military operations would be carried out principally by indigenous forces. Nixon was clearly attempting to reconcile the conflicting political and military needs that dictated resistance against a Communist takeover of all Vietnam, while at the same time signaling an "exit strategy," an eventual withdrawal of American troops from the prolonged *Vietnam War.

After nearly three decades of Cold War "containment," the president was eager to promote the revised emphasis as a way to preserve anti-Communist governments while minimizing the cost to American lives. He spelled out the Nixon Doctrine in detail on several occasions, most formally in a special message to Congress on 15 September 1970. Skeptics scoffed that it essentially prescribed a war of "Asians against Asians" and became the justification for the politically more palatable "Vietnamization" policy. Other critics alleged—as subsequent events would confirm—that it was inadequate for achieving what some still thought might be an American victory. The additional limitations of the Nixon Doctrine were confirmed by the character of international responsibilities after the end of the Cold War.

[See also Cold War: External Course; Cold War: Domestic Course; Pacification.]

• Richard Nixon, *RN: The Memoirs of Richard Nixon*, 1978. Henry Kissinger, *The White House Years*, 1979. Robert Litwak, *Detente and the Nixon Doctrine*, 1984. Stephen E. Ambrose, *Nixon: The Triumph of a Politician, 1962–1972*, 1989. Herbert S. Parmet, *Richard Nixon and His America*, 1996. Raymond L. Garthoff, *Detente and Confrontation: American-Soviet Relations from Nixon to Reagan*, 1985; rev. ed. 1994.   —Herbert S. Parmet

NON-PROLIFERATION OF NUCLEAR WEAPONS, TREATY ON THE (1968). This treaty prohibits the five countries that had *nuclear weapons by 1967—China, France, Great Britain, the Soviet Union (now Russia), and the United States—from giving them to other countries, and it prohibits all other countries that join the treaty from acquiring them. All countries with significant nuclear activities have joined except for India, Israel, and Pakistan.

The treaty requires inspection of significant nuclear activities in all member countries other than the five that had weapons in 1967. It has also become the cornerstone for international cooperation (not always effective) to prevent the export of nuclear-related materials for use in countries such as India, Israel, and Pakistan. Finally, it forms the basis for international efforts by the *United Nations Security Council and ad hoc groups of countries to prevent terrorists, or treaty members such as Iraq and North Korea, from acquiring nuclear weapons.

The treaty has created three growing international norms: no more countries should get nuclear weapons; the five that had nuclear weapons by 1967 should negotiate agreements to stop improving them and producing them and, ultimately, to get rid of them; and the five should not use their nuclear weapons against any member without such weapons unless that member attacks them with the assistance of a country that has nuclear weapons.

The treaty helped implement the first norm in Argentina, Australia, Brazil, Iraq, Kazakhstan, North Korea, South Africa, South Korea, Sweden, Switzerland, Taiwan, and Ukraine. Each of these countries once possessed nuclear weapons or had begun exploring how to make them. Each gave them up. In the case of North Korea, the norm may not yet be fully effective, but international inspections and negotiations continue. In the cases of India and Pakistan, which refused to join the treaty and tested nuclear explosives in 1998, the norm failed. Israel also refused to join the treaty and is believed to have nuclear weapons, though it has not tested or otherwise declared that it has them. In all three cases, international efforts to achieve compliance have not ended.

The second norm—negotiations on nuclear weapons—has had more effect than many realize. At the treaty's review conferences every five years beginning in 1975, members that do not have nuclear weapons have pressed hard for an end to all nuclear weapons testing and for further steps—particularly by Russia and the United States—to reduce their nuclear weapons. The *START Treaties to reduce American and Russian long-range nuclear *missiles were given an impetus as a result. At a conference in 1995, the five gained broad agreement to make the treaty permanent, but they had to promise to achieve a Comprehensive Test Ban Treaty by 1996 and to agree that the goal of the nuclear negotiations obligation was "eliminating" nuclear weapons. A Comprehensive Test Ban Treaty was signed by the end of 1996, but further cuts in long-range nuclear weapons beyond the START Treaties have not so far been negotiated. Future review conferences are expected to pressure the five to go further.

The third norm resulted from the demands of members without nuclear weapons that, if they were to continue abjuring them, the five should promise not to use such weapons against them. Each of the five has made that promise, though all but China say they retain the right to respond with nuclear weapons to an attack by a member not having such weapons if assisted by a nation that does have them.

The treaty has gone beyond the original U.S. idea of preventing the spread of nuclear weapons to any additional countries, coming to symbolize, rather, an international determination to rid the world of nuclear weapons.

[See also Arms Control and Disarmament: Nuclear Arms Race; Cold War: External Course.]

• Glenn T. Seaborg with Benjamin S. Loeb, *Stemming the Tide: Arms Control in the Johnson Years*, 1987. George Bunn, *Arms Control By Committee: Managing Negotiations with the Russians*, Chaps. 4 and 5, 1992. Rebecca Johnson, *Indefinite Extension of the Non-Proliferation Treaty: Risks and Reckonings, Acronym No. 7*, 1995.

—George Bunn

NONVIOLENCE is both an ethical tradition of conflict behavior and a historical method of resistance to coercion. Ethical nonviolence is rooted in the philosophies of Jainism, Buddhism, and Christian pacifists such as *Quakers and Anabaptists, all of whom hold human life inviolable. Nonviolence as method, however, has been guided not so much by ethical restraint as by practical necessity. Conscientious and pragmatic nonviolence have often overlapped in their historical development, but are conceptually distinct. In Gandhian nonviolence, they converged in a single movement.

Nonviolence combines numerous principles and techniques of individual and collective action. Civil disobedience, or breaking law on principle (Thoreau), and *conscientious objection to participation in war (Tolstoy) are perhaps the most influential. A third conceptual pillar is *satyagraha* or "firmness in truth" (Gandhi), the seeking of truth through nonviolent conflict. A range of nonviolent methods are commonly used in social conflict: the strike; the boycott; the fast or hunger strike; the sit-in or other physical obstruction; picketing; and marches. The theoretical foundation of nonviolence is the necessity of mass cooperation for exercising political power. Political scientist Gene Sharp's concept of power as a socially based form of political action has guided numerous theoretical analyses of nonviolence.

The increase in nonviolent action since 1900 has been a response to the growth of the state. As government's control over the individual expanded through taxation, military *conscription, colonial occupation, and targeting of civilians, so did nonviolent resistance to it. By the 1980s, when *nuclear weapons were threatening the very extinction of life on earth, tens of millions of persons were responding with nonviolent action.

Mohandas K. Gandhi was the first to use nonviolence in mass political action, to win India's independence from Great Britain. In fusing the ethic of nonviolence with the practice of mass noncooperation in the 1930s and 1940s, he created a model of empowerment that has inspired movements throughout the world. In the United States, the labor, civil rights, peace, and environmental movements all drew heavily on the Gandhian experience. Women suffragists were also early users of militant nonviolence. Alice Paul and her Congressional Union for Woman Suffrage (later the National Woman's Party) invented techniques of nonviolent action still in use today.

North American social history is replete with leaders and organizations inventing nonviolent action for peaceful change and war prevention: Jane *Addams and the *Women's International League for Peace and Freedom; Abraham J. *Muste and the *War Resisters League; Walter Reuther and the United Auto Workers; Martin Luther *King, Jr., and his Southern Christian Leadership Conference; Dorothy Day and the *Catholic Worker;* Cesar Chavez and the United Farm Workers of America; Elizabeth McAllister and Daniel and Philip *Berrigan of the Plowshares movement; and Greenpeace. Some, such as American folk singer Joan Baez and the German Green Party leader Petra Kelly, transcended national boundaries as icons of a global nonviolence culture.

Latin American nonviolence expanded notably after 1970 in response to three historical forces: (1) militarization of the state to protect entrenched elites; (2) the spread of liberation theology in the Catholic Church; and (3) nonviolence training throughout the continent by Servicio de la Paz y Justicia (SERPAJ). Certain figures symbolized this flowering of nonviolence: the martyrs Archbishop Oscar Romero and the environmentalist Chico Mendes; and three Nobel Peace laureates, Oscar Arias, Rigoberta Menchu, and Adolfo Perez Esquivel.

Nonviolence is supported by training and research programs. One line of inquiry, into disciplined nonviolence as a means to resist military conquest, began with the British Commander Sir Stephen King-Hall in the late 1950s. The theory of civilian-based defense emerging from that research proposes nonviolent resistance as an integral part of a nation's security policy. Citizens would be prepared for it with the same planning and discipline used in military training. Nonmilitary defense theory has particularly influenced national governments adopting nonprovocative defense—a security policy with no offensive military capability to threaten neighboring states. Such a policy would deter attack partly through civilian readiness to resist it with mass noncooperation. Theorists prominent in this field include Gene Sharp, Adam Roberts, Anders Boserup, and Theodor Ebert. The governments of Sweden, Denmark, and the Netherlands have explored the feasibility of nonviolent defense.

The theoretical and practical significance of nonviolence is threefold: (1) it has stimulated the use of extra-institutional politics where formal institutions could not respond to the demand for change; (2) it addresses military institutions directly, as both a means to resist the militarization of national governments and an alternative or supplement to military security; (3) as political and economic power becomes more concentrated in governments and corporations, nonviolence offers an effective "weapon of the weak," providing for democratic empowerment and fuller political participation of low-power groups. Among those are women, who have been especially prominent users of nonviolence. As armed struggle becomes ever more costly, nonviolence presents itself as an alternative strategy for both social change and national defense.

[See also Aggression and Violence; Militarism and Antimilitarism; Nuclear Protest Movements; Pacifism; Peace and Antiwar Movements.]

• Staughton Lynd, ed., *Nonviolence in America*, 1966. Gene Sharp, *The Politics of Nonviolent Action*, 3 vols., 1973. Joan Bondurant, *Conquest of Violence: The Gandhian Philosophy of Conflict*, 1988. Philip McManus and Gerald Schlabach, eds., *Relentless Persistence: Nonviolent Action in Latin America*, 1991. Paul Wehr, Heidi Burgess, and Guy Burgess, eds., *Justice Without*

Violence, 1994. Paul Downton, Jr., and Paul Wehr, *The Persistant Activist*, 1997.

—Paul Wehr

NORIEGA, MANUEL (1936–), Panamanian general and dictator. A Creole born of humble origins in Panama City, Manuel Noriega was an opportunist who joined Panama's National Guard in 1962. As a protégé of Panamanian leader Omar Torrijos, Noriega took classes at the U.S. Army School of the Americas in the Canal Zone. In August 1970, he became commander of G2, the Guard's intelligence branch. G2 maintained close ties with U.S. Army Intelligence, the *Central Intelligence Agency, and the Drug Enforcement Administration (DEA). Soon after Torrijos's death in 1981, General Noriega became the most powerful man in Panama.

Though suspected by the DEA of collusion with Colombian drug lords, Noriega proved immensely useful to the United States. He guaranteed a safe haven for the shah of Iran, who went into exile in 1979; then, in 1983, he agreed to help the counterrevolutionary Nicaraguan Contras destabilize the Sandinista government. He also worked closely, though selectively, with the DEA—all the while enhancing his own power.

By late 1989, in the wake of the *Iran-Contra Affair, Noriega's usefulness as a security asset had ended. President George *Bush attempted various measures to undermine his regime and finally, following a contested election in Panama, sent in U.S. forces to overthrow the Panamanian dictator on the immediate grounds that Noriega had authorized hostile acts against U.S. military personnel. Subsequently, a U.S. court convicted Noriega on money-laundering and other charges related to drug trafficking. July 1992, he was sentenced to forty years in a U.S. prison.

[*See also* Caribbean and Latin America, U.S. Military Involvement in the; Panama, U.S. Military Involvement in.]

• John Dinges, *Our Man in Panama*, 1990. R. M. Koster and Guillermo Sánchez, *In the Time of the Tyrants*, 1990.

—William O. Walker III

NORMANDY, INVASION OF (1944). On the morning of 6 June 1944, a radio broadcast announced the start of the invasion of Normandy: "Under the command of General Eisenhower, Allied naval forces, supported by strong air forces, began landing Allied armies this morning on the northern coast of France."

But this was not the beginning of the operation. Its roots can be traced back to September 1941, when, after the British evacuation from Dunkirk in northern France, Winston S. *Churchill and the British chiefs of staff directed Adm. Lord Louis Mountbatten to begin planning for the invasion of Europe. This mission was transferred in March 1943 to British Lt. Gen. Frederick Morgan, who was appointed chief of staff to the Supreme Allied Commander (Designate). He assembled a joint British-American planning staff, which became known as COSSAC.

For another year, COSSAC continued to refine and develop plans for an assault landing in France. While the Pas de Calais appeared to be the logical target—closest to England, its beaches were easily defensible—the Germans had heavily fortified the area, and no large ports were nearby. Normandy had relatively undefended beaches and Cherbourg was an excellent port. Thus the choice was made.

Initially, it was hoped to make the landings in 1942, but over Russian objections the *North Africa Campaign was chosen instead. Despite American objections in 1943, a lack of landing craft and the need for troops for the Italian campaign postponed Operation Overlord, the code name for the liberation of northwestern Europe.

The Normandy invasion was a joint enterprise. In December 1943, Gen. Dwight D. *Eisenhower was named Supreme Allied Commander. He asked Gen. Bernard Law *Montgomery to be the ground force commander during the invasion phase. Sir Bertram Ramsay would be the naval commander; Air Chief Marshal Sir Arthur Tedder became Eisenhower's deputy and would coordinate the air effort.

Montgomery felt that the projected three- to five-division assault was inadequate for the task and the beaches were too far from Cherbourg (its capture essential to secure a flow of supplies). Eisenhower agreed. However, he lacked landing craft to expand the attack. The landing day was postponed from May to early June, allowing the accumulation of landing craft and aircraft to support an expanded assault and follow-up forces.

Two field armies would make the assault (see map of the Normandy invasion) Lt. Gen. Omar N. *Bradley's First American Army, consisting of VII Corps and V Corps, on the west and the Second British Army to the east. On the American beaches, the Fourth U.S. Infantry would assault on Utah Beach (V Corps). Behind Utah Beach, the U.S. 82nd and 101st Airborne Divisions would land to protect the west flank and secure causeways crossing the flooded area inland from the beach.

Meanwhile, Field Marshal Erwin *Rommel, commanding German Army Group B and responsible for repelling any invasion of northwestern Europe, had been feverishly strengthening the beach defenses. But the Allies' deception plan, Operation Fortitude, which included a phantom army near Dover, commanded by Gen. George S. *Patton, complete with false radio messages and inflatable rubber tanks, had convinced Hitler and his General Staff that the Allies would land at the Pas de Calais, the most direct route to Germany. This belief was so strong that when the Normandy landings occurred, they were considered diversionary, and important reinforcements—including *Panzer* divisions—remained idle in the north until long after the *D-Day landing.

The invasion started shortly after midnight on 6 June 1944, when units of the British Sixth Parachute Division landed and captured two bridges over the Orne River and Caen Canal. The other British and American airborne units were not so immediately successful. Low clouds, flak, errors in map reading at night—all conspired to scatter them widely. This led the Germans to believe the airborne attack a diversion, thus hampering their countermeasures. Most of the airborne units' objectives were eventually achieved.

Rommel's superior, Field Marshal Gerd von Rundstedt, commanding *Oberbefehshaber West*, and responsible for the defense of Western Europe, at 0400 ordered two *Panzer* divisions to head for Caen. However, Hitler had kept personal control of the principal western reserve forces, and his permission had to be secured. This delay undoubtedly contributed to the comparatively easy landings on the British beaches.

In the American area, on Utah Beach, the landings went well. The enemy troops manning this portion of the West Wall (or Siegfried Live) surrendered after only three hours and inflicted only 197 *casualties among the 23,000 men who came ashore on D-Day.

On Omaha Beach, a different story unfolded. Preliminary bombardment by heavy bombers was mostly ineffective as low-lying clouds led them to overshoot the targets for fear of hitting Allied assault troops. Many of the landing craft sank in heavy seas on their ten-mile run to shore. Only about one-third of the first landing wave reached the beach and practically none of the amphibious *tanks did. Ashore, men huddled behind the sea wall. The situation became so chaotic that at one point General Bradley contemplated withdrawing the troops and diverting succeeding assaults to other beaches. But by nightfall things had greatly improved. Individual acts of heroism, the initiative taken by small units, and the accurate fire and close-in support of Allied destroyers and other naval vessels suppressed enemy fire, enabling units to scale the cliffs and clear the enemy from the high ground. Thirty-four thousand troops landed that day, but at a high cost, for over 2,500 became casualties.

In the British sector the landings were successful, but one of the principal objectives, the strongly defended communications hub of Caen, was not captured for another month.

By the end of D-Day, more than 130,000 men had landed from the air and the sea at the cost of some 9,000 casualties. But the beachhead now had to be expanded to make room for supplies en route, airfields had to be built, the port of Cherbourg had to be captured and rehabilitated, and the lodgment area had to be made secure for the breakout to win northwestern Europe.

The U.S. VII Corps on 8 June attacked toward Cherbourg along the St. Mère Eglise–Montebourg highway, but stout German resistance with strong *artillery support slowed their advance. Although the attack to the north continued, the emphasis shifted to the west. The veteran 9th Infantry Division cut the west coastal road by the 18th, and on the 19th, it joined the Corps attack to the north.

The Cherbourg defenses, in a rough semicircle about five miles in radius, were reached by the 4th, 79th, and 9th Infantry Divisions by the evening of 21 June and by the 9th Infantry Division a day later. But it took six more days of hard fighting, assisted by naval bombardment, before organized resistance in the city ceased. By the end of June the area was cleared and the American units were moving south, where VIII Corps had been holding a line across the base of the peninsula.

The Germans had so wrecked Cherbourg Harbor that it would be many months before appreciable tonnage could be landed there. Meanwhile, two artificial harbors (codenamed "mulberries") and over-the-beach landings would have to suffice. On 19 June, a storm hit the coast and wrecked the mulberries: the American one was damaged beyond repair and the British one put out of action for several weeks. Still, over-the-beach operations proceeded better than expected, and by the end of June, over 1 million men and supplies to sustain them had been landed.

The successful lodgment in Normandy provided the base for the breakout at *St. Lô on 25 July and the rapid clearing of German forces in France and Belgium. Had the invasion of Normandy failed, the defeat of Germany could have been delayed several years. This was a decisive battle in the history of the West.

[See also France, Liberation of; World War II: Military and Diplomatic Course.]

• E. Bauer, The History of World War II, 1966; repr. 1984. Charles B. MacDonald, Mighty Endeavor, 1969; rev. ed. 1986. John Keegan, Six Armies in Normandy, 1982. Carlo D'Este, Decision in Normandy, 1983. Max Hastings, Overlord: D-Day and the Battle for Normandy, 1984. David D. Chandler and James Lawton Collins, Jr., eds., The D-Day Encyclopedia, 1994.
—James L. Collins, Jr.

NORTH AFRICA CAMPAIGN (1942–1943). Operation Torch, the invasion of French North Africa by American and British forces in November 1942, was the first major joint Allied offensive operation in World War II. It was the largest amphibious military operation undertaken until then. More than 500 American and British warships, troop transports, supply vessels, and landing craft took part. Over 100,000 troops, mostly Americans, sailed from the United States and Britain to Morocco and Algeria in the opening phase of the invasion.

The decision to invade North Africa ran counter to the U.S. War Department's desire to invade German-occupied France across the English Channel in 1943. The Soviet Union also wanted the West to open a second front. The British feared that a cross-Channel invasion would be premature and would lead to a slaughter on the beaches of France, while Allied control of the North African coast, the ultimate objective of Operation Torch, would expose what Winston *Churchill called the "soft underbelly" of occupied Europe. Facing pressure from President Franklin D. *Roosevelt for a bold, uncostly military move in the European area before November congressional elections, and British objections to an early cross-Channel operation, U.S. Army Chief of Staff Gen. George C. *Marshall reluctantly agreed to the invasion of Vichy French–held North Africa.

Marshall picked U.S. Gen. Dwight D. *Eisenhower to be supreme commander, and British Adm. Sir Andrew Cunningham was chosen to be naval commander. They assembled forces, supplies, and naval and maritime support. Eisenhower also sent Gen. Mark *Clark on a secret submarine mission to negotiate with local Vichy forces not to oppose the landings. Beginning on 8 November, four days after the British stopped German general Erwin *Rommel at El Alamein in Egypt, the Anglo-American landings commenced with commando port assaults and nighttime beach landings. The Allies aided Free French rebels and overwhelmed Vichy French resistance, which was relatively light. The Vichy military commander, Adm. François Darlan, visiting Algiers, was captured and persuaded on 11 November to order a cease-fire. U.S. forces sustained 1,400 *casualties, 526 of which were fatalities. As a result of the invasion, Nazi leader Adolf *Hitler ordered the German Army to occupy Vichy France and rushed troops to Tunisia before the Americans could conquer it. On 14 February 1943, the U.S. II Corps, commanded by Maj. Gen. Lloyd Fredendall, was surprised in the Kasserine Pass by a German counterattack and temporarily thrown back. Fredendall was replaced by Maj. Gen. George S. *Patton, Jr., and his deputy, Maj. Gen. Omar *Bradley, and they resumed the offensive. The U.S. First Army and Gen. Bernard Law *Montgomery's British Eighth Army contained the Germans in Tunisia in April, and 250,000 German and Italian troops surrendered on 13 May 1943, marking the end of the North Africa Campaign. The U.S. casualties amounted to about 18,500.

[See also World War II: Military and Diplomatic Course.]

• George F. Howe, *Northwest Africa: Seizing the Initiative in the West,* 1957. Carlo D' Este, *World War II in the Mediterranean, 1942–1945,* 1990. —Norman Gelb

NORTH ATLANTIC TREATY. *See* NATO.

NORTH ATLANTIC TREATY ORGANIZATION. *See* NATO.

NORTHWEST TERRITORY, MILITARY ACTIONS IN THE OLD (1783–94). In the 1780s, Indians and Americans in the Ohio Valley fought what amounted to a border war over the future of the region. War parties raided enemy villages, killing hundreds of people. The conflict involved neither major battles nor grand strategy. Still, encouraged by British officials in posts such as Detroit (which the British refused to surrender in violation of the Treaty of *Paris), the Miami, Shawnee, Delaware, and other Indians were able temporarily to stymie American expansion.

The U.S. government initially responded to this conflict by constructing forts along the Ohio River with the intention of intimidating both Indian and white *banditti* into peace. These actions failed to stop the raids, however, and pressure from settlers forced a reluctant government into military action.

In the fall of 1790, the Washington administration sent Brig. Gen. Josiah Harmar with 1,500 men, mostly militia, north from Cincinnati against Indian villages on the Maumee River. Harmar achieved his objective of destroying fields and homes. But on 18 October, the Miami chief Little Turtle ambushed a small party of Americans; other Indians attacked some of Harmar's men at present-day Fort Wayne, killing many regular troops, frightening the militia, and forcing Harmar to retreat.

A year later, the Americans tried another expedition, but the 1,400 men under the command of Maj. Gen. Arthur St. Clair never made it to the Maumee. On 4 November 1791, Indians ambushed and completely routed the army, inflicting a staggering 913 *casualties in the worst defeat ever suffered by an American army at the hands of Indians. Convinced that the losses were the result of inept leadership and a reliance on undisciplined militia, the Washington administration committed itself to restoring the military reputation of the United States with a major demonstration of power. To this end, Congress created the Legion of the United States in 1792.

In 1793, after devoting months to preparation, Maj. Gen. Anthony *Wayne began a methodical advance toward the Indian villages on the Maumee. On 20 August 1794, the Legion defeated about 1,000 warriors in a brief but violent action later dubbed the Battle of Fallen Timbers. As important, the retreating Indians found the gates of the nearby British post, Fort Miami, closed to them. Although willing to aid Indians in harassing the Americans, the British refused to risk war with the United States in order to save them.

A decisive military engagement, Fallen Timbers ended decades of struggle over the Ohio Valley. In the 1795 Treaty of Greenville, the Indians recognized the right of the Americans to settle the southern two-thirds of the Ohio Territory. In the same year, as part of Jay's Treaty, Great Britain agreed to abandon its forts on the southern shores of the Great Lakes. No less significant, the triumph of the Legion persuaded many white settlers in the Ohio Valley of the value of the federal government. In the eyes of both its enemies and its own citizens, the Legion had secured the Ohio Valley for the United States.

[*See also* Militia and National Guard; Native Americans: Wars Between Native Americans and Europeans and Euro-Americans.]

• Paul David Nelson, *Anthony Wayne, Soldier of the Early Republic,* 1985. Wiley Sword, *President Washington's Indian War: The Struggle for the Old Northwest, 1790–1795,* 1985. Harvey Lewis Carter, *The Life and Times of Little Turtle,* 1987. Richard White, *The Middle Ground: Indians, Empires, and Republics in the Great Lakes Region, 1650–1815,* 1991. —Andrew R. L. Cayton

NUCLEAR PROLIFERATION. *See* Arms Race: Nuclear Arms Race.

NUCLEAR PROTEST MOVEMENTS. Protest against *nuclear weapons began even before they were built. In 1913, the British writer H. G. Wells wrote a startling novel, *The World Set Free,* which depicted a war fought with "atomic bombs"—a conflict so devastating that humanity established a world government and abolished war. Leo *Szilard, a Hungarian physicist deeply impressed by Wells's novel, conceived the idea of a chain reaction in 1933, but sought to keep the process secret, thus ensuring that it did not fall into the hands of Germany's Nazi government. Nevertheless, in 1939, when scientists in Germany seemed close to a breakthrough, Szilard—by then a refugee in America—mobilized his mentor, Albert Einstein, to warn President Franklin D. *Roosevelt of this ominous development.

Although the Szilard-Einstein initiative helped launch the *Manhattan Project, the Anglo-American program to build the atomic bomb, many *atomic scientists viewed their development of the weapon as a deterrent to its use, presumably by Germany. Therefore, when Szilard and other scientists, principally at the project's Chicago Metallurgical Lab, recognized that it would be employed against a virtually defeated Japan, they urged higher authorities to forgo its use. In the Franck Report of June 1945 (named after the chemist James Franck and written largely by Eugene Rabinowitch), they argued that employment of the weapon would shock world opinion, begin an atomic armaments race, and undermine the possibility of securing an international agreement for nuclear *arms control and disarmament.

When the U.S. government went ahead with the atomic bombing of Japan, it created an enormous furor around the world, and especially in the United States. Whether or not they supported the U.S. government action, most Manhattan Project scientists recognized that the world now faced the prospect of total annihilation. In the fall of 1945, they established the Federation of Atomic Scientists—quickly changed to the Federation of American Scientists—a group that at its height had some 3,000 members. Two other new entities, the Emergency Committee of Atomic Scientists (a small group of prominent scientists headed by Einstein) and the *Bulletin of the Atomic Scientists* (edited by Rabinowitch), became close allies. Pacifist groups like the *Fellowship of Reconciliation, the *War Resisters League, and the *Women's International League for Peace and Freedom also worked to publicize nuclear dangers, as did the burgeoning world federalist movement. Arguing that people faced the prospect of "one world or none," they worked together to champion nuclear disarmament, usually through limitations upon national sovereignty that ranged from international control of nuclear weapons to world government.

Similar movements, often modeled on the American, emerged elsewhere—particularly in Western Europe, Canada, Australasia, and Japan. In addition, a Communist-led movement developed; unlike the other, nonaligned movement, it assailed Western (but not Eastern) nuclear policy. Its best known project was the Stockholm peace petition campaign, a massive antinuclear venture that purportedly drew 2.5 million signatures in the United States.

As the *Cold War advanced in the late 1940s and early 1950s, the nuclear protest movement lost much of the support it had enjoyed. Public opinion grew more hawkish and increasingly amenable to meeting Communist challenges with military might. Administration officials turned from fostering plans for disarmament to winning the *Korean War and developing the most destructive weapon yet: the hydrogen bomb. Buffeted by the Cold War and often confused with their Communist-led rivals, nonaligned nuclear disarmament groups declined precipitously in influence and membership. Even so, by publicizing the nightmarish quality of nuclear war, they did help to stigmatize the atomic bomb, thereby making it more difficult for governments to use it again in war. They also slowed the development of nuclear weapons programs in some nations and made them unthinkable in others.

A second wave of public protest against nuclear weapons began to emerge in 1954, in the United States and around the world. That year, when a U.S. H-bomb test at Bikini atoll sent vast clouds of nuclear fallout surging across the Pacific and irradiated the crew members of a Japanese fishing boat, the *Lucky Dragon*, it highlighted the dangers of nuclear testing. The power of the weapon also illustrated the vast destructiveness of nuclear war. In 1955, Einstein joined the British philosopher Bertrand Russell in issuing a widely publicized appeal to the leaders of the great powers to halt the nuclear *arms race. As pacifists and other antinuclear activists stepped up their protests against nuclear testing, in 1957 concerned scientists launched a series of Pugwash conferences (named for the original meeting site in Pugwash, Nova Scotia), bringing together scientists from both Cold War camps to discuss arms control and disarmament measures. That same year, Norman Cousins and other leading critics of nuclear testing formed the *National Committee for a Sane Nuclear Policy (SANE), whose startling antinuclear ads helped catalyze an organization of some 25,000 members, with chapters around the country. Meanwhile, in 1958, the chemist Linus Pauling released a petition, signed by 11,000 scientists from 49 nations (including 2,875 from the United States), urging the signing of a nuclear test ban treaty.

In contrast to the first wave of public protest against nuclear weapons, students' and women's groups played a very prominent role in this one. Organized in 1959, the Student Peace Union established chapters on dozens of college campuses, and in early 1962, staged the largest disarmament vigil yet seen at the White House. In 1961, women's peace activists launched Women Strike for Peace, which, like SANE, organized picketing, petitions, lobbying, and rallies to secure a test ban treaty and other multilateral measures toward nuclear disarmament.

Despite its remarkable efflorescence, the nuclear protest campaign began to fade after 1963. To a large extent, this reflected its success: the *Limited Test Ban Treaty had been signed (1963), the Soviet Union and the United States seemed on the road to detente, and many activists felt they could return to their private concerns. This mood of relaxation was reinforced by the signing of the Treaty on the *Nonproliferation of Nuclear Weapons in 1968. Furthermore, nuclear disarmament activists were almost invariably peace activists, and with the Johnson administration's escalation of the *Vietnam War in early 1965, many shifted their focus to a vigorous campaign against American participation in that conflict. By this time, however, the nuclear protest movement had made important headway in altering government policy. Thanks to the widespread public clamor in the United States and around the world, it had contributed substantially to a Soviet-British-American moratorium on nuclear testing in 1958, to the decision of numerous nations to not develop or use nuclear weapons, and to the signing of the first nuclear arms control treaties.

In the late 1970s and early 1980s, the nuclear protest movement flared up once again. The collapse of Soviet-American detente, the Soviet Union's deployment of SS-20 *missiles in Eastern Europe, the *NATO decision to deploy cruise and Pershing missiles in Western Europe, and especially the advent of the hawkish Reagan administration, with its glib talk of nuclear war, convinced millions of Americans that their lives were once more in peril. New groups like Mobilization for Survival and Physicians for Social Responsibility grew rapidly, as did older ones, like SANE, that had fallen into decay. In June 1982, nearly a million Americans flocked to a New York City rally against nuclear weapons—the largest demonstration in U.S. history. Meanwhile, there emerged a broadly gauged Nuclear Freeze Campaign. Designed to halt the nuclear arms race through bilateral action, it drew the backing of major churches, unions, and the Democratic Party. Despite the best efforts of the Reagan administration to discredit the Freeze movement, polls found that it garnered the support of 70 percent or more of the American public. In the fall of 1982, a majority of voters backed the Freeze in nine out of ten states where it appeared on the ballot. Although rejected by the U.S. Senate, a Freeze resolution passed the House by a comfortable margin and became a key part of the Democratic presidential campaign of 1984.

Although the nuclear protest movement ebbed substantially in the late 1980s, it could once again point to some important successes. To be sure, the Freeze proposal never became official U.S. policy and President Ronald *Reagan easily won a second term in the White House. Nevertheless, public policy began to shift noticeably. The administration, which had disdained to enter arms control and disarmament discussions with the Soviet government, suddenly started to pursue active negotiations. And when Reagan, to steal the thunder of antinuclear forces in Western Europe and the United States, made arms control and disarmament proposals, the Soviet government startled U.S. officials by accepting them. Part of this sudden accord reflected the shift in Soviet policy under the reform leadership of Mikhail Gorbachev. But Gorbachev too was influenced by Western disarmament groups, and even initiated a nuclear testing moratorium at their suggestion. The result was a burst of diplomatic activity that produced the *INF Treaty (removing U.S. and Soviet intermediate-range nuclear weapons from central Europe) and a number of other nuclear disarmament measures. As the editors of the *Bulletin of the Atomic Scientists* pushed the hands of their famous "doomsday clock" further back from midnight, the nuclear protest campaign deserved some of the credit.

[*See also* Helsinki Watch; Nuclear Weapons and War, Popular Images of; Peace and Antiwar Movements; SALT Treaties; Strategic Defense Initiative; Vietnam Antiwar Movement.]

• Alice Kimball Smith, *A Peril and a Hope: The Scientists' Movement in America, 1945–47*, 1965. Joseph Rotblat, *Scientists in the Quest for Peace for Peace: A History of the Pugwash Conferences*, 1972. Milton S. Katz, *Ban the Bomb: A History of SANE, the Committee for a Sane Nuclear Policy, 1957–1985*, 1986. David S. Meyer, *A Winter of Discontent: The Nuclear Freeze and American Politics*, 1990. Amy Swerdlow, *Women Strike for Peace*, 1993. Allan M. Winkler, *Life Under a Cloud: American Anxiety About the Atom*, 1993. David Cortright, *Peace Works: The Citizen's Role in Ending the Cold War*, 1993. Lawrence S. Wittner, *One World or None: A History of the World Nuclear Disarmament Movement Through 1953*, 1993. Lawrence S. Wittner, *Resisting the Bomb: A History of the World Nuclear Disarmament Movement, 1954–1970*, 1997.

—Lawrence S. Wittner

NUCLEAR STRATEGY. *See* Strategy: Nuclear Warfare Strategy.

NUCLEAR WAR, PREVENTION OF ACCIDENTAL. The outbreak of accidental nuclear war has been a looming fear in both popular and governmental circles since World War II. American efforts to avert accidental nuclear war have focused on four possible scenarios: unauthorized use of *nuclear weapons; mechanical failure leading to detonation; false warning of imminent enemy attack; and misperception of an international incident or within an international crisis escalating to nuclear exchanges.

Avoiding unauthorized use of nuclear weapons is part of the larger issue of whether control of America's nuclear arsenal should rest in civilian or military hands. President Harry S. *Truman institutionalized civilian control in the 1946 Atomic Energy Act, fearing that in the event of crisis or war the military might use nuclear weapons without civilian approval. To some degree, civilian control of nuclear weapons eroded in the 1950s, as global stationing of nuclear weapons and desires for military flexibility encouraged greater delegation of nuclear control to the military.

By the end of the administration of President Dwight D. *Eisenhower (1953–61), civilians moved to reassert greater control and reduce the possibility of unauthorized use. In the late 1950s, the so-called "two-man rule" was installed, which required the simultaneous actions of two individuals to fire any nuclear weapon, thereby reducing the risk that a single deranged officer or unauthorized civilian would detonate a nuclear weapon. In 1962, most nuclear weapons were fitted with Permissive Action Links (PALs), which were essentially combination locks: entering the proper sequence of numbers was required to arm the warhead. PALs guard against unauthorized use by limiting the number of people who can physically detonate a nuclear weapon. Significantly, PALs were not installed on all nuclear weapons, naval nuclear weapons being the notable exception. Other policies have been implemented to reduce the risks of unauthorized use or mechanical accident, including the Personnel Reliability Program, which is designed to weed out unstable or unreliable individuals with nuclear weapons responsibilities, and the Enhanced Nuclear Detonation System, which provides mechanical safeguards to reduce the possibility of accidental or unauthorized detonation.

In preparing systems to warn of an enemy nuclear attack, American policymakers have pursued two goals: reducing the possibility that a nuclear attack on the United States would go undetected while at the same time avoiding false warnings of such an attack. The United States has invested substantial resources in warning systems, such as the DEW (distant early warning) line, a chain of radar installations across Alaska, Greenland, and Canada, which became operational in 1957 to detect a Soviet nuclear attack on North America. As the arms race escalated, American policymakers became increasingly concerned with the vulnerability of U.S. nuclear forces, worrying specifically that short warning of a Soviet nuclear attack would mean the destruction of U.S. nuclear forces before they could be used. Some critics argued that in response to these fears, the United States in the later years of the Cold War adopted a de facto policy of launch on warning (LOW), which called for American nuclear retaliation on the basis of only the warning of an impending Soviet attack, that is, before the confirmed detonation of Soviet nuclear weapons on American territory. Though the American military has taken some actions to reduce the probability of false warning of incoming nuclear attack through, for example, redundant systems, many argue that LOW introduces grave risks of accidental war, as nonmilitary events (such as a passing flock of geese) might be mistaken for an incoming nuclear attack, forcing a decision to retaliate before a warning could be confirmed. The dangers of LOW demonstrate that the two goals of a warning system, providing timely alert of an attack and avoiding false alarms, can be at odds with each other.

Decision makers have also been concerned that an international crisis or incident might inadvertently escalate to war. The United States has signed a number of international agreements designed to facilitate communication between nations to reduce the chances that one side will misinterpret the actions of another side as hostile or threatening. Most famously, a hot line providing direct communication between the United States and the Soviet Union was established after the *Cuban Missile Crisis (1962–63). It was used during the 1973 Yom Kippur War. Additionally, a number of confidence-building measures have been established to increase the transparency of each side's intentions and forces and to facilitate the resolution of minor but potentially dangerous incidents. Two examples are the 1971 Agreement on Measures to Reduce the Risk of Outbreak of Nuclear War and the 1972 Agreement on the Prevention of Incidents at Sea. The 1972 agreement was directed at the specific problem of naval encounters during the Cold War; peacetime naval maneuvers of the two superpowers produced a number of incidents that might have led to real armed clashes.

The end of the Cold War saw an acceleration of activity aimed at reducing the threat of accidental nuclear war. In 1991, the United States began to implement the Cooperative Threat Reduction (CTR) program to assure that nuclear weapons and radioactive materials in the former Soviet Union were handled safely and securely. The United States and Russia agreed in 1994 to "detarget" their nuclear forces, reducing the chances that an accidental missile launch would hit the other country and touch off a nuclear war. The United States also moved to expand its security dialogue with the People's Republic of China, in 1997, gaining a Chinese-American Incidents at Sea agreement and establishing a China-U.S. hot line.

Significantly, scholars are divided on the usefulness of measures to prevent accidental nuclear war. Some point to successes in a number of areas; others argue that the risks of accidental or preemptive nuclear war are extraordinarily low; still others argue that some measures taken to reduce the risks of accidents are ineffective or may even cause potentially dangerous episodes. Advocates of this last position propose, for example, that attempts to build redundancy into nuclear weapons systems can produce excessive complexity and unexpected interactions that can generate incidents raising the risks of accidental nuclear detonation. Accidental nuclear war remains a frightening specter.

[See also Air and Space Defense; Arms Control and Disarmament: Nuclear; Cold War: External Course; On-Site Inspection Agency; Strategy: Nuclear Warfare Strategy.]

• Paul Bracken, The Command and Control of Nuclear Forces, 1983. Daniel Ford, The Button: The Pentagon's Strategic Command and Control System, 1985. Ashton B. Carter, John D. Steinbruner, and Charles A. Zraket, eds., Managing Nuclear Operations, 1987. Peter Douglas Feaver, Guarding the Guardians: Civilian Control of Nuclear Weapons in the United States, 1992. Bruce G. Blair, The Logic of Accidental Nuclear War, 1993. Scott D. Sagan, The Limits of Safety: Organizations, Accidents, and Nuclear Weapons, 1993.

—Dan Reiter

NUCLEAR WEAPONS. The possibility of creating nuclear weapons of almost unimaginable destructive power was first realized in the 1930s as physicists developed a fundamental understanding of the nucleus of the atom. A nuclear explosion is created when heavy nuclei are split—or fissioned—into several of their component parts that are smaller and more stable.

Impact of Nuclear Weapons. Nuclear fission is a fundamentally different process from chemical explosions that occur in conventional high-explosive or incendiary *bombs. In chemical explosions, larger molecular structures are broken apart and rearranged into smaller parts, but the individual atomic nuclei remain untouched. A chemical explosion produces a sudden release of energy that generates an explosive blast, whose resulting high air pressures and strong winds can crush and knock down nearby structures and people. In the case of early nuclear weapons based on the fission process, the energy release, which occurs in microseconds, is enormously larger because the nuclear bonds that hold nuclei together and are broken during fission are so much stronger than the chemical bonds that bind atoms into molecules. Since the nuclear forces are typically 100,000 to 1 million times stronger than the electrical ones responsible for molecular structures, the resultant energy releases are correspondingly larger.

The nuclear blast is so powerful that it can crush objects many miles away with high winds in excess of 150 mph generated at distances greater than a mile. The release of the enormous energy in a nuclear explosion leads to extremely high temperatures, comparable to those that occur at the center of the Sun, causing massive and deadly fires. As a measure of comparison, the temperatures generated by nuclear weapons are hundreds to thousands of times higher than the temperatures on the surface of the Sun, which heats the surface of the Earth from a distance of more than 90 million miles. Dangerous radioactive fallout

is also spread over large distances by the resulting nuclear radiation emerging with the nuclear debris.

The ability to release such enormous energy from single weapons, on a scale unparalleled in human history, profoundly alters the very nature of *war, as well as its consequences. An appreciation of the consequences of a nuclear explosion can be learned from the experience of the only nuclear weapons used in war, the atomic bombs dropped by U.S. air forces on Hiroshima and Nagasaki in 1945. These two weapons devastated two entire cities. They had yields of 15–20 kilotons. That measure simply means that the energy release was the same as that from detonating 15,000–20,000 tons of TNT (TNT is an acronym for the chemical formula of dynamite). By way of comparison, the largest conventional bombs used in World War II—the so-called blockbusters used by the Royal Air Force (RAF)—detonated 10 tons (20,000 pounds) of TNT.

Those fission bombs of 1945 are no more than primitive versions of the first stage, or triggers, of modern nuclear weapons, whose yields range into the megatons, or millions of tons of TNT equivalent, and whose deadly devastating impact ranges over many miles. (One kiloton is equivalent to 2 million pounds of TNT; 1 megaton is equivalent to 2 billion pounds of TNT.) In modern nuclear weapons, such fission triggers are known as the *primaries*. They ignite a secondary stage by creating very high temperatures in order to generate still larger quantities of energy by driving together, or fusing, light nuclei into more stable ones. This is known as *fusion*. Such modern weapons are commonly referred to as *thermonuclear weapons*—or more simply, *H-bombs*.

The effect of a 1-megaton thermonuclear weapon has an energy release 100,000 times greater than the largest 10-ton blockbusters of World War II; the area destroyed by blast would be several thousand times larger than that leveled by such blockbusters. Collateral destruction and *casualties due to fires and radioactive fallout would extend even further than the area destroyed by blast.

Soon after World War II, it was realized that the existence of nuclear weapons posed a new and fearsome threat to modern civilization and that it was vital to treat them differently from "conventional"—nonnuclear—weapons. Serious initiatives during the decade immediately following WWII tried to bring these terrifying new weapons under international control. These efforts failed as the confrontation between the Western powers and the Soviet Union and its allies grew into a cold war. Fueled by this dangerous competition during the 1960s, the individual nuclear arsenals of the United States and the Soviet Union accumulated to tens of thousands of warheads. In addition, France, England, and China acquired their own, albeit much smaller, nuclear arsenals. Furthermore, the newly developed delivery systems of intercontinental-range, and in particular, land-based intercontinental ballistic *missiles (ICBMs)—and long-range ballistic missiles on *submarines (SLBMs) moving about invisibly under the surface of the oceans—brought the threat of nuclear annihilation very close to home, less than thirty minutes away from a nation's borders.

Difficulty of Protection Against Nuclear Weapons. It also became clear before long that there was no known or prospective technology that could provide a defense against a determined nuclear attack. In contrast to previous wars, essentially nothing would be left of a large urban "target"—its population and industry—if just one, or at most a few, nuclear warheads exploded over it. Witness the bombings of *Hiroshima and Nagasaki.

A defense would have to be essentially perfect to provide protection against nuclear weapons, and that is neither a realistic standard of performance today nor a prospective one for future military systems. In World War II, during the Battle of Britain, the RAF defense system managed to destroy no more than one in ten of the attacking planes. At such a rate, the German Air Force was reduced faster than it could replace its losses. At the same time, cities like London could put out the fires and rebuild after the damage. Human defenselessness is a basic fact of the nuclear age. It is also troubling since it denies one of the most basic instincts of the human race: to defend ourselves, our families, our friends, our vital interests. Recognition of the ineffectiveness of defenses against the almost unimaginable destructive potential of a massive attack by nuclear bombs led the United States and the former Soviet Union to acknowledge that their very survival was based on mutual *deterrence—ensuring that nuclear weapons were not used.

Basic Physical Processes in Nuclear Weapons. The first step in detonating a thermonuclear weapon is to ignite the high explosive that causes a shock wave to travel inward and compress the nuclear material the explosive surrounds, known as the *pit*. At the same time, a strong source of neutrons is activated to flood the compressed pit.

If the material in the compressed pit reaches a condition known as *criticality*, the neutrons initiate a strong fission chain reaction. This is the fission, or primary, stage of a thermonuclear explosion. In a chain reaction, an incoming neutron splits the nucleus of fissile material (either an isotope of uranium, U^{235}, that occurs in nature, or of plutonium, Pu^{239}, that is man-made), releasing at least two neutrons, which then run into other fissile material, producing more neutrons, which then run into other fissile material, and so on. Thus, in successive steps, or "generations," of fission, the neutrons will multiply: $2, 2 \times 2, 2 \times 2 \times 2, \ldots$ After very roughly 100 generations, if the fissile material can be held together long enough, (i.e., for microseconds), enough nuclei will have fissioned and enough energy will have been created to generate an explosive equivalent to 10 kilotons or so of TNT.

Several years after the development of such first-generation fission bombs, weapons designers concentrated on improving their performance by using the material more efficiently. U.S. and Soviet weapons technology advanced rapidly after the first Soviet nuclear detonation, "Joe 1," in 1949. The biggest advance occurred when the process of fusion was introduced into the explosive process. Fusion, in contrast to fission, involves combining, or fusing together, several nuclei of the lightest elements, such as hydrogen isotopes, to form more stable heavy ones. High temperatures are required to ignite the fusion process effectively. This is because at high temperatures, individual nuclei acquire high speeds, and move sufficiently rapidly to push their way though their mutual electric repulsion and get near enough to each other to collide and "fuse" together. The new nucleus thus formed is generally more stable, leading to the release of a large energy, plus more neutrons. Fusion is the process fueling the Sun's burning.

Modern weapons with both fission and fusion stages are called *thermonuclear* or *hydrogen bombs*. In a thermonuclear weapon, the primary, or fission, stage creates the necessary high temperatures to ignite the fusion stage, which provides additional neutrons to initiate still more fission, thereby releasing much more energy. A thermonuclear weapon can be built with virtually no limit on the amount of fusion materials it contains. Such weapons generate explosions as large as tens of megatons of TNT, or the equivalent of billions of pounds of TNT. In thinking about the totality of destruction in a nuclear war waged with modern thermonuclear weapons of such enormous yield, it is well to keep in mind that many of the destructive effects of nuclear weapons were not anticipated, and were discovered with surprise by *atomic scientists when they were used or tested. This calls for great humility when it comes to predicting the consequences of nuclear warfare.

Since 1945, the total number of known nuclear tests, worldwide, adds up to some 2,000. A major purpose of testing has been to validate and confirm appropriate performance specifications for new weapons types designed in response to military needs formulated during the Cold War. Starting in the mid-1950s, U.S. weapons were designed and built "ready to go." They conserved special nuclear materials (SNM)—the fissile materials Pu^{239} and U^{235}—and were essentially *maintenance-free, ready to go at any time. "Ready" means that no *physical* changes or steps such as inserting the SNM had to be made in order to detonate a bomb. One merely had to launch and detonate the warhead by signal.

In response to growing worldwide concerns about radioactive fallout from continued nuclear testing, the United States, the Soviet Union, and the United Kingdom joined in 1963 in a *Limited Test Ban Treaty that forbade testing aboveground, in the atmosphere, underwater, and in outer space. Only underground testing was allowed. A further restriction on testing was negotiated in 1974, limiting the yields of underground tests to a maximum of 150 kilotons, roughly ten times the yield of the Hiroshima bomb. This so-called Threshold Test Ban Treaty was generally obeyed henceforth, though it was not ratified until 1990.

In 1992, progress in negotiated reductions in the nuclear arsenals, and further progress in reducing reliance on nuclear weapons after the end of the Cold War, led President George *Bush to rule out nuclear weapons tests for new warheads and to declare a nine-month moratorium on all nuclear testing. This moratorium was continued by his successor and has also been honored by Russia and the United Kingdom. On 11 August 1995, President Bill *Clinton announced U.S. support for negotiating a comprehensive test ban treaty in 1996. The treaty would be of unending duration, and would include, as do all such tests, a "supreme national interest" clause should unanticipated circumstances present compelling arguments for renewed tests. Such arguments might arise if there were serious reversals from the present progress toward reducing nuclear danger in the world, or if unforeseen technical problems arose over time in the enduring nuclear stockpile.

By the best current technical judgment, U.S. weapons appear to be safe, reliable, age-stable, and fully adequate for deterrence; but it will be a new challenge to maintain that confidence without being able to conduct tests that produce any nuclear yield. Under its recently formulated program for stockpile stewardship and management, the United States has accepted this challenge, following a comprehensive scientific review of prospects and needs for its nuclear arsenal. So have the United Kingdom, Russia, France, and China.

On September 1996 President Clinton was the first world leader to sign the Comprehensive Test Ban Treaty at the United Nations in New York. Soon thereafter the other declared nuclear powers—England, France, China, and Russia—also signed, and as of November 1998 150 nations have signed the Treaty and twenty-one have ratified it. For it to go into effect it must be ratified by all forty-four nuclear capable nations, i.e., nations with nuclear reactors for research or for civilian energy production, in addition to those with nuclear weapons. A Comprehensive Test Ban after more than 2,000 tests over a 50-year period would be a tremendous achievement. Efforts to accomplish that goal are currently in progress, together with continuing efforts to reduce the size of the nuclear arsenals at the Strategic Arms Reduction Talks (START) underway between the U.S. and Russia.

[*See also* Arms Control and Disarmament: Nuclear; Cold War: External Course; Cold War: Domestic Course; War Plans; Weaponry; World War II: Military and Diplomatic Course.]

• Margaret Gowing, *Britain and Atomic Energy, 1939–1945,* 1964. Samuel Glasstone and Philip J. Dolan, eds., *The Effects of Nuclear Weapons,* 3rd ed. 1977. Richard Rhodes, *The Making of the Atomic Bomb,* 1986. Robert Serber, *The Los Alamos Primer: The First Lectures on How to Build an Atomic Bomb,* 1992. David Holloway, *Stalin and the Bomb,* 1994. Richard Rhodes, *Dark Sun: The Making of the Hydrogen Bomb,* 1995. —Sidney Drell

NUCLEAR WEAPONS AND WAR, POPULAR IMAGES OF. From the dawn of the atomic age through the end of the Cold War, *nuclear weapons, nuclear testing, and fears of global thermonuclear war loomed large in the popular mind, profoundly affecting American culture. President Harry S. *Truman's announcement of the atomic bombing of Hiroshima on 6 August 1945 unleashed a wave of nervous media speculation about the new weapon. Editorial writers and radio commentators offered grim scenarios of atomic menace. In "The Thirty-Six Hour War" (19 November 1945), *Life* magazine described a missile attack on U.S. cities and presented graphic drawings of New York City reduced to smoldering rubble. John Hersey's *Hiroshima* (1946) moved beyond generalized images of a destroyed city to offer sharply etched narratives of six survivors' experiences.

Simultaneously, other media voices and cultural outlets, encouraged by Washington, took a more hopeful view, picturing a utopian future powered by limitless atomic energy. The advent of the bomb also generated an outpouring of atomic trivia as songwriters exploited the theme and hundreds of businesses from the "Atomic Taxicab Company" to the "Atomic Exterminators" appropriated the potent word. The 1946 U.S. atomic test at Bikini atoll in the Pacific inspired a French fashion designer to underscore the explosive effect of his new line of shockingly revealing women's swimsuits by calling them "bikinis," further expanding the lexicon of the atomic age. While jewelry makers advertised "atomic-inspired" pins and earrings, the General Mills Corporation in 1947 offered kids an "Atomic 'Bomb' Ring" for 50 cents and a Kix cereal boxtop.

In *The Day the Earth Stood Still* (1951), the best of the early atomic-inspired movies, benevolent space aliens urged global cooperation as the only alternative to global annihilation. In general, however, cultural attention to the bomb diminished in the late forties and early fifties, superseded by the Cold War and by anti-Communist hysteria. But a series of U.S. and Soviet hydrogen bomb tests reawakened public fears, this time focused on the specter of radioactive fallout. From the mid-1950s through the early 1960s, as organizations such as the *National Committee for a Sane Nuclear Policy demanded a test ban, fallout worries permeated the mass media. Many science fiction stories, most notably Ray Bradbury's *Fahrenheit 451* (1953) and Walter Miller, Jr.'s, classic *A Canticle for Leibowitz* (1959), spun chilling fantasies of the nuclear future. Popular magazines such as the *Saturday Evening Post* warned of fallout dangers and a wave of Hollywood "mutant" movies exploited the issue. In *Them!* (1954), giant ants spawned from the New Mexico atomic test site go on a deadly rampage in their search for sugar. The unfortunate hero of *The Incredible Shrinking Man* (1957) gradually dwindles to microscopic proportions after his exposure to radioactive fallout.

The new medium of television, while mainly offering escapist fare, sometimes addressed nuclear fears as well. Science fiction TV shows of the fifties and early sixties such as *The Outer Limits* and Rod Serling's *The Twilight Zone* frequently featured stories related to nuclear war themes.

As for Hollywood, a few movies preached *patriotism and preparedness as America's best hope for nuclear-age survival. *Strategic Air Command* (1955), starring James Stewart and June Allyson, for example, celebrated the nation's armada of supersonic bombers capable of raining nuclear devastation on the Soviets. More typically, as in *On the Beach* (1959) and Stanley Kubrick's brilliant black comedy *Dr. Strangelove* (1964), filmmakers offered a far bleaker view of the nuclear arms race and its possible outcome.

Federal civil defense authorities, meanwhile, promised survival from nuclear attack through fallout shelters and citizen readiness. As chronicled in the later documentary *Atomic Café* (1982), this campaign too generated its share of sometimes bizarre cultural by-products. In one animated civil defense film, cheerful Bert the Turtle taught children to "Duck and Cover" if atomic bombs began to fall.

The *Limited Test Ban Treaty of 1963 and later arms limitation agreements such as SALT I (1972) again served for a time to moderate nuclear fear and its cultural manifestations. By the late 1970s, however, anxiety once more intensified, now focused not only on the superpowers' ever-growing nuclear arsenals but also on the spread of nuclear power plants at home. The film *China Syndrome* (1979), whose release coincided with a serious accident at the Three Mile Island nuclear power plant in Pennsylvania, helped crystallize the deepening opposition to nuclear power.

The military buildup and belligerent presidential rhetoric of the early 1980s intensified this resurgence of nuclear fear, triggering yet another round of activism and cultural attention to the bomb. While Jonathan Schell's *The Fate of the Earth* (1982) pondered the meaning of the potential end of all life, artists, poets, dramatists, and photographers also addressed the issue. Tim O'Brien's novel *Nuclear Age* (1985) and a new round of science fiction stories probed aspects of the nuclear reality and imagined nuclear futures. The movie *War Games* (1983) drew upon computer technology to update the scary premise of *Dr. Strangelove:* a nuclear holocaust unleashed by technological systems that break free of human control. A 1984 ABC-TV special, *The Day After,* portrayed the effects of a nuclear attack on Kansas City. The complex reciprocal relationship between the nuclear arms race and popular culture was underscored in 1983, when President Ronald *Reagan's futuristic *Strategic Defense Initiative (SDI) was immediately ridiculed as "Star Wars" by its critics—a derisive nickname drawn from a popular science fiction movie of the 1970s.

The Cold War's demise in the late 1980s brought decades of U.S.-Soviet nuclear rivalry to a sudden and unexpected close. The threat of regional proliferation and the long-term hazard of radioactive waste disposal remained, but the more apocalyptic nightmare of an all-destroying nuclear Armageddon faded from public awareness. As it did, nuclear menace largely vanished as a cultural motif as well. But for more than forty years, few arenas—from literature and the visual arts to advertising, TV, and the movies—had remained unaffected by the nuclear terrors and obsessions that were the unintended by-products of President Truman's fateful decision in August 1945.

[See also Cold War: External Course, Cold War: Domestic Course; Culture, War, and the Military; Fashion, Military Influences on; Hiroshima and Nagasaki, Bombing of.]

• Jim Schley, ed., *Writing in a Nuclear Age,* 1983. Paul Boyer, *By the Bomb's Early Light: American Thought and Culture at the Dawn of the Atomic Age,* 1985; repr. 1994. Paul Brians, *Nuclear Holocausts: Atomic War in Fiction,* 1987. Mick Broderick, *Nuclear Movies: A Filmography,* 1988. Spencer R. Weart, *Nuclear Fear: A History of Images,* 1988. Catherine Caufield, *Multiple Exposures: Chronicles of the Radiation Age,* 1989. Edward T. Linenthal, *Symbolic Defense: The Cultural Significance of the Strategic Defense Initiative,* 1989. Allan M. Winkler, *Life Under a Cloud: American Anxiety About the Atom,* 1993. Guy Oakes, *The Imaginary War: Civil Defense and American Cold War Culture,* 1994. Albert E. Stone, *Literary Aftershocks: American Writers, Readers, and the Bomb,* 1994.   —Paul S. Boyer

NUCLEAR WINTER. Although there had been earlier antecedents, the widespread public debate about nuclear winter began in 1982 with the suggestion by Paul Crutzen, at the University of Colorado, and John Birks, at the Max Planck Institute, that a large-scale nuclear war could produce such conflagrations of forests that a smoke pall covering perhaps half the northern hemisphere would develop. This would absorb enough of the light from the Sun that there could be serious and prolonged reductions in photosynthesis and in temperatures over that part of the planet, resulting in catastrophic agricultural failure. The work was quickly picked up by R. P. Turco, O. B. Toon, T. P. Ackerman, J. B. Pollack, and Carl Sagan, who, on the basis of quantitative modeling, concluded that a large-scale nuclear war could be expected, mainly as a result of the burning of cities rather than forests, to cause temperatures to drop by 36° C. (65° F.) and to remain below freezing for several months. Their work, commonly referred to as the TTAPS study, provided the basis for a number of other publications that appeared in the next three years bearing Sagan's name and the appellation "nuclear winter," which he and Turco coined to describe the phenomenon.

Not surprisingly, these publications caused a considerable stir, given their wide circulation and some of the apocalyptic visions presented: that a major nuclear exchange would produce "the greatest biological and physical disruption of the planet in its last 65 million years" (a period that included the four great ice ages) and that the number of survivors would be reduced to prehistoric levels (presumably a fraction of 1% of those now alive). All of this was buttressed by claims that the TTAPS results were insensitive to wide variations in assumptions about parameters used in modeling. In fact, the results were anything but robust, as subsequent studies would make clear.

There were basically two kinds of problems. First, TTAPS was based on the simplifying assumption that the burning of cities would produce an instantaneous homogeneous distribution of smoke over the entire northern hemisphere, when in reality it would take some days for such spreading to occur, during which time much of the smoke would likely be removed by natural processes. Moreover, the modeling took no account of the warming effects of the infusion of relatively warm air from oceanic and tropical areas to continental interiors. More refined later modeling that did take account of these phenomena, and used comparable assumptions about amounts and characteristics of the smoke from fires, led to radically smaller temperature effects.

Second, there were a number of uncertainties in key areas which, if resolved, could plausibly lead at one extreme to no significant climatic effects, or at the other, to effects as dire as those discussed in 1983, a range of outcomes largely conceded by Turco and Sagan in a characterization of five different classes of nuclear winter by 1989.

The nuclear winter controversy was perhaps as much about policy as about geophysics. Advocates of enlarged programs for *deterrence of nuclear attacks and for defense against them seized on the possibility of nuclear winter to buttress their case for such programs. In contrast, the most vocal proponents of the nuclear winter theory generally argued that it strengthened the case for reducing nuclear stockpiles and foregoing the development and acquisition of new *nuclear weapons; and some argued that even if there were doubts about the phenomenon, it would be wise to base policy on "worst-case analysis." Others argued that war involving enough nuclear explosions to trigger nuclear winter would likely have consequences so catastrophic, at least for the nuclear weapons states, as to overshadow the possibility of nuclear winter in concerns about policy. (And some of those skeptical about the more dire prognostications warned particularly against worst-case analysis being used as a basis for mitigative actions by countries not likely to be directly attacked, noting that such actions could well involve the use of scarce resources sorely needed for other purposes.)

By the early 1990s, nuclear winter was no longer a salient issue in geophysics or from a policy perspective, very likely because the geophysical case for it seemed questionable; because the initiation of massive oil fires in Kuwait during the *Persian Gulf War did not lead to significant climatic effects, as some had predicted; and probably most important, because concern about large-scale nuclear attacks had largely dissipated with the end of the *Cold War.

[*See also* War Plans.]

• Paul J. Crutzen and John W. Birks, "The Atmosphere After a Nuclear War: Twilight at Noon," *Ambio,* Vol. II, no. 2–3 (1982), p. 114. Paul R. Ehrlich, Carl Sagan, Donald Kennedy, and Walter Orr

Roberts, *The Cold and the Dark: The World After Nuclear War*, 1984. National Academy of Sciences, *The Effects on the Atmosphere of a Major Nuclear Exchange*, 1985. *Nuclear Winter*, Vol. 1, no. 2 (1985), p. 112. A. Barrie Pittock, et al., *The Environmental Consequences of Nuclear War*, Vol. I; and Mark A. Harwell and Thomas Hutchinson, Vol. II, 1985. Stanley L. Thompson and Stephen H. Schneider, "Nuclear Winter Reappraised," *Foreign Affairs*, Vol. 64, no. 5 (Summer 1986), p. 981.
—George W. Rathjens

NUNN, SAM (1938–), U.S. senator. Nunn was born in Perry, Georgia. After attending Georgia Tech, he enlisted as a seaman in the Coast Guard for a year's active duty, followed by several years in the reserves. Meanwhile, he graduated from Emory University, receiving a law degree (1962). In 1963, he served as legal counsel to the House Armed Services Committee, and then returned to the family farm to practice law in Perry.

In 1972, Nunn won the U.S. Senate seat formerly held by Richard Russell of Georgia, longtime head of the Armed Services Committee. He served on that committee (1973–96), and as chair (1987–94), becoming one of the most influential senators on military and arms control issues.

A conservative southern Democrat, Nunn was often at odds with liberal Democrats and Republicans. In the late 1970s, he urged major increases in *NATO's conventional firepower and advocated the neutron bomb and the adoption of national service. He was also a significant critic of SALT II. Building bipartisan alliances, Nunn obtained several key weapons systems and blocked the Clinton administration's plan for equal rights for *gay men and lesbians in the military.

Reflecting concerns in the military, Nunn initially opposed the idea of a ground war against Iraq in 1991, and he helped avert a military invasion of Haiti in 1994. For more than a decade, before he retired in 1996, Nunn was the dominant voice in the Senate on defense policy.

[*See also* Haiti, U.S. Military Involvement in; SALT Treaties.]
—John Whiteclay Chambers II

NURSE CORPS, ARMY AND NAVY. Both men and women served as nurses for the army in various capacities beginning in 1775, but it was not until 1901 that an official Army Nurse Corps was created as part of the Medical Department of the U.S. Army. The Corps was exclusively female. Distinguished contributions of women contract nurses during the *Spanish-American War provided the justification for this permanent female nurse corps. Although today's Corps is no longer exclusively female, its purpose endures: to provide nursing care for service members. The organization has a dual significance. It is the oldest military nursing service and the first military branch to admit women.

Army Nursing. When the United States entered World War I in 1917, there were only 403 army nurses on active duty. By November 1918, there were 21,460, 10,000 of whom were serving overseas. During the war, nurses worked primarily in base, evacuation, and mobile surgical hospitals in the United States, France, Hawaii, Puerto Rico, and the Philippines. They also provided care on hospital trains in France and transport ships carrying wounded home across the Atlantic.

More than 57,000 nurses served during World War II. In May 1942, after the Battles of *Bataan and Corregidor, sixty-seven army nurses became prisoners of war of the Japanese. For the thirty-seven-month captivity, the women endured primitive conditions and starvation rations, but still they continued to care for the ill and injured. Nurses landed with troops in the *North Africa campaign on invasion day in November 1942. They also waded ashore at Anzio five days after initial assault landings.

Army nurses supported combat troops when President Harry S. *Truman ordered U.S. forces into Korea in June 1950. During the three-year *Korean War, approximately 550 nurses served abroad, the majority of them in mobile army surgical hospitals (M.A.S.H. units).

More than 5,000 army nurses served in Vietnam during that conflict. Evacuation by *helicopters brought the wounded to medical units located within minutes' flying time of the battlefield. Mobility and large numbers of severely injured patients characterized service in the *Vietnam War. Eight women nurses were killed in action.

During Operation Desert Shield-Desert Storm, approximately 2,200 nurses served in 44 hospitals within the theater of operations. Two of every three nurses in the *Persian Gulf War were from the U.S. Army National Guard or were army reservists. By the late 1990s, 4,200 active duty nurses were providing nursing care to soldiers, retirees, and their families.

Navy Nursing. An act of Congress established the Navy Nurse Corps on 13 May 1908. Soon thereafter, the first twenty nurses, later known as the "Sacred Twenty," reported for duty. Nurses were not new to the navy, however. During the *Civil War, several volunteer nurses served on the Mississippi River aboard *Red Rover*, a captured Confederate sidewheeler converted by Union forces into a floating hospital.

The Navy Nurse Corps remained a small organization until World War I, when it grew to a peak strength of 1,386 in 1918. Navy nurses served at hospitals in the United States, Britain, and France, and even with some army field units in France. No navy nurses died in action, but thirty-six succumbed to other causes.

In 1920, the first nurses reported to the hospital ship USS *Relief*. The Navy Nurse Corps shrank dramatically after the end of the war, averaging only 400–500 personnel during the 1930s.

Navy nurse involvement in World War II began immediately on 7 December 1941. Nurses aboard the hospital ship USS *Solace* in Hawaii treated the first *casualties of the Japanese attack on *Pearl Harbor. The Navy Nurse Corps reached its all-time peak strength with 11,086 nurses on active duty by 1945, serving at 40 naval hospitals, 176 dispensaries, and 6 hospital corps schools in the United States. Overseas, navy nurses served aboard hospital ships, participated in aerial evacuation of casualties, and were stationed at land-based facilities across the Pacific and throughout the Atlantic theater. The war prompted the navy to assign relative rank to nurses on 1 July 1942. In 1944, actual rank was established to last throughout the war plus six months. In April 1947, the Army-Navy Nurses Act established the Nurse Corps as a permanent staff corps of the U.S. Navy bringing permanent commissioned rank and equal pay.

In November 1964, male nurses entered the Navy Nurse Corps for the first time. Currently, they comprise 25 percent of the Corps' overall strength. The 1960s also saw navy nurses serving ashore and aboard hospital ships in Vietnam.

In 1972, the first Navy Nurse Corps officer, Alene Duerk, was appointed to the rank of rear admiral, becoming the first woman appointed to flag rank in the U.S. Navy. The tradition of excellence continues. In Operation Desert Shield/Desert Storm, navy nurses served on land and aboard two hospital ships. By the late 1990s, there were over 5,000 active duty and reserve nurses in the U.S. Navy.

[*See also* Medical Practice in the Military; Women in the Military.]

• Page Cooper, *Navy Nurse*, 1946. *History of the Medical Department of the United States Navy in World War II*, 1953. Mary Roberts, *The Army Nurse Corps: Yesterday and Today*, 1955. Robert Piedmonte and Cindy Gurney, *Highlights in the History of the Army Nurse Corps*, 1987. Elizabeth Norman, *Women at War: The Story of Fifty Military Nurses Who Served in Vietnam*, 1990.

—Constance J. Moore *and* Jan Herman

NYE, GERALD P. (1892–1971). Born in rural Wisconsin, Nye spent fifteen years as a country editor in Wisconsin, Iowa, and North Dakota. A progressive Republican, he was appointed U.S. senator from North Dakota in 1925 to fill a vacancy; he won elections on his own in 1926, 1932, and 1938. During the 1930s, Nye was to the left of the New Deal on domestic policy. In 1934–36, he gained national prominence as chairman of the Special Senate Committee Investigating the Munitions Industry. The committee probed into the close ties between the U.S. and Allied military and the arms manufacturers and financiers, focusing in particular on the Dupont and Morgan interests and their enormous profits in the World War I era, the so-called merchants of death. He unsuccessfully called for heavy taxation of war profits and governmental power to take over industries.

A strong isolationist, Nye sought to limit U.S. military defense to the western hemisphere, endorsing more air-power but curbing battleship production. Influential in the drafting and adopting of the *Neutrality Acts of 1935–37, he vigorously opposed President Franklin D. *Roosevelt's interventionist policies of 1939–41, speaking frequently for the America First Committee. So extreme was his rhetoric that in 1941 he called Britain "the greatest aggressor in modern times." He lost his Senate seat in 1944 in a three-way race.

[*See also* Isolationism; World War I: Domestic Course.]

• Wayne S. Cole, *Senator Gerald P. Nye and American Foreign Relations*, 1962. John Edward Wiltz, *In Search of Peace: The Senate Munitions Inquiry, 1934–36*, 1963.   —Justus D. Doenecke

O

OAS (est. 1948). The United States joined with the twenty Latin American nations to form the Organization of American States in 1948. During the 1970s, the English-speaking Caribbean nations were added, and Canada became a member in 1990. The OAS was established to resolve regional disputes and to promote democracy, human rights, and social and economic progress. The OAS charter also codified the nonintervention pledge of Franklin D. *Roosevelt's "Good Neighbor" policy of the 1930s. The charter did, however, permit collective action by a two-thirds majority.

During the *Cold War, the United States largely bypassed the OAS, because Latin Americans refused to compromise the nonintervention principle in the name of anti-communism. Acting unilaterally, the United States covertly destabilized allegedly Communist governments in Guatemala (1954), Brazil (1964), and Chile (1970–73), and invaded the Dominican Republic (1965). At the time of the U.S. military involvement in the *Dominican Republic, President Lyndon B. *Johnson publicly repudiated the OAS charter, declaring in the Johnson Doctrine that the United States would not permit the establishment of a Communist government in the western hemisphere. During the 1980s, the Reagan administration withheld financial support from the OAS because members refused to support U.S. *guerrilla warfare against the Sandinistas of Nicaragua. OAS members also condemned President George *Bush's invasion of Panama (1989). To be sure, during 1960s, two-thirds of the Latin American nations had followed the U.S. lead and supported sanctions against Fidel Castro's Cuba, because the Cuban revolutionary meddled in the affairs of his neighbors. But by the mid-1970s, the majority of OAS members began to lift those sanctions.

In the post–Cold War era, the United States has shown renewed interest in the OAS on issues of democracy and human rights. In 1991, members developed a basis of action for when popularly elected leaders are overthrown, and the OAS subsequently imposed economic sanctions against Haiti when President Jean-Bertrand Aristide was forcibly removed from office by the Haitian military. In 1994, the United States again acted unilaterally in restoring President Aristide to power by military means, although the OAS did not formally denounce the intervention.

[*See also* Caribbean and Latin America, U.S. Military Involvement in the; Cuba, U.S. Military Involvement in; Haiti, U.S. Military Involvement in; Inter-American Treaty of Reciprocal Assistance; Nicaragua, U.S. Military Involvement in; Panama, U.S. Military Involvement in.]

• G. Pope Atkins, *Latin America in the International Political System,* 1977; 3rd. ed. 1995. Gaddis Smith, *The Last Years of the Monroe Doctrine, 1945–1993,* 1994.　　　　　—Stephen G. Rabe

OFFICE OF SCIENTIFIC RESEARCH AND DEVELOPMENT. *See* Science, Technology, War, and the Military.

OKINAWA, BATTLE OF (1945). Landing day for Okinawa, the final land battle of the Pacific War, was Easter Sunday, 1 April 1945. The Landing force was the new Tenth Army under Army Lt. Gen. Simon Bolivar Buckner. He commanded two corps, XXIV Corps, with five army divisions, and III Amphibious Corps, with three Marine divisions, all told some 182,000 troops. In overall charge was Vice Adm. Raymond A. *Spruance, commander of the Fifth Fleet.

Okinawa, sixty miles long and from two to twenty-eight miles wide, is the largest and most important of the Ryukyu Islands. The 500,000 Okinawans were not then considered to be Japanese.

Japanese Lt. Gen. Mitsuru Ushijima commanded the Thirty-second Army, strength of 77,000 troops, who with naval forces and some 20,000 Okinawan conscripts provided about 100,000 defenders. Ushijima planned a defense in depth, with his main strength in the heavily populated south, and three major defense lines following east-west ridgelines.

Buckner landed his two corps, each with two divisions in the assault, across surprisingly undefended beaches near Hagushi village on the western side of the narrow waist of the island. The III Corps on the left and XXIV Corps on the right crossed the island almost without enemy contact. The Marines then turned northward and the army headed south. On 6 April, XXIV Corps ran into the outer rings of Ushijima's first major defense line running along Kakazu ridge.

Ushijima's plan was to delay his counterattack until much of the supporting U.S. invasion fleet of some 1,200 ships was crippled by massive combined sea and air action, including suicide kamikaze tactics. The first major kamikaze attack came on 6 April. Joining the air action, the giant 18-inch-gun battleship *Yamato* sortied from the home islands, but was destroyed by U.S. Navy aircraft. Ashore, Ushijima's companion counterattack, not launched until 12 April, was easily absorbed by XXIV Corps. Meanwhile, III Corps had overrun most of central and northern Okinawa. Buckner, to overcome Ushijima's stiffening resistance, began shifting the III Corps to the south.

Ushijima's second major counterattack, timed to coincide with the fifth kamikaze attack, went off piecemeal on 3 May and accomplished nothing.

Buckner went forward with a two-corps attack on 11 May. Ushijima's second line, which passed through Shuri, was broken on both of his flanks. He elected to fall back to his third and final line on the southern tip of Okinawa.

Buckner launched his final large-scale attack on 18 June. The general was killed by a Japanese shell while watching the action from a forward observation post. Command of Tenth Army passed to Marine Maj. Gen. Roy S. Geiger of III Corps, who declared the island "secured" on 21 June. That same day, Ushijima committed ceremonial suicide. The last of the ten major air attacks came on 22 April. Next day, Gen. Joseph *Stilwell arrived and took command.

Although liked by his subordinates, army and Marine, Buckner was considered an inexperienced commander. He was criticized by, among others, Administrative Spruance and Gen. Douglas *MacArthur for his unimaginative and costly frontal assaults and his refusal to try a second amphibious landing on the southern end of the island, which might have broken the stalemate. Tenth Army *casualties were 7,613 killed or missing in action and 31,800 wounded. Close to 5,000 U.S. sailors died and as many more were wounded. Seven U.S. carriers had been badly damaged and many other smaller ships were sunk or damaged. Estimates of Japanese casualties ran over 142,000, including many hapless Okinawan civilians.

[See also Marine Corps, U.S.: 1914–45; World War II: U.S. Naval Operations in: The Pacific.]

• Roy E. Appleman, et al., Okinawa: The Last Battle, 1948. Samuel Eliot Morison, Victory in the Pacific, 1960. Benis M. Frank and Henry I Shaw, Jr., History of U.S. Marine Corps Operations in World War II: Victory and Occupation, 1968. Hiromichi Yahara, The Battle for Okinawa, 1997.   —Edwin Howard Simmons

ON-SITE INSPECTION AGENCY. On-site inspection, a long-term demand of the United States for verification of nuclear *arms control and disarmaments agreements, was finally accepted by the Soviet Union under Mikhail Gorbachev in 1987. The verification provisions of the *INF Treaty of December 1987 between the United States and USSR authorized on-site inspectors to monitor and record the elimination of *missiles. Consequently, the Department of *Defense established a small, 40-person agency to conduct and receive INF Treaty inspections; more than 230 on-site inspections were conducted in the first year. In 1990, President George *Bush signed the Threshold Test Ban Treaty, the Conventional Forces in Europe Treaty, and the Wyoming Memorandum of Understanding on the Prohibition of Chemical Weapons, each stipulating on-site inspections. The On-Site Inspection Agency expanded from 40 to 250 people. American inspection and escort teams consisted of military officers, noncommissioned officers (NCOs), and civilian specialists. The officers had experience as military attachés, foreign area officers, and/or weapons specialists. The NCOs served as translators.

In July 1991, Bush and Gorbachev signed the START I Treaty; nine months later, twenty-seven nations concluded the Open Skies Treaty. Within a year, the United States had signed the START II Treaty (5 nations) and the Chemical Weapons Convention (153 nations). Each agreement included provisions for extensive monitoring through on-site inspections. The On-Site Inspection Agency expanded to 760 persons between 1991 and 1994.

[See also Chemical and Biological Weapons and Warfare; START (1982).]

• Joseph P. Harahan, On-Site Inspections Under the INF Treaty, 1993.   —Joseph P. Harahan

OPERATIONAL ART is a twentieth-century concept dealing with the direction of military forces in conceiving and executing operations to attain strategic objectives. It involves joint and combined forces and apportioning resources to tactical units. Operational art forms a bridge between *strategy, defining the political aims of a war, and *tactics, fighting the battles of a war. While not neglecting the strategic objectives of belligerents in war and their tactical doctrines, it concentrates on a level between them. For this reason, some analysts have seen its origins in the eighteenth-century idea of campaign strategy.

In analyzing operational art, it is helpful to conceptualize strategy, operations, and tactics as "perspectives on war" rather than the more accepted "levels of war." Conceptualized as levels, the strategic, operational, and tactical tiers invariably overlap, while if viewed as perspectives, the different analyses can be better outlined to complement one another.

As an example, one might consider the Allied invasion of *Normandy, France, in June 1944. The Allied strategic aim was to enter the Continent of Europe and conduct operations into Germany to destroy Berlin's armed forces. Viewed from this perspective, the endeavor was one of coordinating land, naval, and air forces; apportioning resources between them; conducting military and political *intelligence operations; promoting harmony between the Allied forces participating; and planning campaigns to be carried out over an extended period to destroy Germany's armed forces. From the perspective of the tactical land forces employed in the assault on the French coast, the task became, at its most basic, merely to get ashore, secure the beachhead, and survive until reinforcements were landed. Between these perspectives, the operational perspective included tasks such as apportioning resources to provide a balance between assault forces and follow-on reinforcements; providing for naval and air support of the landings; coordinating the massive *logistics requirements of the invasion; ensuring proper command and control to react to enemy actions; and planning the subsequent campaign for the breakout from the beachhead. Although the perspectives share some aspects, each clearly had definable tasks that are the primary responsibility of commanders at a given level. And commanders from each perspective have the task of apportioning resources; for example, the strategic commander must apportion resources among the Allied nations and their land, naval, and air arms of service, the operational commander among his various tactical units, and the tactical commander among his small units and their assigned beaches.

Soviet military theorists were the first to coin the term operational art and to analyze the concept, institutionalizing it by the mid-1920s. Some saw its genesis in the Russian civil war and World War I, while others saw it as an outcome of the Napoleonic Wars and the revolutionary development of the *levée en masse*, when campaigns followed one another toward the attainment of a strategic goal.

U.S. thinkers began concentrating on operational art by the 1980s. They saw it as the purview of the theater commander, who must determine what sequence of campaigns would be necessary to accomplish the strategic goal and how resources should be apportioned to execute them.

[*See also* France, Liberation of; Germany, Battle for; World War II: Military and Diplomatic Course.]

• Clayton R. Newell, *The Framework of Operational Warfare*, 1991. U.S. Department of the Army, *U.S. Army Field Manual 100–5: Operations*, 1993. —Kenneth E. Hamburger

OPERATIONS RESEARCH. In defense analysis, operations research uses statistics and mathematics to optimize the use of a weapon. To set up a *radar/fighter defense against *bomber aircraft, for example, the traditional method would be to draw advice from war-experienced experts or apply current military *doctrine. An operations researcher, however, starts with a numerical measure of effectiveness—perhaps the number of bombers expected to get through, or the warning time provided, or some combination. The next step is to analyze statistics from past systems, and feed these into a mathematical model combining scanning rates, the decision-making speed of radar operators, and the average number of operational fighters. The best design might be found by pencil and paper analysis, or a computer program that simulates the system under various attacks.

Operations research was first used widely in Britain in 1939–40 at the start of World War II. It spread to the United States, where it solved problems such as the placement of bomber-dropped naval *mines to destroy Japanese shipping. Another question involved a patrol plane coming upon a submarine on the surface—the submarine dives and the patrol plane must set an optimal detonation depth for its depth charge. Operations researchers also improved the likelihood that bombers would destroy an industrial target. They recommended reducing the size of a flight to about a dozen planes, assigning the best bombardier to the lead plane and have the rest follow his cue, and minimizing the time between successive *bombs released from each plane. Photo reconnaissance showed an approximately fourfold improvement

Sometimes operations research has exposed an important simple truth, but sometimes it has oversimplified an essentially complex situation. Starting in the late 1960s, it figured in the public debate over antimissile defenses and the survivability of the Minuteman intercontinental ballistic missile. The problem was construed as Soviet *missiles destroying American missiles in their silos, but it became clear that the adversary would attack communications and control centers, and that U.S. policy was not to wait and "ride out" such an attack. The scenario of missiles attacking silos received attention partly because it was simple enough to solve.

Historically, there has been tension between the mathematical/scientific training of operations researchers and the military background of those implementing their ideas. In the early 1960s, officers generally resented Department of *Defense secretary Robert S. *McNamara's civilian whiz kids. Organizational savvy and the proven worth of the

method have bridged this gap, and today any major campaign, such as Desert Storm, in the *Persian Gulf War, would be preceded by extensive computer simulations.

[*See also* Disciplinary Views of War: History of Science and Technology; Disciplinary Views of War: Peace History; Game Theory; Neumann, John von; Science, Technology, War, and the Military; World War II: Military and Diplomatic Course.]

• Philip Morse and George Kimball, *Methods of Operations Research*, 1951. Jerome Bracken, Moshe Kress, and Richard Rosenthal. *Warfare Modeling*, 1995. —Barry O'Neill

OPPENHEIMER, J. ROBERT (1904–1967), physicist. Perhaps the most controversial scientist of this century, J. Robert Oppenheimer was awarded kudos in the 1940s for his contributions to the war effort and censure for allegedly betraying the country of his birth. Born in New York City and educated at Harvard and Görringen, Oppenheimer earned his Ph.D. in 1927 and quickly became recognized as a leader in theoretical physics, simultaneously rising through the academic ranks at the California Institute of Technology and the University of California at Berkeley, and gathering large numbers of the best scientific minds in the United States to his seminars and laboratories. In so doing, he became the catalyst for the emergence of American theoretical physics as preeminent in the world.

At the National Academy of Scientists in 1941, Oppenheimer led a group of scientists in theoretical discussions of nuclear bombs. Although intensely ambivalent about the creation of such weapons of mass destruction, he was concerned that the Nazis might produce one first, so he accepted an offer from Gen. Leslie Groves to serve as director of a highly classified U.S.-led effort to build an atomic bomb. This effort, the *Manhattan Project, was headquartered at Los Alamos, New Mexico. Many *atomic scientists gathered there between 1942 and the first detonation of an atomic bomb on 16 July 1945.

Even though the dropping of atomic bombs on *Hiroshima and Nagasaki ended World War II and kept the Russians from invading Japan, Oppenheimer was overwhelmed by the devastation he had wrought. He called for a cessation of atomic research or for international guidelines on the use of atomic weaponry. Both during the war and later he became associated with Communist Party members and others with strong leftist political positions. Although no clear violations of security were ever proven, there had been instances of negligence and indiscretion. During the McCarthy investigations and purges of alleged Communists in the U.S. government in the 1950s, Oppenheimer lost his security clearance and was forced to resign from the seven atomic committees he chaired. He became director of the Institute for Advanced Study in Princeton and was later at least partially vindicated when President Lyndon B. *Johnson presented him with the Enrico *Fermi Award in 1962.

[*See also* Cold War: Domestic Course.]

• Michel Rouze, *Robert Oppenheimer: The Man and His Theories*, trans. Patrick Evans, 1962. Peter Michelmore, *The Swift Years: The Robert Oppenheimer Story*, 1969. Peter Goodchild, *J. Robert Oppenheimer: Shatterer of Worlds*, 1981. —Peter J. McNelis

ORDER OF BATTLE refers to listings that count and categorize military forces in terms of unit type (e.g., armor, infantry, brigade, division) and quality and quantity of armament. Sometimes order of battle *intelligence analysis* offers estimates of military units' *combat effectiveness by extrapolating from recent events. Units engaged heavily in combat might be rated less effective—because of recent personnel and equipment losses—than experienced full-strength units.

Order of battle information is crucial to battlefield success: a commander who is unaware of the number, type, and quality of opposing units risks disaster. Attacks are more likely to succeed if they are directed against inexperienced units or units weakened by combat. Movement of experienced units to a given sector can indicate that an attack is imminent.

Because of its importance, operational security and deception often focus on order of battle information. Before the invasion of *Normandy, France, in World War II, the Allies staged a massive deception operation, code-named "Fortitude South," to confuse German intelligence about the Allied order of battle. A variety of ruses were used— phony bases, rubber tanks, simulated radio traffic—to create evidence that a fictional formation, First United States Army Group (FUSAG), actually existed. Nominally "commanded" by George S. *Patton, one of America's best general officers, FUSAG was located in Dover and helped tie down German units in the Pas de Calais as real Allied units stormed ashore 170 miles southwest at Normandy.

Order of battle intelligence also can be controversial. During the *Vietnam War, analysts at the Military Assistance Command Vietnam (MACV) and the *Central Intelligence Agency debated the size and composition of enemy units operating in South Vietnam. The debate continued after the war and was the subject of a federal libel case— *Westmoreland V. CBS*—in 1985.

[*See also* Intelligence, Military and Political; Tactics.]

• David Eisenhower, *Eisenhower at War 1943–1945*, 1986. Renatta Adler, *Reckless Disregard*, 1986.   —James J. Wirtz

ORGANIZATION OF AMERICAN STATES. *See* OAS.

OSCEOLA (Maskóki—Black Drink singer, ca. 1804–1838), Native American war leader. Osceola was born into the Tallassee tribe of Maskóki speakers (called *Creeks* by the British), whose village was near present-day Tuskegee, Alabama. He was never a chief.

Dispossessed by Andrew *Jackson's settlement of the Creek War of 1813–14, he and part of his family migrated southward into the Spanish Floridas. His plight and passion captured the imagination of the U.S. press, which romanticized Osceola as a symbol of Indian resistance to forced removal. Acquisition of the territory by the United States in 1821 increased tensions, and the young warrior spoke vehemently against the treaties by which the United States sought to confine Florida Indians to peninsular reservations. Imprisoned for several days by U.S. Indian agent Wiley Thompson in 1835, Osceola determined to fight removal. Along with tribal leaders, he planned the opening gambits of the Second Seminole War.

On 28 December 1835, Osceola murdered Agent Thompson at Fort King (Ocala) as his compatriots were attacking a U.S. Army column under Maj. Francis Dade en route there. Two days later, he was one of the leaders of the Battle of the Withlacoochee, in which U.S. regulars and volunteers were routed by the numerically inferior Indian forces. He led warriors throughout 1836–37 although his health declined.

On 21 October 1837, Osceola was captured by U.S. troops, while under a white flag of truce, near St. Augustine, East Florida. He was transferred from Fort Marion (St. Augustine) to Fort Moultrie, South Carolina, where he died a prisoner on 30 January 1838.

[*See also* Native Americans, U.S. Military Relations with; Native American Wars: Wars Between Native Americans and Europeans and Euro-Americans; Seminole Wars.]

• John K. Mahon, *History of the Second Seminole War*, 1967; reprint 1991. Patricia R. Wickman, *Osceola's Legacy*, 1991.

—Patricia R. Wickman

OSRD. *See* Science, Technology, War, and the Military.

P

PACIFICATION is a controversial and complex issue in American military history. It is controversial because it denotes U.S. policy toward hostile populations that are either the primary or secondary object of war itself. It is complex because it describes simultaneous military, political, and economic activities to protect, control, appease, or coerce civilians and to reform governments besieged by insurgency or external subversion. It can also refer to efforts to suppress anticolonial movements. Because it is overtly political and targeted at civilians, American officers have viewed pacification equivocally, sometimes treating it as a tertiary mission in a given campaign. Pacification policies have also served as a rallying point for American *peace and antiwar movements, even though these policies often produce less death and destruction than other military operations.

Depending on the nature of the insurgency, pacification can take a variety of forms. From a military perspective, it often involves protecting civilians from *guerrilla warfare depredations (confiscation of property, assassination, torture, and other forms of political coercion) or denying guerrillas access to material and psychological assistance provided by civilian supporters. Government control of the local economy through resettlement, disruption of traditional production methods, or other programs intended to deny civilian surpluses to insurgents weakens both the political appeal and the military capability of insurgencies. By disrupting the guerrillas' logistical infrastructure (i.e., the civilian population), the scope and intensity of an insurgency can be reduced. For police and intelligence operatives, pacification involves the identification and arrest of clandestine cadres that form shadow governments within civilian populations. These operations often involve the interrogation and detention of suspects, maintenance of databases on insurgent networks, or the provision of identification credentials to entire populations. Reform of besieged governments sometimes plays a part by addressing the economic and political grievances that fuel unrest. By reducing or eliminating the economic, social, and political inequities that motivate indigenous support of insurgents, governments can sometimes entice guerrillas and their supporters to abandon military activity and participate in reform.

For many Americans, the term *pacification* is linked to the Vietnam War. Pacification remains a key point in the debate over the sources of the U.S. debacle in Southeast Asia. Harry Summers has criticized U.S. policy for focusing too much on the struggle for the "hearts and minds" of the South Vietnamese peasant and for not destroying the source of the southern insurgency, which he locates in North Vietnam. By contrast, Andrew Krepinevich has sug-

gested that the U.S. military virtually ignored pacification, focusing instead on the "Big-unit war" against North Vietnam. Pacification also served as a source of interservice rivalry during the war. The Marine Corps' Operation Golden Fleece, an effort to deny the rice harvest to Viet Cong forces, and Marine Corps combined action platoons, which stationed small Marine units in Vietnamese villages, reduced Marine participation in large-scale search and destroy operations favored by U.S. Army officers.

American pacification efforts took on many forms and consumed enormous resources during the Vietnam War. In 1959, Ngo Dinh Diem's government launched a program to move South Vietnamese peasants into strong rural settlements named *agrovilles*. This initiative was followed in 1961 by the *strategic hamlet program,* shaped by Sir Robert Thompson, who had helped plan the successful British *counterinsurgency effort in Malaya in the 1950s. Because of mismanagement and conflicting priorities between the Diem regime, which wanted a mechanism to control the southern population, and its Western advisers, who saw physical security and prosperity as a way of winning peasant sympathies from the Viet Cong, both programs foundered. Building these settlements also relied heavily on peasant labor and produced much disruption of rural life, which increased village dissatisfaction with the Saigon regime. Both programs also failed to protect villagers from the Viet Cong. By contrast, one element of the strategic hamlet initiative, the *Chieu Hoi* ("Open Arms") program to offer clemency to insurgents, produced positive results throughout the war. Viet Cong defectors, commonly referred to as "ralliers," even served as "Kit Carson" scouts for U.S. forces.

In 1964, a revised pacification plan called *Chien Thang* ("Will to Victory") was implemented by the South Vietnamese and their American advisers. Based on the "oil-spot concept," *Chien Thang* was intended slowly to increase areas considered pacified. Military and paramilitary units would occupy a central village for a time, clear it of Viet Cong influence, then move on to an adjacent area. Pacified areas would thus spread out from a central village like an ever-expanding drop of oil on water. *Hop Tac* ("Victory"), which also began in 1964, was an effort to apply this oil-spot philosophy to the area surrounding Saigon. Again, this program failed to live up to expectations because of poor execution and a lack of support from conventional military units.

In the aftermath of the January 1968 *Tet Offensive, pacification was given renewed emphasis in U.S. policy. The efforts of many U.S. agencies that contributed to pacification were now coordinated by CORDS (Civil Operations and Revolutionary Development Support). Created in 1967 by a Johnson administration eager to improve U.S. prosecution of the "other war" (pacification), CORDS was headed by Robert "Blowtorch" Komer, known for his determination and bureaucratic savvy. Komer's efforts at coordinating competing civilian programs with military operations yielded results. CORDS efforts to destroy the Viet Cong infrastructure (VCI) by identifying and arresting clandestine cadres in southern villages produced two infamous initiatives: ICEX (infrastructure coordination and exploitation), which was started in mid-1967 to support South Vietnamese police units; and Phoenix, which was started in 1969, to coordinate American and South Vietnamese military, intelligence, and police operations against the VCI. Although Phoenix was criticized as a thinly veiled terror and assassination program, its operations emphasized intelligence collection. Dead suspects were of no use in rolling up the VCI. After the war, Communist observers and American supporters of pacification both agreed that the Phoenix and the *Chieu Hoi* programs were effective, but that pacification had taken too long and had cost too much. The more important battle for the "hearts and minds" of the American public was lost long before the Communists' Great Spring Victory of 1975.

By contrast, in earlier wars American pacification efforts had twice been effective in the Philippines in the twentieth century. In the 1950s, CIA agent Edward G. *Lansdale, a U.S. Air Force officer with a background in advertising, organized an effective response to a revolt of the Communist faction of the Hukbalahap (a Tagalog acronym for "People's Anti-Japanese Army"). Working with the young and charismatic Ramon Magsaysay, who would eventually become president of the Philippines, Lansdale orchestrated a textbook pacification effort. Magsaysay launched reforms that curtailed military and landlord harassment of the peasantry; American aid was used to help satisfy the "land hunger" that motivated many Huks. When Huk leaders were rounded up in a raid of their Manila headquarters, reforms continued to reduce the economic and political concerns motivating rank-and-file Huks, slowly ending the insurgency.

Half a century earlier, Filipino resistance to the U.S. occupation of the archipelago following the *Spanish-American War was ended by harsher methods. After driving the Philippine Army from the field in a series of conventional battles, the U.S. Army ultimately suppressed guerrilla resistance by "concentrating" the rural population into specified areas. Destroying the guerrillas' rural food supplies and tax base, U.S. forces starved the nationalists into submission. The promise of limited self-rule also reduced some of the political motivation behind the guerrilla movement.

Almost from the beginning of the English North American colonies, colonists and later the U.S. government pacified Native Americans, who had been weakened by a horrific demographic shock produced by the introduction of Eurasian diseases. In pre-Revolutionary America, when European settlers and Indian nations were more evenly matched in military capability, pacification took the form of punitive expeditionary raids intended to drive Indian settlements away from areas populated by Europeans or to deny Indians the logistics needed to launch raids against colonists. Later, when westward migration, briefly interrupted by the *Civil War, brought American settlers and western Indian nations into repeated conflict, the U.S. government forced Indians onto reservations and fought to keep them there, making them dependent on government subsidies. Even though the reservation policy, intended to "civilize" Native Americans, destroyed traditional lifestyles, at the time it was often depicted as a humanitarian approach to the "Indian problem." By contrast, many settlers objected to humanitarian efforts advocated by eastern groups (e.g., *Quakers) and simply called for the extermination of Native Americans.

Pacification operations conducted by loyalist forces during the American *Revolutionary War were often brutal. British commanders, however, chose not to adopt a scorched-earth policy to combat the Revolution. Many British officers believed that a deliberate policy of brutality would drive "fence-sitters" to support the rebel cause.

Because pacification often involves the denial of economic or cultural independence to civilian populations or military intervention in the domestic politics of other nations, the policy conflicts with the political and philosophical principles that underlie American political culture. As a result, many Americans view U.S. pacification campaigns as dark chapters in the nation's history.

[See also Native American Wars: Wars Between Native Americans and Europeans and Euro-Americans; Philippine War; Philippines, U.S. Military Involvement in the; Vietnam War: Military and Diplomatic Course; Vietnam War: Changing Interpretations.]

• John Shy, *A People Numerous and Armed: Reflections on the Military Struggle for American Independence*, 1976. Harry Summers, *On Strategy*, 1982. Robert M. Utley, *The Indian Frontier of the American West 1846–1890*, 1984. Andrew Krepinevich, *The Army and Vietnam*, 1986. D. Michael Shafer, *Deadly Paradigms: The Failure of U.S. Counterinsurgency Policy*, 1988. Glenn A. May, *Battle for Batangas: A Philippine Province at War*, 1991. Harold E. Selesky, *War and Society in Colonial Connecticut*, 1991. Douglas J. Macdonald, *Adventures in Chaos: American Intervention for Reform in the Third World*, 1992. Tom Hatley, *The Dividing Paths, Cherokees and South Carolinians Through the Era of Revolution*, 1993. Richard A. Hunt, *Pacification: The American Struggle for Vietnam's Hearts and Minds*, 1995.
—James J. Wirtz

PACIFISM is the principled rejection of war. It has found expression in American history through individuals who acted upon basis of personal conscience and through groups who acted out of a corporate sense of peoplehood. Pacifism has involved the refusal to participate in war or military service, as well as organized activities to promote *peace and to give witness to the power of love in social and political relationships. Degrees of pacifist expression and commitment have varied widely, from a total renunciation of war by separatist religious sects to a general secular bias against militarism. Pacifism has had a role both at the sectarian fringes and at the public center of American life. By the broadest definition of the term—the desire to avoid war—in the words of John Dewey in 1917, "the American people is profoundly pacifist."

Some Native North American tribes had developed corporate pacifist traditions before contacts with the Europeans. In the early fifteenth century, Deganawidah, semi-mythical founder of the Iroquois confederacy, taught a gospel of disarmament, social cooperation, and the rule of law. Sweet Medicine, legendary founder of the Cheyenne, established a "Peace Chief" tradition that counseled chiefs to suffer nonviolently rather than to take violent revenge.

The Lenni Lenape (Delaware) had traditions of peacemaking and mediation which, together with the pacifism of William *Penn and the *Quakers, helped the colony of Pennsylvania for seventy years to avoid the scourge of war that afflicted Indian-white relations elsewhere.

The pacifist Quaker movement began in the mid-seventeenth century in the separatist wing of the Puritan dissent against the Church of England. The Quakers taught that all people, not just "the elect," could be saved and live a life of righteousness through the guidance of the "inner light" from God, without the mediation of priest or sacrament. The Quakers took the Bible seriously, especially the teachings of Jesus in the New Testament, but gave primary emphasis to the universal light within. William Penn made liberty of conscience and the renunciation of war central to his "Holy Experiment" in social and cultural pluralism in the Delaware Valley. Social order in Pennsylvania was not guaranteed by militia, imposed creeds, or social hierarchy, but by an ideal of social harmony and mutual forbearance among different groups. From the founding of Pennsylvania in 1682 to the withdrawal of Quakers from political control in 1750, this experiment evolved a set of pacifist-oriented social ideals and institutions that worked a lasting influence upon American life. After 1750, Quaker pacifism became a more marginal and perfectionist movement, but it remained a continuing source of humanitarian reform impulses for movements against slavery, militarism, and other social ills.

Among the groups Penn attracted to his colony were German-speaking pacifists of Anabaptist and Pietist origin, notably the Mennonites, Amish, and Dunkers (Church of the Brethren). The Mennonites originated in the left wing of the Protestant Reformation on the European Continent and held to a doctrine of two kingdoms that separated church and state. The state was "outside the perfection of Christ" and ordained by God to maintain order in the world. The church was a body of disciplined adult believers who literally followed the teachings of Jesus, including the commandment to love one's enemies. Mennonites and their cousins, the Amish, generally stayed aloof from politics. The Dunkers, of eighteenth-century radical Pietist origin, expressed a warmer evangelical piety than the Anabaptists, but also maintained a strictly disciplined church life of nonresistance, simplicity, and separation from the world. The Quakers, Mennonites, and Brethren eventually became known as the "historic peace churches." Other church and communitarian groups also developed pacifist stances based upon varying apostolic, eschatological, and reform visions (Shakers, Jehovah's Witnesses, Seventh-Day Adventists, Churches of Christ, Church of God in Christ, and others).

The classical republican political philosophy that guided the founders and leaders of the early American republic contained significant elements of pacifist antimilitarism. Classical republicanism, derived from scholars of the French Enlightenment and from English Whig opponents of monarchy, assumed that warfare resulted from the alliance of the ruling aristocracy with their national military forces. This alliance produced standing armies, which encouraged despotism and threatened the freedoms of the people. To maintain public order, classical republicans counted upon the superior virtue of citizens in a republic and upon the efficacy of well-regulated local militia. Classical republicanism, in its acceptance of militia and of defensive wars, was far from absolute pacifism. But it was a "halfway pacifism" opposed to professional military training academies, to a standing army in peacetime, and to national military *conscription in wartime. In the early American republic, it also informed peace initiatives such as President John *Adams's decision for peace with France in the wake of the *XYZ Affair (1799–1800) and President Thomas *Jefferson's use of a trade embargo as an alternative to war (1808). Also in the classical republican tradition were rapid disarmament and reduction of the army after wars, strong opposition to military conscription in the *Civil War and World War I, and alarm over the power of the *military-industrial complex in the *Cold War.

The first nonsectarian peace societies in the United States emerged in the wake of the *War of 1812. In 1828, the local and state peace societies joined to form the *American Peace Society. The peace societies were deeply religious and primarily Christian, believing that God was revealed in Christ, and that Jesus' ethic of love required the rejection of violence and war. The relationship of the peace reform to movements against slavery and for women's rights was especially important in this reform-minded era. In 1838, some radical pacifists, led by William Lloyd *Garrison, formed the New England Non-Resistance Society and called for righteous people to separate themselves from an evil world, particularly the slave-owning South. The peace societies opposed the *Mexican War (1846–48), but when the Civil War broke out (1860) they nearly all supported the North's military effort as a justifiable police action to end slavery and preserve the Union.

Between the Civil War and World War I, the pacifist-anarchist teachings of the Russian author Leo Tolstoy added a new dimension to the peace movement, even as the movement adapted to the new challenges created by urbanization and industrialization. Tolstoy taught a universal nonresistant gospel based upon a law of love common to all world religions. In the first decades of the twentieth century, the secular theme of *internationalism became especially prominent, with proposals for international law and for arbitration of disputes. In 1910, the philosopher and psychologist William James wrote an influential essay, "The Moral Equivalent of War," which argued that the apparent opposites, killing and service, were both expressions of a universal impulse to heroic self-sacrifice. James's essay gave new psychological depth to pacifist thought and fostered alternative service programs to military service. Jane *Addams, founder of the *Women's International League for Peace and Freedom, envisioned benevolent social work on a grand scale as a means of achieving world peace.

Pacifism in the twentieth century addressed the problems of total international warfare and ultimately of a thermonuclear *arms race. During wartime, the historic peace churches continued their *conscientious objection to war and refused military service. The numbers of men who went to prison or to alternative service programs remained small, reduced through acculturation to American *patriotism. But the peace church precedent of conscientious objection provided a wedge for massive challenges to the military draft during the unpopular *Vietnam War, when the Selective Service System almost broke down. Some pacifists worked together with socialists and labor movement leaders in direct action for social justice—sometimes involving civil disobedience.

The nonviolent teachings and methods of Mohandas K.

Gandhi, expressed in the popular movement for Indian independence from British imperial rule, influenced American pacifists with their integration of personal and social ethics, their unity of means and ends, and their combination of Hinduism and Christianity. Martin Luther *King, Jr., adapted Gandhi's methods in leading the civil rights movement from 1956 to 1968 as head of the Southern Christian Leadership Conference. King's pacifism extended to opposition to the Vietnam War at a time when that stance seemed to threaten the civil rights coalition. A boycott on behalf of striking grape pickers in California, organized by Cesar Chavez, (1965–70), was a form of pacifist nonviolent direct action.

During the Cold War, pacifist activity waxed and waned according to recurrent crises in the competition between Communist powers and the West. The threat of atomic destruction produced a position known as "nuclear pacifism"—reflected in the *National Committee for a Sane Nuclear Policy, and held by people who could justify winnable or "just" wars but who in principle opposed nuclear warfare because of its consequences. Pacifist ideals gained expression through activist organizations as well as through the growing academic discipline of peace and conflict resolution studies. A government agency, the United States Institute of Peace, was founded in 1985. National problems of escalating violence led to creative new movements for peer mediation in public schools and victim-offender reconciliation programs in local communities. These new initiatives drew upon a long history of pacifist idealism in the American experience.

[See also Just War Theory; Militarism and Antimilitarism; Nonviolence; Nuclear Protest Movements; Peace and Antiwar Movements; Vietnam Antiwar Movement.]

• Peter Brock, Pacifism in the United States: From the Colonial Era to the First World War, 1968. Charles Chatfield, For Peace and Justice: Pacifism in America, 1914–1941, 1971. Charles DeBenedetti, The Peace Reform in American History, 1980. Lawrence S. Wittner, Rebels Against War: The American Peace Movement, 1933–1983, 1984. Valarie H. Ziegler, The Advocates of Peace in Antebellum America, 1992. Charles Chatfield and Robert Kleidman, The American Peace Movement: Ideals and Activism, 1992. Matthew Dennis, Cultivating a Landscape of Peace: Iroquois-European Encounters in Seventeenth-Century America, 1993. Louise Hawkley and James C. Juhnke, eds., Nonviolent America: History Through the Eyes of Peace, 1993. Charles C. Moskos and John Whiteclay Chambers II, eds., The New Conscientious Objection: From Sacred to Secular Resistance, 1993. Staughton Lynd and Alice Lynd, eds., Nonviolence in America: A Documentary History, 1995.

—James C. Juhnke

PALMER, JOHN McAULEY (1870–1955), U.S. Army officer, manpower specialist. Born in Carlinville, Illinois, Palmer was a U.S. Military Academy graduate of 1892 who served on the Indian frontier, in China, and in the Philippines. The Army Staff School at Fort Leavenworth broadened his horizons and led to service on the U.S. Army General Staff, where in 1915–17 he helped prepare plans for an American mass army and for its deployment overseas in World War I. Accompanying Gen. John J. *Pershing to France, he was the first chief of operations, *American Expeditionary Force. Following service as a brigade commander near Verdun, he returned to the United States as Pershing's emissary on the postwar reorganization of the U.S. Army. In this capacity he became special adviser to the Senate Military Affairs Committee, where he helped write the Defense Act of 1920. He unsuccessfully advocated peacetime Universal Military Training. His wartime experience, however, led him to a lifelong belief in the efficacy of the *citizen-soldier, including the National Guard (the constitutional militia) and the reserve components (under army rather than state control).

After retirement as a brigadier general, Palmer wrote several books promulgating his views on the military manpower problem, especially America in Arms (1941). During World War II, his friend, chief of staff Gen. George C. *Marshall, called him to active service as an adviser.

[See also Army, U.S.: 1900–41; Militia and National Guard; World War I: Military and Diplomatic Course; World War II: Military and Diplomatic Course.]

• Irving B. Holley, Jr., General John M. Palmer, Citizen Soldiers and the Army of a Democracy, 1970.   —I. B. Holley, Jr.

PANAMA, U.S. MILITARY INVOLVEMENT IN. U.S. military involvement in Panama began even before the Central American nation won its independence from Colombia in 1903. With the 1846 Bidlack-Mallarino Treaty, the United States agreed to defend Colombia's rule over Panama in exchange for the rights of free transit across the isthmus. In order to uphold the treaty and to protect American interests in the region, U.S. forces landed in Panama as many as ten times before the turn of the century. In 1885, President Grover Cleveland dispatched more than 1,000 Marines and sailors to put down a nationalist uprising, thus launching the largest U.S. expeditionary force since the *Mexican War. The other interventions were usually smaller affairs, but their frequency as well as the regular presence of the U.S. Navy in Panamanian waters were harbingers of what would come in the next century.

American military and naval leaders had long dreamed of a Central American canal that would allow them to project U.S. power over two oceans using only one naval fleet. The lengthy voyage of the USS Oregon around Cape Horn during the *Spanish-American War strengthened their resolve to secure an interoceanic passage. Secessionist rumblings in Panama provided the opportunity. In violation of the 1846 treaty, the United States deployed warships and landed Marines in order to block Colombian troops from putting down the Panamanian rebellion. Panama became an independent nation on 3 November 1903, but the Hay-Bunau-Varilla Treaty penned two weeks later made the new republic a U.S. protectorate. In addition to the right to intervene militarily in Panama, the treaty gave the United States the right to build a canal through a ten-mile-wide "zone" leased in perpetuity. These generous concessions would be the major source of tension in U.S.-Panama relations for decades.

By the time the Panama Canal opened in 1914, the U.S. military had already established a firm foothold on the isthmus. A U.S. military administration presided over the waterway, which was guarded by U.S. ground troops, naval vessels, and coastal *artillery batteries. All *transportation and communication in the country came under the watchful eyes of the U.S. forces. This strong military presence served the dual function of defending the canal against interlopers from outside Panama and eliminating threats from within the country. The latter project came to dominate U.S. activities in Panama. At different times the

United States wielded its power to help disband the Panamanian Army, supervise elections, halt urban rioting, and pressure political leaders. The United States eventually renounced its right to intervene, but it had amply demonstrated a willingness to subordinate Panama to the needs of canal security.

The presence of the U.S. military in Panama reached its peak during World War II, when the United States operated 14 bases, established more than 100 defense sites, and stationed as many as 67,000 troops there. Although the canal remained physically unscathed, it would never again be the linchpin of American hemispheric *strategy. While the Panamanians objected more vocally to the U.S. presence, Washington found the canal too narrow for the U.S. Navy's new supercarriers and too vulnerable to air and atomic attack. Postwar military involvement therefore included converting the Panamanian National Guard into a quasi-military force, training soldiers in *jungle warfare, and maintaining intelligence operations in the region. U.S. forces were deployed when riots over which nation's flag would be flown in the Canal Zone erupted in 1959 and again in 1964. Although the canal itself became vital to U.S. strategic interests, it remained a potent political symbol to both countries.

Exclusive control of the canal had once been axiomatic in U.S. strategic thought. But Washington began to reconsider its policy toward Panama in the aftermath of the 1964 flag riots. A new treaty signed in 1977 promised to turn over the canal to Panamanian control on 31 December 1999. Despite some resistance from elements within the defense community, the *Pentagon officially endorsed the treaty and agreed to scale back its activities in Panama. To help stabilize the nation after the American withdrawal and to maintain an important pipeline to the Nicaraguan Contras in the 1980s, the United States funneled aid to the Panamanian Defense Forces (PDF; formerly the National Guard). When President George *Bush decided he could no longer countenance PDF chief Gen. Manuel *Noriega, who was accused of election fraud and drug trafficking, he launched the massive Operation Just Cause to capture Noriega in December 1989. The invasion resulted in hundreds of U.S. *casualties and possibly more than 1,000 Panamanian deaths; it also made clear that the United States would not easily sacrifice its historic prerogatives over Panama and its canal.

[See also Caribbean and Latin America, U.S. Military Involvement in the; Nicaragua, U.S. Military Involvement in.]

• Larry LaRae Pippin, The Remon Era, 1964. William D. McCain, The United States and the Republic of Panama, 1970. Walter LaFeber, The Panama Canal, 1978. John Major, "Wasting Asset: The U.S. Re-Assessment of the Panama Canal, 1945–1949," Journal of Strategic Studies, 3 (September 1980), pp. 123–46. Michael L. Conniff, Panama and the United States, 1992.

—Matthew Abramovitz

PANAY INCIDENT (1937). An important, if short-lived, crisis in U.S.-Japanese relations occurred in the 1930s as Japan launched the Second Sino-Japanese War in July 1937. The Japanese had quickly conquered Beijing, Shanghai, and Nanjing, and blockaded the coastline. On 12 December 1937, Japanese warplanes sank the U.S. Navy's gunboat Panay on the Yangtze River, killing three Americans and wounding nearly thirty. In the daylight attack, many of the escaping survivors were repeatedly machine-gunned. Three Standard Oil tankers being convoyed by the Panay were also sunk.

President Franklin D. *Roosevelt's advisers believed Japanese officers in China had authorized the attack on the clearly marked ships, and the president and his cabinet considered an embargo and possible naval action. However, while condemning the attack, congressional and press opinion concluded that no vital American interests were involved.

When the foreign ministry in Tokyo soon offered a formal apology and agreed to U.S. demands for an indemnity of $2 million, the crisis subsided, but it increased anti-Japanese sentiment in the United States and helped persuade the president to take a firmer stand toward Japan, including in 1938 imposing a "moral embargo" on the sale of aircraft to the Japanese military and increasing U.S. Navy.

[See also China, U.S. Military Involvement in; Japan, U.S. Military Involvement in; World War II: Causes.]

• Manny T. Koginos, The Panay Incident, 1967. Hamilton Perry, The Panay Incident, 1969.   —John Whiteclay Chambers II

PARAMILITARY GROUPS. The Oxford English Dictionary defines the term paramilitary as "ancillary to and similarly organized to military forces." Almost all paramilitary organizations in American history developed in response to a threat of real or perceived violence from social groups or institutions. These organizations have varied from bands of frontier horse thieves to agencies of the U.S. government. Paramilitary organizations, both legal and extralegal, were based on the assumption that violence must be met with violence, mobilized either offensively or defensively, to protect a way of life. They have shared several characteristics. At its most basic, a paramilitary group was structured to resemble or imitate a command or military organization. Though it may have been hired or even organized by the state, a paramilitary group was not a direct extension of the state, differentiating it from a government's regular armed forces, militias, or police forces. Paramilitaries have varied in size from half a dozen to several thousand members, and maintained their structure and existence over an extended period of time, differentiating them from such ad hoc violent associations as lynch mobs, which disbanded after achieving their purpose. Paramilitary groups possessed a belief system to which their adherents subscribed, expressed in a constitution, manifesto, or a collection of articles in the most structured organizations. Some dressed in *uniforms or displayed a symbol (a flag or armband) for identity or to communicate their beliefs to outsiders. Some also included weapons or guerilla-style training, or identified with a geographic location where meetings and/or training took place.

One early category developed on the American frontier (from the late eighteenth century into the mid-nineteenth century), a product of the vigilantism that arose in response to the absence of law enforcement and social organization in those areas. Another grew up during the *Civil War and *Reconstruction, in response to both racial and political strife and the continued lack of effective law enforcement throughout the country. A third form, overtly political, emerged in the latter half of the twentieth century when militant groups, often engaged in terrorist activities, pursued political goals on both the left and the right.

Paramilitary groups first arose in any number just before the *Revolutionary War. The Revolution spawned violent resistance to Britain organized in mobs by popular leaders. The structure of the patriot movement was thoroughly connected to Boston's associational or "club" life and to the patriot organizations themselves, including the Loyal Nine, which gave birth to and served as the executive committee for the Sons of Liberty in Massachusetts. Though the Sons of Liberty was not necessarily paramilitary itself, its members and other patriot leaders steered and "politicized" the activities of the numerous clubs, eventually directing them toward more organized violence for revolutionary purposes. Their crucial maneuver by the patriot leaders was to forge a bond between two of the most prominent Boston mobs, composed of lower-class workingmen and artisans, and to direct their hostility, previously aimed at each other, toward the British government. The resulting violence led to several organized riots (one during opposition to the Stamp Act of 1765 and another during the anticustoms resistance of 1768) and finally to the evacuation of two British regiments after the *Boston Massacre (1770).

This loose model of one of the first paramilitary organizations in U.S. history served as a structural and ideological framework for organizations to follow, not only in other colonies before independence but later as well. The tradition of vigilantism became a sporadic feature of American life from the Revolution to about 1900. Sometimes called *regulators*, vigilantes were citizens who formed extralegal organizations to deal with the lawlessness and general disorganization that occurred during late revolutionary, Civil War, and Reconstruction times, and on the frontier. Vigilante movements could be identified by two basic characteristics: their regular organization and their existence over a defined, though sometimes short, period of time. They could be distinguished from more ad hoc mobs, including lynch mobs, by their structured nature and their semipermanence. Vigilante movements were often organized by prominent members of a community and reflected their social and moral values. Thus vigilantism could often be considered a socially conservative form of violence. Though vigilantes of the revolutionary period did contribute to the violence that spurred anti-British sentiment (one of the most prominent groups was the South Carolina Regulators, 1767–69, who became Whigs during the actual Revolution), the vigilante tradition became more firmly rooted in American history and imagination on the frontier, where pioneers and settlers were often organized into extralegal groups who rounded up, flogged, or quickly tried and sometimes hanged the outlaws who plagued these areas before effective law enforcement was in place.

Historians have counted 326 organized vigilante movements in the two centuries since U.S. independence: there may have in fact been at least 500. Their ideology was fourfold: the notion of self-preservation; the right to revolution; the idea of popular sovereignty; and the doctrine of vigilance against crime and disorder. Four waves of vigilantism occurred: in the early 1830s; the early 1840s; the late 1850s; and the late 1860s.

In the mid-nineteenth century, several kinds of legal organizations emerged, also in response to the absence of effective law enforcement and exclusive of the militias. The years 1844–77 saw the rise of the modern urban police system (in direct response to the urban riots of the 1830s and 1840s), but police departments were often undermanned, corrupt, or even incompetent. In the early 1850s, Allan Pinkerton started the Pinkerton National Detective Agency in Chicago. In lieu of a centralized, federal police agency, the Pinkertons essentially became an armed, private police force that could move across local, county, and state lines to deal with small- and large-scale criminal activities or industrial disruption. Pinkertons were trained to solve robbery and assault cases, protect railway trains from looting, break labor strikes, and even to aid the U.S. government against post office theft. From a force of less than a dozen men in 1860, the Pinkertons grew into a late twentieth-century organization of 13,000 full-time and more than 9,000 part-time employees.

One of the most worrisome aspects of frontier life for settlers was conflict with American Indians; several kinds of legal paramilitary organizations developed to defend against and attack Indians. The Comanches of Texas in the mid-1800s, themselves engaging in *guerrilla warfare, were so effective that ranging companies, federal troops, and finally the Texas Rangers were used to deal with the problem. The Texas Rangers (like the Arizona Rangers) were historically situated somewhere between a paramilitary organization and a police force created by the state government; they were mobilized for special circumstances such as Indian attacks and the extreme disorder of the southwestern frontier. The Frontier Battalion of the Texas Rangers, established in 1874, was a thoroughly professional paramilitary organization that was finally able to end the warfare between settlers and Indians in that year in a ruthless and bloody campaign.

The labor movement also led to some illegal organizations to combat terrible working conditions, low wages, and long hours during the expansion of the Industrial Revolution. Beginning in the 1870s, many laborers, from railroad workers to miners, used the strike as their major weapon against industry. Management often used lockouts and strikebreakers in response. These conflicts could lead to violence. The "Molly Maguires," a secret organization of Irish immigrant miners who attempted to unify labor in the coalfields of Pennsylvania throughout the early 1870s, fought their employers with terrorist tactics, engaging in intimidation and assassination. The Pinkertons were sent in to investigate and eventually break this particularly violent organization, and most Molly Maguire gunmen were tried and hanged in 1877. Pennsylvania industrialists employed a private iron and coal police, a paramilitary force, in the late nineteenth century.

One of the most powerful and well known extralegal paramilitary organizations has been the Ku Klux Klan (KKK). Three different waves of Klan activity each represented a phase of history and organizational ideology, though each also reflected some continuity in ritual and regalia. The first movement arose in the South during Reconstruction. This Klan was created by a group of Confederate *veterans as a secret social club in Tennessee in 1866 and grew in direct response to Reconstruction policy. The organization used violence and intimidation against blacks and white Republicans in the South to achieve dominance for the Democratic Party and white supremacy. Though it did not become centralized, the first Klan spread throughout the South; it waned after elite sponsorship withdrew and the U.S. government sought to suppress the Klan under the Enforcement Acts (1870–71).

A second Klan emerging during World War I and in the 1920s was more widespread and composed of between 3 and 6 million followers. This Klan skillfully exploited racism and paranoia, particularly against the foreign-born, and spread throughout the South, Midwest, and West. It not only continued to use force and intimidation but began to wield considerable political power as well. The complex ideology of this more popular and politically adept Klan catered to notions of family and community values, the necessity of protecting the sanctity of the white race, and small-town America.

The third Klan, in the 1950s and 1960s, was a considerably less popular but no less racist, anti-Semitic, paranoid, and militant organization responding to changing race relations, particularly desegregation. The continual acts of *aggression and violence, including the murders of three civil rights activists in Mississippi in 1964, finally forced the federal government to take action. The KKK today remains dedicated to white supremacy and radical nativism and has ties to other Fascist and neo-Nazi groups, including the Aryan Nations and the Order.

Radical political ideology drove some terrorist paramilitary organizations of the extreme Left and Far Right in the late twentieth century. In the 1960s, two offshoots of the New Left Students for a Democratic Society, the Revolutionary Youth Movement and the Weathermen (later the Weather People and Weather Underground), engaged in deliberately violent acts against symbols of authority and U.S. policy in denunciation of social injustice and racism at home and abroad. In 1969 and 1970, the Weather groups staged riots in downtown Chicago, attacked "imperialist" targets like schools and police stations, and finally set off bombs in New York City and elsewhere, killing some civilians and some of their own members. Though the Black Panthers did not begin as a paramilitary organization, local urban police forces found the Panthers' militant separatist ideology and exhibition of weapons quite threatening, and police harassment eventually forced violent confrontations in such cities as Oakland and Chicago in the late 1960s and early 1970s.

Also on the radical Left, the Symbionese Liberation Army was a small (a dozen members) but radical and violent organization of the early 1970s composed of mostly middle-class university radicals with a revolutionary ideology that sanctioned bank robbery, murder, and kidnapping, including the abduction of one of the young members of the Hearst publishing family. Their rampage ended in Los Angeles in a shootout with a Los Angeles SWAT team in 1974. This group served as the archetype for other militant groups, including the Black Liberation Army, which also engaged in intensive terrorist tactics.

On the radical Right, extralegal paramilitary groups in the late twentieth century maintained an ideology based on white supremacy, anti-Semitism, and staunch *nationalism that gained national attention in the late 1980s and early 1990s. One of these, the Aryan Nations, based in Idaho, hosted national conferences to spread the propaganda of intolerance. This organization and others like it, including the Order and the Posse Comitatus, rallied not simply around racism but also the issues of gun control and government intrusion in American life, to which almost all these groups were radically opposed. These paramilitary organizations were part of a growing self-styled "militia movement" of the 1980s and 1990s, which made its opposition to gun control, its hatred of big government, and its defense of self-asserted "constitutional rights" the more public ideological message. Some of the most visible acts committed by individuals or groups who linked their ideology to this so-called militia movement included the bombing of the Alfred P. Murrah federal building in Oklahoma City in 1995 and the actions of the Montana-based Freemen, whose tax evasion and acts of intimidation instigated the federal government's retaliation and an FBI siege in 1996. Other militia groups also engaged in weapons and warfare training, called "paramilitary training," preparing for what they believed would be an apocalypse—a massive crackdown by the federal government or even a full-scale race war.

Despite the enormous variety of their views and membership, paramilitary groups have had an extensive, if sporadic, history in the United States, though their premises have changed with social and political conditions. The first most prominent groups were concerned with maintaining law and order: these included both the extralegal vigilante organizations and the legally sanctioned Pinkertons and Frontier Battalion. The second type arose in response to the social and political disruption of the end of slavery following the Civil War and massive immigration and urbanization in the early twentieth century. Extralegal organizations like the Ku Klux Klan emerged and then spawned similar organizations, which continued to exist in the late twentieth century. A third type, overtly political, has included the terrorist groups of the late 1960s to the 1990s. Rightist groups like the Aryan Nations and the modern Ku Klux Klan bridge two categories by combining racist orientation with ideologically driven activity in pursuit of political goals.

The United States was born in violent revolution, and developed through rapid territorial expansion, urbanization, industrialization, and immigration, frequently at times of limited or ineffective local and national law enforcement. These determinants may have contributed to the national characteristics of voluntarism/associationalism (seen in the tendency to join clubs or voluntary organizations) as well as vigilantism. Paramilitary groups may also be linked with specific periods of social and political unrest, and the perception on the part of the American people that federal and local government is incapable of or unwilling to respond to the needs of the general public. This perception, combined with a widespread ownership of guns and a pervasive belief in individualism and personal freedom, has provided the social, political, and historical impulses behind many paramilitary groups.

[See also Citizen-Soldier; Militia and National Guard; Native American Wars: Wars Between Native Americans and Europeans and Euro-Americans; Patriotism; Posse Comitatus Act; Rangers, U.S. Army.]

• James D. Horan, *The Pinkertons: The Detective Dynasty that Made History,* 1967. Richard Maxwell Brown, *Strain of Violence: Historical Studies of American Violence and Vigilantism,* 1975. Richard Maxwell Brown, "The American Vigilante Tradition," in *Violence in America: Historical and Comparative Perspectives,* Hugh Davis Graham and Ted Robert Gurr, eds., 1979. Richard Maxwell Brown, "Historical Patterns of American Violence," in *Violence in America,* Hugh Davis Graham and Ted Robert Gurr, eds., 1979. Richard

Maxwell Brown, "The History of Extralegal Violence in Support of Community Values," in *Violence in America*, Thomas Rose, eds., 1979. J. Bowyer Bell and Ted Robert Gurr, "Terrorism and Revolution in America" in *Violence in America*, Hugh Davis Graham and Ted Robert Gurr, eds., 1979. David Bennett, *The Party of Fear: From Nativist Movements to The New Right in American History*, 1988. Leonard J. Moore, *Citizen Klansmen: The Ku Klux Klan in Indiana, 1921–1928*, 1991. Eric Foner and Olivia Mahoney, *America's Reconstruction: People and Politics After the Civil War*, 1995. Kenneth S. Stern, *A Force Upon the Plain: The American Militia Movement and the Politics of Hate*, 1996.   —Abigail A. Kohn

PARIS, TREATY OF (1783). The Treaty of Paris, signed on 3 September 1783, ended the American Revolutionary War and represented a major diplomatic triumph for the young nation. Following the decisive victory of the American and French forces at the Battle of *Yorktown (1781), the British recognized that they could not defeat the rebellious colonists on the battlefield. After a change of government brought in a ministry devoted to ending the conflict, the British opened talks with the delegates from the Continental Congress: John *Adams, John Jay, and Benjamin Franklin. The Americans declined the guidance of their French allies and negotiated their own settlement, signing the initial articles on 30 November 1782. The final document was agreed to by all parties in September 1783. The treaty recognized the independence of the United States, generously fixed its western boundary at the Mississippi River (a move that doubled the size of the United States), and gave the new country fishing rights off Newfoundland. The United States agreed to terminate reprisals against loyalists and to return their property.

The Continental Congress ratified the pact in 1784. Issues arising from the treaty would trouble Anglo-American relations in the 1790s, but the team of Adams, Franklin, and Jay had made the most of what their countrymen had won in the battles of the Revolution.

[*See also* Franco-American Alliance; Revolutionary War: Military and Diplomatic Course.]

• Jonathan R. Dull, *A Diplomatic History of the American Revolution*, 1985. Ronald Hoffman and Peter Albert, eds., *Peace and the Peacemakers: The Treaty of 1783*, 1986.   —Lewis L. Gould

PARIS, TREATY OF (1898). The Treaty of Paris, signed on 20 December 1898, between Spain and the United States, ended one war and set the stage for another. Following the U.S. military victories at Manila Bay in May 1898 and in Cuba in early July, Madrid asked for an armistice that began in August. Peace negotiations followed in Paris, the main sticking point being the future of the Philippine Islands, a Spanish colony since 1564. President William *McKinley insisted that Spain cede sovereignty to the United States. The treaty gave the United States temporary control over Cuba (Congress had rejected annexation in the *Teller Amendment when it declared war) and actual possession of Puerto Rico, Guam, and the Philippines. Spain received $20 million.

The U.S. Senate ratified the treaty in February 1899 by one vote more than the necessary two-thirds. By that time, some Filipino nationalists, angry at U.S. intentions, had launched attacks that opened the *Philippine War, which lasted several years, became a bitter guerrilla struggle, and ended in defeat for the native fighters. The Treaty of Paris marked the high tide of late nineteenth-century colonialism in the United States. The euphoria of victory over Spain turned into significant popular unhappiness and doubt about a protracted war against the Filipinos.

[*See also* Caribbean and Latin America, U.S. Military Involvement in; Cuba, U.S. Military Involvement in; Spanish-American War.]

• Lewis L. Gould, *The Presidency of William McKinley*, 1980.
—Lewis L. Gould

PARIS PEACE AGREEMENT (1973). The "Agreement on Ending War and Restoring Peace to Vietnam," signed in Paris, 27 January 1973, concluded America's direct military participation in the Vietnam War. Following a decade of conflict and abortive negotiations, only in October 1972 did North Vietnam signal readiness to accept a cease-fire, return U.S. *prisoners of war (POWs), and allow negotiations among the Vietnamese parties. President Richard M. *Nixon had been gradually withdrawing U.S. combat forces since June 1969 so that he could engage in detente with the Soviet Union and normalization of relations with the People's Republic of China. Nixon's aim was to reach an accord that would allow South Vietnam to defend itself in the hope that attacks from North Vietnam would lessen over time. The aim of the Communist government in Hanoi was to force the cessation of all U.S. military activity in order to position Communist forces (which had suffered severe losses in 1968–72) for renewed hostilities later.

"Backchannel" negotiations between Nixon's national security adviser, Henry *Kissinger, and the special adviser to the North Vietnamese Politburo, Le Duc Tho, took place in 1970–71. On 8 October 1972, Hanoi offered a draft in which, according to Kissinger, the North Vietnamese "dropped their demand for a coalition government" and for the removal of the South Vietnamese leaders. Nixon temporarily halted the bombing of North Vietnam. But Kissinger failed to convince South Vietnamese president Nguyen Van Thieu to accept the text or Hanoi's timetable. On 26 October, Kissinger declared that since Washington and Hanoi were close to a final agreement, "peace is at hand." He spoke also of further negotiations to accommodate Saigon's objections, but refused to elaborate. After Nixon was reelected, further talks with Hanoi led nowhere, convincing Kissinger to cable President Nixon to "increase pressure enormously through bombing and other means."

U.S. round-the-clock bombing, including the use of B-52 *bomber aircraft, began on 18 December. The attacks ended 30 December and negotiations resumed in early January 1973. On 27 January, the agreement was signed in Paris—although on separate pages in order to accommodate Nguyen Van Thieu's refusal to recognize the political status of Hanoi's arm in the South, the Provisional Revolutionary Government of the Republic of South Vietnam (PRG). President Nixon also secretly indicated to Hanoi that the United States was prepared to consider supporting a postwar reconstruction program, assuming the peace held.

The agreement provided for an immediate, internationally supervised cease-fire, the withdrawal of all foreign military forces from South Vietnam, the exchange of POWs, limitations on what military assistance could be provided to Communist and non-Communist forces in the South, and formation of a National Council of Reconciliation and Concord.

Kissinger and Tho were jointly awarded the Nobel Peace Price for 1973, but the latter declined to accept it. The agreement met with skepticism both in the United States and in South Vietnam, where there was much bitterness that the United States had abandoned its ally. By the fall of 1973, the cease-fire was being violated on both sides, local Communist forces refused to cooperate in the search for U.S. soldiers listed as missing in action, and high-level U.S.–North Vietnamese contacts ceased. The Paris Peace Agreement was swiftly overtaken by a "postwar war."

[See also Bombing of Civilians; Vietnam War: Military and Diplomatic Course; Vietnam War: Changing Interpretations.]

• Allan E. Goodman, *The Lost Peace: America's Search for a Negotiated Settlement of the Vietnam War,* 1978. William S. Turley, *The Second Indochina War: A Short Political and Military History,* 1986. David L. Anderson, ed., *Shadow on the White House: Presidents and the Vietnam War, 1945–1975,* 1993. —Allan E. Goodman

PATRIOTISM, in the most elementary sense of the term (the word derives from the Latin *patria* or "fatherland"), suggests the loyalty that all citizens owe to their country or nation. With varying degrees of intensity, nearly all Americans claim to be patriotic citizens of the republic. But the term also has a narrower, more specific history, with sharper political implications. In the two centuries since the *Revolutionary War, patriotism has tended to shift from a left-wing to a right-wing cause.

The term first achieved prominence in Anglo-American politics during the second quarter of the eighteenth century. The British ministry of Sir Robert Walpole, which admitted only Whigs to office and castigated all Tories as disloyal to the Hanoverian dynasty, alienated a number of prominent Whigs, who took the name "Patriots" to distinguish themselves from the Tory opposition. But some prominent Tories, such as Henry St. John, Viscount Bolingbroke, saw an opportunity to create a combined Tory and Whig opposition strong enough to topple Walpole, and also appropriated the label "Patriot" for that goal. By 1750, even Frederick, Prince of Wales, claimed to be a patriot prince, an ambition he bequeathed to his son, who inherited the throne as *George III in 1760. To everyone invoking a patriot identity, the label implied placing loyalty to one's country ahead of personal interest or factional causes.

North American spokesmen jubilantly hailed the accession of George III as a "Patriot King," only to find that his ministers threatened their liberties through direct parliamentary taxation of the colonies. As the resistance movement gained coherence and grew more militant, its members called themselves "Sons of Liberty," "Whigs," and "Patriots." Their enemies were "Tories," who preferred the softer name of "Loyalists." The launching of American independence identified American patriots as republicans and enemies of monarchy, a radical position in the eighteenth century that would become associated with "left" politics during the French Revolution a few years later. That association persisted into the early national period. Democratic-Republicans called their opponents "Tories" and "monocrats" (champions of monarchy), not "Federalists." By 1800, the Federalists seemed to oblige them by increasingly refusing to celebrate the Fourth of July (they preferred Washington's Birthday as their national festival) and above all by refusing to read the Declaration of Independence in public lest it offend Great Britain. Well into the nineteenth century, the term *patriot* retained these radical associations.

The *veterans' movements that followed the *Civil War probably marked a shift toward a more conservative definition of *patriot.* In the former Confederate states, secret paramilitary societies such as the Ku Klux Klan drew heavily on Confederate veterans and their younger kin to undermine Radical *Reconstruction through terrorist acts. They saw themselves as patriots committed to "redeeming" the South for white supremacy from "black Republican" rule. The Union counterpart was much less militant, but over time the veterans' group known as the *Grand Army of the Republic grew less eager to celebrate emancipation and more inclined to glory in the triumph of the Union, while agitating for bonuses and other veterans' benefits.

That trend has continued in the twentieth century. *Veterans' organizations, such as the *American Legion and the Veterans of Foreign Wars, have at times almost claimed a monopoly on American patriotism and have often questioned the loyalty of citizens who disagreed with their objectives. The word *patriot* was becoming strongly associated with the Right in politics, partly because the Left often advocated such internationalist causes as the republican side in the Spanish Civil War and decolonization movements after World War II, both of which also had strong Communist support.

The *Vietnam War sealed these identities. The Left opposed the war and tried to end it; the Right denounced such efforts as disloyal and appropriated all the symbols of American patriotism. By the 1972 presidential election, President Richard M. *Nixon, who had served in the U.S. Navy during World War II, but without seeing combat, successfully invoked his own patriotism while overwhelming his Democrat opponent, George McGovern, who had survived twenty-five missions as a bomber pilot in the European theater of World War II but never used his Army Air Force record to win votes in the campaign.

The label "Patriot," at least in its partisan sense, is recently shifting even further to the right. It has been actively appropriated by paramilitary militia movements around the country, which now seem to equate "Patriot" with white supremacy and a fierce hatred for most actions of the federal government. The ability to capture the label remains an important touchstone in American public life.

[See also Commemoration and Public Ritual; Culture, War, and the Military; Militarism and Antimilitarism; Nationalism; Public Opinion, War, and the Military; Religion and War.]

• Pauline Maier, *From Resistance to Revolution: Colonial Radicals and the Development of American Opposition to Britain, 1765–1776,* 1972. George C. Rable, *But There Was No Peace: The Role of Violence in the Politics of Reconstruction,* 1984. William Pencak, *For God & Country: The American Legion, 1919–1941,* 1989. Christine Gerrard, *The Patriot Opposition to Walpole: Politics, Poetry, and National Myth, 1725–1742,* 1994. Richard Abanes, *American Militias: Rebellion, Racism & Religion,* 1996. Simon P. Newman, *Parades and the Politics of the Street: Festive Culture in the Early American Republic,* 1997. —John M. Murrin

PATTON, GEORGE S. (1885–1945), U.S. Army general. A charismatic and flamboyant aristocrat, Patton excelled in training and leading soldiers into battle, obtaining the utmost from them, and employing them with audacity and speed against the enemy.

Descended from an old Virginia family and a pioneer Californian, Patton was born in San Gabriel, California. Afflicted with dyslexia as a child, he struggled to read and write and overcome his own feelings of worthlessness. After a year at the Virginia Military Academy, he graduated from West Point as a cavalry lieutenant in 1909. In 1910, he married Beatrice Ayer, daughter of a wealthy Boston family.

Patton was highly athletic as well as an outstanding fencer and horseman. In the Mexican Punitive Expedition in 1916, Patton served as an aide to John J. *Pershing, upon whom he modeled himself. In 1917, when the United States entered World War I, Patton accompanied Pershing to France, took command of the U.S. Army's light tank brigade, and led it at St. Mihiel and the *Meuse-Argonne offensive, where he was wounded.

During World War II, Patton headed the I Armored Corps in the successful invasion of *North Africa in November 1942. After the American defeat at Kasserine Pass, Patton was given command of the II Corps in Tunisia in March 1943. He quickly restored morale and won the Battle of El Guettar.

Patton's Seventh U.S. Army and Sir Bernard Law *Montgomery's Eighth British Army undertook the invasion of *Sicily in July 1943. Despite a subsidiary mission, Patton dashed to Palermo, then seized Messina ahead of Montgomery. Competition between the two generals then and later was largely inspired by the media, which contrasted Montgomery's caution with Patton's aggressiveness, backed by his ivory-handled pistols and scowling face.

In Sicily, Patton physically abused two sick soldiers he mistakenly believed were malingering. For his loss of personal control, he was reprimanded by Dwight D. *Eisenhower, who subsequently elevated Omar N. *Bradley, Patton's immediate subordinate, to be Patton's immediate superior in command of the 12th U.S. Army Group for the invasion of *Normandy.

Patton was used in England to deceive Adolf *Hitler about the place of the cross-Channel invasion. After the American breakthrough at *St. Lô, Patton's Third U.S. Army became operational on the Continent on 1 August 1944, and drove rapidly eastward and then north seeking to encircle most of the German troops in Normandy. Stopped from closing the Falaise pocket, Patton's forces swept across the Seine River and northeastern France.

Reacting to the German counterattack at the Battle of the *Bulge in December 1944, Patton pivoted the Third Army 90 degrees to the north, an extraordinary maneuver, and relieved the surrounded American forces at Bastogne. In March 1945, Patton crossed the Rhine and headed across southern Germany. When the war ended, his advance units were in Pilsen, Czechoslovakia, and he was a full, four-star general.

An outspoken critic of the Soviets and of postwar U.S. policies toward Germany, Patton failed as head of the occupation of Bavaria and was reassigned to command the Fifteenth U.S. Army. On 9 December 1945, near Mannheim, he was fatally injured in an automobile accident. He was the most aggressive senior American military commander in World War II and respected by the Germans as the best.

[See also France, Liberation of; Germany, Battle for; World War I: Military and Diplomatic Course; World War II: Military and Diplomatic Course.]

• Martin Blumenson, *The Patton Papers*, 2 vols., 1972, 1974. Martin Blumenson, *Patton: The Man Behind the Legend*, 1985. Carlo D'Este, *Patton: A Genius for War*, 1995.

—Martin Blumenson

PAX CHRISTI USA (1972–), an association of Roman Catholics committed to *nonviolence. Gordon Zahn, a sociologist and a Catholic conscientious objector during World War II, and Eileen Egan, an official in Catholic Relief Services, founded Pax Christi USA in 1972. They secured support from Bishop Thomas Gumbleton of Detroit and Bishop Carroll Dozier of Memphis, and then obtained affiliation with Pax Christi International. Pax Christi USA is organized in seven regions, with a national board, national assemblies, and a wide range of peace activities. By its twentieth anniversary in 1992, Pax Christi USA had over 12,000 members in 300 local chapters.

A turning point for the organization occurred from 1979 to 1982 under the leadership of Mary Evelyn Jegen, SND. She established a national executive council to establish policy, a newsletter, a press service, reflection/action groups, annual liturgies, vigils, and demonstrations. All of these activities kept the organization's aim of education for *peace in the forefront. She also maintained close contact with other Catholic groups as well as with broader *peace and antiwar movements, especially religious pacifist groups. While enabling all concerned Catholics to come together, she gradually moved the organization away from the "just war" tradition and toward *pacifism as the most viable Catholic attitude toward peacemaking.

Pax Christi USA's criticisms of U.S. government policies, particularly in the 1970s and 1980s, were more farreaching than those of mainline Catholics and the hierarchy. They focused on three main areas: the draft (until its end in 1973); Central America; and nuclear warfare, *arms control and disarmament. Pax Christi USA also focused attention on the National Conference of Catholic Bishops' pastoral letter on war and peace issues. When *The Challenge of Peace; God's Promise and Our Response* was issued (1983), Pax Christi USA affirmed it as the strongest moral renunciation of nuclear war and weaponry by any Catholic hierarchy, and vowed to assume responsibility for making the letter and its teachings known and accepted by the broader Catholic community.

[See also Conscientious Objection; Just War Theory; Nuclear Protest Movements; Vietnam Antiwar Movement.]

• *Pax Christi USA*, 17 (Spring–Summer 1992): Gerard Vanderhaar, "The Early Years: 1972–78," pp. 4–10; Patricia McNeal, "The Chicago Years 1979–1984," pp. 11–17, and "Erie Years 1985–Present," pp. 17–25. Patricia McNeal, *Harder Than War: Catholic Peace Making in Twentieth Century America*, 1992.

—Patricia McNeal

PEACE. Perhaps one of the most complex concepts in human history, peace has been used to refer to everything from "absence of war" to "equilibrium" to "a utopian state of spiritual and social harmony devoid of conflict." These widely differing images are indicators of essential differences in ideology, culture, and perceptions of history. Understanding peace requires an acknowledgment of these different contexts as well as a willingness to explore those meanings with which we are less familiar.

Ironically, the most familiar images of peace are perhaps the least helpful, as they consist of stereotypical assumptions that do not invite further examination of a complex phenomenon. These highly idealistic images generally depict peace either as the condition that exists when wars are suspended or terminated, or, conversely, as a harmonious world devoid of conflict. At best, such images provide faint shadows of peace rather than illuminate its essence. More often than not, they serve to lessen any interest in peace as a desirable or achievable state, either by devaluing it (a simple interlude between wars) or by ascribing unattainable, utopian preconditions to it (a world in total harmony without conflict).

Shadows of Peace. In the West, a common understanding of peace originates from the Latin *pax*, meaning "a pact or settlement to deter or end hostilities." This meaning arises primarily in historical, political, and military contexts, which appear to be closely related. Given the fascination of Western historians with war, it is understandable that many continue to envision human history as a series of wars and respites from wars, and salient historical figures as warriors, military leaders, or heads of state who declare and prosecute wars against other states. Within this context, peace has come to be narrowly understood as the absence of war, the end of war, interludes between wars, or nonwar.

Accordingly, in American military history, the word *peace* essentially means "the absence of war." Thus, militaries fight wars to "win the peace"—to bring about periods of nonwar through the use of force. In military paradigms, peace is seen as an ultimate or ideal goal rather than a means to an end. Those engaged in such wars tend to believe theirs will be the last, that the subsequent nonwar period of peace will be enduring, or that moments of nonwar are only interludes that will ultimately give way to future wars.

Related to this is what the Norwegian peace scholar Johan Galtung has termed *negative peace,* that is, the absence of war and "direct" violence. Under this kind of peace, many forms of "structural" violence (indirect, institutionalized violence) such as economic exploitation, racism, sexism, oppression, hunger, and poverty still exist.

Such narrow notions of peace say nothing about what peace is—only what peace *is not.* And they describe what it is not in terms of something with which we appear to be quite familiar: violence and war. Among other conclusions, we might infer from this that our knowledge about peace is at best very limited, since we seek to define it in terms of what it is not rather than what it is.

Related to this is the idyllic image of a world without conflict, pain, suffering, and struggle. Yet at all levels of human existence—from the interpersonal to the global—peace includes, rather than precludes, conflict. Conflict is a basic fact of life; thus, a world at peace will be full of conflict. What distinguishes a peaceful world, among other qualities, is the extent to which unnecessary conflict is prevented and all other conflict is managed in nonviolent ways. This idyllic image often arises out of a fundamental confusion surrounding conflict and violence. *Conflict* and *violence* are not synonymous terms: conflict can be violent, but it also can be nonviolent; it can be destructive and painful, but it also can be constructive and useful. Clarification of these concepts allows movement beyond the normative fear of conflict and negative associations with it. The existence of conflict in the future then becomes an understandable and acceptable fact of life, and the idyllic image of peace becomes unnecessary and unrealistic.

Although these shadow images of peace seem antithetical (i.e., they could be easily juxtaposed at opposite ends of a continuum depicting ideological views of peace), in fact, they have much in common with one another. Both types attempt to define peace in terms of (1) what is missing rather than what is present; and (2) one or two basic components (e.g., violence and conflict).

Once outside (Western) historical, political, and military contexts, however, peace means much more than the absence of a specific phenomenon, which it is not. For many scholars in peace studies and peace research, peace is much more than not-war; it is much more than not-violence; and it is never seen as not-conflict.

Essential Peace. If, instead, we begin with equally valid definitions of *pax*—and with *pacific* (from the Latin *pacifico* and *pacificus,* and the French *pacifique*)—we see a different face of peace altogether: one involving reaching agreement by negotiation (as opposed to the use of force); mediation; reconciliation; amity; calm; tranquility; or order—even "rejecting force as a means of achieving policy objectives." Here it is important to acknowledge that peace can exist at every level of existence, from the intrapersonal (psychological, spiritual, etc.) to the global (political, sociological, environmental). Thus, generic definitions of peace become extremely problematic. Nonetheless, there is general agreement in peace research and peace studies on the broad parameters of peace.

Some peace researchers approach an understanding of what peace is by identifying the conditions necessary for it to exist. The following ideological and infrastructural conditions are not exhaustive by any means, but represent what many experts believe to be essential for peace to develop in the world: the presence of cultures of peace (vs. cultures of violence); the presence of justice (economic, social, and political); the shared democratic use of power (economic, social, and political) among people who govern themselves ("power with") rather than the governance of the many by the few who have "power over" the many; the presence of economic and ecological sustainability; the nonviolent (vs. violent) management and resolution of conflict; the development of common security that does not rely on the threat or use of violence; the pursuit of collective and individual ends through *nonviolence rather than violence; and the elimination of violence in all its myriad forms (including the "war systems" inherent in many nations). Each of these conditions requires a brief explanation.

The *presence of cultures of peace* refers to the social and cultural components (values, belief systems, ideologies, philosophies, theories, societal norms, etc.) that undergird and legitimate everyday life and the infrastructures we create to carry us into the future. Wars are not fought without ideologies that tell us that it is acceptable and justifiable to conduct them. The ubiquitous violence that exists in the media, in entertainment, in our schools, in our streets, and in our homes does not exist without belief systems that legitimate and encourage it. Similarly, peaceful relationships among individuals, groups, genders, classes, nations—as well as relationships between human beings and the rest of the nonhuman world—cannot exist without cultural values and ideologies that promote nonviolence, respect, and tolerance for everyone, especially those who are somehow different from us. In a culture of peace, for example, people would not be entertained by violence (nor would they seek to be entertained by it).

A fundamental ideological cornerstone of the violence surrounding us today is the idea that one's identity is primarily related to one's gender, race, national origin, political affiliation, economic status, religious ideology, or socioeconomic class. The result of this kind of *identity formation* is the grouping of people into "us" and "them." Once a person or an ethnic group or a country is a "them," they are less valuable, less important, and somehow less human than "us." This is the first step toward dehumanizing "the other," which in turn is the first step toward *aggression and violence. Cultures of violence inculcate ideologies that give rise to the formation of these kinds of mutually exclusive identities. Cultures of peace, on the other hand, would embrace "species identity" and other inclusive forms of identifications with humanity, which Elise Boulding and Robert Jay Lifton have so eloquently examined in their research and writings.

The *presence of justice* at all levels (economic, social, and political) refers to the ways in which individuals and groups are treated by society and one another. While *justice* is a highly debated term, there is little disagreement that peace can exist without it. In particular, this is true because the existence of injustice implies ongoing structural violence against certain peoples or groups. As Johan Galtung notes, the Greek *eirene*, the Hebrew *shalom*, and the Arab *salam* take us beyond the Roman *pax* to an understanding of peace that includes "justice." In this view, peace is not only the absence of all violence (including underlying structures of violence) but also the presence of justice (Galtung calls this *positive peace*).

The *shared democratic use of power* is relevant to all personal and social relationships, but especially to those in the arenas of governance, business, international relations, and global security. In his groundbreaking work *Three Faces of Power*, the American economist Kenneth Boulding identifies three basic forms of power ("threat," "exchange," and "integrative" power) and argues that integrative power is the most important of the three, as it is what gives rise to relationships of respect, love, friendship, and so on.

The *presence of economic and ecological sustainability* is essential because economic or ecological development that is not sustainable assumes dysfunctional levels of injustice and violence in the present moment and ultimately will lead to conflict, violence, and systemic imbalance. A peaceful world requires basic levels of security, which are ensured, in part, by stable economic systems and viable ecological relationships with the natural world.

The remaining four conditions fall within the category of *nonviolence*. While *nonviolence* can refer to anything (change, transformation, revolution) that happens not to be violent (as in the case of "nonprincipled nonviolence"), this term is used most often in peace studies to refer to the waging of conflict and the transformation of society through the power of active love. Mahatma Gandhi's nonviolence (*ahimsa* and *satyagraha*) was "the pursuit of truth through love." The strength of nonviolence emanates from an understanding of the origins of power: all power derives from the consent of the governed. The political scientist Gene Sharp carefully explains that known histories of successful nonviolent struggle and conflict resolution date back to the fifth century B.C.

Peace requires the nonviolent management and resolution of conflicts for many reasons, not least of which is found in the shadow of peace, which defines peace as the absence of violence. *Violence* (from the Latin verb *violare*) means "to violate." Violence can be verbal, psychological, emotional, and spiritual—as well as physical. It can be collective as well as individual.

As Duane Friesen makes clear, to do violence to someone is to violate the integrity of that person. Gandhi saw life as one long "experiment with truth," wherein each person possesses a small piece of the truth and conflicts are the moments in which we learn from one another about our separate and collective truths. Waging conflicts violently, then, is the antithesis of being interested in the truth; it is a means to "win" a conflict temporarily—not to be right in the long run. For most in peace studies, violence cannot be seen as conflict resolution: it is, instead, only the violent waging of conflict for reasons that are legitimated by cultures of violence.

For the same reasons that nonviolent conflict resolution is necessary, peace also requires the development of nonviolent systems of common security; the nonviolent pursuit of collective and individual ends; and, ultimately, the elimination of all forms of violence, whether direct or indirect. Thus, for example, personal growth and individual success, interpersonal relationships, social change and transformation, and the conduct of international relations will need to be reenvisioned as nonviolent means and ends rather than accepted as status quo violent means and ends.

Peace Development. In the languages of Western culture, *peace* is a noun, not a verb. It is an object, a goal, a future state of being to be passively wished for and waited upon. No one "does" peace. Yet peace, like *war, requires intensive preparation, organization, training, and education. It also requires immense resources and commitment. Peace will not exist without being developed and built from the ground up.

Peace development requires leaders: those who can envision a world without violence and design its blueprints. Peace development also requires actors who will transform the elements of nonpeace into the fabric of peace. The shadow of peace assumes that geopolitical entities called *nation-states* are the fundamental units of analysis, and that the political and military leaders of these nation-states are the primary actors and leaders. The development of essential peace, on the other hand, is not limited to nation-states and their leaders. Rather, essential peace requires the effort of individuals, communities, local and regional governments, teachers, nongovernmental organizations, international nongovernmental organizations, networks, and the nontraditional loci of nonviolent power.

Since essential peace can exist at all levels of existence, from the spiritual to the global, the paths to its successful development are many: there is no one "right" path to peace and there is no one "right" leader who will take us to it. This awareness allows for everyone to contribute to the building of peace in their lives and in their communities. According to many Eastern religions and philosophies, peace at all levels of existence is interconnected. Therefore, the development of peace in one arena of the world may contribute to the development of peace in many arenas of the world.

[*See also* Pacifism; Peace and Antiwar Movements; Quakers.]

• Louis Fischer, *The Life of Mahatma Gandhi*, 1950. Mohandas K. Gandhi, *An Autobiography: The Story of My Experiments with Truth*, 1957. Joan V. Bondurant, *Conquest of Violence: The*

Gandhian Philosophy of Conflict, 1958. Gene Sharp, *The Politics of Nonviolent Action*, 3 vols., 1973. Ira Sandperl, *A Little Kinder*, 1974. Kenneth Boulding, *Stable Peace*, 1978. James A. Schellenberg, *The Science of Conflict*, 1982. Duane Friesen, *Christian Peacemaking and International Conflict: A Realist Pacifist Perspective*, 1986. Ervin Laszlo and Jong Youl Yoo, eds., *World Encyclopedia of Peace*, 1986, 1989. Robert J. Lifton, *The Future of Immortality and Other Essays for a Nuclear Age*, 1987. Elise Boulding, *Building a Global Civic Culture: Education for an Interdependent World*, 1988. Sissela Bok, *A Strategy for Peace*, 1989. Kenneth Boulding, *Three Tales of Power*, 1989. David P. Barash, *Introduction to Peace Studies*, 1991. Michael Shuman and Julia Sweig, eds., *Conditions of Peace: An Inquiry*, 1991. Johan Galtung, *Oxford Companion to Politics of the WSVW*, 1993.

—Robin J. Crews

PEACE AND ANTIWAR MOVEMENTS. Members of peace and antiwar movements have commonly seen their cause as the antithesis of military force and war. In the context of evolving social values and institutions, however, military and nonviolent responses to conflict and insecurity may also be seen in a dialectical relationship with one another. Both approaches have changed markedly during the past two centuries. Taken together, military and nonviolent approaches to conflict are interrelated facets of societal and cultural change. Considered separately, organized *peace efforts have affected military institutions, policies, and values by challenging specific conflicts and by advancing alternatives to war.

The legal terms of *conscription, the mobilizing of human resources for military ends, changed because of the exigencies of modern warfare and also in response to civilian pressures, first from religious groups and then from secular ones. Moreover, from mid-nineteenth century on, organized peace advocates in Europe and the United States helped to build constraints on the conduct of war into international law and to legitimate mediation and arbitration as alternatives to warfare. They challenged the cultural glorification and romantization of warfare, especially in the context of disillusionment following World War I. Some peace advocates opposed military-based imperialism. Many promoted international organization, hoping to secure change with order at the interstate level. Some of them endorsed collective military security under international auspices, and many promoted *arms control and disarmament in order to limit military confrontation. There were even experiments with alternative missions for the military. Finally, challenges from organized peace advocates affected public policy on specific wars, notably in the debates over intervention in World Wars I and II, and on the terms of withdrawal from Vietnam. In all these respects, the influence of citizen groups on policy governing war and military institutions has been conditioned by their organizational bases and rationales.

Peace and antiwar movements derive from at least three sets of complex historical phenomena with varying sources, principles, goals, and constituencies. Two of them have roots in the ancient and medieval world: modern peace advocacy, which inherited and adapted the "Just War" tradition, and absolute *pacifism as expressed in religious nonresistance. A third source of antimilitarism has been grounded in modern political economy.

Regional economic and political interests characterized opposition to some specific U.S. wars—New England Federalists in the *War of 1812, for example; northern Whigs in the *Mexican War of 1846–48; Northern Peace Demo-

crats and Southern Democrats in the *Civil War—but regional economic groupings were not against war per se, and they are not normally included in histories of peace movements. Some economic movements were very much related to organized peace advocacy, though: the free trade campaigns of Richard Cobden and John Bright; anti-imperialism in Britain and the United States; socialist class consciousness; and a pervasive suspicion of banking and business interests such as that which surfaced in the "merchants of death" rhetoric of the 1930s.

Nonetheless, the primary carriers of antiwar ideology and action have been religious nonresistants and internationalist peace advocates. In this regard, it is useful to delimit the word *pacifists*. Coined in Europe at the turn of the century, it originally referred to all those who sought to mitigate, limit, and eventually end warfare through various forms of *internationalism. During World War I, however, *pacifist* was increasingly narrowed to denote those who on grounds of principle refused altogether to sanction war or participate in it. The word retains that sense in common American usage, although the broader sense is sanctioned by dictionaries and is common in European usage. For the purpose of this essay, the broad program of creating alternatives to war is called *peace advocacy*, while *pacifism* is used in its narrower sense, as the rejection of war or military service altogether.

Such pacifism has characterized the so-called peace churches—the Mennonites, Brethren, and Society of Friends (*Quakers). They cultivated a religious commitment to refuse military service and to reject warfare, *aggression and violence being the way of the unredeemed world. Quaker principles including religious rejection of violence were broadly influential in eighteenth-century England and America. In 1815, following the Napoleonic Wars and the *War of 1812, religious nonresistance was given an institutional base in the London, New York, and Massachusetts peace societies. The constituency of the Massachusetts society was limited to Christian nonresistants, and it soon waned; the London and New York societies included a broad spectrum of peace advocates, and they endured. In the United States, the peace cause achieved national status when the *American Peace Society was formed in 1829 (although in fact it remained essentially northern). Indeed, Charles DeBenedetti interprets the peace movement as the longest continuous American reform movement.

Constraining Military Institutions and Missions. Twentieth-century U.S. military institutions and missions were to some extent constrained by organized peace advocacy and nonresistant pacifism, the clearest impact of which was with respect to the administration of conscription.

The nonresistance tenet of Quakers, Mennonites, Brethren, and members of some other sects had been tested during the *Civil War, and it divided them. In the Confederacy, conscientious objectors (COs) to military service were persecuted and deprived. In the Union, objection on the basis of religious authority was recognized through military exemption, subject to various conditions such as the payment of fines.

The World War I provision for COs under the Selective Service System was based on the Civil War precedent and on prevailing British policy. It was implemented, however, largely in response to pressure from the peace churches, other pacifists, and the National Civil Liberties Bureau (subsequently *American Civil Liberties Union), which pacifists created. There were about 4,000 COs in World War I (about .001% of all men inducted). Exemption was limited to members of recognized sects and organizations in which war in any form was rejected on principle, and it applied only to combat service. Excluded were men whose principles forbade military service itself, whose position was based on a mainstream religious conviction or on secular principles, or who objected to a particular war but not necessarily all wars. Such men, if they persisted in their resistance, were confined in army camps or imprisoned, except for a small number who were furloughed for civilian work.

In anticipation of U.S. entry into World War II, conscription was modified, again largely in response to organized pressure from peace churches and other pacifist groups (aligned as the National Service Board for Religious Objectors). The government formed a working arrangement with them to administer Civilian Public Service projects for men whose objection was based on religious training and belief. They were assigned to projects of so-called national importance such as conservation, hospital service, and farming. The work projects were ill defined, and no provision was made for secular objectors or those who rejected the system of military service itself, so that the pacifist coalition experienced dissension and withdrawals. Still, Civilian Public Service administered camps and other service units for about 11,000 COs who came from some 200 religious bodies or had no religious affiliation.

After World War II, the peace churches and other pacifist groups lobbied for a broad, tolerant interpretation of *conscientious objection. They also led a mainstream coalition that defeated President Harry S. *Truman's proposal for universal military service. By that time, exemption from military service on the grounds of conscientious objection had become a legal right that subsequently was broadened by the courts to include both religious and secular principles. During the *Vietnam War, several pacifist organizations and some churches even endorsed so-called selective conscientious objection to specific wars (on the basis of Just War tradition), while thousands of men made the draft the focal point of demonstrable antiwar resistance. When President Richard M. *Nixon ended conscription in favor of a voluntary military, the decision was at least as much political as it was professional.

The history of conscientious objection most clearly registers the impact of religious nonresistance and absolute pacifism on the military institution of conscription, but it also illustrates the secularization of principled objection, the broadening provisions of the law, and finally the focusing of antiwar activism both on the legitimacy of a specific war and on military conscription in general.

Peace advocacy, a broader tradition than religious nonresistance, addressed the apparent anarchy of the nation-state system in an age of growing economic, intellectual, and political interdependence. Peace advocates came from the rising professional classes of the nineteenth and twentieth centuries. They focused on incremental steps to undercut the idealization of war, and they developed approaches to conflict that might eventually supplant warfare, in particular: international law including a law of war, mediation, arbitration, and international organization.

One approach was to restrict the conduct of war through international conventions. By 1873, when international law associations appeared (in large measure the work of peace activists), the laws of war had been defined in the 1864 international convention of Geneva. As subsequently revised and widely ratified, the *Geneva Conventions on warfare demonstrated that even when locked in battle, governments had a mutual interest in the welfare of their respective military and civilian personnel. Twentieth-century conventions proscribed specific classes of weapons (such as poison gas) and acts of war (such as massacre of the defenseless). The fact that such conventions have been violated only underscores the existence of international norms that influence military conduct. Wars of aggression were prohibited by the 1928 Kellogg-Briand Pact (which owed its existence to initiative taken by peace advocate and internationalist James T. Shotwell). Although widely denigrated as a futile gesture, the Kellogg-Briand Pact was cited along with other international law as grounds for the Nuremberg War Trials following World War II.

Related to international law was the process of arbitration, for which there was an international campaign before the Civil War. The idea acquired prestigious support in both the British Parliament and the U.S. Senate. Spurred by the arbitral settlement of the *Alabama* case (1872), the campaign expanded to other nations, notably Switzerland and France. Delegates to the intergovernmental Hague Peace Conference of 1899 drew upon plans articulated by peace and lawyers' associations when they endorsed mediation and arbitration in a "Convention for the Pacific Settlement of International Disputes" and created the Permanent Court of Arbitration. In the decade before World War I, arbitration was a rallying point for proliferating peace societies in Europe and America.

World War I dramatized the value of permanent international organization, and arbitration became the key to *League of Nations procedures for conflict resolution. This vision of the League was largely a result of organized peace advocacy, mainly British and American. Its charter invoked the threat of diplomatic, economic, and even military sanctions to ensure that nations would attempt mediation and arbitration before resorting to war. Those provisions predicated a change in military mission from unilateral to collective security. The change was not institutionalized by the United States, which rejected League membership, or even in Europe, where League members failed to link the pacific resolution of conflict to disarmament and collective security.

World War II was a consequence of that failure, and out of the *United Nations alliance there emerged a UN organization with strengthened collective security provisions. By the time they were invoked, however, the world had become polarized in a cold war, so that even the UN-sanctioned *Korean War was actually a U.S.-based alliance system. The experience of peacetime military alliances such as *NATO no doubt expanded the political dimensions of military command, while at the same time the United Nation experimented with limited *peacekeeping operations, sometimes in conjunction with initiatives from nongovernmental organizations. By the end of the century, arbitration and mediation enforced with sanctions had become established procedures in international conflict—so much so that during the *Bosnian Crisis in the 1990s, U.S. troops were deployed within a multinational military force to enforce a mediated settlement in a civil war in which *war crimes were explicitly recognized and condemned.

All this is to suggest that organized peace advocacy contributed to changes in the conduct of war and in military mission insofar as it helped to initiate and shape international law on the conduct of war, arbitration and other processes of conflict resolution, and international organization—including even the threat of collective force. This is not to suggest a simple cause-and-effect relationship, but rather to note that citizen activism has been one of the factors shaping modern international and military systems.

Constraining Foreign and Military Policy. Peace and antiwar movements have constrained U.S. policy on the use of military force in at least three respects: intervention in foreign wars; disarmament and arms control; and unilaterally initiated warfare. In a political context, modern peace advocacy must be distinguished from *isolationism. Both peace advocates in the general sense and progressive pacifists have been overwhelmingly internationalist insofar as they advocated U.S. leadership in economic and peace efforts; but when faced with the prospect of war, they have divided between neutralist nonintervention and reluctant support for military forces. In any case, the controversy over U.S. intervention in World War I established the rationale and organizational basis for subsequent peace and antiwar campaigns.

By 1914, there was an established peace movement in the United States that was part of an international phenomenon. Its leadership came primarily from middle-class professionals; but a major sponsor and chief financial constituency was the business community, which provided backing for groups like the American Peace Society, the *Carnegie Endowment for International Peace, the World Peace Foundation, and active local peace societies in New York and Chicago. Those groups had friends in the foreign policy establishment as well as in business. Many of them avoided controversial measures like Theodore *Roosevelt's enlargement of the navy, and supported arbitration, conciliation, and international law. They were internationalists who valued order and stability on a world scale, which they thought would come through good management: commerce and communication, cultural understanding, the cultivation of mutual interests, and a prudent use of power.

The fury with which Europe was swept into war in 1914 profoundly shocked these peace advocates. A few of them concluded with Hamilton Holt, editor of *The Independent*, a progressive journal of the time, that internationalism needed an authoritative international base, which they promoted through the Association for a League to Enforce Peace (1915). Most established peace advocates avoided political issues, however, especially the question of intervening in the European War. When the country did intervene, the established movement overwhelmingly supported what was billed as the "war to end war."

The resulting vacuum of leadership left space for new peace leaders. They were progressives accustomed to political action, who viewed the informed middle class as their primary constituency, and who included outstanding women reformers like Jane *Addams and Lillian Wald. They proposed to end the war through mediation, and they resisted the sharply increased military budget recommended by President Woodrow *Wilson. The campaign for mediation was promoted especially by the Woman's

Peace Party (1915) in active cooperation with European women (the basis for the *Women's International League for Peace and Freedom, 1919). The idea was for the United States to lead a neutral bloc of nations in a standing offer to mediate a peace settlement. Meanwhile, the American Union against Militarism (1915) coordinated a political campaign against President Wilson's military preparedness program, arguing that preparation for war would make military intervention more likely. Two other constituencies completed the new peace advocacy: absolute pacifists from mainstream denominations joined the American *Fellowship of Reconciliation (FOR, 1915), while the Socialist Party of America articulated a strong antiwar position. A coalition of these elements tried to rally opposition to intervention as late as the spring of 1917. The political significance of this politically active coalition was to reinforce American *neutrality by reconciling it with an internationalist orientation and to distinguish military intervention from other forms of engagement abroad.

In wartime, the new progressive peace advocacy was reduced to absolute pacifists, many of whom found refuge in the FOR, and adamant socialists whose antiwar position gave their opponents an excuse for political persecution. Even nonpacifist critics of war policies became politically vulnerable and socially alienated. Thomas Knock has concluded that the wartime administration alienated those very constituencies, like progressive peace advocates and socialists, whose support Wilson needed to carry the League of Nations to victory.

The significance of the antiwar movement of 1914–19, then, was twofold. In the first place, the establishment-oriented prewar peace movement became divided between what might be called conservative and liberal internationalists: the former supported commercial and cultural involvement abroad but clung to political unilateralism; the latter advocated membership in the League of Nations and the World Court. This division was carried into the politics of the postwar era. Secondly, organized peace advocacy acquired a progressive leadership that distinguished military intervention from internationalism per se and created an organizational base for politically oriented pacifists.

That base became operational in the context of the Washington Conference on Naval Arms Limitation (1921–22). Pacifists and peace advocates formed the National Council for Prevention of War (1921) as an agency for information on the conference, and it became an ongoing lobby on disarmament and peace issues. In turn, it developed a citizen network that included constituencies like the League of Women Voters, Future Farmers of America, church denominations, and the YMCA-YWCA, as well as peace groups. The Women's International League for Peace and Freedom, although part of the National Council, put its own lobbyist (Dorothy Detzer) on Capitol Hill. Public pressure was generated against military spending and for international disarmament efforts such as the League-sponsored conference of 1932. Separate committees mobilized opposition to military training in schools and colleges. Thus, peace advocates acquired a political role in the 1920s. Their influence was proportionate to their unity of purpose, however, and the constituent groups in the movement differed sharply over the priorities of the League of Nations, the World Court, international law, disarmament, and peace education.

That changed in the next decade. Beginning with the

Japanese invasion of Manchuria in 1931, war threatened Asia and Europe, while the nations that dominated League policy proved unable to coordinate a collective security response. In consequence, the various elements of the U.S. peace movement forged a common front that briefly united liberal internationalists with progressive pacifists.

Pacifists in the National Council, Women's International League, and FOR played key roles in organizing and popularizing the 1934 Senate investigation of the munitions industry's role in World War I (the Nye Committee), thus tapping into a longstanding populist identification of foreign war with special interests. The following year, the progressive pacifists mobilized political support for strict neutrality legislation. They also gained the initiative in the Emergency Peace Campaign (1936–37), a coalition forged with liberal internationalists of the League of Nations Association (which succeeded the League of Nations Non-Partisan Association in 1929). The basis of the coalition was a platform that included legislation to constrain special interests, reforms to open up and stabilize the world economy, closer cooperation with the League of Nations, and strict neutrality (an impartial embargo against trade and credit on all belligerents). Strict neutrality was valued by pacifists, who hoped that it would prevent U.S. military intervention, and by liberal internationalists, who assumed that it would assure the League powers of U.S. noninterference with strong collective security measures. Once more, then, neutralism was coupled with internationalism to define U.S. military policy. Strict neutrality legislation was adopted in 1935 and refined two years later.

By 1937, the Emergency Peace Campaign was breaking apart. Liberal internationalists like Clark Eichelberger and James T. Shotwell had grown increasingly uncomfortable with strict neutrality and absolute pacifism. In 1938, they broke with pacifists over the proposed Ludlow constitutional amendment for a referendum on war. Creating their own political coalition, they campaigned against that legislation, for neutrality revision, and after 1939 for all aid to the European Allies "short of war." In 1940, their group coalesced into the Committee to Defend America by Aiding the Allies. For a brief time, on the other side, pacifists found themselves uncomfortably aligned with isolationists such as the America First Committee; by 1941 pacifists had largely left the political arena to strengthen their own non-resistant communities for wartime trial, especially regarding COs.

Thus, in order to understand the divisions and realignments over national policy on the use of military force in the decade before 1941, it is necessary to appreciate several things: the distinction within the peace movement between neutralism and isolation; the shift of liberal internationalists from neutralism to wartime alliance (hopefully short of military deployment); and the resulting brief alignment of pacifist internationalists with isolationists, from which pacifists withdrew. Above all, it is important to remember that the policy debate was carried on within the broad peace movement, and that the League of Nations wing consciously functioned as a political ally of the Roosevelt administration, from at least 1939 on.

The political role of liberal internationalists extended into wartime because the administration explicitly relied on them—as by then a well-organized coalition—to build public consensus for a United Nations organization. Growing out of the military exigencies of the UN alliance,

the United Nations was thus subject to both the geopolitical apprehensions of political leaders and, in some measure, the internationalist expectations of a citizen peace movement. Moreover, much of the public hope invested in the United Nations was transferred to a new and Western alliance, NATO, as the United Nations became polarized in the *Cold War.

Public support for arms control and disarmament was generated by a resurgent peace movement that grew out of the nuclear *arms race fueled by the Cold War. This took place in two phases: the test ban movement of 1957–63, and the Nuclear Freeze Campaign of the early 1980s.

The test ban movement grew out of concern over the radioactive fallout from the atmospheric testing of *nuclear weapons by the United States, the Soviet Union, Britain, France, and China. It was initiated by *atomic scientists who challenged the sanguine assurances of the Atomic Energy Commission. As public apprehension rose, liberal internationalists like Norman Cousins joined progressive pacifists like Abraham J. *Muste in the *National Committee for a Sane Nuclear Policy (SANE, 1957). SANE mounted a strong program of national education and mobilized support for an international ban on the atmospheric testing of nuclear weapons. Meanwhile, some pacifists applied techniques of direct, nonviolent action with which they had experimented in race relations since 1942: they sailed into Pacific testing zones, picketed tests in the United States, and demonstrated at weapons-producing sites and elsewhere—not only against nuclear testing but for disarmament.

The test ban campaign lost a measure of focus when the Eisenhower administration and the Soviet Union put unilateral moratoriums on testing; but it continued to add organized public constituencies, notably women and young people. Those constituencies were activated when testing was resumed by both sides early in the Kennedy administration, soon under the threatening cloud of the *Cuban Missile Crisis. Norman Cousins personally helped pave the way for the negotiated treaty of 1963 banning atmospheric testing, and Kennedy recruited the SANE network to mobilize public support for ratification.

Nearly two decades later, and despite arms control agreements initiated by the Nixon administration, attempts to achieve detente between the Soviet Union and the United States broke down. A new round in the spiraling nuclear arms race began under President Jimmy *Carter and accelerated sharply under Ronald *Reagan. Large-scale protest gathered force in Europe, while in the United States a coalition of peace groups backed the idea of a mutual, verifiable freeze in nuclear weapons. Although coordinated by a national organization, the Nuclear Freeze Campaign, the freeze reflected grassroots activism that was elicited by growing public awareness of the destructive realities of a nuclear exchange. An important result of the Nuclear Freeze Campaign was to provide essential political support for arms control, which had been greatly weakened early in Reagan's administration. A second consequence was the existence of informed resistance to Reagan's *Strategic Defense Initiative, itself quite possibly a response to the popularity of the Freeze; and a third was to lay the groundwork for enthusiastic public support of the disarmament initiatives eventually worked out between Presidents Gorbachev and Reagan.

The *Vietnam War presented a different case of antiwar

opposition from the conflicts involving European Allies in the two world wars. It was different because, although initiated by the U.S., the 1965 air war against North Vietnam and the direct, massive engagements of U.S. troops in the South were not preceded by a period of extensive national debate. It was different in that national policy was challenged on a large scale during wartime.

After an initial period of strong public support, Lyndon B. *Johnson's administration faced growing, sullen resistance that became active political opposition in 1968. Richard M. *Nixon entered office as a peace candidate. Despite his withdrawal of U.S. troops under the policy of "Vietnamization," the fact that he continued the war through 1972 and in some respects expanded it into Laos and Cambodia elicited further organized opposition on the home front. Both presidents sought the support of the political center, and each attempted to push antiwar opposition to the political margin. Both administrations treated the *Vietnam antiwar movement as an alien force, despite the repetitive conclusion from major intelligence probes that even the movement's radical wing was independent of foreign or Communist direction. The unresponsiveness of the Johnson administration and active harassment under Nixon strengthened tendencies toward confrontational politics within the antiwar movement. Nonetheless, the political contest increasingly shifted from the streets to the Congress, as antiwar efforts were invested ever more in electoral politics and lobbying.

Opposition accompanied every step of the escalating war in Vietnam. It represented a shifting, unstable coalition of political, pacifist, and cultural currents in the 1960s. Still, the various parts of the coalition espoused one or more of five positions on the war: (1) that it was unfeasible, the cost not being justified by U.S. interests, and the United States not being able to impose self-government on Vietnam; (2) that it destabilized the region and distanced U.S. allies; (3) that the support of repressive government in the South undermined U.S. ideals and interests; (4) that in some measure it represented the arrogance of *imperial wars; and (5) that its level of destruction was immoral. Opposition to the war varied greatly in rationale and tactics.

At its core, the organized antiwar movement clustered around two poles. One was a very tenuous alliance of the surviving Old Left, a youthful New Left, and direct-action pacifists who folded opposition to war into their various agendas (for the Socialist Workers Party the war was a single issue, but they aligned with the diversified Left anyway). Their tactics included political confrontation: large-scale demonstrations, draft resistance, and civil disobedience; they attracted something of the counterculture, and the resulting media coverage largely stereotyped the whole movement in their image. This wing crested in 1968–69 and quickly declined thereafter. The other pole was an informal coalition of liberals with a single-issue antiwar focus. They were the initial source of "teach-ins" in the spring of 1965, and in the next few years they attracted numerous constituencies—from religion, labor, health care, sciences, and business. Their tactics were public education and debate, petitions, lobbying, and electoral politics. Increasingly, this wing of the movement moved into mainstream politics, into the Congress and the 1968 and 1972 presidential elections. In so doing, it lost a measure of visibility because the dominant media image of antiwar effort was street politics. Associated with the liberal wing, however, were growing antiwar veterans' groups—notably the Vietnam Veterans Against the War—that achieved a good deal of credible visibility by their public campaigns.

The movement cannot itself be credited or blamed for the withdrawal of public support from at least 1968 onward. It did, however, keep before the public the issue of whether the war in Vietnam was morally or practically acceptable. It probably exacerbated popular anxiety about social and cultural instability and linked it to the war. Taken quite seriously by Johnson and Nixon, organized opposition may well have elicited some of their duplicity and extralegal harassment. Certainly, it strengthened the congressional role in policymaking. In all these respects, antiwar protest helped to provide a check on the prosecution of war essentially on the terms of the executive branch.

About two decades later, in the 1980s, a fresh, largely grassroots coalition emerged in solidarity with Central American liberation movements, especially in Nicaragua, El Salvador, and Honduras. There were national organizations, notably the Committee in Solidarity with the People of El Salvador, or CISPIES (1980–81), which lobbied effectively with the Congress; but these were supplemented by a loose network of innumerable citizens' groups having contacts in Central America. Often the transnational contacts were along professional lines—farmers, lawyers, educators, editors, religious leaders, and politicians. The Solidarity movement, it was called, thus indicating its main focus and grassroots base.

This movement, and its lobbying agents, challenged the Reagan policies of aggressive support for the Nicaraguan Contras to overthrow the Sandinista revolution, and for the largely military government in El Salvador, which was fighting a revolutionary challenge. The history of the U.S. Solidarity movement has yet to be written; but it seems reasonably clear that it contributed significantly to congressional checks on presidential initiatives that were essentially, if covertly, military. In contrast to this, unilateral military force was employed suddenly and briefly in Panama and Grenada, perhaps on the understanding that quick closure would preclude political debate. Public discussion did foreshadow the *Persian Gulf War against Iraq; even so, military strategy there was designed to control information and avoid protracted engagement, and the war ended relatively quickly.

"No more Vietnams!" That phrase connotes positions that range from no more military intervention abroad to no more military operations subject to public debate and political pressure. In either case, it suggests the extent to which military institutions and missions are responsive to citizen pressure in a democratic society. Insofar as peace and antiwar movements have contributed to public attitudes and values, to alternative means of resolving international conflict, or to political constraints on the conduct of warfare, to that extent they have proved relevant to American military history.

[See also Grenada, U.S. Intervention in; Hague Peace Conferences; Just War Theory; Militarism and Antimilitarism; Nicaragua, U.S. Military Involvement in; Nye, Gerald; Panama, U.S. Military Involvement in; Veterans: Vietnam War; War Crimes.]

• Robert A. Devine, Second Chance: The Triumph of Internationalism in America During World War II, 1967. Sondra R. Herman, Eleven Against War: Studies in American Internationalist Thought,

1898–1921, 1969. Warren F. Kuehl, *Seeking World Order: The United States and International Organization to 1920*, 1969. Charles Chatfield, *For Peace and Justice: Pacifism in America, 1914–1922*, 1971. Roland Marchand, *The American Peace Movement, 1887–1914*, 1972. Charles DeBenedetti, *The Peace Reform*, 1980. Lawrence S. Wittner, *Rebels Against War: The American Peace Movement, 1933–1983*, 1984. Melvin Small, *Johnson, Nixon, and the Doves*, 1988. Charles DeBenedetti, with Charles Chatfield, *An American Ordeal: The Antiwar Movement of the Vietnam Era*, 1990. Charles F. Howlett, *The American Peace Movement: References and Resources*, 1991. John Whiteclay Chambers II, ed., *The Eagle and the Dove: The American Peace Movement and U.S. Foreign Policy, 1900–1922*, 2nd ed. 1991. Charles Chatfield, *The American Peace Movement: Ideals and Activism*, 1992. Thomas Knock, *To End All Wars*, 1992. Harriet Hyman Alonso, *Peace as a Women's Issue: A History of the U.S. Movement for World Peace and Women's Rights*, 1993. Robert Kleidman, *Organizing for Peace: Neutrality, the Test Ban, and the Freeze*, 1993. Lawrence Wittner, *One World or None: A History of the World Nuclear Disarmament Movement Through 1953*, 1993. Robert David Johnson, *The Peace Progressives and American Foreign Relations*, 1995.   —Charles Chatfield

PEACE HISTORY. *See* Disciplinary Views of War: Peace History.

PEACEKEEPING. One consequence of the end of the *Cold War and the demise of the Soviet Union was a burst of joint efforts aimed at resolving armed conflicts. Between 1990 and 1994, fifteen international peacekeeping operations were initiated through the *United Nations. At their peak in 1994, there were over twenty such active operations.

Modern peacekeeping efforts began with the *League of Nations, which employed military forces twice in Germany, in Upper Silesia (1921) and in the Saar (1935). One of the first UN efforts was the United Nations Special Committee on the Balkans (UNSCOB). Emphasizing fact finding and mediation, it also employed "peace observation," with military observers who reported on the conflict to the General Assembly. The first mission employing more than a few military personnel was the United Nations Truce Supervision Organization (UNTSO), operating in the Middle East since 1948.

Early UN operations received such descriptive labels as *peace observation* and *truce supervision*. The term *peacekeeping* was coined by Canadian prime minister Lester Pearson for the United Nations Emergency Force deployed in the Middle East after the 1956 Arab-Israeli War. It was developed to distinguish this larger operation (which deployed 3,600 personnel in military units) from individual observer missions such as UNTSO.

In the early 1960s, the controversial United Nations Operation in the Congo (ONUC), an unprecedentedly large operation, strained the "peacekeeping" concept and the strength of the United Nations. In part as a result, peacekeeping operations underwent a period of retrenchment until the late 1980s. One exception was the 1981 start of the U.S.-manned Multinational Force and Observers (MFO) in the Sinai, the product of the *Camp David Accords. Despite its non-UN origins, it serves as an example of a "chapter six" of the UN Charter, featuring military forces—with the consent of belligerents—monitoring the implementation of an established truce.

In the late 1980s, the member states, through the United Nations, started a new series of peacekeeping operations.

Many of these missions (particularly in Namibia and Cambodia) were very complex, and covered activities ranging from civilian police through election administration and refugee resettlement.

In the 1990s, operations were undertaken in which the central tenets of "classic" peacekeeping (consent by all parties and the restricted use of force by peacekeepers) no longer seemed appropriate. These operations, including the UN and U.S. military involvement in *Somalia and the former Yugoslavia, were mounted in the face of ongoing conflicts. The terms *peace enforcement*, "muscular" *peacekeeping*, and *"chapter seven" operations* reflect U.S. political and military concerns, and imply more aggressive ideas about the use of force. The American domestic debate over such a U.S. role has generated a new dynamic: as operations (rightly or wrongly) were judged failures in domestic debate, new labels were invented to distance new missions from past failures. Operation Joint Endeavor, begun in 1995 in the former Yugoslavia, was called a "peace implementation" mission, not because its tasks are unique but because the mission had to be differentiated from past efforts. The frequently changing labels applied to these operations reflect the lack of consensus within the United States about how to—and indeed whether to—conduct such operations.

[*See also* Bosnian Crisis: Civil-Military Relations; Middle East, U.S. Military Involvement in the.]

• David W. Wainhouse, *International Peacekeeping at the Crossroads: National Support—Experience and Prospects*, 1973. David W. Wainhouse, *International Peace Observation: A History and Forecast*, 1986. Paul F. Diehl, *International Peacekeeping*, 1993. William J. Durch, ed., *The Evolution of UN Peacekeeping: Case Studies and Comparative Analysis*, 1993. David R. Segal and Mady W. Segal, *Peacekeepers and Their Wives: American Participation in the Multinational Force and Observers*, 1993. Barbara Benton, *Soldiers for Peace: Fifty Years of United Nations Peacekeeping*, 1996. Andrew J. Goodpaster, *When Diplomacy Is Not Enough: Managing Multinational Military Interventions*, 1996. William J. Durch, ed., *Peacekeeping, American Politics and the Uncivil Wars of the 1990s*, 1996. United Nations Department of Public Information, *The Blue Helmets: A Review of United Nations Peace-keeping*, 3rd ed. 1997.
                                    —Dana Eyre

PEA RIDGE, BATTLE OF (1862). The Battle of Pea Ridge, 6–8 March 1862, resulted from a *Union army campaign to clear Missouri of Confederate forces during the Civil War and to begin a major offensive down the Mississippi River valley. Brig. Gen. Samuel R. Curtis's Army of the Southwest drove Maj. Gen. Sterling Price's Missouri State Guardsmen from southwestern Missouri into northwestern Arkansas in February 1862. Reinforced by Brig. Gen. Benjamin McCulloch's division and placed under the command of Maj. Gen. Earl Van Dorn, the entire Confederate force was designated the Army of the West. With 16,500 men, Van Dorn attacked Curtis's 10,250 men. Limited fighting occurred on 6 March as Confederate units harassed a Union detachment marching from Bentonville to join Curtis at Pea Ridge. On 7 March, Van Dorn completely outflanked Curtis's army and attacked in two columns, cutting the Federal line of communications. Curtis changed the front of his entire army from south to north.

Fierce fighting occurred on two separate battlefields: McCulloch's division was crushed near Leetown village; McCulloch and his immediate subordinate were killed, nearly destroying the chain of command. Near a hostelry called Elkhorn Tavern, Price's division almost crushed Col. Eugene Carr's Federal division in the bloodiest fighting of the battle, but Carr held firm. After concentrating his army that night, Curtis drove off the remainder of Van Dorn's men on 8 March. Curtis's victory was the turning point of Union efforts to dominate the Trans-Mississippi region. Van Dorn's army was transferred east of the Mississippi River, and Curtis marched across Arkansas, nearly capturing Little Rock. Pea Ridge, which Southerners named the Battle of Elkhorn Tavern, involved the Confederate use of Native American troops, with Cherokee recruits scalping several Federals. The Confederate *casualties were 2,000; Union losses, 1,384.

[See also Civil War: Military and Diplomatic Course; Confederate Army; Native Americans, U.S. Military Relations with.]

• William L. Shea and Earl J. Hess, *Pea Ridge: Civil War Campaign in the West*, 1992.

—Earl J. Hess

PEARL HARBOR, ATTACK ON (1941). The Japanese surprise attack on the U.S. Navy's base at Pearl Harbor and on Oahu in the Hawaiian Islands on Sunday morning, 7 December 1941, destroyed much of the American Pacific Fleet and brought the United States into World War II. What President Franklin D. *Roosevelt called a "day which will live in infamy" led Congress to declare war on Japan on 8 December.

The attack followed the decision of the government of Premier Hideki *Tojo that the Roosevelt administration would not abandon China and Southeast Asia to the Japanese military nor continue to supply Tokyo with oil and other vital supplies. Thus, while negotiating with Washington, Tokyo also planned a major Japanese offensive into British Malaya, the Dutch East Indies, and the American Philippines.

The major opposing naval force in the Pacific would be the U.S. *Navy, which had moved to its forward base at Pearl Harbor in May 1940. As part of the Japanese offensive, Adm. Isoroku *Yamamoto, commander in chief of the Combined Japanese Fleet, devised a secret plan for a preemptive air strike against the American fleet in order to give Japan time to fortify its newly conquered territories.

It was an extremely risky gamble—projecting a naval task force composed of six of Japan's nine *aircraft carriers 3,400 miles across the northern Pacific without discovery or major loss. The strike force, commanded by Vice Adm. Chuichi Nagumo, was composed of two fleet carriers, two converted carriers, and two light carriers, along with two *battleships, and a number of *cruisers, *destroyers, and support ships.

Between 10 and 18 November, Nagumo's ships left separately from Kure Naval Base, assembling 22 November by the Kurile Islands. The force departed on 26 November. To avoid detection, it followed a storm front and maintained strict radio silence, while Tokyo used signals deception from other sites to disguise the true location of the carriers. Consequently, although the U.S. Navy was monitoring Japanese naval radio traffic (they did not break the naval code until 1942), naval intelligence did not know where Japanese carriers were but knew that they had gone on radio silence on earlier deployments.

The United States had secretly broken the Japanese diplomatic codes in a system called *MAGIC, and the few authorities in Washington who were informed of them understood that relations between the two countries had reached a final crisis as the Japanese envoys received Tokyo's last negotiation offer and were told to destroy their code machines and deliver the proposal to the secretary of state on Sunday morning, 7 December. Americans saw Japanese naval vessels and troops ships headed south in the China Sea. But while recognizing that war might be imminent, Washington and Pacific commanders did not know whether this would include an attack on American territories; if it did, they assumed it would be on the Philippines. So did the two American commanders on Oahu, Rear Adm. Husband E. Kimmel, commander in chief of the U.S. Pacific Fleet, and Lt. Gen. Walter Short, U.S. Army commander in Hawaii. Both considered sabotage from among the sizable Japanese population to be the main threat in Hawaii.

On 7 December, Nagumo's force arrived 275 miles northwest of Oahu, and at 6:00 A.M. it launched the first attack wave, consisting of 49 bombers, 40 torpedo planes, 51 dive-bombers, and 43 *fighter aircraft; this was followed by a second wave of 54 bombers, 78 dive-bombers, and 36 fighters. The first wave arrived over Pearl Harbor at 7:55 A.M. (1:20 P.M. in Washington, D.C.), and the attack continued until 9:45 A.M.

While Japanese fighters strafed the Army Air Corps' planes at Hickman Field, the torpedo planes and dive-bombers attacked the navy ships. Along Battleship Row, the *Arizona*, the *California*, and the *West Virginia* were sunk; the *Oklahoma* capsized; the *Nevada* was grounded; and the three others were damaged. (The Japanese had secretly developed aerial *torpedoes that could operate in such shallow water and *bombs that could penetrate deck armor.) In all, the Japanese attack sank or disabled nineteen ships, including all eight battleships, three light cruisers, three destroyers, and several support vessels. At the airfields, 164 planes were destroyed and 128 damaged. Among American sailors, Marines, and soldiers, *casualties were 2,335 killed, along with 68 civilians, and 1,178 persons wounded.

Yamamoto's plan called for a third wave to destroy the repair facilities as well as the storage tanks containing 4.5 million gallons of fuel oil. But despite losing only twenty-nine planes, Nagumo feared a counterattack and turned for home.

News of the surprise attack at Pearl Harbor shocked Americans, ended the prewar isolationist-interventionist debate, and unified the country. Yamamoto had misjudged the effect on a previously divided public. His attack, which was an extraordinary tactical success, failed in its larger military goal of destroying the U.S. Navy in the Pacific. Although the battleships were damaged, Nagumo's failure to destroy the repair yards enabled the Americans eventually to return six of the eight battleships and all but one of the other vessels to active duty (the wreckage of the *Arizona* remains there today as a monument). The fuel reserves enabled the remainder of the fleet to continue to operate, and failure to destroy the submarine base allowed *submarines to play a major role in the Pacific War.

Equally important, the two aircraft carriers normally based at Pearl Harbor—the *Lexington* and the *Enterprise*—were undamaged. Escorted by heavy cruisers and destroyers, they were out delivering planes to Midway and Wake Islands.

Later on 7 December (8 December, Far Eastern Time), the Japanese launched assaults on British forces in Hong Kong and in the Malay peninsula, and U.S. forces on Midway Island, Guam, and the Philippines, where the Japanese also caught American planes on the ground.

The Pearl Harbor attack led to eight investigations between 22 December 1941 and 15 July 1946, to establish responsibility for the disaster. On 24 January 1942, a presidential commission headed by Supreme Court Justice Owen J. Roberts attributed the effectiveness of the Japanese attack to the failure of the military commanders in Hawaii, Admiral Kimmel and General Short, to institute adequate defense measures; it found them guilty of "dereliction of duty."

The Roberts Commission concluded that there had been enough advance warnings for the local commanders to have been on the alert instead of maintaining Sunday routine. Among these were reports to Kimmel in March and August 1941 from the Army Air Corps' commanders and the naval aviation commander in Hawaii indicating the possibility of a Japanese naval air attack from that direction and on a Sunday morning (reports that Kimmel filed away). In addition, as the crisis with Japan had mounted, Washington, on 27 November, notified Kimmel and Short, and all other Pacific commanders, that the Japanese ships and troops were moving south and that war was imminent (although the Hawaii commanders assumed on their own that this meant they should be alert to sabotage). More directly, about 4:00 A.M. on 7 December, the American destroyer *Ward* spotted a Japanese midget submarine trying to enter Pearl Harbor, although it did not report the sighting until it sank the submarine at 6:40 A.M., and even then the army was not informed. Finally, at 7:10 A.M., the new Opana *radar station on Oahu picked up a large blip approaching from the northwest, but the control center concluded erroneously that it was a flight of B-17 *bomber aircraft due in that morning from the mainland, even though those American planes would be arriving from the northeast.

Kimmel was relieved of his command and succeeded on 17 December by Adm. Chester *Nimitz, and both Kimmel and Short were forced into retirement. During the war, the army and navy held several inquiries. Some held the two local commanders derelict in their duty; others concluded that they were simply guilty of errors of judgment. But all left some questions unanswered, and the controversy continued.

After the war, a joint committee of Republicans and Democrats from both houses of Congress held an investigation from 15 November 1945 to 15 July 1946, which obtained additional testimony and previously classified information about the deciphering of the Japanese diplomatic codes and monitoring of naval radio traffic. In the committee's final report, the minority Republicans tended to criticize the Roosevelt administration, the service secretaries, and Gen. George C. *Marshall, the army chief of staff, for misjudgments, interservice rivalry, and poor communication; the majority Democrats blamed Kimmel and Short, although for errors of judgment rather than dereliction of duty. Like its predecessors, the congressional inquiry failed to resolve who was ultimately responsible. Kimmel and Short were never court-martialed. Short

died soon after the investigation; Kimmel lived until 1968.

Although new evidence continues to emerge, particularly about intelligence gathering by the United States and the Allies, no credible evidence has been produced to support the conspiracy thesis of a few writers that Roosevelt had foreknowledge of the attack and "allowed" it to occur so that he could take the United States into World War II. Nor have the president and his subordinates ever been shown to have been guilty of misconduct. No solid evidence has yet emerged to support a recent allegation that British intelligence was reading the Japanese naval code JN25 in 1941 and that, therefore, Prime Minister Winston S. *Churchill knew of the impending attack.

The overwhelming scholarly opinion from the American perspective views the Pearl Harbor attack as an unforeseen tragedy. Scholars have stressed the difficulty in extracting *in advance* the relevant information from masses of intelligence data. Most accounts also note the communication problems caused by interservice and interdepartmental rivalries. Recent evidence has added the FBI, which unfortunately downgraded information from a British double agent, Dusko Popov, who reported that Berlin had asked him in 1941 to obtain detailed information about Pearl Harbor. Nor was information supplied to Kimmel and Short about the reports of spies at the Japanese Consulate in Honolulu transmitting detailed information about ship deployments at Pearl Harbor.

Many scholars also emphasize the distortion of the interpretation of data caused by preexisting perspectives in December 1941; the American underestimation of the Japanese operational ability; and the overriding belief that the targets of Japanese attack were in the western Pacific and Southeast Asia. Indeed, these were the main targets of Japanese *expansionism.

[See also Intelligence, Military and Political; Isolationism; World War II, U.S. Naval Operations in: The Pacific; World War II: Changing Interpretations.]

• *Congressional Record*, U.S. Congress, Hearings and Reports, Vols. 87–104, 1941–58. Robert A. Theobald, *The Final Secret of Pearl Harbor*, 1954. Husband E. Kimmel, *Admiral Kimmel's Story*, 1955. Gwen Teraski, *Bridge to the Sun*, 1957. Roberta Wohlstetter, *Pearl Harbor, Warning and Decision*, 1962. Ladislas Farago, *The Broken Seal*, 1967. David Kahn, *The Codebreakers*, 1967. H. Agawa, *The Reluctant Admiral: Yamamoto and the Imperial Navy*, 1979. John Toland, *Infamy: Pearl Harbor and Its Aftermath*, 1982. Gordon W. Prange, with Donald Goldstein and Katherine V. Dillon, *December 7, 1941: The Day the Japanese Attacked Pearl Harbor*, 1984. Edwin T. Layton, Roger Pineau, and John Costello, *And I Was There*, 1985. Hilary Couroy and Harry Wray, eds., *Pearl Harbor Reexamined: Prologue to the Pacific War*, 1990. Gordon W. Prange, with Donald Goldstein and Katherine V. Dillon, *At Dawn We Slept: The Untold Story of Pearl Harbor*, 1991. Gordon W. Prange, with Donald Goldstein and Katherine V. Dillon, *Pearl Harbor: The Verdict of History*, 1991. Henry C. Clausen and Bruce Lee, *Pearl Harbor: Final Judgment*, 1992. Donald Goldstein and Katherine V. Dillon, *The Pearl Harbor Papers*, 1993. Edward L. Beach, *Scapegoats: A Defense of Kimmel and Short at Pearl Harbor*, 1995.

—Donald M. Goldstein

PEARL HARBOR NATIONAL MONUMENT. Located at the Pearl Harbor Naval Base at Oahu, Hawaii, the overturned hull of the sunken battleship USS *Arizona* is one of the most important American memorials to World War II in the Pacific. On 7 December 1941, in the attack on *Pearl

Harbor, Japanese bombers sank the 1912 battleship with a direct hit on its forward ammunition magazine. Within minutes, the ship rolled over and sank in the shallow harbor; many of the crew were entombed in the wreckage. In 1949, the Hawaiian territorial government's Pacific War Memorial Commission made the ship's wreckage the focal point of efforts to create a permanent monument to the dead at Pearl Harbor. A year later, the U.S. Navy attached a flagpole to the protruding mainmast of the sunken ship and erected a temporary floating platform over the vessel.

In 1958, Congress authorized the commission to raise private funds for a memorial, which was completed four years later. Designed by Alfred Preis, it consists of a 180-foot modernistic building that straddles part of the exposed hull of the *Arizona*.

During the *Cold War, U.S. leaders used the *Arizona* memorial to emphasize military preparedness and the need to guard against a similar surprise attack. Controversy remained, however, over how to interpret Japanese responsibility for the war, as well as tension over whether the memorial would encourage continued animosity between the United States and Japan. In 1991, on the fiftieth anniversary of the Pearl Harbor attack, President George *Bush, himself a naval veteran of the Pacific War, delivered a major address at the memorial urging support for American military preparedness but also stressing the need for friendly relations between the two countries.

[*See also* Battlefields, Encampments, and Forts as Public Sites; Commemoration and Public Ritual.]

• Edward Tabor Linenthal, *Sacred Ground: Americans and Their Battlefields*, 1991. G. Kurt Piehler, *Remembering War the American Way*, 1995.

—G. Kurt Piehler

PENINSULAR CAMPAIGN. See Seven Days' Battle (1862).

PENN, WILLIAM (1644–1718), religious leader, pacifist, social philosopher, and colonial proprietor. Born in London the son of Adm. William Penn, conqueror of Jamaica, and Margaret (née Jasper) van der Schuren Penn, young William was given a rigorous classical education evident in his adult writings. He entered Oxford in 1660 but was dismissed for refusing to attend chapel, an early example of his religious rebellion. He studied theology briefly at a Protestant seminary in France, then read law at Lincoln's Inn, London, for a year. Managing the family estates in Ireland, he became converted in 1667 to Quakerism, a radical, pacifist, Protestant way of thought. He zealously published books and pamphlets, was repeatedly jailed, but never ceased advocating liberty of conscience, which could only be realized through an official policy of tolerating dissent. A pragmatic young man, Penn sought to defend his fellow *Quakers through official channels, using the courts and becoming involved in politics. Resented by some older, purer Friends and facing a fading Whig cause, Penn turned to America to institutionalize his religious and political principles. Charles II granted him proprietorship of Pennsylvania in 1681 in part to repay a loan by Penn's father to the crown, but also to help fill a sparsely populated gap on the Atlantic seaboard.

In visits to America, Penn set up his "holy experiment," which included peaceful relations with the Indians. Subsequently, Penn was caught between the demands of the English government and Scotch-Irish frontier dwellers for military support and the intransigence of the Quaker Pennsylvania legislators. Pennsylvania had no militia until 1755. His own commitment to *pacifism was evident in his publication of *An Essay towards the Present and Future Peace of Europe, by the Establishment of an European Dyet, Parliament or Estates* (1693).

[*See also* Militia and National Guard.]

• Joseph E. Illick, *William Penn, the Politician*, 1965. Richard S. and Mary Maples Dunn, eds., *The Papers of William Penn*, 1986.

—Joseph E. Illick

PENNYPACKER, GALUSHA (1844–1916), youngest general in the Union army. Born near Valley Forge, Pennsylvania, Pennypacker grew up in the house that George *Washington had used as his headquarters. When the Civil War broke out, the sixteen-year-old youth gave up reading law and joined a Chester County militia company as a private. The 97th Pennsylvania Volunteer Regiment was organized in August 1861; Pennypacker joined and was elected a captain.

Pennypacker and the unit participated in the Siege of *Fort Wagner at Charleston, and subsequently in actions at Swift Creek, Drewry's Bluff, Chester Station, and Green Plains, where Pennypacker, appointed a lieutenant colonel in April 1864 at age nineteen, was wounded three times. In August 1864, he was appointed colonel in command of the regiment, and the following month was given a brigade, which he led in operations around Petersburg and Richmond. He was wounded again in an assault on Fort Gilmer.

On 15 January 1865, in the Union attack on Fort Fisher near Wilmington, North Carolina, Pennypacker led the first troops in a charge over the parapet and personally planted the flag of the 97th Pennsylvania Volunteers on the wall. At that moment, he was hit in the side by a bullet and severely wounded. The colonel was caught by Sgt. Jeptha Clark (great-great-grandfather of editor in chief John W. Chambers). Hospitalized for ten months, Pennypacker was awarded the Congressional Medal of Honor for bravery in capturing the fort. In June 1865, the twenty-year-old colonel was promoted to brigadier general, becoming the youngest general in the *Union army. After the war, Pennypacker served in the South and then the West as a colonel of infantry in the U.S. Army until his retirement in 1883 at thirty-nine.

[*See also* Civil War: Military and Diplomatic Course.]

• Isaiah Price, *History of the Ninety-seventh Pennsylvania Volunteer Regiment*, 1875. Patricia L. Faust, ed., *Historical Times Illustrated Encyclopedia of the Civil War*, 1986. Rod Gragg, *Confederate Goliath: The Battle of Fort Fisher*, 1991.

—John Whiteclay Chambers II

The **PENTAGON** is the building that houses the U.S. Department of *Defense, located in Arlington, Virginia, just across the Potomac River from Washington, D.C. As the name indicates, it is a five-sided building, composed of five concentric pentagons interconnected by corridors.

The Pentagon was constructed by the U.S. *Army Corps of Engineers between 1941 and 1943 to consolidate various offices in the War Department, which was expanding rapidly during World War II. Covering an area of thirty-four acres, with four stories aboveground, the reinforced concrete building was designed to provide 5 million square feet of floor space for 40,000 employees. When completed, the Pentagon was the world's largest office building. In 1947, it became the headquarters of the newly established Department of *Defense. The term "the Pentagon" often refers to the Defense Department.

• Lenore Fine and Jesse Remington, *The Corps of Engineers: Construction in the United States*, in *Office of the Chief of Military History, U.S. Army in World War II: The Technical Services*, 1972.
—John Whiteclay Chambers II

PENTAGON PAPERS (1971). On 13 June 1971, the *New York Times* began publication of a secret Department of *Defense history of Vietnam War decision making commissioned by Defense Secretary Robert S. *McNamara toward the end of the Johnson administration. Leaked by former Defense Department analyst Daniel *Ellsberg, who believed the revelation might alter the course of the war, the story outraged President Richard M. *Nixon, already suspicious of the press, particularly by threatening the president's hoped-for opening to China. As Nixon's national security adviser, Henry *Kissinger, observed in his memoir, *The White House Years*, "Our nightmare was that ... the massive hemorrhage of state secrets was bound to raise doubts [in Peking] about our reliability." When the *Times* declined to suspend further publication on its own, Nixon's lawyers won a temporary restraining order from the 2nd Circuit Court in New York. At that point, Ellsberg approached the *Washington Post*, which picked up and ran the story. Nixon's lawyers sued again in the District of Columbia Circuit Court but failed to demonstrate any substantial damage to national security and lost. On 23 June, they appealed to the Supreme Court, which agreed to review the case in an unprecedented Saturday morning sitting. In the end, the Court likewise found in favor of the newspapers, but despite widespread public belief it set no solid precedents in support of freedom of the press by doing so. Ruling that prior restraint of the press imposed a heavy burden of proof, which the Nixon administration had failed to carry out, it left the possibility open that the government or the military might pursue similar litigation in the future with greater success.

[*See also* Supreme Court, War, and the Military; Vietnam War: Changing Interpretations.]

• Sanford Ungar, *The Papers and the Papers*, 1972. Lucas A. Powe, Jr., *The Fourth Estate and the Constitution, Freedom of the Press in America*, 1991.
—William M. Hammond

PEQUOT WAR. *See* Native American Wars: Wars Between Native Americans and Europeans and Euro-Americans.

PERIODICAL PUBLICATIONS ON WAR AND THE MILITARY. The appearance of professional or occupational periodicals is usually a sign that a field has matured. This has certainly been the case for military and defense journals in the United States. From a slow and fitful start in the early days of the republic, serial publications devoted to war and the military have evolved into a number of forums that cover diverse aspects of this broad topic. Unlike other periodicals that cover trades or professions, military publications (which comprise the bulk of this category) are not the prime vehicles that formulate theories and major advancements. Rather, they explain and disseminate officially determined policy. Debate then takes place over details and implementation. These journals also can be a means of spreading specialized military information to the general media.

Prior to the *Civil War, military journals were short-lived. A small and dispersed officer corps, rudimentary mail and *transportation systems, and a core belief that talented men could rapidly master the arts of war created an insurmountable barrier to successful periodicals. The first American military journal, *Military Repository*, set the pattern. It was created during a short-term interest in military affairs in 1796 and folded the following year. A number of similar efforts met the same fate during the *War of 1812. The most successful publication of the antebellum era was the *Army and Navy Chronicle*, which lasted from 1835 to 1844. It was a reflection of a "military enlightenment" of the 1830s. No military periodical appeared during the *Mexican War.

The Civil War saw the rise of several military journals. The large number of new officers created a need for publications that covered military operations and provided basic instruction and counsel for these civilians in uniform. Several addressed this audience, the most prominent being the *Army and Navy Journal* (now the *Armed Forces Journal International, AFJI*). This publication quickly gained the confidence of senior officers and was the only such periodical to continue after the war. It settled into a routine of covering congressional appropriations, military deployments, and the social aspects of officers' lives.

The next spurt began in the 1870s. Officers in the army and navy began to address the basic tenets of their profession by forming societies. Their journals, following the model of the British *Journal of the Royal United Service Institution*, provided sounding boards for these officers' thoughts. The U.S. Navy was first in 1874 with the *U.S. Naval Institute Proceedings*, followed in 1879 by the U.S. Army's *Journal of the Military Service Institution*. The army's branches quickly began producing their own periodicals, such as *Cavalry Journal*, which weakened a desire for a "one-army" voice. Both uniformed and civilian writers also addressed military topics in mainstream publications.

War had two contradictory effects on these publications. Small editorial staffs of regular officers were quickly depleted by the demands for more pressing activities. On the other hand, the influx of thousands of new dues-paying officers who were "encouraged" to join the branch societies rapidly filled the associations' coffers. New publications arose, addressing the concerns of wartime volunteers and conscripts. The most popular enlisted ranks' periodicals have been *Yank* (World War II) and *Stars and Stripes* (both world wars and the postwar period to the present).

The post–World War II period ushered in a golden age of American military and defense journals. Each year between 1945 and 1985 saw the establishment of at least one periodical devoted to war and the military. This development was the direct result of the Cold War. The United States was fielding a large permanent military establishment for the first time in its history, creating a substantial audience in uniform and in industry. Three main sources continue to meet the needs of this readership.

The largest is the military establishment itself. The Department of *Defense and its various military bodies have created a number of publications. Most attempt to disseminate official doctrine, impart useful career information, and inculcate an esprit de corps. Some address the concerns of a particular branch, such as *Infantry*, while others provide information to all the ranks of a single service, such as *Airman*. Of special interest are the journals of the various war colleges (*Parameters, Naval War College Review, Airpower Journal*, etc.), which provide a scholarly venue for uniformed and civilian authors. Aside from these, most of the government periodicals contain limited criticism of official policy. Over the years, there have been attempted cutbacks of service-sponsored periodicals from both the congressional and executive branches, but the publications have endured. In fact, emerging trends spawn new journals, such as *Joint Forces Quarterly.*

Professional organizations are the smallest sources of defense and military journals but arguably the most influential. These groups either form around the major services, such as the Air Force Association (*Air Force*), or activities, such as the Armed Forces Communications and Electronics Association (*Signal*). Their journals display an independence of thought and often reflect what the services actually feel about policies and developments. Many associations have corporate membership, providing a conduit for the views of defense contractors. Unlike their government counterparts, which cannot receive advertisements, these magazines are filled with promotions for the latest products and services of the *military-industrial complex.

"Independent" publishers form the final source of military journals and are the most diverse. Commercial publications such as *Aviation Week and Space Technology* and *Defense News* usually emphasize military equipment and the related aspects of the federal budget. As with their association counterparts, these commercial magazines carry defense contractor advertisements, sometimes in conjunction with special editorial sections that deal with the *weaponry being advertised.

There are some exceptions. The first are the tabloid newspapers of the Army Times Publishing Company (*Army Times, Air Force Times,* and *Navy Times*), which provide articles that uniformed personnel need to succeed in their careers—information on pay, promotions, education, benefits, and so on. Founded during World War II, this company was so successful that it usurped the role that *Armed Forces Journal International* had played. For its part, *AFJI* in the late 1960s successfully repositioned itself to cover defense policy issues in a lively format. It has been joined by a few other commercial publications, notably those of the British Jane's Publishing Company.

Military history journals have a solid niche in popular and academic publishing. Titles aimed at a general audience such as *Military History, World War II, Vietnam, Naval History,* and *MHQ* have received an enthusiastic popular reception. More scholarly offerings such as the *Journal of Military History* and *Air Power History* have been well received in the academic community. The focus of the commercial and academic journals has been on modern (since 1400) Western military history.

The Civil War has generated a myriad of publications that address the interests of its devotees. In the decades that followed the war, most showed a decidedly regional bias, such as *Confederate Veteran*. Almost all of these journals had ceased by the Great Depression, but the war's centennial in 1961 sparked a popular interest that has not

flagged. *Civil War History* is a well-respected academic journal that covers not only military topics but all aspects of the "middle period" of American history. *Civil War Times Illustrated, The Blue and the Gray,* and *America's Civil War* service an apparently insatiable popular market. There are a wide variety of specialty Civil War serials, such as *Lady Reenactor* and *Civil War Token Journal.*

Over the years since World War I, and accelerating with the intellectual ferment during the Robert S. *McNamara era at the Department of Defense, several independent scholarly journals joined the war college and branch journals in examining wider military and defense issues. Periodicals with a social science emphasis, such as Harvard University's *International Security* (political science) and the Inter-University Seminar on Armed Forces and Society's *Armed Forces and Society* (sociology and political science), have established scholarly niches.

The final group of independent publishers consists of those dealing with *peace and *arm control and disarmament issues. Such publications generally arise in periods before or after conflicts and are usually organs of *peace and antiwar movements. The Cold War amplified this phenomenon: a wide variety of peace and disarmament publications appeared, ranging from the semischolarly *Bulletin of the *Atomic Scientists* to the tabloid *Ground Zero.* A related type has been produced by organizations devoted to peace studies, such as *Journal of Conflict Resolution* (University of Michigan), *Peace and Change* (Peace History Society), and *World Affairs* (*American Peace Society). There is not much cross-fertilization between the peace journals and the rest of the military publications, a reflection of the lack of middle ground between their sponsors.

[*See also* Cold War: Domestic Course.]

• Leslie Anders, "Retrospect: Four Decades of Military Journalism," *Military Affairs*, 41 (April 1977), pp. 62–66. Robert B. Sims, *The Pentagon Reporters*, 1983. Grant Burns, "Stopping the War Before It Starts: North American Periodicals of the Peace and Disarmament Movement," *Serial Librarian*, 10 (Summer 1986), pp. 117–42. Michael E. Unsworth, ed., *Military Periodicals: United States and Selected International Journals and Newspapers*, 1990.

—Michael E. Unsworth

PERRY, MATTHEW (1794–1858), naval diplomat and reformer. Perry entered the U.S. Navy in 1809 as midshipman under his brother, Oliver Hazard *Perry, then served on the frigate USS *President* during the *War of 1812, and was wounded when it exchanged fire with the *Belvidera*. In the 1830s, Perry became a leader in the movement to improve naval education and training and to have the navy adopt *steamships. During the *Mexican War he directed attacks on Frontera, Tabasco, and Carmen in 1846, and after assuming command of the Home Squadron in March 1847, Perry conducted the U.S. Army's amphibious landing at Vercruz; he also supervised the capture of Tuxpan and the blockade of Mexico's east coast.

After the war, in his famous expedition to open the closed society of Japan, Perry led four U.S. warships into Tokyo Bay on 8 July 1853 and delivered an invitation from President Millard Fillmore to the emperor to open relations with the United States. Returning in February 1854, he signed the Treaty of Kanagawa, providing for friendship and limited trade between the two nations. Ill health overtook the man known as "Old Bruin"; he returned to the

United States and spent a year writing his account of the mission before retiring from the navy. Perry died in New York City on 4 March 1958.

• Samuel E. Morison, *Old Bruin: Commodore Matthew C. Perry, 1794–1858,* 1967. John Schroeder, "Matthew Calbraith Perry: Percursor of the Steam Navy," in *Captains of the Old Steam Navy,* ed. James C. Bradford, 1986.   —James C. Bradford

PERRY, OLIVER HAZARD (1785–1819), U.S. naval officer. Born of a naval family, Perry served as a midshipman toward the end of undeclared naval war with *France (1789–1800) and as a midshipman and acting lieutenant during the *Tripolitan War (1801–05). After being promoted to lieutenant, he helped enforce the embargo, which prohibited American ships and goods from leaving port, and protected the American coast from *privateering. During the *War of 1812, he directed construction of a small fleet on Lake Erie, and on 10 September 1813, used it decisively to defeat a British squadron at Put-in-Bay. The Battle of Lake Erie secured for the United States control over the lake and changed the balance of power in the western theater of operations, but now is best remembered as the occasion of Perry's report to Gen. William Henry Harrison: "We have met the enemy and they are ours." That same year Perry provided naval support for Winfield *Scott's capture of Fort George, and aided Harrison in the reoccupation of Detroit, as well as at the Battle of the Thames. In 1814, he played a minor role in the defense of the Chesapeake Bay area when the British invaded the region. He died of yellow fever in 1819 while on a naval and diplomatic mission in South America. A younger brother, Matthew C. Perry, led the naval expedition that opened Japan in 1853.

[*See also* Navy, U.S.: 1783–1865.]

• Alexander S. Mackenzie, *The Life of Commodore Oliver H. Perry,* 2 vols., 1840. Charles J. Dutton, *Oliver Hazard Perry,* 1935. David Curtis Skaggs and Gerard T. Altoff, *A Signal Victory: The Lake Erie Campaign, 1812–1813,* 1997.   —Donald R. Hickey

PERRYVILLE, BATTLE OF (1862). The largest Civil War battle fought in Kentucky occurred near Perryville on 8 October 1862. The engagement climaxed a campaign begun when *Confederate army forces entered Kentucky earlier that summer. Confederate commander Braxton *Bragg mistakenly believed that he faced one Union corps at Perryville, but there were actually 58,000 Federal troops in the area. For his part, Union Gen. Don Carlos Buell erred in believing that Bragg's entire force was in his front.

Bragg took the initiative by ordering his 16,000 men into action in the early afternoon. The main blow fell on the Federal left, where a corps commanded by Alexander McCook was shattered and driven back nearly a mile until Union reinforcements and nightfall ended the carnage. Despite this tactical success, Bragg decided to withdraw after belatedly learning that he confronted the bulk of Buell's army. Bragg's army took over 3,000 *casualties; *Union army totals exceeded 4,000. The Confederates retreated first to Harrodsburg and shortly thereafter into Tennessee. Buell was soon replaced as Union commander by William S. *Rosecrans, but the Confederates had little to celebrate in the wake of Perryville. The hard fighting done there proved strategically inconsequential, and Bragg's boldly conceived Kentucky invasion failed.

[*See also* Civil War: Military and Diplomatic Course.]

• Kenneth A. Hafendorfer, *Perryville: Battle for Kentucky,* 1981. James Lee McDonough, *War in Kentucky: From Shiloh to Perryville,* 1994.   —Christopher Losson

PERSHING, JOHN J. (1860–1948), commander of the American Expeditionary Forces (AEF) in World War I, graduated from the U.S. Military Academy in 1886. Cavalryman Pershing served in various Indian campaigns in the West and then became professor of military science at the University of Nebraska in the 1890s, where he took a law degree and thought of another profession. But he stayed in the army and in the black Tenth Cavalry.

Staff assignment to army headquarters in Washington, D.C., in 1896 was followed by appointment to the tactical staff at West Point in 1897. There, Pershing's discipline and his African American regiment earned him the nickname "Black Jack" among the cadets.

In the *Spanish-American War, Pershing distinguished himself in Cuba. Sent to the Philippines in 1899, he led important expeditions against hostile Moros. In 1905, Captain Pershing became military attaché in Tokyo and observed the Russo-Japanese War.

These services induced President Theodore *Roosevelt to promote Pershing to brigadier general in 1906. Becoming governor of the Philippine Moro province in 1909, he subdued the warlike people by 1913. While at Fort Bliss, Texas, Pershing lost his wife and three daughters in a fire at San Francisco's Presidio, 27 August 1915—only his son, Warren, survived.

Throwing himself into work, Pershing led the Punitive Expedition into Mexico in pursuit of Francisco (Pancho) Villa's irregulars in March 1916. Pershing did not capture Villa but did drive away his bands and restore peace to the border. In February 1917, Major General Pershing and his troops were withdrawn from Mexico.

With America's entry into World War I, April 1917, President Woodrow *Wilson bypassed several more senior officers and selected Pershing to command the American Expeditionary Forces. Given wide authority by Wilson and Secretary of War Newton D. *Baker, Pershing was to build a separate American army as soon as possible.

Pershing's duties in France were heavily managerial. He had to organize, train, and supply an army that finally numbered more than 2 million men. He waged two wars— one against the Germans, the other against Allies who tried always to siphon his men into their woefully depleted ranks. Pershing stressed "open warfare" tactics in training, as opposed to the *trench warfare favored by the Allies. Historians argue whether he was right, but when the western front broke open in late 1918, events seemed to validate his program. There is no doubt that his discipline, organization, and iron will made the AEF a vital factor in the final victory. Pershing thought the Allies should push on to Berlin, convince Germany of defeat, and perhaps forestall another war, but he accepted Wilson's decision for an armistice in November 1918.

Congress created the rank of "General of the Armies" for Pershing in 1919. Pershing accepted a five-star insignia but declined the option of wearing it. He served as chief of staff of the U.S. Army from 1921 until his retirement from the service in 1924.

[See also Academies, Service: U.S. Military Academy; Army, U.S.: 1900–41; World War I: Military and Diplomatic Course.]

• John J. Pershing, My Experience in the World War, 2 vols., 1931; repr. 1995. Donald Smythe, Guerrilla Warrior: The Early Life of John J. Pershing, 1973. Frank E. Vandiver, Black Jack: The Life and Times of John J. Pershing, 2 vols., 1977. Donald Smythe, Pershing: General of the Armies, 1986. —Frank E. Vandiver

The **PERSIAN GULF WAR** (1991) was caused by Iraq's invasion of Kuwait on 2 August 1990, and had two major phases. The first phase was Operation Desert Shield—a largely defensive operation in which the United States and Saudi Arabia rushed to build up the defensive forces necessary to protect Saudi Arabia and the rest of the gulf, and the United Nations attempted to force Iraq to leave Kuwait through the use of economic sanctions. The United States then led the UN effort to create a broad international coalition with the military forces necessary to liberate Kuwait, and persuaded the United Nations to set a deadline of 15 January 1991 for Iraq to leave Kuwait or face the use of force.

The second phase, known as "Desert Storm," was the battle to liberate Kuwait when Iraq refused to respond to the UN deadline. The fighting began on 17 January 1991 and ended on 1 March 1991. The UN Coalition liberated Kuwait in a little over six weeks, and involved the intensive use of airpower and armored operations, and the use of new military technologies. The Gulf War left Iraqi leader Saddam *Hussein in power, but it destroyed nearly all of Iraq's conventional forces and allowed the United States to destroy most of Iraq's long-range *missiles and chemical weapons and capabilities to develop *nuclear weapons.

Desert Shield. Saddam Hussein almost certainly saw the seizure and annexation of Kuwait as a means of solving Iraq's economic problems, of greatly increasing Iraq's share of world oil reserves, and as a means of demonstrating that Iraq had become the dominant power in the region. Kuwait was capable of adding at least 2 million barrels a day of oil to Iraq's exports of roughly 3.5 million, and offered the opportunity to double Iraq's total oil reserves, from 100 billion to 198 billion barrels (representing nearly 20% of the world's total reserves).

Although he continued to negotiate his demands on oil revenues and debt relief from the Persian Gulf Arab nations, Saddam Hussein ordered his troops to the Kuwait border in July 1990, built up all of the support capabilities necessary to sustain an invasion, and then ordered his forces to invade on 2 August 1990. Kuwait had not kept its forces on alert, and Iraq met little resistance. It seized the entire country within less than two days; within a week, Iraq stated that it would annex Kuwait as its nineteenth province. Iraqi forces also deployed along Kuwait's border with Saudi Arabia, with more than five Iraqi divisions in position to seize Saudi Arabia's oil-rich Eastern Province. Saudi Arabia had only two brigades and limited amounts of airpower to oppose them.

Saddam Hussein may have felt that the world would accept his invasion of Kuwait or would fail to mount any effective opposition. However, Saudi Arabia and the other gulf states immediately supported the Kuwaiti government-in-exile. The Council of the Arab League voted to condemn Iraq on 3 August and demanded its withdrawal from Kuwait. Key Arab states like Algeria, Egypt, and Syria

supported Kuwait—although Jordan, Libya, Mauritania, the Sudan, and the Palestine Liberation Organization (PLO) supported Iraq. Britain, France, the Soviet Union, and most other European nations as well as the United States, Canada, and Japan condemned the invasion. U.S. president George *Bush announced on 7 August that the United States would send land, air, and naval forces to the gulf.

Equally important, the end of the *Cold War allowed the United Nations to take firm action under U.S. initiative. On the day of the invasion, the Security Council voted 14–0 (Resolution 660) to demand Iraq's immediate and unconditional withdrawal from Kuwait. The United States, Britain, and Saudi Arabia led the United Nations in forming a broad military coalition under the leadership of U.S. Army Gen. H. Norman *Schwarzkopf that deployed the military forces necessary to enforce the United Nations' sanctions and to defend Saudi Arabia. This was the defensive military operation code-named "Desert Shield."

On 29 November 1990, the United States obtained a Security Council authorization for the nations allied with Kuwait "to use all necessary means" if Iraq did not withdraw by 15 January 1991. Key nations like the United States, Britain, France, Egypt, Saudi Arabia, Syria, and several others began to deploy the additional forces necessary to drive Iraq out of Kuwait.

In 1990–91, the United States deployed a total of 527,000 personnel, over 110 naval vessels, 2,000 *tanks, 1,800 fixed-wing aircraft, and 1,700 *helicopters. Britain deployed 43,000 troops, 176 tanks, 84 combat aircraft, and a naval task force. France deployed 16,000 troops, 40 tanks, attack helicopters, a light armored division, and combat aircraft. Saudi Arabia deployed 50,000 troops, 280 tanks, and 245 aircraft. Egypt contributed 30,200 troops, 2 armored divisions, and 350 tanks. Syria contributed 14,000 troops and 2 divisions. Other allied nations, including Canada, Italy, Oman, Qatar, and the United Arab Emirates deployed a significant portion of their small forces.

Iraq responded by building up its military forces in the Kuwait theater of operations to a total of 336,000 troops and a total of 43 divisions, 3,475 battle tanks, 3,080 other armored vehicles, and 2,475 major *artillery weapons. This buildup on both sides made full-scale war steadily more likely and triggered a number of political debates within the West and the Arab world over the need for war. The most important of these debates took place within the United States; largely because of President Bush's political leadership, the Congress, after Bush gained UN endorsement, requested such authorization on 8 January 1991. On 12 January the House of Representatives by 250 to 183 and the Senate by 52 to 47 voted to authorize the use of force.

Though a number of new efforts were made to persuade Iraq to leave Kuwait in late December and early January, Saddam Hussein refused to withdraw under any practical conditions. Baghdad also continued to expand its military capabilities in Kuwait and along the Iraqi border with Saudi Arabia, and continued its efforts to convert Kuwait into an Iraqi province. As a result, the UN Security Council voted to ignore yet another effort to negotiate with Iraq. On that date, 15 January 1991, President Bush ordered the military offensive to begin.

Desert Storm: The Air War. The Gulf War began early in the morning on 17 January when the United States exploited its intelligence and targeting assets, cruise missiles, and offensive airpower to launch a devastating series of air attacks on Iraqi command and control facilities, *communications systems, air bases, and land-based air defenses. During the first hour of the war, U.S. sea-launched cruise missiles and F-117 stealth aircraft demonstrated they could attack even heavily defended targets like Baghdad.

Within three days, a mix of U.S., British, and Saudi *fighter aircraft had established near air superiority. In spite of Iraq's air strength, UN air units shot down a total of thirty-five Iraqi aircraft without a single loss in air-to-air combat. Although Iraq had a land-based air defense system with some 3,000 surface-to-air missiles, the combined U.S. and British air units were able to use electronic warfare systems, antiradiation missiles, and precision air-to-surface weapons to suppress Iraq's longer-range surface-to-air missiles. As a result, Coalition air forces were able rapidly to broaden their targets from attacks on Iraq's air forces and air defenses to assaults on key headquarters, civil and army communications, electronic power plants, and Iraq's facilities for the production of weapons of mass destruction.

Victory in the air was achieved by 24 January, when Iraq ceased to attempt active air combat. A total of 112 Iraqi aircraft fled to Iran, and Iraq virtually ceased to use its ground-based *radar to target UN aircraft. This created a safe zone at medium and high altitudes that allowed U.S. and British air units to launch long-range air-to-surface weapons with impunity. The UN air forces were also able to shift most of their assets to attacks on Iraqi ground forces. For the following thirty days, UN Coalition aircraft attacked Iraqi armor and artillery in the Kuwaiti theater of operations, as well as flying into Iraq itself to bomb Iraq's forward defenses, elite Republican Guard units, air bases and sheltered aircraft, and Iraq's biological, chemical, and nuclear warfare facilities.

Iraq's only ability to retaliate consisted of launching modified surface-to-surface Scud missiles against targets in Saudi Arabia and Israel, which had remained outside the war: forty Scud variants against Israel and forty-six against Saudi Arabia. U.S.-made Patriot missiles in Israel shot down some Scuds, but although the United Nations carried out massive "Scud hunts" that involved thousands of sorties, it never found and destroyed any Scud missiles on the ground, which demonstrated the risks posed by the proliferation of mobile, long-range missiles.

Iraq's Scud strikes could not, however, alter the course of the war. Iraqi ground forces were struck by more than 40,000 air attack sorties; U.S. authorities estimated that airpower helped bring about the desertion or capture of 84,000 Iraqi soldiers and destroyed 1,385 Iraqi tanks, 930 other armored vehicles, and 1,155 artillery pieces before the United Nations launched its land offensive. They also estimated that air attacks severely reduced the flow of supplies to Iraqi ground forces in Kuwait and damaged 60 percent of Iraq's major command centers, 70 percent of its military communications, 125 ammunition storage revetments, 48 Iraqi naval vessels, and 75 percent of Iraq's electric power–generating capability.

Desert Storm: The Land War. By 24 February 1991, airpower had weakened Iraq's land forces in Kuwait to the point where the UN commander, General Schwarzkopf, felt ready to launch a land offensive. Early that morning,

UN land forces attacked along a broad front from the Persian Gulf to Rafha on the Iraqi-Saudi border. This attack had two principal thrusts: a massive, highly mobile "left hook" around and through Iraqi positions to the west of Kuwait to envelop the elite Republican Guard; and a thrust straight through Iraq's defenses along the Kuwaiti border designed to fix the forward Iraqi divisions.

The "left hook" was carried out by a mix of U.S., British, and French armored and airborne forces. The armored VII Corps deployed four armored divisions, one of them British, for the main thrust. Its western flank was protected by the U.S. XVIII Airborne Corps, composed of three U.S. divisions—the 82nd Airborne, the 101st Air Mobile, and the 24th Infantry (Mechanized)—and the French 6th Light Armored Division. They advanced toward the Iraqi cities of Salman, west of Kuwait, and Nasiriya on the Euphrates River, and attacked in an arc to the northeast toward the main routes of communication leading north from Kuwait toward Basra in Iraq. French forces led the attack toward the Iraqi lines of communication along the Euphrates. U.S. armored, mechanized, and attack helicopter forces advanced rapidly toward Basra in the leading edge of the "left hook." British forces guarded the U.S. flank and attacked to the northeast across the gorge of al-Batin along the Iraqi-Kuwaiti border.

The other thrust—directly north through the Iraqi positions along the Kuwaiti border—was carried out by the I Marine Expeditionary Force, and an all-Arab corps composed primarily of the Saudi Army and Egyptian units. These forces rapidly penetrated Iraq's forward defenses and advanced so swiftly that Iraq's shattered ground forces in Kuwait could only launch scattered counterattacks. As a result, the allies rushed toward Kuwait City, Wafrah, and Jahrah.

Though some Iraqi Republican Guard units fought well, the bulk of Iraq's army consisted of poorly trained conscripts with low morale and little motivation. Many Iraqi troops fled after putting up only brief resistance and others were taken prisoner. As a result, UN forces reached their major objectives in Kuwait in half the time originally planned. At the same time, the Coalition continued its air attacks, dropping a total of 88,500 tons of ordnance. U.S. and British air units used 6,520 tons of precision-guided weapons and destroyed or damaged 54 bridges. These attacks helped to end the war by cutting off Iraqi land forces from the roads along the Tigris River north of Basra, although UN forces did not have time to encircle fully or cut off all Iraqi forces, or to use airpower to destroy the retreating Iraqi forces around Basra.

By 26 February, Coalition land forces were in Kuwait City, and U.S. forces had advanced to positions in Iraq to the south of Nasiriya. Many of these advances had taken place at night and all occurred in spite of major rainfalls, substantial amounts of mud, and weather problems hampering the ability to provide air support. These advances effectively ended the war.

Baghdad radio announced on 26 February that all Iraqi forces would withdraw from Kuwait in compliance with UN Resolution 660. A day later, President Bush declared that the United States would halt military operations early in the morning of 28 February, a week after the land offensive had begun. A cease-fire was negotiated on 3 March and formally signed on 6 April. Iraq agreed to abide by all the UN resolutions.

The Aftermath of the War. The Gulf War achieved the United Nation's original objectives of liberating Kuwait while producing remarkably one-sided losses. Iraqi military casualties totaled an estimated 25,000 to 65,000, and the United Nations destroyed some 3,200 Iraqi tanks, over 900 other armored vehicles, and over 2,000 artillery weapons. Some 86,000 Iraqi soldiers surrendered. In contrast, UN forces suffered combat losses of some 200 personnel from hostile fire, plus losses of 4 tanks, 9 other armored vehicles, and 1 artillery weapon. U.S. battle deaths among the 532,000 Americans included 122 from the army and Marines (35 to *friendly fire) and 131 noncombat fatalities. The navy losses were 6 and 8; in the air force 20 were killed in action and 6 in other deaths. The allied forces of 254,000 suffered 92 combat deaths. Although Coalition aircraft flew a total of 109,876 sorties, the allies lost only 38 aircraft versus over 300 for Iraq. This was not only the lowest loss rate in the history of air warfare but a lower loss than the normal accident rate in combat training. The terms of cease-fire were designed to enable UN inspectors to destroy most of Iraq's remaining missiles, chemical weapons, and nuclear weapons facilities.

The Gulf War reshaped the face of modern warfare. It demonstrated a dramatic increase in the importance of joint operations, high-paced air and armored operations, precision strike systems, night and all-weather warfare capabilities, sophisticated electronic warfare and command and control capabilities, and the ability to target and strike deep behind the front line, marking what might be the beginning of a revolution in military affairs. It also demonstrated the growing importance of the mass media in shaping the conduct of operations, and the need to carefully consider collateral damage, *casualties, and the impact of instant TV coverage of military operations.

The Gulf War did not, however, bring stability to the gulf or drive Saddam Hussein and the Ba'ath Party elite from power. Indeed, he suppressed Kurdish and Shi'ite rebellions in 1991. In 1998, Iraq still had the largest army in the gulf region. It seemed to retain some long-range missiles, some ability to deliver chemical weapons, and most of its prewar biological weapons capability. Though it had lost most of its nuclear weapons production facilities, it retained much of its nuclear weapons technology. Baghdad was also able to launch terrorist activities against Kuwait and drive most of the UN mission in Iraq out of the country. Iraqi agents plotted to assassinate President Bush when he visited Kuwait on 14–16 April 1993, and Iraq conducted a major military buildup near the Kuwaiti border in October 1994.

The failure to drive Saddam Hussein from power, and Iraq's actions since the war, have led many to argue that the United Nations should have expanded its war-fighting objectives and invaded Iraq to force Saddam Hussein from power. Some military analysts have argued that even a few days of additional fighting would have proved decisive in overthrowing Saddam Hussein. There is no way to resolve such debates, but it seems unlikely that a few days of additional fighting would have done more than kill more Iraqis, since many of the Republican Guards had already escaped to the north of Basra and half the Iraqi Army and most of Saddam Hussein's security forces remained intact. Expanding the goals of the war might have driven Saddam Hussein from power, but it might also have caused an Iraqi civil war and divided the country, led to bloody urban warfare, and forced a lengthy UN occupation of a sovereign and hostile state. Instead, the United Nations maintained economic sanctions and an embargo on military supplies against Iraq for years after the Persian Gulf War.

[*See also* Chemical and Biological Weapons and Warfare; Middle East, U.S. Military Involvement in the; News Media, War, and the Military.]   —Anthony H. Cordesman

PETERSBURG, SIEGE OF (1864). The Siege of Petersburg, Virginia, began in June 1864 when the Union Army of the Potomac, led by Maj. Gen. George Gordon *Meade but closely supervised by Lt. Gen. Ulysses S. *Grant, crossed the James River after failing to destroy Confederate Gen. Robert E. *Lee's Army of Northern Virginia during a series of battles from the Wilderness to Cold Harbor. From 15–18 June, the Federals made repeated efforts to seize Petersburg, an important railroad center twenty miles south of Richmond. When these failed, Grant initiated siege operations, which continued until 2 April 1865.

To some extent the term *siege* is a misnomer, since the Union forces neither surrounded the city nor made systematic attempts to breach its defenses by regular approach. Instead, Grant used the trench system to hold an extended line economically while he dispatched mobile forces to cut the three railroads that connected Petersburg with the rest of the Confederacy. Lee used the trenches in identical fashion to send mobile forces of his own to block these ventures. To keep Lee on his toes, however, Grant occasionally resorted to direct attacks on the Petersburg defenses.

The most famous of these attacks was the Battle of the Crater (30 July 1864), when Union forces exploded a huge mine beneath a Confederate earthwork called Elliott's Salient. The mine shaft, 511 feet long, ran to a point 20 feet under the enemy work, and when finished, was packed with 8,000 pounds of black powder that when detonated created an enormous crater 30 feet deep. But the subsequent Union infantry assault was wretchedly coordinated, and counterattacking Confederate troops quickly sealed the breach.

Other major actions during the siege included the Battles of Reams Station (25 August 1864) and New Market Heights (28–30 September). These and other engagements were costly but indecisive. By early 1865, however, their incremental effect was to stretch Lee's lines near the breaking point. Aware that a powerful additional Union army under Maj. Gen. William Tecumseh *Sherman was thrusting northward through the Carolinas, Lee understood that when Sherman arrived, the situation would be hopeless. Therefore, on 25 March 1865, he attacked Fort Stedman, hoping to force Grant to contract his line enough so that Lee could slip away to the south, join a scratch Confederate force in eastern North Carolina, and stop or destroy Sherman's army. This desperate bid resulted only in the loss of 5,000 sorely needed infantry. On 1 April, Union forces finally crushed the extreme western end of Lee's line at the Battle of Five Forks. Lee then made preparations to evacuate Petersburg, but a general Union assault in the predawn hours of 2 April severely punished his army before he could get away. Richmond fell once Lee's army left Petersburg. Closely pursued by Grant, Lee surrendered a week later at Appomattox Courthouse. *Casualties for the ten-month siege totaled about 42,000 Union troops and 28,000 Confederates.

[See also Civil War: Military and Diplomatic Course; Confederate Army; Union Army; Wilderness to Petersburg Campaign.]

• Richard J. Sommers, *Richmond Redeemed*, 1979. Noah Andre Trudeau, *The Last Citadel: Petersburg, Virginia, June 1864–April 1865*, 1991.   —Mark Grimsley

PHILIP, or Metacomet (also known as King Philip) (c. 1640–1676), Wampanoag sachem and leader in *King Philip's War. Son of the powerful Massasoit, who had helped early Plymouth Colony survive, Metacom accepted the English name Philip when he replaced his deceased brother as the Wampanoags' principal sachem in 1662. His resistance to English territorial expansion and judicial authority offended Plymouth officials, who subjected him to accusations and humiliating rebukes before 1675, when Wampanoag warriors launched the raids that escalated into King Philip's War. The operational role that he played in this costly struggle is not clear; several capable leaders were involved in the guerrilla action that stunned the New England colonies. Philip did travel long distances through the forests, encouraging bands from various Algonquian tribes to join the desperate rebellion. A mixed force of Indians and English militiamen finally killed him in 1676. According to eyewitness Benjamin *Church, an Indian executioner making a speech over Philip's body said that "he had been a very great man and had made many a man afraid of him." Even in defeat, Philip remained a fearsome symbol of Native American resistance and military prowess.

[See also Native American Wars: Wars Between Native Americans and Europeans and Euro-Americans.]

• Russell Bourne, *The Red King's Rebellion*, 1990. Jill Lepore, *The Name of War: King Philip's War and the Origins of American Identity*, 1998.   —Patrick M. Malone

PHILIPPINES, LIBERATION OF THE (1944–45). The assault on the island of Leyte on 20 October 1944, toward the end of World War II, marked the beginning of the reconquest of the Philippines. Military and naval chiefs in Washington had not shared Gen. Douglas *MacArthur's determination to return to the Philippines, but the logistical realities of the Pacific War gave weight to his demand that the U.S. colony be liberated and that Luzon (rather than Formosa) be seized as a base for further operations against the Japanese home islands. On 8 September 1944, the *Joint Chiefs of Staff authorized the Leyte invasion, and on 3 October they acknowledged that an attack on Luzon would follow.

Shielded by Adm. William F. *Halsey's Third Fleet and Vice Adm. Thomas C. *Kinkaid's Seventh, Lt. Gen. Walter Krueger's Sixth Army (X and XXIV Corps) of MacArthur's Southwest Pacific Area command streamed ashore against light opposition on 20 October. MacArthur and his aides waded ashore, fulfilling his 1942 pledge, "I shall return." Convinced that the naval Battle of *Leyte Gulf (24–25 October) had seriously weakened the Americans, the local Japanese Army commander, Lt. Gen. Suzuki Sosaku, slipped 45,000 reinforcements onto Leyte. The fighting dragged on into early 1945, far longer than MacArthur had expected, and inflicted heavy *casualties: 3,504 Americans dead and 11,991 wounded. Perhaps 50,000 Japanese died on Leyte.

Japanese resistance, heavy rains, and unsuitable terrain limited Leyte's development as a major air and supply base and delayed the Luzon landing, originally scheduled for 20 December 1944. Japanese suicide planes had made their first devastating appearance at Leyte Gulf and now struck hard at ships leading the Luzon invasion force, sinking or seriously damaging eighteen vessels. The Sixth Army (now comprised of I and XIV Corps) landing at Lingayen on 9 January 1945, however, went unopposed.

The depletion of Japanese air and naval power in the defense of Leyte convinced Gen. Tomoyuki Yamashita, commander of the 14th Area Army in the Philippines, that he could no longer contest American landings. He divided his soldiers into three groups and positioned them in the mountains of northern, eastern, and western Luzon. The Japanese were to make the enemy conquest of Luzon as costly and time-consuming as possible.

MacArthur had justified the Luzon operation by arguing that the island's central plain, ideal for base sites, and Manila's port facilities could be seized within six weeks. He urged Krueger forward, despite his subordinate's concern that Yamashita might counterattack along the Sixth Army's overextended flanks. A "flying column" of the First Cavalry Division reached Manila's northern suburbs on 3 February, and 37th Division troops entered the city the following day. The 11th Airborne Division had been approaching Manila from the south. By 11 February, American troops encircled the city.

Yamashita had not intended to defend Manila, but the commander of naval forces in the city, Rear Adm. Sanji Iwabuchi, was determined to do so. To limit damage and civilian casualties, MacArthur forbade the use of air strikes against Japanese positions in the old walled city and concrete government buildings, but he acquiesced in the use of *artillery. In the month-long battle to retake the now devastated capital, more than 1,000 Americans died. Few of the 17,000 Japanese defenders survived, and civilian deaths totaled 100,000, victims of Japanese *atrocities and American bombardment.

While the U.S. Sixth Army turned its attention to the still substantial enemy forces on Luzon, Lt. Gen. Robert Eichelberger's Eighth Army swept the central and southern islands of Japanese troops. Isolated and poorly equipped, Yamashita's soldiers posed little threat to the buildup of American forces on Luzon in preparation for the planned invasion of Japan, but lengthy and difficult fighting remained to neutralize the 14th Area Army. More than 300,000 Filipino guerrillas assisted the army in this task. They gathered intelligence, ambushed enemy soldiers, and mopped up remnants of the Japanese forces. In all, the liberation of the Philippines cost the U.S. Army 13,884 killed and 48,541 wounded. Japanese military and civilian dead numbered over 250,000, and 114,010 others still remained to surrender at the end of the war on 15 August 1945.

[See also Philippines, U.S. Military Involvement in the; Philippine Sea, Battle of the; World War II, U.S. Naval Operations in: The Pacific.]

• M. Hamlin Cannon, *Leyte: The Return to the Philippines*, 1954. Robert Ross Smith, *Triumph in the Philippines*, 1963. D. Clayton James, *The Years of MacArthur*, Vol. 2, 1975. Edward J. Drea, *MacArthur's ULTRA: Codebreaking and the War Against Japan, 1942–1945*, 1992. Alfonso J. Aluit, *By Sword and Fire: The Destruction of Manila in World War II*, 1994.

—Richard B. Meixsel

PHILIPPINES, U.S. MILITARY INVOLVEMENT IN THE

began with Adm. George *Dewey's stunning victory over the Spanish Pacific Fleet in the Battle of *Manila Bay on 1 May 1898, at the beginning of the *Spanish-American War. The situation was complicated by the presence of a Filipino colonial rebellion, which declared independence from Madrid and created a national government under the leadership of Gen. Emilio *Aguinaldo. Both Americans and Filipino nationalists besieged Manila, but the Spanish surrendered to the U.S. forces, which excluded Aguinaldo's forces from the capital.

President William *McKinley decided to ask Spain to cede the Philippines to the United States in the Treaty of *Paris (1898). Annexation was opposed by most Democrats and some Republicans, but supported particularly within the Republican Party for a variety of reasons, commercial as well as strategic. At Manila, fighting, largely provoked by the U.S. commanding general, Elwell S. Otis, broke out between American and Filipino forces on 4 February 1899, two days before the U.S. Senate narrowly ratified the treaty annexing the archipelago.

The *Philippine War lasted from 1899 to 1902. Conventional unit warfare the first year, resulting in heavy Filipino casualties, was succeeded by substantial *guerrilla warfare until Aguinaldo was captured by Frederick Funston in 1901. *Atrocities occurred on both sides in the guerrilla war.

The U.S. military commander, Gen. Arthur MacArthur, who succeeded Otis in May 1900, continued to hold executive power even after a commission headed by federal Judge William Howard Taft arrived and began exercising legislative authority in September 1900. When Gen. Adna Chaffee relieved MacArthur in July 1901, McKinley transferred executive authority from MacArthur as military governor to Taft as civil governor. One of the civil government's first moves was to establish a Philippine Constabulary, consisting of American officers and Filipino enlisted men to maintain order in pacified areas while the U.S. Army and *Philippine Scouts and Constabulary concentrated against the guerrilla bands.

American enthusiasm for formal overseas colonies diminished after the war, in part because of the price of more than 4,000 American deaths and 20,000 Filipino soldiers killed, along with a huge number of civilian *casualties. American farmers worried over competition from Filipino produce while U.S. Army officers felt increasingly vulnerable in defending these distant islands against Japanese expansion. By 1907 a Philippine legislature, dominated by *independistas*, controlled the archipelago's internal affairs, and only the timing of full independence divided America's two main political parties. The Jones Act (1916) promised independence as soon as the Filipinos were ready.

But under the Republicans, progress slowed. From 1921 to 1927, the appointed governor general was U.S. Maj. Gen. Leonard *Wood, who ruled with a heavy hand. The Great Depression and the Democratic administration of Franklin D. *Roosevelt led in 1934 to the Tydings-McDuffie Act, which provided for a ten-year transition to Philippine independence under a commonwealth government. Manuel Quezon was elected commonwealth president in 1935.

With the growing threat from Japan, Quezon sought to build up the Philippine military. With President Roosevelt's permission, Quezon hired recent U.S. Army chief of staff Gen. Douglas *MacArthur (son of Arthur MacArthur) as a military adviser with the rank of field marshal, the only American ever to hold that title. When the Japanese invaded the islands in December 1941, they overwhelmed both the U.S. and the Philippine military. General MacArthur and Quezon left before the surrender of the besieged American forces on the island fortress of Corregidor in the Battle of *Manila Bay. Three years later, despite the navy's plan to bypass the Philippines, MacArthur obtained Roosevelt's permission to liberate the archipelago, and in October 1944 he and American troops waded ashore after the Battle of *Leyte Gulf. Less than a year after the end of the war, the Philippines was granted independence on 4 July 1946.

Particularly because of the *Cold War, the American military presence continued in the Philippine Republic. Americans provided assistance to President Ramon Magsaysay (1953–57) and others in the suppression of the Communist-led Huk rebellion (1946–54). In 1947, the United States was granted leases on several military bases there, including Clark Air Base and the U.S. Navy base at Subic Bay. President Ferdinand Marcos (1965–86) renegotiated those leases, and, at the urging of President Lyndon B. *Johnson, sent a battalion of Philippine Army Engineers to South Vietnam.

In the post-Marcos era, President Corazon Aquino (1986–92) survived the most serious attempted coup against her, in December 1989, through the help of U.S. military aircraft. The end of the Cold War made the U.S. military bases in the Philippines less crucial. As Filipino opposition to them mounted and the Philippine legislature increased its demands for lease renewals, the eruption of Mt. Pinatubo in June 1991 covered Clark Air Base with volcanic ash, and the Philippine Senate rejected a proposed treaty, the U.S. Air Force and U.S. Navy abandoned the bases they had held for nearly a century.

[See also Philippines, Liberation of the.]

• Theodore Friend, *Between Two Empires: The Ordeal of the Philippines*, 1965. Peter W. Stanley, *A Nation in the Making: The United States and the Philippines, 1899–1921*, 1974. Richard Welch, *Response to Imperialism: The United States and the Philippine-American War, 1899–1902*, 1979. Stuart C. Miller, *"Benevolent Assimilation": The American Conquest of the Philippines, 1899–1903*, 1982. Stanley Karnow, *In Our Image: America's Empire in the Philippines*, 1989. Glenn Anthony May, *Battle for Batangas: A Philippine Province at War*, 1991.   —Stuart Creighton Miller

PHILIPPINE SCOUTS AND CONSTABULARY.

Challenged by the climate and terrain of the Philippines and by the linguistic diversity of its inhabitants, the U.S. *Army recruited Filipino collaborators into its ranks soon after the outbreak of the *Philippine War in 1899. Organized into companies commanded by American enlisted men holding local commissions, these Philippine Scouts after the war garrisoned isolated parts of the islands, freeing American soldiers to concentrate near Manila. Provisional Scout regiments took the place of U.S. troops withdrawn for service in World War I. Financial constraints made these regiments the mainstay of the garrison thereafter. Raised from a peacetime strength of 6,000 to 12,000 early in 1941, the well-trained and long-serving Scout units proved to be the greatest obstacle to Japanese victory on Bataan during World War II. After the liberation of the *Philippines in 1944–45, the organization was reformed and considerably enlarged. These "New Scouts" performed garrison duty in the western Pacific until disbanded following Philippine independence on 4 July 1946.

Filipinos had been eligible for Scout commissions since 1901, and in 1908 the U.S. Congress authorized West Point to accept Filipinos. But when it became evident that routine promotions would lead Filipinos to command regular officers, the army ceased commissioning Filipino officers (1933).

The Philippine Constabulary was the Philippine government's national police force, established in August 1901. The constabulary's initial duties were similar to those of the Scouts: suppressing bandits and the remnants of guerrilla forces. Under the command of U.S. Army officers until 1917, the constabulary was headed thereafter by Filipinos. Although its law enforcement duties came to predominate over its military functions, the constabulary formed the nucleus of the Philippine Army, created in 1936, and contributed the Second Regular Division to the Bataan campaign.

[See also Bataan and Corregidor, Battles of; World War II, U.S. Naval Operations in: The Pacific.]

—Richard B. Meixsel

PHILIPPINE SEA, BATTLE OF THE. Much larger than the Battle of *Midway and the Battle of the *Coral Sea combined, the Battle of the Philippine Sea was the largest carrier duel of World War II. The invasion of Saipan on 15 June 1944 brought out the Japanese Mobile Fleet, under Vice Adm. Jisaburo Ozawa, to seek a "decisive" battle with the Americans. Ozawa's fleet was formidable—9 carriers, including the big new armored-deck Taiho; 450 planes; 5 *battleships; 13 cruisers; and 33 destroyers. But Ozawa was saddled with inexperienced and ill-trained air groups.

Ozawa's operational plan, A-GO, envisioned fighting in the Palaus and western Carolines because the Japanese Navy was short of refined fuel. If the Americans attacked the Marianas, the Japanese would use 172 land-based aircraft in the Marianas, along with planes flown from the home islands through Iwo Jima, and the Fleet would use unprocessed Borneo fuel.

Indeed, the battle took place off the Marianas. On 11 June, the Americans attacked Saipan, wiping out a third of the enemy planes there. Vice Adm. Raymond A. *Spruance's Fifth Fleet covered the landings. His main striking force, Task Force (TF) 58, under the command of Vice Adm. Marc A. Mitscher, included 5 task groups, 15 carriers with 902 aircraft, 7 fast battleships, 21 cruisers, and 67 destroyers. Backing them up were seven old battleships and their screening cruisers and destroyers responsible for shore bombardment. Eight escort carriers carrying 201 planes were assigned to the Saipan invasion, while another 3 "jeeps" with 93 aircraft aboard were available from the Guam invasion force.

American *submarines spotted Ozawa's ships leaving Tawitawi on the 13th and again on the 15th as they exited San Bernardino Strait into the Philippine Sea. The Japanese Mobile Fleet was again spotted on the 17th by the submarine Cavalla. That afternoon, Mitscher proposed to move west and flank the Japanese. Spruance concurred, but also issued his own aggressive plan, urging his forces to destroy the Japanese Mobile Fleet completely. But worried about a diversionary attack, the next day Spruance reconsidered; he directed TF 58 to advance westward, but to retire eastward at night so that the Japanese could not flank

him and attach the American transports invading Saipan.

The Battle of the Philippine Sea opened on 19 June, as Ozawa launched 197 aircraft against the Americans, a force larger than Admiral Nagumo had sent against Midway. But in 1944, the odds heavily favored the Americans. Shortly before 10:00 A.M., Japanese planes were picked up on *radar 140 miles away. The ensuing battle became known as the "Marianas Turkey Shoot." Ozawa started the day with 430 carrier aircraft and 43 floatplanes, and launched 355 carrier planes and 19 floatplanes. Only 130 returned to the Mobile Fleet. To the 244 planes that Ozawa lost should be added 50 more land-based aircraft. The Americans lost only twenty-two *fighter aircraft in dogfights or to flak over Guam; nine more planes were lost operationally or on search missions. Fifty-eight aircrewmen or sailors died.

Ozawa's losses were not just over TF 58. The Cavalla sank the Shokaku, which took over half of her crew of 2,000 and 9 planes with her. Another submarine, the Albacore, hit Ozawa's flagship, the big new Taiho, with one torpedo. Poor damage control and the volatile Borneo fuel she used proved fatal. She took almost 1,700 men of her crew of 2,200, plus another 13 planes, to the bottom.

Shortly before 4:00 P.M. on the 20th, searchers finally sighted Ozawa's ships 275 miles from TF 58. It was a long way to fly and night would fall before the planes could return to their carriers. But Mitscher launched 240 aircraft, of which 14 aborted. The rest pressed on and were over the Mobile Fleet by 6:30 P.M. In growing darkness, the Americans attacked, damaging several vessels and sinking three, the carrier Hiyo and two oilers. Besides the need to attack quickly because of low fuel, the attackers' apparent lack of success was a result of the fact that only 24 of the 54 Avengers engaged carried *torpedoes. Nevertheless, Japanese carrier aviation was finished for the remainder of the war. Ozawa had just 35 planes left out of the 430 he started with two days before.

The flight back to TF 58 at night and the recovery of the planes was as chaotic as the attack on the Mobile Fleet. Because many planes were almost out of fuel, Mitscher ordered his ships to turn on their lights to guide his aviators in. Of the 226 planes that reached the Mobile Fleet, 99 were lost. Only about 17 went down in combat; the rest succumbed to ditchings and deck crashes. Thanks to extensive search and rescue efforts, only forty-nine aircrewmen were lost.

The victory brought little satisfaction to the U.S. Navy. Some critics blamed Spruance for wasting the opportunity to destroy the enemy fleet. Others defended him stoutly. Nonetheless, no one can deny that the Japanese Mobile Fleet had been grievously hurt and its aviation arm never recovered from the losses sustained in the Philippine Sea.

[See also Carrier Warfare; World War II, U.S. Naval Operations in: The Pacific.]

• Theodore Taylor, The Magnificent Mitscher, 1954; rev. ed. 1991. Samuel Eliot Morison, History of United States Naval Operations in World War II, Vol. VIII: New Guinea and the Marianas, 1964. Clark G. Reynolds, The Fast Carriers, 1968; rev. ed. 1992. Thomas B. Buell, The Quiet Warrior, 1974; rev. ed. 1987. William T. Y'Blood, Red Sun Setting: The Battle of the Philippine Sea, 1981.

—William T. Y'Blood

The **PHILIPPINE WAR** (1899–1902) was a direct result— an almost inevitable aftermath—of the *Spanish-American War. After a U.S. *Army expedition captured Manila on 13 August 1898, Spain ceded the Philippine archipelago to the United States in the Treaty of *Paris. Seeking to reconcile the Filipinos to American rule by political and social reforms, President William *McKinley ordered a policy of "benevolent assimilation." But Filipino nationalists, who had been fighting for independence since 1896, proclaimed the Philippine Republic on 21 January 1899, with Emilio *Aguinaldo as its president. The Republican Army, a disparate collection of volunteers, conscripts, and former Spanish soldiers, maintained a semisiege over the 12,000 U.S. soldiers in Manila; on 4 February a skirmish between patrols escalated into heavy fighting.

For the remainder of 1899, the war was a conventional conflict between the American and Republican armies. Although Filipino troops often fought with great personal courage, they were poorly armed and abysmally led. Within the first three months, Maj. Gen. Elwell S. Otis's brigade columns swept the countryside in a thirty-mile radius of Manila and captured the republican capital of Malolos on 31 March. Aguinaldo proved an indifferent general, unable either to control his subordinates or to delegate authority; his leadership was further compromised by his complicity in the assassination of his rival, Gen. Antonio Luna. The U.S. Army, however, undermanned by the discharge of volunteers whose enlistments expired with the end of the Spanish-American War and ravaged by sickness and fatigue, could not hold territory or sustain an offensive. Only after a five-month hiatus could Otis launch a three-pronged attack into north-central Luzon; the Republican Army melted away and Aguinaldo barely escaped. By February 1900, virtually every important town in the archipelago lay under the U.S. flag.

From December 1899 until its official termination on 4 July 1902, the war continued as a series of localized campaigns of *counterinsurgency and *pacification. Conceding that his partisans could not prevail on the battlefield, Aguinaldo proclaimed a policy of continued resistance through *guerrilla warfare. Henceforth, the insurgents were to avoid open battle and rely on irregular tactics and intimidation; the American public, faced with a long and brutal war, would reject McKinley in the forthcoming 1900 election and choose the antiannexationist William Jennings *Bryan. Beyond this, there was little central direction. Aguinaldo remained in hiding, and leadership devolved upon provincial warlords such as Miguel Malvar in Batangas and Vicente Lukban in Samar. Leading small partisan bands, local chieftains relied on consanguinity and terror to maintain clandestine control over the residents of American-occupied towns and thereby gain food, shelter, and information. Their guerrillas became adept at harassment, firing on army patrols and then blending into the population.

The U.S. High Command was slow to recognize the depth of the resistance. Convinced the war was over, Otis reorganized the army for occupation duties, breaking up his brigade commands and stationing them in dozens of towns throughout the archipelago. He supported McKinley's policy of benevolent assimilation, ordering his officers to establish local governments, restore trade, build schools, and otherwise demonstrate America's good intentions. Otis's successor, Maj. Gen. Arthur MacArthur, was alert to the guerrilla threat but lacked the manpower or administrative support to combat it. In the absence of suitable instruction from Manila, garrison and provincial commanders began to develop their own pacification policies. With impressive resourcefulness, they devised new tactics, learned how to sustain military operations in the jungles and mountains, created intelligence networks, and formed working alliances with Filipinos. The war became a series of regional struggles, differing greatly from island to island and even village to village.

In December 1900, bolstered by reinforcements and McKinley's reelection, MacArthur instituted a comprehensive pacification campaign aimed at disrupting the connections between the guerrillas and their civilian supporters. American forces, often aided by Filipino auxiliaries, accelerated military operations, attacking guerrilla strongholds and destroying supplies. Military courts imprisoned, deported, or executed those who continued to resist; collaborators received pardons and often were given positions in the civil government. Defections and surrenders increased, especially after Brig. Gen. Frederick Funston's daring capture of Aguinaldo in March 1901. By July, when William H. Taft became governor, only a few provinces remained under military control and the war appeared all but over.

The massacre of an American infantry company at Balangiga, Samar, on 28 September 1901 provoked severe countermeasures. Brig. Gen. Jacob H. Smith, urging one subordinate to make Samar a "howling wilderness," conducted a brutal campaign that inflicted terrible hardships on the population. In southern Luzon, Brig. Gen. J. Franklin Bell destroyed crops, harried guerrillas with soldiers and Filipino auxiliaries, and confined much of the population within protected zones. By April 1902, the last important guerrilla leaders had surrendered; on 4 July 1902, President Theodore *Roosevelt declared the "insurrection" over.

In some respects the war was one of the least costly the United States ever fought. Army *casualties were comparatively light: between 4 February 1899 and 4 July 1902, 1,037 soldiers were killed in action, 2,818 were wounded, and a total of 4,374 died of all causes. Postwar disorder took years to suppress; sporadic military campaigns against bandits, rebels, and Muslim tribesmen, or Moros, continued until 1913.

From its inception, the American conquest was highly controversial. The government and imperialists claimed annexation was necessary for both economic and humanitarian reasons. Arguing that the Filipinos were incapable of self-government, they portrayed Aguinaldo as a Tagalog bandit and his supporters as criminals or dupes. A small but vocal group of anti-imperialists condemned the war as immoral and unconstitutional; they accused American soldiers of looting, arson, and torture. The public supported annexation, although revelations of isolated *atrocities by U.S. soldiers caused some outrage in 1902. Recent scholarship has focused on the regional nature of the war: it emphasizes the resourcefulness of the guerrilla tactics and army countermeasures—a diversity that made this conflict unique.

[See also Jungle Warfare; Philippines, U.S. Military Involvement in the.]

• James A. LeRoy, The Americans in the Philippines, 2 vols., 1914. John M. Gates, Schoolbooks and Krags: The United States Army in the Philippines, 1898–1902, 1973. Richard E. Welch, Response to Imperialism: The United States and the Philippine-American War, 1899–1902, 1979. Brian M. Linn, The U.S. Army and Counterinsur-

gency in the Philippine War, 1899–1902, 1989. Glenn A. May, *Battle for Batangas: A Philippine Province at War*, 1991.

—Brian M. Linn

PHOTOGRAPHY, WAR AND THE MILITARY IN. The perfection of the daguerreotype process by 1839 brought the new science of photography to a stage the modern viewer would recognize: the formation by the physics of light, and its development by the chemistry of silver, of an image on a more or less permanent, portable surface. During the 1840s, the science came from France and England to America and immediately found acceptance amid much experimentation, foreign and domestic, with variations of chemistry and surface. Portraits, landscapes, and architecture, the most frequent early subjects of photography, had obvious military counterparts. There is no record that anyone set out systematically to photograph the scenes and participants in the *Mexican War (1846–48). However, several images exist by chance, depicting groups of U.S. soldiers in camp or en route.

James Robertson and Roger Fenton of Great Britain began the systematic photography of war with their work in the Crimea (1854–55) and at the British staging grounds at Constantinople. Having an eye to commercial sale as well as period sensitivities, they photographed no dead bodies, concentrating instead on soldier groups, officers' portraits, and both close and panoramic views of camps and battle sites. Some photographs, published in periodicals as engravings, fueled a rancorous public debate over army conditions and an inefficient London administration.

In 1854, *The Practical Mechanics Journal* asserted that cameras could ensure "undeniably accurate representation of the realities of war and its contingent scenery, its struggles, its failures and triumphs." The art debate of the day, in general, was between photographic accuracy and painterly license, yet the statement also foreshadowed the ongoing debate over the objective versus subjective depiction of war and its emotions.

By the outbreak of the *Civil War, photography was fully established as an art form and documentary record. Images, both negative and positive, existed on paper, glass, and metal in many variants, and while not yet a do-it-yourself process, original photographs were within the financial reach of many Americans. They could be printed in books and newspapers only as some form of line engraving until the invention of the halftone printing plate in the 1880s, but thousands of original prints were for sale by dealers. Mathew B. Brady, one of the most astute and successful prewar photographers, was already offering his Gallery of Illustrious Americans, including military heroes. In the two decades of photography thus far, the technological curve had risen steeply and quickly, so that images were sharp and clear and workmanship careful even where composition was often unsophisticated. Family portraits could be proudly displayed; they had special meaning in an era of strong family values and high mortality, especially of children. Indeed, some photographers advertised a specialty in pictures of the recently deceased.

Many citizens had limited visual access to their vast country, and a high curiosity, coupled with *patriotism, values, and sentimentality, made for a strong market in war-related imagery. Civil War photographers were of three types. A few practiced their craft while in uniform, such as Andrew Russell, who enlisted in a New York regi-

ment in 1862 and became a photographer of installations, architecture, and battlefield landscapes for the U.S. Military Railroads. His work, lost for years amid that of Brady, only regained its proper identity in the 1980s.

A second group consisted of camp photographers, professionals either unknown or with limited name recognition, who toured camps on pass to do soldier portraits to send home. Tolerated for their contribution to entertainment and troop *morale, they produced an immense quantity of work, often in the form of cartes-de-visite. These were taken as a series of single negatives on a glass plate coated with wet collodion, printed on paper, and cut apart into rectangular pictures modeled on the calling cards of the day (not unlike modern sports cards). The format was so popular it became the vehicle for mass-producing collectible images of generals and politicians.

Mathew Brady was the best known of the prominent commercial photographers who added war scenes to their formal print catalogues. Among others were Alexander Gardner and Timothy O'Sullivan, who worked for Brady before becoming independent in 1863. These men worked on battlefields and in dangerous situations, yet their bulky equipment limited them. Slow exposure times and the absence of movable shutters precluded photography of infantry assaults and cavalry charges in favor of more static scenes. The photographers were not at all squeamish about dead bodies, and some of the best known death studies were compositionally enhanced rather than depicted as found. This fact, however, seems never to have diminished the attraction of pictures like Gardner's "Home of a Rebel Sharpshooter" from Gettysburg. Civil War work was popular for a time but interest soon waned, and *Gardner's Photographic Sketch Book of the Civil War*, published in 1866, was a commercial failure. The modern photo historian William Frassanito has identified hundreds of Civil War images and rephotographed the identical scenes as they look at present.

Major improvements in photographic equipment between 1865 and 1930 brought only limited improvements in the depiction of war and military subjects. Civil War photographers working in the West posed soldier groups in routine surroundings. Edward S. Curtis did outstanding portraits of Indian warriors. The short-lived *Spanish-American War produced much that was reminiscent of the Civil War, as well as two new categories. Marching soldiers now actually marched, but the charge up San Juan Hill was still beyond the limits of clarity. And the availability of small hand cameras—the famous Kodak box—led to snapshots by troops in the field and especially by mischievous sailors prowling the decks. World War I, lengthy, grim, and brutal though it was for soldiers and civilians alike, did not produce a long roster of well-known photographers or a group of memorable individual images. The official work is simply that; the journalistic work was highly controlled; and much of the whole is anonymous, repetitive, and lacking in dimension. Just before the Italian invasion of Ethiopia (1935), Alfred Eisenstaedt, using the new photo essay concept, did a noteworthy series on the harshness of life there, and from the Spanish Civil War (1936) came American photojournalist Robert Capa's remarkable but oft-doubted "Moment of Death."

By any standard, the photographic legacy of World War II is enormous in quantity and importance. In the most photographed war in history, through countless millions of images, photographers brought the use of photography for combat-related purposes to the highest level yet. The interpretation of aerial and reconnaissance images became a vital specialty within high-level command staffs. Of American wars, more World War II imagery circulates in the collectible fine art photography market than from any other conflict. Not only is this work highly evocative and expressive but it also exhibits the meticulousness of style, composition, and craftsmanship that typified the fine art photography of the 1930s and 1940s. Established artists like Eisenstaedt, Margaret Bourke-White, Dorothea Lange, Horace Bristol, Lou Stoumen, Peter Stackpole, Carl Mydans, and many others produced significant war-related work. They succeeded because they were able to combine fine art and documentary styles in a single vision.

Volunteers and draftees alike who had basic photographic knowledge often found themselves in assignments where they could use their skills. The U.S. Navy had a separate rating for photographers; the army and Marines grouped them with other technical personnel. Their work became commingled with that of countless others and identified upon publication only as "official" photography. Anonymity oft repeated equals fame of sorts, as in the familiar image of the destroyer USS *Shaw* exploding at Pearl Harbor, taken by an unknown navy photographer.

In 1942, the well-known New York photographer Edward Steichen, a reserve officer and World War I veteran, at age sixty-three was recommissioned in the navy and authorized to recruit a team of men to receive commissions and photograph the Pacific War. The group, which included Fenno Jacobs, Wayne Miller, Horace Bristol, Victor Jorgensen, Charles Kerlee, Bruce Gallagher, and Paul Dorsey, made the war personal and immediate by concentrating on the enlisted men and junior officers they met while deployed with carrier task forces or on captured islands. Steichen supervised the processing, printing, and media release of the pictures, which were vital links binding war front to home front.

Many photojournalists served with American forces as civilians but were subject to military censorship. World War II was America's most heavily censored war, at least until its final year. The popular newsreel theaters showed live action footage, but the first photograph showing dead American troops where they fell—George Strock's picture of three soldiers on the beach at Buna, New Guinea—did not appear until September 1943. There had been earlier photos showing blanket-covered bodies and flag-draped caskets. *Life* published the Strock photo with a careful editorial to prepare Americans for the shock, fearing a negative effect on morale. The caution was unnecessary. Americans accepted the photo and those to follow.

Home front activities to support the war effort not only utilized official photos supplied by the Office of War Information and other agencies but also produced a variety of published images. War bond drives required advertising and posters, which in turn led to photo contests. One in 1943 invited citizens to submit snapshots on the theme "The American Boy Under Japanese Rule." This kind of informal imagery at home had its counterpart in war zones. As the war progressed, personal cameras were more and more numerous, especially among American troops in Europe after D-Day. In the visual imagery of the war are thousands of snapshots of buddies, prostitutes, townspeople, bombed cities, and landscapes. At the opposite end of

the scale are the great well-known compositions, usually by professionals, such as Joe Rosenthal's picture of the second flag-raising by the Marine Corps on Iwo Jima; Alfred Eisenstaedt's picture of a sailor kissing a nurse in Times Square on V-J Day; and W. Eugene Smith's image of a soldier carrying a small baby found under a rock on Saipan.

The aftermath of the war remained in the public eye for a long time. One of Steichen's crew was among the first cameramen to see the devastation of Hiroshima. Margaret Bourke-White accompanied American troops who liberated concentration camps. One after another, photo essays depicting the conduct of life amid physical and economic ruin appeared in news magazines.

Korea—in a war that Americans tolerated but did not support as enthusiastically as World War II—came across visually as bloody, freezing, and endless, with little of traditional glory and much of individual suffering for American Marines and soldiers. The *Vietnam War, brought live into homes every night both as jungle fighting and urban rioting, offers the best modern example of how blurred and indistinct are the various categories of war scenes, first defined for the Crimean conflict by *The Practical Mechanics Journal*. The visual record became not merely documentation of what was happening but advocacy for what ought to happen. A tight composition of the sweat-streaked face of a teenage Marine, if perhaps a study in courage, also got captioned "Bring Him Home" by war protestors. What may have happened ten minutes before the frame, and in fact defined the frame, is lost in projection of the future. The increasing political complexity of late twentieth-century warfare has a profound effect on its visual record.

Two other realities are also at work. The nightly news emphasis on violence and death at home inures the viewer to scenes of distant combat, even by Americans in brush-fire wars. And the virtual disappearance of the uniform from city streets and depots as a consequence of the Vietnam War has created a distance, both visual and real, from the American people. The boy next door of World War II is now, along with so many other photographic subjects, a part of history.

[*See also* Culture, War, and the Military; Film, War and the Military in; Illustration, War and the Military in.]

• Margaret Bourke-White, *They Called It "Purple Heart Valley": A Combat Chronicle of the War in Italy*, 1944. Frank Freidel, *The Splendid Little War*, 1958. Roy Meredith, *Mr. Lincoln's Camera Man: Mathew B. Brady*, 1976. Jorge Lewinski, *The Camera at War: War Photography from 1848 to the Present Day*, 1978. Christopher Phillips, *Steichen at War*, 1981. Alan Trachtenberg, *Reading American Photographs: Images as History, Mathew Brady to Walker Evans*, 1989. Peter Maslowski, *Armed with Cameras: The American Military Photographers of World War II*, 1993. George H. Roeder, Jr., *The Censored War: American Visual Experience During World War Two*, 1993. Ken Conner and Debra Heimerdinger, *Horace Bristol: An American View*, 1996.
—James E. Sefton

PICKETT'S CHARGE. *See* Gettysburg, Battle of.

PISTOLS. *See* Side Arms, Standard Infantry.

PITCHER, MOLLY (1744?/1754?–1832), Revolutionary War heroine. The legend of "Molly Pitcher" is based at least in part on the actions of Mary (Molly) Ludwig Hays McCauley; the nickname may have applied to her alone, or may have been used collectively to describe all female *"camp followers" who assisted the *Continental army.

The daughter of German immigrants who settled in New Jersey, by 1769 Mary Ludwig was a servant of Dr. William Irvine in Carlisle, Pennsylvania. In that year she married a barber, John Casper Hays. He initially served in Col. Thomas Proctor's First Pennsylvania Artillery (1775–76), then reenlisted, in January 1777, as a private in Dr. (now Col.) Irvine's Seventh Pennsylvania Regiment. Sometime later, Mary joined him in camp.

On 28 June 1778, Mary Hays made a name for herself in the Battle of *Monmouth, in New Jersey. She had been carrying buckets, or pitchers, of water to her husband's *artillery crew; when he fell wounded, she replaced him at the cannon, helping to serve the gun for the remainder of the engagement.

John Hays died several years later, and Mary Hays married another veteran, John (possibly George) McCauley, around 1792. After being widowed a second time and experiencing increasing financial difficulties, she petitioned for a soldier's widow's pension; the Pennsylvania legislature on 21 February 1822 instead awarded her a $40 annuity in recognition of her own services during the Revolution. After her death she became a legendary figure, and a monument was later erected at her burial site in Carlisle.

[See also Revolutionary War: Military and Diplomatic Course; Women in the Military.]

• William Davison Perrine, *Molly Pitcher of Monmouth County, New Jersey, and Captain Molly of Fort Washington, New York, 1778–1937.* 1937. Linda Grant De Pauw, "Women in Combat: The Revolutionary War Experience," *Armed Forces and Society*, 7 (1981), pp. 209–26. Janice E. McKenney, "'Women in Combat': Comment," *Armed Forces and Society*, 8 (1982), pp. 686–92.

—Holly A. Mayer

PITTSBURGH LANDING. *See* Shiloh, Battle of (1862).

PLAINS INDIAN WARS (1854–90). The wars between the Indian tribes of the Great Plains and the U.S. *Army grew out of the westward movement of Americans. The territorial accessions of the *Mexican War of 1846–48, followed by the discovery of gold in California, set off a migration across the plains that ended only in the final decades of the nineteenth century as farmers and stockmen began to occupy the plains themselves. Plains warfare, however, centered mainly on securing the transcontinental travel routes and protecting travelers rather than actual residents from Indian aggressions. Indian hostility arose from resentment over the inroads of travelers on such Indian resources as game, timber, and grass. Typically, the major wars with the Plains tribes followed treaties negotiated by government commissioners that bound the Indians to settle on a designated reservation. The military was then called in to make them go, or to make them return once they had moved, discovered the misery of reservation life, and bolted.

The Plains tribes that fought the United States most intensively were the Sioux (Lakota), Cheyenne, and Arapaho on the northern plains and the Cheyenne, Arapaho, Kiowa, and Comanche on the southern plains. All these tribes had traditions of constant warfare with other tribes—the Sioux and Cheyennes against the Crows and Shoshones, for example. Thus, military operations occurred against a backdrop of constant intertribal fighting, with Indians often serving as scouts or auxiliaries for the federal troops.

Army and Indian warred in different styles. The army maintained a system of forts at strategic locations and fielded heavy offensive columns burdened by slow-moving supply trains. The Indians fought with hit-and-run tactics that exploited environmental factors and avoided open engagement unless the risk was small. The individual warrior excelled over the typical regular in virtually every test of combat proficiency, but in open battle this was offset by military organization, discipline, command, and firepower. In general, the army prevailed when the Indians abandoned their orthodoxy and fought by white rules, or when commanders abandoned their orthodoxy and fought by Indian rules.

After the Mexican War, Indian wars erupted along the Oregon-California Trail, the Santa Fe Trail, and the various trails across Texas. Sioux and Cheyennes slipped into hostilities in 1854–55. Near Fort Laramie, the Grattan Massacre of 19 August 1854, caused by the imprudent actions of a young officer, led to Brig. Gen. William S. Harney's campaign of 1855. At the Battle of Bluewater, 3 September 1855, Harney destroyed a Sioux village and killed Chief Little Thunder. To the south, Kiowas, Comanches, and Cheyennes threatened the commerce with Santa Fe and raided deep into Texas.

The *Civil War years intensified fighting, with federalized volunteer units replacing the regulars. The Minnesota uprising of 1862 spread west into Dakota Territory, where Sioux resented gold seekers crossing their homeland to newly opened mines in western Montana. In the summers of 1863, 1864, and 1865, Brig. Gen. Henry H. Sibley and Brig. Gen. Alfred Sully fought successful engagements with the Sioux. Most notable was Sully's victory over *Sitting Bull and Inkpaduta at the Battle of Killdeer Mountain, 28 July 1864.

On the central plains during the summer of 1864, Indian unrest threatened the trails from the east to Denver, Colorado, and led to the tragic and treacherous attack by Col. John M. Chivington on Black Kettle's Cheyenne village at Sand Creek, 29 November 1864. Sand Creek set off a general war that spread over the plains country in 1865. A three-pronged offensive on the northern plains directed by Brig. Gen. Patrick E. Connor failed when columns encountered bad weather and ran out of supplies.

With the end of the Civil War, regulars returned to the plains. Red Cloud's Sioux closed the Bozeman Trail to the Montana mines and besieged the three forts erected to protect travelers. On 21 December 1866, warriors wiped out an eighty-man force under Capt. William J. Fetterman near Fort Phil Kearny, Wyoming. The following summer, however, in the Wagon Box and Hayfield fights, new breech-loading rifles helped beat back massed Indian assaults. The Fort Laramie Treaty of 1868 ended the Red Cloud War and provided for abandoning the three forts along the Bozeman Trail.

On the southern plains, a war in 1868–69 forced Cheyennes, Kiowas, and Comanches to new reservations. The highlight of this conflict was the Battle of the Washita, 27 November 1868, in which Lt. Col. George Armstrong *Custer fell on the Cheyenne village of Black Kettle, who had survived Sand Creek but now died. In 1874, these tribes, discontented with reservation life, fled to the west. The Red River War of 1874–75, featuring operations by Col. Nelson A. Miles and Col. Ranald S. Mackenzie, ended warfare on the southern plains and along the Texas frontier.

On the northern plains, new tensions arose as railroads aimed for the Sioux country and gold was discovered in the Black Hills, part of the Sioux reservation. The Great Sioux War of 1876 resulted, as the army sought to force Sitting Bull, *Crazy Horse, and other chiefs to go to the reservation. Three columns converged on the Sioux hunting grounds under Brig. Gen. George Crook, Brig. Gen. Alfred H. Terry, and Col. John Gibbon. Riding with Terry was Custer and his Seventh Cavalry Regiment. On 25 June 1876, Custer attacked a great village of Sioux and Cheyennes on Montana's Little Bighorn River. He and the force under his immediate command, 212 men, were wiped out. The Custer disaster so stunned Americans that large armies took the field, and by the spring of 1877, most of the Sioux and Cheyennes had surrendered. Sitting Bull sought refuge in Canada, but gave up in 1881.

The Red River War and the Great Sioux War ended major warfare on the Great Plains, although fighting went on elsewhere in the West until the final surrender of the Apache *Geronimo in 1886. One final bloodletting occurred at the Battle of Wounded Knee, South Dakota, on 29 December 1890. This was hardly war, however, but rather a spiritual revival that blew up in unintended and unexpected violence. Wounded Knee was the last important encounter between U.S. soldiers and American Indians and coincided with the passing of the western frontier.

[See also Native American Wars.]

• Robert M. Utley, *Frontiersmen in Blue: The United States Army and the Indian, 1848–1865,* 1967. Robert M. Utley, *Frontier Regulars: The United States Army and the Indian, 1866–1890,* 1974.

—Robert M. Utley

PLATT AMENDMENT (1901). In 1901, U.S. Senator Orville Platt introduced an amendment to the U.S. Army appropriations bill specifying several conditions for the American military evacuation of Cuba. The two key provisions of the Platt Amendment, first proposed by Secretary of War Elihu *Root, required that Cuba cede territory for American military and naval bases and also grant the United States the right to intervene in the island to preserve order, life, property, and liberty. In Congress, even proponents of Cuban independence like Senators Joseph Foraker and George Hoar supported the amendment, which President William *McKinley signed into law on 2 March. In early June, the Cuban Constitutional Convention acceded to American demands, and the amendment came to regulate Cuban-American relations until it was abrogated in 1934.

The Platt Amendment addressed a fundamental problem for the expanding United States. In 1898, the U.S. government had pledged under the *Teller Amendment to withdraw from Cuba once Spain had been defeated in the *Spanish-American War. But after the U.S. military victory, Washington wished to maintain the strategic gains of 1898 and did not trust the Cubans to establish a government friendly to American interests. The Platt Amendment resolved this contradiction by in essence making Cuba a U.S. protectorate. However, the amendment also poisoned Cuban-American relations and encouraged U.S. *expansionism in the Americas in the early twentieth century.

[See also Caribbean and Latin America, U.S. Military Involvement in the.]

• David F. Healy, *The United States in Cuba, 1898–1902: Generals,* Politicians, and the Search for Policy, 1963. Louis A. Perez, *Cuba Under the Platt Amendment, 1902–1934,* 1986.

—John Lawrence Tone

POLITICAL SCIENCE. *See* Disciplinary Views of War: Political Science and International Relations.

POLK, JAMES K. (1795–1849), eleventh president of the United States. Born in Mecklenburg County, North Carolina, on 2 November 1795, Polk moved to Tennessee with his family in 1806, and graduated from the University of North Carolina. He studied law and was admitted to the bar in 1820. An active Jacksonian Democrat, he served in Congress from 1825 to 1839, was speaker of the house and later governor of Tennessee.

In 1844, Polk—known as "Young Hickory"—was elected president. He entered the White House with a clear and aggressive foreign policy agenda, and as president he employed the threat of war and war itself as instruments to achieve his territorial objective: the West Coast and especially its ports.

The United States annexed Texas in 1845, and Polk provoked the *Mexican War a year later by making use of a climate of hostility, existing border disputes, and Mexican unwillingness and inability to accept U.S. offers to purchase its northern provinces. Polk proved to be a determined, tough, and successful commander in chief. Although he lacked military experience or training, he made many key military decisions and played a direct role in organizing and planning the war effort. Despite opposition from Whigs and some Democrats, Polk never wavered in his determination to use the war to acquire the territories of New Mexico and upper California.

Polk was not a popular president with his contemporaries. He was intensely partisan and had a proclivity for secrecy and evasiveness. He was constantly at odds with his two Whig generals, Zachary *Taylor and Winfield *Scott. Moreover, the Mexican War proved unpopular in the Northeast, and territorial expansion into the Southwest was a highly controversial political issue. Polk, however, is generally recognized as the first effective wartime president. Unlike James *Madison during the *War of 1812, Polk aggressively employed presidential power to conduct the military effort and achieve administration war goals, thus setting an example upon which Abraham *Lincoln would expand during the *Civil War.

[See also Commander in Chief, President as.]

• Paul H. Bergeron, *The Presidency of James K. Polk,* 1987. Sam W. Haynes, *James K. Polk and the Expansionist Impulse,* 1997.

—John H. Schroeder

PONTIAC (c. 1720–1769), Ottawa war leader. Championed as the "great chief" who headed *Pontiac's Rebellion, Pontiac's significance lies in the way he reflected, rather than created, intertribal militancy following the Seven Years' War.

Sources first mention Pontiac at Fort Duquesne (Pittsburgh) in 1757, but definitively he appears in the record only in May 1763. Foiled in his attempt that month to surprise and capture British Fort Detroit, Pontiac and his multitribal allies besieged it until October. Pontiac may have directed, though he certainly did not lead, the successful attacks on the British forts Sandusky (Ohio) and St. Joseph (Michigan). These actions inspired frontier raiding, the elimination of seven other British posts by July 1763, and the Delaware and Shawnee siege of Fort Pitt.

By late 1763 and throughout 1764, Pontiac endeavored to draw support from French garrisons in Illinois. Failing again, he retreated with the British at Detroit in July 1765, confirming peace at Oswego a year later.

By 1768, his reputation among Ottawas had fallen and he became an exile in lower Illinois. There, at Cahokia in April 1769, perhaps in retaliation for his killing of an Illinois Indian in 1766, a Peoria clubbed and stabbed Pontiac to death.

[*See also* Native American Wars.]

• Howard H. Peckham, *Pontiac and the Indian Uprising*, 1947. Richard White, *The Middle Ground: Indians, Empires, and Republics in the Great Lakes Region, 1650–1815*, 1991.

—Gregory Evans Dowd

PONTIAC'S REBELLION (1763–66). This multitribal assault on British western posts after the *French and Indian War resulted from several factors: trade disputes; the Delaware Prophet's millennial teachings; Gen. Jeffrey *Amherst's termination of customary gift distributions to Indians; settlers' encroachment; and the new British forts.

The Ottawa war leader *Pontiac opened the conflict on 9 May, attacking Fort Detroit with warriors from several tribes. The 120-man garrison held out under Maj. Henry Gladwin, but Indians soon captured six forts and forced the abandonment of Fort Edward Augustus. Senecas took two other forts, Venango and Le Boeuf; Le Boeuf's garrison escaped to Fort Pitt, joining the command of Capt. Simeon Ecuyer, to fight off further Indian attacks. At one point, Ecuyer tried to weaken the besiegers by distributing smallpox-contaminated blankets during a parley, which may have caused an epidemic.

In the next phase, fighting centered on the supply lines of Detroit and Fort Pitt. Indians inflicted heavy losses on the British in a surprise attack at Point Pelee, Ontario (28 May), and won a signal victory at Devil's Hole near Niagara Falls, 14 September, when 300–500 Senecas overwhelmed 2 British companies and a convoy, killing 72. Nonetheless, the British armed vessels *Huron* and *Michigan* retained control of Lake Erie, bringing reinforcements to Detroit between June and November, and sustaining the post until the Indians raised their siege. Indians attacked Col. Henry Bouquet's relief force of 460 men at Bushy Run (5 August). Bouquet reached Fort Pitt, but his 110 casualties prevented him from beginning offensive operations.

The final phase began in 1764, when Colonel Bouquet led 1,200 men into the Delaware heartland in October, securing the release of 200 captives and a promise of peace. Pontiac failed to secure assistance from the remaining French garrisons in Illinois and finally sought peace in late 1764. Hostilities were formally concluded at Oswego, July 1766.

The war exacerbated Indian-hating in the colonies, as both the resort to smallpox at Fort Pitt and the "Paxton Boys" massacre in 1763 of twenty peaceful Indians in Pennsylvania show. The British promised to enforce the Royal Proclamation of October 1763 prohibiting colonization west of the Appalachian ridge, and restored the prewar patterns of trade and gift giving. Indians ceded no extensive lands, and the British reestablished none of their abandoned forts. Some 450 British regulars and provincials lost their lives. Indian and settler losses remain unknown.

[*See also* Native American Wars: Wars Between Native Americans and Europeans and Euro-Americans.]

• Howard H. Peckham, *Pontiac and the Indian Uprising*, 1947. Richard White, *The Middle Ground: Indians, Empires, and Republics in the Great Lakes Region, 1650–1815*, 1991.

—Gregory Evans Dowd

PORTER, DAVID DIXON (1813–1891), American admiral. Born in Chester, Pennsylvania, Porter was the son of David Porter, naval hero in the *War of 1812. A midshipman in the U.S. Navy at sixteen, young Porter commanded his first ship at thirty-three during the *Mexican War. In the *Civil War, he became one of the leading commanders in the *Union Navy. In April 1862 during the *Siege of New Orleans, he led a flotilla of twenty-one small gunboats each with a 13-inch heavy mortar, which bombarded the forts guarding the narrow channel, enabling Adm. David *Farragut's fleet of warships to get upriver and successfully besiege the city itself. During the following year, Porter, in charge of the gunboats, ironclads, and supply ships on the Mississippi north of Vicksburg, aided Gens. Ulysses S. *Grant and William Tecumseh *Sherman in their long and ultimately successful Siege of *Vicksburg (1862–1863) and establishment of Union control of the entire Mississippi River. Promoted to rear admiral—after Farragut, the second in U.S. history to hold that rank—Porter assumed command of the North Atlantic Blockading Squadron and the naval portion of two joint land-sea expeditions in the winter of 1864–1865 against Fort Fisher, guarding the port of Wilmington, North Carolina. After Gen. Benjamin F. *Butler failed in his assault, Gen. Alfred Terry succeeded with the support of Porter's sizable fleet, which bombarded the fort and sent 2,000 sailors and marines to join 8,000 soldiers in storming the parapets, achieving the only successful large-scale amphibious attack against a strongly fortified position in the Civil War. After the war, Porter served as superintendent (1865–1869) of the U.S. Naval Academy. He was promoted to vice admiral (1866) and full admiral (1870) on the death of Farragut. The two officers, aggressive and successful in their coordinated efforts with the *Union Army, were the leading Union naval commanders of the Civil War.

• Richard S. West, Jr., *The Second Admiral: A Life of David Dixon Porter, 1813–1891*, 1937; Chester G. Hearn, *Admiral David Dixon Porter: The Civil War Years*, 1996.

—John Whiteclay Chambers II

The **POSSE COMITATUS ACT** (1878) prohibited use of the U.S. Army to aid civil officials in enforcing the law or suppressing civil disorder unless expressly ordered to do so by the president. Southern Democratic members of the House who resented widespread use of federal troops during *Reconstruction introduced the law. Some northern congressmen supported the law due to the army's role in suppressing disorders during the 1877 railroad strike.

In the past, soldiers had occasionally served as posses to assist U.S. marshals or judges without reference to the president. During the 1850s, U.S. Attorney General Caleb Cushing ruled that U.S. marshals could call upon federal soldiers, Marines, and sailors to help enforce the Fugitive Slave Act in the North. Such troops performed similar duties when called on by territorial governors in Kansas and Utah. Regulars routinely acted as posses during Reconstruction in the South, particularly during election disorders. Troops suppressing the 1877 railroad riots took orders from state governors and even municipal officers.

Use of federal troops as a posse comitatus placed them outside the military chain of command and the commander in chief's direct authority. Too often the practice turned regulars into policemen serving the interests of locals directly involved in the disputes provoking disorder. Army officers welcomed the Posse Comitatus Act and the new regulations it engendered, for they felt more comfortable performing their duty safely within the chain of command. The provisions of the act have governed army regulations and civil disorder doctrine to the present.

[See also Civil-Military Relations; Commander in Chief, President as.]

• Robert W. Coakley, *The Role of Federal Military Forces in Domestic Disorder, 1789–1878*, 1988. Jerry M. Cooper, "Federal Military Intervention in Domestic Disorders," in Richard H. Kohn, ed., *The United States Military Under the Constitution of the United States, 1789–1989*, 1991.

—Jerry Cooper

POST EXCHANGES. *See* Commissaries and Post Exchanges.

POST TRAUMATIC STRESS DISORDER. *See* Aggression and Violence; Combat Trauma.

POTSDAM CONFERENCE (1945). On 17 July 1945, Josef *Stalin, Harry S. *Truman, and Winston S. *Churchill (who was replaced on 28 July by Clement Attlee) met for eleven days at Potsdam near Berlin. They faced two related issues: ending the war against Japan and restructuring Germany and Eastern Europe.

Germany ranked high on everyone's list of problems. Truman's goal was to create principles to guide the proposed Allied Control Council in preparing for unification of Germany. Stalin was concerned about reparations and Germany's border with Poland. Accepted were the American principles, including denazification, demilitarization, and democratization, and the Soviet desire for the Oder and Neisse Rivers as Germany's eastern border. Agreeing on reparations was difficult and was resolved only at the end of the conference by a formula calling for each power to take reparations from its zone, with the Soviets receiving some from other zones.

As for Japan, Stalin agreed to Soviet entry into the war by mid-August, while Truman informed Stalin in vague terms about a new weapon to be used against Japan, but failed to specify that it was an atomic bomb. At the end of the meeting, Truman and Attlee issued the Potsdam Declaration, calling upon Japan to surrender unconditionally or face destruction.

Specifics about reparations and issues of Soviet-occupied Eastern Europe were deferred to a newly created Council of Foreign Ministers, which was to draft the peace treaties. This allowed general agreement, and left each power partially satisfied. Much was left undone, and the Big Three's ability to cooperate and work toward similar postwar goals was still unknown. Potsdam remains a transition point as the former Allies moved from World War II to the *Cold War.

[See also World War II: Postwar Impact; World War II: Changing Interpretations.]

• Herbert Feis, *Between War and Peace: The Potsdam Conference,* 1960. Charles Mee, Jr., *Meeting at Potsdam,* 1975.

—James Gormly

POWELL, COLIN (1937–), twelfth chairman of the *Joint Chiefs of Staff (JCS). Born 5 April 1937 in the Harlem section of New York City and raised in the South Bronx, Colin L. Powell, the son of Jamaican immigrants, rose to become the first African American chairman of the JCS. After his 1958 graduation from City College, New York, where he had been a member of the *ROTC, Powell received a commission in the regular army.

As a young officer in the recently integrated army, he had opportunities for leadership not then generally available to blacks in segregated civilian society. He received accelerated promotions to major and colonel, and in 1979 became at forty-two the youngest general then in the army.

A turning point in Powell's career was his 1972 selection as a White House Fellow. Assigned to the Office of Management and Budget, he learned firsthand the workings of the federal bureaucracy and met individuals who later played key roles in his career. He served in the Office of the Secretary of Defense during both Democratic and Republican administrations, and in 1983 became military assistant to the secretary. Appointed President Ronald *Reagan's deputy national security adviser in 1987, he soon became national security adviser.

Selected by President George *Bush, Powell became chairman of the JCS on 1 October 1989. In addition to being the first African American, he was the first ROTC graduate and the youngest man to hold the position. Powell was also the first chairman to serve his entire tenure under the 1986 *Goldwater-Nichols Act that made the chairman, rather than the corporate chiefs, the nation's principal military adviser.

During his four years in office, Powell made full and unprecedented use of the chairman's enhanced authority. He directed the reorientation of U.S. military strategy at the end of the *Cold War and introduced the concept of a "base force" that reduced the size of the armed forces while maintaining U.S. superpower status. He played a central role during the 1991 *Persian Gulf War. The army's experience in Vietnam, where he served two tours, profoundly affected Powell's approach to the use of military force. He advocated deploying U.S. forces in combat only for clear political objectives, and then applying overwhelming force to achieve quick victory.

Powell's active exercise of the chairman's authority greatly strengthened the position. As a result, his tenure became the subject of press and scholarly debate about the proper role of the military in policy formulation.

[See also African Americans in the Military.]

• Colin L. Powell with Joseph E. Persico, *My American Journey,* 1995.

—Lorna S. Jaffe

PRECISION-GUIDED MUNITIONS (PGMs) are generally characterized as weapons with terminal guidance systems. In addition to "smart" bombs, the term is applied to a wide variety of weapons, from air-to-air and air-to-ground *missiles to wire-guided *torpedoes.

One of the most enduring images of the *Persian Gulf

War of 1991 are the videotapes played on CNN and other news networks of "smart" bombs in action. These tapes showed, from bomb-mounted TV cameras, the munitions rapidly and accurately approaching their targets, followed by the picture turning black and then into static when it hit. This popular memory persists despite the fact that a mere 9 percent of the bombs dropped by the Americans during the conflict were of the "smart" type. Weapons such as these fall into the category of precision-guided munitions.

Despite the publicity surrounding the "smart" bomb, *antitank weapons are the type most associated with precision-guided munitions. The Soviets had the best early success in the 1960s with their AT-1, AT-2, and most of all the AT-3 "Sagger" antitank missiles. The United States had its start with anti-armor PGMS in the 1970s with the first generation of TOW (*t*ube-launched, *o*ptically sighted, *w*ire-guided missile), ushering in a period of emphasis on PGMs. These two weapons systems saw their first widespread use in combat during the 1973 Yom Kippur War. Egyptian units equipped with Soviet AT-3s destroyed 180 of 290 Israeli *tanks in just one day of combat on the Sinai front. By the conclusion of the seven days of fighting, Israel had lost 420 tanks—25 percent of its inventory. This devastating result would not go unnoticed by military theorists.

The paramount driving force behind the development of PGMs is efficiency. The massive bombing campaigns and artillery barrages of World War II caused a great deal of collateral damage, but very often failed to destroy the intended target. The actual objectives of many of these attacks could have been neutralized using only a fraction of the explosive tonnage delivered, but the lack of an accurate delivery method required the use of "area bombing" with a large tonnage of munitions. This technique, along with specific targeting of civilians in "terror bombing" campaigns, was at best morally questionable. Furthermore, the belief that bombing would break the enemy's spirit to fight seems to have been unfounded.

The measurement used to determine bombing efficiency is known as *circular error probable* or CEP. The CEP is the radial distance from a target inscribing an imaginary circle with an area large enough so that 50 percent of the bombs dropped fall within it. The CEP during World War II was 3,300 feet; in the *Vietnam War and the Persian Gulf War, it was 6 feet.

The drawback with PGM is cost. A iron "dumb" bomb or an unguided rocket is much less expensive than a precision-guided bomb or missile. Concerns about the costs and reliability and the expenditure in training with these munitions were the subject of congressional hearings in 1984.

Although the Persian Gulf War of 1991 brought headlines to "smart" bomb PGMs, such weapons had been used by the United States five years before in a 1986 raid on Libya and nearly twenty years earlier in Vietnam. Primitive PGMs had even seen some use by Germany in World War II. It was in the Vietnam War, however, that PGMs saw their first success. One of the early PGMs was the navy's "Walleye" electro-optic guided bomb (EGOB). The Walleye is little more than a TV camera mounted on the weapon's nose. As the munition descends, the television relays the bomb's view to a monitor viewed by a weapons officer who remotely steers the bomb electronically by controlling its tail fins. A U.S. Air Force approach, developed by Col. Joseph Short and Weldon Wood of Texas Instruments, involved laser energy. Known as "Paveway," this laser-guided bomb (LGB) involves an attacking aircraft that finds a target via a TV camera and then fires a "Pave Knife" laser designator to "paint" the object to hit. The bomb then follows the beam through a laser seeker unit. This technique required only a single aircraft, but when used against targets in North Vietnam, it was found to be more effective for two aircraft to conduct attacks. One would locate and designate the target while the other dropped the bomb. The first successful PGM attacks in North Vietnam using both Walleye and Paveway-type munitions were against the Paul Dormier Bridge and Than Hoa Bridge in April and May of 1972.

The social and political ramifications of PGM—especially bombs and missiles—has been significant. Post–Gulf War punitive raids on Iraq, strikes on Serbian positions in Bosnia, and the 1998 U.S. retaliatory raids on terrorist facilities in Afghanistan and the Sudan have all been carried out with PGMs in order to minimize damage to civilians and risk to U.S. service people. "Standoff" weapons fitting into the PGM category provide the United States with the means to strike adversaries from a distance with little or no risk to U.S. forces.

[*See also* Bombing of Civilians; Bombs; Heat-Seeking Technology; Lasers.]
—David E. Michlovitz

PRINCIPLES OF WAR. *Objective, Offensive, Mass, Economy of Forces, Maneuver, Unity of Command, Security, Surprise,* and *Simplicity* are the principles of war most often found in military manuals. They have been a part of strategic thinking since China's war philosopher, Sun Tzu (500 B.C.), admonished commanders to *surprise* the enemy by making a noise in the west and striking in the east.

A modern list was developed around 1800, when Napoleon Bonaparte began fighting his way across Europe. Under the influence of the Enlightenment and its credo that life was governed by rational laws, some scholars tried to translate military strategy into a precise science. Prussia's Heinrich von Bülow (1757–1808), for instance, declared that triangle-based geometrics governed all military maneuvers and therefore all strategic decisions.

Yearning to repeat Sir Isaac Newton's discoveries, Antoine Henri *Jomini (1779–1869) suggested that all operational decisions could be rationally determined. After joining the French Army and fighting in several major campaigns, including Napoleon's war against Russia (1812), Jomini ascertained that battle successes were often based on a few pre-engagement principles.

In *The Art of War* (1838), Jomini outlined several Principles of War, of which three were essential. First, keeping in mind the military objective, one should carefully select a theater of war that provides all the offensive advantages. Second, before engaging the enemy, rivers, mountains, and other topographical features must be used to gain added leverage. Third, the enemy must be maneuvered into a vulnerable position; one should then launch a massive and concentrated attack upon this critical point.

Jomini, who lived to be ninety years old, witnessed the rapid rise of railroads, telegraph, and other technologies. Yet, claiming that his precepts were perennial truths, he shunned these advances. He argued that his principles had brought victories to Hannibal, Caesar, and Napoleon; therefore, no matter how warfare changed, they would always prevail. Like other Enlightenment philosophers, Jomini tried to reduce war—a very complex human phenomenon—to a rational science.

In the first part of the nineteenth century, the American military thinker Dennis Hart Mahan introduced Jominian logic to the United States after spending four years in France analyzing *Napoleonic warfare. Mahan joined the U.S. Military Academy in 1830, and for the next forty years taught engineering and operational strategy to a host of future *Civil War generals. Robert E. *Lee, Henry W. Halleck, George B. *McClellan, and other commanders became very familiar with Jominian concepts.

Both as a student and as one of West Point's commandants, General Lee was aware of Jomini's principles, and when the opportunity arose, he applied them. For example, during the Battle of *Chancellorsville—outnumbered nearly two to one—Lee reconfigured his forces to block the *Union army's left and center flanks. Then, finding the enemy's critical point, he sent Gen. "Stonewall" *Jackson around the Union's right and successfully defeated them. Chancellorsville was reminiscent of the way Jomini described Napoleon's use of these same maneuvers in the Marengo campaign in Italy of 1800.

During the later half of the nineteenth century, Jomini's theories became popular at the U.S. Naval War College. Dennis Mahan's son, Alfred T. *Mahan, joined the college in 1885 and a year later became its president. From this pulpit, he lectured and wrote about a blue-water *strategy that included frequent references to Jomini's principles. Never divide the fleet, Mahan admonished. Seek out your opponent and strike him down in an overwhelming display of massive and concentrated seapower.

Among naval officers, Mahan's seapower themes remained popular well into the twentieth century. During World War II, operational plans called for the U.S. *Navy to concentrate its fleet in the mid-Pacific and defeat the Japanese Imperial Navy in decisive Mahanian-style sea battle. For the most part, not until the demise of the Soviet Navy in the late 1980s did the U.S. Navy begin looking beyond Jomini and Mahan for other strategic concepts.

On occasion, strict adherence to the Mahanian principles proved to be unproductive. During the Battle of *Leyte Gulf (1944), Adm. William F. *Halsey elected to sail his main fleet from the San Bernadino Straits and throw it, in mass, upon the Japanese carriers, which proved to be decoys. In an effort never to divide the fleet, Halsey vacated San Bernadino, allowing a second Japanese force to sail through the straits, defeated surprisingly by a small if aggressive U.S. force.

During the early twentieth century, the Principles of War slowly became an essential part of the military's lexicon. British Gen. J. F. C. Fuller, in an attempt to establish a science of war, was one of the first to codify Jomini's postulates into short, easy to understand concepts. Writing in various military journals, Fuller helped popularize their use.

Urged on by the rise of corporate scientific management, American officers also searched for new ways to make warfare subject to a rational analysis. Thus, in the 1920s, for the first time, the War Department included these principles in its training manuals. Because they were practical, logical, teachable, and above all easy to test, the principles quickly became preferred classroom topics. Today, these lessons remain an important part of the military's educational process.

Despite their popularity, some claimed the principles were not adequate in explaining war. Prussia's Karl von *Clausewitz affirmed that any attempt to rationalize war into postulates was flirting with fantasy. War, he said in his unfinished work On War (1830), was too involved with immeasurable moral and other factors to be reduced to a science. Two centuries later, America's Bernard Brodie observed that the principles provided an inappropriate insight into war's ambiguities. Too often, they were simply bantered around as high-sounding slogans.

Finally, a few scholars claimed that violation of the principles has prompted more successful operations than when they were rigidly observed. Had Halsey not insisted on concentrating his fleet leaving San Bernadino Strait undefended, for example, he might have prevented a vicious Japanese attack against American escort carriers off Samar Island. Despite criticisms, the Principles of War remain popular because they provide strategic planners with some basic considerations.

[See also Strategy; War: Nature of War.]

• A. T. Mahan, The Influence of Sea Power Upon History, 1660–1783, 1890. Brevet Colonel J. F. C. Fuller, "The Application of Recent Developments in the Mechanics and other Scientific Knowledge to Prepartaion and Training for Future War on Land," The Journal of the Royal United Service Institution, LXV (May 1920), pp. 239–74. Bernard Brodie, Strategy in the Missile Age, 1959. Russell F. Weigley, The American Way of War: A History of United States Military Strategy and Policy, 1977. Carl von Clausewitz, On War, trans. by Michael Howard and Peter Paret, 1976. John I. Alger, The Quest for Victory: The History of the Principles of War, 1982. U.S. Armed Forces, Joint Warfare of the U.S. Armed Forces, 1991. Antoine Henri de Jomini, The Art of War, 1992.   —Donald D. Chipman

PRISONER-OF-WAR CAMPS, CIVIL WAR. Before 1861, Americans had never had to face the problem of internment of large numbers of captured enemy soldiers. British and Hessian soldiers had been exchanged or sent to farms on the frontier. The Civil War abruptly changed that situation. In four years of fighting, over 409,000 men became prisoners of war. That figure is at least four times more American soldiers captured than in all of the nation's other wars combined.

Neither side knew how to address the problem; neither made a concerted effort to do so. In place of badly needed attention and compassion were inexperience, clumsiness, and indifference. Suffering and the neglect of prisoners of war were present in both Union and Confederacy. Prison camp administrations were patchwork systems usually manned by second-rate officials. Lack of resources was an impairment; so were inadequate facilities, overcrowded conditions, and general mismanagement. The few efforts at prisoner exchange during the war were bungled and short-lived.

Of the 150 compounds established in the North and South, 25 could be termed major prisons or prison camps. Each had the same characteristics: poor food, lack of sanitation, often callous guards, and inadequate protection from the elements. Such ills produced epidemic outbreaks of sickness, malnutrition, mental depression, and—for thousands of helpless men—slow but certain death.

Totally divorced from the outside world, Civil War prisoners endured an unchanging routine. They arose from whatever bedding they had at dawn, answered roll call, and received something to eat. The rest of the day passed in boredom. A second meal came in late afternoon, along with another roll call. Then the men waited for some degree of sleep to blot out reality. Each succeeding day was the same.

No prison had sufficient medicines. Physicians were in short supply and not always attentive to enemy soldiers. Since many of the men had been captured because they were too wounded or sick to escape, and since prison life offered no curatives for recovery, death was a daily occurrence in every Civil War prison. In all, 56,000 captured soldiers perished in the crude compounds of the North and the South.

The two most infamous Civil War compounds went into operation in 1864, when prison authorities should have learned from mistakes and omissions earlier in the war. The South's Andersonville prison (officially known as Camp Sumter, Georgia) was the largest of all. It began receiving inmates before construction was completed. Some 52,300 Federal enlisted men were sent there; more than 13,200 perished from disease, exposure, and lack of medicines.

In the North, at a prison camp for Confederates at Elmira, New York, such scourges as diarrhea and pneumonia killed almost one-fourth of the captured soldiers (of 12,123 inmates, 2,963 died) over the course of the prison's twelve-month existence.

During and especially after the Civil War, each side pointed fingers of guilt at the other. Subsequently, hundreds of "memoirs of prison life" flowed from printing presses as soldiers (many seeking disability pensions) vied in converting questionable facts into dramatic fiction. As a consequence, no aspect of the bitter Civil War has triggered more accusations, more violent passions, and more unresolved controversy than the mistreatment of captured Billy Yanks and Johnny Rebs.

[*See also* Civil War: Domestic Course.]

• Clayton W. Holmes, *The Elmira Prison Camp*, 1912. William B. Hesseltine, *Civil War Prisons: A Study in War Psychology*, 1930; rep. 1962. James I. Robertson, Jr., "The Scourge of Elmira," *Civil War History*, VIII (1962), pp. 184–201. Lonnie R. Speer, *Portals to Hell: Military Prisons of the Civil War*, 1997.

—James I. Robertson, Jr.

PRISONERS AND CAPTIVES OF WAR, COLONIAL.

Prisoners were taken in all North American wars, but contrasting values affected their capture, treatment, and cultural roles. Treatment of captives was a barometer of conflict and change in Indian, European, and colonial martial values.

Indian warriors regarded being taken prisoner as synonymous with death. Captives usually belonged to their individual captors, so a capture ended participation in a raid. Despite some tribal amalgamations and notable adoptions to replace specific dead, comparatively few adult male prisoners were incorporated into communities, and some were ritually tortured to death. Women and young captives were readily adopted to rebuild declining populations, but wholesale adoptions could be divisive, as when Huron adoptees outnumbered native Mohawks after 1650. Ransom and sale of captives to white slavers gradually transformed Indian taking of prisoners into a spasmodic but valuable trade for societies as disparate as the Abenaki and the Cherokee.

Initially, all European intruders captured Indians as informants, hostages, slaves, curiosities, or potential interpreters. Once intercultural warfare began in America, Europeans readily applied the brutal attitudes their wars of religion had encouraged toward prisoners seen as heretics or heathens. Although Christians had a well-developed sense of noncombatant status, they seldom afforded it to Indian women and children. European settlers captured few Indians, rarely adopted them or even held them for exchange, and usually spared combatants only when they could be sold profitably into slavery. As "White Indians" became more numerous than "Red Europeans," most interpreters, traders, and cultural brokers were whites.

After 1755, to the consternation of most colonists and Indians, European regulars introduced the "honors of war" to some American battlefields. Under these new rules, those enemies who surrendered were to be taken prisoner, fed, housed, and guarded, while waiting to be exchanged. Colonial societies had treated European officers this way, but "farmed out" captured soldiers to earn their keep while awaiting exchange. The European professionals also allowed surrendering garrisons deemed valiant to keep their weapons, kit, and battle flags, sometimes releasing them in return for promises not to fight for a specified length of time. Colonials and Indians found these new conventions unprofitable and incomprehensible, resulting in "violations" like the "massacre" at Fort William Henry (1757).

British and French colonials gradually conformed to the humane new martial system, often without enthusiasm. Indians, whose warfare was increasingly deemed comparable to that of European irregulars, were similarly excluded from the "honors of war." Indians found new British demands for the return of all prisoners, a precondition for peace after 1760, particularly oppressive because they regarded the adoption of prisoners as permanent.

Colonial accounts of Indian captivity became popular, using Christian metaphors to demonize Indians and reinforce prevailing definitions. Hundreds of surviving accounts have provided historians and anthropologists with valuable, if coded, information about Indian cultures.

[*See also* Imperial Wars; King Philip's War; Native American Wars.]

• Alden Vaughan and Daniel K. Richter, "Crossing the Cultural Divide: Indians and New Englanders, 1605–1763," *American Antiquarian Society Proceedings*, 90 (1980), pp. 23–99. Ian K. Steele, *Betrayals: Fort William Henry and the "Massacre,"* 1990.

—Ian K. Steele

PRISONERS OF WAR.

This essay consists of three articles that examine different aspects of the history of prisoners of war. U.S. Soldiers as POWs *describes the treatment of American servicepeople as POWs from the Revolutionary War to the present.* Enemy POWs *examines the history of how enemy prisoners of war have been treated during America's wars.* The POW Experience *uses narratives written by American POWs, particularly in recent times, to help understand the experience of modern American POWs.*

PRISONERS OF WAR: U.S. SOLDIERS AS POWS

Although in ancient times wartime captives who were not rich enough to be held for ransom were usually enslaved as laborers by the victors as laborers, by the early modern era, with the emergence of centralized states and regular, professional armies, the practice had changed to regular exchange of prisoners, either during or after war.

In the *Revolutionary War (1775–83), although higher-ranking officers were usually exchanged during the war, the majority of soldiers were not. Because the British government considered the Americans rebels and refused during the war to recognize the Continental Congress as a sovereign government, captured American fightingmen were often treated like criminals. American sailors or seamen from privateers were imprisoned in Britain, sometimes accused of piracy. The majority of American prisoners of war (POWs), however, were soldiers who were confined under wretched conditions in floating British prison hulks around New York City. Many died, some escaped, but few accepted British offers to switch sides. Survivors were exchanged after the war. No accurate count was made, but perhaps more than 18,000 Americans became POWs. During the *War of 1812, the legal status of the United States and its servicemen was not an issue; American POWs were generally treated properly and were repatriated following the peace.

The *Texas War of Independence (1836) proved particularly brutal. Viewing Texans as rebels, the Mexican leader Gen. Antonio Lopez de *Santa Anna refused to take prisoners. Texans captured at the Battle of the *Alamo and at Goliad were executed.

During the *Mexican War (1846–48), although native Texans captured serving with the U.S. *Army were executed as rebels, the Mexican treatment of other North American POWs was fair and humane.

The *Union army and the *Confederate army in the *Civil War were modern mass armies of citizen soldiers. In modern wars of intense *nationalism and mass citizen armies, civilians identified more closely with the *citizen soldier than with the hired professional. Furthermore, the stakes of war became less subject to compromise. Consequently, the practice of prisoner exchange during hostilities declined. During the Civil War, at first, Union and Confederate POWs were regularly exchanged; in 1863, the Union army issued General Order Number 100, *The Rules of Land Warfare*, detailing regulations for treatment of POWs and enemy civilians in occupied territory. In 1864, however, because prisoner exchange was helping to sustain the Southern war effort and because the Confederacy refused to recognize former slaves serving as African American soldiers in the Union army, Gen. Ulysses S. *Grant stopped the regular exchange of POWs. Consequently, both sides were swamped with POWs.

In all, there were some 220,000 Confederate POWs in the North and 211,000 Union POWs in the South, and the makeshift Civil War *prisoner-of-war camps became notorious on both sides. A total of more than 50,000 Union and Confederate POWs died on both sides. After the war, a U.S. military commission convicted the commander of the camp in Andersonville, Georgia, Capt. Henry Wirz, for the maltreatment and death of 14,000 Union POWs. Although probably guilty of inefficiency rather than the conspiracy for which he was convicted, Wirz was hanged in 1865, the only Confederate official to be executed.

By the time of World War I, the major powers had agreed to the *laws of war, which included the treatment of prisoners of war. Drawing on the U.S. Army's 1863 regulations, delegates at the *Hague Peace Conferences (1899, 1907) agreed that each other's POWs should receive decent treatment. After the *Spanish-American War of 1898, the United States quickly repatriated thousands of captured Spanish soldiers, and the Spanish returned their limited number of U.S. POWs. In contrast, the *Philippine War (1899–1902) eventually degenerated into *guerrilla warfare, and *counterinsurgency measures were taken in which prisoners on both sides were sometimes tortured and killed.

The enormity of World War I overwhelmed the major powers with millions of POWs. However, since most of the American fighting occurred only in the final months of the war, just 4,120 American soldiers wound up in German POW camps. U.S. diplomats and the American *Red Cross sought successfully to ensure decent treatment. Only 147 American prisoners died in the German camps, most of them from previous wounds.

By contrast, World War II was characterized by the mistreatment and even murder of Allied prisoners and civilians by Germany—especially on the eastern front—and by Japan throughout Asia and the Pacific. This led to the postwar trial and execution of some German and Japanese officials and military officers for *war crimes. The 1929 Geneva Convention further elaborated details for treatment of POWs. While subjecting many captured civilians and others to slave labor, torture, or death, Nazi Germany usually treated American (and West European) military POWs within the Geneva rules.

Before December 1944, the majority of American soldiers held in *Stalags* (German POW camps) were captured airmen. In the ground war, only a few G.I.'s were captured before December 1944, but in the surprise German Ardennes offensive, known as the Battle of the *Bulge, thousands of Americans were surrounded and captured. In the Malmédy massacre in Belgium, eighty-six captured G.I.'s were executed by a German SS unit on 17 December. During the bitter winter of 1944–45, the Germans force-marched thousands of Allied POWs across the country in an attempt to keep them from the armies invading from the east and west. Several thousand American POWs in the east were therefore liberated by the Red Army and held for a while, after the German surrender on 8 May 1945, and through the *Potsdam Conference in July, although they were eventually repatriated before the end of 1945. Of the 93,941 American POWs held in the European theater during the war, only 1 percent died in captivity, most of them from combat wounds.

In contrast, Japan's treatment of POWs was brutal. Influenced by the military, Tokyo had not signed the 1929 Geneva Convention, and Japanese military leaders instilled in their soldiers the belief that surrender was a betrayal of the emperor and a disgrace to the individual and his family. Pursuing a policy disdainful of Allied servicemen who surrendered, the Japanese military treated Allied POWs viciously. Some POWs, such as captured American airmen who bombed Japan, were beheaded. The majority of American POWs had been captured when the Japanese conquered the Philippine Islands in the winter of 1941–42.

In the infamous Bataan Death March of April 1942, some 78,000 American and Filipino POWs led by Gen. Jonathan *Wainwright, many already starving and weak from malaria, were beaten, clubbed, and bayoneted as they were forced to walk sixty-five miles with little or no food, water, or shelter to the prison camp near Cabanatuan. Between 7,000 and 10,000 people died or were killed on the march. (After the war, Japanese Gen. Masaharu Homma was held responsible and executed. In the Philippines, homage is paid annually to the American and Filipino victims on Bataan Day, 9 April, when Filipinos rewalk parts of the death route.)

After the Americans began the liberation of the *Philippines in October 1944, the Japanese put surviving POWs onto ships to take them to Japan as hostages. There were orders to kill them if the Americans invaded the home islands. Nearly 4,000 American POWs died in unmarked transport ships sunk by American planes or *submarines, but others survived the journey in filthy holds to be worked in mines and other hazardous facilities in Japan until the Japanese surrender in August 1945. (Indeed, after the emperor's call for surrender, several dozen captured American airmen were beheaded by imperial military units in Japan.) Of the 25,600 American POWs held in the Pacific during the war, 10,650 or nearly 45 percent died, most of starvation and disease since they were worked incessantly and given little food, clothing, shelter, or medical treatment.

In the postwar era, despite the trials in Nuremberg and Tokyo of Germans and Japanese for *war crimes, several Communist states refused to accept the 1949 Geneva Conventions, which further developed the laws of war. In the *Korean War (1950–53), North Korean forces executed many G.I.'s in the field, their bodies later recovered with their hands tied behind their backs. A report to Congress in 1954 concluded that this was a deliberate tactic of psychological warfare. Many more Americans were captured during the winter of 1950–51 when *United Nations forces retreated following the massive Chinese intervention.

Of the more than 7,000 Americans captured by the Communists during the Korean War, only 3,800 returned alive. An estimated 1,000 were murdered, and at least another 1,700 died of sickness and malnutrition. When the Chinese Communists took control, the prisoners' physical conditions improved slightly, but they now underwent indoctrination efforts. Under torture, a number of American airmen "confessed" to germ warfare and other atrocities. Twenty-one Americans and one Englishman renounced their citizenship and decided to remain in China following the armistice in 1953. Although only one out of every twenty-three American POWs was ever suspected of serious misconduct, the so-called "brainwashing" of POWs who denounced the United States led to a public outcry. In 1954, President Dwight D. *Eisenhower issued Executive Order 10631, prescribing a code of conduct for American POWs designed to forge captive Americans into a unified community through a common standard of behavior.

In the *Vietnam War (1965–73), North Vietnam and the National Liberation Front in the South refused to consider any requests from the International Red Cross Commission regarding POWs. In effect, Vietnamese Communists viewed American servicepeople as having been criminals before they were captured and thus as without the status of POWs. In the ground war in South Vietnam, some Americans were shot while trying to surrender. Others were taken north to POW camps. Many of the navy and air force aviators captured during the bombing of North Vietnam were held in a prison known sarcastically as the "Hanoi Hilton." Most of the POWs suffered considerable mental and physical abuse and some were tortured, but only a few agreed to issue anti-American propaganda.

Between 1964 and 1972, of the known American POWs

held in North Vietnam, 114 died in captivity. After the *Paris Peace Agreements (1973), 651 POWs returned to American control. However, the status of over 2,000 Americans missing in action (MIAs) and the question of whether the Socialist Republic of Vietnam had retained some American POWs remained controversial for years afterward.

During the *Persian Gulf War (1991), although Iraq, like the United States, had signed the 1949 Geneva Conventions, Saddam *Hussein refused to allow the International Red Cross Commission to inspect Iraq's POW facilities. In captivity, the twenty-three American POWs, including two female soldiers, suffered physical mistreatment that ranged from sexual abuse of the women to electric shocks and bone-breaking for the men.

• Pat O'Brien, *Outwitting the Hun: My Escape from a German Prison Camp*, 1918. Ralph E. Ellinwood, *Behind German Lines: A Narrative of the Everyday Life of an American Prisoner of War*, 1920. Clifford Milton Markle, *A Yankee Prisoner in Hunland*, 1920. William B. Hesseltine, *Civil War Prisons: A Study in War Psychology*, 1930; repr. 1962. U.S. Department of the Army, *Communist Interrogation, Indoctrination and Exploitation of Prisoners of War*, 1956. Stanley L. Falk, *Bataan: The March of Death*, 1962. John G. Hubbell, et al., *P.O.W.: A Definitive History of the American Prisoner of War Experience in Vietnam, 1964–1973*, 1976. David Foy, *For You the War Is Over: American POWs in Nazi Germany*, 1984. Marion R. Lawton, *Some Survived: An Epic Account of Japanese Captivity During World War II*, 1984. John Dower, *War Without Mercy: Race and Power in the Pacific War*, 1986. Richard B. Speed III, *Prisoners, Diplomats, and the Great War: A Study in the Diplomacy of Captivity*, 1990. Susan Katz Keating, *Prisoners of Hope: Exploiting the POW/MIA Myth in America*, 1994. Dwight Messimer, *Escape*, 1994. S. P. MacKenzie, "The Treatment of Prisoners of War in World War II," *Journal of Modern History*, 66 (September 1994), pp. 487–520.
—Robert C. Doyle

PRISONERS OF WAR: ENEMY POWS

Four principles have guided American treatment of enemy POWs: military customs and tradition of the time; internal American military law such as the *Rules of Land Warfare* (1863 to the present); international agreements on the *law of war such as the Hague (1899) and Geneva Conventions (1929, 1949); and, most important, American responses to the practical dynamic that if one side treated its prisoners humanely, the other side was expected to do the same so far as its means allowed.

The first European POWs taken in the British colonies were French prisoners, who, according to custom, were either paroled or exchanged for British or colonial military prisoners held in French Canada. (Indian prisoners, if taken at all, were often sold into slavery before the *Civil War, or afterwards, like *Geronimo, made prisoners for life.) The Americans took more than 16,000 British, Hessian, and loyalist POWs during the *Revolutionary War. Officers were exchanged; enlisted men were generally sent to work on farmland in the frontier, particularly in western Pennsylvania. Captured loyalist became political prisoners and were sent back to their own regions for internment. All prisoners were released by 1783; some assimilated into American society, especially expatriate Hessians; others, including loyalists, returned to England or settled in Canada. During the Revolution, despite the lack of formal British recognition of American POW status until 1783, few enemy POWs perished in American captivity. In the *War of 1812, POW status was recognized and Americans kept enemy POWs under similar conditions to the way that Americans were kept by the British.

During the *Mexican War (1846–48), the U.S. *Army took over 40,000 Mexican POWs, most of whom were paroled in the field. The practice of field parole survived in the first year of the Civil War but proved impractical. Both sides established a system of facilities: Union camps held more than 220,000 Confederates, and the Confederacy held more than 211,000 Union soldiers. In practice, both sides paroled prisoners until 1864. Although Abraham *Lincoln issued General Order 100, *Rules of Land Warfare*, to the *Union army in 1863, over 56,000 Americans on both sides died in captivity, mainly in 1864–65. In the *Spanish-American War (1898), thousands of Spanish troops who surrendered in Cuba, Puerto Rico, and the Philippines were returned home upon the conclusion of hostilities.

Only a handful of German POWs, mostly merchant marine and political internees, were held in the United States during World War I. In Europe, the American Expeditionary Force held over 40,000 German POWs by November 1918; all were freed in 1919. In World War II, the U.S. Army held more than 325,000 German, 50,000 Italian, and 5,000 Japanese Army POWs (the last mostly Koreans and Formosan drafted to work for the Japanese Army) in some 500 prison camps in the United States. The militant Bushido Code required Japanese soldiers to commit suicide rather than surrender until the emperor himself ordered his armed forces to surrender in August 1945.

Treatment of enemy POWs in the United States was proper, just, and humane, and generally consistent with the 1929 Geneva Convention. The most significant problem for American authorities was distinguishing between kind of Axis prisoners: political opportunists, German nationalists, nonpolitical POWs (mostly draftees), and dedicated Nazi Party members, who did distinguish among the other three groups. A total of 1,000 German POWs escaped, but most were soon returned by the FBI, military, or local police, and the last German POWs sailed for Europe in July 1946. American military intelligence initiated programs directed toward reeducation and denazification.

After Germany's surrender in May 1945, Allied powers established a vast system of POW camps for millions of surrendered German soldiers known as "Disarmed Enemy Forces" (DEF). Spread along the Rhine Valley, the meadow camps operated by the American Military Police were filled beyond capacity, and large numbers of former German soldiers, already weakened from long combat and diminished rations, died of starvation, exposure, and disease. By 1947, realities of the *Cold War descended on Europe, and the American occupation discharged most DEFs except for members of the SS, SD, Gestapo, and others held for *war crimes trials.

During the *Korean War, the largest prison facilities for North Korean and Chinese POWs were on Koje and Pongam-do Islands south of the mainland. In Korea, Cold War issues changed American policy from accepting forced repatriations of all POWs to admitting defectors as political refuges. In May and June 1952, the *United Nations Command witnessed the results of that policy change: Communist resisters in the camps staged one of the most successful uprisings in POW history. Rioting lasted for nearly two months. The Americans answered with force and also began separating Communist and non-Communist prisoners upon arrival. No real solution was ever

found, and only the 1953 armistice ended disputes over POW conditions and treatment on both sides.

In the Vietnam War, especially from 1965 to 1971, thousands of Viet Cong and North Vietnamese soldiers fell into American hands. If North Vietnamese soldiers were captured in uniform, they were protected by the 1949 Geneva Convention with oversight by the International *Red Cross, and repatriated in 1973 after the Paris accords. However, a political war raged and more than one prison system operated in secret on both sides. Special units like the Province Reconnaissance Unit (PRU) arrested civilians suspected as Communist Party members and incarcerated these political detainees without habeas corpus or international inspection in notorious conditions such as those at Con Son Island.

Following the *Persian Gulf War in 1991, captured Iraqi soldiers fell into two categories: those who participated in a failed rebellion against the dictator Saddam Hussein, and those who helped him repress their country's minorities. With recent wartime experiences in mind, American authorities conducted rigorous screening of thousands of Iraqi POWs to determine which ones would likely suffer political retribution and imprisonment following repatriation. Many of those POWs were granted political asylum.

• Lucy Leigh Bowie, "German Prisoners in the American Revolution," *Maryland Historical Magazine* (September 1945), pp. 185–200. William Best Hesseltine, *Civil War Prisons*, 1930; repr. 1962. Ovid L. Futch, *History of Andersonville Prison*, 1968. Charles H. Metzger, S. J., *The Prisoner in the American Revolution*, 1971. Judith M. Gansberg, *Stalag USA: The Remarkable Story of German POWs in America*, 1977. Howard S. Levie, ed., *Documents on Prisoners of War*, Vol. 60 of *Naval War College International Law Studies*, 1979. Arnold Krammer, *Public Administration of Prisoner of War Camps in America Since the Revolutionary War*, 1980. James Bacque, *Other Losses: An Investigation into the Mass Deaths of German Prisoners at the Hands of the French and Americans After World War II*, 1989. Günter Bischof and Stephen Ambrose, eds., *Eisenhower and the German POWs: Facts Against Falsehood*, 1992.
—Robert C. Doyle

PRISONERS OF WAR: THE POW EXPERIENCE

American POW experiences began in the colonial past and continue as part of the human legacy of war. For three centuries, American POWs have examined their experience by writing personal histories that search for a sense of social, legal, historical, and personal order in the midst of captivity. In a corpus of American literature, POWs' accounts reveal cultural conflicts of ideologies, international conflicts in law, and stressful human tensions that require life-or-death choices. They also ask ethical and moral questions.

Former POWs often wrote accounts in which they reflected on their experiences as a chaotic hell on earth. These are our best guides to the POW experience. Simple and unadorned, POW narratives contain anecdotal evidence of brutality, torture, stress, and a strong sense of moral outrage. More important, they contain readily identifiable political, social, religious, or military purposes. With a strong sense of mission, some POWs like Ethan Allen during the *Revolutionary War designed their stories to generate both emotional response and renewed commitment to armed political struggle. Other POWs followed the Puritan jeremiad model and reinforced the power of religious faith. Modern POW literature such as the accounts of the war in Southeast Asia by James N.

Rowe, *Five Years to Freedom* (1971), Dieter Dengler, *Escape from Laos* (1979), and James B. Stockdale, *In Love and War* (1984), bear witness to an experience that affected not just the authors but an entire class of Americans whose human rights were denied in wartime. In effect, POW narratives lie beyond the documented statistical histories of war; instead, they tell highly personalized, extremely painful stories about a world consisting of seven commonly recurring events that structure experience and give it meaning.

Precapture guides the reader through personal memories before the POW experience took place. The POW identifies the core value systems—family, comrades-in-arms, God, institutions, country—that later help to establish and maintain the will to survive. *Capture* describes how, where, and when the POW was taken by the enemy. The victim can be man or woman, a civilian caught in the battle's center or in the throes of a political crisis, an individual soldier, sailor, or an entire military garrison that was forced to surrender as a unit. This event dramatizes the battle's loss: a person has nothing more than the moment at hand in which to make decisions. All is lost but life itself, and one's future depends on luck and the whim of one's captor. The *long march* describes the dangerous journey from the place of capture to the place of permanent internment, with intermittent stops along the way. The experience removes the outer layers of the prisoner's cultural veneer as POWs are executed for such trifles as wanting water, walking too slowly, or falling down.

POWs describe the *prison landscape* as the permanent prison facility where chronological time stood still. Simple affairs of life are transformed into time-marked events. Food becomes an obsession, and no POW forgets the cell, filth, rats, or the hunger. In *resistance or assimilation*, the POW begins to understand his or her captors better. No longer stereotypes, captors become real people who demand absolute obedience. POWs describe physical torture and psychological pressure made to change their way of thinking, or at least to change their overt behavior. As a result, many POWs undergo deep personal transformations when they are confronted with basic decision making. Beginning this process as one person, the POW ends as another.

POWs describe *release* as the happy-sad return (or attempted return through escape) to the world from which they came. Escape takes place in this phase of the experience; however, most escapees suffer recapture and receive severe punishment for their efforts. Consequently, there are ever-intensifying social, ethical, and moral conflicts among POWs about the efficacy of escape, especially when the well-being of the entire captive community is at stake. This phase focuses also on the joy of anticipation, the oddities of renewed personal freedom, and the shock of homecoming.

The *lament* allows the POW to reflect on and grieve for what was lost in captivity. As witness bearers, most narrators grieve the cost of the sacrifice in terms of the loss of those who died needlessly or who suffered greatly. POWs also grieve the loss of irreplaceable time—especially time away from home, family, and cultural institutions that put them into another unique class where they have more in common with other POWs than with those people closest to them.

Each scenario contains varied examples of what POWs view as dramatic events that reinforced or destroyed the will to live. Capture is usually individual, whereas long marches tend to be group events. The act of resistance takes place as both a group and an individual event, depending on the nature of the captivity. Interrogation and torture are individual acts of resistance. Assimilation, if it occurs at all, tends to be an individual decision. Escapes are usually individual or small-group ventures, whereas *release/repatriation* are often group experiences. POWs, once part of a community of prisoners, become individuals again after their repatriation, alone with their memories, but with little support from those other POWs on whom they depended for so long. The lament gives them the opportunity to grieve for the time wasted in captivity; for the material opportunities lost over time; and most often for the dead.

For individual POWs, the act of writing about their experience often serves as a catharsis for personal feelings, an ethical forum to tell the world what happened to them and why. Most important, in their expressions of outrage, POWs serve their respective communities as witnesses against willful and often illegal acts of inhumanity. Because writing a memoir terminates an extended act of violence that nearly consumed them, they also achieve a sense of closure. The common denominator remains the moral judgments that test an individual's ability to withstand the unexpected when the chips fall about as low as they can go.

• Michael Walzer, "Prisoners of War: Does the Fight Continue After the Battle?" *American Political Science Review,* 63 (1969), pp. 777–86. Robert F. Grady, *The Evolution of Ethical and Legal Concern for Prisoners of War,* 1971. A. J. Barker, *Prisoners of War,* 1975. John G. Hubbell, *A Definitive History of the American Prisoner of War Experience in Vietnam, 1964–1973,* 1976. Richard Garrett, *POW: The Uncivil Face of War,* 1981. Pat Reid and Maurice Michael, *Prisoners of War,* 1984. Sydney Axinn *A Moral Military,* 1989. Robert C. Doyle, *Voices from Captivity: Interpreting the American POW Narrative,* 1994.

—Robert C. Doyle

PRIVATEERING. Throughout the seventeenth and eighteenth centuries, Great Britain, Spain, France, and other European powers augmented the power of their navies on the high seas by mobilizing businesspeople to fit out their own vessels as warships. Americans continued to dispatch such private warships during the *Revolutionary War and the *War of 1812. European and American officials supported privateering because it threatened enemy commerce inexpensively; European and American merchants sent out vessels, aboard which thousands of mariners served, in hopes of making patriotic windfall profits. American privateering expanded in each imperial conflict. As Britain's New World possessions matured into populous, prosperous provinces, privateering became America's leading contribution to Britain's war efforts. Disrupting an adversary's commerce continued to dominate American naval thinking well into the nineteenth century because of the prohibitive cost of building a battle fleet comparable to Britain's Royal Navy.

Privateering has often been confused with *piracy,* but there were major differences between them. Privateering was a legal enterprise, conducted under state licenses called *letters of marque and reprisal;* governments subjected it to increasing regulation as it grew in scope and importance. Piracy, on the other hand, was a capital crime that European states had largely eliminated by the early 1700s. There was also a substantial difference in the types of people who participated in each endeavor. Some of the most important merchants in Europe and America invested heavily in private men-of-war, whereas piracy principally attracted disgruntled sailors and other marginal people.

Privateering had played an important role in the founding of England's New World empire. The Caribbean exploits of John Hawkins and Francis Drake prompted interest in colonization among England's governing circles. Walter Raleigh partially financed his Roanoke settlement by privateering expeditions against the Spanish, and indeed selected the site because it seemed to offer an ideal privateering base. Similarly, in 1607, the Virginia Company employed a veteran privateering captain, Christopher Newport, to convey settlers to Jamestown.

Privateers operated within the political economy of mercantilism, which recognized the expansion or protection of a nation's trade as a legitimate purpose of war. Acquisitive impulses did not have to be suppressed, but could be harnessed to increase national wealth and inhibit the enemy's ability to wage war simultaneously. Hence the inability of Britain, Spain, and the other European powers—and later the United States—to afford the staggering expenditures necessary for powerful navies prompted the rise of privateering.

Large seaports dominated American privateering because only the major cities possessed the requisite resources. Privateering voyages required entrepreneurial ability, shipping, and manpower. Experienced merchants, men unafraid of risk and who commanded sufficient capital to acquire, arm, and victual a strong vessel, were as necessary to successful cruises as skilled captains, whose reputations could attract large crews. Once a privateer captured an enemy merchantman, the owners' business skills were again crucial, because no income was earned until the prize was condemned in a vice admiralty court and the vessel and cargo were sold at a profit. Business correspondents, warehouse facilities, and market information were all necessary for success.

In addition to business skills, shipping and manpower were also more available in the larger ports. Although some vessels were constructed specifically for privateering, most private men-of-war were converted merchant ships; thus, ports with substantial merchant fleets could dispatch more privateers than their smaller neighbors. Because privateers captured and did not sink their prey, large crews for boarding parties were essential, and the principal ports more easily supplied the necessary numbers of men. All these factors made Newport, New York, Boston, Philadelphia, Baltimore, and Charleston centers of American privateering during the colonial and early national periods.

American privateers hunted the Atlantic from Newfoundland to the Spanish Main, but concentrated on the Caribbean, where the pickings were richest. American warships captured thousands of vessels, earning investors, captains, and crews substantial income; successful privateers generated profits of nearly 150 percent during the eighteenth century.

From the sixteenth century through the early 1800s, so long as naval fleets could not control wartime shipping lanes, privateering dominated Atlantic maritime conflict and exerted a major influence on commerce. Privateering disappeared only when steam power ended the age of fighting sail. Steam warships were simply too costly to be owned by private investors. Although the European powers signed a treaty ending privateering only in 1857 and a few private warships saw action in the American *Civil War, privateering largely ended at the conclusion of the War of 1812.

[*See also* Confederate Navy; Continental Navy; Naval Militia; Sea Warfare.]

• Richard Pares, *War and Trade in the West Indies, 1739–1763*, 1936. James G. Lydon, *Pirates, Privateers, and Profits*, 1970. Gerome R. Garitee, *The Republic's Private Navy: The American Privateering Business as Practiced by Baltimore During the War of 1812*, 1977. Kenneth R. Andrews, *Trade, Plunder and Settlement: Maritime Enterprise and the Genesis of the British Empire, 1480–1630*, 1984. David J. Starkey, *British Privateering Enterprise in the Eighteenth Century*, 1990. Carl E. Swanson, *Predators and Prizes: American Privateering and Imperial Warfare, 1739–1748*, 1991.

—Carl E. Swanson

PROCUREMENT

Overview
Aerospace Industry
Government Arsenals
Influence on Industry
Military Vehicles and Durable Goods Industry
Munitions and Chemical Industry
Nuclear Weapons Industry
Ordnance and Arms Industry
Shipbuilding Industry
Steel and Armor Plate Industry (1865–1918)

PROCUREMENT: OVERVIEW

Military procurement necessarily stands apart from the mainstream of the American economy. This owes partly to the uniqueness of much military equipment, which requires special design, development, and production facilities, and partly to the military's *mobilization needs, which often dictate maintenance of reserve production tooling and supplies. Uniqueness has grown more significant with the advance of technology, and especially with the American military's *Cold War push for technological superiority. Military mobilization needs have grown less important with the invention of *nuclear weapons, which made a long conventional war inconceivable, and with the development of conventional weapons too complex to be produced rapidly in any case.

Neither of these factors explains why the American military buys even simple things in complicated ways, however. While reports of $465 hammers, $10,000 coffeemakers, and sixteen-page technical specifications for sugar cookies prompt cries of fraud or stupidity, more often they result from the fact that defense is a public good, financed by a large federal bureaucracy dispensing public money advanced by a pluralistic political process.

Historically, military procurement has involved three major sets of arrangements, in proportions that have changed over time. The simplest arrangement has involved the purchase from commercial vendors of commercial items, perhaps slightly modified for military use. This was the principal mode of military procurement in the early years of the republic, when military technology differed little from the muskets and saddles people normally owned. The procurement challenge then lay in meeting the military's need for large production quantities and interchangeable parts. As weaponry has grown more sophisticated, the military has moved to other modes of procurement. But today's military still buys office supplies, computers, and some motor vehicles from commercial vendors.

The development, production, and maintenance of military equipment has also been carried out by government-owned laboratories, arsenals, and depots. The "arsenal system" originated early in the 1800s and grew over the following century into an elaborate array of specialized facilities. Arsenals contributed production techniques as well as weapons; work on mass-production techniques at the Springfield and Harpers Ferry arsenals, for example, contributed to the nation's initial industrial development—an early example of so-called spin-off, wherein defense research produces items of commercial value.

But the arsenals also became famous for their stodginess and resistance to technologies they did not themselves invent—the "not-invented-here" syndrome. As technology became more important to military power, the arsenals came under increasing attack. Most of the original arsenals were closed in the twentieth century. Although some labs and depots still operated, these too were disappearing, or at least shrinking in size, as the defense budget fell and the military services "outsourced" such activities to private firms or operators. Although a new set of government-owned facilities grew up during and after World War II to develop and build nuclear weapons, with the end of the Cold War the nuclear weapons facilities too were shrinking and scrambling for new missions.

The most pronounced break with the older arsenals came in the years just after World War I, as the services sought to explore the new aircraft technologies demonstrated during that war. Government arsenals were unable to keep up with these relatively fast-moving technologies; in the time it took a government facility to draw up specifications for a new aircraft engine, for example, still newer models would render those specifications obsolete. The army and naval air arms thus turned to the era's aircraft entrepreneurs, who were eager for government contracts to help finance their fledgling companies. Contracting procedures were complex and never wholly satisfactory, since the exploratory nature of the work made it almost impossible to specify costs in advance, or to run formal competitions against established specifications. Thus, there was far more prototyping than actual production of aircraft in the interwar years. Still, almost all of the aircraft used during World War II were prototyped by private aircraft firms before the war began.

The Cold War saw a massive expansion of this mode of military procurement, stemming partly from the importance of aircraft and missile procurement and partly from the presumption that these firms were far more innovative than the arsenals. In the 1960s, for example, Secretary of Defense Robert S. *McNamara forced the army to shift from what remained of its arsenals to private contractors for much of its procurement. During the Cold War, military procurement came to be highly concentrated in such large aerospace giants as Boeing, Lockheed, and General Dynamics; normally, the top twenty-five defense contractors won nearly half of all procurement dollars awarded annually. It was this form of military procurement that President Dwight D. *Eisenhower referred to as the "*military-industrial complex."

What worried Eisenhower was the political clout such firms seemed to wield. The pioneer aircraft entrepreneurs excelled at lobbying Congress as well as designing innovative aircraft, and thus managed to pull down more than half of all military research and development money allocated in the years between World Wars I and II. Lobbying activities grew in the 1950s. Although the arsenals had always maintained close ties to their local legislators, commercial firms could lobby more aggressively. They could also spread the award of subcontracts widely, at least partly to seek broader political support on Capitol Hill. Although the literature on defense contractors questions the effectiveness of these tactics—permanent installations like arsenals or depots seem always to have had more clout with legislators—there is no denying a political dimension to defense contractors' activity.

The political nature of their market slowly shaped these "private" firms into a form more properly labeled "quasi-socialized." Lacking the competition or price signals found in a real market, and facing steadily growing government regulation, defense firms generally acquired layers of bureaucracy that mirrored the military bureaucracy they served. Commercial firms owning defense facilities have tended to keep these divisions quite separate within the firm, for example, if only because defense accounting techniques differ substantially from those used commercially. More important, the military's drive for technological superiority slowly pushed many defense firms to levels of technical sophistication well beyond what could be marketed commercially. As defense spending fell in the wake of the Cold War, few defense firms were able to "convert" to commercial production except by simply buying commercial subsidiaries. Thus, the nation's defense giants sold out (General Dynamics), purchased their way into commercial sectors (Rockwell), or merged into huge defense conglomerates (Lockheed-Martin, Northrup-Grumman).

Americans want these firms to be both efficient and creative. But no one can measure their efficiency, since no one knows what the world's best fighter aircraft or tank "should" cost (although one credible study comparing the cost of U.S. and European military aircraft concluded that American weapons cost more but performed better). On the other hand, these firms have clearly been creative; in the nineteenth century, U.S. military technology often lagged behind Europe's; during the Cold War, it moved into first place worldwide in many categories. Overall, Americans seem to have paid a premium for premium technology.

Yet it remains to be seen whether the dominant Cold War mode of military procurement can handle the challenge posed by modern information technologies. Like aircraft technologies in the 1920s, today's electronics technologies have military utility but are advancing much faster than the established procurement apparatus can handle. Thus, the commercial world now leads the military in many electronics sectors, and defense procurement reform seeks to forge links from its own process over to commercial electronics firms. Procurement routines are deeply ingrained and difficult to change, of course, raising questions about whether such reform will succeed. If it does, it will shift the mode of military procurement back toward the early years of the republic: the purchase of military technologies from commercial vendors.

[See also Industry and War.]

• Merton J. Peck and Frederic M. Scherer, *The Weapons Acquisition Process: An Economic Analysis*, 1962. Thomas L. McNaugher, *New*

Weapons, Old Politics: America's Military Procurement Muddle, 1989. Kenneth R. Mayer, *The Political Economy of Defense Contracting,* 1991. Paul A. C. Koistinen, *Beating Plowshares into Swords: The Political Economy of American Warfare, 1606–1865,* 1997. Paul A. C. Koistinen, *Mobilizing for Modern War: The Political Economy of American Warfare, 1865–1919,* 1997. Paul A. C. Koistinen, *Planning War, Pursuing Peace: The Political Economy of American Warfare, 1920–1939,* 1997.

—Thomas L. McNaugher

PROCUREMENT: AEROSPACE INDUSTRY

The relationship between the U.S. aircraft industry and the military has always been close. Fixed-wing piloted flight was technologically demanding and required large sums of capital. Early inventors turned to the military services for markets, and the U.S. Army Signal Corps ordered its first craft from the Wright brothers in 1908. Although American capabilities lagged behind those in Europe, the U.S. government spent $350 million during World War I to produce 14,000 military airplanes. It also created the National Advisory Committee for Aeronautics (NACA) to explore aircraft science and advise the military.

Military patronage produced an unusually cooperative structure in the early aircraft industry. The government engineered the formation of the Manufacturers Aircraft Association to moderate ferocious competition and avoid patent battles that might delay wartime production by pooling patents and sharing plane-making methods. After World War I, orders collapsed by over 80 percent. The association successfully pressed for government sponsorship of airmail services and an infrastructure of airports, weather reporting, and flight control, as well as continued military contracts to develop new aircraft. During World War II, President Franklin D. *Roosevelt's call for 40,000 aircraft led to the expansion of small companies like Boeing, Douglas, North American, Consolidated (later General Dynamics), McDonnell, and Grumman by tenfold or more. Aircraft accounted for more than 12 percent of all U.S. wartime manufacturing output.

After World War II, when aircraft orders plunged from a peak of $16 billion to $1 billion, the aircraft industry campaigned vigorously with the newly independent U.S. Air Force for a public commitment to air defense systems, expansion of domestic and international air transport, and the preservation of a strong aircraft manufacturing industry. Close ties with military strategies were relied upon to help shape military markets and government notions of defense necessities. Some scholars have argued that this "technology push" contributed to the development of the *arms race of the *Cold War.

Contracts ballooned in the Cold War and were welcomed by economists advocating "military Keynesianism" to achieve full employment via public spending. Competition between the piloted bomber and the ballistic missile groups within the air force, and between army and navy bids for *helicopters and their own *fighter aircraft, resulted in the production of a broad array of aviation weapons systems, which kept most of the major aircraft companies in business. In 1958, NACA became the National Aeronautics and Space Administration (NASA), with huge additional projects for the industry. The size, speed, and aggressiveness of the industry's development led President Dwight D. *Eisenhower in 1961 to warn the nation about the dangers of a permanent "*military industrial complex."

The renamed "aerospace" industry has been favored by this de facto but unofficial industrial policy. The military acted as the underwriters of aerospace development after World War II, encouraging development of the jet engine and the communications satellite. In 1989, the *Pentagon paid for 82 percent of the aerospace industry's research and development effort and purchased 65 percent of its output. As a result, aircraft remain the nation's strongest manufacturing export, and U.S. companies dominate the world market for commercial as well as military aircraft. Since the end of the Cold War, the industry has undergone deep retrenchment, consolidating into fewer and larger firms (Northrop-Grumman, Lockheed-Martin), and relying more heavily on arms exports.

[*See also* Industry and War.]

• John Rae, *Climb to Greatness: The American Aircraft Industry, 1920–1960,* 1968. G. R. Simonson, ed., *The History of the American Aircraft Industry: An Anthology,* 1968. Martin van Creveld, *Technology and War,* 1989. Ann Markusen, Peter Hall, Scott Campbell and Sabina Deitrick, *The Rise of the Gunbelt,* 1992.

—Ann Markusen

PROCUREMENT: GOVERNMENT ARSENALS

As industrial products, weapons have unique requirements: production rates must radically increase in times of war and rapidly decrease in peacetime; cost, although a significant factor, matters less than uniformity, precision, and performance; manufacturing often involves a mix of mass and batch production uncommon in commercial markets. To meet these special demands, the U.S. government sometimes maintained its own production facilities—armories for small arms, and arsenals for guns, carriages, powder, and other equipment.

Why should government compete with private industry? Critics argued that lower production costs at arsenals represented unfair competition (for they need not make a profit), while conversely, higher costs represented inefficiency. Proponents of arsenals pointed to government production as a "yardstick" to gauge costs in private industry, and to arsenals' ability to nurture costly new technologies for long periods. Military arsenals, as state-owned factories in a capitalist system, have historically raised problems over the government's relationship to technology.

Prior to 1794, the U.S. Army procured arms solely from private contractors, an arrangement that proved expensive and unreliable. Following the *War of 1812, Congress placed the Army Ordnance Department in charge of production at five government-owned arsenals of construction, Allegheny (Pittsburgh); Frankford (Philadelphia); Washington D.C.; Watervliet (upstate New York); and Watertown (outside Boston); and at the two armories, Springfield (Massachusetts) and Harpers Ferry (Virginia). These establishments operated as a cross between industrial plants and military facilities: managers and executives were ordnance officers (usually trained as engineers) but the workforce was civilian. Officers had duties similar to industrial managers but with no worries of marketing, sales, or profits and losses. Thus, they could focus their efforts on production, efficiency, and technical management. Ordnance officers tended to rotate through their assignments every few years, but workers remained at the arsenals for much longer periods. Hence the core of technical and manufacturing expertise resided in highly skilled machinists and workmen. This "armory practice," through a difficult but steady path, laid the foundations of the so-called American System of Manufacturing, which became key to the late nineteenth-century era of large-scale industrialization. By the 1850s, the armory system, characterized by highly mechanized precision production, manufactured rifles with genuinely interchangeable parts—a goal inventor Eli *Whitney had promised forty years before but could not deliver. Government-owned manufacturing facilities provided a stable institutional environment for technology to mature over several decades, despite uncertain economic returns.

This slow, expensive development process proved essential to meeting the *Civil War's unprecedented demand for arms, especially with the loss of the Harpers Ferry Armory in 1861. Between 1860 and 1865, the Springfield Armory produced over 800,000 weapons, more than it had produced in all its previous 67-year history. This accomplishment depended on extensive subcontracting to private firms, made possible by the armory's hard-earned expertise with interchangeable parts. When the war ended, the entire system shrank substantially, but the private contractors had been seeded with the American System. Many failed for lack of government business, but others applied the new manufacturing techniques to sewing machines, typewriters, agricultural equipment, business machines, and even bicycles, thus spurring the great wave of American mass production.

Despite these feats, the armories and the arsenals were often subject to criticism. Because of their unique organization, they tended to focus innovative energies on production and not on design, hence the Ordnance Department's often remarked failure to introduce breechloaders or repeating rifles for the common soldier in the Civil War. This technical conservatism owed less to narrow-mindedness than to the Ordnance Department's appreciation for the difficulty of producing new weapons in large numbers. Still, the austerity of the post–Civil War military budget induced stagnation. By 1900, the U.S. Army's small arms were at least a decade behind those of European militaries, which depended on private companies like Krupp and Vickers for new technology. Even in production, the arsenals could not keep up. In the early twentieth century, ordnance officers introduced new techniques, such as *scientific management,* to streamline operations, but they ran headlong into political and labor opposition. Arsenals, unlike private industry, were subject to congressional oversight, and arsenal workers, unlike their counterparts in companies, could seek redress of their grievances by appealing to political patrons.

World War I caught the arsenal system unprepared, and only heavy reliance on weapons from the British and French saw the United States through the critical period of *mobilization. While the Ordnance Department learned important lessons from the experience, peacetime budgets between the world wars meant that it could do little to implement improvements. Still, the army did accomplish some critical procurement planning during the 1930s, with the consequence that production ramped up more smoothly for World War II, although greatly aided by America's delayed entry into the war. By the 1940s, the increasing complexity and scientific sophistication of weapons tended to favor government laboratories and private companies instead of the older arsenals. Even with small arms, the armory had difficulty introducing new

technology; the debacle over the *M-16 rifle resulted in the closing of the Springfield Armory in 1968. During the *Cold War, the military gradually came to rely on large, diversified corporations, what some analysts have called "private arsenals." These institutions have proven technically innovative, if expensive, the government having lost the arsenals' yardstick function. The end of the Cold War, however, highlighted one great advantage of the arsenal system, conspicuous in its absence: the ability to cut back rapidly in peacetime.

[*See also* Industry and War.]

• Felicia Johnson Deyrup, *Arms Makers of the Connecticut Valley,* 1948. Constance M. Green, Harry C. Thompson, and Peter C. Roots, *The Ordnance Department: Planning Munitions for War,* 1955. Hugh Aitken, *Scientific Management in Action: Taylorism at the Watertown Arsenal,* 1960. Merritt Roe Smith, *Harpers Ferry Armory and the New Technology: The Challenge of Change,* 1977. Edward Clinton Ezell, *The Great Rifle Controversy,* 1984. James J. Farley, *Making Arms in the Machine Age: Philadelphia's Frankford Arsenal 1816–1870,* 1994.   —David A. Mindell

PROCUREMENT: INFLUENCE ON INDUSTRY

In the United States after World War II, a *military-industrial complex developed, quite unlike its counterparts in other advanced industrial countries. A distinctive set of firms in a select set of industries emerged as dominant suppliers to the *Pentagon, and in turn were beneficiaries of a de facto industrial policy. During World War II, the Pentagon appropriated the strongly centralized and strategically planned New Deal state apparatus, creating a permanent security state that endured throughout and even beyond the *Cold War. Traditional "hot war" suppliers such as the auto and machinery industries turned their sights back on commercial markets following the war, but the newly expanded aircraft, *communications, and electronics (ACE) industries remained dependent upon military markets for both research monies and sales.

The ACE complex centered on a set of firms that subsequently climbed the ranks of the Fortune 500 biggest corporations—aerospace companies like Grumman, Rockwell, Northrop, General Dynamics, and Lockheed, and communications/electronics firms like Hughes, TRW, and Raytheon. Boeing, successful in both commercial and military markets, was an exception. As commercial shipbuilding declined, shipyards like Newport News, Bath Iron Works, Litton, and Todd also became increasingly defense-dedicated. In a market that operated as a bilateral monopoly (defined as one buyer and one seller, each dominating its "side of the market"), these firms flourished under military patronage and were kept afloat by "follow-on" procurement practices. Pentagon oversight practices generated a specialized business culture that stressed high performance and timeliness over cost-consciousness, rendering military contractors increasingly ill-equipped to compete for commercial sales.

During the early postwar period, advances in jet engines, navigation and guidance systems, and new forms of rocket propulsion yielded significant technologies for the commercial sector, giving American aircraft, communications, and electronics industries a head start in international competition. Through the end of the century, U.S. net exports remained dominated by these sectors plus arms and agricultural goods. Increasingly, however, the esoteric nature and exorbitant cost of military requirements curtailed spin-off, while commercially oriented economies like Japan and Germany were able to capitalize on U.S. defense-underwritten inventions in electronics, robots, and computers.

In the past few years, scholars have begun to question the contribution of the Cold War military-industrial effort to the American economy. Consuming more than $4 trillion since the 1950s, on average 5 percent and 7 percent of GNP annually, much of it deficit-financed, the military-industrial complex has siphoned off a large portion of the nation's scientific and engineering talent and its capital investment funds. The relatively poor postwar performance of American auto, metals, machinery, and consumer electronics industries can be attributed in part to this relative starvation of resources and the absence of similar industrial incentives.

Its costliness has been exacerbated by the spatial segregation of much of the complex from the traditional industrial heartland, inhibiting cross-fertilization and requiring new public infrastructure in "Gunbelt" cities and areas such as Los Angeles, San Diego, Silicon Valley, Seattle, Colorado Springs, Albuquerque, and Huntsville. The dependency of these firms, industries, and regions on the Pentagon budget has made it more difficult to adjust to post–Cold War realities, especially with associated geopolitical shifts in political representation.

[See also Consultants; Economy and War; Industry and War.]

• Merton J. Peck and Frederick W. Scherer, The Weapons Acquisition Process, 1962. Seymour Melman, The Permanent War Economy: American Capitalism in Decline, 1974. Gregory Hooks, Creating the Military-Industrial Complex, 1992. Ann Markusen and Joel Yudken, Dismantling the Cold War Economy, 1992.

—Ann Markusen

PROCUREMENT:
MILITARY VEHICLES AND DURABLE GOODS INDUSTRY

The maxim, "In war the best is always the enemy of enough," describes the U.S. Army's experience with the wagon and truck industries. The army has relied historically on a mix of large public arsenals, armories and depots, and a number of civilian producers to meet its needs. But procurement of wagons and trucks, its primary transport vehicles, has never followed that pattern. During the nineteenth century, American wagon makers were a mature industry—high-volume manufacturers of quality goods—with sufficient political power to prevent the establishment of competing public production facilities. (American automobile manufacturers occupied a similar position in the twentieth century.) Following the *War of 1812, the Quartermaster Bureau, which procured most of the army's general-purpose vehicles, established standard specifications for wagons and bought them from large private wagon makers like Studebaker, Espenschied, and Murphy. After 1840, certain assemblies and parts like wheels and axles were interchangeable, but industry practice was to adapt off-the-rack commercial lines to military demands. They were not the best wagons to be had, but they were good enough, and could be procured in time and in sufficient numbers to meet military needs.

Between 1906, when the army began to experiment with motor transport, and 1937, there were two attempts to modify those traditional procedures. In 1913, the Quartermaster Bureau developed a working relationship with the new Society of Automotive Engineers (SAE), and in mid-1916, a team of Quartermaster, Ordnance, and SAE specialists designed a fleet of standardized, noncommercial military trucks that the government attempted to place in production after entering the war in 1917. The idea was to contract components throughout the industry and assemble the trucks at central locations. Only the 3-ton Standard B "Liberty" truck reached production before the armistice. Resistance to an independent design was widespread in the automobile industry. Manufacturers like the Four Wheel Drive Company, Marmon, Reo, White, and Ford argued that their own commercial models were sufficient, and often refused Liberty B contracts. Parts and subassemblies from less experienced manufacturers would not interchange. Assembly of completed vehicles was slow to get underway, and as a result, the American Expeditionary Forces were forced to use much Allied equipment. In comparison with the British and French, the Americans were often short of truck transport.

After the war, the Quartermaster Bureau complained that it had not been able to get the kind of trucks it needed from private producers and spent over a decade designing its own Quartermaster Standard Fleet. The automobile industry insisted that its trucks were adequate and lobbied successfully to prevent the introduction of the Quartermaster designs. A compromise in 1937 brought a return to traditional practices. The army set general standards and specifications, and truck makers—General Motors, Dodge, Studebaker, Ford, and others—supplied "modified commercial" vehicles like the 2.5-ton general-purpose truck ("Deuce and a Half") in quantities sufficient to meet wartime needs, while specialized producers like Mack, Diamond T, and Reo built 4- and 6-ton trucks and semitractors. (Ironically, Willys-Overland, according to many the original developer of the 1/4-ton General Purpose Vehicle "Jeep," built relatively few of these wartime vehicles itself, allegedly because of its modest engineering and production capability.) Ultimately, American industry produced approximately 3 million military trucks during the war, and Gen. George C. *Marshall asserted in 1945 that American truck transport, especially the Deuce and a Half and the Jeep, was "the greatest advantage in equipment" the United States possessed.

Since 1945, the practice of building on industry strength to supply general-purpose vehicles economically and in adequate quantity has remained most effective. But military-industrial institutional memories have, on occasion, failed. Again, specially designed trucks like the complex low-pressure-tired, flex-bodied, mid-engined, deafening "GOER" (built by Caterpillar) have proved less successful than anticipated, and off-the-rack vehicles have not held up well. It remains to be seen whether the specially designed "Hummer"—a stocky, wide-stanced, low-profile, state-of-the-art vehicle built of space-age materials and intended to replace the Jeep—will secure a place in the civilian market sufficient to reduce its costs of production.

[See also Industry and War.]

• Erna Risch, Quartermaster Support of the Army: A History of the Corps 1775–1939, 1962. Fred Crismon, U.S. Military Wheeled Vehicles, 1983.

—Daniel R. Beaver

PROCUREMENT: MUNITIONS AND CHEMICAL INDUSTRY

The chemical industry has been strategically important to the U.S. military since World War I. As late as the *Spanish-American War in 1898, the only military explosive was black powder, the ancient Chinese mixture of charcoal, saltpeter (postassium nitrate), and sulfur. Only a year later, the British employed two powerful new chemical-based explosives, smokeless powder and picric acid, in the Boer War in South Africa. Smokeless powder, made from nitrocellulose obtained by reacting cotton fibers with nitric acid, was a powerful propellant that did not generate the smoke that previously had revealed the firer's position. The second new explosive, picric acid, was used as a high explosive in artillery shells; it was derived from chemicals that are found in coal and had been used as a yellow dye for textiles. By the beginning of World War I, the Germans developed another high-explosive compound, trinitrotoluene (abbreviated as TNT), which soon became the most widely used high explosive.

The American military, especially the navy with its large-gunned *battleships, had been experimenting with smokeless powder and high explosives since the 1890s. The Dupont Company, the nation's leading producer of black powder and dynamite, had worked with the army and navy on smokeless powder. Dupont hoped to transfer the skills it had acquired in nitrating glycerine to make dynamite to nitrating cotton to make smokeless powder. When World War I began in 1914, Dupont was the only company in the United States that manufactured smokeless powder. Over the next several years, Dupont and a few other American companies—most notably, Hercules, split off from Dupont in an antitrust suit settlement—built large new plants to supply the Allies with smokeless powder. In two years Dupont sales increased from $25 million to $318 million and profits soared from $5.6 million to $82 million. Dupont used these profits to diversify its business into dyestuffs, plastics, and paints.

When the United States entered the war in April 1917, the government made contracts with Dupont and other companies on terms much more favorable to the purchasing agency than the desperate Europeans had received. Dupont even built two huge smokeless powder plants for the government in Tennessee and Virginia. Many other smaller chemical companies, such as Dow Chemical and Allied Chemical, grew and prospered by producing chemicals used to make high explosives and poison gases during the war.

The mutual dependence of the American munitions industry and the Allies in World War I led some critics in the mid-1930s to attribute American participation in the war to the influence of the munitions industry on the U.S. government. After Senate hearings chaired by Gerald *Nye of North Dakota, Congress passed a series of *neutrality acts prohibiting the sale of munitions to belligerent nations.

When the United States entered World War II, the now mature American chemical industry became a key component of the arsenal of democracy. It turned out explosives in much greater quantities than in World War I; contributed new materials such as nylon and synthetic rubber; and played a critical role in building atomic bombs. The synthetic rubber project was critical to the war effort because the Japanese had cut off the supply of natural rubber from Asia. Within two years, a massive government-sponsored cooperative program, including oil, chemical, and rubber companies, established a new synthetic rubber industry. In the *Manhattan Project, companies such as Dupont, Union Carbide, and Tennessee Eastman helped contruct and operate the nuclear materials plants at Oak Ridge, Tennessee, and Hanford, Washington. In the 1950s, the government contracted with Dupont and Dow to build and operate nuclear facilities at Savannah River, South Carolina, and Rocky Flats, Colorado.

[See also Industry and War; Nuclear Weapons.]

—John Kenly Smith

PROCUREMENT: NUCLEAR WEAPONS INDUSTRY

The *nuclear weapons industry developed after the end of World War II at facilities built for the *Manhattan Project. The industry soon spread to seventeen isolated sites across the United States. These sites became the main economic support for their host regions, and this in turn created continuous political pressure for nuclear weapons spending.

The early U.S. lead in nuclear weapons began to disappear in the 1950s as the Soviet Union built a nuclear force of its own, patterning its research laboratories and early delivery systems directly on U.S. sites and models. For the next thirty years, the United States and the USSR engaged in a massive nuclear arms race that pumped huge sums of money into the U.S. nuclear weapons complex. The total amount paid by the United States for nuclear weapons from 1940 through 1996 was almost $5 trillion in 1996 dollars. This spending made nuclear weapons one of the two most expensive government projects in the history of the United States (the other being Social Security).

After *START I was ratified and nuclear testing stopped, the weapons production complex shrank to four sites by 1998: warhead pits are developed and produced at Los Alamos National Laboratory in New Mexico and Livermore National Laboratory in California; the remaining warhead parts are produced at Sandia National Laboratory in New Mexico, and warheads are assembled at the Pantex plant in Texas. This put significant economic pressure on the remaining sites in the nuclear production network, and a number of those sites—Oak Ridge (Tenn.), Savannah River (S.C.), the Idaho National Engineering Laboratory (Idaho), and Hanford (Wash.)—attempted to salvage a nuclear mission by using or reprocessing nuclear materials for other applications such as energy production. None of these attempts is economical and each would require major government subsidies to survive.

With the continued ban on nuclear testing and likely future cuts in nuclear warheads, the remaining nuclear weapons facilities and the regions in which they reside are threatened with large job losses. In response to these threats, the weaponeers in the national laboratories, in conjunction with their political representatives, proposed a new program to manage existing warheads and to design and computer-test new ones. This "Science-Based Stockpile Stewardship" program was funded in 1998 at an annual level equal to two Manhattan Projects.

Environmental and safety pressures from federal and local sources, as well as loss of mission for the nuclear weapons industry, have caused the remaining sites in the nuclear weapons complex to concentrate on cleaning up the massive amounts of nuclear waste produced during the *arms race. As a result, about $4.5 billion was spent in 1998 to clean up contaminated sites. Massive amounts are also dedicated to building storage sites in New Mexico and Nevada for nuclear waste. These cleanup and storage programs will eventually consume hundreds of billions of dollars and are expected to continue for forty years. At many sites they will provide as much employment and economic stimulus as the original weapons programs that created the waste.

[*See also* Consultants; Economy and War; Industry and War; Nuclear Weapons.]

• William J. Weida, *Regaining Security—A Guide to the Costs of Disposing of Plutonium and Highly Enriched Uranium*, 1997. Steven Schwartz, ed., *Atomic Audit*, 1998.   —William J. Weida

PROCUREMENT: ORDNANCE AND ARMS INDUSTRY

Since the 1790s, the American army has procured ordnance through a mixed system of government and private manufacturers. Anxious to have a domestic source of weapons, it established early government arsenals to turn out muskets. These arsenals produced only a small quantity of weapons when the nation faced possible war with France in 1798. As a result, the army contracted for additional firearms from private entrepreneurs. Only a few of the manufacturers completed their contracts, but a precedent had been established for utilizing the private sector to supplement government production.

In the first part of the nineteenth century, the army adopted a policy of expanding its arsenals and of retaining private firms on a long-term basis. The Ordnance Department evolved an ideology of uniformity in the manufacture of arms in both arsenals and private firms that developed and spread the principles of the so-called "American System of Manufacturing," characterized by mass production of standardized interchangeable parts and tighter management control and supervision.

In the *Civil War, because of the rapid buildup of the *Union army, government arsenals and private contractors were unable to meet initial goals, forcing the army to purchase firearms in Europe. By 1863, however, the combination of profitable contracts for private firms and increased production at arsenals enabled domestic production to exceed demand. After the Civil War, government contracts for weapons were practically suspended and the army depended upon its arsenals.

In the two world wars, the army relied heavily on private firms for its weapons once its arsenals lacked the capacity to meet the demands of modern war and it was not deemed wise to build expensive huge arsenals for war production that would largely stand idle in peacetime. During *World War II, private arms firms like the Winchester Company and the Remington Arms Company were major suppliers of weapons, as were firms not usually involved in arms production like the Chrysler Corporation, the General Electric Company, the General Motors Corporation, and the Singer Sewing Machine Company.

During the 1960s, the Department of *Defense, in an effort to end the long-standing rivalry between combat soldiers and military technicians by separating design and doctrine development from production, drastically reduced the army's own production capacity. Since then, the army has relied primarily on a group of quasi-public industrial suppliers for weapons (the army still produces weapons today at the Rock Island, Illinois, and Waterville, New York, arsenals). These suppliers, such as the General Dynamics Corporation and the United Defense Company, while private corporations, often use government-owned equipment and depend heavily on government contracts.

The mixed system has generally worked well in ordnance procurement. Government arsenals set production standards, improved production methods, trained technicians, and provided data on costs, while private firms contributed improved designs and production methods and the industrial base for large-scale production in wartime. But in recent years the expanded reliance on private firms has prompted concern that undue pressure can be exercised in favor of special economic interests in the selection of weapons.

[*See also* Industry and War; Military-Industrial Complex; Weaponry.]

• James A. Huston, *The Sinews of War: Army Logistics, 1775–1953*, 1966. Merritt Roe Smith, "Military Arsenals and Industry Before World War I," in B. Franklin Cooling, ed., *War Business, and American Society: Historical Perspectives on the Military-Industrial Complex*, 1977.   —John Kennedy Ohl

PROCUREMENT: SHIPBUILDING INDUSTRY

The shipbuilding industry includes new construction as well as modernization, overhaul, and repair of existing ships. Naval warships average a thirty-year life, while commercial ships may last longer. Most ships require several major overhauls or modernizations during this lifetime.

The first commercial ship built in America was a 30-ton bark in 1607, and the first oceangoing vessel was launched in 1631. Mercantilist England saw New England as a source of naval stores and fishing. Because the colonies had all the natural resources required to build ships, they soon became England's major provider. By 1750, there were more than 125 shipyards in America producing faster ships at costs 30 to 50 percent less than in England.

The indigenous shipbuilding industry was also fueled by local demand for fishing boats, water transport between colonies, and delivery of American raw materials and produce to England and the Caribbean to exchange for needed manufactured goods. Tobacco, cotton, molasses, and then slave trade all helped sustain the industry, as did the China trade after 1783.

Robert *Fulton produced the first commercially viable steamboat in 1807, and by 1820 steamships were crossing the Atlantic. The first iron hull was floated in 1825, but American shipping and shipbuilding peaked in 1855 and then began a decline broken only by wartime spending programs during the *Civil War and the *Spanish-American War.

As vessels turned from the graceful clipper ship of the 1850s to steel, the competitiveness of U.S. shipyards declined because the Europeans took this new technology more seriously than the Americans. U.S. iron works put their energy and innovation into building railroads. Consequently, the price of American steel never became internationally competitive, and shipyards languished. Shipbuilding had spectacular growth in the 1890s and early 1900s because of large navy orders for the new steel-hulled "Great White Fleet," coupled with commercial fleet replacement. The decline set in again rather quickly, however.

World War I caused a major rush to build the "bridge of ships" to Europe. Established firms were booked solid with warships, while new yards were started to undertake a crash merchant fleet building program. Bureaucratic delays were such that most of the ships (80%) were completed after the war was over. Postwar depression dropped prices and shipbuilding stagnated as idle commercial ships became common and warships were limited by the *Washington Naval Arms Limitation Treaty of 1922.

The almost sixty years following the Civil War offered

minimal hope for a sustained revival in shipbuilding. It was obvious that political leadership would not consider expending massive public funds to support an American-flag merchant fleet. This required shipbuilders to fall back on naval warship production.

Spasmodic congressional intervention with subsidies beginning in 1924 was required to build even a few commercial ships. In preparation for World War II, a second "emergency" shipbuilding program, the Liberty ships, was begun in 1939. Some 4,732 easy-to-build and simple-to-operate maritime ships were built between 1942 and 1945. A major naval shipbuilding program lasted from 1938 to 1945. A massive movement of labor to shipyards on the East, West, and Gulf Coasts was undertaken to complete this effort successfully.

At the end of World War II, the United States owned 60 percent of the world's tonnage, yet decline of the merchant marine began immediately. By 1948, the sale of 1,746 ships to U.S. and international operators had been completed. During the *Cold War, a 1970 law authorized subsidies for building 300 new merchant vessels over the next 10 years, but a world economic slump driven by rising oil prices hindered this program, and only 83 ships were delivered.

Even new technologies and designs pioneered in the United States could not make American yards competitive for commercial ships because of high material and labor costs (outmoded shipyard processes) in construction and exorbitant operating costs. South Korea, Japan, and Taiwan developed highly automated shipyards that U.S. industry simply could not match. Nevertheless, American shipyards were busy during the 1980s, as President Ronald *Reagan presided over one of the largest peacetime expansions of the navy in U.S. history.

[See also Navy, U.S.]

• Clinton H. Whitehurst, Jr., The U.S. Shipbuilding Industry, 1986. K. Jack Bauer, A Maritime History of the United States, 1988.
—William D. Smith

PROCUREMENT: STEEL AND ARMOR PLATE INDUSTRY

(1865–1918). The battleship era between the *Civil War and World War I brought about an intensification of business-government relationships, the origins of what some historians term the "*military-industrial complex" or "command economy." Intense interaction between naval officials and leading steelmakers was necessary to procure the latest and most effective armor, especially when its possession was a necessity for major warships. Certainly, no private-sector market existed for huge steel plates up to 22 inches in thickness, costing fifteen to twenty times more than steel rails. America's building of a "Great Power" navy, then, required its mastering this technology. However, government incentives given to private steelmakers fanned Populist and Progressive criticism of big business. In these ways, armor procurement became entwined with debates about the nation's foreign and domestic policies.

The armor trade resulted from successive waves of technical change in shipbuilding and steel manufacture. While Britain began building large iron ships in the 1840s, and there were iron gunboats in the Civil War, most American warships were constructed of wood through the 1860s. In the 1870s, the U.S. Navy's Ordnance Bureau found itself unable to obtain the heavy, rifled, breech-loading steel guns then finding favor in Europe. At the navy's behest,

Midvale Steel became the country's leading manufacturer of ordnance steel. In the next decade, large appropriations for steel warships extended the navy's scope of interaction with private industry.

Multi-million-dollar contracts for steel armor plate began with Bethlehem Iron in 1887 and Carnegie Steel in 1890. Initially, the navy helped these two private firms transfer the necessary armor-making technology from France and heavy forging technology from England. The two steel companies soon found it indispensable to hire ex-naval officers (and at least one sitting U.S. senator) to deal effectively with the U.S. government. Finally, the two companies effected a pact of splitting contracts and maintaining high prices, extended to Midvale after its entry into armor plate in 1903. Proponents of the early "military-industrial complex" thesis such as Benjamin Franklin Cooling also cite a series of congressional inquiries about high armor prices and recurrent public scandals about low armor quality. Furthermore, there was a massive procurement following the *Spanish-American War (armor contracts increased fivefold between 1898 and 1900), which could be seen as an instance of a command economy.

The already byzantine politics of armor received an outlandish international twist after 1895, just as Anglo-German antagonism entered a critical phase. Until this time, the great power navies simply chose one of three types of armor; none could be proven definitively superior. But in the mid-1890s, a clearly superior armor was developed whose glass-hard face shattered incoming shells. This armor was invented in America by Hayward A. Harvey, improved in Germany by the Krupp concern, and came to be controlled by an international patent pool based in London (1895–1912). Precisely during the peak years of the global naval arms race, then, warships of all the great powers used the same armor.

From 1887 to 1915, the U.S. Navy purchased from the Bethlehem, Carnegie, and Midvale steel companies a total of 233,400 tons of armor plate (85% of which came after 1898) costing $102 million, and from 1916 to 1920 an additional 121,000 tons of armor plate costing about $65 million. The 1916 Naval Expansion Act authorized a government armor plant to limit private profit. It was built at Charleston, West Virginia, but its first 60-ton armor ingot was not cast until 1921, and it was closed by the Republican administration of Warren Harding. The proper significance of armor plate is to be found not in the battleship itself (which was largely rendered obsolete by the submarine, aerial warfare, and naval disarmament treaties of the 1920s), but in the characteristic entanglement of public and private entities concerning the promotion and procurement of new military technologies.

[See also Battleships; Industry and War; Navy, U.S.: 1866–98.]

• Benjamin Franklin Cooling, Gray Steel and Blue Water Navy: The Formative Years of America's Military Industrial Complex, 1881–1917, 1979. Thomas J. Misa, A Nation of Steel: The Making of Modern America, 1865–1925, 1995.
—Thomas J. Misa

PROPAGANDA AND PUBLIC RELATIONS, GOVERNMENT.

Propaganda is a deliberate attempt to persuade people to think and then behave in a manner desired by the source; public relations, a branch of propaganda, is a related process intended to enhance the relationship between an organization and the public. Both, in turn, are related to *advertising*. Bill Backer, in *The Care and Feeding of Ideas* (1993), suggests that advertising and propaganda are half brothers. An advertisement connects something with human desires; propaganda shapes the infinite into concrete images.

Propaganda has always been a strategm of government and the military. It has always been part of military recruitment, albeit in an earlier era restricted to colorful uniforms or military parades. Propaganda has always been a necessity for any government actively seeking to mobilize its citizens. The American Revolution, for example, would have been inconceivable without making the case for revolution generally known. Thomas Paine's pamphlet *Common Sense* (1776) sold perhaps 500,000 copies in a country with 3 million inhabitants. Nearly four score and seven years later, "Lincoln freed the slaves." It does not trivialize the *Emancipation Proclamation to remember it partly as a piece of political propaganda, originally restricted by Abraham *Lincoln solely to those parts of the South already under Union control. The proclamation was more than a statement of government policy toward slaves; its promulgation assisted the recruitment of black soldiers and helped deter British recognition of the Confederacy, and as such, it served military ends.

Not surprisingly, propaganda came of age in World War I, as all major combatants created agencies to regulate and censor the flow of information, aid in recruitment, and sell the moral validity of the war effort to those on the home front and battlefront. The most effective recruiting device for the American military in World War I was arguably James Montgomery Flagg's recruiting poster, "Uncle Sam Wants You." American war propaganda was shaped through the efforts of President Woodrow *Wilson's Committee on Public Information, headed by journalist George Creel. A Speaker's Bureau (a pre-radio necessity) of 75,000 "Four-Minute Men" visited schools, churches, and other public places, combining up-to-the-minute news from the battlefront with brief patriotic appeals to support the war effort.

The war saw the emergence of pejorative connotations that have surrounded the concept of propaganda up to the present. Instead of realizing the close relationship among morale, education, and propaganda, Americans considered propaganda a synonym for government lies, and that interpretation has remained to today.

The 1920s saw the emergence of public relations, a term first used in 1807 by Thomas *Jefferson in a message to Congress. Edward L. Bernays introduced *public relations counsel* in his *Crystalizing Public Opinion* (1923), and the decade saw the general acceptance of the profession by business and government, if not by every military commander.

New Deal America institutionalized propaganda and public relations within American society. President Franklin D. *Roosevelt promoted his policies directly through public press conferences and "fireside chats," radio addresses to the American people. His promotion of the *Lend-Lease Act and Agreements in 1940–41 is an example. At a press conference in December 1940, Roosevelt introduced the idea of giving away war material to those fighting Nazi Germany with a simple analogy: "Suppose my neighbor's house is on fire and I have a length of garden hose ..." In a "fireside chat" two weeks later, the

president invoked a larger moral purpose: "America must be the great arsenal of democracy." Here was the selling of policy using the talents of the propagandist and public relations counsel.

The documentary filmmaker Pare Lorentz made films for the New Deal about social problems—the Dust Bowl and flooding in the Mississippi Valley—both depicting natural disasters as the result of unchecked individual actions, both offering the New Deal as uniquely capable of solving physical or natural disasters through enlightened state policies. Roosevelt's appeal to those better off than the "one-third of a nation ill-housed, ill-clothed, ill-fed" was documented by photographers of the Farm Security Administration (FSA), whose depiction of rural poverty helped justify federal relief programs and made people aware of the role of photography in public relations campaigns.

The military got the picture. During *World War II, the army's Bureau of Public Relations did a better job of managing news from the battlefront than a competing civilian agency, the Office of War Information (OWI). All newsreel footage shot in various theaters of war was first subject to military censorship; and all photographs were subject to censorship, particularly if they showed the faces of American dead.

Army Chief of Staff George C. *Marshall commissioned Hollywood director Frank Capra to explain the war to millions of soldiers in a series of seven hour-length orientation films entitled *Why We Fight*. The first, *Prelude to War*, was released in 1942; an eighth film, *War Comes to America, Part II*, survives only as a final shooting script. Capra's propaganda films divide the world neatly into forces of light and darkness; enemy footage is reedited to make clear the dangers of totalitarianism. Though the precise impact of the films is hard to gauge, the *Why We Fight* series was the most elaborate statement of war aims produced by any part of the federal government in World War II.

The *Cold War proved a boom time for informational materials aimed at the hearts and minds of the "captive" peoples of Eastern Europe. The Voice of America, created in 1950 to broadcast controlled information to countries "behind the Iron Curtain," was soon joined by Radio Free Europe and Radio Liberty. The United States Information Agency (USIA) became a separate agency of Cold War propaganda in 1953; the end of the Cold War has also meant that the USIA is to be reunited with the Department of State, reflecting its lesser importance, or perhaps the realization that official messages are more successfully transmitted through nongovernmental agencies. In the 1950s, the USIA produced a large number of informational films, shown generally in 16mm in nontheatrical distribution with foreign-language soundtracks; it also sponsored libraries of American literature in USIA branches all over the world. Cold War radio and television broadcasting still survives as Radio Marti and TV Marti, broadcasts from Miami sponsored by the *Central Intelligence Agency and intended to undermine Fidel Castro in Cuba.

The *Vietnam War showed the problems of military information management in an unpopular war, one ostensibly free of overt censorship of civilian news organizations, though military *helicopters were certainly not obliged to take hostile newsmen (and women) wherever they wished to go. The biggest source of complaint was the military's contribution to President Lyndon B. *Johnson's handling of the war, the so-called "credibility gap." The discrepancy between official optimism and what reporters saw as "actual" battlefield failure led the official Vietnam Joint United States Public Affairs Office to hold daily afternoon briefings for news representatives, soon derisively known as the "Five O'Clock Follies." *Pentagon spokesmen reported astronomical numbers of enemy dead—always far higher than the numbers of Americans killed. Nowhere was less done to coordinate military battlefield information needs with the citizens' right to know than in these ill-conceived briefings. Indeed, it might seem in retrospect that Daniel Boorstin's book *The Image* (1962) in which the "pseudo-event"—a non-event that occurs primarily in order to be reported—was tailor-made for the information handed out at the "Five O'Clock Follies."

The Vietnam War taught lessons to the military about the value of censorship, overall management of the news, and the need for more sophisticated public relations personnel. The 1991 *Persian Gulf War reflected these changes. Media coverage often missed what was actually happening, contributing to battlefield victory by reinforcing Saddam *Hussein's (incorrect) belief that the main Allied Coalition attack was sure to come through Kuwait City from the gulf, instead of around fixed desert positions. News management now seems a well-established military policy, even if at the cost of absolute freedom of the press; it also underscores a new importance of propaganda and public relations to the military commander.

As Philip M. Taylor points out in his *Global Communications* (1997), in October 1995, the U.S. *Air Force created its first Information Warfare Squadron (the 609th Squadron, stationed in South Carolina). Enemies today target civilian airlines; they slip bombs into checked luggage; today's terrorists can also engage in chemical, biological, or electronic warfare and be capable of greater destruction than an entire regiment in the field, impervious to attack by conventional armed troops. Accordingly, one now sees the addition of Information Warfare to the military arsenal. No longer is there a clear dividing line between public information and military psychological operations; "infowar" entails all of the following: command and control warfare, intelligence-based warfare, electronic warfare, psychological warfare, computer hacker warfare, economic information warfare, and cyberwarfare. In such an interconnected military environment, one can predict a vastly enhanced role for propaganda and public relations, a decline in the disdain with which many hold such practitioners, and a realization that the military commander becomes ever more dependent on the weaponry of an electronic world—a world in which one side's disinformation is another's information; one side's "flack" another's public relations officer.

[*See also* Enemy, Views of the; Film, War and the Military in: Newsfilms and Documentaries; Film, War and the Military in: Feature Films; News Media, War, and the Military; Public Opinion, War, and the Military; Psychological Warfare.]

• Edward L. Bernays, *Crystalizing Public Opinion*, 1923. Philip Davidson, *Propaganda and the American Revolution, 1763–1783*, 1941; repr. 1973. Allan M. Winkler, *The Politics of Propaganda: The Office of War Information, 1942–1945*, 1977. Stephen Vaughn, *Holding Fast the Inner Lines: Democracy, Nationalism and the Committee on Public Information*, 1980. Terence H. Qualter, *Opinion Control in the Democracies*, 1985. Michael Schudson, *Advertising, the Uneasy Persuasion: Its Dubious Impact on American Society*, 1986. Bill Backer, *The Care and Feeding of Ideas*, 1993. Jacqueline Sharkey, *Under Fire: U.S. Military Restrictions on the Media from Grenada to the Persian Gulf*, 1993. Stuart Ewen, *PR!: A Social History of Spin*, 1997. Philip M. Taylor, *Global Communications, International Affairs and the Media Since 1945*, 1997. —David Culbert

PSYCHIATRY, MILITARY. Most psychiatric illness among soldiers in the eighteenth and nineteenth centuries was called *nostalgia.* In the early nineteenth century, Baron Dominique Larrey, Napoleon's chief surgeon, had treated nostalgia by subjecting soldiers to an interesting, predictable training regimen featuring gymnastics and music. In 1862, Surgeon General William A. Hammond tried unsuccessfully to limit nostalgia in the *Union army by screening out teenagers, the recruits thought to be most susceptible. Twenty years after the war, Hammond wrote that nostalgia could best be treated with a program similar to Larrey's and conducted close to the soldier's unit.

Early in World War I, the term *shell shock* emerged to describe the array of psychiatric symptoms soldiers manifested. French and British psychiatrists learned that the symptoms were not the result of a physical shock to the central nervous system, but were psychological reactions to combat experiences. They also learned that the further a psychological casualty was removed from the front, the more intractable his condition became.

Thomas Salmon, surgeon general of the U.S. *Army, concluded that soldiers perceived that it was better to be sick than a coward, and shell shock offered an honorable way out of combat. Once evacuated, it became progressively more essential psychologically for the soldier to persevere in his symptoms. Salmon organized psychiatric services for the *American Expeditionary Forces along four principles: *proximity*—treat psychiatric casualties close to the battle zone; *simplicity*—treat with rest, food, and a shower; *immediacy*—begin treatment at once; and *expectancy*—assure the soldier that he would soon return to his unit. Baron Larrey's regimen was resurrected.

At the beginning of World War II, the thrust of military psychiatry was to screen out those susceptible to psychiatric breakdown prior to their entering the armed forces. Examining stations rejected 1.6 million registrants for mental or educational reasons—a rate 7.6 times as high as in World War I. Nonetheless, soldiers were discharged for psychiatric reasons at a rate 2.4 times as high as in World War I. Salmon's doctrine of forward treatment had disappeared from military psychiatric practice. Not until 1943 did Capt. Fred Hanson, applying Salmon's principles, demonstrate that he could return more than 70 percent of battle fatigue casualties to their units with forty eight hours of rest in forward areas.

Wartime research revealed that the incidence of psychiatric casualties usually paralleled the number of soldiers wounded; that every man had his breaking point; and that the intensity of combat, duration of exposure, and quality of social supports in the unit were crucial mediating factors. G. W. Beebe and J. W. Appel found that the average soldier's breaking point was eighty-eight days of combat during which his company suffered one or more *casualties. The days need not be consecutive; the effects were cumulative. Concurrently, social psychologists under the leadership of J. A. Stouffer found that cohesive units with competent and supportive leaders had fewer psychiatric casualties, and soldiers endured longer without breaking down.

During the *Korean War, Col. Albert J. Glass organized a system of forward treatment by battalion surgeons or medical aidmen. In an effort to prevent psychiatric casualties, the Far East command rotated soldiers in combat units out of Korea after nine months of service, and all service members in Korea received at least one two-week rest and recuperation leave during their tours. These measures were effective: psychiatric casualties were few, and 90 percent were returned to duty after forward treatment.

By the mid-1960s, psychoanalytic thinking had penetrated military medicine. But attributing behavior to childhood experiences or unconscious processes was antithetical to military values of responsibility and discipline. Consequently, the primary role of military psychiatrists became examining soldiers prior to court-martial or administrative discharge. Soldiers who voluntarily sought psychiatric treatment were usually discharged; those who wanted to stay in the army learned that it was unwise to acknowledge that they had symptoms.

During the period of major American involvement in the *Vietnam War (1965–72), military psychiatry expanded the range of behavior it addressed. Though the incidence of acute combat fatigue was the lowest in any war up to that time, psychiatrists recognized that substance abuse, some misconduct, and postbattle depression had psychological origins. Alcoholism and drug abuse ceased to be disciplinary matters and were taken over by military medicine. Treatment programs, again reminiscent of those devised by Baron Larrey, were designed for execution by paramedical personnel. Some misbehavior was handled on a quasi-medical basis; soldiers were eliminated from the service administratively rather than being punished. Service members with persistent psychiatric symptoms that were classified as Post Traumatic Stress Disorder were discharged. Many received treatment from psychiatrists in the *Veterans Administration.

With the advent of the *All-Volunteer Force in 1973, senior commanders revised organization, training, and leadership to enhance small-unit cohesion as one means of strengthening resistance to combat stress. To identify lessons to be learned from combat and training events, after-action reviews were developed to draw out all of the participants' actions and perceptions. In some units the reviews included emotions as well, and proved effective in reducing Post Traumatic Stress reactions. Military psychiatrists were not involved in these measures. Most military personnel of all ranks continued to fear psychiatrists.

Since the *Cold War ended in 1991, U.S. forces have conducted an average of one major armed intervention per year. Military personnel were likely to experience repeated exposure to combat in a single enlistment. Research between 1991 and 1996 revealed that short-duration combat experiences and noncombat interventions can produce stress reactions. To preserve the psychological readiness of units, it became essential that mental health professionals come out of the hospitals to practice proactive preventive psychiatry. Some psychiatrists took the initiative in peacetime by consulting with commanders and training mental health specialists to provide outreach services in units. As a consequence, during the *Persian Gulf War, some combat stress control teams achieved moderate levels of acceptance in line units. They participated in after-action reviews, conducted post-trauma debriefings for members of units subjected to severe stress, and trained unit leaders in managing homecoming processes to minimize the likelihood of Post Traumatic Stress Disorder.

[*See also* Combat Trauma.]

• W. A. Hammond, *A Treatise on Insanity in Its Medical Relations,* 1883. P. Bailey, et al., eds., *Neuropsychiatry,* Vol. 10: *The Medical Department of the United States Army in the World War,* 1929. Samuel A. Stouffer, et al., *The American Soldier,* 4 vols., 1949. Albert J. Glass and R. Bernucci, eds., *Zone of the Interior,* Vol. 1: *Neuropsychiatry in World War II,* 1966. Albert J. Glass, ed., *Overseas Theaters,* Vol. 2: *Neuropsychiatry in World War II,* 1973. Franklin D. Jones, et al., eds., *War Psychiatry,* Part I, Vol. 6, and *Military Psychiatry: Preparing in Peace for War,* Part I, Vol. 7, 1995. Eric T. Dean, Jr., *Shook Over Hell: Post-Traumatic Stress, Vietnam, and the Civil War,* 1998.

—Faris R. Kirkland

PSYCHOLOGICAL WARFARE is war propaganda directed at enemy audiences to induce surrender, insurrection, or disruption. It is most effective when based on military realities or likelihoods. It is intertwined with twentieth-century mass media, which allows the dissemination and reception of information behind enemy lines through leaflets, radio, and television. Traditionally, one distinguishes among three kinds of psychological warfare: *white, gray,* and *black.* White propaganda openly admits origin, and is disseminated openly by clearly identifiable sources; gray indicates no source; black disguises its source or purports to come from somewhere other than its true source. Black propaganda trades in *disinformation,* that is, misinformation or untrue statements deliberately spread to sow confusion. Today, disinformation has eclipsed black propaganda as a technique of psychological warfare; it works because it plays on recipients' darkest suspicions: it trades in prejudice and bias.

Psychological warfare may be synonymous with the twentieth century, but it is hardly new to the conduct of warfare. The Chinese military specialist Sun Tzu noted in his fourth-century B.C. *Art of War* that "to subdue the enemy without fighting is the acme of skill." In 1400 B.C., Joshua used the techniques of psychological warfare when he marched around the city of Jericho seven times sounding his trumpet to intimidate the enemy. The role of deception in siege warfare is famously part of the Siege of Troy. Thanks to the wooden horse in which Greek soldiers were hidden, we consider the Trojan Horse synonymous with "Greeks bearing gifts." In short, intelligent military commanders have frequently resorted to strategem, particularly in siege warfare, and this is part of what today we consider psychological warfare.

World War I saw the first use of modern propaganda techniques on a large scale. Woodrow *Wilson used the tactics of white propaganda in promoting his *Fourteen Points (1918) as a basis for ending the war. The enemy was depicted through *atrocities propaganda, as the "Brutish Hun," destroyer of civilization, an enemy who did not scruple to kill innocent women and children in the sinking of the *Lusitania (1915). Civilians at home, and doughboys in the trenches, knew it was Germans who bombed the cathedral at Reims. Adolf *Hitler paid careful attention to Allied propaganda successes in some of the shrewdest parts of his autobiography, *Mein Kampf* (1925–26).

World War II led to the advent of "psyops" as a distinct

part of military operations and planning. Correctly understood, psychological warfare does not treat home morale or concern itself with public relations involving friendly countries. It is, rather, concerned with the enemy and enemy-controlled countries. Military force (the alternative to psychological warfare) concerns itself with threats, promises, subversion, and destruction; psychological warfare trades in warnings, alternatives, compassion, and the presumptive surcease of strategic rather than terrorist bombings.

Arguments as to the effectiveness of psychological warfare in World War II turn on what role, if any, these techniques had in persuading the German soldier to surrender before 8 May 1945. Gen. Dwight D. *Eisenhower stressed the significance of psyops to modern warfare in an oft-quoted statement in the spring of 1945: "Without doubt, psychological warfare has proved its right to a place of dignity in our military arsenal." Most military historians recognize the import of this statement but feel that the doctrine of "Unconditional Surrender" fatally undermined the possibility of effective psyops in World War II by precluding the effective utilization of alternatives and compassion. One must conclude that we know an enormous amount about tricks and ruses (often concocted by brilliant practitioners) but very little about demonstrable impact.

The *Korean War introduced a new sort of psyops, the concept of *brainwashing*, first mentioned in 1950, a translation of the Chinese term for "thought reform." To brainwash is to change drastically someone's outlook. It involves convincing someone thoroughly, usually through nefarious means. Twenty-one American prisoners of war refused repatriation in 1953; *Cold War hysteria in America led many to believe that they were the victims of totalitarian practitioners with superhuman skills in indoctrination. Though the word *brainwashing* is part of everyday speech, today it is used to describe the techniques of those who create religious cults; the American military, after exhaustive analysis, concluded that in terms of troop *morale, there was no such thing as brainwashing; instead, the problem had to do with a captured soldier's inner psychological strength or emotional vulnerability.

The *Vietnam War made substantial—and notorious—use of psyops. Persons trained in civil and political affairs joined Special Operations *Forces to bring about so-called *pacification, and to aid in the defection of the Viet Cong to the South Vietnamese side, all part of Civil Operations and Rural Development Support (CORDS). Certainly, psyops operations were mistrusted by conventional soldiers and their commanders, but Vietnam systematized the phrase coined by Gen. Sir Gerald Templer as the goal of British efforts to undermine guerrilla activity in Malaya in the 1950s, "the battle for hearts and minds"—surely the central concern of psychological warfare in all of its guises.

More recently, the *Persian Gulf War (1991) made stunning use of disinformation as a tool of military policy, suggesting that future psyops will make the control of information a central concern. Gen. H. Norman *Schwarzkopf was happy to let television commentators and newspaper correspondents repeat endlessly the inevitability of an assault on Kuwait City from the sea. Saddam *Hussein and his advisers assumed this must be official doctrine and arranged their forces for such an eventuality. When this proved not the case, "the mother of all battles" came to a quick conclusion. Further, the advent of satellite television broadcasting, allowing CNN correspondent Peter Arnett

to broadcast from the enemy's capital while the war progressed, suggests that psyops and information policy are more than ever subjects no modern military commander can ignore. Successes in deception may make fascinating reading, but the real success of psyops entails techniques more white than black in an effort "to subdue the enemy without fighting."

[*See also* Bombing of Civilians; News Media, War, and the Military; Propaganda and Public Relations, Government.]

• Harold D. Lasswell, *Propaganda Technique in World War I*, 1927; repr. 1971. Daniel Lerner, *Psychological Warfare Against Nazi Germany: The Sykewar Campaign, D-Day to VE-Day*, 1949; repr. 1971. Terrence H. Qualter, *Propaganda and Psychological Warfare*, 1962. Philip M. Taylor, *War and the Media: Propaganda and Persuasion in the Gulf War*, 1992. Philip M. Taylor, *Munitions of the Mind: A History of Propaganda from the Ancient World to the Present Day*, 1995. Robert Cole, *Propaganda in Twentieth Century War and Politics: An Annotated Bibliography*, 1996.   —David Culbert

PUBLIC FINANCING AND BUDGETING FOR WAR.

America's great wars—the *Civil War, *World War I, and *World War II—have been the most important events shaping the federal government's approach to public finance. Along with the political crisis of the 1780s and the Great Depression of the 1930s, these wars created distinctive public finance regimes that were crucial not only to the war efforts but also to the subsequent peacetime expansions of the federal government. At the core of these regimes were distinctive systems of taxation, each with its own characteristic tax base, rate structure, administrative apparatus, and social intention.

To mobilize for wars of unprecedented scale required vast new revenues, and this in turn freed American leaders to reexamine the nation's financial options. In so doing, they faced issues that far transcended the technicalities of war finance. Because each great military crisis involved the meaning or survival of the nation, it stimulated debate over fundamental national values, even as it intensified ideological and distributional divisions within American society. And because each war required the sacrifice of lives as well as treasure, it provoked social division and political conflict, which often centered on issues of taxation. The politics of taxation has, therefore, both expressed contested national values and furnished a means to resolve the social and ideological conflicts intensified by war.

Within the conflicted politics of each wartime emergency, the architects of national mobilization worked to persuade Americans to accept new taxes as a necessary form of sacrifice. In the Civil War and each of the two world wars, federal leaders designed new tax programs both to implement sacrifice and to convince the mass of taxpayers that their sacrifices were fair. In the process, the new tax systems came symbolically to express the goals of American society.

Before the Civil War, a system of low tariffs, a borrowing capability that Alexander *Hamilton's financial program had helped establish, and the enormous landed resources of the federal government had been adequate to finance almost all of the activities of the federal government. Only the *War of 1812, because it disrupted the foreign commerce on which tariffs were based, forced the federal government to adopt temporary excise and property taxes. The financial system of the early republic would probably have remained adequate, had not a great national emergency intervened.

In no sense was the Civil War more truly a modern war than in its enormous requirements for capital. Union war costs drove up government spending from less than 2 percent of the gross national product to an average of 15 percent, close to the 20 percent level of the early 1990s. This evoked a program of emergency taxation and borrowing unprecedented in scale and scope.

The Union placed excise taxes on virtually all consumer goods, license taxes on a wide variety of activities (including every profession except the ministry), special taxes on corporations, stamp taxes on legal documents, and inheritance taxes on estates. Each wartime Congress also raised the tariffs on foreign goods, doubling the average tariff rate by the end of the war. Finally, the government levied its first income tax—graduated tax reaching a maximum rate of 10 percent.

Taxes funded about 20 percent of the Union's war costs, leaving the government to finance the rest by running deficits and borrowing money through the sale of Treasury bonds. Secretary of the Treasury Salmon P. Chase and Jay Cooke, a Philadelphia banker, marketed the bonds cleverly, by making interest on them payable in gold, and thus giving investors a hedge against inflation; they also reassured the wealthy by keeping income tax rates low. Most innovatively, they sold bonds not just to the wealthy and to financial institution, but to the middle class. Although banks and rich people in America and Britain bought most of the securities, Cooke's newspaper advertisements and his 2,500 subagents persuaded nearly a million northerners— a quarter of all families—to by them too. The administration of President Abraham *Lincoln pioneered the propaganda techniques that would become essential to funding the major wars in the twentieth century.

In order to persuade Americans to make financial and human sacrifices for World War I, President Woodrow *Wilson and his supporters in Congress had to introduce progressive income taxation on a grand scale. Passed in 1916 as a preparedness measure and expanded significantly after American entry into the war, the World War I income tax was an explicit "soak-the-rich" instrument. It imposed the first significant levies on corporate profits and personal incomes, while avoiding the extensive taxation of wages and salaries. In adopting the concept of taxing corporate "excess profits," the United States—alone among the belligerent powers—placed at the center of wartime finance a graduated tax on all profits above a government-specified "normal" rate of return. Excess-profits taxation generated most of the revenues raised during the war. Taxes produced a larger share of total revenues for the United States than any other belligerent, despite the fact that by the end of 1918 the daily average of war expenditures in the United States was almost double that in Great Britain and far greater than that in any other combatant nation. Thus, wartime public finance was based on the taxation that Democratic political lenders, including President Wilson, regarded as monopoly profits—in effect, ill-gotten gains.

Closely related to the Wilson administration's tax program was its sale of war bonds to middle-class Americans. Rather than tax ordinary citizens at high levels, the Wilson administration sought to mobilize their savings, a strategy that Secretary of the Treasury William G. McAdoo called "capitalizing patriotism." He attempted to persuade ordinary Americans to reduce consumption, increase savings, and become creditors of the state; so that after the war these middle-class bondholders would be repaid by tax dollars raised from corporations and the wealthiest Americans.

Selling bonds directly to average Americans on a multi-billion-dollar scale required marketing campaigns far greater in scope than those used anywhere else in the world. Largely through trial and error, the Wilson administration devised a vast array of marketing techniques, including the sophisticated analysis of national income and savings. Financing by the new Federal Reserve system, which McAdoo turned into an arm of the Treasury, was important, but not as much as McAdoo's efforts to shift private savings into bonds. In promoting the four "Liberty Loans," McAdoo's Treasury armed itself with modern techniques of mass communication, and succeeded in placing its loans deep in the middle class—far deeper than during the Civil War. In the Third Liberty Loan campaign (conducted in April 1918), at least one-half of all American families subscribed. Thus the new public-finance regime installed by the Wilson administration encompassed a revolution in borrowing strategy as well as tax policy.

While the Wilson administration and the military did not always agree on what resources were necessary, the administration never allowed political or economic concerns to influence the setting of financial objectives. By 1918, the financial commitment to the war effort had become substantial; federal military expenditures reached nearly 25 percent of national product. The pay-off would have been even more evident had the war lasted into 1919, as the administration expected.

The most radical tax initiative—excess-profits taxation—did not survive the postwar reaction of the 1920s, but Democratic tax politics retained its "soak-the-rich" thrust into early mobilization for World War II. Like Wilson, President Franklin D. *Roosevelt was committed to generating the revenues required to prosecute the war through taxes that bore heavily on corporations and upper-income groups. "In time of this grave national danger, when all excess income should go to win the war," Roosevelt told a joint session of Congress in 1942, "no American citizen ought to have a net income, after he has paid his taxes, of more than $25,000."

But opposition to radical war-tax proposals strengthened in the face of the revenue requirements of full mobilization. One source of opposition came from a diverse group of military planners, foreign-policy strategists, financial leaders, and economists. One of these was Russell C. Leffingwell, who had been Assistant Secretary of the Treasury during World War I and a partner in J. P. Morgan and Company since the early 1920s. Throughout the turbulence of the 1920s and 1930s, experts like Leffingwell had marshaled the economic lessons of World War I and its aftermath. Now they wanted to mobilize even greater resources, to do so more smoothly and predictably, and to reduce inflationary pressures. They promoted mass-based taxation, based either on a general sales tax or an income tax that produced most of its revenue from wages and salaries. The second source of opposition to Roosevelt's radical tax proposals came from Democrats in both Congress and the administration itself; they worried that stringent corporate taxation might turn a postwar slump into another major depression.

In October of 1942, Roosevelt and Congress compromised by dropping the general sales tax, as Roosevelt wished, and adopting a progressive income tax, although a less progressive one than Roosevelt wanted. The act greatly reduced personal exemptions, enabling the federal government to acquire huge revenues from the taxation of middle-class wages and salaries. Just as important, the rates on individuals incomes—including a surtax graduated from 13 percent on the first $2,000 to 82 percent on income over $200,000—made the personal income tax more progressive than at any other time in its history.

Under the new system the number of individual taxpayers grew from 3.9 million in 1939 to 42.6 million in 1945, and federal income-tax collections leaped from $2.2 billion to $35.1 billion. By 1945 nearly 90 percent of American workers submitted income-tax returns, and about 60 percent of the labor force paid income taxes, usually in the form of withheld wages and salaries. In 1944 and 1945, individual income taxes accounted for roughly 40 percent of federal revenues. Corporate income taxes provided only about one-third, or half their share during World War I. *Mass* taxation had become more important than *class* taxation.

In making the new individual income tax work, the Roosevelt administration and Congress relied heavily on payroll withholding, deductions that sweetened the new tax system for the middle class, the progressive rate structure, and the popularity of the war effort. It was unnecessary to encourage popular support and sacrifice for the war by redistributing wealth through the tax system: Americans who believed their nation's security was at stake concluded that victory required both personal sacrifice and indulgence of the corporate profits that helped fuel the war machine. The Roosevelt administration reinforced this spirit of patriotism and sacrifice by employing an extensive propaganda program. The Treasury, its Bureau of Internal Revenue, and the Office of War Information made elaborate calls for civic responsibility and patriotic sacrifice, building on the arguments that the Wilson administration had crafted during the bond campaigns of World War I.

Because of the buoyant revenues produced under the new regime, during the last two years of World War II tax revenues covered roughly half of government expenditures. The federal deficit, after increasing from $6.2 billion in 1941 to $57.4 billion in 1943, held at about the 1943 level for the remainder of the war. These were impressive feats because the wartime expenditures represented a more massive, faster, and more prolonged shift of resources from peacetime endeavors than had been the case during World War I. The average level of wartime federal expenditures, which increased from 1942 through 1945, amounted to roughly half the national product—more than twice the average ratio during World War I. Moreover, by hitching taxation firmly to expenditure needs and dramatically broadening the tax base, federal policies also restrained wartime price inflation.

Thus, during World War II, as well as in World War I and even in the Civil War, a liberal democratic state demonstrated the fiscal power of a trusting and wealthy public. That trust, nurtured by the federal government, permitted and encouraged the adoption of income taxation—one of the most coercive and statist means of raising revenue. In a fiscal sense, the adoption of mass-based income taxation during World War II, and the victory of a taxpaying culture, represented a triumph for both the republican virtue and the national strength the framers of the Constitution had sought to advance.

Cumulatively, the two world wars revolutionized federal public finance. Policy architects had seized the opportunity to modernize the tax system, adapting it to new economic and organizational conditions and making it a more efficient producer of revenue. (The income tax, for example, enabled the federal government to utilize the financial apparatus of the modern corporation to monitor income flows and collect taxes on them.) No process of "modernization" dictated the selection of options—for example, of income taxation over consumption taxation—but in each crisis policymakers discovered that the organizational maturation of industrial society had created a new menu of feasible options. Exploiting the new tax options during emergencies provided a structure and an administrative apparatus that allowed the federal government to take fiscal advantage of postcrisis economic expansion.

By contributing to the resolution of wartime social crises, the emergency-driven policies of progressive taxation acquired legitimacy and cultural force. The tax regimes of the two world wars did not produce a social revolution but did establish tax policy that was far more progressively redistributional than it had been before World War I, affirmed government's right to redistribute income according to ideals of social justice, and powerfully expressed the nation's democratic ideals.

By creating systems of taxation that had acquired an independent legitimacy and were administratively more robust, each crisis enabled proponents of expanded government programs to advance their interests after the emergency ended. Postwar leaders could forge new expenditure program—both direct and indirect—without raising taxes or introducing new ones. The popularity of the expenditure programs, in turn, reinforced the popularity of the tax system behind the programs.

The tax system created in World War II proved to have a great capacity for expanding federal programs after the war. Persistent inflation and economic growth helped extend the life of the World War II tax regime by making it highly elastic, allowing the federal government to create new programs without enacting politically damaging tax increases. The World War II tax system paid for the strategic defense programs of the Cold War and, without any general or permanent increases in income taxation, for the Korean and Vietnam War mobilizations as well. Because the size of the defense budget relative to the GNP tended to decline through the 1970s (except during the *Korean and *Vietnam Wars), post–World War II increases in federal revenues went largely for the expansion of domestic programs.

In the absence of a new national emergency, the World War II tax regime remains in place today. Beginning in the late 1970s, however, stagnant economic productivity eroded its fiscal force and an antigovernment movement undermined its political legitimacy. Whether or not Americans will devise a new tax system to replace that created during World War II, the creation of the three great wartime regimes suggests that Americans can embrace drastic changes in taxation and public finance if the right political and economic circumstances converge.

• Robert A. Love, *Federal Financing: A Study of the Methods Employed by the Treasury in Its Borrowing Operations*, 1931. Roy G. Blakey and Gladys C. Blakey, *The Federal Income Tax*, 1940. Randolph Paul, *Taxation in the United States*, 1954. Milton Friedman and Anna J. Schwartz, *A Monetary History of the United States, 1867–1960*, 1963. Sidney Ratner, *Taxation and Democracy in America*, 1967. Charles Gilbert, *American Financing of World War I*, 1970. John Witte, *The Politics and Development of the Federal Income Tax*, 1985. W. Elliot Brownlee, *Federal Taxation in America: A Short History*, 1996. W. Elliot Brownlee, ed., *Funding the Modern American State, 1941–1995: The Rise and Fall of the Era of Easy Finance*, 1996.   —W. Elliot Brownlee

PUBLIC OPINION, WAR, AND THE MILITARY. The relationship between American public opinion and foreign affairs, particularly the military dimension, can be divided into three aspects. Those aspects are the public's attention—or inattention—to international affairs; the way Americans evaluate and react to wars and international affairs; and the degree to which wars have lingered in the public mind after they are over. Since extensive public opinion polling data are only available for the period since the mid-1930s, the focus is primarily on that era.

Attention. Because of its size and wealth, the United States has been for most of its history an important country, and in the last century at least, a great power by most conventional standards. At the same time, its peculiar geographical position—bordered by militarily weak neighbors, situated in a hemisphere that has seen remarkably little international war (though much revolution and civil war), and separated from militarily significant countries by two vast oceans—has often allowed it the luxury of standing back from clashes that have engulfed other countries.

The American public, not surprisingly, has reflected this reality and has not been inclined to spend much time worrying about foreign and international matters unless there appears to be a clear, present, and direct threat. Moreover, once international problems involving the United States appear to be resolved, the public can turn back to domestic matters with a virtuosity that is impressive.

This can been seen clearly in the results generated by the poll question, "What do you think is the most important problem facing this country today?, which has been asked with considerable regularity since the mid-1930s. In the 1930s, domestic concerns dominated international ones even as war dangers grew in Europe and Asia, and this changed only when war actually broke out in Europe in 1939. International concerns dropped precipitously again at the end of World War II in 1945 but came to dominate domestic concerns two years later when the *Cold War became fully activated. Attention escalated again during the *Korean War in the early 1950s and during various Cold War crises of the 1950s and early 1960s. But when tensions mellowed in mid-1963 with the Soviet-U.S. detente surrounding the signing of the Partial Test Ban Treaty, public attention to foreign affairs again dropped substantially. By 1966, the *Vietnam War came to dominate the public's concerns, but there was some decline in attention by the 1970s as American casualty rates dropped and as U.S. troops began to be withdrawn. Few foreign events have been able to capture the public's sustained attention since. Indeed, at no time since the *Tet Offensive in early 1968—not even during the *Persian Gulf War of 1991—have foreign policy issues outweighed domestic ones in the public's priorities.

Although the media are often given great credit for setting the political agenda, the chief determinant of public concern has usually been the often overwhelming weight and drama of the events themselves. Beyond this, the principal American actor has been the president—who is, after all, in charge of U.S. foreign policy. In particular, when the president orders American troops into action abroad, there is often a "rally 'round the flag" effect. Americans also seem to be influenced by other prominent members of the political leadership. However, even the president's impact can be limited: after the Gulf War, it was clearly to George *Bush's electoral advantage to keep the war and foreign policy as lively political issues during his reelection campaign. But despite his efforts and despite the advantage of his enormous postwar popularity, the public abruptly shifted its agenda, wanting now to focus on the sagging economy. The media might be seen in all this not so much as agenda-setters but rather as purveyors or entrepreneurs of tantalizing information. If they give an issue big play, it may arrest attention for awhile, but this is no guarantee the issue will take hold. Like any business enterprise, the media follow up on those items that stimulate their customer's interest. In that very important sense, the media do not set the agenda; ultimately the public does.

It is often argued that the public is particularly likely to respond to pictures in our television age: the so-called CNN effect. But this suggests that people are so unimaginative that they only react when they see something visualized. Yet in December 1941, Americans were outraged at and mobilized over the attack on *Pearl Harbor weeks—or even months—before they saw pictures of that event. Moreover, the Vietnam War was not noticeably more unpopular than the Korean War for the period when the wars were comparable in American *casualties, despite the fact that the later war is often seen to be a "television war" while the earlier one was fought during the medium's infancy. And, although the deluge of pictures of horrors during the *Bosnian Crisis in the 1990s may have influenced some editorial writers and columnists, there was remarkably little public demand to send American troops to fix the problem. On those rare occasions when pictures have—or seem to have—an impact, people espy the CNN effect. When pictures have no impact, they fail to notice.

Evaluation. In general, the American public seems to apply a fairly reasonable, commonsensical standard of benefit and cost when evaluating foreign affairs and the participation of its citizens in war. Potential American casualties loom as particularly important in its evaluation.

After Pearl Harbor, the public had no difficulty accepting the necessity, and the costs, of confronting the threats presented by Japan and Germany. And after World War II, most Americans came to accept international communism as a threat and were willing to accept increased defense spending and to enter the wars in Korea and Vietnam as part of a perceived necessity to confront that threat. However, as these wars progressed, reevaluation continued, and misgivings mounted about the wisdom of the conflicts—something that appears primarily to have been a function of the accumulating American casualties.

It seems unlikely that there has been an essential change of standards since the end of the Cold War. There is a clear public reluctance to risk lives to police small, distant, perennially troubled and unthreatening places. But this reluctance does not seem to signal a new isolationist impulse. Americans were willing, at least at the outset, to send troops to risk death in Korea and Vietnam; but that was because they subscribed to the notion that communism was a threat that needed to be stopped wherever it was advancing. Polls from the time make it clear that the public had no interest in losing American lives simply to help the South Koreans or South Vietnamese. Thus, an unwillingness to send Americans to die for purposes that are essentially humanitarian rather than for national defense is hardly new.

Although there is an overwhelming political demand that casualties be extremely low when American troops are sent to deal with a problem that does not seem to be vital or direct, there seems to be little problem about keeping occupying forces in place as long as they are not being killed. There was small public or political support for sending U.S. troops to Haiti in 1994, but almost no protest arose about keeping them there—as long as there were no casualties.

Americans place a high value on the lives of their countrymen, yet their reaction when Americans are killed varies considerably. After Pearl Harbor, the outraged call for revenge against the attackers was overwhelming. At other times, the public has shown a willingness to abandon an overextended or untenable position after American lives have been lost. It accepted, with little regret, the decision to withdraw policing troops from Lebanon in 1983 after a terrorist bomb killed over 200 U.S. Marines, and the killing of 18 U.S. Rangers in a single incident in Somalia in 1993 led to demands for withdrawal, not calls to revenge the humiliation. Unlike the problems in the Pacific War in 1941, the situations in Lebanon and Somalia did not present a wider threat to American interests, and the public was quite willing to support measures to cut losses and leave.

Although Americans are extremely sensitive to U.S. casualties, they seem to be remarkably insensitive to casualties suffered by foreigners, including essentially uninvolved civilians. The Gulf War furnishes an extreme example. Polls make clear there was little animosity toward the Iraqi people, yet this did not translate into much sympathy within the American public for well-publicized civilian casualties caused by bombing attacks. Images of the "highway of death" and reports at the end of the war that as many as 100,000 Iraqis may have been killed scarcely dampened the enthusiasm of postwar celebrations.

Long-Range Impact. The degree to which wars have a long-range impact on opinion varies. Some wars continue to linger in the public consciousness, some vanish almost immediately, some linger and then disappear, and some diminish for awhile but then become revived in memory. Neither the scope nor the objective historical importance of a war seems precisely to determine its long-range impact on opinion.

The best example of an international event that continued uninterruptedly to live in memory long after it was over is undoubtedly World War II. It was, of course, a massive affair, affecting all strata of society, and it continued—and continues—to affect popular perceptions. (On the domestic side, something comparable could probably be said for the Great Depression—an event that had a long, lingering impact.)

The Gulf War seems prototypical of international events that subsequently disappear from public memory.

At the time, the gulf crisis often seemed all-consumingly important: on the eve of the war, half of the American people said they thought about the crisis at least once an hour. But when it was over, it quickly lapsed from public recall. In this, opinion may appropriately be reflecting historical judgment: from the standpoint of world history, that war may well prove to have been quite a minor event. However, the Cold War and its concomitant nuclear fears cannot so easily be dismissed as historical sideshows. Yet the Cold War seems already to be picking up a patina of quaintness as it recedes from memory, and few seem any more able to recall the fear *nuclear weapons once inspired as they were brandished by glowering Cold War contestants.

Wars can have a lingering impact in their immediate aftermath, but then fade from view. Cases in point are the Korean War and the much earlier *War of 1812. Korea, the most costly war since 1945, essentially crystallized the Cold War, and it importantly affected public perceptions throughout the 1950s. A century earlier, the War of 1812 ended rather inconclusively, but the Republicans, who had begun it, were able to fashion an appealing myth that the war had been a glorious triumph, something that subsequently helped them and destroyed the opposition Federalist Party. Yet, both these wars, despite their contemporary importance and their resonance in the immediate postwar period, eventually sagged from the public consciousness and both, interestingly enough, have inspired books with titles proclaiming them to be "forgotten" conflicts.

Finally, some wars are neglected for awhile and then come back to haunt the public consciousness. The Vietnam War was the great nonissue of the 1976 election campaign conducted a year after it was over, and it was neglected in most public memory for several years: Americans, it seemed, did not want to think about it. Yet by the 1980s, Vietnam had became a haunting event in the American consciousness, and it seems likely to remain one for a long time. Something similar happened with the *Civil War—probably the most important event in American history. For years after that conflict, as Gerald Linderman observes, there was considerable desire to forget it. But after some twenty years, the building of War *memorials and monuments—and of myths—began, and the war has no doubt become the most popularly memorable event in American history.

[See also Bombing of Civilians; Haiti, U.S. Military Involvement in; Isolationism; Middle East, U.S. Military Involvement in the.]

• Hadley Cantril and Associates, *Gauging Public Opinion,* 1944. James Rosenau, ed., *Domestic Sources of Foreign Policy,* 1967. Milton J. Rosenberg, Sidney Verba, and Philip E. Converse, *Vietnam and the Silent Majority,* 1970. John Mueller, *War, Presidents and Public Opinion,* 1973. Daniel C. Hallin, *The "Uncensored War": The Media and Vietnam,* 1986. Gerald Linderman, *Embattled Courage,* 1987. Bruce Russett, *Controlling the Sword: The Democratic Governance of National Security,* 1990. Eugene Wittkopf, *Faces of Internationalism: American Public Opinion and Foreign Policy,* 1990. Benjamin I. Page and Robert Y. Shapiro, *The Rational Public: Fifty Years of Trends in American Policy Preferences,* 1992. John Mueller, *Policy and Opinion in the Gulf War,* 1994.
—John Mueller

PUBLIC RITUAL. *See* Commemoration and Public Ritual.

PUBLIC SITES. *See* Battlefields, Encampments, and Forts as Public Sites; Cemeteries, Military; Gettysburg National

Military Park; Memorials, War; Museums, Military History; Pearl Harbor National Monument; Valley Forge National Park.

PUEBLO INCIDENT (1968). On 23 January 1968, the USS *Pueblo*—gathering intelligence on the military strength of North Korea—steamed into the Sea of Japan outside the twelve-mile territorial limit of the Communist nation. Without warning, North Korean warships converged on the *Pueblo* and ordered her crew to heave to or be fired upon. As crewmen began to burn classified documents, the North Koreans opened fire, wounding several American sailors, one mortally. Commander Lloyd M. Bucher ordered an end to resistance.

The U.S. Pacific Command dispatched air and naval forces into the Sea of Japan, but they arrived too late to help the *Pueblo* and her eighty-two-man crew. Meanwhile, the Communists had boarded the *Pueblo,* confiscated intelligence equipment and documents, and brought the ship into Wonsan port. Washington protested North Korea's brazen attack in international waters, but the North Koreans refused to release ship or crew.

Over the next few months, the Communists tortured Bucher and his men to make them admit "guilt" for spying and violating North Korea's territorial waters. Pyongyang made it clear the Americans would not be released until Washington apologized for infringing on North Korean sovereignty and promised not to do so again.

American diplomats met with Communist officials ashore at Panmunjom, in the demilitarized zone between North and South Korea. Finally, President Lyndon B. *Johnson directed his representatives to sign the necessary statement. At the same time, his officials publicly disavowed the document's validity. On 22 December, the North Koreans released the American prisoners and the body of their slain shipmate. They did not return the *Pueblo*. In 1969, a U.S. *Navy court of inquiry recommended that Bucher be court-martialed, but the Johnson administration declined.

[*See also* Korea, U.S. Military Involvement in.]

• Lloyd Bucher, *My Story,* 1970. Daniel V. Gallery, *The Pueblo Incident,* 1970. Robert W. Love, Jr., *History of the U.S. Navy,* Vol. II, 1992.
—Edward J. Marolda

PUERTO RICAN UNITS. Puerto Rico has a long history with the U.S. military. Some Puerto Ricans participated as auxiliary troops in the U.S. invasion of 1898. After taking the island from Spain, the United States initiated new units with native personnel: the Porto Rico Battalion (1899) of infantry (cavalry was added in 1900) to assist in repressing armed peasants, and the Porto Rico Regiment, U.S. Volunteers Infantry (1900). This force—U.S. officers and native troops comprising 900 men—replaced the 700 regular U.S. troops sent to help suppress the Philippine insurrection. In 1901, it became the Provisional Puerto Rican Infantry Regiment, which was integrated into the regular army (1908) as the Porto Rican Infantry Regiment, U.S. Army.

During World War I, an enlarged regiment was assigned to protect the Panama Canal. In 1916, an *ROTC program was established at the University of Puerto Rico. In 1917, soon after the Jones Act extending U.S. citizenship to Puerto Ricans, military *conscription was introduced. Some 18,000 Puerto Ricans were drafted or enlisted and a National Guard unit was created in 1919. In 1920, the Puerto Rican regiment was renamed the 65th Infantry Regiment, but this colonial unit, similar to the Philippine Scouts, was never fully integrated into the U.S. Army structure.

At the onset of World War II, the 65th Infantry was sent to guard the Panama Canal. In 1944, it transferred to the Mediterranean and European theaters and saw some combat, suffering 348 *casualties. More than 65,000 Puerto Ricans served in the U.S. armed forces during the war, most of them as soldiers garrisoning U.S. bases in the Caribbean.

During the *Korean War, the 65th Infantry engaged in intensive combat duty, suffering 743 combat and 186 non-combat casualties in the winter of 1950–51. All told, some 49,200 Puerto Ricans were conscripted or enlisted. Since 1952, when the 65th Infantry was disbanded, Puerto Ricans have served in regular U.S. Army units or the Puerto Rican National Guard. During the *Vietnam War, 23,350 Puerto Ricans participated, suffering 1,300 casualties. Numerous Puerto Rican military personnel also served in the *Persian Gulf War.

[*See also* Philippine Scouts and Constabulary; Spanish-American War; World War II: Military and Diplomatic Course.]

• Jorge Rodríguez Beruff, *Política military dominiación, Puerto Rico en al contexto latinamericano,* 1989. Maria Eugenia Estades, *Intereses estratégicos y dominación colonial,* 1989.
—Jorge Rodríguez Beruff

PULLER, "CHESTY" [LEWIS B.] (1898–1971), Marine Corps combat leader. Born in the peaceful village of West Point, Virginia, where his father had a wholesale grocery business, Puller was reared on tales of Confederate glory. His grandfather, Maj. John Puller, a heroic cavalryman, was killed in 1863. Determined on a military career, Puller completed one year at the Virginia Military Institute (VMI) before enlisting in the U.S. Marine Corps in August 1918. VMI may have given him the exaggerated military bearing for which he was nicknamed, but it was during more than four years as a Marine NCO and concurrent lieutenant of the *Gendarmerie d'Haiti* (1919–23) that Puller developed his distinctive leadership techniques: perfectionism; mission overachievement; and fearless, inspirational conduct under fire. Varied assignments followed his commissioning in 1924, including two tours in Nicaragua, in each of which he was awarded the Navy Cross. His third and fourth Navy Crosses came during World War II at the Battle of Guadalcanal and at Cape Gloucester on New Britain Island; and the fifth in Korea where Puller commanded the 1st Marine Regiment in the assault landing at Inchon, the seizure of Seoul, and the fighting at the Chosin Reservoir.

Fuller was promoted to brigadier general in 1951 and to lieutenant general upon retirement in 1955. During the 1950s, the colorful and outspoken Puller gained attention as a champion of tough, realistic training; a defender of the basic soundness of American youth; and a critic of higher leadership. His legend continued to grow; photographs of his bulldog visage hung in homes and service clubs across the country as a symbol of invincible heroism and fidelity to traditional military standards.

[*See also* Marine Corps, U.S.: 1914–45; Marine Corps, U.S.: Since 1945.]

• Burke Davis, *Marine! The Life of Lt. Gen. Lewis B. (Chesty) Puller, USMC (Ret.)*, 1962.   —Gerald C. Thomas, Jr.

PYLE, ERNIE (1900–1945), American journalist of World War II. A native of Dana, Indiana, Pyle worked on a local paper before joining the *Washington [D.C.] Daily News* in 1923, initially covering aviation and later serving as managing editor. In 1935, Pyle began a syndicated column for the Scripps-Howard organization, describing his experiences motoring around the United States. Over the next four years, his stories focused on the lives of average citizens.

In 1940, Pyle received his first wartime assignment from Scripps-Howard, covering the Blitz in England. Two years later, he started reporting on the *North Africa Campaign and followed U.S. combat troops to Sicily, Italy, and France. Widely respected by both the public and the average G.I., Pyle succeeded in conveying a sense of the hardship, fear, and endurance of the individual soldier, with a special focus on the combat infantryman. At the height of his fame, his columns were carried by over 400 daily newspapers. In 1944, he won the Pulitzer Prize, and *Time* magazine featured him on its cover.

In 1945, Pyle, at the behest of the navy, shifted to covering the Pacific theater. He was killed by enemy fire on the island of Ie Shima near Okinawa on 18 April 1945.

[*See also* News Media, War, and the Military.]

• Frederick S. Voss, *Reporting the War: The Journalistic Coverage of World War II*, 1994. James Tobin, *Ernie Pyle's War: America's Eyewitness to World War II*, 1997.

—G. Kurt Piehler

Q

QUAKERS. The Religious Society of Friends, commonly called Quakers (so dubbed derisively by a seventeenth-century judge who said they quaked before the power of the Lord), has opposed war and violence from its inception, and has sought instead to do away with the causes of war and alleviate the suffering it causes.

George Fox (1624–1691), usually regarded as the founder of the Friends, preached in the 1640s, during the English Civil War, that there was a divine spark within each person, which means that all human beings are infinitely precious in God's sight and no one is justified in taking the life of another.

After the restoration of Charles II in 1660, radical religious groups stirred up rebellion, which led Friends, in 1661, to issue a declaration beginning,: "We utterly deny all outward wars and strife and fightings with outward weapons....". Eventually, this Peace Testimony became fundamental to Quakerism.

In 1682, William *Penn founded his "holy experiment" in Pennsylvania, based on the belief that a province that had no army, treated Native Americans as equals, and offered religious liberty could make the Peace Testimony a living reality. Penn published his *Essay Towards the Present and Future Peace of Europe* (1693), which offered a plan for bringing peace and justice. Although Pennsylvania was drawn into two wars between England and France, the colonists avoided deep involvement, and peace returned in 1713 with the Treaty of Utrecht. When the *French and Indian War broke out in 1754, most of the Quaker politicians resigned from government rather than support the war.

Two decades later, at the start of the *Revolutionary War, Friends took a neutral position and were persecuted by both British loyalists and American Whig revolutionaries. Quakers raised money and sent supplies to assist civilians, first in Boston in 1775, later elsewhere. In 1777, seventeen Philadelphia Quaker leaders were unfairly accused of treason and exiled to Virginia by the Whigs, but the following spring the fourteen who survived were released without trial. Several hundred Friends, including Betsy Ross, were strongly drawn to the revolutionary cause, and many of them joined the armed forces, notably Gen. Nathanael *Greene from Rhode Island. When disowned by their Meetings, they organized a new group known as Free Quakers, but this group died out by the 1830s. A few Friends also joined the British cause as loyalists.

Friends turned their humanitarian efforts to opposition to slavery and other reforms, including the peace movement. When the *Civil War broke out (1861), many Quakers were troubled by their desire to use the conflict as a way to end slavery, for such action ran counter to the Peace Testimony. The official position of Quakers remained un-

changed, but some Friends were tolerant toward those who supported the war for the Union and emancipation and allowed members who joined the armed forces to remain. President Abraham *Lincoln's government was more lenient toward *conscientious objection than the Confederate government, but some conscientious objectors (COs) on both sides suffered for their refusal to fight.

After the Civil War, individual Friends were active for peace. Benjamin F. Trueblood served as secretary of the *American Peace Society; Hannah J. Bailey, a New England Quaker, edited magazines for adults and children on peace education; and Albert K. Smiley sponsored the Mohonk Conferences on International Arbitration in New York.

When the United States entered World War I in 1917, Quakers organized the American Friends Service Committee (AFSC) to assist COs and engage in relief work in Europe. The government recognized COs who belonged to traditional peace churches such as Quakers and Mennonites, but they were expected to serve in the army as noncombatants, usually in the medical corps. Many Quaker COs refused. Some were furloughed to do farm work; a few were imprisoned.

Through the AFSC, Quaker volunteers did relief work in France and Germany—eventually feeding 1 million children daily—in Central Europe, and then in Russia during the famine there. Herbert C. *Hoover and other Friends raised several million dollars for such work.

Quaker organizations strongly advocated the Peace Testimony between the two world wars. In contrast to isolationists, they supported the *League of Nations and conducted peace education in churches and schools; they also helped bring persecuted German Jews to the United States. However, the Friends joined other pacifist groups in opposing *conscription, rearmament, and entrance of the United States into World War II.

The Selective Service Act of 1940 included a provision that COs might be assigned to do "civilian work of national importance" in Civilian Public Service units administered by the peace churches under Selective Service regulations. Some 12,000 men worked in forestry camps, agricultural projects, mental hospitals and institutions for the mentally deficient, and as "guinea pigs" in medical experiments. They received no pay and none of the benefits provided veterans of the armed forces. Deeply stirred by outrageous conditions in mental hospitals, some of the COs created the National Mental Health Foundation in 1946, and four years later this body merged with two others to create the National Association for Mental Health.

In 1947, the AFSC and the Friends Service Council of Britain received the Nobel Peace Prize for their work in Europe and Asia during and after the war.

Quakers opposed the nuclear *arms race and the reintroduction of conscription (1948). The Friends Committee for National Legislation lobbied in Washington, D.C., for Quaker principles.

During the *Vietnam War, when antiwar feeling swept over the nation, Quakers, a tiny minority of the *Vietnam Antiwar Movement, sought to prevent violence and the use of force in antiwar protests. Most young Friends of draft age opposed the war, the first time in the twentieth century that the official Quaker position matched the wartime practices of most of its members of military age. Many Friends' organizations strongly supported members who resisted conscription, and offered help to those imprisoned; at the same time, the AFSC and others provided relief and medical supplies to civilians in Vietnam during and after the war. Similarly, they opposed the *Persian Gulf War and aided its civilian victims.

The AFSC and other Quaker bodies continue to support peace and humanitarian work around the world.

[See also Nonviolence; Peace and Antiwar Movements; Rustin, Bayard; Woolman, John.]

• Mary Hoxie Jones, Swords into Ploughshares, 1937. Mulford Q. Sibley and Philip E. Jacob, Conscription of Conscience, the American State and the Conscientious Objector, 1940–1947, 1952. Edwin B. Bronner, William Penn's "Holy Experiment," 1962. Peter Brock, Twentieth Century Pacifism, 1970. John Ormerod Greenwood, Quaker Encounters, Vol. 1: Friends and Relief, 1975. Lawrence S. Wittner, Rebels Against War: The American Peace Movement 1933–1983, 1984. Peter Brock, The Quaker Peace Testimony, 1660–1914, 1990. Charles C. Moskos and John Whiteclay Chambers, eds., The New Conscientious Objection: From Sacred to Secular Resistance, 1993. Alex Sareyan, The Turning Point, How Men of Conscience Brought About Major Change in the Care of American Mentally Ill, 1994. Arthur J. Mekeel, The American Revolution, 1996.
—Edwin B. Bronner

QUASI-WAR WITH FRANCE. See France, Undeclared Naval War with (1798–1800).

QUÉBEC, BATTLE OF (1759). In the *French and Indian War, conquest of New France presupposed the capture of Québec, the citadel controlling access to the St. Lawrence River. Late in June 1759, 141 British warships and transports brought nearly 9,000 regulars and provincials, commanded by Maj. Gen. James Wolfe, to challenge nearly 16,000 defenders under Gen. Louis-Joseph, marquis de Montcalm. For more than two months the British bombarded the city, destroyed farms, and attempted landings, without luring the French from their formidable defenses.

On 13 September, a desperate General Wolfe led 4,400 troops in a risky night landing, scaled a 150-foot cliff, and secured an exposed position. On the Plains of Abraham outside the fortress, Montcalm, acting with uncharacteristic haste, attacked with forces that barely outnumbered the British. The battle lasted half an hour and killed 658 British and 644 French, with Wolfe among the dead and Montcalm among the dying, but it proved a British victory.

With British control of the Plains of Abraham, four days later the French surrendered the still-defensible city. Viewed by some as a coup de grâce to a crippled empire, and by others as a preliminary victory, the battle is generally seen as the poignant climax of the Anglo-French struggle for North America.

• C. P. Stacey, Quebec, 1759: The Siege and the Battle, 1959.
—Ian K. Steele

R

RACE IN THE MILITARY. *See* African Americans in the Military; Ethnicity and Race in the Military; Native Americans in the Military.

RACE RELATIONS AND WAR. Race relations have helped shape, and in turn have been shaped by, the conduct of American wars; and the dominant pattern of American military race relations was traditionally castelike. Racial status defined how individuals of color were commanded, mobilized, and treated; discrimination has thereby jeopardized military efficiency and claims of "equal" sacrifice. The more inclusive military service was, however, the more it destabilized racial hierarchy and exacerbated racial tensions.

People of color fought for equality and inclusion but usually experienced their opposites. The persistence of castelike approaches, and the conflicts generated, reflected both the power of racism and the important function that military service (or exclusion) played in the development of American society.

Many non-Caucasians demanded inclusion and resisted inequality (or opportunistically asserted their self-interest), while many Caucasians demanded exclusion, white control, and symbolic supremacy. Political and military exigencies resolved this contest. Laws frequently limited participation of non-Caucasians, or mandated segregation; and people of color entered or exited the military differently from Caucasians.

Minorities often were segregated or performed lower-status roles within the military; sometimes they received less pay. They experienced harassment by soldiers and civilians; poor living conditions; prejudicial evaluations of their skill, bravery, and contribution; marginalization at ceremonies; and lack of access to command. Most often serving under white officers, individuals of color, even when commissioned, were frequently prevented from commanding white troops. The assertiveness of soldiers of color challenged the self-image and position of whites, fueling harassment and violence.

Prejudice also affected how many Americans perceived Native American, Latino, and Asian enemies, as well as the military tactics employed and the treatment of American citizens who looked like the "enemy." Compared to European enemies, non-Caucasians were dehumanized and often subjected to harsher tactics. The racial context of warfare sometimes affected the treatment of individuals of color at home (e.g., Japanese Americans in World War II), as well as the willingness of political leaders to employ individuals of color, and the willingness of those individuals

to serve in the military or carry out actions viewed as having racial overtones.

The key periods and their defining characteristics in terms of race relations in the military were 1608–1763: semi-exclusion; 1763–87: revolutionary inclusion; 1787–1862: increasing exclusion; 1862–65: segregated inclusion; 1865–1945: segregation; and 1945–present: increasing integration.

1608–1763: Semi-Exclusion. Blacks and Indians aligned themselves with colonial governments (or enemies) based on self-interest. Governments feared this self-interest, but, needing men, employed troops of color, sometimes unarmed and almost always under white officers. When the need ceased or where fear of servile insurrection became too great, colonies disarmed blacks and Indians or excluded them from the militia. For example, South Carolina enlisted slaves beginning in 1707, but ended this policy after the Stono Rebellion of 1739, in which slaves seized arms, burned plantations, and killed whites. Many colonies, however, modified exclusionary policies to allow non-Caucasians to serve in expeditionary forces as substitutes for white militiamen or as volunteers.

1763–87: Revolutionary Inclusion. Republican ideology, manpower shortages, and British appeals to Indian and black self-interest set the stage for inclusion. Nonetheless, racist and pro-slavery concerns limited the use of black troops everywhere before 1776, and in southern states thereafter.

African Americans, appropriating revolutionary republicanism, enlisted with a self-consciousness reflected in the surnames some of them took: "Liberty," "Freedom," and "Freeman." Although blacks contributed to the early stages of the *Revolutionary War, many revolutionaries opposed their participation, curtailing recruitment until 1775. However, manpower needs and British recruitment of slaves soon caused a policy reversal.

Black and Indian soldiers fought in integrated and segregated units, some serving as volunteers, others as substitutes or draftees. Some states enrolled slaves as well as free blacks; others refused to recruit slaves. Overall, however, the Revolution destabilized slavery. Some slaves achieved freedom by fighting for the Americans, others were freed by the British and emigrated as loyalists. Still others, both free and unfree, applied republican ideology to their social and political struggles.

1787–1862: Increasing Exclusion. Increasing exclusion of individuals of color from the militia and army, and thus from the political and social benefits of military service, marked the early national period. Though the availability of white manpower made it possible to exclude men of

584

color here, the situation was different in the navy, which employed and integrated black sailors from 1812 through 1862, whenever skilled seamen could not be recruited in sufficient numbers.

Congress excluded men of color from the national militia in the Militia Act of 1792, which defined the militia of the United States as being made up of "white-male citizens." Although federal action did not preclude states from including men of color in state militias, all states did so by 1835. Because some states legislatively, and all states symbolically, linked militia service to voting and citizenship, exclusion barred men of color from legal privileges, as well as from the major public source of military training, civic ritual, male bonding, and social control.

Men of color were excluded from the navy and Marines in 1798. The navy soon admitted black sailors and Congress legitimated this practice in 1813, but the Marines remained "white" until 1942. Army statutes of 1790, 1811, 1812, and 1814 did not contain racial restrictions, but biased practices prevented many blacks from serving. Louisiana, which maintained a black militia until after the war, was an exception. Blacks owning $300 in property served in the militia under white and black officers, and 600 free blacks served under black line officers in two black battalions during the Battle of *New Orleans (1815).

Postwar policy consolidated exclusion. The government banned slaves from navy ships and shipyards in 1816, and Secretary of War John C. *Calhoun excluded blacks from the army in 1820. In 1839, the navy instituted a 5 percent quota on black recruits.

1862–65: Segregated Inclusion. The *Civil War reversed the exclusionary trend. Black manpower was important to both Union and Confederate war efforts, and the Union's liberal nationalist ideology supported formal equality of sacrifice. Although black and Indian volunteers had been excluded from "a white man's war" in 1861 and early 1862, the new Militia Act (1862) and the Enrollment Act (1863) contained no racial exclusions, while the Confiscation Act of 1862 and the 1863 Emancipation Proclamation supported military use of former slaves. The Union and Northern state governments aggressively recruited black soldiers, sometimes as volunteers or through *conscription, other times through military press gangs that targeted Southern blacks. The Confederacy began to recruit black troops in March 1865.

Black activists demanded the right to fight and played a key role in Northern recruiting efforts, and they also sought equality. Except for the navy, this did not happen. Black soldiers received less pay and fewer bounties than their white counterparts, and were likelier to receive both harsh punishments and assignment to labor duties. Many former slaves also performed work traditionally done by soldiers, but without being accorded the *uniforms, status, or perquisites of military service.

Blacks served in segregated units, and contact with white units was controlled. With the exception of Louisiana in 1862–63 and a few units near the end of the war, blacks served under white officers. Most black units were demobilized later than their white counterparts, and none participated in the May 1865 Grand March down Pennsylvania Avenue that symbolized the achievements of the nation's citizen soldiers.

Although unequal conditions limited the willingness of

some black activists to serve or recruit, many African Americans self-consciously fought to end slavery and gain political rights. Black soldiers, veterans, and families faced harassment and prejudice, yet their valor and sacrifice did much to change attitudes and official behavior. In 1864 and 1865, the government equalized pay and started to commission black men as line officers. Black soldiers also played a visible role in the liberation of Charleston, Petersburg, and Richmond, and provided manpower and officers for reconstructed state militias. Black military and militia service contributed to black militancy during Reconstruction.

1865–1945: Segregation. Between 1865 and 1880, conservative forces disarmed most black militia, contained the number of black troops, and curtailed access to command positions. Black troops were removed from the South and their service was limited to four segregated regiments in 1866. By the 1880s, black sailors were refused promotions and increasingly assigned to service duties (where Asians would later join and sometimes replace them). After the *Spanish-American War, the army employed Filipinos and Puerto Ricans, treating them similarly to black troops.

Non-Caucasian access to officer positions was rare until 1916. Although the Army Reorganization Act of 1866 lacked racial prohibitions and twelve blacks entered West Point between 1870 and 1886, army examiners rejected all black officer candidates, and black students were segregated and harassed at West Point. Only three graduated. (None of the three blacks who were appointed to Annapolis during the period survived their "hazing.") While the three West Point graduates gained positions within black regiments, there were no more black nominees during the nineteenth century. Some blacks did serve successfully as volunteer line officers during the Spanish-American War, but none was nominated by their colonel for examination for appointment in the regular army. When the army reorganized in 1901, not one of the 1,135 regular army officer vacancies was initially filled by an African American. Only after protests were three black men appointed.

The need for troops and mass support as well as racially inclusive Selective Service legislation structured the employment of troops of color during both world wars. Indians were sometimes integrated into units, and civilian color lines were challenged, but military segregation remained the norm. In spite of protests by black soldiers and civilians, the government created separate training camps for black officers, segregated black and Asian troops, denied promotions to black officers, controlled the number of black troops, billeted blacks away from some southern cities, disparaged black officers and men, and assigned non-Caucasians disproportionately to labor duty. However, black political pressure in the 1940s set the stage for integration: for example, the first black general was appointed one month before the 1940 election, and in 1941, Executive Order 8802 (which prohibited racial discrimination in defense industries, opening up defense plant positions to individuals of color) was issued to prevent a threatened protest march on Washington. While racial segregation remained the policy, the need for infantry replacements led to the inclusion.

1945–Present: Increasing Integration. Increasing civil rights activism, racial tensions within the armed forces, the inefficiencies of segregation, the continued need for manpower, and the challenge of combatting an ideologically antiracist USSR all propelled integration. The army and navy experimented with integration in 1945; a 1948 executive order mandated equality of treatment; and in 1950, Congress repealed the 1866 law that had mandated four segregated regiments. The armed forces were formally integrated in the 1950s, but prejudice and passive resistance at both the staff and line levels persisted through the *Vietnam War. This resistance (along with civilian racial turmoil) generated anger, violence, and support for *peace and antiwar movements among some soldiers of color.

Slow as it was, military integration proceeded faster than did civilian or even National Guard integration (ten states excluded blacks as late as 1963). Organizational integration required leadership and command accountability. Responding to civil rights investigations, the secretary of war in 1963 mandated command responsibility in civil rights matters. Following outbreaks of racial violence in 1969, the army instituted a program to increase racial harmony, equality of opportunity, and the ability of the army to perform its mission.

The pace of change accelerated in the *post-Vietnam Volunteer Force, and leadership integration contributed to racial integration. A black man, Clifford Alexander, was appointed secretary of war in 1977, and Colin *Powell, another African American, was named chairman of the *Joint Chiefs of Staff in 1989. The percentage of black senior noncommissioned officers rose from 14 percent in 1970 to 31 percent in 1990, and the percentage of black commissioned officers rose from 3 percent in 1970 to 11 percent in 1990. Beginning in the 1980s, the armed forces' military academies and command structure began—at last—to reflect the nation's diversity.

[See also African Americans in the Military; Militia Acts; Native Americans in the Military; Puerto Rican Units.]

• Samuel A. Stouffer, et al., The American Soldier: Adjustment During Army Life, 2 vols., 1949. James R. Woolard, "The Philippine Scouts: The Development of America's Colonial Army." Ph.D. diss., 1975. Morris J. MacGregor and Bernard C. Nalty, eds., Blacks in the United States Armed Forces: Basic Documents, 13 vols., 1977. Bernard C. Nalty, Strength for the Fight: A History of Black Americans in the Military, 1986. Morris J. MacGregor, Integration of the Armed Forces, 1940–1965, 1988. Benjamin Quarles, Black Mosaic: Essays in Afro-American History and Historiography, 1988. James A. Thomas, ed., Race Relations in the U.S. Army in the 1970s: A Collection of Selected Readings, 1988. David Osher, "Soldier Citizens for a Disciplined Nation: Union Conscription and the Construction of the Modern American Army." Ph.D. diss., 1992. Ronald Takaki, A Different Mirror: A History of Multicultural America, 1993.

—David Osher

RADAR, an acronym for RAdio Detection And Ranging, is based on German scientist Heinrich Hertz's 1880s discovery that a beam of radio energy that strikes an object of sufficient density will be reflected by it. If that reflected energy is then captured by a receiver at the beam's origin it can be analyzed. Another German scientist, Christian Hulsmeyer, patented the first radio echo device in 1904. Because radio energy travels at a constant speed (the speed of light) the length of time between sending and receiving the energy can thus be used to calculate the object's distance. The direction from which the energy is received can be used to determine the object's bearing. Combining distance and bearing indicates the object's location on/above the surface of the Earth. Modern radars belong to one of two general types. Pulse radars emit a short, intense burst of radio energy, while continuous-wave radars emit a steady signal. The latter, often called Doppler radar, cannot track the range to the object but instead measures the Doppler shift caused by the object's movement, from which the direction and speed of its movement can be determined. There are several other specific types of radars, such as Synthetic Aperture Radar, which electronically focus or shape the radar beam.

The Italian Guglielmo Marconi first demonstrated radio reflection for detection in the 1920s. In the United States, Gregory Breit and Merle A. Tuve discovered the principle of pulse ranging in 1925. Research and development was underway simultaneously in Germany, Great Britain, and the United States by the early 1930s. The Germans initially had better equipment aboard warships that began radar-aided commerce raiding in September 1939. In 1937 the British began deploying the Chain Home early warning network along the Channel coast, which would provide the decisive advantage in the Battle of Britain. Early World War II radars used radio pulses of low frequency and long (a meter or more) wavelength, but these required large antennas, suitable only for large ships or ground stations and were imprecise compared to the next generation radars. With the invention in Great Britain of the cavity magnetron in 1940, however, much smaller sets employing centimeter wavelengths capable of much greater precision were possible. In 1940 Henry Tizard led a mission to the United States that successfully enlisted American industrial aid, and the Germans fell behind, never to regain parity. In the Pacific, the Japanese never even came close to it, and most Japanese radar systems were based on early ones captured from the British and Americans in 1942.

At sea, Allied naval radar was key in the defeat of the U-boat threat in 1943, and radar-directed naval gunfire was decisive in several sea battles, including the Battle of *Leyte Gulf in October 1944, in which US battleships in the Surigao Straits using radar-directed gunfire at night destroyed a Japanese fleet. In the air, the radar struggle between countermeasure and counter-countermeasure was dynamic, deadly, and decisive. In July 1943 the Royal Air Force first used "window" (American term: "chaff"), small strips of reflective tinfoil, to negate German air defenses of Hamburg (Operation "Gomorrah") in a raid that killed approximately 40,000 inhabitants. American bombers equipped with radar jamming transmitters (called "Carpet") blocked German "Wurzburg" anti-aircraft gun-laying radars and assisted in a deceptive spoof on the night of the Normandy landings. Offensively, American and British aircraft carried increasingly sophisticated navigational radars, such as the H2S and H2X ("Mickey") sets that portrayed ground features with greater and greater detail and enabled bombing at night or through cloud cover. Night fighters equipped with small radar sets such as the German "Lichtenstein" hunted enemy aircraft in the darkness and located them entirely by radar. Specialized aircraft ("ferrets") gathered radar intelligence while electronic warfare operators ("ravens") waged an invisible but critical war in what was then called "the ether," and might today be called "cyberspace."

During the Cold War both the U.S. and Russians erected radar networks such as the Distant Early Warning or "DEW" line across Canada to warn of enemy aircraft. Strategic Air Command (SAC) warplans from the 1950s through the 1980s depended on radar to accurately navigate to and identify targets, and electronic countermeasures (ECM) such as radar jamming and chaff were the key to negating enemy defenses. Intercontinental ballistic missiles forced both sides in the 1960s to develop even more sophisticated radar nets such as the Ballistic Missile Early Warning System (BMEWS) to warn of missile attack. Perhaps the ultimate were radars devised to support antimissile defenses, capable of not only detecting enemy missiles in space but also of tracking them for interception and destruction by defensive missiles. Radars belonging to the Space Detection and Tracking System (SPADATS) keep constant track of the thousands of objects orbiting the earth.

The air war over Vietnam was dominated by radar controlled air defenses, as North Vietnam successfully employed Russian radar-guided surface-to-air missiles (SAMs) against American air operations. American countermeasures included not only traditional ECM, but also direct attacks on radar control systems. This technique, called "Wild Weasel", had been tried in WW II, but not until the 1960s were detection and homing systems sufficiently advanced to be successful. Anti-radar electronic warfare EW) was so important by the Persian Gulf War of 1991 that virtually no Coalition aerial attacks were mounted without EW support. Since the 1940s, designers have sought aircraft undetectable by enemy radars. This effort came to fruition with the F-117 "Stealth Fighter" and B-2 "Stealth Bomber", both of which used Low Observable technology to make them almost invisible to enemy radars.

Modern military radars have become increasingly sophisticated, and those mounted in surveillance aircraft such as the Airborne Warning and Control System ("AWACS") or Joint Surveillance and Tracking Radar System ("JSTARS") provide virtually a three-dimensional portrayal of a battlespace the size of a small country. Radar has also had an enormous effect in the civilian world. From radar astronomy, to traffic control, to weather and storm warning, to air and maritime navigation, radar has become an indispensable facet of modern life.

• Alfred Price, *Instruments of Darkness* (1977). Alfred Price, *The History of US Electronic Warfare, Volumes I and II* (1984, 1989). Henry E. Guerlac, *Radar in World War II* (1987). David Pritchard, *The Radar War* (1989). Robert Buderi, *The Invention That Changed the World* (1996). Alan Beyerchen, "From Radio to Radar: Interwar Military Adaptation to Technological Change in Germany, the UK, and the US," in Alan R. Millet and Williamson Murray, editors, *Military Innovation in the Interwar Period,* (1996).

—Daniel T. Kuehl

RADFORD, ARTHUR (1896–1973), World War II admiral and chairman of the *Joint Chiefs of Staff (JCS). Born in Chicago, Arthur Radford graduated from the U.S. Naval Academy in 1916. Following his designation as a naval aviator in 1920, Radford was assigned to a variety of aviation-related positions in the interwar years.

From 1941 until 1943, he served as director of aviation training in the Bureau of Aeronautics. In this assignment, Radford skillfully directed a program of intensive expansion of all phases of naval aviation training that enabled the U.S. *Navy to fulfill its enormous requirement for combat pilots. Other wartime assignments included command in combat of two different *aircraft carrier divisions.

In 1947, Radford was selected by chief of naval operations Louis E. Denfeld to be vice chief of naval operations. He quickly gained a reputation as naval aviation's staunchest defender against attacks from other services. In 1949, while serving as commander in chief, Pacific and Pacific Fleet, Radford spearheaded the navy's testimony before the House Armed Services Committee in the so-called Revolt of the Admirals. Although this incident put a temporary cloud over his career, he continued to serve ably throughout the *Korean War as the unified commander in the Pacific.

Having impressed President-elect Dwight D. *Eisenhower and incoming Secretary of Defense Charles E. *Wilson during their visit to the Pacific in 1952, Radford was appointed the second chairman of the JCS in 1953. In his four years as chairman, Radford served as a strong supporter of Eisenhower's "New Look" defense policy, which relied upon the threat of *nuclear weapons to deter Soviet actions while holding down requirements for larger U.S. conventional forces.

Radford retired from active duty in 1957. He died in 1973. A thoughful proponent of military preparedness, Radford served ably in positions of increasing trust during World War II and the first decade of the Cold War.

[*See also* Bradley, Omar N.; Lemnitzer, Lyman.]

• Stephen Jurika, Jr., ed., *From Pearl Harbor to Vietnam: The Memoirs of Admiral Arthur W. Radford,* 1980. Jeffrey G. Barlow, *Revolt of the Admirals: The Fight for Naval Aviation, 1945–1950,* 1994.

—Jeffrey G. Barlow

RADIO AND TELEVISION SERVICE, ARMED FORCES. Since 1942, the mission of the Armed Forces Radio and Television Service (AFRTS) has been to provide information, education, and entertainment to U.S. military forces everywhere. AFRTS personnel brought American music, news, and network programming (without commercials) to the front lines during World War II and during the *Korean War, the *Vietnam War, and the *Persian Gulf War. Just as valuable, broadcasters relieved the boredom of peacetime military duty around the world.

Begun as unofficial radio stations before World War II in the Panama Canal Zone, the Philippines, and Alaska, the Armed Forces Radio Service (AFRS) was founded in August 1942, at the direction of the army chief of staff, George C. *Marshall. Relying on the advice of movie director Frank Capra, Marshall selected advertising executive Tom Lewis to create a broadcast unit to provide the same information and service Capra was to do with the film series *Why We Fight.* Very quickly, Lewis and his staff concluded he could best attract military personnel for the educational broadcasts by airing the same programs they knew back home. In addition, AFRS produced its own programming in Hollywood, such as *Command Performance,* with the help of the entertainment industry.

Lewis immediately established the principle that AFRTS would not censor news programs (except for security purposes), or broadcast propaganda messages. Consequently, troops as well as foreign nationals have always been able to listen to criticism of the U.S. government. The broadcast service quickly proved a better purveyor of the American way of life than the more propagandistic Voice of America.

Television became an integral part of the operation in the 1950s after Gen. Curtis E. *LeMay established a television station at one of his SAC bases in Maine. Since then, AFRTS has followed the troops wherever they were stationed, carrying the most popular radio and television programs. AFRTS can legitimately be seen as the representative of democracy to the world, as well as the predecessor of Cable News Network (CNN), since foreign nationals have always been able to listen to the over-the-air broadcasts. Most important, AFRTS has provided the U.S. armed forces with a familiar voice and image—whether in the jungles of Vietnam, peacetime Europe, or the Pacific Rim.

[See also Proganda and Public Relations, Government.]

—Lawrence Suid

RANDOLPH, A. PHILIP (1889–1979), labor and civil rights leader. Born the son of a minister in the African Methodist Episcopal Church, Randolph was raised in Jacksonville, Florida. Graduating from Cookman Institute in 1911, he moved to New York's Harlem, working and attending City College. In response to increasing segregation and discrimination against blacks, Randolph shunned moderate reform and racial integration, as advocated by W. E. B. *Du Bois, and emphasized instead socialism and trade unionism. In 1917, he founded and co-edited the *Messenger,* a radical monthly magazine, which campaigned against lynching, opposed U.S. participation in World War I, urged African Americans to resist being drafted to fight for a segregated society, and recommended that they join radical unions. In 1918, Woodrow *Wilson's postmaster general, Albert Burleson, revoked the *Messenger's* second-class mailing privileges.

During the interwar years, Randolph organized the Brotherhood of Sleeping Car Porters Union. In 1941, when blacks were excluded from many defense industry jobs as the United States prepared for World War II, Randolph threatened a mass protest march on Washington. The demonstration was called off when President Franklin D. *Roosevelt issued an executive order (25 June 1941), establishing the Fair Employment Practices Committee to try to prevent such racial discrimination. In 1948, Randolph's advice helped convince President Harry S. *Truman to issue an executive order banning racial segregation in the military.

[See also African Americans in the Military.]

• Jarvis Anderson, *A. Philip Randolph: A Biographical Portrait,* 1973. Paula F. A. Pfeffer, *A. Philip Randolph: Pioneer of the Civil Rights Movement,* 1990.
—Clement Alexander Price

RANGERS, U.S. ARMY. "Rangers Lead the Way" is the motto of the U.S. Army Rangers. Traditionally spearheaders, raiders, and scouts, they have adapted to quick response airborne operations. (In contrast, Special Forces handle covert missions.) Ranger insignia is the black and gold shoulder tab, though in World War II and Korea, they wore a black, red, and white tab. The Ranger Hall of Fame includes Robert Rogers (*French and Indian War); Francis *Marion, the "Swamp Fox" (*Revolutionary War); and John Mosby (*Civil War), among others. All represented the fearless ranger spirit.

U.S. Army Rangers actually originated during World War II, when Gen. George C. *Marshall, army chief of staff, authorized units comparable to British Commandos. In 1942, William Darby was made commander of the 1st Ranger Battalion—only 450 men—volunteers from U.S. divisions in Great Britain. Commandos trained them and took them on raids against "Fortress Europe." In 1943, rangers landed in Algeria ahead of American forces, and

spearheaded Gen. George S. *Patton's corps in Tunisia.

Darby organized the 3rd and 4th Battalions in North Africa. The three battalions were first to land in Sicily and Italy (1943). The rangers were being used, however, as shock troops, and at the Battle of *Anzio (January 1944), they were overcommitted. The Germans wrecked the 1st and 3rd Battalions and bloodied the 4th; the survivors were shipped home and disbanded.

The U.S.-trained 2nd and 5th Ranger Battalions took part in the invasion of *Normandy (6 June 1944). Under fire, rangers scaled 130-foot cliffs to seize 155mm guns atop Pointe du Hoc at Omaha Beach. These battalions engaged in heavy fighting in Europe—averaging 50 percent *casualties in major actions. In the Pacific, the 6th Ranger Battalion, formed in 1944 in New Guinea, fought in the Philippines and rescued American prisoners of war, survivors of the Bataan Death March.

"Merrill's Marauders" (led by Frank Merrill) in Burma were also recognized as rangers. Trained by British Gen. Orde Wingate, of the "Chindits" (Long-Range Patrol troops), the Marauders were key to the capture of Myitkyina, helping to doom the Japanese in Burma, but were reduced from 3,000 to 600 by combat and disease. They were demobilized in 1945 with the 75th Infantry Regiment when all ranger battalions were deactivated.

Seven Airborne Ranger companies served in the *Korean War (1950–53). The Eighth Army Company was trained in Korea; the others were schooled by the new Ranger Training Command (established in September 1950) at Fort Benning, Georgia. All upheld the ranger tradition. The Eighth Army Company (with the 25th Division) was among the first to engage Chinese troops. Of forty-eight rangers, twenty-eight were casualties, including the commander, Ralph Puckett, who was wounded four times. In February 1951, the 1st Ranger Company (ninety men, with the 2nd Division) stopped a Chinese breakthrough at Chipyong-ni, but was almost annihilated. The Far East Command disbanded all ranger companies by October 1951. Only the Ranger School survived—as the Ranger Department, Infantry School, now the Ranger Training Brigade.

Initially, there were no U.S. Ranger units in the *Vietnam War. Special Forces dominated, training counterguerrilla units, but "Green Berets" were often also rangers. And as the U.S. advisory role turned into open combat, commands formed Long-Range Patrols and Long-Range Reconnaissance Patrols. Between 1969 and 1974, they were converted to ranger companies of the 75th Ranger Regiment (Airborne).

In the post-Vietnam era, "Desert One" (1980) was a turning point for American irregulars. Delta Force, organized by Special Forces Col. Charles Beckwith (a former ranger), was to rescue hostages held by Iranians at the U.S. Embassy in Teheran. Rangers were poised in Egypt to assist. But Desert One turned to catastrophe when *helicopters collided at the desert rendezvous.

The failure emphasized the need for an all-service quick response unit. The army led with SOCOM (Special Operations Command), including U.S. Rangers and Special Forces. The air force and navy organized AFSOCOM (Air Force Special Operations Command) and USNSWC (U.S. Navy Special Warfare Command). In 1987, USSOCOM (U.S. Special Operations Command) was created.

Meanwhile, in 1983, the 75th Regiment (two ranger battalions) participated in the U.S. intervention in *Grenada. In 1984, the 75th got a third battalion. The ranger regiment fought in Panama (1989), but had little part in the *Persian Gulf War (1991) because the commanding general, H. Norman *Schwarzkopf, distrusted irregulars. In December 1991, one battalion parachuted into Kuwait in a show of force. Since then, rangers have been deployed in Somalia (1993), Haiti (1995), and in various *United Nations *peacekeeping missions.

The rangers have risen to prominence in recent years as a ready strike force. In the 1990s, they were vital to the army component—30,000 out of 46,000—of the U.S. Special Operations Command.

[See also Special Operations Forces: Army Special Forces.]

• James Altieri, The Spearheaders, 1960. William O. Darby and William H. Baumer, Darby's Rangers: We Led the Way, 1980. Robert W. Black, Rangers in Korea, 1989. Robert W. Black, Rangers in World War II, 1992. Susan L. Marquis, Unconventional Warfare: Rebuilding U.S. Special Operations Forces, 1997. Mark Bowden, Black Hawk Down: A Story of Modern War, 1999.   —Owen Connelly

RANK AND HIERARCHY. Armed forces are based on rank and hierarchy, formal structures of positions designed to ensure command, control, and support in the pursuit of the mission. This entry consists of four articles that explain very briefly the structure of ranks from top to bottom in each of the four major services:

Rank and Hierarchy: Army
Rank and Hierarchy: Navy
Rank and Hierarchy: Air Force
Rank and Hierarchy: Marine Corps

RANK AND HIERARCHY: ARMY

Armies are hierarchical by design, both in terms of organizational elements and in terms of the individuals expected to perform specific functions at each echelon—privates and specialists; corporals and sergeants who lead squads (noncommissioned officers); warrant officers with particular technical abilities; lieutenants who head platoons and captains who command companies (company grade officers); majors and lieutenant colonels who head battalions or act as executive officers, and colonels who command brigades (field grade officers); and brigadier generals who head separate brigades or are assistant division commanders, major generals commanding divisions, lieutenant generals overseeing corps, and generals supervising armies (the executive level). The rank of General of the Armies was created by Congress for John J. *Pershing in 1919 (Pershing accepted the title, but declined the fifth star) and posthumously for George *Washington in 1978. Congress has bestowed the five-star rank of General of the Army upon Dwight D. *Eisenhower, Douglas *MacArthur, George C. *Marshall, and "Hap" *Arnold (all in 1944), and Omar N. *Bradley (in 1950).

Armies are functionally dependent upon chains of command, with appointed leaders at each organizational level. The chain of command is used for disseminating information and issuing directives downward, as well as to receive timely information and reports upward.

The need to identify leaders in the *Continental army and distinguish their ranks was recognized by General Washington from his experience with the British army. In

1775, he ordered the use of stripes to designate rank for officers and noncommissioned officers. Since then, U.S. *Army *insignia have undergone numerous alterations, to include various types and numbers of epaulets to designate rank, as well as colors to designate a functional branch (e.g., artillery red, cavalry yellow, or infantry blue). In 1821, regulations prescribed a cloth stripe or chevron to be worn on the sleeve of the uniform, point upward, to designate noncommissioned officer rank. This method of identifying noncommissioned officers remains to this day for dress *uniforms; for the field uniform, insignia are worn on the collar. Officers wear insignia of rank on the shoulder epaulets of the dress uniform and on the collar of the field uniform.

To attain rank and greater responsibility in the army's hierarchy, a sophisticated military *education and selection process has been institutionalized. To attain a more senior position, defined standards of military training, skills, on-the-job performance, and formal schooling have to be met. Senior noncommissioned officers and officers compete for a limited number of higher-level positions and are chosen by centralized selection boards. Particularly in the twentieth century, seniority has been only one of the many criteria for selection to the next higher rank.

• Mark M. Boatner, Military Customs and Traditions, 1976. William Gardner Bell, Commanding Generals and Chiefs of Staff, 1775–1991, 1992. Lawrence P. Crocker, Army Officer's Guide, 46th ed. 1993.
          —James D. Blundell

RANK AND HIERARCHY: NAVY

U.S. *Navy personnel are divided into commissioned line or staff officers, warrant officers, and enlisted ratings. Unrestricted line officers are eligible to assume command at sea or command of aircraft squadrons, fleets, and shore bases; restricted line officers are designated for engineering and other special duties. Staff officers (commissioned officers assigned to a commander's staff) may command designated shore facilities. Naval officers are selected for promotion by promotion boards composed of senior officers.

Officers are ranked as admiral (four stars); vice admiral (three stars); rear admiral (originally the admiral in command of the rear of the fleet) higher rank (two stars) and lower rank (one star); captain; commander; lieutenant commander; lieutenant; lieutenant junior grade; and ensign. The five-star rank of fleet admiral was created in 1944 and bestowed on only four men: William D. Leahy, Ernest J. *King, and Chester *Nimitz in 1944, and William F. *Halsey in 1945. Until July 1862, when Congress established the ranks of rear admiral and commodore, the highest rank held by an American naval officer was that of captain. The status of commodore has changed over time, but is now considered a position, usually held by a captain, in command of a formation of ships.

The navy retains the traditional warrant officer structure. The former warrant officer or W-1 has been eliminated, and all warrant officers in the 1990s were commissioned as chief warrant officers in grades W-2, W-3, and W-4. They are former enlisted personnel selected for their professional ability and demonstrated qualities of leadership, loyalty, and devotion to duty. Warrant officers are specialists in certain areas such as aviation, *communications, supply, seamanship, and engineering. Enlisted personnel are rated from seaman recruit, seaman apprentice, and seaman, to petty officer third, second, first class, through chief petty officer, senior chief petty officer, to master chief petty officer. In addition to being rated, they are given training at navy service schools to qualify them for various specialty ratings in deck, weapons/ordnance, electronics, and precision equipment, or administrative and clerical categories. Advancement is determined by time in grade and by competitive examinations.

• Leland P. Lovette, *Naval Customs: Traditions and Usage,* 1939. *Bluejackets Manual,* 1990. Naval Education and Training Command, *Basic Military Requirements,* April 1992.

—Barbara Brooks Tomblin

RANK AND HIERARCHY: AIR FORCE

The U.S. *Air Force retained much of its army heritage of rank and hierarchy since it was part of the U.S. *Army until 1947. There were four grades of general officer: brigadier general, major general, lieutenant general, and general; three field grades: major, lieutenant colonel (squadron commander), and colonel (wings commander); and three company grades: second lieutenant, first lieutenant, and captain. All pilots are commissioned officers. However, because of the nature of its technical specialties and missions, the distinction between officer and enlisted personnel in the air force is less pronounced than in the other services. Over time, the air force has adjusted rank and hierarchy to fit its own needs.

The enlisted grades maintained the traditional army enlisted ranks of private through master sergeant. In the early 1950s, the air force created an enlisted grade structure that was a compromise between the position of supervisor and technician. These new grades of airman basic and airman third, second, first class, and senior airman, corresponded to apprentice technicians whose promotion was based on increasing skill in their specialty, and to a lesser extent on military bearing.

The noncommissioned officers (NCOs) in the grades of staff, technical, and master sergeant were expected to be experts in their specialty and front-line supervisors. In 1958, two new grades of senior master sergeant and chief master sergeant were added to the enlisted rank structure. These "supergrades" allowed the other NCO grades to remain focused on technical expertise.

Unlike the other branches of the armed forces, the air force phased out its warrant officer ranks in the early 1960s, arguing that these ranks duplicated both the duties of officers and the supervisory positions of the noncommissioned officer corps. In actuality, the warrant grades significantly cut into the congressional quotas for officers, were far too specialized, and suffered from the stigma of simply not fitting into the air force's rapidly expanding technological environment.

• Mark R. Grandstaff, " 'Neither Fish Nor Fowl': The Demise of the United States Air Force's Warrant Officer Program," *Airpower History,* 42 (Spring 1995), pp. 40–51. Mark R. Grandstaff, *Foundation of the Force: Air Force Enlisted Personnel Policy, 1907–1956,* 1997.

—Mark R. Grandstaff

RANK AND HIERARCHY: MARINE CORPS

While officially part of the Department of the Navy, the Marine Corps, as a ground force, has an organization and rank structure similar to that of the U.S. *Army. General officer ranks include: general—held only by the commandant and the assistant commandant of the Marine Corps; lieutenant general—held by those selected to hold particu-

lar "type" or specially designated commands; major general—in command of either a Marine Expeditionary Force or division; and brigadier general—held normally by commanders of installations, or brigades.

Colonels in the Marine Corps command regiments, function as chiefs of staff, or hold other key billets. Lieutenant colonels usually command battalions or squadrons. Majors normally serve as battalion executive officers. Captains generally lead companies, while lieutenants are often platoon commanders. Besides these commissioned officers there are warrant officers, promoted to officer rank due to their technical or administrative expertise.

The top enlisted rank is sergeant major of the Marine Corps, who advises and assists the commandant in all matters pertaining to enlisted Marines. Sergeant majors normally will be found at all levels in the Fleet Marine Force and other administrative and technical positions. Other staff noncommissioned officer ranks range downward from first or master sergeant to gunnery sergeant and staff sergeant. Due to the low officer-to-enlisted ratio, staff noncommissioned officers (SNCOs) are considered to be the "backbone" of the Marine Corps.

Noncommissioned officers (NCOs) include sergeants and corporals, who act as squad leaders, section heads, and instructors. Junior enlisted grades include lance corporal, private first class, and private.

• *A Brief History of U.S. Marine Corps Officer Procurement,* 1958. Bernard C. Nalty, et al., *United States Marine Corps Ranks and Grades, 1776–1969,* 1970.

—Leo J. Daugherty III

RANKIN, JEANNETTE (1880–1973), pacifist, suffragist, and congresswoman. After successfully leading the suffragist movement in Montana, Jeannette Rankin became the first woman elected to Congress. A progressive Republican and a pacifist, Rankin joined fifty-six other members of Congress on 4 April 1917 in voting against U.S. entry into World War I. This vote contributed to her defeat when she sought election to the U.S. Senate in 1918.

Rankin continued to work for world *peace. In 1919, she served as a U.S. delegate to the Second International Congress of Women in Zurich. In 1929–39, she worked as a Washington lobbyist for the National Council for the Prevention of War. She ran a blistering campaign against President Franklin D. *Roosevelt's foreign policy in 1940; Montana voters returned her to Congress. Still committed to *pacifism, Rankin voted unsuccessfully against the *Lend-Lease Act and Agreements, the draft, the repeal of the *Neutrality Acts, and increased military expenditures. Despite the attack on *Pearl Harbor in December 1941, Rankin cast the sole vote against U.S. entry into World War II, the only member of Congress to vote against U.S. entry in both world wars. She was not reelected in 1942.

After World War II, Rankin decried the *Cold War, opposed the *Korean War, and denounced U.S. involvement in Vietnam. In 1967, a broad anti-*Vietnam War coalition of pacifists, feminists, and students organized the Jeannette Rankin Brigade and urged the eighty-eight-year-old Rankin to run for Congress in 1968. Ill health forced her out of the race, but she continued to speak out against the Vietnam War until her death from a heart attack in Carmel, California, on 18 May 1973.

[*See also* Vietnam Antiwar Movement.]

• Hannah Josephson, *First Lady in Congress: Jeannette Rankin,* 1974.

—Justin D. Murphy

RAPE BY MILITARY PERSONNEL has been notoriously common throughout the history of warfare, leading many to view rape as an inevitable concomitant of war. Gen. George S. *Patton remarked during the American occupation of Morocco in 1942 that "in spite of my most diligent efforts, there would unquestionably be some raping." In recent years, however, change has begun to be seen in American military attitudes and policy on rape. By the early 1990s, each service had announced a policy of "zero tolerance" of sexual assault or harassment by personnel. The long-term effects of such policy change remain to be seen.

Historical Incidence. Relatively little is known about the actual historical incidence of rape by American military personnel. No systematic compilations exist of rape incidence prior to *World War II. However, individual records of rape prosecutions dating back to the earliest years of the republic can be found. George *Washington's notes for 22 July 1780 indicate that a Thomas Brown of the Seventh Pennsylvania Regiment was sentenced to death for rape. The few historians who have commented on the subject suggest that the rape incidence during the *Civil War was relatively low. Rape by non-Americans during World War I has been written about frequently, yet rape by U.S. personnel in that war has not been explored in any comprehensive way.

For World War II, comprehensive statistics of prosecutions of American military personnel are available for the European theater of operations. Those statistics indicate that rape was extensive. Indeed, rape of French women was sufficiently pervasive to cause Gen. Dwight D. *Eisenhower's headquarters to issue a directive to U.S. Army commanders announcing the general's "grave concern," and instructing that speedy and appropriate punishments be administered.

Court-martial statistics are available also for the *Korean War and the *Vietnam War. From 31 May 1951 through 30 May 1953, twenty-three U.S. Army personnel in Korea were convicted of rape, and nine of assault with intent to rape. In Vietnam, from 1 January 1965 to 31 January 1973, twenty army personnel and one air force man were convicted of rape, and fourteen army personnel were convicted of attempted rape or assault with intent to commit rape. In Vietnam (1970–73), one navy serviceman and thirteen Marine Corpsmen were convicted of rape. According to many reports, however, these conviction numbers in no way reflect the actual number of incidents.

During the *Persian Gulf War, twenty-four female American military personnel were subjected to rape, attempted rape, or sexual assault by American military men, according to official records.

Comparing Military and Civilian Rape Rates. To place military rape rates in context, it is valuable to compare them with civilian rates. Comparisons of the crime rates of civilian and military populations during peacetime periods in 1986–92 reveal that contemporary peacetime rates of rape by American military personnel are actually *lower* (controlling for age and gender) than civilian rates. However, the data also indicate that peacetime military rape rates are diminished far less from civilian rates than are military rates for other violent offenses. This "rape differential" is also reflected in the World War II data: U.S. Army rape rates in Europe climbed to several times the U.S. civilian rates for that period, while military rates for other vio-

lent crimes were roughly equivalent to civilian rates. Thus, in both contexts studied, a rape differential exists: the ratio of military rape rates to civilian rape rates is substantially larger than the ratio of military rates to civilian rates for other violent crimes.

Legal Provisions. Rape by military personnel has been criminalized and carried serious penalties, including capital punishment, throughout American history. Rape was specifically prohibited in the English army as early as 1385. The American *Continental army observed the customary prohibition and applied severe penalties, including the death penalty, for committing rape.

From 1950 to 1992, rape was defined by the Uniform Code of Military Justice as "an act of sexual intercourse with a female not [the accused's] wife, by force and without her consent." In 1992, that definition was amended to include rape of a male and rape within marriage. Current military rules of evidence include a rape shield provision that excludes from evidence most testimony regarding the sexual history of the alleged victim.

Despite the clear, long-standing prohibition of rape in military codes, there is anecdotal evidence of some continuing failure to enforce those laws. Witnesses at Senate hearings in 1992 testified that such failures are common. Legislation instituting centralized recordkeeping and oversight of military sexual misconduct cases to ensure consistent enforcement has been introduced in Congress in 1993 and 1994, but none has been adopted to date.

In addition to American domestic law criminalizing rape by military personnel, multiple provisions of international law prohibit rape by military personnel. Rape is incontrovertibly a war crime. Both the fourth Geneva Convention and Protocols I and II to the *Geneva Conventions explicitly prohibit rape, and there is clear movement toward interpreting the Geneva Conventions' grave breach provisions to cover rape. When committed on a mass and systematic basis, rape can constitute a crime against humanity. Rape also can, under certain conditions, constitute a part of the crime of *genocide. In addition to prohibiting rape under international laws of war, provisions of international human rights law, such as the International Covenant on Civil and Political Rights, also proscribe rape by military personnel or others when their acts are attributable to the state.

Historically, rape has not been a focus of international *war crimes prosecutions. Scant attention was paid to rape in the international prosecutions after World War II. Rape was not mentioned in the Nuremberg Charter and was not prosecuted as a war crime at the *Nuremberg Trials. It received some but still rather limited treatment at the International Military Tribunal for the Far East. The International Criminal Tribunals for the former Yugoslavia and for Rwanda are currently beginning their work; there have been indications that these tribunals will prosecute rape vigorously.

[*See also* Culture, War, and the Military; Society and War.]

• Susan Brownmiller, *Against Our Will: Men, Women, and Rape*, 1975. Peter Karsten, *Law, Soldiers, and Combat*, 1977. George C. Rable, *Civil Wars: Women and the Crisis of Southern Nationalism*, 1989. Theodor Meron, "Rape as a Crime Under International Humanitarian Law," *American Journal of International Law*, 87 (1993), pp. 424–28. Christine Chinkin, "Peace and Force in International Law," in *Reconceiving Reality: Women and International Law*, ed.

Dorinda G. Dallmeyer, 1993. Madeline Morris, "By Force of Arms: Rape, War, and Military Culture," *Duke Law Journal*, 45, 1996, pp. 651–781.
                                                                    —Madeline H. Morris

REAGAN, RONALD (1911–), actor, governor, U.S. president. Reagan grew up in Dixon, Illinois, in an impoverished family, and worked his way through Eureka (Ill.) College. From a radio station in Des Moines, Iowa, he left for Hollywood, where he worked as a film and TV actor, 1937–66. A captain during World War II, he made training films for the Army Air Forces. Later, as a TV spokesman for General Electric Company, he became an active Republican. Urged by conservative Southern California businesspeople, Reagan entered politics and was elected governor of California, serving from January 1967 to January 1975. A champion of the GOP's conservative wing, Reagan defeated Democrat Jimmy *Carter to become president in 1980. He was reelected in 1984.

As president (1981–89), Reagan sought to reduce the federal government's domestic programs. Initially, his administration adopted the "supply side" theory to stimulate production and control high inflation through tax cuts and sharp reductions in federal spending. Following a major recession in 1982, economic growth resumed, fueled in part by massive defense spending and a dramatic increase in the national debt.

Reagan's foreign policy was defined by his antipathy toward the Soviet Union, which he called the "evil empire." He and his security advisers, especially Defense Secretary Caspar *Weinberger, called for preparedness for war with the Soviet Union and its allies on a global scale. Exhorting *patriotism, Reagan presided over the largest military buildup in peacetime U.S. history: probably around $2.4 trillion on the armed forces, of which an estimated $536 billion represented increases over previous projected trends for the decade. The largest (in inflation-adjusted dollars) single-year defense budget was $296 billion in fiscal year 1985.

The massive investment in new weapons systems—from *missiles, ships, planes, and *tanks to the speculative *Strategic Defense Initiative or "Star Wars"—was designed not simply to build American strength but also to push the Soviet Union toward economic bankruptcy. In addition, the Reagan Doctrine offered support to anti-Soviet guerrillas anywhere. CIA director William Casey provided covert aid in Central America, Africa, the Middle East, and Afghanistan. Reagan sent Marines to Beirut, Lebanon, to aid Christian militias, but he withdrew them after a truck-bomb killed 241 persons on 23 October 1983. On 25 October, he ordered the U.S. invasion of Grenada in the Caribbean, where pro-Castro military officers had seized power and were thought to endanger American students. In Central America, Reagan was determined to support the government of El Salvador in its battle with leftist guerrillas and to overthrow the Soviet-leaning Sandinista regime in Nicaragua by providing direct (or, when Congress prohibited this, covert) aid to anti-Communist Contra guerrillas. Congressional hearings in 1987 revealed the illegal *Iran-Contra Affair, in which a group in the *National Security Council covertly sold weapons to Iranians to help finance the Contra operation. Reagan's popularity plummeted.

When he and Soviet leader Mikhail Gorbachev agreed to reduce short- and intermediate-range missiles, much of his popularity was restored. The *INF Treaty (1988) was the first time the two countries had agreed to destroy an entire category of strategic weapons.

As the Cold War ended, Reagan and his supporters insisted that the Soviet Union collapsed as a result of U.S. military spending and *covert operations, an assertion contested by those who credit, instead, long-term structural problems of the Soviet economy and the reformism of Gorbachev.

[*See also* Cold War: Changing Interpretations; Grenada, U.S. Intervention in; Lebanon, U.S. Military Involvement in; Nicaragua, U.S. Military Involvement in.]

• John Lewis Gaddis, *The United States and the End of the Cold War*, 1992. Michael Schaller, *Reckoning with Reagan: America and Its President in the 1980s*, 1992. Daniel Wirls, *Buildup: The Politics of Defense in the Reagan Era*, 1992.   —Michael Schaller

RECONSTRUCTION. When the Confederate forces surrendered in April 1865, the U.S. Army embarked on a mission unparalleled in its history: the postwar occupation of a rebellious section of its own country as the enforcer of a politically determined process of reconstruction. No previous war had required such duty. During the *Civil War, reconstruction had begun haltingly in 1862 in those parts of Louisiana, Tennessee, Arkansas, and Virginia under Union military control. However, Abraham *Lincoln's "ten percent" plan for the restoration of individual loyalty and government functions was at best experimental. Military efforts remained focused on victory rather than postwar expectations.

Confederate surrender changed the picture entirely. Many parts of the South had by now experienced the presence of Union troops. Neither soldiers nor civilians knew how long that presence might last, nor what policies would govern the relationship between victor and vanquished. The Constitution, not having anticipated a breakup of the Union by force, gave little specific guidance for the aftermath of such an effort. Federal statutes were equally uninformative on the peacetime use of military power in support of federal political processes. The American tradition of civil control of military institutions was well developed, yet that tradition would not provide clear answers to the many specific questions of power soon to arise. Other complicating factors were the clamor of volunteer troops to go home as soon as possible; the legislative need to establish a peacetime size for the regular army; the resumption of patrol and Indian-fighting duties in the West; and the need for troops to support diplomatic moves against the French presence in Mexico.

During the twelve years of Reconstruction (1865–77), the army's experience in the South evolved significantly as its powers, functions, and problems changed. Five distinct phases can be identified. An initial period of six weeks extended from mid-April 1865 to the end of May. The Confederate national government had collapsed and in many states there were no civil governments functioning. Legislators, governors, judges, aldermen, sheriffs, and other local officials were not at their posts. Thus the army, by default, assumed the task of local government.

Applying to civil government its familiar pattern of military administration, the army established departments, districts, and subdistricts throughout the South. Commanding officers of troops doubled as executive officers of government, or sought to find loyal and trustworthy civilians whom they could temporarily appoint to vacant positions. Considerations of workload as well as personal ability led army officers to prefer a pattern of civilian office-holders working under military orders.

The broad category of regulation called the police power, focusing on the health, safety, welfare, and morals of the community, came under military supervision. Specific subjects varied widely depending on local conditions. Typical regulations applied to collection of garbage, disinfecting alleys and streets with lime, naked children in public, dogs running at large, public profanity, speed limits for carriages, whitewashing of tree trunks, vagrancy, prostitution, distribution of food relief, and reopening of schools. Some commanders required proof of having taken the loyalty oath as a qualification for certain services, including receipt of mail or obtaining a marriage license. Approximately 250,000 troops remained in the South in the weeks immediately following the surrender. They performed a wide variety of different duties without adequate training. Commanding generals, some of whom were not regulars, often had to act on their own judgment or a highly general letter of instruction from superiors. The war had ended with a military surrender, not a treaty of peace, and the future policy of the government was initially unsettled.

On 29 May 1865, President Andrew *Johnson issued two proclamations that would begin a period of "presidential Reconstruction." One prescribed a loyalty oath, established the terms of a general amnesty, and specified a process whereby those excluded from the general amnesty could apply for individual pardon. The second appointed a provisional governor for North Carolina and set forth a process for the reestablishment of a permanent state government and election of local officials. Thus began the second phase of the army's role in the South, which would extend until December 1865. Johnson shortly issued proclamations establishing provisional governments in South Carolina, Georgia, Florida, Alabama, Mississippi, and Texas. In Tennessee, Arkansas, Louisiana, and Virginia, the provisional governments established during the war continued.

The army's presence in the South now had a specific focus. The provisional governors were to reestablish civil government by the participation of loyal voters. The army was to "aid and assist the said provisional governor in carrying into effect this proclamation." Johnson also ordered soldiers "to abstain from in any way hindering, impeding, or discouraging the loyal people from the organization of a State government." Yet much remained unclear. A provisional governor of a state appointed by the president was an anomaly in American constitutional practice. A military force placed to whatever degree at the call of such an official was equally anomalous.

Controversies were bound to occur. Governors wrote to President Johnson complaining about military interference. Officers wrote to the Commanding General, Ulysses S. *Grant, asking for instructions about the limits of their authority. In Mississippi, Governor William L. Sharkey and Gen. Henry W. Slocum clashed over the governor's desire to form a state militia independent of military control. A widespread subject of controversy was military arrests: Could commanders arrest civilians on their own initiative, or only in pursuance of a request from civilian officials for aid in effecting an arrest in a dangerous area? Law enforcement was made more complex by jurisdictional conflicts among (a) military commissions, (b) special Freedmen's Bureau courts designed to resolve labor contract disputes, and (c) local courts reopened by provisional governors. General Grant and Secretary of War Edwin M. *Stanton supported the army in these conflicts, while President Johnson often sided with his political appointees, the provisional governors.

By September 1865, the number of troops in the South was down to 187,000. Distribution varied from 8,700 in Florida to 16,000 in Tennessee to 24,000 in Louisiana to 45,000 in Texas. A growing problem was the desire of white volunteer regiments to be mustered out, which left an increasing proportion of black regiments, organized late in the war, with a year or more left on their enlistments. By the end of 1865, when total troop strength had dropped to 88,000, black regiments outnumbered white ones by 11 to 1 in Mississippi, 6 to 1 in Tennessee, and 9 to 5 in Louisiana. There was a slight preponderance of black troops in Arkansas and Florida, and equal numbers in Alabama and Texas. Complaints from governors about mutual racial antipathy as well as negative reports about discipline from some commanding generals led to an increased discharge rate for black volunteer regiments during 1866.

In December 1865, Congress (which had been out of session since March) met for its new term, expressed dissatisfaction with the results of Johnson's program, and refused to readmit any seceded states to representation. This initiated a legislative struggle with Johnson over control of policy that lasted until March 1867. In consequence of the confusion in Washington, the army's role entered its third phase. The provisional governments remained in place, but congressional Republicans wanted more military supervision of them. Conflict with governors over appointment and removal of local officials increased. Passage of the Freedmen's Bureau Act meant continued military aid for that agency. Passage of the Civil Rights Act, signifying a congressional desire to supersede discriminatory state legislation and judicial practices, meant greater use of military courts, or at least military protection, for former slaves and white unionists. All the while numbers declined, from 39,000 troops in the South in April to 20,000 at year's end. In 1866, the total peacetime strength of the regular army was set at 58,000.

On 2 March 1867, Congress passed the First Reconstruction Act over Johnson's veto, thus establishing a program of "congressional Reconstruction." The army's role entered its fourth phase, which would continue in each state until such time, between the summer of 1868 and the spring of 1871, as the particular state gained readmission to Congress. During this phase, the army's direct power over civil affairs and southern politics reached its greatest extent. The First Reconstruction Act superseded all of the existing state governments, required the election of conventions to rewrite state constitutions, and mandated a new registration of voters under specified qualifications and the election of new governors and legislators. This political process occurred under total military supervision. Congress established five military districts and required the president to assign an army general to the command of each district.

That officer had the duty "to protect all persons in their rights of persons and property, to suppress insurrection, disorder, and violence, and to punish, or cause to be punished, all disturbers of the public peace and criminals." In a clarification of previous uncertainties, the commanding generals had specific permission to try civilians by military commission. Subsequent legislation allowed the generals to appoint the registration boards and control other aspects of the electoral process. They could also remove any civil official and need not accept the U.S. Attorney General's interpretation of their powers under the law.

Gen. Philip H. *Sheridan in Louisiana and Gen. John Pope in Georgia removed governors as well as lesser officials. Pope gerrymandered electoral districts in order to control the results and sought to regulate the press by requiring official notices to be published only in papers that did not oppose congressional Reconstruction. The administration of Gen. John Schofield in Virginia was by comparison much less contentious.

By this legislation as well as other contemporary provisions, Congress had assigned the army an overtly political function. It had also made certain that the army would implement its views on Reconstruction and not those of the president. During the summer of 1867, Johnson removed Generals Sheridan, Pope, and Dan *Sickles from their commands. His subsequent efforts to get Edwin M. *Stanton out of the War Department led to his impeachment.

Congress readmitted several states to representation in the summer of 1868. Others followed in 1870 and 1871. Readmission began the fifth and last phase of army duties in the South, which would continue until the inauguration of Rutherford Hayes in the spring of 1877. Troop strength dropped from 18,000 in October 1868 (one-third on the Texas frontier) to 6,000 in the fall of 1876 (half in Texas). In 1869, a retrenchment-minded Congress once again cut the size of the regular army to less than 40,000 men.

Duties were more intermittent than continuous. Detachments went out to accompany federal revenue officers in search of illicit whiskey stills. General suppression of crime was also a task for the army, but now only at the request of civil authorities, federal or state. The amount of discretion left to the army in honoring these requests caused controversy; often the requests ended up in Washington for review and approval. In 1871, Gen. Alfred H. Terry reported that in the six states of his command, there had been more than 200 expeditions in aid of law enforcement that year. The army also provided the force behind a major effort to break the Ku Klux Klan in South Carolina during 1870–72. Around election time, military activity increased as small detachments visited troubled areas of the state to guard polls and discourage intimidation of voters. Congressional Reconstruction brought Republican state regimes to power, which often called for military aid in the period following readmission. The most continuous use of troops for this purpose was the protracted party struggle in Louisiana from 1872 to 1877.

The twelve years of Reconstruction saw frequent changes in policy, and with them, changes in the army's legal powers and functions. As an institution, the army was able to adjust to these changes, largely because officers saw themselves as administering policy rather than establishing it. This fit the established American tradition in civil-military relations, in spite of the executive-legislative conflict over army control in the Johnson years. The *Posse Comitatus Act of 1878, reflecting the Reconstruction experience, further limited military enforcement of civil law. On the whole, military administration of federal policy was creditable to the institution of the U.S. Army despite errors of judgment and highly unusual circumstances.

[See also African Americans in the Military; Army, U.S.: 1866–99; Civil-Military Relations; Colored Troops, U.S.]

• Otis Singletary, The Negro Militia and Reconstruction, 1957. Max L. Heyman, Prudent Soldier: A Biography of Major General E. R. S. Canby, 1959. Benjamin P. Thomas and Harold Hyman, Stanton: The Life and Times of Lincoln's Secretary of War, 1962. James E. Sefton, The United States Army and Reconstruction, 1865–1877, 1967. Jack D. Foner, The United States Soldier Between Two Wars: Army Life and Reforms, 1865–1898, 1970. James E. Sefton, Andrew Johnson and the Uses of Constitutional Power, 1980. Joseph G. Dawson III, Army Generals and Reconstruction: Louisiana, 1862–1877, 1982. William L. Richter, The Army in Texas During Reconstruction, 1865–1870, 1987.
—James E. Sefton

RECRUITMENT. The military manpower policy of the United States has been marked by sharp contrasts between principles and realities. Universal service has often been the ideal, but the militias and conscript armies have never been equally representative of society.

America's early military traditions were heavily influenced by Great Britain's, and included a predisposition toward militia organization and a distrust of centralized standing peacetime forces. The militias—military organizations composed of civilians enrolled and trained as defensive forces against invaders—developed from medieval notions of the duty of all free men to help the king defend the realm. The colonists, threatened by Native Americans and rival colonial powers, organized as *citizen-soldiers in order to protect themselves and their interests.

When troops were needed for a campaign, legislatures assigned quotas to local militia districts. Local officials then called for volunteers and could draft men when necessary. Thus, the militia—in theory composed of all able-bodied free white men—served as the *mobilization base for the colonies, with volunteers, usually called provincials, providing the troops for campaigning. A considerable proportion of the citizenry was exempted from service by over 200 militia laws. For instance, the Massachusetts Militia Act of 1647 exempted officers, fellows, and students of Harvard College; church elders and deacons; schoolmasters; physicians; surgeons; captains of ships over twenty tons; fishermen employed year-round; people with physical problems; and many others. When the militia failed to produce a sufficiently large number of volunteers, or when legislative calls for additional volunteers failed to expand the force sufficiently, men could be drafted, or impressed. During the colonial period, impressment was rarely successful, and avoided in most provinces because of its potential to create desertion or even riot. For this reason, impressed men were always given the option of paying a fine or hiring substitutes to serve in their stead.

During the *Revolutionary War, the Continental Congress allocated manpower quotas for the *Continental army to the states, and left *conscription policy up to them. At the conclusion of the war, George *Washington urged Congress to accept the principle of universal national military obligation and establish a small peacetime army backed by a national militia. Congress declared that standing armies in times of peace were inconsistent with the principle of republican government, and discharged virtually the entire Continental army.

This tug-of-war between national military need and national thought on standing armies has influenced the whole of military history. One day after it had dismissed the Continental army, Congress requested that the states of Connecticut, New Jersey, New York, and Pennsylvania recruit a total of 700 militiamen for a year of service on the frontier. The term of frontier service was extended to three years, and then the militiamen were replaced by regular soldiers.

With the adoption of the Constitution, the federal government acquired the power to raise and support armies, to provide and maintain a navy, and to make rules for the regulation of the land and naval forces. The right of the states to control their militias was confirmed, and the state forces were to be the country's major land force in the event of a crisis.

A standing army did not fit naturally into the ideological landscape of the new republic. Necessary or not, the armed forces were typically kept small and often suffered from neglect. Soldiers were often untrained, poorly housed and fed, and not always paid. In 1812, as America faced a war, the regular army consisted of less than 7,000 men and was dispersed throughout the expanding country. Older regiments were commanded by aging revolutionary veterans, training was lax, and supply and staff were inadequate even in peacetime. The war effort was built upon volunteer companies and the amorphous state militias behind them. Congress approved enlistment bounties totaling $40 for regular recruits plus three months pay in advance and 160 acres of land. The next year, Congress invited members of volunteer militia organizations to join the regular army for one year. The actual turnout was disappointing. In order to raise necessary manpower in wartime, Congress created the U.S. *Volunteers, locally raised troops for national service for the duration of a conflict.

Recruitment suffered from all the impediments to men leaving their homes for war. Popular indifference always hampered raising and supporting troops. In the early years of the republic, there was strong opposition to any exercise of armed force on the part of the United States—opposition that arose from the fear that the government would come to depend upon the force and from disagreement over whether the Constitution actually allowed it. Historically, the quality of men who would sign up with the army, in a country of expanding economic opportunities, was poor. Until the turn of the nineteenth century, visitors to army posts spoke of the men's low intelligence, loose morals, and habitual drunkenness, and described frontier posts as dirty, dusty, and remote. Desertion was common. The army was barely growing, promotion prospects were dismal, and there was no retirement system.

The patriotic angst that brought the *Civil War fueled its armies as well, composed primarily of U.S. and Confederate volunteers. In a few weeks, *nationalism produced the first mass armies in American history. The U.S. Army grew to twenty-seven times its original strength in the four months following the capture of *Fort Sumter (1861). Both Federal and Confederate forces swelled with volunteers in the early months—and both turned to conscription to augment their mass armies.

Conscription was rationalized on the grounds that the rights guaranteed to the individual by the government implied an obligation upon him to defend his rights by defending the government that assured them. Exemptions were commonplace and the hiring of substitutes remained lawful.

In 1916, with eyes on the war in Europe, Congress passed the National Defense Act, which provided for an expanded peacetime regular army—the National Guard—a reserve force, and a volunteer army to be raised in time of war. That summer, mobilization of the National Guard failed to recruit the Guard to full strength. This convinced the Wilson administration of the inadequacy of voluntary enlistments to raise an army for the Great War. A conscription bill, the Selective Service Act of 1917, was passed immediately after the declaration of war. The regular army and the National Guard continued to recruit volunteers, and the draft was held to remedy any deficiencies.

Having learned lessons from the Civil War, for *World War I there were no substitutes and no bounties. Students under the age of twenty-one, however, were able to defer service by enrolling in the Student Army Training Corps for three years. Otherwise, each eligible person was required to register as an obligation of citizenship or residence in the United States. Conscription was based on the principle of universal obligation to service. The World War I draft supplied close to 67 percent of the total force. It acted as a spur to voluntary enlistment, and the enlistment rate fluctuated with conscription policy. The draft lapsed at the end of the war, and precedents were set not only for a national draft and for student deferments but also for those deferments to expand into exemptions from service.

Although distinctly concerned by the onset of *World War II, the Roosevelt administration hesitated to ask for conscription before a declaration of war for fear of arousing isolationist sentiment. In the summer of 1940, however, public and congressional sentiment outran President Franklin D. *Roosevelt and conscription was enacted. Later that summer, a joint resolution called for *mobilization of the National Guard and reserves.

With the end of World War II and the onset of the *Cold War, the whole landscape changed. Neither life nor war would ever be the same again. Many Americans, including some in the armed forces, believed that an atomic monopoly had brought an end to the era of mass armies. *Demobilization proceeded at great speed: by 1948, the army's combat effective strength was reduced to two and one-third divisions. In June 1948, however, in response to growing tensions between the United States and the Soviet Union, Congress passed a new Selective Service Act, with a two-year limit. The revival of the draft encouraged voluntary enlistments among men who wished to choose service and branch rather than to leave themselves at the mercy of local draft boards. The act was extended for the *Korean War. As voluntary enlistment increased, inductions under Selective Service dropped, from more than a third of accessions during the mid-1950s to less than 10 percent during the early 1960s.

Had it not been for the *Vietnam War, the draft might have been phased out a decade earlier than it was. Opposition to the war and the draft, and the perceived inequities of Selective Service, contributed significantly to the advent of the *All-Volunteer Force in the early 1970s. Critics of the force warned that it would weaken *patriotism, attract the economically disadvantaged, and attenuate the relationship between the armed forces and civilian society. In January 1973, peacetime conscription ended in the United States.

The resulting All-Volunteer Force has surpassed all national concerns. Solely dependent upon volunteers, the force has attracted recruits from across a broad social spectrum, is well trained, well equipped, and well led.

To paraphrase a contemporary recruiting slogan, it is all that it can be.

[See also Militia and National Guard; National Defense Acts; Naval Militia; Reserve Forces Act; Selective Draft Cases.]

• Jerome Johnston and Jerald G. Bachman, Young Men and Military Service, 1972. John K. Mahon, History of the Militia and the National Guard, 1983. John W. Chambers, To Raise an Army, 1987. Christopher Duffy, The Military Experience in the Age of Reason, 1988. Mark J. Eitelberg, Manpower for Military Occupations, 1988. David R. Segal, Recruiting for Uncle Sam, 1989. Martin Binkin, Who Will Fight the Next War? 1993. Mark J. Eitelberg and Stephen L. Mehay, eds., Marching Toward the Twenty-first Century, 1994.

—Susan Canedy

RED CLOUD (1822–1909), Oglala Sioux leader. Born near the forks of the Platte River, Nebraska, Red Cloud became a leader (shirt-wearer) in the "Bad Faces" military lodge for his exploits against enemy Pawnees, Utes, and Crows. Concerned about white encroachments, he launched "Red Cloud's War" in 1866–67 against the army's Bozeman Trail posts. During several engagements, especially the annihilation of William J. Fetterman's eighty-man column outside Fort Phil Kearny, his followers proved a match for the bluecoats.

In the Treaty of Fort Laramie (1868), the government conceded to Red Cloud's demands that the Bozeman Trail forts be abandoned. Thereafter he adopted a more conciliatory stance, apparently convinced that his people stood little chance of winning a war against the United States. Made a "chief" by federal officials, he was in 1876 stripped of this position, only to regain government recognition the following year after helping to convince *Crazy Horse to surrender. Red Cloud sought to maintain traditional ways among his people while demanding that the U.S. government honor its treaty obligations. Controversial for both his decision to abandon military methods and his stubborn determination to preserve tribal customs, his diplomacy was aimed at mitigating the effects of the Oglalas' transition to reservation life.

[See also Plains Indians Wars.]

• James C. Olson, Red Cloud and the Sioux Problem, 1965. Robert W. Larson, Red Cloud: Warrior-Statesman of the Lahota Sioux, 1997.

—Robert Wooster

RED CROSS, AMERICAN. The American Red Cross has served the U.S. military since 1898. Founded on 21 May 1881 by Clara *Barton, who had done humanitarian work in the *Civil War, the society is part of the more than 175-member International Red Cross and Red Crescent movement.

The movement was born in Geneva, Switzerland, in October 1863. Despite centuries of war in Europe and the Civil War raging in America, the humanitarian aspects of war had been largely ignored by most governments. Swiss entrepreneur Jean Henri Dunant brought about a change in that attitude when he volunteered to help the wounded, after a battle between French-Italian and Austrian armies in northern Italy in June 1859. His Memory of Solferino (1862) graphically portrayed the agonies of the 40,000 neglected wounded, influencing governments to consider establishing voluntary relief societies to supplement the work of army medical units.

In February 1863, the International Committee for Relief to the Wounded, precursor to the International Committee of the Red Cross (ICRC), was established. In October 1863, the first Red Cross societies were formed and a red cross was adopted as a neutral symbol; and in 1864, twelve governments signed the first Geneva Convention. The United States acceded to the treaty in 1882 after years of lobbying by Clara Barton.

The four *Geneva Conventions protect the wounded and sick on the battlefield (1863), shipwrecked military personnel (1906), *prisoners of war (1929), and civilians (1949). Protocols added in 1977 protect civilians caught in internal conflicts. ICRC primarily monitors the conventions.

The International Red Cross and Red Crescent movement follows seven fundamental principles: Humanity, Impartiality, Neutrality, Independence, Voluntary Service, Unity, and Universality. In addition to the societies, it consists of the Geneva-based ICRC and the International Federation of Red Cross and Red Crescent Societies, which was founded in 1919 by American Henry P. Davison to address peacetime needs.

During the *Spanish-American War, American Red Cross nurses and volunteers served in Cuba, the Philippines, and at U.S. camps. In 1911, President William H. Taft authorized the organization as "the only volunteer society" to render aid to the military in wartime. The U.S. Army began providing transportation and subsistence for attached Red Cross personnel in 1912. The Red Cross sent 8,000 workers to Europe during World War I, providing medical, recreational, and welfare services. It operated fifty-eight domestic and overseas base hospitals for the military, twenty-four of them in France. Eight million volunteers at home provided welfare services and produced supplies.

During World War II, the American Red Cross collected 14 million units of blood and produced blood plasma, but provided no other medical services. Aided by 7.5 million volunteers at home, some 40,000 staff worldwide supplied emergency *communications, welfare and recreational services, and produced 28 million food packages for U.S. and Allied prisoners of war.

Similar services were provided during the *Korean War and the *Vietnam War, with the military meeting its own blood needs in Vietnam. The Red Cross continues to staff U.S. bases in Europe and elsewhere; it accompanied military units on missions to Somalia, Haiti, the Persian Gulf, and Bosnia.

In 1998 the American Red Cross had over 1,300 volunteer-led chapters, providing disaster relief, meeting half of the nation's blood needs, and conducting community programs designed to help Americans prevent, prepare for, and respond to emergencies. Over 30,000 staff and 1.4 million volunteers supplied support. The nongovernmental, nonprofit organization has had a congressional mandate since 1900 to provide disaster relief, and emergency communication between the military and their families. A fifty-member board of governors, eight appointed by the U.S. president, governs the American Red Cross. Past presidents include Clara Barton, William Howard Taft, and George *Marshall.

[See also Bosnian Crisis; Caribbean and Latin America, U.S. Involvement in the; Persian Gulf War.]

• Foster Rhea Dulles, The American Red Cross—a History, 1950. Hans Haug, Humanity for All, 1993.

—Patrick F. Gilbo

REED, WALTER (1851–1902), medical officer and research scientist. After receiving his M.D. degree in 1869 from the University of Virginia and spending several years working in the field of public health in New York City, Reed joined the Army Medical Department (1875). In 1898, he headed a board that identified typhoid fever as the cause of much sickness and death at the camps where troops gathered to train for the *Spanish-American War. By establishing human waste as the source of contamination, the board made possible effective public health measures to prevent future epidemics. When, in 1900, another board headed by Reed proved that yellow fever, much dreaded by soldiers sent to Cuba, was carried by a mosquito and identified the specific mosquito, successful efforts to reduce this threat to public health also became possible.

Reed's accomplishments resulted not only from his personal skills as a research scientist but from the disciplined world in which he worked: medical officers were often better able than their civilian counterparts to conduct the studies necessary to identify both major diseases that threatened public health and the means by which they spread in civilian and military communities alike. The Walter Reed Army Medical Center in Washington, D.C., is named for him.

[*See also* Cuba, U.S. Military Involvement in; Disease, Tropical.]

• William B. Bean, *Walter Reed*, 1982. Albert E. Truby, *Memoir of Walter Reed*, 1943.
—Mary C. Gillett

REENACTMENTS, MILITARY. The vibrant subculture of battle reenactment is too often thought of as merely a hobby or as activity unworthy of sustained analytical attention. Americans have commemorated wars in a number of ways. Patriotic rhetoric, for example, reinforces the primal themes of patriotic orthodoxy: war as holy crusade that brings new life to the warrior and the nation. It asks the living to rededicate themselves to the ideals for which the warrior died. Monument building is designed to instill the lesson of sacrifice in the civic consciousness, and preservation of battlefields is designed to "freeze" the message in a commemorative environment. Battle reenactment claims to offer participants—and to a lesser extent observers—imaginative entry into a heroic past. Such reenactments are important cultural rituals, and the activities and motivations of reenactors—ranging from those who offer "impressions" of *Revolutionary War and *Civil War soldiers in public events to those who participate in reenactments of World War II battles on abandoned military bases—deserve serious attention, as does the impact of such spectacles on audiences.

There were many kinds of battle reenactment in the late nineteenth century. At commemorative events, Confederate veterans subsequently retraced their steps in the Pickett-Pettigrew charge during the Battle of *Gettysburg, but shook hands with Union veterans at the angle, the High-Water Mark of the Confederacy. Such events would become an enduring feature of *Gettysburg National Military Park commemorative events, celebrating the ideology of reconciliation between white veterans of both sides. The U.S. *Army occasionally used Civil War battlefields for war games, and in the early twentieth century—the era of great historical pageants—battle reenactments were common.

The modern era of battle reenactment, with its emphasis on large numbers of participants (10,000 at the 125th anniversary of Gettysburg in 1988) and on historical accuracy in troop movements, *uniforms, and other details of nineteenth-century life, was sparked by the centennial of the Civil War (1961–65), and subsequently by bicentennial celebrations of 1776 in 1976. Experienced reenactors recall the first major reenactment of the Civil War—the First Battle of *Bull Run in July 1961—as lacking in accuracy, but by September 1962 and the reenactment of the Battle of *Antietam, specific units—the Ninth New York Zouaves, for example—had begun to appear, and attention to historical detail had improved. By the mid-1970s, reenactors had formed the Brigade of the American Revolution, and distinct groups within the reenactment community had formed, distinguished by their commitment to authenticity. "Farbs" (reenactors who practice twentieth-century behaviors during reenactments) were looked upon with contempt because of their "weekend warrior" attitude, specifically their failure to attend to historical accuracy. More diligent reenactors would study their unit's battle tactics and activities, while still others were concerned with "absolute" authenticity, including minute attention to detail in clothing and equipment.

The large-scale reenactments that have occurred since the Civil War centennial of the 1960s have sparked controversy. An eminent historian of the war, Bruce Catton, worried that such spectacles both romanticized war and obscured the issue of slavery over which it was fought. Likewise, John Hope Franklin, prominent historian of African Americans, viewed such activity as a form of memorialized forgetting. Much of Civil War commemorative activity, he believed, celebrated glorious battles and heroic lives of the nineteenth century, while enduring forms of racism continued to shatter lives in the present.

There are revealing cultural attitudes encoded in battle reenactments. Southern events celebrated the ideology of the Lost Cause, and at least some Confederate reenactors offer an implicit objection to modern racial integration. Similarly, commemorative events at the site of the Battle the *Little Bighorn—which would often include reenactments—solidified the classification of Native Americans as barbarians and savages, while George Armstrong *Custer and his men were celebrated as sacrificing themselves for the opening of the West. In 1976, the Confederate air force sparked widespread controversy in the United States and in Japan when during their World War II Airpower Demonstration in the United States, they offered a simulation of the dropping of the atomic bomb on Hiroshima before 40,000 spectators.

Reenactors believe their activities are valuable for a number of reasons. Some offer a "civic virtue" argument, emphasizing educational merit and the opportunity to spark the public's imagination. Some speak of the opportunity for personal transformation, to enter into the world of the past, if only briefly. Some speak of reenactment as a form of commemorative respect, to recall and honor the sacrifice of those who died. Clearly, battle reenactment can mean all of these things to participants, and it may signify yet another protest against modernity and the concomitant urge to recover an illusory and idealized past.

[*See also* Battlefields, Encampments, and Forts as Public Sites; Hiroshima and Nagasaki, Bombings of; Memorials, War; Patriotism.]

• Jay Anderson, *Time Machines: The World of Living History*, 1984. John Bodnar, *Remaking America: Public Memory, Commemoration, and Patriotism in the Twentieth Century*, 1992. Edward T. Linenthal, *Sacred Ground: Americans and Their Battlefields*, 1993. Dennis Hall, "Civil War Reenactors and the Postmodern Sense of History," *Journal of American Culture*, 17 (Fall 1994), pp. 7–11. Jim Cullen, *The Civil War in Popular Culture: A Reusable Past*, 1995. Tony Horowitz, *Confederates in the Attic: Dispatches from the Unfinished Civil War*, 1998.

—Edward T. Linenthal

REFERENCE BOOKS ON WAR, PEACE, AND THE MILITARY. A field as large as military history and the study of war and peace has many specialized reference tools. This provides an introduction. The present writer's *American Military History: A Guide to Reference and Information Sources* (1995) offers a longer, selectively annotated guide.

Among bibliographies, Jack C. Lang, *America's Military Past: A Guide to Information Sources* (1980), while including reference books, has more annotated entries for monographs, journal articles, and government documents. Robin Higham edited a collection of bibliographic essays, *A Guide to the Sources of United States Military History* (1975, with supplements in 1981, 1986, and 1993). The best guide for military periodicals is the extensive and annotated *Military Periodicals: United States and Selected International Journals and Newspapers* (1990), edited by Michael Unsworth. Lenwood G. Davis and George Hill compiled *Blacks in the American Armed Forces, 1776–1983: A Bibliography* (1984). On peace history, John Lofland compiled *Peace Movement Organizations and Activists in the U.S.: An Analytical Bibliography* (1990).

Journal articles are often difficult to locate. Useful in locating pertinent ones are the quarterly *Air University Library Index to Military Periodicals* (1949–), and the quarterly *America: History and Life* (1964–), which abstracts many history journals.

Atlases are especially valuable in military history. The best general one for this subject is Vincent Esposito, *West Point Atlas of American Wars* (1995). For the naval history, see Craig Symonds, comp., *The Naval Institute Historical Atlas of the U.S. Navy* (1995). There have been many reprint editions of the U.S. War Department's *Official Military Atlas of the Civil War* (1983 repr.). On World Wars I and II, see Anthony Livesay, *The Historical Atlas of World War I* (1994) and *The [London] Times Atlas of the Second World War* (1989).

Chronologies list events; for example, Walt Lang, *United States Military Almanac* (1989), lists military events from 1636 to 1988. James W. Atkinson compiled *The Soldier's Chronology* (1993), which provides details about changes in *uniforms, *weaponry, regulations, and other aspects of military life. Developments in the U.S. Navy and Marines are listed in Jack Sweetman, *American Naval History: An Illustrated Chronology of the U.S. Navy and Marine Corps, 1775–Present* (2nd ed. 1991). For some specific wars, see E. B. Long and Barbara Long, *Civil War Day by Day: An Almanac, 1861–1865* (1971); Randal Gray with Christopher Argyle, *Chronicle of the First World War*, 2 vols. (1990–1991); Robert Goralski, *World War II Almanac, 1931–1945: A Political and Military Record* (1981); and John S. Bowman, ed., *The Vietnam War: An Almanac* (1985).

Biographical dictionaries provide useful information. The most complete is the three-volume *Dictionary of American Military Biography* (1984), edited by Roger J.

Spiller, et al.; although see also Stewart Sifakis, *Who Was Who in the Civil War* (1988). On peace leaders, see Harold Josephson, ed., *Biographical Dictionary of Modern Peace Leaders* (1985).

The most used reference works are encyclopedias and historical dictionaries. A global approach is Trevor N. Dupuy, ed., six-volume *International Military and Defense Encyclopedia* (1993). For the United States, Charles R. Shrader, *Reference Guide to United States Military History* (1991–94), has five volumes, each of which covers developments within a particular time period. John E. Jessup and Louise B. Ketz have edited the three-volume *Encyclopedia of the American Military: Studies of the History, Traditions, Policies, Institutions, and Roles of the Armed Forces in War and Peace* (1994), which contains extended essays. Charles D. Bright has edited the *Historical Dictionary of the U.S. Air Force* (1992). For individual histories of particular ships, see the U.S. Navy's official *Dictionary of American Naval Fighting Ships*, 8 vols. (1959–81).

*Peace and disarmament encyclopedias include Christine A. Lunardini's *ABC-Clio Companion to the American Peace Movement in the Twentieth Century* (1994) and Richard Dean Burns's three-volume *Encyclopedia of Arms Control and Disarmament* (1993).

For particular wars, the following are useful reference works: John Mack Faragher, ed., *The Encyclopedia of Colonial and Revolutionary America* (1990); Richard L. Blanco, ed., *The American Revolution, 1775–1783: An Encyclopedia*, 2 vols. (1993); Patricia L. Faust, et al., *The Historical Times Illustrated Encyclopedia of the Civil War* (1986); Benjamin R. Beede, ed., *The War of 1898 and U.S. Interventions, 1898–1934: An Encyclopedia* (1994); Anne C. Venzon, ed., *The United States in the First World War: An Encyclopedia* (1995); Norman Polmar and Thomas B. Allen, eds., *World War II: America at War, 1941–1945* (1991); I. C. B. Dear and M. R. D. Foot, eds., *The Oxford Companion to World War II* (1995); James I. Matray, ed., the *Historical Dictionary of the Korean War* (1991); Stanley I. Kutler, ed., *The Encyclopedia of the Vietnam War* (1995); and Sheikh R. Ali, ed., *Encyclopedia of the Persian Gulf War* (1994).

—Daniel K. Blewett

REGIONALISM AND THE MILITARY. Regional differences involving the military have been related to attitudes as well as other circumstances. Along the eastern seaboard, colonial governments in the English North Atlantic responded to Indians and rival Europeans by building forts and training white males to become the *citizen-soldiers of their local militias. Yet, over time, militiamen in New England faced different circumstances from their southern and western counterparts, and by the *Revolutionary War, competing military traditions had arisen. In the South and landlocked West, the army was a preferred form of military service, whereas maritime New England emphasized the navy.

In the colonial era, the whole eastern seaboard faced European and Native-American threats. In the South, however, the danger of hostilities lasted several decades longer, and outbreaks of warfare were more frequent than in the North. Until the Spanish crown received Louisiana in 1763, the French had long threatened southern borderlands. Thereafter, Spanish occupation of Florida, Mexico, and Louisiana posed a constant threat until Florida's annexation in 1821. Beginning with a series of Anglo-

Powhatan wars in seventeenth-century Virginia, campaigns against southeastern Indians did not cease in the South until the *Seminole Wars ended in 1842. Most Indians successfully resisted dispossession until they were forcibly removed to Oklahoma in the 1830s. Black slavery and the concomitant necessity for whites to control black slaves sustained violence in the culture and the need for active militia as slave patrols. The southern landowning aristocracy's emphasis on martial virtues also contributed to the inclination for the army tradition.

Northerners faced entirely different circumstances. After a series of colonial wars with French Canadians and Indians, the Seven Years' War (1754–63) ended the threat. Lacking a need for slave patrols, and with Indians already removed from their domain, the northern militia lost its chief functions. After the *Revolutionary War, volunteers for the newly formed national army and navy drew upon their past experiences. In New England, this prior training occurred as Atlantic seafarers—fishermen, whalers, and merchant seamen—pursued their livelihoods on the open seas. Although the American navy was small, its ranks were largely drawn from these New England sources. In like fashion, southern militiamen and aristocrats were natural candidates for army service. With their stress upon the ethic of honor, southerners often aspired to the titles of general and colonel, and considered leaders such as Andrew *Jackson to be the highest representation of military valor. To that end, southerners attended college military academies such as the Citadel in South Carolina.

Until the *Civil War, the two traditions became ever more entrenched in regional life. Army officers were predominantly southern or western, while navy officers were mostly from the Northeast. In proportion to their percentage of the national population, southerners were overrepresented by a third at West Point. Southerners and westerners also had regional interests in supporting the military. They rejoiced at the chance to support Texan independence in the Revolution of 1836 and eagerly joined the U.S. Army to conquer territory from Mexico in 1846 to expand the borders of a slaveholding empire. The tendency of southerners to outnumber northerners in the army continued to the outbreak of civil war. In the 1850s, southerners served as two of the three brigadier generals and all but one of the commanders of the army's geographical divisions.

Once the Civil War began, the regional divergence of military interests became apparent. Several army officers who were trained at West Point and raised in the South, such as the Confederate generals Robert E. *Lee and Joseph E. *Johnston, chose between the competing loyalties created by birth and fostered by training. Few naval officers faced such a conflict. With rare exceptions, the officers and enlisted men of the navy swore their allegiance to the Union. Not surprisingly, the first Confederate cities to fall were taken from the water, and the Northern strategy relied heavily on *blockades of Southern ports.

Unlike the North, the West initially followed a pattern similar to the South. With concerns for Indians and western outlaws continuing throughout the nineteenth century, the West and its cycle of conquest became a society deeply embedded in the military. Army forts and posts, crucial to the defense and settlement of the frontier, dominated the region's social and economic life. Often they served as trading posts and points of defense. The military was not only a solution to the violence associated with the frontier—it was also a respectable outlet for it.

In the twentieth century, regional correlations to the armed forces continued, but they have not remained as strong. In 1910, however, 93 percent of army generals' officers still had a southern heritage, and during World War II, southern enlistment in both the army and navy exceeded the national average. New Englanders continued to serve disproportionately in the navy, but their commitment to the military remained weaker than the South's. In the West, where the aviation industry refocused the region's martial spirit, a new regional tendency has emerged. When the Air Force Academy was established in Colorado in 1954, westerners turned to the air force in disproportionate numbers.

Recently, the regional connection to particular branches of the military has diminished. The nationalization of American culture, increased migration among regions, the modernization of the South, and the desegregation of the military have all diminished if not eliminated the old regional patterns. The federal government has ended many of the sectional divisions through its intervention into regional development, and its recruiting quotas and strategies.

[*See also* Academies, Service; Militia and National Guard.]

• John Hope Franklin, *The Militant South*, 1956. Marcus Cunliffe, *Soldiers and Civilizans: The Martial Spirit in America*, 1968. Bertram Wyatt-Brown, *Southern Honor*, 1982. Richard White, *"It's Your Misfortune and None of My Own": A History of the American West*, 1991.
                                                      —Andrew K. Frank

RELIGION AND WAR. Religion has played many, often contradictory, roles in the history of American warfare. With the conquistadors came Roman Catholic priests and brothers to bless, or challenge, Spanish attacks upon indigenous peoples. Two of the most notable of those clerics based enduring theoretical contributions on their knowledge of colonial warfare: the Dominican Bartolomé de Las Casas (1474–1566) concerning the humanity of Native Americans, and his fellow Dominican Francisco de Vitoria (1483–1546) concerning the ethics of international relations. Warfare between the first generation of English settlers and Native Americans brought out the worst and the best in the colonists' religious leaders. The much respected first minister of Cambridge, Massachusetts, Thomas Shepard, could yet herald "the divine slaughter of the Indians at the Hand of the English" after battle with the Pequots of Connecticut in 1637; the Rev. John Eliot of Roxbury, Massachusetts, experienced his finest hour as "apostle to the Indians" in defending his converts from reprisals after *King Philip's War (1675–76). During the eighteenth century, Moravian Brethren carried out humanitarian missionary work in Pennsylvania, New Jersey, and the Ohio Territory, where they repeatedly tried to shield their converts (usually pacifists like themselves) from the ravages of war.

Deep, if ambiguous, connections between war and religion continue to the present day. Religious values supported American ideology in the *Cold War and offered President Ronald *Reagan a vocabulary to define the Soviet Union as the "evil empire." Religious motives often fueled opposition to the *Vietnam War, as with the Baptist senator from Oregon, Mark Hatfield, or the efforts of the Catholic priest Daniel Berrigan, the Jewish rabbi Abraham Heschel, and the Lutheran minister Richard John Neuhaus, who in 1965 founded Clergy and Laity Concerned About Vietnam. On the other side, religious motives also led Francis Cardinal Spellman, Catholic archbishop of New York, and the Protestant evangelist Billy Graham to support the war. In the *Persian Gulf War, President George *Bush consulted the leaders of his own Episcopal Church and invited his longtime friend, Billy Graham, to the White House the night before hostilities commenced. The Episcopalian bishops leaned against considering the conflict a "just war"; Graham offered general support.

Religion Affecting Warfare. The most visible connection between war and religion in American history is the intensification of commitment that religious faith brought to combatants and the promoters of war. This link was a particular bequest of the Anglo-French wars that began in 1689 and ended only with the final defeat of Napoleon. As Linda Colley argues (1992), warfare with France raised the Protestant identity of the British empire to remarkable salience. During King George's War (1744–48) and the *French and Indian War (1754–63), colonists from Massachusetts (like the Congregationalist Thomas Prince) to Virginia (like the Presbyterian Samuel Davies) joined their compatriots across the Atlantic in picturing the military struggle as an apocalyptic contest between the universal truth of Protestantism and the corrupt tyranny of Catholicism. With such preparation, it was a relatively easy matter for patriots in the 1770s to depict the struggle for American independence as, in the words of the Presbyterian Abraham Keteltas, "the cause of heaven against hell—of the kind Parent of the universe against the prince of darkness" (*God Arising and Pleading His People's Cause*, 1777). Loyalists were usually somewhat more restrained in rhetoric, but colonial Anglicans like Charles Inglis of New York and Jonathan Boucher of Maryland were just as convinced that their cause was the cause of God. In hundreds of sermons during the *Revolutionary War, Americans became skilled at interpreting biblical passages as types, or anticipations, of realities fulfilled on contemporary fields of battle.

Religious convictions supported political ideology in all major national conflicts through World War I. During the *War of 1812, New England Congregationalist ministers could show how Scripture called warmaking into question, while their Protestant confreres in southern and western states could show just the reverse. Before the *Civil War, Protestants of both the North and the South sanctified sectional controversy with theological rhetoric; during the war itself, a host of rhetorically accomplished ministers, led by Henry Ward Beecher in the North and Robert Lewis Dabney in the South, grounded their respective causes in universal scriptural imperatives. In World War I, fundamentalists and modernists alike linked German aggression to religious error. According to the revivalist Billy Sunday, "If you turn hell upside down, you will find 'Made in Germany' stamped on the bottom." By comparison with these earlier conflicts, the religious support for World War II was muted. In all American wars, the practice of "civil religion," especially when presidents employ a general religious vocabulary to reassure or inspire their fellow Americans, has always flourished.

Much less frequently, the universal values of religion have worked against rather than for the military purposes of a particular conflict. During the Revolutionary War, the "father of American Lutheranism," Henry Melchior Mühlenberg, denounced the armies of both sides for sacrificing Christian principle to military expediency. At the start of the Civil War, the Northern Presbyterian theologian Charles Hodge was called a heretic for suggesting that the formation of the Confederacy was not sufficient ground for expelling Southern Presbyterians from the denomination. At the end of that same war, an anonymous correspondent to a Jewish periodical, *The Occident*, generated a storm of controversy among his fellow religionists when he wrote that, although Abraham *Lincoln was a worthy president, he hardly deserved to be compared with Moses as several rabbinical memorials had recently done.

Beyond acting to sanction or check national bellicosity, religion has frequently influenced strategy and policy. In early 1776, the Continental Congress sent two Roman Catholic cousins, John Carroll and Charles Carroll, with Benjamin Franklin on a mission to Montréal to persuade the Catholic Québecois to join the revolt. The effort failed, in large part because Catholics there were satisfied with the provisions of Britain's Quebec Act (1774), which guaranteed certain traditional privileges to their church. During World War I, the presence in America of both Protestants and Catholics of German stock complicated Woodrow *Wilson's diplomatic maneuvering. The international humanitarianism that determined Wilson's war aims originated in nineteenth-century liberal Calvinism.

Religious influences on the direct experiences of war have often featured the ministry of chaplains. From 1775, when the Continental Congress authorized chaplains for the army and the navy, through the Civil War, when the chaplaincy began to look like a profession, to World War II, when the four army chaplains (two Protestants, one Catholic, and one Jew) who sacrificed their lives to save servicemen at the sinking of the *Dorchester* in February 1943 inspired the nation, and finally to the efficient mobilization of the chaplaincy in the *Vietnam War and the Gulf War, chaplains have largely avoided the glare of publicity while offering a wide range of spiritual and humane assistance to troops on active duty. During the Civil War, an unusually intense series of revivals spread through the camps of both Northern and Southern armies. According to many participants, these revivals acted as an antidote to dissipation, and—especially in Southern armies during the last eighteen months of the war—to despair.

Warfare Affecting Religion. The impact of war on American religion has, if anything, exceeded the effects of religion on war. The American Revolution, and the revolution in social values it accelerated, crippled the Episcopal Church and substantially hindered the Congregationalists, the two major denominations in colonial America; Methodists, Baptists, and indigenous denominations soon prevailed as the nation's most numerous churches. Insofar as the Revolution lay behind the Constitution and its First Amendment guaranteeing religious freedom, that war was also responsible, however inadvertently, for opening up the United States to peaceful settlement by non-English-speaking Protestants, non-Protestant Christians (especially Roman Catholics), non-Christian adherents of other religions, and finally the nonreligious.

The long-term religious effects of the Civil War were different. As two authors, George M. Frederickson (1965) and Anne C. Rose (1992), have shown, disillusionment with traditional Protestant faiths and an openness to skepticism grew rapidly among Northern intellectuals as a result of the war. The war's failure to usher in the millennium, as many on both sides had hoped, also contributed to the expansion of otherworldly forms of pietism where the emphasis shifted from the Christianization of society to a fascination with speculative prophecy or a concentration on private as opposed to public morality.

World War I played a direct role in fomenting the fundamentalist-modernist controversies of the 1920s. George Marsden (1980) has demonstrated that the intensity of that war mobilized populist revivalists who felt that a crisis had been reached in the progress of Christian civilization as well as in the integrity of the Protestant churches. In response, they mounted a defense of endangered "fundamentals," eliciting outrage from moderates and liberals who hardly appreciated being lumped with the kaiser.

Religious responses to warfare have created institutions of enduring significance. For the profession of nursing, still in the nineteenth century very much a religious vocation for Protestants and Catholics, the Civil War provided a decisive impetus. During World War I, American Roman Catholics founded their first permanent national organization, the National Catholic War Council. This institution later became the National Catholic Welfare Conference (1922–66), which in turn made way for the two federal structures of Catholic organization that exist today, the National Conference of Catholic Bishops and the United States Catholic Conference. For more sectarian and traditional Protestants, World War II hastened the formation of the National Association of Evangelicals (1943) by adding a concern for representation in the chaplaincy to longstanding disquiet with the theological drift of the more ecumenical Federal Council of Churches. More broadly, the massive commitment of American military forces around the world led to the establishment of a host of U.S.-based mission and relief agencies.

Because it tends to inflame passions and demand action, warfare only occasionally deepens theological perspective. In the aftermath of World War I, and sometimes as an act of expiation for jingoism, several important religious thinkers, including the Protestant Harry Emerson Fosdick and the Catholic Dorothy Day, published provocative arguments against warfare in any of its modern forms. Another important voice won to virtual *pacifism in the wake of World War I was Reinhold Niebuhr; he would, however, return to a defense of *Just War theory because of the Fascist threats of World War II and the anti-Communist crusades thereafter. Reactions to the Holocaust have produced painful theological reflection for Jews and many others. Among Roman Catholics, the experience of both bloody fighting and *Cold War nuclear *deterrence led to a concentration of sophisticated ethical reasoning that culminated in the Bishops' Pastoral Letter on War and Peace of 1983. That document's acceptance of *nonviolence on a par with traditional "just war" claims was controversial among Catholics, in the same way that, among Protestants, the pacifism of John Howard Yoder and careful defense of just war from Paul Ramsey and James T. Johnson were controversial. What these proposals shared was serious ethical reasoning, first-level theology, and intense analysis of twentieth-century warfare.

The most notable instance of American warfare deepening theology, however, comes not from an academic theologian or a synod of bishops, but from the sixteenth president of the United States. Abraham *Lincoln, who was never a church member, did not espouse traditional Christian faith; yet during the Civil War, his thought grew in biblical depth until, at his second inaugural address in March 1865, he could articulate a more sublime trust in divine providence, and a more charitable attitude to his foes, than virtually any other public figure of his day.

Religious Rejection of War. Rejection of warfare also enjoys a long American history. During the Revolutionary War, neutralism prevailed among New England immigrants in Nova Scotia because the revivals of Henry Alline created what amounted to a pietist *pacifism. In the thirteen mainland colonies, Mennonites, German Brethren, some Moravians, and numerous Quakers remained faithful to their pacifist principles, despite fines, imprisonment, and confiscation of property. What would later be called "selective conscientious objection" was also at work among some Methodists, Anglicans, Congregationalists, and Baptists, who concluded that neither patriots nor loyalists convincingly demonstrated the necessity for conflict. A similar phenomenon occurred among some Reformed Presbyterians and Calvinist Baptists in the American South during the Civil War.

The most prominent voices raised against warfare in American history have come from the historically pacifist denominations. World War I proved a particular trial to Mennonites, Quakers, and the German Brethren, since it combined a universal draft with inflamed public sentiment. Members of newer American denominations, including Seventh-Day Adventists and some Pentecostals, also refused induction and support of the war effort in this same conflict. During World War II, the Selective Service System granted *conscientious objection to military service from members of the historic peace churches, but dealt more harshly with newer religious bodies. Members of the Jehovah's Witnesses, who refused both to register for the draft and to swear allegiance to the United States, met with especially severe reprisals. Definite enumerations are elusive, but as many as three-fourths of the perhaps 6,000 Americans imprisoned for failing to register for the draft or report for military service were Jehovah's Witnesses.

The Vietnam War, which began without the clear-cut call to arms that the attack on *Pearl Harbor provided for World War II, and which occurred during a period of cultural unrest, produced much religiously grounded opposition to warfare. Yet questions about the legality of this particular war, a resurgence of selective conscientious objection, and arguments for the recognition of conscientious objection not based on religion, at once magnified public debate concerning the morality of war and obscured specifically religious considerations.

Since the Vietnam period, historians have joined other academics in documenting the breadth and depth of antiwar sentiment in American history. Nonetheless, religious support for warfare, or the accommodation of religious beliefs to the exigencies of war, has been much more common in American history than religiously inspired rejection of war.

[See also Aggression and Violence; Berrigan, Daniel and Philip; Militarism and Antimilitarism; Patriotism; Peace and Antiwar Movements; Religion in the Military; Vietnam Antiwar Movement.]

• Bertram W. Korn, *American Jewry and the Civil War,* 1951; 2nd ed. 1976. George M. Frederickson, *The Inner Civil War,* 1965. Peter Brock, *Pacifism in the United States: From the Colonial Era to the First World War,* 1968. Nathan O. Hatch, *The Sacred Cause of Liberty: Republican Thought and the Millenium in Revolutionary New England,* 1977. George Marsden, *Fundamentalism and American Culture,* 1980. Ronald A. Wells, ed., *The Wars of America: Christian Views,* 1981. John F. Piper, Jr., *The American Churches in World War I,* 1985. Melvin B. Endy, Jr., "War and Peace," *Encyclopedia of the American Religious Experience,* 1988. Linda Colley, *Britons: Forging the Nation, 1707–1837,* 1992. Anne C. Rose, *Victorian America and the Civil War,* 1992. Richard J. Carwardine, *Evangelicals and Politics in Antebellum America,* 1993. Gerald Sittser, *A Cautious Patriotism: The American Churches and the Second World War,* 1997. Randall M. Miller, Henry S. Stout, and Charles R. Wilson, eds., *Religion and the American Civil War,* 1998. —Mark A. Noll

RELIGION IN THE MILITARY. For more than 220 years, religion and religious leaders have provided a source of strength and faith for a total of 55 million Americans who have served in the military forces of the United States. The rigorous demands of military duties—separation from friends and family, training in remote locations, battle, and the possibility of violent death—have mandated support for those who serve and who may potentially lay down their lives for their country.

The initial involvement of chaplains as voluntary, noncombatant religious leaders within the American military was an answer to the pressing needs of commanders and soldiers. Religion provided moral direction and spiritual assurance to those who bore the burden of the nation's wars. When George *Washington assumed command of the *Continental army on 2 July 1775, he found twenty-three regiments of soldiers, with fifteen chaplains among them, posted around Boston. From the service of the 220 chaplains of the *Revolutionary War to that of the 12,000 chaplains of World War II and the 5,000 U.S. Army, Navy, and Air Force chaplains who today perform pluralistic ministries at U.S. bases in 65 countries around the world, religion has been a traditional support and a guaranteed right for American military personnel.

The organization of the military chaplaincy began in July 1775, when the Continental Congress appropriated funds to pay officers in the army. Chaplains were authorized $20 a month. Chaplains received no military training, were not eligible for regular promotion above their pay grade of captain, wore no standardized *uniforms, and were endorsed by no particular ecclesiastical agency except the congregations and soldiers they served. After 1776, when Benjamin Balch became the first chaplain in the *Continental navy, chaplains performed their tasks on sea as well as on land.

With the advent of the *Civil War in 1861, ministry in the military widened its base. In 1862, the army authorized the first Jewish chaplains, the first African American chaplains, the first Native American chaplain, and the first hospital chaplains. The navy adopted the Latin cross as the cap insignia for Christian chaplains in 1863, the first faith-specific insignia approved for wear in the U.S. armed forces.

When 2,300 army chaplains volunteered for duty during the early months of World War I, it became clear to Gen. John J. *Pershing and to Congress that a large chaplaincy in a world conflict required more centralized direc-

tion than could be provided by unit commanders. In 1920, the National Defense Act reorganized the armed forces and provided for chiefs of chaplains to direct ministries in each of the services. President Woodrow *Wilson selected Chaplain John T. Axton as the first army chief of chaplains and Chaplain John B. Frazier as the first navy chief of chaplains. Although three chaplains had performed duty in the air service in 1918, it was not until after World War II that the air force chaplaincy was established as a separate service. President Harry S. *Truman appointed Chaplain Charles I. Carpenter the first air force chief in 1948.

Historically, American soldiers and sailors have reflected about the same degree of religious commitment as the civilian communities from which they came. Units that were recruited in areas characterized by strong religious institutions tended to include larger numbers of religious servicemen. In a U.S. Army survey taken in 1994, some 80 percent of the soldiers polled stated that they believed in God and had a specific religious preference. More than 100 religious denominations and faith groups were represented among soldiers, with Protestants and Roman Catholics constituting 85 percent of the total number. Chaplains from an equal number of separate denominations provided ministry for these soldiers.

Religious life in the military centers on opportunities for voluntary worship, counseling, religious education, moral leadership training, pastoral support, religious retreats, child and youth ministries, and holiday observances. Religious activities for military personnel, in garrison or in the field, are approved by the commander of the unit involved. The chaplain serves as a staff officer, qualified by education, ordination, and endorsement to implement the command religious program for the welfare of service members and their families, and to facilitate the free exercise of religion guaranteed to them by the First Amendment.

Worship services are held in a wide variety of settings. Military chapels, mess halls, decks of ships, aircraft hangars, tents, and open field assembly areas are frequently utilized. Chaplains may encourage service members to participate as lay readers, choir members, eucharistic ministers, and ushers, as well as in other roles. In combat, services are frequently conducted in small groups with abbreviated orders of worship. Most chaplains have combat kits available that contain worship supplies suitable for field services. Enlisted chaplain assistants in the army, chaplain service support personnel in the air force, and religious program specialists in the navy, Marine Corps, and Coast Guard assist chaplains in performing their duties.

Since 1973, when the navy commissioned Lt. Dianna Pohlman as its first female chaplain, women have provided increasing religious leadership in the military. By 1993, thirty female chaplains were serving on active duty in the army, navy, and air force. According to some estimates, women perform as much as 65 percent of the volunteer religious work accomplished on military installations.

Since 1775, more than 400 chaplains have given their lives for their country, 7 have been awarded the Congressional Medal of Honor, and hundreds have been decorated for bravery and outstanding service. Recent interest by former *Warsaw Pact countries in developing military chaplaincies based on the U.S. model may be evidence of the respect other nations have for the way religion functions in the American military establishment.

[*See also* Conscientious Objection; Culture, War, and the Military; Militarism and Antimilitarism; Religion and War.]

• Dom Aidan H. Germain, *Catholic Military and Naval Chaplains, 1776–1917*, 1929. Roy J. Honeywell, *Chaplains of the United States Army*, 1958. Daniel B. Jorgensen, *The Service of Chaplains to Army Air Units, 1917–1946*, 1961. Herman A. Norton, *Struggling for Recognition: The United States Army Chaplaincy, 1791–1865*, 1977. Clifford M. Drury, *The History of the Chaplain Corps, USN*, 2 vols., 1983. John E. Groh, "Lively Experiment: A Summary History of the Air Force Chaplaincy," *Military Chaplains' Review* (Winter 1990), pp. 67–114.   —John W. Brinsfield

RESERVE ASSOCIATIONS. *See* Armed Services Lobbying Associations.

RESERVE FORCES ACT (1955). President Dwight D. *Eisenhower's "New Look" defense strategy emphasized nuclear-armed air power, stronger reserve forces, and a greater reliance on conventionally-armed allies. To correct the weaknesses of all of the reserve components of the U.S. armed services, his administration convinced the Congress to pass the Reserve Forces Act of 1955. It amended the *Armed Forces Reserve Act of 1952 and the Universal Military Training and Service Act of 1951. The 1955 legislation increased the size of the Ready Reserve from 1.5 million to 2.9 million personnel and authorized the president to mobilize up to 1 million ready reservists in a declared national emergency without congressional action. For those who agreed to spend two years on active duty and four years in a reserve component, the total military commitment was reduced from eight to six years. The legislation required all those who entered the armed forces after 9 August 1955 to participate in reserve training following completion of active service and authorized specific sanctions for those who failed to participate. It also allowed direct enlistments in the reserve components for nonprior service youths as an alternative to the draft and established a system of continuous screening for members of the Ready Reserve to ensure their availability for active duty. The act did not authorize universal military training, mandatory basic training with the active forces for National Guard recruits, or authority to induct men into the reserve components if sufficient numbers could not be obtained voluntarily. Despite his own grave misgivings about those omissions, President Eisenhower signed the bill on 5 August 1955.

The 1955 act failed to produce the highly capable reserve forces its proponents envisioned. While the numbers of drill pay reservists and Guardsmen climbed dramatically, use of *conscription (or the threat of it) often filled the ranks with less than enthusiastic soldiers, sailors, Marines, and airmen. Funding, equipment, and training remained below par for most of the reserve components until the 1980s. To deal with that problem Secretary of Defense Robert S. *McNamara attempted to shrink the size of the nation's large reserve establishment and merge the federal reserve components of the army and air force into their National Guard counterparts in the early 1960s. When those efforts were blocked on Capitol Hill, he used his administrative authority to create a selected reserve force in each of the military services that was given priority access to training beyond what was normally authorized for Guard and reserve units. McNamara's program provided most of the nation's strategic military reserve in the continental United States while a growing portion of the active duty force was engaged in the *Vietnam War. Although successful, the program was shelved in the early 1970s for budgetary reasons.

With the elimination of the draft and the *Cold War's end, the Reserve Forces Act of 1955 lost much of its relevance. Although the basic legal structure of the reserve components remains unchanged, economics has replaced the draft as the principal incentive for providing reserve components manpower under the all-volunteer force. The president was granted additional authority by the Congress during the 1970s to involuntarily recall limited numbers of Guardsmen and reservists to active duty for specified periods without either a declaration of war or a national emergency. The size of the ready reserve had shrunk to barely over 1.45 million personnel by 30 September 1997 due to the end of the Cold War and cuts in defense expenditures.

[*See also* All-Volunteer Force.]

• Eileen Galloway, *History of U.S. Military Policy on Reserve Forces, 1775–1957*, 1957. Robert L. Goldich, "Historical Continuity in the U.S. Military Reserve System," *Armed Forces and Society*, Fall 1980, pp. 9–16. Charles J. Gross, *Prelude to the Total Force: The Air National Guard, 1943–1969*, 1985. Gerald T. Cantwell, *Citizen Airmen: A History of the Air Force Reserve, 1946–1994*, 1997. "Reserve Component Programs: The Annual Report of the Reserve Forces Policy Board," Office of the Secretary of Defense, March 1998.   —Charles J. Gross

RESERVE OFFICER TRAINING CORPS. *See* ROTC.

REVENUE CUTTER SERVICE. *See* Coast Guard, U.S.

REVOLUTIONARY WAR (1775–83)

Causes
Military and Diplomatic Course
Domestic Course
Postwar Impact
Changing Interpretations

REVOLUTIONARY WAR (1775–83): CAUSES

The roots of the Revolutionary War ran deep in the structure of the British empire, an entity transformed, like the British state itself, by the Anglo-French wars of the eighteenth century. After the fourth of these conflicts, the Seven Years' (or *French and Indian) War, the British government tried to reform the now greatly expanded empire. The American colonists resisted, creating a series of crises that culminated in the armed rebellion of 1775.

The Imperial Background. With the Glorious Revolution (1688), England's foreign policy took the anti-French path it followed until 1815—a path that led to four wars before 1775. These conflicts spawned a British nationalism with powerfully anti-Catholic overtones. They also transformed the British state into the most powerful fiscal-military agency in Europe.

Britain's greatest weapon was its funded national debt, which harnessed private savings to military ends. British financiers, managing the joint stock corporations—the Bank of England, the South Seas Company, the East India Company—loaned the government money in wartime; the government used postwar tax revenues to pay interest on what became a perpetual debt. The demand for revenues stimulated the growth of another fiscal engine, the Treasury. A "Real Whig" (or "Country") political ideology emerged, which denounced this powerful state as the enemy of liberty, stressed the dangers of standing armies, and insisted that consent to taxation was the property holder's sole bulwark against "enslavement" by would-be tyrants in the government. "Country" ideology dominated the language of political opposition, but barely slowed the growth of the state. Each war's demands—and the stability of a securities market underwritten by tax monies—overrode the objections of those who feared expansion of state power.

The third Anglo-French War (1739–48) brought America back in to British strategic calculations for the first time. New England colonists attacked Canada, conquering Louisbourg, the naval base that controlled access to the St. Lawrence. This prevented French reinforcement and resupply, and would have led to the conquest of Canada, had not merchants in Albany traded overland with Québec and kept New York neutral in the fighting. This independent foreign policy outraged British administrators, especially Lord Halifax. Between 1748 and 1754, Halifax and his associates at the Board of Trade planned reforms to ensure that in future wars the empire would function as a unit.

The Seven Years' War (1754–63) Destabilizes Imperial Relations. The French and Indian War, which became the Seven Years' War in Europe, created unprecedented problems of finance and control for Britain. In the war's early years, before 1758, the colonists traded with the enemy and refused to pay for British military operations. The ministry of William Pitt (1757–61) solved the first problem by offering to reimburse the colonies for part of their war expenses; the second solved itself as Britain conquered French colonies in Canada and the Caribbean. Pitt's victories and policies, however, doubled the national debt and made his successor determined to contain costs and reform the empire.

Beginning with George Grenville in 1763, a series of British ministers tightened the bonds of empire while trying to spread some of the costs of imperial defense to the colonies. They revived Halifax's plans to increase metropolitan supervision over imperial trade and the internal polities of the colonies, but also responded to the urgent legacies of war. As early as 1762, Whitehall planned to station fifteen regular army battalions permanently in America, with the colonists paying the bill. When the Peace of Paris in 1763 added all France's holdings east of the Mississippi River to the empire, the army became the de facto administrator of the conquests.

Ministerial efforts to stamp out illegal trade (which resumed after the peace treaty returned to France its richest sugar islands) coincided with attempts to subordinate the colonies to the metropolis. Colonists who believed that Anglo-American cooperation and shared sacrifice had achieved the victory were outraged, and the patriotic fervor of the war evaporated in the face of postwar reforms. Chaos ensued when Parliament tried to extract money directly from the colonies with the Stamp Act of 1765.

The Stamp Act protests expressed outrage at British control. Adapting "Real Whig" ideology to their own needs, Americans insisted that as long as they remained unrepresented in the House of Commons, Britain had no right to tax them; submission to taxation without consent would enslave the colonists to whatever faction controlled Parliament. In the face of virtual anarchy, Parliament repealed the Stamp Act in March 1766, but rejected the American understanding of taxation. According to British constitutional conceptions, taxation was a function of sovereignty (the state's ultimate power to take property and life), which the Glorious Revolution had vested in the king in Parliament. Parliament made its claims explicit by asserting its sovereignty over the colonies in a Declaratory Act that preceded the Stamp Act repeal.

After 1766, Parliament searched for ways to assert its authority. A new set of trade regulations and taxes, the Townshend Duties—named for Chancellor of the Exchequer Charles Townshend, one-time protégé of Lord Halifax—aroused a second wave of colonial opposition beginning in 1767. Deliberation and nonviolence marked this phase of resistance as radical leaders in several provinces clarified American political principles and promoted intercolonial cooperation. The result, a reasonably effective boycott of British imports in 1769, demonstrated the colonies' ability to dispense with the empire.

Unable to retreat in any way that would grant the validity of colonial arguments, Parliament in the spring of 1770 opted (at the urging of a new prime minister, Lord North) to repeal all but one of the Townshend Duties. Retaining a single tax, on tea, kept up Parliament's claim to authority while conciliating the colonists. This concession came none too soon.

On 5 March 1770, the same day North proposed partial repeal in Parliament, a squad of British soldiers fired into a taunting Boston crowd, killing five men. Troops had garrisoned Boston since October 1768 to protect customs officials, and had encountered little opposition before this so-called "*Boston Massacre." To people who accepted the "Real Whig" maxim that standing armies were tyrants' tools, the "massacre" proved Britain's determination to rule by force. In the face of uncontrollable riots, Gen. Thomas *Gage, the British commander in chief, handed over the soldiers for trial and withdrew the troops from Boston.

Before trials could be held, news arrived of the partial repeal of the Townshend Duties. Merchants jumped at the chance to end the unprofitable boycott; by fall, when the juries returned verdicts of manslaughter against two soldiers and acquitted the rest, the nonimportation movement had dissolved. The colonists continued to boycott tea, but otherwise business as usual resumed within the empire.

Yet business as usual in 1771 was not what it had been in 1750. The conquests—Canada, East and West Florida, and the vast trans-Appalachian realm that stretched to the Mississippi—beckoned land-hungry Britons and colonists alike. The Proclamation of 1763, the crown's attempt to separate white settlement from Indian country by a line drawn at the crest of the Appalachians, had failed; western army units had been withdrawn to the seaboard colonies until by late 1771 only one significant detachment remained, in Illinois. Squatters swarmed into the Ohio Valley, and Indian-white relations drifted ever closer to war.

The growing chaos in the west revealed an empire in disarray. Yet empires can exist for centuries in decayed forms without creating revolutions, and British authority in North America might merely have declined indefinitely had not seeds of imperial conflict, planted by the Seven Years' War, borne fruit.

The Tea Crisis and the Dissolution of Empire: 1773–75. British army and naval forces, together with the

East India Company's private army, had seized France's East Indian trading stations during the war; thereafter, the company opportunistically gained control of northeastern India. The costs of government and defense, however, outran the company's revenues, and by 1773 it faced bankruptcy. This would wreck British financial markets, but the Treasury had no funds to bail the company out. The only solution was to turn the company's vast inventory of tea into money, so the ministry granted the company a monopoly on tea sales in America.

But colonists saw the Tea Act of 1773 as an effort to force them to consume a taxed commodity, and no colonial port would allow the tea to be landed. Bostonians actually destroyed three shiploads on 16 December 1773, an action that goaded North's ministry into regarrisoning Boston and proposing a set of Coercive Acts. As passed by Parliament in May and early June 1774, these measures closed the port of Boston until the town paid for the tea; rewrote the Massachusetts charter to give the governor great power over local affairs and protect royal officials—including soldiers—from prosecution in colony courts; and authorized the quartering of troops in private homes. General Gage was appointed governor of the province.

Meanwhile, Parliament also tried to sort out the problems in the west by attaching much of trans-Appalachia to the province of Quebec. The Quebec Act protected Roman Catholicism within the province and sanctioned French legal procedures in its courts, which made it look as if thousands of western settlers would be governed by a cryptopapist regime. The Protestant colonists lumped the Quebec Act and the Coercive Acts together as "Intolerable Acts" and resolved to stand fast.

The result was the most effective intercolonial resistance movement yet. On 5 September 1774, representatives of the colonies convened in a Continental Congress to protest the Intolerable Acts and create a nonimportation measure called the Continental Association. The association empowered local committees of safety to enforce the agreement, creating a crude intercolonial union and vesting police powers in radical hands. Agreeing to meet again on 10 May 1775 if the British government had not yet repealed the Intolerable Acts, Congress adjourned on 26 October.

By then, Massachusetts patriots had created an extralegal government called the Provincial Congress, taken control of the province's arms, and organized self-defense forces. The ministry ordered General Gage to take military action to forestall rebellion. Receiving these orders too late to capture the Provincial Congress, Gage tried to seize munitions stockpiled at Concord. This triggered the Battles of *Lexington and Concord on 19 April 1775, and grew into a general New England uprising. When Congress reconvened on 10 May, its only alternatives were to disavow rebellion and disband or to take control of the incipient war on behalf of all thirteen colonies. It chose the latter course, adopting the New England forces as a *Continental army and appointing George *Washington as commander in chief on 15 June 1775. Although it would be a year before the colonies declared independence from Britain, the Revolutionary War had begun.

• Bernard Bailyn, *The Ideological Origins of the American Revolution*, 1965. John Shy, *Toward Lexington*, 1965. Merrill Jensen, *The Founding of a Nation*, 1968. Pauline Maier, *From Resistance to Revolution*, 1972. P. D. G. Thomas, *British Politics and the Stamp Act Crisis*, 1975. P. D. G. Thomas, *The Townshend Duties Crisis*, 1987. John

Brewer, *The Sinews of Power*, 1989. P. D. G. Thomas, *Tea Party to Independence*, 1991. Linda Colley, *Britons: Forging the Nation, 1707–1837*, 1992. Thomas Fleming, *Liberty! The American Revolution*, 1997.
—Fred Anderson

REVOLUTIONARY WAR (1775–83): MILITARY AND DIPLOMATIC COURSE

In proportion to contemporary population and wealth, the Revolutionary War destroyed more lives and property than any American conflict except the *Civil War; in duration it exceeded all American wars until the one in Vietnam. It was also highly complex. It was a civil war, a war for political independence, and finally a European war conducted on a global scale. Only as a struggle for independence could it be said to have had merely two sides. As a civil war, its active parties were British and German ("Hessian") regulars, American loyalist militias, and British-allied Indians, who fought American patriot regulars (the *Continental army), American patriot militias, and some American-allied Indians. The uncommitted, however, comprised approximately two-fifths of the population, and the outcome of the war ultimately depended on them. As a European conflict and a worldwide war for empire, Britain opposed the United States, France, Spain, and the Netherlands. American social conditions and British strategy shaped the course and determined the outcome of the civil war; but logistical and diplomatic factors governed the war's global phase, and these would strongly influence the nature of American independence.

By 1775, the population of British North America was doubling every twenty-six years. High birth rates and heavy immigration bespoke easily available land, widely distributed among the farming population. The colonists' dispersion and ethnic diversity helped produce the fragmentation and political instability that became pronounced as populations spread westward after the *French and Indian War (known in Britain as the Seven Years' War). The easy availability of land weakened American elites; lacking the ability to live off rents, gentlemen also lacked a secure economic and political base. The southern colonies had stable aristocracies, based on slave ownership; but even the greatest planters lived in fear of slave rebellions. Nor did colonial institutions create stability: governments were small, poor, unbureaucratized, and lacked permanent constabularies; neither a unified market economy nor a universally established church existed. Institutional weakness magnified American parochialism, and most colonists were suspicious of any authority not rooted in their own localities. Americans both distrusted and envied Europe, emulating British styles and institutions while resenting British sophistication. As provincials, colonists saw themselves as morally superior, yet culturally inferior, to the English.

British officers who had served in America during the Seven Years' War believed these conditions made Americans leaderless, lazy, and militarily ineffectual. Remembering the high rates of desertion and mutiny among provincial troops in 1755–60, in 1775 British commanders assumed a lack of toughness in the rebels, who—they thought—would collapse at the first application of force.

A CIVIL WAR AND A WAR FOR INDEPENDENCE: 1775–78

Popular Insurrection and a Failed Police Action: 1775–76. From the tea crisis of 1774 through the evacuation of Boston in March 1776, the British faced massive popular resistance among New Englanders. Insofar as even patriot leaders lagged behind public opinion after the so-called "Intolerable Acts," it is not surprising that the British commander in chief, Gen. Thomas *Gage, failed to understand that the thousands of men who turned out on 19 April 1775 were not armed mobs, but property holders and their sons, who represented communities convinced that the British intended to enslave them. So popular was the rebellion that within a week of the Battles of *Lexington and Concord, 20,000 New England militiamen were besieging the British in Boston, without anyone ordering them to do it.

When news of the fighting in Massachusetts reached the Second Continental Congress at Philadelphia, the delegates assumed responsibility for the New England militia—which on 15 June they designated a *Continental army—and appointed a commander in chief from Virginia, George *Washington. Provincials to the core, the delegates wanted a European-style regular army to conduct a civilized war. The last thing they—or Washington—wanted was for *guerrilla warfare to continue.

Meanwhile, Gage and his officers assumed that they were conducting a police action against agitator-inspired mobs. Thus, when the Americans fortified a Charlestown hilltop on 17 June, the British decided to attack frontally. As Maj. Gen. John *Burgoyne explained, they believed government authority "depends in a great measure upon the idea that trained troops are invincible against any numbers or any position of untrained rabble; and this idea was a little in suspense since the 19th of April." The ensuing carnage and the realization that the rabble had not dispersed, but reorganized, compelled the British to reassess their assumptions. Between the Battle of *Bunker Hill and the evacuation of Boston (17 March 1776), British commanders lost the illusion that they were involved in a police action, and the British ministry replaced Gage with Gen. William *Howe, who understood the war as a confrontation between opposing armies. Howe's plans for 1776 ushered in the second stage of the war, which would last until Burgoyne's defeat at the Battles of *Saratoga (September and October 1777).

Conventional War and Failed Negotiations: 1776–77. Howe moved his base of operations in New York to regain the initiative against Washington. If he thrashed the rebel army, he reasoned, most Americans would return to the imperial fold; as popular enthusiasm waned, Congress would become willing to make peace. Howe wanted negotiation more than outright victory because he was not only commander in chief but (together with his brother, Adm. Lord Richard Howe) peace commissioner in America. This schizoid role handicapped him both as military leader and as diplomat; yet events of summer and fall 1776 suggested that he would succeed.

After the British evacuated Boston, defeats and disaster filled the rest of 1776. The army Congress had sent to invade Canada in June 1775 collapsed in the summer of 1776. After capturing Montréal, the Continentals failed to take Québec, and were forced to raise their siege when British reinforcements arrived by ship in May. By July, the Americans had retreated to Lake Champlain and—desperately hoping to slow the advance of Gen. Guy Carleton's powerful army on New York—built a small fleet of gunboats. At the Battle of Valcour Island (10 October 1776), Brig. Gen. Benedict *Arnold succeeded in stalling Car-

leton's invasion, but had to withdraw to Fort Ticonderoga.

Meanwhile, the fervor of 1775 faded as General Washington tried to transform the Continentals into a regular army capable of holding New York against Howe. He had less than 20,000 troops on Long Island, Manhattan, and the lower Hudson on 25 June 1776 when Howe landed at Staten Island. Howe tried first to negotiate, but found that Congress's representatives, Benjamin Franklin and John *Adams, would settle for nothing less than independence. Howe then used his 32,000 troops, together with his brother's fleet and 10,000 sailors, to drive Washington off Long Island (27–30 August). Following him to Manhattan in mid-September, Howe attacked again in October, compelling Washington to withdraw to White Plains. In November, Howe captured the critical posts of Fort Washington, New York, and Fort Lee, New Jersey. Washington retreated across New Jersey with a disintegrating army. He crossed the Delaware on 7 December with perhaps 5,000 troops fit for duty, and most of their enlistments would expire on 31 December.

Howe's strategy seemed to have worked brilliantly. The Continental army was collapsing; colonists in New York and New Jersey were eagerly swearing allegiance to the king, provisioning his forces, and enlisting in loyalist units. Howe saw popular support for the Revolution evaporating and assumed that Congress would soon negotiate. Yet two features of his campaign were about to produce the opposite effect. First, Howe's troops—particularly the Hessians and the loyalist irregulars—had handled civilian populations roughly. Every incident of rape and theft helped to crystallize popular opposition. Second, on 13 December, Howe sent his men into winter quarters, scattering them across central New Jersey in small cantonments—and thus exposing them to attack.

Venturing everything, Washington used what was left of his army to attack enemy units at Trenton, in late December 1776, and Princeton, in January 1777, and thus began to restore Continental morale. Howe, realizing the mistake of dispersing his units, reconcentrated them in the Lower Raritan Valley, allowing patriot militia to regain control of the province and nullify his recent successes. Howe did not yet see how counterproductive his approach had been, however, and planned to pursue Washington through Pennsylvania in 1777. The ministry, meanwhile, authorized Burgoyne to renew the invasion from Canada. Howe and Burgoyne assumed that loyalist support would emerge wherever the redcoats appeared. They were mistaken.

Burgoyne captured Fort Ticonderoga on 5 July, then pursued the fleeing Continentals through the woods south of Lake Champlain rather than proceeding to the Upper Hudson Valley via Lake George. Reaching the Hudson, he found that his Indian and Hessian allies had turned New Yorkers against him. When the supplies and loyalist supporters he expected never materialized, he found himself trapped. The northern Continental army under Maj. Gen. Horatio *Gates, reinforced by militiamen from New England and New York, defeated Burgoyne at the two Battles of Saratoga (17 September and 5 October 1777). On 17 October, he signed a Convention that allowed him to return to England, but left his army prisoner. Saratoga cost the British over 6,000 casualties and captives. The prisoners of war, called the Convention army, were shifted from colony to colony for the rest of the war.

Meanwhile, Howe defeated Washington in Pennsylvania

at the Battle of the Brandywine (11 September 1777), but again failed to destroy his army. He seized Philadelphia at the end of September. Washington counterattacked unsuccessfully at Germantown (4 October), then lost the Delaware River forts that commanded Philadelphia's water approaches (15–21 November). Unlike the previous year, defeat did not threaten to dissolve the army, which went into winter quarters at Valley Forge on 11 December. Thanks to Friedrich Wilhelm von *Steuben, who improved the army's training during the winter, and to Nathanael *Greene, who as quartermaster general reformed the supply system, the Continentals emerged from Valley Forge tougher and better organized than ever.

Thus, Howe's conventional war strategy failed again. Congress refused to negotiate; redcoat, loyalist, and Hessian abuse of civilians reanimated popular resistance; and patriot militiamen controlled whatever territory the British could not occupy.

Howe failed because he misinterpreted civilian attitudes. What he took for incipient loyalism was no more than the reluctance of many Americans—in the Middle Colonies probably a majority—to take sides. He never understood how the very arrival of the British army (and especially its loyalist, Hessian, and Indian auxiliaries) drove neutrals into alliance with the patriots. By contrast, Washington used enormous restraint in dealing with civilians, refusing to confiscate food and clothing even when his men at Valley Forge were starving. Above all, he deferred to Congress's wishes in order to demonstrate the army's subordination to civil authority.

State governments employed their militia forces with similar restraint. On the whole, prosecutors and militia units tolerated neutral behavior as a manifestation of localism, not loyalism. Knowing that Americans distrusted centralized power, they required only minimal support: anyone who paid his taxes, kept his mouth shut, and turned up for militia duty would be left alone. The practice of allowing men drafted for military duty to hire substitutes, and the parsimonious, quasi-legal use of force in making examples of notorious Tories helped win the acquiescence, if not the hearts and minds, of neutrals. Finally, governments retained the goodwill of property holders by hesitating to confiscate supplies for the army. This restraint had two effects: the Continental army remained chronically undermanned and undersupplied; and neutrals were not driven to loyalism.

THE FRENCH ALLIANCE AND A WORLD WAR: 1778–83

Turning Point: 1777–78. Howe's indecisive campaign and Burgoyne's spectacular defeat convinced the French, who heretofore had offered only covert aid, to enter into open alliance with the United States. Congress had first sent delegates to Paris in 1776; Benjamin Franklin and his colleagues had raised money and publicized America's cause, but France's foreign minister, the comte de Vergennes, had remained cautious. The events of 1777, however, changed his mind. On 17 December 1777, France recognized the United States diplomatically, and soon thereafter it presented drafts of two treaties to the American commissioners. The first of these, the Treaty of Amity and Commerce, offered the United States preferential trading privileges in France. The second, the Treaty of Alliance, was to take effect at the beginning of hostilities between France and Britain; it promised that France would not press any fur-

ther claims to Canada, would refrain from negotiating peace with Britain on any grounds other than American independence, and guaranteed to the United States any territories French troops might conquer in North America during the war. Signed on 6 February 1778, both treaties were ratified in Congress on 4 May 1778.

Hoping to nullify the alliance, the British ministry dispatched the earl of Carlisle to negotiate with Congress. The Carlisle Commission could promise anything short of independence, but Congress would settle for no less. While Carlisle made overtures until November 1778 and military activity in North America came to a standstill, naval warfare broke out between France and Britain. War in Europe transformed a colonial fight for independence into a larger—ultimately worldwide—struggle that the British could not win.

From June 1778 onward, the British had to defend the home islands against invasion, protect Gibraltar, and shield the valuable, vulnerable West Indian sugar islands (especially Jamaica) from attack. This meant that Howe's successor, Gen. Henry *Clinton, would have fewer men and bigger logistical problems than ever, and that he could no longer assume the Royal Navy's superiority in American waters. His response, a new strategy, reflected these new circumstances, as well as his estimate of American social conditions.

Conquest, Pacification, and Civil War in the South: 1778–81. Clinton knew that in Georgia and South Carolina, low country rice planters lived in fear that their slaves (two-thirds of the population) would rebel, and that long-standing animosities divided lowland whites from the poorer, more numerous backcountry farmers. This convinced him that his best hope of victory lay in the Lower South; he also understood that to retain control of even this region, he would have to win the support, or at least the compliance, of the uncommitted population. Clinton therefore decided to move the war to the South, using loyalist units *not* as auxiliaries in conventional operations, but as pacification forces. Once the regulars cleared the countryside of rebels, loyalist units would organize local self-defense forces to keep the patriot militia at bay. When law and order had been established, they would hand control over to civilians, who would reinstitute civil government under crown auspices.

Pacification began promisingly with the invasion of Georgia in the winter of 1778–79. Savannah fell to a 3,500-man British force under Lt. Col. Archibald Campbell on 29 December 1778; hundreds of Georgians volunteered as loyalist irregulars, and quickly garrisoned what the regulars conquered. Redcoats took Augusta on 29 January 1779, then stood off two Continental attempts to retake the town. American forces withdrew to Charleston. By the end of July 1779, royal government had been reinstituted under a civilian governor. A Franco-American force under Admiral d'Estaing and Maj. Gen. Benjamin Lincoln besieged Savannah in October 1779, but d'Estaing soon withdrew to the West Indies and Lincoln returned to Charleston. Georgia became Clinton's base for carrying the war to South Carolina.

The invasion began in the spring of 1780 with a spectacular success: Clinton came from New York with over 8,000 men to direct the campaign, trapping Lincoln in Charleston, which fell on 12 May. The surrender of Lincoln's 2,600-man garrison obliterated the Continental presence in the Lower South. Clinton established outposts throughout the countryside and recruited loyalists to hold them, making every effort to avoid repeating past mistakes. After forbidding looting and appointing an inspector general to keep the loyalists in line, he left Charleston in early summer, taking a third of his troops back to New York.

Clinton did not know it, but his pacification program would engulf the Lower South in a sanguinary civil war. He had already alienated most of the planter gentry by encouraging slaves to run away to the British lines and offering them refuge; he even permitted a black unit, the Carolina Corps, to be formed of ex-slaves, alarming Southern whites fully as much as Burgoyne had alarmed New Yorkers by employing Indians as auxiliaries. Thus even before he left for New York, Clinton had begun to alienate would-be neutrals, and had given patriot planters a reason not to lay down their arms and sit out the remainder of the war. The bands of patriot partisans who retreated to the swamps and mountains could no more be rooted out than the loyalists could be restrained from settling old scores. Patriot irregulars like Thomas Sumter and Francis Marion made terrorist attacks on loyalists and regular detachments, and the Tory legions of Banastre Tarleton and Patrick Ferguson answered terror with terror. Patriot militiamen, for example, massacred many of Ferguson's loyalists after the Battle of *King's Mountain (7 October 1780), retaliating for Tarleton's earlier massacre of patriots at the Battle of Waxhaws (29 May); these were, however, only the best known atrocities in a savage guerrilla war.

Loyalist attacks swelled patriot ranks with former neutrals throughout the backcountry during the summer and fall of 1780. Meanwhile in the low country, Clinton's policy of encouraging slaves to run away brought tens of thousands of them to British camps in search of freedom. Planters lost sympathy with the British as their labor forces vanished. By year's end, pacification was doomed in low country and backcountry alike. Clinton was perhaps the last to know. Back in New York he expected an attack by the French fleet and an expeditionary force under the comte de Rochambeau, France's new commander in chief in America.

Clinton had left behind about 8,000 men under the command of Lord Charles *Cornwallis, whose inability to control a chaotic region intensified his dislike of Clinton and pacification. He preferred action, and with a field army of about 4,000 men responded decisively when a Continental force under Horatio Gates attempted to invade South Carolina. After routing Gates at the Battle of Camden (16 August 1780), Cornwallis concentrated on defeating the next Continental general to appear, Nathanael Greene.

Greene assumed command of a shattered Continental force at Charlotte, North Carolina, on 2 December 1780, and immediately took the offensive. He daringly divided his 2,000 Continentals and militiamen into two bodies, taking about 1,500 men under his own command and assigning the rest to Brig. Gen. Daniel *Morgan. Morgan struck southwest into the backcountry and defeated Tarleton's loyalist legion at the Battle of *Cowpens, 17 January 1781; then he retreated to North Carolina and rejoined Greene at the Catawba River. Cornwallis gave chase; Greene withdrew northeastward toward the Dan River, near the Virginia border. Cornwallis lacked the boats to cross the Dan and halted on 17 February 1781, turning to-

ward Hillsborough to replenish his provisions. Greene crossed back into North Carolina and sent detachments to harass his enemy. On 25 February 1781, the cavalry legion of Lt. Col. Henry *Lee ("Light-Horse Harry") annihilated a loyalist unit at the Haw River, leading Cornwallis's loyalists to abandon him. When Greene finally joined forces on 15 March at the Battle of *Guilford Courthouse, Cornwallis had just 1,600 redcoats to attack 4,450 Continentals and militia.

Cornwallis's superbly disciplined regulars carried the day at Guilford, but a third were killed or wounded while Greene sustained losses of perhaps 10 percent. Cornwallis headed for Wilmington, where he could be resupplied by sea. After a brief rest, he marched north to Virginia. There he hoped to trap the Continentals of the marquis de *Lafayette, who had been fencing with a 3,000-man British force under the turncoat American general, Benedict Arnold. (Arnold had accepted a British command and a large payment in return for his promise to hand over the fortress of West Point, New York, in 1780. The plot failed, but Arnold escaped to fight for the British.) Arnold had picked up substantial loyalist support, and Cornwallis convinced himself that taking Virginia would somehow secure the Carolinas and Georgia. Greene, he assumed, would move to support Lafayette.

But Greene returned to South Carolina and attacked the scattered British garrisons there. Thus, while Cornwallis pursued Lafayette, British commanders in South Carolina and Georgia found themselves forced to withdraw to the coastal enclaves of Wilmington, Charleston, and Savannah. Behind them, patriot militia units reasserted control over the countryside.

Clinton sent troops from New York, giving Cornwallis over 7,000 men to bring Lafayette's 1,200 Continentals (and variable numbers of militiamen) to bay. When Lafayette refused to be trapped, Cornwallis used cavalry units and loyalist auxiliaries to attack rebel property. The more successful these raids were—and some, like Tarleton's Charlottesville raid in June and his 400-mile swing through the Southside in July, were spectacular—the more Lafayette's support grew. Reinforced by Continentals from Pennsylvania, Lafayette shadowed Cornwallis down the York peninsula in August, as he moved to establish a base with access to the sea: Yorktown.

After three years of bungled or thwarted operations, the French Navy finally exerted a decisive effect on land operations. From the beginning of the alliance, French admirals had preferred to cruise the Caribbean whenever possible; they entered North American waters only when the hurricane season made West Indian operations hazardous. Rochambeau's expeditionary force, in America since July 1780, had so far sat in Newport, Rhode Island. Washington and Rochambeau had planned to attack New York, but the arrival of Admiral de Grasse's fleet and the news that Cornwallis had moved to Yorktown changed everything. When de Grasse announced that he would operate in the Chesapeake until 15 October, Washington decided to trap Cornwallis. He marched south with half his army and most of the French expeditionary force on 20 August. On 14 September, he joined forces with Lafayette on the York Peninsula.

De Grasse had already debarked troops and sailed back to the bay's entrance. There, on 5 September, he met the British fleet of Adm. Thomas Graves. In the ensuing battle off the Chesapeake Capes, de Grasse repelled Grave's fleet, inflicting damage that forced it back to New York. This decided the outcome of the campaign, and—in a sense—the war. Within days, Admiral de Barras's squadron arrived from Newport with supplies and siege artillery. Cornwallis was doomed.

The Franco-American army marched to Yorktown on 28 September and prepared to lay siege. Formal operations opened on 6 October and lasted until Cornwallis had endured a week of bombardment. When he surrendered on 20 October, the allies took charge of a quarter of the British army in America—8,000 troops—and a mountain of equipment.

The Battle of *Yorktown did not deal a death blow to British military strength, but it made the ministry's position in Parliament untenable. The prime minister, Lord North, had long hoped to resign; he left office early in 1782. Clinton was recalled and replaced by Gen. Guy Carleton. Pressed by demands in other theaters, Whitehall suspended military activity in America.

Endgame: 1782–83. Carleton reached New York in May 1782 and ended offensive operations until the political settlement could be negotiated in Europe. The British had already abandoned Wilmington (January 1782); they would soon evacuate Savannah (July) and Charleston (December). Washington observed Carleton from his Hudson River fortifications, but took no further action.

Meanwhile, the war went from bad to worse for Britain. Following Yorktown, de Grasse had sailed up the Caribbean, where he seized Nevis, St. Christopher, and Montserrat. In April 1782, he threatened the grandest prize of all, Jamaica; and although Adm. George Romney thwarted that attempt in a battle off the Isles des Saintes near Guadeloupe, it remained possible that a combined Franco-Spanish force would mount a new invasion once the hurricane season had passed. Spain, indeed, had become a critical actor in the war. Following the declaration of war in June 1779, Spanish forces had attacked British posts in West Florida, taking Natchez (5 October 1779), Mobile (14 March 1780), and Pensacola (8 May 1781). Worse, from Britain's perspective, was Spain's conquest of Minorca (5 February 1782) and its repeated threats to Gibraltar. After blockading the fortress in 1779–80 and 1781–82, Spanish naval and land forces besieged it in 1782, trying to storm it in September. The attack failed, but Spain could still seal the straits and starve out the garrison. Finally, Dutch trade had been so valuable to America, Spain, and France that the British had declared war against Holland in December 1780. Dutch belligerency made it virtually impossible for the Royal Navy to operate in the North Sea and raised the possibility that Holland's East Indies fleet would aid the French against British forces in India, where by 1782 the situation looked grave.

Peace commissioners met in Paris as early as April 1782, but only in October did Britain's representatives agree to recognize American independence. Thereafter, the U.S. commissioners—Benjamin Franklin, John Adams, and John Jay—quickly agreed on articles with the British. The French, nearly bankrupt, were also willing to make peace, having revenged the humiliation of 1763 by depriving Britain of thirteen valuable colonies. Spain, however, refused to parley while it might still take Gibraltar, and it was not until 20 January 1783 that preliminary articles were signed. On 4 February, Britain announced the cessation of hostilities. Congress ratified the treaty on 15 April; the formal articles were concluded at the Peace of Paris on 3 September.

The peace treaty strongly favored the United States. Britain recognized American independence, agreed to boundaries between the Great Lakes and the 31st parallel as far west as the Mississippi River, recognized American fishing rights off Newfoundland, and promised to evacuate its posts on American territory "with all convenient speed." The United States in turn agreed to pay all debts due to British creditors and compensate loyalists for their confiscated property. The states proved slow to compensate the loyalists, and the British retained posts in the Northwest until 1796; but in other respects the peace restored amity with remarkable speed, given the length and ferocity of the war.

It was not British benevolence but desperation that accounted for the character of the Peace of Paris. Reeling militarily and isolated diplomatically, Britain faced severe financial peril and a public sick of war. In the end, Britain made peace on generous terms because it needed to trade with its former colonies, just as the United States—bankrupt and facing economic collapse—needed to reestablish the commercial connections war had severed.

Wherever the British army went between 1775 and 1781, it invariably alienated the people whose support it needed most, the neutrals. When the fighting started in 1775, only New England had a patriot majority; elsewhere, local minorities of armed patriots intimidated smaller loyalist minorities, and most colonists avoided committing themselves. No British commander in chief ever found a way to turn the neutrals into active supporters—or keep his troops from providing endless object lessons in British "tyranny."

Thus, over a long and bitter war, the neutrals dwindled in number everywhere. No matter how many battles the British army won, it could not maintain control—and protect its supporters—outside of ports like New York, Charleston, and Savannah. Whenever the army left an area, its collaborators had to choose between fleeing as refugees and remaining to face the patriot militias that reasserted control as soon as the last redcoat had departed. Clinton's recognition of this pattern led both to his southern pacification plan and to the opening of the war's most destructive phase, which nullified the promise of his strategy. Even before Yorktown, Americans were war-weary; but even the most apathetic of them could see that the British government would never sustain its presence in America, and sooner or later the patriots would return. Thus the war educated Americans in the practical politics of self-interest and survival. Ultimately, the neutrals, and many loyalists, chose patriot rule over exile.

This is not to minimize the role of republican ideology in influencing the shape of Revolutionary events, but only to contextualize it. Far from being an autonomous intellectual construct, revolutionary republicanism was a dynamic ideological response to changing conditions, and was itself shaped by the war—particularly insofar as the coercion of populations by armed force gave immediate meaning to the concept of tyranny and encouraged patriot leaders to take stringent steps toward subordinating military to civil authority in the postwar era.

Nor does the recognition of the war as decisively shaped by social factors diminish the importance of French intervention. Even in the indecisive first years of the alliance, the French Navy denied the Royal Navy supremacy on the Atlantic, making the American war difficult to sustain; French matériel and money enabled the Continental army to survive overwhelming difficulties. By denying Cornwallis his escape route, the French Fleet allowed a Franco-American army to besiege Yorktown; French cannon, fired from emplacements laid out by French engineers, persuaded Cornwallis to surrender. The imminent threat of further losses to French, Spanish, and Dutch forces gave British opposition politicians sufficient leverage to end the war. French participation thus determined when and how the war ended; but it did not make the difference between winning and losing for the British. American society itself had rendered the Revolutionary War a fight that Britain could not win.

• Christopher Ward, *The War of the Revolution*, 1952. Piers Mackesy, *The War for America, 1775–1783*, 1964. Mark Mayo Boatner III, *Encyclopedia of the American Revolution*, 1966. Don Higginbotham, *The War of American Independence*, 1971. John Shy, ed., *A People Numerous and Armed*, 1976. Charles Royster, *A Revolutionary People at War*, 1979. Ronald Hoffman, et al., eds., *Diplomacy and Revolution*, 1981. James Kirby Martin and Mark Lender, *A Respectable Army*, 1982. Robert Middlekauff, *The Glorious Cause*, 1982. Ronald Hoffman, et al., eds., *Arms and Independence*, 1984. Jonathan R. Dull, *A Diplomatic History of the American Revolution*, 1985. Ronald Hoffman, et al., eds., *An Uncivil War*, 1985. Ronald Hoffman, et al., eds., *Peace and Peacemakers*, 1986. John Ferling, ed., *The World Turned Upside Down*, 1988. Don Higginbotham, ed., *War and Society in Revolutionary America*, 1988. Russell F. Weigley, *The Age of Battles*, 1991.   —Fred Anderson

REVOLUTIONARY WAR (1775–1783): DOMESTIC COURSE

The War of Independence, the *Pennsylvania Centinel* suggested in 1785, had removed that "great reluctance to innovation, so remarkable in old communities." The *Centinel* did not exaggerate. Between 1776 and 1783, American patriots had to organize new governments, raise and supply a substantial army, create a system of public finance, and manufacture goods once imported from Europe. Beyond these sizable tasks, they had to deal with pressing problems: tens of thousands of loyalists ready to fight for their king; 500,000 enslaved Africans and African Americans, who might themselves revolt for liberty; and a farm economy increasingly dependent on the labor of women and youth. The task was formidable; the stakes high. The war might be fought by soldiers and generals, but it would be won or lost by civilians and civic leaders.

Political Innovation and Conflict. Patriot leaders acted swiftly to establish the legitimacy of their rule. On 10 May 1776, Congress urged patriots to suppress royal authority and establish institutions based on popular rule. By the end of 1776, Virginia, Maryland, North Carolina, New Jersey, Delaware, and Pennsylvania had written new constitutions, and Connecticut and Rhode Island had transformed their colonial charters into republican documents by deleting all references to the king.

The Declaration of Independence stated the republican principle of popular sovereignty, and the Delaware Constitution interpreted that to mean the exercise of political power: "the Right of the People to participate in the Legislature." But most patriots gave a narrow definition to the political nation, restricting voting and office holding to propertied white men. Conservative patriots were more

adamant, denying that popular sovereignty meant rule by men who owned only a little property.

In the heat of revolution, radical patriots embraced a democratic outlook: every citizen who supported the rebellion—property owner or not—had "an equal claim to all privileges, liberties and immunities," declared an article in the *Maryland Gazette*. This democratic republicanism received fullest expression in Pennsylvania, where Scots-Irish farmers, Philadelphia artisans, and Enlightenment-influenced intellectuals cooperated to create the most democratic institutions of government in America or Europe. The Pennsylvania Constitution of 1776 abolished property owning as a qualification for political participation, giving all men who paid taxes the right to vote and hold office.

Pennsylvania's radical constitution alarmed leading patriots in other states, who feared that ordinary citizens would use their numerical advantage to levy heavy taxes on the rich. They insisted on constitutions that would keep the "better sort" in power. Thus, the New York Constitution of 1777, written chiefly by John Jay, used property qualifications to exclude one-half of the white men from voting for the governor and the upper house of the legislature, while the South Carolina Constitution of 1778 restricted membership in the state legislature to the richest 10 percent of the white population.

Nonetheless, the Revolutionary War democratized American politics. The new states constitutions apportioned seats in the legislatures on the basis of population, giving yeomen farmers in western areas more equal representation. Moreover, republican ideology raised the political consciousness of ordinary Americans. During the war, many patriot militiamen claimed the right to elect their officers; subsequently, many veterans, whether or not they had property, demanded the franchise. And when they voted, they chose different sorts of leaders. Before the war, about 85 percent of the assembly were wealthy men; by 1784, however, middling farmers and artisans controlled the lower houses of most northern states and formed a sizable minority in the southern states.

Political innovation also took place on the national level as the Continental Congress devised the first national constitution. The Articles of Confederation, approved by Congress on 15 November 1777, provided for a loose confederation in which "each state retains its sovereignty, freedom, and independence" and all powers and rights not "expressly delegated" to the United States. The Confederation government had the authority to declare war and make peace, to conclude treaties with foreign nations, to borrow and print money, and to requisition funds from the states "for the common defense or general welfare." The body charged with exercising these powers was the Congress, in which each state had one vote, regardless of its population. Because of disputes among the states over the title to western lands, the articles were not ratified until 1781. Threatened by the army of Gen. Charles *Cornwallis, Virginia finally ceded its land claims to Congress in 1781, and Maryland, the final holdout, ratified the articles.

Wartime Finance. Congress's main problem was not land but money. Because opposition to taxes had fueled the independence movement, patriot officials hesitated to impose taxes. To finance the war, the states first borrowed money, in gold or silver or British currency, from wealthy individuals. These funds quickly ran out, so the states created a new paper currency—the dollar—and issued notes with a face value of $260 million, using it to pay soldiers and purchase supplies. Since the new notes were printed in huge quantities and not backed by gold or silver or by tax revenues or mortgages on land, they quickly depreciated. Indeed, North Carolina's paper money came to be worth so little that the state government itself refused to accept it.

The monetary system created by the Continental Congress collapsed as well, despite the efforts of Robert *Morris, the Philadelphia merchant who became superintendent of finance in February 1781. To raise domestic loans, Congress borrowed $6 million from France and pledged it as security; wealthy Americans promptly purchased $27 million in Continental loan certificates. Congress also financed the war by printing money—some $191 million to 1779. By that time, so much currency had been printed that it took $42 in Continental bills to buy goods worth $1 in gold or silver. And things got worse, with the ratio increasing to 100 to 1 in 1780 and 146 to 1 in 1781. At that point, not even the most virtuous patriot farmers would sell food to the American army.

The failure of wartime finance nearly doomed the patriot cause. In 1780, Gen. George *Washington called urgently for a national system of taxation, warning that otherwise "our cause is lost." However, unanimous consent was required to amend the articles, and in 1781 Rhode Island rejected Superintendent Morris's proposal for a national tariff, an import duty of 5 percent on foreign goods. Two years later, New York blocked another proposed national tariff.

Consequently the war was financed through inflated currency, a hidden system of taxation that bore particularly hard on the farmers, artisans, and soldiers who received paper money for supplies and military pay. As soon as these men or their families received the currency, it lost purchasing power—literally depreciating in their pockets. Individually, these losses were small, amounting to a tiny "tax" every time an ordinary citizen received a paper dollar, kept it for a week, and then spent it. But collectively these "currency taxes" paid for the struggle for independence.

The Limits of Republican Virtues. Patriots knew that winning the war depended on *patriotism, and were at first optimistic that their republican ideology would inspire public virtue and self-sacrifice. "The word republic," wrote Thomas Paine, "means the public good, or the good of the whole." And, continued Philadelphia patriot Benjamin Rush: "Every man in a republic is public property. His time and talents—his youth—his manhood—his old age—nay more, life, all belong to his country."

But rhetoric could not create an army. Because yeoman farmers and militiamen preferred to serve in local units near their fields and families, few propertied Americans volunteered for service in the enlisted ranks of the *Continental army. Consequently, except for the officers, most of its recruits were drawn from the lower ranks of society. For example, most troops commanded by Gen. William Smallwood of Maryland were either poor American-born youths or older foreign-born men—British ex-convicts or former indentured servants. Historians continue to debate motivation for enlistment and continued service—the roles of economic gain (a bonus of $20 cash and the promise of 100 acres), belief in the cause of liberty and republicanism, and psychological commitments to their

comrades. Confronted by a reluctant citizenry and a lack of funds, Congress fell far short of its goal of a regular army of 75,000 men; the total Continental force never reached half that number.

As economic hardship brought the war closer to home, civilians also lost their zeal for self-sacrifice. The British naval blockade nearly eliminated the New England fishing industry and cut off the supply of European manufactured goods to American consumers. Domestic trade and production declined as well. The British occupation of Boston, New York, and Philadelphia put thousands of people out of work; the population of New York City declined from 21,000 in 1774 to less than half that at war's end. In the Chesapeake, the British blockade denied tobacco planters access to European markets, forcing them to turn to the cultivation of wheat, corn, and other foodstuffs. All across the land, ordinary commercial activity slackened as farmers and artisans adapted to a war economy.

The scarcity of imported goods brought a sharp rise in prices and widespread appeals for government regulation. Consumers decried merchants and traders as "enemies, extortioners, and monopolizers." In 1777, a convention of New England states tried to limit the price of domestic commodities and imported goods to 175 percent of their prewar level. To enforce this directive, the Massachusetts legislature passed an "Act to Prevent Monopoly and Oppression," but so many farmers and artisans refused to sell at the established prices that consumers had to pay the market price "or submit to starving."

The upward movement of prices—for grain and meat as well as manufactures—stimulated the economy. Army contractors roamed the countryside, offering farmers high prices for food, horses, and wagon transport. State governments encouraged artisans and entrepreneurs to manufacture military clothing, guns and gunpowder, and other scarce items—and with good results. By the end of the war, artisans in the town of Lynn, Massachusetts, were producing over 50,000 pairs of shoes each year. As Alexander *Hamilton noted, the northern countryside had become "a vast scene of household manufacturing." With financial self-interest supplementing republican virtue, Americans laid the basis for economic as well as political independence.

Women and the War Effort. Women workers played a large part in the expansion in production, particularly in the cloth industry. When the war cut off imports from Europe, government officials requisitioned clothing directly from the people. In Connecticut, officials called upon the citizens of Hartford to provide 1,000 coats and 1,600 shirts, and assessed smaller towns on a proportionate basis. Soldiers added their own pleas. Capt. Edward Rogers lost "all the shirts except the one on my back," at the Battle of Long Island and wrote to his wife, "the making of cloath … must go on."

Patriot women stepped into the breach, increasing production of homespun cloth. One Massachusetts town claimed an annual output of 30,000 yards of cloth, while women in Elizabeth, New Jersey, promised "upwards of 100,000 yards of linnen and woolen cloth." With their husbands and sons away, many women also assumed the burden of farm production. Some went into the fields themselves, plowing fields or cutting and loading grain. Others supervised hired laborers or slaves, acquiring a taste for decision making in the process. "We have sow'd our oats as you desired," Sarah Cobb Paine wrote to her absent husband; "had I been master I should have planted it to Corn."

Some upper-class women also entered into political debate, filling their letters and diaries (and undoubtedly their conversations) with opinions on public issues. "The men say we have no business [with politics]," Eliza Wilkinson of South Carolina complained in 1783; "they won't even allow us liberty of thought, and that is all I want." Other women, such as Abigail Adams, asked men to create a republican legal order to replace the common law rules of coverture that completely subordinated married women to their husbands. And a few women, inspired by revolutionary ideology, repudiated prevailing assumptions of women's inferiority. In 1779, Judith Sargent Murray, daughter of a wealthy New England merchant, wrote "On the Equality of the Sexes." In this essay, Murray systematically compared the intellectual faculties of men and women, arguing that women had a capacity for memory equal to that of men, and more imagination; any inferiority in judgment and reasoning, she argued, was due to lack of training.

A few men paid some attention to women's requests for greater social and legal equality. In Massachusetts, the state's attorney general persuaded a jury that girls had equal rights under the state's constitution and should not be deprived of schooling. Benjamin Rush, in his *Thoughts on Female Education* (1787), advocated the intellectual training of women, so they would "be an agreeable companion for a sensible man." Rush likewise praised "republican mothers" who instructed "their sons in the principles of liberty and government." But most patriots viewed women as inferior and subordinate. Politics remained a male preserve, with most state constitutions explicitly restricting suffrage to men. Because of deeply ingrained cultural assumptions of female inferiority, women entered the new republics as second-class citizens.

Slavery Weakened. For enslaved African Americans, as for women, war and republicanism brought new opportunities. Taking advantage of the disruptions of war, many blacks fled from their patriot owners and sought freedom behind British lines. Two white neighbors of Richard Henry Lee, a signer of the Declaration of Independence, lost "every slave they had in the world," as did nearly "all those who were nearly the enemy." More than 5,000 blacks left Charleston, South Carolina, with the departing British army. Other enslaved African Americans used wartime loyalty to their patriot masters to bargain for their liberty. Under a Manumission Act of 1782, Virginia planters granted freedom to more than 10,000 slaves.

Equally important was the intellectual attack against slavery. In Virginia, a Methodist conference declared slavery "contrary to the Golden Law of God on which hang all the Law and Prophets, and the unalienable Rights of Mankind, as well as every Principle of Revolution." Such arguments prompted black emancipation in the northern states, where there were relatively few slaves. By 1784, Massachusetts, Connecticut, and Rhode Island had abolished slavery. To protect white property rights, the Pennsylvania Emancipation Act awarded freedom only to slaves born after 1780—and then only after they had served their mothers' masters for twenty-eight years. Such economic concerns among whites, as well as racial prejudice, prevented emancipation in the South, where slaves accounted for 30 to 60 percent of the population and represented a huge financial investment. But those blacks who had won their freedom during the Revolutionary War began to develop churches, social institutions, and a partly autonomous African American culture.

The Fate of the Loyalists. Even as most free African Americans chose to remain in the land of their birth, tens of thousands of loyalists emigrated to Canada and other British possessions. As early as 1765, many wealthy Americans—and thousands of ordinary colonists—had feared that resistance to Britain would end in mob rule, and the violent activities of the Sons of Liberty seemed to prove the point.

Once war came, it quickly turned into a civil conflict. Patriot committees of safety backed by armed militiamen collected taxes, sent food and clothing to the Continental army, and imposed fines or jail sentences on those who failed to support the patriot cause. "There is no such thing as remaining neutral," declared the Committee of Safety of Farmington, Connecticut, and mobs of New England patriots beat suspected loyalists or destroyed their property. In the Middle Colonies, the contest between loyalists and patriots was more even. In New Jersey, most New Light members of the Dutch Reformed Church—enthusiastic Protestants—actively supported the American cause, but the more conservative Old Lights became loyalists. As the British and American armies marched back and forth across the state, those with reputations as patriots and loyalists fled from their homes to escape arrest—or worse. Soldiers and partisans looted farms, seeking plunder or revenge. Beginning in 1778, British strategies relied heavily on southern loyalists, mobilizing recent immigrants, such as the Scottish Highlanders in North Carolina, and using them to hold territory won by the British army. Their strategy turned the South into an arena of bitter partisan warfare, with *atrocities on both sides.

As the war turned in favor of the patriots, loyalists feared for their lives—especially since more than 55,000 loyalists had fought for the British as regular soldiers or militia. More than 100,000 loyalists emigrated to Canada, the West Indies, or Britain. Those who moved to Canada—where they became known as the United Empire Loyalists—assumed the leadership of the English-speaking colonies of Nova Scotia, New Brunswick, and Ontario.

Some patriots wanted to confiscate the property of the departed "traitors," and the passions of war lent urgency to their arguments. When the British army invaded the South, the North Carolina assembly confiscated loyalists' estates outright. Officials in New York also seized loyalists' lands and goods. However, many patriots opposed these seizures as contrary to republican property rights. Consequently, most states seized only a limited amount of property—that owned by notorious loyalists—so that, unlike France after 1789 or Russia after 1917, the revolutionary upheaval did not drastically alter the structure of American society.

Still, the loyalist exodus disrupted the established social order in many states as upwardly mobile patriot merchants climbed to the top of the economic ladder. In Massachusetts, the Lowell, Higginson, Jackson, and Cabot families filled the vacuum created by the departure of the Hutchinsons and Apthorps and their friends. Small-scale traders in Philadelphia and its environs likewise stepped into vacancies created when loyalist Anglican and neutral/pacifist Quaker mercantile firms collapsed during the war. These changes replaced a conservative economic elite—one that invested primarily in foreign trade and urban real estate—

with a group of more entrepreneurial-minded republican merchants.

In economic life, as in politics, finance, and gender and racial relations, the Revolutionary War was just that: a dramatic disruption of established life that demanded innovation and changed forever the course of American history.

• Willi Paul Adams, *The First American Constitutions: Republican Ideology and the Making of the State Constitutions in the Revolutionary Era*, 1980. Richard Buel, Jr., *Dear Liberty: Connecticut's Mobilization for the Revolutionary War*, 1980. William G. Anderson, *The Price of Liberty: The Public Debt of the American Revolution*, 1983. Ira Berlin and Ronald Hoffman, eds., *Slavery and Freedom in the American Revolution*, 1983. Ronald Hoffman, Thad W. Tate, and Peter J. Albert, eds., *An Uncivil War: The Southern Backcountry during the American Revolution*, 1985. Robert M. Calhoon et al., *The Loyalist Perception*, 1989. Ronald Hoffman and Peter J. Albert, eds., *Women in the Age of the American Revolution*, 1989. Gary B. Nash, *Race and Revolution*, 1990. Alfred F. Young, ed. *Beyond the American Revolution: Explorations in the History of American Radicalism*, 1993. Jean Butenhoff Lee, *The Price of Nationhood: The American Revolution in Charles County*, 1994.   —James A. Henretta

REVOLUTIONARY WAR (1775–83): POSTWAR IMPACT

The new nation still faced critical unresolved issues even after the peace was signed in the Treaty of *Paris in 1783. Some were social and political issues opened in the decade before the war broke out, such as who should vote or what defined the public good, occasionally raising questions for long-term consideration such as the future of slavery or the place of women in society. Others were problems created by the war itself. Effective control over much of the landmass ceded by Britain had yet to be achieved; acceptance by the nations of the world required diplomacy and a clear articulation of American national interests; economic adjustments had to be made to compensate for lost privileges in the British market; and internal differences of opinion about how best to govern the nation had to be resolved. The American Revolution entered its final phase with both leaders and the people asking themselves what kind of country they wanted and how best to achieve it. The ringing phrases of the Declaration of Independence promised much, but what did they mean?

All of the nations involved in the Revolutionary War— both the allies and the adversaries of the United States— made the postwar adjustment difficult. The British were eager enough to end the war; indeed, British public opinion demanded it. But in surrendering the vast terrain south of the Great Lakes, and west of the Appalachians to the Mississippi River, the British negotiators signed away the very land *George III, in his famous Royal Proclamation of 1763, had promised to protect as Indian hunting grounds. Britain's Indian allies, a decided majority of the Indians who chose sides in the Revolutionary War, felt betrayed. When American settlers, unchecked by the United States, began streaming across the Appalachians into the Ohio, Kentucky, and Tennessee regions even before the war ended, bitter clashes with the Indians ensued. Claiming that they sought only to maintain order on a lawless frontier, the British reneged on their treaty promise and maintained British troops on American soil. They remained at Detroit and other western forts until the mid-1790s, encouraging the Indians to believe that they would protect them against the American onslaught, and arguing that the trade in skins and furs (to which the British were entitled) required policing.

America's allies were almost as difficult. France and Spain both hoped that the United States would get less than it got: the French were dissatisfied with the privileged position given American fishermen in the North Atlantic cod fishery, while the Spanish resented the American western boundary at the Mississippi. Spain insisted that Americans had no right to navigate the Mississippi River, and tensions persisted between the two nations until 1795, when a compromise was reached. Meanwhile, Spain, behaving like the British in the Northwest, encouraged Indians on the southwest frontier to defy the Americans.

The United States dealt with these issues both militarily and diplomatically. Even though Congress had disbanded the *Continental Army, reduced the military establishment to the 1st American Regiment, and sold off the ships of the navy, troops were assigned to the frontier, where they negotiated the first new treaties with the western Indians. For their part, the Indians sought compromise and retention of their land rights and created a confederacy to present a united front. But the contradiction between official American promises and unrestrained settler violence created divisions among the native leaders, and in the end the war hawks on both sides won out. The task of bringing peace to the Northwest forced Congress to increase the size of the army, and, in a series of frontier battles, to resolve the matter by force of arms.

Meanwhile, American diplomats, led by Thomas *Jefferson and John *Adams, promoted American interests in Europe. Jefferson went to France (where he remained until the early months of the French Revolution), working to preserve the outward friendship of the wartime alliance, while retaining American freedom of action. With Jefferson's help, France became the chief trading partner of the United States. Adams arrived at the Court of St. James in 1785 as the first American official to confront George III on behalf of the new nation. Both Jefferson and Adams disliked European social distinctions and economic disparities, but each also formed strong attachments to which they later clung, and which helped define their subsequent political followings in the United States, especially in the 1790s when Americans responded to the progress of the French Revolution.

The relations of the United States with the rest of the world depended in large measure on American success in adjusting to new economic imperatives. In 1783, a good many Americans hoped to restore their economic links with Britain, and for a few months after the war, trade was reopened and vigorously pursued. But the British ministry soon decided to cut Americans out of the preferential marketplace of the British empire while merchants tightened credit when it became apparent that Americans lacked the cash to pay for British manufactures. Congress struggled with the problems of economic adjustment. From his position as superintendent of finance, Robert *Morris tried to reorganize credit in the country by establishing a Bank of North America (BNA) as a private bank with a public mandate to serve the Congress and the nation as a central bank. The first American banks were chartered in several states during the 1780s, although the BNA itself ran into trouble politically and financially and lost its Pennsylvania charter before the decade was out. Alexander *Hamilton of New York argued that Morris had taken the right track, and that the United States must solve its economic problems by consolidating the national debt and creating a national bank. Meanwhile, Congress sought most-favored-nation treaties with European nations, and individual merchant houses pressed to open new markets that included the Far East.

The problems of economic adjustment created antagonisms among Americans themselves, and contributed substantially to the political and social division eventually expressed in a debate over the constitution. Nationalists who were to become identified as Federalists argued that the central government needed strengthening, and eventually they insisted that only a new constitution could give the United States the energy it needed to attain economic stability and national respectability. Localists who preferred the decentralized structure provided by the Articles of Confederation rejected the notion of complete constitutional revision and became Anti-Federalists, although most agreed that Congress might need additional powers to tackle the difficult problems of the time.

These were more than superficial disagreements over how best to govern a young republic experiencing short-term economic problems. The divisions represented fundamental differences of opinion about what the American Revolution was about and what independence was meant to accomplish. The war had created some of the divisions and sharpened others. In many states, local antagonism toward Tories or loyalists persisted; 60,000–80,000 loyalists fled the United States as refugees, and legislatures were divided over whether to let Tories return. Most that had confiscated Tory estates refused compensation. States denied Tory and British creditors the right to collect old debts, despite the article in the peace treaty requiring it and Congress's urging the states to comply. The U.S. *Army itself was divided at war's end between an officer class that had sought and won promises of a postwar pension, and men in the ranks who had been paid in depreciated government script and vague promises. When, after the war, the officers organized the Society of Cincinnati to promote their right to a commutation, or lump-sum payment in lieu of pensions, many Americans, including rank-and-file *veterans, complained about the emergence of aristocracy in American society. The war had created other tensions not easily dissipated: wartime shortages of provisions, inflation caused by the printing of paper money, and fears about the manipulation of prices by hoarders and forestallers pitted rural against urban dwellers and farmers against merchants. After the war, a short-lived burst of consumer spending fueled by loose credit arrangements set the stage for bitter social resentments when merchants suddenly contracted credit and called for payment of debts. Many states saw violent demonstrations against debtor courts in 1785–86; Massachusetts faced armed rebellion.

What has been called *Shays's Rebellion, an armed protest by farmer-regulators in western Massachusetts in the fall and winter of 1786–87, was in reality only the most visible sign of a widespread discontent. Forced court closures were common throughout New England; in New Hampshire, protestors for a short time held the legislature hostage; and throughout Massachusetts, farmers complained to the legislature about tax laws, the shortage of money, and the greed of merchants. But only 2,000 or so actually took up arms in the Connecticut River Valley towns of western Massachusetts, and were forcibly suppressed by a hastily recruited government force of about 5,000 under Benjamin Lincoln. Capt. Daniel Shays, a veteran of the Revolutionary War, and other leaders of the uprising, managed to escape into neighboring Vermont, and the rest of the rebels were dispersed. The Massachusetts government eventually provided reprieves or pardons for all, but the experience left Americans divided.

It is too simple to equate the divisions of Shays' Rebellion with Federalist–Anti-Federalist divisions over the Constitution of 1787, but a good many Americans at the time did so; both sides used divisive rhetoric and identified antagonistic interests. Federalists claimed to be merchants, creditors, and commercial farmers, all sound money people who sought order and stability both in the economy and in the larger society, and portrayed their opponents as poor farmers, debtors, or localists who failed to understand the needs of a nation. Anti-Federalists saw themselves as honest husbandmen who were up against rapacious merchants and monied holders of public securities. America's urban-rural split curiously lumped a good many commercial farmers on the urban side of the divide, but also united urban artisans with merchants in the Federalist effort to strengthen the American economy through a revitalized national policy. Even if the divisions were not as precise as contemporaries suggested, the debate over the Constitution shows that there were divisions in American society created or perhaps sharpened by the American Revolution, and in particular by the war. Writing in the famous *Federalist Papers*, James *Madison was to argue that the new Constitution made sense in such a society: it was designed to steer conflicting interests into reasoned debate and compromise.

In practice, not even the new federal Constitution could resolve all of the questions the Revolution had opened. It did, however, provide a democratic framework for resolving such issues in the future, and as Madison envisaged it, it provided a forum for the enormous diversity of condition and opinion that already existed in the United States and was to continue. George *Washington's first administration and the statesmen of the First Congress strengthened popular acceptance of the new Constitution, convincing Americans that their diverse views were fairly represented in government and that their rights were adequately protected. The Revolution, however, had also left a legacy of healthy skepticism about government. Americans argued variously that evangelical religion held better answers, that families must protect values, that women had a special role in nurturing "virtuous" citizens, that both public and private education must be expanded, or that the complexities of modern life required an informed citizenry well served by a free press. There was paradox in the new American culture; there was also vibrancy and excitement and enormous optimism.

[See also Civil-Military Relations; Native American Wars: Wars Between Native Americans and Europeans and Euro-Americans; Newburgh "Conspiracy" (1783); Society and War.]

• Merrill Jensen, *The New Nation: A History of the United States during the Confederation*, 1950. Wallace Brown, *The Good Americans: The Loyalists in the American Revolution*, 1969. Richard H. Kohn, *Eagle and Sword*, 1975. Paul H. Smith, ed., *Letters of Delegates to Congress, 1774–1789*, 25 vols., 1976–98. Jack N. Rakove, *The Beginnings of National Politics*, 1979. David P. Szatmary, *Shays' Rebellion*, 1980. Jonathan R. Dull, *A Diplomatic History of the American Revolution*, 1985. Robert A. Gross, ed., *In Debt to Shays*, 1993. Colin G. Calloway, *The American Revolution in Indian Country*, 1995.
—Stephen E. Patterson

REVOLUTIONARY WAR (1775–83): CHANGING INTERPRETATIONS

It has been argued that the American Revolution is the central event of American history, and it has occasioned more scholarship than any other episode save the *Civil War. Yet, when former President John *Adams asked Thomas McKean in 1815 who would write the Revolution's history, he posed a challenge that historians still confront. The secret sessions and debates, now lost along with other critical information that vanished when the participants died, leave many vital gaps in our understanding. What was the real story?

Historians, of course, have not hesitated to offer accounts of the Revolution. Several key questions have defined their interpretations. How and when did the Americans come to consider themselves a nation different from Great Britain? Was the Revolutionary War inevitable? To what degree was the Revolutionary War a civil war? Was there a struggle for power among the factions in the United States during the war? Why independence? Could the British government have prevented the separation? Why did the British pursue the measures they did?

Military historians have often focused on George *Washington's overall strategy and have debated whether the American victory could have been achieved without the *Continental army, which was its centerpiece. Was the French Alliance critical, or not? To what extent did British strategy and tactics work against an imperial victory by politicizing the American population? Why did the British devastate so much of Scotland in warfare thirty years earlier but do so little, comparatively, to the rebellious colonies in North America?

Finally, how should we interpret the U.S. Constitution? Was it a counterrevolutionary document created to serve the class interests of its framers, or did it realize and embody the ideological promise of revolutionary republicanism? Perhaps most intriguing of all, why did the Revolution not turn upon itself and devour its own as in so many other revolutions? There was no terror—once the war ended, its violence was soon forgotten, and its effects dissipated; unlike most other revolutionary peoples in the Americas, those of the United States escaped militarization or dictatorship by their War of Independence.

The Revolution's first historians witnessed the events they described. Their highly colored, contingent, localized, and biased narratives made impassioned arguments for the justice of their cause, whether loyalist or Whig. Two valuable loyalist accounts are Peter Oliver's violently partisan Origin and Progress of the American Rebellion (1781; published 1961), and the third and fourth volumes of Thomas Hutchinson's History of the Colony and Province of Massachusetts Bay (1767, 1828), which provide a more balanced and insightful view. Their Whig counterparts are Mercy Otis Warren's three-volume History of the Rise, Progress and Termination of the American Revolution (1805), which gives a contemporary woman's view of politics and a relatively balanced account; and Dr. David Ramsay's History of the American Revolution (1789), the only contemporary narrative to focus on the Revolution outside New England. The most significant work published in the immediate post-Revolutionary period, Mason Locke Weem's Life of Washington (1809), treated Washington's as an exemplary life, and fictionalized shamelessly to make its

points. It influenced more Americans than any of the other early accounts.

The first significant school of interpretation on the Revolution, the Nationalist school, emerged in the mid-nineteenth century. These historians collected thousands of documents and built the first archives of Revolutionary writings; their narratives stressed the inevitability of the American victory and endowed the story with providential significance. Jared Sparks, the librarian of Harvard College, was the first great figure of this school, publishing some 100 volumes on the Revolutionary period, including a 12-volume Life and Writings of George Washington (1833–39) and a 10-volume Works of Benjamin Franklin (1836–40). The dominating writer of Nationalist history, George Bancroft, published a ten-volume History of the United States (1834–74), the last six volumes of which detail the events of the Revolution. For the Nationalists, the Revolution was above all a moral tale, acted out by great men whose virtue ensured America's progress toward its destiny of freedom.

The first academic interpreters of the Revolution, the Imperial school, appeared at the end of the nineteenth century. Writing principally from British documents and employing the critical methods pioneered by the German historian Leopold von Ranke, the Imperial historians scorned the providentialism of the Nationalists. Their version of the Revolution emphasized institutional factors and tended to empathize with the British; the most ardent among them regarded the Revolution as the result of a series of unfortunate misunderstandings—a colossal mistake. The most important figures and works in this school include Charles McLean Andrews, The Colonial Background of the American Revolution (1931); Lawrence Henry Gipson, The British Empire Before the American Revolution, fourteen vols. (1936–69); and Leonard Woods Larabee, Royal Government in America (1930).

Twentieth-century historians can be grouped into three major schools: the Progressives, the Neo-Whigs, and the Modernists. The Progressives emphasized social science methods, embraced the frontier theory of Frederick Jackson Turner, and tended to explain the Revolution in terms of class conflict—a struggle not only for home rule but over who (as Carl Becker put it) "should rule at home." They rejected the institutional focus and anglophilia of the Imperial historians and created a Revolution that was preeminently a struggle between common men with democratic aspirations, and their aristocratic, would-be masters. Charles A. Beard, An Economic Interpretation of the Constitution of the United States (1913), Carl Becker, The Declaration of Independence (1922), Arthur M. Schlesinger, Sr., The Colonial Merchant and the American Revolution (1918), John Franklin Jameson, The American Revolution Considered as a Social Movement (1926), and John C. Miller, Samuel Adams (1936) are some of the more significant works by members of this school.

The post–World War II generation of scholars, called Neo-Whigs, reacted against the Progressives' class conflict–based interpretation and described a revolutionary movement that emerged from a broadly shared republican (or "Real Whig") political ideology. Concerned with decision making and explaining human behavior in conflict situations, these historians generally view the Revolution as a conservative movement to protect American rights from the acts of Parliament after 1760. The most influential figure in this school, Bernard Bailyn, has produced several books and essays, most notably *The Ideological Origins of the American Revolution* (1967) and *The Ordeal of Thomas Hutchinson* (1974). Other significant representatives include Daniel Boorstin, *The Americans: The Colonial Experience* (1958); and Edmund and Helen Morgan, *The Stamp Act Crisis* (1953), Bernhard Knollenberg, *Origins of the American Revolution* (1960), Pauline Maier, *From Resistance to Revolution* (1972), Richard D. Brown, *Revolutionary Politics in Massachusetts* (1970), and Jack Rakove, *The Beginnings of National Politics* (1979).

Modernists carry on the interpretative debates of earlier historians. Gordon S. Wood, in two of the most important works on the era, *The Creation of the American Republic* (1969) and *The Radicalism of the American Revolution* (1992), synthesizes the Progressive argument for a counterrevolutionary Constitution with the ideological analysis of the Neo-Whigs, and argues that the Revolution represented a real change in colonial society, not a conservative reaction. In *A Struggle for Power* (1996), Theodore Draper provides a detailed synthesis covering the ten years before the war began, and explicitly downplays the ideological quality of the Revolution in favor of the political pragmatism of the revolutionaries. Draper's lack of interest in ideology as opposed to power mirrors the earlier work of James Kirby Martin, *Men in Rebellion* (1973).

The war itself has received increasing notice as an agent of revolutionary change. John Shy's suggestive essays in *A People Numerous and Armed* (1976), first pointed the way toward interpreting the Revolution as dynamically related to the War of Independence; two other distinguished collections of articles edited by Ronald Hoffman and Peter Albert, *Arms and Independence* (1984) and *An Uncivil War* (1985), offer valuable case studies of the war in local contexts. E. Wayne Carp explains the roles of localism and political culture as they influenced the supply and support of the Continental army in his *To Starve the Army at Pleasure* (1984). Charles Royster describes the interactions between the war, republicanism, and the Continental army in *A Revolutionary People at War* (1979). R. Arthur Bowler explores an important cause of the British failure to crush the rebellion in *Logistics and the Failure of the British Army in America* (1975), while Sylvia R. Frey describes the British army's social character in *The British Soldier in America* (1981). In *The Military Experience in the Age of Reason* (1988), Christopher Duffy develops a clear perspective on how war and society intertwined in the eighteenth century. Other significant works on the British forces and the war include Piers Mackesy, *The Way for America* (1964); John Shy, *Toward Lexington* (1965); William Seymour, *The Price of Folly* (1995); John Tilley, *The British Navy and the American Revolution* (1987); and Nathan Miller, *Sea of Glory* (1974). The secret and intelligence aspects of the war are covered in John Bakeless's *Turncoats, Traitors and Heroes* (1959) and Carl Van Doren's *Secret History of the American Revolution* (1941).

One notable trend in modern scholarship is to include the story of common people and minority groups. Sylvia R. Frey's *Water from the Rock* (1991) and *Slavery in North Carolina* (1995) by Marvin L. Michael Kay and Lorin Cary explore the African American role in war and society. *The Price of Nationhood* (1994), by Jean B. Lee, studies Charles County, Maryland, as transformed by the war; while Robert Gross, *The Minutemen and Their World* (1976), examines Concord, Massachusetts. David Hackett Fisher recounts the coming of the war in Boston in *Paul Revere's*

Ride (1994). John Selby, *The Revolution in Virginia* (1988), and Richard Buel, *Dear Liberty: Connecticut's Mobilization in the Revolutionary War* (1981), are strong colonywide studies of the war's impact.

Two classics in the history of Revolutionary-era women are Mary Beth Norton, *Liberty's Daughters* (1980) and Linda Kerber, *Women of the Republic* (1980); Ronald Hoffman and Peter Albert, eds., *Women in the Age of the American Revolution* (1989), collects several excellent essays.

Native Americans have lately received notable treatments in Richard White, *The Middle Ground* (1991); Gregory Evans Down, *A Spirited Resistance* (1992); Tom Hatley, *The Dividing Paths* (1993); and Colin Calloway, *The American Revolution in Indian Country* (1995), all of which depict Native Americans not as mere victims, but historical actors.

In general, there are two areas where further scholarship is needed. Apart from works on diplomacy and Lee Kennett's *French Forces in America* (1977), the French role remains largely unexplored. Finally, the hidden war that John Adams hinted at remains to be researched. Though its sources are few, it is now, as then, the greatest gap in our knowledge of an era that marks a turning point not only in American history but in the history of the world.

• James Kirby Martin, *A Respectable Army: The Military Origins of the Republic, 1763–1789,* 1982. Colin D. Calloway, *The American Revolution in Indian Country,* 1995. Martin V. Kwasny, *Washington's Partisan War, 1775–1783,* 1996. Holly A. Mayer, *Belonging to the Army: Camp Followers and Community During the American Revolution,* 1996. Charles P. Neimeyer, *America Goes to War: A Social History of the Continental Army,* 1996. Richard Buel, Jr., *In Irons: Britain's Naval Supremacy and the American Revolutionary Economy,* 1998.

—Paul J. Sanborn

REVOLVERS. *See* Side Arms, Standard Infantry.

RICKENBACKER, EDDIE (1890–1973), born Edward Vernon Rickenbacher in Columbus, Ohio, changed the spelling of his name in 1918.

A famed racing car driver before World War I, he joined the army after the United States entered the war in 1917. After serving as Gen. John J. *Pershing's personal driver and an engineering officer, he became a combat pilot. Rickenbacker shot down twenty-two German planes and four balloons and became America's Ace of Aces. To younger aviators, "Captain Eddie" loomed an intriguing hero, neither cold nor overly friendly, one who inspired by simple grace in action. As commander of the famous 94th ("Hat-in-the-Ring") Squadron, he flew against Baron Manfred von Richthofen's "Flying Circus."

After the war, Rickenbacker worked with automobile companies and shared ownership of the Indianapolis Speedway (1927–45). He became president of Eastern Airlines, 1938–59, and chairman of their board of directors, 1954–63.

A civilian air base inspector during World War II, Rickenbacker toured overseas installations. On one of these missions in 1942, his plane went down in the Pacific. He and six others survived for twenty-four days on rafts before being found.

Rickenbacker wrote two autobiographical books, *Fighting the Flying Circus* (1919) and *Seven Came Through: Rickenbacker's Full Story* (1943).

• Finis Farr, *Rickenbacker's Luck: An American Life,* 1979.

—Frank E. Vandiver

RICKOVER, HYMAN G. (1900–1986), U.S. naval officer. Hyman George Rickover is generally known as the "father of the atomic submarine," having been head of the U.S. Navy's nuclear submarine program from 1948 until his retirement in 1982.

Born in Makow (now Maków Mazowiecki), Poland, then a province of Czarist Russia, Rickover came to America at age four, his family settling in Chicago. A good student, he earned an appointment to the U.S. Naval Academy. Although Jewish in a highly prejudiced service, he was generally liked at the academy. (Later, would he renounce Judaism and became an Episcopalian.) He graduated in 1922 and as a young officer served in a destroyer and then a battleship. He received a postgraduate degree in electrical engineering and in 1929 entered the submarine service. Though qualified to command a submarine, Rickover was not given a command and in 1935 returned to surface ship duty.

For less than three months in 1937, he commanded a minesweeper operating in China. He then became a specialized engineering duty officer. Rickover was assigned to the Bureau of Ships in Washington, D.C., in August 1939, and remained there through World War II until mid-1945, most of the time responsible for the electric equipment installed in navy ships.

After the war, Rickover was one of several naval officers and civilian engineers sent to Oak Ridge, Tennessee, to study nuclear energy. Returning to Washington, he was assigned to the navy's nuclear propulsion program (begun as early as 1939). On 4, August 1948, Rickover was named head of the nuclear power branch in the Bureau of Ships. The following February, he was also appointed director of naval reactors in the new Atomic Energy Commission, making him "double-hatted" in naval terminology.

Under Rickover's direction, the navy developed the world's first nuclear propulsion plant, which was installed in the submarine *Nautilus*. She got underway for the first time on 3 January 1955, and in 1958 became the first ship to reach the North Pole (traveling submerged under the arctic ice pack). Rickover subsequently directed a large number of nuclear submarine and surface ship projects.

After being passed over for selection to rear admiral by navy selection boards, Rickover used the press and his congressional contacts to force his selection to rear admiral (1953). He was subsequently promoted to vice admiral (1958), and when he reached the statutory age for retirement, he was retained on active duty by order of the secretary of the navy. He was later promoted to full admiral (1973).

Rickover took exclusive control of the selection and training of all officers for nuclear-propelled *submarines and of engineers for surface ships. His interviews became notorious, often pitting a four-star admiral against a midshipman or junior officer in his twenties. The admiral was frequently bombastic and rude as he sought to determine what made the candidate "tick." Answerable to no one because of his support in Congress, the admiral attacked his peers when their programs threatened funding for his own; he also attacked members of the administration, seniors in the Department of *Defense, and even officials of the shipyards that built the nuclear fleet.

His efforts resulted in a high degree of safety in the U.S. submarine force and, initially, a high degree of innovation as new designs and concepts were developed and innovative nuclear submarines were built. Rickover-trained offi-

cers and enlisted men were soon in high demand by America's nuclear power industry. His close relationship with members of Congress who had submarine shipyards, submarine bases, or nuclear facilities in their states led to extensive support and funding of navy nuclear programs.

Under Rickover's direction the United States initially led the world in nuclear submarine development. However, in the 1960s, following the loss of the U.S. nuclear submarine *Thresher*, Rickover became increasingly conservative in his approach to submarine design. Subsequently, the Soviet Union overtook the United States in numbers of submarines and in many areas of submarine technology.

Rickover's self-centered, petulant, and tactless attitudes earned him the contempt of many naval officers and officials of the government. After the retirement of most of his congressional supporters, the Reagan administration in 1981 ended Rickover's tenure. He left active duty on 31 January 1982 after sixty-four years of naval service.

Rickover received numerous citations for his efforts in the field of nuclear propulsion. He was awarded a Gold Medal by Congress (1959), was the first nonengineer to receive the prestigious Enrico Fermi Award from the Atomic Energy Commission (1965), and was a recipient of the Presidential Medal of Freedom (1980), as well as numerous military decorations, including the Legion of Merit for his wartime work in the Bureau of Ships. The main engineering building at the Naval Academy is named Rickover Hall (1974) and a nuclear-propelled submarine is named the *Hyman G. Rickover* (1983).

[*See also* Atomic Scientists; Navy, U.S.: 1899–1945; Navy, U.S.: Since 1946; Navy Combat Branches: Submarine Forces.]

• Richard G. Hewlett and Francis Duncan, *Nuclear Navy, 1946–1962*, 1974. Elmo R. Zumwalt, Jr., *On Watch*, 1976. Norman Polmar and Thomas B. Allen, *Rickover: Controversy and Genius*, 1982. Francis Duncan, *Rickover and the Nuclear Navy*, 1982. Theodore Rockwell, *The Rickover Effect*, 1992.

—Norman Polmar

RIDGWAY, MATTHEW B. (1895–1993), general, World War II and Korea; Supreme Commander, *NATO; presidential adviser. Ridgway graduated from West Point in 1917 and rose through the ranks as an infantry officer. He served in a score of military and diplomatic assignments, graduated from the Command and General Staff School (1935) and the Army War College (1937), and was on staff with George C. *Marshall, army chief of staff, in 1941.

During World War II, General Ridgway commanded the 82nd Airborne Division in Europe (1943–44), dropping at Sicily, on *D-Day, and at Bastonge. In 1944, he assumed command of the Allied XVIII Airborne Corps. After the war, he served in a variety of command and staff positions, and in 1950 was appointed deputy army chief of staff. In December 1950, he assumed command of Eighth Army during the *Korean War when *United Nations forces were being attacked by the Communist Chinese. His wearing of hand grenades on his jacket symbolized his determination to resist.

Ridgway moved quickly to provide motivation and halt the Chinese south of Seoul. In "Operation Meatgrinder," he counterattacked and established line Kansas, the United Nations' main line of defense across Korea. In April 1951, he replaced Gen. Douglas *MacArthur as commander of UN forces. Reluctantly accepting the stalemate in Korea, Ridgway decided it would be too costly to take the war into China. Under orders from Washington, he initiated the truce talks which, in 1953, produced the armistice.

Ridgway succeeded Dwight D. *Eisenhower as Supreme Commander, NATO, in May 1952. Later, as chief of staff, U.S. Army (1954–55), he advocated a strong ground army, warning against Eisenhower's emphasis on airpower and *nuclear weapons. He was an opponent of America's early involvement in Vietnam (1954) and again in the 1960s. As one of President Lyndon B. *Johnson's "Wise Men" in 1968, he advocated U.S. withdrawal from the *Vietnam War.

A highly successful, if often underrated, military officer, Ridgway was a gifted organizer, strategic planner, and political-military coalition leader.

[See also World War II: Military and Diplomatic Course.]

• Matthew B. Ridgway, Soldier: The Memoirs of Matthew B. Ridgway, 1956. Paul M. Edwards, Comp., General Matthew B. Ridgway: An Annotated Bibliography, 1993. Jonathan M. Soffer, Matthew B. Ridgway, 1998.
—Paul M. Edwards

RIFLES. See M-1 Rifle; M-16 Rifle; Side Arms, Standard Infantry.

RIGHTS IN THE MILITARY, CITIZENS'. In 1962, Earl Warren, then Chief Justice of the United States, lectured at New York University on "The Bill of Rights and the Military" and expressed his conviction that the guarantees of the Bill of Rights were not antithetical to military discipline. In doing so, he acknowledged that military service would affect the exercise of those rights, and he also alluded to a perennial problem: deciding who would be subject to military law and thus within the jurisdiction of courts-martial.

The military codes and justice systems were intended to ensure discipline in the land and naval forces. What of civilians accompanying the forces? British tradition, carried over into American law, provided that "retainers to the camp, and persons serving with the army in the field," although not enlisted, were in time of war subject to military discipline. These provisions were routinely applied in all American wars until Vietnam, when two of the three members of the U.S. Court of Military Appeals ruled that the "war" had to have been formally declared by Congress. This ruling was extended to civilian paymasters' clerks and other navy employees who had been traditionally subject to military law as "persons in the naval service." Since the 1960s, civilian employees of the Department of *Defense, and of government contractors, have not been subject to military trial for offenses committed overseas, even though the offense was committed in a designated war zone like Somalia or the Persian Gulf. Precedent for this decision was a series of 1950s U.S. Supreme Court rulings which held that the military could not court-martial dependents of American military personnel for crimes committed overseas. The same series of decisions prohibited the recall from civilian life and court-martial of persons who had committed crimes while in military service. These decisions relied on World War II precedent, which held that U.S. civilians in Hawaii could not, in the years following the attack on *Pearl Harbor, remain subjected to martial law. The World War II martial law cases relied in turn on the precedent of Ex parte *Milligan, a *Civil War–era decision in which the Supreme Court ruled 5 to 4 that military

tribunals could not exercise their jurisdiction over civilians as long as civil courts were open. Thus, in the past century, the classes of persons subject to military law—and whose civil rights are therefore limited—have been severely curtailed by judicial decisions.

The focus here is on members of the armed forces who are indisputably subject to court-martial jurisdiction and who have asserted claims either that their military status should protect them from some consequence of civil law or that civil rights doctrines should protect them from the military. Cases in the first (immunity) category are rare. In Little v. Barreme (1804), the Supreme Court ruled that immunity would not protect a naval officer who had relied on President Thomas *Jefferson's illegal orders and seized a neutral ship. Congress has, on occasion, provided that service members be indemnified for civil legal liability, as it did when Andrew *Jackson, then military governor of New Orleans, was successfully sued for imprisoning an editor without legal authority. In 1940, Congress passed the Soldiers and Sailors Civil Relief Act, which still protects service members from some civil actions, and in 1988 Congress provided that the United States, not government employees (including members of the armed forces), would be civilly liable for official acts of those employees. Thus, service members gain few rights by virtue of their status.

When members of the armed forces claim a violation of rights, they point either to a statute that grants the right or to the U.S. Constitution. If the right is based on a statute, courts have routinely "second-guessed" the military's interpretation of the law and protected the right. In Brooks v. United States (1949), the Supreme Court rejected the government's interpretation of the Federal Tort Claims Act, which would have precluded service members' claims; but in Feres v. United States (1950), the Court ruled that claims incident to service were barred by the Tort Claims Act. In Bell v. United States (1961), the Court concluded that the military could not refuse to pay *Korean War "turncoats" as *prisoners of war otherwise eligible under the Missing Persons Act.

The most difficult cases arise, however, when the service member claims the protection of a constitutional right. The Constitution itself speaks only once of the rights of members of the armed forces. The Fifth Amendment, which grants the right of a grand jury indictment for serious crimes, makes an exception for courts-martial. Therefore, all other constitutional claims involve assertions by the individual that members of the armed forces should have the same civil rights accorded other citizens, while the executive branch argues that military requirements warrant disparate treatment. Nineteenth-century constitutional challenges that claimed that a court-martial had failed to grant the petitioner the due process guaranteed by the Fifth Amendment uniformly failed. The Supreme Court ruled that as long as the court-martial had jurisdiction over the person and the offense, and the power to authority to impose the sentence, civil courts should not interfere.

In the aftermath of World War II, several subordinate courts did question the fairness of a serviceman's court-martial conviction. The Supreme Court routinely rejected such collateral attacks. Similarly, claims—particularly common during the *Vietnam War—that the armed forces were infringing on a service member's constitutional rights of speech and worship were consistently rejected by the Supreme Court on the rationale that "due deference" should be given to commanders' discretionary judgments because the judiciary was ill-suited to second-guess those decisions. The military was seen as a "separate community," which would appropriately be judged by standards different from those applied in the civilian world. Deference reached its apogee in *Goldman* v. *Weinberger* (1986) when, by a 5–4 vote, the Supreme Court sustained the conviction of a Jewish officer who had violated regulations by wearing his yarmulke while in uniform. Deference may also grant certain benefits, as in *Katcoff* v. *Marsh* (1985), in which an intermediate appeals court concluded that the Constitution's establishment clause was not violated by funding and support for military chaplains.

There have, however, been exceptions to the doctrine of deference. On occasion, as in *Anderson* v. *Laird* (1972), when a subordinate court held that compulsory chapel attendance at the service academies was unconstitutional, the Supreme Court would not hear the government's appeal. In others, deference will not be granted because the judgment involved was neither military nor discretionary. In *Frontiero* v. *Richardson* (1973), the Supreme Court decided that a congressional pay statute which discriminated against military females claiming compensation for dependents was unconstitutional. In *Ryder* v. *United States* (1995), the Court ruled that the Coast Guard acted in violation of the appointments clause of the Constitution in staffing its Court of Military Review.

Any historical survey of service members' rights must conclude that the Supreme Court has consistently deferred to executive branch judgments that did not violate a statute or regulation but that would have been unconstitutional had a civilian been affected. Pending constitutional challenges to the military's treatment of homosexuals must be evaluated in that light.

[*See also* "Camp Followers"; Gay Men and Lesbians in the Military; Religion in the Military; Supreme Court, War, and the Military; Women in the Military.]

• Frederick B. Wiener, *Civilians Under Military Justice*, 1967. Joseph W. Bishop, Jr., *Justice Under Fire, a Study of Military Law*, 1974. John M. Lindley, *"A Soldier Is Also a Citizen": The Controversy Over Military Justice, 1917–1920*, 1990. Allan R. Millett, "The Constitution and the Citizen Soldier," *Revue internationale d'historire militaire*, 69 (1990), pp. 97–119. Jonathan Lurie, "The Role of the Federal Judiciary in the Governance of the American Military: The U.S. Supreme Court and Civil Rights Supervision Over the Armed Forces," in *The United States Military under the Constitution of the United States*, ed. Richard H. Kohn, 1991.

—Michael Noone

RIGHT TO BEAR ARMS. *See* Arms, Right to Bear.

RIO PACT. *See* Inter-American Treaty of Reciprocal Assistance (1947).

RIVALRY, INTERSERVICE. Clearly, the chief adversary of a nation's army should be another nation's army. But in practice, it often seems that the chief adversary of a nation's army is that nation's own navy or air force, and vice versa. Military services engage not only in international rivalry but also in interservice rivalry. These latter conflicts are fought not with lethal arms or over territory, but through lobbying and over "turf"—over the allocation of military roles, missions, and budgetary shares; they are fought not with weapons but over weapons; and they are fought not just in wartime but in peacetime as well.

Interservice rivalry has existed as long as there have been different military organizations employing different means of fighting. It has been especially pronounced, however, in maritime powers, where the navy has long been equal to or superior in status to the army. These were joined in the twentieth century by a third independent service, the air force. In the United States, interservice rivalry has been further institutionalized by the peculiar nature of the American political system, particularly the separation of powers in the federal government, which has given the services opportunities to protect their rival interests. Each U.S. military service has been supported by particular constituencies in Congress and in American society.

Traditionally, support for the army was centered upon the South, with its military bases suitable for training throughout the year, and upon the Midwest, with its heavy industry producing *artillery, *tanks, and military vehicles. Support for the navy, conversely, was centered upon the East and the West Coast, with their ports and their shipbuilding industries. The air force was centered upon the Southwest, the location of the best bases for all-weather flying and of the majority of the major aircraft manufacturers. During the long *Cold War era, however, these regional distinctions largely faded, and the military services became more national in their constituencies.

Interservice rivalry has been most intense in the immediate aftermath of a major war, when the large wartime military budgets are contracting but the large wartime scale of the military services is still in place. In addition, the development of new weapons technologies that occurred during wartime has had unequal impact upon the different services, and this has shifted the balance of power between the services or even within them. Interservice rivalry was intense after both wars and has revived since the Cold War.

During World War II, the U.S. military services fought the war against Germany and Japan according to their own doctrines. Each had its own version of the war. The army focused on a "Europe-first" strategy, a ground war against the German Army; the navy's role was transporting and supporting the army. Conversely, the navy focused on a "Pacific-first" strategy. There, the navy would be the dominant service, with the army in a peripheral role of conquering islands, a role that could be duplicated by the Marines, "the Navy's Army." The U.S. Army Air Corps used the experience of World War II as an opportunity to obtain its independence from the army. In 1947, it became an autonomous third military service. Its emphasis in the 1930s had been on strategic bombing—seen as a war-winning strategy—rather than on tactical airpower, which would make it primarily a ground support arm.

The aftermath of World War II was an especially intense period of interservice rivalry. Within three years, the gigantic military forces and military budgets of the United States were reduced by more than 80 percent. In this context, the struggle between the services over roles and missions was fierce, consuming far more of their time and energy than the emerging Cold War struggle with the Soviet Union.

With the full and formal independence of the U.S. *Air Force in 1947, the army lost its major air mission. Indeed, in the *Key West Agreement among the services in 1948, it lost any fixed-wing combat aircraft and was left with only *helicopters. For a time, the army sought to compensate for this loss of air combat forces by achieving a monopoly of land combat forces, that is, by seeking to eliminate the Marines. The Marines, however, were solidly entrenched in public opinion and Congress and were able to maintain themselves, although on a reduced scale. Throughout the 1950s, the army tried to reenter the realm of airpower by exploiting the new technology of ballistic *missiles. It had some initial success, but this route back into airpower was finally blocked by President Dwight D. *Eisenhower, who canceled the army intercontinental ballistic missile program, giving land-based missiles solely to the air force.

In the same postwar period, the navy saw the air force's aspirations to a monopoly of airpower and the delivery of nuclear and conventional *bombs and warheads to be a threat to its *aircraft carriers, which had become the core force of the navy. It quickly moved to make carriers capable of the strategic bombing mission by proposing a supercarrier, the USS *United States*. But, deferring to the air force, President Harry S. *Truman canceled this ship in 1949, leading to public protests and enforced resignations of several top-ranking naval officers, an episode that was dubbed "the Revolt of the Admirals."

The air force was the chief winner in these interservice conflicts of the late 1940s. During the next decade, through the Strategic Air Command (SAC), it continued to monopolize the strategic bombing mission, and under the Eisenhower administration it normally received fully half of the defense budget. The air force was supported by the new and politically influential aerospace industry. But the navy's development in the late 1950s of the submarine-launched ballistic missile (SLBM) broke the air force monopoly of strategic *nuclear weapons.

Similarly, the army's development in the late 1950s of a conventional war doctrine for the defense of Western Europe (termed *Flexible Response*) was aimed at breaking the air force monopoly of ways in which to defeat the Soviet Union. President Eisenhower rejected the new doctrine, leading to the public protests and forced resignations of its principal advocates, Gen. Maxwell *Taylor and Gen. James Gavin, or a "Revolt of the Generals." This revolt and its doctrine, however, had powerful supporters, first the leading Democrats in Congress and later the next president, John F. *Kennedy, and this gave final victory to the army. These successes by the navy and the army in their struggles with the air force meant that since the early 1960s the budgetary shares of the three services have proved far more equal.

The aftermath of the Cold War produced renewed interservice rivalry over allocation of roles, missions, and budgetary shares. The army rapidly sought to become the premier service in the new conflicts characterizing the post–Cold War era, again seeking to reduce its combat competitor, the Marines. The intervention in Panama (1989) was commanded and largely monopolized by the army. The *Persian Gulf War (1991) was also fought under army command, with that service largely monopolizing the ground war and delegating a peripheral role to the Marines. The air war was largely monopolized by the air force, with the navy playing a peripheral role (via cruise missiles). Once again, the air force claimed to have made the other services obsolete.

It is now a half century since the modern tripartite allocation of roles and missions—what might be termed the *military constitution*—in the aftermath of World War II.

Although there were a few major amendments to that constitution in the course of the Cold War (the navy acquiring a strategic nuclear mission with its SLBMs; the army briefly acquiring in the late 1960s a missile defense mission with its antiballistic missile system and in the 1990s seeking it again with ballistic missile defense), the fundamental structure has remained the same, firmly institutionalized, grounded in the support provided by Congress and by the economic interests and political associations of the wider society. The prospects are that interservice rivalry in the foreseeable future will be conducted on the margins of budgetary shares.

The existing balance of power between the services is largely a product of military technologies that date from World War II and the early Cold War. However, the services are now developing and deploying new weapons systems that are based upon the most advanced integration of computers, telecommunications, and *lasers. In the future, these weapons systems will integrate and even transcend the old distinctions between land, sea-, and airpower, and they may not readily fit into the old services of the army, navy, and air force.

Predictably these established services will seek to master the new technologies, and each will try to demonstrate that it is more suited to shape the future than its rivals. But the victor is likely to discover that the price of nurturing such a radical new technology may be utterly to change the nature of the service itself.

[See also Air Force, U.S.: Since 1947; Army, U.S.: Since 1941; National Security Act (1947); Navy, U.S.: Since 1946; Panama, U.S. Military Involvement in; World War II: Military and Diplomatic Course.]

• Samuel P. Huntington, *The Common Defense: Strategic Programs in National Politics*, 1961. Graham T. Allison, *Essence of Decision: Explaining the Cuban Missile Crisis*, 1971. Richard A. Gabriel, *Military Incompetence: Why the American Military Doesn't Win*, 1985. David C. Kozak and James M. Keagle, eds. *Bureaucratic Politics and National Security: Theory and Practice*, 1988. Michael E. Brown, *Flying Blind: The Politics of the U.S. Strategic Bombing Program*, 1992.

—James Kurth

RIVER CRAFT. Small, shallow draft vessels have played supporting roles in virtually every American conflict since the *Revolutionary War. Pole boats, said to be 60 feet long, 8 feet wide, and drawing 2 feet or less when fully loaded, ferried George *Washington's army across the Delaware.

In the *Civil War, Gen. George B. *McClellan's Army of the Potomac was saved, barely, by Union gunboats pushing up the James River to cover his retreat from before Richmond in the ill-fated Peninsula campaign. On the western rivers, small steamboats outfitted with cannon, mortars, and protective armor contributed greatly to Union victories at Fort Henry, Fort Donelson, Island Number 10, the Battle of *Shiloh, and the Siege of *Vicksburg.

The first three Union gunboats on the Mississippi were converted side-wheelers, averaging 180 feet in length, with 42-foot beams, and drawing about 6 feet of water. They carried 8-inch and 32-pounder guns. These were followed quickly by seven stern-wheelers (Eads boats or "Pook's turtles"), armored at the bow and outboard of propulsion machinery by 2.5-inch iron plate. These had a length of 175 feet, 51-foot beams, and also drew 6 feet—the maximum thought practical for operations on the upper rivers. This was the nucleus of the Union's western flotilla, a river fleet that would number in the hundreds by war's end and include boats outfitted with monstrous 15-inch siege guns.

An interesting variant of the Union river gunboat was the "tin-clad," armored with thin sheets of iron for protection from small-arms fire. It carried 24-pound howitzers and a small number of sharpshooters. About seventy of these were built; they were used primarily to patrol the smaller tributaries of the Mississippi.

The South, seriously deficient in shipbuilding facilities, machine shops, and mills capable of rolling iron plate, still managed to put scores of gunboats on the western rivers. Virtually all were converted from civilian use. Some Confederate boats were "cotton-clads" whose crews and vital engine spaces were shielded by tightly compressed bales of cotton. Armed rams achieved the most notable of the few Southern successes in the losing campaign for control of the Mississippi basin.

In the *Vietnam War, river craft were assigned a more prominent role than in any war since the one on the American western rivers a century before. In the virtually roadless Mekong Delta, whoever controlled the waterways controlled the land, and the U.S. "Brown Water Navy" patrolled a vast network of rivers and canals throughout the country, from the demilitarized zone in the North to the Ca Mau peninsula in the South.

River craft that saw service in Vietnam fell roughly into two categories: World War II *landing craft conversions; and new construction patrol boats adapted from commercial designs.

The LCM (landing craft, mechanized) provided the hull and machinery for a wide variety of "heavy" boats assigned to the Riverine Assault Force, the naval arm of the joint Army-Navy Mobile Riverine Force. These 56-foot, diesel-powered craft displaced more than 60 tons and had a draft of about 3.5 feet. On the rivers they could make little better than 6 knots, a terrible handicap when operating in adverse currents and tides. The LCM conversions included the "monitor," the armored troop carrier (ATC), and the command and control boat (CCB).

The monitor, so called because of its slight resemblance to the Civil War ironclad, carried a 40-mm cannon and a .50-caliber machine gun in a forward turret. An 81-mm mortar and two M-60 *machine guns were mounted amidships, with one 20-mm cannon and two .50-caliber and four M-60 machine guns aft. A few monitors had powerful *flamethrowers mounted forward—from the name of the popular cigarette lighter, these were called "Zippo" boats.

The ATC was designed to carry forty fully armed combat troops. It mounted two 20-mm cannon and two .50-caliber and four M-60 machine guns. Some ATCs were decked over to permit the landing and takeoff of *helicopters. Several carried water cannon capable of washing away bankside bunkers; these, inevitably, were nicknamed "douche boats" by the sailors who crewed them.

The armament on the CCB closely paralleled that of the monitor. Sometimes called a *commandement* (a name borrowed from an earlier French boat), it was designed as an afloat command post and came equipped with additional communications and *radar gear.

The 50-foot assault support and patrol boat (ASPB) was the only new construction craft built for the Riverine Assault Force. It displaced about 35 tons and could make 15 knots in ideal water conditions. It mounted one 20-mm cannon, one 81-mm mortar, two .50-caliber machine guns, and two automatic grenade launchers. Due to low freeboard and numerous other design flaws, the ASPB was not well received by the Brown Water Navy.

The principal craft employed by the navy's River Patrol Force was the 31-foot patrol boat, river (PBR). Adapted from a recreational design, its fiberglass hull had a 10-foot, 6-inch beam, and it drew only 9 to 18 inches. It was powered by two 220-horsepower diesel engines driving Jacuzzi high-speed jet pumps. Having neither rudder nor screws, the PBR was maneuvered by altering the direction of the jet nozzles; its speed rated at 25 knots. It carried twin .50-caliber machine guns forward and .30-caliber machine guns and a grenade launcher aft.

As U.S. participation in the Vietnam War drew to a close, virtually all of the river craft comprising America's Brown Water Navy were transferred to a Vietnamese Navy ill-prepared and ill-equipped to receive them. Relatively few are still operational, either in the U.S. Navy's inventory or in that of the victorious Communist government of Vietnam.

[*See also* Navy, U.S.; Swift Boats; Union Navy.]

• E. B. Potter, ed., *Sea Power—A Naval History*, 1960. Bern Anderson, *By Sea and by River, the Naval History of the Civil War*, 1962. Frank Donovan, *River Boats of America*, 1966. Thomas J. Cutler, *Brown Water, Black Berets*, 1980. Edward L. Beach, *The United States Navy—200 Years*, 1986. R. L. Schreadley, *From the Rivers to the Sea*, 1992. R. Thomas Campbell, *Gray Thunder*, 1996.

—R. L. Schreadley

RIVERS, L. MENDEL (1905–1970), South Carolina congressman and House Armed Services Committee chairman. Rivers, raised in poverty, was a lawyer with the U.S. Justice Department during the depression. In 1940, he began a thirty-year career representing Charleston, South Carolina, and surrounding counties in the U.S. House. He was a member of the Armed Services Committee for most of that time, serving as chairman from 1965 until his death. Rivers was an enthusiastic proponent of a strong military and was unmistakably "hawkish" in the political debates of the *Cold War. He was unrestrained in his advocacy of increased military expenditures and the use of American power, including support for all-out prosecution of the *Vietnam War.

Rivers's constituents were well rewarded with a large number of military bases placed in his district. At the height of his career, at least one-third of all income in the First District came from the military and defense-related industries. Critics labeled his efforts "pork barrel" politics with little regard for actual national security needs.

Rivers was a traditional segregationist, though the one-time Dixiecrat had reconciled with the national Democratic Party by the time he became Armed Services chairman.

• Will F. Huntley, "Mighty Rivers of Charleston." Ph.D. diss., University of South Carolina, 1993. Marion Rivers Ravenel, *Rivers Delivers*, 1995.

—Luther Faggart

RODMAN, THOMAS JACKSON (1815-1871), U.S. *Army officer and ordnance innovator. Born near Salem, Indiana, Rodman graduated seventh in his class at West Point in 1841. He entered the artillery. Distressed by the fatal bursting of the USS *Princeton*'s flawed experimental "Peacemaker" cannon, he proposed in 1845 a novel system of casting smoothbore heavy ordnance. Unlike conventional castings, which cooled from the outside in, Rodman cast cannon on a hollow core, cooling from the inside out. As the outer layers cooled, they compressed the inner layers, giving the cannon greater tensile strength. After initially dismissing the idea, the army's Ordnance Bureau finally approved it in 1859. The United States and European nations immediately adopted it as the method of choice until the 1880s, when steel cannon became too large to cast in one piece. Rodman also introduced mammoth, perforated cake powders, whose larger grains burned more uniformly than earlier gunpowders. He published his work in *Reports of Experiments on the Properties of Metals for Cannon, and the Qualities of Cannon Powder* (1861). During the Civil War, while the Union army made a number of "Rodman guns," Rodman himself supervised the government's Watertown Arsenal. He commanded the Rock Island Arsenal after the war and died on active duty, having reached the rank of brevet brigadier-general.

[*See also* Artillery.]

—Kurt Henry Hackemer

ROGERS, ROBERT. *See* Rangers, U.S. Army.

ROMMEL, ERWIN (1891–1944), German general. Born in Germany, Rommel served with distinction in World War I, winning the coveted Pour le Mérite medal. Rising from infantry captain in 1918 to general during the interwar years, the author of a best-selling book on infantry warfare, and increasingly an admirer and favorite of Adolf *Hitler, Rommel commanded the Führer's headquarters in the Polish campaign of 1939. As commander of the Seventh *Panzer* Division in World War II, he then performed brilliantly in France in 1940, and commanded the Afrika Korps from February 1941 to March 1943 in the *North Africa Campaign. Having achieved the position of a highly decorated and much admired field marshal, Rommel was finally defeated by Gen. Bernard Law *Montgomery at El Alamein, and was recalled from his post before his corps were wiped out in May. In July 1944, Rommel was put in charge of German forces along the "Atlantic Wall" in the Netherlands, Belgium, and France. He disagreed with his superior, Field Marshal Gerd von Rundstedt, advocating impregnable beach defenses rather than reliance upon a mobile reserve to repel the threatened Allied amphibious invasion. The Germans tried to do both. Following the successful Allied invasion of *Normandy, Rommel was severely wounded in an aerial attack in mid-July. Partly implicated in the plot against Hitler, Rommel committed suicide on 14 October to avoid trial and was buried with military honors as a German hero.

Like many of his generation, Erwin Rommel was a gifted, ambitious, patriotic, and politically naive officer. As long as Hitler seemed to offer him personal glory and to lead Germany toward national greatness, Rommel followed him enthusiastically. Belatedly recognizing the looming catastrophe, Rommel halfheartedly communicated with the conspirators. Made into an immensely popular figure of German soldiering by Nazi propaganda, Rommel was preserved from the humiliating fate of the more decisive plotters. For several decades after World War II, Rommel's reputation as a brilliant tactician, the "Desert Fox," and a staunch anti-Nazi made him into something of

a cult figure among military historians in Britain and the United States. More recent studies have shown him to have been much more typical of the majority of the Wehrmacht's generals who knowingly employed their professional skills in the service of an odious regime. He remains a partly tragic, partly pathetic figure who played a major role in Hitler's savage war on civilization. Rommel lacked the strength and courage to act decisively against the regime even when it had clearly become both militarily and morally bankrupt.

[*See also* Germany, Battle for; World War II: Military and Diplomatic Course.]

• Desmond Young, *Rommel*, 1965. David Irving, *The Trail of the Fox: The Life of Field-Marshal Erwin Rommel*, 1978.

—Omer Bartov

ROOSEVELT, ELEANOR (1884–1962), first lady, diplomat, journalist, and activist. Eleanor Roosevelt struggled to reconcile an intense abhorrence of war with a realpolitik commitment against totalitarianism. This caused her to weigh deeply held but often conflicting beliefs. In World War I, as wife of Assistant Secretary of the Navy Franklin D. *Roosevelt, she worked with shell-shocked sailors at St. Elizabeth's Hospital and the American *Red Cross Canteen, and this introduced her to some of the ravages of war. Later she joined the *Women's International League for Peace and Freedom and chaired the Bok Peace Prize Committee. Her second monograph, *This Troubled World*, was a plea for economic *deterrence instead of war. However, by late 1939, Adolf *Hitler's actions led her to support U.S. military intervention in *World War II. As the wife of the president, she urged women to enlist and join defense industries, corresponded with hundreds of military personnel, and used her daily newspaper column to defend the war effort while supporting civil liberties at home. She was a strong critic of Japanese American internment and the administration's policy of limiting the acceptance of refugees, and publicly supported those conscientious objectors who chose medical service and jail over enlistment.

After her husband's death in office in April 1945, as the European War ended, the former first lady urged full employment, a comprehensive *veterans benefit package, and a strong *United Nations. She supported the atomic bombing of Hiroshima but was silent about Nagasaki. Appointed a UN delegate by President Harry S. *Truman, she orchestrated support for the Universal Declaration of Human Rights and oversaw refugee policy. Opposing Truman, she urged early recognition of Israel and UN oversight of the *Marshall Plan, and only reluctantly supported the creation of NATO. As the Cold War intensified in the 1950s, she supported an economic rather than a military emphasis on containment, and in the 1960s, she opposed U.S. military involvement in Vietnam and lobbied against the stockpiling of *nuclear weapons. She died still convinced that effective democracy was the most effective deterrence to both communism and war.

[*See also* Hiroshima and Nagasaki, Bombings of; Japanese-American Internment Cases; World War II: Military and Diplomatic Course.]

• Allida Black, *Casting Her Own Shadow: Eleanor Roosevelt and the Shaping of Postwar Liberalism*, 1996. Allida Black, ed., *Courage in a Dangerous World: Political Writings of Eleanor Roosevelt*, 1999.

—Allida Black

ROOSEVELT, FRANKLIN D. (1882–1945), thirty-second president of the United States. Born to the Hudson River aristocracy of upstate New York, Roosevelt attended Groton, Harvard College, and Columbia Law School before marrying his distant cousin Eleanor *Roosevelt in 1905. Following election to the New York State Senate (1911–13), he served as assistant secretary of the navy in Woodrow *Wilson's administration (1913–21). A devotee of Alfred T. *Mahan's writings, the young FDR championed "Big Navy" preparedness prior to American entry into World War I, instituted "Naval Plattsburg" battleship cruises to recruit civilian reservists, and advocated a system of universal military training. After a three-month tour of the battle zones in 1918, he said that "the last thing this country should do is ever to send an army to Europe again."

An unsuccessful candidate for vice president in 1920, Roosevelt overcame crippling polio to win the New York governorship in 1928 and attain the White House in 1932. Espousing isolationist views during his first two terms, FDR gave priority to New Deal reforms over foreign policy, accepted congressional revision of neutrality laws, and reacted hesitantly to Axis aggression in Asia and Europe. Notwithstanding his "Arsenal of Democracy" speech in December 1940, he had urged moderate rearmament until Adolf *Hitler's conquest of France and supported the Selective Service Act of 1940 only after political opponents had introduced it. While promising to protect the hemisphere from war, he employed the neutrality patrol, the *Destroyers-for-Bases Agreement, Lend-Lease, and economic embargoes primarily to assist potential Allies (Britain, China, Soviet Union) in steps short of full belligerency. Emphasizing naval power and airpower instead of a second *American Expeditionary Force, FDR proceeded to "wage war, but not declare it."

After Japan's attack on *Pearl Harbor in December 1941 catapulted the United States into World War II, some isolationist historians later charged that Roosevelt had provoked the Japanese into firing the first shot so as to overcome American *isolationism and thus ensure support, via the Pacific "back door," for war against Japan's ally, Nazi Germany. Most scholars reject conspiracy and explain Pearl Harbor as the consequence of intelligence errors, missed clues, overconfidence, and plain bad luck. Nonetheless, Japan's attack and Hitler's subsequent declaration of war gave FDR the political leeway to implement a "Europe-first" military strategy. Fearful that mounting American *casualties in the Pacific would focus public resentment against Japan, the president reaffirmed Anglo-American plans to defeat Hitler first. Against recommendations of the *Joint Chiefs of Staff to concentrate forces in England for a cross-Channel invasion by spring 1943, he accepted Winston S. *Churchill's alternative plan, Operation Torch, for the *North Africa Campaign in November 1942. This decision led logically to the invasion and conquest of *Sicily and *Italy in 1943 and effectively postponed the liberation of *France (Operation Overlord) until 1944. Apart from Roosevelt's desire for Americans to fight Germans somewhere in 1942, British strategy predominated in the two years after Pearl Harbor because England had fully mobilized, whereas America had not, and any combined operation had to depend largely on British troops, shipping, and casualties.

Despite the European emphasis, Roosevelt did reinforce the Pacific theater after victories at the Battle of *Coral Sea and the Battle of *Midway (1942) and oversaw a controversial two-prong strategy in which the navy and Marines "leapfrogged" toward Tokyo across Micronesian atolls while U.S.-Australian forces under Gen. Douglas *MacArthur battled northward from New Guinea to the Philippines. FDR's expectation that China would figure decisively in defeating Japan and policing postwar Asia was undermined by Japan's conquest of Burma and internal bickering between Chinese Communists and Nationalists.

Because Roosevelt sought to win the war with minimal American casualties, the country never fully mobilized its population for military service. With no threat of invasion and the bulk of Axis forces engaged in Russia and China, the president gambled that "an air war plus the Russians" meant that ninety U.S. Army divisions would be sufficient for military and political goals.

Such calculations increased dependence on Soviet Russia. With the Red Army "killing more Axis personnel . . . than all other twenty-five United Nations put together," Roosevelt sent the Soviets $11 billion in Lend-Lease supplies, made promises for an early second front, and used personal diplomacy at Teheran (November 1943) and Yalta (February 1945). "Unconditional Surrender" assured a suspicious Josef *Stalin that there would be no separate peace with Hitler or his underlings. It also underscored FDR's belief that Germany deserved punishment for Hitler's crimes, including permanent partition, demilitarization, and dismantling of heavy industry. The president's postwar plans envisaged a disarmed, decentralized, and decolonized Europe initially policed by British and Soviet armies; U.S. forces would patrol the western hemisphere and replace Japanese power in the western Pacific. Because Red Army victories guaranteed Soviet hegemony over Eastern Europe, FDR urged "open" spheres and free elections and hoped that increased contacts would make the Russians "less barbarian."

Aiding the Soviets reflected Roosevelt's military advice. Despite "assured Russian military dominance" after the war, the joint chiefs invariably opposed "get tough" policies because of military necessity, including the need for Soviet help against Japan. According to Secretary of War Henry L. *Stimson in 1945, "in the big military matters the Soviet Government have kept their word." Only after the end of the war did the predominant U.S. military view of the Soviet Union change from ally to adversary.

That the cooperation with the Kremlin had limits was shown in the *Manhattan Project, the secret Anglo-American effort to acquire an atomic weapon before the Germans. Despite Danish physicist Niels *Bohr's plea in 1944 that the Russians be brought into the partnership to prevent a postwar nuclear *arms race, Roosevelt and Churchill chose to maintain their monopoly, partly as a hedge against Russian misbehavior.

The booming U.S. economy (the gross national product had jumped from $90.5 billion in 1939 to $211.9 billion in 1945) also provided insurance against future uncertainties, as did FDR's support for new international institutions—the *United Nations, *World Bank, and International Monetary Fund—designed to maintain peace and prosperity after the war.

The commander in chief died of a cerebral hemorrhage in April 1945, shortly after the *Yalta Conference, on the eve of final victory.

[*See also* Lend-Lease Act and Agreements; World War II: Military and Diplomatic Course.]

• Eric Larrabee, *Commander in Chief: Franklin Delano Roosevelt, His Lieutenants and Their War,* 1987. Frank Freidel, *Franklin D. Roosevelt: A Rendezvous with Destiny,* 1990. Doris Kearns Goodwin, *No Ordinary Time: Franklin and Eleanor Roosevelt: The Homefront in World War II,* 1994. Warren F. Kimball, *Forged in War: Roosevelt, Churchill, and the Second World War,* 1997.

—J. Garry Clifford

ROOSEVELT, THEODORE (1858–1919), assistant secretary of the navy, governor of New York, vice president, and twenty-sixth president of the United States. Born to a wealthy New York family, a puny, asthmatic, and near-sighted child, Theodore Roosevelt seemed destined for a sheltered life. Instead, he developed his body and an appetite for public service in an obsessive quest to prove his masculinity and to assert his independence. He became a dynamic political leader.

Roosevelt embraced things military from an early age. Two years after graduating from Harvard in 1880, he published *The Naval War of 1812,* reflecting the navalist thinking later codified by Capt. Alfred T. *Mahan. Roosevelt developed his political skills as a New York State legislator, U.S. Civil Service Commissioner, and New York police commissioner. In 1897, he became assistant secretary of the navy in the McKinley administration.

An ardent advocate of the *Spanish-American War, Roosevelt used his political connections to secure an appointment in 1898 as lieutenant colonel in the First U.S. Volunteer Cavalry regiment, the "Rough Riders." His friend Col. Leonard *Wood commanded the unit initially, but he left for a higher command. Roosevelt's most famous military exploit came when he led a charge in the Battle of *San Juan Hill (actually Kettle Hill) outside Santiago, Cuba. The well-publicized exploit helped him win the New York governorship in 1898 and vice presidency in 1900.

Roosevelt became president in September 1901 after President McKinley's assassination. A moralist in tone but realist in practice, Roosevelt worried about competition with Germany in the Caribbean and, later, about tensions with Japan. Diplomatically, he acted as a mediator and won a Nobel Peace Prize for negotiating an end to the Russo-Japanese War in 1905.

A fervent believer in the Mahanian doctrine of sea power, Roosevelt paid particular attention to the U.S. Navy as the first line of defense and a primary instrument of American foreign policy. He used the navy to signal American concern during the Venezuelan crisis of 1902–03 and deployed naval forces to block Colombian suppression of the Panamanian revolt in 1903, clearing the way for construction of the Panama Canal. Roosevelt operated in effect as his own secretary of the navy. A competitor in the international naval *arms race of the day, he won congressional approval for sixteen *battleships, including new, powerful dreadnoughts, and he increased the naval budget by 60 percent.

Roosevelt also pushed for more realistic and frequent training exercises. He united the navy's battleships in a true fleet formation and then sent the "great white fleet" on a world cruise from 1907 to 1909 to test its ability to operate coherently and to demonstrate U.S. naval power.

With Secretary of War (and later State) Elihu *Root, Roosevelt also sought to enlarge and modernize the army.

He supported the *General Staff Act, endorsed larger unit training, elevated able officers, and approved reform legislation in 1903 and 1908 to make the National Guard a more reliable federal reserve. He also pushed for the development of aviation and the machine-gun service.

Roosevelt left office in 1909 and lost a bid for the presidency in 1912 on the Progressive Party ticket. As a former president, he played a leading role in the military "Preparedness" movement in 1915–17 for universal military training and for a larger navy. He assailed Woodrow *Wilson's foreign and military policies, urging the United States to enter the war after the sinking of the *Lusitania in 1915. Upon American intervention in 1917, Roosevelt asked to lead a volunteer division, but President Wilson refused. During World War I, Roosevelt denounced dissenters and urged a postwar coalition with Britain. He died shortly after the end of the war.

[*See also* Caribbean and Latin America, U.S. Military Involvement in the; Roosevelt Corollary to the Monroe Doctrine.]

• Howard Beale, *Theodore Roosevelt and the Rise of America to World Power,* 1956. William Henry Harbaugh, *Power and Responsibility: The Life and Times of Theodore Roosevelt,* 1961; rev. ed., 1975. Richard Collin, *Theodore Roosevelt's Caribbean: The Panama Canal, the Monroe Doctrine, and the Latin American Context,* 1990. Lewis L. Gould, *The Presidency of Theodore Roosevelt,* 1991.

—Matthew Oyos

ROOSEVELT COROLLARY TO THE MONROE DOCTRINE (1928). Threats by European powers to occupy the customshouses of defaulting governments in such nations as Venezuela and the Dominican Republic, coupled with the specter of foreign acquisition of military bases in the western hemisphere, led President Theodore *Roosevelt to declare in his annual message of December 1904 that "chronic wrongdoing" or "impotence" on the part of neighboring countries might force the United States to exercise "an international police power," his so-called Corollary to the *Monroe Doctrine.

Roosevelt proceeded to exercise such power in Santo Domingo without injury to the national reputation, and William Howard Taft did the same in Nicaragua. But when Woodrow *Wilson mounted successive military interventions aimed at installing democratic government in Mexico and elsewhere, U. S. prestige began to erode.

Wilsonian intervention left hard feelings on both sides of the Rio Grande contributing to the *isolationism of the 1920s, and one casualty of this shift in sentiment was the Roosevelt Corollary. Impugned by Republicans on the basis of a technicality as outlined by Herbert Hoover's Undersecretary of State, J. Reuben Clark, in a memorandum of December 17, 1928, it was further repudiated by sweeping Democratic pledges of non-intervention at Montevideo (1933) and Buenos Aires (1936).

Disinterested benevolence was the order of the day. However, the principal reason for the Corollary's demise was geopolitical. No longer was it a matter of forestalling an Anglo-German naval demonstration such as had occurred in the Caribbean during the years 1902–03 to force payment of the Venezuelan debt. New international machinery for the adjudication of default was in place; Berlin had tasted defeat and London was friendly. The problem facing Franklin *Roosevelt and his successors was how to deal with socialist subversion based on a portrayal of the

United States as grasping and overbearing. Since such a threat was covered, at least indirectly, by Monroe's original dictum (1823), latter-day intervention by Lyndon B. *Johnson and Ronald *Reagan could be carried out without reference to, or revival of, the Roosevelt Corollary. And so it was.

[See also Caribbean and Latin America, U.S. Military Involvement in the.]

• Dexter Perkins, Hands Off: A History of the Monroe Doctrine, 1955; Samuel Flagg Bemis, The Latin American Policy of the United States, 1967.   —Frederick W. Marks III

ROOT, ELIHU (1845–1937), Wall Street lawyer, secretary of war, secretary of state, U.S. senator. Root was a Wall Street lawyer, familiar with corporate reorganization and international law, when President William *McKinley appointed him secretary of war in 1899. In the wake of the *Spanish-American War, McKinley wanted a secretary who could handle the complexities of administering the new overseas possessions in the Caribbean and Pacific and also reorganize and modernize the War Department following the chaotic mobilization of 1898.

This conservative Republican proved to be not only a competent administrator of Colonial policy in the Philippines and *Cuba, but also a reformer who propelled the U.S. Army into the twentieth century. The "Root Reforms," accomplished while he was secretary of war (1899–1904) under Presidents McKinley and Theodore *Roosevelt, mark him as one of the most important secretaries of war in United States history. Responding to modernizers in the officer corps, Root expanded the army's postgraduate schools, organized them into a coherent system, and established the Army War College in 1900. He also enlarged the peacetime army to meet overseas responsibilities; rotated officers assigned to the War Department's staff bureaus to freshen departmental administration; and helped modernize the National Guard according to federal standards. Finally, he led the legislative campaign for the *General Staff Act to provide for central army direction and planning, which Congress approved in 1903.

He later served as Theodore Roosevelt's secretary of state (1905–09), as Republican senator for New York (1909–15), and as president of the *Carnegie Endowment for International Peace (1910–25), winning the Nobel Peace Prize in 1912. He was a delegate (1921–22) to the conference that led to the Washington Naval Arms Limitation Treaty and an advocate of the World Court.

• Phillip C. Jessup, Elihu Root, 2 vols., 1938. Richard W. Leopold, Elihu Root and the Conservative Tradition, 1954.

—Matthew Oyos

ROOT REFORMS. See General Staff Act (1903).

ROSECRANS, WILLIAM S. (1819–1898), Civil War general, businessman, and politician. Ohio-born and largely self-educated, Rosecrans graduated from West Point in 1842. Resigning his commission after twelve uneventful years, he pursued a variety of unsuccessful business ventures. Rejoining the army in 1861 as a brigadier general in the Civil War, he conducted the critical operations that ejected Confederate forces from western Virginia. In 1862 he moved to the western theater, leading part of the *Union army that seized Corinth, Mississippi. Thereafter,

as a district commander, he held his own in the indecisive battles of Iuka and Corinth.

Promoted to major general, Rosecrans assumed command of the Army of the Cumberland in late October 1862. Charged with regaining middle and eastern Tennessee for the Union, he advanced from Nashville in December and precipitated the Battle of *Stones River. After two days of intense fighting, he successfully held the field, thereby winning the Union's only military triumph at the end of 1862.

Six months later, Rosecrans resumed his advance toward Chattanooga, Tennessee. Clearing middle Tennessee in the masterful Tullahoma campaign, he next lunged across the Tennessee River into Georgia, driving Confederate forces from Chattanooga. Incautiously continuing his advance until confronted by a reinforced Army of Tennessee, he was attacked on Chickamauga Creek—the Battle of *Chickamauga—in late September. Nearing exhaustion, he issued a faulty order that collapsed his line and forced him from the field while much of his army still resisted. Relieved of command in October, he was given the Department of Missouri in 1864 but did not distinguish himself during a Confederate raid.

Postwar, Rosecrans served variously as minister to Mexico, register of the Treasury, congressman, and California rancher. Brilliant but erratic, touted before Chickamauga as a potential general in chief or presidential candidate, Rosecrans saw his military career essentially ended by a single error in judgment on 20 September 1863.

[See also Civil War: Military and Diplomatic Course.]

• William M. Lamers, The Edge of Glory: A Biography of General William S. Rosecrans, 1961. Peter Cozzens, This Terrible Sound: The Battle of Chickamauga, 1992.   —William Glenn Robertson

ROSIE THE RIVETER. See Gender and War.

ROSTOW, WALT W. (1916–), U.S. national security adviser, 1966–69. Walt Rostow was one of the leading American strategists during the *Vietnam War. Throughout the conflict, he maintained a pro-war position. A prominent and well-respected professor of economic history at the Massachusetts Institute of Technology, Rostow was brought to the White House by President John F. *Kennedy in January 1961 as deputy national security adviser. He later developed the "Rostow thesis," which held that an externally supported insurgency could be defeated only by military action against the external source of support. The thesis called for a series of escalating military measures designed to raise the cost of supporting the insurgency. As the number of American ground troops in Vietnam increased by early 1966, Rostow emerged as the leading proponent of President Lyndon B. *Johnson's Vietnam policy. In March 1966, Johnson named him national security adviser; he became one of the president's closest foreign policy advisers and a major advocate of bombing North Vietnam.

Rostow left government service at the end of the Johnson administration in 1969. His strong association with Vietnam policy left him estranged from some in the American academic community. He accepted a teaching position at the University of Texas, where he continued to teach and to write books on history, economics, and international affairs.

[See also Vietnam War: Domestic Course; Vietnam War: Changing Interpretations.]

• Lyndon B. Johnson, The Vantage Point: Perspectives of the Presidency, 1963–1969, 1971. Walt W. Rostow, The Diffusion of Power: An Essay in Recent History, 1972.   —Herbert Y. Schandler

ROTC—the Reserve Officers Training Corps—is the program for training students in American universities, colleges, high schools, and academies to serve as officers in the U.S. armed forces. Since World War II it has provided the majority of active duty and reserve officers, particularly junior officers, for the armed forces.

Although the ROTC program was established in 1916, the idea of obtaining military officers from civilian institutions dates back to the *citizen-soldiers of the colonial militia units. In the new republic, while the federal government founded its own military and naval academies for officering the regular forces, and a few states had private military academies, most officers in the state militias (later National Guard) and the ad hoc wartime units of volunteers were civilians temporarily in uniform. Their preparation came from prior military experience, militia membership, or simply by reading military manuals.

The *Civil War expansion of the army showed the need for a more widespread training of such citizen-officers. The idea of including military training in public colleges was incorporated into the Morrill Act of 1862, which granted public lands for the establishment of colleges and provided that military tactics should be offered as part of the curriculum in these land-grant institutions. The federal government provided some funding and the War Department assigned some active duty or retired officers as professors of military science and tactics. By 1893, some seventy-nine colleges and universities provided such military instruction, varying by state or institution as to whether it was voluntary or compulsory for male students. Between 1865 and 1919, West Point continued to be the main source of commissioned officers for the regular army. The graduates who had taken military courses at the land-grant colleges were neither commissioned nor registered with the War Department.

The growing size of armies and the emergence of the United States as an active world power in the early twentieth century led some military planners, businesspeople, and college presidents to advocate a regularized system of commissioning reserve officers from the citizenry. In 1913, Gen. Leonard *Wood, the army chief of staff, with several college presidents established summer military training camps for college students. After the outbreak of World War I, these formed the model for summer military training camps, held at Plattsburg, New York, and elsewhere in 1915 and 1916, for some 13,000 business and professional men. General Wood, former President Theodore *Roosevelt, and former Secretary of War Elihu *Root obtained federal funding for the camps and the commissioning of their graduates in the army's new Officers Reserve Corps.

The National Defense Act of 1916 also authorized the creation of a campus-based Reserve Officers Training Corps in its modern form. Students would take a two-year basic course plus a two-year advanced course; in addition to their regular academic courses, they would also participate in summer field training, and some would be eligible for scholarships and living allowances. Those who completed the four-year program would become commissioned officers with the regulars or the reserves. U.S. entry into the war in 1917 came as ROTC was just being established. Although ROTC provided some wartime officers, the majority came from the enlisted ranks of the regular army and National Guard, from Plattsburg camp graduates, and from civilians who went through ninety-day officer training camps established by the army during the war. Reserve officers provided 43 percent of the World War I officers, yet the army still obtained only half the 200,000 officers it desired to lead 3.5 million men.

Because the war had demonstrated the shortage of pretrained citizen-officers, the National Defense Act of 1920 expanded the two main programs for preparing reserve officers: the summer camp–oriented Civilian Military Training Corps and the larger, campus-based ROTC. By 1928, there were ROTC units in 225 colleges and universities, 100 high schools and academies, with a total enrollment of 85,000 students. ROTC commissioned about 6,000 graduates each year. In addition, the U.S. Navy created Naval ROTC (NROTC) in 1926 with the units initially at six colleges and universities.

In the antiwar and antimilitary mood of the 1920s and early 1930s, peace activists, educators, and clergy, including John Dewey and Oswald Garrison Villard, formed the Committee on Militarism in Education, to challenge ROTC and military drill programs in high schools. The committee was more successful at the secondary schools than in higher education, for the Supreme Court upheld the right of states to make military training compulsory in state colleges.

With the adoption of the draft and the buildup of the army in 1940–41, ROTC graduates provided many of the required junior officers. During American participation in World War II, as the army expanded to 8.3 million men and women, the largest number of officers came from the enlisted ranks and received three to four months' training at Officer Candidate Schools run by the army. About 120,000 also came through ROTC, but the wartime army fell far short of its desired quota of officers. The navy and Marines obtained wartime officers through NROTC units at two dozen colleges and universities plus special officer training programs at dozens of schools.

Since World War II, ROTC has been the primary source of officers for all the armed forces. (A separate air force ROTC program, AFROTC, was established in 1947.) During the *Korean War, 70 percent of the 26,800 lieutenants called to active duty by the army between 1951 and 1953 were ROTC graduates. The program also supplied a high percentage of the junior officers for the *Vietnam War in the 1960s and early 1970s. Even though the compulsory basis of ROTC had been ended at all public institutions after 1961, the unpopularity of the Vietnam War led to protests and demonstrations on many campuses against the program. Still, in 1968 there were 150,000 students in the initial two-year course. Antiwar and antimilitary sentiment led several colleges and universities to drop their ROTC units.

In the 1980s, however, the number of units grew again, and by the end of the decade, there were army ROTC units at 300 colleges and 800 high schools, AFROTC at 150 colleges and 300 high schools, and NROTC at 65 colleges and 230 high schools. A smaller military in the post-Vietnam and post–Cold War eras required fewer officers. The ROTC programs of the army, navy, and air force had a total enrollment of about 100,000 students in the 1990s.

[*See also* Air National Guard; Army Reserves and National Guard; Education, Military; Marine Corps Reserve; Militia and National Guard; National Defense Acts (1916, 1920); Naval Reserve; Service Academies.]

• Gene M. Lyons and John W. Masland, *Education and Military Leadership: A Study of the R.O.T.C.,* 1959; 2nd ed., 1975. John Garry Clifford, *The Citizen Soldiers: The Plattsburg Training Camp Movement, 1913–1920,* 1972. Robert F. Collins, *Reserve Officers Training Corps,* 1986. Martin Binkin and William W. Kaufman, *U.S. Army Guard and Reserve,* 1989.   —John Whiteclay Chambers II

RULES OF ENGAGEMENT (ROE) are directives issued by commanders that control the use of military force. Basic standards for the use of force have been with the U.S. military since the *Revolutionary War. The classic example was: "Don't shoot until you see the whites of their eyes." Although basic standards for the use of force have long been used, the term *Rules of Engagement* is of recent origin. Detailed ROE standards were developed during the *Cold War era, partly in response to the changing technology and increasing lethality of weapons.

The *Laws of War (LOW) include international treaties and customary practices that guide civilized nations. The basic LOW principles of necessity, proportionality, and avoiding collateral damage are the fundamentals that guide the drafting of ROE for all U.S. military operations.

In the 1980s, a series of incidents caused a reexamination of ROE for U.S. forces. The multinational force ROE in Beirut in 1983 restricted sentries from loading their weapons without instructions from a commissioned officer. This rule was in effect when a suicide truck-bomber ran the gate of the U.S. compound at the Beirut airport, destroying the Marine barracks and killing 241 Marines. In another incident, ambiguous ROE for the warship USS *Vincennes* contributed to the destruction of a civilian Iranian airliner and the death of all aboard on 3 July 1988. After an extensive review, the *Joint Chiefs of Staff in 1994 approved new Standing Rules of Engagement (SROE) to replace the Peacetime Rules of Engagement (PROE) in use since 1988. The SROE provide for self-defense whenever U.S. forces are subjected to a hostile act or when there is clear evidence of hostile intent.

Military lawyers are usually involved in the preparation and dissemination of ROE, but guidance on the use of force is ultimately the commander's responsibility. When U.S. forces engage in multinational or *United Nations–sponsored operations, U.S. policy now requires effective ROE that provide adequately for both mission accomplishment and self-defense.

[*See also* Peacekeeping.]

• Major Mark S. Martins, U.S. Army, "*Rules of Engagement for Land Forces: A Matter of Training,* Not Lawyering," *Military Law Review* (Winter 1994). Colonel F. M. Lorenz, U.S. Marine Corps, "Forging Rules of Engagement," *Military Review* (November–December 1995), p. 17.   —F. M. Lorenz

RUSH-BAGOT AGREEMENT (1817). After the *War of 1812, an Anglo-American arms race threatened the peace. Fearing U.S. encroachments, Canada stationed warships on the Great Lakes and demanded that Great Britain follow suit. America responded with its own vessels. Britain preferred, however, to focus its naval energies on the high seas, while America—confident that it could construct ships quickly if crisis loomed—wished to avoid an expensive naval race. A mutual disarmament treaty therefore appealed to both nations. In notes exchanged between British minister Charles Bagot and Acting Secretary of State Richard Rush, America and Britain pledged to maintain no more than one ship each on Lakes Champlain and Ontario, and only two on the remaining Great Lakes. This accord neither completely nor immediately disarmed the lakes, nor did it address land forces; but it did constitute the first qualitative disarmament treaty in history. No more warships were introduced, the Anglo-American "era of good feelings" continued, and tensions eased along the border. Responding to war threats in 1940, both Canada and the United States modified Rush-Bagot to permit naval construction and training.

• Edgar W. Mcinnis, *The Unguarded Frontier: A History of American-Canadian Relations,* 1942. Bradford Perkins, *Castlereagh and Adams: England and the United States, 1812–1823,* 1964. Kenneth Bourne, *Britain and the Balance of Power in North America, 1815–1980,* 1967.   —Thomas W. Zeiler

RUSSELL, RICHARD (1897–1971), governor of Georgia and U.S. senator. A widely respected political figure, Russell, a Democrat, served in the U.S. Senate from 1933 to 1971. As chairman of the Armed Services Committee from 1951 to 1968, he greatly influenced American military and foreign policy in the post–World War II era.

A leader of southern senators against civil rights, Russell unsuccessfully opposed President Harry S. *Truman's 1948 integration of the military. In 1951, his deft leadership helped assuage the outcry over Truman's dismissal of Gen. Douglas *MacArthur, commander of *United Nations forces in the *Korean War. As chairman of a Senate inquiry into MacArthur's dismissal, Russell provided Truman's congressional opponents an outlet for their anger and prevented expansion of the war and cancellation of armistice negotiations.

Although a strong supporter of Truman's Korean policy, Russell opposed America's initial involvement in Southeast Asia in 1954. By the mid-1960s, he became a reluctant supporter of Presidents Johnson and Nixon's escalation of the *Vietnam War, although he expressed strong concerns that neither man was willing to pursue a decisive victory over North Vietnam. In 1968, Russell relinquished his Armed Services chairmanship in order to head the Appropriations Committee, where he secured continued funding for the war.

[*See also* Vinson, Carl.]

• Gilbert C. Fite, *Richard B. Russell, Jr., Senator from Georgia,* 1991. John A. Goldsmith, *Colleagues: Richard B. Russell and His Apprentice, Lyndon B. Johnson,* 1993.   —Robert Mann

RUSSIA, U.S. MILITARY INTERVENTION IN, 1917–20. American intervention in Russia developed in response to the political turmoil and great power competition triggered by the Russian Revolution and civil war. President Woodrow *Wilson and his advisers enthusiastically welcomed the revolution of March 1917, seeing the overthrow of the incompetent and allegedly pro-German Czarist regime as a triumph of American political principles, an opening to displace German and British rivals for Russian markets, and an opportunity to revitalize Russia's military effort against the Central Powers at the moment when the United States was entering the Great War on the side of the Allies. However, in the following months, Bolsheviks and other antiwar radicals challenged the Russian provisional government's continuation of the war and stimulated socialist and pacifist agitation in foreign countries. In response, in the summer and fall of 1917, American officials offered financial and political support to the liberal and moderate socialist leaders of the provisional government and approved publicity campaigns to counter Bolshevik and German propaganda.

The American loans and pro-war propaganda did not prevent the Bolsheviks from seizing power in Petrograd (now St. Petersburg) in November 1917. Five weeks later, on 12 December 1917, President Wilson and Secretary of State Robert Lansing authorized covert financial support for anti-Bolshevik forces then gathering in southern Russia. American leaders hoped the Cossacks and Russian officers would be able to block German access to Russian resources and would serve as a nucleus from which a democratic Russia could be regenerated.

While Wilson was willing to provide money and moral encouragement to anti-Bolshevik groups, in the first half of 1918 he repeatedly declined British and French proposals for direct military intervention in Russia. Wilson and his top advisers feared that Allied intervention, particularly by Japanese soldiers, would cause Russians to rally around the Soviet government and seek protection from Germany. American leaders also believed that the war was going to be won on the western front, that diverting forces from France would be unwise, that Allied proposals to recreate an eastern front were impractical, and that condoning or participating in expeditions to Russia would undermine American popular support for the war.

After the Bolsheviks ratified the Treaty of Brest-Litovsk with the Central Powers and Germany launched a new western offensive in March 1918, Allied leaders intensified their pressure for military intervention in Russia. In the United States, Congress and the American people grew more favorable to action that might keep German forces in the east. At the same time, anti-Bolshevik leaders outside Russia issued numerous appeals for the liberation of their country from Bolshevik and German domination.

By the end of May, Wilson agreed to contribute American soldiers to an Allied expedition to northern Russia, and in early July he consented to Allied requests for an American expedition to Siberia. On 17 July 1918, Wilson issued an aide-mémoire that explained to Allied leaders that he remained opposed to military intervention directed at the unrealistic objective of restoring an eastern front. American forces, he declared, could only be used to guard military stockpiles at Archangel and Vladivostok, to assist pro-Allied Czechoslovakian soldiers who had come into conflict with Red forces along the Trans-Siberian Railway, and to aid patriotic Russians who were attempting to organize armies and regain control of their affairs.

Despite Wilson's strictures, American forces became involved in fighting Bolsheviks. In early August, shortly after anti-Bolshevik forces overthrew the local Soviet government at Archangel, the USS Olympia sailed into the port and deployed fifty bluejackets, twenty-five of whom immediately joined Allied soldiers in chasing Bolsheviks retreating to the south. On 4 September, the 4,500 men of the 339th Infantry Regiment arrived at Archangel. While Lt. Col. George E. Stewart lacked clear instructions about the deployment of his command, the U.S. ambassador to Russia, David R. Francis, authorized the assignment of American soldiers to the front lines along the Dvina River and the Archangel-Moscow railway. In the following months, the American North Russian Expeditionary Force suffered more than 500 total *casualties, including 100 killed in combat with numerically superior Red Army units. The Wilson administration's failure to provide a convincing explanation for why American troops remained in northern Russia after fighting against Germany ceased in November 1918 exacerbated declining troop *morale among the Americans and provoked demands by their relatives for the return of the expedition. In February 1919, facing persistent criticism from Republican senator Hiram Johnson of California and many other members of Congress, President Wilson ordered the withdrawal of the expeditionary force, which was carried out in June 1919.

Though the Archangel expedition involved "doughboys" from the Great Lakes region, most of the American soldiers dispatched to Siberia were from the West Coast. In August 1918, the 27th and 31st Infantry Regiments sailed from the Philippines to Vladivostok. On 1 September, they were joined by 5,000 men from the Eighth Division. Although some American diplomats and officers hoped to provide active military assistance to anti-Bolshevik armies, Gen. William S. Graves, commander of the Siberian expedition, followed a strict interpretation of President Wilson's aide-mémoire and tried to keep American forces largely neutral in the civil war. In patrolling the railway between Vladivostok and Lake Baikal, however, American soldiers safeguarded the route over which American and Allied supplies were shipped to anti-Bolshevik armies under Adm. Alexander Kolchak in western Siberia. Consequently, American forces clashed both with Red partisans who attacked the railroad and with Cossacks who contested Kolchak's authority in eastern Siberia.

As in the case of the Archangel expedition, the Wilson administration faced demands to bring American soldiers home. Yet Wilson and his advisers had committed themselves to supporting Kolchak, and they worried that withdrawing the American expedition while 70,000 Japanese soldiers remained in eastern Siberia would lead to the establishment of an exclusive Japanese sphere of influence. American officials decided to evacuate the U.S. forces only after the Red Army drove Kolchak's troops eastward across Siberia in the fall of 1919. American soldiers completed their departure from Vladivostok in April 1920.

The limited American interventions in Russia failed to sustain democracy, protect American loans and investments, revive Russian military resistance to Germany, or prevent the Red victory in the Russian civil war of 1917 to 1920. While aid to anti-Bolshevik armies and an economic blockade of Soviet Russia did not eliminate the menace of Bolshevism, they aggravated Bolshevik suspicions of the West and provided Soviet leaders with major themes for anti-American propaganda over seven decades. Wilsonian policy toward Russia also had lasting repercussions in the United States, where senators like Hiram Johnson and many other progressives and socialists viewed the "secret" interventions as dangerous precedents of presidential usurpation of war powers and ominous signs that membership in the *League of Nations would entail further interventions around the world to suppress revolutionary change.

Intervention in Russia has been a subject of enduring controversy among American historians. "Orthodox" or traditional scholars have tended to portray the military expeditions to northern Russian and Siberia as reluctant aberrations in Wilsonian foreign policy caused by the exigencies of waging war against Germany. "Revisionist" or "New Left" historians, on the other hand, have tended to view the expeditions as parts of a wider effort to contain the ideological threat of Bolshevism and overthrow the Soviet government.

[See also Russia, U.S. Military Involvement in, 1921–95; World War I: Military and Diplomatic Course.]

• George F. Kennan, Soviet-American Relations, 1917–1920, 2 vols: Russia Leaves the War, 1956, and The Decision to Intervene, 1958. N. Gordon Levin, Jr., Woodrow Wilson and World Politics: America's Response to War and Revolution, 1968. Lloyd C. Gardner, Safe for Democracy: The Anglo-American Response to Revolution, 1913–1923, 1984. Benjamin D. Rhodes, The Anglo-American Winter War with Russia, 1988. Betty M. Unterberger, The United States, Revolutionary Russia, and the Rise of Czechoslovakia, 1989. David S. Foglesong, America's Secret War Against Bolshevism: United States Intervention in the Russian Civil War, 1917–1920, 1995.
—David S. Foglesong

RUSSIA, U.S. MILITARY INVOLVEMENT IN, 1921–95.
By 1921, the United States had withdrawn its military forces from Russia and entered a long period of official noninvolvement. After opening diplomatic relations with the Soviet Union in 1933, the only military involvement was the usual stationing of military attachés and Marine guards at the U.S. Embassy in Moscow.

In World War II, as a cobelligerent with the Soviet Union against Germany and Italy, the United States provided extensive material military assistance to the Soviet Union under the *Lend-Lease Act and Agreements. And in 1944, some U.S. aircraft flying bombing missions against targets in German-occupied or German-allied Central and Eastern Europe landed on airfields in the Soviet Union. U.S. military personnel were thus involved in the military supply effort (by sea in Murmansk, by air through Alaska, and by land through Iran) and to a limited extent in direct support of U.S. air combat operations.

After this cooperative engagement in World War II, as U.S.-Soviet relations plummeted into the *Cold War during the years after 1945, there was again no direct U.S. military involvement in Russia. There was, however, an active U.S. military role in air and sea reconnaissance along the borders of the Soviet Union. Sometimes inadvertently, and sometimes deliberately, such forays transgressed into illegal incursions into Soviet coastal water and air space. There were also some military, as well as *Central Intelligence Agency, deep air penetrations. This led to dozens of incidents and the shooting down of thirty-one U.S. military aircraft along Soviet borders between 1950 and 1970. Some minor accidental collisions of U.S. *submarines and Soviet ships took place in or near Soviet waters, and there was one deliberate minor collision between surface warships in Soviet territorial waters in 1983.

In only one instance during the Cold War did the United States engage in direct military combat action against a target in the Soviet Union, and then not deliberately. During the *Korean War, in 1950, an American fighter-bomber by error bombed and strafed a military airfield in the Soviet Union near North Korea.

As the Cold War drew to a close, such incidents declined sharply. Moreover, new forms of cooperative and even collaborative contacts emerged. The Intermediate Nuclear Forces (*INF) Treaty in 1987 provided for inspection of intermediate-range missile facilities in the two countries, and U.S. military inspectors thereafter visited many locations in the Soviet Union. This pattern expanded under the START Treaty of 1990, both treaties going beyond the SALT agreements of 1972 in providing exchanges of military information as well as on-site inspection.

Following a meeting of Soviet minister of defense Dmitry Yazov and U.S. secretary of defense Frank Carlucci in 1987, a series of bilateral high-level military contacts took place. The respective military chiefs of staff, Marshal Sergei Akhromeyev and Adm. William *Crowe, reciprocated visits in 1988–89. Many military exchanges at lower levels, including from respective War Colleges, ensued. Ships of the two navies also carried out courtesy calls.

Such cooperative relations continued between Russia and the United States after the Soviet Union dissolved at the end of 1991. By 1995, perspective collaboration in *peacekeeping operations during the *Bosnian Crisis was planned with Russian troops under a senior American commander. A new era had arrived.

[See also Russia, U.S. Military Intervention in, 1917–20; SALT Treaties; START Treaty (1982); World War II: Military and Diplomatic Course.]   —Raymond L. Garthoff

RUSTIN, BAYARD (1910–1987), pacifist and civil rights activist. Born in Westchester, Pennsylvania, Rustin was raised by his grandparents as a Quaker. As an African American of developing political consciousness, Rustin joined the Young Communist League in New York City in the early 1930s, but quit in 1941. He then joined the *Fellowship of Reconciliation, and in 1942, helped form the Congress of Racial Equality (CORE). Rustin spent two years in prison as a conscientious objector during World War II. Afterwards, he joined various anticolonial organizations, including the Free India movement and the Committee to Support South African Resistance. In 1947, he participated in CORE's Journey of Reconciliation, precursor to the 1960s Freedom Rides. Rustin also served as executive director of the *War Resisters League (1953–55).

Best known for his work in the civil rights movement, Rustin joined the Montgomery Bus Boycott, helped conceive the Southern Christian Leadership Conference, and was a key organizer of the 1963 March on Washington. Although one of Martin Luther *King, Jr.'s, closest advisers on *nonviolence and political strategy, Rustin remained on the periphery because of his homosexuality and his ties to the Left. In the mid-1960s, he was among few who urged King to take a political stand against the *Vietnam War. Subsequently, he sought to minimize King's stance to preserve the fragile civil rights coalition.

In six decades of political activism, Rustin shifted from a racially conscious leftist to a more humanist-oriented pacifist and advocate of coalition politics.

[See also Conscientious Objection; Pacifism; Quakers.]

• Taylor Branch, Parting the Waters: America in the King Years, 1954–63 (1988). Jervis Anderson, Bayard Rustin: Troubles I've Seen, 1997.
—Martin A. Summers

S

SADDAM HUSSEIN. *See* Hussein, Saddam.

SAIGON, BATTLE FOR (1968). On 31 January 1968, during the Vietnam War, the North Vietnamese and their Viet Cong (VC) allies in South Vietnam launched the massive *Tet Offensive. Timed to exploit reduced South Vietnamese vigilance during lunar New Year celebrations ("Tet"), the offensive was intended to spark an insurrection by disaffected southern civilians and military units against the American-backed regime with its capital in Saigon. Given the offensive's overtly political purpose, attacking prominent targets in Saigon was key to Hanoi's plans to spark a southern revolt.

At about 3:00 A.M., just as the last volley of Tet celebratory fireworks was set off, a variety of targets were attacked in and around Saigon: air bases, southern military and police headquarters, U.S. military command and billeting facilities, and television and radio studios. Although Communist forces had tipped their hand by mistakenly attacking Hué and others cities to the north of Saigon on 30 January, Americans were shocked by the realization that about 4,000 VC could infiltrate the capital and launch vicious attacks.

The most spectacular engagement in Saigon occurred when the VC C-10 Sapper Battalion penetrated the U.S. Embassy compound, prompting a desperate shootout with security guards and embassy staff. The VC were cleared from the embassy grounds by 9:00 A.M., but American reporters, who had witnessed the fight, were shocked by Gen. William *Westmoreland's assertion that this was a VC publicity stunt and militarily meaningless. The American public was also shocked by television, film, and still photographs of the summary street execution of a suspected VC commando by Nguyen Ngoc Loan, the South Vietnamese chief of Saigon's security forces.

Westmoreland's prediction was accurate militarily; within forty-eight hours, allied forces in Saigon were hunting down the VC, and by 16 February, the battle for Saigon was over. But politically the Tet attacks, especially the VC success in turning Saigon into a battlefield and the false news reports that the VC had actually penetrated the embassy building itself, produced a political uproar in the United States, particularly because they seemed to clash with previous government and military assurance that the VC had been crushed. The summary street execution also revolted many Americans. The credibility gap resulting in part from the Tet Offensive and the Battle for Saigon ultimately prompted President Lyndon B. *Johnson not to run for reelection and American officials to reduce U.S. military involvement in Southeast Asia.

[*See also* Vietnam War: Military and Diplomatic Course.]

• Don Oberdofer, *Tet!*, 1971. James J. Wirtz, *The Tet Offensive: Intelligence Failure in War*, 1991.

—James J. Wirtz

SAILING WARSHIPS. The infant U.S. republic was blessed in that the premier naval weapons system of the day was one it could produce well and use effectively. Modern designers might well pine for a vessel with the nearly unlimited range, comparatively low construction cost, and ease of repair and resupply offered by the sailing man-of-war. Sailing vessels needed only the wind to move them and the food and water to support their crews. Range and endurance depended on how much food and water a given ship needed to get to the next source of supply. Effective repairs of even the most severe damage to a wooden vessel could be and often were carried out on the beach, with tools of the crudest sort.

Building Sailing Warships. The technology of the sailing warship itself was relatively stable from 1775 to 1862, requiring no expensive research and redevelopment each decade or so. Sails, ropes, timber, and guns were the components of the vessels themselves. Hemp for cordage and sails was an early crop in the colonies, and one useful for more than warship construction. Timber, the most basic and vital component of the wooden sailing warship, was present in profusion. Cannon were the most difficult component to produce in the colonies, but the United States produced simple iron smoothbore tubes and round shot as early as 1777. Stable gunpowder would prove most difficult to manufacture, but at least that was a commodity widely available on the international market.

British naval architects quickly realized that the naval stores to be found in the New World were of superior quality to the gleanings centuries of deforestation had left in the British Isles themselves. New England pines and cedars offered masts and spars of such great strength and height as often to negate the need to construct the composite masts that His Majesty's larger ships otherwise required. Moreover, North America produced over seventy-five species of oak, which offered the greatest strength and damage resistance to wooden vessels. The squat and hardy southern live oak (*Quercus virginiana*) offered more advantages for wooden ship construction than many British shipwrights were equipped to employ. The wood grew in useful shapes and was fantastically strong—so much so that it discouraged the builders whose tools it dulled and who found it difficult to work. American shipwrights would come to understand that it could be soaked in brine and made workable, and it soon became apparent that salt water had a tremendous preservative effect on the wood. Thus, after two centuries of naval service, the USS *Constitution*, "Old Ironsides," retains 20 percent of her original timber: a remarkable fact given that the life span of a man-of-war might be considered long at forty years.

The timber itself prompted strains that would contribute to the independence of the United States and play a role in the nature of its earliest navy. British law dictated that prime trees would be marked with the "broad arrow" of the crown and could not be used except for naval construction. It made considerably more economic sense to construct completed vessels in the colonies, as soon became the case for merchant vessels. Colonial shipwrights came to resent the preemption of the finest local timber for the Royal Navy and the British policy of constructing vessels no larger than the welterweight frigates of the era in American yards. In at least subordinate ways, these forces would contribute to American resentment of the crown in the 1760s and 1770s.

The nurturing environment that had led to the construction of the very large colonial merchant marine allowed the *Continental navy, and its successor, the U.S. *Navy, to build or convert functional vessels effectively and quickly. Even the earliest vessels of the fleet could be tremendously effective. The tiny sloop *Providence*, built as *Katy* and armed with cannon stolen from a British fort in 1774, would bedevil the British until 1779, raiding British commerce until finally trapped and burned in the face of overwhelming force. American shipwrights during the *Revolutionary War and the *War of 1812 constructed entire fleets of warships on Lake Champlain and the Great Lakes from imported fittings and standing timber, in as little as nine weeks. The relationship of civilian to military ship technology was sufficiently close to allow privateers— armed vessels outfitted by merchants—to wage a devastating campaign against the British merchant marine in two wars. The Americans built well. The frigates authorized by the Continental Congress in 1775 would perform as creditably as conditions and the varying skills of the commanders allowed, and their designers would be available when the U.S. Navy placed its first orders for purpose-built men-of-war in 1794.

The skills of the wooden shipwright were largely a matter of genius and intuition. Once again, the infant country was fortunate. Joshua Humphreys of Philadelphia designed frigates in the Revolution and had observed their fates when overhauled by powerful British squadrons or larger vessels. The designs he submitted to Congress embodied Secretary of War Henry Knox's brilliant concept that a ship should be able to outrun any opponent it could not outfight, and influenced American naval architecture until well past the advent of steam. Among Humphrey's other creations was the *Constitution*. Humphrey's son, Samuel, and rivals such as Henry Eckford and Adam and Noah Brown were profitable civilian designers and successful military naval architects. Costs stayed low enough for the cities of Boston, New York, and Philadelphia to build ships with local contributions and present them gratis to the infant navy.

Types and Performance of Sailing Vessels. The ratings system most widely used in all navies of the period depended on the number of cannon a given vessel could carry into battle, whether she carried them or not. The system was inexact. The *Constitution's* official rating was 44, the number that followed her name in contemporary records and histories. In fact, the vessel carried a mixed battery of up to fifty guns, including a main battery of long 24-pounders and short carronades, which could fire a heavier 32-pound ball for a much shorter distance. The Royal Navy's somewhat more accurate system never became established in the U.S. Navy since that arm's ships did not conform to its standards, but it provides perspective on the range of vessels in use of the time.

Ships "of the line," expected to participate in the battle line at fleet actions, ranged as low as "5th Rate," such as HMS *Serapis*, which fell victim to John Paul *Jones, rated at forty-four guns but classed as a small ship of the line because she carried them on two gun decks, unlike the heavy frigate *Constitution*, which would have made short work of her. The larger, workhorse "seventy-fours" celebrated during the Napoleonic era were "3rd Rates" under this system; among these, the U.S. Navy boasted Henry Eckford's beautiful USS *Ohio* of 1820. Nelson's *Victory*, 103 guns, was officially a 1st Rate, although a monster larger than she would appear in the U.S. Navy, Humphrey's *Pennsylvania*, of 1840, designed to carry 132 long "32-pounders."

Lighter vessels ranged upward from the *cutter*, a single-masted schooner with as little as one cannon on the open deck, or nothing but swivel guns mounted on her railings. Thomas *Jefferson's navy experimented with gunboats, colloquially named *Jeffs*, of one or two heavy guns—tiny ships that had little to offer in terms of seakeeping ability and endurance. The term *sloop* was used to denote almost any sort of vessel, from the single-masted *Providence* with her battery of twelve 4-pounders to the formidable *Cumberland* of 1862, with a three-masted "ship" rig, armed with a battery of twenty-four tremendous cannon. A *corvette* was a sloop with her guns mounted on an open spar deck. One tremendously successful ship design was the two-masted *brig of war*, with two masts and varying battery, easy to work and fight with a smaller crew. *Niagara*, a restored veteran of the Battle of Lake Erie (1814), remains today a superb vessel of this type, with a single battery of carronades on her spar deck and a shallow, fresh-water hull.

Larger still were the famous frigates, the commerce-raiding cruisers and scouts of the era. These vessels had a full set of square-rigged sailing, three masts, weapons as heavy as "long" 32-pounders or the massive Dahlgren guns of the *Civil War era on a heavy gun deck.

The range of even the smallest sailing vessel was practically unlimited, given basic seaworthiness and intact stores. A fast sailer such as *Constitution* could make as much as 14 knots (16 miles per hour) under sail, but heavier vessels tended to be much slower, a fact to which the *Constitution* owed her life on more than one occasion.

The Sailing Ship in U.S. Service. Privateers, commissioned as warships by the government, made both the Revolution and the War of 1812 tremendously costly to British commerce and so performed a great service to the new nation before massive British *blockades reduced their ability to operate. The early challenges faced by the U.S. Navy included chastising raiders sent from France in the Quasi-War of 1798–1800, and the suppression of Muslim corsairs operating out of North Africa in the decade following. The celebrated U.S. frigate victories of the War of 1812 did much for the navy and the country's prestige, while the twin fleet victories by Americans on Lake Erie and Lake Champlain effectively forestalled British advances from Canada and led to the stabilization of the northern frontier.

The great endurance and qualities of sailing vessels proved useful in the U.S. Navy's sporadic efforts to suppress the African slave trade at its source, starting in 1820. In 1820–33, U.S. vessels worked to suppress piracy in the Caribbean, while ships of the fleet also operated off the coast of revolutionary South America and off the Chinese coast.

The age of the sailing ship as a warship began to end with Robert *Fulton's development of steam-powered ships beginning in the *War of 1812. Yet sailing ships as well as combination steam and sail frigates remained part of the U.S. Navy for several decades. During the Civil War, the destruction of the becalmed *Cumberland* and *Congress* by a steam-only ironclad in 1862 did not prevent other sailing vessels from effective service in Abraham *Lincoln's blockade, but unmistakably signaled the end of the sailing warship in American service. In the decades of decline after the Civil War, the navy would emphasize sail (combined with steam propulsion) for reasons of economy and range; but the last sail-only vessel for the U.S. Navy was constructed in 1855.

[See also France, Undeclared Naval War with; Dahlgren, John; Privateering.]

—Rob S. Rice

ST. LÔ, BREAKOUT AT (1944).

After the successful *D-Day landing, by early July 1944 the World War II fighting in Normandy had become a costly slugging match. The British Second Army was still stalled in front of Caen and the American First Army was mired in the swamps and *bocage* (hedgerows) of the lower Cotentin Peninsula.

The First Army commander, Gen. Omar *Bradley, in consultation with Gen. Dwight D. *Eisenhower, Gen. Bernard Law *Montgomery, and the U.S. VII Army Corps (under Maj. Gen. J. Lawton Collins) devised a plan to attack on a narrow front following massive air bombardment of the enemy lines.

Scheduled for 24 July, the bombers were launched, but bad weather in the target area—a rectangle 5,000 yards by 2,500—forced a postponement to the next day. A few planes did not receive the message and bombed anyway. Some *bombs fell short, killing 25 and wounding 130 in the 30th Division.

On July 25—a bright, clear day—the attack of 2,000 heavy and medium *bomber aircraft and 700 fighter bombers started about noon. Many bombs fell short and over 600 American *casualties resulted. Lt. Gen. Leslie J. McNair, commander of army ground forces in the United States, on an observation visit to the front, was killed.

Despite the disorganization, only one regiment and one battalion were unable to attack on time.

The German *Panzer Lehr* Division and remnants of the German Fifth Parachute Division put up spirited resistance. By the end of the first day, the American infantry was only halfway through the bombed area, but the defense seemed uncoordinated and General Collins ordered the exploitation force to attack the next day. The breakthrough at St. Lô (25 July) and then at Coutances (28 July) opened the way for Lt. Gen. George S. *Patton's Third Army to slash into Brittany and toward the Seine. Thus, the invasion of *Normandy led to the liberation of *France.

[See also World War II: Military and Diplomatic Course.]

• J. Lawton Collins, *Lightning Joe*, 1979. Martin Blumenson, *Breakout and Pursuit*, 1984.

—James L. Collins, Jr.

ST. MIHIEL, BATTLE OF (1918).

This battle was the first independent operation of the newly organized U.S. First Army during World War I. The objective for the American offensive was a German salient into the Allied positions at St. Mihiel, south of Verdun, in northern France. The commander, Gen. John J. *Pershing (who also retained command of the entire American Expeditionary Forces), demanded that the Allied leadership allow the U.S. Army to conduct an independent operation. French general Ferdinand Foch, Supreme Allied Commander, reluctantly agreed. Pershing also requested and received 3,000 Allied *artillery pieces and 430 *tanks (about half of these weapons manned by Americans). In addition, 640 Allied and American aircraft, commanded by U.S. Col. Billy *Mitchell, supported the operation. First Army planned a converging attack by fourteen U.S. and colonial French divisions, striking both sides of the salient.

The offensive began early on 12 September, after a four-hour artillery bombardment. It was a mixed success. The salient was cut off within twenty-four hours, but had already begun a tactical withdrawal to stronger positions; as a result, the number of Germans captured—about 15,000—was less than Pershing had sought. American *casualties were about 7,000 out of 550,000 troops engaged. The operation showed the Americans the difficulty of sustaining a massive infantry attack much beyond four days or ten miles because of difficulties of resupply. However, the First Army's success brought much praise from Allied leaders, who had been skeptical about the state of planning and élan of the U.S. forces.

• John Toland, *No Man's Land: 1918—The Last Year of the Great War*, 1980. Paul F. Braim, *The Test of Battle: The American Expeditionary Forces in the Meuse-Argonne Campaign*, 1987, rev. ed., 1997.

—Paul F. Braim

SALT TREATIES (1972; 1979).

Over the decade from November 1969 to June 1979, the United States and the Soviet Union conducted strategic arms limitation talks (known as SALT). The first set of accords, called SALT I, were reached in less than three years and signed at the first summit meeting of President Richard M. *Nixon with Soviet leader Leonid I. Brezhnev in Moscow on 26 May 1972. It took seven years before a follow-on treaty was reached, SALT II, signed at the only summit meeting between President Jimmy *Carter and Brezhnev, in Vienna on 18 June 1979.

These were the first substantial arms control agreements between the two countries. Originally proposed by the United States in December 1966, the Soviet Union equivocated until May 1968, when the Soviets had numerical strategic parity in sight. A planned opening of SALT at a summit meeting in September 1968 was derailed by the Soviet-led *Warsaw Pact occupation of Czechoslovakia in August. With the defeat of the Democrats in the 1968 presidential election, SALT had to await a new administration and its review of defense and foreign policies. The delay of the opening of SALT from fall 1968 to late fall 1969 had one significant adverse effect: during that year, the United States successfully tested and developed deployable MIRV (multiple, independently targeted reentry vehicle) warheads for its strategic *missiles—five years ahead of the Soviet Union. As a result, the negotiations placed no restrictions on these missiles and a significant continuing growth in numbers of warheads, seriously undercutting the value of the SALT I and SALT II agreements limiting strategic offensive delivery vehicles.

The two SALT I accords reached in May 1972 were the Anti-Ballistic Missile (ABM) Treaty, which severely limited defenses against ballistic missiles (ABM defenses), and an Interim Agreement on the Limitation of Strategic Offensive Arms, which froze the total number of strategic offensive missile launchers pending further negotiation of a more comprehensive treaty limiting strategic missiles and bombers. (A separate agreement on measures to avert accidental use of *nuclear weapons had been concluded in September 1971.) The ABM Treaty, of indefinite duration, restricted each party to two antiballistic missile sites, with 100 ABM launchers at each. In the only later amendment to the treaty, a 1974 protocol, the two parties agreed to forgo one of those sites, so that each was thereafter limited to a single deployment location. Further constraints included a ban on the testing and deployment of land-mobile, sea-based, air-based, and space-based systems. Only fixed, land-based ABM systems could be deployed at the one allowed site. The Soviet Union kept its existing ABM deployment around Moscow. The United States completed its deployment at a site for defense of intercontinental ballistic missile (ICBM) launchers near Grand Forks, South Dakota, but in 1975 "mothballed" the complex as too expensive.

The ABM Treaty was a significant achievement in arms limitation, although agreement had been facilitated by doubts on both sides as to the cost-effectiveness of available ABM systems. Although the treaty headed off a costly and useless ABM deployment race, it did not have the desired effect of also damping down deployment of strategic offensive missiles, especially because MIRVs were not constrained.

The Interim Agreement froze the level of land- and sea-based strategic missiles (permitting completion of launchers already under construction). The Soviet Union had a quantitative advantage with 2,348 missile launchers to 1,710 for the United States. This was, however, offset in two important ways. First, neither strategic bombers nor forward-based nuclear delivery systems were included, and the United States had a significant advantage in both categories. Second, although the Soviet Union had more missile launchers and deployed missiles, the United States had a larger number of strategic missile warheads and by 1972 had already begun deploying MIRV warheads. Overall, the Interim Agreement placed only modest limits on strategic missiles. In contrast to the ABM Treaty, it was not significant as an arms control measure.

President Gerald R. *Ford and Soviet leader Leonid Brezhnev reached an agreement at Vladivostok in November 1974 to place a cap of 1,320 on the number of MIRV warheads and equal overall levels of strategic nuclear delivery vehicles at 2,400, including strategic bombers. This was not, however, a formal agreement and efforts to reach a SALT II Treaty to replace the SALT I Interim Agreement remained stalemated for another five years.

Another abortive attempt to conclude an early SALT II Treaty was made by President Jimmy *Carter in March 1977, soon after assuming office. He attempted to set aside the Vladivostok accord and plunge into deeper cuts, but the attempt failed because it abandoned the earlier basis for agreement by seeking reductions of Soviet intercontinental systems not covered in the proposed treaty. The negotiations got back on track, but by that time other geopolitical differences between the two sides made agreement more difficult and the negotiations more protracted.

The SALT II Treaty was finally signed at the summit meeting of President Carter and President Brezhnev at Vienna in June 1979. It provided equal levels of strategic arms (2,400, to be reduced over time to 2,200, strategic delivery vehicles) and included strategic bombers as well as strategic missiles. Intended to be in effect for ten years, during which a third SALT negotiation for further reductions was envisaged, the SALT II Treaty fell afoul of the collapse of the Soviet-American detente of the 1970s after the Soviet occupation of Afghanistan in 1979, and was never ratified. Its major constraints, however, were formally observed by both sides until 1986, and for all practical purposes even thereafter.

Pursuant to the SALT I agreements a Standing Consultative Commission (SCC) was established to resolve questions regarding the meaning of and compliance with the SALT agreements. It was also stipulated that there would be no interference with the use of national technical means of verification, such as observation *satellites. SALT thus helped at least to stabilize, if not greatly reduce, the military balance. The SALT process and the agreements reached, while causing some friction and disagreements, did contribute to the overall political detente of the 1970s. Although not sufficient to sustain that detente, the SALT process helped ensure that even under renewed tension the risk of nuclear war remained low.

The SALT process was a success in demonstrating that adversaries could reach arms limitation agreements. Nonetheless, owing to the very cautious and conservative approaches of both sides, the limitations on strategic offensive arms were unable to keep up with the military technological advances given precedence by the two countries. The SALT I Interim Agreement and the unratified SALT II Treaty did, however, bridge the period until later strategic arms reduction treaties (START) were reached in the early 1990s.

The ABM Treaty proved surprisingly durable over at least a quarter of a century. To be sure, it was challenged in the 1980s by advocates of President Ronald *Reagan's *Strategic Defense Initiative, and especially by an ill-conceived attempt by the Reagan administration at unilateral reinterpretation to allow greater testing of space-based ABM systems through a "broad interpretation" of the treaty, later repudiated. In the 1990s, a renewed interest in limited defense of the United States against possible missile proliferation or accidental missile launchings, and difficulty in defining the dividing line between strategic ABM systems limited by the treaty and tactical or theater ABM systems not limited by it, again posed a serious challenge. The ABM Treaty continues to be in effect and constitutes an important consideration in making possible the deep reductions in strategic offensive arms under the existing and contemplated START Treaties.

Overall, the SALT Treaties made a significant contribution to containing the dangers of the Cold War and provided a foundation for continuing arms control measures to reduce the risk of nuclear war.

[See also Arms Control and Disarmament; Cold War: External Course; Cuban Missile Crisis; Nuclear War, Prevention of Accidental.]

• John Newhouse, Cold Dawn: The Story of SALT, 1973. Strobe Talbott, Endgame: The Inside Story of SALT II, 1979. Gerard C. Smith, Doubletalk: The Story of SALT I, 1980. Coit D. Blacker and Gloria Duffy, eds., International Arms Control: Issues and Agreements, 2nd ed., 1984.
—Raymond L. Garthoff

SAMOAN INCIDENT (1888–89). The Samoan Islands, which lay on an important sealane, were the site of a war scare in the 1880s between Germany and the United States as both nations expanded into the Pacific. Some historians see the crisis as a critical turning point in U.S. foreign policy, a harbinger of American overseas *expansionism.

In 1878, Washington secured a coaling station at the harbor of Pago Pago on Tutuila in exchange for protection against other foreign powers. However, Berlin also sought territory, particularly Apia Harbor on Upolu, and in December 1888, when German ships shelled Apia, British and American warships confronted them. Expansionist secretary of state James Blaine threatened Germany, and Congress voted $500,000 to protect U.S. interests. But early in March 1889, the three nations agreed to a conference in Berlin.

On 16 March, a hurricane hit Apia, destroying all three U.S. ships and the three German vessels, with heavy loss of life. Consequently, the Berlin conference agreed on 14 June 1889 to a three-power protectorate over the Samoan Islands, with nominal Samoan rule.

After the *Spanish-American War and U.S. acquisition of the Philippines, Guam, Hawaii, and Puerto Rico, the Samoan archipelago was formally divided in 1889. The United States obtained Tutuila, administered by the U.S. Navy, and all except two of the western islands, which went to Germany. New Zealand seized the German islands in 1914 and held them until their independence in 1962. The other islands remained under American control.

[See also Navy, U.S.: 1866–98.]

• G. H. Ryden, The Foreign Policy of the United States in Relation to Samoa, 1933. John A. C. Gray, American Samoa: A History of American Samoa and Its United States Naval Administration, 1960. Paul M. Kennedy, The Samoan Tangle: A Study in Anglo-German-American Relations, 1878–1900, 1974.

—John Whiteclay Chambers II

SAMPSON, WILLIAM (1840–1902), naval officer. Born in Palmyra, New York, Sampson graduated first in his class at Annapolis (1861). After service in the *Civil War, he alternated between commands at sea and staff positions. Becoming superintendent of the Naval Academy (1886), he sponsored educational reforms. As an ordnance specialist, he championed technological modernization. In 1898, he headed the inquiry that erroneously attributed the sinking of the USS *Maine to external causes.

Sampson became commander of the North Atlantic Squadron in March 1898. Promoted to admiral when the *Spanish-American War began (21 April), he immediately blockaded Havana. Transferring to Santiago de Cuba after a Spanish squadron under Adm. Pascual Cervera arrived there, his blockade and plans to foil a sortie by Cervera led to the complete destruction of the Spanish squadron (3 July 1898), forcing Spain to negotiate peace.

Unfortunately, Sampson had left the blockade when Cervera attempted to escape, leaving Commodore William Schley in command. This circumstance engendered a postwar controversy about credit for the victory at Santiago, which divided the navy for many years. Debilitating illness, probably Alzheimer's disease, increasingly compromised Sampson's efficiency between 1897 and his death.

[See also Caribbean and Latin America, U.S. Military Involvement in the.]

• David F. Trask, The War with Spain in 1898, 1981.

—David F. Trask

The **SAND CREEK MASSACRE** (1864) was a tragedy inflicted on the Cheyenne village of Chief Black Kettle by local Colorado troops. Antagonized by Colorado officials, Cheyenne and other Plains tribes had raided settlements and travel routes throughout the summer of 1864. With the approach of winter, the peace chiefs, of whom Black Kettle was the foremost, sought terms. The commander of the military district was Col. John M. Chivington, a former Methodist clergyman with political ambitions who had entered the volunteer service at the outbreak of the *Civil War. He directed the chiefs to camp on Sand Creek until further arrangements could be made. Here Black Kettle believed himself at peace and under military protection.

Chivington, however, had raised a regiment of 100-day militia to fight Indians, and citizens expected it to do so. With great secrecy, he concentrated a force of 700 men, consisting of the territorial militia and units of federalized volunteers, and at daybreak on 29 November, he launched a surprise attack on Black Kettle's village. On Chivington's orders, the troops took no prisoners and indiscriminately shot down men, women, and children. Of some 500 people in the village, 200 were killed and their bodies scalped and mutilated. About two-thirds of the dead were women and children. A few, including Black Kettle, survived.

Sand Creek set off Indian warfare that engulfed the Great Plains through 1865 and 1866. It also prompted official investigations that exposed the perfidy of Chivington's actions and led to new Indian policies emphasizing diplomacy rather than war. Chivington, however, escaped courtmartial by leaving the service.

[See also Militia and National Guard; Plains Indians Wars.]

• Stan Hoig, The Sand Creek Massacre, 1963.

—Robert M. Utley

SANE. See National Committee for a Sane Nuclear Policy.

SANITARY COMMISSION, U.S. (1861–65). Shortly after the outbreak of the *Civil War, New York minister Dr. Henry W. Bellows led a delegation of physicians to Washington, where they lobbied for improved sanitation and medical care in the Union camps. In June 1861, this voluntary group received official status as the United States Sanitary Commission (USSC), charged with inspecting the camps, collecting medical supplies, and advising a somewhat reluctant Medical Bureau. President Abraham *Lincoln accepted the plan with skepticism, fearing that the USSC would become the "fifth wheel on the coach." Before long, the Sanitary Commission's agents were a familiar and welcome sight to Union soldiers. The commission played a crucial role in promoting the appointment in 1862 of a progressive surgeon general, William Hammond, and in breaking army resistance to the use of female nurses.

Under the direction of executive secretary Frederick Law Olmsted, the commission proclaimed a deep passion for order and efficiency and insisted that those goals could only be achieved through careful centralized control. Seven thousand local auxiliaries throughout the North raised funds and shipped food, medicine and clothing to ten regional depots. As the financial demands continued, the USSC turned to nearly thirty local sanitary fairs (1863–65), which netted $4.4 million.

The Sanitary Commission can be interpreted as evidence of the emergence of a more centralized, modernizing society. But although many local bodies eventually affiliated with the commission, others sent their own agents into the field. And even those local branches of the "Sanitary" retained some traditional practices.

The USSC also raises interesting questions about wartime gender roles. Although men dominated the national leadership, women made up the vast majority of local volunteers, and Chicagoans Mary Livermore and Jane C. Hoge became central figures in the commission's midwestern branch. Even if the activities of the Sanitary Commission rarely challenged traditional gender roles, the local bodies provided new opportunities for women to hone public skills.

[See also Nurse Corps, Army and Navy; Union Army.]

• William Quentin Maxwell, *Lincoln's Fifth Wheel: The Political History of the U.S. Sanitary Commission*, 1956. Robert H. Bremner, *The Public Good: Philanthropy and Welfare in the Civil War Era*, 1980.

—J. Matthew Gallman

SAN JACINTO, BATTLE OF (1836). The Battle of San Jacinto, fought near present-day Galveston, Texas, on 21 April 1836, was shaped to a large degree by the mistakes of Mexican president and general Antonio Lopez de *Santa Anna, who after his costly victory at the Battle of the *Alamo divided his remaining forces into four units. Driven by an incautious determination to capture the Texas government's leaders, his command pursued ahead of his army's other branches. He missed his political adversaries by a few hours on 19 April.

Emboldened by his numerical advantage, Texas Gen. Sam Houston and his 900 men at last turned toward the enemy's advance units and began skirmishing on 20 April. The encamped Mexican forces, trapped by a swamp to their rear, had been reinforced to twice their previous numbers and were lulled into unpreparedness by that and the lateness of the hour. Houston's *order of battle in the late afternoon the next day was a thin line, supported by *artillery in the middle and cavalry on its right. The assault turned into a mad rush of hand-to-hand combat; the engagement lasted for fewer than twenty minutes, followed by several hours of individualized killing dominated by revenge-seeking Texans. Santa Anna was captured, along with about half of his force of over 1,300. Houston and thirty others in the army were wounded; only nine of the Texans died in battle.

San Jacinto became a turning point when the Mexican president's retreat orders were obeyed by his next in command. It proved to be the decisive battle of the Texas revolution (San Jacinto Day is a Texas holiday) as the captured Santa Anna signed a treaty pledging recognition of an independent Texas.

[See also Mexican Revolution, U.S. Military Involvement in the.]

—Paul D. Lack

SAN JUAN HILL, BATTLE OF (1898). Probably the best known U.S. battle in Cuba during the *Spanish-American War because of the media coverage of Theodore *Roosevelt, the Battle of "San Juan Hill" is more accurately the Battle of San Juan Heights, and Roosevelt's famous charge occurred on nearby Kettle Hill.

On 1 July 1898, the U.S. Expeditionary Forces under Maj. Gen. William R. Shafter assaulted the Spanish defenses of Santiago, where the Spanish squadron lay protected in the harbor. After sending one division to attack Spanish fortifications at El Caney on his right flank, Shafter ordered the Fifth Corps to attack San Juan Heights, where Gen. Arsenio Linares had established a forward defensive line 4,000 yards long anchored on San Juan Hill, the largest elevation in the area.

In the difficult terrain below the heights, U.S. troop concentrations, located by their *artillery's smoke and their observation balloon, came under Spanish fire. The main attack finally began at 1:00 P.M. The key to the assault on San Juan Hill by a U.S. infantry division was the effective fire of a battery of three Gatling (machine) guns that swept the summit and forced most of the Spanish defenders to flee as the infantry in some disarray secured the heights.

To the right, meanwhile, elements of a dismounted cavalry division moved against Kettle Hill. Without benefit of artillery or the *Gatling gun, and in the face of heavy enemy fire, the dismounted troopers of two regular army cavalry regiments, the First and the Ninth (the latter one of the army's black regiments), and the First U.S. Volunteer Cavalry Regiment, moved up the slopes and drove the Spanish soldiers from the entrenchments at the top.

Although U.S. Army regulars provided the bulk of the force, the press and the American public focused primarily on the exploits of Lt. Col. Theodore Roosevelt, a New York politician, and his First Volunteer Cavalry Regiment, a group of western cowboys and eastern elites known as the "Rough Riders."

In the fighting of 1 July, the U.S. attacking forces sustained 205 killed and 1,180 wounded, the Spanish defenders 215 killed and 376 wounded. Because of the *casualties, Shafter did not assault the next and primary Spanish defensive line, but the Spanish governor general ordered the squadron out of the harbor, where it was destroyed on 3 July by waiting U.S. naval forces. Santiago surrendered on 17 July 1898.

[See also Colored Troops, U.S., Cuba, U.S. Military, Involvement in; Santiago, Battle of.]

• David F. Trask, *The War with Spain in 1898*, 1981. Paul H. Carlson, *"Pecos Bill": A Military Biography of William R. Shafter*, 1989. Michael L. Collins, *That Damned Cowboy*, 1989.

—David F. Trask

SANTA ANNA, ANTONIO LOPEZ DE (1794–1876), Mexican general and politician. An opportunist, Santa Anna shifted allegiance from party to party in Mexico. As dictator, his consolidation of power in 1835 prompted resistance in several Mexican regions, including Texas. Santa Anna took personal command of an army of 6,000 in early 1836. He made significant strategic and tactical errors in the campaign against the *Texas War of Independence, which ultimately resulted in his defeat and capture at the Battle of *San Jacinto.

Despite his slaughter of the defenders of the Battle of the *Alamo, and the execution of those captured around Goliad, Santa Anna survived death threats and imprisonment. He returned to Mexico in time to lead resistance against the French in 1838, made a triumphal return from exile in 1846, and recruited an army of 25,000 to face the United States in the *Mexican War.

Again, Santa Anna displayed more talent for rallying support and planning a campaign than for executing strategy. His only offensive of the war failed at the Battle of *Buena Vista (1847), due mainly to superior U.S. *artillery under Gen. Zachary *Taylor.

He then implemented a plan to defend easternmost

mountain passes, confining the enemy to unhealthy coastal areas. However, at Cerro Gordo (1847), Santa Anna failed to reinforce positions that were turned, resulting in a rout. He managed to collect a considerable force in retreat to Mexico City but was unable to inspire the confidence necessary for a strong resistance. Mexico City fell to Gen. Winfield *Scott's army, and Santa Anna was exiled once more. He returned to rule as "perpetual dictator" from 1853 to 1855, when revolutionaries finally drove him from power.

Santa Anna's failure as a military commander resulted from a character susceptible to delusions of grandeur but lacking in trust sufficient to delegate details to subordinates.

[See also Mexican Revolution, U.S. Military Involvement in the.]

• Antonio Santa Anna, Ann Fears Craw Ford, ed., The Eagle: The Autobiography of Santa Anna, 1988.   —Paul D. Lack

SANTIAGO, BATTLE OF (1898). Early in the *Spanish-American War, President William *McKinley on 26 May 1898 dispatched an army force to help the U.S. Fleet under Rear Adm. William *Sampson destroy Spain's Atlantic Battle Squadron, which had taken refuge in the harbor of Santiago de Cuba, and which was thought capable of raiding the North American coast or endangering American invasion forces bound for Cuba. The 15,000-man army expedition, commanded by Maj. Gen. William R. Shafter, disembarked near Santiago between 22 and 24 June. Following a preliminary action at Las Guasimas on the 24th and a week's delay to bring supplies and equipment ashore, Shafter's army on 1 July assaulted and captured Santiago's outer defenses at El Caney and then fought the Battle of *San Juan Hill, at the cost of more than 1,000 U.S. troops killed and wounded.

Adm. Pascual Cervera, his ships in range of U.S. *artillery fire, now considered Santiago untenable and on 3 July attempted to escape the harbor. His four poorly maintained armored *cruisers and two torpedo boat destroyers were no match for Sampson's five *battleships and two armored *cruisers. In less than three hours, Sampson's squadron, at a cost of one man killed, destroyed all of Cervera's vessels. More than 300 Spanish sailors died. On 17 July, the Spanish land force commander surrendered Santiago, 28,000 troops, and the entire eastern end of Cuba to General Shafter.

The destruction of its Atlantic Fleet and the capture of Cuba's second largest city induced Spain to sue for peace. The campaign was hailed as a triumph for the modern, steel-built U.S. *Navy, as well as for the U.S. Army and Theodore *Roosevelt's famous volunteer cavalry regiment, the "Rough Riders," although the army suffered supply problems and subsequent outbreaks of malaria and yellow fever.

[See also Cuba, U.S. Military Involvement in; Disease, Tropical.]

• Graham A. Cosmas, An Army for Empire: The United States Army in the Spanish-American War, 1971; 2nd ed., 1994. David F. Trask, The War with Spain in 1898, 1981.   —Graham A. Cosmas

SARATOGA, BATTLES OF (1777). The plan to isolate rebellious New England, adopted by British secretary of state for the colonies George Germain midway into the Revolutionary War, stipulated a Lake Champlain–Hudson River campaign under Gen. John *Burgoyne and a sweep through Lake Ontario under Lt. Col. Barry St. Leger, both to join, at Albany, with Gen. William *Howe's army, advancing north from New York City. Burgoyne's army included 4,135 British regulars, Friedrich von Riedesel's 3,116 Germans, and large numbers of authorized *"camp followers." Approximately 500 Indians and 500 French Canadian militia also accompanied the expedition, but most soon departed. Fort Ticonderoga fell to Burgoyne when its commander, Arthur St. Clair, left it unprotected against *artillery fire from southwest Sugar Loaf Hill and northwest Mount Hope. The Americans escaped across the lake.

Burgoyne, running short of food, sent a detachment of Germans under Lt. Col. Friedrich Baum to Bennington, Vermont, for supplies; there they were routed by John Stark's militia on 16 August 1777. Howe, meanwhile, sailed for Philadelphia instead of Albany, and St. Leger's army of loyalists and Indians, although victorious at Oriskany, 6 August, withdrew to Canada. Burgoyne, instead of turning back, declared his orders mandatory and crossed the Hudson; this effectively severed his Canadian supply line.

Horatio *Gates, as commander of the 10,277 American troops, replaced Philip Schuyler, who was blamed for the loss of Ticonderoga. At Freeman's Farm, 19 September, Burgoyne's three-pronged attack was stalled by Col. Daniel *Morgan's riflemen and thrown back by a charge under Gen. Benedict *Arnold. British losses were 566, American 313. At Bemis Heights, 7 October, Burgoyne's 1,723-man spearhead was repulsed by an unauthorized but successful attack led by Arnold, who was wounded in the leg. British losses were 631, American 130.

Gen. Henry *Clinton, Howe's successor in command at New York, declined to send reinforcements, and Burgoyne had waited too long to turn back. He retreated to Saratoga, and on 17 October surrendered his force of 5,895 men. The defeat of a major army led the British government to restrict operations to the southern coast. More important, the American success at Saratoga led France to sign the *France-American Alliance and provide the forces that ultimately helped win the Revolutionary War.

[See also Militia and National Guard; Revolutionary War: Military and Diplomatic Course.]

• Hoffman Nickerson, The Turning Point of the American Revolution, 1928; repr. 1967. Max M. Mintz, The Generals of Saratoga, 1990. Richard M. Ketchum, Saratoga: Turning Point of America's Revolutionary War, 1997.   —Max M. Mintz

SATELLITES, RECONNAISSANCE. American reconnaissance satellites provide images of the Earth and monitor electronic emissions of terrestrial and airborne communications and *radar systems. These automated spacecraft normally are positioned about the Earth in circular, low-altitude polar orbits; in highly eccentric orbits (with a low perigee and extremely high apogee); or in geosynchronous equatorial orbits, in which a satellite remains fixed over a given spot above the equator.

In the years after World War II, America's political leaders sought to prevent the recurrence of an intelligence failure like the attack on *Pearl Harbor and to obtain advance knowledge of any attempt at an atomic surprise attack on the United States. The U.S. *Navy and *Air Force first examined Earth satellites between 1946 and 1949. In 1950, the Research and Development Board of the Department of *Defense (DoD) assigned jurisdiction for military satellites to the air force. Study participants agreed that the most valuable use of satellites was as a platform from which to observe and record activity on Earth.

By late 1954, President Dwight D. *Eisenhower embraced "strategic reconnaissance" as a national policy: the United States would acquire reliable intelligence about the economic and military activities and resources of a potential foreign adversary through periodic, high-altitude overflight in peacetime. Eisenhower and his advisers crafted the legal rationale for this policy in the spring of 1955. Because international law denied airplanes of one state the right to enter the airspace of another without authorization, Eisenhower first sought agreement to permit aerial reconnaissance at a four-power summit conference in July. After Soviet leaders rejected this approach to reducing *Cold War tensions, the president, on his return to the United States, announced that America would launch scientific Earth satellites as part of the nation's contribution to the International Geophysical Year (IGY) planned by the international scientific community in 1957–58. Because international law did not yet apply in outer space, the administration determined to keep that region open to all, where the spacecraft of any state might overfly all states. It intended to use scientific satellites to establish the precedent of "freedom of space," with all that that implied for the eventual overflight of reconnaissance satellites.

Meanwhile, the RAND Corporation had completed studies of a potential reconnaissance satellite for the air force in 1954. In 1956, the air force contracted with the Lockheed Aircraft Corporation to build these satellites. Lockheed already held a secret contract for Project AQUATONE that produced an aerial precursor, *U-2 spy planes. The air force satellite project, eventually termed SAMOS, was an open secret. As reported in the press, this satellite's camera would view the Earth from a circular polar orbit and produce images of surface features of about 20 feet resolution. The exposed film would be scanned electronically and the pictures transmitted to ground stations as the satellite passed overhead. The DoD, however, restricted funding of this "follow-on" satellite system, and little more than design studies had been completed by the time the Soviet Union launched Sputnik 1, the world's first artificial satellite, into Earth orbit on 4 October 1957.

In response, early in February 1958, President Eisenhower approved a secret, high-priority reconnaissance satellite effort known as Project CORONA. Similar in many respects to its SAMOS cousin, CORONA employed the same spacecraft, but was designed to return exposed film to Earth in a special atmospheric reentry capsule that could be recovered in midair or on the ocean's surface. Organized like Project AQUATONE in a partnership between the *Central Intelligence Agency (CIA) and the U.S. Air Force, the first Project CORONA satellite was launched in 1959. President Eisenhower received the first CORONA pictures of the Soviet Union in August 1960, four months after the *U-2 incident in which an American spy plane was shot down. Late in August, Eisenhower approved formation of a new civilian-led organization in the DoD to control and direct the air force SAMOS Project. This organization reported to the secretary of defense and soon became a partnership between the CIA and the military services, acquiring responsibility for all of America's strategic reconnaissance assets; in 1961, it was formally named

the National Reconnaissance Office (NRO). Finally, just before leaving office in 1961, Eisenhower established the civilian-led National Photographic Interpretation Center (NPIC) to receive, process, and distribute reconnaissance film. NPIC reported to the director of Central Intelligence (DCI).

More than 100 CORONA missions were flown over the next 12 years until the project terminated in 1972. Equipped with Itek cameras that produced an image with a resolution at the Earth's surface of about 25 feet on average and, pointed at nadir, eventually about 6 feet at best, CORONA was employed for wide area searches. These satellites proved so successful that the struggling SAMOS project was canceled in the early 1960s after several SAMOS satellites failed to transmit to Earth even one usable picture of the Soviet Union. Other reconnaissance satellites augmented CORONA in the early 1960s, all of them featuring film capsule recovery systems. Project ARGON launched seven successful camera-equipped satellites to support U.S. Army mapping and charting. Collectively, in the years that followed, reconnaissance satellites provided the United States with an overhead "inspection system" that warned of imminent hostilities and permitted international agreement on arms reduction treaties with verification. They continue today to provide America's leaders with information vital to national security.

[See also Intelligence, Military and Political; Space Program, Military Involvement in the.]

• James R. Killian, Jr., *Sputnik, Scientists, and Eisenhower: A Memoir of the First Special Assistant to the President for Science and Technology,* 1977. John Prados, *The Soviet Estimate: U.S. Intelligence Analysis and Russian Military Strength,* 1982. Merton E. Davies and William R. Harris, *RAND's Role in the Evolution of Balloon and Satellite Observation Systems and Related U.S. Space Technology,* 1988. Cynthia M. Grabo, "The Watch Committee and the National Indications Center: The Evolution of U.S. Strategic Warning, 1950–1975," *International Journal of Intelligence and Counterintelligence,* 3 (Fall 1989). Robert A. Divine, *The Sputnik Challenge,* 1993. R. Cargill Hall, "The Eisenhower Administration and the Cold War: Framing American Astronautics to Serve National Security," *Prologue,* 1 (Spring 1995). R. Cargill Hall, "Postwar Strategic Reconnaissance and the Genesis of CORONA," in Dwayne A. Day, et al., eds., *Eye in the Sky: The Story of the CORONA Spy Satellites,* 1998.

—R. Cargill Hall

SCHENCK AND ABRAMS CASES (1919). Under the 1917 Espionage Act, Charles T. Schenck, a high official in the Socialist Party of America, was arrested for urging resistance to the draft. His pamphlet, sent to draftees, condemned *conscription as despotic and unconstitutional. In sustaining Schenck's conviction, Justice Oliver Wendell Holmes, Jr., based his standard for expression on the common law rule of proximate causation. His "clear and present danger" test became the starting point for subsequent free speech cases until the 1960s. Critics, however, deplored the subjectivity of the rule and Holmes's insensitivity to its larger implications for free speech.

The subsequent *Abrams* case, brought under the 1918 Sedition Act, involved the trial of an anarchist Russian immigrant, Jacob Abrams, and his supporters for distributing pamphlets, mainly in Yiddish, calling for a general strike to protest the presence of U.S. troops in Siberia during the Russian Revolution. The Supreme Court sustained conviction following a "bad tendency" test, but Holmes, responding to his critics, dissented. He saw no clear and present danger, but he also took the occasion to argue that free speech served broad social purposes and that the national interest would suffer more from restricting speech, however controversial, than from allowing it to be injected into the marketplace of ideas.

[*See also* Espionage and Sedition Acts of World War I; Supreme Court, War, and the Military.]

• Paul L. Murphy, *World War I and the Origin of Civil Liberties in the United States,* 1979. Richard Polenberg, *Fighting Faiths: The Abrams Case, the Supreme Court, and Free Speech,* 1987.

—Paul L. Murphy

SCHLESINGER, JAMES R. (1929–), economist, strategic analyst, secretary of defense, and first secretary of energy. Schlesinger served as secretary of defense during 1973–75, a turbulent period marked by the final stages of the *Vietnam War, severe cuts in the defense budget, the end of *conscription, and the beginning of the *All-Volunteer Force. A Phi Beta Kappa and 1950 summa cum laude graduate of Harvard College, he subsequently earned a Ph.D. at Harvard, then taught economics at the University of Virginia (1955–63). Next came service at the RAND Corporation as a senior staff member (1963–67) and director of strategic studies (1967–69). He entered government in 1969 as assistant director of the Bureau of the Budget, in 1971 became chairman of the Atomic Energy Commission, and in 1973 was appointed Director of Central Intelligence.

Moving later that same year to the Department of *Defense, Schlesinger forthrightly portrayed the impact of declining budgets, inflation, and spiraling personnel costs on force structure, modernization, and readiness. He laid before Congress a series of hard choices and the likely consequences of each. The United States, Schlesinger maintained, could not escape great responsibilities in a world where "military power remains relevant." He offered a vision of continued American involvement in world affairs based on strength, prudence, and reliability. Because of his background at RAND, Schlesinger was perhaps the secretary of defense most accomplished as a nuclear strategist. He claimed that it was "a dangerous illusion" to think that in the 1990s, when the United States no longer dominated in *nuclear weapons, that *deterrence of the Soviet Union could be based on the ability to inflict "unacceptable" retaliatory damage. "Deterrence is not a substitute for defense," he stressed. Instead, he maintained, deterrence, defense, and also detente "are inextricably bound up with one another in the maintenance of an equilibrium of power."

In 1976, Schlesinger was named assistant to the president to develop a national energy policy; when the Department of Energy was established the following year, he became its first secretary.

[*See also* Consultants; Nixon, Richard M.; Strategy: Nuclear Warfare Strategy.]

• James Schlesinger, *The Political Economy of National Security,* 1960. James Schlesinger, *America at Century's End,* 1989.

—Lewis Sorley

SCHOOLS, POSTGRADUATE SERVICE. Each of the armed services has its own system of postgraduate service schools for the indoctrination, training, and education of officers. Although each system is different, particularly at the lower levels, all military postgraduate schools fall into one of five main categories: service schools, staff colleges, senior service colleges, joint colleges, and specialist training schools. Service schools prepare newly commissioned officers for duties in operational units and aboard ship and senior company-grade officers for small unit command and staffwork. Staff colleges prepare selected midcareer officers for command and staff postings at intermediate echelons. Senior service colleges prepare selected senior field-grade officers for the highest command and staff positions. Joint service colleges teach joint operations and seek to improve interservice cooperation. Specialist training schools impart technical knowledge and manual skills.

U.S. Army. The army was the first of the services to recognize a need for postgraduate officer education. In April 1824, Secretary of War John C. *Calhoun established the Artillery School of Practice at Fortress Monroe, Virginia, to disseminate knowledge of elementary tactics and administration. By 1880, the Artillery School, under the influence of Emory *Upton, had become the model for the service schools later established for each of the army's branches (Infantry, Transportation Corps, etc.). Since 1973, the army service schools have been controlled by the U.S. Army Training and Doctrine Command (TRADOC).

In 1881, Gen. William Tecumseh *Sherman established the School of Application for Infantry and Cavalry. In its early years the service school at Fort Leavenworth, Kansas, prepared lieutenants for company-level duties and was often derided as "the army's kindergarten." The Leavenworth school was transformed between 1890 and 1910 by Arthur L. Wagner, Eben Swift, John F. Morrison, and other officers convinced of the need for an officer corps educated in both theory and practice and imbued with a sense of responsibility, reliability, intellectual acuity, and teamwork. These military educators introduced the systematic study of *strategy, *tactics, and military use of *history, as well as a broad range of other professional subjects using the so-called applicatory method, which called for active student involvement in the learning process by way of participation in the individual or group solution of strategic, tactical, and logistical problems using maps, indoor war games, or outdoor exercises known as *tactical rides.*

Beginning in 1887, a second year of study was provided for the best graduates of the School of Application. The second-year program evolved into the Army Staff College. Renamed the Army Command and General Staff College in 1928, the Leavenworth school thrived in the period between the two world wars and is often credited with being the principal educational influence on the men who led U.S. forces to victory in World War II. In the early 1980s, two new levels of instruction were added to the traditional staff college curriculum. The new Combined Arms and Services Staff School was established to prepare senior company-grade officers for service in battalion- and brigade-level staff positions, and a new School of Advanced Military Studies was created to provide a second year of advanced study for selected Command and General Staff College graduates.

The poor coordination of army forces in the 1898 *Spanish-American War prompted Secretary of War Elihu *Root to act on the ideas expressed by Emory Upton some twenty years before and to establish the Army War College in Washington, D.C., in November 1901. Until 1917, the Army War College was a not entirely successful adjunct of the newly created General Staff. Closed during World War I, the college reopened in 1919 with a regular curriculum stressing strategy, the command and management of large units, and military history. From 1919 to 1940, the Army War College formed the professional officers who held the most senior army commands in World War II. Classes were again suspended in 1940, but the army's senior service college was reestablished at Fort Leavenworth in 1950 and moved to Carlisle Barracks, Pennsylvania, the following year. Since 1950, the Army War College curriculum has focused on the study of national military policy and has become a center for strategic studies, the development of ground warfare doctrine, and international *peacekeeping.

U.S. Navy. For many years, the navy relied on experience at sea as the principal means of officer development. However, the immense changes in naval technology and naval doctrine in the post–*Civil War era prompted the establishment of the Naval War College at Newport, Rhode Island, in October 1884 to provide "an advanced course of professional study for naval officers." The creation and early development of the Naval War College—the first of the senior service colleges—was due primarily to the efforts of Rear Adm. Stephen B. *Luce. As president of the college from 1884 to 1886, Luce was responsible for bringing Alfred T. *Mahan, the great theorist of seapower, to the faculty in 1885. In 1890, William H. Little introduced the applicatory method, and the Naval War College subsequently became a center for the development of war games and naval tactics and strategy. Today, the navy has its own fully developed system of service schools and specialist training institutions, and the navy's own staff college—the College of Naval Command and Staff—is co-located with the Naval War College at Newport. The navy also has a unique high-level technical school, the Naval Postgraduate School, established in California, February 1913, to provide advanced instruction in naval ordnance and engineering subjects.

U.S. Marine Corps. A School of Application for newly commissioned Marine Corps lieutenants was opened in Washington, D.C., in May 1891, and in 1910 an Advance Base School was established at New London, Connecticut. However, before World War I, formal postgraduate education at these service schools took second place to expeditionary service abroad for most Marine Corps officers. In 1920, the Marine Corps School was established at Quantico, Virginia. Recently redesignated the Marine Corps University, it consists of an array of service and specialty schools and the Marine Command and Staff College. There is no Marine Corps senior service college; instead, Marine Corps officers attend the war colleges of the other services or one of the senior joint service colleges such as the National War College.

U.S. Air Force. Since 1947, the air force also has developed its own system of postgraduate professional education. Today, the Air University at Maxwell Air Force Base, Alabama, oversees the service school–level Squadron Officers School, the Air Command and Staff College, and the Air War College, as well as a number of specialist schools and the Air Force Institute of Technology at Wright-Patterson Air Force Base, Ohio, which conducts specialized educational programs, mostly of a technical nature.

Interservice Education. There are also a number of joint service colleges that bring together officers of all services to study joint operations and improve interservice cooperation. Since January 1976, these joint institutions have been part of the National Defense University. The two joint senior service colleges, the National War College and the Industrial College of the Armed Forces, are both located at Fort McNair in Washington, D.C. The National War College was created in 1946 to perpetuate the effective interservice cooperation developed during World War II. Its curriculum is similar to that of the other senior service colleges, but with greater emphasis on joint matters. The Army Industrial College, created in 1924, became a joint activity after World War II and was renamed the Industrial College of the Armed Forces. It focuses on mobilization and military-industrial preparedness. Since 1981, the Armed Forces Staff College in Norfolk, Virginia, established in 1946, has also been part of the National Defense University. Its six-month course concentrates on the functions and capabilities of the various services and on joint operations.

There is a wide variety of specialist training schools, many of which train students from more than one service. Some are designed to teach specific individual skills, such as flying or parachuting; others prepare officers for specific types of warfare, such as amphibious or nuclear operations, or teach technical subjects, such as *communications and computer technology. In addition, a number of joint postgraduate schools provide instruction in such fields as languages, medicine, intelligence, and resource management.

Recent Trends. Each year a limited number of officers from each of the services is selected to attend the military schools of other nations. A few American students also attend the six-month course at the *NATO Defense College in Rome, considered the equivalent of a U.S. senior service college. Officers can be selected to attend graduate degree programs or short courses at civilian universities. Training with industry is yet another alternative, especially for those in technical fields.

In recent years, postgraduate service schools have been greatly influenced by two trends. The first, and most influential, has been the growing demand for greater interservice cooperation, or "jointness," which has resulted in a greater emphasis on attendance at the joint colleges and on the study of joint operations at the various postgraduate institutions. The second important trend has been the growing interest in computer-assisted simulations. War games have a long history in American military education, and recent advances in computer technology have permitted the construction of complex, multifaceted games. Today, computer-assisted simulations are used for officer training at every level of the integrated, progressive system of postgraduate military education in the United States.

[See also Academies, Service; ROTC; Schools, Private Military.]

• John W. Masland and Laurence I. Radway, *Soldiers and Scholars: Military Education and National Policy,* 1957. James C. Shelburne and Kenneth J. Groves, *Education in the Armed Forces,* 1965. Lawrence J. Korb, ed., *The System for Educating Military Officers in the U.S.,* 1976. Martin van Creveld, *The Training of Officers: From Military Professionalism to Irrelevance,* 1990.

—Charles R. Shrader

SCHOOLS, PRIVATE MILITARY. The disciplined environment of West Point has provided one model for civilian schools established to educate intellectually and morally responsible citizens.

The earliest military-style academies in the United States offered practical and technical curricula quite unlike the classical education of contemporary universities. At Norwich University, opened as the private American Literary, Scientific, and Military Academy in New England in 1819, cadets studied engineering, navigation, and agriculture, along with composition and Latin. The Virginia Military Institute (VMI), which opened at Lexington in November 1839, took West Point's engineering curriculum as its model. In 1843, The Citadel Academy at Charleston began a similar course of practical studies for indigent South Carolina boys.

Graduation from these military-style schools did not lead automatically to army commissions, but during the *Civil War, *citizen-soldiers educated at these and other antebellum military academies served under arms, many as commissioned officers. A number of Northern academies, including Norwich, survived the war, but many Southern military schools—VMI excepted—did not. The Citadel remained closed through *Reconstruction; the Georgia Military Institute never reopened; and the University of Alabama's antebellum corps of cadets languished and finally disbanded. The military department of the Howard English and Classical School in Alabama bucked the trend, reemerging postwar as the Marion Military Institute, a two-year school still operating today.

The Morrill Land Grant Act of 1863 extended military-style education to land-grant colleges. By law, these schools had to provide male students with basic military instruction, but they remained essentially civilian institutions. A few land-grant schools initially organized their entire student bodies into military-style formations. Some, such as Clemson University, disbanded their corps of cadets years ago. Others—most notably Texas A&M and the Virginia Polytechnic and State University—still support a corps of cadets, but the military school environment they provide exists only as part of larger state universities. Today, only one school with a land-grant heritage—North Georgia College, opened in 1873 as a mining and technical school in the University of Georgia system—still adopts a military-style organization for the bulk of its student body.

At modern accredited four-year military colleges, cadets no longer find themselves limited to technical or practical majors, and they must meet the same standards for graduation required at comparable civilian institutions. But they still adhere to a tightly structured lifestyle. Although hazing is banned, freshmen endure an emotionally, physically, and intellectually rigorous first year. An Honor Code remains at the heart of the cadet experience. Time has brought change: regulations on *uniforms have relaxed at some schools; certain institutions now allow cadets to marry; others no longer require cadets to live in barracks; cadets may still be required to take *ROTC courses, but they do not necessarily accept a commission to graduate. Most recently, female cadets have begun to appear in the ranks. North Georgia College admitted women to cadet companies in the early 1970s when ROTC programs accepted female cadets, and Norwich did the same when it merged in 1972 with the all-female Vermont College. The Citadel and VMI were forced to open their ranks to women in the 1990s.

Two other types of private military schools exist. The Department of the Army supports an early commissioning program at six military-style academies, which include junior colleges such as Valley Forge Military Academy in Wayne, Pennsylvania. Since the 1880s, military-style schools, some now modeled on the navy, Marine Corps, and air force, also have filled a small niche in secondary education.

The *Vietnam War destroyed much of the attraction of military-style schools. Of 169 secondary and college-level schools open in 1945, only 50 remained in 1975. In the 1990s, however, a slight resurgence of interest in military-style schools has been observed around the country. Today, many of the surviving institutions belong to the Association of Military Colleges and Schools in the United States.

[See also Academies, Service; Education, Military; Schools, Postgraduate Service; Women in the Military.]

—Carol Reardon

SCHROEDER, PATRICIA (1940–), member of Congress (1972–97). Patricia Schroeder, a graduate of Harvard Law School, campaigned as an antiwar, liberal Democrat and won the congressional seat representing the racially diverse Denver, Colorado, district in 1972. When she entered the House of Representatives in the 92nd Congress, there were just thirteen women members. By 1996, when Schroeder announced she would not seek reelection, there were forty-seven women, though still barely 11 percent of the House. Schroeder's period of greatest influence on military issues came in the 1992–94 103rd Congress when the Democrats controlled the House; she chaired a House Armed Services subcommittee; there was a large, politically cohesive Congressional Caucus for Women's Issues and a network of sophisticated women's lobbying groups. Several of these groups focused on military issues (e.g., Women's Action for New Directions and the Defense Advisory Committee on Women in the Services).

Among the issues that Schroeder influenced were: ensuring that military wives and female personnel had access to abortion services at U.S. overseas military hospitals; reversing a Department of *Defense policy that had allowed divorced military men to exclude military retirement benefits from alimony calculations; opening up more "near-combat" and "combat" jobs to women; and insisting that *sexual harassment be taken seriously by senior Defense Department officials. On general questions, Schroeder joined all the other Democratic women in the House in voting against the "Don't ask, don't tell" formula for maintaining the *gay men and lesbians in the military ban. She also voted against funding the B-2 bomber for U.S. participation in *United Nations *peacekeeping.

[See also Gender and War; Gender: Female Identity and the Military; Women in the Military.]

• Debra L. Dodson, et al., Voices, Views, Votes: The Impact of Women on the 103rd Congress, 1995. WAND [Women's Action for New Directions] Bulletin, vol. 15, no. 2 (Spring 1996). Pat Schroeder, 24 Years of House Work . . . and the Place is Still a Mess: My Life in Politics, 1998.

—Cynthia Enloe

SCHWARZKOPF, H. NORMAN (1934–). U.S. Army general. Born in Trenton, New Jersey, the son of a professional army officer, Schwarzkopf graduated from West Point in 1956. After serving with an airborne unit, he returned to the academy as an instructor. But he interrupted that assignment to serve during the *Vietnam War as an adviser (1965–66) to a South Vietnamese Airborne brigade, winning two Silver Stars and a Purple Heart. After completing his faculty assignment and a year at the Army Command and General Staff College, he returned to Vietnam in 1969, soon taking command of the First Battalion, Sixth Infantry Regiment in the American Division along the northern coast near Chu Lai. In 1970, he earned another Silver Star and Purple Heart.

Back in the United States, Schwarzkopf graduated from the Army War College, then commanded an infantry brigade. As a brigadier general in 1978, he served as an assistant division commander in Germany, later as director of military personnel management at the *Pentagon, and in 1983–85 as commander of the 24th Infantry Division (Mechanized). In October 1983, he became deputy commander of the U.S. intervention in *Grenada, but was highly critical of the operation's shortcomings.

Between 1985 and 1988, Schwarzkopf served two tours in the Pentagon in operations and plans and also commanded a corps for a year. In 1988, as a full general, he took charge of the U.S. Central Command, with responsibility for possible deployment to the Middle East from its headquarters in Tampa, Florida.

In August 1990, after Saddam *Hussein's invasion of Kuwait, Schwarzkopf was given overall command of all U.S. and non-Arab Coalition forces, responsible for the massive *mobilization and deployment to the Persian Gulf, and for the planning and execution of the containment and then defeat of the Iraqi forces in Kuwait. The burly general hailed by the press as "Stormin' Norman" developed the so-called fast envelopment—the flanking ground offensive that led to the liberation of Kuwait in February 1991. Subsequently, he retired and wrote his memoirs, explaining his strategy and defending the controversial decision to halt at the Iraqi border.

[See also Persian Gulf War.]

• Roger Cohen and Claudio Gatti, *In the Eye of the Storm: The Life of General H. Norman Schwarzkopf,* 1991. Bob Woodward, *The Commanders,* 1991. H. Norman Schwarzkopf, *It Doesn't Take a Hero,* 1992.
— John Whiteclay Chambers II

SCIENCE, TECHNOLOGY, WAR, AND THE MILITARY. World War II transformed the relationship between war and the military on the one hand and science and technology on the other. What had been a fitful and uncomfortable relationship before the war became continuous and consistent thereafter. Important ties existed before 1941, but they were nothing like the intimate conjunction of these two fields in the last half of the twentieth century.

Engineers initiated that conjunction early in the nineteenth century. President Thomas *Jefferson modeled West Point, the first school of engineering in the United States, on the French state technical schools. The goal of the military academy was not only to train officers for technical service in the army but also to cultivate a pool of engineering talent for the young republic. West Point graduates, both in and out of the service, worked on roads, canals, bridges, and other elements of infrastructure. While the country quadrupled its territory in the nineteenth century, these engineers designed, built, and operated the railroad network that tied the new nation together. In the process, the army divided its personnel into combat and civil engineers, the latter taking up a dominant role in the development of America's water resources.

The military, science, and technology also found themselves jointly engaged in other enterprises in the nineteenth and early twentieth centuries. Both army and navy led exploring expeditions, such as the *Lewis and Clark expedition for the Louisiana Purchase (1804–06) and the Charles Wilkes expedition of 1838–42 to the Antarctic and Pacific Oceans. The army developed a meteorology branch that would become the nucleus of the National Weather Bureau. The American System of Manufacture, which caused a stir in Europe after a strong showing at the Great Exhibition of 1851 in London, was based on techniques of large-scale factory production first developed in government arsenals and private factories producing small arms. Beginning in the nineteenth century, manufacturing standards and contracting protocols were established by army and navy agencies buying goods and services in the private sector. The National Academy of Sciences was created during the *Civil War to help the federal government deal with the avalanche of inventions and proposals that poured into Washington, many having to do with military matters.

As the nineteenth century gave way to the twentieth, the relationship deepened between war and science and between the military and technology. War and the military contributed significantly to the development of such technologies as steel, radio, and aviation. Though none of these fields had their roots in the military, all were shaped by military developments and in turn became indispensable components of military capability.

In spite of this historically close relationship, the military services kept technology at arm's length in World War I. Some science and technology was institutionalized during the war. For example, the National Research Council (NRC) was formed as the working arm of the National Academy of Sciences to assist the services in the war effort. And the National Advisory Committee for Aeronautics (NACA) was created in 1915 to keep aviation developments apace with the hothouse activity in Europe precipitated by the war. But generally, when the services wanted scientific and technical talent, they simply inducted into uniform the individuals deemed necessary. Nobel laureate Robert Millikan, for example, left his academic post at the California Institute of Technology first to serve the navy as a civilian member of the NRC and then to accept a major's commission in the U.S. Army Reserves to head the Signal Corps Science and Research Division. He and others like him helped the services make significant advances in *submarines, radio, aviation, sound-and-ranging techniques for *artillery firing, and other areas. Nonetheless, the services emerged from World War I feeling that science and technology had served them poorly. The famed Naval Consulting Board, for example, chaired by Thomas Alva *Edison, fell into hopeless wrangling over the creation of a naval research laboratory and contributed little to the war effort. Better institutional arrangements were clearly necessary if the military in the future was to realize the full potential of science and technology.

Just such arrangements appeared in World War II. This conflict was the first in history in which the weapons deployed at the end of the war were significantly different from those that opened it. Many of the new developments—*radar, jet propulsion, ballistic *missiles, the atomic bomb—were developed largely or entirely in the course of the war. For all the major combatants, this required the mobilization of the full resources of the state, including, of course, its scientific and technical talent.

In the United States, an entirely new institution sprang up to meet the need. Clearly, much technical work continued to be done in the traditional way through contracts with industry and through research and testing in government laboratories and arsenals. But a significant portion of the most innovative and important research and development in World War II was done through the Office of Scientific Research and Development (OSRD). This small, independent branch of government was the responsibility of Vannevar *Bush—an inventor, teacher, and former dean of engineering at MIT. Originally constituted as the National Defense Research Committee (NDRC) and modeled on the NACA, which Bush had chaired, OSRD soon took shape as a clearinghouse of scientific and technical talent that could be applied to military problems.

The principles behind OSRD, which were to continue into the postwar world, were three. First, instead of trying to do all its own research, the government contracted with scientists and engineers to perform some of it. Second, instead of inducting them into service, as had been done during World War I, the government left its contractors in place, usually in university research laboratories. Third, developments sprang from two different sources: scientists and engineers might respond to military requests for new techniques or devices, or they might propose new developments themselves.

The entire range of research, from basic research through development of working prototypes, was open to exploration. The OSRD examined proposals from scientists and funded those with merit, and the office also took on problems from the military services and sought out researchers and laboratories to work on them. Radar, for example, the largest area of wartime research outside the atomic bomb project, was divided into more than 100 separate research undertakings and distributed to laboratories and test centers around the United States. OSRD scientists actually flew combat missions with prototype equipment to test it out and bring field results back to the laboratory for further refinement.

Just before war's end, Bush and his colleagues submitted to President Franklin D. *Roosevelt a manifesto entitled *Science, the Endless Frontier,* calling on the government to perpetuate the wartime experience of OSRD in a national research establishment. The purpose was to guarantee the economic and military security of the country by keeping its scientific and technical talent funded and focused on projects of national interest. The proposal ran afoul of political concerns over the autonomy that Bush wanted the scientists to have in setting their own agenda. Only in 1950 did the proposal finally become law, creating the National Science Foundation (NSF). Not the peacetime OSRD that Bush had recommended, NSF left military and medical research and development to other agencies and concentrated on basic, civilian research.

Meanwhile, the military services—the army, navy, and after 1947 the air force as well—took independent steps to institutionalize the scientific and technical assistance that had proved so critical in World War II. While uniformed officers in the United States and other countries had historically been skeptical of technological innovation, they now embraced research and development as the key to national security. The world wars may have been wars of industrial production, but the dramatic weapons innovations of the last conflict, culminating in the atomic bombs

dropped on Hiroshima and Nagasaki, led many officers to believe that quality would displace quantity as the determinant of victory in the future.

The services empaneled their own technical consultants, such as the Scientific Advisory Board of the air force; created or continued their own research laboratories, such as the Naval Research Laboratory; and supported research arms at universities around the country, such as the army's Applied Physics Laboratory at the Johns Hopkins University. The developments flowing from these sources resulted in new weapons that succeeded each other in the nation's arsenal at a rate never before seen in peacetime. As the United States slid into a cold war with its former ally, the Soviet Union, a standing military establishment emerged for the first time in the nation's history. Within that establishment, the services competed with each other for the right to develop and deploy ever newer and more sophisticated weapons and thus secure a place on the nation's front line of defense.

Soon this formula produced what President Dwight D. *Eisenhower called the "*military-industrial complex." In his farewell address in 1961, Eisenhower warned of "the unwarranted influence, whether sought or unsought," of contractors grown dependent on military funding. In private, he spoke of a "delta of power" linking the Department of *Defense, Congress, and industry in a mutually reinforcing conflict of interest that shaped U.S. foreign and defense policy and threatened the future of the country. Along with this danger, Eisenhower cautioned that "public policy could itself become the captive of a scientific-technological elite."

Eisenhower's warning did not significantly divert the military-industrial complex. In 1960, more than half the research and development done in the United States—government, corporate, and university-based—was military. The military services, or defense-related agencies such as the Atomic Energy Commission, became the principal supporters of research in nuclear physics, computers, microelectronics, space, and other scientific and technical fields. Furthermore, military considerations had second order consequences in seemingly nonmilitary areas of scientific and technical development. The National Defense Education Act, for example, funded graduate study in science and technology for thousands of American students. More broadly, military funding supported a significant percentage of university research in the *Cold War and helped to shape these institutions. The national interstate highway system was instituted in the Eisenhower administration in part to facilitate the *mobilization and movement of military forces in the event of national emergency. The national space program was launched on military missiles and took its rationale from the Cold War competition with the Soviet Union for the hearts and minds of the world's people. Even social sciences such as psychology and international relations were mobilized in the name of national security.

Preparation for strategic war with the Soviet Union engaged most of the scientific and technical research bent to the Cold War. *Nuclear weapons competition dominated the entire conflict, moving from the U.S. monopoly after World War II through the Soviet explosion of its first nuclear device in 1949 followed by the race to thermonuclear weapons in the early 1950s and other innovations such as tactical nuclear weapons and the neutron bomb in the years to follow. At first, airplanes were the delivery vehicles for these weapons, spawning enormous research and development efforts in aircraft development, antiaircraft defense, early warning systems, and electronic countermeasures. By the end of the 1950s, however, ballistic missiles had become the delivery system of choice, and research and development turned to more powerful launch vehicles, improved guidance systems, multiple independently targetable reentry vehicles (MIRVs), ballistic missile defense, and other esoteric technologies of strategic warfare. Throughout the Cold War, U.S. science and technology proved generally superior to that of the Soviet Union, and yet the Soviets displayed a remarkable capability to mimic U.S. achievements and keep the *arms race close.

The contest finally climaxed in the midst of the most far-reaching and expensive gambit of all, a program by the United States to develop a nationwide ballistic missile defense system. President Ronald *Reagan's *Strategic Defense Initiative (1983–93) invested some $40 billion in ballistic missile defense that critics said could not work; its supporters claimed that the Soviet Union finally had to admit defeat when faced with the prospect of trying to match the effort. In any case, the collapse of the Soviet Union in the late 1980s ended the Cold War and initiated a scaling back of the military-industrial complex, the end of which is not yet in sight.

Beginning with the *Vietnam War, a large amount of attention became focused on conventional and unconventional war. Precision-guided munitions and "smart" bombs employed advanced microelectronics to achieve unprecedented levels of accuracy and discrimination, seeking not only to hit the desired target but to avoid collateral damage. Sensing devices such as night-vision scopes and *heat-seeking technology helped combatants find and target the enemy. New types of *antipersonnel weapons such as cluster bombs and claymore mines entered the deadly arena of unconventional *jungle warfare and other nontraditional fighting environments. Even psychology and social sciences were enlisted in the struggle against enemies who chose not to fight in the traditional Western style.

Weapons and equipment developed for strategic war with the Soviet Union came to be enlisted in nonnuclear war against enemies around the world. Thus the F-117 stealth fighter, an attack airplane virtually invisible to traditional radar, played a role in both the U.S. invasion of Panama in 1989 and in the *Persian Gulf War of 1991. The latter conflict witnessed a rout of the Iraqi Army by *United Nations Coalition forces because the sophisticated arsenal of the United States was able to virtually eliminate the command, control, and *communications of the Iraqis before the ground engagement began. In the minds of some advocates, the Gulf War witnessed the apotheosis of airpower that had been predicted in some quarters since the 1920s.

The tremendous impact of science and technology on war during the second half of the twentieth century mirrored the equally momentous impact that war had on science and technology. In addition to the phenomena already mentioned, military demand created the discipline of operations research, pioneered the techniques employed in the commercialization of nuclear power, introduced many important medical practices and products, and developed technologies such as high-resolution photography

and the global positioning navigation system that subsequently entered the civilian economy.

[See also Atomic Scientists; Consultants; Hiroshima and Nagasaki, Bombings of; Industry and War; Panama, U.S. Military Involvement in; World War I: Domestic Course; World War I: Postwar Impact; World War II: Domestic Course.]

• Harvey M. Sapolsky, The Polaris System Development: Bureaucratic and Programmatic Success in Government, 1972. Merritt Roe Smith, ed., Military Enterprise and Technological Change: Perspectives on the American Experience, 1985. Michael S. Sherry, The Rise of American Air Power: The Creation of Armageddon, 1987. Richard Rhodes, The Making of the Atomic Bomb, 1988. Donald A. Mackenzie, Inventing Accuracy: An Historical Sociology of Nuclear Missile Guidance, 1990. Stephen Peter Rosen, Winning the Next War: Innovation and the Modern Military, 1991. Stuart W. Leslie, The Cold War and American Science: The Military-Industrial Complex at MIT and Stanford, 1993. Paul N. Edwards, The Closed World: Computers and the Politics of Discourse in Cold War America, 1996. Paul A.C. Koistinen, Beating Plowshares into Swords: The Political Economy of American Warfare, 1606–1865, 1997.   —Alex Roland

SCOTT, WINFIELD (1786–1866), U.S. *Army officer and commanding general. Born in Virginia, Scott entered the army in 1807. In the *War of 1812, promoted to brigadier general, he trained his troops superbly and led his brigade ably in battle, defeating British regulars in 1814 at the battles of Chippewa and Lundy's Lane where Scott was severely wounded and became a national hero. To this day, West Point cadets wear gray 1814 uniforms in honor of the American victory over British regulars. After the war, he prepared a three-volume manual on infantry tactics that endured throughout the smoothbore era. He served in the *Black Hawk War and in the campaigns against the Seminoles and Creeks, and in 1838, he supervised the removal of the Cherokees to the West. Scott had a talent for peacemaking, demonstrated first in 1832 when President Andrew *Jackson sent him to Charleston and he helped negotiate the Nullification crisis. Later, he helped restore peace on the Canadian border during the Caroline crisis in 1838 and during the so-called Aroostook war over the Maine border in 1839. In 1841, as a major general, Scott was appointed commanding general of the U.S. Army, a position he held until 1861.

During the *Mexican War of 1846–48, Scott achieved the most spectacular success of any U.S. commander, but his pompous attitude and his squabbles with subordinates and superiors marred his effort and contributed to his sobriquet, "Old Fuss and Feathers." While Zachary *Taylor led the invasion of northern Mexico, Scott in 1847 personally led the southern expedition.

Scott's campaign began with the first major amphibious landing in U.S. history: more than 12,000 U.S. troops were put ashore by the U.S. *Navy without loss of life near the Mexican port of Veracruz in surfboats specifically requested by Scott. The city surrendered after an 88-hour bombardment by Scott's siege guns, which killed between 1,000 and 1,500 Mexicans. At the beginning of the campaign, Scott had issued General Order No. 20, responding to atrocities committed by some of the volunteer troops; in it he required U.S. troops to respect the rights and property of Mexicans, local government, and the Roman Catholic Church.

To avoid yellow fever on the coast and to capture the

Mexican capital, Scott then led the expedition on a long, overland campaign across mountainous terrain to Mexico City. He broke through Gen. Antonio Lopez de *Santa Anna's defense at the strategic pass of Cerro Gordo and then paused at Puebla to await replacements for the twelve-month volunteers whose enlistments expired. When Scott departed from his line of supply and decided to live off the countryside, the Duke of Wellington in Britain declared he would be lost. But Scott successfully led the U.S. troops to Mexico City, first winning victories at Contreras and Churubusco, where Scott's *casualties were one-tenth that of the Mexicans, largely because of his use of superior *artillery and flanking maneuvers. U.S. troops at Churubusco captured members of the San Patricio Battalion, Irish American soldiers who had changed sides when Mexico offered them land and protection of their rights as Roman Catholics. Scott ordered the survivors executed as traitors.

Arriving in front of Mexico City, Scott agreed to Santa Anna's request for an armistice, hoping for a negotiated peace. But when the Mexicans sought to rebuild their army, Scott resumed the offensive, defeating the Mexicans at Molino del Rey in an uncharacteristic frontal attack that cost nearly 800 U.S. *casualties and 2,000 Mexicans killed and wounded. Attacking Mexico City, Scott's forces bombarded, then stormed the Castillo de Chapultepec, overcoming the defenders—including the young cadets, "los Niños," of the military academy there, who died defending the Mexican capital.

President James K. *Polk recalled Scott from Mexico in early 1848 after the disagreements and suspicion between the Democratic president and the Whig general were compounded by the myriad disputes that erupted between Scott and his fellow officers, some of whom filed charges against him. A court of inquiry dismissed these, however, and Scott became a national hero. In 1852, Congress brevetted Scott a lieutenant general and he ran poorly as the Whig Party candidate for president against Democrat Franklin Pierce. In the mid-1850s, Scott's squabbles with Secretary of War Jefferson *Davis were legendary.

Despite his Virginia birth, Scott remained loyal to the Union when the South seceded. In declining health, he still formulated the much derided but thoughtful "Anaconda Plan" for a long, strangling blockade and siege of the Confederacy to preserve the Union while keeping casualties low. After the First Battle of *Bull Run, which he opposed, he retired in November 1861; he died at West Point in 1866.

[See also Mexican War; Native American Wars: Wars Between Native Americans and Europeans and Euro-Americans.]

• Winfield Scott, Memoirs, 2 vols., 1864. Charles Winslow Elliott, Winfield Scott: The Soldier and the Man, 1937. Arthur D. Howden Smith, Old Fuss and Feathers: The Life and Exploits of Lt.-General Winfield Scott, 1937. John S. D. Eisenhower, Agent of Destiny: The Life and Times of General Winfield Scott, 1997. Timothy D. Johnson, Winfield Scott: The Quest for Military Glory, 1999.

—John M. Hart

SDI. See Strategic Defense Initiative.

SEALS. See Special Operations Forces: Navy Seals.

SEA POWER. See Mahan, Alfred T.; Strategy: Naval Warfare Strategy.

SEATO (est. 1954). On 8 September 1954, the United States, Britain, France, Australia, New Zealand, the Philippines, Thailand, and Pakistan signed the Southeast Asia Collective Defense Treaty in Manila. Sometimes referred to as the Manila Pact, this agreement created the Southeast Asia Treaty Organization (SEATO). The Eisenhower administration and especially Secretary of State John Foster *Dulles had worked to establish this loose alliance after the *Geneva Agreement on Indochina ended the French war in Southeast Asia in 1954. Under the prevailing strategy of containment, Dulles envisioned SEATO as a "no trespassing" sign warning Beijing and Moscow not to threaten Southeast Asia. Also, congressional leaders had opposed unilateral U.S. military assistance to France during the siege of Dienbienphu in Vietnam in the spring of 1954. With SEATO, Dulles believed, Congress would support the use of U.S. military forces in any future crisis in Southeast Asia.

Unlike *NATO in Europe, SEATO did not create its own military structure, nor did it obligate its members to respond if one was attacked. In the event of aggression or subversion in the treaty area, the signatories were to consult and to meet the common danger in accordance with their own constitutional processes. South Vietnam, Laos, and Cambodia could not be members because of prohibitions in the Geneva Agreements, but those Indochinese states could request SEATO protection under a separate protocol to the treaty. India, Burma, and Indonesia preferred to maintain a neutral stance toward China and the USSR and declined to join SEATO.

Despite the purposefully vague wording of the SEATO charter, the administration of President Lyndon B. *Johnson claimed in 1965 that SEATO allowed and even required the build-up of U.S. forces in South Vietnam. However, only Australia, New Zealand, and Thailand among the SEATO nations joined the United States in sending combat troops to the *Vietnam War. Pakistan withdrew from the alliance in 1972. After the Democratic Republic of Vietnam prevailed in the Vietnam War, SEATO dissolved completely in 1977.

• David L. Anderson, Trapped by Success: The Eisenhower Administration and Vietnam, 1953–1961, 1991.

—David L. Anderson

SEA WARFARE in the history of the American Republic has consisted of two missions—control of sea lanes and projection of power ashore. During the *Revolutionary War, a great many American merchant ships were outfitted as privateers and preyed on the commerce of Great Britain. According to the records of Lloyds, between 1775 and 1781 American privateers captured 2,600 British merchantmen. The financial impact of these captures on the most influential Britons was an important factor in bringing about American independence. With higher priorities in Europe and India, the British navy attempted to blockade American ports with little success. American projection of power ashore was limited to small raids, but the brief blockade of the Yorktown peninsula by the French fleet under the Comte de Grasse in 1781 was crucial to Gen. George *Washington's victory over Gen. Charles *Cornwallis.

In the *War of 1812, the principal operations of the U.S. *Navy and privateers were in preying on British commerce, which they did with great success. They were much less successful in preventing the Royal Navy from capturing more that 100 American merchantmen, or in preventing the repeated projection ashore by the Royal Navy of successful invasion forces, including those which captured Washington, D.C., in August 1814.

During the American *Civil War, the *Union navy's principal mission was to prevent the use of the seas for resupply and commerce by the Confederacy. A secondary mission was to split the Confederacy in two by taking control of the Mississippi River and using its tributaries and other major systems to interdict communications and commerce with the Confederacy itself. The *Confederate navy devoted its efforts to attempting to break the very effective strangulation of the Union blockade and to raiding Yankee commerce around the world. The nineteen Confederate raiders, most notably the *Alabama*, which took sixty union prizes under Capt. Raphael Semmes, were sail- or steam-powered, heavily armed packets, some, like the *Alabama*, purpose-built in England.

Following the Civil War, the U.S. Navy entered a period of considerable intellectual ferment and technological innovation. Alfred T. *Mahan revolutionized thinking about naval strategy and marine warfare throughout the world; Mahan's *The Influence of Seapower Upon History* changed the course of world history and helped fuel the German-British naval rivalry leading to *World War I. It was a maxim of Mahan's theories that in addition to the classic naval tasks of raiding enemy commerce and protecting one's own and projecting power ashore, the U.S. Navy must have "a navy powerful enough not just to fend off the enemy, but to smite him down" and thereby achieve "command of the seas." This doctrine of maritime superiority became the reigning orthodoxy in the navy from the late nineteenth century to the present.

Before American entry into World War I, the strategic attention of the navy had come to focus on the growing naval power of Japan. Beginning in 1911, "Plan Orange" was a strategy to fight a naval war against Japan and became the central planning focus of the U.S. Navy until 1945. There was virtually no plan for the war with Germany that came in 1917. The official "Plan Black" was an unrealistic scenario of Germany attacking the Caribbean. In the event, the navy focused almost entirely on fighting the German U-boat threat in the North Atlantic and on conducting the transport of munitions and men to Europe. Despite another period of post-war budget slashing, the 1920s and 1930s saw a great deal of technological innovation in the navy. Advanced versions of naval guns and *torpedoes were developed, and American *submarine design was brought forward. The most far-reaching innovation was the introduction of *aircraft carriers to the fleet, beginning with the commissioning of the USS *Langley* in 1922.

*World War II was the largest naval war ever fought. While *battleships fought important engagements and were indispensable in providing the naval gunfire for amphibious assaults in Europe and the Pacific, they were rapidly replaced as the central weapons system by seaborne air power. The sinking of the *Bismarck* by British carrier aircraft and the *Repulse* and the *Prince of Wales* by Japanese aircraft demonstrated that surface combatants, including the largest battleships, could not survive without the protection of air superiority. The Battles of the *Coral Sea and *Midway in 1942 made clear that aircraft would dominate

the war at sea. Thereafter the war unfolded predictably with the U.S. submarine and then surface Pacific fleets interdicting Japanese logistics and blockading the home islands, while multiplying carrier and battleship task forces hunted down and destroyed the remaining elements of the Japanese battle fleet. Simultaneously, Gen. Douglas *MacArthur in the Southwestern Pacific and Adm. Chester W. *Nimitz in the Central Pacific retook the Japanese conquests closing in for the final invasion of Japan planned for late 1945.

The submarine emerged also as a devastating weapons system. For the first two years of the war, despite the fact that the United States was turning out two merchant ships a day, the Germans were able to sink shipping faster than it could be replaced. Once again, however, Allied air cover, and the lack of German air cover, turned the tide. Germany lost 827 submarines and did not pose a serious threat by the end of 1942.

In the Pacific, the American submarine force was enormously effective throughout the war in destroying Japanese commerce and military transport. Japanese submarines, by contrast, equipped with better torpedoes and some better designs, were never used effectively and had no impact on the outcome of the war. When final victory came in 1945, the U.S. Navy had 105 aircraft carriers, 5,000 ships and submarines, and 82,000 vessels and landing craft deployed around the world, manned by experienced citizen-sailors on a ration of seventy reservists to each regular navy individual.

The emergence of nuclear weapons at the end of the war set the stage for a bitter struggle between the navy and the Air Force over roles and missions in the era of nuclear deterrence. The Air Force sought primacy with its long-range bombers and the navy with its carrier-based aircraft. Ultimately, both were relied upon, but they were eclipsed as delivery systems by the emergence of both land-based and sea-based *missiles. In 1960, the first Polaris submarine was deployed on missile patrol with sixteen nuclear-tipped missiles capable of launching while submerged and flying to targets in the Soviet Union. This strategic deterrent mission remains a fundamental part of the navy. Throughout the *Cold War, naval aircraft carriers carried nuclear weapons and, beginning in the mid-1980s, the Tomahawk cruise missile contributed to nuclear deterrence.

Sea warfare in the *Korean War and the *Vietnam War was limited to projection of power ashore. Korea saw the first use of jet-powered aircraft flying combat missions from aircraft carriers. The strategic use of American carrier aircraft in bombing and mining North Vietnam is well chronicled and was the overwhelming bulk of U.S. Navy effort in the war.

After the end of the Vietnam War, the focus of the U.S. Navy swiftly returned to the growing Soviet naval threat to the sealines of communication and the threat of Soviet fleet ballistic missile submarines. This focus was called sea control and had the highest priority in naval planning through the 1970s. Because of the numerical superiority of the Soviet fleet of some 1,700 ships (compared to some 500 ships in the U.S. fleet plus an additional 500 in *NATO and Allied navies), naval strategy took on a fundamentally defensive posture. *Anti-submarine warfare became the highest priority mission with research and development on surveillance, detection, and offensive and defensive weapons systems. Naval strategy was driven by the central importance of resupplying NATO in the event of an attack by the *Warsaw Pact, and preventing Soviet submarines from interdicting the North Atlantic sea-bridge below the "GIUK" gap (Greenland, Iceland, United Kingdom).

In the 1980s, with the adoption of a more assertive foreign policy toward the Soviet Union by the administration of President Ronald *Reagan, the navy, led by Secretary John Lehman, fundamentally shifted its strategy to a more forward posture emphasizing immediate offensive operations in the event of a war initiated by the Warsaw Pact. To a continuing emphasis on sea control and anti-submarine warfare was added a reassertion of projection by naval forces of strike power ashore in support of the land battle and deep into the Warsaw Pact. Naval task forces were trained and redeployed to enable the launch of Tomahawk cruise missiles from submarines and surface ships and air strikes from carrier-based air wings. The integrated Reagan military strategy enabled the threat of significant offensive operations from the sea against Warsaw pact vulnerabilities.

After the collapse of the Soviet Union and the end of the Cold War, the Soviet naval threat rapidly disappeared. Sea control and anti-submarine warfare has remained a top priority of sea warfare because relatively low-cost, effective diesel electric submarines have proliferated around the world, and all naval operations in the future are likely to encounter that threat. Nevertheless, the emphasis has again shifted to the projection of power ashore for crisis management and in support of land forces and peacekeeping efforts.

Whether the naval mission requirement is controlling or interdicting sealanes or the projection of power ashore, the same platforms, electronic systems, and weapons are employed. The foundation of sea warfare today is the aircraft carrier. These large, robust mobile air bases provide the protective bubble of air supremacy without which commercial and military surface ships cannot survive in conflict. The aircraft embarked on these ships include ten difference types of specialized platforms engaged in anti-submarine, anti-surface warfare, electronics, surveillance, intelligence, air combat, and surface strike.

Cruisers, destroyers, frigates, and corvettes are designed to engage simultaneously in anti-submarine, anti-aircraft, anti-ship, and projection of power ashore through naval gunfire and Tomahawk cruise missiles. To this capability is now being added theater area missile defense using the *Aegis radar system and the vertical missile launch tubes on cruisers and destroyers. All submarines in the American navy are nuclear powered and are either fleet ballistic missile submarines or attack submarines designed to detect and destroy enemy submarines and surface ships.

Navy and marine amphibious forces are designed and trained to transport and put ashore substantial marine land and air combat forces against enemy opposition. This involves the use of specialized ships that can simultaneously launch helicopter forces and seaborne landing craft and LCAC air cushion landing craft. The landed forces are provided direct fire support from guns and missiles aboard naval surface combatants, and from navy and marine aircraft flying from aircraft carriers, including the marine VS-TOL Harriers flying from the amphibious ships. In the 1990s the Atlantic Fleet pioneered joint operations using aircraft carriers and amphibious ships to land entire army divisions, integrating army and air force aircraft with navy

and marine. With the earth covered two-thirds by water, space-based systems for communications and intelligence are essential to sea warfare. Their product is integrated in all naval tactical planning and satellite navigation, and communications are primary resources for the fleet.

[*See also* Strategy: Naval Warfare Strategy.]

• Alfred Thayer Mahan, *The Influence of Seapower on History*, 1892. Samuel E. Morison, *History of United States Naval Operations in World War II*, 15 vols., 1947-62. C. S. Forester, *The Age of Fighting Sail*, 1957. Hiroyuki Agawa, *The Reluctant Admiral: Yamomoto and the Imperial Navy*, 1979. John F. Lehman, Jr., *Command of the Seas*, 1988.   —John F. Lehman, Jr.

SELECTIVE DRAFT CASES (1918). In World War I, the Supreme Court upheld the constitutionality of the Selective Draft Act of 1917 and national *conscription in general in the Selective Draft Law Cases (officially, *Arver et al. v. United States*, 245 U.S. 366).

In a unanimous decision written by Chief Justice Edward White, the Court rejected arguments that the draft was not authorized by the Constitution and violated the Thirteenth Amendment's prohibition against involuntary servitude. Citing Southern court rulings upholding conscription in the *Civil War (the Northern judiciary had divided), White—a Confederate veteran and former Louisiana judge and senator—declared that the power to compel military service was inherent in any state for its defense. The Constitution permitted national conscription as "necessary and proper" to implement the specific congressional authority "to raise and maintain armies." Although the judiciary modified some Selective Service procedures, particularly during the *Vietnam War, the Supreme Court has never reexamined the constitutionality of national conscription.

[*See also* Conscientious Objection; Supreme Court, War, and the Military.]

• Paul L. Murphy, *The Constitution in Crisis Times, 1918–1969*, 1972. John Whiteclay Chambers II, *To Raise an Army: The Draft Comes to Modern America*, 1987.
                                        —John Whiteclay Chambers II

SELECTIVE SERVICE. *See* Conscription.

SEMINOLE WARS (1818; 1835–42; 1855–58). The southeastern border of the United States was continuously turbulent during the early nineteenth century. Runaway slaves escaped into Spanish Florida, while Indian bands and white bands marauded unrestrained. Open war finally broke out on 27 November 1817, when Maj. Gen. Edmund P. Gaines sent a detachment to Fowltown, a Seminole village, to arrest its chief, Neamathla, for defying the authority of the United States.

Maj. Gen. Andrew *Jackson took over command on 26 December 1817. With an army of about 4,000 men, half of them Creek Indians, he invaded Spanish Florida and destroyed Seminole power west of the Suwannee River. He went on to take St. Marks and Pensacola, offending Spain; then offended Great Britain by executing two British citizens for aiding the Seminoles. The war seemed over to him, and on 30 May 1818, he left Florida. The next year, because of Jackson's conquests, the Spanish government transferred Florida to the United States by the *Adams-Onís Treaty.

For the Seminoles, American acquisition ended an era of

prosperity and began one of deprivation. The first U.S. policy, initiated in 1823, confined them to a reservation of 4 million acres of poor land. There were numerous violent confrontations, many of them disputes over the ownership of blacks. U.S. slaveholders, Creek Indians, Seminoles, and the blacks themselves harried each other over slave property.

As Americans shoved into Florida in the years after the war, the Seminoles, a loose association of diverse bands, prepared to fight once more. In 1834, however, their leadership came not from hereditary chiefs but from *Osceola, a part-white warrior without ancestral or tribal standing, whose courage and determination inspired the bands to act together. Miccosukees ravaged the plantations east of the St. Johns River, while Alachuas and others killed the Indian agent, Wiley Thompson, and annihilated Maj. Francis L. Dade's detachment of 108 men on 28 December 1835. Dade's defeat began the undeclared Second Seminole War, 1835–42.

By September 1836, the Seminoles controlled all of North Florida east of the Suwannee River except Newnansville, Micanopy, and Garey's Ferry. But when Osceola sickened in the late summer, cooperation among the bands slackened. Leadership passed from Osceola to Wildcat (Coacoochee), Alligator (Halpatter Tustenuggee), Jumper (Ote Emathla), Halleck Tustenuggee, Billy Bowlegs (Holata Mico), and Sam Jones (Arpeika). These men led not a nation but disparate bands that sometimes cooperated.

For the United States, Brig. Gen. Duncan L. Clinch commanded first, followed by Maj. Gen. Winfield *Scott. After Scott, the civilian governor of Florida, Richard K. Call, took charge for six months. Then the sequence of ranking general officers recommenced: Maj. Gen. Thomas S. Jesup, Brig. Gen. Zachary *Taylor, Brig. Gen. Walker K. Armistead, and Brig. Gen. William J. Worth.

Scott's Napoleon-like strategy failed. Jesup, frustrated, began to seize key leaders when they came in to negotiate; his most notorious capture was of Osceola on 27 October 1837. Zachary Taylor directed the notable battle near Lake Okeechobee on Christmas Day, 1837. He threw his 800 men head-on against a position meticulously prepared by the three bands of Seminoles waiting there. He finally dislodged them but sustained 138 *casualties.

About 400 blacks, effective fighters, stood with the Seminoles until the spring of 1838. In March of that year, General Jesup reversed previous policies and promulgated his order that all blacks who joined the U.S. force would become free. Thereafter, the blacks shifted allegiance, ceasing to serve alongside the warriors.

The last two U.S. commanders relied on small detachments led by junior officers. Blacks or captured Indians guided them to the ultimate hideaways of the Indians, where they destroyed the remaining Seminole means of subsistence. Ragged, hungry, and short of ammunition, hostile bands began to surrender; in August 1842, General Worth was able to declare the Second Seminole War ended. About 350 Indians remained south of Lake Okeechobee and Pease Creek.

For a few years, Billy Bowlegs and Sam Jones strove to keep the peace; but the United States, pressed by settlers, began to build roads and survey within the Indian preserve. Escalating white encroachments brought an attack on an army camp on 20 December 1855. It was the catalyst for the Third Seminole War. U.S. volunteers rather than regulars provided the main military force this time. The last fight took place on 5 March 1857. Billy Bowlegs, convinced that the cause was lost, accepted several thousand dollars to emigrate, taking with him 165 followers. About 120 Seminoles remained behind. One of them was Sam Jones, who never left, but died in Florida in 1867, one hundred eleven years old. The United States declared the Third Seminole War officially ended on 8 May 1858.

[See also Native American Wars.]

• John K. Mahon, History of the Second Seminole War, 1835–1842, 1967. James W. Covington, The Billy Bowlegs War, 1855–1858, 1981. Virginia Bergman Peters, The Florida Wars, 1979. Kenneth W. Porter, The Black Seminoles, 1996. Frank Laumer, Dade's Last Command, 1995. John K. Mahon, "The First Seminole War, 1817–1818," Florida Historical Quarterly, Summer 1998.
—John K. Mahon

SERMONS AND ORATIONS, WAR AND THE MILITARY IN. The role of religious ideology in military history is often overlooked. Military matters are frequently touched on in connection with religious history, but only to reinforce the prevalence of religious trends, not to demonstrate religion's impact on military operations. Yet throughout American history, religion has served distinctive militaristic purposes as preachers have conjoined military action with piety to foster a sense of duty, mission, and historic connection to God's will.

In seeking to justify war, ministers in colonial America emphasized conflict as a natural consequence of sin. The Puritan minister Urian Oakes examined the internal struggle with sin and its external manifestation in war. In his 1672 military sermon ("The Unconquerable, All-Conquering, and More-Than-Conquering Souldier"), Oakes superimposed the metaphysical struggle between good and evil onto the military necessities of colonial New England. In the aftermath of *King Philip's War, Samuel Nowell emphasized a more practical theme, self-preservation, in "Abraham in Arms" (1678). He argued that God was a man of war and concluded that the colonists should resist both Indians and European nations. Such messages promoted a sense of military obligation to God and the *state, linking civil religion to *patriotism and military training.

Religious ideology emphasized the orderly, manly, and godly aspects of European-style war. The colonial militia trained in linear European tactics, despite the fact that the Indian forest warfare made them useless. In this instance, religious ideology hindered effective operations. The Puritan minister John Richardson ("The Necessity of a Well Experienced Souldiery") noted in 1675 that learning the art of war gave much glory to God, "the author of every commendable art or science." The pursuit of reason and order through the militia training may have encouraged God's favor, but it did little to prepare colonists for irregular warfare.

A second, functional level of military activity responded to shifts in the conduct of operations. The reality of non-European opponents fighting in unorthodox and "unmanly" ways caused colonists to learn, at great cost, new ways of fighting in dense forests: that maneuver was as important as volley and fire. Without open fields, small units composed of light, mobile troops became the most effective means of combatting the Indians. Such warfare was at odds with both Puritan theology and accepted military practices. In a sermon entitled "Military Duties Laid

Before a Trained Band" (1686), the eminent Puritan minister Cotton Mather addressed Indian tactics and God's will, emphasizing the Christian aspects of military duty and likening the Puritan-Indian struggles to those of the Israelites and the Philistines. New England's success in King Philip's War, he concluded, proved the justness of war and the efficacy of prayer.

In defining accepted behavior, most ministers emphasized the just causes of war. In an election sermon preached to the Honorable Artillery Company of Boston during King William's War ("Good Souldiers a Great Blessing," 1700), Benjamin Wadsworth argued that war was not only lawful, but necessary. Obedience to God and resistance to Indian treachery were the reasons to learn war; like Mather, he reinforced historic connections to Israel and urged participation in militia training. Both Mather and Wadsworth fostered a kind of religious *nationalism by praising military action.

Preachers in the evangelistic era of the Great Awakening (1740–45) suffused this religious ideology with a growing awareness of political rights and liberties. As their sermons reveal, motives for war were no longer strictly religious and defensive; rather, war could be seen as a guarantor of civil liberties.

At the outset of the *French and Indian War, the Presbyterian minister Samuel Davies insisted that warfare was both a civic responsibility and a Christian duty. In August 1755, Davies preached to a company of independent volunteers from Hanover County, Virginia, on the theme "Religion and Patriotism the Constituents of a Good Soldier." Davies rebuked the congregation for unmanliness in failing to support the frontier army, which as members of the body politic they had a responsibility to do. Three years later, Davies preached "The Curse of Cowardice" to a general militia muster, taking his text from Jeremiah 48:10: "Cursed be he that doeth the work of the Lord deceitfully, and cursed be he that keepeth back his sword from blood." Davies used associations with Israel to define the condition of service as something owed both to God and to country. Thus, between the 1740s and the 1780s, many preachers fused political patriotism with religious nationalism. The result was a religious ideology that defined godliness and manliness through the performance of military obligation.

The rise of the political oration in the *Revolutionary War era marked the first shift away from the military sermon. The *Boston Massacre Day orations serve as partially secularized functional equivalents to New England artillery sermons. In 1774, John Hancock ("An Oration Delivered . . . to Commemorate the Bloody Tragedy of the Fifth of March 1770") employed traditional religious imagery to convey an essentially political message: that colonists "fight pro aris & focis, for their liberty, and for themselves, and for their God." Key to his message was his order of delineation: liberty, self, and God. By contrast, John Lathrop, pastor of the Second Church in Boston ("A Discourse Preached on March the Fifth, 1778"), based his commemoration on the biblical text of Genesis 6:13: ". . . The earth is filled with violence." Lathrop argued that North America had been "reserved in divine providence as the last retreat" for those who placed God above "the will of any temporal monarch." These examples bridge the gap between artillery sermons and quasi-religious commemorative speeches, and they mark the beginning of a shift in the control of popular ideology from the pulpit to the political platform.

In the post-Revolutionary era and beyond, these trends became more pronounced. On the one hand, sermons serving to articulate military and political values and to mobilize public sentiment declined generally; yet in times of crisis or impending war, clergy often integrated familiar themes that reinforced cultural attitudes about God's will and just war.

The *Civil War was perhaps the last example of overwhelming ministerial unity on the propriety of war, with sectional interests serving as the justification. Although denominations split along sectional lines, both Northern and Southern ministers used the pulpit to promote their region's cause, and each employed similar themes to reinforce the intended message. When, in 1862, the Northern Congregationalist minister James D. Liggett ("Our National Reserve") preached to a crowd in Leavenworth, Kansas, he relied on historic connections to Israel and the justness of the antislavery cause. Meanwhile, Joel W. Tucker ("God's Providence in War"), a Southern Presbyterian preacher from Fayetteville, North Carolina, made similar connections to Israel and declared that God had ordained the war for Southern independence despite human efforts to prevent it.

At the same time, new and varied ways to express political values contributed to decline of the traditional military sermon. Public orations increasingly expressed familiar themes in this secularized form, linked to religious themes but not denominational affiliation. During the Civil War, President Abraham *Lincoln employed this style in his speech dedicating the cemetery at Gettysburg (1863). In his address, Lincoln made clear that those who had perished in the fight to preserve the Union did not die in vain, for through their sacrifice the nation would have "a new birth of freedom." Here, Lincoln relied on ingrained Christian beliefs to make his point without a formal exegesis of their religious underpinnings. Lincoln had at his disposal an entire history of engendered religious attitudes to carry his meaning home to his audience.

In the late nineteenth century, increased secularism and the waning of providentialist reasoning hastened the decline of clerical consensus on the question of just war, particularly among Protestant clergy. Though both the establishment of religious freedom and the disestablishment of state churches had emerged as consequences of the Revolution and American independence, ministers maintained the power to help influence public opinion. By the turn of the twentieth century, however, the public oration clearly predominated. In 1898, the New York reformer Theodore *Roosevelt appealed to "muscular Christianity" and its values of manly self-sacrifice to encourage participation in the *Spanish-American War; in 1917, President Woodrow *Wilson acted as a moralizing evangelist to stir public sentiment in support of American involvement in World War I.

The linking of religious ideology to military action and public support for war necessitates a reassessment of American civil-military relations. Religion encouraged, if not demanded as a Christian duty, military participation. This, in turn, helped prepare Americans for war. Religion established a just war model and often equated a just war with a holy war. Many ministers joined a sense of religious nationalism to notions of civic republicanism, and transformed both into a political nationalism tinged with highly charged religious metaphors. Thus, emerged a civil religion that defined both religious identity and citizenship through war. Public orators adapted the sermon style to play on traditional themes with the added emphasis of state support. Although the clergy split over several American wars, such as the Revolutionary War, the *War of 1812, and the *Mexican War, this trend has persisted into the modern period.

[*See also* Commemoration and Public Ritual; Militarism and Antimilitarism; Religion and War.]

• Babette May Levy, *Preaching in the First Half Century of New England History,* 1945. Emory Elliott, *Power and Pulpit in Colonial New England,* 1975. Richard Slotkin and James K. Folsom, eds., *So Dreadful a Judgment: Puritan Responses to King Philip's War, 1676–1677,* 1978. David M. Kennedy, *Over Here: The First World War and American Society,* 1980. Marie Ahearn, *The Rhetoric of War: Training Day, the Militia, and the Military Sermon,* 1989. Harry Stout, *The New England Soul: Preaching and Religious Culture in Colonial New England,* 1989. Eric Carlton, *War and Ideology,* 1990. David B. Chesebrough, ed., *"God Ordained This War": Sermons on the Sectional Crisis, 1830–1865,* 1991.

—Edward D. Ragan

SERVICE ASSOCIATIONS. The establishment of service associations or societies for military personnel is a key milestone in the development of professionalism in the U.S. armed forces. America's first military society, the U.S. Naval Lyceum (1833–39), addressed a small audience with an underdeveloped sense of professional identity, dispersed around the globe. The next effort was more enduring and set the pattern for later groups. In 1873, the U.S. Naval Institute was formed by officers who were interested in advancing naval thought and doctrine, even though their service was moribund after the post–*Civil War drawdown. The institute consciously patterned itself after the British Royal United Services Institute, which in turn had imitated the activities of medical and engineering societies. It published a journal, sponsored lectures, symposia, and prize competitions for essays, and lobbied uniformed and civilian authorities.

The army quickly followed the lead of its maritime counterpart with the establishment of the Military Service Institution of the United States (MSIUS) in 1878. However, the various army branches eventually established their own societies, such as cavalry (1885), infantry (1904), and field artillery (1910). This fragmentation eventually proved fatal to MSIUS, which in 1917 succumbed to the frantic World War I buildup. Attempts to gain a "one-Army" voice floundered in the interwar period and were successful only in the early 1950s with the merger of the infantry, field artillery, and coast artillery bodies into the Association of the United States Army.

The U.S. Navy avoided this fragmentation, though the naval engineering corps formed the American Society of Naval Engineers, which addressed technical concerns. Marine Corps officers formed a Marine Corps Association in 1913, and the Air Force Association was established in 1946. Over the years, other associations for various military branches and activities were organized, such as the Reserve Officers Association and the Non-Commissioned Officers Association. These societies generally sponsor journals, book ordering services, meetings, writing competitions, and financial services (insurance, charge cards, job placement, etc.). Moreover, they cultivate government and industry contacts to advance the members' agendas, which often (but not always) parallel the concerns of the relevant armed service. Some academic critics contend

that the officers' societies are not true professional bodies that define expert knowledge but are merely lobbying or "backstop" groups that promote the military's interests in the federal government.

Another type of association is the military-industrial trade group, which often consists of uniformed and civilian members. One of the earliest was the Navy League (1902), which initially tried to become a major grassroots pressure group like its British and German counterparts. After several decades of searching for a workable identity, it adopted a more realistic mission of championing the maritime industry in the federal government. The periods after both world wars saw the emergence of groups that initially focused on army activities but quickly expanded to address similar concerns of the other services. Most prominent of these are the American Defense Preparedness Association, the Armed Forces Communication and Electronics Association, and the American Logistics Association.

Normally, the activities of the societies are fairly low-keyed, but there is an inherent tension in having government officials as members of private bodies that try to influence government activities. From time to time, the congressional and executive branches have tried to distance official military activities from the societies. In 1973, Congress passed a ban on active duty personnel working on associations' staffs, and Navy Department assistance to the Tailhook Association declined rapidly in the 1990s following the notorious Tailhook Convention (1991). Despite such actions, the existence of military societies is well established; they will continue to examine defense issues, provide services for their members, and champion their interests.

• Samuel P. Huntington, *The Common Defense: Strategic Programs in National Politics,* 1961. Gordon Adams, *The Iron Triangle: The Politics of Defense Contracting,* 1982.   —Michael E. Unsworth

SEVEN DAYS' BATTLE (1862). In response to Union Gen. George B. *McClellan's Peninsular Campaign in spring 1862, after brief engagements at Yorktown and Williamsburg, Confederate Gen. Joseph E. *Johnston withdrew to Richmond. They leisurely pursued McClellan along the north bank of the Chickahominy River, arriving at the city's outskirts on 17 May 1862. Although McClellan believed Richmond could best be taken from the south, he held his army north of the Chickahominy in order to receive reinforcements from Gen. Irvin McDowell, advancing from the north via Fredericksburg. A bridgehead across the river was maintained by a single Union corps under Erasmus Keyes at Seven Pines. As McDowell approached, Johnston realized he could not defend Richmond against two armies, and decided to attack McClellan in hopes of forcing him to withdraw. The obvious point of attack was Keyes's exposed position at Seven Pines.

Johnston's assault was bungled, but it discouraged McClellan from further offensive action. Erroneously convinced that he was outnumbered by an enemy of 200,000 troops (the actual number was 85,000), McClellan opted to prepare for a siege of Richmond. He also reversed the disposition of his army relative to the Chickahominy, moving all but Fitz John Porter's corps of 30,000 men south of the river. Porter's task was to protect communications across the river and receive McDowell, if and when he should arrive. In the meantime, Confederate Gen. Robert E. *Lee replaced Johnston, who had been wounded in battle. Lee faced a situation identical to Johnston's, with McClellan in front and McDowell behind. His solution was likewise similar. Rather than defend against a significantly reinforced enemy, Lee prepared to strike McClellan, hoping to defeat him, and then turn on McDowell. Lee summoned "Stonewall" *Jackson, who had been operating in the Shenandoah Valley, to join him. Intelligence informed McClellan that Jackson was en route and headed straight for Porter's corps, yet McClellan did nothing to strengthen his exposed flank.

Lee concentrated 55,000 soldiers against Porter, leaving only 30,000 troops to guard against McClellan's 70,000 men south of the Chickahominy. On 26 May he attacked, driving Porter from his position at Mechanicsville east along the river. Fortunately for McClellan, the Confederate attack was poorly handled and Porter ably defended himself, despite the absence of any help from McClellan. However, Lee's assault threatened McClellan's line of communications, prompting him to shift his base of operations south to the James River.

Again, Lee attempted to destroy Porter on the 27th at Gaines' Mill, with similar disappointing results. Porter was nonetheless obliged to withdraw across the river, which reunited the Army of the Potomac. With the change of base, and with the Chickahominy between him and Lee, McClellan might well have held his ground. But he was convinced that Lee now had 250,000 men (nearly three times Lee's actual strength) and could see only imminent disaster if he stayed put. On the 28th, McClellan began a full-scale retreat. Bridges over the Chickahominy were burned, as were tons of supplies that could not be carried away, delaying Lee's pursuit one day. The withdrawal was hastily executed and without the benefit of McClellan's personal guidance. He had ridden ahead to Harrison's Landing and failed to appoint a second in command. Only Lee's momentary confusion about McClellan's intentions saved the *Union army from immediate attack.

Once apprised that McClellan was moving south, Lee sent two divisions on a circuitous route to strike the Union right, while the rest of Lee's army came down on its rear. Confederate forces caught up with the Union rearguard at Savage's Station on the 29th. Lee's flanking elements failed to appear, and the Federal army escaped.

As the Union retreat continued, a mammoth bottleneck developed at Frayser's Farm, halting the withdrawal. There Lee attempted to concentrate his forces and envelop the Federal line, but again his subordinates were slow, and the Union army escaped. On 1 July, McClellan's force held an impressive defensive position atop Malvern Hill. Frustrated by his previous inability to engage McClellan successfully, Lee ordered an imprudent and costly frontal attack against the closed lines and massed artillery of the Federals.

When the Army of the Potomac reached Harrison's Landing, Lee ended his counteroffensive. During seven days of fighting, the Confederates suffered about 20,500 *casualties to the Union's 16,500. Despite the higher casualties, Lee was proclaimed a hero in the South, for he had taken the offensive and driven a larger army away from Richmond. McClellan, believing he had saved his army from a larger force, criticized Washington for not giving him more support.

[See also Civil War: Military and Diplomatic Course.]

• Clifford Dowdey, *The Seven Days*, 1964. Stephen W. Sears, *To the Gates of Richmond: The Peninsular Campaign*, 1992.
—T. R. Brereton

SEVERSKY, ALEXANDER DE (1894–1974), airpower activist. Born in Tiflis, in Georgian Russia, de Seversky served in the Imperial Russian Naval Air Service during World War I. A combat accident in 1915 claimed his right leg, but he continued flying. The Russian Revolution made de Seversky's temporary assignment to the United States permanent in 1917. Four years later, he sold an new bombsight to the U.S. government. He also met Billy *Mitchell, and for the rest of his life would champion Mitchell's doctrine that strategic air power could win wars, rendering armies and navies superfluous.

In 1939, de Seversky began writing full time. *Victory Through Air Power*, his most influential work, was published in April 1942, following a string of Allied defeats. Readers eager for an antidote to Axis domination bought at least 350,000 hardcover and paperback copies. *Reader's Digest* released a condensed version and many newspapers carried installments. Walt Disney was inspired to make a film using animation to transfer de Seversky's theories to the screen. In his book, Seversky extended Mitchell's vision of airpower to argue that even if bombing could not achieve quick victory, it could obtain total victory through unconditional surrender. He also openly criticized military leaders for slowing development of very long-range *bomber aircraft in order to promote more conventional weapons such as *aircraft carriers and fighter airplanes. Army air force and navy leaders and public relations officers campaigned to discredit de Seversky, his book, and the film. They were largely unsuccessful. By war's end, de Seversky had stimulated popular awareness and driven the national debate on strategic airpower further than any previous writer.

[See also Douhet, Giulio; World War II, U.S. Air Operations in.]

• Russell E. Lee, "Impact of *Victory Through Air Power*—Part I: The Army Air Forces Reaction," *Air Power History* (Summer 1993), pp. 3–33.
—Russell E. Lee

SEWARD, WILLIAM H. (1801–1872), secretary of state during the Civil War. An 1820 graduate of Union College, Seward became a lawyer in Auburn, New York, and was active in the Anti-Masonic Party. He subsequently led the Whig Party in the state. Elected governor in 1838, he entered the U.S. Senate in 1849 and established himself as a promoter of America's mission in the world and a leading opponent of slavery. In 1850, he appealed to a "higher law than the Constitution" in condemning slavery, and in 1858, by then a Republican, spoke of an "irrepressible conflict" between freedom and slavery.

After losing the party's 1860 presidential nomination to Abraham *Lincoln, Seward was offered the State Department as a consolation prize. He accepted only in the false hope of thereby becoming president in all but name. Initially, he proposed going to war with France and Spain in order to reunite the country and avert the Civil War. But his subsequent achievements were considerable.

He worked successfully to keep the European powers out of the Civil War, smoothed relations with Great Britain after the Trent Affair, ended French intervention in Mexico through persuasion and the moving of American troops to the Rio Grande in 1866, and laid the groundwork for the so-called *Alabama* claims for damages done by Confederate commerce raiders. He purchased Alaska from Russia in 1867 and annexed Midway in the same year, concluded a treaty with Great Britain for the suppression of the African slave trade, and opened diplomatic relations with the black republics of Haiti and Liberia. In his eight years in office, he negotiated more treaties with foreign nations than had all his predecessors combined.

With his vision of an American commercial hegemony that would spread democracy throughout the world, Seward was clearly ahead of his time. Such proposals as acquiring Hawaii, the Dominican Republic, and the Danish West Indies came to nothing at the time, as did plans for an isthmian canal and a worldwide telegraphic communications network. But they clearly foreshadowed the shape of things to come.

[*See also* Civil War: Domestic Course.]

• Glyndon Van Deusen, *William Henry Seward*, 1967. Norman B. Ferris, *Desperate Diplomacy: William H. Seward's Foreign Policy, 1861*, 1976. —Manfred Jonas

SEX AND THE MILITARY. The sexual behavior of those in the military, and attitudes and policies related to that behavior, provide important vantage points from which to examine the interactions between civil society and the military society. In the United States, sexual stereotypes are powerful and have helped guide the creation of military policies and regulations. "Natural" and generally different sexual behaviors and attitudes are often associated with being male or female. These understandings, to some degree, have changed over time and certainly are influenced by such factors as culture, race, and age. In times of crisis, particularly wartime, established norms may be contradicted by expediency or military needs and thus force the adoption of quite different practices, regardless of stated ideals.

During the *Revolutionary War, it was common for armies to rely on accompanying wives of soldiers, military *families, or "*camp followers" to provide a range of support services, including sexual ones. During the *Civil War, prostitutes were allowed into army camps and probably performed other than sexual "chores" as well. As Estelle Freedman and John D'Emilio have argued in *Intimate Matters* (1988), the Civil War "facilitated the expansion of prostitution," increasing the number of women set adrift socially by the war who had few other options for survival, and providing a mass market of men in training and camp. Officials of the *Union army became concerned about exposure of soldiers to sexually transmitted *diseases, and therefore experimented with regulating prostitution through medical examinations.

By the last decades of the nineteenth century, prostitution had become a focus of social reformers and public health officials. There was, however, disagreement as to whether prostitution posed primarily a moral or a health threat to American society. As U.S. entry into World War I drew closer, the War Department sought to make military camps safe from both immorality and venereal diseases. As Allan Brandt notes in *No Magic Bullet* (1987), Secretary of War Newton Baker believed that it was the government's responsibility to maintain order and heighten "soldier's moral rectitude." In April 1917, Baker created the Commission on Training Camp Activities, which used education and organized recreational activities to keep soldiers morally and physically fit. Additionally, a moral reform section of the Conscription Act of 1917 prohibited prostitution or the sale of liquor near training camps; this resulted in new attempts to control prostitutes, who were described as "disease spreaders and friends of the enemy," and led to government closing of bordellos in New Orleans, Memphis, and a host of other cities.

In this case, military needs and policies carried into the civilian sphere. By March 1918, thirty-two states had passed laws requiring compulsory medical exams for prostitutes. However, once American troops reached France, the issue of health and efficiency overcame moral goals, and eventually preventive medical programs against sexual diseases were instituted and prophylaxis mandated. As Brandt concludes, these policies "unhinged the alliance with moral reformers at home."

During World War II, educational programs much like those of the previous war were utilized, and vice activities near medical installations were made a federal offense under the May Act of 1941. Training films showed the ravages of advanced syphilis and gonorrhea. However, officials also recognized that they could not fully control sexual behavior and thus provided condoms, as well as subsequent treatment for infections (especially effective after the introduction of penicillin in 1944). At first the army rejected anyone with venereal disease, but by 1942 it changed the policy to allow induction if the cases were not complicated. The military also abandoned the regulation that imposed penalties on those with venereal disease.

Reflecting postwar prudery, the military in the 1950s returned to an emphasis on education and moral exhortations, but these did not create substantive changes. The target in subsequent decades would be the health and efficiency of the armed forces. This would be complicated when *AIDS became a nationally recognized health issue; in 1985, the Department of *Defense mandated screening of new recruits for the HIV antibody and rejection of those infected.

Just as military responses to prostitution and sexually transmitted diseases resembled a balancing act between social values and institutional needs, so military attitudes toward and treatment of homosexuality also illustrated the contradictions between theory and practice. Most social historians agree that it was not until the late nineteenth or early twentieth century that homosexuals were "scientifically" defined as personality "types" and individuals self-identified as homosexuals. In the World War I era, both the army and the navy punished "sodomists" for their criminal acts. In 1916, assault with intent to commit sodomy was made a felony, and, in 1919, sodomy, the act itself, usually defined as anal and sometimes oral sex between men, became a crime, meriting appropriate court-martial and five or more years of imprisonment. Publicity and protest surrounding several such cases brought congressional investigations in 1920 and a report in 1921 that mandated an end to such punishments because "perversion" was not a crime but a disease.

Between the end of World War I and the beginning of World War II, the medical world, and society more generally, adopted the view of homosexuality as "abnormal" and therefore an illness. During World War II, questioning and psychiatric tests were used to prevent homosexuals from entering the services, with limited success. By 1942, the first restrictions on inducting homosexuals were enacted, and a year later a complete ban on homosexuals in the services became the rule. Those already in uniform "found" to be homosexual were deemed unsuitable for military service and received undesirable discharges. Alan Berube argues that, regardless of policy, because of manpower shortages during World War II, most homosexuals were tolerated. Scholars of gay and lesbian history point to an unintended result of this wartime focus on homosexuality—the creation of homosexual identity and subcultures among these military personnel that lasted long after the war ended.

During the 1970s and 1980s, legal challenges to the ban on homosexuals increased, and in 1993, President Bill *Clinton sought to use his executive authority to allow homosexuals in the armed forces. However, strong public and military opposition to that stand left the ban in place, modified somewhat by Senator Sam Nunn's "Don't Ask, Don't Tell" compromise policy.

Separate spheres for men and for women generally kept women out of the more permanent and institutionalized military structures of the nineteenth century, but by World War I, with the establishment of a permanent Army and Navy *Nurse Corps, and particularly with the establishment of the Women's Army Corps (*WAC) in World War II, certain matters of sexual behavior had to be addressed. Primary among these would be women's sexual activity, marriage, and reproductive roles. Before World War II, the Army Nurse Corps would not accept married women, and discharge was automatic if a nurse married. Illegitimate pregnancy and morals offenses were causes for dishonorable dismissal.

World War II brought large numbers of women into all the services and prompted a reexamination of some of the existing sexual regulations. Married women could enter the women's uniformed services (the WAC, *WAVES, and *SPARS), and single women who married in the service could leave voluntarily, a decision not available to men. Women, unlike men, had to provide proof that their spouses and children were dependents in order for them to receive support benefits. Women could still be discharged from the service for pregnancy (or for adopting or for acquiring stepchildren), but the decisions were left up to each service and waivers were possible. At one point during World War II, the surgeon general proposed full sexual instruction and distribution of condoms to all women in the newly formed Women's Army Corps. WAC director Col. Oveta Culp *Hobby rejected the plan as undermining her efforts to keep the women sexless and "respectable." During the war, WACs did receive training lectures condemning sexual relationships between women. However, officers were instructed not to engage in witch-hunts of lesbians. This was consistent with Culp Hobby's effort to protect the reputations of service women and to counter misogynous sexual stereotyping of military women as lesbians or prostitutes.

In the 1960s and 1970s, many of the traditional military policies toward women came under attack, and reforms were instituted. The changes were the result first of civil rights legislation, feminist politics, and sexual revolution. Second, by 1973, the adoption of an *All-Volunteer Force created new and sometimes different "manpower" needs (women soon comprised more than 10% of the armed forces). Certain technological and strategic changes also altered many traditional gender exclusions in military occupation specialties in most of the services. (The navy generally remained the most resistant to change, the air force generally the most amenable.) A series of court cases and DoD investigations and policy changes in the 1970s resulted in women obtaining the same dependent rights as men and made discharge for pregnancy voluntary. It is now common for lectures on pregnancy and sexual awareness to be a part of command indoctrination programs. As the controversies surrounding the navy's 1991 "Tailhook" Convention demonstrate, the military's continuing discharges of gays and lesbians, issues of sexual harassment and sexual stereotyping, differential treatment for men and women, and debate over segregated training and combat exclusion all remain problems within military institutions, as they do within society at large.

[See also Gay Men and Lesbians in the Military; Gender and War; Gender: Female Identity and the Military; Gender: Male Identity and the Military; Sexual Harassment; Women in the Military.]

• Jeanne Holm, Women in the Military, 1982; 2nd ed., 1992. David R. Segal and H. Wallance Sinaiko, eds., Life in the Rank and File, 1986. Allan Brandt, No Magic Bullet, 1987. Estelle Freedman and John D'Emilio, Intimate Matters, 1988. Alan Berube, Coming Out Under Fire: History of Gay Men and Women in World War Two, 1990. Catherine Clinton and Nina Silber, eds., Divided Houses: Gender and the Civil War, 1992. Leisa D. Meyer, Creating G.I. Jane: Sexuality and Power in the Women's Army Corps During World War II, 1996. Nancy Bristow, Making Men Moral: Social Engineering During the Great War, 1996.
—Jane Slaughter

SEXUAL HARASSMENT. In the early 1990s, sexual harassment in the military made headlines as decades of mistreatment of military women became known. The initial spotlight followed the public revelation of the events of the U.S. Navy's annual Tailhook Convention at the Las Vegas Hilton in September 1991. Hundreds of navy and Marine aviators attended the convention, where male aviators assaulted their female colleagues and both men and women took part in inappropriate activities. Naval leadership did not respond to a formal complaint about the event, which only worsened its reputation when the abuses were exposed in the national media. The ripple effects of Tailhook were felt for years within the navy, until another event overtook the public's attention.

In November 1996, allegations of rape, sexual assault, sexual harassment, and fraternization on the part of drill sergeants at the army's Aberdeen Proving Ground training facility in Maryland rekindled public outrage. Tailhook, Aberdeen, and numerous other incidents brought considerable media attention to gender relations in the military. This, in turn, led to commissioned studies, panels, and congressional hearings on the topics of sexual harassment and, more generally, the role of *women in the military.

As revised in 1995, the Department of *Defense defines sexual harassment as a form of sex discrimination that involves unwelcome sexual advances, requests for sexual favors, and other verbal or physical conduct of a sexual nature when (a) submission to such conduct is made either explicitly or implicitly a term or condition of a person's job, pay, or career; (b) submission to or rejection of such conduct by a person is used as a basis for career or employment decisions affecting that person; or (c) such conduct has the purpose or effect of unreasonably interfering with an individual's work performance or creates an intimidating, hostile, or offensive working environment.

People commonly use the term *sexual harassment* to refer to an even wider range of behaviors, including sexual discrimination, sexual assault, and gender harassment. The concept of sexual harassment is particularly problematic because what offends one individual may not faze another. Research has shown that people are more likely to define a behavior as sexual harassment if it comes from someone in a position of power over them, or if it comes from someone of a different race or class background.

In an article entitled "How Women Handle Sexual Harassment: A Literature Review," published in *Sociology and Social Research* (1989), James E. Gruber classified victims' individual responses to harassment into four categories: *avoidance* of the harasser or the place of harassment; *defusion* of the incident, such as making a joke of the issue or discussing it only with friends; *negotiation,* which includes telling the harasser that his behavior is offensive and asking him to stop; and *confrontation,* in which women use more forceful language and may issue an ultimatum or threat.

At the organizational level, military personnel have been reluctant to file formal complaints of sexual harassment for a number of reasons: they do not believe the organization will respond; they believe there will be a "backlash" against them for filing a complaint; they believe the incident was minor and dealt with satisfactorily on the individual level; they are afraid that a minor complaint will be blown up into a major public issue; or there were no witnesses and they do not believe they will win a "he-said, she-said" case. In the 1990s, as harassment received more publicity and women's complaints were taken more seriously, many military men became afraid that they might be falsely accused. The degree to which this actually occurs, however, has not yet been measured.

The targets of sexual harassment can suffer a number of negative effects: poor physical and mental health, drug or alcohol abuse, work dissatisfaction, alienation from coworkers, tardiness and absenteeism, decreased work performance and poor evaluations, job loss or career disruption, and the costs of legal fees, health care, and counseling.

In some ways, the military environment fosters sexual harassment. Military culture has traditionally emphasized aggression and the masculine role, and many of the men who join hold traditional beliefs about gender. Moreover, women have always been and are still a small and very visible minority, historically excluded from some of the most powerful and prestigious military roles. At the same time, the military is a large-scale formal organization with explicit methods for communicating and enforcing its rules and regulations. Its members are trained to be highly disciplined and to uphold a high moral code. Therefore, the military might also be the workplace most able to stamp out sexual harassment, much as it was more successful than the civilian world in integrating racial minorities.

Studies of sexual harassment rates in the civilian workforce typically find that about 50 percent of women have been harassed at work, although some organizations' rates are considerably higher. Rates in the military have been measured at similar levels—noteworthy because soldiers live and work together twenty-four hours a day, seven days a week, and see each other not only "on the job" but in dining facilities, in the gym, in the barracks, and in the base shops and clubs. Harassment rates tend to be higher in the ground combat services—the Marines and the army—and lowest in the air force, which is more technically oriented, has the highest percentage of women overall, the highest percentage of women officers, and the greatest percentage of positions open to military women.

Sexual Harassment in the Workplace (1996), a synthesis of the literature, reports the estimated cost of sexual harassment to the U.S. Army in 1988 to be $533 million (in 1993 dollars). These lost funds derive from reduced productivity; absenteeism; separation, transfer, and replacement of harassers and/or victims; and other miscellaneous costs. The estimate does not account for the expenses of litigation or medical and counseling services.

Because women are not likely to be banned from serving in the armed forces ever again, and because their numbers are increasing under the public's watchful eye, sexual harassment will have to be dealt with effectively by the military. Eliminating the abusive treatment of any soldier will reduce military costs and assist soldiers in maximizing their ability to fight and win wars.

[*See also* Gender: Female Identity and the Military; Gender and War.]

• Barbara A. Gutek, *Sex and the Workplace: The Impact of Sexual Behavior and Harassment on Women, Men, and Organizations,* 1985. Lisa D. Bastian, Anita R. Lancaster, and Heidi E. Reyst, *Department of Defense 1995 Sexual Harassment Survey,* 1995. Defense Equal Opportunity Council, *Report of the Task Force on Discrimination and Sexual Harassment,* Vols. I and II, 1995. Margaret S. Stockdale, ed., *Sexual Harassment in the Workplace,* 1996. Laura L. Miller, "Not Just Weapons of the Weak: Gender Harassment as a Form of Protest for Army Men," *Social Psychology Quarterly,* vol. 60, no. 1 (March 1997), pp. 32–51. Richard J. Harris and Juanita M. Firestone, "Subtle Sexism in the U.S. Military," in *Subtle Sexism,* ed. Nijole V. Benokraitis, 1997. United States Department of the Army, *The Secretary of the Army's Senior Review Panel Report on Sexual Harassment,* Vols. I and II, 1997.   —Laura L. Miller

SHARPSBURG, BATTLE OF. *See* Antietam, Battle of (1862).

SHAYS'S REBELLION (1786–87). After the Revolutionary War, soldiers of the *Continental army were demobilized with little or no pay; whatever "Continental notes" they received could be exchanged only at an enormous discount, and the very states that had approved their issue did not accept them as payment of taxes. Officers eventually received compensation, including land in the Ohio Territory, but by 1786 the plight of the former soldiery was dire, especially in rural Massachusetts, where veterans and farmers suffered most from both the postwar depression and the radical deficit reduction plan of the conservative new governor, James Bowdoin. That year, in western Massachusetts, where many believed they had lost significant political representation under the state constitution of 1780, scores of rural towns petitioned for relief but received none.

In September 1786, a movement called "the Regulation" began across western Massachusetts: whenever the circuit courts were scheduled to meet, between 500 and 2,000 men gathered and marched in a military manner on each court, with the stated aim of postponing the seizure of properties until after the next gubernatorial election. Over the next five months, under an indeterminate, changing leadership, the "Regulators," armed with clubs and muskets, converged upon Northampton, Springfield, Worcester, and other towns where the courts were scheduled to sit, surrounding the courthouses to keep them closed. Until the last of these protests, there were no casualties.

This widespread movement resembled traditional protests, but those who wanted to establish a national constitution depicted it as anarchy. Gen. Henry *Knox, Massachusetts-born secretary of war for the Continental Congress, traveled to Springfield after the first Regulation to consider the safety of the weapons stored there in the undefended Continental Arsenal. It was Knox, writing to Congress, who first declared that this "rebellion" was led by former Capt. Daniel Shays. Knox, like other nationalists, welcomed an opportunity to demonstrate the necessity of a federal government and a permanent standing army; he proclaimed to Congress and to his mentor, Gen. George *Washington, that the "rebels'" goal was to share all private property as "the common property of all," "to annihilate all debts, public and private," and to foment a "civil war." Since the treasuries of both Massachusetts and Congress were empty, Knox helped Bowdoin solicit wealthy Boston merchants to finance an expeditionary force of 4,400 volunteers led by Gen. Benjamin Lincoln to quell the "rebellion." At the Springfield Arsenal on 24–25 January 1787, Lincoln's forces overwhelmed some 1,500 Regulators, led by Captains Daniel Shays, Luke Day, and Eli Parsons. With the first cannon fired, three Regulators were killed and the rest fled. In pursuit, Lincoln captured a number of Regulators for trial; later, two were hanged.

These mostly peaceable protests provoked alarm that the movement could spread across the thirteen states. This concern helped persuade the states to send delegates to the Constitutional Convention in Philadelphia in May 1787, and to create a central U.S. government better equipped to deal with similar economic and social problems.

[See also Revolutionary War: Postwar Impact.]

• Robert Feer, Shays' Rebellion, 1958; repr. 1988. David Szatmary, Shays's Rebellion, 1980.

—Rock Brynner

SHERIDAN, PHILIP H. (1831–1888), Civil War general and frontier army commander. Sheridan was born in Albany, New York; his Irish Catholic family soon moved to Somerset, Ohio, where his father worked as a laborer. Receiving only modest schooling, Sheridan still obtained an appointment to the U.S. Military Academy, graduating in 1853. Typical frontier assignments found him posted as lieutenant of infantry in Oregon in 1861.

After the outbreak of the Civil War, Sheridan served first in the western theater, demonstrating skills as an operational combat commander in several positions. After starting as a cavalry commander, Sheridan led an infantry division in the Battle of *Perryville, Kentucky (8 October 1862) and the Battle of *Stones River, Tennessee (31 December 1862–3 January 1863), and was promoted to major general in the volunteers. In the Battle of *Chickamauga, Georgia (19–20 September 1863), a Confederate attack battered Sheridan's division, and it suffered heavy *casualties. Under the eye of Gen. Ulysses S. *Grant, Sheridan performed well in the fighting around Chattanooga, Tennessee, including an outstanding role in the victorious

Union assault in the Battle of *Missionary Ridge (25 November 1863).

In 1864, Grant as general in chief selected Sheridan to lead the cavalry corps of the Army of the Potomac in the eastern theater. During May and June 1864, Sheridan's cavalry participated in raids supporting the Union offensive toward Richmond, Virginia. Grant next assigned Sheridan to command the Federal Army of the Shenandoah, with about 40,000 soldiers. As part of the new economic warfare, Sheridan devastated crops in the Shenandoah Valley (the Confederacy's "breadbasket"); he also defeated the *Confederate army operating under Gen. Jubal A. Early. The campaign culminated at the Battle of Cedar Creek (19 October 1864), a victory that helped reelect President Abraham Lincoln and made Sheridan one of the top three Northern heroes of the war, ranking behind Grant and William Tecumseh *Sherman. At the end of the war, Sheridan's victory at Five Forks (1 April 1865) prevented Robert E. *Lee's army from escaping from Virginia and led to Lee's surrender at Appomattox.

After the war, Sheridan supervised *Reconstruction in Louisiana and Texas, insisting on basic rights for black soldiers and freedmen. Sheridan's military government and enforcement of congressional Reconstruction policies put him at odds with President Andrew *Johnson, who reassigned him to the Great Plains in 1867.

During the next decade, from the field and headquarters in Chicago, Sheridan directed major campaigns against Indian tribes in the vast area of the Military Division of the Missouri, from Montana to Texas. During the *Plains Indians Wars, those campaigns included devastating clashes with the Sioux, Cheyennes, and Comanches. Sheridan employed railroads in his military operations and winter campaigns that caught the tribes off guard. He adamantly supported Grant as president, even returning for another controversial assignment in Louisiana to enforce federal laws there after the presidential election of 1876. He served as commanding general of the army from 1884 until his death in 1888.

To some, Sheridan appeared radical for his day, especially in Reconstruction politics. In many ways traditional, he also appeared innovative by using railroads in military *logistics, endorsing development of western lands, supporting specialized officer training schools, and testing new firearms for the army. A great combat commander, Sheridan was determined in defense and relentless in attack. As a measure of respect, Congress voted to promote him to the four-star rank of general of the army shortly before he died.

[See also Civil War: Military and Diplomatic Course.]

• Raymond O'Connor, Sheridan the Inevitable, 1953; Robert M. Utley, Frontier Regulars: The U.S. Army and the Indian, 1866–1891, 1973. Joseph G. Dawson III, Army Generals and Reconstruction, 1982. Paul Andrew Hutton, Phil Sheridan and His Army, 1985. Roy Morris, Jr., Sheridan, 1992.

—Joseph G. Dawson III

SHERMAN, FORREST (1896–1951), naval officer. One of the most intellectually gifted and effective military leaders of his generation, Sherman spent most of his career in naval aviation. After participating in the Atlantic Charter Conference of August 1941, he was captain of the aircraft carrier Wasp during World War II until she was sunk in the Guadalcanal campaign in September 1942. He played such a major role in forging Pacific Fleet aviation doctrine as chief of staff to its air commander, Adm. John H. Towers, that he was transferred to the staff of Adm. Chester *Nimitz, Pacific Fleet commander, late in 1943. Promoted to rear admiral and deputy chief of staff for planning, Sherman functioned as Nimitz's alter ego in helping direct the Central Pacific offensive that defeated Japan.

After Nimitz's appointment as chief of naval operations (CNO), Sherman, now a vice admiral, served as deputy CNO for operations during 1945–47. He helped devise early U.S. *Cold War strategy and was the navy's representative in hammering out the compromise that unified the armed forces in 1947. He commanded U.S. naval forces in the Mediterranean until called upon in the wake of "the Revolt of the Admirals" to be CNO in the rank of admiral in November 1949. Sherman restored navy morale and mobilized the navy for the *Korean War and Cold War rearmament. He died on active duty while engaged in a diplomatic mission to strengthen the new North Atlantic Treaty Organization, *NATO.

[*See also* Navy, U.S.: 1899–1945; Navy, U.S.: Since 1946; Navy Combat Branches: Naval Air Forces; World War II, U.S. Naval Operations in: The Pacific.]

• Clark G. Reynolds, "Forrest Percival Sherman," in Robert William Love, ed., *The Chiefs of Naval Operations,* 1980. Michael A. Palmer, *Origins of the Maritime Strategy: American Naval Strategy in the First Postwar Decade,* 1988. Clark G. Reynolds, *Admiral John H. Towers: The Struggle for Naval Air Supremacy,* 1991.

—Clark G. Reynolds

SHERMAN, WILLIAM TECUMSEH (1820–1891), Civil War general and commanding general of the U.S. Army. Born in Lancaster, Ohio, the sixth child of Charles R. and Mary Hoyt Sherman, Sherman was named for the Shawnee Indian leader *Tecumseh. William was not added until 1830: after his father's sudden death and his mother's inability to provide for the family, he was baptized into the Catholic Church upon his entry into the home of a famous Whig politician, Thomas Ewing.

Sherman studied at the U.S. Military Academy, graduating sixth in the class of 1840. He would have ranked fourth except for demerits received because of his unwillingness to follow regulations. Instead of gaining a slot in the prestigious *Army Corps of Engineers, therefore, he settled for the artillery, serving in Florida during the Second Seminole War (1840–42), in Alabama at Fort Morgan (1842), and in South Carolina at Fort Moultrie (1842–46).

With the outbreak of the *Mexican War in 1846, Sherman sailed to California. He saw no combat, doing administrative work and policing the gold-mining areas. Returning to the East (1850), he married his foster sister, Ellen Ewing, and served in the Commissary Corps in St. Louis and New Orleans. In 1853, he left the army to become a banker in San Francisco (1853–57) and New York (1857), a lawyer and real estate entrepreneur in Kansas (1858–59), and superintendent of the Louisiana Military Seminary (1859–61). When Louisiana seceded from the Union in 1861, Sherman reluctantly left the state, taking a position as president of a St. Louis street railway company.

After the Confederate capture of *Fort Sumter, which began the Civil War, he rejoined the army as colonel of the 13th U.S. Infantry Regiment. At age forty-one, Sherman brought with him not only wide experience but also anxious concerns. The death of his father, his entry into the

Ewing family as a young ward, and later his marriage had been crucial factors in his life. He carried a lifelong fear about family-destroying financial failure and an equally important determination to impress his successful foster father. He had spent most of his adult life in the South and developed a genuine affection for its people; his successful tenure as a popular Louisiana educator made his departure wrenching. His lack of combat experience also played on his mind, as did his conviction that Northern political leaders and people did not understand the importance of the Southern threat of secession. To Sherman, the Union represented the order that both he and the nation needed to avoid the catastrophe of public anarchy and personal failure.

Though his leadership abilities stood out at the July 1861 First Battle of *Bull Run (Manassas), the Union failure there convinced him that his fears about Northern unpreparedness were accurate. Later, commanding in Kentucky, he was so overwhelmed by the dangers he saw around him that he fell into a deep depression that came close to incapacitating him. His subordinates believed he had lost his mind and supported his demand to be relieved of command. In early 1862, he was training recruits in a backwater of the war.

The beginning of Sherman's successful association with Gen. Ulysses S. *Grant and his well-praised performance at the Battle of *Shiloh in April 1862 propelled him back into the mainstream of the conflict. From June to December 1862, he successfully governed Memphis, Tennessee, where the idea for another kind of warfare began to form in his mind. Confederate guerrillas and uncooperative civilians led him to realize that the war involved not just organized armies but supporting civilians as well. In retaliation for guerrilla sniping at Mississippi riverboats, he ordered the destruction of Randolph, Tennessee; he then issued Special Order Number 254 calling for the expulsion of ten families from Memphis for every boat fired on.

In December 1862, Sherman led a failed Union attack at Chickasaw Bayou, near Vicksburg, but he later helped Grant capture Vicksburg in July 1863. That November, Sherman became commander of the Army of the Tennessee and participated in Grant's victory at Chattanooga.

In early 1864, Sherman led 25,000 troops from Vicksburg, through Jackson, to Meridian, Mississippi, destroying property along the way in order to diminish civilian support for the war. When Grant moved east, Sherman became commander of the western theater. Using conventional warfare, he repeatedly outflanked Confederate Gen. Joseph E. *Johnston. Defeating Gen. John Bell *Hood, Sherman captured Atlanta in September, his victory helping to ensure Abraham *Lincoln's reelection in November. He inflicted severe damage on the city, but he did not burn it to the ground.

Hoping to end the war quickly and with the least number of *casualties, Sherman, with Grant's authority, decided he had to make another direct assault on civilian and material support for the war. He marched from Atlanta to the sea and then north through the Carolinas, inflicting severe property destruction but few casualties. He brought terror into the heart of the Confederacy while positioning his army to join Grant against Lee in Virginia. The Confederate will to continue the fight diminished and the inevitability of Union *victory became clear. Demonstrating that he had been truthful in promising a soft peace once his hard war had overwhelmed his Southern friends, Sherman gave General Johnston such mild peace terms that his own government accused him of *treason.

In the postwar years, Sherman used his office as commanding general to try to protect the army's place in American life by insisting on its professionalization. He had limited success, but he did establish the concept of service schools for what he hoped would be a more intelligently prepared officer corps. He supervised the hard war against the Indians, determined to make them productive members of society according to white standards. He was a leading Northern opponent of Republican Reconstruction. When Republicans regularly asked him to run for president, he always declined.

Sherman's impact on American military history was substantial. He pushed warfare away from the increasingly old-fashioned approach of masses of soldiers attacking in gigantic frontal assaults and toward the concept of war between entire societies: total war.

[See also Atlanta, Battle of; Civil War: Military and Diplomatic Course; Civil War: Postwar Impact; Seminole Wars; Sherman's March to the Sea; Vicksburg, Siege of.]

• Robert G. Athearn, *William Tecumseh Sherman and the Settlement of the West*, 1956. William T. Sherman, *Memoirs of General William T. Sherman*, 2 vols., 1875; repr. 1990. Charles Royster, *The Destructive War: William Tecumseh Sherman, Stonewall Jackson, and the Americans*, 1991. Albert Castel, *Decision in the West. The Atlanta Campaign of 1964*, 1992. Lloyd Lewis, *Sherman, Fighting Prophet*, 1932; repr. 1993. John F. Marszalek, *Sherman: A Soldier's Passion for Order*, 1993.
                                                          —John F. Marszalek

SHERMAN'S MARCH TO THE SEA (1864–65). After capturing Atlanta in September 1864, a victory that guaranteed the reelection of Abraham *Lincoln and the continuation of the Civil War, Gen. William Tecumseh Sherman, Union commander in the west, turned his thoughts to the most direct assault he could imagine on the heart of the Confederacy, one that targeted Southern morale. Despite some misgivings on the part of Lincoln and Ulysses S. *Grant, the overall Union commander and Sherman's closest friend, Sherman decided to send a blocking force under George H. *Thomas to stop Confederate moves northward. Breaking his lines of communication, he would fan out his army and set off for Savannah, Georgia, on a giant raid that became known as the march to the sea, carving a wide swath through the Georgia countryside on his way.

Uniquely among Union generals, Sherman had the intellectual and emotional capacity to understand *psychological warfare, a war of mass civilian terror. He was quite explicit about the deeper meanings of his march even before he started. "I propose to demonstrate the vulnerability of the South, and make its inhabitants feel that war and individual ruin are synonymous terms," he wrote to one associate, while adding to another, "I am going into the very bowels of the Confederacy, and will leave a trail that will be recognized fifty years hence." In a cooler and more analytic vein, Sherman also recognized that as the South lacked a military force to oppose his destruction of its infrastructure and agricultural supplies, his *victory would be "proof positive" to all Southerners and to the world that the North had an overwhelming power that the South could not resist. "This may not be war, but rather statesmanship," Sherman concluded, thus making his own political analysis of

war. If civilian morale crumbled, so would the Southern army and state.

In their march of 285 miles, which lasted 5 weeks, Sherman's army of 60,000 men cut a swath of between 20 and 60 miles through Georgia, destroying fences and crops, killing livestock, burning barns and factories as well as some houses, particularly those deserted by the planter class. It must be emphasized that Sherman's forces refrained from raping white women and from killing civilians. Although many historians have rather carelessly called Sherman's campaign total war, it never became genocidal, nor had Sherman intended it to become so. Such limits were, of course, of scant comfort to the impoverished and malnourished civilians Sherman's army left in its wake.

On 22 December 1864, the day after the Confederate garrison of 10,000 had escaped the city, Sherman's army marched into Savannah on the sea, which Sherman announced to Lincoln and to the Union with his usual rhetorical vivacity: "I beg to present you as a Christmas gift, the city of Savannah, with 150 heavy guns and plenty of ammunition, and also about 25,000 bales of cotton." A week earlier, George H. Thomas's force had destroyed John Bell *Hood's *Confederate army at Nashville, triumphantly completing the other half of Sherman's post-Atlanta strategy. As Grant's Army of the Potomac was bogged down in *trench warfare before Petersburg, Virginia, it was the Christmas victories of Thomas and Sherman that lifted Union spirits.

On 1 February 1865, Sherman's army set off on its even longer sequel to the march to the sea, a campaign of over 400 miles up through the Carolinas, to come up behind Lee's army for one last, climactic battle if it was needed. As much of South Carolina was a swamp during winter, this part of Sherman's march was more an engineering than a fighting marvel: his troops cut down trees to make roads, bridges, and causeways at a pace of ten miles per day. Incapable of opposing Sherman militarily, Confederates could only watch in horror as Sherman's troops laid waste to the countryside at an even greater level of intensity than they had evinced in Georgia. Now almost all civilian homes were destroyed, and several cities were burned, including Columbia, the capital of South Carolina, although Confederates began the blaze by burning cotton bales in the street before departing. Many of Sherman's men broke ranks and joined in a night of burning and looting before they were disciplined; other Union troops extinguished the flames the next day. At Columbia, Sherman's men reached an apotheosis of destructiveness.

Sherman had realized the potential for terror his army would bring to bear on the state that was the cradle of the Confederacy. "The truth is the whole army is burning with an insatiable desire to wreak vengeance on South Carolina," he had written on Christmas Eve, 1864. "I almost tremble at her fate but feel she deserves all that seems in store for her." Sherman's men—his "bummers," as they styled themselves—shared in this contempt for Confederates, especially those of the South Carolina gentry. "Nearly every man in Sherman's army say they are ready for destroying everything in South Carolina," one private wrote home from Savannah before the campaign resumed, while another confirmed after they had finished that "in South Carolina, there was no restraint whatever in pillaging and foraging. Men were allowed to do as they liked, *burn and destroy*" (Fellman, *Citizen Sherman,* 222–24). Sherman and his men were attuned to one another and acted accordingly. They wanted to create a legend of invincible destructiveness, and they succeeded, landing a devastating blow on Southern morale as they marched and destroyed.

When his army reached North Carolina in March 1865, Sherman reined in the behavior of his troops to a certain extent, because he would soon link up with the Union and feared potential condemnation of his extremism in the press; because he conceived of North Carolinians as poor whites more attuned to Unionism than South Carolina planters; and because he was aware that as the war was nearing an end, violence could decrease. When Lee's lines collapsed at the end of March 1865, Sherman's men were not needed for a final push into Virginia.

But their march would live on in history and in legend. Seven years after the war, Sherman testified that he had not ordered the burning of Columbia, but that "If I [had] made my mind to burn Columbia I would have burnt it with no more feeling than I would a common prairie dog village." Southerners were not mistaken in their hatred of Sherman, who really had intended them as much destruction as he felt might be needed to end the war. Defeated Confederates also testified, despite themselves, to Sherman's effectiveness, for they realized he was the general who had broken their hearts. His march probably shortened the war and made the Southern defeat more comprehensive; therefore the moral meanings of Sherman's march are complex and moot. The march was terrible, but it worked, and it might even have saved lives.

Sherman himself never doubted the efficacy of the destructiveness he had brought to bear. In his 1875 *Memoirs,* he wrote, "My aim then was to whip the rebels, to humble their pride, to follow them to their inmost recesses, and make them fear and dread us." For cold calculation, rage, and ruthlessness, no Union general had a better understanding of the kind of war against civilians that could defeat a democracy such as the Confederacy.

[*See also* Civil War: Military and Diplomatic Course; Civil War: Postwar Impact.]

• William T. Sherman, *Memoirs of General William T. Sherman.* 2 vols., 1875. Lloyd Lewis, *Sherman, Fighting Prophet,* 1932. John T. Barrett, *Sherman's March Through the Carolinas,* 1956. Marion B. Lucas, *Sherman and the Burning of Columbia,* 1976. Joseph T. Glatthaar, *The March to the Sea and Beyond: Sherman's Troops in the Savannah and Carolina Campaigns,* 1986. John F. Marszalek, *Sherman: A Soldier's Passion for Order,* 1993. Lee Kennett, *Marching Through Georgia: The Story of Soldiers and Civilians During Sherman's Campaign,* 1995. Michael Fellman, *Citizen Sherman: A Life of William Tecumseh Sherman,* 1995.   —Michael Fellman

SHILOH, BATTLE OF [Pittsburg Landing, Tennessee] (1862). The prelude to the Shiloh campaign occurred months earlier in the Civil War, in February 1862, when Union Maj. Gen. Ulysses S. *Grant captured Forts Henry and Donelson. The successful Union offensive along the Cumberland and Tennessee Rivers resulted in the evacuation of Nashville and forced Confederates under Gen. Albert S. Johnston to cede much of middle and western Tennessee.

Grant massed his 40,000 troops at Pittsburg Landing, on the Tennessee River twenty-two miles north of Corinth,

Mississippi, a vital rail junction and Grant's next operational target. Union theater commander Maj. Gen. Henry W. Halleck ordered Maj. Gen. Don Carlos Buell, who had occupied Nashville, to leave the capital with 35,000 troops and rendezvous with Grant's force of 40,000 near Pittsburg Landing, Tennessee.

The potential concentration of Grant and Buell alarmed Confederate Gen. P. G. T. *Beauregard, Johnston's second in command, who boldly took charge in the wake of the loss of two forts in February. Beauregard proceeded to issue appeals, collect and organize troops at Corinth, and wield influence over Johnston when the latter arrived. Problems abounded for the *Confederate army. Most of the soldiers were inexperienced, some were poorly trained, and there was a general lack of familiarity between the various components. In spite of the difficulties, Beauregard recommended an offensive strike against Grant near Pittsburg Landing before Buell arrived. Johnston assented.

The movement commenced 3 April, but Beauregard's timetable was too ambitious for the green troops. The plan called for an attack the next day, but rain, rough terrain, and logistical difficulties prevented an attack on either the 4th or the 5th. Convinced that the element of surprise was gone, Beauregard urged Johnston to return to Corinth; but Johnston demurred. Battered by critics for the past several months, Johnston was psychologically unwilling to abandon the offensive. As a result, a massive two-day battle opened early on 6 April near a Methodist meetinghouse called Shiloh Church.

Beauregard's overly intricate *order of battle arranged the 44,000-man army into four lines, commanded successively by William J. Hardee, Braxton *Bragg, Leonidas Polk, and John C. Breckinridge. Hardee's men collided with Federal skirmishers before daylight, and the Confederates soon struck three Union divisions without fieldworks under Brig. Gen. Benjamin M. Prentiss, Brig. Gen. William Tecumseh *Sherman, and Maj. Gen. John A. McClernand. The Confederates achieved tactical surprise and steamrolled one Union position after another. Some Northern units fought tenaciously, while others fell back and reorganized; many of the raw recruits fled, panic-stricken. After three hours of hard fighting, the Confederates had forced the Union right back nearly a mile. Yet success came at an awful price, as *casualties and confusion blunted the Southern momentum.

Prentiss rallied his Union troops along a sunken wagon road, and this spot in the Union center became a magnet for uncoordinated Confederate assaults. At least eleven separate efforts were made against what bloodied Confederates dubbed the "Hornets' Nest." Preoccupation with the Hornets' Nest stalled the Confederate attack for hours. It also prevented the Southerners from massing an effort against Grant's left, closer to Pittsburg Landing. Although the Confederate battle plan called for the primary blow to be made here, the fighting had swirled predominately along Grant's right and center. Johnston rode near the front lines throughout the day, exhorting his men and sending units into the fray. By early afternoon he began probing for the Union left, in order to turn that flank. However, struck by a stray ball that severed an artery in his leg, Johnston died around 2:30 P.M., and Beauregard assumed command. The Hornets' Nest finally gave way after the Southerners assembled sixty-two guns and blasted the position. Surrounded, Prentiss and the last survivors surrendered around 5:30 P.M.

Despite the carnage on his right and center, Grant's hold on Pittsburg Landing was never seriously threatened. The Confederates never marshaled enough men for a knockout punch to drive the Federals away from the river. By the time dusk arrived, it was too late. Johnston's son later accused Beauregard of squandering a brilliant victory by calling off the action at sunset, but evidence suggests that this is untrue. The disorganized blows delivered against the Union left were easily repulsed, and by late afternoon a line of over fifty Federal cannon crowned the heights above Pittsburg Landing. By the end of the day, the assaulting Southerners faced insuperable problems. Hunger, fatigue, command disorder, and high losses helped check the Confederates.

Beauregard had received a telegram asserting that Buell was near Decatur, in northern Alabama. As a result, he evidently expected Grant to retreat across the river that night or remain in place for a renewed Confederate assault the next morning. Yet the vanguard of Buell's army began crossing the river in late afternoon on 6 April. The reinforcements from Buell and the belated arrival of one of his own divisions more than made up for Grant's losses. At dawn on 7 April, Grant assumed the offensive. Beauregard's troops resisted the onslaught but without reinforcements could do little more than launch isolated counterattacks. By midafternoon Beauregard realized the precariousness of his situation and began withdrawing to Corinth, Mississippi.

Both sides claimed Shiloh as a victory, but the Federals had a far stronger case. They retained possession of the battlefield, and in addition, the strategic situation in the west remained unaltered despite the bloodletting. The Confederates had not dealt a mortal blow to either Grant or Buell. Nor had they driven the invaders from Tennessee or reversed the Union's victories in the winter campaign. Instead, Memphis and the remainder of western Tennessee fell into Union hands after the Confederates evacuated Corinth in late May.

The lengthy casualty lists from Shiloh stunned both North and South. Union losses included 1,754 dead, 8,408 wounded, and 2,885 missing, for a total of 13,047 casualties; the corresponding Confederate figures were 1,723, 8,012, and 959, for a total of 10,694. Shiloh disabused both sides of the notion that the war would be short-lived. Grant's failure to fortify, and his heavy losses, injured his reputation until the capture of Vicksburg in July 1863 redeemed him.

[See also Civil War: Military and Diplomatic Course; Union Army; Vicksburg, Siege of.]

• Shelby Foote, *The Civil War: A Narrative*, 3 vols., (1958–74), Vol. 1: *Fort Sumter to Perryville*. Thomas Connelly, *Army of the Heartland: The Army of Tennessee, 1861–1862*, 1967. Wiley Sword, *Shiloh: Bloody April*, 1974. James Lee McDonough, *Shiloh—In Hell Before Night*, 1977. Steven E. Woodworth, *Jefferson Davis and His Generals: The Failure of Confederate Command in the West*, 1990. Larry J. Daniel, *Shiloh: The Battle that Changed the Civil War*, 1997.

—Christopher Losson

SHIPS. See Aircraft Carriers; Amphibious Ships and Landing Craft; Battleships; Cruisers; Destroyers; River Craft; Sailing Warships; Steamships; Submarines; Support Ships; Swift Boats.

SHOUP, DAVID (1904–1983), general and Marine Corps commandant. The son of an Indiana farmer, Shoup graduated from DePauw University in 1926 with an *ROTC commission. After a month as a lieutenant in the U.S. Army Reserve, he was transferred to the Marines. He served on expeditionary duty in Tientsin, China, in 1927–28, and returned to China on various duties, 1934–36. In 1941, he accompanied a Marine brigade to Iceland.

In the Pacific during World War II, Colonel Shoup was twice wounded in action and won the Congressional Medal of Honor for rallying his troops and leading a charge at Betio atoll, Tarawa, in the Gilbert Islands in 1943. He was chief of staff of the 2nd Marine Division in the battles of Saipan and Tinian.

After the war, Shoup served in logistical, fiscal, and training positions. In 1956, he led an investigation of the drowning of six Marine recruits on a disciplinary night march at Parris Island, South Carolina. President Dwight D. *Eisenhower appointed him Marine Corps commandant in 1960. Always outspoken, Shoup criticized attempts to indoctrinate troops with anticommunism, chastised the services for overemphasizing their own interests, argued against introducing U.S. ground forces in the crises with Cuba in 1961 and 1962, and advised against a massive buildup of U.S. forces in Vietnam. In retirement after 1963, he became an outspoken critic of the *Vietnam War.

[See also Cuba, U.S. Military Involvement in; World War II, U.S. Naval Operations in: The Pacific.]

• David M. Shoup, *The Marines in China, 1927–1928*, 1987. Robert Buzzanco and Asad Ismij, *Informed Dissent: Three Generals and the Viet Nam War*, 1988.   —John Whiteclay Chambers II

SICILY, INVASION OF (1943). The invasion of Sicily on 10 July 1943, a combined American and British operation, was the first major Allied attempt to seize a foothold on homeland territory of an Axis power. Code named "Operation Husky," it followed total *victory over Axis forces in the *North Africa Campaign two months earlier. It was undertaken because success in North Africa had made pressing on with the British-backed Mediterranean strategy strategically logical for the Allies. But the U.S. War Department regretted that it delayed for another year the war-winning invasion of occupied France across the English Channel from Britain.

Operation Husky's invasion armada, consisting of 2,500 ships sailing to Sicily from North Africa, Britain, and the United States, was the largest assembled to that time. Two armies—the U.S. Seventh Army on the left, commanded by Gen. George S. *Patton, and the British Eighth Army on the right, under Gen. Bernard Law *Montgomery—effected the landings on an 85-mile front between Licata and Syracuse on the southeast corner of Sicily. *Landing craft for *tanks and infantry that were to feature prominently in subsequent Allied *amphibious warfare were employed for the first time.

The invasion, under the overall command of Gen. Dwight D. *Eisenhower, was to be spearheaded by airborne operations, but U.S. paratroopers and British gliderborne forces were dispersed by gale-force winds. The amphibious landings, preceded by powerful naval and air bombardments, proved successful. The 180,000 troops put ashore on the first day met little initial resistance from warweary Italian defenders. But mounting a fierce counterattack the following morning, German armored forces almost drove the Americans back into the sea at Gela. Nevertheless, within forty-eight hours of the first landings, all the beachheads were secured. Subsequent operations in Sicily proved the fighting abilities of American troops as well as General Patton's aggressive combat leadership, demonstrated by Patton's success in achieving final victory on the island by capturing Messina, across from the Italian mainland, while Montgomery remained bogged down short of the city.

Enemy resistance in Sicily was totally crushed by 17 August—though not before faulty tactical planning by the Allied command permitted most of the German forces on the island to escape. The conquest of Sicily, and control of its air bases, led to the invasion and conquest of *Italy a month later.

Allied *casualties in the Sicily operation were: U.S. Army, 8,781 killed and wounded; U.S. Navy, 1,030. British, 11,843 army, 729 navy. Estimated German casualties totaled 29,000; the Italian estimated total was 145,000, including those captured.

[See also World War II: Military and Diplomatic Course.]

• Omar Bradley, A General's Life, 1983.   —Norman Gelb

SIDE ARMS, STANDARD INFANTRY.

In the national imagination, an armed infantryman stands for all America's warriors, past and present. From the musket-wielding Minuteman in the Revolution to the M-16-toting "grunt" in the *Vietnam War, the image is apt: Until the twentieth century, infantry was the primary combat arm, and even now, infantry continues to play a vital role in modern warfare. The evolution of *weaponry reflects fundamental historical changes in America's military, both as an institution and as a war-fighting entity.

A nation's weapons reveal much about its industry and technology, its commitment to preparedness, and how its military fights. After all, peacetime weapons development determines wartime fighting capabilities. When hostilities begin, a military draws from existing arsenals; new weapons, especially small arms, must often await the next war. Taking a weapon from blueprint to servicewide usage cannot be done overnight. Production lines need retooling; new weapons necessitate fresh tactics (for weapons generally dictate tactics, not vice versa); and end users (infantrymen) must fully accept the new arms. All this requires time, a precious commodity in war.

Arms procurement was much simpler in April 1775. Roused by William Dawes and Paul Revere, Massachusetts Minutemen at the onset of the *Revolutionary War took personal weapons (mostly muskets and fowling pieces) from the mantle and assembled at Lexington Green and Concord Bridge. Such diverse weaponry created ammunition resupply problems, so when the *Continental army was formed, the muzzle-loading, smoothbore flintlock musket was its basic infantry weapon.

Smoothbore muskets remained standard American (and British, Prussian, and French) infantry side arms well into the nineteenth century. During the Revolutionary War, Continentals were armed with French and Dutch imports, British muskets gleaned from battlefields and left over from the Seven Years' War, and a few American manufactures modeled upon Britain's short land service musket, or "Brown Bess." Typical of most contemporary muskets,

the Revolutionary-era "Bess" weighed about 13 pounds, featured a 42-inch smoothbore (unrifled) barrel set on a wooden stock, used black powder, fired a .75-caliber (3/4-inch-diameter) soft lead 1-ounce ball (or round), and mounted a 17-inch socket bayonet. Contemporary drill manuals dictated twenty separate steps to load and fire the Bess, including five just to replace the ramrod.

Mastering these exercises so that a soldier could continue reloading and firing as the enemy closed demanded endless drill and harsh discipline. European doctrine required that troops fire four unaimed rounds per minute—unaimed, because volume of fire, not accuracy, won eighteenth-century battles, and because smoothbore muskets were notoriously inaccurate beyond 50 yards. (A 1779 English test pitted a Bess sharpshooter against a longbowman. At 100 yards, a musketeer with a Bess hit a 4-foot-square target 57 percent of the time; his opponent hit the same target with 74 percent of his arrows.) During the Revolution, however, chronic shortages of gunpowder forced Americans to change doctrine. Officers and noncommissioned officers called for aimed fire to conserve powder (hence Gen. Israel Putnam's Battle of *Bunker Hill injunction "not to fire until you see the whites of their eyes").

For skirmishing and sniping, American light infantry employed "Pennsylvania" or "Kentucky" long rifles. Rifles had spiraled grooves cut inside the barrel—rifling—which imparted spin to the musket ball for greater distance and accuracy. One of Daniel *Morgan's frontier marksmen could pick off a British officer at 300 yards or more. Rifles, however, needed a full minute to load and could not accept bayonets, which made them unsuitable infantry weapons. Nevertheless, the image of a sharpshooting American rifleman exerted powerful influence on subsequent weapons development.

After the Revolutionary War, Congress established national armories in Springfield, Massachusetts, and Harpers Ferry, Virginia. Beginning in 1795 and 1801, respectively, these armories manufactured muskets based upon a .69-caliber French 1777 design. Production and inventiveness initially suffered from a lack of precision machinery and ineffective management by political appointees; but by the 1840s, interchangeable parts production of the American-designed Model 1841 musket began. Percussion caps (invented in 1805 but heretofore little used) now replaced flints, but the basic weapon remained a smoothbore musket. This soon changed.

Marrying a rifle's accuracy and range with a smoothbore's speed in loading was achieved when French Capt. Claude Minié perfected the minié ball in the 1840s. The minié ball—in fact, a cylindro-conoidal bullet—was muzzle-loaded like a round ball, but its hollow base expanded when fired to fit the rifling of even a powder-fouled barrel. Springfield and Harpers Ferry arsenals began producing .58-caliber rifled weapons capable of firing this new ammunition in the mid-1850s. Revised after Britain's Enfield rifle, Springfield Models 1861 and 1863 rifled *muskets became standard Federal (and Confederate, from post-battle harvests) infantry side arms during the *Civil War. Unfortunately, tactics lagged behind technology.

Rifled muskets increased the average infantryman's effective killing range to 250–300 yards. But Confederate and Union generals raised in the smoothbore era and influenced by *Napoleonic warfare persistently sent massed troops in frontal assaults across open fields. Battlefields became slaughterhouses. The battles of *Fredericksburg, *Gettysburg, *Franklin, and the *Wilderness were just a few examples where nineteenth-century weaponry shattered eighteenth-century tactics. That frontal assaults sometimes succeeded despite enormous *casualties speaks more of soldierly courage and fortitude than any general's brilliance.

The bloodletting would have been infinitely worse if repeating rifles had become standard issue. In the 1850s, American gunsmiths Samuel *Colt, Benjamin Tyler Henry, and Christopher Spencer began developing breech-loading, repeating rifles. Colt's, Henry's (later Winchester), and Spencer's rifles used rim-fire, copper-clad cartridges (from .44 to .56), and in the Civil War were primarily carried by Union cavalrymen. Thus armed, 100 men replicated the firepower of a regiment. Why, then, were not all Federal troops in the *Union army armed with repeaters, at least toward war's end?

Military institutionalization had paralleled industrialization, creating a weapons procurement bureaucracy that valued inertia and infighting over fresh ideas and inventiveness. Though field commanders clamored for added firepower, army ordnance bureaucrats believed in long-range, deliberately aimed, ammunition-conserving fire. Only President Abraham *Lincoln's direct intervention forced the army to adopt the seven-shot Spencer repeaters near war's end. Modified and improved, repeating rifles were sometimes employed as U.S. Cavalry weapons in post–Civil War campaigns in the *Plains Indians wars. (But not always; at the Battle of the *Little Bighorn in 1876, George Armstrong *Custer's men fought with single-shot rifles.) The war between aimed fire and firepower advocates, however, had only begun.

After the Civil War, small-arms technology evolved rapidly, but a penurious Congress and an intractable ordnance board balked at rearming an entire army. For instance, in 1866, rather than producing a new weapon utilizing the repeater's efficient breech-loading mechanism, muzzle-loading Springfields were converted to breechloaders with a "trap door" action so imperfect that it was capable of ripping the heads off fired cartridges, leaving the weapon hopelessly jammed. (Many of the rifles from Custer's command were recovered from the Little Bighorn in this condition.) When a new weapon was adopted in 1893, it satisfied no one, least of all soldiers in the field. This was the Krag-Jorgensen, a poor Scandinavian version of the German Paul Mauser's advanced bolt action rifle. Its modern features included a five-shot box magazine and a powerful, .30-caliber smokeless powder round; but the Krag was a Mauser copy, not the real thing. Standard issue during the *Spanish-American War (1898), the Krag was unpopular among the troops. In 1903, the famous *Springfield Model 1903 rifle replaced it.

The Springfield '03 resulted from servicewide modernizing reforms initiated by Secretary of War Elihu *Root. Its adoption was a victory for aimed fire advocates since the bolt action rifle (.30/06) was accurate to well over 600 yards. But it so closely duplicated Mauser's latest rifle that patent infringement charges almost prevented its introduction. Although millions were eventually produced, arsenal production was slow. Many World War I "doughboys" trained with broomsticks, not rifles. The Springfield '03 remained America's basic field weapon until the late 1930s.

World War I *trench warfare demonstrated the need for lightweight, semiautomatic/automatic (self-loading) infantry weapons. Competitions were held featuring two notable weapons designers, J. D. Pederson and John M. Browning. Browning's designs dominated early twentieth-century American automatic arms. His 1911 .45 automatic pistol (M1911A1) remained standard issue until replaced in the 1980s by a 9-millimeter, fifteen-shot Beretta (*NATO designation M-9). The *Browning Automatic Rifle, or BAR, a lightweight .30/06-caliber machine gun, earned kudos from soldiers from World War I to Korea. But after extensive testing, the winner was the little known Springfield Arsenal designer John C. Garand.

Garand's superb rifle was adopted in 1936 and carried into battle by millions of G.I.'s during World War II. Designated the *M-1 rifle, the Garand was a gas-operated, magazine-fed weapon. Propellant gases forced back the bolt, ejected the empty cartridge, and recocked the hammer. The M-1 weighed 9.5 pounds and fired .30/06 rounds in eight-shot clips. The Garand was the only battleworthy semiautomatic produced by any major combatant during World War II, but other nations began eschewing long-range, aimed fire for the increased, if less accurate, firepower of shoulder-fired machine pistols, or submachine guns. These weapons included German Schmeisser "burp" guns capable of firing 450 to 550 rounds per minute, the American Thompson submachine gun, and Britain's Sten gun. All had a major influence on the next generation of infantry arms, the assault rifles.

The first and most influential post–World War II assault rifle was the Soviet Union's Avtomat Kalashnikova 47 or AK-47. Invented in 1947 by Mikhail Kalashnikov, the gas-operated AK-47 (7.62mm, later 5.45mm) weighed 10.6 pounds (later 8.3 pounds), and was capable of semiautomatic or automatic fire at a rate of 600 rounds per minute. Cheap and durable, millions of Kalashnikovs were manufactured and distributed to revolutionary movements worldwide.

America's response was, as usual, a compromise. The semiautomatic M-1 was converted into an automatic, the M-14. The M-14 was a good weapon, but in automatic fire, its 7.62mm round made the recoil too powerful and unstable. Following the *Korean War (1950–53), experiments began with a .22 (or 5.56mm) cartridge with high muzzle velocity (over 3,000 feet per second). To fire this small but powerful round, the army chose a weapon developed by Eugene M. Stoner of Fairchild Aircraft's ArmaLite Division, the AR-15. This 7.6-pound weapon with its plastic stock was capable of semi- and fully automatic fire (700–900 rounds per minute). The U.S. Air Force purchased the AR-15 in 1961, but the army, after extensive testing and controversial modifications, delayed adopting it until 1967 as the *M-16 rifle (technically, the M-16-A1).

The AR-15 was an excellent weapon, the American equivalent (or better) of the Soviet AK-47 and perfect for the mixed terrain of Vietnam; the M-16 was not its equal. Like the AK-47, the AR-15 could take incredible punishment (dirt, rain, poor care) and still keep firing; moreover, Stoner's innovative rifling made it lethal at long range. Infighting between army bureaucrats and a progressive Department of *Defense, however, delayed adoption and forced uncalled-for changes. Perfectly clean and with an M-79 grenade launcher attached, the M-16 was a fine combat weapon; in the mud and dust, jungles and mountains, and rivers and rice paddies of Vietnam, it proved unreliable.

After the *Vietnam War, a new, heavier round was developed, and a remodeled M-16 (the M-16-A2) became standard issue in 1980. This would be the weapon American infantrymen carried in the *Persian Gulf War in 1991 and as *peacekeeping troops during the *Bosnian crisis. Development of laser-type infantry weapons may eventually revolutionize U.S. military arms, but one certainty exists: as long as the current costly, time-consuming procurement process continues, the choice is sure to be controversial.

[See also Army Combat Branches: Infantry; Army Combat Branches: Cavalry; Machine Guns; Procurement: Government Arsenals; Procurement; Ordnance and Arms Industry; Weaponry, Army.]

• Harold L. Peterson, The Book of the Continental Soldier, 1968. Russell F. Weigley, History of the United States Army, 1967; rev. ed. 1984. Trevor N. Dupuy, The Evolution of Weapons and Warfare, 1980. Edward C. Ezell, The Great Rifle Controversy: Search for the Ultimate Infantry Weapon from World War II Through Vietnam and Beyond, 1984. William H. Hallahan, Misfire: The History of How America's Small Arms Have Failed Our Military, 1994. Edward C. Ezell, Small Arms of the World: A Basic Manual, 12th rev. ed., 1983.

—John Morgan Dederer

SIMS, WILLIAM S. (1858–1936), admiral, supporter of reforms to modernize the navy, especially technological innovation and organizational change. Sims graduated from Annapolis in 1880. During the *Spanish-American War, he served as naval attaché in Paris, organizing espionage to report Spanish ship movements. Later he advocated improved gunnery, popularizing the techniques of the Englishman Sir Percy Scott. He commanded two *battleships, *Minnesota* (1909–11) and *Nevada* (1915–16), but his most important command was the Atlantic Torpedo Flotilla (1913–15). He was president of the Naval War College when in March 1917 he was sent to London to coordinate the navy's role in World War I. He later became commander in chief of U.S. naval forces in European waters.

Admiral Sims immediately sensed the necessity for antisubmarine operations to counter Germany's adoption of unrestricted undersea warfare, a maritime strategy intended to force *victory before the United States could make its presence felt. He recommended construction and deployment of antisubmarine craft to European waters to serve under British admirals such as Sir Lewis Bayley at Queenstown, Ireland. This course meant suspension of American naval construction intended to create a unified battle fleet. His views prevailed despite initial opposition from Secretary of the Navy Josephus Daniels and the chief of naval operations, Adm. William Benson, who concluded that Sims was unduly influenced by the British Admiralty. Sims emphasized protection of supply shipments to the Allies; the Navy Department stressed protection of troopships transporting the *American Expeditionary Force to France. Sims generally supported Admiralty views, which made him popular in Britain but suspect at home.

After the war, an angry Sims sparked a congressional inquiry into naval affairs in 1917–18, arguing that the Navy Department's effort had been slow and misdirected. This investigation led to long-term divisions within the officer corps. In 1920, he published *The Victory at Sea*, an account of his wartime service, which won the Pulitzer Prize.

[See also Navy, U.S.: 1899–1945; World War I: Military and Diplomatic Course.]

• Elting E. Morison, Admiral Sims and the Modern American Navy, 1952.
—David F. Trask

SITTING BULL (1831?–1890), Hunkpapa Lakota Sioux chief. One of the most significant of all Indian leaders, Sitting Bull achieved distinction not only as a war leader but as a political chief and spiritual leader as well. His record in war with enemy tribes was exemplary even before he came to the notice of whites in the 1860s. Sitting Bull played a leading role in the fighting with the forces of U.S. Army generals Henry H. Sibley, Alfred Sully, and Patrick E. Connor, who led strong columns into Sioux ranges of Dakota and Montana in 1863–65. After the Treaty of 1868, Sitting Bull was principal leader of the bands that scorned the reservation and came to be known as *hostiles*. He was present at the Battle of the *Little Bighorn, 25–26 June 1876 but as an "old man" chief did not take a conspicuous part in the fighting. As Sitting Bull's coalition fell apart under military pressure, in 1877 he and a small following sought refuge in Canada. Dwindling buffalo resources forced his surrender and return to the United States in July 1881. At the Standing Rock Reservation he feuded with the reservations agent and assumed a prominent role in the Ghost Dance troubles of 1889–90. On 15 December 1890, while attempting his arrest, Indian policemen shot and killed him.

[See also Crazy Horse; Plains Indians Wars; Wounded Knee, Battle of.]

• Robert M. Utley, The Lance and the Shield: The Life and Times of Sitting Bull, 1993.
—Robert M. Utley

SLAVERY. See Civil War: Causes of; Emancipation Proclamation.

SMART BOMBS. See Bombs.

SOCIETY AND WAR. Research on the intersection of social history and the history of warfare has concentrated on four specific areas: social stratification, family forms, veterans' benefits, and taxation.

War and Social Stratification. The effect of war on social inequality is a matter of considerable debate. From the *Revolutionary War onward, the issue of profiteering—of making a fortune out of war provisioning—has come to the fore time and again. The effects on economic organization are evident: war benefits industries able to tie into the munitions trade. These industries emerge stronger after the conclusion of hostilities, and can use the experience and capital generated in wartime to perform more efficiently in peacetime. Thus, war creates wealth and benefits one fraction of the wealthy.

Other property owners may not do so well. The reason is inflation. Those living on fixed incomes, investments, or rent can be devastated by war, since their return on capital loses its real value during periods of spiraling prices. Land as property may produce good profits in wartime, but if rented out over the long term, its capacity to generate annual incomes is compromised by price inflation.

The same mixed fortunes affect wage earners. Those able to transfer their skills to munitions production can do much better in wartime than in peacetime. Hostilities usually eliminate unemployment. They also promote corporate solutions to industrial relations, leading to the temporary recognition of workers as partners in management. This is in everybody's interest because it achieves maximum productivity with a minimum of strikes.

Other workers are not so lucky. Those who work at producing nonessential goods or those unable to move to areas of munitions production are either thrown out of work or earn an inadequate wage at a time of price inflation. Those not central to the tasks of waging war can go to the wall during it. This is a form of economic triage, separating workers whose activities are essential from those the economy (and the nation) can spare. Many of the latter are elderly.

On balance, though, there is a tendency for war to reduce the distance between classes and between strata within classes. This leveling effect may not be long-lasting, and it does create expectations hard to realize in the aftermath of war. Social gains during a war can create a deep sense of anger about their disappearance when the shooting stops.

War and Family Forms. The effects of war are profoundly evident in terms of family forms and behavior. *Mobilization separates families; *casualties destroy them. In the aftermath of war, millions of families are reconstituted. These processes have had significant long-term effects. For example, the cult of domesticity underlying the post-1945 "Baby Boom" is related to the vast upheaval of war and its effects on family life. An inner migration to domesticity happened in most major combatants after World War II; the United States was no exception.

War also changes ideas about divorce. At the outbreak of hostilities, many unfortunate people marry hastily. Over time they see the error of their choice, or grow apart, or find other partners during a spouse's absence. Sexual loyalty is the exception, not only in wartime but perhaps especially during such anxious and emotionally charged periods.

During wartime, civilian migration increases—not only to get out of the way of the fighting, as in the *Civil War, but also to take up new jobs in new places. At the same time, international immigration is suspended. After World War I, that change was made permanent. Reactions to the war, and the supposed radical ideas of European immigrants, helped close the doors to immigration in the 1920s. Before the war, such action was contemplated; after the war, it was realized.

The growing importance of families in the shadow of war had profound effects, too, on the discussion of women's rights. In America as in other countries, women's contribution to postwar recovery was always configured in terms of their domestic work: childbearing; organizing and maintaining the home; and caring for the husband, defined as the key breadwinner and figure of authority. In this network of social tasks, women's outside lives or aspirations had little place. Thus, the irony of war is that it encourages women to leave home to help produce the goods and services needed for victory, and then encourages them to go home again because their primary obligation is not to produce but to reproduce. When wars destroy families, it is their reconstruction that takes precedence over women's rights. This has been as true in the United States as it was for other combatant countries of the major wars of this century. If there is increased recognition of women's talents and services in wartime, that recognition is with-

drawn as soon as the shooting stops. One step forward, two steps back is one way to characterize the impact of war on this aspect of family life.

War and Veterans' Benefits. A third area of fundamental interest for social historians is veterans' history. The first question is pensions: How much and for how long? No country in the world matches the generosity of the *Veterans Administration in the United States, but free access to its medical facilities is not always the pathway to the best medical care. There is less doubt about the positive effects of the *G.I. Bill of Rights, for example, in expanding opportunities for higher education among many men and women who would not have had it in the absence of war.

Veterans form associations, and the history of these groups—by no means restricted to the *American Legion or the *Veterans of Foreign Wars—has drawn much attention in recent years. Their activities in promoting such projects as the Vietnam Veterans' Memorial or the Korean War Memorial in Washington reflect the self-consciousness of veterans that their experience has given them a voice—and a conscience.

The reintegration of veterans into peacetime society is also important. What to do about the handicapped—crippled in mind or in body—has been a preoccupation of many Americans throughout their history. The worry has existed that men trained to kill will turn to crime in peacetime. The "taint" of military or naval service was therefore something soldiers and sailors had to contend with in many different periods. One solution was to move from soldiering to policing or similar service activities.

War and Taxation. The question of pensions for veterans is central to another critical part of the literature on war and social organization. As Theda Skocpol has shown, after the Civil War, pensions' provision constituted the single largest item of the federal budget. The inflection of federal expenditure and taxation in the twentieth century therefore is an extension of nineteenth-century precedent. The expansion of state activity in wartime creates both a concentration effect—bringing to the center activities done at the periphery—and a threshold effect—making the government's share of gross national product rise. Just as in Europe, state expenditure as a proportion of national income doubled after World War I. The same upward inflection happened after 1945 and after the *Vietnam War. The need for states to expand in wartime is self-evident; not so clear is their tendency to stay expanded in peacetime.

When they do, they tend to be in the business of servicing deficits produced in wartime. As current expenditure has to go into paying back past wartime expenditure, the sums available for peacetime projects dwindle. The shadow of war therefore restricts or truncates the capacity of the peacetime federal government to meet wartime expectations for improvements following hostilities.

[*See also* Memorials, War]

• Anthony Lake, ed., *The Vietnam Legacy: The War, American Society, and the Future of American Foreign Policy,* 1976. David Kennedy, *Over Here: The First World War and American Society,* 1980. Theda Skocpol, *Protecting Soldiers and Mothers: The Political Origins of Social Policy in the United States,* 1992. Norman S. Sherry, *In the Shadow of War. The United States Since the 1930s,* 1995. Jay M. Winter and Blaine Baggett, *The Great War and the Shaping of the Twentieth Century,* 1996.

—Jay M. Winter

SOCIETY, MILITARY ORGANIZATION AND. *War has been one of the great learning mechanisms in human history. In the nineteenth century, as war took on its large-scale form, involving enormous numbers of individuals in both combat and support roles, organization became a decisive factor in national survival. Nations able to administer large bodies of men had a tremendous military advantage. Lessons of organization and administration learned in the military field were transferred to civilian society, especially to large-scale business enterprise; they played important roles in the industrialization of the United States and Europe. In the twentieth century, military organization has continued to influence business and economic organization, but now in a mutually reinforcing way, with developments and innovations from the civilian economy increasingly adapted by the military.

The *Civil War was the first large-scale national administrative effort undertaken by the U.S. government. The horrendous logistical experiences in the *Mexican War had been endured by junior officers who later took command of Union and Confederate armies; more than any other factor, this alerted military leadership to the new organizational demands of administering large bodies of men. The demand for millions of *uniforms by the *Union army placed entirely new requirements for speedy mass production of clothing. Uniforms had to be made to fit certain standard sizes, and for the first time serious attention was given to collecting statistics on basic clothing measurements for the American male population. The firms granted these contracts—companies such as the suit manufacturer Hart, Schaffner, and Marx—later used this knowledge to mass-produce men's business suits, the uniform of the rising class of office workers and middle managers in America's industrial age.

The Civil War also produced major administrative advances in railroad management, arms production, food rations, and recordkeeping—for payrolls, for example. Operation at larger scale, over an enlarged geographic space, and with more stringent quality requirements revolutionized American management in ways that were later copied by business. Railroads are a particularly interesting example of how military needs shaped commercial organization. Railroad construction was long dominated by West Point–trained engineers. But railroad operation was different from construction. Making the trains run on time, and making sure they did not collide on the single-track lines of nineteenth-century America, became far more demanding with the increased traffic of the Civil War. Gen. Ulysses S. *Grant's famous War Order Number 1 of 1864, requiring that offensives in the eastern and western fronts be coordinated, was really an order about railroad scheduling: that it had to be centrally controlled. The central control of signals and schedules later contributed to concentrated ownership of railroad companies. Giant organizations in oil, coal, and meatpacking, which precipitated the antitrust movement, had their origins in the efficiency gains learned in centralized railroading during the Civil War.

At the turn of the century, the military lagged behind corporate organizational development. The *Spanish-American War was a logistical disaster for the United States. Even in World War I, the U.S. military remained logistically deficient because factories in America were not properly coordinated for war production. In 1917–18, not a single artillery piece manufactured in the United States made it to Europe in time to be used in action. The army and the government learned that lesson.

World War II, with its requirement for war on an entirely new scale and its mobilization of the national economy, transformed organizational life. The war saw the introduction of such innovations as federal support of institutionalized research in universities, statistical quality control, the scientific study of military actions known as *operations research*, coordination of complex multi-plant factories, and the industrialization of what were once considered activities not suitable to this form of management, such as airplane manufacture. While each of these existed in the 1930s, all were applied on such a large scale and with such success during the war that they were almost immediately adapted after the war ended, becoming the accepted form of organization and management for America's rise in world business in the 1950s. For example, Robert S. *McNamara, assistant to the secretary of war, took his entire unit of statistical control analysts to the Ford Motor Company immediately after the war, where new methods were used to control costs and quality for a major expansion of output to meet the driving needs of a mobile public in the 1950s.

The principal organizational innovations of the *Cold War were *systems engineering* and large-scale coordination of geographically separated units. Systems engineering was used to coordinate the complex technological projects that dominated the Cold War, involving *radar warning systems, *missiles, and airplanes. Large-scale principles were used to gain the maximum performance from the regional commands of the armed forces, for example, to coordinate *antisubmarine warfare operations in the Atlantic and Pacific Oceans. Operations research methods such as linear programming were used to achieve this, and these were quickly copied by airlines and automobile producers, who also faced complicated scheduling problems. Most notable was the speed with which this military-to-business transfer took place.

Skills in coordinating multi-plant factory outputs were used in America's business foray into the new European Common Market of the 1950s and 1960s. European business before the war focused on relatively small national markets, rather than on continental-scale markets as American competitors had done. This was one major reason behind the tremendous resentment displayed toward American multinational firms so prominent in Europe during the 1960s. U.S. companies were constructing continental-scaled markets from local ones in Europe, something they had earlier pioneered and perfected in their own country.

Since the period of the Civil War through the 1970s, the principal impact of military organization on American society was to contribute to the trend of grouping people into increasingly large hierarchies. Whether in the military or in business, large organizations dominated. But in the late 1970s a partial reversal of this trend began, with a move toward small, decentralized structuring of human activity. The disadvantages of centralization and big organization were increasingly recognized. The tendency toward bureaucratic inertia, indifference to costs, loss of flexibility, and lack of innovation were met by a major move toward downsizing, not only as a way to reduce costs but also as a way to increase flexibility and organizational agility. A technological revolution greatly reinforced this trend: management of information moved from centralized mainframe computers to small, decentralized personal computers. With the Internet, originally created by the *Pentagon's Advanced Research Projects Agency, an even greater capacity to decentralize became available.

The results have revolutionized American business enterprise, and these changes have in turn been quickly copied by the military. The U.S. military is copying business organization by emphasizing smaller size and decentralized decision making as keys to flexibility, and by removing strong departmental boundaries in favor of building organizations around processes—known as *reengineering*. The army emphasizes dispersed small units coordinated by shared information. The navy has developed more flexible groupings of ships that are no longer centered on the aircraft carrier. In both instances, the decentralized format of the Internet is being used as an organizational model for the armed forces.

[*See also* Economy and War; Science, Technology, War, and the Military.]

• Alfred D. Chandler, Jr., *The Visible Hand: The Managerial Revolution in American Business*, 1977. Stephen Skowronek, *Building a New American State*, 1982. Karen A. Rasler and William R. Thompson, *War and State Making: The Shaping of the Global Powers*, 1989.

—Paul Bracken

SOMALIA, U.S. MILITARY INVOLVEMENT IN. In 1988, civil war broke out in Somalia in East Africa. The dictator, Siad Barre, was expelled, but power remained divided among local leaders. In the capital of Mogadishu, Mohamed Farah Aideed and Ali Mahdi Mohamed struggled for control; regional groups fought among themselves. In April 1992, the *United Nations established the United Nations Operations in Somalia (UNOSOM I), with a few unarmed troops and Mohamed Sahnoun, an Algerian diplomat, as political coordinator. Sahnoun established good relations with both sides but alienated UN headquarters and soon resigned. In July 1992, the secretary general estimated that 1 million Somali children were malnourished and another 4.5 million people urgently needed food aid. Under pressure from the media, members of Congress, and the international community, President George *Bush decided to airlift food to Somalia in August. However, it was impossible to deliver sufficient quantities of food by air.

Troops of the United Nations Task Force (UNITAF) landed in December 1992. UNITAF was a U.S. military operation, although troops from 30 countries were included; at its peak it numbered about 38,000 troops, of which 25,000 were American. Its mission was confined to relief; the United Nations would conduct political negotiations and prepare a force to replace it. UNITAF succeeded in stopping famine throughout the country within five months.

UNOSOM II had about the same troop strength but a more ambitious task: to establish a Somali government. Somali factions attacked UNOSOM troops, and the conflict escalated. U.S. Delta Force commandos and rangers were sent to Somalia to capture Aideed. Instead, on 3 October 1993, they were ambushed and lost eighteen men. Television cameras showed one of the dead Americans being dragged through the streets. The Clinton administration decided to negotiate with Aideed. U.S. troops were

withdrawn, and the rest of the UN forces left Somalia in March 1995. The famine had been ended, but UN *peacekeeping had been discredited in the United States.

• John L. Hirsch and Robert B. Oakley, *Somalia and Operation Restore Hope*, 1995. Jonathan Stevenson, *Losing Mogadishu*, 1995. Mark Bowden, *Black Hawk Down: A Story of Modern War*, 1999.

—Roy Licklider

SONAR (underwater sound navigation ranging) can be either of the *passive* or *active* type. Passive sonars were developed first and rely upon listening for noise generated by the target vessel, usually *submarines (however, submarines also use sonar to detect other ships). The most difficult aspect of passive sonar use is distinguishing *target noise* from that of the surrounding sea (referred to as *ambient noise*) and particularly that of the searching platform. Active sonars are popularly characterized by the famous *ping* known to anybody who has ever watched a Hollywood submarine movie. The *ping* is a sound wave generated by the searcher that is bounced back off the objects, thus giving the sonar operator a picture of the object in the path of the sound wave.

U.S. sonar development began before World War I when the Submarine Signal Company, formed in 1901, developed steam-operated underwater warning bells that could be heard for up to 10 nautical miles. By 1912, warning bells were used to supplement the work of lighthouses in marking hazards to navigation off the coasts of North America, South America, Europe, and Asia.

In February 1917, the U.S. Navy Consulting Board created a Subcommittee on Submarine Detection. Two passive sonar detectors developed by a staff member of the Submarine Signal Company, Professor R. A. Fessenden, were installed on navy destroyers, but their performance proved disappointing.

World War II saw active sonar systems predominate in U.S. ships and submarines, in contrast to the Germans, who concentrated on large fixed passive array systems. The American approach helped mitigate the effect of ocean noise that proved such a problem with passive sonars. Navy General Board guidelines of 1938 called for two sonars per destroyer and one unit for lesser craft. However, wartime demands for escort vessels and the low rate of sonar production prevented these guidelines from being followed. Instead, the scarce equipment was put out among destroyer escorts. U.S. submarines typically carried a passive device along with a combined ranging and sounding set.

During the *Cold War, passive developments included large arrays of hydrophones mounted conformally along submarine hulls to achieve very well defined and very long range receiving beams; systems for passive range finding; PUFFS (Passive Underwater Fire Control Feasibility Study, a short range triangulation device using three passive sonars mounted along the length of a submarine); and submarine-towed arrays. The towed array came into use to mitigate the effect of a vessel's own noise upon passive sonar systems; it consists of a string of passive hydrophones towed at some distance behind the ship. A further advantage of the towed array is that it can be made as long as necessary to detect sounds with long (very low frequency) wavelengths.

Today's most advanced U.S. submarines, the SSN-688I and the SSN-21, use the AN/BSY-1 integrated sonar and fire control system that includes both active and passive sonar types. In addition to MAD (magnetic anomaly detector) sensors (a means of locating submarines by detecting changes in the earth's magnetic fields caused by large metal objects), aircraft use small sonobuoys as a means of detecting submarines. *Helicopters hover above the ocean surface and dip scanning sonars that emit a *ping* in all directions at once.

[*See also* Antisubmarine Warfare Systems; Destroyers and Destroyer Escorts.]

• Norman Friedman, *U.S. Naval Weapons Systems*, 1982; repr. 1985, 1988.   —David E. Michlovitz

SOUTHEAST ASIA TREATY ORGANIZATION. *See* SEATO.

SPAATZ, CARL A. (1891–1974), World War II general. A 1914 graduate of the U.S. Military Academy, one of the earliest U.S. military aviators, commanded a pilot training center in France during World War I. He also managed one tour at the front and shot down three aircraft. After the war he showed his moral and physical courage by testifying at the Mitchell courts-martial and in pioneering in-flight refueling. As a special observer in England, in 1940, his optimistic reports helped ensure continued U.S. aid. After participating in *World War II planning, he took the Eighth Air Force to England in 1942 and established a cordial working relationship with the Royal Air Force (RAF). Gen. Dwight D. *Eisenhower called him to North Africa in late 1942 as Allied Air Forces commander. Again Spaatz established a sound relationship with the RAF and also helped correct U.S. air-ground cooperation difficulties. Upon returning to England in 1944 he became the senior U.S. air officer in Europe. At his insistence the United States began the highly successful bombing of the German synthetic oil industry. After the victory in Europe, he transferred to the Pacific and was the senior operational officer in the atomic bomb drops on *Hiroshima and Nagasaki. In 1946, as Gen. "Hap" *Arnold's successor, he played a leading role in the creation of the U.S. *Air Force (USAF) as a separate military service and in the division of roles and missions between the services. He became USAF Chief of Staff in 1947 and retired the next year.

• David R. Mets, *Master of Airpower, General Carl A. Spaatz*, 1988. Richard G. Davis, *Carl A. Spaatz and the Air War in Europe, 1940–1945*, 1993.   —Richard G. Davis

SPACE PROGRAM, MILITARY INVOLVEMENT IN THE. The U.S. space program began with military studies of instrumented Earth satellites in 1945. Ten years later, American political leaders approved and subsequently organized a space program expressly for purposes of national security. Because the "space age" began amid the superpower tensions of the 1950s, the tone, tempo, and direction of America's astronautical enterprise in the years afterward would be impressed with the near-indelible seal of the *Cold War.

The U.S. *Navy, *Army, and *Air Force first examined the military applications of Earth satellites between 1945 and 1950. The air force continued these studies in the early 1950s, primarily through contracts with the RAND Corporation, an independent consultant organization established and funded by the service.

On 4 October 1957 the Soviet Union launched the world's first satellite, Sputnik I, and in November, its heavier companion, Sputnik II, followed. The public outcry in the United States after the launches prompted various measures from the administration. In February 1958, President Dwight D. *Eisenhower established the Advance Research Projects Agency (ARPA) in the Department of *Defense (DoD), assigning to it temporary responsibility for directing all U.S. space projects—civil and military. Early in that same month, he authorized Project CORONA, a secret reconnaissance satellite effort that might more quickly return images of the Soviet Union. Because of its national security applications, Eisenhower was inclined to assign all of America's burgeoning civil and military space programs to ARPA, but Vice President Richard M. *Nixon and Eisenhower's science adviser, James R. Killian, Jr., persuaded him otherwise. On 2 April 1958, they submitted to Congress draft legislation that would establish the National Aeronautics and Space Administration (NASA). Except for military space flight, for which the DoD remained responsible, the statute declared that all nonmilitary aeronautical and space endeavors would be directed by this civilian agency. The 1958 legislation divided American space activities between civilian space science and applications missions and military defense support missions, for which the air force eventually became the lead service. In 1960, after one of the *U-2 spy planes was shot down over the Soviet Union, Eisenhower completed the framing of American astronautics in a house of three wings: civil space science and applications (NASA); DoD military support missions (such as communication, navigation, and missile early warning); and reconnaissance satellites, now directed by a civilian National Reconnaissance Office in the DoD.

A few months later, on 6 March 1961, Secretary of Defense Robert S. *McNamara confirmed this division of labor when he issued Directive 5160 on the "Development of Space Systems." If loss of the strategic reconnaissance mission had been a bitter pill for air force leaders to swallow, the directive at least offered a sugar coating: the air force was given responsibility for running all DoD space development programs. Among the most prestigious of space endeavors at that time, military or civil, was manned space flight.

The air force first sought a role in the nation's manned space flight program with a rocket bomber entrant known as "Dyna-Soar" (for Dynamic Soaring). The winged space vehicle, carrying one man, would be mounted atop an ICBM and launched into Earth orbit. Later, after completing its mission, Dyna-Soar would reenter the Earth's atmosphere and glide to a landing. But just what its manned mission would be remained a serious stumbling block because, in 1958–59, administration officials refused to consider weapons in orbit. The Kennedy administration in December 1963 canceled Dyna-Soar in favor of a military space station, termed the Manned Orbital Laboratory (MOL).

With Project Apollo (the manned lunar landing) well underway at NASA, the DoD sought with MOL to determine and test the military usefulness of human beings in Earth orbit. Exactly what military duties astronauts might perform, however, continued to dog the enterprise. The most likely mission appeared to be one of reconnaissance. In the years that followed, MOL's technical problems multiplied and its costs soared. A few weeks before NASA's Project Apollo landed men on the Moon, in July 1969,

President Richard M. *Nixon canceled MOL. His defense secretary, Melvin *Laird, cited funding constraints and recent advances in the performance of instrumented military satellites that performed the same missions planned for MOL. The president's decision ended air force attempts to create a separate military manned space program.

Having lost the strategic reconnaissance mission to a civilian DoD agency in 1960, the armed services still held responsibility for the remaining defense support missions identified in the 1950s. In fact, the DoD had assigned responsibility for instrumented navigation satellites to the navy and communication satellites to the army before Secretary of Defense McNamara's 1961 dictum named the air force the lead service in space affairs. But in May 1962, McNamara canceled the army communications satellite project, known as Advent, which featured a set of satellites to be placed in geosynchronous orbit 22,300 miles above the equator.

In place of Advent, McNamara authorized a larger number of small communications satellites in medium-altitude orbits of about 6,000 miles. He designated the air force responsible for procuring the launch vehicles and satellites, and the army for developing the ground terminals. Known at first as the Interim (or Initial) Defense Communications Satellite Program (IDCSP), after worldwide operations began between fixed bases, it was renamed the Defense Satellite Communications System I (DSCS I). Beginning in June 1966, clusters of seven or eight satellites were launched simultaneously; a final launch in June 1968 brought the operational system to twenty-six DSCS I satellites.

In 1968, the DoD approved a follow-on military strategic communications satellite program, similar in many respects to Advent and called DSCS II. These larger communication satellites began to be launched into geosynchronous orbits in 1972, and, after some early spacecraft problems, a set of four was declared operational in late 1978. More advanced DSCS III satellites followed in the 1980s, and the DoD declared this military space communications system operational in 1993. The first of four even more advanced and complex satellites, called Milstar and designed to use extremely high frequencies, was launched into geosynchronous orbit in 1994.

Meanwhile, a navy program known as Transit began to launch instrumented satellites in 1960 to improve terrestrial military navigation. When declared operational in 1964, Transit consisted of five satellites in offset polar orbits circling the Earth at an altitude of about 670 miles. By combining the calculated satellite positions, the range difference measurements between these positions as the satellite moved overhead, and information on vessels' speed, ships or *submarines receiving Transit radio signals could obtain a two-dimensional position fix accurate to about 650 feet in latitude and longitude. Although widely employed at sea, Transit proved useless for aircraft, which moved at too high a speed; nor could it determine altitude. However, the navy and the air force began investigations of an improved three-dimensional system—one that would provide a terrestrial vehicle's position in tens of feet, its velocity at all speeds, and its altitude above the Earth's surface.

In 1974, the DoD combined the best features of the navy and air force navigation satellite proposals, assigned the air force responsibility for the project, and identified it as the Navstar Global Positioning System (GPS). When declared operational in 1994, the GPS consisted of 24 satellites that circle the Earth every 12 hours at a height of 12,524 miles. Four satellites are located in each of six planes inclined 55 degrees to the equator, creating a satellite "bird cage" around the world. Each GPS satellite, equipped with atomic clocks, continuously transmits pseudorandom codes at two frequencies that provide synchronized time signals and data about its own position. Integrating the signals from four satellites, a vehicle equipped with a GPS receiver can determine its location, velocity, and altitude with extreme precision. Although American military leaders were slow to procure GPS receivers, the 1991 *Persian Gulf War demonstrated the extraordinary advantages of this space system for military forces in navigating, mapping, and directing artillery fire.

Two other important defense support missions—early warning of missile launches and the detection of nuclear detonations—have roots in the 1950s, when these issues consumed the U.S. leadership. The first of them, called MIDAS (for Missile Detection and Alarm System), began as a part of Lockheed's reconnaissance satellite contract in 1956. The concept called for mounting infrared sensors and a telescope on an instrumented satellite that pointed them at the Earth. The instrument, turned at about 6 rpm, swept a given field of view and detected the hot exhaust flames of rockets as they ascended under power through the atmosphere. The time of a missile's launch, its location, and direction of flight would be radioed to an Earth station within moments, allowing the air force time to scramble its alert bombers before the warhead struck.

Not until the mid-1960s did Lockheed demonstrate beyond question the performance and reliability of the MIDAS concept in space operations. At that time, the DoD *put the operational system out to bid with industry.* Known as the Defense Support Program (DSP), it would employ three or four satellites in geosynchronous orbits instead of the twelve or fourteen satellites in 6,000-mile-high polar orbits planned for MIDAS. TRW prevailed in this competition, and the air force launched the first DSP satellites in the early 1970s. The performance of these instrumented satellites exceeded expectations and the system was declared operational in the mid-1970s. Employed in 1991 during Operation Desert Storm, DSP satellites gave Allied Coalition forces in the Persian Gulf and citizens of Israel crucial advance warning of Iraqi Scud ballistic missile launches. This allowed people to seek cover and Patriot missiles to be pointed and fired at an incoming Scud.

Back in the late 1950s, the DoD had also approved development of a second, related space system that could detect nuclear detonations on Earth and in space. A variety of national concerns promoted this project, known as Vela Hotel. In the mid-1950s, President Eisenhower initiated negotiations with leaders of the Soviet Union and Great Britain to secure agreement on a nuclear test ban treaty. Administration leaders then demanded a space system that would police compliance with its terms.

Representatives of the United States, Great Britain, and the Soviet Union signed a *Limited Nuclear Test Ban Treaty in August 1963 that prohibited testing of nuclear devices in the atmosphere, underwater, and in outer space. The air force began to launch Vela Hotel satellites before month's end. Placed in 70,000-mile-high elliptical orbits that rose far above the Van Allen radiation belts, and located on opposite sides of the Earth, the initial satellites provided complete coverage of outer space. Later satellites with improved optics also looked earthward to detect the flash of a nuclear explosion. Eventually, Vela instruments were carried on board other military satellites, such as DSP and GPS vehicles, and the effort was renamed the Integrated Operational Nuclear Detection System (IONDS). But however named, for over thirty years this space system detected numerous atmospheric atomic tests and verified, contrary to the fears of some, that all states party to the Nuclear Test Ban Treaty had abided by its terms.

The last of the major military application satellite systems, the Defense Meteorological Satellite Program, or DMSP, also began in the late 1950s. Originally, NASA was to develop a single civil-military satellite system, one that would serve both the DoD and the Commerce Department's Weather Bureau. Because NASA's design was so complex, the DoD authorized the air force to develop a simplified, low-altitude military weather satellite. The resulting spacecraft, first launched in 1962, proved so effective that the Weather Bureau soon advised NASA it would buy copies of the military satellite system.

Shortly after these classified military weather satellites became operational, U.S. forces began military operations in the *Vietnam War. DMSP satellites in 450-nautical-mile polar orbits, equipped to provide day- and nighttime images of cloud cover, were employed to assist both air and surface military activity. The cloud cover photos, widely distributed in Southeast Asia, made DMSP an open secret by the early 1970s. In 1973, Secretary of the Air Force John McLucas publicly announced the program's existence, and DMSP images were released for civilian use.

Operation Desert Storm, the military campaign in the Persian Gulf War to liberate Kuwait from Iraqi occupation in January–February 1991, became the first major contest of arms in which all military space systems were integrated into both planning and operations. It has been called "the first space war" because communication, navigation, weather, early warning, and reconnaissance satellites provided information indispensable to combat operations. These military space assets, pre-positioned in Earth orbit, permitted the Allied Coalition leaders to wield terrestrial forces in concert and multiplied their effects on the battlefield so enormously that without them, an enemy in the twenty-first century has little hope of prevailing in combat.

[See also Air and Space Defense; Communications; Missiles; Satellites; Reconnaissance; Strategic Defense Initiative (SDI).]

• Thomas S. Moorman, Jr., "The Space Revolution," in Jacob Neufeld et al., eds., Technology and the Air Force: A Retrospective Assessment, 1997. Curtis Peebles, High Frontier: The United States Air Force and the Military Space Program, 1997. William E. Burrows, This New Ocean: The Story of the First Space Age, 1998. David N. Spires, Beyond Horizons: A Half Century of Air Force Space Leadership, 1998. R. Cargill Hall and Jacob Neufeld, eds., The U.S. Air Force in Space, 1945 to the Twenty-first Century, 1998.

—R. Cargill Hall

SPANISH-AMERICAN WAR (1898). In 1895, the Cuban patriot José Martí renewed his homeland's attempt to achieve independence from Spain, triggering a guerrilla war that eventually brought about U.S. intervention. The Spanish government tried to suppress the insurgency, but the Cubans, led by Maximo Gomez and Antonio Maceo, managed to remain in the field. One Spanish general, Valeriano Weyler, adopted a policy of reconcentration of the civilian population in detention camps, but this measure backfired when it aroused international concern, notably in the United States. Presidents Grover Cleveland and William *McKinley both extended good offices to Spain, eventually urging a policy of home rule. This campaign proved successful. The Spanish premier Práxedes Sagasta granted a form of autonomy to Cuba and Puerto Rico beginning 1 January 1898, but the insurgents, sensing weakness, rejected it.

U.S. opinion gradually coalesced in favor of the insurgent cause, but only the mysterious sinking of the USS *Maine in Havana Harbor on 15 February 1898 led to vast popular support for armed intervention on behalf of the Cubans. McKinley proved reluctant to go to war. He attempted to obtain Cuban independence by diplomatic measures. The Spanish government balked. It recognized that the United States would most likely prevail in battle, but Sagasta and his colleagues, after unsuccessfully seeking assistance from other European powers, decided that failure to defend the Pearl of the Antilles might lead to revolution at home. An unsuccessful war appeared preferable to overthrow of the established order. On 25 April, the United States declared war, retroactive to 21 April.

Spain had a large army in Cuba and a strong garrison in its other insular possession, the Philippine Islands, but its navy was largely based in home ports. A weak squadron defended Manila. There were no significant naval forces in Cuban waters. In an attempt to retain its principal overseas colonies, Spain adopted a defensive strategy, depending on troops already in the field to fend off American attacks. The navy would reinforce and resupply threatened locations.

The United States fielded a small regular army of only 28,000 men, although it would eventually mobilize an impressive volunteer army to support the efforts of its modest but well-prepared navy. Prewar preparations envisioned a naval blockade of Cuba and command of the Caribbean Sea—an achievement that would permit land operations when the U.S. Army was sufficiently mobilized to take such action. A secondary naval campaign would take place in the western Pacific. The Asiatic Squadron would attack the Spanish Squadron at Manila to preclude commerce raiding and to exert maximum pressure on Spain.

On 21 April, Adm. William *Sampson took the North Atlantic Squadron to Havana and established a blockade, and on 1 May, Commodore George *Dewey smashed Adm. Patricio Montojo's squadron in Manila Bay. Sampson extended his blockade to other Cuban ports while awaiting the arrival of a Spanish squadron under Adm. Pascual Cervera. Dewey remained in Manila Bay, unable to take further action until land forces came to his assistance. Early in May, the McKinley administration decided to send troops under Gen. Wesley Merritt to seize Manila and to prepare for eventual land operations at Havana. The Eighth Army Corps assembled at San Francisco finally reached Manila.

Plans for operations in Cuba changed when Cervera's squadron, reduced to six vessels, arrived at Santiago de Cuba, only to be blockaded in port by 28 May. This event led McKinley to organize a force at Tampa composed mainly of regular army regiments. It was ordered to Santiago de Cuba to help destroy Cervera's squadron.

Gen. William Shafter hastily transferred the Fifth Army Corps, 17,000 men strong, to Santiago de Cuba, arriving there on 20 June. Admiral Sampson urged him to attack the batteries defending the entrance to the harbor. When these were reduced, he could sweep naval *mines from the channel and steam in to engage Cervera. Shafter had different ideas. He decided upon an interior line of operation, proceeding westward from a beachhead in the Daiquirí-Siboney area to Santiago de Cuba, depriving himself of much needed naval gunnery support. After landing virtually unopposed, the Fifth Corps moved toward the San Juan Heights, the principal bulwark in the first of three defensive lines around the city. Spanish artillery supported this position from a second line of defenses. The only opposition to the advance occurred at Las Guásimas, where a small skirmish gave the Fifth Corps its baptism of fire (24 June).

Shafter chose to form three divisions in line for the attack on the San Juan Heights, which would roll over the hills and move on to capture Santiago de Cuba. To protect his right flank, he asked Gen. Henry Lawton, commanding one of his divisions, to seize the Spanish fortifications at El Caney before moving into the line of battle at the heights. The Spanish commander, Gen. Arsenio Linares, played into Shafter's hands: he distributed his force of 10,000 at various points around the perimeter of Santiago de Cuba instead of concentrating at probable points of attack. Only 500 men defended the heights.

Shafter attacked on 1 July, but the engagement did not develop as expected. Lawton encountered difficulty from a garrison of a mere 500 Spaniards at El Caney. After considerable delay, Shafter decided to attack the heights without Lawton. After a difficult deployment under Spanish artillery fire, the dismounted cavalry division under Gen. Joseph Wheeler attacked up the northeastern extension of the heights, a rise known as Kettle Hill, and the infantry division to its left commanded by Gen. Jacob Kent assaulted the principal elevation to the southwest. Fortunately, a battery of *Gatling guns positioned at El Pozo about 600 yards to the rear was able to drive the Spanish defenders off the heights. Fifth Corps struggled into the Spanish positions and hastily entrenched. All thought of continuing on to Santiago de Cuba was forgotten. American *casualties for the day were 1,385, with 205 killed, about 10 percent of the troops engaged. The Spanish suffered less—593 casualties, with 215 killed, about 35 percent of some 1,700 troops in good defensive positions. Theodore *Roosevelt's ability to publicize his exploits as a commander of The First U.S. Volunteer Cavalry Regiment—the Rough Riders—during the Battle of *San Juan Hill helped propel him into the governorship of New York and later the vice presidency.

After the action of 1 July, Cervera received orders to leave Santiago de Cuba. On 3 July, the reluctant admiral complied. His six ships—four *cruisers and two destroyers—began their exit from the channel at 9:00 A.M. Sampson had left the blockade to meet Shafter, leaving Commodore William Schley as the senior officer present. The American vessels were able to concentrate their fire on each Spanish ship as it emerged from the channel. Only one, the Cristóbal Colón, managed to avoid immediate destruction or beaching. It fled for about seventy miles westward toward Cienfuegos, but the pursuing Americans finally obtained its range, and the Spanish commander drove his vessel onto the shore. After the war, a controversy erupted over credit for the victory between Schley and Sampson, dividing the officer corps for many years.

Shafter decided to besiege the city, a measure that forced its capitulation on 17 July. The Fifth Corps meanwhile fell victim to tropical *diseases. Early in August, it was evacuated to Long Island for recuperation and other troops arrived to continue the occupation.

The victory at Santiago de Cuba forced the Spanish government to inaugurate peace negotiations, but during this process, the army undertook two more campaigns. One was an expedition to Puerto Rico, led by the Commanding General of the Army, Gen. Nelson Miles, which landed on the south shore of the island and advanced against token opposition toward San Juan. The other was an attack on the city of Manila. The land operations of the Eighth Corps amounted to a sham battle because Admiral Dewey managed to arrange a Spanish capitulation that took place after a brief engagement satisfied Spanish honor. A third operation, a naval sortie into Spanish waters by a detachment of Sampson's fleet designated the Eastern Squadron, did not occur because Spain finally agreed to a protocol signed on 12 August that ended hostilities.

The protocol settled all major issues except the disposition of the Philippine Islands. Early in June, the United States signaled its war aims to Madrid through a third party. They included independence for Cuba, the cession of Puerto Rico in lieu of a monetary indemnity, the cession of a port in the Ladrones (Marianas), and a port in the Philippines. In the protocol, Spain agreed to the first three demands. A peace conference was arranged to confirm this agreement and to decide the disposition of the Philippines. McKinley eventually instructed the American peace commission to obtain the entire archipelago, responding both to a burst of annexationist sentiment and to the lack of a viable alternative. Spain reluctantly accepted a payment of $20,000,000. On 6 March 1899, the Senate gave its consent to the treaty, and on 19 March, the queen regent of Spain overrode opposition in the Cortes and agreed to ratification. Ratifications were exchanged on 11 April 1899.

The acquisition of the Philippines led to a long insurgency that was finally quelled by July 1902. McKinley and his successor, Theodore Roosevelt, were able to exert sufficient force to bring down the Filipino insurgents while overcoming an active but ultimately ineffective protest from anti-imperialists who offered constitutional, political, economic, and even racial arguments against annexation. The imperialist impulse proved short-lived. As early as 1916, Congress began preparations for Philippine independence, a process that was completed in 1946.

Although the United States triumphed during the Spanish-American War, inefficiency, waste, and even scandal characterized the army's *mobilization efforts, especially the supplying of troops. Widely investigated by the newspapers and the Dodge Commission, appointed by the McKinley administration, these problems prompted calls for a restructuring of the War Department and reconsideration of the relationship between the regular army and the National Guard. During the tenure of Secretary of War Elihu *Root, a series of reforms were implemented.

[See also Caribbean and Latin America, U.S. Military Involvement in the; Cuba, U.S. Military Involvement in; Militia and National Guard; Philippine War]

• Chadwick, French Ensor. The Relations of the United States and Spain: The Spanish-American War, 2 vols., 1911. Reprinted New York: Russell & Russell, 1968. May, Ernest R. Imperial Democracy: The Emergence of America as a Great Power, New York: Harcourt,

Brace, and World, 1961. Rickover, Hyman G. *How the Battleship Maine Was Destroyed*, 1976. Offner, John L. *An Unwanted War: The Diplomacy of the United States and Spain Over Cuba, 1895–1898*. Chapel Hill: University of North Carolina Press, 1992. Trask, David F. *The War with Spain in 1898*, N.Y.: Macmillan, 1981. Reprinted Lincoln: University of Nebraska Press, 1996. Cosmas, Graham A. *An Army for Empire: The United States Army and the Spanish-American War*, Columbia: University of Missouri Press, 1971. Reprinted College Station: Texas A & M University Press, 1998. Louis A. Pérez, Jr., *The War of 1898: The United States and Cuba in History and Historiography*, 1998.
—David F. Trask

SPARS. The Women's Reserve of the Coast Guard was created by an act of Congress signed into law on 23 November 1942. It was modeled on the one the U.S. Navy had created a few months earlier, with similar restrictions: women could not (a) serve in combat; (b) be stationed outside the continental United States; or (c) be given command authority over men.

Capt. Dorothy C. Stratton, former dean of women at Purdue University, served throughout the war as director of the Coast Guard Women's Reserve. She suggested that its official nickname—SPARS—be based on the Coast Guard motto: "*Semper paratus*—Always Ready."

During World War II, the SPARS recruited about 12,000 women, including 955 officers. SPARS and female civilian employees did most of the clerical work in the Coast Guard's Washington headquarters. Other specialties gradually were opened to enlisted SPARS, who eventually held forty-three ratings from boatswain's mate to yeoman. Twelve SPARS staffed the Chatham, Massachusetts, LORAN station, part of a highly secret electronic navigation system. In September 1944, Congress lifted the ban on stationing women outside the contiguous states; about 200 SPARS were sent to Alaska and 200 more to Hawaii.

SPARS enlisted for "duration plus six"—the length of the war plus six months. After the surrender of Japan in August 1945, the women's reserve branches of all the services were disbanded, though the label SPARS continued to be applied informally to female Coast Guardsmen. In 1956, twenty-one women were serving in the *Coast Guard Reserve. Though it continued to accept a few female recruits, the service made no further systematic effort to recruit women until the 1970s when women were admitted into all of the U.S. armed forces.

[*See also* Women in the Military.]

• U.S. Coast Guard Public Information Division, *The Coast Guard at War*, Vol. 22: *Women's Reserve*, 1946 (one of a series of unpublished monographs available through the Coast Guard Historian's Office, Washington, D.C.). Mary C. Lyne and Kay Arthur, *Three Years Behind the Mast: The Story of the United States Coast Guard SPARS*, n.d. Malcolm Willoughby, *The U.S. Coast Guard in World War II*, 1957. Jeanne Holm, *Women in the Military: An Unfinished Revolution*, 1992.
—John A. Tilley

SPECIAL FORCES. *See* Special Operations Forces.

SPECIAL OPERATIONS FORCES

SPECIAL OPERATIONS FORCES: OVERVIEW

Functionally, American special operations forces have existed since the seventeenth century, but they were only formally institutionalized in the late twentieth century. Habitually comprising a very small portion of the military services, these diverse units perform unusual tasks requiring extensive training and particular skills. The U.S. *Army has six types of special operations forces: Special Forces, Psychological Operations, Civil Affairs, Delta Force, Special Operations Aviation, and U.S. Army *Rangers. The Navy has the SEALs (Sea, Air, Land) and the air force has the Special Operations Wing. The Marine Corps has no such permanent forces but contained special operations units during World War II, and it periodically conducts training.

Special operations forces share some common characteristics. Unlike conventional combat units, these forces are not organized, equipped, or trained to conduct sustained combat. They depend on stealth, surprise, and speed to achieve their aims and usually operate deep within enemy held territory. In contrast, army psychological operations forces and civil affairs units are not combat units: they perform their missions from rear areas or in conjunction with combat units. Psychological operations units attempt to influence enemy attitudes and those of indigenous populations. Civil affairs units work with civilian governments and nonmilitary organizations to further the aims of American commanders.

Rangers were the first American special operations organization. Skilled woodsmen capable of Indian-style fighting, Rangers, as early as 1676, were employed in small groups to scout ahead of colonial militia and later British infantry forces. Robert Roger's Rangers were particularly useful in the *French and Indian War and Daniel *Morgan's Rangers during the *Revolutionary War conducted long-range raids and reconnaissance tasks. Similarly, John S. Mosby's Confederate partisans plagued Union forces from 1863 until the end of the *Civil War.

Despite proven utility, these kinds of American units were disbanded after each conflict, only to be recreated during the next one. American Rangers prized independence and individual initiative, bridled at parade ground obedience, and were thus often suspect to professional soldiers. Additionally, these units required a special style of commander and often held loyalties untransferrable to other leaders.

The cycle of wartime creation and peacetime disbandment was tempered after the *Korean War. Although Rangers were once again formed, employed, and disestablished, the army retained military government (now civil affairs) and psychological operations units after war's end. In 1952, the *guerrilla warfare support function was embodied in a new organization called Special Forces. The latter are mature soldiers, averaging thirty-two years of age and possessing ten years' military experience, who advise, train, assist, and sometimes lead indigenous irregulars against enemy forces. Special operations forces were rapidly expanded during the *Vietnam War, but were just as quickly reduced when American forces were withdrawn from Southeast Asia. President John F. *Kennedy had become an enthusiastic supporter of the army's Special Forces (called the "Green Berets" because of their distinctive headgear) and encouraged the other services to create companion elements. In the early 1960s, the navy established the SEALs and the air force organized the Air Commandos, later redesignated the Special Operations Wing. However, in the wake of America's disillusionment with that war, special operations forces were cut back far below pre-Vietnam levels. In 1978, Special Forces and the Special Operations Wing were at only 60 percent of their 1964 strengths.

Congressional legislation in the aftermath of the failed special operations attempt to rescue U.S. hostages in Iran in 1980 resulted in the reform and expansion of special operations forces. It also led to a wholly new four-star command, a Department of *Defense office to represent these forces, and a separate, enhanced budget. After more than three centuries, America's special operations forces achieved permanence.

• Frank R. Barnett, B. Hugh Tovar, and Richard H. Shultz, eds., *Special Operations in U.S. Strategy*, 1984. Ross S. Kelly, *Special Operations and National Purpose*, 1989. Lucien S. Vandenbroucke, *Perilous Options: Special Operations as an Instrument of U.S. Foreign Policy*, 1993. John M. Collins, *Special Operations Forces: An Assessment, 1986–1993*, 1994. Joel and J. R. Wright, *Special Men and Special Missions: Inside American Special Operations Forces, 1945 to the Present*, 1994. Susan L. Marquis, *Unconventional Warfare: Rebuilding the U.S. Special Operations Forces*, 1997.

—Rod Paschall

SPECIAL OPERATIONS FORCES: ARMY SPECIAL FORCES

Organized in 1952, the U.S. *Army's Special Forces, identified by their distinctive, world-famous green berets, perform guerrilla support, reconnaissance, raids, and other kinds of behind-the-lines missions that require experience, maturity, and special skills. Additionally, these forces are capable of training, advising, and assisting foreign military and paramilitary organizations in *counterinsurgency. The employment of a few Special Forces troopers has often provided U.S. decision makers a middle course between the use of American combat units or doing nothing militarily.

Conducting small-unit, clandestine operations deep in an opponent's territory has been a part of the American military tradition since the colonial era. During the *French and Indian War, Robert Rogers's "Rangers" staged effective frontier actions against Indians allied with the French. There were also Rangers in the *Revolutionary War and *Civil War. But it was not until World War II that an organized, behind-the-lines American military system was created and employed. This was mostly achieved by the uniformed arm of the Office of Strategic Services (OSS), operating under the direction of the *Joint Chiefs of Staff. In the Southwest Pacific area, Gen. Douglas MacArthur encouraged highly effective Filipino guerrilla support operations without OSS aid. Elsewhere, from 1942 until 1945, OSS led, advised, or supported partisan operations in Burma, China, France, Italy, and Yugoslavia. OSS was dissolved after the war, although some of its activities and personnel were carried over to the *Central Intelligence Agency.

During the *Korean War, an ad hoc Eighth U.S. Army organization recruited, organized, and employed the more than 22,000 Korean partisans who fought the Communists in North Korea. But in 1952, the first contingent from the newly formed Special Forces began arriving in Korea. Not long after the conflict had begun, the 10th Special Forces Group, an organization created to support guerrilla warfare in Soviet bloc countries in the event of another European war, had been formed. In 1953, the 77th (later redesignated the 7th Group) had been activated at Fort Bragg, North Carolina. Soon thereafter, the 1st Special Forces Group was deployed to a Pacific Ocean base, the island of Okinawa.

Under President John F. *Kennedy, Army Special Forces attained its greatest notoriety. Seeking an unobtrusive, less costly means of battling Communist-inspired *guerrilla warfare in the Third World, Kennedy settled on Special Forces. By 1963, the newly formed 8th Special Forces Group was assisting Latin American governments in five separate counterinsurgency campaigns; the 5th Special Forces Group was performing the same task in Vietnam; and the 3rd and 6th Special Forces Groups were being organized for Middle East and African contingencies. Kennedy had overruled the army's hierarchy, which was suspicious of this special elite force, and granted the wearing of the green beret at the request of the Special Forces commander, Brig. Gen. William P. Yarborough. Although Special Forces organization was reduced after the *Vietnam War, it recovered much of its former strength during the 1980s and performed liaison, rescue, and reconnaissance tasks during the 1991 *Persian Gulf War.

The popularity of Special Forces among recent U.S. decision makers is due to their maturity, secretiveness, and ability to achieve substantial aims with small numbers. Special Forces recruits chiefly noncommissioned officers. The average age of troopers is 32—ten years older than the average army infantryman or Marine. Troopers therefore have already had considerable experience, extensive training, the ability to teach, and are likely to command more respect than would a younger, less experienced soldier. Additionally, Special Forces troopers are parachutists; they are also required to speak at least one foreign language.

Special Forces units traditionally shun publicity in their missions. They have often worked abroad in civilian clothes. Using a low-visibility approach, they allow indigenous forces to take credit for achievements. Typically, the unit that Special Forces employs on an independent mission is the twelve-man "A" Detachment, composed of a captain, a warrant officer, and ten noncommissioned officers. The members of this small contingent possess highly developed communications, medical, engineering, weapons, and intelligence skills. A full-strength Special Forces Group contains fifty-four "A" detachments.

The most important advantage offered by Special Forces is the ability of the "A" detachment to extend its influence far beyond its small numbers. Each of these units can train, assist, or if need be lead an indigenous unit of 300–500 members. It is this "force multiplier" effect that has attracted U.S. policy makers. By employing Special Forces units, an American ally may solve its own military problems with minimal use of U.S. manpower and resources.

• Charles M. Simpson III, *Inside the Green Berets: The First Thirty Years*, 1983. Shelby L. Stanton, *Green Berets at War: U.S. Army Special Forces in Southeast Asia, 1956–1975*, 1985. Aaron Bank, *From OSS to Green Berets*, 1986. Terry White, *Swords of Lightning: Special Forces and the Changing Face of Warfare*, 1992. Greg Walker, *At the Hurricane's Eye: U.S. Special Forces from Vietnam to Desert Storm*, 1994. Ed Evanhoe, *Dark Moon: Eighth Army Special Operations in the Korean War*, 1995.

—Rod Paschall

SPECIAL OPERATIONS FORCES: NAVY SEALS

Youngest of the American special operations forces, U.S. *Navy Sea-Air-Land (SEAL) teams, SEAL Vehicle Delivery teams, Special Boat Squadrons, and Light Attack Helicopter Squadrons perform a wide variety of maritime, shoreline, and riverine special operations. The nautical arm of U.S. Special Operations Forces has experienced growth, often over the objections of traditionalist senior naval leadership. In a short time, naval special operations units have developed a distinct culture.

In December 1962, at the insistence of President John F. *Kennedy's secretary of defense, Robert S. *McNamara, the navy initiated its special operations forces with the primary aim of accomplishing "limited counterinsurgency civic action tasks incidental to counterguerilla operations." Additional goals were to conduct shallow-water and riverine boat operations and to "organize, train, assist and advise friendly military or paramilitary forces." The central focus of this development was the growing American involvement in Southeast Asia. The first naval special operations force was a SEAL team: an organization of ten 16-man platoons, each composed of two officers and ten enlisted men. As parachute-qualified underwater swimmers, the SEALs quickly found themselves employed along the littoral and riverine sections of the Republic of Vietnam.

Navy special operations forces have always pushed the outer limits of technology. SEAL teams have been equipped with steadily improving bubbleless, closed-circuit breathing equipment and underwater communications devices and weapons. During the late 1960s and early 1970s, SEALs were joined by SEAL Delivery Vehicle teams and Special Boat Squadrons. The delivery teams are equipped with free-flooding mini-*submarines that can carry six SEALs and are themselves launched from a submerged submarine. They are capable of transporting their passengers into an enemy harbor for sabotage missions. The Special Boat Squadrons possess a mix of fast surface craft, inflatable boats, and pump jet propulsion craft capable of rapid movement in shallow water. In the 1980s, small helicopter gunships and transport units were added.

Naval special warfare units experienced some reduction in strength in the post-Vietnam era, but during the 1980s these forces were substantially enhanced, and they gained their own senior command. In April 1987, the Naval Special Warfare Command, headed by an admiral, was established with the mission to "organize, equip, train, and provide naval Special Operations Forces that specialize in maritime and riverine operations." SEAL strength grew from twenty platoons in 1981 to sixty in 1993.

U.S. naval special operations forces experienced hard luck during the 1980s in combat operations. At the outset of the 1983 U.S. intervention in *Grenada, four SEALs lost their lives in an attempted air-sea rendezvous with a U.S. naval combatant in heavy seas. However, in a successful operation six years later during Operation Just Cause in Panama, five SEAL platoons under Cmdr. Tom McGrath denied the Panamanian defense forces use of their own patrol craft, isolated some of these forces on an island, and prevented the Panamanian leader, Manuel *Noriega, from using his personal jet at Paitilla Airport.

• Darryl Young, *The Element of Surprise: Navy Seals in Vietnam*, 1990. Richard Marcinko, *Rogue Warrior*, 1992. Bill Fawcett, *Hunters and Shooters: An Oral History of the U.S. Navy SEALs in Vietnam*, 1995. James Watson, *Walking Point: The Experiences of a Founding Member of the Elite Navy Seals*, 1997.

—Rod Paschall

SPECIAL OPERATIONS FORCES: MARINE SPECIAL UNITS

In World War II, the Marine Corps formed a number of special units, only two of which remained in combat until the end of the war. These were the "war dogs" and "rocket platoons," both of which saw action on Okinawa, the final major campaign of the Pacific War. The other disparate organizations were the defense, Raider, and parachute battalions, and the glider and barrage balloon squadrons. Of these, two obtained lasting fame—the parachute and Raider units.

Marine parachutists, or Paramarines, began training in the fall of 1940. The 1st Parachute Battalion came into being on 15 August 1941; the 2nd Parachute Battalion became active 2 September. They were used as infantry in the Solomon Islands campaign because the Corps did not have an adequate lift capability to use them as parachutists. The parachute program was formally disbanded on 29 February 1944, and its Marines were reassigned primarily to the newly organized Fifth Marine Division.

Several Marine Raider battalions formed in the war from volunteers met the apparent need for specially trained commando units that would conduct hit-and-turn raids on Japanese-controlled islands of the Pacific and keep the Japanese off balance. Raider training began 6 January 1942, when the 1st Battalion, Fifth Marines, an infantry unit commanded by Lt. Col. Merritt A. Edson, was redesignated the 1st Separate Infantry Battalion, and then the 1st Raider Battalion on 16 February. Before the war, Edson's reputation had been established by his antibanditry exploits in the early 1930s. On the West Coast, on 4 February 1942, the 2nd Separate Battalion was activated under command of Lt. Col. Evans F. Carlson. It became the 2nd Raider Battalion on 19 February. Carlson had been an observer in China with Mao Zedong's Eighth Route Army during the Sino-Japanese War. Carlson's executive officer was Capt. James Roosevelt, son of President Franklin D. *Roosevelt.

The 1st Raiders joined the 1st Marine Division in the Battle of *Guadalcanal on 31 August 1942. The Raiders suffered heavy losses in the Battle of Bloody (or Edson's) Ridge and were no longer an effective unit when they were withdrawn from the island on 17 October. Carlson's 2nd Raider Battalion went to Hawaii for training in landing from *submarines and rubber boat handling. Two companies reinforced the garrison at Midway in the successful repulse of the Japanese attack in early June 1942.

On 8 August 1942, the 2nd Battalion boarded submarines and set out for the Gilberts for a raid on Makin Island on the 17th. The greatest asset of the raid was its effect on home front morale. Carlson's battalion then moved to Guadalcanal, landing there in early November to begin a 20-day combat patrol, fighting more than a dozen actions and killing nearly 500 Japanese soldiers. In September, a 3rd Raider Battalion was formed in Samoa; and a 4th Battalion was formed on the West Coast that October. Eventually, two Raider regiments were formed. The 1st took part in the capture of the Russell Islands and later participated in the New Georgia operation. The 2nd Raider Regiment (Provisional) reinforced the Third Marine Division in its assault of Bougainville in November. As with the parachute units, Raider regiments siphoned off manpower needed elsewhere; they proved to be a luxury the Marine Corps could not afford. The Raiders also were too small in organization, too lightly armed, and too specialized in their tables of organization and equipment. Unlike the parachutists, they did conduct at least one operation of a type for which they had been trained—the raid on Makin. In early 1944, the Raider organizations were disbanded and redesignated as components of the new Fourth Marines.

The Marine Corps established no lasting special units in the post-World War II period, during the *Korean War, or during the *Vietnam War, except for reconnaissance companies and battalions that were organic to larger organizations. In 1985, the Marine Amphibious/Expeditionary Units (MAU/MEU) assigned to the navy's afloat amphibious ready groups were trained for "special operations capabilities." The tasks assigned to these units centered on the security requirements following a decade of low intensity conflicts instead of war, and they trained for such assignments as raids, hostage recovery, evacuation of civilians from areas of conflict, and humanitarian efforts. The Marine Corps also established surveillance-reconnaissance-intelligence groups (SRIG) that combined various units with like missions. The SRIG also operated the surveillance and reconnaissance centers that coordinated the similar assignments during the *Persian Gulf War, *in Somalia, *Haiti, and in *Panama during Operation Just Cause.

• Frank O. Hough, Verle E. Ludwig, and Henry I. Shaw, Jr., *Pearl Harbor to Guadalcanal*, Vol. I: *History of U.S. Marine Corps Operations in World War II*, 1958. Henry I. Shaw, Jr., and Douglas T. Kane, *Isolation of Rabaul*, Vol. II: *History of U.S. Marine Corps Operations in World War II*, 1963; Benis M. Frank and Henry I. Shaw, Jr., *Victory and Occupation*, Vol. V: *History of U.S. Marine Corps Operations in World War II*, 1969. Charles L. Updegraph, Jr., *United States Special Marine Corps Units in World War II*, 1972. Jon T. Hoffman, *From Makin to Bougainville: Marine Raiders in the Pacific War*, 1995.   —Benis M. Frank

SPECIAL OPERATIONS FORCES:
AIR FORCE SPECIAL FORCES

The U.S. *Air Force's involvement in unconventional warfare has been episodic, and special operations aviators have operated on the fringes of air force organization and culture.

During World War II, the Army Air Forces organized the 1st Air Commando Group in early 1944 to support Allied irregular operations in North Burma against the Imperial Japanese Army. The "air commandos"—named after Lord Mountbatten's British Commandos—used C-47s and gliders to transport the troops and P-51s to fly close air support. They also pioneered in rescuing downed pilots and waging psychological warfare. Flamboyant and unconventional, air commandos adopted the motto, "Any Place, Any Time, Any Where." Other U.S. airmen in Europe supported Allied unconventional warfare operations by the Office of Strategic Services (OSS) and the British Special Operations Executive, such as the 60th Troop Carrier Group that operated in the Balkans in 1943–44.

After 1945, the air force eliminated the air commandos, but they lived on in the public's imagination through Milton Caniff's popular comic strip, "Terry and the Pirates." In 1951, the U.S. Air Force organized three "air resupply and communications" wings that supported U.S.–South Korean partisan operations in Korea, Chinese Nationalist

forces against the Chinese Communists, and the French against the Viet Minh in Indochina. But these units fell victim to air force reorganization in 1953.

The air force entered the *counterinsurgency field in 1961, when it organized the 4400th Combat Crew Training Squadron ("Jungle Jim," renamed 1st Air Commando Squadron in 1963), and deployed a detachment ("Farm Gate") to South Vietnam. In 1962, the Special Air Warfare School (later Special Operations School) opened at Hurlburt Field, Florida.

Air force special operations forces grew rapidly in Southeast Asia, while the *Central Intelligence Agency created "Air America," a similar civilian organization that specialized in aerial resupply of irregular forces and rescue of downed American airmen. In 1965, air commandos began using unusual aerial gunships: AC-47s, AC-119s, and later AC-130s (nicknamed "Spooky," "Spectre," or "Puff the Magic Dragon"), armed with rapid-firing mini-guns and even side-firing 105mm cannon. Air commandos supported other special operations forces and conducted search and rescue, reconnaissance, direct action, and psychological operations. At the height of the *Vietnam War, the air force had in the region 4 special operations wings (as they were renamed in 1968) with 500 aircraft. By then, more modern A-37s and AC-130s had replaced the venerable A-1s, B-26s, T-28s, and AC-47s. Five air crew received the Medal of Honor as air commandos.

After the Vietnam War, the air force dismantled most of its special operations formations and reduced the 1st Special Operations Wing to twenty aircraft. But the air force once again rebuilt its capabilities after 1980 under the 23rd Air Force, procuring the MH-53J Pave Low helicopter and other sophisticated equipment. A new generation of air commandos played important roles in Grenada, Panama, the "War on Drugs," and undeclared wars in Central America. In 1990, the 23rd Air Force became Air Force Special Operations Command, a component of U.S. Special Operations Command. In 1991, during the *Persian Gulf War, 1st Special Operations Wing pilots of *helicopters led the first strike against Iraqi *radar sites and hunted mobile missile launchers. Since then, air force special operations forces have seen extensive service in various post–*Cold War military operations.

• R. D. Van Wagner, *1st Air Commando Group*, 1986. Philip D. Chinnery, *Any Time, Any Place: Fifty Years of the USAF Air Commando and Special Operations Forces, 1944–1994*, 1994. Orr Kelly, *From a Dark Sky: The Story of U.S. Air Force Special Operations*, 1996.
                                          —James C. McNaughton

SPOTSYLVANIA, BATTLE OF. *See* Wilderness to Petersburg Campaign (1864).

THE SPRINGFIELD MODEL 1903 rifle was developed at the Springfield National Armory in Massachusetts between 1900 and 1903 in order to provide a magazine-loaded, bolt action rifle more robust than the U.S. *Army's previous standard infantry rifle, the Danish-made Krag-Jorgenson, adopted in 1892. Based on the German Mannlicher system, the Springfield used a five-round clip instead of the single-round clip used by the Krag. The weapon weighed 9 lbs., 8 oz., and fired 220-grain round propelled by 43.3 grains of smokeless powder. An 18-inch knife bayonet was added to the weaponry in 1905. The "Springfield '03," as it was called, saw favorable service through World War I. However, the American Expeditionary Forces (AEF) made only limited use of the 1903 rifle because the British 1917 Enfield was already in wartime mass production and was adopted as the M-1917 for the American army. In 1936, the Model 1903 rifle was replaced by the M-1 gas-operated, semi-automatic Garand rifle as the standard infantry weapon. The Model 1903 continued to be used, however, as a limited standard weapon, particularly as a sniper rifle and a grenade launcher. The "Springfield '03" ultimately was made by a variety of manufacturers and had a reputation as one of the most accurate military rifles ever produced.

[*See also* M-1 Rifle; Weaponry, Army.]

• James E. Hicks, *U.S. Firearms, 1776–1956,* 1957.

—Stephen J. Allie

SPRUANCE, RAYMOND A. (1886–1969), World War II U.S. *Navy admiral. Born in Baltimore, Maryland, the son of a reclusive father, Raymond was reared by his mother and three spinster aunts; he showed an early talent for writing poetry. The shy young man graduated from the U.S. Naval Academy in 1907, and first sailed around the world with the "Great White Fleet," returning to study electrical engineering at the General Electric Company in 1909. His first command at sea was the Philippines-based destroyer *Bainbridge* in 1913. Promoted to lieutenant commander in August 1917, Spruance never saw action during World War I.

Regarded as a superb ship handler, Spruance advanced between the wars, rising to the rank of rear admiral in 1940 after commanding a battleship. Taking command of Cruiser Division Five at Pearl Harbor in September 1941, he served as the surface screen commander for Adm. William F. *Halsey during the early months of the war. When his friend Halsey was temporarily ill, Spruance took command of the American carrier force that fought and won the most crucial and decisive naval engagement of World War II: the June 1942 Battle of *Midway.

Afterward, Spruance served as chief of staff to Adm. Chester *Nimitz in Pearl Harbor, but he returned to battle in 1943 commanding the Fifth Fleet. His command of this force during the Battle of the *Philippine Sea in 1944 attracted some criticism because the Japanese fleet escaped. However, it was during this battle that Japan lost the bulk of its remaining naval airpower, and Spruance's primary mission was to protect the transports carrying the troops to invade Saipan. After the war, he served as the president of the Naval War College until his retirement. Called out of retirement, Spruance served as the U.S. ambassador to the Philippines (1952–55) before retiring once again. Spruance's near-flawless performance of command during two critical battles in World War II marked him as one of the U.S. Navy's great commanders.

• Emmet P. Forrestel, *Admiral Raymond A. Spruance, USN: A Study in Command,* 1966. Thomas B. Buell, *The Quiet Warrior: A Biography of Admiral Raymond A. Spruance,* 1974.

—Rod Paschall

STALIN, JOSEF (1879–1953), Communist leader of the Soviet Union for a quarter of a century, including World War II and the formative years of the Cold War. *Stalin,* the pseudonym adopted by a young underground revolutionary and former Orthodox seminary student in Czarist Russia, means "man of steel." This quality indeed marked the career of Josef Vissarionovich Djugashvili, who was born in obscurity in Russian Georgia in December 1879 and died a feared autocrat and world leader in March 1953.

Stalin rose within Lenin's Bolshevik faction of the Russian Communist Party from 1898 through the Russian Revolution in 1917 and beyond. Following Lenin's death, he outmaneuvered Trotsky and other rivals and by 1929 became the sole leader of the ruling Communist Party of the Soviet Union. A shrewd and ruthless political infighter, he built a tyrannical but powerful totalitarian state. Millions were "liquidated" in massive "purges." In international affairs, although Stalin's outlook was shaped by belief in a historically destined global victory for communism, he was also a realist and pragmatist.

When World War II came to the USSR in 1941, despite Stalin's political machinations to avoid German invasion (including the Nazi-Soviet Pact of August 1939), the Soviet Union was ill-prepared. Stalin, who had become prime minister as well as chief of the ruling party, also became commander in chief of the armed forces. For many Russians, he symbolized successful determination to win the war. The Soviet Union entered a grand alliance with Great Britain and the United States against the Axis powers (although against Japan only in the final weeks of the war). Stalin concentrated on winning the war, but not at the expense of constant calculation of how to enhance the international role and power of the Soviet Union in the postwar world. He dealt shrewdly with Western leaders, including Winston S. *Churchill of Great Britain and Presidents Franklin D. *Roosevelt at the *Yalta Conference and Harry S. *Truman at Potsdam. Despite *victory and the founding of the *United Nations, the very success of the wartime coalition ended the common interest that had brought the USSR and the Western democracies together. The end of World War II thus quickly led to the emergence of a new so-called Cold War, dividing the former Allies.

Stalin's ideological predispositions, reinforced by personal suspiciousness, if not paranoia, led him to pursue an aggressive postwar course in foreign relations that constituted a central element in the unleashing of the Cold War. His reliance on a personal dictatorship within his own Communist Party, and a totalitarian state structure within the Soviet Union, required severe limitations on contact with the outside world. It also contributed to a conduct of relations with other states that soon resulted in the sharp drawing of lines between the bloc he controlled and the outside world.

Stalin sought to expand Communist rule, Soviet influence, and his own control in those places and under circumstances where it was possible. Unlike Adolf *Hitler, however, he was not driven to advance where it was inexpedient, much less to court or initiate war. This was true even the most apparent exception—the *Korean War. Archival documents released in the 1990s showed that the principal impetus for a North Korean military attack on South Korea came from Kim Il Sung, although Stalin (and Chinese leader Mao Zedong) were led to approve and provide support for the attack and thus bear responsibility. Initially, however, Stalin refused to approve Kim's plans, and did so only when he mistakenly concluded that the United States would not intervene. The Korean attack was neither Stalin's test of Western resolve nor precursor to a possible Soviet attack in Western Europe, as was widely feared at the time.

In his last years, Stalin's paranoia grew, and he was about to launch a new purge of his henchmen when he suffered a stroke and died. Ironically, he had imagined or invented a plot by Kremlin doctors against Soviet leaders and removed long-trusted doctors, aides, and guards; some of his threatened surviving entourage may then have hastened his death by denying medical assistance. In any event, succeeding leaders soon stopped virtually any mention of his name, a striking contrast to the ubiquitous glorification of Stalin that had emerged after the war. By 1956, his successor, Nikita Khrushchev, not only condemned "the cult of the individual" that had been built up by Stalin, but in a secret speech denounced his crimes against the people and the party. The lot of the people, while still subordinated to the interests of the state, improved. Stalin's successors also moved to reduce frictions with the rest of the world.

Thus, after Stalin's death, a general lessening of tension ensued. The Cold War, however, continued with varying intensity for another thirty-six years, until a Soviet leader—Mikhail Gorbachev—came to power prepared to discard the "Stalinist" world view and so end the division of Europe and the world.

[See also Cold War: External Course; Cold War: Changing Interpretations.]

• Adam B. Ulam, *Stalin: The Man and His Era,* 1973. Robert C. Tucker, *Stalin in Power,* 1990. Dmitri Volkogonov, *Stalin: Triumph and Tragedy,* 1991.
—Raymond L. Garthoff

STANTON, EDWIN M. (1814–69), secretary of war under President Abraham *Lincoln, was born in Steubenville, Ohio, 19 December 1814. Admitted to the bar in 1836, Stanton made a quick reputation for brilliance. Moving to Pittsburgh in 1847, he won national attention by representing Pennsylvania before the Supreme Court in an interstate commerce suit. A growing Supreme Court practice took him to Washington, D. C. in 1857.

In 1858, Stanton exposed a conspiracy to defraud the government of some $150 million worth of land in California. This catapulted him into the office of U.S. Attorney General when President James Buchanan reorganized his cabinet in December 1860. Democrat Stanton opposed slavery and supported the Wilmot Proviso, but accepted the Dred Scott decision. He tried to strengthen Buchanan's policy against secession and to reinforce Fort Sumter.

Stanton returned to private life when Buchanan's term ended. He distrusted Lincoln and befriended Gen. George B. *McClellan when he took charge of army operations and openly derided Lincoln and his administration. Nevertheless, Lincoln invited him to replace Simon Cameron as Secretary of War in January 1862. Inheriting an administrative shambles, Stanton soon restored honesty and order.

Brusque and intemperate with people, rigid and vigorous in pursuit of victory, Stanton made few friends in his department or the cabinet, but he and the president gradually forged mutual admiration. Lincoln trusted Stanton's judgment and came to rely heavily on his advice. An active war secretary, Stanton lost faith in McClellan. In September 1863, Stanton's dispatch of 23,000 men from east to west in less than seven days to reinforce Gen. William S.

*Rosecrans ranks as a logistical marvel. An early admirer of Gen. Ulysses S. *Grant, he pushed his advancement, and enthusiastically approved his appointment as general-in-chief of the Union armies in 1864.

Meddling in civil affairs, Stanton censored newspapers and had citizens arrested for suspicion of disloyalty. Although Stanton and Grant got along well, the general disliked the secretary's abrupt and severe rebuke of Gen. William Tecumseh *Sherman for his proposed surrender terms to Gen. Joseph E. *Johnston.

Lincoln's assassination released a fanatical streak in Stanton, who pushed the execution of Mrs. Mary Surratt and tried to implicate Jefferson *Davis in the assassination plot. President Andrew *Johnson kept Stanton at his post—an error he soon regretted. Although Stanton did a masterful job in demobilizing the Union armies, he joined the Republican Radicals against presidential reconstruction policies. He did, however, oppose the *Tenure of Office Act (aimed at keeping him in office).

When Johnson asked for his resignation in August 1867, the secretary refused to leave office until Congress reconvened in December (he argued that since the Tenure of Office Act had been passed over Johnson's veto, it was law). Johnson suspended him but was overridden by the Senate in January 1868. The president dismissed Stanton in February 1868, but Stanton held on and even ordered the arrest of Adjutant-General Lorenzo Thomas, whom Johnson had named as secretary ad interim. Stanton resigned when Johnson's impeachment failed. Appointed by President Grant to the Supreme Court, Stanton died on December 24, 1869, four days after his confirmation.

• Frank A. Flower, *Edwin McMasters Stanton: The Autocrat of Rebellion, Emancipation, and Reconstruction,* 1905. Benjamin P. Thomas and Harold M. Hyman, *Stanton: The Life and Times of Lincoln's Secretary of War,* 1962.
—Frank E. Vandiver

START. In 1982, under the administration of President Ronald *Reagan, a new series of negotiations, the Strategic Arms Reduction Talks (START), succeeded the negotiations that had led to the *SALT Treaties of the 1970s. In July 1991, the START I Treaty was signed in Moscow by President George *Bush and Soviet president Mikhail Gorbachev. In January 1993, the START II Treaty was also signed in Moscow, by Bush and Russian president Boris Yeltsin. Both treaties involved substantial reductions; even so, START I brought the level of strategic warheads down only to about the level prevailing when SALT II was signed, and START II would bring it down to the level when SALT I was signed.

The START I Treaty, signed just months before the dissolution of the Soviet Union, could only be ratified by Russia and the United States after agreements were reached with Ukraine and Belarus, also successors to the Soviet Union, that those states would relinquish Soviet strategic nuclear arms on their territory and commit themselves to join the Treaty on the *Nonproliferation of Nuclear Weapons as nonnuclear weapons states. The START I Treaty then went into effect in December 1994. Under this treaty, the United States reduced its ballistic missile warheads by about one-third, and Russia by about one-half, to totals (not specified) of about 8,000–10,000 for each side.

The START II Treaty is more ambitious, not only providing for considerably deeper reductions but also for the elimination of all MIRV warheads on land-based intercontinental ballistic *missiles (ICBMs). Overall, each side would be limited to no more than 3,500 strategic warheads. Bomber *nuclear weapons are also counted on a more realistic basis, and hence its warhead levels were real rather than nominal.

At present, the START II Treaty has yet to be ratified by Russia, not so much owing to its terms (although some Russians object to the need to scrap all existing land-based MIRV missile systems due to uncertainties with respect to continued U.S. observance of the ABM Treaty and a general deterioration of U.S.-Russian relations). In addition, the START I reductions, and still more the prospective additional large START II reductions in Russian ICBM systems, pose a heavy burden in dismantling and destroying such systems under START procedures intended to assure verification.

Further reductions in Russian strategic forces, and to a much lesser extent U.S. systems, will proceed even without ratification of START II, given the inevitable obsolescence and the lack of ready replacements. But the elimination of land-based MIRV systems, especially in Russia, and the large reduction in submarine-launched ballistic missiles (SLBMs), especially in the United States, will not take place for some years unless START II is ratified or until there is at least tacit agreement to proceed as though it had been ratified (as occurred with the SALT II Treaty).

[See also Arms Control and Disarmament; Arms Race: Nuclear Arms Race; INF Treaty.]

• Kerry M. Kartchner, *Negotiating START: Strategic Arms Reduction Talks and the Quest for Strategic Stability,* 1992.

—Raymond L. Garthoff

STAR WARS. *See* Strategic Defense Initiative.

STATE, THE. The American concepts of state and state power have since colonial times been shaped by national security interests and by experience in the management and use of the American military. Insofar as a sovereign state holds a monopoly on the legitimate use of violence, state power must be defined with reference to the raising and employment of armed forces. The logic is Hobbesian. The state provides order; the alternative is anarchy and a life both "brutish and short." Given this choice, the citizen opts for order and accepts the rule of Hobbes's Leviathan— the state.

Historical development has distanced the American state from this view but never quite overcome it. The nation's founding myth—that a dispute with the crown over contractual rights and responsibilities caused the Revolution—follows John Locke's contrary postulate that the social contract grants limited power to the state. The Constitution itself confirmed the relevance of Locke's version of the contract metaphor to the U.S. government and its constitution.

The Internal Security Dilemma and the Nineteenth-Century American State. This conception of limited state power poses special problems with respect to national security. National security becomes a vital issue when survival of the state is threatened; then the Hobbesian (or realpolitik) understanding of the state and state power clashes with the Lockean (or liberal) conception. This clash creates what can be called the "internal security dilemma." In the realpolitik view, the state cannot provide the blessings of liberty unless it can assure its own survival. In the liberal view, the powers of the state must be so disposed as to protect citizens. Hence the dilemma: The state must somehow cope with threats to itself while maintaining the liberties and rights of citizens.

From the end of the *War of 1812 to the close of the nineteenth century, state survival was not a question of external threat. Survival emerged as a serious sectional issue, which the *Civil War settled; otherwise, policies and disputes associated with the security of the American state centered on providing the United States with strategic space. By denying the western hemisphere to rival powers, the *Monroe Doctrine (declared in 1823 but an unfinished project until the twentieth century) laid claim to an enormous strategic space for the United States. The quarrel with Britain over the Oregon Country, settled diplomatically in 1846, and the disputes with Mexico that led to the *Mexican War in that same year, actualized American state claims to territory on the basis of strategic considerations no less than by invoking "manifest destiny." The Civil War, however, definitively established the nineteenth-century American understanding of the state's power to ensure its survival, as the federal government held a continent-wide country-qua-empire together by force of arms. The scale and violence of the Civil War tested the limits of war itself, while its political stresses took a heavy toll on civil liberties—the federal courts proving particularly ineffective guardians against martial law's encroachments on freedom of speech and assembly.

The exercise of political opposition and the employment of military force furnish two major reference points for defining the state. Democracy requires the possibility of legitimate opposition to government, while nation-states under threat to their survival or security, and states that vastly expand their military activity, usually give priority to security considerations and seek to limit political partisanship. Such tensions were particularly evident in the early- and mid-nineteenth-century United States, where army officers, and to a lesser extent navy officers, often cultivated political connections and acted as partisan figures. In 1846, for example, the Senate rejected President James K. *Polk's attempt to appoint Senator Thomas Hart Benton, a civilian with no military experience and a fellow Democrat, as the top general commanding the campaigns against Mexico. Polk had to content himself with two Whig generals, Zachary *Taylor and Winfield *Scott, both aspirants to their party's presidential nomination in 1848, as leading officers in the campaigns. In 1864, Gen. George B. *McClellan, once Abraham *Lincoln's general in chief, ran against Lincoln as Democratic nominee for the presidency. For his own part, Lincoln did not hesitate to appoint brigadier generals and allot military contracts as a means of cultivating local interests and winning their political support.

Partisanship and "pork" persisted after the Civil War, but preferment gradually diminished. The army, deployed in the West during the *Plains Indians Wars, became more isolated from American society and thus susceptible to reforms, adopted after the *Spanish-American War, that made it more professional and less political. Up to that point, however, political considerations generally tended to place American state power—and the services of the U.S. Army—at the disposal of local interests. This was largely true in the Mexican War and in westward expansion. In the

Spanish-American War, the Cuban campaign was essentially a projection of land power partly in response to the demands of Cuban exiles in New York and Florida.

The army reforms of 1899–1904, largely under Secretary of War Elihu *Root, reinforced civilian authority over the army, with a chief of staff, the army's leader-manager, answering to the president as *commander in chief, and depending upon the civilian secretary of war to be effective in his own job. This structure reduced the autonomy of the army bureaus and weakened their links to congressional interests, while centralizing authority in such a way as to strengthen professionalism. Despite a certain amount of resistance at the top, officers tended to embrace the new managerial ideals, which facilitated the planning and coordination fundamental to modern warfare, and thus rejected older, populist views of military leadership, which stressed romantic, intuitive qualities and fostered partisan political activity. The navy followed suit, achieving its reforms by more informal means.

Professionalism has usually advanced at the expense of local politics in the American military establishment and has strengthened civilian leadership based on the power and authority of the president as commander in chief. Significant advances occurred during the first two decades of the twentieth century, although localism remained evident at the end of the century when post–*Cold War budget cutbacks led to military base closings that were opposed by local interests.

During the twentieth century, American armed forces took part in four major wars—World War I, World War II, the *Korean War, and the *Vietnam War—and several minor conflicts, the largest of which was the *Persian Gulf War. None of these five occurred in the western hemisphere: two took place in Europe, two in Asia, and one in the Middle East. Local interests played either a negligible role or no role at all in any of them. Military power was associated with "high politics," a phrase commonly used during the Cold War to refer to the way Congress and the executive branch handled *national security in the nuclear age—in particular, the way Congress deferred to the president—and the way the public rallied to support state power in times of crisis.

When the United States entered World War I, President Woodrow *Wilson chose a professional officer to command the American Expeditionary Forces. Though Gen. John J. *Pershing was son-in-law to a senior Republican senator, he avoided partisan politics, and after the war, he scotched a movement to run him for president on the Republican ticket.

During World War II, President Franklin D. *Roosevelt minimized political controversy about the conduct and purpose of the war effort by two means. One was to promote bipartisanship; the other, to delay the resolution of contentious issues about war aims until the return of peace. The first he accomplished by bringing two prominent Republicans into his wartime cabinet (Henry L. *Stimson as secretary of war and Frank Knox as secretary of the navy) and appointing other Republicans to administer war agencies. The second he accomplished by declaring, as he did at the Casablanca Conference in 1942, that unconditional surrender was the Allied military objective of the war.

But important issues about the employment of the armed forces as the principal instruments of state power in war remained. One had to do with strategic priorities. Roosevelt adopted the army's favored strategy of defeating Germany first (before Japan). Command links to the European theater from Roosevelt through Army Chief of Staff George C. *Marshall to Gen. Dwight D. *Eisenhower in Europe worked nearly perfectly. No field commander in American history caused his commander in chief less trouble or delivered more results than did Eisenhower. Although Japan surrendered sooner than expected, the Pacific War was a different matter, for Asia's lower priority left two military scores to be settled after 1945—one with the navy and one with Gen. Douglas *MacArthur. Both had important consequences for the state and its control over the armed forces.

The navy's priority lay in the Pacific theater, where it could demonstrate its seaborne striking power. Only after the defeat of Germany did it gain first priority, and then the Pacific War ended quickly. In the immediate aftermath of the war, as the administration of Harry S. *Truman sought to restructure the U.S. military, the navy bitterly opposed the force integration that modern warfare required. This dispute was settled by the *Key West Agreement of 1948 and other compromises, delaying the development of combined arms warfare and perpetuating interservice *rivalry that handicapped military operations and distorted military advice during the Vietnam War.

MacArthur proved in some ways a more difficult problem. Charismatic and personable, he was a virtual throwback to the nineteenth century; as army commander in chief of the Pacific theater, he proved an uneasy partner to the admiral commanding the Pacific Fleet, Chester *Nimitz. With the defeat of Japan, MacArthur became the virtual American proconsul in Tokyo, often ignoring instructions from Washington on occupation policy. The problem worsened when it fell to him to lead the *United Nations (predominantly American) forces in the Korean War. His relations with Washington deteriorated into mutual mistrust until President Truman dismissed him in 1951, when MacArthur sought the support of congressional Republicans in a ploy reminiscent of the Partisan Politics of the Mexican War or the Civil War.

This, the second score to be settled from World War II, showed that Eisenhower's example was now the rule. A general might have presidential aspirations, but not a hint of them may show until he takes off his uniform. American military activities in the last half of the twentieth century would scarcely be isolated from business interests or shielded from political controversy, but whatever personal political ambitions arose within the officer corps were strictly channeled.

The Truman administration's political fortunes suffered because of the Korean War, which put any candidacy by Truman for a second elected term as president beyond consideration. In broader terms, Truman had invoked crises too often in his efforts to build a permanent and stable Cold War posture. Eisenhower profited by his predecessor's hard lesson that presidents could overplay their hand in the "high politics" of state power. Elected in part to end the Korean War, Eisenhower resisted the temptation to use crises to win political support for military programs and military actions. Yet his calmer leadership style with respect to "high politics" had its own problems. When the Soviets launched Sputnik, the first of the space *satellites, in 1957, his administration came under attack for its seeming unconcern about competing with Soviet military technology. John F. *Kennedy employed charges of a "missile gap" in his successful presidential campaign in 1960 (only to learn later, and admit, that it never existed).

No twentieth-century war drew the American state into more domestic dissent than the Vietnam War. President Lyndon B. *Johnson's decisions about the war added up to an unsuccessful military policy, with disastrous domestic effects. As with Truman and Korea, they led to a turnover of the White House to a Republican president. Richard M. *Nixon, who succeeded Johnson, expanded the war in the course of ending it, leaving the Democrats in bitter opposition and the American state burdened with failures in both security policies and the handling of its military leaders and forces. Yet if Vietnam raised the political costs of engaging American military forces abroad, it did not end the practice. It had little effect on *NATO; if anything, the ending of the American engagement in Vietnam enabled the United States to strengthen its forces in Europe. Meanwhile, the nation's postwar *isolationism proved only temporary. Jimmy *Carter was elected president in 1976 at the head of a Democratic Party that espoused moderately anti-internationalist and antimilitary policies. But Carter reversed himself and started a rearmament program that became the Ronald *Reagan rearmament policy of the 1980s. The Vietnam War's more permanent legacy, a reduced confidence in America's leaders in their employment of force, led Reagan to try to restore popular confidence in U.S. military power. In this he proved only partially successful.

"Vietnam" remained shorthand for a warning against committing American military forces without an exit strategy. But strategy alone was not the issue: the way the American state handled "high politics" was.

As the management of the armed forces in relation to Congress, the executive branch, and society, "high politics" defined the degree of consensus on national security issues and hence the dimensions of American state power. Defined in this inclusive way, the Cold War's high politics shifted dynamically over time to reflect changes in threat perceptions, in the perceived need for the armed forces, and in their successes and failures. State power expanded and contracted accordingly, growing during the first half century, declining briefly in the early fifties as a result of the Korean War and the Communist scare, then recovering and reaching its high point of consensus on security issues in the early sixties. It was never the same again. The manifest errors of the Vietnam War reduced public and elite confidence in the employment of force to achieve political goals and sharply curbed the expression of state power. Eventually, the early seventies watchword, "No more Vietnams," faded from use; but the skepticism it reflected remained. By the late eighties and nineties, policymakers concerned with security and the state were looking increasingly to economic leverage as a substitute for military power.

Nuclear Danger and the Definition of the Powers of the Commander in Chief. Before the United States acquired *nuclear weapons, U.S. political leaders regarded the state's military function as synonymous with its capacity to mobilize for and conduct large-scale warfare. Nuclear weapons did not displace this role because conventional war-fighting capabilities continued to be regarded as necessary in maintaining stable *deterrence and in minimizing the danger of a catastrophic nuclear war. Yet nuclear weapons irrevocably altered the way the American state employed force to achieve security. Three interrelated factors shaped the change.

The first was World War II's impact on the balance of power. The war severely damaged the military capacity of all participants except the United States, which emerged as the world's first superpower. This eliminated the prospect that America could confine itself to the role of power balancer of last resort, for other states could no longer reliably stabilize the international political order. Specifically, Western Europe could not balance the Soviet bloc without an explicit and tangible U.S. commitment from the beginning. For the first time in its history, the American state had to maintain massive military forces in the absence of active hostilities.

The second factor that shaped the American state's military power after World War II was the American view of the Soviet Union during the Cold War. U.S. leaders saw it as a threat to the military and political security of Western Europe and to American interests there. They took the Soviet bloc as a given; in the interest of stability, they did not challenge it—which in turn meant containing it, not defeating it. For a European statesman, the point was self-evident, but those who wielded American state power found it an unfamiliar idea. Only for the leaders of the American state was it necessary to decouple the identification of a rival from the course of the action the United States had taken in two world wars: to mobilize and defeat it.

The third factor was the American development of nuclear weapons systems—the warheads themselves and the technologies for warning and target acquisition, for aiming and delivering and guiding weapons, for safeguarding them and for commanding and controlling their employment—that could deter enemies from attacking at locations remote from U.S. territory; and finally, the doctrines that explained how these vast, complicated systems should be positioned and employed. All of this placed an enormous burden on the military *command and control process, beginning at the top, with the commander in chief. President Kennedy, appalled at the "spasm war" scenarios for which the nuclear air force had planned, took steps in 1961 to provide himself, as commander in chief, with options in a *Flexible Response doctrine, expanding the range of choices available to presidents for employing nuclear weapons. But the Vietnam War produced a quite different approach to options, based on a critique that placed much of the blame for the U.S. defeat on civilian leaders—in particular, on the president—for overextending American power and micromanaging the war with catastrophic consequences.

This criticism has persisted. President Reagan's secretary of defense, Caspar *Weinberger, issued guidelines for military interventions that assured maximum autonomy to the generals in determining how they might fight. In substance, President George *Bush followed these guidelines in the *Persian Gulf War.

Criticisms of the Vietnam War also led to the Congressional *War Powers Resolution of 1973. Intended by its authors to increase congressional participation in decisions that might lead to war under circumstances that did not directly threaten the survival of the United States, this act has been opposed by every president since its passage. Presidential concern for preserving the prerogatives of the commander in chief, however, have been no more significant in rendering the act inconsequential than has congressional reluctance to follow through on the claim to a decisive role in determining whether or not forces should be introduced in dangerous situations. The law claims for Congress a resolve it has in actual practice lacked: to share in presidential decisions regarding the employment of conventional forces.

At the end of the twentieth century, divergent views about security threats, the military forces needed to meet them, and the employment of those forces have left the American concept of the state, in relationship to security and the military, unfocused and in flux. Congress avoids showdowns over military issues with the president; legislators avoid partisan showdowns among themselves over military policies. Meanwhile, the military itself enjoys a voice in security policy—and is called upon to participate in quasi-police activities like the "war on drugs"—to a degree unanticipated by military professionals at midcentury.

Looking back from an era of total war and nuclear standoff, one is struck by the prominence the U.S. Constitution gave (and still gives) to executive power by combining in the presidency the offices of chief of state and commander in chief. This solution reflected British experience as it was understood at the Constitutional Convention in Philadelphia in 1787, and addressed the internal security dilemma in two enduring respects. One was to avoid the potential tyranny of an Oliver Cromwell (the English military dictator in the mid-seventeenth century) by conferring the highest military authority on a civilian, whose authority did not derive solely from the Congress. The other was to combine the offices of chief of state and commander in chief as a means of avoiding "Caesarism," the despotism of a military commander insulated by popularity from control by civil authorities. The men who drafted the Constitution were aware of an internal security dilemma when international threats to the survival of the American state were taken seriously. This dilemma remains. After more than 200 years, it continues to impose stress on a government of limited powers that, when dealing with the issues of its citizens, ultimately depends upon the survival of the state.

[See also Civil Liberties and War; Congress, War, and the Military; Constitutional and Political Basis of War and the Military; Nationalism; Supreme Court, War, and the Military.]

• Edward S. Corwin, Total War and the Constitution, 1947. Samuel P. Huntington, The Soldier and the State; The Theory and Politics of Civil-Military Relations, 1957. Ernest R. May, ed., The Ultimate Decision; The President as Commander in Chief, 1960. Paul Y. Hammond, Organizing for Defense: The American Military Establishment in the Twentieth Century, 1961. Allan R. Millett and Peter Maslowski, For the Common Defense; A Military History of the United States of America, 1984. Henry Bartholomew Cox, War, Foreign Affairs, and Constitutional Power: 1829–1901, Report of the American Bar Association Steering Committee on War, Foreign Affairs, and Constitutional Power, Vol. 2, 1984. Robert Previti, Civilian Control Versus Military Rule, 1988. Daniel P. Franklin, Extraordinary Measures: The Exercise of Prerogative Powers in the United States, 1991. John Hart Ely, War and Responsibility, 1993. John T. Rourke, Presidential War and American Democracy: Rally 'Round the Chief, 1993. Barbara Hinckley, Less Than Meets the Eye; Foreign Policy Making and the Myth of the Assertive Congress, 1994.

—Paul Y. Hammond

STEALTH AIRCRAFT. The term "stealth" is commonly applied to aircraft or missile systems that have been de-signed to produce as small a radar signature as is practicable. In fact, stealth technology goes beyond this to include reducing as many "observables" of an aircraft or missile system as possible—for example, its visual, noise, and heat signatures, as well as its electromagnetic ones. Stealth technology is applicable to other systems as well, particularly to ship design. Overall, while the term "stealth" is convenient shorthand, a more precise and all-encompassing term used in the military community is "low observables."

Interest in reducing the observable characteristics of aircraft dates to *World War I, when various of the warring powers experimented with both camouflage paint schemes and even see-through fabric coatings applied to airplanes. Theoretical studies in *World War II indicated that it might be possible to reduce the radar signature of an airplane; in related work, the Germans developed radar-absorbent materials to shield *radar return from submarines' Schnorkels when these retractable air pipes were raised above the surface of the water. Flight tests of flying wing designs in the late 1940's indicated that they had minimal radar return characteristics, but this was serendipitous, and not the result of a deliberate attempt to develop low observable technology. In the late 1950's, with the growing sophistication of radar and missiles, the United States developed a comprehensive series of radar test ranges, where models could be suspended from cables or mounted on poles, and then radiated by radar emitters to assess their "signature" characteristics. Such "pole testing" played an important part in developing both a knowledge base on reducing radar signature and in assessing what portions of an aircraft typically offer the greatest strength of radar return. The strength of return determines the radar cross section (RCS) of the aircraft; it is the apparent size of an aircraft as it appears to search and fire control radars, and has no relationship to the actual physical cross section of an airplane.

The first aircraft designed to have a greatly reduced radar signature was the Lockheed A-12, the predecessor of the SR-71 Blackbird strategic reconnaissance airplane. It made use of the three major means of radar cross-section reduction: shaping, structural absorption via special materials, and specialized coatings. During the *Vietnam War, such technology was also exploited on small jet-propelled drones launched over North Vietnam on photo reconnaissance and electronic intelligence missions during the late 1960's and early 1970's. This experience, coupled with the lessons from the 1973 Arab-Israeli war (which demonstrated the vulnerability of conventional aircraft to radar-guided *missiles and gunfire, as well as heat-seeking missiles) greatly encouraged development of larger special-purpose radar-defeating "stealth" aircraft.

Ironically, given the Soviet Union's failure to exploit stealth technology, the key breakthrough in developing a stealth airplane came from theoretical studies by Pytor Ufimtsev, the chief scientist at the Moscow Institute of Radio Engineering. Ufimtsev's conclusions, published in the West, were studied by Lockheed engineer Denys Overholser, who recognized that they enabled the systematic analysis of an aircraft's shape to assess its radar reflectivity. Overholser discussed his findings with Ben R. Rich, the chief of Lockheed's famed "Skunk Works" advanced development team. Rich ordered developmental tests and, in September 1975, pole tests on a slender delta configuration having a faceted surface configuration (like a diamond) confirmed that such a shape could have a remarkably reduced radar return. The next step was development of a true airplane.

The first true "stealth" airplane—an aircraft designed primarily to defeat radar—was the Lockheed Have Blue technology demonstrator. Two of these aircraft, first flown in 1977, demonstrated that an aircraft company could design and build a potentially militarily useful airplane incorporating low observable principles. In 1978, the Air Force contracted with Lockheed for a special purpose stealth attack airplane. This airplane, the Lockheed F-117, first flew on June 18, 1981, entering service with the Air Force in 1983; 59 were subsequently built. During the *Persian Gulf War, F-117's shattered Iraq's air defense control centers, opening up the country to attack by conventional non-stealthy strike airplanes. Because of their survivability and ability to undertake precision attacks using laser-guided bombs, they were the only strike aircraft operated over Baghdad throughout the war.

Development of the first stealth aircraft encouraged the development of the Northrop B-2 stealth bomber (which entered Air Force service in December 1993), and an advanced stealthy cruise missile, the General Dynamics AGM-129. Stealth is an important development in military aerospace, for it renders an aircraft or missile difficult to detect, and virtually impossible to track, engage, and destroy. The success of these early stealth efforts has spawned interest both in counter-stealth studies and in a variety of other stealth designs. But as of this writing, only the United States possesses stealth aircraft and missiles in operational service.

[*See also* Bombs; Fighter Aircraft; Intelligence, Military and Political.]

—Richard Hallion

STEAMSHIPS. In his classic study, *Sea Power in the Machine Age,* Bernard Brodie observed that navies were relatively late in utilization of the technological advances of the machine age. Progress in steampower development was followed closely by the various admiralties—Great Britain, France, and the United States being most active. During the nineteenth century, the steam warship was by far the most important of the great naval revolutions, the most significant such innovation in warships since the fifteenth century. Steampower completely revised naval tactics and strategy; now ships could go anywhere, any time. During a transition period at midcentury, the largest warships retained masts and sails while adding steampower and either paddle wheels or screw propellers. Actually, the transition from the warfare of *sailing ships to modern naval warfare involved multiple technological developments: steam propulsion, iron (later, steel) construction, armor plate, replacement of paddle wheels with screw propellers, advances in naval ordnance such as the shell gun and rifling, the development of *torpedoes and *mines, and even some experimentation with the ram. Former reliance on wind and weather for the sailing ships was superseded by dependence on fuel sources—first the burning of wood, then coal, and finally oil. Logistical supplies of these sources became decisive factors. Naval steampower used on a global basis made overseas bases essential.

The earliest steam-powered engines, initially developed in Great Britain through the collaboration of James Watt and Matthew Bolton in the late eighteenth century, were crude, inefficient, and bulky. They were initially used to pump water to facilitate mining at deeper levels. Installation of increasingly efficient engines in vehicles for water transport took place in Great Britain, France, and the United States in the early nineteenth century. Key contributions were made by James Rumsey, John Fitch, Robert *Fulton—all Americans—and a Swedish immigrant to America, John *Ericsson. For the steam engine, reciprocation into rotary motion, compound pressurization, and separation of the condenser as a detached unit contributed to efficiency, portability, and use at sea.

Fulton's "North River Steamboat," erroneously dubbed *Clermont,* was the first unqualified commercial success, operating on the Hudson River from New York to Albany beginning in 1807. Fulton also designed the first steam-powered warship, "Fulton Steam Frigate," to be used for harbor defense and as a blockade runner during the *War of 1812. Fulton died in early 1815, and the steam warship was completed too late for use during the war. Its paddle wheel arrangement was centered amidships, a less vulnerable location. *Fulton I,* as it was later named, was diverted for use as a receiving ship in New York Harbor, where it accidentally blew up in 1829.

In the continuous naval competition between the British and French, invasion panics arose in Great Britain in the early 1840s when the French announced advances in steam warship design. In 1845, the British Admiralty sponsored a demonstration to determine which was superior, the paddle wheel or screw propeller; the latter clearly won. Steam warships proved their effectiveness and capability irrespective of wind and weather when used by the British and French during the Russian (Crimean) War, 1854–56. The French *Gloire* of 1859 was the first seagoing armored warship, built of wood with a covering of iron plate. The following year, the British response, HMS *Warrior,* contained an iron hull. Metal hulls facilitated larger size. In the next decade, the British entry, HMS *Devastation,* contained turrets and no sails. (HMS *Warrior* has been restored. Along with the ultimate sailing ship-of-the-line, HMS *Victory,* Lord Nelson's flagship of 1805, it is on display at Portsmouth, England.)

For the U.S. *Navy, the transition from the first steam warship to the modern battle fleet occurred between the 1840s and 1880s, led by Benjamin Franklin Isherwood, engineer-in-chief. The USS *Princeton,* designed and built by Ericsson, qualified as the first steam-powered, screw propeller warship, but a fatal gun accident in 1844 caused delays in its development. The expedition of Adm. Matthew *Perry to Japan in 1854 included steam warships. Meantime, the American gun developed by John *Dahlgren in 1856 proved temporarily superior. More important, Ericsson designed and built the USS *Monitor* just in time to participate in the famous Battle of *Hampton Roads, Virginia, in March 1862, against the *Confederate navy's *Virginia* (formerly USS *Merrimac*), a converted ironclad steam vessel. *Monitor* contained the first turret gun arrangement. The battle was a draw but nevertheless revolutionized naval warfare. *Monitor* was unstable and later sank off North Carolina. The USS *Michigan* was the first iron-hulled, paddle wheel steamship of the U.S. Navy, in service for eighty years. Another advance was Isherwood's USS *Wampanoag,* completed in the late 1860s, a steam and sail cruiser capable of 18 knots speed.

Further advances in steampower, metal boilers, expansion systems utilizing high pressures, reduction gears, and more efficient propeller designs followed. By the 1880s, the navy had converted entirely to steampower and the age of sail was over. Steam remains the basis of propulsion for sea transportation, generated today by petroleum or nuclear fuel.

• Bernard Brodie, *Sea Power in the Machine Age*, 1941; 1969. Edward W. Sloan, *Benjamin Franklin Isherwood, Naval Engineer*, 1965; 1980. K. T. Rowland, *Steam at Sea*, 1970. Wallace Hutcheon, Jr., *Robert Fulton*, 1981. Andrew Lambert, ed., *Steam, Steel and Shellfire: The Steam Warship, 1815–1905*, 1993.

—Eugene L. Rasor

STEUBEN, FRIEDRICH WILHELM VON [BARON] (1730–1794), Revolutionary War general. Born at Magdeburg, Friedrich Steuben followed his father's path into the Prussian Army, eventually serving as an infantry officer, staff officer, and aide under Frederick the Great. Court life lured the young captain from the army in 1764, but the American *Revolutionary War drew him back to military service. In 1777, the self-proclaimed Lt. Gen. "Baron von" Steuben—who was neither a general nor a nobleman—arrived in Philadelphia and requested a commission in the *Continental army. Americans soon found that if the Prussian had misrepresented his credentials, he did not exaggerate his talents.

After Congress accepted Steuben's offer to serve without rank in January 1778, he found the beleaguered Continentals at Valley Forge lacking the skill and knowledge of European regulars. Steuben consequently developed a system of drill that customized European methods to American needs, demonstrated its effectiveness on his personally trained "model company," and eventually published its principal elements in *Regulations for the Order and Discipline of the Troops of the United States* (1779). By May 1778, he became inspector general, with the rank of major general. Though he also served in the field, Steuben's most significant military contribution remained the greater degree of professionalism he gave to Continental forces.

• John M. Palmer, *General von Steuben*, 1937; repr. 1966.

—J. Mark Thompson

STEVENS, THADDEUS (1792–1868), radical Republican and leader of the House of Representatives. Stevens was born in Danville, Vermont, graduated from Dartmouth, and established himself as a lawyer in Gettysburg and later in Lancaster, Pennsylvania. He was an excellent parliamentarian who served (with few interruptions) in 1833–42 as an Anti-Mason in the Pennsylvania legislature, where he was instrumental in saving the bill for compulsory free education. Elected to Congress in 1848 as a Whig, he took a determined antislavery stand and retired in 1853, only to be reelected in 1858 as a Republican.

As a strong opponent of the secessionists, in 1861, Stevens became chairman of the Ways and Means Committee, a position that enabled him to frame and implement important legislation during the Civil War. Stevens constantly pressured President Abraham *Lincoln to institute an antislavery policy. He believed that only the laws of war, not the Constitution, applied to the seceded states, which he considered conquered provinces and in which he advocated confiscation of rebel property. His adept congressional leadership enabled him to raise the necessary funds for the Union forces, particularly by the introduction of paper currency "greenbacks," which he favored throughout his career.

After the war, Stevens was the main proponent in the House of Radical Reconstruction. Largely responsible for denying seats to Southern members and for the establishment of the Joint Committee of Fifteen on Reconstruction, he became the principal author of the Fourteenth Amendment; the Reconstruction Acts, which initially remanded the Southern states to military rule; and the impeachment of Andrew *Johnson. Often called vindictive and a dictator of Congress, Stevens was in fact opposed to the death sentence and did not succeed with many of his measures that fell short of his desires. Nevertheless, his advocacy for equal rights for the freedmen was an important inducement for Republican Reconstruction measures. He died in 1868, disappointed at his failure to procure the conviction and removal of President Johnson.

[*See also* Civil War: Domestic Course.]

• Fawn M. Brodie, *Thaddeus Stevens, Scourge of the South*, 1959. Hans L. Trefousse, *Thaddeus Stevens: Nineteenth Century Egalitarian*, 1997.

—Hans L. Trefousse

STILWELL, JOSEPH (1883–1946), U.S. general in World War II. Graduating from West Point in 1904, Stilwell's first assignment, to the Philippines, began a military career that would be closely associated with Asia, especially China. After service as an intelligence officer during World War I, Stilwell was sent to China—the first of several assignments that eventually included a stint as military attaché (1935–39), when he observed the Sino-Japanese War.

Highly regarded by Gen. George C. *Marshall, Stilwell, who was fluent in Chinese, was appointed U.S. commander of the *China-Burma-India theater of operations in 1942. Although allotted minimal resources, Stilwell strived to encourage the Nationalist leader, Chiang Kai-shek, to build an effective military force to counter Japanese advances in China and Burma. Stilwell's relationship with Chiang was strained, given the latter's unwillingness to reform the corrupt and poorly led Chinese armies. Nicknamed "Vinegar Joe" for his blunt manner, Stilwell proved unable to use Chinese troops to halt the 1942 conquest of northern Burma, which cut the only viable land link between China and India. Relying largely on Chinese forces trained by his American staff, he succeeded two years later in recapturing a large part of northern Burma and was promoted to lieutenant general. This campaign eventually paved the way for the reopening of the Burma Road in 1945.

Recalled by President Franklin D. *Roosevelt in October 1944 at the behest of Chiang, Stilwell returned to the United States to resume his career in Washington, D.C., as commander of army ground forces. He was slated to command the Tenth Army for the planned invasion of Japan before the surrender of Tokyo in August 1945.

• Barbara W. Tuchman, *Stilwell and the American Experience in China, 1911–1945*, 1970. Eric Larrabee, *Commander in Chief: Franklin Delano Roosevelt, His Lieutenants, and Their War*, 1987.

—G. Kurt Piehler

STIMSON, HENRY L. (1867–1950), lawyer, secretary of state, secretary of war. The grandson of a New York stockbroker and son of a doctor, Stimson was educated at Phillips Andover Academy, Yale College, and the Harvard

Law School. He practiced law in New York as a partner of Elihu *Root, later, like him, secretary of both war and state.

Stimson's long career spanned the entire history of modern American warfare, from Indian fighting to the atomic bomb. As an undergraduate, he saw Indian warfare in Colorado. As secretary of war in the Taft administration, he visited the army posts of the Old West in the last years of their existence. He saw active service in France during World War I as an artillery officer with the American Expeditionary Forces.

In early 1902, while riding in Washington, Stimson was spotted by President Theodore *Roosevelt, who jokingly ordered him to swim Rock Creek. Stimson took the order literally and nearly drowned as he forded the creek. Within a year, Teddy Roosevelt, who liked that kind of man, tapped Stimson as U.S. Attorney in New York, where he made a great record as a prosecutor.

Appointed secretary of war by President Taft, Stimson helped to modernize the army's structure, ending the isolation of the privileged staff corps. His reforms infuriated conservatives, led by the adjutant general, Maj. Gen. Fred C. Ainsworth, who called Stimson and his supporters, in writing, "incompetent amateurs." After consulting Root, who said when a man pulls your nose you must hit him, Stimson fired Ainsworth for gross insubordination.

Stimson ran unsuccessfully for governor of New York in 1910; then, after the war, practiced law in New York until he was asked by Coolidge to impose a settlement in Nicaragua and in 1927 to serve as governor general of the Philippines. As Herbert C. *Hoover's secretary of state, he was involved in the London Naval Conference of 1930 and in the 1931–32 Manchuria crisis, in which he formulated the "Stimson Doctrine" of nonrecognition of conquered countries.

He was prominent among the internationalist Republicans who argued for American "preparedness" in the late 1930s. In 1940, President Franklin D. *Roosevelt appointed him secretary of war. Stimson worked closely with Gen. George C. *Marshall and assembled an able team of civilian advisers, including Robert C. Lovett and John J. McCloy. He helped to steer through the decision to give first priority to the war in Europe; he also presided over the *Manhattan Project, which built the atomic bomb.

Although he chaired the meetings at which the decision to use the bomb was taken, after the bombings of *Hiroshima and Nagasaki, Stimson had second thoughts. At his last cabinet meeting in September 1945 he argued that the United States should enter into an agreement with the Soviet Union to control the use of *nuclear weapons.

[See also Nicaragua, U.S. Military Involvement in; Philippines, U.S. Military Involvement in; World War II: Domestic Course.]

• Henry L. Stimson and McGeorge Bundy, *On Active Service in Peace and War*, 1948. Elting E. Morison, *Turmoil and Tradition*, 1960. Godfrey Hodgson, *The Colonel: The Life and Wars of Henry L. Stimson*, 1990.   —Godfrey Hodgson

STONES RIVER, BATTLE OF (1862–63). Stones River—also known as the Battle of Murfreesboro—was one of the costliest engagements of the Civil War in Tennessee. Following the failure of his Kentucky campaign the previous fall, Confederate Gen. Braxton *Bragg positioned his Army of Tennessee (34,000 strong) to protect the railroad line

running southeastward from Nashville into the heart of the Confederacy. Union Maj. Gen. William S. *Rosecrans's Army of the Cumberland (44,000 strong) advanced from Nashville 30 miles to meet Bragg's army at Murfreesboro in late December. Rosecrans and Bragg both planned to attack with their left wings, but Bragg moved first at dawn, 31 December, catching the Federals by surprise. Rosecrans's extreme right wing quickly retreated, offering scattered resistance. The Federal center fought more steadily, particularly Brig. Gen. Philip H. *Sheridan's division, which slowed the Confederate advance several hours.

The flat terrain, rocky outcroppings, and intermittent cedar forests also confused and delayed the Confederates. In the center, Col. William B. Hazen's brigade held a wooded area called the Round Forest against repeated and fierce attacks. The Forest spanned the Nashville Pike and the Nashville & Chattanooga Railroad, Rosecrans's lines of communication. Hazen's stand saved the Federal army, allowing the right wing to retreat by pivoting on his position.

By nightfall, Rosecrans had managed to patch together a final stand along the pike. When the fighting died down, the Confederates hastily constructed breastworks to protect their gains. The bitter cold caused great suffering for the thousands of wounded men of both armies who littered the field that night. The next day, the two exhausted armies maintained their positions without moving.

The stalemate was temporarily broken on 2 January 1863, when Rosecrans moved a division under Col. Samuel Beatty across Stones River at McFadden's Ford to threaten Bragg's extreme right wing. Confederate Maj. Gen. John C. Breckinridge's division counterattacked, driving Beatty's men back across the river, but was halted by the concentrated fire of nearly sixty Federal field guns. This engagement demonstrated the effectiveness of Union *artillery as a decisive factor on the battlefield. After five days of maneuvering and bitter fighting, neither army had gained an advantage. On 3 January, Bragg was given evidence that Rosecrans was receiving substantial reinforcements, and he decided to give up the field. The Confederates began to retreat that night, but Rosecrans chose not to pursue. He consolidated his position at Murfreesboro, digging extensive *fortifications, while Bragg fortified towns a few miles further south along the rail line. The two armies had so exhausted themselves that neither resumed active campaigning for nearly six months.

Stones River was both a tactical and a strategic *victory for the North. Occurring after costly Federal defeats at Fredericksburg, Virginia, and Chickasaw Bayou, Mississippi, the morale of the Northern public needed a victory, even one bought at such a dear cost in lives. Confederate and Federal *casualties amounted to approximately 13,000 men apiece, roughly one-third of those engaged.

[See also Civil War: Military and Diplomatic Course.]

• James Lee McDonough, *Stones River: Bloody Winter in Tennessee*, 1980. Peter Cozzens, *No Better Place to Die: The Battle of Stones River*, 1990.   —Earl J. Hess

The **STRATEGIC DEFENSE INITIATIVE** (SDI) was a major program for defense against Soviet *missiles championed by President Ronald *Reagan beginning in 1983.

The U.S. missile defense program began in March 1946 in response to Germany's World War II missile program that included plans for an intercontinental ballistic missile

(ICBM). By the mid-1950s, when intelligence indicated the Soviets were developing their own ICBM, both the army and air force were pursuing missile defense programs. In 1958, to end squabbling that had developed between the two services, the secretary of defense assigned responsibility for missile defenses to the army.

After its Nike Zeus missile achieved the first successful intercept of a dummy ICBM warhead in July 1962, the army pushed for the deployment of national missile defenses. Secretary of Defense Robert S. *McNamara successfully resisted such a deployment until September 1967. By then, the Soviets were deploying their own system around Moscow; in response, President Lyndon B. *Johnson ordered the fielding of Sentinel to provide limited protection for U.S. cities.

Following his election in 1968, President Richard M. *Nixon switched the focus of Sentinel to defense of deterrent forces and renamed it Safeguard. In August 1969, about two months after Nixon had invited the Soviets to discuss reductions in strategic arms, Congress approved the Safeguard deployment.

The first phase of the Strategic Arms Limitation Talks (SALT) produced the Anti-Ballistic Missile Treaty in May 1972. It restricted the signatories to two missile defense sites, each having up to one hundred interceptors. A 1974 protocol reduced to one the number of sites each nation could deploy.

About a year after the protocol, the United States completed its Safeguard site at Grand Forks, North Dakota. A few months later, Congress ordered the Department of *Defense (DoD) to close the facility. The Soviet missile defense system near Moscow remains operational.

After the closure of Safeguard, the army concentrated its missile defense efforts on developing hit-to-kill (HTK) missiles to replace the nuclear-tipped interceptors required by Safeguard. In June 1984, this new interceptor concept was successfully demonstrated.

In the meantime, the Soviets were improving their nuclear forces. By the early 1980s, some strategic analyses showed the Soviets could cripple U.S. retaliatory forces and still have enough missiles to devastate American cities. As a result, in a February 1983 meeting with President Reagan, the *Joint Chiefs of Staff (JCS) recommended greater emphasis on strategic defenses.

Already supportive of missile defenses, Reagan was receptive to this message. In a nationally televised speech on 23 March 1983, he announced his decision to initiate an expanded research and development program to assess the feasibility of strategic defenses. In April 1984, following a year of technical and strategic studies, DoD chartered the Strategic Defense Initiative Organization under the leadership of Air Force Lt. Gen. James A. Abrahamson. This organization was to conduct the research to resolve the feasibility issue.

After two and a half years of work, the president and Secretary of Defense Caspar *Weinberger decided at the end of 1986 to enter the Strategic Defense System (SDS) Phase I Architecture into the defense acquisition process. This architecture had two major deficiencies: it was expensive, and its space-based elements were vulnerable to Soviet antisatellite weapons (ASATs). These difficulties were epitomized in the space-based interceptor (SBI), one of the architecture's six subsystems.

SBI was a large, garagelike satellite housing ten hit-to-

kill interceptors. About 300 SBIs were to orbit the Earth. In case of a Soviet attack, the SBIs would launch their interceptors at Soviet missiles, destroying many of them before they could release their multiple warheads and decoys. Because of its complexity, SBI was costly; because of its size, it was an easy target for ASATs.

The solution to these problems was to use miniaturized sensors and computers to give individual interceptors the ability to operate without support from a garage. Instead of several hundred large targets, Soviet ASATs would now confront several thousand small, hard-to-find interceptors. Because these Brilliant Pebble interceptors (BP) were to be mass-produced, they would be relatively inexpensive, thereby lowering the cost of SDS Phase I.

The decision to integrate BP into the architecture came in 1989, as the Soviet empire began to crumble. This dramatically changed the strategic situation, prompting President George *Bush to initiate a review of U.S. strategic requirements. The SDI portion of this review was completed in March 1990 by Ambassador Henry Cooper, who had served as America's chief negotiator during the defense and space talks. Cooper's report argued that the most dangerous threat to the United States was now unauthorized or terrorist attacks by limited numbers of missiles. Moreover, deployed U.S. forces would increasingly face threats from shorter-range theater missiles as the technology of ballistic missiles and weapons of mass destruction proliferated. Cooper recommended refocusing SDI to concentrate on defenses against these new threats.

Shortly after Cooper took over the SDI organization, his report proved prophetic. In August 1990, Iraq invaded Kuwait, touching off a crisis that led to the *Persian Gulf War of 1991. This war produced the first operational engagement between a ballistic missile (an Iraqi Scud) and a missile defense system (the American Patriot). Furthermore, the danger of theater missiles was graphically illustrated on 25 February when a single Scud killed twenty-eight Americans and injured one hundred.

Responding to the new world situation, on 29 January 1991, President Bush had announced a reorientation of the SDI program away from developing strategic defenses to a new system known as GPALS for Global Protection Against Limited Strikes. GPALS consisted of three main components: a ground-based national missile defense (NMD), a ground-based theater missile defense (TMD), and a space-based global defense. In this scheme, the space-based element complemented TMD and NMD.

The emphasis on TMD reflected in GPALS was reinforced under President Bill *Clinton, whose secretary of defense, Les *Aspin, Jr., changed the name of the Strategic Defense Initiative Organization to the Ballistic Missile Defense Organization. In announcing this change on 13 May 1993, Aspin hailed the end of the *Cold War and credited SDI with helping to end it.

In September 1993, a new shape for America's missile defense program emerged from the Bottom-Up Review (BUR), the Clinton administration's study of America's post–Cold War defense needs. The BUR laid out a three-part, $18 billion missile defense program covering the six years of the future years defense plan. The top priority was to be a $12 billion TMD component focused on three programs: improvements to the Patriot missile system; upgrading the navy's *Aegis air defense system so it could intercept theater ballistic missiles; and a new army system known as Theater High Altitude Area Defense to complement Patriot. The second element of the plan was a $3 billion "technology readiness" program to shorten NMD's deployment time. Finally, a $3 billion technology program was to support both national and theater defenses.

Over the next few years, the Clinton administration would find it necessary to expand the TMD program and increase its funding. Additional funding was also required for NMD, which had to be transformed into a deployment readiness program to permit rapid fielding of defenses as the missile threats to the U.S. homeland suddenly emerge. Nevertheless, the BUR had provided the broad framework that guided the U.S. missile defense program into the new millennium.

[See also Air and Space Defense; Arms Control and Disarmament: Nuclear; Deterrence; SALT Treaties; Space Program, Military Involvement in the; Weapons, Evolution of.]

• B. Bruce-Briggs, The Shield of Faith: A Chronicle of Strategic Defense from Zeppelins to Star Wars, 1988. Donald R. Baucom, The Origins of SDI, 1944–1983, 1992. David B. H. Denoon, Ballistic Missile Defense in the Post–Cold War Era, 1995.

—Donald R. Baucom

STRATEGY

Fundamentals
Historical Development
Land Warfare Strategy
Naval Warfare Strategy
Air Warfare Strategy
Nuclear Warfare Strategy and War Plans

STRATEGY: FUNDAMENTALS

To ancient Greeks, strategos, from which we derive strategy, meant simply the general's art; a modern definition, however, would generalize the meaning to a reasoned relationship among military means and the ways they might be used to reach the ends of national policy. For the senior commander of a theater of war, the battle tactics of lower echelons blend into operational strategy in which he uses their combat in the conduct of campaigns designed to achieve war's politically defined purposes. The national military headquarters also uses the means-ways-ends calculation while devising a national military strategy, establishing campaign objectives, and building armed forces as one of several instruments contributing to grand strategy, often called national security policy.

Dimensions. In On War, Carl von *Clausewitz helped push the domain of strategy beyond the battlefield when he acknowledged that the tactical and operational successes sought by military commanders are but means to political ends. At the highest level, therefore, military strategy and national policy overlap, with the latter shaping and directing military operations and force development. As Clausewitz warned, however, political leaders should not ask their generals to pursue goals unattainable through organized violence, beyond their forces' capacity to attain, and either imposing disproportionate costs or requiring methods so destructive as to preclude a satisfactory *peace—summarized as the tests of suitability, feasibility, and acceptability. From the French Revolution, Clausewitz concluded that the strategic calculations of the government and armed forces depend not simply on the *State

and the army, but also on a sound estimate of popular attitudes—the existence of a national will to carry war to a successful conclusion.

The twentieth century's expanded governmental bureaucracies and financial systems—and revolutions in production and *transportation—have added new dimensions to strategy. A government able to mobilize overwhelming human and material resources and convey them to the theater of war can, for example, enable its generals to defeat even opponents more skilled in the operational aspects of strategy. As World War I demonstrated, the capacity to mobilize massive military resources includes the danger that modern industrial powers with sound logistical strategies might fall into a mutually destructive war of attrition that continues until even the victors have paid too great a price for *victory.

Though technological superiority may enable a belligerent to escape attrition's blind alley, the *Cold War demonstrated that two technologically superior powers possessing the means and the will to destroy one another may create a long-term strategic impasse that precludes fighting—except through proxies—until one of the powers suffers internal collapse. Because the development and production of increasingly sophisticated modern weapons (and training armed forces in their use) takes years, major powers must also devise peacetime force development strategies that economically build forces for wars they can only anticipate.

Strategy also has a psychological dimension, which may enable a power skilled in propaganda or with a reputation for great resolve and military skill to undermine its opponent's will to resist and gain its political ends with a minimum of combat. As Sun Tzu observed more than two millennia ago, the "acme of skill" is overcoming your enemy's resistance "without fighting," or, failing that, accepting battle only when strategic success makes victory certain. Although that psychological dimension of warfare may lead to great strategic efficiency, a strategist who overrates his nation's military reputation or underrates his opponent's resolve may so miscalculate the means-ways-ends relation as to increase the risk of defeat if threats and reputation do not suffice.

Strategic Concepts. Because strategic concepts represent ways that military and other means might be employed in pursuit of political ends, their principal forms deserve brief description.

In the broadest terms, strategies may be either direct or indirect and sequential or cumulative. Military force supplies the paramount element of a direct strategy whose focus is violent, perhaps sequential assaults on the enemy's main strength with the aim of overcoming his forces in decisive battle and thus rendering him vulnerable to coercion. In the extreme, the destruction becomes so complete as to lead to his political overthrow and might be characterized as a strategy of annihilation. Should a decisive victory prove impossible, the direct approach may end in exhausting the enemy's forces or will through attrition.

Indirect strategies, championed by Basil Liddell Hart, often involve less violence and typically include a series of military, economic, diplomatic, or psychological actions completed in no fixed order but aimed at enemy weaknesses, often locations on his periphery. If successful, the cumulative effect of the attacks will so unbalance the enemy as to cause him to yield or, at least, render him vulnerable to direct assault. Though more passive in nature, the *containment* strategy of the Cold War era represents another form of indirect approach, one leading to an opponent's internal collapse as prelude to victory.

Maritime and airpower strategies also have an indirect character in that they aim to undermine the enemy's will to resist or deny his armed forces the means to make war. Seapower strategy, whose best known advocate is Alfred T. *Mahan, seeks those ends by gaining control of the seas—perhaps in a decisive fleet engagement—and imposing an economy-strangling blockade. To the same end, weaker naval powers raid an enemy's commerce. To avoid costly ground campaigns, airpower strategists, beginning with Giulio *Douhet and Billy *Mitchell, advocated bombardment of an enemy's military and industrial base, or, by attacking cities, terrorizing citizens into surrender.

Although *deterrence, seeking to prevent war by making even victory unacceptably costly, has long been a factor in strategy, nuclear-tipped intercontinental *missiles made it the distinguishing strategic concept of the Cold War. The nuclear powers typically sought deterrence by threatening an enemy's cities (*countervalue strategy*), but a desire to limit war's costs should deterrence fail led to consideration of *counterforce strategies* (attacks on military facilities).

Revolutionary strategy, developed in its modern form by Mao Zedong, aims to overthrow an existing government through a long struggle during which the revolutionaries develop a covert political base amongst the population and strengthen it with propaganda, terrorism, and guerrilla attacks (hence the use of *guerrilla warfare for this strategy) designed to discredit and demoralize the government before launching assaults by the rebels' conventional troops on its weakened armed forces. In response, the leading Western powers developed equally multifaceted *counterinsurgency strategies.

With the collapse of the former Soviet Union, the United States entered a new strategic environment in which it needed to assess the contribution of armed forces to maintaining regional balances and Third World *peacekeeping at a time of public reluctance to pay for forces sufficient to either purpose.

[*See also* Tactics.]

• Basil H. Liddell Hart, *Strategy.* 1954; 2nd rev. ed. 1967. Andre Beaufre, *An Introduction to Strategy,* 1965. Michael Howard, *War in European History,* 1976. Peter Paret, ed., *Makers of Modern Strategy: From Machiavelli to the Nuclear Age,* 1986. Edward N. Luttwak, *Strategy,* 1987. Williamson Murray, MacGregor Knox, and Alvin Bernstein, eds., *The Making of Strategy: Rulers, States, and War,* 1994.

—James L. Abrahamson

STRATEGY: HISTORICAL DEVELOPMENT

Shielded by broad oceans and neighbors presumptively friendly but certainly weak, the United States has scarcely needed the ingenuities of strategy since it survived a most bloody civil war to acquire the world's richest economy. It is those who fight against the odds, outweighed defenders or overambitious attackers, who must try to circumvent enemy strengths and exploit enemy weaknesses by obeying the paradoxical (seemingly contradictory) logic of strategy, as opposed to commonsense "linear" logic.

At each level, the paradoxical logic of strategy usually precludes the most efficient action, for the latter is inherently predictable and can therefore be anticipated, blocked, or circumvented. At each level, the paradoxical logic entails risks, possibly catastrophic (e.g., long, thin, deep penetration offensives can be cut off and encircled). But at each level, the high-risk/high-payoff methods inspired by the paradoxical logic can allow the weak to prevail over the strong, though never reliably.

At the *tactical* level, paradoxical action, i.e., the deliberately "bad" move, can be the good move if it yields surprise, thus reducing the enemy to a nonreacting object—if only temporarily, if only partially. Surprise is thus the supreme advantage, for it suspends the entire predicament of warfare, characterized precisely by the presence of a reacting enemy.

At the *operational* level, the logic favors the disruption of the enemy's physical or mental preparations by maneuver over the systematic destruction of his forces by head-on combat, for in the latter ("attrition"), sheer strength must prevail.

At the level of *theater strategy*, narrow-deep penetrations and outflanking thrusts on the offensive, or elastic maneuvers on the defensive, are likewise favored over broad-front advances or firm defenses, both of which require a superiority of means to yield victory. In nonterritorial *force strategies*, there are the aerial, maritime, or space equivalents, where again ingenuity can prevail over sheer strength.

Finally, at the level of *grand strategy*, the logic favors artful combinations of intelligence, diplomacy (the leveraging of force by threatening or reassuring), material inducements, deception and subversion (undermining the enemy by terror, propaganda, and substitution), as well as concrete military strength, as opposed to strength alone or accompanied by material inducements, whereby the results obtained depend on the military and economic resources expended.

The United States and its armed forces have by contrast generally been able to prevail in modern times by straightforwardly efficient and correspondingly reliable methods, which obey only the "linear" logic of common sense. At every level—tactical, operational, theater strategic, or grand strategic—the sheer strength of U.S. military forces and an abundance of economic means have usually sufficed to yield success at low risk, though not at low cost.

There have been exceptions, of course, as in the case of Gen. Douglas *MacArthur's very bold theater-level outflanking maneuver of September 1950: North Korea's victorious invasion forces were cut off and destroyed by the U.S. forces inserted into their deep rear by the high-risk/high-payoff *Inchon landing.

In the 1991 *Persian Gulf War, by contrast, an overwhelming technical superiority was applied to an enemy virtually incapable of reacting, except by flight. With the paradoxical logic of strategy mostly irrelevant, there was no need to deviate from reliable, efficient, predictable managerial methods. After thirty-nine days of systematic air bombardment that hollowed out Iraq's entire military structure, there followed a simple, broad-front 100-hour ground offensive, neither bold nor quick, yet quite sufficient to induce Iraq's withdrawal from Kuwait (no deep outflanking maneuver to cut off Iraq's army was attempted). As for the one ingenuity later claimed—the non-landing of U.S. Marine amphibious forces that supposedly pinned down Iraqi troops on the Kuwaiti shore—it was not a planned deception but rather the result of prudence: the Iraqis had scattered sea *mines, and losses of ships and *landing craft were feared. (In any case, Iraq's forces in Kuwait were already immobilized by the impact of the air campaign.)

Earlier, during the *Vietnam War, on the other hand, a vast superiority of means was outmaneuvered by an enemy that stubbornly refused to concentrate into efficiently targetable mass formations—and no strategical remedy was found when sheer firepower was thus frustrated.

The origin of Western strategical thought is unambiguously found in the words attributed to Heracleitus of Ephesus (c. 500 B.C.): "Men do not understand ... [the coincidence of opposites]: there is a 'back-stretched connection' like that of the bow....." and "the equilibrium of all things existent is due to the clash of opposing forces." Deemed obscure by the ancients, Heracleitus has been made transparent by our experience of nuclear *deterrence, whereby the peaceful had to be constantly ready to attack, and *nuclear weapons could only be useful if unused. That fully uncovered for all the paradoxical logic of strategy, the "back-stretched" connection that unites opposites. Long before Heracleitus, many a cunning fighter had won by surprising his enemy—something only possible when better ways of attacking, hence expected ways, are deliberately eschewed. In war's coincidence of opposites, the bad move is good because it is bad, and vice versa.

Carl von *Clausewitz, *the* modern strategist, extended the logic beyond the coincidence of opposites, revealing the dynamics of reversal: *victory turns into *defeat after its culminating point by exhausting the will to fight and/or overstretching the until-then victorious forces and/or frightening neutrals into enmity and allies into neutrality. *War itself is transformed into *peace beyond its culminating point, by consuming the means and the will to fight, and/or because the costs of warmaking (human, material) devalue the perceived losses of war termination (thus, the abandonment of South Vietnam was accepted when too many American lives were lost). Again, because the destructive capacity of nuclear weapons exceeded the culminating point of advantageous destruction, they were too effective (militarily) to be effective (politically). Their season of maximum importance was therefore short (1945–69), and their significance in world politics has not ceased to decline since then—only hollow great power pretenders such as India and Pakistan and second-rate countries of the Iran/Iraq type still strive to acquire them.

Enemies react, therefore straightforward "engineering" methods routinely fail in war. But they are persistently seductive, because war is so much simpler when the enemy is ignored. In World War II, both the British Bomber Command and the U.S. "strategic" air forces (then under the U.S. Army) kept asking for the means (additional thousands of bombers) in order to destroy physically the industrial sources of German and Japanese military power and thus win the war by airpower alone. But, as Prime Minister Winston *Churchill kept pointing out, if the bombing *did* begin to succeed, Germans and Japanese would not passively await defeat, but would instead strengthen their air defenses and disperse their industries, for in war, "all things are always on the move simultaneously."

Eventually, bombing proved very effective (in part by forcing the diversion of German and Japanese resources to air defense) but quite insufficient on its own. This did not stop Robert S. *McNamara from repeating exactly the same error in the 1960s with his Mutual Assured Destruc-

tion policy, which was meant to stabilize *deterrence and stop the nuclear *arms race. McNamara began with the very sound claim that a reliable ability to destroy half the Soviet Union's population and three-quarters of its industrial capacity was ample to deter, but he ignored the possibility that Soviet leaders might not want what he wanted, the paralysis of mutual deterrence. In fact, they kept aiming for a nuclear superiority that was entirely meaningless according to McNamara—but not according to them. In the end, it was the open-ended technological challenge of President Ronald *Reagan's *Strategic Defense Initiative (SDI) that forced the Soviet leadership to give up military accumulation to try domestic reforms instead—with fatal results for their system.

Conflict unfolds at the several distinct levels, which interpenetrate much more easily downward than upward. In World War II, all German tactical-, operational-, or even theater-level victories (notably over France in 1940) were nullified by Adolf *Hitler's choice of the wrong allies (Italy, Romania, Hungary, Slovakia) and the wrong enemies (the Anglo-American-Soviet coalition) at the level of grand strategy. Even if the *D-Day landing had been repulsed and the Soviet army had ceased to fight, Germany would still have been ultimately defeated—by the fission bomb. As for Japan, given its utter inability to march on Washington to impose a favorable peace, the brilliant success of the surprise *attack on Pearl Harbor was worse than useless: had the pilots of the Japanese navy failed miserably, evoking ridicule instead of hatred, American public opinion might not have been so aroused and the United States might have dealt less harshly with Japan.

Different grand strategies can be evaluated by the degree of their reliance on force. It was the high strategic achievement of the United States that it successfully protected numerous allies throughout the Cold War by relying primarily on the "armed suasion" of nuclear deterrence, while having to fight seriously only in Korea and Indochina. That was only possible because an American diplomatic elite that had been very small, and military elites that had been very provincial, were able to develop rapidly an entire culture of multilateral diplomacy and alliance management, notably to create *NATO and preserve its unity in the face of constant difficulties and frequent crises. The precondition of that historic success was, however, the extraordinary evolution of American public opinion, from the isolationist presumption that lasted until 7 December 1941 to a remarkably sophisticated understanding of the value of allies—even inconstant, demanding, and deliberately irritating allies.

It was only when the diplomatic and military elites persisted in pursuing diplomatic and military priorities *after* the Cold War had ended (c. 1990) that American public opinion started to withdraw its consent from their aims and methods. Symptomatic of this divergence, while much of elite opinion still saw Japan as a valuable ally, popular opinion recognized it as a direct economic competitor. But the more obvious change was the collapse of public support for military intervention. Having correctly understood that, in Cold War conditions, any locality could be important once it became the scene of Soviet-American contention, no matter how worthless economically or lacking in any sort of American presence or connections, public opinion reacted to the end of the Cold War by generally refusing to sanction large "discretionary" military interventions in the absence of immediate and compelling justifications for the same.

[*See also* Land Warfare; Tactics.]

• M. Marcovich, ed., *Heraclitus: Greek text with a short commentary*, 1967. Carl von Clausewitz, *On War*, ed. and trans. by Michael Howard and Peter Paret, 1976. George T. Dennis (Transl.) *Maurice's Strategikon: Handbook of Byzantine military strategy* (Philadelphia Pa.: Pennsylvania University Press, 1984). Edward N. Luttwak, *Strategy: The Logic of War and Peace*, 1987; 2nd ed. 1992. Williamson Murray, MacGregor Knox, and Alvin Bernstein, eds., *The Making of Strategy: Rulers, States, and War*, 1994. N. P. Milner, *Vegetius: Epitome of military science* 2nd rev. ed. 1996.
—Edward N. Luttwak

STRATEGY: LAND WARFARE STRATEGY

For almost four centuries, American land warfare has tested nearly the full range of strategies: direct strategies pursuing decisive battles of *annihilation* to overthrow the enemy army; somewhat less direct efforts to overcome an enemy's forces through *attrition and exhaustion*; strategies of *maneuver* seeking, with a minimum of bloodshed, to control important territories; more explicitly *indirect approaches* and multifaceted strategies such as *containment*; as well as *guerrilla warfare* and *counterinsurgency*. In addition to strategies focused on combat, American strategists have given careful thought in peacetime to defense of the coasts, sizing the army, and fixing its relation to the militia. Until the *Cold War, moreover, the United States followed a *mobilization* strategy, relying on distance and sometimes allies for security while it prepared for war.

Strategies of Annihilation. Beginning with the seventeenth-century Indian Wars, American strategists have usually preferred to act directly against an enemy's armed forces, somehow bringing them to battle and seeking in a single decisive action or campaign to destroy them so thoroughly as to force terms on a disarmed opponent.

Despite the possibility of an armed European descent on their ports, the first colonists principally feared the normally hospitable Indians. Aware of the defensive inadequacies of militia and blockhouses in an age when both messages and men moved slowly, colonials favored short offensives that quickly returned them to farms and families. Indians, however, refused to fight in the European manner, and militiamen generally lacked the skill and patience for tribal warfare. The colonists therefore overcame their foes by attacking, usually in winter, their food supplies and villages in order to force a decisive battle that would annihilate the hostile tribe as an independent polity, as in the Tidewater Wars, the Pequot War, and *King Philip's War—a strategy also used in the *Plains Indians Wars.

Facing European opponents, colonists applied strategies of annihilation in a regional context. During the imperial conflicts culminating in the *French and Indian War, Americans displayed little strategic variation as they held to a single goal: permanent security by driving France off the continent. With the aid of the British army and navy, they finally achieved this in 1763.

Early in the *Revolutionary War, George *Washington made similar efforts to drive Great Britain from the continent. He threatened its forces with destruction if they did not evacuate Boston, and later dispatched forces under Richard Montgomery and Benedict *Arnold in an unsuccessful attempt to seize Québec. Washington even attempted to turn back the British invasion of New York, un-

til a series of lost battles around Manhattan convinced him to abandon so direct a strategy in favor of exhausting the British and exploiting the revolutionary role of the militia.

In the *War of 1812, similarly unable, except through commerce raiding, to strike at the sources of British power, the United States chose to invade Canada, which if successful might add new territory and eradicate British power in North America. Due to antiwar sentiment in New England, the army unwisely failed to concentrate in northern New York for an overwhelming descent on Montréal and Québec. Until forced on the defensive by Napoleon's 1814 defeat, the army instead launched a series of indecisive offensives in the West.

During the *Civil War, Robert E. *Lee, commander of the Army of Northern Virginia, and Union commanders George B. *McClellan and George Gordon *Meade pursued decisive battlefield victories in the Napoleonic manner—victories so complete as to break an opponent's will to continue. With the introduction of rifled weapons to armies that still moved on foot and by horse, battles became more bloody even as decisive *victory became less likely.

Considering the Confederacy's vast land and maritime frontier, lack of a navy, small population, and industrial inferiority, Lee wisely rejected the strategy of perimeter defense initially employed in the western theater. But the Confederacy proved unable to replace the losses resulting from an aggressive strategy in which his army sought to break the Union's will through the defeat of its armies or victories on its soil, which eluded Lee at Antietam and Gettysburg.

In the end, Lee could not withstand Ulysses S. *Grant's use (in 1864–65) of unremitting pressure, campaigns of constant battles rather than a few decisive engagements. Driven back on Petersburg, Virginia, Lee accepted a siege he knew to be fatal before being overwhelmed by Union forces as he attempted escape. In the western theater, Grant sent William Tecumseh *Sherman in similar grim pursuit of the Army of the Tennessee, which Sherman destroyed. Those Union victories, historian Russell Weigley has asserted, established annihilation as the army's preferred strategy.

In World War II, though initially forced by the British and lack of resources to follow a peripheral strategy, American forces in Europe finally launched their preferred cross-Channel attack in June 1944, and in conjunction with British forces and (on the eastern front) the Red Army, commenced a concentrated mass assault on German forces, aimed at their annihilation and imposition of unconditional surrender.

In the *Korean War, annihilation of the enemy's forces, following an envelopment, also influenced Douglas *MacArthur's *Inchon landing—though attrition became the strategy following Chinese intervention and increasing American fear of a Soviet attack in Europe.

During the *Persian Gulf War, the army planned a campaign of annihilation calling on airpower to isolate the battlefield and weaken Iraqi forces in Kuwait, which only an early armistice saved from being enveloped and destroyed by ground and air attack. That campaign also benefited from recent American preparations for the defense of Western Europe without relying on the early use of *nuclear weapons. Aiming to win, though fighting outnumbered, the U.S. Army intended to annihilate the Red Army not through the unremitting direct pressure of superior force (in the manner of Grant) but by increasing the pace of combat beyond what the Soviets could match, using violent maneuver that would send American forces into rear areas, disrupting Soviet *command and control, service support, and reserves.

Strategies of Attrition and Exhaustion. When unwilling or unable to win through annihilation, U.S. strategists have sometimes resorted to gradual and often indirect efforts to wear down their opponent's military forces or exhaust his will to resist.

The superiority of British regulars led Washington to alter his initial strategy in 1777, keeping his *Continental army largely concentrated and employing it principally to shadow and harass the British. His forces sought battle only when they could safely retreat from failure or overwhelm detachments from their opponent's main body—as at Trenton and Princeton, Saratoga, Monmouth, and, during 1781, in the Carolinas and at Yorktown. That strategy wore down British forces, and when combined with French forces, also Britain's will to continue the war. With American militia units retaining control of most of the countryside and the population—as in a revolutionary strategy—Britain had little to show for its expensive military efforts.

Confederate president Jefferson *Davis favored a similar defensive strategy in the *Civil War, concentrating Confederate forces in a few large armies that would avoid decisive battles, maintain Southern independence, and exhaust Union will. That meant, however, leaving more areas of the Confederacy vulnerable to occupation than Davis could tolerate politically—opening the door for Lee's offensives in the East. Only Joseph E. *Johnston—too late in the war and with too little room for maneuver—skillfully employed that strategy against Sherman's advance on Atlanta.

Early on, Abraham *Lincoln, preferring the more rapid results seemingly promised by direct methods, rejected Winfield *Scott's "Anaconda" Plan for undermining Confederate will through naval *blockades and army-navy riverine assaults to isolate major sections of its territory. In the last twelve months of the war, however, Grant encouraged *Sherman to exhaust Confederate will by marching his army across Georgia and through the Carolinas, destroying the supplies and lines of communication upon which Lee depended and making Confederates feel war's "hard hand." Drained by combat losses, suffering naval blockade, and terrorized by Sherman's capacity to ravage rear areas, Confederate will collapsed, and both Lee and Johnston refused Davis's order to commence guerrilla operations.

Strategies of Maneuver and Indirect Approaches. If American ground forces have most often employed strategies of annihilation and various types of attrition, they have also used traditional maneuver strategies aimed either at forcing an enemy's withdrawal with a minimum of fighting or gaining control of points whose possession might lead to *peace. Acting even less directly, they have fought limited battles at weak points along an enemy's periphery and employed economic, political, and psychological methods designed to undermine his strength or will to resist.

In the *Mexican War, for example, President James K. *Polk directed his generals to seize Mexican territory—the northern tier of provinces bordering Texas, and ultimately the capital itself—in order to pressure Mexico to cede New Mexico and Upper California to the United States. Win-

field Scott's seizure of Veracruz and movement on Mexico City, with a minimum of costly combat, represent classic American use of maneuver warfare.

In 1846, Henry W. Halleck and his mentor, Dennis Hart Mahan, published the first American works on strategy. Both rejected Napoleonic offensives in favor of fortification, tactical defense, and maneuver-oriented strategies characteristic of the eighteenth century and Scott's campaign. Although most (strategically unschooled) Civil War commanders knew only that the great Napoleon had won military fame in decisive but bloody battles, the Union produced one advocate of maneuver who was sympathetic to the need for both speedy *victory and minimal *casualties: George B. McClellan, unsuccessful commander of the Army of the Potomac.

The *Spanish-American War better illustrates that American land war strategy has taken limited forms. The army initially planned to assist Cuban independence only by providing military assistance to the insurrection, perhaps through some remote port seized by a few regulars. Meanwhile, it would defend coastal cities and carefully raise, arm, and train volunteer units, if necessary, to occupy the island. With the president impatient for victory and the navy leading the way, the army captured Guam en route to occupation of Manila, seized Puerto Rico, and stormed El Caney and the San Juan Heights in order to take Santiago and drive the Spanish fleet into the navy's guns. This tactic forced Spain to recognize the futility of further resistance and eliminated any need directly to overcome its main army in Cuba.

In World War I, initially convinced that neither maneuver nor a single battle could decisively overcome a major power, John J. *Pershing expected his American Expeditionary Forces in 1918 to employ frontal assaults, modified by open field tactics, only to penetrate German positions before descending on its objective, the rail center at Metz. That strategic maneuver, Pershing hoped, would force a general German withdrawal from France. Fighting on a front without flanks and as part of a multinational force, however, Pershing had to accept his Allies' reliance on bloody frontal assaults to push German forces back all along the line, a strategy more in keeping with the Grantian tradition.

During the first years of World War II, the United States, possessing few mobilized, trained military forces, had no alternative but to adopt Winston S. *Churchill's peripheral strategy, a classically indirect approach. The British opposed a prompt cross-Channel invasion and favored weakening Germany with indirect attacks: strategic bombardment, supplying the Soviets, assistance to resistance movements, and seizure of territory on the periphery of the German conquests. But President Franklin D. *Roosevelt was eager to involve American forces in the fighting. His planners reluctantly agreed, first, to the invasion of French North Africa, then Sicily, and finally Italy, before insisting, with Soviet support, that Churchill abandon his Balkan schemes and agree to invade northern France in mid-1944.

The Pacific War was an American war of strategic maneuver, even if for unlimited ends and involving many bloody tactical assaults. In the face of Japan's rapid advance in the winter of 1941–42, the United States and Great Britain sought to secure their lines of communication to Australia and India. Although unconditional surrender seemingly required the annihilation of Japan's armed forces, the United States thereafter bypassed and isolated many Japanese strongholds en route to gaining control of a vast oceanic territory. Using land, sea, and air forces, the U.S. Army pushed north from Australia, while the navy led the drive through the central Pacific, a two-front advance culminating in the conquest of the Philippines, Okinawa, and Iwo Jima. With its navy sunk, its economy prostrate, and half its army isolated overseas, after the bombings of *Hiroshima and Nagasaki, Japan surrendered before American plans for combined assaults on its home islands could be implemented.

Cold War Strategies. The Cold War and nuclear weapons changed the strategic position of the United States and the emphasis of its land warfare tradition. The country lost the protection offered by European rivalries, and technology undermined the security of vast oceans. Facing an enemy threatening America's very survival, U.S. planners dared not rely on weakened allies to buy time for *mobilization.

Although containment emerged in 1947 as America's grand strategy, the next four decades demonstrated great variation in its means (economic, political, and military) and intermediate ends (protecting vital areas or securing all the nations along the Sino-Soviet perimeter). To overcome the Red Army's numerical superiority in Europe, the United States relied on nuclear *deterrence while also employing military assistance, German rearmament, tactical nuclear weapons, and new maneuver strategies later tested, as noted above, in the Persian Gulf.

During periods when containment emphasized perimeter defense, the army engaged in limited conflict in Korea and in revolutionary war in Vietnam. Although not unaware of the nature of the *Vietnam War and the elements of successful counterinsurgencies, the army—aided by the marines and the other services' air forces—too often fought in traditional ways. Commanders hoped to bring the enemy's main forces to decisive combat, used firepower lavishly to limit U.S. casualties, and relied on airpower to isolate the battlefield, destroy the enemy's economy, and break his will. Fearful of prompting Chinese intervention, the United States applied its power incrementally—discounting the psychological impact of sustained powerful blows and rejecting direct assault on North Vietnam—and made a negotiated settlement its war aim. All of this meant that its opponent could set the pace and intensity of the war at levels it found endurable. "Vietnamization"—turning the war over to the South Vietnamese—showed initial promise, but without lavish American aid, the strategy could not resist North Vietnam's 1975 cross-border invasion.

[See also Enemy, Views of the; Land Warfare; Napoleonic Warfare; Native American Wars: Wars Between Native Americans and Europeans and Euro-Americans; Philippines, U.S. Military Involvement in the; Tactics: Land Warfare Tactics.]

• Russell F. Weigley, *American Military Thought: From Washington to Marshall*, 1962. Walter Millis, ed., *American Military Thought*, 1966. Russell F. Weigley, *The American Way of War: A History of United States Military Strategy and Policy*, 1973. John Lewis Gaddis, *Strategies of Containment: A Critical Appraisal of Postwar American National Security Policy*, 1982. Allan R. Millett and Peter Maslowski, *For the Common Defense: A Military History of the United States of America*, 1984. Archer Jones, *Elements of Military Strategy: An Historical Approach*, 1996.
                                                  —James L. Abrahamson

On the surface, Alfred T. *Mahan embodies American thinking about the uses of a navy and the exploitation of the nation's maritime geography. Captain (later Admiral) Mahan, ship commander, historian, and teacher, explored earlier wars for their lessons about sea power. He wrote and lectured for his fellow naval officers, found an international hearing among navalists, and gathered a large public audience. His ideas guided the generations who built the navies before and after *World War I, and his emphasis on the battle fleet still dominates the American naval culture. Mahan, like Carl von *Clausewitz, typifies the strategist we expect to instruct us: a military professional whose rigorous thinking illuminates basic truths about war.

In Mahan's formulation, "strategy decides where to act." Yes, but the American strategic tale transcends the historian's record of admirals and sea fights. With the exception of the pre- and post-World War I decades and part of the Pacific War in World War II, the history of American naval strategy is not Mahanian and only intermittently about full-scale war. The makers of strategy have often been civilian officials; their regular problem has been how to use the navy day to day in peacetime and in small, distant skirmishes. When planning for war they have worked closely with the army. Invariably, domestic priorities and partisan politics entangle military and naval logic. Why? Because navies are expensive. They take time to build and train. And once built, they last a long time. The fleet cruising on a distant station has been wrestled into place by a struggle among many participants, each favoring a different strategic calculus, few of them ship captains, fewer likely to have foreseen the contingency at hand.

An inattentive strategic culture was visible in our earliest days: "A disposition seems rather to prevail among our citizens to give up all ideas of navigation and naval power and lay themselves consequently on the mercy of foreigners, even for the price of their produce," wrote John *Adams from London to Thomas *Jefferson in Paris. Exchanging letters between their ambassadorial posts in 1786, a year before the Constitutional Convention in Philadelphia, the two future presidents were discussing ways to resolve the threat to American commerce from the pirates of Algiers. Jefferson—later to lead a political party fiercely opposed to a standing navy—proposed an armed naval force. Adams—later as president to shepherd the bill establishing a small peacetime navy—judged that an attack on the Barbary ports was not likely to eradicate the threat. He held that, however unsavory, discussions and tribute payments were the better *modus vivendi*. "I agree in opinion of the wisdom and necessity of a navy for other uses," wrote Adams, ". . . [but] I perceive that neither force nor money will be applied."

His skepticism was sound. It was to be fourteen years before Adams, as president, sailed the USS *George Washington* with a "peace offering" to the Dey of Algiers. A year later, with Adams defeated for reelection and the situation worsening, newly installed President Jefferson shifted policies. In a show of force, he dispatched America's first "squadron of observation"—half the decaying naval establishment he had been left by Adams—with instructions to "superintend the safety of our commerce there, and to exercise our seamen in their nautical duties." Jefferson advised the Dey that it was "the first object of our solicitude to cherish peace and friendship with all nations with whom it can be held of terms of equality and reciprocity."

Thus are evident from our earliest days some durable traits: in the political arena, subtle, foresighted thinking by individual leaders, a shallow reservoir of public support, and party politics that confuse positions and delay action. Also foreshadowed are a perennial preference for influence by peaceful indirection, for sailing fairly large, well-armed task forces in troubled waters with politically ambiguous instructions to cruise for "observation" and "training," and a preference for operations mounted far from U.S. coasts. Other inclinations rise from the inevitable gap between the politics which create the fleet and the circumstances demanding its use. The construction of flexible, multipurpose forces is preferred over investment in smaller, single-use systems; the ability to invent winning tactical combinations with the forces at hand is valued above the rote execution of preplanned doctrine.

As Adams cautioned, we should not find too much rigor in these instincts for the use of a navy and the exploitation of the nation's maritime geography. Inattention more than ingenuity, politics more than policy have husbanded America's naval resources. Frustrating as this intermittent attention may be to navalists, it accords with the national psyche. Save for the anomalous half-century of the *Cold War, American security strategy has been marked by a preference for other, more domestic concerns and by a parallel bias against the apparatus of standing forces, be they military and naval or latterly aerial and space-based. That bias has extended to thinking about the use of force. In over two centuries, the United States has seen only a few theoreticians gain a public audience, and they often appeared as propagandists aiming to create popular support for the funding of one kind of military force over another, e.g., Gen. Billy *Mitchell's campaign to supplant battleships with bombers. In the assessment of one naval historian, the writings of Mahan himself were "weapons in rough-and-tumble debates between proponents and opponents of naval expansionism, colonialism, and aggressive mercantile capitalism."

Secretaries and assistant secretaries of the navy, occasionally even presidents, have thought about making naval strategy their job. Benjamin Stoddert, Gideon *Welles, *Theodore *Roosevelt, Franklin D. *Roosevelt, and Josephus Daniels were among those secretaries or assistants to exercise their office vigorously toward a strategic design. Recently, Secretary John Lehman reprised that role but the Cold War rise of a national security establishment with a strong Secretary of Defense, a *primus inter pares* Chairman of the *Joint Chiefs of Staff, and the *National Security Council staff in the White House have seen the political locus of strategy making shift upward from the Navy Department and the process become more leaderless than ever.

Among naval officers Mahan's emphasis on the primacy of the battle fleet helps fuel an enduring belief that the navy is best used independently, that it must be kept separate from the army. Without minimizing inter-service rivalry for funding, the record shows much more Army-Navy—and latterly Air Force-Navy—cooperation than myth would have it. Joint planning has been common and army generals have sometimes had much useful to say about Navy's employment. Listen to Gen. George *Washington during the *Revolutionary War: "In any operation, and under all circumstances," he declared, "a decisive naval

superiority is to be considered as a fundamental principle and the basis on which every hope of success must ultimately depend." This was not mere theory. Though the rebel's navy never rose much above haphazard operations by individual ships, the course of the Revolutionary War hinged repeatedly on the duel between Washington's army and mobile, sea-borne British forces. Washington climaxed the struggle at the Battle of *Yorktown with the timely aid of a French fleet that blocked the threatening British ships. Stranded, Gen. Charles *Cornwallis offered the decisive surrender. Army officers ever since have closely attended their naval flanks, giving rise to a lasting struggle between two different visions of U.S. naval power. A requirement for the nation to go to war has usually found the army devising ways for the navy to transport and support land forces while naval officers instinctively incline to blue water schemes to defeat the enemy's navy and interdict his shipping.

Pick up the narrative at the *Civil War. President Abraham *Lincoln's successful "Anaconda Plan," by which the navy would help encircle and split the Confederacy, was advanced very early in the war by army Commanding Gen. Winfield *Scott. The concept drew on Scott's success during the *Mexican War when he and accompanying naval commanders innovated a huge amphibious landing at Vera Cruz. At the end of the nineteenth century, Mahan famously pushed the balance the other way with his arguments drawn from history that the central purpose of a navy was to defeat the enemy's navy. Illustrated by Horatio Nelson's victory over the French fleet at Trafalgar, a successful sea fight led to "sea control," which delivered a decisive political outcome. Mahan-inspired battle fleets proliferated, but for the United States the Atlantic battles of World War I and World War II were shaped by the priorities of getting troops and supplies to Europe in the face of German *submarine attack. As foreseen in years of prior war gaming at the Naval War College, fleet vs. fleet fighting dominated the naval campaigns of World War II in the Pacific. But even in the Pacific, naval operations were also tied closely to the progress of Gen. Douglas *MacArthur's island-hopping land forces. The *Korean War saw the navy back in close support of the land war; the *Vietnam War drew naval forces into riverine and coastal operations not seen since the Anaconda campaign a hundred years earlier.

At the height of the Cold War in the early and mid-1980s these tendencies to favor "ship vs. land" over "ship vs. ship" strategy reached their apotheosis in the "Maritime Strategy." Devised by naval officers, the Maritime Strategy laid out in considerable detail the expected battles at sea when, at the beginning of a hypothetical World War III, the navy and its allies would attack the Soviet forces defending the seaward approaches to the USSR homeland. The Strategy made it clear, however, that the purpose of the ocean fighting was to clear the way rapidly for direct naval attacks on the Soviet Union. By doing so, the Strategy argued, naval forces operating far forward on several fronts would both diffuse the Soviet focus on Western Europe and forestall Soviet attempts to repeat World War-style battles for control of the Atlantic logistics lanes. The Strategy delivered two key benefits: extrapolating back from the successful battles it proposed in a future world war, it found its central purpose as a deterrent against the outbreak of that war. And with that portrait of present and future success, the Strategy provided a politically credible template for the budget. Controversial as it was—the army, especially, doubted that the far forward campaign would indeed safeguard its cross-ocean logistics—the Maritime Strategy was widely influential. U.S. and *NATO military planners adopted its concepts until the end of the Cold War rendered it obsolete, closing what some had called a renaissance in naval strategic thinking.

With both the Soviet navy and the specter of World War III dissolved, the machinery of strategy making reverted to its habitual, diffused state. Funding for the fleet derived more from domestic politics and traditional preferences for big, flexible units; forward peace support missions, now labeled "operations other than war," resumed their central place in fleet tasking. What did not change was the focus of war planning on the battle of the fleet against the shore. Absent any significant high seas competitor, the post-Cold War naval strategy, titled ". . . From the Sea," could, at least *ad interim,* tie its offensive capabilities into multi-service operations ashore and base its defensive requirements on landward threats.

From the pure, Mahanian world of fleet-on-fleet warfare, the U.S. naval profession has gone deeper and deeper into matters of peace and war ashore. Mahan's canonical world of seamanship, marine technology, and tactical competence, which held sway more in myth than history, has given way to a much more complex professional reality. At century's end profound changes in the international geostrategic climate promise to draw naval strategy still further away from self-contained battle plans. Ahead is an even more messy world where international political calculations and the civil, humanitarian dimensions of international security policy are added to domestic political and inter-service dynamics and all is infused with torrents of information. Also ahead is a world of space-based systems, long-range aircraft, and remotely controlled devices that invade the navy's traditional sea space. Reliance on strategy by muddling through in the era ahead—however much that might be the national style—seems unlikely to deliver the coherently designed and effectively deployed forces needed if the navy is to continue to be central to American security.

[*See also* Navy, U.S.; Navy Combat Branches; Sea Warfare; Tactics: Naval Warfare Tactics; Weaponry, Naval.]

• Edward L. Beach, *The United States Navy: 200 Years,* 1986. Wayne P. Hughes, *Fleet Tactics: Theory and Practice,* 1986. J. C. Wylie, *Military Strategy: A General Theory of Power Control,* 1990. Edward S. Miller, *War Plan Orange: The U.S. strategy to defeat Japan, 1897–1945,* 1991. David Alan Rosenberg, "Process: The Realities of Formulating Modern Naval Strategy," James Goldrick and John B. Hattendorf, eds., *Mahan is not Enough,* 1993. George W. Baer, *One Hundred Years of Sea Power: the U.S. Navy, 1890–1990,* 1994. Colin S. Gray and Roger W. Barnett, *Seapower and Strategy,* 1996. N. A. M. Rodger, ed., *Naval Power in the Twentieth Century,* 1996. Jon Tetsuro Sumida, *Inventing Grand Strategy and Teaching Command: The Classic Works of Alfred Thayer Mahan Reconsidered,* 1997.

—Larry Seaquist

STRATEGY: AIR WARFARE STRATEGY

The military advantages of being able to fly above an enemy were evident from the earliest times, and strategies of aerial warfare had their origins in the musings of such science fiction writers as H. G. Wells. Their apocalyptic visions, however, outstripped the operational capabilities of early aircraft, and the emergence of air strategy had to await the development of flying machines that could carry significant destructive payloads and institutions willing to expend the resources needed to exploit their capabilities. That combination appeared in 1915, when French and German airmen perceived that they could bomb targets whose destruction would affect the enemy's strategic potential directly, rather than indirectly by influencing the outcome of a land or naval battle. This generally meant attacks on industrial targets close behind the front, for example, German munitions factories in the Saar, though the German Naval Air Service proposed to bring Britain to its knees by Zeppelin attacks on London targets such as the Bank of England, the city's gasworks, and the Admiralty radio transmitter.

These schemes were frustrated by the feeble means available—inadequate bombloads and range in the first instance, and the vulnerability of hydrogen-filled Zeppelins in the second—but aircraft capabilities kept improving. The Italians bombed strategic Austrian targets from 1916, and in the spring of 1917, the German army attempted to destroy London with conventional bombers in a campaign that failed to achieve its primary purpose, but forced the British to shift significant air assets from the western front to home defense. The newly formed Royal Air Force mounted a strategic bombing offensive against German industry in 1918, the first to be formally labeled as such. Ambitious in concept, it achieved little.

While strategic airpower had little impact in World War I, airpower enthusiasts saw promise, notably in the panic sparked by the 1917 German raids on London. The indecisiveness of slaughter in the trenches was evident, as was the stalemate of Dreadnought battleship fleets. It was in this context that in 1921, Italian Lt. Col. Giulio *Douhet published *Command of the Air,* the first formal treatise on air strategy. Douhet received little attention beyond Italy, and his impact on American air strategists is uncertain; he was important mainly in articulating in extreme form ideas current among contemporary airmen. He argued that armies and navies had become irrelevant, and that a nation could be defeated by a single, massive air attack that destroyed its cities and centers of production under a rain of high-explosive, incendiary, and poison gas bombs, shattering civilian morale and producing *victory. There was no defense, he wrote, against such an attack, delivered by a fleet of swift battle planes, and victory would go to the side that got in the first blow. While Douhet's arguments were extreme, heavy emphasis on bombardment was common among early airpower pioneers, notably Gen. Hugh Trenchard, the first head of the Royal Air Force.

Meanwhile, in America, Brig. Gen. Billy *Mitchell, drawing on his experience as commander of the American Expeditionary Force's air component in 1917–18, had conceived a more pragmatic theory. While Mitchell, like Douhet, believed that airpower would be decisive in future wars, he considered bombardment as part of a spectrum in which the traditional missions—pursuit, observation, ground attack, and reconnaissance—retained their value, and saw a role for transport aviation and parachute troops. He believed, moreover, that defeat of the enemy air force was an air force's first task. His main contribution was to argue that airpower was indivisible, and that all air assets should be concentrated under a single air commander rather than parceled out to the army and navy. Mitchell's calls for the establishment of an independent air force produced a strongly negative official response, and his predictions and opinions, widely published in popular magazines, became increasingly extreme. He eventually accused senior military leaders of criminal incompetence, leading to his court-martial in 1925 and dismissal from service in 1926.

Whether because or in spite of Mitchell's activism, the U.S. Army granted its airmen increasing autonomy, and 1920 saw the formation of the Air Corps Tactical School (ACTS) which, its name notwithstanding, became the first formally chartered air warfare strategic planning group. The ACTS approached war as an essentially economic phenomenon, and from the mid-1920s focused increasingly on the strategic use of heavy bombers. Implicitly rejecting the notion that victory could be achieved with a single, paralyzing blow, the ACTS planners sought ways in which attacks on carefully selected nodes of the industrial network could cause economic collapse. Refining their theories by analyzing the vulnerabilities of America's economy, they concluded by the mid-1930s that attacks on the appropriate node—electric power generation, for instance, or petroleum refining—could achieve the desired result. They concluded, moreover, that it could be done within the means available. The key caveat was that the requisite accuracy could be achieved only in daylight, which, in turn, meant high-altitude attacks to minimize the effectiveness of anti-aircraft artillery and fighter interception. In retrospect, their assumptions concerning bombing accuracy and, above all, the ability of unescorted bombers to protect themselves against fighter attack, were overoptimistic.

Applied by the U.S. Army Air Forces (USAAF) in mid-1943 against German ball-bearing production during World War II, the ACTS concepts produced major operational defeat; more remarkably, they provided a viable intellectual framework that, with the addition of long-range escort fighters, led to the defeat of the Luftwaffe. Though not strategically decisive in isolation, attacks on two nodes, petroleum production and the rail net, conducted from early 1944 in conjunction with RAF's Bomber Command, were pivotal in the defeat of the Third Reich. The other attempts of note to use airpower "strategically" in World War II were RAF Bomber Command's campaign against German cities and by the Luftwaffe, implicitly in the Battle of Britain and explicitly in 1943 on the eastern front, using a strategy much like that of the ACTS, though with grossly inadequate resources. Airpower proved decisive in the war at sea, but as an adjunct to battle fleets and in the *antisubmarine role. Indeed, air superiority was a decisive element of victory in virtually every campaign involving industrialized opponents, vindicating the validity of Mitchell's operational insight.

During World War II, the enormity of the strategic stakes and the totality of resources committed effectively erased the distinction between civilian and military targets, validating a central point of Douhet's theory. This appeared most dramatically in RAF Bomber Command's area bombing campaign against German cities from 1942 and in the USAAF's 1945 firebombing of Japanese cities; it found its ultimate expression in the atomic bombings of *Hiroshima and Nagasaki.

Influenced by the awesome power of nuclear and thermonuclear weapons, air strategies in the postwar era evolved along two distinct paths: nuclear and conventional. After the Soviet Union ended the United States's nuclear monopoly in 1949, American nuclear strategy revolved around two interlocked concepts: *massive retaliation,* aimed at deterring Soviet expression, especially in Western Europe; and *deterrence,* intended to discourage a preemptive nuclear attack on the United States. The latter found definitive, if not final, expression in John F. *Kennedy's administration's concept of "Mutual Assured Destruction" (MAD). The manned bomber's monopoly as a nuclear delivery system was broken by intercontinental ballistic missiles (ICBMs) in the late 1950s and by submarine-launched ballistic missiles (SLBMs) in the mid-1960s, erasing the distinction between nuclear air strategy and nuclear strategy. It is worth noting, however, that the United States was unique in vesting responsibility for the planning and execution of nuclear strategy in its air force, all strategic *nuclear weapons coming under the operational control of the Strategic Air Command (SAC) from its inception in 1947 until it was disbanded in 1993.

In conventional air strategy, the USAF has followed the trajectory of Mitchell's ideas, arguing for the indivisibility of airpower and that all air forces should be placed under a single air force commander. That insistence on unity of command and a continued belief in the decisiveness of strategic bombing were hallmarks of the air force's approach to the Korean and Vietnam Wars, with at best uncertain results. The navy and Marine Corps, drawing on their successful experience in World War II, viewed aviation as an extension of naval and land forces, and resisted what they considered air force attempts to usurp their internal unity of command. The air force's insistence on indivisibility has yielded important strategic dividends in airlift and aerial refueling, two areas in which the USAF has been in a class by itself since the 1950s. Both capabilities played a large part in the *Cold War and in the 1991 *Persian Gulf War. In the latter conflict, newly matured technologies—laser-guided bombs, electronic warfare, electronic *communications, and stealth bombers—prompted adoption of a radical air strategy developed in the late 1970s by Air Force Col. John Warden. Rejecting the attritional gradualism used in the *Vietnam War, Warden's strategy was "inside out," targeting Iraqi command centers, communications, *radar, and power generation first, with attacks on traditional military and economic targets coming only after strategic paralysis was achieved. While the strategic decisiveness of the air campaign in the Persian Gulf War is hotly debated, its tactical and technological success is widely acknowledged.

[See also Air Warfare; Tactics: Air Warfare Tactics.]

—John F. Guilmartin, Jr.

STRATEGY: NUCLEAR WARFARE STRATEGY AND WAR PLANS

Within months of the atomic bombings of *Hiroshima and Nagasaki that devastated those two cities in early August 1945, the basic questions that have bedeviled nuclear strategists and war planners ever since became evident in congressional testimony and published treatises. The United States itself would be vulnerable to air attack in future war, Congress was told in November 1945 by Gen. Carl A. *Spaatz, head of U.S. Army Air Forces in Europe. Gen. "Hap" *Arnold, commanding general of the Army Air Forces, warned Congress that since air attack could arrive without warning, the basic defense against such an attack would have to be the ability to launch a rapid, powerful air offensive against the source of the attack. "But, better still," Arnold declared, "the actual existence of these weapons ... in sufficient quantities and so located that a potential aggressor knows we can use them effectively against him, will have a very deterring effect, particularly if the aggressor does not know the whole story and only knows *part* of the story."

Within these assertions lay the roots of U.S. strategic doctrine that were to permeate the *Cold War: the concepts of *deterrence on one hand and defense by destruction of the enemy's capacity for offensive action on the other; the vulnerability of the United States to surprise attack through the air; the need for extensive forces, variously deployed and capable of rapid action; and the perceived need for secrecy. These initial military concerns were mirrored by two civilian theorists—Bernard Brodie and William Borden.

Brodie, a Yale scholar who had first studied war at sea and now turned his attention to war from the air, wrote a paper in November 1945 entitled "The Atomic Bomb and American Security," which was later included in expanded form as two chapters of The Absolute Weapon (1946), the first book published on nuclear strategy. In the paper, he staked out deterrence as the dominant concept of nuclear strategy. As he put it famously: "Thus far the chief purpose of our military establishment has been to win wars. From now on its chief purpose must be to avert them. It can have almost no other purpose." To achieve such deterrence, however, would require the United States "to take measures to guarantee to ourselves in case of attack the possibility of retaliation in kind." For the next two decades, particularly in 1951–66, while he worked at the RAND Corporation, a newly established national security research institution in Santa Monica, California, Brodie set the pace among civilian theorists of nuclear strategy. His next book, Strategy in the Missile Age (1959), remains even today the only true classic on the essential questions of nuclear force structure (how much is enough? and hence, enough for what?) and force postures (offensive, defensive, retaliatory, preemptive, and air-, land-, or sea-based).

In contrast to Brodie's emphasis on deterrence were the views of a colleague at Yale, William Borden, who wrote There Will Be No Time: The Revolution in Strategy (1946). Borden believed that atomic war was inevitable and would likely be fought by nuclear-tipped intercontinental-range rockets based in underground "hedgehogs" located far from cities and "on undersea platforms scattered throughout the world's oceans." These would be aimed against the enemy's military forces rather than cities. Borden concluded that such a war could be won decisively and with only limited civilian damage. However, because of the secrecy surrounding preparations for such a war and the unprecedented powers the president would be granted in peacetime, Borden surmised that American democracy would be inevitably diminished. As noted by Gregg Herken, "with minor variations, the positions taken by Brodie and Borden endured as the opposite poles of a debate that would rage for the next forty years...."

Thus, even before the end of 1946, most major issues, except those resulting from such unforeseen technological developments as antiballistic missile (ABM) defenses and satellite reconnaissance, were already recognized. These included deterrence as an end in itself; offensive readiness and threatened retaliatory capability (eventually including *missiles housed in silos in areas remote from popula

tion centers or aboard *submarines in the ocean's depths) as the answer to defensive vulnerability; and the potential emergence of a "national security state." Still, very few Americans read Brodie or Borden or otherwise became engaged in questions of "atomic strategy." Most focused on the more pressing immediate problems of economic prosperity.

Within the military, during the administration of President Harry S. *Truman (1945–51), war planning for what some called the "air atomic age" was initially incoherent. It was severely limited by the extreme secrecy governing nuclear matters, incessant interservice *rivalry (such as the B-36 bomber vs. the supercarrier controversy of 1949), and the ambivalent attitude of Truman regarding the *nuclear weapons themselves. The planning process that evolved by the early 1950s was complex and variable, but can be sketched in broad outline. Initially, a Joint War Plans Committee (JWPC) in the *Pentagon had the lead, but following passage of the *National Security Act of 1947 and the creation of a U.S. Air Force separated from the army, an elaborately structured process of nuclear war planning emerged.

At its apex was the *National Security Council (NSC), chaired by the president, which spelled out national security objectives and provided overall guidance regarding nuclear weapons. Below that were the *Joint Chiefs of Staff (JCS), who were responsible for translating generalized NSC guidance into specific strategic plans. The Joint Strategic Capabilities Plan (JSCP) covered global war planning for the coming year and was prepared annually. In addition, the Joint Strategic Objectives Plan (JSOP) projected a four- to six-year time frame and was also prepared each year. The crucial elements of the nation's nuclear war plan—general guidance regarding target categories and desired damage levels—were contained in Annex C of the JSOP.

At the third level (below the NSC and JCS), the task was to identify specific targets and prepare operational plans detailing the means and timing of delivering the nuclear weapons to their targets. Until the late 1950s, identification of specific targets was the province of the Air Targets Division within the U.S. Air Force Directorate of Intelligence. Operational planning fell to the Strategic Air Command (SAC), which was moved in 1948 away from Washington, D.C., to the vicinity of Omaha, Nebraska.

Factors external to this formal planning process included intelligence estimates regarding the capability and vulnerability of the Soviet Union and technological change, especially as it affected the numbers, availability, and delivery modes of U.S. nuclear weapons. Also largely external to this process were the thoughts of the nuclear war theorists both within and outside the government, whose ideas, although they could affect public perceptions, were least important to the operational planners, whose work was directed essentially at pragmatic problem solving.

Nuclear war planning in the late 1940s and the 1950s can be summarized as follows: The people in the intelligence community, especially within the air force but also including the *Central Intelligence Agency (CIA), looked for targets, all the while fearing they might miss important ones and hence listing all they could find. The people who worked on development of nuclear weapons, especially those people in the Atomic Energy Commission, focused on reducing the size of warheads, improving their yield (destructive power), and increasing their number to keep up with the growing target list. The people who planned the military operations—planners at SAC and later at the European, Atlantic, and Pacific unified commands (EU-COM, LANTCOM, and PACOM)—sought to match the available weapons to the designated targets.

Inevitably, given the compartmentalized secrecy governing the artificially separate elements of the nuclear war planning process, a certain dynamic arose. More targets required more weapons, which in turn required more delivery systems (aircraft, missiles, submarines). As a result, the day-to-day work of the operations planners had little to do with any subtleties of either nuclear strategy or deterrence theory. Rather, it had to do with deploying as effectively and efficiently as possible the weapons available against the targets assigned; in sum, pragmatic problem solving. It took a decade for the formal system to become fully institutionalized.

At first, however, prior to the 1949 test explosion of the first Soviet atomic bomb, things were simpler. During the years between 1946 and 1949, the war planners in the U.S. military envisioned that war with the Soviet Union would be like World War II but on a more destructive scale. The United States then had few atomic weapons, let alone aircraft equipped to carry what were then extremely large and heavy nuclear bombs. The atomic-capable *bomber aircraft and their weapons would be "seeded" among normal B-29 bombers at one of the American forward overseas bases. The detailed war plans remained secret until the end of the *Cold War, when the early plans were declassified and published (1990) in fifteen volumes, edited by Steven T. Ross and David Alan Rosenberg, and entitled *America's Plans for War Against the Soviet Union, 1945–1950*. Plans since 1950 remain generally classified.

The initial scarcity of nuclear weapons was soon overcome. (The U.S. nuclear weapons stockpile grew from only a couple of warheads in 1945 to more than 500 in 1951, then exponentially to more than 1,000 in 1952, the last of which included 720 loadings on 660 bombers; by 1955, there were 2,250 warheads stockpiled with 1,755 loadings on 1,260 bombers.) The prodigious increase in the number of U.S. nuclear weapons resulted from a combination of technological breakthroughs and a dramatic surge in military spending, first by the Truman administration as a result of the *Korean War (1950–53) and then as a result of a decision by President Dwight D. *Eisenhower to emphasize the strategic nuclear forces while cutting back on the other armed services and reducing the overall defense budget.

In January 1954, following a year-long review of defense policy by the administration, Secretary of State John Foster *Dulles announced the doctrine of "Massive Retaliation": the administration would rely upon the threat of nuclear escalation, including massive destruction of the Soviet Union, to deter or stop Soviet-inspired local wars in the future. The policy was driven by the frustrations of the Korean War and Eisenhower's fears about the impact of increased defense spending upon the American economy. Essentially, it was an economic rather than a strategic decision, one that sought "more bang for the buck over the long haul."

Massive retaliation provoked immediate debate. Some theorists of nuclear strategy questioned the credibility of the threat of a full-scale nuclear attack on the Soviet Union

as the result of any conflict less than a Soviet invasion of Europe. Some questioned the sanity of introducing an "age of overkill," arguing instead that the ability to deliver with certainty a relatively few nuclear weapons would be sufficient for the needs of deterrence. The "finite deterrence" school, however, despite a strong effort by the U.S. Navy in 1957, was never really accepted in the United States, even though Eisenhower's own view was that it was not necessary to be able to destroy the entire Soviet Union in order to deter Moscow.

Despite Eisenhower's personal view, other matters intervened, always with political overtones, to increase the U.S. nuclear stockpile. This included 3,550 nuclear warheads in 1956, with 2,123 loadings on 1,470 bomber-based launchers, to 23,000 warheads stockpiled in 1961, with 3,153 loadings, including 3,083 on bombers, 57 on intercontinental ballistic missiles (ICBMs), and 80 on submarine-launched ballistic missiles (SLBMs). Among the developments that contributed to the increase were the test explosion of the first Soviet hydrogen bomb in 1953; a 1954 RAND study, led by theorist Albert Wohlsetter, on the perceived vulnerability of SAC's forward bases overseas; intelligence failures positing a "bomber gap" with the Soviets outproducing the Americans in bombers; the 1957 Gaither Report warning of an impending "missile gap" in favor of the USSR, followed immediately by the Soviet launching of Sputnik (the first space satellite), falsely taken to demonstrate such a gap (which in fact favored the Americans); and the shooting down by the Soviets of one of the American *U-2 spy planes over the USSR in 1960. Still, by the end of the 1950s, the open threat of massive retaliation became muted, and steps were begun at the end of the decade to improve conventional forces as an alternative to nuclear confrontation.

The increased emphasis on conventional forces under the doctrine of *Flexible Response was accelerated under President John F. *Kennedy, but the Kennedy administration (1961–63) also escalated the buildup of strategic nuclear forces to previously undreamt-of levels. Under Kennedy, this occurred primarily by switching from the emphasis on bombers to land- and sea-launched ballistic missiles, amounting to 1,000 Minuteman and 54 Titan land-based intercontinental ballistic missiles and a fleet of 41 Polaris-type submarines, each armed with 16 submarine-launched ballistic missiles. Kennedy used the overwhelming American strategic superiority to help convince Moscow to back down in the *Cuban Missile Crisis, leading the Soviets in the aftermath to increase dramatically their own strategic forces.

From 1948 through 1965, from President Truman to President Lyndon B. *Johnson, the most important nuclear strategist in the United States was Gen. Curtis E. *LeMay, who was commander of SAC (1948–57), U.S. Air Force vice chief of staff (1957–61), and air force chief of staff (1961–65). LeMay was absolutely determined to avoid a "nuclear Pearl Harbor" and was convinced that massive numerical superiority, with instant readiness, was the essence of deterrence. On several occasions, LeMay made it clear to his superiors that a preemptive attack option by the United States was written into the secret war plans (secret even from the JCS from 1951 to 1955). Furthermore, he had no interest in "this launch-under-attack business," but instead, he planned to launch on *warning* (never formally defined), and with virtually the entire SAC nuclear force.

By 1960, SAC planners had identified some 8,000 targets to be destroyed in a nuclear strike on the Soviet Union. Also by that date, the navy's Polaris missile had been successfully tested. In an attempt to impose order on the target planning process (and incessant wrangling among the services), the president established the multiservice Joint Strategic Target Planning Staff (JSTPS), which was directed to prepare a coordinated U.S. Single Integrated Operational Plan (SIOP). Its first edition, formally designated SIOP-62, became effective on 1 July 1961.

When briefed on the plan, President Kennedy and his defense secretary Robert S. *McNamara found the existing SIOP wholly unacceptable, and they demanded changes to provide the president with a variety of options from which he could choose in a nuclear confrontation. As a result, the new "declared policy" emphasized the destruction of the enemy's military forces, not his civilian population; it was quickly dubbed the "counterforce" option as opposed to the previous "countervalue"—or city-destroying—strategy. Although General LeMay disagreed with the new emphasis, he went along, especially once he realized that a counterforce strategy would mean an increased number of targets and, therefore, increased strategic forces.

In actuality, despite the change in declared policy, the war plan was not radically changed but merely provided with more options. The so-called no-cities strategy was, in truth, a sham, given the location of key military targets in or near cities and given the residual effects of nuclear detonations. Indeed, before leaving office in 1967, McNamara abandoned counterforce in favor of a capability to threaten the "assured destruction" of "one-quarter to one-third of [the Soviet Union's] population and about two-thirds of its industrial capacity." To be sure, the SIOP would now list several lesser options that a president might choose, but assured destruction was surely massive retaliation by another name. Given the enormous strategic nuclear forces in both the United States and the Soviet Union, "Mutual Assured Destruction" (MAD), while never a formal policy, was an apt description.

Subsequent presidents, secretaries of defense (especially James R. *Schlesinger, Harold *Brown, and Caspar *Weinberger), and national security advisers (particularly Henry *Kissinger) made fitful attempts to modify the targeting criteria and options of the SIOP. Three such instances that were leaked to the public involved the Nuclear Weapons Employment Policy (NUWEP-1) signed by Schlesinger in April 1974; the Nuclear Targeting Policy Review of 1978; and Presidential Directive 59 (PD-59), signed by President Jimmy *Carter in July 1980. In each case, the changes were more declaratory than substantive, although this was difficult to discern given all the hoopla generated by the press, especially regarding an alleged new emphasis on targeting the "recovery capability" of the Soviet Union.

Most attention during the 1970s focused on the extent to which technological advances appeared to undermine any hopes for the stability of emerging arms control efforts. The first Strategic Arms Limitation Treaty (SALT I), an attempt to cap the number of ICBMs and ABM defense systems, was signed by President Richard M. *Nixon and Soviet premier Leonid I. Brezhnev in 1972. But it sidestepped the newly crucial issue of multiple, independently targetable reentry vehicles (MIRVs), whereby a single large ICBM could now carry as many as a dozen warheads that could, within trajectory limits, strike different targets. The

Soviet emphasis on large ICBMs, especially the SS-18 armed with MIRVs, quickly led to fears that the U.S. land-based missile force had suddenly become vulnerable to a disarming first (or surprise) strike. Why the Soviets might decide to attempt such a strike was an irrelevant question in the war planning culture. If they could, they might, so capabilities rather than intentions or likelihoods were important. And for those concerned with a Soviet first strike there was always the fear that Moscow's true goal might not be a disarming first strike at all, but rather a new ability in a crisis to impose "nuclear blackmail" based on U.S. perceptions of the vulnerability of its own forces and their allied mechanisms of *command and control.

Abetted by exaggerated claims regarding the accuracy of Soviet missiles, the United States, it was argued, would soon face an emerging "window of vulnerability" unless drastic measures were taken to "modernize" its forces. This meant the production of the B-1 and B-2 bombers, the MX missile, Trident submarines, the "hardening" of command and control networks, and replacement of the existing inventory of nuclear warheads with new and improved models. (The number of warheads in the U.S. nuclear weapons stockpile had grown to 26,500 in 1962, 29,000 in 1963, 31,000 in 1964, and 31,500 in 1965 and 1966; it reached a peak of 32,000 in 1967; then began to drop, as older warheads were eliminated, to between 28,000 and 25,000 during the 1970s, where it remained until well into the 1980s. Meanwhile, the number of nuclear warheads loaded on various types of launchers averaged about 6,000 during the 1960s.) Critics of the argument about the need for such modernization to meet an alleged window of vulnerability were appalled. Their view was best encapsulated by Lord Solly Zuckerman, the British scientist, in his Nuclear Illusion and Reality (1982): "Once the numbers game took over, reason flew out the window."

President Ronald *Reagan took office in 1981 fully committed to the direst possible view of the capabilities as well as the intentions of the Soviet Union. The SALT II talks, envisaging significant reductions, had begun in 1974, leading to a treaty signed by Carter and Brezhnev in June 1979. But divided American opinion led the Senate to delay action, and the Soviet invasion of Afghanistan in December 1979 effectively killed the treaty, at least until after the 1980 election.

The apparent enthusiasm with which the Reagan administration (1981–89) initially adopted the long dominant and prevailing views among war planners regarding "nuclear warfighting," "countervailing strategy," and other mantras going back to Herman Kahn's On Nuclear War (1960) frightened many Americans. Vice President George Bush's statement that a nuclear war was winnable, Secretary of State Alexander M. *Haig's comment about "a nuclear demonstration shot," and the president's own musings on a European nuclear war, along with outlandish remarks by civil defense officials on the survivability of nuclear war—all had the unforeseen effect of capturing the attention of a public accustomed to ignoring such issues for the previous twenty years. Despite the protest from a sizable and vocal segment of the public, the Reagan administration's position on nuclear war planning was not significantly different from that of its predecessors. However, it had brought to the declarative level, and thus made openly public, the assumptions upon which the operational level planners had been working for years—and that had shocked a considerable and influential segment of the public.

The reaction that set in during 1982–83, symbolized by the Nuclear Freeze Campaign and an unusual pastoral letter against nuclear war from the Roman Catholic bishops' conference in America, may well have played some part in leading the Reagan administration to shift focus to an improbable antimissile defense, the so-called *Strategic Defense Initiative (SDI), and move to reconsider the SALT II treaty by reopening the talks, soon relabeled *START (Strategic Arms Reductions Talks). It was also during the Reagan administration that civilians began to assert somewhat more control over the war planning process, although the fundamentals were not changed.

In their analysis of the six Single Integrated Operational Plans (SIOPs) for U.S. nuclear strategy in effect from 1960 to 1985, Desmond Ball (with Jeffrey Richelson) concluded that the general categories and particular types of targets had remained remarkably resilient. They were the Soviet Union's military forces, its urban-industrial structure, and its leadership centers. "Two developments have occurred, however," Ball advised. "One is that the number of potential target installations ... increased enormously, from ...4,100 in 1960 ... to some 50,000.... Second, these targets have been increasingly divided into a larger array of 'packages' of varying sizes and characteristics, providing ... 'customized' options for an extremely wide range of possible contingencies." In 1986, Ball saw little reason to expect these developments to change markedly.

But then came the dramatic events of 1989–91: the fall of the Berlin Wall, the disintegration of the *Warsaw Pact, and the collapse of the Soviet Union. The end of the Cold War threw all earlier calculations of nuclear war planning into doubt. In the initial transition, President George *Bush (1989–93) ordered a nuclear targeting review. Conducted in 1989–91, it did not result in any radical changes but did lead to significant reductions in the number of targets. In the Bush administration, nuclear arms control efforts moved to the forefront, initially confounded by the location of Soviet ICBMs in at least four of the "successor republics" to the Soviet Union. In 1991, the United States and the Russians signed the first Strategic Arms Reduction Treaty (START I). Under that treaty, the United States reduced its arsenal of strategic nuclear warheads loaded on launchers from 13,700 in 1987 down to about 7,000 in 1996. On his last day in office in January 1993, President Bush sent a second treaty, START II, to the Senate (which did not ratify it until January 1996; by the end of 1998, the Russian Duma still had not ratified the START II Treaty).

When President Bill *Clinton took office in 1993, the entire U.S. military establishment was in a state of flux, undergoing radical reductions in personnel and weapons, coincident with a wholesale reorganization of the armed services, especially the air force. In 1992, the Strategic Air Command was transformed into a joint command. This new Strategic Command was headed first by Air Force Gen. George Lee Butler, former head of SAC, and subsequently by either an air force general or navy admiral.

Considerable pressure mounted in the late 1990s for reducing the nuclear arsenal. In December 1996, sixty retired generals and admirals from a number of countries, including the former Soviet Union and the United States (the latter including General Butler, now retired), issued a call for long-term nuclear planning to be based on the assumption of eventual complete elimination of nuclear weapons. In March 1997, President Clinton and Russian president Boris N. Yeltsin agreed that if and when the Russian legislators approved START II, the two nations would begin talks on further reductions, to perhaps 2,000–2,500 warheads. In November 1998, with the Russian Duma still delaying ratification of the START II Treaty, Pentagon officials, driven as much by budgetary constraints as by reduced security risks, recommended that the Clinton administration consider unilateral reductions in the U.S. nuclear arsenal, either reducing the number of loaded warheads from the approximately 7,000 that existed at the end of 1998 or eliminating some categories of strategic weapons.

The state of affairs in Eastern Europe and the former Soviet Union remained so uncertain and unpredictable that in the late 1990s, preexisting nuclear war plans, although placed in a tentative hold status, remained, as it were, on the shelf. Although the information is classified, it is possible that major changes in strategy and targeting have occurred or will occur. The principal concern of nuclear theorists, strategists, and war planners had become the proliferation—both real and potential—of nuclear capabilities around the world. President Clinton gave few indications that nuclear issues were high on his agenda, causing the very small percentage of the American public that pays attention to such matters considerable concern.

[*See also* Air and Space Defense; Air Force Combat Organizations: Strategic Air Forces; Arms Control and Disarmament: Nuclear; Arms Race: Nuclear Arms Race; Deterrence; Nuclear Protest Movements; Nuclear War, Prevention of Accidental; Nuclear Weapons and War, Popular Images of; Procurement; SALT Treaties (1972, 1979); Theorists of War.]

• Lawrence Freedman, *The Evolution of Nuclear Strategy*, 1981; rev. ed. 1989. Fred Kaplan, *The Wizards of Armageddon*, 1983. David Alan Rosenberg, "The Origins of Overkill: Nuclear Weapons and American Strategy, 1945–1960," *International Security*, 7 (Spring 1983), pp. 1–71. David MacIsaac, "The Nuclear Weapons Debate and American Society," *Air University Review*, 35 (May–June 1984), pp. 81–96. Thomas B. Cochran, William M. Arkin, and Milton M. Hoenig, *Nuclear Weapons Data Book.* Vol. I: *U.S. Nuclear Forces and Capabilities*, 1984. Robert Jervis, *The Illogic of American Nuclear Strategy*, 1984. Charles W. Kegley, Jr., and Eugene R. Wittkopf, eds., *The Nuclear Reader: Strategy, Weapons, War*, 1985. Gregg Herken, *Counsels of War*, 1985; enl. ed. 1987. Desmond Ball and Jeffrey Richelson, eds., *Strategic Nuclear Targeting*, 1986. A. B. Carter et al., eds., *Managing Nuclear Operations*, 1987. Steven Ross, *American War Plans, 1945–1950*, 1988. Janne E. Nolan, *Guardians of the Arsenal: The Politics of Nuclear Strategy*, 1989. Scott Sagan, *Moving Targets: Nuclear Strategy and National Security*, 1989. Samuel R. Williamson, Jr., and Steven L. Reardon, *The Origins of U.S. Nuclear Strategy, 1945–1953*, 1993. Robert S. Norris and Thomas B. Cochran, *US-USSR/Russian Strategic Offensive Nuclear Forces, 1945–1996*, 1997. Stephen I. Schwartz, ed., *Atomic Audit: The Costs and Consequences of U.S. Nuclear Weapons Since 1940*, 1998.

—David MacIsaac

STRATIFICATION AND LABOR MARKET DYNAMICS IN THE MILITARY. When the United States ended military *conscription in 1973 and moved to an *All-Volunteer Force, some commentators suggested that labor market dynamics had been substituted for civic virtue as a means of manning the force. In fact, such dynamics have always affected the composition and rank structure of the military. An understanding of internal and segmented labor markets helps explain variations in the social composition of the armed forces.

Military Forces as Internal Labor Markets. Neoclassical economics sees employment decisions controlled by labor supply and demand. The internal labor market perspective, by contrast, attributes variations in employment to organizations that control access to their labor force, start people at entry-level jobs, and promote them to higher-level positions along prescribed career paths. These processes characterize the armed forces.

In obtaining the bulk of enlisted personnel through conscription (e.g., during World War I and from World War II to 1973), the government controlled this market, drafting some people for military service and channeling others to essential civilian occupations through deferments and exemptions. Under volunteer conditions, the forces use recruiting resources to gain personnel with the characteristics they seek in competition with other potential employers. Within the force, the promotion system determines who moves up and who leaves the military. The services operate as independent internal labor markets, each recruiting at the entry level and promoting personnel internally. A person in one service is unlikely to transfer to another for career advancement. Each of the services can be regarded as a two-tiered internal labor market, with separate tracks and desired characteristics, entry points, and career structures for enlisted personnel and for commissioned officers.

The 85 percent of the force who enter military service as recruits (usually as high school graduates currently, and most commonly from working-class backgrounds) will serve in the enlisted ranks of that service, and some may progress to the highest noncommissioned officer grades. The 15 percent of personnel who come into the service as officers are most commonly commissioned as second lieutenants or ensigns through accession programs currently associated with receipt of a college degree (*ROTC or the service *academies) and are likely to come from middle-class backgrounds. If they are successful and choose to remain in service, they will progress through the ranks. Otherwise they will return to civilian life.

The Military Workforce as a Segmented Labor Market. Internal labor markets are related to segmented labor markets, which identify distinct sectors of jobs and workers. The primary sector consists of appealing jobs, with high wages, good working conditions, chances for advancement, equity, and employment stability. Jobs in the secondary sector are low-paying, with poor working conditions, little chance of advancement, absence of equity, and little employment stability. Internal labor markets operate in the primary sector. Though it was not conventional to think of military service as a good job under conscription, the services have attempted to establish primary sector status in the transformation to a large All-Volunteer Force. They tried to compete effectively for personnel with the characteristics they sought by offering good jobs, competitive wages, high quality of work life, attractive benefits—including support for higher education—and opportunities for training, travel, advancement, and supervisory responsibility at a relatively young age.

Organizations that function as internal labor markets possess market power, usually because of the desirability of their jobs or the level of their wages. However, the most successful internal labor market in terms of control of entry-level recruiting may have been the wartime military, which was based on selective conscription. It would take those people with the characteristics it wanted, largely independent of their volition, and could reject others. As an internal labor market, it would then seek to retain, through compensation and promotion, those it wanted to keep.

Workers, as well as jobs, are segmented into market sectors. Desirable workers may be defined in terms of their skills and the price of their labor, as well as other characteristics such as gender and race. Members of minority groups, historically relegated to the secondary labor market, must frequently have had to settle for jobs characterized by unpleasant working conditions, low prestige, and low potential for advancement. However, when primary sector employers cannot recruit sufficient primary sector employees, they will broaden their recruitment base.

Ability is a primary definitive characteristic of labor market sector. Since World War I, the armed forces have used tests to screen out the bottom of the mental aptitude distribution, and recruitment screening today takes into account both educational level, which is related to social class, and mental aptitude test scores. However, during World War II, the criterion of literacy was relaxed to expand the induction base and obtain a massive force.

Gender has also been important in segmenting the labor force. Military service, and particularly involvement in combat, has historically been primarily a male pursuit; women have traditionally been relegated to the secondary market. The numbers and roles of *women in the military have increased dramatically when the requisite numbers of men were not available, either because of the magnitude of mobilization (World War II), or because in the absence of conscription since 1973, sufficient numbers of men could not be recruited for a large standing force. Internally, women have done well in those career fields to which they have been admitted.

For most of American history, African Americans were regarded as a secondary source of labor, and the military was segregated from the early nineteenth century until the mid-twentieth century. Integration took place under the pressure to mobilize for the *Korean War from the small Depression generation and the World War II veterans. African Americans are now overrepresented in the enlisted grades, although underrepresented in the officers' grades.

In short, the military has historically defined young, white, unmarried, heterosexual males of high mental aptitude as its primary labor market, and has used these variables to segment the remainder of the market. When market conditions precluded filling all of the positions from the primary market, the services made decisions as to which segments to tap next. The services turned first to older married white men, then to African American men, then to women, ignoring sexual orientation until very recently. Even when secondary labor force segments are drawn upon for entry-level personnel, the people so recruited are disadvantaged. Their characteristics operate against them in competition for jobs that offer greater opportunity for retention and promotion, although there has been an increasing emphasis on ability and decreasing concern for secondary characteristics.

[*See also* Class and the Military; Gender; Gender and War; Rank and Hierarchy.]

• Neil D. Fligstein, "Who Served in the Military, 1940–73?" *Armed Forces and Society*, 6 (Winter 1980), pp. 297–312. Sue E. Berryman, *Who Serves? The Persistent Myth of the Underclass Army*, 1986. David R. Segal, *Recruiting for Uncle Sam*, 1989.

—David R. Segal

STUART, J. E. B. (1833–1864), Confederate cavalry commander. Virginia-born James Ewell Brown (Jeb) Stuart graduated from West Point in 1854, served on the Great Plains and in Kansas, and then helped capture John Brown at Harper's Ferry.

In 1861, he resigned from the U.S. Army to become a Confederate colonel of cavalry. Winning early distinction by protecting the Confederate left at the First Battle of *Bull Run, he became a brigadier general. In 1862, during Gen. George B. *McClellan's Peninsular Campaign, Stuart covered Robert E. *Lee's initial withdrawal, then gained enduring fame in a daring reconnaissance raid completely around McClellan's army, burning supplies and capturing documents on the Union forces' strength and employments that enabled Lee to plan his offensive in the *Seven Days' Battle.

As a major general in Lee's Army of Northern Virginia, Stuart continued to stage morale-boosting raids and performed well at the Second Battle of *Bull Run and at Fredericksburg. At the Battle of *Chancellorsville, he found Gen. Joseph *Hooker's flank exposed, and once "Stonewall" *Jackson fell, mortally wounded, he swiftly assumed temporary command of Jackson's corps.

In 1863, Stuart suffered a number of setbacks. Union cavalry surprised him in the Battle of *Brandy Station, Virginia, in June. Most controversially, in Lee's second invasion of the North, Stuart allowed himself to be diverted from his primary mission of providing intelligence for the army. Riding behind Union lines, he became cut off for three days by the *Union army in motion, leaving Lee without information and arriving at the Battle of *Gettysburg after it was well underway.

In May 1864, when Union Gen. Philip H. *Sheridan threatened Richmond, Stuart met him at Yellow Tavern, just north of the capital. During a fierce encounter, Stuart turned back Sheridan, but was mortally wounded. He died the next day, 12 May 1864.

A highly romantic and spectacular figure, Stuart will always be remembered as the dashing cavalier—indeed, one of the finest cavalry commanders.

[*See also* Civil War: Military and Diplomatic Course.]

• D. S. Freeman, *Lee's Lieutenants*, 1942–44. Emory Thomas, *Bold Dragon*, 1986.

—Brian S. Wills

STUDENTS FOR A DEMOCRATIC SOCIETY. First organized in 1960 as the rejuvenated student arm of the venerable League for Industrial Democracy, Students for a Democratic Society (SDS) burst on the national scene in 1962 with its Port Huron Statement. Comparable to Karl Marx's *Communist Manifesto*, the statement laid out the organization's analysis of contemporary America and explained how through "participatory democracy" SDS would reform capitalism. The most important and influential of the New Left groups on college campuses in the 1960s, with as many as 400 chapters by 1968, SDS led the first mass *Vietnam Antiwar Movement demonstration on 17 April 1965 in Washington, D.C. After that point, despite

the fact that the organization strongly opposed the war, U.S. imperialism, and the Selective Service System, its leaders chose not to play a major role in other mass demonstrations. They and their members, however, were deeply involved in many other antiwar activities, including Stop the Draft Week in October 1967 and the riots at the Democratic National Convention in Chicago in 1968. SDS self-destructed in 1969 as a result of sectarian infighting and after the nihilistic and violent Weathermen faction gave the organization—and the antiwar movement—a bad name.

[*See also* Draft Resistance and Evasion; Peace and Antiwar Movements; Vietnam War: Domestic Course.]

• Kirkpatrick Sale, *SDS: Ten Years Toward a Revolution*, 1973.

—Melvin Small

SUBMARINES are special purpose naval vessels that use their submerged capability for protection. A submarine must possess a hull strong enough to withstand substantial water pressure; tanks for taking on and holding water to adjust buoyancy and facilitate diving below the water's surface; and a means of underwater propulsion. Typically, submarines carry *torpedoes as weapons, but some have carried ballistic *missiles.

David Bushnell's human-powered *Turtle* launched the first (unsuccessful) submarine attack in New York Harbor in September 1776 during the *Revolutionary War. In the *Civil War, Horace Hunley built the *David* craft for the *Confederate navy, one of which sank the USS *Housatonic* in July 1864, in Charleston, South Carolina, sinking itself in the process. In the late nineteenth century, John Holland, an Irish immigrant and inventor from Paterson, New Jersey, privately built a series of experimental craft culminating in a gasoline-powered submersible, *Holland VI* (1896). Due to its oxygen requirements, the boat's engine could only operate while it cruised on the surface, so the vessel also had an electric battery to provide submerged propulsion. Holland's design became the basis for submarines of the U.S. Navy, and the Royal Navy bought his design as well.

European technical developments paralleled U.S. efforts, especially in Germany and France. French naval theorists of the so-called young school (*jeune école*) provided submerged weapons for submarines by first combining them in 1893 with the self-propelled torpedo. In the view of most naval officers, submarines would be especially useful to defend a coast or for a relatively weak naval power to attack an enemy line of *battleships. Due to their low submerged speed, most submarines operated as temporarily submersible *torpedo boats, largely sailing and often attacking while surfaced.

During World War I, the submarines, and especially the German *Untersee* boats (U-boats), achieved prominence. Submarine crews gained a reputation as élite personnel who endured real hardships; few survived the sinking of a submarine. The submarines of all navies had internal combustion engines (usually diesel), a periscope, and a deck gun for surface combat, as well as torpedoes or mines. Early in the war, a submerged German U-boat torpedoed and sank three British *cruisers in one day; another was responsible for the sinking of *Lusitania* (1915). Against Allied merchant shipping, the long-range U-boat came into its own, evading the larger Royal Navy, and sometimes attacking even while surfaced until deterred by the U.S.

convoy system and vigorous U.S. antisubmarine efforts in 1917–18. Allied submarines, including American boats sent to Britain in 1918, focused upon attacking enemy surface ships but faced few targets due to the enemy's caution. Since the force almost succeeded in starving Britain, the Treaty of *Versailles forbade German possession of U-boats.

After World War I, the Washington Naval Arms Limitation Conference (1922) considered a complete ban on submarines. But opposition from the Italian and French governments guaranteed that submarines remained in the inventories of most navies, and they returned in Germany after 1935. Interwar developments included improved construction, more sophisticated torpedoes, better torpedo fire control systems, and even air conditioning in U.S. vessels. Submarine doctrine remained divided between those who desired to use the boats for commerce warfare, the German goal, and those who emphasized fleet reconnaissance and attacks on *warships, the policy in the U.S. and Imperial Japanese navies.

World War II saw accelerated building of submarines by both the Axis and the Allied sides, with almost 2,000 vessels serving. Overwhelmingly, submarines attacked enemy merchant shipping, despite prewar doctrines emphasizing fleet operations. Their patrols succeeded in sinking over 20 million tons of shipping, one-quarter by 300 American boats, which provided an effective naval blockade of Japan. U.S. design innovations included improved torpedoes and the addition of *radar for surface operations. Changes from 1943 onward in Germany included series construction, the snorkel, an air tube for submerged diesel use, and improvements in submarine battery power and submerged speed. All postwar diesel submarine designs made use of these German innovations.

During the *Cold War, submarine design incorporated *nuclear weapons and propulsion, as well as improved *sonar and reduced noise signatures. Nuclear weapons entered use as torpedoes, cruise missiles, and as the strategic ballistic missiles that the United States, Soviet Union, France, Britain, and the People's Republic of China added to their fleets. Ballistic missile submarines were a prominent nuclear deterrent. Nuclear propulsion, first introduced in the U.S. Navy by Adm. Hyman *Rickover, gave submarines virtually unlimited range and radically more underwater capability due to their power plants' independence of air supplies. With improved range and weapons, both diesel and nuclear submarines fully realized their capabilities, emerging as a versatile branch of modern navies.

[See also Mines, Naval; Washington Naval Arms Limitation Treaty.]

• John Moore, Jane's Pocket Book of Submarine Development, 1976. Ulrich Gabler, Submarine Design, 1986. Gary Weir, Building American Submarines 1914–1940, 1991. Gary Weir, Forged in War, 1993. Norman Friedman, U.S. Submarines Since 1945, 1995. Norman Friedman, U.S. Submarines Through 1945, 1995.

—Sarandis Papadopoulos

SUBMARINE WARFARE. Modern navies employed submarines in combat, using their ability to proceed submerged, although not necessarily for an entire cruise. Their concealment meant that submarines were also ideal for allowing a weaker naval power to attack a stronger one. Smaller, less heavily armed, slower, and less expensive than many surface warships, submarines could nonetheless employ a sort of guerrilla warfare at sea, using surprise and attacking the weakest points of their opponents' navies and maritime trade to great effect.

The large-scale use of submarines against surface warships began in World War I; both sides employed them in that role. German successes overshadowed those of the Allies, primarily because there were few German surface ships, which robbed Allied craft of targets. Still, both sides succeeded in sinking opposing warships, and the threat of submarines caused commanders to exercise greater caution in using their fleet units.

But it was the attack on Allied merchant shipping by German submarines (Untersee boats or U-boats) that drew the most attention during World War I. The U-boats' ability to slip past the Allied naval *blockades of German ports allowed them to gain access to British sealanes, attacking shipping headed for Great Britain. When Royal Navy defensive measures made it difficult for surfaced U-boats to stop merchant ships at sea and board them, the German Navy resorted to "unrestricted submarine warfare," that is, sinking merchant shipping without warning. Such a German sinking of the *Lusitania, in 1915, led to a dramatic worsening of relations with the neutral United States, and the return of the more limited submarine attacks. Germany's political and military leadership gambled in 1917 on a resumption of unrestricted submarine warfare to win the war quickly on neutral as well as belligerent shipping. This prompted the United States to enter on the Allied side in April 1917. Though the Germans sank over 11 million tons of ships, the submarine offensive failed to strangle trade with Britain due to the introduction of protected convoys of merchant ships by the Allies, and the availability of merchant vessels from neutral countries to help replace losses. The threat of submarine attack did compel the U.S. Navy to defend its troopship convoys across the Atlantic, a task accomplished without loss.

The U-boat campaign of World War II again raised the question of neutral American shipping and the possibility of German attacks. In response, President Franklin D. *Roosevelt extended a "neutrality zone" eastward from the North American coast ultimately to Iceland, patrolled by U.S. Navy warships before the official American entry in the war. On several occasions, U-boats clashed with American warships, in one case sinking the destroyer Reuben James in October 1941. After American entry into World War II, U-boats initially decimated American East Coast shipping almost with impunity. With the introduction of adequate antisubmarine forces, convoying, and decryption of German naval signals, however, American losses fell dramatically, and the U.S. Navy and Allied forces took the war to the U-boats in the central Atlantic with deadly effect.

Perhaps the most effective submarine campaign in history was the American Pacific Ocean submarine operation in World War II. This entailed many difficulties initially, including a dearth of bases, faulty *torpedoes, and many cautious submarine commanders. Submarine crews spent eight weeks at a time on patrol under cramped conditions and with few amenities. Still, submarines played a vital reconnaissance role from the start of the conflict. Eventually aided by *radar, the decryption of Imperial Japanese Navy radio signals (*MAGIC), and improved torpedoes, the greatly expanded submarine force scored notable sinkings, destroying one Japanese battleship, eight *aircraft carriers, and eleven *cruisers. More significantly, the U.S. Navy's submarines crippled Japan's merchant marine, sinking 5.3 million tons, or over half of its ships, in the most successful campaign of the war. Groups of U.S. Navy submarines also emulated the German Navy's "wolf-pack" tactics to great effect against Japanese convoys. In the war's last days, American submarines ranged over the entire Pacific, even entering the Japanese Inland Sea. But these accomplishments came at a price; 22 percent of submarine personnel died during the conflict, the highest of any American service.

Following World War II, submarines gained new propulsion—nuclear-fueled. One of the new roles was in *antisubmarine warfare, using their own concealed operations, as well as improved *sonar and radar, to find opposing submarines. Another was submarine-launched ballistic *missiles as a part of the nuclear deterrent of the superpowers. Submarine combat operations remained limited after 1945, however. Just one ship—an Argentine cruiser—was sunk by a Royal Navy submarine during the Falkland War in 1982.

[See also Navy Combat Branches: Submarine Forces; Submarines.]

• Edward Beach, *Run Silent, Run Deep,* 1955. Clay Blair, *Silent Victory,* 1975. Mark P. Parillo, *The Japanese Merchant Marine in World War II,* 1993. I. J. Galantin, *Submarine Admiral,* 1995. Clay Blair, *Hitler's U-Boat War,* 1996. Peter Padfield, *War Beneath the Sea,* 1996.
—Sarandis Papadopoulos

SUBSTANCE ABUSE. The Department of *Defense (DoD) defines substance abuse as the use of tobacco, illicit drugs, or excessive amounts of alcohol. Responsibility for controlling substance abuse has oscillated between the command structures and the medical departments of the services.

Political interest in regulating alcohol consumption in the United States emerged in the mid-nineteenth century, when eighteen states passed prohibition laws. Temperance organizations subsequently made drinking a national issue. In 1862, the traditional rum ration for naval personnel was discontinued, and in 1914, drinking by officers aboard navy ships was prohibited. The Prohibition Amendment was ratified in 1919. After Prohibition was repealed in 1933, drinking in the armed services became an almost obligatory social ritual. Command-sponsored club happy hours, airborne forces' "Prop Blast" parties, and naval aviators' Tailhook Conventions were organized around heavy drinking.

In 1970, PL 91-616, the Comprehensive Alcohol Abuse and Alcoholism Prevention, Treatment, and Rehabilitation Act, defined alcoholism as a disease and mandated that military alcohol abusers receive treatment in a nondiscriminatory and confidential context. The following year, Title V of the Selective Service Act, PL 92-129, required DoD to identify, treat, and rehabilitate alcoholics to prevent the loss of experienced personnel. The medical departments treated physiological and psychiatric conditions associated with drinking, and command conducted rehabilitation programs.

In 1980, DoD announced that alcohol abuse was incompatible with military discipline, performance, and readiness. Commanders were to deglamorize drinking, ed-

ucate service members on its harmful effects, punish drunken driving severely, and deemphasize alcohol at social functions. The 1986 DoD Health Promotion Program, designed to improve the quality of service members' lives and to enhance readiness, included programs to reduce the use of alcohol, tobacco, and drugs. By 1987, the services were operating the world's largest integrated occupational health program, with 47,000 enrollees. But alcoholic service members, suspecting that their careers would be compromised, were reluctant to ask for rehabilitation.

The DoD-sponsored *Worldwide Survey of Substance Abuse and Health Behaviors Among Military Personnel* began in 1980. Between 1980 and 1992, the proportion of drinkers among service members declined from 86.5 percent to 79.6 percent, and heavy drinkers declined from 20.8 percent to 14.5 percent. In contrast, 9.5 percent of civilians in 1991 were heavy drinkers.

Cigarettes became a ritual of relaxation during World War II. In 1964, Surgeon General Luther Terry made public the deleterious effects of smoking on health. In 1982, DoD began to track smoking on its *Worldwide Surveys.* As part of the 1986 Health Promotion Program, DoD limited smoking in workplaces; in 1994, it banned smoking indoors. Between 1980 and 1992, the proportion of military smokers declined from 51 percent of the force to 35 percent. During the same period, civilian smoking declined from 30 percent to 25 percent.

Use of illegal drugs and abuse of medicinal drugs became a problem in the armed forces in the late 1960s as a consequence of expanding drug use in the civil sector and easy availability of drugs in Vietnam. During the *Vietnam War, drug users were classified as addicts and evacuated through medical channels. In 1971, treatment and rehabilitation of drug as well as alcohol abusers was mandated.

The Boys in the Barracks, a landmark study of drug use in the U.S. Army in 1973–74 by L. H. Ingraham and F. J. Manning, revealed the psychological purposes served by drug abuse. Soldiers in dysfunctional units used drugs as a basis for establishing trust among themselves and bonding against authority. These findings led to initiatives to enhance cohesion around military values and to train leaders to care for and empower their subordinates. The first *Worldwide Survey* (1980) indicated that drug abuse was volitional rather than addictive behavior, and a 1980 DoD directive made commanders rather than the medical departments responsible for its control.

In 1984, random urinalysis made it difficult for drug users to escape detection, and in 1986 the Health Promotion Program introduced zero tolerance for drug use. Officers and noncommissioned officers caught using drugs were eliminated from the service. Commanders had discretion to give junior enlisted personnel a second chance by authorizing rehabilitation. Drug use fell from 27.6 percent of military personnel in 1980 to 3.4 percent in 1992. The latter figure compares favorably with 10 percent use in 1991 in the general population.

Since the mid-1980s, substance abuse has declined as commanders, supported by the medical departments, have assumed responsibility for promoting healthy behavior. Emphasis on cohesion, focus on wartime missions, and improved leadership have reduced the psychosocial needs for drugs, alcohol, and tobacco. The military population has become older and better educated, and more members are married—demographic characteristics negatively correlated with substance abuse. Drug abuse has been almost eliminated. But both drinking and smoking—which military traditions define as characteristics of a fighting man—persist, particularly among the young, unmarried, and poorly educated.

• Marvin R. Burt, et al., *Worldwide Survey of Nonmedical Drug Use and Alcohol Use Among Military Personnel: 1980,* 1982. Robert M. Bray, et al., *1982 (1985, 1988, 1992) Worldwide Survey of Substance Abuse and Health Behaviors Among Military Personnel,* titles vary; 1983, 1986, 1989, 1992. Larry H. Ingraham and Frederick J. Manning, *The Boys in the Barracks,* 1984. U.S. Department of the Army, *Alcohol and Drug Abuse Prevention and Control Program,* Army Regulation 600–85, 1988. Henry J. Watanabe, Paul T. Harig, Nicholas J. Rock, and Ronald J. Koshes, "Alcohol and Drug Abuse and Dependence" in Franklin D. Jones, et al., eds., *Textbook of Military Medicine,* Part I, Vol. 7: *Military Psychiatry—Preparing in Peace for War,* 1994. Robert M. Bray, Larry A. Kroutil, and Mary Ellen Marsden, "Trends in Alcohol, Illicit Drug, and Cigarette Use Among U.S. Military Personnel: 1980–1992," *Armed Forces and Society,* 21 (Winter 1995), pp. 271–93.   —Faris R. Kirkland

SUPPORT SHIPS, as their name implies, are generally defined as noncombatant or defensively armed ships whose mission is to assist the fighting forces. While support ships are perhaps best known for their role in naval warfare, they have been employed since the American Revolution, have been operated by both the army and navy, and have provided support to all of the military services. During the *Revolutionary War and *Civil War, support ships were used primarily by the army as troop transports and logistical supply ships. In the Civil War, by early 1865 the Quartermaster Corps of the *Union army operated almost all of the nation's commercial vessels.

Prior to World War I, the U.S. *Navy utilized a small number of support ships, known as naval auxiliaries and consisting primarily of colliers and supply ships. These were manned by civilian crews but maintained by the navy and under naval control when operating with the fleet. After the United States entered World War I in April 1917, these auxiliaries were placed in full naval status under the Naval Overseas Transport Service (NOTS), which grew to over 450 ships by war's end. Even prior to the establishment of NOTS, the navy had acquired a number of noncombatant ships, including captured German vessels, ships taken over from the Shipping Board, and others received for the U.S. *Army. The army, which had established its own Transport Service in 1898 during the *Spanish-American War, continued to operate support ships and to maintain responsibility for overseas troop movements during both World Wars I and II.

By the end of World War I, NOTS ships had carried approximately 6 million tons of cargo, including over 3 million tons of supplies for the Army Expeditionary Force in France, 1 million tons for naval bases overseas, over 1 million tons of coal for the fleet, and food for all the Allies. While the majority of NOTS ships were general cargo, a substantial numbers of tankers, colliers, and refrigerator ships were also included, as well as four hospital ships.

Perhaps the best known ship operated by NOTS in 1917–18 was the collier USS *Jupiter.* Owned by the Shipping Board, received by NOTS in April 1918, and at war's end operated in the U.S. Navy's Pacific Train, the *Jupiter* was recommissioned in March 1922 as the USS *Langley* (CV 1), the first of the navy's *aircraft carriers, serving in

this capacity until 1936, when she was converted to a seaplane tender.

In the interwar years the navy established a base force that evolved into the Atlantic and Pacific Service Forces, which provided mobile logistic support squadrons in both oceans as the fleets increased their ability to maintain themselves at sea for increasingly long periods. In addition, specialized ships such as aircraft, submarine, and destroyer tenders were added to the inventory.

World War II saw the advent of the fast carrier task force and with it the development of the doctrine of underway replenishment: supplies provided by ships of the mobile logistic support force allowed combat ships to stay at sea and fight for long periods of time far away from their advanced naval bases. Fast attack transports and cargo ships were added for use in the amphibious assaults of the Pacific War.

After World War II, the Army Transport Service and the Naval Transportation Service were combined to form the Military Sea Transport Service (MSTS). MSTS ships supplied U.S. forces overseas and, augmented by commercial ship charters and vessels from the Reserve Fleet, provided sealift support in every national emergency from the *Korean War to the *Vietnam War. MSTS was renamed the Military Sealift Command (MSC) in 1970 under the Department of *Defense (DoD), a single operating agency for sealift for all the military services.

As warfare doctrines and weapon systems evolved, support ships became more specialized. Ships for military research were added: oceanographic research ships (AGOR); missile range instrumentation ships (AGM); and exotic deep submergence research vessels such as the NR-1, a nuclear-propelled submarine, developed in great secrecy during the *Cold War and now made available to technical institutions and to the National Science Foundation for research. Vessels were configured for specific duties; for example, command ships (AGF, CC, CLC); guided missile ships (AVM); and for less obvious purposes, such as the ill-fated USS *Pueblo,* which was designated an environmental research ship (AEGR) but used for signals intelligence collection until captured by the North Koreans in the *Pueblo* Incident in 1968.

To meet the challenges of military logistic support in the post–Cold War era, the Defense Transportation System has been established to coordinate requirements for sealift, scheduling, and shipping during routine operations. When an overseas deployment, such as Operation Desert Shield in 1990, is ordered, all elements—air, ground, and shipping—including the Military Sealift Command, are drawn together under the DoD's Transportation Command to deliver the necessary forces and material.

In 1991, during Desert Shield/Desert Storm combat operations in the *Persian Gulf War, ships of the Military Sealift Command transported 95 percent of the supplies needed by U.S. forces in the most massive sealift operation since World War II. First to arrive were ships of the Strategic Sealift Force, pre-positioned in the Indian Ocean and fully loaded to support immediate combat operations, followed shortly thereafter by fast sealift ships and hospital and aviation support ships from U.S. ports. Additional support ships were drawn from the Ready Reserve Force and were chartered from U.S. and foreign shipowners as required.

Desert Storm demonstrated a particular need for roll

on/roll off–type support ships that could be loaded, held in an overseas area for immediate dispatch, and rapidly unloaded upon arrival. As the U.S. Navy shifts strategic emphasis from preparing for war at sea to seaward support of joint operations on land, the importance of support ships in the twenty-first century will become ever greater, with increased emphasis on afloat pre-positioning of fast sealift support ships. Budget constraints, declining numbers of U.S. flag merchant ships, and the real possibility that for political reasons foreign flag vessels may not be available for charter in future crises, combine to make the availability of support ships key in future military operations.

[See also Logistics; Transportation.]

• Worrall R. Carter, *Beans, Bullets and Black Oil*, 1953. Samuel Eliot Morison, *History of United States Naval Operations in World War II*, vol. VII (1951) and vol. VIII (1953). Lewis P. Clephane, *History of the Naval Overseas Transportation Service in World War I*, 1969. Richard T. Ackley, "Sealift and National Security," *Naval Institute Proceedings* (July 1992), pp. 41–47. Charles Dana Gibson and E. Kay Gibson, comps., *Dictionary of Transport and Combatant Vessels Steam and Sail Employed by the Union Army, 1861–1868*, 1995.

—Alan Harris Bath

SUPREME COURT, WAR, AND THE MILITARY. Since its founding (1789), the U.S. Supreme Court generally has avoided questions of war, peace, and foreign affairs. In the relatively few such cases, the justices have usually supported the president over the Congress. Congress has generally acquiesced, and the Court sanctioned, presidential warmaking. However, in several dramatic exceptions the Court restrained the president's authority as commander in chief of the nation's armed forces.

Though the Constitution allocates all of the war powers to Congress, it confers the office of commander in chief on the president. In addition to the power to declare war, Congress has the constitutional authority to create and regulate the armed forces, allocate funds for the military, make rules of military conduct, and provide for organizing, arming, and disciplining the militia (the National Guard). Congress possesses all of the auxiliary war powers—the various powers necessary to wage war effectively. Constitutionally, Congress has the authority to decide when to wage war, to control the conduct of war, and to restore the nation to peace.

In granting the president the office of commander in chief, the framers of the Constitution had two basic objectives. First, they intended to secure civilian control over the military. Second, as the debates of the Constitutional Convention suggest, they gave the president authority to respond to sudden attacks on U.S. territory as well as U.S. citizens and the military at home and abroad. But they did not intend to grant the president authority to initiate war and hostilities. By separating the war powers from the office of commander in chief, the framers hoped to make it more difficult to go to war than to keep the peace.

Apparently, the framers believed in a distinction between aggressive or offensive war and defensive military measures. They recognized the necessity for dispatch in responding to sudden attacks, but wanted to assure democratic control over the decision to commit the nation to foreign wars. In a constitutional democracy, the separation and sharing of foreign affairs and other powers of external sovereignty was the best way to hold government accountable to the people. Despite the framers' intentions, a succession of strong presidents have presented Congress with military fait accomplis, which the justices generally have legitimized when called upon. The Marshall Court confirmed Congress's plenary authority to initiate and control the scope of hostilities during the Undeclared Naval War with *France (1798–1800) and the *War of 1812, but various presidents, beginning with Thomas *Jefferson, have initiated military actions without consulting Congress. In the wars against the Barbary powers (1801–05), Jefferson dispatched a naval squadron to protect American shipping in the Mediterranean, waiting nine months to inform Congress of his actions. In response, Congress passed a resolution (1802) authorizing the president to protect American seamen. Apparently, Jefferson began the now well accepted practice of presidential initiative, subsequent communication with Congress, and expectation of pliant legislative approval.

Between 12 April and 4 July 1861, following the Confederate capture of *Fort Sumter, Abraham *Lincoln waged "war" against the Confederacy without calling Congress into session. He proclaimed a blockade of the belligerent states, increased the army, and expended public funds without congressional approval. When Lincoln suspended the *Habeas Corpus Act, Chief Justice Roger Taney ordered the commanding general at Fort McHenry to release a military prisoner held without trial. Lincoln simply ordered General Cadwalader to ignore Taney's request (*Ex parte *Merryman*, 1861). Lincoln defended these actions as defensive measures necessary to the preservation of the Union and its government, and therefore essential to the salvation of the Constitution.

In the *Prize Cases* (1862), the Supreme Court sustained the president's maritime seizures. Speaking for a narrow majority, Justice Robert Grier argued that the chief executive had a constitutional duty to meet force with force. Justice Samuel Nelson dissented that only Congress has the authority to initiate war and authorize belligerent measures. Only after the *Civil War had ended, in *Ex parte *Milligan* (1866), did the Court attempt to curb the president's wartime power by denying that he had the constitutional authority to suspend the writ of habeas corpus and substitute military tribunals for civilian courts outside the military theater. Similarly, during World War II, the Supreme Court upheld the evacuation (*Hirabayashi* v. *U.S.*, 1943) and detention (*Korematsu* v. *U.S.*) of 112,000 Japanese Americans and legal resident aliens without civilian trials on charges of disloyalty or espionage (*Ex parte Endo*, 1944).

As the majority and dissenting opinions in the *Prize Cases* suggest, the distinction between defensive and offensive warfare is elusive. During the twentieth century, the emergence of *guerrilla warfare, insurgency and *counterinsurgency movements, wars of national liberation, and international *terrorism has all but erased the framers' differentiation between aggression and defensive warfare. How far can the president go in defending the nation's strategic interests without intruding on congressional authority to initiate and control military hostilities? The Supreme Court's *Curtiss-Wright* (1936) opinion holds that the president has inherent, extraconstitutional authority to protect the nation's military security, yet in *Youngstown Sheet & Tube* v. *Sawyer* (1952), the Court ruled that President Harry S. *Truman could not seize the nation's steel mills, contrary to congressional policy, even to assure the delivery of essential war material during the *Korean War. But *Youngstown* stands as an isolated curb on presidential warmaking power.

The Supreme Court has evaded an authoritative response, but Congress has attempted to clarify the boundaries. In the *War Powers Resolution (1973), Congress sought to limit presidential authority to employ armed forces abroad without prior authorization. The resolution requires the president to report the commitment of armed forces to hostilities within forty-eight hours and to withdraw such forces within sixty to ninety days, unless Congress authorizes continuing operations. In effect, Congress delegated the war power to the presidency but reserved the right to force removal of the troops. The Supreme Court has not decided the constitutionality of delegating authority to initiate hostilities for such a limited period of time.

Despite congressional attempts to rein in presidential warmaking, virtually every president since Richard M. *Nixon has evaded the essential objective of the War Powers Resolution. By claiming that their actions were defensive, that hostilities were not present or imminent, or that U.S. forces were engaged in *peacekeeping operations, recent presidents have circumvented the reporting requirements. In the *Persian Gulf War, after Desert Shield, President George *Bush obtained congressional consent for the offensive, Operation Desert Storm, in January 1991. As a result, the clock did not begin to toll on the time limit for withdrawing troops. With military forces in the field committed to combat, Congress has been reluctant to challenge the authority of the president as *commander in chief.

At the beginning of the 104th Congress (1995–99), Senate majority leader Robert Dole suggested that the War Powers Resolution should either be amended or repealed because it had not restored legislative control over warmaking. Although Dole's argument was logically persuasive, unless Congress asserts its authority over foreign policy decisions, it is unlikely that lawmakers will alter the basic pattern of presidential initiative, legislative acquiescence, and judicial legitimation.

[See also Civil-Military Relations; Japanese-American Internment Cases; Selective Draft Cases.]

• Abraham D. Sofaer, *War, Foreign Affairs, and Constitutional Power,* 1976–84. W. Taylor Reveley III, *War Powers of the President and Congress: Who Holds the Arrows and Olive Branch,* 1981. Abraham D. Sofaer, "The War Powers Resolution," U.S. Department of State, Bureau of Public Affairs, Office of Communication, 1988. Edward Keynes, *Undeclared War: Twilight Zone of Constitutional Power,* 1982; rev. ed. 1991. Edward Keynes, "The War Powers Resolution: A Bad Idea Whose Time Has Come and Gone," *University of Toledo Law Review* 23 (Winter 1992), pp. 343–62. John Hart Ely, *War and Responsibility: Constitutional Lessons of Vietnam and Its Aftermath,* 1993.
—Edward Keynes

SURVEILLANCE, DOMESTIC. U.S. military surveillance operations within the United States have always been controversial because of the American tradition of individual liberty and civilian supremacy over the military. The public generally condones such counterintelligence operations only in wartime, and then only against enemy aliens or others involved in military espionage or sabotage.

Domestic military surveillance, first used on a significant scale under President Abraham *Lincoln during the Civil War, emerged in its modern form under the adminis-

tration of Woodrow *Wilson in World War I. The army General Staff's Military Intelligence Division (MID) was created in 1917, in part to locate German spies or saboteurs. It found few enemy agents; but under its creator, Capt. (later Maj. Gen.) Ralph H. Van Deman, it turned during the war and postwar period to investigate Americans whom MID considered "dangerous." These included not simply enemy aliens and other immigrants but citizens who were labor unionists, pacifists, socialists, or civil rights activists. In the antiradicalism of the postwar era, MID, working with the newly created Federal Bureau of Investigation (FBI), as well as local police and vigilante groups, conducted illegal raids, made illegal arrests, and subjected many U.S. citizens to interrogation. It also developed an elaborate filing system for its dossiers on thousands of American citizens, and it helped local authorities crush major labor strikes and suppress racial disturbances.

In the 1920s, military intelligence sought, without real evidence, to link pacifist groups, including liberal women's and religious organizations, to an alleged Communist threat to U.S. internal security. Indeed, MID prepared "Emergency Plan White"—a detailed outline for army intervention to suppress what the conservative planners feared would be Communist-led civil disorder and armed insurrection in the United States.

In 1932, the U.S. Army used a modified version of Plan White against the unemployed veterans encamped in Washington, D.C., petitioning Congress for relief. Based upon an MID report that the veterans were led by Communists (an allegation denied by the Washington police chief), President Herbert C. *Hoover authorized the army to drive the men from the capital. Fear of foreign aggression and radicalism in the 1930s led MID to expand its domestic operations, increasing the surveillance of unionists, pacifists, civil rights activists, and Communists. Van Deman retired in 1938, but the agency continued to pursue radical specters at home more than foreign espionage and intelligence evaluations, a lesson brought home by the unanticipated attack on *Pearl Harbor in 1941.

During World War II, domestic military surveillance expanded substantially. President Franklin D. *Roosevelt gave military intelligence (now G-2) responsibility for protecting defense plants, and it established a network of thousands of informants. Although the FBI had primary jurisdiction over domestic investigation of civilians, it eventually cooperated with G-2 and with the army's new Counter Intelligence Corps (CIC). Almost half of CIC's 5,000 civilian agents operated undercover among various groups of civilians—particularly disaffected minority or political groups. In addition, G-2 continued to assemble data for Plan White, reporting on radical labor and political groups and what it called "semiradical" groups concerned with *pacifism and civil liberties. Military intelligence continued that policy throughout much of the *Cold War era.

In the 1950s, President Dwight D. *Eisenhower restricted the use of military-intelligence personnel in monitoring civil disturbances until a presidential authorization indicated that the use of federal troops was imminent. Only after the decision to use federal troops to enforce desegregation did G-2 and CIC join the FBI in monitoring groups of whites and blacks in Little Rock, Arkansas, in 1957–58. In the desegregation crisis at the University of Mississippi in 1962, however, military intelligence agents violated regulations and conducted investigations of civilians without specific authorization from President John F. *Kennedy.

Domestic military surveillance expanded to an unprecedented extent in peacetime in the 1960s with the concern of Presidents Lyndon B. *Johnson and Richard M. *Nixon, among others, over threats to internal security in the United States as a result of the civil rights movement, the *Vietnam antiwar movement, and the urban disturbances. In 1965, a new intelligence command was established at Fort Holabird, Maryland. It began coordinating the work of counterintelligence agents at G-2 offices at each army command within the United States, preparing daily civil disturbance situation reports on right-wing and racial activists and on left-wing and antiwar dissidents. The widespread dissent, civil disorder, and violence in the 1960s led to the pre-positioning and occasionally active intervention of units of the army in American cities under President Johnson—Detroit in 1967 and Washington, D.C., Chicago, and Baltimore in 1968. President Nixon deployed troops at both the Democratic and Republic National Conventions in Miami Beach in 1972, and at his second inauguration in 1973.

By 1966, the U.S. Army's Intelligence Command at Fort Holabird had broadened its civilian surveillance, including operations violating regulations and probably done without knowledge of senior army commanders. By 1968, renamed Continental United States Intelligence (CONUS Intel), the Holabird center had computerized field reports on civilians composed by more than 1,000 plainclothes army agents, who monitored civil rights and antiwar organizations, infiltrated radical groups like the *Students for a Democratic Society, and sometimes engaged in provocative and illegal acts to discredit them.

Military intelligence crossed the dividing line into illegal, unconstitutional activity between 1963 and 1972, as it had in the period 1917–21. Violating laws and regulations restricting federal domestic investigatory activity to civilian agencies, primarily the FBI, the military's investigation of civilian protest went beyond immediate use in tactical operations. Instead, it intimidated and sometimes restrained legitimate exercise of civil and political rights. The use of the military against political criticism of the central government was precisely the kind of abuse of standing armies feared by Americans since the mid-eighteenth century.

The extent of domestic military surveillance became the center of controversy when it was exposed in *Washington Monthly* magazine in January 1970 by a former military intelligence officer. This led to the first full-scale public debate on the subject in America. Although the Supreme Court in *Laird* v. *Tatum* (1972) upheld the legitimacy of military surveillance for national security, a widespread public and congressional belief that the surveillance had become excessive, if not illegal, led the army to exercise greater control over its domestic military intelligence system.

[See also Civil-Military Relations: Civilian Control of the Military; Vietnam War: Domestic Course.]

• U.S. Congress, Senate Subcommittee on Constitutional Rights, Committee on the Judiciary, *Military Surveillance of Civilian Politics: A Report*, 1973. Christopher H. Pyle, *Military Surveillance of Civilian Politics, 1967–1970*, 1986. Joan M. Jensen, *Army Surveil-*

lance in America, 1775–1980, 1991. Roy Talbert, Jr., *Negative Intelligence: The Army and the American Left, 1917–1941*, 1991.

—John Whiteclay Chambers II

SWAMP FOX. *See* Marion, Francis.

SWIFT BOATS. The U.S. Navy swift boat, or patrol craft, fast (PCF), was used extensively during the Vietnam War to inhibit the movement of enemy troops and supplies in the coastal waters and rivers of South Vietnam. Adapted from a civilian crew boat used to transport workers to and from offshore oil rigs in the Gulf of Mexico, this twin-screwed, aluminum-hulled vessel had an overall length of 50 feet, a beam of 13.5 feet, and at full load a draft of 4 feet 10 inches. It displaced 22.5 tons. Two 475-horsepower diesel engines gave it a maximum speed of 28 knots. Armament consisted of twin .50-caliber *machine guns mounted over the pilot house forward, and a single .50-caliber machine gun "piggy-backed" over an 81-mm mortar aft. It carried a crew of one officer-in-charge (ordinarily a lieutenant, junior grade) and five enlisted men. Despite the rigorous and often dangerous duty these men performed, swift boat sailors in Vietnam displayed unusually high morale and esprit de corps.

Principal swift boat bases in Vietnam were located at Da Nang, Chu Lai, Cam Ranh Bay, Qui Nhon, Cat Lo, and An Thoi. Originally employed almost exclusively in offshore waters, the SEALORDS strategy of Vice Adm. Elmo R. *Zumwalt, Jr., sent them increasingly into the rivers and canals of South Vietnam in the 1968–70 period on barrier patrols designed to interdict enemy supplies crossing from Cambodia.

During the course of the war, some 125 swift boats were built. Of these, 104 were transferred to the South Vietnamese Navy as U.S. Navy combat operations in the war were phased out.

[See also Navy, U.S.: Since 1946; Vietnam War, U.S. Naval Operations in the.]

• Thomas J. Cutler, *Brown Water, Black Berets*, 1980. R. L. Schreadley, *From the Rivers to the Sea*, 1992.

—R. L. Schreadley

SZILARD, LEO (1898–1964), physicist, molecular biologist, and arms control activist. Szilard was born in Budapest, Hungary. Educated at Budapest's Technical University, he earned a Ph.D. in physics at the University of Berlin in 1922. Fleeing to London in 1933, he conceived the nuclear chain reaction, which he patented in 1934 and assigned to the British Admiralty as a military secret. He pursued chain reaction research at Oxford until 1938, then emigrated to the United States.

At Columbia University in 1939, he codesigned with Enrico *Fermi the world's first nuclear reactor, and drafted for Albert Einstein the 2 August 1939 letter to President Franklin D. *Roosevelt that warned about German *nuclear weapons research. This letter eventually led to the American effort in 1942, known as the *Manhattan Project, to build the atomic bomb. Despite feuds over science and administration with the director, Gen. Leslie R. Groves, Szilard worked in 1942 and 1943 on reactor design, and by 1944 initiated postwar control schemes for atomic energy.

In 1945, Szilard organized an unsuccessful petition to President Harry S. *Truman, urging that the atomic bomb be demonstrated before use against Japanese cities. He led the successful lobbying by scientists in 1945 to shift the atom's control from the army to the new, civilian Atomic Energy Commission, and thereafter worked against the proliferation of nuclear weapons.

In nuclear strategy, Szilard postulated in 1945 the concept of a "preventive" nuclear war, and in 1961 he proposed the balance of nuclear weapons necessary to assure minimal *deterrence among armed states. He met privately in 1960 with Nikita S. Khrushchev, gaining the Soviet leader's assent to a Moscow-Washington hot line. A founding participant from 1957 in the *arms control and disarmament activities of the Pugwash Conferences on Science and World Affairs, Szilard created the first political action committee for arms control, the Council for a Livable World (1962). He also published both fiction and nonfiction positing wildly original and later useful techniques for nuclear arms control and verification.

[See also Atomic Scientists; Hiroshima and Nagasaki, Bombings of.]

• Gertrud Weiss Szilard and Spencer Weart, eds., Leo Szilard: His Version of the Facts, 1978. Helen Hawkins, G. Allen Greb, and Gertrud Weiss Szilard, eds., Toward a Livable World: Leo Szilard and the Crusade for Nuclear Arms Control, 1987. William Lanouette, Genius in the Shadows: A Biography of Leo Szilard, the Man Behind the Bomb, 1993.   —William Lanouette

T

TACTICS

Fundamentals
Land Warfare Tactics
Naval Warfare Tactics
Air Warfare Tactics

TACTICS: FUNDAMENTALS

Tactics are the art of using armed forces to fight battles. They include all actions taken in preparing for battle, including preliminary disposition, actual arrangement of forces and weapons systems, and combat actions. Tactics are the battlefield culmination of actions taken at the strategic and operational levels. They are both an art and a science, and writings on the subject have been in existence since the time of Sun Tzu, the unidentified Chinese author who wrote *The Art of War* (c. 500–320 B.C.). Tactics are executed by human beings who suffer fear, fatigue, hunger, exhilaration, and a multitude of other emotions. Psychological aspects are as important as physical ones.

At the basic level, tactics combine both offensive and defensive operations. Through history, tactics have been in a constant state of change, influenced by technology and leadership. Innovations and technology have had great impact throughout the ages: The stirrup allowed the mounted armored knight to dominate the battlefield for years. Gunpowder and the invention of reliable shoulder-fired weapons, in turn, afforded significant tactical advantage to the dismounted soldier, enabling infantry to replace the armored horseman as the dominant force. Refinements such as rifled *muskets and light field *artillery changed tactics. Later technological innovations such as *machine guns, rapid-firing artillery, *tanks, airplanes, *submarines, and *aircraft carriers have caused tactics to continue to evolve.

According to the great Prussian military writer Carl von *Clausewitz (1780–1831), and his book *On War*, tactics are the use of armed forces to win battles; strategy is the use of battles to win the war. Warfare can be considered at three levels, with inexact lines of distinction between those levels: *strategic, operational,* and *tactical.* Strategy is the concerted, coordinated use of all resources available to a nation in order to win a war. *Operational art lies between strategy and tactics: it orchestrates battlefield tactical actions into major operations and campaigns that can achieve the strategic goals. The strategic level is normally the realm of politicians and their senior advisers. The tactical level is that of the military. The operational level is a combination of political and military influences.

Although tactics are at the micro-level, the loss of a tactical battle can reverse well-designed strategic and operational-level plans. During the *Civil War, Maj. Gen. Joseph *Hooker devised an operational campaign in 1863 to outflank Gen. Robert E. *Lee's Army of Northern Virginia entrenched around Fredericksburg. Although the Union had overwhelming numerical superiority and initial surprise, Confederate Gen. "Stonewall" *Jackson's tactical attack against the open Union right flank caused Hooker to halt the campaign and retreat back to his original positions.

Similarly, tactical victory can be negated by failure at the operational and strategic levels. In World War I, for example, the German offensives of spring 1918, using new "infiltration tactics," had great tactical success. However, the German Army could not follow up at the operational level because of an ultimate lack of mobility and reserves. In the *Vietnam War, the United States never suffered a major tactical defeat, yet it lost the war at the strategic and political level.

At the beginning of the nuclear age, some futurists thought nuclear "super weapons" would bring an end to tactical operations. However, human ingenuity persevered, tactics were again modified, and battles at the tactical level continue to this day. The historical continuity of terrain, weather, "frictions" of war, and the indomitability of the human spirit cause tactics to change but still remain a critical element in warfare. Despite the advances of technology through the ages, tactical victory still goes to the force that is best able to combine technology with leadership, discipline, esprit, and moral force.

[*See also* Strategy; Victory; War: Levels of War.]

• Carl von Clausewitz, *On War*, 1832; Michael Howard and Peter Paret, eds., 1984. C. E. Callwell, *Small Wars: Their Principles & Practice*, 3rd ed. 1906; Introduction by Douglas Porch, 1996. Ardant Du Picq, *Battle Studies: Ancient and Modern Battle*, John Greely and Robert Cotton, trans., 1946. Sun Tzu, *The Art of War*, Samuel B. Griffith, trans., 1984. Hans Delbruck, *History of the Art of War Within the Framework of Political History*, 4 vols., Walter J. Renfroe, Jr., trans., 1990. John A. English, and Bruce I. Gudmundsson, *On Infantry*, 1994.
—Stephen Bowman

TACTICS: LAND WARFARE TACTICS

Tactics are the specific techniques used by military forces to win battles and engagements. Though the term is sometimes associated with the entire art of fighting, military theorists usually associate land warfare tactics with the organization and disposition of troops, use of weapons and equipment, and execution of movements in offense or defense. For much of the nineteenth and twentieth centuries, theorists distinguished between minor and grand tactics, and today they continue that distinction by associating grand tactics (or *strategy) with the *operational art of war and minor tactics with the tactical level. Such a distinction leaves the tactician concerned primarily with the employment of small units in combat and focused on leading soldiers and solving problems amid the uncertainty and unpredictability of battle.

The first conclusive evidence of the use of ground warfare tactics comes from the Neolithic Age. Primitive warfare consisted of ambushes, raids, and skirmishes and relied on techniques and weapons closely associated with hunting. Although primitive warriors understood the importance of numbers, they knew little about tactical formations and less about command and control. These warriors nonetheless adopted the bow, sling, dagger, and mace between 12,000 and 8,000 B.C. and began deploying troops in column and line, firing arrows in volleys, and enveloping the flanks of an enemy line. Rough paintings of such actions from the Neolithic Age clearly indicate the existence of tactics in this early period.

By the fourth millennium B.C., tactics had advanced considerably. As the extraction and smelting of metals improved, bronze weapons became common, and battleaxes and metal arrowheads influenced many battles. The introduction of the wheel also permitted the invention of the war chariot, a vehicle that improved considerably in succeeding centuries. In the third millennium B.C., the Sumerians in the Euphrates Valley left written evidence of formally organized troop formations, with infantry equipped with body armor, spears, and shields and chariots occupied by soldiers carrying javelins. By 1468 B.C., the Egyptians had mastered the weapons of the Bronze Age and demonstrated the value of superior tactics in the Battle of Megiddo against the armies of Syria and Palestine.

The Greeks and Romans brought tactics to new levels of sophistication. The Greeks relied on the phalanx, which consisted of infantrymen carrying long spears, short swords, and heavy shields. By advancing shoulder to shoulder and presenting a massive array of overlapping shields and spear points, the Greeks could rupture an opponent's front and crush him. Philip of Macedonia and Alexander the Great achieved great success by skillfully employing the phalanx with cavalry, archers, and other lightly armed troops. To obtain greater flexibility, the Romans modified the phalanx and used the maniple and the cohort in their legions; but they did not abandon the idea of placing highly trained troops in carefully organized and equipped formations. Superior tactical methods and organizations proved essential for the establishment of the Greek and Roman empires.

Numerous changes occurred in tactics during the next 1,000 years, but none had a greater effect than the introduction of gunpowder. From the sixteenth to the nineteenth century, commanders adapted their tactics and made significant advances with formations such as the *tercio*, which combined hand-powered weapons with chemically powered ones. During the Thirty Years' War (1618–48), the Swedish king Gustavus Adolphus armed his infantry with muskets and pikes, his cavalry with wheellock pistols and sabers, and his artillery with mobile guns. Gustavus then created innovative tactics that relied on close cooperation between infantry, *artillery, and cavalry, exploited firepower and shock, and performed well on the offense or defense. His methods demonstrated how the flexible adaptation of technology could profoundly affect battlefield tactics.

In the era of the French Revolution at the turn of the eighteenth century, the French developed tactics that enabled them to capitalize on the initiative and commitment of their highly motivated soldiers. Though some historians have dismissed these as "horde tactics," French commanders learned through trial and error how to change their formations quickly from column to line and from line to column; they also learned to precede their infantry with swarms of skirmishers and support their advance with concentrated artillery. The result was not an army prepared for the parade ground but one prepared to fight against Europe's best professional armies and defeat them. When Napoleon came to power, he made few changes in French tactics and relied on many of the innovations achieved in previous years, although he received credit for so-called *Napoleonic warfare. His eventual defeat came from his failed strategy and his inflated ego, not from the aggressive tactics he inherited from his predecessors.

Tactics continued to change in the nineteenth century. In the United States, Gen. Emory *Upton emerged as the most notable American thinker on the subject. A much decorated and wounded veteran of the *Civil War, Upton searched during that war for an alternative to the close order, linear tactics practiced by most units with resulting high *casualties. In 1867, the U.S. *Army adopted Upton's system of tactics, which included commands and formations enabling infantry, artillery, and cavalry to work together more closely. Recognizing the accuracy of the rifled *musket and the rapid fire of the breechloader, Upton proposed organizing the infantry in a single line, rather than two or three lines, and taking advantage of their breechloader's greater firepower. He also proposed making groups of four soldiers the basis of all infantry formations and training infantry to march in columns composed of "fours" and move quickly into line. Such an organization could face in any direction after receiving simple orders. Additionally, Upton emphasized the use of skirmishers to precede and protect the main body of the infantry. These tactics placed a premium on the initiative of individual soldiers and made infantry formations more flexible, but they were only a small step forward in the effort to develop new tactics for a battlefield increasingly dominated by firepower.

Numerous important innovations in tactics occurred during World War I. Many of these changes came from the changing relationship between artillery and infantry. As the artillery changed from a direct-fire to an indirect-fire role, and as the volume of fire increased dramatically, the coordination of infantry and artillery proved to be one of the most complex and enduring problems of the war. In essence, artillery support dictated the movement of the infantry and created conditions that made maneuver extremely difficult. The Germans became the most tactically innovative of the belligerents and eventually devised an elastic defense-in-depth and infiltration tactics. In both the offensive and defense, the Germans achieved excellent coordination of infantry and artillery, and relied on the maneuver of small units and the initiative of lower-level commanders. When the Americans entered the war in 1917, Gen. John J. *Pershing resolved to abandon *trench warfare and restore mobility to the battlefield; but the exhaustion of the belligerents and the tactical innovations of the Germans did more to restore mobility than the vast resources and new energy of the Americans in the brief period of major U.S. involvement.

Tactics continued to evolve prior to and during World War II. The most notable advances again came from the

Germans, this time with the integration of *tanks and aircraft into the battle. During the May–June 1940 campaign against the French, the Germans combined their infantry, artillery, tanks, and aircraft into a highly mobile, combined-arms team and drove quickly through Poland's and France's linear defenses. Ironically, the tanks and aircraft received most of the publicity, particularly after the invention of the term *Blitzkrieg* (lightning war) to describe the operation; but infantry and artillery proved vital to the Germans' success in many of the campaigns' key encounters. The 1940 defeat of France nonetheless marked the flourishing of mechanized tactics and provided a long-lived model of three-dimensional mobile warfare. Other innovations during World War II came with the development of *airborne warfare and *amphibious warfare; but once landed, the forces involved in such operations used tactics similar to those employed by standard infantry units.

In the decades following 1945, commanders faced many new questions about tactics. With the introduction of *nuclear weapons, the superpowers developed new methods for fighting on nuclear battlefields. In the United States, the army developed the "Pentomic" division and "checkerboard tactics," which permitted the dispersal and rapid concentration of units on a nuclear battlefield, but the transition from the doctrine of massive retaliation to that of *flexible response eventually resulted in the abandonment of methods appropriate only for a nuclear environment. The outbreak of revolutionary wars around the globe resulted in the development of tactics for *guerrilla warfare and *counterinsurgency, both of which relied on the initiative of small-unit commanders and the mobility of all units. In this environment, air–mobile operations proved useful, but neither the Americans in Vietnam nor the Russians in Afghanistan achieved strategic success, even though they won numerous tactical victories. By the end of the *Cold War, advances in technology had produced sophisticated weapons and equipment that promised many future modifications in tactics.

Through thousands of years, land warfare tactics have evolved as commanders have modified their methods, developed different organizations, and adopted new weapons. Though tactics remained subservient to strategy, the greatest tacticians have been those who recognized the constantly changing nature of tactics—and the unpredictability of battle.

[*See also* Strategy: Land Warfare Strategy.]

• Mao Tse-tung, *Guerrilla Warfare*, 1962. John R. Galvin, *Air Assault: The Development of Airmobile Warfare*, 1969. Robert A. Doughty, *The Evolution of U.S. Army Tactical Doctrine, 1946–1976*, 1979. Steven T. Ross, *From Flintlock to Rifle: Infantry Tactics, 1740–1866*, 1979. Timothy T. Lupfer, *The Dynamics of Doctrine: The Changes in German Tactical Doctrine During the First World War*, 1981. Paul H. Herbert, *Deciding What Has to be Done: General William E. DePuy and the 1976 Edition of FM 100-5, Operations*, 1988. James S. Corum, *The Roots of Blitzkrieg: Hans von Seeckt and Germany Military Reform*, 1992. Perry D. Jamieson, *Crossing the Deadly Ground: United States Army Tactics, 1865–1899*, 1994.
—Robert A. Doughty

TACTICS: NAVAL WARFARE TACTICS

Tactics are the handling of forces in battle. *Maneuver*, meaning movement, was once a near synonym for *tactics*, but over the past half century naval "maneuvers" have come to mean any set of tactical actions intended to gain a

combat advantage. Currently encompassed in the term *naval tactics* are effective search and detection (or scouting), the command and control of forces, and countermeasures that neutralize or degrade enemy actions, all of which have become as important as formations and firepower.

For roughly 400 years, guns were a fighting fleet's decisive weapon and a tightly spaced column was its advantageous formation. The tactical aim was to bring the maximum number of guns to bear on the enemy; massed forces was the tactical means. Then, in the twentieth century, aircraft introduced the possibility of massing the striking power without physically concentrating the *aircraft carriers that launched the planes. To that end, in World War II the Imperial Japanese Navy developed tactics based on separated carrier formations, sometimes supplemented with strikes from island airfields.

Nevertheless, by 1944, both sides in the Pacific War saw that concentration was still the superior tactic, principally for purposes of antiaircraft defense based on counterfire from air and sea rather than primary reliance on protective armor plate. American ship defenses became so formidable that the Japanese resorted to kamikazes: manned aircraft acting as missiles on suicidal one-way missions.

At the end of World War II, defense through counterfire ended abruptly with the threat of air-dropped nuclear bombs. Dispersed formations were designed to conceal warships amid merchant shipping long enough for them to launch their own nuclear strikes. By the 1960s, this desperate tactic that was modified as counterfire was resumed through surface-to-air *missiles of the Terrier, Talos, and Tarter programs, and air-to-air missiles such as those of jet fighters like the F-14 "Tomcat." Tactics were further altered as the likelihood of nuclear war at sea waned and the principal threat to ships became conventional warheads in air-to-surface missiles instead of aerial gravity bombs.

By the 1960s, Soviet *submarines were armed with AS-CMs of such great range (some more than 300 miles) that American fleet defenses developed many layers, beginning with aerial surveillance and protection. But survival depended on adequate warning, plenty of sea room, depth of fire, and the absence of neutral aircraft and shipping.

As the reach and lethality of firepower increased, so did the need to detect the enemy at longer and longer ranges. In fact, the threat of large pulsed attacks from *torpedoes, aircraft, and missiles made apparent the enormous advantage of finding the enemy first and attacking before he could respond. In World War II, nothing but aerial scouts could hope to reach far enough to find the enemy, target him, and strike first. Submarines off enemy ports and straits gave strategic warning of enemy movements (and attacked if they could), but tactical detection and tracking were achieved by an unstinting aerial search. After World War II, aircraft continued their crucial scouting role, but concurrently highly sophisticated earth-orbiting satellites grew in significance, as did electronic search, both active and passive, conducted by ships, submarines, and land sites. Some sensors are able to detect ships and aircraft far over the horizon at ranges of thousands of miles. The moves and countermoves across the electromagnetic spectrum have become so intricate that the tactics of nonlethal "information warfare" have become as important as the missiles themselves in determining who will attack effectively first.

All naval warfare since World War II has been closely connected with conflict ashore. Thus, joint littoral operations have consistently defined modern naval warfare. Land-sea missile attacks such as a 1982 attack during the Falklands/Malvinas War on British warships by an Exocet missile launched from a land site in Argentina have added to the already prevalent strikes by aircraft to blur the tactical distinction between sea and land combat. More such littoral engagements seem certain, for the U.S. *Navy's most important contribution to future war overseas will be, as in the past, the safe delivery and sustainment of army, air force, and Marine elements that will engage the enemy on the land.

Because missiles are swift, accurate, lethal, and long-ranged, naval battle maneuvering has shifted from warship to weapon. Survivability is now largely dependent on quick defeat of attacking missiles. Counterfire with defensive missiles has had an insignificant effect, but chaff, jamming, and other defensive countermeasures have been highly successful when a defender was alerted. Thus, a scouting advantage and application of superior electronic tactics and technology has become vitally important as an advantage.

Over 400 guided missiles have been fired at merchant vessels and warships since 1967, when an Egyptian patrol craft launched 4 Soviet-made Styx missiles and sank the Israeli destroyer *Eilat*. Since 1967, torpedoes, *mines, aerial bombs, or shellfire have had considerable consequences, but ASCMs have inflicted by far the most damage and are the central weapon of naval tactics today.

Many in American policy circles believe that naval operations have changed radically since the collapse of the Soviet Union. Contemporary operations as disparate as the *Persian Gulf War, the interdiction of shipping in the Adriatic, and efforts to intercept both drugs and illegal immigrants in the Caribbean have all taken place in littoral waters. Consequently, a new concept called *joint littoral warfare* has developed, in which army, navy, air force, and Marine forces are concerted by joint commanders who conduct wide-ranging operations in the coastal regions of the world. The focus of U.S. naval operations has returned to its roots because throughout history most naval battles have been fought within 100 miles of land. Furthermore, during the Cold War, a dichotomy existed between U.S. Navy *war plans and actual force deployment. War plans were drawn to gain sea control, support a major *NATO war in Europe, and attack the Soviet homeland directly, with or without *nuclear weapons. The plans envisioned battles fought against Soviet submarines, long-range aircraft, and surface warships over the vastness of the ocean. Simultaneously, and paradoxically, the actual profitable deployment of American naval forces took place close inshore in a wide variety of circumstances and locales, involving air strikes, amphibious landings, and sustainment of forces fighting on land. The "new" littoral warfare tasks of the U.S. Navy at the end of the twentieth century are no different from those actually carried out in coastal waters by naval forces for the past fifty years, such as air strikes against North Vietnam and Libya, amphibious landings in Korea, Lebanon, and Grenada, coastal *blockades, and naval gunfire support.

Changes in tactics wrought by missiles are as far-reaching tactically as the shift from sail to steam or from battleship to aircraft carrier. Moreover, the great range of missiles coupled with the proximity to land creates a combat environment of intensified tactical interaction between the sea and the land in which force on force is no longer exclusively, or even primarily, fleet against fleet.

Starting in World War I, mines, *torpedo boats, and coastal submarines forced surface fleets to back away from close coastal blockade. In World War II, aircraft extended the air-land interaction, as ships used planes to attack land targets and land-based planes attacked ships. In the missile age, while ships become targets of land-based missiles, ship-based missiles are used against land sites. Since the 1950s, submarines armed with nuclear ballistic missiles have been capable of striking deep inland. In the Persian Gulf War of 1991, nearly 300 American sea-launched cruise missiles struck military targets in Iraq with conventional warheads.

The revolution in naval tactics wrought by missiles, however, is far more extensive than a change in the principal weapon. Until World War II, fleet maneuvers were designed to achieve a positional advantage relative to the enemy. In the age of fighting sail, the weather gauge (upwind of the opposing fleet) was such a crucial advantage. In the battleship era, crossing the "T" (alignment of one's column across the head of the enemy's column) was the relative position sought. Then, in World War II, maneuvers by ships in formation were supplanted by the swifter movement of raids by aircraft carrying *bombs and torpedoes or salvos of torpedoes launched from destroyers and light *cruisers. These outperformed gunfire from heavy cruisers and *battleships. Today, small maneuverable missile craft have the capacity to put much larger warships out of action, especially in confined coastal waters; large salvos of fifty or more missiles can be rapidly and accurately launched against land targets from a comparatively small warship, as they were in the U.S. retaliatory attacks on purported terrorist sites in the Sudan and Afghanistan in August 1998. Aircraft carriers—so fragile and frequently sunk in World War II—now use their mobility to position themselves out of danger, yet where their aircraft can deliver telling, repeated attacks.

[*See also* Strategy: Naval Warfare Strategy.]

• Sir Julian S. Corbett, *Some Principles of Maritime Strategy*, 1911; reissued 1988. Wayne P. Hughes, *Fleet Tactics: Theory and Practice*, 1986. Eric Grove, *The Future of Sea Power*, 1990. Brian Tunstall, *Naval Warfare in the Age of Sail: The Evolution of Fighting Tactics 1650–1815*, 1990. John C. Schulte, *An Analysis of the Historical Effectiveness of Antiship Cruise Missiles in Littoral Warfare*, 1994. Wayne P. Hughes, Jr., "A Salvo Model of Warships in Missile Combat Used to Evaluate Their Staying Power," *Naval Research Logistics*, 1995. Craig Symonds, *Historical Atlas of the U.S. Navy*, 1995. Martin S. Navias and E. R. Hooton, *Tanker Wars: The Assault on Merchant Shipping During the Iran-Iraq Conflict, 1980–1988*, 1996.

—Wayne P. Hughes, Jr.

TACTICS: AIR WARFARE TACTICS

Tactics in air warfare consist of fundamental methods, skills, and techniques designed to lead to success in aerial combat. Subject to change as the result of the rapid and continuing improvements in aircraft, *weapons, and support technology over the last eighty years, *air warfare tactics nevertheless remain a natural outgrowth of the earliest use of military aircraft by the major belligerents during World War I.

The classic goal of air warfare is to deny an enemy the use of airspace and to exploit that airspace for *victory. Typically, this mandates the destruction of enemy aircraft—either in the air or on the ground—and winning and maintaining air superiority. Success in the battle for air superiority permits one's aircraft to attack enemy ground or naval forces, deny the enemy logistic support, resupply friendly forces, collect photographic intelligence, and bring an enemy's country under long-range strategic bombardment. Scores of other missions exist as well, and are not confined to the atmosphere immediately surrounding the Earth. Space is a new arena for air warfare. At a fundamental level, military aviators create and modify air warfare tactics to maximize the impact and effectiveness of aircraft or aerospace vehicles—manned or unmanned—whatever the objective.

At the beginning of World War I, Germany and Britain used aircraft largely for straightforward reconnaissance, observation, and artillery-spotting purposes. In its earliest forms, air combat developed as an outgrowth of these missions. It was not long before airmen who had greeted each other with smiles and waves began shooting at each other with rifles and pistols. These weapons quickly gave way to *machine guns synchronized to fire through propellers. The German fighter pilot Max Immelmann is generally credited with developing in 1915 the first aerial maneuver designed to give an attacking aircraft a relative advantage over another. The 180-degree climbing turn that soon bore his name might accurately be thought of as the genesis of aerial tactical development. Another German aviator, Oswald Boelcke, developed seven fundamental rules of air combat, several of which survive to this day. The most enduring admonitions were to surprise the enemy and to maintain the offensive advantage. Boelcke was also among the earliest proponents of formation flying. Eschewing "lone-eagle" patrols, he believed aircraft attacking in pairs offered mutual support and enjoyed a greater chance of success against the enemy.

Boelcke's notions and techniques found widespread acceptance on both sides of the lines during World War I. At its most basic tactical level, fighter air combat consisted largely of seeing the enemy, deciding whether or not an attack was possible, closing by maneuver, firing, and escaping. If the original attack was unsuccessful, further maneuver was necessary either to reengage or to avoid further attack and survive. With allowances for vast increases in speed, target acquisition, and accuracy of weapons, these tenets are just as valid today as they were between 1914 and 1918.

By the end of World War I, air warfare tactics were remarkably sophisticated, and included concepts for the employment of large numbers of bombing and reconnaissance aircraft. All sides employed mass formations; aircraft attacked targets both on the immediate battlefield and deep within enemy country. Using lighter-than-air Zeppelins and large, specially designed long-range airplanes, the Germans undertook the first sustained strategic bombing campaign in history against London. Although it caused only minimal physical damage, its psychological impact was important. Moreover, the campaign spurred many of the doctrinal and tactical developments during the interior period.

The 1920s and 1930s were a fertile time for those thinking about the potential use of airpower. Airpower advocates in Britain and the United States, like Sir Hugh Trenchard and Gen. Billy *Mitchell, and Giulio *Douhet in Italy, suggested that large independent air forces, built around long-range bombers, could have a winning impact. At a tactical level, they assumed that bombers were fast enough, well enough defended, and could fly high enough to avoid or defeat enemy interceptors. In their minds, this reduced or virtually eliminated the need for armed escort of fighter planes. Moreover, the most optimistic zealots confidently predicted that bombers would be able to obliterate their targets and terrorize civilian populations with little difficulty. Americans, less comfortable than their British counterparts with the notion of *bombing of civilians in cities, believed accurate U.S. bombsights and well-protected aircraft such as the B-24 and B-17 were capable of precision against industrial targets. A few, such as Claire *Chennault, advocated increased emphasis on *fighter aircraft.

The Germans developed their own views on the uses of airpower during this period. They were particularly impressed with the concept of terror bombing. Their success in the Spanish Civil War convinced them that bombers might play a significant role in reducing an enemy's morale and willingness to resist. Nevertheless, the Germans' principal contribution here related to the importance of ground support aviation. In the earliest campaigns of World War II, the *Luftwaffe* became a true extension of the German Army, and in many ways operated like mobile *artillery. German fighters, flying in flexible and mutually supporting formations, attacked first to sweep an enemy air force from the ground and sky. Subsequent waves of high- and low-altitude bombers attacked enemy airfields, transportation centers, fuel storage areas, and troop installations. Finally, highly accurate dive-bombers assisted the swift-moving columns of German *tanks as they swept through enemy defenses in deep, encircling penetrations. The rapid German victories in 1939 and 1940 astonished the world.

The Allies were also able to put the principal tactical elements of their air warfare doctrine to the test. Beginning in 1942, British and American bombers undertook an offensive against German-occupied Europe and the Nazi homeland. In an attempt to reduce casualty rates, the British bombed area targets largely by night. The Americans, convinced that high-altitude, daylight formation bombing was possible, attacked a succession of more precise industrial and military targets. Unfortunately, both air forces suffered huge *casualties, while German armament production rates actually increased. Employing *radar and an increasingly effective nighttime air and ground defense network, the *Luftwaffe* battled the British over the largest German cities. In the daytime, German fighters used heavier armament and increasingly sophisticated tactics to blast hundreds of U.S. bombers out of the sky. It was not until early 1944 and the employment of sizable numbers of new, long-range escort fighters like the P-51, that the American bomber formations became truly effective. Given the attritional nature of the air war in the proceeding months, it took an amazingly short time for the *Luftwaffe* to suffer the effects. In just six months American fighters largely swept the Germans from the skies, while Allied bombers finally concentrated on the target arrays that would bring the German military machine to a virtual halt—oil and *transportation.

Amphibious island-hopping actions and naval aviation dominated the Pacific War. Naval air warfare tactics were largely built around carrier-borne aircraft whose main mission was to attack enemy ships. The primary targets in most engagements were enemy *aircraft carriers, and the best way to attack them was with coordinated formations of dive-bombers and torpedo planes. Navy fighter aircraft, in a way similar to their land-based counterparts, supported offensive air operations or flew in air defense roles. Long-range strategic bombing by the army air forces in the Pacific fell mainly to the American B-29. This aircraft, which eventually carried out the first atomic bomb attacks, was capable of large bomb loads and inflicted huge damage on Japanese cities in a series of incendiary raids between 1944 and 1945.

The development of *nuclear weapons appeared to fulfill the most visionary projections of the air power advocates. During many of the years of the *Cold War, the potential use of atom bomb–laden aircraft dominated the thinking of many leaders in the military and government. According to various airpower historians, the focus on strategic nuclear warfare in the U.S. *Air Force caused a corresponding atrophy in developments with regard to ground support or tactical aviation. High-altitude, long-range bombers like the Boeing B-52 and the medium-range, supersonic Convair B-58 came to symbolize the Cold War. Soviet air defense improvements predictably forced U.S. Air Force planners to develop increasingly sophisticated penetration tactics. At the same time, intercontinental ballistic *missiles (ICBMs) gradually took the place of the great masses of bombers at U.S. Cold War air bases. But the events of the *Korean War and the *Vietnam War also demonstrated that an air force organized and equipped mainly for a strategic nuclear mission was ill-suited for the demands of low-intensity conflict.

Vietnam validated the need for a well-balanced air force as well as principles that encompassed a broader base of air warfare tactics. The young U.S. Air Force aviators who had witnessed American defeat in Vietnam, and later rose to high rank, concentrated on doctrinal, organizational, technological, and tactical developments that would make their air force the most effective in the world. Both the air force and the navy established fighter weapon schools where classic air-to-air combat training with gun and missile could be conducted by experts. American aircraft industry produced a new generation of highly maneuverable and sophisticated jet aircraft, such as the Grumman F-14, the McDonnell-Douglas F-15, and the General Dynamics F-16. *Precision-guided munitions, the use of artificial intelligence, and the full exploitation of the electromagnetic and space environments all became part and parcel of the modern air battlefield. The air force devoted significant resources to data and intelligence collection as it became increasingly apparent that accurate targeting was the key to airpower's effectiveness. At intellectual resource centers like the U.S. Air Force Academy, Air Command and Staff College, the Air War College, and the National War College, officers began to think more critically about airpower. These myriad elements came together in the *Persian Gulf War of 1991, affording the world a powerful demonstration of the impact of modern airpower.

Despite the apparent technological domination of contemporary war, air warfare tactics show an unbroken human thread back to 1914–18. At its most fundamental level, air warfare continues to require a human being to shoot down an enemy aircraft or put munitions on target. As long as nations threaten each other, military airmen will ponder the requirements for seizing control of the air and subsequently exploiting that control, much as they did during World War I.

[See also Strategy: Air Warfare Strategy.]

• Keith Ayling, Combat Aviation, 1943. Barry D. Watts, The Foundation of U.S. Air Doctrine: The Problem of Friction in War, 1984. Richard P. Hallion, Rise of Fighter Aircraft: 1914–1918, 1984. Robert L. Shaw, Fighter Combat: The Air and Science of Air-to-Air Warfare, 1985. Michael S. Sherry, The Rise of American Air Power, 1987. R. A. Mark Clodfelter, The Limits of Air Power: The American Bombing of North Vietnam, 1989. John Warden, The Air Campaign: Planning for Combat, 1989. John Gooch, ed., Airpower: Theory and Practice, 1995.

—Mark K. Wells

TAFT, ROBERT (1889–1953), U.S. senator, isolationist. Born in Cincinnati, the son of William Howard Taft, later secretary of war and president, young Taft graduated from Yale University and Harvard Law School. He practiced law in Ohio and served in the state legislature before being elected to the U.S. Senate in 1938.

A conservative, isolationist midwestern Republican, Taft opposed most of the domestic and international policies of Democratic presidents Roosevelt and Truman. Favoring hemispheric rather than forward defense, he voted against the prewar draft in 1940 and Lend-Lease and the *Destroyers-for-Bases Agreement with Britain in 1941.

In the postwar era, he was not converted to *internationalism like former Republican isolationist Arthur Vandenberg of Michigan. Instead, although Taft voted for the establishment of the *United Nations, he came to believe it unsound and voted against U.S. participation in it. Taft opposed *NATO as a provocative and expensive act that would stimulate the *arms race and eventually force the United States to send troops to Europe. He later condemned President Harry S. *Truman's *Korean War policy, opposed his stand on Formosa, and challenged Secretary of State Dean *Acheson. Like former President Herbert C. *Hoover, Taft favored *neutrality and nonintervention, and recommended a defense policy based largely upon naval and airpower (called the "cavalry of the sky") rather than the deployment of U.S. ground forces.

Taft, "Mr. Republican," sought the presidential nomination in 1952 but lost to Dwight D. *Eisenhower, representing the GOP's eastern, internationalist wing. Taft extracted concessions for his support of Eisenhower, but he died within six months of becoming Senate majority leader.

[See also Isolationism; Lend-Lease Act and Agreements.]

• Robert A. Taft, Foreign Policy for Americans, 1951. James T. Patterson, Mr. Republican: A Biography of Robert A. Taft, 1974.

—John Whiteclay Chambers II

TAIWAN STRAIT CRISES (1955; 1958). Several small, obscure island groups in the 100-mile-wide Taiwan Strait, which separates the Chinese mainland from Taiwan Island (also known as Formosa), twice became the center of world attention in the 1950s when conflicts between the Chinese Communists and the Chinese Nationalists threatened to draw the United States and other countries into wide-scale military conflict, including the use of *nuclear weapons. The U.S. handling of the crises also became an important issue in domestic politics, particularly during the 1960 presidential contest between John F. *Kennedy and Vice President Richard M. *Nixon.

After the triumph of the Communists over the Nationalists in 1949 on the mainland, the Chinese civil war continued in the offshore islands. The Nationalist forces of Chiang Kai-shek, in addition to holding Taiwan and Pescadores Island, also controlled several smaller islands, many just off the China coast, of which the most important were Quemoy and Matsu. The contending Chinese forces regularly fought for these small bits of territory, which were sparsely populated, economically unimportant, and of questionable military value.

During and after the *Korean War, the Nationalists used the islands as staging areas for harassment of the mainland and Communist shipping lanes. U.S. policy under both Truman and Eisenhower supported the Nationalists' retention of all territory under their control. Washington wanted no further territory to fall to the Communists. Elements of the U.S. Seventh Fleet had patrolled the strait since 1950 and U.S. military advisers were stationed on the islands.

The first major crisis began in September 1954, when Communist shore batteries heavily shelled Quemoy. The Nationalists retaliated with punishing air raids against the mainland and strengthened their island fortifications. Communist pressure on the islands continued, and top-level officials in President Dwight D. *Eisenhower's administration began to believe that the Communists were preparing to assault all the offshore islands and possibly even Taiwan itself. Washington strengthened its commitment to Chiang Kai-shek with a mutual defense treaty and congressional passage of the "Formosa Resolution," which allowed the president to commit U.S. forces to Taiwan's defense.

The crisis came in April 1955, when the United States threatened to use *nuclear weapons in the event of a Communist assault on Quemoy and Matsu. Simultaneously, Chinese premier Zhou Enlai signaled Beijing's willingness to negotiate with the United States. Tensions rapidly dissipated and direct talks between the two sides began in Warsaw. It does not appear, however, that the Communists were actually deterred by the nuclear threat.

In August 1958, during an international crisis in the Middle East, another U.S.-China confrontation broke out over Quemoy and Matsu, after the Communists again bombarded the islands from onshore batteries. This confrontation was shorter but more intense than the first one. For several weeks, it again appeared that the United States, which sent several carrier groups to the region, might be drawn into a war with China, and possibly with the Soviet Union, which publicly supported Beijing's "Liberate Taiwan" campaign. But like the first crisis, tensions broke as Washington and Beijing resumed negotiations and Beijing backed away from an assault.

Over the years, Beijing seized most of the offshore islands, except Quemoy and Matsu, which remain in Nationalist hands.

[See also China, U.S. Military Involvement in; Chinese Civil War, U.S. Military Involvement in the; Cold War: External Course; Middle East, U.S. Military Involvement in the.]

• Alexander L. George and Richard Smoke, *Deterrence in American Foreign Policy: Theory and Practice*, 1974. Gordon H. Chang, *Friends and Enemies: The United States, China and the Soviet Union, 1948–1972*, 1990.
—Gordon H. Chang

TANK DESTROYERS were the U.S. Army's response to Germany's *Blitzkrieg* armored victories over Poland and France in the early years of World War II. Lt. Gen. Lesley J. McNair, head of army doctrine and training, decided that mobile, powerfully gunned antitank units were the best way to defeat enemy tanks. In November 1941, the War Department ordered the creation of such units, designated "tank destroyer" battalions.

Tank destroyer weapons could be either towed or self-propelled. The towed weapons were 3-inch *artillery pieces pulled by half-tracks. Self-propelled tank destroyers had 3-inch, 76mm or (late in the war) 90mm guns mounted on tank chassis within fully rotating, open-topped turrets. These carried less armor and mounted more powerful guns than the standard M-4 Sherman tank.

Tank destroyer units were trained to operate aggressively and en masse to destroy enemy armor. In combat, however, they were usually dispersed among front-line units, where they provided their most valuable service as mobile artillery directly supporting the infantry. Paradoxically, U.S. tank destroyers that did encounter heavy German tanks were generally outgunned.

After World War II, the army decided that there was no functional difference between a tank destroyer and a medium tank. Thereafter, the tank destroyer's fire support and antitank missions were officially assigned to *tanks. The last tank destroyer units were disbanded in 1946.

[See also Armored Vehicles; Weaponry, Army; World War II: Military and Diplomatic Course.]

• Charles M. Bailey, *Faint Praise: American Tanks and Tank Destroyers During World War II*, 1983. Christopher R. Gabel, *Seek, Strike, and Destroy: U.S. Army Tank Destroyer Doctrine in World War II*, 1985.
—Christopher R. Gabel

TANKS. The tank, invented in *World War I out of military necessity, immediately captured the popular imagination. The machine's raw power, gadgetry, speed, and size, along with the secrecy with which it was developed, created for it a mystique. Initially, the very name *tank* was employed as part of a deception to shroud its true nature as a weapon.

The British first developed this mobile, armored war machine in a program initiated by E. D. Swinton and Maurice Hankey; Winston S. *Churchill, then first lord of the Admiralty, also supported the program. The first British tank, the Mark I, was a rhomboid-shaped, tracked heavy vehicle weighing 26 tons, with two 57mm guns and a speed of 3.7 mph. On 15 September 1916, at the Battle of the Somme, after horrific infantry losses, forty-nine Mark I tanks were sent in to support infantry attack across no-man's-land. Early critics charged they were committed in insufficient numbers to make a difference. In September 1917, the French introduced their Renault FT 17, a smaller (6-ton), lighter-armed (one 37mm gun), faster (4.8 mph) tank, with what became the classic tank design of a swivel turret. The Americans used mainly Renault tanks in France.

During the interwar years, the limited role assigned to tanks by U.S. infantry generals, as well as budget limitations, imposed serious constraints on design and development in the United States. J. Walter Christie, an American automotive engineer, developed a suspension system that allowed tanks high speed and overland performance. His

M1919 tank, which evolved into the M1928/1930 or T-3 medium tank, weighed 9 tons, carried a 37mm gun, and attained speeds of 27 mph. But the U.S. Army failed to continue Christie's contract.

In contrast, the Soviet Union used Christie's design and production techniques to develop by 1939–40 the T-34, a highly reliable and balanced tank weighing 29 tons, armed with a 76.2mm gun, and reaching a maximum speed of 34 mph. It became the Red Army's main battle tank in World War II and was used by North Korean forces in the *Korean War.

In Great Britain, military theorists J. F. C. Fuller and Basil H. *Liddell Hart envisioned a small but mobile army with tanks as the centerpiece. After many problems, the British introduced the Crusader (22 tons, 57mm gun, and 26 mph maximum speed), used early in World War II. But defects and battle experience led to its replacement in 1943 by the Cromwell (31 tons, 75mm gun, 31 mph).

French experimentation before 1939 developed the Heavy B (CHAR) tank, probably the best in the world at the onset of World War II. Huge for its day, it was heavily armored, weighing 34 tons, had a 75mm gun mounted on the front hull and a 47mm gun on the turret, but sacrificed maximum speed to only 17 mph. The tank's firepower and armor advantage were, however, offset in 1940 by French doctrinal and organizational failures.

In September 1939, when the German Army invaded Poland, it had not yet accepted Gen. Heinz Guderian's ideas about armored warfare and used tankette-type vehicles more suitable for training. But before invading France in May 1940, the Germans achieved great advances in doctrine, unit reorganization, and tank manufacture, incorporating superior *Panzer* tanks (23 tons, 24 mph, and guns increased from 37mm in the *Panzer* III to 75mm in the *Panzer* IV tanks). To counter the Soviet's effective T-34s, the Germans produced the *Panzer* V. This "Panther" tank, probably the best overall German tank, weighed 50 tons in later versions, with speeds of up to 28 mph and armed with a 75mm gun.

By 1942, the Germans fielded the Tiger tank, which challenged established ideas about armored warfare. Despite problems in maneuverability, serviceability, and speed (23 mph on roads, 12 mph cross-country), this heavy tank provided extraordinary armor protection (63 tons) and firepower with its 88mm gun.

In the United States, the M4-A Sherman replaced the awkward Grant early in World War II to become the main American battle tank. More than 45,000 of these reliable, rugged, and versatile medium tanks were produced for the U.S. Army, as well for Great Britain and the Soviet Union. The early model weighed 33 tons, had a speed of 23 mph, and was armed with a 75mm gun. Subsequent modifications in the A-3 increased weight to 35 tons, speed to 29 mph, and the gun to 76.2mm. Though the Sherman was no match individually with any German tank, and its gasoline rather than diesel fuel was highly explosive, it proved highly successful, due to the numbers committed and its reliability. In various forms Shermans were used by the United States in the *Korean War and by the Israel Defense Force in the Six-Day War of 1967 when a "Super Sherman" was mounted with a 105mm gun.

In 1945, the British produced a remarkable tank based on their war experiences, the Centurion, which became the backbone of British armored forces for a quarter of a century. This tank was noted for its reliability and proved itself in combat in the Korean War. The Centurion I mounted a 17-pound gun and was produced in thirteen versions, the last manufactured in Israel. It was considered the best all-around tank in the West in the 1950s and 1960s. The final Israeli version weighed 54 tons, sported a 105mm gun, and traveled at 21 mph.

Tank design was revolutionized in 1945 by the new Soviet JS-3 Stalin heavy tank. This eventually evolved to the T-10 heavy in the 1950s. Its design allowed a tank of 51 tons at 23 mph and supported armament of a 122mm gun. During the *Cold War, the JS-3's low, sleek design was perpetuated by the West German Leopard, the French AMX 30, and the British Chieftain. The same turtle turret design characterized the Soviets' medium tanks, evolving from the 1950s through the 1970s from T-54/55, T-62, and T-64 to T-80. Weight increased from 42 to 46 tons, speed from 31 to 46 mph, and armament from 100mm to 114mm and finally 125mm on the T-64 and T-80.

The United States pursued a different design approach. Its M-48 (1952) and M-60 (1960) main battle tanks sacrificed low weight and silhouette in favor of an excellent 105mm gun system and reliability. The M60A-3 version weighed 57 tons and attained 30 mph.

In 1973, man-packed wire-guided missiles caused massive tank losses in the Arab-Israeli War, which, along with *NATO's new "Active Defense" doctrine demanding high-speed lateral movement, resulted in major changes in tank tactics and development. When first produced in the mid-1970s, the U.S. Army's M-1 Abrams tank weighed 68 tons and was unique in using a multifuel turbine power plant and innovative suspension system allowing speeds over 45 mph. Initially armed with the reliable M-68 105mm gun, the Abrams in its subsequent models increased combat weight and armament to mount a smoothbore 120mm gun. The Abrams proved its technological superiority in NATO war games and in actual battle during the *Persian Gulf War.

In the 1990s, the tank of the future was being designed using such techniques as automatic loaders to reduce crew size, more efficient power plants, new reactive armor to defeat larger gun size and anti-tank *missiles, and special armor to increase protection and reduce weight for faster deployment.

[*See also* Armored Vehicles; Army Combat Branches: Armor; Tank Destroyers.]

• Ralph E. Jones, George H. Rarey, and Robert J. Icks, *The Fighting Tanks Since 1916,* 1969. Duncan Crow and Robert J. Icks, *Encyclopedia of Tanks,* 1975. Chris Elliot and Peter Chamberlain, *The Great Tanks,* 1975. R. E. Simpkin, *Tank Warfare,* 1979. Christopher F. Foss, *Jane's Main Battle Tanks,* 1983. Richard M. Ogorkiewicz, *Technology of Tanks,* Vol. 1, 1991. Christopher Chant, *World Encyclopaedia of the Tank,* 1994.
—George J. Mordica II

TARAWA, BATTLE OF (1943). In June 1943, the *Joint Chiefs of Staff ordered Adm. Chester W. *Nimitz, Commander in Chief, Pacific Ocean Areas/Pacific Fleet, to invade the Japanese-held Gilbert Islands with a target date of November 15. The immediate objective of the Fifth Fleet would be Tarawa Atoll, with the target Betio Island. The Fifth Amphibious Force, under Rear Adm. Richmond Kelly Turner, would carry and support the V Amphibious Corps (VAC) under Marine Maj. Gen. Holland M. Smith. The landing force would be the 2d Marine Division. Betio was two miles long, 500 yards wide at its broadest, and in no place more than 10 feet above sea level. Most of it was filled with an airstrip; the rest was comprised of fortifications and more than 200 guns including two British-made eight-inch naval rifles. The commander of the 5,000-man island garrison was Rear Adm. Keichi Shibasaki. The United States decided to land three battalions abreast on the northern, or lagoon, side of the island. The transports would have to stand outside the atoll, there would be a long approach of ten miles for the landing craft, and it was questionable if there would be enough water over the reef to allow them to get to the beach. As a result, the Marines would have to depend on thin-skinned amphibian tractors, or amtracs, barely tested at Guadalcanal. Just 100 were available, enough for the first three waves. In the assault was the 2d Marines, reinforced by the 8th Marines, also an infantry regiment. The 6th Marines, the third infantry regiment of the 2d Division, was held in corps reserve. H-hour was 8:30, November 20. The first waves touched down ashore at 9:14. Behind them, ordinary landing craft were stopped at the edge of the reef and Marines on board had to wade in a half mile under heavy fire. By nightfall, Marines held a shallow box-shaped perimeter with elements of four battalions, and another battalion held a tiny beachhead on the western end of the island. The remaining assault battalion was still afloat beyond the reef. On the morning of November 21, the Marines jumped off in the attack, and by evening reached the south side of the island. Sometime during the day, Admiral Shibasaki died in his bunker. On the west end of the island, a fresh battalion was landed. By the evening of November 22, the Marines held the western two-thirds of Betio. The next day, another previously uncommitted battalion continued the attack eastward. Maj. Gen. Julian C. Smith, commander of the 2d Marine Division, declared the island secured. His division, which had begun the battle with 18,600 Marines, counted 990 dead and 2,391 wounded. Four Marines were awarded the Medal of Honor, three posthumously. The Tarawa operation was the first assault in the Pacific War against a heavily defended island, and many lessons were learned from it, including the need for many more amtracs. The operation was extensively recorded on 35mm news film, subsequently shown in theaters across the country. Shots of dead Marines floating along the Tarawa beaches brought the war home graphically to the American people.

[See also Marine Corps, U.S.: 1914–1945; World War II: Military and Diplomatic Course.]

• Joseph H. Alexander, Across the Reef: The Marine Assault of Tarawa, 1993.   —Benis M. Frank

TAYLOR, MAXWELL (1901–1987), *World War II and *Korean War Veteran, chairman Joint Chiefs of Staff (JCS), ambassador to Vietnam. Maxwell Taylor graduated from West Point in 1922, being commissioned first in the engineers and subsequently in the field artillery. He spent thirteen of the interwar years in schools, either as teacher or student, culminating in his graduation from the Army War College in 1940.

In September 1943, while part of the 82nd Airborne Division during World War II, he entered Italy behind German lines on a secret mission for Gen. Dwight D. *Eisenhower to assess the ability of the Italians to support an American airborne drop near Rome. On Taylor's advice, Eisenhower canceled the plan as a potential disaster.

In March 1944, Taylor assumed command of the 101st Airborne Division and at the *D-Day landing and parachuted with his division behind enemy lines, becoming the first American general to land in Nazi-occupied France. After the war, Taylor was appointed superintendent of West Point (1945–49) and thereafter held a series of increasingly important assignments until he assumed command of the U.S. Eighth Army in February 1953 during the Korean War. He served as chief of staff, 1955–59, during the Eisenhower presidency. At the end of his tour as he retired from the army, Taylor published The Uncertain Trumpet, a book critical of the Eisenhower administration's emphasis on reduced defense budgets and on airpower and nuclear *weaponry over ground forces.

But Taylor is best known for his involvement in the Vietnam War. In 1961, President John F. *Kennedy recalled Taylor to active duty as his military representative and also named him chairman of the Special Group Counterinsurgency. Taylor participated in JFK's decision sharply to increase the scale of U.S. support for South Vietnam. Subsequently, after the president named him chairman of the JCS, Taylor was unsuccessful in opposing the U.S. decision to support the overthrow of Ngo Dinh Diem, the South Vietnamese chief of state.

In 1964, Lyndon B. *Johnson appointed him ambassador to South Vietnam. Taylor strongly supported U.S. air strikes against North Vietnam, but unsuccessfully opposed LBJ's 1965 decision to introduce U.S. combat troops into the war. From 1965 to 1969, he served as special consultant to the president on Vietnam.

Maxwell Taylor was one of the major American military figures of the twentieth century. He was a transition figure—the last of the World War II heroic generals and the first of a new breed, the managerial generals. More soldier than statesman, his major involvement in the American political scene took place during the Vietnam War, in which his role was central but not decisive.

[See also Army, U.S.: Since 1941; Vietnam War: Military and Diplomatic Course; Vietnam War: Domestic Course.]

• Maxwell Taylor, Swords and Plowshares, 1972. Douglas Kinnard, The Uncertain Trumpet, 1991.   —Douglas Kinnard

TAYLOR, ZACHARY (1784–1850), *Mexican War general and U.S. president. Elected president in 1848, Zachary Taylor served only sixteen months in office before his death in 1850. Despite holding the highest office in the land, Taylor is best remembered as a general in charge of the first campaign by the American forces against Mexico during the Mexican War.

Born in Virginia, the son of a prosperous landowner, Taylor grew up in Louisville. In 1808, he gained a commission and served in the *War of 1812. For the next three decades he participated in Indian wars and gained the rank of general with the nickname "Old Rough and Ready" during the *Seminole Wars. As commander of the U.S. troops on the Mexican frontier with Texas, Taylor directed a series of battles near the Rio Grande. After victories at Palo Alto and Resaca de la Palma in May 1846, he pressed on into Mexico, eventually capturing Monterrey in September after a vigorous fight. In February 1847, his army barely repelled a powerful attack at Buena Vista.

A hero throughout the United States, Taylor was passed over as commander for the invasion of Mexico at Veracruz.

In 1848, Taylor ran for president as a Whig and was elected, only to die early in his term.

• Henry B. Montgomery, *The Life of Major-General Zachary Taylor, Twelfth President of the United States,* 1847. Edward J. Nichols, *Zach Taylor's Little Army,* 1963. K. Jack Bauer, *Zachary Taylor: Soldier, Planter, Statesman of the Old Southwest,* 1985.

—John M. Hart

TECUMSEH (c. 1768–1813), Shawnee chief and leader of an Indian confederation. Born when the Shawnee Indians were fighting to defend their Kentucky and Ohio lands, Tecumseh lost his father at the Battle of Point Pleasant (1774), a brother in the American *Revolutionary War, and another in the wars that followed. He fought against Josiah Harmar (1790), Arthur St. Clair (1791), and Anthony Wayne (1794). He refused to sign the Treaty of Greenville (1795), which ceded most of Ohio to the United States, and in the next decade emerged as the leading opponent of American expansion.

In 1805, following a vision, Tecumseh's brother, Tenskwatawa, began to preach a return to traditional ways and rejection of white influences. Tecumseh broadened and directed the religious movement into a multitribal confederation opposed to further land cessions. A gifted orator, he carried his message of Indian unity from Canada to Florida.

In 1811, while Tecumseh was spreading his message in the South, William Henry Harrison, governor of Indiana Territory, attacked and burned Tenskwatawa's village at Tippecanoe, costing the Indian confederation much unity and momentum.

In the *War of 1812, Tecumseh allied with the British and assisted Gen. Isaac Brock in capturing Detroit. After Brock's death, however, the British-Indian alliance began to falter. Tecumseh despised the caution of the new commander, Col. Henry Proctor, but accompanied the British army on its retreat to Canada after the Americans won control of Lake Erie. He was killed during the Battle of the Thames in October 1813.

Tecumseh was not the first Indian to preach united resistance on the part of the tribes, but he was the most effective, forging a confederation of unprecedented range. Intratribal divisions—as many opposed as supported him among the Shawnees and other Indian nations—undermined his efforts to resist U.S. power. His death killed hopes for a united Indian state and ended major Indian resistance north of the Ohio River.

[*See also* Native American Wars.]

• R. David Edmunds, *Tecumseh and the Quest for Indian Leadership,* 1984. John Sugden, *Tecumseh, A Life,* 1998.

—Colin G. Calloway

TELEVISION. *See* Film; News Media, War and the Military.

TELLER, EDWARD (1908–), nuclear physicist. The Hungarian-born physicist earned his Ph.D. in physical chemistry in Germany after academic study and research in Munich and Leipzig. In Germany during the Weimar years, Teller taught at the University of Göttingen while studying atomic physics under Niels *Bohr in Copenhagen. In 1935, he went to the United States to teach at George Washington University.

Teller worked with Enrico *Fermi at the University of Chicago to create the first self-sustaining nuclear chain reaction. In 1943, he was recruited to work with J. Robert *Oppenheimer on the fission bomb at the *Manhattan Project in Los Alamos, New Mexico. While at Los Alamos, Teller began his own research on the feasibility of a thermonuclear or hydrogen fusion bomb. The USSR's explosion of an atomic bomb in 1949 galvanized Teller strongly to advocate U.S. development of the hydrogen bomb. After President Harry S. *Truman approved the H-bomb project in 1950, Teller returned to Los Alamos to begin work on the new weapon. The collaboration between Teller and the physicist S. M. Ulam proved successful. The fusion concept was successfully tested in the Pacific at Enewetok atoll on 1 November 1952.

As the *Cold War intensified, Teller gave testimony at government hearings in 1954 that contributed to the removal of Oppenheimer's security clearance. After helping in 1952 to create the Lawrence Livermore nuclear laboratory in Berkeley, California, Teller divided his time between working at Livermore and teaching physics at Berkeley.

Teller has been a powerful policy advocate for many years. His strong anti-Communist views led him to oppose the 1963 *Limited Test Ban Treaty and to influence President Ronald *Reagan to propose the *Strategic Defense Initiative in 1983.

[*See also* Atomic Scientists; Nuclear Weapons.]

• Louis G. Panos, *Edward Teller,* 1990.

—Mark Polelle

The **TELLER AMENDMENT** (1898), sponsored by Republican senator Henry M. Teller of Colorado, was adopted along with congressional authorization, 20 April 1898, for the use of U.S. military force to establish Cuban independence from Spain, following President William *McKinley's request for force on 11 April. In the amendment, the United States disclaimed any "intention to exercise sovereignty, jurisdiction or control over [Cuba] except for the pacification thereof, and asserts its determination when that is accomplished to leave the government and control of the island to its people."

Teller was a friend of Cuban independence and had unsuccessfully supported U.S. recognition of the Cuban insurgents. The unanimous adoption of his amendment reflected considerable opposition to the annexation of Cuba on various grounds—racial, cultural, and economic (competition with U.S. sugar growers). It did not apply to other Spanish possessions such as Puerto Rico, Guam, and the Philippines. While foreclosing forcible annexation of Cuba, it did not prevent the postwar establishment of a U.S. protectorate over the island under Senator Orville Platt's amendment to the Army Appropriations Bill of 2 March 1901 (the *Platt Amendment), which was made part of the Cuban Constitution, 1901–34, and authorized U.S. military intervention in Cuba when deemed necessary.

[*See also* Cuba, U.S. Military Involvement in; Spanish-American War.]

• John L. Offner, *An Unwanted War: The Diplomacy of the United States and Spain Over Cuba, 1895–1898,* 1992. Jose M. Hernandez, *Cuba and the United States, Intervention and Militarism, 1898–1933,* 1993.

—Jorge Rodríguez Beruff

TENURE OF OFFICE ACT (1867). This statute resulted from a fear on the part of congressional Republicans that

President Andrew *Johnson, in the course of a bitter dispute over *Reconstruction policy, would make sweeping removals of federal officeholders and replace them with Democrats. The law sought to protect officials appointed with Senate consent "until a successor shall have been in like manner appointed and duly qualified." Cabinet officers were to remain in place "for and during the term of the President by whom they may have been appointed, and for one month thereafter."

The latter provision appeared to protect Secretary of War Edwin M. *Stanton, who had allied himself with the congressional position on Reconstruction. Since the U.S. Army was the chief enforcement agency for federal policy in the South, control of the army, through the War Department, was vital to both Johnson and Congress. Johnson vetoed the measure as unconstitutional; Congress overrode the veto on 2 March 1867.

In February 1868, Johnson appeared to violate the act by removing Stanton. The House of Representatives impeached Johnson, citing his violation of the Tenure of Office Act as one reason. At the trial, the president's defense team raised serious questions about the statute's constitutionality. They also raised doubts that it even applied to Stanton, who had been appointed not by Johnson but by Abraham *Lincoln. These doubts, together with other considerations, caused enough senators to vote not guilty that Johnson escaped conviction by a single vote. Efforts to repeal the law began in 1869 and succeeded in 1887. In 1926, the Supreme Court, reviewing the presidential removal power in *Myers* v. *United States,* held unconstitutional the Tenure of Office Act and an 1876 successor.

[*See also* Commander in Chief, President as.]

• James E. Sefton, *The United States Army and Reconstruction, 1865–1877,* 1967. Hans L. Trefousse, *Andrew Johnson: A Biography,* 1989.
—James E. Sefton

TERRORISM AND COUNTERTERRORISM. Terrorism is defined in Title 22 of the United States Code, Section 2656f(d) as "premeditated, politically motivated violence perpetrated against noncombatant targets by subnational groups or clandestine agents, usually intended to influence an audience." Terrorism falls into the spectrum of low intensity conflict, relying upon the methods and strategies of unconventional warfare in targeting businesspeople, tourists, and other civilians to gain exposure, pressure governments, and extort concessions.

It is important to differentiate among state terrorism, state-supported terrorism and sub-state terrorism.

"State terrorism" refers to the use of terror by a government, using the resources of the state—including the police, judiciary, military—against its own citizens to quell domestic opposition to its policies, as exemplified by the "dirty war" in Argentina during the 1970s and early 1980s in which an estimated 15,000 to 30,000 regime opponents were killed or disappeared. "State-supported terrorism" refers to situations where states provide logistical, financial and training support for a terrorist organization. In 1998, the U.S. Department of State designated Cuba, Iran, Iraq, Libya, North Korea, Sudan, and Syria as state sponsors of terrorism. Sub-state terrorism refers to acts of terrorism perpetrated by non-state actors.

In considering sub-state terrorism, one can distinguish between five principal varieties:

Social revolutionary terrorism, also known as terrorism of the left, includes those acts perpetrated by groups seeking to overthrow the capitalist economic and social order and was typified by the European "fighting communist organizations" active throughout the 1970s and 1980s (e.g., the Red Army Faction in Germany and the Red Brigades in Italy), though social revolutionary groups have been active around the world, including the Shining Path in Peru and the Japanese Red Army Faction in Japan.

Religious extremist terrorism is characterized by groups seeking to maintain or create a religious social and political order and has included groups representing established religious doctrines as well groups representing "new religions." Traditional groups include Christian, Jewish, and Islamic extremists, while new religions include groups like Aum Shinrikyo, responsible for the 1995 subway sarin attack in Tokyo, Japan.

Nationalist-separatist terrorists, also known as ethno-nationalist terrorists, includes those groups fighting to establish a new political order or state based on ethnic dominance or homogeneity. The Irish Republican Army, the Liberation Tigers of Tamil Eelam (LTTE) of Sri Lanka, the Basque Fatherland and Liberty (ETA) in Spain, and the various groups representing Palestinian causes are prominent examples.

Right-wing terrorists comprise those groups seeking to maintain an extant political order or to return society to an idealized "golden age" of the past. Examples include neo-Nazi terrorist groups and groups espousing fascist ideology.

Single-issue terrorism, as the label suggests, represents groups acting on a single issue, such as the environment or animal rights.

The era of modern terrorism was ushered in by the dramatic slaying of Israeli athletes by the Palestinian group Black September during the globally televised 1972 Olympics in Munich, Germany. While terrorism prior to 1972 principally had been a domestic phenomenon, the Munich attack emphasized the expansion of tactics and targets to include exploitation of global mass communications networks and international aviation, internationalizing terrorism.

The relationship between terrorism and the media has been extensively studied (Nacos, 1994), and has been found to influence the tactics and strategies of modern terrorist groups. According to one estimate (Jenkins, 1985: 12), 95% of all terrorist attacks are designed to maximize exposure and influence through the media. The hijacking of airlines ("skyjackings") was particularly prevalent during the 1970s and early 1980s, as were hostage taking episodes. All received extensive media coverage.

The terrorist threat to the United States has traditionally come from two distinctly different strains of political terrorism: the leftist social revolutionary terrorists of Western Europe, attacking representatives of the United States as symbols of capitalism and Western militarism in the form of the North Atlantic Treaty Organization (NATO); and the national-separatist and religious fundamentalist groups of the Middle East—especially those connected with the liberation movements in Palestine—who attack U.S. forces and civilians first as supporters of Israel and second in connection with the rise of Islamic fundamentalism.

The German Red Army Faction (RAF) was responsible for numerous bombings of U.S. military installations. U.S. forces have also been targeted in Italy by the Red Brigades and in Greece by the Revolutionary Organization "November 17." Apart from bombings, European social revolutionary groups have been engaged in assassination and kidnapping attempts against U.S. military and NATO leaders stationed in Europe.

While terrorism committed by the European leftist groups against U.S. targets in Europe remained fairly localized, terrorists operating out of the Middle East, especially those organizations supported by states hostile to U.S. interests, such as Syria, Libya, and Iran, have operated on a more global setting, taking advantage of air travel and modern mass communications to pressure the United States and its allies into withdrawing support for Israel and diminishing U.S. and Western influence in the region.

America's first prolonged experience with terrorism began in 1979 with the seizure of the U.S. Embassy in Tehran, Iran, and the ensuing hostage crisis in which U.S. diplomats were held for 444 days. U.S. airliners have been susceptible to skyjackings, such as the 1985 Trans World Airlines (TWA) flight 847 skyjacking by Abu Nidal terrorists resulting in the deaths of 2 Americans, and bombings, the most spectacular of which was the 1988 bombing of PAN AM flight 103 by suspected Libyan terrorists.

Terrorists operating out of the Middle East frequently target U.S. military personnel. PLO splinter groups were responsible for the 1983 bombing of the U.S. Embassy in Beirut, killing 86 and wounding 100, and the car-bombing of the U.S. Marine barracks at Beirut airport, resulting in the deaths of 241 U.S. servicemen. U.S. servicemen were targeted by Libyan terrorists in the 1986 bombing of a nightclub in Berlin, Germany. Following the *Persian Gulf War in 1991, U.S. military bases in Saudi Arabia have become targets of Islamic groups heavily opposing U.S.-Saudi Arabian cooperation and the continued presence of U.S. forces on Saudi Arabian soil. The bombing of the Khobar Towers military residence in Dhahran, Saudi Arabia, resulted in 19 deaths and 500 wounded.

Evidence suggests changing trends in terrorism as the twentieth century draws to a close. First, there is a trend toward fewer, but more lethal acts. Second, there are fewer claims of responsibility being made for attacks, perhaps reflecting the growing prevalence of religious extremist terrorism and transnational terrorism. Third, the collapse of the Soviet Union has raised concern that poorly guarded nuclear, chemical, and biological materials might find their way into the hands of terrorists. Finally, international terrorists have for the first time attacked targets within the territorial United States with the World Trade Center bombing in 1993 and the subsequent conspiracy to bomb several other New York City landmarks by Middle East terrorists. The U.S. has also experienced its most devastating case of domestic anti-government terrorism with the 1995 bombing of the Alfred P. Murrah Federal Building in Oklahoma City, resulting in 168 deaths.

To combat terrorism, the United States' counterterrorism policy follows three general rules: the U.S. does not negotiate with terrorists; the U.S. will treat terrorists as criminals and pursue them aggressively; and the U.S. will apply maximum sanctions upon states supporting terrorism and encourage other states to do so as well (U.S. Department of State, 1996:iv). Accordingly, the U.S. has responded to the threat of modern international terrorism with a multi-tracked approach, including diplomatic and legal efforts and military interdiction and deterrence. The United States

is a party to nine major multilateral conventions that define states' responsibilities toward countering terrorism. Among them are treaties protecting diplomatic personnel and the safety of civil aviation and maritime navigation; outlawing the taking of hostages; the physical protection of nuclear materials; and the marking of explosives for identification.

Following the passage of the "long arm" anti-terrorism statute in 1984, the Department of Justice has been empowered to arrest foreign nationals who have committed acts of terrorism against U.S. citizens for trial in the U.S. court system. Fawaz Younis (1987) and Mohammed Al Rezaq (1995) were arrested abroad by agents of the Federal Bureau of Investigation and successfully tried in the U.S. The Department of Defense and U.S. military forces have played a mixed role in support of the United States' counterterrorism policy. Delta Force, the United States' secretive military unit specifically designed to counter terrorism, was founded during the Carter Administration (1976–1980). Modeled on the British Secret Air Services (SAS), Delta Force is comprised of elite commandos skilled in hostage rescue and incident interdiction. However, Delta Force's first deployment, Operation Eagle Claw (1980) to rescue the U.S. diplomats held hostage in Iran, proved a disastrous failure. Delta Force was joined in 1980 by a Navy counterpart, Seal Team 6, also tasked primarily with hostage rescue.

In addition to hostage rescue, U.S. military forces have been used to retaliate against states which have sponsored terrorist attacks against U.S. targets, such as the 1986 bombing raid on the Libyan capitol Tripoli in response to Libyan involvement in several dramatic acts of international terrorism in 1985 and 1986.

In a triumph of timely intelligence and coordination with the U.S. military, the aircraft carrying the hijackers of the Achille Lauro was intercepted by U.S. warplanes and forced to land at a U.S. Air Force base in Italy in October, 1985. The standoff at the airport between Italian and U.S. forces claiming jurisdiction over the captured terrorists, however, emphasizes the difficulties of pursuing U.S. counterterrorism policies abroad.

• James M. Poland, *Understanding Terrorism: Groups, Strategies, and Responses*, 1988. Alex P. Schmid and Albert J. Jongman, *Political Terrorism*, 1988. Martha Crenshaw, "The Logic of Terrorism: Terrorist Behavior as a Product of Strategic Choice," in Walter Reich, ed., *Origins of Terrorism: Psychologies, Ideologies, Theologies, States of Mind*, 1990. Jerrold M. Post, "Terrorist Psycho-Logic: Terrorist Behavior as a Product of Psychological Forces," in Walter Reich, ed., *Origins of Terrorism: Psychologies, Ideologies, Theologies, States of Mind*, 1990. R. Kingston, "The American Approach to Combating Terrorism," *Terrorism and Political Violence*, Autumn 1992, pp. 102–106. M. Gunter, "Countering Terrorism: The Reagan Record," *Conflict Quarterly* Spring 1994, pp. 7–10. Brigitte L. Nacos, *Terrorism and the Media: From the Iran Hostage Crisis to the Oklahoma City Bombing*, 1994. Jerrold M. Post, E. Shaw, and Keven G. Ruby, "From Car Bombs to Logic Bombs: Information Systems Terrorism," in John Harrald and G. Shaw, eds., *Disaster and Emergency Management: International Challenges for the Next Decade*, 1998. U.S. Department of State, *Patterns of Global Terrorism, 1997*, 1998.

—Jerrold M. Post *and* Keven G. Ruby

TET OFFENSIVE (1968). The attacks by Communist forces inside South Vietnam's major cities and towns that began around the Vietnamese New Year ("Tet") of 1 February 1968 were the peak of an offensive that took place over a period of several months during the Vietnam War. Gen. William C. *Westmoreland, the American commander in Vietnam, believed the attacks to be a last "throw of the dice" by the losing side. The attacks that Americans dubbed the "Tet Offensive" were just part of what the Communists called a "General Offensive and Uprising," designed to jolt the war into a new phase. The offensive ultimately achieved the Communists' aim, but at a price many of them thought excessive.

The offensive had long-term conceptual origins in Vietnam's August Revolution of 1945, in which the Communist-led Viet Minh had instigated popular uprisings in the cities to seize power from a puppet government Japan had installed before its defeat. Two decades later, as American commitment to the anti-Communist government in Saigon deepened in the early 1960s, the Communists looked to that earlier event for inspiration. Lacking the military power to inflict outright defeat on the American military, the Communists had somehow to destroy American confidence that "limited war" could eventually bring victory for the United States. By sending armed forces directly into the South's cities and fomenting rebellion there, the Communists hoped to pull down the Saigon government or facilitate the rise to power of neutralists who would demand the withdrawal of U.S. forces. Even if the offensive did not bring immediate victory, the Communists calculated it would allow rural forces to disrupt the *pacification program, destroy the American illusion of success, and induce the United States to enter negotiations in which Hanoi could bargain from a position of strength.

The plan formally approved by the Communist Party political bureau in Hanoi in July 1967 recognized that American, allied, and Saigon forces constituted a much more formidable foe than the shaky regime the August Revolution had toppled in 1945. The offensive therefore actually began in September 1967, with artillery-supported assaults by the People's Army of Vietnam (PAVN), supported from the North, on the U.S. combat bases located along route 9 just south of the demilitarized zone, and then with operations in the central highlands, to test American reactions. The tests revealed that the Americans would remain in defensive positions; and although PAVN troops would face devastating firepower, massing for attack on these positions in remote areas could lure significant forces away from population centers.

The American response encouraged the Communists to position up to 40,000 regulars of Divisions 304, 320, 325, and 324B in December 1967 around Khe Sanh, a U.S. Marine outpost near the western end of route 9. The outpost was an attractive target because it lay only fourteen kilometers beyond the terminus of an improved road over which the PAVN could move heavy equipment. Upon detecting the Communist buildup, the American command increased forces defending the base to 6,000 troops, including a battalion of Saigon's Army of the Republic of Vietnam (ARVN). After the PAVN opened the attack with a massive artillery barrage on 21 January, the United States shifted 15,000 more troops from the South's 5 northern provinces to route 9. Fifty thousand U.S. troops eventually fought at or supported the base.

Despite superficial similarities between the situation at Khe Sanh and Dien Bien Phu, where the PAVN had overrun a French force in 1954, PAVN commanders knew they could not duplicate that feat in the face of massive American air and ground firepower. The battle was worth the effort to them because of the attention and resources it drew from the lowlands. Still, their orders were to destroy if possible one or more of the route 9 bases to facilitate the movement of PAVN regulars into the South. Although unable to create a major breach, a PAVN regiment overran the Special Forces/Civil Indigenous Defense Group camp at Lang Vei, eight kilometers west of Khe Sanh, on 7 February. Soviet-supplied PT-76 light amphibious tanks of the People's Army made their first appearance of the war at Lang Vei.

Meanwhile, U.S. intelligence had detected preparations for attacks on urban centers, and in a few localities commanders had taken precautionary measures. But analysts did not believe the Communists were capable of achieving, or bold enough to attempt, what the evidence indicated they were planning. With General Westmoreland and Saigon's President Nguyen Van Thieu convinced that Khe Sanh was the Communists' primary target, Communist forces had begun attacking outposts around cities and towns. A mixed force of maneuver and guerrilla troops estimated at around 60,000 and composed largely of troops recruited and trained in the South, had then slipped past these outposts to enter 5 municipalities, 36 province capitals, and 64 district capitals.

In the night of 29 January, assault forces attacked government offices in Qui Nhon, Kontum, Pleiku, Darlac, and Nha Trang. Attacks in other cities began over the next two days. In Saigon, the sapper team that blasted into the U.S. Embassy compound captured the headlines, but attacks on Tan Son Nhut airfield, the ARVN general staff compound, government ministries, and the presidential palace involved larger forces and took greater effort to beat back. *Tanks and helicopter gunships striking a battalion-sized unit in Cholon leveled several city blocks. The attacks sputtered out in days, except in Hué, where a force of 7,500 Communist troops held out behind the walls of the old city until 24 February.

Only in scattered places did people join the Communists in demanding the establishment of "revolutionary administrations." Despite initial disarray, the ARVN and Saigon government rallied rather than disintegrated. Perhaps half of the assault forces died in the attacks or retreat. Although the Communists increased control in rural areas when U.S. and Saigon forces redeployed to route 9 and the cities, they were unable to defend these gains when U.S. and ARVN units returned to the countryside.

The Communists launched follow-up attacks against the cities in May and August, but the PAVN had taken such heavy casualties along route 9 that it could not move forward to support them, and forces attacking the lowlands suffered further grave depletion. The reasons for these disappointing results remained for years a source of controversy among the Communists themselves, who blamed inadequate PAVN involvement, too little time to organize popular participation, and decisions that left lowland forces too long in exposed positions. PAVN Gen. Tran Van Tra admitted in his memoir, Concluding the Thirty Years War (1982), that the offensive caused a decline in strength from which Communist forces did not recover for two years. With better planning, the Communists believed, the offensive could have brought the war to an end more quickly.

In the aftermath, General Westmoreland saw an opportunity to seize the initiative and requested 206,000 more troops, but for many Americans both the offensive and the request discredited claims that the war could be won soon or at an acceptable cost. Westmoreland's defenders blamed media coverage for turning public opinion against the war, but in fact the press generally accepted the official interpretation of Tet as a major military defeat for the Communists. It was evident nonetheless that the United States could not control the war's scope and duration. President Lyndon B. *Johnson sought the advice of dovish civilians, announced he would not seek nomination for another term, declared a bombing halt over most of North Vietnam, and called for peace talks, which opened in May 1968. The offensive thus titled the United States away from expanding involvement and toward eventual withdrawal.

[See also News Media, War, and the Military; Vietnam War: Military and Diplomatic Course; Vietnam War: Changing Interpretations.]

• Peter Braestrup, Big Story, 1977. David Hunt, "Remembering the Tet Offensive," Radical America (November 1977–February 1978), pp. 79–96. Don Oberdorfer, Tet! The Turning Point in the Vietnam War, 1984. Gabriel Kolko, Anatomy of a War, 1985. Daniel Hallin, The Uncensored War, 1986. William S. Turley, The Second Indochina War, 1986. Philip B. Davidson, Vietnam at War, 1988. Larry Berman, Lyndon Johnson's War, 1989. James Wirtz, The Tet Offensive: Intelligence Failure in War, 1991. Ngo Vinh Long, "The Tet Offensive and Its Aftermath," in Jayne Werner and David Hunt, eds., The American War in Vietnam, 1993. Ronnie E. Ford, Tet 1968: Understanding the Surprise, 1995.   —William S. Turley

TEXAS WAR OF INDEPENDENCE (1836). The origins of the Texas War for Independence were directly linked to the growth of the province following Mexico's own national independence in 1821. Mexican liberals bent on economic progress opened the borders to immigrants and provided them generous land grants and considerable local authority. The population grew tenfold by 1835 and the central government soon became concerned over the Anglo-American majority in the province. Disputes arose over Mexico City's efforts to govern Texas more firmly and prohibit the importation of more slaves. In 1835, President Antonio Lopez de *Santa Anna centralized the government, abolishing the 1824 constitution and snuffing out provincial rebellions. Many Anglo and Mexican residents of Texas protested. Resistance to the central government in turn created in Mexico a determination to rule Texas firmly and to reduce the malcontents to obedience by force.

Mexico City dispatched troops to Texas in the late summer of 1835, and fighting broke out that October. The campaign focused on the town of San Antonio de Béxar, which contained Mexico's major military garrisons and political offices. Hastily assembled Texas forces were organized loosely under colonizer Stephen F. Austin, who had difficulty disciplining the democratic-minded volunteers. Hostilities interrupted efforts to establish a stable provisional government and accentuated problems of supply and strategy. A "Consultation" held in November endorsed a compromise view of the purpose of the war (maintaining Texas rights under the 1824 constitution, including the right to import slaves) and created an unworkable interim political structure. The rebel Texan forces at Béxar, including a unit organized in the United States as the New Orleans Greys, conducted a loose siege spiced by a couple of skirmishes, and continued debates, until 5 December, when commander Edward Burleson ordered an assault.

Five days of house-to-house warfare ended with capitulation by the Mexican commandant, Martin Perfecto de Cos.

Most of the Texas residents returned home in the knowledge that volunteers were streaming in from the United States. A handful remained at Béxar, but most concentrated around Goliad near the coast. Sam Houston, a dynamic former governor of Tennessee who had moved to Texas in 1833, was appointed commander of the Texan revolutionary army and gave defensive orders.

Into this setting in February 1836, Santa Anna led an army of 5,000 regulars and conscripts to Texas on a march through cold, wet, and wind. This force had superiority in officer training, discipline in the ranks, and professional cavalry, as well as numbers, although the conscripted peasants were ill-prepared. The rebel army suffered from smaller numbers, disjointed command, and a defensive line stretching 200 miles, from Béxar to the coast. The Texans always fought better where terrain gave the advantage to accurate rifled weapons and minimized close order drill, horse, and *artillery. Such conditions did not prevail when 550 men under Mexican Gen. José de Urrea arrived from Matamoros and slashed up details of the Texas volunteers in engagements at the towns of San Patricio and Refugio, and at Agua Dulce creek in late February and March 1836.

These men, under command disputed between James Bowie and William Barrett Travis, concentrated in a walled mission in Béxar called the Alamo on 23 February 1836, when the advance units of Santa Anna's main army were first sighted. Both sides probably made significant errors. Travis ignored the consensus that the town was a death trap and relied on reinforcements from the ranks of unorganized settlers and the addled Fannin. Santa Anna yielded to his desire to avenge the Mexicans' December defeat and decided not to bypass Béxar. Further, he set aside the likelihood that siege guns and time would reduce the fortress. For twelve days the opponents squared off, pilloried surrender demands, and exchanged a few shots.

During the early morning assault of 6 March, both sides displayed remarkable courage, one in bitter defense against overwhelming odds and the other in open assault against fortified sharpshooters and about twenty artillery pieces. All 187 of the defenders died, including David Crockett and a few others who were executed after being captured at the end of the battle. Mexican losses totaled around 600 killed and wounded out of 3,000 troops.

On the political front, four days before the Alamo fell, a Texan convention 300 miles away adopted a Declaration of Independence and worked on a constitution. At Goliad, Col. James W. Fannin dispersed his men in vain efforts to save elements of his army, this time engaged at Refugio, 12–14 March. Not until 19 March did Fannin begin an ill-planned retreat, only to be caught by Urrea's cavalry on open ground short of Coleto Creek. After an afternoon of bloody fighting, he agreed to surrender on the morning of 20 March. On 27 March, the prisoners were executed; more than 340 Texans were killed in the Goliad massacre.

Houston took command of the new volunteers who assembled for renewed fighting. He confirmed the fate of the Alamo and began an unpopular retreat eastward, moving ever deeper into the Anglo population centers rather than making a stand on the Brazos or Colorado Rivers. Santa Anna divided his army into four and set off not after Houston's army but the leaders of the interim Texas government, barely missing them at Harrisburg as they left for

Galveston Island. This advance placed Santa Anna and 700 of his men further east than the rest of his army, except for a reinforcement of 350 on 20 April. Houston at last turned from the road leading to the United States to one approaching the Mexican Army, thoughtlessly placed with the San Jacinto River and marshlands barring retreat.

The 800 or so members of the vengeful Texas Army attacked in a long, thin line on the late afternoon of 21 April. The Battle of *San Jacinto took fewer than twenty minutes, but was followed by several hours of close order clubbing, knifing, and shooting. Santa Anna was captured and wrote out orders for his second in command to take the rest of his army out of Texas. He also signed a treaty pledging recognition of Texas, an act repudiated by the Mexican Congress.

The victory at San Jacinto gave the new republic a semblance of security and an opportunity to build a nation, though most of its citizens favored annexation. Sam Houston became president of the Republic of Texas in October 1836. Eight years later, annexation of Texas by the United States led to the *Mexican War.

[See also Alamo, Battle of the.]

—Paul D. Lack

TEXTBOOKS, WAR AND THE MILITARY IN. Five-sixths of all Americans never take a course in U.S. history beyond high school, so it is in high school, where textbooks dominate the teaching of history, that most Americans learn about their American military history.

Supporters of American history courses often claim that these courses lead to a more enlightened citizenry. A major duty of U.S. citizens is "to analyze issues and interpret events intelligently," one textbook says. Indeed, eighteen-year-olds (especially males) may be expected to fight, so such classes might encourage young people to understand why and how America has fought its wars.

Textbooks do give considerable coverage to war. *Triumph of the American Nation*, probably the best-selling high school textbook of the 1980s and early 1990s, devotes about 17 percent of its text (150 pages) to U.S. military history. Another 2.5 percent relates closely to war. Included are 15 pages on the *Revolutionary War, 9 pages on the *War of 1812, 8 pages on the Texan and Mexican Wars, 29 pages on the *Civil War, 5 pages on the *Plains Indians Wars, 6 pages on the *Spanish-American War, 17 pages on World War I, 41 pages on World War II, 3 pages on the *Korean War, and 12 widely scattered pages on the *Vietnam War. This coverage is typical and the proportions are similar to coverage in shorter, easier texts. There is an almost complete lack of coverage of Indian wars in the colonial and early national periods.

Textbooks do make efforts to include various racial groups, but such attempts are often clumsy, probably because publishers want to win adoptions and avoid offense. Thus, 5,000 black soldiers fought alongside whites in the *Continental army, "with courage and skill," says *Triumph of the American Nation*. In reality, of course, some fought "with courage and skill"—like some white recruits—and some did not fire their guns and ran off—like some white recruits. A more important point would be that the British recruited African Americans, especially slaves, more easily than did the colonists, but this is not covered, presumably because it might offend some textbook adoption committees. Authors do a somewhat better job on *gender and war and *gender and the military.

Textbooks provide useful detail and good maps—particularly for the Revolutionary War and the Civil War. However, coverage on the home front is not nearly as good. The topic of internal opposition to the Confederacy, for example, gets little attention.

Layout editors often contribute a further obstacle by assuming that students have short attention spans and making frequent random topic changes. *Triumph of the American Nation* interrupts the outbreak of World War I to treat "The World's Ocean." And while describing the dismemberment of Poland in 1939 by Germany and the Soviet Union, the authors insert over a page on irrigation in the Western United States. Another popular textbook, *The American Pageant*, by Thomas Bailey and David Kennedy (1994), avoids such pitfalls. But some texts aimed at less advanced readers offer no coherent narrative of the Civil War, simply a series of boxed topics.

Who are the authors of most high school American history textbooks? According to Hillel Black, whose *The American Schoolbook* (1967) is probably still the most important study of this topic, the names on the cover of a textbook rarely represent the people who actually wrote it. Lewis Todd and Merle Curti may have written the first draft of *Rise of the American Nation* in 1949, but when its title changed to *Triumph of the American Nation* in 1986, Curti was almost ninety and Todd was dead. (For the latest incarnation, the title becomes *Todd and Curti's The American Nation*, 1994, with a new author listed.) In an article entitled "The Ghost Behind the Classroom Door" in *Today's Education* (April 1978), a person who never taught a history class or earned a history degree tells of writing textbooks and ancillary material for publishers. Since the history profession does not review high school texts, errors by these ghostwriters or even by professional historians may go uncorrected for years, including the claim by one text that Truman ended the Korean War by dropping the atomic bomb!

Two omissions loom even larger. First, coverage is often sanitized. The poet Walt Whitman wrote of the Civil War, "The real war will never get into the books." Certainly, the true nature of war does not get into most high school textbooks. James W. Loewen's analysis, in *Lies My Teacher Told Me* (1995), of the photographs used to illustrate the Vietnam War, demonstrates this clearly: rather than the famous photographs of the *My Lai Massacre or the napalmed girl running naked toward the camera, many publishers choose nondescript images of soldiers walking through rice paddies in Southeast Asia.

Second, authors and publishers often avoid moral and strategic issues. On 8 December 1941, the day after the attack on *Pearl Harbor, the United States in the Pacific War abandoned all international rules governing submarine warfare and began attacking Japanese shipping—military or commercial—without warning. This policy is defensible, but the defense might make awkward discussions in U.S. textbooks of Berlin's unrestricted submarine warfare as one of the reasons the United States entered World War I against Germany.

Similarly, America's atomic bombings of *Hiroshima and Nagasaki in World War II remain controversial. Because high school texts often avoid controversy, a typical account of the ending of World War II maintains that "Japan rejected [the call] for its unconditional surrender" on 29 July; "the United States dropped the atomic bomb on

Hiroshima" and "two days later" (actually three) "dropped a second atomic bomb on Nagasaki"; "on August 10 the Japanese government asked for peace"; and "on August 14, 1945, President Truman announced by radio that Japan had accepted the Allied peace terms." The clear implication is that the bombs alone forced Japan to accept unconditional surrender (from Todd and Curti, *Triumph of the American Nation*, 1986).

There are issues here of both fact and morality. What role did the announcement of Soviet entry in the war against Japan have in precipitating surrender? Given that Gen. Douglas *MacArthur acceded to Japan's condition that Emperor *Hirohito remain on the throne, is the surrender best understood as unconditional? Did the United States drop the Hiroshima bomb partly to influence the Soviet Union in the postwar period? Was it correct to drop either the first or second bomb? *The American Pageant* summarizes the bomb as "a fantastic ace up [America's] sleeve." Having witnessed the Smithsonian Institution's reversal on its *Enola Gay* display, most textbook publishers are unlikely to explore this controversy further.

As their titles imply, high school textbooks take a generally triumphal view of American history. They treat war as they do other topics, supplying detail about individual campaigns but little analysis and no moral judgments. Students memorize facts for exams but often forget most of them by the time they graduate. According to Diane Ravitch and Chester Finn in *What Do Our 17-Year-Olds Know?* (1987), two-thirds of American seventeen-year-olds cannot place the Civil War in the right half century. High school history textbooks currently fall for short in developing an adequate understanding of U.S. history, let alone America's military history.

[*See also* Disciplinary Views of War: Military History; Public Opinion, War, and the Military.]

—James W. Loewen

THAYER, SYLVANUS (1785–1872), army engineer and putative "Father of the Military Academy." A native of Braintree, Massachusetts, Thayer attended Dartmouth for three years, then entered West Point, graduating in 1808. After coastal fortification service and participation in the *War of 1812, he spent two years in Europe studying military institutions. He became superintendent of the U.S. Military Academy in 1817. Backed by Secretary of War John C. *Calhoun, Thayer overhauled the academic and disciplinary systems. His reforms included organizing the corps of cadets into a battalion, establishing an academic board to oversee curricular matters, dividing classes into sections according to merit, and holding semiannual examinations. He also recruited several professors who achieved distinction, especially Dennis Hart Mahan. After a dispute with President Andrew *Jackson, Thayer resigned his office in 1833 and returned to coastal fortification duty. Upon retirement, he established an engineering school at Dartmouth.

Having created what he considered a perfect structure at the military academy, Thayer resisted all subsequent attempts at modification, blasting other reformers with his vitriolic pen despite their contributions to the institution. In some respects he succeeded. Key elements of the Thayer system remain in force at West Point today.

[*See also* Academies, Service.]

• Sidney B. Forman, *West Point, A History of the United States Military Academy*, 1950. Joseph Ellis and Robert Moore, *School for Soldiers: West Point and the Profession of Arms*, 1974. James L. Morrison, Jr., *"The Best School": West Point, 1833–1866*, 1998.

—James L. Morrison, Jr.

THEORISTS OF WAR. All warfare requires thought. Even the most primitive battle demands mental preparation, and it is not possible to control armed forces of any size without preconceived methods of organization and action. It is difficult, and perhaps unnecessary, to distinguish categorically between this kind of instrumental thinking and military theory more strictly understood, as a systematic attempt to link or subordinate the conduct of war to abstract analytic concepts or to broader social, political, or geographic relationships of which war is but a part. Such theorizing may aim at practical knowledge of how war can be conducted or averted, in which case its concerns may approach those of the strategist or military planner. Or, a theorist of war may simply seek understanding for its own sake. Yet these are not mutually exclusive impulses, and both are evident in varying degrees in the work of most serious students of war.

Until the end of the nineteenth century, military theory in the United States was dominated by European models, of which the most imposing was that provided by Antoine Henri *Jomini. Jomini, a staff officer in the French Army during the Napoleonic Wars, sought to codify the basic tenets of modern war in terms of a small number of timeless principles. He stressed the advantages of fighting on interior lines; of maintaining secure communications while seeking to attack those of the enemy; and above all, of concentrating one's forces at what he called "the decisive point." Jomini's work suggested that the chaos and uncertainty of war could be mastered by means of a positivistic social science, and also that the precise mental habits and systematic approach of the engineer and the industrial manager could find a use on the battlefield.

Jomini's ideas permeated the curriculum of the U.S. Military Academy at West Point in the antebellum era, and shaped the basic outlook of officers on both sides of the *Civil War. The protracted destructiveness of that conflict caused his reputation to recede, in part because he was thought to have held out a false promise: that war conducted on scientific principles would be more readily controlled than in the past. Yet no modern army has felt able to dispense with the notion, however tenuous, that there are in fact enduring Principles of War that matter to the conduct of operations and the education of officers. In this respect, Jomini remains among the most influential of modern military theorists.

The most creative of Jomini's American disciples was a naval officer, Alfred T. *Mahan, whose self-proclaimed intention was to do for naval warfare what Jomini had done for war on land. Mahan argued that "sea power," an expression he claimed to have coined, was the ultimate arbiter of world affairs. Its principal instrument was the battle fleet, built for the sole purpose of defeating or intimidating others of its kind. Mahan was among the first to articulate a comprehensive strategic vision for the steam-and-steel navies of the industrial era. In relation to the wooden-hulled vessels they displaced, the tactical superiority of such ships was absolute. Yet, because of their dependence upon a global infrastructure of coaling stations and secure ports of call, their capacity to conduct traditional operations of close blockade, commerce raiding, and *amphibious warfare seemed far beneath what had been possible in the age of sail. Mahan, however, argued that all such techniques were secondary to, and dependent upon, the clash of battle fleets, whose outcome would decide any war in which a naval power might engage.

Like Jomini, Mahan's reputation suffered because the future failed to conform to his expectations. The battle fleets of the great powers did not determine the results of World War I, in part because new underwater weapons were already transforming combat at sea, in part because the belligerents were reluctant to risk the irreplaceable fleets they had built up at such great expense. The early twentieth century was also marked by a growing realization, stimulated in part by the work of the English geographer Halford Mackinder, that the saliency of seapower was being eroded by the spread of railroads, paved highways, and modern *communications. Certainly, these developments reduced the relative advantages of movement over water compared to land, and contributed to the growth of integrated continental economies relatively resistant to the effects of *blockades. At the same time, the attendant confidence that armies would be able to "outflank the sea," by reaching decisions on land before the attritional effects of naval war could be felt, would prove almost entirely illusory. Seapower thus remains an important theoretical conception, less because its possession ensures military success than because its absence continues to be disproportionately associated with military failure.

Jomini and Mahan exemplify theories of war based on a didactic reading of what they considered to be the relevant historical record—chiefly war in the West, particularly Europe, from the middle of the eighteenth century to the fall of Napoleon. This general point of view continues to prevail among students of what has increasingly been called "conventional" war, meaning combats between the organized forces of established states. In this arena, intellectual mastery includes a strong sense of historical continuity, and a pronounced respect for the "lessons" of at least the recent past. At the same time, technological and political developments have seemed sufficiently unprecedented to cast doubt on the continuing validity of such an approach.

In the decades between the world wars, for instance, proponents of strategic airpower argued that the advent of *bomber aircraft had rendered historical experience obsolete. Billy *Mitchell, a general in the U.S. Army Air Corps and the most prominent American champion of this new kind of war, regarded armies, navies, and civilian populations as equally vulnerable to air attack, against which neither geographic isolation nor human art could offer a defense. World War II demonstrated that this latter impression was mistaken, even as it inspired the development of weapons whose destructive power fully vindicated Mitchell's intuition of a world made new by technology. No country has relied more heavily on *nuclear weapons than the United States, and it is unsurprising that American nuclear war theorists like Herman Kahn, Thomas Schelling, and Bernard Brodie should occupy a preeminent place among those who have sought to analyze principles governing their use.

A comparable sense of novelty has prevailed among theorists of what in America is termed *revolutionary insurgency* or *low-intensity conflict*. Here, too, the distinction between armed forces and civil society, on which theories of "conventional" war depend, has threatened to dissolve. In Mao Zedong's famous (and often misunderstood) phrase, political power in revolutionary war grows out of the barrel of a gun, in the sense that it is through military effort that political authority is constituted and legitimized. The guerrilla fighter is accordingly conceived as a fish swimming in the sea of his countrymen, without the distinguishing marks that have allowed soldiers to recognize each other in the past.

America's encounters with *guerrilla warfare have given rise to an academic and professional literature that resembles the work of the nuclear theorists in being marked by deep pessimism and frustration and a strong sense that the best solution to conflicts of this kind is to avoid them. It has also contributed to a revival of interest in one of the greatest of all theoretical works on war, Sun-tzu's *The Art of War*. Sun-tzu's treatise dates from the Warring States period of Chinese history (c. 403–221 B.C.) and has been known in the West since the eighteenth century. Only since the 1960s, however, has it received sustained attention, by virtue of the inspiration it afforded Mao, and for the insight it offers into Asian ideas about war. These considerations do not exhaust Sun-tzu's contemporary appeal. By reaffirming the importance of intellect and technique in war, the central value of discipline and generalship, and the vital importance of avoiding escalation and attrition, *The Art of War* speaks to the dilemmas of modern war with a directness that few contemporary works can match.

Contemporary military theory thus finds itself confronted by three distinct modalities of conflict—conventional, nuclear, and revolutionary—that have proven strongly resistant to intellectual synthesis. One measure of the perplexity that has resulted is the exceptional status still accorded Carl von *Clausewitz's classic treatise *On War* (1832), whose intellectual range transcends the fragmentation of modern military experience. This Prussian military intellectual approached the theory of war by way of comprehensive historical study combined with a rigorous theoretical focus on war's fundamental elements. In Clausewitz's work, attack and defense, risk and decisiveness, combat and maneuver, politics and violence, appear not as static characteristics to be weighed up and accounted for once and for all, but as dynamic concepts that define and react upon each other. It is a method ill-suited to the development of prescriptive theory, but remarkably powerful as a means of grasping what Clausewitz called the chameleonlike nature of organized *violence.

[*See also* War.]

• Alfred Thayer Mahan, *The Influence of Sea Power upon History*, 1890. William Mitchell, *Winged Defense*, 1925. Giulio Douhet, *The Command of the Air* [*Il dominio dell'aria*, 1921], trans. Dino Ferrari, 1942. Antoine-Henri Jomini, *Summary of the Art of War* [*Précis de l'art de la guerre*, 1838], trans. J. D. Hittle, 1947. Bernard Brodie, *Strategy in the Missile Age*, 1959. Herman Kahn, *On Thermonuclear War*, 1960. Thomas Schelling, *Arms and Influence*, 1966. Carl von Clausewitz, *On War* [*Vom Kriege*, 1832], trans. Michael Howard and Peter Paret, 1976. Peter Paret, ed., *Makers of Modern Strategy*, 1986. Sun-Tzu, *The Art of Warfare* [*Ping-fa*] trans. Roger Ames, 1993. Lawrence Freedman, ed., *War*, 1994.

—Daniel Moran

THOMAS, GEORGE H. (1816–1870), Civil War general. A native of Southampton County, Virginia, Thomas graduated from the U.S. Military Academy in 1840. Commissioned as an artilleryman, he won brevet promotions as a captain and major at Monterey and Buena Vista in the *Mexican War. Transferring to the cavalry in 1855, he served on the Texas plains until 1861. In the secession crisis, Thomas spurned a Virginia state commission and remained loyal to the Union. Promoted to brigadier general of volunteers in August 1861 and ordered to Kentucky, he gained public attention with a minor victory at Mill Springs in January 1862. Thereafter, he commanded a division in the Army of the Ohio at Shiloh and Corinth, rising to major general in April 1862. Offered command of that army in September, he declined and acted as Don Carlos Buell's deputy at the Battle of Perryville, Kentucky. Following Buell's relief, Thomas loyally served the new commander, William S. *Rosecrans, formerly his junior. Commanding the center of Rosecrans's Army of the Cumberland at the Battle of *Stones River, he performed brilliantly.

Subsequently, Thomas commanded the XIV Corps in the Tullahoma and Chickamauga campaigns in 1863. At the Battle of *Chickamauga, he and his command stood firm while Rosecrans and other corps commanders fled the field. Nicknamed the "Rock of Chickamauga," Thomas led the Army of the Cumberland to victory at Missionary Ridge and in the Atlanta campaign of 1864. Sent to Nashville at the time of *Sherman's march to the sea, Thomas destroyed John B. Hood's Army of Tennessee in December 1864. Postwar, he remained in the regular army, until his death in 1870 as commander of the Military Division of the Pacific.

Although Thomas's record in the Civil War as a consistently competent and tenacious tactician was unsurpassed, his unwillingness to promote himself meant he received less credit than was his due. Nevertheless, few Union officers made a greater contribution to the ultimate *victory.

[See also Civil War: Military and Diplomatic Course; Union Army.]

• Francis F. McKinney, Education in Violence: The Life of George H. Thomas and the History of the Army of the Cumberland, 1961. Peter Cozzens, This Terrible Sound: The Battle of Chickamauga, 1992.

—William Glenn Robertson

THOMAS, NORMAN (1884–1968), minister, antiwar and civil rights activist, leader of the Socialist Party of America, and social critic. Preeminently in his generation, Norman Thomas secularized the pacifist impulse and criticized militarism in relation to social systems: ideology and institutions tending to impose military responses on political challenges.

Thomas was introduced to the religious Social Gospel at Union Theological Seminary and was immersed in the urban reality of an immigrant parish in New York. In World War I, he joined progressive peace organizations to prevent U.S. intervention. During U.S. belligerency, he resigned his pastorate, became the founding editor of the World Tomorrow (1918), and helped organize the National Civil Liberties Bureau, primarily to defend conscientious objectors.

He also joined the Socialist Party because of its social vision and antiwar stance. In the 1920s, Thomas became the party's acknowledged leader, its presidential candidate from 1928 to 1948. From that base he criticized the New Deal as inadequate and opposed the nation's rearmament and drift toward war.

Thomas gave critical support to the Roosevelt administration in World War II, but condemned internment of Japanese Americans and policies such as the *bombing of civilians and unconditional surrender. He lobbied for a postwar foreign policy that would address real conflicts of power by institutionalizing mutual interests. He advocated measuring power politics against social reconstruction and flexible and realistic policies against democratic and just principles. Skeptical of both unilateral disarmament and arms control, he helped to form the *National Committee for a Sane Nuclear Policy (1957).

Norman Thomas was significant precisely because he put military issues in their social context, warning that military approaches both reflect and reify arbitrary institutions and unjust social orders. War is therefore the crisis of democracy, and, whatever the merit of a specific conflict, does not offer a realistic or acceptable solution for political problems. In speeches, articles, and books, Thomas insisted that the alternative to war is social change that increases equity, democracy, and stability.

[See also Conscientious Objection; Japanese-American Internment Cases; Militarism and Antimilitarism; Peace; Peace and Antiwar Movements; War.]

• James C. Duram, Norman Thomas, 1974. W. A. Swanberg, Norman Thomas: The Last Idealist, 1976. Charles Chatfield, "Norman Thomas: Harmony of Word and Deed," in Peace Heroes in Twentieth-Century America, ed. Charles DeBenedetti, 1988, pp. 85–121.

—Charles Chatfield

THOREAU, HENRY DAVID (1817–1862), transcendentalist, writer, war protester. Henry David Thoreau was born in Concord, Massachusetts. A shy, quiet boy who loved the outdoors, Thoreau graduated from Harvard College in 1837, taught school intermittently until 1841, then turned to writing as a career. He subsequently led a simple life as one of the New England transcendentalists, writing poems, essays, and two books while trying to earn a living.

Although Thoreau may well have been the best remembered antiwar dissenter of his time, his protest against the *Mexican War had no discernible effect on public opinion, the antiwar effort, or the conduct of the war. In July 1846, Thoreau, who had not paid his Massachusetts poll tax for several years, denounced the war in his annual brush with the tax collector, refused again to pay, and spent one night in jail before one of his friends paid the tax without his consent and Thoreau was released. Though he believed the war an immoral conflict to extend slavery, Thoreau viewed his own dissent as an individual act of protest, not an effort to work with or mobilize others to end the war. To Thoreau, it was the duty of each honest citizen directly to resist his government when it condoned or perpetuated an evil such as slavery or war to extend slavery.

Thoreau immortalized his protest in the essay "Resistance to Civil Government," popularly known as "Civil Disobedience," which was published in 1849. Although his actions attracted only local attention at the time, his essay achieved fame as the clear, well-reasoned justification of an honest citizen protesting an immoral policy of his government. As such, "Civil Disobedience" became an influential manifesto for subsequent antiwar protesters and freedom fighters such as Mohandas K. Gandhi and Dr. Martin Luther *King, Jr.

[See also Conscientious Objection; Peace and Antiwar Movements.]

• John H. Schroeder, *Mr. Polk's War: An American Opposition and Dissent, 1846–1848,* 1973. Richard Lebeaux, *Thoreau's Seasons,* 1984. —John H. Schroeder

TIDEWATER WARS. *See* Native American Wars: Wars Between Native Americans and Europeans and Euro-Americans.

TOJO, HIDEKI (1884–1948), Japanese general of the army and prime minister. Tojo, a graduate of the Japanese Military Staff College, was promoted to lieutenant general in 1936. By that time, he had become both pro-German and an ardent advocate of Japanese military *expansionism in China. In 1937, Tojo became chief of staff of the Kwantung Army in China, and in October 1941, he forced out and succeeded Prince Fumimaro Konoye as Japanese prime minister. Tojo took his country into World War II with the United States with the surprise attack on *Pearl Harbor in December 1941, and he remained prime minister until July 1944, after the fall of Saipan. In 1945, he attempted suicide, but was brought before the International Military Tribunal, Far East, for *war crimes and hanged in 1948.

Historians depict Tojo as a militant and expansionist nationalist who underestimated the United States's determination and industrial capacity to fight total war to defeat Japan. In a narrow sense, Tojo was a competent administrator (nicknamed "Razor Tojo"), but he was neither an imaginative strategist nor a skillful political leader. He accelerated Japan's atomic research, worshipped the emperor, and to the end clung to his belief in the innate spiritual strength and *victory of the Japanese.

• Robert J. C. Butow, *Tojo and the Coming of the War,* 1961. —Saki Dockrill

TORPEDO BOATS. Functionally descended from Federico Gianibelli's sixteenth-century fireships, torpedo boats first emerged in the United States as semisubmersible bearers of "infernal machines," directed by David Bushnell's *Turtle* and Robert *Fulton's *Mute* against British blockaders during the *Revolutionary War and the *War of 1812. Advances in spar torpedo technology during the *Civil War spawned additional craft. Their capabilities were demonstrated in the historic attack by the Confederate submersible *H. L. Hunley* against the USS *Housatonic* off Charleston, and by Lt. W. B. Cushing's sinking of CSS *Albemarle* with a picket boat carrying a spar torpedo.

Commercial introduction of the Whitehead self-propelled torpedo in 1875 triggered rapid development of coastal and seagoing torpedo boats in Europe. "Jeune Ecole" enthusiasts in France hailed growing squadrons of *torpilleurs* as effective counters to British naval superiority; yet by 1890, Britain, Germany, and Japan had acquired comparable flotillas. The U.S. Navy, amid post–Civil War doldrums, engaged yacht designer Nathaniel Herreshoff to construct swift torpedo craft, including the spar torpedo boat *Lightning* (1876); the *Stilletto* (1887), armed with John Howell's automotive torpedo; and finally the USS *Cushing* (1890), the navy's first steel-hulled torpedo boat.

Britain's introduction in 1893 of the torpedo boat destroyer, direct antecedent of the more seaworthy destroyer, dimmed prospects for the torpedo boat, whose influence on fleet operations during the *Spanish-American War proved less impressive than at Tsushima in the Russo-Japanese War. During World War I, German torpedo boats, torpedo-armed destroyers, U-boats, and naval *mines combined to inhibit British Grand Fleet operations severely, but postwar naval designers showed little interest in the prevailing torpedo boat configuration. Torpedo attacks by surfaced U-boats accounted significantly for Allied merchant ship losses. Torpedo boats also reappeared during World War II in a smaller configuration, as wooden-hulled motor torpedo boats, swift launches active notably in the English Channel, Mediterranean, and (against Japanese supply barges) the Southwest Pacific. In postwar years, these short-lived craft were rapidly replaced by missile launches, terminating a century of torpedo boat development.

[*See also* World War I: Military and Diplomatic Course.]

• Larry R. Smart, "Evolution of the Torpedo Boat," *Military Affairs,* vol. 22, no. 2 (Summer 1959), pp. 97–101. Alex Roland, *Underwater Warfare in the Age of Sail,* 1978. E. W. Jolie, *A Brief History of U.S. Navy Torpedo Development,* 1978. —Philip K. Lundeberg

TORPEDOES. The torpedo, a self-propelled and self-guided underwater explosive device, was invented in 1866 by Robert Whitehead, a British engineer working for the Austro-Hungarian Navy. The U.S. Navy evinced early interest in the device and established in 1869 the Torpedo Station at Newport, Rhode Island. After pursuing a technological dead-end in the flywheel-driven Howell type, the navy turned back to the Whitehead in 1892. Improved models soon followed, with turbine propulsion introduced in 1905 and an air heater in 1910 that quintupled the range to 4,000 yards.

As the torpedo increased in capability, it naturally grew in size: by 1912, the 18-inch Mark 7 measured 17 feet in length, weighed 1,628 pounds, and carried a warhead of 326 pounds of TNT to a range of 6,000 yards at 35 knots. In 1914, the navy settled on a diameter of 21 inches for most of its new torpedoes—a standard that endured for the rest of the century.

Over the interwar period, Newport, under the guidance of the talented mechanical engineer and submariner Ralph Waldo Christie, pushed ahead with a number of advanced concepts: exotic propulsion systems using oxygen, hydrogen peroxide, or electric motors to give wakeless runs; large, air-dropped torpedoes; and magnetic exploders to increase lethality by detonating the torpedo under its target. As financial constraints prevented the navy from pursuing all of these promising leads, it concentrated on the last two. Introduced in 1936 was the Mark 13 air-dropped weapon, which imposed severe speed and altitude restrictions on the aircraft carrying it. Also flawed was the new Mark 6 magnetic exploder. Expensive and highly secret, it entered the inventory in the 1930s, but was neither tested extensively nor issued to the fleet until 1941.

World War II put U.S. torpedoes to the operational test for the first time, and they were found wanting. Following the Japanese attack on *Pearl Harbor, U.S. destroyers, *submarines, and aircraft were all hobbled by torpedo problems. American torpedo bombers at Midway suffered appalling losses as they made their low-level attacks. The Mark 6 exploder frequently failed, and its backup contact pistol proved too fragile. The Mark 14 submarine torpedo, introduced in 1931, left a prominent wake, tended to run deep, and sometimes even circled. A series of distressing incidents highlighted the problems. *Tang,* one of the most successful submarines, was sunk by its own weapon. Two destroyers, ordered to scuttle the damaged *Hornet* after the Battle of Santa Cruz, fired sixteen torpedoes at the carrier without sinking it. In a particularly damning episode on 24 July 1943, the submarine *Tinosa* shot fifteen torpedoes into the largest tanker in the Japanese merchant fleet; only four exploded.

Hurried remedial measures developed by the navy, the scientific community, and industry resolved the difficulties. Aircraft torpedoes were modified so that they could be dropped at much faster speeds and higher altitudes. The Mark 6 magnetic exploder was deactivated. New types of torpedoes were hurried into production, the most important being the Mark 18 electric and the homing types. The former, built by Westinghouse and introduced in September 1943, offered the great advantage of leaving no bubble trail. By 1945, 65 percent of all shots were by electrics. Also strikingly successful was the acoustic homing torpedo developed by Bell Labs, General Electric, and Harvard for antisubmarine work. Dubbed for security reasons the Mine Mark 24, the torpedo followed sound pulses to its underwater target. Beginning in May 1943, the air-dropped Mark 24, nicknamed "Fido," sank thirty-one submarines; its surface ship variant claimed thirty-three additional victims.

Wartime expenditure of torpedoes was prodigious. U.S. submarines fired 14,748 torpedoes, sinking 214 warships and 1,178 merchant vessels. U.S. aircraft made 1,287 attacks, scoring 514 hits. Overall, about 33 percent of torpedoes fired hit their targets. The navy kept up with mushrooming demand by reopening its World War I facility at Alexandria, Virginia, and by contracting with private firms (Bliss, Pontiac, and Westinghouse). Overall production totaled 57,655 torpedoes between 1 January 1939 and 1 June 1946.

Although the last U.S. operational use of torpedoes came on 1 May 1951, when navy planes breached the Hwachon dam in North Korea during the *Korean War, development of the weapon continued apace, largely to match increasingly capable Soviet nuclear submarines. On operational service from 1958 to 1977 was the Mark 45 Astor, with a nuclear warhead. By the 1990s, two types remained in service: the 3,450-pound Mark 48 (range 35,000 yards, speed 55 knots, depth over 2,500 feet) and the Mark 46 lightweight torpedo for close-in use by aircraft or surface ships.

[*See also* Navy, U.S.: 1899–1945; Navy, U.S.: Since 1946; Navy Combat Branches: Submarine Forces.]

• Buford Rowland and William B. Boyd, *U.S. Navy Bureau of Ordnance in World War II*, 1953. Norman Friedman, *U.S. Naval Weapons*, 1983. John Campbell, *Naval Weapons of World War Two*, 1985. Edwyn Gray, *The Devil's Device: Robert Whitehead and the History of the Torpedo*, 1991. Robert Gannon, *Hellions of the Deep: The Development of American Torpedoes in World War II*, 1996.
—Malcolm Muir, Jr.

TOXIC AGENTS

Atomic Radiation Exposure
Agent Orange Exposure

TOXIC AGENTS: ATOMIC RADIATION EXPOSURE

From 1945 to 1963, radioactive fallout from U.S. aboveground *nuclear weapons tests exposed over 200,000 military personnel, as well as a large but indeterminate number of civilian test workers and and so-called downwinders,

people living near the test sites. Most exposures were very low, however, and clear evidence of injury was lacking.

Three military groups received the bulk of relatively high exposures: uniformed members of the test organizations (1945–63); members of the task forces required for Pacific testing (1946–62); and participants in Desert Rock training exercises for a nuclear battlefield, held in Nevada (1951–57).

Military members of the test organizations and Pacific task forces observed the same safety standards and procedures as other test workers, except for the crews of aircraft sampling clouds for radioactivity. Assigned much higher exposure limits than others, they occasionally received much higher doses as well. Consistently, the most heavily exposed among those without special limits were radiation monitors, military and civilian, chiefly because their work often placed them where fallout was most likely. Statistical analysis of evidence, however, does not indicate that aircrews or monitors suffered long-term deleterious effects.

When thermonuclear weapons testing began in 1952, the fallout problem intensified. The worst overexposure of civilians in test history, and the only documented instances of fallout-caused injury, followed the 1954 Castle Bravo test at Bikini atoll in the Pacific. Unexpectedly heavy fallout hit two groups 100 miles from ground zero: the 23-man crew of the Japanese fishing boat *Lucky Dragon* and 82 Marshallese on Rongelap in the Marshall Islands. One of the fishermen died six months later from complications of treatment, but the rest recovered without incident. Although all the Marshallese likewise recovered, thyroid problems attributed to fallout radioiodine surfaced two decades later among those who had been infants and children at the time. Heavy fallout from Bravo also dusted a twenty-eight-man U.S. Air Force weather unit on Rongerik and hundreds of other Marshallese on more distant atolls, none of whom displayed any symptoms of radiation injury.

The same absence of observable effects marked the very much lower doses associated with Desert Rock training exercises in Nevada. Expecting nuclear field training to be a onetime experience for any individual, the *Pentagon negotiated special rules to enhance its realism. Despite somewhat higher limits than test workers, however, few troops approached, or exceeded, normal test standards. Only one subgroup at Desert Rock, officers who volunteered to entrench relatively close to ground zero for some tests, received some sizable doses.

In addition, there is no unambiguous evidence of long-term radiation injury to participants in the Desert Rock exercises. The author of a widely publicized medical report claiming excess leukemia linked to the 1957 Smoky test (at the Nevada Test site) later corrected his initial findings. No other nuclear weapons test has shown any apparent linkage.

Evidence of injury to other exposed groups, test site workers and downwinders, is even less clear. The problem is that it is extremely difficult to tease out the possible effects of exposure to low-level radiation from other causes of illness. At present, the issue remains unresolved within the medical community.

• J. Newell Stannard, *Radioactivity and Health: A History*, 1988. Barton C. Hacker, *Elements of Controversy: The Atomic Energy Commission and Radiation Safety in Nuclear Weapons Testing, 1947–1974*, 1994.
—Barton C. Hacker

TOXIC AGENTS: AGENT ORANGE EXPOSURE

Agent Orange, the toxic plant killer named after the color-coded stripe that was painted around the 55-gallon barrels in which it was stored, is a combination of two commercial herbicides: 2-4-D (n-buytl-2,4-dichlorophenoxacetate) and 2,4,5-T (n-butyl-2,4,5-trichlorophenoxyacetate). First developed by the U.S. Army as an instrument of chemical warfare at Fort Detrick, Maryland, Agent Orange was so successful in destroying broad-leaf plants that Secretary of Defense Robert S. *McNamara suggested further testing be done on jungle vegetation during the *Vietnam War. In 1962, the Department of *Defense commenced a program of systematically defoliating millions of acres of Vietnamese forests and croplands. By the time the program was called to a halt in 1971, herbicides had destroyed an estimated 4.5 million acres of countryside.

Agent Orange contains TCDD-dioxin, a substance so toxic to animals and humans that Dr. Jacqueline Verrett of the Food and Drug Administration called it "100,000 times more potent than thalidomide as a cause of birth defects in some species." Before he died of cancer in 1978 at the age of twenty-eight, Vietnam veteran Paul Reutershan concluded that his terminal cancer could be traced to his extensive exposure to Agent Orange in Vietnam. Reutershan founded Agent Orange Victims International, and began a $100 million damage claim against Dow Chemical and other Agent Orange manufacturers. Reutershan's claim became a much larger class action lawsuit in which many Vietnam veterans and their families attempted to force Dow Chemical, Monsanto, Uniroyal, Diamond Shamrock, and Hercules to concede that Agent Orange had injured thousands of veterans, and to assume financial responsibility for manufacturing and selling a hazardous product.

Plaintiffs in the Agent Orange class action suit asked for a ban on all advertising, promotion, distribution, marketing, and sale of contaminated herbicides; for chemical companies to reveal all they knew about the dangers of contaminated herbicides; and for a tax-exempt fund to be set up to cover damages from exposure to herbicides.

In 1984, the Agent Orange class action suit was settled out of court for the sum of $180 million. A number of plaintiffs were outraged that the case was not heard in court. At "Fairness Hearings" held in five American cities to ascertain the plaintiffs' reactions to the out-of-court settlement, Vietnam veterans and their wives denounced their own lawyers and the agreement, and demanded that the case be heard before a jury of their peers. Federal judge Julius Weinstein refused the plaintiffs' appeals, arguing that the settlement was fair and just.

Five years later, a decision was reached on how the $180 million, ballooned by interest, would be distributed. The payment plan confirmed the fears expressed at the Fairness Hearings. A totally disabled Vietnam veteran would receive a maximum of $12,000, spread out over a period of ten years. Further, disabled veterans receiving these payments could become ineligible for food stamps, public assistance, and government pensions. A widow of a Vietnam veteran who died from exposure to Agent Orange would receive $3,700.

After years of stonewalling on the issue, the *Veterans Administration agreed to compensate certain illnesses related to exposure to dioxin. Nevertheless, the legacy is a deep bitterness among those who fought in Southeast Asia,

including Adm. Elmo *Zumwalt, whose son died from exposure to Agent Orange in Vietnam. The Agent Orange issue remains one of the great tragedies of American military history.

[See also Veterans: Vietnam War.]

—Fred A. Wilcox

TRACY, BENJAMIN F. (1830–1915), soldier, jurist, secretary of the navy. A small-town lawyer and Republican politician from Tioga County, New York, Tracy served in the state legislature before raising and commanding troops in the Civil War. He received a Medal of Honor (1897) for gallantry at the Battle of the *Wilderness despite subsequent controversial administration of the Elmira, New York, prison camp. Elmira, with its prisoner death rate of 25 percent, held the distinction of being the worst Union prison, although more as a result of War Department policy and bureaucracy than Tracy's management. Moving to Brooklyn in 1865, he served as federal district attorney from 1866 to 1873, and chief justice of the state court of appeals in 1881 and 1882. Tracy's major contribution to national security came as secretary of the navy (1889–93) during Benjamin Harrison's presidency.

Tracy publicly championed Alfred T. *Mahan's doctrine of seapower. He launched the navy upon battle fleet construction in support of that doctrine, as well as introducing a prototype *military-industrial complex through close relationships between government and the steel industry. He encouraged technology transfer from Europe, and shrewdly negotiated with Congress for increased naval budgets. He modernized operational planning through establishment of a policy board, organized the first tactical squadron of evolution for fleet maneuver training, and abolished the spoils system in navy yards in order to reform the shore establishment. His ventures in overseas naval base acquisitions in Samoa, Haiti, and Santo Domingo, as well as his response to revolutions in Chile and Hawaii, proved more controversial than successful. Tracy's active retirement included service in the boundary dispute over British Guiana and chairman of the greater New York Charter Commission in 1897.

[See also Navy, U.S.: 1866–98; Prisoner-of-War Camps, Civil War.]

• B. Franklin Cooling, *Benjamin Franklin Tracy; Father of the Modern American Fighting Navy,* 1979. Paola E. Coletta, "Benjamin F. Tracy," in Coletta, ed., *American Secretaries of the Navy,* 1980.

—B. Franklin Cooling

TRADE, FOREIGN. *This essay on foreign trade as an instrument of foreign and defense policy is divided into three sections:* Wartime *provides an overview of the role of foreign trade in U.S. strategic and economic policies in wartime;* Trade Restrictions *examines the use of embargoes and economic sanctions as instruments of U.S. security policy against hostile nations; and* Neutral Trade *explores America's assertion of commercial rights when it was a neutral nation affected by other countries' wars.*

TRADE, FOREIGN: WARTIME

The drive for American national economic security has existed since 1776, and foreign trade has played a strategic and economic role in U.S. policy. The interaction of commerce and defense was necessary and obvious. Historians have long argued over the relative importance of economic and strategic concerns in foreign policy, with revisionists emphasizing the profitability of trade expansion and realists stressing strategic defense imperatives. Regardless of this debate, the trade/security linkage has prevailed throughout the nation's history.

International commerce was central to the American search for independence in the *Revolutionary War. The alliance with France, 1778–1800, allowed trade to serve political purposes. As president, George *Washington perceived national security in terms of commercial relations and a military establishment, not entangling alliances, yet trade discrimination, mercantilism, and pirates threatened the security of the new nation. In response, Secretary of State Thomas *Jefferson issued a Report on Commerce in 1793 that would reflect trade ideology for the next two centuries. Recommending specialization at home, Jefferson demanded reciprocity treaties and equal access to markets abroad to enhance national defense. American commerce flourished in the early nineteenth century, but was inevitably vulnerable to reprisals from warring Europeans. Terminating the commercial alliance with France in 1800, the country still developed North Atlantic and western frontier trade. *Neutrality and trade expansion collided with British maritime coercion and led to mutual sanctions. The nearly disastrous *War of 1812 convinced U.S. policymakers further that trade and military power were complementary.

Although American diplomacy was "altogether, of a commercial character," as the historian Theodore Lyman wrote in 1828, the dimension of power was integrated into the trade/security formula in the late nineteenth century. While it still neglected the merchant marine fleet, the government funded a modern navy in the 1880s to promote commercial penetration overseas. Seapower and vigorous trade were complementary, wrote Alfred T. *Mahan in promoting American greatness through imperialism, and pursuit of an interoceanic canal became part of this equation. By 1890, tariff policy shifted from protectionism to export expansion through reciprocity treaties as a way to boost American power. And trade and security—essential elements of international status—fused after the *Spanish-American War of 1898, as America acquired territories in the Caribbean and stepping-stone islands across the Pacific to the fabled China market.

Officials did not necessarily elevate trade over diplomatic issues, yet they understood that trade policy meshed with global strategic objectives. President Theodore *Roosevelt recognized the limits of American power in Asia, for instance, but viewed export growth as a component of military might, industrial strength, and domestic social order. Maintaining a balance of power in Europe, predominance in Latin America, and a presence in Asia all hinged on expanding and defending trade routes to U.S. possessions and markets. The building of the Panama Canal exemplified this coupling of commerce and security.

By World War I, this bond was inseparable. President Woodrow *Wilson's *Fourteen Points proposed that *peace and prosperity could exist only by equal access to markets and an end to trade conflict. In the 1920s, American officials such as Secretary of Commerce Herbert C. *Hoover also realized that America depended on foreign supplies of raw materials for its industrial production, which strengthened the country's military. Oil imports, for

instance, became a priority. Thus, the commercial retaliation of the early depression gave way to mutually beneficial negotiations under the Reciprocal Trade Agreements Act of 1934, the brainchild of Secretary of State Cordell Hull. Protectionism led to political strife, he claimed, and his proof was that no trade agreement signee ever fought America. In the movement toward World War II, the administration of Franklin D. *Roosevelt looked on German trade autarchy as a threat to U.S. commerce and peace, while American security required an export embargo to slow Japanese aggression in Asia. By the end of World War II, Washington planned for a cooperative, multilateral trade system based on nondiscriminatory commercial practices as the economic means to assure peace and security.

Multilateralism was a pillar of national security policies in the *Cold War. With unparalleled economic power, America forged a trade system under the General Agreement on Tariff and Trade (GATT) in 1947 that boosted the recovery and prosperity of its Cold War allies. GATT promoted trade liberalization among the capitalist nations, strengthened their economies, and thereby brought them political stability, rendering them invulnerable to Soviet penetration. Liberal trade with American allies, and commercial restrictions against Communist rivals, were hallmarks of the Cold War until the demise of the Soviet bloc by 1991. Every president since Harry S. *Truman has pursued liberal trade as a weapon against aggression and instability. Multilateralism built world trade equilibrium and interdependence among like-minded nations, continuing the service of trade to security imperatives.

• Cordell Hull, *The Memoirs of Cordell Hull,* 1948. Peggy Liss, *Atlantic Empires: The Network of Trade and Revolution, 1713–1826,* 1983. William H. Becker and Samuel F. Wells, Jr., *Economics and World Power: An Assessment of American Diplomacy Since 1789,* 1984. Robert Pollard, *Economic Security and the Origins of the Cold War, 1945–1950,* 1985. Walter LaFeber, *The American Search for Opportunity, 1865–1913,* 1993.

—Thomas W. Zeiler

TRADE, FOREIGN: TRADE RESTRICTIONS

A priority in U.S. wartime foreign policy has always been to restrict trade with the enemy; yet as America's global power changed, so too did the nature and scope of these constraints and their efficacy. Commercial sanctions usually hurt American enemies in wartime, but were often difficult to maintain effectively. Nonetheless, sanctions and embargoes were readily used tools of warfare, not as substitutes for, but usually complements to, military measures.

Trade with the enemy in the *Revolutionary War hinged on international law. The U.S. Model Commercial Treaty of 1776 and the Treaty of Amity and Commerce with France in 1778 struck at British control of the seas by asserting the rights of neutral trade from capture by belligerents. This "free ships make free goods" doctrine served military purposes. Joining with other small-navy nations to demand neutral rights, Americans sought to undercut Britain's maritime dominance and imperial power. This defensive approach helped win the war; thereafter, the doctrine of *neutrality remained an American trade weapon.

More aggressive approaches to trade restriction as a means of coercing other nations, however, became the policy rule, and frequently created equivocal or even detrimental results. Trade sanctions against Britain from 1806, in response to London's coercive Orders of Council on

U.S. shipping, helped cause the *War of 1812. But rather than unduly hurting Britain with its sanctions, America incurred losses as its merchants were driven from the seas and the Royal Navy blockaded the coast. Later in the century, the brevity of the *Mexican War and the *Spanish-American War made trade restrictions irrelevant; but the Union used sanctions successfully against the Confederacy in the *Civil War. A naval blockade hurt the southerners by cutting them off from cotton markets in Europe. Hindered by British acquiescence in the blockade, Confederate blockade runners tried to evade the U.S. *Navy. Although these missions were initially successful, the blockade took an increasing toll after 1862.

A Trading with the Enemy Act passed in 1917 and modified ever since has formed the legal basis for policies on trade coercion since World War I. Congress's authorization of an embargo on American exports—in tandem with a British blockade—was instrumental in strangling the central powers in 1917–18. Before and during World War II, the administration of Franklin D. *Roosevelt relied on the act to deny scarce materials to the Axis, utilizing export controls and other economic warfare measures to wield its trade restrictions effectively. Even so, some neutral nations had no incentive to cooperate with the Allied blockade of Germany until the tide of battle turned. Thus, the Nazis were able to stockpile supplies of iron ore and wolfram from neutral Sweden, Spain, and Portugal, better surviving the blockade in this world war than in the first. By contrast, the American embargo hurt Japan badly. America imposed a gradual embargo in the fourteen months leading up to the attack on *Pearl Harbor, as Japanese forces marched through China and Indochina. Designed to restrict Japan, the embargo helped drive Tokyo to war with the United States; but during the conflict, Japan could never capitalize on its conquests in Southeast Asia to ship home enough oil, tin, and other commodities. World War II thus revealed both the successes and the limitations of trade sanctions.

The realization of these limits, and pressure from America's *Cold War allies, led to a more flexible approach to trade with the enemy after 1945. Anti-Communist sentiment prompted Congress to restrict trade severely with the Soviet bloc under the Export Control Act of 1949. But U.S. allies depended on trade with the Communist nations, and with their recovery from the war stagnant, America allowed for the sale of nonstrategic goods to the East from the early 1950s onward. The Soviet Union's ability to develop substitute goods also weakened export control policy. American leaders realized that trade sanctions oftentimes alienated friends, diverted trade to other nations, and took away the country's leverage with the satellite nations. These problems, and the possibility of shaping Soviet behavior by economic contacts, resulted in a moderation of U.S. policy. Still, China remained under economic quarantine until 1972, while America used its Trading with the Enemy Act and other measures to halt commerce with Vietnam, Cuba, North Korea, and other hostile powers in the Cold War.

After the Cold War, the United States led the *United Nations to embargo Iraq's oil and other trade goods in an attempt to force that nation's retreat from Kuwait. In 1991, while most Democrats in Congress preferred economic sanctions to military measures, the country nonetheless fought the *Persian Gulf War. Regardless of their effectiveness, then, trade sanctions in wartime have been viewed as necessary and natural complements to military efforts.

• Stuart L. Bernath, *Squall Across the Atlantic: American Civil War Prize Cases and Diplomacy,* 1970. U.S. Congress, House Subcommittee on International Trade and Commerce of the Committee on International Relations, *Trading with the Enemy: Legislative and Executive Documents Concerning Regulation of International Transactions in Time of Declared National Emergency,* 1976. Richard J. Ellings, *Embargoes and World Power: Lessons from American Foreign Policy,* 1985. Reginald Horsman, *The Diplomacy of the New Republic, 1776–1815,* 1985. Philip Funigiello, *American-Soviet Trade in the Cold War,* 1988. Homer Moyer, Jr., and Linda Mabry, *Export Controls as Instruments of Foreign Policy: The History, Legal Issues, and Policy Lessons of Three Recent Cases,* 1988.

—Thomas W. Zeiler

TRADE, FOREIGN: NEUTRAL TRADE

The United States has historically interpreted neutral commercial rights both legalistically and pragmatically as a tool of business and diplomacy. Entrepreneurs demanded an impartiality in international politics that permitted them freedom to export and import goods, while the government interpreted the *neutrality doctrine broadly to help friendly nations threatened by aggressors. Views of neutral trade policy, therefore, became entangled in debates over the proper role of commerce in wartime. In general, however, America exercised its neutral rights to enhance profits and security.

Beset with threats to U.S. commerce due to the European war led by Britain against France, President Thomas *Jefferson in 1803 sanctioned the practice of the broken voyage by which French West Indian goods were Americanized and then re-exported to British enemies as neutral trade. The United States held that neutrals had the right to trade noncontraband goods with belligerents, but such indirect trade naturally provoked Britain, which began taxing this neutral commerce and impressing American sailors into its navy. America nonetheless prospered from its clever policy, although an infuriated Congress passed the Non-Importation Act of 1806 to counter British violations of neutrality. When Britain attacked the USS *Chesapeake* in 1807, Jefferson implemented both the act and an embargo on shipping and exports. Assertive action ultimately failed, however, and the *War of 1812 resulted largely from resentments that had accumulated over neutral rights.

World War I placed neutral trade again at the center of Anglo-American relations. During the *Civil War, Britain had honored the Union trade quarantine against the Confederacy, and in 1914, London expected Washington to follow this precedent of respecting a belligerent's blockade. Shutting down neutral trade to the central powers in 1914, Britain seized U.S. ships, expanded the list of contraband goods, and even flew the American flag on some of its merchant ships to avoid attacks from German *submarines. President Woodrow *Wilson largely acquiesced in these tactics, but they sparked debate over the character of neutrality. Germany had good cause to cry foul. U.S. exports to France and Britain rocketed to $2.75 billion in 1916, aided by banking arrangements under which the House of Morgan loaned the Allies $2.3 billion before 1917. By contrast, exports to Germany plummeted to $2 million in 1916, and loans totaled only $27 million in 1914–17. Trade and credit profited the United States as New York City came to dominate world finance by 1916. Improved Anglo-American relations, British propaganda, and the huge English market for U.S. goods helped generate sympathy for the Allied war effort, while German aggression seemingly threatened U.S. power in the western hemisphere and on the seas. Wilson and his advisers, especially Edward House and Secretary of State Robert Lansing, clearly wanted Allied victory; Lansing developed a pro-British neutrality policy to secure it.

America maintained an increasingly technical neutrality. Wilson protested restraints on American trade, but because Britain controlled the seas, U.S. products ended up in Allied ports. Whether the United States pursued its neutral policies as a moneymaker for private interests remains a matter of debate. At any rate, German efforts to use *submarine warfare to curb the trade flowing to Britain and France eventually brought America into the war.

In the 1930s, isolationists wanted stricter neutrality as war loomed again in Europe. Congress imposed an arms embargo and prohibited loans in the first of the *Neutrality Acts (1935). Isolationists claimed that the selfish economic interests of merchants and bankers had dragged America into World War I, but President Franklin D. *Roosevelt pressed for fewer restraints on arms and commercial trade, until by 1939, the most onerous provisions of the Neutrality Acts had been repealed. Despite U.S. neutrality in the event of war, foreign nations could buy U.S. goods as long as they paid in cash (which circumvented restrictions on loans) and carried the products away on their own ships (which kept American merchants out of the war zone). The revision of the acts allowed the United States to aid allies at war and maintain commercial profits, while remaining legally neutral. America had once again bent the concept of neutrality to suit its economic and political interests.

Unlike Wilson in World War I, however, Roosevelt tried to prevent private interests from trading with aggressors. Unfortunately for many victims of *aggression and violence, the neutral trade policies of the United States worked all too well. Republicans fighting Franco's Fascist-backed forces in Spain, and Ethiopians struggling against Mussolini's Italian invasion, could not obtain vital war supplies. American exports of petroleum reached Mussolini's army in increasing amounts, while goods were denied to Ethiopia. Roosevelt sought an embargo against Italy, but American business saw no reason to curb sales with a nation at peace with the United States. Once war broke out in Europe, America remained neutral until the attack on *Pearl Harbor in December 1941, but Roosevelt bent the rules even further to aid the Allies through loans, Lend-Lease assistance, and other means. Once again, the exercise of neutrality meant that trade would serve the economic, diplomatic, and military interests of the United States.

• Louis Martin Sears, *Jefferson and the Embargo*, 1966. Jeffrey J. Safford, *Wilsonian Maritime Diplomacy, 1913–1921*, 1978. Robert Dallek, *Franklin D. Roosevelt and American Foreign Policy, 1932–1945*, 1979. Kathleen Burk, *Britain, America, and the Sinews of War, 1914–1918*, 1985. Robert W. Tucker and David C. Hendrickson, *Empire of Liberty: The Statecraft of Thomas Jefferson*, 1990.

—Thomas W. Zeiler

TRAIL OF TEARS (1838–39). In the late eighteenth century, the Cherokees led all other tribes in responding to George *Washington's policy of assimilation, establishing a written constitution, a bicameral legislature, and a supreme court. White Americans, however, sought their removal in order to use their land "more efficiently," and

President Andrew *Jackson asked Congress to remove them west of the Mississippi. The Removal Bill and the failure to enforce the *Worcester v. Georgia* (1832) decision sealed the Cherokees' doom. A few unauthorized headmen signed away the nation's remaining land at New Echota, in present day Georgia, in December 1835, and the government gave them two years to remove themselves.

By May 1838, only 2,000 of approximately 16,000 Cherokees had moved, and Maj. Gen. Winfield *Scott entered Cherokee territory with about 2,200 federal troops and nearly 5,000 state volunteers from Georgia, Alabama, North Carolina, and Tennessee. They herded the Cherokees into stockades, and then, in June, forced three groups—approximately 2,745 men, women, and children—to begin the 850-mile march from Tennessee to Indian territory. Sickness and death in the stockades led Chief John Ross to request a delay until cooler weather. The remainder were removed, in thirteen detachments, between 23 August and 5 December 1838. Approximately 4,000 died as a result of their ordeal, most not on the trail itself.

Cherokee removal—the Trail of Tears—remains one of the greatest tragedies that the United States has inflicted upon a minority population. Removal and assimilation, however, remained incomplete. Remnants of the tribe comprise the Eastern Bank of Cherokees today, and many preserve traditional culture.

[*See also* Native Americans, U.S. Military Relations with.]

• William L. Anderson, ed., *Cherokee Removal Before and After*, 1991. Theda Perdue and Michael D. Green, *Cherokee Removal: A Brief History with Documents*, 1994.

—William L. Anderson

TRAINING AND INDOCTRINATION. The military has always recognized the importance of training in accomplishing its missions; indeed, training is often seen as decisive in combat. Considerable attention has therefore been paid to both collective and individual training. For most of the past 350 years, military leaders in, first, the American colonies and then the United States gave thought only sporadically to what constituted military training, defined as the inculcation of skills aimed at achieving maximum efficiency on the battlefield. When doing so, military and political leaders assumed that the task was straightforward. Training was drill, and drill embodied everything that soldiers needed in order to function in battle. However much the intricacies of drill might be enshrouded in arcane language and symbols, for the individual soldier and the unit of which he was a part, training was the mechanics of marching and firing.

At one level, this approach remains true today. Basic training, the preparation of individuals from civilian life for the demands of military life, provides physical conditioning and military fundamentals and imbues recruits with their particular service's point of view. Since military service requires fitness, discipline, and the ability to live and work in a highly structured organization, recruit training emphasizes military rules, discipline, social conduct, physical conditioning, self-confidence, and pride in being a member of the military.

Subsequently, individuals also go through a progression of skills training, depending on their roles and military occupational specialties. (This entry deals primarily with enlisted personnel; education and leadership training for officers is examined mainly in the entries on Service *Academies and *ROTC.) Collective training, from unit field training exercises to complex, joint, or even multinational maneuvers, is designed to prepare cohesive groups to accomplish their missions.

In the colonial period, militia training days were a regular part of the calendar, particularly when the danger of war seemed imminent. Training of farmer militiamen involved mainly military drill and volley fire, often on the village green or nearby field. In the *Revolutionary War, the national *Continental army of longer service soldiers had little systematic training and discipline until Gen. Friedrich Wilhelm von *Steuben, formerly of the Prussian army, instituted regular training in marching, firing, and tactical maneuvers during the Valley Forge encampment in the winter of 1777. Steuben's *Regulations for the Order and Discipline of the Troops of the United States* (1778–79) remained the army's basic training manual for three decades. Smaller and less centralized, the *Continental navy drew upon experienced seamen and where necessary relied on training on shipboard.

Under the Constitution of 1787, military training was divided, as were the nation's military institutions, between the state militias and the regular army. The Constitution and the Uniform Militia Act (1792) prescribed standardized organization and training procedures for the state militias, but these were not enforced until the twentieth century. Uniform procedures were enforced, however, in the regular army and navy and Marines, where training was patterned largely along European lines. In the northern states, universal militia training was gradually abolished and the common militia was replaced by volunteer units of the *militia and National Guard; however, compulsory militia training continued in the white South until the *Civil War.

Primary reliance upon the ad hoc U.S. *Volunteers during the wars of the nineteenth century meant that the locally raised temporary wartime units of citizen-soldiers of the *War of 1812, the *Mexican War, the Civil War, and the *Spanish-American War were trained by their junior officers and noncommissioned officers from the same locale, many of whom had little more military knowledge than the enlisted men. Consequently, training and discipline were often haphazard. Regular forces, however, continued strict training and discipline by veteran NCOs, usually following European models. In the Mexican War, training took place at camps of instruction operated under the General Recruiting Service using Gen. Winfield *Scott's *Instructions for Field Artillery, Horse and Foot,* which became the standard training manual in 1845. The War Department never developed a comprehensive training program in the Civil War; instead, training depended upon the initiative of individual officers or division commanders.

Traditionally, the U.S. Navy relied on an apprentice system of shipboard training to produce able-bodied seamen; given the pattern of long-term shipboard assignments, that approach proved adequate. But in the late nineteenth century, creation of the steel-hulled, big-gun navy led to specialized training on shore for enlisted men, beginning with gunnery school in 1883 and electricity schools in 1899. In the 1890s, nativist fears caused by mass immigration and concerns of potential disloyalty by aliens in wartime led the military services to establish special training and "Americanization" schools for recruits who had not yet become naturalized U.S. citizens. An enlarged modern fleet led the navy to create a series of specialized schools. Between 1901 and 1916, training programs for forty different trades, from bakers to woodworkers, were established at Norfolk or Newport. Collectively, the navy conducted squadron and fleet exercises in conformity to new naval doctrines.

The U.S. Army began systematic training as part of its modernization programs in the early twentieth century. Abandoning the little posts in the West, the army held its first division-sized maneuver in peacetime in 1911. However, training of recruits in peacetime remained a responsibility of the unit to which the fledgling soldier was assigned. The norm was customarily a nine-month apprenticeship. With U.S. entry into World War I and the rapid creation of a mass army, the War Department reduced the training of recruits to four months before new infantrymen were sent overseas. This "basic" training occurred in large, hastily erected training cantonments, drawing initially on French and British training and technical manuals; audiovisual aids (such as the motion picture series *The Training of a Soldier*) also were employed. (Because the army was racially segregated, training of blacks and whites took place in different locations.)

As a result, American troops and units reached France poorly prepared, and special schools were established to give infantrymen further training in military demeanor, marksmanship, and Gen. John J. *Pershing's offensively oriented tactics before being committed to combat. The army also established additional programs to train enlisted men in the use of new technology: *artillery, *machine guns, field telephones, trucks, *tanks, and airplanes. Similarly, the wartime navy expanded its training stations at Newport, Norfolk, the Great Lakes, and San Francisco, and compressed the normal training period so that "boot" camp became merely a brief introduction to navy life and discipline, with the majority of training occurring afterwards.

In the interwar period, the navy's training system included boot camp for new recruits, followed by shore schools for advanced instruction in specialties for non-rated enlisted personnel, advanced training for petty officers, and schools for such special duty assignments as submarines and aviation. Marine Corps drill instructors imbued recruits with discipline, traditions, and basic skills, while advanced units engaged in practice landings for the Marines' new mission: amphibious assaults. In World War II, both the navy and the Marine Corps greatly expanded their training facilities and programs.

Army proposals for short-term universal military training were rejected by Congress in the *National Defense Act of 1920; instead, while reducing the regular army, Washington put primary military reliance on the organized reserve and National Guard, which took their training on weekends and in the summer. The army retained its specialized schools. In particular, the Infantry School at Fort Benning, Georgia, and the Army War College gave attention to training issues.

During the period of prewar expansion (1940–41), the army conducted recruit training in Replacement Training Centers (RTCs) modeled on an improved version of World War I training and often using reactivated cantonments that featured precisely scripted instruction (typically thirteen weeks) in drill, military courtesy, hygiene, use and care of weapons, and small unit tactics. However, after U.S. entry into World War II in December 1941, this approach was abandoned. For the remainder of the war, almost all draftees and volunteers underwent a battery of vocational and psychological tests in RTCs, then were assigned directly to a division or other large unit for eight weeks of basic training and participation in battalion, regimental, and divisional exercises. The aim was to match precisely individual capabilities with the rapidly proliferating requirements of modern warfare.

Following detailed training manuals and instructions, army drill sergeants taught the new recruits the rudiments of military discipline, familiarized them with their weapons and equipment, and sought to forge them into soldiers. Thereafter, individual training occurred in a specialized skill or branch or by happenstance for the bulk of infantry and artillery soldiers. The acute shortage of weapons and equipment for training in 1940–41 was eventually overcome; early neglect of tactical proficiency was to some degree corrected through intensive small unit training. Training manuals and films were revised throughout the war. Because the World War II U.S. Army was a mass citizen force raised primarily through *conscription, the War Department also sponsored educational programs to maintain health and troop *morale and to inform soldiers about why the United States had gone to war (most prominently in the *Why We Fight* film series). How best to motivate (indoctrinate) individual soldiers remained unresolved, with many asserting that combat performance was a function of leadership, others arguing that ideology was preeminent, and still others (including most *veterans) insisting that loyalty to one's buddies was pivotal. Again in World War II, the army enforced rigid racial segregation, with black soldiers being trained separately and mostly commanded by white officers.

Rapid increase of the number of pilots and planes in the Army Air Corps led to the creation in 1941 of a formal training program for technicians and ground and air crews to support them. To teach more than 300 skills, the Army Air Forces Training Command offered 80 courses, ranging from 4 to 44 weeks, and including airplane repair and maintenance, aviation engineering, armaments and equipment, weather, and photography.

Belated changes in training accompanied technological and structural developments in the U.S. armed forces during the *Cold War period and afterward. Evidence of inadequate training during the first weeks and months of the *Korean War led to important reforms affecting individual training, assignment, and motivation, and unit rotation policies. Racial desegregation, ordered by President Harry S. *Truman in 1948 and implemented during the Korean War, meant that blacks and whites now trained together. Creation of the North Atlantic Treaty Organization (*NATO) meant that by the late 1950s U.S. air, land, and naval forces engaged in joint training maneuvers and exercises with those of other NATO countries. In addition, increasingly sophisticated weaponry demanded that all the services develop expanded technical specialization training. Yet the U.S. armed forces also sought in the 1960s and 1970s to emphasize traditional military values and the sense that military service was more than simply an occupation. The army established the Non-Commissioned Officers Academy in 1966, created the position of sergeant major of the army, and in 1973 created a Sergeants Major Academy at Fort Bliss, Texas, to provide advanced leader-

ship training. In the 1980s, the air force created Project Warrior to emphasize the fighting spirit in an organization dominated numerically by support personnel.

After the military's problems in the *Vietnam War and the creation of the *All-Volunteer Force, the army in 1973 established the Training and Doctrine Command (TRADOC) at Fort Monroe, Hampton, Virginia, to improve the preparation of soldiers from basic training to such special centers for combat training and advanced courses as the First Special Operations Command (SOCOM), created at Fort Bragg, North Carolina, in 1982. TRADOC established prerequisites for all NCO and commissioned officer courses. Subsequently, the army set up a number of technologically sophisticated advanced training facilities, such as its National Training Center, established in 1982 at Fort Irwin in California's Mojave Desert. There on 1,000 square miles, battalion-sized combat units of armor and mechanized infantry rotated in up to a month of fighting scenarios, including force-on-force maneuvers and live fire missions. In the 1990s, faced with force reductions, the army emphasized training designed to be realistic, difficult, and performance-oriented, and it developed a program to enhance the combined training of active army and reserves.

Difficult issues remained unresolved. Efforts to confront the complex question of combat performance continued. Racial tensions were not entirely eradicated from promotion hearings and shipboard relationships. The integration into basic training of women, who by 1998 comprised 14 percent of the armed forces, remained as controversial as the assignment of women to combat roles. Integration of the sexes had varied by service since women had entered the regular military in large numbers in the 1970s. The air force integrated men and women in basic training in 1976; but the army, after conducting a short-lived trial in the late 1970s and early 1980s, did not do so until 1993, and the navy not until 1994. (The Marine Corps continued to retain sexually segregated basic training.) Debate persisted over basic training and the importance of male bonding and directed aggression for unit cohesion in ground combat. Following a series of highly publicized rape and assault charges at an army training facility in Maryland, a special panel recommended that men and women be separated in basic training. Although Secretary of Defense William S. Cohen rejected the recommendation in 1998, the issue of sexually integrated basic training remained controversial.

[See also African Americans in the Military; Bases, Military: Development of; Citizen-Soldier; Combat Effectiveness; Education, Military; Ethnicity and Race in the Military; Gender; Ideals, Military; Justice, Military; Language, Military; Recruitment; Women in the Military.]

• Marvin A. Kreidberg, and Merton G. Henry, *History of Military Mobilization of the United States Army, 1775–1945*, 1955. Alfred Goldberg, ed., *A History of the United States Air Force, 1907–1957*, 1957. Russell F. Weigley, *The History of the U.S. Army*, 1967; enl. ed. 1984. Maurice Matloff, *American Military History*, 1969. Frederick S. Harrod, *Manning the New Navy: The Development of a Modern Naval Enlisted Force, 1899–1940*, 1978. Allan R. Millett, *Semper Fidelis: The History of the United States Marine Corps*, 1980; 2nd ed. 1991. Anthony Kellett, *Combat Motivation*, 1982. Edward M. Coffman, *The Old Army*, 1986. U.S. Department of Defense, Office of the Secretary, Force Management and Personnel Training Policy,

Military Manpower Training Report, 1991. Anne W. Chapman, *The Origins and Development of the National Training Center, 1976–1984,* 1992. Anne W. Chapman, *The Army's Training Revolution, 1973–1990: An Overview,* 1994. Mark Grandstaff, *Foundations of the Force,* 1997. Theodore Wilson, *Building Warriors: Selection and Training of Ground Combat Troops in World War II,* 1999.

—Theodore Wilson

TRANSPORT AND SUPPLY AIRCRAFT. The U.S. Army Air Corps' interest in transport airplanes started in 1925 by acquiring the Douglas C-1, a single engine biplane with a maximum takeoff weight (Mtow) of 7400 pounds. In an airplane the figure for Mtow is similar to that of displacement tonnage for an oceangoing ship; it is the one figure that provides a definite measure of size and probable productivity. An airplane's payload is typically about 20 percent of its Mtow.

Built to Air Corps specifications, a C-1 had seats for eight passengers; alternatively, it could carry 2000 lbs of cargo. A C-1's range was 380 miles; its cruising speed 85 mph. This was the last transport prepared to an Air Corps specification for more than 15 years. Prior to World War II transport planes served the Air Corps' internal needs and rarely the Army at large so it was expedient to buy transports that had been designed for civilian airlines.

The demonstrated success of Nazi Germany's use of airborne troops in lightning conquests of Norway, Belgium, and the Netherlands in early 1940 moved the Air Corps to create an increasingly large transport force. The backbone of this force was the immediately available Douglas DC-3 and the Curtiss CW.20 then under development. Both were twin-engine civil airliners. The DC-3, 28,000 lb Mtow, became the military C-47 or C-53, the former being the cargo version, the latter a troop carrier. More than 10,000 C-47/C-53s were procured during World War II. The CW.20, 40,000 lb Mtow, became the C-46; more than 3,000 were procured.

A shortcoming of both types was that they had been designed in the mid-1930s, too soon to take advantage of the innovation of tricycle landing gear. The C-47, C-53, and C-46 were "taildraggers"; on the ground they sat on a tailwheel with their noses up at an angle. This made the loading of heavy cargo difficult and unloading awkward. The Douglas DC-4 airliner which became available after 1942 as the C-54, 62,000 lb Mtow, was a versatile airplane but left something to be desired as a military transport. It sat up on tricycle gear which provided a level cabin on the ground, but like most airliners it was a low wing airplane. This required a tall landing gear to maintain propeller clearance with the ground, a result being an airplane that was so high off the ground that forklifts, elevated platforms, and other devices were necessary to gain access to its cabin for loading and unloading.

In 1947 the U.S. *Air Force was established as a separate service. Although the Air Force continues to adapt airline equipment to its transport needs, these airplanes only indirectly meet the Army's combat airlift requirements. Ideally, a military transport plane is a high wing airplane, its fuselage slung beneath the wing resulting in minimum clearance between its cabin floor and the ground. This facilitates loading and unloading, including roll-on and roll-off of wheeled vehicles with a bare minimum of auxiliary equipment. In 1941 a specification was prepared for such an airplane. This was the Fairchild C-82 known as the "Flying Boxcar," a twin engine airplane, 54,000 lb Mtow, but the prototype did not fly until late 1944; more than 200 were produced but they were too late for World War II.

The C-82 was redesigned in a larger and more powerful version, the C-119, 72,700 lb Mtow, more than 900 built. Both types were used in the Korean War and in Vietnam. After 1954, however, they were gradually supplanted by the ubiquitous 4-engine Lockheed C-130 Hercules. Whereas the C-82 and C-119 were powered by piston engines, the C-130 has turbine driven propellers. And the main element of the C-130's tricycle landing gear consists of four wheels "nested" into the sides of the fuselage. This distributes the airplane's weight across a broader "footprint," facilitating operations from unimproved airfields.

Initially 124,200 lb Mtow, with increases in engine power the C-130 has grown to more than 155,000 lb and built in more than four dozen variants for the U.S. Air Force, *Navy, *Marines, and *Coast Guard, and more than 60 of the world's air forces. More than 2100 C-130s have been built, and by the year 2004 it will have been in production for a half century.

By the late 1950s there was clearly a requirement for a high-speed transatlantic trooplift capability to reinforce NATO and it produced the Lockheed C-141A which flew in 1963. The C-141A was a 4-engine turbojet of 323,000 lb Mtow capable of lifting 138 equipped troops or 62,000 lb of cargo across 4100 miles. A total of 285 were built. In 1976 the fuselages of C-141As were "stretched" by some 23 feet to increase hull volume, were modified to be receivers of inflight refueling, and redesignated C-141Bs. In 1995 most C-141Bs were 30 years old; by the year 2005 it is expected that C-141Bs will have been replaced by the new McDonnell Douglas C-17A.

Although the C-141 met the requirements for trooplift and most cargo, it could not carry heavy tanks and other less heavy but bulky loads, such as Army troop-carrying *helicopters, all of which would be required in a reinforcement of NATO. The result was the Lockheed C-5A, 769,000 lb Mtow, which flew in 1968. Whereas the cabin cross-section of C-141B is 124 inches, that of a C-5A is 228 inches; usable cubic volumes of cargo spaces are 11,399 and 34,796 cubic feet, respectively. A versatile aspect of the C-5A is cargo doors in both the nose and tail permitting straight-through loading and unloading. An upper deck has seats for 75 troops who may be necessary to handle the cargo at terminal points.

The C-5A is the first U.S. military transport equipped to receive inflight refueling, a feature that proved invaluable in the resupply of Israel in the Arab-Israeli War of 1973. A specification for a transoceanic transport airplane usually described a range of 4000 miles, roughly the distance from bases in northeastern United States to bases in West Germany. It could be assumed that if operations were to be extended to the Eastern Mediterranean they could be staged through Western Europe. But the distance from the U.S. to Israel is about 6000 miles and during the 1973 War the Arabs pressured the nations of Western Europe to deny refueling services to the U.S. airlift to Israel. Although a C-5A could fly 6000 miles nonstop it could do so only with a reduced payload. However, refueled in flight by Boeing KC-135 tankers based in Spain and the Azores, C-5As were able to fly full loads from North America to Israel nonstop.

Flight operations revealed a flaw in the C-5A's wing structure that limited the wing's fatigue lift to less than expectations and in the 1980s all C-5As were re-winged. Concurrently, 50 C-5Bs were procured. Built with the new wing, they are essentially the same as the C-5A and increase the C-5 fleet to more than 120 airplanes.

With the C-141 fleet more than 30 years old and approaching the end of their fatigue lives, they are being replaced by the McDonnell Douglas C-17, a 4-engine jet transport of 580,000 lbs Mtow that is equipped for inflight refueling. The C-17 was first flown in 1991 and in 1995 it started to equip its first squadrons. At the turn of the century the backbone Air Force's Air Mobility Command will consist of C-5s, C-17s, and C-130s, served by some 500 KC-135 and 50 KC-10 tankers which provide the force with global range.

[*See also* Air Force, U.S.: Overview; Air Force, U.S.: Predecessors of, 1907 to 1946; Air Force, U.S.: Since 1947.]
—Richard K. Smith

TRANSPORTATION is the key to successful military operations in peace and war. At both the strategic and the tactical level—on land and sea and in the air—transportation provides the essential means for assembling men, equipment, and supplies at the critical time and place. Military transportation includes planning and executing the movement of personnel, equipment, and supplies to the theater of operations (*strategic* transportation), within the theater (*operational* transportation), and on the battlefield (*tactical* transportation). Effective and efficient transportation involves *movement control* and the use of all modes of transportation: human and animal, transoceanic and inland water transport, rail, motor, air, and such other methods as pipelines and aerial tramways.

Movement control encompasses the planning, coordination, and supervision of military movement of all types and includes such subfunctions as scheduling personnel and cargo movement to maximize the use of available carriers and ensure that men and materiel arrive when and where needed; tracking the progress of movement; and regulating the frequency, speed, and density of movement in order to avoid congestion at any point along the route.

Human and animal transport have been used to move military forces since prehistoric times. Well into the twentieth century, most armies relied almost entirely upon human and animal bearers. Even today in more primitive areas, porters and pack animals are still the most effective means of moving military supplies. Able to operate under most weather conditions on all sorts of terrain, a human bearer can carry 60–80 pounds for fifteen miles in a day. Pack animals (horses, mules, bullocks, and camels) can carry about 200–250 pounds, and the standard U.S. Army four-horse wagon of the *Civil War period could haul over 1 ton of cargo. Human and animal transport is often critical to the success or failure of a military campaign. The terrible privations suffered by Washington's *Continental army at Valley Forge in the winter of 1777–78 during the *Revolutionary War were due more to the lack of adequate teams, wagons, and teamsters than to any absolute lack of food, clothing, and fuel in the rebellious colonies. However, by the end of the Civil War less than 100 years later, wagon transport had become a particularly effective means of moving supplies under the control of competent logisticians.

Water transport is essential to move men and materiel overseas, and both transoceanic and inland water transport can move large numbers of troops and supplies in bulk over long distances. However, most water transport is relatively slow, and its effective utilization depends upon adequate loading and unloading facilities. Water transport has played an important role in all America's wars, especially since 1898, when overseas campaigns became the norm for U.S. forces. Beginning in 1948, the U.S. Navy assumed responsibility for managing water transport for all military services, but until after World War II, the army operated its own fleet of seagoing transports and cargo vessels under the direction of the Quartermaster Corps and, after 1942, the Transportation Corps.

Rail transport can haul large tonnages over great distances in all sorts of weather, but it is manpower-intensive, restricted to established routes, and quite vulnerable to enemy attack. Railroads were first used for military transportation in the United States during the *Mexican War of 1846–48, and they became an important factor in strategic and operational mobility during the Civil War. American railroads carried almost all military troops and cargo within the continental United States in World Wars I and II, but in recent years military rail movements have been largely supplanted by motor and air transport. Until the formation of the Army Transportation Corps in 1942, U.S. military railroads were operated by the U.S. *Army Corps of Engineers.

Motor transport is now the principal mode of military movement at the operational and tactical level. Such transport is flexible but requires a high expenditure of manpower and other resources, not only to operate and maintain the vehicles themselves but also to maintain roads capable of handling sustained military traffic. Motor transport is also relatively vulnerable to the effects of weather and enemy interdiction. The U.S. Army, which purchased its first motor vehicles in the 1890s, was one of the first armies in the world to achieve full mechanization of its tactical and logistical forces. Until 1942, motor transport was the responsibility of the Quartermaster Corps, although a distinct Motor Transport Corps existed for a short time in World War I.

Air transport first became a factor in modern warfare during World War II and has since assumed great importance. The rapid long-distance movement of substantial numbers of men and large quantities of cargo by air has revolutionized the strategic mobility of military forces. At the same time, tactical mobility has been enormously improved by the use of *helicopters. But air transport is very expensive and generally requires improved terminal facilities. The air force provides U.S. military forces with worldwide strategic airlifts and tactical airlifts of men and materiel, effecting deliveries by both air landing and parachute drop. The other services also operate their own tactical airlifts, principally in the form of troop and cargo-carrying helicopters. The *Persian Gulf War demonstrated the capabilities of adequate and properly managed air transport.

Pipelines, aerial tramways, hovercraft, and other means of transport supplement the principal modes. Pipelines, operated by the Army Quartermaster Corps, are particularly useful for the movement of bulk liquids and solids suspended in liquid (e.g., coal dust). They are, however, relatively inflexible, vulnerable to enemy action, and require substantial resources to build and maintain.

Since most modern military movement of any consequence involves more than one service, management at the highest levels is a joint undertaking. The U.S. Transportation Command, a joint headquarters established in 1987, provides movement control and the allocation of strategic transportation resources for all the services. Close links are maintained with civilian enterprises (shipping and trucking companies, the railroads, and commercial air carriers), which in fact own and operate under government contract most of the equipment and facilities needed to meet military requirements, particularly within the United States and to the overseas theaters.

Modern military forces possess great destructive power, but that power must be positioned at the decisive time and place if *victory is to be attained. The only means for achieving the necessary concentration is transportation—by land, sea, or air. A military force without adequate transportation cannot achieve overwhelming superiority on the battlefield and is thus doomed to failure.

[See also Armored Vehicles; Logistics.]

• Headquarters, Department of the Army, Field Manual 55-15: Transportation Reference Data, 1963. James A. Huston, The Sinews of War: Army Logistics, 1775–1953, 1966. Headquarters, Department of the Army, Field Manual 54–10: Logistics—An Overview of the Total System, 1977; Headquarters, Department of the Army, Field Manual 700–80: Logistics, 1982.

—Charles R. Shrader

TREASON—betraying the nation-state that the American military was created to defend—is among the most odious of crimes. Yet American history suggests how fine the line can be between patriot and traitor.

The founding fathers had to become traitors to their king in order to create the United States. The Declaration of Independence articulated the conditions—tyranny—under which a people might legitimately renounce their allegiance to one sovereign authority and transfer it to another.

Efforts to punish disloyalty to the new nation predated its independence. On 24 June, 1776, the Continental Congress adopted a motion by its Committee on Spies recommending that individual colonies punish those "who shall levy war against any of the said colonies ... or be adherent to the King of Great Britain...." Thus authorized, the revolutionary factions in the individual colonies punished as traitors avowed Tories, along with those who uttered favorable opinions about the king, had contact with the British, or entered British-controlled territories. The emphasis was on protecting the new nation, not the rights or intent of the accused. Punishment most often involved confiscation of property and exile. The revolutionaries justified such severity by the presumption that, as the Virginia treason statute suggested, "all countries have a Right to the personal services" of their inhabitants.

Treason was given an enduring symbol in 1780 when Gen. Benedict *Arnold, disillusioned with the revolutionary cause, unsuccessfully schemed to surrender the army garrison at West Point to the British, fleeing to the British after his plot was discovered. Arnold's name remains synonymous with betrayal in American history.

The excesses of the Revolution prompted the framers of the Constitution to restrict the definition of treason to "levying war against" the United States and providing "aid and comfort" to its enemies, and to require the testimony of two witnesses "to the same overt act" and the establishment of treasonous intent for conviction. They limited punishment to the person charged, and abjured the attainder of the traitor's relatives or heirs. Thus the framers hoped to balance the security of the state with the protection of private property and individual rights and to prevent the charge of treason from becoming an instrument of political repression.

The first application of the Constitution's treason provisions occurred in 1794 with the *Whiskey Rebellion. Federal troops led by George *Washington quashed this challenge to central authority, and a federal circuit court condemned to death two men—whom Washington later pardoned—for treason.

A major landmark in the evolution of treason law occurred in the 1807 trial of Aaron Burr, who stood accused of attempting to establish an independent trans-Appalachian empire. Although circumstantial evidence pointed toward the defendant's guilt, the government's inability to prove that an overt act of treason had occurred resulted in Burr's acquittal. In a victory for a narrow interpretation of the law of treason, Chief Justice John Marshall ruled that "the difficulty of proving a fact will not justify conviction without proof."

During the *Mexican War (1846–48), religious allegiance took precedence over national loyalty for several hundred Irish immigrant U.S. troops who deserted to the Mexican Army when the Mexican government appealed to them to defend Catholicism and promised them land. The "San Patricio Brigade" put up fierce resistance against U.S. units at the Battle of Churubusco before surrendering to Gen. Winfield *Scott, who executed fifty of them for treason.

In 1859, John Brown and his followers, in the name of God and slave liberation, seized the Federal arsenal at Harpers Ferry, Virginia, as part of a plan to establish a free guerrilla state. Although Brown had attacked U.S. property, Governor Henry Wise had the conspirators tried for treason against Virginia. This assertion of state jurisdiction reflected the assumptions that soon produced the secession of the Southern states in 1861, the most significant act of treason in American history. Suppression of the rebellion was based on the assumption that the Union was permanent and that secession from it could never be justified.

Although the Constitution defines treason strictly, Congress has expanded the definition of treasonous behavior by legislation such as the *Alien and Sedition Acts of 1798 and and the *Espionage and Sedition Acts of World War I (1917; 1918), which punished political expression deemed hazardous to the state. Both sets of legislation proved controversial. The acts of 1798 provoked the violent opposition of the emerging Jeffersonian Republican Party and facilitated the election of Thomas *Jefferson as president in 1801. The acts of 1917–18 legitimated a government crackdown on dissent of all kinds and foreshadowed the crisis atmosphere of the Red Scare of the 1920s.

The *Cold War saw the charge of treason used to build political careers and silence dissent. Congressman Richard M. *Nixon first came to prominence in 1948 investigating a State Department employee, Alger Hiss, for his alleged activities as a Communist Party contact in the 1930s. In 1952, Senator Joseph McCarthy, alleging "twenty years of treason," launched his campaign to eliminate alleged traitors in the federal government. McCarthyism made dissent tantamount to treason. Julius and Ethel Rosenberg, who were convicted and executed in 1953 for passing secrets to the Soviets, were condemned by many for being traitors.

Jonathan Pollard, a Defense Department analyst convicted in 1985 of passing vital secrets to Israel, remains incarcerated in spite of continued pressure from the Israeli government for his release. The quantity and importance of the information Pollard leaked constitutes one of the most significant security breaches in U.S. history.

In recent years, treason has tended to be committed for monetary gain rather than ideological commitment. Typical of this trend are *Central Intelligence Agency (CIA) officials Aldrich Ames and Harold James Nicholson. Ames, before being discovered in 1994, passed extensive information on U.S. intelligence operatives abroad to Soviet and Russian agents. Nicholson, who confessed in March 1997 to passing secrets to the Russians, is the highest ranking CIA employee to be caught spying.

[See also Patriotism.]

• Nathaniel Weyl, *Treason: The Story of Disloyalty and Betrayal in American History*, 1950. Bradley Chapin, *The American Law of Treason: Revolutionary and Early National Origins*, 1964. James Willard Hurst, *The Law of Treason in the United States: Collected Essays*, 1971.
—William Earl Weeks

TRENCH WARFARE in the form of siege operations was already a developed art by the seventeenth century. The master of this form of warfare was the French marshal Vauban (1633–1707). His system set the stage for two centuries of siege warfare, and was used during the Crimean War (1854–56).

An American observer of that war, George B. *McClellan, noted the improved power of the entrenched defense, while the outstanding American military theorist of the time, Dennis Hart Mahan, advocated before the *Civil War an entrenched but active defense, and expressed doubts about the frontal assault of fortified positions. Mahan and his supporters represented one school of thought, and their concerns were reinforced by the introduction of the rifled musket in the mid-1850s. However, an opposite and more popular school of thought emphasized offensive *Napoleonic warfare. This approach also benefitted from successful American assaults in the *Mexican War (1846–48).

Thus, in the first two years of the Civil War, entrenchments were often ignored. However, from 1863 on, as the rifled musket made an even greater impact, as infantry dominated the battlefield, as the cost of offensive warfare in *casualties climbed steeply, and as the *Confederate army went more frequently onto the defensive, entrenchments became much more significant. These often consisted of breastworks of logs, since engineers and digging tools were in short supply. But where possible, those who believed in the value of trenches used them, although others deprecated their use, believing that they lowered *troop morale. Still others, like Gen. Ulysses S. *Grant, were inconsistent in their attitude toward entrenchments.

This move toward trench warfare can be seen in sieges such as at Vicksburg (1863) and Petersburg (1864). At the Siege of *Vicksburg, for example, General Grant penned in a Confederate army, which constructed strongpoints and forts every few hundred yards for the *artillery, and linked these strongpoints with rifle pits and trenches. Grant tried two attacks upon these defenses, and both failed, with heavy loss of life. Grant then turned to Vauban-style be-

sieging tactics and began sapping and mining toward the defensive works. So close did the trench lines approach each other that the night pickets were able to fraternize. But with daylight it was "Watch out, Johnnie, and hunt your hole." Eventually, Grant wore down the defenders. Similarly, at the Siege of *Petersburg, the lengthy siege with trenchworks and mining failed to take the city, which only surrendered through lack of supplies and attrition.

Vicksburg and Petersburg showed the power of defensive entrenchments during sieges when protected by artillery and rifles. Equally, in the last three years of the Civil War, both offensive and defensive entrenchments revealed their value in battle, for example, at Cold Harbor (1864), and at Kennesaw Mountain (1864). Dennis Mahan's school of thought had been vindicated by the Civil War. However, other armies did not appreciate the change in warfare, as the shadow of Napoleon continued to emphasize offensive ideas. Thus, the Franco-Prussian War, the Boer War in South Africa, and the Russo-Japanese War all demonstrated the problems of taking entrenchments that were defended by improved rifles, long-range artillery, and increasingly, *machine guns.

Trench warfare of World War I continued the nineteenth- and early twentieth-century trend toward increased power of the entrenched defense. Weapons were now even more powerful, and these forced the infantry underground into long lines of trenches, which spread across the entire western front by late 1914. The United States entered the war in April 1917, under the command of Gen. John J. *Pershing, who hindered his troops' efficiency by advocating "open warfare." Pershing believed the French and British had bogged down in defeatist trench warfare, and that the American Expeditionary Forces (AEF) could break through enemy trenches and achieve open warfare by the use of initiative, the rifle, and the bayonet. Pershing stated that *victory "could not be won by the costly process of attrition, but it must be won by driving the enemy out into the open and engaging him in a war of movement." However, Pershing ignored the power of trench defenses, and so AEF troops frequently suffered heavy losses, such as the attack in June 1918 at the Battle of *Belleau Wood, where the U.S. Second Division took nearly 9,000 casualties.

Nevertheless, Pershing felt vindicated by the AEF success at the Battle of *St. Mihiel in September 1918, where rapid advances did overrun trenches and barbed wire. Next, the AEF took part in the *Meuse-Argonne Offensive. This ran into logistical problems, but inexperience also led to underuse of hand grenades and gas masks, while frontal attacks against German trenches and positions created severe losses among the Americans. In fact, the AEF was actually waging costly attrition warfare, despite Pershing's ideas. Late in October 1918, the AEF reorganized and assimilated trench warfare lessons. Assault teams were created to deal with German machine guns, while the main offensive bypassed these strongpoints. This tactic, plus the use of other weapons, produced a combined arms approach to dealing with German defenses. In the early morning of 1 November 1918, the AEF's First Army attacked in this fashion and broke through all German defenses. Pershing's wish was finally achieved: open warfare had arrived.

Trench warfare, defined as combat with both sides in trenches, apparently came to an end with the armistice in 1918. However, dug-in positions remained a feature of warfare, as the later twentieth century showed. During World War II, in Normandy after the *D-Day landing, the defenses of the *bocage* (hedgerow) countryside slowed down Allied forces until an American sergeant devised steel teeth mounted on a Sherman tank to cut through the roots of the thick hedges. In the Pacific War, Japanese soldiers on Iwo Jima and Okinawa had to be driven out of their entrenchments and caves with artillery, *tanks, rockets, *flamethrowers, and dynamite. Then, in the *Korean War, especially between November 1951 and July 1953, both sides dug in and resumed a static World War I form of trench warfare on hilltops and mountain ridges, complete with "no-man's-land." During the *Vietnam War, U.S. forces occasionally came across remarkable series of enemy trenches and underground systems, such as the tunnels at Cu Chi. Finally, in the *Persian Gulf War, the Iraqi Army dug in with extensive defenses of sand berms, trenches, foxholes, and minefields. Led by American divisions, *United Nations forces used bulldozers and antimine tank plows to cut lanes through the defenses, as well as plowing under trenches that contained infantry resisters.

Recent conflicts show that trench warfare still continues. Yet the basic contradiction of this style of fighting remains—trench warfare is essentially defensive, but armies continually seek offensive success.

[*See also* Engineering, Military; Iwo Jima, Battle of; Okinawa, Battle of; World War I: Military and Diplomatic Course; World War II: Military and Diplomatic Course; World War II, U.S. Naval Operations in: The Pacific.]

• Tom Mangold and John Penycate, *The Tunnels of Cu Chi*, 1985. Bill Ross, *Iwo Jima: Legacy of Valour*, Vanguard, New York, 1985. Paul Braim, *The Test of Battle: The American Expeditionary Forces in the Meuse-Argonne Campaign*, 1987. Tim Travers, *The Killing Ground: The British Army, the Western Front, and the Emergence of Modern Warfare, 1900–1918*, 1987. Edward Hagerman, *The American Civil War and the Origins of Modern Warfare*, 1988. David Trask, *The AEF and Coalition Warmaking, 1917–1918*, 1993.

—Tim Travers

TRENTON AND PRINCETON, BATTLES OF (1776–77). When George *Washington's army captured the Hessian garrison of Trenton, New Jersey, on 26 December 1776, and parried the British relief column at Princeton on 3 January 1777, it won victories that marked the turning point of the Revolutionary War. Since August, Gen. William *Howe had forced the American army out of New York and hounded it across northern New Jersey in November, and might have destroyed it altogether, had not Washington crossed to the western shore of the Delaware River in mid-December, seizing all available boats as he went. Nearly destitute of food, clothing, and ammunition, with enlistments expiring and men abandoning what looked like a lost cause, the *Continental army was about to fade away. But Washington, unwilling to let the cause die without one last effort, was able to keep together a force large enough to attack a vulnerable part of the overextended British army as it settled down for the winter.

On Christmas night, in a storm of rain, hail, and snow, Washington led his remaining 2,400 men back across the Delaware, and just as dawn broke on the 26th, surprised and captured the 1,000-man Hessian garrison at Trenton.

Careful not to attempt too much with too little, Washington's army retraced its steps back across the Delaware, only to appear on 3 January 1777 at Princeton, ten miles northeast of Trenton, outflanking British forces that had advanced to reclaim the town. The American army, reduced to 1,600 men, attacked 1,200 disorganized British troops at Princeton with modest success. Washington risked his life leading a charge against a British position, but kept his head and broke off the engagement before British reinforcements under Charles *Cornwallis arrived from Trenton. The Continentals withdrew to the northwest and went into winter quarters at Morristown in mid-January. Washington and his little army had foiled the British conquest of northern New Jersey and showed the world that the rebellion was not dead yet.

[*See also* Revolutionary War: Military and Diplomatic Course.]

• William S. Stryker, *The Battles of Trenton and Princeton*, 1898. Alfred H. Bill, *The Campaign of Princeton*, 1948. Douglas S. Freeman, *George Washington, Leader of the Revolution*, 1951.

—Harold E. Selesky

TRIPOLITAN WAR (1801–05). Late eighteenth-century European powers paid the Barbary states (Morocco, Algiers, Tunis, and Tripoli, called *Barbary* for the Berber people of North Africa) to capture their competitors' ships. Sometimes known as "Barbary pirates," the North African sea raiders seized ships for both profit and political reasons. The raiding was an organized government activity, not piracy; the United States and other powers negotiated treaties with the North African states to protect their commerce. In 1785, Great Britain encouraged Algiers to capture two ships from the newly independent United States.

While the captive American sailors languished, the U.S. minister to France, Thomas *Jefferson, tried to enlist Portugal, Naples, Sardinia, and Russia in an alliance against Algiers. France refused to cooperate. In 1793, Britain promulgated a fraudulent treaty between Algiers and Portugal, after which Algiers captured a dozen American ships and over 100 American sailors. American envoys negotiated a treaty in 1795, pledging an annual tribute in naval supplies, and a frigate as a gift to the dey, or ruler, of Algiers. Richard O'Brien, captive in Algiers since 1785, negotiated similar treaties with Tunis and Tripoli.

But the United States was slow to send tribute. When Jefferson became president in 1801, Tripoli's Pasha Yusuf Qaramanli, demanding his tribute, had all but declared war. Although Jefferson, determined to cut military spending, had sold or decommissioned most of the U.S. Navy's ships, he sent what was left to the Mediterranean with instructions to cooperate with Sweden, Sicily, Malta, Portugal, and Morocco against Tripoli. This coalition forced Qaramanli to back down, ultimately giving the United States a victory, even with a minimal navy.

For two years a small U.S. squadron (one frigate and its consorts) patrolled the Tripolitan coast. When the frigate USS *Philadelphia* ran aground in October 1803, Tripoli captured the 300 men on board and prepared to use the ship against the Americans. Jefferson's political opponents accused him of fighting a war without sufficient resources, but Lt. Stephen *Decatur silenced the critics in February 1804 when he entered Tripoli Harbor with a small crew and burned the *Philadelphia*. Decatur, promoted to captain, became a national hero; the navy increased its bombardments of Tripoli.

William Eaton, American consul to Tunis, proposed an alliance with Ahmed Qaramanli, Yusuf's brother, whom the pasha had deposed in 1795. Eaton organized an army of Arabs, Greeks, and U.S. Marines to reinstall Ahmed as ruler, in the expectation that he would make a favorable treaty with the United States. Jefferson neither supported the plan nor discouraged it. Eaton's force marched from Egypt to the city of Derne, which it captured in June 1805, just as the United States made peace with Yusuf. The government ransomed the *Philadelphia*'s crew, and Tripoli promised not to attack American ships. The diplomatic results were less impressive than the patriotic effusions in the United States: paintings, songs, poems, plays, and statues celebrated America's victory over its Muslim enemies.

In 1807, Algiers declared war on the United States, but the embargo and the *War of 1812 kept American shipping out of the Mediterranean. In 1815, the Madison administration sent Decatur to settle the dispute. Algiers promised not to take American ships, and a few months later an English fleet forced Algiers to renounce attacks on European shipping. Great Britain no longer needed Algiers to fight its enemies. In 1830, France invaded Algiers, beginning a century of European colonization in North Africa.

[*See also* Marine Corps, U.S.: 1775–1865; Navy, U.S.: 1783–1865.]

• Kola Folayan, *Tripoli During the Reign of Pasha Yusuf Qaramanli*, 1979. Robert J. Allison, *The Crescent Obscured: The United States and the Muslim World 1776–1815*, 1995.

—Robert J. Allison

TRUMAN, HARRY S. (1884–1972), thirty-third U.S. president. Born in Lamar, Missouri, a poor farmer's son, Harry Truman abandoned hope of a West Point education because of poor eyesight, but joined the National Guard in 1905. In World War I, 1917–18, Captain Harry Truman commanded Battery D, 129th Field Artillery, 35th Division, at the Battle of *St. Mihiel, Varennes, the *Meuse-Argonne Offensive, and Metz. Back home as a protégé of the Democratic Pendergast machine of Kansas City, Truman won several local elections before his election as a U.S. senator in 1934. During World War II, in 1941–44, he chaired a special Senate committee investigating defense spending. He became President Franklin D. *Roosevelt's vice presidential running mate in 1944, and succeeded to the presidency upon Roosevelt's death, 12 April 1945.

After the successful test of the atomic bomb in New Mexico in July 1945, Truman maintained the unconditional surrender demand toward Japan and took an increasingly hard line toward the Soviet Union. He approved the bombings of *Hiroshima and Nagasaki that brought about the end of the war.

As president, 1945–53, Truman shaped U.S. foreign and defense policy in the early *Cold War. His *internationalism—more accurately, militant *nationalism—depended heavily on military preparedness, a result of his belief in dealing from strength and his own combative personality. He relied upon particularly cosmopolitan, hard-line advisers, especially Secretaries of State George C. *Marshall and Dean *Acheson and the U.S. ambassador to Moscow, W. Averell Harriman; but he prided himself on making the final decisions.

Responding to Josef *Stalin's imposition of Soviet control in Eastern Europe and American fears of a global expansion of communism, the Truman administration sought to create a postwar order of democracy, self-government, and expanding world trade. But the *Truman Doctrine of "containment" announced originally in 1947 as political and economic soon because militarized, as did the *Marshall Plan of 1948 and *NATO, created in 1949. The administration began to support a variety of anti-Communist efforts in Europe and Asia.

U.S.-Soviet relations had became confrontational in 1946. By 1948, in a dispute over Germany, Stalin blockaded Berlin; Truman responded with the Berlin airlift. In 1949, after the Soviet A-bomb test, Truman ordered U.S. development of the hydrogen bomb.

The Truman administration in the late 1940s had sought an expanded military within a restricted budget. It failed to achieve universal military training for the army and in 1948 accepted a selective draft. In 1949, when it canceled the navy's supercarrier, it faced a "Revolt of the Admirals." Primary reliance was placed on atomic *bomber aircraft of the U.S. Air Force, made independent by the *National Security Act of 1947.

The *Korean War changed the budget picture and led to the enormous expansion of all the armed services. It also led to desegregation of the armed services, ordered by Truman in 1948. Yet the frustrations of this limited war precipitated a major crisis in civil-military relations: Gen. Douglas *MacArthur's public challenge to the administration's restrictions against attacking China itself. Consequently, President Truman relieved him of command.

Although the Truman administration was highly unpopular when it left office in 1953, admiration for Truman rose in the 1970s over his plain and honest style, decisiveness, and many of his Cold War policies, which some in the 1990s credited with ultimately defeating the Soviet Union. Yet a number of scholars believe that Truman's get-tough style and hard-line policies interacting with Stalin's paranoia and ruthlessly blunt policies served to escalate rather than diminish the Cold War.

[*See also* Berlin Crises; Civil Military Relations: Civilian Control of the Military; Manhattan Project; World War I: Military and Diplomatic Course; World War II: Military and Diplomatic Course.]

• Richard F. Haynes, *The Awesome Power: Harry S. Truman as Commander in Chief*, 1973. Melvyn Leffler, *Preponderence of Power: National Security, the Truman Administration, and the Cold War*, 1992. David McCullough, *Truman*, 1992. Alonzo L. Hamby, *Man of the People: A Life of Harry S. Truman*, 1995.

—Richard F. Haynes

TRUMAN DOCTRINE. In 1947, Soviet-American tensions developed along the "northern tier" of the Mediterranean and culminated in the Truman Doctrine. The Soviet Union, recently rebuffed in Iran, seemed determined to stage a Communist takeover in Greece and wrest the Dardenelles Straits—connecting the Black Sea with the Mediterranean—from Turkey. Although it is doubtful that the Soviets were either directly involved in the Greek troubles or actually prepared to take military action against Turkey, the perception of danger distorted reality. The Truman administration feared that the Soviets sought access to the Persian Gulf, the Mediterranean, and ultimately the entire Middle East. Soviet hegemony in this oil-rich region could promote the collapse of Western Europe.

The immediate concern was Greece. The British supported the restoration of the monarchy after World War II, but opposition came from numerous groups, including the Greek Communist Party. Fighting had broken out in

Athens in late 1944, which resulted in an uneasy truce in February 1946; but in August, Greek guerrillas raided a number of villages and towns, and soon received assistance from the Communist regimes in Yugoslavia, Albania, and Bulgaria. By the spring of 1947, the U.S. government regarded Greece as the supreme test of the free world.

Turkey was also crucial. Located along the Soviet border, it controlled the Dardanelles and was vital to the Soviets' push for a warm-water link to the Middle East. By early 1947, Soviet troops had amassed along the common border, causing a war of nerves that forced the Turkish government into military preparations.

The crisis in the Mediterranean became an American problem in February 1947, when the British government declared itself financially incapable of maintaining longstanding commitments in Greece and Turkey. Secretary of State George C. *Marshall had already instructed his undersecretary, Dean *Acheson, to prepare an economic and military assistance plan for Greece. Congressional members from both parties received invitations to the White House to join the administration in halting a Communist drive allegedly engineered by the Kremlin. Because of traditional American *isolationism, what lay ahead, President Harry S. *Truman remarked, was "the greatest selling job ever facing a President."

The result was the Truman Doctrine. Before a joint session of Congress on 12 March 1947, the president outlined the dangers in Greece and Turkey. "I believe," he emphasized, "that it must be the policy of the United States to support free peoples who are resisting attempted subjugation by armed minorities or by outside pressures." To save Greece and Turkey, he called on Congress to authorize a military and economic aid program of $400 million.

Widespread resistance arose against this policy. Marshall and State Department adviser George F. *Kennan thought the anti-Communist tone of the message too severe. Isolationist Republican senator Robert *Taft argued against assuming Britain's responsibilities, and columnist Walter Lippmann warned that the administration had not distinguished which areas were vital to U.S. interests and was heading toward a worldwide ideological crusade. Containment, Lippmann asserted, was a "strategic monstrosity." Acheson insisted that the Truman Doctrine applied specifically to Greece and Turkey, and that the administration would consider aid to other countries only on their "individual merits."

The arguments continued for weeks, but in May 1947 Congress approved the Greek-Turkish aid bills by a wide, bipartisan margin, and American aid was soon en route to both countries.

The Truman Doctrine stabilized Greece and Turkey, thereby appearing to establish the credibility of containment. Nearly 300 U.S. military and civilian personnel provided advisory assistance to the Greek Army in its war against the guerrillas. American weaponry also proved essential to the government's victory, although the growing rift between Yugoslav leader Marshal Tito (Josip Broz) and the Soviet Union played an important role. A year after his defection from the Cominform in July 1948, Tito closed the border and effectively denied the Greek guerrillas further refuge and assistance. In October 1949, the royalist army scattered them into the northern mountains of Greece and into Albania, and the fighting came to an end. The crisis in Turkey likewise passed as America's military assistance and advice bolstered the country against Soviet pressure.

Containment brought mixed results. It yielded a monumental triumph in the Near East, and hence in the Cold War. Yet the administration's rhetoric and emergency tactics encouraged a Red Scare during the 1950s, known as *McCarthyism*. More far-reaching, American policymakers later ignored the restraints implanted in the Truman Doctrine to launch the global crusade Lippmann had warned against. Indeed, containment became heavily military in orientation, as exemplified by the establishment of *NATO in 1949 and the later U.S. involvement in Vietnam.

[*See also* Cold War: External Course; Cold War: Domestic Course.]

• John L. Gaddis, *The United States and the Origins of the Cold War, 1941–1947*, 1972. Bruce R. Kuniholm, *The Origins of the Cold War in the Near East: Great Power Conflict and Diplomacy in Iran, Turkey, and Greece*, 1980. Lawrence S. Wittner, *American Intervention in Greece, 1943–1949*, 1982. Howard Jones, *"A New Kind of War": America's Global Strategy and the Truman Doctrine in Greece*, 1989. Peter J. Stavrakis, *Moscow and Greek Communism, 1944–1949*, 1989. Melvyn P. Leffler, *A Preponderance of Power: National Security, the Truman Administration, and the Cold War*, 1992. Randall B. Woods and Howard Jones, *Dawning of the Cold War: The United States' Quest for Order*, 1991.

—Howard Jones

TWINING, NATHAN F. (1897–1982), World War II general. Twining was a 1918 graduate of U.S. Military Academy and served in U.S. National Guard during *World War I. Throughout his career, from private to Chairman of the *Joint Chiefs of Staff (JCS), Twining never lost touch with his great fund of common sense or his ability to work with others. After becoming a pilot in 1924, Twining served in various postings until joining the Air Corps Staff in 1940. In January 1943 Twining became commander of the Thirteenth Air Force, in the south Pacific—a job that placed him, for practical purposes, under U.S. *Navy command. General Twining almost died when he and fourteen others spent six days in a life raft after crashing into the ocean. In January 1944, he assumed command of the Fifteenth Air Force in Italy, in a theater dominated by the British. This posting reinforced his belief in strategic bombing. After V-E Day he returned to the Pacific to take charge of the Twentieth Air Force. He ordered both atomic bomb missions. In 1950 the service promoted him to USAF Vice Chief of Staff—the person responsible for the day-to-day operations of the U.S. *Air Force (USAF). In 1953 he became USAF Chief of Staff and in 1957 President Dwight D. *Eisenhower appointed him Chairman of the JCS. Twining's views on strategic deterrence and cooperation among the armed services meshed perfectly with the administration's emphasis on collegiality and a defense strategy based on atomic weapons. Twining retired in 1960.

• Nathan F. Twining, *Neither Liberty Nor Safety*, 1966. Donald J. Mrozek, "Nathan F. Twining: New Dimensions, a New Look," in John L. Frisbee, ed., *Makers of the United States Air Force*, 1987.

—Richard G. Davis

U

ULTRA became the code word the Allies used to identify intelligence produced by decrypting enemy communications during World War II. The British Admiralty first used the term in May 1940 to enable commanders to evaluate the source of the intelligence dispatched to them. By 1945, ULTRA was in official use by American, Australian, Canadian, and British intelligence agencies and field armies and navies worldwide. ULTRA's sources were mainly decrypted German and Japanese military and naval ciphers, although some codebreaking successes were achieved against the Italian armed forces as well. In general terms, the Germans relied on numerous machine-generated ciphers, while the Japanese resorted to multiple book-based cipher systems. Success in reading one code did not translate into a wholesale breakthrough into all existing code systems. Nor did breaking one code guarantee continual solution of the system because the enemy introduced changes on a routine basis to preclude just such a possibility.

The first German code penetrated was the German *Luftwaffe* (Air Force) system. It relied for security on an ENIGMA machine to encrypt messages. The British began their uninterrupted reading of this cipher in May 1940 and used its secrets to great advantage during the Battle of Britain. Of greater importance was the breaking of the German U-boat cipher. Some penetrations were made in the system in 1940, but not until April 1943 did sustained and timely decryption of German submarine messages became possible. ULTRA's contribution to victory in the Atlantic cannot be overstated. By enabling the Allies to know where German *submarines lurked, ULTRA allowed commanders to reroute convoys around the wolf packs or to direct aircraft and warships to attack the submarines. Depriving the U-boats of their greatest advantage, stealth, ULTRA made possible the great trans-Atlantic convoys that first kept Britain in the war, then fed the buildup for the *D-Day landing, and finally nourished the Allied drive across Western Europe.

ULTRA's role in the ground war in the west was a mixed one. The Allies deciphered few German Army messages until the summer of 1942. By reading the porous *Luftwaffe* ciphers, however, they gained significant intelligence about ground dispositions. Yet it required a frustrating learning period to develop a system to distribute ULTRA where it was most needed—into the hands of the field commanders. In 1941, for instance, ULTRA revealed in precise detail the German plan to attack the Mediterranean island of Crete. Without a distribution system for the precious intelligence, London could order immediate action, but field commanders hesitated, either unsure about the reliability of the source or fearful of betraying it by acting on its revelations. The story in the seesaw *North Africa Campaign of the western desert against Erwin *Rommel's Afrika Korps between November 1941 and June 1942 was initially similar until the British deployed ULTRA intelligence analysts to field commands and institutionalized a system for distributing ULTRA to operational headquarters.

Perhaps ULTRA's greatest contribution to *victory in the west was its cumulative accretion of details about the German *order of battle. This priceless intelligence, communicated unwittingly in the Germans' own words, enabled the Allies to make accurate assessments of German strengths and weaknesses; to exploit German preconceptions; and sometimes to disrupt German plans.

In European war, ULTRA was never distributed to field commanders below army level. Each army headquarters had an assigned special liaison officer or special security officer. They received ULTRA intelligence from Bletchley Park in Buckinghamshire, northwest of London, and hand-carried it to the army commander as well as his immediate staff. A series of Anglo-American arrangements concluded in 1942 and 1943 also made ULTRA the universal code word for such intelligence and established the distribution system used in the western theater throughout the war. Furthermore, the major Allies divided the ULTRA world between themselves. The British took responsibility for ULTRA in the *China-Burma-India theater; the Americans in the Pacific; and both shared the Atlantic, Mediterranean, and European theaters.

In the Pacific, the situation was far less centralized. American, British, and Australian naval cryptanalysts worked against Imperial Japanese Navy book codes. The U.S. Army's cryptanalytic arm, the Signal Intelligence Service, attacked Japanese Army code systems and foreign ministry communications from Arlington Hall in the Washington, D.C., suburbs. German ciphers were the main British targets, but Bletchley Park and the Wireless Experimentation Center in India also played major roles in solving the Japanese Army Air Force's ciphers and air-ground codes. And a combined American, Australian, British, and Canadian organization, Central Bureau, served as Gen. Douglas *MacArthur's independent cryptanalytic agency. Since the Japanese Army and Navy used different cryptologic systems, there was little exchange of technical cryptanalytic data. ULTRA intelligence, however, was exchanged on a routine basis.

Before the Japanese attack on *Pearl Harbor, in December 1941, both the U.S. Army and Navy were devoting most of their slim cryptanalytic resources to solving Japanese diplomatic ciphers, notably the foreign ministry's PURPLE machine. The U.S. Navy, together with British cryptanalysts at Singapore, was analyzing the Japanese naval cipher and indeed had broken into the system in

September 1940. A change to the key register in 1941 prevented further exploitation of the initial success. Thus, at the time of Pearl Harbor, the Allies were not breaking any Japanese high-level military ciphers.

Because of its prewar experience, the U.S. Navy was able to solve portions of the Japanese Navy's main administrative code, JN-25, in early 1942. Intelligence gleaned from this source proved crucial to the Allies' deflection of the Japanese naval thrust against Port Moresby, Papua New Guinea, in May 1942, and decisive in the Battle of *Midway the following month. Sustained and timely reading of the naval cipher, with occasional periods of blackout, typified the next three years of the naval war in the Pacific. ULTRA uncovered numerous Japanese seaborne reinforcement schemes for eastern New Guinea and the Solomons. In March 1943, ULTRA forewarning led to the Battle of the Bismarck Sea, where the loss of sixteen ships crammed with Japanese reinforcements shifted the strategic initiative to the Allies in the southwest Pacific. ULTRA was especially valuable to the American submarine campaign in the Pacific. The Allies' ability to read the Japanese Army and Navy water transport codes enabled them to pinpoint convoy routes, times, and locations for Japanese convoys.

In the early days of the war, Central Bureau received responsibility for solving Japanese naval land-based aircraft codes and ciphers. Within nine months of its establishment in April 1942, Central Bureau cryptanalysts had solved the naval land-based air cipher; the army air force's air-ground code; and the Japanese weather cipher. This intelligence enabled Allied air commanders to marshal their forces to meet enemy raiders and later to catch Japanese aircraft on the ground.

Allied success in the great air battles over Guadalcanal, the central Solomons, and Papua, New Guinea in late 1942 and early 1943 owed much to alerts provided by ULTRA. Probably the most notable example was to shoot down the aircraft carrying Adm. Isoroku *Yamamoto after a decrypted message betrayed the admiral's itinerary. Other major success included the destruction of the Japanese air forces in eastern New Guinea, at Wewak in August 1943 and at Hollandia in March 1944.

The main Japanese Army codes, both strategic and tactical, resisted all cryptanalytic attempts to break them. Then, in January 1944, Australian troops pursuing the retreating Japanese in eastern New Guinea discovered a steel box containing the complete cryptologic library of the Japanese 20th Infantry Division. These captured codebooks enabled the Allies to read the Japanese Army's main code system until April 1944, when changes appeared. By that time, however, MacArthur had capitalized on this newly available source to put forces ashore some 200 miles behind the main Japanese units in eastern New Guinea. His surprise landings at Hollandia and Aitape in April 1944 severed Japanese forces in New Guinea, completely isolated Rabaul, and opened the route for his return to the Philippines.

In the Philippines and the Central Pacific campaigns, ULTRA enabled U.S. submarines to interdict Japanese reinforcements. Heavy losses of troops and supplies intended for Saipan, Okinawa, Luzon, Leyte, and Iwo Jima weakened those garrisons, although the Japanese still exacted a terrible toll of U.S. *casualties in those grim struggles. ULTRA's contribution to British Gen. William J. C. Slim's brilliant campaigns in India and Burma is less certain, awaiting further declassification of pertinent documents. There can be no doubt about ULTRA's prowess in the summer of 1945. By that time, the Allies could solve all major Japanese Army and Navy code systems. ULTRA uncovered the massive Japanese reinforcement of Kyushu, the next target on the Allied drive to Tokyo, thereby certainly influencing the decision to use atomic *bombs against Japan.

The release of ULTRA documents in 1977 opened the way for numerous historical reassessments of generalship and strategic decision making in World War II. Revisionists initially emphasized the spectacular intelligence coups ULTRA provided; but subsequent scholarship, by placing codebreaking triumphs in a larger context, makes more modest claims for the cryptanalytic warriors. The continuing declassification of records and firsthand published accounts is helping to fill still significant gaps about this marvelous intelligence source. Even without complete documentation, however, ULTRA surely shortened the war in east and west, enabling the Allies to win it with fewer losses than might otherwise have been the case.

[See also World War II: Military and Diplomatic Course; World War II: Changing Interpretations; World War II, U.S. Naval Operations in: The North Atlantic; World War II, U.S. Naval Operations in: The Pacific.]

• Ralph Bennett, ULTRA in the West: The Normandy Campaign of 1944–45, 1979. F. H. Hinsley, et al., British Intelligence in the Second World War: Its Influence on Strategy and Operations, 3 vol. in 4 parts, 1979–88. W. J. Holmes, Double Edged Secrets: U.S. Naval Intelligence Operations in the Pacific During World War II, 1979. Thomas Parrish, The ULTRA Americans: The U.S. Role in Breaking the Nazi Codes, 1986. David Kahn, Seizing the Enigma: The Race to Break the German U-Boat Codes, 1939–1943, 1991. Edward J. Drea, MacArthur's ULTRA: Codebreaking and the War against Japan, 1942–1945, 1992. F. H. Hinsley and Alan Stripp, eds., Codebreakers: The Inside Story of Bletchley Park, 1993.   —Edward J. Drea

UNDECLARED NAVAL WAR WITH FRANCE. See France, Undeclared Naval War with (1798–1800).

UNIFICATION OF THE ARMED SERVICES. See National Security Act.

UNIFORM CODE OF MILITARY JUSTICE. See Justice, Military: Uniform Code of Military Justice.

UNIFORMS. In the modern sense, uniforms appeared in seventeenth-century Europe with the development of professional armies; functionally, they identify members of the military, distinguish units, and help establish group cohesion. They reflect the hierarchial structure of the military, and they entice recruits to join the service.

The United States provides clothing to enlisted members of the armed forces, while officers outfit themselves. Although tradition remains central, uniforms constantly evolve: cost, efficiency, fashion, comfort, and critical materials all affect pattern and use.

Although the U.S. *Army is the oldest service, its uniforms include some of the newest. They reflect frequent changes in mission, *logistics, and public opinion. During the *Revolutionary War, blue was chosen as the primary color for the uniforms of *Continental army soldiers, in contrast to British red and Royal French white. In the eighteenth century, the American soldiers' blue coats had button-back lapels and cuffs forming contrasting facings, adapted from gentleman's attire by European armies, with artillery yellow or infantry white metal buttons and lace and crossed white shoulder belts to attach cartridge box and bayonet. The influence in the next century of *Napoleonic warfare reduced the coat with a cut-in skirt and exchanged the three-cornered or cocked hat for a cap (*shako*), on which metal branch *insignia appeared in 1832.

Sky blue trousers replaced white to avoid the winter mud, and the French full-skirt frock coat with black accoutrements added branch colors by 1851. During the *Civil War, the Union forces continued to wear blue, but the Confederate forces chose gray, the economical color of state units and West Point since 1816. From the *Union army, the blue sack-coat fatigue blouse and French forage cap emerged as postwar duty wear, with officers adding the national eagle to their caps in 1895, and moving branch insignia to their collars, along with "U.S." for the regular army.

In 1902, need for a seasonal service uniform and enhanced concealment from rapid and smokeless-rifle fire led to field uniforms of cotton khaki and wool olive drab, limiting army blue to dress uniforms only. The forage cap became the service cap, and the blouse became the pocketed service coat, worn with pegged breeches, leggings, and russet footwear.

World War I added the colorful shoulder-sleeve insignia, British-pattern steel helmet, and French pocket-size overseas or garrison cap. Britain shared the belt created and named for one-armed Gen. Sam Browne and the contrasting-shade officer uniform, "pinks and greens."

World War II G.I.s had the M-1 steel helmet and liner, cargo pocket "fatigues," parachute-jumper combat boots, and the olive drab-7 cotton M-1943 field jacket with its layering arrangement.

Beginning in 1956, Army Green-44 replaced olive drab, while seasonal khaki lasted until 1985. The 1946 Doolittle Board ended distinctive officer and enlisted uniforms, and the 1949 Uniform Board separated garrison from field uniforms. Black accessories now matched the other services, and a black trouser stripe, with gold chin strap and visor cap embroidery, identified officers. The *Cold War saw starched olive green-107 fatigues, with name tapes and US ARMY added by 1954. Tropical combat clothing with subdued insignia was adopted for the *Vietnam War. A military beret in green distinguished the Special Forces by 1961, followed by ranger black in 1975, and airborne maroon in 1980.

Navy uniforms, which vary in cut according to rank, resemble the dress of other seafarers rather than any national identity. Their dark blue and summer white reflects British influence. Traditionally similar, Coast Guard uniforms, identified by a national shield, changed to a distinctive light blue in 1973.

Naval officers dress as military commanders. Prescribed a blue coat faced red in the *Continental navy, they obtained blue with gold lace in 1802. Their service dress evolved from an 1852 jacket into the double-breasted blue coat by 1919, adding the line star to the gold cuff stripes in 1863. The cloth cap replaced the cocked hat for duty in 1841, displaying the current device by 1883 and the gold-embroidered visor in 1897. The summer white coat with shoulder marks appeared in 1901. Finally, shipboard officers had khaki working dress by 1941.

Sailors in the U.S. *Navy, except for senior petty officers,

dressed in open-neck occupational clothing. Early *slops* (wide-legged breeches) stores provided blue jackets, vests, shirts, trousers, black neckerchiefs, and canvas hats. Their frocks or jumpers had deep collars decorated with white tape by 1879. An overcoat (Dutch "pea coat") eased out the round jacket in 1885. The blue broadfall trousers gained their 13 buttons in 1902. The stitched white hat arrived in 1885, replacing the 1859 blue cloth cap ("flat hat") by 1963. World War II brought blue denim and chambray dungarees for working seamen, while the postwar bell-bottom ("cracker jack") uniform yielded to a coat and tie in 1975, only to return, by sailor demand, in 1978.

Marines are seagoing soldiers whose dress reflects both military and naval service. Nicknamed "Leathernecks" (soldier's neck stock) by open-collar sailors, the U.S. *Marine Corps is a small, proud organization that has helped maintain its identity by establishing strong uniform traditions.

Continental Marines wore green coats faced white or red; but since 1797, French-inspired blue, faced red, with yellow-metal buttons has been the custom. The current enlisted blue dress coat with slash cuff appeared in 1892, gaining pockets by 1949. Officers had the blue coat by 1909, now worn with a cloth belt, plus the 1839 sixteen-button mess jacket and 1825 Mameluke sword from the Barbary Wars.

Since 1912, the Marine Corps has worn a forest green service uniform with pointed cuffs, and cloth belt after 1943. Officers have the quatrefoil on their service caps, and all wear the bronze 1868 globe and anchor and khaki shirts with neckties. The camouflage helmet cover and USMC-monogrammed utilities appeared for World War II, while the 1944-pattern utility ("cover") cap still distinguishes a Marine.

The uniforms of the U.S. *Air Force, separated from the army in 1947, look to the future. Like the navy, their uniforms have a stronger affiliation to air forces in general than to national identity. Individual, independent, and often engaged in dangerous missions, pilots have affected rakish appearances since World War I. By 1942, the Army Air Forces permitted the "50-mission crush" for a pilot's service cap by removing its grommet, and crews decorated their leather A-2 and B-3 shearling-lined flying jackets.

In 1950, the air force selected a distinctive uniform of lighter blue (blue-84) wool, with notched lapels, bellows pockets, and silver insignia. Senior officers had silver visor ornamentation of lightning bolts, and aircraft markings formed the noncommissioned-officer blue and gray chevrons. Changes have been few, except for darker shades of blue and the elimination of bellows pockets in 1969. But in 1993, the Air Force Chief of Staff introduced a novel business suit uniform, with silver cuff stripes for officer grades.

The entry of women into the armed forces led to special uniforms that reflect common factors rather than service differences. The challenge remains to comply with male traditions and fashion while reflecting the changing roles and images of women in American society and the military.

For women in World War I, the need for street uniforms was met by the roll-collar Norfolk suit, worn with felt or straw hat. Army and navy nurses and navy female yeomen wore blue, while female Marines wore forest green uniforms. By World War II, each service chose distinctive headgear. The army nurse had a soft visor cap, and *WACs the stiff olive drab or khaki "Hobby hat" (named after the first head of the WACS). The navy nurse wore a visorless cap, while *WAVES and Coast Guard *SPARS received Mainbocher-designed sailor hats. Women Marines matched the cords of their forest green service caps with Montezuma red lipstick.

In 1947, Christian Dior's "New Look" calf-length skirt showed uniforms a need for fashion. Designer Hattie Carnegie created an army taupe-shade ensemble in 1951, and Mainbocher revised the Marine wardrobe. In 1950, the air force gave WAFS the blue-84 uniform, with a stitched flight cap, but the 1970s brought a modern double-breasted box jacket, short skirt, and felt beret. The army changed to green in 1959, adding the "pot hat" in 1963, while the Coast Guard switched to a light blue uniform designed by Edith Head.

Modern armed forces uniforms utilize synthetic materials, nonseasonal schemes, and increased informality, doffing the coat and tie for open-collar casualness. A common Department of *Defense supply system has standardized many items, such as the "wooly-pully" sweater, zipper windbreaker, shoulder marks, camouflage Battle Dress Uniform, and the female overblouse and maternity uniform.

The future looks both to "one service–one uniform" and to gender-neutral clothing. Conflicts over tradition and function will continue. But the principles of recognition will surely remain as the appropriate appearance of soldiers, sailors, flyers, and Marines continues to evolve.

[See also Awards, Decorations, and Honors; Doolittle, James; Fashion, Military Influences on; Rank and Hierarchy; Women in the Military.]

• James C. Tily, The Uniforms of the United States Navy, 1964. John R. Elting, ed. Military Uniforms in America, Vols. 1–4, 1974–88. C. G. Sweeting, Combat Flying Clothing, Army Air Forces Clothing During World War II, 1984. Donald L. Canney and Barbara Voulgaris, Uniforms of the United States Coast Guard, 1990. Jim Moran, U.S. Marine Corps Uniforms and Equipment in World War II, 1992. Shelby Stanton, U.S. Army Uniforms of the Cold War, 1948–1973, 1994.
—Walter H. Bradford

UNION ARMY. Although the United States had a regular army of 16,000 career soldiers when the Civil War began, throughout the conflict it placed chief reliance on an ad hoc force of U.S. *Volunteers, the Union army. On 15 April 1861, President Abraham Lincoln summoned 75,000 militia to serve for three months. (Oversubscribed, 91,816 were actually accepted.) Then, without legal authority, he increased the regular army by 22,714 men and called for 42,034 three-year volunteers. In July 1861, the U.S. Congress sanctioned Lincoln's extralegal acts and authorized 500,000 additional volunteers.

The Union army grew steadily throughout the war, from 186,751 in July 1861 to 1,000,516 in May 1865. By war's end, about 2 million men had served in the army, a figure that includes 179,000 African Americans and 100,000 white unionist Southerners from the Confederate states. However, at any given time as many as one-third of Union soldiers might be absent through illness, transfer, or some other cause—including desertion, which accounted for about 200,000 men absent during the course of the war.

Like its Confederate counterpart, the Union army was one of the first great military formations created by mass politics. States and localities played a critical role in its recruitment. Typically, a community leader such as a lawyer or politician with the volunteer rank of captain would encourage men to join his company, which when filled would be offered to the state governor. The governor then assigned ten companies to a numbered regiment and appointed a colonel (frequently yet another community leader) to command the regiment. At that point the new regiment would be mustered into federal service and thenceforth paid, fed, and equipped at national expense.

The system had pronounced strengths and weaknesses. On the positive side, it tended to maximize popular support, and the decentralized nature of American society made it practically the only workable system anyway. But the governors tended to see it as a vast opportunity for political patronage, which meant that as regimental numbers diminished through battle *casualties and disease, the tendency was to create new regiments rather than make good losses in existing ones. Only Wisconsin maintained an efficient system of replacements to keep veteran units up to strength.

Politics also played a significant role in the motivation of Union soldiers. Although they might have many reasons to enlist, surviving letters and diaries strongly suggest that many were politically aware and had a strong grasp of the stakes of the struggle, which most understood to be the future of self-government (a much smaller percentage were animated by antislavery views). This political commitment to the Union cause was one of the most important factors holding the army together during four bloody and often discouraging years of war.

The first wave of Union volunteers achieved significant success in early 1862. But military reversals during the summer of 1862 spurred a call for 300,000 additional three-year volunteers (which actually produced 421,000 new troops). This outpouring was assisted by the Militia Act of 17 July 1862, which empowered the president to set quotas of troops to be raised by each state, and authorized him to enforce the quota through a special militia draft if a given state failed to supply enough volunteers.

The threat of *conscription as a tactic to secure more volunteers was applied systematically in the Enrollment Act of 3 March 1863, by which all able-bodied males between twenty and forty-five became liable for military service. But under terms of the act, conscription would be applied only to communities that failed to supply their quota of volunteers. As a result, most communities adopted the practice of paying a cash bounty to men willing to enlist. By 1864, a typical recruit could pocket as much as $1,000 in local, state, and federal bounties. Unsurprisingly, this system was flamboyantly abused. Numerous "bounty jumpers" deserted their units at first opportunity and repeatedly reenlisted, each time pocketing a bounty.

The Union conscription system had three other bad features. First, although the draft law nominally permitted few exemptions, over 50 percent of Northern draftees exploited the exemption categories that did exist and thereby escaped service. Second, it was possible for a man to pay $300 (a year's wages for a worker) and avoid being drafted in any given call-up. Third, a man could also gain permanent exemption by hiring a substitute to serve in his place. Both the $300 commutation fee and the hiring of substitutes fueled bitter complaints that it was "a rich man's war and a poor man's fight." Draft riots and other significant disorders resulted, and at least thirty-eight federal provost marshals were killed trying to enforce the draft. Conscription directly accounted for only 13 percent of Union soldiers, but by the last two years of the war it undoubtedly encouraged a large number of voluntary enlistments.

The basic organization of the Union army was the regiment, theoretically composed of just under 1,000 men but usually operating at half strength or less. Four or five regiments generally made up a brigade, and two or three brigades typically comprised a division. Two or more divisions comprised a corps; several corps comprised an army. The principal Union field armies, named after major rivers in their area, were the Army of the Potomac, the Tennessee, the Cumberland, the Ohio, and the James. But these formations never contained even half the total strength available because many troops garrisoned strategic points or guarded important railroads.

Presiding over the Union army was the secretary of war. Simon Cameron initially held the post, but he resigned in January 1862 amid charges of corruption and incompetence. He was replaced by Edwin M. *Stanton, who served forcefully and effectively for the rest of the war. The top military leader was the general in chief, of whom there were four: Lt. Gen. Winfield *Scott (April–November 1861); Maj. Gen. George B. *McClellan, Jr. (November 1861–March 1862); Maj. Gen. Henry W. Halleck (July 1862–March 1864); and Lt. Gen. Ulysses S. *Grant (March 1864–May 1865). Of these, only Grant exercised sustained control over the army; the others tended to plan, propose, and advise, but not direct. President Abraham Lincoln was, of course, commander in chief.

Equipping and supplying the Union army was a formidable task that demanded high professionalism and efficiency. Fortunately, Quartermaster General Montgomery *Meigs performed ably, as did David C. McCallum, superintendent of the U.S. Military Railroads, which proved quite successful in its vital *transportation task of ferrying troops and supplies within the sprawling war zone. All in all, the Union army possessed an impressive *logistics network, and the Union soldier was so lavishly equipped and supplied that European observers, to say nothing of his *Confederate army counterpart, frequently expressed amazement.

Of the 583 Union generals, only 217 were West Point graduates, but most had previous military experience. Quite a few owed their appointments to political considerations, particularly their influence over important constituencies. Such "political generals" seldom won battlefield success, although Gen. John *Logan, an Illinois congressman who commanded a corps in William Tecumseh *Sherman's Army of the Tennessee, was an able exception. They often had substantial administrative abilities and popularity with their troops—no mean consideration in a civil war. Maj. Gen. Nathaniel P. Banks, for example, was a former Speaker of the House and an important Democrat. Although a poor combat commander, he performed a considerable service by presiding over a crucial experiment in wartime *Reconstruction in Louisiana.

Although at first the goal was primarily to capture Richmond, the Confederate capital, Union strategy eventually focused on the destruction of Confederate armies and (after 1863) the destruction of Confederate war resources, including crops and livestock. The Union army's battlefield performance varied. The Army of the Potomac proved un-able to win a decisive victory in Virginia until the closing days of the war, leading some historians to speculate that it suffered from a cultural inferiority complex. The Army of the James's record was even more dismal. But in the western theater, the Army of the Tennessee went from success to success, while the Armies of the Cumberland and the Ohio also achieved significant victories. In every case, however, success or failure owed mainly to the quality of the senior leadership. The rank and file fought with determination and élan in almost every engagement.

Officially, total Union army deaths from all causes are placed at 360,222. Of these, 110,100 were killed or mortally wounded in battle. Most of the rest died of disease. Indeed, a Union soldier stood a 1 in 13.5 chance of dying of illness as opposed to a 1 in 65 risk of being killed in action. An additional 275,175 Union troops were wounded, while some 211,411 became *prisoners of war. Proud of their efforts, Union army veterans created the Grand Army of the Republic (GAR) in 1868. By the 1880s, it was a potent force in American politics, and remained so for the rest of the century. Unlike most similar organizations, membership in the GAR was open neither to veterans of other wars nor to the veterans' own sons. Their service to the country in saving the Union, Northern veterans believed, was unique.

[See also African Americans in the Military; Civil War: Military and Diplomatic Cause; Militia Acts; New York City Antidraft Riots; Veterans: Civil War.]

• Bell Irvin Wiley, The Life of Billy Yank: The Common Soldier of the Union, 1951. Ezra Warner, Generals in Blue: Lives of the Union Commanders, 1964. Carl L. Davis, Arming the Union, 1973. Michael C. C. Adams, Our Masters the Rebels: A Speculation on Union Military Failure in the East, 1861–1865, 1978. Stephen Z. Starr, The Union Army, 1861–1865: Organization and Operations, 2 vols., 1989. James W. Geary, We Need Men: The Union Draft in the Civil War, 1991. Mark Grimsley, The Hard Hand of War: Union Military Policy Toward Southern Civilians, 1861–1865, 1995.

—Mark Grimsley

UNION NAVY. The Civil War caught the U.S. Navy unprepared. President Abraham *Lincoln proclaimed a blockade of Southern ports the week after *Fort Sumter fell; but the U.S. Navy had no more than ninety ships, about half that number in service. Commanding general of the army Winfield *Scott proposed an "Anaconda plan" to constrict the Confederacy between the army on land and a blockade by sea; however, eight ships comprised the Home Squadron, only four of them screw steamers. Other squadrons routinely assigned to protect American commerce around the globe could not be recalled for months. Thus, as states seceded, the Union could not halt the seizure of ports, ships, and naval facilities from Norfolk to New Orleans.

Union unpreparedness did not prevent a "paper blockade" of Southern ports. Official proclamations were published in Southern papers, and ships were dispatched to give due notice of the Union policy to neutrals and Confederates in the most populous of 189 harbors, rivers, and inlets along 3,500 miles of Southern coast.

An "effective blockade"—actually preventing entry and exit at Southern ports—would require 600 ships. As the Union tripled the navy's manpower with a call for 18,000 *volunteers, 21 percent of U.S. naval officers joined the fledgling *Confederate navy.

*Mobilization on that scale required new navy secretary Gideon *Welles to appoint Gustavus V. Fox assistant secretary for operations to work with the chief clerk and naval bureaus. Boards to plan blockade strategy and ironclads soon followed. Construction was authorized for 52 new ships: ironclad "turtles," monitors, and steamers; 136 vessels were acquired, including merchantmen, tugs, and ferries.

The blockade strategy evolved as four blockading squadrons: North Atlantic on the Virginia–North Carolina coast; South Atlantic from Charleston and Savannah to Key West; East Gulf from Key West to St. Andrews Bay; and the West Gulf from Pensacola past Mobile, New Orleans, and Galveston to the Rio Grande. Union commanders David *Farragut, David Dixon *Porter, and John *Dahlgren were especially successful, and within a year after the Blockade Proclamation, the Union had recaptured Norfolk, Pensacola, and New Orleans as the Anaconda plan tightened the blockade.

Union blockaders pursued blockade runners and searched out any vessels to be found in coastal and inland waters, always examining ships' papers to distinguish neutrals from Confederates. Blockade activities came to include destroying sand forts and saltworks ashore; receiving and transferring refugees, escaping slaves, and Confederate deserters; volunteering medical aid, purchasing supplies, and hiring local civilians.

This change in naval operations brought endless frustrations of operating seagoing vessels in shallow coastal waters. Pursuit of blockade runners often ran them aground, costing officers and crew the prize money awarded for captures. Mastering new steam and ironclad technologies placed complex demands on crews; added peril came from engaging new Confederate technologies, including ironclad ships, mined harbors and rivers, spar *torpedo boats, and the primitive submarine *Hunley* at Mobile and Charleston. Sheer numbers of ships and men taxed Union naval resources—all told, 600 ships and 51,000 men at full strength, though a total of 120,000 were enlisted in 1861–65, at least 20,000 of them African Americans.

For all the promise of prize money, the *blockades added increments of difficulty to a service already known for hardships and deprivation. Serving on sweltering ironclads and steamers or on marginally seaworthy vessels required increased attention to medical care, nutrition, and morale for volunteer citizen-sailors. Malaria and yellow fever were special concerns in Southern waters. Temperance replaced the time-honored daily grog ration. Boredom was an ever-present enemy.

The Union strategy combined army-navy expeditions on a large scale. The numbers engaged at Port Royal would not be matched until World War II. On the Potomac and the James Rivers, naval bombardment reinforced army field artillery. On the Mississippi, Tennessee, and Cumberland Rivers, combined army-navy operations at Forts Henry and Donelson, at Vicksburg, and elsewhere added dramatic chapters to riverine history.

A civil war in home waters in no way diminished the navy's international role. The United States ran afoul of Britain's neutral rights when Confederate officials were removed from the British vessel *Trent.* Diplomatic tensions continued into the 1870s with U.S. claims against England because British-built Confederate commerce raiders preyed upon American merchantmen and whalers. Despite those losses, the Union won one of history's most famous sea battles when the *Kearsarge* sank the *Alabama* in the English Channel.

The Union navy's response to the Civil War was heroic in its rapid mobilization and in combining a traditional blockade with innovative administration, operations, and weaponry.

[*See also* African Americans in the Military; Civil War: Military and Diplomatic Course; Fort Wagner, Siege of (1863); Hampton Roads, Battle of (1862); Mobile Bay, Battle of (1864); Navy, U.S.: 1783–1865; New Orleans, Siege of (1862); Vicksburg, Siege of (1862–63).]

• Allen A. Gosnell, *Guns on the Western Waters: The Story of River Gunboats in the Civil War,* 1949. Berne Anderson, *By Sea and by River: The Naval History of the Civil War,* 1962. Rowena Reed, *Combined Operations in the Civil War,* 1978. William M. Fowler, Jr., *Under Two Flags: The American Navy in the Civil War,* 1990. Robert M. Browning, Jr., *From Charles to Cape Fear, the North Atlantic Blockade Squadron During the Civil War,* 1993. Robert John Schneller, *A Quest for Glory: A Biography of Rear Admiral John A. Dahlgren,* 1994. Ivan Musicant, *Divided Waters, the Naval History of the Civil War,* 1995.
—Maxine T. Turner

UNIT COHESION. See Combat Effectiveness.

UNITED KINGDOM, U.S. MILITARY INVOLVEMENT IN THE. Following the U.S. entry into World War II, the United Kingdom became a springboard for Allied bombing offensives against the Axis countries as well as the assembly point for Allied invasion forces prior to the *D-Day landing (1944). A series of Anglo-American military operations, such as the *North Africa Campaign, paved the way for D-Day and the final assault on Germany in June 1944. The joint U.S.-British invasion of *Normandy (Operation Overlord) marked the largest combined operation in the history of warfare. By 11 days after D-Day, 641,170 British, Canadians, and Americans had crossed the English Channel and landed in northwest France. The United Kingdom's role as a deployment base for operations on the Continent was to continue after the war when, in Churchill's words, the United Kingdom became an unsinkable aircraft carrier for U.S. forces.

During the *Cold War, before development of the B-52 intercontinental bomber in the early 1950s, the United Kingdom was of crucial strategic importance for USAF bombers defending Western Europe. The first B-29s capable of carrying atomic munitions arrived in the summer of 1949 in East Anglia. This and the outbreak of the *Korean War in 1950 led to British demands for more formal understandings about U.S. basing. Meetings between Prime Ministers Clement Attlee and Winston S. *Churchill with President Harry S. *Truman in 1950 and 1952, respectively, resulted in the controversial understanding that the use of the bases would be a "matter for joint decision" by the two governments "in the light of the circumstances prevailing at the time." American concerns centered on whether this implied a British veto; British concerns centered on the possible use of U.S. *nuclear weapons without consultation.

Throughout the 1950s, the number of air bases grew. Strategic Air Command (SAC) operations in Britain were overseen by the Seventh Air Division (headquarters in Omaha, Nebraska), while the Third Air Force (headquarters at RAF Mildenhall) assumed responsibility for all tactical and logistical activities. The number of U.S. military personnel grew to around 30,000 deployed on 9 major bases and 30 smaller locations.

The growing importance of *missiles was stressed in

1957, when intermediate-range ballistic missiles were introduced into Britain, as well as into Italy and Turkey, to balance a perceived Soviet advantage in the number of intercontinental ballistic missiles. Special emphasis was placed on low-level penetration of *Warsaw Pact nations' air defenses, a role assumed by the Third Air Force and the F-111 aircraft based in Oxfordshire and East Anglia. The advent of longer-range missiles also raised concerns about the vulnerability of air bases and heavy *bomber aircraft, which led to the deactivation of the Seventh Air Division in 1965.

The U.S. *Navy assumed a significant role in 1960 in an agreement between President John F. *Kennedy and Prime Minister Harold Macmillan to use Holy Loch in Scotland for deployment of nuclear-armed Polaris (later Trident) *submarines. In spite of the cutback in SAC operations, the number of U.S. military personnel remained constant, due to the naval presence and the influx of U.S. military personnel from France in 1967 following withdrawal of French forces from *NATO.

Public opposition to the U.S. military presence in the United Kingdom was primarily antinuclear (with the British Campaign for Nuclear Disarmament taking a leading role), notably against the Thor missiles, Polaris and Trident submarines, and the deployment of ground-launched Pershing cruise missiles following the 1979 North Atlantic Council decision. The use of U.S. bases in East Anglia for the 1986 air strike against Libya also prompted public opposition, although the raid had the full support of Margaret Thatcher's government.

The end of the Cold War and the dissolution of the Warsaw Pact saw a reduction in the number of American service personnel in the United Kingdom. By mid-1995, there were 18 U.S. bases or facilities in the United Kingdom and nearly 14,000 active duty personnel, 2,384 civilian personnel, and 10,281 dependents.

[See also France, Liberation of; Germany, Battle for; Middle East, U.S. Military Involvement in the; World War II: Military and Diplomatic Course.]

• Duncan Campbell, The Unsinkable Aircraft Carrier, 1984. Robert Jackson, Strike Force: The USAF in Britain Since 1948, 1986. Simon Duke, U.S. Defence Bases in the United Kingdom, 1987. Simon Duke and Wolfgang Krieger, eds., U.S. Military Forces in Europe: The Early Years, 1945–60, 1993. David Reynolds, Rich Relations: The American Occupation of Britain, 1942–5, 1995.   —Simon Duke

UNITED NATIONS (est. 1945). President Franklin D. *Roosevelt foresaw the need for "Four Policemen"—the United States, the Soviet Union, Britain, and China (France was added later)—to order the post–World War II world and repel all attempts at *aggression and violence. Meeting in San Francisco in 1945, the founders of the *United Nations tried to fulfill that vision by creating a Security Council with five permanent members charged with saving "succeeding generations from the scourge of war."

The UN Charter set up a military staff committee—consisting of the chiefs of staff or their representatives from the five permanent members—to take over the strategic direction of any military operation of the Security Council. Although this committee has met regularly for more than a half century, it has never directed any UN military operation. During the *Cold War, the United States and the Soviet Union could never agree sufficiently on military issues to share a joint command. Even after the Cold War, this kind of cooperation proved impractical. Yet, despite an inert military staff committee, the United Nations has been heavily involved in military action.

In one instance, the North Korean invasion of South Korea in June 1950, the Security Council did act like a team of Roosevelt-inspired policemen. The Council condemned North Korean aggression, called on the world to aid South Korea, and authorized a UN command under U.S. Gen. Douglas A. *MacArthur. But the United Nations managed to do all this only because the Soviet Union was boycotting sessions of the Security Council to protest the denial of a Council seat to Communist China. Although fifteen other countries dispatched troops or air support to Korea under a UN flag, the Americans commanded and dominated the UN force and fought the three-year *Korean War as if it were their own.

Aside from the accident of the Soviet boycott during the initial Korean crisis, the United Nations had no significant role in dealing with the Cold War. During the *Cuban Missile Crisis of 1962, for example, the United Nations served as no more than a theater as U.S. ambassador Adlai Stevenson displayed photographic evidence of the Soviet Union installing missiles and launchers in Cuba. And Secretary General U Thant earned only contempt from President Lyndon B. *Johnson during the late 1960s for trying to mediate an end to the *Vietnam War.

The United Nations dealt instead with crises on the periphery of the Cold War. A major innovation in UN work arose from the Suez Canal crisis of 1956. Looking for a way to ease the British, French, and Israeli troops out of Egypt after their ill-fated intervention, Dag Hammarskjold, the urbane Swedish bureaucrat who headed the United Nations as secretary general, persuaded all sides to accept UN troops in their place. That had never been done before. In a remarkable feat of management and energy, Hammarskjold and his chief aide, the African American Nobel Peace Prize laureate Ralph Bunche, put together in one week the United Nations' first *peacekeeping force—6,000 troops from 9 countries. The United States offered surplus helmets, which were quickly painted blue and passed to the troops, the first "Blue Helmets," as UN peacekeepers would come to be known.

In 1960, the United Nations dispatched Blue Helmets to the former Belgian Congo (now the Democratic Republic of the Congo) to restore law and order out of bloody chaos and replace the Belgian troops, who no longer had any place in an independent African country. Hammarskjold, who would die in a plane crash while on a Congo mission, interpreted Security Council resolutions as broadly as possible and directed his troops to put down the secession of Katanga. The suppression was so controversial and bloody, however, that UN peacekeepers would not engage in military offensives for another thirty years. Quiet patrolling of cease-fire lines in trouble spots like Cyprus (between Greek and Turkish Cypriots), the Sinai (between Egyptians and Israelis), and the Golan Heights (between Syrians and Israelis) would become the hallmark of UN peacekeepers, earning them the Nobel Peace Prize in 1988.

The character of UN peacekeeping was transformed by the collapse of the Berlin Wall in 1989 and the end of the Cold War. Euphoria over the *Persian Gulf War of 1991 contributed to the change. Although this war was not officially declared a UN war as the Korean War had been, the

Security Council played a key role with resolutions authorizing the United States and its Coalition partners to drive Iraq out of Kuwait. The war persuaded UN diplomats and bureaucrats that the Security Council, as long as the United States and Russia agreed, could now literally attempt anything. Some analysts felt that Franklin Roosevelt's dream would be realized at last.

The United Nations found itself dealing with a host of crises in different ways: monitoring human rights violations, supervising elections, creating democratic institutions, feeding the hungry, as well as policing the peace in such flashpoints as El Salvador, Cambodia, Angola, Haiti, and Rwanda. But its new confidence was swiftly shattered by ill-fated missions to Somalia and Bosnia.

When eighteen U.S. Army Rangers died in Mogadishu in October 1993 during their abortive manhunt for a Somali warlord, President Bill *Clinton decided to withdraw all U.S. troops, crippling the mission. Although the fallen rangers had operated outside UN command, aides of Clinton unjustly put the blame on Secretary General Boutros Boutros-Ghali, despoiling the image of the United Nations in American eyes. That image worsened in the *Bosnian crisis (1992–95). The United Nations proved incapable of halting Serb aggression and protecting Muslim civilian populations from massacre in towns that had been designated "safe areas" by the Security Council. This impotence stemmed from the failure of the United States and its European allies to agree on a strategy for dealing with Serb aggression. UN peacekeepers found themselves patrolling Bosnia under the authority of scores of contradictory toothless resolutions from the Security Council. When the United States brokered a peace agreement at Dayton, Ohio, in 1995, NATO troops supplanted the UN peacekeepers and enforced the agreement.

The animosity toward the United Nations so intensified in the United States that Congress refused to pay all the assessments that Washington owed, precipitating a financial crisis. UN diplomats and officials commemorated the fiftieth anniversary in October 1995 in a depressed mood, convinced that the United Nations no longer would have the funds or public support to mount many peacekeeping missions.

[See also Berlin Crises; Internationalism; Somalia, U.S. Military Involvement in.]

• Brian Urquhart, Hammarskjold, 1972. John Bartlow Martin, Adlai Stevenson and the World, 1977. Robert J. Donovan, Tumultuous Years: The Presidency of Harry S Truman, 1982. Brian Urquhart, A Life in Peace and War, 1991. Brian Urquhart, Ralph Bunche: An American Life, 1993. Stanley Meisler, United Nations: The First Fifty Years, 1995.   —Stanley Meisler

UPTON, EMORY (1838–1881), *Civil War general, military educator and reformer. Emory Upton, born in Batavia, New York, graduated eighth in the U.S. Military Academy's Class of May 1861. In four years, during the Civil War, he rose from second lieutenant to brevet (temporary) major general. First commanding a Regular Army artillery battery and later serving as divisional chief of artillery, he became colonel of the 121st New York Infantry in October 1862. Upton won special distinction at Spotsylvania on 10 May 1864 when his twelve-regiment assaulting column successfully pierced the Confederate salient, the deployment offering an alternative to traditional and costly linear tactics; he won promotion to brigadier general two days later. After recovering from a wound suffered in September 1864, Upton actively led a cavalry division at war's end.

After the war, Upton became an articulate advocate of military efficiency and effectiveness. He drew upon his own broad experience to begin substantial revisions of the army's infantry, cavalry, and *artillery tactics, an ambitious and contentious effort he continued to supervise while commandant of cadets at West Point (1870–75). The protégé of Gen. William Tecumseh *Sherman, he went on a multinational tour of military establishments and published his observations in The Armies of Asia and Europe (1878), in part to suggest ways in which organizational and personnel reforms might create a more professional U.S. army.

As superintendent of the Artillery School at Fort Monroe (1877–80), Upton introduced combined arms training and theory-based case studies to add intellectual rigor to its limited practical curriculum. His institution became the model for advanced officer education throughout the army. Years after Upton committed suicide in March 1881 (the reasons for which remain uncertain) the reformist secretary of war Elihu *Root published Upton's most enduring work, The Military Policy of the United States (1904), a treatise that challenged contemporary notions of the "minuteman tradition," arguing instead for a professional army, headed by a General Staff, to be the proper foundation for national defense.

[See also Academies, Service; Army Combat Branches; Militia and National Guard.]

• Peter S. Michie, The Life and Letters of Emory Upton, 1885. Stephen E. Ambrose, Upton and the Army, 1964.
                    —Carol Reardon

USO—the United Service Organizations—is a civilian, voluntary, nonprofit organization serving the morale needs of U.S. military personnel and their families worldwide. Although congressionally chartered, it is not a government agency and is supported by individual and corporate donations, United Way, and Combined Federal Campaign. USO was created on 4 February 1941 by President Franklin D. *Roosevelt, who determined that private organizations should handle the on-leave recreation of the rapidly growing U.S. military. Six civilian agencies—the Salvation Army, Young Men's Christian Association (YMCA), Young Women's Christian Association (YWCA), National Catholic Community Services, National Travelers Aid Association, and National Jewish Welfare Board—coordinated their civilian war efforts to form the USO.

During World War II, USO became the G.I.'s "home away from home," and began a tradition of entertaining the troops that continues today. Comedian Bob Hope presented his first USO tour in 1942, a practice he continued into the 1990s. USO regrouped in 1950 for the *Korean War, after which it was recommended that USO also provide peacetime services. During the *Vietnam War, USOs were located in combat zones.

USO began a new era of social services in the 1970s and 1980s. A 1987 Memorandum of Understanding between USO and the Department of *Defense named USO as the principal channel representing civilian concern for American forces worldwide. In the 1990s USO delivered services to 5 million active duty service members and their families. Through 125 airport, fleet, family and community centers, mobile canteens, and celebrity entertainment, USO continues to be a touch of home to America's troops.

• Frank Coffey, *Always Home: 50 Years of the USO,* 1991.

—Jennifer L. Blanck

U-2 INCIDENT (1960). On 1 May 1960, a U.S. spy plane—a U-2—departed from Peshawar, Pakistan, on a reconnaissance mission over the Soviet Union. It never arrived at its destination—Bodo, Norway. On 6 May, Soviet premier Nikita Khrushchev announced that the aircraft had been shot down by a surface-to-air missile deep inside Soviet territory. Washington countered by saying that the aircraft was on a weather research mission when it strayed off course after the pilot's oxygen system failed. Khrushchev then revealed that the U-2's film magazines had been recovered and that the pilot, Francis Gary Powers, was alive and in Soviet custody.

The incident created a sensation and threatened to scuttle the Soviet-American summit conference scheduled to convene in Paris on 16 May. In a controversial move, President Dwight D. *Eisenhower accepted responsibility for the flights rather than let the world believe that lower-level functionaries had such authority. He also promised an end to the missions, but refused to apologize. The overflights, he asserted, had been necessary to safeguard American security. An angry Khrushchev refused to attend the summit conference.

The summit's cancellation was both a public humiliation and a personal blow to Eisenhower. He had hoped to make what would have been his final summit meeting a fitting capstone to his presidency by reaching agreement on a number of critical issues. The president even spoke of resigning, but soon changed his mind.

Powers was convicted of espionage by a Soviet court and sentenced to ten years' "deprivation of liberty," the first three to be served in prison. He served less than two years before being exchanged in January 1962 for a Soviet agent in Western custody. He died in a helicopter crash in 1977.

[*See also* Cold War: External Course; Cold War: Domestic Course; Intelligence, Military and Political; U-2 Spy Planes.]

• Michael R. Beschloss, *Mayday: Eisenhower, Khrushchev, and the U-2 Affair,* 1986.

—Vance O. Mitchell

U-2 SPY PLANES. To avert a surprise nuclear attack, some American intelligence analysts immediately after World War II believed that "pre-hostilities reconnaissance" over potential enemy territory would be prudent. But since the Soviet Union, the only nation capable of threatening the United States, had few long-range *bomber aircraft and no *nuclear weapons, American reconnaissance aircraft were ordered to respect Soviet air space.

The deepening *Cold War and Moscow's growing inventory of nuclear weapons changed attitudes in the early 1950s. In 1954, Lockheed Aircraft Corporation began work on an aircraft that could fly above Soviet air defenses. Modifying an F-104 interceptor fuselage and giving it a wingspan of almost 100 feet, Lockheed first tested the U-2 aircraft in August 1955. Essentially a powered glider, the U-2 could climb over 70,000 feet and had a range of 3,000 miles. The *Central Intelligence Agency exercised operational management, but overflights of Soviet air space needed presidential approval. In all, the U-2 flew twenty-four missions over the Soviet Union.

In June 1956, American U-2s began periodic flights over the Sino-Soviet bloc, carrying cameras as their main sensors, supplemented by communications and electronic intercept equipment. The Royal Air Force also flew overflight missions under the authority of the British prime minister.

The overflights ended in May 1960 after the Soviets shot down a U-2, but the U-2's service continued. Several planes were given to the Nationalist Chinese for missions over the People's Republic of China. In October 1962, a U-2 discovered Soviet offensive missiles in Cuba, precipitating the *Cuban Missile Crisis. U-2s flew missions during the *Vietnam War, collected radioactive debris from other nations' nuclear tests, monitored the cease-fire that ended the 1973 Yom Kippur War, and served in the *Persian Gulf War. They will fly well into the next century.

[*See also* Intelligence, Military and Political; Satellites, Reconnaissance; U-2 Incident (1960).]

• Chris Pocock, *Dragon Lady: The History of the U-2 Spyplane,* 1989.

—Vance O. Mitchell

V

VALLANDIGHAM, CLEMENT L. (1820–1871), Democratic congressman, leading critic of the Lincoln administration during the *Civil War. A lawyer and editor active in Democratic party politics from the 1840s, Vallandigham entered Congress in 1858. During the Civil War, he stridently opposed slave emancipation, the growth of central government power, and a harsh war policy against the South, demanding instead a negotiated peace to save the Constitution from Republican depredations. His opponents claimed that he was so militantly antiwar that he espoused *treason. He came under military surveillance and was arrested by Gen. Ambrose *Burnside after a speech in 1863 whose General Order No. 38 forbade any "habit of declaring sympathies for the enemy" in Ohio. He was tried and convicted by a military commission, not a civil court, and sentenced to prison.

President Abraham *Lincoln, sensitive to the potential political damage of a civil liberties martyr, ordered him deported to Confederate territory. Vallandigham went on to Canada, from where he ran for governor of Ohio in 1863; he was soundly beaten. In 1864, his continued peace advocacy cost the Democrats dearly. Whatever their commitment to constitutional liberties, Northern voters were hostile to the Democrats' apparent support for the nation's enemies. The issues of free expression and opposition to wartime policies, even the war itself, raised by Vallandigham's experiences were to reappear in America's later wars and have never been comfortably settled to everyone's satisfaction.

[*See also* Black Hawk War.]

• Frank L. Klement, *The Limits of Dissent: Clement L. Vallandigham and the Civil War,* 1970. Joel H. Silbey, *"A Respectable Minority": The Democratic Party in the Civil War,* 1977. Mark E. Neely, Jr., *The Fate of Liberty: Abraham Lincoln and Civil Liberties,* 1991.

—Joel H. Silbey

VALLEY FORGE NATIONAL PARK. Although the 1777–78 winter encampment at Valley Forge is a familiar metaphor for the sufferings of the *Continental army during the Revolutionary War and a part of the nation's folklore, other winter ordeals were probably worse. Valley Forge's reputation for misery arose because Gen. George *Washington, hoping for greater support, stressed the Continentals' sufferings there in his correspondence with Congress. However, during that same winter, the army made significant progress in discipline under Friedrick Wilhelm von *Steuben's tutelage, and Nathanael *Greene greatly improved its *logistics system. In this sense, the encampment marked a turning point for the army; more broadly, its popular importance remains symbolic of endurance in adversity.

Pennsylvania created the Valley Forge State Park on 30 May 1893. It remained a state institution until the mid-1970s, when individuals and citizens' groups, fearing deterioration, urged its transfer to the U.S. Park Service. This was accomplished when President Gerald *Ford signed the legislation creating Valley Forge National Historical Park on 4 July 1976, emphasizing the site's mythic character by making it a focus for bicentennial observances. With the new focus on social history, Park Service interpreters now treat the site less as a shrine to democracy than as a venue for describing the daily life of Revolutionary-era soldiers to the approximately 4 million people who visit the park annually.

[*See also* Revolutionary War: Military and Diplomatic Course.]

• Lorett Treese, *Valley Forge: Making and Remaking a National Symbol,* 1995.
—Thomas A. Thomas

VANDENBERG, HOYT (1899–1954), air force general. A 1923 graduate of West Point, Vandenberg was handsome, affable, and the nephew of a senator. He began his career in ground support aviation. In the mid-1930s, he attended professional schools, including the Command and General Staff School at Leavenworth, where he met Carl A. *Spaatz, a senior air officer. In 1939, Spaatz assigned Vandenberg to the Plans Section, the key office in Air Corps expansion. Vandenberg spent eight months in headquarters, in 1942, before becoming chief of staff, Twelfth Air Force, in August. He served in North Africa and the Mediterranean until summoned to Washington. In November 1943, in Moscow, he negotiated to obtain Soviet bases for shuttle flights for American *bomber aircraft. As a result of Dwight D. *Eisenhower's appeal, Vandenberg received the post of deputy commander of the Allied Expeditionary Air Force in March 1944. This position required tact and a personality forceful enough to defend U.S. interests. Vandenberg succeeded, and in August 1944 he took command of the Ninth Air Force, the world's most powerful tactical air force. The Ninth supported Bradley's Twelfth Army Group, through the Battle of the *Bulge and victory in the battle for *Germany.

In 1946, Vandenberg became the assistant chief of staff, Intelligence, and then director, Central Intelligence Group, the *Central Intelligence Agency's predecessor. He worked aggressively to improve intelligence collection and the CIA's status. In October 1947, during the *Cold War, he became the first vice chief of staff, U.S. Air Force. After General Spaatz's brief tenure, Vandenberg was appointed USAF's second chief of staff in April 1948, a position he occupied until retirement, June 1953. He proved an able officer for the rapid expansion of the air force. His relationships with important army officers eased negotiations within the *Joint Chiefs of Staff, while his knowledge of personnel enabled him to make key appointments, such as Curtis E. *LeMay to the Strategic Air Command. Vandenberg maintained excellent relations with Congress in a time of first budget cuts and interservice squabbles and then military buildup. He also led the independent service through the *Korean War. He died prematurely, of cancer, at age fifty-five.

[See also Air Force, U.S.: Predecessors of, 1907–46; Air Force, U.S.: Since 1947; World War II, U.S. Air Operations in.]

• Philip Meilinger, *Hoyt S. Vandenberg: The Life of a General*, 1989.
—Richard G. Davis

VENEREAL DISEASES. See Diseases, Sexually Transmitted.

VERSAILLES, TREATY OF (1919). The Treaty of Versailles ended World War I between Germany and the Allied nations. On 6 October 1918, Prince Max von Baden, the Reich Chancellor, appealed to President Woodrow *Wilson to take steps leading to an armistice based on Wilson's *Fourteen Points. The Allies had never endorsed this progressive peace program; they acceded to most of it, however, because in the armistice negotiations Wilson had managed the confiscation or internment of virtually all Germany's machines of war.

At the Paris Peace Conference, the president's priority was the inclusion of the Covenant of the *League of Nations as an integral part of the treaty. Despite grave reservations, the British, French, and Italian leaders bowed to the massive public support Wilson's proposal enjoyed throughout Europe. But the peacemakers used their acceptance as a lever to gain concessions from him on other vital issues. For example, Australia, New Zealand, and South Africa coveted the captured colonies of (respectively) New Guinea, Samoa, and German Southwest Africa. These claims defied the idea of "mandates," the League's arrangement for guiding incipient states along the path to self-government. In this, as in other quarrels, Wilson found himself in a minority of one. The territories were designated as mandatories but were ultimately assigned on the basis of military occupation.

At another juncture, Georges Clemenceau, implying that he might withdraw his endorsement of the League, demanded for France the coal-rich Saar basin and military occupation of the Rhineland. Vittorio Orlando claimed for Italy the Yugoslav port city of Fiume and left when Wilson refused to indulge him. Japan, too, threatened to bolt as it insisted on retaining economic control over Shantung. Wilson was able to moderate some of these demands, albeit in less than satisfactory compromises. From Japan, he wrung a pledge (honored in 1922) to restore Chinese sovereignty in Shantung through mediation by the League. In the case of France, he and Clemenceau settled on a fifteen-year occupation of the Rhineland. The crisis over Fiume, alas, was never resolved at Paris.

The acrimony came to a head when British prime minister David Lloyd George added military pensions to the already astronomical reparations bill that France had presented against Germany. On the verge of physical collapse, Wilson at last capitulated. Then came Article 231—a dec-

laration saddling Germany with the moral responsibility for allegedly having started the war. The reparations section and the "war-guilt" clause would spark unending controversy. In all of this, Wilson anticipated that, once wartime passions had cooled, the League could redress the injustices.

Because he had so many difficulties in keeping faith with the spirit of the Fourteen Points, and because (largely for other reasons) the Senate refused to ratify the Treaty of Versailles, Wilson, in his own time and in history, would bear the main burden for its shortcomings. Yet many scholars today contend that the territorial provisions were not nearly as bad as disillusioned contemporaries and revisionist historians believed them to be; and that, without the president's intermittent heroic exertions, some of the settlement's 440 conditions would have been far more severe. Nevertheless, this remains the most controversial peace treaty of the twentieth century.

[See also World War I.]

• Thomas A. Bailey, *Woodrow Wilson and the Lost Peace*, 1944. Arno J. Mayer, *Politics and Diplomacy of the Peacemaking: Containment and Counterrevolution at Versailles, 1918–1919*, 1967. Arthur Walworth, *Wilson and His Peacemakers*, 1986. Manfred F. Boemeke, Gerald D. Feldman, and Elizabeth Glaser, eds., *The Treaty of Versailles: A Reassessment after 75 Years*, 1998.

—Thomas J. Knock

VERTICAL TAKEOFF AND LANDING AIRCRAFT (known as VTOL aircraft) debuted in the *Korean War primarily in the medevac role. The venerable piston-powered Bell 47 (H-13) helicopter provided the U.S. *Army with an unprecedented ability to rapidly evacuate wounded personnel for lifesaving treatment. VTOL technology was first used in a significant combat role by U.S. forces during the *Vietnam War. This was made possible by the advent of a practical turbine engine, providing excellent horsepower-to-weight ratios, coupled with advances in lightweight aluminum honeycomb construction techniques and epoxies that made strong, lightweight airframes possible, and rotor systems vastly improved over the older wooden blades. These technologies culminated in the Bell UH-1 (Huey), OH-58 (Kiowa), and AH-1 (Cobra), the Boeing Vertol CH-47 (Chinook), the Sikorsky CH-54 (SkyCrane), and the Hughes OH-6 (Cayuse). The civilian helicopter fleet during and after the Vietnam War was an outgrowth of the technology pioneered by the military, in which many aircraft were nearly indistinguishable from their military cousins.

One unique VTOL aircraft is the USMC single-pilot Harrier ground attack/fighter aircraft. Developed by British Aerospace in the 1960s, the Harrier flies in the vertical flight mode solely by vectored thrust from a single engine, allowing overflight with transition to forward jet flight at the flick of a wrist. While rather fuel-inefficient and very noisy, the Harrier stands alone as the only operational VTOL jet worldwide.

VTOL aircraft have revolutionized combat for the ground forces over the last fifty years, and the technology developed has found numerous uses in the civilian world. Improvements in VTOL technology, such as the U.S. Navy/Marine V-22 "Osprey" tilt-rotor aircraft, may someday make VTOL aircraft the rule and eliminate the need for runways in either military or civilian aviation.

[See also Helicopters.]
—Mark Cannon

VESSEY, JOHN (1922–), army general and chairman of the *Joint Chiefs of Staff (JCS). Vessey hailed from Minnesota. After high school, he enlisted in the National Guard and was called to active duty in 1941. He served as an artillery sergeant in the *North Africa Campaign and received a battlefield commission at the Battle of *Anzio in 1944. After the war he remained in the army, rising to deputy chief of staff, operations and plans, and commander of the Eighth Army during the *Korean War. Vessey was army vice chief of staff when President Ronald *Reagan named him tenth chairman of the JCS in 1982. He saw no need for the major changes in the joint system proposed by his predecessor, Gen. David *Jones. Instead, he moved to improve the system within the existing framework. Plainspoken and with a ready wit, he often induced his JCS colleagues to rise above service positions on controversial issues. To improve advice to the president, Vessey arranged quarterly meetings for the chiefs with the president and brought the major operational commanders into the budget and strategic planning process. Nevertheless, U.S. intervention in *Grenada and the terrorist bombing of the U.S. Marine barracks in Lebanon (both in 1983) raised criticisms about poor service cooperation and a cumbersome chain of command, which helped to bring about passage of the *Goldwater-Nichols Act in 1986, a year after Vessey's retirement.

[*See also* Lebanon, U.S. Military Involvement in; World War II: Military and Diplomatic Course.]

• JCS Biography, *General John W. Vessey, Jr.,* Willard J. Webb and Ronald H. Cole, *The Chairmen of the Joint Chiefs of Staff,* 1989.
—Willard J. Webb

VETERANS

Overview
Revolutionary War
Civil War
World War I
World War II
Korean War
Vietnam War

VETERANS: OVERVIEW

Two major changes have taken place in the relation of the American veteran to civilian society, especially since 1865: the growth of veterans' groups as nationalist lobbies, and the rapid expansion of a military pension system that some scholars see as the template for the twentieth-century American welfare state. Even before the *Revolutionary War ended, however, questions of veteran/civilian relations had arisen. In 1776, the Continental Congress pensioned veterans disabled in war, but beyond this step (which had long colonial and English precedents) there was sharp disagreement. Some representatives embraced the ideal of the civilian volunteer, and argued that the service pensions Congress had promised in 1778 represented an entering wedge for standing armies. Such worries were heightened when officers of Washington's army encamped at Newburgh, New York, demanded pensions or a cash equivalent as the price of their disbandment in 1783, and formed a hereditary order, the Society of the *Cincinnati. Among enlisted personnel, indigent veterans would finally be pensioned in 1818, but full service pensions did not arrive until 1832. Thus, from its inception, the U.S. military

pension system drew distinctions between three classes of the deserving: war invalids; indigent "dependents"; and soldiers whose only claim to benefits was their service.

As a result of the Newburgh remonstrances, Congress, in the Commutation Act of 1783, provided officers with five years' full pay in lieu of half-pay pensions for life. Because the federal government continued in default until 1791, however, many officers sold their commutation certificates for as little as 12 1/2 cents on the dollar, a fate that also befell many enlisted veteran holders of Continental land warrants. Under acts of 1776 and 1780, Congress had promised the veterans large tracts of the public domain, mostly in the Northwest and Southwest territories; land-rich states such as Virginia and New York made additional grants. But conflicting state land claims, wars with Indian nations, and land sales restrictions made land warrants of small value to most veterans until the late 1790s, by which time most had sold their warrants to speculators. Eventually, title to 2,666,080 acres of public lands was issued on the basis of Revolutionary claims.

Revolutionary War veterans never organized for mass politics and had little public visibility in the early republic. Many of the estimated 232,000 men who served had been militiamen, whose irregular, seasonal war service produced scant national consciousness (it also excluded them from pension benefits, much to the disgust of those who saw volunteer militias as bulwarks of liberty). Even Continental regulars often had little contact with soldiers from states other than their own, and consequently Revolutionary veterans' organizations were limited in scope. The Society of the *Cincinnati declined to only six state chapters, all in the Northeast, by 1832; the Society of St. Tammany, founded by New York City veterans in 1789, quickly evolved into a Democratic political club.

The wars of the early nineteenth century likewise produced few veterans' groups, in part because they produced few veterans: 28,186 were demobilized from the *War of 1812, 139,036 from the *Mexican War. A tiny Society of the War of 1812 led a fitful existence from 1853 into the 1890s, when it became a hereditary order; the National Association of *Mexican War Veterans was not formed until 1874, and lasted barely into the twentieth century. Veterans of both wars benefited immediately from federal land grants and invalid pensions, but dependent and service pensions came only as part of the tremendous pension rush following the *Civil War—to War of 1812 veterans in 1871 and to Mexican War veterans in 1887 (dependent) and 1907 (service). Because most Mexican War volunteers had been southerners, there was great resistance to pensioning them in the post–Civil War era, and the law of 1887 excluded those whose wounds had been sustained in Confederate service or who were politically disbarred by the Fourteenth Amendment.

The Civil War revolutionized the relationship of veteran to society. The number of troops involved was unprecedented: at least 2 million men fought for the Union, some 750,000 for the Confederacy. More important, veterans of the *Union army in 1866 created a powerful mass organization, the *Grand Army of the Republic (GAR), to lobby for their interests and promote loyalty to the nation-state. Nearly every Northern town had a GAR post, and with more than 400,000 members by 1890, the GAR was a voting machine for the Republican Party. Politicians of both parties vied for the veterans' favor with generous pension legislation, especially the Arrears Act (1879) and Dependent Pension Act (1890), the latter granting a virtual service pension to Union veterans at a time when many were still in their fifties. By 1891, military pensions accounted for one dollar of every three spent by the federal government, and at the peak in 1902, 999,446 persons (including widows and dependents) were on the pension rolls. By 1917, the nation had spent approximately $5 billion on Civil War pensions. Reformers attacked the frauds that riddled this system.

Beyond pensions, Civil War veterans occupied the center of a postwar culture that in each region venerated its ex-soldiers. In the North, cities erected expensive monuments; Gettysburg was preserved as a historical park; and Grand Army men lectured schoolchildren on patriotic holidays, including Memorial Day, first proclaimed by GAR commander in chief John Logan in 1868 to honor the Union dead. By 1888, twelve northern states and the federal government had erected soldiers' homes. Union veterans won land grants, special treatment under the Homestead Act, and preference in hiring—by law in some states, de facto in federal agencies such as the Pension Bureau. The most important aspect of Union veteran culture, however, was its intensely conservative *nationalism, visible in the GAR's crusades against anarchy, flag desecration, and "impure" school textbooks in the 1890s. Veterans of the Union army were the first to assert a privileged relation to the national state.

In the South, Confederate veterans organized late, at least partly in reaction to the GAR. Barred from federal entitlements, they obtained pensions and soldiers' homes from most southern states, though such benefits usually were quite modest. (Georgia's Confederate disability pensions, for example, averaged 14% of the federal rate.) The United Confederate Veterans (1889) presided over a veteran culture that shifted ground from intransigence in the 1870s to a romantic "Lost Cause" sensibility in the 1890s that even Union veterans could accept with some reservations.

The legacy of Civil War veterans was immense. First, the Civil War pension system provided the United States's first significant encounter with entitlement spending. When other groups—mothers, workers, the unemployed—sought state aid after 1900, their claims were evaluated in light of the partisanship, nationalistic rhetoric, and fraud that had characterized the Civil War system. Second, the GAR provided an organizational model and political agenda that twentieth-century veterans' groups copied. Founded after World War I, the *American Legion adopted the GAR's internal structure and consulted with aging GAR members on political strategy. All veterans' organizations until the *Vietnam War continued the GAR program of flag ritualism, "patriotic instruction," and unqualified nationalism.

The Spanish-American War produced only two significant organizations: the United Spanish War Veterans (1904), which soon faded, and the *Veterans of Foreign Wars (VFW), founded in 1913. Unlike the GAR and United Confederate Veterans, the VFW admitted all overseas veterans, not just those from one war, a policy that has allowed it to persevere to the present. On the other hand, the VFW policy of limiting membership to overseas veterans initially hampered the organization in competition with the more inclusive American Legion.

The approximately 4 million veterans of World War I returned to a situation markedly different from that following the Civil War. High unemployment marked both periods, but the soldiers of 1865 came back mostly to farms, while those of 1919 returned primarily to cities, where joblessness was acute and vocational training scarce. Rural land grants proposed by Interior Secretary Franklin Lane in 1919 proved impracticable in any case, since most arable public land had already been given away. Meanwhile, labor and political strife were rampant—revolution in Russia, chaos in Germany, a general strike in Seattle, a race riot in Chicago, and indices of class and racial turmoil elsewhere in the United States.

Under such circumstances, the American Legion (founded at Paris in 1919) came out immediately against "Bolshevism" and other radicalism, which it defined broadly to include everyone from the Communist Party to the League of Women Voters. Legion members helped break strikes of Kansas coal miners and Boston police in the summer of 1919, and from the 1920s through the 1950s made a war on "reds" one of their main activities. Legionnaires helped bring a House Un-American Activities Committee into existence in 1938 and aided FBI probes of subversion thereafter. The interwar Legion was strongest in smaller cities and among prosperous members of the middle class. Like the GAR, it left racial matters largely to localities, which in practice usually meant segregated posts.

The War Risk Act of 1917 was intended to avoid the expense and abuses of the Civil War pension system by allowing World War I soldiers to pay small premiums in return for life insurance and future medical care. Administration of the act was inefficient, however, and veterans' hospitals proved too few in number and unable to cope with late-developing disabilities and shell shock. The first vocational training and rehabilitation programs for veterans, established in 1917, similarly suffered from underfunding, poor teaching, and the tendency of veterans to treat "training" grants as pensions. Veteran protests brought about the consolidation of medical and educational programs in the Veterans Bureau (1921), which in 1930 became the Veterans Administration (VA). It was not until Frank Hines replaced the corrupt Charles Forbes in 1923, however, that the bureau began to function effectively.

World War I veterans never received service pensions and were eligible for nonservice-related disability pensions only briefly, from 1930 to 1933. Instead, attention focused on "adjusted compensation," a bonus approved by Congress in 1924 and payable in 1945, designed to make up for wartime inflation and lost earnings. Veterans were seriously divided on the propriety of the bonus, even after depression hardships drove 20,000 of them to march on Washington in 1932 as a "Bonus Army" demanding its immediate payment. Although troops led by Gen. Douglas *MacArthur violently expelled the veterans from the city, the bonus was finally paid in 1936.

The rise of a general social welfare system under the New Deal decreased the need for military pensions and made aid to ex-soldiers seem less like "special benefits." Thus, when the 12 million veterans of World War II returned home, debate was minimal over the largest package of veterans' benefits in American history. The *G.I. Bill (1944), drafted by former Legion commander Harry Colmery, provided

World War II veterans with free college education and medical care, unemployment insurance for one year, and guaranteed loans up to $4,000 to buy homes or businesses. Other legislation guaranteed farmers loans on crops, reinstituted vocational training, and tried to safeguard the jobs of returning employees. By the 1970s, VA spending was greater than all but three cabinet departments (it achieved cabinet status in 1989). By 1980, benefits distributed under the G.I. Bill totaled $120 billion, an enormous investment in "social capital" and social mobility.

Unlike previous wars, World War II was fought mostly by conscripts, which may have made taxpayers more willing to compensate them for "forced labor." These veterans were slightly younger and better educated than World War I veterans; they were mustered out into considerably less class and racial strife than the veterans of 1919. Still, they joined older veterans' groups rather than forming significant new ones: American Legion membership, which had fluctuated between 600,000 and 1 million before 1941, reached a record 3.5 million in 1946, while VFW membership rose from 300,000 to 2 million. Among liberal alternative groups founded in 1945, only AMVETS reached 250,000 members.

The Korean and Vietnam conflicts produced none of the triumphalism that followed World War II. Although the VA continued to grow—its 1995 budget was $37.4 billion, more than half of it earmarked for benefits—the Legion and VFW struggled throughout the 1960s and 1970s to attract new veterans. After the *Vietnam War, which the older organizations supported fiercely, young veterans felt alienated from a society that often ignored or pitied them. In 1967, they formed the first significant antiwar veterans' group, the Vietnam Veterans Against the War (VVAW; after 1983, the Vietnam Veterans of America, VVOA). With less than 20,000 members, the VVAW publicized war *atrocities and lobbied for American withdrawal. In the 1980s, more Vietnam veterans began to join the Legion and VFW, bringing those groups up to their 1995 memberships of approximately 3 million and 2 million, respectively. Yet the Vietnam Veterans War Memorial, dedicated at Washington in 1982, remains starkly noncelebratory: a sunken black granite wall listing names of the dead.

More recent health problems of *Persian Gulf War veterans have highlighted the special needs of servicemen and women.

[See also Battlefields, Encampments, and Forts as Public Sites; Memorials, War; Newburgh "Conspiracy."]

• William Glasson, Federal Military Pensions in the United States, 1918. Dixon Wecter, When Johnny Comes Marching Home, 1944. Mary R. Dearing, Veterans in Politics: The Story of the G.A.R., 1952. Wallace Davies, Patriotism on Parade: The Story of Veterans' and Hereditary Organizations in America, 1783–1900, 1955. Paul Starr, The Discarded Army: Soldiers After Vietnam, 1973. Peter Karsten, Soldiers and Society: The Effects of Military Service and War on American Life, 1978. William Pencak, For God and Country: The American Legion, 1919–1941, 1989. Stuart McConnell, Glorious Contentment: The Grand Army of the Republic, 1866–1900, 1992. Theda Skocpol, Protecting Soldiers and Mothers: The Political Origins of Social Policy in the United States, 1992. R. B. Rosenberg, Living Monuments: Confederate Soldiers' Homes in the New South, 1993. Laura S. Jensen, "The Early American Origins of Entitlements," Studies in American Political Development, 10 (1996). Eric T. Dean, Jr., Shook Over Hell: Post-traumatic Stress, Vietnam and the Civil War, 1997.

—Stuart McConnell

VETERANS: REVOLUTIONARY WAR

Because inadequate records were kept, the exact number of Americans who fought in the *Continental army and in state militia units during the *Revolutionary War (1775–83) is unknown. Most former members of the Continental army officer corps became ardent nationalists as a result of their military service and pressed to replace the Articles of Confederation with a new constitution. President George *Washington placed a number of his former Continental army officers in executive positions in the new federal government.

Continental officers created the Society of the *Cincinnati for themselves, but no national veterans' organizations emerged for the common soldiers. Many veterans of the Revolution continued to serve in the militia after 1783, and for numerous Americans the militia embodied the republican ideals of the *citizen-soldier. The heightened *nationalism that emerged after the *War of 1812 helped turn the aging and shrinking ranks of Revolutionary War veterans into symbols of civic virtue in the eyes of politicians and the public. In communities across the country, these gray-haired ex-soldiers often received honored places at the head of Fourth of July parades and other rituals honoring the Revolution and the Republic.

In 1818, responding to the public's growing esteem for the Revolutionary veteran, the U.S. Congress for the first time offered pensions to any veteran of the Continental army who had demonstrated financial need and had served for at least nine months. This differed from previous pensions offered only to officers and also to those soldiers permanently injured in battle. In 1832, Congress further liberalized these requirements and granted pensions to all living veterans, including militia members, regardless of financial need, if they had served for six months. This pension system set important precedents for the relationship of the veteran and the federal government. Subsequently, after every major war, veterans often received pensions and other benefits by virtue of their wartime service.

[See also Revolutionary War: Postwar Impact; Revolutionary War: Changing Interpretations.]

• John C. Dann, ed., The Revolution Remembered: Eyewitness Accounts of the War for Independence, 1980. John P. Resch, "Politics and Public Culture: The Revolutionary War Pension Act of 1818," Journal of the Early Republic, 8 (Summer 1988), pp. 139–58.

—G. Kurt Piehler

VETERANS: CIVIL WAR

The Civil War produced more than 2 million veterans of both armies; as late as 1890, the federal census found 1,034,073 surviving Union ex-soldiers and 432,020 former Confederates. At the war's close, both groups faced dim employment prospects, civilian indifference, and the lingering effects of wounds and disease—13.9 percent of Union veterans and probably 20 percent of ex-Confederates suffered from wounds alone. Union veterans in 1866 organized the *Grand Army of the Republic (GAR), which grew to more 400,000 members by 1890 and became probably the most powerful political lobby of the Gilded Age. Smaller groups included the Union Veteran Legion, the Veterans Rights Union (VRU), and the officers-only Military Order of the Loyal Legion of the United States (MOLLUS). Union veteran political pressure helped bring about the Arrears Act of 1879, which doubled pension expenditures in less than two years, and the Dependent Pension Act of 1890, which created a service pension system in all but name. The number of Union pensioners (including widows) reached a peak of 969,711 in 1901. In 1874, Congress mandated preference for disabled veterans in federal hiring, and New York and Kansas enacted general veteran preference laws; twelve new state soldiers' homes opened between 1879 and 1888. Federal largess to veterans, which represented the United States's first foray into social welfare spending, drew the fire of genteel reformers such as E. L. Godkin in the 1890s.

Confederate veterans organized much later. The largest Confederate veterans' group, the United Confederate Veterans (UCV), was founded in 1889, and had an estimated 80,000 members by 1903; before 1885, the more exclusive Association of the Army of Northern Virginia (AANV) predominated. Ex-Confederates were ineligible for federal pensions and hiring preferences, though individual southern states erected sixteen soldiers' homes to care for the wounded and indigent, and some provided modest pensions. Much of Confederate veteran culture, especially after 1890, was tied to a developing Lost Cause mythology that helped southerners cope with defeat while reintegrating themselves within the nation.

The attitudes of Civil War veterans toward each other, and toward noncombatants, were exceedingly complex. Wartime hatreds never really disappeared, as suggested by Grover Cleveland's hasty retraction, under GAR pressure, of an 1887 order to return captured Confederate battle flags to the South, or by ex-Confederate veneration of Jefferson *Davis and his daughter Varina Anne Davis on their tour of the South in 1886. Union and Confederate veterans also skirmished throughout the 1890s over the proper telling of Civil War history in school textbooks. But veterans of both sides also were prone to idealize each other at the expense of "civilians." Between 1884 and 1887, the *Century*'s widely read "Battles and Leaders of the Civil War" avoided politics and balanced northern and southern viewpoints, while local Blue-Gray reunions beginning in the 1880s culminated in a gigantic fiftieth anniversary reunion at Gettysburg in 1913. In their memoirs, veterans from both sides tended to emphasize Union, states' rights, and personal heroism and to downplay slavery and race.

[*See also* Civil War: Postwar Impact.]

• Gaines M. Foster, *Ghosts of the Confederacy: Defeat, the Lost Cause, and the Emergence of the New South*, 1987. Stuart McConnell, *Glorious Contentment: The Grand Army of the Republic, 1866–1900*, 1992.   —Stuart McConnell

VETERANS: WORLD WAR I

There were approximately 4.5 million veterans of the eighteen-month U.S. participation in World War I. The average had served twelve months. About half went overseas for an average of 5.5 months. Some 1.1 million actually saw combat; of these, 204,000 were wounded or otherwise disabled. Veterans were simply mustered out of service from their bases in the United States. The government was unprepared to deal with the problems faced by returning veterans, especially unemployed or disabled veterans. A brief postwar recession in which unemployment reached 16 percent ended by 1921, the year in which the Veterans Bureau (forerunner of the *Veterans Administration) was created. A system of veterans' hospitals was established

that provided long-term care especially for war-related wounds and illnesses, tuberculosis caused by poison gas, and mental illness caused by "shell shock."

Throughout the 1920s, veterans' benefits averaged $650 million per year, about 20 percent of the federal budget. In 1924, Congress, under pressure, acknowledged that the dollar per day enlisted men received had been outpaced by wartime inflation and voted World War I veterans an "adjusted compensation" ("the Bonus"), to be paid in 1945. During the Great Depression, unemployed veterans, calling themselves the "forgotten men," demanded immediate payment of the bonus. Congress agreed, but President Herbert C. *Hoover vetoed it. When many "Bonus Army" marchers remained camped in Washington, D.C., U.S. Army troops under Gen. Douglas *MacArthur used tanks and tear gas to clear the capital of the protestors.

In the 1936 election year, the bonus was paid ahead of schedule at a cost of $3.9 billion of a total federal budget of $8.4 billion. In addition to the "Bonus," hospitals, and disability benefits, World War I veterans also received civil service preference at all levels of government. Between one-fifth and one-third of surviving veterans belonged to the *American Legion, formed by World War I veterans in 1919. Having served briefly and gloriously in the Great War, most veterans valued their experience in uniform for comradeship and travel, especially as three-quarters of the veterans had never seen combat.

[*See also* Veterans of Foreign Wars.]

• William P. Dillingham, *Federal Aid to Veterans, 1917–1941*, 1952. William Pencak, *For God and Country: The American Legion, 1919–1941*, 1989.   —William Pencak

VETERANS: WORLD WAR II

Over 16 million American men and women served in World War II, and their return home had a profound impact on them and on society. The sudden end of the war in September 1945 complicated *demobilization. A shortage of transports as well as the need to maintain occupation forces in Japan and Germany meant long delays in bringing some troops home, especially from the Pacific theater. G.I.s staged demonstrations in Manila, Calcutta, Paris, and several other cities, demanding an immediate return. They were supported by their families. As portrayed in films like *The Best Years of Our Lives* (1946), once they returned to the United States, they sought in various ways to resume their civilian lives and put the war behind them.

Despite the fears expressed by some social commentators about the destructive influences of war on combatants, the reintegration of veterans into American society produced neither economic upheaval nor a dangerous new class of men unable to accept the norms of civilian life. Returning G.I.s and their families faced a severe shortage of housing; consumer goods also remained in short supply in 1946 and 1947. The generous adjustment allowances provided by the *G.I. Bill smoothed the transition of many ex-servicemen and -women into civilian life. Military service did take a significant emotional toll on a number of former servicepeople, especially those who had been in combat. There were also many disabled veterans. But the majority of veterans returned successfully to a society that vindicated their efforts on behalf of the "Good War." In turn, many returning veterans expressed the strong desire to "get on with their lives," and after V-J Day both marriage and birth rates soared as scores of former servicepeople started families.

As a political force, the impact of the World War II veterans on American politics remained important, if often elusive. Their numbers as a potential voting bloc helped explain why politicians showered such an array of benefits, including property tax breaks, educational benefits, and preferences of public employment. Every U.S. president from 1953 to 1992 had served in World War II, and veterans of this conflict also made up a significant portion of both houses of Congress in the period.

The *American Legion, the *Veterans of Foreign Wars, and the Disabled American Veterans attracted a significant share of eligible former servicemen and -women. Efforts on the part of some liberal left veterans to create a new mass-based veterans' organization, the American Veterans Committee (AVC), failed. Tarred by critics for being a Communist front organization, the AVC won the allegiance of only a small fraction of veterans. Even after the "Good War," the majority of veterans never joined any established veterans' organization. Furthermore, in contrast to veterans of the *Civil War, World War I, and later the *Vietnam War, the World War II veterans expressed little interest in sponsoring or lobbying for either local or national monuments marking their service, at least until the fiftieth anniversary of the war in the 1990s, when many of its veterans were already passing from the scene.

[See also Memorials, War; World War II: Postwar Impact.]

• Davis R. B. Ross, *Preparing for Ulysses: Politics and Veterans During World War II,* 1969. Richard Severo and Lewis Milford, *The Wages of War: When America's Soldiers Came Home—From Valley Forge to Vietnam,* 1989.   —G. Kurt Piehler

VETERANS: KOREAN WAR

Over 6 million Americans served in the armed forces during the era of the *Korean War (1950–53), but they represented a smaller cohort demographically than their counterparts in World War II and they failed to garner the same public attention and acclaim. An unpopular war with limited *mobilization, the Korean conflict ended in a stalemate instead of total *victory. In 1952, the U.S. Congress enacted a Veterans' Readjustment Assistance Act providing Korean veterans with educational benefits similar to but less than those offered World War II veterans under the *G.I. Bill.

Further tarnishing the image, a handful of American servicemen captured by the enemy renounced their U.S. citizenship and a small number of American *prisoners of war who participated in anti-U.S. propaganda were put on trial by the U.S. government after their exchange for collaborating with the enemy. Some political commentators voiced concerns that captured American soldiers had been "brainwashed" by their Communist captors and now posed a threat of internal infiltration. This theme would be reflected in a controversial 1962 film, *The Manchurian Candidate.*

By the 1970s, the Korean War became "the forgotten war," but during the 1980s restored pride in the armed forces and the dedication of the national Vietnam Veterans Memorial (1982) sparked renewed interest among Korean War veterans and political leaders to build a similar national monument honoring those who served in Korea. Authorized by the U.S. Congress in 1986, built with private funds by the American Battle Monuments Commission, the Korean War Veterans Memorial was dedicated in Washington, D.C. in 1995.

[See also Memorials, War; Veterans Administration.]

• Richard Severo and Lewis Milford, *The Wages of War: When America's Soldiers Came Home—From Valley Forge to Vietnam,* 1989. Charles S. Young, "Missing Action: POW Films, Brainwashing and the Korean War, 1954–1968," *Historical Journal of Film, Radio, and Television,* 18 (1998), pp. 49–74.   —G. Kurt Piehler

VETERANS: VIETNAM WAR

The Department of *Defense (DoD) and the Department of Veterans' Affairs (DVA) define the 9,656,000 men and 178,000 women who served on active duty in the armed forces between August 1964 and May 1975 as Vietnam-era veterans. Of these, 2,586,152 men and 7,848 women served in the war in Vietnam.

Public attitudes toward veterans of the Vietnam War shifted from respect in 1965–67 to disdain following an antiwar movement that developed in 1968–70. Veterans and their problems became an embarrassment to the voters and the government as reminders of a war that had lost much popular support. The press highlighted veterans who engaged in violent crime, though they were not significantly overrepresented in crime, drinking, or drug use compared to nonveterans in their age cohort. In the early 1980s, popular sentiment began to change again. The dedication of the Vietnam Veterans Memorial in Washington in 1982 marked the beginning of a national commitment to honoring veterans of the war.

Veterans who served in Vietnam faced unique biological and psychological problems. The most serious and widespread biological matter was exposure to dioxin in Agent Orange, a defoliant sprayed by aircraft. The effects of dioxin poisoning, which appeared several months after exposure, included chloracne (skin lesions), peripheral neuropathy (loss of feeling in the extremities), hepatic dysfunction (liver failure), non-Hodgkin's lymphoma and soft tissue sarcomas (cancers), and porphyrinuria and hypertriglyceridemia (metabolic disorders). None of these conditions was amenable to cure; treatment could only alleviate symptoms.

Approximately 30 percent of veterans of the war suffered from posttraumatic stress disorder (PTSD). Symptoms appeared gradually, and could include recurrent intrusive dreams and memories, feelings of estrangement from others, flat affect, survival guilt, impaired memory and concentration, exaggerated startle response, and sleep disorders. Veterans experienced higher than expected mortality rates from motor vehicle wrecks, suicide, homicide, and drug-related medical conditions. PTSD resulted principally from the abrupt rupture of powerful emotional relationships when servicemembers left their comrades in the war zone, the lack of opportunity to process traumatic events with those who had shared them, and hostile or indifferent responses to veterans and their experiences by civilians back home. PTSD was most common among the psychologically vulnerable.

Vietnam veterans made up small minorities (24–28 percent) within the memberships of the existing veterans' organizations. The *Veterans of Foreign Wars opposed measures that would benefit Vietnam veterans if those programs competed for dollars with programs to improve benefits for veterans of earlier wars. The *American Legion was passive until 1982 with respect to programs for Vietnam veterans. The Disabled American Veterans, the most active advocate of Vietnam veterans' needs, took positive action to support veterans' mental health with storefront clinics.

The Veterans' Education and Training Amendments Act of 1970 (PL 91-219) was the first of a series of acts to enhance educational benefits for Vietnam-era veterans. Others include Public Laws 92-540, 93-508, 94-502, and 95-202. In 1979, 740,000 veterans were enrolled in education or vocational training under these programs. PL 93-508 also required federal contractors to take affirmative action to hire disabled and Vietnam-era veterans. Health benefits lagged until popular feelings toward veterans became more favorable in the 1980s. The DoD and DVA were slow to recognize dioxin poisoning and PTSD as service-connected.

A measure to provide readjustment counseling to victims of PTSD was held up for several years in the House Veterans' Affairs Committee before it was enacted in 1979 (PL 96-22). In 1981, the Congress gave the Veterans Administration discretionary authority to treat victims of dioxin poisoning, and in 1984, PL 98-542 established standards for compensation. Not until 1991 was a presumption of service connection established for chloracne, non-Hodgkin's lymphoma, and soft tissue sarcomas (PL 102-4). In 1993, DVA established a presumptive service connection for porphyria, Hodgkin's disease, and other cancers.

[*See also* Toxic Agents: Agent Orange Exposure; Vietnam War.]

• David E. Bonier, Steven M. Champlin, and Timothy S. Kolly, *The Vietnam Veteran: A History of Neglect*, 1984. Joel Osler Brende and Erwin Randolph Person, *Vietnam Veterans: The Road to Recovery*, 1985. Ghislaine Boulanger and Charles Kadushin, *The Vietnam Veteran Redefined*, 1986.   —Faris R. Kirkland

The **VETERANS ADMINISTRATION** (VA) is an independent federal agency administering benefits and programs to veterans; it achieved cabinet-level status as the Department of Veterans Affairs in 1988. Established by Congress in 1930, the VA absorbed three separate agencies: the Bureau of Pensions, established in 1833; the National Homes of Disabled Volunteer Soldiers, founded in 1866; and the Veteran's Bureau, created in 1921.

Brig. Gen. Franklin T. Hines served as the first administrator of the VA in 1930–45. Originally called to Washington in 1923, this Utah native reformed the Veterans' Bureau, which had been mired in scandal under Charles R. Forbes, a political crony of President Warren G. Harding. Hines's longevity in office stemmed from his nonpartisanship, hard work, and efficiency, as well as his ability to maintain good relations with Congress and national veterans' organizations, especially the *American Legion.

In 1944, Congress vested the agency with responsibility for administering the *G.I. Bill for over 16 million eligible veterans. In 1945, President Harry S. *Truman named Gen. Omar N. *Bradley to head the agency and carry out a series of much needed reforms for its larger roles. Under Bradley's three-year tenure as administrator, the agency embarked on a massive program of hospital construction and made major improvements in the delivery of medical

care to disabled veterans, including the establishment of a Department of Medicine within the agency and the formal affiliation of VA Hospitals with major medical schools.

In 1953, President Dwight D. *Eisenhower implemented the recommendation of a private consultant to streamline the VA and created three major departments within the agency: Medicine and Surgery; Insurance; and Benefits. This newly configured VA administrated less generous packages of *G.I. Bill benefits for veterans of wars in Korea and later Vietnam. In 1973, the VA also assumed responsibility from the Department of the Army for military *cemeteries.

During the late 1960s, the VA, geared to serving an aging population of veterans from two world wars, came under criticism for failing to provide adequate acute care for servicemen and -women injured in the *Vietnam War and for a general insensitivity to the particular needs of veterans of that war. For example, many veterans and their supporters protested the reluctance of the agency to acknowledge the long-term effects of the herbicide Agent Orange. In 1977, President Jimmy *Carter appointed Max Cleland, a double amputee, as the first Vietnam veteran to head the VA.

In 1988, Congress elevated the VA to a cabinet-level department, and in 1989, Republican congressman Edward J. Derwinski of Illinois became the first secretary of Veterans Affairs. After the *Persian Gulf War (1991), the Department of Veterans Affairs, along with the Department of *Defense, was criticized for failing to recognize or treat "Gulf War syndrome," allegedly caused by exposure to biological and chemical weapons.

[*See also* Toxic Agents; Veterans: Overview.]

• Davis R. B. Ross, *Preparing for Ulysses: Politics and Veterans During World War II*, 1969. Richard Severo and Lewis Milford, *The Wages of War: When America's Soldiers Come Home—From Valley Forge to Vietnam*, 1989.   —G. Kurt Piehler

The **VETERANS OF FOREIGN WARS** (VFW) was organized in 1913 with the emergence of two organizations of *Spanish-American War veterans. Formed as an association of *veterans who served overseas, its membership, which consisted of over 1 million in the aftermath of World War II, includes veterans from every war in the twentieth century. Its headquarters is in Kansas City. Like its chief rival organization, the *American Legion, the VFW established local posts throughout the United States and wielded political influence in Washington as a voice for veterans and a strong foreign and military policy.

The VFW saw its lobbying efforts in the context of peacetime *patriotism that called the nation not to forget the soldiers who defended American freedom and to be vigilant against internal as well as external threats. Contradictions between the celebration of soldier solidarity and individual heroism, between collective responsibility for veteran welfare and extremist individualism, and between pervasive antistatist rhetoric and arguments for expanded state benefits for veterans permeate the history of veteran groups in general and of the VFW in particular.

In one of its most successful political efforts, the VFW achieved in 1924 what was called "the Soldier's Bonus": the World War Veterans Adjusted Compensation Act. This act granted veterans a cash payment for the sacrifice of wages due to wartime service. The VFW also was instrumental in the passage in 1946 of the Servicemen's Adjustment Act, or *G.I. Bill, under which World War II veterans received unprecedented employment preference, education, and loan guarantees.

• Rodney G. Minott, *Peerless Patriots: Organized Veterans and the Spirit of Americanism*, 1962. Bill Bottoms, *The V.F.W.: An Illustrated History of the Veterans of Foreign Wars of the United States*, 1991.

—Elizabeth Faue

VICHY FRANCE. *See* France, U.S. Military Involvement in.

VICKSBURG, SIEGE OF (1862–63). During the Civil War, Vicksburg, a port city above the Mississippi River at the mouth of the Yazoo, was a key link between the eastern and the trans-Mississippi areas of the Confederacy. In May 1862, 3,000 Confederate troops under Brig. Gen. Martin L. Smith occupied the town. Smith began fortifying the 200-foot bluffs. With the siege of *New Orleans and the fall of Memphis, Vicksburg quickly became the only bastion on the Mississippi blocking Union river traffic.

On 28 May 1862, the USS *Oneida* arrived and opened fire upon Vicksburg. Additional vessels under Flag Officer David *Farragut joined the bombardment in the coming weeks, augmented by mortar schooners under Cmdr. David Dixon *Porter. Lacking sufficient forces for a land assault, the Federals attempted to dig a canal across the peninsula opposite the town. On 28 June, Farragut's ships steamed upstream and joined Charles H. Davis's gunboat squadron. On 15 July, however, the CSS *Arkansas*, an iron-clad riverboat, ran the gauntlet of Union vessels to anchor safely below Vicksburg. Farragut's vessels failed to destroy the *Arkansas* when they returned downstream that night. Low water ended construction on the canal and threatened to strand the deep-draft vessels.

When the Union fleets departed on 25 July, both sides understood that only a Union army could capture Vicksburg. To prevent that possibility, Smith's successor, Maj. Gen. Earl Van Dorn, ringed Vicksburg with earthworks and fortified Port Hudson. On 14 October, Confederate Maj. Gen. John C. Pemberton assumed command of Mississippi and eastern Louisiana.

Ulysses S. *Grant marched southward on 2 November from Grand Junction with 30,000 men and outmaneuvered Pemberton, who fell back to Grenada. While Grant continued overland, William Tecumseh *Sherman moved via the Mississippi to Vicksburg. Grant's advance stalled after Confederate cavalry disrupted his rail communications and destroyed his supply base at Holly Springs on 20 December. The following week, Sherman's 32,000 troops landed near Vicksburg, but in fighting 27–29 December they suffered a repulse at Chickasaw Bluffs. Sherman withdrew on 2 January 1863.

Undeterred, Grant decided to isolate Vicksburg from the east while supplying his entire army via the Mississippi. However, that required Union transports below or behind Vicksburg. Attempts to complete the canal and to create an all-water route west of the Mississippi proved fruitless. Fort Pemberton prevented Union vessels from entering the Yazoo River above Vicksburg, and attempts to bypass the fort failed.

On 31 March, Grant started two corps down the west side of the Mississippi. To distract Pemberton, Sherman's corps remained near Vicksburg and 1,700 Union cavalrymen under Col. Benjamin H. Grierson conducted a raid that disrupted Confederate *communications throughout Mississippi. On the night of 16 April, nine Federal gunboats and two Union troop transports steamed past Vicksburg, followed six nights later by five transports and six barges of supplies. From 30 April through 1 May, 23,000 Union soldiers crossed the Mississippi and disembarked at Bruinsburg.

Grant's maneuvering baffled Pemberton, who was further impaired by conflicting orders. His immediate superior, Joseph E. *Johnston, instructed him to concentrate and defeat Grant; but Pemberton focused on Grierson's cavalry and followed President Jefferson *Davis's mandate to hold Vicksburg and Port Hudson. Pemberton's confusion enabled Grant to defeat Confederate detachments at Port Gibson and Grand Gulf. After securing the latter on 3 May and being joined by Sherman, Grant marched toward Jackson, Mississippi. He encountered no serious resistance until 12 May, when Confederates made a stand near Raymond. Fearing an enemy concentration, Grant sent James B. McPherson's corps and Sherman's to Jackson; John A. McClernand's corps remained in reserve to block any Confederate advance from Vicksburg.

That same day, General Johnston arrived in Jackson and took command of all Confederate forces in Mississippi; but Grant's deployment prevented him from establishing reliable communications with Pemberton. Pemberton finally led 17,500 Confederates from Vicksburg on 12 May, but when he failed to join Johnston, Grant proceeded to defeat the two Confederate armies, one at a time. After driving Johnston's 6,000 troops from Jackson on 14 May Grant turned and defeated Pemberton at Champion Hill on 16 May and at Big Black River on 17 May. Pemberton then withdrew to Vicksburg.

Eager to avoid a lengthy siege, Grant launched several unsuccessful assaults against the bastion, but his troops suffered heavy *casualties. Union engineers began constructing 12 miles of earthworks, about 600 yards from the 9-mile-long Confederate *fortifications. By 1 June, Grant had 50,000 troops surrounding 30,000 Confederates; an additional 27,000 Union soldiers arrived by mid-June.

Anxious to aid Pemberton, Johnston organized an army near Jackson. When he claimed his 24,000 troops were insufficient, he received 7,000 reinforcements. A trans-Mississippi division also attempted to destroy Grant's supply base at Milliken's Bend. On 15 June, Johnston notified President Jefferson that he could not save Vicksburg. Grant deployed Sherman with 34,000 men east of Vicksburg to block Johnston.

Believing that Pemberton could hold out until 10 July, Johnston dispatched a courier to notify Pemberton that he would make a diversionary attack to enable the garrison to escape. Johnston could do no more because of *transportation and *logistics problems, unreliable communications, and inferior numbers against an entrenched enemy.

However, Pemberton never received the message, and conditions at Vicksburg deteriorated more rapidly than anticipated. Dwindling foodstuffs, insufficient water, and daily bombardments took a heavy toll on civilians and soldiers alike. Pemberton concluded his men were too weak to fight their way out.

On 3 July, he met with Grant and agreed to surrender the following day. At the surrender on 4 July 1863—the same week as The Battle of *Gettysburg—the garrison consisted of 2,166 officers, 27,230 enlisted men, 115 civilian employees, 172 cannon, and 60,000 long arms. Casualties during the Vicksburg campaign totaled about 9,000 for the Union and 10,000 for the Confederacy, not counting Confederate prisoners. The victory further elevated Grant's prominence. Johnston learned of the surrender on 5 July, and after skirmishing with Sherman, withdrew. On 9 July, Port Hudson surrendered, giving the Union complete control of the Mississippi and dividing the Confederacy in half.

[*See also* Civil War: Military and Diplomatic Course; Confederate Army; Union Army.]

• Gilbert E. Govan and James W. Livingood, *A Different Valor: The Story of General Joseph E. Johnston, C.S.A.*, 1956. Peter F. Walker, *Vicksburg: A People at War, 1860–1865*, 1960. Edwin C. Bearss, *Rebel Victory at Vicksburg*, 1963; repr. 1989. Edwin C. Bearss, *The Vicksburg Campaign*, 3 vols., 1985–86. Mary D. McFeely and William S. McFeely, eds., *Memoirs and Selected Letters: Ulysses S. Grant*, 1990. Michael B. Ballard, *Pemberton: A Biography*, 1991.

—Lawrence Lee Hewitt

VICTORY. Although it can denote simply success in a single engagement or operation, victory is one of the most basic yet elusive concepts in military thought when applied to war. American experience reaffirms Carl von *Clausewitz's argument in *On War* (1832) that victory in the broader sense results from a balance between war's inner logic of force begetting more force, pushing a conflict toward a "war of annihilation," and the limitations imposed by friction and political objectives. For most of American history, factors such as geographic isolation and a small professional military have acted as friction.

From the seventeenth to the twentieth century, victory was achieved in two separate phases: limited military operations and diplomatic negotiations. As colonists, Americans witnessed their wars of empire settled in Europe, often well after hostilities ended in North America. The signing of the Treaty of *Paris in 1783, ending the *Revolutionary War, occurred two years after major military operations ceased. Perhaps most famously, Andrew *Jackson's defeat of the British in the Battle of *New Orleans occurred after the Treaty of Ghent concluded the *War of 1812. Similarly, negotiations ended the *Mexican War and the *Spanish-American War after the United States achieved strategic advantage in limited military operations.

There were notable exceptions: the *Civil War and wars with Native Americans. Both belligerents entered the Civil War hoping to achieve victory quickly and with limited engagements. Initially, the opponents' conceptions of victory mirrored one another: for the Confederacy, independence; for the Union, reunion. Steadily, however, the war evolved into a protracted struggle. This led to an expansion of the Union's aims to include the elimination of slavery. President Abraham *Lincoln as commander in chief integrated these political objectives with military *strategy. Although scholars debate whether the Civil War was the first "modern" or "total war," the combination of Ulysses S. *Grant's campaign of attrition against the Army of Virginia and William Tecumseh *Sherman's strike at the heart of the Confederacy's economy and civilian morale with his drive to Atlanta and then his *march to the sea represented means to victory hitherto unprecedented in American history. Despite his expressed willingness to negotiate

with the Confederacy, Lincoln's insistence on reunion and abolition of slavery as preconditions for any settlement linked "unconditional surrender" to the end of the war in popular memory.

In their wars against Native American nations, Americans rejected limited objectives and sought instead the forcible relocation or elimination of entire peoples. Therefore, from the Pequot War to the slaughter at the Battle of *Wounded Knee, South Dakota, on 29 December 1890, America's pursuit of victory against Native Americans approached wars of annihilation by means of bounties, fire, opportunistic alliances, and eventually superior firepower and mobility.

After the outbreak of World War I, President Woodrow *Wilson hoped that the United States could serve as an impartial mediator to end the conflict. In this context, Wilson sought in his "Peace Without Victory" address (1917) to redefine "victory" as the imposition of a settlement by the victor upon the vanquished, a condition that inevitably bred resentment and undermined prospects for long-term peace. Wilson juxtaposed against this portrait of traditional victory his vision of *peace based upon the interests of all nations and the repudiation of traditional power politics. Although after the United States entered the war, he embraced "complete victory" and oversaw a *mobilization that eclipsed the Civil War experience, Wilson nonetheless conceived of an American victory in the distinctive terms of creating a new international order as suggested in his *Fourteen Points. But the compromises of the Treaty of *Versailles, the American failure to join the *League of Nations, and the subsequent deterioration of European stability all disenchanted Americans, until the entire experience seemed not a "peace without victory" but a military victory without meaningful peace.

This bitter experience shaped Americans' views of victory during World War II. President Franklin D. *Roosevelt proclaimed the objective of "absolute victory." He then supervised the formulation of American strategy as Lincoln had. "V for Victory" symbolized a hybrid Wilsonian idealism and realpolitik. Such pronouncements as FDR's "Four Freedoms" Speech (6 January 1941), the Atlantic Charter (14 August 1941), and the *United Nations Declaration (2 January 1942) linked victory to both the elimination of the military and ideological threat posed by the Axis powers and the creation of a new international order. Yet the United Nations' prospects for success were predicated on the continued leadership and cooperation of the Grand Alliance. For rhetorical and policy reasons, FDR resurrected "unconditional surrender" at the Casablanca Conference (1943) as a vital prerequisite for victory. To win such a victory, the United States adopted means approaching pure total war by expanding the boundaries of what Americans considered militarily legitimate—for example, the atomic bombings of *Hiroshima and Nagasaki.

After World War II, the United States confronted a new strategic environment dominated by the *Cold War with the USSR. The idea of seeking unconditional surrender in any future war with the USSR appeared fantastic. Against this backdrop, the United States intervened in the *Korean War in June 1950, sought the reunification of the peninsula by force, and then changed its objectives to a return to the status quo ante bellum and circumscribed its means following the Communist Chinese intervention in late 1950. A new class of civilian strategists developed theories of Limited War, which postulated the Korean War as the likely norm in a world of two nuclear-armed superpowers. Such ideas provided the intellectual foundation for the Kennedy and Johnson administrations' *Flexible Response strategy. When applied to Vietnam, however, a policy emerged that did not emphasize American victory but rather the denial of victory to the Vietnamese Communists. President Lyndon B. *Johnson's strategy led to a prolonged attrition of American will and ultimate failure.

This failure stimulated a reassessment of the relationship between military and political factors in war. As articulated in the so-called Weinberger and Powell Doctrines and implemented in Panama (1989–90) and the *Persian Gulf War (1991), current U.S. strategy emphasizes the application of overwhelming military force to terminate a conflict swiftly and decisively. Yet, despite the unmistakable battlefield triumph in the Gulf War, many doubt whether the final outcome constituted a true victory because of the perseverance of Saddam *Hussein's regime. Therefore, even though the United States approached the end of the twentieth century as the world's sole superpower, it still confronted the central dilemma of achieving victory: finding the proper balance between political objectives and military means.

[See also Defeat; Limited War, Joint Chiefs of Staff and; Native American Wars: Wars Between Native Americans and Europeans and Euro-Americans; Powell, Colin; War; Weinberger, Caspar.]

• Fred Iklé, *Every War Must End,* 1971; rev. ed. 1991. Bernard Brodie, *War and Politics,* 1973. Russell F. Weigley, *The American Way of War: A History of United States Military Strategy and Policy,* 1973. Christopher M. Gacek, *The Logic of Force: The Dilemma of Limited War in American Foreign Policy,* 1994.

—Andrew P. N. Erdmann

VIETNAM ANTIWAR MOVEMENT. Though the first American protests against U.S. intervention in Vietnam took place in 1963, the antiwar movement did not begin in earnest until nearly two years later, when President Lyndon B. *Johnson ordered massive U.S. military intervention and the sustained bombing of North Vietnam. In the spring of 1965, "teach-ins" against the war were held on many college campuses. *Students for a Democratic Society (SDS) organized the first national antiwar demonstration in Washington; 20,000 people, mainly students, attended.

As the war expanded—over 400,000 U.S. troops would be in Vietnam by 1967—so did the antiwar movement, attracting growing support off the campuses. The movement was less a unified army than a rich mix of political notions and visions. The tactics used were diverse: legal demonstrations, grassroots organizing, congressional lobbying, electoral challenges, civil disobedience, *draft resistance, self-immolations, political violence. Some peace activists traveled to North Vietnam. *Quakers and others provided medical aid to Vietnamese civilian victims of the war. Some G.I.s protested the war.

In March 1967, a national organization of draft resisters was formed; the Resistance would subsequently hold several national draft card turn-ins. In April 1967, more than 300,000 people demonstrated against the war in New York. Six months later, 50,000 surrounded the *Pentagon, sparking nearly 700 arrests. By now, senior Johnson administration officials typically encountered demonstrators when speaking in public, forcing them to restrict their outside appearances. Many also had sons, daughters, or wives who opposed the war, fueling the sense of besiegement. Prominent participants in the antiwar movement included Dr. Benjamin Spock, Robert Lowell, Harry Belafonte, and Rev. Martin Luther *King, Jr. Encouraged by the movement, Senator Eugene McCarthy announced in late 1967 that he was challenging Johnson in the 1968 Democratic primaries; his later strong showing in New Hampshire was seen as a major defeat for Johnson and a repudiation of his war policies.

The Johnson administration took numerous measures to the antiwar movement, most notably undertaking close surveillance and tarnishing its public image, sending speakers to campuses, and fostering pro-war activity. Many administration officials felt foreign Communists were aiding and abetting the movement, despite the failure of both the *Central Intelligence Agency and the FBI to uncover such support.

In 1965, a majority of Americans supported U.S. policies in Vietnam; by the fall of 1967, only 35 percent did so. For the first time, more people thought U.S. intervention in Vietnam had been a mistake than did not. Blacks and women were the most dovish social groups. Later research found that antiwar sentiment was inversely correlated with people's socioeconomic level. Many Americans also disliked antiwar protesters, and the movement was frequently denounced by media commentators, legislators, and other public figures.

By 1968, faced with widespread public opposition to the war and troubling prospects in Vietnam, the Johnson administration halted the bombing of North Vietnam and stabilized the ground war. This policy reversal was the major turning point. U.S. troop strength in Vietnam would crest at 543,000.

The antiwar movement reached its zenith under President Richard M. *Nixon. In October 1969, more than 2 million people participated in Vietnam Moratorium protests across the country. The following month, over 500,000 demonstrated in Washington and 150,000 in San Francisco. Militant protest, mainly youthful, continued to spread, leading many Americans to wonder whether the war was worth a split society. And other forms of antiwar activity persisted. The Nixon administration took a host of measures to blunt the movement, mainly mobilizing supporters, smearing the movement, tracking it, withdrawing U.S. troops from Vietnam, instituting a draft lottery, and eventually ending draft calls.

Two long-standing problems continued to plague the antiwar movement. Many participants questioned its effectiveness, spawning dropouts, hindering the organization of protests and the maintenance of antiwar groups, and aggravating dissension over strategies and tactics. And infighting continued to sap energy, alienate activists, and hamper antiwar planning. The strife was fanned by the U.S. government, but it was largely internally generated.

In the spring of 1970, President Nixon's invasion of Cambodia and the Kent State shootings (followed by those at Jackson State) sparked the greatest display of campus protest in U.S. history. A national student strike completely shut down over 500 colleges and universities. Other Americans protested in cities across the country; many lobbied White House officials and members of Congress. Over 100,000 demonstrated in Washington, despite only a week's prior notice. Senators John Sherman Cooper and Frank

Church sponsored legislation (later passed) prohibiting funding of U.S. ground forces and advisers in Cambodia. Many labor leaders spoke out for the first time, and blue-collar workers joined antiwar activities in unprecedented numbers. However, construction workers in New York assaulted a group of peaceful student demonstrators, and (with White House assistance) some union leaders organized pro-administration rallies.

Despite worsening internal divisions and a flagging movement, 500,000 people demonstrated against the war in Washington in April 1971. Vietnam Veterans Against the War also staged protests, and other demonstrators engaged in mass civil disobedience, prompting 12,000 arrests. The former Pentagon aide Daniel *Ellsberg leaked the *Pentagon Papers to the *New York Times*. Meanwhile, the morale and discipline of U.S. soldiers in Vietnam was deteriorating seriously: drug abuse was rampant, combat refusals and racial strife were mounting, and some soldiers were even murdering their own officers.

With U.S. troops coming home, the antiwar movement gradually declined between 1971 and 1975. The many remaining activists protested continued U.S. bombing, the plight of South Vietnamese political prisoners, and U.S. funding of the war.

The American movement against the Vietnam War was the most successful antiwar movement in U.S. history. During the Johnson administration, it played a significant role in constraining the war and was a major factor in the administration's policy reversal in 1968. During the Nixon years, it hastened U.S. troop withdrawals, continued to restrain the war, fed the deterioration in U.S. troop *morale and discipline (which provided additional impetus to U.S. troop withdrawals), and promoted congressional legislation that severed U.S. funds for the war. The movement also fostered aspects of the Watergate scandal, which ultimately played a significant role in ending the war by undermining Nixon's authority in Congress and thus his ability to continue the war. It gave rise to the infamous "Huston Plan"; inspired Daniel Ellsberg, whose release of the Pentagon Papers led to the formation of the Plumbers; and fed the Nixon administration's paranoia about its political enemies, which played a major part in concocting the Watergate break-in itself.

[See also Bombing of Civilians; Peace and Antiwar Movements; Vietnam War: Domestic Course.]

• Kirkpatrick Sale, SDS, 1973. Fred Halstead, Out Now!, 1978. Nancy Zaroulis and Gerald Sullivan, Who Spoke Up?, 1984. Todd Gitlin, The Sixties, 1987. Charles DeBenedetti with Charles Chatfield, An American Ordeal, 1990. Tom Wells, The War Within, 1994.

—Tom Wells

VIETNAM VETERANS OF AMERICA. *See* Veterans: Vietnam War.

VIETNAM WAR (1960–1975)

Causes
Military and Diplomatic Course
Domestic Course
Postwar Impact
Changing Interpretations

VIETNAM WAR (1960–75): CAUSES

Most American wars have obvious starting points or precipitating causes: the Battles of *Lexington and Concord in 1775, the capture of *Fort Sumter in 1861, the attack on *Pearl Harbor in 1941, and the North Korean invasion of South Korea in June 1950, for example. But there was no fixed beginning for the U.S. war in Vietnam. The United States entered that war incrementally, in a series of steps between 1950 and 1965. In May 1950, President Harry S *Truman authorized a modest program of economic and military aid to the French, who were fighting to retain control of their Indochina colony, including Laos and Cambodia as well as Vietnam. When the Vietnamese Nationalist (and Communist-led) Vietminh army defeated French forces at Dienbienphu in 1954, the French were compelled to accede to the creation of a Communist Vietnam north of the 17th parallel while leaving a non-Communist entity south of that line. The United States refused to accept the arrangement. The administration of President Dwight D. *Eisenhower undertook instead to build a nation from the spurious political entity that was South Vietnam by fabricating a government there, taking over control from the French, dispatching military advisers to train a South Vietnamese army, and unleashing the *Central Intelligence Agency (CIA) to conduct psychological warfare against the North.

President John F. *Kennedy rounded another turning point in early 1961, when he secretly sent 400 *Special Operations Forces–trained (Green Beret) soldiers to teach the South Vietnamese how to fight what was called *counterinsurgency* war against Communist guerrillas in South Vietnam. When Kennedy was assassinated in November 1963, there were more than 16,000 U.S. military advisers in South Vietnam, and more than 100 Americans had been killed. Kennedy's successor, Lyndon B. *Johnson, committed the United States most fully to the war. In August 1964, he secured from Congress a functional (not actual) declaration of war: the Tonkin Gulf Resolution. Then, in February and March 1965, Johnson authorized the sustained bombing, by U.S. aircraft, of targets north of the 17th parallel, and on 8 March dispatched 3,500 Marines to South Vietnam. Legal declaration or no, the United States was now at war.

The multiple starting dates for the war complicate efforts to describe the causes of U.S. entry. The United States became involved in the war for a number of reasons, and these evolved and shifted over time. Primarily, every American president regarded the enemy in Vietnam—the Vietminh; its 1960s successor, the National Liberation Front (NLF); and the government of North Vietnam, led by *Ho Chi Minh—as agents of global communism. U.S. policymakers, and most Americans, regarded communism as the antithesis of all they held dear. Communists scorned democracy, violated human rights, pursued military aggression, and created closed state economies that barely traded with capitalist countries. Americans compared communism to a contagious disease. If it took hold in one nation, U.S. policymakers expected contiguous nations to fall to communism, too, as if nations were dominoes lined up on end. In 1949, when the Communist Party came to power in China, Washington feared that Vietnam would become the next Asian domino. That was one reason for Truman's 1950 decision to give aid to the French who were fighting the Vietminh.

Truman also hoped that assisting the French in Vietnam would help to shore up the developed, non-Communist nations, whose fates were in surprising ways tied to the preservation of Vietnam and, given the domino theory, all of Southeast Asia. Free world dominion over the region would provide markets for Japan, rebuilding with American help after the Pacific War. U.S. involvement in Vietnam reassured the British, who linked their postwar recovery to the revival of the rubber and tin industries in their colony of Malaya, one of Vietnam's neighbors. And with U.S. aid, the French could concentrate on economic recovery at home, and could hope ultimately to recall their Indochina officer corps to oversee the rearmament of West Germany, a *Cold War measure deemed essential by the Americans. These ambitions formed a second set of reasons why the United States became involved in Vietnam.

As presidents committed the United States to conflict bit by bit, many of these ambitions were forgotten. Instead, inertia developed against withdrawing from Vietnam. Washington believed that U.S. withdrawal would result in a Communist victory—Eisenhower acknowledged that, had elections been held as scheduled in Vietnam in 1956, "Ho Chi Minh would have won 80% of the vote"—and no U.S. president wanted to lose a country to communism. Democrats in particular, like Kennedy and Johnson, feared a right-wing backlash should they give up the fight; they remembered vividly the accusatory tone of the Republicans' 1950 question, "Who lost China?" The commitment to Vietnam itself, passed from administration to administration, took on validity aside from any rational basis it might once have had. Truman, Eisenhower, and Kennedy all gave their word that the United States would stand by its South Vietnamese allies. If the United States abandoned the South Vietnamese, its word would be regarded as unreliable by other governments, friendly or not. So U.S. credibility seemed at stake.

Along with the larger structural and ideological causes of the war in Vietnam, the experience, personality, and temperament of each president played a role in deepening the U.S. commitment. Dwight Eisenhower restrained U.S. involvement because, having commanded troops in battle, he doubted the United States could fight a land war in Southeast Asia. The youthful John Kennedy, on the other hand, felt he had to prove his resolve to the American people and his Communist adversaries, especially in the aftermath of several foreign policy blunders early in his administration. Lyndon Johnson saw the Vietnam War as a test of his mettle, as a southerner and as a man. He exhorted his soldiers to "nail the coonskin to the wall" in Vietnam, likening *victory to a successful hunting expedition.

When Johnson began bombing North Vietnam and sent the Marines to South Vietnam in early 1965, he had every intention of fighting a limited war. He and his advisers worried that too lavish a use of U.S. firepower might prompt the Chinese to enter the conflict. It was not expected that the North Vietnamese and the NLF would hold out long against the American military. And yet U.S. policymakers never managed to fit military *strategy to U.S. goals in Vietnam. Massive bombing had little effect against a decentralized economy like North Vietnam's. Kennedy had favored counterinsurgency warfare in the South Vietnamese countryside, and Johnson endorsed this strategy, but the political side of counterinsurgency—the effort to win the "hearts and minds" of the Vietnamese peasantry—was at best underdeveloped and probably doomed. Presidents proved reluctant to mobilize American society to the extent the generals thought necessary to defeat the enemy.

As the United States went to war in 1965, a few voices were raised in dissent. Within the Johnson administration, Undersecretary of State George *Ball warned that the South Vietnamese government was a functional nonentity and simply could not be sustained by the United States, even with a major effort. Antiwar protest groups formed on many of the nation's campuses; in June, the leftist organization *Students for a Democratic Society decided to make the war its principal target. But major dissent would not begin until 1966 or later. By and large in 1965, Americans supported the administration's claim that it was fighting to stop communism in Southeast Asia, or people simply shrugged and went about their daily lives, unaware that this gradually escalating war would tear American society apart.

[See also Commander in Chief, President as; Counterinsurgency; Guerrilla Warfare; Peace and Antiwar Movements.]

• George C. Herring, America's Longest War, 1979; 3rd ed. 1996. Stanley Karnow, Vietnam: A History, 1983; rev. ed. 1991. George M. Kahin, Intervention, 1986. Andrew J. Rotter, The Path to Vietnam, 1987. Lloyd Gardner, Approaching Vietnam: World War II Through Dienbienphu, 1988. Neil Sheehan, A Bright Shining Lie: John Paul Vann and America in Vietnam, 1988. David Anderson, Trapped by Success: The Eisenhower Administration and Vietnam, 1953–1961, 1991. Marilyn B. Young, The Vietnam Wars, 1991. Lloyd Gardner, Pay Any Price: Lyndon Johnson and the Wars for Vietnam, 1995. John Prados, The Hidden History of the Vietnam War, 1995. Robert Buzzanco, Masters of War: Military Dissent and Politics in the Vietnam Era, 1996. Robert D. Schulzinger, A Time for War: The United States and Vietnam, 1941–1975, 1997.   —Andrew J. Rotter

VIETNAM WAR (1960–1975): MILITARY AND DIPLOMATIC COURSE

The Vietnam War was the longest deployment of U.S. forces in hostile action in the history of the American republic. Although there is no formal declaration of war from which to date U.S. entry, President John F. *Kennedy's decision to send over 2,000 military advisers to South Vietnam in 1961 marked the beginning of twelve years of American military combat. U.S. unit combat began in 1965. The number of U.S. troops steadily increased until it reached a peak of 543,400 in April 1969. The total number of Americans who served in South Vietnam was 2.7 million. Of these, more than 58,000 died or remain missing, and 300,000 others were wounded. The U.S. government spent more than $140 billion on the war. Despite this enormous military effort, the United States failed to achieve its objective of preserving an independent, noncommunist state in South Vietnam. This failure has led to searching questions about why and how the war was fought and whether a better diplomatic and military outcome was possible for the United States.

Escalation. By 1961, guerrilla warfare was widespread in South Vietnam. Communist-led troops of the National Liberation Front (NLF) of South Vietnam, commonly referred to as Vietcong, were initiating hundreds of terrorist and small unit attacks per month. Saigon's military, the Army of the Republic of Vietnam (ARVN), was not able to contain this growing insurgency. During the administration of President Dwight D. *Eisenhower, a small U.S. Military Assistance Advisory Group (MAAG), never numbering more than 740 uniformed soldiers, had provided training and logistics assistance to the ARVN. The Kennedy administration determined that the size and mission of the U.S. advisory effort must change if the U.S.-backed government of Ngo Dinh Diem in Saigon was to survive. Some of Kennedy's aides proposed a negotiated settlement in Vietnam similar to that which recognized Laos as a neutral country. Having just suffered international embarrassment in Cuba and Berlin, the president rejected compromise and chose to strengthen U.S. support of Saigon.

In May 1961, Kennedy sent 400 U.S. Army Special Forces (Green Beret) troops into South Vietnam's Central Highlands to train Montagnard tribesmen in counterinsurgency tactics. He also tripled the level of aid to South Vietnam. A steady stream of airplanes, helicopters, armored personnel carriers (APCs), and other equipment poured into the South. By the end of 1962, there were 9,000 U.S. military advisers under the direction of a newly-created Military Assistance Command Vietnam (MACV), commanded by U.S. Army Gen. Paul Harkins. Under U.S. guidance, the Diem government also began construction of "strategic hamlets." These fortified villages were intended to insulate rural Vietnamese from Vietcong intimidation and propaganda.

U.S. and South Vietnamese leaders were cautiously optimistic that increased U.S. assistance finally was enabling the Saigon government to defend itself. On 2 January 1963, however, at Ap Bac on the Plain of Reeds southwest of Saigon, a Vietcong battalion of about 320 men inflicted heavy damage on an ARVN force of 3,000 equipped with troop-carrying helicopters, new UH-1 ("Huey") helicopter gunships, tactical bombers, and APCs. Ap Bac represented a leadership failure for the ARVN and a major morale boost for the antigovernment forces. The absence of fighting spirit in the ARVN mirrored the continuing inability of the Saigon regime to win political support. Indeed, many South Vietnamese perceived the strategic hamlets as government oppression, not protection, because people were forced to leave their ancestral homes for the new settlements.

While Vietcong guerrillas scored military successes, leaders of Vietnam's Buddhist majority protested against what they saw as the Diem regime's religious persecution. In June, a monk dramatically burned himself to death at a busy Saigon intersection. The "Buddhist crisis" and dissatisfaction with Diem by top Vietnamese Army leaders made U.S. officials receptive to the idea of a change in South Vietnam's leadership. Ambassador Henry Cabot *Lodge and the Central Intelligence Agency (CIA) did not interfere as a group of ARVN officers plotted a coup. On 1 November 1963, the generals seized power, and Diem and his unpopular brother Ngo Dinh Nhu were murdered. Three weeks later, President Kennedy was assassinated, and U.S. policy in Vietnam was again at a crossroads. If the new government in Saigon failed to show progress against the insurgency, would the United States withdraw its support from a lost cause, or would it escalate the effort to preserve South Vietnam as an anticommunist outpost in Asia?

Lyndon B. Johnson inherited the Vietnam dilemma. As Senate majority leader in the 1950s and as vice-president, he had supported Eisenhower's and Kennedy's decisions to aid South Vietnam. Four days after Kennedy's death, Johnson, now president, reaffirmed in National Security Action Memorandum (NSAM) 273 that the U.S. goal was to assist South Vietnam in its "contest against the externally directed and supported communist conspiracy." U.S. policy defined the Vietnam War as North Vietnamese aggression against South Vietnam. North Vietnam infiltrated troops and matériel into South Vietnam by sea and along the so-called Ho Chi Minh Trail in Laos. Throughout his administration, Johnson insisted that the only possible negotiated settlement of the conflict would be one in which North Vietnam recognized the legitimacy of South Vietnam's government. Without such recognition, the United States would continue to provide Saigon as much help as it needed to survive.

The critical military questions were how much U.S. assistance was enough and what form it should take. By the spring of 1964, the Vietcong controlled vast areas of South Vietnam, the strategic hamlet program had essentially ceased, and North Vietnam's aid to the southern insurgents had grown. In June, Johnson named one of the army's most distinguished officers, Gen. William C. *Westmoreland, then commandant of West Point, as commander U.S. MACV. Westmoreland immediately asked for more men, and by the end of 1964 U.S. personnel in the South exceeded 23,000. Increasingly, however, the U.S. effort focused on the North. Secretary of Defense Robert S. *McNamara, Secretary of State Dean Rusk, and other key White House aides remained convinced that the assault on South Vietnam originated in the ambitious designs of Hanoi backed by Moscow and Beijing.

Throughout 1964, the United States assisted South Vietnam in covert operations to gather intelligence, disseminate propaganda, and harass the North. On the night of 2 August, North Vietnamese gunboats fired on the USS Maddox, a destroyer on an intelligence-collecting mission, in the same area of the Gulf of Tonkin where South Vietnamese commandos were conducting raids against the North Vietnamese coast. Two nights later, under stormy conditions, the Maddox and another destroyer, the Turner Joy, reported a gunboat attack. Although doubts existed about these reports, the president ordered retaliatory air strikes against the North Vietnamese port of Vinh. The White House had expected that some type of incident would occur eventually, and it had prepared the text of a congressional resolution authorizing the president to use armed force to protect U.S. forces and to deter further aggression from North Vietnam. On 7 August 1964, Johnson secured almost unanimous consent from Congress (414–0 in the House; 88–2 in the Senate) for his Gulf of Tonkin Resolution, which became the principal legislative basis for all subsequent military deployment in Southeast Asia.

Johnson's decisive but restrained response to the *Gulf of Tonkin incidents helped him win the 1964 election, but Saigon's prospects continued to decline. The president wanted to concentrate on his ambitious domestic program, the Great Society, but his political instincts told him that his leadership would be damaged fatally if America's client state in South Vietnam succumbed. Instability mounted in South Vietnam as rival military and civilian factions vied for power and as Vietcong strength grew. A consensus formed among Johnson's advisers that the United States would have to initiate air warfare against North Vietnam. Bombing could boost Saigon's morale and might persuade the North to cease its support of the insurgency. The *Joint Chiefs of Staff (JCS) favored a massive bombing campaign, but civilians in the State and Defense Departments preferred a gradual escalation.

Using as a pretext a Vietcong attack on 7 February 1965 at Pleiku that killed eight American soldiers, Johnson ordered retaliatory bombing north of the Demilitarized Zone along the 17th parallel that divided North and South Vietnam. Within a week, the administration began ROLLING THUNDER, a gradually intensifying air bombardment of military bases, supply depots, and infiltration routes in North Vietnam. Flying out of bases in Thailand, U.S. Air Force fighter-bombers—primarily F-105 Thunderchiefs and later F-4 Phantoms—joined U.S. Navy Phantoms and A-4 Skyhawks from a powerful carrier task force located at a point called Yankee Station, seventy-five miles off the North Vietnamese coast in the Gulf of Tonkin. In 1965, U.S. aircraft flew 25,000 sorties against North Vietnam, and that number grew to 79,000 in 1966 and 108,000 in 1967. In 1967 annual bombing tonnage reached almost a quarter million. Targets expanded to include the Ho Chi Minh Trail in Laos and factories, farms, and railroads in North Vietnam.

From the beginning of the bombing, American strategists debated the effectiveness of air power in defeating a political insurgency in a predominantly agricultural country. Despite the American bombs, dollars, and military advisers, the Vietcong continued to inflict heavy casualties on the ARVN, and the political situation in Saigon grew worse. By June 1965, there had been five governments in the South since Diem's death, and the newest regime, headed by General Nguyen Van Thieu and Air Marshall Nguyen Cao Ky, inspired little confidence. To stave off defeat, the JCS endorsed Westmoreland's request for 150,000 U.S. troops to take the ground offensive in the South. When McNamara concurred, Johnson decided to commit the forces. The buildup of formal U.S. military units had begun on 8 March 1965, when two battalions of Marines landed at Da Nang. In June, Marine and army units began offensive unit operations—"search and destroy" missions. On 28 July, Johnson announced that 50,000 U.S. troops would go to South Vietnam immediately. By the end of the year, there were 184,300 U.S. personnel in the South.

Although Johnson's actions meant that the United States had crossed the line from advising the ARVN to actually fighting the war against the Vietcong, the president downplayed the move. The JCS wanted a mobilization of the reserves and National Guard, and McNamara proposed levying war taxes. Such actions would have placed the United States on a war footing. With his ambitious social reform program facing crucial votes in Congress, the president wanted to avoid giving congressional conservatives an opportunity to use mobilization to block his domestic agenda. Consequently, he relied on other means. Monthly draft calls increased from 17,000 to 35,000 to meet manpower needs, and deficit spending, with its inherent inflationary impact, funded the escalation.

With U.S. bombs pounding North Vietnam, Westmoreland turned America's massive firepower on the southern insurgents. Johnson's choice of gradual escalation of bombing and incremental troop deployments was based upon the concept of limited warfare. Risks of a wider war with China and the Soviet Union meant that the United States would not go all out to annihilate North Vietnam. Thus, Westmoreland chose a strategy of attrition in the South. Using mobility and powerful weapons, the MACV commander could limit U.S. *casualties while exhausting the enemy, that is, inflicting heavier losses than could be replaced.

Escalation of the air and ground war in 1965 provoked

Hanoi to begin deploying into the South increasing units of the regular North Vietnamese Army (NVA), or People's Army of Vietnam (PAVN), as it was called. In October, Gen. Vo Nguyen *Giap, the PAVN commander, launched a major offensive in the Central Highlands, southwest of Pleiku. Westmoreland responded with the 1st Air Cavalry Division (Air Mobile). Through much of November, in the Battle of the *Ia Drang Valley, U.S. and North Vietnamese forces engaged each other in heavy combat for the first time. The Americans ultimately forced the NVA out of the valley and killed ten times as many enemy soldiers as they lost. Westmoreland used helicopters extensively for troop movements, resupply, medical evacuation, and tactical air support. USAF tactical bombers and even huge B-52 strategic bombers attacked enemy positions. The battle convinced the U.S. commander that "search and destroy" tactics using air mobility would work in accomplishing the attrition strategy. Soon after the PAVN departed the battlefield, however, so too did the American air "cavalry." Clearly, control of territory was not the U.S. military objective.

During 1966 Westmoreland requested more ground troops, and by year's end the U.S. ground force level "in country" reached 385,000. These were organized into seven divisions and other specialized airborne, armored, special forces, and logistical units. With U.S. aid, the ARVN also expanded to eleven divisions, supplemented by local and irregular units. While MACV was getting men and munitions in place for large-unit search and destroy operations, army and marine units conducted smaller operations. Although the "body count"—the estimated number of enemy killed—mounted, attrition was not changing the political equation in South Vietnam. The NLF continued to exercise more effective control in many areas than did the government, and Vietcong guerrillas, who often disappeared when U.S. forces entered an area, quickly reappeared when the Americans left.

In 1967, Westmoreland made his big push to win the war. With South Vietnam's forces assigned primarily to occupation, pacification, and security duties, massive U.S. combat sweeps moved to locate and destroy the enemy. In January, Operation Cedar Falls was a 30,000-man assault on the Iron Triangle, an enemy base area forty miles north of Saigon. From February through April, Operation Junction City was an even larger attack on nearby War Zone C. There was major fighting in the Central Highlands, climaxing in the battle of Dak To in November 1967. U.S. forces killed many enemy soldiers and destroyed large amounts of supplies. MACV declared vast areas to be "free-fire zones," which meant that U.S. and ARVN artillery and tactical aircraft, as well as B-52 "carpet bombing," could target anyone or anything in the area. In Operation RANCH HAND, the USAF sprayed the defoliant Agent Orange to deprive the guerrillas of cover and food supplies. Controversy about the use of Agent Orange erupted in 1969 when reports appeared that the chemical caused serious damage to humans as well as to plants.

Late in 1967, with 485,600 U.S. troops in Vietnam, Westmoreland announced that, although much fighting remained, a cross-over point had arrived in the war of attrition; that is, the losses to the NVA and Vietcong were greater than they could replace. This assessment was debatable, and there was considerable evidence that the so-called "other war" for political support in South Vietnam was not going well. Corruption, factionalism, and continued Buddhist protests plagued the Thieu-Ky government. Despite incredible losses, the Vietcong still controlled many areas. A diplomatic resolution of the conflict remained elusive. Several third countries, such as Poland and Great Britain, offered proposals intended to facilitate negotiations. These formulas typically called upon the United States and DRV to coordinate mutual reduction of their military activities in South Vietnam, but both Washington and Hanoi firmly resisted even interim compromises with the other. The war was at a stalemate.

De-escalation. The decisive year was 1968. In the early morning of 30 January, Vietcong forces launched the *Tet Offensive, named for the Vietnamese holiday then being observed. In coordinated attacks throughout South Vietnam, the Vietcong assaulted major urban areas and military installations in an attempt to spark a popular uprising against the Saigon regime and its American backers. Heavy fighting ensued for three weeks, some of the most brutal at Hué. Westmoreland claimed victory because no cities were lost and thousands of casualties were inflicted upon the attackers. Indeed, the Vietcong lost so many soldiers that thereafter the PAVN took over much of the conduct of the war. The *Tet Offensive, however, was a great strategic gain for North Vietnam and its southern adherents. U.S. and ARVN losses were high, and the fighting generated thousands of refugees that further destabilized the South. Most importantly, as a result of the massive surprise attack and the pictures from Saigon, the U.S. press and public began to challenge the Johnson administration's assurances of success and to question the value of the increasingly costly war.

At the same time as the Tet Offensive, the siege of Khe Sanh underscored the image of the war as an endless, costly, and pointless struggle. From 20 January to 14 April 1968, 30,000 to 40,000 NVA forces surrounded 6,000 U.S. Marines and ARVN at the remote hilltop outpost of Khe Sanh in the northwest corner of South Vietnam. Using artillery and air power, including B-52 strikes, the United States eventually broke the siege and forced an NVA withdrawal. At the end of June, however, the Marines abandoned the base to adopt a more mobile form of fighting in the DMZ area. Once again, a major engagement left seemingly intangible results.

In March 1968, Johnson decided that the size of the U.S. effort in Vietnam had grown as large as could be justified. Prompted by a request from Westmoreland and JCS Chairman General Earle G. *Wheeler for 206,000 more men, the president asked his new secretary of defense, Clark *Clifford, for a thorough policy review. Johnson's sense that a limit had been reached seemed confirmed when the "Wise Men," a group of outside advisers including such elder statesmen as former Secretary of State Dean *Acheson and Gen. Omar *Bradley, recommended against further increases. The president authorized only 13,500 more soldiers and bluntly informed Thieu and Ky that their forces would have to carry more of the fighting. He then announced on television on 31 March 1968 that the United States would restrict the bombing of North Vietnam and pursue a negotiated settlement with Hanoi. Johnson also revealed that he would not seek reelection.

Meanwhile, combat raged in South Vietnam. Over 14,000 Americans were killed in action in Vietnam in 1968, the highest annual U.S. death toll of the war. The worst U.S. war crime of the conflict occurred on 16 March 1968 (although not revealed in the press until 6 November

1969) when American infantrymen massacred some 500 unresisting civilians, including babies, in the village of *My Lai. In April and May 1968 the largest ground operation of the war, with 110,000 U.S. and ARVN troops, targeted Vietcong and NVA forces near Saigon. Peace talks began in Paris on 13 May but immediately deadlocked. On 10 June 1968, Gen. Creighton *Abrams succeeded Westmoreland as MACV commander. In the fall Abrams began to shift U.S. strategy from attrition to a greater emphasis on combined operations, pacification area security, and what was called "Vietnamization," that is, preparing the ARVN to do more of the fighting.

When Richard M. *Nixon became president in 1969, the U.S. war effort remained massive, but the basic decision to de-escalate had already been reached. Nixon owed his political victory to voter expectation that somehow he would end the war. He and his principal foreign policy adviser, Henry *Kissinger, rejected precipitate U.S. withdrawal. With the ground war stalemated, the new administration turned increasingly to air bombardment and secretly expanded the air war to neutral Cambodia. Publicly the White House announced in June the first withdrawal of 25,000 U.S. troops and heralded Vietnamization as effective. In fact, South Vietnam's armed forces remained problem-plagued. To bolster the South, the administration leaked to the press dire threats of a "go for broke" air and naval assault on the North—possibly including nuclear weapons. Kissinger also began secret meetings with North Vietnamese representatives in Paris hoping to arrange a diplomatic breakthrough.

The morale and discipline of U.S. troops declined in 1969 as the futility of the ground war and the beginnings of U.S. withdrawal became more obvious. After an intense ten-day battle in May, infantrymen of the 101st Airborne Division (Air Mobile) took a ridge in the A Shau Valley that they had dubbed *Hamburger Hill. Having fought bravely and suffered significant losses, the soldiers were bitter when the site soon was abandoned. Such inability to see progress, and an awareness among the troops that politicians back home were giving up on the war, helped undermine military effectiveness. Simple survival of their twelve-month tour of duty became the only motivation for many soldiers. Incidents of insubordination, mutiny, fatal assaults on officers, drug use, racial tensions, and other serious problems increased.

Faced with mounting public dissatisfaction, the slow pace of Vietnamization, and diplomatic frustration, Nixon boldly sent U.S. units into Cambodia in April 1970. U.S. military leaders had long complained about the sanctuary that neutral Cambodia provided Vietcong and NVA forces. This Cambodian incursion lasted until the end of June and provided some tactical gains, but it also sparked sharp controversy and demonstrations by the *Vietnam antiwar movement in the United States over what seemed an expansion of the war to another country. U.S. troop reductions continued with only 334,600 in the South as 1970 ended.

Nixon stuck with more of the same in 1971. Responding to domestic critics, he continued to order U.S. troops home, leaving only 156,000 by December. To support Vietnamization, heavy U.S. air attacks continued against Communist supply lines in Laos and Cambodia, and so-called protective-reaction strikes hit military targets north of the Demilitarized Zone and near Hanoi and its port city of

Haiphong. Tactical air support continued, with the heaviest coming in March during a South Vietnamese assault into Laos. Code named Lam Son 719, this operation ended in a confused retreat by the ARVN that further sullied the notion of Vietnamization.

During 1971, Kissinger made progress in the secret negotiations by offering to separate the arrangement of a ceasefire from discussion of the future of the Saigon government. In 1972 Nixon traveled to China and the USSR in diplomatic initiatives, trying to isolate Hanoi from its suppliers. With the shrinking American forces nearing 100,000 (only a small portion being combat troops), General Giap launched a spring 1972 offensive by Communist forces against the northern provinces of South Vietnam, the Central Highlands, and provinces northwest of Saigon. In most of the battles, the ARVN was saved by massive B-52 bombing. Nixon also launched the heavy bombers against North Vietnam itself in a campaign called Linebacker, and the United States mined the harbor at Haiphong. Over the course of the war, total U.S. bombing tonnage far exceeded that dropped on Germany, Italy, and Japan in World War II.

Wearied by the latest round of fighting, the United States and North Vietnamese governments agreed in October on a ceasefire, return of U.S. prisoners of war (POWs), at least the temporary continuation of Thieu's government, and, most controversially, permission for NVA troops to remain in the South. Objections from Thieu caused Nixon to hesitate, which in turn led Hanoi to harden its position. In December, the United States hit North Vietnam again with repeated B-52 attacks, codenamed Linebacker II and labeled the Christmas Bombing by journalists. On 27 January 1973, the United States, North Vietnam, South Vietnam, and the Provisional Revolutionary Government representing the NLF signed the *Paris Peace Agreements Ending the War and Restoring Peace in Vietnam, which basically confirmed the October terms.

By 1 April 1973, U.S. forces were out of Vietnam (except for a few embassy guards and attaches) and 587 POWs had returned home (about 2,500 other Americans remained missing in action). Congress cut off funds for the air war in Cambodia, and bombing there ended in August. Over Nixon's veto, Congress passed the *War Powers Resolution in November 1973. It limited presidential power to deploy U.S. forces in hostile action without congressional approval.

Nixon characterized the Paris Peace Agreements of 1973 as "peace with honor," but primarily they allowed the U.S. military to leave Vietnam without resolving the issue of the country's political future. Without U.S. air and ground support, South Vietnam's military defenses steadily deteriorated. In the spring of 1975, an NVA thrust into the Central Highlands turned into an ARVN rout. On 30 April, as NVA and Vietcong soldiers entered the city, the last remaining Americans abandoned the U.S. embassy in Saigon in a dramatic rooftop evacuation by *helicopters.

The United States failure in Vietnam raised important questions. Should the United States have fought the war at all? Did the United States fight the war the wrong way? Many analysts believe that the strategic importance of Vietnam was vastly exaggerated and, furthermore, that the nationalism driving Vietnam's history and politics could not be altered by U.S. military power, no matter how great. An alternative view is that even if the odds were poor for U.S. success, the United States had to make the effort to maintain its moral and strategic credibility in the world. On the question of how the war was fought, the debate centers on whether the United States used its military power adequately and effectively. Assuming that more is better, some critics argue that a greater use of U.S. force, either against North Vietnam or to isolate the battlefield in South Vietnam, would have produced victory. Throughout the conflict, however, the Saigon regime proved incapable of translating military success into political success. Also, massive U.S. assistance seemed to prove North Vietnam's and the Vietcong's claims that South Vietnam was not a Vietnamese but an American creation. Finally, a larger war would have risked a dangerous military conflict with China and the Soviet Union. Most scholars conclude that the Vietnam War was a tragic event whose costs far exceeded any benefits for the United States.

• Raphael Littauer and Normal Uphoff, eds., The Air War in Indochina, 1972. Edwin Hooper, et al., The United States Navy and the Vietnam Conflict, 1976. Harry G. Summers, Jr., On Strategy: A Critical Analysis of the Vietnam War, 1982. Stanley Karnow, Vietnam: A History, 1983. Bruce Palmer, Jr., The 25-Year War: America's Military Role in Vietnam, 1984. John S. Bowman, ed., The World Almanac of the Vietnam War, 1985. James William Gibson, The Perfect War, 1986. Gary R. Hess, Vietnam and the United States, 1990. David L. Anderson, ed., Shadow on the White House: Presidents and the Vietnam War, 1945–1975, 1993. Ronald H. Spector, After Tet, 1993. George Donelson Moss, Vietnam: An American Ordeal, 2nd ed., 1994. George C. Herring, America's Longest War: The United States and Vietnam, 1950–1975, 3rd ed., 1995.

—David L. Anderson

VIETNAM WAR (1960–75): DOMESTIC COURSE

When President Lyndon B. *Johnson made the war in Vietnam an American war in 1965, he worried about the impact of his policies on the home front. He could have rallied support for his decisions to bomb North Vietnam and assume the dominant ground combat role by telling the nation that it faced a crisis vital to its national security. But he feared that in response to such a message, the public would demand a full-scale, no-holds-barred war that could have led to Chinese and Russian intervention. For Johnson and his advisers, the Vietnam War was the prototype for future limited wars in the Third World that would have to be fought without arousing public passion. However, by underselling the war, the president presented an opening to critics who asked why he was expending so much human and material treasure in such a remote conflict.

Johnson had another motive for playing down the commitment in Southeast Asia. After the Democrats won by a landslide in the 1964 election, the president believed he had a two-year window of opportunity to push through Congress legislation for his Great Society, the most ambitious set of reforms since the New Deal. He was painfully aware of what happened to Woodrow *Wilson's and Franklin D. *Roosevelt's comparable reform programs when they fell victim to "guns-over-butter" decisions. Escalating by stealth in Vietnam, Johnson was able to have "guns and butter" without increasing taxes to pay for both projects. This irresponsible decision had a profound impact on the American economy.

Johnson's failure to rally the public around the commitment in Vietnam led to the growth of the largest and most effective antiwar movement in American history. Beginning in 1966, through mass demonstrations, petitioning, teach-ins, electoral politics, civil disobedience, and countless other individual and collective forms of protests, millions of Americans challenged administration policies. Although a majority of the population found aspects of the campus-based movement repellent, it did attract support in many important sectors of the society and contributed to the collapse of the bipartisan *Cold War consensus that had held since 1947.

Moreover, on at least two occasions, the antiwar movement dramatically affected policy. After 35,000 mostly young people besieged the *Pentagon on 21–22 October 1967, Lyndon Johnson launched a public relations campaign that emphasized how well the war was going. When the Communists launched their seemingly successful nationwide *Tet Offensive on 30 January 1968, most Americans felt that they had been deceived by their own government. That widespread public disaffection led to Johnson's decision on 31 March 1968 not to escalate further and not to stand for reelection. He also faced serious challenges for the nomination from antiwar senators Eugene McCarthy (D-Minn.) and Robert F. Kennedy (D-N.Y.).

A little more than a year later, Republican president Richard M. *Nixon sent an ultimatum to Hanoi to alter its bargaining position at the Paris Peace Talks by 1 November or confront a major escalation. The North Vietnamese called Nixon's bluff, and he did not escalate, in good measure because of the depth and breadth of antiwar sentiment reflected in the largest antiwar activity of the period, the 15 October 1969 Moratorium, a peaceful and dignified protest involving many middle-class adults. Nixon's decision was also influenced by his advisers' determination that no matter what form the proposed escalation (Operation Duck Hook) took, it was unlikely to end the war.

Finally, both Johnson and Nixon were convinced that the perceived popularity of the antiwar movement influenced the Vietnamese Communists. Thus, both presidents' policies were affected, to some degree, by how they thought Hanoi interpreted the success of the movement. That relative success led Johnson, and especially Nixon, to take extralegal and illegal actions against antiwar critics and organizations. Some of those actions became part of the Watergate scandal, the series of crimes and misdemeanors that ultimately led to Nixon's resignation. For example, Nixon first authorized illegal wiretaps in May 1969 to find the leaker who told a New York Times reporter that the United States was secretly bombing Cambodia.

Johnson and Nixon also confronted spirited challenges to their foreign policymaking authority on Capitol Hill. Beginning in the winter of 1966 with hearings held by Senate Foreign Relations Committee Chairman J. William Fulbright (D-Ark.), and increasing to a crescendo after 1968 when the Democratic legislature confronted a Republican president, Congress began to rein in what had come to be called the "imperial presidency." It was true that 95 percent of those legislators present and voting approved of war-related appropriation bills from 1965 through 1972. Nevertheless, during the invasion of Cambodia in the spring of 1970, the Senate voted to repeal the Gulf of Tonkin Resolution and to cut off funds for the operation after 30 June. Moreover, from 1973 through 1975, Congress passed several resolutions that restricted the use of troops and airpower in Southeast Asia and rejected presidential requests

for further aid to South Vietnam. Most important, in 1973 it passed, over Nixon's veto, the *War Powers Resolution, which sought to restrict the president's ability to send American troops into combat without informing Congress or obtaining its approval for an extended commitment.

The war affected as well the presidential elections of 1968 and 1972. In 1968, the candidacy of Hubert H. Humphrey was significantly weakened by the bloody confrontations in Chicago at the Democratic National Convention between youthful critics of the war and the police. In addition, Lyndon Johnson announced a complete bombing halt one week before the election in an "October Surprise," which aided his vice president. For his part, Richard Nixon suggested obliquely that he had a plan (it did not exist) to end the war. In a law and order campaign, he also appealed to those who abhorred antiwar and other unruly demonstrators.

After Nixon was unable to end the war on his terms during his first year in office, he and his aides encouraged the growth of the POW-MIA movement, which was concerned about the treatment of the known prisoners of war (POWs) in Communist captivity and the whereabouts of those classified as missing in action (MIA), some of whom were also suspected to be among those languishing, undocumented, in camps in North and South Vietnam and Laos. Nixon then contended from 1970 through 1972 that during the extended public and secret peace talks, the North Vietnamese were recalcitrant on the emotional POW-MIA issue. Undoubtedly, the president was concerned about how the sort of peace he obtained in Vietnam would affect his prospects in his reelection campaign.

One week before the 1972 election, Nixon's national security adviser, Henry *Kissinger, offered a Republican "October Surprise" when he announced that "peace is at hand." The North Vietnamese forced Kissinger to make this statement when they announced on 25 October that they and the Americans had finally agreed on terms for ending the war. Hanoi went public with the arrangements because it feared, correctly, that Washington and especially Saigon were reneging on the provisional agreement reached on 21 October. What the national security adviser did not reveal then—or even after the election—was that he had been unable to convince the South Vietnamese government to accept the terms he had negotiated with the North Vietnamese. Nonetheless, Kissinger's announcement effectively took away Democratic antiwar candidate George McGovern's most important issue. McGovern had obtained the nomination in good measure because of reforms adopted by his party in the wake of the Chicago riots.

Some of those who opposed the war were driven by the fact that as Johnson's policy escalated, more and more young people were drafted into the armed services and sent to Vietnam. By 1967, almost 50 percent of the enlisted men in the army were draftees. By 1969, draftees comprised over 50 percent of all combat deaths and 88 percent of army infantrymen in Vietnam.

No war since the *Civil War produced so much opposition to the draft. Part of the problem had to do with its perceived unfairness. Undergraduates and, until 1968, graduate students could defer military service until they completed their programs. In addition, many young men, often from the middle class, joined the National Guard and Reserves on the likely gamble that they would not be called up for duty in Southeast Asia. Consequently, the Vietnam

War appeared to many to be a "working-class war," with draftees and enlisted men coming disproportionately from blue-collar backgrounds. At first, from 1965 through 1967, African Americans especially served and died in Vietnam in disproportionate numbers. By the end of the war, however, they accounted for 12 percent of the combat deaths, a figure close to their actual percentage in the population.

Of the 27 million men eligible for *conscription during the Vietnam era, 8,720,000 enlisted, often to beat the draft; 2,215,000 were drafted; and almost 16 million never served. Of that 16 million, 15,410,000 were deferred, exempted, or disqualified, and an estimated 570,000 were draft offenders. Of that number, over 209,517 were accused of draft violations, 8,750 were convicted, and 3,250 were imprisoned. The number of violators swamped the judiciary system.

During the war, the Selective Service System, prodded by the Supreme Court, relaxed its definition of *conscientious objection. As a consequence, 170,000 men received that status, of whom close to one-third evaded alternate service. Between 60,000 and 100,000 young men chose exile to avoid the draft, with Canada and Sweden the favorite sanctuaries. The prospect of the draft also affected millions of eligible males' decisions to marry, have children, or continue their education.

Widespread draft resistance—including flamboyant acts of civil and not so civil disobedience that impeded the operation of the system—and severe discipline problems posed by obstreperous and poorly motivated draftees in the field led to dramatic reform. First, on the eve of the Moratorium in October 1969, Nixon removed the unpopular Gen. Lewis B. Hershey, who had been in charge of the Selective Service System since World War II. The president instituted a lottery system two months later in an attempt to make the system somewhat fairer. In September 1971, Congress passed his proposal for an *All-Volunteer Force, and in July 1973, Nixon terminated the draft.

As important as these reforms were to the American military and society in general in the years from 1973 to the present, the impact of the Vietnam War on the economy during the same period was even more important. For many economists, the last truly good years for the economy were 1962–65, with almost full employment; very low inflation; respectable growth in productivity, gross national product, and national income; and a favorable balance of trade.

On the last issue, an increasingly unfavorable balance of trade, related in part to spending for the war abroad, contributed to an international monetary crisis involving a threat to U.S. gold reserves in 1967–68. That threat helped convince some administration officials and Wall Street analysts that the United States could no longer afford the war.

As early as the winter of 1965, Lyndon Johnson's economic advisers, who worried about the imminent overheating of the economy, recommended a tax increase to help pay for the increasingly expensive war and to hold down inflation. For domestic political reasons, Johnson refused to accept their advice until 1968, when he introduced a 10 percent income tax surcharge, which economists now claim, was too little and too late.

For most of Johnson's term, however, the inflation figures remained relatively low, reaching 4 percent in 1968. Nixon had to deal with the economic problems caused in part by war spending. His attempts to solve the unique "stagflation," rising inflation and rising unemployment, included a variety of fiscal and monetary adjustments, and ultimately wage and price controls in August 1971 through April 1973. That Democratic solution, which was influenced by Nixon's decision to end the convertibility of the dollar to gold, was one way to stabilize the economy until the 1972 election.

As early as the Johnson administration, the Vietnam War, which civil rights leader Martin Luther *King, Jr., called "America's tragic distraction," began significantly to affect domestic reform. Although critics continue to disagree about the design and relative success of the vast array of Great Society programs, there is no doubt that Johnson would have spent more on them had he not had to pay for the war. In fact, Congress would not give him his 1968 surcharge until he agreed to cut $6 billion from nondefense programs.

Inflation, sparked by the war, contributed to the rise in oil prices in 1973 because of the impact of the devaluation of the dollar on oil producers. It also led to the real estate boom of the 1970s, and because of the built-in expectation of inflation, the introduction of variable interest rates and certificates of deposit by banks and offshore banking.

The Department of *Defense placed the direct costs of the Vietnam War at $173 billion. To that could be added potential veterans' benefits costs of $220 billion and interest of $31 billion. Of course, veterans did receive educational and other benefits; research and design in certain fields were enhanced; and expenditures in the defense industry provided jobs for millions that might not have been there in other circumstances.

Despite its limited scope, in many ways the Vietnam War influenced the future course of events on the home front as dramatically as the two world wars. Whether the focus is on domestic politics, the economy, the armed services, or even the way presidents have thought about future military interventions, the war profoundly affected all aspects of American life.

[See also Bombing of Civilians; Commander in Chief, President as; Draft Resistance and Evasion; Economy and War; Prisoners of War: U.S. Soldiers as POWs; Veterans: Vietnam War; Vietnam Antiwar Movement.]

• Robert Warren Stevens, Vain Hopes, Grim Realities: The Economic Consequences of the Vietnam War, 1976. Lawrence M. Baskir and William A. Strauss, Chance and Circumstance: The Draft, the War, and the Vietnam Generation, 1978. P. Edward Haley, Congress and the Fall of South Vietnam and Cambodia, 1982. Melvin Small, Johnson, Nixon, and the Doves, 1988. Charles DeBenedetti with Charles Chatfield, An American Ordeal: The Antiwar Movement of the Vietnam Era, 1990. Anthony S. Campagna, The Economic Consequences of the Vietnam War, 1991. Christian P. Appy, Working Class War: American Combat Soldiers and Vietnam, 1993. George Q. Flynn, The Draft, 1940–1973, 1993. H. Bruce Franklin, M.I.A. or, Mythmaking in America, 1993.   —Melvin Small

VIETNAM WAR (1960–75): POSTWAR IMPACT

Following the end of America's combat role in Vietnam in 1973, and the subsequent fall of Saigon to the North Vietnamese Army (NVA) in 1975, the often prophesied and much feared resurgence of McCarthyite Red-baiting, the bitter accusations of "who lost Vietnam?" barely transpired. Rather than massive recriminations, a collective amnesia took hold. The majority of Americans, it appeared, neither wanted to talk or think about their nation's longest and most debilitating war—the only war the United States ever lost. That forgetfulness gave way in the early 1980s to a renewed interest in the war: Hollywood, network television, and the music industry made Vietnam a staple of popular culture; and scholars, journalists, and Vietnam veterans produced a flood of literature on the conflict, especially concerning its lessons and legacies. Much of it, emphasizing the enormity of the damage done to American attitudes, institutions, and foreign policy by the Vietnam ordeal, echoed George F. *Kennan's depiction of the Vietnam War as "the most disastrous of all America's undertakings over the whole two hundred years of its history."

Initially, the humiliating defeat imposed by a nation Secretary of State Henry *Kissinger had described as "a fourth-rate power" caused a loss of pride and self-confidence in a people that liked to think of the United States as invincible. An agonizing reappraisal of American power and glory dampened the celebration of the Bicentennial birthday in 1976. So did the economic woes then afflicting the United States, which many blamed on the estimated $167 billion spent on the war. President Lyndon B. *Johnson's decision to finance a major war and the Great Society simultaneously, without a significant increase in taxation, launched a runaway double-digit inflation and mounting federal debt that ravaged the American economy and eroded living standards from the late 1960s into the 1990s.

The United States also paid a high political cost for the Vietnam War. It weakened public faith in government, and in the honesty and competence of its leaders. Indeed, skepticism, if not cynicism, and a high degree of suspicion of and distrust toward authority of all kind characterized the views of an increasing number of Americans in the wake of the war. The military, especially, was discredited for years. It would gradually rebound to become once again one of the most highly esteemed organizations in the United States. In the main, however, as never before, Americans after the Vietnam War neither respected nor trusted public institutions.

They were wary of official calls to intervene abroad in the cause of democracy and freedom, and the bipartisan consensus that had supported American foreign policy since the 1940s dissolved. Democrats, in particular, questioned the need to contain communism everywhere around the globe and to play the role of the planet's policeman. The Democratic majority in Congress would enact the 1973 *War Powers Resolution, ostensibly forbidding the president from sending U.S. troops into combat for more than ninety days without congressional consent. Exercising a greater assertiveness in matters of foreign policy, Congress increasingly emphasized the limits of American power, and the ceiling on the cost Americans would pay in pursuit of specific foreign policy objectives. The fear of getting bogged down in another quagmire made a majority of Americans reluctant to intervene militarily in Third World countries. The neo-isolationist tendency that former President Richard M. *Nixon called "the Vietnam syndrome" would be most manifest in the public debates over President Ronald *Reagan's interventionist policies in Nicaragua and President George *Bush's decision to drive Iraqi forces out of Kuwait. Despite the victorious outcome of the *Persian Gulf War for the United States and its allies, and President Bush's declaration in March 1991—"By God, we've kicked the Vietnam syndrome once and for all!"—the fear of intervention would reappear in the pub-

lic debate over President Bill *Clinton's commitment of U.S. *peacekeeping forces in Somalia and Bosnia. Quite clearly, for at least a quarter of a century after the Vietnam War ended, that conflict continued to loom large in the minds of Americans. Accordingly, a new consensus among foreign policy makers, reflecting the lessons learned from the Vietnam War, became manifest: the United States should use military force only as a last resort; only where the national interest is clearly involved; only when there is strong public support; and only in the likelihood of a relatively quick, inexpensive victory.

Another consensus also gradually emerged. At first, rather than giving returning veterans of the war welcoming parades, Americans seemed to shun, if not denigrate, the 2 million-plus Americans who went to Vietnam, the 1.6 million who served in combat, the 300,000 physically wounded, the many more who bore psychological scars, the 2,387 listed as "missing in action," and the more than 58,000 who died. Virtually nothing was done to aid veterans and their loved ones who needed assistance in adjusting. Then a torrent of fiction, films, and television programs depicted Vietnam vets as drug-crazed psychotic killers, as vicious executioners in Vietnam and equally vicious menaces at home. Not until after the 1982 dedication of the Vietnam Veterans Memorial in Washington, D.C., did American culture acknowledge their sacrifice and suffering, and concede that most had been good soldiers in a bad war.

Yet this altered view of the Vietnam veterans as victims as much as victimizers, if not as brave heroes, was not accompanied by new public policies. Although most veterans did succeed in making the transition to ordinary civilian life, many did not. More Vietnam veterans committed suicide after the war than had died in it. Even more—perhaps three-quarters of a million—became part of the lost army of the homeless. And the nearly 700,000 draftees, many of them poor, badly educated, and nonwhite, who had received less than honorable discharges, depriving them of educational and medical benefits, found it especially difficult to get and keep jobs, to maintain family relationships, and to stay out of jail. Although a majority of Americans came to view dysfunctional veterans as needing support and medical attention rather than moral condemnation, the *Veterans Administration, reluctant to admit the special difficulties faced by these veterans and their need for additional benefits, first denied the harm done by chemicals like Agent Orange and by the posttraumatic stress disorder (PTSD) afflicting as many as 700,000, and then stalled on providing treatment.

Although diminishing, the troublesome specter of the Vietnam War continued to divide Americans and haunt the national psyche. It surfaced again in 1988 when Bush's running mate, Dan Quayle, had to defend his reputation against revelations that he had used family political connections to be admitted into the Indiana National Guard in 1969 to avoid the draft and a possible tour of duty in Vietnam. It emerged four years later when Bill *Clinton, the Democratic candidate for president, faced accusations that he had evaded the draft and then organized antiwar demonstrations in 1969 while he was a Rhodes scholar in England. In each instance, such charges reminded Americans of the difficult choices young Americans had to make in what many saw as at best a morally ambiguous war.

Mostly, remembrances continue to be stirred by the

Vietnam Veterans Memorial, the most visited site in the nation's capital. Its stark black granite reflecting panels, covered with the names of the more than 58,000 American men and women who died in Vietnam, is a shrine to the dead, a tombstone in a sloping valley of death. Lacking all the symbols of heroism, glory, *patriotism, and moral certainty that more conventional war memorials possess, the Vietnam Veterans' Memorial is a somber reminder of the loss of too many young Americans, and of what the war did to the United States and its messianic belief in its own overweening virtue.

[*See also* Economy and War; Memorials, War; Toxic Agents: Agent Orange Exposure; Veterans: Vietnam War.]

• James F. Veninga and Harry A. Wilmer, eds., *Vietnam in Remission,* 1985. John Hellman, *American Myth and the Legacy of Vietnam,* 1986. Nayan Chanda, *Brother Enemy: The War After the War,* 1986. Ellen Frey-Wouters and Robert S. Laufer, *Legacy of a War,* 1986. Bob Greene, *Homecoming,* 1989. Bill McCloud, *What Should We Tell Our Children About Vietnam?,* 1989.

—Harvard Sitkoff

VIETNAM WAR (1960–75): CHANGING INTERPRETATIONS

Interpretations of the Vietnam War have departed significantly from typical patterns both during and after most of America's previous wars. Instead of reflecting, defending, and bolstering official accounts of the war, as occurred with World Wars I and II, early historical assessments of the Vietnam conflict were for the most part highly critical of U.S. policy. The most widely read works on the Vietnam War during the late 1960s and early 1970s—including those of journalists Bernard Fall, Robert Shaplen, and David Halberstam, and historians Arthur M. Schlesinger, Jr., and George McT. Kahin and John W. Lewis—indicted government policy, often quite harshly. Those works presented a radically different version of the war's origins, purpose, and efficacy than that offered by Washington officialdom. Only in the late 1970s, following North Vietnam's military triumph and the extended soul-searching it occasioned throughout the United States, did a revisionist school of thought emerge. Ironically, the Vietnam revisionists mounted a belated defense of the American war effort, venting much of their anger at the prevailing liberal orthodoxy, which, they insisted, wrongly considered the Indochina war to be unwinnable or—even more egregious from their perspective—immoral.

Despite the broad agreement among early writers that the Vietnam War represented a colossal mistake for the United States, and that American policy was plagued persistently by errors, blunders, misperceptions, and miscalculations, significant interpretive differences still existed within that literature. In their influential book, *The Irony of Vietnam: The System Worked* (1979), Leslie H. Gelb and Richard K. Betts identified no less than nine distinct explanations advanced by experts during the 1960s and 1970s for America's failed intervention in Vietnam. They ranged from economic imperialism to idealistic imperialism, from bureaucratic politics to domestic politics, and from misperceptions and ethnocentrism to ideological blinders and the imperatives of international power politics. Analysts disagreed from the first, then, not just about the reasons for the U.S. failure in Vietnam, but about the relative weight of the factors that precipitated and sustained American commitment.

Two sharply differentiated views emerged in that first wave of scholarship about the Vietnam War, views that continue to be echoed in today's debates. The first characterizes American involvement in the war as an avoidable tragedy. American policymakers, according to this liberal realist perspective, foolishly exaggerated Vietnam's importance to the United States. Had they more soberly assessed its true value to the economic and security interests of the United States, recognized the popular appeal of revolutionary *nationalism within the country, and appreciated the limits of American power, then the ensuing tragedy might well have been averted.

That view remains the dominant interpretation of the Vietnam War. Most books and articles about American involvement, for all the different emphases that naturally distinguish the work of individual authors, fall within its wide boundaries. Major overviews of the war by such experts as George C. Herring, Stanley Karnow, Gary R. Hess, George McT. Kahin, William S. Turley, Neal Sheehan, and William J. Duiker take as a basic point of departure the notion that the Vietnam conflict was a tragic misadventure that could have been avoided had American leaders only been wiser, more prudent, and less wedded to the assumptions of the past. The former defense secretary Robert S. *McNamara's memoir, *In Retrospect* (1995), also falls within this interpretive school.

The other major interpretive approach offers a far more radical critique of American intentions and behavior. It depicts the United States as a global hegemony, concerned primarily with its own economic expansion, and reflexively opposed to communism, indigenous revolution, or any other challenge to its authority. Authors writing from this perspective typically characterize American intervention in Indochina as the necessary and logical consequence of a rapacious superpower's drive for world dominance. Although scholarly and polemical treatments of the war have been written in this vein since the late 1960s, Gabriel Kolko's seminal *Anatomy of a War* represents the most sophisticated and comprehensive formulation of the radical perspective. Kolko sees U.S. intervention in Vietnam as a predictable consequence of the American ruling class's determination to exert control over the world capitalist system. The U.S. political economy's need for raw materials, investment outlets, and the integration between capitalist core states and the developing regions of the periphery set Washington on a collision course with revolutionary nationalist currents throughout the Third World.

By the early 1980s, a conservative revisionism had emerged that, at least temporarily, shifted the terms of a debate that up to then had largely pitted liberal realists against radical neo-Marxists. The Vietnam revisionist perspective was spearheaded by three former U.S. Army officers, Harry G. Summers, Jr., Bruce Palmer, Jr., and Philip B. Davidson, all veterans of the war. In separate books, each vehemently criticized U.S. policy. Summers, Palmer, and Davidson asserted that military and civilian leaders failed to develop realistic plans for achieving American politico-military objectives in Vietnam, failed to assess accurately the capabilities and intentions of their adversaries, and failed to coordinate specific battlefield tactics with an overall strategy for securing *victory. The conservative critique of America's Vietnam policy scored points with academic and nonacademic audiences alike, while calling attention to fundamental shortcomings in the American approach to warfare in Southeast Asia. Another group of conservative revisionists also emerged during the 1980s. This group, which included such diverse authorities as R. B. Smith, Larry Cable, Andrew Krepinevich, Walt W. Rostow, and William Colby, insisted that real benefits accrued to the non-Communist nations of Southeast Asia as a result of U.S. intervention, and argued that the "pacification" campaign pursued by the United States could have succeeded.

For all the attention accorded it by the media and by politicians, the conservative revisionist wave has not fundamentally altered our understanding of the Vietnam War. The revisionists may, ironically, have bolstered the central premises of the liberal realists more than they have overturned them. The chief faultline in the literature continues to lie between the liberal realists, on the one hand, and their left radical critics on the other—much as it has for the past three decades. That faultline will not soon be closed since the core issues at stake concern matters much broader than the mere origins and outcome of a war. They encompass as well such fundamental questions as the purpose of American foreign relations, the nature of American society, and the meaning of the American historical experience. That is why, perhaps, debates about the Vietnam conflict remain as hotly contested years after the war's end as they were at the height of U.S. involvement in the late 1960s.

• George McT. Kahin and John W. Lewis, *The United States in Vietnam*, 1969. George C. Herring, *America's Longest War*, 1979; 3rd rev. ed. 1996. Harry G. Summers, Jr., *On Strategy: A Critical Analysis of the Vietnam War*, 1982. Gabriel Kolko, *Anatomy of a War*, 1985. George McT. Kahin, *Intervention*, 1986. Robert J. McMahon, "U.S.-Vietnamese Relations: A Historiographical Survey," in *Pacific Passage*, ed. Warren I. Cohen, 1996.

—Robert J. McMahon

VIETNAM WAR, U.S. AIR OPERATIONS IN THE. During the Vietnam War, airpower commanded more American resources than any other aspect of the struggle. More than half of the hundreds of billions of dollars America invested in the war was devoted to U.S. *Air Force, Army, and Navy air operations. The United States dropped over 8 million tons of bombs on Vietnam, Laos, and Cambodia from 1962 to 1973 and lost over 8,588 fixed-wing aircraft and *helicopters. U.S. military air crew losses totaled 4,302 by 1973. For all this investment, airpower, while occasionally influential, was never decisive.

The U.S. Air Force dates its involvement in Vietnam to the summer of 1950, when it sent advisers to help France maintain and operate U.S.-manufactured aircraft in the war with the Viet Minh. After the Viet Minh victory and the partitioning of the country into North and South in 1955, America continued sending air advisers to Vietnam. By 1961, six South Vietnamese squadrons were ready for combat, supported by an American combat training detachment known as "Farm Gate." The boundary between fighting and training for U.S. Air Force personnel during the early 1960s was never clearly defined. The Farm Gate commandos believed they were primarily to fly close air support missions for the Army of the Republic of Vietnam (ARVN), but their official rules of engagement precluded them from engaging in combat without a member of the South Vietnamese Air Force in the aircraft or in self-defense.

By the end of 1962, more than 3,000 U.S. Air Force advisers were serving in Vietnam. American pilots flew air support and reconnaissance missions; they also transported ARVN troops around the country, and defoliated jungle areas with C-123 "Ranch Hand" aircraft. During the latter program, which lasted over ten years, the air force sprayed 19.22 million gallons of herbicides and defoliants over approximately 5.96 million acres of the country.

After the Tonkin Gulf incidents in August 1964 and a surprise Viet Cong sapper attack on the U.S. air base at Bien Hoa in November, President Lyndon B. *Johnson slowly began to raise the intensity of the air war. He initiated Operation Barrel Roll, a series of interdiction missions flown along the infiltration routes developing in the Laotian panhandle. When the Viet Cong attacked a second air base at Pleiku in February 1965, Johnson retaliated with raids against targets just north of the demilitarized zone (DMZ). Initially known as Flaming Dart, these reprisal missions evolved into a sustained air campaign, Operation Rolling Thunder, beginning in March 1965.

Rolling Thunder was the longest air campaign in American military history. Between March 1965 and November 1968, navy, air force, and Marine aviation flew 2 million sorties and dropped 1 million tons of *bombs on North Vietnam. Rolling Thunder had several objectives. One was to persuade Hanoi to abandon its support of the southern insurgency; another was to raise the morale of military and political elites in South Vietnam; and the third was interdiction—strikes against *logistics targets such as bridges, roads, and railroads designed to reduce Hanoi's ability to support the war in the South.

Though Rolling Thunder attacked strategic targets such as electric plants and fuel storage facilities, the limited number of these targets and restrictions against bombing near Hanoi, Haiphong, and the Chinese border made interdiction its prime focus. Throughout the campaign, American pilots clamored to "go downtown" (bomb Hanoi), but President Johnson, who approved and sometimes picked the targets, constantly turned down these requests. He believed the threat of more intensive destruction implicit in limited, incremental bombing would have a greater impact on Hanoi's willingness to negotiate than an all-out terror offensive. He also believed that this gradualist approach would stave off possible Chinese intervention.

For pilots, the most frustrating aspect of the bombing restrictions was that most North Vietnamese fighter bases and surface-to-air missile (SAM) batteries fell within restricted areas. To cope with these defenses, the services developed elaborate "strike packages" consisting of fighter-bombers, fighter escorts, electronic warfare aircraft, search and rescue planes, and airborne command and control aircraft. Yet North Vietnamese air defenses claimed over 900 American aircraft during Rolling Thunder. Most of these aircraft were downed by simple 23–100 mm antiaircraft *artillery. The North used high-altitude SAMs to compel American aircraft to fly low, thereby bringing them within range of their guns. Russian-built MiGs were used sparingly, generally making just one pass before retreating home. These "guerilla" tactics yielded meager results: only seventy-six planes shot down during the war, or about 7 percent of U.S. fixed-wing losses over the North. On the other hand, such caution made the U.S. kill ratio just 2.5 to 1 from 1965 to 1973; consequently only five Americans qualified as aces (with five or more "kills").

Overall, Rolling Thunder failed to accomplish its major objectives. Although the bombing caused an estimated

$600 million worth of damage to North Vietnam, it did not prevent the Communist forces from launching the *Tet Offensive in 1968, nor did it bring about a negotiated peace settlement.

Most histories of the air war focus on the bombing of North Vietnam; yet the United States dropped far more tonnage in the South over the course of the war. By 1973, the year of U.S. withdrawal, the "in-country" war claimed 4 million tons. By contrast, only 1 million tons had been dropped on North Vietnam. To begin this effort, 21,000 air force personnel and 500 aircraft were deployed to South Vietnam in 1965.

The impetus behind this massive buildup was close air support. These missions were generally flown by small fighters like the F-100 Supersabre, but beginning in June 1965, B-52s (U.S. strategic bombers) being flown from Guam were used as well. By the end of the war, 75 percent of all B-52 "Arc Light" strikes had flown against targets in South Vietnam, 20 percent to Laos, and 5 percent against the North. During the siege of Khe Sanh, B-52s dropped 60,000 tons of bombs on North Vietnamese positions just outside the Marine base. This joint operation, dubbed Niagara, is generally credited with compelling the North Vietnamese to lift their siege of the beleaguered outpost.

Besides close air support, B-52s also flew interdiction missions in Cambodia and Laos during 1968–72. President Richard M. *Nixon employed B-52s to pulverize supply storage areas along the Ho Chi Minh Trail in Cambodia. Beginning on March 1969, these secret "Menu" bombings in Cambodia lasted 14 months, during which B-52s flew 3,630 sorties into Cambodia and dropped 100,000 tons of bombs. In Laos, B-52s created landslides in mountain passes vital to Ho Chi Minh's logistical system. These missions fell under the rubric of Operation Commando Hunt, an interdiction campaign that lasted from November 1968 to April 1972.

The many exotic weapons used during Commando Hunt included an elaborate sensor system known as Igloo White, antipersonnel mines, and AC-130 Specter gunships. B-52s established blocking belts by creating landslides and sewing roads with mines. After mines were laid and major passes blocked, air force planners would send in Specter gunships to blast resulting traffic bottlenecks with their 20- and 40mm cannons and 105mm howitzers. The Specters even located trucks and personnel at night, using low-light television cameras and infrared *heat-seeking technology.

For all its wizardry, Commando Hunt had little impact upon the Communist ability to wage war. In fact, the North launched its biggest offensive to date in 1972, with over 120,000 regulars and 200 armored vehicles. President Nixon responded to this *Easter Offensive by launching a new wave of air attacks against North Vietnam. The resulting Linebacker I raids were designed to hinder the North Vietnamese invasion of the South by destroying its petroleum storage facilities, power-generating plants, and major bridges. This campaign became a watershed in airpower history because it was the first to place heavy reliance on *precision-guided munitions. Laser- and television-guided bombs enabled small numbers of aircraft to destroy heavily defended targets from extreme distances. By the end of June, the air force and navy had demolished or damaged 400 bridges in North Vietnam, including ones, such as the Paul Doumer Bridge, Hanoi, that had been bombed repeatedly earlier to no effect.

In October 1972, peace seemed close at hand and Nixon halted the bombing of the North. Le Duc Tho, the North's chief negotiator, had presented substantially new terms and a settlement seemed imminent. However, South Vietnamese demands for changes stalled the talks. By early December, agreement was in shambles, and Nixon launched a second series of Linebacker attacks. Known as the "Christmas bombings," the eleven-day Linebacker II campaign in late December was the most intense air assault of the war. Tactical aircraft flew more than 1,000 sorties and B-52s about 740 against targets in the heart of Hanoi and Haiphong. The North Vietnamese fought back with everything available and destroyed twenty-seven American aircraft, including eighteen B-52s; but by the end of the campaign, Hanoi had expended its entire supply of antiaircraft *missiles and B-52s could fly over the North Vietnamese cities with impunity.

The eleven-day air campaign and its impact upon the peace negotiations is still a point of controversy in Vietnam War historiography. "Revisionist" histories of the war, mostly written by participants, argue that such a campaign early in the struggle could have yielded an American victory. Recently, a second group of historians has challenged this conventional wisdom. Mark Clodfelter (1989) argues that the Linebacker campaigns "worked" in 1972 because Nixon's political goals were limited to securing an American withdrawal and a cease-fire. Moreover, the nature of the ground war in 1972 was conventional. Such an approach, maintains Clodfelter, could not have been replicated earlier on during the guerrilla struggle, when America's goal was to defeat a popular insurgency in the South. Earl H. Tilford (1991) takes the argument a step further. He contends that, in the final analysis, "it was the Air Force and Navy's very own leaders that failed to develop a strategy appropriate for the war at hand." Could any air strategy, though, have won the conflict? *Joint Chiefs of Staff chairman Maxwell *Taylor's response in 1975 was an unequivocal no. According to him, "we didn't know our ally. Secondly, we knew even less about the enemy. And the last, most inexcusable of our mistakes, was not knowing our own people."

[See also Army Combat Branches: Aviation; Bombing of Civilians; Marine Corps Combat Branches: Aviation Forces; Vietnam War: Military and Diplomatic Course; Vietnam War: Changing Interpretations.]

• Ulysses S. Grant Sharp, Strategy for Defeat: Vietnam in Retrospect, 1978. Robert F. Futrell, The United States Air Force in Southeast Asia: The Advisory Years to 1965, 1981. John B. Nichols and Barrett Tilman, On Yankee Station: The Naval Air War Over Vietnam, 1987. John Schlight, The United States Air Force in Southeast Asia: The Years of Offensive, 1965–1968, 1988. Earl H. Tilford, Setup: What the Air Force Did in Vietnam and Why, 1991. Mark Clodfelter, The Limits of Air Power: The American Bombing of North Vietnam, 1989. Kenneth H. Bell, 100 Missions North, 1993. John Trotti, Phantom Over Vietnam: Fighter Pilot, USMC, 1993. Marshall L. Michel III, Clashes: Air Combat Over North Vietnam 1965–1972, 1997.

—John Darrell Sherwood

VIETNAM WAR, U.S. NAVAL OPERATIONS IN THE. The U.S. Navy's ability to project its combat power ashore in Southeast Asia, control the coastal waters off Vietnam, and provide logistic support for a major U.S. overseas military commitment mandated its heavy involvement in the Vietnam War. Naval operations took place in the South

China Sea, among myriad islands, along the coastline of Vietnam, and on thousands of nautical miles of rivers and canals.

The first significant U.S. naval engagement of the war was the famous Tonkin Gulf incident of 1964. On the afternoon of 2 August, three North Vietnamese motor *torpedo boats attacked the destroyer *Maddox* in the Gulf of Tonkin with gunfire and *torpedoes. On the night of 4 August, *Maddox* and another destroyer, *Turner Joy,* reported fighting a running battle with hostile patrol craft in the middle of the gulf. Communications intercepts and other relevant information convinced Washington that an attack had taken place. At President Lyndon B. *Johnson's direction, on 5 August navy carrier forces bombed North Vietnam. Two days later, the U.S. Congress overwhelmingly passed the Tonkin Gulf Resolution, which Johnson thereafter used to wage war in Vietnam.

Even though Washington did not pursue a traditional military victory in the war, the navy made a major effort on the operational and tactical levels. Carrier aircraft of the Seventh Fleet executed round-the-clock bombing of enemy *logistics facilities, fuel and supply depots, power plants, bridges, and railroads in Laos, North Vietnam, and after 1970, Cambodia. The air campaigns produced no decisive results, and they cost the navy 900 aircraft lost and 881 pilots and other air crew killed or captured. These operations, however, hindered the enemy's resupply efforts and shortened Hanoi's ground offensives in South Vietnam. In addition, the navy–air force bombing and the navy's simultaneous mining of North Vietnam's ports during 1972 and 1973 helped ease the U.S. withdrawal from the conflict.

Navy and Marine Corps aircraft also flew close air support for allied units battling Viet Cong and North Vietnamese Army forces in South Vietnam. Carrier-based search and rescue *helicopters retrieved hundreds of American aviators whose aircraft were shot down ashore or at sea.

The battleship *New Jersey* and numerous *cruisers and destroyers shelled bridges, rail lines, *radar sites, *artillery batteries, and small vessels along the North Vietnamese coast and Communist troops, fortifications, and supply caches along the coasts and waterways of South Vietnam. During the Communist *Easter Offensive of 1972, U.S. naval gunfire devastated enemy armor and infantry units on the northern coast of South Vietnam.

The U.S. Coastal Patrol Force and South Vietnamese naval units mounted Operation Market Time, which limited Communist seaborne infiltration of supplies into South Vietnam. The allied forces destroyed or turned back all but two of the fifty Communist steel-hulled trawlers discovered heading for the South Vietnamese coast between 1965 and 1972.

Navy–Marine Corps amphibious units exploited the fleet's mobility to carry out assaults from the sea along the coast of South Vietnam. In 1967 and 1968, naval leaders increasingly used the amphibious force as a floating reserve for Marine units fighting near the demilitarized zone.

Commander U.S. Naval Forces, Vietnam (COMNAVFORV) also took advantage of the waterways that crisscrossed the Mekong Delta region to deploy combat forces deep into enemy-controlled territory in South Vietnam. The *Swift boats (river patrol craft) and SEAL commandos of COMNAVFORV's River Patrol Force, in Operation

Game Warden, disrupted Communist supply traffic on the main rivers. Also important to the inland effort was the army-navy Mobile Riverine Force of heavily armed and armored monitors. Both forces prompted the Communists to divert their sampans and other supply craft to smaller rivers and canals.

In 1968, an energetic COMNAVFORV, Vice Adm. Elmo R. *Zumwalt, Jr., adopted an innovative strategic approach, which he called SEALORDS. In a comprehensive campaign, U.S. and Vietnamese river forces put the enemy on the defensive by setting up patrol boat barriers along the Cambodian border and by penetrating areas deep in the Mekong Delta. Hence, the Communists were unable to mount a major attack there during the Easter Offensive.

The navy also directed the seaborne logistic operation that sustained the American forces and their allies in Southeast Asia. The merchantmen of the navy's Military Sealift Command delivered 95 percent of the vehicles, ammunition, fuel, equipment, and other military supplies that entered the ports of South Vietnam. In addition, navy Seabee construction units developed enormous logistic support bases at Da Nang and Saigon.

The decade of heavy commitment to the war in Southeast Asia, which ended on 30 April 1975, cost the U.S. Navy dearly. Of the 1,842,000 Navy men and women who served in the combat theater, over 2,600 were killed in action and 10,000 were wounded. The navy also had to contend with serious morale, drug abuse, and disciplinary problems. Racial conflict hampered operations on board two Pacific Fleet carriers, *Kitty Hawk* and *Constellation.*

Equally serious, the war's high operating costs limited the funds available for needed repairs and for the design and construction of newer and better ships. To help pay for the war, the Ford and Carter administrations reduced the navy's Vietnam era fleet of 769 ships to just over 450.

In some ways, however, the Vietnam experience strengthened the navy. The conflict reaffirmed the critical importance of naval forces to the conduct of warfare in distant waters. Vietnam influenced a whole generation of midlevel naval officers, many of whom rose to prominent command in later years, to recommend to political leaders that they use force judiciously when faced with crises in Central America, Africa, and the Middle East.

[*See also* Navy, U.S.: 1946 to the Present; Vietnam War: Military and Diplomatic Course.]

• Edward J. Marolda and Oscar P. Fitzgerald, *From Military Assistance to Combat,* 1986. Thomas J. Cutler, *Brown Water, Black Berets: Coastal and Riverine Warfare in Vietnam,* 1988. R. L. Schreadley, *From the Rivers to the Sea: The United States Navy in Vietnam,* 1992. Edward J. Marolda, *By Sea, Air, and Land: An Illustrated History of the U.S. Navy and the War in Southeast Asia,* 1994.

—Edward J. Marolda

VILLARD, OSWALD and FANNY GARRISON, pacifists, antiracists, and feminists. This mother and son team carried on the political tradition of Fanny Garrison Villard's father, reformer William Lloyd *Garrison.

Fanny Garrison (1844–1928) married the German-born business entrepreneur and newspaperman Henry Villard in 1866. Her adult political work had begun with efforts to help newly freed slaves during *Reconstruction. She continued her charity work through the Diet Kitchen Association (dedicated to improving nutrition for the poor), the New York Infirmary for Women and Children, and the Woman's Exchange. In 1898, both she and her youngest son, Oswald (1872–1949), spoke against the imperialist position taken by the United States in the *Spanish-American War. In 1914, both became active in the anti–World War I movement. Fanny acted through the Woman's Peace Party and the suffrage movement; Oswald, for a time, through the *Fellowship of Reconciliation. More notably, Oswald, like his grandfather, voiced his antiwar sentiment as a journalist and publisher, first via the *New York Evening Post* and then the *Nation* (founded in part by his uncle, Wendell).

Fanny's voice continued from 1919 to her death in 1928 through the Women's Peace Society, an "absolutely" pacifist organization. Oswald also stood for *pacifism to his death in 1949. Both were also among the founders and activists of the National Association for the Advancement of Colored People.

[*See also* Peace and Antiwar Movements.]

• D. Joy Humes, *Oswald Garrison Villard: Liberal of the 1920's,* 1960. Michael Wreszin, *Oswald Garrison Villard: Pacifist at War,* 1965. (There is currently no biographical study of Fanny Garrison Villard.)   —Harriet Hyman Alonso

VINSON, CARL (1883–1981), Chair, House Naval Affairs Committee and Armed Services Committee. A rural Georgia lawyer and Democrat, Vinson was elected to the House of Representatives in 1914. He was appointed to the House Naval Affairs Committee in his first term, and throughout his fifty-year career in the House, he would remain an advocate of strong military defense. In 1931, Vinson became chair of the committee and worked, with the support of President Franklin D. *Roosevelt, for naval expansion. The *Vinson-Trammel Act (1934) authorized construction of 102 warships. The Naval Act (1938) provided for a ten-year, $1.1 billion building program, including all categories of ships, and a doubling of the U.S. Navy's airplanes. In July 1940, Vinson won an emergency "Two Ocean Navy" act, doubling the size of the combat fleet and including the new fast carriers and *battleships that would begin to join the fleet in 1943. During World War II, Vinson sponsored bills to curb strikes in defense industries and called for a ban on employment in those industries for anyone suspected of un-American activities.

Vinson remained head of the Naval Affairs Committee until 1947, and from 1949 to his retirement in 1964, he chaired the House Armed Services Committee, a strong advocate of national defense and containment of communism. A stern taskmaster and skillful legislator, Vinson lost only three floor fights on bills reported by his committee between 1940 and 1964. The navy named a nuclear carrier after him.

[*See also* Navy, U.S.: 1899–1945; Navy, U.S.: 1946 to the Present.]   —John Whiteclay Chambers II

The **VINSON-TRAMMEL ACT** (1934), cosponsored by Georgia Democrat Carl *Vinson, chair of the House Naval Affairs Committee, was part of the naval expansion program of the administration of President Franklin D.

*Roosevelt during the Great Depression. Elected in 1932, ten years after the *Washington Naval Arms Limitation Treaty, Roosevelt issued an executive order in 1933 allowing $238 million in emergency public works funds to be used to build thirty-two warships over the next three years. Undeterred by critics' accusations that the United States was initiating another naval arms race, Vinson crafted the Vinson-Trammel Naval Act of 1934, which authorized the navy to construct 102 new warships over the next eight years. This would bring the U.S. Navy up to the full strength authorized by the treaty. By 1937, the year after Japan renounced any treaty limitations, the U.S. Navy had under construction three new *aircraft carriers, ten *cruisers, forty-one destroyers, and fifteen *submarines, most of which would join the fleet at the end of the decade. By 1939, the United States had fifteen *battleships, the Japanese ten, but Japan had six aircraft carriers compared to five in the U.S. Navy. Congress authorized further naval construction in 1938 and 1940.

[*See also* Navy, U.S.: 1899–1945.]

—John Whiteclay Chambers II

VIOLENCE. *See* Aggression and Violence.

VOLUNTEERS, U.S. The U.S. Volunteers was the federal government's primary mechanism in the nineteenth century for raising large forces of *citizen-soldiers needed in wartime to augment the small regular army and organized *militia and National Guard. These ad hoc units were locally raised and led, but funded by the federal government and under the overall command of U.S. Army generals.

With congressional authorization, governors nominated local notables whom the president commissioned as temporary officers. These recruited local men into temporary units up to regiments. In keeping with militia traditions, enlisted men elected the junior officers.

The system drew upon the essentially local basis of American society in the nineteenth century in order to serve national purposes. It enabled the central government to raise a sizable wartime force in a country where political power was fragmented by federalism.

Raised only when needed, the U.S. Volunteers did not exist in peacetime. Unlike the militia, which, by law, could not be kept in federal service for more than nine months nor sent outside the country, the U.S. Volunteers were enlisted for terms of one to three years, and between 1794 and 1902 fought outside the country in the *Mexican War, the Spanish-American War, and the *Philippine-American War. Within the United States, they fought in the Indian wars, the *War of 1812, and the *Civil War.

Use of U.S. Volunteers ended in the twentieth century when a strong federal government drew draftees and volunteers into a truly national army.

[*See also* Army, U.S.: 1783–1865; Army, U.S.: 1866–99; Conscription.]

• John Whiteclay Chambers II, *To Raise an Army: The Draft Comes to Modern America,* 1987.

—John Whiteclay Chambers II

WAC. Half a year before the attack on *Pearl Harbor, Congresswoman Edith Nourse Rogers of Massachusetts introduced a bill in Congress on 28 May 1941, to establish a Women's Army Auxiliary Corps (WAAC) within the U.S. Army. Mrs. Rogers's bill aroused immediate controversy: most men in Congress and the War Department opposed the idea of women in the military.

To gain passage, Mrs. Rogers had to accept changes in the WAAC bill. When it was finally passed on 14 May 1942, it provided for a corps of 25,000, to be an auxiliary to the U.S. Army without military status. Later that year, the corps was authorized to increase to 150,000. The WAACs would serve under women commanders, be given duty at army posts in the United States and overseas, have separate grade titles and pay schedules from men, be noncombatants, wear *uniforms, and serve under WAAC rather than army regulations. The head of the corps would have the title of colonel but receive the lower pay of an army major. Ironically, bills enacted later in 1942 permitted women to serve in the U.S. Navy and Marine Corps as reservists on active duty with the same military status, pay, and benefits as men.

On 1 September 1943, Congress gave the WAACs military status and eliminated "Auxiliary" from the title. (Over 60,000 members were on active duty then; 937 in North Africa and England.) Members of the new Women's Army Corps (WAC) now had the same grade titles, pay, benefits, and privileges as men in the army. But they could not command men's units, participate in combat, rise to a grade higher than lieutenant colonel, or automatically receive pay and benefits for their dependents as men did. One woman, the director, Oveta Culp *Hobby, received the title and pay of a full colonel.

Initially, as WAACs, women were limited to work as clerks, cooks, drivers, and telephone operators. After receiving military status, the WACs were assigned to an increasing variety of army jobs. By war's end, they were serving in all theaters of war and almost every noncombat job. Nearly 100,000 were on active duty on 30 April 1945–over 16,000 serving overseas.

After World War II, the new chief of staff of the army, Gen. Dwight D. *Eisenhower, asked Congress to enact legislation to make the Women's Army Corps part of the Regular Army and the Organized Reserve Corps (later U.S. Army Reserve). He wanted WACs permanently in the army to do the work they had done so well in wartime. The bill was enacted 12 July 1948. The WAC then became a separate corps (or branch) of the Regular Army. WAC officers and NCOs commanded units of enlisted women, who were housed in separate detachments, companies, or battalions on army posts. WAC officers and enlisted women

were assigned, sent to schools, discharged, and retired by Department of the Army orders.

When the *Korean War began on 25 June 1950, WAC strength was 7,300, but it increased to 12,000 a year later. In Korea, the combat zone was so fluid and unpredictable that a noncombatant WAC unit could not be assigned in the country. Only a half-dozen WAC officers and enlisted women served as stenographers and interpreters.

After the war ended (1953), WAC strength fell to 7,800. The corps was rejuvenated when the army built a permanent WAC training center and school (1954) at Fort McClellan, Alabama. (Today, the Women's Army Corps is located there.) New opportunities opened for women officers and enlisted women in *communications, intelligence, *logistics, and *transportation.

During the Berlin crisis (1961) and the *Cuban Missile Crisis (1962), both active duty and reserve WACs participated in logistical efforts. In June 1962, WAC strength was 11,113; following the pattern after crises, it fell to 8,700 by June 1964.

Early in the 1960s, South Vietnam requested and obtained U.S. advisers to help train defense forces. In January 1965, the U.S. Army began sending one WAC officer and one NCO to Saigon each year for a one-year tour. They helped the South Vietnam government organize and train a Women's Armed Forces Corps. In 1967, a WAC unit of 100 arrived for duty with the U.S. Army, Vietnam, at Long Binh; others worked in Saigon as clerk-typists, stenographers, finance and supply clerks, intelligence technicians, and communications specialists. By 1972, opposition to the war caused President Richard M. *Nixon to order the withdrawal of U.S. forces from Vietnam. The WAC detachment left in October 1972.

For years, directors of the WAC and heads of the other women's services had tried to obtain equality of promotion and retirement for women officers. Finally, on 8 November 1967, Congress enacted a bill to equalize retirement eligibility and remove restrictions, making women officers eligible to compete for promotion to general and flag rank. On 10 June 1971, WAC director Elizabeth P. Hoisington, was the first WAC officer to be promoted to brigadier general.

After 1967, WAC directors obtained other important policy and statutory changes. Women could command men's units, serve in *ROTC, be assigned to combat support positions, become pilots of noncombat planes, remain on active duty while pregnant, and attend senior service colleges. Separate WAC units and the position of WAC staff adviser were eliminated in 1973 and 1974, respectively. Except in combat units and combat jobs, army men and women were assigned interchangeably to positions in the United States and overseas. In 1974, WAC officers were released from WAC branch and assigned to other noncombat branches of the army. In 1976, women entered the U.S. Military Academy at West Point, New York.

The remaining vestiges of the Women's Army Corps were eliminated by Congress in 1978 so that women in the army could be more fully assimilated into the overall army structure. The positions of director and deputy director were abolished, April 1978; Congress then disestablished the WAC as a separate corps of the army, October 1978. Corps strength at that time was 52,997.

The action taken by Congress was not popular with the majority of corps members. They missed the cohesiveness of their units, the esprit fostered by individual and unit achievements, their role models, and the camaraderie of working together as a unit. By the 1990s, women served in most units and branches of the army except Infantry, Armor, and short-range Artillery.

[See also Berlin Crises; Families; Military; Gender: Female Identity and the Military; WAVES; Women in the Military.]

• Mattie E. Treadwell, The Women's Army Corps in World War II, 1954. Bettie J. Morden, The Women's Army Corps, 1945–1978, 1990.
—Bettie J. Morden

WADE, BENJAMIN FRANKLIN (1800–1878), radical Republican senator in the *Civil War. Born in Massachusetts, Wade settled in Jefferson, Ohio, to practice law, was elected to the legislature as a Whig, and rose to become a presiding judge of the third Ohio district. In 1850, he was sent to the U.S. Senate by a combination of Whigs and Free Soilers.

An outspoken opponent of slavery, when the Civil War broke out, Wade, now chairman of the Committee on Territories, attempted to arrest the rout at the First Battle of *Bull Run by putting his carriage across the road and turning back the retreating troops with his rifle, an experience that caused him to develop a great mistrust of West Point leadership. Also serving as chairman of the Joint Committee on the Conduct of the War, he sought to further the antislavery cause by badgering President Abraham *Lincoln to dismiss conservative generals in favor of their radical counterparts. In investigations of the battles of Bull Run, Balls Bluff, and the *Seven Days' Battle, he attempted to induce Lincoln to dismiss Gen. George B. *McClellan, and (unsuccessfully) in later hearings to retire Gen. George Gordon *Meade, while vigorously defending Joseph *Hooker, Dan *Sickles, Benjamin F. *Butler, and others. Wade also chaired investigations of the Fort Pillow Massacre and of Confederate *atrocities against *prisoners of war, the results of which were published as powerful propaganda for the Union cause.

In 1864, the senator was the co-author of the Wade-Davis Reconstruction bill, which was more radical than Lincoln's plan. As president pro tem of the Senate, Wade would have become president had Andrew *Johnson been convicted in his impeachment trial. Wade was forced to retire in 1869 after the Democrats captured the Ohio legislature.

[See also For Pillow, Battle of; Reconstruction.]

• Hans L. Trefousse, Benjamin Franklin Wade, Radical Republican from Ohio, 1963.
—Hans L. Trefousse

WAINWRIGHT, JONATHAN (1883–1953), U.S. general in World War II. Graduating from West Point in 1906,

Wainwright served in World War I as a captain. In 1940, as major general, he assumed command of the Philippines Division. Commanding North Luzon forces during the opening days of the Japanese invasion in December 1941, he redeployed American forces to defensive positions on the Bataan Peninsula.

On 11 March 1942, after Gen. Douglas *MacArthur left for Australia, Wainwright assumed command of U.S. forces on Bataan and the island fortress of Corregidor in Manila Bay. Promoted to lieutenant general and put in command of all U.S. forces in the Philippines, Wainwright proved unable to prevent the collapse of resistance on Bataan on 8 April. In order to ensure continued resistance of U.S. forces in other areas of the Philippines, he released them from his control shortly before he surrendered the U.S. forces on Corregidor on 6 May. Gen. Homma Masahura, commander of a Japanese force invading Corregidor, refused to accept this partial surrender. Out of concern for those already in captivity, Wainwright ordered the capitulation of all U.S. forces, and more than 80,000, Americans and Filipinos then surrendered to the Japanese.

Wainwright spent the remainder of the war in a series of Japanese prisoner-of-war camps. Liberated in Manchuria in 1945, the frail, emaciated general took part in the formal surrender ceremonies aboard the USS Missouri in Tokyo Bay. Greeted with a hero's welcome upon his return to the United States, Wainwright resumed active service for a brief time before retiring in 1947.

[See also Bataan and Corregidor, Battles of; World War II, U.S. Naval Operations in: The Pacific.]

• Louis Morton, The Fall of the Philippines, 1953. Duane P. Schultz, Hero of Bataan: The Story of General Jonathan M. Wainwright, 1991.
—G. Kurt Piehler

WAR. This essay consists of five articles, which deal broadly with different large aspects of war. The first provides an interpretation of the changing Nature of War from ancient times to the present. The second examines Levels of War—tactical, operational, strategic—comparing recent historical examples with modern American military thought. The third explores the degree to which there has been an American Way of War. The fourth, which shows American perspectives on the Causes of War, assesses historic interpretations of the causes of war by American policymakers, scholars, and activists. The fifth, examining the American experience, probes the debate over the Effects of War on the Economy.

WAR: NATURE OF WAR

Definitions of war have varied, but any attempt to understand it must include the following critical elements. First, war is an organized violent activity, waged not by individuals but by men (sometimes joined by women) in groups. Second, war is a mutual activity; whatever takes place in it relates, or should relate, primarily to the enemy's movements with the aim of defeating him and avoid being defeated oneself. Third, the conduct of war is conditioned on the hope for *victory, or at the very least self-preservation. Where that hope does not exist there can be no war, only suicide.

War being an organized activity, the best way to classify it is neither by *tactics nor by *weaponry but by the nature of the human communities that wage it. Thus we find that some very small and very loosely organized communities, such as the South African Bushmen or Arctic Eskimo, did not have war but merely more or less violent duels among individuals. More complex "tribes without rulers," such as the Indians of the North American Plains, did engage in war; yet there was still no specialized organization for waging it, since every healthy adult male was a warrior by definition. Probably the first individuals who were in any sense specialized warriors were the retainers of tribal chiefs such as still existed in areas of Africa until recently. The classical Mediterranean city-states were, in this respect, less advanced: they did not have armies but only militias that were mustered as war broke out and went home as it ended. The task of building standing forces was left to empires, like those of ancient Egypt or Assyria or China or Rome. For a long time these remained the strongest military-political organizations.

The characteristic modern way of organizing war, which grew out of the transformation of feudal into modern society, is to entrust it to be directed by the *state. For 300 years, since the Treaty of Westphalia in 1648 ended the Thirty Years *War, states alone have been authorized to wage war; conversely, whenever *aggression and violence were used by individuals, or by other groups and organizations, it was known as crime, uprising, rebellion, or civil war. Inside each state a distinction was drawn between the government, which alone could conduct the war at the highest level; the armed forces, whose task was to fight; and the civilian population, whose assigned role was to pay and sustain the effort. By setting up an organization whose members, even at the higher levels, were selected for their professionalism rather than their loyalty (which had been the case in empires and feudal societies) and who were dedicated solely to war, the state and its resources led the way to unprecedented technological development in the military field. So great were the modern state's military and warmaking capabilities that by 1914, some half-dozen industrialized states had come virtually to dominate the world.

Not only did the modern state wage war more effectively than any other organization, but war itself played a great role in the construction of the modern state. First came the establishment of civilian bureaucracies, whose primary function was to obtain resources for war and extract the taxes that would be used to pay the troops. Next came such institutions as the national debt and paper money, both of which had their origin in the need to finance war. During the nineteenth century, the advent of railways and telegraphs for the first time enabled large states to begin to harness virtually their entire resources for military purposes; this culminated in the era of "total war" (1914–45) when such governments took over control of almost every aspect of their citizens' lives from the wages that they were paid to the temperature of the water in which they could bathe. These trends affected the United States, which was relatively isolated and safe, much later than they did the main European powers, which confronted each other directly. Still, even in the United States the task of building a strong centralized state was linked to war, initially in the *Civil War, but more dramatically in World War I and World War II. In the long run, the United States built a *military-industrial complex larger than any other in the world.

As the warmaking communities developed and became more sophisticated, so did the scale on which they fought

and the methods they used. Early tribal societies counted their warriors in the dozens and knew only the raid, the ambush, the skirmish, and sometimes the setpiece encounter (agreed upon in advance) that can be seen as part war, part sport. With the establishment of chiefdoms, there appeared forces numbering in the hundreds or at most thousands, as well as battle and siege operations, whereas empires could count their troops in the hundreds of thousands and were capable of conducting sophisticated operations that lasted for years on end. However, all premodern political entities were hampered in their conduct of war by problems of both *logistics and *communications. The former meant that armed forces spent more time looking after their supplies than actively campaigning, and indeed that war itself was usually a seasonal activity—in the summer. The latter not only prevented the coordination of operations from the capital but made it virtually impossible for the armed forces of any one state to cooperate with each other on anything larger than a tactical scale once they had been united on the battlefield.

Modern technology during the late eighteenth and early nineteenth century put an end to these limitations. Instead of coming about by tacit agreement between the commanders on both sides, battles could be developed into coherent campaigns; campaigns waged in different theaters could be integrated with the conduct of war as a whole, and the latter coordinated from the national capital, which also controlled the *mobilization of demographic and economic resources. The different *levels of war—from minor tactics through tactics and the *operational art and *strategy all the way to grand strategy—made their appearance. More and more, war came to be waged by vast powers or coalitions of powers, each counting their subjects in the dozens if not hundreds of millions. Once unleashed by the Industrial Revolution, military technology mushroomed. Between 1815 and 1945, it took war from flintlocks to *tanks and from foot-slogging soldiers to long-range *bomber aircraft and the first ballistic *missiles.

Throughout these millennia of organizational and technological growth, the character of war as a mutual activity remained unchanged. War involves the use of organized violence to achieve one's end, often to the maximum extent possible; but that violence is directed against a living, reacting enemy, who in turn uses violence to achieve *his* ends. Hence, the real essence of war, in whatever form and at whatever level, is the interplay between the two sides' moves and countermoves.

Assuming that the force on one side is not overwhelming—in which case little or no military art will be required—to achieve victory it is necessary to strike at a point that is both vital and vulnerable. To force the enemy to expose his vulnerable point, it is necessary to deceive him as to one's intentions. To deceive him, it is usually necessary to pretend to strike at some other point or points; but this in turn means diverting force for the purpose, which will weaken one's ability to launch the decisive stroke as well as to defend oneself.

In this way, war is subject to a peculiar logic of its own, which has been aptly called "paradoxical." It differs from engineering activities, whose object is to mold inorganic matter, but in some ways resembles games such as football or chess; like them, it consists of action, counteraction, and counter-counteraction, all of which are accompanied by a bodyguard of secrecy, lies, feints, and sometimes even espionage. The resulting uncertainty, the friction that is inherent in the activity of large bodies of people, and the sheer risk to life and limb that is involved, combine to make the conduct of war extraordinarily difficult. As Napoleon once said, intellectually it poses problems worthy of a Newton or an Euler; however, the character attributes that it demands—such as courage, endurance, determination, the ability to keep one's mind clear in a crisis—are, if anything, even greater.

Still, assuming a rough balance between opposing sides, in theory, victory goes to the side that, reading the enemy's intentions while concealing its own, is able to strike hardest at the decisive point without exposing itself. In practice, the necessary calculations are often much too complicated for any one brain or combination of brains, with the result that, as in the case of many games, the outcome depends on making the fewest mistakes, as well as pure chance.

With the advent of *nuclear weapons—themselves made possible by the tremendous scientific and industrial resources at the disposal of the modern state—warfare seems to have undergone a decisive change. Hitherto, it had often been possible for one side to use some combination of force and guile in order to achieve victory at a cost acceptable to itself. Now, the prospect had to be faced that victory, instead of guaranteeing one's existence, would lead to annihilation as the defeated side fell on the nuclear button. Indeed, the more resounding the victory, the more acute the danger that this would happen. Under such circumstances, it is scant wonder that those states that possessed nuclear weapons—meaning, by and large, the most powerful ones—generally began taking very good care not to commit suicide and to avoid escalating conflicts between each other. The more nuclear weapons proliferated, the less important and less powerful the states against which large-scale, conventional warfare (as in the period 1648–1945) could still be fought.

Reflecting these developments, military organization and military technology reversed direction. Throughout the years since A.D. 1000, armies and navies had been getting larger and larger, culminating in the tens of millions of uniformed personnel who served during World Wars I and II; now, all of a sudden, they began to shrink as the most important states abandoned the system of mass mobilization of the kind that initially appeared after 1789. For the first time in history, some weapons—specifically, the most important ones by far—were deliberately made less, rather than more, powerful. Neither the most powerful missiles, such as the American Titan, nor the monster hydrogen bomb of 58 megatons (58 *million* tons of TNT) that the Soviets exploded in 1961 had successors. Research and development were redirected in an effort to develop more accurate delivery systems such as multiple independent reentry vehicles (MIRVs) and cruise missiles carrying more limited warheads: Both reflected the feeling that their city-destroying predecessors had grown too indiscriminate and too dangerous to serve any useful purpose.

As nuclear weapons put a ceiling on the size and violence of wars between nations, such wars became rarer at the end of the twentieth century. Beginning in the so-called Third World and spreading to the Second, their place as an agent of political change was increasingly taken by another form of war. This new form of war was not based on the customary division of labor among government, armed forces, and people. Since it did not require a large, continuous, statelike territorial basis, it was immune to those weapons and could be waged even in their presence. *Guerrilla warfare and *terrorism and counterterrorism were, in fact, anything but new phenomena; however, the fact that they were directed against the occupying Axis powers during World War II had given them a new respectability as well as legitimacy in international law. As Europe's overseas *expansionism shows, until 1914 its armies had usually been able to confront with overwhelming force peoples who did not have states, governments, or regular armed forces. But from the moment Adolf *Hitler invaded Yugoslavia in 1941, this clearly ceased to be the case, as the Yugoslav partisans prevented even the German Wehrmacht from conquering all of their country.

Though the forces at their disposal were usually small and their weapons primitive, guerrillas and terrorists in dozens upon dozens of cases since 1945 have defeated the most modern armies and the most powerful modern states that ever existed. In the 1990s, they continued to resist successfully the armed forces of many states around the world, nor, to judge by cases from Algeria to Bosnia to Somalia, does it appear modern states know how to deal with them. For those states and their armed forces, the writing is on the wall. Under the shadow of the mushroom cloud, a new form of war that is simultaneously very old is reemerging and asserting itself. Either modern states learn to cope with it, or they themselves will soon disappear into the dustbin of history.

• Sun Tzu, *The Art of War*, 1963. Carl von Clausewitz, *On War*, 1976. Edward Luttwak, *Strategy: The Logic of War and Peace*, 1987. Martin van Creveld, *The Transformation of War*, 1991.

—Martin van Creveld

WAR: LEVELS OF WAR

Modern military analysts view warfare as an undertaking that can be broadly examined on three complementary and somewhat overlapping levels: *tactics, *operational art, and *strategy. Recent American military thinking, influenced by the *Vietnam War and then accelerated by the *Goldwater-Nichols Act of 1986, has matured and become much more sophisticated in its analysis and understanding of the nature and conduct of war. With the notable exceptions of Alfred T. *Mahan and Billy *Mitchell, until recently civilian defense analysts have done the majority of innovative theoretical thinking in the United States about warfare. There is now, however, an intellectual renaissance within the ranks of the government defense community. Still prodded by civilian thinkers and critics, the American military establishment has recently developed a paradigm that views warfare as an activity to be conducted and understood on the three levels: tactical, operational, and strategic. The latest and least-developed concept concerns the nature and conduct of war at the strategic level.

The United States's military *education system, particularly its Senior Service Colleges (War Colleges), provides a thorough grounding in the classics of military thinking. Sun Tzu, Antoine Henri *Jomini, Carl von *Clausewitz, and others are studied in depth for applicable lessons for current military practitioners. Learning from the past, from recent military experiences, and from a study of foreign armies, particularly in the former Soviet Union, American military thinkers have begun to view war in somewhat overlapping constructs. These *levels of war* are useful in framing activities by military echelons within a theater of operations and in establishing a structure for ordering activities in time and space. They provide civilian decision-makers and military commanders with a method to visualize an orderly sequence of operations, the resources necessary, and the specific tasks to be accomplished. Each level of warfare is defined by the intended outcome and not by the size of the specific unit tasked to accomplish it.

The most basic and thoroughly understood is the *tactical level* of warfare. It is concerned with the planning and executing of battles and engagements to accomplish military objectives that are assigned to tactical units or to task forces. With army and Marine forces, these are normally division-size units or smaller; in the air force and navy, the force size is roughly the squadron and battle group level, respectively. At the tactical level, the focus of activities is the ordered arrangement and maneuver of combat elements to achieve combat objectives. Actions here are focused on specific missions, and *victory in battle and engagements is attained by achieving superiority over an enemy by exercising adroitly the *principles of war: objective, initiative, maneuver, mass, surprise, security, simplicity, economy of force, and unity of command. Success or failure at this level may determine victory or defeat at the operational and ultimately strategic levels. Tactics employ both the art and science of warfare to use all available means to defeat the enemy; normally, there is more emphasis on the science and less on the art of warfare. In essence, the tactical level of warfare involves battlefield problem solving.

The *operational level* of warfare is the level at which campaigns and major operations are planned and conducted. It provides the linkage between the tactical level, where individual battles and engagements are fought, and strategic-level objectives. The operational level focuses on conducting joint (multiservice) operations through the design, structure, and execution of subordinate campaign plans and major operations. Emphasis here is on operational art, which the *Joint Chiefs of Staff (JCS) define as "the skillful employment of military forces to attain strategic and/or operational objectives within a theater through the design, organization, integration, and conduct of theater strategies, campaigns, major operations and battles." The essence of operational art is to determine when, where, and for what end forces will fight. At this level, warfare is more an art than a science as senior commanders seek to balance the ends sought with the ways to accomplish those ends in light of the resources available.

The study of the *strategic level* of war is the most recent area of development in American military thinking. At this level, there is the closest linkage between military and civilian leaders in defining and articulating national objectives. Military leaders must then translate national objectives into national security objectives attainable by military means. The pursuit of these military objectives is often done as a member of a coalition of nations. The strategic level then determines national or multinational security objectives and guidance, and uses national resources to achieve these aims. According to the JCS, the strategic level of warfare includes activities to "sequence initiatives; define limits and assess risks for the use of military and other instruments of national power; develop global plans or theater war plans to achieve these objectives; and provide

military forces and other capabilities in accordance with strategic plans."

At the strategic level, again, warfare is much more an art than a science. Contemporary analysts are still debating and refining the concept of strategic art. In 1995, the JCS had yet to publish an accepted definition of what constitutes "strategic art." Because of the level at which it is applied, practitioners of the strategic level of warfare must have an appreciation for all the realms of national power—economic, diplomatic, and informational, as well as the purely military dimension. Those who would master the strategic art must embody three complementary roles: leader, practitioner, and theorist.

The strategic leader is one who *exercises* strategic art, or in military parlance, "makes it happen." A strategic leader provides vision and focus of effort; applies leadership and consensus-building skills in ambiguous, often multicultural associations; coordinates ends, ways, and means; and inspires others to think and to act. Recent historic examples include the American generals Dwight D. *Eisenhower and George C. *Marshall, and the British leaders Gen. William J. Slim and Prime Minister Winston S. *Churchill.

The practitioner of strategic art can be defined as one who *translates* political and military guidance into broad, attainable military objectives. A strategic practitioner both develops and executes strategic plans. Such an individual must have a thorough mastery of all the levels of war and must be able to employ force and the other dimensions of military power. A list of recent strategic practitioners might include Erwin *Rommel, Matthew B. *Ridgway, and H. Norman *Schwarzkopf. All were adept at the art of applying ends, ways, and means to solve military problems in a variety of strategic environments.

The strategic theorist, as the name implies, is one who *develops* strategic concepts and theories. Such an individual would be a student of the history of warfare who also might have practical experience in war, although this would not be a *sine qua non*. The theorist's understanding of warfare would permit him to analyze and synthesize concepts of war to develop even finer understanding and distinctions. Examples of strategic theorists would include Thucydides, Sun Tzu, and Carl von Clausewitz.

Contemporary American military thinking views military operations as a continuum. This spectrum extends from general war to large-scale combat operations, possibly including weapons of mass destruction (nuclear, biological, and chemical), down through military operations other than war. Under this last rubric are a number of operations that have become the most prevalent types of warfare conducted in the last decade of the twentieth century. They include noncombatant evacuation operations, strikes and raids, support to insurgency, counterdrug operations, antiterrorism, disaster relief, civil support, peace operations (peace enforcement, *peacekeeping, and peace building), and nation assistance. Each of these operations can be viewed through the prism of the three levels of war: tactical, operational, and strategic. Some involve the destruction of enemy forces; many do not. All represent the use of the military element of power in pursuit of national objectives.

This paradigm of warfare as a tiered and interlocking system will be particularly useful as our understanding of warfare continues to evolve. Military operations other than war have already begun to blur the traditional understanding of the uses of military power. Military observers in the future will have to analyze such disparate acts as electronically crippling a nation's banking system, or the insertion of a virus into the computer-controlled mass transit system of a city, and then decide whether these are acts of war. Their level of analysis—tactical, operational, strategic—will be important for the conclusions they draw about the ever-changing nature of war.

• Michael Howard, *The Theory and Practice of War,* 1965. Russell F. Weigley, *The American Way of War,* 1973. Peter Paret, Gordon Craig, and Felix Gilbert, eds., *Makers of Modern Strategy,* 1986. Michael I. Handel, *Masters of War: Sun Tzu, Clausewitz, and Jomini,* 1992. Joint Chiefs of Staff, *Joint Pub 1-02: Department of Defense Dictionary of Military and Associated Terms,* 1994. Richard Chilcoat, *Strategic Art: The New Discipline for 21st Century Leaders,* 1995.
—John D. Auger

WAR: AMERICAN WAY OF WAR

Like shadows on a parade field, military institutions and war reflect in part the society that creates them. Although many Americans view themselves as a peace-loving people and war as an aberration, war has been a regular part of American history, integral to the way the nation developed.

Despite divisions among Americans, the United States has justified its wars as in defense of American lives, property, or ideals. Policymakers have also taken the nation into war for various strategic, economic, and political reasons. But since the idea of Old World balance-of-power wars or wars of subjugation over other nations has been anathema to Americans' self-image, the United States has usually mobilized for war in highly idealistic crusades—for liberty or democracy.

America views itself as antimilitaristic because for most of its history, the nation relied in wartime on *ad hoc* citizen armies rather than large standing forces, and because civilian control of the military is seen as a fundamental principle. This antimilitarism was reinforced by isolationism. Secure behind vast oceans, the United States did not develop large peacetime standing forces until the *Cold War.

Another paradox is that although Americans generally view themselves as peaceloving, they have been capable of engaging in the most devastating kind of warfare—war aimed at total *victory and complete elimination of the enemy threat, sometimes of the enemy themselves. This view of warfare emerged from European Americans' wars with Native Americans.

Eastern woodland Indians' warfare was originally much less bloody than that of Europeans, who were accustomed to vicious religious crusades and to the savage subjugation of peoples from Ireland to the Indies. Even as the horrors of religious wars were replaced in the Old World by limited warfare using newly organized professional armies, they were repeated in the New World by amateur soldiers of the militia.

Throughout the seventeenth and eighteenth centuries, colonial militiamen were mobilized in terms of crusades against the "heathen savages." Unable to entice Indian warriors, who preferred raiding, sniping, and ambushing, into open-field European-style combat, frustrated militiamen turned to complete destruction of Native Americans' crops and villages, killing men, women, and children, or selling them into slavery. Although the Indians responded with escalating violence, the superior numbers and resources of the colonists ultimately led to the destruction or removal of entire Indian nations. An American view emerged that military threats to society could indeed be eliminated by the extirpation of the enemy—a result that was impossible among European nations.

This American view of war was reinforced in the eighteenth and nineteenth centuries. In the *French and Indian War (1756–1763), the Americans claimed credit for aiding the British army and navy drive the French out of Canada and the trans-Appalachian West. Later, in the *Revolutionary War, Americans won complete independence from Great Britain. The apparent British threat to American interests and liberties was again defeated in the *War of 1812.

Throughout the nineteenth century, the United States remained free from any external threat (the Civil War was internal and viewed as an aberration). The country was protected by its geographical isolation, the balance of power in Europe, and relatively weak and nonaggressive neighbors. Its formative experiences with war had produced a dichotomy in which the nation was perceived as either wholly secure or wholly insecure. In the latter case, a crusade could be waged that would eliminate the threat and thus restore Americans to total security.

A pattern had emerged in America's wars. War usually began with setbacks, largely because the nation, although willing to go to war, was militarily unprepared. Early defeats were followed by preparation and retaliation, and ultimately decisive redeeming victories—at Quebec, at Saratoga and Yorktown, at New Orleans, and at Gettysburg (at least for the Union). The belief in the inherent righteousness of the cause, in the natural fighting ability of the American *citizen-soldier, and in the nation's ability to mobilize its resources gave Americans an extraordinary optimism about what they could achieve militarily. Wars against Indians, Mexicans, and Spaniards in the nineteenth century reinforced these views, as with relatively small loss of life suffered by U.S. citizens the United States gained enough territory to claim overwhelming, if not always total, victory. In World War I, President Woodrow *Wilson called for a crusade to "end all wars" and to make the world "safe for democracy." The American war effort helped defeat the German empire, create a German republic, and make the United States the financial capital of the world.

The *Civil War had led the United States to adopt the warfighting doctrine of Gen. Ulysses S. *Grant, which emphasized overwhelming and continual military force applied directly against the enemy army and indirectly through deprivation of the enemy's civilian population and resources. In the twentieth century, during two world wars, and limited wars in Korea and Vietnam, the U.S. Army would pursue this strategy against the enemy forces, while the air force and navy pursued the indirect campaign, through bombing and blockade, against the enemy's material resources and political will.

As the United States industrialized, optimism about America's fighting ability focused on superior weaponry. At the turn of the century, Adm. Alfred T. *Mahan's doctrine of Sea Power emphasizing the use of a modern fleet promised swift and total victory. In the 1920s and 1930s, Gen. Billy *Mitchell of the Army Air Service helped develop the doctrine of Strategic Airpower as a technological means to achieve quick and total victory. In World War II, in response to the Japanese attack on *Pearl Harbor and in a crusade against fascism, Americans waged war on land, sea, and air, including conventional and ultimately nuclear bombing of urban areas to achieve decisive victory and unconditional surrender of the enemy.

The *Cold War posed a major challenge to American views of war and the military. Containment of the Soviet Union led to large standing military forces, but even these did not produce a sense of military security, for the USSR also developed intercontinental ballistic missiles and thermonuclear weapons. Before it ended in 1991, with the total collapse of the Soviet empire, the forty-year Cold War represented an unprecedented period of U.S. uncertainty over national security.

During the Cold War, the U.S. government refrained from the use of total military force in Korea and Vietnam. But the policy of limited war clashed with the traditional goal of total victory. The *Korean War ended in a frustrating stalemate, the *Vietnam War ultimately in defeat. After the United States had fought for more than seven years to prevent it, the Communist victory in Vietnam was a severe blow to Americans' optimism, sense of righteousness, and sense of military prowess, which did not return until the collapse of the USSR and the American victory in the *Persian Gulf War of 1991.

The U.S.-led coalition assault in Operation Desert Storm seemed quite justified and resulted in a quick, decisive victory that drove the forces of Iraqi dictator Saddam *Hussein out of Kuwait. Although the Baghdad regime continued in power, its threat to the region was dramatically curtailed. More than any other U.S. military engagement since World War II, the Gulf War to liberate Kuwait conformed to the traditional American way of war.

[See also Civil-Military Relations; Internationalism; Isolationism; Strategy; War: Causes of War; War: Levels of War; War: Nature of War.]

• Russell F. Weigley, The American Way of War: A History of United States Military Strategy and Policy, 1973. John Shy, A People Numerous and Armed: Reflections on the Military Struggle for American Independence, 1976. Michael Howard, War and the Liberal Conscience, 1978. Lloyd C. Gardner, A Covenant with Power: America and World Order from Wilson to Reagan, 1984. Stephen Watts, The Republic Reborn: War and the Making of Liberal America, 1790–1820, 1987. Geoffrey Perret, A Country Made by War: From the Revolution to Vietnam—The Story of America's Rise to Power, 1989. John E. Frehling, Struggle for a Continent: The Wars of Early America, 1993. Michael Sherry, In the Shadow of War: The United States since the 1930s, 1995. John Whiteclay Chambers II and G. Kurt Piehler, eds., Major Problems in American Military History, 1999.

—John Whiteclay Chambers II

WAR: CAUSES OF WAR

Americans' assumptions about the causes of war have shaped important U.S. foreign and security policies. However, these assumptions were often poorly grounded and sometimes simply wrong.

Ideas on the causes of war held by various American *peace and antiwar movements, for example, often had little basis in reality. Since the early nineteenth century, these movements have, at various times, offered eight main prescriptions that embody their central ideas: (1) arbitration treaties and an international court to arbitrate disputes (popular ideas from the 1840s until 1914); (2) treaties forbidding resort to force (such as the 1920s movement for the "outlawry of war"); (3) disarmament or quantitative

arms reductions; (4) collective security (popular during and after World War I); (5) some form of world government; (6) U.S. *isolationism or strict *neutrality (popular in the late 1930s); (7) pacifist noncooperation with national military programs; (8) dovish U.S. policies toward U.S. adversaries (e.g., Vietnamese Communists or Nicaraguan Sandinistas). Some peace groups have also emphasized the need to cultivate pacific values through public moral education and by emphasizing the horrors of war.

When tried, these prescriptions usually proved infeasible or ineffective. Many arbitration treaties were signed before 1914, but they proved useless: governments freely ignored arbitration rulings that went against them. The Kellogg-Briand Treaty supposedly "outlawed" war in 1928, yet it proved to be an empty stunt that had no political effects. Quantitative disarmament rests on a proposition— that the incidence or intensity of warfare increases with the quantity of modern weapons available—that remains unproven and seems wrong. (Ancient history offers evidence against it, recording many immensely destructive wars fought wholly without modern weapons.) The collective security idea, embodied in the *League of Nations, proved ineffective in the 1930s while distracting Americans from more feasible ways to prevent World War II, such as early U.S. moves to deter or contain Germany and Japan. World government is now among those ideas so discredited they are no longer seriously discussed. U.S. neutrality, codified in the U.S. *Neutrality Acts of 1935–39, helped embolden Adolf *Hitler to start World War II while failing to keep the United States out of that war, and thus must be reckoned as more a cause of war than *peace. *Pacifism also helped embolden Hitler, who saw British and American pacifism as easing his road to European hegemony. Pressure for dovish policies did end one or two wars (e.g., the Indochina and Nicaraguan Contra wars), but only after these wars had burned for years. Overall, peace movements' main prescriptions seem generally unsound in retrospect.

Another misdirected approach to the causes of war has come in the twentieth century from anti-Communist conservatives. Their analysis rested on two main hypotheses: (1) communism causes war because Communist states will seek to expand by force against capitalist states; and (2) appeasement of communism causes war by emboldening Communist states in their *expansionism. Their second hypothesis was arguably valid, at least in some situations, but their first was not. Communist states proved to be only modestly aggressive. The USSR was an opportunistic but cautious aggressor, not a Hitlerian juggernaut. Soviet leaders committed vast crimes against their own people but only modest international aggressions.

After three great victories—in the wake of World War I and World War II, and after the *Cold War, which ended in 1991—the United States has sought to shape a durable peace based on its assumptions about the causes of war. Twice the United States failed, but its third attempt has had some success.

Woodrow *Wilson's post–World War I policies rested on poor theories of war's causes. Wilson offered six main prescriptions, framed in his famous *Fourteen Points: (1) Replace balance-of-power politics and competitive alliance making (which Wilson believed caused war) with a collective security system. But collective security was infeasible, as the League's later failure showed. (2) Reduce armaments to "the lowest level consistent with national safety." Here

Wilson was misled by the myth that quantitative disarmament could reduce violence between states. (3) End secret diplomacy in favor of "open covenants . . . openly arrived at," a change Wilson believed would bolster popular control of foreign policy, promoting peace. This soon-forgotten notion was a false corollary to the stronger hypothesis that democracy promotes peace. (4) Grant self-determination to freedom-seeking peoples. But this was infeasible in a post-1919 Europe of much intermingled ethnicities. (5) Remove trade barriers. This was a sound economic idea but a poor peace program, because free trade can cause war as well as peace, as illustrated by the way U.S. trade with the Allies helped draw the United States into World War I. (6) End colonialism. This was a humane idea that addressed a non-cause of the world war (European colonial rivalries had largely ended by 1914).

In World War II, President Franklin D. *Roosevelt's ideas about the causes of war and peace echoed Wilson's in part and differed in part. Like Wilson, Roosevelt believed that arms reductions, free trade, and national self-determination would promote peace. Unlike Wilson, Roosevelt also believed that aggressor states could best be tamed by completely defeating, disarming, and occupying them. His core belief, however, was that the best cornerstone of peace would be a concert system resembling the 1815 Concert of Europe, run through the cooperation of the "four policemen" (the United States, Britain, Nationalist China, and the Soviet Union). Roosevelt's concert scheme failed because a concert requires an underlying consensus among the great powers—something rare in history and absent after 1945.

In the 1990s, the administrations of George *Bush and Bill *Clinton built their post–Cold War peace on better ideas and got better results. They continued U.S. security guarantees to primary U.S. allies in Europe and Asia, backed by a continued overseas U.S. military presence. They pressed Europe's newly freed states to respect the rights of ethnic minorities. Echoing Wilson, they pressed Europe's dictatorships to democratize, believing that democracies seldom fight each other. Finally, they pushed former Communist states to "marketize" their economies, believing that marketization would promote prosperity, which would bolster democracy and peace. These post–Cold War policies, produced a softer landing than the policies of 1919 and 1945.

Social scientists have developed a large body of theories on the causes of war since World War II, some of them useful and influential. Two major theories have identified military factors as key causes of war and implied military-related prescriptions. What became known as "stability theory" warned that the risk of war increased with the size of the military advantage accruing to the side that struck first. With a large first-strike advantage, a "reciprocal fear of surprise attack" could set in, with each side thinking that "they fear we fear they will attack; so they might attack; so we must." Developed by nuclear strategists of Albert Wohlstetter and Thomas Schelling in the 1950s and 1960s, the theory led some strategists to advise against deploying strategic nuclear forces that were designed for surprise attack on the adversary's nuclear forces. However, the theory had only modest influence on policy, largely because the U.S. *Air Force rejected it.

What became known as "offense-defense theory" warned that the risk of war increased as offensive forces grew stronger and conquest grew easier. When conquest is easy, this theory holds, aggressors are tempted to attack by prospects of easy gain, and *status quo* powers grow more aggressive because they desire more defensible borders. The theory drew mention before the 1970s but was first developed by the political scientist Robert Jervis in 1978, and then elaborated by others. It is now widely accepted in academe and in many policy circles, although the U.S. military remains skeptical. Its proponents have used it to explain historical events, such as the outbreak of World War I, and as a guide for policy, warning against unduly offensive military doctrines and force postures, and recommending giving security guarantees to others as a way to preserve peace in other regions. It influenced the European peace movement to call for a more defensive *NATO conventional military posture during the mid-1980s; it helped persuade the Soviet reform government of Mikhail Gorbachev to adopt a more defensive military posture in late 1980s; and it encouraged the decisions of the Bush and Clinton administrations to extend defensive security guarantees in Europe and Asia.

What could be called "misperception theory" has warned that governments are subject to a wide range of war-causing misperceptions. Its dominant version, also developed in the 1970s by Robert Jervis and others, argues that national misperceptions stem from the cognitive errors of policymakers. These psychological errors lead governments to underestimate their own role in provoking others' hostility, to learn slowly, to exaggerate the order and coherence of others' actions, and to fall into spirals of self-reinforcing mutual hostility. Another variant of the theory, elaborated by Geoffrey Blainey in the 1970s, warned that wars of false optimism erupt when states underestimate others' capacity or will to fight.

During the 1970s and 1980s, scholars also explored the hypothesis, asserted in the eighteenth century by the German philosopher Immanuel Kant but never tested, that democracies are more peaceful than other types of government. This led to the growth of "democratic peace theory," and the discovery that while democracies are as war-prone as other states, they almost never fight each other. Democratic peace theory informed official policy in the 1980s and 1990s, fueling a return to Woodrow Wilson's goal of fostering democracy overseas. Most notably, Congress created the National Endowment for Democracy to support democracy abroad, and the Bush and Clinton administrations put priority on supporting democracy in the former Soviet empire.

Other recent scholarly theories of war have had less policy impact. A "structural realist" school argued that a bipolar world of two superpowers is more peaceful than a multipolar world of three or more great powers. A "liberal institutional" school argued that international institutions and regimes ease international cooperation, and, its proponents implied, promote peace. Others offered a "power transition" theory, positing that wars break out during transitions from the leadership of one great power to another. However, these theories are controversial within academe and have had little impact outside it.

Theories of war that drove U.S. policy for much of American history have often proved erroneous. Both the left and the right have frequently treated war's causes as a question to be settled by reference to movement dogma rather than by study. Americans have paid in blood for mistaken policies that stemmed from these errors. On the other hand, social science has made progress on the problem of war in recent years, and this progress may promise better policies in the future.

[*See also* Disciplinary Views of War: Political Science and International Relations.]

• Robert Jervis, *Perception and Misperception in International Politics*, 1976. Robert Jervis, "Cooperation Under the Security Dilemma," *World Politics*, 30 (January 1978), pp. 167–214. Geoffrey Blainey, *The Causes of War*, 3rd ed. 1988. Alexander L. George, "Domestic Constraints on Regime Change in U.S. Foreign Policy," in G. John Ikenberry, ed., *American Foreign Policy*, 1989, pp. 583–608. Jack Levy, "The Causes of War: A Review of Theories," in Philip E. Tetlock, et al., eds., *Behavior, Society, and Nuclear War*, 1 (1989), pp. 209–333. Nils Petter Gleditsch, "Democracy and Peace," *Journal of Peace Research*, 29 (1992), pp. 369–76. Greg Cashman, *What Causes War? An Introduction to Theories of International Conflict*, 1993.

—David Mendeloff *and* Stephen Van Evera

WAR: EFFECTS OF WAR ON THE ECONOMY

The most persistent and perhaps most important question relating to the effects of America's wars and their related costs on the U.S. economy is whether military expenditures have been a prop or a burden for economic growth. This question has continued relevance because the United States in the 1990s spent a larger part of its gross domestic product (GDP) on defense (3.8% in 1995) than any other G7 industrial nation, almost four times Japan's expenditure and nearly twice as much as Germany's—America's two most important economic competitors. The fact that Russia in the 1990s spent almost three times more of its GDP on defense—and was in economic chaos—only strengthened this concern.

Historians and economists have waxed and waned with regard to the effect of military expenditures on the U.S. economy. Charles and Mary Beard in *The Rise of American Civilization* (1927) and Louis Hacker in *The Triumph of American Capitalism* (1940) argued that the *Civil War destroyed not only slavery but also the Southern slaveocracy, thus allowing the balance of political power to shift to Northern industrialists and hence spurring American economic growth. Prior to these accounts, the classical economists (Adam Smith, David Ricardo, and Thomas Malthus) were concerned with the effects of war on aggregate demand. The eighteenth and early nineteenth centuries saw very high levels of military expenditures in Britain, for example, which these economists believed had a negative impact on industrial growth. The national debts resulting from war, Smith believed, "enfeebled every state ... enriching in most cases the idle and profuse debtor at the expense of the industrious and frugal creditor."

Critics of the capitalist system in more recent years have argued that capitalist societies are prone to periodic stagnation, and that only wars of the magnitude of World War II are capable of curing massive unemployment. Alternatively, liberal economists argue that war, and particularly World War II, was the strongest influence establishing Keynesian economics as a guideline and a justification for U.S. government fiscal policies for the postwar era—policies that led to widespread employment, high earnings, and a modest measure of income redistribution. Even some strong opponents of the *Vietnam War began to argue in the mid-1990s that full employment was only possible in the late 1960s because of that war.

Paul Kennedy, in his widely read *Rise and Fall of the Great Powers* (1987), is perhaps the best known historian for the view that persistent and high military expenditures have played an important role in the relative economic decline of major nations since 1500. In this and subsequent works, he argues that the United States now runs the risk of "imperial overstretch"; that America's global commitments are greater than its capacity to fund them. For him, war is not only a burden, but continuous high levels of defense spending can and generally have turned major nations into minor ones. Although his is a popular view, he had yet to persuade the experts that the United States was well down the road to relative economic decline.

The most sophisticated studies on the prop v. burden issue—whether defense spending contributes to economic growth and well-being by stimulating the economy, or whether defense spending uses up scarce resources and diverts resources into less productive channels—tend to emphasize that growth in the GDP has been rather constant, with little lasting impact from the nine major wars America has fought since independence. Wars temporarily reduce long-run productive capacity by reducing the growth of population and the inflow of immigrants; but the general burden of any given war falls largely on the current generation, according to Chester Wright in a seminal study on the more enduring economic consequences of American wars to 1940. More recently, Todd Sandler and Keith Hartley demonstrated that defense spending generally inhibits economic growth in developed countries by crowding out public and private investment, and siphoning off of R & D resources. Indeed, since the late 1980s, world military expenditures as a percentage of GDP have decreased dramatically without any evidence of harmful effects on the world economy. In truth, the overall economic burden of America's wars is less significant than the inequitable manner in which so much of that burden has been placed upon the working class and those with modest education, while others largely escape or even profit from such wars.

If the effect of military spending during the war years is the most obvious point of impact on the economy, the most lasting one has to do with veterans' benefits paid after the war to *veterans and their dependents. Veterans' benefits have been paid for every war since the American Revolution. They amounted to about two-thirds of the total dollar cost of the *Revolutionary War; more than half the cost of the *War of 1812; and 3.7 times the cost of mobilizing the Union forces in the *Civil War. Surprisingly, these benefits continued to rise for about forty to sixty years after the end of each of these wars and did not cease until well over a century later. Benefits for Civil War veterans and spouses ceased only in the 1980s; World War II benefits will be paid until sometime after 2070. To date, World War II veteran's benefits have amounted to more than $300 billion, only somewhat less than the original cost of that war in current dollars. Clearly, veterans' benefits have been a major infusion of funds into the economy, and were the major direct federal subsidy to families prior to the welfare state. Compared to other countries, American soldiers and their dependents received benefits much earlier (since 1783) and in more generous amounts than elsewhere. The average payment to a still-living World War I veteran, for example, was $6,500 in 1992. Confederate soldiers, of course, received no federal veterans benefits, although some southern states sought to add them.

The most troubling problem concerning the impact of war on the economy has to do with rapidly rising public debt. Large but temporary public debts have occurred in all of America's wars; all were paid off in time until the 1970s, when U.S. public debt rose dramatically owing to large defense increases and major tax cuts under President Ronald *Reagan. In the 1990s, U.S. net public debt (most of which is war-related) was at an unprecedented peacetime level. High public debt levels—a problem in all G7 nations—boost real interest rates, retard the accumulation of private capital, and limit gains in living standards, according to the International Monetary Fund. Reducing this unsustainable public debt, the most significant legacy of recent American wars, will be one of the United States's greatest challenges in the twenty-first century.

[See also Disciplinary Views of War: Economics; Economy and War; Industry and War; Military-Industrial Complex; Public Financing and Budgeting for War].

• Charles and Mary Beard, The Rise of American Civilization, 1927. Louis Hacker, The Triumph of American Capitalism, 1940. Chester W. Wright, "The More Enduring Economic Consequences of America's Wars," in the Journal of Economic History (1943). James L. Clayton, ed., The Economic Impact of the Cold War, 1970. Steven Rosen, ed., Testing the Theory of the Military-Industrial Complex, 1973. Paul Kennedy, The Rise and Fall of the Great Powers, 1987. Paul Kennedy, Preparing for the Twenty-First Century, 1993, esp. chaps. 13 and 14. Todd Sandler and Keith Hartley, The Economics of Defense, 1995. International Monetary Fund, World Economic Outlook May 1996, "Focus on Fiscal Policy," 1996.

—James L. Clayton

WAR COLLEGES. See Schools, Postgraduate Service.

WAR CRIMES. Defined largely by international treaties, conventions, and tribunals, war crimes generally fall into one of three categories: crimes against peace; crimes against humanity; and conventional war crimes, which involve egregious violations of the customs and *laws of war. They are based on the assumptions that aggressive war and certain actions by civilian officials or military personnel in war can be limited or at least punished.

War crimes differ from conventional military crimes, criminal violations of codes of military law, or military justice prosecuted by a country's military against violators in its own military service. Few countries have tried their own military personnel for war crimes (although armed services have tried their own members for violations which in other circumstances would be called war crimes).

Enemy soldiers and political leaders have long been punished with or without trial by the victors for heinous acts. However, only in modern times have war crimes been formally defined and made statutory offenses. Murder and maltreatment of *prisoners of war (POWs) was declared a crime in 1792 by the National Assembly in Revolutionary France. In the American *Civil War, the U.S. War Department in 1863 issued General Order No. 100, a code of military conduct toward enemy civilians and POWs (drafted by Professor Francis Lieber of Columbia College). During the war, both sides punished some of their own soldiers for military crimes, but only one person was tried and executed for war crimes—Confederate Capt. Henry Wirz, commander of the infamous POW camp at Andersonville, Georgia, who was held responsible for the deaths of thousands of captured Union soldiers.

In the *Philippine War (1899–1902), the U.S. *Army tried several officers by courts-martial for offenses that were violations of the laws and customs of war. There was a congressional investigation of U.S. Army officers for allegedly mistreating prisoners. (Fighting in the Philippines had devolved into *guerrilla warfare not greatly dissimilar to that of the Plains Indians Wars in the United States a few decades earlier.)

The international community began to codify the laws of war in the nineteenth and early twentieth centuries as weapons grew more destructive, mass armies were created, and industrialized warfare began to blur the lines between combatant and noncombatant. The *Geneva Conventions (1864) adopted agreements to protect wounded soldiers; the *Hague Peace Conferences (1899, 1907) prohibited the use of certain weapons; subsequent Geneva Conventions in 1906, 1929, and 1949 expanded the laws of war as they applied to civilians, POWs, and sick and wounded military personnel.

In 1919, following World War I, the victorious Allies created a Commission on the Responsibility of the Authors of the War and on Enforcement of Penalties. Article 227 of the Treaty of *Versailles (1919) arraigned the former German emperor, *Wilhelm II, "for a supreme offense against international morality and the sanctity of treaties," and provided for his trial by a special Allied court. But since Wilhelm had abdicated and fled to the neutral Netherlands, which refused to surrender him, the trial never occurred. In Article 228 of the peace treaty, Germany recognized the Allies' right to try those suspected of war crimes (such as the alleged *atrocities in Belgium). The Allies allowed the new Weimar Republic to try the cases. Although the results in the polarized German republic were farcical, the Allied action of 1919 of deciding to hold individuals accountable to an international body set an important precedent.

During World War II, the barbarities perpetrated by Nazi Germany led the Allies in the Declaration of Moscow (1943) to assert firmly that those responsible for atrocities committed during the war would be tried and punished. In August 1944, the Allies signed the London Agreement establishing an International Military Tribunal to try accused Axis war criminals not only for conventional war crimes, such as brutal treatment of POWs, but also for waging aggressive war and committing crimes against peace and against humanity.

The International Military Tribunal, composed of members from Britain, France, the Soviet Union, and the United States, sat in Nuremberg, a former center of Nazi Party activity, from November 1945 to October 1946. The original twenty-four defendants at the *Nuremberg Trials included many of the surviving leaders of the Nazi regime. (Adolf *Hitler, Propaganda Minister Joseph Goebbels, and Gestapo chief Heinrich Himmler had committed suicide.) Only three defendants were acquitted; of the rest, twelve were sentenced to death and hanged (the most prominent among them, Hermann Goering, a longtime Nazi leader and commander of the German air forces, committed suicide by swallowing cyanide hours before he was to be hanged). Three were sentenced to life imprisonment. And four others, including Albert Speer, the armaments minister, were given sentences of ten to twenty years in Spandau Prison, Berlin. Sentences for the indicted German military commanders included: Gens. Wilhelm Keitel and Alfred

Jodl, death by hanging; Adm. Erich Raeder, life imprisonment; and Adm. Karl Doenitz, ten years in prison. In addition, in 1945–49, separate military tribunals by each of the Allied occupying powers tried others accused of war crimes. The U.S. military tribunal meeting in Nuremberg tried another 185 prominent Nazis in that period.

At the *Potsdam Conference in July 1945, American, British, and Soviet leaders had warned Japan that war criminals would be punished. Consequently, in January 1946, an International Military Tribunal for the Far East was established in Tokyo by the Supreme Commander Allied Powers, Gen. Douglas *MacArthur. With judges from each of the eleven countries at war with Japan, the Far Eastern tribunal tried twenty-eight major Japanese military and civilian leaders between May 1946 and November 1948. The most famous defendant was Gen. Hideki *Tojo, prime minister in 1941–44, who had failed in a suicide attempt in August 1945. The others included thirteen generals, a colonel, three admirals, five diplomats, three government bureaucrats, one politician, and an ultranationalist (later declared insane and unfit for trial). Controversially, Emperor *Hirohito, in whose name the war had been fought, was exempted because MacArthur believed his trial would trigger massive Japanese resistance to the American occupation. The court held all except two of the defendants guilty of conspiracy to wage aggressive war and all were convicted on other charges of responsibility for war crimes. Tojo and six others were hanged in December 1948. Sixteen defendants were sentenced to life in prison, one man to twenty years, and one to seven years in prison.

Unlike the Nuremberg Trials, some elements of the Tokyo War Crimes Trials remain legally controversial. One was the conviction and execution of Gen. Tomoyuki Yamashita, who was held responsible for barbarous acts against civilians in the defense of Manila in 1944, despite the fact that he had ordered Japanese soldiers to leave the city in an orderly manner and had no idea the atrocities occurred, and regardless of the fact that most of these barbarities had been committed by naval ground troops not under his direct command. MacArthur and the U.S. Supreme Court refused his appeal.

Above all, however, the Tokyo trials have remained controversial for a version of history that even some of the judges admitted was based on a seriously flawed interpretation of Japanese *expansionism since the late 1920s, blaming it on a conspiracy of the defendants rather than an essentially incremental, *ad hoc* expansionism, vigorously debated within Japan, up to the decision for war with the West at the end of 1941.

The Nuremberg Trials had a profound impact on the evolution of international law and concepts of responsibility for war and behavior in war. The tribunal rejected the argument that the trials were *ex post facto,* asserting that the acts of which the defendants were accused had been considered crimes long before World War II. Furthermore, the results of the trials clearly held individuals, military or civilian, responsible for conduct leading to or during war. The tribunal rejected the contention that the state, not individuals, was responsible for war and other national policies. The tribunal also rejected the defense that the accused were only following orders issued by others. Instead, individuals were held responsible for their actions, although for those found guilty, the tribunal indicated that a person's place in the hierarchy of authority and the nature of those orders could be considered as mitigating circumstances in the determination of sentencing. Consequently, no one was convicted of responsibility for the German bombing of Allied cities or for waging unrestricted *submarine warfare.

The Nuremberg principles were upheld by the newly formed *United Nations in 1946. Indeed, the UN Charter of 1945 limited resort to war to self-defense and to UN actions to enforce international security. In 1948, the United Nations prepared a Convention on the Prevention and Punishment of the Crime of Genocide. In 1968, it adopted a convention that removed the statute of limitations from war crimes and crimes against humanity.

In the postwar period, the international community sought to define and codify by treaty the nature of war crimes. The Geneva Conventions of 1949 listed among what were considered "grave breaches" of the laws of war torture and other inhuman treatment. The 1977 Protocol to the Geneva Conventions of 1949 added making civilian populations or individual civilians the object of attack or launching an indiscriminate attack affecting the civilian population.

The 1977 Geneva Protocol provided for the establishment of fact-finding commissions to investigate reported grave breaches of international law. Some allegations of war crimes have been made since World War II. In the *Korean War, they concerned "death marches," the torture and killing of American POWs by the North Korean military, and maltreatment by Chinese soldiers. In the *Vietnam War, the allusions were to the torture and execution of captive soldiers by the Communist Viet Cong and North Vietnamese and of suspected Communists by the South Vietnamese. In violation of the Geneva Convention prohibitions against deliberately exposing POWs to insults and public curiosity, Hanoi authorities also marched captured American aviators through the streets of Hanoi to bolster North Vietnamese morale. But there were also accusations of atrocities committed by U.S. forces. In the Iran-Iraq War, atrocities were again claimed, including the use of poison gas by Saddam *Hussein's army.

None of these or other accusations led to an international fact-finding commission under the 1977 Geneva Protocol. Rather, if armed forces responded at all to such allegations, they tended to do so by trying individuals in their organizations by court-martial for breach of their own military or civilian criminal law. In 1971, for example, U.S. Army courts-martial tried 5 soldiers for murder and 2 officers for murder and dereliction of duty for covering up a massacre of 347 civilians during a military operation in the village of My Lai in South Vietnam in 1968. Only one, Lt. William L. Calley, was convicted. For premeditated murder, he was sentenced to life imprisonment in 1971, but in 1974 a federal court overturned the conviction. An investigation by the army confirmed that the *My Lai massacre had occurred and been covered up within the division before being exposed in 1969 by some of the American soldiers who saw it.

With the end of the *Cold War, the United Nations began to establish war crimes tribunals to investigate some of the grave breaches of the rules and customs of war in the ethnic and civil wars that erupted during the 1990s. In 1993, the United Nations set up the first UN War Crimes Tribunal in the Hague to try war crimes cases stemming from the civil wars in areas of the former Yugoslavia. In the

*Bosnian Crisis (1992–95), the tribunal indicted several Bosnian Serbs for war crimes—primarily against Bosnian Muslims—including torture and execution of prisoners of war, the forced relocation ("ethnic cleansing") and murder of large numbers of civilians. Several of the indicted were arrested by *NATO *peacekeeping forces, including U.S. troops; however, as late as 1998, the most important of the indicted war criminals, former Bosnian Serb leader Radovan Karadzic, remained at large.

In Africa, as a result of the 1994 slaughter in Rwanda of perhaps 500,000 Tutsi and moderate Hutu civilians and prisoners of war by an extremist Hutu government and military, a UN tribunal sitting in neighboring Tanzania in 1998 handed down the first guilty verdict by an international court for the crime of genocide, and for the first time defined rape as genocidal. Following four years of proceedings, the three-judge court convicted former Rwandan mayor Jean-Paul Akayesu of responsibility for the death of more than 2,000 persons and the rape of dozens of Tutsi women in his city, Taba, even though the actual attacks had been carried out by police officers, soldiers, and Hutu militiamen. The court sentenced him to life in prison.

The UN tribunal dismissed several charges against Akayesu that he had violated the Geneva Conventions on the treatment of victims of war, stating that the mayor was not a military figure who could be held accountable under those treaties. However, the establishment of war crimes trials in the late 1990s for Bosnia and Rwanda clearly marked a pivotal moment in international law and laid the legal groundwork for future war crimes prosecutions in UN courts.

[*See also* Genocide; Holocaust, U.S. War Effort and the; Justice, Military; Laws of War; Prisoner-of-War Camps, Civil War; War.]

• Morris Greenspan, *The Soldier's Guide to the Laws of War*, 1969. Richard Hammer, *The Court-Martial of Lieutenant Calley*, 1971. R. H. Minear, *Victor's Justice: The Tokyo War Crimes Trial*, 1971. S. D. Baily, *Prohibitions and Restraints in War*, 1972. Seymour Hersh, *Cover-up*, 1972. James F. Willis, *Prologue to Nuremberg: The Politics and Diplomacy of Punishing War Criminals of the First World War*, 1981. C. Hosoya, et al. eds., *The Tokyo War Crimes Trial: An International Symposium*, 1986. Telford Taylor, *Anatomy of the Nuremberg Trials: A Personal Memoir*, 1992. George J. Andreopoulos and Mark R. Shulman, eds., *The Laws of War: Constraints on Warfare in the Western World*, 1994. Geoffrey Best, *War and Law Since 1945*, 1994. Theodor Merron, "Comments: War Crimes in Yugoslavia and the Development of International Law," *American Journal of International Law*, 88 (January 1994), p. 78. Joseph E. Persico, *Nuremberg: Infamy on Trial*, 1994. Michael R. Marrus, ed., *The Nuremberg War Crimes Trial: A Documentary History*, 1997.

—Rod Paschall

WAR OF 1812. The War of 1812 is often referred to as the United States's second war of independence because, like the *Revolutionary War, it was fought against Great Britain. The Conflict resulted from the clash between American *nationalism and the war Britain and its allies were waging against the empire of Napoleonic France. Many Americans believed that England sought to humiliate the United States, limit its growth, and perhaps even impose a quasi-colonial status upon its former colonies.

Background. Throughout the wars between Revolutionary and Napoleonic France and Great Britain

(1793–1801 and 1803–15), the belligerent powers of Europe repeatedly violated the maritime rights of neutral nations. The United States, endeavoring to market its own produce while also asserting the right to profit as an important neutral carrier in the Atlantic commercial system, was particularly hard hit. In order to man the Royal Navy, British naval officers impressed seamen from American vessels, claiming that they were either deserters from British service or British subjects, irrespective of whether they had been naturalized by the United States. The United States defended its right to naturalize foreigners and rejected Britain's claim that it could legitimately practice impressment on the high seas. Relations between the two countries reached breaking point on this issue in June 1807, when the frigate HMS *Leopard* fired on the USS *Chesapeake* inside American territorial waters in order to remove, and later execute, four of its crew.

The exact number of Americans affected by impressment is difficult to ascertain—American newspapers on the eve of the war claimed that it was in excess of 6,000—and Great Britain and the United States were never able to resolve the dispute. Over time the issue became the most flagrant example of Great Britain's reluctance to respect the sovereignty of the United States, and this was one of the reasons why President James *Madison cited impressment in his 1 June 1812 message to Congress as the first major grievance that had to be settled by war.

Equally offensive to the United States was the British practice of issuing executive orders in council, particularly those of November 1807 and April 1809, in order to establish *blockades of the European coast. The Royal Navy then seized neutral vessels bound for the Continent that did not first call at a British port to pay duties and unload cargo. By these means, Great Britain could simultaneously wage economic warfare against France and control American trade to its advantage. British ministries justified these tactics as fair retaliation against Napoleon's equally antineutral Berlin and Milan decrees, promulgated in December 1806 and December 1807, respectively; but American merchantmen suffered more heavily from British seizures than from French, and the administrations of Thomas *Jefferson and James Madison never accepted British blockading practices as valid under the law of nations. It was the seriousness of this dispute that ultimately raised the question of whether the United States should go to war to defend its neutral rights.

At first, the United States responded with policies of economic coercion rather than war. At the suggestion of President Jefferson, Congress passed a series of embargo laws between December 1807 and January 1809. These laws prohibited virtually all American ships from putting to sea and eventually banned any overland trade with British and Spanish colonial possessions in Canada and Florida. Because the legislation failed to change British policy and seriously harmed the U.S. economy as well, it was replaced by the Non-Intercourse Act in March 1809. This measure forbade trade with European belligerents until it was replaced in May 1810 by Macon's Bill No. 2. This law reopened American trade with all nations subject to the proviso that in the event of either France or Great Britain repealing its antineutral policies, the United States would then enforce nonintercourse against whichever nation failed to follow suit by lifting the remaining restrictions on trade.

In August 1810, Napoleon announced he would repeal the Berlin and Milan decrees on the understanding that the United States would also force Great Britain to respect its neutral rights. President Madison accepted this as proof that French policy had changed, and in November 1810 he imposed nonintercourse against Great Britain. He then demanded the repeal of the orders in council as a condition for the resumption of Anglo-American trade. When Great Britain refused to comply, Madison, in July 1811, summoned the Twelfth Congress into an early session in November to prepare for war. After eight months of debate, Congress responded to the president's initiatives by declaring war on 18 June 1812. The decision was bitterly controversial and was carried by Republican Party majorities alone. In the House of Representatives, the vote was 79 to 49 for war; in the Senate, 19 to 3. The Federalists, whose constituents (especially in New England) depended heavily on trade with Great Britain, believed that France had equally offended against American neutrality; they opposed the declaration of war and, thereafter, its prosecution.

Military and Naval Events. The principal theater of operations in the war was the American-Canadian frontier between Detroit and Lake Champlain. Upper and Lower Canada were the closest British imperial possessions that were vulnerable to U.S. military and naval power. The rapid growth of their economies in the early nineteenth century, particularly in the timber trade, had transformed them into a significant resource for Great Britain during its protracted maritime struggle against France; this reinforced the American desire to seize them, and fostered a strategy of invasion. To the extent that the British were able to carry the war to the Americans, it was by sea; thus, especially after the summer of 1814, the theater of operations expanded to include the mid-Atlantic coast and the American territories around the Gulf of Mexico. For this reason, a war that commenced as an invasion of Canada in 1812 concluded in a defense of the city of New Orleans in the early months of 1815.

Over the summer and fall of 1812, U.S. forces, under the commands of Brigs. Gen. William Hull, Alexander Smyth, and Stephen Van Rensselaer, and Maj. Gen. Henry Dearborn, were directed to invade Canada at Detroit, Niagara, and Montréal; but inadequate preparations, poor leadership, and untrained troops undermined the invasions. The British general Sir Isaac Brock, together with *Tecumseh and the Shawnee, Delaware, and other northwestern Indians who had their own complaints about American territorial expansion, captured Detroit in August 1812. In September and October, Brock and Maj. Gen. Roger Sheaffe defeated two American invading armies on the Niagara peninsula, while Dearborn's invasion of Lower Canada was called off after only one minor engagement in November. American efforts made at the same time by Maj. Gen. William Henry Harrison and Brig. Gen. James Winchester to retake Detroit were also unsuccessful; the latter officer surrendered his army to British and Indian forces on the Raisin River in Michigan Territory in January 1813.

The only American victories in the opening months of the war occurred on the ocean as the heavy frigates of the tiny U.S. Navy took to the seas to protect American trade and to harass the vastly superior naval forces of their enemy. In August 1812, the USS *Constitution*, under Capt. Isaac Hull, destroyed HMS *Guerrière*; in October, Capt.

Stephen *Decatur's USS *United States* captured HMS *Macedonian*; and in December, the *Constitution*, now under Capt. William Bainbridge, defeated HMS *Java* in an engagement off the coast of Brazil.

Between May and November 1813, the U.S. Army attempted to invade Canada across the Great Lakes and down the St. Lawrence River. American forces were successful inasmuch as they captured Fort George and York (now Toronto) in Upper Canada in May, but subsequent efforts to extend American control in the province were thwarted by British victories at Stony Creek and Beaver Dams in June. A major thrust from Sacketts Harbor down the St. Lawrence toward Montréal under Maj. Gen. James Wilkinson was also aborted, first by British resistance at Crysler's Farm in November 1813, then by Wilkinson's decision to end his offensive after learning that he would be unable to join forces with U.S. troops below Montréal. On the northwest frontier, American naval forces under Commodore Oliver Hazard *Perry defeated a British squadron at Put-in-Bay on Lake Erie in September. Thereafter, Harrison and his U.S. and Kentucky troops were able first to retake Detroit, and then, in October, to destroy the alliance between the British and the Indians with a victory at the Battle of the Thames.

There were no other major American victories in 1813. The Royal Navy avenged the defeats of 1812 by capturing the USS *Chesapeake* in June 1813, and throughout the year British frigates steadily extended their blockade of U.S. ports, annoying coastal communities and disrupting trade. Yet another setback for the American war effort came in the fall of 1813 when "Redstick" factions in the Creek Nation, who like the Shawnees and Delawares had ample grievances against the United States, attacked forts and settlements on the southwestern frontier. Georgia and Tennessee mobilized troops in response and Tennessee forces under Maj. Gen. Andrew *Jackson eventually defeated the Creeks at Horsehoe Bend, Mississippi Territory, in March 1814.

By 1814, American land forces had improved in both quality and leadership. Disciplined troops under Maj. Gen. Jacob Brown and Brig. Gen. Winfield *Scott resumed efforts from the previous year to expel the British from Niagara, and between July and September they fought the enemy on even terms in three major engagements at Chippewa, Lundy's Lane, and Fort Erie. But the defeat of Napoleon in Europe in the spring of 1814 allowed Great Britain to send more troops to North America, and by late summer, the United States had to contend with invasions by combined army and navy forces at Lake Champlain and in Chesapeake Bay. Capt. Thomas Macdonough's victory over a British squadron on Lake Champlain in September compelled one invading army to withdraw to Canada. Meanwhile, another British force had taken and burned the White House, the U.S. capitol, and most other government buildings in Washington, D.C. (in August), and a third had occupied the northeastern section of the District of Maine. Efforts to seize Baltimore failed as Maryland militiamen inflicted heavy losses on the British regulars of Gen. Robert Ross, and the harbor defenses of Baltimore withstood a heavy naval bombardment. It was during the shelling of Fort McHenry on 13–14 September that the poet Francis Scott Key composed the work that became "The Star-Spangled Banner" as a tribute to the American defense.

Conclusion. Efforts to end the war lasted almost as long as the conflict itself. Great Britain, in fact, repealed its orders in council in June 1812 before it had learned of the declaration of war, but President Madison decided to continue the struggle in order to obtain a comprehensive settlement of American grievances. For this purpose, he accepted in March 1813 a Russian offer to mediate the conflict and dispatched a five-man negotiating team to St. Petersburg. Britain rejected mediation in July, but later offered to open separate peace negotiations. Madison accepted this offer in January 1814; the opening of the talks was delayed until July, however, because of changes in venue resulting from the defeat of Napoleon. At Ghent, Belgium, Great Britain initially made unrealistic demands, seeking not only to establish a neutral Indian buffer state in the American Northwest but to revise both the Canadian-American boundary and the terms of the 1783 Treaty of *Paris that had established the United States as an independent nation. The United States, which had originally wanted an end to all objectionable British maritime practices and cessions of Canadian territory as well, forbore to press any claims at this time. Its diplomats parried Great Britain's demands until the British ministry, rebuffed by the duke of Wellington (who refused to take command in Canada) and fearing the expense of a long continuation in hostilities decided to settle for a peace based on the status quo ante bellum. Between the signing of the treaty, on 24 December 1814 and the time the news arrived in the United States, the last major battle, the Battle of *New Orleans, had been fought on 7–8 January 1815.

Neither the War of 1812 nor the Treaty of Ghent secured American maritime rights on a firm basis; but a century of peace in Europe after 1815 meant that they were not seriously threatened again until World War I. Nor did Great Britain pursue its future disputes with the United States to the point of risking war. And though the United States failed to obtain any Canadian territory, the campaigns of the war destroyed Indian opposition to U.S. expansion on the northwestern and southwestern frontiers. Both the United States and Canada emerged from the war with a heightened sense of national purpose and awareness, and particularly in the American case, the war consolidated the nation's military and naval establishments on more secure bases than before 1812.

In other respects, though, the war was as much a mixed blessing as an unqualified gain for the United States. The immediate domestic impact of the conflict was to heighten tensions between the northern and the southern states, on the one hand, and the Federalist and Republican parties, on the other. These strains became so serious that in November 1814, New England Federalists met in convention at Hartford, Connecticut, to consider measures to nullify the war effort. The ending of the war shortly afterwards left the Federalists marked with the stigma of disloyalty, and this undoubtedly contributed to the party's rapid demise after 1815.

The economic impact of the war was equally complex. The disruptions it entailed on America's international commerce were, to some extent, offset by greater governmental expenditures, an increased demand for domestic manufacturing, and the deflection of capital from shipping to the first large-scale American industries, especially in New England. Yet not all of the resulting gains survived the unstable economic conditions of the postwar period; and

even the American belief that the war marked a significant stride toward cultural, economic, and political independence would ultimately be overshadowed by the *Civil War, which profoundly altered the meaning of all America's earlier conflicts in the shaping of the nation's identity and purposes.

[See also Neutrality; Rush-Bagot Agreement; Trade, Foreign.]

• Henry Adams, *The History of the United States During the Administrations of Thomas Jefferson and James Madison*, 9 vols., 1891; 1986. Alfred T. Mahan, *Sea Power in Its Relations to the War of 1812*, 2 vols., 1905. Frank Updyke, *The Diplomacy of the War of 1812*, 1915. Bradford Perkins, *Prologue to War: England and the United States, 1805–1812*, 1961. Bradford Perkins, *Castlereagh and Adams: England and the United States, 1812–1823*, 1964. J. C. A. Stagg, *Mr. Madison's War: Politics, Diplomacy, and Warfare in the Early American Republic, 1783–1830*, 1983. George F. Stanley, *The War of 1812: Land Operations*, 1983. Steven Watts, *The Republic Reborn: War and the Making of Liberal America, 1790–1820*, 1987. Donald Hickey, *The War of 1812: A Forgotten Conflict*, 1989.

—J. C. A. Stagg

WAR OF INDEPENDENCE. See Revolutionary War (1775–1783).

WAR PLANS. An effective war plan must reflect the goals of the *state and enable a nation's armed forces to fight on favorable terms. Strategic plans have to deal with numerous factors, including force generation, logistics intelligence, the power and intentions of the enemy, and when necessary the strength and interests of allies. No plan can eliminate the unexpected, described by Carl von *Clausewitz as *friction*, and many commanders believe that no plan can survive the first contact with the enemy—when it must be immediately modified. War plans are nonetheless indispensable, both for *mobilization and for establishing the broad outlines of specific military operations. A war plan must not only meet the general requirements of effectiveness but also respond to particular national and historical contexts. U.S. war plans have been in large part shaped by American history and culture, by American attitudes toward war.

Bordered by oceans and militarily weak neighbors, the United States was traditionally safe from invasion. On the other hand, in the early twentieth century the creation of an overseas empire consisting of distant insular possessions posed serious strategic dilemmas because of an American characteristic—popular suspicion of large standing forces, coupled with a reluctance to assume heavy defense expenditures in time of peace.

During most American wars, mobilization took place after hostilities began. In 1812, 1846, 1861, and 1898, Congress declared war and at the same time called for large numbers of U.S. *volunteers to supplement the small regular army. In 1917, the United States declared war on Germany and then instituted *conscription. The nation did maintain large standing forces during the *Cold War, but force levels fluctuated widely in response to particular local conflicts. Moreover, postwar *demobilization was usually quite rapid. In 1945, for example, the U.S. *Army contained eighty-nine divisions; by 1947, the number had fallen to nine, only one of which was combat-ready. After the *Vietnam War, the government not only reduced conventional force levels but also abolished the draft. The expansion of the *All-Volunteer Force in the 1980s came to an end with the collapse of the USSR in 1991.

Americans have also become fascinated by technology, seeking technological means that will produce *victory with very low U.S. *casualties. Concepts such as strategic aerial bombardment and the *Strategic Defense Initiative (SDI), indicate that the desire for a painless strategy is pervasive.

These considerations have influenced national war plans. From the *Revolutionary War to the end of World War I, war planning, like mobilization, usually took place after war began. In 1846, President James K. *Polk met with his secretary of war and the commanding general of the army to discuss strategy the day after the declaration of war. Both sides in the *Civil War began to devise strategy after the firing of the first shot. In the *Spanish-American War, the navy did have existing war plans, but the army did not.

By the turn of the century, however, the United States had begun to create a prewar planning system. Staff officers at both the Naval War College and the Army War College had among their missions the preparation of war plans. In 1903, Congress established an Army General Staff, and in the same year the government created the Joint Army and Navy Board. The Joint Board was to discuss and reach common conclusions on matters concerning both services, including war plans. The board did not have its own planning staff but acted as coordinating authority for plans submitted by the individual services.

The board did produce a number of war plans—known as *color plans* since potential adversaries were designated by color. However, failure of the two services to agree on their ability to defend a naval base in the Philippines against the Japanese (Orange) soon undermined the board's influence. Presidents William H. Taft and Woodrow *Wilson made little use of the board, which played a marginal role in World War I.

In 1919, the services decided to strengthen the Joint Board by providing it with its own planning staff. The board resumed writing war plans. Some addressed realistic contingencies that could be handled with existing forces; others dealt with major wars and several as training exercises for staff officers. Before the late 1930s, only one plan dealt with a two-ocean war (Plan Red-Orange, against Britain and Japan). In that case, the board concluded that a European foe posed the greater threat; the United States would have to fight defensively in the Pacific until the European enemy was defeated.

The rise of German, Italian, and Japanese aggression and violence compelled the Joint Board to begin contemplating the prospect of a real war against one or more major enemies. The Rainbow Plans (so-called because of the different colors), written between 1939 and 1941, initially focused on defense of the western hemisphere and a war against either Japan or Germany. After the German victories of 1940, America slowly began to rearm and to supply assistance to Britain.

When Franklin D. *Roosevelt was reelected in 1940, the chief of naval operations submitted a paper to the president. Known as Plan Dog, it recommended secret staff talks with the British and a Germany-first strategy in case of a two-ocean war. Early in 1941, American and British staff officers met secretly in Washington. The ABC-1 Conference accepted the Germany-first approach and agreed to create a permanent structure for Allied decision making. In November 1941, the Americans revised Rainbow-5 into a two-ocean war plan with a Germany-first strategy and a defensive strategy in the Pacific until the fate of Germany was sealed.

The Joint Board also wrote an estimate of requirements for a global war. The army's Victory Program, prepared by September 1941, called for massive forces (a wartime army and air force of 8.7 million men) that would ensure complete destruction of the Axis powers and avoid the perceived mistakes of 1918. For the first time in the nation's history, the United States had established a grand strategy and had agreed to participate in a coalition prior to the outbreak of hostilities.

American and Allied strategy in World War II did not, however, follow prewar plans. The initial success of Japan's offensive forced Washington to commit major forces to the Pacific and to mount major operations in the region. In Europe, British reluctance to mount an early cross-Channel attack and the overriding need to retain Allied unity led to Anglo-American operations in North Africa, Sicily, and Italy. This imposed a long delay on the Allied invasion of France. By June 1944, the United States was waging major offensives in both Europe and the Pacific. Rome fell on 4 June; the Allies staged the invasion of *Normandy on 6 June; and a few days later U.S. forces stormed Saipan and fought the Battle of the *Philippine Sea.

After Japan's surrender and rapid American demobilization, the Joint Chiefs of Staff (JCS, established in 1942 with the Joint Board as its core) began to devise war plans for a possible conflict with the Soviet Union. The JCS presumed that the USSR possessed overwhelming conventional superiority. Since neither the government nor the public was willing to bear the cost of matching Soviet conventional forces, the military planners sought a technological response in the form of *nuclear weapons, the start of a nuclear arms race that would last for half a century.

The arms race in turn spawned a class of civilian nuclear strategists ranging from those who believed that nuclear war was winnable to advocates of unilateral nuclear disarmament. Military planners, however, always presumed that nuclear weapons were war-fighting instruments and made plans to use them in war. From the Pincher Plans of 1946 to the post-1960 Single Integrated Operational Plans (SIOP), targeting was always strategic. The number of nuclear warheads grew from 13 in 1947 to more than 20,000 by the early 1980s. By this time, many thought the United States had an "overkill" capability—more weapons than could be usefully targeted. Elaborate nuclear war plans notwithstanding, Washington and Moscow understood that a nuclear war involving thousands of nuclear explosions on their home territories would be catastrophic.

Moreover, focus on a total war with the Soviet Union and China left the United States unprepared to wage limited war. The nation was not ready for the *Korean War and equally unready for the type of warfare it had to face in the *Vietnam War. Nevertheless, the conventional expansion of the 1980s, designed to fight the Soviets in Germany, was applicable to the *Persian Gulf War of 1991.

After nearly a century of organized war planning, it is clear that the United States had won most of its major wars and worked effectively with allies. Such victories have rested in part on effective war planning. Whether strategic planners are prepared to face the problems of the post-Cold War world remains to be seen.

[See also Arms Race; Joint Chiefs of Staff; Nuclear Weapons; Strategy; War.]

• Steven T. Ross and David A. Rosenberg, eds., American War Plans 1945–1950, 15 vols., 1990. Steven T. Ross, ed., American War Plans 1919–1941, 5 vols., 1992. Steven T. Ross, American War Plans 1945–1950, 1996. Steven T. Ross, American War Plans 1941–1945, 1997.
—Steven T. Ross

The **WAR POWERS RESOLUTION** was passed by Congress, vetoed by President Richard M. *Nixon on 23 October 1973, and repassed over his veto on 7 November 1973. Enacted in the aftermath of the *Vietnam War and in the midst of the Watergate crisis, its purposes were to check the "imperial presidency" by ensuring that the collective judgment of both the Congress and the president would apply to the introduction of the military into potential or actual combat.

Section 3 of the resolution requires presidential consultation with Congress before sending U.S. armed forces into hostilities. Section 4 requires the president to report to Congress within forty-eight hours after the introduction of U.S. forces into hostilities or imminent hostilities, and every six months thereafter. Section 5 provides that within sixty days after issuing the initial report, the president must receive either a declaration of war or a specific statutory authorization, or else an extension of the sixty-day period; if Congress refuses, the president has thirty days to remove U.S. forces from hostilities. Section 5 also allowed Congress at any time to direct removal of the forces by concurrent resolution. Since 1983, an amendment has specified that removal of forces is directed by a joint resolution that must be submitted to the president and is subject to presidential veto.

Richard Nixon and all his successors have argued that the law undercuts U.S. credibility with its allies, gives adversaries reason to doubt U.S. determination to use force, and infringes on presidential prerogatives. Presidents have routinely ignored, evaded, or otherwise minimized the reach of the law, and by the end of the Reagan administration, Congress had abandoned it.

Federal courts have indicated their doubts about the constitutionality of many provisions of the law in Crockett v. Reagan, Lowry v. Reagan, Dellums v. Bush, and Ange v. Bush. The effect of these cases, and congressional unwillingness to use the procedures in the act, has essentially nullified it, although there appears to be significant public support for the concept behind it.

[See also Civil-Military Relations: Civilian Control of the Military; Commander in Chief, President as; Congress, War, and the Military.]

• The War Power After 200 Years: Congress and the President at a Constitutional Impasse, Hearings Before the Special Subcommittee on War Powers, Committee on Foreign Relations, U.S. Senate, 100th Cong., 2nd Sess., 1988. The Constitutional Roles of Congress and the President in Declaring and Waging War, Hearings Before the Committee on the Judiciary, U.S. Senate, 102nd Cong., 1st Sess., 1991. Louis Fisher, Presidential War Power, 1995.
—Richard M. Pious

The **WAR RESISTERS LEAGUE,** an American pacifist organization, was founded in 1923 by Jessie Wallace Hughan, New York City teacher and socialist. Hughan believed the

League should encourage the growth of *pacifism and provide a home for secular pacifists who could not fit into church-based peace groups.

In literature and street meetings, the War Resisters League spread the message that "wars will cease when men refuse to fight." In the 1930s, increasingly alarmed by the rise of fascism and Nazi brutality, the League demonstrated against anti-Semitism and worked to rescue its victims. During World War II, Evan Thomas, himself a resister in World War I, and the brother of Norman *Thomas, Socialist Party leader, chaired the League when many of its male members were enrolled in alternative civilian service or incarcerated for resisting *conscription. Imprisoned members used work stoppages and hunger strikes to protest prison injustices such as racial segregation.

After World War II, the League led demonstrations against continued conscription and for amnesty for conscientious objectors. It also opposed the militarization of America, especially the nuclear *arms race. In the 1950s and 1960s, its members included the writer Grace Paley, folk singers Joan Baez and Pete Seeger, the former Pentagon scholar Daniel *Ellsberg, and the poet Allen Ginsburg.

The League is affiliated with the War Resisters International (WRI), founded in 1921, with current headquarters in London. The WRI has more than seventy affiliates in at least thirty countries. During the 1960s, the War Resisters League allied with other organizations in the civil rights campaign, and it played an important role in the *Vietnam antiwar movement, organizing demonstrations and training participants in nonviolent activism for *peace and justice.

[See also Conscientious Objection; Peace and Antiwar Movements.]

• War Resisters League, History of the War Resisters League, 1980. Lawrence S. Wittner, Rebels Against War: The American Peace Movement, 1933–1983, 1984. Scott H. Bennett, " 'Pacifism Not Passivism: The War Resisters League and Radical Pacifism, Nonviolent Direct Action, and the Americanization of Gandhi, 1915–1963." Ph.D. diss., Rutgers University, 1998.
—Larry Gara

WARSAW PACT (est. 1955). The Warsaw Pact was created by the Soviet Union on 14 May 1955 as a political-military alliance of European Communist states to counter the North Atlantic Treaty Alliance (*NATO), particularly the entry of West Germany into NATO in 1955. Officially called the Warsaw Treaty Organization, the original eight members were Albania, Bulgaria, Czechoslovakia, East Germany, Hungary, Poland, Romania, and the Soviet Union. However, unlike NATO, the Warsaw Pact was a multinational rather than a multilateral military defense organization.

Following Soviet suppression of the Hungarian uprising in October 1956, Moscow reduced the influence of the pact's governing body, the multinational Political Consultative Council (PCC), and tightened its own central control. In the subsequent strains, some southern-tier nations withdrew: Albania, which supported China in the Sino-Soviet split, stopped military cooperation in 1961 and left the pact in 1968 (following the invasion of Czechoslovakia by the pact's forces). Romania excluded Soviet troops and refused to participate in military exercises after 1965.

The Soviet Union controlled the alliance, provided 80 percent of the manpower, and bore more than 90 percent of the pact's defense expenditures for forces, which in the early 1980s reached 5.4 million troops. The USSR alone had *nuclear weapons and strategic forces, and all nuclear warheads were in Soviet custody.

With declining economies, the shift in Soviet policy under reformer Mikhail Gorbachev, and the increasing independence of the East European nations, the Warsaw Pact lost cohesion in the 1980s. In 1987–88, the pact's doctrine was changed from offensive defense to one that emphasized nonoffensive defense. Following a Soviet proposal in 1987, NATO and the Warsaw Pact agreed in 1990 to substantial reduction of forces.

In 1990, responding to popular demand and the ending of the *Cold War, Poland, Hungary, and Czechoslovakia demanded the removal of Soviet troops and refused to participate in future military exercises. East Germany left the pact that year with German unification. The military structure was officially ended by the PCC in March 1991; the political organization was terminated in July 1991.

• R. W. Clawson and L. S. Kaplan, eds., *The Warsaw Pact: Political Purpose and Military Means*, 1982. W. J. Lewis, *The Warsaw Pact: Arms, Doctrine and Strategy*, 1982. J. Simon, *Warsaw Pact Forces: Problems of Command and Control*, 1985. Neil Fodor, *The Warsaw Treaty Organization: A Political and Organizational Analysis*, 1990.
—John Whiteclay Chambers II

WASHINGTON, GEORGE (1732–1799), *Revolutionary War commander in chief and first president of the United States. Born into a family on the margins of the Virginia aristocracy, Washington advanced rapidly to local prominence owing to his brother Lawrence's brief career in the British military establishment and to Lawrence's marriage into the powerful Fairfax family. Ambitious and intelligent, though lacking formal education, Washington obtained the office of regional militia adjutant, the assignment of warning the French in the Ohio Valley to depart from lands claimed by Virginia, and afterward the position of special aide to Gen. Edward *Braddock. Washington's heroic performance during *Braddock's defeat on the Monongahela helped earn him the command of Virginia's frontier defenses during the *French and Indian War. Hampered by problems of inadequate manpower and supplies, he performed well, though displaying a lack of respect for higher civil and military authority. His regiment won the praise of crown officers for its training and degree of professionalism, although Washington failed in repeated efforts to have his forces taken into the British army.

Washington's drive and determination, essential qualities for any military commander and revolutionary leader, manifested themselves before 1775 in acquiring still other public posts: county surveyor, vestryman, and legislator. As a planter, he had already shown skill in obtaining land before he inherited Mount Vernon after his brother Lawrence's death. Recognizing the hazards of tobacco growing, he profitably converted much of his acreage to wheat prior to the Revolution, and he continued to accumulate western lands through claims based on his colonial military service.

An early critic of Britain's new colonial policy after 1763, Washington strongly supported boycotting British goods and advocated other forms of nonviolent resistance. Beginning in 1774, he played the leading role in organizing and reforming the Virginia militia, and as a member of the Continental Congress he wore his Virginia uniform to indicate his willingness to serve after hostilities erupted at Lexington and Concord. Because of his military background and experience in dealing with legislative bodies, the highly visible Washington was the obvious choice, and Congress appointed him commander in chief of the *Continental army in June 1775.

Sensitive to *civil-military relations and to the problems of conducting warfare without the resources of a strong government, Washington had learned much since his earlier wartime service in the 1750s. He communicated regularly with the state governors and with the Congress, aware that he was something of a diplomat in a coalition war involving a weak central authority and thirteen sovereign states. His patience and deference added enormously to his stature and respect, as did certain symbolic acts during the war, such as his refusal to accept military pay and his repeatedly expressed wish to retire quietly to Mount Vernon and eschew subsequent honors and office.

During the first major phase of the Revolutionary War, 1775–78, the conflict was fought largely in the northern and middle states, and Washington's immediate command bore the brunt of the British efforts to crack the rebellion. After Washington's siege of the British in Boston, he moved south to meet the enemy at New York in the summer of 1776. His army fought stubbornly but suffered a succession of defeats before Washington retreated and regrouped on the Pennsylvania side of the Delaware River. Counterattacks that picked off British posts at Trenton and Princeton in New Jersey during the Christmas season reinvigorated the American cause, but the army suffered important defeats the following year at Brandywine and Germantown in Pennsylvania. Yet Washington was a fighter, not a Fabian, as often portrayed, and he learned from his mistakes. He kept coming back, as when he battered the rear guard of the British army at Monmouth when it moved from Philadelphia back toward New York in 1778.

With the war stalemated in the North, Washington capitalized on France's entry into the conflict. Since the British dispersed some regiments to the West Indies and turned increasing attention to the American South, Washington spent the next three years keeping close watch on British forces in New York City and endeavoring to keep his own army up to strength, annual tasks that never eased. His opportunity for a bold stroke did not come again until 1781, when he raced south to cooperate with French military and naval forces in capturing Charles *Cornwallis's army on the Virginia Peninsula at the Battle of *Yorktown, 19 October 1781.

Washington's stature actually increased during the war's final two years. He dramatically upstaged a band of conspiratorial officers at Newburgh, New York, in 1783, shaming them for their threatening behavior toward a weak Congress. He also wrote two of the great, if neglected, state papers of the Revolution: his "Circular to the States" on the need for a firmer union, and his "Sentiments on a Peace Establishment," in which he advocated ideas about regular and militia forces that contributed to the debate on national defense in the Constitutional Convention.

Consistently a nationalist in 1775–76, Washington presided at that convention in 1787, threw his weight behind the Constitution's ratification, and accepted (albeit reluctantly) the presidency in 1789, serving two terms. He worked to build a viable peacetime military structure and federalized the militia to put down the *Whiskey Rebellion in 1794, at the same time avoiding a war with Britain over neutral rights, a conflict that he considered the country ill-prepared to fight.

Washington always recognized that governments needed power to perform effectively. As general and president, he employed the power available to him but with moderation and restraint. In both his military and his civilian capacities, he set precedents that successful American generals and presidents still follow.

[*See also* Commander in Chief, President as; Revolutionary War: Military and Diplomatic Course.]

• Douglas Southall Freeman, *George Washington*, 7 vols., 1948–57. Marcus Cunliffe, *George Washington: Man and Monument*, 1958. James Thomas Flexner, *George Washington*, 4 vols., 1965–72. Edmund S. Morgan, *The Genius of George Washington*, 1980. Don Higginbotham, *George Washington and the American Military Tradition*, 1985. John E. Ferling, *The First of Men*, 1988.

—Don Higginbotham

WASHINGTON NAVAL ARMS LIMITATION TREATY

(1922). After World War I, fear that an unrestrained naval race would lead to another world war, the corollary hope that arms limitation would ensure peace, and the demand for domestic economy combined to generate the pressures and incentives that led to the Washington Conference of 1921–22, the most ambitious pre-nuclear effort to limit arms in the history of the United States. The conference produced a series of agreements intended to end naval competition between the United States, Great Britain, and Japan, and to stabilize the political situation in East Asia. The Washington Naval Treaty established tonnage ratios for *battleships and *aircraft carriers of the United States, Great Britain, Japan, France, and Italy 5, 5, 3, 1.75, and 1.75, respectively. The United States, Great Britain, and Japan also agreed not to build more fortifications on certain islands in the western Pacific.

The treaty powers linked the naval settlement with political settlements reached at the conference. The Nine Power Treaty pledged to uphold the "open door" policy in China, but contained no enforcement mechanism. The Four Power Treaty replaced the Anglo-Japanese Military Alliance of 1902, anathema to the United States, with a diffuse consultative pact between the United States, Great Britain, Japan, and France. Under the Mandates Treaty, the United States recognized Japan's trusteeship over former German colonies in the western Pacific in exchange for a Japanese pledge not to fortify those islands.

Subsequent efforts at naval arms control achieved only modest and fleeting success. The London Treaty of 1930 extended the ratio system to include *cruisers, destroyers, and *submarines, but was limited to the United States, Great Britain, and Japan. A Second London Naval Conference (1935–36) ended in failure when Japan refused to accept anything less than parity with Great Britain and the United States. In 1938, the Japanese declined to give assurances that their new super-battleships were within treaty size limits, and efforts to limit naval arms collapsed entirely; henceforth, the United States and Great Britain slowly resumed their major building programs.

Despite the indisputably positive impact of the Washington Treaties on the overall tenor of Anglo-American relations, events largely confounded lofty expectations. The treaties failed to achieve their goal of "positively ending the arms race," or freezing the naval balance indefinitely. The Japanese kept building warships even when the United States and Great Britain reduced their building programs significantly. According to some scholars (see Kaufman, 1990), America's restraint in naval building during the interwar years enticed the Imperial Japanese Navy to engage in an unrestrained naval race that ultimately culminated in Japan's decision to undertake the attack on *Pearl Harbor in December 1941.

The political assumptions underpinning the Washington Treaties also proved transitory. China did not develop peacefully as hoped, but descended into chaos that simultaneously frightened and emboldened Japanese militarists. Japanese constitutionalism did not become more robust, but collapsed under the combined weight of the Great Depression and a badly flawed constitution that put the forces of moderation at a severe disadvantage. The determination of Japanese militarists to dominate China made the failure of the treaties inevitable during the 1930s, just as the ascendance of Japanese moderates who preferred conciliation to conquest had made the treaties' success possible during the 1920s.

Some scholars, among them Emily Goldman (1994), view the Washington Treaties' accomplishments more positively, primarily because they consider that they were essential in averting Anglo-American enmity. There is agreement, however, that the experiment with naval arms limitation made sense during the 1920s when detente prevailed among the United States, Great Britain, and Japan. But such arms limitation became unrealistic in the 1930s, when the United States and Great Britain persisted in such attempts despite the fact that the world situation had manifestly changed for the worse.

[*See also* Arms Control and Disarmament: Nonnuclear; World War II: Causes.]

• Robert Gordon Kaufman, *Arms Control During the Pre-Nuclear Era: The United States and Naval Limitation Between the Two World Wars*, 1990. Emily O. Goldman, *Sunken Treaties: Arms Control Between the Wars*, 1994.

—Robert Gordon Kaufman

WAVES.

President Franklin D. *Roosevelt signed Public Law 625 establishing a program for women in the U.S. Navy, as an integral part of the naval reserve, on 30 July 1942. The navy's newest members served for the duration of the war plus six months. On 2 August, Mildred McAfee, president of Wellesley College, became the director of the navy's female reserve and the first female naval officer with the rank of lieutenant commander. To avoid nicknames such as "sailorette," Elizabeth Raynard, a member of the Naval Advisory Council that developed the women's program, recommended the official nickname WAVES, an acronym for Women Accepted for Volunteer Emergency Service.

Women were recruited from nearly every state. Officers were trained at Smith College in Northampton, Massachusetts. The navy organized training schools for yeomen, radiomen, and storekeepers, located respectively at Oklahoma A&M College, the University of Wisconsin, and Indiana University in Bloomington. In February 1943, a naval station for enlisted recruits was commissioned at Hunter College in New York. WAVES could apply for more billets and were assigned to more locations than their predecessors, the 11,275 yeomen (female) who served temporarily during World War I. WAVES worked at naval shore establishments across the United States as chauffeurs, cryptologists, recruiters, and stenographers. They also filled nontraditional billets as air traffic controllers, link trainers, mechanics, and parachute riggers. About one-third of the WAVES served in the communications and aviation communities. By 1944, the need to relieve men stationed in Alaska and Hawaii led the navy to amend the original bill that had limited WAVES to duty within the continental United States.

Nothing in the legislation prevented the recruiting of black women, yet the navy did not admit them into the WAVES until 19 October 1944. The next day, the U.S. *Coast Guard also announced that African Americans could join its female reserve program, but the Women's Marines Corps remained all-white until 1949. Two black women, Frances E. Wills and Harriet Ida Pickens, were sworn into the U.S. Navy on 13 November 1944 and were added to the last class of WAVES officer candidates to be trained. Receiving their commissions on 25 December, they became the first black female officers in the navy. The first black enlisted recruits reported to Hunter in January 1945. By 30 July, the WAVES had reached a peak strength of 86,000.

The performance of the WAVES and the other 150,000 women serving in the military services—*SPAR, *WAC (Women's Army Corps), WASP (Women Air Service Pilots), and the U.S. *Marine Corps Women's Reserve—persuaded officials that women should have a permanent place in the peacetime military. Senator Margaret Chase Smith of Maine achieved that goal with the Women's Armed Services Act of 1948. WAVES continued to serve, particularly during the *Korean War and the *Vietnam War. In 1972, Capt. Robin Quigley, assistant chief of naval personnel for women, wrote a memo discontinuing the navy's official use of the term WAVES, recommending the more accurate description Women in the Navy. This change reflected the navy's policy of integrating women. By then, the women-in-ships program had begun and the aviation community was opening up more jobs to women.

[See also African Americans in the Military; Women in the Military.]

• Joy B. Hancock, Lady in the Navy, 1972. Jean Ebbert and Marie-Beth Hall, Crossed Currents, Navy Women from World War I to Tailhook, 1993.
—Regina T. Akers

WAYNE, ANTHONY (1745–1796), Revolutionary War general; commander of the Legion of the United States. An imposing Pennsylvanian, Wayne was a commissioned colonel in the *Continental army in 1776 and took part in the unsuccessful American invasion of Canada. Promoted brigadier general in 1777, he served with George *Washington in Pennsylvania, suffering defeat at Paoli on 20 September. He fought gallantly at the Battle of *Monmouth, 28 June 1778; on 15 July 1779, he seized an important British fortified position on the Hudson River, Stony Point, in a brilliantly executed light infantry assault. He suppressed two mutinies among his soldiers in early 1781 before joining the marquis de *Lafayette's army in Virginia and following Gen. Charles *Cornwallis's withdrawal to Yorktown. After the British surrender there (19 October), he commanded troops in Georgia and South Carolina before resigning from the army in 1782.

Frustrated in civilian pursuits, Wayne gladly accepted Washington's offer in 1792 to command the Legion of the United States, with the rank of major general. His mission was to end the formidable Indian resistance in the Northwest Territory. Over the next two years, he created a tough, disciplined army, and—despite secret attempts by his subordinate James Wilkinson to ruin him—decisively defeated a Delaware, Shawnee, and Canadian force at the Battle of Fallen Timbers, 20 August 1794. After establishing a number of military posts, Wayne concluded the Treaty of Greenville in 1795, pacifying the region. He died on duty at Presque Isle late the following year, at the height of his fame. Known for his vanity, fearlessness, and violent temper, he was popularly called "Mad Anthony" Wayne—a nickname that his troops bestowed in admiration of his audacity in battle.

[See also Native American Wars: Wars Between Native Americans and Europeans and Euro-Americans; Revolutionary War: Military and Diplomatic Course.]

• Paul David Nelson, Anthony Wayne: Soldier of the Early Republic, 1985.
—Paul David Nelson

WEAPONRY, EVOLUTION OF. Weapons are instruments designed to harm, kill, or otherwise disable other human beings, to destroy other military resources, or to deter an enemy's ability to make war through the actual or threatened destruction of crucial components of their society. Broadly conceived, weapons include not only the instruments themselves and their munitions but also their delivery vehicles—so-called weapons platforms: *tanks, ships, aircraft, missile launchers. Today, the combinations are often labeled weapons systems.

Because weapons, like other physical objects, operate under natural laws, discoveries in chemistry, physics, quantum mechanics, and other areas of science and technology have helped propel both the industrial revolution and the dramatic expansion of weaponry in the nineteenth and twentieth centuries. Thus, as shown in the accompanying articles on the development of weaponry in the army, marine corps, navy, and air force, the U.S. armed forces have followed and sometimes originated major developments in science and technology.

Improvements in metallurgy, for example, created stronger gun barrels. These could withstand more powerful explosive charges, themselves the result of chemical discoveries. Stronger rifled barrels in turn provided more accuracy and longer range for standard infantry *side arms, *artillery, and *naval guns. Mechanical improvements eventually produced automatic weapons, including self-loading, magazine rifles and *machine guns. The internal combustion engine led to the development of *submarines, *tanks, and aircraft in the twentieth century. At sea, steam power, iron, and steel transformed naval warships in the nineteenth century. Later, submarines were transformed by new alloys, shapes, and nuclear propulsion. Aircraft made the transition from fabric and wood to aluminum in the 1930s, then more recently in some cases to titanium, carbon-fibre composites and high-strength plastics. Experiments in rocketry combined with developments in guidance mechanisms and gas-turbine engines led to jet aircraft and to ballistic and cruise *missiles. Computer technology and electronic sensing and guidance systems have dramatically improved fire control and accuracy, leading eventually to *precision-guided munitions designed to make corrections in flight and on final approach to the target.

Weapons of mass destruction are in a class by themselves. Choking and burning forms of poison gas first developed in World War I were later augmented by nerve agents. Stocks of infectious microbes and other toxins were accumulated for *chemical and biological weapons and warfare, but the controversy over the use of Agent Orange and other defoliants in the Vietnam War led President Richard *Nixon to renounce biological and toxin weapons, to begin destroying the stocks of *toxic agents, and to ratify an international agreement prohibiting them. In 1997, the United States ratified a treaty banning poison gas weapons.

The development of nuclear fission weapons and later thermonuclear fusion weapons represented an incomparable revolution in weaponry. Yet their enormous lethality contributed to a universal refusal to use the weapons after the bombing of *Hiroshima and Nagasaki. Thus nuclear weapons have become predominantly instruments of threat, operating in a nuclear strategy described as *deterrence. The proliferation of such weapons to additional countries and possibly eventually to terrorist groups has long threatened to weaken the tabu against their use. Attempts to curtail weapons of mass destruction have been offset in part by the growing lethality and destructiveness of conventional arms.

But the evolution of weaponry has not been simply a narrow history of scientific invention or technological development. Weapons are artifacts both of the armed forces and of the societies that create them. Essential to the conduct of *war, they can in part be understood through the functions they are expected to perform in warfare on the land, at sea, or in the air. But a fuller understanding of their evolution derives from the recognition that their origins and development derive from particular inventions and also from larger cultural attitudes and ideology and political, military, economic and other institutional structures in society which help to define national security and allocate resources for defense.

Technology—the purposeful, systematic manipulation of the material world—encompasses, of course, inventions for both civilian and military use. Increasingly in the past two centuries, radically new science-based technologies—inventions providing new power sources and means of transportation and communication, for example—have had a transformative effect on society, and on warfare. But despite widespread popular belief in technology as a determinative agent of change, indeed as part of the culture of modernity, a debate continues over the inevitability of the social consequences of particular major inventions. While some see technology as a virtually autonomous agent of change, others contextualize it in larger socio-cultural processes. The latter emphasize that material innovation is initiated and developed, or not developed by human beings with particular abilities and resources (the gun was largely banned from feudal Japan, for example, for more than two centuries; see Noel Perrin, *Giving up the Gun: Japan's Reversion to the Sword, 1543–1879,* 1979). Despite the power of a technological development once it has begun, the beginning and end of every such sequence, as Robert L. O'Connell (*Of Arms and Men,* 1989) has said, is a point when human choice can and does exert itself.

Dedicated to the idea of progress and heirs of the Enlightenment, Americans have traditionally embraced science and technology as instruments for human and material betterment as well as national security. Ingenuity and invention have been valued attributes, protected legally and rewarded economically. All of this encouraged technological development and change.

The military, however, has traditionally not sought nor often welcomed change. Virtually all the most important military devices invented in nineteenth-century Europe or America—the breech-loading rifle; built-up steel, rifled cannon; effective armored warships; the automatic machine gun; the modern submarine—originated with civilians who brought them uninvited to the military. None of the most important weapons transforming warfare in the twentieth century—the airplane, tank, *radar, jet engine, *helicopter, electronic computer, not even the atomic bomb—owed its initial development to a doctrinal requirement or request of the military.

Despite their desire for *more* weapons, most admirals and generals until World War II had been reluctant to adopt *new and unproven* weapons. The U.S. Army initially rejected development of the revolver, the repeating rifle, and the machine gun in the mid-nineteenth century. It suppressed generations of available improvements in artillery in the nineteenth and twentieth centuries. And until the eve of World War II, it delayed development of the tank, which later became its most favored weapon. The U.S. Navy rejected or resisted pivotal inventions by David Bushnell, Robert *Fulton, Samuel *Colt, and John *Ericsson, and it suppressed and sometimes even persecuted such uniformed technological reformers as John *Dahlgren, William Sims, and Hyman *Rickover. Even in its comparatively short history, the U.S. Air Force, with its dedication to piloted planes, initially resisted liquid fueled missiles, sold fuel missiles, cruise missiles, and unmanned spacecraft.

The armed forces tend to be even less flexible than most other large bureaucratic organizations. In part, this results from their compartmentalization, need for standardization, innate conservatism, and the limitations imposed on them by Congress. Partly it is because military organizations, designed to operate at great risk in a medium of enormous uncertainty—the unpredictability and chaos of war—have emphasized discipline and subordination in a rigidly hierarchical command structure. But the reluctance of the military bureaucracy to innovate has other sources as well. Traditionally, it reflected a dedication to an existing weapon already proven in combat and integrated into doctrine and training (and deployed at great expense) over uncertainties about a projected weapon, which might or might not eventually prove itself in combat. The new weapon's failure, of course, might well mean the deaths of many of those relying on it. High-ranking officers with the power to make such decisions often owe their lives and their careers to particular weapons and doctrines. The officer corps of each branch is a community, and as Elting Morison (*Men, Machines, and Modern Times,* 1967) suggests, communities, particularly to the degree that they are autonomous and isolated from external influence, are often resistant to change. Particularly with radical innovation, resistance may stem from concerns about the costs of purchasing an expensive but unproven technology or fears of potential impact upon the structure, status, and traditions of the organization. Officers of the *sailing ship navy in the mid-nineteenth century were correct in their fears that the replacement of sails by steam propulsion would mean the end to an entire way of life.

Civilian leaders have often been more receptive to radical new weapons technologies than the military. Consequently, uniformed reformers, civilian inventors, or corporate manufacturers have often circumvented the military bureaucracy through political connections. Frustrated, Samuel Colt sent his proposal for underwater mines directly to Congress; Dahlgren took his ideas about a new naval gun to President Abraham *Lincoln; and William Sims relayed his proposals for rapid-firing gunnery directly to President Theodore *Roosevelt. Less successfully, Billy *Mitchell took his case for air power to the public in an abortive attempt to exert public pressure on Congress and President Calvin Coolidge.

Although traditionally not the initiator of new weapons (since World War II, this has been reversed and the military has become the initiator), the military has often been quite successful in developing those that it became convinced were warranted. In time of war or continuing danger to national security, the government has mobilized enormous financial resources for the military, particularly for weaponry. Before World War II, most of America's wars were too short to be fought with weapons other than those on hand or in development at the beginning of the conflict (the lead time on research and development of modern sophisticated weapons can run 15 years or more). The atomic bomb, developed in a massive effort under the supervision of the Army *Corps of Engineers' *Manhattan Project in three years (1943–45), was an exception.

Once invented and adopted, military weapons have been produced in the United States either by government facilities or more commonly in the twentieth century by corporate manufacturers under government contract. The new republic used its own national armories at Springfield, Massachusetts, left from the *Revolutionary War, and Harper's Ferry, Virginia, newly constructed by 1801. After decades of producing small arms by hand, by 1842 the armories introduced large-scale assembly of muskets from uniform, interchangeable parts. Together with their private competitors, such as Colt's factory in Hartford, Connecticut, the federal armories became important centers of technological and manufacturing innovation, contributing to what arms makers and others around the world soon called the "American system of manufactures." To make cannon, caissons, gunpowder, and other military supplies, the government possessed five federal arsenals, in or near Boston, upstate New York, Philadelphia, Pittsburgh, and Washington, D.C. (with later additions at Rock Island, Illinois, and Fayetteville, North Carolina).

Thus in the nineteenth century, government manufacturing for the military provided a means to continue technological development, when private manufacturers feared uncertain economic returns in a market environment offering large-scale profits for such items mainly in wartime. During the Civil War, the military-run government facilities ran at full capacity while also providing the specifications and techniques for private subcontractors to mass produce arms for the *Union Army. The first ships of the U.S. Navy were built in half a dozen private shipyards along the Atlantic Coast in the 1790s. Later government navy yards were erected to repair the fleet and for some new construction, but the Navy Department always relied more on private contractors than on its own yards

for the construction of new vessels whether in the wooden, iron, or steel navy.

After the Civil War, the spending cutbacks and other factors resulted by 1900 in the U.S. Army being a decade behind European militaries in the development of small arms and artillery. The increasing complexity of weaponry in the twentieth century and the possibilities of sustained high economic profits, first in research and development for the navy, then for the air service, and finally for the ground forces, led corporations to become continuing military contractors and the government to phase out most of its own armories, arsenals, and shipyards for conventional weapons. The U.S. government continued, however, to underwrite *National Laboratories for research and development of nuclear weapons.

Production of weapons has always been profitable for private entrepreneurs in wartime, but the *Cold War (1947–1991) produced a market of unprecedented duration and size for weapons. Scholars debate the origins of what President Dwight D. *Eisenhower in 1961 called the *"Military-Industrial Complex," some seeing its antecedents in the steel and steam naval construction program of the late nineteenth and early twentieth centuries others with the nexus established between the army air service, aircraft manufacturers and Congress in the 1920s and 1930s. Whatever the origins, the scale of industrial development and production of weaponry on a sustained basis has grown extraordinarily in the last sixty years, a period when, as Michael Sherry has written, Americans since 1939 lived *Under the Shadow of War* (1995).

The politically influential, triangular relationship between the military, defense contractors, and Congress, meant that a comparatively few giant corporations that dominated the defense contracting industry were essentially guaranteed a sustained market by the U.S. government. During the Cold War, the arms race between the United States and its *NATO allies and the Soviet Union and the other *Warsaw Pact nations encompassed conventional and nuclear weapons. The threat of nuclear war and the concept of deterrence meant a sustained condition of constant readiness for war, which led the U.S. military to modify some of its traditional resistance to declaring proven weapons obsolete or at least obsolescent. Instead, in concert with Congress, the Department of *Defense kept research institutes, national laboratories, and defense contractors busy with requests for new and improved generations of weapons.

U.S. defense spending for most of the Cold War averaged about 7 percent of the Gross National Product (GNP), surging briefly during the administration of President John F. *Kennedy to 10 per cent. As a result for more than forty years, the armed forces exerted an unprecedented continuing influence on the American economy. Domestically, such massive defense spending beginning in 1950 may have helped prevent a post-war World War II depression as followed the cancellation of war orders after World War I, but such continued "military Keynesianism," skewed the operation of the market system in allocation of human, financial, and material resources, a phenomenon, William H. McNeill (*The Pursuit of Power*, 1982) linked to a "command economy" in which the state drives the economy through the development and production of the technology of war.

Such unprecedented defense spending, particularly the

development and acquisition of weaponry, was eventually challenged. Criticism and protest against certain weapons systems was hardly new. Theodore Roosevelt's battleship building program had been curtailed by public and congressional outcries against its cost. Immediately after World War I, big business joined the peace movement in stopping a second naval arms race. Development of chemical weapons was restrained in the 1920s by public outrage on moral grounds as well as protests from old-line army leaders on the basis of tradition and ineffectiveness. In the 1950s, *nuclear protest movements lobbied for restriction or elimination of nuclear weapons on various grounds: moral, health, ecological, and humanitarian. Such protests helped produce in 1963 an end to the testing of nuclear weapons above ground (with its airborne radioactive fallout). The *SALT Treaties (1972, 1979) and the *START negotiations reversed the nuclear arms race even before the end of the Cold War in 1991 (indeed the end of the Cold War has paradoxically made it difficult to complete START). The general downturn in arms expenditures, both in the United States and the world at large, began in 1987, before the final collapse of the Soviet Union and the official end of the Cold War.

The *Vietnam War (1965–73) divided Americans and raised questions about failure of the U.S. military. Americans' belief in technological progress was also challenged by a series of setbacks including problems with nuclear energy plants and the space program as well as increased concerns about environmental and health damage from new technologies and their products. These contributed to some skepticism about technological progress and inevitability and a belief that politics, markets, and organizational structures could also condition outcomes, implying that some aspects of technological development can be controlled by political and economic decisions.

Militarily in the 1960s and 1970s, rapidly rising prices and the clear numerical superiority in conventional forces in Europe of the Warsaw Pact ignited major debates in the United States over the armed forces, their force structure, strategy, and weaponry. These debates involved issues of military effectiveness and also of civilian contractors' cost-overruns, waste, fraud, and abuse, revealed in congressional and journalistic investigations.

A military reform movement, originating in a controversy over a new fighter plane for the air force, began a debate which spread through Congress and each of the services, prompting a searching examination of the Cold War focus on new, larger, more sophisticated, and more expensive weaponry. It raised the possibility of less expensive yet adequate alternatives, many small *aircraft carriers instead of a few supercarriers, for example, or a single type of *fighter aircraft that could be used with modifications by the air force, navy, and marines. The reformers liked to point out that cutting-edge technology was not always the most appropriate, not always decisive or even victorious in war, as evidenced arguably by the failure of the Germans in Russia in World War II, the French and Americans in Vietnam, and the Russians in Afghanistan.

Beginning in 1979, Soviet actions and resurgent anti-communism in the United States led President Jimmy *Carter reluctantly and President Ronald *Reagan enthusiastically to increase U.S. defense spending dramatically. The Reagan administration achieved the largest peacetime military buildup in U.S. history (approximately $2.4 tril-

lion spent overall in 1981–89). The focus was on weapons, and each military service obtained long-delayed and often controversial weapons systems, including the B-1 bomber, the MX intercontinental ballistic missile (ICBM), new vehicles and helicopters, the Trident II submarine-launched ballistic missile (SLBM), and many new warships to build toward a goal of a 600 ship navy.

The escalating arms race and the bellicosity of the Reagan administration triggered considerable opposition. The largest protest demonstrations since the Vietnam War failed to prevent the deployment of new, nuclear-tipped, intermediate range ballistic missiles in Europe. But dissent within the scientific community and skepticism in the media limited research on President Reagan's proposed missile defense project, the *Strategic Defense Initiative (SDI), known as "star wars" after a popular science fiction movie of the time. Debate continues over the reasons for the collapse of the Soviet Union in 1989–91. Some link it to economic pressures resulting from the arms race resumed by the United States a decade earlier; others attribute the failure to accumulating systemic problems in Russia and its empire.

In the U.S. armed forces, the reform plans of the 1970s and the buildup of the 1980s produced American forces in Europe which had shifted from a strategy emphasizing overwhelming firepower including nuclear weapons to the "AirLand Battle" focusing on more effective use of conventional air and ground forces to outmaneuver and defeat the greater numbers of the Warsaw Pact. Modified for different conditions, the concept and weapons were used successfully in the *Persian Gulf War in 1991. Its aircraft and precision-guided munitions were employed again in the *Kosovo Crisis of 1999.

The end of the Cold War in 1991 did result in cutbacks in defense spending, even if not as much as many had expected. Although some defense contractors went out of business, merged, or shifted to other production, a military-industrial complex, decidedly smaller, continued to exist. The American market had shrunk. U.S. defense spending in 1995 was down to 4.3 percent of Gross National Product. Defense contracting still remained lucrative to some, however. At beginning of 2000, Lockheed-Martin and Boeing were competing against each other for the largest military contract in history, nearly one-third of a trillion dollars, to design a Joint Strike Fighter plane, capable with modifications of serving the needs of the air force, navy, and marines, and to build 5,000 them, replacing most of the existing fighter planes (not the F-15s or F-18s, however) in the U.S. armed forces.

American defense contractors also turned again to foreign markets. There, limited only by certain legal constraints designed to keep the most sensitive military secrets secure from potential enemies (a continuing challenge), they competed with other arms makers. In the international arms marketplace, the new weaponry was often valued as much for the prestige that such weapons, for example, the latest most sophisticated fighter planes, seem to provide for a nation and its government and armed forces as for their contribution to that nation's security.

In the U.S. experience, as Alex Roland suggested (*Journal of Military History*, 1991), the development of military technology in relationship to strategy and to ground warfare, for example, has been shaped in part by fundamental American views and practices as well as the technology itself. The value put on the individual human life and labor of U.S. citizens, a concept rooted in early labor scarcity and reinforced by American democracy, has contributed to an emphasis on citizen-soldiers, trying to protect them against usually greater enemy numbers through superior technology, especially weapons of greater firepower and accuracy. Additionally, fear of standing armies and an insistence on civilian control of the military, a reaction to British policies, contributed, directly through the Constitution's two-year limit on military appropriations, to inhibiting long-term development projects for the army. The navy and the air force are by definition technology-dependent services and have required by necessity long-term development of their ships, planes, and missiles.

For most of the nineteenth century and even the early twentieth century, the United States enjoyed freedom from threats of sudden attack by a foreign foe. This allowed the nation to be generally free from the need to prepare massive ground forces or to some extent even major naval forces in advance of war. In concert with foreign policies of *neutrality and *isolationism, the majority of Americans came to view this situation of comparatively free security as a natural condition for the United States. With the exception of certain expansionist-minded industrialists and navalists at the turn of the century, no influential group saw the need or desirability to have large and expensive stocks of the latest weapons on hand. To convince Americans to build one of the largest navies in the world at the turn of the century, navalists like Theodore Roosevelt, had to link the gleaming battleships and armored cruisers of the "Great White Fleet" with the prestige of the world's newest and most powerful industrialized nation.

The era of comparatively free security was suspended with the Japanese attack on *Pearl Harbor and U.S. entry into World War II, and it certainly stopped for nearly half a century during the Cold War. The commitment to containing the threat from the Soviet Union and communism, meant the development of a sustained, enormous market for weaponry, which was supplied by American defense contractors.

American decisions in the Cold War to push for the most advanced technologies and to build big, sophisticated, expensive weapons, however, over more smaller, less complex weapons, even if it meant fewer rather than more weapons, involved many factors: military, economic, political, and also cultural. For such decisions, like those at the turn of the century to build more battleships and fewer smaller warships like submarines and *destroyers, can also reflect images of national identity. As the "Great White Fleet" was said to represent America's emergent status as a "world power," so the giant *bomber aircraft and supercarriers of the Cold War reinforced its image as the leader and protector of the "free world." Even after the end of the Cold War, as economic competition surpassed military conflict as the primary continuing concern of industrialized nations, the image of America's most sophisticated weaponry—the *Stealth aircraft and precision-guided munitions were most prominent at the end of the twentieth century—remained linked in many minds to the prestige of the United States.

Yet for purposes of self-image as well as self-interest, Americans have sometimes sought to limit the development of certain weapons. The United States, for example, curtailed battleship development in the *Washington Naval Arms Limitation Treaty of 1922. It restricted aspects of the development of nuclear weapons in the *Limited Test Ban Treaty of 1963 and the Comprehensive Test Ban Treaty signed in 1996 (although still not ratified in the summer of 1999). There was also a major international movement to ban the use of land *mines, but because of their use to defend South Korea and the U.S. naval base at Guantanamo, Cuba, the U.S. government had not yet joined the international agreement to prohibit land mines as the century ended. Some attempts were made to limit weaponry in outer space, but such technology has grown dramatically since the late 1950s, particularly the increasing use of military satellites in earth orbit. The development of weapons systems for attacking satellites and proposals for ballistic missile defense systems such as SDI have extended the dangers of warfare to outer space.

At the dawn of the twenty-first century, future directions of weaponry and warfare are unclear in the post–Cold War world and the military missions of preparing for regional and littoral conflict, anti-terrorism, and peacekeeping operations. But requests from the U.S. military for satellite global positioning systems, microcomputers, superconductors, fiber optics, and biotechnical materials suggest that the cyber revolution has led to new forms of vulnerability, for example, the electronic network upon which postmodern societies and their military depend. Such dual-use technology also suggests the degree to which the American economic and technological infrastructure has come to be seen as a backbone of national security. Whatever the weaponry of the future, decisions about its development or nondevelopment will be shaped by technological innovation and by cultural attitudes and political, economic, and military institutions as well as dominant perceptions of the international situation.

[See also Arms Control and Disarmament; Arms Race; Civil-Military Relations: Civilian Control of the Military; Disciplinary Views of War: History of Science and Technology; Economy and War; Industry and War; Military-Industrial Complex; Nuclear Weapons; Procurement; Public Financing and Budgeting for War; Science, Technology, War and the Military; Space Program, Military Involvement in the; War: American Way of War.]

• Walter Millis, Arms and Men, 1956; Arthur A. Ekirch, The Civilian and the Military: A History of the American Antimilitarist Tradition, 1956; Ralph Lapp, Arms Beyond Doubt: The Tyranny of Weapons Technology, 1970; Merritt Roe Smith, Harpers Ferry Armory and the New Technology: The Challenge of Change, 1977; Alex Roland, Underwater Warfare in the Age of Sail, 1978; Trevor N. Dupuy, The Evolution of Weapons and Warfare, 1980; William H. McNeill, The Pursuit of Power: Technology, Armed Force, and Society since A.D. 1000, 1982; Martin van Creveld, Technology and War: From 2000 B.C. to the Present, 1989; Robert L. O'Connell, Of Arms and Men: A History of War, Weapons, and Aggression, 1989; Thomas L. McNaughter, New Weapons: Old Politics: America's Procurement Muddle, 1989; Donald MacKenzie, Inventing Accuracy: An Historical Sociology of Nuclear Missile Guidance, 1990; Alex Roland, "Technology, Ground Warfare, and Strategy: The Paradox of American Experience," Journal of Military History (October 1991,): 447–468; Bhupendra Jasani, ed., Outer Space: A Source of Conflict or Co-Operation?, 1992; James G. Burton, The Pentagon Wars: Reformers Challenge the Old Guard, 1993; Merritt Roe Smith and Leon Marx, eds., Does Technology Drive History? The Dilemma of Technological Determinism, 1994; Michael S. Sherry, In the Shadow of War: The United States Since the 1930s, 1995; Paul A.C. Koistinen, Beating Plowshares into

Swords: The Political Economy of American Warfare, 1606–1865, 1996; Paul A.C. Koistinen, *Mobilizing for Modern War: The Political Economy of American Warfare, 1865–1919*, 1997; and John Whiteclay Chambers II, "The American Debate over Modern War, 1871–1914," in Manfred F. Boemeke, Roger Chickering and Stig Foerster, eds., *Anticipating Total War: The German and American Experience, 1871–1914*, 1999.
—John Whiteclay Chambers II

WEAPONRY, AIR FORCE. One of the principal tasks of an air force in war is the destruction of selected enemy targets. In the achievement of this aim, air force weapons have evolved from hand-held guns and *bombs into a vast inventory, which includes rapid-firing cannon, guided *missiles for use against air and surface targets, "smart" bombs, weapons dispensers, mines, and cruise and ballistic missiles.

Americans were the first to take weapons into the air in heavier-than-air flying machines. In June 1910, Glenn Curtiss, flying his "Golden Flyer" biplane, aimed tennis ball–sized dummy bombs at a target shaped like a battleship. The following year, Lt. Myron Crissy dropped small high-explosive bombs by hand from a Wright biplane during army exercises near San Francisco. The first shots were fired from an airplane in August 1910, when Lt. Jacob Fickel aimed a rifle from the leading edge of a Curtiss biplane's wing and hit a small ground target. In June 1912, Capt. Charles Chandler successfully air-tested a Lewis machine gun mounted on a Wright B Flyer at College Park, Maryland.

The high command remained generally unimpressed by these unofficial experiments. As a result, American development of the air weapon was neglected before 1917 and the U.S. Army Air Service entered World War I with almost no combat capability. American squadrons in France had to use British or French armament and equipment, even though one of the most effective Allied weapons was the Lewis gun, an American design manufactured in Europe. By the end of the war, an excellent lightweight machine gun, the Browning, was in production in the United States, but too late for combat.

Between the wars, most advances in airborne weapons design were led by Germany and the Soviet Union; elsewhere progress was relatively insignificant. The U.S. Army Air Forces entered World War II using weapons that were mostly updated versions of those available in 1918. The majority of combat aircraft carried *machine guns of 0.3-inch or 0.5-inch caliber, or 20mm cannon. The 0.3-inch gun was found to be generally inadequate, but the higher calibers proved effective against enemy aircraft and soft-skinned surface targets. A 75mm gun was fitted to a few B-25 medium bombers for attacks on shipping, and some *bomber aircraft also carried *torpedoes. (The air force still retains a commitment to support naval operations by minelaying.) During the latter part of the war, tactical aircraft began to attack surface targets with unguided rockets.

The principal American bombs used in World War II were high-explosive, weighing from 100 to 4,000 pounds, and small incendiaries, usually of 2.2 pounds. The devastating effect of these unsophisticated weapons delivered in large numbers was exemplified by the destruction of cities like Hamburg, Dresden, and Tokyo. Some attempts were made to use radio-guided bombs against pinpoint targets, but the experiments were not generally successful. Although the war did see considerable development in aerial weapons, the only revolutionary change in weapons technology came in 1945, with the B-29 atomic bombings of *Hiroshima and Nagasaki, which effectively destroyed both cities and ended the war in the Pacific. The debate over the morality of *nuclear weapons has persisted ever since.

The *Vietnam War highlighted both the folly of attempting close political management of the air campaign and the inefficiency of using massive weights of free-fall ("dumb") bombs, including huge quantities of napalm, against a relatively unsophisticated but well-armed enemy. Such notable successes as were achieved from the air were mostly associated with the advent of the first reliable guided ("smart") weapons. (The Than Hoa Bridge near Hanoi defied over 800 "dumb" attacks, but was destroyed by four F-4 Phantoms on the first sortie with "smart bombs.")

Since the Vietnam War, air force weaponry has increased greatly in variety and power. None of the weapons are entirely new in concept, but technological advances have dramatically improved their accuracy and effectiveness. Large stocks of free-fall nuclear, chemical, and high-explosive bombs are retained. The high-explosive types, including cluster bomb units, can still be used to considerable effect—during the *Persian Gulf War they were deployed by B-52s against Iraqi troop concentrations—but the proportion of guided weapons in the inventory is increasing as guidance systems become smaller and cheaper. As the Gulf War demonstrated, munitions guided by *radar, infrared, or electrooptical (TV and laser) systems greatly enhance the effectiveness of attacking aircraft, one bomb often accomplishing what would have taken hundreds in World War II. The precision of the initial air assault on Iraq in 1991, although not as accurate as was first thought, was still such that the national command and control system was devastated within hours. Guided high-explosive bombs can be extremely effective both tactically, in providing support to surface forces, and strategically, against the fabric of an enemy state.

Short-range air-to-surface missiles, some introduced during the Vietnam War, carry high-explosive warheads and are used by tactical aircraft against pinpoint targets. Similar weapons are available for use against shipping. The next generation of these missiles, with improved "seeker" heads and employing "stealth" technology, should be operational by the end of the century.

Although they represent the ultimate in destructive capacity, in the aftermath of the *Cold War the air force's nuclear weapons occupy a less commanding position than previously in American airpower doctrine. Nevertheless, the air force retains the capability to deliver nuclear warheads of varying yields both as free-fall bombs and in guided vehicles. B-1, B-2, and venerable B-52 bombers carry cruise-guided missiles, which can be launched at ranges of less than 100 to over 1,000 miles from their targets. The air force is also responsible for the intercontinental ballistic missiles deployed in silos in the western United States. During the Cold War, these various nuclear weapons were central to the policy of *deterrence employed in containing the Soviet Union. They still have an important if less well defined role in deterring international aggression at the highest level.

The primary air force weapons in air-to-air combat are guided missiles, typically using infrared or radar homing and achieving in-flight speeds of up to Mach 4. Some are designed for relatively short ranges, others can be fired at targets more than thirty miles away. The guided missile is now sufficiently reliable to be dominant in air-to-air combat, but guns are still mounted in aircraft like the F-15 and F-16, and will be fitted to the next-generation air superiority fighter, the F-22. They are retained because they are effective at very close range, relatively cheap, and, once fired, "dumb" bullets cannot be fooled by enemy countermeasures. Modern fighter aircraft guns are usually multibarrel weapons of 20–30mm caliber, in which several barrels rotate in *Gatling gun style. Rates of fire can reach over 6,000 rounds per minute, with muzzle velocities of 3,400 feet per second. The combination of these weapons is intended to ensure that air superiority can be achieved by U.S. fighter aircraft wherever required in future conflicts involving American forces.

[See also Air Force, U.S.; Air Warfare; Bombs; Fighter Aircraft; Heat-Seeking Technology; Weaponry, Army; Weaponry, Marine Corps; Weaponry, Naval; Weaponry, Evolution of: World War I, U.S. Air Operations in; World War II, U.S. Air Operations in: The Air War in Europe; World War II, U.S. Air Operations in: The Air War Against Japan.]

• John W. R. Taylor, A History of Aerial Warfare, 1974. Bill Gunston, The Illustrated Encyclopedia of Aircraft Armament, 1988. Ron Dick, American Eagles, 1997.　　　　　　　　　　　　—Ron Dick

WEAPONRY, ARMY. The technology of war can best be examined in the light of two interrelated triangular relationships. The first of these is Carl von*Clausewitz's curious trinity of reason, chance, and violence, which are respectively manifested by the government, the army, and the people. Although Michael Handel (1986) has argued that twentieth-century warfare demands that technology be added as a fourth pole to the Clausewitzian paradigm, it is far more useful to think of it as an implicit factor in each. This interpretation was suggested, though not specifically addressed, by Alex Roland (1991), who argues that technology is a paradoxical factor in the American military experience. It lurked within each of several enduring issues of that experience before World War II and has tended to obscure them since. In turning from politico-strategic questions on the nature of *war to the operational and tactical issues of combat itself, however, there is no such ambivalence. Here, technology is clearly a major ingredient of a long-standing triad of men, ideas, and weapons. How armies have or have not been able to balance the relations among these three factors and adapt them to particular circumstances of terrain and adversary has almost always been a major determinant of their *combat effectiveness. In short, though weapons themselves are usually not decisive in warfare, they constitute a significant and at times crucial component of a larger framework.

The development of army weapons progressed through three overlapping but fairly distinct periods: the craft era, from the colonial period through the early nineteenth century; the industrial era, from the early nineteenth century through World War II; and the technological era, from World War II to the present.

The Craft Era. The early colonists were armed with weapons made by small groups of craftsmen. The necessity for these weapons was driven by the need to tame a wilderness inhabited by natives not amenable to conversion. The colonists originally armed themselves with armor and pikes, which soon proved their lack of utility in hostile terrain against bows and arrows. Matchlocks worked somewhat better, but their unreliability, particularly in wet weather, led to the development of flintlocks, the most famous of which was the "Pennsylvania" or "Kentucky" rifle. The serious role of individual armament in colonial society was evident in legislation prescribing the weaponry each militia soldier had to provide and in the establishment of public arsenals to supplement the supply of private arms.

At the beginning of the *Revolutionary War, weapons were a major concern. The scarcity of powder caused Gen. George *Washington great anxiety; small arms were often defective; and *artillery was almost nonexistent. Powder was at a premium throughout the Revolution, but the combination of a number of small mills in patriot hands and imports from France kept the supply adequate. Muskets were in short supply in the New York campaign of 1776, but the militia's practice of retaining their personal weapons put a number of British army "Brown Bess" muskets in American hands, which were supplemented as the war progressed by importing French Charlevilles. Thus, throughout most of the war, both the *Continental army and the militia were supplied with adequate individual weapons equal in quality to those of their British adversaries. The one unresolved deficiency, common to almost all revolutionary armies, was that the wide variety of types greatly complicated problems of maintenance and supply.

The lack of artillery was made good by the boldness, initiative, and genius of a single individual: Henry *Knox. Knox not only captured Fort Ticonderoga; he transported some sixty liberated guns by sled to Washington's army. He also developed improved carriages that allowed light guns to accompany troops into battle, giving the Continentals a decided tactical advantage at the Battles of *Trenton and Princeton. The American Revolution was not won by superior weaponry, but it would not have been won without a usually reliable supply of adequate weapons—the best that a craft system and human ingenuity could produce.

The Industrial Era. Daniel Shays's *Rebellion of 1786 demonstrated the weakness of the Articles of Confederation and led the new Constitutional government to provide more effectively for the common defense. One of its provisions was the establishment of government arsenals for the manufacture of powder, small arms, and gun carriages. At least equally significant, perhaps more so, was its policy to issue contracts for weapons manufacture. This sponsorship did a great deal to nurture the idea of standard manufacturing processes and the concomitant concept of interchangeable parts, particularly in the case of the most notable weapons contractor, Eli *Whitney. Like the Revolutionary War, the *War of 1812 was not won by superior weapons. It did, however, bring to an end an almost two-century period of concern with national survival, ushering in a century of virtual freedom from external aggression and violence. It also demonstrated the utility of standardized weapons manufactured to government specification.

By the *Mexican War of 1846, American troops were supposed to be armed with the 1841 percussion musket, but many still carried flintlock models of 1822 and 1840. Despite their standardization and the increased reliability of the percussion cap over the flintlock, each of these weapons shared two common characteristics with their Revolutionary War forebears: a smoothbore, and an effective range of about 100 yards. American artillery employment, however, had advanced dramatically. At the Battle of Palo Alto, Maj. Samuel Ringold demonstrated that light artillery maneuvered aggressively in the defense could break up an infantry attack made by superior forces.

On the eve of the *Civil War, many American officers thought Ringold's tactics could be used in the attack as well as the defense. This calculation was upset by a significant advance in small-arms technology: the development for the rifled *musket of a lead projectile—the minié ball—that expanded into the grooves of the rifling and spun out of the barrel with a stability that made it accurate to ranges of up to 500 yards and lethal up to 1,000. This capacity, combined with developments in artillery that allowed it progressively to engage attacking infantry formations with rifled shell, solid shot, and canister, tilted the tactical equation firmly in the favor of the defense.

The weapons issue during the Civil War thus quickly became which side could arm itself with the most rifles and artillery pieces the fastest. The Confederacy was at a decided disadvantage. But the capture of the manufacturing capacity of Harpers Ferry; the expansion of factories in Richmond and Fayetteville, North Carolina; and the limited importation of weapons from Europe allowed it to arm the men available for *mobilization and to develop ratios of artillery pieces to soldiers roughly comparable to those of the Union. The problem, of course, was that in absolute terms the Confederacy was significantly outnumbered. The South produced 600,000 rifles during the course of the war; the North imported about that number and manufactured another 1,700,000. Neither side solved the tactical problem of countering the power of the defense. This led to horrendous *casualties, which, in the long run, the Union could afford to absorb better than could the Confederacy. It would be foolish to argue that the Union prevailed simply because of numerical superiority. Nevertheless, the American Civil War was demonstrably the first war whose outcome was significantly influenced by the relative industrial capacity of the two sides to produce weapons.

This lesson, however, was soon forgotten. After a long period of constabulary duties, a short war with Spain, and a punitive expedition into Mexico, the U.S. Army found itself almost completely bereft of the tools of modern warfare.

In 1917, when the United States entered World War I, American soldiers were armed with the very effective *Springfield Model 1903 rifle; but there were only 890,000 in the arsenals. They also possessed in the 3-inch gun an artillery piece comparable in quality to the French 75mm. Here, too, the problem was one of supply. Of the roughly 2,250 artillery pieces in the hands of the *American Expeditionary Force in 1918, only 100 were made in the United States. The U.S. Army had not neglected the machine gun, and the *Browning Automatic Rifle was among the best in the world. But it was in short supply as well and not issued to divisions departing for France until July 1918. *Tanks were another problem entirely. All U.S. tank units were equipped with French tanks; even so, both British and French tank units were needed to help support the American infantry. In short, though the U.S. Army provided a much needed infusion of manpower to the Allied cause in

World War I, its lack of suitable weapons placed a significant constraint on its *combat effectiveness.

The period between the wars was ambivalent. On one hand, a combination of severe resource deprivation and military conservatism inhibited the army from developing a modern force. Tank development languished and operational concepts of armored warfare were constrained by an infantry-artillery mind-set. On the other hand, the army consciously studied the question of industrial mobilization; further refined its relatively progressive education system, which encouraged its small officer corps to study issues of large-scale war; and developed a sophisticated system for artillery fire control.

Nevertheless, the U.S. Army entered World War II in 1941 unprepared. Troops deploying for the *North Africa Campaign were issued antitank rockets, known as bazookas, with no previous instruction as to their technical or tactical employment. At the Battle of Kasserine Pass in February 1943, the light and medium tanks of the First Armored Division, armed with 37mm and low-velocity 76mm guns, respectively, were devastated by the heavier-gunned, better-protected, and more skillfully employed Panzers and antitank guns of Erwin *Rommel's Afrika Korps. The American 37mm tank destroyer was an equal disappointment. The one bright spot was the Garand *M-1 rifle, which proved to be a superb infantry weapon throughout the war.

By late 1944, things had changed. Although the Sherman tank was still outgunned by the German Tigers and Panthers, the tank destroyer's armament had been enhanced to 90mm and its role changed from offensive to defensive, recognizing the tank as one of the principal *antitank weapons. Equally important, through trial and error, American units had significantly enhanced their techniques of combined arms tactics. After the initial surprise wore off in the Battle of the *Bulge, U.S. troops stopped the Germans in their tracks with the sophisticated integration of rifle and machine-gun fire; land *mines; tank destroyers; tanks; and closely coordinated volleys of accurate artillery, augmented by *radar-controlled fuses. Furthermore, all were in adequate quantity. The last observation raises an important point. It is possible to argue that the United States won the war solely through the might of its industrial capacity. However, with the exception of tank development, which never really caught up to the demands of European warfare, the American soldier was well armed; and, of equal significance, by the end of the war his tactics were as good as his weapons.

The Technological Era. World War II marked a watershed in the U.S. Army's approach to weapons. Technological breakthroughs such as high-frequency radio, radar-controlled fuses, and shaped-charge antitank munitions had clearly demonstrated the benefits of scientific advances for ground warfare. Yet the army's initial postwar experiences were disappointing.

In June 1951, Task Force Smith, a battalion-size force commanded by Lt. Col. Charles B. Smith, deployed to the *Korean War with an inadequate number of World War II weapons. Its antitank capacity was nonexistent: it had no mines, no recoilless rifles, no tanks; and the rounds from its 2.36-inch rocket launchers failed to penetrate the North Koreans' Soviet T-34 tanks just as they had failed to penetrate the German's Tigers. The task force's Company K carried two 81mm mortar baseplates and two tubes, but lacked both bipods and sights. It soon lost radio contact with its supporting artillery and was forced to conduct a hasty withdrawal. After a seesaw battle up and down the peninsula, the lines stabilized. Gen. Matthew B. *Ridgway reinfused the Eighth Army with a fighting spirit that employed massive amounts of air and artillery, combined with aggressive infantry tactics to take the high ground. The war ended in a stalemate that was driven primarily by the exigencies of limited war in the nuclear era.

These same constraints shaped the war in Vietnam. But the *Vietnam War was also affected by the army's checkered weapons development and lack of operational acumen. The infantryman's principal weapon was by now the *M-16 rifle. It had the advantage of either semiautomatic or automatic fire, but its fine tolerances made it unsuitable to a jungle environment. *Helicopters provided an initial advantage in tactical mobility, but this advantage dissipated as soon as infantrymen dismounted. The artillery used improved versions of the 105mm and 155mm howitzer of World War II. The "beehive" canister round was devastatingly effective in repulsing enemy attacks, as were large volumes of indirect fire. But the artillery's overall effectiveness was hostage to the willingness of Viet Cong and North Vietnamese units to present suitable targets, which they tended to do only if they could gain the element of surprise. This led to development of sophisticated instruments for locating enemy units in *jungle warfare. Never very effective, the effort caused U.S. Army leaders to become extremely interested in sensor and *heat-seeking technology.

This interest paid off handsomely in the post-Vietnam reform era. After surveying the Arab-Israeli War of 1973, the U.S. Army promulgated a concise and startling epigram: What can be seen can be hit; what can be hit can be killed. It also worked consciously to fashion its doctrine, training, education, and equipment to repulse a Soviet offensive into Western Europe. The equipment manifestations were the Bradley infantry fighting vehicle; the Abrams tank; the multiple launch rocket system; the Blackhawk and Apache helicopters; and a sophisticated sensor and information distribution system, developed in conjunction with the air force. Rather than being employed on the plains of Europe, these weapons were used in the 1991 *Persian Gulf War to liberate Kuwait. And although one must note the ineptitude of the Iraqi High Command, a strong argument can be made that Operation Desert Storm represents a case in which an adequate number of superior weapons in the hands of well-led, well-trained troops indeed helped to turn the tide of battle.

Conclusion. The experience of U.S. Army weapons development has been at best uneven, with World War I representing the nadir and the Gulf War the apogee. The key variables appear to have been the American people's willingness to provide for the nation's security; the government's ability to articulate a convincing rationale for such provision and to channel America's productive capacity; and the army's foresight in war preparation and acumen in war conduct. In other words, with minor adaptation, Clausewitz's trinity retains its explanatory power. The future of army weapons development rests on how well these elements are kept in balance with each other and with the exigencies of a constantly changing world.

[See also Armored Vehicles; Army Combat Branches; Army, U.S.; Flamethrowers; Gatling Gun; Weaponry, Air Force; Weaponry, Marine Corps; Weaponry, Naval; Weaponry, Evolution of.]

• Maurice Matloff, ed., *American Military History*, 1969. Carl von Clausewitz, *On War*, trans. and ed. Michael Howard and Peter Paret, 1976. John Shy, "The American Military Experience: History and Learning," in John Shy, *A People Numerous and Armed*, 1976. Allan Millett and Peter Maslowski, *For the Common Defense*, 1984. Russell Weigley, *History of the United States Army*, 1984. Michael Handel, "Clausewitz in the Age of Technology," in Michael Handel, ed., *Clausewitz and Modern Strategy*, 1986. Charles Heller and William Stofft, eds., *America's First Battles*, 1986. Alex Roland, "Technology, Ground Warfare, and Strategy: The American Paradox," *Journal of Military History*, 55 (October 1991), pp. 447–67.

—Harold R. Winton

WEAPONRY, MARINE CORPS. The Marine Corps from its beginnings was smaller in numbers than other services and was often thrown into action against larger forces. This fact led to a constant search for superior firepower. The result was adoption of more effective weapons ahead of both enemies and sister services.

During the *Revolutionary War, the Continental Marines were armed with British and French muskets of the day. These were variations known as "sea service" models. They were shorter for use in tight spaces aboard ship and aloft, with brass fittings, and the barrel and lock were tin-plated to resist corrosion from salt air and spray. Use of these arms continued well into the nineteenth century, with new developments such as percussion cap locks replacing flint ignition and rifled barrels replacing smoothbores. The Hall breech-loading rifle was used in a 1832 campaign against pirates in Sumatra. Early models of Colt revolving rifles were used in the Seminole Wars of the 1830s.

During the *Civil War, in addition to obsolete Springfield rifled *muskets, Spencer seven-shot repeating rifles (tin-plated for sea service) were used, as well as single-shot Sharps rifles. After the Civil War, many breech-loading and repeating rifles were tried, including the Remington rolling block and the five-shot Remington-Lee bolt action; the army's single-shot "trapdoor" Springfield was finally adopted. The multibarreled, hand-cranked *Gatling gun provided additional firepower during the 1870s to 1890s.

The development in the 1880s of smokeless powder of greater power enabled the firing of smaller (6mm to 8mm or .24- to .31-caliber) bullets at much higher velocities and thus greater ranges. The Marine Corps adopted the Winchester-Lee "straight-pull" five-shot rifle and the Colt-Browning machine gun in 1895, both firing 6mm cartridges. Marines fighting in the *Spanish-American War (1898) were armed with these weapons. In 1900, the accurate .30-caliber Krag-Jorgenson replaced the Winchester-Lee. At this time, the Marine Corps began to stress rifle marksmanship. All Marines were expected to achieve a high order of skill, a policy that has continued to the present.

Marine aviators began training in 1911 on Curtiss pusher biplanes; by 1913, an aircraft unit with Curtiss seaplanes was integrated into the Advance Base Force as the first air-ground team. Every overseas deployment since has been as an integrated ground and aviation team. In 1916, the Marines adopted the King armored car, armed with a light machine gun. The first of the *armored vehicles adopted for regular service, it continued in use until 1921.

Marine rearmament began in the early twentieth century with the army M1903 .30-caliber rifle replacing the Krag in 1912. In the constant search for superior firepower, the Benét-Mercié light machine gun was adopted as the navy Mark II. The Lewis light machine gun, rejected by the army, was adopted by the Marines in 1916. When the Marines joined the U.S. Army's Second Division in France during World War I, they left their Lewis guns behind and were armed like the rest of the division with French Hotchkiss heavy *machine guns and Chauchat light machine guns. After the armistice, these were replaced by the new Browning M1917 heavy machine gun and the M1918 *Browning automatic rifle (BAR). The Brownings continued in use through the *Korean War—one to three BARs in each squad.

Seeking a firepower edge for close quarters fighting, Marines adopted the Thompson submachine gun, firing .45-caliber pistol cartridges, in the early 1920s. They were the first service to adopt the submachine gun as a regular weapon.

The *Springfield Model 1903 rifle continued in use until early in World War II, when it was replaced by the eight-shot Garand *M-1 rifle. The M-1 was replaced by the improved twenty-shot M-14 rifle in the early 1960s. The M-14, which fired the new *NATO standard 7.65mm cartridge, in turn, was replaced during the *Vietnam War by the lightweight *M-16 rifle in 5.56mm or .223 caliber.

By the early 1990s, the Belgian-designed M249 squad automatic rifle (SAW) in 5.56mm was adopted to fulfill the role of the BAR and the automatic M-14. Shortly thereafter, also from Belgium's Fabrique Nationale, the M240 general-purpose machine gun in 7.65mm replaced the M60. The Mark 19 40mm automatic grenade launcher, developed by the U.S. Navy and Marine Corps, added to the firepower.

Sniper rifles included an M1903 equipped with an 8-power Unertl telescope used in World War II and Korea. In Vietnam and the *Persian Gulf War, a bolt action M-40 rifle with telescope was used; in the Gulf War, a Barrett 30-pound M-82 .50-caliber semiautomatic rifle for very long range work was used with great effect.

A weapon unique to the Marine Corps is the amphibian tractor—or landing vehicle tracked—introduced in World War II for ship-to-shore movement and to cross coral barrier reefs in the Pacific Islands. All carried machine guns, with some variants armed with cannon. Modern versions as the LVTP-5 of the Vietnam War and the LVTP-7 of the Gulf War continue in their original purpose and are used as troop carriers inland.

Also unique to the Corps from the late 1980s is the light armored vehicle (LAV), an eight-wheeled armored car carrying an infantry squad and mounting a 25mm automatic gun.

Heavy supporting weapons, *artillery, *mortars, *antitank weapons, and *tanks were procured from the army. Here, too, the U.S. *Marine Corps often participated in their development.

[See also Armored Vehicles; Army Combat Branches; Marine Corps, U.S.; Weaponry, Air Force; Weaponry, Army; Weaponry, Naval; Weaponry, Evolution of.]

• Robert Debs Heinl, Soldiers of the Sea: The U.S. Marine Corps, 1775–1962, 1962. Robert H. Rankin, Small Arms of the Sea Services, 1972. W. H. B. Smith and Joseph E. Smith, Small Arms of the World, 10th rev. ed. 1973. Edwin H. Simmons, The United States Marines: The First Two Hundred Years, 1775–1975, 1976. Allan R. Millett, Semper Fidelis: The History of the United States Marine Corps, 1980. Norman A. and Roy F. Chandler, Death from Afar: Marine Corps Sniping, Vols. 1–3, 1992–94.   —Brooke Nihart

WEAPONRY, NAVAL. The history of U.S. naval weaponry embraces not just the weapons themselves and the sensors that point them to their targets. It also includes the so-called platforms—the ships, aircraft, and even unmanned aerial vehicles—that carry the weapons and sensors into battle.

The navy's record of dealing with new weaponry and platform technology is not uniformly bright. There have been periods of hidebound conservatism and willful refusal to understand new developments. But more often the U.S. Navy has sought out technological opportunity and exploited it with vigor, showing itself capable of striking innovations from the early years of American independence to the dawn of the information revolution.

The Fledgling Navy. When the *Revolutionary War began, naval armaments had remained essentially unchanged for over a century. Wooden *sailing warships mounted inaccurate smoothbore cannon along each side and fought each other at close range. The most decisive battles were between massive "ships of the line" with two or three decks of guns.

The colonies had few advantages in weaponry. Their foundries produced guns of uneven quality, and their ships relied heavily on foreign guns. Their fledgling navy had only a few small vessels, whereas the Royal Navy of 1775 possessed more than 131 ships of the line and 139 other warships. Overwhelming power enabled the Royal Navy to blockade any port not occupied by British troops.

But America had abundant oak and softwood for hulls, tall timber for masts and spars—and resins to make critical naval stores like tar to protect standing rigging. It also had a large merchant fleet with fine ships, skilled sailors, and experienced captains. American *privateering scourged British commerce during the Revolution, and some U.S. Navy skippers like John Paul *Jones won famous single-ship victories.

The subsequent *War of 1812 played out along similar lines. By then, however, the U.S. Navy had begun its distinguished history of technological innovation. Not all of it turned out well. The decision to arm the frigate Essex exclusively with carronades—a short piece invented in Europe that could deliver as heavy a ball at short range as a much heavier "long gun"—proved disastrous when a British frigate used the greater range of its long guns to batter the helpless American vessel into submission.

But a new class of "big frigates," among them the famous USS Constitution, proved more than a match for their Royal Navy counterparts and prompted Britain to build similar vessels. The forty-four-gun frigates were cleverly designed, with the speed to escape from any ship of the line but more firepower than most other frigates and a much stronger hull. In addition, they carried a particularly effective mix of long guns and carronades, the latter greatly increasing the firepower on their upper deck, where minimizing weight was critical.

The Young Republic. The Industrial Revolution that had originated in Britain spread to the United States, bringing with it the potential for great innovations in ordnance and ships. For several decades, the United States played a leading role in exploiting that potential.

Explosive shells entered service in Europe in the 1830s, and European navies began to experiment with more accurate, rifled guns firing elongated projectiles. In 1844, the U.S. Navy commissioned its first steam warships, the side-wheel frigates *Missouri* and *Mississippi,* which were considered the equal of any European warship then in service. They mounted only two 10-inch and eight 8-inch shell guns, a reduced main battery that illustrates the general trend from a large number of relatively small pre-industrial cannon to a handful of the much larger, longer-range guns made possible by advances in metallurgy, and other related technologies.

The U.S. frigate *Princeton,* which followed in 1844, was the world's first warship with a screw propeller. This eliminated paddle wheels and allowed machinery to be located well within the ship and below the waterline, making it less vulnerable and freeing topside space for guns. The *Princeton* carried twelve 42-pound carronades and two 12-inch wrought-iron guns that fired a 225-pound shot.

However, during a demonstration on the new wrought-iron guns, one of them exploded, killing the secretary of the navy and the secretary of state. The resulting scandal prompted the navy to turn away wrought-iron ordnance. Instead, under the technical leadership of Cmdr. (later Rear Adm.) John *Dahlgren, it subsequently chose to concentrate on safer cast-iron smoothbore guns, in which it became the acknowledged leader.

The Civil War. France and Britain were already pursuing armor and iron hulls for seagoing warships when the *Civil War began. The Confederacy, unable to match the Union fleet, also turned to armor, rebuilding the damaged U.S. steam frigate *Merrimac* as the ironclad ram *Virginia.* Other rams followed, often armed with rifled guns that could fire elongated, steel-cored iron "bolts" for piercing Union ship armor.

The Union countered armor with ever more powerful smoothbores, eventually up to 15 inches in bore diameter, firing solid shot. Many were mounted in revolving turrets in low-freeboard armored coastal ships called Monitors, after the original *Monitor* that confronted the *Virginia* at the Battle of *Hampton Roads in 1862. The only seagoing armored ship of the war, the Union's *New Ironsides,* mounted its guns on the broadside. The Confederacy ordered several seagoing armored rams from European shipyards, but the war ended before any reached the South.

Both sides experimented with the predecessors of today's fast attack craft: steam-powered boats with a "spar torpedo," an explosive charge on a pole, protruding from the bow. Private Confederate citizens built the *Hunley,* a primitive submarine powered by a hand crank. Taken over by the *Confederate army at Charleston, South Carolina, and armed with a spar torpedo, it became the first submarine to sink a warship, the Union sloop *Housatonic.* However, the *Hunley* also sank, drowning its crew.

Both sides used naval *mines, the "torpedoes" famously damned by Adm. David *Farragut at the Battle of *Mobile Bay (1864). These were detonated either by contact or by wires connected to primitive electric batteries ashore.

Postwar Apathy. America turned to its western frontier after the Civil War, scrapping the Union's 700-ship fleet and laying up its ironclads to rust. The seagoing fleet ossified, with wooden ships and antiquated guns. A new fast cruiser, the *Wampanoag,* became the first ship to use superheated steam, achieving an unprecedented 17.7 knots in 1868 sea trials; but a special board of line admirals, fearing the rise of naval engineers, ordered her boilers removed, and she rotted away at the pier. An 1869 general order required all U.S. naval vessels to have "full sail power" in addition to steam.

In Europe, meanwhile, innovation accelerated. Breech-loading guns entered naval service in the 1870s, rapid-firing guns using cordite charges in the 1880s, and armor-piercing high-explosive shells in the 1890s. In 1866, British engineer Robert Whitehead invented the self-propelled torpedo, which provided the first effective weapon for fast attack craft and, later, for *submarines. Contact and magnetic mines, which did not require remote detonation, also appeared.

American Naval Resurgence. Stimulated in part by the seapower theories of Capt. (later Rear Adm.) Alfred T. *Mahan, the U.S. Navy began to revive. In the 1880s, it built its first all-steel ships, forerunners of the oceangoing steel fleet that emerged in the 1890s. That fleet no longer reflected a vibrant maritime culture, America's merchant marine having declined; rather, it reflected the industrial might of a nation that had become the world's leading steelmaker by the mid-1890s.

Europe continued to lead in naval technology, with the United States playing catch-up. Work carried out at the Washington Naval Shipyard gave the U.S. Navy the ability to cast ever larger rifled guns, and the service encouraged steelmakers to produce first-rate armor and shells. As improved guns, optical rangefinders, mechanical calculators, and electrical distribution systems increased effective gunnery ranges from 6,000 yards in 1898 to more than 20,000 yards in World War I, the United States kept pace.

In 1906, Britain built the *Dreadnought,* the revolutionary "all-big-gun" battleship designed to take advantage of this technology. The first U.S. "dreadnought," was actually funded before the *Dreadnought,* but was not completed until 1909. Like the *Dreadnought,* the *Michigan* had 12-inch guns but its design was much more advanced, with superfiring turrets and all turrets on the centerline. Britain completed the first battleship with 14-inch guns in 1911; America matched it with the *battleships *New York* and *Texas* in 1912. By the end of World War I, Britain had settled on a 15-inch standard for capital ships, while America adopted a 16-inch standard.

American pursuit of newer naval technologies was more uneven. The first true submarine, propelled by a gasoline engine on the surface and an electric battery when submerged, was built in America in 1881 by Irish immigrant John *Holland. In 1893, he built the *Holland,* the first truly practical sub, which the U.S. Navy acquired two years later. But the navy lost its early lead in submarine technology as European navies forged ahead with such innovations as diesel propulsion.

U.S. torpedo development also lagged. In 1907, after decades of depending on foreign suppliers, the navy finally built its first torpedo factory, in Newport, Rhode Island, but the factory continued to produce variants of foreign torpedo designs until the 1920s. During World War I, the service absorbed early British antisubmarine technology, such as the depth charge and hydrophones.

The navy had also shown early interest in aircraft, another American invention. In 1910, it fitted the scout cruiser *Birmingham* with a temporary wooden flight deck so that civilian aviator Eugene Ely could make the first landing on a ship. In 1911, Ely not only landed on the armored cruiser *Pennsylvania*, but also took off again. Yet, as with the submarine, Europe once more took the lead, and it was Britain that operated the first experimental aircraft carrier (1917) and commissioned the first true carrier, the *Argus* (1918).

The U.S. Navy Comes of Age. By the end of World War I, America's naval building program dwarfed that of any other power, particularly in battleships and battlecruisers. The other powers therefore reluctantly agreed to the 1922 *Washington Naval Arms Limitation Treaty, which left only the Royal Navy equal to the U.S. Navy. Limitations on capital ships were the heart of the treaty, although it limited other ship types as well. Ironically, however, the battleship's supremacy was nearly at an end, and the U.S. Navy was taking a leading role in the aviation technology that would seal its fate.

In 1922, the navy commissioned its first aircraft carrier, the *Langley*, a converted collier. Two half-built *battle cruiser hulls to be scrapped under the new treaty became instead the world's largest *aircraft carriers: the *Lexington* and the *Saratoga*. Aircraft carriers built for the purpose soon followed. The torpedo bomber, developed by the British in World War I, and the dive-bomber, developed in the 1920s by the U.S. *Marine Corps, would become the carriers' great offensive weapons of World War II.

Also from the Royal Navy the United States obtained "Asdic," which it christened *Sonar. The British and the U.S. Naval Weapons Laboratory in Washington, D.C., each developed *radar independently, but the two countries subsequently collaborated on its perfection. One key U.S. Navy radar innovation was the "plan position indicator"—the familiar radar scope.

The shipboard combat information center (CIC), developed during World War II, used radar data to control *fighter aircraft defending the carrier task force. Closer in, the ships defended themselves with antiaircraft guns and dual-purpose 5-inch guns firing shells equipped with newly invented proximity fuses—miniature radars that detonated the shells as they neared enemy aircraft.

The U.S. fleet *submarines of World War II could not dive as deep as German submarines, but they had long range and good surface speed. They also had radar to help locate and target Japanese ships. Like several other navies, the U.S. Navy had developed a magnetic exploder to detonate its *torpedoes lethally directly beneath the keel of enemy ships. However, while other countries quickly abandoned those unreliable devices, the U.S. Navy's reluctance to do so initially hindered its submarine campaign against Japan.

For *antisubmarine warfare the navy continued to develop sonar, weapons, and tactics. Mortars for projecting charges ahead of the ship supplemented depth charges rolled off the stern and projected over the side of *destroyers and destroyer escorts. Aircraft equipped with radar drove submarines beneath the surface, where they could less readily intercept Allied convoys.

U.S. Preeminence in Naval Weaponry. The United States emerged from World War II with by far the most powerful fleet, but *nuclear weapons delivered by long-range *bomber aircraft seemed destined to render fleets irrelevant. When the Soviet Union obtained nuclear

weapons, the resulting stalemate placed a premium on *deterrence. The navy deployed nuclear-armed Regulus I cruise missiles on diesel-electric submarines in the 1950s, but it did not obtain a significant share of the deterrence mission until the 1960s, when the marriage of the long-range ballistic missile and the nuclear-powered submarine enabled it to provide the least vulnerable leg of America's nuclear "triad," which also included land-based *missiles and bombers.

In conventional war, which continued to exist, guided missiles were slower to rival aircraft. The Soviet Navy fielded land attack and antiship missiles from the 1950s, but they tended to be inaccurate or vulnerable to countermeasures. By the 1970s, missile technology had advanced, and the U.S. Navy developed two subsonic cruise missiles: the Harpoon antiship missile, for launch by either aircraft or ships; and the ship- and submarine-launched Tomahawk, which came in nuclear, conventional land attack, and antiship versions.

The missile also became the preeminent defensive weapon, since only a missile had the range and homing capability to intercept supersonic aircraft and cruise missiles. In the 1950s, the navy fielded Tartar, Terrier, and Talos—the so-called 3-T missile systems. However, the unprecedented complexity of these shipboard systems made them unreliable, despite several "get-well" programs. The only solution was to treat the entire ship as a single weapon "platform," with all of its war-fighting equipment integrated into a single system. Such "total system engineering" became the hallmark of the successful *Aegis program, which, starting in the late 1970s, oversaw all development and building of guided-missile cruisers and destroyers.

The same level of integration increasingly characterized submarine programs as well. Nuclear propulsion gave the submarine high underwater speed and unlimited submerged endurance, making it not only an unprecedented threat to surface ships but also the foremost weapon against enemy submarines. The Mk-48 torpedo reflected that new priority, being designed primarily for antisubmarine warfare and secondarily for use against surface ships.

Antisubmarine warfare necessarily became much more sophisticated. Aircraft now dropped sonobuoys for detection and lightweight *torpedoes for attack. Surface ships mounted powerful bow-mounted active sonars and carried antisubmarine rockets and *helicopters. Beginning in the 1970s, the fleet relied increasingly on Tow-ed passive sonar arrays. From early in the *Cold War, extensive arrays of passive receivers were also emplaced on the ocean bottom. However, the post–Cold War threat of diesel submarines in shallow coastal waters has posed a new challenge that may require a return to active sonar, or "bistatic" sonar, which employs a remote sound source.

The U.S. Navy in the Twenty-First-Century. Just as technological developments in the post–World War II period led inexorably to the concept of total system engineering for entire ships, so the increasing complexity of data processing and communications in the new century will lead to "systems of systems" in which many ships and aircraft must be able to act swiftly and reliably as a single entity. Increasingly, all platforms will have access to a common picture of the "battle space," permitting an aircraft to control an air defense missile launched by a distant cruiser, or an unmanned aerial vehicle (UAV) to control a cruise missile launched from a submarine.

This "network-centric warfare," as the navy calls it, will not be easy to master. Like steampower, armor, and long-range guns in the nineteenth century, or aircraft and submarines in the twentieth, it promises revolutionary increases in *combat effectiveness. But to obtain that capability, the U.S. Navy will have to summon up the best attributes of its most progressive eras: the boldness to make mistakes, the discipline to study those mistakes impartially, and the unfailing ambition to seek out solutions.

[See also Navy, U.S.: 1866–98; Navy, U.S.: 1899–1945; Navy, U.S.: Since 1946; Navy Combat Branches; Weaponry, Evolution of; Navy, U.S.: 1783–1865.]

• Richard Hough, Dreadnought: A History of the Modern Battleship, 1964. John D. Alden, The American Steel Navy, 1972. Clay Blair, Jr., Silent Victory: The U.S. Submarine War against Japan, 1975. Nathan Miller, The U.S. Navy: An Illustrated History, 1977. Henry E. Gruppe, The Frigates, 1979. Robert Gardner, ed., Navies in the Nuclear Age, 1993. Ivan Musicant, Divided Waters: A Naval History of the Civil War, 1995. Raimundo Luraghi, A History of the Confederate Navy, 1996. Robert J. Schneller, A Quest for Glory: A Biography of Rear Admiral John A. Dahlgren, 1996. Norman Friedman, U.S. Naval Weapons, 1997.   —John J. Patrick

WEDEMEYER, ALBERT C. (1896–1989), World War II general and diplomat. A native of Omaha, Nebraska, Wedemeyer graduated from West Point in 1919. His service in the regular army included tours in the Philippines and China (1923–25, 1930–34). Two years as an exchange student at the German Kriegsakademie in Berlin (1936–38) gave him insight into the Blitzkrieg.

Brought to the War Plans Division of the U.S. Army General Staff by Gen. George C. *Marshall in 1941, Wedemeyer became the primary author of the "Victory Plan"— the prophetic prewar document that visualized mobilizing U.S. resources for all-out war with the Axis, and outlined the broad operational *strategy that eventually brought *victory. As a member and then head of the Strategy and Policy Group of the wartime Operations Division of the General Staff, he participated in the joint councils that managed the war.

Upon the recall of Gen. Joseph *Stilwell in 1944, Wedemeyer assumed the twin posts of U.S. China theater commander and Allied chief of staff to Chiang Kai-shek, the Nationalist president of China. He achieved effective working relations with China; after the war, he recommended continued U.S. support of Chiang's Nationalist government in its struggle with Mao Zedong's Communists. When a postwar effort by the Truman administration to arrange a political coalition of China's warring factions failed, Wedemeyer again was dispatched to East Asia (1947) on a fact-finding mission.

In the wake of the Communist victory in China (1949), Wedemeyer held that, although China had indeed not been "ours to lose," it had been ours to push over the brink. Had China remained friendly to the West, neither the *Korean War nor the *Vietnam War would have occurred.

Wedemeyer retired from the army in 1951. His memoirs (1958) sharply criticized U.S. and British war policies, arguing that better leadership might have altered a costly struggle in which one set of tyrants—the Nazis and Fascists—were thoroughly defeated, only to facilitate the rise of another—the Communists.

[See also China-Burma-India Theater.]

• Albert C. Wedemeyer, Wedemeyer Reports!, 1958. John Keegan, Six Armies in Normandy, 1982. Keith E. Eiler, ed., Wedemeyer on War and Peace, 1987.   —Keith E. Eiler

WEINBERGER, CASPAR (1917–), lawyer, government official, secretary of defense. President Ronald *Reagan appointed Weinberger, a former California and federal official, as secretary of defense in 1981. Weinberger worked to implement Reagan's defense program, stressing armed forces modernization, readiness, and sustainability to counter the threats of the Soviet Union, which Reagan labeled the "evil empire." Weinberger pushed for a broad strategic weapons program, including B-1B bombers, a stealth aircraft, the Trident II submarine-launched ballistic missile, and the MX "Peacekeeper" ICBM. He backed development of Reagan's space-based system to defend against missile attack—the *Strategic Defense Initiative or "Star Wars" program.

Weinberger persuaded Congress to approve large increases in the defense budget, which increased from about $176 billion (total obligational authority) in fiscal year 1981 to over $276 billion in fiscal year 1985, the largest peacetime defense buildup in U.S. history. After that, he was less successful in getting his budget requests through Congress. Between 1981 and 1985, there was substantial real growth; after 1985, although the dollar amount of the defense budget continued to increase slowly, there was negative real growth.

Weinberger was cautious about committing military forces in trouble spots around the world, but while he was at the *Pentagon, U.S. forces joined an international peacekeeping force in Lebanon (August 1982) and invaded Grenada (October 1983) to oust a Communist-controlled government. Responding to tension in the Persian Gulf, the Department of *Defense created the unified Central Command for Southwest Asia. During Weinberger's term, Congress passed the *Goldwater-Nichols Act (1986), which strengthened the control of the chairman of the *Joint Chiefs of Staff over the JCS organization and increased his influence as adviser to the president on military matters. Weinberger showed little enthusiasm for the U.S.-USSR arms control negotiations (*START and the *INF Treaties), which Reagan accorded high priority during his second term (1985–89). Although within the administration, he opposed the activities leading to the *Iran-Contra Affair (1986). Weinberger was later indicted on a charge that he had not disclosed to an independent counsel the existence of notes he kept on the matter; President George *Bush pardoned him in 1992 shortly before his trial was to begin.

After serving longer than any secretary of defense except Robert S. *McNamara, Weinberger left office in November 1987.

[See also Grenada, U.S. Intervention in.]

• Caspar W. Weinberger, Fighting for Peace: Seven Critical Years in the Pentagon, 1990. Roger R. Trask and Alfred Goldberg, The Department of Defense, 1947–1997: Organization and Leaders, 1997.   —Roger R. Trask

WELLES, GIDEON (1802–1878), secretary of the navy, 1861–69. A prominent political leader from Connecticut, Welles first served in the Navy Department during the Polk administration as chief of the navy's Bureau of Provisions and Clothing.

As Lincoln's secretary, he resisted public demands of ships for the Northern coastline while concentrating on blockading and strangling the Confederacy during the *Civil War. Welles used monitors for Southern harbors and ironclad riverboats for the Mississippi River. In July 1861, he allowed ships to keep contrabands on board. By September, he authorized enlisting contrabands under the same regulations as other enlistments. And in July 1862, he ordered the East Gulf Blockading Squadron actively to recruit contrabands (runaway slaves).

Administratively, through Congress, Welles reorganized the navy. In July 1861, he established the post of assistant secretary and temporary volunteer officers to fill wartime needs. That August, he retired older, infirm officers. Automatic officer retirement for over-age and service limits began in December. In July 1862, line officers received nine ranks, and staff bureaus were raised to eight. The bureau changes reflected the new technologies developing in gunnery and steam engineering. With minor modifications, Welles's administrative changes would remain in place until newer technologies after World War II demanded further reorganization.

[See also Navy, U.S.: 1783–1865; Navy, U.S.: 1866–1898; Union Navy.]

• Gideon Welles, Diary, 3 vols., 1911. John Niven, Gideon Welles, 1973.
—George E. Buker

WESTMORELAND, WILLIAM C.

WESTMORELAND, WILLIAM C. (1914–), U.S. general. One of the most controversial figures in American military history, William Westmoreland, by his own appraisal, was "the most vilified man in America" during the 1970s. A military leader of the U.S. buildup in the Republic of South Vietnam from 1964 until 1968, the general exuded confidence, only to undergo a devastating Communist attack during the 1968 *Tet Offensive. Critics cited this attack as reason to withdraw U.S. forces and proof that Westmoreland had followed a failed strategy.

Born in Spartanburg County, South Carolina, and graduated from West Point in 1936, Westmoreland held Field Artillery assignments until World War II. Promoted to lieutenant colonel, he participated in the *North Africa Campaign in 1942, landed in Sicily in 1943, and landed on the Normandy coast in 1944. Westmoreland gained a reputation for superb staff work and sound battle leadership during the war.

After the war, Westmoreland joined the infantry, became a paratrooper in 1946, and commanded the only U.S. airborne infantry regiment to participate in the Korean War. After attending an advanced management program at Harvard University, he commanded the 101st Airborne, (1958–60) and served as Superintendent of the U.S. Military Academy (1960–63), after which he took command of the XVIII Airborne Corps. Westmoreland's era of high notoriety began when, as a full general, he was assigned to head the United States Military Assistance Command, Vietnam (MACV) in 1964, an advisory and support effort to the South Vietnamese Army. He saw that the infusion of increasing numbers of North Vietnamese troop units into the small Southeast Asian country was transforming a guerrilla war into a stand-up contest between conventionally organized regulars. Convinced that U.S. forces would have to enter the war as offensive units, Secretary of Defense Robert S. *Mac-

Namara and President Lyndon B. *Johnson received a proposal from Westmoreland that would have the new U.S. Army airmobile force, the 1st Cavalry Division, cut the Communist line of communications by establishing mobile bases in the Laotian Panhandle. Rebuffed and faced with the task of defending all of South Vietnam, Westmoreland devised a scheme of "search and destroy" offensive missions by U.S. forces to locate, engage, and defeat Communist forces in South Vietnam. Following the surprise *Tet Offensive (1968) by the Communists and the erosion of American support, despite its defeat, Westmoreland was succeeded in Vietnam by Gen. Creighton *Abrams.

Returning to the United States in 1968, Westmoreland became chief of staff of the army and retired in 1972. After an unsuccessful run for the governorship of South Carolina in 1974, he became embroiled in a failed 1985 suit against CBS for portraying himself and his staff as falsifying enemy strength and casualty reports during the *Vietnam War.

[See also Westmoreland v. CBS.]

• William C. Westmoreland, A Soldier Reports, 1976. Samuel Zaffiri, Westmoreland: A Biography of General William C. Westmoreland, 1994.
—Rod Paschall

WESTMORELAND v. CBS (1985). On 22 January 1982, CBS Television broadcast a 90-minute documentary, CBS Reports: The Uncounted Enemy: A Vietnam Deception. The program was produced by George Crile and based in large part on reporting by Sam Adams. Crile was the co-author. The narrator—who also conducted some of the interviews—was Mike Wallace of 60 Minutes.

The program charged that Gen. William C. *Westmoreland, while U.S. military commander during the Vietnam War, had led a conspiracy prior to the surprise *Tet Offensive (1968) to keep down official intelligence estimates of enemy strength, thereby deceiving President Lyndon B. *Johnson, the rest of the military, and the American public. Further, such a "reduction" in enemy strength resulted in the surprise at Tet, with greater troops losses. Most important, public support for the war plummeted.

Three days later, General Westmoreland held a press conference challenging the program and asking for an apology. CBS stood by the broadcast, but an article in TV Guide charged the program with at least eight major errors and violations of CBS procedures.

On 13 September 1982, Westmoreland brought suit against CBS for libel, asking $120 million. The trial—Westmoreland v. CBS—lasted from October 1984 to February 1985. On 17 February 1985, just as it was to go to the jury, the two sides settled, each stating that it had proven its major points.

Burton Benjamin, longtime CBS News executive, was also asked to produce an internal evaluation. After an exhaustive investigation, he concluded the program was "seriously flawed": it was out of balance; "conspiracy" had not been proven; friendly witnesses had been coddled and those opposing the thesis treated harshly. Mike Wallace stood by the program, but later said that it took him two years to get his confidence back.

The controversy provided an ironically fitting epilogue to arguments between the press and the military over Vietnam.

[*See also* Culture, War, and the Media; Film, War and the Military in: Newsfilms and Documentaries; Vietnam War.]

• Don Kowet, *A Matter of Honor: General William C. Westmoreland versus CBS*, 1984. Burton Benjamin, *Fair Play: CBS, Westmoreland, and How a Television Documentary Went Wrong*, 1988.

—Lawrence W. Lichty

WHEELER, EARLE G. (1908–1975), general, U.S. Army; chairman, *Joint Chiefs of Staff (JCS), 1964–79. Gen. Earle Wheeler's tenure as the nation's top military officer spanned the height of America's involvement in the Vietnam War. President Lyndon B. *Johnson appointed Wheeler chairman of the JCS in July 1964 to succeed Gen. Maxwell *Taylor. Wheeler oversaw and supported the expanding U.S. military role in the conflict in the mid-1960s, consistently backing the field commander's requests for additional troops and operating authority. Concerned that the U.S. buildup in Vietnam depleted U.S. military capabilities in other parts of the world, he urged the president to mobilize American reserve forces. In February 1968, after the *Tet Offensive, Wheeler extracted from Gen. William C. *Westmoreland, the U.S. military commander in Vietnam, a request for some 200,000 additional ground troops to be gained by mobilizing reserve forces. However, Wheeler intended to use most of these troops to reconstitute a general reserve in the United States. His request was not approved and, together with the Tet offensive and shifts in U.S. public opinion, resulted finally in President Johnson's decision to de-escalate the war.

After the election of President Richard M. *Nixon, Wheeler oversaw the implementation of the "Vietnamization" program, whereby South Vietnamese forces assumed increasing responsibility for the war as U.S. forces were withdrawn. He retired from the army in July 1970 and died in 1975.

[*See also* Army Reserves and National Guard; Mobilization; Vietnam War.]

• Herbert Y. Schandler, *The Unmaking of a President: Lyndon Johnson and Vietnam*, 1977. Mark Perry, *Four Stars*, 1989.

—Herbert Y. Schandler

The **WHISKEY REBELLION** (1794) originated in a dispute over the role of taxation in the United States. Many citizens of the new republic assumed that the *Revolutionary War meant they would never be made to pay direct taxes to support a distant government. But Washington's secretary of the treasury, Alexander *Hamilton, wanted to tax Americans to help finance the national debt and to support a relatively large national government. Hamilton's plan to override the parochialism of local authorities and to make the United States stable and prosperous prevailed in Congress, which passed an act (3 March 1791) creating an excise tax on spirits distilled in the United States. Opposition to the act was widespread, but centered in western Pennsylvania, where local politicians denounced the tax and citizens attacked it in public meetings. Opponents tarred and feathered tax collectors and their collaborators, including distillers who cooperated with federal officials.

In the summer of 1794, mounting tensions exploded. On 16 July, some 500 men attacked the home of Gen. John Neville, local inspector of the excise in Allegheny County. Neville and his household mounted a defense with the aid of a few regular soldiers, killing two men and wounding six

others. When Neville and his men escaped, the attackers looted and burned his house. Emboldened, the insurgents called a meeting at Braddock's Field, southeast of Pittsburgh, for 1 August. Approximately 6,000 men attended. But after two days of talking about further resistance, they dispersed.

President George *Washington refused to tolerate the escalating defiance of federal authority. On 7 August, he announced that he was calling out the militia to restore order and enforce the law. At the same time, he sent commissioners to western Pennsylvania to offer amnesty to the insurgents in return for oaths of submission to the United States. When that strategy failed, the president, on 25 September, ordered 12,950 militia and volunteers from Pennsylvania, New Jersey, and Maryland to march to Pittsburgh. They arrested a handful of insurgents. Two were convicted of treason, but Washington later pardoned them. Many of the leaders simply fled.

If the Whiskey Rebellion had little military significance, its political importance was tremendous. It demonstrated the willingness of federal officials to use the potentially enormous power of the national government to enforce national law. Coupled with the American victory over the Indians of the Old Northwest in August 1794, the suppression of the Whiskey Rebellion marked the emergence of the national government as a significant presence west of the Appalachians. On the other hand, the rebellion showed the depth of American citizens' hostility to central government intent upon taxing them and regulating their lives. This hostility was part of the more peaceful political rebellion that climaxed in the 1800 election of Thomas *Jefferson as president. Under Jefferson, Congress repealed the Whiskey Tax.

[*See also* Commander in Chief, President as; Militia and National Guard.]

• Thomas P. Slaughter, *The Whiskey Rebellion, Frontier Epilogue to the American Revolution*, 1986. Stanley Elkins and Eric McKitrick, *The Age of Federalism: The Early American Republic, 1788–1800*, 1993.

—Andrew R. L. Cayton

WHITNEY, ELI (1765–1825), inventor and firearms manufacturer. In debt from futile litigation against piracy of his cotton-gin patent, this Massachusetts-born Yale alumnus (class of 1792) obtained a federal contract in 1798 to make 10,000 military muskets. Unhampered by gunsmithing experience, Whitney built a water-powered factory in Hamden, Connecticut, where he devised production methods later adopted into "armory practice." His initially unskilled workers used specialized jigs and fixtures to shape ostensibly uniform gun parts before fitting them together for shipment to the Springfield Armory.

Declining an offer in 1806 to head the Harpers Ferry Armory, Whitney continued to receive contract extensions despite production delays, for his persuasively expressed plan agreed with the desire of French-influenced ordnance officers to standardize weapons. Meeting with Whitney in 1815, they established interchangeability of parts as the goal for military musket production. That required coordination of effort among Springfield, Harpers Ferry, and contractors by a system of inspection and production gauges, which did not operate effectively until the late 1840s. Despite Whitney's fame, his muskets, like others of his era, lacked interchangeable parts.

[*See also* Musket, Rifled.]

• Constance McLaughlin Green, *Eli Whitney and the Birth of American Technology*, 1956. Merritt Roe Smith, "Army Ordnance and the 'American system' of Manufacturing, 1815–1861," in Merritt Roe Smith, ed., *Military Enterprise and Technological Change*, 1985.

—Carolyn C. Cooper

WILDERNESS, BATTLE OF THE (1864). The Battle of the Wilderness, fought on 5 and 6 May 1864, was the first Civil War confrontation between Lt. Gen. Ulysses S. *Grant and Gen. Robert E. *Lee. Now heading the Union war effort, Grant sought to destroy Lee's Army of Northern Virginia, which numbered about 65,000 soldiers and occupied strong earthworks below the Rapidan River. Grant planned to send Maj. Gen. George Gordon *Meade's Army of the Potomac, supplemented by Maj. Gen. Ambrose *Burnside's 9th Corps, directly against Lee, while Maj. Gen. Benjamin F. *Butler's Army of the James advanced up the James River into Richmond, and another army under Maj. Gen. Franz Sigel threatened Lee's western flank. Hampered by shortages in food, horses, and supplies, Lee decided to bide his time and strike Grant when he crossed the Rapidan.

At midnight on 3–4 May, Grant's main force of 120,000 began moving around Lee's eastern flank, crossing the Rapidan at two fords and camping in the forested Wilderness of Spotsylvania. Lee reacted by dividing his army, already outnumbered two to one, and thrusting Lt. Gen. Richard Stoddert *Ewell's 2nd Corps east toward Grant along Orange Turnpike and Lt. Gen. A. P. *Hill's 3rd Corps east along Orange Plank Road. Lee's purpose was to pin Grant in place with Ewell and Hill, then swing his 1st Corps under Lt. Gen. James *Longstreet into Grant's southern flank. The scheme entailed risk, but Lee counted on the Wilderness's dense underbrush to offset Grant's considerable advantage in troops and weaponry.

Early on 5 May, Ewell deployed along the western edge of a clearing named Saunders' field. Meade ordered Maj. Gen. Gouverneur K. Warren's 5th Corps to attack immediately, but the troops were unable to form in the woods until early afternoon. Well entrenched, Ewell repulsed first Warren's 5th Corps, then Maj. Gen. John Sedgwick's 6th Corps. Hill's Confederates meanwhile advanced along Orange Plank Road, but were stopped at the Brock Road intersection by a detachment under Brig. Gen. George W. Getty. Hill constructed a defensive line a few hundred yards west of Brock Road. Late in the afternoon, Getty and Maj. Gen. Winfield S. Hancock's 2nd Corps attacked. With only two divisions, Hill fought a stubborn defensive action against overwhelming odds and was saved by the arrival of night.

Grant now rearranged his army to concentrate overwhelming numbers against Hill. Hancock, augmented by Getty, was to attack Hill frontally, while four brigades under Brig. Gen. James S. Wadsworth slammed Hill's northern flank. Warren and Sedgwick meanwhile were to keep Ewell occupied, and Burnside was to march between Ewell and Hill and attack Hill's rear. Recognizing Hill's perilous situation, Lee ordered Longstreet to abandon his flanking movement and hurry to relieve Hill. Lee assumed that Longstreet would arrive before daylight and so permitted Hill's tired men to rest without repairing their lines.

Early on 6 May, however, before Longstreet's troops arrived, Hancock and Wadsworth overwhelmed Hill and

poured into Widow Tapp's field, where Lee had his headquarters. At the last moment, Longstreet's Confederates reached the clearing. "Lee to the rear!" they shouted, refusing to advance until Lee retired to safety. Saving the day for the Confederates, Longstreet first repulsed Hancock, then launched a surprise attack against the southern Union flank from an unfinished railroad gradient. Longstreet was accidentally wounded by his soldiers, and the Confederate offensive ground to a halt.

Ever aggressive, Lee once again attacked Hancock, who had entrenched along Brock Road. A portion of Hancock's works ignited, and Southerners poured through the breach, only to be driven back by well-placed Union artillery. Fighting sputtered to a close around 6:00 P.M. Shortly before dark, Confederate Brig. Gen. John B. Gordon assaulted the northern end of Grant's line and overran a portion of Sedgwick's corps. Darkness ended the attack.

Lee had fought Grant to impasse and occupied a strong position along high ground. Instead of renewing his attacks, Grant decided to try to maneuver Lee onto more favorable terrain. After dark, Grant started south toward the crossroads hamlet of Spotsylvania Courthouse, intending to interpose between Lee and Richmond.

During the two-day battle, Grant took approximately 18,000 *casualties, Lee 11,000. Neither could claim victory. Grant had suffered a tactical defeat, but he persisted in his strategic goal of attempting to destroy Lee's army, exhibiting a measure of tenacity previously unknown in the east. For his part, Lee had thwarted a well-provisioned force twice as large as his own, but his grievous loss in men had gutted his offensive capacity. Henceforth, the Army of Northern Virginia would fight defensively. The *Wilderness to Petersburg Campaign, which began with the Battle of the Wilderness, would last five weeks and include the bloody battles of Spotsylvania Courthouse and Cold Harbor.

[*See also* Civil War: Military and Diplomatic Course; Confederate Army; Union Army.]

• Andrew A. Humphreys, *The Virginia Campaign of '64 and '65*, 1883. Morris Schaff, *The Battle of the Wilderness*, 1910. Edward Steere, *The Wilderness Campaign*, 1960. Gordon C. Rhea, *The Battle of the Wilderness: May 5–6, 1864*, 1994.

—Gordon C. Rhea

WILDERNESS TO PETERSBURG CAMPAIGN (1864). On 4 May 1864, Lt. Gen. Ulysses S. *Grant initiated a campaign with the Union's Army of the Potomac to defeat Gen. Robert E. *Lee and the Confederate's Army of Northern Virginia. For forty days, Grant hammered and maneuvered. Lee deftly fended off Grant's force, which was double his own. The series of battles, from the Battle of the *Wilderness to the siege of *Petersburg, was called the "Overland Campaign" to distinguish it from Maj. Gen. George B. *McClellan's Peninsular Campaign (*Seven Days' Battle), in 1862, which had involved an approach by water. The Overland Campaign cost 60,000 Union *casualties and perhaps 35,000 Confederate losses. Strategically, it was a Union success, ending in June with Lee's army backed against Petersburg and Richmond, unable to maneuver.

Grant began by crossing the Rapidan River west of Lee and stopping for the night in the timbered Wilderness near Spotsylvania, Virginia. On 5 May, Lee surprised Grant in the Wilderness and fought him to impasse in a bloody two-day battle costing 18,000 Federal and 11,000 Confederate casualties. Undeterred, Grant swung southeast, hoping to interpose between Lee and Richmond and draw the Confederates out of the Wilderness. While J. E. B. *Stuart's cavalry delayed Grant's progress, a portion of the *Confederate army beat Grant to Spotsylvania Court House.

The Confederates constructed a formidable line of earthworks above the hamlet. On 8 May, the Battle of Spotsylvania Court House began when Grant battered Lee's left wing at Laurel Hill. On 10 May, he attacked Lee's flank on the Po River and orchestrated a massive assault against the entire entrenched Confederate line. None of these efforts succeeded. On 12 May, Grant assailed a bulge in Lee's formation known as "the Mule Shoe" and broke through, but the Confederates rallied and repulsed the attackers. For twenty-two hours, fearsome combat raged unabated at a bend in the Confederate earthworks called the "Bloody Angle."

Lee constructed a new line across the base of the Mule Shoe. For several days, the Union forces probed for weak points. Following a bloody repulse by Confederate artillery on 18 May, Grant gave up trying to overrun Lee's earthworks and once again swung east and south. Lee countered by deploying his army into an inverted "V" below the North Anna River, its tip resting on the river. Grant crossed the stream in pursuit, only to find that Lee's V had divided his army. Sickness left Lee too debilitated to exploit his ingenious trap.

On 26 May, Grant circled southeast across the Pamunkey River and advanced toward Richmond. Lee parried by drawing a strong line along Totopotomoy Creek. 30 May, Lee attacked part of Grant's army near Bethesda Church, and on 1 June, the armies clashed in the Battle of Cold Harbor. Both sides rushed in reinforcements, and on the morning of 3 June, Grant launched a concerted assault to break Lee's line. The frontal attack across open land against entrenched positions was repulsed with 12,000 Union soldiers killed or wounded. Thwarted in his frontal attacks, Grant again resorted to maneuver. On 12–14 June, he marched to the James River and crossed his army on ferries and a pontoon bridge, heading for Petersburg, the railroad center serving Richmond.

[See also Civil War: Military and Diplomatic Course.]

• Edward Steeve, *The Wilderness Campaign*, 1960. Gordon C. Rhea, *The Battle of the Wilderness: May 5–6, 1864*, 1994. Gordon C. Rhea, *The Battles for Spotsylvania Courthouse and the Road to Yellow Tavern, May 7–12, 1864*, 1998.   —Gordon C. Rhea

WILHELM II (1859–1941), grandson of Wilhelm I, was the last German kaiser, 1888–1918. He dismissed Bismarck as chancellor and took a dominant role in making Germany a world power, enlarging its army, navy, and empire. His belligerent policy provoked brushes with U.S. naval forces at Samoa (1889) and Manila (1898), and he authorized naval contingency plans for *blockades of the U.S. coast and assaults in the Caribbean.

Wilhelm had little accurate knowledge of the United States when he authorized the German Navy during World War I to begin unrestricted submarine warfare in February 1917. By so doing, this insecure and garrulous narcissist brought America into the war against Germany, tipping the perilous balance against his country.

Although considered one of the dominant players on the world stage in 1913, from 14 August 1914—when he told the German High Command that it was their job to run the war, not his—until approximately 1967, Wilhelm II's importance in world affairs was downplayed. Recent historiography, however, has reestablished him as a key player in his era. He died in exile in the Netherlands.

[See also World War I: Causes; World War I: Military and Diplomatic Course: World War I: Changing Interpretations.]

• Arden Bucholz, *Moltke, Schlieffen and Prussian War Planning*, 1991. Thomas Kohut, *Wilhelm II and the Germans*, 1991.
                  —Arden Bucholz

WILPF. *See* Women's International League for Peace and Freedom.

WILSON, CHARLES E. (1890–1961), industrialist and secretary of defense. Wilson received an engineering degree in 1909 at Carnegie Tech University. A distinguished career in industry led to his appointment as vice president of General Motors (GM) in 1928 and president in 1941. During World War II, Wilson directed GM's outstanding performance in producing *tanks, aircraft engines, trucks, and munitions.

President Dwight D. *Eisenhower selected Wilson as his secretary of defense in 1953, and he remained in office for almost five years. Since the president formulated national defense policy, Wilson's principal responsibility was managing the Department of *Defense.

Wilson's years in office were troubled ones. The outspoken secretary of defense made a habit of needlessly offending others. During his Senate confirmation hearings in January 1953, for example, a beleaguered Wilson insisted that his heavy stockholding in GM could constitute *no* conflict of interests "because for years I thought that what was good for our country was good for General Motors and vice versa." More important, he was indecisive and failed to grow in his job. As a result, the services squabbled among themselves, and Wilson expected the White House to provide him with both general guidelines and assistance in resolving technical matters. Finally, while knowing little about foreign affairs or strategic doctrine, Wilson acted as chief spokesman for the administration's "New Look" defense policies, which emphasized airpower and *nuclear weapons over conventional forces. This strategy came under severe attack from within and outside Congress, and from the armed services—particularly the army. Critics charged that the nation was no longer able flexibly to meet its strategic obligations.

Under Wilson, military budgets declined by over 10 percent. These cuts stemmed from Eisenhower's desire to protect the civilian economy and curb the growth of a *military-industrial complex, goals shared by Wilson. However, reduced military spending was complicated by the administration's strident anticommunism, which led to growing commitments abroad—commitments the administration proposed to meet through policies labeled "brinkmanship" and "massive retaliation."

Wilson was in part a victim of circumstances beyond his control. Effectively managing the Defense Department without having a voice in strategic doctrine was nearly impossible. Moreover, justifying military cutbacks would have been easier had the administration seized various opportunities to reduce Cold War tensions.

[*See also* Cold War; Commander in Chief, President as; Flexible Response.]

• Douglas Kinnard, *President Eisenhower and Strategy Management*, 1977. E. Bruce Geelhoed, *Charles E. Wilson and Controversy at the Pentagon, 1953 to 1957*, 1979.   —Paul A. C. Koistinen

WILSON, WOODROW (1856–1924), scholar, president of Princeton University, governor of New Jersey, twenty-eighth president of the United States. The son of a Presbyterian minister, Wilson was born in Staunton, Virginia, grew up in Georgia and South Carolina, graduated from Princeton University, attended the University of Virginia law school, and earned a Ph.D. in history and political science from the Johns Hopkins University (1885). He was a professor at Bryn Mawr College and Wesleyan and Princeton universities, and in 1902 he became president of Princeton, serving until 1910, when he was elected governor of New Jersey. In 1912, he secured the Democratic nomination for the presidency, was elected, and served two terms.

As president, Wilson was often accused by his political enemies of being cowardly and pacifistic, but he used armed force in support of diplomatic goals seven times between April 1914 and November 1918—more often than any other president. Most historians recognize that he had a sophisticated understanding of the value and limitations of force in international relations, and that he was an effective commander in chief.

Wilson thought that the United States must take an active part in promoting the worldwide spread of democratic ideals, international law, and the cooperation of peaceloving nations. He preferred to achieve these goals through diplomacy and moral persuasion, but he did not shrink from the use of military force. He believed that the president must absolutely control foreign policy, including the decision to use or refrain from using armed force, but he also believed that policymakers should not meddle in military operations once they had begun, just as military commanders should not dictate policy.

Wilson's first uses of force were in Latin America, a region traditionally viewed by the United States as within its sphere of influence. In April 1914, he authorized the occupation of Veracruz, Mexico, to avenge an insult to some American sailors and to pressure the Mexican dictator into resigning. He refused to allow the expansion of intervention beyond this one city, however, and relied mainly on negotiations to achieve his aims. Two years later, he authorized a punitive expedition into Mexico in search of border raiders but again entrusted his main objective—restraining the Mexican Revolution—to negotiators rather than soldiers. Other U.S. military involvement, in *Haiti in 1914 and the *Dominican Republic in 1915, was limited to the minimum force necessary to establish order while American occupiers tried to develop local support for democratic self-government.

When World War I began in August 1914, Wilson at first shared the feeling of most Americans that *neutrality was the proper policy for the United States. He also hoped, by keeping America neutral, to have an opportunity to mediate the conflict. He opposed expansion of the army and navy and employed his diplomatic skills to maximize American trade. In 1915 and 1916, he sent his friend Edward M. House to Europe to promote peace talks.

The beginning of German submarine warfare early in 1915 undermined the president's optimism, and that autumn he came out for enlarging the army and navy. In May 1916, he suggested that the United States might join a postwar association of nations dedicated to collective security. That autumn, after his reelection, he launched a new peace effort in Europe, and upon its failure, proposed his own peace terms in the "Peace Without Victory" speech on 22 January 1917. This initiative also failed when the Germans announced unrestricted submarine warfare.

Wilson severed diplomatic relations with Germany on 3 February 1917, but before seeking a declaration of war he first explored armed neutrality. On 2 April, he at last asked Congress for a declaration of war on Germany, justifying the request as a defense of neutral rights and, more important, as an opportunity for the United States to defeat autocracy and mold a peace based on democracy and collective security.

After Congress declared war on 6 April, Wilson named Gen. John J. *Pershing commander of the *American Expeditionary Force to be sent to France, and gave him full authority to decide when, where, and how American troops were to be used. Likewise, the president gave his full backing to the plans of Adm. William S. *Sims to concentrate virtually the whole naval effort on developing a convoy system to defeat the German submarine threat. To coordinate U.S. military policy with that of the British and French, he appointed Edward House and the retiring chief of staff of the army, Gen. Tasker H. Bliss, to sit on a permanent inter-Allied conference. House and Bliss understood that their role was to smooth differences with the Allies and to give U.S. military commanders maximum freedom within the coalition.

In April 1917, German leaders were confident that American armies would arrive too late to affect the outcome of the conflict. They were wrong. Within a year the United States had mobilized and transported a large army of fresh troops to Europe in time to help deal the decisive blow. That achievement was partly a testimony to Wilson's decision to let his commanders do their jobs without political interference, but even more it was proof of the enormous productivity of the American economy.

Wilson was keenly aware that *victory in the war depended upon the maintenance of solidarity among the Allies. To promote unity, he agreed to the creation of an Inter-Allied Supreme War Council to coordinate military policy, and to the appointment of French Gen. Ferdinand Foch as supreme military commander over all Allied forces. He also agreed to allow expeditions of American soldiers to take part in Allied forces that landed at Murmansk, Archangel, and Vladivostok. At first, they were intended to help keep Russia in the war, then to protect Allied military supplies from German seizure after the Bolsheviks made a separate peace with Germany, and to support the withdrawal of Czech prisoners of war for assignment to the western front. Although hostile to the Bolsheviks, Wilson was skeptical of this intervention because he believed it would arouse Russian hostility. He eventually yielded to maintain Allied solidarity and to restrain the ambitions of the other Allies, who seemed interested in territory (Japan) or counterrevolution (Britain and France).

By October 1918, German leaders realized that they had catastrophically underestimated the importance of American intervention. Faced with imminent defeat, they suggested to President Wilson an armistice on the basis of his "*Fourteen Points" speech of 8 January 1918. Wilson used the German overture to force the Allies and General Pershing to agree that the Fourteen Points would be the basis for a cease-fire and the starting point for negotiation of the peace treaty. Thus by November 1918, when the armistice was signed, it appeared that Wilson had been remarkably successful in using American military power not only to force his peace program on the enemy but to impose it on the Allies as well. Only later, after the guns fell silent, would many of his hard-won gains slip away.

Wilson led the American delegation to the peace talks in Paris in the spring of 1919 and submitted the resulting Treaty of *Versailles to the U.S. Senate in July. But the Senate rejected it, and the president, crippled by a stroke that October, served out the last years of his term an embittered invalid isolated in the White House.

[See also Caribbean and Latin America, U.S. Military Involvement in the; Commander in Chief, President as; Mexican Revolution, U.S. Military Involvement in the; World War I: Military and Diplomatic Course; World War I: Postwar Impact.]

• Arthur S. Link, Wilson, 5 vols., 1947–65. Robert H. Ferrell, Woodrow Wilson and World War I, 1917–1921, 1985. Frederick S. Calhoun, Power and Principle: Armed Intervention in Wilsonian Foreign Policy, 1986. Arthur S. Link and John Whiteclay Chambers II, "Woodrow Wilson as Commander in Chief," in The United States Military Under the Constitution of the United States, 1789–1989, ed. Richard H. Kohn, 1991. Thomas J. Knock, To End All Wars: Woodrow Wilson and the Quest for a New World Order, 1992. Kendrick A. Clements, The Presidency of Woodrow Wilson, 1992.

—Kendrick A. Clements

WOMEN IN THE MILITARY. The role of women in the U.S. military has changed significantly over the last 200 years, but the greatest change has come since the initiation of the *All-Volunteer Force in 1973. Throughout American history, the expansion of women's roles has come about when the military faced a shortage of male recruits, usually in times of war. Historically, women's participation has occurred mainly in medical and administrative support positions, thus releasing male soldiers from desk jobs to fight in combat. However, the excellent performance of women in support roles in combat zones during the 1980s and 1990s spurred extensive public debates about opening combat positions to women and about women's duties and rights as citizens. This debate focused attention specifically on the contribution women soldiers have made to military readiness and efficiency, rather than simply on the older notion that a woman's military role was to free up men to fight.

From the *Revolutionary War to the present day, women have served in the armed forces. Until World War I, however, their roles—as laundresses or nurses, for example—were generally informal and seldom institutionalized. A handful of women disguised themselves as men and fought alongside male soldiers in the eighteenth and nineteenth centuries. In World War I, 21,000 women served in the U.S. Army and Navy *Nurse Corps, and another 13,000 volunteered for clerical positions in the U.S. Navy and Marine Corps. All except the nurses held a quasi-military status and were discharged from active duty immediately after the war ended. At the outbreak of World War II, the shortage of military personnel led to the first large-scale recruitment of women and the formation of the women's auxiliary military branches. During that war, more than 350,000 women served primarily in the medical and administrative fields, although the services also employed women as pilots, mechanics, truck drivers, gunnery instructors, and electricians. Women were not used in combat roles, but rather to fill support positions and thus release male soldiers for combat.

The end of World War II brought the *demobilization of large numbers of servicemen and -women and a corresponding diminution in women's roles. In 1948, Congress passed the Women's Armed Services Integration Act, which provided the first ever legal basis for and legal limits to a permanent role for women in the military. Allowing for women to hold full military rank and privilege, the 1948 act also placed caps on women's enlistment and promotion, and excluded them from combat service. Women were not to exceed 2 percent of active duty personnel in each service and could not be promoted beyond lieutenant-colonel or commander. The combat exclusion requirement remained more or less in effect into the late 1990s (aside from exceptions in the early 1990s for female pilots), but the enlistment and promotion ceilings were repealed in 1967, when the Department of *Defense again needed to ease a recruitment deficit at the height of the unpopular *Vietnam War. Coinciding with the expanding role of women in the labor force and calls for equal rights more broadly, women's participation in the services grew gradually over the next few years (in 1971, 1.6% of active duty personnel were women; in 1976, 5%), and the first women were promoted to general officers in 1970.

When the end of U.S. involvement in Southeast Asia resulted in the elimination of the draft in 1973 and the initiation of the All-Volunteer Force, the military began planning how to recruit more women to compensate for expected shortages of qualified male volunteers. Congressional passage of the Equal Rights Amendment (1972), as well as a number of court rulings in favor of equal treatment across gender lines in the services, led to changes in personnel policies that allowed women to command units composed of both men and women; eliminated rules that required the automatic discharge of pregnant women soldiers; ended segregated training of male and female recruits; and equalized dependents' entitlements for married servicewomen and servicemen. In 1973, the first women naval aviators earned their wings (followed by women pilots in the army in 1974 and air force in 1977). In 1976, the first women cadets were admitted to service academies; in 1978, President Jimmy *Carter signed a new law allowing navy women to be assigned to sea duty aboard noncombat ships.

During the 1990s, women participated in all major military deployments of U.S. forces, and some combat specialties opened up to them. In 1989, 800 women soldiers served among the 18,400 U.S. troops sent to Panama for Operation Just Cause. From August 1990 to February 1991, 41,000 military women were deployed to the Persian Gulf for Operations Desert Shield and Desert Storm. In the *Persian Gulf War, women constituted 7 percent of all U.S. military personnel deployed; 13 U.S. women were among the 375 U.S. soldiers who died, and 2 women were captured and held as prisoners of war. In April 1993, Air Force 1st Lt. Jeannie Flynn was the first woman to complete a combat training course to fly advanced *fighter aircraft.

By 1996, 197,693 women were serving in the armed forces, constituting 13.4 percent of all active duty personnel. At the junior officer levels, women were represented relatively proportional to their numbers in the services. However, there remained a "glass ceiling" inhibiting promotion at the senior levels. In 1996, no women held three- or four-star rank, and only 2 of the 277 two-star officers and 14 of the 430 one-star officers were women.

Media coverage in the 1990s led to increased public debate about the role of women in the armed forces. In arguing for equal treatment of all individuals in the military, some senior women military officers and liberal feminists, including Congresswoman Pat *Schroeder of the Armed Services Committee, have pressed for opening combat roles to women as part of a larger program to give women full citizenship rights and responsibilities. Furthermore, women's advocates note that combat exclusion reinforces the glass ceiling that blocks promotion to the most senior ranks in a system that favors combat experience over support roles as a condition for advancement. Those opposing women's assignment to combat roles argue that *combat effectiveness will be compromised because men will be more likely to defend their female colleagues than to destroy the enemy; that unit cohesion might be undercut by tensions between the sexes; and that the problem of pregnancy makes women soldiers not deployable in times of emergency. Some observers have suggested that the line between combat and noncombat roles will become increasingly arbitrary as support functions put women in the line of fire (as in the Persian Gulf) and as the armed forces prepare to fight noninfantry, high-technology wars.

The issue of *sexual harassment has caught public attention in recent years. Starting with the 1991 Tailhook Conference, at which at least 83 women were assaulted by drunken male navy fighter pilots, harassment scandals have rocked the services. In 1997, a number of female soldiers at the Aberdeen Proving Ground in Maryland alleged that their army drill instructors harassed them during their training. Subsequently, a sexual harassment hotline set up to field anonymous calls from women in the armed forces yielded hundreds of reports of abuse of rank and privilege by senior male noncommissioned officers and commissioned officers. The sexual harassment issue remains controversial as the armed forces attempt to establish fair procedures to adjudicate complaints in organizational environments hostile to change.

[See also Families, Military; Gender: Female Identity and the Military; Gender and War; SPARS; WAC; WAVES.]

• Jeanne Holm, Women in the Military: An Unfinished Revolution, 1982; rev. ed. 1992. Presidential Commission on the Assignment of Women in the Armed Forces, Report to the President, 1992. Martin Binkin, Who Will Fight the Next War? The Changing Face of the American Military, 1993. Ruth H. Howes and Michael R. Stevenson, eds., Women and the Use of Military Force, 1993. Laura Miller, Feminism and the Exclusion of Army Women from Combat, 1995. Richard D. Fisher, et al., Keeping America Safe and Strong: Keeping the Armed Forces Focused on the Military Mission, 1996. Office of the Secretary of Defense, Department of Defense Selected Manpower Statistics, Fiscal Year 1996, 1996.   —Mary P. Callahan

The **WOMEN'S INTERNATIONAL LEAGUE FOR PEACE AND FREEDOM** (WILPF) was founded in Geneva, Switzerland, in 1919, an outgrowth of the International Committee of Women for Permanent Peace, formed at the Hague during World War I. Composed primarily of white, educated, middle-class women, the U.S. Section began as the Woman's Peace Party, organized by the social worker Jane *Addams in 1915. Still functioning with international headquarters in Geneva, the WILPF has branches in countries across the globe.

With a peak membership of approximately 16,000 in the mid-1930s, the U.S. Section was an active and influential organization in the American peace movement between the two world wars. This was due largely to the astute leadership of first president Addams, as well as that of the former Wellesley economics professor Emily Greene *Balch and the Quaker activist Hannah Clothier Hull, and the administrative talents of executive secretary Dorothy Detzer and organization secretary Mildred Scott Olmsted. Addams and Balch were awarded the Nobel Peace Prize (1931 and 1946, respectively), the only American women so far to be so honored.

Only a minority of WILPF antiwar activists were absolute pacifists, but all were committed to a world that repudiated *aggression and violence as a way of resolving disputes among nations. Erroneously accused by critics of *isolationism, the interwar WILPF endorsed all cooperative endeavors internationally that did not involve war or preparation for war. It supported disarmament, consultative pacts, arbitration, and the World Court, and advocated aid to Jewish and other victims of Nazi persecution, but opposed U.S. involvement in World War II.

After 1945, the U.S. Section became alarmed by the *Cold War, with its escalating *arms race and *nuclear weapons proliferation. Now led by Olmsted, the WILPF opposed American involvement in the *Korean War and the *Vietnam War; continued its longtime support of equal rights for women as well as for ethnic and racial minorities; and protested American low-intensity warfare in Asia, Africa, and Latin America.

[See also Nonviolence; Pacifism; Peace and Antiwar Movements; Quakers.]

• Harriet Hyman Alonso, Peace as a Women's Issue: A History of the U.S. Movement for World Peace and Women's Rights, 1991. Margaret Hope Bacon, One Woman's Passion for Peace and Freedom: The Life of Mildred Scott Olmsted, 1993. Carrie Foster, The Women and the Warriors: The U.S. Section of the Women's International League for Peace and Freedom, 1915–1946, 1995.   —Carrie Foster

WOOD, LEONARD (1860–1927), army officer and colonial administrator. Educated at Harvard and Harvard Medical School, Wood joined the army as a contract surgeon in 1885. Although he entered the line in 1898 as the colonel in command of his friend Theodore *Roosevelt's First U.S. Volunteer Cavalry (the "Rough Riders"), Wood was considered an outsider by most career officers. Remaining in Cuba after the *Spanish-American War, Wood, as a brigadier general, was appointed military governor and implemented a program of wide-ranging progressive reforms. Later, in the Philippines, as governor of the Moro province, he directed the bloody campaign to pacify the Moros. In 1910, President William H. Taft appointed Major General Wood army chief of staff.

Wood sought to modernize the U.S. Army. As chief of staff (1910–14), he worked to break the authority of the War Department bureau system, to reform the General Staff, and to reorganize the field army. He also encouraged the formation of the Army League, a supportive group of business, foreign policy, and education elites. After war broke out in Europe in 1914, Wood became, with former President Theodore Roosevelt, one of the chief architects of the "Preparedness" movement, advocating compulsory, short-term military training for all able-bodied young men, as well as reserve officer training to prepare a mass reserve army. Wood's highly visible role in the controversial Republican-led campaign to drum up popular support for military preparedness did little to endear him to Democratic president Woodrow *Wilson. Established as a partisan figure, the army's senior general spent the period of U.S. involvement training recruits in Kansas.

Resentment at having been denied command in France during World War I pushed Wood further into politics. Afterward, he claimed Roosevelt's mantle as leader of the Republican Party's progressive wing, yet also ran a "law and order" campaign for the presidential nomination in 1920 while on active duty. The convention chose Senator Warren Harding, who after election sent Wood to the Philippines as governor general, a position that he held until his death from a brain tumor.

Wood's restless energy and monumental ambition made him an innovator who adapted the progressive spirit of the age to military affairs. He was also a maverick, ruthlessly attacking anything that thwarted his ambitions, and exempting himself from traditional strictures excluding professional soldiers from politics.

[See also Army, U.S.: 1900–41; Philippine War.]

• Hermann Hagedorn, *Leonard Wood: A Biography*, 2 vols., 1931. Jack C. Lane, *Armed Progressive: General Leonard Wood*, 1978.

—Andrew J. Bacevich

WOOLMAN, JOHN (1720–1772), American Quaker and reformer. Born near Mt. Holly, New Jersey, Woolman traveled as a minister through the colonies and England. Best known for his *Journal* and for his antislavery efforts, he became involved in peace issues during the *French and Indian War, becoming a war tax refuser, and joining others in 1755 in signing "An Epistle of Tender Love and Caution." In 1759, he wrote a second letter, sometimes called the "Pacifist Epistle." In response to the draft, Woolman emphasized principled objection, decrying objectors who merely "pretend scruple of conscience." He did not refuse to quarter soldiers, but would not accept pay, explaining that he acted "in passive obedience to authority." During the frontier violence after the war, he visited the Indians at Wyalusing, Pennsylvania, "to feel and understand the spirit they live in" and to promote peaceful relations. His essay "A Plea for the Poor" shows unusual insights into the causes of war, urging people to look at their possessions and "try whether the seeds of war have any nourishment in them."

[See also Conscientious Objection; Nonviolence; Pacifism; Quakers.]

• Edwin H. Cady, *John Woolman*, 1965. Phiilips P. Moulton, *The Journal and Major Essays of John Woolman*, 1971.

—Sterling P. Olmsted

WORLD BANK (est. 1944). At the July 1944 Bretton Woods Conference in Bretton Woods, New Hampshire, forty-four nations, including the United States, Great Britain, and the Soviet Union, agreed to establish the International Monetary Fund (IMF) and the International Bank for Reconstruction and Development (IBRD, but called the World Bank) to provide loans to governments for postwar economic reconstruction. The IBRD officially came into existence on 27 December 1945, when states holding 65 percent of the bank's shares approved the agreement. The bank's headquarters are in Washington, D.C. Each of the 179 member states has one representative on the board of governors. Each state's voting power, however, depends on the number of bank shares held by the state. The United States as the single largest investor currently holds 16.53 percent of the shares.

The World Bank's membership and objectives were affected by the *Cold War. The Soviet Union never joined the bank; post–Soviet Russia, however, became a member on 1 June 1992. In 1948–52, the European Recovery Program—the *Marshall Plan—superseded the IBRD as the primary reconstruction aid provider for Western Europe. The bank's main objective became making or guaranteeing loans to developing states. Since the early 1990s, aid to Eastern European countries, including member states of the former Soviet Union, has become an increasingly important aspect of the bank's work. In January 1996, the IBRD granted Bosnia a $150 million loan to aid rebuilding after the end of its civil war.

From its inception to 30 June 1998, the World Bank has granted 7,112 loans to 168 recipients, totaling $425 billion. African states received 18 percent of that amount, Asian and Pacific countries 42 percent, Near Eastern states 3 percent, European countries (including Russia) 12 percent, and Latin American and Caribbean states 25 percent.

[See also Bosnian Crisis.]

• Robert W. Oliver, *International Economic Cooperation and the World Bank*, 1975. Michael D. Bordon and Barry Eichengreen, eds., *A Retrospective on the Bretton Woods System*, 1993.

—Georg Schild

WORLD WAR I (1914–18)

Causes
Causes of U.S. Entry
Military and Diplomatic Course
Domestic Course
Postwar Impact
Changing Interpretations

WORLD WAR I (1914–18): CAUSES

Although the United States did not enter World War I until 1917, the outbreak of that war in 1914, and its underlying causes and consequences, deeply and immediately affected America's position both at home and abroad. In the debate on *neutrality and later on peace aims, much was made of European secret diplomacy, which was rejected on the U.S. side of the Atlantic, of militarism and the escalating arms race before 1914, and of the impact of colonialism. Undoubtedly, all these factors contributed to the origins of the European catastrophe, but they do not explain why the war broke out when it did. This question can only be answered more precisely by looking at the political and military decision-making processes in the last months, weeks, and days of peace in 1914.

After decades of debate about whether Europe "slithered over the brink" (David Lloyd George's phrase) owing to general crisis mismanagement among all participant nations or because of the actions of a clearly identifiable group of people, the overwhelming majority consensus has emerged among historians that the primary responsibility rests in Berlin and Vienna, and secondarily perhaps on St. Petersburg. Judging from the documents, it has become clear that the German kaiser and his advisers encouraged Vienna to settle accounts with Serbia following the assassinations of the heir to the Austro-Hungarian throne, Archduke Ferdinand, and his wife at Sarajevo in Bosnia-Herzegovina on 28 June 1914.

By issuing a "blank check" to Austria-Hungary on 5 July 1914, the German government took the first step in escalating a crisis that involved the risk of a world war among the great powers. This risk was high not only because these powers had been arming over the previous years, but also because they had regrouped into two large camps: the Triple Alliance (Germany, Austria-Hungary, Italy) and the Triple Entente (Britain, France, Russia). And when, after various diplomatic maneuvers, it became clear toward the end of July that such a world war might indeed be imminent, Berlin refused to deescalate although the decision makers were in the best position to do so.

The Czarist government, as Serbia's protector, also had a role in this development; but it was primarily a reactive one after Vienna had delivered a stiff ultimatum in Belgrade and subsequently began to invade its smaller Balkan neighbor. So, while the main responsibility for the outbreak of war is therefore to be laid at the kaiser's door, the question of why he and his advisers pushed Europe over the brink continues to be a matter of debate. The German historian Fritz Fischer has argued that the kaiser's government saw the Sarajevo crisis as the opportunity for aggressively achieving a *Griff nach der Weltmacht (Breakthrough to World Power Status)*, as the 1961 German version of Fischer's first, and highly controversial, book on the subject was entitled. The American historian Konrad Jarausch and others, by contrast, have asserted that Berlin's and Vienna's initial strategy was more limited. By supporting Austria-Hungary against the Serbs, the two powers hoped to weaken Slav nationalism and Serb expansionism in the Balkans and thus to restabilize the increasingly precarious position of the ramshackle Austro-Hungarian empire with its many restive nationalities. According to this interpretation, the assumption was that Russia and its ally, France, would not support Serbia, and that, after a quick localized victory by the central powers in the Balkans, any larger international repercussions could be contained through negotiation following the fait accompli.

It was only when this strategy failed owing to St. Petersburg's resistance that the German military got its way to launch an all-out offensive, the first target of which would be Russia's ally, France. This was the sole military operations plan, the "Schlieffen Plan," first developed by Gen. Alfred von Schlieffen, that the kaiser still had available in 1914. The alternative of an eastern attack on Russia had been dropped several years before. Worse, since the German Army was not strong enough to invade France directly through Alsace-Lorraine, Helmut von Moltke, chief of the General Staff, had further reinforced the right flank of the invasion force with the aim of reaching Paris swiftly from the north. However, this could only be achieved by

marching through Belgium, and it was this violation of Belgian neutrality that brought Britain into the conflict, definitely turning it into a world war.

In a further radicalization of his argument, Fischer asserted in his second book, *War of Illusions* (1973), that the German decision to start a world war had been made at a "War Council" on 8 December 1912, and that Berlin used the next eighteen months to prepare it. However, this view has not been generally accepted by the international community of scholars. Unless new documents supporting Fischer emerge, possibly from the Russian archives, the most plausible argument seems to be the one developed by Jarausch and others of a miscalculated "limited war" that grew out of control.

While diplomatic historians and political scientists have dominated the debate on the outbreak of World War I, social historians have more recently begun to examine the attitude of the "masses" in that summer of 1914. The older view has been that there was great enthusiasm all-round and that millions in all participant countries flocked to the colors expecting to achieve victory no later than Christmas 1914. No doubt there was strong popular support, reinforced by initial serious misconceptions about the nature of modern industrialized warfare. But there have been recent challenges to this view, and it appears that divisions of contemporary opinion were deeper and more widespread than previously believed. French social historians have shown that news of the *mobilization was received in some parts of the country with tears and consternation rather than joy and parades. In Germany, too, feeling was more polarized than had been assumed. Thus, there were peace demonstrations in major cities to warn Austria-Hungary against starting a war with Serbia. And when the German mobilization was finally proclaimed, the reaction of large sections of the population was decidedly lukewarm. As one young trade unionist wrote after watching cheerful crowds around him near Hamburg's main railroad station on 1 August 1914: "Am I mad or is it the others?"

Considering the unprecedented slaughter that began shortly thereafter in the trenches of the western front as well as in the east, this was certainly a good question, and further research may well open up new perspectives on the mentalities of the men and women in 1914 and on the socioeconomic and political upheavals that followed, which ultimately also involved the United States as a participant.

• Fritz Fischer, *Germany: War Aims in the First World War*, 1967. Konrad Jarausch, *The Enigmatic Chancellor*, 1972. Volker R. Berghahn, *Germany and the Approach of War in 1914*, 1973. Fritz Fischer, *War of Illusions*, 1973. James Joll, *The Origins of the First World War*, 1984. John W. Langdon, *July 1914, The Long Debate 1918–1990*, 1991. Samuel R. Williamson, Jr., *Austria-Hungary and the Origins of the First World War*, 1991.

—Volker R. Berghahn

WORLD WAR I (1914–18): CAUSES OF U.S. ENTRY

Like the origins of World War I itself, the causes of U.S. entry on 6 April 1917 have been much debated. The 1930s emphasis on economic motivations—the desire of American munitions makers and financiers to protect their stake in Allied victory—has been superseded by two new interpretations. One, a broad view enunciated first by historians William Appleman Williams and N. Gordon Levin, emphasizes the desire of President Woodrow *Wilson and many among America's economic and foreign policy elites to ensure a liberal, capitalist world order in contrast to reactionary militarism and colonialism or widespread revolution and communism. The other reflects a greater focus on Wilson's decision making and is put forward by Arthur S. Link, Ernest May, Robert H. Ferrell, and Thomas J. Knock. They emphasize variously the strategic situation of the United States as the leading neutral industrial and financial power; and the influence upon Wilson of the German *submarine warfare, the predominantly pro-British attitude of American elites, and the president's own appropriation of the leadership of the liberal movement toward a just and lasting peace based upon a league of nations.

In 1914, Wilson proclaimed U.S. *neutrality in keeping with American tradition. He was also aware of the great divisions over the war: although perhaps a bare majority of Americans favored Britain, nearly as many were hostile to the Allies because of ethnic loyalties or suspicions of Britain, the world's most powerful empire and financial center, or hostility toward czarist Russia with its autocracy and pogroms.

Both Germany and Britain violated U.S. neutral maritime rights, as Wilson strictly defined them, but German submarine warfare seemed more ruthless, particularly with the sinking of the *Lusitania, a British passenger liner, in 1915. American trade with the Allies tripled to $3 billion a year between 1914 and 1916 and helped economic recovery in the United States. Pro-British elites and the urban press increasingly emphasized German immorality—the invasion of neutral Belgium and alleged *atrocities there and later the barbarity of submarine warfare. Seeking to avoid being drawn into the war but also insisting on Americans' right to aid the Allies, Wilson held Germany to "strict accountability" for its submarine warfare, and for a while caused Berlin to restrict its U-boats.

After his reelection in 1916, Wilson offered to mediate a peace; but both sides refused. Berlin then decided on unrestricted submarine warfare, beginning 1 February 1917, to starve Britain into terms. Wilson severed diplomatic relations on 3 February. American public opinion was also inflamed by the Zimmermann note, in which Germany sought a military alliance with Mexico against the United States. When submarines sank three American merchant ships, Wilson abandoned temporary armed neutrality and decided to take the United States into the war, in part because his strict accountability policy had failed and in part because he wanted the United States to help shape a treaty for peace.

In his powerful war message of 2 April 1917, Wilson condemned the German submarine campaign as "warfare against mankind," and urged Americans to fight, in his famous phrase, to make the world "safe for democracy." By a vote of 82–6 in the Senate (4 April) and 373–50 in the House (6 April), Congress adopted a resolution declaring that a state of war existed between the United States and Germany.

[See also Germany, U.S. Military Involvement in.]

• William Appleman Williams, The Tragedy of American Diplomacy, 1959. Ernest R. May, The World War and American Isolation, 1914–1917, 1959. Arthur S. Link, Wilson: Campaigns for Progressivism and Peace, 1916–1917, 1965. N. Gordon Levin, Jr., Woodrow Wilson and World Politics: America's Response to War and Revolution, 1968. Ross Gregory, The Origins of American Intervention in the First World War, 1971. Robert H. Ferrell, Woodrow Wilson and World War I, 1917–1921, 1985. Thomas J. Knock, To End All Wars: Woodrow Wilson and the Quest for a New World Order, 1992.

—John Whiteclay Chambers II

WORLD WAR I (1914–18): MILITARY AND DIPLOMATIC COURSE

"The situation is extraordinary. It is militarism run stark mad." Col. Edward House, President Woodrow *Wilson's closest adviser, did not exaggerate when he wrote these words. The Europe he described in the spring of 1914 was divided into two armed camps: the Triple Entente (Russia, France, and Great Britain) and the Triple Alliance (Germany, Austria-Hungary, and Italy). An unprecedented arms race was underway that coincided with revolutionary advances in the technology of warfare. Magazine-loading rifles, belt-fed *machine guns, and improved *artillery dramatically increased the firepower of armies. Relying on an expanding network of railways, the general staffs of the major European powers devised elaborate *mobilization and offensive schemes. The smallest details were covered, including the preparation of exact railway timetables and even the registration of farmers' horses for possible use. Universal *conscription fostered militarism. Governments identified and registered able-bodied males of military age. Approximately 4 million men were in uniform when the war started in August 1914; that number had risen to a staggering 20 million by the end of the month.

Europe's military elite, accepting Carl von *Clausewitz's military principles of "the decisive force, at the decisive place, at the decisive time," were committed to an offensive strategy designed to climax in one or two great decisive battles. Clausewitz's ideas on war may also have influenced society. The historian John Keegan argues that Europe had been transformed into a warrior society by the acceptance of Clausewitz's maxims that *war was a continuation of political activity and that "war is an act of violence pushed to its utmost bounds."

A month after House's letter, the assassination on 28 June 1914 of Archduke Franz Ferdinand, the heir to the Austro-Hungarian throne, precipitated a general European crisis that quickly became unmanageable. The Austrians, given unequivocal support by their ally, Germany, blamed Serbia for the archduke's death and decided to crush Serbia's challenge to the fragile Austro-Hungarian empire. Vienna's determination to go to war triggered a general conflict. The illusion that modern industrialized wars would be short made this decision easier. Few believed the Polish banker and economist, Ivan S. Bloch, the author of The Future of War in Its Economic and Political Relations: Is War Now Impossible? (1898), who argued that modern military technology had made unlimited war mutually destructive for the participants.

Germany's "Schlieffen Plan," designed to achieve victory over France within six weeks by a gigantic flanking movement through neutral Belgium, came to grief during the First Battle of the Marne (5–9 September). An ominous portent was that the French, Germans, and British had suffered over half a million *casualties in three weeks of fighting. Meanwhile, the Russian offensive in East Prussia was checked and thrown back, with an entire Russian army destroyed at Tannenberg (26–30 August).

Following the opening battles, the armies in the west

dug in. An almost continuous line of parallel defensive systems was constructed from the North Sea to Switzerland. Protected by barbed wire, usually 50 or more feet deep, these earthworks were frequently built in depth. The front resembled a spiderweb, consisting of thousands of miles of connecting and parallel trenches. *Trench warfare also existed to some extent of other fronts—in some areas of Russia, Italy, the Balkans, and Palestine—though nowhere did it become as prominent as in France and Flanders.

Europe's military leaders sought to return to a war of maneuver by rupturing the enemy's front. To restore the offensive, new weapons such as *tanks and chemical warfare were eventually introduced. High-explosive shells, recoilless carriages, optical sights, improved communications, and cannon ranges of 20 or more miles made indirect artillery bombardment the dominant force of the battlefield. The application of massive and increasingly sophisticated artillery fire proved to be the most effective means of reducing fortifications. But the western defenses, bolstered by dramatic advances in firepower, were so strong and thickly defended that it was possible to break into them but not through them prior to 1918. When breakthroughs were successful, there remained limitations to the advance. The 1916–18 version of the tank lacked the speed and reliability to maintain the momentum of an attack over battle-torn ground before defenders dug in again. Nor could the heavy guns be moved forward rapidly to support a continued advance of the infantry.

The 1930s view, which lingers still among many, is that the generals of the western front were inept and their approaches to winning the war futile. "A war of attrition was substituted for a war of intelligence," is the way that Lloyd George, British prime minister and a leading critic of attempts to win the war on the western front, put it. The historian Tim Travers has emphasized that many commanders had difficulty abandoning their nineteenth-century vision of warfare, which emphasized the *élan* of the individual soldier over the new weapons technology. But recent studies of the evolution of tactics by Paddy Griffith and Robin Prior and Trevor Wilson have demonstrated that the western front during the last half of the war was not tactically stagnant. The Germans are often considered the most innovative with their elastic defense-in-depth and stormtrooper tactics of infiltration. But the British, with more offensive experience than the enemy in 1916–17, also perfected all-arms assaults and advanced techniques of trench raiding prior to the tactical successes of the Germans in the spring of 1918.

Germany, relying on strong support from Austria-Hungary, concentrated its resources on the eastern front in 1915. The vastness of that front, and the clear superiority of German artillery and leadership, made possible an advance of some 300 miles. Although Italy joined the Allies in 1915, by the end of the year, Berlin dominated Central and southeastern Europe, had a bridge to Asia and Africa through its Turkish ally, and retained Belgium and the most industrial part of France. Serbia had been defeated and Bulgaria enlisted as an ally. British efforts to find a "way around" the western front ended in dismal failure in the Dardanelles and Gallipoli campaigns. The central powers, with a more unified command because of Germany's dominant position, interior lines, and a good system of railways, held a formidable position despite their inferiority in warships, manpower, and industrial capacity.

In 1916, Germany sought to break the stalemate in the west in the ten-month Battle of Verdun, deliberately seeking a decisive battle of attrition and will. To relieve Verdun, a massive Anglo-French offensive was launched on the Somme in July. When winter brought the fighting to a close, the western front had little changed: Verdun remained in French hands, and the Allies had captured no position of strategical importance on the Somme. Combined German-Allied casualties exceeded 2 million. Despite the carnage, the warring coalitions faced a bleak future of continued stalemate and exhaustion.

Compared to the great powers of Europe, the United States was a profoundly peaceful and unmilitaristic nation. Prior to America's entry into the war in April 1917, Wilson's secretary of the navy, Josephus Daniels, was decidedly antiwar if not pacifistic, and Newton Baker, secretary of war since 1916, was an ardent antimilitarist. The U.S. Navy had expanded to defend American shores and trade routes, but the U.S. Army ranked seventeenth in the world. The United States was the world's number one industrial power, but the army lacked modern weaponry, including tanks, poison gas, aircraft, heavy artillery, and trench mortars. War *mobilization, 1917–18, failed to remedy this deficiency: the American Expeditionary Forces (AEF) largely fought with foreign weapons.

Although legally neutral, the United States had become a vital factor for the Allies with their growing dependence on American credit and material. Caught between the effective Allied naval blockade and Germany's *submarine warfare campaign, America's right to trade overseas was jeopardized. To keep the United States from being drawn into the global conflict, Wilson attempted mediation. With the European belligerents unable to take the U.S. military seriously, he had little diplomatic leverage except for American economic might. The European nations wanted a peace to reflect their immense sacrifices in blood and treasure. But an acceptable peace to one side represented defeat to the other.

Wilson's mediation efforts implied that he was prepared to accept a global role for the United States to obtain a compromise peace, but he certainly never imagined any circumstances that would involve American forces in what he referred to as the "mechanical game of slaughter" in France. Nor apparently could he identify any strategic interest for the United States in the total defeat of Germany, which he believed would result in an unbalanced peace of victors. His formula for a satisfactory end to the fighting as he announced in January 1917 was "peace without victory."

Pressed into the war in April 1917 by Germany's gamble for quick victory through unrestricted submarine warfare, Wilson initially believed that American belligerency would largely be economic and psychological and that the central powers could be forced to the peace table without U.S. troops becoming involved on European battlefields. Pressure from London and Paris and the realization that his voice in any peace conference would be small without an American military presence in Europe changed his mind.

Only once before, during the American Revolution, had the United States fought as part of a military alliance. The General Staff in the War Department, however, quickly concluded that the only way that the United States could fight in Europe was through a collective military enterprise with the British and French on the western front. Nonetheless, America's leadership was determined to maintain a distinct military and political position. Wilson immediately disassociated himself from the entente's controversial war objectives by insisting that the United States was an "associate power," with freedom to conduct independent goals.

The commander in chief of the AEF, John J. *Pershing, proved an excellent choice to defend a separate and distinct U.S. military role in the war. The AEF commander tenaciously adhered to his goal of an independent U.S. force with its own front, supply lines, and strategic goals. His preparations for a win-the-war American breakthrough to occur in 1919 in Lorraine to the east and west of Metz profoundly influenced America's military participation. The United States supported unity of command and the selection of Gen. Ferdinand Foch as generalissimo; but Pershing resisted anything but the temporary amalgamation of American units into French and British divisions, even during the grave military crisis confronting the Allies in the spring of 1918. The German High Command, with Russia knocked out of the war in the winter of 1917–18, attempted to destroy the French Army and drive the British from the Continent through a series of offensives. Pershing resisted the only means of immediately assisting the depleted Allied forces: the inclusion of American units in British and French divisions. Small numbers of American soldiers, however, began to enter combat under the American flag in May and June. On 28 May, 14 months after the United States entered the war, a reinforced U.S. regiment (about 4,000 men) captured the village of Cantigny. Several days later, the Second Division (which included a Marine brigade) took up a defensive position west of Château-Thierry and engaged the advancing Germans.

Pershing rebuffed efforts by Allied soldiers to share their increasingly sophisticated tactical techniques with his forces. Revisionists have been critical of his emphasis on riflemen, the American frontier spirit, and open field tactics, arguing that he did not comprehend how science and the machine age had revolutionized warfare.

After gaining reluctant approval from Foch for the formation of an independent American force, the U.S. First Army, Pershing went forward with plans to eliminate the threatening salient of St. Mihiel, as a prelude to his Metz offensive. The Battle of *St. Mihiel (12–16 September 1918) proved to be an impressive but misleading U.S. victory because German forces were in the process of withdrawing to a new and shorter defensive line when the Americans attacked and cut off the salient.

The pressing demands of coalition warfare, however, forced Pershing to delay preparations for his 1919 Metz campaign. Complying with Foch's strategy, he reluctantly shifted most of his troops some sixty miles northward to the Meuse-Argonne sector, where he was expected to participate in simultaneous and converging Allied attacks against the large German salient. Logistical chaos, flawed tactics, and inexperienced men and officers contributed to a disastrous start to the *Meuse-Argonne offensive (26 September–11 November 1918). Pershing hoped to advance ten miles on the first day; his front, however, had moved just thirty-four miles by the armistice six weeks later, much of the ground gained only during the last phase of the offensive when Germany had exhausted its reserves.

Although only involved in heavy fighting for 110 days, the AEF made vital contributions to Germany's defeat. With tens of thousands of "doughboys" crossing the Atlantic to reinforce the Allies, and with the AEF emerging as a superior fighting force, the exhausted and depleted Germans had no hope of avoiding total defeat if the war continued into 1919.

Before Berlin's appeal in early October for a peace based on Wilson's *Fourteen Points, the United States was on the verge of brilliantly coordinating its participation in the land war in Europe with its political plans to reshape the postwar world. If the war had continued into the spring of 1919, Pershing's plan to deliver a knockout blow to the German Army probably would have been achieved. Gen. Jan C. Smuts, the South African statesman who served in the British War Cabinet, warned the British government in October: if the war continued another year, the United States would become the "diplomatic dictator of the world."

In contrast to Pershing's wishes for total *victory, Wilson hoped to avoid placing Germany at the mercy of the Allies. American participation had not been designed to further the British empire, strengthen French security, or even maintain the European balance of power. Wilson stood not with the interests of the nation-states, but with the rights of humankind. He thus attempted with mixed results to use separate negotiations with Berlin over an armistice to impose his Fourteen Points on the Allies as well as Germany.

As the Great War concluded with the armistice on 11 November 1918, American policy was directed toward the repudiation of power politics and the erection of a "permanent" peace. Wilsonianism promised an end to war primarily through democratic institutions, the end of secret diplomacy, the self-determination for ethnic minorities, and most especially through a *League of Nations. It has been argued that this visionary approach raised expectations that were impossible to meet. The war had destroyed the old balance of power in Europe, and the peace settlement made revisionist nations out of the two states that would soon dominate the Continent, Germany and the Soviet Union. The United States, the greatest economic beneficiary of the war, helped make the peace, but with its rejection of the Treaty of *Versailles refused responsibility for maintaining it.

A war in which over 65 million troops had been mobilized by the belligerents ended in a twenty-year truce instead of "permanent peace." The failure to achieve Wilson's unrealistic though desirable goal was hardly surprising. But another general war was not inevitable. World War II was caused by many factors, including the flawed peace settlement of 1919, the Great Depression of the 1930s, and the psychological scars of World War I, which enfeebled the democracies. But the inability of the victorious powers, especially Great Britain and the United States, to work together to prevent the resurgence of German military power, was certainly one of the most important reasons for the resumption of war in 1939.

• B. H. Liddell Hart, The Real War 1914–1918, 1930. Edward M. Coffman, The War to End All Wars: The American Military Experience in World War I, 1968. Donald Smythe, Pershing: General of the Armies, 1985. Tim Travers, The Killing Ground: The British Army, the Western Front and the Emergence of Modern Warfare, 1900–1918, 1987. Allan R. Millett, "Over Where? The AEF and the American Strategy for Victory, 1917–1918," in Allan Millett and

Williamson Murray, eds., *Against All Enemies: Interpretations of the American Military from Colonial Times to the Present*, 1988. Timothy K. Nenninger, "American Military Effectiveness in the First World War," in *Military Effectiveness*, Vol. 1: *The First World War*, Allan Millett and Williamson Murray, eds., 1988. David Stevenson, *The First World War and International Politics*, 1988. Robin Prior and Trevor Wilson, *Command on the Western Front: The Military Career of Sir Henry Rawlinson 1914–18*, 1992. John Keegan, *A History of Warfare*, 1993. David F. Trask, *The AEF and Coalition Warmaking, 1917–1918*, 1993. David R. Woodward, *Trial by Friendship: Anglo-American Relations, 1917–1918*, 1993. Paddy Griffith, *Battle Tactics of the Western Front: The British Army's Art of Attack, 1916–18*, 1994. D. Clayton James and Anne Sharp Wells, *America and the Great War, 1914–1920*, 1998.

—David R. Woodward

WORLD WAR I (1914–18): DOMESTIC COURSE

With its dynamic economy, its large population, and its stable government, the United States was well suited to the kind of total conflict that was raging overseas in World War I. But to realize its potential as a belligerent, it had to overcome several obstacles. Unity was vital in a war that pitted whole nations against one another; yet in the months that followed the country's entry into the war in April 1917, the country remained divided. Faults ran through American society along lines of race, ethnicity, and economic class. The declaration of war had not eliminated *isolationism apathy, pockets of *pacifism and antimilitarism, and even sympathy in some quarters for the people America was fighting. Although American factories, farms, and mines had been producing materials for the Allies for many months, the task of converting the economy to war production promised to be complex and difficult. The method for raising and supporting an army of the size that would have to fight had barely been sketched out.

President Woodrow *Wilson's administration improvised a series of solutions to these problems. It exhorted Americans to work and sacrifice for the war and to submerge their differences. It isolated and punished the war's opponents and rewarded people and organizations whose cooperation it needed. The result of its efforts was what has been called a wartime welfare state, in which government and interest groups sought to manage one another; in which *patriotism and idealism and sacrifice existed alongside the determined pursuit of self-interest; in which those with the greatest power, the strongest organization, or the most badly needed resources tended to secure the largest benefits from Congress and the Wilson administration.

To control domestic public opinion, the administration established a Committee on Public Information, which supplied American media with overwhelming quantities of facts and propaganda. Together with the Department of Justice and the Post Office, the Committee on Public Information defined what Americans were permitted to say in wartime. Notable dissenters, including the Socialist leader Eugene V. *Debs and hundreds of others whom government officials felt had opposed government policies or interfered with war production, were sent to prison. The government's portrayal of a monstrous enemy and its attacks on dissenters, together with the reports of *casualties suffered in battle at enemy hands, helped promote a frenzy of anti-German and anti-German American feelings in parts of the nation.

Appealing to liberals, at that time a very large faction, the administration made the war, in some respects, a continuation of the prewar Progressive movement. It depicted the struggle against the central powers as a campaign for worldwide reform. It endorsed a federal women's suffrage amendment as a reward for women's war work. It extended disability benefits to members of the armed forces, provided financial support to their dependents, and created occupational health and safety standards for war workers. It tried to limit alcohol consumption and abolish prostitution, goals of many reformers. To assure the cooperation of pro-war labor unions, the administration approved collective bargaining for the duration of the conflict, provided federal mediation of labor disputes, and gave union officials an opportunity to sit on boards that managed the economy—but not to determine the policies of those boards. To the small and weak contingent of racial equality reformers, however, it offered only modest concessions, including positions in government as intelligence workers so that civil rights leaders could inform the government of possible disaffection among African Americans.

American corporations made large gains in wartime. The government enabled business groups to regulate themselves. Executives of leading companies dominated agencies, such as the Council of National Defense and the War Industries Board, that coordinated war production and distribution and arranged prices. It could hardly have been otherwise. Without a large, experienced regulatory bureaucracy of its own, the U.S. government needed not only the products of factories run by these businessmen but also their expert knowledge of how their industries operated. The president and Congress provided some checks on abuses by businesses. They declined for several months to give precise authority to the Council of National Defense and the War Industries Board; for a long time they failed to stop the War Department from resisting control over procurement by the business-dominated agencies. Congress passed legislation that in principle outlawed conflicts of interest. In some cases, the administration even used federal agencies to run important segments of the war economy, such as the railroad system. Yet the bureaucracy that managed railroads for the Railroad Administration was recruited from executives who had managed the railroads before the government took them over, so even that organization—a supposed example of "war socialism"—continued the practice of self-regulation.

The economic war agencies operated largely through a system of incentives, often using indirect methods rather than overt commands to achieve their objectives. They established a priority system in which companies that volunteered to manufacture war goods were given greater access to raw materials, workers, fuel, and *transportation than those whose activities were deemed less essential. (To put it another way, companies that chose not to cooperate might receive barely enough of what they needed to keep them going). These agencies offered cooperating businesses the chance to earn very large profits, partly because prices for whole industries were set at a level that could make the most inefficient producers profitable. Because the people who awarded contracts and negotiated their terms came from the industries that received the awards, executives who sought those contracts could feel confident that they were dealing with knowledgeable persons, not insensitive government officials. Businesses could engage in collusion without fear of being prosecuted. Although producers in the lumber, steel, automobile, and other industries drove very hard bargains with the war agencies, and in some cases threatened to refuse contracts for vital war products, American capitalists used publicity about their war work to restore an image of private enterprise that had been seriously tarnished in the prewar years. Certain large business leaders also appreciated the wartime opportunity to substitute cooperation for competition—a change some of them hoped would be permanent.

Incentives and publicity played significant parts in other areas of war *mobilization. To induce farmers to expand production, the federal government set a minimum price for wheat. It ran massive propaganda campaigns encouraging citizens to conserve food and fuel and to help pay for the war by purchasing government Liberty bonds. The Committee on Public Information and the Treasury Department staged Liberty bond rallies at which movie stars, war heroes, politicians, and other celebrities appeared to promote bond sales. Government publicity encouraged men of military age to join the armed forces and promoted a public climate in which able-bodied "slackers" felt extremely uncomfortable. Though thousands held back out of *conscientious objection or for other reasons, plenty of Americans wanted to enlist. Still, the government decided not to rely on volunteers alone. It instituted *conscription, administered by a Selective Service System, which sent sent two and three-quarter million men to the armed forces. The Selective Service System also promoted economic mobilization, inducing essential civilian workers to stay where they were by exempting them from the draft, but warning them that they must work or fight.

From women suffragists to civil rights leaders, from union officials to corporate executives, American civilians sought to turn the war to their advantage or to the advantage of the groups to which they belonged. Their political leaders and representatives did the same. After announcing that "politics is adjourned," President Wilson asked the voters to elect candidates from the Democratic Party in 1918 as a referendum on his war leadership. (They responded by giving Republicans control of both houses of Congress.) Several of the state councils of defense, which had been established to foster mobilization, became political organizations, usually dominated by Republicans. Many wartime measures were intensely political—for example, the decisions to fix minimum prices for certain products and not others, and to pay part of the cost of the war by progressive taxation and by taxes on "excess" profits.

The wartime welfare state, created for temporary purposes and staffed largely by volunteers rather than by a standing bureaucracy, dissolved at the end of the war. But the memory of the wartime system remained in the minds of those who had run it, and some of its components persisted in the 1920s—such as a federal system of medical benefits to *veterans and government-sponsored cooperation among businesses. During the Great Depression, several wartime agencies were resurrected with new names and altered purposes, including the War Finance Corporation, restored in Herbert C. *Hoover's administration as the Reconstruction Finance Corporation, and a host of New Deal organizations such as the National Recovery Administration, which traced its origins to the War Industries Board. Short-lived though it may have been, the wartime

system for managing America's home front in 1917 and 1918 contained some of the germs of the late twentieth-century welfare state, and was a progenitor of modern big government.

[*See also* Agriculture and War; Civil Liberties and War; Economy and War; Industry and War; Public Financing and Budgeting for War.]

• David M. Kennedy, *Over Here: The First World War and American Society,* 1980. Robert H. Ferrell, *Woodrow Wilson and World War I: 1917–1921,* 1985. David R. Woodward and Robert Franklin Maddox, *America and World War I: A Selected Annotated Bibliography of English-Language Sources,* 1985. John Whiteclay Chambers II, *To Raise an Army: The Draft Comes to Modern America,* 1987. Ronald Schaffer, *America and the Great War: The Rise of the War Welfare State,* 1991.
                                                        —Ronald Schaffer

WORLD WAR I (1914–18): POSTWAR IMPACT

World War I marked a turning point in world history. It reduced the global influence of Europe, destroying some of its monarchies and empires and diminishing the strength of others. It enabled new nations to emerge. Shifting economic resources and cultural influences away from Europe, the war encouraged nations in other areas of the world, notably the United States, to challenge Europe's international leadership.

Essentially a civil war in Europe with global implications, World War I destroyed some empires and weakened others. The 1917 Revolution in Russia, following the czarist regime's collapse, culminated in the Bolshevik seizure of power. With military defeat in 1918, the Ottoman and Austro-Hungarian Empires disintegrated, while Germany replaced the kaiser's government with the Weimar Republic. New nations such as Poland, Czechoslovakia, and Yugoslavia emerged from former empires. Victory for the European Allies came at a high price. They owed over $11 billion to the United States, which was transformed from a net debtor to a net creditor. New York replaced London as the world's financial center. The European Allies also faced increasing demands for self-rule from their colonies. They no longer controlled sufficient military and economic resources to shape world affairs as before.

By war's end, the United States and Japan were among the victorious powers at the Paris Peace Conference of 1919, along with the United Kingdom, France, and Italy, with U.S. president Woodrow *Wilson playing a leading role. He made the *League of Nations an essential part of the Treaty of *Versailles with Germany. The United States and the Allies, refusing to recognize the Bolshevik government in Russia, excluded the Soviet Union from Paris. Still, the specter of Bolshevism loomed over the conference.

Wilson sought a peace settlement that would protect democratic and capitalist nations. Affirming the principle of national self-determination, he called for a postwar League of Nations to provide collective security for its members. He expected the League, under American leadership, to protect its members' territorial integrity and political independence against external aggression, and thereby preserve the peace.

Within the belligerent countries, the war had enhanced the *state's role in the economy and society, but it also generated a backlash. Democratic governments in Western Europe retained civilian control, while autocratic governments in Central and Eastern Europe had succumbed to both military rule and revolution. Western democratic governments lost authority after the war. British elections in 1918 that kept Prime Minister David Lloyd George in office also registered Irish demands for self-rule. France experienced political instability after Premier Georges Clemenceau's resignation following his defeat in the presidential election.

Americans likewise reacted against Wilson's strong wartime leadership. The 1918 elections reduced the Democrats to the minority in Congress. After the war, as wartime agencies removed regulations, the United States experienced rapid inflation, labor strikes, and economic recession. The American Expeditionary Forces returned from France and quickly demobilized. Congress reorganized the armed forces with the *National Defense Act of 1920, reducing the regular army to nearly its prewar level.

Rapid readjustment and *demobilization produced social unrest in the United States in 1919–20. Regardless of their wartime *patriotism, African Americans were primary victims of urban race riots and rural lynchings, while socialists and other radicals, whether immigrants or native-born, were targets of the Red Scare. Wilson was partly responsible for this postwar impact, given his negative attitudes toward black people, new immigrants, and labor strikes, and his international focus, resulting in a neglect of postwar reconstruction at home. He contributed to the Red Scare, too, by advocating the League of Nations as a barrier against Bolshevism. Nevertheless, under Henry Cabot *Lodge's leadership, the Republican Senate kept the United States out of Wilson's League by rejecting the Treaty of Versailles.

Americans reacted against the wartime regulatory state and international involvement. Voters in 1920, including women who had just gained the suffrage under the Nineteenth Amendment, elected Republican senator Warren G. Harding to the presidency. Promising less government at home and less entanglement abroad, he epitomized one postwar alternative to Wilsonianism.

The postwar legacy of World War I was very different from Wilson's hopes. The League of Nations failed to maintain peace when aggressive nations—notably Communist Russia, Fascist Italy, Nazi Germany, and Imperial Japan—later challenged the Versailles peace. These revisionist powers rejected democracy and capitalism and challenged the status quo. They exploited the Anglo-American revisionism of the treaty's critics, such as John Maynard Keynes in *The Economic Consequences of the Peace* (1920), to justify their aggression. During the Great Depression of the 1930s, which resulted in part from the postwar failure to create a sustainable world economy, they turned modern *nationalism into a hostile force that culminated in World War II.

Yet the long-term impact of World War I also included the enduring legacy of Wilsonianism. Wilson had emphasized the principle of national self-determination in the peacemaking. To curb nationalist excesses and aggression, he had advocated collective security through the League of Nations, hoping to enable free nations to participate in a new world order of peace and prosperity. He had endeavored to shape public opinion in favor of democracy and capitalism as well as internationalism. Despite his failure after World War I, Wilson's ideals deeply influenced the statecraft of future generations. Wilsonianism would continue to shape the international history of the twentieth century.

• Burl Noggle, *Into the Twenties: The United States from Armistice to Normalcy,* 1974. Barry D. Karl, *The Uneasy State: The United States from 1915 to 1945,* 1983. Robert H. Ferrell, *Woodrow Wilson and World War I, 1917–1921,* 1985. Klaus Schwabe, *Woodrow Wilson, Revolutionary Germany, and Peacemaking, 1918–1919: Missionary Diplomacy and the Realities of Power,* 1985. Arthur Walworth, *Wilson and His Peacemakers: American Diplomacy at the Paris Peace Conference, 1919,* 1986. Lloyd E. Ambrosius, *Woodrow Wilson and the American Diplomatic Tradition: The Treaty Fight in Perspective,* 1987. Manfred F. Boemeke, Gerald D. Feldman, and Elisabeth Glaser-Schmidt, eds., *The Treaty of Versailles: A Reassessment after 75 Years,* 1998.
—Lloyd E. Ambrosius

WORLD WAR I (1914–18): CHANGING INTERPRETATIONS

Historical opinion about the causes of World War I, American entry, and the making of peace has changed sharply over the years, with the publication of documentary collections, the opening of archives, and the appearance of memoirs and collections of personal papers, as well as changing theories and international circumstances. There is now general agreement on the causes of the war and of American entry; but disagreement remains over the American role in the peace.

During the years between the two world wars, contentions abounded between the adherents of Sidney B. Fay of Harvard University and Bernadotte Schmitt of the University of Chicago, who took respectively the sides of the central powers and the Allies, and based their books and articles on the national documentary collections and memoirs. At the end of World War II, the American and British governments took control of the German Foreign Office files and opened them, which revealed the bias of the earlier German documentary collection, *Die Grosse Politik der Europaeischen Kabinette: 1871–1914.* Opinion now is that German *nationalism bears primary responsibility for starting the war.

American entrance into the great European conflict, which made it a true world war, produced an argument in the 1930s between Charles Seymour of Yale University and the popular historian Charles A. Beard, in which Seymour singled out German *submarine warfare, especially the resort to unrestricted use of submarines beginning 1 February 1917, contrary to historical American neutral rights, as the cause of President Woodrow *Wilson's decision to move from *neutrality to intervention. Beard belittled such a monocausal contention, writing that the cause of any large event is necessarily complex, akin to a chemist pouring reagents into a test tube and obtaining a precipitate—but the latter is not the cause. Historical opinion now favors multicausality within a larger cultural and economic context provided by U.S. ties with the Allies.

In the making of the peace it is possible to say that the Wilsonian internationalists, the champions of the American president, such as historians Arthur Link and Arthur Walworth, have held the field. But questions remain, notably about whether the American people were prepared in 1919 for, if not a world government, then a world organization. Historians have agreed that Wilson himself was not his own best advocate. Thomas J. Knock has argued that Wilson undermined the progressive internationalist coalition by wartime repression. There is particular concern about the Wilson design of the Covenant of the *League of Nations, which was neither fish nor fowl—neither a general scheme to promote international law and arbitration, which was in the American diplomatic tradition, nor a design for a postwar alliance of the victorious powers, which such conservative senators as Henry Cabot *Lodge of Massachusetts might have approved on a short-term basis. Historians have remarked on the extraordinary nationalism of post-1918 America, the inchoate but ardent desire to promote peace, and the victory of *isolationism. They are unsure that any American president, seeking an acceptable peace, could have done anything other than what President Warren G. Harding did, which was to declare agreement with the nonpolitical provisions of the Treaty of *Versailles.

[*See also* Disciplinary Views of War.]

—Robert H. Ferrell

WORLD WAR I, U.S. AIR OPERATIONS IN. The U.S. declaration of war on April 6, 1917, found American aviation in an embryonic and woefully unprepared state. The army air service had some 1,400 officers and men; naval aviation, 300.

America's first operational unit in Europe, a naval air detachment, began flying seaplane escort for French coastal convoys in September. The first army flight candidate landed in France in June 1917, while those arriving in Italy in the fall included New York congressman Fiorello La Guardia.

In France the command of the embryonic U.S. Air Service remained in flux into 1918, as frontline commander Col. William "Billy" *Mitchell emerged as the key leader. Mitchell determined to undertake a tactical aerial offensive on the Western Front with an air arm of new recruits from America and a nucleus of veterans from the Lafayette Escadrille and Lafayette Flying Corps, who had flown with the French since the battle of Verdun in 1916.

U.S. units entered action in the quiet sector around Toul in the spring, and in early June thirteen squadrons joined the struggle over Chateau-Thierry during the Aisne-Marne offensive.

When the First Army AEF attacked the *St. Mihiel salient on September 12 to 16, Billy Mitchell commanded 1,481 airplanes, the largest wartime concentration of Allied air forces, nearly half of which were American. Despite poor weather conditions, this overwhelming mass seized aerial control as fighters penetrated over German airfields and day bombers struck targets on the battlefield and in the rear. St. Mihiel also marked the meteoric ascent of balloon-busting ace Frank Luke, who shot down 18 Germans in 17 days before meeting his death. The impetuous Luke won the Medal of Honor, as would American ace of aces Eddie *Rickenbacker, who ultimately gained 26 victories and survived the war.

In the climactic *Meuse-Argonne Offensive from September 26 to the end of October, Mitchell successfully continued his massed offensive tactics. By the Armistice the intensive fighting combined with supply problems to reduce the air service to 45 squadrons with 457 serviceable airplanes, nearly two hundred fewer aircraft than in September. Yet the air service had grown to 195,024 officers and men by war's end. More than 2,000 American flight personnel had reached the front. 681 aviators died, 75 percent of them in accidents and 25 percent in combat.

By October 1918 the navy had some 900 seaplanes for convoy duties, 400 of which were stationed abroad at 27 U.S. naval air stations from Ireland to Italy. A few naval aviators flew bombers from Calais-Dunkirk, while army aviators in Italy manned bomber units there.

American industry delivered Curtiss flying boats, the standardized Liberty engine, and copies of the British DH4 bomber to American combat units. Yet inadequate overall aviation production necessitated American reliance primarily on allied aerial equipment. The U.S. Air Service's significance lay in its support of the army through reconnaissance and attacks on enemy troops and supplies at and behind the front, while fighter aviation protected observation and bomber craft, engaged in ground attack, and provided the public with heroic aces.

[*See also* Air Force, U.S.: Predecessors of, 1907 to 1946; Strategy: Air Warfare Strategy; World War I (1914–1918): Military and Diplomatic Course.]

• James J. Hudson, *Hostile Skies: A Combat History of the American Air Service in World War I,* 1968. Adrian O. Van Wyen, *Naval Aviation in World War I,* 1969.

—John H. Morrow, Jr.

WORLD WAR I, U.S. NAVAL OPERATIONS IN. As a direct response to the war in Europe, the Naval Act of 1916 required the United States to construct a battle fleet equal to that of Britain and able to gain command of the sea. President Woodrow *Wilson hoped that this radical change in naval policy would strengthen his hand in efforts to arrange a negotiated peace. The United States entered the war in 1917 before this ambitious program was very far advanced. Thereafter, the peculiar exigencies of naval operations caused its abandonment. Germany's resumption of unrestricted *submarine warfare against neutral and noncombatant merchant shipping on the high seas (attack without warning) led to the U.S. intervention. German leaders expected this response, but believed that a maritime strategy, interrupting the flow of supplies to the Allies, would force a decision on the western front within six months, long before U.S. assistance could affect the outcome. This challenge led the United States to concentrate on naval construction to thwart the submarine offensive—building antisubmarine craft to engage the German U-boats and merchant ships to replace those destroyed at sea. This program forced postponement in constructing *battleships and *cruisers, the most important elements of a battle fleet.

Adm. William S. Benson, the chief of naval operations, and others wished to continue the 1916 building program, seeking to gain postwar political leverage, but Adm. William S. *Sims, sent to London to establish liaison with the British Admiralty, offered counsel that helped fix naval policy for the remainder of the war. Soon grasping the severity of the submarine depredations, Sims urged immediate support of the antisubmarine war. Following British strategy, he became a strong advocate of the convoy, that is, forming groups of merchant ships and escorting them with naval vessels through submarine-infested waters. This recommendation was accepted in Washington, forcing suspension of the 1916 building program in favor of antisubmarine craft and merchant vessels.

The first move of the Navy Department was to send available reinforcements to European waters. Six *destroyers were sent to Queenstown, Ireland, to join the British antisubmarine force there. Others soon followed, helping to escort merchantmen to British ports. U.S. destroyers were later dispatched to the Mediterranean Sea, assisting the Allied fleet there to protect communications with Asia. Beside destroyers, the United States built small submarine chasers, of which 235 reached European waters. In all cases, ships under Sims's control operated under Allied commanders. Thus, American vessels were effectively integrated into the Allied navies, especially the Royal Navy. This approach meant that the U.S. Navy, unlike the army, which resisted integration into European commands, was able to make an early, sustained, and significant contribution to the Allied cause.

In 1918, Admiral Benson pushed for the development of a strong escort service based at the French port of Brest to cover the arrival of the American Expeditionary Force. This force soon became larger than the one at Queenstown that protected commerce. The British continued to stress escort of merchant shipping, but the U.S. Navy Department concerned itself primarily with American army troop transports. Sims supported the Admiralty view, which strengthened the impression that his was unduly pro-British. Fortunately, conflicts over this questions were kept within reasonable bounds; sufficient resources were found to maintain both types of escort duty. No loaded American troop transports were sunk en route to Europe, although several empty vessels were torpedoed while returning to the United States.

The inter-Allied antisubmarine campaign eventually contained the German undersea offensive, although the U-boats were never defeated decisively. Allied tonnage losses were cut from 875,000 tons in April 1917 to about 260,000 tons in April 1918. Effective management techniques and merchant ship construction were sufficient to preserve maritime communications.

During 1918, Admiral Sims devoted considerable attention to the Allied Naval Council, founded to coordinate inter-Allied naval campaigns. Allied shipping losses in the Mediterranean, especially to Austrian submarines operating from the Adriatic ports of Pola and Cattaro, led Sims to urge offensive naval operations in that theater, particularly raids on enemy bases and barrages to interdict the passage of submarines through choke points such as the Strait of Otranto at the southern end of the Adriatic. This endeavor led to nothing because the Italian Navy effectively opposed operations that might endanger its ships. The Italian government wished to preserve its fleet as leverage in support of postwar territorial claims. Nevertheless, U.S. naval vessels, including thirty-six submarine chasers, supported the barrage between Otranto and Corfu.

During 1918, the U.S. Navy made two other contributions to the naval war. U.S. super-battleships (Dreadnoughts) were sent to the North Sea, becoming the Sixth Battle Squadron of the British Grand Fleet. These vessels helped to continue to contain the German High Sea Fleet in its bases. A more ambitious enterprise was the construction of the huge North Sea Mine Barrage, which the Navy Department sponsored despite initial British resistance. The Anglo-American Mining Squadron laid a belt of 75,000 naval *mines between the Orkney Islands and the coast of Norway. About 240 miles long and 15 to 35 miles wide, it was intended to force U-boats to proceed to the Atlantic Ocean through the English Channel, a dangerous passage. The barrage was not completed until just before the armistice of November 11, too late for a thorough test. Four U-boats were confirmed lost, and perhaps an equal number more were also destroyed.

Although the U.S. Navy did not conduct independent operations and maneuvered few vessels other than those on antisubmarine duty, it lent notable support to the victory at sea in World War I. Admiral Sims, critical of his superiors' skepticism about his recommendations, precipitated a postwar congressional investigation of the Navy Department, complaining that it had moved slowly and inefficiently during the crises of 1917. Nevertheless, because of its effective antisubmarine work and the protection of the troopships, the U.S. Navy emerged from the war with enhanced prestige and valuable experience that would prove useful during World War II despite the naval disarmament treaties of the interwar years.

[See also Sea Warfare: Strategy: Naval Warfare Strategy; World War I: Military and Diplomatic Course.]

• Elting E. Morison, *Admiral Sims and the Modern American Navy,* 1942. E. David Cronon, *The Cabinet Diaries of Josephus Daniels, 1913–1921,* 1963. Thomas G. Frothingham, *The Naval History of the World War,* 3 vols., 1971. David F. Trask, *Captains and Cabinets: Anglo-American Naval Relations, 1917–1918,* 1972. William S. Sims, *The Victory at Sea,* ed. David F. Trask, 1984. Mary Klachko with David F. Trask, *Admiral William Shepherd Benson: First Chief of Naval Operations,* 1987. Paul G. Halperin, *A Naval History of World War I,* 1994.   —David F. Trask

WORLD WAR II (1939–45)

Causes
Military and Diplomatic Course
Domestic Course
Postwar Impact
Changing Interpretations

WORLD WAR II (1939–45): CAUSES

The entry of the United States into World War II came formally as a consequence of the Japanese naval air attack on *Pearl Harbor on 7 December 1941. But although overtly committed to *neutrality, the U.S. government had been involved in the conflict, both morally and effectively, for over a year before that fateful date.

World War II was a conjunction of two geographically separated armed conflicts. The one that began with the German attack on Poland on 1 September 1939, and the British and French declarations of war on 3 September, was provoked by Adolf *Hitler's commitment of the state of Germany, whose machinery he had completely captured for himself and his Nazi Party, to a drive for world hegemony. In this drive, Hitler saw, after the destruction of the Soviet Union and the annexation of its agricultural and energy resources, the United States as the ultimate enemy. Britain and France (up to the latter's defeat in 1940) recognized Hitler's drive to be incompatible with and inimical to their conception of a peaceable world based on consensus and mutual respect between the major, especially the European, powers. This conception they called "civilization," seeing the alternative as chaos or "barbarism." The attack on Poland was thus the occasion, not the cause, of the outbreak of armed conflict in Europe.

The second conflict arose from Japanese militarism and Japan's ambition to establish exclusive domination over greater East Asia, including Southeast Asia and the western Pacific, an ambition with strong racialist overtones. The first target of Japanese military *expansionism was China, with whom conflict broke out in 1937. Britain and the

United States became the second targets, since Japanese military opinion saw Western support for Nationalist China as the cause of the Chinese failure to acknowledge defeat. Britain, followed by the United States, attempted to contain Japan by diplomacy, backed by increasing economic pressure on the nation's need for imported metals and petroleum. Japan exploited German success against Britain and France to expand into Southeast Asia. U.S. economic pressure led the extreme nationalist elements in Japan to support war against the United States, accompanied by an all-out assault on and capture of the French-, Dutch-, and British-controlled areas in Southeast Asia and on the U.S.-protected Philippines.

The two aggressor states had common enemies, including Britain and the United States—the latter, under the leadership of President Franklin D. *Roosevelt, unwilling to see universalism destroyed by two cultures so antagonistic to consensual "world order" as those of Nazi Germany and militaristic-nationalist Japan. In practice, Japan's relative weakness in the face of possible joint Anglo-American resistance led successive Japanese governments to act only when events in Europe—the German defeat of France and occupation of the Netherlands in 1940, and the German occupation of southeastern Europe and invasion of the Soviet Union in 1941—seemed to open the way for a progressive takeover of French Indochina as an open threat to the oil, tin, rubber, and other mineral resources of Malaysia and the East Indies. President Roosevelt's decision in the winter of 1938–39 to strengthen Britain and France as the first barrier to the threat to the United States he recognized Hitler's Germany as constituting—a decision reiterated in the autumn of 1940, when British determination to continue the war against Germany was underlined by their victory in the Air Battle of Britain—made the progressive application of economic pressure on Japan inevitable. The United States was largely unprepared for war. Furthermore, the loss of British Malaysia to Japan might well prove fatal to Britain's ability to continue the war against Hitler in Europe.

Roosevelt had already shown his judgment that Germany constituted a greater threat to U.S. security than did Japan as early as 1936. To this he added a confidence in British and French military strength, suitably backed by American industry, which events were to prove quite inadequate. But apart from a moment of doubt in the summer of 1940, he never changed his policy of perceiving Germany as the main threat. The *destroyers-for-bases agreement (1940), the *Lend-Lease Act and Agreements (1941), the denial of the western Atlantic by U.S. naval patrols to German U-boat warfare in 1941, and the takeover of the occupation of Iceland from the British that year were all backed by a secret decision made in late 1940 that if America were to find itself at war with both Germany and Japan (wrongly believed to be coordinating their actions), priority would be given to the defeat of Germany in Europe.

American public opinion was divided, with Roosevelt somewhat restricted by isolationists, particularly in Congress. The belief that American entry into World War I had been secured by a combination of unscrupulous British propaganda, U.S. arms manufacturers, and New York bankers, bound by the scale of British purchases and borrowings to the defeat of Germany, reinforced traditional *isolationism. War in Europe was a spectator sport. Most Americans supported Britain; but intervention necessitat-

ing the *conscription of American youth to fight overseas was something else. Opinion on the West Coast was vigorously hostile to Japan. Yet for the bulk of Americans, war in China was likewise a spectator sport with Nationalist China the hero and militarist Japan the villain. A Japanese attack on the United States seemed inconceivable. Japan's ability to project its power across the Pacific and defeat American forces on their own territory was underestimated by both American military and civilian opinion, just as the ability of Japanese spiritual *élan* to overcome American technological superiority and productivity was overestimated in Japan.

By the beginning of 1941, the Japanese expansionists had already taken their moderate colleagues well on the way to war. The year 1940, believed to be the 2,600th anniversary of the founding of the Japanese empire, filled them with a millennialist, now-or-never spirit. In June 1940, with France defeated and invasion threatening Britain, Tokyo decided on Japanese expansion southward, rather than in China or against the Soviet Union, irrespective of any Western resistance. In August, the establishment of the "Greater East-Asian Co-Prosperity Sphere" was announced. In September, with American opposition hardening, Japan signed the Tripartite Pact with Fascist Italy and Nazi Germany. Direct military action forced the French to accept Japanese occupation of northern Indochina.

America stood largely aside from all this, offering little aid to the French or British, forced that summer to agree to close the route by which Nationalist China received Western arms supplies. But once Roosevelt had been reelected president in November, American economic pressure on Japan resumed. With most of its forces involved in containing Fascist Italy in the Mediterranean, Britain welcomed American leadership in the Far East, as a realization of something sought since the mid-1930s. Staff talks between American, British, Chinese, and Dutch commanders in Southeast Asia were followed by close coordination of British and American economic pressure on Japan. The culmination was reached at the end of July 1941. The German attack on the Soviet Union on 22 June 1941 led the Japanese, freed from fears of the USSR, to occupy southern Indochina, outflanking the American-protected Philippines and directly threatening Malaya. In response, the United States froze all Japanese assets in America and embargoed all oil and petroleum exports to Japan. Without American (or East Indian) oil, Japan's air forces and navy would be paralyzed.

There followed a dual-track set of events for Japan. Internally, a series of imperial and ministerial/military liaison conferences drove the nation toward the decision for war. Externally, those opposed were driven to a succession of increasingly desperate attempts to negotiate an end to the embargo on terms that would not provoke a military coup in Tokyo. Had the United States leadership been willing to accept a modus vivendi by which Japan withdrew from southern Indochina in return for an end to the embargo and a free hand in China, the decision for war would have been abandoned. But neither President Roosevelt nor his secretary of state, Cordell Hull, let alone their British and Chinese allies, were ready for such a compromise, which could at best have been seen as only a postponement of conflict.

The actual Japanese decision to open hostilities by attacking Pearl Harbor only emerged as a plan in the summer of 1941 and was only adopted reluctantly in October. But it followed logically from the strategic position of the American forces in the Philippines across the flank of Japanese expansion into Malaya and the East Indies. By a narrow margin, the problem of supply was taken to rule out an actual invasion of Hawaii. U.S. strategic myopia, separate service commands, and failures in intelligence, analysis, and *communications gave the Japanese total strategic and tactical surprise in their attack on Pearl Harbor; only the absent *aircraft carriers, vital to America's naval victories later in 1942, escaped destruction.

President Roosevelt declared 7 December a "day of infamy," and Congress declared war on Japan on 8 December 1941. On 11 December, under the Tripartite Pact, Hitler's Germany and Mussolini's Italy declared war on the United States. The two separate conflicts had become one global war.

—Donald Cameron Watt

WORLD WAR II (1939–45):
MILITARY AND DIPLOMATIC COURSE

Officially, the United States remained neutral during the first two years of World War II and did not enter the conflict until December 1941, when it was forced to do so in response to both the Japanese attack on *Pearl Harbor and a German declaration of war. In reality, however, it became an unofficial belligerent and ally of England in mid-1940, and by the fall of 1941 it was engaged in an undeclared naval war with Germany.

The fundamental reason for this shift in U.S. policy was the series of dramatic German military victories in the spring of 1940, culminating in the June conquest of France. The speed and totality of these victories, largely the result of a very effective use of mechanized forces and airpower commonly referred to as *Blitzkrieg*, or "lightning war," led many Americans to question their traditional belief that the Atlantic Ocean constituted a defensive moat that freed them from concern with the European balance of power and provided extensive time to prepare for any threat. German power now appeared to pose such a threat, one capable of crossing the Atlantic at will and easily defeating the meager U.S. military forces then in existence.

President Franklin D. *Roosevelt proposed a twofold response to this perceived menace: national rearmament and sufficient aid to maintain British resistance and thereby keep the Germans preoccupied in Europe. Congress quickly agreed to rearmament with the first peacetime *conscription and billion-dollar defense bills in U.S. history, but aid to England aroused much more controversy. Consequently, Roosevelt used his executive powers in September to transfer fifty overage destroyers to Britain in return for ninety-nine-year leases on British bases in the western hemisphere, and justified the agreement as a net strategic gain.

British prime minister Winston S. *Churchill soon made clear that such aid was insufficient, however, and that Britain was running out of money to purchase American supplies. Roosevelt responded in December 1940 by proposing that Congress agree to lend or lease London extensive war material on the grounds that England constituted the first line of American defense and that its continued survival could preclude U.S. entry into the war. His critics maintained that such unneutral activities would bring about U.S. entry, but in March 1941 they were outvoted as Congress passed the *Lend-Lease Act and Agreements.

Determined to force a favorable end to the Sino-Japanese War that had been raging since 1937 and achieve hegemony in the Far East, Japan during this time period decided to take advantage of the German victories by extending its influence into the European colonies of Southeast Asia. The British, French, and Dutch authorities were powerless to act against Tokyo due to the military events in Europe, but the United States responded with economic sanctions and the movement of its fleet to Hawaii. Japan in turn responded with the Tripartite Pact with Germany and Italy, a defensive military alliance asserting that an attack by a present neutral on one of them would be considered an attack on all. In actuality, this pact was a diplomatic bluff, never supported by actual military collaboration, to scare the United States out of assistance to England and China via the threat of a two-front war. It failed to do even that, however, and in effect only hardened the American opposition to all three nations while convincing U.S. strategists of the need to plan for a two-front, global war against all three Axis powers.

This thought had actually begun to dominate U.S. strategic planning as early as 1939 with the inception of the RAINBOW *war plans. Yet throughout that year and most of 1940, attention had centered on continental and hemispheric defense. Then in late 1940, Chief of Naval Operations Adm. Harold E. Stark proposed in his "Plan Dog" memorandum that the United States focus instead on a scenario in which it would be allied with England and would concentrate its forces in the Atlantic/European theater to defeat Germany first, while assuming the strategic defensive against Japan. Secret Anglo-American staff conversations in Washington during early 1941 led to agreement in the so-called ABC-1 accord, and then the revised U.S. RAINBOW 5 plan, that this would constitute Anglo-American global strategy should the two powers find themselves at war with the Axis.

The German attack on the Soviet Union in June 1941 only reinforced the validity of this strategic approach while providing Britain and the United States with another ally, albeit one perceived as weak and not to be trusted. Nevertheless, Churchill and Roosevelt quickly welcomed Soviet leader Josef *Stalin and promised him material assistance. In July, Moscow and London signed an accord pledging mutual assistance and no separate peace. Then, in August, Churchill and Roosevelt met off the coast of Newfoundland in their first wartime summit conference and issued the Atlantic Charter, a statement of lofty war aims focusing on national self-determination and eschewing any territorial desires.

Roosevelt still refused to commit the United States to entering the conflict, however, or even to convoying Lend-Lease material to England. Yet he did create a de facto convoy system via the gradual extension of his definition of the western hemisphere "security zone," including the occupation of Greenland in April and Iceland in July, and naval cooperation with the British fleet. By September this had resulted in a German U-boat attack upon the U.S. destroyer *Greer* and a subsequent presidential "shoot on sight" order against German *submarines. By late November, Congress had agreed to requested revisions of the U.S. *Neutrality Acts that enabled Roosevelt to send Lend-Lease supplies on armed and escorted U.S. merchant vessels, and the United States found itself engaged in a full-scale if undeclared naval war with German submarines in the Atlantic.

War officially came in the Pacific when Japan responded to increasing U.S. economic sanctions, including a total freeze in the summer on Japanese assets, with a decision to go to war against Britain and the United States in an effort to obtain economic self-sufficiency before the sanctions crippled its warmaking potential. The 7 December surprise naval air attack on Pearl Harbor was designed to remove the naval threat to the flank of the Japanese invasion forces moving into the resource-rich Southeast Asia, thereby assuring military *victory. It did so, but at the cost of infuriating the American people and guaranteeing Japan the unlimited war it could not win instead of the limited, colonial war it desired.

Adolf *Hitler's decision to declare war on the United States three days later formally globalized the conflict. It also enabled Roosevelt and Churchill to reaffirm their "Germany First" strategy during the ensuing Arcadia summit conference in Washington. At that conference, they further agreed to the creation of a Combined Chiefs of Staff organization to run the global war and report directly to them; additional combined boards to meld their war efforts; full unity of command of all British and American land, naval, and air forces in all theaters; specific priorities for those theaters; and a combined Anglo-American invasion of French North Africa (Gymnast) in 1942. In March 1942, they further agreed to a global division of responsibility whereby the U.S. *Joint Chiefs of Staff (JCS) assumed primary responsibility for the Pacific and the British chiefs for the Middle East, while the European theater remained a combined responsibility.

The Arcadia decisions would create a very special and unparalleled wartime relationship between Britain and the United States within the framework of a larger coalition. That so-called Grand Alliance officially came into existence on 1 January 1942, when all the nations at war with any of the Axis powers signed the Declaration of the United Nations, pledging themselves to military victory and the creation of a postwar world based on the principles of the Atlantic Charter. The Soviet Union insisted upon retaining the Baltic States and portions of Poland and Romania that it had obtained as a result of the 1939 Ribbentrop-Molotov Pact, however, and in meetings with British foreign secretary Anthony Eden in December, Stalin pressed for recognition of this frontier shift as well as other postwar territorial agreements. Eden was ready to consider such accords as a means of strengthening the alliance, but Roosevelt disagreed vehemently. Remembering the disastrous impact of the World War I secret treaties, he feared that territorial discussions would lead to acrimony within the alliance and endanger public support for the war effort; consequently, postponement of all such discussions would remain a fundamental U.S. policy until 1945.

The Arcadia decisions were accompanied and followed by a series of Allied military defeats, which called into question the very survival of the coalition and some of its members. In the Pacific, Japanese forces quickly destroyed all Allied resistance and conquered the Dutch East Indies, Singapore, Malaya, the Philippines, and Burma. They also appeared capable of conquering India as well as Australia and New Zealand, and of forcing a Chinese withdrawal from the war. In Libya and Egypt, German forces under Gen. Erwin *Rommel advanced to within sixty miles of Alexandria and striking distance of the Suez Canal by June 1942. Simultaneously, German forces in Russia, checked in December for the first time in front of Moscow, now launched an offensive in the south that brought them to the Caucasus oil fields and Stalingrad on the Volga River. A complete Soviet collapse was widely predicted.

The American military response to these defeats was to propose the strategic defensive in all theaters except Europe and the immediate concentration of all available Anglo-American forces in England for a cross-Channel invasion in late 1942 or early 1943 in order to relieve the hard-pressed Red Army and prevent its collapse, as well as to force the Germans into a two-front war. Roosevelt concurred in March and Churchill in April, but in June the prime minister came to Washington once again and argued that the Channel could not be successfully crossed in 1942; rather than remain idle, Anglo-American forces should invade French North Africa, as originally planned during the Arcadia Conference, and in conjunction with a British offensive in Egypt trap Rommel's forces. The JCS objected vehemently to such a strategic shift, and the conference ended inconclusively. A few weeks later, however, London vetoed cross-Channel operations in 1942 and pressed for a North African substitute. Intent upon some 1942 offensive to bolster both public opinion and Soviet morale, Roosevelt concurred, and in mid-July sent his dissenting military advisers to London for a second time to reach accord. The result was an Anglo-American agreement to invade North Africa instead of northern France in the fall of 1942 (Torch).

Stalin, however, had been promised a cross-Channel operation. Indeed, Roosevelt had used this operation as a means of obtaining Soviet agreement not to press for any territorial agreements during the negotiations that led to the Anglo-Soviet Alliance of May 1942. Churchill therefore flew to Moscow in August to inform Stalin personally of the shift in Anglo-American plans for 1942. Simultaneously, he promised a large cross-Channel operation in 1943. With German forces at the gates of Stalingrad, the Soviet leader's response was frosty at best.

So, too, was the response of the JCS. From their perspective, Torch was a dangerous diversion and part of a badly flawed, politically inspired, peripheral strategy. Roosevelt had forced them to agree to it, but they now fought to limit its scope and free resources for Asia and the Pacific, where Japanese successes had created political as well as military crises. Most notable in this regard were continued Japanese movements into the South Pacific to cut Allied lines of communication to Australia and New Zealand, leading to pleas for assistance from those two governments and threats to remove their forces from the Middle East. Equally if not more ominous were warnings from Nationalist Chinese leader Chiang Kai-shek that collapse was imminent unless additional U.S. aid was forthcoming. Such aid was quickly sent and temporarily quieted the crisis on the mainland. The Pacific crisis, however, would lead to a series of major battles.

In the spring of 1942, U.S. forces had first succeeded in blunting the Japanese Pacific threat in two pivotal naval air engagements. The Battle of the *Coral Sea on 7–8 May, the first naval battle in which the opposing fleets did not even see each other, was tactically a draw but strategically a U.S. victory since the Japanese Navy halted its southern advance. The Battle of *Midway on 4 June was a much more decisive victory, one of the most decisive of the war and of naval history in general. Rather than surprising and destroying the remnants of the U.S. Fleet as planned, the Japanese were themselves surprised as U.S. forces broke their naval code and destroyed 4 of their aircraft carriers as well as 253 planes. Tokyo was never able to recover from this loss of capital ships, aircraft, and trained pilots. Nevertheless, Japanese forces continued their advance southward by launching a land offensive along the northeastern coast of New Guinea and by seizing Tulagi and Guadalcanal in the Solomons astride the U.S.-Australian lines of communication. Finding this intolerable, the JCS ordered the retaking of these islands at the same time the British were vetoing cross-Channel operations and proposing the North African substitute.

The fall of 1942 witnessed the end result of all these decisions—a series of major battles and campaigns that, taken together, constitute what is usually referred to as the "turning point" of the war. In October, British Gen. Bernard Law *Montgomery defeated Rommel at El Alamein and forced the latter to retreat westward. A few weeks later, on 8 November, combined Anglo-American forces under the command of Gen. Dwight D. *Eisenhower invaded Casablanca, Oran, and Algiers in French North Africa, secured French surrender, and drove eastward toward Tunisia, effectively trapping Rommel. Simultaneously, Australian, New Zealand, and U.S. forces halted the Japanese offensive on New Guinea and counterattacked while U.S. forces took Guadalcanal and in a six-month campaign of attrition succeeded in holding it against numerous Japanese counterattacks. In November, the Red Army counterattacked and succeeded in first isolating and then forcing the January surrender of the entire German Sixth Army in Stalingrad. Taken together, these victories ended all Axis hopes of total victory and gave the strategic initiative to the Allies. The Axis still controlled enormous populations, resources, and territory, however, and their defeat was far from secured or predetermined. Indeed, Allied forces were badly dispersed in numerous theaters, and future military stalemate remained a distinct possibility.

In January 1943, Roosevelt, Churchill, and their advisers met once again to plan future strategy, this time in the recently captured Casablanca. Once again the British were able to win American acquiescence in their strategy, now in the form of an invasion of Sicily (Husky) after Rommel had been cleared from Tunisia and the probable postponement of cross-Channel operations until 1944. In return, the Americans under the prodding of naval chief Adm. Ernest J. *King insisted that more attention be given to the war against Japan, both in the Pacific and via operations in Burma to reopen supply lines to China. Both nations further agreed that first priority had to be given to the war against German submarines in the Atlantic, and that a combined bomber offensive should be launched against Germany from the United Kingdom.

The Casablanca Conference is best known not for these strategic decisions, but for Roosevelt's announcement at a press conference of the Allied policy of "Unconditional Surrender." Actually, this had long been the unstated policy of and lowest common denominator within the Grand Alliance. Roosevelt verbalized it on this occasion for multiple political reasons: to reassure Stalin in the continued absence of a second front; to reassure Chiang in the continued absence of a major military effort in the China theater; and to reassure British and American public opinion in the aftermath of controversial compromises that Eisenhower had made with the Vichy French official, Adm. Jean Darlan, in North Africa. In doing so, however, Roosevelt made Unconditional Surrender *the* official Allied policy and thereby indirectly reinforced his own policy of postponing territorial issues until war's end.

Anglo-American forces in 1943 obtained most of the objectives outlined at Casablanca, albeit not as rapidly as anticipated nor with the decisive results desired. Simultaneously, and to an extent consequently, serious military and political disputes arose once again within the Grand Alliance and threatened to disrupt the coalition. These disputes were successfuly resolved in a series of high-level conferences at year's end, thereby establishing both an agreed-upon strategy for the duration of the war and a framework for establishing a postwar peace.

The greatest Allied successes in 1943 were on the eastern front and in the Atlantic. In July, Soviet intelligence enabled the Red Army to prepare for and halt, in the largest tank battle of the war, Hitler's thrust at the Kursk salient; German forces never recovered from the ensuing destruction of their armor. Simultaneously, Anglo-American forces made effective use of their own intelligence breakthroughs, most notably cryptographic intercepts from the Enigma Machine (*ULTRA), as well as new naval and air tactics to turn the tide against German submarines in the Battle of the Atlantic. In other areas, however, Anglo-American successes were far more limited.

Unable to reconcile U.S. precision daylight bombing with British nighttime area bombing, the Combined Chiefs of Staff in effect allowed each nation to pursue its favored approach simultaneously under the umbrella of the Combined Bomber Offensive. While German cities were devastated and civilian *casualties mounted, this controversial campaign also resulted in very high Allied casualties and destroyed neither German industrial capacity nor the civilian will to resist. In that sense it was a failure and revealed serious shortcomings in the strategic bombing concept. It did force the German Luftwaffe into an extensive war of attrition, however, one it could not win due to the enormous U.S. productive capacity. The result would be complete Anglo-American control of the air by the time their forces invaded France in June 1944.

In Tunisia, Rommel in February 1943 was able to inflict a stinging defeat on the still green U.S. forces at Kasserine Pass. The Germans were soon overwhelmed by British forces under Montgomery coming from the south and the revived American forces under Gen. George S. *Patton and Gen. Omar N. *Bradley coming from the west, however, and on 13 May they surrendered in Tunis. Then, on 10 July, Anglo-American forces under Eisenhower's overall command succeessfully invaded Sicily. Consequently, the Italians deposed Benito Mussolini and began secret peace negotiations that culminated in a 3 September surrender. Simultaneously, Eisenhower's forces invaded the toe and heel of the Italian "boot" and Salerno just below Naples.

In the Pacific, U.S. naval forces completed their victory at Guadalcanal and moved up the chain of Solomon Islands, while Gen. Douglas *MacArthur's forces stopped the Japanese advance in New Guinea and in a series of "leapfrogging" moves along the northern coast dealt

Japanese forces a series of stinging defeats. By year's end these dual lines of advance had isolated the major Japanese base at Rabaul and precluded the necessity of a costly invasion. Where to go next aroused heated controversy. Reverting to their prewar ORANGE war plan, naval planners called for a major thrust across the central Pacific toward Formosa. MacArthur disagreed and argued instead for a major offensive in his Southwest Pacific theater aimed at liberation of the Philippines. The JCS temporarily resolved this dispute by sanctioning both offensives, a resolution made possible by U.S. productive capacity and the subsequent availability of resources, with the final territorial objectives remaining undetermined. While MacArthur's forces continued their leapfrogging along the New Guinea coast, U.S. naval and Marine forces under Adm. Chester *Nimitz began their central Pacific advance in November with bloody but successful assaults on Tarawa and Makin in the Gilbert Islands. The availability of resources did not extend to Southeast Asia, however, and the Burma invasion had to be canceled.

While American preoccupation with the Pacific deeply disturbed the British, their own preoccupation with the Mediterranean at the expense of cross-Channel operations deeply upset the Americans. This strategic disagreement was heatedly debated and compromised during the May Trident and August Quadrant summit conferences in Washington and Quebec. At these meetings, the Americans agreed to the Italian campaign but only within limits that would allow for a May 1944 cross-Channel assault (Overlord) under an American commander. In September and October, Churchill requested additional delays in the movement of landing craft and troops from the Mediterranean to England so as to take advantage in the Aegean of the Italian surrender, reinforce Eisenhower's forces in the wake of Hitler's rescue of Mussolini and decision to hold the Italian peninsula, and break the resulting military stalemate south of Rome.

Along with this Anglo-American conflict came continuing problems with the Chinese due to the cancellation of the Burma operation and a very serious split with the Soviets over both Poland and cross-Channel operations. In April 1943, Stalin broke diplomatic relations with the Polish government-in-exile, supposedly over Polish demands for investigation of the recently revealed Katyn Forest massacre of Polish officers, but actually due to Polish refusal to cede eastern Poland to Russia. Less than two months later, Stalin angrily denounced the further postponement of cross-Channel operations until 1944. Secret low-level German-Soviet contacts took place during the spring, but without any concrete results. By the summer, separate peace rumors were filling the air.

All of these conflicts were resolved in a series of high-level Allied conferences held between October and December 1943. The first of these was the Tripartite Foreign Ministers' Conference in Moscow, during which the British and Americans reaffirmed their intention to cross the Channel in the spring of 1944 and the Soviets responded with formal agreement to the Unconditional Surrender policy, Allied occupation of Germany, and a postwar collective security organization. Then, in November, Roosevelt met with Chiang as well as Churchill in Cairo and mollified the former with promises of an amphibious operation in the Bay of Bengal as well as postwar return of territory and equality as a great power. Immediately thereafter, Roosevelt

and Churchill flew to Teheran for the first "Big Three" meeting, during which Roosevelt and Stalin finally forced Churchill to abandon additional Mediterranean campaigns and agree to lanch Overlord across the Channel in May 1944, with forces in Italy shifted to a supporting invasion of southern France (Anvil). Stalin in turn promised a simultaneous Soviet offensive in the east and entry into the war against Japan once Germany had been defeated. Informal political talks also took place, most notably over a possible shift in Polish boundaries westward and the future status of Germany. Churchill and Roosevelt then returned to Cairo for yet another conference, during which the Burma operation was once again postponed so as to provide Overlord with sufficient landing craft and Roosevelt appointed Eisenhower to command the operation.

This series of conferences would prove critical, both militarily and politically. It by no means ended Allied conflicts and differences, but it did result in an agreed-upon *strategy that would preserve the alliance and lead to total military victory. It also established the essential prerequisites for a new postwar order based on Allied dominance and cooperation, verbalized by Roosevelt as the "Four Policemen," within a global collective security framework. Additionally, it marked both a decline in British power and the rise of the Soviet Union and the United States. Henceforth, these two emerging superpowers would exercise more and more control over both the war effort and postwar plans.

The year 1944 witnessed the results of these 1943 accords in an extraordinary series of Allied military victories. The most notable of these involving U.S. forces was Operation Overlord, the largest amphibious invasion in history. After meticulous preparation, including an extensive deception plan, it was successfully launched on 6 June 1944 against the Normandy coast under Eisenhower's overall command. Progress was extremely slow, however, even after the launching a few weeks later of the promised and massive Soviet offensive in Byelorussia, and only in late July did Allied forces break out of the bridgehead. Their progress after that date was extremely rapid, however, partially because Hitler's simultaneous decision to counterattack at Avranches enabled them to form a pincer that almost destroyed his entire army in the west. In the ensuing debacle, Anglo-American forces were able to sweep through France very rapidly, liberating Paris on 25 August and moving into the Low Countries. But large numbers of German forces managed to escape before the pincers closed around the so-called Falaise pocket, and they would effectively regroup in the fall to fight again.

The Anglo-American sweep through France was aided not only by the Soviet offensive in the east, but also by a breakthrough in Italy that culminated in the capture of Rome on 4 June and the subsequent invasion of southern France in August. These took place long after they were supposed to, however, and were subjects of great controversy. Seeking to break the Italian deadlock in late 1943, Churchill had pressed for an amphibious landing at Anzio. Although successfully launched in January 1944, it remained an isolated and endangered bridgehead until May–June, when Allied forces under Gen. Mark *Clark finally broke through the main German lines. Clark's decision to take Rome enabled the main body of German troops to escape northward and thus to fight on until the spring of 1945.

The Anzio fiasco delayed preparations for Anvil and reinforced Churchill's desire to cancel that operation in favor of a movement eastward into Yugoslavia. Fed up with the prime minister's continued interest in the Balkans, and aware of Eisenhower's desperate need for additional port facilities, the Americans bluntly refused such a shift and insisted that a delayed Anvil be launched, even after Overlord. Churchill was forced to accede to the renamed Operation Dragoon, and on 15 August, Allied forces landed in southern France and quickly advanced up the Rhône Valley, where they joined Eisenhower's forces moving eastward. Those forces now included nine armies organized into three army groups: the British-Canadian 21st under Montgomery, the American 12th under Bradley, and the Franco-American 6th under Gen. Jacob Devers.

A similar string of military successes took place in the Pacific during 1944 as the "dual advance" picked up momentum. While MacArthur's forces continued to leapfrog along the northern coast of New Guinea and nearby islands, Nimitz took Kwajalein in the Marshall Islands. During the summer his forces conquered Saipan, Tinian, and Guam in the Marianas, and destroyed what remained of the Japanese naval air forces in the Battle of the *Philippine Sea. In October, the joint chiefs finally decided to invade the Philippines rather than Formosa, and MacArthur's forces landed at Leyte Gulf. In the ensuing naval Battle of *Leyte Gulf, the largest naval engagement in history, the Japanese surface fleet was virtually destroyed. Simultaneously, U.S. submarines sank much of the Japanese merchant fleet.

The first nine months of 1944 were also marked by substantial progress in postwar planning. In July, representatives of forty-four nations meeting in Bretton Woods, New Hampshire, established the basis of a new postwar economic order, including a *World Bank and an International Monetary Fund. Then from August to October, British, Chinese, Soviet, and U.S. diplomats meeting at the Dumbarton Oaks estate in Washington, D.C., reached agreement on the essentials of a postwar collective security organization. In September, Churchill, Roosevelt, and their advisers met for a second time in Quebec (Octagon), both to plan their next military moves and to consider numerous postwar issues. As Churchill noted at the beginning of this conference, virtually everything the Allies had touched in the last nine months had turned to gold.

The luster was quickly tarnished, however. Throughout 1944, the China theater and Burma had remained notable exceptions to the string of Allied victories, with the Japanese repelling Allied ground and air offensives and launching major counteroffensives of their own. By May, the Allies had successfully halted an invasion of India; but in China, the Japanese overran the U.S. air bases that had recently been established by Gen. Claire *Chennault and precipitated a near collapse of Chinese forces. U.S. Gen. Joseph *Stilwell, who had been sent to China in 1942 to serve as Chiang's chief of staff, blamed the Chinese leader for the fiasco. So did his superiors in Washington, who now demanded that control of Chinese forces be ceded to Stilwell. Chiang, however, insisted that Stilwell was the problem and in the fall demanded his recall. Roosevelt complied and replaced him with Gen. Albert C. *Wedemeyer, but the combination of success in the Pacific and failure on the Asian mainland led the JCS to downgrade the future importance of the China theater, put increased emphasis on obtaining Soviet entry into the Far Eastern war, and focus even more intently on the naval advance in the Pacific. By October that advance was running into problems of its own, largely as a result of new Japanese suicidal tactics (most notably but far from excusively the kamikaze air attacks) that increased both the length of battles and the number of U.S. casualties.

The situation in the European theater during the fall was not much better. In August, German forces had appeared to be on the brink of collapse, but they were able to rally in the fall and postpone total defeat—most significantly when they checked Montgomery's September attempt to use airborne forces to cross the Rhine River defenses in the Netherlands (Market-Garden). Thereafter, Eisenhower's controversial "broad-front" approach, involving a series of slower, methodical offensive operations to bring his entire front to the Rhine defenses, dominated Anglo-American strategy despite heated protests by his subordinates, each of whom insisted he could end the war if given all the supplies. Then, in December, Hitler launched a counteroffensive against the thin U.S. forces in the Ardennes in an effort to reach Antwerp and thereby split the British and American armies. The resulting "bulge" in the American lines gave this largest U.S. engagement of the war its name, and led Eisenhower to temporarily transfer control of two U.S. armies north of the German advance to Montgomery. The bulge never developed into an open break, largely because of fierce resistance by the outnumbered Americans, combined with reinforcements and counterattacks by Patton in the south and Montgomery in the north, the return to good weather and with it Allied airpower, and a massive Soviet offensive that brought the Red Army to within thirty-five miles of Berlin. In the end, Hitler wasted the last of his reserves on this operation. Its only accomplishment was to delay further Anglo-American advances until the spring and thereby guarantee that the Red Army would reach Berlin before the British or the Americans.

By early 1945 this probability, along with the extent of Soviet conquests in Eastern and Central Europe, had begun to worry numerous American as well as British officials. Stalin's August–September halting of the Red Army on the east bank of the Vistula River and abject refusal to assist the Polish Home Army in its uprising against the Germans in Warsaw appalled these individuals and led to deep worries over the extent of Soviet territorial conquests and postwar goals. With American vetoes foreclosing his proposed military operations to secure some postwar influence in the Balkans, Churchill in October flew to Moscow for a second time and arranged with Stalin for British and Soviet spheres of influence in the Balkans; two months later, he made use of this agreement to suppress forcibly a Communist uprising in Greece.

Given this fait accompli as well as military events and the deterioration in Allied relations, Roosevelt realized that he could no longer avoid discussion of postwar issues. Such issues, as well as strategy for termination of the war, would dominate the second Big Three conference, held in February 1945 at Yalta in the Crimea. There the Big Three were able to reach agreement on operations for the final defeat of Germany, military occupation zones in Germany and Berlin, a shift of Polish boundaries westward and a Communist-dominated Polish provisional government, free postwar elections for all of Europe, the outline of a charter for what would become the *United Nations, and Soviet entry into the war against Japan within three months of German defeat in return for territorial concessions focusing on reacquisition of Russian losses from the Russo-Japanese War of 1904–05. The advent of the *Cold War after 1945 led to severe condemnation of Roosevelt for many of these agreements, most notably those concerning Poland and the Far East. At the time, however, he and his advisers believed that they had guaranteed both total victory in the war and a stable postwar peace, and in the ensuing years his supporters defended the accords as both understandable and unavoidable in light of the power, position, and continued importance of the Red Army to the war effort.

The post–*Yalta Conference euphoria proved to be totally justified militarily but largely unjustified diplomatically. In March, U.S. First Army forces captured an intact Rhine River bridge at Remagen, leading Eisenhower to alter his plans and allow these forces rather than Montgomery's to seize the initiative. When Montgomery did cross a few weeks later, the two forces linked up and trapped 350,000 German troops in the Ruhr. After another heated Anglo-American debate, Eisenhower then ordered a limited U.S. movement southeastward to the Elbe River rather than a move by Montgomery against Berlin, on the grounds that he needed to prevent a collision with the Red Army and a Nazi movement into the Bavarian Alps for protracted *guerrilla warfare, and that the German capital was no longer a military objective or worth U.S. casualties—especially in light of the fact that by the Yalta accords the city would be divided into zones of occupation anyway. Meanwhile, Soviet behavior in Poland and Romania led Churchill and Roosevelt to accuse Stalin of breaking the Yalta accords, while the Soviet leader in turn accused them of trying to negotiate a separate peace on the Italian front. Amidst bitter recriminations, Roosevelt died unexpectedly on 12 April, leaving a host of unresolved military and diplomatic issues to his unprepared successor, Harry S *Truman. A few weeks later, Soviet and American forces met along the Elbe at Torgau, splitting Germany in half. On 30 April, Hitler committed suicide in his Berlin bunker as Red Army forces took the city, and on 7–8 May his successor, Adm. Karl Doenitz, surrendered unconditionally.

With the common enemy totally defeated, Soviet-American relations continued to deteriorate throughout the spring. Some differences were resolved by Harry Hopkins's June visit to Moscow and the July Big Three summit conference in the Berlin suburb of Potsdam, but only partially and temporarily as the two nations' definitions of a secure postwar world began to collide and mutual suspicions increased. The method by which the war against Japan came to an end both reflected and reinforced those collisions and suspicions.

American forces made substantial progress in the Pacific War during the first half of 1945, liberating the Philippines, destroying what remained of the Japanese merchant fleet, conquering the islands of Iwo Jima and Okinawa, and launching a devastating strategic bombing campaign against Japanese cities from their bases in the Marianas. Nevertheless, the Japanese used their new suicide tactics to exact a heavy toll on American troops and naval forces in the Philippine, Iwo Jima, and Okinawa campaigns. Although Japan's position was clearly hopeless, its armed forces fought on fanatically in the hope of forcing a negoti-

ated peace with the Americans. Simultaneously, American scientists successfully developed and in July successfully tested the first nuclear weapon. Seeing this weapon as a means of shocking the Japanese into a quick surrender and obtaining the "diplomatic bonus" of impressing the Soviets with this new, awesome power, Truman and his advisers ordered the use of atomic weapons against Japanese cities. On 6 August, Hiroshima was destroyed, and on 9 August, Nagasaki. In between, on 8 August, the Soviet Union entered the war, thereby fulfilling its Yalta pledge and depriving Japan of all hopes for a mediated end to the war. On 14 August, Japanese leaders agreed to surrender, albeit with the proviso that the emperor be retained, and on 2 September, they signed the official surrender documents.

World War II thus ended militarily. Diplomatically, however, continued friction within the Grand Alliance would preclude the possibility of any general peace treaty and would lead instead to the forty-five-year Cold War between the Soviet Union and the United States.

[See also Air Force, U.S.: Predecessors of, 1907–46; Army, U.S.: Since 1941; China-Burma-India Theater; Holocaust, U.S. War Effort and the; Marine Corps, U.S.: 1914–45; Navy, U.S.: 1899–1945; World War II, U.S. Air Operations in: The Air War in Europe; World War II, U.S. Air Operations in: The War Against Japan; World War II, U.S. Naval Operations in: The North Atlantic; World War II, U.S. Naval Operations in: The Pacific.]

• Center for Military History, U.S. Army, United States Army in World War II, 79 vols., 1947–. Samuel E. Morison, History of U.S. Naval Operations in World War II, 15 vols. 1947–62. Wesley F. Craven and James L. Cate, eds., The Army Air Forces in World War II, 7 vols., 1948–1958. William H. McNeill, America, Britain and Russia: Their Cooperation and Conflict, 1941–1946, 1953. U.S. Marine Corps, History of U.S. Marine Corps Operations in World War II, 5 vols., 1958–1971. John L. Snell, Illusion and Necessity: The Diplomacy of Global War, 1939–1945, 1963. Herbert Feis, Churchill, Roosevelt and Stalin: The War They Waged and the Peace They Sought, 1967. Peter Calvocoressi, Guy Wint, and John Pritchard, Total War, rev. ed., 2 vols., 1989. Gaddis Smith, American Diplomacy in World War II, 1941–1945, 2nd ed. 1985. H. P. Willmott, The Great Crusade, 1989. Martin Kitchen, A World in Flames: A Short History of the Second World War in Europe and Asia, 1939–1945, 1990. Robin Edmonds, The Big Three: Churchill, Roosevelt, and Stalin in Peace & War, 1991. Robert J. Maddox, The United States and World War II, 1992. David Reynolds, Warren F. Kimball, and A. O. Chubarian, Allies at War: The Soviet, American and British Experience, 1939–1945, 1994. Gerhard Weinberg, A World at Arms: A Global History of World War II, 1994. Richard Overy, Why the Allies Won, 1995. Stephen E. Ambrose, American Heritage New History of World War II, 1997. Stephen E. Ambrose, Citizen Soldiers: The U.S. Army from the Normandy Beaches to the Bulge to the Surrender of Germany, 1997. Tom Brokaw, The Greatest Generation, 1998.

—Mark A. Stoler

WORLD WAR II (1939–45): DOMESTIC COURSE

The early stages of American *mobilization before its entry into World War II in December 1941 were halting and gave little indication of the prodigious efforts to come. A critical step was massively to expand the U.S. *Army. After France fell in June 1940, this could no longer be delayed. But President Franklin D. *Roosevelt, who was soon to run for an unprecedented third term, did not wish to offend antiwar voters—often called isolationists—so, in the end both sponsors of the *conscription program known as Selective

Service were Republicans, Senator Edward R. Burke of Nebraska and Congressman James W. Wadsworth of New York. Among the other Republicans who provided essential support were two Wall Street lawyers with a longtime interest in the military, Grenville Clarke and Henry L. *Stimson, the latter a distinguished statesman who soon became secretary of war.

On 2 August, Roosevelt finally endorsed Selective Service, and so did Wendell Willkie, the Republican candidate for president. Burke-Wadsworth's Selective Training and Service Act received majority votes of 58–31 in the Senate and 263–149 in the House, and was signed into law 16 September 1940. America's first peacetime draft provided for the registration of men aged twenty-one to thirty-five who might be called up for twelve months of training and service within the United States. The first call inducted 1.2 million men, while 800,000 reservists were mobilized as well. Owing to the high degree of public support, there was no wholesale refusal to register for the draft, unlike during World War I, although there was some *conscientious objection by pacifists and others. The main difficulty was that a U.S. Army numbering only 270,000 officers and men could not more than triple in size during one year without having serious problems.

In the end, these problems were solved, however. Even the extension in 1941 of the term of enlistment from one year to two and a half provoked little more than angry protests from the men—although it was almost derailed in the House, which extended service by a margin of one vote. If late in coming, the draft—later stretched to include men aged eighteen to forty-four and service for the duration—worked well. A total of more than 16 million men and women served in the military during the war, approximately 11 million in the army and Army Air Force, 4 million in the navy, 670,000 in the Marines, and 330,00 in women's military units. Most were draftees, although 5 million volunteered for service, primarily in the navy and Army Air Force. The army, stretched thin around the world, could have used even more people. But women were not drafted for noncombat assignments, as in Britain. The military also lost large numbers of men who were declared "4-F," that is, mentally or physically unfit for service. Others were given occupational deferments to keep them on critical jobs in defense plants.

Mobilizing the civilian economy proved to be more difficult than raising an army. Even after his reelection in 1940, President Roosevelt was reluctant to make demands on the public, and refused also to hand over the direction of mobilization to a single head, or "czar." Thus, he created a series of agencies with limited mandates, commonly referred to as "monstrosities" at the time, while shortages of commodities and disputes over priorities made a farce of prewar mobilization.

After the Japanese attack on *Pearl Harbor and the U.S. formal entry into the war, Roosevelt established the War Production Board. He also created an Office of Economic Stabilization under James Byrnes, an ex-senator, which began to bring order out of chaos. A Controlled Materials Plan finally established an effective method of allocating critical commodities. The rubber shortage, caused by Japan's seizure of most of the world's rubber trees, was solved by building synthetic rubber plants and rationing gasoline. The rationing, which politicians feared people would reject, won popular acceptance after a distinguished panel led by the financier Bernard *Baruch issued a report proving beyond doubt that there was no way to conserve rubber except by limiting automobile use. Consequently, in 1942 a national speed limit of 35 miles per hour was established, and most drivers were given a weekly limit of 3 gallons of gas.

War financing was an outstanding success, thanks in important part to the work of Beardsley Ruml, the treasurer of Macy's Department stores. He led a group of businessmen who argued that the income tax should be extended to all workers, instead of the affluent few, and that taxes should be collected "at the source," in the form of payroll deductions. This effort resulted in the Revenue Act of 1942, which raised the number of taxpayers from 7 to 42 million. It cost the United States $318 billion to wage World War II, 45 percent of which came from current revenues—a much higher percentage than in any previous war. The balance was paid for by borrowing from banks, bond sales to financial institutions, and also to the general public—which bought $49 billion worth of Liberty bonds.

The manufacture of automobiles, home appliances, and many other products was suspended for the duration. Meanwhile, industrial wages rose by 22 percent and net farm income doubled. With more money chasing fewer goods, inflation would have soared had not the government imposed wage and price controls, which were resented but largely effective. So, too, was the elaborate system of rationing food, clothing, and other consumer goods, in which stamps or coupons worth various "points" were required in addition to cash to make a purchase. As availability and the number of points required for any given item changed constantly, shopping could be a nightmare. Still, despite some black marketeering, rationing did the job, aided by backyard "Victory Gardens," which in 1943 produced 8 million tons of produce—more than half the nation's total.

The United States never fully mobilized, despite achieving full employment. There was no labor draft, for example, though Roosevelt suggested one in 1944—much later than he should have. Congress refused to act even then, so industry was forced to rely on incentives that varied greatly from firm to firm, resulting in local labor deficits. Often these were caused by housing shortages, which neither government nor private enterprise did much to ease. With so many men in uniform, industry was forced, against its will at first, to hire women, including married women with children. Yet it was rare for government at any level, or for industry itself, to provide the child-care and support services that mothers required. Despite all obstacles, women flocked to defense plants. Their symbol, "Rosie the Riveter," was based on fact. America could not have produced what it did without the millions of women who took the hardest jobs in shipyards, steel mills, aircraft plants, and every heavy industry except mining.

Yet, even without going flat out, America stunned the world by arming and equipping not only its own armed forces but, to a considerable extent, those of its Allies as well. Before Pearl Harbor, Roosevelt had said that the United States would become the "arsenal of democracy," and so it did. Some $50 billion in Lend-Lease aid flowed to all corners of the world. Britain and its Commonwealth received about half of this; the Soviet Union $10 billion. At war's end, the Soviet Union possessed 655,000 motor vehicles, of which 400,000 were made by Americans; the

United States also supplied the USSR with 2,000 locomotives, 11,000 freight cars, and 540,000 tons of rail. In addition, the Soviets received from their allies, chiefly the United States, over 20,000 combat aircraft and 11,500 *tanks and self-propelled guns.

Predictably, national elections were determined by military events. In the 1942 congressional elections, after a string of American defeats in the Pacific War, and before the successful invasion of North Africa, voters elected so many Republicans that, together with conservative Democrats, they gained effective control of Congress. Although it gave Roosevelt great discretion over military and diplomatic affairs, the conservative coalition in Congress did all it could to destroy the New Deal—ending many useful social agencies, such as the Civilian Conservation Corps and the National Youth Administration. In the 1944 presidential election, with the war going well, Republicans took a beating at the polls. FDR, and his new vice president, Harry S. *Truman, defeated Governor Thomas E. Dewey of New York, winning 25 million votes to his 22 million. The New Deal, however, remained curtailed.

Although the mass media were filled with war news and exhortations of every kind, government did not establish a ministry of propaganda, despite considerable pressure to do so. Instead, when Roosevelt established the Office of War Information, he gave it a limited mandate, and did not react strongly in 1943 when Congress abolished all of its domestic functions except for the Bureau of Motion Pictures—which attempted, with little success, to make films more progressive. Hollywood did crank out an enormous number of war-related movies, a few of which, such as Casablanca, live on still. For the most part they were ephemeral; many of the most successful films of the period, such as Going My Way and National Velvet, had nothing to do with the war.

There was no ministry of science either, yet weapons development was one of the great successes of the war. In 1941, FDR created an Office of Scientific Research and Development (OSRD) to coordinate, rather than direct, advancements in *weaponry. Headed by Dr. Vannevar *Bush, the OSRD brought cooperation between military, industrial, and educational experts to a level never before seen in the United States. Under OSRD direction, *radar was improved, the radio proximity fuse was developed, and many other innovations created for military use. And it was OSRD that persuaded Roosevelt to back what became the atomic bomb—which entailed not only building an entire industry from scratch, but persuading Congress to finance a secret effort, the *Manhattan Project, without being told what it was paying for.

Popular entertainments of every kind flourished, partly because of the need for diversion, partly because there was little to buy at a time when workers were earning more money than ever. Ball parks, racetracks, and similar facilities prospered, as did the music industry. Perhaps more than films, the popularity of certain types of songs says much about the national mood in wartime. The biggest hits were not about the war itself, but spoke to the emotions that *war inspired. The most popular song of 1944 was the touching "I'll Be Seeing You." Another hit was "I'll Be Home for Christmas," with its melancholy epilogue— "if only in my dreams." The biggest seller of the war years was Irving Berlin's nostalgic "White Christmas."

Although civil rights and liberties were not suspended entirely, as during World War I, they took the usual beating. A great miscarriage of justice occurred in 1942 when the entire Japanese and Japanese American population of the West Coast was transported to internment camps. Despite receiving a clean bill of health from the FBI following a roundup of suspected aliens, more than 100,000 of them would spend much of the war behind barbed wire in so-called "relocation" camps, an action upheld by the Supreme Court in the *Japanese American internment cases. Racism further disfigured the national effort when minorities sought work in the booming war industries. Attacks against Mexican Americans took place in Southern California, and against blacks in many places. The worst race riot broke out in Detroit on 20 June 1943, leaving 35 dead and 700 wounded—most of them African Americans.

Yet, despite all the difficulties and heartbreaks, and the ugly outbursts of racism, war made life seem more precious, which is probably why the suicide rate fell by a third. Similarly, the birth and marriage rates, which had reached new lows in the thirties, started their fateful rise—early signs of the baby boom that would transform the nation.

Although America suffered less than any other major warring nation, *victory did not come without sacrifice. In addition to the 400,000 uniformed personnel who died, hundreds of thousands more were disabled. All who served lost, as most felt at the time, on average three years of their lives—as did their wives, sweethearts, and children. Americans did everything that was asked of them, and would have done more if more had been wanted, as polls repeatedly showed. At war's end they were right to feel proud: in saving their country from defeat, they also helped to save democracy, putting all free peoples in their debt.

[See also Demography and War; Economy and War; Ethnicity and War; Film; Gender and War; Internment of Enemy Aliens; Music, War and the Military in; Propaganda and Public Relations, Government; Public Financing and Budgeting for War; Public Opinion, War, and the Military; Race Relations and War; Science Technology, War, and the Military; Society and War; Women in the Military.]

• Richard M. Dalfiume, Desegregation of the U.S. Armed Forces: Fighting on Two Fronts, 1939–1945, 1969. Geoffrey Perrett, Days of Sadness, Years of Triumph: The American People, 1939–1945, 1973. Paul A. C. Koistinen, The Military-Industrial Complex, 1980. H. G. Nichols, ed., Washington Dispatches 1941–1945: Weekly Political Reports from the British Embassy, 1981. Nelson Lichtenstein, Labor's War at Home: The CIO in World War II, 1982. Peter Irons, Justice at War, 1983. Harold G. Vatter, The U.S. Economy in World War II, 1985. Paul Fussell, Wartime: Understanding and Behavior in the Second World War, 1989. Doris Weatherford, American Women and World War II, 1990. William L. O'Neill, A Democracy at War: America's Fight at Home and Abroad in World War II, 1993.

—William L. O'Neill

WORLD WAR II (1939–45): POSTWAR IMPACT

Insulated from the war's destructiveness, most Americans foresaw that World War II would shape their future, but not how it would. Alone among major combatants, the United States was physically undamaged and economically vitalized by the war. Even its loss of 400,000 uniformed personnel in combat was censored in visual culture and small compared to other countries' losses. Just as most Americans had to imagine the war itself, they had to imagine its consequences.

To do so, they projected the past into the future. Above all, they felt stung by World War I's tragic aftermath, traumatized by the Great Depression, and transfixed by mighty enemies in World War II. Uncertain, secretive, exhausted by the war, President Franklin D. *Roosevelt gave them only a few signals about what to expect, but did voice their broad desire for a better life and for "security"—a word inscribed in the names of countless postwar agencies and acts of Congress. Thus, most Americans saw the war's impact as rising steeply during hostilities, then receding sharply until some ill-defined, worrisome normality resumed. Enormous focus on returning 16 million *veterans to civilian life exhibited that expectation—almost magically, the veterans' readjustment would be the nation's—even as the tool for achieving readjustment, the *G.I. Bill (1944), broke sharply from the past. The postwar economy attracted fear and hope, nourished by the depression and by propaganda promising an economic reward for wartime sacrifices. Thanks partly to the G.I. Bill, the hope was largely met.

In contrast, few foresaw the war's consequences for social relations. In fact, the war undermined the existing racial system by extending federal power into the Jim Crow South, inspiring the aspirations and tactics of African Americans, and reshaping national priorities. Pushed by black spokesmen like A. Philip *Randolph, leaders increasingly saw racial discrimination as an anachronism that squandered resources needed to wield power abroad and mocked the claim of defending freedom against Fascist and Communist oppression. Though cautious on racial matters, FDR sounded this theme: a nation facing "totalitarianism" should strengthen its "unity and morale by refuting at home the very theories which we are fighting abroad."

President Harry S. *Truman's 1948 order banning segregation and discrimination in the military flowed from forces set in motion by the war, which also eroded religious and ethnic barriers. The war reworked systems of gender and sexuality in more complex ways. Prizing both male virtue and women's contributions, wartime culture set the stage for a virtual invention of the "traditional family," to the detriment of many women and homosexuals. However varied their fortunes, social groups nonetheless had something in common: their fate was now shaped by America's global power and the national government's resultant additional authority. As world war faded into cold war, this temporary change turned into a lasting one that few anticipated.

Expectations were nearer the mark regarding international relations: Americans knew their nation was a superpower; most expected it to act like one, and few yearned for the *isolationism that purportedly had led to World War II. Axis aggression, the Depression, and the war's startling technological advances, all seemed to forecast a seamless postwar world presenting new threats to America's economic and military security. Against those threats, most leaders argued, the United States would have to mobilize power even in peacetime, just as wartime *victory gave many Americans confidence that they could do so, alone or through the new *United Nations. As Gen. George C. *Marshall warned in 1945, the vast "ocean distances" that once protected America had evaporated; reliance on such outdated factors would put "the treasure and freedom of this great Nation in a paper bag."

Initially, many Americans feared renascent German and Japanese power, but Americans' brittle mix of anxiety and arrogance, stoked by their possession and use of atomic weapons, shaped perceptions of the Soviet Union. Many soon regarded Stalinist Russia as the old Axis wolf in bear's clothing—"Red fascism" was a common term eliding the two. Likewise, for decades, leaders defending their *Cold War policies cited failure to foresee Axis aggression and violence, symbolized by the 1938 Munich Conference and the 1941 attack on *Pearl Harbor. While scholars dispute the Cold War's causes, World War II certainly created an institutional and imaginative apparatus in America that at least initially exaggerated—with help from a ruthless Stalinist regime—the Soviet menace to the United States. The war's greatest legacy was Americans' newfound sense of permanent peril and the Cold War it helped to nourish.

Thus, too, postwar developments extended the impact of World II into an indeterminate future. The Cold War gave permanence to temporary wartime improvisations in national governance—secrecy, *conscription, repression, industrial and scientific mobilization, and high levels of defense spending. Because of the Cold War, or under its guise, America exercised awesome military, economic, and political power in the postwar world. World War II alone did not make that happen, but it set the stage for it to happen, as did many of America's war-weakened European allies, who nervously encouraged its postwar role and joined it in *NATO (the North Atlantic Treaty Organization, 1949). Since victory impresses leaders and institutions, American technological and logistical supremacy in World War II also shaped how Americans would wage later wars—including, disastrously, the *Vietnam War. Seen that way, World War II accelerated America's militarization—pervasive military and defense influence—in a historical process as defining as industrialization and urbanization earlier had been.

Its handmaiden was a more powerful national government, a development often erroneously attributed solely to the New Deal. Indeed, national security imparted to the federal government a size, reach, and legitimacy never decisively achieved under the New Deal. Its broad mandate embraced social programs—the G.I. Bill, initiatives in civil rights, and federal aid to education, for example—seen variously as rewards for Americans' sacrifices in war, expressions of national vitality, and necessities for tapping all available resources. Rather than imposing sharp choices between "welfare" and "warfare," the Cold War "militarized" national security and blurred the two, at least as long as national abundance and credible threats abroad allowed. The war taught a related lesson that few leaders would forget: massive government spending promoted prosperity. Only in the 1980s and 1990s did the system dissolve and with it much of national government's legitimacy.

Until then, it helped to sustain Americans' impressive prosperity and economic power. And since the system served "national security," it largely escaped the stigma of "welfare" or "social engineering" attached to the New Deal. Because it prized military and technological strength, it sent prosperity flowing above all to men, institutions, and corporations in the "gunbelt," particularly to the south, southwest, and the West Coast—to the long-run detriment of trade unions, women, minorities, older industrial regions, and the nation's economic competitiveness. But with defense spending so huge, and economic competitors so damaged by the world war, a majority of Americans initially shared in midcentury prosperity.

World War II also forged a new sense of *patriotism and nationhood that lingered into the Cold War era. To be sure, unity was defined as well by exclusion—of conscientious objectors, right-wing zealots, and Japanese Americans during the war, and pacifists, leftists, gay people, racial militants, and others after it. Ethnic, racial, and religious tensions remained. Yet crusades against enemies abroad prized inclusiveness at home, if only to mobilize all the nation's resources. Catholics and Jews (especially those of Southern and Eastern European background), refugees fleeing fascism and communism, African and Asian Americans, and others generally, though unequally, tapped into and benefited from the assimilationist mood.

World War II also shaped postwar culture. Again, national pride—a conviction that America was now the world's cultural capital—swelled. But a darker sensibility—skeptical, tragic, or apocalyptic—characterized fiction, religious writing, and movie genres like film noir. Pearl Harbor, the Nazi Holocaust, and the atomic bomb generated a pervasive iconography of the horrors of modern warfare. Their symbols first served to dramatize not what the United States did to others—as in the atomic bombings of *Hiroshima and Nagasaki—but what others—a nuclear Soviet Union—could do to the United States, and thus to undergird Washington's Cold War policies. But it measured the war's staying power that these symbols were recycled decades later to different purposes—by the antinuclear, anti-*Vietnam War, anti-abortion, and *AIDS action movements, among others.

The war's most lasting impact was as benchmark of national greatness. As Dwight D. *Eisenhower demonstrated, military service in World War II became a virtual requirement for the presidency during the Cold War, just as most leaders invoked World War II when framing Washington's great postwar initiatives at home and abroad. During the war's fiftieth anniversary celebrations in the United States, only a celebratory stance seemed possible—as indicated by the outcome of a bitter debate over the 1990s Smithsonian Institution exhibit of the B-29 bomber, *Enola Gay*, that attacked Hiroshima—one that honored the real virtue and unity while dismissing the complexities and conflicts in America's conduct of the war.

Both reassuring and disquieting, the celebratory stance registered national pride, but also the gnawing sense that World War II was the nation's finest hour, its moment of greatest unity and purposefulness, with everything after it more dubious, complex, or tragic. Placing it at the center of their modern history, Americans were left to wonder how, outside the arena of war, they might restore past unity and glory.

[*See also* China, U.S. Military Involvement in; Gender and War; Germany, U.S. Military Involvements in; Japan, U.S. Military Involvement in; United Kingdom, U.S. Military Involvement in; War and Society.]

• Ernest R. May, *"Lessons" of the Past: The Use and Misuse of History in American Foreign Policy*, 1973. John M. Blum, *V Was for Victory: Politics and American Culture During World War II*, 1976. Richard Polenberg, *One Nation Divisible: Class, Race, and Ethnicity in the United States Since 1938*, 1980. Susan Hartmann, *The Home Front and Beyond: American Women in the 1940s*, 1982. William S. Graebner, *The Age of Doubt: American Thought and Culture in the 1940s*, 1991. Ann Markusen, Scott Campbell, Peter Hall, and Sabina Deitrick, *The Rise of the Gunbelt: The Military Remapping of Industrial America*, 1991. William L. O'Neill, *A Democracy at War: Americans Fight at Home and Abroad in World War II*, 1993. George H. Roeder, Jr., *The Censored War: American Visual Culture During World War Two*, 1993. Michael S. Sherry, *In the Shadow of War: The United States Since the 1930s*, 1995. —Michael S. Sherry

WORLD WAR II (1939–45): CHANGING INTERPRETATIONS

For over half a century, a general consensus has existed on the fundamental cause of World War II in Europe: on 1 September 1939, Adolf *Hitler attacked Poland without provocation in order to obtain *Lebensraum* (expanded territory for Germany), his stated goal from the time he wrote *Mein Kampf* (1925). Often corollary was the claim that Hitler not only preached aggressive war against France and the Soviet Union but followed a carefully timed blueprint of *expansionism. As revealed in the Hossbach Memorandum of 5 November 1937, the Führer had made Austria and Czechoslovakia his immediate targets. Winston S. *Churchill said in the House of Commons on 14 March 1938, well over a year before war broke out, "Europe is confronted with a program of aggression, nicely calculated and timed, unfolding stage by stage." From the *war crimes prosecutors at Nuremberg to Walter Hofer's book *War Premeditated, 1939* (1955), few disagreed.

By the sixties, the matter of a timetable was being challenged. Only a minute group of people, often rooted in neo-Nazism, took seriously David Hoggan's *The Forced War: When Peaceful Revisionism Failed* (1961; English translation, 1989), an attempt to absolve Hitler of all aggressive designs. Far more formidable was *Origins of the Second World War* (1961), written by the provocative British historian A. J. P. Taylor. Hitler—claimed Taylor—was governed primarily by opportunism and improvisation, a position challenged in the many works of Gerhard L. Weinberg, for example, *The Foreign Policy of Hitler's Germany* (2 vols., 1970, 1980). Many historians—such as Alan Bullock in his *Hitler: A Study in Tyranny* (1952) and Gordon Brook-Shepherd in *The Anschluss* (1963)—long held that Hitler kept his options open until the last minute.

Even prominent German historians, however, share in the consensus that any ad hoc method to Hitler's diplomacy operated within such long-standing goals as Germany's control of Europe, mastery of the seas, internal warfare against the Jews, and external warfare against the Slavs—see, for example, Eberhard Jäckel, *Hitler's Weltanschauung* (1969; English translation, 1972); Andreas Hillgruber, *Hitlers Strategie: Politik und Kriegführung, 1940–1941* (1975); Klaus Hildebrand, *The Foreign Policy of the Third Reich* (1970; English translation, 1973); and Karl Dietrich Bracher, *The German Dictatorship* (1969; English translation, 1970). Some German historians, participating in the *Historikerstreit* (historians' debate) of the 1980s, sought to "relativize" Hitler's *genocide by pointing to other global *atrocities and stressing the anti-Bolshevik nature of Nazism; see for example, Ernst Nolte, *Der europäische Bürgerkrieg, 1917–1945: Nationalsozialismus und Bolshewismus* (1987), a position strongly criticized in Richard J. Evans, *In Hitler's Shadow: West German Historians and the Attempt to Escape from the Nazi Past* (1989). Nonetheless, few historians took seriously Hitler's claim that the attack on Russia of 21 June 1941 was a mere preventive strike before Josef *Stalin attacked; and a major 1995 study confirmed the traditional picture: James Barros and Richard Gregor, *Double Deception: Stalin, Hitler, and the Invasion of Russia* (1995).

As to Asia, rarely did historians ever see a Japanese master plan at work. If David Bergamini's *Japan's Imperial Conspiracy* (1971) asserted that Emperor *Hirohito masterminded Japan's aggression of the 1930s, no serious historian today finds any specific blueprint in that decade to conquer all East Asia. Even the famous Marco Polo Bridge incident of 7 July 1937, an event near Peking (Beijing) that triggered the Sino-Japanese War of 1937–45, did not result from any planned Japanese campaign.

If, however, Japan had blundered into the bridge incident, Japan's leaders increasingly perceived that their nation's security and prosperity, indeed very survival, depended upon domination of East Asia. To Japan's leaders, such mastery increasingly relied upon the ability ultimately to fight the Soviets and the Americans and to destroy Nationalist China. Michael A. Barnhart's *Japan Prepares for Total War: The Search for Economic Security, 1919–1941* (1987) stresses the Imperial Japanese Army's desire for resources in Manchuria, northern China, and possibly the Southwest Pacific. By the 1970s, some Japanese historians were acknowledging their country's aggressive policies; see, for example, (Japanese contributors to Dorothy Borg and Shumei Okamoto, eds., *Pearl Harbor as History: Japanese-American Relations, 1931–1941* (1973), and James W. Morley, ed., *Japan's Road to the Pacific War*, 4 vols. (1976–84, translated from *Taiheiyo senso e no michi*, a multivolume work by Japanese scholars).

The historiographical debate over U.S. entry into World War II was in many ways a replay of the isolationist-interventionist debate of 1939–41. During the pre–Pearl Harbor debate over such Roosevelt policies as Lend-Lease and armed convoys in the Atlantic and embargoes against Japan in the Pacific, isolationist historians called the president's measures warlike and provocative, and their postwar histories were efforts to support their case—Charles A. Beard, *President Roosevelt and the Coming of the War, 1941* (1948), and Harry Elmer Barnes, ed., *Perpetual War for Perpetual Peace: A Critical Examination of the Foreign Policy of Franklin D. Roosevelt and Its Aftermath* (1953).

The most extreme writers, a mere handful, argued without credible evidence that the Roosevelt administration possessed specific foreknowledge of the Japanese attack on *Pearl Harbor, but—seeking a "back door" to full-scale U.S. participation in the European War—permitted the deliberate loss of American lives and ships: Charles Callan Tansill, *Back Door to War: Roosevelt Foreign Policy, 1933–1941* (1952), and John Toland, *Infamy: Pearl Harbor and Its Aftermath* (1982). A British and an Australian writer recently levied a similar unsubstantiated accusation against the British prime minister, Winston Churchill: James Rusbridger and Eric Nave, *Betrayal at Pearl Harbor: How Churchill Lured Roosevelt into World War II* (1991). A less extreme argument by a respected scholar, Paul W. Schroeder, *The Axis Alliance and Japanese-American Relations, 1941* (1958), claimed that U.S. intransigence over China led to the conflict; this still finds adherents, but most scholars believe American leaders were less committed to liberating China than Schroeder suggests.

Interventionist historians were quick to supply rejoinders to the isolationist polemics, the standard work for many years being William L. Langer and S. Everett Gleason's two-volume *The World Crisis and American Foreign Policy* (1952–53). Waldo Heinrichs's *Threshold of War: Franklin D. Roosevelt and American Entry into World War II* (1988) in many ways updates their findings. Accusations of conspiracy and deceit concerning Pearl Harbor have long been rejected by all major scholars. Gordon W. Prange, *At Dawn We Slept: The Untold Story of Pearl Harbor* (1981), and Roberta Wohlstetter, *Pearl Harbor: Warning and Decision* (1962), emphasize *communications and intelligence analysis failures. Currently debated are such matters as the wisdom of America's Far Eastern diplomacy, in particular, the levying of economic sanctions on Japan on 25 July 1941—Jonathan G. Utley, *Going to War with Japan, 1937–1941* (1985); the responsibility of the American commanders in Hawaii—Edward L. Beach, *Scapegoats: A Defense of Kimmel and Short at Pearl Harbor* (1995); blundering diplomats—R. J. C. Butow, *The John Doe Associates: Back Door Diplomacy for Peace, 1941* (1974), and Hilary Conroy and Harry Wray, eds., *Pearl Harbor Reexamined: Prologue to the Pacific War* (1990); and multinational oil companies—Irvine Anderson, *The Standard-Vacuum Oil Company and United States East Asian Policy, 1933–1941* (1975).

By the 1960s, the interventionist interpretation had so strongly swept the historical profession that not a single major professional historian defended the isolationists' conspiratorial view. Revisionism itself, however, did not die; rather, it took a different form. In 1959, William Appleman Williams's *Tragedy of American Diplomacy* (rev. ed. 1962) presented World War II as "the war for the American frontier," an effort to preserve the U.S. democratic and capitalistic system by eliminating the closed economic blocs of Germany and Japan. A few economically oriented writers asserted that overproduction led the United States into the war in order to keep open foreign markets—Patrick J. Hearden, *Roosevelt Confronts Hitler: America's Entry into World War II* (1987)—or to secure the wealth of Southeast Asia—Jonathan Marshall, *To Have and Have Not: Southeast Asian Raw Materials and the Origins of the Pacific War* (1995).

The *Cold War led to more bitter controversy about World War II, this time centering on wartime diplomacy. Over the years, four schools have emerged. Defenders of Franklin D. *Roosevelt, if they differed with the president on particulars, saw the president's wartime diplomacy as usually pragmatic and realistic; he was a man much attuned to the realities of power. Examples include Robert A. Divine, *Roosevelt and World War II* (1969); James MacGregor Burns, *Roosevelt: Soldier of Freedom, 1940–1945* (1970); and Robert Dallek, *Franklin D. Roosevelt and American Foreign Policy, 1932–1945* (1979). Conversely, a "realist" school portrayed the president understandably, if unfortunately, as too attached to universalistic and unattainable Wilsonian goals; see, for example, Gaddis Smith's *American Diplomacy During the Second World War, 1941–1945* (1965; 2nd ed. 1985). A few right-wing isolationist critics, such as William Henry Chamberlain, *America's Second Crusade* (1950), opposed unconditional surrender of Germany, saw Japan as a bastion against the USSR, and found FDR needlessly solicitous of Stalin, going so far as to betray Poland and China. Although such an isolationist critique never attained scholarly standing, it was long prevalent in right-wing political circles. A left-wing "revisionist" school, represented by Gabriel Kolko—*The Politics of War: The World and United States Foreign*

Policy, 1943–1945 (1968)—described the Roosevelt administration as relentlessly pursuing open capitalistic markets and sources of raw materials at the expense of Britain, the Soviet Union, and even the Third World. Although Kolko enjoyed some popularity in the 1960s, the pragmatic and idealist schools retained the most adherents. An important subdebate, prompted by the Cold War revisionist Gar Alperovitz, centered on the claim that the Truman administration undertook the atomic bombings of *Hiroshima and Nagasaki primarily to intimidate the Soviets—*Atomic Diplomacy: Hiroshima and Potsdam* (1965; 2nd, expanded ed. 1994)—a motive most historians see as decidedly secondary to winning the war as rapidly as possible.

The terms of debate over the war, however, are currently being altered by new forms of investigation, including comparative cultures—Akira Iriye, *Power and Culture: The Japanese-American War, 1941–1945* (1981); bureaucratic politics—Theodore A. Wilson, *The First Summit: Roosevelt and Churchill at Placentia Bay, 1941* (1969; rev. ed. 1991), and Mark M. Lowenthal, *Leadership and Indecision: American War Planning and Policy Process, 1937–1942* (1988); public opinion—Michael Leigh, *Mobilizing Consent: Public Opinion and American Foreign Policy, 1937–1947* (1976); and definitions of American national security—Lloyd C. Gardner, *Spheres of Influence: The Great Powers Partition Europe, From Munich to Yalta* (1993).

[*See also* Disciplinary Views of War.]

• Gerald K. Haines and J. Samuel Walker, eds., *American Foreign Relations: A Historiographical Review,* 1981. P.M.H. Bell, *The Origins of the Second World War in Europe,* 1986, Part 1. Mark A. Stoler, "Historiography: U.S. World War II Diplomacy," *Diplomatic History,* 18 (Summer 1994), pp. 375–403. Barton J. Bernstein, "Understanding the Atomic Bomb and the Japanese Surrender: Missed Opportunities, Little Known Near Disaster, and Modern Memory," *Diplomatic History,* 19 (Spring 1995), pp. 227–73. Justus D. Doenecke, "Historiography: U.S. Policy and the European War, 1939–1941," *Diplomatic History,* 19 (Fall 1995), pp. 669–98. Michael A. Barnhart, "The Origins of World War II in Asia and the Pacific," *Diplomatic History,* 20 (Spring 1996), pp. 241–60.

—Justus D. Doenecke

WORLD WAR II, U.S. AIR OPERATIONS IN: THE AIR WAR IN EUROPE. U.S. air operations in the Mediterranean and Europe evolved into two distinct fields of effort: the strategic air campaign against the German war economy and the tactical air support of American ground forces. In both arenas the U.S. Army Air Forces (AAF) began hostilities with untested doctrine. In the strategic sphere, the AAF believed that it could attack and destroy German war industries, with accuracy and in daylight, without the benefit of friendly fighter escort, while suffering acceptable losses. In the tactical sphere, using methods based on British combat experience in 1940–41, Field Manual 35-31 laid out a scheme for the command and control of tactical air power that usually placed airmen in control of their own forces.

U.S. Tactical Air Operations in Europe. Tactical air power requires the cooperation and understanding of two combat arms, each with a unique perspective on ground operations. The United States' initial ground campaign in Tunisia demonstrated the difficulties inherent in orchestrating ground and air efforts. At the outset neither ground nor air understood the U.S. *Army's air support doctrine, but both were forced, unprepared, into combat. As a result,

"teething" problems, such as lack of *radar for early warning and excessive fear by ground units of air attack, hampered cooperation. In mid-February 1943, the placement of all Anglo-American tactical air power under the command of an experienced air officer, Air Marshal Arthur T. Conningham of the British Royal Air Force (RAF), coincided with air reinforcements and the solution of air logistics problems. By the campaign's end, tactical air power had contributed greatly to the Axis defeat on the ground. Likewise, tactical air power assisted in repelling Axis counterattacks on the beachheads of Sicily and Salerno in Italy. In the winter of 1943–44, tactical air aided the fruitless Allied assaults on the Cassino Line and the defense of the Anzio Beachhead. In the spring of 1944, the U.S. Twelfth Air Force and British First Tactical Air Force began Operation STRANGLE, a campaign designed to interdict German supplies, and in the winter of 1944–45, tactical air operations in Italy followed much the same pattern.

In the European theater, the AAF established the Ninth (Tactical) Air Force in October 1943 in Great Britain under the command of Lieut. Gen. Lewis H. Brereton. By June 1944, it had become the most powerful tactical air force in World War II. Initially, Ninth Air Force fighters flew escort for strategic *bomber aircraft attacking into Germany. As the needs of the Anglo-American invasion forces increased the Ninth gradually switched its emphasis to air/ground training and to an attritional air attack on the Belgian and French transportation systems. The Allied high command expected the transportation plan to hinder the post-invasion movement of German reinforcements and logistics to oppose the beachhead. On the day of the landings in *Normandy on 6 June 1944, the Ninths' medium bombers struck invasion beaches, its fighters supplied air cover, and its troop transports delivered the bulk of the Allied parachute forces. Allied fighter bombers made daylight movement by German ground forces almost impossible and entirely thwarted German air force tactical operations. After assisting in the breakout at *St. Lô on 25 June 1944, the Ninth worked closely with the U.S. Twelfth Army Group assigning a Tactical Air Command to each of its armies; AAF pilots literally rode in the turrets of the most advanced American armored spearheads in order to call upon tactical air power when needed. With the invasion of southern France on 25 August 1944, the AAF established the First Provisional Air Force to assist the Sixth Army Group. In the winter of 1944–45, Germany purposely launched their Ardennes counteroffensive in poor flying weather in hopes of negating Allied air power. This ploy ultimately failed and tactical air pushed back the Germans and then assisted the Allied drive into Germany in the spring.

U.S. Strategic Air Operations in Europe. On and increasing scale from mid-1942 through May 1945, U.S. strategic air contributed to the defeat of Germany. Along with the British strategic effort, U.S. bombing constituted a second or third front against the enemy. In a significant diversion of strength and resources, Germany was forced to disperse its aircraft and ball bearing industries, devote two million troops to air defenses, skew aircraft production toward interceptors, and divert high velocity artillery and vital communications equipment to home defense. This drain increased throughout the conflict, constituting a significant, if somewhat intangible, achievement of strategic bombing.

Responding to a promise to British prime Minister Winston *Churchill, U.S. strategic air operations began on

4 July 1942, with a raid of six U.S. Eighth Air Force light bombers on Dutch airfields. The Eighth's first heavy bomber raid of twelve B-17s hit marshalling yards at Rouen, France on 17 August 1942. The raid came after pressure from AAF headquarters in Washington and criticism of American methods in the British press. On 27 January 1943, fifty-five aircraft made the first American air attack on Germany—the naval base at Wilhelmshaven. Once again, the attack followed promises made to Churchill and the Combined Chiefs of Staff. Throughout the war, U.S. strategic air power would be the focus of intense political, diplomatic, military, and bureaucratic pressures.

Pre-war plans specified that the U.S. air force in Britain would be the AAF's largest overseas contingent and gave it the task of conducting an offensive against the German war economy. However, shifting priorities (such as the invasion of *North Africa) slowed the rate of the Eighth's growth. By the second Schweinfurt Raid of 14 October 1943, the Eighth had failed to gain air superiority over Germany. Its short-ranged fighters could not accompany the bombers deep into Germany, where the bombers suffered crushing losses, while the European weather allowed only a slow rate of operations. Wartime crew training could not produce sufficient personnel capable of duplicating pre-war bombing accuracies. The Eighth had inflicted no permanent damage to the German war effort.

By the end of February 1944, however, the Eighth's fortunes reversed. In November 1943, the Eighth introduced the H2X radar bombing device, which permitted the bombing of large targets through clouds and, consequently, allowed an increase in attacks. Long-range escort fighters, P-51s, P-38s, and P-47s with drop tanks arrived in large numbers, while a change in tactics, instigated by the Eighth's new commander. Lieut. Gen. James H. *Doolittle, required American fighters to attack German aircraft rather than passively protect bombers. Constant combat increased the attrition of German pilots to catastrophic levels. In addition, an influx of new bomb groups almost doubled the Eighth's bomblift, and the creation in Italy of a new U.S. strategic air force, the Fifteenth, opened new areas to attack and spread German air defenses.

Just as the Eighth gained air superiority over Germany, a dispute arose in London as to how strategic air could best aid the coming invasion of France. Lieut. Gen. Carl A. *Spaatz, commander of the Eighth and Fifteenth Air Forces, wished to attack the German synthetic oil industry, while Gen. Dwight D. *Eisenhower's air commanders favored an attritional attack on the French and Belgian rail systems. Eisenhower chose transportation bombing, but allowed two oil attacks in May 1944. The success of those attacks, confirmed by Allied code breakers, made oil the first priority air target in the month before the invasion. Both tactical and strategic air power mangled the French railways, but strategic air power's chief contribution to the Normandy landings was the elimination of the German day fighter force. From landing to breakout, the invasion never encountered significant air opposition.

For the remainder of the war, synthetic oil was the primary U.S. strategic target. By September 1944, bombing temporarily halted production entirely. The oil campaign, which deprived the German air force of flight and training time, severely hampered the mobility of ground forces, and even limited fuel to the U-boats, was the finest achievement of U.S. strategic bombardment. It destroyed a vital,

compact, target system with minimal damage to the civilian population. However, the harsh weather of the winter of 1944–45 rendered the refineries safe even to the H2X. Consequently, the Eighth devoted the majority of its effort to hitting the German rail system, especially after the German Ardennes counteroffensive. The key components of the rail system, marshalling yards, were physically located in the midst of German urban areas. Given the inaccuracy of bombing in severely overcast conditions, rail yard bombing meant that many bombs would fall among the civilian population. The Eighth further increased destruction by employing large numbers of incendiary bombs in rail yard raids. At the end of January 1945, at Churchill's urging, the Allied strategic bombing effort began an offensive against eastern Germany to aid Soviet ground forces and demonstrate Allied solidarity. Strategic raids on Berlin and other cities followed, including the RAF's controversial attack on Dresden on 13 and 14 February. The Eighth bombed the center of the city on 15 February. Ironically, the transportation bombing achieved its aim. By the end of February 1945, it had ruined the rail system, shattering Germany's ability to sustain its war economy.

[See also Air Force, U.S.: Predecessors of, 1907 to 1946; Air Warfare Strategy; World War II: Military and Diplomatic Course.]

• Stephen McFarland and Wesley Newton. *To Command the Sky: The Battle for Air Superiority over Germany, 1942–1944,* 1991. Conrad Crane, *Bombs, Cities, and Civilians: American Airpower Strategy in World War II,* 1993. Thomas A. Hughes, *Overlord: General Pete Quesada and the Tactical Air Power in World War II,* 1995.

—Richard G. Davis

WORLD WAR II, U.S. AIR OPERATIONS IN: THE AIR WAR IN JAPAN. On 18 April 1942, sixteen B-25 bombers under the command of Army Lt. Col. James *Doolittle took off from U.S. *Navy *aircraft carriers 650 miles off the coast of Japan. Their raid on Tokyo and other Japanese cities caused little material effect but a significant psychological one, boosting American morale while embarrassing Japanese leaders into accelerating operations that would lead to the Battle of the *Coral Sea and the Battle of *Midway later that year. But it would be more than two years before new American bomber aircraft returned to hit the Japanese home islands again.

In 1944–45, long-range B-29 Superfortresses were used to carry out the strategic air campaign against Japan. Eventually, over 1,000 were deployed in the 20th Air Force, subdivided into the XXth and XXIst Bomber Commands. The Army Air Forces (AAF) commanding general, H. H. "Hap" *Arnold, retained direct command of the 20th Air Force, to prevent diversion of its resources to theater commanders. Feeling pressure to get results from his expensive Very Heavy Bomber (VHB) project, he fielded the new B-29s even before testing had been completed, gambling that they could achieve decisive results while correcting any technical deficiencies.

In June 1944, B-29s from Maj. Gen. Kenneth Wolfe's XXth Bomber Command staged from India to China, and began bombing Japan as part of Operation Matterhorn. Wolfe was plagued by *logistics and mechanical problems, however, which grew worse when Japanese ground troops in Operation Ichigo overran advanced U.S. airfields in China. Arnold relieved Wolfe and brought in Maj. Gen. Curtis E. *LeMay, the AAF's premier problem solver and the most innovative air commander of World War II. However, except for a successful incendiary raid on Hankow, even LeMay achieved poor results with Matterhorn.

Arnold's greatest hopes for *victory through airpower over Japan rested with the XXIst Bomber Command, under the command of Brig. Gen. Haywood "Possum" Hansell, which began operations from the Marianas in November 1944. Hansell was one of the architects of precision-bombing doctrine, but his operations also had little success. Poor facilities, faulty training, aircraft engine failures, cloud cover, and jet stream winds at bombing altitudes made precision methods impossible. Hansell seemed unwilling to change his tactics, and Arnold feared that he would lose control of the heavy bombers to Asian theater commanders Douglas *MacArthur, Chester *Nimitz, or Louis Mountbatten without better results. Arnold decided to consolidate both Bomber Commands in the Marianas under LeMay and relieved Hansell.

LeMay instituted new training and maintenance procedures but still failed to achieve useful results with daylight high-altitude precision attacks. So he resorted to low-level incendiary raids at night. Although area firebombing went against dominant American Army Air Forces doctrine, flying at low altitude reduced engine strain, required less fuel, improved bombing concentration, avoided high winds, and took advantage of weaknesses in Japanese defenses. LeMay's systems analysts predicted that he could set large enough fires to leap firebreaks around important industrial objectives. His first application of the new tactics, Operation Meetinghouse on the night of 9 March 1945, resulted in extraordinary destruction: 334 B-29s incinerated 16 square miles of Tokyo, destroying 22 key targets and killing 80,000–90,000 civilians in the deadliest air raid of the war.

Once enough incendiaries were stockpiled, the fire raids began in earnest. Warning leaflets were also dropped; their primary purpose was to terrorize Japanese civilians into fleeing from cities. Eight million did so. When Gen. Carl A. *Spaatz arrived in July 1945 to take command of Army Strategic Air Forces in the Pacific (including the 20th Air Force and Doolittle's 8th Air Force redeploying from Europe) and to coordinate air operations supporting the invasion of Japan, he was directed to shift the air campaign from cities to *transportation. But there was too much momentum behind the fire raids—sustained by operational tempo, training programs, and bomb stocks—for strategy to change.

By the time Spaatz arrived, naval carrier strikes were also hitting key industrial objectives in Japan. More important, the navy's submarine blockade had crippled the Japanese economy, and the Russians were about to attack Manchuria. Spaatz maintained direct command over the 509th Composite Group of B-29s specially modified to carry atomic bombs. Directed by Washington to deliver these weapons as soon as possible after 3 August, Spaatz ordered the bombings of *Hiroshima and Nagasaki. Along with the incendiary campaign, these different elements composed the series of blows that produced immediate Japanese surrender.

As with the atomic bomb, there is still debate over the effects and morality of the fire raids. LeMay's bombers burned out 180 square miles of 67 cities, killed at least 300,000 people, and injured over 400,000 more. His 313th Bomb Wing also sowed 12,000 naval *mines in ports and waterways, sinking almost 1 million tons of shipping in about four months. LeMay remained convinced that

his conventional bombing could have achieved victory by itself, without need for a ground invasion of the Japanese or the atomic bombs. He even briefed Arnold and the *Joint Chiefs of Staff in July 1945 that the war would have to end by 1 October, when the 20th Air Force would run out of targets.

[See also Air Force, U.S.: Predecessors of, 1907–46; Bombing of Civilians; China-Burma-India Theater; Strategy: Air Warfare Strategy; World War II: Military and Diplomatic Course.]

• Wesley Frank Craven and James Lea Cate, The Army Air Forces in World War II. Vol. 5: The Pacific: Matterhorn to Nagasaki, June 1944 to August 1945, 1953. Carroll V. Glines, Doolittle's Tokyo Raiders, 1964. Curtis LeMay with MacKinley Kantor, Mission with LeMay, 1965. Haywood S. Hansell, Jr., Strategic Air War Against Japan, 1980. Conrad C. Crane, Bombs, Cities, and Civilians: American Airpower Strategy in World War II, 1993. Kenneth P. Werrell, Blankets of Fire: U.S. Bombers Over Japan During World War II, 1996.

—Conrad C. Crane

WORLD WAR II, U.S. NAVAL OPERATIONS IN: THE NORTH ATLANTIC.

During World War II (1939–1945), Germany attempted to isolate Great Britain by severing the North Atlantic sealanes by *submarine warfare. Initially, the Kriegsmarine Untersee-Waffe commander, Adm. Karl Doenitz deployed submarines into England's southwestern approaches, where they nearly crippled Allied shipping. The effectiveness of this operation increased substantially when France and the Low Countries capitulated in spring 1940, giving the Germans U-boat bases on the Atlantic. During the war's first two years, German submarines sank more than 1,200 Allied ships and severely hampered England's supply systems.

In the fall of 1941, with U.S. Lend-Lease supplies to Britain in jeopardy, President Franklin D. *Roosevelt ordered U.S. naval warships to begin escorting Allied convoys. On 4 September, after evading a torpedo from a German submarine, the destroyer USS Greer launched a depth charge attack against the U-boat. Roosevelt then ordered the navy not to wait until attacked but to shoot German submarines on sight. Eight weeks later, after several other confrontations, a German submarine sank the USS Reuben James. Before the attack on *Pearl Harbor, U.S. naval forces were fighting in a major if undeclared naval war with Germany in the North Atlantic.

After the United States entered the war in December 1941, U-boats began patrolling off the American East Coast and in the Gulf of Mexico, where they unleashed Operation Paukenschlag (Drumbeat) to destroy American shipping. In four months the Germans sank more than 360 ships, including the destroyer USS Jacob Jones. Caught off guard, the U.S. Navy had failed adequately to protect commercial coastal vessels, which were often gunned down by surfaced U-boats using East Coast city lights to silhouette their targets.

Because U.S. naval forces were spread thin across the Atlantic and Pacific, the chief of naval operations, Adm. Ernest J. *King, decided against using a coastal convoy system. Instead, in what was later called the "Bucket Brigade," merchant captains were advised to sail close to America's shorelines by day and to dash into the nearest harbor at night.

The British criticized King for not providing proper antisubmarine warfare (ASW) defenses. After carefully convoying ships across the Atlantic and into American waters, the U.S. Navy was allowing too many merchant ships to fall prey to the enemy along the coast. Upon transferring several British ASW escort ships to the U.S. Navy, Prime Minister Winston S. *Churchill suggested that America inaugurate a coastal convoy system.

In May 1942, after continued losses, King did institute such a system, and assigned land-based airplanes and blimps to patrol along the Atlantic seaboard. As these pressures increased, the U-boats withdrew from East Coast waters and reconcentrated in the Gulf of Mexico and Caribbean Sea, where they sank another 160 ships.

During the fall of 1942, Doenitz ordered his submarines into the mid-Atlantic, which was free of Allied air cover. Here, in an area called the "Black Pit," the Germans in their continuing assault against convoys instituted *Rudeltaktik* (wolf pack tactics). Initially, these attacks on convoys by groups of submarines were quite successful. However, by the summer of 1943, improved ASW tactics, better training, and new technology began extracting a toll on the U-boats.

The Battle of the Atlantic was ultimately a conflict of attrition: numbers of vessels sunk versus new ships constructed, and numbers of U-boats sunk versus new submarines constructed. As time passed, the Allies amassed great quantities of merchant ships, war vessels, ASW weapons, and sophisticated equipment. Improved *radar, *sonar, and radio direction-finding systems, coupled with extensive use of airpower, slowly turned the tide of war against the U-boats.

Intelligence gathered from *ULTRA and the decoding of U-boat and other German radio transmissions allowed the rerouting of convoys around the wolf packs. *Destroyers equipped with radio direction finders located U-boats, drove them underwater, and dropped depth charges on them. Airborne and shipborne radar was significant in spotting surfaced submarines. U.S. patrol planes flying over the Bay of Biscay used radar to find and attack surfaced U-boats transiting in and out of French ports.

In addition to these technical advances, organizational reforms aided the U.S. Navy's effort. During the spring of 1943, Admiral King consolidated all ASW research, training, weapons procurement, and strategy under one command, the Tenth Fleet. Under his authority, the Tenth Fleet coordinated and streamlined all Atlantic operations.

A turning point in the Battle of the Atlantic occurred in the spring of 1943, when the U.S. Navy began using long-range, land-based aircraft and escort carriers to patrol the mid-Atlantic. Planes such as PBY Catalinas and B-24 Liberators provided extensive convoy coverage across the "Black Pit." Flying from Iceland, a B-24 Liberator (with depth charges aboard) could enter the mid-Atlantic and patrol above Allied vessels for nearly four hours. Many of these planes successfully attacked and destroyed U-boats. On occasion, patrolling aircraft forced U-boats into deep water dives, where for extended periods they were unable to threaten the convoys. In May 1943 alone, the Germans lost more than forty submarines.

American hunter-killer groups, typically composed of one escort carrier and three destroyers, substantially enhanced the U.S. Navy's ability to defend the convoys. Often, in the mid-Atlantic, after forcing U-boats to crash-dive, carrier planes dropped homing *torpedoes on the submarines. One particular success occurred on 4 June 1944, when the crew of the escort carrier *Guadalcanal* cap-

tured U-boat *505* on the surface, along with all of its code-books and sophisticated equipment.

In part because of these successes. Germany was unable to block the men and material necessary for the invasion of *Normandy and the *D-Day landing. By war's end, Doenitz's *U-Waffe* was depleted. While his submarines sank more than 2,700 Allied ships, they also lost nearly 800 U-boats and 28,000 sailors. Yet there were no spectacular, Midway-style decisive battles for the U.S. Navy in the Atlantic as there were in the Pacific. Instead, for U.S. naval forces, the battle consisted of endless days of searching for elusive U-boats and once one was found, of launching a prolonged attack upon the submerged enemy.

After the war, because most documents remained long classified, a myth of the highly successful U-boat campaign developed. However, newly declassified documents have indicated that because of torpedo and other technical problems, U-boats were much more vulnerable to ASW attacks than previously thought. The evidence also reveals that the submarines destroyed only a very small percentage of the ships crossing the Atlantic. This new evidence, however, has not distracted from the difficulties and the bitterness of one of history's longest and most complex naval campaigns.

[*See also* Antisubmarine Warfare Systems; Submarines; World War II: Military and Diplomatic Course; Strategy: Naval Warfare Strategy.]

• Samuel Eliot Morison, *The Battle of the Atlantic: September 1939–May 1943*, Vol. 1, 1947; and *The Atlantic Battle Won: May 1943–May 1945*, Vol. X, 1956. Dan Van der Vat, *The Atlantic Campaign: World War II's Great Struggle at Sea*, 1988.

—Donald D. Chipman

WORLD WAR II, U.S. NAVAL OPERATIONS IN: THE PACIFIC. In *The Armed Forces of the Pacific: A Comparison of the Military and Naval Power of the United States and Japan,* published early in 1941, retired Capt. William D. Puleston, former Director of Naval Intelligence, concluded that a war between the two countries would end with an American victory in a climactic naval battle somewhere in the western Pacific. Carrier-based aircraft would be important, but the decisive element would be the battle line of heavy surface ships. Such thinking was widespread in the pre-World War II navy.

The circumstances and aftermath of the Japanese attack on *Pearl Harbor, 7 December 1941, radically altered the character and course of World War II in the Pacific. Since the three carriers of the U.S. Pacific Fleet were out of the harbor and the eight *battleships were heavily damaged, air power would dominate naval action for the first six months of 1942 and would heavily influence strategic planning for the entire war. When surface combat began in August 1942, American heavy *cruisers had to do the work of battleships against Japanese capital ships. The battleships damaged at Pearl Harbor would slowly return, along with their newer, faster sisterships, but their chief functions would be gunfire support for landings and escort of carrier task forces. Only twice, at Guadalcanal in November 1942 and at Surigao Strait in the Battle for *Leyte Gulf two years later, would there be classic gun duels with Japanese battleships in the manner anticipated by every fresh young ensign of the late 1930s.

Following Pearl Harbor, destruction of small British and Dutch naval forces (along with the inadequate United States Asiatic Fleet) meant that the Allied effort in the

Pacific war would become almost exclusively American. President Franklin D. *Roosevelt and his advisors, reacting more to public pressure and political considerations than to geographical realities, the need for unity of command, and clear administration, assigned to Army Gen. Douglas *MacArthur the Southwest Pacific Area, comprising Australia, the Solomons, New Guinea, and the Philippines, while Adm. Chester W. *Nimitz commanded all the remaining Pacific Ocean Area. Interservice *rivalry and bickering, especially by the more image-conscious MacArthur, flared repeatedly during the war.

The first, or defensive, phase of the Pacific war lasted from Pearl Harbor until August 1942. *Submarines harassed Japanese military and commercial shipping. The celebrated carrier raid on Tokyo (18 April) by James *Doolittle's B-25s proved that Japan was vulnerable and buoyed American spirits. A defensive line, protecting vital communications with Australia, stretched from the Aleutians to Midway to Samoa to New Guinea. Above all, Japanese expansion to the east and southeast had to be stopped. The major engagements of this phase came as Americans blunted each prong of a three-part Japanese expansion plan for the spring and summer of 1942.

A Japanese effort at a seaborne invasion of Port Moresby in southeastern New Guinea as a base from which to attack Australia led to the Battle of the *Coral Sea (4–8 May). Fought entirely between carrier fleets 95 miles apart and tactically unfortunate, the battle accomplished its strategic purpose of preventing the invasion. A month later the Japanese sought to spread the northern end of the defensive perimeter by attacking the Aleutians and to draw the American fleet into a destructive battle by threatening Midway with a large invasion fleet. Once again, air-to-air and air-to-surface action replaced ship-to-ship combat. The Battle of *Midway (4–6 June), one of the war's most decisive victories, cost the Japanese four carriers, plus 250 planes and experienced pilots. The United States lost one carrier.

The third part of the overall Japanese plan, a move through the southern Solomons against New Caledonia, Fiji, and Samoa to cut the communication line to Australia, ended the purely defensive phase of the war. On 7 August 1942 United States Marines invaded Guadalcanal in the southern Solomons to prevent completion of a vital Japanese airfield. The invasion marked the beginning of the second or offensive phase of the Pacific War by the Americans. The centerpiece of this offensive phase was the recapture of the Philippines, preceded by an island-hopping campaign to get there, and followed by another one to position American forces for the expected seaborne invasion of Japan.

The Solomons campaign lasted from August 1942 until January 1943. It included three major land battles on Guadalcanal and six naval engagements in the southern and eastern Solomons, most of them extremely fierce night surface actions, fought at close range. The Japanese prided themselves on night fighting with searchlights; the Americans had *radar, a new weapon not always available and not always well used in combat. Most Japanese cruisers, unlike American cruisers, carried *torpedoes. Lingering controversies over tactics and command arose from several engagements, most notably the loss of three American and one Australian heavy cruiser at Savo Island in August 1942. More effective torpedoes increased the efficiency of U.S. submarine raids on Japanese shipping during 1943.

The securing of *Guadalcanal on 9 February 1943 focused full attention on Rabaul, a major Japanese base on New Britain, which stood in the way of any approach to the Philippines via the islands to the southeast. Six more naval engagements occurred in the central and northern Solomons and the Bismarck Sea before Rabaul, neutralized and bypassed, ceased to be a threat in January 1944.

The encirclement of Rabaul had clearly required a joint army-navy strategic effort, although MacArthur had pressed for army dominance in a hopscotch campaign along island chains and the north coast of New Guinea. The assault on the Philippines, whose personal significance to MacArthur matched its strategic significance, also required joint effort to avoid a dangerously unprotected eastern flank. The navy and marine corps, with some army troops as well, swept westward across the central Pacific, beginning with Tarawa in the Gilberts in November 1943, continuing with Kwajalein in the Marshalls, and ending with Saipan, Guam, and Tinian in the Marianas in mid-1944. The Japanese attempted to destroy the American fleet with air attacks in the Battle of the *Philippine Sea (19–20 June) but lost three carriers and nearly 500 planes. From this defeat the Japanese naval air arm never recovered.

October 1944 brought the long-awaited invasion of the Philippines. The Battle for Leyte Gulf (23–26 October), the world's last great naval battle, secured and protected the congested landing beaches. A multi-phase response to a complex Japanese plan, the battle included the destruction in Surigao Strait of one battleship formation by the gunfire of several repaired Pearl Harbor battleships, heavy air attacks on other Japanese ships in several locations, and the luring away of Adm. William F. *Halsey's Third Fleet by a decoy Japanese carrier force. In light of a near disaster, Halsey's judgment has been controversial ever since. The Japanese lost four carriers, three battleships, ten cruisers, and eleven destroyers, permanently ending their ability to challenge the U.S. Navy for control of the seas.

Only the kamikaze or suicide plane remained a major weapon. First used in the Philippines, this desperate sacrifice of both plane and pilot was a terror weapon designed to maximize loss of life among sailors stationed topside on the destroyers and cruisers that screened the carriers, and most importantly to cause as many fires as possible on the carrier. Kamikazes sank 34 ships, none larger than a destroyer, and damaged 368 others, including some carriers, in a failed attempt to prevent the capture of *Okinawa (April–June, 1945). But the failure was bloody: nearly 5000 sailors died, more than double the number killed at Pearl Harbor and comprising nearly 15 percent of the navy's total World War II battle deaths in all theaters. Following American use of the atomic bomb against *Hiroshima and Nagasaki, Japan agreed to surrender on 14 August, executing the final documents on board the battleship USS *Missouri* in Tokyo Bay on 2 September 1945.

The greatest naval war in history had ended with victory for a naval force of unprecedented size and power. The Marianas campaign alone, for example, required 800 ships manned by 250,000 sailors, transporting 150,000 Marines and soldiers. From Pearl Harbor to Tokyo Bay, the U.S. Navy lost 128 combatant vessels in the Pacific and only 29 in the Atlantic. To a much greater degree than the Atlantic phase, the Pacific phase of World War II evolved into the world's first three-dimensional format of the traditional navy war, with large formations of ships engaged in surface, submarine, and air combat. Only superior American human and industrial resources made such an effort possible.

• Samuel E. Morison, *History of United States Naval Operations in World War II*, 15 vols., 1947–1963. E. B. Potter and Chester Nimitz, eds., *Sea Power: A Naval History*, 1960. S. E. Smith, ed., *The United States Navy in World War II*, 1966. Thomas B. Buell, *The Quiet Warrior: A Biography of Admiral Raymond A. Spruance*, 1974. James M. Merrill, *A Sailor's Admiral: A Biography of William F. Halsey*, 1976. E. B. Potter, *Nimitz*, 1976. Ronald Spector, *Eagle Against the Sun: The American War with Japan*, 1985. B. Mitchell Simpson, *Admiral Harold R. Stark: Architect of Victory, 1939–1945*, 1989. Craig L. Symonds, *The Naval Institute Historical Atlas of the U.S. Navy*, 1995.
—James E. Sefton

WOUNDED KNEE, BATTLE OF (1890). The final major encounter between Indians and the U.S. Army, Wounded Knee grew out of the revitalization movement known as the Ghost Dance that swept western Indian reservations in 1889–90. On the Sioux reservations of North and South Dakota, people embraced the new religion with fervor. Fearful of violence, agents called for military assistance, and strong forces were dispatched. The overall commander, Maj. Gen. Nelson A. Miles, pressed for the imprisonment of such "troublemakers" as *Sitting Bull and Big Foot.

On 15 December 1890, Sitting Bull was killed while resisting arrest by Indian policemen. Big Foot eluded arrest when he led his band of Lakota Sioux in a trek toward Pine Ridge Agency; his intent was not hostile, as assumed, but peaceful. Intercepted, the band was escorted to Wounded Knee Creek to be disarmed. Col. James W. Forsyth and the Seventh Cavalry, about 500 strong and bolstered by four small-caliber cannon, surrounded the Indian village of about 350 people. Neither side intended a fight, but the disarming process built tension and suspicion. A rifle accidentally discharged touched off battle.

After a brief exchange of close range fire and hand-to-hand fighting, the Indians scattered and the artillery opened fire. The village was flattened, and Indians fleeing in all directions were cut down. About 200 of Big Foot's people, including women and children, were killed or wounded, while the troops lost 25 killed and 39 wounded. After Wounded Knee, General Miles maneuvered his forces in such fashion as to bring about the surrender of the Ghost Dancers. The Indians, and even General Miles, accused the troops of indiscriminate massacre. Although few such incidents can be documented, the tragedy at Wounded Knee poisoned relations between whites and Indians; today, it still symbolizes the wrongs inflicted by one race on the other.

[*See also* Plains Indians Wars.]

• Robert M. Utley, *The Last Days of the Sioux Nation*, 1963. Richard E. Jensen, R. Eli Paul, and John E. Carter: *Eyewitness at Wounded Knee*, 1991.
—Robert M. Utley

WRIGHT, ORVILLE and **WILBUR,** inventors of the airplane and pioneer aviators. Wilbur and Orville Wright went to local schools in Ohio, Indiana, and Iowa; neither attended college. In 1889, the brothers established a printing shop in their home town of Dayton, Ohio. In addition to providing normal printing services, they launched two unsuccessful newspapers and built presses for other local printers. They expanded in 1892, establishing a bicycle sales and repair facility. By 1896, they were manufacturing bicycles of their own design.

The Wrights first became interested in heavier-than-air flight between 1896 and 1899. They built and flew one kite (1899); three gliders (1900, 1901, 1902); and three powered machines (1903, 1904, 1905). The disappointing performance of the first two gliders led them to undertake a series of key experiments with a wind tunnel (1901). Their clarity of vision, capacity to solve the most difficult problems (particularly with regard to roll controls), and their determination to design their machine through solid experimentation set them apart from their contemporaries.

The Wright brothers made the world's first powered, sustained, and controlled flights with a heavier-than-air machine near Kitty Hawk, North Carolina, on the morning of 17 December, 1903. They returned to Dayton, where they continued their experiments quietly in a local cow pasture for two more years. By fall 1905, they had built the world's first practical airplane. In the summer and fall of 1908, they won world fame with their first demonstration flights in Europe and America.

The Wrights never doubted that world governments would be their primary customers. They signed their first contract for the sale of a military airplane to the U.S. Army in 1908. In 1909, in cooperation with a group of financiers, they founded the Wright Company to build and sell airplanes in the United States, and licensed various manufacturers to produce their machines in Europe. That same year, they trained the first group of U.S. military airmen. The Wrights taught many officers to fly, including Lt. Kenneth Whiting, the U.S. Navy aviator who commanded the first U.S. military unit to arrive in France during World War I, and "Hap" *Arnold, who would command U.S. Army Air Forces in World War II.

Wilbur and Orville Wright achieved an extraordinarily difficult technical goal that had eluded engineers for over a century. The airplane, a product of their combined inventive genius, would reshape the history of the twentieth century, redefine the notion of battle, and open the way to total war.

[*See also* Air Warfare.]

• Marvin W. McFarland, ed., *The Papers of Wilbur and Orville Wright*, 1953. Charles Harvard Gibbs-Smith, *The Wright Brothers and the Rebirth of European Aviation*, 1974. Tom D. Crouch, *The Bishop's Boys: A Life of Wilbur and Orville Wright*, 1989. Peter Jakob, *Visions of a Flying Machine: The Wright Brothers and the Process of Invention*, 1990.
—Tom D. Crouch

Y

YALTA CONFERENCE (1945). In 1945, the "Big Three" of World War II—Franklin D. *Roosevelt, Winston S. *Churchill, and Josef *Stalin—had not met since December 1943. Because of Allied landings in France and the Soviet thrust across Poland and into Germany, by the summer of 1944 a second meeting of the three men was deemed necessary. But arguments over the time and place of their meeting delayed the conference until 4–11 February 1945, when they met at Yalta in the Crimea because Stalin refused to leave the Soviet Union.

Each man traveled to Yalta for different reasons. Roosevelt came because of his desire to create a *United Nations before World War II ended. Churchill feared the growing power of the Soviet Union in a devastated Europe. Stalin was intent on protecting the Soviet Union against another German invasion. The major problems facing the three leaders included Poland, Germany, Soviet entry into the war against Japan, and the United Nations.

At Yalta, Roosevelt attained his goal in an agreement for a conference on the United Nations to convene in San Francisco, 25 April 1945. In addition, Stalin accepted the American proposal on the use of the veto in the Security Council and the number of Soviet states represented in the General Assembly.

Much time was spent on Poland because Stalin insisted on a "friendly" Poland. The three men agreed to move the Polish eastern boundary westward to the 1919 Curzon Line and to restore western Byelorussia and the western Ukraine to the Soviet Union. At Stalin's insistence, a Communist Polish provisional government would be reorganized to include primarily Polish leaders from within Poland, but he agreed to some from abroad to placate Roosevelt. Stalin promised free elections there within a month on the basis of universal suffrage and the secret ballot.

Stalin demanded $20 billion in reparations from Germany, half of this sum to be destined for the Soviet Union. Churchill rejected this amount while Roosevelt accepted the sum as a basis for future discussion. Germany would be temporarily divided into three zones of occupation, with France invited to become a fourth occupying power.

Stalin promised that the Soviet Union would enter the war against Japan after the fighting ended in Europe. Stalin's terms for this were accepted: the southern Sakhalin and adjacent islands to be returned to the Soviet Union; Darien to be internationalized; Port Arthur to be leased as a naval base to the Soviet Union; Chinese-Soviet companies to operate the Chinese-Eastern and the South Manchurian railroads; Outer Mongolia to remain independent of China; and the Kurile Islands to be handed over to the Soviet Union. China would be sovereign in Manchuria.

In a Declaration on Liberated Europe, proposed by Roosevelt, the three governments pledged jointly to assist liberated people in forming temporary governments representing all democratic elements and pledged to free, early elections. When the three governments thought action necessary, they would consult together on measures to fulfill their responsibilities. There could be no action without the agreement of all three governments.

Roosevelt probably hoped that in the United States, the Declaration would project an acceptable image of the Yalta Conference as the protector of the rights of liberated peoples. It could also be a standard against which Stalin's policies in Eastern Europe could be judged. However, when put to the test, Declaration proved ineffective. After the Yalta Conference, the Western powers accepted a Polish government in which two-thirds of the members were Communists. When elections finally came in 1947, they were not democratic.

In the Far East, Soviet armies went to war against Japan two days after the atomic bomb was dropped on Hiroshima. The Soviet entry into the war accelerated the Japanese surrender. However, in February 1945, American military planners had expected the war against Japan to drag on into 1946 or even 1947.

As the *Cold War heated up, anti-Communist American critics, particularly in the Republican Party, condemned Yalta as a symbol of appeasement and a diplomatic defeat for the United States. Poland and Eastern Europe had been betrayed. The United States should avoid negotiating with the Soviet Union. Some critics later insisted that China had gone Communist because of the Yalta Conference. The severest claimed that Roosevelt was either too sick to deal with Stalin or was duped by him.

The reality of Yalta was that the location of armies determined the final outcome. Soviet armed forces decided the politics of Eastern Europe; Allied forces influenced politics in Western Europe. China became Communist because the armies of Chiang Kai-shek were defeated, not because Roosevelt had abandoned Chiang.

Yalta was an attempt to transform a temporary wartime coalition into a permanent agency for peace. Roosevelt apparently hoped to modify Stalin's behavior through the United Nations and postwar U.S. policies. Agreements had been negotiated while war was in progress when unity was vital. After the enemies were vanquished, however, the victors quarreled and their fundamental disagreements emerged.

[*See also* Hiroshima and Nagasaki, Bombings of; World War II: Postwar Impact; World War II: Changing Interpretations.]

• Edward R. Stettinius, Jr., *Roosevelt and the Russians. The Yalta Conference*, ed. Walter Johnson, 1949. *Foreign Relations of the United States. Diplomatic Papers. The Conference at Malta and Yalta*, 1955. John L. Snell, ed., *The Meaning of Yalta: Big Three Diplomacy and the New Balance of Power*, 1955. Diane Shaver Clemens, *Yalta*, 1970. Athan G. Theoharis, *The Yalta Myth: An Issue in American Politics, 1945–1955*, 1970. Richard F. Fenno, Jr., ed., *The Yalta Conference*, 1972. Russell D. Buhite, *Decision at Yalta. An Appraisal of Summit Diplomacy*, 1986.   —Keith Eubank

YAMAMOTO, ISOROKU (1884–1943), Japanese admiral and champion of naval aviation; as Combined Fleet commander in chief (1941), carried out the air attack on *Pearl Harbor. No Imperial Japanese Navy officer of his age knew more about the United States than Yamamoto. He had served as a language officer and special student at Harvard (1919–21) and as naval attaché in Washington (1926–28). When navy vice minister (1936–39), Yamamoto opposed Japan's alignment with Germany and Italy, warning that the United States was not the weak-willed nation pictured by Tokyo's hard-liners. He also warned fellow officers that the industrial might of America posed a great threat. But when he was ordered to fight the United States, he took bold action.

The orthodox strategy of the Japanese naval General Staff was to wait for the U.S. Fleet to steam into the western Pacific and destroy it there in a battleship contest. To Yamamoto, a pioneer of naval aviation and a long-standing lover of games of chance, this was a weak-hearted approach. He insisted on a preemptive carrier strike on Pearl Harbor to destroy the U.S. Fleet at the outset. The navy staff opposed him, and only his immense moral stature allowed him to prevail.

The attack on 7 December 1941 proved a brilliant tactical success, and strategically it achieved its objective of protecting Japan's Southeast Asian offensives. But the wave of American public anger that it aroused made impossible a limited settlement of the war. Yamamoto continued to command the fleet in 1942 and 1943, but less successfully. The disastrous Japanese defeat at the Battle of *Midway was his responsibility, and his air offensives in the Solomons wore down Japanese naval airpower relentlessly. On 18 April 1943, Yamamoto was on his way to visit forward units in the Solomon Islands when his plane was shot down by U.S. P-38s, alerted to his route by reading the Japanese naval codes.

[*See also* MAGIC; World War II, U.S. Naval Operations in: The Pacific.]

• Hiroyuki Agawa, *The Reluctant Admiral. Yamamoto and the Imperial Navy*, 1979. Shinjimbutsu Oraisha, *Yamamoto Isoruku no subete*, 1985.   —David C. Evans

YAMASEE WAR. See Native American Wars: Wars among Native Americans.

YORK, ALVIN (1887–1964), American soldier and World War I hero known as "Sergeant York." A semieducated Tennessee mountaineer and sharpshooter, York in his late twenties joined a fundamentalist pacifist sect. In 1917, when his draft board rejected his claim for deferment as a conscientious objector, York went off to war, convinced, after a second conversion experience, that God wanted him to fight for his country.

During the *Meuse-Argonne offensive in France in an engagement on 8 October 1918, York's small detachment from the 82nd Division was pinned down by German fire. He personally shot and killed 25 German soldiers, captured 132 more, and put 35 enemy *machine guns out of action. Promoted from corporal to sergeant, he was awarded the highest decorations of the American and French governments, and became, as "Sergeant York," the most renowned doughboy of the war.

York rejected offers of commercial ventures and returned to Pall Mall, Tennessee, to a farm partially funded by public subscription. He founded a vocational school for the undereducated mountain children.

In 1940–41, York became an ardent interventionist, endorsing U.S. defense measures and aid to the Allies. He approved a Warner Bros. film, *Sergeant York* (1941), starring Gary Cooper.

A plain-talking mountaineer combining religious piety and deep-rooted *patriotism, York was a latter-day descendant of the American frontier and perfect hero for the new popular press and for a United States fighting its first war in Europe.

[*See also* Conscientious Objection; World War I: Military and Diplomatic Course.]

• Alvin C. York, *Sergeant York: His Own Life Story and War Diary*, ed. Tom Skeyhill, 1928. David D. Lee, *Sergeant York: An American Hero*, 1985.   —John Whiteclay Chambers II

YORKTOWN, BATTLE OF (1781). The entry of France into the Revolutionary War in May 1778 gave Americans hope that they might achieve *victory rather than just stave off defeat, for French naval power could impede the flow of British resources across the Atlantic and help to trap British forces in the seaports from which they operated. Yet it was not until the autumn of 1781 that four factors combined to produce a decisive victory.

First, Gen. George *Washington kept the *Continental army in the field despite shortages of money, clothing, food, and ammunition. Second, the leaders of the French army (Rochambeau) and fleet (de Grasse) were competent commanders, willing to cooperate with one another and with Washington. Third, the British had concentrated their resources in home waters to forestall invasion. Ships sent across the Atlantic were responsible for protecting both the West Indies and British coastal enclaves in North America. Fourth, Britain's efforts to use loyalists to reestablish royal control in the South failed to eliminate rebel activity in South Carolina. Charles Lord *Cornwallis, commander of the last British mobile force in America, invaded North Carolina and then Virginia, to eliminate support for the rebels further south.

Cornwallis's operations in Virginia during the summer of 1781 put his 10,000-man army within range of Franco-American forces based in southern New England and New York. Washington saw the opportunity Cornwallis had presented, and Rochambeau and de Grasse agreed to attempt a joint operation. Leaving half the American army to pin Sir Henry *Clinton's forces at New York City, Washington with 2,300 Continentals and Rochambeau with 4,000 Frenchmen began moving south on 20 August. They reached Williamsburg on the 26th, having traveled down Chesapeake Bay by ship. There they joined 3,400 Continentals and 3,200 Virginia state and militia troops already operating against Cornwallis, who had withdrawn to York-town, on the York River, to await resupply.

The plan's key element was de Grasse's fleet, which arrived on 26 August from the West Indies, established control of the coastal waters inside the Capes of Virginia, and contributed 4,800 more men to the besieging force. Ten days later, de Grasse fought a strategically decisive engagement with a British squadron sent by Clinton to evacuate Cornwallis's force. The British failure to penetrate past de Grasse, plus Cornwallis's inertia, allowed Washington and Rochambeau to spring their trap.

The allies closed in on Yorktown on 28 September, and on 6 October began formal siege operations, which would have been impossible without French heavy *artillery. By 14 October, the cannonade had weakened British positions sufficiently to allow the allies to capture key outposts: 400 American light infantry, led by Alexander *Hamilton, took the smaller Redoubt No. 10 sooner and with fewer *casualties than the French at Redoubt No. 9. Cornwallis and 8,000 men surrendered on 17 October.

Yorktown's most decisive effect was on political opinion in Britain. The British still had substantial forces in North America, but all were tied down defending coastal enclaves; Cornwallis's army was the last force surplus to garrison requirements they had been able to scrape together. Britain could have continued the war, but its political leaders had lost the will to fight.

[See also Revolutionary War: Military and Diplomatic Course.]

• Henry P. Johnston, *The Yorktown Campaign and the Surrender of Cornwallis, 1781,* 1881; repr. 1979. Douglas S. Freeman, *George Washington: Victory with the Help of France,* 1955. William B. Will-cox, *Portrait of a General: Sir Henry Clinton in the War of Independence,* 1964.
                                              —Harold E. Selesky

YOUNG, CHARLES (1864–1919), U.S. Army colonel, military attache. The son of slaves, Young was born in Kentucky and educated in Ohio. He became the ninth African American appointed to West Point, and only the third to graduate (1889). Young's military career was consistently marked by his achievement in mixing combat, command, and intelligence assignments with teaching, administrative, and diplomatic duties at home and abroad. He served for nearly three decades (1889–1917), experiencing combat in the *Spanish-American War, the *Philippine War, Haiti, Liberia, and Mexico. On the eve of World War I, he was sixth in line for promotion to brigadier general.

Although genuine physical aliments (high blood pressure and kidney inflammation) constituted the official reasons for his removal from active duty, Colonel Young was also the victim of the 1890s and early twentieth-century white redefinitions of manhood, gender, and race. The African American successes as combatants during the Spanish-American War helped spark debate within the military on the suitability of using blacks for combat. The cultural attempt by African Americans to define their independence as citizens came into play in the enforced retirement of Colonel Young as the nation prepared for entry into World War I.

[See also African Americans in the Military.]

• Gerald W. Patton, *War and Race: The Black Officer in the American Military, 1915–1941,* 1981. Robert Ewell Greene, *Colonel Charles Young, Soldier and Diplomat,* 1985.
                                              —Gregory L. Mixon

Z

ZUMWALT, ELMO R., JR. (1920–), U.S. Navy admiral and chief of naval operations, 1970–74. Born in San Francisco, Zumwalt was valedictorian of his high school class and graduated with distinction from the U.S. Naval Academy (1942). He attended the Naval War College in 1952–53 and the National War College in 1961–62.

During World War II, he served in the Pacific on destroyers and fought in the Battle of *Leyte Gulf. His subsequent service at sea included commands of USS *Tills*, USS *Isbell*, and USS *Dewey*. Zumwalt served tours, as a captain, in the Department of *Defense (International Security Affairs), and as executive assistant and senior aide to the secretary of the navy (Paul *Nitze). Selected for rear admiral in 1964, he was ordered to command of Cruiser-Destroyer Flotilla Seven. In 1966, he returned to Washington to become director of the chief of naval operations Systems Analysis Group.

In 1968, Vice Adm. Zumwalt reported for duty in the Vietnam War as commander, Naval Forces, Vietnam. Promoted to three-star rank, at age forty-seven he was the navy's youngest vice admiral. His employment of the "Brown-Water Navy" in the rivers and canals of South Vietnam was imaginative and daring. Under President Richard M. *Nixon's program of "Vietnamization," Zumwalt's accelerated transfer of U.S. Navy ships, craft, bases, and operational responsibilities to the Vietnamese

Navy only increased his standing. In 1970, leapfrogging many more senior officers, he was promoted to four-star rank and named chief of naval operations (CNO).

Admiral Zumwalt's tour as CNO was marred by serious disciplinary problems and related racial disturbances in the navy. He issued a series of "Z-Grams" to the fleet, dealing with personnel matters (haircuts, liberty, *uniforms, etc.) traditionally the province of local commands. His popularity with the junior enlisted community soared, but the "mod navy" he ushered in did not meet with general approval in the officer corps or with many conservatives in Congress.

After retirement, Zumwalt published two books: *On Watch* (1976) and *My Father, My Son* (1986).

Admiral Zumwalt's son, LTJG Elmo R. Zumwalt III, served as officer in charge of a *swift boat in the Vietnam War. He later contracted and perished from cancer, which he and his father believed was caused by exposure to chemical defoliants used extensively in the war.

[*See also* Navy, U.S.: Since 1946; Pacification; Vietnam War: Military and Diplomatic Course.]

• Elmo R. Zumwalt, Jr., *On Watch*, 1976. Thomas J. Cutler, *Brown Water, Black Berets*, 1980. Elmo R. Zumwalt, Jr., *My Father, My Son*, 1986. R. L. Schreadley, *From the Rivers to the Sea*, 1992.

—R. L. Schreadley

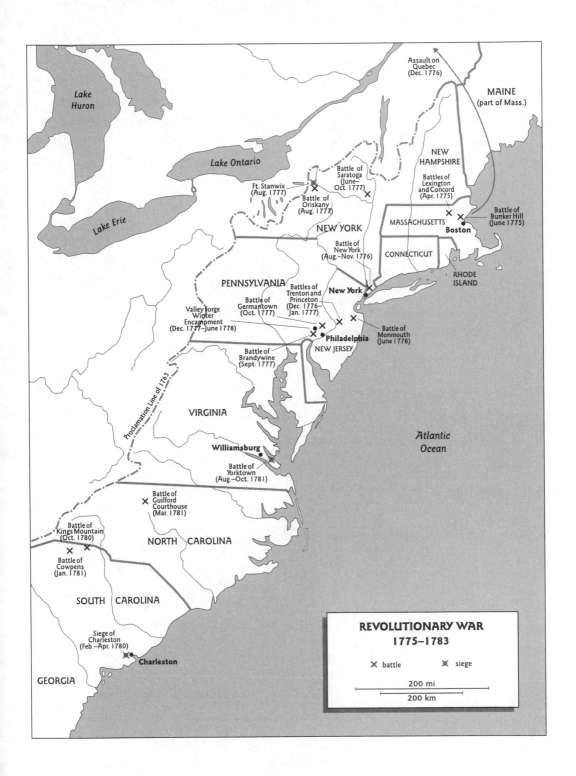

Lake Huron

Lake Ontario

Lake Erie

Assault on Quebec (Dec. 1776)

MAINE (part of Mass.)

NEW HAMPSHIRE

Ft. Stanwix (Aug. 1777)

Battle of Saratoga (June–Oct. 1777)

Battle of Oriskany (Aug. 1777)

Battles of Lexington and Concord (Apr. 1775)

Battle of Bunker Hill (June 1775)

NEW YORK

MASSACHUSETTS

Boston

Battle of New York (Aug.–Nov. 1776)

CONNECTICUT

RHODE ISLAND

PENNSYLVANIA

Battle of Germantown (Oct. 1777)

Battles of Trenton and Princeton (Dec. 1776–Jan. 1777)

New York

Valley Forge Winter Encampment (Dec. 1777–June 1778)

Philadelphia

Battle of Monmouth (June 1778)

NEW JERSEY

Battle of Brandywine (Sept. 1777)

Proclamation Line of 1763

VIRGINIA

Atlantic Ocean

Williamsburg

Battle of Yorktown (Aug.–Oct. 1781)

Battle of Guilford Courthouse (Mar. 1781)

Battle of Kings Mountain (Oct. 1780)

NORTH   CAROLINA

Battle of Cowpens (Jan. 1781)

SOUTH   CAROLINA

Siege of Charleston (Feb.–Apr. 1780)

Charleston

GEORGIA

REVOLUTIONARY WAR 1775–1783

✕ battle   ⊠ siege

200 mi

200 km

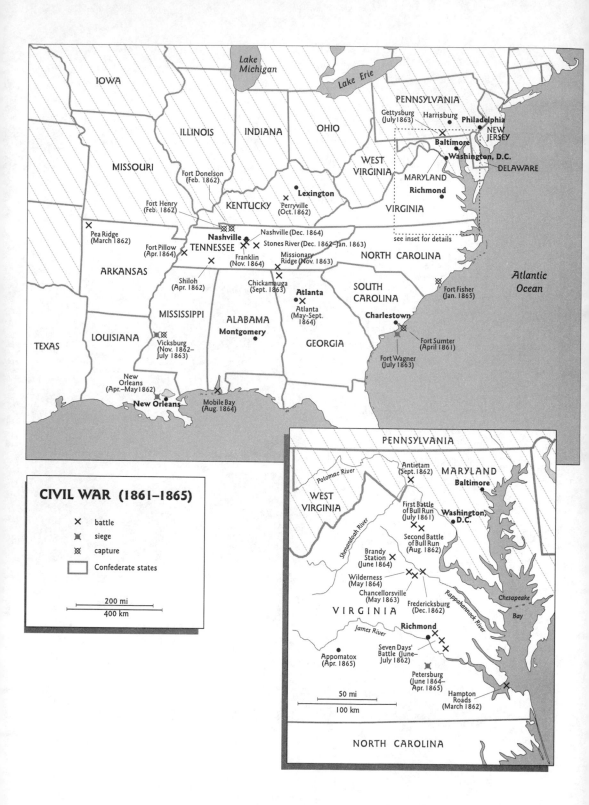

CIVIL WAR (1861–1865)

- ✕ battle
- ⬟ siege
- ⊠ capture
- ▭ Confederate states

200 mi
400 km

Main map labels:

IOWA

Lake Michigan

Lake Erie

ILLINOIS INDIANA OHIO

PENNSYLVANIA

Gettysburg (July 1863) Harrisburg **Philadelphia**

MISSOURI

WEST VIRGINIA

MARYLAND

Baltimore

NEW JERSEY

Washington, D.C.

DELAWARE

Fort Donelson (Feb. 1862)

Lexington

Perryville (Oct. 1862)

Richmond

Fort Henry (Feb. 1862)

KENTUCKY

VIRGINIA

see inset for details

✕ Pea Ridge (March 1862)

Nashville (Dec. 1864)

Nashville Stones River (Dec. 1862–Jan. 1863)

NORTH CAROLINA

Atlantic Ocean

Fort Pillow (Apr. 1864)

TENNESSEE

ARKANSAS

Franklin (Nov. 1864)

Missionary Ridge (Nov. 1863)

Shiloh (Apr. 1862)

Chickamauga (Sept. 1863)

Atlanta

SOUTH CAROLINA

Fort Fisher (Jan. 1865)

MISSISSIPPI

ALABAMA

Atlanta (May–Sept. 1864)

Charlestown

Montgomery

GEORGIA

Fort Sumter (April 1861)

TEXAS

LOUISIANA

Vicksburg (Nov. 1862–July 1863)

Fort Wagner (July 1863)

New Orleans (Apr.–May 1862)

New Orleans

Mobile Bay (Aug. 1864)

Inset map labels:

PENNSYLVANIA

Potomac River

Antietam (Sept. 1862)

MARYLAND

Baltimore

WEST VIRGINIA

First Battle of Bull Run (July 1861)

Washington, D.C.

Shenandoah River

Second Battle of Bull Run (Aug. 1862)

Brandy Station (June 1864)

Wilderness (May 1864)

Chancellorsville (May 1863)

Fredericksburg (Dec. 1862)

Rappahannock River

Chesapeake Bay

VIRGINIA

James River

Richmond

Seven Days' Battle (June–July 1862)

Appomatox (Apr. 1865)

Petersburg (June 1864–Apr. 1865)

Hampton Roads (March 1862)

50 mi
100 km

NORTH CAROLINA

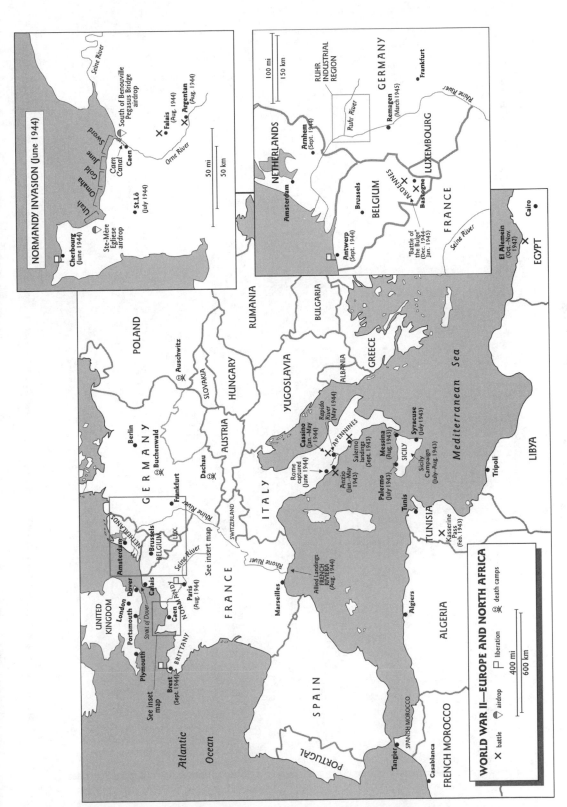

NORMANDY INVASION (June 1944)

Cherbourg (June 1944)

Ste-Mère Église airdrop

St. Lô (July 1944)

Utah / Omaha / Gold / June / Sword

Caen Canal

South of Benouville Pegasus Bridge airdrop

Caen

Falaise (Aug. 1944)

Argentan (Aug. 1944)

Orne River

Seine River

50 mi

50 km

Amsterdam

NETHERLANDS

Antwerp (Sept. 1944)

Brussels

BELGIUM

Arnhem (Sept. 1944)

RUHR INDUSTRIAL REGION

Ruhr River

GERMANY

Remagen (March 1945)

Frankfurt

"Battle of the Bulge" (Dec. 1944–Jan. 1945)

ARDENNES

Bastogne

LUXEMBOURG

FRANCE

Seine River

100 mi

150 km

El Alamein (Oct.–Nov. 1942)

Cairo

EGYPT

Atlantic Ocean

UNITED KINGDOM

London

Portsmouth

Plymouth

Dover

Calais

Brest (Sept. 1944)

See inset map

BRITTANY

Caen

NORMANDY

Paris (Aug. 1944)

Strait of Dover

F R A N C E

Rhine River

Seine River

Rhône River

Allied Landings FRENCH RIVIERA (Aug. 1944)

Marseilles

Amsterdam

NETHERLANDS

Brussels

BELGIUM

Lux.

See insert map

SWITZERLAND

Berlin

G E R M A N Y

Buchenwald

Frankfurt

Dachau

AUSTRIA

SLOVAKIA

HUNGARY

POLAND

Auschwitz

RUMANIA

BULGARIA

YUGOSLAVIA

ALBANIA

GREECE

I T A L Y

APENNINES

Cassino (Jan.–May 1944)

Rapido River (May 1944)

Rome captured (June 1944)

Anzio (Jan.–May 1943)

Salerno landings (Sept. 1943)

Messina (Aug. 1943)

Palermo (July 1943)

SICILY

Syracuse (July 1943)

Sicily Campaign (July–Aug. 1943)

Tunis

TUNISIA

Kasserine Pass (Feb. 1943)

Algiers

ALGERIA

Tripoli

LIBYA

Mediterranean Sea

S P A I N

PORTUGAL

SPANISH MOROCCO

Tangier

Casablanca

FRENCH MOROCCO

WORLD WAR II—EUROPE AND NORTH AFRICA

✕ battle ◊ airdrop ☐ liberation ⊛ death camps

400 mi

600 km

845

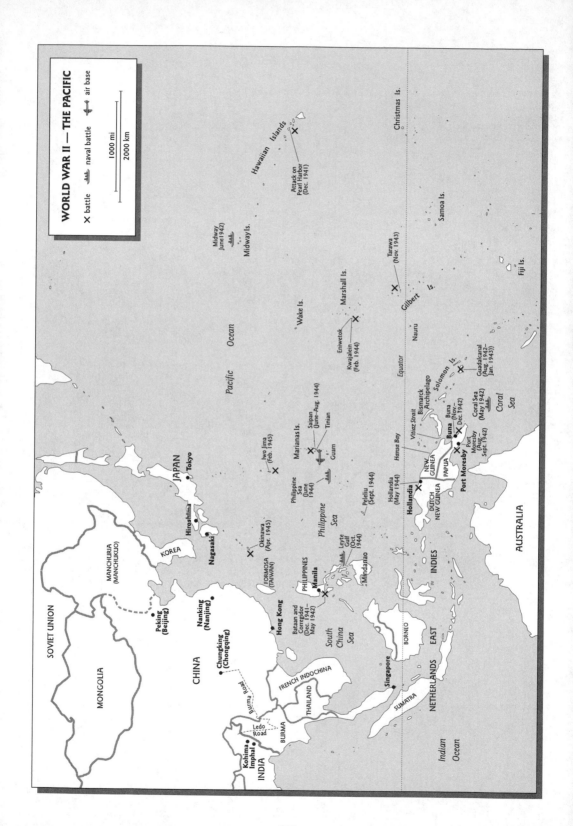

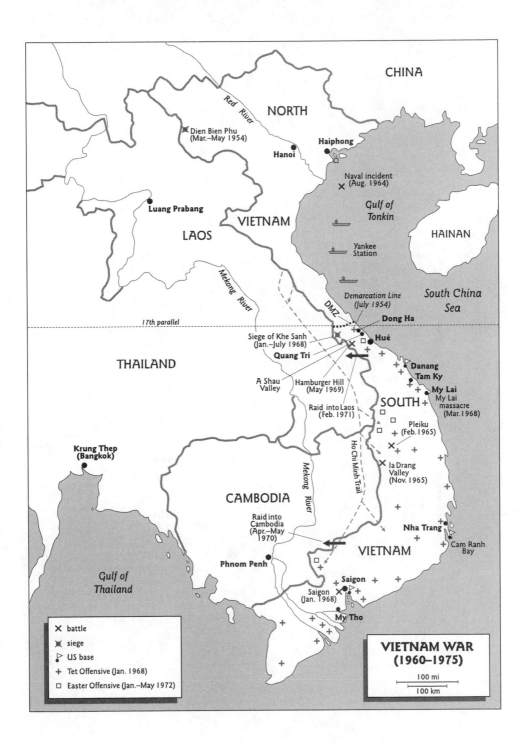

CHINA

Red River

NORTH

Dien Bien Phu
(Mar.–May 1954)

Haiphong

Hanoi

Naval incident
(Aug. 1964)

VIETNAM

Gulf of
Tonkin

HAINAN

Luang Prabang

LAOS

Yankee
Station

Mekong River

Demarcation Line
(July 1954)

South China
Sea

17th parallel

DMZ

Dong Ha

Siege of Khe Sanh
(Jan.–July 1968)

Hué

Quang Tri

THAILAND

Danang
Tam Ky

A Shau
Valley

Hamburger Hill
(May 1969)

My Lai
My Lai
massacre
(Mar. 1968)

Raid into Laos
(Feb. 1971)

SOUTH

Pleiku
(Feb. 1965)

Krung Thep
(Bangkok)

Ho Chi Minh Trail

Ia Drang
Valley
(Nov. 1965)

Mekong River

CAMBODIA

Nha Trang

Raid into
Cambodia
(Apr.–May
1970)

Cam Ranh
Bay

VIETNAM

Phnom Penh

Gulf of
Thailand

Saigon

Saigon
(Jan. 1968)

My Tho

× battle
⚔ siege
▷ US base
✛ Tet Offensive (Jan. 1968)
☐ Easter Offensive (Jan.–May 1972)

**VIETNAM WAR
(1960–1975)**

100 mi

100 km

U.S. Military Service and Casualties in Major Wars and Conflicts, 1775–1991

Conflict	Total Serving	Battle Deaths	Other Deaths	Wounded
Revolutionary War (1775–1783)	ca. 290,000	6,824	ca. 18,500	8,445
War of 1812 (1812–1815)	286,730	2,260	*	4,505
Mexican War (1846–1848)	78,718	1,733	11,550	4,152
Civil War (1861–1865)				
Union	2,213,363	140,414	224,097	281,881
Confederate[a]	600,000–1,500,000	74,524	59,297	*
Indian Wars (1865–1898)	106,000	919	*	1,025
Spanish-American War (1898–1899)	306,760	385	2,061	1,622
Philippine War (1898–1902)	127,068	1,020	3,176	2,930
World War I (1917–1918)[b]	4,734,991	53,402	63,114	204,002
World War II (1941–1945)[c]	16,112,566	291,557	113,842	670,846
Korean War (1950–1953)[d]	5,720,000	33,746	*	103,284
Vietnam War (1964–1973)[e]	8,744,000	47,355	10,796	153,303
Persian Gulf War (1990–1991)	467,159	148	151	467

* Reliable figures not available.

[a] Estimates based on incomplete returns in *Final Report of the United States Army Provost Marshal General, 1863–1866.* Another 26,000–31,000 Confederates died in Northern POW camps.

[b] *Battle Deaths* and *Wounded* include North Russia to 25 August 1919 and Siberia to 1 April 1920; *Other Deaths* cover the period 1 April 1917 to 31 December 1918; 4,120 U.S. servicemen were captured during World War I, and 3,350 were listed missing in action.

[c] Covers the period 7 December 1941–31 December 1946, when hostilities were officially ended by presidential proclamation. *Total Serving* is for the period 7 December 1941 through 14 August 1945 inclusive. *Battle Deaths* and *Wounded* include casualties due to hostile action in October 1941; 130,201 U.S. servicemen were captured in World War II, and 30,314 were listed missing in action.

[d] 7,140 U.S. servicemen were captured in Korea, and 8,177 were listed missing in action.

[e] *Wounded* includes 150,322 personnel not requiring hospitalization; 826 U.S. servicemen were captured in Vietnam, and as of September 1993, 2,489 were listed missing in action.

Sources:
Francis B. Heitman, *Historical Register and Dictionary of the United States Army from Its Organization, September 29, 1789 to March 2, 1903,* Vol. 2, 1903. Armed Forces Information School, *The Army Almanac,* 1950. U.S. Department of Defense, Statistical Service Center, *Principal Wars in Which the United States Participated: U.S. Personnel Serving and Casualties,* 1957. H. H. Peckham, ed., *The Toll of Independence,* 1974. Edna J. Hintner, "Combat Casualties Who Remained at Home," *Military Review,* Vol. 60, no. 1 (January 1980), p. 37. Allan R. Millett, *Semper Fidelis: The History of the United States Marine Corps,* 1980. Madeline Sapienza, *Peacetime Awards of the Purple Heart in the Post-Vietnam Period,* 1987. "U.S. Casualties in Previous Wars," *Washington Post,* 1 March 1991, p. A32. U.S. Department of Defense, *Defense 94–Almanac,* Issue 5 (September–October 1994).

Table compiled by Charles R. Shrader

Grade	Army		Navy	
Officers				
O-11[1]	General of the Army		Fleet Admiral	
O-10	General		Admiral	
O-9	Lieutenant General		Vice Admiral	
O-8	Major General		Rear Admiral (upper)	
O-7	Brigadier General		Rear Admiral (lower)	
O-6	Colonel		Captain	
O-5	Lieutenant Colonel	[SILVER]	Commander	[SILVER]
O-4	Major	[GOLD]	Lieutenant Commander	[GOLD]
O-3	Captain		Lieutenant	
O-2	First Lieutenant	[SILVER]	Lieutenant Junior Grade	[SILVER]
O-1	Second Lieutenant	[GOLD]	Ensign	[GOLD]

Compiled from information found in the following websites:
Army: www.inxpress.net/~rokats/toda_era.html,
www-perscom.army.mil/tagd/tioh/rank/orank.html, and
www-perscom.army.mil/tagd/tioh/rank/erank.html
Navy: www.chinfo.navy.mil/navpalib/allhands/ranks/officers/o-rank.html
and www.chinfo.navy.mil/navpalib/allhands/ranks/rates/rates.html

Rank and Insignia

Grade	Air Force	Marine Corps
Officers		
O-10	General	General
O-9	Lieutenant General	Lieutenant General
O-8	Major General	Major General
O-7	Brigadier General	Brigadier General
O-6	Colonel	Colonel
O-5	Lieutenant Colonel [SILVER]	Lieutenant Colonel [SILVER]
O-4	Major [GOLD]	Major [GOLD]
O-3	Captain	Captain
O-2	First Lieutenant [SILVER]	First Lieutenant [SILVER]
O-1	Second Lieutenant [GOLD]	Second Lieutenant [GOLD]

Air Force: www.af.mil/news/airman/0199/ngrades.html
Marine Corps: www.usmc.mil/rank.nsf/ranks

[1] The five-star rank has been bestowed, by act of Congress, on the following: **Army:** George Washington (posthumously), John J. Pershing, Dwight D. Eisenhower, Douglas MacArthur, George C. Marshall, H. H. "Hap" Arnold of the Army Air Forces, and Omar N. Bradley; **Navy:** William D. Leahy, Ernest J. King, Chester W. Nimitz, and William F. Halsey.

Grade	Army		Navy	
Enlisted personnel				
E-9	Sergeant Major of the Army		Master Chief Petty Officer of the Navy	
	Command Sergeant Major		Master Chief Petty Officer	
	Sergeant Major			
E-8	First Sergeant		Senior Chief Petty Officer	
	Master Sergeant			
E-7	Sergeant First Class		Chief Petty Officer	
E-6	Staff Sergeant		Petty Officer First Class	
E-5	Sergeant		Petty Officer Second Class	
E-4	Corporal		Petty Officer Third Class	
E-3	Private First Class		Seaman	
E-2	Private		Seaman Apprentice	
E-1	Private Recruit (no rank insignia)		Seaman Recruit	

Rank and Insignia

Grade	Air Force		Marine Corps	
Enlisted personnel				
E-9	Chief Master Sergeant of the Air Force		Sergeant Major of the Marine Corps	
	Command Chief Master Sergeant		Sergeant Major	
	Chief Master Sergeant		Master Gunnery Sergeant	
E-8	Senior Master Sergeant		First Sergeant	
			Master Sergeant	
E-7	Master Sergeant		Gunnery Sergeant	
E-6	Technical Sergeant		Staff Sergeant	
E-5	Staff Sergeant		Sergeant	
E-4	Senior Airman		Corporal	
E-3	Airman First Class		Lance Corporal	
E-2	Airman		Private First Class	
E-1	Airman Basic (no rank insignia)		Private (no rank insignia)	

INDEX